A NEW LANDMARK
IN LATIN-ENGLISH DICTIONARIES
FOR THE MODERN STUDENT!

This totally revised and enlarged Latin-English dictionary is the first Latin dictionary ever to be compiled on the basis of modern lexicographical principles.

COMPREHENSIVE—More than 70,000 words and phrases.

DEFINITIVE—Based on the foremost Classical authorities and organized to achieve the utmost clarity, precision, and convenience.

MODERN—Obsolete definitions have been replaced by fresh translations that correspond to current English usage.

THE BANTAM NEW COLLEGE DICTIONARY SERIES

JOHN C. TRAUPMAN, Ph.D. in Classics, Princeton University, was chairman of the Department of Classics at St. Joseph's University (Philadelphia). He is the author of *The New College German & English Dictionary* (Bantam Books, 1981; Amsco School Publications, Inc., 1981), *Latin Is Fun: Lively Lessons for Beginners* (Amsco School Publications, Inc., Book I 1989), *Latin Is Fun: Lively Lessons for Advancing Students* (Amsco School Publications, Inc., Book II 1994), and *Conversational Latin for Oral Proficiency* (Bolchazy-Carducci Publishers, Inc., 2006). He is an associate editor of *The Scribner-Bantam English Dictionary* (Scribner's, 1977; Bantam Books, 1979). He served as a member of the Board of American Consultants to Lexus, Ltd., Glasgow, Scotland, and as editor in chief of the Wimbledon Publishing Co., Ltd., London.

The Bantam New College

LATIN & ENGLISH DICTIONARY

Third Edition

JOHN C. TRAUPMAN, Ph.D.
St. Joseph's University, Philadelphia

BANTAM BOOKS

THE BANTAM NEW COLLEGE LATIN & ENGLISH DICTIONARY
A Bantam Book

PUBLISHING HISTORY
Bantam mass market edition published April 1966
Bantam mass market revised edition / May 2007

Published by Bantam Dell
A Division of Random House, Inc.
New York, New York

Cover design by Beverly Leung

ISBN 978-0-553-59012-8

Printed in the United States of America
Published simultaneously in Canada

www.bantamdell.com

OPM 10 9 8 7 6 5 4

Contents

Preface to the Third Edition

This totally revised and expanded edition, with over 70,000 words and phrases, in addition to all the features of the second edition, reflecting the increased interest in oral Latin, includes many neologisms in the English–Latin section in order to deal with subjects such as house and furniture, daily activities, health and physical fitness, classroom activities, sports and other leisure activities, modern means of transportation, and modern technology, such as computers. This dictionary also provides a wide range of historical, mythological, and geographical names as they would have been known in ancient times. Where appropriate, the modern geographical name is provided, e.g., Brundisium (*modern Brindisi*).

Since current Latin textbooks use the consonantal *i* in place of the *j*, this edition has also adopted the consonantal *i*. Variant spellings of Latin words are provided within the entries. In the Latin–English section, long vowels in closed syllables are indicated by a macron. The transitive and intransitive functions of verbs have been clearly presented, with the transitive uses always preceding the intransitive uses. Illustrative phrases within the entries are all translated and arranged in alphabetical order.

The level of usage of Latin words and phrases is faithfully reflected in the level of usage of the English translations, so that, if the Latin word is colloquial, slang, or vulgar, the English translation corresponds, even when the result might be words which would not be used in American polite society.

The author gratefully acknowledges the kind support of Donald Reis, formerly of Bantam Books, under whose direction the first edition of this dictionary was undertaken, and Philip Rappaport, Senior Editor, Bantam Dell Publishing Group, under whom the present edition was undertaken. Special thanks are due to Dr. Dominic M. Roberti, chemistry professor turned desktop publisher, who gave much helpful advice; he is responsible for the page design and typesetting of this book. The author also wishes to express his thanks to Dr. James McDonough for his critical comments and to Steven Earl Heinsz and Gary Varney for pointing out various typographical errors.

Abbreviations

abbr.........abbreviation
abl..........ablative
acc..........accusative
adj..........adjective
adjl.........adjectival
adv..........adverb
advl.........adverbial
anat.........anatomy
archit.......architecture
astr.........astronomy
bot..........botany
biol.........biology
c............circa, about
cf...........confer, compare
cent.........century
coll.........colloquial
com..........commerce
comp.........comparative
comput.......computer
conj.........conjunction
d............died
dat..........dative
defect.......defective verb
dim..........diminutive
E............East(ern)
eccl.........ecclesiastical
educ.........education
euphem.......euphemism
esp..........especially
expr.........expressed
f............feminine noun
fem..........feminine
fig..........figurative
fin..........finance
fl...........floruit, flourished
fpl..........feminine plural noun
fut..........future
gen..........genitive
geog.........geography
geol.........geology
gram.........grammar
hum..........humorous
imperf.......imperfect
impers.......impersonal verb
impv.........imperative
indecl.......indeclinable
indef........indefinite
indic........indicative
inf..........infinitive
interj.......interjection
interrog.....interrogative
intr.........intransitive
leg..........legal
lit..........literal
loc..........locative
m............masculine noun
masc.........masculine
math.........mathematics
mech.........mechanics
med..........medicine
mf...........masculine or feminine noun
mil..........military
mpl..........masculine plural noun
mus..........music
n............neuter noun
N............North(ern)
naut.........nautical
neg..........negative
neut.........neuter
nom..........nominative
npl..........neuter plural noun
opp..........opposite of
p............participle
pass.........passive
pej..........pejorative
perf.........perfect
phil.........philosophy
pl...........plural
poet.........poetry
pol..........politics
pp...........past participle
pref.........prefix
prep.........preposition
pres.........present
pron.........pronoun
pros.........prosody
prov.........proverb
refl.........reflexive
rel..........relative
relig........religion
rhet.........rhetoric
s............substantive
S............South(ern)
sc...........scilicet
singl........singular
sl...........slang
s.o..........someone
spl..........substantive plural
s.th.........something
subj.........subjunctive
suf..........suffix
superl.......superlative
theat........theater
topog........topography
tr...........transitive verb
usu..........usually
vbl..........verbal
v defect.....defective verb
v impers.....impersonal verb
vulg.........vulgar
w............with
W............West(ern)

A Guide to the Dictionary

The main entry, its inflected forms, spelling variants, and illustrative phrases are set in boldface. Part-of-speech labels are set in italics. In the Latin-English section long vowels are marked in the entry word as well as in the illustrative phrases within the entry.

Centered periods within entry words indicate division points at which inflectional elements are to be added, without regard to syllabification, e.g.,

ōrd·ō -inis = ōrdō, ōrdinis

Compound words are generally given in their assimilated forms, e.g., **accurrō** rather than **adcurrō.** Cross-references are provided as guides for those using texts which employ the unassimilated forms, e.g.,

adc- = acc-

adn- = ann-

exf- = eff-

sēpiō *see* **saepīō**

Spelling variants are indicated in bold type in parentheses after the part-of-speech abbreviation, e.g.,

affīnit·ās -ātis *f* **(adf-)** affinity, connection; relationship by marriage

However, nouns with both Greek and Latin endings are shown in full, e.g.,

troch·us *or* **troch·os -ī** *m* hoop

Tened·os *or* **Tened·us -ī** *f* Tenedos *(island off the coast of Troy)*

Adjectives of three endings, whether of the first and second or of the third declension, are shown with three endings; adjectives with a single ending are shown in the nominative, followed by the genitive ending, e.g.,

curv·us -a -um *adj* curved

simil·is -is -e *adj* similar

dīlig·ēns -entis *adj* careful; diligent

When constructions are provided, cases are not shown with the most common prepositions **ab, ad, ex,** *or* **cum.** For all other prepositions, the case that the preposition governs is shown, e.g.,

stō stāre stetī statum *intr* to stand; *(w.* **ex)** to consist of; *(w. abl or* **in** *+ abl)* to depend on; *(w.* **per** *+ acc)* to be due to, thanks to

Synonymous meanings are separated by commas; distinct meanings are separated by semicolons. When a grammatical construction applies to several distinct meanings, thus extending beyond semicolons, the distinct meanings are numbered, e.g.,

perfugiō *intr (w.* **ad** *or* **in** *+ acc)* **1** to flee to for refuge; **2** to desert to; **3** to have recourse to

Discriminations between two or more meanings of an entry word are often shown by means of English words in parentheses, coming before or after the English meaning, e.g.,

argūt·us -a -um *adj* bright, smart *(person);* rustling *(leaves);* babbling *(brook);* chirping *(bird, cricket);* pungent *(smell);* expressive *(eyes, gestures)*

aspect·ō -āre -āvī -ātus *tr* **(ads-)** to look at, gaze at; *(of a place)* to face; to obey *(orders)*

However, words in parentheses, but not in italics, coming before or after a meaning are optional additions to the word in the target language, e.g.,

avuncul·us -ī *m* (maternal) uncle

abi·ēs -etis *f* fir (tree)

Level of usage of Latin words, indicated by the abbreviations *(coll)* for "colloquial," *(sl)* for "slang," and *(vulg)* for "vulgar," is reflected in the level of usage of the English translation of the Latin word, e.g.,

admutil·ō -āre *tr* to clip close; *(coll)* to clip, cheat

ab·eō -īre -īvī *or* **-iī itum** *vi* to go away, depart; **abī in malam rem!** *(sl)* go to hell!

cōle·ī -ōrum *mpl (vulg)* balls

Subject labels are given in italics and listed in alphabetical order, e.g.,

concurs·us -ūs *m* a running together, concourse; *(astr)* conjunction; *(gram)* juxtaposition *(of letters)*; *(leg)* joint-right; *(mil)* charge, clash

When an entry word is a proper noun, the proper noun is not repeated in English if the form is the same in Latin and in English; but when the proper noun has two possible endings, the form used in English is provided, e.g.,

Eurīpid·ēs -is *m* Athenian tragic playwright *(480-406 B.C.)*

Eurōp·a -ae *or* **Eurōp·ē -ēs** *f* Europa *(daughter of the Phoenician king Agenor)* **‖** (continent of) Europe

Substantives formed from adjectives are generally listed under the adjectives from which they are derived and are separated by vertical parallel bars, e.g.,

dialectic·us -a -um *adj* logical **‖** *m* logician **‖** *f* logic **‖** *npl* dialectics

Proper nouns derived from adjectives or from common nouns are subsumed, in short entries, under the adjective and common noun respectively, e.g.,

daedal·us -a -um *adj* skillful, artistic; intricately constructed **‖ Daedal·us -ī** *m* builder of the Labyrinth in Crete

Tarquini·us -a -um *adj* Tarquinian **‖** *m* Tarquinius Priscus *(fifth king of Rome, c. 616-579 B.C.)* **‖** Tarquinius Superbus *(seventh and last king of Rome, c. 534-510 B.C.)*

cast·or -ōris *m* beaver **‖ Castor** *son of Tyndareus, twin brother of Pollux*

Vertical parallel bars are used to separate different parts of speech of the entry word, for instance, pronominal adjectives from pronouns, e.g.,

alt·er -era -erum *adj* one *(of two)*; a second, the second; the next **‖** *pron* one *(of two)*, the one, the other; a second one

Vertical parallel bars are used to separate past participles, when occurring as separate entries, from adjectives and substantives derived from them, e.g.,

impēns·us -a -um *pp of* **impendō** **‖** *adj* high, costly, expensive; **‖** *f see* **impēnsa** **‖** *n* high price

Vertical parallel bars are used to separate nouns in the singular from nouns in the plural when the plural of the nouns carries a special meaning, e.g.,

aed·ēs *or* **aed·is -is** *f* room; apartment; shrine, temple **‖** *fpl* house, home

Vertical parallel bars are used to separate common nouns from proper nouns, e.g.,

urs·a -ae *f* she-bear **‖ Ursa Māior** *(astr)* Great Bear; **Ursa Minor** *(astr)* Little Bear

Vertical parallel bars are used to separate verb functions. Transitive *(tr)*, reflexive *(refl)*, passive (with intransitive sense) *(pass)*, intransitive *(intr)*, and impersonal *(impers)* functions of verbs with their dependent constructions are clearly differentiated and are presented in the fixed order as listed above, e.g.,

ēmer·gō -gere -sī -sus *vt* to raise *(from the water)* **‖** *refl or pass* to rise **‖** *intr* to emerge; to rise *(in power)*

Illustrative phrases are provided at the end of entries in strict alphabetical order. However, when a Latin phrase illustrates a specific meaning, for instance, when the main entry is a prefix, suffix, or preposition, the phrase is placed immediately after that meaning and introduced by a colon, e.g.,

-i·cō -āre *vbl suf* **1** used to form verbs from adjectives: **claudicāre** to be lame, to limp; **2** used to form verbs from other verbs: **fodicāre** to stab *(from* **fodere)**

For the sake of clarity, optional variants in illustrative phrases are placed in parentheses, e.g.,

vēra et falsa *(or* **vēra falsīs) dīiūdicāre** to distinguish truth from falsehood

When a noun may be either masculine or feminine, the abbreviations are written together, but when a noun is generally, say, masculine but only rarely feminine or neuter, the rarer gender is shown in parentheses, e.g.,

serp·ēns -entis *mf* serpent

pampin·us -ī *m (f)* vine shoot

sāl salis *m (n)* salt

Past participles are listed as separate entries when difference in form from the first person singular present indicative warrants such listing, provided they fall alphabetically more than one word before or after their verb, e.g.,

vīs·us -a -um *pp of* **videō**

Similarly, the perfect form of a verb is listed as a separate entry in its alphabetical position, e.g.,

trīvī *perf of* **terō**

On the English-Latin side, Latin vowels are marked to distinguish:

1. words otherwise spelled alike: **lēvis** (smooth), **levis** (light); **esse** (to be), **ēsse** (to eat)
2. the ablative singular from the nominative singular of nouns of the first declension.
3. the infinitive of verbs of the second conjugation from the infinitive of verbs of the third conjugation
4. the genitive singular and nominative and accusative plural from the nominative singular of the fourth declension.

On the English-Latin side, a boldface dash represents the vocabulary entry, e.g.,

awake *adj* vigil, vigilans; **to be —** vigilare

PRONUNCIATION

Vowels

Classical Method

a	*a* in ago: **comp*a*rō**
ā	*a* in father: **im*ā*gō**
e	*e* in pet: **prop*e*rō**
ē	*a* in late: **l*ē*nis**
i	*i* in hit: ***i*dem**
ī	*ee* in keen: **am*ī*cus**
o	*o* in often: **m*o*dus**
ō	*o* in hope: **n*ō*men**
u	*u* in put: ***u*t**
ū	*u* in rude: ***ū*tor**
y	*ü* in German Hütte: **m*y*rta**
ȳ	*ü* in German über: **T*ȳ*deus**

Ecclesiastical Method

Generally the same as the Classical Method. However, in practice the different values of the vowels are frequently not rigidly adhered to.

Diphthongs

	Classical Method		Ecclesiastical Method
ae	*y* in by: ***ae*cus**...	**ae**	*a* in late: **c*ae*cus**
au	*ow* in now: **n*au*ta**	**au**	as in Classical Method
e͡i	*ey* in they: **h*e͡i***	**ei**	as in Classical Method
e͡u	*eu* in feud: **Orph*e͡u*s**	**eu**	*eu* in Italian neutro: ***eu*ge**
o͡e	*oi* in oil: **c*o͡e*pit**	**oe**	*a* in late: **c*oe*pit**
u͡i	*uey* in gluey: **c*u͡i*;** after **q,** *wee* in week: **quī**	**ui**	same as Classical Method

Consonants

	Classical Method		Ecclesiastical Method
b	English **b**	**b**	English b
c	always *c* in can: ***c*īvis, *c*antō, *c*edō**	**c**	before **e, i, ae,** or **oe** = *ch* in cherry: ***c*elsus, *c*ivis, *c*aelum, *c*oepit,** but before other letters, *c* in can: ***c*antō, a*c*tus**
d	English **d**	**d**	English d
f	English **f**	**f**	English f
g	always *g* in go: ***g*allīna, *g*enus, *g*rātus, *g*ula**	**g**	before **e** or **i** = *g* in gentle: ***g*enus, re*g*īna,** but before other letters except **g** and **n** (see under Consonant Groups) = *g* in go: ***g*allīna, *g*rātus, *g*ula, ro*g*ō**
h	English **h**	**h**	English h
i	*y* in yes: ***i*am, *i*ungō**	**j**	*y* in yes: ***j*am, *J*ēsūs, *j*ūstus**
k	English **k,** but unaspirated	**k**	English k

l	English **l**	**l**	English l
m	English **m**, but in verse (and probably in prose) final **m** seems to have beem reduced to a nasalization of the preceding vowel	**m**	English m
n	English **n**	**n**	English n
p	English **p**, but unaspirated	**p**	English p
q	English **q**	**q**	English q
r	trilled **r** as in the Romance languages	**r**	as in Classical Method
s	always **s** in sing: **mi*s*er, mor*s***	**s**	*s* in sing: ***s*alū*s*,** but when standing between two vowels or when final and preceded by a voiced consonant = *z* in dozen: **mi*s*er, mor*s***
t	English **t**, but unaspirated	**t**	as in Classical Method
u	*w* in **w**ine, when unaccented, preceded by q, sometimes by s, and sometimes by g, and followed by a vowel: **q*u*i·a, s*u*ā·vis** (but **s*u*·ō·rum), dis·tin·g*u*ō** (but **ex·i·gu·*us*)**	**u**	in Classical Method
v	*w* in **w**ine: ***v*ī*v*ō**	**v**	English v
x	*x* (= **ks**) in si**x**: **e*x*trā**	**x**	*x* (as **ks**) in si**x**: **pā*x*;** but in words beginning with **ex** and followed by a vowel, **h,** or **s,** = *x* (as **gz**) in e**x**haust: **e*x*audī, e*x*hālō, e*x*solvō**
z	*dz* in a**dz**e: ***z*ōna**	**z**	as in Classical Method

Consonant Groups

	Classical Method		Ecclesiastical Method
bs	*ps* in a**ps**e: **o*bs*idō, ur*bs***	**bs**	**bs** in o**bs**ession: **o*bs*idō,** but in the final position = **bs** (= **bz**) in o**bs**erve: **ur*bs***
bt	*pt* in ca**pt**ain: **o*bt*inēre**	**bt**	*bt* in o**bt**ain: **o*bt*inēre**
cc	*kk* in boo**kk**eeper: **e*cc*e, o*cc*īdō, o*cc*āsum, o*cc*lūdō**	**cc**	before **e** or **i** = *tch* in ca**tch**: **e*cc*e, o*cc*īdō;** but before other letters = *kk* in boo**kk**eeper; **o*cc*āsum, o*cc*lūdō**
ch	*ch* in **ch**aotic: **pul*ch*er**	**ch**	as in Classical Method
gg	*gg* in le**g g**uard: **a*gg*er**	**gg**	before **e** or **i** = *dj* in a**dj**ourn: **a*gg*er;** but before other letters = *gg* in le**g g**uard: **a*gg*regō**
gn	*ngn* in ha**ngn**ail: **di*gn*us**	**gn**	*ny* in ca**ny**on: **di*gn*us**
gu	see consonant **u**	**gu**	as in Classical Method
ph	*p-h* in to**p-h**eavy: ***ph*ōca**	**ph**	*ph* in **ph**oenix: ***ph*ōca**
qu	see consonant **u**	**qu**	as in Classical Method

sc	*sc* in scope: **sciō, scūtum**	**sc**	before **e** or **i** = *sh* in **shin: ascendō, sciō;** but before other letters = **sc** in scope: **scandō, scūtum**
su	see consonant **u**	**su**	as in Classical Method
th	*t* in take: ***th*eātrum**	**th**	as in Classical Method
ti	*ti* in English patio: **nā*tiō***	**ti**	when preceded by **s, t,** or **x,** or when followed by a consonant = *ti* in English patio: **hos*ti*a, admix*tiō*, for*ti*ter;** but when unaccented, followed by a vowel, and preceded by any letter except **s, t,** or **x** = *tzy* in ritzy: **nā*tiō*, pre*ti*um**

Syllabification

1. Every Latin word has as many syllables as it has vowels or diphthongs: **ae·ger, fī·li·us, Bai·ae**
2. When a word is divided into syllables:
   - **a)** a single consonant between two vowels goes with the following syllable (**h** is regarded as a consonant; **ch, ph, th, qu,** and sometimes **gu** and **su** are regarded as single consontants)*; **a·ger, ni·hil, a·qua, ci·hor·rē·um**
   - **b)** the first consonant of a combination of two or more consonants goes with the preceding vowel: **tor·men·tum, mit·tō, mon·strum**
   - **c)** a consonant group consisting of a mute **(b, c, d, g, p, t)** followed by **l** or **r** is generally left undivided and goes with the following vowel: **pa·trēs, a·cris, du·plex.** In Classical poetry this combination is often treated like any other pair of consonants: **pat·rēs, ac·ris, dup·lex**
   - **d)** prefixes form separate syllables even if the division is contrary to above rules: **ab·est, ob·lā·tus, abs·ti·nē·ō, ab·stō**
3. A syllable ending in a vowel or diphthong is called *open;* all others are called *closed*
4. The last syllable of a word is called the *ultima;* the next to last is called the *penult;* the one before the penult is called the *antepenult*

---

* The double consonant **x** goes with the preceding vowel: **dīx·it**

Quantity of Vowels

1. A vowel is *long* **(lēvis)** or *short* **(levis)** according to the length of time required for its pronunciation

2. A vowel is long:

a) before **ns, nf: ingēns, īnfāns**

3. A vowel is short (with some rare exceptions):

a) before another vowel or **h: dea, trahō**

b) generally before **nd** and **nt: portandus, portant**

4. Diphthongs are long: **causa**

Quantity of Syllables

1. Syllables are distinguished as *long* or *short* according to the length of time required for their pronunciation
2. A syllable is long:
   - **a)** if it contains a long vowel or a diphthong: **vē·nī scrī·bō, caus·ae** (such a syllable is said to be *long by nature)*
   - **b)** if it contains a short vowel followed by **x, z,** or any two consonants except a mute (**b, d, g, p, t, c**) followed by **l** or **r: sax·um, Ma·zentius, mit·tō, cur·sor** (such a syllable is said to be *long by position,* but the vowel is pronounced *short)*
3. A syllable is short:
   - **a)** if it contains a short vowel followed by a vowel or by a single consonant (**h** is regarded as a consonant; **ch, ph, th, qu,** and sometimes **gu** and **su** are regarded as single consonants): **me·us, ni·hil, ge·rit, a·qua**
   - **b)** if it contains a short vowel followed by a mute (**b, d, g, p, t, c**) plus **l** or **r**, but it is sometimes long in verse: **fla·grāns, ba·ra·thrum, ce·le·brō** (such a syllable is said to be *common)*

Accent

1. Words of two syllables are accented on the first syllable: **ómnēs, tángō, gérit**
2. Words of more than two syllables are accented on the penult if it is long: **amícus, regúntur,** and on the antepenult if the penult is short: **família, géritur**
3. These rules apply to words with enclitics appended (**-ce, -dum, -met, -ne, -que, -ve**): **vósmet, laudátne, déaque** (nominative), **déāque** (ablative). Some Latin grammarians argued that the vowel before such enclitocs is accented, whether long or short; thus: **deā́que** and **deáque**
4. In the second declension, the contracted genitive and the contracted vocative of nouns in **-ius** and the contracted genitive of those in **-ium** retain the accent of the nominative: **Virgílī, ingénī**
5. Certain words which have lost a final **-e** retain the accent of the complete forms: **illíc** for **illíce, tantṓn** for **tantṓne**
6. Certain compounds of **faciō,** in which a feeling for the individuality of the components was preserved, retain the accent of the simple verb: **benefácit**

Guide to Latin Grammar

Nouns

	First Declension Singular	Second Declension Singular		
	rosa *f*	**sonus** *m*	**puer** *m*	**ager** *m*
	rose	*sound*	*boy*	*field*
Nom	ros**a**	son**us**	puer	ager
Gen	ros**ae**	son**ī**	puer**ī**	agr**ī**
Dat	ros**ae**	son**ō**	puer**ō**	agr**ō**
Acc	ros**am**	son**um**	puer**um**	agr**um**
Abl	ros**ā**	son**ō**	puer**ō**	agr**ō**

	First Declension Plural	Second Declension Plural		
Nom	ros**ae**	son**ī**	puer**ī**	agr**ī**
Gen	ros**ārum**	son**ōrum**	puer**ōrum**	agr**ōrum**
Dat	ros**īs**	son**īs**	puer**īs**	agr**īs**
Acc	ros**ās**	son**ōs**	puer**ōs**	agr**ōs**
Abl	ros**īs**	son**īs**	puer**īs**	agr**īs**

Second Declension Singular

	vir *m*	dōnum *n*	**servos** *m*	**fīlius** *m*	**ingenium** *n*
	man	*gift*	*servant*	*son*	*talent*
Nom	vir	dōn**um**	serv**os**	fīl**ius**	ingeni**um**
Gen	vir**ī**	dōn**ī**	serv**ī**	fīl·**iī** *or* **-ī**	ingen·**iī** *or* **-ī**
Dat	vir**ō**	dōn**ō**	serv**ō**	fīli**ō**	ingeni**ō**
Acc	vir**um**	dōn**um**	serv**om**	fīli**um**	ingeni**um**
Abl	vir**ō**	dōn**ō**	serv**ō**	fīli**ō**	ingeni**ō**

Second Declension Plural

Nom	vir**ī**	dōn**a**	serv**ī**	fīli**ī**	ingeni**a**
Gen	vir**ōrum**	dōn**ōrum**	serv**ōrum**	fīli**ōrum**	igeni**ōrum**
Dat	vir**īs**	dōn**īs**	serv**īs**	fīli**īs**	ingeni**īs**
Acc	vir**ōs**	dōn**a**	serv**ōs**	fīli**ōs**	ingeni**a**
Abl	vir**īs**	dōn**īs**	serv**īs**	fīli**īs**	ingeni**īs**

Notes
(a) The vocative singular of **-us** nouns ends in **-e: amīce**. The vocative singular (and sometimes the genitive singular) of **-ius** nouns ends in **-ī: fīlī, Tiberī**. But the vocative of **deus** is **deus**.
(b) The earlier inflection of masculine nouns of the second declension, down to Caesar and Cicero, followed the pattern of **servos.**

Third Declension Masculine/Feminine Nouns Singular

	rēx *m* *king*	**mīles** *m* *soldier*	**prīnceps** *m chief*	**māter** *f* *mother*
Nom	rēx	mīles	prīnceps	māt**er**
Gen	rēg**is**	mīlit**is**	prīncip**is**	mātr**is**
Dat	rēg**ī**	mīlit**ī**	prīncip**ī**	mātr**ī**
Acc	rēg**em**	mīlit**em**	prīncip**em**	mātr**em**
Abl	rēg**e**	mīlit**e**	prīncip**e**	mātr**e**

Third Declension Masculine/Feminine Nouns Plural

Nom	rēg**ēs**	mīlit**ēs**	prīncip**ēs**	mātr**ēs**
Gen	rēg**um**	mīlit**um**	prīncip**um**	mātr**um**
Dat	rēg**ibus**	mīlit**ibus**	prīncip**ibus**	mātr**ibus**
Acc	rēg**ēs**	mīlit**ēs**	prīncip**ēs**	mātr**ēs**
Abl	rēg**ibus**	mīlit**ibus**	prīncip**ibus**	mātr**ibus**

Third Declension Masculine/Feminine Nouns Singular

	hostis *m enemy*	**custōs** *m guard*	**vigil** *m* *fireman*	**nox** *f* *night*
Nom	host**is**	custōs	vigil	nox
Gen	host**is**	custōd**is**	vigil**is**	noct**is**
Dat	host**ī**	custōd**ī**	vigil**ī**	noct**ī**
Acc	host·**em** *or* **-im**	custōd**em**	vigil**em**	noct**em**
Abl	host·**e** *or* **-ī**	custōd**e**	vigil**e**	noct**e**

Third Declension Masculine/Feminine Nouns Plural

Nom	host**ēs**	custōd**ēs**	vigil**ēs**	noct**ēs**
Gen	host**ium**	custōd**um**	vigil**um**	noct**ium**
Dat	host**ibus**	custōd**ibus**	vigil**ibus**	noct**ibus**
Acc	host·**ēs** *or* **-īs**	custōd**ēs**	vigil**ēs**	noct**ēs**
Abl	host**ibus**	custōd**ibus**	vigil**ibus**	noct**ibus**

Third Declension Neuter Nouns Singular

	nōmen *n* *name*	**caput** *n* *head*	**opus** *n* *work*	**iter** *n* *road*	**mare** *n* *sea*	**animal** *n* *animal*	**cor** *n* *heart*
Nom	nōmen	caput	opus	iter	mar**e**	animal	cor
Gen	nōmin**is**	capit**is**	oper**is**	itiner**is**	mar**is**	animāl**is**	cord**is**
Dat	nōmin**ī**	capit**ī**	oper**ī**	itiner**ī**	mar**ī**	animāl**ī**	cord**ī**
Acc	nōmen	caput	opus	iter	mar**e**	animal	cor
Abl	nōmin**e**	capit**e**	oper**e**	itiner**e**	mar**ī**	animāl**ī**	cord**e**

Third Declension Neuter Nouns Plural

Nom	nōmin**a**	capit**a**	oper**a**	itiner**a**	mar**ia**	animāl**ia**	cord**a**
Gen	nōmin**um**	capit**um**	oper**um**	itiner**um**	mar**ium**	animāl**ium**	—
Dat	nōmin**ibus**	capit**ibus**	oper**ibus**	itiner**ibus**	mar**ibus**	animāl**ibus**	cord**ibus**
Acc	nōmin**a**	capit**a**	oper**a**	itiner**a**	mar**ia**	animāl**ia**	cord**a**
Abl	nōmin**ibus**	capit**ibus**	oper**ibus**	itiner**ibus**	mar**ibus**	animāl**ibus**	cord**ibus**

Notes **(a)** Masculine and feminine **i**-stem nouns, such as **hostis,** regularly end in **-is** in the nominative singular, and always have **-ium** in the genitive plural. The accusative singular ends in **-em** *or* **-im**, and the ablative in **-e** *or* **-ī**, and the accusative plural in **-ēs** *or* **-īs.**

(b) A number of monosyllabic nouns with mute stems (like **cor**) lack the genitive plural.

	Fourth Declension Singular			**Fifth Declension Singular**	
	fructus *m* *fruit*	**manus** *f* *hand*	**genū** *n* *knee*	**diēs** *m* *day*	**rēs** *f* *thing*
Nom	fruct**us**	man**us**	genū	di**ēs**	r**ēs**
Gen	fruct**ūs**	man**ūs**	gen**ūs**	di**ēī**	r**eī**
Dat	fruct**uī**	man**uī**	gen**ū**	di**ēī**	r**eī**
Acc	fruct**um**	man**um**	gen**ū**	di**em**	r**em**
Abl	fruct**ū**	man**ū**	gen**ū**	di**ē**	r**ē**

	Fourth Declension Plural			**Fifth Declension Plural**	
Nom	fruct**ūs**	man**ūs**	gen**ua**	di**ēs**	r**ēs**
Gen	fruct**uum**	man**uum**	gen**uum**	di**ērum**	r**ērum**
Dat	fruct**ibus**	man**ibus**	gen**ibus**	di**ēbus**	r**ēbus**
Acc	fruct**ūs**	man**ūs**	gen**ua**	di**ēs**	r**ēs**
Abl	fruct**ibus**	man**ibus**	gen**ibus**	di**ēbus**	r**ēbus**

Notes (a) Nouns of the fourth declension are mostly masculine nouns. The following nouns in **-us** are feminine: **acus** needle; **domus** house; **manus** hand; **porticus** colonnade; **tribus** tribe; **īdūs** *(pl)* Ides; also most names of trees, such as **quercus** oak.

(b) All fifth-declension nouns are feminine, except **diēs** *m* "day" and **merīdiēs** *m* "midday, noon." But **diēs** is sometimes feminine in the singular, especially in phrases indicating a fixed time, and regularly when used of time in general, e.g., **constitūtā diē** "on the appointed day"; **longa diēs** "a long time."

Greek Nouns

First Declension

Greek nouns that end in **-ē** are feminine; those that end in **-ās** and **-ēs** are masculine. In the plural, when found, they are declined like regular Latin nouns of the first declension.. In the singular they are declined as follows:

	Aenēās *m* *Aeneas*	Anchīsēs *m* *Anchises*	Pēnelopē *f* *Penelope*	Persēs *m* *Persian*
Nom	Aene**ās**	Anchīs**ēs**	Pēnelop**ē**	Pers**ēs**
Gen	Aenē**ae**	Anchīs**ae**	Pēnelop**ēs**	Pers**ae**
Dat	Aenē**ae**	Anchīs**ae**	Pēnelop**ae**	Pers**ae**
Acc	Aenē·**am** *or* **-ān**	Anchīs·**ēn, -am**	Pēnelop**ēn**	Pers·**ēn** *or* **-am**
Abl	Aenē**ā**	Anchīs·**ē** *or* **-ā**	Pēnelop**ē**	Pers·**ē** *or* **-ā**
Voc	Aenē·**ā** *or* **-a**	Anchīs·**ē** *or* **-ā** *or* **-a**	Pēnelop**ē**	Pers·**ē** *or* **-a**

Second Declension

Greek nouns of the second declension end in **-os** *or* **-ōs** and are masculine or feminine; those ending in **-on** are neuter. In the plural, when found, they are declined like regular Latin nouns. They are mostly proper names and are declined as follows in the singular:

	Lesbos *f* *Lesbos*	**Athōs** *m* *Athos*	**Īlion** *n* *Ilium*	**Panthūs** *m* *Panthus*
Nom	Lesb·**os** *or* **-us**	Ath·**ōs** *or* **-o**	Īli·**on** *or* **-um**	Panth**ūs**
Gen	Lesb**ī**	Ath·**ō** *or* **-ōnis**	Īli**ī**	Panth**ī**

Dat	Lesbō	Athō		Īliō	Panthō
Acc	Lesb·on *or* -um	Ath·ōn *or* -ōnem		Īli·on *or* -um	Panthūn
Abl	Lesbō	Ath·ō *or* -ōne		Īliō	Panthō
Voc	Lesbō	Athōs		Īli·on *or* -um	Panthū

Third Declension Singular

	hērōs *m*	basis *f*	nāïs *f*	tigris *mf*	lampas *f*
	hero	base	naiad	tiger	torch
Nom	hērōs	basis	nāïs	tigris	lampas
Gen	hērōïs	bas·eōs *or* -idos	nāïd·os *or* -is	tigr·is *or* -idis	lampados
Dat	hērōï	basī	nāïdī	tigrī	lampadī
Acc	hērōa	bas·in *or* -ida *or* -im	nāïda	tigr·in *or* -idem	lampada
Abl	hērōë	basī	nāïde	tigr·ī *or* -ide	lampade

Third Declension Plural

Nom	hērōes	basēs	nāïdes	tigrēs	lampades
Gen	hērōum	bas·eōn *or* -ium	nāïdum	tigrium	lampadum
Dat	hērōïbus	basibus	nāïdibus	tigribus	lampadibus
Acc	hērōas	basīs *or* -eīs	nāïdas	tigr·īs *or* -idas	lampadas
Abl	hērōïbus	basibus	nāïdibus	tigribus	lampadibus

Third Declension Proper Names

Nom	Dīdō	Capys	Paris		Orpheûs
Gen	Dīdōnis *or* Dīdūs	Capyos	Paridis		Orph·eī *or* -eōs
Dat	Dīdōnī *or* Dīdō	Capyī	Paridī		Orph·eō *or* -eī
Acc	Dīdō *or* Dīdōnem	Capyn	Parid·em *or* -im *or* -in		Orphe·um *or* -a
Abl	Dīdōne *or* -ō	Capyë	Paridē *or* Parī		Orpheō
Voc	Dīdō	Capy	Pari		Orpheû

Nom	Periclēs	Simoïs	Atlās	Selīnūs
Gen	Pericl·is *or* -ī	Simoënt·is *or* -os	Atlantis	Selīnuntis
Dat	Pericl·ī *or* -i	Simoëntī	Atlantī	Selīnuntī
Acc	Pericl·em *or* -ea *or* -ēn	Simoënta	Atlanta	Selīnuntā
Abl	Pericle	Simoënte	Atlante	Selīnunte
Voc	Pericl·ēs *or* -ē	Simoïs	Atlā	Selīnūs

Notes (a) The regular Latin forms may be used for most of the above.

(b) Most stems in **id-** *(nom: -*is**)**, as **tigris**, often have also the forms of **i**-stems: *gen:* **-idis** *or* **-idos** *or* **-is**; *acc:* **-idem** *or* **-ida** *or* **-im** *or* **-in**; *abl:* **-ide** *or* **-ī**. However, most feminine proper names have *acc* **-idem** *or* **-ida**, *abl:* **-ide**, — not **-im** *or* **-ī**.

(c) Stems in **ant-, ent-,** and a few in **unt-** follow the model of **Simoïs, -entis, Atlās, -antis** and **Selīnūs -untis**.

(d) Many Greek names, of the third declension in Latin, pass over into the first declension in the plural, as, **Hyperid·ae -ārum**, etc.

(e) Many names in **-ēs** belonging to the third declension have also genitive in **-ī**, e.g., **Pericl·ēs -is** *or* **-ī**.

(f) Greek names in **-eûs**, like **Orpheûs**, have forms of the second and third declensions.

(g) Greek nouns of the third declension end in **-es** in the nominative plural, as **Phryges** Phrygians, and end in **-as** in the accusative plural, as **Phrygas** Phrygians.

Pronouns

Personal Pronouns

	ego *I*	**tu** *you*	**is** *he*	**ea** *she*	**id** *it*
			SINGULAR		
	1st Pers	*2nd Pers*		*3rd Pers*	
NOM	ego	tū	is	ea	id
GEN	meī	tuī	ēius	ēius	ēius
DAT	mihi *or* mī	tibi	ī	eī	eī
ACC	mē	tē	eum	eam	id
ABL	mē	tē	eō	eā	eō
			PLURAL		
	1st Pers	*2nd Pers*		*3rd Pers*	
NOM	nōs	vōs	eī *or* iī	eae	ea
GEN	nostrum	vestrum	eōrum	eārum	eōrum
	nostrī	vestrī			
DAT	nōbīs	vōbīs	eīs	eīs	eīs
ACC	nōs	vōs	eōs	eās	ea
ABL	nōbīs	vōbīs	eīs	eīs	eīs

NOTES (a) The forms **nostrum** and **vestrum** are used partitively, e.g., **ūnusquisque nostrum** each one of us; otherwise, the forms **nostrī** and **vestrī** are used, e.g., **meminit vestrī** he remembered you.

(b) The form **mī** is sometimes used in poetry instead of **mihi.**

Reflexive Pronouns

		SINGULAR	
	1st Pers	*2nd Pers*	*3rd Pers*
NOM	——	——	——
GEN	meī	tuī	suī
DAT	mihi	tibi	sibi
ACC	mē	tē	sē *or* sēsē
ABL	mē	tē	sē *or* sēsē

NOTES (a) The reflexive of the third person serves for *all genders* of both singular and plural. Thus, **suī** may mean "of himself," "of herself," "of itself," or "of themselves;" **sibi** may mean "to himself," "to herself," or "to themselves," etc.

(b) All of the reflexive pronouns can serve as reciprocal pronouns, e.g., **inter sē culpant** they blame each other (one another).

		PLURAL	
	1st Pers	*2nd Pers*	*3rd Pers*
NOM	——	——	——
GEN	nostrī	vestrī	suī
DAT	nōbīs	vōbīs	sibi
ACC	nōs	vōs	sē *or* sēsē
ABL	nōbīs	vōbīs	sē *or* sēsē

Demonstrative Pronouns

hic this (one) **haec** this (one) **hoc** this (one)

SINGULAR

	masc	*fem*	*neut*
NOM	hīc	haec	hōc
GEN	hūius	hūius	hūius
DAT	huic	huic	huic
ACC	hunc	hanc	hōc
ABL	hōc	hāc	hōc

PLURAL

	masc	*fem*	*neut*
NOM	hī	hae	haec
GEN	hōrum	hārum	hōrum
DAT	hīs	hīs	hīs
ACC	hōs	hās	haec
ABL	hīs	hīs	hīs

ille that (one) **illa** that (one) **illud** that (one)

SINGULAR

	masc	*fem*	*neut*
NOM	ille	illa	illud
GEN	illīus	illīus	illīus
DAT	illī	illī	illī
ACC	illum	illam	illud
ABL	illō	illā	illō

PLURAL

	masc	*fem*	*neut*
NOM	illī	illae	illa
GEN	illōrum	illārum	illōrum
DAT	illīs	illīs	illīs
ACC	illōs	illās	illa
ABL	illīs	illīs	illīs

NOTES (a) **Iste, ista, istud** ("that") is declined like **ille.**

(b) **Ille** and **iste** appear in combination with the demonstrative particle **-c,** shortened from **-ce** (giving the sense "that there") in the following forms:

SINGULAR

	masc	*fem*	*neut*
NOM	illic	illaec	illuc *or* illoc
ACC	illunc	illanc	illuc *or* illoc
ABL	illōc	illāc	illōc

PLURAL

	masc	*fem*	*neut*
NOM	——	——	illaec
ACC	——	——	illaec

	masc	fem	neut
	SINGULAR		
NOM	istic	istaec	istuc *or* istoc
ACC	istunc	istanc	istuc *or* istoc
ABL	istōc	istāc	istōc
	PLURAL		
NOM	——	——	istaec
ACC	——	——	istaec

	īdem the same	**eadem** the same	**idem** the same
	SINGULAR		
	masc	*fem*	*neut*
NOM	īdem	eadem	idem
GEN	ēiusdem	ēiusdem	ēiusdem
DAT	eīdem	eīdem	eīdem
ACC	eundem	eandem	idem
ABL	eōdem	eādem	eōdem
	PLURAL		
	masc	*fem*	*neut*
NOM	eīdem *or* iīdem	eaedem	eadem
GEN	eōrundem	eārundem	eōrundem
DAT	eīsdem *or* īsdem	eīsdem *or* īsdem	eīsdem *or* īsdem
ACC	eōsdem	eāsdem	eadem
ABL	eīsdem *or* īsdem	eīsdem *or* īsdem	eīsdem *or* īsdem

Intensive Pronouns

	ipse -self	**ipsa** -self	**ipsum** -self
	SINGULAR		
	masc	*fem*	*neut*
NOM	ipse	ipsa	ipsum
GEN	ipsīus	ipsīus	ipsīus
DAT	ipsī	ipsī	ipsī
ACC	ipsum	ipsam	ipsum
ABL	ipsō	ipsā	ipsō
	PLURAL		
	masc	*fem*	*neut*
NOM	ipsī	ipsae	ipsa
GEN	ipsōrum	ipsārum	ipsōrum
DAT	ipsīs	ipsīs	ipsīs
ACC	ipsōs	ipsās	ipsa
ABL	ipsīs	ipsīs	ipsīs

Relative Pronouns

	quī who, that	**quae** who, that	**quod** which, that
		SINGULAR	
	masc	*fem*	*neut*
NOM	quī	quae	quod
GEN	cūius	cūius	cūius
DAT	cui	cui	cui
ACC	quem	quam	quod
ABL	quō	quā	quō
		PLURAL	
	masc	*fem*	*neut*
NOM	quī	quae	quae
GEN	quōrum	quārum	quōrum
DAT	quibus	quibus	quibus
ACC	quōs	quās	quae
ABL	quibus	quibus	quibus

NOTE (a) The interrogative adjective **quī, quae, quod** (what? what kind of? which?), is declined throughout like the relative pronoun.

Interrogative Pronouns

	quis who?	**quid** what?
	masc & fem	*neut*
NOM	quis	quid
GEN	cūius	cūius
DAT	cui	cui
ACC	quem	quid
ABL	quō	quō

NOTES (a) The rare form of the plural follows the declension of the relative pronoun.

(b) **Quī** is sometimes used for **quis** in indirect questions.

(c) **Quis,** when modifying words denoting persons, is sometimes an adjective: **quis homō** = what man? whereas **quī homō** = what sort of man?

(d) The pronoun **quis** and the pronominal adjective **quī** may be strengthened by adding **-nam,** e. g., **quisnam** just who? exactly who?; **quidnam** just what?, exactly what?; **quīnam, quaenam, quodnam** of exactly what kind?

Indefinite Pronouns

	aliquis somone	**aliqua** someone	**aliquid** something
		SINGULAR	
	masc	*fem*	*neut*
NOM	aliquis (aliquī)	aliqua	aliquid (aliquod)
GEN	alicūius	alicūius	alicūius
DAT	alicui	alicui	alicui
ACC	aliquem	aliquam	aliquid (aliquod)
ABL	aliquō	aliquā	aliquō
		PLURAL	
	masc	*fem*	*neut*
NOM	aliquī	aliquae	aliqua
GEN	aliquōrum	aliquārum	aliquōrum
DAT	aliquibus	aliquibus	aliquibus
ACC	aliquōs	aliquās	aliqua
ABL	aliquibus	aliquibus	aliquibus

NOTES (a) The indefinite adjective **aliquī** "some" is declined in the same way as the indefinite pronoun **aliquis** "someone" except in the three cases indicated above in parentheses: nominative masculine singular, neuter nominative singular, and neuter accusative singular.

(b) **Quis** is used instead of **aliquis** after **nē, sī, nisi,** and **num,** e.g., **sī quis** "if anyone."

	quīdam, quaedam a certain person		**quiddam** a certain thing
		SINGULAR	
	masc	*fem*	*neut*
NOM	quīdam	quaedam	quiddam
GEN	cūiusdam	cūiusdam	cūiusdam
DAT	cuidam	cuidam	cuidam
ACC	quendam	quandam	quiddam
ABL	quōdam	quādam	quōdam
		PLURAL	
	masc	*fem*	*neut*
NOM	quīdam	quaedam	quaedam
GEN	quōrundam	quārundam	quōrundam
DAT	quibusdam	quibusdam	quibusdam
ACC	quōsdam	quāsdam	quaedam
ABL	quibusdam	quibusdam	quibusdam

NOTES (a) The corresponding pronomimal adjective differs only in these forms: **quoddam** for **quiddam.**

(b) There are two indefinite relative pronouns: **quīcumque** and **quisquis** "whoever." **Quīcumque** declines only the first part; **quisquis** declines both but has only **quisquis, quidquid,** and **quōquō** in common use.

Adjectives

First and Second Declensions Singular

	bonus good			**tener** tender		
	masc	*fem*	*neu*	*masc*	*fem*	*neut*
Nom	bon**us**	bon**a**	bon**um**	tener	tener**a**	tener**um**
Gen	bon**ī**	bon**ae**	bon**ī**	tener**ī**	tener**ae**	tener**ī**
Dat	bon**ō**	bon**ae**	bon**ō**	tener**ō**	tener**ae**	tener**ō**
Acc	bon**um**	bon**am**	bon**um**	tener**um**	tener**am**	tener**um**
Abl	bon**ō**	bon**ā**	bon**ō**	tener**ō**	tener**ā**	tener**ō**

First and Second Declensions Plural

	masc	*fem*	*neu*	*masc*	*fem*	*neut*
Nom	bon**ī**	bon**ae**	bon**a**	tener**ī**	tener**ae**	tener**a**
Gen	bon**ōrum**	bon**ārum**	bon**ōrum**	tener**ōrum**	tener**ārum**	tener**ōrum**
Dat	bon**īs**	bon**īs**	bon**īs**	tener**īs**	tener**īs**	tener**īs**
Acc	bon**ōs**	bon**ās**	bon**a**	tener**ōs**	tener**ās**	tener**ā**
Abl	bon**īs**	bon**īs**	bon**īs**	tener**īs**	tener**īs**	tener**īs**

First and Second Declensions Singular

	sacer sacred		
	masc	*fem*	*neut*
Nom	sacer	sacr**a**	sacr**um**
Gen	sacr**ī**	sacr**ae**	sacr**ī**
Dat	sacr**ō**	sacr**ae**	sacr**ō**
Acc	sacr**um**	sacr**am**	sacr**um**
Abl	sacr**ō**	sacr**ā**	sacr**ō**

First and Second Declensions Plural

	masc	*fem*	*neut*
Nom	sacr**ī**	sacr**ae**	sacr**a**
Gen	sacr**ōrum**	sacr**ārum**	sacr**ōrum**
Dat	sacr**īs**	sacr**īs**	sacr**īs**
Acc	sacr**ōs**	sacr**ās**	sacr**a**
Abl	sacr**īs**	sacr**īs**	sacr**īs**

Nine Irregular Adjectives

alter the other . . . .*see below*
alius another . . . .*see below*
nūllus none . . . . .same as tōtus
neuter neither . . . . . . .same as uter
sōlus alone . . . . .same as tōtus
tōtus whole . . . .*see below*
ūllus any . . . . .same as tōtus
ūnus one . . . . .same as tōtus
uter which (of two)? . . . .*see below*

First and Second Declension Irregular Adjectives

They are declined in the singular as follows (the plural is regular):

	masc	*fem*	*neut*	*masc*	*fem*	*neut*
Nom	ali**us**	ali**a**	ali**ud**	alter	alter**a**	alter**um**
Gen	alter**īus**	alter**īus**	alter**īus**	alter**īus**	alter**īus**	alter**īus**
	al**īus**	al**īus**	al**īus**			
Dat	ali**ī**	ali**ī**	ali**ī**	alter**ī**	alter**ī**	alter**ī**
Acc	ali**um**	ali**am**	ali**ud**	alter**um**	alter**am**	alter**um**
Abl	ali**ō**	ali**ā**	ali**ō**	alter**ō**	alter**ā**	alter**ō**

	masc	*fem*	*neut*	*masc*	*fem*	*neut*
Nom	uter	utr**a**	utr**um**	tōt**us**	tōt**a**	tōt**um**
Gen	utr**īus**	utr**īus**	utr**īus**	tōt**īus**	tōt**īus**	tōt**īus**
Dat	utr**ī**	utr**ī**	utr**ī**	tōt**ī**	tōt**ī**	tōt**ī**
Acc	utr**um**	utr**am**	utr**um**	tōt**um**	tōt**am**	tōt**um**
Abl	utr**ō**	utr**ā**	utr**ō**	tōt**ō**	tōt**ā**	tōt**ō**

THIRD DECLENSION ADJECTIVES OF THREE ENDINGS: SINGULAR

alacer lively

	masc	*fem*	*neut*
NOM	alacer	alacr**is**	alacr**e**
GEN	alacr**is**	alacr**is**	alacr**is**
DAT	alacr**ī**	alacr**ī**	alacr**ī**
ACC	alacr**em**	alacr**em**	alacr**e**
ABL	alacr**ī**	alacr**ī**	alacr**ī**

THIRD DECLENSION ADJECTIVES OF THREE ENDINGS: PLURAL

	masc	*fem*	*neut*
NOM	alacr**ēs**	alacr**ēs**	alacr**ia**
GEN	alacr**ium**	alacr**ium**	alacr**ium**
DAT	alacr**ibus**	alacr**ibus**	alacr**ibus**
ACC	alacr·**ēs** *or* **-īs**	alacr·**ēs** *or* **-īs**	alacr**ia**
ABL	alacr**ibus**	alacr**ibus**	alcr**ibus**

THIRD DECLENSION ADJECTIVES OF TWO ENDINGS: SINGULAR

	fortis brave		**fortior** braver	
	masc & fem	*neut*	*masc & fem*	*neut*
NOM	fort**is**	fort**e**	fortior	fortius
GEN	fort**is**	fort**is**	fortiōr**is**	fortiōr**is**
DAT	fort**ī**	fort**ī**	fortiōr**ī**	fortiōr**ī**
ACC	fort**em**	fort**e**	fortiōr**em**	fortius
ABL	fort**ī**	fort**ī**	fortiō·**re** *or* **-rī**	fortiō·**re** *or* **-rī**

THIRD DECLENSION ADJECTIVES OF TWO ENDINGS: PLURAL

	masc & fem	*neut*	*masc & fem*	*neut*
NOM	fort**ēs**	fort**ia**	fortiōr**ēs**	fortiōr**a**
GEN	fort**ium**	fort**ium**	fortiōr**um**	fortiōr**um**
DAT	fort**ibus**	fort**ibus**	fortiōr**ibus**	fortiōr**ibus**
ACC	fort·**ēs** *or* **-īs**	fort**ia**	fortiōr·**ēs** *or* **-īs**	fortiōr**a**
ABL	fort**ibus**	fort**ibus**	fortiōr**ibus**	fortiōr**ibus**

THIRD DECLENSION ADJECTIVES OF ONE ENDING: SINGULAR

	audāx bold		**potēns** powerful		**vetus** old	
	masc & fem	*neut*	*masc & fem*	*neut*	*masc & fem*	*neut*
NOM	audāx	audāx	potēns	potēns	vetus	vetus
GEN	audāc**is**	audāc**is**	potent**is**	potent**is**	veter**is**	veter**is**
DAT	audāc**ī**	audāc**ī**	potent**ī**	potent**ī**	veter**ī**	veter**ī**
ACC	audāc**em**	audāx	potent**em**	potēns	veter**em**	vetus
ABL	audāc**ī**	audāc**ī**	potent**ī**	potent**ī**	veter**e**	veter**e**

THIRD DECLENSION ADJECTIVES OF ONE ENDING: PLURAL

	masc & fem	*neut*	*masc & fem*	*neut*	*masc & fem*	*neut*
NOM	audāc**ēs**	audāc**ia**	potent**ēs**	potent**ia**	veter**ēs**	veter**a**
GEN	audāc**ium**	audāc**ium**	potent**ium**	potent**ium**	veter**um**	veter**um**
DAT	audāc**ibus**	audāc**ibus**	potent**ibus**	potent**ibus**	veter**ibus**	veter**ibus**
ACC	audāc·**ēs -īs**	audāc**ia**	potent**ēs**	potent**ia**	veter**ēs**	veter**a**
ABL	audāc**ibus**	audāc**ibus**	potent**ibus**	potent**ibus**	veter**ibus**	veter**ibus**

Comparison of Irregular Adjectives

Positive	*Comparative*	*Superlative*
bonus, *good*	mel**ior,** *better*	opt**imus,** *best*
exter, *external*	exter**ior**, *outer*	extr**ēmus**, *outermost*
frūgī, *thrifty*	frūgāl**ior,** *thriftier*	frūgāl**issimus**, *thriftiest*
magnus, *big*	mā**ior,** *bigger*	max**imus**, *biggest*
malus, *bad*	pē**ior,** *worse*	pess**imus**, *worst*
multus, *bad*	plūs, *more*	plūr**imus**, *most*
nēquam, *worthless*	nēqu**ior,** *worse*	nēqu**issimus**, *worst*
posterus, *following*	poster**ior**, *later*	postr**ēmus**, postu**mus**, *last*
superus, *upper*	super**ior,** *higher*	supr**ēmus**, sum**mus**, *highest*
————	dēter**ior,** *worse*	dēter**rimus**, *worst*
————	īnfer**ior**, *lower*	īnf**imus, īmus**, *lowest*
————	inter**ior,** *inner*	int**imus,** *innermost*
————	ōc**ior,** *swifter*	ōc**issimus,** *swiftest*
————	pot**ior,** *preferable*	pot**issimus,** *most important*
————	pr**ior,** *former*	prī**mus,** *first*
————	prop**ior,** *nearer*	prox**imus,** *nearest*
falsus, *false*	————	fals**issimus,** *most false*
fīdus, *faithful*	————	fīd**issimus**, *most faithful*
novus, *new*	(recent**ior**), *more recent*	nov**issimus**, *latest, newest*
parvus, *small*	minor, *smaller*	minimus, *smallest*
sacer, *sacred*	————	sacer**rimus**, *most sacred*
vetus, *old*	(vetust**ior**), *older*	veter**rimus**, *oldest*

Notes **(a)** For the declension of the comparative degree, see **fortior, fortius** above.

(b) Adjectives in **-er** form the superlative by adding **-rimus** to the nominative of the positive. The comparative is regular. Thus:

ācer, *sharp*	ācr**ior,** *sharper*	ācer**rimus,** *sharpest*
celer, *swift*	celer**ior**, *swifter*	celer**rimus**, *swiftest*
miser, *wretched*	miser**ior,** *more w.*	miser**rimus**, *most w.*

(c) Five adjectives in **-ilis** form the superlative by adding **-limus** to the stem of the positive. The comparison is regular. Thus:

facilis, *easy*	facil**ior,** *easier*	facil**limus**, *easiest*
difficilis, *difficult*	difficil**ior,** *more d.*	difficil**limus** *most d.*
similis, *similar*	simil**ior,** *more s.*	simil**limus,** *most s.*
dissimilis, *unlike*	dissimil**ior,** *more u.*	dissimil**limus**, *most u.*
humilis, *low*	humil**ior,** *lower*	humil**limus,** *lowest*

Adverbs

Comparison of Irregular Adverbs

bene, *well*	mel**ius,** *better*	opt**imē**, *best*
diū, *long*	diūt**ius,** *longer*	diūt**issimē**, *longest*
magnopere, *greatly*	mag**is,** *more*	max**imē**, *most*
male, *badly*	pē**ius,** *worse*	pess**imē**, *worst*
multum, *much*	plūs, *more*	plūr**imum**, *most*
nēquiter, *worthlessly*	nēqu**ius,** *more w.*	nēqu**issimē**, *most w.*
nūper, *recently*	————	nūper**rimē**, *most r.*
parum, *little*	min**us,** *less*	min**imē**, *least*
prope, *near*	prop**ius,** *more c.*	prox**imē,** *most c.*
saepe, *often*	saep**ius,** *oftener*	saep**issimē,** *most o.*
secus, *otherwise*	sēt**ius,** *less*	————
————	pot**ius,** *rather*	pot**issimum,** *especially*
————	pr**ius,** *previously*	prī**mum,** *first*

First Conjugation Verbs

Principal parts:	**amō**	*I love, am loving*
	amāre	*to love*
	amāvī	*I loved, I have loved*
	amātus	*(having been) loved*

Indicative Mood

Active Voice		*Passive Voice*	
Singular	*Plural*	*Singular*	*Plural*
PRESENT			
amō	amāmus	amor	amāmur
amās	amātis	amā·ris *or* -re	amāminī
amat	amant	amātur	amantur
IMPERFECT			
amābam	amābāmus	amābar	amābāmur
amābās	amābātis	amābā·ris *or* -re	amābāminī
amābat	amābant	amābātur	amābantur
FUTURE			
amābō	amābimus	amābor	amābimur
amābis	amābitis	amābe·ris *or* -re	amābiminī
amābit	amābunt	amābitur	amābuntur
PERFECT			
amāvī	amāvimus	amātus sum	amātī sumus
amāvistī	amāvistis	amātus es	amātī estis
amāvit	amāvē·runt *or* -re	amātus est	amātī sunt
PLUPERFECT			
amāveram	amāverāmus	amātus eram	amātī erāmus
amāverās	amāverātis	amātus erās	amātī erātis
amāverat	amāverant	amātus erat	amātī erant
FUTURE PERFECT			
amāverō	amāverimus	amātus erō	amātī erimus
amāveris	amāveritis	amātus eris	amātī eritis
amāverit	amāverint	amātus erit	amātī erunt

Subjunctive Mood

Active Voice		Passive Voice	
Singular	*Plural*	*Singular*	*Plural*
PRESENT			
amem	amēmus	amer	amēmur
amēs	amētis	amē·ris *or* -re	amēminī
amet	ament	amētur	amentur
IMPERFECT			
amārem	amārēmus	amārer	amārēmur
amārēs	amārētis	amārē·ris *or* -re	amārēminī
amāret	amārent	amārētur	amārentur
PERFECT			
amāverim	amāverimus	amātus sim	amātī sīmus
amāveris	amāveritis	amātus sīs	amātī sītis
amāverit	amāverint	amātus sit	amātī sint
PLUPERFECT			
amāvissem	amāvissēmus	amātus essem	amātī essēmus
amāvissēs	amāvissētis	amātus essēs	amātī essētis
amāvisset	amāvissent	amātus esset	amātī essent

Imperative Mood

Active Voice		Passive Voice	
Singular	*Plural*	*Singular*	*Plural*
PRESENT			
amā *(2nd pers)*	amāte *(2nd pers)*	amāre *(2nd pers)*	amāminī *(2nd pers)*
FUTURE			
amātō *(2nd pers)*	amātōte *(2nd pers)*	amātor *(2nd pers)*	———
amātō *(3rd pers)*	amantō *(3rd pers)*	amātor *(3rd pers)*	amantor *(3rd pers)*

Infinitive	**Participle**	**Infinitive**	**Participle**
PRESENT			
amāre	am·āns, -antis	amārī	———
PERFECT			
amāvisse	———	amātus esse	amātus
FUTURE			
amātūrus esse	amātūrus	amātum īrī	amandus *(gerundive)*

	Gerund	**Supine**
GEN	amandī	———
DAT	amandō	———
ACC	amandum	amātum
ABL	amandō	amātū

Second Conjugation Verbs

Principal parts:	**moneō**	*I advise, am advising*
	monēre	*to advise*
	monuī	*I advised, have advised*
	monitus	*(having been) advised*

Indicative Mood

Active Voice		*Passive Voice*	
Singular	*Plural*	*Singular*	*Plural*
PRESENT			
mone**ō**	monē**mus**	mone**or**	monē**mur**
monē**s**	monē**tis**	monē**·ris** *or* **-re**	monē**minī**
mone**t**	mone**nt**	monē**tur**	mone**ntur**
IMPERFECT			
monē**bam**	monē**bāmus**	monē**bar**	monē**bāmur**
monē**bās**	monē**bātis**	monē**bā·ris** *or* **-re**	monē**bāminī**
monē**bat**	monē**bant**	monē**bātur**	monē**bantur**
FUTURE			
monē**bō**	monē**bimus**	monē**bor**	monē**bimur**
monē**bis**	monē**bitis**	monē**be·ris** *or* **-re**	monē**biminī**
monē**bit**	monē**bunt**	monē**bitur**	monē**buntur**
PERFECT			
monu**ī**	monu**imus**	monitus **sum**	monitī **sumus**
monu**istī**	monu**istis**	monitus **es**	monitī **estis**
monu**it**	monu**ē·runt** *or* **-re**	monitus **est**	monitī **sunt**
PLUPERFECT			
monu**eram**	monu**erāmus**	monitus **eram**	monitī **erāmus**
monu**erās**	monu**erātis**	monitus **erās**	monitī **erātis**
monu**erat**	monu**erant**	monitus **erat**	monitī **erant**
FUTURE PERFECT			
monu**erō**	monu**erimus**	monitus **erō**	monitī **erimus**
monu**eris**	monu**eritis**	monitus **eris**	monitī **eritis**
monu**erit**	monu**erint**	monitus **erit**	monitī **erunt**

Subjunctive Mood

Active Voice		*Passive Voice*	
Singular	*Plural*	*Singular*	*Plural*
PRESENT			
moneam	moneāmus	monear	moneāmur
moneās	moneātis	moneā·ris *or* -re	moneāminī
moneat	moneant	moneātur	moneantur
IMPERFECT			
monērem	monērēmus	monērer	monērēmur
monērēs	monērētis	monērē·ris *or* -re	monērēminī
monēret	monērent	monērētur	monērentur
PERFECT			
monuerim	monuerimus	monitus sim	monitī sīmus
monueris	monueritis	monitus sīs	monitī sītis
monuerit	monuerint	monitus sit	monitī sint
PLUPERFECT			
monuissem	monuissēmus	monitus essem	monitī essēmus
monuissēs	monuissētis	monitus essēs	monitī essētis
monuisset	monuissent	monitus esset	monitī essent

Imperative Mood

Active Voice		*Passive Voice*	
Singular	*Plural*	*Singular*	*Plural*
PRESENT			
monē *(2nd pers)*	monēte *(2nd pers)*	monēre *(2nd pers)*	monēminī *(2nd pers)*
FUTURE			
monētō *(2nd pers)*	monētōte *(2nd pers)*	monētor *(2nd pers)*	———
monētō *(3rd pers)*	monentō *(3rd pers)*	monētor *(3rd pers)*	monentor *(3rd pers)*

Infinitive	**Participle**	**Infinitive**	**Participle**
PRESENT			
monēre	mon·ēns, -entis	monērī	———
PERFECT			
monuisse	———	monitus esse	monitus
FUTURE			
monitūrus esse	monitūrus	monitum īrī	monendus *(gerundive)*

	Gerund	**Supine**
GEN	monendī	———
DAT	monendō	———
ACC	monendum	monitum
ABL	monendō	monitū

Third Conjugation Verbs

Principal parts:	**regō**	*I rule, am ruling*
	regere	*to rule*
	rēxī	*I ruled, have ruled*
	rēctus	*(having been) ruled*

Indicative Mood

Active Voice		*Passive Voice*	
Singular	*Plural*	*Singular*	*Plural*
PRESENT			
regō	regimus	regor	regimur
regis	regitis	rege·ris *or* -re	regiminī
regit	regunt	regitur	reguntur
IMPERFECT			
regēbam	regēbāmus	regēbar	regēbamur
regēbās	regēbātis	regēbā·ris *or* -re	regēbāminī
regēbat	regēbant	regēbātur	regēbantur
FUTURE			
regam	regēmus	regar	regēmur
regēs	regētis	regēr·is *or* -re	regēminī
reget	regent	regētur	regentur
PERFECT			
rēxī	rēximus	rēctus sum	rēctī sumus
rēxistī	rēxistis	rēctus es	rēctī estis
rēxit	rēxē·runt *or* -re	rēctus est	rēctī sunt
PLUPERFECT			
rēxeram	rēxerāmus	rēctus eram	rēctī erāmus
rēxerās	rēxerātis	rēctus erās	rēctī erātis
rēxerat	rēxerant	rēctus erat	rēctī erant
FUTURE PERFECT			
rēxerō	rēxerimus	rēctus erō	rēctī erimus
rēxeris	rēxeritis	rēctus eris	rēctī eritis
rēxerit	rēxerint	rēctus erit	rēctī erunt

Subjunctive Mood

Active Voice		*Passive Voice*	
Singular	*Plural*	*Singular*	*Plural*
PRESENT			
regam	**regāmus**	**regar**	**regāmur**
regās	**regātis**	**regā·ris** *or* **-re**	**regāminī**
regat	**regant**	**regātur**	**regantur**
IMPERFECT			
regerem	**regerēmus**	**regerer**	**regerēmur**
regerēs	**regerētis**	**regerē·ris** *or* **-re**	**regerēminī**
regeret	**regerent**	**regerētur**	**regerentur**
PERFECT			
rēxerim	**rēxerimus**	**rēctus sim**	**rēctī sīmus**
rēxeris	**rēxeritis**	**rēctus sīs**	**rēctī sītis**
rēxerit	**rēxerint**	**rēctus sit**	**rēctī sint**
PLUPERFECT			
rēxissem	**rēxissēmus**	**rēctus essem**	**rēctī essēmus**
rēxissēs	**rēxissētis**	**rēctus essēs**	**rēctī essētis**
rēxisset	**rēxissent**	**rēctus esset**	**rēctī essent**

Imperative Mood

Active Voice		*Passive Voice*	
Singular	*Plural*	*Singular*	*Plural*
PRESENT			
rege *(2nd pers)*	**regite** *(2nd pers)*	**regere** *(2nd pers)*	**regiminī** *(2nd pers)*
FUTURE			
regitō *(2nd pers)*	**regitōte** *(2nd pers)*	**regitor** *(2nd pers)*	———
regitō *(3rd pers)*	**reguntō** *(3rd pers)*	**regitor** *(3rd pers)*	**reguntor** *(3rd pers)*

Infinitive	**Participle**	**Infinitive**	**Participle**
PRESENT			
regere	**reg·ēns, -entis**	**regī**	—
PERFECT			
rēxisse	—	**rēctus esse**	**rēctus**
FUTURE			
rēctūrus esse	**rēctūrus**	**rēctum īrī**	**rēgendus** *(gerundive)*

	Gerund	**Supine**
GEN	**regendī**	———
DAT	**regendō**	———
ACC	**regendum**	**rēctum**
ABL	**regendō**	**rēctū**

Third Conjugation Verbs in *-io*

Principal parts:	**capiō**	*I take, am taking*
	capere	*to take*
	cēpī	*I took, have taken*
	captus	*(having been) taken*

Indicative Mood

Active Voice		*Passive Voice*	
Singular	*Plural*	*Singular*	*Plural*
PRESENT			
capiō	**capimus**	**capior**	**capimur**
capis	**capitis**	**cape·ris** *or* **-re**	**capiminī**
capit	**capiunt**	**capitur**	**capiuntur**
IMPERFECT			
capiēbam	**capiēbāmus**	**capiēbar**	**capiēbāmur**
capiēbās	**capiēbātis**	**capiēbā·ris** *or* **-re**	**capiēbāminī**
capiēbat	**capiēbant**	**capiēbātur**	**capiēbāntur**
FUTURE			
capiam	**capiēmus**	**capiar**	**capiēmur**
capiēs	**capiētis**	**capiē·ris** *or* **-re**	**capiēminī**
capiet	**capient**	**capiētur**	**capientur**
PERFECT			
cēpī	**cēpimus**	**captus sum**	**captī sumus**
cēpistī	**cēpistis**	**captus es**	**captī estis**
cēpit	**cēpē·runt** *or* **-re**	**captus est**	**captī sunt**
PLUPERFECT			
cēperam	**cēperāmus**	**captus eram**	**captī erāmus**
cēperās	**cēperātis**	**captus erās**	**captī erātis**
cēperat	**cēperant**	**captus erat**	**captī erant**
FUTURE PERFECT			
cēperō	**cēperimus**	**captus erō**	**captī erimus**
cēperis	**cēperitis**	**captus eris**	**captī eritis**
cēperit	**cēperint**	**captus erit**	**captī erunt**

Subjunctive Mood

Active Voice		Passive Voice	
Singular	*Plural*	*Singular*	*Plural*
Present			
capiam	capiāmus	capiar	capiāmur
capiās	capiātis	capiā·ris *or* -re	capiāminī
capiat	capiant	capiātur	capiantur
Imperfect			
caperem	caperēmus	caperer	caperēmur
caperēs	caperētis	caperē·ris *or* -re	caperēminī
caperet	caperent	caperētur	caperentur
Perfect			
cēperim	cēperimus	captus sim	captī sīmus
cēperis	cēperitis	captus sīs	captī sītis
cēperit	cēperint	captus sit	captī sint
Pluperfect			
cēpissem	cēpissēmus	captus essem	captī essēmus
cēpissēs	cēpissētis	captus essēs	captī essētis
cēpisset	cēpissent	captus esset	captī essent

Imperative Mood

Active Voice		Passive Voice	
Singular	*Plural*	*Singular*	*Plural*
Present			
cape *(2nd pers)*	capite *(2nd pers)*	capere *(2nd pers)*	capiminī *(2nd pers)*
Future			
capitō *(2nd pers)*	capitōte *(2nd pers)*	capitor *(2nd pers)*	———
capitō *(3rd pers)*	capiuntō *(3rd pers)*	capitor *(3rd pers)*	capiuntor *(3rd pers)*

Infinitive	Participle	Infinitive	Participle
Present			
capere	cap·iēns, -entis	capī	———
Perfect			
cēpisse	———	captus esse	captus
Future			
captūrus esse	captūrus	captum īrī	capiendus *(gerundive)*

	Gerund	Supine
Gen	capiendī	———
Dat	capiendō	———
Acc	capiendum	captum
Abl	capiendō	captū

Fourth Conjugation Verbs

Principal parts:	**audiō**	*I hear, am hearing*
	audīre	*to hear*
	audīvī	*I heard, have heard*
	audītus	*(having been) heard*

Indicative Mood

Active Voice		*Passive Voice*	
Singular	*Plural*	*Singular*	*Plural*
PRESENT			
audi**ō**	aud**īmus**	aud**ior**	aud**īmur**
aud**īs**	aud**ītis**	aud**ī·ris** *or* **-re**	aud**īminī**
aud**it**	aud**iunt**	aud**ītur**	aud**iuntur**
IMPERFECT			
audi**ēbam**	audi**ēbāmus**	audi**ēbar**	audi**ēbāmur**
audi**ēbās**	audi**ēbātis**	audi**ēbā·ris** *or* **-re**	audi**ēbāminī**
audi**ēbat**	audi**ēbant**	audi**ēbātur**	audi**ēbantur**
FUTURE			
aud**iam**	audi**ēmus**	aud**iar**	audi**ēmur**
audi**ēs**	audi**ētis**	audi**ē·ris** *or* **-re**	audi**ēminī**
audi**et**	audi**ent**	audi**ētur**	audi**entur**
Perfect			
audīvī	audīv**imus**	audītus **sum**	audītī **sumus**
audīv**istī**	audīv**istis**	audītus **es**	audītī **estis**
audīv**it**	audīv**ēr·unt** *or* **-re**	audītus **est**	audītī **sunt**
PLUPERFECT			
audīv**eram**	audīv**erāmus**	audītus **eram**	audītī **erāmus**
audīv**erās**	audīv**erātis**	audītus **erās**	audītī **erātis**
audīv**erat**	audīv**erant**	audītus **erat**	audītī **erant**
FUTURE PERFECT			
audīv**erō**	audīv**erimus**	audītus **erō**	audītī **erimus**
audīv**eris**	audīv**eritis**	audītus **eris**	audītī **eritis**
audīv**erit**	audīv**erint**	audītus **erit**	audītī **erunt**

Subjunctive Mood

Active Voice		*Passive Voice*	
Singular	*Plural*	*Singular*	*Plural*
PRESENT			
aud**iam**	aud**iāmus**	aud**iar**	aud**iāmur**
aud**iās**	aud**iātis**	aud**iā·ris** *or* **-re**	aud**iāminī**
aud**iat**	aud**iant**	aud**iatur**	aud**iantur**
IMPERFECT			
aud**īrem**	aud**īrēmus**	aud**īrer**	aud**īrēmur**
aud**īrēs**	aud**īrētis**	aud**īrē·ris** *or* **-re**	aud**īrēminī**
aud**īret**	aud**īrent**	aud**īrētur**	aud**īrentur**
PERFECT			
audīv**erim**	audīv**erimus**	audīt**us sim**	audīt**ī sīmus**
audīv**eris**	audīv**eritis**	audīt**us sīs**	audīt**ī sītis**
audīv**erit**	audīv**erint**	audīt**us sit**	audīt**ī sint**
PLUPERFECT			
audīv**issem**	audīv**issēmus**	audīt**us essem**	audīt**ī essēmus**
audīv**issēs**	audīv**issētis**	audīt**us essēs**	audīt**ī essētis**
audīv**isset**	audīv**issent**	audīt**us esset**	audīt**ī essent**

Imperative Mood

Active Voice		*Passive Voice*	
Singular	*Plural*	*Singular*	*Plural*
PRESENT			
aud**ī** *(2nd pers)*	aud**īte** *(2nd pers)*	aud**īre** *(2nd pers)*	aud**īminī** *(2nd pers)*
FUTURE			
aud**ītō** *(2nd pers)*	aud**ītōte** *(2nd pers)*	aud**ītor** *(2nd pers)*	———
aud**ītō** *(3rd pers)*	aud**iuntō** *(3rd pers)*	aud**ītor** *(3rd pers)*	aud**iuntor** *(3rd pers)*

Infinitive	**Participle**	**Infinitive**	**Participle**
PRESENT			
aud**īre**	aud**i·ēns, -entis**	aud**īrī**	———
PERFECT			
audīv**isse**	———	audīt**us esse**	audīt**us**
FUTURE			
audīt**ūrus esse**	audīt**ūrus**	audīt**um īrī**	aud**iendus** *(gerundive)*

	Gerund	**Supine**
GEN	aud**iendī**	———
DAT	aud**iendō**	———
ACC	aud**iendum**	audīt**um**
ABL	aud**iendō**	audīt**ū**

Conjugation of *sum*

Principal parts:	**sum**	*I am*
	esse	*to be*
	fuī	*I was, have been*
	futūrus	*about to be*

Indicative Mood

Singular	*Plural*
PRESENT	
sum	**sumus**
es	**estis**
est	**sunt**
IMPERFECT	
eram	**erāmus**
erās	**erātis**
erat	**erant**
FUTURE	
erō	**erimus**
eris	**eritis**
erit	**erunt**
PERFECT	
fuī	**fuimus**
fuistī	**fuistis**
fuit	**fuē·runt** *or* **-re**
PLUPERFECT	
fueram	**fuerāmus**
fuerās	**fuerātis**
fuerat	**fuerant**
FUTURE PERFECT	
fuerō	**fuerimus**
fueris	**fueritis**
fuerit	**fuerint**

Subjunctive Mood

Singular	*Plural*
PRESENT	
sim	**sīmus**
sīs	**sītis**
sit	**sint**
IMPERFECT	
essem	**essēmus**
essēs	**essētis**
esset	**essent**
PERFECT	
fuerim	**fuerīmus**
fuerīs	**fuerītis**
fuerit	**fuerint**
PLUPERFECT	
fuissem	**fuissēmus**
fuissēs	**fuissētis**
fuisset	**fuissent**

Imperative Mood

Singular	*Plural*
PRESENT	
es *(2nd pers)*	**este** *(2nd pers)*
FUTURE	
estō *(2nd pers)*	**estōte** *(2nd pers)*
estō *(3rd pers)*	**suntō** *(3rd pers)*

Infinitive	**Participle**
PRESENT	
esse	———
PERFECT	
fuisse	———
FUTURE	
futūrus esse	**futūrus**

Conjugation of *vōlō, nōlō, mālō*

Principal parts:

volō	*I wish*	velle	*to wish*	voluī	*I wished*
nōlō	*I do not wish*	nōlle	*to be unwilling*	nōluī	*I did not wish*
mālō	*I prefer*	mālle	*to prefer*	māluī	*I preferred, have preferred*

Indicative Mood

PRESENT	volō	nōlō	mālō
	vīs	nōn vīs	māvīs
	vult	nōn vult	māvult
	volumus	nōlumus	mālumus
	vultis	nōn vultis	māvultis
	volunt	nōlunt	mālunt
IMPERFECT	volēbam	nōlēbam	mālēbam
FUTURE	volam	nōlam	mālam
PERFECT	voluī	nōluī	māluī
PLUPERFECT	volueram	nōlueram	mālueram
FUTURE PERFECT	voluerō	nōluerō	māluerō

Subjunctive Mood

PRESENT	velim	nōlim	mālim
	velīs	nōlīs	mālīs
	velīt	nōlīt	mālit
	velīmus	nōlīmus	mālīmus
	velītis	nōlītis	mālitis
	velint	nōlint	mālint
IMPERFECT	vellem	nollem	mallem
PERFECT	voluerim	nōluerim	māluerim
PLUPERFECT	voluissem	nōluissem	māluissem

Imperative Mood

PRESENT	nōlī; nōlīte *(2nd pers)*
FUTURE	nōlītō; nōlītōte *(2md pers)*
	nōlītō; nōluntō *(3rd pers)*

Infinitive

PRESENT	velle	nōlle	mālle
PERFECT	voluisse	nōluisse	māluisse

Participle

PRESENT	vol·ēns, -entis	nōl·ēns, -entis	———

Conjugation of *eo*

Principal parts:	**eō**	*I go, am going*
	īre	*to go*
	īvī *or* **iī**	*I went*
	itum (est)	*people went*

Indicative Mood

	Singular	*Plural*
PRESENT	eō	īmus
	īs	ītis
	it	eunt
IMPERFECT	**ībam**	**ībāmus**
FUTURE	**ībō**	**ībimus**
PERFECT	**īvī** *or* **iī**	**īvimus** *or* **iimus**
PLUPERFECT	**īveram** *or* **ieram**	**īverāmus** *or* **ierāmus**
FUTURE PERFECT	**īverō** *or* **ierō**	**īverimus** *or* **ierimus**

Subjunctive Mood

PRESENT	**eam**	**eāmus**
IMPERFECT	**īrem**	**īrēmus**
PERFECT	**īverim** *or* **ierim**	**īverīmus** *or* **ierīmus**
PLUPERFECT	**īvissem** *or* **iissem**	**īvissēmus** *or* **iissēmus**

Imperative Mood

PRESENT	**ī** *(2nd pers)*	**īte** *(2nd pers)*
FUTURE	**ītō** *(2nd pers)*	**ītōte** *(2nd pers)*
	ītō *(3rd pers)*	**euntō** *(3rd pers)*

	Infinitive	**Participle**
PRESENT	**īre**	**iēns, euntis**
PERFECT	**īvisse** *or* **isse**	———
FUTURE	**itūrus esse**	**itūrus**
		eundum *(gerundive)*

	Gerund	**Supine**
GEN	**eundī**	———
DAT	**eundō**	———
ACC	**eundum**	**itum**
ABL	**eundō**	**itū**

Conjugation of *fīō*

Principal parts:	**fīō**	*I am made, become*
	fierī	*to be made, become*
	factus sum	*I was made, became*

Indicative Mood

	Singular	*Plural*
PRESENT	fīō	fīmus
	fīs	fītis
	fit	fīunt
IMPERFECT	fīē**bam**	fīē**bāmus**
FUTURE	fī**am**	fī**ēmus**
PERFECT	factus **sum**	factī **sumus**
PLUPERFECT	factus **eram**	factī **erāmus**
FUTURE PERFECT	factus **erō**	factī erimus

Subjunctive Mood

PRESENT	fī**am**	fi**āmus**
IMPERFECT	fi**erem**	fi**erēmus**
PERFECT	factus **sim**	factī **sīmus**
PLUPERFECT	factus **essem**	factī **essēmus**

Imperative Mood

Singular	*Plural*
fī	fī**te**

	Infinitive	**Participle**
PRESENT	fierī	———
PERFECT	factus **esse**	factus
FUTURE	factum **īrī**	faciendus *(gerundive)*

Roman Numerals

	Cardinal	Ordinal	
1	ūnus, ūna, ūnum	prīmus	I
2	duo, duae, duo	secundus	II
3	trēs, tria	tertius	III
4	quattuor	quārtus	IV
5	quīnque	quīntus	V
6	sex	sextus	VI
7	septem	septimus	VII
8	octō	octāvus	VIII
9	novem	nōnus	IX
10	decem	decimus	X
11	ūndecim	ūndecimus	XI
12	duodecim	duodecimus	XII
13	tredecim	tertius decimus	XIII
14	quattuordecim	quārtus decimus	XIV
15	quīndecim	quīntus decimus	XV
16	sēdecim	sextus decimus	XVI
17	septendecim	septimus decimus	XVII
18	duodēvīgintī	duodēvīcēsimus	XVIII
19	ūndēvīgintī	ūndēvīcēsimus	XIX
20	vīgintī	vīcēsimus	XX
21	vīgintī ūnus ūnus et vīgintī	vīcēsimus prīmus	XXI
22	vīgintī duo duo et vīgintī	vīcēsimus secundus	XXII
30	trīgintā	trīcēsimus	XXX
40	quadrāgintā	quadrāgēsimus	XL
50	quīnquāgintā	quīnquāgēsimus	L
60	sexāgintā	sexāgēsimus	LX
70	septuāgintā	septuāgēsimus	LXX
80	octōgintā	octōgēsimus	LXXX
90	nōnāgintā	nōnāgēsimus	XC
100	centum	centēsimus	C
101	centum ūnus centum et ūnus	centēsimus prīmus	CI
200	ducentī, -ae, -a	ducentēsimus	CC
300	trecentī, -ae, -a	trecentēsimus	CCC
400	quadringentī, -ae, -a	quadringentēsimus	CCCC
500	quīngentī, -ae, -a	quīngentēsimus	D
600	sēscentī, -ae, -a	sēscentēsimus	DC
700	septingentī, -ae, -a	septingentēsimus	DCC
800	octingentī, -ae, -a	octingentēsimus	DCCC
900	nōngentī, -ae, -a	nōngentēsimus	DCCCC
1,000	mīlle	mīllēsimus	M
2,000	duo mīlia	bis mīllēsimus	MM
10,000	decem mīlia	deciēs mīllēsimus	CCIↃↃ
100,000	centum mīlia	centiēs mīllēsimus	CCCIↃↃↃ

NOTES (a) **-ēnsimus** and **-iēns** are often written in the numerals instead of **-ēsimus** and **-iēs.**
(b) The declension of **ūnus, ūna, ūnum** is indicated under "Nine Irregular Adjectives," p. 17.

DECLENSION OF DUO AND TRES

	masc	*fem*	*neut*	*masc*	*fem*	*neut*
NOM	duo	duae	duo	trēs	trēs	tria
GEN	duōrum	duārum	duōrum	trium	trium	trium
DAT	duōbus	duābus	duōbus	tribus	tribus	tribus
ACC	duōs, duo	duās	duo	trēs (trīs)	trēs (trīs)	tria
ABL	duōbus	duābus	duōbus	tribus	tribus	tribus

LATIN – ENGLISH

A

A, a *(supply* littera) *f* first letter of the Latin alphabet; letter name: **a**

A. *abbr* **Aulus** *(Roman first name, praenomen); (leg)* **Absolvō** I acquit; *(pol)* **Antīquō** I vote "no" *(on the bill)*

-ā *advl suf* forms adverbs which are also used as prepositions, *e.g.*, **suprā** above

-a *masc suf* indicating occupation or profession, *e.g.:* **agricola** one who tills a field, farmer; **scrība** one who writes, scribe

ā *or* **āh** *interj* ah!

ā- *or* **ab- abs-** *pref (before initial* **f** *becomes* **au-: auferre** to take away; *before* **p** *becomes* **as-: asportāre** to take away, carry off, *with the sense of:* **1** from, away, away from: **abdūcere** to lead away; **2** off: **abscīdere** to cut off; **3** at a distance: **abesse** to be at a distance, be absent; **4** completely, thoroughly: **abūtī** to use up, exhaust by using; **5** the absence of what the noun implies: **āmēns** demented; **6** a more remote degree of relationship: **abnepōs** great-great-grandson

ā *or* **ab** *prep (w. abl)* **1** *(of agency)* by, at the hands of: **ā Caesare in servitūtem redāctus** reduced to slavery by Caesar; **2** *(of time)* since, from, after: **ā puerō** since childhood; **ā somnō** after a sleep; **3** *(of space)* from, away from: **ā castrīs perfuga** a deserter from the camp; **4** *(named)* after: **oppidum ā Latīnī fīliā appellātum** a town named after the daughter of Latinus; **5** on: **ā dextrō latere** on the right side; **6** in: **ā tergō** in the rear; **ab ūnā parte corporis** in one part of the body; **7** *(of cause, motive)* out of, from: **ab singulārī amōre** out of unparalleled love; **8** *(designating an office):* **ab epistulīs** secretary; **ā ratiōnibus** accountant; **9** *(in respect to):* **dolēre ab stomachō** to have a stomachache (to ache in respect to the stomach); **10** on the side of: **ab senātū stāre** to side with the Senate (to stand on the side of the Senate)

abāctus *pp of* **abigō**

abac·us -ī *m* cupboard; game board; abacus *(calculator);* panel; tray

abaliēn·ō -āre -āvī -ātus *tr* to alienate, estrange; to sell; to separate; **alicūius animum ā sē abaliēnāre** to turn s.o. else's attention away from oneself

Abantiad·ēs -ae *m* descendant of Abas

Ab·ās -antis *m* 12th king of Argos, father of Acrisius, and grandfather of Perseus

abav·us -ī *m* great-great-grandfather *(a grandfather's grandfather)*

Abdēr·a -ōrum *npl or* **Abdēr·a -ae** *f* town in S. Thrace, notorious for the alleged stupidity of its people

abdicāti·ō -ōnis *f* abdication, renunciation, resignation; disowning; disinheriting

abdic·ō -āre -āvī -ātus *tr* to abdicate, renounce, resign; to disinherit **II** *refl* **sē magistrātū abdicāre** to resign from office

ab·dīcō -dīcere -dīxī -dictus *tr (in augury)* to disapprove of, forbid

abditē *adv* secretly, privately

abdit·us -a -um *adj* hidden, secret; secluded; abstruse; **abditus ā cōnspectū** hidden from view

ab·dō -dere -didī -ditus *tr* to hide; to remove, withdraw; to banish; to plunge *(e.g., a sword)* **II** *refl* to hide; **in litterīs sē abdere** to bury oneself in literature

abdōm·en -inis *n* abdomen, belly; *(fig)* gluttony, greed

ab·dūcō -dūcere -dūxī -ductus *tr* to lead away, take away; to withdraw *(troops);* to seduce; to alienate; *(w.* **ab)** to distinguish from; **animum abdūcere** to distract attention

Abell·a -ae *f* town in Campania, abounding in filbert nuts

ab·eō -īre -iī -itum *intr* to go away, depart; to disappear: **ab oculīs** *(or* **ē cōnspectū) abīre** to disappear from sight; to pass away, die; *(of time)* to pass, elapse; to change, be changed; to retire; **abī in malam rem**! *(sl)* go to hell!

abequit·ō -āre -āvī *intr* to ride off

aberrāti·ō -ōnis *f* wandering; escape, relief

aberr·ō -āre -āvī -ātum *intr* to wander, go astray; to get lost; to make a mistake, go wrong; to do wrong; to digress; *(of a stream)* to overflow; *(w.* **ab) 1** to disagree with; **2** to get one's mind off *(e.g., sadness);* **3** to deviate from; **4** to differ from

abesse *inf of* **absum**

abhinc *adv (w. acc or abl of time)* ago; **abhinc annōs centum** a hundred years ago

abhorr·eō -ēre -uī *intr* to shrink back; *(w.* **ab) 1** to be averse to; **2** to be inconsistent with; **3** to differ from; **4** to be free from

ab·iciō -icere -iēcī -iectus *tr* to throw away, throw down; to push away; to understate; to belittle, slight; to give up; to humble, debase; to cow, reduce to despair; to sell cheaply, sacrifice; to express carelessly *or* perfunctorily; to discard; to cease to wear, take off; to expose *(a child to die);* to leave *(a corpse)* unburied; to turn down *(an offer);* to give up *(practices, intentions, attitudes);* **animam** *(or* **vītam) abicere** to give up (this) life; **arma**

abicere to throw down one's arms **||** *refl* to throw oneself down, fall down; **sē ad pedēs alicūius abicere** to throw oneself down at s.o.'s feet; **sē in herbā abicere** to fall down on the grass

abiectē *adv* negligently; unworthily

abiect·us -a -um *adj* dejected, downhearted; undistinguished; unimportant; despicable; groveling

abiēgn·us -a -um *adj* fir, made of fir wood

abi·ēs -etis *f* fir (tree); ship; spear; writing tablet

ab·igō -igere -ēgī -āctus *tr* to drive away, get rid of; to banish, expel; to dispel

abit·us -ūs *m* departure; outlet; end

abiūdic·ō -āre -āvī -ātus *tr* to take away *(by judicial decree);* to reject

ab·iungō -iungere -iūnxī -iūnctus *tr* to unyoke; to detach **||** *refl (w.* **ab)** to detach oneself from, give up *(an activity);* **sē ab hōc refrāctāriolō dīcendī genere abiungere** to give up this quibbling style of speaking

abiūr·ō -āre -āvī -ātus *tr* to deny under oath

ablātīv·us -a -um *adj & m* ablative

ablāt·us -a -um *pp of* **auferō**

ablēgāti·ō -ōnis *f* sending off; banishment

ablēg·ō -āre -āvī -ātus *tr* to send away; to remove, banish; to dismiss, get rid of

abligū(r)r·iō -īre -īvī *or* **-iī** *tr* to eat up; *(coll)* to gobble up, waste, squander

abloc·ō -āre -āvī -ātus *tr* to lease, rent out

ab·lūdō -lūdere -lūsī lūsum *intr* to be out of tune; to be unlike; *(w.* **ab)** to differ from, fall short of

ab·luō -luere -luī -lūtus *tr* to wash away, cleanse, remove; to flush *(a toilet); (poet)* to bathe, refresh

abneg·ō -āre -āvī -ātus *tr* to refuse, turn down

abnep·ōs -ōtis *m* great-great-grandson

abnept·is -is *f* great-great-granddaughter

abnoct·ō -āre -āvī *intr* to spend the night, stay out all night

abnōrm·is -is -e *adj* irregular, unorthodox

ab·nuō -nuere -nuī *tr* to refuse *(to do s.th.);* to deny *(an assertion, allegation, one's guilt);* to repudiate responsibility for *(a crime);* to reject, refuse *(an offer);* to refuse to grant *(e.g., an interview);* to refuse to submit to *(authority);* to forbid, rule out *(e.g., hope);* to decline *(battle);* to refuse to perform *(a duty, task);* to disown *(children); (w. acc & inf)* to forbid *(the occurrence of an event);* **nōn abnuere** to admit, not to deny **||** *intr* to say "no"; *(w.* **dē** *+ abl)* to say "no" to; **dē societāte haud abnuērunt barbarī** the barbarians did not say "no" to (the idea of) an alliance

abnūt·ō -āre *intr* to keep saying "no" *(with a nod)*

abol·eō -ēre -ēvī -itus *tr* to abolish, efface; to destroy, obliterate; to banish from the mind, efface the memory of; to allow *(a practice)* to lapse, drop; to prohibit, ban; to put an end to *(an institution);* to rescind *(a law);* **abolēre memoriam** *(w. gen)* to blot out the memory of *(s.th. unpleasant);* **abolēre reum** *(leg)* to give up prosecuting a defendant

abol·ēscō -ēscere -ēvī *intr* to decay, vanish, die out; *(of things)* to be forgotten; *(of a memory)* to fade

aboliti·ō -ōnis *f* abolition, rescinding *(of a law, sentence);* amnesty

aboll·a -ae *f* cloak; *(fig)* wearer of a cloak, soldiers, philosophers

abōminand·us -a -um *adj* ill-omened; detestable, abominable

abōmin·or -ārī -ātus sum *tr* to loathe, detest; to seek to avert *(e.g., a bad omen, destruction)* by prayer

aborīgin·ēs -um *mpl* aborigines, original inhabitants, natives

ab·orior -orīrī -ortus sum *intr* to miscarry; to fail; *(of stars, etc.)* to set

aborti·ō -ōnis *f* miscarriage, abortion

abortīv·us -a -um *adj* prematurely born **||** *n* drug causing abortion

abort·us -ūs *m* miscarriage; **abortum facere** to have *or* to cause a miscarriage

ab·rādō -rādere -rāsī -rāsus *tr* to scrape off, shave; *(fig)* to squeeze out, extort

ab·ripiō -ripere -ripuī -reptus *tr* to take away by force, kidnap; to seize *(as booty);* to squander; *(of the wind)* to blow, drive *(off course);* to rescue *(from a bad situation);* **abripere mordicus** to bite off **||** *refl* to hurry away, get away

ab·rōdō -rōdere -rōsī -rōsus *tr* to gnaw off

abrogāti·ō -ōnis *f* repeal

abrog·ō -āre -āvī -ātus *tr* to repeal, annul

abroton·um -ī *n* **(hab-)** southernwood *(aromatic medicinal plant)*

ab·rumpō -rumpere -rūpī -ruptus *tr* to break off; to tear, sever; to burst apart *(e.g., the clouds);* to rupture *(a body part);* to put an end to, cut short **||** *refl (w. abl)* to dissociate oneself from

abruptē *adv* abruptly; rashly

abrupti·ō -ōnis *f* breaking off *(of relations);* divorce

abrupt·us -a -um *pp of* **abrumpō ||** *adj* abrupt, steep **||** *n* precipice

abs- *pref see* **ā-, ab-, abs-**

abs *prep (w. abl, confined almost exclusively to the combination* **abs tē)** by, from

abs·cēdō -cēdere -cessī -cessum *intr* **(aps)** to go away, depart; to vanish; to retire *(from work);* to desist; *(w. dat)* to cease to support; *(of feelings, illness)* to pass; *(of heavenly bodies)* to move farther away; *(mil)* to retreat; **nōn abscēdere ā corpore**

not to leave the body *(of a deceased person)*

abscessi·ō -ōnis *f* diminution, loss

abscess·us -ūs *m* departure; absence; remoteness

abs·cīdō -cīdere -cīdī -cīsus *tr* **(aps-)** to cut off, chop off; to cut short; to destroy *(hope);* to banish *(from the mind)*

ab·scindō -scindere -scidī -scissus *tr* to tear off, break off; to renounce; to divide

abscīs·us -a -um *pp of* **abscīdō ‖** *adj* steep, precipitous; concise; abrupt

abscissus *pp of* **abscindō**

absconditē *adv* secretly; obscurely; profoundly

abscondit·us -a -um *adj* concealed, secret; abstruse, profound

abscon·dō -dere -dī *or* **-didī -ditus** *tr* to hide; to keep secret, conceal; to lose sight of, leave behind; to shroud (in darkness); *(w.* **in** *+ acc)* to plunge *(weapon)* into **‖** *refl & pass* to hide

abs·ēns -entis *pres p of* **absum ‖** *adj* absent; in spite of being absent; non-existent; **mē absente** in my absence; **praesēns absēns** whether present or absent

absenti·a -ae *f* **(aps-)** absence; non-appearance in court

absil·iō -īre -(i)ī *intr* to jump away

absimil·is -is -e *adj (w. dat)* unlike

absinth·ium -(i)ī *n* wormwood *(plant yielding bitter extract, used in flavoring wine)*

abs·is -idis *f* **(aps-)** vault, arch; orbit *(of a star)*

ab·sistō -sistere -stitī *intr* to stand back, retire, withdraw, depart; to cease

absolūtē *adv* absolutely, perfectly, completely

absolūti·ō -ōnis *f* exhaustiveness, completeness; perfection; acquittal; release *(from an obligation)*

absolūtōri·us -a -um *adj* of acquittal, granting acquittal

absolūt·us -a -um *adj* perfect, complete, unqualified

absol·vō -vere -vī -ūtus *tr* **(aps-)** to release, set free; to detach; to acquit; to get *(s.o.)* acquitted; *(of single juror)* to vote for the acquittal of; to complete, finish *(task, transaction, book);* to put the finishing touches to *(an operation);* to pay off, discharge *(an account, debt); (w. gen or abl of the charge)* to prove *(s.o.)* innocent of; **verbō** *(or* **paucīs** *or* **breviter) absolvere** to sum up, put in a nutshell

abson·us -a -um *adj* **(aps-)** discordant, harsh *(sound);* unpleasant, jarring; *(w. dat or abl)* inconsistent with

absor·beō -bēre -buī *(or* **-psī) -ptus** *tr* **(aps-)** to swallow, devour; to absorb; to engross; to engulf

absque *prep* **(aps-)** *(w. abl)* without, apart from, but for: **absque mē foret** had it not been for me; **absque ūnā hāc foret** but for this one thing

abstēmi·us -a -um *adj* abstemious, temperate, sober

abster·geō -gēre -sī -sus *or* **absterg·ō -ere** *tr* **(aps-)** to wipe off, wipe dry; to expel, banish; **flētum abstergēre** to wipe away tears

absterr·eō -ēre -uī -itus *tr* **(aps-)** to scare away; to deter

abstin·ēns -entis *adj* temperate; forbearing; chaste; *(w. gen or abl)* showing restraint in respect to, not greedy for

abstinenter *adv* with restraint, incorruptibly

abstinenti·a -ae *f* restraint, self-control; integrity; *(w. gen or abl)* **1** restraint in respect to; **2** abstinence from

abs·tineō -tinēre -tinuī -tentus *tr* **(aps-)** to withold, keep away, hold back; to restrain **‖** *refl (w. abl or* **ab)** to refrain from, keep oneself from **‖** *intr* to abstain, refrain; *(w. gen, abl or w.* **ab,** *w. inf, w.* **quīn** *or* **quōminus)** to refrain from

abst·ō -āre *intr* **(aps-)** to stand at a distance, stand aloof

abstra·hō -here -xī -ctus *tr* **(aps-)** to pull away, draw away, remove; to detach; to split; to deduct, subtract; to distract, divert; to exclude, except

abstrū·dō -dere -sī -sus *tr* **(aps-)** to push away; to conceal, suppress **‖** *pass* to be concealed *(by intervening object)*

abstrūs·us -a -um *pp of* **abstrūdō (aps-) ‖** *adj* hidden, concealed, secret; profound, abstruse; reserved *(person);* secluded

abstulī *perf of* **auferō**

absum abesse āfuī āfutūrus *intr* to be away, be absent, be distant; to be missing; to be unsuitable, be inappropriate; to be wanting; *(w. abl or* **ab)** to be removed from, keep aloof from, be disinclined to; *(w.* **ab) 1** to be different from; **2** to be inconsistent with; **3** to be free from; **4** to be unsuitable for, be unfit for; *(w. dat)* to be of no help to; **ab hōc cōnsiliō abesse** to have no part in this strategy; **ā culpā abesse** to be free of guilt; **ā perīculīs abesse** to avoid dangers; **lēgātōs haud procul āfuit quīn violārent** they came close to outraging the ambassadors; **nōn multum aberat ab eō quīn** he was not far from, he was almost on the point of; **tantum aberat ā bellō, ut** he was so averse to war that

absūm·ō -ere -psī -ptus *tr* to take away, diminish; to consume, use up, waste; to exhaust; to destroy; to spend *(time);* to cause the death of, carry off **‖** *pass (w.* **in** *+ acc)* to disappear into

absurdē *adv* **(aps-)** out of tune; absurdly

absurd·us -a -um *adj* **(aps-)** out of tune; absurd, illogical, senseless, silly
Absyrt·us -ī *m* brother of Medea and son of Aeëtes, the king of Colchis
abund·āns -antis *adj* abundant, overflowing; affluent; more than enough; *(of rivers)* in flood; *(w. gen or abl)* abounding in, rich in
abundanter *adv* abundantly; profusely
abundanti·a -ae *f* abundance; affluence; lavishness; profusion
abundē *adv* abundantly, amply
abūsi·ō -ōnis *f* incorrect use *(of words)*
abūsque *prep (w. abl)* all the way from
ab·ūtor -ūtī -ūsus sum *intr (w. abl)* **1** to use up; **2** to misuse, abuse; **alicūius patientiā abūtī** to try s.o.'s patience
Abȳd·os *or* **Abȳd·us -ī** *f* town on the Hellespont
ac *conj (usually before consonants)* and, and also, and moreover; *(connecting a more emphatic sentence element)* and in particular, and what is more; *(connecting a sentence element which strengthens or corrects the first element)* and in fact; *(in comparisons)* than, as
Acadēmi·a -ae *f* Academy *(where Plato taught);* Platonic philosophy; Cicero's villa near Puteoli
Acadēmic·us -a -um *adj* Academic **II** *m* Academic philosopher **II** *npl* Cicero's treatise on Academic philosophy
acalanth·is -idis *f* goldfinch *(bird)*
acanth·us *or* **acanth·os -ī** *m (bot)* acanthus *(plant on whose leaves the architectural ornament of capitals of Corinthian columns was patterned)*
Acarnāni·a -ae *f* district in N.W. Greece
Acast·us -ī *m* son of Pelias
ac·cēdō -cēdere -cessī -cessum *tr* **(adc-)** to come up to, approach **II** *intr* to approach; *(w.* **ad***)* to come up to, approach; *(w. dat or* **ad***)* **1** to agree with, approve of, to go along with; **2** to be like, resemble; *(w.* **ad** *or* **in** *+ acc)* to enter upon, undertake; **accēdit ut** *or* **quod** there is the additional fact that
acceler·ō -āre -āvī -ātus *tr* to speed, quicken **II** *intr* to hurry
accen·dō -dere -dī -sus *tr* to light *(a fire, lamp);* to set on fire; to arouse *(emotions);* to aggravate *(conditions);* to work up, incite *(people);* to raise *(prices);* to light up, brighten; **accēnsa lūmina** lamp-lighting time, dusk
accēns·eō -ēre -uī -us *tr* to regard; to assign *(as attendant)*
accēns·us -a -um *pp of* **accendō II** *adj* on fire
accēns·us -ī *m* attendant, orderly **II** *mpl* rear-echelon troops
accent·us -ūs *m* accent, intonation
accepti·ō -ōnis *f* accepting, receiving
accept·ō -āre -āvī -ātus *tr* to accept, receive *(regularly);* to be given *(a name)*
accept·or -ōris *m* recipient; approver
acceptr·īx -īcis *f* recipient *(female)*
accept·us -a -um *pp of* **accipiō II** *adj* welcome, pleasing, acceptable **II** *n* receipt; credit side *(in account books);* **acceptum facere** *(or* **ferre***)* to treat *(a debt)* as paid off; **acceptum fierī** *(w. dat)* to be set down to the credit of; **acceptum referre** *(w. dat)* to set down to the credit side, have *(him, her, etc.)* to thank for
accersō *or* **arcess·ō -ere -īvī** *or* **-iī -ītus** *tr* to call, summon; to bring, procure
accessi·ō -ōnis *f* approach; addition, increase; additional payment, bonus; intensification; appendage, accessory; addition to one's resources; **accessiōnem facere** to make progress, gain ground; **accessiō temporis** *(leg)* extra time *(added to possessorship)*
access·us -ūs *m* act of approaching, approach; attack; rising *(of heavenly bodies);* blowing *(of the wind);* going at, tackling *(a task);* right to approach, access; entry, way in, passage; **accessus et recessus aestuum** flow and ebb of the tide
Accher·ūns -untis *mf* lower world
ac·cī·dō -cīdere -cīdī -cīsus *tr* to cut down; to impair, weaken; to decimate
ac·cidō -cidere -cidī *intr* to happen, occur, come to pass; *(w. dat of person affected)* to happen to, befall; *(w. adv)* to turn out; *(w. abl of cause)* to happen as the result of; *(w. dat)* to strike *(s.o. as), e.g.:* **hōc tibi īnsolentia praeter opīniōnem accidēbat** this struck you as exceptional insolence; *(w.* **in** *+ acc)* **1** to fall upon; **2** to be applicable to; *(w. dat or* **ad***)* to fall at *(e.g., s.o.'s feet);* **aurēs** *(or* **auribus** *or* **ad aurēs***)* **accidere** *(w. gen)* to reach the ears of; **accidit ut** *(w. subj or* **quod** *w. indic)* it happens that; **sī quid mihi acciderit** if anything should happen to me
ac·cingō -cingere -cīnxī -cīnctus *tr* to gird; to gird up, tuck up *(one's clothing)* **II** *refl and pass (w. abl)* to arm oneself with, equip oneself with; **accingī** *or* **sē accingere** *(w. dat or* **ad** *or* **in** *+ acc)* to prepare oneself for, to enter upon, to undertake; **ferrō accingī** to put on the sword
ac·ciō -cīre -cīvī -cītus *tr* to call, send for, invite; **mortem sibi accīre** to commit suicide
ac·cipiō -cipere -cēpī -ceptus *tr* to take, receive, accept; to welcome, entertain; to hear, learn, understand; to interpret, explain; to undertake *(a task);* to assume *(a responsibility);* to take *(medicine, food);* to incur *(a wound, loss);* to accept *(a post, office);* to borrow *(money);* to

approve of, agree to; to have room for, accommodate; to welcome, entertain; to accept as valid, admit; to learn, hear, be told of; to infer, conclude; *(geol)* to let in *(the sea);* **accipere dareque** to exchange; **āctiōnem accipere** *(leg)* to be granted a hearing; **auribus accipere** to hear, learn by listening; **initium** *(or* **orīginem** *or* **ortum)** **accipere** to begin; **fīnem accipere** to come to an end

accipi·ter -tris *m* hawk

accīs·us -a -um *pp of* **accīdō** ‖ *adj* impaired, ruined; troubled, disordered

accītus *pp of* **acciō**

accīt·us -ūs *m* summons, call

Acc·ius -(i)ī *m* Roman tragic poet *(170–85? B.C.)*

acclāmāti·ō -ōnis *f* **(adc-)** shout *(of approval or disapproval)*

acclām·ō -āre -āvī -ātus *tr* to hail, acclaim ‖ *intr* to shout *(in approval); (w. dat)* to shout at

acclār·ō -āre -āvī *tr* **(adc-)** to clarify

acclīnāt·us -a -um *adj* prostrate; sloping; *(w. dat)* **1** leaning on; **2** inclined toward, disposed to

acclīn·ō -āre -āvī -ātus *tr* **(adc-)** *(w. dat or* **in** *+ acc)* to lean *or* rest *(s.th.)* against ‖ *refl (w.* **ad)** *(fig)* to be inclined toward

acclīv·is -is -e *adj* **(adc-)** sloping upwards, uphill, steep

acclīvit·ās -ātis *f* **(adc-)** slope, ascent

accol·a -ae *mf* **(adc-)** neighbor

ac·colō -colere -coluī -cultus *tr* **(adc-)** to dwell near

accommodātē *adv* **(adc-)** suitably, fittingly; comfortably

accommodāti·ō -ōnis *f* **(adc-)** adjustment; compliance, accommodation

accommodāt·us -a -um *adj* **(adc-)** *(w. dat or* **ad)** fit for, adapted to, suitable for

accommod·ō -āre -āvī -ātus *tr* **(adc-)** *(w. dat or* **ad)** to adjust *or* adapt *or* apply *(s.th.)* to ‖ *refl (w.* **ad)** to apply *or* devote oneself to

accommod·us -a -um *adj* **(adc-)** *(w. dat)* fit for, adapted to, suitable for

accrē·dō -dere -didī -ditum *intr* **(adc-)** *(w. dat)* to believe, put faith in, trust

accr·ēscō -ēscere -ēvī -ētum *intr* **(adc-)** to grow larger, increase; to be added

accrēti·ō -ōnis *f* **(adc-)** increase

accubiti·ō -ōnis *f* **(adc-)** reclining *(at meals)*

accub·ō -āre *intr* to lie nearby; to recline at table; *(w. dat)* to lie near

accūd·ō -ere *tr* **(adc-)** to coin

ac·cumbō -cumbere -cubuī -cubitum *intr* **(adc-)** to take one's place at table; *(w.* **cum)** to lie down with

accumulātē *adv* **(adc-)** abundantly

accumulāt·or -ōris *m* **(adc-)** hoarder

accumul·ō -āre -āvī -ātus *tr* **(adc-)** to heap up, accumulate, amass; to load, overwhelm

accūrātē *adv* **(adc-)** carefully, accurately, exactly, meticulously

accūrāti·ō -ōnis *f* **(adc-)** carefulness, accuracy

accūrāt·us -a -um *adj* **(adc-)** careful, accurate, exact; studied

accūr·ō -āre -āvī -ātus *tr* **(adc-)** to take care of, attend to; *(w. subj,* **ut, nē)** to see to it (that, that not)

ac·currō -currere -currī *or* **-cucurrī -cursum** *intr* **(adc-)** to run up; *(w.* **ad** *or* **in** *+ acc)* to run (up) to

accurs·us -ūs *m* **(adc-)** running, concourse; *(mil)* attack, charge

accūsābil·is -is -e *adj* reprehensible

accūsāti·ō -ōnis *f* accusation; *(leg)* (bill of) indictment

accūsātīv·us -a -um *adj & m* accusative

accūsāt·or -ōris *m* accuser, prosecutor; informant

accūsātōriē *adv* like an accuser, as a prosecutor

accūsātōri·us -a -um *adj* accuser's, prosecutor's

accūsātr·īx -īcis *f* accuser *(female)*

accūsit·ō -āre -āvī -ātus *tr* to keep on accusing

accūs·ō -āre -āvī -ātus *tr* to accuse; to prosecute; to reproach, blame; *(w. gen of the charge or w.* **dē** *+ abl)* to accuse of

ā·cer -cris -cre *adj* sharp, pointed; alert, vigilant; shrewd; energetic, active; excited, eager, enthusiastic; strict, stern, hard; pinched, sharp *(features);* strong *(drink);* fierce, sharp *(bite);* bright, vivid *(color);* strong, pungent *(odor);* strong, bitter *(taste);* wild, savage *(animal);* fierce, relentless *(enemy);* violent *(storm);* biting *(cold);* strong, high *(wind);* swift *(river);* intense *(hunger, pain);* drastic *(remedy);* strong, powerful *(incentive);* serious, critical *(situation); (coll)* huge, terrific; **nāribus ācer** keen-scented

ac·er -eris *n* maple tree; maple wood

acerbē *adv* bitterly, harshly

acerbit·ās -ātis *f* bitterness, harshness, sharpness, sourness; distress, painful experience; ill-feeling, bitterness; satirical quality *(of writing)*

acerb·ō -āre -āvī -ātus *tr* to embitter; to exacerbate; to render *(s.th.)* disagreeable

acerb·us -a -um *adj* bitter, harsh, sour *(flavor, taste);* unripe, green *(fruit);* cruel, hostile, pitiless *(enemy);* harsh *(speech, remark);* untimely, premature *(death);* bitter *(feelings; cold);* rough *(winter);* strict, severe *(person in authority); (in a weakened sense)* troublesome, disagreeable

acern·us -a -um *adj* maple

acerr·a -ae *f* incense box
acersecom·ēs -ae *m* young man
acervātim *adv* in heaps; briefly
acerv·ō -āre -āvī -ātus *tr* to heap *or* pile up
acerv·us -ī *m* heap, pile; multitude; *(in logic)* sorites
acēscō acēscere acuī *intr* to turn sour
Acest·ēs -ae *m* king of Sicily
acētābul·um -ī *n* vinegar bottle
acēt·um -ī *n* sour wine, vinegar; *(fig)* sharp tongue
Achaemen·ēs -is *m* first king of Persia, great-grandfather of Cyrus
Achaemenid·ēs -ae *m* follower of Ulysses who was left behind in Sicily
Achaemeni·us -a -um *adj (poet)* Persian; Parthian
Achae·us -a -um *adj & m* Achaean; Greek
Achai·a *or* **Achāï·a -ae** *f* province in N. part of Peloponnesus on Gulf of Corinth; Greece
Achāï·cus -a -um *adj & m* Achaean; Greek
Achāt·ēs -ae *m* companion of Aeneas ‖ river in Sicily
Achelō·is -idis *f* daughter of Acheloüs; a Siren; a water nymph
Achelōï·us -a -um *adj* of the river Acheloüs; of Acheloüs *(the river god);* descended from Acheloüs
Achelō·üs -ī *m* river in N.W. Greece, flowing between Aetolia and Acarnania; god of this river
Acher·ōn -ontis *or* **Acher·ūns -untis** *m (f) or* **Acher·os -ī** *m* Acheron *(river in Hades);* god of this river; lower world; river in Epirus; river in S. Italy
Acheruntic·us -a -um *adj* of Acheron, of the lower world; **senex Acheruntīcus** old man with one foot in the grave
Acherūsi·us -a -um *adj* of the river Acheron, of the lower world
Achill·ās -ae *m* Egyptian who murdered Pompey
Achill·ēs -is *or* -ī *or* -eī *m* Greek warrior, son of Peleus and Thetis
Achillē·us -a -um *adj* of Achilles
Achillīd·ēs -ae *m* son *or* descendant of Achilles *(esp. his son Pyrrhus)*
Achīv·us -a -um *adj* Achaean, Greek
Acīdali·a -ae *f* Venus
acid·us -a -um *adj* sour, tart; *(of sound)* harsh, shrill; sharp, keen; pungent; unpleasant, disagreeable
aci·ēs -ēī *f* sharpness, sharp edge; keenness of vision; glance; eyesight, eye; pupil *(of the eye);* mental power; battle line, battle array; battlefield; battle; debate
acīnac·ēs -is *m* scimitar *(used by the Persians, Medes, and Scythians)*
acin·um -ī *n or* **acin·us -ī** *m* berry; grape; seed in the berry
acipēns·er -eris *or* **acipēns·is -is** *m* sturgeon
Āc·is -idis *m* son of Faunus, loved by Galatea, changed after his death into a river in Sicily
acl·ys -ydis *f* small javelin
aconīt·um -ī *n (bot)* wolfsbane; strong poison
ac·or -ōris *m* sour taste, sourness
acqui·ēscō -ēscere -ēvī -ētum *intr* **(adqu-)** to become quiet; to rest; to die; *(w. abl, dat, or* **in** + *abl)* **1** to find rest in; **2** to acquiesce in, be content with; **3** find pleasure in, rejoice in
acquī·rō -rere -sīvī -sītus *tr* **(adqu-)** to acquire, obtain, gain, win
Acrae·us -a -um *adj (title of Jupiter and Juno)* on the heights, on high
Acrag·ās -antis *m* town on S.W. coast of Sicily *(poetic and Greek for Agrigentum)*
acrātophor·um -ī *n* vessel for holding unmixed wine
acrēdul·a -ae *f* bird *(species unknown; perhaps owl or nightingale)*
ācricul·us -a -um *adj* irritable, peevish
ācrimōni·a -ae *f* sharpness, pungency; irritation; energy
Ācrisiōn·ē -ēs *f* daughter of Acrisius *(Danaë)*
Ācrisiōnē·us -a -um *adj* of Acrisius
Ācrisiōniad·ēs -ae *m* descendant of Acrisius *(Perseus)*
Ācris·ius -(i)ī *m* king of Argos, father of Danaë, grandfather of Perseus
ācriter *adv* sharply, keenly; clearly, in a distinctive manner; closely, attentively; with vigor, with enthusiasm; severely; vehemently; bitterly, hard
ācroām·a -atis *n* entertainment; comic actor; actor
ācroās·is -is *f* public lecture; recital
Ācroceraunī·a -ōrum *npl* promontory in Epirus on the Adriatic Sea
Ācrocorinth·us -ī *f* citadel of Corinth
Ācr·ōn -ōnis *m* a king of the Caeninenses *(killed by Romulus)*
Ācrot·a -ae *m* a king of Alba *(brother of Romulus Silvius)*
act·a -ae *f* seashore; seaside resort; beach party
āct·a -ōrum *npl see* **āctum**
Actae·ōn -onis *m* grandson of Cadmus, changed into a stag and devoured by his own dogs
Actae·us -a -um *adj* Attic, Athenian; **Actaea virgō** Athena
āctāri·us -ī *m* registrar of state documents; shorthand writer
Actē -ae *f* early name of Attica
Actiac·us -a -um *adj* of Actium; celebrating the victory of Actium
Acti·as -adis *fem adj* Attic
ācti·ō -ōnis *f* doing, performance, action, activity; proceedings; act, deed; proposal, measure; delivery *(of orator or actor);*

plot, action *(of play); (leg)* suit, right to bring a suit; **grātiārum āctiō** expression of gratitude; **nātūrālēs āctiōnēs** physiological functions

āctit·ō -āre -āvī -ātus *tr* to do *(repeatedly);* to plead *(cases regularly);* to act *(often)* in *(plays)*

Acti·um -ī *n* promontory in Epirus *(where Octavian defeated Antony and Cleopatra in 31* B.C.*)*

āctiuncul·a -ae *f* short law-court speech

āctīv·us -a -um *adj* practical *(philosophy); (gram)* active

Act·or -oris *m* companion of Aeneas

āct·or -ōris *m* doer, performer; agent, manager; actor, player; herdsman; *(leg) (with or without* **causae) 1** defense counsel; **2** prosecutor; **āctor summārum** cashier, accountant

āctuāriol·um -ī *n* small, fast boat

āctuāri·us -a -um *adj* swift **II** *m* stenographer **II** *f* swift passenger ship *(having both sails and oars)*

āct·um -ī *n* act, deed; transaction **II** *npl* great deeds, exploits, achievements; official records *(of events; of business transacted by the Senate, emperors, etc.);* decrees *(of a magistrate, general, etc.);* **ācta diurna** day-by-day record of events; **ācta Herculis** labors of Hercules; **ācta mittere** to publish the news

āctuōsē *adv* actively, energetically

āctuōs·us -a -um *adj* active, energetic

āct·us -a -um *pp of* **agō II** *adj* finished, past

āct·us -ūs *m* act, performance; physical movement; driving *(of cattle or wagon);* right of way; cow path; wagon track; path, course *(of sun);* linear land measure *(120 ft.);* sequence *(of numbers);* drawing *(of breath);* transaction *(of business);* performance *(of a play);* act *(of a play);* delivery *(of a speech);* **dēdūcere in āctus** to dramatize; **in āctū esse** to be active

āctūtum *adv* instantly, immediately

acul·a *or* **aquol·a** -**ae** *f* small stream

aculeāt·us -a -um *adj* prickly; *(of insects)* having a sting; *(fig)* stinging, barbed

acule·us -ī *m* sting, proboscis *(of insects);* barb *(of arrow);* spike; sharp point; sarcasm; **aculeum ēmittere** *(fig)* to shoot one's wad, spend all one's money

acūm·en -inis *n* point, sharpness; sting *(of insects);* cunning; clever trick; **ingeniī acūmen** mental acumen

acuō acuere acuī acūtus *tr* to sharpen, make pointed; to whet; to tune *(musical instruments);* to stir emotionally; to stimulate; to quicken *(one's pace)*; to accent *(syllable)*

ac·us -ūs *f* needle, pin; hairpin; curling iron; **ab aciā et acū** in great detail; **acū rem tangere** to hit the nail on the head

acūtē *adv* acutely, sharply, keenly

acūtul·us -a -um *adj* somewhat sharp, rather subtle

acūt·us -a -um *pp of* **acuō II** *adj* sharp, pointed; shrill *(sound);* keen *(senses, mind);* shrewd, intelligent *(person);* piercing *(cold);* fiercely hot *(sun);* nimble *(movement);* pungent *(smell, taste);* subtle *(distinction)*

ad- *pref* **1** at: **adclāmāre** *(or* **acclāmāre)** to shout at; **2** toward, aiming at: **adīre** to go toward; **3** bringing things together: **adstringere** *(or* **astringere)** to tie up; **4** toward a purpose: **adiūrāre** to swear to, swear by; **5** of increase or addition: **addere** to add; **6** of intensity: **adamāre** to love deeply

ad *prep (w. acc) (of space)* to, toward, at, near; *(often w.* **ūsque)** reaching to, as far as; for the purpose of, to; according to; in consequence of; with respect to; compared with; at the house of, with; in the company of; before *(judge, magistrate); (of time)* toward, about, until, at, on, by; *(with numbers)* about, almost; **ad Capuam** toward Capua, in the direction of Capua; **ad diem** on the right day, promptly; **ad extrēmum** to the very end; **ad haec** *or* **ad hōc** besides; **ad locum** on the spot; **ad manum** on hand, available; **ad omnia** in all directions; to crown all; **ad praesēns** for the moment; **ad prīma** to the highest degree; **ad summam** in short; **ad summum** at most; **ad tempus** on time, in time; **ad ultimum** utterly; **ad ūnum** one and all; **ad unguen** exactly, to the tee; **ad verbum** word for word; **ad vesperum** toward evening

adācti·ō -ōnis *f* administering *(an oath)*

adāctus *pp of* **adigō**

adāct·us -ūs *m* bringing together; snapping *(of jaws)*

adaequē *adv* equally

adaequ·ō -āre -āvī -ātus *tr* to make level; to equal, match, come up to the level of; *(fig)* to put on the same level; **adaequāre solō** to level to the ground **II** *intr* to be on the same level, be equal; *(of votes)* to be equally divided *(for acquittal and for condemnation); (w. dat)* to be level with; *(w. abl)* to be on a par with, be equal to *(in some respect)*

adamantē·us -a -um *adj* made of steel

adamantin·us -a -um *adj* hard as steel, adamantine; **saxa adamantina** diamonds

adam·ās -antis *m* adamant; steel; diamond; anything inflexible

adambul·ō -āre *intr (w. dat or* **ad)** to walk beside, walk up to

adam·ō -āre -āvī -ātus *tr* to love deeply; to fall in love with; to take a fancy to

adaper·iō -īre -uī -tus *tr* to uncover, throw open; to open up; to disclose to view, make visible; to open wide *(mouth,* *door);* to uncover *(head as sign of respect); (med)* to loosen *(bowels)*

adapertil·is -is -e *adj* that can be opened

adapert·us -a -um *adj* open *(door, flower)*

adaptāt·us -a -um *(w. dat)* adjusted to

adapt·ō -āre -āvī -ātus *tr* to adapt, modify; *(w. dat)* to fit to

adaqu·ō -āre *tr* to water ‖ *intr* to fetch water

adauctus *pp of* **adaugeō**

adauct·us -ūs *m* further growth, increase

adau·geō -gēre -xī -ctus *tr* to increase; to increase the number of; to exaggerate; *(w. abl)* to crown with

adaugēsc·ō -ere *intr* to begin to grow

adbib·ō -ere -ī *tr* to begin to drink; to listen attentively to

adbīt·ō -ere *intr* to approach

adc- = acc-

addec·et -ēre *v impers* it is proper

addēns·eō -ēre *or* **addēns·ō -āre** *tr* to close *(ranks)*

ad·dīcō -dīcere -dīxī -dictus *tr (w. dat)* **1** *(leg)* to assign *(property)* to; **2** to give custody of *(debtor)* to *(creditor);* **3** to sell *(by sale or auction)* to; **4** to award *(prizes, provinces)* to; **5** to ascribe to *(author);* **6** to condemn, doom to ‖ *refl & pass (w. dat)* to give one's support to ‖ *intr (in augury)* to be favorable

addict·us -a -um *adj (w. dat)* addicted to, a slave of; *(w. inf)* bound to *(do s.th.)* ‖ *mf* person enslaved for debt or theft

ad·discō -discere -didicī *tr* to learn in addition

additāment·um -ī *n* addition, increase

ad·dō -dere -didī -ditus *tr* to add; to give additionally; to add by way of exaggeration; to increase; to quicken *(one's pace);* to impart; to insert; to put *(into a container); (w. dat)* **1** to attach to, fit onto; **2** to serve *(a drink)* to; **3** to give to, confer on, inflict on; **4** to attribute to; **5** to intensify *(feelings);* **manūs in vincula addere** to tie one's hands

addoc·eō -ēre -uī *tr* to teach in addition, teach new *(skills, etc.)*

addubit·ō -āre -āvī -ātus *tr* to call into doubt ‖ *intr* to begin to feel doubt; to hesitate

ad·dūcō -dūcere -dūxī -ductus *tr* to lead up, bring up; to bring with one, bring along; to import; to bring up *(reinforcements);* to lead *(the mind to);* to introduce *(arguments);* to draw together, wrinkle; to induce; to sail *(a ship to);* to bring *(water to a town);* to shut *(door);* to shorten *(rein);* to draw back *(bowstring);* to bend *(bow); (of time, conditions)* to bring on; *(leg)* to prosecute, bring to trial; **(in iūdicium) addūcere** to take to court

adduct·us -a -um *adj* drawn tight, strained; narrow, tight *(place);* strict, serious *(character)*

ad·edō -edere *or* **-ēsse -ēdī -ēsus** *tr* to nibble at; to eat up; to waste; *(of fire)* to scorch; *(of water)* to erode

adempti·ō -ōnis *f* a taking away; confiscation

ademptus *pp of* **adimō**

adeō *adv* to such a degree, so; even, indeed, truly; very, extremely; for that matter; *(following pronouns and numerals, to give emphasis)* precisely, exactly; quite, just, chiefly; *(at the beginning of sentence)* thus far, to such an extent; *(w.* **ut** *+ subj)* to the end that; *(w.* **nē** *+ subj)* to the end that … not; *(w.* **dum, donec,** *etc.)* to the point of time when; **adeō nōn** much less

ad·eō -īre -iī *or* **-īvī -itus** *tr* to approach; to attack; to consult; to visit; to undertake, set about, undergo; to consult *(an oracle)* ‖ *intr* to go up, come up; *(w.* **ad) 1** to go up to, approach; **2** to enter upon, undertake, set about; **3** to meet *(danger);* **ad rem pūblicam adīre** to go into politics

ad·eps -ipis *mf* fat; corpulence

adepti·ō -ōnis *f* obtaining, acquisition

adeptus *pp of* **adipīscor**

adequit·ō -āre -āvī -ātum *intr* to ride up; *(w. dat or* **ad)** to ride up to, ride toward

adesse *inf of* **adsum**

adēsse *inf of* **adedō**

adēsur·iō -īre -īvī *intr* to be very hungry

adēsus *pp of* **adedō**

adf- = aff-

adfuī *perf of* **adsum**

ad·haereō -haerēre -haesī -haesum *intr (w. dat, abl,* **ad** *or* **in** *+ acc)* **1** to cling to, stick to; **2** to keep close to, hang on to; **3** *(anat)* to be attached to; **4** *(of land)* to be contiguous with, be near; **laterī adhaerēre** to stick to *(a person's)* side; **memoriae adhaerēre** to stick in one's memory

adhae·rēscō -rēscere -sī -sum *intr* to stick; to falter; *(w. dat, abl,* **in** *+ abl, or* **ad) 1** to stick to, cling to; **2** to be devoted to; **3** to correspond to, accord with; **4** *(of weapons)* to become lodged in; **5** to run aground on

adhaesi·ō -ōnis *f* clinging, adhesion

adhaes·us -ūs *m* clinging, adhesion

Adherb·al -alis *m* son of Micipsa *(king of Numidia),* murdered by Jugurtha; Carthaginian general in the 2nd Punic War

adhib·eō -ēre -uī -itus *tr* to stretch out *(hands);* to apply *(remedies, fetters, treatment);* to administer *(medicine);* to call in *(as advisor, witness, expert);* to cite *(an authority); (w. abl)* to supply *(s.o.)* with; **animum adhibēre** *(w. dat)* to turn one's attention to; **fidem adhibēre** *(w. dat)* to lend credence to; *(w. adv)* to treat; *(w.* **ad)** to invite *(to a meal)*; **||** *refl* to conduct oneself, behave

adhinn·iō -īre -iī *or* **-īvī -ītus** *tr* to whinny after; to lust after **||** *intr (w. dat or* **ad** *or* **in** + *acc)* **1** to whinny after; **2** to lust after, crave; **3** to chuckle in delight at

adhortāti·ō -ōnis *f* exhortation, encouragement; pep talk

adhortāt·or -ōris *m* fan, supporter

adhort·or -ārī -ātus sum *tr* to cheer on, encourage

adhūc *adv* thus far, hitherto; till now; as yet, still; besides, in addition, moreover; to a greater degree, still further; *(w. numerals)* besides; **nihil adhūc** nothing as yet

adiac·eō -ēre -uī *tr* to adjoin **||** *intr (w. dat or* **ad)** to lie near; to border

ad·iciō -icere -iēcī -iectus *tr* to add; to increase; *(w. dat or* **ad) 1** to hurl *(weapon, insults)* at; **2** to add *(s.th.)* to; **3** to turn *(eyes, attention)* to; *(w.* **in** + *acc)* to hurl *(weapon)* at

adiecti·ō -ōnis *f* addition; annexation

adiectīv·us -a -um *adj* adjectival **||** *n* adjective

ad·igō -igere -ēgī -āctus *tr* to drive *(cattle);* to move up *(siege engine);* to assemble *(ships);* to hurl *(weapon);* to inflict *(wound);* to plunge *(weapon)* into; **aliquem iūs iūrandum adigere** to have s.o. swear allegiance; **prōvinciam in verba sua et Pompēiī iūs iūrandum adigere** to have the province swear allegiance to himself and Pompey

ad·imō -imere -ēmī -emptus *tr (w. dat of separation)* to take away from; **alicui vītam** *(or* **lībertātem) adimere** to deprive s.o. of life *or* liberty

adipātus -a -um *adj* fatty, greasy; gross, bombastic **||** *n* pastry *(made in fat)*

ad·ipīscor -ipīscī -eptus sum *tr* to get, obtain; to arrive at, reach; to inherit; to win *(victory);* **mortem adipīscī** to commit suicide

aditiāl·is -is -e *adj* inaugural

aditi·ō -ōnis *f* a going to

aditus *pp of* **adeō**

adit·us -ūs *m* doorway, entrance, passage; extent to which a door is opened, opening; approach; arrival; access; entrance; right of entry, admittance; right to hold *(an office);* audience, interview; beginning, commencement; chance, opportunity; hostile approach, attack; chance of attacking, an "opening"; **prīmus aditus** first encounter *(with a person)*

adiūdic·ō -āre -āvī -ātus *tr* to adjudge, award; to ascribe, assign

adiūment·um -ī *n* help, support

adiūnct·a -ōrum *npl* attendant circumstances; **ad nōmina adiūncta** epithets, nicknames

adiūncti·ō -ōnis *f* joining, union; addition; *(rhet)* repetition

ad·iungō -iungere -iūnxī -iūnctus *tr (w. dat)* **1** to yoke *or* harness *(animal)* to; **2** to add *(ingredients)* to; **3** to ascribe *(qualities)* to; **4** to bestow *(praise, honor)* on; *(w. dat or* **ad) 1** to add, attach *(s.th.)* to; **2** to apply, direct *(mind, attention, etc.)* to; **uxōrem adiungere** to get married **||** *refl (w. dat)* to join

adiūr·ō -āre -āvī -ātus *tr* to swear to; to swear by **||** *intr* to swear

adiūtābil·is -is -e *adj* helpful

adiūt·ō -āre -āvī -ātus *tr* to help **||** *intr (w. dat)* to be of assistance to

adiūt·or -ōris *m* helper, assistant; aide, adjutant, deputy; supporting actor

adiūtōr·ium -(i)ī *n* help, support

adiūtr·īx -īcis *f* helper *(female)*

ad·iuvō -iuvāre -iūvī -iūtus *tr* to help; to encourage; to keep *(the fire)* going; *(med)* to relieve; *(w.* **ad** *or* **in** + *acc)* to contribute to **||** *v impers* it helps, it is advantageous, it is useful

adl- = **all-**

admātūr·ō -āre *tr* to bring to maturity, ripen; to speed up, expedite

ad·mētior -mētīrī -mēnsus sum *tr (w. dat)* to measure *(s.th.)* out to

Admēt·us -ī *m* king of Pherae in Thessaly, husband of Alcestis

admigr·ō -āre *intr (w.* **ad)** to move to

adminicul·ō -āre -āvī -ātus *tr* to prop up

adminicul·um -ī *n* prop, support, stake, pole; rudder; aid; assistant

adminis·ter -trī *m* assistant; server, waiter

administr·a -ae *f* assistant, handmaid; waitress

administr·ō -āre -āvī -ātus *tr* to administer, direct, manage, run; to rule; to execute *(orders);* to govern *(a province);* to conduct *(a war)* **||** *intr* to manage

administrāti·ō -ōnis *f* handling, administration, management, government; method of dealing with **||** *fpl* administrative functions *or* duties; administrative qualities

administrāt·or -ōris *m* administrator, director, manager

admīrābil·is -is -e *adj* admirable, wonderful; strange, surprising; **admīrābile est** it is remarkable

admīrābilit·ās -ātis *f* admiration, wonder; wonderfulness

admīrābiliter *adv* admirably; astonishingly

admīrāti·ō -ōnis *f* admiration, wonder; surprise

admīrāt·or -ōris *m* admirer

admīr·or -ārī -ātus sum *tr* to admire, wonder at; to be surprised at

admī·sceō -scēre -scuī -xtus *tr* to mix in, add; to involve, implicate; to join, mingle; *(w. dat, w.* **ad** *or* **in** + *acc or* **cum)** to add *(s.th.)* to, to mix *or* mix up *(s.th.)* with **||** *refl* to get involved

admissār·ius -(i)ī *m* stallion; *(fig)* stud

admissi·ō -ōnis *f* audience, interview

admiss·um -ī *n* fault, crime

ad·mittō -mittere -mīsī -missus *tr* to let in, admit; to allow; to let loose; to listen to; to put at a gallop; to let *(water, hair)* flow; to allow; to commit *(error, crime)*; **facinus in sē admittere** to commit a fault, error, crime; **ad animum admittere** to consider; **auribus** (*or* **ad aurēs**) **admittere** to listen to **||** *intr (in augury)* to be propitious

admīxti·ō -ōnis *f* admixture

admīxtus *pp of* **admīsceō**

admoderātē *adv* appropriately

admodum *adv* to the limit; very, quite, fully; *(w. numbers)* just about; *(w. negatives)* at all; *(in answers)* quite so, yes

admoen·iō -īre -īvī -ītus *tr* to besiege

admol·ior -īrī -ītus sum *tr* to pile up; **manūs admolīrī** *(w. dat)* to lay violent hands on **||** *intr (w.* **ut** *+ subj)* to struggle to

admon·eō -ēre -uī -itus *tr* to admonish, remind, suggest; to warn; *(w. acc or gen)* to recall

admoniti·ō -ōnis *f* admonition, reminder, suggestion

admonit·or -ōris *m* reminder, one who admonishes

admonit·um -ī *n* advice, warning, suggestion

admonit·us -ūs *m* advice; suggestion; warning; command *(given to an animal)*; **admonitū** *(w. gen)* at the suggestion of

admord·eō -ēre *(no perf)* **admorsus** *tr* to bite at; *(fig)* to fleece

admōti·ō -ōnis *f* moving, movement

ad·moveō -movēre -mōvī -mōtus *tr* to move up, bring up, bring near; to lead on, conduct; to promote, advance; to employ *(fear, flattery)*; *(w. dat or* **ad)** **1** to move *or* bring *(s.th.)* to; **2** to apply *(s.th.)* to; **3** to direct *(attention, etc.)* to; **aurem admovēre** to give heed; **calcar** *(or* **stimulum)** **admovēre** *(w. dat)* to spur

admūg·iō -īre *intr (w. dat)* to bellow to

admurmurāti·ō -ōnis *f* murmuring

admurmur·ō -āre -āvī -ātum *intr* to murmur *(in approval or disapproval)* **||** *impers pass* **admurmurātum est** people murmured

admutil·ō -āre -āvī -ātus *tr* to clip close; *(coll)* to clip, cheat *(of money)*

adn- = ann-

ad·oleō -olēre *intr* to smell

ad·oleō -olēre -oluī -ultus *tr* to burn *(ritually)*; to make burnt sacrifices to, worship; to cremate; to light *(pyre)*; to destroy by fire, burn; **adolēre altāria dōnīs** to pile the altar high with gifts; **flammīs adolēre penātis** *(fig)* to light the hearth; **honōrēs adolēre** *(dat)* to make burnt offerings to

adolēsc·ēns -entis *m* young man **||** *f* young lady

adol·ēscō -ēscere -ēvī adultum *intr* **(adul-)** to grow up; to become mature; to increase; *(of habits, etc.)* to become established

Adōn·is -is *or* **-idis** *m* son of Cinyras *(king of Cyprus)*, loved by Venus, killed by a wild boar

adoper·iō -īre -uī -tus *tr* to cover up; to close

adopert·us -a -um *adj* covered; veiled; hiding; shut, closed; *(poet)* clothed

adopīn·or -ārī -ātus sum *tr* to suppose, conjecture further

adoptāti·ō -ōnis *f* adoption *(into a family)*

adopti·ō -ōnis *f* adoption *(into a family)*

adoptīv·us -a -um *adj* adoptive

adopt·ō -āre -āvī -ātus *tr* to adopt; to select; to graft *(plants)*

ad·or -ōris *or* **-oris** *n* spelt *(hardy European type of wheat)*

adōrāti·ō -ōnis *f* adoration, worship

adōre·a -ae *f (a gift of grain as)* reward for valor; praise, glory

adōre·us -a -um *adj* of spelt, of wheat

ad·orior -orīrī -ortus sum *tr* to rise up against, attack; to attempt; to undertake

adōrn·ō -āre -āvī -ātus *tr* to adorn; to equip, get ready

adōr·ō -āre -āvī -ātus *tr* to implore, entreat; to ask for; to adore, worship

adp- = app-

adq- = acq-

adr- = arr-

ad·rādō -rādere -rāsī -rāsus *tr* to shave close

Adrast·us -ī *m* king of Argos, father-in-law of Tydeus and Polynices

Adri- = Hadri-

adsc- = āsc-

adsi- = assi-

adso- = asso-

adsp- = asp-

adst- = ast-

adsu- = assu-

ad·sum -esse -fuī -futūrus *intr* to be present; to appear; *(of conditions)* to exist; *(of time, events)* to be at hand; to be of assistance; *(of an assembly)* to convene; *(w. dat)* **1** to share in, participate in; **2** to assist, stand by; **3** *(leg)* to serve as attorney to; **4** *(of gods)* to look favorably on; **adesse animō** (*or* **animīs**) to pay attention; to cheer up; **adest illī corporis pulchritūdō** he has a handsome physique

adt- = att-

adūlāti·ō -ōnis *f* flattery; fawning, cringing
adūlāt·or -ōris *m* flatterer
adūlātōri·us -a -um *adj* flattering
adulēsc·ēns -entis *m* **(adol-)** young man ‖ *f* young lady
adulēscenti·a -ae *f* **(adol-)** youth, young people
adulēscentul·a -ae *f* girl
adulēscentul·us -ī *m* boy
adūl·ō -āre *tr* to fawn on *(like a dog)*
adūl·or -ārī -ātus sum *tr* to fawn on ‖ *intr* *(w. dat)* to kowtow to
adult·er -era -erum *adj* adulterous, unchaste; cross-bred *(plants);* debased *(coinage);* **adultera clāvis** skeleton key ‖ *m* lover, adulterer ‖ *f* adulteress
adulterīn·us -a -um *adj* adulterous; counterfeit
adulter·ium -(i)ī *n* adultery; adulteration
adulter·ō -āre -āvī -ātus *tr* to defile, corrupt; to adulterate; to counterfeit; to falsify *(documents)* ‖ *intr* to commit adultery
adult·us -a -um *adj* grown, mature, adult
adumbrātim *adv* in outline
adumbrāti·ō -ōnis *f* sketch, outline
adumbrāt·us -a -um *adj* shadowy, sketchy; spurious
adumbr·ō -āre -āvī -ātus *tr* to shade; to obscure *(truth);* to sketch; to counterfeit
aduncit·ās -ātis *f* curvature
adunc·us -a -um *adj* curved, hooked
adurg·eō -ēre *tr* to be in hot pursuit of
ad·ūrō -ūrere -ūssī -ūstus *tr* to scorch, singe; to cause a burning sensation in, to burn; to nip, freeze; to desiccate; *(med)* to cauterize
adūsque *prep (w. acc)* all the way to, right up to
adūsti·ō -ōnis *f* burning; *(med)* burn; heatstroke
adūst·us -a -um *pp of* **adūrō** ‖ *adj* scorched; **nivibus adūstus** frostbitten; **sōle adūstus** sunburned
advectīci·us -a -um *adj* imported, foreign
advect·iō -ōnis *f* transportation
advect·ō -āre *tr* to import
advectus *pp of* **advehō**
advect·us -ūs *m* importation
adve·hō -here -xī -ctus *tr* to convey; to ship; to import ‖ *pass* to ride; **equō advehī (ad** *or* **in** + *acc)* to ride to; **nāvī advehī (in** + *acc)* to sail to
advēl·ō -āre *tr* to veil; to wreathe
adven·a -ae *mf* stranger, foreigner
ad·veniō -venīre -vēnī -ventum *intr* to arrive; *(of periods of time, events)* to draw near, approach, be imminent; *(w.* **ad** *or* **in** *+ acc, or acc of limit of motion)* to arrive at, come to, reach; *(w. dat) (of possession)* to come into the hands of; *(pres p)* at *or* upon my (your, his, her, etc.) arrival; **advenientem īlicō ad cēnam addūxī** immediately upon his arrival I took him to dinner
adventīci·us -a -um *adj* foreign; imported; extraneous; unusual; migratory *(birds);* **cēna adventīcia** reception; **ex adventīciō** from an extraneous source
advent·ō -āre -āvī -ātum *intr* to keep coming closer; to turn up *(at a place); (of tide)* to come in; *(of time, events)* to draw near
advent·or -ōris *m* visitor, guest; customer
advent·us -ūs *m* arrival, approach; visit; (official) visitation
adversāri·us -a -um *adj* **(-vors-)** *(w. dat)* turned toward, opposed to, opposite ‖ *mf* adversary ‖ *npl* journal, notebook, memoranda; assertion *(of opponent)*
adversātr·īx -īcis *f* **(-vors-)** opponent *(female)*
adversi·ō -ōnis *f* directing
advers·ō -āre -āvī -ātus *tr* **(-vors-)** to turn, direct; **animum adversāre** to direct attention; *(w.* **nē)** to be careful not to
advers·or -ārī -ātus sum *intr* **(-vors-)** to put up opposition; to be unfavorable; *(w. dat)* **1** to oppose, resist; **2** to be incompatible with; **3** to be inconsistent with
adversum *or* **adversus** *adv* **(-vors-)** in the opposite direction ‖ *prep (w. acc)* facing, opposite, toward; in the direction of; in the opposite direction to, against; compared with, in comparison with; to the disadvantage of; *(after verbs expressing hostile intent)* to meet, face; compared with; contrary to; in the eyes of; in criticism of; in reply to, in response to; **adversus clīvum** *(or* **collem)** uphill
advers·us -a -um *adj* **(-vors-)** opposite, in front; facing; unfavorable; hostile; *(astr)* diametrically opposite; **adversā viā** up the road; **adversō flūmine** upstream; **frontibus adversīs** head-on; **rēs adversae** misfortunes, adversities; **ventus adversus** head wind ‖ *n* trouble, adversity, misfortune; the opposite; **ex adversō** *(w. dat)* opposite to; **in adversum** forwards; to meet face to face; *(of several things)* in the opposite direction; **in adversum subīre** to go uphill; **per adversum** in the opposite direction
adver·tō -tere -tī -sus *tr* **(-vor-)** *(w. acc or dat or* **in** *+ acc)* **1** to turn *or* direct *(s.th.)* toward; **2** to steer *(ship)* toward; **animōs** *(or* **aurēs** *or* **oculōs)** **advertere** to attract attention; **animum advertere** *(w. dat or* **ad)** to pay attention to, heed, observe ‖ *intr* to land; *(w.* **in** *+ acc)* to punish
advesper·āscit -āscere -āvit *v impers* evening approaches
advigil·ō -āre -āvī -ātum *intr* to be vigilant, keep watch; *(w. dat)* to keep watch over, bestow attention on; *(w.* **prō** *+ abl)* to watch out for
advocāt·a -ae *f* supporter *(female)*

advocāti·ō -ōnis *f* legal assistance; legal counsel; the bar; period of time allowed to procure legal assistance; delay, adjournment

advocāt·us -ī *m* helper, supporter; *(leg)* attorney

advoc·ō -āre -āvī -ātus *tr* to call; to convoke; to invoke; to invoke the help of; to invite *(to a meal);* to consult; to cite; *(leg)* to adjourn

advol·ō -āre -āvī -ātum *intr* (*w. dat or* **ad**) **1** to fly toward; **2** to rush at; **3** *(mil)* to swoop down on

advol·vō -vere -vī -ūtus *tr (w. dat or* **ad)** to roll *(s.th.)* to *or* toward ‖ *refl* **sē advolvere ad genua** (*or* **genibus**) *(w. gen)* to fall prostrate before

advor- = **adver-**

adyt·um -ī *n* sanctuary; *(fig)* tomb

Aeacidēi·us -a -um *adj* of the descendants of Aeacus; **Aeacidēia rēgna** Aegina

Aeacid·ēs -ae *m* descendant of Aeacus

Aeac·us *or* **Aeac·os -ī** *m* king of Aegina, father of Peleus, Telamon, and Phocus, and judge of the dead

aed·ēs *or* **aed·is -is** *f* room, apartment; shrine, temple ‖ *fpl* house; **in ūnīs aedibus** in one house

aedicul·a -ae *f* chapel, shrine; small room, closet; small house ‖ *fpl* small house

aedificāti·ō -ōnis *f* constructing, building; structure, building

aedificātiuncul·a -ae *f* tiny building

aedificāt·or -ōris *m* builder, architect; **aedificātor mundī** creator of the world

aedific·ium -(i)ī *n* building, edifice

aedific·ō -āre -āvī -ātus *tr* to build; **locum aedificāre** to erect buildings on a site ‖ *intr* to erect a building

aedīlici·us -a -um *adj* aedile's ‖ *m* ex-aedile

aedīl·is -is *m* **(ēd-)** aedile *(Roman magistrate charged with the supervision of public buildings, markets, grain supply, games, and theatrical productions);* magistrate in Italian and other towns; **aedīlis cereālis** aedile in charge of the grain supply

aedīlit·ās -ātis *f* aedileship

aedis *see* **aedēs**

aeditu·us *or* **aeditim·us** *or* **aeditum·us -ī** *m* sacristan

Aedu·ī -ōrum *mpl* **(Haed-)** Gallic tribe occupying the territory between the Saône and the Loire

Aeētae·us -a -um *adj* of Aeëtes

Aeēt·ēs *or* **Aeēt·ās** *or* **Aeēt·a -ae** *m* Aeëtes *(king of Colchis and father of Medea)*

Aeēti·as -adis *f* daughter of Aeëtes *(Medea)*

Aegae·us -a -um *adj* **(Aegē·us, Ēgē·us)** Aegean ‖ *n* Aegean Sea

Aegāt·ēs -um *fpl* Aegatian Islands *(three islands off the W. coast of Sicily where the Carthaginians were defeated, thus ending the First Punic War in 241 B.C.)*

ae·ger -gra -grum *adj* sick; *(w. abl of cause or* **ex)** sick from; diseased; weary, exhausted; depressed; depraved *(character, mind);* labored *(breathing, words);* corrupt *(institutions)* ‖ *mf* patient

Aeg·eus -eī *m* king of Athens and father of Theseus

Aegīd·ēs -ae *m* son of Aegeus *(Theseus)*

Aegīd·ae -ārum *mpl* descendants of Aegeus

Aegīn·a -ae *f* island off Attica ‖ mother of Aeacus

aeg·is -idis *f* shield of Minerva and of Jupiter; aegis, protection

Aegisth·us -ī *m* son of Thyestes and murderer of Agamemnon

aegrē *adv* painfully; with difficulty; reluctantly; hardly, scarcely; **aegrē esse alicui** *or* **aegrē facere alicui** to annoy s.o.; to hurt s.o.; **aegrē ferre** (*or* **patī**) to take (it) hard; to resent

aegr·eō -ēre *intr* to be sick

aegrēsc·ō -ere *intr* to become sick; to get worse; to be distressed

aegrimōni·a -ae *f* distress, trouble

aegritūd·ō -inis *f* sickness; sorrow

aegr·or -ōris *m* illness

aegrōtāti·ō -ōnis *f* sickness, disease; sorrow

aegrōt·ō -āre -āvī -ātum *intr* to be sick; **animō aegrōtāre** to be mentally ill

aegrōt·us -a -um *adj* sick; love-sick

Aegypti·us -a -um *adj* of Egypt, Egyptian

Aegypt·us -ī *f* Egypt ‖ *m* mythical king of Egypt, whose 50 sons married the 50 daughters of his brother Danaüs

aelinon *interj* exclamation of sorrow, said to signify "alas for Linus"

aelin·os -ī *m* a dirge

Aëll·ō -ūs *f* one of the Harpies; a swift dog

Aemiliān·us -a -um *adj* of the Aemilian gens; Scipio Aemilianus Minor, son of L. Aemilius Paulus

Aemili·us -a -um *adj* name of a Roman clan *(nomen), esp.* Lucius Aemilius Paullus, who defeated Perseus at Pydna in 168 B.C.; **Via Aemilia** road from Ariminum to Placentia

Aemilius Macer a poet from Verona, friend of Vergil and Ovid

Aemoni·a -ae *f* **(Hae-)** Thessaly

aemul·a -ae *f* rival *(female);* rival city

aemulāti·ō -ōnis *f* emulation, rivalry

aemulāt·or -ōris *m* rival, imitator

aemulāt·us -ūs *m* emulation, rivalry

aemul·or -ārī -ātus sum *or* **aemul·ō -āre** *tr* to emulate, rival ‖ *intr (w. dat or* **cum)** to be jealous of

aemul·us -a -um *adj (w. gen or dat)* **1** jealous of, striving after; **2** *(of things)* similar to, comparable to ‖ *m* rival ‖ *f* rival
Aenari·a -ae *f* island on the Campanian coast, where Aeneas made landfall *(modern Ischia)*
Aenead·ēs -ae *m* descendant of Aeneas; Trojan; Roman; Augustus
Aenē·ās -ae *m* son of Venus and Anchises, and hero of Vergil's epic
Aenē·is -idis *or* **-idos** *f* the *Aeneid*
aēne·um *or* **ahēne·um** *or* **aēn·um -ī** *n* bronze vessel, cauldron, pot
aēne·us *or* **ahēne·us** *or* **a(h)ēn·us -a -um** *adj* bronze; hard as bronze; bronze-colored
Aenīd·ēs -ae *m* son of Aeneas *(Ascanius)*
aenigm·a -atis *n* enigma, riddle, puzzle
aēni·pēs -pedis *adj* bronze-footed
aēnum *see* **aēneum**
aēnus *see* **aēneus**
Aeoli·a -ae *f* realm of Aeolus *(king of winds);* group of islands off Sicily
Aeolid·ēs -ae *m* a descendant of Aeolus *(esp. his sons Sisyphus and Athamas)*
Aeoli·ī -ōrum *or* **Aeol·ēs -um** *mpl* Aeolians *(in N.W. Asia Minor)*
Aeol·is -idis *or* **-idos** *f* Aeolia *(N.W. part of Asia Minor)*
Aeol·us -ī *m* god of winds *(son of Jupiter, ruler of the Aeolian islands)*
aequābil·is -is -e *adj* equal; alike; consistent, uniform; fair, impartial
aequābilit·ās -ātis *f* equality; uniformity; impartiality
aequābiliter *adv* evenly, equally; uniformly
aequaev·us -a -um *adj* of the same age, coeval
aequāl·is -is -e *adj* equal; of equal importance; even, level; of the same age; contemporary; symmetrical; affecting all equally, universal, general; *(of conditions, etc.)* comparable; uniform *(in consistency, shape, color, content, style);* homogeneous; *(of natural phenomena)* regular, continuous; *(of weather)* settled; equally balanced *(contest); (w. dat)* level with, on a level with, on a par with; *(w.* **ad)** equally disposed to ‖ *mf* comrade; contemporary
aequālit·ās -ātis *f* equality *(of age, status, merit);* regularity; evenness; smoothness
aequāliter *adv* equally; evenly
aequanimit·ās -ātis *f* calmness, patience; kindness; impartiality
aequāti·ō -ōnis *f* equal distribution
aequē *adv* equally; justly, fairly; **aequē ... ac** *or* **atque** *or* **et** just as if; **aequē ... quam** as ... as, in the same way as
Aequ·ī -ōrum *mpl* a people of central Italy
aequilībrit·ās -ātis *f* balance
aequilībr·ium -(i)ī *n* horizontal position; equilibrium
aequinoctiāl·is -is -e *adj* equinoctial
aequinoct·ium -(i)ī *n* equinox
aequiperābil·is -is -e *adj (w. dat or* **cum)** comparable to
aequiper·ō -āre -āvī -ātus *tr* **(-par-)** to compare; to equal, rival, come up to; *(w. dat, w.* **ad** *or* **cum)** to compare *(s.th.)* to ‖ *intr (w. dat)* to become equal to, be equal to
aequit·ās -ātis *f* evenness; conformity; symmetry; equity; calmness; **animī aequitās** equanimity, calmness
aequ·ō -āre -āvī -ātus *tr* to make level; to smooth (out); to equalize; to equal, match, rival; to reach as high *(or* as deep) as; to keep pace with; to balance *(scales); (w. dat)* to liken to; **gradūs aequāre** to keep pace; **solō aequāre** to raze to the ground; **sortēs aequāre** to shake up the lots fairly
aequ·or -oris *n* level surface; plain; sea
aequore·us -a -um *adj* of the sea, marine
aequ·us -a -um *adj* level, even, flat, smooth; on a level *(with),* as tall *or* as high *(as);* fair-minded, impartial, just, reasonable; evenly balanced; *(of laws, treaties)* giving equal rights, fair; *(of persons)* on an equal footing, equal *(in strength, etc.); (of qualities)* matching, equal, alike; *(of love)* reciprocated; *(of verse)* regular, uniform; *(of movement)* steady, calm; *(of the mind)* calm, resigned; *(of things)* favorable, advantageous; *(w. dat)* **1** inclined toward; **2** sympathetic to, favorable to; **3** content with; **aequā mente** with calmness, patiently; **aequa pars** a half; **aequā parte** on a basis of equality; **aequī facere** to regard as immaterial, regard as a matter of indifference; **aequīs manibus** *(of battles)* equally balanced; **aequō animō** with calmness, patiently; **aequō campō** *(mil)* on a level field *(offering advantage to neither side);* **aequō fronte** *(mil)* in a straight line, in line; **aequō Mārte** *(of battles)* evenly balanced; **aequō pede** on even terms, on an equal footing; **aequum est** it is right (that); **aequum solō pōnere** to raze to the ground; **ex īnferiōre locō loquitur sīve ex aequō sīve ex superiōre** whether he speaks before the judges on the bench or in the Senate, or from the rostra ‖ *n* level, plain; justice, fairness; **ex aequō** from the same level; *(fig)* equally
ā·ēr -eris *m* air; atmosphere; climate; sky; weather; mist
aerāment·um -ī *n* bronze utensil
aerāri·us -a -um adj copper, bronze; of mines; financial, fiscal ‖ m coppersmith; low-class Roman citizen ‖ f mine; smelting furnace ‖ n treasury; funds contained

in the treasury; (specifically) public treasury at Rome, kept in the temple of Saturn in the Forum; aerārium mīlitāre treasury for veterans' benefits; aerārium sānctius a reserve fund (to be touched only in an emergency)

aerāt·us -a -um *adj* copper, bronze; rich

aere·us -a -um *adj* bronze; bronze-armored; bronze-beaked *(ships)*

āëre·us -a -um *adj see* **āërius**

aerif·er -era -erum *adj* carrying (bronze) cymbals

aerip·ēs -edis *adj* bronze-footed

āëri·us -a -um *adj* aerial, lofty; airy; airborne; **āërium mel** dew

Āërop·ē -ēs *or* **Āërop·a -ae** *f* Aërope *(wife of Atreus, mother of Agamemnon and Menelaus)*

aerūginōs·us -a -um *adj* rusty

aerūg·ō -inis *f* copper rust, verdigris; money; corroding passion, envy, greed

aerumn·a -ae *f* trouble; distress; task; labor *(of Hercules)*

aerumnābil·is -is -e *adj* distressing

aerumnōs·us -a -um *adj* full of troubles, distressed; causing distress, calamitous

aes aeris *n* copper, bronze; bronze object; armor; statue; utensil; trumpet; money, cash; bronze coin, a copper; inscribed bronze tablet; payment; reward; **aes album** *(or* **candidum)** brass; **aes aliēnum** debt; **aes et lībra** *(leg)* (symbolical) copper coin and scales *(used in transactions over property, emancipation of slaves, etc.);* **aes mīlitāre** military pay; **in meō aere sum** I am free of debt

Aeschin·ēs -is *m* famous Athenian orator and opponent of Demosthenes ‖ Milesian orator contemporary of Cicero ‖ follower of Socrates

Aeschyl·us -ī *m* Athenian tragic poet *(525–456 B.C.)*

Aesculāp·ius -(i)ī *m* god of medicine

aesculēt·um -ī *n* **(ēsc-)** oak forest

aescule·us -a -um *adj* oak

aescul·us -ī *f* **(ēsc-)** Italian oak

Aeserni·a -ae *f* town in Samnium

Aesernīn·us -a -um *adj* of Aesernia

Aes·ōn -onis *m* Aeson *(father of Jason)*

Aesonid·ēs -ae *m* son of Aeson *(Jason)*

Aesoni·us -a -um *adj* of Aeson, of Jason

Aesōp·us -ī *m* Aesop

aest·ās -ātis *f* summer; summer heat, summer weather

aestif·er -era -erum *adj* sultry; *(of a constellation)* that brings on the hot weather

aestimābil·is -is -e *adj* valuable

aestimāti·ō -ōnis *f* **(-tum-)** appraisal, assessment; esteem; worth, value; **lītis** *(or* **lītium)** **aestimātiō** *(leg)* assessment of damages *or* penalty; **possessiōnum et rērum aestimātiō** real estate appraisal

aestimāt·or -ōris *m* appraiser

aestim·ō -āre -āvī -ātus *tr* **(-tum-)** to appraise, rate, value, estimate; to esteem highly; to judge; to consider, think; *(w. gen or abl of value)* to consider worth; **lītem (lītēs) aestimāre** *(leg)* to assess the damages; **magnī** *(or* **parvī)** **aestimāre** to consider *(s.th. or s.o.)* worth much *(or* little)

aestīv·a -ōrum *npl* summer camp; campaign season, campaign; summer pastures; cattle

aestīvē *adv* scantily *(clad)*

aestīv·ō -āre -āvī -ātum *intr* to spend the summer

aestīv·us -a -um *adj* summer; **occāsus aestīvus** northwest; **oriēns aestīvus** northeast

aestuār·ium -(i)ī *n* estuary, lagoon; marsh; air shaft

aestu·ō -āre -āvī -ātum *intr* to boil, seethe; to burn, glow; to undulate, swell; to be tossed, heave; to waver; to be in heat, be all worked up

aestuōsē *adv* hotly, impetuously

aestuōs·us -a -um *adj* sultry; billowy; raging, seething; passionate; wavering

aest·us -ūs *m* agitation, anxiety, restlessness; glow, heat, sultriness; surge, billows; tide; **minuente aestū** at low tide

aet·ās -ātis *f* lifetime, age; period of life; generation; passage of time; age group; era; **aetātem agere** to spend one's life; **aetātem exigere** to live out one's life; **id** *(or* **hōc)** **aetātis** at this time of life; **media** *(or* **cōnstāns,** *or* **firmāta)** **aetās** middle age; **prōvecta aetās** old age

aetātul·a -ae *f* tender age

aeternit·ās -ātis *f* eternity; immortality; *(of things)* durability; courtesy title of the Emperor

aeternō *adv* forever

aetern·ō -āre *tr* to perpetuate, immortalize

aeternum *adv* forever; constantly

aetern·us -a -um *adj* eternal, everlasting, immortal; imperishable; durable; permanent, enduring a lifetime; *(of events)* remembered for ever; **in aeternum** forever

aeth·ēr -eris *m* upper air *(opp:* **āër);** sky, heaven; upper world *(opp:* Hades)

aetheri·us -a -um *adj* ethereal, heavenly; of the upper world; **ignēs aetheriī** inspiration

Aethiopi·a -ae *f* Ethiopia

Aethi·ops -opis *m* Ethiopian; black man; *(poet)* Egyptian

aethr·a -ae *f* pure air, serene sky; air, sky, heavens

Aethr·a -ae *f* wife of Aegeus and mother of Theseus ‖ daughter of Oceanus and mother of Hyas ‖ wife of Hyperion

Aetn·a -ae *or* **Aetn·ē -ēs** *f* Mt. Etna

Aetnae·us -a -um *adj* of Etna; **frātrēs Aetnaeī** the Cyclopes

Aetōli·a -ae *f* district in N.W. Greece
Aetōlic·us *or* **Aetōli·us -a -um** *adj* Aetolian
Aetōl·us -a -um *adj* of Aetolia, Aetolian; of Diomedes; of Meleager, like those of Meleager; of Tydeus ‖ *mpl* Aetolians
aevit·ās -ātis *f* age, lifetime
aev·um -ī *n or* **aev·us -ī** *m* age, lifetime, life; time, period; generation; eternity; **ad hōc aevī** hitherto; **aevō** *(or* **aevīs)** for ages; **aevum agere** *(or* **agitāre, dēgere, exigere)** to spend one's life; **ex ineunte aevō** from one's earliest years; **in** *(or* **per) (omne) aevum** forever; **prīmum aevum** early youth
Ā·fer -fra -frum *adj* African; **Āfer turbō** S.W. Wind ‖ *m* African ‖ Publius Terentius Afer *(i.e., Terence, playwright, d. 159 B.C.)* ‖ *mpl* Africans; inhabitants of the Roman province of N. Africa
affābil·is -is -e *adj* **(adf-)** affable; kind
affābilit·ās -ātis *f* **(adf-)** affability
affabrē *adv* **(adf-)** skillfully, ingeniously
affatim *or* **ad fatim** *adv* **(adf-)** sufficiently, enough
affātur (adf-) *see* **affor**
affātus *pp of* **affor**
affāt·us -ūs *m* **(adf-)** address, discourse
affectāti·ō -ōnis *f* **(adf-)** disposition, state of mind; affectation, conceit
affectāt·or -ōris *m* **(adf-)** *(w. gen)* aspirant to
affectāt·us -a -um *adj* **(adf-)** affected
affecti·ō -ōnis *f* **(adf-)** frame of mind, mood; feeling; attitude, point of view; inclination, partiality; affection
affect·ō -āre -āvī -ātus *tr* **(adf-)** to grasp; to strive after, aim at, aspire to *(power);* to try to win over; to affect, feign; *(w. inf)* to aim to; **dextrā affectāre** to lay one's hand on, seize; **iter** *(or* **viam) affectāre** to set out on a journey; **spem affectāre** to cherish a hope
affectus *pp of* **afficiō (adf-)**
affect·us -a -um *adj* **(adf-)** furnished, provided; gifted; weakened, sick; affected, moved, touched
affect·us -ūs *m* **(adf-)** state, disposition, mood; feeling, emotion; affection
afferō afferre attulī allātus *tr* **(adf-)** to bring; to carry, convey; to report, announce; to introduce; to quote; to apply, employ, exert, exercise; to produce, cause, occasion; to impart; to allege; to assign; to contribute; to help; to offer for sale; **auxilium** *(or* **opem) afferre** to bring help; **causam afferre** *(w. gen or dat)* to be the cause of; **in iūdicium causam afferre** to prefer charges; **manūs afferre** *(w. dat)* to lay violent hands on, attack
af·ficiō -ficere -fēcī -fectus *tr* **(adf-)** to treat, handle, manage; to influence, move; to attack, afflict; to impair; *(w. adv)* to treat *(in a certain way); (abl and verb may be rendered by the English verb corresponding to the Latin abl):* **cruce afficere** to crucify; **honōribus afficere** to honor; **suppliciō afficere** to punish
af·fīgō -fīgere -fīxī -fīxus *tr* **(adf-)** *(w. dat or* **ad)** to fasten, attach, nail to; to apply *(as a remedy);* **animō affīgere** to impress on the mind
af·fingō -fingere -fīnxī -fictus *tr* **(adf-)** to form, fashion besides; to make up, invent *(in a bad sense); (w. dat)* **1** to attach, affix, add, join, contribute *(s.th.)* to; **2** to connect with, associate with; **3** to ascribe to, impute to
affīn·is -is -e *adj* **(adf-)** adjoining, neighboring; related by marriage; *(w. dat or* **ad)** taking part in, privy to, associated with; subject to *(an affliction)* ‖ *mf* neighbor; in-law
affīnit·ās -ātis *f* **(adf-)** affinity, connection; relationship by marriage
affirmātē *adv* **(adf-)** with solemn assurance, positively
affirmāti·ō -ōnis *f* **(adf-)** affirmation, assertion, declaration; emphasis
affirm·ō -āre -āvī -ātus *tr* **(adf-)** to strengthen; to confirm, encourage; to assert
affīx·us -a -um *pp of* **affīgō (adf-)** ‖ *adj (w. dat)* **1** *(of guards, attendants)* assigned to; **2** attached to, devoted to; **3** intent on
afflāt·us -ūs *m* **(adf-)** blast, breeze; breath; inspiration
affl·eō -ēre *tr* **(adf-)** to weep at
afflīctāti·ō -ōnis *f* affliction
afflīct·ō -āre -āvī -ātus *tr* **(adf-)** to strike repeatedly; *(of storms)* to toss about; to shatter, damage; to trouble, distress, torment; *(mil)* to harass ‖ *refl & pass* to be troubled
afflīct·or -ōris *m* **(adf-)** subverter
afflīct·us -a -um *adj* **(adf-)** damaged, shattered; downhearted; vile
af·flīgō -flīgere -flīxī -flīctus *tr* **(adf-)** to knock down; to batter; to injure, damage; to distress, afflict; *(fig)* to crush
affl·ō -āre -āvī -ātus *tr* **(adf-)** to blast *(w. heat, lightning); (w. dat)* **1** to breathe on, blow on; **2** to impart to ‖ *intr (of winds)* to blow; *(of smells)* to be wafted; to blow favorably ‖ *pass (of sounds or smells)* to carry toward
afflu·ēns -entis *adj* **(adf-)** flowing; affluent; abounding, numerous
affluenter *adv* **(adf-)** lavishly, abundantly
affluenti·a -ae *f* **(adf-)** flow; abundance; extravagance
afflu·ō -ere -xī -xum *intr* **(adf-)** *(w. dat or* **ad)** **1** to flow to *or* toward, glide by; **2** to flock to; *(w. abl)* to abound in

af·for -fārī -fātus sum *tr* **(adf-)** *(of this defective verb, the chief forms in use are pres indic* **affātur, affāminī, affantur;** *pres impv* **affāre;** *inf* **affārī;** *pp* **affātus)** to address, accost ‖ *pass* to be destined

affore = adfutūrus esse *(fut inf of* **adsum)**

afforem = adessem *(imperf subj of* **adsum)**

afformīd·ō -āre *intr* **(adf-)** to get scared

afful·geō -gēre -sī *intr* **(adf-)** to shine, beam; to dawn; to appear; *(w. dat)* to shine on

af·fundō -fundere -fūdī -fūsus *tr* **(adf-)** *(w. dat)* **1** to pour, sprinkle *(s.th.)* on; **2** to send *or* dispatch *(s.o.)* to ‖ *refl & pass (w. dat)* to prostrate oneself before

aflu·ō -ere -xī *intr* **(abf-)** to flow away; to be abundant; *(w. abl)* to abound in; *(w.* **ex)** to issue from, come from

āfore = āfutūrus esse *(fut inf of* **absum)**

āforem = abessem *(imperf subj of* **absum)**

Afrāni·us -a -um *adj* Roman clan name *(nomen), esp.* Lucius Afranius *(comic poet)* ‖ Lucius Afranius *(one of Pompey's generals)*

Āfric·a -ae *f* originally the district of Carthage, made a Roman province after the 3rd Punic War in 146 B.C.; continent of Africa; *(fig)* inhabitants of Africa

Āfricān·us -a -um *adj* African ‖ *m* Roman honorary name *(agnomen)* conferred upon the two Scipios

Āfric·us -a -um *adj* African ‖ *m* S.W. wind

āfuī *perf of* **absum**

āfutūrus *fut p of* **absum**

Agamēmn·ōn -onis *m* king of Mycenae, son of Atreus and Aërope, brother of Menelaus, murdered by his wife Clytemnestra

Agamēmnonid·ēs -ae *m* son of Agamemnon *(i.e., Orestes)*

Agamēmnoni·us -a -um *adj* of Agamemnon, descended from Agamemnon

Aganipp·ē -ēs *f* fountain on Mt. Helicon sacred to the Muses

agās·ō -ōnis *m* stable boy; driver; lackey

Agathocl·ēs -is *m* king of Sicily, son of a potter, famous for his war with Carthage over the possession of Sicily *(361–287 B.C.)*

Agāv·ē -ēs *f* wife of Echion, king of Thebes, and mother of Pentheus

agedum *interj* come on!; well!

agell·us -ī *m* little field, plot

agēm·a -atis *n (mil)* honor guard

Agēn·or -oris *m* son of Belus, king of Phoenicia, father of Cadmus and Europa, and ancestor of Dido

Agēnorid·ēs -ae *m* descendant of Agenor *(esp. Cadmus, Perseus)*

ag·ēns -entis *pres p of* **agō** ‖ *adj* powerful, striking ‖ *mpl* secret police *(under the Empire)*

a·ger -grī *m* (arable) land, (tilled) field *(opp:* **campus** = untilled, open land); ground; soil; farm, estate; territory, land, district; country *(opp:* **urbs); ager pūblicus** state-owned land; **in agrum** in depth *(opp:* **in fronte** in frontage) ‖ *mpl* countryside

agg·er -eris *m* rubble; soil; rampart; breakwater; dike, dam; fortification; ramp; pile, heap, collection; ridge, mound, hill; funeral pyre; **— rīpae** bank *(of river);* **— (viae)** causeway

agger·ō -āre -āvī -ātus *tr* to pile up, fill up; to amass; to increase; *(fig)* to stimulate, intensify

ag·gerō -gerere -gessī -gestus *tr* **(adg-)** to bring forward; to pile up; *(w. dat)* to heap *(accusations, benefits)* on

aggest·us -ūs *m* **(adg-)** accumulation; terrace

agglomer·ō -āre -āvī -ātus *tr* **(adg-)** to gather together ‖ *refl & intr* to gather

agglūtin·ō -āre -āvī -ātus *tr* **(adg-)** to glue, paste; to solder ‖ *refl (w.* **ad)** to stick close to

aggravēsc·ō -ere *intr* **(adg-)** to grow heavy; *(of diseases)* to get worse

aggrav·ō -āre -āvī -ātus *tr* **(adg-)** to weigh down; to make *(conditions)* worse, aggravate; to increase the force of *(a blow); (fig)* to burden, oppress

ag·gredior -gredī -gressus sum *tr* **(adg-)** to approach; to address; to attack; *(w. inf)* to undertake to ‖ *intr (w.* **ad)** *(fig)* to tackle

aggreg·ō -āre -āvī -ātus *tr* **(adg-)** to assemble; *(w.* **in** *acc)* include (in); to implicate; *(leg) (w. dat)* to lump together with ‖ *refl & pass* to flock together; *(w. dat or* **ad)** to join

aggressi·ō -ōnis *f* **(adg-)** attack; *(rhet)* introduction

aggressus *pp of* **aggredior (adg-)**

agil·is -is -e *adj* agile, nimble, quick; busy, active; easily moved, mobile

agilit·ās -ātis *f* agility, nimbleness, quickness; activity; mobility

agitābil·is -is -e *adj* mobile

agitāti·ō -ōnis *f* motion, movement, agitation; activity; waving *(of arms)*

agitāt·or -ōris *m* driver; charioteer

agit·ō -āre -āvī -ātus *tr* to set in motion; to drive on, impel; to hunt; to scour *(for game);* to brandish, wave *(weapon);* to pursue *(an objective);* to shake *(reins);* to drive *(vehicle);* to ride *(horse);* to tend *(flocks);* to urge, support, insist on; to practice *(justice, a trade)*; to exercise *(the body);* to engage in *(conversation);* to enjoy *(peace, fame);* to observe, celebrate; to obey, carry out; to spend, pass *(time);* to toss, disturb; to distress; to stimulate, arouse *(the mind, emotions);*

to deride, insult; to criticize; to discuss; to cherish *(hope);* **sēcum** *(or* **animō** *or* **mente) agitāre** to think about, consider, ponder; *(w. indirect question)* to debate *(in one's mind)* ‖ *intr* to live, spend one's life

Āglaur·ōs -ī *f* daughter of Cecrops

agm·en -inis *n* herd, flock, troop, crowd; body, mass; army column; procession; retinue, escort; course, flow *(of a stream);* movement *(of oars);* **agmen claudere** *(or* **cōgere)** to bring up the rear; **agmen dūcere** to form the van; **agmen prīmum** the van; **agmine** *(or* **ūnō agmine** *or* **agmine factō)** in marching formation; in a body

agn·a -ae *f* lamb *(female)*

ag·nāscor -nāscī -nātus sum *intr* to be born subsequently *(after the father has made his will);* **testāmentum agnāscendō rumpitur** a will is broken by the subsequent birth (of a son)

agnāti·ō -ōnis *f* blood relationship *(on the father's side)*

agnāt·us -ī *m* relative *(on the father's side)*

agnell·us -ī *m* little lamb

agnīn·a -ae *f* mutton, lamb

agniti·ō -ōnis *f* recognition, acknowledgement, admission; knowledge

ag·nōscō -nōscere -nōvī -nitus *tr* to recognize, identify; to acknowledge; to own up to, admit to

agn·us -ī *m* lamb

agō agere ēgī āctus *tr* to drive, lead, conduct; to chase, hunt; to drive away, steal; to spend *(time);* to do; to manage, administer, carry on; to transact; to discuss; to play, act the part of; to plead *(a case);* to exercise, practice; to hold *(an office);* to celebrate *(triumph);* to work at, be busy on; to have in mind, plan; to push *(siege works)* forward; to emit *(smoke, flames);* to trace *(one's descent);* *(fig)* to dispel *(fear, hunger, etc.);* to spend, pass *(time, life);* *(of plants)* to put forth *(roots, sprouts);* to drive *(chariot);* to sail *(ship);* to construct *(anything linear: rampart, tunnel);* **agere fūrtī** to accuse of theft *or* robbery; **agere reum** to indict a defendant; **aliud** *(or* **aliam rem) agere** not to attend to one's business; **animam agere** to breathe one's last; **grātiās agere** to thank; **in crucem agere** to crucify; **iter** *(or* **cursum) agere** to make one's way; **nūgās agere** to act foolishly; **praedam** *(or* **bovēs) agere** to rustle cattle; **prīmās partēs agere** to play the lead role; **proelium agere** to do battle; **quid agis?** how do you do? **quō agis?** what's your point?; **satis agere** to have more than enough to do; **spūmās agere** to foam *(at the mouth)* ‖ *refl* to go, come; to grow; to behave, comport oneself ‖ *pass* to be done, happen, occur, come to pass; to be involved, be at stake; **bene agitur** things turn out well; **quid agitur?** what's going on? ‖ *intr* to take action, act; to be busy; to bargain; to live, dwell; *(theat)* to act; **age**! come on!; *(in assent)* O.K., very well; **bene (male) agere cum aliquō** to treat s.o. well (badly); **cum populō** *(or* **ad populum) agere** to address the people; **quō tū agis?** where are you off to?

-āg·ō -inis *fem suf* mostly formed from verbs in **-āre: imāgō** image; also from other sources: **cartilāgō** cartilage

ag·ōn -ōnis *m* contest

agrāri·us -a -um *adj* agrarian, land ‖ *mpl* land-reform party

agrest·is -is -e *adj* rustic, country; boorish; wild, uncultivated *(plants);* savage; uncivilized ‖ *m* peasant, rustic

agricol·a -ae *m* farmer, peasant

Agricol·a -ae *m* Gnaeus Julius Agricola *(father-in-law of Tacitus)*

agricultūr·a -ae *f* agriculture

Agrigent·um -ī *n* city on S. coast of Sicily *(modern Agrigento)*

agripet·a -ae *m* colonist, settler

Āgripp·a -ae *m* Marcus Vipsanius Agrippa *(son-in-law of Augustus, husband of Julia, and father of Agrippina)*

Āgrippīn·a -ae *f* Vipsania Agrippina *(daughter of Agrippa, wife of Tiberius and mother of Drusus, d.* A.D. *20)* ‖ Vipsania Agrippina Major *(wife of Germanicus and mother of Caligula, d.* A.D. *33)* ‖ Julia Agrippina Minor *(daughter of the previous Agrippina and Germanicus, and mother of Nero, (murdered by Nero in* A.D. *59)*

āh *interj (denoting various feelings: distress, pity, regret; surprise, joy; contempt; entreaty)* ah!, ha!, oh!

aha *interj (denoting surprise, irony)* aha!

ai *interj (denoting grief)* ah!

Āi·āx -ācis *m* son of Telamon *(king of Salamis)* ‖ son of Oïleus *(king of the Locri)*

āin = aisne *(see* **āiō)**

āiō *tr & intr (used mainly in pres and imperf indic; opp:* **negō**) I say; I say yes, I say so; I assert, tell relate; **ain (= aisne) tandem?** *(or* **ain tū?** *or* **ain tūte** *or* **ain vērō?)** *(coll) (expressing surprise)* do you really mean it?, you don't say!, really?

-al -ālis *neut suf* forms neuter nouns: **animal** animal; **cubital** elbow cushion

āl·a -ae *f* wing; armpit; squadron *(of cavalry);* flank *(of battle line);* reef *(of a sail)*

alabas·ter -trī *m,* **alabastr·um -ī** *n* perfume box

ala·cer *or* **ala·cris -cris -cre** *adj* lively, brisk; quick; eager; active; cheerful

alacrit·ās -ātis *f* liveliness, briskness; quickness; eagerness; cheerfulness
alap·a -ae *f* slap; ceremonius slap given to a slave at emancipation
ālār·is -is -e *adj (mil)* consisting of auxiliary cavalry
ālāri·us -a -um *adj* consisting of auxiliary troops ‖ *mpl* auxiliaries, allies
ālāt·us -a -um *adj* winged
alaud·a -ae *f* lark
Alb·a -ae *f* town *(also called Alba Longa)* founded by Ascanius
Albān·ī -ōrum *mpl* inhabitants of Alba Longa
Albān·um -ī *n* Alban estate; Alban wine
albāt·us -a -um *adj* dressed in white
alb·eō -ēre -uī *intr* to be white
albēsc·ō -ere *intr* to turn white, whiten; to dawn; *(of hair)* to turn grey
albic·ō -āre -āvī -ātum *or* **albic·or -ārī -ātus sum** *intr* to be white, be whitish
albid·us -a -um *adj* white, whitish
Albi·ōn -ōnis *f* Britain
albitūd·ō -inis *f* whiteness
Albul·a -ae *f* earlier name of the Tiber River
albul·us -a -um *adj* whitish
alb·um -ī *n* white; record, list, register; white tablet: **1** = the Annales Maximi *(the record of the year's event, kept by the Pontifex Maximus;* **2** the tablet on which the edicts of the praetor were posted in public; **3** list or register of names, e.g., of senators or jurors, etc.
Albune·a -ae *f* fountain at Tibur; nymph of that fountain
alb·us -a -um *adj* flat white; bright, shining, clear *(sky, light, sun, etc.);* favorable; clad in white; light-skinned, fair; whitened, made white; favorable, auspicious; grey *(hair);* pale *(from fear, sickness);* **album opus** stucco work; **albus āterne sit nēscīre** not to know a person from Adam *(literally, not to know whether he is white or black)* ‖ *m* white man
Alcae·us -ī *m* Greek lyric poet from the Island of Lesbos *(fl. 610 B.C.)*
alcēd·ō -inis *f* kingfisher, halcyon
alcēdōni·a -ōrum *npl* halcyon days; *(fig)* deep calm, tranquillity
alc·ēs -is *f* elk
Alcēst·is -is *or* **Alcēst·ē -ēs** *f* Alcestis *(loyal wife of Admetus, king of Pherae, who gave up her life to save the life of her husband; she was rescued by Hercules and given back to Admetus)*
Alc·eūs -eī *and* **-eos** *m* father of Amphitryon and grandfather of Hercules
Alcibiad·ēs -ae *or* **-is** *or* **-ī** *m* Athenian politician, disciple of Socrates *(450?–404 B.C.)*
Alcīd·ēs -ae *m* descendant of Alceus *(esp. Hercules)*
Alcimed·ē -ēs *f* wife of Aeson and mother of Jason
Alcino·ūs -ī *m* king of the Phaeacians, who entertained Ulysses
Alcitho·ē -ēs *f* daughter of Minyas of Thebes, changed into a bat for ridiculing Bacchic rites
Alc(u)mēn·a -ae *or* **Alcmēn·ē -ēs** *f* Alcmene *(wife of Amphitryon and mother of Hercules by Jupiter)*
alcy·ōn -onis *f* **(hal-)** halcyon *(bird believed to build its nest on the sea)*
Alcyon·ē -ēs *or* **Alcyon·a -ae** *f* **(Hal-)** Alcyone (daughter of Aeolus and wife of Cyex *(both of whom were changed into halcyons)* ‖ wife of Meleager ‖ one of the Pleiades
āle·a -ae *f* dice game; gambling; die; risk, gamble; **āleā lūdere** to gamble; **iacta ālea est** the die is cast
āleāri·us -a -um *adj* gambling
āleāt·or -ōris *mf* gambler
āleātōri·us -a -um *adj* gambling
ālēc *see* **allēc**
Ālect·ō -ūs *f* one of the three Furies
āle·ō -ōnis *m* gambler
āl·es -itis *adj* winged ‖ *mf* winged creature, bird ‖ *m* poet; Cupid ‖ *f* augury, omen
alēsc·ō -ere *intr* to grow up
Alexan·der -drī *m* Paris *(son of Priam and Hecuba)* ‖ Alexander the Great *(son of Philip II and Olympias, and king of Macedonia, 356–323 B.C.)* ‖ son of Perseus *(king of Macedonia)* ‖ a tyrant of Pherae in Thessaly ‖ a king of Epirus
Alexandrē·a -ae *f* **(-drī·a)** Alexandria (Greek city of N. Egypt, founded by Alexander the Great)
Alexandrīn·us -a -um *adj* Alexandrine; characteristic of Alexandria *(i.e., luxurious)*
alg·a -ae *f* seaweed
alg·ēns -entis *adj* cold; **algēns toga** thin toga
alg·eō -ēre ālsī *intr* to be cold; to feel cold; to endure cold; *(fig)* to be left out in the cold
al·gēscō -gēscere ālsī *intr* to catch a cold
algid·us -a -um *adj* cold
Algid·us -a -um *adj* of Mt. Algidus ‖ *m* mountain in Latium, S. of Tusculum
alg·or -ōris *m* cold; fit of shivering
alg·us -ūs *m* the cold
ali- *a stem meaning* else, different, other, *e.g.,* **alius;** *but when combined with* **quis, quam, cubi,** *etc., is translated* some or other, *e.g.,* **aliquis** someone or other, **alicubi** somewhere or other
aliā *adv* by another way
aliās *adv* at another time, at other times; previously; subsequently; in other circumstances, otherwise; apart from this, in

any case, besides; all the same, nevertheless; **aliās** ... **aliās** at one time ... at another, sometimes ... sometimes
āliāt·um -ī *n* food flavored with garlic
alibī *adv* elsewhere; otherwise, in other respects; in another passage *(in a book, speech);* **alibī** ... **alibī** in one place ... in another, here ... there; **alibī aliter** differently in different places; **alius alibī** one in one place, another in another
alic·a -ae *f* emmer *(type of wheat)*
alicāri·us -a -um *adj* of emmer ‖ *f* prostitute
ali-cubi *adv* somewhere or other; anywhere (at all); occasionally
ālicul·a -ae *f* light cape
ali-cunde *adv* from somewhere; from someone else
aliēnāti·ō -ōnis *f* transfer *(of property);* alienation; aversion; **aliēnātiō mentis** insanity
aliēnigen·a -ae *m* foreigner, stranger *(born in another country)*
aliēn·ō -āre -āvī -ātus *tr* to transfer, sell; to give up *(children)* for adoption; to alienate, set at variance; to treat as an enemy; to remove, separate; to drive mad; **ā sēnsū aliēnāre** to deprive of feeling; **paene aliēnātā mente** almost driven mad ‖ *pass* to fall into s.o. else's hands; *(mil)* to fall into the enemy's hands; *(w.* **ab)** to recoil from
aliēn·us -a -um *adj* another's; foreign; contrary; hostile; strange; unsuitable; incongruous, inconsistent; inconvenient; **aliēnum est** it is out-of-place, it is amiss ‖ *m* stranger, foreigner ‖ *n* another's property; foreign soil ‖ *npl* another's affairs
ālif·er *or* **ālig·er -era -erum** *adj* winged, wearing wings
alimentāri·us -a -um *adj* **(alum-)** relating to welfare
aliment·um -ī *n* **(alum-)** nourishment, food, provisions; fuel ‖ *npl* means of livelihood; alms
alimōni·a -ae *f or* **alimōn·ium -(i)ī** *n* nourishment, food; support; cost of living
aliō *adv* to another place, elsewhere; to another topic; to another policy; for another purpose; **aliō** ... **aliō** in one direction ... in another; **alius aliō** one in one direction, another in another
aliōquī(n) *adv* otherwise, in other respects, for the rest; apart from these considerations; besides; in general; in any case
aliōrsum *or* **aliōvorsum** *adv* **(-sus)** in another direction; in a different manner; in a different sense
ālip·ēs -edis *adj* wing-footed, swift-footed
alipt·ēs *or* **alipt·a -ae** *m* wrestling trainer, rubdown man
aliquā *adv* somehow; to some extent
aliquam *adv* to some degree; **aliquam multī** fairly many
aliquamdiū *adv* **(-quan-)** for some time; for a considerable distance
aliquandō *adv* sometime or other, once; at any time, ever; now and then; for once, now; finally, now at last; someday *(in the future)*
aliquantill·um -ī *n* a bit
aliquantisper *adv* for a while
aliquantō *adv* somewhat, to some extent, a little, rather
aliquantulum *adv* somewhat
aliquantul·us -a -um *adj* little ‖ *n* a small amount
aliquantum *adv* somewhat, a little, rather
aliquant·us -a -um *adj* considerable ‖ *n* a certain amount *(of);* a certain degree *(of);* a bit, a part
aliquātenus *adv* for some distance; to a certain extent; in some respects, partly; up to a point
ali·quī -qua -quod *adj* some; *(after a negative,* **sī**, *etc.)* any at all
aliquid *adv* to some extent
ali·quid -cūius *pron* something, anything; something important; **ad aliquid esse** *(of a term)* to be relative; **aliud aliquid** something else; **aliquid vīnī** some wine; **est aliquid** *(w. inf)* it is something to ‖ *adv* to some degree
ali·quis -cūius *pron* someone, somebody, anyone; someone important
aliquō *adv* to some place, somewhere
aliquot *indecl adj* some, several
aliquotiēns *adv* several times
aliquōvorsum *adv* in one direction or another
aliter *adv* otherwise, else; **aliter** ... **aliter** in one way ... in another; **aliter atque aliter** now in one way, now in another; **aliter esse** *or* **aliter sē habēre** to be different; **nōn** *(or* **haud) aliter quam** *(or* **ac) sī** just as if
alitus *pp of* **alō**
aliubi *adv* elsewhere; **aliubi** ... **aliubi** here ... there
āl·ium -(i)ī *n* **(āli-)** garlic
aliunde *adv* from another place; **aliunde** ... **aliunde** from one place ... from another; **alius aliunde** one from one place, another from another
ali·us -a -ud *adj (gen singl is generally* **alterīus;** *dat:* **alterī)** another, other, different; *(w.* **ac, atque, et, nisi, quam)** other than ‖ *pron* another; **aliī** ... **aliī** some ... others; **alius** ... **alius** one ... another, the one ... the other; **alius atque alius** first one person, then another; **alius ex aliō** one after another
al·lābor -lābī -lāpsus sum *intr* **(adl-)** to glide toward, slide toward, slip; *(of liq-*

uids) to flow toward, appraoch; *(of missiles)* to fly toward, go sailing toward
allabōr·ō -āre *intr* **(adl-)** to work hard
allacrim·ō -āre *intr* **(adl-)** to weep
allāps·us -ūs *m* **(adl-)** slithering
allātr·ō -āre -āvī -ātus *tr* **(adl-)** to bark at; *(fig)* to revile; *(of sea)* to break against
allāt·us -a -um *pp of* **afferō (adf-)**
allaudābil·is -is -e *adj* praiseworthy
allaud·ō -āre *tr* **(adl-)** to praise highly
all·ēc -ēcis *n* **(hall-)** fish sauce
allēcti·ō -ōnis *f* **(adl-)** promotion, advancement
allect·ō -āre *tr* **(adl-)** to allure, entice
Allect·ō -ūs *f* **(Ālec-)** Alecto *(one of the three Furies)*
allēgāti·ō -ōnis *f* **(adl-)** intercession; allegation
allēgāt·us -ūs *m* **(adl-)** prompting, instigation **II** *mpl* deputies
allēg·ō -āre -āvī -ātus *tr* **(adl-)** to commission; to deputize; to put up; to dispatch; to allege; to instigate; *(w. dat)* to lay *(prayers)* before
al·legō -legere -lēgī -lēctus *tr* **(adl-)** to select; to appoint *(to an office)*
allēgori·a -ae *f* allegory
allevāment·um -ī *n* **(adl-)** alleviation
allevāti·ō -ōnis *f* lifting; alleviating, easing
allev·ō -āre -āvī -ātus *tr* **(adl-)** to lift up, raise; to alleviate; to comfort; to lighten
Alli·a -ae *f* tributary of the Tiber where the Gauls defeated the Romans in 390 B.C.
allice·faciō -facere -fēcī -factus *tr* to entice, allure
al·liciō -licere -lexī -lectus *tr* **(adl-)** to attract; to bring on *(sleep)*; to attract the attention of; to win over
allī·dō -dere -sī -sus *tr* **(adl-)** *(w. dat or* **ad** *or* **in** *+ acc)* to dash *(s.th.)* against **II** *pass* to be shipwrecked
Alliēns·is -is -e *adj* of the Allia River; of the battle at the Allia River
allig·ō -āre -āvī -ātus *tr* **(adl-)** to bind; to bandage *(wounds)*; to tie up; to grip firmly; to hold together; to freeze solid; to curdle *(milk)*; to curb, restrict; to fetter; to hinder, detain; to involve, implicate; *(w.* **ad)** to bind *(s.th.)* to; *(of laws)* to be binding on
al·linō -linere -lēvī -litus *tr* **(adl-)** to smudge; *(w. dat)* to smear *(s.th.)* on
all·ium -(i)ī *n* garlic
Allobrog·ēs -um *mpl* Gallic tribe in Gallia Narbonensis
allocūti·ō -ōnis *f* **(adl-)** address; pep talk
alloqu·ium -(i)ī *n* **(adl-)** address; conversation; reassuring words
allo·quor -quī -cūtus sum *tr* **(adl-)** to speak to, address; to invoke *(gods)*; to console, comfort
allubēsc·ō -ere *intr* **(adl-)** to be lovely
allūc·eō -ēre -xī *intr* **(adl-)** *(w. dat)* to be a light for
allūdi·ō -āre *intr* **(adl-)** to play, frolic
allū·dō -dere -sī -sus *tr* **(adl-)** to play with **II** *intr* to play, joke; *(of waves) (w. dat)* to lap; *(w. dat or* **ad)** to allude playfully to
allu·ō -ere -ī *tr* **(adl-)** *(of rivers, the sea)* to flow past, lap, touch; *(of water)* to touch, wet *(a part of the body)*
alluvi·ēs -ēī *f* **(adl-)** pool *(left by flood waters)*; silt
alluvi·ō -ōnis *f* **(adl-)** flood; alluvial land
alm·us -a -um *adj* nourishing; kind, gracious; bountiful *(earth)*
aln·us -ī *f* alder tree; *(fig)* ship
al·ō -ere -uī -tus *or* **-itus** *tr* to nurse, breastfeed; to feed, nourish; to promote the growth of; to raise *(children, animals)*; to support *(family, etc.)*; *(of places, employment)* to provide a livelihood for; to foment *(discord)*; to encourage; to promote the interests of; to increase; to strengthen
alo·ē -ēs *f (bot)* aloe *(whose bitter juice was used as a purgative)*; bitterness
Alō·eus -eī *m* a son of Poseidon and Canace
alogi·a -ae *f* folly, nonsense
Alōïd·ae -ārum *mpl* the giants Otus and Ephialtes *(sons of Poseidon and Iphimedeia, the wife of Aloeus)*
Alp·ēs -ium *fpl* the Alps
alpha *indecl n* alpha *(first letter of the Greek alphabet)*
Alphē·us *or* **Alphī·us** *or* **Alphē·os -ī** *m* Alpheus *(chief river of the Peloponnesus)*
Alpic·us -a -um *adj* Alpine
Alpīn·us -a -um *adj* Alpine
alsī *perf of* **algeō** *and* **algēscō**
als(i)·us -a -um *adj* chilly, cold
altār·ia -ium *npl* altar; altars, high altars; burnt-offerings
altē *adv* high, on high, highly; from a great height; deeply, far, remotely; intensely, profoundly
alt·er -era -erum *adj* one *(of two)*; a second, the second, the next **II** *pron* one *(of two)*, the one, the other; a second one, the second one, the next one; anyone else; another *(one's fellow man)*; **alter ... alter** the one ... the other, the former ... the latter; **ūnus et** *(or* **aut) alter** one or two
alterās *adv* at another time
altercāti·ō -ōnis *f* altercation, dispute, argument; *(phil)* debate
altercāt·or -ōris *m* disputant, debater
alterc·ō -āre *or* **alterc·or -ārī -ātus sum** *intr* to argue, wrangle; to argue back and forth *(in court)*
alternīs *adv* by turns, alternately
altern·ō -āre -āvī -ātus *tr* to do by turns; to alternate, arrange in alternating order; to exchange **II** *intr* to alternate

altern·us -a -um *adj* one after another, alternate; mutual; every other; **alternā vice** *(or* **alternīs vicibus)** alternately; in turn, successively; **in alternum** for one another, reciprocally; **īre per alternās vicēs** to go back and forth
alteru·ter -tra -trum *(fem also* **altera utra;** *neut also* **alterum utrum)** *adj* one *(of two),* either, one or the other ‖ *pron* one, either one, one or the other
Althae·a -ae *f* wife of Oeneus, king of Calydon, and mother of Meleager
alticīnct·us -a -um *adj* energetic
altil·is -is -e *adj* fattened, fat; *(fig)* rich ‖ *f* fattened fowl
altison·us -a -um *adj* sounding from on high; sublime
altiton·āns -antis *adj* thundering on high
altitūd·ō -inis *f* height; depth; *(fig)* profundity *(of mind);* loftiness *(of style);* **ad** *or* **in altitūdinem** vertically ‖ *fpl* the heights
altiusculē *adv* rather high
altiuscul·us -a -um *adj* rather high
altivol·āns -antis, altivol·us -a -um *adj* high-flying
alt·or -ōris *m* foster father
altrim secus *adv* on the other side
altrīnsecus *adv* on the other side
altr·īx -īcis *f* foster mother; wet nurse; *(of the earth)* nourisher; motherland
altrōvorsum *adv* **(-sus)** on the other hand
alt·us -a -um *adj* high; tall; deep; profound *(wisdom);* deep, loud *(sound);* intense *(heat, cold);* thick *(fog);* high-born, ancient *(lineage)* ‖ *n* high seas, the deep; heaven; **ab altō** from on high, from heaven; **ex altō** far-fetched; **ex altō petere** *(or* **repetere)** to go far afield for
ālūcin·or -ārī -ātus sum *intr* **(hāl-, allūc-)** to ramble on; to rave; to daydream
alumn·a -ae *f* foster daughter
alumn·us -ī *m* foster son
alūt·a -ae *f* soft leather; shoe; purse
alv(e)ār·ium -(i)ī *n* beehive
alveol·us -ī *m* bowl, basin; bathtub; river bed; game board
alve·us -ī *m* hollow; tub; bathtub; riverbed; hull of boat; game board; beehive
alv·us -ī *f (m)* belly, bowels, stomach; womb; rectum; boat; beehive; **alvum purgāre** (*or* **solvere)** to move the bowels; **alvus fūsa** *(or* **cita)** diarrhea
am- *pref see* **ambi-**
amābil·is -is -e *adj* lovable, lovely, attractive; delightful
amābilit·ās -ātis *f* attractiveness
amābiliter *adv* lovingly, delightfully
Amalthē·a -ae *f* nymph who fed infant Jupiter with goat's milk ‖ Cumaean sibyl
āmandāti·ō -ōnis *f* sending away
āmand·ō -āre -āvī -ātus *tr* **(amend-)** to send away
am·āns -antis *adj* loving, affectionate; **amāns patriae** patriotic ‖ *mf* lover
amanter *adv* lovingly, affectionately
āmanuēns·is -is *m* secretary
amārac·us -ī *mf and* **amārac·um -ī** *n* marjoram *(aromatic plants whose leaves are used as seasoning)*
amarant·us -ī *m* amaranth *(imaginary flower that never fades)*
amārē *adv* bitterly
amāriti·ēs -ēī *f* bitterness
amāritūd·ō -inis *f* bitterness; tang; sadness
amār·or -ōris *m* bitterness
amār·us -a -um *adj* bitter, pungent, tangy; shrill; brackish; **nux amāra** almond
Amaryll·is -idis *f* conventional name for a shepherdess
amāsi·ō -ōnis *m* lover
amāsiuncul·a -ae *f* darling
amāsiuncul·us -ī *m* lover
amās·ius -(i)ī *m* lover
amāt·a -ae *f* loved one
Amāt·a -ae *f* mother of Lavinia
Amath·ūs -untis *f* town in Cyprus
Amathūsiac·us -a -um *adj* of Amathus
Amathūsi·us -a -um *adj* of Amathus ‖ *f* Venus
amāti·ō -ōnis *f* love affair
amāt·or -ōris *m* lover; friend; **amātor patriae** patriot
amātorcul·us -ī *m* poor little lover
amātōriē *adv* lovingly
amātōri·us -a -um *adj* erotic, love ‖ *n* love charm
amātr·īx -īcis *f* mistress, girlfriend
Amāz·ōn -onis *or* **Amāzon·is -idis** *f* Amazon
Amāzonic·us -a -um *adj* Amazonian
Amāzoni·us -a -um *adj* Amazonian
amb- *pref see* **ambi-**
ambact·us -ī *m* vassal
ambāg·ēs -is *f* a winding, labyrinth; double talk; roundabout way; digression; ambiguity, obscurity; **per ambāgēs** enigmatically
amb·edō -ēsse -ēdī -ēsus *tr* to eat up; to waste, squander; *(of fire)* to char
ambestr·īx -īcis *f* gluttonous woman
ambi- *pref (before vowels usually* **amb-;** *before consonants* **ambi-, am-, an-)** around
ambig·ō -ere *tr* to go around, avoid; to call into question, debate ‖ *intr* to waver, hesitate, be undecided; to argue, debate, wrangle ‖ *v impers* **ambigitur** it is uncertain
ambiguē *adv* indecisively; ambiguously; in an untrustworthy manner
ambiguit·ās -ātis *f* ambiguity
ambigu·us -a -um *adj* wavering, changeable; uncertain; disputed; unreliable, untrustworthy; ambiguous, dark, obscure ‖ *n* doubt, uncertainty; paradox

amb·iō -īre -īvī *or* **-iī -itus** *tr* to go the round of; to go around, encircle; to throng; to go round, go past; to embrace; to include; *(pol)* to campaign for ‖ *intr* to move in an orbit; to rotate

ambiti·ō -ōnis *f* ambition *(in good and bad sense);* popularity; flattery; partiality, favoritism; pomp, ostentation; *(pol)* campaigning *(by lawful means)*

ambitiōsē *adv* ambitiously; ostentatiously; from a desire to please

ambitiōs·us -a -um *adj* winding; publicity-conscious; ambitious; ostentatious; eager for popularity

ambit·us -ūs *m* winding, revolution; circuit, circumference, border; orbit; ostentation; circumlocution; *(pol)* illegal campaign practices, bribery; **ambitus verbōrum** *(or* **ōrātiōnis)** phrase; *(rhet)* rounded and balanced sentence, period

ambiv·ium -(i)ī *n* road junction

amb·ō -ae -ō *adj (dat & abl:* **ambōbus, ambābus;** *acc:* **ambō** *&* **ambōs)** both, two ‖ *pron* both, the two

Ambraci·a -ae *f* district of Epirus

Ambraciēns·is -is -e *adj* of Ambracia

Ambraciōt·ēs -ae *m* an Ambracian

Ambraci·us -a -um *adj* of Ambracia

ambrosi·a -ae *f* ambrosia *(food of the gods; imaginary healing plant)*

ambrosi·us -a -um *adj* **(-e·us)** ambrosial, divine

ambūbāi·a -ae *f* Syrian singer and courtesan ‖ *(bot)* wild endive

ambulācr·um -ī *n* walk, avenue

ambulāti·ō -ōnis *f (act; place)* walk

ambulātiuncul·a -ae *f* short walk; small promenade

ambulāt·or -ōris *m* stroller *(person);* idler, loafer; peddler

ambulātōri·us -a -um *adj* movable

ambul·ō -āre -āvī -ātus *tr* to traverse, travel ‖ *intr* to walk, take a walk; to march; to travel; to strut; *(of things)* to extend, run; **bene ambulā**! bon voyage!

amb·ūrō -ūrere -ūssī -ūstus *tr* to burn up; to scorch, char; to scald; to cremate; *(of cold)* to numb, nip

ambūstulāt·us -a -um *adj* half-roasted

ambūstus *pp of* **ambūrō** ‖ *n* a burn

amell·us -ī *m (bot)* wild aster *(plant having daisylike flowers of various colors)*

ām·ēns -entis *adj* insane; foolish, stupid

āmenti·a -ae *f* insanity; folly

āment·ō -āre -āvī -ātus *tr* **(amm-)** to fit *(a javelin)* with a strap

āment·um -ī *n* **(amm-)** strap, thong

Ameri·a -ae *f* town in Umbria, noted for its osiers *(modern Amelia)*

Amerīn·us -a -um *adj* of Ameria; produced in Ameria ‖ *m* Amerian

am·es -itis *m* pole for fowler's net; fence rail

amethystināt·us -a -um *adj* dressed in violet-blue

amethystin·us -a -um *adj* violet-blue; set with amethysts ‖ *npl* violet-blue garments

amethyst·us -ī *f* amethyst

amfrāctus *see* anfrāctus

amīc·a -ae *f* girlfriend, lady friend; mistress

amīcē *adv* in a friendly way

am·iciō -icīre -icuī *or* **-īxī -ictus** *tr* to wrap around; to cover, clothe, wrap

amīciter *adv* in a friendly way

amīciti·a -ae *f* friendship; alliance, ties of friendship *(between nations);* **amīcitiam comparāre** *(or* **contrahere, iungere, facere)** cum *(w. abl)* to form an alliance *(or* league of friendship) with; **amīcitiam gerere** to carry on a friendship; **amīcitiam dīrumpere** to break off a friendship, sever ties of friendship; **in amīcitiā esse** to be on terms of friendship

amīciti·ēs -ēī *f see* **amīcitia**

amictori·um -ī *n* wrap

amictus *pp of* **amiciō**

amict·us -ūs *m* wrap, cloak; clothing; fashion *(in dress),* style *(in dress)*; headdress used in worship

amīcul·a -ae *f* girlfriend, mistress

amicul·um -ī *n* wrap, mantle ‖ *npl* clothing

amīcul·us -ī *m* dear friend; pal, buddy

amīc·us -a -um *adj* friendly; supportive; favorable, congenial; helpful; dear, welcome; **amīcus reīpūblicae** patriotic ‖ *m* friend; lover; partisan, supporter; companion, disciple; **amīcus reīpūblicae** patriot ‖ *f see* **amīca**

āmigr·ō -āre *intr* to move (away)

Amilcar *see* **Hamilcar**

āmissi·ō -ōnis *f* loss

āmissus *pp of* **āmittō**

āmiss·us -ūs *m* = **āmissiō**

amit·a -ae *f* aunt *(father's sister; mother's sister is* **mātertera); magna amita** great aunt

Amitern·um -ī *n* town in the Sabine district, birthplace of Sallust

ā·mittō -mittere -mīsī -missus *tr* to lose; to let slip, miss; to let go, release; to let fall, drop; **animam** *(or* **spīritum) āmittere** to lose one's life; **fidem āmittere** to break one's word; **spē āmissā** having given up hope

amm- = adm-

amment·ō -āre *see* **āmentō**

amment·um -ī *n* **(āmen-)** strap

Amm·ōn *or* **Hamm·ōn -ōnis** *m* an Ethiopian god, identical with Jupiter and represented as a ram

amnicol·a -ae *mf* riverside plant

amnicul·us -ī *m* brook

amn·is -is *m (f)* river; river water; **adversō amnī** upstream; **secundō amnī** downstream

am·ō -āre -āvī -ātus *tr* to love, like, be fond of; to fall in love with; **amābō (tē)** *(coll)* please **II** *intr* to be in love
amoenē *adv* charmingly, pleasantly
amoenit·ās -ātis *f* charm
amoen·us -a -um *adj* charming, pleasant *(esp. to sight)* **II** *npl* pleasant places
āmōl·ior -īrī *tr* to remove; to put aside, put away; to get rid of, shake *(a person);* to put out of the way, dispose of *(a person);* to refute **II** *refl* to remove oneself, clear out
amōm·um -ī *n (bot)* spice plant; spice obtained from this plant
am·or -ōris *m* love; affection; object of affection, love; liking, fondness, attachment; strong desire, yearning; love song; Cupid; *(w.* **in** *+ acc,* **ergā** *+ acc)* affection for, love of; **amor patriae** patriotism **II** *mpl* love affair
āmōti·ō -ōnis *f* removal
ā·moveō -movēre -mōvī -mōtus *tr* to remove; to withdraw, put away; to lay aside *(suspicion, etc.);* to get rid of; to banish; to deprive of rights; to dispel *(fear);* to steal; **ex animō āmovēre** to put out of one's mind **II** *refl* to retire, withdraw
Amphiarā·üs -ī *m* famous Greek seer, son of Oecle(u)s *(or* Apollo) and Hypermestra, one of the Seven against Thebes
Amphiárēïad·ēs -ae *m* descendant of Amphiaraüs, his son Alcmaeon
amphiboli·a -ae *f* ambiguity, double meaning
Amphictyon·es -um *mpl* the representatives of the confederated Greek states who met in Thermopylae, later at Delphi
Amphilochi·a -ae *f* small district at the E. end of the Ambracian Gulf
Amphiloch·us -ī *m* son of Amphiaraüs, and founder of Argos Amphilochium *(the chief town of Amphilochia)*
Amphī·ō(n) -onis *m* son of Zeus and Antiope, twin brother of Zethus, and husband of Niobe
Amphīoni·us -a -um *adj* of Amphion
Amphipol·is -is *f* town in Macedonia near the mouth of the Strymon
amphitheātr·um -ī *n* amphitheater
Amphitrīt·ē -ēs *f* wife of Neptune; *(fig)* the sea
Amphitry·ō(n) *or* **Amphitru·ō -ōnis** *m* husband of Alcmena
Amphitryōniad·ēs -ae *m* Hercules
amphor·a -ae *f* amphora; liquid measure *(c. 7 gallons)*
ampl·a -ae *f* opportunity
amplē *adv* amply; grandly, splendidly
am·plector -plectī -plexus sum *tr* to embrace, hug; to cling to; to accept gladly, welcome; to comprise, extend over, cover, include; to encircle *(enemy forces);* to grasp, grip; to understand; *(of serpent)* to coil itself around; *(mil)* to occupy
amplex·ō -āre *or* **amplex·or -ārī -ātus sum** *tr* to embrace; to welcome; to cling to, grasp; to espouse, cherish
amplex·us -ūs *m* circuit; embrace, caress; coil *(of snake)*
amplificātiō -ōnis *f* extension, enlargement; *(rhet)* amplification
amplificāt·or -ōris *m* amplifier, enhancer
amplificē *adv* splendidly
amplific·ō -āre -āvī -ātus *tr* to enlarge, extend, widen; to increase; to extol; *(rhet)* to enlarge upon, develop
ampli·ō -āre -āvī -ātus *tr* to widen, enlarge; to enhance; to postpone *(judgment);* to adjourn *(court in order to gather more evidence);* to magnify, glorify; *(leg)* to postpone *(trial)*
ampliter *adv* splendidly; fully, very
amplitūd·ō -inis *f* width, size, bulk, extent; greatness, dignity, importance; high rank; *(rhet)* amplification, development
amplius *adv* any further, any more, any longer; besides; further, more, longer; more than *(without quam);* **amplius centum cīvēs Rōmānī** *(without quam)* more than a hundred Roman citizens; **amplius hōc** what is more, in addition; **amplius ūnō diē** one day longer; **nec amplius** no longer; **nēmō amplius** no one else; **nihil amplius** nothing else; **quid amplius (quam)** what else (than) **II** *n* more, a larger amount *or* number; **amplius negōtī** more trouble
ampliusculē *adv* rather more freely
ampl·us -a -um *adj* ample, large, wide, spacious; strong, great, powerful; grand, imposing; eminent, prominent, illustrious; **amplissimō genere nātus** born from an eminent family; **amplissimus** *(as title for persons of high office)* his Eminence; **amplissimus ōrdō** senatorial rank; **amplus ōrātor** a powerful speaker; **parum amplus** *(w. dat)* insufficiently large (for); **spēs ampla** high hopes; **vīrēs amplae** great strength
Ampsanct·us -ī *m* valley and lake in Samnium with toxic exhalations, regarded as an entrance to the lower world
ampull·a -ae *f* bottle, flask; *(fig)* bombast
ampullār·ius -(i)ī *m* bottle-maker
ampull·or -ārī -ātus sum *intr* to be bombastic
amputāti·ō -ōnis *f* pruning
amput·ō -āre -āvī -ātus *tr* to lop off, prune; to curtail, shorten; **amputāta loquī** to speak disconnectedly
Amūl·ius -(i)ī *m* king of Alba Longa, brother of Numitor, and granduncle of Romulus and Remus
amurc·a -ae *f* dregs of oil

Amycl·ae -ārum *fpl* town in Laconia, the birthplace of Castor and Pollux
Amyclae·us -a -um *adj* of Amyclae
Amyclīd·ēs -ae *m* Hyacinthus *(worshiped at Amyclae)*
amygdal·a -ae *f* almond tree
amygdal·um -ī *n* almond
amyst·is -idis *f* drinking bottoms up
an *conj (introducing the second or further part of a multiple question, direct or indirect)* or, or whether; **haud sciō an** I am inclined to think, probably
anabathr·a -ōrum *npl* bleachers
Anacre·ōn -ontis *m* lyric poet of Teos *(fl 540 B.C.)*
anadēm·a -atis *n* headband
anaglypt·a -ōrum *npl* work in bas-relief
anagnōst·ēs -ae *m* reader, reciter
analect·a -ae *m* slave who cleaned up the crumbs after a meal
analectr·is -idis *f* shoulder pad *(to improve the figure)*
analogi·a -ae *f* ratio; *(gram)* analogy *(similarity in inflection and derivatives of words); (phil)* method of reasoning from similar cases
anancaec·um -ī *n* large cup that must be emptied "bottoms up"
anapaest·us -a -um *adj (pros)* anapestic **‖** *m* anapest (⏑⏑—) **‖** *n* poem in anapestic meter; anapestic line *or* passage
Anāp·us -ī *m* river in Sicily
an·as -atis *f* duck
anaticul·a -ae *f* **(anet-)** *(sometimes as term of endearment)* duckling
anatīn·us -a -um *adj* **(anet-)** duck's
anatocism·us -ī *m* compound interest
Anaxagor·ās -ae *m* Greek philosopher, teacher of Pericles and Euripides *(500?–428 B.C.)*
Anaximan·der -drī *m* Greek philosopher of Miletus *(610–547 B.C.)*
Anaximen·ēs -is *m* Greek philosopher of Miletus *(fl 544 B.C.)*
an·ceps *or* **ancip·es -cipitis** *adj* two-headed, facing in two directions; exposed on both sides; two-edged; twin-peaked; amphibious; of doubtful allegiance, untrustworthy; unreliable, unpredictable; *(of a person)* undecided, wavering; *(of a battle)* fought on two fronts; *(of enemies)* attacking on both sides; *(of dangers, evils)* arising from two sources, double, twofold; *(of roads)* leading in two directions; *(of battles)* indecisive; *(of words)* ambiguous; *(of situations)* hazardous, critical **‖** *n* danger, peril
Anchīs·ēs -ae *m* son of Capys, lover of Venus, and, by her, father of Aeneas
Anchīsē·us -a -um *adj* of Anchises
Anchīsiad·ēs -ae *m* son of Anchises *(Aeneas)*
ancīl·e -is *n* small figure-eight shield *(esp. one of twelve such kept by the Salii in the shrine of Mars and carried in religious processions)*
ancill·a -ae *f* slave girl
ancillār·is -is -e *adj* having the status of a slave girl
ancillul·a -ae *f* little slave girl
Ancōn·a -ae *f* seaport in N. Picenum
ancor·a -ae *f* **(anch-)** anchor
ancorāl·e -is *n* anchor cable
ancorāri·us -a -um *adj* of an anchor
Anc·us Mārci·us -ī *m* the fourth king of Rome
Ancȳr·a -ae *f* Ankara, capital of Galatia
andabat·a -ae *m* blindfolded gladiator
And·ēs -ium *fpl* village near Mantua, birthplace of Vergil
Andri·us -a -um *adj* of the Greek island of Andros **‖** *mpl* people of Andros **‖** *f* woman from Andros
Androge·ōs -ō *or* **Androge·ōn -ōnos** *or* **Androge·us -ī** *m* Androgeüs *(son of Minos and Pasiphaë, whose death Minos avenged by attacking Athens)*
androgyn·us -ī *m or* **androgynē -ēs** *f* hermaphrodite
Andromach·ē -ēs *or* **Andromach·a -ae** *f* Andromache (Hector's wife)
Andromed·a -ae *or* **Andromed·ē -ēs** *f* daughter of Cepheus and Cassiope, rescued from a sea monster by Perseus
andr·ōn -ōnis *m* corridor
Andronīc·us -ī *m* Livius Andronicus *(fl 241 B.C., first epic and dramatic poet of Latin literature)*
Andr·os *or* **Andr·us -ī** *f* Aegean island
ānell·us -ī *m* little ring
anēt(h)·um -ī *n (bot)* dill *(aromatic herb whose seeds and leaves were used as seasoning)*
-āne·us -a -um *adjl suf* chiefly from nouns denoting a place: **circumforāneus** connected with (the business of) the forum
anfrāct·us -ūs *m* curve *(of road, seashore);* spiral, coil; *(astr)* orbit; *(rhet)* circumlocution
angell·us -ī *m* small angle, small corner
angin·a -ae *f* tonsillitis; throat infection
angiport·us -ūs *m or* **angiport·um -ī** *n* alley
ang·ō -ere *tr* to choke, strangle; to distress; to tease; to trouble
ang·or -ōris *m* strangling, suffocation; anguish, distress
anguicom·us -a -um *adj* snake-haired
anguicul·us -ī *m* small snake
anguif·er -era -erum *adj* snaky, having snakes in place of hair, snake-haired; *(of places)* snake-infested
anguigen·a -ae *m* offspring of a dragon; Theban
anguill·a -ae *f* eel

anguine·us -a -um *adj* snaky; serpent-like
anguīn·us -a -um *adj* snaky
anguip·ēs -edis *adj* serpent-footed
angu·is -is *mf* snake, serpent ‖ **Anguis** *m* Dragon, Serpent, Hydra *(constellations)*
Anguiten·ēns -entis *m* Ophiuchus *(constellation)*
angulār·is -is -e *adj* angular
angulāt·us -a -um *adj* **(angl-)** angular
angul·us -ī *m* angle, corner; nook, recess; **ad parēs angulōs** *(or* **rēctīs angulīs)** at right angles
angustē *adv* within narrow limits; closely; hardly, scarcely; briefly, concisely
angusti·ae -ārum *fpl* narrow place; defile; narrow passage, strait; shortage, scarcity, want, deficiency; difficulty, tight spot; limitations; distress, straits; narrow-mindedness; poverty of vocabulary; **angustiae spīritūs** shortness of breath
angusticlāvi·us -a -um *adj* wearing a tunic with a narrow purple stripe *(a sign of equestrian rank)*
angust·ō -āre -āvī -ātus *tr* to narrow down; to reduce in size *or* amount; to choke
angust·us -a -um *adj* narrow, close; short, brief *(time);* scanty *(means);* tight *(reins);* difficult, critical; narrow-minded; base, mean; short, limited *(time, money, suppplies);* curt *(style)* ‖ *n* a confined space; narrowness; critical condition, danger; **in angustum addūcere** *(or* **cōgere, conclūdere, dēdūcere)** to narrow down, compress, reduce
anhēlāti·ō -ōnis *f* panting
anhēlit·us -ūs *m* panting, difficulty in breathing, puffing; breath, breathing; vapor; **anhēlitum recipere** to catch one's breath; **vīnī anhēlitus** breath that reeks of wine
anhēl·ō -āre -āvī -ātus *tr* to breathe out, to pant after ‖ *intr* to pant, puff; to exhale; *(of fire, sea)* to roar
anhēl·us -a -um *adj* panting
anicul·a -ae *f* little old lady
Aniē(n)s·is -is -e *or* **Aniēn·us -a -um** *adj* of the Anio *(Tiber tributary)*
anīl·is -is -e *adj* of an old woman; **anīlēs fābulae** old wives' tales
anīlit·ās -ātis *f* old age *(of women)*
anīliter *adv* like an old woman
anim·a -ae *f* air, wind, breeze; breath; breath of life, life; soul *(as principle of life, opposed to* **animus** *as principle of thought and feelings);* spirit, ghost; **animam agere** to gasp for breath; **animam dūcere** to draw a breath; **animam ēdere** *(or* **efflāre** *or* **ēmittere** *or* **exspīrāre)** to breathe one's last; **animam trahere** to struggle to breathe
animadversi·ō -ōnis *f* attention, observation; mention; remark; criticism; punishment
animadvers·or -ōris *m* observer
animadver·tō -tere -tī -sus *tr* **(-vort-)** to pay attention to, attend to; to notice, observe, realize; to criticize; to punish
anim·al -ālis *n* animal; living creature
animāl·is -is -e *adj* consisting of air; animate, living ‖ *mfn* living creature; animal
anim·āns -antis *adj* living, animate ‖ *mfn* living thing; animal
animāti·ō -ōnis *f* the bestowal of life; *(fig)* living being
animāt·us -a -um *adj* courageous; inclined, disposed; *(w.* **ergā** *or* **in** + *acc)* disposed toward
anim·ō -āre -āvī -ātus *tr* to make alive, animate; to encourage
animōsē *adv* courageously; eagerly
animōs·us -a -um *adj* courageous; energetic; violent *(wind, fire)*; spunky *(horse); (w. causal abl)* proud of
animul·a -ae *f* little soul, little life
animul·us -ī *m* darling; **mī animule** my darling
anim·us -ī *m (cf* **anima)** intellect, understanding; mind; state of mind; thought, reason; memory; knowledge; sense, consciousness; *(mostly in the abl)* judgment, opinion; imagination; heart, feelings, passions; spirit, courage, morale; disposition, character; pride, haughtiness; will, purpose, desire, inclination; pleasure, delight; confident hope; **aequō animō** patiently, calmly; **animī causā** for amusement; **animō libentī** gladly; **animum advertere** *(w. dat) or* **adiungere** *or* **adhibēre** *or* **applicāre** *or* **attendere** *or* **intendere** to apply the mind to, turn attention to, pay attention to: **animus aeger** sick feeling; **bonō animō esse** to take heart, be of good cheer; **commūnī animō** unanimously; **compos animī** in control of oneself; **ex animō** from the bottom of the heart, sincerely; **ex animō effluere** to slip one's mind; **ex animī tuī sententiā** in your opinion; **animīs fingite** imagine; **in animō habēre** *or* **esse** *(w. inf)* to have in mind to, intend to; **impos, inops animī** lacking self-control; **meō quidem animō** at least in my opinion; **ūnō animō** unanimously
Ani·ō -ōnis *m* tributary of the Tiber
Ani·us -ī *m* king and priest on Delos
ann- = adn-
Ann·a -ae *f* sister of Dido ‖ **Anna Perenna** goddess of the returning year
annāl·is -is -e *adj* lasting a year, annual; **lēx annālis** law fixing the minimum age for holding public offices ‖ *mpl* annals, chronicle
annat·ō -āre -āvī -ātum *intr* **(adn-)** *(w. dat or* **ad)** to swim to
anne *conj (alternate form of* **an)** or, or whether

anne·ctō -ctere -xuī -xus *tr* **(adn-)** *(w. dat or* **ad)** to tie, connect, annex *(s.th.)* to; *(w. dat)* to apply *(s.th.)* to
annex·us -ūs *m* connection
annicul·us -a -um *adj* **(-ucul-)** one year old; lasting only one year
annī·tor -tī -sus *or* **-xus sum** *intr* **(adn-)** to try one's hardest; to give support; *(w. dat or w.* **ad)** to lean on; *(w.* **ut** *or inf)* to strive to
anniversāri·us -a -um *adj* employed annually, renewed annually; occurring every year, growing every year; *(of games, festivals, sacrifices)* celebrated annually, annual
ann·ō -āre -āvī -ātum *intr* **(adn-)** *(w. dat, w.* **ad,** *w. acc of limit of motion)* to swim to *or* toward; *(w. dat)* to swim along with
annōn *conj* or not; **suntne dī annōn?** are there gods or not?
annōn·a -ae *f* year's crop; grain; price of grain; cost of living; high price; **annōna cāra** high prices
annōs·us -a -um *adj* aged, old
annotāti·ō -ōnis *f* **(adn-)** notation, remark
annōtin·us -a -um *adj* last year's, a year old
annot·ō -āre -āvī -ātus *tr* **(adn-)** to note *(in writing),* put on record; to observe, notice; to comment on; to register, designate
annumer·ō -āre -āvī -ātus *tr* **(adn-)** *(w. dat)* to count out *(money)* to; *(w. dat or* **in** *+ acc)* to add *(s.th.)* to, include *(s.o.)* among
annūnti·ō -āre -āvī -ātus *tr* **(adn-)** to announce, make known, bring the news, proclaim
an·nuō -nuere -nuī -nūtus *tr* **(adn-)** to designate by a nod; to indicate, declare; *(w. dat)* to promise, grant *(s.th.)* to ‖ *intr* to nod assent; *(w. dat)* to nod assent to, be favorable to, smile on
ann·us -ī *m* year; season; age, time of life; year of office; year's produce, crops; circuit *(e.g., of a planet);* **ad annum** for the coming year, a year from now; **annō** *(advl phrase)* a year ago, last year; **annō exeunte** *(or* **annō plēnō)** at the end of the year; **annum** *(or* **in annum)** for a year; **annus meus (tuus,** *etc.)* my (your, *etc.)* year of office; my (your, *etc.)* birthday; **annus solidus** a full year; **per annōs** year by year
annu·us -a -um *adj* lasting a year; annual, yearly ‖ *npl* yearly pay, pension
an·quīrō -quīrere -quīsīvī -quīsītus *tr* to search carefully; to examine, inquire into; *(w. gen or abl of the charge)* to accuse *(s.o.)* of ‖ *intr* to hold an inquest
āns·a -ae *f* handle; *(fig)* opportunity
ānsāt·us -a -um *adj* having handles; **homō ānsātus** man with arms akimbo
āns·er -eris *m* goose *(male),* gander
Āns·er -eris *m* a poet, friend of the triumvir Antonius
Antae·us -ī *m* Libyan giant, son of Earth, killed by Hercules ‖ name of a Carthaginian general
ante *adv* before, previously, in the past; in front; forwards; **ante … quam** before; **annō ante** a year ago; **multīs annīs ante** many years before that
ante- *pref (used in the senses of the adv)*
ante *prep (w. acc)* **1** before, in front of: **ante urbis portās** before the city gates; **2** before *(in time):* **ante diem** before the due date, too early; *(in dates):* **ante diem quārtum Īdūs Mārtiās** *(instead of* **quārtō diē ante Īdūs Mārtiās)** *or abbr* **a.d. IV Id. Mart.** three days before the Ides of March; **ante tempus** before time, prematurely; **3** *(in preference, choice)* more than, above; **ante omnia** first of all; above all
anteā *adv* before, previously, formerly; **iam anteā** already in the past
anteāct·us -a -um *adj (of time)* that has passed
anteambul·ō -ōnis *m* one who runs before *(to clear the way),* blocker
ante·capiō -capere -cēpī -ceptus *tr* to receive beforehand; to take possession of beforehand, preoccupy; to anticipate
ante·cēdō -cēdere -cessī -cessus *tr* precede; to outdo, surpass ‖ *intr (w. dat)* **1** to have precedence over; **2** to excel, surpass
antecell·ō -ere *tr* to surpass ‖ *intr (w. dat) (w. abl of respect or* **in** *+ abl)* to surpass *(s.o.)* in
antecessi·ō -ōnis *f* antecedent cause
antecess·or -ōris *m (mil)* scout ‖ *mpl* advance guard
antecurs·or -ōris *m (mil)* scout ‖ *mpl* vanguard
ante·eō -īre -īvī *or* **-iī** *tr* to precede; to surpass; to anticipate, prevent ‖ *intr* to precede; to take the lead; *(w. dat)* **1** to go before; **2** to surpass
ante·ferō -ferre -tulī -lātus *tr* to prefer; to anticipate
antefīx·um -ī *n* antefix *(image, statue, etc., affixed to roofs and gutters of temples or homes)*
ante·gredior -gredī -gressus sum *tr* to precede
antehab·eō -ēre -uī *tr* to prefer
antehāc *adv* before now, formerly, previously; before that (time)
antelātus *pp of* **anteferō**
antelogi·um -ī *n* introduction, prologue
antelūcān·us -a -um *adj* pre-dawn
antemerīdiān·us -a -um *adj* before noon
ante·mittō -mittere -mīsī -missus *tr* to send out ahead

Antemn·ae -ārum *fpl* ancient town in Latium

Antemnāt·ēs -ium *mpl* the people of Antemnae

antenn·a *or* **antemn·a -ae** *f* yardarm, sail yard, sail

Antēn·or -oris *m* Trojan founder of Patavium *(Padua)*

Antēnore·us -a -um *adj* Patavian, Paduan

Antēnorid·ēs -ae *m* descendant of Antenor; native of Patavium *(Padua)*

anteoccupāti·ō -ōnis *f (rhet)* anticipation of an opponent's arguments, objection

antepart·um -ī *n* **(-pert-)** thing *or* property acquired in the past

ante·pēs -pedis *m* forefoot

antepīlān·ī -ōrum *mpl* front ranks *(soldiers drawn up in the first two lines of a battle formation)*

antepoll·eō -ēre *tr* to surpass in strength **||** *intr (w. dat)* to be superior to *(s.o.)* in strength

ante·pōnō -pōnere -posuī -positus *tr* to place *or* station in front of; to place before *(in time);* to prefer, esteem more highly; *(w. dat)* to give *(a person)* preference over *(another);* to serve *(food);* to put *(a word, prefix, or letter)* before *(a word)*

antepot·ēns -entis *adj* very wealthy

antequam *or* **ante ... quam** *conj* before; sooner ... than

anteri·or -ōris *adj* anterior; previous *(time); (of place)* in front

Anter·ōs -ōtis *m* avenger of unrequited love *(son of Venus and Mars)*

ant·ēs -ium *mpl* rows *(of vines, soldiers, etc.)*

antesignān·us -ī *m* soldier fighting in front of the standards to defend them; leader, prominent man, protagonist

ante·stō *or* **anti·stō -stāre -stitī** *intr* to excel; *(w. dat)* to be superior to

antest·or -ārī -ātus sum *tr (leg)* to call as witness

antetulī *perf of* **anteferō**

ante·veniō -venīre -vēnī -ventus *tr* to come before, arrive ahead of; to anticipate, thwart; to surpass **||** *intr* to arrive first; to become more distinguished; *(w. dat)* **1** to anticipate; **2** to get ahead of; **3** to be better than, surpass

antever·tō -tere -tī -sus *tr* **(-vort-)** to go *or* come before; to anticipate; to prefer **||** *intr* to act first; to go out first, set out first; *(w. dat)* to outweigh

antevol·ō -āre *intr* to dash out ahead

Antiānus -a -um *adj* of Antium *(very ancient coastal town in Latium)*

Antiās -ātis *adj* of Antium **||** *mpl* people of Antium

Antiātīnus -a -um *adj* of Antium

Anticat·ō -ōnis *m* title of the books which Caesar wrote in answer to Cicero's panegyric *Cato*

anticipāti·ō -ōnis *f* preconception

anticip·ō -āre -āvī -ātus *tr* to anticipate; to have a preconceived idea of; **viam anticipāre** to take the lead *(in a race)*

antīc·us -a -um *adj* front, foremost

Anticyr·a -ae *f* name of several Greek towns famous for their hellebore *(used to cure insanity)*

antideā, antideō, antidhāc *adv* old forms for **anteā, anteō, antehāc**

antidot·um -ī *n or* **antidot·os** *or* **antidot·us -ī** *f* antidote

Antigon·ē -ēs *or* **Antigon·a -ae** *f* Antigone *(daughter of Oedipus* **||** *daughter of Laomedon, changed into a stork)*

Antigon·us -ī *m* Greek name, *esp.* one of the generals of Alexander the Great **||** Antigonus Doson

Antiloch·us -ī *m* son of Nestor

Antiochī·a -ae *f* **(-chē·a)** Antioch *(chief city of Syria)*

Antioch·us -ī *m* name of seven kings of Syria **||** Academic philosopher, teacher of Cicero and Brutus

Antiop·a -ae *or* **Antiop·ē -ēs** *f* Antiope *(mother, by Jupiter, of Amphion and Zethus)*

Antipa·ter -trī *m* a general and successor of Alexander the Great, father of Cassander **||** his grandson, son of Cassander, and son-in-law of Lysimachus **||** name of several philosophers

Antiphat·ēs -ae *m* king of the Laestrygonians **||** son of Sarpedon, killed by Turnus

antiquāri·us -a -um *adj & m* antiquarian

antīquē *adv* in former times; in the good old style

antīquit·ās -ātis *f* antiquity; the ancients; the good old days

antīquitus *adv* in former times, of old; from ancient times; in the old style

antīqu·ō -āre -āvī -ātus *tr* to reject *(law, bill) (the letter A was used = Antiquo, I vote against the bill)*

antīqu·us -a -um *adj* **(-tic-)** old, ancient; old-fashioned, venerable; long-standing *(friendship);* located *or* lying in front **||** *mpl* ancients, ancient authors **||** *n* antiquity; old custom

antisophist·ēs -ae *m (rhet)* opponent in argument

antist·ēs -itis *m* high-priest *(of temple or deity);* authority *(of an art, philosophical school)* **||** *f* high-priestess

Antisthen·ēs -is *or* **-ae** *m* pupil of Socrates and founder of Cynic philosophy *(455?–360 B.C.)*

antistit·a -ae *f* high-priestess

antithet·on -ī *n (rhet)* antithesis

Ant·ium -(i)ī *n* coastal town in Latium *(modern Anzio)*
antli·a -ae *f* pump; treadmill
Antōni·us -a -um *adj* Roman clan name *(nomen), esp.* Marcus Antonius *(orator, consul in 99 B.C.)* ‖ Marcus Antonius *(triumvir, consul in 44 B.C.)*
antr·um -ī *n* cave, cavern, grotto; *(fig)* hollow *(of a tree)*
Anūb·is -is *or* **-idis** *m* jackal-headed Egyptian god of hunting
ānulār·ius -(i)ī *m* ring maker
ānulāt·us -a -um *adj* wearing a ring
ānul·us -ī *m* ring, signet ring
-ān·us -a -um *adjl suf* **1** from common nouns: **urbānus** of the city; **2** from place names: **Rōmānus** from *or* of Rome, Roman; **3** from personal names: **Claudiānus** of Claudius, Claudian
ān·us -ī *m* anus, rectum; ring
an·us -ūs *f* old woman; *(pej)* hag
anxiē *adv* uneasily
anxiet·ās -ātis *f* anxiety, worry; meticulousness
anxif·er -era -erum *adj* disquieting, worrisome
anxitūd·ō -inis *f* anxiety, worry
anxi·us -a -um *adj* worried, anxious, uneasy; meticulous
Anx·ur -uris *m & n* coastal town of Latium *(modern Terracina)*
Anyt·us -ī *m* one of Socrates' three accusers
Āonid·ēs -um *fpl* Muses *(named after the section of Boeotia, called Aonia, where Mt. Helicon is located)*
Āoni·us -a -um *adj* Boeotian; Theban; of the Muses; of Helicon; poetic ‖ *f* Boeotia
Aorn·os -ī *m* Lake Avernus *(meaning: having no birds)*
apage *interj* go!; scram!
Apamē·a -ae *f* name of several towns in Asia Minor, *esp.* that in Syria and that in Phrygia
apēliōt·ēs -ae *m* east wind
Apell·ēs -is *m* Greek painter *(fl 4th cent. B.C.)*
Āpennīnicol·a -ae *m* **(App-)** inhabitant of the Apennines
Āpennīnigen·a -ae *adj (masc only)* **(App-)** born on the Apennines
Āpennīn·us -a -um *adj* **(App-)** Apennine ‖ *m* Apennine Mountains
a·per -prī *m* wild boar; meat of wild boar as food
aper·iō -īre -uī -tus *tr* to open, uncover, lay bare, disclose, reveal; to prove, demonstrate; to explain; to recount; to cut open, split; to usher in *(a new year);* to introduce *(a subject); (mil)* to spread out *(forces); (topog)* to bring into view; **locum aperīre** *(w. dat)* to open the way to, afford an opportunity for ‖ *refl (of flowers)* to open; to come into view
apertē *adv* openly, frankly, candidly
apert·ō -āre *tr* to bare
apert·us -a -um *pp of* **aperiō** ‖ *adj* bare, uncovered, exposed; without decks; clear *(style);* frank, candid; plain, evident; accessible, unobstructed ‖ *n* open space; **in apertō** in the open; **in apertō esse** to be clear, evident, well known, notorious
ap·ex -icis *m* point, tip; top, summit; conical flamen's hat; cap, crown; crowning glory; long mark over a vowel, macron
ap(h)eliōt·ēs -ae *m* the E. wind
aphract·us -ī *f or* **aphract·um -ī** *n* cargo ship without a deck
Aphrodīsi·a -ōrum *npl* festival in honor of Aphrodite
aphronit·um -ī *n* washing soda, sodium carbonate
apiār·ius -iī *m* beekeeper
apiastr·um -ī *n* a variety of balm
Apīc·ius -iī *m* gourmet of the 1st cent. A.D.
apicul·a -ae *f* little bee
apin·ae -ārum *fpl* trifles, nonsense
ap·is -is *f (gen pl:* **-um** *&* **-ium**) bee
Āp·is -is *or* **-idis** *m* Egyptian sacred bull
ap·īscor -īscī -tus sum *tr* to pursue; to get, reach, gain; to get, obtain; *(lit & fig)* to grasp; to get hold of; **lītem apīscī** to win a lawsuit
ap·ium -iī *n* celery; parsley
aplustr·e -is *or* **aplustr·um -ī** *n (naut)* curved ornamental stern
Apoclēt·ī -ōrum *mpl* select committee *(of Aetolian League)*
apodytēr·ium -(i)ī *n* dressing room *(of a bath)*
apolactiz·ō -āre *tr* to kick aside; to scorn
Apollinār·is -is -e *adj* of Apollo; **lūdī Apollinārēs** games in honor of Apollo, instituted after the victory at Cannae ‖ *n* place sacred to Apollo
Apoll·ō -inis *m* son of Jupiter and Latona, twin brother of Diana, god of the sun, divination, archery, healing, poetry, and music
Apollodōr·us -ī *m* rhetorician, teacher of Augustus
Apollōni·a -ae *f* name of several cities: on the S. coast of Illyricum; on the S. coast of the Black Sea; in Crete
apolog·us -ī *m* story, fable
Apon·us -ī *m* warm spring near Padua
apophorēt·a -ōrum *npl* presents for departing house guests
apoproēgmen·a -ōrum *npl* things that have been rejected
aposphrāgism·a -atis *n* device on signet ring, seal
apothēc·a -ae *f* warehouse, storeroom
apparātē *adv* **(adp-)** sumptuously
apparāti·ō -ōnis *f* **(adp-)** preparation

apparāt·us -a -um *adj* **(adp-)** getting *or* making ready, preparing; providing; well supplied; splendid

apparāt·us -ūs *m* equipment, apparatus, gear; equipping, organization; armaments; stock, store; rhetorical devices; pomp, display, magnificence

appār·ēns -entis *adj* **(adp-)** visible

appāreō -ēre -uī -itum *intr* **(adp-)** to appear, become visible, be visible; to be seen, show oneself, show up; to materialize, take shape; to appear, look *(e.g., unhappy);* to be perceptible *(to the senses);* to be clearly ... , be seen to be; *(of facts)* to be clear, be evident, be obvious; *(w. dat)* **1** to wait on, serve; **2** to obey *(laws);* **nec caput nec pēs appāret mihi** I can make neither head nor tail of it; **nūsquam appārēre** to have disappeared **II** *v impers* it is evident, it is clear; **ut appāret** apparently

appāriti·ō -ōnis *f* **(adp-)** attendance, service; provision **II** *fpl* household servants

appārit·or -ōris *m* servant; attendant *(of public official, e.g., aide, lictor, secretary)*

appar·ō -āre -āvī -ātus *tr* **(adp-)** to prepare; to provide; to organize *(weddings, public games, war); (w. inf or* **ut)** to get ready to **II** *refl (w.* **in** *+ acc)* to prepare oneself for, equip oneself for

appellāti·ō -ōnis *f* **(adp-)** addressing; *(w.* **ad)** appeal to *(in general; to higher authority);* naming, calling by name; designation, name, title; pronunciation; *(gram)* common noun

appellāt·or -ōris *m (leg)* one who appeals, appellant

appell·ō -āre -āvī -ātus *tr* **(adp-)** to speak to, address, accost; to appeal to, call on, beseech; to make overtures to, approach; to invoke *(god as witness);* to demand payment of; to call up *(to pay a debt or obligation);* to recognize (as), style officially; to name, call; to mention by name, use the name of, mention; to pronounce; to designate, term, call; to demand payment of; *(leg)* to sue; **imperātōrem appellāre** to hail as "Imperator" **II** *intr* to appeal

ap·pellō -pellere -pulī -pulsus *tr* **(adp-)** *(w. dat or* **ad)** **1** to drive *(s.th.)* to; **2** to move *(military equipment, personnel)* to; **3** to steer *(ship)* to **II** *pass (w.* **ad)** *(of a ship)* to put in at **II** *intr (of a ship)* to land

appendicul·a -ae *f* small addition

append·ix -icis *f* addition, appendage; related topic; hanger-on; *(anat)* appendix

appen·dō -dere -dī -sus *tr* **(adp-)** to hang; to weigh; to pay out; *(fig)* to weigh, consider

Appenn- = **Āpenn-**

appet·ēns -entis *adj* **(adp-)** greedy; *(w. gen)* eager for, craving

appetenter *adv* **(adp-)** greedily, avidly

appetenti·a -ae *f* **(adp-)** *(w. gen)* the craving for, desire for; **cibī appetentia** appetite (for food)

appetīti·ō -ōnis *f* **(adp-)** grasping; desire, appetite; *(w. gen)* **1** the craving for; **2** the reaching out for; **appetītiō nātūrālis** *(or* **ex nātūrā** *or* **animī)** instinctive desire, appetite *(for),* impulse *(toward)*

appetīt·us -ūs *m* **(adp-)** desire, appetite *(esp. natural or instinctive)* **II** *mpl* the appetites, passions *(opp:* **ratiō** reason)

appet·ō -ere -īvī *or* **-iī -ītus** *tr* **(adp-)** to try to reach; to lay hold of; to strive after, aim for; to seek the friendship of; to court; to make for, head for; to attack, assault; to have an appetite for *(food)*; to tackle *(a job)* **II** *intr (of events)* to approach, draw near

Appiān·us -a -um *adj* of Appia, a town in Phrygia **II** of Appius Claudius the decemvir **II** *m* Appian of Alexandria *(historian of the 2nd cent.* A.D.*)*

Appi·as -adis *f* a nymph of the Appian fountain, near the temple of Venus Genetrix **II** title of Venus

Appiet·ās -ātis *f* the rank *or* status of an Appius

apping·ō -ere *tr* **(adp-)** to paint; to write *(s.th.)* in addition *(to a verbal picture)*

Appi·us -a -um *adj* Appian; **aqua Appia** Appian Aqueduct *(built by Appius Claudius Caecus);* **via Appia** Appian Way *(road between Rome and Capua, built by the same man)* **II** *m* Roman first name, *esp.* of the Claudian clan: Appius Claudius Crassus *(consul and decemvir in 451* B.C.*)* **II** Appius Claudius Caecus *(censor in 312* B.C.*)* **II** Appius Claudius Caudex *(consul in 264* B.C.*)* **II** Appius Claudius Pulcher *(consul in 54* B.C.*, censor in 50* B.C.*)* **II** **Appī Forum** town in Latium on the Appian Way

applau·dō -dere -sī -sus *tr* **(adp-)** to strike, slap; **terrae applaudere** to dash to the ground **II** *intr* to applaud

applicāti·ō -ōnis *f* **(adp-)** application

applicāt·us -a -um *adj* **(adp-)** *(w.* **ad)** inclined to; *(w. dat)* lying close to, attached to

applicit·us -a -um *adj* **(adp-)** *(w. dat)* adjacent to

applic·ō -āre -āvī *or* **-uī -ātus** *or* **-itus** *tr* **(adp-)** to bring into close contact; *(w. dat or* **ad)** **1** to apply, attach, add, join *(s.th.)* to; **2** to steer *(ship)* toward; **3** to apply *(mind, attention)* to; *(w.* **ad)** to place *(geographically)* near to **II** *refl* to lean (against); to sit down (on); *(w.* **ad)** to devote oneself to, apply oneself to **II** *intr (of ships)* to put in *(at)*, land

applōdō *see* **applaudō**
applōr·ō -āre -āvī *intr* **(adpl-)** to lament
ap·pōnō -pōnere -posuī -positus *tr* **(adp-)** to serve *(food); (w. dat or* **ad)** to put or lay *(s.th.)* near, at, *or* beside; *(w. dat)* **1** to set *(food)* before; **2** to appoint, assign *(s.o.)* to; **3** to reckon *(s.th.)* as; **modum appōnere** *(w. dat)* set a limit to
apporrēct·us -a -um *adj* **(adp-)** stretched out near *or* beside
apport·ō -āre -āvī -ātus *tr* **(adp-)** to carry, bring (to); to bring along, bring with one; to import; to present *(a play);* to bring in its train, cause; *(w. dat)* to carry *(s.th.)* to
apposc·ō -ere *tr* to demand in addition
appositē *adv* **(adp-)** appropriately
apposit·us -a -um *pp of* **appōnō** ‖ *adj (w.* **ad)** suited to; *(w. dat)* situated near, bordering on
appōt·us -a -um *adj* **(adp-)** drunk
apprec·or -ārī -ātus sum *tr* **(adp-)** to pray to, worship
apprehen·dō *or* **appren·dō -dere -dī -sus** *tr* **(adp-)** to grasp, seize, take hold of; to arrest; to take up *(topic); (mil)* to occupy
apprīmē *adv* **(adp-)** chiefly, especially; very
ap·primō -primere -pressī -pressus *tr* **(adp-)** *(w. dat)* to press *(s.th.)* close to
approbāti·ō -ōnis *f* **(adp-)** approbation, approval; proof; decision
approbāt·or -ōris *m* **(adp-)** one who seconds *or* approves
approbē *adv* **(adp-)** very well
approb·ō -āre -āvī -ātus *tr* **(adp-)** to approve; to prove; to prove *(statement)* true
apprōmitt·ō -ere *tr* **(adp-)** to promise in addition
apprōn·ō -āre -āvī -ātus *refl* **(adp-)** to lean forward
approper·ō -āre -āvī -ātus *tr* **(adp-)** to hasten, speed up ‖ *intr* to hurry
appropinquāti·ō -ōnis *f* **(adp-)** approach
appropinqu·ō -āre -āvī *intr* **(adp-)** to approach; *(w. dat or* **ad)** to come near, approach
appugn·ō -āre -āvī -ātus *tr* **(adp-)** to fight, attack
appulsus *pp of* **appellō**
appuls·us -ūs *m* **(adp-)** landing; approach; influence, impact
aprīcāti·ō -ōnis *f* sunbathing
aprīc·or -ārī -ātus sum *intr* to sunbathe
aprīc·us -a -um *adj* sunny ‖ *n* sunny spot; sunshine, light of day
Aprīl·is -is -e *adj* of April; **mēnsis Aprīlis** April ‖ *m* April *(second month of the old calendar until 153 B.C.)*
aprūgn·us -a -um *adj* of a wild boar
aps = abs
apsinth·ium -(i)ī *n* **(abs-)** *(bot)* wormwood *(yielding a bitter abstract used in flavoring wine)*
apsūmēd·ō -inis *f* a devouring
aptē *adv* closely; suitably
apt·ō -āre -āvī -ātus *tr* to fasten, fit, adjust; to make ready, equip
apt·us -a -um *adj* tied, bound, fastened; fitted together; suitable, adapted; neat, orderly, in good order, in good condition; handy, convenient; *(w. abl)* provided with; *(w.* **ex** *or adv)* following from, dependent on; *(w.* **ad** *or* **in** + *acc)* **1** equipped for, ready for; **2** efficient at, good at; **3** convenient for; **4** useful for; **5** favorable for; **causae inter sē aptae** connected causes
apud *prep (w. acc)* at, by, near, among; at the house of; in *(a building, town);* in the care of, in the hands of, in possession of; before, in the presence of; in the writings of; (with influence) over; **apud gentēs** *(or* **hominēs)** in the whole world; **apud mē (tē)** in my (your) care; at my (your) house; **apud mēnsam** at table; **apud prīncipia** on parade; **apud sē esse** to be in one's right mind
Āpūli·a -ae *f* region in S.W. Italy
Āpūlic·us -a -um *adj* Apulian
Āpūl·us -a -um *adj* Apulian
aqu·a -ae *f* water; rain, rainfall; aqueduct; **aquā et ignī interdīcere** to outlaw *(literally, to keep (away) from water and fire);* **aquam praebēre** *(w. dat)* to entertain *(guests)* ‖ *fpl* spa, baths
aquaeduct·us -ūs *m* aqueduct
aquāliculus -ī *m* potbelly
aquāl·is -is -e *adj* water ‖ *mf* washbasin
aquāri·us -a -um *adj* of water ‖ *m* water-conduit inspector ‖ *n* water supply
Aquār·ius -(i)ī *m (astr)* Aquarius *(constellation and sign of the zodiac)*
aquātic·us -a -um *adj* growing in water; watery, moist, humid ‖ *npl* well-watered places; marshes
aquātil·is -is -e *adj* living *or* growing in water, aquatic; watery
aquāti·ō -ōnis *f* fetching water; water hole
aquāt·or -ōris *m* water carrier
aquil·a -ae *f* eagle *(bird; Roman legionary standard); (fig)* legion; gable *(of house)*
Aquilēi·a -ae *f* town in Venetia at head of the Adriatic
aquil·ex -egis *m* water finder, dowser; water conduit inspector
aquilif·er -erī *m* standard-bearer
aquilīn·us -a -um *adj* eagle's
aquil·ō -ōnis *m* north wind; North
aquilōni·us -a -um *adj* northerly
aquil·us -a -um *adj* swarthy
Aquīn·ās -ātis *adj* of Aquinum ‖ *m* citizen of Aquinum

Aquīn·um -ī *n* town of the Volsci, birthplace of Juvenal
Aquītāni·a -ae *f* province in S.W. Gaul
aquol·a *or* **acul·a -ae** *f* **(aquu-)** brook; small amount of water
aqu·or -ārī -ātus sum *intr* to fetch water
aquōs·us -a -um *adj* well-watered; rainy; humid; *(med)* dropsical
aquul·a -ae *f* brook
ār·a -ae *f* altar; altar tomb; *(fig)* sanctuary *(of protection)* ‖ **Āra** *(astr)* Altar *(constellation)*
arabarch·ēs -ae *m* customs officer in Egypt
Arab·ī -ōrum *mpl* Arabs
Arabi·a -ae *f* Arabia
Arabic·us *or* **Arabi·us** *or* **Arab·us -a -um** *adj* Arabian
Arab·s -is *m* Arab
Arachn·ē -ēs *f* Lydian girl whom Minerva changed into a spider
arāne·a -ae *f* spider; cobweb
arāneol·a -ae *f* small spider
arāneol·us -ī *m* small spider
arāneōs·us -a -um *adj* full of cobwebs; resembling cobwebs
arāne·us -a -um *adj* spider's ‖ *m* spider ‖ *n* spider web
Ar·ar -aris *(acc:* **Ararim)** *m* Rhone tributary *(modern Saône)*
arāti·ō -ōnis *f* cultivation, tilling; agriculture; arable land
arātiuncul·a -ae *f* small plot; small farm
arāt·or -ōris *m* farmer ‖ *adj* plow
arātr·um -ī *n* plow
Arāt·us -ī *m* Greek author, from Soli in Cilicia, of poem on astronomy *(fl 270 B.C.)*
Arax·ēs -is *m* river in Armenia ‖ river in S. Persia, now Iran
arbi·ter -trī *m* eyewitness, spectator; judge; *(leg)* arbitrator *(with wider discretionary power than a* **iūdex);** ruler, director, controller
arbitr·a -ae *f* eyewitness
arbitrāriō *adv* uncertainly
arbitrāri·us -a -um *adj* discretionary; arbitrary
arbitrāt·us -ūs *m* decision; inclination, pleasure, choice; **arbitrātū** *(w. gen)* at the discretion of; *(leg)* according to the decision of *(an official arbitrator);* **arbitrātū meō, tuō** *(coll)* to my (your) heart's content
arbitr·ium -(i)ī *n* (process of) arbitration *(before an arbitrator);* independent judgment; settlement *(of a matter);* mastery, power, control; wishes, desires; whim, caprice; **ad arbitrium nostrum** as much as we please; **meī arbitriī est** it is in my power; **suī arbitriī esse** to be one's own master; **suō arbitriō** on one's own initiative
arbitr·ō -āre -āvī -ātus *tr* to think, judge; *(w. a predicate)* to consider ‖ *pass (of a dispute)* to be settled
arbitr·or -ārī -ātus sum *tr & intr* to decide *or* judge *(as an arbitrator);* to consider, judge, think; to reckon, suppose, imagine; to infer; to be a witness of; to award as an arbiter; *(w. inf)* to think it proper
arb·or *or* **arb·ōs** -**oris** *f* tree; mast, oar, ship; gallows; **arbor Iovis** oak tree; **arbor Palladis** olive tree; **arbor Phoebī** the laurel; **Herculea arbor** the poplar
arborēt·um -ī *n* plantation of trees
arbore·us -a -um *adj* of a tree; tree-like
Arbuscul·a -ae *f* Arbuscula *(actress in the time of Cicero)*
arbuscul·a -ae *f* small tree, sapling
arbust·us -a -um *adj* wooded, planted with trees ‖ *n* orchard; vineyard planted with trees ‖ *npl* trees
arbute·us -a -um *adj* of arbutus
arbut·um -ī *n* wild strawberry *(fruit of arbutus)*
arbut·us -ī *f* arbutus, strawberry tree
arc·a -ae *f* chest, cupboard; money box *(also the money itself),* safe, coffer; coffin; prison cell
Arcadi·a -ae *f* district in central Peloponnesus, famed for its pastoral beauty
Arcadic·us *or* **Arcadi·us -a -um** *adj* Arcadian
arcānō *adv* in secret; in confidence
arcān·us -a -um *adj* secret, concealed; private; trustworthy *(friend)* ‖ *n* secret; sacred mystery
Arc·as -adis *m* inhabitant of Arcadia, Arcadian ‖ Arcas *(son of Callisto by Jupiter, eponymous hero of Arcadia)* ‖ Mercury *(who was born on Mt. Cyllene in Arcadia)*
arc·eō -ēre -uī *tr* to shut up, enclose; to keep out *(rain, cold);* to keep at a distance, keep off; to hinder, prevent; to control, govern; to prevent, stop; *(w. abl)* to protect from, rescue from
arcer·a -ae *f* ambulance
Arcesil·ās -ae *or* **Arcesilā·ūs -ī** *m* philosopher of the 3rd cent. B.C., founder of the Middle Academy
arcessīt·us -a -um *pp of* **arcessō (accers-)** ‖ *adj* foreign; far-fetched; self-inflicted *(death)*
arcessīt·us -ūs *m* call, summons
arcess·ō *or* **accers·ō -ere -īvī** *or* -**iī -ītus** *tr* to send for, summon; to raise *(money);* to drag in *(gratuitously);* to induce *(sleep, tears)*; to bring upon oneself *(troubles);* to derive; to import; *(leg)* to arraign
archetyp·us -a -um *adj* original, autograph ‖ *n* original
Archiloch·us -ī *m* Greek iambic and elegaic poet of Paros *(c. 714–676 B.C.)*
archimagīr·us -ī *m* chef

Archimēd·ēs -is *or* -ī *m* Greek scientist of Syracuse *(287?–212 B.C.)*
archipīrāt·a -ae *m* pirate captain
architect·ō -āre -āvī -ātus *tr* to design
architect·ōn -onis *m* architect
architect·or -ārī -ātus sum *tr* to design; to build; *(fig)* to devise
architectūr·a -ae *f* architecture
architect·us -ī *m* architect; designer, deviser
arch·ōn -ontis *m* archon *(a chief magistrate of Athens)*
Archyt·ās -ae *m* Pythagorean philosopher *(from Tarentum)* of the 4th cent. B.C.
arcisell·ium -(i)ī *n* chair *(with rounded back)*
arciten·ēns -entis *adj* holding a bow; **dea arcitenēns** Diana ‖ **Arcitenēns** *m* Apollo; *(astr)* Sagittarius *(constellation and sign of the zodiac)*
Arctophyl·ax -acis *m (astr)* Boötes *(constellation)*
arct·os -ī *m* North Pole; North; north wind; night ‖ **Arctos** *m (astr)* the Great and Little Bear *(double constellation)*
arctūr·us -ī *m (astr)* brightest star in Boötes
arcuāt·us -a -um *adj* bow-shaped; covered *(carriage)*
arcul·a -ae *f* small box *(for perfumes, jewels)*
arculār·ius -(i)ī *m* maker of small jewel boxes
arcu·ō -āre -āvī -ātus *tr* to curve
arc·us -ūs *m* bow; rainbow; curve; arch; triumphal arch; one of the five zones of the sky; halo *(of the sun)*
ardeli·ō -ōnis *m* busybody, meddler
arde·a -ae *f* heron ‖ **Ardea** town in Latium
Arde·ās -ātis *adj* of Ardea ‖ *mpl* the people of Ardea
Ardeātīn·us -a -um *adj* of Ardea
ārd·ēns -entis *adj* blazing, burning, hot, fiery; gleaming; intense *(emotions);* zealous, eager; high *(fever);* bright *(colors, stars)*
ārdenter *adv* ardently, passionately; eagerly
ārdeō ārdēre ārsī ārsūrus *tr* to be in love with ‖ *intr* to be on fire, burn, blaze; to flash, glow; to smart, burn; *(of countries)* to be in turmoil; *(of corpses)* to be cremated; *(of seas)* to be rough
ārdēsc·ō -ere *intr* to catch fire; to gleam, glitter; *(of passions)* to become more intense, flare up
ārd·or -ōris *m* heat, flame; flashing, brightness; heat *(of passions);* loved one, flame
Arduenn·a -ae *f* forest in the N. of Gaul *(Ardennes)*
ardu·us -a -um *adj* steep, high; uphill; erect; difficult; *(of hopes)* difficult to realize ‖ *n* height; difficulty; **in arduum** *(or* **per arduum)** upwards, uphill; high into the air
āre·a -ae *f* open space; forecourt *(of temple);* park, playground; building site; threshing floor; bald spot
āre·faciō -facere -fēcī -factus *tr* to dry up
Arelāte *indecl n* town in S. Gaul *(Arles)*
arēna *see* **harēna**
ār·ēns -entis *adj* dry, parched; parching *(thirst)*
ār·eō -ēre *intr* to be dry; to be thirsty
Arēopagīt·ēs -ae *m* member of the Areopagus
Arēopag·us -ī *m* criminal court in Athens; hill where this court met
Ar·ēs -is *m* Greek god of war *(counterpart of Mars)*
ār·ēscō -ēscere -uī *intr* to become dry; to wither; *(of streams)* to run dry
aretālog·us -ī *m* teller of tall tales
Arethūs·a -ae *f* nymph pursued by river god Alpheus in the Peloponnesus and changed into a fountain ‖ fountain in Syracuse
Argē·ī -ōrum *mpl* figures of men made of straw and thrown annually into the Tiber in place of earlier human sacrifices
argentāri·us -a -um *adj* silver; silvery; financial; banker's ‖ *m* banker ‖ *f* banking; bank; silver mine
argentāt·us -a -um *adj* silver-plated; *(hum)* concerned with money
argenteol·us -a -um *adj* **(-tiol-)** silver
argente·us -a -um *adj* silver, silvery; *(hum)* of money ‖ *m* silver coin
argent·um -ī *n* silver; silver plate; money, cash; **argentum bīgātum** silver coin stamped with a two-horse chariot; **argentum signātum** silver coin; **argentum vīvum** mercury, quicksilver
Argē·us *or* **Argei·us** *or* **Argī·us -a -um** *adj* Argive; Greek
Arg·ī -ōrum *mpl or* **Argos** *n (only nom and acc)* Argos *(town in N.E. Peloponnesus)*
Argīlēt·um -ī *n (also* **Argī lētum)** district in Rome between the Quirinal and Capitoline Hills
argill·a -ae *f* potter's clay
Arginūs(s)·ae -ārum *fpl* group of three islands off the coast of Asia Minor, the scene of an Athenian naval victory in 406 B.C.
argīt·is -idis *f* vine with white grapes
Argīv·us -a -um *adj* Argive; Greek
Arg·ō -ūs *(acc & abl:* **Argō)** *f* Jason's ship
Argolic·us -a -um *adj* Argive; Greek
Argol·is -idis *adj (fem only)* Argive ‖ Argive woman ‖ the Argolid *(district around Argos)*
Argonaut·ae -ārum *mpl* Argonauts
Argos *n (only nom & acc)* Argos *(see* **Argī)**
Argō·us -a -um *adj* of the Argo

argūmentāti·ō -ōnis *f* argumentation; proof

argūment·or -ārī -ātus sum *tr* to adduce as proof; to support by arguments; *(w.* **dē** + *abl)* to conclude from ‖ *intr* to adduce arguments, argue

argūment·um -ī *n* evidence, proof; argument; theme, plot; topic, subject; motif *(of artistic representation);* **ex argūmentō** from the facts of the case

arg·uō -uere -uī -ūtus *tr* to prove; to reveal, betray; to accuse, charge, impeach *(person);* to find fault with *(thing);* to denounce as wrong; to prove guilty, convict

Arg·us -ī *m* many-eyed monster set over Io and killed by Mercury

argūtāti·ō -ōnis *f* creaking

argūtē *adv* shrewdly

argūti·ae -ārum *fpl* subtlety; sophistry; wit

argūt·ō -āre -āvī *tr* to say childishly

argūt·or -ārī -ātus sum *intr* to chatter

argūtul·us -a -um *adj* somewhat subtle

argūt·us -a -um *adj* clearcut, bright, distinct; piercing; bright, smart, witty *(person);* clear-voiced, melodious; rustling *(leaves);* babbling *(brook);* chirping *(birds, crickets);* pungent *(smell);* expressive *(eyes, gestures)*

argyrasp·is -idis *adj* wearing a silver shield

-āri·a -ae *fem suf* forms nouns **1** denoting a place: **argentāria** a bank; **2** a female agent: **librāria** female secretary

Ariadn·a -ae *or* **Ariadn·ē -ēs** *f* Ariadne (*daughter of King Minos; she extricated Theseus from the Labyrinth*)

Arīci·a -ae *f* town in Latium on the Via Appia

āridul·us -a -um *adj* somewhat dry

ārid·us -a -um *adj* dry, parched; withered; meager; dry *(style)*

ari·ēs -etis *m* ram; battering ram; bulwark *(used as breakwater);* **ariete crebrō** with constant ramming ‖ **Ariēs** Aries *(sign of Zodiac)*

ariet·ō -āre -āvī -ātus *tr* to batter, ram; **inter sē arietārī** to collide ‖ *intr* to collide; to trip; *(w.* **in** + *acc)* to ram against

Ariobarzān·ēs -is *m* king of Cappadocia

Arī·ōn -onis *m* early Greek poet and musician, rescued from drowning by a dolphin

Ariovist·us -ī *m* king of Germanic tribe

-ār·is -is -e *adjl suf* collateral with **-ālis** but used when the stem contains an **l: cōnsulāris** consular

arist·a -ae *f* ear of grain

Aristae·us -ī *m* son of Apollo and Cyrene *(said to have taught man beekeeping and to have been the first to plant olive trees)*

Aristarch·us -ī *m* Alexandrine critic and scholar *(fl 156 B.C.);* stern critic

Aristīd·ēs -ae *m* Athenian politician and general in the time of Persian Wars, famous for his honesty ‖ author from Miletus

aristolochi·a -ae *f (bot)* birthwort *(plant believed to aid in childbirth)*

Aristophan·ēs -is *m* Greek comic playwright *(c. 450?–385? B.C.)*

Aristotel·ēs -is *or* -ī Aristotle *(384–322 B.C.)*

arithmētic·us -a -um *adj* of numbers ‖ *f or npl* arithmetic

āritūd·ō -inis *f* dryness

-ār·ium -(i)ī *n suf* denoting a place, *e.g.,* **armāmentārium** place for keeping arms, arsenal

-ār·ius -(i)ī *m suf* denoting "dealer in," *e.g.,* **librārius** bookseller

arm·a -ōrum *npl* armor, defensive arms *(opp* **tēla** weapons to throw or thrust); war, warfare; camp life; armed men, troops; equipment, tools; utensils; nature's arms *(teeth, claws, etc.)*; **ab armīs dēcēdere** *or* **discēdere** to lay down one's arms, stop fighting; **ad arma adīre** *(or* **venīre)** to resort to military force; **arma capere (movēre, sūmere,** *etc.)* to take up arms; **arma cōnferre cum** to clash with; **arma ferre contrā** *or* **in** *(w. acc)* to fight against; **arma īnferre** *(dat)* to make war on; **arma pōnere** *(or* **dēpōnere)** to lay down one's arms; **arma vēnātōria** hunting gear; **in armīs** *(or* **sub armīs)** under arms, monbilized; **levia arma** light-armed troops; *(applied to the wings made by Daedalus)* **umerīs arma** equipment for his shoulders

armamax·a -ae *f* a Persian travel carriage for women

armāment·a -ōrum *npl* ship's gear; equipment

armāmentār·ium -(i)ī *n* arsenal, armory

armāriol·um -ī *n* small cabinet, chest, closet

armār·ium -(i)ī *n* cupboard, chest; bookcase; safe

armātūr·a -ae *f* outfit, equipment; armor; light-armed troops

armāt·us -a -um *adj* armed; equipped ‖ *m* armed man, soldier

armāt·us -ūs *m* armor; **gravis armātī** heavy-armed troops

Armeni·a -ae *f* **(-min-)** country in N.E. Asia Minor

Armeniac·um -ī *n* apricot

Armeniac·us -ī *f* apricot tree

Armeni·us -a -um *adj* Armenian; **prūnum Armenium** apricot ‖ *m* an Armenian

armentāl·is -is -e *adj* of the herd

armentār·ius -(i)ī *m* herdsman

arment·um -ī *n* herd *(of oxen, horses, stags, sea monsters)*

armif·er -era -erum *adj* arms-bearing, armed, warlike; **deus armifer** Mars; **dea armifera** Minerva

armig·er -era -erum *adj* armed; producing warriors; *(of a field sown with dragon's teeth)* producing armed men **II** *m* armed man; bodyguard; armor-bearer **II** *f* armor-bearer *(female)*; **Iovis armigera** Jove's armor-bearer *(i.e., the eagle)*

armill·a -ae *f* armlet, bracelet

armillātus -a -um *adj* wearing a bracelet

Armilūstr·um -ī *n* ceremony of purifying arms

armipot·ēns -entis *adj* powerful in arms, valiant

armison·us -a -um *adj* reverberating with arms

arm·ō -āre -āvī -ātus *tr* to arm; to rouse to arms; to equip *(ships)* for war

arm·us -ī *m* shoulder, shoulder blade, upper arm; flank *(of animal)*

Arniēns·is -is -e *adj* name of one of the tribes in Rome

ar·ō -āre -āvī -ātus *tr* to plow, till

Arpīn·ās -ātis *adj* of Arpinum **II** *mpl* inhabitants of Arpinum

Arpīn·um -ī *n* town in Latium, birthplace of Marius and Cicero

arq- = arc-

arquāt·us -a -um *adj* jaundiced

arr- = adr-

arrab·ō -ōnis *m* down payment, deposit; **arrabō amōris** token of love; **centum dēnāriōs arrabōnī dare** to make a down payment of one hundred denarii

arrēct·us -a -um *pp of* **arrigō II** *adj* upright; steep

arrēp·ō -ere -sī *intr* **(adr-)** *(w. dat or* **ad)** to creep toward, steal up on

Arrēt·ium -(i)ī *n* town in Etruria, known for its pottery

arrēxī *perf of* **arrigō**

arrī·deō -dēre -sī -sus *tr* **(adr-)** to smile at **II** *intr (w. dat)* **1** to smile at, smile on; **2** to laugh with; **3** to be favorable to; **4** to please

ar·rigō -rigere -rēxī -rēctus *tr* **(adr-)** to erect; to arouse, excite; to prick up *(ears)*; **animum arrigere** to arouse courage; **in digitōs arrēctus** on tiptoe; **oculī arrēctī** staring eyes

ar·ripiō -ripere -ripuī -reptus *tr* **(adr-)** to snatch, seize eagerly; to get hold of; to obtain, acquire; to head eagerly for *(destination)*; to jump at *(a chance, excuse)*; *(of disease)* to attack; to assail, attack suddenly; *(fig)* to grasp quickly; *(leg)* to arrest, arraign

arrīsī *perf of* **arrideō**

arrō·dō -dere -sī -sus *tr* **(adr-)** to gnaw at, nibble away part of

arrog·āns -antis *adj* **(adr-)** arrogant

arroganter *adv* **(adr-)** arrogantly

arroganti·a -ae *f* **(adr-)** arrogance; presumption

ar·rogō -āre -āvī -ātus *tr* **(adr-)** to question; to lay claim to, arrogate; to claim to possess; to assign, attribute

arrōsī *perf of* **arrōdō**

arrōsus *pp of* **arrōdō**

Arrūn·s -tis *m* Etruscan proper name, traditionally given to the younger sons

ars artis *f* skill; craft, trade; craftsmanship, art; work of art; invention, device; trick, stratagem; *(mil)* tactic; profession, occupation; method, way, manner, means; artificial means, artificiality; science; theory *(opp:* **ūsus** practice); manual, textbook; **arte** cunningly; **bonae** *(or* **līberālēs) artēs** liberal arts; **ex arte** systematically; **istae artēs** evil practices, bad habits

Arsac·ēs -is *m* first king of the Parthians; title of his successors

ārsī *perf of* **ārdeō**

Artaban·us -ī *m* name of several Parthian kings

artē *adv* closely, tightly; *(to love)* deeply, dearly; *(to sleep)* soundly

Artem·is -idis *f* Greek counterpart of Diana

artēri·a -ae *f* windpipe; artery

arthrītic·us -a -um *adj* arthritic

articulātim *adv* piecemeal; *(to speak)* articulately, distinctly

articul·ō -āre *tr* to articulate

articul·us -ī *m* joint, knuckle; finger; toe; limb; point of time, juncture; *(gram)* single word *(of a sentence)*; *(gram)* clause; *(gram)* (definite, indefinite) article; *(gram)* pronoun, pronominal adjective; **in articulō temporis** in the nick of time

artif·ex -icis *adj* **(-tuf-)** skilled, ingenious, professional; creative, productive; cunning; skillfully made, cunningly wrought; *(w. gen,* **ad** *or* **in** *+ acc)* skilled in, expert in; broken, trained *(horse)*

artif·ex -icis *m* craftsman, artist, master, professional; performer, actor, musician; author *(of book)*; originator, contriver; *(w. gen or* **ad** *or* **in** *+ abl)* expert in

artificiōsē *adv* skillfully; systematically

artificiōs·us -a -um *adj* skillful, ingenious, accomplished; artificial

artific·ium -(i)ī *n* skill, talent; work of art; trade, profession; cleverness, cunning; theory

arti·us -a -um *adj* sound in mind and body

art·ō -āre -āvī -ātus *tr* **(arct-)** to pack closely; to compress, contract; to limit; to tighten

artolagan·us -ī *m* pancake *(made of meal, pepper, wine, milk, oil, lard)*

artopt·a -ae *m* bread pan; baker

artu·a -ōrum *npl* limbs

art·us -a -um *adj* close, tight; confined, restricted; narrow; dense; firm; scanty, small; needy; parsimonious, stingy; strict; sound *(sleep)* ‖ *n* narrow space; tight spot, difficulty; **in artum colligere** to summarize

art·us -ūs *m* joint; limb

ārul·a -ae *f* small altar

arund·ō -inis *f* reed; shaft, arrow; pipe, flute; pen; fishing rod; hobby-horse; *(in weaving)* comb

arvīn·a -ae *f* grease

arv·us -a -um *adj* arable, plowed ‖ *n* arable land, soil, land; plain; region; grain

arx arcis *f* citadel; fortress, stronghold; place of refuge; hilltop, peak; *(fig)* mainstay, protection; summit, pinnacle; **arcem facere ē cloācā** *(prov)* to make mountains out of molehills; **arx caelī** height of heaven; **arx corporis** head; **Rōmae septem arcēs** seven hills of Rome

-ās *advl suf:* **aliās** elsewhere

ās assis *m* pound *(divisible into 12 ounces);* bronze coin, penny; jugerum *(c. 3/5 of an acre);* undivided estate; **hērēs ex asse** sole heir; **nōn assis facere** not to give a hoot about

-ās -ātis *adjl suf* **1** originally used in ethnic adjectives from the names of Italian towns: **Arpīnās** of *or* connected with Arpinum; **2** extended to other stems to form adjectives and substantives: **optimās** aristocratic; **optimātēs** artistocrats

Ascan·ius -(i)ī *m* son of Aeneas and Creusa and founder of Alba Longa

ascen·dō -dere -dī -sus *tr* **(ads-)** to climb; to mount *(horse);* to board *(ship)* ‖ *intr* to climb up, ascend; *(of voice, river)* to rise; *(w.* **ad** *or* **in** *+ acc)* to climb, climb up to; *(w.* **super** *or* **suprā** *+ acc)* to rise above, surpass; **per gradūs ascendere** to climb the stairs

ascēnsi·ō -ōnis *f* climbing up, ascent

ascēns·us -ūs *m* **(ads-)** ascent; means of ascending, approach; step, degree; flight of stairs; *(fig)* climb, rise

asci·a -ae *f* ax, hatchet; mason's trowel; **sub asciā** while still under construction

asc·iō -īre *tr* **(ads-)** to associate with oneself

asc·īscō -īscere -īvī -ītus *tr* **(ads-)** to adopt; to approve *(a bill);* to assume, arrogate; to select, to receive, admit *(as ally, citizen, etc.);* to hire; *(w.* **in** *+ acc)* to admit *(to citizenship, the senate);* **inter patriciōs ascīscere** to admit to the patrician order

ascīt·us -a -um *adj* acquired *(as opposed to innate)*

Asclēpiad·ēs -is *m* famous doctor of Prusa in Bithynia, who practised in Rome and was a friend of Crassus *(d. 40 B.C.)*

āscop·a -ae *f* small leather pouch

Ascr·a -ae *f* birthplace of Hesiod in Boeotia, near Mt. Helicon

Ascrae·us -a -um *adj* of Ascra; **Ascraeus poēta** *or* **senex** Hesiod

ascrī·bō -bere -psī -ptus *tr* **(ads-)** to add *(by writing);* to impute, ascribe; to enroll, register; to reckon, number, class

ascrīptīci·us -a -um *adj* **(ads-)** enrolled, registered

ascrīpti·ō -ōnis *f* **(ads-)** addition *(in writing)*

ascrīptīv·us -ī *m* **(ads-)** *(mil)* reserve

ascrīpt·or -ōris *m* **(ads-)** supporter

Asc(u)l·um -ī *n* chief town of Picenum in N. Italy

Asculān·us -ī *m* inhabitant of Asculum

asell·a -ae *f* ass *(female)*

asell·us -ī *m* ass, donkey

Āsi·a -ae *f* Asia; Asia Minor *(modern Turkey);* kingdom of Troy

Āsiān·us -a -um *adj & m* Asian

Āsiātic·us -a -um *adj* connected with Asia or the East *(esp. Asia Minor and the Roman province of Asia);* **mare Āsiāticum** Carpathian Sea

asīl·us -ī *m* horsefly, gadfly

asin·a -ae *f* ass

asināri·us -a -um *adj* connected with asses; **via asināria** a road S.E. of Rome ‖ *m* ass-driver

asin·us -ī *m* ass; *(coll)* ass, fool

Ās·is -idis *f* Asia; Asia Minor

Āsi·us -a -um *f* of Asia, of Asia Minor

Āsōp·us *or* **Āsōp·os -ī** *m* a river in Boeotia, personified as the father of Aegina

asōt·us -ī *m* playboy, rake

asparag·us -ī *m* asparagus

aspargō *see* **aspergō**

aspectābil·is -is -e *adj* visible

aspect·ō -āre -āvī -ātus *tr* **(ads-)** to look at, gaze at; to look with respect at; *(of a place)* to face; to obey *(orders)*

aspectus *pp of* **aspiciō**

aspect·us -ūs *m* **(ads-)** look, sight, glance; sense of sight; eyes, expression in the eyes, look; range of vision, view; appearance, aspect; sight, vision; **prīmō aspectū** at first sight; **sub oculōrum aspectum cadere** to come into view; **ūnō aspectū** at a glance

aspell·ō -ere *tr* to drive away

asp·er -era -erum (asprīs = asperīs) *adj* rough, uneven; harsh, severe, stormy *(climate);* grating, hoarse *(sound);* pungent, strong *(odor);* rough, hard; unkind, cruel, bitter, rude *(character);* austere, rigid *(person);* wild, fierce *(animal);* rough, annoying, adverse *(circumstances);* embossed *(cup, etc.);* craggy; rugged *(style)*

asperē *adv* roughly; harshly, sternly, severely

asper·gō -gere -sī -sus *tr* **(ads-) (-spar-)** to sprinkle, scatter; to taint; *(w. dat)* to sprinkle *(s.th.)* on

asperg·ō -inis *f* **(ads-) (-spar-)** sprinkling; spray
asperit·ās -ātis *f* unevenness, roughness; severity, fierceness; difficulty, trouble
āspernāti·ō -ōnis *f* disdain
āspern·or -ārī -ātus sum *tr* to disdain, spurn, reject
asper·ō -āre -āvī -ātus *tr* to make rough *or* uneven, roughen; to exasperate; to make worse
aspersi·ō -ōnis *f* sprinkling
aspiciō aspicere aspexī aspectus *tr* **(ads-)** to catch sight of, spot; to look at; to inspect, look over; to look *(a person)* in the eye; to visit; to consider; to picture
aspīrāti·ō -ōnis *f* **(ads-)** breathing; exhalation; *(gram)* aspiration *(making an h sound)*
aspīr·ō -āre -āvī -ātum *intr* to breathe, blow; *(w. dat or* **ad** *or* **in** *+ acc)* to aspire to, desire to reach *or* obtain, come near to obtaining; *(w. dat)* to favor; *(w.* **ad)** to rival; *(w. acc & dat)* to instil *(e.g., love)* in
asp·is -idis *f* asp *(poisonous snake of N. Africa)*
asportātiō -ōnis *f* removal
asport·ō -āre -āvī -ātus *tr* to carry away, remove; *(of vehicles)* to haul away
asprēt·a -ōrum *npl* rough terrain
Assarac·us -ī *m* king of Troy, son of Tros, and grandfather of Aeneas
assecl·a -ae *m* **(ads-)** hanger-on
assectāti·ō -ōnis *f* **(ads-)** (political) support
assectāt·or -ōris *m* **(ads-)** attendant, companion; disciple; devotee; *(pol)* supporter
assect·or -ārī -ātus sum *tr* **(ads-)** to follow closely; to escort; to be an adherent of, follow
assecul·a -ae *m* **(ads-)** hanger-on
assēnsi·ō -ōnis *f* **(ads-)** approval, applause; agreement, belief **‖** *fpl* expressions of approval
assēns·or -ōris *m* **(ads-)** backer, supporter
assēns·us -ūs *m* **(ads-)** assent, approval; agreement; belief
assentāti·ō -ōnis *f* **(ads-)** assent, agreement; flattery
assentātiuncul·a -ae *f* **(ads-)** bit of flattery
assentāt·or -ōris *m* **(ads-)** yes-man
assentātōriē *adv* **(ads-)** flatteringly
assentātr·īx -īcis *f* **(ads-)** flatterer *(female)*
assen·tiō -tīre -sī -sum *or* **assen·tior -tīrī -sus sum** *intr* **(ads-)** to agree; *(w. dat)* assent to, agree with, approve
assent·or -ārī -ātus sum *intr* **(ads-)** to agree always; *(w. dat)* **1** to agree always with; **2** to humor
asse·quor -quī -cūtus sum *tr* **(ads-)** to pursue, go after; to catch up to, reach; to gain, obtain, procure; to achieve, attain, win *(wisdom, citizenship, etc.)*; to come up to, equal, match; to comprehend, understand

ass·er -eris *m* pole; joist, rafter; pole on which a litter was carried
asser·ō -ere -uī -tus *tr* **(ads-)** to set free, liberate *(slave)*; to protect, defend; to claim, appropriate; **in servitūtem asserere** to claim *(s.o.)* as one's slave
as·serō -serere -sēvī -sītus *tr* **(ads-)** *(w. dat)* to plant *(s.th.)* close to
asserti·ō -ōnis *f* **(ads-)** declaration of civil status
assert·or -ōris *m* **(ads-)** defender, protector, champion; *(leg)* claimant *(who claims a person as his slave)*
asserv·iō -īre -īvī *or* **-iī** *intr* **(ads-)** *(w. dat)* to apply oneself to
asserv·ō -āre -āvī -ātus *tr* **(ads-)** to preserve; keep *(records)*; to watch; to keep in custody; *(mil)* to guard
assessi·ō -ōnis *f* **(ads-)** company (legal) support, standing by
assess·or -ōris *m* **(ads-)** adviser; *(leg)* counselor
assess·us -ūs *m* **(ads-)** legal assistance
assevēranter *adv* **(ads-)** emphatically
assevērāti·ō -ōnis *f* **(ads-)** assertion; emphasis; earnestness; firmness; *(rhet)* emphasizing particle *(e.g.,* **eheu)**
assevēr·ō -āre -āvī -ātus *tr* **(ads-)** to assert emphatically; *(of things)* to give clear evidence of; to be serious about **‖** *intr* to be serious
as·sideō -sidēre -sēdī -sessus *tr* **(ads-)** to sit near; *(mil)* to besiege **‖** *intr* to sit nearby; *(w. dat)* **1** to sit near, stand by, take care of, keep *(s.o.)* company; **2** to be busily engaged in; **3** *(of places)* to be situated close to; **4** to attend to, mind; **5** to resemble; **6** *(mil)* to encamp near; **7** *(mil)* to set up a blockade against
as·sīdō -sīdere -sēdī *intr* **(ads-)** to sit down; *(of birds)* to land, alight
assiduē *adv* **(ads-)** assiduously, continually
assiduit·ās -ātis *f* **(ads-)** constant presence; persistence, frequent recurrence
assiduō *adv* **(ads-)** continually
assidu·us -a -um *adj* **(ads-)** constantly present; persistent, incessant; tireless, busy; restless *(sea)* **‖** *m* taxpayer; rich man
assignāti·ō -ōnis *f* **(ads-)** allotment *(of land)*
assign·ō -āre -āvī -ātus *tr* **(ads-)** to mark out, allot, assign *(land)*; *(w. dat)* **1** to confer *(honors)* on; **2** to ascribe to, impute to; **3** to attribute to; **4** to entrust to the care of
as·siliō -silīre -siluī -sultum *intr* **(ads-)** to jump; *(w. dat)* **1** to jump upon, leap at; **2** *(mil)* to make a sudden assault on; *(w.* **ad)** **1** to jump to; **2** to have recourse to
assimil·is -is -e *adj* **(ads-)** *(w. gen or dat)* similar to, like
assimiliter *adv* **(ads-)** in like manner

assimulāti·ō -ōnis *f* **(ads-)** similarity; comparison; pretense
assimulāt·us -a -um *adj* **(ads-)** similar; counterfeit
assimul·ō -āre -āvī -ātus *tr* **(ads-) (-mil-)** to pretend; to resemble, imitate; *(w. dat)* to compare to
as·sistō -sistere -titī *intr* **(ads-)** to stop; to stand nearby; *(w.* **ad)** to stand at *or* near; *(w. dat)* to assist, defend; *(mil) (w.* **in** + *acc)* to take up a position against; *(leg)* to assist in court; *(leg) (w. dat)* to assist, defend
assitus *pp of* **asserō**
assol·eō -ēre *intr* **(ads-)** to be usual
asson·ō -āre *intr* **(ads-)** *(w. dat)* to echo
assūctus *pp of* **assūgō** sucked in
assūdēsc·ō -ere *intr* **(ads-) (-āsc-)** to break out into a sweat
assuē·faciō -facere -fēcī -factus *tr* **(ads-)** to train; *(w. dat or* **ad** *or inf)* to accustom *(s.o.)* to, get *(s.o.)* used to
assu·ēscō -ēscere -ēvī -ētus *tr* **(ads-)** *(w. dat)* to accustom *(s.o.)* to, make *(s.o.)* familiar with **||** *intr (w. dat,* **ad,** *or w. inf)* to become used to; *(w. dat)* to become intimate with
assuētūd·ō -inis *f* **(ads-)** habit, custom; intimacy
assuēt·us -a -um *pp of* **assuēscō ||** *adj* accustomed, customary, usual; *(w. abl)* trained in; *(w. dat,* **ad** *or* **in** + *acc or inf)* accustomed to, used to; *(w. dat)* intimate with
assū·gō -gere -xī -ctus *tr* **(ads-)** to suck in
assul·a -ae *f* splinter, chip, shaving
assulātim *adv* into splinters
assult·ō -āre -āvī -ātus *tr* **(ads-)** to assault **||** *intr (w. dat)* to jump at, jump to
assult·us -ūs *m* **(ads-)** assault
assūm·ō -ere -psī -ptus *tr* **(ads-)** to take in addition, add; to adopt; to usurp; to claim, assume; to employ, hire; to derive, borrow; to gain, acquire *(qualities);* to take *(food, drink, bait);* to take along *(as companion);* **sibi assūmere** to lay claim to
assūmpti·ō -ōnis *f* **(ads-)** assumption; adoption; acquisition; claim; *(in logic)* minor premise; *(rhet)* taking up *(of a point)*
assūmptīv·us -a -um *adj* **(ads-)** resting on external evidence, extrinsic
assu·ō -ere *tr* **(ads-)** *(w. dat)* to sew *(e.g. patch)* on
assur·gō -gere -rēxī -rēctum *intr* **(ads-)** to stand up; to rise; to increase, swell; *(of hair)* to stand on end; *(w. dat)* to rise out of respect for
ass·us -a -um *adj* roasted; dry *(sunbathing without anointing)* **||** *n* roast
assūxī *perf of* **assūgō**
Assyri·a -ae *f* Assyria
Assyri·us -a -um *adj* Assyrian **||** *mpl* Assyrians
ast *conj (old form of* **at)** but
Astart·ē -ēs *f* Syro-Phoenician goddess, counterpart of Venus
Asteri·a -ae *f* sister of Leto, who was metamorphosed into a quail at Delos
astern·ō -ere *tr* **(ads-)** to strew **||** *pass* to prostrate oneself
astic·us -a -um *adj* city, urban
astipulāt·or -ōris *m* **(ads-)** legal assistant; supporter, adherent
astipul·or -ārī -ātus sum *intr* **(ads-)** *(w. dat)* to side with
astit·uō -uere -uī -ūtus *tr* to place near; *(w.* **ad)** to make *(s.o.)* stand near
ast·ō -āre -itī *intr* **(ads-)** to stand erect, stand up; to stand nearby, stand by; *(w. dat)* **1.** to stand by; **2.** to assist; **astā**! stand still!, stop!
Astrae·a -ae *f* goddess of justice
Astrae·us -a -um *adj* of Astraeus; **frātrēs Astraeī** the winds **||** *m* a Titan, husband of Aurora and father of the winds
astrep·ō -ere -uī *tr* **(ads-)** *tr* to assail *(with shouts)* **||** *intr* to shout in support; *(w. dat)* to applaud
astrīctē *adv* **(ads-)** concisely; strictly
astrīct·us -a -um *pp of* **astringō ||** *adj* drawn together, tight; stingy; concise
astrif·er -era -erum *adj* starry
astr·ingō -ingere -īnxī -īctus *tr* **(ads-)** to tighten, bind fast; to obligate; to restrain; to freeze; to pledge; *(fig)* to numb; *(fig)* to compress, abridge; to occupy *(attention);* to embarrass; to implicate *(in a crime);* **fidem astringere** to give one's word; **inter sē astringere** to fasten together
astrologi·a -ae *f* astronomy; astrology
astrolog·us -ī *m* astronomer; astrologer
astr·um -ī *n* star; constellation **||** *npl* stars; sky, heaven
astr·uō -uere -uxī -uctus *tr* **(ads)** to build as an additional structure; **nōbilitātem alicui astruere** to add nobility to s.o.
astu *indecl n the* city *(i.e., Athens)*
astup·eō -ēre -uī *intr (w. dat)* to be amazed at, be enthralled by
ast·us -ūs *m* cunning; trick
astūtē *adv* slyly
astūti·a -ae *f* cunning, slyness; astuteness; **astūtiae** sly tricks
astūt·us -a -um *adj* clever, astute; *(usu. pej)* cunning
Astyag·ēs -is *m* king of Media and grandfather of Cyrus; an enemy of Perseus changed by him into a stone by means of the head of Medusa
Astyan·ax -actis *m* son of Hector and Andromache
asyl·um -ī *n* refuge, asylum
at *conj* but; *(in a transition)* but on the other hand; *(in anticipation of an opponent's*

objection) but, it may be objected; *(in an ironical objection)* but really, but after all; *(after a negative clause, to introduce a qualification)* but at least; **at contrā** but on the contrary; **at tamen** but at least

Atābul·us -ī *m* sirocco, S.E. wind

Atalant·a -ae *or* **Atlant·ē -ēs** *f* daughter of King Schoeneus, defeated by Hippomenes in a footrace ‖ daughter of Iasius and participant in the Calydonian boar hunt

atat *(or* **attat)** *interj (expressing surprise or fear)* aha!, uhoh!

atav·us -ī *m* great-great-great-grandfather; ancestor

Ātell·a -ae *f* Campanian town

Ātellān·a -ae *f* comic farce *(originated in Atella)*

ā·ter -tra -trum *adj* flat black *(different from* **niger** glossy black); dark; gloomy; malicious; poisonous; unlucky, ill-omened

Atham·ān -ānis *m* inhabitant of Athamania

Athamāni·a -ae *f* district in Epirus

Athamantē·us -a -um *adj* of Athamas *(referring to Phrixus or Palaemon)*

Atham·ās -antis *m* king of Thessaly, father of Helle and Phrixus by Nephele, and of Learchus and Melecertes by Ino

Athēn·ae -ārum *fpl* Athens

Athēniēns·is -is -e *adj* Athenian

Athēnodōr·us -ī *m* Stoic philosopher, teacher of Augustus

athe·os -ī *m* atheist

āthlēt·a -ae *m* athlete; boxer; wrestler

āthlēticē *adv* athletically; like an athlete

āthlētic·us -a -um *adj* athletic ‖ *f* athletics

Ath·ōs *or* **Athō** *or* **Ath·ōn** *(no gen) m* mountain on the peninsula of Acte in Chalcidice

Ātīn·a -ae *f* town in Latium ‖ town in Lucania (now Basilicata)

Ātīn·ās -ātis *m* of Atina ‖ *mpl* the people of Atina

Atl·ās -antis *m* Atlas *(giant supporting the sky, son of Iapetus and Clymene)* ‖ Mt. Atlas *(on N.W. coast of Africa)*

Atlantē·us -a -um *adj* Atlantic

Atlantiad·ēs -ae *m* grandson of Atlas (Mercury) ‖ great-grandson of Atlas (Hermaphroditus)

Atlantic·us -a -um *adj* Atlantic

Atlant·is -idis *or* **-idos** *f* daughter *or* female descendant of Atlas

atom·os -ī *f* atom *(an indivisible element)*

atque *conj (used before vowels and "h" and sometimes consonants; see* **ac)** and, and also, and besides; *(in adding a more important word)* and indeed, and in particular

atquī *conj* but yet, and yet; however, rather, and yet

ātrāment·um -ī *n* ink; **ātrāmentum sūtōrium** black shoe polish

ātrāt·us -a -um *adj* dressed in black *(for mourning)*

Atr·eus -eī *m* son of Pelops, brother of Thyestes, father of Agamemnon and Menelaus

ātricol·or -ōris *adj* black

Atrīd·ēs -ae *m* descendant of Atreus

ātriēns·is -is *m* butler

ātriol·um -ī *n* small hall, anteroom

ātrit·ās -ātis *f* blackness

ātrīt·us -a -um *adj* blackened

ātr·ium -(i)ī *n* atrium *(first main room of Roman house);* hall *(of temple or public building)* ‖ *npl* house; palace

atrōcit·ās -ātis *f* hideousness; fierceness, brutality, cruelty; severity, rigor

atrōciter *adv* atrociously, horribly; cruelly

Atrop·os -ī *f* one of the three Fates whose function it was to cut the thread of human life

atrōt·us -a -um *adj* invulnerable

atr·ōx -ōcis *adj* atrocious, horrible; hideous; frightful; cruel, fierce; harsh, stern, unyielding, grim

attāctus *pp of* **attingō**

attāct·us -ūs *m* **(adt-)** touch, contact

attag·ēn -ēnis *m* woodcock *(game bird)*

attagēn·a -ae *f* woodcock *(game bird)*

Attalic·us -a -um *adj* of Attalus; Pergamean; rich, splendid; covered with gold brocade ‖ *npl* gold brocade

Attal·us -ī *m* king of Pergamum

attamen *conj* but still, but yet

attat *or* **attatae** *interj* uhoh!

attegi·a -ae *f* hut, cottage

attemperātē *adv* **(adt-)** on time, at the right time; in the nick of time

attempt·ō -āre -āvī -ātus *tr* **(adt-)** to attempt; to test; to tempt, try to seduce; to call into question; to attack

atten·dō -dere -dī -tus *tr* **(adt-)** to notice, mark; to pay attention to, mind, consider; **animō attendere** to listen to; **animum attendere** to pay attention; **aurēs attendere** to listen closely ‖ *intr* to pay attention, listen

attentē *adv* **(adt-)** attentively

attenti·ō -ōnis *f* attention

attentō *see* **attemptō**

attent·us -a -um *pp of* **attendō** ‖ *adj* attentive; careful; frugal; industrious

attenuātē *adv* plainly, in a plain style

attenuāt·us -a -um *adj* weak, weakened; shortened, brief; over-refined, affected; plain, bald *(style)*

attenu·ō -āre -āvī -ātus *tr* **(adt-)** to weaken; to thin; to lessen, diminish; to impoverish ‖ *pass* to become thinner, shrink

at·terō -terere -trīvī -trītus *tr* **(adt-)** to rub (against), wear away, wear out; to reduce in dimensions, diminish; to impair *(facul-*

ties, qualities); to reduce *(military forces);* to weaken, exhaust; to waste, fritter away; to destroy ‖ *pass* **atterī** to lose face by being outdone

attest·or -ārī -ātus sum *tr* **(adt-)** to attest

attex·ō -ere -uī -tus *tr* **(adt-)** to add *(by weaving);* to add on

Atth·is -idis *f* Attica

Attic·a -ae *f* district of Greece, with Athens as its capital

Atticē *adv* in the Athenian style

Atticiss·ō -āre *tr & intr* to speak in the Athenian (Attic) manner

Attic·us -a -um *adj* Attic, Athenian ‖ *m* Titus Pomponius Atticus *(friend of Cicero, 109–32* B.C.*)* ‖ *f* daughter of Atticus

attigō *see* **attingō**

at·tineō -tinēre -tinuī -tentus *tr* **(adt-)** to hold tight, hold on to, hold back; to reach for ‖ *intr (w.* **ad)** to pertain to, relate to, refer to, concern; **quod ad mē attinet** as far as I am concerned

at·tingō -tingere -tigī -tāctus *tr* **(adt-)** to touch, come in contact with; to reach, arrive at; to touch *(food),* taste; to touch, lie near, border; to touch upon, mention lightly; to touch, strike, attack; to touch, affect; to undertake, engage in; to take in hand, manage; to resemble; to concern, belong to

Att·is -idis *m* priest of Cybele

attoll·ō -ere *tr* **(adt-)** to lift up, raise; to erect; to stir up *(dust, sea);* to cause *(river)* to rise; to hold aloft, carry; to exalt; to uplift; to extol; **īrās atollere** to rouse anger ‖ *refl & pass* to rise; to appear; to grow

atton·deō -dēre -dī -sus *tr* **(adt-)** to clip, shave, shear; to prune; to crop; *(fig)* to fleece, cheat, clip

attonit·us -a -um *adj* **(adt-)** thunderstruck, stunned, dazed, astonished; inspired; frantic, frenzied

atton·ō -āre -uī -itus *tr* **(adt-)** to strike with lightning; to drive crazy; to shock

attorqu·eō -ēre *tr* **(adt-)** to wind up *(before hurling),* hurl up

at·trahō -trahere -trāxī -trāctus *tr* **(adt-)** to attract; to drag in; to cause to happen, bring on; to draw toward oneself; to bend *(a bow);* to draw up *(the feet);* to contract, draw together

attrect·ō -āre -āvī -ātus *tr* **(adt-)** to touch, handle; to appropriate to oneself

attrepid·ō -āre *intr* **(adt-)** to hobble along

attrib·uō -uere -uī -ūtus *tr* **(adt-)** to allot, assign; to appoint *(to a post);* to put under the command of; to attribute; to bestow, give; to impose *(taxes)*

attribūti·ō -ōnis *f* **(adt-)** *(gram)* predicate; *(leg)* transference of a debt *(to another person, obligating him)*

attribūt·um -ī *n* **(adt-)** *(gram)* predicate

attrīt·us -a -um *pp of* **atterō** ‖ *adj* worn away, wasted; thin; hardened

au *interj* ouch!

au·ceps -cupis *m* fowler, bird trapper; poulterer; spy, eavesdropper

auctār·ium -(i)ī *n* addition, overweight *(in a purchase)*

auctific·us -a -um *adj* increasing

aucti·ō -ōnis *f* increase; auction; **auctiōnem cōnstituere** *or* **facere** to hold an auction; **auctiōnem prōscrībere** to advertise an auction

auctiōnāri·us -a -um *adj* auction

auctiōn·or -ārī -ātus sum *intr* to hold an auction

auctit·ō -āre *tr* to keep increasing

auct·ō -āre *tr* to increase; *(w. abl)* to bless with *(children)*

auctor -ōris *m* originator, author; writer, historian; reporter, harbinger *(of news);* acknowledged expert, authority *(for statement or theory)*; proposer *(of a law);* supporter, backer; vendor, seller; progenitor *(of a clan, family, race);* founder *(of city);* model, example; adviser, counselor; teacher; guarantor, security; leader, statesman; source, thrower, dealer *(of missile, wound, death);* **auctor esse** *(w.* **ut, nē** + *subj)* to advocate, advise; to move that, propose that; **faenoris auctor** lender; **mē auctōre** on my initiative, at my suggestion; **pecūniae auctor** person responsible for or owing a sum of money; **rērum omnium auctor parēnsque** the Creator *(literally, the author and parent of all things);* **sine auctōre** anonymous

auctōrāment·um -ī *n* contract; pay

auctōrit·ās -ātis *f* origination, source, cause; view, opinion, judgment; advice, encouragement; power, authority, weight, influence, prestige; leadership; importance, significance, worth, consequence; example, model, precedent; authority *(for establishing a fact);* document, record; decree *(of senate);* right of ownership, title

auctōr·ō -āre -āvī -ātus or **auctōr·or -ārī** *tr* to hire out, sell ‖ *refl & pass* to hire oneself out

auct·us -a -um *pp of* **augeō** ‖ *adj* blessed *(with children, good omens)*

auct·us -ūs *m* increase, growth; abundance, prosperity

aucup·ium -(i)ī *n* fowling; trap; eavesdropping; **aucupia verbōrum** quibbling

aucup·ō -āre -āvī -ātus *or* **aucup·or -ārī -ātus sum** *tr* to lie in wait for, watch for; to chase, strive after, catch ‖ *intr* to trap birds

audāc(i)ter *adv* boldly

audāci·a -ae *f* boldness, courage, daring; recklessness, effrontery, audacity; bold deed ‖ *fpl* adventures

aud·āx -ācis *adj* bold, daring; reckless

aud·ēns -entis *adj* bold, daring

audenti·a -ae *f* boldness, daring

audeō audēre ausus sum *tr* to dare, risk; **vix ausim** *(old perf subj active)* **crēdere** I could scarcely dare to believe ‖ *intr* to dare, be bold

audi·ēns -entis *m* hearer, listener ‖ *mpl* audience

audienti·a -ae *f* hearing, attention; **audientiam facere** to command attention, command silence

aud·iō -īre -īvī *or* **-iī -ītus** *tr* to hear, listen to; to be taught by, learn from; to grant; to accept, agree with, yield to; to obey; to be called, be named; to be reported, be regarded

audīti·ō -ōnis *f* hearsay, rumor

audīt·ō -āre -āvī *tr* to hear

audīt·or -ōris *m* hearer; student

audītōr·ium -(i)ī *n* lecture hall; the audience

audīt·us -ūs *m* hearing, sense of hearing; hearsay

auferō auferre abstulī ablātus *tr* to take away, bear off; to remove, withdraw; to steal; to sweep away, kill, destroy; to gain, obtain; to learn, understand; to mislead; to lead into a digression; to abduct; to captivate; **pedēs auferre** to go away ‖ *pass* **ē cōnspectū auferrī** to disappear from sight ‖ *refl* to go away

Aufid·us -ī *m* river in Apulia

au·fugiō -fugere -fūgī *tr* to shun, flee from ‖ *intr* to run away, escape

Aug·ē -ēs *f* mother of Telephus by Hercules

Augē·ās -ae *m* king of Elis, whose stables were cleaned by Hercules

au·geō -gēre -xī -ctus *tr* to increase, enlarge, augment, spread; to magnify; to exalt; to exaggerate; to emphasize; to enrich; to honor, advance, promote; to reinforce; to feed *(flame);* to raise *(voice);* to endow

augēsc·ō -ere *intr* to begin to grow; to become larger, increase; to prosper; *(of river)* to rise

aug·ur -uris *mf* augur *(priest who foretold future by observing birds);* seer

augurācul·um -ī *n* place of augury *(later known as the* **arx)**

augurāl·is -is -e *adj* augural, augur's ‖ *n* area in a Roman camp where the general took the auguries

augurāti·ō -ōnis *f* prophesying

augurātō *adv* after taking the auguries

augurāt·us -a -um *adj* consecrated after taking the auspices

augurāt·us -ūs *m* office of augur

augur·ium -(i)ī *n* observation of omens, interpretation of omens, augury; sign, omen; prophecy; foreboding

auguri·us -a -um *adj* of augurs; **iūs augurium** the right to take auguries

augur·ō -āre -āvī -ātus *or* **augur·or -ārī -ātus sum** *tr* to consult by augury; to consecrate by augury; to predict, prophesy; to conjecture, imagine ‖ *intr* to act as augur; to take auspices

August·a -ae *f* title of wife, mother, grandmother, daughter, or sister of the emperor

Augustāl·is -is -e *adj* of Augustus; **sodālēs Augustālēs** priests of deified Augustus ‖ *npl* games in honor of Augustus

Augustān·us -a -um *adj* of Augustus, Augustan; of an emperor, imperial ‖ *mpl* knights appointed by Nero

augustē *adv* reverently, solemnly

Augustiān·ī -ōrum *mpl* Nero's claque in the theater

Augustīn·us -a -um *adj* of Augustus

august·us -a -um *adj* august, sacred, venerable; majestic

August·us -a -um *adj* Augustan, imperial; **mēnsis Augustus** August ‖ *m* honorary cognomen of Octavius Caesar after 27 B.C. and of subsequent emperors

aul·a -ae *f* inner court, hall *(of house);* palace; royal court; people of the royal court, the court; royal power

aulae·um -ī *n (more frequently used in the pl)* bed coverings; canopy; curtain *(which was let down below the stage when the play began, and was raised again when the play ended; hence,* **aulaea premuntur** *or* **aulaeum mittitur** the curtain is lowered *(i.e.,* the performance is beginning); **aulaeum tollitur** the curtain is raised *(i.e.,* the play is over) ‖ *npl* curtain; tapestries

aulic·us -a -um *adj* courtly, princely ‖ *m* courtier

Aul·is -is *or* **-idis** *f* port in Boeotia from which Greeks sailed for Troy

auloed·us -ī *m* singer accompanied by reed pipe

aur·a -ae *f* breeze; breath of air, wind; air, atmosphere; heights, heaven; upper world; odor, exhalation; daylight, publicity; **ad aurās ferre** to make known, publicize; **ad aurās venīre** to come to the upper world; **aura aurī** the gleam of gold; **auram captāre** to sniff the air; **aura populāris** popular favor; **aurās fugere** to hide; **aura speī** breath of hope; **sub aurās** to light, into the air; into the open air

aurāri·us -a -um *adj* gold, golden ‖ *f* gold mine

aurāt·us -a -um *adj* made of gold; gold-plated; golden; glittering; **aurāta pellis** the Golden Fleece

Aurēli·us -a -um *adj* Roman clan name *(nomen), esp.* Marcus Aurelius *(Roman Emperor* A.D. *161–180)* ‖ named after an Aurelius, *esp.* Via Aurelia *(running along the Etruscan coast to the Maritime Alps)*
aureol·us -a -um *adj* gold, golden; splendid; very precious
aure·us -a -um *adj* gold, golden; gilded, gilt; beautiful, magnificent; brilliant ‖ *m* gold coin
auricom·us -a -um *adj* golden-haired; with golden foliage
auricul·a -ae *f* **(ōr-)** outer ear; earlobe; *(leg)* **auriculam tangere** *or* **appōnere** to agree to be a witness
aurif·er -era -erum *adj* producing *or* containing gold; *(of trees)* bearing golden apples
aurif·ex -icis *m* **(auru-)** goldsmith
aurīg·a -ae *mf* **(ōr-)** charioteer; *(fig)* pilot ‖ **Aurīga** *m* Auriga *(constellation)*
aurīgāti·ō -ōnis *f* chariot-driving
aurigen·a -ae *m* offspring of gold *(i.e., Perseus)*
aurig·er -era -erum *adj* gold-bearing; gilded
aurīg·ō -āre -āvī -ātum *intr* to drive a chariot; to compete in a chariot race
aur·is -is *f* ear; **aurem admovēre** to listen; **auribus servīre** to flatter; **aurēs adhibēre** to pay attention; **in aurem dextram** *(or* **in aurem utramvīs) dormīre** to sleep soundly, be unconcerned; **in** *or* **ad aurem** *or* **in aure dīcere, admonēre,** *etc.* to whisper in the ear
aurīscalp·ium -(i)ī *n (med)* earpick, probe
aurītul·us -ī *m* "little long-ears" *(i.e., an ass)*
aurīt·us -a -um *adj* long-eared; attentive; nosey; **testis aurītus** witness by hearsay only ‖ *m* rabbit, hare
aurōr·a -ae *f* dawn, daybreak; the East ‖ **Aurora** goddess of dawn
aur·um -ī *n* gold; color of gold, golden luster; gold cup; gold necklace; gold jewelry; gold plate; golden fleece; gold money; Golden Age
Aurunc·a -ae *f* town in Campania, birthplace of the poet Lucilius
Aurunc·us -a -um *adj* of Arunca ‖ *mpl* people of Arunca
auscultāti·ō -ōnis *f* obedience; a listening
auscultāt·or -ōris *m* listener
auscult·ō -āre -āvī -ātus *tr* to listen to; to overhear ‖ *intr (w. dat)* to obey, listen to
ausim *see* **audeō**
Auson·es -um *mpl* Ausonians *(ancient inhabitants of central Italy)*
Ausoni·a -ae *f (poet)* Italy
Ausonid·ae -ārum *mpl (poet)* Italians
Ausoni·us -a -um *adj (poet)* Ausonian, Italian ‖ *mpl (poet)* Ausonians, Italians
ausp·ex -icis *mf* augur, soothsayer; *(fig)* guide, director, protector ‖ *mpl* witnesses *(at a marriage ceremony)*
auspicātō *adv* after taking the auspices; auspiciously
auspicāt·us -a -um *adj* consecrated *(by auguries);* auspicious, lucky
auspic·ium -(i)ī *n (often used in the plural)* auspices *(from behavior of birds or chickens);* right to take the auspices; sign, omen; command, leadership, authority; inauguration; **auspicia incerta** ambiguous auspices; **auspicium habēre** to have the right to take auspices; **auspicium facere** *(of birds)* to give a sign; **pullārium in auspicium mittere** to send the keeper of chickens to take the auspices; **tuīs auspiciīs** under your command *(or* leadership)
auspic·ō -āre -āvī *intr* to take the auspices
auspic·or -ārī -ātus sum *tr* to inaugurate, make a ceremonial beginning of; to enter upon ‖ *intr* to take auspices; to make a start
aus·ter -trī *m* south wind; the South
austērē *adv* austerely, severely
austērit·ās -ātis *f* austerity
austēr·us -a -um *adj* austere, stern, harsh *(person);* pungent *(odor);* harsh *(taste);* drab, dark *(color);* serious *(talk);* gloomy, hard *(circumstances);* dry *(wine)*
austrāl·is -is -e *adj* southern; **cingulus** *(or* **regiō** *or* **ōra) austrālis** torrid zone
austrīn·us -a -um *adj* southerly, from the south; southern
aus·us -a -um *pp of* **audeō** ‖ *n* daring attempt, enterprise, venture; outrage
aut *conj* or; *(correcting what precedes)* or rather, or else; *(adding emphatic alternative)* or at least; **aut … aut** *(introducing two or more logically exclusive alternatives)* either … or; **ūnus aut alter** one or two
autem *conj (regularly follows an emphatic word)* but, on the other hand, however; *(in transitions)* now
autheps·a -ae *f* cooker *(utensil)*
autograph·us -a -um *adj* written with one's own hand, autograph
Autolyc·us -ī *m* father of Anticlea, maternal grandfather of Ulysses
automat·on *or* **automat·um -ī** *n* automaton
automat·us -a -um *adj* automatic, spontaneous, voluntary
Automed·ōn -ontis *m* charioteer of Achilles; a charioteer
Autono·ē -ēs *f* daughter of Cadmus, wife of Aristaeus, and mother of Actaeon
autumnāl·is -is -e *adj* autumnal, fall
autumn·us -a -um *adj* autumn ‖ *m* autumn
autum·ō -āre -āvī -ātus *tr* to assert, state, say; *(w. acc & inf)* to say that

auxiliār·is -is -e *adj* auxiliary **||** *mpl* auxiliary troops, auxiliaries
auxiliāri·us -a -um *adj* auxiliary
auxiliāt·or -ōris *m* helper
auxiliāt·us -ūs *m* help, aid
auxili·or -ārī -ātus sum *intr (w. dat)* **1** to give help to; **2** *(of things)* to be helpful to, be of use to; **3** *(med)* to relieve, heal, cure
auxil·ium -(i)ī *n* help; *(med)* relief, remedy; **auxiliō esse** *(w. dat)* to be of assistance to **||** *npl* auxiliary troops; reinforcements
avārē *adv* greedily
avāriter *adv* greedily
avāriti·a -ae *f* avarice, greed; gluttony
avār·us -a -um *adj* greedy, avaricious; *(w. gen)* eagerly desirous of, greedy for
avē! *see* **aveō**
āve·hō -here -xi -ctus *tr* to haul away **||** *pass* to ride off; to sail away
ā·vellō -vellere -vellī *(or* **-vulsī** *or* **-volsī) -vulsus** *(or* **-volsus)** *tr* to pull *or* pluck away; to tear off; to separate, remove **||** *refl & pass (w.* **ab)** to tear oneself away from, withdraw from
avēn·a -ae *f* oats; reed, stem, stalk, a straw; shepherd's pipe
Aventīn·us -a -um *adj* Aventine **||** *m & n* Aventine Hill *(one of the Seven Hills of Rome)* **||** *m* son of Hercules
av·eō *or* **hav·eō -ēre** to desire, long for, crave; *(w. inf)* to long to **||** *intr* to say goodbye; **avē!**, **avēte!** hello!, farewell!, goodbye!; **aliquem avēre iubeō** I send greetings to s.o.
Avernāl·is -is -e *adj* of Lake Avernus
Avern·us -a -um *adj* birdless; of Lake Avernus **||** *m* Lake Avernus *(near Cumae, reputed entrance to the underworld)*
āverr·ō -ere -ī *tr* to sweep away
āverrunc·ō -āre *tr* to avert
āversābil·is -is -e *adj* abominable
āvers·or -ārī -ātus sum *tr* **(-vor-)** to repulse, reject, refuse; to shun, avoid; to send away **||** *intr* to turn away *(in displeasure, shame, contempt)*
āvers·or -ōris *m* embezzler
āvers·us -a -um *pp of* **āvertō** **||** *adj* turned back, reversed; rear, in the rear; *(of blows)* coming from the rear; distant, remote; out-of-the-way; disinclined, alienated, unfavorable, hostile; *(w. dat or* **ab)** averse to, hostile to, opposed to, estranged from **||** *n* the back part, the back; **in āversum** backwards **||** *npl* the back; hinterland
ā·vertō -vertere -vertī -versus *tr* **(-vor-)** to turn away, avert; to embezzle, misappropriate; to divert, distract; to alienate **||** *refl* to retire **||** *intr* to withdraw, retire
avi·a -ae *f* grandmother; old wives' tale
āvi·a -ōrum *npl* wasteland
aviāri·us -a -um *adj* of birds, bird **||** *n* aviary; haunt of wild birds
avidē *adv* eagerly, greedily
avidit·ās -ātis *f* eagerness, longing; avarice
avid·us -a -um *adj* eager, earnest; greedy; voracious, gluttonous; *(w. gen or dat or* **in** *acc)* eager for
av·is -is *f* bird; sign, omen; **avis alba** *(or* **rāra)** rarity
avīt·us -a -um *adj* grandfather's; ancestral; *(wine)* old
āvi·us -a -um *adj* pathless; out-of-the-way, lonely; untrodden; wandering, straying; going astray
āvocāment·um -ī *n* diversion, recreation, hobby
āvocāti·ō -ōnis *f* distraction
āvoc·ō -āre -āvī -ātus *tr* to call away; to divert, remove, withdraw; to amuse; to distract *(attention);* to interrupt *(work)*
āvol·ō -āre -āvī -ātum *intr* to fly away; to dash off
āvulsus *pp of* **āvellō**
avuncul·us -ī *m* (maternal) uncle; **avunculus magnus** granduncle
av·us -ī *m* grandfather; forefather
-āx -ācis *suf* implying tendency, ability: **capāx** ability to hold, **dīcāx** tendency to talk, **pertināx** tendency to hold on
Axen·us -ī *m* Black Sea
axici·a -ae *f* pair of scissors
āxill·a -ae *f* armpit
ax·is -is *m* axle; wagon, chariot; the earth's axis; north pole; vault of heaven; region, climate, country; board, plank

B

B, b *(supply* littera) *f* second letter of the Latin alphabet; letter name: **be**
babae *interj* great!, wonderful!
Babyl·ō -ōnis *m* Babylonian; rich man
Babyl·ōn -ōnis *f* city on the Euphrates River
Babylōni·a -ae *f* country between Tigris and Euphrates
Babylōnic·a -ōrum *npl* Babylonian tapestry
Babylōniēns·is -is -e *adj* Babylonian
Babylōni·us -a -um *adj* Babylonian **||** *mpl* Babylonians
bāc·a -ae *f* berry; olive; fruit; pearl
bācāt·us -a -um *adj* adorned with pearls; **monīle bācātum** pearl necklace
bacc·ar -aris *n* cyclamen *(plant with showy white, pink, or red flowers)*
Bacch·a -ae *f* Bacchante *(female member of the orgiastic cult of Bacchus)*
bacchābund·us -a -um *adj* raving
Bacchān·al -ālis *n* site sacred to Bacchus **||** *npl* Bacchanalian orgies
bacchant·ēs -(i)um *fpl* Bacchantes
bacchāti·ō -ōnis *f* orgy, revelry

Bacchē(i)·us, Bacchic·us, Bacchi·us -a -um *adj* Bacchic
bacch·or -ārī -ātus sum *intr* to celebrate the rites of Bacchus; to revel, rage, run wildly about; *(of a place)* to be the scene of Bacchanalian orgies; *(of a rumor)* to run wild
Bacch·us -ī *m* god of wine; *(fig)* vine, wine
baceol·us -a -um *adj (coll)* nutty
bācif·er -era -erum *adj* bearing berries; bearing olives
bacill·um -ī *n* small staff, wand; lictor's staff
Bactr·a -ōrum *npl* Bactra *(capital of Bactria, a province of Parthia)*
Bactriān·us -a -um *adj* Bactrian **II** *mpl* Bactrians
Bactri·us -a -um *adj* Bactrian
bacul·um -ī *n or* **bacul·us -ī** *m* a cane; (lictor's) staff; scepter
badiz·ō -āre *intr* to go, walk
Baeticāt·us -a -um *adj* dressed in clothes of Baetican wool
Baetic·us -a -um *adj* of the Baetis river **II** *mpl* the people of Baetica **II** *f* Baetica *(Roman province in S. Spain, modern Andalusia)*
Baet·is -is *m* river in Spain *(modern Guadalquivir)*
Baeturi·a -ae *f* part of the province of Baetica
Bagō·ās -ae *m* eunuch *(used to guard women's quarters)*
Bagrad·a -ae *m* river in N. Africa *(modern Majerda)*
Bāi·ae -ārum *fpl* resort town at N. end of Bay of Naples **II** villa at Baiae
Bāi·ānus -a -um *adj* of Baiae
bāiul·ō -āre *tr* to carry, bear
bāiul·us -ī *m* porter
bālaen·a *or* **ballaen·a -ae** *f* **(bālēn-)** whale
balanāt·us -a -um *adj* anointed with balsam; embalmed
balan·us -ī *mf* acorn; date; balsam; type of shellfish
balatr·ō -ōnis *m* jester, buffoon
bālāt·us -ūs *m* bleating *(of sheep)*
balb·us -a -um *adj* stammering, stuttering **II Balbus** *m* Roman family name, *cognomen, esp.* Lucius Cornelius Balbus (*a supporter of Caesar, defended by Cicero in 56* B.C.)
balbūt·iō *or* **balbutt·iō -īre** *tr & intr* to stammer, stutter; to babble
Baliāric·us -a -um *adj* **(Bale-)** Balearic
Baliār·is -is -e *adj* **(Bale-)** Balearic; **Baliārēs īnsulae** Balearic Islands *(Majorca and Minorca)*
baline·um -ī *n* bath
ballēna *see* **bālaena**
Balli·ō -ōnis *m* actor playing the worthless fellow; worthless fellow
ballist·a -ae *f* **(bālis-)** artillery piece *(for hurling stones and other missiles)*
ballistār·ium -(i)ī *n* artillery emplacement
balne·ae -ārum *fpl* **(balin-)** baths
balneāri·us -a -um *adj* **(balin-)** of a bath **II** *npl* baths
balneāt·or -ōris *m* **(balin-)** bath superintendent
balneol·ae -ārum *fpl* baths
balneol·um -ī *n* small bath
balne·um -ī *n* **(balin-)** *(pl also:* **balne·ae -ārum)** bathroom; public baths; bathing, taking a bath
bāl·ō -āre -āvī -ātum *intr* to bleat
balsam·um -ī *n* fragrant gum of the balsam tree **II** *npl* balsam *(used as perfume)*
balte·us -ī *m or* **balte·um -ī** *n* belt; shoulder strap; woman's belt
bal·ūx -ūcis *f* gold dust
Bandusi·a -ae *f* pleasant fountain on Horace's Sabine farm
Bantīn·us -a -um *adj* of the town of Bantia in Apulia
baptistēr·ium -(i)ī *n* swimming pool
barāthr·um -ī *n* abyss, chasm, pit; lower world; maw, stomach *(of a greedy man)*
barb·a -ae *f* beard *(of man or animals);* **barbam dēmittere** to grow a beard; **barbam vellere** to tuck on the beard *(as a sign of insult)*
barbar·a -ae *f* foreign woman
barbarē *adv* in a foreign language; savagely; *(of diction, etc.)* rudely
barbari·a -ae *or* **barbari·ēs -ēī** *f* foreign country; strange land; rudeness, lack of culture; barbarity, brutality
barbaric·us -a -um *adj* barbarian; barbaric; foreign, outlandish
barbariēs *see* **barbaria**
barbarism·us -ī *m* barbarism *(error in pronunciation or expression)*
barbar·us -a -um *adj* foreign; barbarous **II** *mf* foreigner; barbarian **II** *n* barbarism
barbātul·us -a -um *adj* wearing a short beard
barbāt·us -a -um *adj* bearded; adult; old-time **II** *m* old-timer
barbig·er -era -erum *adj* bearded
barbit·os -ī *m (f)* lyre; lute; music of the lute
barbul·a -ae *f* short beard
Barc·a -ae *m* name of Carthaginian family to which Hamilcar, Hannibal, and Hasdrubal belonged
Barcae·ī -ōrum *mpl* the people of Barce *(city of Cyrenaica)*
barcal·a -ae *m* simpleton
Barcīn·us -a -um *adj* of the Barca family, Barcan
Bardae·ī -ōrum *mpl* Illyrian tribe
Bardaïc·us -a -um *adj* **(Var-)** Bardaean; **Bardaïcus calceus** a soldier's boot
bard·us -a -um *adj* stupid, dull

bār·is -idos *f* flat-bottomed boat
barīt·us -ūs *m* **(barr-)** the war cry of the Germans
Bār·ium -(i)ī *n* coastal town in Apulia *(modern Bari)*
bār·ō -ōnis *m* dunce, blockhead
barrīt·us -ūs *m* trumpeting *(of elephants);* war cry
barr·us -ī *m* elephant
bāscaud·a -ae *f* basin *(of British origin)*
bāsiāti·ō -ōnis *f* kissing; kiss
bāsiāt·or -ōris *m* one who kisses
basilic·a -ae *f* basilica, courthouse
basilicē *adv* royally
basilic·us -a -um *adj* royal; splendid **II** *n* princely robe
bāsi·ō -āre -āvī -ātus *tr* to kiss
bāsiol·um -ī *n* little kiss, peck
bas·is -is *f* base, support; pedestal; base *(of a triangle)*
bās·ium -(i)ī *n* kiss
Bassar·eūs -eī *m* Bacchus
Bassaric·us -a -um *adj* of Bacchus
Bassar·is -idos *f* Bacchante
Bastarn·ae -ārum *mpl* **(Bat-)** Germanic tribe close to the mouth of the Danube
bā(t)tu·ō -āre *tr* to beat, pound; *(vulg)* to screw **II** *intr* to fence
Batāv·us -a -um *adj* of the Batavi, Batavian **II** *mpl* people of Lower Germany *(modern Holland)*
batioc·a -ae *f* drinking cup
batiol·a -ae *f* drinking vessel
Bat·ō -ōnis *m* Illyrian rebel leader
Battiad·ēs -ae *m* inhabitant of Cyrene *(esp.* the poet Callimachus)
Batt·us -ī *m* legendary founder of Cyrene
Bauc·is -idis *f* wife of Philemon
Baul·ī -ōrum *mpl* town between Baiae and Misenum
baxe·a -ae *f* kind of sandal
beātē *adv* happily **II** *interj* great!; bravo!
beātit·ās -ātis *f* happiness
beātitūd·ō -inis *f* happiness
beātul·us -a -um *adj (of a deceased person)* of blessed memory
beāt·us -a -um *adj* happy; prosperous; fertile; abundant; wealthy, rich; sumptuous **II** *mpl* the blessed (people) **II** *n* happiness
Bebryci·a -ae *f* territory of the Bebryces in Asia Minor
Bebryci·us -a -um *adj* of Bebrycia *or* of the Bebryces
Bēdriāc·um -ī *n* **(Bētr-)** village between Mantua and Cremona
Belg·ae -ārum *mpl* inhabitants of N. Gaul
Belgic·us -a -um *adj* of the Belgae; **Gallia Belgica** N. part of the province of Gallia Comata, occupied by the Belgae
Belg·ium -iī *n* country of the Belgae
Bēlīd·ēs -ae *m* descendant of Belus
Bēlīd·ēs -um *fpl* Danaids *(descendants of Belus)*
bellāri·a -ōrum *npl* sweets, dessert
bellāt·or -ōris *adj (masc only)* warlike; **bellātor equus** war horse **II** *m* warrior, fighter
bellātōri·us -a -um *adj* warlike
bellātr·īx -īcis *f* warrior *(female)*
bellē *adv* prettily, nicely, well; **bellē esse** to have a nice time; **bellē est** all is well *(of health);* **cētera bellē** the rest is all right; **sē bellē habēre** to be in good health
Belleroph·ōn -ontis *or* **Bellerophont·ēs -ae** *m* slayer of Chimaera and rider of Pegasus
Bellerophontē·us -a -um *adj* of Bellerophon
belliātul·us -a -um *adj* pretty little
belliāt·us -a -um *adj* pretty
bellicōs·us -a -um *adj* warlike
bellic·us -a -um *adj* war, military; warlike, fierce **II** *n* bugle; bugle call
bellig·er -era -erum *adj* warring, warlike; war
belliger·ō -āre -āvī -ātum *or* **belliger·or -ārī -ātus sum** *intr* to fight a war, be at war, fight
bellipot·ēns -entis *adj* mighty *or* valiant in war **II** *m* Mars
bell·ō -āre -āvī -ātum *or* **bell·or -ārī -ātus sum** *intr* to wage war, be at war; to fight
Bellōn·a -ae *f* **(Duell-)** goddess of war
bellul·us -a -um *adj* pretty, cute
bell·um -ī *n* **(duell-)** war; warfare; **bellī** *(loc)* at war, abroad; **bellī domīque** at home and abroad, on the war front and the home front; **bellō** *or* **in bellō** in war, in times of war; **bellum administrāre** to conduct a war *(as a general);* **bellum agere** *or* **gerere** to fight a war, wage war; **bellum compōnere** to settle a war *(by diplomacy);* **bellum cōnficere** *or* **perficere** to bring an end to the war *(by victory);* **bellum dēnūntiāre** *or* **dīcere** to declare war; **bellum dūcere** *or* **trahere** to drag out, protract a war; **bellum īnferre alicui** to go to war with someone; **bellum movēre** to stir up a war
bell·us -a -um *adj* pretty; fine, nice
bēlu·a -ae *f* beast, brute, monster
bēluāt·us -a -um *adj* embroidered with figures of beasts
bēluōs·us -a -um *adj* full of monsters
Bēl·us -ī *m* Baal **II** king of Tyre and father of Dido **II** king of Egypt, father of Danaüs and Aegyptus
Bēnāc·us -ī *m* lake near Verona *(modern Lago di Garda)*
bene *adv* well; thoroughly, very, quite; elegantly; **bene ambulā**! bon voyage!; **bene audīre** to be well spoken of; **bene dīcere** to speak well, sensibly, correctly, to the point; **bene dīcite**! hush!; **bene emere** to buy at a bargain; **bene esse** *(w. dat)* to be well with, to be doing all right; **bene est**

it's O.K.; **bene ferre** to put up with in good spirits; **bene habet** it's O.K.; **bene sum** *or* **mihi bene est** I am content; **bene sentīre dē** (+ *abl)* to have sound views about; **bene spērāre** to be optimistic; **bene vēndere** to sell at a good price; **satis bene** fairly well; **sē bene habēre** to be happy, be content; to do well; **‖** *interj (w. acc or dat) (in drinking to health)* here's to you!

benedicē *adv* with friendly words, kindly

benedī·cō -cere -xi -ctus *intr (w. dat)* to speak well of, praise; *(eccl)* to bless

bene·faciō -facere -fēcī -factus *tr* to do *(s.o.)* a service, confer a benefit on; **multa ergā** (+ *acc)* **benefacere** to do many kindnesses to

beneficenti·a -ae *f* beneficence, kindness

beneficiāri·ī -ōrum *mpl* soldiers exempt from menial tasks

benefic·ium -(i)ī *n* **(benif-)** kindness, favor, benefit, service; help, support; promotion; right, privilege; **beneficiō** *(w. gen)* thanks to; **beneficium accipere et reddere** to receive and return a favor

benefic·us -a -um *adj* generous, liberal, obliging

Benevent·um -ī *n* town in Samnium in S. Italy *(modern Benevento)*

benevolē *adv* **(beniv-)** kindly

benevol·ēns -entis *adj* **(beniv-)** kind-hearted, benevolent, obliging

benevolenti·a -ae *f* **(beniv-)** benevolence, kindness, goodwill; favor

benevol·us -a -um *adj* **(beniv-)** kind, benevolent **‖** *m* well-wisher

benignē *adv* kindly, courteously; mildly; generously, liberally; **benignē**! *(both in accepting and declining an offer)* thank you!; much obliged!; no, thank you!

benignit·ās -ātis *f* kindness, friendliness, courtesy; generosity

benign·us -a -um *adj* kind-hearted; mild; liberal; favorable; bounteous

be·ō -āre -āvī -ātus *tr* to make happy; to bless; to enrich; to refresh

Berecynt(h)i·us -a -um *adj* Berecyntian; epithet of Cybele

Berecynt·us -ī *m* mountain in Phrygia sacred to Cybele *or* Magna Mater

Berenīc·ē -ēs *f* female name, *esp.* the daughter of the Jewish King Agrippa I; **crīnis Berenīcēs** "hair of Berenice" *(constellation, named after the wife of Ptolemy Euergetes)*

bēryll·us -ī *m* beryl *(precious stone)*

bēs bē(s)sis *m* two thirds; **bēs alter** one and two thirds; **faenus bēssibus** interest at ⅔% per month *or* 8% per year

bēsāl·is -is -e *adj* comprising two-thirds

Bess·ī -ōrum *mpl* a people of Thrace

Bessic·us -a -um *adj* of the Bessi

bēsti·a -ae *f* beast, wild beast

bēstiāri·us -a -um *adj* of wild beasts **‖** *m* wild-beast fighter

bēstiol·a -ae *f* insect

bēt·a -ae *f* beet

bēta *indecl n* beta *(second letter of the Greek alphabet)*

bētāce·us -a -um *adj* of a beet

bētiz·ō -āre *intr* to be listless

bi- *pref* consisting of, having, measuring two of the things named, *e.g.:* **bimar·is -is -e** situated between two seas

bibliopōl·a -ae *m* bookseller

bibliothēc·a -ae *f* library; study *(room)*

bibliothēcār·ius -(i)ī *m* librarian

bib·ō -ere -ī *tr* to drink; to visit, live near *(river); (fig)* to take in, absorb **‖** *intr* to drink; to guzzle

bibul·us -a -um *adj* fond of drinking; absorbent; thirsty; *(of ears)* eager to hear

bi·ceps -cipitis *adj* two-headed; twin-peaked

biclīn·ium -(i)ī *n* table for two

bicol·or -ōris *adj* two-colored, of two colors

bicorn·is -is -e *adj* two-horned; two-pronged

bicorp·or -oris *adj* double-bodied

bid·ēns -entis *adj* with two teeth; with two points; two-pronged **‖** *m* hoe, mattock; sacrificial animal; sheep

bident·al -ālis *n* place struck by lightning

Bidīn·us -a -um *adj* of Bidis *(town in Sicily)*

bīdu·um -ī *n* two-day period; two days

bienn·ium -(i)ī *n* two-year period; two years; **in** *(or* **per)** **biennium** for two years

bifāriam *adv* on both sides, twofold; in two parts; in two ways; in two directions

bifāri·us -a -um *adj* double, twofold

bif·er -era -erum *adj* bearing (fruit *or* flowers) twice (a year)

bifid·us -a -um *adj* split in two, forked, cloven

bifor·is -is -e *adj* having two doors; having two holes *or* openings; *(of sound)* double, coming from double pipes

bifōrmāt·us -a -um *adj* double, having two forms

bifōrm·is -is -e *adj* double, having two forms

bifr·ōns -ontis *adj* two-faced

bifurc·us -a -um *adj* two-pronged **‖** *n* crotch

bīg·ae -ārum *fpl* two-horse chariot; team of horses

bīgāt·us -a -um *adj (of a coin)* stamped with the image of a two-horse chariot

biiug·is -is -e *or* **biiug·us -a -um** *adj* two-horse

Bilbil·is -is *f* town in Hispania Tarraconensis, birthplace of Martial

bilībr·a -ae *f* two pounds

bilībr·is -is -e *adj* two-pound

bilingu·is -is -e *adj* two-tongued; bilingual; deceitful, two-faced

-bil·is -is -e *adjl suf* denoting ability, *e.g.:* **terribilis** able to frighten

bīl·is -is *f* bile; wrath; **bīlis ātra** melancholy; insanity; **bīlem movēre** *(w. dat)* to get *(s.o.)* angry

bil·īx -īcis *adj* with a double thread *or* wire

bilūstr·is -is -e *adj* lasting for two lustra *(i.e., ten years)*

bimar·is -is -e *adj* situated between two seas

bimarīt·us -ī *m* bigamist

bimāt·er -ris *adj* having two mothers, twice-born *(Bacchus)*

bimembr·is -is -e *adj* half-man, half-beast **II** *m* centaur

bimēstr·is -is -e *adj* two-month-old; lasting two months

bīmul·us -a -um *adj* two-year-old

bīm·us -a -um *adj* two-year-old; lasting two years

bīn·ī -ae -a *adj* two by two, two each; two at a time; two *(per day, year, etc.);* a set of, a pair of; double, twofold; **inter bīna castra** between the two camps

binoct·ium -(i)ī *n* period of two nights

binōmin·is -is -e *adj* having two names

Bi·ōn -ōnis *f* Greek philosopher, noted for his sharp sayings

Biōnē·us -a -um *adj* typical of Bion, satirical

bipalm·is -is -e *adj* two palms long *or* broad

bipartītō *adv see* **bipertītō**

bipat·ēns -entis *adj* opening in two directions

bipedāl·is -is -e *adj* two-foot (long, broad, *or* high)

bipennif·er -era -erum *adj* wielding a two-edged ax

bipenn·is -is -e *adj* two-edged **II** *f* two-edged ax

bipertītō *adv* **(-part-)** in two parts; **bipertītō esse** to be divided

bipertīt·us -a -um *adj* **(-part-)** divided into two parts, bipartite

bip·ēs -edis *adj* two-footed, biped

birēm·is -is -e *adj* two-oared; with two banks of oars **II** *f* ship with two banks of oars

bis *adv* twice; doubly; **bis tantō** *or* **tantum** twice as much

Bīsalt·ae -ārum *mpl* a people of Macedonia

Bīsalt·is -is *f* Theophane, daughter of Bisaltes *(changed by Neptune into a crane)*

Biston·es -um *mpl* fierce tribesmen in Thessaly

bisulc·us -a -um *adj* split; forked; cloven

Bīthȳni·a -ae *f* a district, later a Roman province, on the N.W. coast of Asia Minor

Bīthȳnic·us -a -um *or* **Bīthȳn·us -a -um** *adj* Bithynian

bīt·ō -ere *intr* to go

bitūm·en -inis *n* asphalt, pitch

bivi·us -a -um *adj* two-way **II** *n* crossroads, intersection

blaes·us -a -um *adj* lisping; slurring

blandē *adv* flatteringly; coaxingly, seductively, charmingly

blandidic·us -a -um *adj* smooth-spoken, using flattering words

blandiloquentul·us -a -um *or* **blandiloqu·us -a -um** *adj* smooth, smooth-tongued

blandīment·um -ī *n* flattery, compliment; charm

blandi·or -īrī -ītus sum *intr* (*w. dat*) **1** to flatter; **2** to coax; **3** to allure; **4** to charm, please; **5** *(of dogs)* to fawn on; *(w.* **ut** *+ subj)* to coax, persuade with blandishments to **II** *refl (w. dat)* to delude oneself

blanditer *adv* flatteringly

blanditi·a -ae *or* **blanditi·ēs -ēī** *f* flattery, compliment; charm

bland·us -a -um *adj* smooth; flattering; fawning; alluring, charming, winsome, pleasant

blater·ō -āre -āvī -ātus *tr* to utter *(in a babbling way)* **II** *intr* to babble

blat·iō -īre to talk foolishly, babble

blatt·a -ae *f* cockroach; *(insect)* bookworm; clothes-moth

blenn·us -ī *m (coll)* idiot, blockhead

blite·us -a -um *adj* silly; tasteless **II** *n* worthless stuff, trash

blit·um -ī *n* tasteless vegetable *(kind of spinach)*

boāri·us -a -um *adj* **(bov-)** cattle; **forum boārium** cattle market

Boc(c)h·us -ī *m* king of Mauretania, who betrayed Jugurtha to the Romans **II** king of Mauretania in the time of Julius Caesar

Boeb·ē -ēs *f* lake in Thessaly

Boeōti·a -ae *f* district N. of Attica

Boeōti·us -a -um *or* **Boeōt·us -a -um** *adj* Boeotian **II** *mpl* Boeotians

bōi·a -ae *f* collar *(worn by criminals)*

Boi·ī -ōrum *mpl* Celtic people who migrated from Gaul into N. Italy

bōlēt·us -ī *m* mushroom

bol·us -ī *m* throw *(of the dice);* cast *(of the net); (fig)* haul, piece of good luck, gain; choice morsel

bombax *interj (of surprise)* strange!; indeed!

bomb·us -ī *m* booming; buzzing, humming

bombȳcin·us -a -um *adj* silk, silken **II** *npl* silk clothes

bomb·ȳx -ȳcis *m* silkworm; silk; silk garment

Bon·a De·a -ae *f* Roman goddess of chastity and fertility, worshipped by women
bonit·ās -ātis *f* goodness, integrity, good behavior; excellence, high quality *(of things)*
Bonn·a -ae *f* city in Lower Germany *(modern Bonn)*
Bonōni·a -ae *f* city of Cisalpine Gaul *(modern Bologna)*
Bonōniēns·is -is -e *adj* of Bologna
bon·us -a -um *adj* good; *(morally)* good; cheerful *(face)*; sound, valid, well-founded *(arguments)*; pretty, shapely; *(w. dat)* good for; *(w.* **ad)** good at; *(w. dat or* **ad)** good, kind toward; **bona aetās** prime of life; **bonae artēs** liberal arts, liberal education; **bonae reī esse** to be wealthy; **bonae rēs** good things, desirable things; wealth; **bonae vīrēs** full strength; **bona fōrma** good appearance; **bone vir**! sir!; my good fellow!; **bonō animō esse** *(or* **bonum animum habēre)** to be of good cheer, be in a good mood; to be well-disposed; **bonō modō** in moderation; **bonō perīculō** with little risk; **bonum est** *(w. inf)* it is good to; **bonus ā tempestātibus** free from storms, fine; **bonus stomachus** good humor; **cum bonā pāce** *(w. gen)* with the full consent of; **(cum) bonā veniā tuā** with your kind permission; **virī bonī** decent citizens; *(pol)* conservatives ‖ *mpl* decent people; brave men; *(pol)* conservatives ‖ *n* good thing, good; **bonō esse alicui** to be good for s.o., be profitable to s.o.; **cui bonō?** for whose benefit? ‖ *npl* goods, property
bo·ō -āre *or* **-ere** *intr* to bawl; to bellow, roar
Boōt·ēs -ae *m* Boötes *(constellation)*
bore·ās -ae *m* north wind; the North ‖ **Boreās** god of the north wind
borē·us -a -um *adj* north, northern
Borysthen·ēs -is *m* Scythian river *(modern Dnieper)*
bōs bovis *m (gen pl:* **boum** *or* **bovum;** *dat & abl pl:* **bōbus** *or* **būbus)** ox, bull ‖ *mpl* cattle ‖ *f* cow
Bosp(h)or·us *or* **Bosp(h)or·os -ī** *m* strait between Thrace and Asia Minor, connecting Propontis and Black Sea
botell·us -ī *m* small sausage
botul·us -ī *m* a black pudding
bovīl·e -is *n* ox stall, cow stable
Bovill·ae -ārum *fpl* town in Latium on the Appian Way, about 12 miles S. of Rome
bovill·us -a -um *adj* cattle
brabeut·a -ae *m* umpire
bracchiāl·is -is -e *adj* of the arm
bracchiol·um -ī *n* dainty arm
bracch·ium -(i)ī *n* arm, lower arm; *(cf.* **lacertus** *the upper arm)*; claw; branch; tendril; arm of the sea; *(naut)* yardarm
brāc·ae -ārum *fpl* pants, trousers
brācāt·us -a -um *adj* wearing trousers; foreign, barbarian; effeminate
brācil·is -is -e *adj (esp. of a tunic)* to be worn with trousers
bracte·a -ae *f* **(bratt-)** gold leāf; gold foil
bracteol·a -ae *f* **(bratt-)** very thin gold leaf
brassic·a -ae *f* cabbage
bratt- = bract-
Brenn·us -ī *m* Celtic chieftain who captured Rome about 390 B.C. ‖ Galatian chieftain who invaded Greece in 279 B.C.
brevī *adv* briefly, in a few words; shortly, in a short time; **brevī ante (post)** shortly before (afterwards)
breviār·ium -(i)ī *n* abridgment, summary
brevicul·us -a -um *adj* rather short
breviloqu·ēns -entis *adj* concise, of few words
breviloquenti·a -ae *f* conciseness
brevi·ō -āre -āvī -ātus *tr* to shorten; to abbreviate; to pronounce *(a syllable)* short
brev·is -is -e *adj* short, little; low; stunted *(trees)*; *(of depth)* shallow; brief; transient; short-lived; compressed, concise *(style)*; small *(amounts, weights)*; modest, simple; small, narrow, confined *(space)*; **ad** *(or* **in)** **breve tempus** for (only) a short time ‖ *f (gram)* short syllable ‖ *n* a short space of time; **ad** *(or* **in)** **breve** for (only) a short time; **brevī** in a few words, briefly; in a short time, soon; for (only) a short time; after a lapse of a short space of time; **brevī ante** shortly before; **brevī post** shortly after; **in brevī** in a few words, briefly ‖ *npl* shallow water, shallows
brevit·ās -ātis *f* brevity; smallness; shortness; stunted size *(of trees)*; short period of time; shortness of life; *(pros)* short quantity; *(rhet)* conciseness, terseness
breviter *adv* for (only) a short time; within a short space of time, quickly; in (only) a few words, briefly; to (only) a short distance; *(pros)* short
Brigant·es -um *mpl* a people of N. Britannia
Brīsē·is -idos *f (acc:* **Brīsēida)** slave and concubine of Achilles
Britann·ī -ōrum *mpl* Britons
Britanni·a -ae *f* **(Britt-)** Britain
Britannic·us -a -um *adj* British ‖ *m* surname of the emperor Claudius after his victory in Britain; name taken by Germanicus, son of Claudius and Messalina
Britann·us -a -um *adj* British
Brit(t)·ō -ōnis *m* Briton
Brixi·a -ae *f* town in Cisalpine Gaul *(modern Brescia)*
brocch·us -a -um *adj* buck-toothed
Brom·ius -(i)ī *m* epithet of Bacchus "the roaring god"

Bront·ēs -ae *m* Brontes *(a Cyclops)*
brūm·a -ae *f* winter solstice, shortest day; (dead of) winter; winter's cold
brūmāl·is -is -e *adj* wintry
Brundis·ium -(i)ī *n* port in S.E. Italy on the Adriatic Sea *(modern Brindisi)*
Bruti·ī -ōrum *mpl* inhabitants of Apulia, the toe of Italy
brūt·us -a -um *adj* heavy, unwieldy; dull, stupid
Brūt·us -ī *m* Roman family name, *cognomen, esp.* Lucius Iunius Brutus *(drove out Tarquinius Superbus)* **‖** Marcus Iunius Brutus *(one of the murderers of Julius Caesar)*
būbīl·e -is *n* cow stable
būb·ō -ōnis *mf* owl
būb(u)l·us -a -um *adj* ox, bull's, cow's; **corius būbulus** oxhide, oxhide whip; **oculus būblus** bull's-eye
būbul·a -ae *f* beef
bubulcit·or -ārī *intr* to tend cattle, be a herdsman; to ride herd
bubulc·us -ī *m* herdsman
būcaed·a -ae *m (coll)* flogged slave
buc(c)ul·a -ae *f* little cheek; visor
bucc·a -ae *f* cheek; loudmouth; trumpeter; parasite; mouthful; **dīcere quidquid in buccam venerit** to say whatever came into his head
buccell·a -ae *f* small mouthful; morsel
bucc·ō -ōnis *f (coll)* fathead
bucculent·us -a -um *adj* having fat cheeks; loud-mouthed
būcer(i)·us -a -um *adj* horned
būcin·a -ae *f (curved)* trumpet *(used to proclaim the watches of the day and night; also used for summoning a public meeting);* war trumpet; shepherd's horn; Triton's trumpet shell
būcināt·or -ōris *m* trumpeter
būcin·us -ī *m* trumpeter
būcolic·us -a -um *adj* pastoral, bucolic **‖** *npl* pastoral poetry, bucolics
būcul·a -ae *f* heifer
būf·ō -ōnis *m* toad
-bul·a -ae *fem suf* forms feminine nouns denoting instrument or agent, *e.g.:* **fībula** safety pin
bulb·us -ī *m* bulb; onion
būl·ē -ēs *f (Greek)* council, senate
būleut·a -ae *m* councilor
būleutēr·ium -(i)ī *n* meeting place of a Greek council
bull·a -ae *f* bubble; boss, stud, knob; amulet; locket *(hung around neck of children)*
bullāt·us -a -um *adj* inflated, bombastic; studded; wearing a bulla *(i.e., still a child)*
bull·iō -īre *intr* to bubble, boil
bullul·a -ae *f* little bubble
-bul·um -ī *neut suf* denoting instrument or place, *e.g.:* **vēnābulum** hunting instrument, spear; **stabulum** place for cattle to stand, stable
būmast·us -a -um *adj* having large grapes
būr·a -ae *or* **būr·is -is** *f* curved handle of plow
Busīr·is -idos *or* **-idis** *m* king of Egypt who sacrificed strangers and was killed by Hercules
būstirap·us -ī *m* tomb robber
būstuāri·us -a -um *adj* of a tomb, of a pyre; **gladiātor būstiārius** gladiator who fought at a tomb in honor of the dead
būst·um -ī *n* pyre; grave mound, tomb; *(pej) (applied to a person)* ruination
būte·ō -ōnis *m* buzzard
Būt(h)rōt·um (·on) -ī *n or* **Būt(h)rōt·os -ī** *f* town on the coast of Epirus
buxēt·um -ī *n* plantation of boxwood trees
buxif·er -era -erum *adj* producing boxwood trees
bux·um -ī *n (bot)* boxwood tree; *(object made of the hard wood of the boxwood tree):* (spinning) top, comb, writing tablet, flute
bux·us -ī *f* boxwood tree
Bybl·is -idis *f* daughter of Miletus and Cyaneë, changed into a fountain
Byrs·a -ae *f* **(Bur-)** citadel of Carthage
Byzant·ium -(i)ī *n* city on the Bosporus, later named Constantinople *(modern Istanbul)*
Byzanti·us -a -um *adj* Byantine **‖** *mpl* Byzantines

C

C, c *(supply* littera*)* *f* third letter of the Latin alphabet; letter name: **ce**
C *abbr* **centum** (one hundred)
C. *abbr* **Gāius** *(Roman first name, praenomen)*
caballīn·us -a -um *adj* horse's; **fōns caballīnus** *(pej)* "nag's spring" *(i.e., Hippocrene)*
caball·us -ī *m* horse, nag; packhorse; riding horse; **Gorgoneus caballus** Pegasus *(sprung from the blood of the Gorgon Medusa)*
Cabīr·us -ī *m* deity worshiped on Lemnos and Samothrace *(e.g., Bacchus)*
cacātur·iō -īre -iī *intr (vulg)* to want *or* need to shit
cachinnāti·ō -ōnis *f* horselaugh
cachinn·ō -āre -āvī -ātum *intr* to laugh loud, roar *(with laughter)*
cachinn·us -ī *m* loud laugh; *(fig)* rippling *(of waves)*
cac·ō -āre -āvī -ātus *tr & intr (vulg)* to shit

cacoēth·es -is *n* malignant, incurable disease; *(fig)* itch; **cacoēthes scrībendī** an itch to write

cacozēli·a -ae *f* bad taste *(in style)*

cacozēl·os -on *adj (of style)* in bad taste

cacul·a -ae *m (sl)* soldier's slave, "dog robber"

cacūm·en -inis *n* point, tip, top, peak; young shoot; **extrēmum cacūmen** outer limit

cacūmin·ō -āre -āvī -ātus *tr* to point, make pointed

Cāc·us -ī *m* giant son of Vulcan, living on the Aventine Hill and slain by Hercules

cadāv·er -eris *n* corpse, carcass

cadāverōs·us -a -um *adj* cadaverous, ghastly

Cadmē·is -idos *adj (fem only)* of Cadmus ‖ *f* daughter of Cadmus

Cadmē·us -a -um *adj* Cadmean, Theban; **Tyros Cadmēa** Tyre, home city of Cadmus ‖ *f* citadel of Thebes

Cadm·us -ī *m* son of Phoenician king Agenor, brother of Europa, and founder of the citadel of Thebes; **Cadmī terra** Phoenicia

cadō cadere cecidī cāsum *intr* to fall, sink, drop; to be slain, die, be sacrificed; to happen, occur, turn out, come to pass; to belong, refer, be suitable, apply; to flag, decline, decay; to vanish, fail, cease; to derive *(from a source); (of parts of the body)* to fall out, be shed; *(of heavenly bodies)* to sink, set; *(of wind, sea, noise)* to die down; *(of words)* to fall from one's lips; *(of efforts)* to come to nothing; *(w.* **in** *+ acc)* **1** to come upon, arrive at by chance; **2** to fall upon *(the enemy);* **3** to coincide with *(a time, period);* **4** to fall due on *(a date);* **5** to be consistent *or* compatible with, fit; **6** *(of words, clauses)* to end, terminate in *(e.g., a long syllable);* **7** to fall into *(a category); (w.* **ad** *or* **in** *+ acc)* to lapse into, degenerate into; **aptē cadere ad** to be exactly adapted to; **causā cadere** *(leg)* to lose one's case, be convicted; *(fig)* to be in the wrong; **fōrmulā cadere** to lose one's case on a technicality; **hūc cadere** to fall so low; **numerōsē cadere** to sound rhythmical

cādūceāt·or -ōris *m* herald

cādūce·us -ī *m* herald's staff, caduceus

cādūcif·er -era -erum *adj* with herald's staff

cādūc·us -a -um *adj* falling; fallen; inclined to fall, tottery, unsteady; frail, perishable, transitory; *(of hopes, words)* futile; *(of persons)* destined to die, doomed; *(of fire)* likely to go out; *(of streams)* likely to dry up; *(of vines)* drooping; *(leg)* lapsed, without heir; *(mil)* fallen in battle

cadurc·um -ī *n* coverlet; *(fig)* marriage bed

cad·us -ī *m* (large) jar, keg *(mostly of clay)*

Cadūsi·ī -ōrum *mpl* the people of Cadusia *(near the Caspian Sea)*

caecigen·us -a -um *adj* born blind

Caecili·us -a -um *adj* Roman clan name, *nomen*

caecit·ās -ātis *f* blindness; **caecitās animī** moral blindness; **caecitās mentis** mental blindness, lack of discernment

caec·ō -āre -āvī -ātus *tr* to blind; to obscure the judgment of; **astū caecāre** *(fig)* to pull the wool over *(s.o.'s)* eyes

Caecub·um -ī *n* Caecuban wine *(from Caecubum in S. Latium)*

Caecul·us -ī *m* son of Vulcan and founder of Praeneste

caec·us -a -um *adj* blind; invisible; vague, random, aimless; uncertain, unknown; unsubstantiated; blinding; obscure, mysterious; dark, gloomy; concealed, disguised; unforeseeable *(dangers)*; **diē caecō emere** to buy on credit *(i.e., to buy with no definite date of payment)*

caed·ēs -is *f* murder, slaughter, massacre; bloodshed, gore; the slain

caedō caedere cecīdī caesus *tr* to hack at; to chop; to strike, beat; to fell; to cut off, cut to pieces; to cut through, sever; to kill, murder; to crack, smash, break; to use up, consume; *(hum)* to devour; **sermōnēs caedere** to exchange chitchat

caedu·us -a -um *adj* ready for felling

caelām·en -inis *n* engraving, bas-relief

caelāt·or -ōris *m* engraver

caelāt·um -ī *n* engraved work

caelātūr·a -ae *f* engraving

cael·ebs -ibis *adj* **(-eps)** unmarried, single *(whether bachelor or widower); (of trees)* not supporting vines

cael·es -itis *adj* heavenly ‖ *mpl* gods

caelest·is -is -e *adj* heavenly, celestial; supernatural, divine ‖ *mf* deity; godlike person ‖ *npl* heavenly bodies

caelibāt·us -ūs *m* celibacy

caelicol·a -ae *mf* denizen of heaven *(god or goddess)*

caelif·er -era -erum *adj* supporting the sky

Caelimontān·us -a -um *adj* located on the Caelian Hill

caelipot·ēns -entis *adj* powerful in heaven

caelit·ēs -um *mpl* gods in heaven

Caeli·us -a -um *adj* Roman clan name *(nomen)*

Caeli·us Mōns *(gen:* **Caeliī Montis)** *m* Caelian Hill *(in Rome)*

cael·ō -āre -āvī -ātus *tr* to engrave in relief, emboss; to carve; to cast; to fashion, compose; to adorn

cael·um -ī *n* engraver's chisel

cael·um -ī *n* sky, heaven(s); air, climate, weather; universe, world; **caelum apertum** *(or* **patēns)** the open air; **in caelō**

esse to be in seventh heaven; **positiō caelī** *(geog)* latitude
caement·um -ī *n* **(cēm-)** *(also used in pl)* crushed stone
Caen·eūs -eī *or* **-eos** *m* child of Elatus, born a girl, but changed by Neptune into a boy
Caenīn·a -ae *f* ancient city of Latium *(defeated by Romulus)*
Caen·is -idis *f* child of Elatus, born a girl but changed into a boy
caenōs·us -a -um *adj* filthy, muddy
caen·um -ī *n* **(cēn-)** filth, mud, slime; *(applied to persons) (sl)* scum
caep·a *or* **cēp·a -ae** *f or* **caep·e** *or* **cēp·e -is** *n* onion
Caepi·ō -ōnis *m* Roman family name *(cognomen), esp.* in the *gens Servilia*
Caer·e -itis *or* **-ētis** *n* city in Etruria *(modern Cerveteri)*
Caer·es -itis *or* **-ētis** *adj* of Caere; **dignus Caerite cērā** *i.e.,* without voting rights **ǁ** *mpl* the people of Caere
Caerētān·us -a -um *adj* of Caere
caerimōni·a -ae *f* rite, ceremony; sanctity; awe, reverence **ǁ** *fpl* rites, ceremonies; practices
caerul·a -ōrum *npl* blue expanse *(of the sky);* blue waters *(of the sea)*
caerul(e)·us -a -um *adj* blue; blue-eyed; dark-blue; greenish-blue; dark
Caes·ar -aris *m* Gaius Julius Caesar *(102?–44 B.C.)* **ǁ** honorary title of Octavian and succeeding emperors **ǁ** cognomen of various members of the imperial family
Caesarē·a -ae *f* name of several towns, *esp.* two in Palestine, one in Cappadocia, and one in Mauretania
Caesare·us -a -um *or* **Caesariān·us -a -um** *adj* connected with Julius Caesar; connected with Augustus; imperial
Caesariān·us -i *m* soldier *or* supporter of Julius Caesar; supporter *or* servant of the Roman emperor
caesariāt·us -a -um *adj* long-haired
caesari·ēs -ēī *f* long, flowing hair
caesīci·us -a -um bluish, dark-blue
caesim *adv* by chopping, by cutting; with a slashing blow; *(rhet)* in short clauses, in a clipped style
caesi·us -a -um *adj* bluish-grey; blue-eyed; grey-eyed; cat-eyed **ǁ Caesius** Roman clan name *(nomen)*
Caes·ō -ōnis *m* **(Kaes-)** Roman first name *(praenomen)*
caesp·es -itis *m* sod, turf; grass; altar of sod; rampart made of turf; mound of earth *(esp. as the covering of a grave)*
caest·us -ūs *m* **(cēst-)** boxing glove
caes·us -a -um *pp of* **caedō ǁ** *npl:* **inter caesa et porrēcta** *(fig)* at the eleventh hour *(literally, between the victim being slain and offered)*
caetr·a -ae *f* **(cēt-)** short Spanish shield
caetrāt·us -a -um *adj* armed with a shield **ǁ** *mpl* soldiers armed with a shield; Greek peltasts
Caīc·us -ī *m* **(Cay-)** river in Mysia
Cāiēt·a -ae *f* nurse of Aeneas **ǁ** town on the coast of Latium
cai·ō -āre *tr* to beat, thrash
Cāïus *see* **Gāius**
Cala·ber -bra -brum *adj* Calabrian
Calabri·a -ae *f* region of S.E. Italy
Cala·is -is *m (winged)* son of Boreas and Orithyia, and brother of Zetes
calamāri·us -a -um *adj* for holding pens
Calam·is -idis *m* Greek sculptor of the 5th cent. B.C.
calamis·ter -trī *m* curling iron
calamistrāt·us -a -um *adj* curled *(with a curling iron)*
calamistr·um -ī *n* curling iron
calamit·ās -ātis *f* calamity, disaster; *(mil)* defeat
calamitōsē *adv* disastrously
calamitōs·us -a -um *adj* disastrous; liable to disaster; blighted *(fields);* hit by disaster, ill-starred **ǁ** *m* victim of a disaster
calam·us -ī *m* reed; stalk, shoot *(of a plant);* pen *(for writing on paper, as opposed to* **stilus** *of metal or bone for writing on wax);* arrow; fishing rod; lime rod *(smeared at top with lime to catch birds);* vine prop; *(mus)* reed pipe; *(collectively or pl)* Panpipes
calathīsc·us -ī *m* small wicker basket
calath·us -ī *m* wicker basket; vessel for holding cheese *or* curdled milk; wine bowl
Cālāti·a -ae *f* town in Campania
calāt·or -ōris *m* **(kal-)** servant; priest's attendant
calautic·a -ae *f* type of woman's headdress
calc·ar -āris *n* spur; *(fig)* stimulus
calceāment·um -ī *n* footwear, shoe
calceār·ium -(i)ī *n* shoe allowance
calceāt·or -ōris *m* shoemaker
calceāt·us -ūs *m* footwear, shoes
calce·ō -āre -āvī -ātus *tr* to put shoes on; to shoe *(animals)*
calceolār·ius -(i)ī *m* shoemaker
calceol·us -ī *m* small shoe, half-boot; slipper
calce·us -ī *m* shoe; **calceī mulleī** *(or* **patriciī)** red shoes worn by senators who had held curule office; **calceōs mūtāre** *(fig)* to become a senator *(from the shoes that senators wore);* **calceōs poscere** to leave the table *(literally, to call for one's shoes)*
Calc(h)·ās -antis *m* Calchas *(Greek seer at Troy)*
Calc(h)ēd·ōn -ōnis *f* Calchedon *(town on the Asiatic side of the Bosphorus, opposite Byzantium)*
calci- *see* **calce-**

calcitr·ō -āre -āvī -ātum *intr* to kick; to be recalcitrant, kick up one's heels
calcitr·ō -ōnis *m* kicker; blusterer
calc·ō -āre -āvī -ātus *tr* to trample; to trample on; to tread *(grapes)*; to set foot on; to tread on accidentally, trip upon; *(fig)* to spurn; **viam calcāre** to tread a path
calculāt·or -ōris *m* arithmetic teacher; accountant, bookkeeper
calcul·us -ī *m* pebble, stone; kidney stone; counter of an abacus; piece *(used in games);* **calculus albus** white pebble *(of acquittal);* **calculōs** *(or* **calculum)** **pōnere** *(or* **subdūcere)** to make a calculation *(esp. gains or losses);* **calculus āter** black pebble *(of condemnation);* vote, decision, sentence; **parem calculum pōnere cum** to return an equivalent gift to
calda, caldārius, caldus *see* **calid-**
cal(e)·faciō -facere -fēcī -factus *tr* to warm, heat; to rouse, excite, anger
Calēdoni·a -ae *f* Caledonia, Scotland
calefact·ō -āre -āvī -ātus *tr* to warm, heat
calefierī *pass inf of* **calefaciō**
Calend- *see* **Kalend-**
Calēn·us -a -um *adj* of Cales *(in Campania)* **ǁ** *n* wine from Cales
cal·eō -ēre -uī *intr* to be warm, be hot; to feel warm; to glow; to be flushed *(with wine);* to be hot *(with lust);* to be busy, have one's hands full; to be yet new, be fresh **ǁ** *impers* **calētur** *(of the weather)* it is hot
Cal·ēs -ium *fpl* Campanian town famous for its wine
cal·ēscō -ēscere -uī *intr* to get warm, get hot; to become excited *(with love)*
caliandrum *see* **caliendrum**
calidē *adv* promptly, quickly
calid·us -a -um *adj* **(cald-)** warm, hot; eager, rash; hot-headed; hasty; intoxicating *(wine);* high *(fever);* cold *(cash)* **ǁ** *f* warm water **ǁ** *n* hot drink; heat
caliendr·um -ī *n* **(-lian-)** wig *(for women)*
calig·a -ae *f* army boot; *(fig)* military service
caligāt·us *or* **caligāri·us -a -um** *adj* wearing army boots **ǁ** *m (mil)* private
cālīginōs·us -a -um *adj* misty, foggy
cālīg·ō -āre *tr* to veil in darkness, obscure; to make dizzy **ǁ** *intr* to be dark, be gloomy; to steam, reek; to be wrapped in mist *or* darkness; to be blind, grope
cālīg·ō -inis *f* darkness; mist, fog; dark smoke; gloom; obscurity; mental blindness; dizziness
caligul·a -ae *f* small army boot
Caligul·a -ae *m* nickname given by soldiers to Emperor Gaius, son of Germanicus, when he was a small boy
cal·ix -icis *m* cup, goblet; cooking pot; *(fig)* wine
Callaec·ī -ōrum *mpl* a people in the N.W. corner of Spain
callaïn·us -a -um *adj* turquoise
call·eō -ēre -uī *tr* to know by experience; to have skill in; *(w. inf)* to know how to, be able to **ǁ** *intr* to grow hard, be calloused; *(fig)* to be thick-skinned, be callous; *(w. abl)* to be experienced in, be skilled in
callidē *adv* skillfuly; well; cunningly
callidit·ās -ātis *f* skill, dexterity; shrewdness; cunning **ǁ** *fpl* clever tricks
callid·us -a -um *adj* expert, adroit, skillful; ingenious, clever; cunning, wily; *(w. gen, dat, or* **in** *+ abl)* experienced in; *(w. inf)* skilled at
Callimach·us -ī *m* Alexandrine poet and grammarian *(fl c. 270 B.C.)*
Calliop·ē -ēs *or* **Calliop(ē)·a -ae** *f* Calliope *(Muse of epic poetry)*
Callirrho·ē -ēs *f* daughter of the River Acheloüs, and second wife of Alcmaeon **ǁ** a famous spring in Athens
call·is -is *mf* rough footpath **ǁ** *mpl* mountain pasturage; cattle trails
Callistō -ūs *(dat:* **-ō)** *f* daughter of Lycaon *(king of Arcadia),* changed into a she-bear and then into the constellation Ursa Major
callōs·us -a -um *adj* thick-skinned, calloused; solid, hard
call·um -ī *n or* **call·us -ī** *m* hard skin; *(lit & fig)* callousness; **callum obdūcere dolōrī** to produce insensibility to grief
cal·ō -āre -āvī -ātus *tr* **(kal-)** to proclaim; to convoke *(only in religious matters)*
cāl·ō -ōnis *m* soldier's slave,"dog-robber"; drudge
cal·or -ōris *m* warmth, heat; glow; passion, love; fire, zeal, impetuosity; fever
Calp·ē -ēs *f* Gibraltar
Calpurni·us -a -um *adj* name of a plebeian clan **ǁ** *f* Calpurnia *(wife of Julius Caesar)*
calt(h)·a -ae *f (bot)* marigold
caltul·a -ae *f (woman's)* yellow slip *(tied below the breasts)*
calumni·a -ae *f* **(kal-)** false accusation, malicious charge; frameup; conviction for malicious prosecution; false statement, misrepresentation; trickery; pretext; sham; **calumniam** *or* **dē calumniā iūrāre** to swear that one is not making a false accusation
calumniāt·or -ōris *m* malicious accuser; shyster
calumni·or -ārī -ātus sum *tr* to accuse fasely; to misinterpret, misrepresent; to blame unjustly; to find fault with **ǁ** *intr* to make a false accusation; to practice legal chicanery
calv·a -ae *f* bald head, scalp; skull
calvit·ium -(i)ī *n,* **calviti·ēs -ēī** *f* baldness
calv·us -a -um *adj* bald

cal·x -cis *f* heel; (back of the) hoof; *(fig)* foot, kick; **calcibus caedere** to kick

cal·x -cis *f* lime, limestone; pebble *(used in games);* finish line, goal; **ad calcem pervenīre** to reach the goal; *(prov)* **ad carcerēs ā calce revocārī** to have to do a thing all over again *(lit:* to be called back to the starting gate from the finish line)

Calyd·ōn -ōnis *or* **-ōnos** *f* town in Aetolia, site of the boar hunt led by Meleager

Calydōn·is -idos *adj (fem only)* Calydonian ‖ *f* Calydonian woman *(Deianira, the sister of Maleager)*

Calydōni·us -a -um *adj* Calydonian

Calyps·ō -ūs *f* nymph *(daughter of Atlas)* who entertained Ulysses on the island of Ogygia

camara *see* **camera**

camell·a -ae *f* drinking cup

camēl·us -ī *m* camel

Camēn·a -ae *f* Muse; poem; poetry

camer·a -ae *f* **(-mar-)** vault, arched roof, arch; flat boat with arched covering

Camerīn·um -ī *n* town in Umbria

Camill·a -ae *f* Volscian female warrior, ally of Turnus against Aeneas

Camill·us -ī *m* Marcus Furius Camillus, who liberated Rome from the Gauls in 390 B.C.

camīn·us -ī *m* fireplace; furnace, forge; vent of subterranean fires; **oleum addere camīnō** *(prov)* to pour oil on the fire

cammar·us -ī *m* **(gam-)** lobster

Campāni·a -ae *f* region on E. coast of central Italy below Latium

Campān·us -a -um *adj* Campanian

campes·ter *or* **campes·tris -tris -tre** *adj* flat, level; overland *(march); (of city)* situated in a plain; *(of army)* fighting in a plain; *(of sports, elections)* held in the Campus Martius ‖ *n* loincloth ‖ *npl* flat lands

camp·us -ī *m* open field *(opp:* **ager** tilled field); flat space, plain; level surface; *(fig)* field of action, subject of debate; **Campus Mārtius** Field of Mars *(near the Tiber, used for sports, elections, military exercises)*

cam·ur *or* **cam·urus -ura -urum** *adj* crooked; concave

Canac·ē -ēs *f* daughter of Aeolus, who committed incest with her brother Macareus

canāl·is -is *mf* pipe, conduit; gutter, open drain; channel *(of a river; of the sea);* flow *(of language)*

cancell·ī -ōrum *mpl* railing, grating; barrier *(at sports, public events);* boundaries, limits; **intrā cancellōs** in a confined space

can·cer -crī *m* crab; the South; tropical heat; *(med)* cancer ‖ **Cancer** *(astr)* Cancer, the Crab *(sign of the zodiac)*

cande·faciō -facere -fēcī -factus *tr* to make white; to make white-hot

candēl·a -ae *f* candle, taper; waxed cord

candēlābr·um -ī *n* candlestick, candelabrum; lampstand

cand·ēns -entis *adj* white, shining, glistening; white-hot *(iron)*

cand·eō -ēre -uī *intr* to be shiny white, glitter, shine; to be white-hot

cand·ēscō -ēscere *intr* to become white, begin to glisten; to get white-hot

candidātōri·us -a -um *adj* of a candidate, candidate's

candidāt·us -a -um *adj* clothed in white ‖ *m* candidate

candidē *adv* in dazzling white; clearly, simply, sincerely

candidul·us -a -um *adj* white, gleaming

candid·us -a -um *adj (cf* **albus** flat white) shiny white, white, bright, dazzling, gleaming, sparkling; lucky, favorable, happy; fair *(complexion);* candid, frank *(person);* bright, cheerful *(mood, circumstances);* clear, bright *(day); (of winds)* bringing clear weather; white, silvery *(poplar, hair);* clear, unaffected *(style);* **candidus līmes** Milky Way; **candida sententia** vote of acquittal

cand·or -ōris *m* whiteness, brightness, radiance; fair complexion; candor, sincerity, kindness; clarity *(of style)*

can·ēns -entis *pres p of* **canō**

cān·ēns -entis *adj* grey, white

cān·eō -ēre -uī *intr* to be grey

cānēsc·ō -ere *intr* to turn grey; to grow old; *(of discourse)* to become dull

cān·ī -ōrum *mpl* grey hair(s)

canīcul·a -ae *f* small dog ‖ **Canīcula** *(astr)* Canicula, Sirius, Dog Star

canīn·us -a -um *adj* canine; snarling, spiteful; **canīna littera** the letter R

can·is -is *mf* dog; *(pej)* skunk; worst throw *(in dice)* ‖ **Canis** *m (astr)* Canis Major *or* Sirius

canistr·um -ī *n* wicker basket *(for bread, flowers, etc.)*

cāniti·ēs -ēī *f* greyness; *(fig)* grey hair; *(fig)* old age

cann·a -ae *f* reed; reed pipe, flute

cannab·is -ae *f or* **cannab·um -ī** *n* hemp, marijuana; hempen rope

Cann·ae -ārum *fpl* town in Apulia where Hannibal defeated the Romans in 216 B.C.

Cannēns·is -is -e *adj* of Cannae

canō canere cecinī cantus *tr* to sing; to sing of; to speak in a singsong tone; to sing of; to prophesy, predict; *(mil)* to blow, sound; **signa** *(or* **classicum)** **canere** to sound the signal for battle ‖ *intr* to sing; *(w. abl)* to play *(a musical instrument); (of birds)* to sing; *(of roosters)* to crow; *(of frogs)* to croak; **receptuī canere** to sound the retreat; **surdīs**

canere to preach to deaf ears; **tībiā canere** to play the flute
Canōp·us -ī *m* town on W. mouth of the Nile
can·or -ōris *m* tune, sound, melody, song; tone *(of instruments)*
canōr·us -a -um *adj* melodious, musical; singsong, jingling **ll** *n* melody
Canta·ber -brī *m* Cantabrian; **Cantabr·ī -ōrum** *mpl* the people of Cantabria in N. Spain
Cantabri·a -ae *f* district in N. Spain
cantām·en -inis *n* incantation, spell
cantāt·or -ōris *m* singer
cant(h)ērīn·us -a -um *adj* of a horse
cant(h)ēr·ius -(i)ī *m* gelding; eunuch
canthar·is -idis *f* beetle; Spanish fly
canthar·us -ī *m* wide-bellied drinking vessel with handles, tankard
canth·us -ī *m* iron rim; wheel
cantic·um -ī *n* song; aria in Roman comedy; singing tone *(in an orator's delivery)*
cantilēn·a -ae *f* old song; *(coll)* gossip; **cantilēnam eandem canere** *(fig)* to harp on the same old theme
canti·ō -ōnis *f* singing; incantation, spell, charm
cantit·ō -āre -āvī -ātus *tr* to keep on singing *or* playing
Cant·ium -(i)ī *n* district of Britain *(modern Kent)*
cantiuncul·a -ae *f* catchy tune
cant·ō -āre -āvī -ātus *tr* to sing; to sing of, celebrate; to harp on, keep repeating; to drawl out; to predict; *(of birds)* to sing, crow, warble; *(of actor)* to play the part of **ll** *intr* to sing; *(w. abl)* to play *(a musical instrument)*; *(of instruments)* to sound; to drawl; *(of rooster)* to crow; **ad surdās aurēs cantāre** *(fig)* to preach to deaf ears
cant·or -ōris *m* singer; poet; eulogist; actor, player; musician
cantr·īx -īcis *f* singer, player, musician *(female)*
cant·us -ūs *m* song, tune, melody; incantation; magic spell; prediction; poetry
cān·us -a -um *adj* grey; white; grey-haired; old; age-old *(things)*; whitened, foam-capped *(sea)*; *(of trees, plants)* covered with silvery foliage
Canusīn·a -ae *f* garment made of Canusian wool
Canus·ium -(i)ī *n* Greek town in Apulia *(modern Canosa)*
capācit·ās -ātis *f* capacity
Capan·eūs -eī *m* one of the "Seven against Thebes," killed by lightning
cap·āx -ācis *adj* capacious, spacious, wide, roomy; *(of mind)* able to grasp, receptive; *(w. gen, dat or inf)* big enough for; *(w. gen)* **1** capable of, capable of holding; **2** susceptible of; **3** capable of understanding; **capāx nāvium** navigable
capēd·ō -inis *f* cup, bowl *(used in sacrifices)*
capēduncul·a -ae *f* small cup *or* bowl *(used in sacrifices)*
capell·a -ae *f* she-goat, nanny goat **ll** *(astr)* **Capella** *(star in the constellation Auriga)*
Capēn·a -ae *f* a town of the Veientians in Etruria *(now San Martino)*
Capēn·ās -ātis *adj* of Capena **ll Capēnātēs** inhabitants of Capena
Capēn·us -a -um *adj* of Capena; **Porta Capēna** *(gate in the Servian Wall marking the start of the Via Appia, now the Porta San Sabastiano)*
ca·per -prī *m* he-goat, billy goat
caperr·ō -āre -āvī -ātus *tr & intr* to wrinkle
capess·ō -ere -īvī *or* **-iī -ītus** *tr* **(-iss-)** to try to reach, make for; to seize, get hold of, snatch at; to take up, engage in; **arma capessere** to take up arms, go to war; **cursum** *(or* **viam) capessere** to take the road (to); **flammam capessere** to catch fire; **iūssa capessere** to execute orders; **poenās capessere** to exact punishment; **rem pūblicam capessere** to engage in politics **ll** *refl & intr* to go
Caphēr·eūs -eī *m* **(-phār-)** rocky promontory at the S.E. end of Euboea
capillāment·um -ī *n* wig, toupeé
capillār·e -is *n* hair oil
capillāt·us -a -um *adj* long-haired
capill·us -ī *m* hair *(of the head)*; *(single)* hair; *(of plants)* fibers; hair, fur *(of animals)*
capiō capere cēpī captus *(archaic fut:* **capsō)** *tr* to take hold of, grasp; to occupy; to take up *(arms)*; assume *(office)*; to put on *(clothes, armor)*; to catch, capture; to catch *(fish)*; to bag *(game)*; to captivate, charm; to cheat, mislead, seduce, delude; to trap; to defeat, overcome; to keep under control; to be able to hold, have room for; to convince; to reach, arrive at, land at; to exact *(tribute, penalty)*; to extort, accept as a bribe; to take, obtain, enjoy, reap *(profit, advantage)*; to reap, gather *(crops)*; to cherish, cultivate, adopt *(habits, etc.)*; to form, come to, reach *(conclusions, plans, thoughts, resolutions, purposes)*; to take, derive, draw, obtain *(examples, proofs, instances)*; to receive, experience *(impressions, feelings)*; *(of feeling)* to come over; to suffer, be subjected to *(injury)*; to hold, contain, be large enough for; to comprehend, grasp; **animō capere** to grasp, get, understand; **cōnsilium capere** to form a plan; **fidem capere** to be credible; **fīnem capere** to come to an end; **fugam capere** to take to flight; **honōrem capere** to assume an office; **initium capere** to begin; **īnsulam, portum capere** reach the

island, harbor *(by ship);* **prīncipium capere** to make a beginning, begin; **rādīcem capere** to take root; **quiētem capere** to get some rest; **somnum capere** to go to sleep; **ūsū capere** to acquire, inherit ‖ *refl* **sē nōn capere** not to contain oneself, not to control oneself

cap·is -idis *f* bowl *(with one handle, used in sacrifices)*

capistr·ō -āre -āvī -ātus *tr* to put a halter on, muzzle

capistr·um -ī *n* halter, muzzle

capit·al *or* **capit·āle -ālis** *n* capital offense; crime punishable by death

capitāl·is -is -e *adj* relating to the head *or* life; *(leg)* affecting a person's life *or* civil status; *(of crime)* punishable by death, punishable by loss of civil rights; dangerous, deadly, fatal; mortal *(enemy);* first-class, fine

capitāliter *adv* with bitter hostility

capit·ō -ōnis *m (coll)* bighead

Capitōlīn·us -a -um *adj* Capitoline ‖ *m* Capitoline Hill ‖ *mpl* persons in charge of the Capitoline games ‖ *n see* **Capitōlium**

Capitōl·ium -(i)ī *n* the Capitol *(temple of Jupiter on the summit of Mons Tarpeius);* the Capitoline Hill *(including temple and citadel);* citadel *(of any city)*

capitulātim *adv* briefly, summarily

capitul·um -ī *n* small head; *(as term of endearment)* dear fellow; end, point *(of an instrument, pole, etc.)*

Cappadoci·a -ae *f* country in E. Asia Minor between Cilicia and Pontus

Cappadoc·us -a -um *adj* Cappadocian

Cappad·ox -ocis *m* inhabitant of Cappadocia; *(pej)* Asiatic

cappar·is -is *f* pickled flower bud of the caper plant *(prickly shrub)*

capr·a -ae *f* she-goat ‖ **Capra** *(astr)* star in the constellation Auriga

capre·a -ae *f* wild she-goat; **Capr(e)ae Palūs** Goat's Pool *(in Campus Martius, site of Circus Flaminius)*

Capre·ae -ārum *fpl* Isle of Capri

capreol·us -ī *m* chamois, roebuck; rafter

Capricorn·us -ī *m (astr)* Capricorn

caprific·us -ī *f* wild fig tree

caprigen·us -a -um *adj* of goats; **caprigenum pecus** herd of goats

caprimulg·us -ī *m* country bumpkin *(literally, goat milker)*

caprīn·us -a -um *adj* goat; **dē lānā caprīnā rīxārī** *(fig)* to fight over nothing

caprip·ēs -edis *adj* goat-footed *(poetic epithet of rural dieties)*

caps·a -ae *f* container, holder, box, case *(esp. for scrolls)*

capsō *see* **capiō**

capsul·a -ae *f* small box

capt·a -ae *f* captive *(female)*

captāti·ō -ōnis *f* hunt, quest; **captātiō verbōrum** verbalism

captātor -ōris *m* seeker; legacy hunter; **aurae populāris captātor** publicity hound

capti·ō -ōnis *f* trick, fraud; loss, disadvantage; verbal quibble

captiōsē *adv* slyly, trickily

captiōs·us -a -um *adj* tricky, deceptive; sophistical; harmful, disadvantageous

captiuncul·a -ae *f* quibble, sophism

captīvit·ās -ātis *f* captivity; capture

captīv·us -a -um *adj* captured; captive; prisoner's; caught *(in hunting, fishing)* ‖ *mf* prisoner-of-war

capt·ō -āre -āvī -ātus *tr* to try to catch; to keep reaching for; to chase after; to strive after, long for, desire earnestly; to try to find; to try to trap, lure; to catch *(fish);* to try to get the better of *(in an argument);* to adopt *(plan);* to try to cause *(laughter, response in others);* to watch for *(an opportunity);* to begin *(conversation);* **aure** *(or* **auribus)** **captāre** to try to hear, listen in on, eavesdrop on; **cēnam captāre** to sponge a meal

captūr·a -ae *f* capture; quarry, kill; catch *(in fishing)*

capt·us -a -um *pp of* **capiō** ‖ *adj* captive; **oculīs et auribus captus** blind and deaf; **mente captus** crazy

capt·us -ūs *m* grasping, taking; capacity, potentiality

Capu·a -ae *f* chief city of Campania

capūd·ō -inis *f* primitive sacrificial vessel

capulār·is -is -e *adj (sl)* with one foot in the grave

capul·us -ī *m* coffin; hilt, handle

cap·ut -itis *n* head; top, summit; point; principal point, main item; essential thing, matter of prime importance; end *(of anything, esp. when rounded or resembling a head, e.g., of a pole);* source *(of river);* beginning *(of a road);* root *(of plant);* top *(of tree, poppy);* head, leader; prime mover, ring-leader; individual, person *(e.g.,* **caput līberum** free person); chief city, capital *(of a country, etc.);* main point *(of discourse);* chapter, heading; substance, summary; beginning, first part *(of a speech, action; initial letter, beginning of a word or sentence);* main course; *(com)* capital; *(fin)* principal; *(leg)* life, civil status; **capitis accūsāre** to accuse of a capital crime; **capitis damnāre** to condemn to death; **capitis rēs** matter of life and death; **caput dēmittere** to hang one's head; **dīminūtiō capitis** loss of civil rights; **dīminūtiō capitis maxima** condemnation to death *or* slavery; **dīminūtiō capitis media** loss of citizenship; **dīminūtiō capitis minima**

change of status *(as by adoption, marriage)*; **suprā caput esse** to be imminent

Cap·ys -yos *m* son of Assaracus and father of Anchises ‖ companion of Aeneas ‖ eighth king of Alba Longa

carbase·us -a -um *adj* linen, canvas

carbas·us -a -um *adj* linen ‖ *f* sail, canvas; awning; linen cloth ‖ *npl* linen clothing

carb·ō -ōnis *m* charcoal; piece of charcoal used in writing, drawing, marking; *(fig)* something worthless

carbōnār·ius -(i)ī *m* charcoal burner *(person)*, collier

carbuncul·us -ī *m* (live) coal, ember; garnet; *(med)* carbuncle, tumor

carc·er -eris *m* prison; prisoners; *(coll)* jailbird ‖ *mpl* starting gate *(at racetrack)*; **ad carcerēs ā calce revocārī** to start over from scratch *(literally, to be called back from the chalk line, i.e., finish line, to the starting gate)*

carcerāri·us -a -um *adj* prison

carchēs·ium -(i)ī *n* drinking cup; masthead *(of ship)*

cardiac·us -a -um *adj* suffering from heartburn ‖ *m* dyspeptic

card·ō -inis *m* **(kar-)** pivot and socket; hinge; turning point; axis, pole; boundary; region, district *(of a country)*; the earth *(as pivot of the universe)*; **cardō extrēmus** old age; **cardō rērum** critical juncture; **cardō summus** zenith *(of the sky)*

cardu·us -ī *m* thistle

cārē *adv* at a high price, dearly

cārect·um -ī *n* a bed of sedge *(reed grass, having solid rather than hollow stems)*

car·eō -ēre -uī *intr (w. abl or gen)* **1** to be without; **2** to miss; **3** to be free from *(trouble, pain, blame)*; **4** to keep away from, be absent from; **5** to abstain from; **6** to fail to achieve, be denied; **7** to go without

cār·ex -icis *f* sedge, reed grass *(having solid rather than hollow stems)*

Cāri·a -ae *f* district in S.W. Asia Minor

cari·ēs -ēī *f* decaying; decay, rot; shriveling up

carīn·a -ae *f* keel; ship ‖ **Carīnae** *fpl* the Keels *(district in Rome between the Esquiline and Caelian Hills)*

cārīnār·ius -(i)ī *m* dyer of yellow

cariōs·us -a -um *adj* rotten, decayed; crumbly; wrinkled *(old age)*

cār·is -idis *f* shrimp

cārit·ās -ātis *f* dearness, costliness, high price, high cost of living; affection

carm·en -inis *n* song, tune; poem; poetry; lyric poetry; incantation; oracular utterance; ritual formula; legal formula; adage

Carment·a -ae *or* **Carment·is -is** *f* Roman goddess, mother of Evander

Carmentāl·is -is -e *adj* of Carmenta; **Porta Carmentālis** gate in the Servian Wall in Rome

Carment·is -is *f see* **Carmenta**

carnār·ium -(i)ī *n* meat hook

carnār·ius -(i)ī *m* butcher, dealer in meat

Carnead·ēs -is *m* Greek Academic philosopher of the 2nd cent. B.C.

Carneadē·us -a -um *adj* characteristic of Carneades

carnif·ex -icis *m* **(carnu-)** executioner, hangman; murderer, butcher; scoundrel

carnificīn·a -ae *f* **(carnu-)** execution; *(fig)* torture

carnific·ō -āre -āvī -ātus *tr* to execute, butcher; to mutilate

car·ō -nis *or* **carn·is -is** *f* meat; **carō būbula** beef; **carō ferīna** venison; **carō pūtida** carrion; *(fig)* rotten egg

Carpathi·us -a -um *adj* of the island of Carpathus *(between Crete and Rhodes)*; **Carpathius senex (vātēs)** Proteus

carpatin·a -ae *f* rough-leather shoe

carpent·um -ī *n* two-wheeled covered carriage *(used esp. by women)*

carp·ō -ere -sī -tus *tr* to pluck, pick; to carp at, pick on; to enjoy, make use of; to crop *(grass)*; *(mil)* to harass; to cut to pieces; to card *(wool)*; *(of wild animals)* to tear at; **aurās vītālēs carpere** to breathe the breath of life; **diem carpere** to make the most of the present; **gȳrum carpere** to go in a circle; **iter** *(or* **viam) carpere** to make one's way, travel; **pēnsum** *(or* **vellera) carpere** to spin

carptim *adv* piecemeal, separately; selectively; at different times; at various points; gradually

carpt·or -ōris *m* carver *(at table)*

carrūc·a -ae *f* four-wheeled carriage

carr·us -ī *m*, **carr·um -ī** *n* Gallic type of wagon

Carthae·us -a -um *adj* of Carthaea *(town on the Greek island of Ceos)*

Carthāginiēns·is -is -e *adj* **(Kar-)** Carthaginian

Carthāg·ō -inis *f* **(Kar-)** Carthage *(city in N. Africa, founded in 9th cent. B.C.)*

Carthēi·us -a -um *adj see* **Carthaeus**

caruncul·a -ae *f* scrap of meat

cār·us -a -um *adj* dear, expensive; dear, loving, affectionate

Cār·us -ī *m* Roman family name *(cognomen)*

cas·a -ae *f* cottage, cabin, hut; play house

Cāsc·a -ae *m* Roman family name *(cognomen), esp.* Gaius and Publius Servilius Casca Longus *(two of Caesar's assassins)*

cāsc·us -a -um *adj* old-time, primitive

cāseol·us -ī *m* small piece of cheese

cāse·us -ī *m* cheese

casi·a -**ae** *f* wild cinnamon tree; fragrant shrub

Caspi·us -a -um *adj* Caspian; **mare Caspium** Caspian Sea; **sinus Caspius** Caspian Sea; **Caspiae pylae** *(or* **portae)** name of passes in the Caucasus mountains S. of the Caspian Sea

Cassandr·a -ae *f* prophetic daughter of Priam and Hecuba, believed by no one

cass·ēs -ium *see* **cassis**

cassid·a -ae *f* metal helmet

Cassiop·ē -ēs *or* **Cassiopē·a -ae** *f* wife of Cepheus and mother of Andromeda, afterwards changed into a constellation

cass·is -idis *f* metal helmet *(cf* **galea** leather helmet)

cass·is -is *m (often pl)* hunting net, snare; spider web; **cassēs alicui tendere** to set a trap for s.o.

cassiter·um -ī *n* tin

Cass·ius -(i)ī *m* name of a Roman clan *(nomen), esp.* Gaius Cassius Longinus *(one of Caesar's murderers)*

cass·ō -āre *intr* to totter

cass·us -a -um *adj* empty, hollow; *(fig)* groundless, pointless; *(w. abl)* deprived of, devoid of, without; **cassus lūmine** without life; **in cassum** *(also as one word:* **incassum)** to no purpose, pointlessly

Castali·a -ae *f* spring at Delphi, associated with Apollo and the Muses

Castal·is -idis *adj (fem only)* Castalian; **sorōrēs Castalidēs** Muses ‖ *f* Muse

Castali·us -a -um *adj* of Castalia, of Apollo, of the Muses, of the Delphic oracle, Castalian

castane·a -ae *f* chestnut tree; chestnut

castē *adv* chastely, purely, spotlessly; virtuously; devoutly

castellān·us -a -um *adj* of a fortress ‖ *mpl* occupants of a fortress, garrison

castellātim *adv* one fortress after another; **castellātim dissipātī** (troops) stationed in various fortresses

castell·um -ī *n* fort, fortress; castle; *(fig)* stronghold, refuge; small reservoir *or* center of distribution on an aqueduct

castēri·a -ae *f* rower's quarters *(on a ship)*

castīgābil·is -is -e *adj* punishable

castīgāti·ō -ōnis *f* correction, punishment; censure, reproof

castīgāt·or -ōris *m* castigator

castīgātōri·us -a -um *adj* reproving

castīgāt·us -a -um *adj* small, delicate *(breast)*

castīg·ō -āre -āvī -ātus *tr* to correct, make right; to reprove, find fault with; to restrain, hold in check

castimōni·a -ae *f* purity, morality; chastity; ceremonial purification

castit·ās -ātis *f* chastity, purity

cast·or -oris *m* beaver ‖ **Castor** Castor *(son of Tyndareus, twin brother of Pollux, brother of Helen and Clytemnestra, and patron of sailors)*; **aedes** *(or* **templum) Castoris** temple of Castor (and Pollux)

castore·um -ī *n* strong-smelling secretion of beavers *(used in medicine)*

castr·a -ōrum *npl* camp; day's march; the service, army life; *(pol)* party; *(phil)* school; **bīna castra** two camps; **castra facere** *(or* **munīre** *or* **pōnere)** to construct a camp; **castra habēre** to be encamped; **castra movēre** to break camp; **castra ūnā** one camp

castrēns·is -is -e *adj* camp, military; characteristic of soldiers; **corōna castrēnsis** crown conferred on first soldier to enter an enemy's camp

castr·ō -āre -āvī -ātus *tr* to castrate

castr·um -ī *n* fort, fortress ‖ *npl see* **castra**

cast·us -a -um *adj* chaste, pure, innocent; *(of places)* free from crime; holy, sacred

casul·a -ae *f* little hut, little cottage

cās·us -ūs *m* falling; fall, downfall, overthrow, end; chance, event, occurrence; occasion, opportunity; adventure; emergency; misfortune, accident; plight; eventuality, possible situation, contingency; death; fate; *(gram)* case; **nōn cōnsultō sed cāsū** not on purpose but accidentally

cataclysm·os -ī *m* deluge

catafract- *see* **cataphract-**

catagraph·us -a -um *adj* print *(dress)*

catamīt·us -ī *m* catamite ‖ **Catamītus** Ganymede

cataphag·ās -ae *m* glutton

cataphract·ēs -ae *m* coat of mail

cataphract·us -a -um *adj* clad in mail

cataplūs *m (nom only)* putting into port, ship's arrival

catapult·a -ae *f* catapult

catapultāri·us -a -um *adj* catapulted, shot *(from a catapult)*

cataract·a *or* **catarract·a -ae** *or* **catar(r)(h)act·ēs -ae** *f* rapids, cataract; sluice; portcullis

cataractri·a -ae *f (fictitious)* spice

catast·a -ae *f* platform on which slaves were displayed for sale

catē *adv* skillfully, wisely

catēi·a -ae *f* javelin

catell·a -ae *f* puppy *(female)*; small chain *(worn by women)*

catell·us -ī *m* puppy; small chain

catēn·a -ae *f* chain; series; curb, restraint ‖ *fpl* chains, fetters

catēnāt·us -a -um *adj* chained

caterv·a -ae *f* crowd, throng, band, mob; troop *(of actors)*; *(mil)* troop

catervāri·us -a -um *adj* in a crowd

catervātim *adv* in groups; in companies; in herds

cathedr·a -ae *f* armchair, cushioned seat; sedan chair; teacher's chair
Catilīn·a -ae *m* Lucius Sergius Catiline *(leader of conspiracy in 63 B.C.)*
catīll·ō -ōnis *m* plate licker
catīll·ō -āre -āvī -ātum *intr* to lick the plate
catīll·us -ī *m or* **catill·um -ī** *n* (small) plate
catīn·us -ī *m* plate, bowl, dish
Cat·ō -ōnis *m* Marcus Porcius Cato *(model of Roman aristocratic conservatism, 239–149 B.C.)* **||** Marcus Porcius Cato Uticensis *(grandson of the former, arch-enemy of Julius Caesar, 95–45 B.C.)*
Catull·us -ī *m* Gaius Valerius Catullus *(lyric and elegiac poet of Verona, 86–54 B.C.)* **||** a mime writer
catul·us -ī *m* puppy; cub **|| Catulus** Roman family name *(cognomen), esp.* Quintus Lutatius Catulus *(consul in 78 B.C.)*
cat·us -a -um *adj* clever; sly
Caucasi·us -a -um *adj* of the Caucasus; **portae Caucasiae** pass through the Caucasus Mountains
Caucas·us -ī *m* Caucasus Mountains
caud·a -ae *f* tail **(cōd-)** *(of an animal);* tail-end; *(vulg)* penis; **caudam iactāre** *(w. dat)* to flatter; **caudam movēre** to wag the tail; **caudam trahere** *(to have a tail stuck on)* to be mocked
caude·us -a -um *adj* wooden
caud·ex -icis *m* **(cōd-)** trunk *(of tree);* block *(of wood to which one was tied for punishment);* book, tablet; ledger; *(coll)* blockhead
caudicāl·is -is -e *adj* wood-splitting
Caudīn·us -a -um *adj* of Caudium, Caudine; **Furculae Caudīnae** Caudine Forks *(where Romans suffered a great defeat at the hands of Samnites in 321 B.C.)*
Caud·ium -(i)ī *n* town in Samnium *(near which was the mountain pass where the Romans were defeated)*
caul·ae -ārum *fpl* fence; sheepfold; opening, hole; **caulae corporis** *(anat)* pores
caulicul·us -ī *m* small stalk; small cabbage
caul·is -is *f* stalk, stem; cabbage
caup·ō -ōnis *m* innkeeper
caupōn·a -ae *f* inn, tavern; innkeeper *(female);* retail shop
caupōni·us -a -um *adj* of an inn *or* shop
caupōn·or -ārī -ātus sum *tr* to trade in, traffic in
caupōnul·a -ae *f* small inn; small shop
Caur·us *or* **Cor·us -ī** *m* the northwest wind
caus·a *or* **causs·a -ae** *f* cause, grounds, motive, reason; good reason, just cause; pretext, pretense; inducement, occasion; side, party, faction; condition, situation, position; responsibility, blame; *(leg)* case, trial, plea; *(med)* case, symptoms; *(rhet)* matter of discussion, subject matter; matter, business, concern; **causā** *(postpositive) (w. gen)* for the sake of, because of; **animī causā** for the sake of amusement; **causae amīcitiae** ties of friendship; **causae necessitūdinis** friendly relations; **causam agere** *(or* **dīcere** *or* **ōrāre)** to plead a case; **causam cognōscere** *(of a judge)* to examine a case; **in causā esse** to be responsible; **meā causā** for my sake; as far as I am concerned, for all I care; **nōn sine causā** with good reason; **ob hanc causam** because of this; **per causam** *(w. gen)* under the pretense of; **valētūdinis causā** for reasons of (poor) health; **vestrā causā** in your interests
causāri·us -a -um *adj* sick; **missiō causāria** *(mil)* medical discharge **||** *m* soldier with medical discharge
causi·a -ae *or* **cause·a -ae** *f* wide-brimmed Macedonian hat
causidic·us -ī *m* lawyer; *(pej)* shyster
causific·or -ārī -ātus sum *intr* to make excuses
caus·or -ārī -ātus sum *tr* to give as an excuse, pretend
caussa *see* **causa**
causul·a -ae *f* poor reason; *(leg)* petty lawsuit
cautē *adv* cautiously, carefully; without risk
cautēl·a -ae *f* precaution, caution
caut·ēs -is *f* **(cōt-)** *(usu. pl)* rock, crag, cliff; *(fig)* hard-heartedness
cautim *adv* warily, cautiously
cauti·ō -ōnis *f* caution, wariness; guarantee, provision; *(leg)* bond, bail; **mea** *(or* **mihi)** **cautiō est** I must see to it, I must take care
caut·or -ōris *m* wary person; *(leg)* bondsman
caut·us -a -um *pp of* **caveō ||** *adj* cautious, careful; safe, secure
cavaed·ium -(i)ī *n* inner court of a Roman house
cave·a -ae *f* cavity; enclosure for animals: cage, den, hole, stall, beehive; auditorium *(of a theater);* **prīma cavea** section of auditorium for nobility; **ultima cavea** section for lower classes
caveō cavēre cāvī cautus *tr* to guard against, beware of; to keep clear of; to stipulate, decree, order; to guarantee; **cavē canem**! beware of the dog! **||** *intr* to be careful, look out, be on one's guard; *(w. abl or* **ab)** to be on one's guard against; *(w.* **ab)** to get a guarantee from; *(w. dat)* **1** to guarantee, give a guarantee to; **2** to provide for, take care of; **cavē tangere** (= **nōlī tangere**)! do not touch! **||** *impv with subj* **1** *without* **nē** take care not to, don't; **2** *with* **ut** take care to
cavern·a -ae *f* hollow; cavity *(in tooth);* cavern; hole; den, lair; hold *(of ship);* **caverna caelī** vault of the sky
cavill·a -ae *f* jeering, scoffing
cavillāti·ō -ōnis *f* banter, scoffing; quibbling

cavillāt·or -ōris *m* scoffer; quibbler

cavill·or -ārī -ātus sum *tr* to scoff at, mock, criticize, satirize ‖ *intr* to scoff, jeer; to quibble

cav·ō -āre -āvī -ātus *tr* to hollow out, excavate, dig a hole in; to pierce, run through

cav·us -a -um *adj* hollow, hollowed; concave, vaulted; deep-channeled *(river)* ‖ *m & n* depression; cave, cavern; burrow, hole *(of an animal);* hole, cavity, hollow; aperture, perforation; **cavum aedium** inner court of a house

-ce demonstrative enclitic appended to pronouns and adverbs (like colloquial English *here, there,* with *this* or *that);* **hīce** *(for* **hicce**) this *(here);* **huiūsce** of this *(here);* (when followed by the enclytic **-ne,** the form becomes **-ci: hīcine, sīcine**)

Cē·a *or* **Cī·a -ae** *or* **Cē·os -ī** *f* Ceos *(Greek island in the Cyclades)*

Cecropi·a -ae *f* Athens, the citadel of Athens

Cecropid·ēs -ae *m* descendant of King Cecrops; **Cecropidae** Athenians

Cecrop·is -idis *or* **idos** *f* female descendant of Cecrops; Aglauros; Procne; Philomela; Athenian woman

Cecropi·us -a -um *adj* of Cecrops; Athenian

Cecr·ops -opis *m* first king of Athens

cēd·ēns -entis *adj* unresisting

cedo *(pl:* **cette**) *(old impv)* give here, hand over, bring here; let's hear, tell, out with; look at; **cedo dum**! all right! **cedo ut īnspiciam** let me have a look

cēdō cēdere cessī cessus *tr* to grant, concede, yield, give up ‖ *intr* to go, move, walk, walk along; to go away, depart, withdraw; *(usu. w.* **vītā**) to pass away, die; *(of time)* to pass; *(of events)* turn out; *(w. dat)* **1** to befall, fall to the lot of; **2** to yield to, submit to, give in to; **3** to be inferior to; **4** to comply with, conform to, obey; *(w.* **in** + *acc)* **1** to result in; **2** to be changed into, become; *(w.* **prō** + *abl)* **1** to pass for; **2** to be the equivalent of; **3** to be the price of; **bonīs** *(or* **possessiōnibus**) **alicui cēdere** to give up *or* cede one's property to s.o.; **forō cēdere** to go bankrupt

cedr·us -ī *f* cedar; cedarwood; cedar-wood oil

Celaen·ō -ūs *f* daughter of Atlas and one of the Pleiades ‖ one of the Harpies ‖ greedy woman

cēlāt·um -ī *n* secret

cele·ber -bris -bre *adj* crowded, populous, frequented; well-attended; famous; well-known, common, usual; solemn, festive; numerous, repeated, frequent

celebrāti·ō -ōnis *f* large assembly; festival, celebration; widespread use ‖ *fpl* throngs

celebrāt·us -a -um *adj* crowded, populous; much-frequented; celebrated, famous; solemn, festive; common, current

celebrit·ās -ātis *f* crowd; large assembly; publicity; frequency; fame

celebr·ō -āre -āvī -ātus *tr* to frequent; to crowd, fill; to inhabit; to celebrate, observe; to honor, worship; to escort, attend; to practice, exercise; to announce, publicize; **sermōne celebrāre** to discuss

cel·er -eris -ere *adj* fast; agile, quick; hurried; rash, hasty; passing quickly

celere *adv* quickly

Celer·ēs -um *mpl* mounted bodyguards of Roman kings

celerip·ēs -edis *adj* swift-footed ‖ *m* race horse

celerit·ās -ātis *f* speed; quickness; excessive speed

celeriter *adv* quickly; soon, early

celer·ō -āre -āvī *tr* to quicken, speed up ‖ *intr* to be quick, rush, hurry

celeum·a -atis *n* boatswain's call *(giving time to the rowers)*

Cele·us -ī *m* king of Eleusis and father of Triptolemus

cell·a -ae *f* storeroom; silo; small room; *(coll)* hole-in-the-wall, poor man's apartment; sanctuary *(of temple where statue stood);* cell *(of beehive);* cubicle *(in a bathing establishment or in a brothel);* porter's room

cellāri·us -a -um *adj* of a storeroom ‖ *m* one in charge of the storeroom

cellul·a -ae *f* **(-ola)** small storeroom; small room; porter's lodge; slave's room

cēl·ō -āre -āvī -ātus *tr* to hide, conceal; to keep secret, keep quiet about; to conceal the identity of; *(w. acc of thing and acc of person from whom one conceals)* to keep *(s.o.)* in the dark about *(s.th.),* hide *(s.th.)* from *(s.o.)* ‖ *refl & pass* to pass out of view; **cēlārī dē** *(w. abl)* to be kept in ignorance of

cel·ōx -ōcis *adj* swift, quick ‖ *f* light, fast boat

cels·us -a -um *adj* high, lofty, towering, prominent; erect; lofty *(thoughts);* high *(rank);* proud; *(of head)* held high; tall *(animals, person, trees, buildings)*

Celt·ae -ārum *mpl* Celts

Celtib·ēr -ērī *mpl* a Celtiberian ‖ *mpl* Celtiberians *(early people of central Spain)*

cēn·a -ae *f* dinner; dish, course; **ad cēnam invītāre** *or* **vocāre** to invite to dinner; **caput cēnae** main dish; **cēnam appōnere** to serve dinner; **in cēnā** for dinner; **inter cēnam** at table, during dinner

cēnācul·um -ī *n* dining room *(usually on the upper floor);* upper floor, attic; attic apartment

cēnātic·us -a -um *adj* dinner

cēnāti·ō -ōnis *f* dining room
cēnātōri·a -ōrum *npl* formal wear; dinner apparel
cēnāt·us -a -um *pp of* **cēnō** having dined; stuffed from feasting
cēnit·ō -āre *intr* to dine often
cēn·ō -āre -āvī -ātus *tr* to dine on, eat ‖ *intr* to dine, eat dinner
cēns·eō -ēre -uī -us *tr* to think, believe, suppose, imagine, expect; to esteem, appreciate, value; *(of senator)* to propose, move, vote; to recommend; to suggest, advise; *(of the Senate and other bodies and supreme magistrates)* to decide, resolve; *(of the censor)* to estimate, rate, assess, tax; to register *(possessions); (w. abl)* to measure by; **cēnseō** *(in replies)* I think so; **quid cēnsēs?** what is your opinion? *(formula used by the presiding magistrate to invite a senator to express his opinion)* ‖ *pass (w. abl)* to be valued for, have one's reputation based on; *(as deponent)* to reckon, count (as)
cēnsi·ō -ōnis *f* tax assessment; punishment *(imposed by the censor)*
cēns·or -ōris *m* censor *(one of two magistrates who took the census and exercised general control over morals);* severe judge of morals; critic
cēnsōri·us -a -um *adj* of the censors; subject to censure; rigid, stern; **fūnus cēnsōrium** public funeral; **homō cēnsōrius** ex-censor; **lēx cēnsōria** contract *(drawn up by censors)* for leasing buildings; **opus cēnsōrium** a fault *or* crime punished by the censors
cēnsūr·a -ae *f* office of censor, censorship; censure, criticism
cēns·us -ūs *m* census; register of the census; income bracket; wealth, property; rich presents; **cēnsum agere** *(or* **habēre)** to hold a census; **cēnsū prohibēre** to exclude from citizenship; **in cēnsum referre** to register in the census list
centaurē·um -ī *n* **(-i·um, -i·on)** centaury *(herb)*
Centaurē·us -a -um *adj* of Centaurs
Centaur·us -ī *m* Centaur *(half-man, half-horse); (astr)* Centaurus *(a constellation)*
centēn·ī -ae -a *adj* one hundred each; **deciēns centēna mīlia passuum** ten hundred thousand (one million) paces, one thousand miles
centēsim·us -a -um *adj* hundredth ‖ *f* hundredth part, one percent; *(com)* 1% monthly, 12% annually
centi·ceps -cipitis *adj* hundred-headed
centiēs *adv* **(-iēns)** a hundred times; *(fig)* a good many times
centiman·us -a -um *adj* hundred-handed
cent·ō -ōnis *f* patchwork, quilt
centr·um -ī *n* center
centum *indecl adj* hundred
centumgemin·us -a -um *adj* hundredfold
centumpl·ex -icis *adj* hundredfold
centumpond·ium -(i)ī *n* hundred pounds, hundred-pound weight
centumvirāl·is -is -e *adj* of the centumvirs
centumvir·ī -ōrum *mpl* panel of one hundred *(jurors chosen annually to try civil suits under a quaestor, esp. concerning inheritances)*
centuncul·us -ī *m* piece of patchwork; blanket *(made of patchwork)*
centuri·a -ae *f (mil)* company, century *(nominally 100 soldiers); (pol)* century, voting division; unit of land *(100 heredia, 200 jugera, i.e., c. 133 acres)*
centuriātim *adv (mil, pol)* by companies *or* centuries
centuriāt·us -a -um *adj (mil, pol)* divided into companies *or* centuries; **comitia centuriāta** centuriate assembly *(legislative body that met in the Campus Martius to elect high magistrates, decree war, etc.)*
centuriāt·us -ūs *m* rank of centurion; division into centuries
centuri·ō -āre -āvī -ātus *tr* to divide into centuries *or* companies
centuri·ō -ōnis *m* centurion *(commander of an infantry company)*
centuriōnāt·us -ūs *m* rank of centurion; revision of the list of centurions
centuss·is -is *m* copper coin, worth about one dollar
cēnul·a -ae *f* light dinner
cēnum *see* **caenum**
Ceōs *see* **Cēa**
cēpa *or* **cēpe** *see* **caepa**
Cephallāni·a -ae *f* Greek island in the Ionian Sea
Cephal·us -ī *m* husband of Procris, whom he accidentally killed
Cēphē·is -idos *f* daughter of Cepheus *(Andromeda)*
Cephēi·us -a -um *adj* descended from Cepheus
Cēphēn·es -um *mpl* a people of Ethiopia
Cēphēn·us -a -um *adj* of the Cephenes, Ethiopian
Cēph·eūs -eī *m* king of the Cephenes *(Ethiopia),* father of Andromeda
Cēphīs·os -ī *m* Cephissus *(river in Attica; river in Phocis)*
cēr·a -ae *f* wax; writing tablet *(covered with wax);* wax seal; wax bust of an ancestor; cell *(of beehive);* **prīma cēra** first page
Ceramb·us -ī *m* herdsman, changed into a beetle
Ceramīc·us -ī *m* cemetery of Athens
cērār·ium -(i)ī *n* fee for affixing a seal
cerast·ēs -ae *m* horned serpent
ceras·um -ī *n* cherry
ceras·us -ī *f* cherry tree; cherry
cērāt·us -a -um *adj* waxed ‖ *n* wax-salve *(made of wax and oil)*

Cerber·us -ī *m* three-headed dog guarding entrance to lower world
cercopithēc·us -ī *m* long-tailed monkey
cercūr·us -ī *m* swift-sailing ship
cerd·ō -ōnis *m* (common) laborer
Cereāl·is -is -e *adj* of Ceres; of grain; **arma Cereālia** utensils for grinding and baking **II** *npl* festival of Ceres *(April 10)*
cerebrōs·us -a -um *adj* hot-headed
cerebr·um -ī *n* brain; head, skull; hot temper; *(fig)* brains
Cer·ēs -eris *f* goddess of grain and fruits and mother of Proserpina; grain, wheat; bread; food
cēre·us -a -um *adj* of wax, waxen; wax-colored; soft, pliant **II** *m* taper
cērinth·a -ae *f* wax flower
cērin·us -a -um *adj* wax-colored
Cermal·us -ī *m* **(Germ-)** part of the Palatine Hill in Rome
cernō cernere crēvī crētus *tr* to sift; to distinguish, make out, see; to understand, see; to decide, decree, determine; **hērēditātem cernere** to accept an inheritance formally; **vītam cernere** to decide a question of life or death
cernu·us -a -um *adj* leaning forward; headfirst
cērōm·a -atis *n* wrestler's oil; *(fig)* wrestler
cērōmatic·us -a -um *adj* smeared with oil, oily, greasy
cerrit·us -a -um *adj* possessed by Ceres, crazy, frenzied
certām·en -inis *n* contest, match; rivalry; *(mil)* battle, combat
certātim *adv* with a struggle, in rivalry
certāti·ō -ōnis *f* contest; rivalry, discussion, debate
certē *adv* surely, certainly; of course; *(in answers)* certainly; *(to restrict an assertion)* at least
certō *adv* for sure; in fact, really; **certō scīre** to know for sure
cert·ō -āre -āvī -ātus *tr* to contest **II** *pass* to be fought over **II** *intr (w.* **dē** *+ abl)* to fight over, struggle for; *(w.* **cum)** to fight with, struggle with, compete with; *(w. inf)* to strive to; *(leg)* to debate
cert·us -a -um *adj* certain, sure; fixed; regular; specific, particular, definite; faithful, trusty; unerring; unwavering; **certiōrem facere** to inform; **certum est mihi** *(w. inf)* I am determined to **II** *n* certainty; **certum habēre** to regard as certain; **prō certō** for sure; **prō certō habēre** to be assured, regard as certain
cērul·a -ae *f* piece of wax; crayon; **cērula miniāta** "red pencil" *(of a critic)*
cēruss·a -ae *f* ceruse, white paint
cērussāt·us -a -um *adj* painted white
cerv·a -ae *f* doe
cervīc·al -ālis *n* pillow, cushion
cervīcul·a -ae *f* slender neck
cervīn·us -a -um *adj* of a stag
cerv·īx -īcis *f (often in plural with same meaning as singular)* neck, nape; **in cervīcibus nostrīs esse** *(fig)* to be on our necks; **ā cervīcibus nostrīs āvertere** *(fig)* to get *(s.o.)* off our necks; **cervīcibus sustinēre** to shoulder *(responsibility)*
cerv·us -ī *m* stag, deer; *(mil)* palisade
cessāti·ō -ōnis *f* cessation; letup; delay; idleness, inactivity
cessāt·or -ōris *m* loafer
cessāt·us -a -um *adj* having been in abeyance; *(of land)* having been left fallow; spent in idleness
cessi·ō -ōnis *f (leg)* surrendering
cess·ō -āre -āvī -ātum *intr* to cease; to let up, slack off, become remiss; to be idle, do nothing; to lie fallow; to fail, not function; *(w. inf)* to hesitate to, be slow to; *(of things)* to stop, give out; *(of things)* to be at rest, be motionless; *(of things)* to be neglected, remain unused; *(w. abl or* **ab)** to be free of, be clear of, be wanting in; *(leg)* to fail to take action, default; *(leg)* to fail to appear in court
cessus *pp of* **cēdō**
cest·os *or* **cest·us -ī** *m* brassière
cestrosphendon·ē -ēs *f* artillery piece for hurling stones
cētār·ium -(i)ī *n* fish pond
cētār·ius -(i)ī *m* fishmonger; fisherman
cētē *see* **cētus**
cētera *adv* otherwise, in all other respects, for the rest
cēterōquī(n) *adv* otherwise, in all other respects, for the rest
cēterum *adv* but, still; for the rest, otherwise; however that may be
cēter·(us) -a -um *adj (nom singl masc not in use)* the other, the remaining, the rest of **II** *pron masc pl & fem pl* the others, all the rest, everybody else **II** *n* the rest; **dē cēterō** for the rest; otherwise; for the future; **in cēterum** in the future
Cethēg·us -ī *m* Gaius Cornelius Cethegus *(fellow conspirator of Catiline)*
cette *see* **cedo**
cēt·us *or* **cēt·os -ī** *(nom & acc npl:* **cētē)** *m* large sea animal: whale, shark, dolphin, seal; sea-monster
ceu *conj (in comparisons)* as, just as; *(in comparative conditions)* as if, just as if; **ceu cum** as when
cēv·eō -ēre *intr (cf.* **crīsō)** *(of a male) (sl)* to move the hips, shake it up
Cē·ÿx -ÿcis *m* king of Trachis, changed into a kingfisher *(bird)*
Chaerōnē·a -ae *f* town in Boeotia where Philip of Macedon defeated the Greeks in 338 B.C.
Chalcidic·us -a -um *adj* of Chalchis *(in Euboea);* of Cumae *(in Italy)*

Chaldae·us -a -um *adj* Chaldean ‖ *m* astrologer, fortuneteller
chalybēï·us -a -um *adj* of steel, steel
Chalyb·es -um *mpl* people of Pontus in Asia Minor noted as steel-workers and iron-workers
chal·ybs -ybis *m* steel; iron
Chāon·es -um *mpl* tribe in Epirus
Chāoni·us -a -um *adj* Chaonian; of Epirus ‖ *f* Chaonia *(in Epirus)*
Cha·os -ī *n* chaos, the unformed world; **ā Chaō** from the beginning of the world
char·a -ae *f* wild cabbage (?)
Charit·ēs -um *fpl* the Graces
Char·ōn -ōntis *m* ferryman of the lower world
chart·a -ae *f* sheet of papyrus, paper; thin sheet of metal ‖ *fpl (fig)* writings
chartul·a -ae *f* sheet of papyrus, slip of paper; note
Charybd·is -is *f* whirlpool between Italy and Sicily *(regarded as a female monster); (fig)* cruel person
Chatt·ī -ōrum *mpl* Germanic tribe
Chauc·ī -ōrum *mpl* Germanic tribe
Chēl·ae -ārum *fpl (astr)* the Claws *(of the constellation Scorpio); (astr)* Libra
chelydr·us -ī *m* poisonous water snake
chelys *(gen not in use; acc:* **chelyn)** *f* tortoise; lyre
cheragr·a -ae *f* arthritis in the hand
Cheronēs·us -ī *f* **(Cherson-)** a peninsula, *esp.* **Cheronēsus Thrācia** the Chersonese *(now Gallipoli)*
chīliarch·ēs -ae *or* **chīliarch·us -ī** *m* commander of 1,000 men; Persian chancellor *(highest office next to the king)*
Chimaer·a -ae *f* fire-breathing female monster, with lion's head, goat's body, and dragon's tail
Chimaerifer·a -ae *adj (fem only) (of Lycia)* that produced the Chimaera
Chi·os *or* **Chi·us -ī** *f* Chios *(Greek island off the coast of Ionia)*
chīrograph·um -ī *n* **(-graf-)** one's handwriting; autograph; manuscript; written promise; **falsum chīrographum** forgery
Chīr·ō(n) -ōnis *m* Chiron *(Centaur, tutor of Hercules, Achilles, etc.); (astr)* Chiron *(constellation)*
chīronom·ōn -untos *adj* gesticulating ‖ *mf* gesticulator
chīronom·os -ī *m* pantominist
chīrūrgi·a -ae *f* surgery
chīrūrgic·us -ī *m* surgeon
chīrūrg·us -ī *m* surgeon
Chi·us -a -um *adj & mf* Chian ‖ *n* Chian wine ‖ *npl* Chian cloth
chlamydāt·us -a -um *adj* wearing a military cape
chlam·ys -ydis *f* Greek military cape; gold-brocaded cape
Choeril·us -ī *m* incompetent panegyrist of Alexander the Great
chorāg·ium -(i)ī *n* stage properties
chorāg·us -ī *m* theatrical producer
choraul·ēs -ae *m* flute player *(who accompanied the choral dance)*
chord·a -ae *f* string *(of musical instrument);* cord, rope
chore·a -ae *f* dance
chorē·us -ī *m* trochee (— ⏑)
chorocitharist·ēs -ae *m* one who accompanied a chorus on the cithara
chor·us -ī *m* chorus; choir
Chrem·ēs -ētis *or* **-is** *or* **-ī** *m* miserly old character in plays of Terence
Christiān·us -ī *m* Christian
Christ·us -ī *m* Christ
Chrȳsē·is -idis *or* **-idos** *f* Agamemnon's slave girl, daughter of Chryses
Chrȳs·ēs -ae *m* priest of Apollo
Chrȳsipp·us -ī *m* famous Stoic philosopher *(290–210 B.C.)*
chrȳsolith·os -ī *m* chrysolite, topaz
chrȳs·os -ī *m* gold
cibāri·us -a -um *adj* of food; common, coarse *(food for slaves)* ‖ *npl* rations, provisions, food allowance
cibāt·us -ūs *m* food; feed, fodder
cib·ō -āre -āvī -ātus *tr* to feed
cibōr·ium -(i)ī *n* chalice
cib·us -ī *m* food; feed; meal; nutriment; fuel; **cibum capere** to take food, eat food, eat a meal
cicād·a -ae *f* cicada; harvest fly
cicātrīcōs·us -a -um *adj* scarred, covered with scars
cicātr·īx -īcis *f* scar
cicc·us -ī *m* core of pomegranate; *(sl)* junk
cic·er -eris *m* chickpea; testicle
Cicer·ō -ōnis *m* Cicero *(Marcus Tullius Cicero, orator and politician, 106–43 B.C.)* ‖ Quintus Tullius Cicero *(his brother, 102–43 B.C.)* ‖ Marcus Tullius Cicero *(his son, consul in 30 B.C.)*
cichorē·um *or* **cichōri·um -ī** *n* endive
cicima(li)ndr·um -ī *n* comic name for an imaginary seasoning
Cicon·es -um *mpl* Thracian tribe
cicōni·a -ae *f* stork
cic·ur -uris *adj* tame
cicūt·a -ae *f* hemlock tree; hemlock poison; pipe, flute *(carved from hemlock wood)*
-cīd·a -ae *m suf* denoting one who cuts *or* kills *(e.g.,* **lapicīda** stonecutter; **mātricīda** murderer of one's mother)
cidar·is -is *f* tiara *(of Persian king)*
cieō ciēre cīvī citus *tr* to set in motion, move; to stir up, rouse up, muster; to call for, send for; to summon for help; to invoke, appeal to; to bring about; to cause, make; **lacrimās ciēre** to shed tears; **strāgem ciēre** to wreak havoc

Cilici·a -ae *f* country and Roman province in S.E. Asia Minor
cilic·ium -(i)ī *n* rug *or* blanket of goat's hair
Cilici·us -a -um *adj* Cilician ‖ *n* garment made of goat's hair
Ciliss·a -ae *f* Cilician woman
Cil·ix -icis *adj & m* Cilician
-cill·um -ī *neut suf* forms diminutives: **cor-cillum** little heart
-cill·us -ī *masc suf* forms diminutives from diminutives: **penicillus** (small) painter's brush
Cim·ber -brī *m* Cimbrian ‖ Roman family name *(cognomen)*
Cimbr·ī -ōrum *mpl* Germanic tribe that invaded Gaul and Italy at the end of the 2nd cent. B.C. and was defeated by Marius
Cimbric·us -a -um *adj* Cimbrian
cīm·ex -icis *m* bedbug; *(pej)* vermin
Cimmeri·ī -ōrum *mpl* people in the Crimea ‖ mythical people living in perpetual darkness in caves between Baiae and Cumae
cinaedic·us -a -um *adj* lewd
cinaed·us -ī *m* catamite; homosexual
cincinnāt·us -a -um *adj* curly-haired ‖ **Cincinnātus** *m* Lucius Quinctius Cincinnatus *(Roman war hero, appointed dictator in 458 B.C.)*
cincinn·us -ī *m* a curl, lock of curled hair; *(rhet)* artificial expression
Cinci·us -a -um *adj* name of a Roman gens *(nomen);* L. Cincius Alimentus *(Roman historian of the Second Punic War)*
cīncticul·us -ī *m* small belt *or* sash
cīnctūr·a -ae *f* belt, sash
cīnctus *pp of* **cingō**
cīnct·us -ūs *m* tucking up; belt, sash; **cīnctus Gabinius** Gabinian style of wearing the toga *(usually employed at religious festivals; it was tucked up, its corner drawn over the left shoulder and under the right arm)*
cīnctūt·us -a -um *adj* wearing a belt *or* sash; old-fashioned
Cine·ās -ae *m* a friend of King Pyrrhus, who advised Pyrrhus to make peace with the Romans
cinefact·us -a -um *adj* reduced to ashes
cinerār·ius -(i)ī *m* hairdresser
cin·gō -gere cīnxī cīnctus *tr* to surround, encircle; to escort; to enclose *(a space);* to wreathe *(head);* to tuck up *(garment); (mil)* to cover, protect ‖ *pass* to get dressed; to form a circle; **cingī in proelia** to gear up for battle; **ferrum cingī** to put on one's sword; **Hispānō gladiō cingitur** he puts on a Spanish sword
cingul·a-ae *f* belt; sash; girth; sword belt; chastity belt
cingul·um -ī *n* belt; sword belt; sash; girdle; chastity belt
cingul·us -ī *m* zone *(of the earth)*
ciniflō·ō -ōnis *m* hairdresser
cin·is -eris *m (f)* ashes; ruin, death
-cin·ium -(i)ī *neut suf* denoting activity or profession *(e.g.,* **latrōcinium** robbing, robbery)
Cinn·a -ae *m* Lucius Cornelius Cinna *(notorious consul 87–84 B.C.)*
cinnamōm·um *or* **cinnam·um -ī** *n* cinnamon ‖ *npl* cinnamon sticks
cīnxī *perf of* **cingō**
Cinyr·ās -ae *m* father of Myrrha, and, by her, also father of Adonis
cipp·us -ī *m* stake, post, pillar; gravestone; *(mil)* palisade
circā *adv* around, round about; all around, in the vicinity ‖ *prep (w. acc)* around, surrounding, about, in the neighborhood of, near; through; attending, escorting; concerning, in respect to; *(of time)* around, about, toward; *(w. numbers)* about, nearly, almost
Circa *see* **Circē**
Circae·us -a -um *adj* of Circe
circāmoer·ium -(i)ī *n* area on both sides of a city wall
Circ·ē -ēs *or* **Circ·a -ae** *f* Circe *(famous witch, daughter of Sol and Perse)*
circēns·is -is -e *adj* of the racetrack ‖ *mpl* races
circin·ō -āre -āvī -ātus *tr* to make round; to circle
circin·us -ī *m (geometer's)* compass
circiter *adv* about, nearly, approximately ‖ *prep (w. acc)* about, near
circlus *see* **circulus**
circ(u)l·us -ī *m* circle, circuit; ring, hoop; social circle; *(astr)* orbit
circueō *see* **circumeō**
circuitiō *see* **circumitiō**
circuit·us -ūs *m* circuit; going around, revolution; detour; circumference; beating around the bush; *(rhet)* period
circulātim *adv* in groups
circulāt·or -ōris *m* peddler; itinerant performer
circulātr·īx -īcis *f* peddler *(female);* itinerant performer *(female)*
circul·or -ārī -ātus sum *intr* to gather a crowd around oneself; to stroll about
circum *adv* about, all around ‖ *prep (w. acc)* around, about; in the neighborhood of
circum- *suf* around, about: **circumstāre** to stand around
circu(m)iti·ō -ōnis *f* going around; patrolling; beating around the bush
circum·agō -agere -ēgī -āctus *tr* to turn around; to turn *(e.g., a wheel);* to sway ‖ *refl & pass* to turn around; *(of feelings)* to change; to change *(in form);* to go out of one's way; *(of time)* to pass, roll around
circumar·ō -āre -āvī *tr* to plow around
circumcaesūr·a -ae *f* contour, outline

circumcī·dō -dere -dī -sus *tr* to cut around, trim; to cut short; to cut down on *(expenses);* to abridge, shorten; to circumcise
circumcircā *adv* all around
circumcīs·us -a -um *pp of* **circumcīdō ‖** *adj* steep, inaccessible; abridged
circumclū·dō -dere -sī -sus *tr* to shut in, enclose; *(mil)* to surround; *(fig)* circumvent
circumcol·ō -ere *tr* to live near
circumcurs·ō -āre -āvī *tr & intr* to run around
circum·dō -dare -dedī -datus *tr* to surround, enclose, encircle; *(w. dat)* to place *or* put *(s.th.)* around
circumdū·cō -cere -xī -ctus *tr* lead around, draw around; *(w. double acc)* to lead *(s.o.)* around to; **aliquem omnia praesidia circumdūcere** to lead s.o. around to all the garrisons
circumducti·ō -ōnis *f* perimeter; *(w. gen)* cheating out of; *(rhet)* period
circum·eō -īre -īvī *or* **-iī -itus** *tr* to go around, go around to, visit, make the rounds of; to surround, encircle, encompass; to circumvent, deceive, cheat **‖** *intr* to go around, make a circuit
circumequit·ō -āre *tr* to ride around *(on horseback)*
circumerr·ō -āre -āvi *tr & intr* to wander around, prowl around
circum·ferō -ferre -tūlī -lātus *tr* to carry around, hand around; to publicize, spread around; to purify; **oculōs circumferre** to glance about **‖** *pass* to revolve
circumfle·ctō -ctere -xī -xus *tr* to turn around, wheel about
circumfl·ō -āre *tr* to blow around; *(fig)* to buffet
circumflu·ō -ere -xī *tr* to flow around; to surround; to overflow **‖** *intr* to be overflowing, abound
circumflu·us -a -um *adj* flowing around; surrounded *(by water)*
circumforāne·us -a -um *adj* strolling about from market to market, itinerant; arouhd the forum
circumfrem·ō -ere -uī *intr* to groan all around
circum·fundō -fundere -fūdī -fūsus *tr* to pour around; to surround, cover, envelop **‖** *refl & pass* to crowd around; *(w. dat)* to cling to
circumgem·ō -ere *tr* to growl around *(e.g., a sheepfold)*
circumgest·ō -āre *tr* to carry around
circum·gredior -gredī -gressus sum *tr* to surround *(esp. to attack)*
circumiac·eō -ēre *intr (w. dat)* to lie near, border on, be adjacent to
circumiect·us -a -um *adj* surrounding, encompassing, taking in
circumiect·us -ūs *m* an encompassing
circum·iciō -icere -iēcī -iectus *tr* to throw *or* place around; to surround; *(w. dat)* to throw *(s.th.)* around *(s.o. or s.th.);* **fossam circumicere** to dig a trench all around
circumitus *see* **circuitus**
circumlāt·us -a -um *pp of* **circumferō**
circumlav·ō -āre *or* **-ere** *tr* to wash around, wash the sides of
circumlīg·ō -āre -āvī -ātus *tr* to bind; *(w. dat)* to tie *(s.th.)* to
circum·linō -linere (-lēvī) -litus *tr* to smear all over, to anoint; to cover; *(fig)* to clothe
circumlu·ō -ere *tr* to flow around
circumluvi·ō -ōnis *f* island *(formed by a river flowing in a new channel)*
circum·mittō -mittere -mīsī -missus *tr* to send around
circummūg·iō -īre *intr* to moo around
circummūn·iō -īre -īvī -ītus *tr* **(-moen-)** to fortify *(with wall, moat, etc.)*
circummūnīti·ō -ōnis *f* investment *(of town);* circumvallation
circumpadān·us -a -um *adj* situated along the Po River
circumpend·eō -ēre *intr* to hang around
circumplaud·ō -ere *tr* to applaud from every direction
circumple·ctor -ctī -xus sum *tr* to embrace; to surround
circumplic·ō -āre -āvī -ātus *tr* to wind up; to coil around; *(w. dat)* to wind *(s.th.)* around
circum·pōnō -pōnere -posuī -positus *tr (w. dat)* to place *or* set *(s.th.)* around
circumpōtāti·ō -ōnis *f* round of drinks
circumrēt·iō -īre *tr* to snare
circumrō·dō -dere -sī -sus *tr* to nibble all around; to hesitate to say; to slander
circumsaep·iō -īre -sī -tus *tr* **(-sēp-)** to fence in, enclose
circumscind·ō -ere *tr* to strip off
circumscrī·bō -bere -psī -ptus *tr* to draw a line around, mark the boundaries of; to limit, circumscribe; to set aside; to defeat the purpose of; to trap, defraud
circumscrīptē *adv* concisely; *(rhet)* in periodic style
circumscrīpti·ō -ōnis *f* encircling; circle; limits, boundary; outline, definition; cheating; *(rhet)* periodic sentence
circumscrīpt·or -ōris *m* cheat
circumscrīpt·us -a -um *pp of* **circumscrībō ‖** *adj* restricted; concise; *(rhet)* periodic, rounded-off
circumsec·ō -āre -uī -tus *tr* to cut around; to circumcise
circum·sedeō -sedēre -sēdī -sessus *tr* to beset, besiege, blockade
circumsēpiō *see* **circumsaepiō**
circumsessi·ō -ōnis *f* blockading
circum·sīdō -sīdere -sēdī -sessus *tr* to besiege, surround, invest

circumsil·iō -īre *tr & intr* to hop around
circum·sistō -sistere -stetī *tr* to stand around, surround
circumson·ō -āre -uī *tr* to make resound, cause to re-echo ‖ *intr* to resound everywhere; *(w. dat)* to resound to
circumson·us -a -um *adj* noisy
circumspectātr·īx -īcis *f* spy *(female)*
circumspecti·ō -ōnis *f* looking around; circumspection, caution
circumspect·ō -āre *tr* to watch for, search carefully for; to catch sight of ‖ *intr* to keep looking around, look around anxiously
circumspect·us -a -um *pp of* **circumspiciō** ‖ *adj* well-considered, guarded *(words);* circumspect, cautious
circumspect·us -ūs *m* consideration; commanding view; contemplation
circum·spiciō -spicere -spexī -spectus *tr* to look around at, survey; to catch sight of; to consider, examine ‖ *refl* to think highly of oneself ‖ *intr* to be circumspect, be cautious, be on the watch
circumstant·ēs -ium *mpl* bystanders
circum·stō -stāre -stetī *tr* to surround, envelop; *(of terror, etc.)* to grip ‖ *intr* to stand around
circumstrep·ō -ere -uī -itus *tr* to shout at on all sides, surround with noise *or* shouts
circumsurg·ēns -entis *adj (of mountains)* rising all around
circumtent·us -a -um *adj* tightly covered
circumter·ō -ere *tr* to rub shoulders with, crowd around
circumtext·us -a -um *adj* with embroidered border
circumton·ō -āre -uī *tr* to crash around, thunder around
circumtōns·us -a -um *adj* clipped *or* trimmed all around
circumvā·dō -dere -sī *tr* to attack on every side; *(of terror)* to grip
circumvag·us -a -um *adj* flowing around, encircling
circumvall·ō -āre -āvī -ātus *tr* to blockade ‖ *refl* to form a blockade
circumvecti·ō -ōnis *f* carting around *(of merchandise);* circular course, revolution *(of sun)*
circumvect·ō -āre -āvī -ātus *tr* to carry around ‖ *pass* to travel around, sail around
circumve·hor -hī -ctus sum *tr* to ride around (to), sail around (to), travel around (to); to travel past
circumvēl·ō -āre *tr* to envelop, cover
circum·veniō -venīre -vēnī -ventus *tr* to enclose, surround; to go around to; to distress, beset; to circumvent, cheat; to prosecute *or* convict unjustly
circumver·tō -tere -tī -sus *tr* **(-vor-)** to turn *(s.th.)* around ‖ *pass* to turn around; **rota circumvertitur axem** the wheel revolves around its axle
circumvest·iō -īre *tr* to clothe
circumvinc·iō -īre *tr* to tie up
circumvīs·ō -ere *tr* to look around, glare around at
circumvolit·ō -āre -āvī *tr & intr* to fly around, dash about, rove around; to hover around
circumvol·ō -āre -āvī *tr* to fly around, dart around ‖ *intr* to hover about, hover over, flit about
circumvol·vō -vere -vī -ūtus *tr* to wind, roll around ‖ *refl & pass (w. dat or acc)* to revolve around, wind oneself around
circ·us -ī *m* circle; racetrack; *(astr)* orbit
Circ·us Flāmini·us -ī *m* racetrack built by Gaius Flaminius Nepos in the Campus Martius in 220 B.C.
Circ·us Maxim·us -ī *m* oldest racetrack in Rome, between the Palatine and Aventine Hills
cirrāt·us -a -um *adj* curly-haired
Cirrh·a -ae *f* **(Cyrr-)** town near Delphi, sacred to Apollo
Cirrhae·us -a -um *adj* of Cirrha; of Apollo
cirr·us -ī *m* lock, curl; forelock
Cirt·a -ae *f* town in Numidia
Cirtēns·ēs -ium *mpl* inhabitants of Cirta
cis- *pref* used in the sense of the preposition
cis *prep (w. acc)* on this side of *(on the Roman side of); (of time)* within
Cisalpīn·us -a -um *adj* Cisalpine *(on the Roman side of the Alps)*
cis·ium -(i)ī *n* gig *(light, two-wheeled carriage)*
Cisp·ius -(i)ī *m* **(Cesp-)** one of the summits of the Esquiline Hill
Cisrhenān·us -a -um *adj* dwelling on the W. side of the Rhine
Cissē·is -idis *f* daughter of Cisseus *(i.e., Hecuba)*
Ciss·eūs -eī *m* king of Thrace and father of Hecuba
cist·a -ae *f* box, chest *(esp. of wicker, for clothes, money, books, etc.);* ballot box
cistell·a -ae *f* small box
cistellātr·īx -īcis *f* female slave in charge of the money box
cistellul·a -ae *f* small box
cistern·a -ae *f* cistern, reservoir
cistophor·us -ī *m* Asiatic coin *(with a representation of a bearer of the cista of Dionysus on it)*
cistul·a -ae *f* small box
citātim *adv* quickly, hurriedly
citāt·us -a -um *adj* rapid, speedy; *(of limbs)* moved quickly; *(of pace, actions)* quick, speedy; *(of bowels)* loose; **citātō equō** at full gallop
citāt·us -ūs *m* impulse
citeri·or -or -us *adj* on this side, near *(to Rome);* earlier; *(nearer to the present)*

later, more recent; more down-to-earth, nearer home; *(w. abl)* earlier than

Cithaer·ōn -ōnis *m* Greek mountain range dividing Attica from Boeotia

cithar·a -ae *f* lyre

citharist·a -ae *m* lyre player

citharistri·a -ae *f* lyre player *(female)*

cithariz·ō -āre *intr* to play the lyre

citharoed·us -ī *m* singer *(playing the lyre)*

citim·us -a -um *adj* (lying) nearest

citius *adv* sooner, rather; **dictō citius** no sooner said than done; **sērius aut citius** sooner or later

cito *adv* quickly; soon

cit·ō -āre -āvī -ātus *tr* to excite, rouse; to call, summon; to call to witness, appeal to; to arouse, produce; to cite *(as an authority)*

citrā *adv* on this side, on the near side; **citrā cadere** to fall short ‖ *prep (w. acc)* **1** on this side of, on the near side of: **citrā mare** on this side of the sea, in Italy; **2** *(of time)* since, before: **citrā Trōiāna tempora** before the Trojan period; **3** just short of, less than, except: **peccāvī citrā scelus** I committed a fault just short of a crime; **4** regardless of *(e.g., a person's wishes)*: **citrā senātūs populīque auctōritātem** regardless of *or* without regard for the authority of the senate and the people

citre·us -a -um *adj* of citrus wood

citrō *adv* to this side, this way; **ultrō (et) citrō** *(or* **citrō ultrōque)** to and fro, up and down; mutually

citr·um -ī *n* wood of the citron tree; table *(made of citron wood)*

citr·us -ī *f* citron tree

cit·us -a -um *pp of* **cieō** ‖ *adj* quick

cīvic·us -a -um *adj* civil; civilian; suitable for one as a civilian; **corōna cīvica** civic crown *(given to war hero for saving s.o.'s life)*

cīvīl·is -is -e *adj* civil, civic; civilian; forensic, legal; political; unassuming; **iūs cīvīle** private *or* civil law; civil rights; **ratiō cīvīlis** political science; **rēs cīvīlis** *(or* **cīvīlēs)** politics; **vir cīvīlis** statesman, politician

cīvīlit·ās -ātis *f* politics; courtesy

cīvīliter *adv* like a citizen; as an ordinary citizen should; politely

cīv·is -is *mf* citizen; fellow citizen; private citizen

cīvit·ās -ātis *f* state; community; city; citizenship

clād·ēs -is *f* disaster; loss; *(mil)* defeat, carnage; destruction; ruins; *(of person)* scourge, destroyer

clam *adv* secretly, privately; stealthily; **clam habēre aliquem** to keep s.o. in the dark ‖ *prep (w. abl or acc)* without the knowledge of; **neque clam mē est** nor is it unknown to me; **clam patre** without the father's knowledge

clāmāt·or -ōris *m* loudmouth

clāmitāti·ō -ōnis *f* bawling, racket

clāmit·ō -āre -āvī -ātus *tr & intr* to cry out, yell, to keep yelling

clām·ō -āre -āvī -ātus *tr* to shout, yell; to proclaim; to call upon ‖ *intr* to shout

clām·or -ōris *m* shout; acclamation; applause; battle cry; noise; wailing

clāmōsē *adv* with a shout, loudly

clāmōs·us -a -um *adj* yelling, noisy; loud-barking *(dog)*

clanculum *adv* secretly; privately ‖ *prep (w. acc)* unknown to

clandestīnō *adv* secretly

clandestīn·us -a -um *adj* clandestine

clang·ō -ere *intr (of eagle)* to scream

clang·or -ōris *m* clang, noise; blast *(of trumpet)*; cry, scream *(of bird)*; baying *(of dog)*

clārē *adv* clearly; out loud; brightly; with distinction, honorably; **clārē legere** to read aloud

clār·eō -ēre *intr* to be clear, be distinct, be bright; to be evident; to be famous

clār·ēsco -ēscere -uī *intr* to become clear, become distinct; to become bright; to become famous; *(of sound)* to get loud

clārigāti·ō -ōnis *f* reparation; fine

clārig·ō -āre -āvī -ātum *intr* to demand satisfaction, demand reparation

clārison·us -a -um *adj* clear-sounding

clārit·ās -ātis *f* loudness; clarity; brightness; distinction, renown

clāritūd·ō -inis *f* brightness; fame

Clari·us -a -um *adj* of the island of Claros, *esp.* as epithet of Apollo

clār·ō -āre -āvī -ātus *tr* to clarify, explain; to light up, illuminate; to make famous

Clar·os -ī *f* town in Asia Minor famous for a temple and oracle of Apollo

clār·us -a -um *adj* loud; clear, bright; plain, manifest; famous; notorious; **clāra lūx** broad daylight; **clārior lūce** clearer than daylight; **vir clārissimus** gentleman of the Senate

classiāri·us -a -um *adj* naval ‖ *mpl* marines

classicul·a -ae *f* flotilla

classic·us -a -um *adj* first-class, belonging to the highest class of citizens; classical; naval ‖ *m* trumpeter who summoned the *comitia centuriata* ‖ *mpl* marines, sailors ‖ *n* battle signal; bugle call; **classicum canere** to sound the bugle *(to begin battle; to announce a capital trial or an execution)*

class·is -is *f* fleet; *(social)* class; grade, class *(of pupils)*; band, group; **classī** with a fleet, at sea; in a naval battle

clāt(h)rāt·us -a -um *adj* barred

clāt(h)r·ī -ōrum *mpl* bars; railings

claud·eō -ēre *or* **claud·ō -ere** *intr* to be lame, to limp; to falter; to be imperfect

Claudiān·us -a -um *adj* connected with members of the Claudian clan, *esp.* the Emperor Claudius

claudicāti·ō -ōnis *f* limping

claudic·ō -āre *intr* to be lame, to limp; to incline to one side; to be halting, be defective; to be deficient, fall short

Claud·ius -(i)ī *m* Appius Claudius Caecus *(censor in 312 B.C. and builder of the Appian Way and Appian aqueduct)* **‖** the Roman Emperor Claudius *(Tiberius Claudius Nero Germanicus, reigned 41–54 A.D.)*

clau·dō -dere -sī -sus *tr* to shut, close; to bring to a close, conclude; to shut up; to lock up, imprison; *(mil)* to blockade, hem in; to limit; to cut off, block; to keep secret, suppress *(feelings, thoughts);* **agmen claudere** to bring up the rear; **numerīs** *(or* **pedibus)** **claudere** to put into verse; **trānsitum claudere** to block traffic

claud·us -a -um *adj* **(clōd-)** lame, limping; crippled, imperfect, defective; wavering; untrustworthy

claustell·um -ī *n* **(clos-)** keyhole

claustr·a -ōrum *npl* lock, bolt, bar; gate; dam, dike; barrier, barricade; cage, den; fortress; defenses

clausul·a -ae *f* close, conclusion *(of a letter, speech, argument; of a transaction);* clause *(in a law or document);* end *(of a word, of a line of verse); (rhet)* close of a periodic sentence with particular regard to its rhythm

claus·us -a -um *pp of* **claudō ‖** *adj* closed, inaccessible *(place); (of a person)* impervious to feelings; shut, locked up; enclosed *(in a container)* **‖** *n* enclosure

Claus·us -ī *m* a Sabine chief, reputed ancestor of the *gens Claudia* **‖** *mpl* members of the *gens Claudia*

clāv·a -ae *f* cudgel, club

clāvār·ium -iī *n* soldier's allowance for shoe nails

clāvāt·or -ōris *m* club-bearer

clāvicul·a -ae *f* tendril; key; pivot

clāvig·er -era -erum *adj* carrying a club; carrying keys **‖** *m* club bearer *(Hercules);* key bearer *(Janus)*

clāv·is -is *f* key; hook *(for rolling a hoop);* **clāvīs adimere uxōrī** to take the keys away from a wife, get a divorce

clāv·us -ī *m* nail; rivet; rudder, helm; purple stripe *(worn on the tunic, broad for senators and their sons, narrow for equites);* **clāvō** *(or* **clāvō trabālī)** **fīgere** to nail; *(fig)* to nail down, clinch; **clāvum rēctum tenēre** to keep a steady course; **clāvus annī** beginning of the year; **clāvus trabālis** spike *(large nail)*

clēm·ēns -entis *adj* gentle, mild, kind, compassionate; mild, calm *(weather)*

clēmenter *adv* gently, mildly, kindly, compassionately; at an easy pace; **collēs clēmenter assurgentēs** gently rising hills

clēmenti·a -ae *f* mildness, clemency, compassion

Cle·on -ōnis *m* rhetorician from Halicarnassus

Cleōn·ae -ārum *fpl* small town in Argolis near Nemea

Cleopatr·a -ae *f* daughter of Ptolemy Auletes and queen of Egypt *(d. 31 B.C.)*

clep·ō -ere -sī -tus *tr* to steal, swipe

clepsydr·a -ae *f* water clock; *(fig)* time *(allotted to speakers);* **clepsydram dare** *(w. dat)* to give *(s.o.)* the floor; **clepsydram petere** to ask to have the floor

clept·ēs *or* **·a -ae** *m* thief

clīban·us -ī *m* oven; bread plate

cli·ēns -entis *m* client *(e.g., ex-slave protected by a former owner acting as patron);* follower, retainer; vassal **‖** *mpl* clients *(the citizens of an Italian or other city in their relationship to their Roman patronus)*

client·a -ae *f* client *(female)*

clientēl·a -ae *f* clientele; patronage, protection; clientship *(the relationship of a provincial city or a foreign people to their Roman patronus);* vassalage **‖** *fpl* allies, dependants

clientul·us -ī *m (as term of contempt)* just a poor client

clīnām·en -inis *n* swerve

clīnāt·us -a -um *adj* bent, inclined, sunk

clīnic·us -ī *m* clinical physician *(who tends patients at their bedside)*

Clī·ō -ūs *f* Muse of history

clipeāt·us -a -um *adj* armed with a *(round)* shield

clipe·um -ī *n or* **clipe·us -ī** *m* round bronze shield; medallion; disc *(of sun)*

clītell·ae -ārum *fpl* packsaddle

clītellāri·us -a -um *adj* carrying a packsaddle

clīvōs·us -a -um *adj* hilly; steep

clīv·us -ī *m* sloping ground, incline, hill; slope, pitch; *(fig)* uphill struggle; **adversus clīvum** uphill; **prīmī clīvī** foothills

Clīv·us Sac·er *(gen:* **Clīv·ī Sac·rī)** *m* Sacred Incline *(part of the Via Sacra ascending the Capitoline Hill, also called* **Clīvus Capitōlīnus)**

cloāc·a -ae *f* sewer, drain; **cloāca maxima** main sewer *(draining the area of the Roman Forum)*

Cloācīn·a -ae *f* Venus *(the "purifier")*

Clōdi·a -ae *f* sister of the notorious tribune Clodius

Clōdiān·us -a -um *adj* Clodian, of the Clodian faction

Clōd·ius -(i)ī *m* Publius Clodius Pulcher *(notorious tribune of the plebs, enemy of Cicero, killed in 52 B.C.)*

Cloeli·a -ae *f* Roman girl who was given as hostage to Porsenna and escaped by swimming the Tiber back to Rome

Clōthō *(gen not in use; acc:* **Clōthō)** *f* one of the three Fates

clu·eō -ēre *or* **clu·eor -ērī** *intr* to be spoken of as, be known for; **ut nōmen cluet** as the word implies

clūn·is -is *mf* buttock ‖ *mpl & fpl* buttocks; hind quarters *(of an animal)*

clūr·a -ae *f* ape

clūrīn·us -a -um *adj* of apes

Clūs·ium -(i)ī *n* chief Etruscan town

Clūs·ius -(i)ī *m* Janus

Clymen·ē -ēs *f* mother of Phaëthon

clyst·ēr -ēris *m* an injection; *(fig)* syringe

Clyt(a)em(n)estr·a -ae *f* Clytemnestra *(wife of Agamemnon, sister of Helen, Castor, and Pollux, and mother of Electra, Iphigenia, and Orestes)*

Cn. *abbr* **Gnaeus** *(Roman first name, praenomen)*

Cnid·os *or* **Cnid·us -ī** *f* town in Caria, famous for the worship of Venus (*modern Knossis*)

Cnōss·us (Gnōss·us *or* **-os) -ī** *f* town in Crete, capital of King Minos

Cnōssi·us -a -um (Gnōs-) of Cnossus

coacervāti·ō -ōnis *f* accumulation

coacerv·ō -āre -āvī -ātus *tr* to gather into a heap; to accumulate; to make *(by heaping up)*

coac·ēscō -ēscere -uī *intr* to become sour; *(fig)* to go sour

coācti·ō -ōnis *f* collection *(of money);* abridgment

coāct·ō -āre *tr* to force

coāct·or -ōris *m* collector *(of money, taxes);* **agminis coāctōrēs** rearguard elements

coāct·us -a -um *pp of* **cōgō** ‖ *adj* forced, unnatural, hypocritical ‖ *n* felt cloth ‖ *npl* felt cloak

coāct·us -ūs *m* coercion, compulsion

coaedific·ō -āre -āvī -ātus *tr* to build *(a town);* to build up *(an area),* fill with buildings

coaequ·ō -āre -āvī -ātus *tr* to level off; to treat as equal, equate

coagmentāti·ō -ōnis *f* union; joint

coagment·ō -āre -āvī -ātus *tr* to join together; to glue, cement together; to construct; to fit *(words)* together

coagment·um -ī *n* joint

coāgul·um -ī *n* rennet *(curdled milk taken from the stomach of young mammals);* curds

coal·ēscō -ēscere -uī -itum *intr* **(cōl-)** to grow together, coalesce; *(of wounds)* to close; to become unified; to grow firm, take root; to become established, thrive

coangust·ō -āre -āvī -ātus *tr* **(conang-)** to contract, compress; to limit, restrict

coarct- *see* **coart-**

coargu·ō -ere -ī *tr* to bring out into the open *(usu. s.th. undesirable);* to prove conclusively, demonstrate; to refute, prove wrong *or* guilty; *(w. gen of the charge)* to prove *(s.o.)* guilty of

coartāti·ō -ōnis *f* crowding together; tightening

coart·ō -āre -āvī -ātus *tr* to narrow, make narrower; to crowd together, confine; to pack *(e.g., the Forum);* to shorten; to abridge

coax·ō -āre *intr (of frogs)* to croak

Cōcal·us -ī *m* mythical king of Sicily who protected Daedalus

Cocceï·us -a -um *adj* Roman clan name *(nomen), esp.* Marcus Cocceius Nerva, emperor A.D. 96–98

coccināt·us -a -um *adj* dressed in scarlet

coccin(e)·us -a -um *adj* scarlet ‖ *npl* scarlet clothes; scarlet coverlets

cocc·um -ī *n* scarlet dye, scarlet

coc(h)le·a -ae *f* snail

coc(h)leār·(e) -is *n* spoon

cocilendr·um -ī *n* an imaginary magical seasoning

cocl·es -itis *m* person blind in one eye ‖ **Cocles** Horatius Cocles *(commonly called Horatio and famous for defending the Pons Sublicius against Porsenna's army)*

coctil·is -is -e *adj* baked; brick

coct·or -ōris *m* cook

coct·us -a -um *pp of* **coquō** ‖ *adj* cooked; roasted; baked *(bricks);* ripe; *(fig)* mild ‖ *n* cooked food

coc·us -ī *m* **(coqu-)** cook

Cōcȳt·us -ī *m* river (of wailing) of the lower world

Cōdēt·a -ae *f* piece of ground in the Campus Martius

cōd·ex -icis *m* **(caud-)** trunk *(of tree);* block *(of wood to which one was tied for punishment);* book, tablet; ledger; *(coll)* blockhead

cōdicill·ī -ōrum *mpl* **(-cell-)** fire logs; set of writing tablets; note; petition to the emperor; rescript from the emperor; supplement to a will, codicil

Codr·us -ī *m* last king of Athens

coēgī *perf of* **cōgō**

coel- *see* **cael-**

Coel·ē -ēs *adj (fem only)* **Coelē Syria** "Hollow Syria" *(the S. part of Syria, esp. the region between Lebanon and Antilebanon);* **Coelē Thessalia** the plain of Thessaly

co·emō -emere -ēmī -emptus *tr* to buy up

coëmpti·ō -ōnis *f* fictitious sale of an estate; marriage *(contracted by fictitious sale of contracting parties)*
coëmptiōnāl·is -is -e *adj* of a marriage by fictitious sale
coen- *see* **caen-**
co·eō -īre -iī -itus *tr* **societātem coīre** to form an alliance ‖ *intr* to come together; to meet, assemble; to be united, combine; to mate, copulate; to have sexual intercourse; to congeal, curdle; to agree; to conspire; to clash *(in combat); (of wounds)* to close
coep·ī -isse -tus *(v. defect) tr & intr* to have begun
coept·ō -āre -āvī -ātus *tr* to begin eagerly; *(w. inf)* to try to ‖ *intr* to make a beginning
coept·um -ī *n* undertaking, enterprise
coept·us -ūs *m* beginning; undertaking
coëpulōn·us -ī *m* dinner guest
coërc·eō -ēre -uī -itus *tr* to enclose, confine, hem in; to limit; to restrain, check, control, keep in order
coërciti·ō -ōnis *f* physical restraint, coercion; inflicting of summary punishment by a magistrate; right to inflict summary punishment
coët·us -ūs *m* coming together, meeting; crowd, company; gang; combination
Coe·us -ī *m* Titan, father of Latona
cōgitātē *adv* deliberately, carefully
cōgitāti·ō -ōnis *f* thinking, deliberating; reflection; thought, plan, idea; reasoning power, imagination
cōgitāt·us -a -um *adj* well-considered, deliberate ‖ *npl* thoughts, ideas
cōgit·ō -āre -āvī -ātus *tr* to consider, ponder, reflect on; to imagine; *(w. inf)* to intend to ‖ *intr* to think
cognāti·ō -ōnis *f* relationship by birth; agreement, resemblance, affinity; relatives, family
cognāt·us -a -um *adj* related by birth; related, similar, akin ‖ *mf* relative
cogniti·ō -ōnis *f* learning, acquiring knowledge; knowledge; notion, idea; recognition; *(w. gen)* knowledge of, acquaintance with; *(leg)* inquiry, hearing, trial
cognit·or -ōris *m* attorney; defender, protector; witness
cognitūr·a -ae *f* the duty of an attorney
cognit·us *pp of* **cognōscō** ‖ *adj* acknowledged, known; familiar
cognit·us -ūs *m* act of getting to know; **dignus cognitū** worth knowing; **iucundus cognitū** pleasant to know
cognōm·en -inis *n* surname, family name *(e.g.,* **Caesar;** *a second* **cognōmen,** *called* **agnōmen** *by later grammarians, was given as an honorary name to a person for some achievement, e.g.,* **Āfricānus);** additional title of a god *(e.g.,* **Iupiter Feretrius);** nickname; derived name *(esp. of places);* **ā duce Tarpeiā mōns est cognōmen adeptus** the hill took its name from Tarpeia *(the enemy's)* guide
cognōment·um -ī *n* family name; name
cognōmināt·us -a -um *adj* synonymous; surnamed
cognōmin·is -is -e *adj* like-named, with the same name
cognōmin·ō -āre -āvī -ātus *tr* to give *(s.o.)* a surname *or* nickname
cogn·ōscō -ōscere -ōvī -itus *tr* to become acquainted with, get to know, learn; to recognize, identify; to inquire into, investigate; *(mil)* to reconnoiter; **cognōvisse** to know
cōgō cōgere coēgī coāctus *tr* to gather together, collect; to assemble; to round up; to gather *(crops);* to collect, raise *(money, taxes);* to force, compel; to pressure; to exact, extort; to infer, conclude; to prove conclusively; to compress *(into a mass);* to abridge; to shorten, restrict in time; to form *(e.g., wrinkles by contraction);* to thicken, condense, curdle; **agmen cōgere** to bring up the rear; **in ōrdinem cōgere** to bring to order, bring back into line
cohaer·ēns -entis *adj* adjoining, continuous; consistent; harmonious
cohaerenti·a -ae *f* organic structure
cohae·reō -rēre -sī -sum *intr* to stick *or* cling together, cohere; to be consistent, be in agreement; *(w.* **cum)** **1** to be closely connected with; **2** to be in harmony with; **3** to be consistent with; **inter sē cohaerēre** to be consistent
cohaerēsc·ō -ere cohaesī *intr* to stick together, cohere; to adhere
cohēr·ēs -ēdis *mf* joint-heir
cohib·eō -ēre -uī -itus *tr* to hold together, hold close; to confine; to clothe; to keep *(information, etc.)* secret, suppress; to check the growth of *(e.g., power);* to withold *(assent);* to hold back, repress *(emotions);* to check, stop *(an action, etc.); (w. acc & inf)* to prevent ‖ *refl* to remain, stay *(in a place);* to exercise self-restraint
cohonest·ō -āre *tr* to honor, pay respect to; to make respectable
cohorr·ēscō -ēscere -uī *intr* to shiver all over
cohor·s -tis *f* barnyard; retinue, escort; *(mil)* cohort *(comprising 3 maniples or 6 centuries and forming one-tenth of a legion, or 600 men)*
cohortāti·ō -ōnis *f* encouragement
cohorticul·a -ae *f* small cohort
cohort·or -ārī -ātus sum *tr* to encourage, cheer up, urge on

coïti·ō -ōnis *f* meeting; encounter; conspiracy; coalition
coït·us -ūs *m* meeting; junction, meeting place; sexual intercourse
col- *pref see* **con-**
-col·a -ae *masc suf* denotes a person who inhabits, tills, or worships: **amnicola** one who dwells near the river; **agricola** one who tills the field; **Iūnōnicola** one who worships Juno
colaph·us -ī *m* a punch
Colchic·us, Colch·us -a - um *adj* Colchian, of Colchis
Colch·is -idis *f* country on E. end of the Black Sea **||** Colchian woman, Medea
cōle·ī -ōrum *mpl (vulg)* balls; **sī cōleōs habērēmus** if we had the balls *(i.e., if we dared assert ourselves)*
col·ēns -entis *p of* **colō ||** *adj (w. gen)* devoted to
cōl·is -is *m* stalk; cabbage
collabāsc·ō -ere *intr* **(conl-)** to waver, totter
collabefact·ō -āre *tr* **(conl-)** to shake hard
collabe·fiō -fierī -factus sum *intr* **(conl-)** to collapse, be ruined; to sink down
collā·bor -bī -psus sum *intr* **(conl-)** to fall down, collapse; to sink
collacrimāti·ō -ōnis *f* **(conl-)** weeping
collacrim·ō -āre -āvī -ātus *tr* **(conl-)** to cry bitterly over **||** *intr* to cry together
collacte·a -ae *f* **(-ti·a)** foster sister
collār·e -is *n or* **collār·is -is** *m* collar
Collāti·a -ae *f* old town in Latium
Collātīn·us -ī *m* husband of Lucretia
collāti·ō -ōnis *f* **(conl-)** bringing together; contribution of money, collection, fund; comparison; *(gram)* comparison; **collātiō prīma** comparative; **collātiō secunda** superlative
collāt·or -ōris *m* **(conl-)** contributor
collātus *pp of* **cōnferō**
collaudāti·ō -ōnis *f* **(conl-)** warm praise
collaud·ō -āre -āvī -ātus *tr* **(conl-)** to praise highly
collax·ō -āre *tr* to loosen
collēct·a -ae *f* **(conl-)** contribution of money
collēctāne·us -a -um *adj* **(conl-)** collected from various sources
collēctīci·us -a -um *adj* **(conl-)** hastily gathered
collēcti·ō -ōnis *f* **(conl-)** gathering; recapitulation; inference; *(phil)* syllogism
collēctus *pp of* **colligō** (to collect)
collēct·us -ūs *m* collection
collēg·a -ae *m* **(conl-)** colleague *(in office)*; associate; fellow member
collēg·ium -(i)ī *n* **(conl-)** association in office; official body, board, college; guild, corporation; club, society
collībert·us -ī *m* **(conl-)** fellow ex-slave
collib·uit *or* **collub·uit -uisse -itum** *v impers* **(conl-)** it pleases
collī·dō -dere -sī -sus *tr* **(conl-)** to smash to pieces, crush; to strike together; to cause to clash, set at variance **||** *pass* to be at variance, conflict; *(of teeth)* to chatter
colligāti·ō -ōnis *f* **(conl-)** binding together, connection
collig·ō -āre -āvī -ātus *tr* **(conl-)** to tie together, connect; to stop, restrain, check
col·ligō -ligere -lēgī -lēctus *tr* **(conl-)** to pick up; to gather together, collect; to attain, acquire *(esp. by natural processes)*; to compile *(in a book)*; to build (up) *(a reputation)*; to hitch up, tuck up *(clothing)*; to furl *(sails)*; to gather in *(the reins)*; to harvest *(fruit, crops)*; to summarize, sum up; to contract, compress, concentrate; to acquire gradually, amass; to infer, conclude, gather; *(of numbers, totals)* to amount to; to enumerate; **animum** *(or* **mentem)** **colligere** to compose oneself; **ignēs colligere** to catch fire; **vāsa colligere** *(mil)* to gather up one's gear, break camp **||** *refl & pass* to pull oneself together; to amount to; *(of winds, clouds, dust)* to gather; *(of anger)* to build up
collīne·ō -āre -āvī -ātus *tr* **(-ni·ō) (conl-)** to aim, direct **||** *intr* to hit the mark
col·linō -linere -lēvī -litus *tr* **(conl-)** to smear; to defile
Collīn·us -a -um *adj* of the Quirinal Hill; **Collīna Porta** Colline Gate *(near the Quirinal Hill)*
colliquefact·us -a -um *adj* **(conl-)** melted, dissolved
coll·is -is *m* hill
collocāti·ō -ōnis *f* **(conl-)** arrangement; giving in marriage
collocāt·us -a -um *adj* **(conl-)** *(geog)* located, lying
colloc·ō -āre -āvī -ātus *tr* **(conl-)** to place *(in a particular place)*; to put in order, arrange; to station, deploy *(troops)*; to give in marriage; to lodge, quarter; to occupy, employ; to spend, invest *(money)*; to bestow; *(w.* **in** *+ acc or abl)* to devote *(time, energy)* to; **in tūtō** *(or* **in tūtum)** **collocāre** to make safe **||** *pass* to occur, be found
collocuplēt·ō -āre -āvī -ātus *tr* **(conl-)** to enrich
collocūti·ō -ōnis *f* **(conl-)** conversation; debate, discussion; conference
colloqu·ium -(i)ī *n* **(conl-)** conversation; discussion, conference; interview
collo·quor -quī -cūtus sum *tr* **(conl-)** to talk to **||** *intr (w.* **cum)** talk with, converse with; *(w. acc & inf)* to say in conversation (that)
collubet *see* **collibet**
collūc·eō -ēre *intr* **(conl-)** to shine brightly, be entirely illuminated; *(fig)* to glitter
colluctāti·ō -ōnis *f* **(conl-)** struggling

colluct·or -ārī -ātus sum *intr* **(conl-)** *(w.* **cum)** to wrestle *(with)*
collū·dō -dere -sī -sum *intr* **(conl-)** to play together; to be in collusion; *(w. dat)* to play with
coll·um -ī *n or* **coll·us -ī** *m* neck; bottleneck, neck of a flask
col·luō -luere -luī -lūtus *tr* **(conl-)** to wash out, rinse; to wash away
collūsi·ō -ōnis *f* **(conl-)** collusion
collūs·or -ōris *m* **(conl-)** playmate; fellow gambler
collūstr·ō -āre -āvī -ātus *tr* **(conl-)** to light up; to survey, inspect; *(in painting)* to represent in bright colors
collutulent·ō -āre *tr* **(conl-)** to soil, defile
colluvi·ō -ōnis *or* **colluvi·ēs -ēī** *f* **(conl-)** sewage; dregs; impurities; impure mixture; turmoil; rabble
collyb·us -ī *m* **(collu-)** conversion of currency; rate of exchange
collȳr·a -ae *f* pasta, noodles, macaroni
collȳric·us -a -um *adj* **iūs collȳricum** noodle soup
colō colere coluī cultus *tr* to till *(the soil);* to cultivate *(friendship, other ties);* to live in, inhabit; *(of gods)* to care for, guard, protect; to honor, revere, worship; to adorn, dress; to follow, practice *(religion);* to observe *(laws, customs);* to experience, live *(one's life);* **ārās colere** to bow down before the altars; **sacra colere** to perform the sacred rites
colocāsi·a -ae *f* lotus, water lily
colōn·a -ae *f* peasant woman
colōni·a -āe *f* colony; *(coll)* town; settlers, colonists; **colōniam dēdūcere** *(or* **mittere)** to send out settlers
colōnic·us -a -um *adj* colonial
colōn·us -ī *m* farmer; colonist, settler
Coloph·ōn -ōnis *m* city in Ionia, one of the "birthplaces" of Homer
col·or *or* **col·ōs -ōris** *m* color, tint; external condition; complexion; tone, style; luster; grace; colorful pretext
colōrāt·us -a -um *adj* colored, tinted; tanned; swarthy; trumped up
colōr·ō -āre -āvī -ātus *tr* to color; to tan; *(fig)* to give a certain tone to
colossē·us -a -um *adj* colossal
coloss·us *or* **coloss·os -ī** *m* colossus *(any large statue of a Roman emperor, made to rival the orginal Colossus)* **‖ Colossus Rhodī** the Colossus of Rhodes
colostr·a -ae *f or* **colostr·ūm -ī** *n* **(-lust-)** first milk after childbirth, colostrum
colu·ber -brī *m* snake, adder
colubr·a -ae *f* snake, adder *(female)*
colubrif·er -era -erum *adj* snaky, wearing snakes *(of Medusa)*
colubrīn·us -a -um *adj* cunning, wily
cōl·um -ī *n* strainer
columb·a -ae *f* pigeon, dove *(female)*
columb·ar -āris *n* pigeonhole
columbār·ium -(i)ī *n* pigeonhole; niche in a sepulcher
columbīn·us -a -um *adj* of a dove *or* pigeon **‖** *m* little dove
columb·us -ī *m* pigeon, dove
columell·a -ae *f* small column, pillar
colum·en -inis *n* height, summit, peak; roof; ridgepole; head, leader; *(fig)* "crown," "jewel"; *(fig)* cornerstone *(of an argument); (fig)* very embodiment *(of a quality);* **summum columen** highest point *(of an orbit)*
column·a -ae *f* column, pillar; support; waterspout; *(vulg)* (big) penis; **columnae Herculis** *(or* **Hesperiae)** the Pillars of Hercules; **columna Maenia** whipping post *(in the Forum for thieves and slaves and to which debtors were summoned for trial);* **Prōteī columnae** the Pillars of Proteus, the "borders of Egypt" **‖** *fpl* portico; bookshop
columnār·ium -(i)ī *n* tax on house pillars
columnār·ius -(i)ī *m* debtor *(convicted at the* **Columna Maenia)**
columnāt·us -a -um *adj* supported by pillars; **ōs columnātum** *(fig)* the head supported by one's arms
colurn·us -a -um *adj* of hazelwood
col·us -ī *or* **-ūs** *mf* distaff
colūte·a -ae *f* pod-like kind of fruit
cōlȳphi·a -ōrum *npl* choice cuts of meat, loin cuts
com- *pref see* **con-**
com·a -ae *f* hair *(of head);* mane; fleece; foliage; grass; *(poet)* rays
com·āns -antis *adj* hairy; long-haired; plumed *(helmet);* leafy; **comāns stella** comet
cōmarch·us -ī *m* village chief
comāt·us -a -um *adj* long-haired; leafy; **Gallia Comāta** Gaul other than the province existing after the conquest by Caesar
combib·ō -ere -ī *tr* **(conb-)** to drink up; to absorb; to swallow, engulf; to repress, conceal *(tears);* to absorb *(knowledge)*
combib·ō -ōnis *m* **(conb-)** drinking partner
com·būrō -būrere -būssī -būstus *tr* **(conb-)** to burn up, consume; *(fig)* to ruin
combūstus *pp of* **combūrō**
com·edō -edere *(or* **-ēsse)** **-ēdī -ēsus** *(or* **-ēstus)** *tr* to eat up, consume; to squander **‖** *refl* to pine away; *(fig)* to feast one's eyes on
com·es -itis *mf* companion; fellow traveler; associate, partner; attendant; staff member; concomitant
comēsse *see* **comedō**
comēstus *pp of* **comedō**
comēsus *pp of* **comedō**
comēt·ēs -ae *m* comet
cōmicē *adv* like a comedy

cōmic·us -a -um *adj* of comedy, comic; **cōmicum aurum** stage money ‖ *m* actor, playwright *(of comedy)*
cōminus *see* **comminus**
cōm·is -is -e *adj* polite; kind, friendly; *(w. dat or* **ergā** *or* **in** *+ acc)* kind toward
cōmissābund·us -a -um *adj* riotous; drunken; boozing
cōmissāti·ō -ōnis *f* drinking party
cōmissāt·or -ōris *m* reveler
cōmiss·or -ārī -ātus sum *intr* to carouse, make merry
cōmit·ās -ātis *f* politeness, kindness
comitāt·us -a -um *adj* (by) accompanied *(w. abl);* **comitātior** accompanied by a larger following, better attended
comitāt·us -ūs *m* escort, retinue; court *(of emperor, king);* company *(traveling together),* caravan
cōmiter *adv* politely; kindly
comitiāl·is -is -e *adj* of the assembly; **diēs comitiālis** day on which the comitia could transact business; **morbus comitiālis** epilepsy *(so called because its occurrence could cause an assembly to be adjourned)*
comitiāt·us -ūs *m (pol)* assembly
comit·ium -(i)ī *n* comitium, assembly place, voting place ‖ *npl* popular assembly; elections; **comitia habēre** to hold elections
comit·ō -āre -āvī -ātus *or* **comit·or -ārī -ātus sum** *tr* to accompany; to escort; to share *(a fate);* to attend *(a funeral); (of ancestral busts)* to be carried at *(a funeral)* ‖ *intr (w. dat)* to be present with, attend
comm·a -atis *n (gram)* phrase, part of a line
commacul·ō -āre -āvī -ātus *tr* to spot; to stain, defile
commaníp(u)lār·is -is *m* army buddy
commarīt·us -ī *m* fellow husband
commeāt·us -ūs *m* passage; traffic; convoy; *(mil)* furlough; *(mil)* lines of communication; *(mil)* supplies; **in commeātū esse** to be on furlough
commedit·or -ārī *tr* to practice hard; to imitate
com·mēiō -mēiere -mī(n)xī mī(n)ctus *tr (sl)* to wet, pee
commemin·ī -isse *(v. defect) tr & intr* to remember well
commemorābil·is -is -e *adj* memorable
commemorāti·ō -ōnis *f* **(conm-)** reminder; recollection, remembrance
commemor·ō -āre -āvī -ātus *tr* **(conm-)** to remember; to bring up, mention, relate
commendābil·is -is -e *adj* commendable
commendātīci·us -a -um *adj* of recommendation, of introduction
commendāti·ō -ōnis *f* recommendation; commendation, praise; approval, esteem; excellence
commendāt·or -ōris *m* backer
commendātr·īx -īcis *f* backer *(female)*
commendāt·us -a -um *adj* recommended; acceptable, suitable
commend·ō -āre -āvī -ātus *tr* to entrust; to recommend; to commit *(to writing, posterity);* to commend ‖ *refl (w. dat)* to devote oneself to
commentāriol·um -ī *n* notebook; essay
commentār·ium -(i)ī *n or* **commentār·ius -(i)ī** *m* **(conm-)** notebook, diary, journal; record, register; textbook; (collection of) notes; **ā commentāriīs** official in charge of records
commentāti·ō -ōnis *f* careful study; treatise, commentary; textbook; *(rhet)* argument
commentīci·us -a -um *adj* thought-out; imaginary, fictitious
comment·or -ārī -ātus sum *tr* to think over, consider; to contrive, make up; to write, compose; to discuss; to practice, prepare *(a speech)*
comment·or -ōris *m* inventor, deviser
comment·us -a -um *pp of* **comminīscor** ‖ *adj* fictitious, invented, pretended ‖ *n* invention; fabrication; contrivance, device
comme·ō -āre -āvī -ātum *intr* to come and go; to back and forth; to travel repeatedly; *(of water)* to pass, flow; to travel around; to commute; to pass *(from one state to another)*
commerc·ium -(i)ī *n* trade, commerce; dealing, business; communication, correspondence; exchange *(of goods),* trafficking; goods, merchandise; sexual intercourse; *(leg)* right to engage in trade, commercial rights; *(w. gen)* right to buy and sell *(a commodity), e.g.:* **commercium agrī** right to buy and sell land; **commericium bellī** ransom; **commercium epistulārum** correspondence; **commercium linguae** common language *(shared by various tribes);* **iūs commerciī** trading rights
commerc·or -ārī -ātus sum *tr* **(conm-)** to purchase
commer·eō -ēre -uī -itus *or* **commer·eor -ērī -itus sum** *tr* **(conm-)** to deserve fully, merit; to be guilty of
com·mētior -mētīrī -mēnsus sum *tr* **(conm-)** to measure; *(w.* **cum)** to measure *(s.th.)* in terms of
commēt·ō -āre -āvī *intr* to go often, come and go
commīctus *pp of* **commingō**
commigr·ō -āre -āvī -ātum *intr* to move, migrate
commīlit·ium -(i)ī *n* military comradeship
commīlit·ō -ōnis *m* army buddy
comminātī·ō -ōnis *f* violent threat

com·mingō -mingere -mīnxī -mīctus *tr (sl)* to pee on; to wet *(bed);* **commīctum caenum** *(sl)* dirty skunk

com·minīscor -minīscī -mentus sum *tr* to think up, contrive; to fabricate *(lie);* to state falsely, pretend, allege

commin·or -ārī -ātus sum *tr* to threaten, make a threat of

commin·uō -uere -uī -ūtus *tr* to lessen considerably; to smash, shatter; *(fig)* to crush, humiliate

comminus *adv* hand to hand; near at hand; **comminus cōnferre signa** to engage in hand-to-hand combat

commi·sceō -scēre -scuī -xtus *tr* to mix together; to confuse; to unite, bring together; *(w.* **cum)** to discuss with

commiserāti·ō -ōnis *f (rhet)* appeal for compassion *or* pity

commiserēsc·ō -ere *intr (w. gen)* to feel pity for ‖ *v impers* **mē commiserēscit ēius** I pity him

commiser·or -ārī -ātus sum *tr* to feel sympathy for ‖ *intr (rhet)* to try to evoke sympathy

commīsī *perf of* **committō**

commissi·ō -ōnis *f* commencement

commissūr·a -ae *f* connection; joint

commiss·us -a -um *pp of* **committō** ‖ *n* offense, crime; secret, trust; undertaking; thing confiscated

commītig·ō -āre *tr* **(conm-)** to soften up

com·mittō -mittere -mīsī -missus *tr* **(conm-)** to bring together; to join together, make continuous, connect, combine; to cause to compete, match *(for a fight, etc.);* to begin, commence *(games);* to undertake; to commit *(crime),* do *(s.th. wrong);* to incur *(penalty);* to bring about, effect; to give up, forfeit, hand over; to engage in *(battle, war); (w. dat)* **1** to take *(a person or matter)* before *(s.o.)* for a verdict, decision, *or* approval; **2** to entrust *(a person or thing)* to *(s.o.);* **hostēs pugnae** *(or* **proeliō) committere** to engage the enemy; **memoriae committere** to commit to memory; **omnēs inter sē committere** to set all at variance with one another; **proelium** *(or* **pugnam) committere** to go into action, engage the enemy ‖ *refl (w.* **in** *+ acc)* to venture into ‖ *intr* to commit an offense, break the law

commodē *adv* properly, appropriately; neatly; adequately, satisfactorily; at the right moment; conveniently, readily; helpfully, obligingly; tastefully; comfortably

commodit·ās -ātis *f* timeliness, right time; proportion, symmetry; convenience, comfort; pleasantness, kindness; *(rhet)* aptness of expression

commodō *adv* suitably, conveniently

commod·ō -āre -āvī -ātus *tr* to adjust, adapt; to bestow, supply, lend, give; **aurem** *(or* **aurēs) commodāre** to lend an ear; **manum commodāre** to lend a helping hand ‖ *refl* **mihi tē commodāre** to put yourself at my disposal ‖ *intr* to be obliging; *(w. dat)* to be accommodating to, help

commodulē *or* **commodulum** *adv* nicely, conveniently

commodum *adv* at a good time; in the nick of time; **commodum cum** just at the time when

commod·um -ī *n* convenience; opportunity; profit, advantage; privilege; loan; pay, reward; **commodō tuō** at your convenience; **ex commodō** *(or* **per commodum)** *(w. gen)* at the convenience of

commod·us -a -um *adj* convenient, suitable, fit; timely; opportune, good *(time);* comfortable; advantageous; agreeable, obliging, pleasant *(person);* good *(health);* **quod commodum est** just as you please

Commod·us -ī *m* Roman Emperor *(son of Marcus Aurelius, reigned A.D. 180–192)*

commōl·ior -īrī -ītus sum *tr* to set in motion, move with effort

commōnstr·ō -āre -āvī -ātus *tr* to point out; to show where *(a person, thing, place)* is

commone·faciō -facere -fēcī -factus *tr* to call to mind; *(w. acc of person and gen of thing)* to remind *(s.o.)* of

common·eō -ēre -uī -itus *tr* to remind, warn; *(w. gen or* **dē** *+ abl)* to remind *(s.o.)* of

commoniti·ō -ōnis *f* reminder

commorāti·ō -ōnis *f* stay; delay *(rhet)* dwelling on a point

com·morior -morī -mortuus sum *intr (w. dat or* **cum)** to die with

commor·or -ārī -ātus sum *tr* to stop, detain ‖ *intr* to linger, stay, stop off; **in sententiā commorārī** to stick to an opinion

commōti·ō -ōnis *f* motion; commotion; **animī commōtiō** excitement

commōtiuncul·a -ae *f* slight agitation

commōt·us -a -um *adj* excited, nervous; deranged *(mind);* angry; impassioned; *(rhet)* lively *(style)*

com·moveō -movēre -mōvī -mōtus *tr* to stir up, shake; to disturb, upset; to excite, shake up; to arouse, provoke; to generate, produce; *(fig)* to touch, move; to influence; to impress; to cause, start *(a war, battle);* to dislodge *(an enemy);* to call in *(a debt)*

commūn·e -is *n* common property; community; **in commūne 1** publicly; **2** for the good of all; **3** jointly; **4** in general terms

commūnicāti·ō -ōnis *f* sharing; *(rhet)* deliberating with the audience

commūnic·ō -āre -āvī -ātus *or* **commūnic·or -ārī -ātus sum** *tr* to share; to unite, link; to impart, communicate; to discuss together; to plan together

commūn·iō -īre -īvī *or* **-iī -ītus** *tr* **(-moen-)** to fortify; to build and fortify; *(fig)* to strengthen, fortify

commūni·ō -ōnis *f* sharing; kinship, association

commūn·is -is -e *adj* **(conm-)** common, joint; common, ordinary; public; universal, general; familiar; courteous; democratic; *(of arguments)* applicable to either side; **commūnis est coniectūra** it is open to conjecture; **commūnis est aestimātiō** it is a matter of opinion; **loca commūnia** public places; **locī commūnēs** general topics; **sēnsus commūnis** civic *or* public spirit **||** *n see* **commūne ||** *npl* the common good; *(poet)* common lot

commūnit·ās -ātis *f* sharing, partnership, joint possession; social ties, fellowship, togetherness; affability

commūniter *adv* in common

commūnīti·ō -ōnis *f* road building; *(fig)* preparation, introduction

commurmur·ō -āre *or* **commurmur·or -ārī -ātus sum** *intr* to murmur, grumble

commūtābil·is -is -e *adj* changeable, subject to change; interchangeable

commūtāti·ō -ōnis *f* change, alteration; shift; exchange; reversal

commūtāt·us -ūs *m* change

commūt·ō -āre -āvī -ātus *tr* to change, alter; to interchange, exchange; to barter; to give in exchange; *(w. abl or* **cum)** to exchange *(s.th.)* for; **verba commūtāre** to exchange words, talk

cōm·ō -ere -psī -ptus *tr* to set, do, braid *(the hair);* to adorn, deck out

cōmoedi·a -ae *f* comedy

cōmoedicē *adv* as in comedy

cōmoed·us -a -um *adj* of comic actors **||** *m* comic actor

comōs·us -a -um *adj* with long hair; hairy; leafy

compacīscor *see* **compecīscor**

compācti·ō -ōnis *f* framework

compāct·us -a -um *pp of* **compingō ||** *adj* compact, well-built **||** *n* compact

compāg·ēs -is *f* construction; joint, seam; structure, framework; *(anat)* joint

compāg·ō -inis *f* **(conp-)** (act of) fastening; connection; framework, structure

comp·ār -aris *adj* **(conp-)** similar, alike; equal; *(w. dat)* matching, resembling **||** *mf* buddy; playmate; perfect match; spouse

comparābil·is -is -e *adj* **(conp-)** comparable, similar

comparātē *adv* **(conp-)** comparatively

comparāti·ō -ōnis *f (from* **compar- + ō)** comparison; relative position *(of planets); (gram)* comparative degree; *(rhet)* argument based on the law of probability; **ex comparātiōne** *(w. gen)* in comparison with; **comparātiō prō portiōne** proportion

comparāti·ō -ōnis *f (from* **con- + parō)** preparation; acquisition, procuring, obtaining, provision *(by purchasing or otherwise);* arrangement, settlement

comparātīv·us -a -um *adj* **(conp-)** comparative; *(gram)* that is in the comparative degree

compār·eō -ēre -uī *intr* **(conp-)** to be visible, be plain, be evident; to appear; to be at hand, be present

compar·ō -āre -āvī -ātus *tr (from* **compar- + ō)** to unite; to match, pit; to align; to estimate; to compare *(with or to);* to point out by way of comparison

compar·ō -āre -āvī -ātus *tr (from* **con- + parō)** to prepare, make preparations for; to purchase; to plan, devise; to put together, get together, provide; to match; to set up *(courts, a body of laws);* to procure, get, collect; to appoint; to establish, institute; to raise *(troops);* to compose *(writings);* **comparāre inter sē** *(esp. of consuls)* to arrange, settle

compās·cō -cere — -tus *tr & intr* **(conp-)** to feed together

compāscu·us -a -um *adj* **(conp-)** of public grazing; **compāscuus ager** public pasture land

compect·us -a -um *adj* in agreement **||** *n* agreement, compact; **(dē) compectō** by previous agreement

comped·iō -īre — -ītus *tr* **(conp-)** to shackle

compedīt·us -a -um *pp of* **compediō ||** *adj* shackled **||** *m* shackled slave

compēgī *perf of* **compingō**

compellāti·ō -ōnis *f* **(conp-)** rebuke; *(rhet)* addressing, apostrophizing

compell·ō -āre -āvī -ātus *tr* **(conp-)** to address, speak to; to call upon, appeal to; to challenge; *(w. predicate adj)* to call *(s.o., e.g., disloyal, etc.);* to rebuke, call to account; *(leg)* to arraign

com·pellō -pellere -pulī -pulsus *tr* **(conp-)** to drive together, round up; to crowd together; to compel, drive; *(of wind, waves)* to drive, push, force; *(w.* **in** *+ acc)* to drive *(s.o.)* into; *(w.inf or* **ut** *+ subj)* to compel *(s.o.)* to *(do s.th.);* to coerce, constrain; to reduce by force *(to some state or condition);* to clench *(teeth);* to localize, concentrate *(fighting)*

compendiāri·us -a -um *adj* **(conp-)** short, abridged; **via compendiāria** shortcut

compend·ium -(i)ī *n* **(conp-)** careful weighing; saving *(of money);* profit;

shortening, abridging; shortcut; **compendium facere** *(w. gen)* to save oneself the trouble of; **compendī fierī** to be brief; **compendiō servīre** to serve one's own private interests

compēnsāti·ō -ōnis *f* compensation

compēns·ō -āre -āvī -ātus *tr* **(conp-)** to compensate for, make up for; to balance mentally

comper·cō -cere -sī *tr* **(conp-)** to save up, hoard; *(w. inf)* to refrain from

comperendināti·ō -ōnis *f or* **comperendināt·us -ūs** *m* **(conp-)** *(leg)* two-day adjournment

comperendin·ō -āre -āvī -ātus *tr* **(conp-)** to adjourn *(court)* for two days; to put off *(defendant)* for two days

comper·iō -īre -ī -tus *or* **comper·ior -īrī -tus sum** *tr* **(conp-)** to find out, discover, learn; **compertum habeō** *or* **compertum mihi est** I know for certain

compern·is -is -e *adj* **(conp-)** having thighs close together

compert·us -a -um *pp of* **comperiō ‖** *adj* ascertained; well authenticated; *(w. gen)* convicted of; **compertum habeō** I have verified; **nihil compertī** no certainty; **prō compertō** *(to regard)* as certain; **rēs comperta** *(or* **compertae)** reliable information

comp·ēs -edis *f* **(conp-)** *(usu. pl)* shackles *(for the feet)*, fetters; bond *(of love)*

compēsc·ō -ere -uī *tr* **(conp-)** to confine, restrain; to imprison; to close, block *(entrances);* to check the movement of, steady; to stop, restrain *(activity of any kind);* to calm *(a storm);* to control *(a person);* to subdue, quell, crush *(an enemy, a mutiny);* to curb *(one's tongue, one's words);* to stifle *(feelings, fears, laughter);* to quench *(thirst);* to allay *(hunger);* **compēsce dīcere iniūstē**! stop speaking unfairly!; **compēsce digitō labellum**! put your finger to your lip! *(to indicate silence)*

competīt·or -ōris *m* **(conp-)** competitor; rival claimant *(to the throne);* rival bidder *(at an auction); (pol)* fellow candidate

competītr·īx -īcis *f* **(conp-)** competitor *(female)*

compet·ō -ere -īvī *or* **-iī -ītum** *intr* **(conp-)** to come together, meet; *(of events)* to coincide; to be adequate, be suitable; *(w.* **ad)** to be capable of **‖** *v impers* **sī competit** if it is convenient; *(w.* **ut)** if it happens that

compīlāti·ō -ōnis *f* **(conp-)** plundering burglary; *(of a collection of documents)* compilation

compīl·ō -āre -āvī -ātus *tr* **(conp-)** to pillage; to plagiarize

com·pingō -pingere -pēgī -pāctus *tr* **(conp-)** to put together, construct; to compose; to lock up, put *(in jail)*

compitāl·ia -ium *npl* **(conp-)** festival of the Lares at crossroads, celebrated twice annually at the crossroads with flowers

compitālici·us -a -um *adj* **(conp-)** of the crossroads

compitāl·is -is -e *adj* **(conp-, compet-)** associated with the festival at the crossroads

compit·um -ī *n* **(conp-)** crossroads; *(fig)* crucial decision

complac·eō -ēre -uī *or* **-itum** *intr* **(conp-)** *(w. dat)* to suit just fine

complān·ō -āre -āvī -ātus *tr* **(conp-)** to level; to raze

comple·ctor -ctī -xus sum *tr* **(conp-)** to embrace, hug; to display affection for, display esteem for; to clasp *(the right hand); (of sleep)* to hold in its embrace; *(fig)* to embrace, take up *(a cause, a course of action);* to grip, grasp, cling to; to encircle, surround, enclose; to comprise; to take in, include within its limits *(an area); (of power, reputation, knowledge)* to extend over, embrace; to involve, associate, include *(in a relationship, class, activity);* to include, cover *(in a book or speech);* to state in a concise manner, sum up; to grasp, understand; **animō** *(or* **mente) complectī** to comprehend, take in; **memoriā complectī** to keep in mind

complēment·um -ī *n* **(conp-)** complement, completion

compl·eō -ēre -ēvī -ētus *tr* **(conp-)** to fill, fill up; to fill with sound, make resound; to supply, furnish; to complete; to impregnate; to bring *(a legion)* to full strength; *(mil)* to man

complēt·us -a -um *adj* **(conp-)** complete, perfect

complexi·ō -ōnis *f* **(conp-)** combination, collection, group; *(rhet)* summary; **complexiō verbōrum** a connected series of words, period, sentence

complex·us -ūs *m* **(conp-)** embrace; *(fig)* love, affection; close combat; mental grasp; grouping *(of words);* envelopment

complicāt·us -a -um *adj* **(conp-)** complicated

complic·ō -āre -āvī *(or* **-uī) -ātus** *(or* **-itus)** *tr* **(conp-)** to fold up

complō·dō -dere -sī -sus *tr* **(conp-)** to clap *(the hands)* together

complōrāti·ō -ōnis *f or* **complōrāt·us -ūs** *m* **(conp-)** wailing, lamentation

complōr·ō -āre -āvī -ātus *tr* **(conp-)** to mourn (together *or* deeply)

complūr·ēs -ēs -a *or* **-ia** *adj* **(conp-)** several, a fair number of

complūriēns *adv* **(-iēs) (conp-)** several times, a good many times
complūscul·ī -ae -a *adj* **(conp-)** several
compluv·ium -(i)ī *n* **(conp-)** compluvium *(quadrangular, inward-sloping central part of the roof of a Roman house to direct rain to a pool below, called* **impluvium)**
com·pōnō -pōnere -posuī -positus *tr* **(conp-)** to put together, join; to place *(things together);* to store up, hoard; to lay aside, put away; to build; to compose, write; to arrange, settle, agree upon; to match; to match up *(pairs);* to compare; to treat as comparable; to balance *(e.g., deeds with words);* to lay out *(the dead);* to put in an urn; to bury; to arrange in order, lay out; to arrange systematically; to arrange properly, adjust; to deploy *(troops);* to arrange, plan, organize *(a plan of action);* to make up, fabricate *(a false report, story);* to reconcile; to concoct, contrive; to quell *(a revolt);* to subdue *(rebels);* to calm, soothe, appease *(a person);* to reconcile *(estranged friends);* to settle *(disputes, problems, affairs);* **bellum compōnere** to end a war *(by coming to terms);* **in maestitiam compositus** putting on the appearance of sadness; **vultum compōnere** to put on a false front
comport·ō -āre -āvī -ātus *tr* **(conp-)** to bring together, bring in, collect, accumulate
comp·os -otis *adj* **(conp-)** *(w. gen or abl)* in possession of, master of, having control over; **compos animī** *(or* **mentis)** sane; **compos suī** self-controlled; **compos vōtī** having one's prayer answered
compos(i)tūr·a -ae *f* **(conp-)** structure
compositē *adv* **(conp-)** in an orderly manner; *(of actions)* deliberately; **compositē dīcere** to speak logically
compositi·ō -ōnis *f* **(conp-)** putting together, fitting together, connecting, arranging, composition; matching *(of gladiators, etc.);* reconciliation *(of friends);* orderly arrangement *(of words)*
compositō *adv* **(conp-)** by prearrangement
composit·or -ōris *m* **(conp-)** an arranger; writer
composit·us -a -um *pp of* **compōnō ‖** *adj* compound *(words, etc.);* composite, blended; orderly, tidy; calm *(sea);* composed, calm **‖** *n* compound medication; **dē** *(or* **ex) compositō** by agreement, as agreed **‖** *npl* law and order, settled situation
compōtāti·ō -ōnis *f* **(conp-)** drinking party
compot·iō -īre -īvī -ītus *tr* **(conp-)** *(w. acc of person and abl of thing)* to make *(s.o.)* master of **‖** *pass (w. abl)* to attain
compōt·or -ōris *m,* **compōtr·īx -īcis** *f* **(conp-)** drinking partner
comprāns·or -ōris *m* **(conp-)** dinner companion, fellow guest
comprecāti·ō -ōnis *f* **(conp-)** public supplication
comprec·or -ārī -ātus sum *tr* **(conp-)** to pray earnestly to, implore, invoke; *(w. acc of thing)* to pray for; *(w.* **ut** + *subj)* to pray that
comprehen·dō -dere -dī -sus *or* **compren·dō -dere -dī -sus** *tr* **(conp-)** to bind together, unite; to hold together *(e.g., w. ropes)*; to take hold of, grasp; to catch; to attack; to arrest; to capture; to occupy; to detect; to comprehend; to express; to describe, recount; **animō** *(or* **mente) comprehendere** to apprehend, appreciate; **ignem comprehendere** to catch fire; **memoriā comprehendere** to remember; **numerō comprehendere** to count, enumerate
comprehēnsibil·is -is -e *adj* **(conp-) (-dibilis)** comprehensible, intelligible
comprehēnsi·ō *or* **comprēnsi·ō -ōnis** *f* **(conp-)** seizing; arrest; comprehension, perception; combining; *(rhet)* period
comprendō *see* **comprehendō**
compressi·ō -ōnis *f* **(conp-)** pressing closely; embrace; *(rhet)* compression
compress·or -ōris *m* rapist
compress·us -ūs *m* **(conp-)** compression; embrace; rape
com·primō -primere -pressī -pressus *tr* **(conp-)** to press together, compress; to close; to embrace; to check, curb; to keep back, suppress, withhold, conceal; to rape; to hold *(one's breath);* **compressīs manibus sedēre** to sit on folded hands, not lift a finger; **ōrdinēs comprimere** to close ranks
comprobāti·ō -ōnis *f* **(conp-)** full approval
comprobāt·or -ōris *m* **(conp-)** enthusiastic approver
comprob·ō -āre -āvī -ātus *tr* **(conp-)** to approve, sanction, acknowledge; to prove, establish, verify; to confirm; to justify
comprōmiss·um -ī *n* **(conp-)** *(leg)* compromise *(agreement between the parties to abide by the arbitrator's decision)*
comprō·mittō -mittere -mīsī -missum *intr* **(conp-)** *(leg)* to compromise *(to agree to abide by the arbitrator's decision)*
comptiōnāl·is -is -e *adj (of worn-out goods)* suitable to be sold in batches
cōmpt·us -a -um *pp of* **cōmō ‖** *adj (of hair)* set, neatly arranged; *(of person)* dressed up; *(of speech, writing)* polished
cōmpt·us -ūs *m* hairdo
compulī *perf of* **compellō**
compulsus *pp of* **compellō**
compun·gō -gere compūnxī compūnctus *tr* **(conp-)** to puncture, prick; to tattoo; to prod

comput·ō -āre -āvī -ātus *tr* **(conp-)** to compute, count
computrēsc·ō -ere *intr* **(conp-)** to rot
Cōm·um -ī *n* Como *(town N. of Po River, modern Como)*
con- *pref (also:* **co-, col-, com-, cor-)** **1** together: **coniungere** to join together; **2** up, completely, fully: **cōnsūmere** to use up; **concrēdere** to trust completely; **3** with: **cōnspīrāre** to plot with *(s.o.)*; **4** hard: **conicere** to throw hard, fling
cōnām·en -inis *n* effort, struggle; support; *(often pl)* endeavor, attempt
cōnāt·um -ī *n* effort; venture
cōnāt·us -ūs *m* effort; endeavor; thrust *(with weapon)*
concac·ō -āre -āvī -ātus *tr (vulg)* to soil, shit
concaed·ēs -ium *fpl* log barricade
concale·faciō -facere -fēcī -factus *tr* to warm up, heat
concal·ēscō -ēscere -uī *intr* to grow quite warm; to glow *(e.g., with love)*
concall·ēscō -ēscere -uī *intr* to grow hard; *(fig)* to become insensitive
concamerāt·us -a -um *adj* vaulted
Concān·us -ī *m* one of a Spanish tribe that drank horse's blood
concastīg·ō -āre -āvī -ātus *tr* to dress down; to chastise, punish
concav·ō -āre *tr* to curve, bend
concav·us -a -um *adj* concave, hollow; deep-sunken *(eyes)*; deep *(valley)*
con·cēdō -cēdere -cessī -cessus *tr* to give up; to pardon, overlook; to grant **ll** *intr* to go away; to withdraw, retire; to pass away, die; *(w. dat)* **1** to yield to, succumb to; **2** to submit to, comply with; **3** to make allowances for, pardon; **4** to be inferior to; *(w.* **in** + *acc)* to pass over to, be merged into; **fātō** *(or* **nātūrae** *or* **vītā)** **concēdere** to die
concelebr·ō -āre -āvī -ātus *tr* to frequent; to fill; to pursue *(studies)*; to enliven; to celebrate; to publish, proclaim
concēnāti·ō -ōnis *f* dinner party
concenti·ō -ōnis *f* singing together, singalong, harmony
concenturi·ō -āre *tr* to assemble by centuries *(groups of hundreds)*; *(fig)* to marshal
concent·us -ūs *m* concert; harmony; shouting in unison; blending
concepti·ō -ōnis *f* conception; *(leg)* formula
concept·us -a -um *pp of* **concipiō ll** *adj* **concepta verba** formula
concept·us -ūs *m* conception; embryo, fetus
concerp·ō -ere -sī -tus *tr* to tear up, tear to shreds; *(fig)* to cut up, revile
concertāti·ō -ōnis *f* wrangling
concertāt·or -ōris *m* rival
concertātōri·us -a -um *adj* controversial
concert·ō -āre -āvī -ātus *tr* to quarrel over; to rival **ll** *intr* to fight, quarrel
concessi·ō -ōnis *f* concession; admission *(of guilt with a plea for mercy)*
concess·ō -āre -āvī *intr (w. inf)* to cease to, stop *(doing s.th.)*
concess·us -a -um *pp of* **concēdō ll** *adj* allowable, lawful **ll** *n* concession
concess·us -ūs *m* permission; **concessū Caesaris** with Caesar's permission
conch·a -ae *f* clam, oyster, mussel, murex; clamshell, oyster shell; pearl; purple dye; trumpet *(of Triton)*; vessel *(for ointments, etc.)*; vulva
conch·is -is *f* bean
conchīt·a -ae *m* clam digger
conchul·a -ae *f* a small shellfish
conchȳliāt·us -a -um *adj* purple
conchȳl·ium -(i)ī *n* shellfish, clam, oyster; murex; purple dye, purple **ll** *npl* purple garments
concī·dō -dere -dī -sus *tr* to cut up, cut to pieces, kill; to beat severely; *(fig)* to demolish *(w. arguments)*; *(rhet)* to chop up *(sentences)*
concid·ō -ere -ī *intr* to collapse; to fall *(in battle)*; *(fig)* to decline, fall, fail, decay, perish; *(of winds)* die down
con·cieō -ciēre -cīvī -cītus *or* **con·ciō -cīre -cīvī -cītus** *tr* to assemble; to shake; *(fig)* to stir up
conciliābul·um -ī *n* public meeting place
conciliāti·ō -ōnis *f* union, bond; conciliating; inclination, bent
conciliāt·or -ōris *m* mediator; agent
conciliātrīcul·a -ae *f* madame *(of a brothel)*; dear matchmaker
conciliātr·īx -īcis *f* matchmaker; promoter *(of relationships)*
conciliāt·us -a -um *adj (w.* **ad)** endeared to, disposed toward
conciliāt·us -ūs *m* union, joining
concili·ō -āre -āvī -ātus *tr* to bring together, unite; to win over; to bring about *(by mediation)*; to acquire, win
concil·ium -(i)ī *n* popular assembly *(esp. that of the plebs in Rome)*; private meeting; council; union; association; a hearing in council; deliberation, debate; *(pol)* a league of states; **in ūnō conciliō** together
concin·ēns -entis *adj* harmonious
concinnē *adv* nicely, daintily
concinnit·ās -ātis *or* **concinnitūd·ō -inis** *f* elegance; excessive refinement; symmetry *(of style)*
concinn·ō -āre -āvī -ātus *tr* to prepare for use, make ready; to repair; to touch up; to make up, concoct; to give rise to; to make, drive *(e.g., insane)*; **lacrumentem concinnās tuam uxōrem** you are making your wife cry

concinn·us -a -um *adj* symmetrical; elegant; courteous, nice; polished
concin·ō -ere -uī *tr* to sing of; to prophesy ‖ *intr* to sing *or* play together; *(fig)* to agree
conciō *see* **concieō**
concipil·ō -āre -āvī *tr* to seize and carry off
con·cipiō -cipere -cēpī -ceptus *tr* to take in, absorb; to imagine, think; to understand, perceive; to conceive; to produce, form; *(of things)* to contain, hold; to contract *(disease)*; to catch *(fire)*; to entertain *(hope)*; to frame *(in formal language)*; to announce *(in formal language)*; *(w. abl, adv,* **ab, ex)** to draw, derive from *(a source)*; to utter solemnly; **verba concepta** solemn utterance
concīsē *adv* concisely
concīsi·ō -ōnis *f (rhet)* dividing a sentence into short phrases
concīs·us -a -um *pp of* **concīdō** ‖ *adj* cut up, cut short, terse; minute, very small
concitātē *adv* vigorously, vividly
concitāti·ō -ōnis *f* rapid movement; excitement; disturbance, riot
concitāt·or *or* **concit·or -ōris** *m* instigator, ring-leader; rabble-rouser
concitāt·us -a -um *adj* excited; rapid
concit·ō -āre -āvī -ātus *tr* to stir up, rouse, urge; to spur on *(horses, etc.)*; to agitate, stir up, disturb; to awaken; to summon, assemble; to galvanize into action; to infuriate; to bring about, cause, occasion
concitor *see* **concitātor**
conclāmāti·ō -ōnis *f* loud shouting, yell; acclamation
conclāmit·ō -āre *intr* to keep on shouting, keep on yelling
conclām·ō -āre -āvī -ātus *tr* to shout, yell; to call to *(for help)*; to call repeatedly by name, bewail *(the dead)*; to exclaim; **iam conclāmātum est** *(coll)* all's lost; **vāsa conclāmāre** *(mil)* to give the signal to pack up; **ad arma conclāmāre** to sound the call to arms
conclāv·e -is *n* room; public restroom
conclū·dō -dere -sī -sus *tr* to shut up, enclose; to include, comprise; to round off, conclude *(speech, letter)*; to end rhythmically; to deduce, conclude
conclūsē *adv (rhet)* in a rhythmical cadence
conclūsi·ō -ōnis *f* conclusion; *(mil)* blockade; *(rhet)* summation
conclūsiuncul·a -ae *f* false conclusion
conclūs·us -a -um *pp of* **conclūdō** ‖ *adj* confined, restricted
concol·or -ōris *adj* of the same color
concomitāt·us -a -um *adj* escorted
conco·quō -quere -xī -ctus *tr* to cook thoroughly; to boil down; to digest; to stomach, put up with; to cook up, concoct *(ideas)*; to weigh seriously; to ripen ‖ *intr* to digest one's food
concordi·a -ae *f* harmony, concord
concorditer *adv* harmoniously
concord·ō -āre -āvī -ātum *intr* to be of one mind; to be in harmony, agree
concor·s -dis *adj* of the same mind, agreeing, harmonious
concoxī *perf of* **concoquō**
concrēbr·ēscō -ēscere -uī *intr* to grow strong
concrē·dō -dere -didī -ditus *tr* to entrust; to confide *(a secret)*
concrem·ō -āre -āvī -ātus *tr* to burn to ashes, burn down
concrep·ō -āre -uī *intr* to rattle, creak, grate, clash, sound, make noise; **digitīs concrepāre** to snap the fingers ‖ *tr* to cause to sound *or* to rattle
con·crēscō -crēscere -crēvī -crētum *intr* to grow together; to congeal; to curdle; to clot; to stiffen; to take shape, grow, increase
concrēti·ō -ōnis *f* condensing, congealing; matter, substance
concrēt·us -a -um *pp of* **concrēscō** ‖ *adj* grown together, compounded; solid, hard; frozen; matted; condensed, dense; curdled; inveterate, ingrained; dim *(light)* ‖ *n* hardness; solid matter
concrēvī *perf of* **concrēscō**
concrīmin·or -ārī -ātus sum *intr* to make bitter charges
concruci·ō -āre *tr* to torture
concubīn·a -ae *f* concubine
concubīnāt·us -ūs *m* free love
concubīn·us -ī *m* catamite, homosexual
concubit·us -ūs *m* reclining together; sexual intercourse
concubi·us -a -um *adj* **concubiā nocte** at bedtime ‖ *n* intercourse
conculc·ō -āre -āvī -ātus *tr* trample under foot; to despise, treat with contempt
con·cumbō -cumbere -cubuī -cubitum *intr* to sleep together; *(w.* **cum)** to sleep with, have intercourse with
concup·īscō -īscere -īvī *or* **-iī -ītus** *tr* to long for; to strive for
concūr·ō -āre *tr* to take good care of
concur·rō -rere -rī -sum *intr* to run together, flock together; to unite; to strike one another, crash; to happen at the same time, coincide; *(mil)* to clash; *(w.* **ad)** to have recourse to; *(of jaws)* to snap together; *(of facts, statements)* to agree
concursāti·ō -ōnis *f* running together, assembly; rushing about; *(mil)* skirmish
concursāt·or -ōris *m* skirmisher
concursi·ō -ōnis *f* concourse; *(gram)* collocation *(of vowels)*; *(rhet)* repetition for emphasis
concurs·ō -āre -āvī -ātus *tr* to run around to; **domōs concursāre** to run from house to house ‖ *intr* to rush around excitedly, dash up and down; *(mil)* to skirmish

concurs·us -ūs *m* a running together; concourse, assembly; combination; collision *(of atoms); (astr)* conjunction; *(gram)* juxtaposition *(of letters); (leg)* joint right; *(mil)* charge, clash
concussi·ō -ōnis *f* shaking; earthquake
concuss·us -ūs *m* shaking, shock
concu·tiō -tere -ssī -ssus *tr* to bang together; to convulse; to shake; to shatter; to harass, upset, shock; to stir up; to wave *(weapon, hand);* to weaken, shake *(authority, confidence)*
condal·ium -(i)ī *n* (slave's) ring
condec·et -ēre *v impers* it is quite becoming
condecor·ō -āre -āvī -ātus *tr* to adorn; to grace
condemnāt·or -ōris *m* accuser; *(leg)* prosecutor
condemn·ō -āre -āvī -ātus *tr* to condemn, doom; to blame; *(leg)* to prosecute successfully, convict, sentence
condēns·ō -āre -āvī -ātus *tr* to pack together
condēns·us -a -um *adj* crowded, packed
condici·ō -ōnis *f* contract, arrangement; stipulation, terms, condition; state, situation, circumstances; state of health; legal status; rank, place; marriage contract, marriage; prospective marriage partner, good match; nature, character; choice, option; **eā condiciōne ut** on the condition that; **in condiciōne manēre** to stick to an agreement; **nūllā condiciōne** by no means; **sub condiciōne** conditionally; **vītae condiciō** living conditions
condī·cō -cere -xī -ctus *tr* to talk over, arrange together; **(ad) cēnam condīcere** *(w. dat)* to make a dinner engagement with
condignē *adv* very worthily
condign·us -a -um *adj (w. abl)* fully deserving of, fully worthy of
condīment·um -ī *n* seasoning, spice
cond·iō -īre -īvī *or* **-iī -ītus** *tr* to season; to pickle, preserve; to embalm; *(fig)* to give zest to
condiscipul·a -ae *f* schoolmate *(female)*
condiscipulāt·us -ūs *m* companionship at school
condiscipul·us -ī *m* schoolmate
con·discō -discere -didicī *tr* to learn thoroughly, learn by heart
condīti·ō -ōnis *f* seasoning; method of preserving *(food)*
condit·or -ōris *m* founder, builder; originator *(of a practice; of a product);* organizer; creator; *(as honorary title)* preserver; author, writer
condīt·or -ōris *m* seasoner
conditōr·ium -(i)ī *n* coffin; tomb
condīt·us -a -um *pp of* **condiō** ‖ *adj* seasoned, spicy; elegant *(style)*
condit·us -a -um *pp of* **condō** ‖ *adj* concealed, secret; sunken *(eyes)*
condīxī *perf of* **condīcō**
con·dō -dere -didī -ditus *tr* to build, found; to write, compose; to establish *(a practice, institution);* to store up, hoard; to preserve; to keep safe; to plunge *(a weapon);* to drown out *(a sound);* to put *(in prison, chains);* to put an end to *(a day)*
condoce·faciō -facere -fēcī -factus *tr* to train well
condoc·eō -ēre -uī -tus *tr* to teach thoroughly
condol·ēscō -ēscere -uī *intr* to begin to ache, get very sore; *(fig)* to feel grief
condōnāti·ō -ōnis *f* donation
condōn·ō -āre -āvī -ātus *tr* to give, present; to permit; to deliver over *(to enemy, for punishment);* to adjudge; *(w. double acc)* to make *(s.o.)* a present of *(s.th.); (w. acc of thing and dat of person)* to forgive, pardon *(s.o. an offense)*
condorm·iō -īre *intr* to sleep soundly
condorm·īscō -īscere -īvī *or* **-iī** *intr* to fall soundly asleep
condūcibil·is -is -e *adj* advantageous, profitable; *(w.* **ad** *or* **in** *+ acc)* just right for
condū·cō -cere -xī -ctus *tr* to bring together, collect, assemble; to connect, unite; to rent; to borrow; to induce, bribe; to employ, hire; to contract for, undertake a contract in connection with *(buildings, etc.)* ‖ *intr* to be of use; *(w. dat)* **1** to be useful to, be of use to; **2** to be profitable to; **3** to be fitting for; **4** to be conducive to; *(w.* **ad** *or* **in** *+ acc)* to be conducive to
conductīci·us -a -um *adj* mercenary; rented *(house)*
conducti·ō -ōnis *f* bringing together; recapitulation; the taking of a lease, renting
conduct·or -ōris *m* contractor; lessee, tenant
conduct·us -a -um *pp of* **condūcō** ‖ *mpl* hired men; mercenaries ‖ *n* rented apartment, rented house; lease, contract
conduplicāti·ō -ōnis *f* doubling; *(hum)* embrace
conduplic·ō -āre -āvī -ātus *tr* to double; **corpora conduplicāre** to embrace
condūr·ō -āre -āvī -ātus *tr* to harden
cond·us -ī *m* storeroom manager
cōne·ctō -ctere -xuī -xus *tr* **(conn-)** to tie; to connect, join, link; to state as a conclusion; **nōdum cōnectere** to tie a knot
cōnexi·ō -ōnis *f* logical conclusion
cōnexuī *perf of* **cōnectō**
cōnex·us -a -um *pp of* **cōnectō** ‖ *adj* linked; related, associated; interdependent; **per affīnitātem cōnexus** *(w. dat)* related by marriage to ‖ *n* logical connection, necessary consequence
cōnex·us -ūs *m* connection

cōnfābul·or -ārī -ātus sum *tr* to discuss **||** *intr* to have a talk, chat
cōnfarreāti·ō -ōnis *f* solemn marriage ceremony before the Pontifex Maximus and ten witnesses
cōnfarre·ō -āre -āvī -ātus *tr* to marry with solemn rites; to contract *(marriage)*
cōnfātāl·is -is -e *adj* bound by the same fate
cōnfecti·ō -ōnis *f* preparation; completion; conclusion, end; compiling; mastication
cōnfect·or -ōris *m* finisher, executor; destroyer
cōnfer·ciō -cīre — -tus *tr* to stuff, cram, pack together; to stuff full
cōn·ferō -ferre -tulī -lātus *or* **collātus** *tr* to bring together; to contribute *(money, etc.)*; to condense, compress; to assemble *(ideas, plans, etc.)*; to discuss, talk over; to bear, convey, direct; to devote, apply; to confer, bestow, give, lend, grant; to ascribe, impute, assign; to postpone; *(w.* **in** + *acc)* to change *(s.o. or s.th.)* into; to compare, contrast; **capita cōnferre** to put heads together, confer; **gradum cōnferre cum** to walk together with; **lītēs cōnferre** to quarrel; **pedem cum pede cōnferre** to fight toe to toe; **sermōnēs cōnferre cum** to engage in conversation with; **signa cōnferre** to begin fighting **||** *refl (w.* **in** + *acc)* **1** to go to, head for; **2** to have recourse to; **3** to join *(a group, etc.)*
cōnfertim *adv (mil)* shoulder to shoulder
cōnfert·us -a -um *pp of* **cōnferciō ||** *adj* crowded, packed, thick, dense; *(mil)* shoulder to shoulder
cōnfervēfac·iō -ere *tr* to make glow, make melt
cōnfer·vēscō -vēscere -buī *or* **-vuī** *intr* to begin to boil
cōnfessi·ō -ōnis *f* confession, acknowledgment; admission of guilt; token, proof
cōnfess·us -a -um *pp of* **cōnfiteor ||** *adj* acknowledged, incontrovertible **||** *m* confessed criminal **||** *n* admission; **ex cōnfessō** admittedly, beyond doubt; **in cōnfessum venīre** to be generally admitted
cōnfestim *adv* immediately, suddenly
cōnfici·ēns -entis *adj* productive, efficient; *(w. gen)* **1** productive of; **2** efficient in **||** *npl (w. gen)* sources of
cōn·ficiō -ficere -fēcī -fectus *tr* to make, manufacture, process, refine; to do, perform, accomplish; to carry out, discharge; to celebrate *(a rite, festival)*; to make ready, prepare; to complete, execute, fulfill; to bring about, cause; to bring together, collect; to secure, obtain; to use up, wear out, exhaust; to finish off, destroy, kill; to run through, waste *(money, inheritance)*; to chew *(food)*; to digest *(food)*; to spend, pass *(time)*; to compose, write; to set down in writing, record; to demonstrate; to cover *(a distance)*; *(of grief, worry)* to overwhelm
cōnficti·ō -ōnis *f* fabrication
cōnfictus *pp of* **cōnfingō**
cōnfīd·ēns -entis *adj* trustful; self-confident; presumptuous, smug
cōnfīdenter *adv* confidently; smugly
cōnfīdenti·a -ae *f* confidence; self-confidence, smugness
cōnfīdentiloqu·us -a -um *adj* speaking confidently
cōnfī·dō -dere -sus sum *intr* to have confidence, be confident; *(w. dat)* to confide in, rely on, trust, believe
cōnfī·gō -gere -xī -xus *tr* to fasten, join together; to pierce, transfix; *(fig)* to paralyze
cōn·fingō -fingere -fīnxī -fictus *tr* to make up, fabricate
cōnfīn·is -is -e *adj* having common boundaries, adjoining; *(fig)* akin
cōnfīn·ium -(i)ī *n* common boundary, frontier; border; *(fig)* borderline **||** *npl* limits, confines
cōnfīnxī *perf of* **cōnfingō**
cōn·fīō -fierī *intr* to be accomplished; to occur, happen; *(w.* **ex)** to be made from
cōnfirmāti·ō -ōnis *f* confirmation, encouragement; verification; *(rhet)* presentation of evidence
cōnfirmāt·or -ōris *m* guarantor
cōnfirmāt·us -a -um *adj* resolute, confident, courageous; established, well-attested
cōnfirmit·ās -ātis *f* firmness; stubbornness
cōnfirm·ō -āre -āvī -ātus *tr* to strengthen; to establish on a firm basis; to develop *(mind, character)*; to reinforce; to sanction, ratify; to encourage; to corroborate; to assert positively; *(w. acc & inf)* to prove that; to prove the existence of; to give assurances of, affirm; *(mil)* to strengthen *(a position)* **||** *refl* to recover, gain strength **||** *pass* to become mature
cōnfisc·ō -āre -āvī -ātus *tr* to deposit in a treasury; to confiscate *(for the public treasury)*
cōnfīsi·ō -ōnis *f* confidence
cōnfīsus *pp of* **cōnfīdō**
cōn·fiteor -fitērī -fessus sum *tr* to confess, acknowledge, admit; to reveal **||** *intr* to confess; *(poet)* to admit defeat
cōnfīxī *perf of* **cōnfīgō**
cōnfīxus *pp of* **cōnfīgō**
cōnflagrāti·ō -ōnis *f* conflagration; eruption *(of a volcano)*
cōnflagr·ō -āre -āvī -ātum *intr* to burn, be on fire; to be burnt down; *(fig)* to be utterly destroyed
cōnflīcti·ō -ōnis *f* conflict
cōnflīct·ō -āre -āvī -ātus *tr (usu. used in the passive)* to strike down; to ruin; to afflict, torment; to buffet

cōnflīct·or -ārī -ātus sum *intr* to struggle, wrestle
cōnflīct·us -ūs *m* clash, collision
cōnflī·gō -gere -xī -ctus *tr* to knock together, beat, clap ‖ *intr* to clash, fight, battle; *(w.* **cum)** to come into conflict with, clash with; *(w.* **adversus** + *acc or* **contrā** + *acc)* to fight against; **inter sē cōnflīgere** to collide with one another
cōnfl·ō -āre -āvī -ātus *tr* to kindle, ignite; to inflame *(passions);* to melt down *(metals);* to raise *(army, money, etc.);* to concoct *(a lie);* to run up *(debt);* to bring about, cause; to hatch *(plot);* to organize *(riot)*
cōnflu·ēns -entis *adj* flowing together; flowing into; **ā cōnfluente Rhodānō** from the confluence of the Rhone *(with the Arar)*
cōnflu·ēns -entis *m (often pl)* confluence
cōnflu·ō -ere -xī *intr* to flow together; *(fig)* to flock together, come in crowds; *(of things)* to gather
cōn·fodiō -fodere -fōdī -fossus *tr* to dig up *(soil)*; to stab; *(fig)* to harm
cōnfore = cōnfutūrum esse to be about to happen
cōnfōrmāti·ō -ōnis *f* shape, form; fashion; idea, notion; arrangement *(of words);* expression *(in voice); (rhet)* figure of speech
cōnfōrm·ō -āre -āvī -ātus *tr* to shape, fashion, put together; to describe, delineate; to train, educate; to bring into harmony
cōnfoss·us -a -um *pp of* **cōnfodiō** ‖ *adj* full of holes, punctured
cōnfrāctus *pp of* **cōnfringō**
cōnfragōs·us -a -um *adj* rough, rugged ‖ *npl* rugged terrain
cōnfrem·ō -ere -uī *intr* to grumble
cōnfric·ō -āre *tr* to rub vigorously; to massage
cōn·fringō -fringere -frēgī -frāctus *tr* to smash, crush; to ruin, undo ‖ *pass (of ships)* to be wrecked
cōn·fugiō -fugere -fūgī *intr* to flee, take refuge, run for help; *(w.* **ad) 1** to have recourse to; **2** to appeal to
cōnfug·ium -(i)ī *n* place of refuge, sanctuary, shelter
cōnfulg·eō -ēre -sī *intr* to glitter, sparkle
cōn·fundō -fundere -fūdī -fūsus *tr* to pour together, blend, mingle; to mix up, jumble together, confuse, bewilder; to spread, diffuse
cōnfūsē *adv* in confusion
cōnfūsi·ō -ōnis *f* mixing, blending; confusion, mixup; **cōnfūsiō ōris** blush
cōnfūs·us -a -um *pp of* **cōnfundō** ‖ *adj* confused; troubled *(look)*
cōnfūt·ō -āre -āvī -ātus *tr* to keep from boiling over; to repress, stop; to confute
cōnfu·tuō -tuere -tuī -tūtus *tr (vulg)* to screw; **quidquid puellārum cōnfutuere** to screw any and every girl
congel·ō -āre -āvī -ātus *tr* to cause to freeze up, harden; to curdle; *(fig)* to chill; **in lapidem congelāre** to petrify ‖ *intr* to freeze, freeze up; to become hard; to become inactive
congemināti·ō -ōnis *f* doubling
congemin·ō -āre -āvī -ātus *tr* to double
congem·ō -ere -uī -itus *tr* to deplore deeply ‖ *intr* to gasp, sigh, groan
con·ger -grī *m* eel
congeri·ēs -ēī *f* heap, pile
con·gerō -gerere -gessī -gestus *tr* to bring together; to heap up, build up; to build, erect; to keep up, multiply; to repeat *(arguments); (w.* **in** + *acc)* **1** to shower *(weapons)* on; **2** to heap *(curses, favors)* upon
congerr·ō -ōnis *m* playmate
congestīci·us -a -um *adj* piled up
congestus *pp of* **congerō**
congest·us -ūs *m* heap, mass
congiāl·is -is -e *adj* holding a gallon
congiāri·us -a -um *adj* holding a gallon ‖ *n* gift of one gallon *(e.g., of olive oil apiece to the people);* bonus *(to the army);* gift of money *(to the people);* gift, donation
cong·ius -(i)ī *m* liquid measure *(about 6 pints)*
conglaci·ō -āre -āvī *intr* to freeze up
conglīsc·ō -ere *intr* to blaze up
conglobāti·ō -ōnis *f* massing together
conglob·ō -āre -āvī -ātus *tr* to make round, form into a ball; to mass together
conglomer·ō -āre -āvī -ātus *tr* to roll up; to group together, crowd together ‖ *refl (w.* **in** + *acc)* to crowd into
conglūtināti·ō -ōnis *f* gluing together; *(fig)* combining *(of words)*
conglūtin·ō -āre -āvī -ātus *tr* to glue, cement; *(fig)* to unite closely, to cement
congraec·ō -āre -āvī -ātus *tr* to squander like a Greek
congrātulāti·ō -ōnis *f* congratulations
congrātul·or -ārī -ātus sum *intr* to offer congratulations; *(of several persons)* to express their joy
con·gredior -gredī -gressus sum *tr* to meet, accost, address; to engage ‖ *intr* to come together, meet; *(w.* **cum) 1** to meet with; **2** to associate with; **3** to fight against
congregābil·is -is -e *adj* gregarious
congregāti·ō -ōnis *f* flocking together, congregation, union, association
congreg·ō -āre -āvī -ātus *tr* to herd together; to assemble; to group together ‖ *pass* to flock together; **parēs cum paribus facillimē congregantur** *(prov)* birds of a feather flock together
congressi·ō -ōnis *f* meeting, conference

congressus *pp of* **congredior**
congress·us -ūs *m* meeting, association, society; union, combination; hostile encounter; fight; sexual intercourse
congru·ēns -entis *adj* coinciding, corresponding; suitable; consistent; self-consistent, uniform
congruenter *adv* consistently; *(w. dat or* **ad)** in conformity with; **congruenter nātūrae vīvere** to live in conformity with nature
congruenti·a -ae *f* consistency; similarity; good proportion
congru·ō -ere -ī *intr* to coincide; to correspond, agree, be consistent; *(w.* **ad** *or* **cum)** to correspond to, agree with, be consistent with; *(w. dat or* **in** *+ acc)* to agree with
congru·us -a -um *adj* agreeing, corresponding
coniecti·ō -ōnis *f* hurling, barrage *(of missiles);* conjecture; guesswork; interpretation *(of dreams, etc.);* prophecy; **coniectiōnem facere** to draw a conclusion
coniect·ō -āre -āvī -ātus *tr* **(cōiect-)** to conjecture, infer
coniect·or -ōris *m* interpreter of dreams, seer
coniectr·īx -īcis *f* interpreter of dreams, seeress
coniectūr·a -ae *f* **(cōiect-)** conjecture, guess; inference; interpretation
coniectūrāl·is -is -e *adj* conjectural
coniect·us -ūs *m* throwing together; crowding together; connecting; heap, crowd, pile; throwing, hurling; turning, directing *(eyes);* casting *(a glance);* barrage *(of stones, missiles);* **ad** *(or* **intrā)** **tēlī coniectum venīre** to come within range of a weapon
cōnif·er *or* **cōnig·er -era -erum** *adj* coniferous
con·iciō -icere -iēcī -iectus *tr* **(cō·iciō)** to hurl, cast; to pile together; to conclude, infer; to conjecture; to interpret ‖ *refl* **sē in fugam** *(or* **in pedēs)** **conicere** to take to one's heels
cōnī·tor -tī -xus sum *or* **-sus sum** *intr* to make a great effort, struggle, exert oneself; *(w.* **in** *+ acc)* to struggle toward, try to reach
coniugāl·is -is -e *adj* conjugal
coniugāti·ō -ōnis *f (gram)* etymological relationship *(of words)*
coniugāt·or -ōris *m* uniter *(said of Hymen, god of marriage)*
coniugiāl·is -is -e *adj* marriage
coniug·ium -(i)ī *n* union *(e.g., of body and soul);* marriage, wedlock; mating *(of animals); (fig)* spouse
coniug·ō -āre -āvī -ātus *tr* to join in marriage; to form *(a friendship);* **verba coniugāta** *(gram)* cognates
coniūnctē *adv* conjointly; at the same time; hypothetically; in intimacy
coniūnctim *adv* jointly
coniūncti·ō -ōnis *f* combination, union; association, connection; friendship, intimacy; marriage; relationship *(by blood or marriage);* sympathy, affinity; *(gram)* conjunction
coniūnct·us -a -um *adj (w. dat or abl)* bordering on, near; *(w. dat or abl or* **cum) 1** connected with; **2** agreeing with, conforming with ‖ *n* connection
coniun·gō -gere coniūnxī coniūnctus *tr* to join together; to unite in making *(war);* to join in marriage; to unite *(by bonds of friendship); (w. dat)* to add *(e.g., words)* to *(e.g., a letter)*
con·iūnx -iugis *m* **(-iux)** spouse, husband ‖ *mpl* married couple ‖ *f* spouse, wife; fiancée; bride; the female *(of animals)*
coniūrāti·ō -ōnis *f* plot, conspiracy; alliance
coniūrāt·us -a -um *adj* bound together by an oath, allied, associated; *(mil)* sworn in ‖ *mpl* conspirators
coniūr·ō -āre -āvī -ātum *intr* to take an oath together; to plot, conspire
coniux *see* **coniūnx**
cōn·īveō -īvēre -īvī *or* **-īxī** *intr* **(conn-)** to close the eyes; to blink; *(of sun, moon)* to be eclipsed; to be drowsy; *(w.* **in** *+ acc)* to connive at, overlook
conj- = coni-
conl- = coll-
conm- = comm-
Con·ōn -ōnis *(acc:* **-ōna)** famous Athenian admiral *(fl c. 400 B.C.)* ‖ famous mathematician and astronomer of Samos *(fl c. 230 B.C.)*
cōnōpī·um -ī *n* **(-pē·um)** mosquito net; bed with net, canopy bed
cōn·or -ārī -ātus sum *tr* to try
conquassāti·ō -ōnis *f* severe shaking, disturbance
conquass·ō -āre -āvī -ātus *tr* to shake hard; *(fig)* shatter, upset, disturb
conque·ror -rī -stus sum *tr* to complain bitterly about, deplore ‖ *intr* to complain bitterly
conquesti·ō -ōnis *f* complaint; *(rhet)* appeal for sympathy; *(w. gen, w.* **dē** *+ abl or* **adversus** *+ acc)* complaint about
conquest·us -ūs *m* loud complaint
conqui·ēscō -ēscere -ēvī -ētum *intr* to rest, take a rest; to go to sleep; to find rest, find recreation; to keep quiet, remain inactive; to slacken; to lie dormant; to stop, pause
con·quinīscō -quinīscere -quexī *intr* to crouch down, squat
conquī·rō -rere -sīvī *or* **-siī -sītus** *tr* to search for, look for; to procure, bring together, collect; *(fig)* to go after *(e.g., pleasures)*

conquīsīti·ō -ōnis *f* search *(in order to bring together or obtain),* procuring, collection; *(mil)* recruitment, draft
conquīsīt·or -ōris *m* **(-quist-)** recruiting officer
conquīsīt·us -a -um *pp of* **conquīrō** ‖ *adj* select, choice
conr- = corr-
cōnsaep·iō -īre -sī -tus *tr* **(-sēp-)** to fence in, enclose
cōnsaept·um -ī *n* **(-sēp-)** enclosure
cōnsalūtāti·ō -ōnis *f* exchange of greetings
cōnsalūt·ō -āre -āvī -ātus *tr* to greet *(as a group),* greet cordially ‖ *intr* **inter sē cōnsalūtāre** to greet one another, exchange greetings
cōnsān·ēscō -ēscere -uī *intr* to heal up; to recover
cōnsanguine·us -a -um *adj* related by blood ‖ *m* brother ‖ *mpl* relatives ‖ *f* sister
cōnsanguinit·ās -ātis *f* blood relationship; **cōnsanguinitāte propinquus** closely related
cōnsauci·ō -āre -āvī -ātus *tr* to wound severely
cōnscelerāt·us -a -um *adj* wicked, depraved, criminal; *(fig)* rotten to the core
cōnsceler·ō -āre -āvī -ātus *tr* to stain with guilt, dishonor, disgrace
cōnscen·dō -dere -dī cōnscēnsus *tr* to climb up, ascend; to climb *(tree);* to mount *(horse, chariot);* to board *(ship);* **aequor nāvibus cōnscendere** to go to sea ‖ *intr* to climb up; to climb aboard
cōnscēnsi·ō -ōnis *f* embarkation; **in nāvēs cōnscēnsiō** boarding the ships
cōnscienti·a -ae *f* joint knowledge; consciousness, knowledge; conscience; scruples; remorse
cōn·scindō -scindere -scidī -scissus *tr* to tear up, tear to pieces; *(fig)* to tear apart, abuse
cōnsc·iō -īre -īvī *tr* to have on one's conscience
cōnsc·īscō -īscere -īvī *or* **-iī -ītus** *tr* to decree, decide on; *(w.* **sibi)** to inflict on oneself; **sibi mortem cōnscīscere** to decide on suicide
cōnsci·us -a -um *adj* cognizant, conscious, aware; *(w. gen or dat)* having knowledge of, privy to ‖ *mf* partner; accomplice; confidant(e), confederate
cōnscre·or -ārī -ātus sum *intr* to clear the throat
cōnscrī·bō -bere -psī -ptus *tr* to enlist, enroll; to write up, compose; to prescribe
cōnscrīpti·ō -ōnis *f* record
cōnscrīpt·us -a -um *pp of* **cōnscrībō** ‖ *m* senator; **patrēs cōnscrīptī** gentlemen of the Senate ‖ *n (leg)* deposition
cōnsec·ō -āre -uī -tus *tr* to cut up into small pieces, dismember
cōnsecrāti·ō -ōnis *f* consecration; deification *(of emperors)*
cōnsecr·ō -āre -āvī -ātus *tr* to consecrate; to dedicate to the gods below, doom to destruction; to immortalize; to hallow; to deify
cōnsectāri·us -a -um *adj* conclusive
cōnsectāti·ō -ōnis *f* eager pursuit
cōnsectātr·īx -īcis *f* eager pursuer
cōnsecti·ō -ōnis *f* cutting up
cōnsect·or -ārī -ātus sum *tr* to follow eagerly, go after; to chase, hunt; to overtake; to imitate, follow
cōnsecūti·ō -ōnis *f* effect, consequences; *(rhet)* order, sequence
cōnsen·ēscō -ēscere -uī *intr* to grow old, grow old together; to become grey; to become obsolete; to waste away, fade, decline; to degenerate
cōnsēnsi·ō -ōnis *f* agreement, unanimity; harmony; plot
cōnsēns·us -ūs *m* agreement, unanimity; harmony; plot; **cōnsēnsū** with one accord; **in cōnsēnsum vertere** to become a general custom
cōnsentāne·us -a -um *adj (w. dat or* **cum)** **1** agreeing with; **2** according to, in accord with; **3** proper for; **cōnsentāneum est** it is reasonable ‖ *npl* concurrent circumstances
cōnsenti·ēns -entis *adj* unanimous
cōnsen·tiō -tīre -sī -sus *tr* to agree on; to consent to; **bellum cōnsentīre** to agree on war, vote for war ‖ *intr* to agree; *(w. inf)* **1** to agree to; **2** to plot to; *(w.* **cum) 1** to agree with; **2** *(pej)* to plot with, conspire with; **3** *(of things)* to fit in with, be consistent with, harmonize with
cōnsēp- = cōnsaep-
cōnsequ·ēns -entis *adj* reasonable; corresponding; logical; suitable ‖ *n* consequence, conclusion
cōnsequenter *adv* consequently
cōnsequenti·a -ae *f* consequence; natural sequence; **per cōnsequentiās** consequently
cōnse·quor -quī -cūtus sum *tr* to follow, follow up, pursue, go after; to catch up with, catch; to reach, attain to; to arrive at; *(fig)* to follow, copy, imitate; to obtain, get, acquire; to understand; *(of speech)* to do justice to; *(of time)* to come after, follow; to result from
cōnser·ō -ere -uī -tus *tr* entwine, tie, join, string together; **manum** *(or* **manūs) cōnserere** to fight hand-to-hand; **proelium** *(or* **pugnam) cōnserere** to begin to fight
con·serō -serere -sēvī -situs *tr* to sow, plant
cōnsertē *adv* in close connection
cōnserv·a -ae *f* fellow slave *(female)*
cōnservāti·ō -ōnis *f* preservation

cōnservāt·or -ōris *m* preserver, defender
cōnservātr·ix -īcis *f* protectress
cōnservit·ium -(i)ī *n* fellowship in slavery
cōnserv·ō -āre -āvī -ātus *tr* to keep safe, preserve, maintain; to act in accordance with, observe; *(fig)* to keep intact
cōnserv·us -ī *m* fellow slave
cōnsess·or -ōris *m* neighbor *(one who sits next to another at a feast, assembly, court of justice, public games)*
cōnsess·us -ūs *m* a sitting together, an assembly, a court, an audience
cōnsīderātē *adv* deliberately, with caution
cōnsīderāti·ō -ōnis *f* consideration, examination
cōnsīderāt·us -a -um *adj* cautious; well-considered, deliberate
cōnsīder·ō -āre -āvī -ātus *tr* to inspect, examine; to consider, reflect on
cōnsid·ium -(i)ī *n* court of justice
cōn·sīdō -sīdere -sēdī *or* **-sīdī -sessum** *intr* to sit down, be seated; to hold sessions, be in session; to settle, stay *(in residence)*; to settle, sink; *(fig)* to sink; to subside, calm down; *(mil)* to encamp, take up a position; **cōnsīdere in** (+ *abl*) *(of a bird)* to land on
cōnsign·ō -āre -āvī -ātus *tr* to seal, sign; to certify, vouch for; to record *(in a sealed document)*; to put on record
cōnsil·ēscō -ēscere -uī *intr* to fall silent; to become still, calm down
cōnsiliāri·us -a -um *adj* counseling **‖** *m* counselor, consultant; cabinet member *(of an emperor)*
cōnsiliāt·or -ōris *m* counselor
cōnsiliō *adv* intentionally
cōnsili·or -ārī -ātus sum *intr* to deliberate; to give advice
cōnsil·ium -(i)ī *n* consultation, deliberation; advice; council; council of war; plan, stratagem; measure; decision; purpose, intention; policy; judgment, wisdom, discretion, sense; *(emperor's)* cabinet; **cōnsiliō** *(or* **cōnsiliīs)** **alicūius** on s.o.'s instructions; **cōnsilium capere** *(or* **inīre** *or* **suscipere)** to form a plan, come to a decision; **cōnsilium mihi est** *(w. inf)* I intend to; **in cōnsiliō esse** to be available for consultation; **nōn est cōnsilium mihi** *(w. inf)* I don't mean to; **prīvātō cōnsiliō** for one's own purpose
cōnsiluī *perf of* **cōnsilēscō**
cōnsimil·is -is -e *adj* quite similar; *(w. gen or dat)* just like
cōnsip·iō -ere *intr* to be sane
cōn·sistō -sistere -stitī *intr* to come to a stop, stop, pause, halt; *(w.* **cum)** to talk with; to take a stand; to stand still; to grow hard, become solid, set; *(of ships)* to come to anchorage, to ground; *(of travelers)* to halt on a journey; to be firm, be steadfast, endure; to be, exist; to come into existence; to continue in existence, remain; to occur, take place; *(mil)* to take up a position, be posted, make a stand; *(w. abl or* **in** + *abl)* **1** to consist of; **2** to depend on; **3** to be based on; **4** to base one's case on; *(w. abl, w.* **in** + *abl, w.* **dē** *or* **ex** + *abl)* to be comprised of; **cōnstitit** *(w. acc & inf)* it is a fact that
cōnsiti·ō -ōnis *f* sowing, planting
cōnsit·or -ōris *m* sower, planter
cōnsitūr·a -ae *f* sowing, planting
cōnsōbrīn·a -ae *f* first cousin *(female)*
cōnsōbrīn·us -ī *m* first cousin
cōnsoc·er -erī *m* (a joint) father-in-law
cōnsociāti·ō -ōnis *f* association
cōnsociāt·us -a -um *adj* shared
cōnsoci·ō -āre -āvī -ātus *tr* to join in *(plans, activities)*; to share **‖** *intr* to enter into a partnership
cōnsōlābil·is -is -e *adj* consolable
cōnsōlāti·ō -ōnis *f* consolation, comfort; encouragement; allaying
cōnsōlāt·or -ōris *m* comforter
cōnsōlātōri·us -a -um *adj* comforting; **litterae cōnsōlātōriae** letter of condolence
cōnsōlor -ārī -ātus sum *tr* to console, comfort; to reassure, soothe, encourage; to relieve
cōnsomni·ō -āre -āvī *tr* to dream about
cōnson·ō -āre -uī *intr* to sound together, ring, resound, reecho; *(w. dat or* **cum)** to harmonize with, agree with; **inter sē cōnsonāre** to agree, be in accord
cōnson·us -a -um *adj* harmonious
cōnsōp·iō -īre -īvī *or* **-ītus** *tr* to put to sleep
cōnsor·s -tis *adj* having a common lot; common; shared in common **‖** *mf* partner **‖** *m* brother **‖** *f* sister
cōnsorti·ō -ōnis *f* partnership; association; fellowship
cōnsort·ium -(i)ī *n* community of goods; partnership; participation; *(w. gen)* partnership in
cōnspect·us -a -um *pp of* **cōnspiciō ‖** *adj* visible; in full sight; conspicuous, striking
cōnspect·us -ūs *m* look, sight, view; (sense of) sight; mental view; appearance on the scene; **cōnspectū in mediō** before all eyes
cōnsper·gō -gere -sī -sus *tr* to sprinkle; to splatter
cōnspiciend·us -a -um *adj* worth seeing; distinguished
cōnspicill·um -ī *n* lookout (post)
cōn·spiciō -spicere -spexī -spectus *tr* to look at attentively, observe, fix the eyes on; to catch sight of, spot; to look at with admiration; to face *(e.g., the Forum)* **‖** *pass* to be conspicuous, be noticed, be admired; to attract attention
cōnspic·or -ārī -ātus sum *tr* to catch sight of, spot, see; *(in a passive sense)* to be conspicuous

cōnspicu·us -a -um *adj* visible, in sight; conspicuous, striking, remarkable, distinguished

cōnspīrāti·ō -ōnis *f* agreement, unanimity, harmony; plot

cōnspīrāt·us -a -um *adj* conspiring, conspiratorial

cōnspīr·ō -āre -āvī -ātum *intr* to act in harmony; to agree; to conspire

cōnspōns·or -ōris *m* co-guarantor

cōn·spuō -spuere -spuī -spūtus *tr* to spit on

cōnspurc·ō -āre -āvī -ātus *tr* to defile, mess up; to defile sexually

cōnspūt·ō -āre -āvī -ātus *tr* to spit on

cōnstabil·iō -īre -īvī *or* **-iī -ītus** *tr* to stabilize, put on a firm basis

cōnst·āns -antis *adj* constant, uniform, steady, fixed, stable, regular, invariable, persistent; consistent; *(fig)* faithful, trustworthy

cōnstanter *adv* constantly, steadily, uniformly, invariably; consistently

cōnstanti·a -ae *f* constancy, steadiness, firmness, perseverance; consistency, harmony; steadfastness; self-possession

cōnsternāti·ō -ōnis *f* consternation, dismay, alarm; disorder, disturbance; mutiny; wild rush, stampede

cōnstern·ō -āre -āvī -ātus *tr* to shock; to startle; to stampede; to derange; *(w.* **ad** *or* **in** *+ acc)* to drive *(by fear, etc.)* to *(some action)*

cōn·sternō -sternere -strāvī -strātus *tr* to spread, cover; to pave; to thatch; **cōnstrāta nāvis** ship with deck

cōnstīp·ō -āre -āvī -ātus *tr* to pack together, crowd together

cōnstit·uō -uere -uī -ūtus *tr* to set up, erect; settle *(e.g., people in a place);* to establish; to settle on, fix *(date, price, penalty);* to moor *(a ship);* to arrange, organize; to designate, appoint, assign; to decide, arbitrate, decree, judge; *(mil)* to station, post, deploy; *(w. inf)* to decide to

cōnstitūti·ō -ōnis *f* constitution, nature; disposition; regulation, ordinance; definition; *(rhet)* issue, point of discussion

cōnstitūt·us -a -um *pp of* **cōnstituō** ‖ *adj* ordered, arranged; **bene cōnstitūtum corpus** good constitution ‖ *n* agreement, arrangement; appointment

cōn·stō -stāre -stitī *intr* to stand together; to agree, correspond; to stand firm, be constant; to stand still; to be in existence; *(com)* to tally, be correct; *(w. abl of price)* to cost; **ratiō cōnstat** the account tallies, is correct ‖ *v impers* it is a fact, it is known; **nōn mihi satis cōnstat** I have not quite made up my mind; **satis cōnstat** it is an established fact, all agree

cōnstrāt·us -a -um *adj* paved; *(ship)* with deck ‖ *n* platform; deck *(of ship);* flooring

cōn·stringō -stringere -strīnxī -strictus *tr* to tie together, tie up; to chain; *(fig)* to restrain, inhibit, control; to limit, confine; to limit in time; to knit *(the brow);* to tone up *(the body); (rhet)* to condense

cōnstructi·ō -ōnis *f* building, construction; arrangement *(of words)*

cōnstru·ō -ere -xī -ctus *tr* to heap up; to construct; to arrange in a group; *(gram)* to construct

cōnstuprāt·or -ōris *m* rapist

cōnstupr·ō -āre -āvī -ātus *tr* to rape

cōnsuā·deō -dēre -sī -sus *tr* to advocate ‖ *intr (w. dat)* to try to persuade

Cōnsuāl·ia -ium *npl* feast of Consus *(ancient Italic god of fertility, celebrated on August 21 and December 15)*

cōnsuās·or -ōris *m* adviser

cōnsūcid·us -a -um *adj* very juicy

cōnsūd·ō -āre -āvī *intr* to sweat profusely

cōnsuē·faciō -facere -fēcī -factus *tr* to accustom, inure

cōnsu·ēscō -ēscere -ēvī -ētus *tr* to accustom, inure ‖ *intr* to become accustomed; *(w. inf)* to become accustomed to, get used to; *(w.* **cum***)* to cohabit with

cōnsuēti·ō -ōnis *f* sexual intercourse

cōnsuētūd·ō -inis *f* custom, habit; usage, idiom; social ties; sexual intercourse; **ad cōnsuētūdinem** *(w. gen)* according to the custom of; **(ex) cōnsuētūdine** from habit; **prō meā cōnsuētūdine** as is my habit; **ut fert cōnsuētūdō** as is usual

cōnsuēt·us -a -um *pp of* **cōnsuēscō** ‖ *adj* customary

cōn·sul -sulis *m* consul *(one of the two highest magistrates of the Roman Republic);* **cōnsul dēsignātus** consul-elect; **cōnsulem creāre** *(or* **dīcere,** *or* **facere)** to elect a consul; **cōnsul ōrdinārius** regular consul *(who entered office in January 1);* **cōnsul suffectus** substitute consul *(chosen in the course of the year to fill a vacancy)*

cōnsulār·is -is -e *adj* consular; **aetās cōnsulāris** minimum legal age to be consul *(42 years);* **comitia cōnsulāria** consular elections; **vir cōnsulāris** a man of consular rank ‖ *m* ex-consul

cōnsulāriter *adv* like a consul, in a manner worthy of a consul

cōnsulāt·us -ūs *m* consulship; **cōnsulātum gerere** to hold the consulship; **cōnsulātum petere** to run for the consulship; **sē cōnsulātū abdicāre** to resign from the consulship

cōnsul·ō -ere -uī -tus *tr* to consult; to consider; to advise *(s.th.),* offer as advice; **bonī (optimī) cōnsulere** to think well (very highly) of ‖ *intr* to deliberate, reflect; *(w. dat)* to look after; *(w.* **ad** *or* **in** + *acc)* to reflect on, take into consideration; *(w.* **in** + *acc)* to take measures against; *(w.* **dē** + *abl)* to pass sentence on

cōnsultāti·ō -ōnis *f* mature deliberation, consideration; consulting; inquiry; subject of consultation

cōnsultē *adv* deliberately, with due deliberation, prudently

cōnsultō *adv* deliberately, on purpose

cōnsult·ō -āre -āvī -ātus *tr* to reflect on, consider maturely; to ask *(s.o.)* for advice, consult **||** *intr* to deliberate; *(w. dat)* to look after, take care of; **in medium** *(or* **in commūne)** **cōnsultāre** to look after the common good

cōnsult·or -ōris *m* counselor, consultant; advisee, client

cōnsultr·īx -īcis *f* protectress

cōnsult·um -ī *n see* **cōnsultus**

cōnsult·us -a -um *pp of* **cōnsulō** **||** *adj* skilled, experienced **||** *m* expert; **iūris cōnsultus** legal expert, attorney **||** *n* deliberation, consideration; decree, decision; response *(from an oracle)*; **bene cōnsultum** a good measure; **male cōnsultum** an ill-advised measure; **senātūs cōnsultum** decree of the Senate

cōnsummāt·us -a -um *adj* consummate, perfect

cōnsumm·ō -āre -āvī -ātus *tr* to sum up; *(of numbers)* to add up to; to finish, accomplish, perfect; to complete *(public works)*

cōnsūm·ō -ere -psī -ptus *tr* to consume, use up, exhaust; to devour; to wear out; to waste

cōnsūmpti·ō -ōnis *f* consumption; wasting

cōnsūmpt·or -ōris *m* consumer; spendthrift

con·suō -suere -suī -sūtus *tr* to sew up

cōnsur·gō -gere -rēxī -rēctum *intr* to stand up; to rise in a body; *(w.* **ad** *or* **in** + *acc)* to aspire to

cōnsurrēcti·ō -ōnis *f* rising up, standing up in a body

Cōns·us -ī *m* ancient Italic deity of agriculture and fertility

cōnsusurr·ō -āre -āvī *intr* to whisper to one another

contābē·faciō -facere -fēcī -factus *tr* to wear out; to waste *(fig)* to run *(s.o.)* down

contāb·ēscō -ēscere -uī *intr* to waste away

contabulāti·ō -ōnis *f* flooring; floor, story

contabul·ō -āre -āvī -ātus *tr* to cover with boards; to construct with multiple stories; to bridge, span

contāct·us -a -um *pp of* **contingō**

contāct·us -ūs *m* touch, contact; contagion; *(fig)* infection

contāg·ēs -is *f* touch, contact

contāgi·ō -ōnis *f* touching; touch, contact; contagion, infection

contāg·ium -(i)ī *n* touch, contact; contagion; moral contamination

contāmināt·us -a -um *adj* contaminated, polluted; vile

contāmin·ō -āre -āvī -ātus *tr* to contaminate, pollute; to adulterate; to defile, desecrate; to ruin, spoil

contechn·or -ārī -ātus sum *intr* to devise plots; to think up tricks

conte·gō -gere contēxī contēctus *tr* to cover up; to hide; to protect; to put a roof on; to bury

contemer·ō -āre -āvī -ātus *tr* to defile

contem·nō -nere -psī -ptus *tr* to regard with contempt, look down on, despise; to treat with contempt; to pay no attention to, disregard; to have nothing to do with

contemplāti·ō -ōnis *f* viewing, surveying; contemplation, consideration

contemplāt·or -ōris *m* contemplator, observer

contemplāt·us -ūs *m* contemplation

contempl·ō -āre -āvī -ātus *or* **contempl·or -ārī -ātus sum** *tr* to observe, survey, gaze on, contemplate

contemptim *adv* contemptuously; fearlessly

contempti·ō -ōnis *f* scorn; contempt; disregarding, belittling

contempt·or -ōris *m* despiser

contemptr·īx -īcis *f* despiser *(female)*

contempt·us -a -um *pp of* **contemnō** **||** *adj* contemptible

contempt·us -ūs *m* contempt; **contemptuī esse** to be an object of contempt

conten·dō -dere -dī -tus *tr* to stretch, draw tight; to tune *(instrument)*; to aim, shoot, hurl; to strain, exert; to assert, hold, allege; to compare, contrast; **cursum** *(or* **iter)** **contendere** to make one's way **||** *intr* to exert oneself; to contend, compete, fight; to dispute, argue; to travel, march; to match, contrast; *(w.* **dē** + *abl)* to demand from; *(w. inf)* to be in a hurry to; *(w.* **in** + *acc)* to rush to, head for; *(w.* **ad)** to strive for, aspire to; *(w.* **cum)** **1** to contend with, argue with; **2** to fight with

contentē *adv (from* **contendō)** vehemently, vigorously, earnestly

contentē *adv (from* **contineō)** in a restricted way, sparingly, scantily

contenti·ō -ōnis *f* stretching, tension; exertion, effort; competition; quarrel; contrast, comparison, antithesis; *(gram)* comparison of adjectives; *(rhet)* crescendo; **in contentiōnem venīre** *or* **vocārī** *(or* **in contentiōne pōnī)** to become the subject of a dispute

content·us -a -um *pp of* **contendō** **||** *adj* tense, strained; energetic

content·us -a -um *pp of* **contineō** **||** *adj* content, satisfied

contermin·us -a -um *adj* neighboring; *(w. dat)* adjacent to

con·terō -terere -trīvī -trītus *tr* to grind to powder, pulverize, crush; to wear out; *(fig)* to wear down; *(fig)* to trample on; to expunge, wipe out; to waste *(time, effort);* to exhaust *(topic)*

conterr·eō -ēre -uī -itus *tr* to scare the life out of

contest·or -ārī -ātus sum *tr* to call to witness; *(fig)* to prove, attest; **lītem contestārī** to open a lawsuit by calling witnesses

contex·ō -ere -uī -tus *tr* to weave together; to make by joining, devise, build; to link, join *(words);* to compose *(writings);* to dream up

contextē *adv* in a coherent manner

context·us -a -um *pp of* **contexō** ‖ *adj* interwoven; coherent; continuous, uninterrupted

context·us -ūs *m* joining together; coherence; continuity, connection; structure; plan, course

contic·ēscō -ēscere *or* **contic·īscō -īscere -uī** *intr* to become quite still, fall completely silent; to keep silence; *(fig)* to abate, cease

conticinn·um -ī *n* silence of the night; **conticinnō** in the evening

conticīscō *see* **conticēscō**

contignāti·ō -ōnis *f* floor, story

contign·ō -āre -āvī -ātus *tr* to lay a floor on

contigu·us -a -um *adj* contiguous, touching, adjoining, within reach; *(w. dat)* bordering on, near

contin·ēns -entis *adj* continuous, unbroken; homogeneous; adjacent, close; next, immediately following; successive *(days);* self-controlled, moderate; restrained; *(w. dat)* contiguous with, adjacent to; *(w.* **cum)** bordering on ‖ *f* interior *(of a country);* mainland ‖ *n* main point *(of argument);* **ex continentī** *(or* **in continentī)** without delay

continenter *adv* in unbroken succession; without interruption; *(sitting)* close together; moderately

continenti·a -ae *f* repression; self-control

con·tineō -tinēre -tinuī -tentus *tr* to hold *or* keep together; to keep within bounds, confine; to contain, comprise, include; to control, repress

con·tingō -tingere -tigī -tāctus *tr* to come into contact with; to touch, border on; to reach, attain; to infect; to contaminate; *(fig)* to touch, affect ‖ *intr* to happen, turn out, come to pass; *(w. dat)* to touch, border on ‖ *v impers* it happens, turns out; *(w. dat)* it befalls, happens to

continuāti·ō -ōnis *f* unbroken series, succession; *(rhet)* period

continuō *adv* immediately; right from the first; without more ado; continuously; necessarily

continu·ō -āre -āvī -ātus *tr* to make continuous, join together, connect; to extend *(in time or space);* to continue, carry on, draw out, prolong; to pass, occupy *(time)* ‖ *pass (w. dat)* **1** to be contiguous with, adjacent to; **2** to follow closely upon ‖ *intr* to continue, last

continu·us -a -um *adj* continuous, unbroken; successive; **diēs continuōs quīnque** (for) five days in a row

conti·ō -ōnis *f* meeting, rally; public meeting *(of the people or soldiers);* speech, pep talk; **contiōnem habēre** to give a speech; to give a pep talk

contiōnābund·us -a -um *adj* haranguing, holding forth *(like a demogogue)*

contiōnāl·is -is -e *adj* like in assembly; demogogic

contiōnāri·us -a -um *adj* mob-like

contiōnāt·or -ōris *m* demogogue

contiōn·or -ārī -ātus sum *intr* to hold forth at a rally, to harangue; to come to a rally ‖ *tr (w. acc & inf)* to say at a rally (that)

contiuncul·a -ae *f* small rally

contoll·ō -ere *tr* **gradum contollere** to step up *(to a person)*

conton·at -āre *v impers* it is thundering loudly

contor·qeō -quēre -sī -tus *tr* to twist, whirl; to throw hard; to twist *(words)* around

contortē *adv* intricately

contortiōn·ēs -um *fpl* intricacies *(of language)*

contort·or -ōris *m* perverter; **contortor lēgum** shyster

contortul·us -a -um *adj* terribly complicated

contortuplicāt·us -a -um *adj* all tangled up

contort·us -a -um *pp of* **contorqueō** ‖ *adj* involved, intricate

contrā *adv* in opposition, opposite, in front, face to face; in turn, in return; on the other hand; on the other side; reversely, in the opposite way, the other way; on the contrary, conversely; **contrā atque** *(or* **ac)** contrary to, otherwise than; **contrā dīcere** to reply; to raise objections; **contrā dīcitur** the objection is raised; **contrā ferīre** to make a counterattack; **contrā quam fās est** contrary to divine law; **contrā quam senātus cōnsuluisset** contrary to what the Senate would have decided; **quīn contrā** nay on the contrary

contrā *prep (w. acc)* **1** opposite, opposite to, facing, toward: **contrā septentriōnēs** facing north; **2** *(in a hostile sense)* against, with, in opposition to: **contrā patriam exercitum dūcere** to lead an army against one's country; **3** injurious to, unfavorable to: **quod contrā sē ipsum sit dīcere** to say what is against one's own interests; **4** in defiance of: **contrā senātum proficīscī** to depart in defiance of the Senate; **5** in violation of: **contrā iūs gentium** in violation of international law; **6** contrary to, the reverse of **contrā exspectātiōnem omnium** contrary to universal expectation; **contrā spem** contrary to hope, unexpectedly; **7** in comparison with: **nunc contrā istum librum faveō ōrātiōnī quam nūper dedī** now in comparison with that book I prefer the speech which I recently gave *(you)*

contracti·ō -ōnis *f* contraction; shortening *(of syllable);* **contractiō animī** depression; **contractiō nervōrum** cramp

contractiuncul·a -ae *f* slight mental depression

contract·us -a -um *pp of* **contrahō ‖** *adj* contracted; narrow, limited *(place);* brief; pinching *(poverty);* limited in scope; parsimonious; terse *(style)*

contract·us -ūs *m* contraction

contrā·dīcō -dīcere -dīxī -dictum *tr* to contradict **‖** *intr (w. dat)* **1** to contradict; **2** to speak against, oppose

contrādicti·ō -ōnis *f* objection, refutation

con·trahō -trahere -trāxī -tractus *tr* to draw together; to contract; to collect, assemble; to shorten, narrow, abridge; to lessen; to wrinkle; to bring about, accomplish, cause, produce, incur; to conclude *(a bargain);* to transact *(business);* to settle *(an account);* to complete *(business arrangements)*

contrāposit·um -ī *n* antithesis

contrāriē *adv* in opposite directions; in a different way

contrāri·us -a -um *adj* opposite; contrary, conflicting; hostile, antagonistic; from the opposite direction; reciprocal, mutual; *(w. dat)* opposed to, contrary to **‖** *n* the opposite, the contrary, the reverse; antithesis; **contrāriō** on the contrary; **e(x) contrāriō** on the contrary; on the opposite side; **in contrāriās partes** in opposite directions; **in contrāria versus** changed into its opposite; **in contrārium** in the opposite direction

contrectābiliter *adv* **(-tract-)** appreciably, tangibly

contrectāti·ō -ōnis *f* **(-tract-)** handling, touching; fondling, caressing

contrect·ō -āre -āvī -ātus *tr* **(-tract-)** to touch, handle; *(sl)* to fondle; *(sl)* to have sexual intercourse with; to deal with *(a subject)*

contrem·īscō -īscere -uī *tr* to shudder at **‖** *intr* to tremble all over; to waver

contrem·ō -ere -uī *intr* to tremble all over; to quake

contrib·uō -uere -uī -ūtus *tr* to bring together, enroll together; to associate, unite, incorporate; to contribute, add

contrīst·ō -āre -āvī -ātus *tr* to sadden; to cast gloom over, darken, cloud

contrīt·us -a -um *pp of* **conterō ‖** *adj* worn out; common, trite

contrōversi·a -ae *f* controversy, quarrel, dispute; debate; civil lawsuit, litigation; subject of litigation; contradiction; question

contrōversiōs·us -a -um *adj* controversial

contrōvers·us -a -um *adj* disputed, controversial; questionable, undecided

contrucīd·ō -āre -āvī -ātus *tr* to cut down, massacre; *(sl)* to make a mess of

contrū·dō -dere -sī -sus *tr* to push hard; to crowd together

contrunc·ō -āre -āvī -ātus *tr* to hack to pieces

contubernāl·is -is *m* army buddy; junior staff officer; *(coll)* husband *(of slave);* personal attendant; companion, colleague **‖** *f* wife *(of slave)*

contubern·ium -(i)ī *n* sharing the same tent; wartime friendship; army tent; serving as a junior staff officer; concubinage; marriage *(among slaves);* hovel *(of slave couple)*

contudī *perf of* **contundō**

contu·eor -ērī -itus sum *tr* to look intently at; to catch sight of; to be within sight of *(a place)*

contuit·us *or* **contūt·us -ūs** *m* sight, observation, gaze

contumāci·a -ae *f* insubordination, defiance; *(leg)* contempt

contumāciter *adv* defiantly

contum·āx -ācis *adj* insubordinate, defiant

contumēli·a -ae *f* mistreatment; outrage; abuse; insult, affront

contumēliōsē *adv* abusively; outrageously

contumēliōs·us -a -um *adj* insulting, outrageous, humiliating; abusive, rude

contumul·ō -āre -āvī -ātus *tr* to bury

con·tundō -tundere -tudī -tūsus *tr* to crush, grind, pound; to bruise; *(fig)* to crush, subdue; to baffle; to outdo *(performance)*

conturbāti·ō -ōnis *f* disorder; dismay, consternation

conturbāt·or -ōris *m* a bankrupt person

conturbāt·us -a -um *adj* confused, distracted, in confusion

conturb·ō -āre -āvī -ātus *tr* to confuse, throw into confusion; to disturb; to upset *(plans);* **ratiōnēs** *(or* **ratiōnem) conturbāre** to be bankrupt **‖** *intr* to go bankrupt

cont·us -ī *m* pole

contūsus *pp of* **contundō**

cōnūbiāl·is -is -e *adj* conjugal

cōnūb·ium -(i)ī *n* intermarriage; right to intermarry; marriage; **iūs cōnūbiī** right to intermarry

cōn·us -ī *m* cone; apex *(of helmet)*

convad·or -ārī -ātus sum *tr* to subpoena

conval·ēscō -ēscere -uī *intr* to grow strong, thrive; to convalesce; *(fig)* to improve; *(leg)* become valid

convall·is -is *f* valley

convās·ō -āre -āvī -ātus *tr* to pack, pack up

convect·ō -āre -āvī -ātus *tr* to gather

convect·or -ōris *m* fellow passenger

conve·hō -here -xī -ctus *tr* gather, bring in *(esp. the harvest);* to convey, ship

con·vellō -vellere -vellī -vulsus *tr* **(-vols-)** to tear away, pull off, pluck, wrest; to tear to pieces, dismember; to break, shatter; *(fig)* to turn upside down, subvert, overthrow; **convellere signa** to break camp

conven·ae -ārum *mpl or fpl* strangers; refugees, vagabonds, the homeless

conveni·ēns -entis *adj* agreeing, harmonious, consistent; appropriate; *(w. dat or* **cum)** consistent with, appropriate to; *(w.* **ad)** appropriate for, suitable for

convenienter *adv* consistently; suitably; *(w.* **cum** *or* **ad)** in conformity with

convenienti·a -ae *f* agreement, accord, harmony; conformity

con·veniō -venīre -vēnī -ventus *tr* to meet, go to meet; to interview; *(leg)* to sue; **Rēgulus convēnit mē in praetōris officiō** Regulus met me at the installation of a praetor ‖ *intr* to come together, meet, gather; to make an agreement; to coincide; to converge; to unite, combine; to come to an agreement, agree; to fit; *(w.* **ad)** to fit *(as a shoe fits the foot); (w. dat or* **cum** *or* **ad** *or* **in** *+ acc)* to be applicable to, appropriate to; **bene convenīre** to be on good terms; to fit well; **in mātrimōnium cum virō convenīre** *(of a bride)* to get married; **virō in manum convenīre** *(of a bride)* to come under the control of her husband ‖ *v impers* it is fitting; it is proper; it is agreed; **bene convenit nobīs** we get along well; **convenit inter cōnsulēs** there is agreement between the consuls

conventīci·us -a -um *adj* coming together, met by chance ‖ *n* fee paid for attending the assembly

conventicul·um -ī *n* small gathering; small meeting place

conventi·ō -ōnis *f* assembly; agreement, contract

convent·um -ī *n* contract, agreement

convent·us -ūs *m* gathering, assembly; congress; district court; company, corporation; agreement; **ex conventū** by agreement; of one accord; **conventum agere** to hold court

converber·ō -āre -āvī -ātus *tr* to beat soundly, bash

conver·rō -rere -rī -sus *tr* **(-vorr-)** to sweep out; to brush thoroughly; *(fig)* to scoop up *(e.g., an inheritance)*

conversāti·ō -ōnis *f* familiarity, close association *(with people);* **conversātiō parit contemptum** *(prov)* familiarity breeds contempt

conversi·ō -ōnis *f* rotation; cycle; transposition; inversion; alteration; political change, upheaval; *(rhet)* repetition of word at end of clause; *(rhet)* balancing of phrases; *(rhet)* period

convers·ō -āre -āvī -ātus *tr* to turn around ‖ *refl* to revolve

conver·tō -tere -tī -sus *tr* **(-vor-)** to rotate; to turn back, reverse; *(fig)* to turn, direct *(attention, laughter);* to convert, transform; to translate; to turn upside down; to convulse, shake; to turn *(e.g., horse)* around; to shift, transfer; to transpose, invert *(an arrangement);* to turn aside, divert; to distract *(the mind);* to repulse *(attackers);* **ad sē** *(or* **in sē)** **convertere** to attract *(e.g., attention);* **in fugam convertere** to put to flight; **signa convertere** to face about; **terga convertere** to turn tail ‖ *refl* to turn around; *(mil)* to retreat ‖ *intr* to return; to change, turn; *(w.* **in** *+ acc)* to be changed into, turn into

convest·iō -īre *tr* to clothe, cover

convex·us -a -um *adj* rounded off; arched, convex; concave; sloping down ‖ *n* vault, arch, dome

convīciāt·or -ōris *m* heckler

convīci·or -ārī -ātus sum *intr* to jeer; *(w. dat)* to heckle, jeer at

convīc·ium -(i)ī *n* noise, chatter; wrangling; jeers, heckling, abuse; cry of protest; reprimand; **aliquem convīciīs cōnsectārī** to heckle s.o.; **convīcium habēre** *(coll)* to catch hell

convicti·ō -ōnis *f* socializing, association, companionship; companions

convict·or -ōris *m* bosom pal

convict·us -ūs *m* socializing, association

con·vincō -vincere -vīcī -victus *tr* to refute, prove wrong; *(leg)* to convict; to prove, demonstrate clearly; **dēvōtiōnem convincere** *(of a god)* to grant a request

convīs·ō -ere -ī -us *tr* to examine, search; to go to visit

convīv·a -ae *m (f)* guest; dinner guest

convīvāl·is -is -e *adj* convivial, festive

convīvāt·or -ōris *m* host; master of ceremonies

convīv·ium -(i)ī *n* banquet, dinner party; party; **convīvium agitāre** *(coll)* to throw a party; **convīvium dare** to give a party ‖ *npl* dinner guests

convī·vō -vere -xī -ctum *intr* to live together; to live at the same time; *(w.* **cum)** to dine with
convīv·or -ārī -ātus sum *intr* to feast together, have a party
convocāti·ō -ōnis *f* calling together
convoc·ō -āre -āvī -ātus *tr* to convoke
convol·ō -āre -āvī -ātum *intr* to flock together
convol·vō -vere -vī -ūtus *tr* to roll together; to roll up *(scroll);* to fasten together, interweave; to wrap; **terga convolvere** *(of snakes)* to wiggle ‖ *refl* to roll along; to go in a circle
convom·ō -ere -uī -itus *tr* to vomit all over
convortō *see* **convertō**
convulner·ō -āre -āvī -ātus *tr* **(-vol-)** to wound seriously
convuls·us -a -um *pp of* **convellō**
coöper·iō *or* **cōperi·ō -īre -uī -tus** *tr* **(cōp-)** to cover; to overwhelm
coöptāti·ō -ōnis *f* **(cōp-)** coöptation *(election of a colleague by incumbents)*
coöpt·ō -āre -āvī -ātus *tr* **(cōp-)** to coöpt
coör·ior -īrī -tus sum *intr* to rise (all together *or* all at once; to be born; to originate; to appear suddenly; *(of war)* to break out; *(mil)* to go on the attack
coört·us -ūs *m* rising, originating
Co·os *or* **Co·us -ī** *f* small island in the Aegean, famous for its wine and fine linen *(modern Kos)*
cōp·a -ae *f* barmaid
cophin·us -ī *m* basket
cōpi·a -ae *f* abundance, supply, store; plenty; multitude, large number; wealth, prosperity; opportunity, means; command of language, fluency; *(w. gen)* power over; *(w. dat)* access to; **cōpia dīcendī** *(or* **verbōrum)** command of language, large vocabulary, richness of expression; **prō cōpiā** as one's circumstances allow ‖ *fpl* troops, armed forces; provisions, supplies
cōpiol·ae -ārum *fpl* small contingent of troops
cōpiōsē *adv* abundantly; *(rhet)* fully, at length, eloquently
cōpiōs·us -a -um *adj* plentiful; well-supplied, rich; eloquent, fluent; *(w. abl)* abounding in, rich in
cop·is -idis *f* small, curved sword
cōpō *see* **caupō**
cōp·s -is *adj* rich, well-supplied; *(of the chest)* swelling *(with pride)*
copt·a -ae *f* crisp cake
cōpul·a -ae *f* cord, string, rope, leash; *(fig)* tie, bond
cōpulāti·ō -ōnis *f* coupling, joining, union; combining *(of words)*
cōpulāt·us -a -um *adj* closely connected; compound, complex; close, intimate *(relationship)*
cōpul·ō -āre -āvī -ātus *tr* to couple, join; *(fig)* to unite; *(w. dat or* **cum)** to couple with, join to, combine with ‖ *refl & pass* to unite *(for practical purposes)*
cōpul·or -ārī -ātus sum *tr* to join, clasp; **dextrās copulārī** to shake hands
coqu·a -ae *f* cook *(female)*
coquīn·ō -āre -āvī -ātum *intr* to be a cook
coquīn·us -a -um *adj* of cooked and baked food
co·quō -quere -xī -ctus *tr* to cook; to fry, roast, boil, bake; to brew; to bake *(bricks, bread);* to fire *(pottery);* to smelt *(ore);* to season *(lumber);* to burn, parch; to ripen; to digest *(food);* to disturb, worry; to concoct, dream up; to hatch *(plots)*
coqu·us *or* **coc·us -ī** *m* cook
cor cordis *n* heart *(as the seat of the emotions, as the seat of wisdom);* mind, judgment; dear friend; **aliquid cordī habēre** to take s.th. to heart; **cordī esse** *(w. dat)* to please, be dear to, be agreeable to; **cor habēre** to have common sense; **sī vōbīs nōn fuit cordī** *(w. acc & inf)* if it was not to your liking that ‖ *npl* friends, souls
coracīn·us -ī *m* dark-colored species of fish
cōram *adv* in person, personally; publicly, openly; in someone's presence, face to face ‖ *prep (coming before or after abl)* before, in the presence of, face to face with, before the eyes of
corb·is -is *m (f)* wicker basket
corbīt·a -ae *f* slow-sailing merchant ship
corbul·a -ae *f* small basket
corcōta *see* **crocōta**
corcōtāri·us -a -um *adj* concerned with saffron-colored clothes
corcul·um -ī *n* little heart; sweetheart; poor fellow; the Wise *(name given to Publius Scipio Nasica)*
Corcyr·a -ae *f* island off coast of Epirus, sometimes identified with Scheria, the island of Alcinoüs
cordātē *adv* wisely, prudently
cord·āx -ācis *m* trochaic meter; indecent dance
cordol·ium -(i)ī *n* heartache
Cordub·a -ae *f* town in S. Spain *(modern Cordova)*
cordȳl·a -ae *f* baby tuna
Corfīn·ium -(i)ī *n* town in central Italy, center of the Social War
coriandr·um -ī *n (bot)* coriander *(aromatic herb, used as seasoning)*
Corinn·a -ae *f* Greek lyric poetess *(fl c. 500 B.C.)*
Corinthiac·us -a -um *or* **Corinthiēns·is -is -e** *adj* Corinthian
Corinthi·us -a -um *adj* Corinthian; **aes Corinthium** alloy of gold, silver, and copper used in expensive jewelry ‖ *mpl* Corinthians ‖ *npl* costly Corinthian products

Corinth·us *or* **Corinth·os -ī** *f* Corinth
Coriolān·us -ī *m* Gnaeus Marcius Coriolanus *(notorious Roman general who led the Volsci against Rome)*
cor·ium -(i)ī *n or* **cor·ius -(i)ī** *m* skin, hide; leather; bark; peel, rind; *(sl)* one's hide; **coriō suō lūdere** *(sl)* to risk one's own hide; **corium alicūius petere** *(sl)* to be after s.o.'s hide
Cornēli·us -a -um *adj* Roman clan name *(nomen)* and tribal name; **lēx Cornēlia** a law proposed by any member of the Cornelian clan *(esp. Sulla)*
corneol·us -a -um *adj* made of horn; *(fig)* hard, tough
corne·us -a -um *adj* of horn; of cornel wood; of the cornel tree
cornic·en -inis *m* horn blower
cornīc·or -ārī -ātus sum *tr (sl)* to croak, say in a croaking voice **||** *intr* to caw
cornīcul·a -ae *f* poor little crow
corniculār·ius -(i)ī *m* soldier decorated with horn-shaped medal for bravery; adjutant to a centurion
cornicul·um -ī *n* **(cornu-)** little horn; *(mil)* horn-shaped decoration
cornig·er -era -erum *adj* horned
cornip·ēs -edis *adj* hoofed
corn·īx -īcis *f* crow; *(pej)* old crow
corn·ū -ūs *or* **corn·um -ī** *n* horn *(of animals, insects)*; drinking vessel *(made from a horn)*; funnel *(made from a horn)*; horn, trumpet; lantern; oil cruet; hoof; bill *(of bird)*; horn *(of moon)*; tip *(of a bow)*; branch *(of river)*; arm *(of lake)*; tongue *(of land)*; crest socket *(of helmet)*; roller end *(of scroll)*; *(mil)* wing, flank; **cornua addere** *(w. dat)* to give courage to, add strength to; **cornua sūmere** to gain strength; **cornū cōpiae** cornucopia; **cornū Indicum** ivory
corn·um -ī *n* cornel cherry; spear
corn·us -ī *f* cornel cherry tree; dogwood tree; spear, shaft, javelin
coroll·a -ae *f* small garland
corollār·ium -(i)ī *n* garland; gilt wreath *(given as reward to actors)*; gift, tip
corōn·a -ae *f* crown, garland; circle of bystanders; *(mil)* cordon of besiegers; *(mil)* ring of defense; **corōna cīvica** decoration for a saving a life; **corōna mūrālis** decoration for being the first to scale an enemy wall; **corōna nāvālis** decoration for naval victory; **corōna obsidiālis** decoration for breaking a blockade; **sub corōnā vēndere** to sell *(captives)* as slaves; **sub corōnā vēnīre** *(of captives)* to be sold at auction **||** **Corōna** *(astr)* Ariadne's crown, Corona Borealis
corōnāri·us -a -um *adj* for a crown; **aurum corōnārium** gold collected in the provinces for a victorious general's crown
Corōnē·a -ae *f* town in Boeotia
Corōn·eūs -eī *m* king of Phocis, whose daughter was changed into a crow
Corōnīd·ēs -ae *m* Aesculapius, son of Coronis
Corōn·is -idis *f* mother, by Apollo, of Aesculapius
corōn·is -idis *f* symbol for showing the end of a book, colophon
corōn·ō -āre -āvī -ātus *tr* to crown, wreathe; to enclose, encircle, shut in
corpore·us -a -um *adj* physical, of the body, bodily; corporeal, substantial; of flesh
corpulent·us -a -um *adj* corpulent, stout
corp·us -oris *n* body; matter, substance; flesh; plumpness; trunk *(of tree)*; corpse; person, individual; frame, structure, framework; community; corporation; society, union, guild; particle, grain; sum *(of money)*; *(literary)* corpus; *(in geometry)* a solid; **corporis** *(w. noun)* body, bodily, physical; **corporis custōs** bodyguard; **corpus reīpūblicae** the body politic; **tōtō corpore** with all one's strength
corpuscul·um -ī *n* puny body; particle, atom; *(coll)* little fellow
corrā·dō -dere -sī -sus *tr* **(conr-)** to scrape together, rake up; *(coll)* to scrape *(money)* together
corrēcti·ō -ōnis *f* **(conr-)** correction, improvement, amendment; rhetorical restatement
corrēct·or -ōris *m* **(conr-)** corrector, reformer
corrēct·us -a -um *pp of* **corrigō** **||** *adj* improved, correct
corrēp·ō -ere -sī -tum *intr* **(conr-)** to creep, slink; **in dūmēta corrēpere** *(coll)* to beat around the bush, indulge in jargon
correptē *adv* **(conr-)** with a short vowel *or* syllable
correptius *adv* **(conr-)** more briefly; **correptius exīre** to end in a short vowel
correptus *pp of* **corripiō** **(conr-)** **||** *adj* short *(syllable, vowel)*
corrēxī *perf of* **corrigō**
corrīd·eō -ēre *intr* **(conr-)** to laugh out loud
corrigi·a -ae *f* shoelace
cor·rigō -rigere -rēxī -rēctus *tr* **(conr-)** to straighten out; to smooth out; to correct, improve, reform; to make up for *(delay)*; to make the best of
cor·ripiō -ripere -ripuī -reptus *tr* **(conr-)** to take hold of, snatch up; to seize *(a person)*; to seize unlawfully; *(of a current)* to carry off; to steal, carry off; to enrapture, sweep off one's feet; to attack suddenly; to speed up, rush; to shorten, contract; to

abridge *(a literary work);* to reproach; to cut short *(period of time); (gram)* to pronounce *(a word)* with a short syllable, pronounce *(a syllable)* short; **arma corripere** to go to war; **gradum corripere** to pick up the pace; **igne** *(or* **flammā)** **corripere** to ignite, set on fire; **in sē corripere** to absorb ‖ *refl* to bestir oneself, jump up, hurry off

corrōbor·ō -āre -āvī -ātus *tr* **(conr-)** to strengthen, invigorate; *(fig)* to fortify, encourage; *(mil)* to reinforce ‖ *refl & pass* to become mature

cor·rōdō -rōdere -rōsī -rōsus *tr* **(conr-)** to gnaw, chew up

corrog·ō -āre -āvī -ātus *tr* **(conr-)** to go asking for, collect, drum up, solicit; to invite, summon

corrōsus *pp of* **corrōdō**

corrūg·ō -āre -āvī -ātus *tr* **(conr-)** to wrinkle; **nārēs corrūgāre** *(w. dat)* to turn up one's nose at

cor·rumpō -rumpere -rūpī -ruptus *tr* **(conr-)** to burst, to break to pieces, smash; to destroy completely, ruin, waste; to mar; to corrupt; to adulterate; to falsify, tamper with; to bribe; to seduce

corru·ō -ere -ī *tr* **(conr-)** to shatter, wreck, ruin ‖ *intr* to fall down, tumble, sink; *(fig)* to fall, fail, sink

corruptē *adv* **(conr-)** corruptly, perversely; in a lax manner

corruptēl·a -ae *f* **(conr-)** corruption; seduction; bribery; corrupting influence

corrupti·ō -ōnis *f* **(conr-)** corruption, ruining, breaking up; corrupt condition

corrupt·or -ōris *m or* **corruptr·īx -īcis** *f* **(conr-)** corrupter, seducer, briber

corrupt·us -a -um *pp of* **corrumpō (conr-)** ‖ *adj* corrupt, spoiled, bad, ruined

Corsic·a -ae *f* Corsica

cort·ex -icis *m (f)* bark, shell, hull, rind; cork; **nāre sine cortice** to swim without a cork life preserver; *(fig)* to be on one's own

cortīn·a -ae *f* kettle, caldron; tripod; *(fig)* vault of heaven

corulus *see* **corylus**

cōrus *see* **caurus**

corūsc·ō -āre -āvī *tr* to shake, wave, brandish ‖ *intr* to flit, flutter; to oscillate; to tremble; to flash, gleam

corūsc·us -a -um *adj* oscillating, vibrating, tremulous; flashing, gleaming, glittering

corv·us -ī *m* raven; *(mil)* grapnel

Corybant·ēs -ium *mpl* the Corybantes *(priests of goddess Cybele)*

Corybanti·us -a -ium *adj* of the Corbyantes

Coryb·ās -antis *m* priest of Cybele

Cōrycid·es -um *fpl* **nymphae Cōrycides** the Muses

Cōryci·us -a -um *adj* of the Corycian mountain-caves on Mt. Parnassus

cōryc·us -ī *m* punching bag

corylēt·um -ī *n* cluster of hazel trees

coryl·us -ī *f* **(-rul-)** hazel tree

corymbif·er -era -erum *adj* wearing *or* carrying clusters of ivy berries ‖ *m* Bacchus

corymb·us -ī *m* cluster *(esp. of ivy berries)*

coryphae·us -ī *m* leader, head

cōrӯt·os *or* **cōrӯt·us -ī** *m* quiver

cōs- = cōns-

cōs cōtis *f* whetstone

cosmēt·a -ae *f* slave girl in charge of the wardrobe

cosmic·os -ē -on *adj* worldly, fashionable

cosm·os -ī *m* the universe, cosmos ‖ a chief magistrate of Crete

cost·a -ae *f* rib; *(fig)* side, wall

cost·um -ī *n* perfume

cothurnāt·us -a -um *adj* wearing buskins; suitable to tragedy, tragic

cothurn·us -ī *m* high boot; hunting boot; buskin *(worn by tragic actors);* subject of tragedy; tragedy; lofty style of Greek tragedy

cōtīd- = cottīd-

cottab·us -ī *m* game which consisted of flicking drops of wine on a bronze vessel

cottan·a -ōrum *npl* **(-on·a)** Syrian figs

cottīdiānō *adv* **(cōt-, quōt-)** daily

cottīdiān·us -a -um *adj* **(cōt-, quōt-)** daily; everyday, ordinary

cottīdiē *adv* **(cōt-, quōt-)** daily

coturn·īx -īcis *f* quail

Cot·ys -yis *m* name of several Thracian kings

Cotӯtt·ō -ūs *f* Thracian goddess of orgiastic rites

Cotytti·a -ōrum *npl* festival of Cotytto

Cō·us -a -um *adj* Coan, of Cos ‖ *n* Coan wine ‖ *npl* Coan garments

Coüs *see* **Coos**

covinnār·ius -(i)ī *m* soldier who fought from a chariot

covinn·us -ī *m* war chariot *(of Britons and Belgae, with scythes attached to the axles);* coach *(for travel)*

cox·a -ae *f* hip; haunch *(of an animal)*

coxend·īx -īcis *f* hip; hipbone

crābr·ō -ōnis *m* hornet; **irritāre crābrōnēs** *(fig)* to stir up a hornet's nest

cramb·ē -ēs *f* cabbage; **crambē repetīta** warmed-over cabbage; *(fig)* same old story, hackneyed writing

Crant·or -ōris *m* Greek Academic philosopher *(fl 300 B.C.)*

crāpul·a -ae *f* drunkenness; hangover; **crāpulam obdormīre** to sleep off a hangover

crāpulāri·us -a -um *adj* for getting rid of a hangover

crās *adv* tomorrow

crassē *adv* thickly; rudely, confusedly; dimly

crassitūd·ō -inis *f* thickness, density; dregs
crass·us -a -um *adj* thick, dense; stout, plump; *(fig)* dense, dull
Crass·us -ī *m* Lucius Licinius Crassus *(famous orator, d. 90 B.C.)* **‖** Marcus Licinius Crassus Dives *(triumvir)* *(112?–53 B.C.)*
crāstin·us -a -um *adj* tomorrow's; **diē crāstinī** *(old abl form)* tomorrow **‖** *n* tomorrow; **in crāstinum differre** to put off till tomorrow
crāt·ēr -ēris *m or* **crātēr·a -ae** *f* mixing bowl; bowl; crater of a volcano **‖ Crātēr** *m (astr)* Bowl *(a constellation)*
crāt·is -is *f* wickerwork; lattice work; harrow; ribs of shield; crisscross structure; cage; *(anat)* rib cage; *(mil)* faggots *(for filling trenches)*
creāti·ō -ōnis *f* election, appointment; procreation *(of children)*
creāt·or -ōris *m* creator; procreator, father; founder; one who appoints
creātr·īx -īcis *f* creatress; mother
crē·ber -bra -brum *adj* numerous, crowded; repeated; frequent; luxuriant, prolific *(growth)*
crēbr·ēscō -ēscere -uī *intr* to increase; to become frequent; to become widespread; to gain strength
crēbrit·ās -ātis *f* frequency; density
crēbrō *adv* repeatedly, frequently, again and again; thickly, densely
crēdibil·is -is -e *adj* credible, trustworthy; convincing, plausible; likely; **crēdibile est** *(w. acc & inf)* it is probable that
crēdibiliter *adv* credibly
crēdit·or -ōris *m* creditor, lender
crēd·ō -ere -idī -itus *tr* to lend, loan; to entrust; to believe, accept as true; to believe in; to think, suppose, imagine; *(w. predicate adj)* to believe to be, regard as **‖** *intr (w. dat)* to believe, put faith in, have trust *or* confidence in; **crēdās** one would imagine, you can imagine; **crēde mihi** *(to give assurance)* believe me; **crēdō** *(in replies)* I think so; *(parenthetical)* I suppose **‖** *refl (w. dat)* to entrust oneself to **‖** *v impers* **satis crēditum est** it is believed on good evidence
crēdulit·ās -ātis *f* credulity, trustfulness
crēdul·us -a -um *adj* credulous, trustful; gullible; *(w. dat or* **in** *+ acc)* trusting in
crem·ō -āre -āvī -ātus *tr* to burn; to burn alive; *(of fire)* to consume; to cremate; *(w. dat)* to offer as a burnt offering to
Cremōn·a -ae *f* town in N. Italy
Cremōnēns·is -is -e *adj* of Cremona
crem·or -ōris *m* thick broth; gravy; thickened juice
cre·ō -āre -āvī -ātus *tr* to create; to produce; to elect *or* appoint *(to office);* to cause, occasion; to beget, bear
Cre·ōn -ontis *or* **Cre·ō -onis** *or* **-ōnis** *m* Creon *(brother of Jocasta and brother-in-law of Oedipus)* **‖** Creon *(king of Corinth who gave his daughter in marriage to Jason)*
crep·er -era -erum *adj* dark; *(fig)* obscure, uncertain, doubtful
crepid·a -ae *f* slipper, sandal
crepidāt·us -a -um *adj* wearing sandals *or* slippers
crepīd·ō -inis *f* base, pedestal; pier; dike; curb, sidewalk
crepidul·a -ae *f* small sandal *or* slipper
crepitācill·um -ī *n* small rattle
crepit·ō -āre -āvī -ātum *intr* to make noise, rattle, creak, chatter, rumble, rustle; *(of flames)* to crackle
crepit·us -ūs *m* noise, rattle, creak, chatter, rumble, rustle, crackle; *(vulg)* fart; **crepitum ventris ēmittere in convīviō** *(vulg)* to let a fart at a dinner party; **crepitus digitōrum** snap(ping) of the fingers
crep·ō -āre -uī *tr* to rattle; to talk noisily about, rattle on about **‖** *intr* to make noise, rattle, crackle, creak, chatter, rustle; *(of the stomach)* to rumble; *(of doors)* to creak; *(of flames)* to crackle; *(vulg)* to fart
crepundi·a -ōrum *npl* toy rattle; **in crepundiīs** in earliest childhood
crepūscul·um -ī *n* twilight; dimness, obscurity **‖** *npl* darkness
Crēs Crētis *m* a Cretan; Cretan dog
crēscō crēscere crēvī crētum *intr* to come into being, arise; to grow, grow up; to increase *(in size, amount, numbers, length, quantity, dimensions);* to swell; to expand; *(of rivers)* to rise; *(of period of time)* to advance, progress; to prosper, thrive; to become great; to swell with pride; **crēscunt nōbīs animī** our spirits rise; **diē crēscente** as the day progressed
Crēsi·us -a -um *adj* Cretan
Cress·a -ae *adj (fem only)* Cretan; of chalk **‖** *f* Cretan woman; Ariadne
crēt·a -ae *f* whitish clay; clayey soil; chalk; finish line *(in a chariot race);* **crēta figulāris** *(or* **figlīna)** potter's clay; **crētā fullōnia** fuller's earth; **crēta sūtōria** shoe polish
Crēt·a -ae *or* **Crēt·ē -ēs** *f* Crete; *(fig)* the Cretans
Crētae·us -a -um *adj* Cretan
Crētān·ī -ōrum *mpl* Cretans
crētāt·us -a -um *adj* whitened with chalk *(feet of slaves about to be auctioned off);* dressed in white *(as candidate)*
Crētēns·is -is -e *adj & m* Cretan **‖** *n* Cretan wine
crēte·us -a -um *adj* of chalk, of clay, clayey
Crētic·us -a -um *adj* Cretan **‖** *m (pros)* Cretic (foot) (— ᴗ —)

crēti·ō -ōnis *f (leg)* formal acceptance of an inheritance; *(leg)* terms laid down for making the declaration of acceptance
Crēt·is -idis *adj (fem only)* Cretan
crētōs·us -a -um *adj* clayey
crētul·a -ae *f* white clay
crēt·us -a -um *pp of* **cernō** *and of* **crēscō** ‖ *adj (w. abl or* **ab** *or* **dē**) sprung from
Creūs·a -ae *f* daughter of Priam and wife of Aeneas ‖ daughter of Creon (king of Corinth), and wife of Jason ‖ mother of Ion
crībr·um -ī *n* sieve; **imbrem in crībrum gerere** *(prov)* to swim against the tide *(literally, to carry rain water in(to) a sieve)*
crīm·en -inis *n* indictment; reproach; guilt; crime; **esse in crīmine** to be arraigned; **in crīmen addūcī** *(or* **pōnī** *or* **venīre** *or* **vocārī**) to be indicted; *(of actions)* to be called into question
crīmināl·is -is -e *adj (leg) (opp.* **cīvīlis**) criminal
crīmināti·ō -ōnis *f* indictment; accusation; slander
crīmināt·or -ōris *m* accuser
crīmin·ō -āre *or* **crīmin·or -ārī -ātus sum** *tr* to indict, accuse; to slander; to complain of; to denounce
crīminōsē *adv* by way of accusation, accusingly; slanderously
crīminōs·us -a -um *adj* accusatory, reproachful; shameful
crīnāl·is -is -e *adj* for the hair; **acus crīnālis** hairpin ‖ *n* hairpin
crīn·is -is *m (f)* hair *(of the head);* lock of hair; tail of a comet
crīnīt·us -a -um *adj* long-haired; **crīnīta dracōnibus ōra** *(Medusa's)* snake-haired head; **crīnītae angue sorōrēs** snake-haired sisters; **stella crīnīta** *(or* **sidus crīnītum**) comet
crīs·ō -āre -āvī -ātum *intr (sl) (of a woman)* to wiggle the buttocks, shake it up *(cf.* **ceveō**)
crīsp·āns -antis *adj* curly; wrinkled
crīsp·ō -āre -āvī -ātus *tr* to curl, wave *(hair);* to wave, brandish *(weapons)*
crīspul·us -a -um *adj* having short curly hair
crīsp·us -a -um *adj* curled, waved; curly-headed; wrinkled; tremulous, quivering
crist·a -ae *f* cockscomb; crest, plume
cristāt·us -a -um *adj* crested, plumed
critic·a -ōrum *npl* literary criticism
critic·us -ī *m* critic
croce·us -a -um *adj* of saffron; yellow, golden
crocin·um -ī *n* saffron oil *(used as perfume)*
crōc·iō *or* **grōc·iō -īre** *intr* to croak
crocodīl·us -ī *m* **(-dill-)** crocodile
crocōt·a -ae *f* saffron-colored dress *(worn by women and transvestites)*
crocōtāri·us -a -um *adj* of saffron-colored clothes
crocōtul·a -ae *f* saffron-colored dress
croc·us -ī *m or* **croc·um -ī** *n* saffron; saffron color; saffron oil
Croes·us -ī *m* king of Lydia, famous for his wealth *(590?–546 B.C.)*
crotalistri·a -ae *f* castinet dancer
crotal·um -ī *n* castanet
Crotō(n) -ōnis *or* **Crotōn·a -ae** *f* Crotona *(town in S. Italy)*
cruciābilitāt·ēs -um *fpl* torments
cruciābiliter *adv* with torture
cruciāment·um -ī *n* torture
cruciāt·us -ūs *m* torture; mental torment; instrument of torture
cruci·ō -āre -āvī -ātus *tr* to put on the rack, torture; *(fig)* to torment ‖ *refl or pass* to suffer mental anguish
crūdēl·is -is -e *adj* cruel, hardhearted; *(w.* **in** + *acc)* cruel toward
crūdēlit·ās -ātis *f* cruelty
crūdēliter *adv* cruelly
crūd·ēscō -ēscere -uī *intr* to become fierce; *(of battle, disease)* to get rough
crūdit·ās -ātis *f* indigestion
crūd·us -a -um *adj* bloody, bleeding; uncooked *(food);* raw *(meat; wound);* unripe, green *(fruit);* untanned *(hide);* undigested *(food);* suffering from indigestion; hoarse; hardy, vigorous *(old age);* coarse, rude; fierce, wild, savage
cruent·ō -āre -āvī -ātus *tr* to bloody, stain with blood; *(fig)* to wound
cruent·us -a -um *adj* gory, blood-stained; bloodthirsty; blood-red
-cr·um -ī *neut suf* denoting place or instrument: **ambulācrum** a walk, avenue; **involūcrum** wrapper, envelope
crumēn·a -ae *f* **(-mīn-)** purse, pouch; *(fig)* money supply
crumill·a -ae *f* small purse
cru·or -ōris *m* blood, gore ‖ *mpl* bloodshed, murder
cruppellāri·ī -ōrum *mpl* warriors in full armor
crūrāl·is -is -e *adj* of the shin; **fāsciae crūrālēs** puttees
crūricrepid·a -ae *m (hum) (of one who has chains rattling around his legs)* "rattle-legs"
Crūrifrag·ius -(i)ī *m (comic slave name)* "Broken-shins"
crūs crūris *n* leg; shin; upper support of a bridge
crūscul·um -ī *n* little leg
crusm·a -atis *n* tune
crūst·a -ae *f* crust, shell; peel, rind; inlaid work
crūstul·um -ī *n* cookie
crūst·um -ī *n* pastry

Crustumīnus -a -um *adj* of Crustumerium *or* Crustumium *(town in the Sabine district of Italy)*

crux crucis *f* cross; crucifixion; torment; tormentor; **ī in malam crucem**! *(coll)* go hang yourself!

crypt·a -ae *f* **(cru-)** underground passage, covered gallery; tunnel; crypt

cryptoportic·us -ūs *f* covered walk

crystallīn·us -a -um *adj* **(crus-)** made of crystal **II** *npl* crystal vases

crystall·us -ī *f or* **crystall·um -ī** *n* **(crus-)** crystal

cub·āns -antis *adj* lying down; low-lying

cubiculāri·us -a -um *adj* bedroom **II** *m* chamberlain

cubicul·um -ī *n* bedroom; room; emperor's box in the theater *or* circus; **ā cubiculō** (imperial) chamberlain

cubīl·e -is *n* bed, couch; marriage bed; lair, nest, hole; kennel

cubit·al -ālis *n* elbow cushion

cubitāl·is -is -e *adj* of the elbow; one cubit long *(i.e., 17 to 21 inches)*

cubit·ō -āre -āvī -ātum *intr* to lie down, be in the habit of lying down; *(w.* **cum)** to go to bed with, have intercourse with

cubit·um -ī *n* elbow; forearm; cubit; **cubitum pōnere** *(fig)* to sit down to dinner

cubitūr·a -ae *f* reclining, lying down

cubit·us -ūs *m* lying down; sexual intercourse

cub·ō -āre -uī *or* **-āvī -itum** *intr* to lie, lie down; to recline at table; to lie in bed; to take one's rest, sleep; to be confined to bed; *(of bones)* to rest; *(of roof)* to slope; *(of towns)* to lie on a slope; *(w.* **cum)** to have intercourse with

cub·us -ī *m* cube; lump

cucull·us -ī *m* cowl, hood

cucūl·us -ī *m* cuckoo; *(pej)* ninny

cucum·a -ae *f* large kettle *(for cooking)*

cucum·is -is *or* **-eris** *m* cucumber

cucurbit·a -ae *f* gourd; *(sl)* dolt, dummy; *(med)* cupping glass

cūd·ō -ere *tr* to strike, beat, pound; to thresh; to forge; to coin, stamp

cūi·ās *or* **cūi·ātis -ātis** *interrog pron* from what country?; **Scīpiō eum percontātus est quis et cūiās esset** Scipio asked who he was and from what country he came

cuicuimodī *or* **quoiquoimodī** *adj* of any kind, of whatever sort

cūius *(gen of* **quī, quae, quod, quis, quid)** *pron (interrog)* whose, of whom **II** *(interrog)* whose?

cūiusnam *(gen of* **quisnam, quidnam)** *pron (interrog)* just whose, exactly whose?

cūiuscemodī, cūiusmodī *adj* which kind of?

-cul·a -ae *fem suf* forms diminutives: **uxorcula** dear wife

culcit·a -ae *f* mattress, feather tick; cushion, pillow

culcitell·a *or* **culcitul·a -ae** *f* small cushion

cūleus *see* **culleus**

cul·ex *or* **cul·ix -icis** *mf* gnat

culīn·a -ae *f* kitchen; cuisine

culle·us -ī *m* **(cūle-)** leather bag *(for holding liquids);* leather sack *(in which criminals were sewn and drowned); (sl)* scrotum

culm·en -inis *n* peak; summit; stalk; *(fig)* pinnacle, height; **fabae culmen** bean stalk

culm·us -ī *m* stalk, stem; straw, thatch; hay

culp·a -ae *f* fault, blame; sense of guilt; imperfection, fault, defect; *(poet)* cause of blame; **in culpā esse** *(or* **versārī)** to be at fault

culpit·ō -āre *tr* to blame

culp·ō -āre -āvī -ātus *tr* to blame, reproach; to find fault with, complain of

cult·a -ōrum *npl* standing crops; grain fields

cultē *adv* elegantly, tastefully

cultell·us -ī *m* small knife

cul·ter -trī *m* knife; razor; plowshare

culti·ō -ōnis *f* cultivation, tilling

cult·or -ōris *m* tiller, cultivator, planter, farmer; inhabitant; supporter; worshipper

cultrār·ius -(i)ī *m* one who slew the victim

cultr·īx -īcis *f* cultivator *(female);* worshipper *(female);* inhabitant *(female)*

cultūr·a -ae *f* tilling, cultivating; agriculture; cultivation *(e.g., of the mind, important friendships)*

cult·us -a -um *pp of* **colō II** *adj* tilled, cultivated; neat, prim; refined, civilized, cultured

cult·us -ūs *m* tilling, cultivation; care, tending *(of flocks);* training, education; culture, refinement, civilization; high style of living; luxury; style of dress, fancy clothes; fancy outfit; worship, reverence; cult; management *(of a household);* **cultus corporis** personal grooming; **cultus vītae** standard of living

culull·us -ī *m* drinking cup, goblet

-cul·um -ī *neut suf* **1** denoting places: **cubiculum** place for sleeping; **2** denoting instruments: **curriculum** small chariot

cūl·us -ī *m (sl)* ass, anus

-cul·us -ī *masc suf* **1** forming diminutives: **pisciculus** little fish; **2** nouns ending in **-ō, -ōnis** and **-ō -inis** take the form **-un-** before the suffix **-culus: sermunculus** small talk; **homunculus** little man, puny person

cum *prep (w. abl)* **1** *(accompaniment)* with, together with; **2** *(time)* at the same time with, at the time of, at, with; **3** *(circumstance, manner, etc.)* with, under, in, in the midst of, among, in connection with; **cum eō quod** *or* **cum eō ut** on the condition that; **cum pāce** peacefully; **cum prīmā lūce** at dawn; **cum prīmīs** especially, particularly; **mēcum** at my house; with me

cum, quum, *or* **quom** *conj* when, at the time when; whenever; while, as; since, now that, because; although; **cum maximē** just when; especially when, just while; just then; **cum prīmum** as soon as; **cum ... tum** both ... and, not only ... but also, while ... so too; **praesertim cum** *or* **cum praesertim** especially since; **quippe cum** since of course; **utpote cum** seeing that

Cūm·ae -ārum *fpl* town near Naples, residence of its famous Sibyl

Cūmae·us -a -um *adj* Cumaean

Cūmān·us -a -um *adj* Cumaean **II** *n* Cicero's estate near Cumae

cūmātil·is -is -e *adj* sea-blue

cumb·a *or* **cymb·a -ae** *f* boat

cumer·a -ae *f* bin

cumīn·um -ī *n* cumin *(medicinal plant, said to produce paleness)*

cummi *indecl n or* **cumm·is -is** *f* **(gumm-)** gum

cumque, cunque, *or* **quomque** *adv* at any time

-cumque *suf added to relative pronouns and pronominal adverbs:* **quīcumque** whoever; **ubicumque** wherever

cumulātē *adv* completely, abundantly

cumulāt·us -a -um *adj* heaped; abundant, vast, great; *(w. gen or abl)* abounding in

cumul·ō -āre -āvī -ātus *tr* to heap up, pile up; accumulate; to fill up, overload; to increase, augment; *(fig)* to crown

cumul·us -ī *m* heap, pile; increase; *(fig)* finishing touch, crown; *(fig)* peak, pinnacle; **summus cumulus** highest point

cūnābul·a -ōrum *npl* cradle

cūn·ae -ārum *fpl* cradle; *(poet)* nest

cunctābund·us -a -um *adj* hesitant

cunct·āns -antis *adj* hesitant, slow to act; clinging

cunctanter *adv* hesitantly, slowly

cunctāti·ō -ōnis *f* hesitation, reluctance, delay

cunctāt·or -ōris *m* dawdler, slow-poke, procrastinator **II Cunctātor** Quintus Fabius Maximus Cunctator *(cautious general who constantly avoided battles with Hannibal, d. 203* B.C.*)*

cunct·or -ārī -ātus sum *intr* to hesitate, delay, linger; to be in doubt; **cunctātū brevī** after a moment's hesitation

cūnct·us -a -um *adj* all together, the whole, all, entire

-cund·us -a -um *adj/ suf* denoting a tendency: **īrācundus** inclined toward anger, irascible

cuneātim *adv* in the form of a wedge, in tight formation

cuneāt·us -a -um *adj* wedge-shaped

cune·ō -āre -āvī -ātus *tr* to fasten with a wedge; *(fig)* to wedge in, squeeze in

cuneol·us -ī *m* small wedge; pin

cune·us -ī *m* wedge; wedge-form section of seats in the theater; *(mil)* troops formed in shape of wedge

cunīculōsus -a -um *adj* full of rabbits

cunīcul·us -ī *m* rabbit; burrow, hole; tunnel; water conduit, channel; *(mil)* mine

cunil·a -ae *f (bot)* savory *(aromatic plant used as seasoning)*

cunnu·s -ī *m (vulg)* cunt

cunque *see* **cumque**

cūp·a -ae *f* vat

cūpēd- = cuppēd-

cupidē *adv* eagerly

Cupīdine·us -a -um *adj* Cupid's, charming, alluring

cupidit·ās -ātis *f* eagerness, longing, desire; passion, lust; ambition; greed; object of one's desire

cupīd·ō *or* **cūpēdō** *or* **cuppēdō -inis** *mf* eagerness, desire; carnal desire, lust; greed **II Cupīdō** *m* Cupid, son of Venus

cupid·us -a -um *adj* eager; lecherous; ambitious; *(w. gen)* desirous of, longing for, fond of, enthusiastic about

cupi·ēns -entis *adj* eager, enthusiastic; *(w. gen)* desirous of, longing for, fond of, enthusiastic about

cupienter *adv* eagerly

cup·iō -ere -īvī *or* **-iī -ītus** *tr* to wish, be eager for, long for, desire

cupīt·or -ōris *m* daydreamer

cuppēdenār·ius -(i)ī *m* pastry baker

cuppēdi·a -ōrum *npl or* **cūpēdi·a -ae** *f* sweets; delicacies; sweet tooth

cuppēdinār·ius -(i)ī *m* **(cūpēd-)** confectioner

cuppēd·ō -inis *f see* **cupīdō**

cupp·es -edis *adj* fond of sweets; gluttonous

cupressēt·um -ī *n* cypress grove

cupresse·us -a -um *adj* cypress

cupressif·er -era -erum *adj* cypress-bearing

cupress·us -ī *or* **-ūs** *f* cypress tree

cūr *or* **quor** *adv* why

cūr·a -ae *f* care, concern, worry; carefulness, attention, pains; heartache; object of concern; sweetheart; task, reponsibility, post; administration, management, charge; trusteeship, care; guardian, keeper; study, reflection; literary effort, study, literary work; *(w. gen)* eagerness for, anxiety about, zeal for; *(med)* treatment; *(med)* cure; **in cūrā esse** *(w. dat)* to be a matter of concern to, be dear to; **in cūrā habēre** to hold dear, care dearly about; **cūrā** purposely; **cūrae esse** *(w. dat)* to be of concern to; to be dear to; **cūrae habēre** to hold dear

cūrābil·is -is -e *adj* troublesome; needing medical treatment

cūral·ium -(i)ī *n* coral

cūrāti·ō -ōnis *f* management, administration; office; *(med)* treatment

cūrātius *adv* more carefully

cūrāt·or -ōris *m* superintendent, manager; *(leg)* guardian

cūrātūr·a -ae *f* care, attention; superintendence

cūrāt·us -a -um *adj* well cared-for; anxious, sollicitous, earnest

curculi·ō -ōnis *m* **(gurg-)** weevil; *(vulg)* penis

curculiuncul·us -ī *m* little weevil; *(fig)* trifle

Cur·ēs -ium *mpl* ancient Sabine town

Cūrēt·es -um *mpl* people of Crete who attended Jupiter at his birth

cūri·a -ae *f* senate building; meeting of the senate; curia, ward *(one of the 30 wards into which Romulus had divided the people)*

cūriāl·is -is -e *adj* belonging to a ward **‖** *m* ward member

cūriātim *adv* by wards

cūriāt·us -a -um *adj* composed of wards; passed by the assembly of wards; **comitia cūriāta** assembly of wards, curiate assembly

cūri·ō -ōnis *m* ward boss; **cūriō maximus** chief ward boss

cūriōsē *adv* carefully; curiously

cūriōsit·ās -ātis *f* curiosity, inquisitiveness

cūriōs·us -a -um careful, diligent; curious, inquisitive; careworn

cur·is *or* **quir·is -ītis** *f* spear

cūr·ō -āre -āvī -ātus *tr* to take care of, look after, attend to, trouble oneself about; to worry about; to take charge of, see to; to procure; to provide for the payment of, settle up; to attend to *(the body with food, washing, etc.)*; *(med)* to treat; *(med)* to cure; **cūrā ut** see to it that; *(at end of letter)* **cūrā ut valeās** take care of yourself; **cutem cūrāre** to look after one's appearance

curriculō *adv* at full speed, on the double

curricul·um -ī *n* race; lap; racetrack; racing chariot; *(fig)* career

currō currere cucurrī cursus *tr* to run over, skim over, traverse **‖** *intr* to run, dash; to sail; to move quickly, flow along; to fly; *(of night, day)* to pass

curr·us -ūs *m* chariot, car; war chariot; triumphal car; triumph; racing chariot; *(poet)* plow wheel; *(poet)* ship

cursim *adv* on the double, quickly

cursit·ō -āre -āvī *intr* to keep running around, run up and down; to vibrate

curs·ō -āre -āvī *intr* to run around, run up and down

curs·or -ōris *m* runner, racer; courier; errand boy

cursūr·a -ae *f* running; haste, speed

curs·us -ūs *m* running, speeding, speed; trip; course, direction; suitable time *or* weather for travel; rapid movement, flow; progress; **magnō cursū** at top speed; **cursus honōrum** political career

Curt·ius -a -um *adj* Roman clan name *(nomen), esp.* Quintus Curtius Rufus *(who wrote a history of Alexander the Great's campaigns)* **‖ Lacus Curtius** area of the Roman Forum that was once a pond

curt·ō -āre -āvī -ātus *tr* to shorten; *(hum)* to circumcise

curt·us -a -um *adj* shortened; gelded, castrated; *(hum)* circumcised; broken; defective

curūl·is -is -e *adj* official, curule; **aedīlis curūlis** patrician aedile; **sella curūlis** curule chair, official chair *(inlaid with ivory, used by consuls, praetors, and patrician aediles)*

curvām·en -inis *n* curve, bend

curvātūr·a -ae *f* curvature; **curvātūra rotae** rim of a wheel

curv·ō -āre -āvī -ātus *tr* to curve, bend, arch; *(fig)* to affect, move, stir

curv·us -a -um *adj* curved, bent; crooked; concave, arched; hollow, winding *(stream, shore)*; *(fig)* crooked **‖** *n* wrong, crookedness

-c·us -a -um *adjl suf formed from nouns:* **bellicus** warlike

cusp·is -idis *f* point; bayonet; spearhead; spear, javelin; trident; scepter; sting *(of a scorpion)*

custōdēl·a -ae *f* charge, custody *(of a person or thing)*

custōdi·a -ae *f* protection, safekeeping, defense; preservation *(of a practice, etc.)*; place for safekeeping; watch, care; sentry, guard; sentry post; custody, confinement, prison; prisoner, *(collectively)* prisoners; **custōdiam agitāre** to be on guard; **in līberā custōdiā** under surveillance, under house arrest

custōd·iō -īre -īvī *or* **-iī -ītus** *tr* to guard, watch over, protect, defend; to hold in custody; to keep an eye on; to keep carefully, preserve; **memoriā custōdīre** to keep in mind

cust·ōs -ōdis *m* guard; guardian; watchman; protector; jailer; *(mil)* sentinel; **custōs corporis** bodyguard **‖** *mpl* garrison **‖** *f* guardian; protectress; container

cutīcul·a -ae *f* (thin external) skin, cuticle

cut·is -is *f* skin; **cutem cūrāre** to look after one's appearance; *(fig)* to look after one's own skin

Cyan·ē -ēs *f* a spring in Syracuse; nymph who was changed into that spring
cyathiss·ō -āre -āvī *intr* to ladle out wine
cyath·us -ī *m* ladle; liquid measure *(half pint)*
cybae·a -ae *f* merchant ship
Cybel·ē -ēs *f* **(Cybēbē)** Phrygian goddess of fertility, worshipped in Rome as Ops *or* Magna Mater **‖** mountain of Phrygia
Cybelēi·us -a -um *adj* of Cybele
Cybel·us -ī *m* mountain in Phrygia
cyb·ium -(i)i *n* young tuna
cycladāt·us -a -um *adj* wearing a formal gown
Cyclad·es -um *fpl* Cyclades *(group of islands, roughly forming a circle, in the Aegean Sea)*
cycl·as -adis *f* woman's formal gown
cyclic·us -a -um *adj* cyclic; **poēta cyclicus** cyclic poet *(one of a group of poets treating epic sagas revolving around the Trojan War)*
Cyclōpi·us -a -um *adj* Cyclopean
Cycl·ōps -ōpis *m* one-eyed giant of Sicily, *esp.* Polyphemus
cycn·us -ī *m* **(cyg-)** swan; *(fig)* poet **‖ Cycnus** king of the Ligurians, changed into a swan, and placed among the stars as a constellation **‖** son of Neptune
Cyd·ōn -ōnis *adj* Cydonian, of Cydonea *(a city on the N. coast of Crete)* **‖** *m* inhabitant of Cydonea
Cydōnae·us -a -um *adj* **(-ē·us)** Cydonian; *(esp. as poetic epithet for arrows)* Cretan
Cydōne·a -ae *f* city on the N. coast of Crete
Cydōni·us -a -um *adj* Cretan **‖** *n* quince
cygnus *see* **cycnus**
cylindr·us -ī *m* cylinder; roller *(for rolling the ground)*; cylindrical jewel
Cyllēn·ē -ēs *or* **-ae** *f* mountain in Arcadia where Mercury was said to have been born
Cyllēnē·us *or* **Cyllēni·us -a -um** *adj* of Mt. Cyllene **‖** *m* Mercury
cymb·a -ae *f* **(cum-)** boat
cymbal·um *or* **cymbal·on -ī** *n (usu. pl, esp. as used in the worship of Cybele)* cymbal; *(fig)* tedious speaker
cymb·ium -(i)ī *n* small cup
Cynicē *adv* like the Cynics
Cynic·us -a -um *adj* Cynic, relating to the Cynic philosophy **‖** *m* Cynic philosopher, *esp.* Diogenes, its founder *(412–323 B.C.)*
cynocephal·us -ī *m* dog-headed ape
Cynosūr·a -ae *f (astr)* Cynosure *(the constellation Ursa Minor)*
Cynthi·us -a -um *adj* of Mt. Cynthus; Cynthian **‖** *m* Apollo **‖** *f* Diana
Cynth·us -ī *m* low mountain on Delos, where Latona is said to have given birth to Apollo and Diana
cypariss·us -ī *f* cypress tree
cypress·us -ī *or* **-ūs** *f* cypress tree; box made of cypress
Cypri·us -a -um *adj* Cypriote; **aes Cyprium** copper **‖** *f* Venus
Cypr·us *or* **Cyp·ros -ī** *f* Cyprus *(island off S. coast of Asia Minor)*
Cypsel·us -ī *m* despot of Corinth *(reigned 655–625 B.C.)*
Cȳrēnae·us *or* **Cȳrēnaic·us -a -um** *or* **Cȳrēnēns·is -is -e** *adj* of Cyrene
Cȳrēn·ē -ēs *f or* **Cyrēn·ae -ārum** *fpl* chief city of Greek settlement in N.E. Africa
Cȳrē·us -a -um *adj* of Cyprus
Cyrnē·us -a -um *adj* Corsican
Cyrn·os -ī *f* Greek name for Corsica
Cyr·us -ī *m* father of Cambyses and founder of the Persian monarchy in 559 B.C. *(d. 529 B.C.)* **‖** Cyrus the Younger, son of Darius Nothus, whose famous march against his brother Artaxerxes is recorded by Xenophon *(d. 401 B.C.)*
Cyt·ae -ārum *fpl* town in Colchis, reputed birthplace of Medea
Cytae·is -idis *f* Medea
Cythēr·a -ōrum *npl* island off the S. coast of the Peloponnesus, famous for the worship of Venus
Cytherē·is -idis *f* Venus
Cytherēï·us -a -um *adj* Cytherean; **hērōs Cytherēïus** Aeneas **‖** *f* Venus
Cytherē·us -a -um *adj* Cytherean **‖** *f* Venus
cytis·us -ī *mf or* **cytis·um -ī** *n* clover
Cytōriāc·us -a -um *adj* of Cytorus, Cytorian; **pecten Cytōriācus** comb made of boxwood
Cytōr·us *or* **Cytōr·os -ī** *m* mountain in Paphlagonia, famous for its boxwood
Cȳzicēn·us -a -um *adj* of Cyzicus
Cyzic·um -ī *n or* **Cyzic·us** *or* **Cyzic·os -ī** *f* town on S. coast of Propontis

D

D, d *(supply* littera) *f* fourth letter of the Latin alphabet; letter name: **de**
D *abbr* **quīngentī** five hundred
D. *abbr* **Decimus** *(Roman first name, praenomen)*
Dāc·ī -ōrum *mpl* Dacians
Dāci·a -ae *f* Roman province on the lower Danube *(roughly modern Romania)*
Dācic·us -a -um *adj* Dacian **‖** *m* gold coin struck under Domitian, conqueror of Dacia
dactylic·us -a -um *adj (pros)* dactylic
dactyliothēc·a -ae *f* ring case
dactyl·us -ī *m (pros)* dactyl (— ᴗ ᴗ)
daedal·us -a -um *adj* skillful, artistic; intricately constructed **‖ Daedal·us -ī** *m* builder of the Labyrinth in Crete and the first person to construct wings and fly

Damascēn·us -a -um *adj* of Damascus ‖ *npl* plums from Damascus
Damasc·us *or* **Damasc·os -ī** *f* city in Syria
damm·a *or* **dām·a -ae** *f* deer; venison
damnāti·ō -ōnis *f* condemnation; *(w. gen of the crime)* conviction on the charge of; **damnātiō ambitūs** conviction on illegal campaign practices; **condemnātiō pecūniae** a fine
damnātōri·us -a -um *adj (leg)* guilty *(verdict)*
damnāt·us -a -um *adj (leg)* found guilty; hateful, damn
damnific·us -a -um *adj* harmful
damnigerul·us -a -um *adj* injurious
damn·ō -āre -āvī -ātus *tr (leg)* to find guilty, convict; to sentence, condemn; to secure the condemnation of; to offer as a sacrifice, doom to the gods below; to pass judgment on *(a case)*; *(w. dat of the aggrieved person)* to deliver by judicial sentence to, award *(s.o. s.th.)*; *(w. abl)* to fine *(s.o.)* in the amount of; *(w. gen or abl)* to find fault with for; *(w. gen or abl of the charge)* to find *(s.o.)* guilty of; **aliquem vōtī damnāre** to condemn s.o. to the amount he has vowed; **capite** *(or* **capitis) damnāre** to condemn to death; **dē māiestāte damnāre** to find guilty of treason; **exiliō damnārī** to be sentenced to exile; **vōtī damnāre** to oblige *(s.o.)* to fulfill a vow
damnōsē *adv* ruinously, with great loss
damnōs·us -a -um *adj* damaging, destructive; prodigal; **canēs damnōsī** crap *(worst throw of dice)*
damn·um -ī *n* loss, damage, harm; fine; defect; *(w. gen)* forfeiture of; *(mil)* losses; **damnum explēre** *(or* **sarcīre)** to make good a loss; **damnum facere** to incur a loss; to cause loss *(to another)*; **nātūrae damnum** a natural defect
Dana·ē -ēs *f* daughter of Acrisius and mother, by Zeus, of Perseus
Danaïd·es -um *fpl* fifty daughters of Danaüs
Dana·üs -ī *m* Danaüs *(son of Belus and brother of Aegyptus and king of Argos)* ‖ *mpl* Greeks
danīst·a -ae *m* moneylender, banker
danīstic·us -a -um *adj* moneylending, banking
danō *see* **dō**
Dānuv·ius -(i)ī *m* **(Dānub-)** Upper Danube *(opp:* **Hister** = Lower Danube)
Daphn·ē -ēs *f* nymph *(daughter of the river-god Peneus, pursued by Apollo and changed into a laurel tree)*
Daphn·is -idis *(acc:* **-im** *or* **-in)** *m* handsome young Sicilian shepherd, inventor of pastoral poetry
dapin·ō -āre *tr* to serve *(food)*
dap·s -is *f* ceremonial feast; feast; banquet; feed *(for animals)*
dapsil·is -is -e *adj* sumptuous, costly
Dardanid·ēs -ae *m* descendant of Dardanus; Trojan; Roman
Dardan·is -idis *or* **-idos** *adj (fem only)* Trojan
Dardan·us -a -um *adj* Dardanian, Trojan; Roman *(descendant of Aeneas)* ‖ *m* son of Jupiter and ancestor of the Trojan race ‖ *mpl* Illyrian tribe; a people of Asia Minor
Dārē·us *or* **Dārī·us -ī** *m* Darius *(521–485 B.C., Persian king whose generals were defeated by the Greeks at Marathon in 490 B.C.)* ‖ Darius Nothus *(424–405 B.C., son of Artaxerxes I)* ‖ Darius Codomanus *(last king of Persia, reigned 336–331 B.C.)*
datāri·us -a -um *adj* to be handed out, to be given away
datātim *adv* by giving *or* tossing from hand to hand *(in games)*
dati·ō -ōnis *f* giving, allotting; transfer *(e.g., of property)*
datīv·us -a -um *adj & m (gram)* dative
dat·ō -āre -āvī -ātus *tr* to keep giving
dat·or -ōris *m* giver; *(in playing ball)* passer
dat·us -ūs *m* giving
Daul·is -idis *f* town in Phocis, famous for the fable of Procne and Philomela
Daun·us -ī *m* mythical king of Apulia, the father of Turnus
dē- (de- before vowels and **h)** *pref* indicating: **1** motion down from or away: **dēpendēre** to hang down; **2** removal, deprivation: **dēspolīre** to despoil; **3** left behind: **dērelinquere** to leave behind; **4** reversal of process: **deonerāre** to unload; **5** completely, to the end: **dēpugnāre** to fight it out, fight to the finish; **6** down, from the right path or state or norm: **dēfōrmis** ugly; **7** intensity: **deamāre** to love passionately
dē *prep (w. abl)* **1** *(of space)* down from, from, away from, out of; **2** *(of origin)* from, of, descended from: **Priamī dē stirpe Diōrēs** Diores of Priam's lineage; **3** *(of separation)* from among, out of: **noctem dē diē facere** to make night out of day; **4** *(in partitive sense)* of, out of: **dīmidium dē praedā dare** to give half of the booty; **5** *(of time)* immediately after; **diem dē diē** day after day; **6** *(of reference)* about, on, concerning, of, in respect to: **ōrātiō dē domō suā** a speech concerning his own home; **7** according to, in imitation of: **castae dē mōre puellae** like a chaste girl *(literally, according to the manner of a chaste girl)*; **8** *(of cause)* for, on account of, because of: **quā dē causā** for that reason, wherefore; **9** *(of which*

s.th. is made) **templum dē marmore** a marble temple, a temple (made) of marble; **10** *(indicating persons over whom victory is gained)* over: **dē Samnitibus triumphāvit** he held a triumph for his victory over the Samnites; **11** *(indicating change)* from, out of: **dē templō carcerem facere** to make a prison out of a temple; **dē imprōvīsō** unexpectedly; **dē industriā** on purpose, intentionally; **dē integrō** afresh, all over again; **dē nocte** *(or* **dē vigiliā)** at night; **dē novō** anew

de·a -ae *(dat & abl pl:* **deābus)** *f* goddess

dealb·ō -āre -āvī -ātus *tr* to whiten, whitewash

deambulāti·ō -ōnis *f* strolling, walking about, walk, stroll

deambul·ō -āre -āvī -ātum *intr* to go for a walk

deam·ō -āre -āvī -ātus *tr* to love passionately; to be much obliged to

dearm·ō -āre -āvī -ātus *tr* to disarm

deartu·ō -āre -āvī -ātus *tr* to tear limb from limb, dismember

deasci·ō -āre -āvī -ātus *tr* to smooth with an ax; *(fig)* to cheat, con

dēbacch·or -ārī -ātus sum *intr* to rant and rave

dēbellāt·or -ōris *m* conqueror

dēbell·ō -āre -āvī -ātus *tr* to fight it out with, wear down, subdue **II** *intr* to fight it out to the end; to bring a war to an end

dēb·eō -ēre -uī -itus *tr* to owe; to be responsible for; *(w. inf)* **1** to have to, be obliged to; **2** to be destined to; **dēbeō abīre** I ought to leave **II** *pass (w. dat)* to be due to

dēbil·is -is -e *adj* crippled, frail, feeble; ineffective

dēbilit·ās -ātis *f* lameness; debility, weakness, feebleness

dēbilitāti·ō -ōnis *f* disabling, enfeebling

dēbilit·ō -āre -āvī -ātus *tr* to disable; to debilitate, weaken; to unnerve; *(fig)* to paralyze

dēbiti·ō -ōnis *f* debt

dēbit·or -ōris *m* debtor; person under obligation

dēbit·um -ī *n* debt; obligation

dēblater·ō -āre -āvī -ātus *tr & intr* to blurt out

dēcant·ō -āre -āvī -ātus *tr* to repeat monotonously; to reel off **II** *intr* to sing on to the end; to stop singing

dē·cēdō -cēdere -cessī -cessum *intr* to withdraw, depart, clear out; to retreat; to make way, make room, yield; to disappear; to die; to abate, subside, cease; to go wrong; *(w. dat)* to give in to; *(w.* **dē** *+ abl)* to give up, abandon, relinquish

decem *indecl adj* ten

Decem·ber -bris -bre *adj* December, of December; **mēnsis December** (month of) December *(tenth month of the Roman calendar until 153 B.C.)* **II Decem·ber -bris** *m* December

decemiug·is -is *m* ten-horse chariot

decemped·a -ae *f* ten-foot measuring rod

decempedāt·or -ōris *m* surveyor

decempl·ex -icis *adj* tenfold

decemprīm·ī *or* **decem prīm·ī -ōrum** *mpl* ten-man council *(governing Italic towns)*

decemscalm·us -a -um *adj* ten-oared

decem·vir -virī *m* decemvir *(member of a board of ten)*

decemvirāl·is -is -e *adj* decemviral; **lēgēs decemvirālēs** laws passed by the decemviri

decemvirāt·us -ūs *m* decemvirate

decemvir·ī -ōrum *mpl* board of ten *(appointed in Rome at different times and for various purposes: maintaining Sibylline books, distribution of land; codifying the XII Tables; deciding whether a person was free or slave);* **decemvirī sacrīs faciundīs** commission for attending to religious matters

decenn·is -is -e *adj* ten-year

dec·ēns -entis *adj* decent, proper, becoming; handsome, pretty

decenter *adv* decently, properly

decenti·a -ae *f* decency, propriety

dē·cernō -cernere -crēvī -crētus *tr* to sift, separate; to decide, determine, settle; to resolve, decree, vote; to decide by combat; to fight, combat **II** *intr* to contend, compete, struggle; to put forward a proposal; *(w.* **dē** *or* **prō** *+ abl)* to fight over, fight for *(in court)*

dēcerp·ō -ere -sī -tus *tr* to tear off, break off; to gather *(fruit, grapes);* to pick *(flowers);* to derive *(e.g., benefits, satisfaction);* **aliquid dē gravitāte dēcerpere** to detract somewhat from dignity

dēcertāti·ō -ōnis *f* decisive struggle

dēcert·ō -āre -āvī -ātum *intr* to fight it out, decide the issue

dēcessi·ō -ōnis *f* withdrawing; retirement, departure *(from a province);* decrease; disappearance

dēcess·or -ōris *m* retiring official; predecessor *(opp:* **successor)**

dēcess·us -ūs *m* withdrawal; retirement *(of an official from a province);* decease, death

dec·et -ēre -uit *(used only in inf and 3rd sing & pl)* *tr* to befit; to lend grace to; to adorn **II** *v impers (w. inf)* it is proper for *(s.o.)* to; *(w. dat & inf)* it is proper *or* right for *(s.o.)* to

dē·cidō -cidere -cidī *intr* to fall down; to die; to drop; to sink; *(of things)* to fail, go wrong; to end up, land; *(of plants)* to wilt

dē·cīdō -cīdere -cīdī -cīsus *tr* to cut off, cut away; to cut down; to cut short, terminate; to settle *(a matter);* **pennās**

dēcīdere *(w. dat) (fig)* to clip *(s.o.'s)* wings ‖ *intr (w.* **cum)** to come to terms with

deciēns *adv* **(-iēs)** ten times; **deciēns centēna mīlia** *(or simply* **deciēns)** a million; **bis deciēns** two million

decimānus *see* **decumānus**

decimum *adv* for the tenth time

decim·us -a -um *adj* **(-cum-)** the tenth; **cum decimō** tenfold; **cum decimō effēcit ager** the field produced a tenfold return

dē·cipiō -cipere -cēpī -ceptus *tr* to deceive, cheat; to dupe, mislead; to frustrate, disappoint; to escape the notice of; **aliquem labōrum dēcipere** to make s.o. forget his troubles

dēcīsi·ō -ōnis *f* settlement

dēcīsum *pp of* **dēcīdō**

Dec·ius -(i)ī *m* Publius Decius Mus *(father and son, who gave their lives to save the Roman army)*

dēclāmāti·ō -ōnis *f* practice in public speaking; practice speech; theme *(in a practice speech)*

dēclāmāt·or -ōris *m* student of public speaking, declaimer

dēclāmātōri·us -a -um *adj* rhetorical

dēclāmit·ō -āre -āvī -ātus *tr* to plead *(cases)* ‖ *intr* to practice public speaking

dēclām·ō -āre -āvī -ātus *tr* to recite ‖ *intr* to practice public speaking, declaim

dēclārāti·ō -ōnis *f* declaration, disclosure, announcement; **dēclārātiō amōris** an expression of affection

dēclār·ō -āre -āvī -ātus *tr* to make clear, make evident, disclose; to proclaim, announce officially; to show, prove, demonstrate; to mean, express, signify; to declare *(e.g., s.o. consul)*

dēclīnāti·ō -ōnis *f* deviation, swerve; inclination; avoidance; digression; *(gram)* declension

dēclīn·ō -āre -āvī -ātus *tr* to deflect; to parry, avoid; *(gram)* to decline, conjugate ‖ *intr* to deviate; to digress

dēclīv·e -is *n* slope; **per dēclīve** downwards

dēclīv·is -is -e *adj* sloping, steep, down-hill

dēclīvit·ās -ātis *f* sloping terrain

dēcoct·a -ae *f* cold beverage *(invented by Nero)*

dēcoct·or -ōris *m* a bankrupt person

dēcoct·us -a -um *pp of* **dēcoquō** ‖ *adj* luscious; ripe; over-ripe; mellow, over-sweet *(style)*

dēcoll·ō -āre -āvī -ātus *tr* to behead

dēcōl·ō -āre -āvī *intr* to drain away, come to naught, fail

dēcol·or -ōris *adj* off-color, faded; dark-skinned; degenerate, depraved

dēcolōr·ō -āre -āvī -ātus *tr* to discolor, stain, deface; to disgrace

dēco·quō -quere -xī -ctus *tr* to boil down, boil thoroughly; to bring to ruin; to digest *(food)* ‖ *intr* to go bankrupt

dec·or -ōris *m* beauty, grace, elegance, charm; ornament

decōrē *adv* beautifully, gracefully; suitably, properly

decor·ō -āre -āvī -ātus *tr* to beautify, adorn, embellish; to decorate, honor

decōr·us -a -um *adj* beautiful, graceful; glorious, noble; suitable, proper ‖ *n* grace; propriety

dēcoxī *perf of* **dēcoquō**

dēcrepit·us -a -um *adj* decrepit, broken down, worn out

dē·crēscō -crēscere -crēvī -crētum *intr* to grow less, become fewer, diminish, fade; *(of time)* to grow shorter; *(of water)* to subside, go down

dēcrēt·us -a -um *pp of* **dēcernō** ‖ *n* decree, decision; principle

decum·a -ae *f* **(-cim-)** one-tenth; tithe, land tax; largess to the people

decumān·us -a -um *adj* **(-cim-)** paying tithes; of the tenth legion, of the tenth cohort; subject to the 10% tax; **porta decumāna** main gate of Roman camp on the side turned away from the enemy ‖ *m* tax collector ‖ *mpl* men of the tenth legion ‖ *f* tax collector's wife

decumāt·ēs -ium *pl adj* subject to tithes

dē·cumbō -cumbere -cubuī *intr* to lie down; to recline at table; to fall *(in battle)*

decuri·a -ae *f* decury *(unit in Roman government consisting of ten families);* group of ten *(organized for work, recreation, etc.);* panel *(from which jury members were selected);* social club, society

decuriāti·ō -ōnis *f or* **decuriāt·us -ūs** *m* dividing into decuries

decuri·ō -āre -āvī -ātus *tr (fig)* to divide into groups; *(pol)* to divide into groups of ten

decuri·ō -ōnis *m* squad leader *(in the cavalry or navy in charge of ten men);* councilman *(of a municipality or colony);* chief chamberlain

dē·currō -currere -(cu)currī -cursus *tr* to run down, hurry down *(e.g., a path);* to travel over *(a course),* to cover *(a distance);* to make straight for; to turn to *(s.o.)* for help; to pass through *(life);* to run through *(mentally, in a speech),* discuss, treat ‖ *intr* to run down; to run for exercise, jog; *(of liquids)* to run down, flow down; *(of terrain)* to slope down; *(of rivers, ships)* to run down to the sea; *(of ships, travelers)* to come to land; to travel downstream; *(mil)* to run through a drill, carry out maneuvers, parade ‖ *v impers* **eō dēcursum est ut** it got to the point where

dēcursi·ō -ōnis *f* raid; *(mil)* drill, maneuvers, dress parade
dēcurs·us -ūs *m* running down; downward course; *(mil)* maneuvers; *(mil)* dress parade; *(mil)* attack from higher ground; *(rhet)* the flow *(of a sentence, verse);* **dēcursiō honōrum** completion of a political career
dēcurtāt·us -a -um *adj* cut down, cut off short, mutilated; clipped *(style)*
dec·us -oris *n* beauty, glory, honor, dignity; virtue, worth; source of glory ‖ *npl* achievements
dēcuss·ō -āre -āvī -ātus *tr* to divide crosswise *(in the form of an X)*
dēcu·tiō -tere -ssī -ssus *tr* to shake off, beat off, strike down; to chop off *(head);* to break down *(wall with battering ram)*
dēdec·et -ēre -uit *v impers* it ill befits; *(w. inf)* it is a disgrace to
dēdecor·ō -āre -āvī -ātus *tr* to disgrace, dishonor; to make a sham of
dēdecōr·us -a -um *adj* disgraceful, dishonorable, unbecoming
dēdec·us -oris *n* disgrace, dishonor, shame; vice, crime, outrage; *(mil)* disgraceful defeat; **dēdecorī esse** *(w. dat)* to be a source of disgrace to; **dēdecus admittere** to incur disgrace; **per dēdecus** disgracefully
dēdicāti·ō -ōnis *f* dedication, consecration
dēdic·ō -āre -āvī -ātus *tr* to dedicate, consecrate, set aside; to declare *(property in a census return)*
dēdign·or -ārī -ātus sum *tr* to disdain, look down on; *(w. double acc)* to scorn *(s.o.)* as; **aliquem marītum dēdignārī** to regard s.o. as an unworthy husband
dē·discō -discere -didicī *tr* to unlearn, forget
dēditīc·ius -(i)ī *m* prisoner-of-war
dēditi·ō -ōnis *f* surrender; **aliquem in dēditiōnem accipere** to accept the surrender of s.o.
dēdit·us -a -um *pp of* **dēdō** ‖ *adj (w. dat)* given to, devoted to; addicted to; *(w.* **in** *+ acc)* absorbed in ‖ *mpl* prisoners-of-war
dēd·ō -ere -idī -itus *tr* to give up, surrender; to devote; to apply; to abandon; **dēditā operā** on purpose; **necī** *(or* **ad necem) dēdere** to put to death
dēdoc·eō -ēre -uī -tus *tr* to cause to forget; *(w. inf)* to teach *(s.o.)* not to
dēdol·eō -ēre -uī *intr* to feel pain no more
dēdol·ō -āre -āvī -ātus *tr* to hew into shape
dēdū·cō -cere -xī -ctus *tr* to lead *or* draw down; to launch *(ship);* to accompany, escort; to lead out *(colonists to new colony);* to conduct *(bride to husband),* give *(bride)* away; to evict; to subtract, deduct; to summon *(as witness);* to divert; to mislead; to derive *(name);* to compose *(poetry);* to comb out *(hair);* to draw out *(thread in spinning);* to lure *(into a trap); (leg)* to arraign; *(pol)* to install *(in a position of authority);* **rem hūc** *(or* **eō) dēdūcere ut** to bring things to the point that
dēducti·ō -ōnis *f* draining *(of water);* settling of colonists; subtraction, deduction; inference; *(leg)* eviction; **ratiōnis dēductiō** line of reasoning; **sine ūllā dēductiōne** in full
dēduct·or -ōris *m* escort
dēduct·us -a -um *pp of* **dēdūcō** ‖ *adj* drawn down; bent inwards, concave; lowered, modest; subtle, well-wrought *(poem);* **nāsus dēductus** pug nose
deërr·ō -āre -āvī -ātum *intr* to go astray, wander away, get lost; to stray; to go wrong
dēfaec·ō -āre -āvī -ātus *tr* to remove the dregs of, strain; *(fig)* to clear up
dēfatīgāti·ō -ōnis *f* **(-fet-)** exhaustion
dēfatīg·ō -āre -āvī -ātus *tr* **(-fet-)** to exhaust
dēfatīscor *see* **dēfetīscor**
dēfecti·ō -ōnis *f* failure; defection, desertion; weakening, exhaustion; *(astr)* eclipse; *(gram)* ellipsis; **dēfectiō animī** mental breakdown; **in dēfectiōne esse** to be in revolt
dēfect·or -ōris *m* defector, deserter
dēfect·us -a -um *pp of* **dēficiō** ‖ *adj* weak, worn out
dēfect·us -ūs *m* failing, failure; desertion, defection; *(astr)* eclipse
dēfen·dō -dere -dī -sus *tr* to defend, protect, guard; to repel, beat off, avert; to keep off *(the cold, heat);* to answer *(a charge);* to support, uphold *(argument);* to play the part of *(a character); (leg)* to defend; *(w. dat)* to ward off *(s.th. harmful)* from; **sōlstitium pecorī dēfendere** to ward off the noonday heat from the flock, protect the flock from the noonday heat
dēfēnsi·ō -ōnis *f* defense
dēfēnsit·ō -āre -āvī -ātus *tr* to defend (often); **causās dēfēnsitāre** to be a lawyer
dēfēns·ō -āre -āvī -ātus *tr* to defend, protect
dēfēns·or -ōris *m* defender, protector; champion *(leg)* defense lawyer; *(leg)* guardian
dēfēnsus *pp of* **dēfendō**
dē·ferō -ferre -tulī -lātus *tr* to bring *or* carry down; to carry away; to drive *(ship)* off course; to offer, confer, grant; to inform against, indict; to give an account of; to announce, report; to recommend; to register; **aliquem ad aerārium dēferre** to recommend s.o. for a monetary reward; **ad cōnsilium dēferre** to take into consideration

dēfer·vēscō -vēscere -v(u)ī *or* **-buī** *intr* to stop boiling, cool off; *(fig)* to calm down
dēfess·us -a -um *adj* weary, tired
dēfetīgō *see* **dēfatīgō**
dē·fetīscor -fetīscī -fessus sum *intr* **(-fat-)** to get tired; *(w. inf)* to tire of
dē·ficiō -ficere -fēcī -fectus *tr* to fail, disappoint; to desert, abandon **||** *intr* to fail, be a failure; *(of supplies, etc.)* to run low, run out; *(of strength, morale)* to fail, sink; *(of sun, moon)* to be eclipsed; *(of a family line, race)* to become extinct; *(of fire)* to die out; *(w. dat or* **ad**) to be insufficient for; *(com)* to be bankrupt; *(mil, pol)* to defect; *(pol)* to secede
dēfī·gō -gere -xī -xus *tr* to fix, fasten down; to drive down; to fix, concentrate *(eyes, attention);* to root to the spot, astound; to bewitch; **in terrā dēfīgere** to stick *or* plant *or* set *(s.th.)* up in the ground; to stick *(weapon into s.o.)*
dēfing·ō -ere dēfīnxī *tr* to form, mold; to disfigure
dēfīn·iō -īre -īvī *or* **-iī -ītus** *tr* to mark out the limits of *(a place);* to limit, restrict; to define; to fix, determine, appoint; to bring to a finish, put an end to; to assign, prescribe
dēfīnītē *adv* precisely
dēfīnīti·ō -ōnis *f* boundary; *(fig)* marking out, prescribing; definition
dēfīnītīv·us -a -um *adj* definitive, explanatory; decisive
dēfīnīt·us -a -um *pp of* **dēfīniō ||** *adj* definite, precise
dēfīnxī *perf of* **dēfingō**
dē·fīō -fierī *intr* to fail, be lacking, be in short supply
dēflagrāti·ō -ōnis *f* conflagration
dēflagr·ō -āre -āvī -ātus *tr* to burn down **||** *intr* to burn down; to perish, be destroyed; *(of passions)* to cool off
dē·flectō -flectere -flexī -flexus *tr* to deflect, bend aside, turn away, divert; *(fig)* to modify, twist; to bend *(a bow);* to lead astray **||** *intr* to digress, deviate
dēfl·eō -ēre -ēvī -ētus *tr* to cry bitterly for; to lament; to mourn as lost **||** *intr* to cry bitterly
dēfloccāt·us -a -um *adj (hum)* bald
dēflocc·ō -āre -āvī -ātus *tr* to rub the nap off *(cloth); (fig)* to fleece
dēflōr·ēscō -ēscere -uī *intr* to shed blossoms; *(fig)* to fade, droop
dēflu·ō -ere -xī -xum *intr* to flow *or* float down; to glide down; to slide, fall; to drain off, run dry; to vanish, pass away, cease; to go out of style; *(w.* **ab**) to be descended from
dē·fodiō -fodere -fōdī -fossus *tr* to dig down; to hollow out; to bury, conceal
dēfore = dēfutūrum esse *fut inf of* **dēsum**
dēfōrmāti·ō -ōnis *f* configuration; disfigurement
dēfōrm·is -is -e *adj* shapeless; misshapen, disfigured, ugly; degrading; degraded; humiliating; unbecoming
dēfōrmit·ās -ātis *f* deformity, ugliness, hideousness; vileness; lack of good taste *(in writing)*
dēfōrmiter *adv* without grace; shamefully
dēfōrm·ō -āre -āvī -ātus *tr* to form from a pattern; to sketch, delineate; to deform, disfigure, mar
dēfossus *pp of* **dēfōdiō**
dēfraud·ō *or* **dēfrūd·ō -āre -āvī -ātus** *tr* to defraud, rob; to cheat; **animum** *(or* **sē** *or* **genium suum) dēfraudāre** to deny oneself some pleasure
dēfrēnāt·us -a -um *adj* unbridled
dēfric·ō -āre -uī -tus *or* **-ātus** *tr* to rub down; to brush *(teeth);* to scour; *(fig)* to satirize
dē·fringō -fringere -frēgī -frāctus *tr* to break off, break to pieces
dēfrūdō *see* **dēfraudō**
dēfrut·um -ī *n* new wine
dē·fugiō -fugere -fūgī *tr* to run away from, avoid, shirk; to evade *(e.g., authority, law)* **||** *intr* to run off
dēfūnct·us -a -um *pp of* **dēfungor ||** *adj* finished; dead
dē·fundō -fundere -fūdī -fūsus *tr* to pour out; to empty
dēfun·gor -gī dēfūnctus sum *intr (w. abl)* **1** to perform, carry out; **2** to finish, be done with; **3** to have done with, get rid of; **dēfūnctus honōribus** having ended a public career; **dēfūnctus iam sum** I'm safe now; **dēfungī (vītā)** to die; **quasi dēfūnctus rēgis imperiō** as if carrying out the king's order; **suā morte dēfūnctus est** he died a natural death
dēfūsus *pp of* **dēfundō**
dēfutūt·us -a -um *adj (vulg)* worn out from excessive sex
dēgen·er -eris *adj* degenerate; unworthy; ignoble
dēgener·ō -āre -āvī -ātus *tr* to disgrace, dishonor; to fall short of **||** *intr* to degenerate; *(w.* **ad** *or* **in** *+ acc)* to sink to
dēger·ō -ere *tr* to carry off
dēg·ō -ere *tr* to spend, pass *(time);* to spend one's time in **||** *intr* to spend one's time, live
dēgrandin·at -āre *v impers* it is hailing hard
dēgrav·ō -āre — -ātus *tr* to weigh down; *(fig)* to burden, distress, inconvenience, overpower
dē·gredior -gredī -gressus sum *intr* to march down, go down, walk down, descend; *(from a standard)* to depart; **ad pedēs dēgredī** to dismount
dēgrunn·iō -īre *intr* to grunt loud

dēgust·ō -āre -āvī -ātus *tr* to taste; *(fig)* to taste, sample, try, experience; *(of weapon)* to graze

dehinc *adv* from here, from now on, after this; then, next; hereafter

dehīsc·ō -ere *intr* to part, divide, gape, yawn; to develop a crack; *(w.* **in** *+ acc)* to split open and reveal

dehonestāment·um -ī *n* blemish, disfigurement, dishonor, disgrace

dehonest·ō -āre -āvī -ātus *tr* to dishonor, disgrace

dehort·or -ārī -ātus sum *tr* to dissuade, discourage; **multa mē dehortantur ā vōbīs** many things tell me to keep my distance from you

Dēianīr·a -ae *f* daughter of Oeneus and wife of Hercules

dē·iciō -icere -iēcī -iectus *tr* **(dē·ji-)** to throw down, fling down; to kill *(sacrificial victim); (of winds)* to drive off course; to depose, fire *(from office);* to lower *(eyes);* to banish *(feelings); (leg)* to evict; *(mil)* to dislodge; *(w. abl or* **dē** *+ abl)* to deprive *(s.o.)* of, prevent *(s.o.)* from obtaining, rob *(s.o.)* of; **ā rē pūblicā oculōs dēicere** to take one's eyes off the government; **dē gradū** *(or* **dē locō** *or* **dē statū)** **dēicere** to throw off balance; **mente suā dēiectus** driven out of one's mind; **sortem dēicere** to cast a lot *(into an urn)*

dēiecti·ō -ōnis *f* **(dējec-)** *(leg)* eviction

dēiect·us -a -um *pp of* **dēiciō ‖** *adj* **(dējec-)** low, depressed, sunken *(place);* downhearted, depressed, despondent

dēier·ō -āre -āvī -tum *tr & intr* **(dējer-)** to swear solemnly

dein *see* **deinde**

deinceps *adv* one after another, in succession, in order; without interruption; *(of time)* from now on, from then on, after that, after this, next; *(of space)* beyond that; **et deinceps** and so on

deinde *or* **dein** *adv (of place)* from that place, from there; *(of time)* then, thereafter, thereupon, afterwards; *(in enumerating facts, presenting arguments)* secondly, in the next place

Dēïphob·us -ī *m* son of Priam and Hecuba, and husband of Helen after Paris' death

dē·iungō -iungere -iūnxī -iūnctus *tr* **(dējun-)** to unyoke; to sever

dēiūrō *see* **dēierō**

dēiuv·ō -āre *tr* **(dējuv-)** to refuse to help

dēj- = dēi-

dēlā·bor -bī -psus sum *intr* to slip down, fall down, sink; to glide down, float down; *(of water)* to flow down; *(fig)* to stoop, condescend; *(w.* **ad)** to be inclined toward, be partial to; *(w.* **in** *+ acc)* to sneak in among

dēlacer·ō -āre -āvī -ātus *tr* to tear to pieces

dēlāment·or -ārī -ātus sum *tr* to grieve deeply for

dēlass·ō -āre -āvī -ātus *tr* to tire out, weary

dēlāti·ō -ōnis *f* reporting; informing, denouncing; **nōminis dēlātiō** indicting a person

dēlāt·or -ōris *m* reporter; *(leg)* informant

dēlātus *pp of* **dēferō**

dēlēbil·is -is -e *adj* able to be obliterated

dēlectābil·is -is -e *adj* delightful; delicious

dēlectāment·um -ī *n* delight; amusement, pastime, hobby

dēlectāti·ō -ōnis *f* delight, pleasure, amusement; satisfaction

dēlect·ō -āre -āvī -ātus *tr* to delight; to amuse, charm; to attract, allure; **dēlectārī** *(w. abl)* to delight in **‖** *v impers* **mē īre dēlectat** I like to go, I enjoy going

dēlēct·us -ūs *m* choosing, choice; *(mil)* recruitment; *(mil)* recruits

dēlēgāti·ō -ōnis *f (leg)* assignment to a third party of a creditor's interest in a debt

dēlēg·ō -āre -āvī -ātus *tr* to assign, appoint *(s.o. to a task);* to ascribe *(credit, blame);* to transfer *(ownership of property)*

dēlēnific·us -a -um *adj* soothing, ingratiating

dēlēnīment·um -ī *n* allurement, bait; solace, comfort

dēlēn·iō -īre -iī -ītus *tr* **(-līn-)** to soothe, calm down, console, appease; to allure, win over

dēlēnīt·or -ōris *m* charmer

dēl·eō -ēre -ēvī -ētus *tr* to destroy; to annihilate; to overthrow; to extinguish; to raze; to blot out, erase; to put an end to, abolish

dēlētr·īx -īcis *f* destroyer *(female)*

Dēliac·us -a -um *adj* Delian, of Delos

dēlīberābund·us -a -um *adj* deep in thought

dēlīberāti·ō -ōnis *f* considering, weighing; deliberation, consultation; **habet rēs dēlīberātiōnem** the matter requires thought

dēlīberātīv·us -a -um *adj* deliberative; requiring deliberation

dēlīberāt·or -ōris *m* thoughtful person

dēlīberāt·us -a -um *adj* resolved upon, determined

dēlīber·ō -āre -āvī -ātus *tr* to weigh, think over; to resolve; to consult *(an oracle)* **‖** *intr* to deliberate; *(w.* **dē** *+ abl)* to think over; *(w.* **cum)** to consult

dēlīb·ō -āre -āvī -ātus *tr* to sip, take a sip of; to taste, take a taste of, nibble at; to take away, subtract, remove; to touch on *(subject)*

dēlibr·ō -āre -āvī -ātus *tr* to strip the bark off

dēlibūt·us -a -um *adj* anointed; defiled, smeared, stained; steeped

dēlicātē *adv* delicately; luxuriously

dēlicāt·us -a -um *adj* delicate, dainty, tender; pampered; frivolous; fastidious, squeamish; self-indulgent; luxurious ‖ *mf* favorite
dēlici·a -ae *f* darling, pet
dēlici·ae -ārum *fpl* delight, pleasures; sweetheart, darling; pet, favorite; comforts, luxuries; ornaments; mannerisms, airs; **dēliciās facere** to enjoy oneself; to have fun *(at s.o. else's expense);* **dēliciās facere** *(w. dat) (sl)* to play around with *(a girl);* **esse in dēliciīs** *(w. dat)* to be the pet *or* favorite of; **habēre in dēliciīs** to have as a pet *or* favorite
dēliciol·ae -ārum *fpl* darling
dēlic·ium -(i)ī *n* darling; pet
dēlic·ō -āre *tr* **(-qu·ō)** to make clear
dēlict·um -ī *n* fault, offense, wrong; defect *(in a thing)*
dēlicu·us -a -um *adj* **(-liqu-)** lacking, missing
dēlig·ō -āre -āvī -ātus *tr* **(-leg-)** to tie up, fasten; *(med)* to bandage
dē·ligō -ligere -lēgī -lēctus *tr* to pick off; to pick out, choose, select; to gather; *(mil)* to draft; *(mil)* to hold a draft in *(a place)*
dēlin·g(u)ō -g(u)ere -xī *tr* to lick off; to have a lick of
dēlīni- = dēlēni-
dēlin·ō -ere — -itus *tr* to smudge
dē·linquō -linquere -līquī -lictus *tr (w. neut pron)* to commit *(an offense);* **māiōra dēlinquere** to commit greater wrongs; **sī quid dēlīquerō** if I commit some offense ‖ *intr* to be missing; to be wanting, fall short; to do wrong, commit an offense
dē·liquēscō -liquēscere -licuī *intr* to melt, dissolve; to pine away
dēliqui·ō -ōnis *f* failure; *(w. gen)* failure to get; *(astr)* eclipse
dēliqu·ium -(i)ī *n* failure
dēliquō *see* **dēlicō**
dēlīrāment·um -ī *n* nonsense, delusion, absurdity
dēlīrāti·ō -ōnis *f* silliness, folly, madness; infatuation; dotage
dēlīr·ō -āre *intr* to be off the beam, be crazy; to rave
dēlīr·us -a -um *adj* crazy, silly; senseless; in dotage
dēlit·ēscō -ēscere -uī *intr* **(-tīsc-)** to conceal oneself, lie hidden, lurk
dēlītig·ō -āre *intr* to rant, have it out
Dēli·us -a -um *adj* Delian, of Delos, of Apollo ‖ *m* Apollo
Dēl·os -ī *f* sacred island in the Cyclades, where Apollo and Diana were born
Delph·ī -ōrum *mpl* town in Phocis, in Central Greece, famous for the shrine and oracle of Apollo ‖ people of Delphi
Delphic·us -a -um *adj* of Delphi; of Apollo ‖ *f* three-legged table
delphīn·us -ī *or* **delph·īn -īnis** *m* dolphin ‖ **Delphīnus** *(astr)* Dolphin *(constellation)*
Delph·is -idis *f* Delphic priestess of Apollo
delta *indecl n* delta *(letter of the Greek alphabet)* ‖ **Delta** the Delta *(of the Nile River)*
Deltōt·on -ī *n (astr)* the Triangle *(constellation)*
dēlūbr·um -ī *n* shrine, sanctuary
dēluct·ō -āre -āvī *or* **dēluct·or -ārī -ātus sum** *intr* to wrestle
dēlūdific·ō -āre -āvī -ātus *tr* to make fun of
dēlū·dō -dere -sī -sus *tr* to fool, con
dēlumb·is -is -e *adj* lame
dēlumb·ō -āre *tr* to lame in the loins; *(fig)* to weaken
dēmad·ēscō -ēscere *intr* to become drenched, become wet; to be moistened
dēmand·ō -āre -āvī -ātus *tr* to hand over, entrust
dēmān·ō -āre -āvī *intr* to run down
dēmarch·us -ī *m* demarch *(chief of a village in Attica); (fig)* tribune of the people
dēm·ēns -entis *adj* demented, out of one's mind; senseless, reckless
dēmēns·us -a -um *pp of* **dēmetior** ‖ *n* ration, allowance
dēmenter *adv* insanely
dēmenti·a -ae *f* insanity; folly
dēment·iō -īre *intr* to be insane
dēmer·eō -ēre -uī -itus *or* **dēmer·eor -ērī -itus sum** *tr* to earn, merit, deserve; to serve well, do a service to, win the favor of
dēmer·gō -gere -sī -sus *tr* to sink; to plunge, dip; to bury ‖ *pass (of heavenly bodies)* to set
dēmessus *pp of* **dēmetō**
dēmēt·ior -īrī -mēnsus sum *tr* to measure out
dē·metō -metere -messuī -messus *tr* to mow, reap, harvest; to pick *(flowers, fruit);* to cut off
Dēmētr·ius -(i)ī *m* Demetrius Poliorcetes, son of Antigonus, and king of Macedonia ‖ Demetrius of Phaleron, famous orator and politician at Athens
dēmigrāti·ō -ōnis *f* emigration
dēmigr·ō -āre -āvī -ātum *intr* to migrate, emigrate, move, depart; *(fig)* to pass on, die
dēmin·uō -uere -uī -ūtus *tr* to make smaller, lessen, diminish; to deduct; *(w. abl)* to deprive of; *(w.* **dē** *+ abl)* to deduct from; **capite dēminuere** to deprive of civil rights
dēminūti·ō -ōnis *f* lessening, diminution, abridging; *(leg)* right of disposing of property; **capitis dēminūtiō** loss of civil rights; **prōvinicae dēminūtiō** shortening of term of office
dēmīr·or -ārī -ātus sum *tr* to be surprised at, be amazed at

dēmissē *adv (opp:* **altē)** low; humbly, modestly; abjectly

dēmissīci·us -a -um *adj* allowed to hang down, flowing; *(of clothes)* ankle-length

dēmissi·ō -ōnis *f* letting down, sinking, lowering; **dēmissiō animī** low morale

dēmiss·us -a -um *pp of* **dēmittō ‖** *adj* low, low-lying *(place);* drooping *(lips, etc.);* bent *(head);* flowing, long *(hair); (of clothes)* hanging down, full-length; *(fig)* downhearted, dejected; *(fig)* poor, humble; *(w. abl)* descended from

dēmītig·ō -āre *tr* to calm down

dē·mittō -mittere -mīsī -missus *tr* to drop, let drop, let sink; to lower; to dip; to sink *(a well);* to bring downstream; to shed *(blood);* to land *(ship);* to let down *(hair);* to grow *(beard);* to move down *(troops from a higher place);* **animum** *(or* **mentem)** **dēmittere** to become discouraged; **dēmittere aurēs ad** to deign to listen to **‖** *refl* to descend, go down; to stoop, bend down; *(fig)* to plunge into; *(geog)* to slope downwards **‖** *pass* to descend, go down

dēmiurg·us -ī *m* **(dāmi-)** magistrate in a Greek state

dēm·ō -ere -psī -ptus *tr* to take away, remove, withdraw; *(w. dat or abl or* **ab** *or* **dē** *+ abl)* to take away from, remove from, subtract from, withhold from; **vincla pedibus dēmere** to remove the fetters

Dēmocrit·us -ī *m* philosopher from Abdera in Thrace and founder of the atomic theory *(born c. 460 B.C.)*

dēmōl·ior -īrī -ītus sum *tr* to demolish, pull down

dēmōlīti·ō -ōnis *f* demolishing

dēmōnstrāti·ō -ōnis *f* pointing out; explanation; description

dēmōnstrātīv·us -a -um *adj* showy

dēmōnstrāt·or -ōris *m* one who points out, indicator

dēmōnstr·ō -āre -āvī -ātus *tr* to point out clearly; to state precisely, explain, describe; to mention, speak of; to demonstrate, prove, establish

Dēmopho·ōn -ontis *m* son of Theseus and Phaedra

dēmor·ior -ī -tuus sum *tr* to be dying for **‖** *intr* to die; to die off; to become extinct

dēmor·or -ārī -ātus sum *tr* to delay, detain; to hinder, block **‖** *intr* to wait

Dēmosthen·ēs -is *or* **-ī** *m* greatest Greek orator *(384–322 B.C.)*

dē·moveō -movēre -mōvī -mōtus *tr* to remove, move away; to dispossess, expel; to oust

dēmptus *pp of* **dēmō**

dēmūgīt·us -a -um *adj* bellowing, lowing

dēmul·ceō -cēre -sī *tr* to stroke lovingly, pet

dēmum *adv* at last, finally; not till then; *(to give emphasis)* precisely, exactly, just; *(to give assurance)* in fact, certainly, to be sure, as a matter of fact; **decimō dēmum annō** not till the tenth year; **modo dēmum** only now, not until now; **nunc dēmum** now at last, not until now; **post dēmum** not until afterwards; **tum dēmum** then finally, not until then

dēmurmur·ō -āre *tr* to grumble through *(e.g., a performance)*

dēmūtāti·ō -ōnis *f* transformation

dēmūt·ō -āre -āvī -ātus *tr* to change; to make worse **‖** *intr* to fail; to change one's mind

dēnār·ius -iī *m* denarius *(about $1);* money

dēnārr·ō -āre -āvī -ātus *tr* to recount in detail

dēnās·ō -āre *tr* to bite the nose off *(s.o.'s face)*

dēnat·ō -āre *intr* to swim downstream

dēneg·ō -āre -āvī -ātus *tr* to deny, refuse, turn down **‖** *intr* to say no

dēn·ī -ae -a *adj* in sets of ten, ten each, in tens; tenth

dēnicāl·is -is -e *adj* purifying from death; **fēriae dēnicālēs** purification service *(after death in the household)*

dēnique *adv* finally, at last; in short, in a word; *(for emphasis)* just, precisely; *(ironical)* of course; **octāvō dēnique mēnse** not till after the eighth month; **tum dēnique** then at last, only then, not till then

dēnōmin·ō -āre -āvī -ātus *tr (w.* **ab** *or* **ex)** to name after

dēnōrm·ō -āre *tr* to make crooked *or* irregular; to disfigure, spoil

dēnot·ō -āre -āvī -ātus *tr* to mark down, specify; to take careful note of; to observe closely

dēns dentis *m* tooth; ivory; point, prong; fluke; *(of an elephant)* tusk; **albīs dentibus dērīdēre aliquem** *(prov)* to laugh heartily at s.o.; **dēns Indus** elephant's tusk

dēnsē *adv* closely, thickly, in quick succession, repeatedly

dēnseō *see* **dēnsō**

dēnsit·ās -ātis *f* closeness; thickness

dēns·ō -āre -āvī -ātus *or* **dēns·eō -ēre** *tr* to thicken; to press close together; to close *(ranks);* to condense

dēns·us -a -um *adj* dense, close, thick, crowded; frequent, repeated; intense *(love, cold);* concise *(style)*

dentāl·ia -ium *npl* plow beam

dentāt·us -a -um *adj* toothed; serrated; *(of paper)* polished smooth

dentifrangibul·us -a -um *adj (hum)* tooth-breaking **‖** *m* thug **‖** *n* fist

dentifric·ium -(i)ī *n* tooth powder

dentileg·us -ī *m (hum)* toothpicker *(one who picks up teeth after they have been knocked out)*
dent·iō -īre *intr* to teethe
dentiscalp·ium -(i)i *n* toothpick
dēnū·bō -bere -psī -ptum *intr (of a woman)* to marry beneath her rank; to go through a mock marriage
dēnūd·ō -āre -āvī -ātus *tr* to strip naked, strip bare; to expose, leave unprotected; *(fig)* to lay bare
dēnumer·ō -āre -āvī -ātus *tr* to pay *(money)* in full
dēnūntiāti·ō -ōnis *f* intimation; warning, threat; announcement, proclamation; **senātūs dēnūntiātiō** Senate ordinance; **testimōniī dēnūntiātiō** summons to testify
dēnūnti·ō -āre -āvī -ātus *tr* to intimate; to give notice of; to announce officially; to give official warning to; to warn, threaten; *(mil)* to report to; **dēnūntiāre testimōnium** *(w. dat)* to give *(s.o.)* a summons to testify
dēnuō *adv* anew, once more, all over again; **dēnuō alius** yet another
deoner·ō -āre *tr* to unload
deopt·ō -āre *tr* to choose
deorsum *adv* **(-sus)** downwards, down; *(of position)* down below, underneath
deōscul·or -ārī -ātus sum *tr* to shower with kisses
dēpāct·us -a -um *adj* fastened down
dēparc·us -a -um *adj* very stingy
dēpacīscor *see* **dēpecīscor**
dē·pāscō -pāscere -pāvī -pāstus *or* **dē·pāscor -pāscī -pāstus sum** *tr* to eat up; to feed on; to graze on; to feed the cattle on *(grass, etc.)*; to consume, to destroy, waste; *(fig)* to prune off *(excesses in style)*; **altāria dēpāscere** to consume the flesh on the altar
dēpec·īscor -īscī -tus sum *tr* **(-pac-)** to agree on, come to terms on; to bargain for
dēpe·ctō -ctere — -xus *tr* to comb out; *(fig)* to flog
dēpecūlāt·or -ōris *m* embezzler
dēpecūl·or -ārī -ātus sum *tr* to embezzle; to steal
dē·pellō -pellere -pulī -pulsus *tr* to drive off, drive away; to drive out; to avert; *(mil)* to dislodge; *(w.* **quīn** *or w.* **ab** *or* **dē** *+ abl)* to deter from, dissuade from, wean from **II** *intr* to deviate
dēpend·eō -ēre -ī *intr* to hang down; *(w. abl)* to be derived from; *(w.* **ab** *or* **dē** *+ abl)* to depend on; *(w.* **ex)** to hang down from
dēpen·dō -dere -dī -sus *tr* to pay up; to pay *(penalty)*
dēper·dō -dere -didī -ditus *tr* to lose completely; to ruin, destroy
dēper·eō -īre -iī *tr* to be hopelessly in love with **II** *intr* to go to ruin, perish; to be lost, be finished; **dēperiī**! I'm done for!
dēpexus *pp of* **dēpectō**
dēpilāt·us -a -um *adj* plucked; *(fig)* swindled, gypped
dē·pingō -pingere -pīnxī -pictus *tr* to paint, portray; to embroider; *(fig)* to portray, describe, represent
dēplan·gō -gere -xī *tr* to beat one's breast in mourning over; to grieve over, cry one's heart out over
dēplex·us -a -um *adj* grasping, gripping firmly
dēplōrābund·us -a -um *adj* complaining bitterly; sobbing
dēplōr·ō -āre -āvī -ātus *tr* to cry over, mourn; to despair of **II** *intr* to cry bitterly, take it hard
dēplu·it -ere -it *v impers* it is raining hard, is pouring down
dē·pōnō -pōnere -posuī (-posīvī) pos(i)tus *tr* to put down, put aside; to get rid of; to bet; to deposit; *(w.* **apud** *+ acc)* to entrust to, commit to the care of; **bellum dēpōnere** to give up war; **imperium dēpōnere** to relinquish power
dēpopulāti·ō -ōnis *f* ravaging, pillaging
dēpopulāt·or -ōris *m* marauder
dēpopul·ō -āre -āvī -ātus *or* **dēpopul·or -ārī -ātus sum** *tr* to ravage, pillage, lay waste; *(of diseases)* to ravage; *(fig)* to wreck, destroy
dēport·ō -āre -āvī -ātus *tr* to carry down; to carry away; to bring home, win *(victory)*; to transport; to banish
dē·poscō -poscere -poposcī *tr* to demand; to require, call for; to request earnestly; to challenge
dēposit·us -a -um *pp of* **dēpōnō II** *adj* despaired of **II** *n* deposit *(as down-payment; for safekeeping)*; **dēpositī agere** to sue for breach of trust; **dēpositī damnāre** to convict of breach of trust
dēprāvātē *adv* perversely
dēprāvāti·ō -ōnis *f* distorting; *(fig)* distortion; perversity, perversion
dēprāv·ō -āre -āvī -ātus *tr* to make crooked, distort; to pervert, corrupt, seduce; to misrepresent
dēprecābund·us -a -um *adj* imploring
dēprecāti·ō -ōnis *f* supplication, averting by prayer; invocation, earnest entreaty; *(w, gen)* intercession against *(danger, etc.)*
dēprecāt·or -ōris *m* intercessor; *(w. gen)* champion of
dēprec·or -ārī -ātus sum *tr* to pray against, avert by prayer; to pray for, beg for; to intercede on behalf of; to plead in excuse **II** *intr* to pray; to make an entreaty
dēprehen·dō -dere -dī -sus *or* **dēpren·dō -dere -dī -sus** *tr* to get hold of; to arrest;

to catch, intercept; to surprise, catch in the act; to detect, discover; to perceive, understand; to embarrass

dēprehēnsi·ō -ōnis *f* detection

dēpress·us -a -um *pp of* **dēprimō** ‖ *adj* low *(voice);* low-lying *(land)*

dē·primō -primere -pressī -pressus *tr* to depress, weigh down; to plant deep; to dig *(e.g., trench);* to sink *(ship)* ‖ *pass* to sink

dēproeli·or -ārī *intr* to fight it out, battle fiercely

dēprōm·ō -ere -psī -ptus *tr* to take down; to bring out, produce; **pecūniam ex arcā dēprōmere** to get the money out of the safe

dēproper·ō -āre *tr* to make in a hurry ‖ *intr* to hurry

deps·ō -ere -uī -tus *tr* to knead; *(vulg)* to feel up

dēpud·et -ēre -uit *v impers* **eum dēpudet** he is unashamed, has lost all sense of shame

dēpūg·is -is *adj* **(-pȳg-)** *(masc & fem only)* with thin buttocks

dēpugn·ō -āre -āvī -ātum *intr* to fight hard; to fight it out ‖ *v impers (pass)* **dēpugnātum est** they fought hard

dēpulsī *perf of* **dēpellō**

dēpulsi·ō -ōnis *f* averting; *(rhet)* defense

dēpuls·ō -āre *tr* to push aside; **dē viā dēpulsāre** to push out of the way

dēpuls·or -ōris *m* averter

dēpulsus *pp of* **dēpellō**

dēpung·ō -ere *tr* to mark off *(in an account by punching holes)*

dēpurg·ō -āre -āvī -ātus *tr* to clean (out) thoroughly

dēput·ō -āre -āvī -ātus *tr* to prune; to reckon, consider

dēpȳgis *see* **dēpūgis**

dēque *adv* down, downwards

dērād·ō -ere -rāsī -rāsus *tr* to shave off; to scrape off

dērēct·us -a -um *pp of* **dērigō;** *see* **dīrēctus**

dērelicti·ō -ōnis *f* neglect

dēre·linquō -linquere -līquī -lictus *tr* to leave behind, abandon

dērepente *adv* suddenly, all of a sudden

dērēp·ō -ere -sī *intr* to crawl down

dēreptus *pp of* **dēripiō**

dērī·deō -dēre -sī -sus *tr* to deride ‖ *intr* to laugh it off *(i.e., get off scot-free)*

dērīdicul·us -a -um *adj* quite ridiculous, absurd ‖ *n* derision; absurdity; **dērīdiculō esse** to be the butt of ridicule

dērig·ēscō -ēscere -uī *intr* to grow stiff, grow rigid; to curdle

dērigō *see* **dīrigō**

dē·ripiō -ripere -ripuī -reptus *tr* to tear off; to remove; to seize; to tear down, pull down

dērīs·or -ōris *m* scoffer

dērīs·us -ūs *m* derision

dērīvāti·ō -ōnis *f* diverting *(of streams);* divergence of sense; derivation *(of words)*

dērīv·ō -āre -āvī -ātus *tr* to draw off, divert; to derive

dērō·dō -dere — -sus *tr* to nibble away at

dērog·ō -āre -āvī -ātus *tr* to propose to repeal *(a law)* in part; to restrict, modify; to take away

dērōs·us -a -um *adj* gnawed away, nibbled

dēruncin·ō -āre -āvī -ātus *tr* to plane off; *(fig)* to rip off

dēru·ō -ere -ī *tr* to throw down, demolish; *(w.* **dē** *+ abl)* to detract from

dērupt·us -a -um *adj* rough, steep ‖ *npl* crevasses, crags

dēsaev·iō -īre -(i)ī -ītum *intr* to rage furiously, vent one's rage; to run wild

dēsalt·ō -āre -āvī -ātus *tr* to dance; **canticum dēsaltāre** to dance a number

dēscen·dō -dere -dī -sum *intr* to climb down, descend, come down; to dismount; to fall, sink; to sink in, penetrate; to go down *(to the forum); (fig)* to go down, sink down, penetrate; *(fig)* to lower oneself, stoop, yield; *(mil)* to march down

dēscēnsi·ō -ōnis *f* descent; sailing down; **dēscēnsiō Tiberīna** sailing down the Tiber

dēscēns·us -ūs *m* climbing down, descent; slope

dēsc·īscō -īscere -īvī *or* **-iī -ītum** *intr* to revolt, defect; *(fig)* to depart, deviate; *(w.* **ab)** to deviate from, break allegiance with, revolt from; **ā mē dēsciī** I abandoned my own principles; **in mōnstrum dēscīscere** to degenerate into a monster

dēscrī·bō -bere -psī -ptus *tr* to write out, transcribe, copy; to describe, portray, design, sketch

dēscrīptē *see* **dīscrīptē**

dēscrīpti·ō -ōnis *f* copy; diagram, plan; transcript; description; **dēscrīptiō crīminis** indictment

dēscrīptus *pp of* **dēscrībō**

dēsec·ō -āre -uī -tus *tr* **(-sic-)** to cut off

dēser·ō -ere -uī -tus *tr* to desert, abandon, forsake; *(leg)* forfeit

dēsert·or -ōris *m* deserter

dēsert·us -a -um *pp of* **dēserō** ‖ *adj* deserted; uninhabited ‖ *npl* wilderness, desert

dēserv·iō -īre *intr (w. dat)* to be a slave to, serve devotedly

dēs·es -idis *adj* sitting down, sitting at ease; lazy, idle; apathetic, listless

dēsicc·ō -āre *tr* to dry up; to drain

dē·sideō -sidēre -sēdī *intr* to sit idle, remain inactive

dēsīderābil·is -is -e *adj* desirable

dēsīderāti·ō -ōnis *f* missing, feeling the absence, yearning; **dēsīderātiō voluptātum** yearning for pleasures

dēsīder·ium -(i)ī *n* longing, missing, feeling of loss; want, need, desire; request, petition; **ex dēsīderiō labōrāre** to be homesick; **mē dēsīderium tenet** *(w. gen)* I miss, am homesick for

dēsīder·ō -āre -āvī -ātus *tr* to miss, long for; to call for, require; *(mil)* to lose *(men)* in combat ‖ *pass* to be lost, be missing, be a casualty

dēsidi·a -ae *f* idleness, inactivity; laziness; apathy

dēsidiābul·um -ī *n (coll)* place to lounge, hangout

dēsidiōsē *adv* idly

dēsidiōs·us -a -um *adj* idle, lazy; causing idleness *or* laziness; spent in idleness

dē·sīdō -sīdere -sēdī *or* **-sīdī** *intr* to sink; to subside; to settle down; *(of morals)* to deteriorate; **in īmō dēsīdere** to settle at the bottom

dēsignāti·ō -ōnis *f* specification; layout; appointment; election

dēsignātor *see* **dissignātor**

dēsign·ō -āre -āvī -ātus *tr* to mark out, point out, designate; to outline; to define, trace; *(of words)* to denote, indicate; to earmark; to appoint, elect; **cōnsul dēsignātus** consul-elect

dē·siliō -silīre -siluī *or* **-silīvī** *or* **-siliī -sultum** *intr* to jump down; to dismount

dē·sinō -sinere -sīvī *or* **s(i)ī -situs** *tr* to give up, abandon, finish with; *(w. inf)* to stop *(doing s.th.)*; **furere dēsinere** to stop raging ‖ *intr* to stop, come to a stop, end; to stop speaking; *(w. gen)* to cease from; *(w.* **in** *+ acc)* to end in; **similiter dēsinere** to have similar endings

dēsipi·ēns -entis *adj* foolish, silly

dēsipienti·a -ae *f* foolishness

dēsip·iō -ere *intr* to be silly, fool around

dē·sistō -sistere -stitī *intr* to stop, desist; to get stuck, stick; *(w. abl or w.* **ab** *or* **dē** *+ abl)* to desist from, abandon, give up *(an action begun)*; **dēsistere ā dēfēnsiōne** to give up the defense

dēsitus *pp of* **dēsinō**

dēsōl·ō -āre -āvī -ātus *tr* to leave desolate, leave empty; to strip *(of inhabitants)*; to leave alone, forsake, abandon; **dēsōlātus** left in the lurch; *(w. abl)* deprived of

dēspect·ō -āre *tr* to look down on, overlook, command a view of; *(fig)* to look down on, despise

dēspect·us -a -um *pp of* **dēspiciō** ‖ *adj* contemptible

dēspect·us -ūs *m (with* **in** *+ acc)* commanding view of; contempt,

dēspēranter *adv* dispairingly, hopelessly

dēspērāti·ō -ōnis *f* desperation, despair

dēspērāt·us -a -um *adj* desperate, hopeless; despaired of

dēspēr·ō -āre -āvī -ātus *tr* to despair of ‖ *intr* to despair, give up hope; *(w.* **dē** *+ abl)* to despair of

dēspicāti·ō -ōnis *f* contempt ‖ *fpl* feelings of contempt

dēspicāt·us -a -um *adj* despicable; **aliquem dēspicātum habēre** to hold s.o. in contempt

dēspicāt·us -ūs *m* contempt

dēspici·ēns -entis *adj* contemptuous; *(w. gen)* contemptuous of

dēspicienti·a -ae *f* contempt

dē·spiciō -spicere -spexī -spectus *tr* to despise, look down on ‖ *intr* to look down; *(w.* **in** *+ acc)* to look down on, have a view of

dēspic·or -ārī -ātus sum *tr* to despise, disdain

dēspoliāt·or -ōris *m* robber, plunderer

dēspoli·ō -āre -āvī -ātus *tr* to strip, rob, plunder

dēspon·deō -dēre -dī -sus *tr* to pledge, promise solemnly; to promise in marriage; **animum** *(or* **animōs)** **dēspondēre** to lose heart, despair

dēspōns·ō -āre *tr* to betroth

dēspōns·us -a -um *pp of* **dēspondeō**

dēspūm·ō -āre -āvī -ātus *tr* to skim (off); to work off *(i.e., digest)* ‖ *intr* to stop foaming

dēspu·ō -ere *tr* to spit out, spit down; to avert by spitting; *(fig)* to reject ‖ *intr* to spit on the ground *(to avert evil, etc.)*

dēsquām·ō -āre -āvī -ātus *tr* to scale *(fish)*; *(fig)* to peel off

dēstill·ō -āre -āvī -ātus *tr* to drip, distill ‖ *intr* to drip, trickle down

dēstimul·ō -āre *tr* to goad on

dēstināti·ō -ōnis *f* designation; nomination; purpose, intention; **locus dēstinātiōnis** destination

dēstināt·us -a -um *adj* obstinate; fixed, determined; **animus mortī dēstinātus** a mind set on death; **dēstinātum est mihi** *(w. inf)* I have made up my mind to; **locus dēstinātus** destination ‖ *n* design, intention; mark *(aimed at)*; **ex dēstinātō** according to plan

dēstin·ō -āre -āvī -ātus *tr* to lash down, secure; to fix, determine, resolve; to earmark; to appoint, designate; to arrange the purchase of; to aim at ‖ *intr* to make up one's mind ‖ *v impers* **dēstinātum mihi est** I have made up my mind

dēstit·uō -uere -uī -ūtus *tr* to set apart; to set down, place; to forsake; to leave high and dry, betray, desert; *(w.* **ab)** to rob of, leave destitute of

dēstitūti·ō -ōnis *f* forsaking, abandonment; disappointment

dēstrict·us -a -um *pp of* **dēstringō** ‖ *adj* severe, rigid

dē·stringō -stringere -strīnxī -strictus *tr* to strip; to unsheathe; to give *(s.o.)* a rubdown; to brush gently against, skim; *(of weapon)* to graze; *(fig)* to criticize, satirize

dēstructi·ō -ōnis *f* pulling down *(e.g., of walls)*; destruction, demolition; refutation

dēstru·ō -ere -xī -ctus *tr* to pull down, demolish; *(fig)* to ruin

dēsubitō *or* **dē subitō** *adv* suddenly

dēsūdāsc·ō -ere *intr* to begin to sweat all over

dēsūd·ō -āre -āvī -ātum *intr* to sweat; *(w. dat) (fig)* to sweat over

dēsuē·fīō -fierī -factus sum *intr (w.* **ab***)* to become unused to, get away from

dēsu·ēscō -ēscere -ēvī -ētum *intr (w. inf)* to become unaccustomed to, get away from

dēsuētūd·ō -inis *f* disuse, lack of use

dēsuēt·us -a -um *pp of* **dēsuēscō ‖** *adj* unused, out of use, obsolete; out of practice; *(w. dat)* unused to, unfamiliar with

dēsult·or -ōris *m* circus rider *(who leaps from one horse to another)*; **amōris dēsultor** fickle lover, "butterfly"

dēsultōri·us -a -um *adj* of a circus rider; **equus dēsultōrius** show horse

dēsultūr·a -ae *f* jumping down

dē·sum -esse -fuī -futūrus *intr* to fall short, fail; to fail in one's duty; to be absent, be missing; *(w. dat)* **1** to be absent from, be missing from; **2** to fail to support; **sibi dēesse** to sell oneself short; **temporī dēesse** *(or* **occāsiōnī temporis)** **dēesse** to pass up the opportunity

dēsūm·ō -ere -psī -ptus *tr* to pick out, choose; to undertake; **sibi hostem dēsūmere** to take on an enemy

dēsuper *adv* from above

dēsur·gō -gere -rēxī -rēctum *intr* to rise; **cēnā dēsurgere** to get up from the table; *(euphem)* to go to the toilet, leave the room

dē·tegō -tegere -tēxī -tēctus *tr* to detect, uncover, expose, lay bare; to reveal, disclose, betray

dēten·dō -dere — -sus *tr* to loosen; to strike *(a tent)*

dētentus *pp of* **dētineō**

dēter·geō -gēre -sī -sus *or* **dēter·gō -gere** to wipe off, wipe away; *(fig)* to wipe clean

dēteri·or -or -us *adj* inferior, worse, poorer; lower in value; weaker

dēterius *adv* worse

dēterminūti·ō -ōnis *f* boundary; conclusion, end

dētermin·ō -āre -āvī -ātus *tr* to bound, limit; *(rhet)* to conclude *(sentence, period)*

dē·terō -terere -trīvī -trītus *tr* to rub away, wear away; to wear out; to lessen, weaken, detract from; **calcēs alicūius dēterere** to tread on s.o.'s heels

dēterr·eō -ēre -uī -itus *tr* to deter, frighten away, discourage; *(w. abl or* **ab** *or* **dē** *+ abl, or w.* **nē, quīn,** *or* **quōminus** *w. subj)* to deter *(s.o.)* from, discourage *(s.o.)* from

dētersus *pp of* **dētergeō**

dētestābil·is -is -e *adj* detestable

dētestāti·ō -ōnis *f* detestation; curse; *(leg)* formal renunciation

dētest·or -ārī -ātus sum *tr* to curse; to invoke *(the gods)* to avert; to plead against; to detest; *(w.* **in** *+ acc)* to call *(e.g., vengeance)* upon; **invidiam dētestārī** to avert jealousy, avoid unpopularity

dētex·ō -ere -uī -tus *tr* to weave, finish weaving; *(fig)* to finish (off)

dē·tineō -tinēre -tinuī -tentus *tr* to hold back, keep back; to hold up, detain; to occupy, keep busy; *(w.* **ab** *or* **dē** *+ abl)* to keep back from; *(w. abl or* **in** *+ abl)* to occupy *(day, mind)* with, keep *(s.o.)* busy with

dēton·deō -dēre -dī -sus *tr* to cut off, shear off; *(fig)* to strip off

dēton·ō -āre -uī *intr* to stop thundering; *(of Jupiter)* to thunder down

dētōnsus *pp of* **dētondeō**

dētor·queō -quēre -sī -tus *tr* to twist *or* bend aside; to twist out of shape; to turn aside; to turn, direct; to avert *(eyes)*; to divert, pervert; to distort, misrepresent *(words)*

dētracti·ō -ōnis *f* **(-trect-)** taking away, wresting; removal; *(rhet)* ellipsis

dētractō *see* **dētrectō**

dētract·or -ōris *m* detractor

dē·trahō -trahere -trāxī -tractus *tr* to drag down, drag away, pull down, pull away; to remove, withdraw; to deprive, rob, strip; to induce to come down *(e.g., an enemy from a strong position)*; to disparage, detract, slander; *(w. dat or* **dē** *+ abl)* to rob *(s.o.)* of

dētrectāti·ō -ōnis *f* drawing back, avoidance; **mīlitiae dētrectātiō** draft dodging

dētrectāt·or -ōris *m* detractor; shirker

dētrect·ō -āre -āvī -ātus *tr* **(-trac-)** to draw back from, shirk, decline, reject; to disparage; to demean; **mīlitiam dētrectāre** to dodge the draft

dētrīmentōs·us -a -um *adj* detrimental

dētrīment·um -ī *n* detriment, loss, harm; **dētrīmentum accipere** *(or* **capere)** to incur a loss; **dētrīmentum īnferre** *(or* **afferre)** to cause harm *or* loss

dētrītus *pp of* **dēterō**

dētrīvī *perf of* **dēterō**

dētrū·dō -dere -sī -sus *tr* to push down, push away, push off; to postpone; *(mil)* to dislodge; *(leg)* to evict; **aliquem dē suā**

sententiā dētrūdere to get s.o. to change his mind
dētrunc·ō -āre -āvī -ātus *tr* to cut off, lop off; to mutilate; to behead
dētulī *perf of* **dēferō**
dēturb·ō -āre *tr* to beat down, tear down, strike down; to eject, expel, dispossess; *(mil)* to dislodge; **aliquem dē sānitāte dēturbāre** to drive a person mad
dēturp·ō -āre *tr* to disfigure
Deucali·ōn -ōnis *m* son of Prometheus who, together with his wife Pyrrha, survived the Deluge
deūn·x -cis *m* eleven-twelfths; **hērēs ex deūnce** heir to eleven-twelfths
de·ūrō -ūrere -ussī -ūstus *tr* to burn up, destroy; *(of frost)* to nip
de·us -ī *(nom pl:* **deī, dī** *or* **diī;** *gen pl:* **deōrum** *or* **deum;** *dat and abl pl:* **deīs, dīs** *or* **diīs;** *vocative sg:* **deus)** *m* god, deity ‖ *mpl (of people in high places)* the powers that be; **dī bonī**! good heavens!; **dī hominēsque** all the world; **dī meliōra**! Heaven forbid!; **dīs volentibus** with the help of the gods; **dī tē ament**! bless your little heart!
deūstus *pp of* **deūrō**
de·ūtor -ūtī *intr (w. abl)* to mistreat
dēvast·ō -āre -āvī -ātus *tr* to devastate
dēve·hō -here -xī -ctus *tr* to carry down, carry away, carry off, ship off ‖ *pass* to ride down; to sail down
dēvellō dēvellere dēvellī *or* **dēvolsī dēvulsus** *or* **dēvolsus** *tr* to pluck
dēvēl·ō -āre *tr* to unveil
dēvener·or -ārī -ātus sum *tr* to worship; to avert by prayer
dē·veniō -venīre -vēnī -ventum *intr* to come down, arrive; *(w. acc of extent of motion or w.* **ad** *or* **in** *+ acc)* to arrive at, reach; *(w.* **ad)** to happen to, befall
dēverber·ō -āre -āvī -ātus *tr* to thrash soundly
dēverb·ium -(i)ī *n* spoken parts of a play, unaccompanied by music
dēvers·or -ārī -ātus sum *intr* to stay as a guest; *(w.* **apud** *+ acc)* to stay at the house of
dēvers·or -ōris *m* **(vor-)** guest
dēversōriol·um -ī *n* small inn
dēversōri·us -a -um *adj* **(-vor-)** of an inn, fit to stay at; **taberna dēversōria** inn ‖ *n* inn
dēverticul·um -ī *n* **(-vort-)** side road; detour; digression; refuge; inn, tavern; *(coll)* dive; *(fig)* loophole
dēver·tō -tere -tī -sum *or* **dēver·tor -tī -sus sum** *intr* **(-vort-)** to turn aside, turn away; to stay as guest, spend the night; *(w.* **ad** *or* **apud** *+ acc)* to stay with, stay at the house of; *(w.* **ad)** to have recourse to
dēvex·us -a -um *adj* inclining, sloping, steep; *(w.* **ad)** prone to, inclined to
dē·vinciō -vincīre -vīnxī -vīnctus *tr* to tie up, clamp; *(fig)* to obligate, unite closely ‖ *refl* **sē vīnō dēvincīre** *(coll)* to get tight on wine
dē·vincō -vincere -vīcī -victus *tr* to beat decisively, trounce
dēvīnctus *pp of* **dēvinciō** ‖ *adj (w. dat)* strongly attached to
dēvītāti·ō -ōnis *f* avoidance
dēvīt·ō -āre -āvī -ātus *tr* to avoid
dēvi·us -a -um *adj* out of the way; off the beaten track; living apart, solitary, sequestered; inconsistent ‖ *npl* wilderness
dēvoc·ō -āre -āvī -ātus *tr* to call down; to call off; to recall; to call away; to allure; **deōs ad auxilium dēvocāre** to invoke the gods for help
dēvol·ō -āre -āvī -ātum *intr* to fly down; to fly away; to rush down, rush away
dēvol·vō -vere -vī -ūtus *tr* to roll down; *(w.* **dē** *+ abl);* to roll down from ‖ *pass* to roll down, go tumbling down; *(w.* **ad)** to fall back on
dēvor- = dēver-
dēvor·ō -āre -āvī -ātus *tr* to devour, gulp down; to consume, waste; *(of sea)* to engulf, swallow up; to swallow, mumble *(words);* to repress *(tears);* to bear with patience
dēvorti·a -ōrum *npl* side roads, detour
dēvōti·ō -ōnis *f* self-sacrifice; cursing; outlawing; incantation, spell; **capitis** *(or* **vītae) dēvōtiō** sacrifice of one's life
dēvōt·ō -āre -āvī -ātus *tr* to bewitch, jinx
dēvōt·us -a -um *pp of* **dēvoveō** ‖ *adj* devoted, faithful; accursed; *(w. dat)* **1** devoted to; **2** addicted to
dē·voveō -vovēre -vōvī -vōtus *tr* to devote, vow, sacrifice, dedicate; to mark out, doom, destine; to curse; to bewitch ‖ *refl* **sē (dīs) dēvovēre** to devote onself to death
dēvulsus *pp of* **dēvellō**
dext·āns -antis *m* five-sixths
dextell·a -ae *f* little right hand; right-hand man
dex·ter -tera -terum *or* **-tra -trum** *adj* right, on the right side; handy, dexterous; lucky, propitious, favorable; opportune, right ‖ *f* right hand, right side, the right; **ā dextrā laevāque** to the right and left, right and left, everywhere; **dextrā** with the right hand; *(fig)* with valor; **dextrā** *(w. gen or acc)* to the right of; **dextrae iungere dextram** to shake hands; **dextram dare** *(or* **tendere)** to give a pledge of friendship
dexterē *or* **dextrē** *adv* dexterously, skillfully; **dextrē fortūnā ūtī** *(fig)* to play the cards right
dexterit·ās -ātis *f* dexterity; readiness to help

dextrōrsum *or* **dextrōrsus** *or* **dextrōversum** *adv* **(-vor-)** to the right, toward the right side
dī *see* **deus**
Dī·a -ae *f* ancient name of the island of Naxos ‖ mother of Mercury
diabathrār·ius -(i)ī *m* shoemaker
diadēm·a -atis *n* diadem
diadēmāt·us -a -um *adj* wearing a diadem, wearing a crown
diaet·a -ae *f* room; suite *(of rooms);* cabin *(of ship);* annex *(to the main building); (med)* regimen *(proper exercise, etc.)*
dialecticē *adv* logically
dialectic·us -a -um *adj* dialectical, logical ‖ *m* dialectician, logician ‖ *f* logic, dialectics ‖ *npl* dialectics
dialect·os -ī *f* dialect
Diāl·is -is -e *adj* of Jupiter; of Jupiter's high priest; **apex Diālis** high priest's miter; **flāmen Diālis** high priest of Jupiter
dialog·us -ī *m* dialogue, conversation; literary composition in the form of a dialogue
Diān·a *or* **Diān·a -ae** *f* Diana *(Roman goddess, identified with Artemis); (fig)* Diana's temple; *(fig)* moon; **īrācunda Diāna** lunacy
Diāni·us -a -um *adj* Diana's ‖ *n* enclosure sacred to Diana
diāri·a -ōrum *npl* daily ration
dibaph·us -ī *f* crimson robe; official robe *(of a magistrate or augur)*
dic·a -ae *f (leg)* lawsuit, case, judicial proceedings; **dicam alicuī impingere** to hit s.o. with a lawsuit; **dicam scrībere** *(w. dat)* to sue s.o.; **dicās sortīrī** to select a jury
dicācit·ās -ātis *f* sarcasm
dicācul·us -a -um *adj* witty, sharp; sarcastic
dicāti·ō -ōnis *f* declaration of intent of becoming a citizen
dic·āx -ācis *adj* witty, sharp; sarcastic
dichorē·us -ī *m (pros)* double trochee
dici·ō -ōnis *f* jurisdiction; sway, authority, control, rule, dominion, sovereignty; **in** *(or* **sub)** **diciōne esse** *(w. gen)* to be under the control of, be subject to, be under the jurisdiction of; **in diciōnem redigere** *(w. gen) or* **diciōnī subicere** *(w. gen)* to bring *(s.o.)* under the control of
dicis causā *or* **grātiā** *adv* for show, for the sake of appearances
dic·ō -āre -āvī -ātus *tr* to dedicate, consecrate; to deify; to inaugurate; to set apart, devote; *(w. dat)* to devote *(e.g., time, energy, self)* to
dīcō dīcere dīxī dictus *tr* to say; to tell, relate; to indicate, mention, specify, point out; to nominate, appoint; to fix, set *(day, date);* to speak, deliver, recite; to pronounce, utter, articulate; to call, name; to assert, state; to describe; to predict; *(w. double acc)* to appoint *(s.o.)* as; **causam dīcere** to plead *or* defend a case; **diem dīcere** *(w. dat)* to set a date for; **facētē dictum**! well put!; **sententiam dīcere** to express an opinion; **testimōnium dīcere** to give evidence
dicrot·a -ae *f* bireme
dicrot·um -ī *n* bireme
Dictae·us -a -um *adj* of Mt. Dicte, Dictaean, Cretan
dictamn·us *or* **dictamn·os -ī** *f (bot)* dittany *(aromatic plant, believed to have magical powers)*
dictāt·a -ōrum *npl* lessons, rules; dictation
dictāt·or -ōris *m* dictator *(emergency magistrate in Rome, legally appointed for a maximum six-month term);* chief magistrate *(of Italic town)*
dictātōri·us -a -um *adj* of a dictator
dictātr·īx -īcis *f* mistress of ceremonies
dictātūr·a -ae *f* dictatorship
Dict·ē -ēs *f* mountain in Crete, the alleged birthplace of Jupiter
dicti·ō -ōnis *f* saying, speaking, uttering; diction, style; conversation; oracular response, prediction; **dictiō causae** pleading of a case; **dictiō testimōnī** right to give testimony; **iūris dictiō** administration of justice; jurisdiction
dictit·ō -āre -āvī -ātus *tr* to keep saying, to state emphatically; **causās dictitāre** to practice law
dict·ō -āre -āvī -ātus *tr* to reiterate, say repeatedly; to dictate; to compose; to suggest, remind
dict·us -a -um *pp of* **dīcō** ‖ *n* saying, word, statement; witticism; maxim, proverb; prediction; order, instruction; promise, assurance; derisive remark; **dicta dīcere** to make (witty *or* cutting) remarks; **dictīs manēre** to stick to one's promises
Dictynn·a -ae *f* Cretan goddess Britomartis, identified with Diana
-dicus -a -um *adjl suf;* **-dic·us -ī** *masc suf* denotes one who speaks: **vēridicus** saying the truth; **causidicus** one who pleads cases, lawyer
dī·dō *or* **dis·dō -dere -didī -ditus** *tr* to publicize, disseminate; to distribute, hand out
Dīd·ō -ūs *or* **-ōnis** *(acc:* **Dīdō** *or* **Didōn)** *f* daughter of Tyrian king Belus, and foundress and queen of Carthage
dīdū·cō -cere -xī -ctus *tr* to draw apart, open; to part, sever, separate, split; to undo, untie; to divide, distribute; to scatter, disperse; to untie *(knot);* to break up *(friendships);* to deploy *(forces);* to digest *(food);* to open wide *(mouth); (in mathematics)* to divide; **animus dīductus** *(w. abl)* the mind torn between *(alternatives)*
dīducti·ō -ōnis *f* separation into parts, distribution
diēcul·a -ae *f* a little while

diērēct·us -a -um *adj (coll)* finished, done for; **ābī** *(or* **ī) diērēctus**! *(sl)* go straight to blazes!

di·ēs -ēī *m (but occasionally feminine when referring to a fixed day or time in general)* day; time, period, space of time, interval; daylight; light of day; anniversary; daybreak; season; **dē diē** by day; **diē** in the daytime; **diem dīcere** *(w. dat)* to impeach, bring an accusation against; **diem ex diē** from day to day, day after day; **diem noctemque** day and night; **diēs meus** my birthday; **in diem** for the moment; for a future day; **in diēs** (more and more) every day; **longō diē** throughout the long day; **multō dēnique diē** not till late in the day; **postrīdiē ēius diēī** the day after that; **post tertium ēius diēī** two days after that

Diēspi·ter -tris *m* Jupiter

diffām·ō -āre -āvī -ātus *tr* to spread the bad news of; to defame, slander

differenti·a -ae *f* difference, diversity; distinguishing characteristic; specific difference, species

differit·ās -ātis *f* difference

differō differre distulī dīlātus *tr* to carry in different directions; to scatter, disperse; to publicize; to postpone; to put *(a person)* off; to humor; to get rid of; to bewilder; to disquiet **||** *intr* to differ, be different; *(w.* **ab)** to differ from **||** *v impers* there is a difference; **multum differt** there is a great difference

differt·us -a -um *adj* stuffed; crowded, overcrowded

difficile *adv* with difficulty

difficil·is -is -e *adj* difficult, hard; surly; hard to manage; hard to please

difficiliter *adv* with difficulty, barely

difficult·ās -ātis *f* difficulty, hardship, trouble, distress; surliness; poverty, financial embarrassment

difficulter *adv* with difficulty, barely; grudgingly

diffīd·ēns -entis *adj* diffident, lacking in confidence; anxious, nervous

diffīdenter *adv* without confidence, distrustfully

diffīdenti·a -ae *f* diffidence, mistrust, distrust

diffī·dō -dere -sus sum *intr (w. dat)* to distrust; to despair of; *(w. acc & inf)* to have no confidence that; *(w. inf)* to expect not to

dif·findō -findere -fidī -fissus *tr* to split, divide; **diem diffindere** *(fig)* to put off the day of the trial

diffing·ō -ere *tr* to form differently, remodel; to alter

diffissus *pp of* **diffindō**

diffit·eor -ērī *tr* to disavow, disown

diffl·ō -āre -āvī -ātus *intr* to blow away; to disperse

difflu·ō -ere -xī -ctum *intr* to flow in different directions, flow away; to dissolve, melt away, disappear; *(w. abl)* to wallow in *(e.g., luxury)*

dif·fringō -fringere -frēgī -frāctus *tr* to shatter, break apart, smash

dif·fugiō -fugere -fūgī *intr* to flee in different directions; to disperse; to disappear

diffug·ium -(i)ī *n* dispersion

diffundit·ō -āre *tr* to pour out, scatter; to waste

dif·fundō -fundere -fūdī -fūsus *tr* to pour out; to scatter, diffuse, spread, extend; to bottle *(wine);* to give vent to; to cheer up, gladden

diffūsē *adv* diffusely; fully

diffūsil·is -is -e *adj* diffusive

diffūs·us -a -um *pp of* **diffundō ||** *adj* extending over a wide area; extensive *(writings);* diffuse, expansive *(speech)*

diffutūt·us -a -um *adj (vulg)* exhausted by too much sex

dī·gerō -gerere -gessī -gestus *tr* to distribute in all directions; to spread about, disperse, divide; to arrange; to interpret

dīgesti·ō -ōnis *f* arrangement; *(rhet)* enumeration

dīgestus *pp of* **dīgerō**

digitul·us -ī *m* little finger

digit·us -ī *m* finger; inch *(one sixteenth of a Roman foot);* toe; **digitīs concrepāre** to snap the fingers; **digitō ūnō attingere** to touch lightly, touch tenderly; **digitum intendere ad** to point the finger at; **digitum tollere** to make a bid; **digitus index** index finger; **digitus medius** *(or* **īnfāmis** *or* **obscēnus)** middle finger; **digitus minimus** little finger; **digitus pollex** thumb; **digitus quārtus** ring finger; **in digitōs arrēctus** on tiptoe; **prīmus** *(or* **prīmōris** *or* **prior) digitus** fingertip

dīgladi·or -ārī -ātus sum *intr* to fight in a gladiatorial contest

dignāti·ō -ōnis *f* esteem, respect; dignity, honor; rank, status, social position

dignē *adv* worthily

dignit·ās -ātis *f* worth, worthiness; dignity; authority, rank, reputation, distinction, majesty; self-respect; dignitary; political office

dign·ō -āre -āvī -ātus *or* **dign·or -ārī -ātus sum** *tr (w. abl)* to think worthy of; *(w. inf)* to think fit to; *(w. double acc)* to think *(s.o.)* worthy of being *(e.g., a son)*

dīgnōsc·ō *or* **dīnōsc·ō -ere** *tr* to distinguish, know the difference; *(w. abl)* to distinguish *(s.o.)* from; **dominum ac servum dīgnōscere** to know the difference between master and slave

dign·us -a -um *adj* worthy, deserving; fit, adequate, suitable, deserved, proper; *(w. abl)* worthy of

dīgre·dior -dī -ssus sum *intr* to move apart, separate; to deviate; to digress

dīgressi·ō -ōnis *f* parting, separation; deviation; digression

dīgressus *pp of* **dīgredior**

dīgress·us -ūs *m* departure; digression

diiūdicāti·ō -ōnis *f* decision

diiūdic·ō -āre -āvī -ātus *tr* to decide, settle; **vēra et falsa** *(or* **vēra ā falsīs) diiūdicāre)** to distinguish between truth and falsehood

dī·lābor -lābī -lāpsus sum *intr* to fall apart, break up; *(of ice)* to melt; to disperse; to decay; *(of time)* to slip by; *(of water)* to flow in different directions

dīlacer·ō -āre -āvī -ātus *tr* to tear to pieces

dīlāmin·ō -āre *tr* to split in two; to crack *(nuts)*

dīlani·ō -āre -āvī -ātus *tr* to tear to pieces

dīlapid·ō -āre -āvī -ātus *tr* to demolish *(a structure of stone); (coll)* to squander

dīlāpsus *pp of* **dīlābor**

dīlarg·ior -īrī -ītus sum *tr* to hand out generously, lavish

dīlāti·ō -ōnis *f* postponement, delay; *(leg)* adjournment

dīlāt·ō -āre -āvī -ātus *tr* to dilate, stretch, broaden, extend, enlarge; *(fig)* to amplify, spread, extend; to drawl out

dīlāt·or -ōris *m* procrastinator, slowpoke

dīlātus *pp of* **differō**

dīlaud·ō -āre *tr* to praise enthusiastically

dīlēct·us -a -um *pp of* **dīligō ‖** *adj* beloved, dear

dīlēct·us -ūs *m* selection; *(mil)* selective service, draft; draftees; recruitment; **dīlēctum habēre** to conduct a draft; **legiōnēs ex novō dīlēctū cōnficere** to bring the legions to full strength with new draftees

dīlīd·ō -ere *tr* to smash to pieces

dīlig·ēns -entis *adj* careful, accurate; exacting, strict; thrifty; industrious; *(w. gen)* **1** observant of; **2** devoted to, fond of; *(w.* **ad** *or* **in** + *acc)* **1** careful in, careful to; **2** conscientious about

dīligenter *adv* carefully, diligently; thoroughly, well, in detail

dīligenti·a -ae *f* care, diligence, industry, attentiveness; economy, frugality; *(w. gen)* regard for

dī·ligō -ligere -lēxī -lēctus *tr* to esteem; to like; to value, appreciate; to love

dīlōrīc·ō -āre -āvī -ātus *tr* to tear open

dīlūc·eō -ēre *intr* to be clear, be evident; *(w. dat)* to be obvious to

dī·lūcēscō -lūcēscere -lūxī *intr* to get light, dawn

dīlūcidē *adv* clearly, distinctly

dīlūcid·us -a -um *adj* clear, distinct, plain, evident

dīlūcul·um -ī *n* daybreak, dawn

dīlūd·ium -(i)ī *n* intermission *(between plays, games, etc.)*

dīl·uō -uere -uī -ūtus *tr* to wash away; to break up, separate; to dilute; to get rid of *(worries, annoyances);* to atone for; to explain

dīluvi·ēs -ēī *f* flood, deluge

dīluvi·ō -āre *tr* to flood, inundate

dīluv·ium -(i)ī *n* flood, deluge

dimach·ae -ārum *mpl* (Macedonian) soldiers who fight either on foot or on horseback

dīmān·ō -āre *intr* to flow in different directions; *(fig)* to spread around

dīmēnsi·ō -ōnis *f* measurement, dimensions

dī·mētior -mētīrī -mēnsus sum *tr* to measure out; to count off

dīmēt·ō -āre *or* **dīmēt·or -ārī** *tr* to measure or mark off

dīmicāti·ō -ōnis *f* fight, combat, struggle; contest, rivalry

dīmic·ō -āre -āvī -ātus *intr* to contend, fight, struggle; **dē capite** *(or* **dē vītā)** **dīmicāre** to fight for one's life

dīmidi·a -ae *f* half

dīmidiāt·us -a -um *adj* half, in half

dīmid·ium -(i)i *n* half; **dīmidiō longior** twice as long; **dīmidium mīlitum quam** half as many soldiers as

dīmidi·us -a -um *adj* half; broken (in two); **dīmidius patrum, dīmidius plēbis** half patrician, half plebeian; **parte dīmidiā auctus** twice as large

dīmi·nuō -nuere -nuī -nūtus *tr* to shatter

dīmissi·ō -ōnis *f* dismissal; sending out; *(mil)* discharge

dī·mittō -mittere -mīsī -missus *tr* to send away, let go; to dismiss *(an assembly);* to spread; to set free, release; to let off; to scatter, distribute; to let go of, let loose; to abandon; to let go, let slip, forgo *(a chance, an opportunity);* to divorce *(a wife); (fin)* to settle *(a debt); (fin)* to pay off *(a creditor); (mil)* to discharge *(a soldier),* disband *(an army)*

dimminuō *see* **dīminu·ō**

dī·moveō -movēre -mōvī -mōtus *tr* to move apart, part, separate; to disperse, scatter; to dismiss; to lure away

Dindymēn·ē -ēs *f* Cybele *(named after Dindymus, a mountain in Phrygia sacred to Cybele)*

Dindym·us *or* **Dindym·os -ī** *m* Mt. Dindymus *(in Phrygia)*

dīnōscō *see* **dignōscō**

dīnumerāti·ō -ōnis *f* enumeration, counting up

dīnumer·ō -āre -āvī -ātus *tr* to enumerate, count up; to count out, pay

diōbolār·is -is -e *adj* costing two obols *(about 2¢)*
Diodot·us -ī *m* Stoic philosopher and tutor of Cicero *(d. 59 B.C.)*
dioecēs·is -is *or* **-eōs** *f* district; governor's jurisdiction
dioecēt·ēs -ae *m* treasurer; secretary of revenue
Diogen·ēs -is *m* Ionic philosopher *(5th cent. B.C.)* ‖ Cynic philosopher from Sinope, in Pontus *(412?–323 B.C.)*
Diomēd·ēs -is *m* son of Tydeus and king of Argos, and hero at Troy
Diō(n) -ōnis *m* Dion *(brother-in-law of the elder Dionysius, the tyrant of Syracuse, and a pupil and friend of Plato's)*
Diōn·ē -ēs *or* **Diōn·a -ae** *f* mother of Venus
Dionȳsi·a -ōrum *npl* festival of Dionysus
Dionȳs·ius -(i)ī *m* tyrant of Syracuse *(430–367 B.C.)* ‖ Dionysius the Younger *(397–330? B.C.)*
Dionȳs·us *or* **Dionȳs·os -ī** *m* Greek god of wine and fertility, equated with Bacchus
diōt·a -ae *f* two-handled wine jar
Diphil·us -ī *m* Greek comic writer of Sinope, used by Plautus
diplōm·a -atis *n* travel pass *(to travel free on the Imperial post);* certificate
dips·as -adis *f* poisonous snake whose bite provokes thirst
Dipyl·on -ī *n* N.W. gate at Athens
dipyr·us -a -um *adj* twice burned
Dīr·a -ae *f* Fury *(goddess of revenge)*
dīr·ae -ārum *fpl* bad omens; curses
Dircae·us -a -um *adj* Dircean, Boeotian; **cycnus Dircaeus** Boeotian swan *(Pindar, lyric poet from Boeotia)*
Dirc·ē -ēs *f* famous spring in Boeotia
dīrēctē *adv* **(dēr-)** in a straight line
dīrēctō *adv* **(dēr-)** in a straight line; directly, without intervening procedures
dīrēct·us *or* **dērēct·us -a -um** *pp of* **dīrigō** ‖ *adj* straight, direct; level; upright, vertical, perpendicular; *(fig)* direct, straightforward, simple; **in dīrēctum** *(or* **per dīrēctum)** in a straight line; **in dīrēctō** on a straight stretch *(of road)*
diremptus *pp of* **dirimō**
dirempt·us -ūs *m* separation
dīrepti·ō -ōnis *f* plundering, pillaging ‖ *fpl* acts of pillage; a scramble for a share
dīrept·or -ōris *m* plunderer
dīreptus *pp of* **dīripiō**
dirib·eō -ēre -uī -itus *tr* to sort *(votes taken out of the ballot box)*
diribiti·ō -ōnis *f* sorting *(of votes)*
diribit·or -ōris *m* sorter *(of ballots)*
diribitōr·ium -iī *n* sorting room
dīrigō dīrigere dīrēxī dīrēctus *tr* **(dē-)** to direct; to put in order, arrange, line up, straighten out; to level *(a surface);* to construct *(roads, tunnels, along a given line); (mil)* to deploy
dir·imō -imere -ēmī -emptus *tr* to take apart; to part, separate, divide; to break off, disturb, interrupt; to separate, dissolve; to put off, delay; to break off, end, bring to an end; to nullify, bring to naught
dī·ripiō -ripere -ripuī -reptus *tr* to tear apart, tear to pieces; to lay waste, pillage; to loot, rob; to steal; to snatch away; to whip out *(sword);* to run after, compete for the company of *(person)*
dīrit·ās -ātis *f* frightfulness; dire event
dī·rumpō -rumpere -rūpī -ruptus *tr* to break to pieces, smash, shatter; to break off *(friendship);* to sever *(ties)* ‖ *pass* to burst *(w. laughter, envy, etc.)*
dīru·ō -ere -ī -tus *tr* to pull apart, demolish, destroy, overthrow; to scatter; to bankrupt; *(mil)* to break up *(enemy formation)*
dīr·us -a -um *adj* dire, awful, fearful; ominous, ill-omened; dreadful; cruel, relentless, fierce; **temporibus dīrīs** in the reign of terror; **venēna dīra** deadly poisons ‖ *fpl & npl* ill-boding portents, unlucky signs
dīrutus *pp of* **dīruō**
dīs dītis *adj* rich; fertile; generous; expensive; *(w. abl)* abounding in ‖ **Dīs Dītis** *m* Pluto *(king of the lower world)*
dis- *pref* (unchanged before initial **c p t s; dī-** before **b d g l m n r,** consonantal **u** and sometimes **i; dif-** before **f; dir-** *(by rotacism)* before vowels and **h** *(with rare exceptions);* it commonly signifies **1** separation or dispersion or both: **diffugere** to flee in different directions, disperse; **discēdere** to draw apart; **2** the reversal of a previous process: **disiungere** to disunite, separate; **3** a negative sense: **displicēre** to displease, not please
di(s)iūnctē *adv* in separate words, separately
di(s)iūncti·ō -ōnis *f* separation, alienation; divination; variation; dilemma; *(rhet)* asyndeton *(succession of phrases or clauses without conjunction)*
di(s)iūnct·us -a -um *adj* separate, distinct; distant, remote; disjointed, disconnected, incoherent; logically opposed ‖ *npl* opposites
di(s)iun·gō -gere -xī -ctus *tr* to unyoke; to sever, divide, part, remove; to separate; to alienate
dis·cēdo -cēdere -cessī -cessum *intr* to go away, depart; to separate, be severed; to disperse, be dissipated, disappear; to split open, come apart; *(of wife)* to separate *(from husband);* to deviate, swerve; to pass away, cease; *(mil)* to march off, break camp; *(mil)* to come off *(victorious, etc.); (w. abl)* **1** to forsake *(e.g., friends);* **2** to deviate from, swerve from; *(w.* **ex** *or* **dē** + *abl)* to depart from; *(w.* **ad)** to depart for; *(w.* **in** + *acc)* to vote for; **ā vītā**

discēdere to die; **discēdere in Catōnis sententiam** to vote for Cato's proposal; **ut discēdātur ab** apart from

disc·ēns -entis *m* learner, apprentice, trainee

disceptāti·ō -ōnis *f* dispute, difference of opinion; discussion, debate

disceptāt·or -ōris *m*, **disceptātr·īx -īcis** *f* arbitrator

discept·ō -āre -āvī -ātus *tr* to debate, dispute, discuss, treat; to decide, settle ‖ *intr* to act as judge, arbitrate; to argue; to be at stake

dis·cernō -cernere -crēvī -crētus *tr* to separate, mark off, divide; to keep apart; to distinguish between; to discern, make out

discerp·ō -ere -sī -tus *tr* to mangle, mutilate; *(fig)* to tear apart *(with words, arguments)*

discessi·ō -ōnis *f* separation, division; divorce; *(in the Senate)* division, formal vote; **discessiō sine ūllā varietāte** unanimous vote

discess·us -ūs *m* separation, parting; departure; banishment; marching off

discid·ium -(i)ī *n* parting; discord, disagreement; divorce

discīd·ō -ere -ī *tr* to cut up

discīnct·us -a -um *pp of* **discingō** ‖ *adj* without a belt; dissolute, loose; effeminate, voluptuous

di·scindō -scindere -scidī -scissus *tr* to tear apart, tear open, rend; **amīcitiās discindere** to break off the ties of friendship

dis·cingō -cingere -cīnxī -cīnctus *tr* to take off; to loosen; to disarm

disciplīn·a -ae *f* instruction, training, teaching, education; learning, knowledge, science; discipline, branch of study, subject; custom, habit; system; **mīlitāris disciplīna** basic training; **reīpūblicae disciplīna** statesmanship

discipul·a -ae *f* pupil *(female)*

discipul·us -ī *m* pupil; disciple, follower

discissus *pp of* **discindō**

disclū·dō -dere -sī -sus *tr* to keep apart, shut off; to seal up, seal off; to assign

discō discere didicī *tr* to learn; to get to know, become acquainted with; to be told *(e.g., the truth)*; *(w. inf)* to learn how to

discobol·us -ī *m* discus-thrower

discol·or -ōris *adj* of a different color; of different colors; *(w. dat)* different from

discondūc·ō -ere *intr* to be unprofitable, be prejudicial

disconven·iō -īre *intr* to disagree; to be inconsistent ‖ *v impers* there is disagreement

discordābil·is -is -e *adj* discordant, disagreeing

discordi·a -ae *f* discord, dissension, disagreement; mutiny

discordiōs·us -a -um *adj* prone to discord, mutinous

discord·ō -āre *intr* to quarrel, disagree; *(w. dat or* **ab***)* **1** to be be out of harmony with; **2** to be opposed to

discor·s -dis *adj* discordant; at variance; contradictory, inconsistent; warring *(winds, etc.)*; *(w. abl)* inconsistent with, different from

discrepanti·a -ae *f* discrepancy, dissimilarity, difference

discrepāti·ō -ōnis *f* disagreement, dispute

discrepit·ō -āre *intr* to be completely different

discrep·ō -āre -āvī *or* **-uī** *intr* to be different in sound, sound different; to be out of tune; to disagree; to be different, vary; to be inconsistent; to be disputed; *(w. dat or abl or* **ab** *or* **cum***)* **1** to disagree with; **2** to be different from; **3** to be inconsistent with ‖ *v impers* there is a difference of opinion, it is a matter of dispute, it is undecided

discrī·bō -bere -psī -ptus *tr* to distribute, divide; to classify; to assign, apportion; *(w.* **in** *+ acc)* to distribute among, divide among

discrīm·en -inis *n* dividing line; interval, intervening space, division, distance, separation; discrimination, difference, distinction; critical moment, turning point; crisis, jeopardy, peril, danger, risk; decision, determination; decisive battle; difference in pitch; part *(in the hair)*; **rēs in discrīmine est** the situation is at a critical stage; **parvum discrīmen lētī** narrow escape from death

discrīmin·ō -āre -āvī -ātus *tr* to divide, separate; to apportion

discrīptē *adv* in an orderly way, lucidly, distinctly

discrīpti·ō -ōnis *f* distribution, classification

discrīpt·us -a -um *pp of* **discrībō** ‖ *adj* well-arranged, sorted, classified

discruci·ō -āre -āvī -ātus *tr* to torture; to distress, torment

discumbō discumbere discubuī discubitum *intr (of several)* to take their places at the table; *(of several)* to go to bed

discup·iō -ere *tr (coll)* to want badly; *(w. inf) (coll)* to be dying to

dis·currō -currere -cucurrī *or* **-currī -cursum** *intr* to run in different directions, scamper about, run up and down, dash around

discurs·us -ūs *m* running up and down, running about; *(mil)* pincer movement

disc·us -ī *m* discus

discussus *pp of* **discutiō**

discu·tiō -tere -ssī -ssus *tr* to knock apart; to smash to pieces, shatter; to shake off; to break up, disperse *(an assembly, gath-*

ering); to dispel *(danger, sleep);* to frustrate, bring to naught; to suppress, destroy
disertē *adv* clearly, eloquently
disertim *adv* clearly, distinctly
disert·us -a -um *adj* fluent, eloquent; clear
dis·iciō -icere -iēcī -iectus *tr* to drive apart, scatter; to tear to pieces; to ruin; to frustrate, wreck; *(mil)* to break up *(enemy formation)*
disiect·ō -āre -āvī -ātus *tr* to toss about
disiect·us -a -um *pp of* **disiciō** ‖ *adj* scattered; dilapidated
disiect·us -ūs *m* scattering
disj- = disi-
dispālēsc·ō -ere *intr* to be spread abroad, get around
dispāl·or -ārī -ātus sum *intr* to wander around; to straggle, stray off
dis·pandō pandere — -pānsus *tr* **(-pen-)** to stretch out, extend; to expand
dis·pār -paris *adj* different, unlike; unequal; ill-matched
disparāt·us -a -um *adj* separate, distinct; negatively opposite *(e.g.,* **sapere et nōn sapere** to be wise and not to be wise)
disparil·is -is -e *adj* dissimilar, different
dispariliter *adv* differently
dispar·ō -āre -āvī -ātus *tr* to separate; to make different ‖ *intr* to be different
dispartiō, dispartior *see* **dispertiō**
dispectus *pp of* **dispiciō**
dis·pellō -pellere -pulī -pulsus *tr* to dispel, drive away; to disperse
dispend·ium -(i)ī *n* expense, cost; loss *(as result of a transaction)*
dispendō *see* **dispandō**
dis·pennō -pennere — -pessus *tr* to stretch out, extend; to expand
dispēnsāti·ō -ōnis *f* weighing out, doling out; management, superintendence, administration; office of treasurer
dispēnsāt·or -ōris *m* household manager, chief butler; cashier; treasurer
dispēns·ō -āre -āvī -ātus *tr* to weigh out, pay out; to distribute, manage *(household stores);* to regulate, manage
dispercut·iō -ere *tr* to knock out; **cerebrum dispercutere** *(w. dat)* to knock *(s.o.'s)* brains out
disper·dō -dere -didī -ditus *tr* to spoil, ruin; to squander
disper·eō -īre -iī *intr* to go to ruin; to go to waste; to be undone, perish; **disperiī**! *(coll)* I'm finished!; **dispeream sī** *(coll)* I'll be darned if
disper·gō -gere -sī -sus *tr* **(sparg-)** to scatter about, disperse; to splatter; to distribute, scatter *(e.g., men)* without organization; to spread, extend *(war, rumor, etc.)*
dispersē *adv* here and there; occasionally
dispersus *pp of* **dispergō**
dispers·us -ūs *m* dispersal
dispert·iō -īre -īvī *or* **-iī -ītus** *or* **dispert·ior -īrī -ītus sum** *tr* to distribute, divide; to assign *(e.g., gates, areas)* as posts to be guarded
dispertīti·ō -ōnis *f* distribution, sharing
dispessus *pp of* **dispandō**
di·spiciō -spicere -spexī -spectus *tr* to see clearly, make out, distinguish, detect; to look into, consider carefully, perceive, discover; to reflect on ‖ *intr* to see clearly
displic·eō -ēre -uī -itum *intr* to be unpleasant, be displeasing; *(w. dat)* to displease; **sibi displicēre** to be dissatisfied with oneself; to be in a bad mood
dis·plōdō -plōdere — -plōsus *tr & intr* to burst apart
dis·pōnō -pōnere -posuī -positus *tr* to place here and there; to distribute; to arrange, set in order; to station, post, assign; to adjust; to dispose; **diem dispōnere** to arrange the day's schedule
dispositē *adv* orderly, methodically
dispositi·ō -ōnis *f* orderly arrangement, development *(of a theme)*
dispositūr·a -ae *f* order, arrangement
disposit·us -a -um *pp of* **dispōnō** ‖ *adj* well-arranged; methodical, orderly
disposit·us -ūs *m* order, orderly arrangement
dispud·et -ēre -uit *v impers (w. inf)* it's a great shame to
dispulsus *pp of* **dispellō**
dis·pungō -pungere -pūnxī -pūnctus *tr* to check, audit, balance *(accounts)*
disputāti·ō -ōnis *f* argument, discussion
disputāt·or -ōris *m* disputant
disput·ō -āre -āvī -ātus *tr* to dispute, discuss; *(com)* to estimate; to examine, treat, explain ‖ *intr* to argue, argue one's case
disquīr·ō -ere *tr* to examine closely
disquīsīti·ō -ōnis *f* inquiry, investigation
disrumpō *see* **dīrumpō**
dissaep·iō -īre -sī -tus *tr* to partition, fence off
dissaept·um -ī *n* partition, barrier
dissāvi·or *or* **dissuāvi·or -ārī** *tr* to kiss passionately
dissec·ō -āre -uī -tus *tr* to cut up, dissect
dissēmin·ō -āre -āvī -ātus *tr* to disseminate
dissēnsi·ō -ōnis *f* difference of opinion, disagreement; dissension; conflict, incompatibility
dissēns·us -ūs *m* dissension, discord
dissentāne·us -a -um *adj* disagreeing, dissenting; conflicting; contrary
dissen·tiō -tīre -sī -sum *intr* to dissent, disagree; to differ, be in conflict, be inconsistent; *(w. dat or* **ab** *or* **cum)** to differ with; *(w.* **ab)** to differ from, be opposed to
disserēn·at -āre -āvit *v impers* it is clearing up

disser·ō -ere -uī -tus *tr* to discuss; to examine; to arrange ‖ *intr (w.* **dē** + *abl)* to discuss

dis·serō -serere -sēvī -situs *tr* to scatter; to sow here and there; to stick in the ground at intervals

disserp·ō -ere *intr* to creep around; to spread gradually

disserti·ō -ōnis *f* severance, a disconnecting

dissert·ō -āre -āvī -ātus *tr* to discuss

dissertus *pp of* **disserō** *(to discuss)*

dis·sideō -sidēre -sēdī *intr* to be distant, be remote; to live far apart; to disagree; to differ, be unlike; *(of garment)* to be on crooked; *(w.* **ab** *or* **cum)** to disagree with

dissignāti·ō -ōnis *f* arrangement

dissignāt·or -ōris *m* **(dēsig-)** master of ceremonies; usher *(at theater);* undertaker, mortician

dissign·ō -āre -āvī -ātus *tr* to regulate; to arrange; to contrive

dissil·iō -īre -uī *intr* to fly apart, burst, split, break up; to be dissolved

dissimil·is -is -e *adj* dissimilar, different; *(w. gen or dat or w.* **atque** *or* **ac)** different from

dissimiliter *adv* differently

dissimilitūd·ō -inis *f* difference

dissimulābiliter *adv* furtively

dissimulanter *adv* secretly, slyly

dissimulanti·a -ae *f* faking, hiding

dissimulāti·ō -ōnis *f* dissimulation; Socratic irony; pretended ignorance

dissimulāt·or -ōris *m* dissembler, faker

dissimul·ō -āre -āvī -ātus *tr* to conceal, disguise; to keep secret; to pretend not to see, ignore

dissipābil·is -is -e *adj* **(dissu-)** that may be dissipated

dissipāti·ō -ōnis *f* **(dissu-)** dispersal, dissipation; distribution

dissip·ō *or* **dissup·ō -āre -āvī -ātus** *tr* to scatter, disperse; to demolish, overthrow; to squander, dissipate; to circulate, spread; to drive away *(worries); (mil)* to break up *(enemy formation)*

dissitus *pp of* **disserō** *(to scatter)*

dissociābil·is -is -e *adj* incompatible; irreconcilable

dissociāti·ō -ōnis *f* separation

dissoci·ō -āre -āvī -ātus *tr* to dissociate, separate; to ostracize; to set at variance; to divide into factions; to detach

dissolūbil·is -is -e *adj* dissoluble, separable

dissolūtē *adv* disconnectedly, loosely; carelessly

dissolūti·ō -ōnis *f* dissolution, breakup; abolition; destruction; refutation; looseness, dissoluteness; *(rhet)* asyndeton

dissolūt·us -a -um *adj* disconnected, loose; careless, negligent, remiss; loose, dissolute ‖ *n (rhet)* asyndeton

dissol·vō -vere -vī -ūtus *tr* to dissolve, melt; to dismantle; to disband; to make to disappear; to free, release; to loosen, undo; to solve *(problem);* to break up; to pay *(debt);* to refute; to weaken, wear out; to put an end to, do away with; to refute *(argument);* **animam dissolvere** to die; **lēgem dissolvere** to rescind a law; **poenam dissolvere** to pay the penalty

dissonus -a -um *adj* discordant, jarring, confused *(sounds); (w. abl)* differing from, different from

dissor·s -tis *adj* having a different fate; *(w.* **ab)** unshared by

dissuā·deō -dēre -sī -sus *tr* to advise against; to dissuade ‖ *intr* to argue against an idea

dissuāsi·ō -ōnis *f* dissuasion; *(w. gen)* opposition to, objection to

dissuās·or -ōris *m* opponent

dissuāvior *see* **dissāvior**

dissult·ō -āre *intr* to fly apart, burst

dissu·ō -ere -uī -tus *tr* to take the stitches out of, undo

dissupō *see* **dissipō**

distaed·et -ēre *v impers (w. gen)* it makes *(one)* tired of; **mē distaedet loquī** I'm sick and tired of talking

distanti·a -ae *f* distance, remoteness; difference, diversity

disten·dō *or* **disten·nō -dere -dī -tus** *tr* to stretch apart, stretch out; to distend; to cause to swell *or* bulge; to fill to capacity; to distract; to perplex ‖ *pass* to swell; to bulge

distent·us -a -um *pp of* **distendō** ‖ *adj* distended ‖ *pp of* **distineō** ‖ *adj* busy, occupied, distracted

distermin·ō -āre -āvī -ātus *tr* to serve as a boundary between, separate by a boundary, divide, limit

distich·on -ī *n (pros)* couplet

dīstīnctē *adv* distinctly, clearly

dīstīncti·ō -ōnis *f* distinction, differentiation, discrimination; distinctive quality *(of a thing);* difference; punctuation mark; division, paragraphing

dīstīnct·us -a -um *pp of* **dīstinguō** ‖ *adj* distinct, separate; studded, adorned; varied, diversified; lucid *(speaker);* eminent

dīstīnct·us -ūs *m* distinction, difference

dis·tineō -tinēre -tinuī -tentus *tr* to keep apart, separate; to detain, hold back, hinder; to employ, engage; to divert; to put off, delay; to keep divided; to stand in the way of; to distract

dīstin·guō -guere dīstīnxī dīstīnctus *tr* to mark off; to distinguish; to specify; to set off *(w. colors, gold, etc.);* to punctuate

dīst·ō -āre *intr* to stand apart, be separate, be distant; to differ; *(w. dat or* **ab)** to differ from; *(w. abl)* to be separated by *(a* *period of time)* ‖ *v impers* there is a difference, it makes a difference

distor·queō -quēre -sī -tus *tr* to twist, distort; to curl *(lips);* to roll *(eyes);* **cogitātiōnem distorquēre** to rack one's brains

distorti·ō -ōnis *f* twisting; contortion

distort·us -a -um *pp of* **distorqueō** ‖ *adj* distorted, misshapen, deformed; perverse

distracti·ō -ōnis *f* pulling apart; dividing; discord, dissension

distract·us -a -um *adj* severed; rarefied; distracted, perplexed

dis·trahō -trahere -trāxī -tractus *tr* to pull *or* drag apart, separate forcibly; to tear away, drag away, remove; to distract; to sever; to alienate; to prevent, frustrate; to end, settle *(e.g., disputes);* to sell retail; to sell *(land)* in lots

distrib·uō -uere -uī -ūtus *tr* to distribute

distribūtē *adv* methodically

distribūti·ō -ōnis *f* distribution, apportionment, division

dīstrict·us -a -um *adj* drawn in opposite directions; distracted; busy, engaged

dī·stringō -stringere -strīnxī -strictus *tr* to draw apart; to distract, draw attention to

distrunc·ō -āre -āvī -ātus *tr* to cut in two, hack apart

distulī *perf of* **differō**

disturbāti·ō -ōnis *f* demolition

disturb·ō -āre *tr* to throw into confusion; to demolish; to break up *(a marriage);* to frustrate

dītēsc·ō -ere *intr* to get rich

dīthyrambic·us -a -um *adj (pros)* dithyrambic

dithyramb·us -ī *m* dithyramb *(song in honor of Bacchus)*

dīti·ae -ārum *fpl* riches

dīt·ō -āre -āvī -ātus *tr* to enrich, make rich ‖ *pass* to get rich

diū *adv* by day, in the daytime; long, for a long time; in a long time; **diū noctūque** by day and by night; **iam diū** this long; **satis diū** long enough

diurn·us -a -um *adj* of the day, by day, day, daytime; daily, of each day; day's, of one day; **mērum diurnum** daytime drinking ‖ *n* account book ‖ *npl* record, journal, diary

dī·us *or* **dīv·us -a -um** *adj* godlike, divine; divinely inspired; having the brightness of day

diūtīnē *adv* for a long time

diūtīn·us -a -um *adj* long, lasting, long-lasting

diūtissimē *adv* for a very long time; longest; **iam diūtissimē** long long ago

diūtius *adv* longer, still longer; **paulum diūtius** a little too long

diūturnit·ās -ātis *f* length of time, long duration; durability

diūturn·us -a -um *adj* long, long-lasting; chronic

dīv·a -ae *f* goddess

dīvāric·ō -āre -āvī -ātus *tr* to stretch out, spread ‖ *pass* to stand *or* sit with legs apart

dī·vellō -vellere -vellī -vulsus *or* **-volsus** *tr* to tear apart; to tear away; to untie; to wrest, remove, separate; to estrange

dīvēnd·ō -ere -idī -itus *tr* to sell retail

dīverber·ō -āre -āvī -ātus *tr* to split; to batter; to zip through, fly through

dīverb·ium -(i)ī *n (theat)* dialogue

dīversē *adv* **(-vor-)** in different directions, differently

dīversit·ās -ātis *f* distance; diversity; difference; difference of opinion; difference of method; direct opposite; inconsistency; *(w. gen or* **inter** *+ acc)* difference between

dīvers·us -a -um *adj* **(-vor-)** in different directions; *(of roads)* running *or* leading in different directions; moving from opposite directions, converging; facing *or* turned in two *(or more)* directions; *(w.* **ab**) leading away from; situated at a distance from each other, apart, separate; distant, remote; opposite; of the opposing side *(in war),* hostile; unsettled, irresolute; dissimilar, distinct; inconsistent; different *(from one another in quality, quantity, purpose, degree, effect, etc.); (w. dat or gen or* **ab** *or* **quam**) different from, the reverse of ‖ *mpl* individuals ‖ *n* opposite direction, different quarter, opposite side, opposite view; **ex dīversō** from a different direction; on opposite sides; from *or* on the opposing side; in contrast, on the other hand; on the contrary; from a different point of view, in turn; in reverse, vice versa; **in dīversum** in a different direction; for a different reason; to a different effect; vice versa; **per dīversum** crosswise ‖ *npl* different parts; **in dīversa** in different directions; **per dīversa** for different reasons

dīver·tō -tere -tī -sum *intr* **(-vor-)** to go different ways; to turn off; to stop off, stay

dīv·es -itis *adj* rich; costly; precious, sumptuous; plentiful; *(w. gen or abl)* rich in, abounding in

dīvex·ō -āre -āvī -ātus *tr* to ravage; to harass

dīvidi·a -ae *f* worry, trouble; nuisance; dissension, antagonism

dī·vidō -videre -vīsī -vīsus *tr* to divide; to distribute, share; to break up, destroy; to arrange, apportion; to separate, distinguish; to segregate, keep apart; to accompany *(songs with music);* **dīmidium dīvidere** to go halves *(w. s.o.);* **sententi-**

am dīvidere to break down a proposal *(so as to vote on each part separately)*

dīvidu·us -a -um *adj* divisible; divided, separated; forked

dīvīnāti·ō -ōnis *f* clairvoyance; forecasting, predicting, divination; *(leg)* selection of the most suitable prosecutor

dīvīnē *adv* through divine power; prophetically; divinely, gorgeously

dīvīnit·ās -ātis *f* divinity, godhead; prophetic power, clairvoyance; excellence

dīvīnitus *adv* from heaven, from god; providentially; prophetically; divinely, in a godlike manner; excellently

dīvīn·ō -āre -āvī -ātus *tr* to divine, predict; to guess

dīvīn·us -a -um *adj* divine, heavenly; divinely inspired, prophetic; godlike; gorgeous, excellent; **dīvīnum iūs** natural law; **dīvīnum iūs et hūmānum** natural and positive law; **dīvīnum scelus** sacrilege; **rem dīvīnam facere** to worship; to sacrifice; **rēs dīvīna** rite; **rēs dīvīnae** religious affairs, religion; celestial matters **II** *m* prophet **II** *npl* divine matters; religious duties; **dīvīna hūmānaque** things divine and human, the whole world; **dīvīna hūmānaque agere** to perform religious and secular duties

dīvīsi·ō -ōnis *f* division, distribution

dīvīs·or -ōris *m* distributor; agent hired by a candidate to give out bribes

dīvīs·us -a -um *pp of* **dīvidō II** *adj* separate, distinct

dīvīs·us -ūs *m* division, distribution; **facilis dīvīsuī** easily divided

dīviti·ae -ārum *fpl* riches; richness *(of soil);* costly things

dīvolg- = dīvulg-

dīvor- = dīver-

dīvort·ium -(i)ī *n* divorce; fork *(of road or river);* **dīvortium facere cum** to divorce *(a woman)*

dīvulgāt·us -a -um *adj* common, widespread

dīvulg·ō -āre -āvī -ātus *tr* to divulge, spread among the people; to publish *(book);* to publicize, advertise

dīvulsus *pp of* **dīvellō**

dīv·us *or* **dī·us -a -um** *adj* divine, deified **II** *m* god, deity; title applied to dead emperors **II** *n* sky; the open; **sub dīvō** out in the open; **sub dīvum rapere** to bring out into the open

dō dare dedī datus (danit = dat; danunt = dant; dāne = dāsne; duim, duis, duit = dem, dēs det; *(in Plautus:* **dane = dāsne; datin = datisne; dabin = dabisne; duās = dēs)** *tr* to give; to offer, dedicate; to pay out *(money);* to confer; to permit, grant; to give up, hand over; to communicate, tell; to ascribe, impute, assign; to cause, make; to furnish, afford, present; to admit; to administer *(medicine);* to utter, give expression to, announce; **amplexūs dare** to embrace; **comoediam dare** to present a comedy; **concilium** *(or* **contiōnem) dare** to allow a private person to address the assembly; **cōnspectum dare** to make visible; **damnum dare** to cause damage; **fābulam dare** to present a play; **iūs** *(or* **iūra) dare** to give laws, give a constitution, administer justice; **lētō** *(or* **mortī) dare** to send *(s.o.)* to *(his)* death; **lēgem dare** to enact a law; **litterās dare** to mail a letter; **locum dare** *(w. dat)* to make way for; **manūs dare** to surrender; **nōmen dare** to enlist; **operam dare** *(w. dat)* to pay attention to, devote attention to, look out for; **palam dare** to make clear; **poenam** *(or* **poenās** *or* **supplicium) dare** to pay the penalty; **satis dare** *(w. dat)* to give satisfaction to, satisfy; **senātum dare** to allow a private person to address the Senate; **spatium dare** to make room; **terga dare** to take to one's heels; **vēlum dare** to set sail; **veniam dare** to grant pardon; **vēnum dare** to put up for sale **II** *refl* to present oneself; to plunge, rush; **sē dare mīlitem** *(or* **mīlitiae)** to enlist in the service

doc·eō -ēre -uī -tus *tr* to teach, instruct; to give instructions to; to tell, inform *(s.o. of a fact); (w. double acc)* to teach *(s.o. s.th.);* **fābulam docēre** to produce a play, put on a play

dochm·ius -iī *m (pros)* dochmiac foot *(consisting of iamb and cretic)* (⏑ — — ⏑ —)

docil·is -is -e *adj* easily taught, teachable; ready to listen

docilit·ās -ātis *f* aptitude for learning

doctē *adv* skillfully; learnedly; cleverly

doct·or -ōris *m* teacher

doctrīn·a -ae *f* teaching, instruction, education, training; lesson; erudition, learning; science; **doctrīnā** on principle

doct·us -a -um *pp of* **doceō II** *adj* learned, skilled, experienced, trained; clever, shrewd; *(w. abl or ad or* **in** *+ abl)* skilled in, clever at

document·um -ī *or* **docum·en -inis** *n* **(doci-)** example, model, pattern; object lesson, warning; proof, evidence

Dōdōn·a -ae *f* town in Epirus, famous for the oracular oak tree sacred to Jupiter; *(fig)* the oak grove in Dodona

Dōdōnae·us -a -um *adj* of Dodona

Dōdōn·is -idis *adj (fem only)* of Dodona

dōdr·āns -antis *m* three-fourths; **hērēs ex dōdrante** heir to three-fourths of an estate

dōdrantāri·us -a -um *adj* **tabulae dōdrantāriae** account books connected with the Valerian Law of 86 B.C., which reduced debts by three-fourths

dogm·a -atis *n* doctrine, tenet
Dolabell·a -ae *m* Roman family name *(cognomen)* in the *gens Cornelia, esp.* Publius Cornelius Dolabella, Cicero's son-in-law *(d. 43 B.C.)*
dolābr·a -ae *f* pickax, mattock
dol·ēns -entis *adj* painful, smarting; distressing; grieving
dolenter *adv* painfully; with sorrow
dol·eō -ēre -uī -itūrus *tr* to give pain to, hurt **II** *intr* to feel pain; to hurt, be sore, ache, smart; to grieve, be sorry, be hurt; take offense; *(w. dat)* to give pain to, afflict; **caput mihi dolet** I have a headache
dōliār·is -is -e *adj (coll)* fat, tubby
dōliol·um -ī *n* small barrel
dōl·ium -iī *n* large earthenware barrel
dol·ō -āre -āvī -ātus *tr* to chop; to beat up, drub; *(fig)* to hack out *(e.g., a poem)*
dol·ō -ōnis *m* pike *(having a wooden shaft and a short iron point);* topsail
Dol·ōn -ōnis *m* Dolon *(Trojan spy)*
Dolop·es -um *mpl* tribe of Thessaly
dol·or -ōris *m* pain, ache; grief, distress; indignation, resentment, chagrin; pathos; object of grief; **capitis dolor** headache; **dentium dolor** toothache; **esse dolōrī** *(w. dat)* to be a cause of grief *or* resentment to
dolōsē *adv* shrewdly, slyly
dolōs·us -a -um *adj* wily, cunning
dol·us -ī *m* trick; deceit, cunning; **dolus malus** *(leg)* malice aforethought, fraud
domābil·is -is -e *adj* able to be tamed
domesticātim *adv* at home, by the use of one's domestics
domestic·us -a -um *adj* of the house *or* home; domestic, household; familiar, private, personal; native, of one's own country; **bellum domesticum** civil war **II** *mpl* members of the household, one's staff
domī *see* **domus**
domicēn·ium -(i)ī *n* a meal at home
domicil·ium -(i)ī *n* residence, home
domin·a -ae *or* **domn·a -ae** *f* lady of the house; mistress, owner; lady; sweetheart; wife; *(as a title of courtesy)* Ma'am
domin·āns -antis *adj* ruling, dominant; **nōmen domināns** word in its literal sense, normal word **II** *m* ruler
dominātī·ō -ōnis *f* mastery; tyranny, despotism; dominion, kingdom **II** *fpl* control; supremacy; rulers
dominat·or -ōris *m* arbitrary ruler, lord
dominātr·īx -īcis *f* ruler, mistress
dominat·us -ūs *m* absolute rule, sovereignty; ownership; mastery
dominic·us -a -um *adj* master's; mistress's; owner's; belonging to the emperor **II** **Dominic·a -ae** *f (eccl)* the Lord's day, Sunday
domin·ium -(i)ī *n* rule, dominion; ownership; banquet, feast
domin·or -ārī -ātus sum *intr* to be master, be lord, have dominion; to domineer; *(w.* **in** + *acc or abl)* to lord it over, dominate
domin·us -ī *m* owner, proprietor; employer; master, ruler, lord; tyrant; commander; lover; manager *(of a troupe); (as a courtesy title)* Sir; *(as imperial title)* His Imperial Highness; **convīvī dominus** host **II** **Dominus** *(eccl)* the Lord
domiport·a -ae *f* house-carrier *(snail)*
Domitiān·us -ī *m* Domitian *(Titus Flavius Domitianus, son of Vespasian and Roman emperor, 81–96 A.D.)*
domit·ō -āre -āvī *tr* to train, break in
domit·or -ōris *m* tamer; conqueror
domitr·īx -īcis *f* tamer *(female)*
domit·us -a -um *adj* house-bound, kept at home
domit·us -ūs *m* taming
dom·ō -āre -uī -itus *tr* to tame, break in; to domesticate; to master, subdue, vanquish, conquer
dom·us -ūs *or* **-ī** *(dat:* **domō** *or* **domuī;** *abl* **domō** *or* **domū;** *loc:* **domī,** *rarely* **domō** *or* **domuī;** *gen pl:* **domōrum** *or* **domuum)** *f* house, home; mansion, palace; family, household; school *(of philosophers);* building *(of any sort);* seat *(an an activity);* **domī** at home; by one's own resources; **domī mīlitiaeque** at home and in the field; in peace and in war; **domī meae** at my home; **domī tuae** at your home; **domō** from home; from the house; from one's own resources; at home; **domum** *(to one's)* home; *(coll)* into one's pocket
dōnābil·is -is -e *adj* worthy of a gift
dōnār·ium -(i)ī *n* gift repository of a temple; sanctuary; altar; votive offering
dōnātī·ō -ōnis *f* donation
dōnātīv·um -ī *n (mil)* bonus
dōnec *(also* **dōnicum)** *conj* while; as long as; until
dōn·ō -āre -āvī -ātus *tr* to present, grant; to condone, excuse; to forgive, let off; to give up, sacrifice; **aliquem cīvitāte dōnāre** to present s.o. with citizenship; **cīvitātem alicui dōnāre** to bestow citizenship on s.o.
dōn·um -ī *n* gift, present; votive offering, sacrifice; **ultima dōna** funeral rites, obsequies
dorc·as -adis *f* gazelle
Dōr·ēs *or* **Dōr·īs -um** *mpl* Dorians *(one of the four Hellenic tribes inhabiting the Peloponnese in the classical period; also, the inhabitants of Doris in N. Greece)*
Dōricē *adv* in the Dorian dialect
Dōric·us -a -um *adj* Doric **II** *mpl* the Dorians

Dōr·is -idis *or* **-idos** *adj (fem only)* Dorian, Doric ‖ *f* district in N. Greece ‖ the S.W. tip of Caria with its offshore islands ‖ a sea-goddess, wife of Nereus and mother of fifty sea nymphs

Dōri·us -a -um *adj* Dorian

dorm·iō -īre -īvī *or* **-iī -ītum** *intr* to sleep; to fall asleep; to be idle, be unconcerned

dormītāt·or -ōris *m* night-prowler

dormīt·ō -āre -āvī *intr* to be sleepy, be drowsy; to nod, fall asleep

dormīt·or -ōris *m* sleeper

dormītōri·us -a -um *adj* for sleeping; **cubiculum dormītōrium** bedroom

dors·um -ī *n or* **dors·us -ī** *m* back; ridge; reef; ridge *(of a mountain)*

doryphor·os *or* **doryphor·us -ī** *m* spearman

dōs dōtis *f* dowry; endowment

Dossenn·us -ī *m* hunchback, clown *(well-known character in early Italic comedy)*

dōtāl·is -is -e *adj* of a dowry, given as a dowry, dotal

dōtāt·us -a -um *adj* endowed; **dōtātissimus** richly endowed

dōt·ō -āre -āvī -ātus *tr* to endow

drachm·a *or* **drachum·a -ae** *f* drachma *(Greek coin approximately the value of a denarius, c. $1)*

drachumiss·ō -āre *intr* to work for a drachma a day

drac·ō -ōnis *m* dragon; huge serpent ‖ **Dracō** Draco *(Athenian lawgiver, notorious for his severity, c. 621* B.C.*); (astr)* Dragon *(constellation)*

dracōnigen·us -a -um *adj* sprung from (the teeth of) a dragon; **urbs dracōnigena** Thebes

drāpet·a -ae *m* runaway slave

drauc·us -ī *m* athlete

drom·as -adis *m* dromedary, camel

drom·os -ī *m* parade ground

drōp·ax -acis *m* hair-remover

Druid·ēs -um *or* **Druid·ae -ārum** *mpl* Druids *(priests and sages of the Gauls and Britons)*

Drūsill·a -ae *f* Livia Drusilla *(second wife of Augustus and mother of Tiberius, 58* B.C.*–*A.D. *29)* ‖ sister of Caligula ‖ daughter of Caligula, murdered in infancy

Drūs·us -ī *m* Livius Drusus *(tribune of the people with Gaius Gracchus in 122* B.C.*)* ‖ Marcus Livius Drusus *(former's son, famous orator and tribune of the people in 91* B.C.*)* ‖ Nero Claudius Drusus *(son of Livia, brother of Tiberius, 38* B.C.*–*A.D. *9)*

dry·as -adis *f* dryad *(wood nymph)*

Dryop·ē -ēs *f* mother of Amphissus by Apollo ‖ mother of Tarquinius

Dryop·es -um *mpl* a people of Epirus

dubiē *adv* doubtfully; **haud dubiē** undoubtedly, indubitably

dubitābil·is -is -e *adj* doubtful

dubitanter *adv* doubtingly, hesitantly

dubitāti·ō -ōnis *f* doubt, uncertainty; wavering, hesitancy; hesitation, delay; *(rhet)* pretended embarrassment *(to win over sympathy)*

dubit·ō -āre -āvī -ātus *tr* to doubt; to consider, ponder, wonder about ‖ *intr* to be doubtful, be in doubt, be uncertain, be perplexed; to deliberate; to waver, hesitate, delay

dubi·us -a -um *adj* wavering, doubtful, dubious, uncertain; precarious, critical; adverse, difficult; dim *(light);* overcast *(sky);* indecisive *(battle);* **haud prō dubiō habēre** to regard as beyond doubt; **in dubium venīre** to come into question; **in dubium vocāre** to call into question; **procul dubiō** undoubtedly

ducāt·us -ūs *m* military leadership, command

ducēnāri·us -a -um *adj* receiving an annual salary of 200,000 sesterces *(c. $50,000)*

ducēn·ī -ae -a *adj* two hundred each

ducentēsim·a -ae *f* half-percent tax

ducent·ī -ae -a *adj* two hundred

ducentiēns *adv* **(-iēs)** two hundred times

dūcō dūcere dūxī ductus *tr* to lead, guide, direct, conduct; to command; to march; to draw, pull; to draw out, prolong; to pass, spend *(time);* to stall *(s.o.);* to pull at *(oars);* to mislead, take in, fool; to draw, attract; to draw *(lots);* to draw in, breathe in; to sip, drink; to trace; to construct, form, fashion, shape; to run, build *(a wall or ditch or rampart or road from one point to another);* to drive *(vehicles);* to assume, get *(a name); (of a man)* to marry; to calculate, compute; to regard, consider, hold, account; to derive, trace *(lineage);* to spin *(wool); (of a road)* to lead, take *(s.o.);* **dūcere triumphum** to hold a triumph; **id parvī dūcere** to consider it of little importance; **initium** *(or* **ratiōnem)** **dūcere** to take account *(of),* pay attention *(to);* **prīncipium dūcere** *(w.* **ab)** to start from, originate from, trace to, e.g.: **bellī initium ā fame dūcere** to trace the beginning of the war to hunger; **uxōrem dūcere** *(of the groom)* to get married, take a wife

ductil·is -is -e *adj (of a river)* that is led along a course

ductim *adv* in a continuous stream

ductit·ō -āre -āvī -ātus *tr* to take home, marry *(a woman);* to lead on, trick

duct·ō -āre -āvī -ātus *tr* to lead; to draw; to accompany, escort

duct·or -ōris *m* leader, commander, general; guide; pilot

duct·us -ūs *m* drawing, conducting; line, row; leadership, command; **aquae ductus** aqueduct; **ōris ductus** facial expression

dūdum *adv* a short time ago; just now; once, formerly; **cum dūdum** just as; **haud dūdum** not long ago, just now; **iam dūdum** for some time; **iam dūdum eum exspectō** I have been waiting for him a long time; **quam dūdum** how long; **ut dūdum** just as
Duill·ius *or* **Duīl·ius -(i)ī** *m* Duilius *(Roman consul who won Rome's first naval victory, off Sicily, in 260 B.C.)*
duim, duis duit *see* **dō**
dulcēd·ō -inis *f* sweetness; pleasantness, charm, delightfulness
dulc·ēscō -ēscere *intr* to become sweet
dulciāri·us -a -um *adj* **pīstor dulciārius** confectioner, pastry baker
dulcicul·us -a -um *adj* rather sweet
dulcif·er -era -erum *adj* full of sweetness, sweet
dulc·is -is -e *adj* sweet; pleasant, delightful; dear, affectionate, kind
dulciter *adv* sweetly; pleasantly
dulcitūd·ō -inis *f* sweetness
dūlicē *adv* like a slave
Dūlich·ium -iī *n or* **Dūlichi·a -ae** *f* Dulichium *(island in the Ionian Sea)*
Dūlich·ius -(i)ī *m* Ulysses
dum *adv* up to now, yet, as yet; now; **age dum**! *(pl:* **agite dum**!) come now!; all right!; **nēmō dum** no one (as) yet; **nōn dum** not yet
dum *conj* while; as long as; until; provided that, if only; **dum modo** *or* **dummodo** provided that, if only; **exspectābam dum redīret** I was waiting for him to return
dūmēt·um -ī *n* thicket, underbrush
dummodo *conj* provided that
dūmōs·us -a -um *adj* overgrown with bushes, bushy
dumtaxat *adv (with numbers)* up to, at most, not exceeding; *(with small numbers)* only, just; not less than, at least; *(limiting a statement)* at any rate, at least, strictly speaking; up to a point ‖ *conj* provided that, as long as; **nōn dumtaxat … sed** not just … but also
dūm·us -ī *m* bush, bramble
du·o -ae -o *(dat & abl pl:* **duōbus, duābus, duōbus;** *masc acc pl:* **duo** *or* **duōs)** *adj* two
duodeciēns *adv* **(-ciēs)** twelve times
duodecim *indecl adj* twelve
duodecim·us -a -um *adj* **(-cum-)** twelfth
duodēn·ī -ae -a *adj* twelve each, twelve, apiece; a dozen; **duodēnīs assibus** at 12%
duodēquadrāgēsim·us *adj* thirty-eighth
duodēquadrāgintā *indecl adj* thirty-eight
duodēquīnquāgēsim·us -a -um *adj* forty-eighth
duodēquīnquāgintā *indecl adj* forty-eight
duodētrīciēns *adv* **(-ciēs)** twenty-eight times
duodētrīgintā *indecl adj* twenty-eight
duodēvīcēn·ī -ae -a *adj* eighteen each
duodēvīgintī *indecl adj* eighteen
duoetvīcēsimān·ī -ōrum *mpl* soldiers of the twenty-second legion
duoetvīcēsim·us -a -um *adj* **(-cens-)** twenty-second
duovirī *see* **duumvirī**
dupl·a -ae *f* a double amount of money; double the price
dupl·ex -icis *adj* twofold, double; divided into two; in double rows; double, twice as big; twice as long; complex, compound; two-faced, double-dealing, false
duplicār·ius -iī *m* soldier receiving double pay
dupliciter *adv* doubly; in two ways; into two categories
duplic·ō -āre -āvī -ātus *tr* to double up, bend over; to double *(in size, length, quantity)*
dupl·us -a -um *adj* double, twice as much, twice as large ‖ *f see* **dupla** ‖ *n* double the price; **in duplum** twice the amount; **in duplum īre** to pay twice as much
dupond·ius -(i)ī *m or* **dupond·ium -(i)ī** *n* two-as coin *(worth c. 2¢)*
dūrābil·is -is -e *adj* durable, lasting
dūracin·us -a -um *adj* having a hard berry
dūrām·en -inis *n* hardness
dūrate·us -a -um *adj* wooden
dūrē *or* **dūriter** *adv* hard, sternly, rigorously, roughly; stiffly, awkwardly
dūr·ēscō -ēscere -uī *intr* to grow hard, harden; to become solid
dūrit·ās -ātis *f* hardness, toughness; harshness
dūriter *see* **dūrē**
dūriti·a -ae *or* **dūriti·ēs -ēī** *f* hardness; austerity; strictness, harshness, rigor; oppressiveness; insensibility, callousness
dūriuscul·us -a -um *adj* somewhat hard, rather harsh
dūr·ō -āre -āvī -ātus *tr* to harden, solidify; *(fig)* to harden, inure, toughen up; to make insensible; to dull, blunt ‖ *intr* to be tough, be inured; to become hard; *(of liquids)* to become solid; to endure, last, hold out; to continue unchanged, remain; *(of food)* to keep; *(of hills)* to continue unbroken, extend
dūr·us -a -um *adj* hard; lasting; rough *(to the senses);* tough, hardy; rough, rude, uncouth; shameless, brazen; harsh, cruel; callous, insensitive; severe, oppressive; parsimonious
duum·vir *or* **duo·vir** *or* **II·vir -virī** *m* duumvir *(member of a board of two) (see* **duumvirī)**
duumvirāt·us -ūs *m* duumvirate, office of duumvir
duumvir·ī -ōrum *or* **duovir·ī** *or* **II·virī -ōrum** *mpl* two-man board; **duumvirī ad**

aedem faciendam two-man board for the construction of a temple; **duumvirī iūrī dīcundō** two-man board of colonial magistrates; pair of judges; **duumvirī nāvālēs** two-man board to equip the navy; **duumvirī perduelliōnis** criminal court *(to try cases of treason);* **duumvirī sacrōrum** two-man board in charge of the Sibylline books

dux ducis *m (f)* general; guide; leader, head, ringleader; driver *(of chariot);* captain *(of ship),* commander *(of naval force);* **dux gregis** shepherd

Dymant·is -idos *f* daughter of Dymas *(Hecuba)*

Dym·ās -antis *m* father of Hecuba

dynam·is -is *f* store, plenty

dynast·ēs -ae *m* ruler, (Eastern) prince

Dyrr(h)ach·ium -(i)ī *n* Adriatic port in Illyria, serving as landing place for those sailing from Italy to Greece

dysenteri·a -ae *f* dysentery

dyspepsi·a -ae *f* indigestion

E

E, e *(supply* littera) *f* fifth letter of the Latin alphabet; letter name: **e**

-ē *advl suf* forms adverbs from adjectives: **clārē** clearly; but in prosody, **bene, male**

ē- *pref see* **ex-**

ē *prep* of, out of, from *(see* **ex)**

eā *adv* there; that way

ea ēius *pron* she

eādem *adv* the same way, by the same route; at the same time; likewise, by the same token

eāpropter *adv* therefore

eapse = ipsa *(old feminine emphatic form of* **ipse**)

eātenus *adv* so far; *(followed by* **quod** *or* **ut)** so far ... as (that)

eben·us -ī *f* ebony tree, ebony

ēbib·ō -ere -ī -itus *tr* to drink up, drain; *(of things)* to absorb, swallow up; to spend on drinks

ebiscum *see* **hibiscum**

ēbīt·ō -ere *intr* to go out

ēbland·ior -īrī -ītus sum *tr* to coax out, obtain by flattery

Eborāc·um -ī *n* **(Ebur-)** town in Britain *(modern York)*

eborāt·us -a -um *adj* **(ebur-)** adorned with ivory

ēbriet·ās -ātis *f* drunkenness

ēbriol·us -a -um *adj* tipsy

ēbriōsit·ās -ātis *f* habitual drunkenness, heavy drinking

ēbriōs·us -a -um *adj* addicted to drinking **II** *mf* drunkard

ēbri·us -a -um *adj* drunk; drunken *(acts, words),* of a drunk; *(fig)* intoxicated *(e.g., w. love, power)*

ēbull·iō -īre -iī *or* **-īvī** *tr* to babble about; **animam ēbullīre** *(coll)* to give up the ghost **II** *intr* to bubble up

ebul·um -ī *n or* **ebul·us -ī** *f (bot)* dwarf elder *(small tree having clusters of white flowers and red or blackish berry-like fruit)*

eb·ur -oris *n* ivory; ivory object *(e.g., statue, flute, scabbard);* elephant's tusk; elephant; curule chair *(of a magistrate, ornamented with ivory)*

eburāt·us -a -um *adj* inlaid with ivory

eburneol·us -a -um *adj* made of ivory

eburne·us *or* **eburn·us -a -um** *adj* ivory; white as ivory; **dentēs eburneī** tusks; **ēnsis eburneus** sword with ivory hilt

ec- *pref (prefixed to interrogatives with intensive or indefinite force, e.g.,* **ecquis** is there anyone who?)

ēcastor *interj (used mainly by women)* by Castor!

ecca, eccam, eccās *see* **ecce**

ecce *interj* see!, look!, look here! here!; *(followed by accusative in early literature; also followed by nominative from time of Cicero on)* **ecce mē**! here I am!; **ecce nōs**! here we are!; *(colloquially combined with the pronouns* **is, ille, iste: ecca**! *(i.e.,* **ecce + ea)** *(fem sing)* here she is!; *(neut pl)* here they are!; **eccam**! *(i.e.,* **ecce + eam)** here she is!; **eccilla** *or* **eccistam**! there she is!; **eccillum** *or* **eccum**! here he is!; **eccōs**! here they are!; *(calling attention to something non-visual)* mark this!; *(in vivid narrative, introducing a surprising event)* lo and behold!

eccerē *interj* there!

eccheum·a -atis *n* pouring out

eccill- *see* **ecce**

eccist- *see* **ecce**

ecclēsi·a -ae *f* Greek assembly of the people; *(eccl)* church, congregation

eccōs *interj see* **ecce**

eccum *interj see* **ecce**

ecdic·us -ī *m* public prosecutor; public defender

ecf- = eff-

echidn·a -ae *f* viper **II** **Echidna** Hydra; **Echidna Lernaea** Lernaean Hydra **II** monstrous mother of Cerberus, half woman and half serpent

Echidnē·us -a -um *adj* of Echidna; **canis Echidnēus** Cerberus

Echīnad·es -um *fpl* cluster of small islands off Acarnania

echīn·us -ī *m* sea urchin; hedgehog; dishpan

Echī·ōn -onis *m* hero who sprang from the dragon's teeth sown by Cadmus, married

Agave, and became father of Pentheus ‖ an argonaut

Echīonid·ēs -ae *m* Pentheus, son of Echion

Echīoni·us -a -um *adj* Cadmean, Theban

Ēch·ō -ūs *(acc:* **-ō** *or* **-ōn)** *f* nymph who was changed by Hera into an echo

eclog·a -ae *f* literary selection; eclogue

eclogāri·ī -ōrum *mpl* excerpted literary passages

ecquandō *adv* ever, at any time; *(in indirect questions)* whether ever

ecqu·ī -ae *(or* **-a)** **-od** *interrog adj* any at all, really any

ecquī *conj (in indirect questions)* whether

ec·quid -cūius *pron* anything at all; *(in questions)* whether, if at all

ec·quis -cūius *pron* any at all, anyone at all; *(in indirect questions)* whether anyone

ecquō *adv* anywhere

ecule·us -ī *m* foal, colt; small equestrian statue; torture rack; hobbyhorse

edācit·ās -ātis *f* gluttony

ed·āx -ācis *adj* gluttonous; *(fig)* devouring, destructive

ēdent·ō -āre -āvī -ātus *tr (sl)* to knock the teeth out of

ēdentul·us -a -us *adj* toothless, old

edepol *interj* by Pollux!, gad!

eder·a *or* **heder·a -ae** *f* ivy

ē·dīcō -dīcere -dīxī -dictus *tr* to proclaim; to decree; to appoint

ēdicti·ō -ōnis *f* edict, decree

ēdict·ō -āre -āvī -ātus *tr* to proclaim, publish

ēdict·um -ī *n* edict, proclamation; edict of a praetor listing rules he would follow in his capacity as judge

ē·discō -discere -didicī *tr* to learn by heart, learn thoroughly

ēdisser·ō -ere -uī -tus *tr* to explain in detail, analyze fully

ēdissert·ō -āre -āvī -ātus *tr* to explain fully, explain in detail

ēditīci·us -a -um *adj* set forth, proposed; **iūdicēs ēditīciī** panel of jurors *(subject to challenge by defendant)*

ēditi·ō -ōnis *f* statement, account; publication; edition *(of book)*; *(leg)* declaration *(of the form of judicial procedure to be followed)*

ēdit·us -a -um *adj* high; raised, rising; *(fig)* exalted; **locus ēditus** height, hill ‖ *n* height; ordinance; **ex ēditō** from a height; **in ēditō** on a hill; *(fig)* on a pedestal

edō edere *(or* **ēsse)** **ēdī ēsus** *tr* to eat; *(fig)* to devour, consume, destroy; **pugnōs edere** *(sl)* to be hit with a fist, eat a knuckle sandwich

ēd·ō -ere -idī -itus *tr* to give out, put forth, bring forth, emit; to give birth to, bear; to publish; to tell, announce, disclose; to show, display, produce, perform; to bring about, cause; to bring forward *(witnesses)*; *(leg)* to give the defendant notice of; **animam ēdere** to give up the ghost

ēdoc·eō -ēre -uī -tus *tr* to teach thoroughly; to instruct clearly; to inform; to show clearly; *(w. double acc)* to teach *(s.o. s.th.)* well

ēdol·ō -āre -āvī -ātus *tr* to hew out: *(fig)* to hew into shape

ēdom·ō -āre -uī -itus *tr* to conquer thoroughly; to overcome *(vices, difficulties)*

Ēdōn·ī -ōrum *or* **Ēdōn·es -um** *mpl* Thracian tribe noted for its heavy drinking

Ēdōn·is -idis *adj (fem only)* Edonian ‖ *f* Bacchante.

Ēdōn·us -a -um *adj* Edonian

ēdorm·iō -īre -īvī *or* **-iī -ītus** *tr* to sleep off; to sleep through *(e.g., a lecture)*; **crāpulam ēdormīre** to sleep off a hangover ‖ *intr* to sleep soundly

ēdormīsc·ō -ere *tr* to sleep off *(a hangover)*

ēducāti·ō -ōnis *f* raising *(of children, animals, plants)*

ēducāt·or -ōris *m* fosterer; foster father

ēducātr·īx -īcis *f* foster mother; nurse

ēduc·ō -āre -āvī -ātus *tr* to bring up, raise *(children, animals, plants)*; to produce *(fruit, grain)*

ēdū·cō -cere -xī -ctus *tr* to draw out, to take away; to build high, raise, erect *(tower)*; to drain off *(liquids)*; to draw *(sword)*; to spend *(time)*; to lead out *(army)*; to raise *(children, animals, plants)*; **in iūs ēdūcere** to take to court

edūl·ia -ium *npl* eatables

edūl·is -is -e *adj* edible, eatable

ēdūr·ō -āre *intr* to last, endure

ēdūr·us -a -um *adj* hard, tough; *(fig)* tough

Ēēti·ōn -ōnis *m* father of Andromache and king of Thebe in Cilicia

effarciō *see* **efferciō**

effāt·us -a -um *pp of* **effor** ‖ *adj* solemnly pronounced ‖ *n* pronouncement; axiom, proposition

effecti·ō -ōnis *f* accomplishment, performance; efficient cause

effectīv·us -a -um *adj* effective; practical

effect·or -ōris *m*, **effectr·īx -īcis** *f* producer, author

effect·us -a -um *pp of* **efficiō** ‖ *adj* finished, complete ‖ *n* effect

effect·us -ūs *m* effecting; completion; effect, result; **ad effectum addūcere** to bring to completion; **cum effectū** in fact, actually; **effectū** in effect, to all intents and purposes; **sine effectū** without a decisive result

effēminātē *adv* effeminately

effēmināt·us -a -um *adj* **(ecf-)** effeminate

effēmin·ō -āre -āvī -ātus *tr* **(ecf-)** to make a woman of; to represent as a woman, regard as female; to emasculate ‖ *pass* to become unmanly

efferāt·us -a -um *adj* wild, savage
effer·ciō *or* **effarciō -cīre -sī -tus** *tr* **(ecfer-, ecfar-)** to stuff; to fill in *(e.g., a ditch)*
efferit·ās -ātis *f* wildness, barbarism
effer·ō -āre -āvī -ātus *tr* **(ecf-)** to make wild, brutalize; to exasperate
efferō efferre extulī ēlātus *tr* **(ecf-)** to carry out, bring out, bring forth; to utter, express, to publish, spread *(news);* to carry out for burial, bury; to produce, bear; to name, designate; to lift up, raise; to promote, advance; to bring out, expose; to praise, extol; to sweep off one's feet; *(w.* **ex)** to copy out *(of some text);* **in lūcem efferre** *(of fields)* to produce *(crops);* **gressum** *(or* **pedem) efferre** to go forth **||** *refl* to arise; to be haughty, be conceited **||** *pass (fig)* to be carried away
effert·us -a -um *pp of* **efferciō ||** *adj* chock-full, crammed, bulging
effer·us -a -um *adj* very wild, savage
efferv·eō -ēre *or* **efferv·ō -ere** *intr* to boil over; *(of bees, etc.)* to come pouring out; *(of volcano)* to erupt
efferv·ēscō -ēscere -ī *intr* to boil, boil over; to burst forth; to get all worked up; to seethe; to rage; *(of words) (fig)* to become heated
effēt·us -a -um *adj* worn out, spent; vain, delusive; *(w. gen)* incapable of
efficācit·ās -ātis *f* efficiency
efficāciter *adv* efficiently, effectively
effic·āx -ācis *adj* efficient, effective, efficacious
effici·ēns -entis *adj* efficient, effective; **rēs efficientēs** *(phil)* efficient causes
efficienter *adv* efficiently
efficienti·a -ae *f* efficiency, efficacy, influence
ef·ficiō -ficere -fēcī -fectus *tr* **(ecf-)** to bring about, bring to pass, effect, cause, produce; to make, form; to construct; to finish, complete, accomplish; to show, prove; *(w.* **ut)** to bring it about that; to carry out *(an order); (of component parts)* to constitute; to cover *(a distance in travel); (of numbers)* to amount to, add up to; *(of a field)* to produce, yield; to compose *(a speech, an essay); (w. double acc)* to elect *(s.o., e.g., consul)* **||** *pass* to follow; **ita efficitur ut** thus it follows that
effictus *pp of* **effingō**
effigi·ēs -ēī *or* **effigi·a -ae** *f* effigy, likeness, semblance; opposite number; copy, imitation; image; statue, figure, portrait; ghost, phantom
ef·fingō -fingere -fīnxī -fictus *tr* **(ecf-)** to mold, form, fashion; to imitate; to wipe out, wipe clean; to represent, portray; to imagine
efflō *pass of* **efficiō**
efflāgitāti·ō -ōnis *f* urgent demand
efflāgitāt·us -ūs *m* insistence
efflāgit·ō -āre *tr* to demand, insist on; to pester *(s.o. with requests)*
effl·āns -antis *pres p of* **efflō** *& adj* dying; deadly, fatal
efflīctim *adv* **(ecf-)** passionately
ef·flī·gō -flīgere -flīxī -efflīctus *tr* **(ecf-)** to strike dead, exterminate
effl·ō -āre -āvī -ātus *tr* **(ecf-)** to breathe out; **animam efflāre** to expire
efflōr·ēscō -ēscere -uī *intr* **(ecf-)** to bloom, blossom forth; *(fig)* to flourish
efflu·ō -ere -xī *intr* **(ecf-)** to flow out, flow forth, run out; to slip away, drop out, disappear; *(of rumor)* to get out, circulate; *(of secret)* to leak out; **ex animō** *(or* **memoriā) effluere** to slip one's mind
effluv·ium -(i)ī *n* outlet
ef·fodiō -fodere -fōdī -fossus *tr* **(ecf-, exf-)** to dig up; to gouge out *(eyes);* to hollow out; to root out; to make *(by digging);* to erase; **humum** *(or* **terram) effodere** to dig a hole in the ground
ef·for -fārī -fātus sum *tr* **(ecf-)** to say out loud, tell; *(in augury)* to mark off, consecrate *(an area)* **||** *intr* to speak out
effossus *pp of* **effodiō**
effrēnātē *adv* **(ecf-)** without restraint, out of control
effrēnāti·ō -ōnis *f* impetuosity
effrēnāt·us -a -um *adj* **(ecf-)** unbridled; *(fig)* unbridled, unrestrained
effrēn·us -a -um *adj* unbridled; *(fig)* uncontrolled
ef·fringō -fringere -frēgī -frāctus *tr* **(ecf-)** to break open, smash, break off; to break down *(door)*
ef·fugiō -fugere -fūgī *tr* **(ecf-, exf-)** to escape; to keep away from *(a person or place);* to avoid; to escape the grasp of, slip out of *(the hands);* to escape the notice of **||** *intr* to escape, slip away; *(w. abl or w.* **ab** *or* **ex)** to escape from
effug·ium -(i)ī *n* escape, flight; means of escape; avoidance
efful·geō -gēre -sī *or* **effulg·ō -ere** *intr* to shine forth, gleam, flash, glitter; *(fig)* to shine forth
effult·us -a -um *adj* propped up, supported
ef·fundō -fundere -fūdī -fūsus *tr* **(ecf-)** to pour out, pour away; to emit; to utter *(sounds);* to allow *(rain water)* to run off; to shed *(tears);* to hurl, shower *(weapons); (w.* **in** *+ acc)* to shower *(praises)* on; *(of the stomach)* to throw up; to give up, let go, abandon, resign; to knock down, overturn *(walls, buildings);* to produce in abundance; to lavish, waste *(money, energy); (of tree)* to spread out *(branches);* to empty out *(bags, etc.);* to give vent to, pour out **||** *refl & pass* to come pouring out; *(of rain)* to pour down; *(of a river) (w.* **ab)** to begin to flow from,

have its source at; **super rīpam effundī** to overflow its banks

effūsē *adv* far and wide; at random, in disorder; lavishly; immoderately

effūsi·ō -ōnis *f* **(ecf-)** outpouring, rushing out; shedding; effusion; profusion, lavishness, extravagance **II** *fpl* excesses

effūs·us -a -um *pp of* **effundō II** *adj* spread out, extensive; *(of troops)* thinly spread out *(over a large area);* straggly, disorderly; relaxed, loose; disheveled; lavish; unrestrained; immoderate; *(w.* **in** *+ acc)* very prone to *(some weakness),* passionately devoted to *(some cause);* **effūsissimīs habēnīs** at full speed

effūt·iō -īre -īvī *or* **-iī -ītus** *tr & intr* to blab, babble

effut·uō -uere -uī -ūtus *tr* **(ecf-)** *(vulg)* to wear out through excessive sex

ēgelid·us -a -um *adj* tepid; cool

eg·ēns -entis *adj* needy, poor; *(w. gen)* in need of, needing

egēn·us -a -um *adj* needy, destitute; *(w. gen or abl)* in need of, needing

eg·eō -ēre -uī *intr* to be needy, suffer want; *(w. gen)* **1** to be in need of; **2** to lack, be without; **3** to want, desire, miss

Ēgeri·a -ae *f* nymph whom King Numa visited at night for advice

ē·gerō -gerere -gessī -gestus *tr* to carry out, take away, remove; to discharge, vomit, emit; to express *(grief)*

egest·ās -ātis *f* need, want, poverty; *(w. gen)* lack of

ēgesti·ō -ōnis *f* squandering

ēgestus *pp of* **ēgerō**

ego *pron* I

egomet *pron* I personally, I and nobody else

ē·gredior -gredī -gressus sum *tr* to go beyond, pass; to quit; *(fig)* to surpass **II** *intr* to go out, come out; to march out; to disembark, land; to go up, climb; *(fig)* to digress

ēgregiē *adv* exceptionally, singularly, uncommonly, splendidly

ēgregi·us -a -um *adj* exceptional, uncommon; distinguished, illustrious; **vir ēgregius** *(title given under the Empire to officials of equestrian rank)* the honorable . . .

ēgressus *pp of* **ēgredior**

ēgress·us -ūs *m* way out, exit; departure; disembarking, landing; mouth *(of river);* digression **II** *mpl* comings and goings

ēgurgit·ō -āre *tr* to pour out, lavish

ehem *interj (expressing pleasant surprise)* ha!, aha!

ēheu *interj (expressing pain)* oh!

eho *interj (often expressing rebuke)* look here!, see here!; whoa!; **eho dum**! look here now!

ei *interj* **hei** *(expressing fear or dismay)* ah!; *(expressing pain)* ouch!

ēia *or* **hēia** *interj (expressing joy or surpise)* ah!; ah ha!; good!; *(expressing haste)* quick!, come on!; **ēia age** come on!, up then!; be quick!; **ēia vērō** *(ironic)* nonsense!; oh sure!; oh yeah!

ēiacul·or -ārī -ātus sum *tr* to squirt **II** *refl (of water, etc.)* to squirt

ēiciō ēicere ēiēcī ēiectus *tr* to throw out, drive out, put out, eject, expel; to banish; to utter; to run aground; to reject, disapprove; to boo *(s.o.)* off the stage **II** *refl (of passions)* to come to the fore, break out **II** *pass* to be stranded

ēiectāment·a -ōrum *npl* refuse; jetsam

ēiecti·ō -ōnis *f* ejection; banishment, exile

ēiect·ō -āre -āvī -ātus *tr* to spout forth; to keep throwing up *(e.g., blood)*

ēiect·us -ūs *m* emission

ēier·ō āre -āvī -ātus *tr* **(ēiūr-)** to refuse under oath, abjure, forswear; to deny under oath; to resign, abdicate; to disown, abandon

ēiulāti·ō -ōnis *f* lamenting

ēiulāt·us -a -um *adj* wailing

ēiul·ō -āre *intr* **(hēi-)** to wail, lament

ēiūrō *see* **ēierō**

ēiusdemmodī *see* **modus**

ēj- = **ēi-**

-ēl·a, -ell·a -ae *fem suf* forms diminutives chiefly from verbs: **querēla** complaint *(from* **querī** to complain)

ēlā·bor -bī -psus sum *intr* to glide off; to slip away, escape; to pass away, disappear; *(w. abl or* **super** *+ acc)* to glance off

ēlabōrāt·us -a -um *adj* studied, overdone; elaborate, finished

ēlabōr·ō -āre -āvī -ātus *tr* to work out, elaborate; to produce **II** *intr* to make a great effort, take great pains; *(w. inf)* to strive to

ēlāmentābil·is -is -e *adj* very mournful, pathetic

ēlangu·ēscō -ēscere -ī *intr* to slow down, slacken, let up

ēlāpsus *pp of* **ēlābor**

ēlātē *adv* proudly

ēlāti·ō -ōnis *f* elation, ecstasy

ēlātr·ō -āre *tr* to bark out

ēlāt·us -a -um *pp of* **efferō II** *adj* high, elevated; exalted; haughty, proud

ē·lavō -lavāre -lāvī -lautus *or* **-lōtus** *tr* to wash out; *(coll)* to clean out, rob **II** *intr* to be cleaned out, be wrecked; **ēlavāre bonīs** *(coll)* to be broke

Ele·a -ae *f* town in Lucania in S. Italy *(modern Velia),* birthplace of Eleatic philosophy

Eleāt·ēs -ae *m* inhabitant of Elea *(e.g., Zeno)*

Eleātic·ī -ōrum *mpl* Eleatics, Eleatic philosophers *(Parmenides and Zeno)*

ēlecebr·a -ae *f* **(exl-)** snare; seductress

ēlēctē *adv* tastefully

ēlēctil·is -is -e *adj* choice, dainty
ēlēcti·ō -ōnis *f* choice, selection
ēlēct·ō -āre *tr* to select, choose; to wheedle out, coax out *(a secret)*
Ēlectr·a -ae *f* daughter of Agamemnon and Clytemnestra **‖** Pleiad, daughter of Atlas and mother of Dardanus
ēlectr·um -ī *n* amber; gold-silver alloy **‖** *npl* amber beads
ēlēct·us -a -um *pp of* **ēligō ‖** *adj* select, choice; *(mil)* elite
ēlēct·us -ūs *m* choice
ēleg·āns -antis *adj* elegant; choosy; fine, choice, select; *(pej)* dainty
ēleganter *adv* elegantly, tastefully
ēleganti·a -ae *f* elegance, refinement, taste, propriety; *(pej)* daintiness
elegē·um -ī *n* **(gīum)** elegaic poem
eleg·ī -ōrum *mpl* elegaic verses
elegī·a -ae *f* **(-gē·a** *or* **-gēi·a)** elegy
Elel·eūs -eī *m (epithet of)* Bacchus
elementāri·us -a -um *adj* engaged in learning the rudiments; **senex elementārius** old schoolteacher
element·um -ī *n* first principle, element; atom, particle; letter of the alphabet **‖** *npl* rudiments, elements; beginnings; ABC's
elench·us -ī *m (pear-shaped)* pearl **‖** *mpl* criticisms
elephantomach·a -ae *m* fighter mounted on an elephant
elephant·us -ī *or* **eleph·ās -antis** *m* elephant; *(fig)* ivory
Ēlē·us -a -um *adj* of Elis *(in the Peloponnese)*
Eleus·īn -īnis *f* Eleusis *(town in Attica, sacred to Demeter, the Roman Ceres)*
Eleusīn·us -a -um *adj* Eleusinian; **Eleusīna Māter** Demeter *or the Roman* Ceres
eleutheri·a -ae *f* freedom, liberty
ēlev·ō -āre -āvī -ātus *tr* to lift up, raise; to alleviate; to lessen; to make light of, disparage
Ēli·as -adis *adj (fem only)* Elian, Olympic
ēlic·iō -ere -uī -itus *tr* to elicit, draw out; to lure out, entice; to conjure up
ēlicitus *pp of* **ēliciō**
Ēlic·ius -(i)ī *m (epithet of)* Jupiter
ēlī·dō -dere -sī -sus *tr* to knock out, strike out, tear out, force out; to shatter, smash to pieces, crush; to force out, stamp out
ē·ligō -ligere -lēgī -lēctus *tr* **(-leg-)** to pluck out; to pick out, choose
ēlīmin·ō -āre *tr* to carry outside; to spread abroad
ēlīm·ō -āre -āvī -ātus *tr* to file; to finish off, perfect
ēlingu·is -is -e *adj* speechless; *(fig)* inarticulate; *(rhet)* dull, flat, insipid
ēlingu·ō -āre *tr* to tear out *(s.o.'s)* tongue
Ēl·is -idis *f* town and district on the W. coast of the Peloponnesus in which Olympia is located
-ēl·is -is -e *adjl suf* formed from nouns and adjectives: **crūdēlis** cruel
Eliss·a *or* **Elīs·a -ae** *f* Dido
ēlīsus *pp of* **ēlīdō**
ēl·ix -icis *m* drainage ditch
ēlix·us -a -um *adj* boiled; *(sl)* soused
-ell·a -ae *fem suf* forms diminutives: **cistella** a little box
ellam = ecce + illam there she is!
elleborōs·us -a -um *adj* crazy
ellebor·us -ī *m or* **ellebor·um -ī** *n* **(hell-)** hellebore *(plant used to cure mental illness)*
ellips·is -is *f* ellipsis
ellum = ecce + illum there he is!
-ell·us -ī *masc suf* forms diminutives: **agellus** small plot
ēloc·ō -āre -āvī -ātus *tr* to lease out, rent out
ēlocūti·ō -ōnis *f* style of speaking, elocution, delivery
ēlog·ium -(i)ī *n* saying, maxim; inscription, epitaph; codicil *(in a will);* criminal record
ēloqu·ēns -entis *adj* eloquent
ēloquenter *adv (used in comp & supl degree)* eloquently
ēloquenti·a -ae *f* eloquence
ēloqu·ium -(i)ī *n* eloquence
ēlo·quor -quī -cūtus sum *tr* to speak out, declare; to divulge, tell **‖** *intr* to speak, give a speech
ēlōtus *pp of* **ēlavō**
ēlū·ceō -cēre -xī *intr* to shine forth; to glitter
ēluct·or -ārī -ātus sum *tr* to struggle out of, struggle through *(e.g., deep snow);* to surmount *(difficulties)* **‖** *intr* to force a way out
ēlūcubr·ō -āre -āvī -ātus *or* **ēlūcubr·or -ārī -ātus sum** *tr* to compose by lamplight
ēlū·dō -dere -sī -sus *tr* to elude, parry, avoid; to escape, shun; to delude, deceive; to make fun of; to get the better of, outmaneuver **‖** *intr* to end the game; to behave outrageously with impunity, have free play *(for outrageous conduct)*
ēlū·geō -gēre -xī *tr* to mourn for **‖** *intr* to cease to mourn
ēlumb·is -is -e *adj* **(-bus -a -um)** having a dislocated hip; bland *(style)*
ē·luō -luere -luī -lūtus *tr* to wash off, wash clean; to wash away; to rinse out; *(fig)* to wash away, get rid of **‖** *intr (coll)* to lose one's property, be cleaned out
ēlūsus *pp of* **ēlūdō**
ēlūt·us -a -um *pp of* **ēluō ‖** *adj* watery, insipid; weak

ēluvi·ēs -ēī *f* inundation, overflow; sewage; ravine
ēluvi·ō -ōnis *f* deluge
Elvīn·a -ae *f* **(Hel-)** epithet of Ceres
Ēlys·ium -iī *n* realm of the blessed in the lower world
Ēlysi·us -a -um *adj* Elysian
em *interj* **(hem)** *(in offering some object or fact to s.o., often followed by a dat)* here (there) you are!
emācit·ās -ātis *f* fondness for shopping, mania for buying
ēmad·ēscō -ēscere -uī *intr* to become soaked
ēmancipāti·ō -ōnis *f* **(-cup-)** emancipation; transfer of property
ēmancipāt·us -a -um *adj* transferred; sold
ēmancip·ō -āre -āvī -ātus *tr* **(-cup-)** to transfer; to declare *(a son)* free and independent, emancipate; to surrender, abandon
ēmān·ō -āre -āvī -ātum *intr* to flow down; to trickle out, leak out; to become known **||** *v impers* **ēmānābat** *(w. acc & inf)* word got out that
Ēmathi·a -ae *f* Macedonia; Thessaly, Pharsalus
Ēmath·is -idis *adj (fem only)* Macedonian **||** *fpl* the Pierides
Ēmathi·us -a -um *adj* Macedonian, Thessalian, Pharsalian
ēmātūr·ēscō -ēscere -uī *intr* to begin to ripen; to soften; *(fig)* to mellow
em·āx -ācis *adj* fond of shopping; *(fig) (of a prayer)* bargaining with the gods, haggling
emblēm·a -atis *n* mosaic; inlay
embol·ium -(i)ī *n* interlude; insertion *(in literary work)*
ēmendābil·is -is -e *adj* capable of correction
ēmendātē *adv* faultlessly, pefectly
ēmendāti·ō -ōnis *f* emendation
ēmendāt·or -ōris *m,* **ēmendātr·īx -īcis** *f* corrector, reformer
ēmendāt·us -a -um *adj* faultless
ēmendīc·ō -āre -āvī -ātus *tr* to get by begging
ēmend·ō -āre -āvī -ātus *tr* to emend, correct; to reform, improve, revise; to atone for
ēmēnsus *pp of* **ēmētior**
ēment·ior -īrī -ītus sum *tr* to falsify, fabricate, feign **||** *intr* to tell a lie
ēmerc·or -ārī -ātus sum *tr* to buy up; to obtain through bribery
ēmer·eō -ēre -uī -itus *or* **ēmer·eor -ērī -itus sum** *tr* to earn; to lay under obligation, do *(s.o.)* a favor; *(mil)* to serve out *(term of service)* **||** *intr* to serve out one's time in the army
ēmer·gō -gere -sī *tr* to raise *(from the water)* **||** *refl & pass* to raise oneself up, rise **||** *intr* to emerge; to rise *(in power);* to extricate oneself; *(w.* **ex)** to get clear of
ēmerit·us -a -um *pp of* **ēmereō ||** *adj (mil)* discharged; *(fig)* ready to be let out to pasture **||** *m* veteran
ēmersus *pp of* **ēmergō**
emetic·a -ae *f* an emetic
ē·mētior -mētīrī -mēnsus sum *tr* to measure out; to traverse, travel over; to live through; to impart
ēmet·ō -ere *tr* to mow down; *(w. abl)* to reap from
ēmi- = hēmi-
ēmic·ō -āre -uī -ātum *intr* to dart out, dash out; *(of liquids)* to spurt out; *(of flame)* to shoot out; *(fig)* to stand out, be conspicuous
ēmigr·ō -āre -āvī -ātum *intr* to move out, depart; **ē vītā ēmigrāre** to pass on
ēmināti·ō -ōnis *f* threatening, blustering
ēmin·ēns -entis *adj* projecting, prominent, high; eminent
ēminenti·a -ae *f* projection, prominence; *(in painting)* highlights, foreground
ēmin·eō -ēre -uī *intr* to stand out, project; to be conspicuous; *(in paintings)* to be highlighted, stand out against a background
ēmin·or -ārī *tr* to threaten
ēminus *adv* at long range, at a distance; from afar
ēmīr·or -ārī -ātus sum *tr* to be greatly surprised at, stand aghast at
ēmissār·ium -(i)ī *n* drain, outlet
ēmissār·ius -(i)ī *m* scout, spy
ēmissīci·us -a -um *adj* spying; **oculī ēmissīciī** prying eyes
ēmissi·ō -ōnis *f* discharge, hurling, shooting; releasing, letting off
ēmissus *pp of* **ēmittō**
ēmiss·us -ūs *m* emission, sending forth; hurling, shooting
ē·mittō -mittere -mīsī -missus *tr* to send out; to hurl, shoot; to let go, let slip, let loose, drop, release, let out; to publish; to allow to escape; to emancipate, set at liberty; to utter; to pass up *(opportunity);* **animam ēmittere** to give up the ghost **||** *refl & pass (w.* **ex)** to break out of
emō emere ēmī emptus *tr* to buy; *(w. gen or abl of price)* to buy *(s.th.)* at; to pay for; to gain, obtain; to bribe; **bene emere** to buy at a bargain; **in diem emere** to buy on credit; **male emere** to pay dearly for; **percussōrem emere** to hire a killer
ēmoder·or -ārī *tr* to moderate
ēmodul·or -ārī *tr* to sing the praises of, celebrate in song
ēmōl·ior -īrī -ītus sum *tr* to accomplish with great effort
ēmoll·iō -īre -īvī *or* **-iī -ītus** *tr* to soften; to make mild; to enervate
ēmol·ō -ere — *tr* to grind up

ēmolument·um -ī *n* effort, exertion; reward; achievement, success; profit; advantage, benefit
ēmon·eō -ēre *tr* to admonish earnestly
ēmor·ior -ī -tuus sum *intr* to die; to die off; *(of a fire)* to die down, go out; *(of river)* to peter out; *(fig)* to die out
ēmortuāl·is -is -e *adj* of death
ēmortuus *pp of* **ēmorior**
ē·moveō -movēre -mōvī -mōtus *tr* **(exm-)** to move out, remove, expel; to dislodge; to shake *(e.g., foundations of a wall)*
Empedocl·ēs -is *or* **-ī** *m* philosopher of Sicily who is said to have jumped into the crater of Mt. Etna *(444 B.C.)*
emphas·is -is *f* emphasis, stress
empīric·us -ī *m* empiricist *(physician who relies on experience rather than on scientific theory)*
empor·ium -(i)ī *n* market town; trade mart, market, shopping center
empti·ō -ōnis *f* buying, purchase; thing purchased, purchase
emptit·ō -āre -āvī -ātus *tr* to be in the habit of buying, buy *(regularly)*
empt·or -ōris *m,* **emptr·īx -īcis** *f* purchaser, customer
empt·um -ī *n* a purchase
emptus *pp of* **emō**
ēmūg·iō -īre *tr* to bellow out
ēmul·geō -gēre — -sus *tr* to drain off *(milk);* to drain *(a swamp)*
ēmūnct·us -a -um *adj* refined; snobbish; **nāris ēmūnctae esse** to have discriminating tastes
ē·mungō -mungere -mūnxī -mūnctus *tr* to wipe the nose of; *(fig)* to swindle; *(w. abl)* to cheat *(s.o.)* of ‖ *refl & pass* to blow one's nose
ēmūn·iō -īre -īvī *or* **-iī -ītus** *tr* to build up; to fortify; to make a road through *(woods)*
ēn *interj (in questions)* really?; *(in commands)* come on!; *(to call attention)* hey!
ēnārrābil·is -is -e *adj* explainable, describable, intelligible
ēnārrāti·ō -ōnis *f* description; analysis
ēnārr·ō -āre -āvī -ātus *tr* to explain in detail; to describe; to interpret
ēnāscor ēnāscī ēnātus sum *intr* to grow out, sprout, arise; to be born
ēnat·ō -āre -āvī -ātum *intr* to swim away, escape by swimming; *(fig)* to get away with it
ēnātus *pp of* **ēnāscor**
ēnāvig·ō -āre -āvī -ātus *tr* to sail across, traverse ‖ *intr* to sail away; *(fig)* to escape
encaust·us -a -um *adj* burnt in, painted in encaustic *(i.e., with molten wax as paint)*
Encelad·us *or* **Encelad·os -ī** *m* one of the giants whom Jupiter buried under Mount Etna
endrom·is -idis *f* athlete's bathrobe
Endymi·ōn -ōnis *m* handsome young man with whom Luna fell in love and who was doomed to everlasting sleep on Mt. Patmos; any handsome young man
ēnec·ō *(or* **ēnicō)** **-āre -uī** *(or* **-āvī)** **-tus** *(or* **-ātus)** *tr* to kill, kill off; to exhaust, wear out; *(coll)* to kill, pester to death
ēnervāt·us -a -um *adj* without sinews, without muscles; without energy
ēnerv·is -is -e *or* **ēnerv·us -a -um** *adj* weak, feeble
ēnerv·ō -āre -āvī -ātus *tr* to weaken, enervate, render impotent
ēnicō *see* **ēnecō**
enim *conj* namely, for instance; yes, indeed, certainly; for, you know; in fact, to be sure; *(in replies)* of course, no doubt; for, because
enimvērō *adv* yes indeed, to be sure, certainly; *(ironically)* of course
Enīp·eūs -eī *m* tributary of the River Peneus in Thessaly
ēnīsus *pp of* **ēnītor**
ēnit·eō -ēre -uī *intr* to shine out, sparkle; to be conspicuous
ēnit·ēscō -ēscere *intr* to begin to shine, begin to brighten; to become conspicuous
ēnī·tor -tī -sus *or* **-xus sum** *tr* to work one's way up, climb; to give birth to ‖ *intr* to exert oneself, make an effort; *(w. inf)* to struggle to, strive to
ēnīxē *adv* strenuously, earnestly
ēnīx·us -a -um *pp of* **ēnītor** ‖ *adj* strenuous, earnest
Enni·us -(i)ī *m* father of Latin literature, writer of tragedy, comedy, epic, and satire *(239–169 B.C.)*
Ennosigae·us -ī *m (epithet of Neptune)* Earthshaker
ēn·ō -āre -āvī -ātum *intr* to swim out, swim away, escape by swimming
ēnōdātē *adv* without knots; clearly
ēnōdāti·ō -ōnis *f* solution, explanation
ēnōd·is -is -e *adj* without knots; clear
ēnōd·ō -āre -āvī -ātus *tr* to explain, clarify
ēnorm·is -is -e *adj* abnormal; enormous; shapeless, irregular; ill-fitting *(clothes);* extravagant *(style)*
ēnormit·ās -ātis *f* enormity; irregular shape
ēnōt·ēscō -ēscere -uī *intr* to become known
ēnot·ō -āre -āvī -ātus *tr* to take notes of, note down
ēnsicul·us -ī *m* little sword
ēnsif·er *or* **ēnsig·er -era -erum** *adj* with a sword, wearing a sword
-ēns·is -is -e *adj suf* forms adjectives mainly from words denoting places: **Athēniēnsis** Athenian, from Athens
ēns·is -is *m* sword
enterocēl·ē -ēs *f* hernia of the intestines
enterocēlic·us -a -um *adj* suffering from an intestinal hernia

entheāt·us -a -um *adj* filled with divine frenzy
enthe·us -a -um *adj* inspired; inspiring, that fills with divine frenzy
enthȳmēm·a -atis *n* thought, reflection; *(phil)* condensed syllogism
ēnū·bō -bere -psī *intr (of a woman)* to marry outside her rank
ēnucleātē *adv* precisely
ēnucleāt·us -a -um *adj* precise, to the point; straightforward, simple *(style);* fine-drawn *(arguments)*
ēnucle·ō -āre -āvī -ātus *tr (fig)* to examine carefully; to weigh *(one's decision)*
ēnumerāti·ō -ōnis *f* enumeration
ēnumer·ō -āre -āvī -ātus *tr* to count up; to count out, pay out; to recount, detail, enumerate
ēnūntiāti·ō -ōnis *f* announcement; *(in logic)* assertion; proposition; *(gram)* pronunciation *(of a word or syllable)*
ēnūnti·ō -āre -āvī -ātus *tr* to disclose, reveal, betray; to say, assert, express; to proclaim publicly; *(gram)* to pronounce *(a word or syllable)*
ēnūpti·ō -ōnis *f* right of a woman to marry outside her clan
ēnūtr·iō -īre -īvī *or* **-iī -ītus** *tr* to nourish, raise, bring up
Enȳ·ō -us *f* Greek goddess of war; *(fig)* war
eō *adv* there, to that place; to that end, to that purpose; so far, to such an extent, to such a pitch; on that account, for that reason, with that in view; **eō erō brevior** I will be all the briefer; **eō magis** all the more; **eō maximē quod** especially because; **eō quō** to the place to which; **quō ... eō** the ... the ... ; **quō plūs potestis, eō moderātius imperiō ūtī dēbētis** the more power you have, the more moderately you ought to use that power; **eō quod** because; **eō ... ut** to such an extent ... that
eō īre īvī *or* **iī itum** *intr* to go; to walk, sail, ride; *(of time)* to pass; *(of events)* to go on, happen, turn out; *(of things)* to give way; *(mil)* to march; *(w. abl)* to stem from; **in sententiam īre** *(pol)* to vote for a bill
eōdem *adv* to the same place, purpose, *or* person
Ēōs *(nom only) f* Dawn *(the Latin Aurora, daughter of Hyperion and Theia or Euryphaëssa)*
Ēō·us -a -um *adj* of the dawn; Eastern, oriental ‖ *m* morning star; dawn; an oriental
Ēō·us -ī *m* morning star ‖ inhabitant of the East ‖ one of the horses of the sun ‖ dawn
Epamīnōnd·ās -ae *m* famous Theban general who defeated the Spartans in two great battles *(c. 371 B.C.)*
epaphaeres·is -is *f* a second close clip *(of the hair)*
Epaph·us -ī *m* son of Jupiter and Io
ēpāst·us -a -um *adj* eaten up
Epē·us *or* **Epī·us -ī** *m* builder of the Trojan horse
ephēb·us -ī *m (Greek)* young man
ephēmer·is -idis *or* **-idos** *f* diary; journal
Ephes·us *or* **Ephes·os -ī** *f* city on the coast of Asia Minor with famous temple of Diana
ephippiāt·us -a -um *adj* riding a saddled horse
ephipp·ium -iī *n* saddle
ephor·us -ī *m* ephor *(Spartan magistrate)*
Ephyr·a -ae *or* **Ephyr·ē -ēs** *f* ancient name of Corinth
Epicharm·us -ī *m* Sicilian Greek writer of early comedy *(530?–440 B.C.)*
epichys·is -is *f* wine ladle
epicōp·us -a -um *adj* furnished with oars; **phasēlus epicōpus** rowboat
epicroc·us -a -um *adj* thin yellow *(garment)* ‖ *n* thin yellow garment
Epicūr·us -ī *m* Greek philosopher, born on Samos *(342–270 B.C.)*
epic·us -a -um *adj* epic ‖ **Epic·ī -ōrum** *mpl* epic poets
epidīctic·us -a -um *adj* showy
epidipn·is -idis *f* a dessert
epigramm·a -atis *or* **-atos** *n* inscription, epitaph; short poem, epigram
epilog·us -ī *m* epilogue, peroration
epimēni·a -ōrum *npl* month's rations
Epimēth·eūs -eī *m* son of Iapetus and brother of Prometheus
epinīc·ion -iī *n* victory song
epiraed·ium -(i)ī *n* horse-drawn carriage
Ēpīrōt·ēs -ae *m* native of Epirus
Ēpīr·us *or* **Ēpīr·os -ī** *f* district of N.W. Greece
epistol·ium -(i)ī *n* note
epistul·a -ae *f* **(-tol-)** letter; **ab epistulīs** *(in apposition)* secretary
epistulār·is -is -e *adj* **(-tol-)** concerned with letters; **chartae epistulārēs** writing paper, stationery
epitaph·ium -(i)ī *n* eulogy
epithalam·ium -(i)ī *n* wedding song
epithēc·a -ae *f* addition, increase
epitom·a -ae *or* **epitom·ē -ēs** *f* epitome, abridgment
epitȳr·um -ī *n* olive salad
epoch·ē -ēs *f* suspension of judgment
ep·ops -opis *m* hoopoe *(an Old World bird having a fanlike crest and a slender downward-curving bill)*
epos *(nom & acc only; pl:* **opē)** *n* epic
ēpōt·us -a -um *adj* **(exp-)** drunk dry, drained to the dregs; *(fig)* swallowed up, absorbed
epul·ae -ārum *fpl* courses, dishes; sumptuous meal; **epulae rēgum** dinner fit for a king

epulār·is -is -e *adj* at dinner, of a dinner; **sermō epulāris** talk at dinner, table talk
epulāti·ō -ōnis *f* banqueting
epul·ō -ōnis *m* dinner guest; **Trēsvirī** *(or* **Septemvirī) Epulōnēs** college of priests who superintended the state dinner to the gods
epul·or -ārī -ātus sum *tr* to feast on ‖ *intr* to attend a dinner; *(w. abl)* to feast on
epul·um -ī *n* banquet, feast
equ·a -ae *f* mare
Equ·es -itis *m* knight; capitalist *(member of Roman middle class);* equestrian order, bourgeoisie
equ·es -itis *m* rider; trooper, cavalryman; cavalry ‖ *mpl* cavalry
eques·ter *or* **equest·ris -tris -tre** *adj* equestrian; cavalry; middle-class
equidem *adv* truly, indeed, in any event; of course, to be sure; *(w. first person)* for my part, as far as I am concerned
equīn·us -a -um *adj* horse's
equīri·a -ōrum *npl* **(equirr-)** horse races *(held annually in the Campus Martius in honor of Mars)*
equitāt·us -ūs *m* cavalry
equit·ō -āre -āvī -ātum *intr* to ride, ride a horse
equule·us -ī *m* foal, colt; small equestrian statue; torture rack
equ·us -ī (equos *and* **equom** *in pre-Augustan period,* **ecus** *and* **ecum** *from Aug. period to end of 1st cent.* A.D., **equus** *and* **equum** *after that) m* horse; **equīs virīsque** *(or* **equīs virīs)** *(fig)* with might and main; **equō merēre** to serve in the cavalry; **equō vehī** to ride a horse; **equus bipēs** sea horse; **in equō** mounted ‖ *mpl* chariot
er·a *or* **her·a -ae** *f* lady of the house
ērādīc·ō -āre -āvī -ātus *tr* **(exr-)** to uproot; to destroy utterly
ērā·dō -dere -sī -sus *tr* to scratch out, erase, obliterate
eran·us -ī *m* mutual insurance society *(in Greece)*
Erāt·ō *(nom and voc only) f* Muse of erotic poetry; Muse
Eratosthen·ēs -is *m* Alexandrine geographer, poet, and philosopher *(276–196* B.C.*)*
erc- *see* **herc-**
Ereb·us -ī *m* god of darkness, son of Chaos and brother of Night; lower world
Erechthē·us -a -um *adj* of Erechtheus; *(poet)* Athenian
Erechth·eūs -eī *m* king of Athens, son of Hephaestus ‖ grandson of former and son of Pandion
Erechthīd·ae -ārum *mpl* descendants of Erechtheus; *(poet)* Athenians
ērēct·us -a -um *pp of* **ērigō** ‖ *adj* erect, upright; noble, elevated, lofty; haughty; attentive, alert, tense; resolute, courageous
ērēp·ō -ere -sī *tr* to crawl through *(a field);* to crawl up *(a mountain)* ‖ *intr* to crawl out
ērepti·ō -ōnis *f* robbery
ērept·or -ōris *m* robber
ēreptus *pp of* **ēripiō**
Eretri·a -ae *f* city on the island of Euboea, birthplace of the philosopher Menedemus
Eretriac·ī -ōrum *mpl* philosophers of the school of Menedemus
ergā *(prep) (w. acc)* to, toward; against; next to
ergastul·um -ī *n* prison *(on a large estate where unruly slaves were kept);* chain gang
ergō *adv* therefore, consequently; *(resumptive)* well then, I say, as I was saying; *(w. imperatives)* then, now
ergō *prep (w. preceding gen)* for the sake of, in consequence of; **illīus ergō** for his sake
Erichthon·ius -iī *m* king of Athens ‖ son of Dardanus, father of Tros, and king of Troy
ēric·ius -(i)ī *m* hedgehog; *(mil)* beam with iron spikes
Ēridan·us -ī *m* Greek name of the river Padus *(modern Po); (astr)* constellation
erifug·a -ae *m* runaway slave
ē·rigō -rigere -rēxī -rēctus *tr* to set up straight, straighten out *(e.g., tree);* to set up, erect; to cheer up, encourage; to arouse, excite; *(mil)* to deploy troops on a slope ‖ *refl & pass* to raise oneself, get up
Ērigon·ē -ēs *f (astr)* Virgo *(constellation)*
erīl·is -is -e *or* **herīl·is -is -e** *adj* master's, mistress's
Erīn·ys -yos *f* Fury; *(fig)* frenzy
Eriphȳl·a -ae *or* **Eriphȳl·ē -ēs** *f* wife of the seer Amphiaraus; a treacherous wife
ē·ripiō -ripere -ripuī -reptus *tr* to snatch away, pull out, tear out; to deliver, rescue; to rob; *(w. dat or w.* **ab** *or* **ex)** to take away from, rescue from ‖ *refl* to escape
-ern·us -a -um *adjl suf* forms adjectives denoting times: **hestiernus** yesterday's
ērogāti·ō -ōnis *f* expenditure, outlay, payment
ērogit·ō -āre *tr* to try hard to find out
ērog·ō -āre -āvī -ātus *tr* to allocate, expend; to bequeath; *(w.* **in** *+ acc)* **1** to allocate to, spend on; **2** to bequeath to
Er·ōs -ōtis *m* Love, Cupid, Eros
errābund·us -a -um *adj* wandering, straggling
errātic·us -a -um *adj* erratic, wandering; **stella errātica** planet
errāti·ō -ōnis *f* wandering
errāt·um -ī *n* error, mistake
errāt·us -ūs *m* roving, wandering about

err·ō -āre -āvī -ātum *intr* to wander, roam; to lose one's way, stray; to waver; to err, make a mistake, be mistaken; *(w.* **in** + *abl)* to be mistaken about
err·ō -ōnis *m* vagrant, vagabond
err·or -ōris *m* wandering; wavering, uncertainty; error; cause of error, deception; maze, winding, intricacy
ērubēscendus -a -um *adj* enough to make one blush, shameful
ērub·ēscō -ēscere -uī *tr* to blush at; to be ashamed of; to respect **II** *intr* to grow red, redden; to blush
ērūc·a -ae *f (bot)* cole *(type of cabbage)*
ēruct·ō -āre -āvī -ātus *tr* to belch, vomit; to talk drunkenly about
ērud·iō -īre -iī *or* **-īvī -ītus** *tr* to educate, teach, instruct; *(w. double acc)* to teach *(s.o. s.th.)*
ērudītē *adv* learnedly
ērudīti·ō -ōnis *f* instructing, instruction; erudition, learning
ērudītul·us -a -um *adj* somewhat experienced, somewhat skilled
ērudīt·us -a -um *adj* educated, learned, accomplished
ēruī *perf of* **ēruō**
ē·rumpō -rumpere -rūpī -ruptus *tr* to cause to break out; to give vent to; **īram in hostēs ērumpere** to vent one's wrath on the enemy **II** *intr* to burst out, break out
ēru·ō -ere -ī -tus *tr* to uproot, dig out; to tear out, gouge out *(eyes);* to undermine, demolish, destroy; to draw out, elicit; to churn up *(sea);* to plow up
ērupti·ō -ōnis *f* eruption; *(bot)* sprouting; *(mil)* sortie
ēruptus *pp of* **ērumpō**
er·us *or* **her·us -ī** *m* master of the house, head of the family; lord, owner; *(coll)* boss
ērutus *pp of* **ēruō**
erv·um -ī *n (bot)* vetch *(cultivated for its edible seeds)*
Erycīn·us -a -um *adj* of Mt. Eryx *(in N.W. Sicily);* of Venus; Sicilian **II** *f* Venus
Erymanth·is -idos *f* Callisto *(changed first into a bear and then into a constellation)*
Erymanth·us -ī *m* mountain range in Arcadia, where Hercules killed a boar
Erythē·a -ae *f* small island in the Bay of Gades, home of the giant Geryon
erythīn·us -ī *m* red mullet *(fish)*
Er·yx -ycis *or* **Eryc·us -ī** *m* Eryx *(mountain on N.W. coast of Sicily, famous for its temple to Venus)* **II** son of Venus and Butes, half-brother of Aeneas
ēsc·a -ae *f* dish; food; bait
ēscāri·us -a -um *adj* of food; of bait **II** *npl* dishes, courses
ēscen·dō -dere -dī -sus *tr & intr* to climb, climb up; to sail up
ēscēnsi·ō -ōnis *f* climbing up; hostile raid *(from the coast)*
ēscēns·us -ūs *m* ascent
-ēsc·ō -ere *vbl suf* formed from nouns and adjectives, with inchoative force: **senēscere** to begin to be old, get old
ēsculent·us -a -um *adj* edible **II** *npl* edibles, foodstuffs
ēsculētum *see* **aesculētum**
ēsculus *see* **aesculus**
-ēsim·us *or* **-ēnsim·us -a -um** *suf* used to form ordinal numbers from 20 to 1000
ēsit·ō -āre -āvī -ātus *tr* **(essi-)** to be used to eating
Ēsquili·ae -ārum *fpl* Esquiline Hill
Ēsquilīn·us -a -um *adj* Esquiline **II** *f* Esquiline gate
Ēsquili·us -a -um *adj* Esquiline
esse *inf of* **sum** to be; **ēsse** *inf of* **edō** to eat
essedār·ius -(i)ī *m* soldier *or* gladiator fighting from a chariot
essed·um -ī *n* Gallic war chariot; light traveling carriage
essenti·a -ae *f* essence
essitō *see* **ēsitō**
-ess·ō -ere -īvī *or* **-iī -ītus** *vbl suf* with conative force: **capessere** to try to catch, snatch at, catch at eagerly, strive for
essuri·ō -ōnis *m* a hungry man
ēstr·īx -īcis *f* glutton *(female)*
ēsuriāl·is -is -e *adj* **(ess-)** of hunger
ēsur·iō -īre *tr* **(ess-)** to be hungry for **II** *intr* to be hungry
ēsuri·ō -ōnis *m* a hungry man
ēsurīti·ō -ōnis *f* hunger
ēsus *pp of* **edō**
ēs·us -ūs *m* eating; **ēsū** in the eating
et *adv* besides, also; even, I mean
et *conj* and; *(for emphasis)* and even, yes and; *(antithetical)* however, but; **et ... et** both ... and, not only ... but also
etenim *conj* for, and as a matter of fact
etēsi·ae -ārum *mpl (fpl)* periodic winds *(on the Aegean Sea)*; monsoons
ēthic·ē -ēs *f* ethics
ēthologi·a -ae *f* portrayal of character
ētholog·us -ī *m* impersonator
etiam *adv & conj* also, and also, besides, likewise; *(of time)* yet, as yet, still, even now; *(in affirmation)* yes, yes indeed, certainly, by all means; *(emphatic)* even, rather; *(w. emphatic imperatives)* but just; **etiam atque etiam** again and again
etiamnunc *or* **etiamnum** *adv* even now, still
etiamsī *conj* even if, although
etiamtum *or* **etiamtunc** *adv* even then, till then, still
Etrūri·a -ae *f* district N. of Rome
Etrusc·us -a -um *adj* Etruscan, of Etruria **II** *mpl* the Etruscans
etsī *conj* even if, although

-ēt·um -ī *neut suf* formed mainly from names of plants to denote the place where they grow: **rosētum** rose bed
etymologi·a -ae *f* etymology
eu *interj (sometimes ironic)* fine!, great!
Euān *or* **Euhān** *m* cult title of Bacchus, cult cry
eu·āns *or* **euh·āns -antis** *adj* crying Eu(h)an *(Bacchic cry)*
euax *interj* hurray!
Euboe·a -ae *f* Greek island off E. coast of Attica and Boeotia
Euēn·us -ī *m* a king of Aetolia, father of Marpessa ‖ river in Aetolia
euge *or* **eugepae** *interj* terrific!
euhāns *see* **euāns**
Euhēmer·us -ī *m* Greek writer who attempted to prove that all ancient myths were basically historical events *(c. 316 B.C.)*
Euh·ius -iī *m* Bacchus
Euhoe *or* **Euoe** *interj* ecstatic cry of revelers at festival of Bacchus
Euius *see* **Euhius**
Eumenid·ēs -um *fpl* Eumenides *or* Erinyes *or* Furies *(goddesses of vengeance)*
eunūch·us -ī *m* eunuch
Euoe *see* **Euhoe**
Euphorb·us -ī *m* brave Trojan warrior whose soul Pythagoras asserted had transmigrated to himself
Euphrāt·ēs -is *or* **-ae** *or* **-ī** *m* Euphrates River
Eupol·is -idis *or* **-is** *m* Athenian comic playwright *(446?–411 B.C.)*
Eurīpid·ēs -is *m* Athenian tragic playwright *(485–405 B.C.)*
eurīp·us -ī *m* channel; trench running between the arena and the seats in the Circus Maximus ‖ **Eurīpus** strait between Boeotia and Euboea
Eurōp·a -ae *or* **Eurōp·ē -ēs** *f* Europe ‖ Europa, daughter of Agenor and mother of Sarpedon, Rhadamantus, and Minos by Jupiter, who, in the shape of a bull, carried her off to Crete
Eurōt·ās -ae *m* chief river of Laconia in S. Greece, on which Sparta stood
Eur·us -ī *m* S.E. wind; east wind; wind
Eurydic·ē -ēs *f* wife of Orpheus
Eurysth·eus -eī *m* king of Argos who imposed the Twelve Labors on Hercules
Euryt·is -idos *f* daughter of Eurytus, king of Oechalia *(i.e., Iole)*
-e·us -a -um *adjl suf* formed from nouns, usually to denote material: **ligneus** (made) of wood, wooden
euschēmē *adv* gracefully
Euterp·ē -ēs *f* Muse *(later associated with the reed pipe)*
Euxīn·us Pont·us -ī *m* Black Sea
ēvā·dō -dere -sī -sus *tr* to pass, pass by; to pass through, escape ‖ *intr* to go out; to turn out to be, become, prove to be; to get away; to climb; **quō ēvādis?** *(fig)* what's your point?
ēvag·or -ārī -ātus sum *tr* to stray beyond, transgress ‖ *intr (fig)* to spread; *(mil)* to maneuver
ēval·ēscō -ēscere -uī *intr* to grow strong; to increase; *(of a word or expression)* to gain currency; *(w. inf)* to be able to; *(w.* **in** *+ acc)* to develop into
ēvalid·us -a -um *adj* very strong
Evan·der *or* **Evan·drus -drī** *m* Evander *(Arcadian who founded Pallanteum at the foot of the Palatine Hill)*
ēvān·ēscō -ēscere -uī *intr* to vanish, pass away, die away; to be forgotten; *(of liquids)* to evaporate
ēvānid·us -a -um *adj* vanishing
ēvast·ō -āre -āvī -ātus *tr* to devastate, wreck completely
ēvāsus *pp of* **ēvādō**
ēve·hō -here -xī -ctus *tr* to carry out; to spread abroad; to lift up, raise ‖ *pass* to ride, sail, drift
ē·vellō -vellere -vellī *or* **-vulsī -vulsus** *tr* to pluck out; to eradicate; to extract *(teeth)*
ē·veniō -venīre -vēnī -ventum *intr* to come out, come forth; to come to pass, happen; to turn out, result, end ‖ *v impers* it happens
ēvent·um -ī *n* event, occurrence; result, effect, consequence; fortune; experience
ēvent·us -ūs *m* happening; outcome, event; lot, fate; issue, consequence, result; occurrence, accident; good fortune, success
Evēn·us -ī *m* river in Aetolia
ēverber·ō -āre -āvī -ātus *tr* to hit hard; to beat up
ēverricul·um -ī *n* broom; dragnet
ēver·rō -rere -rī -sus *tr* to sweep out; *(fig)* to clean out, strip
ēversi·ō -ōnis *f* overthrow, subversion, destruction
ēvers·or -ōris *m* destroyer
ēversus *pp of* **ēverrō** *and of* **ēvertō**
ēver·tō -tere -tī -sus *tr* **(-vor-)** to overturn, turn upside down; to overthrow; to expel; to subvert, destroy, ruin
ēvestīgāt·us -a -um *adj* tracked down
ēvictus *pp of* **ēvincō**
ēvid·ēns -entis *adj* evident, visible, plain, clear, obvious
ēvidenter *adv* plainly, obviously
ēvidenti·a -ae *f* obviousness; evidence; *(rhet)* vividness
ēvigil·ō -āre -āvī -ātus *tr* to watch through *(the night);* to work through the night writing *(e.g., books)* ‖ *intr* to be wide-awake; *(fig)* to be on one's toes
ēvīl·ēscō -ēscere -uī *intr* to depreciate, become worthless

ē·vinciō -vincīre -vīnxī -vīnctus *tr* to tie up; to crown, wreathe
ē·vincō -vincere -vīcī -victus *tr* to conquer completely, trounce; to prevail over
ēvīnctus *pp of* **ēvinciō**
ēvirāt·us -a -um *adj* effeminate
ēvir·ō -āre -āvī -ātus *tr* to castrate, emasculate
ēviscer·ō -āre -āvī -ātus *tr* to disembowel, gut, eviscerate; to mangle
ēvītābil·is -is -e *adj* avoidable
ēvītāti·ō -ōnis *f* avoidance
ēvīt·ō -āre -āvī -ātus *tr* to avoid, escape
ēvocāt·ī -ōrum *mpl* veterans called up again, reenlisted veterans
ēvocāt·or -ōris *m* recruiter
ēvoc·ō -āre -āvī -ātus *tr* to call out, summon; to challenge; to evoke, excite, stir; *(mil)* to call up *(for service)*
ēvolgō *see* **ēvulgō**
ēvol·ō -āre -āvī -ātum *intr* to fly out, fly away; to rush out; *(fig)* to soar
ēvolsi·ō -ōnis *f* extraction
ēvolūti·ō -ōnis *f* unrolling a scroll; *(fig)* reading
ēvol·vō -vere -vī -ūtus *tr* to roll out, unroll, unfold; to spread; to read, study; to disclose; to free, extricate; to repel; to evolve, develop
ēvom·ō -ere -uī -itus *tr* to vomit, spew out, disgorge
ēvulg·ō -āre -āvī -ātus *tr* **(-vol-)** to divulge, make public
ēvulsi·ō -ōnis *f* extraction
ēvulsus *pp of* **ēvellō**
ex- or **ē-** *pref* **(ex-** normally before vowels, **c, q, p, s, t; s** is sometimes absorbed, e.g., **expectāre; x** is dropped in **ēscendere, ēpotāre; e-** before **g, b, d, r, l, m, n, i, u;** with **f, ff-** is commonly formed, also **ecf-)** **1** out: **exīre** to go out; **2** away: **ēfugere** to run away; **3** well, thoroughly: **ēdiscere** to learn thoroughly, learn by heart; **4** hard, up: **ēverberāre** to beat hard, beat up; **5** *(negative, deprivation)* -less, un-: **exsanguis** unbloody; **exos** boneless; **6** up: **exaggerāre** to pile up
ex *or* **ē** *prep (w. abl)* **1** *(of space)* out of, from: **ex conciliō īre** to come out of the assembly; **2** *(of space)* down from: **sē ex altissimō praecipitāre** to jump down from a great height; **3** *(of space)* up from: **ē lectō surgere** to get up from his bed; **4** *(of time)* from, from … onward, following, since: **ex eō** *(or* **ex illō** *or* **ex quō)** from that time on, ever since then; **5** *(of time)* right after: **ex imbre** right after the rain; **6** *(of material of which s.th. consists)* of: **statua ex aurō** a statue of gold; **7** *(of parentage, racial origin)* by, from; **trēs fīliōs ex eā generāvit** he had three children by her; **8** *(of cause or origin)* from, through, by, on account of, by reason of: **ex aere aliēnō commōtus** upset because of his debts; **9** *(derivation of a word)* from, after: **appellāta est ex virō virtus** "manliness" is derived from "man"; **10** *(in partitive sense)* of, out of, from among: **paucōs ex suīs dēperdidit** he lost few of his own men; **11** *(indicating extent):* **cōpiae ex parte dēlētae, ex parte captae** troops partly destroyed, partly captured; **12** *(indicating repetition)* after: **bella ex bellīs serere** to sow the seeds of war after war; **diēs ex diē** day after day; **13** *(indicating recovery)* **ex vulnere refectus** recovered from a wound; **14** *(indicating point from which action is performed)* from: **ex equō pugnāre** to fight from a horse *(i.e., on horseback);* **ex itinere pugnāre** to fight en route; **15** *(indicating conformity)* after, according to, in conformity with: **ex cōnsuētūdine cōtīdiānā** according to their daily habit; **17** *(w. verbs of learning)* from: **ex litterīs tuīs intellēxī** I understood from your letter
e(x)sangu·is -is -e *adj* bloodless; pale; feeble; causing paleness
exacerb·ō -āre -āvī -ātus *tr* to exasperate, enrage; to exacerbate, make worse
exācti·ō -ōnis *f* driving out, expulsion; demanding; exaction, collection; supervision *(of public works)*
exāct·or -ōris *m* expeller; collector; supervisor
exāct·us -a -um *pp of* **exigō** ‖ *adj* exact, precise
exac·uō -uere -uī -ūtus *tr* to sharpen; to stimulate, spur, inflame
exadversum *or* **exadversus** *adv* **(-vor-)** on the opposite side ‖ *prep (w. dat or acc)* across from, right opposite
exaedificāti·ō -ōnis *f* construction
exaedific·ō -āre -āvī -ātus *tr* to finish building, build, construct; *(fig)* to complete
exaequāti·ō -ōnis *f* leveling; uniformity
exaequ·ō -āre -āvī -ātus *tr* to level, make level; *(fig)* to equal, regard as equal ‖ *pass (w. dat)* to be put on the same level with
exaestu·ō -āre -āvī -ātum *intr* to seethe, boil; to ferment
exaggerāti·ō -ōnis *f* exaltation; *(rhet)* intensification *(by repetition or piling up);* **animī exaggerātiō** broadening of the mind
exagger·ō -āre -āvī -ātus *tr* to pile up; to enlarge; to enhance
exagitāt·or -ōris *m* critic
exagit·ō -āre -āvī -ātus *tr* to stir up, keep on the move; to scare away; to criticize, satirize; to irritate; to arouse *(feelings)*
exagōg·a -ae *or* **exagōgē -ēs** *f* exportation
exalb·ēscō -ēscere -uī *intr* to turn pale

exām·en -inis *n* swarm; crowd; tongue of a scale; weighing, consideration
exāmin·ō -āre -āvī -ātus *tr* to weigh, balance; to examine ‖ *intr* to swarm
examussim *adv* exactly
exancl·ō -āre -āvī -ātus *tr* to draw off, drain; to go through *(e.g., a war)*
exanimāl·is -is -e *adj* dead, lifeless; deadly
exanimāti·ō -ōnis *f* breathlessness; terror, panic
exanim·is -is -e *or* **exanim·us -a -um** *adj* breathless, terrified; lifeless; fainting
exanim·ō -āre -āvī -ātus *tr* to knock the breath out of; to tire, weaken; to deprive of life, kill; to scare out of one's wits; to dishearten; to agitate
exanimus *see* **exanimis**
exār·dēscō -dēscere -sī -sum *intr* to catch fire; *(lit & fig)* to flare up
exār·ēscō -ēscere -uī *intr* to become quite dry, dry up
exarm·ō -āre -āvī -ātus *tr* to disarm
exar·ō -āre -āvī -ātus *tr* to plow up; to raise, produce; to write *(on wax with a stylus)*, write down, note; to furrow, wrinkle; **frontem rūgīs exarāre** to knit one's brows
exasper·ō -āre -āvī -ātus *tr* to make rough, roughen; to exasperate; to make worse
exauctōr·ō -āre -āvī -ātus *tr (mil)* to discharge; *(mil)* to give a dishonorable discharge to
exaud·iō -īre -īvī *or* **-iī -ītus** *tr* to hear clearly; to discern; to perceive, understand; to listen to; to grant
exaug·eō -ēre *tr* to increase greatly
exaugurāti·ō -ōnis *f* deconsecration
exaugur·ō -āre -āvī -ātus *tr* to deconsecrate
exauspic·ō -āre -āvī *intr (w.* **ex)** *(hum)* to come out of *(e.g., chains)* with good auspices
exb- = ēb-
exballist·ō -āre *tr* to finish off, batter down the defenses of
exbibō *see* **ēbibō**
exc- = exsc-
excaec·ō -āre -āvī -ātus *tr* to blind; to block up *(a river, pipe);* to dim, darken
excalceāt·us -a -um *adj* unshod, barefoot; *(of an actor)* not wearing the buskin, acting in comedy ‖ *mpl* comic actors
excalce·ō -āre *tr* **excalceāre pedēs** take off the shoes
excandēscenti·a -ae *f* mounting anger, outburst of anger
excand·ēscō -ēscere -uī *intr* to grow white hot; to burst into a rage, flare up, reach a pitch *(of emotion)*
excant·ō -āre -āvī -ātus *tr* to charm away
excarnific·ō -āre -āvī -ātus *tr* **(-nu-)** to tear to pieces, torture to death; to torment *(mentally)*
excav·ō -āre -āvī -ātus *tr* to hollow out
ex·cēdō -cēdere -cessī -cessus *tr* to exceed, pass, surpass ‖ *intr* to go out, go away, withdraw, depart, disappear; to die; **ē mediō** *(or* **ē vītā)** **excēdere** to depart this life
excell·ēns -entis *adj* excellent, superior
excellenter *adv* excellently
excellenti·a -ae *f* excellence, superiority; **per excellentiam** par excellence
excell·ō -ere -uī *intr* to excel; *(w. dat or* **super** *+ acc)* to be superior to, surpass; *(w. abl or* **in** *+ abl)* to be superior in, excel in
excelsē *adv* high, loftily
excelsit·ās -ātis *f* loftiness
excels·us -a -um *adj* high, lofty; tall; eminent ‖ *n* height, high ground; high social status; **in excelsō aetātem** *(or* **vītam)** **agere** to be in the limelight
excepti·ō -ōnis *f* exception, restriction, limitation; *(leg)* objection raised by a defendant against an accuser's statement; *(leg)* a limiting clause
except·ō -āre -āvī -ātus *tr* to catch; to pick up
exceptus *pp of* **excipiō**
ex·cernō -cernere -crēvī -crētus *tr* to sift out, separate
excerp·ō -ere -sī -tus *tr* to pick out, extract, to choose; to gather; to leave out, omit
excerpt·um -ī *n* excerpt
excess·us -ūs *m* departure; death; digression
excetr·a -ae *f* water-snake; spiteful woman
excidi·ō -ōnis *f* destruction
excid·ium -(i)ī *n* destruction, overthrow; cause of destruction
ex·cīdō -cīdere -cīdī -cīsus *tr* to cut out, cut off, cut down; to raze, demolish; *(fig)* to banish, eliminate
ex·cidō -cidere -cidī *intr* to fall out; *(of an utterance)* to slip out; to pass away, perish; to degenerate; to disappear; to be forgotten; *(w.* **in** *+ acc)* to degenerate into; *(w. abl or* **ex)** **1** to be deprived of, lose; **2** to forget, miss; *(w. dat or* **dē** *+ abl)* **1** to fall from; **2** to escape from *(lips);* **ē memoriā excidere** to slip one's mind
excieō *see* **exciō**
exc·iō -īre -īvī *or* **-iī -ītus** *or* **-itus** *or* **exci·eō -ēre** *tr* to call *(s.o.)* out, summon; to awaken; to disturb; to frighten; to stir up, excite; to produce, occasion
ex·cipiō -cipere -cēpī -ceptus *tr* to take out, remove; to rescue; to exempt; to take, receive, catch, capture; to follow, succeed to; to intercept; to be exposed to; to incur; to welcome; to take up eagerly; to listen to, overhear; to except, make an exception of; to reach *(a place);* to mention in particular; to take on, withstand
excīsi·ō -ōnis *f* destruction

excīsus *pp of* **excīdō**
excitāt·us -a -um *adj* excited, lively, vigorous; loud
excit·ō -āre -āvī -ātus *tr* to wake up, rouse; to raise, stir up; to erect, construct, produce; to cause, occasion; *(fig)* to arouse, awaken, inspire, stimulate, enliven, encourage; to startle
excītus *or* **excitus** *pp of* **exciō**
excīvī *pp of* **exciō**
exclāmāti·ō -ōnis *f* exclamation
exclām·ō -āre -āvī -ātus *tr & intr* to exclaim, shout, yell
exclū·dō -dere -sī -sus *tr* to exclude, shut out, shut off; to remove, separate; to hatch; *(coll)* to knock out *(an eye);* to prevent
exclūsi·ō -ōnis *f* exclusion
exclūsus *pp of* **exclūdō**
excoctus *pp of* **excoquō**
excōgitāti·ō -ōnis *f* thinking up, inventing, contriving
excōgitāt·us -a -um *adj* carefully thought up; choice
excōgit·ō -āre -āvī -ātus *tr* to think up, devise, contrive
ex·colō -colere -coluī -cultus *tr* to tend, cultivate, work carefully; to refine, ennoble, perfect, improve; to adorn; to worship
ex·coquō -coquere -coxī -coctus *tr* to cook out, boil away; to dry up; to bake thoroughly; to temper *(steel)*
excor·s -dis *adj* senseless, silly
excrēment·um -ī *n* excretion *(spittle, urine, etc.);* excrement
excreō *see* **ex(s)creō**
ex·crēscō -crēscere -crēvī -crētum *intr* to grow out; to grow up, rise up
excruciābil·is -is -e *adj* deserving torture
excruci·ō -āre -āvī -ātus *tr* to torture, torment
excubi·ae -ārum *fpl* standing guard; sentry; watchfire
excubit·or -ōris *m* sentry
excub·ō -ere -uī -itum *intr* to sleep out of doors; to be attentive, be on the alert; *(mil)* to stand guard
excū·dō -dere -dī -sus *tr* to beat out, strike out; to hammer out; to forge; to hatch *(eggs); (fig)* to hammer into shape, write up
exculc·ō -āre -āvī -ātus *tr* to kick out; to tread down on; to stomp
excultus *pp of* **excolō**
excūrāt·us -a -um *adj* carefully attended to
ex·currō -currere -cucurrī *or* **-currī -cursum** *intr* to run out, dash out; *(mil)* to sally forth, make an incursion; to project, extend; *(fig)* to fan out, expand
excursi·ō -ōnis *f* sally, sortie; excursion, short trip *(away from a place);* journey, expedition; digression; outset, opening *(of a speech)*
excurs·or -ōris *m* skirmisher; emissary; courier
excurs·us -ūs *m* sortie, raid, charge; expedition, short trip *(away from a place);* journey; digression; *(geog)* projection
excūsābil·is -is -e *adj* excusable
excūsātē *adv* excusably, without blame
excūsāti·ō -ōnis *f* excuse
excūsāt·us -a -um *adj* free from blame, exempt
excūs·ō -āre -āvī -ātus *tr* to free from blame, excuse; to except; to make excuses for, apologize for; to allege in excuse, plead as an excuse **II** *refl* to apologize
excussus *pp of* **excutiō**
excūsus *pp of* **excūdō**
excu·tiō -tere -ssī -ssus *tr* to shake out, shake off, shake loose; to knock out *(e.g., teeth); (of a horse)* to throw; to shake out *(a garment);* to jilt, give the cold shoulder to; to toss, throw, shoot; to search; to examine, investigate; to discover; *(fig)* to shake off
exd- = ēd-
exdorsu·ō -āre *tr* to fillet *(fish)*
exec- *see* **exsec-**
ex·edō -ēsse *or* **-edere -ēdī -ēsus** *tr* to eat up, consume; to destroy; to prey on; to make hollow; to wear away, corrode; to emaciate
exedr·a -ae *f (semi-circular recess in a wall for sitting, often used for lectures)* sitting room; lecture hall
exedr·ium -(i)ī *n* small sitting room
exempl·ar *or* **exempl·āre -āris** *n* copy; transcript; likeness; pattern, model, ideal
exemplār·is -is -e *adj* following a model **II** *n* copy; transcript
exempl·um -ī *n* sample, example, typical instance; precedent; pattern, make, character; model, pattern *(of conduct);* object lesson; warning; copy; transcript; portrait
exemptus *pp of* **eximō**
exenter·ō -āre -āvī -ātus *tr* **(int-)** to disembowel, gut; *(fig)* to empty *(a purse)*
ex·eō -īre -īvī *or* **-iī -itus** *tr* to pass beyond, cross; to ward off, avoid; *(fig)* to exceed **II** *intr* to go out, go forth; to go away, withdraw, depart, retire; to march out; to disembark; to pour out, gush out, flow out; to escape, be freed; to pass away, perish; *(of time)* to run out; to get out, become public; to burgeon forth; *(of hills)* to rise
exeq- = exseq-
exerc·eō -ēre -uī -itus *tr* to exercise, train; to keep *(s.o.)* busy, keep *(s.o.)* going; to supervise; to cultivate, work *(the soil);* to occupy *(the mind);* to practice *(medicine, patience, skills, etc.);* to carry into effect; to annoy, bother; to worry; to last through *(e.g., winter);* to levy, collect *(taxes);* to

use *(instruments, materials);* to wield *(power, authority);* to run *(a business, a shop);* to carry on *(investigation); (mil)* to drill, train; **aleam exercēre** to gamble; **causidicōs exercēre** to keep the lawyers busy; **faenus exercēre** to lend money at interest; **imperium exercēre** to wield power; **iūstitiam exercēre** to administer justice; **lēgem exercēre** to enforce a law; **medicīnam exercēre** to practice medicine; **negōtium exercēre** to run a business; **quaestiōnem dē sicāriīs exercēre** to conduct prosecutions for murder; **studia līberālia exercēre** to pursue liberal arts; **tabernam exercēre** to run a shop; **vectīgālia exercēre** to levy taxes, collect taxes **ll** *refl* to exercise, do exercises

exercitāti·ō -ōnis *f* exercise, practice, experience, training; cultivation; *(w. gen)* practice in

exercitāt·us -a -um *adj* experienced, trained, disciplined; troubled

exercit·ium -(i)ī *n* exercise, training, practice; written exercise; proficiency

exercit·ō -āre -āvī -ātus *tr* to keep in training, train, exercise; to habituate; to trouble

exercit·or -ōris *m* trainer

exercit·us -a -um *pp of* **exerceō ll** *adj* disciplined; experienced; trying, tough; troubled, harassed

exercit·us -ūs *m* army; infantry; army of followers; swarm, flock, multitude; *(pol)* assembly of the people

exerō *see* **exserō**

exēs·or -ōris *m* corrosive factor, underminer

exēsus *pp of* **exedō**

exf- *see* **eff-**

exhālāti·ō -ōnis *f* exhalation, vapor

exhāl·ō -āre -āvī -ātus *tr* to exhale, give off; **animam** *(or* **vītam) exhālāre** to breathe one's last **ll** *intr* to exhale; to steam

exhau·riō -rīre -sī -stus *tr* to draw out, empty; to drain, exhaust; to deplete; to take away, remove; to drain dry; to bring to an end; to undergo, endure; to carry out *(task);* to discuss fully

exhērēd·ō -āre -āvī -ātus *tr* to disinherit

exhēr·ēs -ēdis *adj* disinherited

exhib·eō -ēre -uī -itus *tr* to hold out; to present, produce; to display, exhibit; to cause, occasion; to render, make

exhilar·ō -āre -āvī -ātus *tr* to cheer up

exhorr·ēscō -ēscere -uī *tr* to shudder at **ll** *intr* to be terrified

exhortāti·ō -ōnis *f* encouragement **ll** *fpl* words of encouragement

exhort·or -ārī -ātus sum *tr* to encourage, exhort

ex·igō -igere -ēgī -āctus *tr* to drive out, push out, thrust out, expel; to demand, exact, collect; to require; to pass, spend, complete *(life, time);* to finish, conclude; to ascertain; to weigh, consider, estimate; to examine; to test; to dispose of

exiguē *adv* slightly, sparingly, barely; briefly

exiguit·ās -ātis *f* shortness, smallness; meagerness, scantiness, scarcity

exigu·us -a -um *adj* slight, small, meager, scanty, poor, paltry, inadequate; a little, a bit of **ll** *n* a bit, a small amount

exiliō *see* **exsiliō**

exīl·is -is -e *adj* thin, small, meager, feeble; *(in wealth)* poor; dreary; depleted *(ranks);* worthless; insincere; *(rhet)* dry, flat, jejune *(style)*

exīlit·ās -ātis *f* thinness; meagerness; dreariness

exīliter *adv* concisely; drearily; parsimoniously; jejunely

exilium *see* **exsilium**

exim *see* **exinde**

eximiē *adv* exceptionally

eximi·us -a -um *adj* excepted; exempt; choice, select; special, exceptional

ex·imō -imere -ēmī -emptus *tr* to take out, take away, remove; to exempt; to free, release, let off; to make an exception of; to waste, lose *(time);* to banish *(worries)*

exin *see* **exinde**

exinān·iō -īre -īvī *or* **-iī -ītus** *tr* to empty; to drain, dry up; to weaken; to strip; *(fig)* to clean out, fleece

exinde *or* **exim** *or* **exin** *adv* from that place, from that point; *(in enumerating)* after that, next, then, furthermore; *(of time)* from that point, after that, then; accordingly

existimāti·ō -ōnis *f* **(-tum-)** opinion, view, judgment, favorable opinion; appraisal; decision, verdict; reputation, good name; *(com)* credit; **vulgī existimātiō** public opinion; **existimātiō tibi est** it is for you to judge

existimāt·or -ōris *m* critic, judge

existim·ō -āre -āvī -ātus *tr* **(-tum-)** to form an opinon of, judge, consider, regard; to think, suppose; **in hostium numerō existimāre** to regard as an enemy

existō *see* **exsistō**

exitiābil·is -is -e *adj* deadly, fatal

exitiāl·is -is -e *adj* deadly, fatal

exiti·ō -ōnis *f* going out, exit

exitiōs·us -a -um *adj* deadly, destructive

exit·ium -(i)ī *n* destruction, ruin; cause of destruction; death

exit·us -ūs *m* going out, exit, departure; way out, outlet; end, close, conclusion; **ad exitum addūcere** to bring to a close

exl- = ēl-

exlecebra *see* **ēlecebra**

ex·lēx -lēgis *adj* without law, exempt from the law; lawless

exm- = **ēm-**
exo- = **exso-**
exobsecr·ō -āre -āvī -ātus *tr* **(exops-)** to beg earnestly, entreat
exocul·ō -āre -āvī -ātus *tr* to knock the eyes out of
exod·ium -(i)ī *n* finale; farce *(presented after the main feature)*
exol·ēscō -ēscere -ēvī -ētum *intr* **(exs-)** to decay, fade; to become obsolete; to grow up, become an adult
exolēt·us -a -um *adj* full-grown **II** *m (fig)* male prostitute
exoner·ō -āre -āvī -ātus *tr* to unload; to empty; *(fig)* to relieve, free
exoptābil·is -is -e *adj* highly desirable, long-awaited
exoptāt·us -a -um *adj* longed-for, welcome, desired
exopt·ō -āre -āvī -ātus *tr* to long for, wish earnestly for, desire greatly
exōrābil·is -is -e *adj* accessible, sympathetic
exōrābul·a -ōrum *npl* enticements, bait, entreaties
exōrāt·or -ōris *m* successful petitioner
exōr·dior -dīrī -sus sum *tr & intr* to begin, start, commence
exōrd·ium -(i)ī *n* beginning, start, commencement; origin; introduction
exor·ior -īrī -tus sum *intr* to come out, come forth, rise, appear; to begin, arise, be caused, be produced
exōrnāti·ō -ōnis *f* embellishment
exōrnāt·or -ōris *m* embellisher
exōrn·ō -āre -āvī -ātus *tr* to fit out, furnish, equip, provide, supply; to adorn, embellish, decorate, set off
exōr·ō -āre -āvī -ātus *tr* to prevail upon, win over; to gain *or* obtain by entreaty; to appease
ex·ors -ortis *see* **exsors**
exōrs·us -a -um *pp of* **exōrdior II** *npl* beginning, commencement; introduction, preamble
exōrs·us -ūs *m* beginning, commencement; introduction
exortus *pp of* **exorior**
exort·us -ūs *m* rising; the East
ex·os -ossis *or* **exoss·is -is -e** *adj* boneless
exōscul·or -ārī -ātus sum *tr* to kiss lovingly, kiss tenderly
exoss·ō -āre -āvī -ātus *tr* to bone, take the bones out of
exōstr·a -ae *f* movable stage; **in exōstrā** in public
exōs·us -a -um *adj* hating, detesting; hateful
exōtic·us -a -um *adj* foreign; exotic; **Graeca exōtica** Magna Graecia *(S. Italy)*
exp- = **exsp-**
expall·ēscō -ēscere -uī *tr* to turn pale at, dread **II** *intr* to turn pale
expalliāt·us -a -um *adj* robbed of one's cloak
expalp·ō -āre -āvī -ātus *tr* to coax out
ex·pan·dō -dere -dī -sus *or* **-passus** *tr* to spread out, unfold, expand
expassus *pp of* **expandō**
expatr·ō -āre -āvī -ātus *tr* to squander
ex·pavēscō -pavēscere -pāvī *tr* to panic at **II** *intr* to panic
expect- = **exspect-**
expecūliāt·us -a -um *adj* stripped of one's savings
exped·iō -īre -īvī *or* **-iī -ītus** *tr* to untie, unwrap; to unfetter; to extricate *(a person from a confined position);* to disentangle; to get ready; to clear for action; to clear *(roads of obstacles);* to solve, clear up *(problems);* to settle *(a debt);* to get *(s.o.)* out of *(troubles);* to put in order, arrange, settle, adjust, set right; to explain, clear up; to disclose; to recount, relate; to supply, provide; to accomplish, achieve **II** *refl* to prepare oneself, get ready **II** *intr* to be useful, be profitable; to set out *(on a military expedition);* to turn out *(in a certain manner); (w. dat)* to be useful to **II** *v impers (w. inf)* it is useful to, is good to
expedītē *adv* freely, nimbly; quickly, expeditiously; unambiguously
expedīti·ō -ōnis *f* (military *or* naval) expedition, campaign; special mission; *(rhet)* proof by elimination
expedīt·us -a -um *adj* unencumbered, unhampered, unobstructed; ready, prompt; ready at hand, convenient; agile; *(of roads)* easy to travel, fast; quick *(mind); (mil)* light-armed; **in expedītō** in readiness, at hand; without hindrance
ex·pellō -pellere -pulī -pulsus *tr* to drive out, expel; to disown
expen·dō -dere -dī -sus *tr* to weigh out; to pay out, pay down, lay out, expend; to rate, estimate; to ponder, consider; to pay *(penalty)*
expēns·us -a -um *adj* paid out, spent **II** *n* payment, expenditure
expergē·faciō -facere -fēcī -factus *tr* to awaken, wake up; to arouse
exper·gīscor -gīscī -rēctus sum *intr* to wake up; to be alert
experg·ō -ere -ī -itus *tr* to wake up
experi·ēns -entis *adj* enterprising, active; *(w. gen)* ready to undergo
experienti·a -ae *f* test, trial, experiment; experience, practice; effort
experīment·um -ī *n* test, experiment, proof; experience; person serving as a test, test-case
exper·ior -īrī -tus sum *tr* to test, try, prove; to experience, endure, find out; to try to do, attempt; to measure strength with **II** *intr* to go to court
experrēctus *pp of* **expergīscor**

exper·s -tis *adj (w. gen)* **1** having no share in, having no part in; **2** devoid of, free from, without
expert·us -a -um *pp of* **experior** ‖ *adj* tried, tested, proved; *(w. gen)* experienced in
expetess·ō -ere *tr* to desire, long for
expet·ō -ere -īvī *or* **-iī -ītus** *tr* to ask for, demand; to exact *(penalty);* to ask about; to aim at, head for; to desire, long for ‖ *intr (w.* **in** + *acc)* to befall; to fall upon, assail
expiāti·ō -ōnis *f* expiation, atonement; satisfaction; purification
expictus *pp of* **expingō**
expīlāti·ō -ōnis *f* pillaging, ransacking, looting
expīlāt·or -ōris *m* plunderer, looter
expīl·ō -āre -āvī -ātus *tr* to plunder, rob, ransack; to plagiarize
ex·pingō -pingere -pīnxī -pictus *tr* to paint; to depict
expi·ō -āre -āvī -ātus *tr* to purify; to atone for, expiate; to avenge; to appease; to avert *(a curse, bad omen)*
expīrō *see* **exspīrō**
expisc·or -ārī -ātus sum *tr* to go fishing for *(information)*
explānātē *adv* plainly, clearly
explānāti·ō -ōnis *f* explanation; clear pronunciation
explānāt·or -ōris *m* interpreter
explānāt·us -a -um *adj* plain
explān·ō -āre -āvī -ātus *tr* to explain, make clear; to flatten out; to pronounce distinctly
explaudō *see* **explōdō**
explēment·um -ī *n* filling, stuffing
expl·eō -ēre -ēvī -ētus *tr* to fill up; to complete; to satisfy *(desires);* to make good *(losses);* to fulfill, perform, accomplish, discharge
explēti·ō -ōnis *f* satisfying, fulfillment
explēt·us -a -um *adj* full, complete, perfect
explicātē *adv* clearly, plainly
explicāti·ō -ōnis *f* unfolding, uncoiling; analysis; interpretation
explicāt·or -ōris *m,* **explicātr·īx -īcis** *f* explainer, interpreter
explicāt·us -a -um *adj* plain, clear-cut, straightforward
explicāt·us -ūs *m* unfolding; explanation, interpretation
explicit·us -a -um *adj* disentangled; simple, easy
explic·ō -āre -āvī *(or* **-uī) -ātus** *(or* **-itus)** *tr* to unfold, unroll; to spread out; to loosen, undo; to set free; to arrange, adjust, settle; to exhibit; to explain; to display
ex·plōdō -plōdere -plōsī -plōsus *tr* **(-plaud-)** to drive off the stage *(by clapping);* to boo; to disapprove of, discredit
explōrātē *adv* after careful examination; for sure, for certain
explōrāti·ō -ōnis *f* exploration, examination
explōrāt·or -ōris *m* scout, spy
explōrāt·us -a -um *adj* sure, certain; safe, secure; *(w. abl)* clear of; **explōrātum** *(or* **prō explōrātō) habēre** to know for sure
explōr·ō -āre -āvī -ātus *tr* to explore, investigate; to probe, search; to test, try, try out; *(w. acc & inf)* to ascertain that; *(w.* **ut, nē)** to ensure (that; that not); *(mil)* to reconnoiter
explōsi·ō -ōnis *f* driving off the stage, booing
expol·iō -īre -īvī *or* **-iī -ītus** *tr* to polish; to finish off *(a building e.g., with plaster); (fig)* to embellish, adorn, refine
expolīti·ō -ōnis *f* polishing, finishing off, embellishing
expolīt·us -a -um *adj* polished, lustrous; refined
ex·pōnō -pōnere -posuī -positus *or* **-postus** *tr* to put out, bring out (into the open); to expose *(children to die);* to leave in an exposed position; to display, exhibit; to make available; to reveal; to publish; to exhibit; to relate; to explain; to offer, tender; to set on shore, land; to send *(s.o.)* sprawling; *(w. dat or* **ad** *or* **adversus** + *acc)* to expose to
expor·rigō *or* **expor·gō -rigere -rēxī -rēctus** *tr* to stretch out, spread (out); **exporge frontem**! *(coll)* quit frowning! ‖ *refl (geog)* to extend, reach
exportāti·ō -ōnis *f* exportation
export·ō -āre -āvī -ātus *tr* to carry out; to export
ex·poscō -poscere -poposcī *tr* to demand, beg, insist upon; to demand the surrender of; *(w. double acc)* to ask *(s.o.)* for *(s.th.)*
expositīci·us -a -um *adj* foundling
expositi·ō -ōnis *f* exposing; *(rhet)* statement, description, explanation
exposit·us -a -um *pp of* **expōnō** ‖ *adj* frank; affable; plain, trite
expostulāti·ō -ōnis *f* insistent demand; complaint
expostul·ō -āre -āvī -ātus *tr* to demand, insist on; to complain of; *(w.* **cum** *of person)* to complain about *(s.th)* to *(s.o.)* ‖ *intr (w.* **cum)** to lodge a complaint with
expostus *pp of* **expōnō**
expōtus *see* **ēpōtus**
express·us -a -um *adj* distinct, clear, express; *(w.* **ad)** closely modeled on
ex·primō -primere -pressī -pressus *tr* to press out, squeeze out; to extort; to press upwards, raise; to model, form, portray; to stamp *(a design on a surface);* to represent; to imitate, copy; *(w.* **ad)** to model on *(a pattern);* to describe; to express; to

translate; to pronounce, articulate; **exprimere in melius** to improve on

exprobrāti·ō -ōnis *f (w. gen)* reproach arising from

exprobr·ō -āre -āvī -ātus *tr* to reproach, find fault with; *(w. dat)* to cast *(s.th.)* up to, put the blame for *(s.th.)* on **||** *intr (w. dat)* to complain to

exprōm·ō -ere -psī -ptus *tr* to bring out, fetch out *(from storage);* to give vent to; to disclose, display, exhibit; to utter, express, state; to bring into play, put to use

expugnābil·is -is -e *adj* vulnerable to attack

expugnāci·or -or -us *adj* more potent

expugnāti·ō -ōnis *f* assault; *(w. gen)* assault on; ruin

expugnāt·or -ōris *m* attacker; **expugnātor pudīcitiae** rapist

expugn·ō -āre -āvī -ātus *tr* to assault, storm; to break into, plunder *(a home);* to defeat; *(fig)* to overcome, sweep aside *(conditions, purposes); (fig)* to achieve, accomplish; *(fig)* to extort, wrest, gain; to persuade, overcome the resistance of

expulsi·ō -ōnis *f* expulsion

expuls·ō -āre -āvī -ātus *tr* to drive out, expel

expuls·or -ōris *m* expeller

expulsus *pp of* **expellō**

expultr·īx -īcis *f* expeller *(female)*

ex·pungō -pungere -pūnxī -pūnctus *tr* to expunge; *(fin)* to cancel *(a debt),* check off the list as paid

expuō *see* **exspuō**

expūrgāti·ō -ōnis *f* **(-pūrig-)** justification, excuse; cleansing

expūrg·ō -āre -āvī -ātus *tr* **(-pūrig-)** to cleanse, purify; to cure; to vindicate; to excuse, justify

expūtēsc·ō -ere *intr* to rot away

exput·ō -āre -āvī -ātus *tr* to prune, lop off; to consider; to figure out

exquīrō exquīrere exquīsīvī exquīsītus *tr* **(-quaer-)** to look into, ask about; to look for; to search, examine, check into; to find out; **pretium exquīrere** to work out a price

exquīsītē *adv* carefully, accurately; exquisitely

exquīsīt·us -a -um *pp of* **exquīrō ||** *adj* carefully considered; meticulous; choice, exquisite

exr- = ēr-

exrādīcitus *adv* utterly

exsar·ciō -cīre -sī -tus *tr* **(exser-)** to patch up, mend

exsati·ō -āre -āvī -ātus *tr* to satisfy fully

exscindō exscindere exscidī exscissus *tr* to annihilate, demolish; to exterminate *(a people)*

exscre·ō -āre -āvī -ātus *tr* to cough up, spit out

exsculp·ō -ere -sī -tus *tr* to carve out; to scratch out, erase; *(fig)* to extort

exsec·ō *or* **exsic·ō -āre -uī -tus** *tr* to cut out, cut away, cut off; to castrate; to deduct

exsecrābil·is -is -e *adj* accursed; bitter, merciless, deadly; amounting to execration

exsecrāti·ō -ōnis *f* curse, execration; solemn oath

exsecrāt·us -a -um *adj* accursed, detestable

exsecr·or -ārī -ātus sum *tr* to curse **||** *intr* to take a solemn oath

exsecti·ō -ōnis *f* cutting out

exsecūti·ō -ōnis *f* execution, performance; administration *(of a province);* development *(of a subject)*

exsecūtus *pp of* **exsequor**

exsequi·ae -ārum *fpl* funeral procession; funeral service; **exsequiās īre** to attend a funeral

exsequiāl·is -is -e *adj* funeral; **carmina exsequiālia** dirges

exse·quor -quī -cūtus sum *tr* to follow out; to accompany to the grave; to perform, execute, carry out; to follow up, investigate; to pursue, go after; to avenge, punish; to say, tell, relate; to describe; to enumerate, go through; *(rhet)* to develop *(a topic);* **verbīs exsequī** to enumerate

exser·ō -ere -uī -tus *tr* to untie, disconnect; to stretch out *(one's arms);* to stick out *(one's tongue);* to bare, uncover

exsert·ō -āre -āvī -ātus *tr* to keep on stretching *or* sticking out

exsertus *pp of* **exserō ||** *adj* uncovered, bare; protruding

exsībil·ō -āre -āvī -ātus *tr* to hiss off the stage

exsiccāt·us -a -um *adj* dry, uninteresting

exsicc·ō -āre -āvī -ātus *tr* to dry up; to drain dry

exsicō *see* **exsecō**

exsil·iō -īre -uī *intr* to jump out; to be startled; **exsilīre gaudiō** to jump for joy

exsil·ium -(i)ī *n* exile; place of exile

ex·sistō -sistere -stitī -stitum *intr* to come out, come forth; to appear, emerge; to exist, be; to arise, proceed; to turn into; to be visible **||** *v impers* it follows as a consequence

exsol·vō -vere -vī -ūtus *tr* to loosen, untie; to release, set free; to discharge, pay; to keep, fufill; to satisfy *(hunger);* to break open, wound; to solve; to explain; to throw off, get rid of; to repay, requite; to give out *(awards, punishment)*

exsomn·is -is -e *adj* sleepless

exsor·beō -bēre -psī *tr* to absorb; to suck up, drain; to gulp down; to exhaust; *(fig)* to gobble up *(wealth, etc.)*

exsor·s -tis *adj* without lots; chosen specially; *(w. gen)* having no share in, free from

exspati·or -ārī -ātus sum *intr* to go *or* wander off course; to flow away from its course; to digress; to expatiate

exspectābil·is -is -e *adj* expected, anticipated

exspectāti·ō -ōnis *f* expectation, anticipation, suspense; **exspectātiōnem facere** to cause suspense

exspectāt·us -a -um *adj* expected, awaited, desired

exspēs *adj (only in nom sing)* hopeless, without hope

exspīrāti·ō -ōnis *f* breathing out, exhalation

exspīr·ō -āre *tr* to breathe out, exhale, emit ‖ *intr* to be exhaled; to expire, breathe one's last; *(fig)* to come to an end, cease

exsplend·ēscō -ēscere -uī *intr* to glitter, shine; to become conspicuous

exspoli·ō -āre -āvī -ātus *tr* to strip; to pillage

exsp·uō -uere -uī -ūtus *tr* to spit out; *(fig)* to banish *(e.g., cares)*

exstern·ō -āre -āvī -ātus *tr* to startle, scare; to terrify; to stampede

exstīll·ō -āre -āvī *intr* to drip, trickle out; to melt

exstimulāt·or -ōris *m* instigator

exstimul·ō -āre -āvī -ātus *tr* to goad; *(fig)* to stir up

exstīncti·ō -ōnis *f* extinction

exstīnct·or -ōris *m* extinguisher; suppressor; destroyer

ex·stinguō -stinguere -stīnxī -stīnctus *tr* to extinguish, put out; to destroy, kill; to abolish, annul ‖ *pass* to die, die out; to be forgotten

exstirp·ō -āre -āvī -ātus *tr* to pull up by the roots, extirpate, root out, eradicate

exst·ō -āre exstitī *intr* to stand out, protrude, project; to stand out, be prominent, be conspicuous; to be visible; to appear; to exist, be extant

exstrūcti·ō -ōnis *f* erection, construction

ex·struō -struere -strūxī -strūctus *tr* to pile up; to build, erect, construct

exsūct·us -a -um *pp of* **exsūgō** ‖ *adj* dried up

exsūd·ō -āre -āvī -ātus *tr* to sweat over; to exude ‖ *intr* to ooze out

exsū·gō -gere -xī -ctus *tr* to suck out; *(fig)* to draw out *(moisture)*

exs·ul -ulis *mf* exile, refugee

exsul·ō -āre -āvī *intr* to be an exile, be a refugee

exsultāti·ō -ōnis *f* exultation, jumping for joy

exsultim *adv* friskily

exsult·ō -āre -āvī *intr* to jump up; to frisk about; *(of horses)* to rear, prance; *(of heart)* to throb; to exult, rejoice, jump for joy; to revel, run riot; to boast; *(of speech)* to jump around

exsuperābil·is -is -e *adj* conquerable

exsuperanti·a -ae *f* superiority

exsuper·ō -āre -āvī -ātus *tr* to surmount; to tower above; to exceed; to be too strong for, overpower; to outdo; to outlive ‖ *intr* to rise; to be superior, excel, to be conspicuous; to gain the upper hand; *(of flames)* to shoot up

exsurd·ō -āre -āvī -ātus *tr* to deafen; to dull *(the senses)*

exsur·gō -gere -rēxī *intr* to get up, rise, stand up; to swell; *(fig)* to recover strength; **forās ex(s)urgere** to get up and go out

exsaev·iō -īre *intr* to lose its fury

exsangu·is -is -e *adj* bloodless; pale; feeble; causing paleness

exsaturābil·is -is -e *adj* appeasable

exsatur·ō -āre -āvī -ātus *tr* to satisfy completely, glut

exsce- = **ēsce-**

exscrī·bō -bere -psī -ptus *tr* to write down; to write out in full; to copy; *(fig)* to take after, resemble

exsign·ō -āre -āvī -ātus *tr* to mark down exactly, write down in detail

exspect·ō -āre -āvī -ātus *tr* to await, wait for, look out for; to hope for, anticipate, long for, expect ‖ *intr* to wait with anticipation

exsper·gō -gere — -sus *tr* to sprinkle, scatter

exstrūct·um -ī *n* platform

exsuscit·ō -āre -āvī -ātus *tr* to rouse from sleep; to fan *(fire);* to excite, stir up

ext·a -ōrum *npl* vital organs *(heart, lungs, liver, spleen)*

extāb·ēscō -ēscere -uī *intr* to waste away; to pine away; to disappear

extār·is -is -e *adj* used for cooking the sacrificial victim; sacrificial

extemplō *adv* immediately, right away; on the spur of the moment

exten·dō -dere -dī -tus *or* **-sus** *tr* to stretch out, spread out, extend; to enlarge, increase; to widen; to prolong, continue; to pass, spend; to exert, strain; **labellum extendere** to pout *(literally, to extend the lip);* **vīrēs omnēs imperiī extendere** to do everything in one's power ‖ *refl* to exert oneself ‖ *pass* to stretch out, extend; to be stretched out at full length

extent·ō -āre -āvī -ātus *tr* to exert, strain

extent·us -a -um *pp of* **extendō** ‖ *adj* extensive, wide; level; **per fūnem extentum īre** to walk a tightrope

extenuāti·ō -ōnis *f* belittlement

extenuāt·us -a -um *adj* thinned, reduced; trifling; weak, faint

extenu·ō -āre -āvī -ātus *tr* to thin out; to lessen; to detract from

exter *or* **exter·us -a -um** *adj* exterior, outward; foreign, strange; **mare exterum** the ocean *(as opposed to the Mediterranean Sea)* ‖ *m* foreigner

exterebr·ō -āre -āvī -ātus *tr* to bore out; to extort

exter·geō -gēre -sī -sus *or* **exter·gō -gere** *tr* to wipe out, wipe away; to wipe clean; *(fig)* to clean out

exteri·or -or -us *adj* exterior, outer

exterius *adv* on the outside

extermin·ō -āre -āvī -ātus *tr* to drive out, banish; to put aside, put away; to dismiss *(from the mind)*

extern·us -a -um *adj* external, outward; foreign, strange ‖ *m* foreigner, stranger, foreign enemy ‖ *npl* foreign goods

ex·terō -terere -trīvī -trītus *tr* to rub out, wear away; *(fig)* to crush

exterr·eō -ēre -uī -itus *tr* to terrify; *(w. abl)* to frighten out of

extersī *perf of* **extergeō**

extersus *pp of* **extergeō**

exters·us -ūs *m* the wiping

exterus *see* **exter**

extex·ō -ere -uī -tus *tr* to unweave; *(fig)* to cheat

extim·ēscō -ēscere -uī *tr* to become terribly afraid of, dread ‖ *intr (w.* **dē** *+ abl)* to become panicky over

extim·us -a -um *adj* outermost, farthest, most remote

extisp·ex -icis *m* soothsayer *(who makes predictions by inspecting the entrails of animals)*

extispic·ium -(i)ī *n* the examination of vital organs as a means of divination

extoll·ō -ere *tr* to lift up; to erect; to postpone; to extol, praise; to raise, exalt; to keep raised, hold up; to beautify; **animōs extollere** to raise the morale ‖ *refl & pass (of heavenly bodies)* to rise

extor·queō -quēre -sī -tus *tr* to wrench, wrest; to dislocate; to extort

extorr·is -is -e *adj* driven out of one's country, banished, exiled

extorsī *perf of* **extorqueō**

extort·or -ōris *m* extortionist

extort·us -a -um *pp of* **extorqueō** ‖ *adj* deformed

extrā *adv* outside, on the outside; from the outside; **extrā quam** except in the case that; **extrā quam sī** unless ‖ *prep (w. acc)* **1** outside, outside of: **extrā nostrum ōrdinem** outside our class; **extrā ōrdinem** outside the usual order, extraordinarily, exceptionally; **extrā sortem** by direct appointment *(literally, outside the casting of lots);* **2** beyond (the limits of): **extrā meum fundum** beyond (the limits of) my farm; **extrā tēlī iactum** beyond the range of the weapon, out of range; **3** beyond the scope of, not subject to: **extrā lēgēs** beyond the scope of the laws, not subject to the laws; **4** free from, without: **extrā modum** immoderately, abnormally *(literally, without measure);* **extrā numerum** not in meter; off-key; **extrā numerum es mihi** *(fig)* you don't count in my eyes; **5** apart from, except: **omnēs extrā mē** everyone except me; **6** aside from: **extrā iocum** all joking aside

ex·trahō -trahere -trāxī -tractus *tr* to pull out, drag out; to draw *(water)* out; to pull up *(to higher ground);* to prolong; to waste *(time);* to extricate, rescue; to remove; to tow *(a ship)* out

extrāne·us -a -um *adj* extraneous, external, irrelevant; foreign ‖ *mf* stranger; foreigner

extrāōrdināri·us -a -um *adj* extraordinary

extrāri·us -a -um *adj* outward, external; unrelated *(by family ties)*

extrēm·a -ōrum *npl* extremities, last measures, last resort; end *(e.g., of life, of strip of land); (mil)* rear elements

extrēmit·ās -ātis *f* extremity, end

extrēmō *adv* finally, at last

extrēmum *adv* finally, at last; for the last time

extrēm·us -a -um *adj* extreme, outermost, on the end; latest, last, hindmost; the last part of, end of; the tip of, the edge of; *(of degree)* utmost, extreme; lowest; **ad extrēmum** at last; at the end; utterly; **extrēma aetās** advanced old age; **extrēma cauda** tip of the tail; **extrēmā līneā amāre** to love at a distance; **extrēma manus** final touches; **extrēmīs digitīs attingere** to touch lightly; to hold tenderly; to touch lightly on; **extrēmō tempore** finally; **extrēmus ignis** flickering flame; **in extrēmō** in mortal danger, in a crisis; **in extrēmō librō secundō** at the end of the second book ‖ *n* end; limit; edge; tip; bottom; extremity; conclusion

extrīc·ō -āre -āvī -ātus *or* **extrīc·or -ārī -ātus sum** *tr* to extricate; to clear up; to obtain with difficulty

extrīnsecus *adv* from the outside, from abroad; outside, on the outside

extrītus *pp of* **exterō**

extrīvī *perf of* **exterō**

extrū·dō -dere -sī -sus *tr* to push out; to eject, expel, drive out; to keep out *(e.g., the sea with dikes)*

extum·eō -ēre -uī *intr* to swell up

ex·tundō -tundere -tudī -tūsus *tr* to beat out, hammer out; to fashion; to devise; to extort

exturb·ō -āre -āvī -ātus *tr* to drive out, chase out, drive away; to divorce; to knock out; to disturb, upset; **mātrimōniō exturbāre** to divorce *(a woman)*

exūber·ō -āre -āvī -ātum *intr* to grow luxuriantly; to abound

exul *see* **exsul**
exulcer·ō -āre -āvī -ātus *tr* to make sore; to aggravate; to exasperate; to wound the feelings of
exulō *see* **exsulō**
exulul·ō -āre -āvī -ātus *tr* to invoke with cries **||** *intr* to howl, ululate
exūnctus *pp of* **exungō**
exund·ō -āre -āvī *intr* to gush up, well up; to overflow; **in lītora exundāre** to wash ashore
ex·ungō -ungere -ūnxī -ūnctus *tr* to rub down with oil
ex·uō -uere -uī -ūtus *tr* to take off, pull off; to shake off; to undress; to strip; to deprive *(of possessions);* to release; to cast aside, cast off; to bare
exurg·eō -ēre *tr* to squeeze out
ex·ūrō -ūrere -ūssī -ūstus *or* **-ūssus** *tr* to burn out; to burn up; to burn down; to dry up; to consume, destroy; to purge away; *(fig)* to inflame; **vīvum** *(or* **vīvam)** **exūrere** to burn alive
exūssus *pp of* **exūrō**
exūsti·ō -ōnis *f* conflagration
exūst·us -a -um *pp of* **exūrō**
exūtus *pp of* **exuō || *adj*** bare; **ūnum pedem exūtus** with one foot bare
exuvi·ae -ārum *fpl* spoils *(stripped from an enemy, such as armor);* souvenir; hide, skin; slough *(of snake);* clothing; symbols of the gods *(e.g., lightning bolt, scepter, etc., carried in procession)*
exuv·ium -(i)ī *n* spoils

F

F, f *(supply* littera*)* *f* sixth letter of the Latin alphabet; letter name: **ef**
fab·a -ae *f* fava, lima bean
fabāl·is -is -e *adj* bean; **stipulae fabālēs** bean stalks
fābell·a -ae *f* short story; fable; play
fa·ber -bra -brum *adj* skilled **||** *m* craftsman; skilled worker; smith; carpenter; builder; **faber aerārius** coppersmith; **faber ferrārius** blacksmith; **faber marmoris** marble worker; **faber nāvālis** ship builder; **faber sandapilārum** maker of (cheap) coffins; **faber tignārius** carpenter
Fab·ius -(i)ī *m* Quintus Fabius Maximus Cunctator *(see* **cunctātor)**
fabrē *adv* skillfully
fabrē·faciō -facere -fēcī -factus to build, construct; to forge
fabrēfact·us -a -um *adj* constructed by craftsmen
fabric·a -ae *f* craft, trade, industry; workshop; workmanship; process of building, construction, production; **fabricam fingere** *(w.* **ad)** *(coll)* to pull a trick on
fabricāti·ō -ōnis *f* construction; structure
fabricāt·or -ōris *m* builder, producer, creator, architect
fabric·or -ārī -ātus sum *or* **fabric·ō -āre -āvī -ātus** *tr* to make, build, construct, produce; to forge; to prepare, form; to coin *(words)*
fabrīl·is -is -e *adj* craftsman's, carpenter's, smith's, builder's, sculptor's; skilled **||** *npl* tools
fābul·a -ae *f* story, tale; talk, conversation; conversation piece; small talk; gossip; affair, matter; myth, legend; drama, play; dramatic poem; **fābula est** *(w. acc & inf)* legend has it that, the story goes that; **fābulae**! *(coll)* baloney!; **fābulam dare** *(or* **docēre)** to present a play; **fābulam nārrāre** to tell a story; **lupus in fābulā**! *(coll)* speak of the devil!; **quae haec est fābula?** *(coll)* what's that you are saying?
fābulār·is -is -e *adj* legendary; **historia fābulāris** mythology
fābulāt·or -ōris *m* story-teller; writer of fables
fābul·or -ārī -ātus sum *tr* to say, invent **||** *intr* to talk, chat, gossip
fābulōs·us -a -um *adj* legendary; incredible; fictitious, mythical **||** *n* myth, legend
fābul·us -ī *m* small bean
facess·ō -ere -īvī *or* **-iī -ītus** *tr* to do eagerly, perform, accomplish; to bring on, cause, create; **negōtium alicui facessere** to cause s.o. trouble; *(leg)* to bring a case against s.o.; **rem facessere** *(leg)* to sue **||** *intr* to go away, depart, take off; *(lit & fig)* to retire; **cubitum facessere** to go to sleep
facētē *adv* facetiously, humorously, wittily, amusingly, brilliantly
facēti·ae -ārum *fpl* clever thing, clever talk, witticism, humor
facēt·us -a -um *adj* witty, humorous; fine, elegant; brilliant
faci·ēs -ēī *f* face; look, facial expression; appearance; make, form, shape, outline; nature, character; pretense, pretext; **ā faciē** in the face, in front; **in faciē** *(w. gen)* in the presence of; **in faciem** *(w. gen)* so as to give the appearance of; into the presence of; **prīmā faciē** at first sight
facile *adv* easily, without trouble; unquestionably, far, by far; generally; quite, fully; promptly, readily, willingly; pleasantly, well; **nōn facile** hardly
facil·is -is -e *adj* easy; nimble; convenient, suitable; ready, quick; easygoing, good-natured; favorable; prosperous; gentle *(breeze);* easily borne, slight *(loss);* tame, obedient *(animals);* **ex** *(or* **ē)** **facilī** easily; **facile est** *(w. inf)* it is easy to; **facile est dē** (+ *abl)* it does not matter about; **facilis vīctū** well-to-do, well-off; **facilius est ut**

it is more likely that; **in facilī esse** to be easy

facilit·ās -ātis *f* facility, ease, easiness; readiness; fluency; aptitude; good nature; courteousness; levity

faciliter *adv (pedantic for* **facile)**

facinorōs·us -a -um *adj & m* **(-ner-)** criminal; wicked

facin·us -oris *n* deed, act; event; crime, outrage; criminal

faciō facere fēcī factus (faxim = fēcerim; faxō = fēcerō) *tr* to make; to do, perform; to fashion, frame, create; to build, erect; to produce, compose; to produce *(young);* to bring about, cause, occasion; to acquire, get, gain; to incur, suffer; to render, grant, give, confer; to assert, say, represent, depict; to choose, appoint; to follow, practice; to regard, prize, value; **aliquem certiōrem facere dē** (+ *abl)* to inform s.o. about; **cōpiam facere** *(w. dat)* to afford *(s.o.)* the opportunity; **diēs facere** to spend days; **fac ita esse** suppose it were so, granted that it is so; **fidem facere** to give one's word; **grātiam facere** to grant pardon, excuse; **grātum (pergrātum) facere** *(w. dat)* to do s.o. a (great) favor; **pecūniam** *(or* **stipendium) facere** to make money, earn money; **pretium facere** to name the price; **prōmissum facere** to fulfill a promise; **sacra facere** to sacrifice, offer sacrifice; **verba facere** to speak; **viam facere** *(w. dat)* to make way for **II** *intr* to do, act; to take part, take sides; *(w. dat or* **ad)** to be satisfactory for, be fit for, do for; *(of medicines)* to work; *(w.* **ad)** to be effective in dealing with; **suā causā** *(or* **suā rē) facere** to act in one's own interests; *(euph. for relieving oneself; supply* **aquam)** to pee

facteon = faciendum

facti·ō -ōnis *f* doing; making; party, faction; partisanship; band, group; troupe *(of actors);* social set, association; **quae haec factiō est?** *(coll)* what's this all about?

factiōs·us -a -um *adj* busy; well-connected; belonging to a faction; factious, subversive, revolutionary

factit·ō -āre -āvī -ātus *tr* to keep doing, keep making; to practice *(e.g., trade); (w. double acc)* to declare *(s.o.)* to be *(e.g., heir)*

fact·or -ōris *m* maker; perpetrator *(of crime);* **factōrēs et datōrēs** pitchers and catchers *(in ballgame)*

factū *abl sing. masc.* **facilis factū** easy to do

fact·us -a -um *pp of* **faciō II** *n* deed, act; accomplishment, exploit; misdeed; **bonum factum**! *(formula of good omen)* knock on wood!; **dictum factum** no sooner said than done

facul·a -ae *f* little torch

facult·ās -ātis *f* opportunity; feasibility; ability, capacity, skill; material resources; *(of things)* power, potency; supply *(of money, ships, men);* convenience; *(w. gen)* **1** power over; **2** skill in; **facultās ingeniī** expertise **II** *fpl* talents; resources

fācundē *adv* eloquently

fācundi·a -ae *f* eloquence

fācundit·ās -ātis *f* eloquence

fācund·us -a -um *adj* eloquent

faece·us -a -um *adj* foul

faecul·a -ae *f* **(fēc-)** wine lees *(when dried, used as medicine or spice)*

faenebr·is -is -e *adj* **(fēn-)** *(fin)* of interest; lent at interest

faenerāti·ō -ōnis *f* **(fēn-)** lending at interest, investment

faenerātō *adv* with *or* at interest

faenerāt·or -ōris *m* **(fēn-)** money lender, investor

faener·or -ārī -ātus sum *or* **faener·ō -āre -āvī -ātus** *tr* **(fēn-)** to lend at interest; to invest *(money)*; to finance; to ruin *(e.g., a province)* through high interest rates **II** *intr* to yield interest, bring profit

faene·us -a -um *adj* made of hay

faenicul·um -ī *n* fennel *(used as seasoning or medicine)*

faenīl·ia -ium *npl* **(fēn-)** hayloft

faenisec·a -ae *m* **(fēn-)** reaper, farmer

faen·um -ī *n* **(fēn-)** hay; **faenum habet in cornū** *(sl)* he's crazy *(literally, he has hay on his horns)*

faen·us -oris *n* **(fēn-)** interest; debt *(as result of heavy interest);* capital; *(fig)* profit, gain, advantage; **faenore** at interest; **in faenore** on loan

faenūscul·um -ī *n* **(fēn-)** a little interest

fae·x -cis *f* wine lees, dregs; sediment; slag; impure mixture; *(fig)* scum

fāgine·us *or* **fāgin·us** *or* **fāge·us -a -um** *adj* beech

fāg·us -ī *f* beech tree

fal·a *or* **phal·a -ae** *f* movable wooden siege tower; scaffold; curtain towers in the Circus

falāric·a -ae *f* **(phal-)** incendiary missile

falcār·ius -(i)ī *m* sickle maker

falcāt·us -a -um *adj* fitted with scythes; sickle-shaped, curved

falcif·er -era -erum *adj* scythe-bearing

falc·ō -ōnis *m* pigeon-toed person

Faleri·ī -ōrum *mpl* city of Etruria

Falern·us -a -um *adj* Falernian; **ager Falernus** district in N. Campania, famous for its wine **II** *n* Falernian wine

Falisc·us -a -um *mpl* Faliscan **II** *mpl* a people of S. E. Etruria

fallāci·a -ae *f* deception, deceit, trick

fallācit·ās -ātis *f* deceptiveness

fallāciter *adv* deceptively; falsely

fall·āx -ācis *adj* deceptive, deceitful; spurious, false

fall·ēns -entis *adj* deceptive

fallō fallere fefellī falsus *tr* to cause to fall, trip; to lead into error, mislead; to deceive, trick, dupe, cheat; to fail to live up to, disappoint; to while away *(time);* to escape the clutches of; to escape the notice of, slip by; to disguise; *(poet)* to swear falsely by; **faciem alicūius fallere** to impersonate s.o.; **fidem fallere** to break one's word; **oculōs fallere** to be invisible; **opīniōnem fallere** *(w. gen)* to fail to live up to the expectations of ‖ *pass* **nisi** *(or* **nī)** **fallor** unless I'm mistaken ‖ *intr* to go unnoticed ‖ *v impers* **mē fallit** I am mistaken

falsār·ius -(i)ī *m* forger

falsē *adv* falsely

falsidic·us -a -um *adj* speaking falsely, lying

falsific·us -a -um *adj* acting dishonestly

falsiiūri·us -a -um *adj* swearing falsely

falsiloqu·us -a -um *adj* lying

falsimōni·a -ae *f* trick, deception

falsipar·ēns -entis *adj* bastard

falsō *adv* mistakenly, wrongly, erroneously; falsely, deceitfully

fals·us -a -um *adj* false, untrue; mistaken, wrong, erroneous; lying, deceitful; vain, groundless, empty; spurious, sham, fictitious ‖ *n* error; lying; lie, falsehood; perjury

fal·x -cis *f* sickle; pruning hook, pruning knife; *(mil)* hook for pulling down walls

fām·a -ae *f* talk, rumor, report, news; saying, tradition; *(w. gen)* reputation *(for)*; fame, renown, name; infamy, notoriety; public opinion

famēlic·us -a -um *adj* famished

fam·ēs -is *f* hunger; starvation; famine; fasting; *(fig)* craving; *(rhet)* bald style, poverty of expression

fāmigerāti·ō -ōnis *f* rumor

fāmigerāt·or -ōris *m* gossip, rumormonger

famili·a -ae *or* **-ās** *f* household slaves, domestics; gang of slaves; retinue of servants; household; house, family; family estate; sect, school; **familia gladiātōrum** stable of gladiators; **familiam dūcere** to head a sect; **pater familiās** head of the family

familiār·is -is -e *adj* domestic, family, household; familiar, intimate; private, personal *(as opposed to public); (in augury)* one's own *(part of the sacrificial animal);* **rēs familiāris** one's private property, estate, patrimony ‖ *m* servant, slave; acquaintance; close friend

familiārit·ās -ātis *f* close friendship, intimacy; familiarity; *(of things)* close relationship

familiāriter *adv* in the manner of a close friend; thoroughly; as if at home, in a familiar manner; familiarly

fāmōs·us -a -um *adj* much talked of; famous, renowned; infamous; slanderous, libelous; **carmen fāmōsum** lampoon

famul·a -ae *f* maid, slave-girl

famulār·is -is -e *adj* of slaves, servile

famulāt·us -ūs *m* slavery, servitude

famul·or -ārī -ātus sum *intr* to be a slave; *(w. dat)* to serve

famul·us -a -um *adj* servile ‖ *m* servant, attendant; slave ‖ *f see* **famula**

fānātic·us -a -um *adj* belonging to a temple; fanatic, enthusiastic, inspired; frantic ‖ *mf* temple attendant

fand·us -a -um *adj* that may be spoken

fān·um -ī *n* shrine, sanctuary; temple

fār farris *n* spelt *(type of wheat);* coarse meal, grits; sacrificial meal; bread; dog biscuit ‖ *npl* grain

far·ciō -cīre -sī -tus *tr* to stuff; to fatten *(birds for table); (w.* **in** *+ acc)* to cram into ‖ *refl* to gorge oneself

farfar·us *or* **farfer·us -ī** *m* coltsfoot *(plant w. heart-shaped leaves)*

-fāriam *advl suf* forms multiplicative adverbs denoting -sided: **multifāriam** many-sided

farīn·a -ae *f* flour; powder; *(fig)* character, quality

farrāg·ō -inis *f* mash *(for cattle); (fig)* medley, hodgepodge

farrāt·us -a -um *adj* filled with grain, made with grain

fart·is -is *f* stuffing, filling; mincemeat; **fartim facere ex hostibus** to make mincemeat of the enemy

fart·or -ōris *m* fattener of poultry

far·tus -us -a -um *pp of* **farciō** ‖ *adj* well-fed; crammed, gorged, stuffed

fās *indecl n* divine law; sacred duty, divine will, fate; right; natural law; **fās est** it is right, it is lawful; it is permissible; **fās tibi est** you have the right; **omne fās est fīdere** there is every reason to trust

fāsci·a -ae *f* bandage; bra; diaper; headband, fillet; wisp of cloud

fāsciātim *adv* in bundles

fāscicul·us -ī *m* small bundle

fāscin·ō -āre -āvī -ātus *tr* to cast an evil eye on, bewitch, jinx; to envy

fāscin·um -ī *n or* **fāscin·us -ī** *m* evil eye; jinx; witchcraft; charm, amulet; *(vulg)* penis

fāsciol·a -ae *f* ribbon; headband

fāsc·is -is *m* bundle, pack, parcel; fagot; load, burden; baggage ‖ *mpl* fasces *(bundle of rods and ax, carried before high magistrates by lictors as symbols of authority);* high office, supreme power, consulship

fassus *pp of* **fateor**

fāst·ī -ōrum *mpl* calendar, almanac; annals; register of higher magistrates ‖ **Fāstī** poem by Ovid
fastīd·iō -īre -īvī *or* **-iī -ītus** *tr* to despise, snub, turn up the nose at ‖ *intr* to feel disgust, feel squeamish; to be snobbish, be haughty
fastīdiōsē *adv* fastidiously, squeamishly; disdainfully, snobbishly
fastīdiōs·us -a -um *adj* fastidious, squeamish; disdainful, snobbish; refined, delicate; nauseating
fastīd·ium -(i)ī *n* fastidiousness, distaste, squeamishness, disgust, loathing; snobbishness, haughtiness; **(in) fastīdiō esse** to be repugnant; **in fastīdium īre** to become repugnant
fastīgātē *adv* sloped, at an angle
fastīgāt·us -a -um *adj* rising to a point; sloping down
fastīg·ium -(i)ī *n* gable; pediment; roof; ceiling; slope; height, elevation; top, edge; depth, depression; completion; rank, dignity; main point, heading; highlight *(of a story, etc.)*
fastīg·ō -āre -āvī -ātus *tr* to make pointed; to taper; to cause to slope, incline ‖ *refl & pass* to taper; to narrow
fastōs·us -a -um *adj* disdainful; *(fig)* magnificent
fāst·us -a -um *adj (of day)* lawful *(for transaction of business);* **diēs fāstus** court day ‖ *mpl see* **fāstī**
fast·us -ūs *m* contempt; arrogance, haughtiness ‖ *mpl* arrogant deeds
Fāt·a -ōrum *npl* the Fates
fātāl·is -is -e *adj* fateful, destined, preordained; fatal, deadly; **deae fātālēs** the Fates
fātāliter *adv* by fate, by destiny
fateor fatērī fassus sum *tr* to admit, acknowledge, confess; to profess, declare; **fatendī modus** *(gram)* the indicative mood ‖ *intr* to admit guilt, confess; to say yes; *(w. inf)* to agree to
fātican·us -a -um *adj* **(-cin-)** prophetic
fātidic·us -a -um *adj* prophetic
fātif·er -era -erum *adj* fatal, deadly
fatīgāti·ō -ōnis *f* fatigue
fatīg·ō -āre -āvī -ātus *tr* to fatigue, weary, tire out; to wear down; to worry, torment, bother; to pray to constantly
fātiloqu·a -ae *f* prophetess
fatīsc·ō -ere *or* **fatīsc·or -ī** *intr* to split, crack, give way; *(fig)* to become exhausted, wear out, grow weary
fātū *abl sing m* in the telling; **haud mollis fātū** not easy to tell
fatuē *adv* foolishly
fatuit·ās -ātis *f* silliness
fāt·um -ī *n* divine utterance, oracle; fate, destiny, doom; calamity; ruin; death; *(fig)* cause of death, cause of ruin; **ad fāta novissima** to the last; **fātō fūnctus** dead; **fātō obīre** to meet death; **fātum est** it is fated; **fātum prōferre** to put off fate, prolong life ‖ *npl* what fate has in store, the future
fātus *pp of* **for**
fatu·us -a -um *adj* silly, foolish; clumsy; tasteless *(food)* ‖ *m* fool; jester
fauc·ēs -ium *(poet: abl singl:* **fauce)** *fpl* throat; gullet; neck; strait, channel; pass, gorge; mouth *(of river);* entrance *(to harbor, home, building, cave, lower world);* jaws, maw *(of wild animals);* crater *(of volcano);* neck *(of vase, jar);* **faucēs premere** *(w. gen)* to throttle s.o.
Faun·us -ī *m* king of Latium, father of Latinus and worshiped as the Italian Pan ‖ *mpl* Fauns, woodland spirits
faustē *adv* favorably, auspiciously
faustit·ās -ātis *f* fertility; good fortune, happiness
Faustul·us -ī *m* shepherd who rescued and raised Romulus and Remus
faust·us -a -um *adj* auspicious, favorable; lucky ‖ **Faustus** personal name *(agnomen)* of the son of the dictator Sulla
faut·or *or* **favit·or -ōris** *m,* **fautr·īx -īcis** *f* patron, supporter, fan
fave·a -ae *f* favorite girl, pet slave girl
faveō favēre fāvī fautum *intr (w. dat)* to be favorable to, favor, support, side with; *(w. inf)* to be eager to; **favēre linguīs** *(or* **ōre)** to observe a reverential silence
favill·a -ae *f* ashes, embers; *(fig)* spark, beginnings
favitor *see* **fautor**
Favōn·ius -(i)ī *m* West Wind *(also called Zephyrus)*
fav·or -ōris *m* favor, support; applause; appreciation *(shown by applause)*
favōrābil·is -is -e *adj* popular
favōrābiliter *adv* in order to win popularity
fav·us -ī *m* honeycomb ‖ *mpl* honey
fax facis *f* torch; wedding torch, wedding; funeral torch, funeral; meteor, shooting star, comet; firebrand; fire, flame; guiding light; instigator; flame of love; stimulus, incitement; cause of ruin *or* destruction; **dīcendī facēs** fiery eloquence; **dolōrum facēs** pangs of grief
faxim, faxō *see* **faciō**
febrīcul·a -ae *f* slight fever
febrīculōs·us -a -um *adj* fever-ridden; prone to fevers
febr·is -is *f* fever
Febru·a -ōrum *npl* Roman festival of purification and expiation, celebrated on February 15
Februāri·us -a -um *adj & m* February *(twelfth month of the Roman calendar until the reform of 153 B.C.)*
febru·um -ī *n* purification

fēcundit·ās -ātis *f* fertility, fruitfulness; *(rhet)* overstatement
fēcund·ō -āre -āvī -ātus *tr* to fertilize
fēcund·us -a -um *adj* fertile, fruitful; abundant, rich; fertilizing; *(w. gen or abl)* rich in, abounding in
fefellī *perf of* **fallō**
fel fellis *n* gallbladder; gall, bile; bitterness, animosity; poison
fēl·ēs *or* **fēl·is -is** *f* cat
fēlīcit·ās -ātis *f* fertility; luck, piece of luck; felicity, happiness
fēlīciter *adv* fruitfully, abundantly; luckily; happily; sucessfully; favorably; *(ellipsis)* **fēlīciter (tibi ēveniat)**! good luck!
fēlis *see* **fēlēs**
fēl·īx -īcis *adj* fruit-bearing; fruitful, fertile; favorable, auspicious; lucky; happy; successful; well-aimed
fellāt·or -ōris *m,* **fellātr·īx -īcis** *f* one who practices oral sex
fell·ō -āre -āvī -ātus *tr* to practice oral sex with **||** *intr* to practice oral sex
fēmell·a -ae *f* girl, young lady
fēmin·a -ae *f* female; woman
feminal·ia -ium *npl* stockings *(to cover the thighs)*
fēmine·us -a -um *adj* woman's; effeminate, unmanly
fēminīn·us -a -um *adj* female; *(gram)* feminine
fem·ur -oris *or* **-inis** *n* thigh
fēn- = faen-
fenestr·a -ae *f* window; hole *(for earrings); (fig)* window of opportunity; *(fig)* loophole; *(mil)* breach *(in a wall);* window *(of the soul)*
-fer -fera -ferum *adj/ suf* denotes bearing, carrying, or bringing: **cōnifer** bearing cones
fer·a -ae *f* wild beast, wild animal; sea monster; **magna minorque ferae** the Great and Little Bear
ferāciter *adv* fruitfully
ferācius *adv* more fruitfully
Fērāl·ia -ium *npl* **(Fer-)** memorial service of the dead, celebrated on February 17th or 21st
fērāl·is -is -e *adj* associated with death *or* the dead; funeral; deadly, fatal, gloomy, dismal; **pāpiliō fērālis** funerary butterfly *(symbolizing the soul)*
fer·āx -ācis *adj* fertile, fruitful; *(w. gen)* productive of
fercul·um -ī *n* food tray; dish; course; float *(for carrying spoils in a victory parade or cult images in a religious procession)*
fercul·us -ī *m* litter bearer
ferē *or* **fermē** *adv* approximately, nearly, almost, about, just about; generally, as a rule, usually; *(w. negatives)* practically; **haud ferē** *(or* **nōn ferē)** hardly ever; **nēmō ferē** practically no one
ferentār·ius -(i)ī *m* light-armed soldier; eager helper
Feretr·ius -(i)ī *m* epithet of Jupiter on the Capitoline Hill
feretr·um -ī *n* litter, bier
fēri·ae -ārum *fpl* holidays, vacation; *(fig)* leisure
fēriāt·us -a -um *adj* vacationing, taking it easy; dressed for the holiday; unemployed; **diēs fēriātus** holiday, day off
fericulum = ferculum
ferīn·us -a -um *adj* of wild animals; brutish; **carō ferīna** venison; **vīta ferīna** life in the wild **||** *f* venison
fer·iō -īre *tr (the forms of the perf and pp are supplied by* **percutiō)** to strike, hit, shoot, knock; to kill; to slaughter, sacrifice *(an animal);* to coin; *(fig)* to strike, reach, affect; *(fig)* to cheat, trick; **cornū ferīre** to butt; **foedus ferīre** to conclude a treaty; *(fig)* to strike a bargain; **sēcūrī ferīre** to behead; **verba ferīre** to coin words
ferit·ās -ātis *f* wildness, fierceness
fermē *see* **ferē**
ferment·um -ī *n* yeast; beer; *(fig)* anger; *(fig)* cause of anger
ferō ferre tulī *or* **tetulī lātus** *tr* to bear, carry; to bear, produce; to bear, endure; to lead, drive, conduct, direct; to bring, offer; to receive, acquire, obtain, win; to carry off, plunder, ravage; to manifest, display; to make known, report, say, tell; to call; to propose, bring forward; to allow, permit; to cause, create; to set in motion; to call, name; *(of circumstances, etc.)* to suggest; *(in accounting)* to enter; to carry *(e.g., a ward in an election);* **aditum ferre** to approach; **aegrē ferre** to be annoyed at; to take it hard; **caelō supīnās manūs ferre** to raise the hands heavenward in prayer; **crīmina ferre in** *(w. acc)* to bring charges against; **cursum** *(or* **iter)** **ferre** to go, proceed, pursue a course; **hunc inventōrem artium ferunt** they call him the inventor of the arts; **in oculīs ferre** *(fig)* to have before one's eyes, have on one's mind; **iūdicem ferre** *(w. dat)* to propose a judge to *(i.e., to go to court with);* **laudibus ferre** to extol; **lēgem ferre** to propose a bill; **molestē ferre** to be annoyed at; **ōre ferre** to show *(by one's looks);* **ōsculum ferre** *(w. dat)* to give *(s.o.)* a kiss; **pedem** *(or* **pedēs)** **ferre** to come, go, move, get going; **prae sē ferre** to display, manifest; **repulsam ferre** to experience defeat *(at polls);* **respōnsum ferre** to get an answer; **sententiam ferre** to pass judgment; to cast a vote; **signa ferre** *(mil)* to begin marching; **suffrāgium ferre** to cast a vote, cast a ballot; **ventrem ferre** to be pregnant **||** *refl* to go, proceed; to rush, flee; *(of*

rivers) to flow; **sē ferre obviam** *(w. dat)* to rush to meet **||** *pass (of things)* to be carried along; to extend; *(of sounds)* to carry **||** *intr* to say *(e.g.,* **ut ferunt** as people say, as they say); to allow, permit *(e.g.,* **sī occāsiō tulerit** if the occasion permit); to lead *(e.g.,* **iter ad oppidum ferēbat** the road led to the town)

ferōci·a -ae *f* fierceness, ferocity; fighting spirit; pride, presumption

ferōc·iō -īre *intr* to rampage

ferōcit·ās -ātis *f* fierceness, ferocity; aggressiveness; presumption

ferōciter *adv* ferociously, aggressively; defiantly, arrogantly

Fērōni·a -ae *f* early Italic goddess of groves and springs, and patroness of ex-slaves

fer·ōx -ōcis *adj* fierce, ferocious; warlike; defiant; arrogant

ferrāment·um -ī *n* tool, implement

ferrāri·us -a -um *adj* iron, of iron; **faber ferrārius** blacksmith; **officīna** *(or* **taberna) ferrāria** blacksmith shop **||** *m* blacksmith **||** *fpl* iron mines; iron works

ferrātil·is -is -e *adj* fit to be chained

ferrāt·us -a -um *adj* iron-plated; iron-tipped; in chains; in armor; **calx ferrāta** spur **||** *mpl* soldiers in armor

ferre·us -a -um *adj* iron, of iron; cruel, hardhearted; firm, unyielding; armored; inexorable, inflexible *(fate, laws);* **ferreus somnus** death

ferricrepin·us -a -um *adj (coll)* clanking with chains

ferriter·ium -(i)ī *n (coll)* brig *(jail)*

ferriter·us -ī *m (coll)* glutton for punishment

ferritrīb·āx -ācis *adj (coll)* chainsore *(from dragging chains)*

ferrūgine·us -a -um *adj* rust-colored, dark, dusky

ferrūg·ō -inis *f* rust, verdigris; dark-red; dark color; gloom

ferr·um -ī *n* iron; tool, implement; iron object: sword, dart, arrowhead, ax, plowshare, crowbar, spade, scissors, stylus, curling iron, *(surgical)* knife; gladiatorial fight; **ferrō atque ignī** with fire and sword; **ferrō dēcernere** to decide by force of arms; **ferrum sūmere** to resort to arms

ferrūm·en -inis *n* adhesive, cement

fertil·is -is -e *adj* fertile, fruitful; productive; fertilizing; life-giving; profitable, lucrative; *(w. gen, dat, or abl)* productive of

fertilit·ās -ātis *f* fertility

ferul·a -ae *f* reed, stalk; rod, whip

fer·us -a -um *adj* wild; uncultivated, untamed; savage, uncivilized; rude, cruel, fierce; wild, bleak *(place)* **||** *m* wild beast; wild horse; lion; stag **||** *f* wild beast, wild animal

fervē·faciō -facere -fēcī -factus *tr* to heat, boil

ferv·ēns -entis *adj* seething, burning, hot; red-hot *(iron); (of mind)* in turmoil; *(fig)* hot, heated, violent, impetuous, ardent; **fervēns īra oculīs** anger sparkling in the eyes

ferventer *adv (fig)* heatedly, impetuously

ferv·eō -ēre ferbuī *or* **ferv·ō -ere -ī** *intr* to boil, seethe, steam; to foam; to swarm; to be busy, bustle about; *(fig)* to burn, glow, rage, rave; **fervet opus** the work goes on at a feverish pace

fervēsc·ō -ere *intr* to become boiling hot, grow hot, begin to boil

fervid·us -a -um *adj* boiling, seething, hot; fermenting *(grapes);* hot, highly spiced; *(fig)* hot, fiery, violent, impetuous, hot-blooded

fervō *see* **ferveō**

ferv·or -ōris *m* heat; boiling; fermenting; fever; raging *(of the sea); (fig)* heat, vehemence, ardor, passion

Fescenni·a -ae *f* town in Etruria

Fescennīn·us -a -um *adj* Fescennine **||** *mpl* Fescennine verses *(coarse, boisterous form of dramatic dialogue)*

fess·us -a -um *adj* tired out, worn out; weakened *(by wounds, disease, etc.); (fig)* demoralized, depressed; *(w. abl)* weary of, sick of

festīnanter *adv* quickly

festīnāti·ō -ōnis *f* hurry, haste

festīnātō *adv* hurriedly

festīn·ō -āre -āvī -ātus *tr* to perform, *(or* make *or* do) without delay; to move *(s.th.)* quickly; to accelerate; **iūssa festīnāre** to carry out orders promptly **||** *intr* to rush, hurry; to bustle; to be in a hurry; *(w. inf)* to be anxious to, lose no time in

festīn·us -a -um *adj* hasty, speedy

fēstīvē *adv* gaily; *(coll)* humorously; *(coll)* delightfully, neatly, nicely

fēstīvit·ās -ātis *f* festivity, gaiety, fun; *(rhet)* humor, liveliness *(of speaker, speech)*

fēstīv·us -a -um festal, of a holiday *or* festival; merry, jolly; humorous

festūc·a -ae *f* **(fis-)** stalk; rod *(with which slaves were tapped when freed)*

fēst·us -a -um *adj* festive, joyous, in holiday mood; **diēs fēstus** holiday **||** *n (often plural in singular sense)* holiday, festival; **fēstum agere** to observe a holiday

fētiāl·is -is -e *adj* negotiating, diplomatic; fetial, of the fetial priests **||** *m* fetial *(member of a college of priests who performed the ritual in connection with declaring war and making peace)*

fētid·us -a -um *adj* **(foet-)** fetid, stinking

fētūr·a -ae *f* breeding, bearing; offspring, young

fēt·us -a -um *adj* pregnant, breeding; fruitful, teeming, productive
fēt·us -ūs *m* childbirth; laying *(of eggs); (of plants)* producing, bearing; offspring, young; fruit, produce; *(fig)* product *(of mind or imagination)*
fī *interj (at a bad smell)* phew!
fi·ber -brī *m* beaver
fibr·a -ae *f* fiber, filament; lobe *(of liver, lungs)* **‖** *fpl* entrails
fībul·a -ae *f* clasp, safety pin, brooch; barrette; clamp; bolt, peg; chastity clamp *(worn through the prepuce to prevent sexual intercourse)*
fīcedul·a -ae *f* **(-cēd-)** beccafico, fig-pecker *(small songbird)*
fictē *adv* falsely, fictitiously
fictil·is -is -e *adj* clay, earthen **‖** *n* jar; clay statue **‖** *npl* earthenware
ficti·ō -ōnis *f* forming, formation; disguising; supposition; fiction
fict·or -ōris *m* shaper, sculptor, molder; attendant of priest who kneaded the sacrificial cake
fictr·īx -īcis *f* maker, molder *(female)*
fictūr·a -ae *f* shaping, fashioning
fict·us -a -um *pp of* **fingō ‖** *adj* false, fictitious; insincere *(person, character, emotions);* false *(witness);* **vox ficta** falsehood **‖** *n* falsehood; pretense; fiction
fīcul·a -ae *f* little fig
fīculn(e)·us -ā -um *adj* of a fig tree
fīc·us -ī *or* **-ūs** *f* fig; fig tree; **prīma fīcus** early autumn **‖** *fpl* hemorrhoids
fidēcommiss·um -ī *n* **(fideī-)** trust fund
fīdēlē *adv* faithfully
fidēli·a -ae *f* earthen pot, bucket; **duo parietēs dē eādem fidēliā dealbāre** *(prov)* to kill two birds with one stone *(literally, to whitewash two walls with one bucket)*
fidēl·is -is -e *adj* faithful, loyal; trustworthy, true, sure; safe *(ship, port, advice, etc.); (w. dat or* **ad)** faithful to **‖** *m* confidant
fidēlit·ās -ātis *f* fidelity, loyalty
fidēliter *adv* faithfully, loyally; securely, certainly
Fīdēn·ae -ārum *fpl* Fidenae *(ancient town near Rome, once the rival of Rome)*
Fīdēn·ās -ātis *adj* of Fidenae, against Fidenae **‖** *mpl* people of Fidenae
fīd·ēns -entis *adj* self-confident; bold; *(w. gen)* confident in
fīdenter *adv* confidently; boldly
fīdenti·a -ae *f* self-confidence; assurance; boldness
fid·ēs -eī *f* trust, faith, reliance, confidence; credence, belief; trustworthiness, conscientiousness, honesty; promise, assurance; word, word of honor; protection, guarantee; safe conduct; confirmation, proof; *(com)* credit; **bonae fideī** in good faith; **bonā fidē** *(or* **ex bonā fidē)** in good faith; really, genuinely; **dē fide malā** in bad faith; **Dī vostram fidem!** for heaven's sake!; **fidē dēcēdere** to cease to be loyal; **fideī causā** as proof of *(one's)* trustworthiness; **fidem dare** to give one's word; **fidem alicūius dēcipere** to deceive s.o. through (misplaced) trust, betray s.o.'s trust; **fidem facere** *(w. dat)* **1** to convince; **2** to place trust in; **fidem fallere** to break one's word; **fidem firmāre** to make good one's word, back up one's promise; **fidem habēre** to be credible, be believed, have credibility; **fidem habēre** *(w. dat)* to have confidence in, give credence to; **fidem obsecrāre** to beg for support *or* protection; **fidem obligāre** to pledge one's word, make a solemn promise, guarantee one's loyalty; **fidem obstringere** *(w. dat)* to pledge one's word to; **fidem praestāre** *(or* **servāre** *or* **tenēre** *or* **retinēre)** to keep one's word; **fidem sequī** *(w. gen)* to seek the protection of; **fidēs pūblica** promise of immunity; safe conduct; **in fidem accipere** to take under one's protection; **in fidē manēre** to remain loyal; **meā (tuā) fidē** on my *(your)* word; **optimā fidē** with the utmost honesty; **prō fidem deum!** for heaven's sake!; **rēs fidēsque** capital and credit
fid·ēs -is *f* string *(of musical instrument)* **‖** *fpl* stringed instrument, lyre; *(fig)* lyric poetry; **fidibus canere** to play the lyre; **fidibus discere** to learn to play the lyre; **fidibus scīre** to know how to play the lyre
fīdī *perf of* **findō**
fidic·en -inis *m* lyre player; *(fig)* lyric poet
fidicin·a -ae *f* lyre player *(female)*
fidicul·a -ae *f* small lyre **‖** *fpl* torture rack
Fid·ius -(i)ī *m* epithet of Jupiter; **medius fidius!** honest to goodness!, so help me God!
fīdō fīdere fīsus sum *intr (w. dat or abl)* to trust, confide in, put confidence in
fīdūci·a -ae *f* trust, confidence, reliance; self-confidence; trustworthiness; security; guarantee; *(w. gen)* confident hope of; *(leg)* deposit, pledge, security; **fīdūciā** *(w. gen)* with reliance on
fīdūciāri·us -a -um *adj* held in trust, fiduciary; of a trustee
fīd·us -a -um *adj* trusty, dependable; certain, sure, safe; *(w. dat)* loyal to; **fīdō animō esse** to be steadfast; **male fīdus** *(w. dat)* treacherous (to *or* for)
figlīn·us -a -um *adj* **(figul-)** potter's
figment·um -ī *n* figment; unreality
figō fīgere fīxī fīxus *tr* to fix, fasten, affix, attach, nail; to drive in; to pierce; to erect, set up; to build; to put up, hang up, post; **crucī** *(or* **in cruce) fīgere** *(or simply* **fīgere)** to crucify; **dicta animō fīgere** to let the words sink in; **lūmine fīgere** *(poet)* to stare at

figulār·is -is -e *adj* potter's
figul·us -ī *m* potter; bricklayer
figūr·a -ae *f* figure, shape, form; phantom, host; nature, kind; figure of speech; *(gram)* form *(of a word by inflexion)*
figūrāti·ō -ōnis *f* forming; form, shape; description, sketch
figūrāt·us -a -um *adj* figurative
figūr·ō -āre -āvī -ātus *tr* to shape, form, mold, fashion; to train; *(w.* **in** *+ acc)* to transform into; *(rhet)* to embellish *(a speech)* with rhetorical figures
fīlātim *adv* thread by thread
fīli·a -ae *f (dat & abl pl:* **fīliābus)** daughter
fīlicāt·us -a -um *adj* engraved with fern patterns
fīliol·a -ae *f* little daughter, dear daughter
fīliol·us -ī *m* little son, dear son
fīl·ius -(i)ī *m* son; **terrae fīlius** a nobody
fil·ix -icis *f* fern
fīl·um -ī *n* thread; string, cord; wick; fillet; figure, shape *(of a woman);* build *(of a person);* texture, quality, style *(of speech); (fig)* character; **fīla lyrae** strings of a lyre; **fīlō pendēre** to hang by a thread, be in a precarious situation
fimbri·ae -ārum *fpl* fringe, edge, border *(esp. if separated into shreds)*
fim·us -ī *m* dung, manure; mire
findō findere fidī fissus *tr* to split **‖** *refl & pass* to fork, split
fingō fingere finxī fictus *tr* to shape, form; to mold, model *(in clay, wax);* to arrange *(esp. the hair),* trim; to imagine, suppose, think; to contrive, invent; to pretend, feign; to train, influence *(s.o.)* to be; to compose *(poetry);* to disguise *(looks);* to trump up *(charges); (w. double acc)* to represent as, depict as; **ars fingendī** sculpture; **linguā fingere** to lick **‖** *refl* to pretend to be; *(w.* **ad) 1** to adapt oneself to; **2** to be subservient to
fīni·ēns -entis *m* horizon
fīn·iō -īre -īvī *or* **-iī -ītus** *tr* to limit; *(fig)* to set bounds to, limit, restrain; to mark out, fix, determine; to put an end to, finish, complete **‖** *pass & intr* to come to an end
fīn·is -is *m (f)* boundary, border, limit; end; purpose, aim; extreme limit, summit, highest degree; starting point; goal; death; **eādem fīnī** within the same period; **fīne** *(w. gen)* up to, as far as; **fīnem facere** *(w. gen or dat)* to put an end to; **in fīne** in conclusion; **quā fīne** *(or* **quā fīnī)** up to the point where; up to what point?; **quem ad fīnem** how long, to what extent **‖** *mpl* boundaries, country, territory, land
fīnītē *adv* to a limited degree; specifically
fīnitim·us -a -um *adj* **(-tum-)** neighboring, bordering; *(w. dat)* **1** bordering on; **2** *(fig)* bordering on, akin to **‖** *mpl* neighbors
fīnīt·or -ōris *m* surveyor
fīnīt·us -a -um *pp of* **fīniō ‖** *adj* limited; *(rhet)* rhythmical
fīō fierī factus sum *intr* to come into being, arise; to be made; to be done; to become, get; to happen, occur; *(of events, festivals, etc.)* to take place, be held; *(of physical phenomena)* to arise, develop; *(w. gen of price)* to be valued at; *(in arithmetic)* to equal; **fīat** so be it; **fierī nōn potest quīn** it is inevitable that; **fierī potest ut** it is possible that; **ita fit ut** *(or* **quō fit ut)** thus it happens that; **plūrimī fierī** to be valued highly; **quid fiet?** *(w. dat)* what's going to happen to?; **quoad fīat** as far as is possible **‖** *v impers* a sacrifice is being offered
firmām·en -inis *n* prop, support
firmāment·um -ī *n* prop, support; mainstay; main point
firmāt·or -ōris *m* promoter
firmē *adv* firmly, steadily
firmit·ās -ātis *f* firmness, stability; strength
firmiter *adv* firmly, tight,; securely, safely; resolutely
firmitūd·ō -inis *f* firmness, strength, durability; vigor; stability; **memoriae firmitūdō** unfaltering memory
firm·ō -āre -āvī -ātus *tr* to strengthen, support, reinforce; to encourage; to assure; to fortify; to put *(laws, institutions)* on a firm footing, establish; to guarantee; to assert, affirm; to substantiate, vouch for *(a statement or its veracity);* **aliquem in sē** *(or* **sibi) firmāre** to make sure of the loyalty of; **animum firmāre** to get up one's courage; **fidem firmāre** to make good one's word, back up one's promise; **gradum firmāre** to walk resolutely; **oculōs** *(or* **vultum) firmāre** to look determined **‖** *refl* to brace oneself
firm·us -a -um *adj* firm, strong; stable; hardy, sound *(health);* solid, substantial *(food);* steadfast, trusty; lasting
fiscāl·is -is -e *adj* fiscal, of the imperial treasury
fiscell·a -ae *f* small basket
fiscin·a -ae *f* wicker basket, wickerwork; **cum porcīs cum fiscinā** *(fig)* lock, stock, and barrel *(literally, with pigs and with wicker basket)*
fisc·us -ī *m* basket; money box; imperial treasury *(distinct from state treasury:* **aerārium);** state revenues
fissil·is -is -e *adj* easily split; split
fissi·ō -ōnis *f* dividing, splitting
fiss·us -a -um *pp of* **findō ‖** *adj* cloven, divided **‖** *n* split
fistūca *see* **festūca**
fistul·a -ae *f* pipe, tube; water pipe; hollow reed; flute; *(med)* fistula
fistulāt·or -ōris *m* one who plays a shepherd's pipe
fistulāt·us -a -um *adj* provided with pipes

fīsus *pp of* **fīdō**

fīx·us -a -um *pp of* **fīgō** ‖ *adj* fixed, immovable; irrevocable; *(w. abl)* fitted with

flābellifer·a -ae *f* female slave who waved a fan

flābellul·um -ī *n* small fan

flābell·um -ī *n* fan

flābil·is -is -e *adj* of air

flābr·a -ōrum *npl* gusts of wind; breezes, winds

flacc·eō -ēre *intr* to be flabby; to lose heart; *(of a speech)* to get dull

flacc·ēscō -ēscere -uī *intr* to become flabby; to wither, droop

flaccid·us -a -um *adj* flaccid, flabby; weak, feeble

flacc·us -a -um *adj* flabby

flagell·ō -āre -āvī -ātus *tr* to whip

flagell·um -ī *n* whip; scourge; riding crop; young shoot, sucker; tentacle *(of polyp);* pang *(of conscience)*

flāgitāti·ō -ōnis *f* demand

flāgitāt·or -ōris *m* persistent demander

flāgitiōsē *adv* shamefully, disgracefully

flāgitiōs·us -a -um *adj* shameful, disgraceful, scandalous

flāgit·ium -(i)ī *n* shame, disgrace, scandal; good-for-nothing

flāgit·ō -āre -āvī -ātus *tr* to demand; *(w. double acc, or w.* **ab)** to demand *(s.th.)* of *(s.o.)*

flagr·āns -antis *adj* blazing, flaming, hot; shining, glowing, glittering; ardent, hot, vehement, eager

flagranter *adv* vehemently, ardently

flagranti·a -ae *f* blaze, glow; passionate love; **flāgitī flagrantia** utter disgrace

flagritrib·a -ae *m (coll) (said of a slave)* victim of constant whipping, whipping boy

flagr·ō -āre -āvī *tr* to burn with love for ‖ *intr* to blaze, be on fire; *(w. abl)* **1** to glow with, flare up in; **2** to be the victim of *(e.g., envy)*

flagr·um -ī *n* whip; whipping

flām·en -inis *m* flamen *(priest of a specific deity);* **flāmen Diālis** priest of Jupiter

flām·en -inis *n* gust, gale; breeze

flāminic·a -ae *f* wife of a flamen; priestess

Flāminīn·us -ī *m* Titus Quintus Flamininus *(consul of 198 B.C, and conqueror of Philip V of Macedon at Cynoscephalae in 197 B.C.)*

flāmin·ium -(i)ī *n* office of flamen, priesthood

Flāmini·us -a -um *adj* Flaminian; **via Flāminia** road leading N. from Rome to Ariminum ‖ *m* Gaius Flaminius *(conqueror of Insubrian Gauls in 223 B.C., and builder of the Circus Flaminius and Flaminian road)*

flamm·a -ae *f* flame, fire, blaze; star; torch; burning fever; glow, passion; sweetheart; danger; flare-up *(of violence);* **flammam adicere** *(or* **suggerere)** *(w. dat)* to fan the flames of; **flammam concipere** to catch fire; **in flammā** in flames, ablaze

flammār·ius -(i)ī *m* maker of bridal veils

flammeol·um -ī *n (flame-colored)* bridal veil

flammēsc·ō -ere *intr* to become inflamed, become fiery

flamme·us -a -um *adj* flaming, fiery; flashing *(eyes);* flame-colored ‖ *n (flame-colored)* bridal veil

flammif·er -era -erum *adj* fiery

flamm·ō -āre -āvī -ātus *tr* to set on fire; *(fig)* to get *(s.o.)* all excited ‖ *pass* to glow, flame

flammul·a -ae *f* little flame

flāt·us -ūs *m* blowing, breathing, breath; breeze, wind; **flātum ēmittere** *(sl)* to break wind ‖ *mpl* haughtiness, arrogance

flāv·ēns -entis *adj* yellow, golden

flāv·eō -ēre *intr* to be yellow, be blond(e)

flāvēsc·ō -ere *intr* to become yellow, become golden-yellow

Flāvi·us -a -um *adj* Flavian; **gēns Flāvia** Flavian clan *(to which the emperors Vespasian, Titus, and Domitian belonged)*

flāv·us -a -um *adj* yellow; blond; reddish-yellow, golden ‖ *m* gold coin

flēbil·is -is -e *adj* pitiful, pathetic, deplorable; tearful

flēbiliter *adv* tearfully, mournfully

fle·ctō -ctere -xī -xus *tr* to bend, curve; to turn, wheel about, turn around; to wind, twist; to curl *(hair);* to direct, avert, turn away *(eyes, mind, etc.);* to double, sail around *(a cape);* to inflect *(voice);* to change *(mind);* to persuade, move, appease; to handle *(reins, tiller);* to guide, steer; **animum** *(or* **mentem)** **flectere** to give way, bend; **viam** *(or* **iter)** **flectere** *(w.* **ad)** to make one's way toward, head toward; **vultum flectere** to change one's expression ‖ *refl & pass (geog)* to wind, curve ‖ *intr* to turn; to go

flēmin·a -um *npl* swollen ankles

fl·eō -ēre -ēvī -ētus *tr* to cry for, mourn (for) ‖ *intr* to cry

flēt·us -ūs *m* crying ‖ *mpl* tears

flexanim·us -a -um *adj* moving, touching, persuasive

flexī *perf of* **flectō**

flexibil·is -is -e *adj* flexible; shifty

flexil·is -is -e *adj* flexible, pliant

flexiloqu·us -a -um *adj* ambiguous

flexi·ō -ōnis *f* bending, turning; winding *(path);* inflection *(of voice)*

flexip·ēs -edis *adj* creeping *(ivy)*

flexuōs·us -a -um *adj* winding

flexūr·a -ae *f* bending, winding

flex·us -a -um *pp of* **flectō ‖** *adj* curved, twisting; involved, obscure *(language); modulated (voice); (of a syllable)* having a circumflex

flex·us -ūs *m* bending, curving, turning, winding; bend, curve; shift, change, transition; curling *(of hair);* inflection *(of voice)*

flīct·us -ūs *m* clashing, banging together, collision

flō flāre flāvī flātus *tr* to blow; to breathe, exhale; to coin *(money);* to play *(flute, songs)* **‖** *intr* to blow; to breathe

flocc·us -ī *m* tuft of wool; down; **floccī facere** *(or* **pendere)** to think little of, not give a hoot about

Flōr·a -ae *f* goddess of flowers *(honored on April 28-May 3)*

Flōrāl·ia -ium *npl* festival of Flora *(on April 28)*

Flōrālici·us -a -um *adj* of the Floralia

Flōrāl·is -is -e *adj* connected with Flora *or* her festival

flōr·ēns -entis *adj* blooming; prosperous; flourishing; illustrious; strong, powerful; vivid *(speaker); (w. abl)* in the prime of, at the height of

flōr·eō -ēre -uī *intr* to blossom, bloom; *(of wine)* to foam, froth, ferment; *(of arts)* to flourish; to be prosperous, be eminent; *(w. abl)* **1** to abound in; **2** to swarm with, be filled with; **aetāte flōrēre** to be in one's prime

flōr·ēscō -ēscere -uī *intr* to begin to bloom; to increase in renown

flōre·us -a -um *adj* flowery; made of flowers

flōridul·us -a -um *adj* flowery; pretty; in the bloom of youth

flōrid·us -a -um *adj* flowery; covered with flowers; fresh, pretty; florid *(style)*

flōrif·er -era -erum *adj* flowery

flōrileg·us -a -um *adj (of bees)* going from flower to flower

flōs flōris *m* flower; bud, blossom; best *(of anything);* prime *(of life);* youthful beauty; innocence, chastity; crown, glory; aroma *(of wine);* best period, heyday, zenith; *(rhet)* literary ornament

flōscul·us -ī *m* little flower; flower, pride, glory; *(rhet)* literary ornament

flūctifrag·us -a -um *adj* surging, wave-breaking *(shore)*

flūctig·er -era -erum *adj* wave-borne

flūctuāti·ō -ōnis *f* wavering, vacillation

flūctu·ō -āre -āvī -ātus *or* **flūctu·or -ārī -ātus sum** *intr* to fluctuate, undulate, wave; to be restless; to waver, vacillate

flūctuōs·us -a -um *adj* rough *(sea)*

flūct·us -ūs *m* wave; flowing, undulating; turbulence, commotion; disorder, unrest; **flūctus in simpulō** *(prov)* tempest in a teacup

flu·ēns -entis *adj* loose, flowing; *(morally)* loose; smooth, fluent *(speech, composition)*

fluent·a -ōrum *npl* flow, stream, river

fluenter *adv* like a wave

fluid·us -a -um *or* **flūvid·us -a -um** *adj* flowing, fluid; soft; relaxing

fluit·ō -āre *intr* to float, swim; to sail; to toss about; to hang loose, flap; to be uncertain, waver; to stagger; *(of fluids)* to flow

flūm·en -inis *n* flowing, stream; river; *(fig)* flood *(e.g., of tears, words);* **flūmine adversō** upstream; **secundō flūmine** downstream

flūmine·us -a -um *adj* river

flu·ō -ere -xī -xum *intr* to flow; to run down, drip; to overflow; to fall gradually, sink, drop, slip; to droop; to pass away, vanish, perish; *(of time)* to slip by; *(of plans)* to proceed, develop; to melt; to be fluent; to be monotonous; *(w.* **ab** *or* **ex) 1** to spring from, arise from, proceed from; **2** *(of words)* to be derived from; *(of crowds)* to stream, flock; *(of branches)* to spread; *(of clothes, hair)* to hang loosely, flow; *(phil)* to be in a state of transition *or* flux

fluviātil·is -is -e *adj* river, found in rivers; **equus fluviātilis** hippopotamus; **fluviātilēs nāvēs** river boats

flūvidus *see* **fluidus**

fluv·ius -(i)ī *m* river; running water; stream

fluxī *perf of* **fluō**

flux·us -a -um *adj* flowing, loose; careless; loose, dissolute; frail, weak; transient, perishable

fōcāl·e -is *n* scarf

fōcil·ō -āre -āvī -ātus *tr* to warm, revive; *(fig)* to foster, cherish

fōcul·um -ī *n* stove

focul·us -ī *m* brazier; *(fig)* fire

foc·us -ī *m* hearth, fireplace; brazier; funeral pile; altar; *(fig)* home, family

fodic·ō -āre -āvī -ātus *tr* to poke, nudge

fodiō fodere fōdī fossus *tr* to dig, dig out; *(fig)* to prod

foecund- = fēcund

foedē *adv* foully, cruelly, shamefully

foederāt·us -a -um *adj* federated, allied

foedifrag·us -a -um *adj* treaty-breaking, treacherous

foedit·ās -ātis *f* foulness, hideousness

foed·ō -āre -āvī -ātus *tr* to make filthy, foul up; to make hideous, disfigure; to mutilate, mangle; to ravage savagely *(land);* to darken, dim *(light);* to pollute, defile; to disgrace

foed·us -a -um *adj* foul, filthy, disgusting; horrible, shocking

foed·us -eris *n* treaty, charter; league; compact, agreement; law; **aequō foedere** on equal terms, mutually; **foedere certō** by fixed law; **foedere pactō** by fixed agreement; **foedus īcere** to conclude a treaty; **foedus rumpere** to break a treaty

foen- = **faen-**

foet·eō -ēre *intr* **(faet-, fēt-)** to stink

foetid·us -a -um *adj* **(faet-, fēt-)** fetid, stinking

foet·or -ōris *m* **(faet-, fēt-)** stink, stench

foetu- = **fētu-**

foliāt·us -a -um *adj* leafy ‖ *n* perfume *(made from aromatic leaves)*

fol·ium -(i)ī *n* leaf; petal; **folium recitāre Sibyllae** *(coll)* to tell the gospel truth *(literally, to read aloud the leaf of the Sibyl)*

follicul·us -ī *m* small bag, sack; shell, skin; eggshell; large inflated ball

foll·is -is *m* bag, sack; punching bag; inflated ball; bellows; moneybag; puffed-out cheeks

follīt·us -a -um *adj* enclosed in a sack

fōment·um -ī *n* compress, dressing; *(fig)* remedy, solace, alleviation

fōm·es -itis *m* tinder

fōns fontis *m* spring, fountain; spring water, water; stream; headwaters, source *(of river)*; *(fig)* source, origin

fontān·us -a -um *adj* spring

fonticul·us -ī *m* little spring, little fountain

for fārī fātus sum *tr & intr* to say, speak

forābil·is -is -e *adj* vulnerable; *(w. abl)* vulnerable to

forām·en -inis *n* hole, opening; socket; pore; stop *(in musical pipe)*

forās *adv (w. verbs implying motion)* out, outside, out of doors; *(w. verbs of selling, lending)* into the hands of outsiders; *(w. verbs of publishing)* into the light of day; **vocātus ad cēnam forās** invited out to dinner; **forās cēnāre** to eat out

forc·eps -ipis *f* tongs; tweezers; pliers; clippers; claw *(of a crab)*

ford·a -ae *f* pregnant cow

fore = **futūr·us -a -um esse** to be about to be

forem = **essem**

forēns·is -is -e *adj* of the Forum, in the Forum; public *(as opp. to domestic)*; forensic, of the lawcourts *(because the lawcourts were located in the Forum)* ‖ *npl* street clothes

forf·ex -icis *f* scissors; tongs, forceps

forficul·ae -ārum *fpl* scissors

foric·a -ae *f* public toilet

forīs *adv* outside, out of doors; outside the Senate, among the people; among strangers, in public life; abroad, in foreign countries; from outside, from abroad; **ā forīs** from outside; **forīs cēnāre** to eat out; **forīs esse** to be bankrupt

for·is -is *f* door; entrance, opening ‖ *fpl* double doors; **in foribus** in the doorway

fōrm·a -ae *f* form, shape, figure; beauty, good looks; image; mold, stamp; shoemaker's last; vision, apparition, phantom; species, form, nature, sort, kind; outline, design, sketch, plan; map

fōrmāl·is -is -e *adj* formal

fōrmāment·um -ī *n* shape

fōrmāt·or -ōris *m* shaper, creator

fōrmātūr·a -ae *f* fashioning, shaping

Formi·ae -ārum *fpl* town on S. coast of Latium

formīc·a -ae *f* ant

formīcīn·us -a -um *adj* ant-like

formīdābil·is -is -e *adj* terrifying, formidable

formīd·ō -āre -āvī -ātus *tr* to dread ‖ *intr* to be afraid

formīd·ō -inis *f* fear, terror; *(religious)* dread, awe; bogy; threats

formīdolōsē *adv* **(-dul-)** dreadfully, terribly

formīdolōs·us -a -um *adj* **(-dul-)** formidable, alarming; fearful, frightened

fōrm·ō -āre -āvī -ātus *tr* to form, shape, mold, build; *(w.* **in** *+ acc)* to transform into, make into; to make, produce, invent; to imagine; to shape, direct; to instruct; to depict, represent; *(gram)* to inflect

fōrmōsē *adv* beautifully, gracefully

fōrmōsit·ās -ātis *f* beauty, good looks

fōrmōs·us -a -um *adj* shapely, beautiful, handsome, good-looking

fōrmul·a -ae *f* nice shape, beauty; list, register; legal position; formula; contract, agreement; rule, regulation; pattern, type; charter *(of a government)*; *(leg)* regular form of judicial procedure; *(leg)* provisions *(of a law)*; *(phil)* principle; **fōrmula quaestiōnis** the rule of evidence; **fōrmulam accipere** to be sued; **fōrmulam ēdere** *(or* **intendere** *or* **scrībere)** to bring an action, bring suit

fornācāl·is -is -e *adj* of an oven

fornācul·a -ae *f* small oven

forn·āx -ācis *f* oven, furnace; kiln; forge

fornicāti·ō -ōnis *f* arch, vaulting

fornicāt·us -a -um *adj* arched

forn·ix -icis *m* arch, vault; arcade; brothel

fornus *see* **furnus**

for·ō -āre -āvī -ātus *tr* to bore, pierce

fors *adv* perhaps, chances are

for·s -tis *f* chance, luck, accident; **forte** by chance, accidentally, by accident; perhaps; **vīdistīne forte eum?** did you happen to see him?

forsan *or* **forsit** *or* **forsitan** *adv* perhaps

fortasse *or* **fortassis** *adv* perhaps

forte *see* **fors**

forticul·us -a -um *adj* quite bold, rather brave

fort·is -is -e *adj* brave, courageous; strong, mighty, powerful; resolute, steadfast, firm; loud, noisy *(sounds)*; *(of cities)* rich in resources *or* manpower; decent, honorable *(conduct)*; drastic *(remedies)*; vigorous *(speakers);* strong, potent *(medicine, wine)*

fortiter *adv* bravely, boldly; strongly, vigorously, firmly; justifiably

fortitūd·ō -inis *f* fortitude, bravery, courage; strength; resolution

fortuītō *adv* fortuitously, by chance, accidentally; haphazardly

fortuīt·us -a -um *adj* fortuitous, accidental; random, haphazard

fortūn·a -ae *f* chance, luck, fate, fortune; good luck, prosperity; bad luck, misfortune; lot; opportunity; circumstances; state, rank, position; property, goods, fortune; **fortūnae mandāre** to leave to chance; **fortūnam alicūius sequī** to follow s.o.'s leadership; **fortūnam suam sequī** to follow one's star; **fortūnam temptāre** *(or* **perīclitārī)** to tempt fate; **in fortūnā positus esse** *(or* **fortūnae subiectus esse)** to be left to chance, be dependent on luck; **per fortūnās**! *(in earnest entreaties)* for heaven's sake! **ll** *fpl* riches, fortune

fortūnātē *adv* happily; prosperously; successfully

fortūnāt·us -a -um *adj* fortunate, lucky, prosperous; happy; rich

fortūn·ō -āre -āvī -ātus *tr* to make happy, make prosperous; to bless

forul·ī -ōrum *mpl* bookshelves

For·um Appiī *(gen:* **Forī Appiī)** *n* town in Latium on the Via Appia

for·um -ī *n* forum, civic center; shopping center, mall, marketplace; market town; trade, commerce; public life, public affairs; jurisdiction; popular assembly; the bar, the courts; game board; **ad forum dēdūcere** to escort *(a young man)* to the Forum to assume the toga of manhood; **cēdere forō** to go bankrupt; **extrā suum forum** beyond his jurisdiction; **Forum Boārium** cattle market; **Forum Olitōrium** produce market; **Forum Piscātōrium** fish market; **Forum Rōmānum** Roman Forum; **in forō** outside one's home, in public; **forum agere** to hold court; **forum attingere** to enter public life; **in forō versārī** to be engaged in business

for·us -ī *m* gangway; tier of seats; tier of a beehive; **forī** bleachers

foss·a -ae *f* ditch, trench; moat; canal; **fossam dēprimere** to dig a ditch

fossi·ō -ōnis *f* digging

foss·or -ōris *m* digger; *(fig)* lout

fossūr·a -ae *f* digging

fossus *pp of* **fodiō**

fōtus *pp of* **foveō**

fove·a -ae *f* small pit; *(lit & fig)* pitfall

foveō fovēre fōvī fōtus *tr* to warm, keep warm; to refresh, soothe; to bathe; to massage; to freshen *(breath);* to nurse *(wounds);* to fondle, caress; to cherish *(hope);* to foster, nurture; to take the side of; to support, encourage; to pamper

frāct·us -a -um *pp of* **frangō ll** *adj* interrupted, irregular; weak, feeble

frāg·a -ōrum *npl* strawberries

fragil·is -is -e *adj* fragile, brittle; crackling; frail, flimsy; unstable; impermanent, uncertain

fragilit·ās -ātis *f* fragility; frailty

fraglō *see* **flagrō**

fragment·um -ī *n* fragment, remnant

frag·or -ōris *m* crash, noise, uproar, din; applause; clap of thunder

fragōs·us -a -um *adj* broken, uneven, rough; crashing, roaring

frāgr·ō *or* **frāgl·ō -āre -āvī** *intr* to smell sweet, be fragrant; to reek

frame·a -ae *f* German spear

frangō frangere frēgī frāctus *tr* to break to pieces, smash to pieces, shatter; to grind, crush *(grain);* to curl *(hair);* to make *(waters)* choppy; to violate, break *(treaty, law, promise); (fig)* to break down, overcome, crush, dishearten, humble; to repress *(feelings);* to weaken, soften; to inflict a crushing blow on *(a nation); (esp. of old age)* to exhaust, wear out; to break the force of; to move, touch; **diem merō frangere** to break up the day with wine; **iter frangere** to force a way; **nāvem frangere** to wreck a ship **ll** *pass* to suffer shipwreck; to relent

frātell·us -ī *m* little brother

frā·ter ·tris *m* brother; cousin; *(euphem) (homosexual)* sex partner; **frāter germānus** full brother; **frāter patruēlis** first cousin *(on father's side)*

frātercul·us -i *m* little brother

frāternē *adv* like a brother

frāternit·ās -ātis *f* brotherhood

frātern·us -a -um *adj* fraternal; brotherly; brother's

frātricīd·a -ae *m* murderer of a brother, fratricide

fraudāti·ō -ōnis *f* swindling

fraudāt·or -ōris *m* swindler, cheat

fraud·ō -āre -āvī -ātus *tr* to swindle, cheat, defraud; to embezzle; *(w. abl)* to cheat *(s.o.)* out of

fraudulenti·a -ae *f* dishonesty

fraudulent·us -a -um *adj* fraudulent, dishonest; deceitful, treacherous

frau·s -dis *f* fraud, deception, trickery; error, delusion; offense, crime; harm, damage; *(person)* fraud, cheat; **sine fraude** without harm to oneself, unscathed; without risk of punishment, with impunity; **fraudem lēgī facere** to violate the law

fraxine·us -a -um *adj* made of ash wood

fraxin·us -a -um *adj* of ash wood

fraxin·us -ī *f* ash tree; spear *(made of ash wood)*
frēgī *perf of* **frangō**
fremibund·us -a -um *adj* **(-meb-)** roaring
fremid·us -a -um *adj* growling
fremit·us -ūs *m* roar, growl, rumble, hum; din, noise; grumbling, muttering; loud buzz of approval
frem·ō -ere -uī -itus *tr* to grumble at, complain loudly about; to demand angrily, clamor for; to declare noisily **II** *intr* to roar, growl, snort, howl; to grumble; to resound
frem·or -ōris *m* roaring, grumbling; murmuring
frend·ō -ere -uī *intr* to gnash the teeth; **dentibus frendere** to gnash the teeth
frēnī *see* **frēnum**
frēn·ō -āre -āvī -ātus *tr* to bridle, curb; *(fig)* to curb
frēn·um -ī *n or* **frēn·a -ōrum** *npl or* **frēn·ī -ōrum** *mpl* reins; bridle, bit; *(fig)* curb, control, restraint; *(poet)* riding *(on horseback);* **frēna** *(or* **frēnōs** *or* **frēnum)** **accipere** *(or* **patī)** to take the bit, learn obedience; **frēna** *(or* **frēnōs) dare** *(or* **effundere** *or* **immittere** *or* **laxāre** *or* **remittere)** to loosen the reins; **frēna (ab)rumpere** to snap the reins, bolt; **frēna** *(or* **frēnōs) tenēre** *(or* **moderārī)** *(w. gen)* to hold the reins of, be in control of; **in frēnīs** *(or* **sub frēnō)** under control
frequ·ēns -entis *adj* crowded, packed, filled; in crowds, numerous; frequent, repeated, usual, common; full, plenary *(Senate session); (of persons)* constant, regular; *(may be rendered adverbially)* often, frequently, *e.g.:* **frequēns et audīvī et adfuī** I was often at your side and heard you speak; *(w. abl)* **1** crowded with; **2** densely covered with; **frequēns emporium** well-stocked market; **frequēns est** *(w. inf)* it is a common practice to
frequentāti·ō -ōnis *f* piling up, concentration
frequenter *adv* in crowds, in large numbers; frequently, in quick succession; commonly, widely; **frequenter habitārī** *(or* **colī)** to be densely populated
frequenti·a -ae *f* crowd; crowded assembly, large attendance; dense mass; populousness; populous district; crowdedness; abundance; multitude; population; frequency; conscientious performance *(of duties);* **frequentia vehiculōrum** heavy traffic
frequent·ō -āre -āvī -ātus *tr* to crowd, people, populate; *(w. abl)* to pack with, stock with, crowd with; to assemble in a crowd; to crowd around *(a person);* to attend *(e.g., games)* in large numbers; to sue frequently; to say over and over again; to do often, repeat; to use frequently; to frequent, resort to; to visit often; to celebrate, observe *(festival, ceremony);* to attend *(a meeting, school, lecture);* to appear on *(the stage);* to inhabit *(a place)* **II** *pass* to become common
fretēns·is -is -e *adj* **mare fretēnse** Strait of Messina *(between Italy and Sicily)*
fret·um -ī *n* strait, channel; sea, the deep; waters; *(fig)* seething flood
frēt·us -a -um *adj (w. dat or abl)* relying on, confident of, depending on; *(w. acc & inf)* confident that
fret·us -ūs *m* strait
fric·ō -āre -uī -tus *or* **-ātus** *tr* to rub; to chafe; to rub down, massage
frictus *pp of* **fricō**
frīctus *pp of* **frīgō**
frīgefact·ō -āre *tr* to cool
frīg·eō -ēre *intr* to be cold, be chilly; to freeze; *(fig)* to be numbed, be lifeless, be dull; *(fig)* to get a cool reception, get the cold shoulder; *(of words)* to fall flat; *(of an old man)* to lack vigor; to have nothing to do, be idle
frīger·ō -āre *tr* to cool off
frīgēsc·ō -ere frīxī *intr* to become cold, become chilled; to become lifeless; *(of a speech)* to fall flat
frīgid·a -ae *f* cold water
frīgidāri·us -a -um *adj* cooling
frīgidē *adv* feebly; coolly
frīgidul·us -a -um *adj* rather cold; rather faint
frīgid·us -a -um *adj* cold, cool; numbed, dull, lifeless; indifferent, unimpassioned; flat, insipid, trivial **II** *f* cold water
frīg·ō frīgere frīxī frīctus *tr* to roast, fry
frīg·us -oris *n* cold, coldness, chill, coolness; frost; cold of winter, winter; coldness of death, death; chill, fever; shudder, chill; cold region; cold reception; coolness, indifference; slowness, inactivity **II** *npl* cold spell
frigutt·iō -īre *intr* to stutter
fringill·a -ae *f* a songbird
fri·ō -āre -āvī -ātus *tr & refl & pass* to crumble
fritill·us -ī *m* dice box
frīvol·us -a -um *adj* frivolous, trifling, worthless, sorry, pitiful **II** *npl* trifles
frīxī *perf of* **frīgēscō** *and* **frīgō** *and* **frīgeō**
frondāt·or -ōris *m* pruner
frond·eō -ēre *intr* to have leaves; *(of places)* to be green with trees
frondēsc·ō -ere *intr* to get leaves
fronde·us -a -um *adj* leafy
frondif·er -era -erum *adj* leafy
frondōs·us -a -um *adj* full of leaves, leafy
frōn·s -dis *f* foliage; leafy bough, green bough; chaplet, garland
frōn·s -tis *f* forehead, brow; front end, front; face, look; façade; vanguard; exte-

rior, appearance; outer end of a scroll; sense of shame; **ā fronte** in front; **frōns firma** *(fig)* a bold front; **frōns prīma** front line; **frontem contrahere** *(or* **addūcere** *or* **cōnstringere** *or* **obdūcere)** to frown; **frontem ferīre** to tap oneself on the forehead *(in annoyance)*; **frontem remittere** *(or* **exporrigere)** to smooth the brow, cheer up, relax; **frontis tenerae vidērī** to seem to blush *(literally, to seem to be of sensitive brow)*; **in fronte** *(in measuring land)* in breadth, in frontage; **salvā fronte** without shame; **tenuis frōns** low forehead

frontāl·ia -ium *npl* frontlet *(ornament for forehead of horse)*

front·ō -ōnis *m* person with bulging forehead

frūctuāri·us -a -um *adj* productive; subject to land tax

frūctuōs·us -a -um *adj* fruitful, productive

frūctus *pp of* **fruor**

frūct·us -ūs *m* fruit, produce; proceeds, profit, income, return, revenue; enjoyment, satisfaction; benefit, reward, results, consequence

frūgāl·is -is -e *adj* thrifty, frugal

frūgālit·ās -ātis *f* frugality, economy; temperance; honesty; worth

frūgāliter *adv* frugally, economically; temperately

frūgēs *see* **frūx**

frūgī *indecl adj* frugal; thrifty; temperate; honest; worthy; useful; proper; **frūgī esse** to do the right thing

frūgif·er -era -erum *adj* fruitful, productive, fertile; profitable

frūgifer·ēns -entis *adj* fruitful

frūgileg·us -a -um *adj (of ants)* food-gathering

frūgipar·us -a -um *adj* fruitful

fruitus *pp of* **fruor**

frūmentāri·us -a -um *adj* of grain, grain; grain-producing; of provisions; **rēs frūmentāria** *(mil)* supplies, quartermaster **||** *m* grain dealer; *(mil)* forager

frūmentāti·ō -ōnis *f (mil)* foraging

frūmentāt·or -ōris *m* grain merchant; *(mil)* forager

frūment·or -ārī -ātus sum *intr (mil)* to forage

frūment·um -ī *n* grain; wheat **||** *npl* grain fields; crops

frūn·īscor -īscī -ītus sum *tr* to enjoy

fruor fruī frūctus sum *or* **fruitus sum** *tr* to enjoy; **||** *intr (w. abl)* **1** to enjoy, delight in; **2** to enjoy the company of; **3** *(law)* to have the use and enjoyment of

frūstillātim *adv* in bits

frūstrā *adv* in vain, uselessly, for nothing; without reason, groundlessly; **frūstrā discēdere** to go away disappointed; **frūstrā esse** to be mistaken; **frūstrā habēre** to have *(s.o.)* confused

frūstrām·en -inis *n* deception, error

frūstrāti·ō -ōnis *f* deception; frustration

frūstrāt·us -ūs *m* deception; **frūstrātuī habēre** *(coll)* to take for a sucker

frūstr·or -ārī -ātus sum *or* **frūstr·ō -āre** *tr* to deceive, trick; to disappoint; to frustrate

frūstulent·us -a -um *adj* full of crumbs

frūst·um -ī *n* crumb, bit, scrap; **frūstum puerī** *(coll)* whippersnapper

frutect·um *or* **fruticēt·um -ī** *n* thicket, shrubbery **||** *npl* bushes

frut·ex -icis *m* shrub, bush; stem, trunk; *(coll)* blockhead

fruticētum *see* **frutectum**

frutic·ō -āre -āvī *or* **frutic·or -ārī** *intr* to sprout; to become bushy; *(fig) (of hair)* to become bushy

fruticōs·us -a -um *adj* bushy, overgrown with bushes

frūx frūgis *f or* **frūg·ēs -um** *fpl* produce; crops; grain; vegetables; bread, meal; barley meal *(for sacrifice)*; fruits, benefit; *(singl)* morality, honesty; **ad frūgem bonam sē recipere** to turn over a new leaf; **bonae frūgī esse** to be honest, be thrifty; **expers frūgis** worthless; **frūgem facere** to do the decent thing

fūcāt·us -a -um *adj* artificial *(color)*; dyed, colored, painted; phony

fūc·ō -āre -āvī -ātus *tr* to dye, tint; to apply makeup to; to disguise, falsify

fūcōs·us -a -um *adj* painted, colored; artificial, spurious

fūc·us -ī *m* (red) paint; rouge; drone; bee-glue; disguise; pretense, deceit; **sine fūcō ac fallāciīs** without mincing words

fūdī *perf of* **fundō**

fue *or* **fu** *interj* phui!

fug·a -ae *f* flight, escape; avoidance; exile; speed, swift passage; disappearance; *(w. gen)* avoidance of, escape from; **fugae sēsē mandāre** *(or* **fugam capere** *or* **fugam capessere** *or* **fugam facere** *or* **sē in fugam cōnferre** *or* **sē in fugam conicere** *or* **sēsē in fugam dare)** to flee; **in fugam cōnferre** *(or* **in fugam conicere** *or* **in fugam dare** *or* **in fugam impellere)** to put to flight; **fugam petere** to look for a means of escape

fugācius *adv* more cautiously, with one eye on flight

fug·āx -ācis *adj* apt to flee, fleeing; shy, timid; swift; transitory; *(w. gen)* shy of, shunning, avoiding, steering clear of, averse to

fugi·ēns -entis *adj* fleeing, retreating; *(w. gen)* avoiding, averse to

fugiō fugere fūgī fugitus *tr* to escape, escape from, get away from; to run away from, shun, avoid; to succeed in avoiding;

to vanish from; to be repelled by; to leave *(esp. one's country);* to be averse to, dislike; to escape the notice of, be unknown to; **fuge** *(w. inf)* do not ... !; **fugere cōnspectum** *(w. gen)* to keep out of sight of; **fūgit mē ratiō** I made a mistake; **fūgit mē scrībere** it slipped my mind to write ‖ *intr* to flee, escape, run away; to go into exile; to vanish; to pass away, perish; to begin to decay; *(w.* **ab)** to keep away from, shrink from; *(of things)* to slip out of one's grasp *or* control

fugit·āns -antis *adj* fleeing; *(w. gen)* averse to

fugitīv·us -a -um *adj & m* runaway, fugitive

fugit·ō -āre *tr* to run away from, shun ‖ *intr* to run away

fug·ō -āre -āvī -ātus *tr* to put to flight, rout, drive away, chase away; to exile, banish; to avert

fulcīm·en -inis *n* support, prop

ful·ciō -cīre -sī -tus *tr* to prop up, support; to sustain, strengthen; **pedibus fulcīre** to tread

fulcr·um -ī *n* bedpost; couch leg; *(fig)* bed, couch

ful·geō -gēre -sī *or* **fulg·ō -ere** *intr* to gleam, flash, blaze, shine, glare; to be conspicuous, be illustrious

fulgid·us -a -um *adj* flashing, shining

fulgō *see* **fulgeō**

fulg·or -ōris *m* flash; flash of lightning, lightning; brightness; splendor, glory; *(astr)* meteor; *(astr)* bright star; **fulgor lūnae** moonlight

fulg·ur -uris *m* flash of lightning; place struck by lightning

fulgurāl·is -is -e *adj* of lightning; *(books)* on lightning

fulgurāt·or -ōris *m* interpreter of lightning

fulgurīt·us -a -um *adj* struck by lightning

fulgur·ō -āre -āvī -ātum *intr* to lighten, send lightning ‖ *v impers* it is lightning

fulic·a -ae *or* **ful·ix -icis** *f* waterfowl *(perhaps the coot)*

fūlīg·ō -inis *f* soot *(used as a cosmetic, in paint, in medications, in ink)*

fulix *see* **fulica**

full·ō -ōnis *m* fuller *(person who shrank, beat, pressed, cleaned, and whitened cloth with chalk)*

fullōni·a -ae *f* fuller's craft, fulling

fullōnic·a -ae *f* fuller's craft, fulling; fuller's shop

fullōni·us -a -um *adj* fuller's

fulm·en -inis *n* thunderbolt, lightning bolt; *(fig)* bolt out of the blue; **fulmine ict·us -a -um** struck by lightning

fulment·a -ae *f* heel

fulmine·us -a -um *adj* of lightning, lightning; shiny, sparkling, flashing

fulmin·ō -āre -āvī -ātum *intr (said of Jupiter)* send lightning; *(fig)* to flash; *(fig)* to spread disaster ‖ *impers* it is lightning

fulsī *perf of* **fulciō** *and* **fulgeō**

fultūr·a -ae *f* support, prop

fultus *pp of* **fulciō**

fulv·us -a -um *adj* yellow, yellowish brown, reddish yellow, tawny; strawberry-blond

fūme·us -a -um *adj* smoky, murky

fūmid·us -a -um *adj* smoky, full of smoke; smoking; steaming

fūmif·er -era -erum *adj* smoking

fūmific·ō -āre -āvī *intr* to smoke; to burn incense

fūmific·us -a -um *adj* smoking, steaming

fūm·ō -āre -āvī *intr* to smoke, fume; to steam; to reek

fūmōs·us -a -um *adj* smoky; grimy from smoke; smoked *(food)*

fūm·us -ī *m* smoke; fume; steam, vapor ‖ *mpl* clouds of smoke

fūnāl·e -is *n* taper of wax-soaked rope; chandelier, candelabrum

fūnambul·us -ī *m* tightrope walker

fūncti·ō -ōnis *f* performance

fūnct·us -a -um *pp of* **fungor** ‖ *adj* dead ‖ *mpl* the dead

fund·a -ae *f* sling; pebble *(used in a sling);* dragnet

fundām·en -inis *n* foundation; **fundāmina pōnere** to lay the foundations

fundāment·um -ī *n* foundation; *(fig)* basis, ground, beginning; **ā fundāmentīs** utterly; **fundāmenta agere** *(or* **iacere** *or* **locāre)** to lay the foundation(s)

fundāt·or -ōris *m* founder

fundāt·us -a -um *adj* well-founded, established

Fund·ī -ōrum *mpl* Fundi *(town in Latium)*

fundit·ō -āre -āvī -ātus *tr* to sling, hurl with a sling; *(fig)* to sling *(e.g., words)* around

fundit·or -ōris *m* slinger

funditus *adv* from the bottom, utterly, entirely

fund·ō -āre -āvī -ātus *tr* to found; to put on a firm basis, establish; to secure, make fast ‖ *pass (w. abl)* to be based on

fundō fundere fūdī fūsus *tr* to pour, pour out; to smelt *(metals);* to cast *(in metal);* to pour in streams, shower, hurl; to pour out, empty; to spread, extend, diffuse; to bring forth, bear, yield in abundance; to throw to the ground, bring down; to give up, lose, waste; to pour out *(words); (mil)* to pour in *(troops); (mil)* to rout

fund·us -ī *m* bottom; farm; estate; *(leg)* sanctioner, authority

fūnebr·is -is -e *adj* funeral, funerary; deadly, murderous

fūnerāt·us -a -um *adj* done in, killed; **prope fūnerātus** almost sent to *(one's)* grave
fūnere·us -a -um *adj* funerary, mourning; deadly, fatal
fūner·ō -āre -āvī -ātus *tr* to bury; to bring *(s.o.)* to his grave, kill
fūnest·ō -āre -āvī -ātus *tr* to defile with murder, desecrate
fūnest·us -a -um *adj* funereal, mourning; lamentable; polluted *(through contact with a corpse);* deadly, fatal, calamitous; sad, dismal, mournful
fungīn·us -a -um *adj* of a mushroom
fun·gor -gī fūnctus sum *tr* to perform, execute; **diem** *(or* **vītam)** **fungī** to die **II** *intr (w. abl)* **1** to perform, execute, discharge, do; **2** to busy oneself with, be engaged in; **3** to finish complete; *(w.* **prō** + *abl)* to act as; **fātō** *(or* **morte** *or* **vītā** *or* **officiō)** **fungī** to die
fung·us -ī *m* mushroom, fungus; candle snuffer; *(fig)* clown
fūnicul·us -ī *m* cord
fūn·is -is *m* rope, cable, cord; rigging; **fūnem redūcere** *(fig)* to change one's mind; **per extentum fūnem īre** *(lit & fig)* to walk a tightrope; **sequī potius quam dūcere fūnem tortum** to follow the lead rather than to lead
fūn·us -eris *n* funeral, funeral rites, burial; corpse; death; murder; havoc, ruin, destruction; **sub fūnus** on the brink of the grave **II** *npl* shades of the dead
fūr fūris *mf* thief; *(fig)* rogue
fūrācissimē *adv* just like a thief
fūr·āx -ācis *adj* thievish
furc·a -ae *f* fork; fork-shaped prop *(for supporting vines, bleachers, etc.);* pillory *(used to punish slaves); (topog)* defile, pass
furcif·er -erī *m* rogue, rascal
furcifer·a -ae *f* rascal *(female)*
furcill·a -ae *f* pitchfork; **furcillā extrūdī** *(coll)* to be given the bum's rush
furcill·ō -āre -āvī -ātus *tr* to support, prop up
furcul·a -ae *f* fork-shaped prop **II** *fpl* narrow pass, defile; **Furculae Caudīnae** Caudine Forks *(mountain pass in Samnium where Roman army was trapped in 321 B.C. and made to pass under the yoke)*
furenter *adv* furiously
furf·ur -uris *m* chaff; bran
furi·a -ae *f* frenzy, madness, rage; remorse; madman **II Furia** Fury *(one of the three goddesses of vengeance: Megaera, Tisiphone, and Alecto)*
furiāl·is -is -e *adj* frenzied, frantic, furious; infuriated; of the Furies
furiāliter *adv* frantically
furibund·us -a -um *adj* frenzied, frantic, mad; inspired
fūrīn·us -a -um *adj* of thieves
furi·ō -āre -āvī -ātus *tr* to drive mad, infuriate
furiōsē *adv* in a rage, in a frenzy
furiōs·us -a -um *adj* frenzied, frantic, mad, furious; maddening
furn·us -ī *m* **(for-)** oven; bakery
fur·ō -ere *intr* to be out of one's mind; to rush furiously around; to rage, rave
fūr·or -ārī -ātus sum *tr* to steal, pilfer; to pillage; to plagiarize; to obtain by fraud **II** *refl* to steal away
fur·or -ōris *m* madness, rage, fury, passion; furor, excitement; prophetic frenzy, inspiration; passionate love
fūrtific·us -a -um *adj* thievish
fūrtim *adv* secretly; imperceptibly
fūrtīvē *adv* secretly, stealthily
fūrtīv·us -a -um *adj* stolen; secret, hidden, furtive
fūrt·um -ī *n* theft, robbery; trick; secret action, intrigue; secret love; **fūrtum facere** to steal **II** *npl* intrigues; secret love affair; stolen goods
fūruncul·us -ī *m* petty thief
furv·us -a -um *adj* black, dark, gloomy, eerie; **diēs furvus** unlucky day
fūscin·a -ae *f* trident
fūsc·ō -āre -āvī -ātus *tr* to darken, blacken
fūsc·us -a -um *adj* dark; dim, ill-lit *(room);* hoarse *(voice);* dark-skinned, swarthy; low, muffled *(sound)*
fūsē *adv* widely, extensively; in great detail; loosely, roughly
fūsil·is -is -e *adj* molten, liquid
fūsi·ō -ōnis *f* outpouring, effusion
fūst·is -is *m* club; stick; beating to death *(as military punishment)*
fūstitudin·us -a -um *adj (hum)* whip-happy
fūstuār·ium -(i)ī *n* beating to death *(as military punishment)*
fūs·us -a -um *pp of* **fundō II** *adj* spread out; broad, wide; diffuse *(style)*
fūs·us -ī *m* spindle
fūtātim *adv* frequently, abundantly
futtilē *adv* uselessly, in vain
futtil·is -is -e *adj* **(fūtil-)** brittle; futile, worthless; trifling
futtilit·ās -ātis *f* **(fūtil-)** futility, uselessness
fut·uō -uere -uī -ūtus *tr (vulg)* to have intercourse with, screw *(a woman)*
futūr·us -a -um *adj* coming, future; impending, imminent; **tempus futūrum** *(gram)* future tense **II** *n* the future; **in futūrum** for the future **II** *npl* future events, the future
futūti·ō -ōnis *f (vulg)* sex, screwing
futūt·or -ōris *m (vulg)* sex partner
futūtr·īx -īcis *adj (fem only) (vulg)* lecherous **II** *f* sex partner *(female)*

G

G, g *(supply* littera) *f* seventh letter of the Latin alphabet; letter name: **ge**
gabat·a -ae *f* plate, dish
Gabi·ī -ōrum *mpl* Gabii *(ancient town just outside Rome)*
Gabīni·us -a -um *adj* of the Gabinian clan
Gabīn·us -a -um *adj* of Gabii **II** *mpl* the people of Gabii
Gād·ēs *or* **Gād·īs -ium** *fpl or* **Gād·is -is** *f* Cadiz *(in S. Spain)*
Gādītān·us -a -um *adj* of Gades **II** *mpl* the people of Gades **II** *fpl* dancing girls from Gades **II** *n* dance by Gades dancing girls
gaes·um -ī *n* (**gēs-**) Gallic spear
Gaetūl·us -a -um *adj* Gaetulian, African **II** *mpl* a people in N.W. Africa along the Sahara Desert
Gāï·a -ae *f* Gaia *(archaic feminine form of Gaius, surviving in ritual and legal language as a name for any woman)*
Gā·ïus -iī Gaius *(Roman praenomen; the names of Gaius and Gaia were formally given to the bridegroom and bride respectively at the wedding ceremony)*
Galat·ae -ārum *mpl* Galatians *(a people of central Asia Minor)*
Galatē·a -ae *f* sea nymph loved by Acis and Polyphemus
Galati·a -ae *f* Galatia *(Roman province in Asia Minor)*
Galb·a -ae *m* Roman emperor *(A.D. 68–69)*
galbane·us -a -um *adj* of galbanum
galban·um -ī *n* galbanum *(resinous sap of a Syrian plant)*
galbe·us -ī *m* armband *(worn as ornament or for medical purposes)*
galbināt·us -a -um *adj* dressed in chartreuse
galbin·us -a -um *adj* chartreuse; yellowish; *(fig)* effeminate **II** *npl* chartreuse clothes
gale·a -ae *f* helmet *(usu. of leather)*
galeāt·us -a -um *adj* helmeted, wearing a helmet
gale·ō -āre *tr* to equip with a helmet
galēricul·um -ī *n* leather cap; toupee
galērīt·us -a -um *adj* wearing a leather cap
galēr·um -ī *n or* **galēr·us -ī** *m* leather cap; ceremonial cap *(worn by pontifices, flamines, etc.)*; wig
gall·a -ae *f* gallnut *(nutlike growth on a plant)* **II** *f* Gallic woman
Gall·ī -ōrum *mpl* Gauls *(inhabitants of modern France, Belgium, and N. Italy)*
Galli·a -ae *f* Gaul
Gallicān·us -a -um *adj* Gallic
gallicin·ium -(i)ī *n* cockcrow, daybreak
Gallic·us -a -um *adj* Gallic; belonging to the priests of Cybele; **canis Gallicus** a breed of hunting dog **II** *f* Gallic shoe
gallīn·a -ae *f* chicken, hen; *(as term of endearment)* chick
gallīnāce·us -a -um *adj* of domestic fowl; **gallus gallīnāceus** rooster; **lac gallīnāceum** *(hum)* hen's milk *(i.e., an impossible thing)*
gallīnār·ius -(i)ī *m* poultry farmer; one who looks after the poultry used in augury
Gallograec·ī -ōrum *mpl* Galatians *(Celts who migrated from Gaul to Asia Minor in 3rd cent. B.C.)*
Gall·us -a -um *adj* Gallic **II** *m* a Gaul; priest of Cybele; Galatian
gall·us -ī *m* rooster, cock
gāne·a -ae *f or* **gāne·um -ī** *n* low-class restaurant, dive; gluttonous eating
gāne·ō -ōnis *m* glutton
gāneum *see* **gānea**
Gangarid·ae -ārum *mpl* an Indian people near the Ganges
Gang·ēs -is *m* Ganges River
Gangētic·us -a -um *adj* Indian
gann·iō -īre *intr* to snarl
gannīt·us -ūs *m* snarling
Ganymēd·ēs -is *m* Ganymede *(handsome boy carried off to Olympus by an eagle to become the cupbearer of the gods and catamite of Zeus)*
Ganymēdē·us -a -um *adj* of Ganymede
Garamant·ēs -um *mpl* tribe in N. Africa
Garamant·is -idos *adj (fem only) (poet)* African
Gargān·us -ī *m* mountain in S.E. Italy
Gargar·a -ōrum *npl* a peak in the Ida mountain range in the Troad; town in that region
garr·iō -īre -īvī *tr* to chatter, prattle; **nūgās garrīre** to talk nonsense **II** *intr* to chatter, chat; *(of frogs)* to croak
garrulit·ās -ātis *f* talkativeness; chattering
garrul·us -a -um *adj* garrulous, talkative; blabbing; *(of birds)* chattering; *(time)* for chattering
gar·um -ī *n* fish sauce
gaud·ēns -entis *adj* cheerful
gaudeō gaudēre gavīsus sum *tr* to rejoice at; **gaudium gaudēre** to feel joy **II** *intr* to rejoice, be glad; *(w. abl)* to be glad about, feel pleased at, delight in; **in sē gaudēre** *(or* **in sinū)** **gaudēre** to be secretly glad
gaud·ium -(i)ī *n* joy, gladness, delight; cause of joy, source of delight; **gaudium nūntiāre** to announce good news; **mala mentis gaudia** gloating
gaul·us -ī *m* bucket
gausap·a -ae *f or* **gausap·e -is** *or* **gausap·um -ī** *n* coarse woolen cloth; felt; shaggy beard
gāvīsus *pp of* **gaudeō**
gāz·a -ae *f* royal treasure; treasure, riches
gelasīn·us -ī *m* dimple
gelidē *adv* coldly; indifferently

gelid·us -a -um *adj* cold, icy, frosty; ice-cold, stiff, numbed **||** *f* ice-cold water
gel·ō -āre -āvī -ātus *tr & intr* to freeze
Gelōn·ī -ōrum *mpl* Scythian tribe
gel·u -ūs *n or* **gel·um -ī** *n* cold; frost; ice; chill, coldness *(of death, old age, fear)*
gemebund·us -a -um *adj* groaning
gemellipar·a -ae *f* mother of twins
gemell·us -a -um *adj & m* twin
gemināti·ō -ōnis *f* doubling; repetition
gemin·ō -āre -āvī -ātus *tr* to double; to join, unite; to pair; to do repeatedly **||** *intr* to become double
gemin·us -a -um *adj* twin; paired, double, twofold, two, both; similar **||** *m* twin
gemit·us -ūs *m* sigh, groan
gemm·a -ae *f* bud; gem, jewel; jeweled goblet; signet ring, signet; eye *(of a peacock's tail);* literary gem; pebble *(for marking days);* a piece in a game-board
gemm·āns -antis *adj* adorned with gems; decorated
gemmāt·us -a -um *adj* set with gems, jeweled
gemme·us -a -um *adj* set with jewels, jeweled; brilliant, glittering, sparkling
gemmi·fer -fera -ferum *adj* containing gems; gem-producing
gemm·ō -āre -āvī -ātum *intr* to sprout, bud; to sparkle
gem·ō -ere -uī -itus *tr* to sigh over, lament **||** *intr* to sigh, groan, moan; to creak
Gemōni·ae -ārum *fpl* steps on the Aventine slope from which the corpses of criminals were thrown into the Tiber River
gen·a -ae *f* cheek; cheekbone; eyelid **||** *fpl* cheeks; region about the eyes, eyes; sockets of the eyes
geneālog·us -ī *m* genealogist
gen·er -erī *m* son-in-law; daughter's fiancé; brother-in-law
generāl·is -is -e *adj* general, universal
generāliter *adv* in general, generally
generāsc·ō -ere *intr* to be generated
generātim *adv* by species, by classes; in general, generally
generāt·or -ōris *m* producer, father
gener·ō -āre -āvī -ātus *tr* to beget, procreate, father; *(of places, of the body)* to produce; to engender, arouse *(emotions)*
generōsē *adv* with dignity, nobly
generōsit·ās -ātis *f* good breeding, nobility of stock
generōs·us -a -um *adj* of good stock, high-born, noble; noble-minded; high-spirited
genes·is -is *f* birth; horoscope
genesta *see* **genista**
genetīv·us -a -um *adj* **(-nit-)** inborn, innate; *(gram)* genitive **||** *m (gram)* genitive case
genetr·īx -īcis *f* **(-nit-)** mother, ancestress
geniāl·is -is -e *adj* nuptial, bridal; genial; joyous, merry, festive
geniāliter *ad* merrily
geniculāt·us -a -um *adj* knotted, having knots, jointed
genist·a -ae *f* **(-nest-)** broom plant
genitābil·is -is -e *adj* productive
genitāl·is -is -e *adj* generative, productive; of birth; **diēs genitālis** birthday **||** *n* genital organ
genitāliter *adv* fruitfully
genitīvus *see* **genetīvus**
genit·or -ōris *m* father; creator; source, cause
genitrīx *see* **genetrīx**
genitūr·a -ae *f* horoscope
genitus *pp of* **gignō**
gen·ius -iī *m* guardian spirit *(of person, place, or thing); (hum)* personification of all natural appetites, natural inclination; talent, wit
gen·ō -ere *see* **gignō**
gēn·s -tis *f (Roman)* clan, extended family *(sharing the same nomen and, theoretically, the same ancestor);* stock; tribe; nation, people; country; class, set, race; species, breed; descendant, offspring; *(poet)* herd, flock, hive **||** *fpl* the peoples of the world; rest of the world *(apart from the Romans),* foreign nations; **longē gentium abīre** to be far, far away; **minimē gentium** by no means; **ubi gentium** where in the world
gentic·us -a -um *adj* tribal; national
gentīlici·us -a -um *adj* of a Roman clan, of the extended family
gentīl·is -is -e *adj* family, hereditary; tribal; national **||** *m* clansman, kinsman
gentīlit·ās -ātis *f* clan relationship
gen·ū -ūs *n* knee; **genibus minor** kneeling; **genibus nīxus** on one's knees; **genuum iūnctūra** knee joint; **sē advolvere ad genua** *(w. gen)* to prostrate oneself before
genuāl·ia -ium *npl* garters
genuī *perf of* **gignō**
genuīn·us -a -um *adj* innate, natural
genuīn·us -a -um *adj* of the cheek; jaw, of the jaw **||** *mpl* back teeth
-gen·us -a -um *adjl suf* forms adjectives meaning "born of": **caeligenus** heaven-born
gen·us -eris *n* race, descent, lineage, breed, stock, family; noble birth; tribe; nation, people; descendant, offspring, posterity; kind, sort, species, class; rank, order, division; fashion, style, way; matter, respect; genus; sex; *(gram)* gender; **aliquid id genus** *(acc of respect instead of gen of quality)* something of that sort; **genus hūmānum** *(or* **genus hominum)** the human race, mankind; **in omnī genere** in every respect; **suī generis** in a class of its *(her, his, their)* own, unique

geōgraphi·a -ae *f* geography
geōmetr·ēs -ae *m* geometer, mathematician
geōmetri·a -ae *f* geometry
geōmetric·us -a -um *adj* geometrical ‖ *f* geometry ‖ *npl* geometry
geōrgic·us -a -um *adj* agricultural ‖ *npl* Georgics *(poems on farming by Vergil)*
ger·ēns -entis *adj (w. gen)* managing, running *(e.g., a business)*
germānē *adv* sincerely
Germān·ī -ōrum *mpl* Germans
Germāni·a -ae *f* Germany
Germānic·us -a -um *adj* Germanic ‖ *m* cognomen of Tiberius's nephew and adoptive son *(15 B.C.–A.D. 19)*
germānit·ās -ātis *f* brotherhood, sisterhood *(relationship between brothers and sisters of the same parents; relationship between colonies of the same mother-city)*
germān·us -a -um *adj* having the same parents; brotherly, sisterly; genuine, real, true ‖ *m* full brother ‖ *f* full sister
germ·en -inis *n* sprout, shoot; bud; embryo
germin·ō -āre -āvī -ātus *tr* to put forth, grow *(hair, wings, etc.)* ‖ *intr* to sprout
gerō gerere gessī gestus *tr* to bear, carry *(in one's hands); (of things)* to have in it, contain; to bear *(fruit);* to bear, carry *(in the womb);* to wear *(clothing);* to hold *(consulship, etc.);* to spend, pass *(time);* to bring; to display, exhibit; to entertain *(feelings);* to assume; to carry on, manage; to govern, regulate, administer; to carry out, transact, do, accomplish; **bellum gerere** to fight a war, carry on a war; **cōnsulātum gerere** to hold the consulship; **dum ea geruntur** while that was going on; **mōrem gerere** *(w. dat)* to gratify; **persōnam gerere** *(w. gen)* to play the part of; **rem gerere** to run a business, conduct an affair; **rēs prosperē gerere** *(mil)* to conduct a successful campaign ‖ *refl* to behave, conduct oneself; *(w.* **prō** + *abl)* to claim to be for; **sē medium gerere** to remain neutral
ger·ō -ōnis *m* porter
gerr·ae -ārum *fpl* trifles; *as interj* nonsense!
gerulifigul·us -ī *m* accomplice; *(w. gen)* accomplice in
gerul·us -ī *m* porter
Gēry·ōn -onis *or* **Gēryon·ēs -ae** *m* Geryon *(three-headed monster of Spain that was slain by Hercules)*
gessī *perf of* **gerō**
gestām·en -inis *n* load; article(s) worn; load, pack, burden; vehicle, litter ‖ *npl* ornaments; accouterments; arms
gestāti·ō -ōnis *f* ride *(on horseback, in litter, in vehicle);* drive *(place),* walk *(place)*
gestāt·or -ōris *m* bearer, carrier
gest·iō -īre -īvī *or* **-iī** *intr* to be delighted, be thrilled; to be eager; *(w. inf)* to be itching to, long to
gesti·ō -ōnis *f* performance
gestit·ō -āre -āvī *tr* to be in the habit of carrying *or* wearing
gest·ō -āre -āvī -ātus *tr* to bear, wear, carry; to take for a ride *(in a litter, in a vehicle, on horseback);* to spread, blab, tell; to cherish, harbor *(thoughts)* ‖ *pass* to ride, drive, sail *(esp. for pleasure)*
gest·or -ōris *m* tattler
gestuōs·us -a -um *adj* gesturing; suggestive
gest·us -a -um *pp of* **gerō** ‖ *adj* **rēs gestae** deeds, accomplishments ‖ *n* business; deed
gest·us -ūs *m* gesture; gesticulation, gestures; posture, bearing, attitude
Get·ae -ārum *mpl* Thracian tribe on the Lower Danube
Geticē *adv* in Getic, in the Getic language
Getic·us -a -um *adj* of the Getae; Thracian
gibb·us -ī *m or* **gibb·a -ae** *f* hump
Gigant·ēs -um *mpl* Giants *(race of gigantic size that tried to storm heaven and were placed under various volcanoes)*
gignō gignere genuī genitus *or* **gen·ō -ere** *tr* to beget, bear, produce; to cause, occasion; to give rise to, bring about; to create, begin ‖ *pass* to be born; *(of faculties, parts of the body)* to be produced; *(w. abl)* to be born of, spring from; *(phil)* to come into being
gilv·us -a -um *adj* pale-yellow; **equus gilvus** palomino
gingīv·a -ae *f* gum *(of mouth)*
-gintā *indecl suf* forms numerals from 30 to 90
glabell·us -a -um *adj* bald; smooth
gla·ber -bra -brum *adj* bald; smooth ‖ *m* young slave, favorite slave
glaciāl·is -is -e *adj* icy, frozen
glaci·ēs -ēī *f* ice
glaci·ō -āre -āvī -ātus *tr* to turn into ice, freeze ‖ *intr* to congeal, harden
gladiāt·or -ōris *m* gladiator; ruffian; assassin ‖ *mpl* gladiatorial combat, gladiatorial show; **gladiātōrēs dare** *(or* **ēdere)** to stage a gladiatorial show
gladiātōri·us -a -um *adj* gladiatorial; **mūnus gladiātōrium** gladiatorial show ‖ *n* gladiator's pay
gladiātūr·a -ae *f* gladiatorial profession
gladiol·us -ī *m* small sword; *(bot)* gladiola
glad·ius -(i)ī *m* sword; murder, death; **gladium ēdūcere** *(or* **stringere)** to draw the sword; **gladium recondere** to sheathe the sword; **iūs** *(or* **potestās) gladiī** right to try and punish a capital crime *(granted by emperor to provincial governors)*
glaeb·a -ae *f* **(glēb-)** lump of earth, clod; soil, land; lump, piece

glaebul·a -ae *f* **(glēb-)** small lump; bit of land, small farm
glaesum *see* **glēsum**
glandif·er -era -erum *adj* acorn-bearing
gland·ium -(i)ī *n* delicate kernel *(esp. of pork)*
glān·s -dis *f* acorn, beechnut, chestnut; pellet, bullet *(for a sling); (anat)* head of the penis
glāre·a -ae *f* gravel
glāreōs·us -a -um *adj* full of gravel, gravelly
glaucōm·a -atis *(acc fem singl:* **glaucumam)** *n* cataract; **glaucumam ob oculōs obicere** *(w. dat)* to throw dust into *(s.o.'s)* eyes
glau·cus -a -um *adj* grey-green, greyish; bright, sparkling ‖ **Glauc·us -ī** *m* leader of the Lycians in the Trojan War ‖ fisherman of Euboea who was changed into a sea deity ‖ son of Sisyphus
glēb- = glaeb-
glēs·um *or* **glaes·um -ī** *n* amber
glī·s -ris *m* dormouse *(small, furry-tailed Old World rodent resembling a small squirrel in appearance and habits)*
glīsc·ō -ere *intr* to grow, swell up, spread, blaze up; to grow, increase
globōs·us -a -um *adj* spherical, round
glob·us -ī *m* ball, sphere, globe; crowd, throng, gathering; clique
glomerām·en -inis *n* ball, globe
glomer·ō -āre -āvī -ātus *tr* to form into a ball; to gather up, roll up; to collect, gather together, assemble ‖ *refl & pass* to gather, assemble
glom·us -eris *n* ball of yarn
glōri·a -ae *f* glory, fame; pride; feeling of pride; source of pride, pride and joy; false pride, vanity, boasting; glorious deed; thirst for glory, ambition
glōriāti·ō -ōnis *f* boasting, pride
glōriol·a -ae *f* bit of glory
glōri·or -ārī -ātus sum *tr (only w. neuter pron as object)* to boast about; **haec glōriārī** to boast about this, be proud of this; **idem glōriārī** to make the same boast, be proud of the same thing ‖ *intr* to be proud; to boast; *(w. abl or w.* **dē** *or* **in** *+ abl)* to take pride in, boast about; *(w.* **adversus** *+ acc)* to boast *or* brag to *(s.o.)*
glōriōsē *adv* gloriously, proudly; boastfully, pompously
glōriōs·us -a -um *adj* glorious, illustrious; eager for glory, ambitious; boastful; proud
glossēm·a -atis *n* word to be glossed
glūb·ō -ere *tr* to peel, skin
glūt·en -inis *n* glue
glūtināt·or -ōris *m* bookbinder
glūtin·ō -āre -āvī -ātus *tr* to glue together; *(med)* to close *(wounds)*
glutt·iō -īre -īvī *or* **-iī -ītus** *tr* **(glūt-)** to gulp down
glutt·ō -ōnis *m* glutton
Gnae·us *or* **Gnē·us -ī** *m* Roman first name *(praenomen, abbreviated Cn.)*
gnār·us -a -um *adj* skilled, expert; known, familiar; *(w. gen)* having knowledge of, familiar with, expert in, experienced in
gnāta *see* **nāta**
gnātus *see* **nātus**
gnōbilis *see* **nōbilis**
Gnō(s)s·us -ī *f* Cnossos *(ancient capital of Crete and residence of King Minos)*
gnōscō *see* **nōscō**
Gnōsi·a -ae *or* **Gnōsi·as -adis** *or* **Gnōs·is -idis** *f* Ariadne *(daughter of King Minos of Cnossos)*
gnōtus *see* **nōtus**
gōb·ius -(i)ī *m* **(cōb-)** goby *(small fish)*
Gorgi·ās -ae *(acc:* **-am** *and* **-ān)** *m* famous orator and sophist from Sicily *(480–c.390 B.C.)*
Gorg·ō -ōnis *f* Gorgon *(one of three daughters of Phorcys and Ceto: Stheno, Medusa, and Euryale)*
Gorgone·us -a -um *adj* Gorgonian; **Gorgoneus equus** Pegasus; **Gorgoneus lacus** the spring Hippocrene *(on Mt. Helicon)*
grabāt·us -ī *m* cot; army cot
Gracch·us -ī *m* Roman family name *(cognomen);* Tiberius Sempronius Gracchus *(social reformer, and tribune in 133 B.C.)* ‖ Gaius Sempronius Gracchus *(younger brother of Tiberius and tribune in 123 B.C.)*
gracil·is -is -e *adj* slim, slender; thin, skinny; poor; slight, insignificant; plain, simple *(style)*
gracilit·ās -ātis *f* slenderness; thinness, leanness, meagerness
grācul·us -ī *m* **(gracc-)** jackdaw *(glossy, black European bird resembling the crow)*
gradātim *adv* step by step, gradually, little by little
gradāti·ō -ōnis *f* flight of steps; tiers of seats *(in theater); (rhet)* series of propositions of ascending emphasis
gradior gradī gressus sum *intr* to go, walk, step
Grādīv·us *or* **Gradīv·os -ī** *m* epithet of Mars
grad·us -ūs *m* step, pace, walk, gait; step, degree, grade, stage; approach, advance, progress; status, rank; station, position; step, rung, stair; footing, stance; **concitō gradū** on the double; **dē gradū deicere** *(fig)* to throw off balance; **gradum celerāre** *(or* **corripere)** to pick up the pace; **gradum cōnferre** *(mil)* to come to close quarters; **gradūs ferre** *(mil)* to charge; **plēnō gradū** on the double; **per gradūs** by degrees; **per gradūs ascen-**

dere to climb the stairs; **suspēnsō gradū** on tiptoe

Graecē *adv* Greek, in Greek; **Graecē discere (legere, loquī, scīre)** to learn (read, speak, know) Greek

Graeci·a -ae *f* Greece; **Magna Graecia** Greek cities along the coast of S. Italy, including Sicily

graeciss·ō -āre *intr* to ape the Greeks; to speak Greek

graec·or -ārī *intr* to go Greek, act like a Greek, live it up

Graecul·us -a -um *adj (pej)* Greek through and through, hundred-percent Greek ‖ *mf (pej)* Greekling, dirty little Greek

Graec·us -a -um *adj & mf* Greek ‖ *n* Greek, Greek language

Grāiugen·a -ae *m* Greek *(by birth)*

Grāi·us -a -um *adj* Greek ‖ *mpl* Greeks

grall·ae -ārum *fpl* stilts

grallāt·or -ōris *m* stilt walker

grām·en -inis *n* grass; meadow, pasture; plant, herb

grāmine·us -a -um *adj* grassy, of grass

grammatic·us -a -um *adj* grammatical, of grammar ‖ *m* teacher of literature and language; philologist ‖ *f & npl* grammar; philology

grammatist·a -ae *m* elementary school teacher

grānāri·a -ōrum *npl* granary

grandaev·us -a -um *adj* old, aged

grandēsc·ō -ere *intr* to grow, grow big

grandicul·us -a -um *adj* rather large; pretty tall

grandif·er -era -erum *adj* productive, producing large crops

grandiloqu·us -ī *m* big talker

grandin·at -āre *v impers* it is hailing

grand·iō -īre *tr* to enlarge, increase

grand·is -is -e *adj* full-grown, grown up, tall; large, great; aged; important; powerful, strong; lengthy *(book, speech);* intense *(emotions);* proud, noble *(words, sentiments);* grand, lofty *(style);* dignified *(person);* loud, strong *(voice);* heavy *(debt);* dignified *(speaker);* **aevō** *(or* **aetāte) grandis** advanced in years, elderly

grandit·ās -ātis *f* grandeur

grand·ō -inis *f (m)* hail, hailstorm

grānif·er -era -erum *adj (of an ant)* grain-carrying

grān·um -ī *n* small particle, grain; seed; kernel; stone *(in fruit);* **grānum piperis** peppercorn

graphiār·ium -(i)i *n* case for holding a stylus, "pencil box"

graphicē *adv* in the manner of a painter; vividly, graphically; *(coll)* perfectly, properly, thoroughly

graphic·us -a -um *adj* artistic; *(coll)* exquisite, first-class

graph·ium -(i)ī *n* stylus

grassāt·or -ōris *m* tramp; bully, hoodlum; mugger, prowler, thug

grassātūra -ae *f* waylaying, mugging

grass·or -ārī -ātus sum *intr* to advance, press on; to prowl; to run riot, rage; *(w.* **adversus** *or* **in** *+ acc)* to attack, waylay, mug

grātē *adv* willingly, with pleasure; gratefully

grātēs *(gen not in use) fpl* thanks, gratitude; **grātēs agere** *(w. dat)* to thank; **grātēs habēre** *(w. dat)* to feel grateful toward

grāti·a -ae *f* grace, charm, pleasantness, loveliness; influence, prestige; popularity; love, friendship; service; favor, kindness; thanks, gratitude; cause, reason, motive; **cum grātiā** *(w. gen)* to the satisfaction of; with the approval of; **eā grātiā ut** for the reason that; **exemplī grātiā** for example; **grātiā** *(w. gen) (postpositive)* for the sake of, on account of; **grātiam facere** *(w. dat of person and gen of thing)* pardon *(s.o.)* for *(a fault);* **grātiās agere** *(w. dat)* to thank; **grātiās habēre** *(w. dat)* to be grateful to; **in grātiam** *(w. gen)* in order to win the favor of, in order to please; **in grātiam habēre** to regard *(s.th.)* as a favor; **meā grātiā** for my sake; **quā grātiā?** why?

Grāti·ae -ārum *fpl* Graces *(Aglaia, Euphrosyne, and Thalia)*

grātificāti·ō -ōnis *f* kindness, favor

grātific·or -ārī -ātus sum *tr* to give up, surrender, sacrifice ‖ *intr (w. dat)* **1** to do *(s.o.)* a favor; **2** to gratify, please *(s.o.);* **3** to humor *(s.o.)*

grātiōs·us -a -um *adj* popular, influential; obliging

grātīs *adv* gratis, free, for nothing

grāt·or -ārī -ātus sum *intr* to rejoice; to express gratitude; *(w. dat)* to congratulate; **invicem inter sē grātārī** to congratulate one another

grātuītō *adv* gratuitously, gratis, for nothing; for no particular reason

grātuīt·us -a -um *adj* done for mere thanks, gratuitous, free, spontaneous; voluntary; unprovoked

grātulābund·us -a -um *adj* congratulating

grātulāti·ō -ōnis *f* congratulation; rejoicing, joy; public thanksgiving

grātulāt·or -ōris *m* well-wisher

grātul·or -ārī -ātus sum *intr* to be glad, rejoice; *(w. dat)* **1** to congratulate; **2** to render thanks to

grāt·us -a -um *adj* pleasing, pleasant, agreeable, welcome; thankful, grateful; deserving thanks, earning gratitude; popular ‖ *n* favor; **grātum (et acceptum) habēre** *(w. dat)* to be grateful to **grātum facere** *(w. dat)* to do *(s.o.)* a favor

gravanter *adv* reluctantly

gravātē *adv* with difficulty; unwillingly, grudgingly
gravātim *adv* with difficulty; unwillingly
gravēdinōs·us -a -um *adj* prone to catch colds, susceptible to colds
gravēd·ō -inis *f* cold, head cold
graveol·ēns -entis *adj* stinking
gravēsc·ō -ere *intr* to grow heavy; *(fig)* to get worse
graviditās -ātis *f* pregnancy
gravid·ō -āre -āvī -ātus *tr* to impregnate
gravid·us -a -um *adj* loaded, filled, full; pregnant; *(w. abl)* teeming with
grav·is -is -e *adj* heavy, weighty; burdensome; grave, serious; troublesome, oppressive, painful, harsh, hard, severe, unpleasant; indigestible *(food);* important, influential; venerable, dignified; grave, serious; pregnant; hostile; relentless; obnoxious *(person);* exorbitant *(prices);* low, deep *(voice);* flat *(note);* harsh, bitter, offensive *(smell, taste);* impressive *(speech);* stormy *(weather);* labored *(breathing);* oppressive *(heat);* unhealthy *(climate, place, season);* dangerous *(animal, person); (mil)* heavy-armed
gravit·ās -ātis *f* weight; severity, harshness; seriousness; importance; dignity, influence, authority; pregnancy; violence, vehemence; offensiveness *(of smell);* unhealthfulness *(of climate, place, season)*
graviter *adv* heavily, ponderously; hard, violently, vehemently; severely, harshly; unpleasantly; sadly, sorrowfully; with dignity, with propriety, with authority; *(to feel)* deeply; *(to smell)* offensive; *(to speak)* impressively; **graviter ferre** to take *(s.th.)* hard
grav·ō -āre -āvī -ātus *tr* to weigh down, load (down); to be burdensome to, be oppressive to; to aggravate; to increase
grav·or -ārī -ātus sum *tr* to feel annoyed at, object to; to refuse, decline; to bear with reluctance, regard as a burden ‖ *intr* to feel annoyed
gregāl·is -is -e *adj* of the herd *or* flock; common; **mīles gregālis** a private; **sagulum gregāle** a private's uniform ‖ *mpl* comrades, companions
gregāri·us -a -um *adj* of the flock *or* herd; common, ordinary; **mīles gregārius** a private ‖ *m (mil)* a private
gregātim *adv* in flocks, in herds, in crowds
grem·ium -(i)ī *n* lap, bosom; womb
gressus *pp of* **gradior**
gress·us -ūs *m* step; course, way
gre·x -gis *m* flock, herd; swarm; school *(of fish);* company, group, crowd, troop, set, clique, gang; theatrical cast, troupe
gruis *see* **grūs**
grunn·iō -īre -īvī *or* **-iī -ītum** *intr* **(grund-)** to grunt
grunnīt·us -ūs *m* grunt, grunting
gru·ō -ere *intr (of a crane)* to honk
grū·s *or* **gru·is -is** *mf* crane
grȳps grȳpis *m* griffin *(fabled monster having the head and wings of an eagle and the body of a lion)*
gubernāc(u)l·um -ī *n* rudder, tiller, helm ‖ *npl (fig)* helm
gubernāti·ō -ōnis *f* navigation
gubernāt·or -ōris *m* navigator, pilot, helmsman; ruler, governor, director
gubernātr·īx -īcis *f* directress
gubern·ō -āre -āvī -ātus *tr* to steer, navigate, pilot; to direct, govern
gul·a -ae *f* gullet, throat; palate, appetite; gluttony
gulōs·us -a -um *adj* appetizing, dainty; fond of fine foods
gurg·es -itis *m* abyss, gulf, whirlpool; waters, flood, depths, sea; spendthrift
gurguli·ō -ōnis *m* gullet; windpipe
gurgust·ium -(i)ī *n* dark hovel; *(fig)* hole in the wall
gustātōr·ium -(i)ī *n* appetizer
gustāt·us -ūs *m* sense of taste; flavor, taste
gust·ō -āre -āvī -ātus *tr* to taste; *(fig)* to enjoy; to overhear ‖ *intr* to have a snack
gust·us -ūs *m* tasting; flavor, taste; appetizer; small portion, taste
gutt·a -ae *f* drop; spot, speck
guttātim *adv* drop by drop
guttāt·us -a -um *adj* spotted
guttul·a -ae *f* tiny drop
gutt·ur -uris *n (m)* gullet, throat, neck ‖ *npl* throat, neck
gūt·us -ī *m* **(gutt-)** cruet, flask
Gy·ās -ae *m* hundred-armed giant
Gȳg·ēs -is *or* **-ae** *m* king of Lydia *(reigned 716–678 B.C.)*
gymnasiarch·us -ī *m* manager of a gymnasium
gymnas·ium -(i)ī *n* gymnasium
gymnastic·us -a -um *adj* gymnastic
gymnic·us -a -um *adj* gymnastic
gymnosophist·ae -ārum *mpl* Hindu Stoics
gynaecē·um -ī *or* **gynaecī·um -ī** *n* women's apartment in a Greek house
gynocōnit·is -idis *f* women's apartment in a Greek house
gypsāt·us -a -um *adj* covered with gypsum, white with gypsum
gyps·ō -āre -āvī -ātus *tr* to whiten with gypsum *(the feet of slaves put up for auction);* to plaster up
gyps·um -ī *n* gypsum; plaster of Paris; *(fig)* figure of plaster
gȳr·us -ī *m* circle, cycle, ring; *(astr)* orbit, course; a place where horses are trained; **in gȳrōs īre** to go in circles; **in gȳrum** in a circle; all around

H

H, h *(supply* littera) *f* eighth letter of the Latin alphabet; letter name: **ha**

ha *interj* expression of joy, satisfaction, *or* laughter

habēn·a -ae *f* strap **‖** *fpl* reins; *(fig)* reins of government; **habēnae rērum** reins of state; **habēnās addūcere** *(or* **dare** *or* **effundere** *or* **immittere)** *(w. dat)* to give free rein to; **habēnās premere** to tighten the reins; **immissīs habēnīs** at full speed

hab·eō -ēre -uī -itus *tr* to have; to hold; to possess; to own; to keep, retain, detain; to have at one's disposal, have available; to have on one's side, have in one's favor; to control, have under one's control; to involve, entail; to have knowledge of *(facts, information);* to afford, give *(e.g., pleasure);* to have on, wear *(clothes);* to treat, handle, use; *(of a vessel)* to hold, contain; to be made up of, consist of; *(of feelings)* to beset, come over, grip; to hold, conduct *(meeting, inquiry, census);* to deliver, give *(speech),* give *(a talk);* to keep, observe *(a law, edict, practice); (of owner, inhabitant)* to occupy, inhabit; to pronounce, utter *(words);* to spend, live *(life, youth);* to hold, manage, govern, wield; to hold, think, consider, believe; to occupy, engage, busy; to occasion, produce, render; to know, be informed of, be acquainted with; to take, accept, endure, bear; **animō habēre** *(w. inf)* to have in mind to, intend to; **certum habēre** to regard as certain; **comitia habēre** to hold an assembly; to hold elections; **contiōnem habēre** to hold a meeting *or* rally; **grātiam habēre** to be grateful; **in animō habēre** to have on one's mind, have in mind; **iūstum habēre** *(w. inf)* to have a duty to; **locum priōrem habēre** to have the lead *(in a race);* **melius habēre** *(w. inf)* to think it better to; **necesse habēre** *(w. inf)* to have an obligation to; **parum habēre** *(w. inf)* to think it a minor matter to; **parum habēre violāsse** to think nothing of having violated; **prō certō habēre** to regard it as certain; **prō explōrātō habēre** to regard it as an established fact; **rūs mē nunc habet** I am now in the country; **sēcum habēre** to have with one *or* in one's possession, have in one's company; **sēcum** *(or* **sibi) habēre** to keep *(s.th.)* to oneself, keep secret **‖** *refl (w. adv)* to be, feel *(well, etc.);* **bene vōs habētis** you are doing fine; **mē male habeō** I'm doing lousy; **quō pactō tē habēs?** how are you doing?; **sīc rēs sē habet** that's the situation, that's the way things are; **singulōs ut sēsē habēret rogitāns** asking each and every one how he was doing **‖** *intr (w. adv or abl)* to be, live, dwell *(in a place);* **habet**! *(said of gladiator receiving fatal wound)* he's had it!; **hīc ego habeō** I live here **‖** *v impers* **bene habet** (that's) fine!, O.K. then!; **sīc habet** that's how it is

habil·is -is -e *adj* handy; easy to handle; suitable, convenient; active; *(of vehicles)* easy to control

habilit·ās -ātis *f* aptitude

habitābil·is -is -e *adj* fit to live in

habitāti·ō -ōnis *f* residence; (cost of) rent

habitāt·or -ōris *m* inhabitant; occupant, tenant *(of house, apartment)*

habit·ō -āre -āvī *tr* to live in, inhabit **‖** *intr* to dwell, live

habitūd·ō -inis *f* condition, appearance; bearing

habitur·iō -īre *tr* to like to have

habit·us -a -um *pp of* **habeō ‖** *adj* in good physical condition; **corpulentior et habitior vidērī** to look stouter and in better physical condition

habit·us -ūs *m* condition *(of the body);* physical make-up, build, looks, form, shape; circumstances; style, style of dress; character, quality; disposition, state of feeling; posture

hāc *adv* this way, in this way

hāctenus *adv* to this place, thus far; until now, hitherto, so far; to this extent, so much; *(in writing)* to this point; **haec hāctenus** enough of this

Hadri·a -ae *f* **(Adr-)** Adriatic Sea

Hadriac·us -a -um *adj* Adriatic

Hadriān·us -a -um *adj* **(Adr-)** Adriatic **‖** *m* Hadrian *(Roman emperor,* A.D. *117–138)*

Hadriātic·us -a -um *adj* Adriatic

haec hōrum *(neut pl of* **hoc)** *adj & pron* these

haec hūius *(older form:* **haece;** *gen:* **huiūsce)** *(fem of* **hic)** *adj* this; the present, the actual; the latter; *(occasionally)* the former; **haec … haec** one … another **‖** *pron* this one, she; the latter; *(occasionally)* the former; **haec … haec** one … another one; **haecine (haec** *w. interrog enclitic* **-ne)** is this … ?

haece *see* **haec**

haecine *see* **haec**

Haed·ī -ōrum *mpl (astr)* the Kids *(pair of stars in the constellation Auriga)*

haedili·a -ae *f* little goat

haedill·us -ī *m (term of endearment)* little goat

haedīn·us -a -um *adj* kid's, goat's

haedul·us -ī *m* little kid, little goat

haed·us -ī *m* young goat, kid

Haemōni·a -ae *f* Thessaly

Haem·us *or* **Haem·os -ī** *m* mountain range in N. Thrace

hae·reō -rēre -sī -sum *intr* to cling, stick; to hang around, linger, stay, remain fixed, remain in place; to be rooted to the spot; to come to a standstill, stop; to be embarrassed, be at a loss, hesitate, be in doubt; *(w. dat or abl or w.* **in** + *abl)* **1** to cling to, stick to, be attached to; **2** to loiter in, hang around in, waste time in *(a place) or* at *(an activity);* **3** to adhere to, stick by *(an opinion, purpose);* **4** to gaze upon; **5** to keep close to; **in terga** *(or* **tergīs** *or* **in tergīs) hostium haerēre** to keep on the enemy's tail

haerēsc·ō -ere *intr* to stick together

haeres·is -is *f* philosophical school

haesitābund·us -a -um *adj* hesitating, faltering

haesitanti·a -ae *f* hesitancy

haesitāti·ō -ōnis *f* hesitation, indecision

haesitāt·or -ōris *m* hesitator

haesit·ō -āre -āvī -ātum *intr* to get stuck; to hesitate; to stammer; to be undecided, be at a loss

hahae, hahahahae *interj* expression of joy, satisfaction, *or* laughter

halagor·a -ae *f* salt market

hāl·āns -antis *adj* fragrant

hāl·ēc *or* **(h)all·ēc -ēcis** *n* **(·ex)** fish sauce; fish soup

haliaeët·os -ī *m* osprey *(large hawk that preys on fish, also called fish hawk)*

hālit·us -ūs *m* breath; steam, vapor

hal(l)ūcin·ō -āre *or* **hālūcin·or -ārī -ātus sum** *tr* to say in a distracted state **II** *intr* to have hallucinations; to daydream; to ramble

hāl·ō -āre *tr* to exhale **II** *intr* to be fragrant

halopant·a -ae *m* scoundrel

halōs·is -is (*acc*: **-in**) *f* capture

halt·ēr -ēris *m* weight held in the hand by an athlete

hālūcinor *see* **hal(l)ūcinō**

ham·a *or* **am·a -ae** *f* bucket

Hamādry·as -adis *(dat pl:* **Hamādryasin)** *f* wood nymph

hāmātil·is -is -e *adj* with hooks

hāmāt·us -a -um *adj* hooked

Hamilc·ar -aris *m* Carthaginian general in the First Punic War, surnamed Barca, and father of Hannibal *(d. 228 B.C.)*

hāmiōt·a -ae *f* fisher(man)

Hamm·ō(n) *or* **Amm·ōn -ōnis** *m* Ammon *(Egyptian god, represented as a ram, who had a famous oracle in Libya and was identified with Jupiter Ammon);* **ultimus Ammon Āfrōrum** deepest Africa

hāmul·us -ī *m* small hook

hām·us -ī *m* hook, fishhook; barb

Hannib·al -alis *m* son of Hamilcar Barca and famous general in the Second Punic War *(240–182 B.C.)*

har·a -ae *f* pen, coop, stye

(h)arēn·a -ae *f* sand; seashore, beach; arena **II** *fpl* desert

harēnāri·a -ae *f* sandpit

harēnōs·us -a -um *adj* sandy

hariol·a -ae *f* fortuneteller *(female)*

hariol·or -ārī -ātus sum *intr* to foretell the future; to talk gibberish

hariol·us -ī *m* fortuneteller

harmoni·a -ae *f* harmony **II Harmonia** wife of Cadmus, founder and first king of Thebes

harpag·ō -āre -āvī -ātus *tr (coll)* to hook *(to steal)*

harpag·ō -ōnis *m* hook; harpoon; grappling hook; greedy person

Harpalyc·ē -ēs *f* Thracian princess, raised as a warrior

harpast·um -ī *n* handball

harp·ē -ēs *f* sickle; scimitar

Harpȳi·a -ae *f* harpy *(creature with head of a woman and body of a bird)*

harundif·er -era -erum *adj* reed-bearing

harundine·us -a -um *adj* of reeds

harund·ō -inis *f* reed; cane; fishing rod; pen; shepherd's pipe; shaft, arrow; fowler's rod; weaver's comb; **harundō Indica** bamboo

harusp·ex -icis *m* soothsayer *(interpreter of internal organs, prodigies, and lightning)*

haruspic·a -ae *f* soothsayer *(female)*

haruspicīn·us -a -um *adj* of divination **II** *f* the art of divination

haruspic·ium -(i)ī *n* divination

Hasdrub·al -alis *m* brother of Hannibal *(d. 207 B.C.)* **II** son-in-law of Hamilcar Barca *(d. 221 B.C.)*

hast·a -ae *f* spear *(weapon; spear stuck into ground at public auction; symbol of the centumviral court, which dealt with cases of property and inheritance);* **sub hastā vēndere** to sell at auction

hastāt·us -a -um *adj* armed with a spear **II** *mpl* soldiers in the first line of a Roman battle formation

hastīl·e -is *n* shaft; spear; rod

hau *or* **au** *interj* oh!, ow!, ouch!

haud *or* **haut** *or* **hau** *adv* hardly; not, not at all, by no means

hau(d)quāquam *adv* by no means whatsoever, not at all

hau·riō -rīre -sī -stus *tr* to draw, draw up, draw out; to drain, drink up; to spill, shed *(blood); (of water)* to swallow up, engulf; *(of flames)* to devour; to consume, use up *(resources);* to scoop up; to hollow out; to derive; *(fig)* to have one's fill of; *(fig)* drink in

haustr·um -ī *n* scoop *(on a water-wheel)*

haustus *pp of* **hauriō**

haust·us -ūs *m* drawing *(of water);* drinking, swallowing; drink, draft; handful; stream *(of blood)*

haut *see* **haud**
haveō *see* **aveō**
hebdom·as -adis *f* week; a group of seven; fever occurring at seven-day intervals
Hēb·ē -ēs *f* goddess of youth, daughter of Juno, and cupbearer of the gods
heben·us -ī *f* ebony tree, ebony
heb·eō -ēre *intr* to be blunt, be dull; *(of light)* to grow dim; *(of anger)* to die down; *(fig)* to be sluggish, be inactive
heb·es -etis *adj* blunt, dull; faint, dim; dull, obtuse, stupid
hebēsc·ō -ere *intr* to grow blunt, grow dull; to become faint *or* dim; to lose vigor
hebet·ō -āre -āvī -ātus *tr* to blunt, dull, dim
Hebr·us -ī *m* principal river in Thrace
Hecat·ē -ēs *f* goddess of magic and witchcraft, identified with Diana
hecatomb·ē -ēs *f* hecatomb *(public sacrifice of 100 oxen to the gods)*
Hect·or -oris *m* son of Priam and Hecuba, husband of Andromache
Hecub·a -ae *or* **Hecub·ē -ēs** *f* **(-cab-)** wife of Priam *(after the destruction of Troy, she became a slave and was metamorphosed into a dog)*
heder·a -ae f ivy
hederig·er -era -erum *adj* wearing ivy
hederōs·us -a -um *adj* overgrown with ivy
hēdycr·um -ī *n* perfume
hei, hēia *see* **ei, ēia**
Helen·a -ae *or* **Helen·ē -ēs** *f* Helen of Troy *(wife of Menelaus, sister of Clytemnestra, Castor, and Pollux)*
Helen·us -ī *m* prophetic son of Priam and Hecuba
Hēliad·es -um *fpl* daughters of Helios and sisters of Phaëthon, who were changed into poplar trees and whose tears were changed into amber
helic·a -ae *f* spiral
Helicā·ōn -onis *m* the son of Antenor and founder of Patavium *(modern Padua)*
Helicāoni·us -a -um *adj* of Helicaon *(i.e., of Patavium)*
Helic·ē -ēs *f (astr)* Big Bear *(constellation Ursa Major); (poet)* northern regions
Helic·ōn -ōnis *m* mountain in Boeotia sacred to Muses and Apollo
Helicōniad·es *or* **Helicōnid·es -um** *fpl* Muses
Helicōni·us -a -um *adj* of Helicon
hēliocamīn·us -ī *m* sun-room
Hell·as -adis *or* **-ados** *f* (mainland of) Greece
Hell·ē -ēs *f* daughter of Athamas and Nephele who, while riding the golden-fleeced ram, fell into the Hellespont *(= Helle's Sea)* and drowned
hellebor- = **ellebor-**
Hell·ēn -ēnis *m* son of Deucalion, and king of Thessaly, from whom the Greeks were said to have been called Hellenes
Hellespont·us -ī *m* Hellespont *(modern Dardanelles)*
hellu·ō -ōnis *m* glutton; squanderer
hellu·or -ārī -ātus sum *intr* to be a glutton
hel·ops *or* **ell·ops -opis** *m* highly prized fish *(perhaps the sturgeon)*
helvell·a -ae *f* delicious herb
Helvēti·us -a -um *adj* Helvetian ‖ *mpl* Helvetians *(a people of ancient Switzerland)*
helv·us -a -um *adj* pale-yellow
hem *interj (expression of surprise)* well!
hēmerodrom·us -ī *m* courier
hēmicill·us -ī *m (pej)* mule, ass
hēmicycl·ium -(i)ī *n* semicircle of seats
hēmīn·a -ae *f* half a sextarius *(half a pint)*
hendecasyllab·ī -ōrum *mpl (pros)* hendecasyllabics *(verses with eleven syllables)*
hēpatiāri·us -a -um *adj* of the liver
heptēr·is -is *f* galley *(perhaps)* with seven banks of oars
Hēr·a -ae *f* Greek goddess, identified with Juno
hera *see* **era**
Hēraclē·a -ae *f* name of numerous towns *(esp. a part of Lucania on the Siris River and, in Sicily, a town between Lilybaeum and Agrigentum)* ‖ epic poem on the subject of Hercules
Hēraclīt·us -ī *m* early Greek philosopher of Ephesus who believed fire to be the primary element *(fl 513 B.C.)*
Hērae·a -ōrum *npl* festival in honor of the Greek goddess Hera
herb·a -ae *f* blade; stalk; herb; plant; grass, lawn; **adhūc tua messis in herbā est** *(prov)* don't count your chickens before they are hatched *(literally, your harvest is still on the stalk)*; **herba mala** weed
herbēsc·ō -ere *intr* to sprout
herbe·us -a -um *adj* grass-green
herbid·us -a -um *adj* grassy; full of weeds
herbif·er -era -erum *adj* grassy, grass-producing; made of herbs; bearing magical herbs
herbigrad·us -a -um *adj (of a snail)* that crawls on the grass
herbōs·us -a -um *adj* grassy; made with herbs; resembling vegetation
herbul·a -ae *f* small plant
hercīsc·ō -ere *intr* to divide an inheritance
herct·um -ī *n* inheritance
hercle *or* **hercule** *or* **ercle** *interj (used for emphasis or to express strong feeling, normally used by the male sex only)* by Hercules!
Herculānēns·is -is -e *adj* of Herculaneum ‖ *m* district of Herculaneum ‖ *mpl* inhabitants of Herculaneum
Herculāne·um -ī *n* town on the Bay of Naples, destroyed by the volcano of Mt. Vesuvius in A.D. 79

Hercul·ēs -is *or* -**ī** *or* -**eī** *m* son of Jupiter and Alcmena, husband of Deianira

Herculēs *or* **Herc(u)le** *interj* by Hercules! *(see* **hercle)**

Herculē·us -a -um *adj* of Hercules

Hercyni·us -a -um *adj* Hercynian, of Hercynia *(a region of the forest-covered mountains extending from the Rhine to the Carpathians)*

here *see* **herī**

hērēdipet·a -ae *m* legacy hunter

hērēditāri·us -a -um *adj* of an inheritance; inherited, hereditary

hērēdit·ās -ātis *f* inheritance; hereditary succession; **hērēditās sine sacrīs** an inheritance without encumbrances

hērēd·ium -(i)ī *n* inherited estate

hēr·ēs -ēdis *m* heir *(to an estate, throne);* **hērēs ex dōdrante** heir to three-quarters of an estate; *(w. ordinal numbers, indicating order of succession):* **hērēs Pelopis tertius** Pelop's heir third in order of succession *(i.e., Agamemnon)* ‖ *f* heiress

herī *or* **here** *adv* yesterday

herif-, herīl- = **erif-, erīl-**

Hermaphrodīt·us -ī *m* son of Hermes and Aphrodite who combined with the nymph Salmacis to become one bisexual person

Hermathēn·a -ae *f* a herm *(i.e., a quadrangular pillar)* with a bust of Athena

Herm·ēs -ae *m* Greek god identified with Mercury; herm *(quadrangular pillar with the bust of Hermes, or later, of other gods)*

Hermion·ē -ēs *or* **Hermion·a -ae** *f* Hermione *(daughter of Helen and Menelaus and wife of Orestes)*

Herm·us -ī *m* gold-rich river in the Greek district of Aeolis

Hērodot·us -ī *m* father of Greek history, born at Halicarnassus on coast of Asia Minor *(484–425 B.C.)*

hērōïc·us -a -um *adj* heroic, epic

hērōïn·a -ae *f* demigoddess, heroine

hērō·is -idis *f* demigoddess, heroine

hēr·ōs -ōis *m* hero *(mythological figure; a man with heroic qualities)*

hērō·us -a -um *adj* heroic, epic ‖ *m* dactylic hexameter; a dactyl

Hersili·a -ae *f* wife of Romulus

herus *see* **erus**

Hēsiod·us -ī *m* Hesiod *(early Greek poet from Boeotia, 8th cent. B.C.)*

Hēsion·ē -ēs *or* **Hēsion·a -ae** *f* Hesione *(daughter of Laomedon, king of Troy, whom Hercules rescued from a sea monster)*

Hesperi·a -ae *f* the land of the evening star *(i.e., Italy and Spain)*

Hesperid·es -um *fpl* daughters of Hesperus who guarded the golden apples beyond Mount Atlas

Hesper·us *or* **Hesper·os -ī** *m* evening star

hestern·us -a -um *adj* yesterday's

hetairi·a -ae *f* secret society

hetairic·ē -ēs *f* Macedonian mounted guard

heū! *interj (expression of pain or dismay)* oh!, ah!

heūs! *interj (to draw attention)* say there!, hey!

hexame·ter -tra -trum *adj (pros)* hexameter, having six metrical feet *(applied esp. to dactylic hexamter)* ‖ *mpl* verse in this meter

hexaphor·um -ī *n* litter carried by six men

hexēr·is -is *f* ship *(perhaps)* with 6 banks of oars

hiāt·us -ūs *m* opening; open mouth; mouthing, bluster; basin *(of a fountain); (w. gen)* greedy desire for; chasm; *(pros)* hiatus

Hibēr·es -um *mpl* Spaniards ‖ tribe south of the Caucasus

Hibēri·a -ae *f* Iberian peninsula *(Greek name for Spain)*

Hibēric·us -a -um *adj* Spanish

hībern·a -ōrum *npl (mil)* winter quarters; winter-quartering

hībernācul·a -ōrum *npl* winter bivouac; winter residence

Hiberni·a -ae *f* Ireland

hībern·ō -āre -āvī -ātum *or* **hībern·or -ārī -ātus sum** *intr* to spend the winter; to stay in winter quarters; *(fig)* to hibernate

hībern·us -a -um *adj* winter, in winter, wintry; designed for winter use

Hibēr·us -ī *m* river in Spain *(modern Ebro)*

hibīsc·um -ī *n (bot)* hibiscus *(plant w. large, showy flowers)*

hibrid·a -ae *mf* **(hyb-)** hybrid, mongrel, half-breed

hic hūius *(older form:* **hice hūiūsce)** *adj* this; the present, the actual; the latter; *(occasionally)* the former; **hic … hic** one … another ‖ *pron* this one, he; this man; myself, yours truly *(i.e., the speaker or writer);* the latter; *(occasionally)* the former; *(in court)* the defendant, my defendant; **hic … hic** one … another; **hicine (hic** + *interrog enclitic* **-ne)** is this … ?

hīc *adv* here, in this place; at this point; in this affair, in this particular

hice *see* **hic**

hicine *see* **hic**

hiemāl·is -is -e *adj* winter, wintry; stormy

hiem·ō -āre -āvī -ātum *intr* to spend the winter; to be wintry, be cold, be stormy

Hiemps·ala -alis *m* name of several N. African kings, *esp.* a grandson of Massinisa and cousin of Jugurtha, by whom he was killed

hiem·s *or* **hiem·ps -is** *f* winter; cold; storm

Hier·ō(n) -ōnis *m* Hieron *(ruler of Syracuse, in Sicily, and patron of philosophers and poets, d. 466 B.C.)* ‖ Hieron

(ruler of Syracuse and friend of the Romans in First Punic War, 306?–215 B.C.)

Hierosolym·a -ae *f or* **Hierosolym·a -ōrum** *npl* Jerusalem

hiet·ō -āre *intr* to keep yawning

hilarē *adv* cheerfully, merrily

hilar·is -is -e *adj* cheerful, merry

hilarit·ās -ātis *f* cheerfulness

hilaritūd·ō -inis *f* cheerfulness

hilar·ō -āre -āvī -ātus *tr* to cheer up

hilarul·us -a -um *adj* cheerful little

hilar·us -a -um *adj* cheerful, merry

hill·ae -ārum *fpl* smoked suasage

Hīlōt·ae -ārum *mpl* Helots *(serfs of the Spartans)*

hīl·um -ī *n (usu. after a neg.)* the least bit

hinc *adv* from here, from this place; on this side, here; for this reason; from this source; after this, from now on, henceforth; *(partitive)* of this, of these; **hinc illinc** from one side to the other

hinn·iō -īre -iī *intr* to whinny, neigh

hinnīt·us -ūs *m* neighing

hinnule·us -ī *m* fawn, young deer

hi·ō -āre -āvī *tr* to mouth, sing with mouth wide open **‖** *intr* to open, be open; to gape; to yawn; to make eyes *(in surprise or greedy anticipation); (rhet)* to be disjointed

hippagōg·os -ī *f* ship for transporting horses

Hipparch·us -ī *m* son of Pisistratus, tyrant of Athens, slain in 514 B.C.

Hippi·ās -ae *m* son of Pisistratus *(tyrant of Athens),* and tyrant of Athens himself *(527–510 B.C.)*

hippocentaur·us -ī *m* centaur

Hippocrat·ēs -is *m* founder of scientific medicine *(c. 460–380 B.C.)*

Hippocrēn·ē -ēs *f* spring on Mt. Helicon, sacred to the Muses and produced when the hoof of Pegasus hit the ground there

Hippodam·ē -ēs *or* **Hippodamē·a** *or* **Hippodamī·a -ae** *f* Hippodamia *(daughter of Oenamaüs, king of Elis, and wife of Pelops)* **‖** Hippodamia *(daughter of Adrastus and wife of Pirithoüs)*

hippodrom·os -ī *m* racetrack

Hippolyt·ē -ēs *or* **Hippolyt·a -ae** *f* Hippolyte *(Amazonian wife of Theseus)* **‖** wife of Acastus, king of Magnesia

Hippolyt·us -ī *m* **(Ipp-)** son of Theseus and Hippolyte

hippoman·es -is *n* discharge of a mare in heat; membrane of the head of a newborn foal

Hippomen·ēs -ae *m* young man who competed with Atalanta in a race and won her as his bride

Hippōn·ax -actis *m* Greek satirist *(fl 540 B.C.)*

hippotoxot·ae -ārum *mpl* mounted archers

hippūr·us -ī *m* goldfish

hīr·a -ae *f* empty gut

hircīn·us -a -um *adj* **(-quīn-)** goat, of a goat

hircōs·us -a -um *adj* smelling like a goat

hirc·us -ī *m* **(-qu·us)** goat

hirne·a *or* **hirni·a -ae** *f* jug

hirsūt·us -a -um *adj* hairy, hirsute, shaggy; bristly; prickly; rude

Hirt·ius -(i)ī *m* Aulus Hirtius *(consul in 43 B.C. and author of the eighth book of Caesar's Memoirs on the Gallic War)*

hirt·us -a -um *adj* hairy, shaggy; uncouth

hirūd·ō -inis *f* leech, bloodsucker

hirundinīn·us -a -um *adj* swallow's

hirund·ō -inis *f* swallow *(bird)*

hīsc·ō -ere *tr* to murmur, utter **‖** *intr* to (begin to) open, gape, yawn; to open the mouth; to split open

Hispān·ī -ōrum *mpl* Spaniards

Hispāni·a -ae *f* Spain

Hispāniēns·is -is -e *adj* Spanish

hispid·us -a -um *adj* hairy, shaggy; rough, rugged *(terrain)*

His·ter -trī *m* Lower Danube *(also applied to the whole river)*

histori·a -ae *f* history; account, story; theme *(of a story)*

historic·us -a -um *adj* historical **‖** *m* historian

histric·us -a -um *adj* theatrical

histri·ō -ōnis *m* actor

histriōnāl·is -is -e *adj* theatrical; histrionic

histriōni·a -ae f dramatics, art of acting

hiulcē *adv* with frequent hiatus

hiulc·ō -āre *tr* to split open

hiulc·us -a-um *adj* split, split open; open, gaping; with hiatus

hōc hūius *(old form:* **hōce;** *gen:* **hūiūsce)** *(neut of* **hic)** *adj* this; the present, the actual; the latter; *(occasionally)* the former **‖** *pron* this one, it; the latter; *(occasionally)* the former; *(w. gen)* this amount of, this degree of, so much; **hōc erat quod** this was the reason why; **hōc est** that is, I mean, namely; **hōcine (hōc +** *interrog enclitic* **-ne)** is this ... ?; **hōc facilius** all the more easily

hōce *see* **hōc**

hōcine *see* **hōc**

hodiē *adv* today; nowadays; still, to the present; at once, immediately; **hodiē māne** this morning; **numquam hodiē** *(coll)* never at all

hodiern·us -a -um *adj* today's; **hodiernus diēs** this day, today

holit·or -ōris *m* grocer

holitōri·us -a -um *adj* vegetable

hol·us -eris *n* vegetable; *(collectively)* vegetables; **holus ātrum** cabbage-like plant growing on the seashore

holuscul·um -ī *n (pej)* vegetables

Homērē·us -a -um *or* **Homēri·us -a -um** *adj* Homeric
Homēric·us -a -um *adj* Homeric
Homēr·us -ī *m* Homer
homicīd·a -ae *m* murderer
homicīd·ium -(i)ī *n* homicide, murder, manslaughter
hom·ō -inis *mf* human being, man, person, mortal; mankind, human race; fellow; fellow creature; member of a military force; **mī homō**! my good man! ‖ *mpl* people; **inter hominēs esse** to be alive; to see the world
homull·us -ī *or* **homunci·ō -ōnis** *or* **homuncul·us -ī** *m* poor guy
honest·a -ae *f* lady
honestāment·um -ī *n* ornament
honest·ās -ātis *f* good reputation, respectability; sense of honor, respect; beauty, grace; integrity; decency ‖ *fpl* respectable persons, decent people
honestē *adv* honorably, respectably, decently; honestly, fairly; **honestē genitus** *(or* **nātus)** high-born
honest·ō -āre -āvī -ātus *tr* to honor, dignify; to grace, adorn; to put a good face on
honest·us -a -um *adj* honored, respected; honorable, decent, respectable; handsome; well-born, of high rank ‖ *n* a virtue, a good
hon·or *or* **hon·ōs -ōris** *m* honor, esteem; (high) position, office, post; mark of honor, reward, prize, acknowledgment; recompense, fee; offering, sacrifice, rites *(to the gods or the dead);* grace, beauty, charm; glory, fame, reputation; **honor mortis** *(or* **sepultūrae)** funeral rites; **honōris causā** out of respect, with all respect; **in honōre esse** to meet general approval; **praefārī honōrem** to begin with an apology; **pugnae honor** military glory; **tempus honōris** term of office
honōrābil·is -is -e *adj* honorable, respectable
honōrār·ium -(i)ī *n* honorarium, fee
honōrāri·us -a -um *adj* complimentary, honorary; **summa (pecūnia) honōrāria** sum of money contributed by a magistrate to the treasury on entering office
honōrātē *adv* with honor, honorably
honōrāt·us -a -um *adj* honored, respected; in high office; honorable, respectable; **honōrātum habēre** to hold in honor
honōrificē *adv* honorably, respectfully
honōrific·us -a -um *adj* conferring honor, complimentary
honōr·ō -āre -āvī -ātus *tr* to honor, respect; to embellish, decorate
honōr·us -a -um *adj* conferring honor, complimentary; deserving honor
honōs *see* **honor**
hoplomach·us -ī *m* heavy-armed gladiator
hōr·a -ae *f* hour; time; season; **ad hōram** on time, punctually; **hōrās quaerere** to ask what time it is; **in diem et hōram** continually; **in hōram vīvere** to live from hand to mouth; **quota hōra est?** what time is it? ‖ *fpl* hours; time; clock; **hōrās īnspicere** to look at the clock; **hōrās quaerere ab aliquō** to ask s.o. the time; **omnibus hōrīs** at all hours, at all times; **omnium hōrārum** suited to all occasions; **quotās hōrās nūntiāre** to say what time it is, tell the time
Hor·a -ae *f* wife of Quirinus *(i.e., of deified Romulus),* called Hersilia before her death
Hōr·ae -ārum *fpl* Hours *(daughters of Jupiter and Themis, who kept watch at the gates of heaven)*
hōrae·us -a -um *adj* pickled; seasoned; in season
Horāt·ius -(i)ī *m* Horace *(Quintus Horatius Flaccus, poet, 65–8 B.C.)* ‖ Horatio *(Horatius Cocles, defender of the bridge across the Tiber in the war with Porsenna)*
horde·um -ī *n* **(ord-)** barley
hōri·a -ae *f* fishing boat
hōriol·a -ae *f* small fishing boat
horiz·ōn -ontos *m* horizon
hornō *adv* this year, during this year
hornōtin·us -a -um *adj* this year's
hōrn·us -a -um *adj* this year's
hōrolog·ium -iī *n* clock, water clock, sundial
hōrōscop·us *or* **hōrōscop·os -ī** *m* horoscope; eastern horizon
horrend·us -a -um *adj* horrendous, horrible; awesome
horr·ēns -entis *adj* dreadful, awful
horr·eō -ēre -uī *tr* to dread; to shudder at, shrink from; to be amazed at; to regard *(gods, etc.)* with awe ‖ *intr* to stand on end, stand up straight; to get gooseflesh; to shiver, tremble; to bristle; to look frightful, look unkempt; to have a gloomy character
horr·ēscō -ēscere -uī *tr* to dread, become terrified at ‖ *intr* to stand on end; *(of the sea)* to become rough; to begin to shake *or* shiver; to start, be startled
horre·um -ī *n* barn, shed; silo, granary; wine cellar; storehouse *(of bees),* beehive
horribil·is -is -e *adj* horrible, terrifying; amazing; rough, uncouth
horridē *adv* roughly, rudely; harshly
horridul·us -a -um *adj* rather shaggy; somewhat shabby; *(rhet)* somewhat unsophisticated *(style)*
horrid·us -a -um *adj* shaggy, prickly; bristly *(pig);* choppy *(sea);* disheveled *(appearance);* rugged, wild *(terrain);* rude, uncouth *(manner);* horrible; shivering *(from cold)*

horrif·er -era -erum *adj* causing shudders; freezing, chilling; terrifying
horrificē *adv* awfully, in a frightening way
horrific·ō -āre -āvī *tr* to make rough, ruffle; to terrify, frighten
horrific·us -a -um *adj* frightful, terrifying
horrison·us -a -um *adj* frightening *(sound),* frightening to hear
horr·or -ōris *m* bristling; shivering, shuddering; horror, dread; awe, reverence; chill; thrill
hōrsum *adv* this way
hortām·en -inis *n* injunction; encouragement; incentive
hortāment·um -ī *n* encouragement
hortāti·ō -ōnis *f* exhortation, encouragement
hortāt·or -ōris *m* backer, supporter, rooter; instigator
hortāt·us -ūs *m* encouragement, cheering, cheer
Hortēns·ius -(i)ī *m* Quintus Hortensius *(lawyer and friendly competitor of Cicero, 114–50 B.C.)*
hort·or -ārī -ātus sum *tr* to encourage, cheer, incite, instigate; to give a pep talk to *(soldiers)*
hortul·us -ī *m* little garden
hort·us -ī *m* garden; garden used by Epicurus as a place of teaching; *(fig)* philosophical system **II** *mpl* park
hosp·es -itis *m* host, entertainer; guest, visitor; friend; stranger, foreigner
hospit·a -ae *f* hostess; guest, visitor; friend; stranger, foreigner; **hospita nāvis** foreign ship
hospitāl·is -is -e *adj* host's; guest's; hospitable **II** *npl* guest room
hospitālit·ās -ātis *f* hospitality
hospitāliter *adv* hospitably, as a guest
hospit·ium -(i)ī *n* hospitality; ties of hospitality, friendship; welcome; guest room; lodging; inn
hospit·or -ārī -ātus sum *intr* to be put up *(as a guest)*
hosti·a -ae *f* victim, sacrificial animal; **hostia māior** full-grown victim
hostiāt·us -a -um *adj* bringing sacrificial victims
hostic·us -a -um *adj* hostile, of the enemy; foreign **II** *n* enemy territory
hostific·us -a -um *adj* hostile, bitter
hostīl·is -is -e *adj* enemy, hostile
hostīliter *adv* like an enemy, in a hostile manner
Hostīl·ius -(i)ī *m* Tullus Hostilius *(third king of Rome)*
hostīment·um -ī *n* compensation
host·iō -īre *tr* to get even with **II** *intr* to get even
host·is -is *mf* (public) enemy; stranger
hūc *adv* here, to this place; to this point, so far; to such a pitch; for this purpose; **hūc atque illūc** here and there, in different directions; **hūcine? (hūc +** *interrog enclitic)* so far?
hui! *interj* wow!
hūius(ce)modī *adj (indecl)* of this sort, this kind of
hūmānē *adv* like a human being; politely, gently, with compassion
hūmānit·ās -ātis *f* human nature; humanity; kindness, compassion, human feeling; courtesy; culture, refinement, civilization
hūmāniter *adv* like a human being; reasonably; gently, with compassion
hūmānitus *adv* humanly; humanely, kindly, compassionately
hūmān·us -a -um *adj* of a human being, human; humane, kind, compassionate; courteous; cultured, refined, civilized
humāti·ō -ōnis *f* burial
hūme- = ūme-
hūmid- = ūmid-
humil·is -is -e *adj* low, low-lying, low-growing; short *(in stature);* humble; lowly, poor, obscure; insignificant; petty, unimportant; small-minded, cheap; humiliated, humbled
humilit·ās -ātis *f* lowness, lack of stature; lowliness, insignificance; small-mindedness; humiliation; humility, subservience
humiliter *adv* low, deeply; abjectly
hum·ō -āre -āvī -ātus *tr* to bury
hum·us -ī *f* ground, earth, soil; land, region, country; **humī** on *(or* in) the ground
hyacinthin·us -a -um *adj* of the hyacinth; crimson
hyacinth·us *or* **hyacinth·os -ī** *m* hyacinth **II Hyacinth·us** *or* **Hyacinth·os -ī** *m* Hyacinth *(Spartan youth who was accidentally killed by Apollo and from whose blood hyacinths sprang)*
Hyad·es -um *fpl* Hyades *(group of 7 stars in the head of the constellation Taurus whose rising indicated rain)*
hyaen·a -ae *f* hyena
hyal·us -ī *m* glass; **color hyalī** glass-green color
Hyantē·us -a -um *adj* Boeotian
Hy·ās -antis *m* son of Atlas; **sīdus Hyantis** the Hyades
Hybl·a -ae *or* **Hybl·ē -ēs** *f* Sicilian town on the slopes of Mt. Aetna, famous for its honey
Hyblae·us -a -um *adj* of Hybla; **Hyblaeus liquor** honey
hybrid·a -ae *mf* hybrid, mongrel, half-breed
Hydasp·ēs -is *m* tributary of the Indus River
Hȳdr·a -ae *f* Hydra *(seven-headed water snake killed by Hercules)* **II** monster guarding the gate to the lower world *(mother of Cerberus)* **II** *(astr)* Hydra *or* Anguis *(constellation)*

hydraulic·us -a -um *adj* hydraulic
hydraul·us -ī *m* water organ
hydri·a -ae *f* water jug, urn
Hydrocho·us -ī *m (astr)* Aquarius
hydrōpic·us -a -um *adj* dropsical
hydr·ops -ōpis *m* dropsy
hydr·us *or* **hydr·os -ī** *m* water snake; snake; dragon
Hygī·a -ae *f* goddess of health
Hȳlae·us -ī *m* centaur who wounded Milanion, the lover of Atalanta
Hyl·ās -ae *m* favorite of Hercules who was carried off by the nymphs
Hyll·us -ī *m* son of Hercules and husband of Iole
Hym·ēn -enis *or* **Hymenae·us** *or* **Hymenae·os -ī** *m* Hymen *(god of marriage);* wedding ceremony; wedding; wedding song
Hymett·us *or* **Hymett·os -ī** *m* mountain in E. Attica, famous for its honey and marble
Hypan·is -is *m* river in Sarmatia *(modern River Bug)*
hyperbat·on -ī n *(rhet)* transposition of words *or* clauses
hyperbol·ē -ēs *f* hyperbole
Hyperbore·ī -ōrum *mpl* people in the land of the midnight sun
Hyperī·ōn -onis *or* **-onos** *m* son of Titan and Earth, father of the Sun
Hypermestr·a -ae *or* **Hypermestr·ē -ēs** *f* only one of the 50 daughters of Danaüs who did not kill her husband on her wedding night
hypocaust·um *or* **hypocaust·on -ī** *n* subfloor heating chamber
hypodidascal·us -ī *m* assitant teacher
hypomnēm·a -atis *n* note, reminder
hypothēc·a -ae *f (fin)* collateral
Hypsipyl·ē -ēs *f* queen of Lemnos at the time of the Argonauts
Hyrcāni·a -ae *f* country on S.E. side of the Caspian Sea
Hyrcān·us -a -um *adj* of Hyrcania; **mare Hyrcānum** Caspian Sea
hysteric·us -a -um *adj* having a gynecological ailment

I

I, i *(supply* littera) *f* ninth letter of the Latin alphabet; letter name: **i**
-i·a -ae *fem suf* forms abstract nouns from adjectives: **audācia** boldness *(from* **audāx** bold)
Iacch·us -ī *m* Bacchus; wine
iac·eō -ēre -uī -itum *intr* to lie, lie down; to recline *(at table);* to lie ill, be sick; to rest; to lie dead, to have fallen *(in battle); (of structures, cities)* to lie in ruins; to linger, stay *(in a place); (of places)* to lie, be situated; *(of places)* to be low-lying, lie low; *(of fields)* to lie idle; *(of prices)* to be low; *(of persons)* to feel low, be despondent; *(of the eyes, face)* to be downcast; *(of hair)* to hang loose; *(of the sea)* to be calm; *(of duties, responsibilities)* to be neglected; to lie prostrate, be powerless; *(of arguments)* to fail, be refuted; to be low in s.o.'s opinion; **amīcī iacentem animum incitāre** to cheer up a friend's despondent mood; **animī mīlitum iacent** the morale of the soldiers is low; **Brundisī iacēre** to linger in Brundisi; **in orbem iacēre** *(of a group of islands)* to lie in a circle, form a circle; **iacēre cum** to have sexual intercourse with; **mihi ad pedēs iācere** to lie prostrate at my feet
iaciō iacere iēcī iactus *tr* to throw, cast, fling; to toss *(head, limbs);* to hurl *(charges, insults);* to lay *(foundations);* to build, establish, set, found, construct; to emit, produce *(heat, light, sparks);* to sow, scatter *(seed);* to throw down; to throw away; to mention, utter, declare, intimate; **contumēliam in aliquem iacere** to hurl the charge of defiance at s.o., charge s.o. with defiance; **fundāmenta iacere** to lay the foundations; **vōcēs iaciuntur** words are uttered **II** *refl* to leap; to rush, burst
iact·āns -antis *adj* boastful, showing off; proud
iactanter *adv* boastfully; ostentatiously; arrogantly
iactanti·a -ae *f* bragging; ostentation
iactāti·ō -ōnis *f* tossing to and fro; swaying; shaking; writhing; bragging, showing off; **iactātiō animī** agitation; **iactātiō corporis** gesticulation; **iactātiō maritima** seasickness
iactāt·us -ūs *m* tossing, waving
iactit·ō -āre *tr* to display, show off
iact·ō -āre -āvī -ātus *tr* to throw, hurl; to toss about, shake; to wave, brandish; to throw away, throw out; to throw overboard; to throw aside, reject; to disturb, disquiet, stir up; to make restless, cause to toss; to consider, discuss; to throw out, mention; to brag about, show off **II** *refl* to boast, show off, throw one's weight around **II** *pass* to toss, rock
iactūr·a -ae *f* throwing away, throwing overboard; loss, sacrifice
iactus *pp of* **iaciō**
iact·us -ūs *m* toss, throw, cast
iaculābil·is -is -e *adj* missile
iaculāti·ō -ōnis *f* hurling
iaculāt·or -ōris *m* thrower, hurler; light-armed soldier; spearman; hunter
iaculātr·īx -īcis *f* huntress
iacul·or -ārī -ātus sum *tr* to throw; to shoot at; *(fig)* to aim at, strive after
iacul·us -a -um *adj* throwing, casting **II** *n* dart, javelin; casting net

iāiūn- = **iēiūn-**
Iālysi·us -a -um *adj* of Jalysos, a town on the island of Rhodes
Iālys·us -ī *m* son of the god Helios, and eponym of the town Jalysos **||** famous portrait of Jalysus by Protogenes
iam *adv (in the present)* now, already; *(in the past)* already, by then, by that time; *(in the future)* very soon, right away; *(in transition)* now, next, moreover; *(for emphasis)* actually, precisely, quite; *(in conclusion)* then surely; **iam ante(ā)** even before that; **iam dūdum** long ago, long since; **iam inde** immediately; **iam inde ab** all the while from, continuously from; **iam iam** *(for emphasis or emotive effect)* at last, now finally **iam ... iam** at one time ... at another; first ... then; **iamiamque** at any time now, now all but ... ; **iam nunc** even now; **iam prīdem** long since; **iam prīmum** to begin with, first of all; **iam tum** even then, even at that time; **quid iam?** *(coll)* what (is the matter) now?
iambē·us -a -um *adj (pros)* iambic
iambic·us -a -um *adj (pros)* iambic
iamb·us -ī *m (pros)* iamb (⏑—); iambic trimeter *(consists of three double feet, i.e., of six iambic feet);* iambic poem; iambic poetry
Iānicul·um -ī *n* Roman hill on right bank of the Tiber
Iānigen·a *adj (masc & fem only)* born of Janus
iānit·or -ōris *m* doorman, porter
iānitr·īx -īcis *f* portress
ianthin·us -a -um *adj* violet **||** *n* the color violet **||** *npl* violet clothes
iānu·a -ae *f* door; doorway, entrance; *(fig)* entrance, approach, gateway; **iānua lētī** gateway of death, gateway to the lower world
Iānuāri·us -a -um *adj* of Janus; **mēnsis Iānuārius** January *(first month, after 153 B.C., of the Roman year)* **||** *m* January
iān·us -ī *m* covered passage, arcade; **iānus īmus, iānus medius, iānus summus** bottom archway, middle archway, top archway *(three archways on the east side of the Forum, where money changers and merchants conducted their business)* **|| Iānus** Janus *(old Italic deity, represented as having two faces)* **||** temple of Janus *(at the bottom of the Argiletum in the Forum)* **|| Iānus Geminus** *(or* **Iānus Quirīnus** *or* **Iānus Quirīnī)** shrine of Janus in the Forum consisting of an archway, with doors at the ends that were closed in times of peace
Iāpyd·es -um *mpl* **(-pud-)** an Illyrian tribe
Iāpydi·a -ae *f* country in the N. part of Illyria
Iāpygi·a -ae *f* Greek name for part of S.E. Italy, including some or all of Calabria and Apulia
Iāp·yx -ygis *adj* Iapygian **||** *m* son of Daedalus who ruled in S. Italy **||** wind that blew from Apulia to Greece
Iāp·yx -ygis *or* **-ygos** *adj* Iapygian **||** *m* son of Daedalus, who gave his name to Iapygia **||** river in Apulia **||** the W.N.W. wind, which favors the crossing from Italy to Greece
Iarb·a(s) -ae *m* Iarbas *(king of the Gaetulians in N. Africa, whom Dido rejected as a suitor)*
Iarbīt·a -ae *m* Mauretanian, Moor
Iardan·is -idis *f* daughter of Jardanus, king of Lydia *(i.e., Omphale)*
Iās·ō(n) -onis *m* Jason *(son of Aeson, leader of the Argonauts, and husband of Medea)*
Iāsoni·us -a -um *adj* Jason's
iasp·is -idis *or* **-idos** *f* jasper
Iās·us -ī *f* town on the coast of Caria
iātralipt·ēs -ae *m* masseur
Iāz·yx -ygis *m* member of a people dwelling near the Danube
ibi *or* **ibī** *adv* there, in that place; then, on that occasion; therein
ibidem *or* **ibīdem** *adv* in the same place, just there; in the place already mentioned, therein, thereon; at that very moment, there and then; at the same time; in the same matter
īb·is -is *or* **-idis** *f* ibis *(bird sacred to the Egyptians)*
Īcariōt·is -idis *adj* of Penelope **||** *f* Penelope *(daughter of Icarius)*
Īcari·us -a -um *adj* of Icarus, Icarian; of the Icarian Sea; **Canis Īcarius** *(astr)* Dog Star; **||** *m* father of Penelope **||** *n* Icarian Sea
Īcar·us -ī *m* son of Daedalus, who, on his flight from Crete with his father, fell into the sea
ichneum·ōn -onis *m* ichneumon *(Egyptian rat that eats crocodile eggs)*
īcī *perf of* **īcō**
-ici·us -a -um *adjl suf* **1** used to form adjectives from nouns denoting officers, relationships, etc.: **tribūnicius** tribunician; **patricius** patrician; **2** denoting the time of birth, of a birthday: **nātālicius** of the time of birth, belonging to a birthday; **3** used to form adjectives from past participles: **expositicius** exposed, foundling; **4** used to form adjectives from nouns denoting materials: **latericius** brick, of brick *(from* **later** brick)
īc·ō -ere -ī -tus *tr* to hit, strike, shoot; to sting, bite; **foedus īcere** to conclude a treaty
-icō *vbl suf* **1** used to form verbs from adjectives: **claudicāre** to be lame, to limp

(*from* **claudus** lame, limping); **2** used to form verbs from other verbs: **fodicāre** to stab (*from* **fodere** to stab, dig)
īc·ōn -onis *f* image
īconic·us -a -um *adj* giving an exact image
icteric·us -a -um *adj* jaundiced
ict·is -idis *f* weasel
ictus *pp of* **īcō**
ict·us -ūs *m* stroke, blow, hit; cut; sting, bite; wound; range; *(musical or metrical)* beat; *(fig)* shock, blow; **sub ictum** within range
id *adv* for that reason, therefore
id ēius *(neut of* **is)** *adj* this, that, the aforesaid ‖ *pron* it; a thing, the thing; **ad id** for that purpose; **aliquid id genus** s.th. of that sort, s.th. like that; **cum eō ut** on condition that, with the stipulation that; **ēo plūs** the more; **ex eō** from that time on; as a result of that, consequently; **id cōnsilī** some sort of plan, some plan; **id temporis** at that time; of that age; **in id** to that end; **in eō esse** to depend on it; **in eō esse ut** to be so far gone that, to get to the point where
Īd·a -ae *or* **Īd·ē -ēs** *f* Mt. Ida *(mountain range near Troy)* ‖ Mt. Ida *(mountain in Crete where Jupiter was brought up)*
Īdae·us -a -um *adj* Idaean, of Mt. Ida *(in Crete or near Troy)*
Īdal·ium -(i)ī *n* city in Cyprus dear to Venus
idcircō *adv* on that account, for that reason, therefore
īdem eadem idem *adj* the same, the very same, exactly this; *(often equivalent to a mere connective)* also, likewise ‖ *pron* the same one
identidem *adv* again and again, continually; over and over again
ideō *adv* therefore
idiōt·a -ae *m* layman, amateur; private individual
īdōl·on -ī *n* apparition, ghost
idōneē *adv* suitably
idōne·us -a -um *adj* suitable, fit, proper; *(w. dat or w.* **ad** *or* **in** + *acc)* fit for, capable of, suited for, convenient for, sufficient for
Īd·ūs -uum *fpl* Ides *(15th day of March, May, July, and October, and 13th day of the other months; interest, debts, and tuition were often paid on the Ides)*
iec·ur -oris *or* **-ineris** *or* **-inoris** *n* liver; *(as the seat of emotions)* anger, lust
iecuscul·um -ī *n* little liver
iēiūnē *adv (fig)* dryly
iēiūniōs·us -a -um *adj* **(iāiūn-)** *(hum)* abounding in hunger, hungry
iēiūnit·ās -ātis *f* **(iāiūn-)** fasting; dryness *(of style);*
iēiūn·ium -(i)ī *n* fasting, fast; hunger, leanness
iēiūn·us -a -um *adj* **(iāiūn-)** fasting; hungry; thin; insignificant, paltry; poor *(land);* jejune *(style)*
iēns euntis *pres p of* **eō**
-iēns *or* **-iēs** *advl suf* forming numerals and adjectives to denote a number of times: **centiēns** a hundred times; **totiēns** so many times, so often
-iēns·is -is -e *adjl suf* used to form ethnic adjectives from place names: **Carthaginiēnsis** Carthaginian
ientācul·um -ī *n* **(iāien-)** breakfast
ient·ō -āre -āvī *intr* to eat breakfast
igitur *adv* then, therefore, accordingly; *(resumptive after parenthetical matter)* as I was saying; *(in summing up)* so then, in short
ignār·us -a -um *adj* ignorant, unaware, inexperienced; unsuspecting; senseless; unknown, strange, unfamiliar; *(w. gen)* unaware of, unfamiliar with, ignorant of
ignāvē *adv* listlessly, lazily
ignāvi·a -ae *f* listlessness, laziness; cowardice
ignāviter *adv* listlessly, lazily
ignāv·us -a -um *adj* listless, lazy, idle, inactive; relaxing; cowardly; unproductive, useless
ignēsc·ō -ere *intr* **(-nis-)** to catch fire, become inflamed, burn; *(fig)* to flare up
igne·us -a -um *adj* of fire, on fire, fiery; red-hot; fiery, ardent *(person)*
ignicul·us -ī *m* small fire, little flame; sparkle; *(lit & fig)* spark
ignif·er -era -erum *adj* fiery
ignigen·a -ae *m* son of fire *(epithet of Bacchus)*
ignip·ēs -edis *adj* fiery-footed
ignipot·ēns -entis *adj* lord of fire *(epithet of Vulcan)*
ign·is -is *m* fire; watch fire, fire signal; torch; lightning, bolt of lightning; funeral pyre; star; brightness, glow, splendor; *(fig)* fire, rage, fury, love, passion; flame, sweetheart; agent of destruction, fanatic ‖ *mpl* love poems
ignōbil·is -is -e *adj* unknown, obscure, insignificant, undistinguished; low-born, ignoble
ignōbilit·ās -ātis *f* obscurity; humble birth
ignōmini·a -ae *f* ignominy, dishonor, disgrace; *(mil)* dishonorable discharge; **ignōminiā afficere** to dishonor, disgrace; **ignōminia senātūs** public censure imposed by the Senate
ignōminiōs·us -a -um *adj* disgraced; ignominious, disgraceful, shameful ‖ *m (person)* disgrace
ignōrābil·is -is -e *adj* unknown
ignōranti·a -ae *f* ignorance
ignōrāti·ō -ōnis *f* ignorance
ignōr·ō -āre -āvī -ātus *tr* to not know, be ignorant of, be unfamiliar with; to be

unaware of, know nothing about; to fail to recognize; to mistake, misunderstand; to ignore, disregard, take no notice of

ignōsc·ēns -entis *adj* forgiving, indulgent

ig·nōscō -nōscere -nōvī -nōtum *intr (w. dat)* to pardon, forgive, excuse; *(w. dat of person and acc of the offense)* to pardon, forgive, excuse *(s.o. a fault)*

ignōt·us -a -um *adj* unknown, unfamiliar, strange; inglorious; unnoticed; low-born, ignoble; vulgar; ignorant

īl·ex -icis *f* holm oak *(European evergreen oak with foliage resembling that of a holly)*

Īli·a -ae f Rhea Silvia *(daughter of Numitor and mother of Romulus and Remus)*

īl·ia -ium *npl* flank, side *(of the body extending from the hips down to the groin)* guts, intestines; belly, groin, private parts

Īliac·us -a -um *adj* Trojan

Īli·as -adis *f Iliad;* Trojan woman

īlicet *adv (ancient form for adjourning an assembly)* you may go; *(expressing dismay)* it's all over!, finished!; at once, immediately

īlicō *adv* on the spot, right then and there, immediately

īlign(e)·us -a -um *adj* of holm oak, oaken

Īl·ios -iī *f* Ilium, Troy

Īlithȳi·a -ae *f* goddess who aided women in childbirth

Īl·ium -iī *n or* **Īl·ion -iī** *n of* **Īl·ios -iī** *f* Ilium, Troy

Īli·us -a -um *adj* of Ilium, Trojan

illā *adv* that way

ill·a -īus *adj fem* that; that famous **II** *pron* that one, she

illabefact·us -a -um *adj* **(inl-)** unbroken, uninterrupted; unimpaired

illā·bor -bī -psus sum *intr* **(inl-)** to flow; to sink, fall; to fall in, cave in; to slip; *(w. dat or w.* **ad** *or* **in** *+ acc)* to flow into, enter into, penetrate

illabōr·ō -āre *intr* **(inl-)** *(w. dat)* to work at, work on

illāc *adv* that way

illacessīt·us -a -um *adj* **(inl-)** unprovoked

illacrimābil·is -is -e *adj* **(inl-)** unlamented, unwept; inexorable

illacrim·ō -āre -āvī *or* **illacrim·or -ārī -ātus sum** *intr* **(inl-)** *(w. dat)* to cry over

ill·aec *(acc:* **-anc;** *abl:* **-āc)** *adj fem* that **II** *pron* she

illaes·us -a -um *adj* **(inl-)** unharmed

illaetābil·is -is -e *adj* **(inl-)** sad, melancholy

illāpsus (inl-) *pp of* **illābor**

illaque·ō -āre -āvī -ātus *tr* **(inl-)** to trap, entangle

illātus (inl-) *pp of* **īnferō**

illaudāt·us -a -um *adj* **(inl-)** unworthy of praise, unpraised

ill·e -īus *adj masc* that; that famous; the former; **ille aut ille** this or that, such and such **II** *pron* that one; he; the former one

illecebr·a -ae *f* **(inl-)** attraction, allurement

illecebrōs·us -a -um *adj* **(inl-)** alluring, seductive

illēct·us -a -um *adj* **(inl-)** unread

illectus (inl-) *pp of* **illiciō**

illect·us -ūs *m* **(inl-)** allurement

illepidē *adv* **(inl-)** inelegantly, rudely

illepid·us -a -um *adj* **(inl-)** inelegant, lacking refinement

illēvī *perf of* **illinō**

ill·ēx -ēgis *adj* **(inl-)** lawless

ill·ex -icis *mf* **(inl-)** lure, decoy

illexī *perf of* **illiciō**

illībāt·us -a -um *adj* **(inl-)** undiminished, unimpaired, intact

illīberāl·is -is -e *adj* **(inl-)** stingy

illīberālit·ās -ātis *f* **(inl-)** stinginess

illīberāliter *adv* **(inl-)** stingily

ill·ic *(acc:* **-unc;** *abl:* **-ōc)** *adj masc* that **II** *pron* he

illīc *adv* there, in that place; in that matter, therein

il·liciō -licere -lexī -lectus *tr* **(inl-)** to allure, attract; to seduce, mislead

illicitāt·or -ōris *m* **(inl-)** hired bidder *(one who bids at an auction to make others bid higher)*

illicit·us -a -um *adj* **(inl-)** unlawful, illicit

illī·dō -dere -sī -sus *tr* **(inl-)** to smash to pieces, crush; *(w. dat or w.* **ad** *or* **in** *+ acc)* to smash *(s.th.)* against

illig·ō -āre -āvī -ātus *tr* **(inl-)** to attach, connect; to tie, bind; to oblige, obligate; to impede; to involve, tie up

illim *adv* from there

illīm·is -is -e *adj* unmuddied, clear

illinc *adv* from there; on that side

il·linō -linere -lēvī -litus *tr* **(inl-)** to cover; to smear; *(w. dat)* to smear *or* spread *(s.th.)* on, cake *(s.th.)* on

illiquefact·us -a -um *adj* **(inl-)** melted

illīsī *perf of* **illīdō**

illīsus *pp of* **illīdō**

illi(t)terāt·us -a -um *adj* **(inl-)** uneducated, illiterate

illitus *pp of* **illinō**

illō(c) *adv* there, at that place; at that point

illōt·us *or* **illaut·us -a -um** *adj* **(inl-)** unwashed, dirty

ill·ūc *(acc;* **-ūc;** *abl* **-ōc)** *adj neut* that **II** *pron* it

illūc *adv* to that place, in that direction; to that person, to him, to her; to that matter; to that point

illūc·eō -ēre *intr* **(inl-)** *(w. dat)* to shine on

illū·cēscō -cēscere -xī *intr* **(inl-)** to grow light, dawn; to begin to shine

ill·ud -īus *adj neut* that; the former **II** *pron* it

illū·dō -dere -sī -sus *tr* **(inl-)** to make fun of, ridicule; to waste, fritter away *(time, life)* ‖ *intr (w. dat) (coll)* to play around with *(sexually)*
illūminātē *adv* **(inl-)** clearly
illūmin·ō -āre -āvī -ātus *tr* **(inl-)** to illuminate, light up, make bright; to illustrate
illūsī *perf of* **illūdō**
illūsi·ō -ōnis *f* **(inl-)** irony
illūstr·is -is -e *adj* **(inl-)** bright, clear, brilliant; plain, distinct, evident; distinguished, famous, illustrious, noble
illūstr·ō -āre -āvī -ātus *tr* **(inl-)** to light up, illuminate; to make clear, clear up, explain; to make famous; to embellish
illūsus *pp of* **illūdō**
illuvi·ēs -ēī *f* **(inl-)** filth, dirtiness; mud; inundation; *(of a person) (pej)* scum
illūxī *perf of* **illūcēscō**
Illyric·us -a -um *adj* Illyrian ‖ *n* Illyria
Illyri·us -a -um *adj & m* Illyrian ‖ *f* Illyria *(on the E. coast of the Adriatic Sea)*
Īl·us -ī m son of Tros, father of Laomedon, and founder of Ilium ‖ Ascanius
-im *advl suf*
imāgināri·us -a -um *adj* imaginary
imāginātiōn·ēs -um *fpl* imaginings
imāgin·or -ārī -ātus sum *tr* to imagine
imāg·ō -inis *f* image, likeness, picture, bust; bust of ancestor; ghost, vision; echo; appearance, semblance, shadow; mental picture, concept, thought, idea; figure of speech, simile, metaphor
imbēcillit·ās -ātis *f* **(inb-)** weakness, feebleness; helplessness
imbēcill·us -a -um *adj* **(inb-)** weak, feeble; helpless; *(of medicine)* ineffective
imbell·is -is -e *adj* **(inb-)** anti-war; unwarlike; peaceful, quiet; ineffective *(weapon); (pej)* unfit for war, soft
im·ber -bris *m* rain, rainstorm; *(lit & fig)* shower; rain cloud; rainwater; water *(in general)*; snowstorm; hail-storm; flood of tears; **maximus imber** very heavy downpour
imberb·is -is -e *or* **imberb·us -a -um** *adj* **(inb-)** beardless
imbib·ō -ere -ī *tr* **(inb-)** to imbibe, drink in; **(animō) imbibere** to absorb, form *(e.g., an opinion)*
imbīt·ō -ere *tr* **(inb-)** to enter
imbr·ex -icis *f* (fluted) tile, gutter tile
imbric·us -a -um *adj* rainy
imbrif·er -era -erum *adj* rainy, bringing rain
im·buō -buere -buī -būtus *tr* to wet, soak; to dip; to moisten; to stain, taint, infect; to imbue, fill, steep; to instruct; *(w.* **ad***)* to introduce to
imitābil·is -is -e *adj* imitable, capable of being imitated
imitām·en -inis *n* imitation, copy; image, likeness
imitāment·um -ī *n* imitation ‖ *npl* pretense
imitāti·ō -ōnis *f* imitation; mimicking, copying; copy, counterfeit
imitāt·or -ōris *m,* **imitātr·īx -īcis** *f* imitator
imitāt·us -a -um *adj* fictitious, copied
imit·or -ārī -ātus sum *tr* to imitate, copy; to portray; to ape
immad·ēscō -ēscere -uī *intr* **(inm-)** to become wet
immāne *adv* **(inm-)** savagely
immān·is -is -e *adj* **(inm-)** huge, enormous, monstrous; inhuman, savage
immānit·ās -ātis *f* **(inm-)** vastness, enormity; savageness, cruelty
immānsuēt·us -a -um *adj* **(inm-)** untamed, savage, wild
immātūrit·ās -ātis *f* **(inm-)** immaturity; prematureness; overanxiousness
immātūr·us -a -um *adj* **(inm-)** immature; unripe; premature
immedicābil·is -is -e *adj* **(inm-)** incurable
immem·or -oris *adj* **(inm-)** forgetful, forgetting; negligent, heedless; **immemor patriae** forgetting (one's) country
immemorābil·is -is -e *adj* **(inm-)** not worth mentioning; untold
immemorāt·a -ōrum *npl* **(inm-)** novelties, things hitherto untold
immēnsit·ās -ātis *f* **(inm-)** immensity ‖ *fpl* immense stretches
immēns·us -a -um *adj* **(inm-)** immense, unending, immeasurable, huge ‖ *n* infinity, infinite space
immer·ēns -entis *adj* **(inm-)** undeserving, innocent
immer·gō -gere -sī -sus *tr* **(inm-)** to immerse, dip, plunge; to overwhelm, drown; *(w.* **in** *+ acc)* to dip *(s.th.)* into ‖ *refl (w.* **in** *+ acc)* **1** to plunge into; **2** to insinuate oneself into
immeritō *adv* **(inm-)** undeservedly, innocently
immerit·us -a -um *adj* **(inm-)** undeserving, innocent; undeserved; **immeritō meō** through no fault of mine
immersābil·is -is -e *adj* **(inm-)** unsinkable
immersī *perf of* **immergō**
immersus *pp of* **immergō**
immētāt·us -a -um *adj* **(inm-)** unmeasured, undivided
immigr·ō -āre -āvī -ātum *intr* **(inm-)** to immigrate; *(w.* **in** *+ acc)* **1** to move into; **2** to invade
immin·eō -ēre *intr* **(inm-)** to project, stick out; to be near, be imminent; to threaten, menace; *(w. dat)* **1** to look out over, overlook *(a view)*; **2** to hover over, loom over, threaten; *(w. dat or* **in** *+ acc)* to be intent on, be eager for
immin·uō -uere -uī -ūtus *tr* **(inm-)** to lessen, curtail; to weaken, impair; to infringe upon, encroach upon, violate, subvert, destroy

imminūti·ō -ōnis *f* **(inm-)** lessening; mutilation; *(rhet)* understatement

im·mīsceō -mīscēre -mīscuī -mīxtus *tr* **(inm-)** to mix in, intermix, blend; *(fig)* to mix up, confuse; **manūs manibus immīscēre** *(of boxers)* to mix it up ‖ *refl & pass (w. dat)* **1** to join, join in with, mingle with, get lost in *(e.g., a crowd)*; **2** to blend with, disappear in *(e.g., the night, a cloud)*

immiserābil·is -is -e *adj* **(inm-)** unpitied

immisericorditer *adv* **(inm-)** unmercifully

immisericor·s -dis *adj* **(inm-)** merciless

immīsī *perf of* **immittō**

immissi·ō -ōnis *f* **(inm-)** letting *(e.g., saplings)* grow

immissus *pp of* **immittō**

immīt·is -is -e *adj* **(inm-)** unripe, sour, green *(fruit)*; sour *(wine)*; harsh; rude; cruel, ruthless, pitiless

im·mittō -mittere -mīsī -missus *tr* **(inm-)** to send *(to or into)*; to steer *(a ship)*; to guide *(a horse)*; to insert; to let in, let go in, admit; to let go of, let drop; to let fly, throw; to let *(death, ills)* loose *(on)*; to direct the flow of *(water, air, etc., into or against)*; **habēnās immittere** to slacken the reins ‖ *refl & pass* to go *(into)*; to leap *(into)*; *(geog)* to extend *(to, into)*

immīxtus (inm-) *pp of* **immīsceō**

immō *or* **immo** *adv (in contradiction or correction of preceding words)* nay, on the contrary, or rather, more precisely; *(in confirmation of preceding words)* quite so, yes indeed; **immō vērō** yes and in fact

immōbil·is -is -e *adj* **(inm-)** motionless, unshaken; immovable; fixed, unalterable; clumsy, unwieldy

immoderātē *adv* **(inm-)** immoderately

immoderāti·ō -ōnis *f* **(inm-)** lack of moderation, excess

immoderāt·us -a -um *adj* **(inm-)** unmeasured, limitless; immoderate, uncontrolled, excessive

immodestē *adv* **(inm-)** immoderately, shamelessly

immodesti·a -ae *f* **(inm-)** lack of self-control; excesses; insubordination

immodest·us -a -um *adj* **(inm-)** immoderate, uncontrolled

immodicē *adv* **(inm-)** excessively

immodic·us -a -um *adj* **(inm-)** huge, enormous; immoderate, excessive; *(w. gen or abl)* given to, excessive in

immodulāt·us -a -um *adj* **(inm-)** unrhythmical

immolāti·ō -ōnis *f* **(inm-)** sacrifice

immolāt·or -ōris *m* **(inm-)** sacrificer

immōlīt·us -a -um *adj* **(inm-)** constructed, erected ‖ *npl* buildings

immol·ō *or* **inmol·ō -āre -āvī -ātus** *tr* **(inm-)** to sprinkle the feet of *(the victim)* with coarse flour in preparation for sacrifice; to immolate, sacrifice

immor·deō -dēre — -sus *tr* to bite into; *(fig)* stimulate

immor·ior -ī -tuus sum *intr* **(inm-)** *(w. dat)* to die in, die upon; *(fig)* to get sick over

immor·or -ārī -ātus sum *intr* **(inm-)** *(w. dat)* to dwell upon

immors·us -a -um *adj* bitten into; excited, stimulated

immortāl·is -is -e *adj* **(inm-)** immortal

immortālit·ās -ātis *f* **(inm-)** immortality

immortāliter *adv (coll)* **(inm-)** infinitely, eternally

immortuus (inm-) *pp of* **immorior**

immōt·us -a -um *adj* **(inm-)** unmoved, immovable; unshaken, undisturbed, steadfast

immūg·iō -īre -īvī *or* **-iī -ītum** *intr* **(inm-)** to bellow; to roar

immulg·eō -ēre *tr* **(inm-)** to milk

immunditi·a -ae *f* **(inm-)** dirtiness, filth

immund·us -a -um *adj* **(inm-)** dirty, filthy

immūn·iō -īre -īvī *or* **-iī** *tr* **(inm-)** to reinforce, fortify

immūn·is -is -e *adj* **(inm-)** without duty *or* office; tax-exempt; free, exempt; pure, innocent; *(w. abl or* **ab)** free from, exempt from; *(w. gen)* **1** free of, free from; **2** devoid of, without; **3** having no share in

immūnit·ās -ātis *f* **(inm-)** immunity, exemption; exemption from tribute

immūnīt·us -a -um *adj* **(inm-)** unfortified; unpaved *(road)*

immurmur·ō -āre *intr* **(inm-)** to grumble; *(w. dat) (of the wind)* to whisper among

immūtābil·is -is -e *adj* **(inm-)** immutable, unchangeable; changed

immūtābilit·ās -ātis *f* **(inm-)** immutability

immūtāti·ō -ōnis *f* **(inm-)** exchange, substitution; *(rhet)* metonymy

immūtāt·us -a -um *adj* **(inm-)** unchanged

immūt·ō -āre -āvī -ātus *tr* **(inm-)** to change, alter; to substitute

impācāt·us -a -um *adj* **(inp-)** unsubdued

impāctus *pp of* **impingō**

impall·ēscō -ēscere -uī *intr* **(inp-)** *(w. abl)* to turn pale at

imp·ār -aris *adj* **(inp-)** uneven, odd *(numbers)*; uneven *(in size or length)*; unlike *(in color or appearance)*; unequal; unfair; ill-matched; crooked; *(w. dat)* **1** not a match for, inferior to; **2** unable to cope with

imparāt·us -a -um *adj* **(inp-)** unprepared

impariter *adv* **(inp-)** unequally

impāst·us -a -um *adj* **(inp-)** unfed, hungry

impati·ēns -entis *adj* **(inp-)** impatient; *(w. gen)* **1** impatient with; **2** unable to endure, unable to take *(e.g., the heat)*; **impatiēns īrae** unable to restrain one's anger

impatienter *adv* **(inp-)** impatiently; intolerably

impatienti·a -ae *f* **(inp-)** *(w. gen)* inability *or* unwillingness to endure

impavidē *adv* **(inp-)** fearlessly

impavid·us -a -um *adj* **(inp-)** fearless, undismayed

impedīment·um -ī *n* **(inp-)** impediment, hindrance; difficulty **‖** *npl* baggage; mule train

imped·iō -īre -īvī *or* **-iī -ītus** *tr* **(inp-)** to entangle; to hamper, hinder; to entwine, encircle; to clasp, embrace; to block *(road);* to hinder, prevent; to embarrass; *(w.* **nē, quīn,** *or* **quōminus)** to prevent *(s.o.)* from

impedīti·ō -ōnis *f* **(inp-)** hindrance **‖** *fpl* cases of obstruction

impedīt·us -a -um *adj* **(inp-)** hampered; obstructed, blocked; difficult, intricate; impassable; busy, occupied

impēgī (inp-) *perf of* **impingō**

im·pellō -pellere -(pe)pulī -pulsus *tr* **(inp-)** to strike against, strike; to reach *(the ears);* to push, drive, drive forward, impel, propel; to urge, persuade; to stimulate, induce; to force, compel; to put to rout; to swell *(sails)*

impend·eō -ēre *intr* **(inp-)** to be near, be at hand, be imminent, threaten; *(w. dat)* to hang over; *(w. dat or* **in** *+ acc)* to hover over, loom over

impendiōs·us -a -um *adj* **(inp-)** extravagant, free-spending

impend·ium -(i)ī *n* **(inp-)** expense, cost, outlay; interest *(paid out);* loss

impen·dō -dere -dī -sus *tr* **(inp-)** to weigh out, pay out; to expend, devote, apply, employ; *(w.* **in** *+ acc)* **1** to spend *(money)* on; **2** to expend *(effort)* on; **3** to pay *(attention)* to

impenetrābil·is -is -e *adj* **(inp-)** impenetrable

impēns·a -ae *f* **(inp-)** expense, cost, outlay; waste; contribution; **impēnsam facere** to incur an expense; **meīs impēnsīs** at my expense

impēnsē *adv* **(inp-)** at a high cost, expensively; with great effort

impēns·us -a -um *pp of* **impendō ‖** *adj* high, costly, expensive; strong, vehement; earnest **‖** *n* high price

imper·āns -antis *m* **(inp-)** master, ruler

imperāt·or -ōris *m* **(inp-)** commander, general; commander in chief; emperor; director; master, ruler

imperātōri·us -a -um *adj* **(inp-)** of a general, general's; imperial

imperātr·īx -īcis *f* **(inp-)** controller, mistress

imperāt·um -ī *n* **(inp-)** command, order

impercept·us -a -um *adj* **(inp-)** unperceived, unknown

imperc·ō -ere *intr (w. dat)* **(inp-)** to spare, take it easy on

impercuss·us -a -um *adj* **(inp-)** noiseless

imperdit·us -a -um *adj* **(inp-)** not killed, unscathed

imperfect·us -a -um *adj* **(inp-)** unfinished; imperfect; undigested *(food)*

imperfoss·us -a -um *adj* **(inp-)** unpierced, not stabbed

imperiōs·us -a -um *adj* **(inp-)** masterful, commanding; imperial; magisterial; tyrannical, overbearing, domineering, imperious

imperītē *adv* **(inp-)** unskillfully, clumsily; in an ignorant manner

imperīti·a -ae *f* **(inp-)** inexperience, awkwardness, ignorance

imperit·ō -āre -āvī -ātus *tr & intr* **(inp-)** to command, rule, govern

imperīt·us -a -um *adj* **(inp-)** inexperienced, unfamiliar, ignorant, unskilled; *(w. gen)* inexperienced in, unacquainted with, ignorant of

imper·ium -(i)ī *n* **(inp-)** supreme administrative power *(exercised by the kings, subsequently by certain magistrates and provincial governors, and later by Roman emperors);* absolute authority *(in any sphere);* dominion, sway, government; empire; command, order; right to command; authority; exercise of authority; military commission, military command; mastery; sovereignty; realm, dominion; public office, magistracy; term of office

imperiūrāt·us -a -um *adj* **(inp-)** sacrosanct

impermiss·us -a -um *adj* **(inp-)** forbidden

imper·ō -āre -āvī -ātus *tr* **(inp-)** to requisition, give orders for, order, demand; *(w. acc of thing and dat of source demanded from)* to demand *(e.g., hostages)* from **‖** *intr* to be in command, rule, be master; *(w. dat)* to give orders to, order, command, govern, master, exercise control over; *(gram)* to express a command

imperterrit·us -a -um *adj* **(inp-)** undaunted, fearless

impert·iō -īre *tr* **(inp-)** *(w. dat)* to impart, communicate, bestow, assign, direct *(s.th.)* to, share *(s.th.)* with; *(w. acc of person and abl of thing)* to present *(s.o.)* with

imperturbāt·us -a -um *adj* **(inp-)** unperturbed, unruffled

impervi·us -a -um *adj* **(inp-)** impassable; *(w. dat)* impervious to

impete *(abl singl) m* with an assault, with a charge

impetibil·is -is -e *adj* **(inp-)** intolerable

impet·ō -ere *tr* **(inp-)** to make for; to attack

impetrābil·is -is -e *adj* **(inp-)** obtainable; successful

impetrāti·ō -ōnis *f* **(inp-)** obtaining one's request

impetr·iō -īre *tr* **(inp-)** to try to obtain through favorable omens
impetr·ō -āre -āvī -ātus *tr* **(inp-)** to obtain, procure *(by asking);* to achieve, accomplish, bring to pass
impet·us -ūs *m* **(inp-)** attack, assault; rush; impetus; impetuosity, vehemence, vigor; violence, fury, force; wide expanse *(of sea, sky); (w. gen)* sudden burst of; *(w. inf or* **ad)** impulse to *(do s.th.);* **animī impetus** impulse, urge; **omnī impetū** with all one's might
impex·us -a -um *adj* **(inp-)** uncombed, unkempt, tangled
impiē *adv* **(inp-)** wickedly
impiet·ās -ātis *f* **(inp-)** impiety, irreverence, lack of respect; disloyalty
impi·ger -gra -grum *adj* **(inp-)** diligent, active, energetic
impigrē *adv* **(inp-)** energetically, actively
impigrit·ās -ātis *f* **(inp-)** energy, activity
im·pingō -pingere -pēgī -pāctus *tr* **(inp-)** *(w. dat or* **in** + *acc)* **1** to fasten to; **2** to pin against, force against, dash against; **3** to press *or* force *(s.th.)* on; **4** to fling at
impi·ō -āre -āvī -ātus *tr* **(inp-)** to make disrepectful **||** *refl* to act disrespectfully
impi·us -a -um *adj* **(inp-)** impious, godless, irreverent, disrespectful; disobedient; disloyal; wicked, unscrupulous; **Tartara impia** Tartarus, the abode of the impious
implācāt·us -a -um *adj* **(inp-)** implacable, inexorable, insatiable
implacid·us -a -um *adj* **(inp-)** restless; rough, wild
impl·eō -ēre -ēvī -ētus *tr* **(inp-)** to fill up; to satisfy; to fatten; to make pregnant; to enrich; to cover with writing, fill up *(a book);* to discharge, execute, implement; to complete, end; to occupy, take up *(time)*; to make up, amount to; to fulfill, satisfy *(wishes, hopes, prophecies, appetites)*
implex·us -a -um *adj* **(inp-)** entwined; involved
implicāti·ō -ōnis *f* **(inp-)** interweaving; network; **implicātiō reī familiāris** financial embarrassment
implicāt·us -a -um *adj* **(inp-)** involved, intricate
implicīsc·or -ī *intr* **(inp-)** to become confused
implicitē *adv* **(inp-)** intricately
implicitus *pp of* **implicō ||** *adj* confused; **implicitus morbō** disabled by sickness
implic·ō -āre -āvī -ātus *or* **-āre -uī -itus** *tr* **(inp-)** to entwine, wrap; to intertwine; to involve; to envelop; to embrace, clasp, grasp; to connect, join, unite; to implicate; to kindle *(a fire)* **||** *refl* **sē dextrae implicāre** to clasp *(s.o.'s)* right hand **||** *pass* to be intimately associated; to be embroiled
implōrāti·ō -ōnis *f* **(inp-)** imploring
implōr·ō -āre -āvī -ātus *tr* **(inpl-)** to implore, appeal to; *(w. double acc)* to beg *(s.o.)* for; *(w.* **ab)** to ask for *(s.th.)* from
impl·uit -uere -uit *or* **-ūvit -ūtum** *intr* **(inp-)** *(w. dat)* to rain on
implūm·is -is -e *adj* **(inp-)** featherless, unfledged; without wings
impluviāt·us -a -um *adj* **(inpl-)** square, shaped liked an impluvium
impluv·ium -(i)ī *n* **(inp-)** impluvium, rain basin *(square basin built into the floor of the atrium to hold rain water; (rarely =* **compluvium:** *square opening in the roof of the atrium of a Roman house to get rid of smoke and let in light and air)*
impolītē *adv* **(inp-)** simply, without fancy words
impolīt·us -a -um *adj* **(inp-)** unpolished, rough; lacking culture; *(of materials)* in the crude state
impollūt·us -a -um *adj* **(inp-)** unsullied
im·pōnō -pōnere -posuī -positus *or* **-postus** *tr* **(inp-)** to impose; *(w. dat or* **in** + *acc)* to place on, lay on, set on; *(w. dat or* **super** + *acc)* to build *(house, bridge, city)* on; *(w. dat or* **ad)** to station *(soldiers)* in *or* at; *(w. dat or* **ad** *or* **in** + *acc)* to apply *(remedies)* to; *(w. dat)* **1** to place *(s.o.)* in command *or* control of, put *(s.o.)* in charge of; **2** to put *(garments)* on *(s.o.);* **3** to impose *(taxes, terms, laws, responsibilites, limits, etc.)* on; **4** to inflict *(wounds, blows, punishment)* on; *(w. dat, w.* **in** + *acc,* **in** + *abl, or* **suprā** + *acc)* to place, put, set, lay *(s.th. or s.o.)* on **||** *intr (w. dat)* **1** to impose upon; **2** to trick, cheat
import·ō -āre -āvī -ātus *tr* **(inp-)** to bring in, import; to introduce; to bring about, cause; *(w. dat)* to inflict *(damage, trouble)* on
importūnit·ās -ātis *f* **(inp-)** importunity, rudeness, insolence; unfitness
importūn·us -a -um *adj* **(inp-)** inconvenient; unsuitable, out of place; troublesome, annoying; lacking consideration for others, rude, ruthless; stormy *(weather);* grim *(looks);* ill-omened
importuōs·us -a -um *adj* **(inp-)** without a harbor
imp·os -otis *adj* **(inp-)** out of control; *(w. gen)* not having control of; **impos animī** *(or* **mentis** *or* **suī)** out of one's mind
impositus (inp-) *pp of* **impōnō ||** *adj* situated, located
impossibil·is -is -e *adj* **(inp-)** impossible
impostus *pp of* **impōnō**
imposuī *perf of* **impōnō**
impot·ēns -entis *adj* **(inp-)** impotent, powerless; lacking self-control, uncontrollable, wild, violent; *(w. gen)* having no

control over; **impotēns suī** *(or* **animī)** out of one's mind

impotenter *adv* **(inp-)** impotently, weakly; without self-control, lawlessly, intemperately

impotenti·a -ae *f* **(inp-)** weakness, helplessness; lack of self-control, violence, fury, lawlessness

impraesentiārum *adv* **(inp-)** for the present, under present circumstances

imprāns·us -a -um *adj* **(inp-)** without breakfast *or* lunch, fasting

imprecāti·ō -ōnis *f* **(inp-)** the calling down of curses, imprecation

imprec·or -ārī -ātus sum *tr* **(inp-)** to call down *(a curse);* to invoke

impressī *perf of* **imprimō**

impressi·ō -ōnis *f* **(inp-)** pressure; attack, charge; rhythmical beat; emphasis; impression *(on the mind)*

impressus *pp of* **imprimō**

imprīmīs *or* **in prīmīs** *adv* **(inp-)** in the first place; chiefly, especially

im·primō -primere -pressī -pressus *tr* **(inp-)** to press down; to impress, imprint, stamp *(a seal, marks, patterns)*; to thrust, drive in *(esp. weapons);* to plant *(the feet, kisses); (fig)* to impress; **animum quasi cēram imprimere** to impress the mind like wax

improbāti·ō -ōnis *f* **(inp-)** disapproval; *(leg)* discrediting *(of a witness)*

improbē *adv* **(inp-)** badly, wickedly, wrongfully; recklessly; persistently

improbit·ās -ātis *f* **(inp-)** wickedness, depravity; roguishness

improb·ō -āre -āvī -ātus *tr* **(inp-)** to disapprove of, condemn, blame, reject

improbul·us -a -um *adj* **(inp-)** somewhat impudent, naughty

improb·us -a -um *adj* below standard, inferior; bad, shameless; rebellious, unruly; restless, indomitable, self-willed; cruel, merciless; disloyal, ill-disposed; *(of language)* offensively rude

improcēr·us -a -um *adj* **(inp-)** undersized

imprōdict·us -a -um *adj* **(inp-)** not postponed

imprompt·us -a -um *adj* **(inp-)** slow

improperāt·us -a -um *adj* **(inp-)** unhurried

impropri·us -a -um *adj* **(inp-)** *(gram)* improper, incorrect

improsp·er -era -erum *adj* **(inp-)** unfortunate

improsperē *adv* **(inp-)** unfortunately

imprōvidē *adv* **(inp-)** without foresight, thoughtlessly

imprōvid·us -a -um *adj* **(inp-)** not foreseeing, not anticipating; *(w. gen)* indifferent to

imprōvīs·us -a -um *adj* **(inp-)** unexpected; **dē imprōvīsō** *(or* **ex imprōvīsō** *or* **imprōvīsō)** unexpectedly **‖** *npl* emergencies

imprūd·ēns -entis *adj* **(inp-)** not foreseeing, unsuspecting; off one's guard; inconsiderate; foolish, imprudent; *(w. gen)* **1** unaware of, ignorant of; **2** heedless of; **3** not experienced in

imprūdenter *adv* **(inp-)** without foresight, thoughtlessly, unintenionally; foolishly, imprudently

imprūdenti·a -ae *f* **(inp-)** thoughtlessness; ignorance, imprudence

impūb·ēs -eris *or* **impūb·is -is -e** *adj* **(inp-)** youthful, young, underage; beardless *(cheeks);* innocent, chaste, celibate, virgin; **annī impūbēs** childhood years

impud·ēns -entis *adj* **(inp-)** shameless

impudenter *adv* **(inp-)** shamelessly, impudently; immodestly

impudenti·a -ae *f* **(inp-)** shamelessness, impudence; immodesty

impudīciti·a -ae *f* immodesty, lewdness, shamelessness

impudīc·us -a -um *adj* **(inp-)** immodest, lewd, shameless

impugnāti·ō -ōnis *f* **(inp-)** assault, attack

impugn·ō -āre -āvī -ātus *tr* **(inp-)** to assault, attack; *(fig)* to impugn; *(w. acc & inf)* to assert in opposition *(that)*

impulsi·ō -ōnis *f* **(inp-)** pressure; impulse

impuls·or -ōris *m* **(inp-)** instigator

impulsus *pp of* **impellō**

impuls·us -ūs *m* **(inp-)** blow, impact, shock; impulse; instigation, incitement

impūnē *adv* **(inp-)** with impunity, unpunished, scot-free; safely, unscathed

impūnit·ās -ātis *f* **(inp-)** impunity

impūnītē *adv* **(inp-)** with impunity

impūnīt·us -a -um *adj* **(inp-)** unpunished; unrestrained; safe

impūrāt·us -a -um *adj* **(inp-)** filthy

impūrē *adv* **(inp-)** impurely

impūrit·ās -ātis *f* **(inp-)** impurity

impūriti·ae -ārum *fpl* **(inp-)** filth

impūr·us -a -um *adj* **(inp-)** impure; unclean, filthy

imputāt·us -a -um *adj* **(inp-)** unpruned, untrimmed

imput·ō -āre -āvī -ātus *tr* **(inp-)** to charge to someone's account, enter in an account; *(w. dat)* **1** to charge to; **2** to ascribe to; **3** to give credit for *(s.th.)* to; **4** to put the blame for *(s.th.)* on

īmul·us -a -um *adj* cute little

īm·us -a -um *adj* deepest, lowest; last; the bottom of, the foot of, the tip of **‖** *n* bottom, depth; **ab īmō** utterly; **ab īmō ad summum** from top to bottom; **ex īmō** utterly, completely **‖** *npl* lower world

in- *pref* **(n** *is assimilated to following* **l, m,** *and* **r;** *becomes* **m** *before* **b** *and* **p;** *disappears before* **gn) 1** *combines, usu. with verbs, in the local or figurative senses of* *the preposition, e.g.,* **inaedificāre** to build in *(a place); also with intensive force, e.g.,* **increpāre** to make a loud noise; **2** *inchoative:* **īnsūdāre** to begin to sweat, break out in a sweat; **3** *negative or privative pref, e.g.:* **incognitus** unknown

in *prep (w. abl)* **1** in, on, upon; **2** among; **3** at; **4** before; **5** under; **6** *(of time)* during, within, in, at, in the course of, on the point of; **7** in case of; **8** in relation to; **9** subject to; **10** affected by; **11** engaged in, involved in; **12** over: **pōns in flūmine** a bridge over a river ‖ *(w. acc)* **1** into; **2** up to, as far as *(a point of space or time);* **3** *(indicating person toward whom feelings are directed)* toward, to, for; **4** until; **5** about, respecting; **6** *(w. verbs of opposition or hostility)* against; **7** for, with a view to; **8** according to, after; *(w. verbs of sending, traveling)* to *(a country, city);* **9** *(w. verbs of spending)* on; **10** *(w. verbs of distributing)* among

inaccess·us -a -um *adj* inaccessible

inac·ēscō -ēscere -uī *intr* to turn sour

Īnachid·ēs -ae *m* descendant of Inachus *(esp.* Perseus and Epaphus)

Īnach·us *or* **Īnach·os -ī** *m* first king of Argos and father of Io

inacuī *perf of* **inacēscō**

inadsc- = ināsc-

inadt- = inatt-

inadūst·us -a -um *adj* unburned, unsinged

inaedific·ō -āre -āvī -ātus *tr* to build on, build as an addition, erect, construct; to wall up, barricade; *(w.* **in** + *abl)* to build *(s.th.)* on top of

inaequābil·is -is -e *adj* uneven

inaequābiliter *adv* unevenly, unequally

inaequāl·is -is -e *adj* uneven, unequal; unlike; changeable, inconstant

inaequālit·ās -ātis *f* unevenness

inaequāliter *adv* unevenly

inaequāt·us -a -um *adj* unequal

inaequ·ō -āre -āvī -ātus *tr* to level off

inaestimābil·is -is -e *adj* inestimable; invaluable; valueless

inaestu·ō -āre *intr* to seethe; to flare up

inaffectāt·us -a -um *adj* unaffected, natural

inamābil·is -is -e *adj* hateful, revolting

inamārēsc·ō -ere *intr* to become bitter

inambitiōs·us -a -um *adj* unambitious

inambulāti·ō -ōnis *f* walking about, strutting about

inambul·ō -āre -āvī *intr* to walk up and down; to stroll about

inamoen·us -a -um *adj* unpleasant

ināni·ae -ārum *fpl* emptiness

inānilogist·a -ae *m* chatterbox

inānīment·um -ī *n* empty space

inanim·us -a -um *adj* inanimate

inān·is -is -e *adj* empty, void; deserted, abandoned, unoccupied; hollow; worthless, idle; lifeless, unsubstantial; penniless; unprofitable; groundless ‖ *n* empty space, vacuum; emptiness; worthlessness

inānit·ās -ātis *f* empty space, emptiness; uselessness, worthlessness

ināniter *adv* uselessly, vainly

inarāt·us -a -um *adj* untilled, unplowed

inār·dēscō -dēscere -sī *intr* to catch fire, burn, glow

inārēsc·ō -ere *intr* to become dry, dry up

inārsī *perf of* **inārdēscō**

ināscēns·us -a -um *adj* not climbed

inassuēt·us -a -um *adj* unaccustomed

inattenuāt·us -a -um *adj* undiminished; unappeased

inaud·āx -ācis *adj* timid

inaud·iō -īre -īvī *or* **-iī -ītus** *tr* **(indau-)** to hear, learn, get wind of

inaudīt·us -a -um *adj* unheard-of, unprecedented; unusual; without a court hearing

inaugurātō *adv* after taking the auspices

inaugur·ō -āre -āvī -ātus *tr* to inaugurate, consecrate, install ‖ *intr* to take the auspices

inaurāt·us -a -um *adj* gilded, gilt, goldplated

inaur·ēs -ium *fpl* earrings

inaur·ō -āre -āvī -ātus *tr* to goldplate, gild; to line the pockets of *(s.o.)* with gold

inauspicātō *adv* without consulting the auspices

inauspicāt·us -a -um *adj* undertaken without auspices; unlucky

inaus·us -a -um *adj* unattempted

inb- = imb-

incaedu·us -a -um *adj* uncut, unfelled

incal·ēscō -ēscere -uī *intr* to get warm, get hot; to get excited

incalfac·iō -ere *tr* to warm, heat

incallidē *adv* unskillfully

incallid·us -a -um *adj* unskillful; stupid, simple, clumsy

incand·ēscō -ēscere -uī *intr* to become white; to get white-hot

incantāt·us -a -um *adj* enchanted

incān·us -a -um *adj* grown grey

incassum *adv* in vain

incastīgāt·us -a -um *adj* unscolded, unpunished

incautē *adv* incautiously, recklessly

incaut·us -a -um *adj* incautious, inconsiderate, thoughtless, reckless; unforeseen, unexpected; unguarded

in·cēdō -cēdere -cessī -cessum *intr* to go, walk, move; to step, stride, strut; to proceed; to come along, happen, occur, appear, arrive; to advance, go on; *(of troops)* to march, advance

incelebrāt·us -a -um *adj* unheralded

incēnāt·us -a -um *adj* supperless

incendiārius -(i)ī *m* agitator; arsonist

incend·ium -(i)ī *n* fire; heat

incen·dō -dere -dī -sus *tr* to light, set on fire, burn; to light up, make bright; *(fig)* to inflame, fire up, excite, enrage
incēn·is -is -e *adj* dinnerless
incēnsi·ō -ōnis *f* burning
incēns·us -a -um *adj* not registered *(w. the censor)*
incēnsus *pp of* **incendō**
incepti·ō -ōnis *f* inception, beginning; undertaking
incept·ō -āre -āvī -ātus *tr* to begin; to undertake
incept·or -ōris *m* beginner, originator
incept·us -a -um *pp of* **incipiō** ‖ *n* beginning; undertaking, attempt, enterprise; subject, theme
in·cernō -cernere -crēvī -crētus *tr* to sift
incēr·ō -āre -āvī -ātus *tr* to wax, cover with wax, coat with wax
incertē *adv* uncertainly
incertō *adv* uncertainly
incert·ō -āre -āvī -ātus *tr* to render doubtful, make uncertain
incert·us -a -um *adj* uncertain; vague, obscure; doubtful; unsure, hesitant ‖ *n* uncertainty, insecurity; contingency; **in incertum** for an indefinite time
incessī *perf of* **incēdō**
incess·ō -ere -ī *or* **-īvī** *or* **-uī** *tr* to fall upon, assault; to reproach, accuse, attack
incess·us -ūs *m* walk, gait, pace; trampling; invasion, attack; advance; procession
incestē *adv* impurely, sinfully; indecently
in·cidō -cidere -cidī -cāsum *intr* to happen, occur; *(w.* **ad** *or* **in** *+ acc)* to fall into, fall upon; *(w.* **in** *+ acc)* **1** to come upon unexpectedly, fall in with; **2** to attack; *(w. dat or* **in** *+ acc)* **1** to occur to *(mentally)*; **2** to fall on *(a certain day)*; **3** to befall, happen to; **4** to agree with
incī·dō -dere -dī -sus *tr* to carve, engrave, inscribe; to cut, sever; *(fig)* to cut into, cut short, put an end to, break off, interrupt
incīl·e -is *n* ditch, trench
in·cingō -cingere -cīnxī -cīnctus *tr* to drape; to wreathe; to invest, surround
incin·ō -ere *tr* to sing; to play
incipessō *see* **incipissō**
in·cipiō -cipere -cēpī -ceptus *tr & intr* to begin, start
incipiss·ō -ere *tr* to begin
incīsē *or* **incīsim** *adv* in short phrases
incīsi·ō -ōnis *f* incision; *(rhet)* short phrase
incīsus *pp of* **incīdō**
incitāment·um -ī *n* incentive
incitāti·ō -ōnis *f* inciting, rousing; speed
incitāt·us -a -um *adj* rapid, speedy; **equō incitātō** at full gallop
incit·ō -āre -āvī -ātus *tr* to incite, urge on, spur on, drive on; to stimulate; to inspire; to stir up, arouse; to increase; **currentem incitāre** *(fig)* to spur a willing horse ‖ *refl* to rush
incit·us -a -um *adj* rapid, swift; immovable; **ad incita** *(or* **ad incitās) adigere** to bring to a standstill
inclāmit·ō -āre -āvī -ātus *tr* to cry out against, revile, abuse
inclām·ō -āre -āvī -ātus *tr* to call out to; to invoke; to shout at, scold, revile ‖ *intr* to yell
inclār·ēscō -ēscere -uī *intr* to become famous
inclēm·ēns -entis *adj* harsh, unmerciful; violent *(movement)*
inclēmenter *adv* harshly; rudely
inclēmenti·a -ae *f* harshness, cruelty
inclīnāti·ō -ōnis *f* leaning; inclination, tendency, bias; change; *(gram)* inflection
inclīnāt·us -a -um *adj* inclined, prone; sinking; low, deep; *(gram)* inflected
inclīn·ō -āre -āvī -ātus *tr* to bend, turn; to turn back, drive back, repulse; to shift *(e.g., blame)*; to change; *(gram)* to inflect *(nouns or verbs)* ‖ *refl & pass* to lean, bend, turn; to change *(esp. for the worse)* ‖ *pass (mil)* to fall back ‖ *intr* to bend, turn, lean, dip, sink; to change, deteriorate; to change for the better
inclit·us -a -um *adj* famous
inclū·dō -dere -sī -sus *tr* to shut in, confine, lock up; to include; to insert; to block, shut off, obstruct; to restrain, control; to close, end *(e.g., a day)*
inclūsi·ō -ōnis *f* locking up, confinement
inclut·us -a -um *adj* famous
incoct·us -a -um *pp of* **incoquō** ‖ *adj* uncooked, raw; undigested
incōgitābil·is -is -e *adj* thoughtless, inconsiderate
incōgit·āns -antis *adj* unthinking, thoughtless
incōgitanti·a -ae *f* thoughtlessness
incōgitāt·us -a -um *adj* thoughtless, inconsiderate
incōgit·ō -āre -āvī -ātus *tr* to think up
incognit·us -a -um *adj* not investigated; unknown, unrecognized, unidentified, incognito; unparalleled
incohāt·us *or* **inchoāt·us -a -um** *adj* only begun, unfinished, imperfect; temporary *(structure)*
incoh·ō -āre -āvī -ātus *tr* to begin
incol·a -ae *mf* inhabitant; resident alien
incol·ō -ere -uī *tr* to live in, inhabit, occupy ‖ *intr* to live, reside
incolum·is -is -e *adj* unharmed, safe and sound, unscathed, alive; *(w. abl)* safe from
incolumit·ās -ātis *f* safety
incomitāt·us -a -um *adj* unaccompanied
incommendāt·us -a -um *adj* unprotected
incommodē *adv* at the wrong time; inconveniently; annoyingly; improperly; unfortunately

incommodestic·us -a -um *adj (coll)* ill-timed, inconvenient
incommodit·ās -ātis *f* inconvenience; unsuitableness; disadvantage
incommod·ō -āre -āvī -ātum *intr (w. dat)* to inconvenience, be inconvenient for, be annoying to
incommod·us -a -um *adj* inconvenient; troublesome, tiresome, annoying; disadvantageous, unfavorable; unpleasant, disagreeable **ll** *n* inconvenience, discomfort; disadvantage; misfortune, trouble; *(med)* ailment; *(mil)* setback, disaster
incommūtābil·is -is -e *adj* unchangeable
incomparābil·is -is -e *adj* unequaled, incomparable
incompert·us -a -um *adj* unknown, undetermined; forgotten
incompositē *adv* in disorder
incomposit·us -a -um *adj* disordered, poorly arranged, poorly written; clumsy, awkward *(movements);* disorganized *(troops)*
incomprehēnsibil·is -is -e *adj* incomprehensible
incompt·us -a -um *adj* unkempt, messy; untidy; simple, unstudied; unpolished *(writing, speech)*
inconcess·us -a -um *adj* forbidden, unlawful
inconcili·ō -āre -āvī -ātus *tr* to deceive, trick; to rob, fleece
inconcinn·us -a -um *adj* clumsy, awkward; absurd
inconcuss·us -a -um *adj* unshaken
inconditē *adv* confusedly
incondit·us -a -um *adj* unorganized, disorderly, confused; irregular; rough, undeveloped *(style);* raw *(jokes)*
incōnsīderātē *adv* thoughtlessly
incōnsīderāt·us -a um *adj* thoughtless
incōnsōlābil·is -is -e *adj* inconsolable; *(fig)* incurable
incōnst·āns -antis *adj* inconsistent, fickle, shifty
incōnstanter *adv* inconsistently
incōnstanti·a -ae *f* inconsistency, fickleness
incōnsultē *adv* indiscreetly
incōnsult·us -a -um *adj* indiscreet, ill-advised; not consulted
incōnsult·us -ūs *m* lack of consultation; **incōnsultū meō** without consulting me
incōnsumpt·us -a -um *adj* unconsumed
incontāmināt·us -a -um *adj* untainted
incontent·us -a -um *adj* loose, untuned *(string)*
incontin·ēns -entis *adj* intemperate
incontinenter *adv* without self-control, intemperately
incontinenti·a -ae *f* lack of self-control
inconveni·ēns -entis *adj* unsuitable, dissimilar
inco·quō -quere -xī -ctus *tr* to boil *(in or with);* to dye; to imbue
incorrēct·us -a -um *adj* uncorrected
incorruptē *adv* honestly, fairly
incorrupt·us -a -um *adj* intact, unspoiled, untainted; uncorrupted; not open to bribes, incorruptible; chaste; genuine, authentic
incoxī *perf of* **incoquō**
incrēb(r)·ēscō -ēscere -uī *intr* to grow; to rise; to increase; to spread
incrēdibil·is -is -e *adj* incredible
incrēdibiliter *adv* incredibly
incrēdul·us -a -um *adj* incredulous
incrēment·um -ī *n* growth, increase; increment, addition; addition to the family, offspring
increpit·ō -āre -āvī -ātus *tr* to scold, rebuke
increp·ō -āre -uī -itus *or* **-āvī -ātus** *tr* to cause to make noise, cause to ring; to rattle; *(of Jupiter)* to thunder at; to scold, rebuke; to protest against; *(of sounds)* to strike *(the ears); (w. acc & inf)* to say reproachfully that, to remark indignantly that **ll** *intr* to make noise; to snap, rustle, rattle, clash; to speak angrily; *(of a bow)* to twang; *(of flying object)* to whiz, whir; **suspiciō tumultūs increpat** the suspicion of a riot sounds the alarm
incr·ēscō -ēscere -ēvī *intr* to grow, increase; *(w. dat or abl)* to grow in *or* upon
incrētus *pp of* **incernō**
incrēvī *perf of* **incernō** *and* **incrēscō**
incruentāt·us -a -um *adj* unbloodied
incruent·us -a -um *adj* bloodless, without bloodshed
incrūst·ō -āre -āvī -ātus *tr* to coat, cover with a coat, encrust
incub·ō -āre -uī -itum *intr (w. dat)* **1** to lie in *or* upon; **2** to lean on; **3** to brood over; **4** to watch jealously over
incū·dō -dere -dī -sus *or* **-ssus** *tr* to indent by hammering; to emboss
inculc·ō -āre -āvī -ātus *tr* to impress, inculcate; *(w. dat)* to force *(s.th.)* upon
inculpāt·us -a -um *adj* blameless
incultē *adv* uncouthly, roughly
incult·us -a -um *adj* untilled, uncultivated; neglected, slovenly; rough, uneducated, uncivilized **ll** *npl* desert, wilderness, the wilds
incult·us -ūs *m* neglect; dirt, squalor
in·cumbō -cumbere -cubuī -cubitum *intr (w. dat or* **in** *+ acc)* **1** to lean on *or* against; **2** to lie down on *(bed, couch);* **3** to bend to *(the oars);* **4** to light on, fall on; **5** *(fig)* to press upon, burden, oppress, weigh down; **6** to apply oneself to, take pains with; **7** to pay attention to; *(w.* **ad** *or* **in** *+ acc)* to be inclined toward, lean toward

incūnābul·a -ōrum *npl* baby clothes; *(fig)* cradle, infancy; birthplace; origin, source
incūrāt·us -a -um *adj* neglected; uncured
incūri·a -ae *f* carelessness, negligence
incūriōsē *adv* carelessly
incūriōs·us -a -um *adj* careless, unconcerned, indifferent; neglected
in·currō -currere -currī *or* **-cucurrī -cursus** *tr* to attack **||** *intr (w. dat or* **in** *+ acc)* **1** to run into, rush at, charge, attack; **2** to invade; **3** to extend to; **4** to meet, run into; **5** to fall on, coincide with
incursi·ō -ōnis *f* incursion, invasion, raid; attack; collision
incurs·ō -āre -āvī -ātus *tr* to attack; to invade **||** *intr (w. dat or* **in** *+ acc)* **1** to attack; **2** to run into, bump against; **3** to strike, meet *(e.g., the eyes);* **4** to affect, touch, move
incurs·us -ūs *m* attack; invasion, inroad, raid; collision, impact
incurv·ō -āre -āvī -ātus *tr* to bend
incurv·us -a -um *adj* bent, crooked
inc·ūs -ūdis *f* anvil
incūsāti·ō -ōnis *f* accusation
incūs·ō -āre -āvī -ātus *tr* to blame, find fault with, accuse
incussī *perf of* **incutiō**
incussus *pp of* **incutiō**
incuss·us -ūs *m* shock
incustōdīt·us -a -um *adj* unguarded; unconcealed; imprudent
incūs·us -a -um *pp of* **incudō ||** *adj* forged; embossed; **lapis incūsus** indented millstone
incu·tiō -tere -ssī -ssus *tr* to throw; to produce; *(w. dat or* **in** *+ acc)* to strike *(s.th.)* on *or* against; *(w. dat)* **1** to strike into, instill in; **2** to throw at, to fling upon; **metum incutere** *(w. dat)* to strike fear into; **scīpiōne in caput alicūius incutere** to beat s.o. over the head with a stick
indāgāti·ō -ōnis *f* investigation, search
indāgāt·or -ōris *m,* **indāgātr·īx -īcis** *f* investigator
indāg·ō -āre -āvī -ātus *tr* to track down, hunt; to investigate, explore
indāg·ō -inis *f* dragnet; **indāgine agere** to ferret out
indaudiō *see* **inaudiō**
inde *adv* from there; from that source, therefrom; from that time on, after that, thereafter; then; from that cause
indēbit·us -a -um *adj* that is not owed, not due
indec·ēns -entis *adj* unbecoming, improper, indecent
indecenter *adv* improperly, indecently
indec·eō -ēre *tr* to be improper for **||** *intr (w. dat)* to be inappropriate to
indēclīnāt·us -a -um *adj* unchanged, constant
indec·or -oris *or* **indecor·is -is -e** *adj* disgraceful, dishonorable; cowardly
indecōrē *adv* indecently, improperly
indecor·ō -āre -āvī -ātus *tr* to disgrace
indecōr·us -a -um *adj* unsightly
indēfēns·us -a -um *adj* undefended
indēfess·us -a -um *adj* tireless; not tired
indēflēt·us -a -um *adj* unwept
indēiect·us -a -um *adj* undemolished
indēlēbil·is -is -e *adj* indestructible, indelible
indēlībāt·us -a -um *adj* undiminished
indemnāt·us -a -um *adj* unconvicted
indēplōrāt·us -a -um *adj* unwept
indēprēns·us -a -um *adj* undetected
indeptus *pp of* **indipīscor**
indēsert·us -a -um *adj* unforsaken
indēspect·us -a -um *adj* unfathomable
indēstrīct·us -a -um *adj* unscathed
indētōns·us -a -um *adj* unshorn
indēvītāt·us -a -um *adj* unavoidable, unerring *(e.g., arrow)*
ind·ex -icis *m* index, sign, mark; indication, proof; title *(of book);* informer, spy; index finger
Indi·a -ae *f* India
Ind·ī -ōrum *npl* Indians, people of India
indicāti·ō -ōnis *f* setting the price; statement, declaration
indīc·ēns -entis *adj* not speaking; **mē indīcente** without a word from me
indic·ium -(i)ī *n* information, disclosure, evidence; indication, proof; permission to give evidence; reward for giving evidence; **indiciō esse** to give evidence; to be an indication *or* proof; **indicium afferre** *(or* **dēferre)** to adduce evidence; **indicium facere** to give away a secret; to give an indication *or* warning
indic·ō -āre -āvī -ātus *tr* to point out; to reveal, disclose; to betray, inform against; to put a price on **||** *intr* to give evidence
in·dīcō -dīcere -dīxī -dictus *tr* to proclaim, announce, publish; to summon, convoke; to impose *(a fine);* **bellum indīcere** to declare war; **diem indīcere** to set a date
indict·us -a -um *adj* unsaid; **causā indictā** without a hearing
Indic·us -a -um *adj* Indian **||** *m* Indian **||** *n* indigo
indidem *adv* from the same place; from the same source, from the same thing
indiffer·ēns -entis *adj* (morally) indifferent; unconcerned, indifferent
indigen·a -ae *adj masc & fem* native
indig·ēns -entis *adj* indigent; *(w. gen)* in need of
indigenti·a -ae *f* indigence, need; craving
indig·eō -ēre -uī *intr (w. gen or abl)* **1** to need, be in need of; **2** to require; *(w. gen)* to crave, desire
indig·es -etis *adj* indigenous, native **||** *m* native god; national hero

indīgest·us -a -um *adj* unarranged, disorderly, confused, in confusion

indignābund·us -a -um *adj* highly indignant

indign·āns -antis *adj* indignant; *(w. gen)* resentful of

indignāti·ō -ōnis *f* indignation, displeasure; provocation, occasion for indignation **II** *fpl* expressions of indignation

indignē *adv* unworthily; undeservedly; shamefully, outrageously; **indignē ferre** *(or* **patī)** to be indignant at

indignit·ās -ātis *f* unworthiness; indignation; indignity, shameful treatment; enormity, shamelessness

indign·or -ārī -ātus sum *tr* to be indignant at, displeased at, angry at, offended by

indign·us -a -um *adj* unworthy, undeserving; undeserved; shameful, scandalous; *(w. abl)* **1** unworthy of; **2** not deserving; **3** not worth; *(w. gen)* unworthy of, undeserving of; **indignum**! shame!

indig·us -a -um *adj* needy, indigent; *(w. gen or abl)* in need of

indīlig·ēns -entis *adj* careless

indīligenter *adv* carelessly

indīligenti·a -ae *f* carelessness

ind·ipīscor -ipīscī -eptus sum *or* **indipīsc·ō -ere** *tr* to obtain, get; to win, acquire **II** *intr (w.* **dē** *+ abl)* to gain one's point about

indīrept·us -a -um *adj* unplundered

indīscrēt·us -a -um *adj* closely connected, inseparable; used indiscriminately; indistinguishable; **indīscrētum est** it makes no difference

indisertē *adv* ineloquently

indisert·us -a -um *adj* without eloquence

indisposit·us -a -um *adj* confused, disordered

indissolūbil·is -is -e *adj* imperishable, indestructible

indistīnct·us -a -um *adj* indistinct; applied without distinction

inditus *pp of* **indō**

indīvidu·us -a -um *adj* indivisible; inseparable; equal, impartial **II** *n* atom, indivisible particle

in·dō -dere -didī -ditus *tr* to put, place; to introduce; to impart, give; *(w.* **in** *+ acc)* to put *or* place *(s. th.)* into *or* on, insert into

indocil·is -is -e *adj* slow to learn; impossible to teach; untrained, ignorant

indoctē *adv* unskillfully

indoct·us -a -um *adj* untaught, untrained; ignorant, uninformed

indolenti·a -ae *f* freedom from pain; insensibility to pain

indol·ēs -is *f* inborn quality, natural quality; nature, character; natural ability, talent; *(w. gen)* natural capacity for, natural tendency toward

indol·ēscō -ēscere -uī *intr* to feel sorry; to feel resentment

indomābil·is -is -e *adj* untamable

indomit·us -a -um *adj* untamed, wild; indomitable; unrestrained; unmanageable

indorm·iō -īre -īvī *or* **-iī -ītum** *intr* to fall asleep; to grow careless; *(w. dat or abl or* **in** *+ abl)* **1** to fall asleep at *or* on; **2** to fall asleep over; **3** to become careless about

indōtāt·us -a -um *adj* without dowry; poor; without funeral rites; **ars indōtāta** *(rhet)* unadorned style

indubitābil·is -is -e *adj* indubitable

indubitāt·us -a -um *adj* undoubted

indubit·ō -āre *intr (w. dat)* to begin to distrust, begin to doubt

indubi·us -a -um *adj* undoubted, certain

indūci·ae *or* **indūti·ae -ārum** *fpl* armistice, truce

in·dūcō -dūcere -dūxī -ductus *tr* to lead in, bring in; to introduce; to induce; to seduce; to overlay, drape, wrap, cover; to put on, clothe; to strike out, erase; to repeal, cancel; to present, exhibit; *(theat)* to stage, put on; to mislead, delude; *(w.* **in** *+ acc)* **1** to lead to, lead into, lead against; **2** to bring into, introduce into; **3** to enter into *(account books)*; *(w. dat or* **super** *+ acc)* to put *(item of apparel, esp. shoes)* on, spread *(s.th.)* over, wrap *(s.th.)* around, draw *(s.th.)* over; **animūm** *(or* **in animum) indūcere** to make up one's mind, convince oneself, be convinced, conclude, suppose, imagine

inducti·ō -ōnis *f* bringing in, introduction, admission; resolution, determination; intention; induction, generalization; **animī inductiō** inclination; **errōris inductiō** deception

induct·or -ōris *m (hum) (referring to a whip)* persuader

induct·us -a -um *pp of* **indūco II** *adj* alien, adventitious

induct·us -ūs *m* inducement

indūcul·a -ae *f* slip, petticoat

indulg·ēns -entis *adj* indulgent, lenient; *(w. dat or* **in** *+ acc)* lenient toward, kind toward

indulgenter *adv* indulgently, leniently, kindly

indulgenti·a -ae *f* indulgence, leniency, kindness

indul·geō -gēre -sī -sus *tr (w. dat)* to grant, concede *(s.th.)* to; **veniam indulgēre** *(w. dat)* to make allowances for **II** *refl* **sibi indulgēre** to be self-indulgent, take liberties **II** *intr (w. dat)* **1** to be lenient toward, be kind to, be tender to; **2** to yield to, give way to; **3** to indulge in, be addicted to; **4** to make allowance for; **5** *(of deities, fate, etc.)* to look favorably on, show kindness to; **6** to take pleasure in; **7** to devote oneself to *(an activity)*

ind·uō -uere -uī -ūtus *tr* to put on *(e.g., a tunic);* to cover, wrap, clothe, array; to envelop; to engage in; to assume, put on; to assume the part of; to involve; *(w. dat)* to put *(e.g., a tunic)* on *(s.o.)*

indup- = imp-

indūr·ēscō -ēscere -uī *intr* to become hard, harden

indūr·ō -āre -āvī -ātus *tr* to harden

indūruī *perf of* **indūrēscō**

Ind·us -a -um *adj* Indian **II** *m* Indian; Ethiopian; mahout

indusāri·us -ī *m* maker of women's underwear

indusiāt·us -a -um wearing underwear

industri·a -ae *f* industry, diligence; **dē** *(or* **ex) industriā** diligently; **industriā** *(or* **dē** *or* **ex industriā** *or* **ob industriam)** on purpose, deliberately

industriē *adv* industriously, diligently

industri·us -a -um *adj* industrious, diligent, painstaking

indūti·ae *or* **indūci·ae -ārum** *fpl* armistice, truce

indūt·us -a -um *pp of* **induō**

indūt·us -ūs *m* putting on, wearing

induvi·ae -ārum *fpl* clothes

inebri·ō -āre -āvī -ātus *tr* to make drunk; *(fig)* to fill *(e.g., the ear with gossip)*

inedi·a -ae *f* fasting; starvation

inēdit·us -a -um *adj* not made known, unknown, unpublished

inēleg·āns -antis *adj* inelegant, undistinguished

inēleganter *adv* without style, poorly; without clear thought

inēluctābil·is -is -e *adj* inescapable

inēmor·ior -ī *intr (w. dat)* to die at the sight of

inempt·us -a -um *adj* unpurchased; without ransom

inēnārrābil·is -is -e *adj* indescribable

inēnārrābiliter *adv* indescribably

inēnōdābil·is -is -e *adj* inexplicable

in·eō -īre -īvī -iī -itus *tr* to enter; to enter upon, undertake, form; to begin, engage in; **ab ineunte pueritiā** from earliest boyhood; **cōnsilium inīre** to form a plan; **in cōnsilium inīre ut** *(or* **quā** *or* **quemadmodum)** to plan how to *(do s.th.);* **ineunte vēre** at the beginning of spring; **inīre numerum** *(w. gen)* to go into an enumeration of, enumerate; **inīre ratiōnem** *(w. gen)* to form an estimate of; **inīre ratiōnem ut** *(or* **quā** *or* **quemadmodum)** to consider, find out, *or* figure out how to *(do s.th.);* **viam inīre** to begin a trip; to find a way, devise a means

ineptē *adv* foolishly, absurdly, inappropriately, pointlessly

inepti·a -ae *f* foolishness **II** *fpl* nonsense; trifles

inept·iō -īre *intr* to be absurd, make a fool of oneself

inept·us -a -um *adj* foolish, silly; inept, awkward, absurd; unsuitable, out of place; tactless, tasteless

inerm·is -is -e *or* **inerm·us -a -um** *adj* unarmed, defenseless; undefended; toothless *(gums);* harmless; peaceful

inerr·āns -antis *adj* not wandering, fixed

inerr·ō -āre -āvī *intr* to wander about

iner·s -tis *adj* unskilled, incompetent; inactive, sluggish; weak, soft, helpless; stagnant, motionless; ineffective; dull, insipid; numbing *(cold);* expressionless *(eyes);* uneventful, leisurely *(time)*

inerti·a -ae *f* lack of skill, ignorance, rudeness; inactivity; laziness

inērudīt·us -a -um *adj* uneducated; crude, inconsiderate

inēsc·ō -āre -āvī -ātus *tr* to bait; *(fig)* to bait, trap; to gorge

inēvect·us -a -um *adj* mounted

inēvītābil·is -is -e *adj* inevitable, inescapable

inexcīt·us -a -um *adj* unexcited, calm

inexcūsābil·is -is -e *adj* without excuse; admitting no excuse

inexercitāt·us -a -um *adj* untrained

inexhaust·us -a -um *adj* unexhausted, not wasted; inexhaustible

inexōrābil·is -is -e *adj* inexorable, relentless; unswerving, strict

inexperrēct·us -a -um *adj* unawakened

inexpert·us -a -um *adj* untried, untested; novel; *(w. abl or* **adversus** *or* **in** *+ acc)* inexperienced in, unaccustomed to

inexpiābil·is -is -e *adj* inexpiable, not to be atoned for; irreconcilable, implacable

inexplēbil·is -is -e *adj* insatiable

inexplēt·us -a -um *adj* unsatisfied, unfilled

inexplicābil·is -is -e *adj* inextricable; inexplicable, baffling; impassable *(road);* involved, unending *(war);* incurable *(disease)*

inexplōrātō *adv* without reconnoitering

inexplorāt·us -a -um *adj* unexplored; unfamiliar; not investigated

inexpugnābil·is -is -e *adj* impregnable, unassailable; invincible

inexspectāt·us -a -um *adj* unexpected, unforeseen

inexsuperābil·is -is -e *adj* insuperable, insurmountable

inextīnct·us -a -um *adj* unextinguished; insatiable

inextrīcābil·is -is -e *adj* inextricable

īnfabrē *adv* unskillfully

īnfabricāt·us -a -um *adj* unshaped, untrimmed, unwrought

īnfacētē *adv* boorishly

īnfacēti·ae -ārum *fpl* crudities

īnfacēt·us -a -um *adj* not witty, not funny, dull, stupid

īnfācund·us -a -um *adj* ineloquent
īnfāmi·a -ae *f* bad reputation; disrepute, disgrace; scandal; *(w. gen)* stigma of; *(pol)* public disgrace *(involving loss of some civil rights)*
īnfām·is -is -e *adj* infamous, notorious, disreputable, disgraceful; disgraced; *(w.* **in** + *acc or abl)* suspected of misconduct with; **īnfāmis digitus** middle finger *(used in obscene gestures)*
īnfām·ō -āre -āvī -ātus *tr* to defame, dishonor, disgrace; to smear *(esp. groundlessly)* ‖ *pass (w.* **in** + *acc)* to be suspected of misconduct with
īnfand·us -a -um *adj* unspeakable, shocking
īnf·āns -antis *adj* speechless, unable to speak; baby, infant, young; childish, silly; *(fig)* tongue-tied ‖ *mf* infant
īnfanti·a -ae *f* infancy; childishness; inability to speak; lack of eloquence; young children
īnfar- = **īnfer-**
īnfatu·ō -āre -āvī -ātus *tr* to make a fool of
īnfaust·us -a -um *adj* ill-omened, unpropitious; unfortunate
īnfect·or -ōris *m* dyer
īnfect·us -a -um *pp of* **īnficiō** ‖ *adj* not made, not done, undone, unfinished; unwrought *(metals);* unachieved; infeasible; **foedere īnfectō** without concluding a treaty; **rē īnfectā** without achieving the objective
īnfēcundit·ās -ātis *f* unfruitfulness
īnfēcund·us -a -um *adj* unfruitful
īnfēlīcit·ās -ātis *f* bad luck, misfortune
īnfēlīciter *adv* unhappily; unluckily, unsuccessfully
īnfēlīc·ō -āre *tr* to make unhappy
īnfēl·īx -īcis *adj* unfruitful; unhappy; unfortunate, unlucky; causing misfortune, ruinous; ill-omened; pessimistic
īnfēnsē *adv* with hostility, aggressively
īnfēns·ō -āre -āvī -ātus *tr* to antagonize; to make dangerous ‖ *intr* to be hostile
īnfēns·us -a -um *adj* hostile, antagonistic; dangerous; *(w. dat or* **in** + *acc)* **1** hostile to; **2** dangerous to
īnfer·a -ōrum *npl* lower world
īnfer·ciō -cīre -sī -ctus *tr* **(-far-)** to stuff, cram
īnfer·ī -ōrum *mpl* the dead; the world below
īnferi·ae -ārum *fpl* rites and offerings to the dead
īnferi·or -or -us *adj* lower, farther down; *(fig)* inferior; subsequent; later, more recent *(period); (w. abl or* **in** + *abl)* inferior, worse in *(some respect)*
īnferius *adv* lower, at a lower level; too low; at a later stage
īnfernē *adv* below, beneath
īnfern·us -a -um *adj* lower; infernal, of the lower world ‖ *mpl* the shades below ‖ *npl* the lower world
īnferō īnferre intulī illātus *tr* to bring in, carry in; to import; to introduce; to bring forward, adduce, produce; *(w. dat)* to cause *(injury, death, delay)* to; to bury, inter; *(w.* **in** + *acc)* to reduce to; *(w. dat)* to pay *(money)* to *(e.g., the treasury);* **arma** *(or* **bellum) īnferre** *(w. dat)* to make war on; **gradum** *(or* **pedem** *or* **signa) īnferre** to advance *(usually to attack);* **conversa signa īnferre** *(w. dat)* to turn around and attack; **facēs** *(or* **ignem) īnferre** *(w. dat)* to set fire to; **honōrēs īnferre** to offer a sacrifice; **manūs īnferre** *(w. dat)* to lay hands on; **nōmen in tabulās īnferre** to enter one's name in the records ‖ *refl & pass* to enter; to rush in *or* on; to go, march, charge, plunge; **sē in perīculum īnferre** to expose oneself to danger ‖ *intr* to infer, conclude
īnfer·us -a -um *adj* lower; southern ‖ *mpl* the dead
īnferv·eō -ēre *intr* to come to a boil
īnfervēsc·ō -ere *intr* to simmer, come to a boil, start to boil
īnfestē *adv* hostilely, violently
īnfest·ō -āre -āvī -ātus *tr* to annoy, harass, bother; to attack; to damage; *(of diseases, pests)* to infest
īnfest·us -a -um *adj* hostile, antagonistic; aggressive, warlike; troubled *(times, conditions); (of weapons)* poised to strike; *(of armies)* taking the offensive; *(of things)* harmful, troublesome; *(of places)* threatened, exposed to danger, insecure; *(w. abl)* **1** dangerous *or* unsafe because of; **2** infested with
īnficēt- = **īnfacēt-**
īn·ficiō -ficere -fēcī -fectus *tr* to dip, dye, tint; to infect; to stain; to corrupt, spoil; to imbue, instruct; *(fig)* to poison, infect
īnfidēl·is -is -e *adj* unfaithful, untrue, disloyal
īnfidēlit·ās -ātis *f* infidelity, disloyalty
īnfidēliter *adv* disloyally
īnfidī *perf of* **īnfindō**
īnfid·us -a -um *adj* untrustworthy, treacherous
īn·fīgō -fīgere -fīxī -fīxus *tr* to drive in, nail, thrust; to imprint, fix, impress; *(w. dat)* **1** to drive into, thrust into; **2** to impale on; **3** to imprint on *or* in; **4** to fasten to, attach to
īnfimātis *see* **īnfumātis**
īnfim·us -a -um *(superl of* **īnferus)** *adj* **(-fum-)** lowest, last; worst; humblest; **ab īnfimō colle** at the foot of the hill; **īnfimum mare** the bottom of the sea ‖ *n* bottom

in·findō -findere -fidī -fissus *tr (w. dat)* to cut *(e.g., furrows)* into

īnfīnit·ās -ātis *f* endlessness, infinity; *(phil)* the Infinite

īnfīnītē *adv* without bounds, without end, infinitely; without exception

īnfīnīti·ō -ōnis *f* boundlessness, infinity

īnfīnīt·us -a -um *adj* unlimited, boundless; without end, endless, infinite; countless; indefinite

īnfirmāti·ō -ōnis *f* invalidation; refutation

īnfirmē *adv* weakly, faintly, feebly

īnfirmit·ās -ātis *f* weakness, feebleness; infirmity; inconstancy

īnfirm·ō -āre -āvī -ātus *tr* to weaken, enfeeble; to refute, disprove; to annul

īnfirm·us -a -um *adj* weak, faint, feeble; infirm, sick; trivial; inconstant

īnfissus *pp of* **īnfindō**

īnfit *v defect* he, she, it begins

īnfiti·ae -ārum *fpl* denial; **īnfitiās īre** *(w. acc)* to deny, refuse to acknowledge as true; to disown, repudiate

īnfitiāl·is -is -e *adj* negative

īnfitiāti·ō -ōnis *f* denial

īnfitiāt·or -ōris *m* repudiator

īnfiti·or -ārī -ātus sum *tr* to deny, repudiate, disown; to contradict

īnfīxī *perf of* **īnfīgō**

īnfīxus *pp of* **īnfīgō**

īnflammāti·ō -ōnis *f* setting on fire; *(med)* inflammation; **animī īnflammātiō** inspiration; **īnflammātiōnem īnferre** *(w. dat)* to set on fire

īnflamm·ō -āre -āvī -ātus *tr* to set on fire, kindle, light up; *(med)* to inflame; *(fig)* to excite

īnflāti·ō -ōnis *f* swelling up; flatulence, gas; **habet īnflātiōnem faba** beans cause gas

īnflātius *adv* rather pompously

īnflāt·us -a -um *adj* blown up, inflated; swollen; haughty; turgid *(style)*

īnflāt·us -ūs *m* puff, blast; inspiration

īnfle·ctō -ctere -xī -xus *tr* to bend, curve, bow; to tilt, slant; to turn aside; to change *(course)*; to influence; to inflect, modulate *(voice)* ‖ *refl & pass* to curve; to change course; to turn around; *(of a person)* to change

īnflēt·us -a -um *adj* unwept

īnflexī *perf of* **īnflectō**

īnflexibil·is -is -e *adj* inflexible

īnflexi·ō -ōnis *f* bending; modification, adaptation

īnflexus *pp of* **īnflectō**

īnflex·us -ūs *m* curve, bend, winding

īnflī·gō -gere -xī -ctus *tr (w. dat)* **1** to strike *(s.th.)* against, smash *(s.th.)* against; **2** to inflict *(wound)* on; **3** to bring *(e.g., disgrace)* to

īnfl·ō -āre -āvī -ātus *tr (of wind)* to blow on; to blow *(horn)*, play *(flute)*; *(of a deity)* to inspire; to inflate, fill with conceit; to puff up *(cheeks)*; to fill *(sails)*; to distend, bloat; to amplify *(sound)*; to inflate *(price)*

īnflu·ō -ere -xī *intr (w.* **in** *+ acc)* **1** to flow into; **2** *(fig)* to spill over into, stream into, pour into; **3** *(of words, ideas)* to sink into, penetrate

in·fodiō -fodere -fōdī -fossus *tr* to dig; to bury

īnfōrmāti·ō -ōnis *f* formation *(of an idea)*; sketch; idea

īnfōrm·is -is -e *adj* unformed, shapeless; ugly, hideous

īnfōrm·ō -āre -āvī -ātus *tr* to form, shape; to sketch *(in words)*, give an idea of; to instruct, educate

īnfor·ō -āre -āvī -ātus *tr* to bring into court

īnfortūnāt·us -a -um *adj* unfortunate

īnfortūn·ium -(i)ī *n* misfortune; *(euphem. for punishment)* trouble

īnfossus *pp of* **īnfodiō**

īnfrā *adv* below, underneath; down south; down the coast; downstream; lower down *(on the page or in the work)*; below the surface; later ‖ *prep (w. acc)* **1** below, beneath, under; **2** inferior *(in quality, rank, etc.)* to; **3** smaller than; **4** lower *(in number)* than; **5** beneath the dignity of, degrading to; **6** submissive to; **7** south of; **īnfrā et suprā Ephesum** south and north of Ephesus; **8** after, later than; **9** falling short of *(a target)*

īnfrācti·ō -ōnis *f* breaking; **animī īnfrāctiō** discouragement

īnfrāct·us -a -um *pp of* **īnfringō** ‖ *adj* broken; disjointed *(words)*; weakened; humble, subdued *(tone)*; **īnfrāctōs animōs gerere** to feel down and out

īnfragil·is -is -e *adj* unbreakable, indestructible; vigorous *(voice)*

īnfrēgī *perf of* **īnfringō**

īnfrem·ō -ere -uī *intr* to growl, bellow, roar; to rage

īnfrēnāt·us -a -um *adj* unbridled

īnfrend·eō -ēre *or* **īnfrend·ō -ere** *intr* to grit the teeth; **dentibus īnfrendere** to grit the teeth, gnash the teeth

īnfrēn·is -is -e *or* **īnfrēn·us -a -um** *adj* unbridled

īnfrēn·ō -āre -āvī -ātus *tr* to bridle; to harness; *(fig)* to curb

īnfrēnus *see* **īnfrēnis**

īnfrequ·ēns -entis *adj* uncrowded, not numerous; poorly attended; thinly populated; unusual, infrequent *(words)*; inconstant; irregular; *(mil)* undermanned, below strength; *(mil)* absent without leave

īnfrequenti·a -ae *f* small number, scantiness; poor attendance; emptiness; depopulated condition *(of a place)*

in·fringō -fringere -frēgī -frāctus *tr* to break; to break in; to bend; to break up *(sentences);* to impair, affect adversely; to subdue; to weaken, break down; to cause to relent; to foil *(an action);* to render null and void

īnfr·ōns -ondis *adj* leafless

īnfructuōs·us -a -um *adj* unfruitful; pointless

īnfūcāt·us -a -um *adj* painted over

īnfūdī *perf of* **īnfundō**

īnful·a -ae *f* bandage; fillet *(worn by priests, by sacrificial victims; displayed as a sign of submission);* festoon *(hung on doorposts at a wedding)*

īnfumāt·is -is *m* **(īnfim-)** one of the lowest *(in rank)*

īnfumus *see* **īnfimus**

īn·fundō -fundere -fūdī -fūsus *tr* to pour in, pour on, pour out; *(w. dat or* **in** *+ acc)* **1** to pour into, pour upon; **2** to administer to; **3** to shower *(gifts)* upon; **4** to rain *(missiles)* upon; **5** to stretch out *(the body)* upon; **6** to instil *(ideas, feelings)* in ‖ *refl & pass (w. dat)* to spread out on, relax on

īnfusc·ō -āre -āvī -ātus *tr* to darken, obscure; to stain, corrupt, sully

īnfūs·us -a -um *pp of* **īnfundō** ‖ *adj* diffused; permeating; fallen *(snow);* crowded; **coniugis īnfūsus gremiō** relaxing on the lap of his spouse; **īnfūsīs humerō capillīs** with his hair streaming over his shoulders

ingemin·ō -āre -āvī -ātus *tr* to redouble; to repeat; **ingemināre vōcēs** to call repeatedly; **ignēs ingemināre** to flash repeatedly ‖ *intr* to increase in intensity, get worse

ingem·īscō -īscere -uī *intr* **(-ēsc-)** to groan, heave a sigh; *(w. dat or* **in** *+ abl)* to groan over, sigh over

ingem·ō -ere -uī *tr* to groan over, sigh over ‖ *intr* to groan, moan; *(w. dat)* to sigh over

ingener·ō -āre -āvī -ātus *tr* to engender, generate, produce; *(fig)* to implant

ingeniāt·us -a -um *adj* naturally endowed, talented

ingeniōsē *adv* ingeniously

ingeniōs·us -a -um *adj* ingenious, clever, talented; *(w. dat or* **ad)** naturally suited to

ingenit·us -a -um *adj* inborn, natural

ingen·ium -(i)ī *n* innate quality; nature, temperament, character; bent, inclination; mood; natural ability, talent, intellect; bright person; gifted writer; skill, ingenuity; clever device

ing·ēns -entis *adj* huge, vast; great, mighty, powerful; a great amount of, a great number of; very important, momentous; proud, haughty, heroic *(character); (w. abl)* outstanding in; **ingēns pecūnia** a lot of money

ingenuē *adv* liberally; frankly

ingenuī *perf of* **ingignō**

ingenuit·ās -ātis *f* noble birth; noble character; frankness

ingenu·us -a -um *adj* native, indigenous; natural; free-born; like a freeman, noble; ingenuous, frank

in·gerō -gerere -gessī -gestus *tr* to carry in, throw in, heap; to ingest *(food, drink, esp. in large amounts);* to hurl, shoot *(missiles);* to pour out *(angry words);* to heap *(abuse);* to rain *(blows); (w. dat)* to force *(unwelcome things)* on *(s.o.);* to say repeatedly

in·gignō -gignere -genuī -genitus *tr* to cause *(plants)* to grow; *(fig)* to implant *(qualities, etc.)*

inglōri·us -a -um *adj* inglorious, without glory, inconspicuous

ingluvi·ēs -ēī *f* crop, maw; gluttony

ingrātē *adv* unpleasantly; unwillingly; ungratefully

ingrātific·us -a -um *adj* ungrateful

ingrātiīs *or* **ingrātīs** *f abl pl* unwillingly, against one's will; against another's will; *(w. gen or poss adj)* against the wishes of

ingrāt·us -a -um *adj* unpleasant, unwelcome; ungrateful; receiving no thanks, unappreciated; thankless

ingravēsc·ō -ere *intr* to get heavier; to become pregnant; *(of troubles)* to grow worse; to become more serious; to become weary; to become dearer *(in price); (of prices)* to become inflated; to become more important

ingre·dior -dī -ssus sum *tr* to enter; to undertake; to begin; to walk in, follow *(footsteps)* ‖ *intr* to go in, enter; to go, walk, walk along; to begin, commence; to begin to speak; *(mil)* to go to the attack; *(w.* **in** *+ acc)* **1** to go into, enter; **2** to enter upon, begin, take up, undertake; *(w. dat)* to walk on; **in rem pūblicam ingredī** to enter politics

ingressi·ō -ōnis *f* entering; walking; gait, pace; beginning

ingress·us -ūs *m* entry; walking; gait; beginning; *(mil)* inroad

ingru·ō -ere -ī *intr* to come, come on, rush on; *(of war)* to break out; *(of rain)* to pour down; *(w. dat or* **in** *+ acc)* to fall upon, attack

ingu·en -inis *n* groin; swelling, tumor ‖ *npl* private parts

ingurgit·ō -āre -āvī -ātus *tr* to pour in; to gorge, stuff ‖ *refl* to stuff oneself; *(w.* **in** *+ acc)* **1** to steep oneself in; **2** to devote oneself to

ingustāt·us -a -um *adj* untasted

inhabil·is -is -e *adj* clumsy, unhandy, unwieldy; *(w. dat or* **ad)** unfit for

inhabitābil·is -is -e *adj* uninhabitable

inhabit·ō -āre -āvī -ātus *tr* to inhabit, occupy ‖ *intr (w. dat or* **in** *+ abl)* to live in

inhae·reō -rēre -sī -sum *intr* to stick, cling, adhere; to be inherent; *(w. dat, w.* **ad** *or* **in** *+ acc)* **1** to cling to; **2** to be closely connected with; **3** to gaze upon

inhae·rēscō -rēscere -sī *intr* to begin to stick, become attached; to become stuck; to become fixed *(in the mind)*

inhal·ō -āre -āvī -ātus *tr (w. dat)* to breathe *(e.g., bad breath)* on *(s.o.)*

inhib·eō -ēre -uī -itus *tr* to hold back, curb, check, control; to use, employ, apply; to inflict *(punishment)*; **retrō nāvem** *(or* **nāvem rēmīs)** **inhibēre** to back up the ship ‖ *intr* to row backwards, backwater; **rēmīs inhibēre** to backwater

inhibiti·ō -ōnis *f* backing up

inhi·ō -āre -āvī -ātus *tr* to gape at; to pore over; to cast longing eyes at ‖ *intr* to stand open-mouthed, be amazed; *(w. dat)* to be eager for

inhonestē *adv* dishonorably, disgracefully; dishonestly

inhonest·ō -āre -āvī -ātus *tr* to dishonor, disgrace

inhonest·us -a -um *adj* dishonorable, disgraceful, shameful; indecent; ugly, degrading

inhonōr·us -a -um *adj* defaced

inhorr·eō -ēre -uī *intr* to stand on end, bristle

inhorr·ēscō -ēscere -uī *intr* to stand on end, bristle; to vibrate; to shiver, tremble, shudder

inhospitāl·is -is -e *adj* inhospitable, unfriendly

inhospitālit·ās -ātis *f* inhospitality

inhospit·us -a -um *adj* inhospitable

inhūmānē *adv* inhumanly; rudely; heartlessly

inhūmānit·ās -ātis *f* inhumanity; churlishness; stinginess; heartlessness

inhūmāniter *adv* impolitely; heartlessly

inhūmān·us -a -um *adj* uncivilized; ill-bred, discourteous; heartless, brutal

inhumāt·us -a -um *adj* unburied

inibi *or* **inibī** *adv* there, in that place; near at hand

in·iciō -icere -iēcī -iectus *tr* to throw, inject; to hurl, discharge *(missiles)*; to impose, apply; to inspire, infuse; to cause, occasion; to furnish *(a cause)*; to bring up, mention *(a name)*; *(w. dat)* to put *(e.g., a cloak)* on *(s.o.)*; **manicās alicui inicere** to put handcuffs on s.o.; **manum inicere** *(w. dat)* **1** to lay hands on; **2** take possession of ‖ *refl (w. dat or* **in** *+ acc)* **1** to throw oneself into, rush into, expose oneself to; **2** to fling oneself down on; **3** *(of the mind)* to turn itself to, concentrate on, reflect on

inimīc·a -ae *f (personal)* enemy *(female)*

inimīcē *adv* with hostility, in an unfriendly way

inimīciti·a -ae *f* unfriendliness, enmity ‖ *fpl* feuds

inimīc·ō -āre -āvī -ātus *tr* to make into enemies, set at odds

inimīc·us -a -um *adj* unfriendly, hostile; harmful ‖ *m (personal)* enemy; **inimīcissimus suus** his bitterest *(personal)* enemy ‖ *f (personal)* enemy *(female)*

inīquē *adv* unequally, unevenly; unfairly

inīquit·ās -ātis *f* unevenness; inequality; disadvantage; unfairness

inīqu·us -a -um *adj* uneven, unequal; not level, sloping; unfair; adverse, harmful; dangerous, unfavorable; prejudiced; excessive; impatient, discontented; **inīquō animō** impatiently, unwillingly ‖ *m* enemy, foe

initi·ō -āre -āvī -ātus *tr* to initiate, begin; to initiate *(into mysteries)*

init·ium -(i)ī *n* entrance; beginning ‖ *npl* elements; first principles; sacred rites, sacred mysteries

initus *pp of* **ineō**

init·us -ūs *m* entrance; beginning

iniūcundit·ās -ātis *f* unpleasantness

iniūcundius *adv* rather unpleasantly

iniūcund·us -a -um *adj* unpleasant

iniūdicāt·us -a -um *adj* undecided

iniun·gō -gere iniūnxī iniūnctus *tr* to join, attach, fasten; *(w. dat)* **1** to join to, attach to, fasten to; **2** to inflict on; **3** to impose *(e.g., taxes)* on

iniūrāt·us -a -um *adj* not under oath

iniūri·a -ae *f* injustice, wrong, outrage; insult, affront; harshness, severity; revenge; injury, damage, harm; ill-gotten goods; **iniūriā** unjustly, undeservedly, innocently; **per iniūriam** unjustly; outrageously

iniūriōsē *adv* unjustly, wrongfully

iniūriōs·us -a -um *adj* unjust, wrongful; insulting; harmful

iniūri·us -a -um *adj* unjust, wrong

iniūr·us -a -um *adj* unjust

iniūssū *(abl only) m* without orders; **iniūssū meō** without my orders

iniūss·us -a -um *adj* unasked, unbidden, voluntary

iniūstē *adv* unjustly

iniūstiti·a -ae *f* injustice

iniūst·us -a -um *adj* unjust

inl- = ill-

inm- = imm-

innābil·is -is -e *adj* unswimmable

in·nāscor -nāscī -nātus sum *intr (w. dat)* **1** to be born in; **2** *(of plant life)* grow in *or* on; *(w.* **in** *+ abl)* **1** to originate in; **2** *(of plant life)* to grow in; **3** *(of minerals)* to occur in, be native to

innat·ō -āre -āvī *tr* to swim ‖ *intr (w. dat)* to swim around in, float on; *(w.* **in** *+ acc)* to swim into

innāt·us -a -um *pp of* **innāscor** ‖ *adj* innate, inborn, natural

innāvigābil·is -is -e *adj* unnavigable

in·nectō -nectere -nexuī -nexus *tr* to entwine; to tie, fasten together; to join, attach, connect; *(fig)* to devise, invent, plan

innī·tor -tī -xus sum *or* **-sus sum** *intr (w. abl)* to lean on, rest on, be supported by

inn·ō -āre *tr* to swim; to sail, sail over ‖ *intr (w. abl)* **1** to swim in, float on; **2** to sail on; **3** *(of the sea)* to wash against *(a shore)*

innoc·ēns -entis *adj* harmless; innocent; upright; unselfish; *(w. gen)* innocent of

innocenter *adv* innocently, blamelessly; harmlessly

innocenti·a -ae *f* innocence; integrity; unselfishness

innocuē *adv* harmlessly; innocently

innocu·us -a -um *adj* harmless, innocuous; innocent; unharmed

innōt·ēscō -ēscere -uī *intr* to become known; to become notorious

innov·ō -āre -āvī -ātus *tr* to renew, restore ‖ *refl (w.* **ad** *+ acc)* to return to

innoxi·us -a -um *adj* harmless; safe; innocent; unhurt; *(w. gen)* innocent of

innub·a -ae *adj (fem only)* unmarried

innūbil·us -a -um *adj* cloudless

innū·bō -bere -psī *intr (of a girl) (w. dat)* to marry into *(a family)*

innumerābil·is -is -e *adj* innumerable

innumerābilit·ās -atis *f* countless number

innumerābiliter *adv* in countless ways; countless times

innumerāl·is -is -e *adj* innumerable

innumer·us -a -um *adj* countless

in·nuō -nuere -nuī -nūtum *intr* to give a nod; *(w. dat)* to nod to

innūpt·a -ae *adj (fem only)* unmarried ‖ *f* unmarried girl, maiden

innūtr·iō -īre -īvī *or* **-iī -ītus** *tr (w. abl)* to bring up in

Īn·ō -ūs *f* daughter of Cadmus and Harmonia, wife of Athamas and mother of Learchus and Melicertes

inoblīt·us -a -um *adj* unforgetful

inobrut·us -a -um *adj* not overwhelmed

inobservābil·is -is -e *adj* unnoticed

inobservanti·a -ae *f* inattention

inobservāt·us -a -um *adj* unobserved

inoccidu·us -a -um *adj* never setting

inodōr·us -a -um *adj* odorless

inoffēns·us -a -um *adj* unobstructed, uninterrupted, unhindered; unimpaired; smooth *(path)*

inofficiōs·us -a -um *adj* irresponsible; unobliging; **testāmentum inofficiōsum** a will passing over the relatives

inol·ēns -entis *adj* odorless

inol·ēscō -ēscere -ēvī *tr* to implant ‖ *intr* to become inveterate; *(w. dat)* to grow in, develop in

inōmināt·us -a -um *adj* ill-starred, inauspicious

inopi·a -ae *f* lack, want, need, poverty; scarcity; helplessness; *(rhet)* barrenness *(of style)*; *(rhet)* lack of subject matter

inopīn·āns -antis *adj* unsuspecting, taken by surprise, off one's guard

inopīnanter *adv* unexpectedly

inopīnātō *adv* unexpectedly, by surprise

inopīnāt·us -a -um *adj* unexpected, unsuspected, surprising ‖ *n* surprise; **ex inopīnātō** by surprise, unexpectedly

inopīn·us -a -um *adj* unexpected

inopiōs·us -a -um *adj (hum) (w. gen)* in need of

in·ops -opis *adj* without means *or* resources; poor, needy, destitute; helpless, weak, forlorn; *(rhet)* bald *(style)*; poor *(expression)*; deficient in vocabulary; pitiful, contemptible; *(w. gen)* destitute of, stripped of, without; *(w. abl)* lacking in, deficient in, poor in

inōrāt·us -a -um *adj* not presented; **rē inōrātā** without presenting one's case

inōrdināt·us -a -um *adj* disordered

inōrnāt·us -a -um *adj* unadorned; unheralded; *(rhet)* plain *(style)*

inp- = imp-

inquam *v defect (the following forms are found: pres:* **inquam, inquis, inquit, inquimus, inquiunt;** *imperfect:* **inquiēbat;** *fut:* **inquiēs, inquiet;** *perfect:* **inquiī, inquistī;** *persent subj:* **inquiat;** *impv:* **inque** *or* **inquitō**) to say; *(after one or more words of direction quotation, e.g.,* **dēsilite, inquit, mīlitēs et** ... "jump down, fellow soldiers," he says, " and ... "); *(in emphatic repetition, e.g.,* **tuās, tuās inquam suspiciōnēs** ... your suspicions, yes I say yours ...); **inquit** it is said, one says, they say

inqui·ēs -ētis *adj* restless

inquiēt·ō -āre -āvī -ātus *tr* to disquiet, disturb

inquiēt·us -a -um *adj* restless, unsettled

inquilīn·us -ī *m* tenant, lodger

inquinātē *adv* filthily

inquināt·us -a -um *adj* filthy, foul

inquin·ō -āre -āvī -ātus *tr* to mess up, defile, contaminate

in·quīrō -quīrere -quīsīvī *or* **-quīsiī -quīsītus** *tr* to search for, inquire into, examine, pry into ‖ *intr* to hold an investigation; to hold a preliminary hearing

inquīsīti·ō -ōnis *f* search, inquiry, investigation; preliminary hearing; *(w. gen)* search for, inquiry into, investigation of

inquīsīt·or -ōris *m* inspector, examiner; spy; *(leg)* investigator

inquīsīt·us -a -um *pp of* **inquīrō** ‖ *adj* not investigated, unexamined
inquīsīvī *perf of* **inquīrō**
inquit *see* **inquam**
inquiunt *see* **inquam**
inr- = **irr-**
īnsalūbr·is -is -e *adj* unhealthy, unhealthful
īnsalūtāt·us -a -um *adj* ungreeted
īnsānābil·is -is -e *adj* incurable
īnsānē *adv* insanely, madly
īnsāni·a -ae *f* insanity, madness, frenzy; rapture; mania; excess; **ad īnsāniam** to the point of madness
īnsān·iō -īre -īvī *or* **-iī -ītum** *intr* to be insane; to be absurd; to be wild, rave; *(w.* **in** *+ acc)* to be crazy about
īnsānit·ās -ātis *f* insanity
īnsānum *adv (coll)* exceedingly, very
īnsān·us -a -um *adj* insane, crazy; absurd, foolish; excessive, extravagant; monstrous, outrageous; inspired; maddening
īnsatiābil·is -is -e *adj* insatiable; voracious; that cannot cloy
īnsatiābiliter *adv* insatiably
īnsatiet·ās -ātis *f* insatiable desire
īnsaturābil·is -is -e *adj* insatiable
īnsaturābiliter *adv* insatiably
īnscen·dō -dere -dī -sus *tr* to climb up; to get up on *(horse, chariot)* ‖ *intr* to climb up; **in arborem īnscendere** to climb a tree; **in currum īnscendere** to climb into a chariot; **in nāvem īnscendere** to board a ship
īnscēnsi·ō -ōnis *f* mounting; **in nāvem īnscēnsiō** embarkation
īnscēnsus *pp of* **īnscendō**
īnsci·ēns -entis *adj* unaware; silly, ignorant, stupid
īnscienter *adv* ignorantly; inadvertently
īnscītē *adv* ignorantly, unskillfully
īnscīti·a -ae *f* ignorance; inexperience; lack of skill; neglect
īnscīt·us -a -um *adj* ignorant; stupid
īnsci·us -a -um *adj* unaware; ignorant, silly, stupid
īnscrī·bō -bere -psī -ptus *tr* to inscribe; to ascribe; to title *(a book); (w. dat)* **1** to assign, attribute to; **2** to apply to; **3** to address *(a letter)* to; *(w. dat or* **in** *+ abl)* to write *(s.th.)* on *or* in; **aedēs vēnālēs** *(or* **mercēde) īnscrībere** to advertise a house for sale
īnscrīpti·ō -ōnis *f* inscribing; branding *(of slaves);* inscription; title *(of book)*
īnscrīpt·us -a -um *pp of* **īnscrībō** ‖ *adj* unwritten; *(of a book)* entitled ‖ *n* inscription; brand (mark); title *(of a book)*
īnsculp·ō -ere -sī -tus *tr* to cut, carve, engrave; *(w. dat or abl or* **in** *+ abl)* to cut, carve, *or* engrave on; **in animō** *(or* **in mente) īnsculpere** to imprint on the mind
īnsectāti·ō -ōnis *f* hot pursuit
īnsectāt·or -ōris *m* persecutor
īnsect·or -ārī -ātus sum *or* **īnsect·ō -āre** *tr* to pursue, chase, attack; to heckle, harass
īnsect·us -a -um *adj* indented, notched; **animālia īnsecta** insects ‖ *n* insect
īnsecūtus *pp of* **īnsequor**
īnsēdābiliter *adv* unquenchably
īnsēdī *perf of* **īnsideō** *and* **īnsīdō**
īnsen·ēscō -ēscere -uī *intr (w. dat)* to grow old amidst, grow old over; *(of the moon)* to wane
īnsēnsil·is -is -e *adj* imperceptible
īnsepult·us -a -um *adj* unburied
īnsequ·ēns -entis *adj* next, following, succeeding
īnse·quor -quī -cūtus sum *tr* to follow (immediately behind); to succeed, follow up; to attack, go for; to persecute; to catch up with; to reproach; to strive after ‖ *intr* to follow, come next; to pursue the point; *(w. inf)* to proceed to
īnser·ō -ere -uī -tus *tr* to insert; to introduce; to include *(in a book, speech);* to involve; to join, enroll, associate; to mingle, blend; **manūs īnserere** *(w. dat)* to lay hands on, seize; **oculōs īnserere** *(w.* **in** *+ abl)* to look into *(e.g., s.o.'s heart)*
īn·serō -serere -sēvī -situs *tr* to sow, plant; to graft on *(a cutting);* to graft a cutting on *(a tree); (lit & fig)* to implant; **singulōs hortōs cūiusque generis surculīs serere** to plant each garden with one kind of cutting
īnsert·ō -āre -āvī -ātus *tr* to insert
īnserv·iō -īre -īvī *or* **-iī -ītus** *tr* to serve, obey ‖ *intr* to be a slave, be a subject; *(w. dat)* **1** to serve, be subservient to; **2** to be subject to; **3** to be devoted to; **4** to pay attention to
īnsessus *pp of* **īnsideō** *and* **īnsīdō**
īnsēvī *perf of* **īnserō** (to plant)
īnsībil·ō -āre -āvī -ātum *intr (of the wind)* to whistle (in *or* among)
in·sideō -sidēre -sēdī -sessus *tr* to hold, occupy ‖ *intr* to sit down; to settle down; to be deep-seated; *(w. abl or* **in** *+ abl)* **1** to sit on; **2** to settle down on *or* in; **3** *(fig)* to be fixed in, be stamped in
īnsidi·ae -ārum *fpl* ambush; plot, trap; **īnsidiās dare** *(or* **collocāre** *or* **parāre** *or* **struere)** *(w. dat)* to lay a trap for
īnsidiāt·or -ōris *m* soldier in ambush; *(fig)* plotter, subversive
īnsidi·or -ārī -ātus sum *intr (w. dat)* **1** to lie in wait for; **2** to plot against; **3** to watch for, be on the lookout for *(e.g., opportunity)*
īnsidiōsē *adv* insidiously, by underhand means
īn·sīdō -sīdere -sēdī -sessus *tr* to occupy, keep possession of, possess ‖ *intr* to sink in, penetrate; *(of diseases)* to become deep-seated; *(w. dat)* to settle in *or* on; *(w.*

in + *abl)* to become fixed in, become imbedded in; *(of a bird)* to land on

īnsign·e -is *n (s.th. worn or carried as an indication of rank or status)* insignia, mark; coat of arms; signal; honor, distinction; brilliant passage, gem; *(mil)* decoration, medal ‖ *npl* insignia, regalia, uniform; outer trappings

īnsign·iō -īre -īvī *or* **-iī -ītus** *tr* to make conspicuous, distinguish, mark

īnsign·is -is -e *adj* conspicuous, distinguished; prominent, eminent, extraordinary, singular

īnsignītē *adv* notably, extraordinarily

īnsigniter *adv* remarkably

īnsignīt·us -a -um *adj* marked, conspicuous, clear, glaring; distinguished, striking, notable

īnsil·ia -ium *npl* treadle *(of a loom)*

īnsil·iō -īre -uī *or* **-īvī** *tr* to jump up on, mount ‖ *intr (w. dat)* to jump on; *(w.* **in** + *acc)* **1** to jump into *or* on(to); **2** to mount; **3** to climb aboard

īnsimulāti·ō -ōnis *f* allegation *(of a crime);* charge, accusation

īnsimul·ō -āre -āvī -ātus *tr* to allege; to charge, accuse

īnsincēr·us -a -um *adj* adulterated; not genuine, insincere

īnsinuāti·ō -ōnis *f (rhet)* winning sympathy *(in a speech)*

īnsinu·ō -āre -āvī -ātus *tr* to bring in secretly, sneak in ‖ *refl (w.* **inter** + *acc)* to wriggle in between, work one's way between *or* among; **sē īnsinuāre in familiāritātem** *(w. gen)* to ingratiate oneself with

īnsipi·ēns -entis *adj* foolish

īnsipienter *adv* foolishly

īnsipienti·a -ae *f* foolishness

īn·sistō -sistere -stitī *tr* to stand on, trample on; to set about, keep at *(a task, etc.);* to follow, chase after; **iter** *(or* **viam) īnsistere** to pursue a course ‖ *intr* to stand, stop, come to a stop; to pause; *(w. dat)* **1** to tread on the heels of, pursue closely; **2** to press on with; **3** to dwell upon; *(w. dat or* **in** + *abl)* to persist in; *(w.* **ad** *or* **in** + *acc)* **1** to keep at, keep after, keep the pressure on; **2** pursue vigorously

īnsiti·ō -ōnis *f* grafting; grafting time

īnsitīv·us -a -um *adj* grafted; *(fig)* spurious

īnsit·or -ōris *m* grafter *(of trees)*

īnsit·us -a -um *pp of* **īnserō** ‖ *adj* inborn, innate; incorporated

īnsociābil·is -is -e *adj* incompatible

īnsōlābiliter *adv* unconsolably

īnsol·ēns -entis *adj* unaccustomed, unusual; immoderate, excessive; extravagant; insolent; *(w. gen or* **in** + *abl)* **1** unaccustomed to; **2** inexperienced in; **in aliēnā rē īnsolēns** free with someone else's money

īnsolenter *adv* unusually; excessively; insolently

īnsolenti·a -ae *f* unusualness, novelty, strangeness, inexperience; affectation; insolence, arrogance

īnsolēsc·ō -ere *intr* to become proud, become insolent; to become elated

īnsolid·us -a -um *adj* soft

īnsolit·us -a -um *adj* unaccustomed; inexperienced; unusual, strange, uncommon ‖ *n* the unusual

īnsomni·a -ae *f* insomnia

īnsomn·is -is -e *adj* sleepless

īnsomn·ium -(i)ī *n* sleeplessness; dream; vision in a dream *or* trance

īnson·ō -āre -uī *intr* to make noise; to sound, resound, roar; **calamīs īnsonāre** to play the reed pipe; **flagellō īnsonāre** to crack the whip; **pennīs īnsonāre** to flap the wings

īns·ōns -ontis *adj* innocent; harmless

īnsōpīt·us -a -um *adj* sleepless

īnsop·or -ōris *adj* sleepless

īnspeciōs·us -a -um *adj* homely

īnspecti·ō -ōnis *f* inspection

īnspect·ō -āre -āvī -ātus *tr* to look at, view, observe, examine ‖ *intr* to look on; **īnspectante Rōsciō** with Roscius looking on, under the eyes of Roscius

īnspectus *pp of* **īnspiciō**

īnspēr·āns -antis *adj* not hoping, not expecting

īnspērāt·us -a -um *adj* unhoped for, unexpected, unforeseen; unwelcome; **(ex) īnspērātō** unexpectedly

īnsper·gō -gere -sī -sus *tr* to sprinkle on

īn·spiciō -spicere -spexī -spectus *tr* to inspect, look into, examine; to look at, watch; to consider; to comprehend, grasp; to investigate; to look at, consult *(books);* to look into *(the mirror)* ‖ *intr (w.* **in** + *acc)* to look into

īnspīc·ō -āre -āvī -ātus *tr* to make pointed

īnspīr·ō -āre -āvī -ātus *tr* to inspire, infuse, enkindle ‖ *intr (w. dat)* to blow on, breathe on

īnspoliāt·us -a -um *adj* undespoiled

īnsp·uō -uere -uī -ūtus *tr* to spit on ‖ *intr (w. dat)* to spit on

īnspūt·ō -āre -āvī -ātus *tr* to spit on

īnstābil·is -is -e *adj* unstable, unsteady; not remaining still; *(fig)* changeable

īnst·āns -antis *adj* present; immediate, threatening, urgent

īnstanter *adv* vehemently, insistently

īnstanti·a -ae *f* presence; earnestness, insistence; concentration

īnstar *indecl n* image, likeness, appearance, resemblance; *(w. gen)* like, equal to, as large as, worth, as good as; **ad īnstar** *(w. gen)* according to the standard of

īnstaurāti·ō -ōnis *f* renewal, repetition

īnstaurātīv·us -a -um *adj* begun anew, repeated

īnstaur·ō -āre -āvī -ātus *tr* to set up; to renew, repeat, start all over again *(esp. games and celebrations because of alleged bad omens in the initial event);* to repay, requite

īn·sternō -sternere -strāvī -strātus *tr* to cover; to lay *(a floor, deck)*

īnstīgāt·or -ōris *m,* **īnstīgātr·īx -īcis** *f* instigator, ringleader

īnstīg·ō -āre -āvī -ātus *tr* to instigate, goad on, stimulate, incite

īnstill·ō -āre -āvī -ātus *tr (w. dat)* to pour *(s.th.)* on, instill *(s.th.)* in

īnstimulāt·or -ōris *m* instigator

īnstimul·ō -āre -āvī -ātus *tr* to stimulate, urge on, goad on

īnstīnct·or -ōris *m* instigator

īnstīnct·us -a -um *adj* aroused, fired up; infuriated; inspired

īnstipul·or -ārī -ātus sum *intr* to bargain

īnstit·a -ae *f* border, flounce; band, ribbon; *(fig)* lady

īnstitī *perf of* **īnsistō** *and* **īnstō**

īnstiti·ō -ōnis *f* standing still

īnstit·or -ōris *m* salesman, huckster

īnstit·uō -uere -uī -ūtus *tr* to set, fix, plant; to set up, erect, establish; to arrange; to build, make, construct; to prepare; to provide, furnish; to institute, organize, set up; to appoint, designate; to undertake, begin; to control, direct, govern; to teach, train, instruct, educate; *(w. inf)* to decide to

īnstitūti·ō -ōnis *f* arrangement; custom; instruction, education; **mōrum īnstitūtiō** established custom **||** *fpl* principles of education

īnstitūt·um -ī *n* plan, program; practice, custom, usage; precedent; principle; decree, regulation, stipulation, terms; purpose, intention; **ex īnstitūtō** according to custom, by convention **||** *npl* teachings, precepts, principles of education

īn·stō -stāre -stitī *tr* to follow, pursue; to work hard at; to menace, threaten **||** *intr* to be at hand, approach, be impending; to insist; *(w. dat or* **in** *+ abl)* to stand on *or* in; *(w. dat)* **1** to be close to; **2** to be on the heels of, pursue closely; **3** to harass

īnstrātus *pp of* **īnsternō**

īnstrāvī *perf of* **īnsternō**

īnstrēnu·us -a -um *adj* lethargic

īnstrep·ō -āre -uī -itum *intr* to creak, rattle

īnstructi·ō -ōnis *f* construction; array, formation; instruction

īnstructius *adv* with better preparation

īnstruct·or -ōris *m* supervisor; preparer

īnstruct·us -a -um *pp of* **īnstruō ||** *adj* equipped, furnished; prepared, arranged; instructed, versed

īnstruct·us -ūs *m* equipment; *(rhet)* stock-in-trade *(of an orator)*

īnstrūment·um -ī *n* instrument, tool, utensil; equipment; dress, outfit; repertory, stock-in-trade; means, supply, provisions; *(leg)* document, deed, instrument

īnstru·ō -ere -xī -ctus *tr* to build up, construct; to furnish, prepare, provide, fit out; to instruct; *(mil)* to deploy

īnsuās·um -ī *n* dark-orange color

īnsuāv·is -is -e *adj* unpleasant, disagreeable

īnsūd·ō -āre -āvī *intr* to sweat, break a sweat; *(w. dat)* to drip sweat on

īnsuēfact·us -a -um *adj* accustomed

īnsu·ēscō -ēscere -ēvī -ētus *tr* to accustom, familiarize **||** *intr (w. dat, w.* **ad** *or w. inf)* to get used to

īnsuēt·us -a -um *adj* unusual; *(w. gen or dat, w.* **ad** *or w. inf)* unused to

īnsuēvī *perf of* **īnsuēscō**

īnsul·a -ae *f* island; apartment building

īnsulān·us -ī *m* islander

īnsulār·ius -(i)ī *m* superintendent *(of an apartment building)*

īnsulsē *adv* in poor taste; insipidly, absurdly

īnsulsit·ās -ātis *f* lack of taste; silliness, absurdity

īnsuls·us -a -um *adj* unsalted, without taste; coarse, tasteless, insipid; silly, absurd; bungling **||** *fpl* silly creatures *(i.e., women)*

īnsult·ō -āre -āvī -ātus *tr* to insult, scoff at, taunt; *(of votaries)* to dance about in **||** *intr* to jump, gambol, prance; to gloat; *(w. abl)* **1** to jump in, cavort in, gambol on, jump upon; **2** to gloat over; *(w. dat or* **in** *+ acc)* **1** to scoff at; **2** to gloat over

īnsultūr·a -ae *f* jumping on *or* in

īn·sum -esse -fuī *intr* to be there, exist; *(w. dat or* **in** *+ acc)* **1** to be in, be on; **2** to be implied in, be contained in, belong to

īnsūm·ō -ere -psī -ptus *tr* to spend, devote, waste; *(w. dat or* **in** *+ acc)* to devote to, apply to; *(w. abl or* **in** *+ abl)* to expend on; **operam īnsūmere** *(w. dat)* to devote effort to, waste effort on

īn·suō -suere -suī -sūtus *tr* to sew up; *(w. dat)* **1** to sew up in; **2** to embroider *(s.th.)* on

īnsuper *adv* above, overhead, on top; from above; moreover, besides, in addition **||** *prep (w. acc)* above, over, over and above; *(w. abl)* in addition to, besides

īnsuperābil·is -is -e *adj* insurmountable; unconquerable

īnsur·gō -gere -rēxī -rēctum *intr* to rise, stand up, stand high, tower; to rise, increase, grow, grow intense; to rise to power; *(of language)* to soar; *(w. dat)* **1** to rise up against; **2** to strain at *(e.g., oars)*

īnsusurr·ō -āre -āvī -ātus *tr (w. dat)* to whisper *(s.th.)* to; **īnsusurrāre in aurem**

(*w. gen*) to whisper in (*s.o.'s*) ear; **sibi cantilēnam īnsusurrāre** to hum a tune to oneself **||** *intr* to whisper; (*of wind*) to blow gently

intāb·ēscō -ēscere -uī *intr* to melt away gradually, dissolve gradually; (*fig*) to waste away, pine away

intāctil·is -is -e *adj* intangible

intāct·us -a -um *adj* untouched; uninjured, intact; unpolluted; untried; unmarried, virgin, chaste

intāct·us -ūs *m* intangibility

intāmināt·us -a -um *adj* unsullied

intēct·us -a -um *pp of* **integō ||** *adj* uncovered; naked; open, frank

integell·us -a -um *adj* fairly pure *or* chaste; in fair condition

inte·ger -gra -grum *adj* whole, complete, intact; unhurt, unwounded; healthy, sound; new; fresh; pure, chaste; untouched, unaffected; unbiased; unattempted; unconquered; unbroken (*horse*); not worn, unused; inexperienced; virtuous, honest, blameless; healthy, sane; (*mil*) having suffered no losses; **ab** (*or* **dē** *or* **ex**) **integrō** anew, all over again; **in integrum restituere** to restore to a former condition; to pardon; **integrum alicui esse** (*w. inf*) to be in someone's power to

in·tegō -tegere -tēxī -tēctus *tr* to cover up; to protect

integrāsc·ō -ere *intr* to start all over again

integrāti·ō -ōnis *f* renewal, new beginning

integrē *adv* wholly, entirely; honestly; correctly

integrit·ās -ātis *f* soundness; integrity; innocence; purity, chastity

integr·ō -āre -āvī -ātus *tr* to make whole; to heal, repair; to renew, begin again; to refresh, reinvigorate

integument·um -ī *n* covering; lid; wrapping; protection

intellēctus *pp of* **intellegō**

intellēct·us -ūs *m* intellect; perception; comprehension, understanding

intelleg·ēns -entis *adj* intelligent; (*w. gen*) appreciative of; (*w.* **in** + *abl*) versed in

intellegenter *adv* intelligently

intellegenti·a -ae *f* intelligence; understanding, knowledge; perception, judgment, discrimination, taste; skill; concept, notion; (*w. gen*) knowledge of, understanding of; (*w.* **in** + *abl*) judgment in

intel·legō -legere -lēxī -lēctus *tr* to understand, perceive, comprehend; to realize, recognize; to have an accurate knowledge of, be an expert in **||** *intr* (*in answers*) I understand, I get it

intemerāt·us -a -um *adj* undefiled, pure, chaste; pure, undiluted

intemper·āns -antis *adj* intemperate, without restraint; lewd

intemperanter *adv* intemperately

intemperanti·a -ae *f* intemperance, lack of self-control; extravagance; (*w. gen*) unrestrained use of

intemperāri·ae -ārum *fpl* wild outbursts; wildness

intemperātē *adv* intemperately

intemperāt·us -a -um *adj* excessive

intemperi·ēs -ēī *f* wildness, excess; outrageous conduct, excesses; **intemperiēs aquārum** heavy rain; **intemperiēs caelī** stormy weather

intempestīvē *adv* at a bad time, at the wrong time

intempestīv·us -a -um *adj* untimely; unseasonable (*weather*); poorly timed

intempest·us -a -um *adj* unseasonable; dark, dismal; unhealthy; **nox intempesta** dead of night

intemptāt·us -a -um *adj* (**-tent-**) unattempted, untried

inten·dō -dere -dī -tus *or* **-sus** *tr* to stretch, stretch out, extend, spread out; to stretch, bend (*e.g., a bow*); to aim, shoot (*weapon*); to spread (*sails*); (*of winds*) to fill (*sails*); to cover (*e.g., with festoons*); to increase, magnify, intensify; to intend; to urge, incite; to aim at, intend; to assert, maintain; to raise (*voice*); to stretch (*truth*); to direct, turn, focus (*mind, attention*); to pitch (*tent*); **cursum** (*or* **iter**) **intendere** to direct one's course **||** *intr* (*w.* **in** + *acc*) **1** to direct one's effort to, apply oneself to; **2** to turn to

intentātus *see* **intemptātus**

intentē *adv* intently, attentively

intenti·ō -ōnis *f* stretching, straining; tension, tautness; attention; effort, exertion; aim, intention; accusation; (*leg*) statement of the charge

intent·ō -āre -āvī -ātus *tr* to stretch out; to aim, direct; to threaten; to brandish threateningly; **arma Latīnīs intentāre** to threaten the Latins with war; **manūs intentāre in** (*w. dat or* **in** (*w. acc*) to shake hands with; **oculōs intentāre** (*w. dat*) to fix one's gaze on, gaze at

intent·us -a -um *pp of* **intendō ||** *adj* tense, taut; intent, attentive; eager; tense, nervous; strict (*discipline*); vigorous (*speech*)

intent·us -ūs *m* stretching out, extending (*of the palms*)

intep·eō -ēre -uī *intr* to be lukewarm

intep·ēscō -ēscere -uī *intr* to get warm, be warmed

inter- *pref* with one of the senses of the preposition

inter *prep* (*w. acc*) **1** between, among, amidst; **2** during, within, in the course of; **inter cēnam** during dinner; **inter haec** during these events, in the meantime; **inter tālia opera** during such frenetic activites; **3** (*in classifying*) among, in, with; **inter sē** each other, one another, mutually

interaestu·ō -āre *intr* to retch

interāment·a -ōrum *npl* framework of a ship

Interamn·a -ae *f* town in Latium on the Liris River ‖ town in Umbria, birthplace of Tacitus

interārēsc·ō -ere *intr* to dry up

interātim *adv* meanwhile

interbib·ō -ere *tr* to drink up

interbīt·ō -ere *intr* to come to nothing

intercalār·is -is -e *adj* intercalary, added *(to the calendar)*

intercal·ō -āre -āvī -ātus *tr* to intercalate, add *(to the calendar)*

intercapēd·ō -inis *f* interruption, break, pause

inter·cēdō -cēdere -cessī -cessum *intr* to come *or* go in between; *(of time)* to intervene, pass, occur; to act as an intermediary; to intercede; *(of tribunes)* to exercise the veto; *(w. dat)* **1** to veto, protest against; **2** to interfere with, obstruct, hinder

intercepti·ō -ōnis *f* interception

intercept·or -ōris *m* embezzler

interceptus *pp of* **intercipiō**

intercessi·ō -ōnis *f* intercession, mediation; *(tribune's)* veto

inter·cīdō -cīdere -cīdī -cīsus *tr* to cut through, sever; to cut off, cut short; to cut the seals of, tamper with *(documents)*

inter·cidō -cidere -cidī *intr* to fall short, miss the mark; to happen in the meantime; to drop out, be lost

intercin·ō -ere *tr* to interrupt with song *or* music

inter·cipiō -cipere -cēpī -ceptus *tr* to intercept; to trap *(animals);* to draw *(water illegally from the aqueduct);* to steal, usurp *(rights, honors);* to interrupt, cut off, cut short *(a conversation)*; to appropriate; to misappropriate; to receive by mistake *(e.g., poison); (mil)* to cut off *(the enemy); (mil)* to capture; *(mil)* to be struck by *(e.g., spear intended for another)*

intercīsē *adv* piecemeal

intercīsus *pp of* **intercīdō**

interclū·dō -dere -sī -sus *tr* to shut off, shut out, cut off; to stop, block up; to hinder, prevent; to blockade, shut in; to cut off, intercept; to separate, divide

interclūsi·ō -ōnis *f* stopping; parenthetical matter; **animae interclūsiō** shortwindedness

interclūsus *pp of* **interclūdō**

intercolumn·ium -(i)ī *n* space between columns, intercolumniation

inter·currō -currere -cucurrī -cursum *intr* to intervene, mediate; to mingle; to rush in

intercurs·ō -āre -āvī -ātum *intr* to crisscross; **inter sē intercursāre** to crisscross each other

intercurs·us -ūs *m* intervention

interc·us -utis *adj* between the skin and flesh; **aqua intercus** dropsy

inter·dīcō -dīcere -dīxī -dictus *tr* to forbid, prohibit ‖ *intr* to issue a prohibition, issue an injunction; **aquā et ignī interdīcere** *(w. dat)* to outlaw *(s.o.)*, banish *(s.o.) (literally, to prohibit s.o. from receiving water and fire)*

interdicti·ō -ōnis *f* prohibiting; **aquae et ignī interdictiō** banishment

interdict·um -ī *n* prohibition; contraband; injunction *(by praetor or pro-magistrate)*

interdictus *pp of* **interdīcō**

interdiū *or* **interdiūs** *adv* by day, in the daytime

interdīxī *perf of* **interdīcō**

inter·dō -dare -dedī -datus *tr* (**·duō**) to place between, place at intervals, interpose; **ciccum** *(or* **floccum** *or* **nihil) interduim** *(sl)* I don't give a hoot

interduct·us -ūs *m* (inter)punctuation

interdum *adv* sometimes, now and then, occasionally; meanwhile

interdu·ō *see* **interdō**

intereā *adv* meanwhile, in the interim; anyhow, nevertheless

interemptus *pp of* **interimō**

inter·eō -īre -iī -itum *intr* to die; to be done for, be finished, perish, be lost; to become extinct

interequit·ō -āre -āvī -ātus *tr* to ride between *(e.g., the ranks or columns)* ‖ *intr* to ride *(on horseback)* in between

interfāti·ō -ōnis *f* interruption

interfecti·ō -ōnis *f* killing

interfect·or -ōris *m,* **interfectr·īx -īcis** *f* killer, murderer

inter·ficiō -ficere -fēcī -fectus *tr* to kill; to destroy

inter·fīō -fierī *intr* to be destroyed

inter·fluō -fluere -flūxī *tr* to flow between ‖ *intr* to flow in between

inter·fodiō -fodere -fōdī -fossus *tr* to pierce, penetrate

inter·for -fārī -fātus sum *tr & intr* to interrupt

interfug·iō -ere *intr* to slip in between

interfulg·eō -ēre *intr (w. abl)* to shine amid *or* among

interfūs·us -a -um *adj* spread here and there; *(w. acc)* flowing between

interiac·eō -ēre *intr (w. dat)* to lie between

interiaciō *see* **intericiō**

interibi *adv* in the meantime

inter·iciō -icere -iēcī -iectus *tr* to interpose; *(w. dat or* **inter** *+ acc)* **1** to throw *or* set *(s.th.)* between; **2** to intermingle *(s.th.)* with, intermix *(s.th.)* with

interiecti·ō -ōnis *f (gram)* interjection; *(rhet)* parenthetical remark *or* phrase
interiect·us -a -um *pp of* **intericiō** ‖ *adj (w. dat or* **inter** *+ acc)* set *or* lying between
interiect·us -ūs *m* interposition; interval
interim *adv* meanwhile; for the moment; sometimes; however, anyhow
inter·imō -imere -ēmī -emptus *tr* to do away with, abolish; to kill
interi·or -or -us *adj* inner, interior; internal; inner side of; more remote *(places, peoples, esp. far from the seacoast);* secret, private; deeper, more profound; more intimate, more personal, more confidential
interiti·ō -ōnis *f* ruin, destruction; *(violent or untimely)* death
interit·us -ūs *m* ruin; *(violent or untimely)* death; dissolution *(of institutions, society, material things);* extinction
inter·iungō -iungere -iūnxī -iūnctus *tr* to join together; to clasp
interius *adv* on the inside; inwardly; in the middle; too short; *(to listen)* closely; more deeply
inter·lābor -lābī -lāpsus sum *intr* to glide in between, flow in between
inter·legō -legere -lēgī -lēctus *tr* to pick *or* pluck here and there
inter·linō -linere -lēvī -litus *tr* to smear; to daub in the gaps *(of a structure);* to tamper with *(a document to falsify it)*
interlo·quor -quī -cūtus sum *intr* to interrupt
interlū·ceō -ēre -xī *intr* to shine through; to be lightning now and then; to be transparent; to be plainly visible
interlūni·a -ōrum *npl* new moon
interlu·ō -ere *tr* to flow between; to wash
intermēnstru·us -a -um *adj* of the new moon ‖ *n* new moon
intermināt·us -a -um *adj* endless
intermin·or -ārī -ātus sum *tr (w. dat)* to threaten *(s.o.)* with *(s.th.)* ‖ *intr* to threaten
inter·mīsceō -mīscēre -mīscuī -mīxtus *tr* to intermingle
intermissi·ō -ōnis *f* intermission, pause, interruption; interval of time; *(leg)* adjournment
inter·mittō -mittere -mīsī -missus *tr* to interrupt, break off, suspend; to omit, neglect; to leave gaps in, leave unoccupied, leave undefended; to allow *(time)* to pass ‖ *intr* to pause, stop
intermīxtus *pp of* **intermīsceō**
inter·morior -morī -mortuus sum *intr* to die suddenly; to faint
intermortu·us -a -um *adj* dead; unconscious; *(fig)* half-dead
intermundi·a -ōrum *npl* outer space
intermūrāl·is -is -e *adj* intermural, between two walls
internāt·us -a -um *adj (w. dat)* growing among *or* between
internecīn·us -a -um *adj* internecine, exterminating, of extermination
interneci·ō -ōnis *f* massacre
internecīv·us -a -um *adj* exterminating; **bellum internecīvum** war of extermination
internec·ō -āre -āvī -ātus *tr* to exterminate
internect·ō -ere *tr* to intertwine
internit·eō -ēre *intr* to shine out
internōd·ium -(i)ī *n (anat)* space between two joints
inter·nōscō -nōscere -nōvī -nōtus *tr* to distinguish, pick out; *(w.* **ab***)* to distinguish *(one thing)* from *(another)*
internūnti·ō -āre *intr* to exchange messages
internūnt·ius -(i)ī *m,* **internūnti·a -ae** *f* messenger, courier; mediator, go-between
intern·us -a -um *adj* internal; civil, domestic
in·terō -terere -trīvī -trītus *tr* to rub in; to crumble up
interpellāti·ō -ōnis *f* interruption
interpellāt·or -ōris *m* interrupter; petitioner
interpell·ō -āre -āvī -ātus *tr* to interrupt, break in on; to disturb, obstruct; to raise an objection; to accost with a request
interpol·is -is -e *adj* patched up, touched up, made like new
interpol·ō -āre -āvī -ātus *tr* to refurbish, touch up; to make like new
inter·pōnō -pōnere -posuī -positus *tr* to insert, interpose, intersperse; to add as an ingredient; to include *(in a speech or book);* to introduce, bring into play; to introduce as witness *or* participant; to admit *(a person);* to let *(time)* pass; to alter, falsify *(writings);* to allege, use as a pretext; *(w.* **inter** *+ acc)* to place between; **auctōritātem interpōnere** to assert one's authority, exert one's influence; **fidem interpōnere** to give one's word; **fidem suam in eam rem interpōnere** to give his word in that matter; **operam** *(or* **studium)** **interpōnere** to apply effort ‖ *refl* to interfere; to intervene in order to veto; *(w. dat or* **in** *+ acc)* to interfere with, meddle with, get mixed up with ‖ *pass (of time)* to elapse in the meantime, intervene; to lie between; *(of writing)* to contain insertions
interpositi·ō -ōnis *f* insertion; introduction; inclusion; parenthetical statement
interposit·us -ūs *m* interposition
interpositus *pp of* **interpōnō**
interpr·es -etis *mf* mediator, negotiator; middleman, broker; interpreter; expounder; translator

interpretāti·ō -ōnis *f* interpretation, explanation; meaning; translation
interpret·or -ārī -ātus sum *tr* to interpret, construe; to infer, conclude; to decide; to translate
inter·primō -primere -pressī -pressus *tr* to squeeze; **faucēs interprimere** to choke
interpūncti·ō -ōnis *f* punctuation
interpūnct·um -ī *n* pause *(between words and sentences);* punctuation mark
interpūnct·us -a -um *adj* well-divided; *(w. abl)* interspersed with
inter·pungō -pungere -pūnxī -pūnctus *tr* to divide *(words)* with punctuation, punctuate; to intersperse
interqui·ēscō -ēscere -ēvī *intr* to rest awhile; to pause awhile
interrēgn·um -ī *n* interregnum *(time between the death of one king and election of another or similar interval between consuls)*
inter·rēx -rēgis *m* interrex, regent
interrit·us -a -um *adj* undaunted
interrogāti·ō -ōnis *f* question; interrogation, cross-examination; argument developed by question and answer
interrogāt·um -ī *n* question; **ad interrogātum respondēre** to answer the question
interrog·ō -āre -āvī -ātus *tr* to ask, question; to interrogate, cross-examine; to sue; to seek information from; **cāsus interrogandī** *(gram)* genitive case; **sententiam interrogāre** tō ask *(a senator's)* opinion; **lēge** *(or* **lēgibus)** **interrogāre** *(leg)* to arraign, indict ‖ *intr* to ask a question, ask questions; to argue, reason
interrumpō interrumpere interrūpī interruptus *tr* to break apart, break in half; to break up, smash; to divide, scatter; to interrupt, break off
interruptē *adv* with interruptions
interruptus *pp of* **interrumpō**
intersaep·iō -īre -sī -tus *tr* to fence off, ēnclose; to stop up, close, cut off
inter·scindō -scindere -scidī -scissus *tr* to tear apart, tear down; to cut off, separate
interscrī·bō -bere -psī -ptus *tr* to write *(s.th.)* in between
interser·ō -ere -uī *tr* to interpose, insert; *(w. dat)* to add *(s.th.)* to
interspīrāti·ō -ōnis *f (rhet)* breathing pause, correct breathing *(in delivering a speech)*
interstīnct·us -a -um *adj* blotchy, spotted
interstin·guō -guere -xī -ctus *tr* to spot, blotch; to extinguish
interstring·ō -ere *tr* to squeeze; to strangle
inter·sum -esse -fuī *intr* to be present, assist, take part; to differ; to be of interest; *(w. dat)* **1** to be present at, attend; **2** take part in; *(w.* **in** *+ acc)* to be present at ‖ *v impers* there is a difference; it makes a difference; it is of importance; it is of interest; *(w.* **inter** *+ acc or* **in** *+ abl)* there is a difference between; *(w. gen or with fem of poss pronouns* **meā, tuā, nostrā,** *etc.)* it makes a difference to, it is of importance to, it concerns (me, you, us, etc.); *(w. gen of value, e.g.,* **magnī, permagnī, tantī,** *or w. adv* **multum, plūrimum, maximē)** it makes a (great, very great, such a great) difference, it is of (great, very great, such great) concern; **nē minimum quidem interest** there is not the slightest difference; **nihil omnīnō interest** there is no difference whatever
intertext·us -a -um *adj* interwoven
intertra·hō -here -xī -ctus *tr (w. dat)* to take *(s.th.)* away from
intertrīment·um -ī *n* wear and tear; loss, wastage
interturbāti·ō -ōnis *f* confusion, turmoil
interturb·ō -āre -āvī *tr* to confuse
intervall·um -ī *n* interval, space, distance; gap, opening; interval of time, spell; pause; break, intermission; contrast, difference *(in degree, quality, etc.);* **ex intervallō** at *or* from a distance; after a while; at intervals; **ex intervallīs** at intervals; **longō intervallō** after a long while, much later; **per intervallum** *(or* **intervalla)** at intervals
inter·vellō -vellere -vulsī -vulsus *tr* to pluck here and there
inter·veniō -venīre -vēnī -ventus *tr* to interfere with ‖ *intr* to happen along, come on the scene; to intervene, intrude; to happen, crop up; *(w. dat)* to interfere with, interrupt, put a stop to, come in the way of, oppose, prevent
intervent·or -ōris *m* intruder, untimely visitor
intervent·us -ūs *m* intervention; intrusion; mediation
interver·tō -tere -tī -sus *tr* **(-vort-)** to divert, embezzle
intervīs·ō -ere -ī -us *tr* to drop in on; to visit from time to time
intervolit·ō -āre -āvī *intr* to flit about
intervom·ō -ere -uī -itus *tr (w.* **inter** *+ acc)* to throw up amongst
intervulsus *pp of* **intervellō**
intestābil·is -is -e *adj* infamous, notorious; detestable, shameful
intestātō *adv* intestate
intestāt·us -a -um *adj* intestate; unconvicted by witnesses
intestīn·us -a -um *adj* internal ‖ *n* alimentary canal; intestine; **intestīnum tenue** small intestine
intēxī *perf of* **integō**
intex·ō -ere -uī -tus *tr* to interweave, interlace; to weave; to embroider; to surround, envelop
intib·um -ī *n* **(inty-)** endive

intimē *adv* intimately, cordially
intim·us -a -um *adj* **(-tum-)** innermost; deepest, most abstruse, most profound; most secret, most intimate **‖** *m* close friend
in·tingō -tingere -tīnxī -tīnctus *tr* to dip, soak; to color *(w. cosmetics)*
intolerābil·is -is -e *adj* intolerable; irresistible
intolerand·us -a -um *adj* intolerable
intoler·āns -antis *adj* intolerable; *(w. gen)* unable to stand, unable to put up with
intoleranter *adv* intolerably, immoderately, excessively
intoleranti·a -ae *f* impatience
inton·ō -āre -uī -itus *tr* to thunder forth **‖** *intr* to thunder
intōns·us -a -um *adj* unshorn, untrimmed; long-haired; rude
intor·queō -quēre -sī -tus *tr* to twist, turn, roll; *(w.* **circum** *+ acc)* to wrap *(s.th.)* around; *(w. dat or* **in** *+ acc)* to hurl *(e.g., spear)* at
intort·us -a -um *adj* twisted; tangled; *(fig)* crooked
intrā *adv* on the inside, inside, within; inward
intrā *prep (w. acc)* **1** inside, within; **intrā parietēs** within the walls, at home, privately; **intrā sē** to oneself, privately; by oneself, alone; in one's own country, at home; **2** inside *(a period of time),* within, during, in the course of, in less than; **intrā hōs diēs** within these (last few) days; **3** within the limits of, without passing beyond, on this side of, short of *(a certain point);* **modicē hoc facere aut etiam intrā modum** to do this with moderation and even keep on the safe side of moderation; **intrā tēlī iactum prōgredī** to come within range; **intrā (et) extrā** inside and out, on both sides
intrābil·is -is -e *adj* approachable
intractābil·is -is -e *adj* intractable, unmanageable; formidable
intractāt·us -a -um *adj* untamed; unbroken *(horse);* unattempted
intrem·īscō -īscere -uī *intr* to begin to tremble
intrem·ō -ere -uī *intr* to shake, tremble, shiver
intrepidē *adv* calmly, intrepidly
intrepid·us -a -um *adj* calm, intrepid, not nervous; untroubled
intrīc·ō -āre -āvī -ātus *tr* to entangle, involve
intrīnsecus *adv (opp:* **extrīnsecus)** on the inside; to the inside, inwards
intrīt·us -a -um *adj* not worn away; *(fig)* not worn out
intrō *adv* inwards, inside, in
intr·ō -āre -āvī -ātus *tr & intr* to enter; to penetrate
intrō·dūcō -dūcere -dūxī -ductus *tr* to bring in, lead in; to introduce; to raise *(a subject, point)*
intrōducti·ō -ōnis *f* introduction
intrō·eō -īre -īvī *or* **-iī -itum** *tr & intr* to enter
intrō·ferō -ferre -tulī -lātus *tr* to carry in; *(w.* **in** *+ acc)* to carry into; **pedem intrōferre** *(w.* **in** *+ acc)* to set foot in
intrō·gredior -gredī -gressus sum *intr* to step inside
introit·us -ūs *m* entrance; hostile entry; invasion; beginning, prelude
intrōlātus *pp of* **intrōferō**
intrō·mittō -mittere -mīsī -missus *tr* to let in, admit; to send in; to introduce
intrōrsum *adv* **(-sus)** inwards, toward the inside; *(fig)* inwardly
intrō·rumpō -rumpere -rūpī -ruptus *tr* to break in, enter by force
intrōspect·ō -āre *tr* to look in on
intrō·spiciō -spicere -spexī -spectus *tr* to look into; to look at, regard; *(fig)* to look into, examine **‖** *intr (w.* **in** *+ acc) (lit & fig)* to look into, inspect
intub·um -ī *n* endive
intu·eor -ērī -itus sum *or* **intu·or -ī** *tr* to look at, gaze at; to consider, take into consideration; to look up to, have regard for; to keep an eye on; to examine visually, inspect **terram intuērī** to look down at the ground
intum·ēscō -ēscere -uī *intr* to swell up, rise; *(of voice)* to grow louder; *(of river)* to rise, become swollen; to become angry; to get a big head, swell with pride
intumulāt·us -a -um *adj* unburied
intuor *see* **intueor**
inturbid·us -a -um *adj* undisturbed, quiet
intus *adv* inside, within; at home, in; to the inside; from within
intūt·us -a -um *adj* unsafe; unprotected, unguarded, defenseless
inul·a -ae *f* elecampane *(tall, coarse plant with yellow flowers)*
inult·us -a -um *adj* unavenged; unpunished
inumbr·ō -āre -āvī -ātus *tr* to shade; to cover
inundāti·ō -ōnis *f* inundation, flood
inund·ō -āre -āvī -ātus *tr* to inundate, flood **‖** *intr* to overflow; **sanguine inundāre** to run red with blood
in·ungō (in·unguō) -ungere -ūnxī -ūnctus *tr* to anoint
inurbānē *adv* impolitely, rudely
inurbān·us -a -um *adj* impolite; unsophisticated, rude, rustic
inur·geō -gēre -sī *intr* to butt
in·ūrō -ūrere -ūssī -ūstus *tr* to burn in, brand, imprint; *(w. dat)* **1** to brand upon, imprint upon, affix to; **2** to inflict upon
inūsitātē *adv* unusually, strangely

inūsitāt·us -a -um *adj* unusual, strange, uncommon, extraordinary

inūstus *pp of* **inūrō**

inūtil·is -is -e *adj* useless; unprofitable; impractical; injurious, harmful

inūtilit·ās -ātis *f* uselessness; harmfulness

inūtiliter *adv* uselessly; harmfully

invā·dō -dere -sī -sus *tr* to come *or* go into, enter; to enter upon, undertake, attempt; to invade, attack, rush upon; *(fig)* to seize, take possession of ‖ *intr* to come *or* go in; to invade; *(w.* **in** + *acc)* **1** to invade; to assail; **2** to seize; **3** to get possession of; **4** to rush to embrace

inval·ēscō -ēscere -uī *intr* to grow stronger; *(fig)* to increase in power; to grow in frequency; to predominate

invalid·us -a -um *adj* weak; feeble; dim *(light, fire);* inadequate; ineffectual

invāsī *perf of* **invādō**

invāsus *pp of* **invādō**

invecti·ō -ōnis *f* importation, importing; arrival by boat

in·vehō -vehere -vēxī -vectus *tr* to carry in, bring in, ship in *(by cart, horse, boat, etc.); (w. dat)* to bring *(e.g., evils)* upon ‖ *refl (w. acc or* **in** + *acc)* to rush against, attack ‖ *pass* to ride, drive, sail; *(w. acc or* **in** + *acc)* **1** to ride into, sail into; **2** to attack; **3** to inveigh against, attack *(w. words);* **invehī equō** to ride a horse; **invehī nāve** to sail

invēndibil·is -is -e *adj* unsaleable

in·veniō -venīre -vēnī -ventus *tr* to come upon, find, come across, discover; to find out; to invent, devise; to learn, ascertain; to get, reach, earn

inventi·ō -ōnis *f* inventiveness; inventing, invention

invent·or -ōris *m,* **inventr·īx -īcis** *f* inventor, author, discoverer

invent·us -a -um *pp of* **inveniō** ‖ *n* invention, discovery

invenust·us -a -um *adj* having no sex appeal; homely, unattractive; unlucky in love

inverēcund·us -a -um *adj* disrespectful, immodest, shameless

inverg·ō -ere *tr (w. dat or* **in** + *acc)* to pour upon

inversi·ō -ōnis *f* inversion *(of words);* irony; allegory

invers·us -a -um *pp of* **invertō** ‖ *adj* turned upside down; turned inside out; **manus inversa** back of the hand

inver·tō -tere -tī -sus *tr* to invert, turn upside down, upset, reverse, turn inside out; to transpose, reverse; to pervert, abuse, misrepresent; to use ironically

invesperāsc·it -ere *v impers* evening is approaching, twilight is falling

investīgāti·ō -ōnis *f* investigation; search

investīgāt·or -ōris *m* investigator

investīg·ō -āre -āvī -ātus *tr* to track, trace, search after; to investigate, search into, search after

inveter·āscō -āscere -āvī *intr* to begin to grow old, get old; to become fixed, become established; to become rooted, grow inveterate; to become obsolete

inveterāti·ō -ōnis *f* chronic illness

inveterāt·us -a -um *adj* inveterate, long-standing

invēxī *perf of* **invehō**

invicem *or* **in vicem** *adv* in turn, taking turns, one after another, alternately; mutually, each other; **dēfatigātīs invicem integrī succēdunt** fresh troops take turns in relieving the exhausted troops

invict·us -a -um *adj* unconquered; invincible

invid·ēns -entis *adj* envious, jealous

invidenti·a -ae *f* envy, jealousy

invideō -vidēre -vīdī -vīsus *tr* to envy, be jealous of ‖ *intr (w. dat)* to envy, begrudge; *(w. dat of person and abl of cause or* **in** + *abl)* to begrudge *(s.o. s.th.),* to envy *(s.o.)* because of *(s.th.)*

invidi·a -ae *f* envy, jealousy; unpopularity; **invidiae esse** *(w. dat)* to be the cause of envy to; **invidiam habēre** to be unpopular

invidiōsē *adv* spitefully; so as to bring unpopularity on an opponent

invidiōs·us -a -um *adj* envious; spiteful; envied; enviable, causing envy

invid·us -a -um *adj* envious, jealous; *(w. dat)* hostile to, unfavorable to

invigil·ō -āre -āvī -ātum *intr* to be alert, be on one's toes; *(w. dat)* to be on the lookout for, keep an eye on, pay attention to, watch over; *(w.* **prō** + *abl)* to watch over

inviolābil·is -is -e *adj* inviolable; invulnerable, indestructible

inviolātē *adv* inviolately

inviolāt·us -a -um *adj* inviolate, unhurt; inviolable

invīsitāt·us -a -um *adj* unusual, strange; not seen before, unknown

invīs·ō -ere -ī -us *tr* to visit, go to see; to look into, inspect; to look after; to catch sight of

invīs·us -a -um *pp of* **invideō** ‖ *adj* unseen; hated, detested; hostile

invītāment·um -ī *n* attraction, allurement, inducement

invītāti·ō -ōnis *f* invitation; challenge

invītāt·us -ūs *m* invitation

invītē *adv* unwillingly, against one's wishes

invīt·ō -āre -āvī -ātus *tr* to invite; to entertain; to summon, challenge; to ask, request; to allure, attract; to encourage, court

invīt·us -a -um *adj* reluctant, unwilling, against one's will; **invītā Minervā**

against one's better judgment, against the grain
invi·us -a -um *adj* without roads, trackless, impassable ‖ *npl* rough terrain
invocāti·ō -ōnis *f* invocation
invocāt·us -a -um *adj* unbidden
invoc·ō -āre -āvī -ātus *tr* to invoke, call upon; to call out *(name of one's girlfriend in rolling dice);* to pray for; to address *(with an honorific title)*
involāt·us -ūs *m* flight
involgō *see* **invulgō**
involit·ō -āre -āvī *intr (w. dat)* (of long hair) to trail over
invol·ō -āre -āvī -ātus *tr* to swoop down on, pounce on ‖ *intr* to swoop down; *(w.* **in** *+ acc)* to swoop down on
involūcr·um -ī *n* wrapper; cover; envelope; *(fig)* cover-up, front
involūt·us -a -um *adj* complicated
invol·vō -vere -vī -ūtus *tr* to wrap up; to involve, envelop; to cover completely, overwhelm; *(w. dat or* **in** *+ acc)* to pile *(s.th.)* on ‖ *refl (w. dat) (fig)* to get all wrapped up in
involvol·us -ī *m* caterpillar *(which rolls up the leaves it infests)*
invulg·ō -āre -āvī -ātus *tr* **(-vol-)** to reveal, publicize ‖ *intr* to give public evidence
iō *interj (expressing joy)* ho!; hurray!; *(expressing pain)* ah!; *(in a sudden call)* yo!
Ī·ō -ūs *or* **-ōnis** *f (acc & abl:* **Īō**) Io *(daughter of Argive King Inachus, loved by Jupiter, changed into a heifer because of fear of Juno, and driven by Juno over the world)*
Iocast·a -ae *or* **Iocast·ē -ēs** *f* Jocasta *(wife of Laius, and mother as well as wife of Oedipus)*
iocāti·ō -ōnis *f* jesting, humor
iocineris *gen of* **iecur**
ioc·or -ārī -ātus sum *or* **ioc·ō -āre** *tr* to say in jest ‖ *intr* to joke, crack a joke, be joking
iocōsē *adv* humorously, as a joke, jokingly
iocōs·us -a -um *adj* humorous, funny; fond of jokes
iocular·is -is -e *adj* humorous, funny
ioculāri·us -a -um *adj* ludicrous
ioculāt·or -ōris *m* joker
iocul·or -ārī -ātus sum *intr* to joke
iocul·us -ī *m* joke; **ioculō** as a joke, in fun
ioc·us -ī *m (pl:* **ioc·ī -ōrum** *mpl,* **ioc·a -ōrum** *npl)* joke; laughing stock; child's play; **iocō remōtō** all joking aside; **per iocum** as a joke
Iolā·us -ī *m* son of Iphicles and companion of Hercules
Iol·ē -ēs *f* daughter of Eurytus, who fell in love with Hercules
Iōn·es -um *mpl* Ionians *(Greek inhabitants of the W. coast of Asia Minor)*
Iōnic·us -a -um *adj* Ionic ‖ *m* Ionic dancer ‖ *npl* Ionic dance
Iōni·us -a -um *adj* Ionian ‖ *f* Ionia *(coastal district of Asia Minor)* ‖ *n* Ionian Sea *(off W. coast of Greece)*
iōta *indecl n* iota *(ninth letter of the Greek alphabet)*
Īphianass·a -ae f Iphigenia
Īphigenī·a -ae *f* daughter of Agamemnon and Clytemnestra, who was to have been sacrificed at Aulis but was saved by Artemis
Īphit·us -ī *m* Argonaut, son of Eurytus and Antiope
ips·a -īus *or* **-ius** *adj* self, very, just, mere, precisely; in person; by herself, alone; of her own accord ‖ *pron* she herself; lady of the house
ips·e *or* **ips·us -īus** *or* **-ius** *adj* self, very, just, mere, precisely; in person; by himself, alone; of his own accord ‖ *pron* he himself; master; host
ipsim·a -ae *f (coll)* boss
ipsim·us -ī *m (coll)* boss
ips·um -īus *or* **-ius** *adj* self, very, just, mere, precisely; by itself, alone; of itself, spontaneously; **nunc ipsum** just then ‖ *pron* it itself, that itself; **ipsum quod . . .** the very fact that
ipsus *see* **ipse**
īr·a -ae *f* wrath, resentment
īrācundē *adv* angrily; passionately
īrācundi·a -ae *f* quick temper; anger, wrath, passion, violence; resentment
īrācund·us -a -um *adj* hot-tempered, irritable; angry; resentful
īrāsc·or -ārī *intr* to get angry, fly into a rage; *(w. dat)* to get angry with
īrātē *adv* angrily
īrāt·us -a -um *adj* irate, angry, enraged; *(w. dat)* angry at
īrōnī·a -ae *f* irony
irrās·us -a -um *adj* unshaven
irratiōnāl·is -is -e *adj* **(inr-)** irrational
irrau·cēscō -cēscere -sī *intr* **(inr-)** to become hoarse
irredivīv·us -a -um *adj* **(inre-)** irreparable
irred·ux -ucis *adj* **(inre-)** one-way *(road)*
irreligāt·us -a -um *adj* **(inre-)** not tied
irreligiōsē *adv* **(inr-)** impiously, blasphemously
irreligiōs·us -a -um *adj* **(inr-)** irreligious, impious
irremeābil·is -is -e *adj* **(inr-)** from which there is no return, one-way
irreparābil·is -is -e *adj* **(inr-)** irretrievable; irreparable *(damage)*
irrepert·us -a -um *adj* **(inr-)** undiscovered, not found
irrēp·ō -ere -sī -tum *intr* **(inr-)** to creep in; *(fig)* to sneak in; *(w.* **ad** *or* **in** *+ acc)* to creep toward *or* into; *(fig)* to sneak up on
irreprehēns·us -a -um *adj* **(inr-)** blameless

irrequiēt·us -a -um *adj* **(inr-)** restless
irresect·us -a -um *adj* **(inr-)** untrimmed
irresolūt·us -a -um *adj* **(inr-)** not loosened, still tied, unrelaxed
irrēt·iō -īre -īvī *or* **-iī -ītus** *tr* **(inr-)** to net, trap in a net
irretort·us -a -um *adj* **(inr-)** not turned back; **oculō irretortō** without one backward glance
irrever·ēns -entis *adj* **(inr-)** irreverent, disrespectful
irreverenter *adv* **(inr-)** irreverently, disrespectfully
irreverenti·a -ae *f* **(inr-)** irreverence, disrespect
irrevocābil·is -is -e *adj* **(inr-)** irrevocable; implacable, relentless
irrevocāt·us -a -um *adj* **(inr-)** not called back, not asked back
irrī·deō -dēre -sī -sus *tr* **(inr-)** to ridicule, laugh at **‖** *intr* to laugh, joke; *(w. dat)* to laugh at
irrīdiculē *adv* **(inr-)** with no sense of humor
irrīdicul·um -ī *n* **(inr-)** laughing stock
irrigāti·ō -ōnis *f* **(inr-)** irrigation
irrig·ō -āre -āvī -ātus *tr* **(inr-)** to irrigate, water; to inundate; *(fig)* to diffuse; *(fig)* to flood, steep, soak
irrigu·us -a -um *adj* **(inr-)** wet, soaked, well-watered; refreshing
irrīsī (inr-) *perf of* **irrīdeō**
irrīsi·ō -ōnis *f* **(inr-)** ridicule, mockery
irrīs·or -ōris *m* **(inr-)** reviler, mocker
irrīsus (inr-) *pp of* **irrīdeō**
irrīs·us -ūs *m* **(inr-)** mockery, derision; laughing stock, object of derision
irrītābil·is -is -e *adj* **(inr-)** easily excited; easily enraged, irritable; sensitive
irrītām·en -inis *n* **(inr-)** incentive; provocation
irrītāment·um -ī *n* **(inr-)** incentive; provocation
irrītāti·ō -ōnis *f* **(inr-)** incitement; irritation, provocation; stimulant
irrīt·ō -āre -āvī -ātus *tr* **(inr-)** to provoke, annoy; to incite; to excite, stimulate; to bring on *(a calamity, etc.)*
irrit·us -a -um *adj* **(inr-)** not valid, null and void; futile, pointless, useless; unsuccessful *(person)*
irrogāti·ō -ōnis *f* **(inr-)** imposition *(e.g., of a fine)*
irrog·ō -āre -āvī -ātus *tr* **(inr-)** to impose, inflict; to object to *(proposals)*
irrōr·ō -āre -āvī -ātus *tr* **(inr-)** to moisten with dew; to sprinkle, water; **aquam capitī irrōrāre** to sprinkle water on (s.o.'s) head
irruct·ō -āre *intr* **(inr-)** to belch
ir·rumpō -rumpere -rūpī -ruptus *tr* **(inr-)** to rush into, break down **‖** *intr* to rush in; *(w. dat or* **in** *+ acc)* **1** to rush into, rush through; **2** *(fig)* to intrude upon
irru·ō -ere -ī *intr* **(inr-)** to rush in, force one's way in; *(w. dat or* **in** *+ acc)* **1** to rush into; **2** to rush on; **3** to invade, attack; **irruere in odium** *(w. gen)* to incur the anger of
irrūpī (inr-) *perf of* **irrumpō**
irrupti·ō -ōnis *f* **(inr-)** bursting in; forcible entry; *(mil)* incursion; assault
irrupt·us -a -um (inr-) *pp of* **irrumpō ‖** *adj* unbroken
is ēius *(see also* **ea** *and* **id)** *adj* this, that, the said, the aforesaid **‖** *pron* he; **is quī** he who, the person who, the one who
Ismari·us -a -um *adj* of Mt. Ismarus in Thrace; Thracian
ista *see* **iste**
istāc *adv* that way
istāctenus *adv* thus far
istaec *see* **istic**
ist·e -a -ud *adj* that of yours; this, that, the very, that particular; such, of such a kind; that terrible, that despicable **‖** *pron* that one; *(in court)* your client
Isthm·us *or* **Isthm·os -ī** *m* Isthmus of Corinth
istīc *adv* there, in that place; herein; on this occasion
ist·ic -aec -oc *or* **-uc** *adj* that, that of yours; *(in form of questions:* **isticine** *and* **istūcine) ‖** *pron* the one, that one
istinc *adv* from there; from your side; from what you have
istīusmodī *or* **istīmodī** *or* **istīus modī** *or* **istī modī** *adj* that kind of; **istīusmodī scelus** that kind of crime
istō *adv* where you are; therefore; in that matter
istōc *adv* there, to where you are
istōrsum *adv* in that direction, that way
istūc *adv* there, to that place, to where you are, that way; **istūc veniam** I'll come to that matter
istūcine *see* **istic**
istud *see* **iste**
ita *adv* thus, so, in this manner, in that way; *(of natural consequence)* thus, accordingly, therefore, under these circumstances; *(in affirmation)* yes, true, exactly; *(in questions)* really?, truly?; **ita … ut** *(in comparisons)* just as … so; *(introducing contrast)* whereas … at the same time; *(as adversative)* although … nevertheless; *(introducing result clauses)* so *or* in such a way that; *(as correlatives)* both … and, both … as well as; *(in restriction)* on the condition that, insofar as, on the assumption that; *(of degree)* to such a degree … that, so much … that, so … that; **nōn ita** not very, not especially; **quid ita?** how so?, what do you mean?

Ītali·a -ae *f* Italy
Ītalic·us -a -um *adj* Italic
Ītal·is -idis *adj* Italian **||** *fpl* Italian women
Ītali·us -a -um *adj* Italian **||** *f see* **Ītalia**
Ītal·us -a -um *adj* Italian
itaque *adv* and so, and thus, accordingly, therefore, consequently
item *adv* likewise, besides, moreover
it·er -ineris *n* journey, trip; walk; march; day's march; day's journey; route; right of way; duct, passage; method, course, way, road; **ex** *(or* **in)** **itinere** en route, on the way; **iter facere** to take a trip; to travel; to make way; *(mil)* to march; **iter flectere** to change course; **iter patefacere** to clear a way; **iter terrestre** overland route; **itinere** en route; **maximīs itineribus** by marching at top speed
iterāti·ō -ōnis *f* repetition
iter·ō -āre -āvī -ātus *tr* to repeat, renew; to plow again
iterum *adv* again, a second time; **iterum atque iterum** repeatedly, again and again
Ithac·a -ae *or* **Ithac·ē -ēs** *f* Ithaca (*island off W. coast of Greece in the Ionian Sea and home of Odysseus*)
itidem *adv* in the same way
itin- *see* **iter**
iti·ō -ōnis *f* going
it·ō -āre -āvī *intr* to go
it·us -ūs *m* going; departure
It·ys -yos *m* son of Tereus and Procne, who was killed by Procne and served up as food to Tereus
iu- = iu-
iub·a -ae *f* mane; crest
iub·ar -aris *n* radiance, brightness; sunshine
iubāt·us -a -um *adj* crested
iubeō iubēre iussī iussus *tr* to order;; to bid, ask, tell; to prescribe *(a task);* to designate, appoint; *(med)* prescribe; *(pol)* to order, decree, ratify; **iubē frātrem tuum salvēre** *(in letters)* best regards to your brother; say good-bye to your brother
iūcundē *adv* pleasantly, delightfully
iūcundit·ās -ātis *f* pleasantness, delight, enjoyment **||** *fpl* favors
iūcund·us -a -um *adj* pleasant, delightful, agreeable
Iūdae·us -a -um *adj* Jewish **||** *mf* Jew **||** *f* Judea, Palestine
Iūdaïc·us -a -um *adj* Jewish; of Judea; *(mil)* stationed in Judea
iūd·ex -icis *m* judge; juror; arbitrator; umpire; critic, scholar; **iūdex mōrum** censor; **mē iūdice** in my judgment
iūdicāti·ō -ōnis *f* judicial investigation; *(fig)* judgment, opinion
iūdicāt·us -a -um *adj* decided, determined **||** *m* condemned person **||** *n* judicial decision, judgment; precedent; fine; **iūdicātum facere** to carry out a decision; **iūdicātum solvere** to pay a fine
iūdicāt·us -ūs *m* judgeship
iūdiciāl·is -is -e *adj* judicial, forensic
iūdiciāri·us -a -um *adj* judiciary
iūdic·ium -(i)ī *n* trial, court; sentence; jurisdiction; opinion, decision; faculty of judging, judgment, good judgment, taste, tact, discretion; criterion; **ad iūdicium īre** to go to court; **in iūdiciō esse** to be under investigation; **in iūdicium dēdūcere** *(or* **vocāre)** to take to court; **in iūdicium venīre** to come before the court; **iūdicium agere** to conduct a trial; **iūdicium dare** *(or* **reddere)** *(of a praetor)* to grant an action; **iūdicium facere (in +** *acc)* to pass judgment against; **iūdicium tenēre** *(or* **vincīre)** to win a case; **iūdicium prīvātum** civil suit; **iūdicium pūblicum** criminal trial; **meō iūdiciō** in my judgment; **suō iūdiciō** intentionally; **suprēma iūdicia** last will and testament
iūdic·ō -āre -āvī -ātus *tr* to judge; to examine; to sentence, condemn; to form an opinion of; to conclude; to declare, proclaim; *(w. dat of person and acc of the offense)* to convict *(s.o.)* of; *(w. gen)* to find *(s.o.)* guilty of; *(w. dat of person and gen of the offense)* to convict *(s.o.)* of
iugāl·is -is -e *adj* yoked together; nuptial
iugāti·ō -ōnis *f* tying up
iūger·um -ī *n* jugerum *(land measure, about ⅔ of an acre)*
iūg·is -is -e *adj* continuous, perennial, inexhaustible
iūgl·āns -andis *f* walnut tree; walnut
iugōs·us -a -um *adj* hilly
Iugul·ae -ārum *fpl (astr)* Orion's Belt *(3 stars in the constellation Orion)*
iugul·ō -āre -āvī -ātus *tr* to cut the throat of, kill, murder; to destroy; to silence
iugul·um -ī *n,* **iugul·us -ī** *m* throat
iug·um -ī *n* yoke, collar; pair, team; crossbar *(of loom);* thwart *(of boat);* common bond, union; wedlock; pair, couple; mountain ridge; *(mil)* yoke *(consisting of a spear laid crosswise on two upright spears, under which the conquered had to pass)* **||** *npl* heights
Iugurth·a -ae *m* king of Numidia *(160–104 B.C.)*
Iūli·a -ae *f* aunt of Julius Caesar and wife of Marius **||** daughter of Julius Caesar and wife of Pompey *(d. 54 B.C.)* **||** daughter of Augustus by Scribonia *(39 B.C.–A.D. 14)*
Iūli·us -a -um *adj* Julian; of July; **mēnsis Iūlius** July **||** *m* Roman first name *(praenomen);* July
Iūl·us -ī *m* son of Aeneas *(also called Ascanius)*
iūment·um -ī *n* beast of burden, horse, mule
iunce·us -a -um *adj* of reeds; slim, slender

iuncōs·us -a -um *adj* overgrown with reeds
iūnctim *adv* side by side; in succession
iūncti·ō -ōnis *f* joining, combination, union
iūnctūr·a -ae *f* joining, uniting, joint, juncture; connection, relationship; combination
iūnct·us -a -um *pp of* **iungō** ‖ *adj* connected, associated, united, attached
iunc·us -ī *m* reed
iungō iungere iūnxī iūnctus *tr* to join, join together, unite, connect; to yoke, harness; to couple, pair, mate; to bridge *(a river);* to bring together, associate, ally; to add; to compose *(poems);* to combine *(words)*
iūni·or -ōris *adj (mas & fem only)* younger ‖ *mpl* younger men *(esp. of military age, between 17 and 46 years)*
iūniper·us -ī *f* juniper
Iūni·us -a -um *adj* June, of June; **mēnsis Iūnius** June ‖ *m* Roman first name *(praenomen);* June
iūn·ix -īcis *f* heifer
Iūn·ō -ōnis *f* daughter of Saturn and wife and sister of Jupiter *(commonly identified with Hera);* woman's tutelary deity *(corresponding to a male's* **genius); Iūnō Lūcīna** goddess of childbirth *(applied to Juno and Diana);* **Iūnō īnferna** name of Proserpina *(queen of the lower world);* **Iūnōnis avis** peacock; **Iūnōnis stella** planet Venus
Iuppiter *(or* **Diēspiter) Iovis** *m* son of Saturn, brother and husband of Juno, and chief god of the Romans *(commonly identified with Zeus)*
iūrāt·or -ōris *m* judge; assistant censor
iūrāt·us -a -um *adj* being under oath; having given one's word
iūre *adv* rightfully; with good reason, deservedly; correctly
iūrecōnsult·us -ī *m* **(iūris-)** legal expert
iūreperītus *see* **iūrisperītus**
iurg·ium -(i)ī *n* quarrel ‖ *npl* reproaches, abuse
iurg·ō -āre -āvī -ātus *tr* to scold ‖ *intr* to quarrel
iūridiciāl·is -is -e *adj* juridical
iūriscōnsult·us -ī *m* **(iūre-)** legal expert, lawyer
iūrisdicti·ō -ōnis *f* administration of justice; jurisdiction
iūrisperīt·us -ī *m* **(iūre-)** legal expert, lawyer
iūr·ō -āre -āvī -ātus *tr* to swear; to swear by, attest, call to witness; to swear to, attest; to promise under oath, vow ‖ *intr* to swear, take an oath; *(w.* **in** *+ acc)* **1** to swear allegiance to; **2** to swear to observe *(the laws, etc.);* **3** to conspire against; **in haec verba iūrāre** to swear according to the prescribed form; **in verba alicūius iūrāre** to swear allegiance to s.o.; **iūrāre calumniam** to swear that the accusation is not false
iūs iūris *n* juice, broth, gravy
iūs iūris *n* law, the laws *(as established by society and custom rather than statute law);* legal system, right, justice; law court; legal right, authority, permission; prerogative; jurisdiction; **in iūs īre** to go to court; **iūra dare** to prescribe laws, administer justice; **iūre** by right, rightfully; **iūs cīvīle** civil law; **iūs dīcere** to sit as judge, hold court; **iūs gentium** law available to aliens as well as to citizens; international law; **iūs patrium** the power of life or death over one's children; **iūs praetōrium** principles of law contained in a praetor's edict; **iūs pūblicum** constitutional law; **meī iūris** subject to my control; **prō iūre suō** without exceeding one's rights, at will, freely; in one's own right; **suī iūris** *(or* **suō iūre)** legally one's own master; **summum iūs** strict letter of the law
iūsiūrandum *or* **iūs iūrandum** *(gen:* **iūr·isiūrand·ī** *or* **iūr·is iūrand·ī)** *n* oath; **aliquem iūreiūrandō adigere** to bind s.o. with an oath, have s.o. take an oath
iūssū *(abl only) m* by order; **meō iūssū** by my order
iūss·us -a -um *pp of* **iubeō** ‖ *n* order, command, bidding
iūstē *adv* justly, rightly
iūstific·us -a -um *adj* righteous
iūstiti·a -ae *f* justice, fairness
iūstit·ium -(i)ī *n* suspension of legal business, legal holiday; period of mourning; *(fig)* standstill
iūst·us -a -um *adj* just, fair; justified, well-founded; formal; in due order, according to protocol, regular ‖ *n* justice; due measure; **plūs quam iūstō** more than due measure, too much ‖ *npl* rights, one's due; regular tasks, formalities; ceremonies, due ceremony; funeral rites, obsequies
Iūturn·a -ae *f* nymph, sister of Turnus, the king of the Rutuli
iūtus *pp of* **iuvō**
iuvenāl·is -is -e *adj* youthful; juvenile ‖ **Iuvenālis** *m* Juvenal *(Decimus Junius Juvenalis, Roman satirist in the time of Domitian and Trajan, c.* A.D. *62–142)*
iuvenc·us -a -um *adj* young ‖ *m* bullock; young man ‖ *f* heifer; girl
iuven·ēscō -ēscere *intr* to grow up; to become young again
iuvenīl·is -is -e *adj* youthful; juvenile; cheerful
iuvenīliter *adv* youthfully, boyishly
iuven·is -is -e *adj* young ‖ *m* young man *(between the ages of 20 and 45);* warrior ‖ *f* young lady

iuven·or -ārī -ātus sum *intr* to act like a kid
iuvent·a -ae *f* youth
iuvent·ās -ātis *f or* **iuvent·ūs -ūtis** *f* youth, prime of life, manhood; *(collectively)* young people, the young, youth
iuv·ō iuvāre iūvī iūtus *tr* to help; *(of terrain)* to give *(one)* an advantage; to back up *(an opinion);* to benefit, do good to; to please, delight **||** *v impers (w. inf)* it helps to; **iuvat mē** it delights me, I am glad, I am relieved
iūxtā *adv* nearby, in close proximity; alike, in like manner, equally; *(w.* **ac, atque, et, quam,** *or* **cum)** as well as, just the same as **||** *prep (w. acc)* **1** close to, near to, next to; **2** next to, immediately after; **3** near, bordering on; **4** next door to
iūxtim *adv* near; equally
Ixīone·us -a -um of Ixion
Ixī·ōn -onis *or* **-onos** *m* Ixion *(king of the Lapiths, who was tied to a wheel by Jupiter for trying to seduce Juno and sent flying into Tartarus)*
Ixīonid·ēs -ae *m* son of Ixion *(esp.* Pirithous)
Ixīoni·us -a -um *adj* of Ixion

J

Note: Following contemporary practice, the letter **j** *has been replaced by the letter* **i** *in this dictionary.*

K

K, k *(supply* littera) *f* tenth letter of the Latin alphabet; letter name: **ka**
K. *abbr* **Kaeso** *(Roman first name, praenomen)*
Kalend·ae -ārum *fpl* **(Cal-)** Kalends *(first day of the Roman month);* **ad Kalendās Graecās solvere** to pay on the Greek Kalends *(i.e., never, since there were no Greek Kalends);* **trīstēs Kalendae** gloomy Kalends *(because interest was due on the Kalends)*
Kalendār·ium -(i)ī *n* account book, ledger
Karthāginiēns·is -is -e *adj* **(Carth-)** Carthaginian
Karthāg·ō -inis *f* **(Carth-)** Carthage

L

L, l *(supply* littera) *f* eleventh letter of the Latin alphabet; letter name: **el**
L *abbr* the number 50
L. *abbr* **Lūcius** *(Roman first name, praenomen)*
labāsc·ō -ere *intr* to wave, totter; to give in, yield
lābēcul·a -ae *f* blemish, stain *(of disgrace)*
labe·faciō -facere -fēcī -factus *tr* to cause to totter; to shake, weaken; *(fig)* to cause to waver, shake; *(fig)* to undermine *(authority, power)*
labefactāti·ō -ōnis *f* loosening
labefact·ō -āre -āvī -ātus *tr* to shake, loosen, make unsteady; to undermine the authority of; to undermine *(loyalty, etc.)*
labe·fīō -fierī *pass of* **labefaciō**
labell·um -ī *n* cute lip
lābell·um -ī *n* small basin
labeōs·us -a -um *adj* thick-lipped
lāb·ēs -is *f* fall, falling down; stroke, blow; disaster; cause of disaster; blot, stain; blemish, defect; disgrace, discredit; *(geol)* subsidence, landslide; **lābem dare** to collapse
labi·a -ae *f and* **labi·um -ī** *n* (thick) lip; **aliquem labiīs ductāre** *(prov)* to lead s.o. by the nose
Labīcān·us -a -um *adj* of the town of Labici; **Via Labīcāna** a road entering Rome from the S.E. **||** *n* territory of the Labici
Labīc·ī -ōrum *mpl* small town about 15 miles S.E. of Rome **||** *mpl* the Labicans
Labiēn·us -a -um *adj* Roman clan name *(nomen), esp.* Titus Labienus *(Caesar's officer who defected to Pompey, d. 45 B.C.)*
labiōs·us -a -um *adj* thick-lipped
lab·ium -(i)ī *n and* **labi·a -ae** *f* (thick) lip
lab·ō -āre -āvī *intr* to totter, wobble; to waver, hesitate, be undecided; to fall to pieces, go to ruin
lābor lābī lāpsus sum *intr* to glide, slide, slip; to fall, sink; to slip away, disappear, escape; *(of time)* to slip by, pass; *(of liquids, rivers)* to flow; *(of the sun)* to sink down; *(of day)* to decline; *(of style)* to run smoothly; *(of words)* to slip out; *(of a building)* to collapse; *(fig)* to fade; *(fig)* to fall into error, go wrong; **memoriā lābī** to have a lapse of memory; **mente lābī** to go out of one's mind
lab·or *or* **lab·ōs -ōris** *m* effort, exertion; work, labor; trouble, distress, suffering; cause of distress; wear and tear; product of work, production; drudgery; **lūnae** *(or* **sōlis)** **labōrēs** eclipse of the moon *(or* sun)
labōrif·er -era -erum *adj* struggling, hard-working
labōriōs·us -a -um *adj* laborious; full of troubles, troublesome; energetic, industrious, hard-working
labōr·ō -āre -āvī -ātus *tr* to work at; to make by toil; to produce *(grain, etc.); (w. internal acc)* to be worried about, be concerned about, *e.g.:* **hoc hominēs timent,**

hoc labōrant people fear this, they are worried about this; **nihil labōrō dē iīs** I am not concerned about them; **nihil labōrō, nisi ut salvus sīs** my only concern is that you are O.K. *(literally, I am concerned as to nothing except that you be well)* ‖ *intr* to work, perform physical work; to suffer, be troubled; to exert oneself; *(w. abl of cause or* **ab** *or* **ex)** **1** to suffer *(physical pain)* from, *e.g.:* **(ā) stomachō** *(or* **ex stomachō)** **labōrāre** to have stomach trouble; **ē dolōre labōrāre** to suffer pain; **ē rēnibus labōrāre** to have kidney problems; **labōrantēs uterō puellae** pregnant girls, girls in labor *(i.e., in giving birth);* **2** to be distressed at, be anxious about, be worried about, be in trouble because of: **labōrat dē aestimātiōne suā** he is anxious *or* worried about his reputation; **ex aere aliēnō labōrāre** to be heavily in debt, be in trouble because of debt; **ē dolōre labōrāre** to be afflicted with grief; **ex īnscientiā labōrāre** to suffer from ignorance; **cūius manū sit percussus, nōn labōrō** I do not concern myself about whose hand struck him; *(w.* **in** *+ abl)* **1** to be in trouble over, be in danger because of, *e.g.:* **in rē familiārī valdē labōrāre** to be in deep trouble over personal finances, be in deep financial trouble; **2** to take pains with, exert oneself on behalf of, *e.g.:* **multō plūs est in reliquā causā labōrandum** much greater pains must be taken with the rest of the case *or* lawsuit; *(w.* **in** *+ acc)* to strive for, work for, *e.g.:* **in dīvitiās luxuriamque labōrāre** to strive for wealth and luxury; *(w. inf or* **ut** *+ subj)* to strive to, try to, take pains to, make an effort to, *e.g.:* **labōrābat ut reliquās cīvitātēs adiungeret** he tried to annex the rest of the communities; *(w.* **dē** *+ abl)* to be anxious about, be worried about; **lūna labōrat** *(astr)* the moon is in eclipse; **silvae labōrantēs** the groaning forests; **suīs labōrantibus succurrere** to help his own people in difficulty

labōs *see* **labor**

lābr·um -ī *n* basin, tub, bathtub

labr·um -ī *n* lip; edge

labrūsc·a -ae *f* wild vine

labrūsc·um -ī *n* wild grape

labyrinthē·us -a -um *adj* labyrinthine

labyrinth·us -ī *m* labyrinth, maze *(esp. that built by Daedalus on Crete)*

lac lactis *n* milk; milky sap of plants

Lacaen·a -ae *f* Spartan woman

Lacedaem·ō(n) -onis *f* Sparta

Lacedaemōni·us -a -um *adj* Spartan

lac·er -era -erum *adj* mangled, lacerated; *(of things)* badly damaged

lacerāti·ō -ōnis *f* laceration, tearing, mangling

lacern·a -ae *f* mantle, cloak

lacernāt·us -a -um *adj* cloaked, wearing a cloak

lacer·ō -āre -āvī -ātus *tr* to lacerate, tear, mangle; to batter, damage; to rack *(w. pain);* to slander, abuse; to waste *(time);* to wreck *(a ship); (fig)* to murder *(a song, speech)*

lacert·a -ae *f* lizard *(female)*

lacertōs·us -a -um muscular

lacert·us -ī *m* lizard; upper arm

lacert·us -a -um *adj* muscular ‖ *m* upper arm; muscle; lizard ‖ *mpl* muscles, brawn ‖ *f* lizard *(female)*

lacess·ō -ere -īvī *or* **-iī -ītus** *tr* to provoke, exasperate; to challenge; to move, arouse

Laches·is -is *f* one of the three Fates

lacini·a -ae *f* flap *(of a garment)*

Lacīn·ium -(i)ī *n* promontory in Bruttium with a temple to Juno

Lac·ō(n) -ōnis *m* Spartan; Spartan dog

Lacōni·a -ae *f* district of the Peloponnesus of which Sparta was the chief city

Lacōnic·us -a -um *adj* Spartan ‖ *n* sweat bath, sauna

lacrim·a -ae *f* **(-rum-)** tear(drop); *(bot)* gumdrop *(from plant)* ‖ *fpl* tears; dirge

lacrimābil·is -is -e *adj* worthy of tears, deplorable

lacrimābund·us -a -um *adj* tearful, about to break into tears

lacrim·ō -āre -āvī -ātus *tr* **(-rum-)** to cry for, shed tears over ‖ *intr* to cry, shed tears

lacrimōs·us -a -um *adj* crying, tearful; causing tears, bringing tears to the eyes

lacrimul·a -ae *f* teardrop, little tear; *(fig)* crocodile tear

lacrum- = **lacrim-**

lact·āns -antis *adj* milk-giving

lactāri·us -a -um *adj* milky

lact·ēns -entis *adj* unweaned, still breast-feeding; milky, juicy, tender; full of milk ‖ *m* suckling

lacteol·us -a -um *adj* milk-white

lact·ēs -ium *fpl* small intestines; *(as a dish)* chitterlings; **laxae lactēs** empty stomach

lactēsc·ō -ere *intr* to turn to milk

lacte·us -a -um *adj* milky, full of milk; milk-colored, milk-white; **lacteus orbis** *or* **lactea via** the Milky Way

lact·ō -āre -āvī -ātus *tr* to cajole, induce

lactūc·a -ae *f* lettuce

lacūna -ae *f* ditch, hole, pit; pond, pool; *(fig)* hole, gap

lacūn·ar -āris *n* paneled ceiling

lacūn·ō -āre -āvī -ātus *tr* to panel

lacūnōs·us -a -um *adj* sunken; pitted

lac·us -ūs *m* vat; tank, pool, reservoir, cistern; lake

lae·dō -dere -sī -sus *tr* to knock, strike; to hurt; to rub open; to wound; to break *(promise, pledge);* to harm *(reputation,*

interests); to offend, outrage, violate; *(w.* **ad)** to smash *(s.th.)* against; *(poet)* to mar
laen·a -ae *f* lined upper garment *(worn by the flamens and by persons of distinction)*
Lāërt·ēs -ae *m* father of Odysseus
laesī *perf of* **laedō**
laesi·ō -ōnis *f* attack, provocation
Laestrȳg·ōn -onis *or* **-onos** *m* Laestrygonian *(one of the mythical races of cannibals in Italy, founders of Formiae)*
Laestrȳgoni·us -a -um *adj* Laestrygonian, of Formiae
laes·us -a -um *pp of* **laedō** ‖ *adj* harmed; **rēs laesae** adversity
laetābil·is -is -e *adj* cheerful, glad
laet·āns -antis *adj* joyful, glad
laetāti·ō -ōnis *f* rejoicing, joy
laetē *adv* joyfully, gladly
Lāërt·ēs -ae *(acc:* **-ēn)** *m* father of Odysseus
Lāërtiad·ēs -ae *m* son of Laërtes *(Odysseus)*
laetific·āns -antis *adj* joyous
laetific·ō -āre -āvī -ātus *tr* to gladden, cheer up ‖ *pass* to rejoice
laetific·us -a -um *adj* joyful, cheerful
laetiti·a -ae *f* joyfulness, gladness, exuberance
laet·or -ārī -ātus sum *intr* to rejoice, be glad
laet·us -a -um *adj* glad, cheerful, rejoicing; happy; fortunate, auspicious; fertile, rich *(soil);* smiling *(grain);* sleek, fat *(cattle);* bright, cheerful *(appearance);* cheering, welcome *(news)*
laevē *adv* awkwardly
laev·us -a -um *adj* left, on the left side; awkward, stupid; ill-omened; lucky, propitious ‖ *f* left hand, left side ‖ *n* the left ‖ *npl* the area on the left
lagan·um -ī *n,* **lagan·us -ī** *m* pancake
lagēna *see* **lagoena**
lagē·os -ī *f* a Greek variety of vine
Lāgē·us -a -um *adj* of Lagus *(i.e., of the Ptolemies),* Egyptian
lagoen·a *or* **lagōn·a** *or* **lagēn·a** *or* **lagūn·a -ae** *f* bottle
lagō·is -idis *f* grouse
lagōna *see* **lagoena**
lagūna *see* **lagoena**
lagucul·a -ae *f* flask
Lāg·us -ī *m* Ptolemy I, King of Egypt
Lāïad·ēs -āe *m* son of Laius *(Oedipus)*
Lāï·us -ī *m* Laius *(father of Oedipus)*
lall·ō -āre *intr* to sing a lullaby
lām·a -ae *f* swamp, bog
lamber·ō -āre *tr* to tear to pieces
lamb·ō -ere -ī *tr* to lick, lap; *(of a river)* to lap, flow by; *(of ivy)* to cling to
lāment·a -ōrum *npl* lamentation
lāmentābil·is -is -e *adj* pitiable; doleful; mournful, sorrowful
lāmentāri·us -a -um *adj* sorrowful, pitiful
lāmentāti·ō -ōnis *f* lamentation
lāment·or -ārī -ātus sum *tr* to lament ‖ *intr* to lament, wail, cry
lami·a -ae *f* witch, sorceress
lāmin·a *or* **lammin·a** *or* **lāmn·a -ae** *f* plate, thin sheet *(of metal or wood);* blade; *(coll)* cash; peel, shell
lamp·as -adis *or* **-ados** *f* torch; brightness; light *(of the sun, moon, stars);* meteor; lamp; *(w. numerals)* day
Lam·us -ī *m* king of the Laestrygonians ‖ son of Hercules and Omphale
lān·a -ae *f* wool; working in wool, spinning; **lāna aurea** golden fleece; **lānam trahere** to card wool; **lānās dūcere** to spin wool; **rīxārī dē lānā caprīnā** *(prov)* to fight over nothing *(literally, to fight over goat wool)*
lānār·ius -(i)ī *m* wool worker
lānāt·us -a -um *adj* woolly ‖ *fpl* sheep
lance·a -ae *f* lance, spear
lancin·ō -āre -āvī -ātus *tr* to squander
lāne·us -a -um *adj* woolen; soft
langue·faciō -facere -fēcī -factus *tr* to make tired
langu·ēns -entis *adj* languid, drooping, listless
langu·eō -ēre *intr* to be tired, be weary; to be weak, be feeble *(from disease);* to be sick; *(fig)* to be listless; to be without energy; *(of water)* to be sluggish; *(of plants)* to droop, wilt
langu·ēscō -ēscere -uī *intr* to become weak, grow faint; to become listless; to decline, decrease; to relax
languidē *adv* weakly; slugglishly
languidul·us -a -um *adj* languid; wilted, drooping *(plants)*
languid·us -a -um *adj* weak, faint; weary; languid, sluggish; listless; lazy; drooping, wilting *(plants)*
langu·or -ōris *m* weakness, faintness, languor; listlessness, sluggishness; apathy; idleness
laniāt·us -ūs *m* mangling ‖ *mpl* mental anguish
laniēn·a -ae *f* butcher shop
lānific·ium -(i)ī *n* weaving
lānific·us -a -um *adj* spinning, weaving, of spinning, of weaving
lānig·er -era -erum *adj* fleecy ‖ *m* sheep *(ram)* ‖ *f* sheep *(ewe)*
lani·ō -āre -āvī -ātus *tr* to tear to pieces, mangle
lanist·a -ae *m* gladiator trainer, fencing master; *(pej)* ringleader
lānit·ium -(i)ī *n* wool
lan·ius -(i)ī *m* butcher; *(pej)* executioner, butcher
lantern·a -ae *f* **(lāt-)** lantern
lanternār·ius -(i)ī *m* guide
lānūg·ō -inis *f* down *(of plants, on cheeks)*
Lānuv·ium -(i)ī *n* town in Latium on the Appian Way

lān·x -cis *f* dish, platter; pan *(of a pair of scales);* **aequā lance** impartially
Lāöco·ōn -ontis *m* son of Priam and priest of Apollo, who, with his two sons, was killed by sea serpents
Lāömedontē·us *or* **Lāömedonti·us -a -um** *adj* Trojan
Lāömedontiad·ēs -ae *m* son of Laomedon (*Priam*) **ll** *mpl* Trojans
lapath·um -ī *n or* **lapath·us -ī** *f* sorrel *(plant)*
lapicīd·a -ae *m* stonecutter, quarry worker
lapicīdīn·ae -ārum *fpl* stone quarry
lapidāri·us -a -um *adj* stone; **lātomiae lapidāriae** stone quarry **ll** *m* stonecutter
lapidāti·ō -ōnis *f* throwing stones, stoning
lapidāt·or -ōris *m* stone thrower
lapide·us -a -um *adj* of stones, stone, stony; **lapideus imber** shower of meteoric stones; **lapideus sum** *(fig)* I am petrified
lapid·ō -āre -āvī -ātus *tr* to throw stones at, stone **ll** *v impers* it is raining stones
lapidōs·us -a -um *adj* full of stones, stony; hard as stone; gritty *(bread)*
lapill·us -ī *m* small stone, pebble; precious stone, gem; piece, counter *(in a game);* voting pebble
lap·is -idis *m* stone; milestone; platform; boundary stone, landmark; tombstone; precious stone, gem, pearl; stone statue; marble table; **lapidēs loquī** to speak harsh words
Lapith·ae -ārum *mpl* mountain tribe in Thessaly that fought the centaurs
lapp·a -ae *f* bur *(prickly head or seed vessel of certain plants)*
lāpsi·ō -ōnis *f* sliding, slipping; *(fig)* tendency
lāps·us -ūs *m* falling, fall, sliding, slipping, gliding, flow, flight; blunder, slip; fall from favor; lapse *(of time);* course *(of the stars);* **lāpsus rotārum** rolling wheels
laqueār·ia -ium *npl* paneled ceiling
laqueāt·us -a -um *adj* paneled, having a paneled ceiling
laque·us -ī *m* noose; snare; *(fig)* snare, trap **ll** *mpl* subtleties
Lār Laris *(gen plur:* **Larum** *or* **Larium)** *m* tutelary deity, household god; hearth, home **ll** *mpl* hearth, home, house, household, family
lard·um -ī *n* bacon
Lārenti·a -ae *f (also* **Acca Lārentia)** wife of Faustulus who reared Romulus and Remus
largē *adv* liberally, generously; in large numbers, in large quantities; to a great extent *or* degree
largific·us -a -um *adj* bountiful
largiflu·us -a -um *adj* gushing
largiloqu·us -a -um *adj* talkative
larg·ior -īrī -ītus sum *tr* to give generously, bestow freely; to lavish; to confer; to grant, concede; to condone, overlook; *(w. dat)* to overlook in favor of: **rogō ut amōrī nostrō plūsculum, quam concedat vēritās, largiāre** I beg you to overlook a little more than truth would allow, in favor of our affection (for each other) **ll** *intr* to give bribes, engage in bribery; *(of time, conditions)* to allow
largit·ās -ātis *f* generosity, bounty
largiti·ō -ōnis *f* generosity; bribery
largīt·or -ōris *m* generous donor; spendthrift; briber
larg·us -a -um *adj* abundant, plentiful, large, much; generous; bountiful, profuse
lārid·um -ī *n* bacon
Lāriss·a -ae *f* **(-rīs-)** town in Thessaly on the Peneus River, famous for its beauty
Lārissae·us -a -um *adj* **(-rīs-)** of Larissa
Lār·ius -(i)ī *m* Lake Como
Lar·s -tis *m* first name *(praenomen)* of Etruscan origin, *usu.* given to the eldest son
larv·a -ae *f* mask; ghost; *(pej)* devil
larvāt·us -a -um *adj* bewitched
lasan·um -ī *n or* **lasan·us -ī** *m* chamber pot
lāsarpīcif·er -era -erum *adj* producing asafetida *(used as an anti-spasmodic)*
lāscīvi·a -ae *f* frisking, playfulness; lewdness, sexual freedom; fun
lāscīvibund·us -a -um *adj* frisky
lāscīv·iō -īre -iī -ītum *intr* to frolic, be frisky; to run riot, run wild; to be in heat
lāscīv·us -a -um *adj* playful, frisky; brash, impudent; licentious, horny; luxuriant *(growth)*
lāserpīc·ium -(i)ī *n* silphium *(plant yielding asafetida, used as an anti-spasmodic)*
lassitūd·ō -inis *f* tiredness, lassitude
lass·ō -āre -āvī -ātus *tr* to tire out, exhaust
lassul·us -a -um *adj* somewhat tired
lass·us -a -um *adj* tired, exhausted
lātē *adv* widely, extensively; profusely; **lātē longēque** far and wide; **lātē patēre** to cover a wide field, have wide application
latebr·a -ae *f* hiding place, hideaway, hideout; *(fig)* loophole
latebricol·a -ae *mf* person who hangs around dives and brothels
latebrōsē *adv* secretly
latebrōs·us -a -um *adj* full of holes; hidden, secret; porous
lat·ēns -entis *adj* hidden, secret
latenter *adv* in secret
lat·eō -ēre -uī *intr* to hide, lie hidden; to lurk; to be out of sight, be invisible; to lie below the surface; to keep out of sight, sulk; to live a retired life, remain in obscurity, remain unknown; to escape notice; to be in safety; to avoid a summons, lie low; to be obscure; to take shelter

lat·er -eris *m* brick, tile; brickwork; **laterem lavāre** *(prov)* to waste effort *(literally, to wash sun-dried bricks of clay);* **laterēs dūcere** to make bricks

laterām·en -inis *n* earthenware

latercul·us -ī *m* small brick; tile; biscuit

laterici·us -a -um *adj* brick, of brick ‖ *n* brickwork

lātern·a -ae *f* **(lant-)** lantern

latēsc·ō -ere *intr* to hide

lat·ex -icis *m* liquid, fluid; water; spring; wine; oil

latibul·um -ī *n* hiding place, hideout, lair, den; *(fig)* refuge

lāticlāvi·us -a -um *adj* having a broad crimson stripe *(distinctive mark of senators, military tribunes of the equestrian order, and of sons of distinguished families)* ‖ *m* senator; nobleman

lātifund·ium -(i)ī *n* large estate, ranch

Latīnē *adv* Latin, in Latin; in proper Latin; in plain Latin; **Latīnē docēre** to teach Latin; **Latīnē loquī** to speak Latin; to speak correct Latin; *(coll)* to talk turkey; **Latīnē reddere** to translate Latin; **Latīnē scīre** to understand Latin

Latīnit·ās -ātis *f* pure Latin, Latinity; Latin rights and privileges

Latīn·us -a -um *adj* Latin; possessing Latin rights and privileges ‖ *m* Latinus *(king of Latium, who gave his daughter Lavinia in marriage to Aeneas)* ‖ *mpl* the Latins, people of Latium ‖ *f* Latin (language) ‖ *n* Latin (language); **in Latīnum convertere** to translate into Latin

lāti·ō -ōnis *f* bringing, rendering; formal proposal *(of a law);* **suffrāgiī lātiō** the franchise

latitāti·ō -ōnis *f* lying in concealment

latit·ō -āre -āvī *intr* to keep hiding oneself; to be concealed, hide, lurk; to lie low *(in order to avoid a summons)*

lātitūd·ō -inis *f* breadth, width; latitude; size, extent; wide area; richness of expression; **lātitūdō verbōrum** drawl; **in lātitūdine** *(or* **per lātitūdinem)** horizontally; **in lātitūdinem** in width

Lati·us -a -um *adj* of Latium, Latin, Roman ‖ *n* Latium *(district in W. central Italy, in which Rome is situated);* **iūs Latiī** *(or* **iūs Latium)** Latin political rights and privileges

lātius *adv* of late

Lātō·is -idis *f* daughter of Latona (*Diana*)

lātom- = lautom-

Lātōn·a -ae *f* mother of Apollo and Diana *(equated with the Greek goddess Leto)*

Lātōnigen·a -ae *mf* child of Latona (*Apollo, Diana*)

Lātōni·us -a -um *adj* of Latona ‖ *f* Diana

lāt·or -ōris *m* bringer, bearer; proposer *(of a law)*

Lātō·us -ī *m* son of Latona (*Apollo*)

lātrāt·or -ōris *m* barker; dog

lātrāt·us -ūs *m* barking

lātrīn·a -ae *f* washroom; toilet

lātr·ō -āre -āvī -ātus *tr* to bark at, snarl at ‖ *intr* to bark; *(fig)* to rant

latr·ō -ōnis *m* mercenary; robber, bandit, brigand; *(of animal or hunter)* predator; *(in chess)* pawn

latrōcin·ium -(i)ī *n* military service *(as a mercenary);* brigandage, banditry, vandalism, piracy; robbery, highway robbery; villany, outrage; band of robbers

latrōcin·or -ārī -ātus sum *intr* to serve as a mercenary; to be a bandit, be a pirate

latruncul·us -ī *m* small-time bandit; piece *(on a battle-game board)*

lātumi·ae -ārum *fpl* stone quarry; prison

lāt·us -a -um *adj* wide, broad; extensive; widespread; drawling *(pronunciation);* **in lātum** in width; **lātus clāvus** broad vertical crimson stripe on the tunic of men of the senatorial class

lat·us -eris *n* side, flank; body, person; lungs; lateral surface; coast; *(mil)* flank; **ā latere** *(mil)* on the flank; **ā latere** *(w. gen)* **1** at the side of, in the company of; **2** from among the friends of; **apertō latere** *(mil)* on the exposed flank; **in latus cubāre** to lie on one's side; **latere tēctō** scot-free; **latus dare** to expose oneself; **latus tegere** *(w. gen)* to walk by the side of, to escort

lātus *pp of* **ferō**

latuscul·um -ī *n* small side

laudābil·is -is -e *adj* laudable

laudābiliter *adv* laudably

laudāti·ō -ōnis *f* commendation; eulogy, panegyric, funeral oration; *(in court)* testimony by a character witness

laudāt·or -ōris *m* praiser; eulogist, panegyrist; *(leg)* character witness

laudāt·us -a -um *adj* praiseworthy, commendable, excellent

laud·ō -āre -āvī -ātus *tr* to praise, commend; to name, quote, cite; to pronounce the funeral oration over, eulogize

laure·a -ae *f* laurel tree; laurel branch; laurel crown, bay wreath; triumph

laureāt·us -a -um *adj* laureate, laureled, crowned with laurel; **litterae laureātae** communiqué announcing victory

Laur·ēns -entis *adj* Laurentian, of Laurentum

Laurent·ēs -um *mpl* Laurentians *(people of Laurentum, a town in Latium)*

Laurentīn·us *or* **Laurenti·us -a -um** *adj* Laurentian

laureol·a -ae *f* little laurel crown; triumph

laure·us -a -um *adj* laurel, of laurel ‖ *f see* **laurea**

lauricom·us -a -um *adj* laurel-covered *(mountain)*

laurif·er -era -erum *or* **laurig·er -era -erum** *adj* producing laurels; crowned with laurels

laur·us -ī *or* **-ūs** *f* laurel tree, bay; laurel branch; triumph

lau·s -dis *f* praise, commendation; fame, glory; reputation; approval; praiseworthy deed; merit, worth; **laus est** *(w. inf or* **ut** *w. subj)* it is praiseworthy to **II** *fpl* eulogy; praises; **laudibus ferre** *(or* **efferre** *or* **tollere) in** *(or* **ad) caelum** to praise to the skies

Laus·us -ī *m* son of Numitor and brother of Rhea Silvia **II** son of Mezentius, killed by Aeneas

lautē *adv* sumptuously, splendidly

lauti·a -ōrum *npl* state banquet *(given to foreign ambassadors and state guests)*

lautiti·a -ae *f* luxury, high living

lautumi·ae *or* **lātomi·ae** *or* **lātumi·ae -ārum** *fpl* stone quarry *(esp. used as a prison)*

laut·us -a -um *adj* expensive, elegant, fine; well-heeled; refined, fashionable

lavābr·um -ī *n* bath

lavāti·ō -ōnis *f* washing, bathing, bath; bathing kit

Lāvīni·us -a -um *adj* Lavinian, of Lavinium **II** *n* town in Latium founded by Aeneas **II** *f* wife of Aeneas

lav·ō lavāre *(or* **lavere) lāvī lautum** *(or* **lavātum** *or* **lōtum)** *tr* to wash, bathe; to wet, drench; to wash away **II** *refl & pass & intr* to wash, wash oneself, bathe

laxāment·um -ī *n* relaxation, respite, letup, mitigation

laxāt·us -a -um *adj* loose, extended *(e.g., ranks)*

laxē *adv* loosely, widely; freely

laxit·ās -ātis *f* roominess; extent, width; freedom of movement

lax·ō -āre -āvī -ātus *tr* to extend, widen, expand; to spread out, scatter; to open up *(passage, hole);* to undo; to loose *(bonds, bolts, doors);* to untie; to relax *(body, mind);* to slacken; to mitigate; *(fig)* to release, relieve; to unstring *(bow)* **II** *refl* to increase in size, spread out **II** *pass* to relax **II** *intr (of prices)* to go down

lax·us -a -um *adj* roomy, wide; loose, slack; prolonged, extended *(time);* far off, distant *(date);* low *(price);* loose-hanging *(clothes);* wide-open *(door);* gaping *(joints, holes); (fig)* relaxed, easygoing

le·a -ae *f* lioness

leaen·a -ae *f* lioness

Lēan·der -drī *m* youth of Abydos who swam across the Hellespont every night to his girlfriend

Learch·us -ī *m* son of Athamas and Ino, killed by his mad father

leb·ēs -ētis *m* cauldron

lectīc·a -ae *f* litter

lectīcār·ius -(i)ī *m* litter bearer

lectīcul·a -ae *f* small litter; small bier

lēcti·ō -ōnis *f* selection; reading, reading aloud; perusal; **lēctiō senātūs** revision of the Senate roll *(by censors)*

lectisterniāt·or -ōris *m* slave who arranged the seating at table

lectistern·ium -(i)ī *n* ritual feast *(at which images of the gods were placed on couches at the table)*

lēctit·ō -āre -āvī -ātus *tr* to read and reread; to like to read

lēctiuncul·a -ae *f* light reading

lēct·or -ōris *m* reader *(esp. a slave who read aloud to his master)*

lectul·us -ī *m* cot; small bed, small couch, settee; humble bier

lēct·us -a -um *pp of* **lēgo II** *adj* select, choice, special, elite

lect·us -ī *m* bed; couch; dining couch; bier; **lectus geniālis** marriage bed *(placed in the atrium)*

Lēd·a -ae *f* mother of Helen, Clytemnestra, Castor, and Pollux

lēgāti·ō -ōnis *f* embassy, mission, legation; members of an embassy; work *or* report of work of a mission; nominal staff appointment; command of a legion; **lēgātiō lībera** junket

lēgāt·um -ī *n* bequest, legacy

lēgāt·us -ī *m* deputy, representative; commander *(of a legion);* commander-in-chief; ambassador, envoy; adjutant *(of a consul, proconsul, or praetor);* **lēgātus Augustī** governor of an imperial province;

lēgī *perf of* **legō** (to read)

lēgif·er -era -erum *adj* lawgiving

legi·ō -ōnis *f* legion *(divided into 10 cohorts and numbering between 4,200 and 6,000 men);* army, active service

legiōnāri·us -a -um *adj* legionary **II** *m* legionary soldier

lēgirup·a -ae *or* **lēgirupi·ō -ōnis** *m* lawbreaker

lēgitimē *adv* legitimately, lawfully; properly

lēgitim·us -a -um *adj* legitimate; lawful; regular, right, just, proper; genuine; professional *(boxers, gladiators)* **II** *npl* legal formalities

legiuncul·a -ae *f* under-manned legion

lēg·ō -āre -āvī -ātus *tr* to commission; to send on a public mission, despatch; to delegate, deputize; to bequeath, will; *(fig)* to entrust

legō legere lēgī lēctus *tr* to read, peruse; to recite, read aloud; to gather, collect, pick; to pick out, choose; to pick one's way through, cross; to sail by, coast along; to pick up, steal; to pick up *(news, rumor);* **fīla legere** to wind up the thread of life; **senātum legere** to read off the Senate roll

lēgulē·ius -(i)ī *m* pettifogger

legūm·en -inis *n* leguminous plant; vegetable; pulse; bean

lemb·us -ī *m* cutter, yacht *(built for speed),* speedboat

lemm·a -atis *n* theme, subject matter; epigram

Lemnicol·a -ae *m* inhabitant of Lemnos *(i.e., Vulcan)*

lēmniscāt·us -a -um *adj* heavily decorated with combat ribbons

lēmnisc·us -ī *m* ribbon which hung down from a victor's wreath

Lemni·us -a -um *adj* Lemnian **||** *m* Lemnian *(i.e., Vulcan)* **||** *mpl* the people of Lemnos

Lemn·os *or* **Lemn·us -ī** *f* large island in the N. Aegean Sea

Lemur·ēs -um *mpl* ghosts

Lemūri·a -ōrum *npl* night festival, held on May 9th, 11th, 13th to drive ghosts from the house

lēn·a -ae *f* madame *(of brothel)*

Lēnae·us -a -um *adj* Bacchic; **laticēs Lēnaeī** wine **||** *m* Bacchus

lēnē *adv* gently

lēnīm·en -inis *n* consolation

lēnīment·um -ī *n* alleviation

lēn·iō -īre -īvī *or* **-iī -ītus** *tr* to soothe, alleviate, calm **||** *intr* to calm down

lēn·is -is -e *adj* mild, gentle, soft, smooth, calm; gentle *(slope);* weak, mild *(medicine);* quiet *(sleep);* mellow *(wine);* tolerable, moderate *(conditions);* kind *(person)*

lēnit·ās -ātis *f* mildness, gentleness, softness, smoothness; tenderness, clemency

lēniter *adv* mildly, gently, softly, smoothly; quietly, calmly; halfheartedly; *(of style)* smoothly

lēnitūd·ō -inis *f* mildness, gentleness, softness, smoothness

lēn·ō -ōnis *m* pimp, brothel keeper

lēnōcin·ium -(i)ī *n* pimping, pandering; allurement; alluring makeup; sexy clothes; flattery

lēnōcin·or -ārī -ātus sum *intr* to be a pimp; *(w. dat)* **1** to play up to, pander to; **2** to stimulate, promote

lēnōni·us -a -um *adj* pimp's

lēn·s -tis *f* lentil

lentē *adv* slowly; indifferently, half-heartedly; calmly, leisurely, deliberately

lentēsc·ō -ere *intr* to get sticky; *(fig)* to soften, weaken

lentīscif·er -era -erum *adj (of a region)* producing mastic trees

lentīsc·us -ī *f* mastic tree *(small evergreen tree that yields an aromatic resin called mastic);* toothpick *(made of mastic wood)*

lentitūd·ō -inis *f* slowness; insensibility, apathy, dullness

lent·ō -āre -āvī -ātus *tr* to bend *(under strain)*

lentul·us -a -um *adj* somewhat slow

lent·us -a -um *adj* sticky, clinging; pliant, limber; slow, sluggish; lingering; irresponsive, reluctant, indifferent, backward; slow-moving; tedious; at rest, at leisure, lazy; calm, unconcerned

lēnul·us -ī *m* little pimp

lēnuncul·us -ī *m* young pimp

lēnuncul·us -ī *m* small boat, skiff

le·ō -ōnis *m* lion **|| Leō** *(astr)* Leo *(constellation and sign of the zodiac)*

Leōnid·ās -ae *m* king of Sparta *(who fell at Thermopylae after a gallant stand in 480 B.C.)*

leōnīn·us -a -um *adj* lion's, of a lion

Leontīn·ī -ōrum *mpl* town in E. Sicily

lep·as -adis *f* limpet *(shellfish)*

lepidē *adv* charmingly, pleasantly, neatly; *(as affirmative answer)* yes; *(of approval)* great!

lepid·us -a -um *adj* charming, delightful, nice, neat; witty, amusing *(writings, remarks)*

lep·ōs *or* **lep·or -ōris** *m* pleasantness, charm, attractiveness

lep·us -oris *m* hare **|| Lepus** *(astr)* Lepus, the Hare *(constellation)*

lepūscul·us -ī *m* little hare

Lern·a -ae *f* marsh near Argos, where Hercules slew the Hydra

Lernae·us -a -um *adj* Lernaean

Lesbi·us -a -um *adj* of Lesbos, Lesbian **||** *f* fictitious name given by Catullus to his mistress Clodia **||** *n* Lesbian wine

Lesb·os *or* **Lesb·us -ī** *f* large island in the N. Aegean, birthplace of Alcaeus and Sappho

less·us *(gen does not occur; acc:* **lessum***)* *m* loud wailing

lētāl·is -is -e *adj* lethal, fatal, mortal

Lēthae·us -a -um *adj* of Lethe; infernal; causing drowsiness

lēthargic·us -ī *m* lazy fellow

lētharg·us -ī *m* lethargy

Lēth·ē -ēs *f* Lethe *(river of forgetfulness in lower world)*

lētif·er -era -erum *adj* deadly, fatal; **locus lētifer** mortal spot

lēt·ō -āre -āvī -ātus *tr* to kill

lēt·um -ī *n* death; ruin, destruction; **lētō dare** to put to death

Leuc·as -adis *f* "White Island," island off W. Greece

leucasp·is -idis *adj* armed with a white shield

Leucipp·us -ī *m* philosopher, teacher of Democritus, and one of the founders of Atomism *(5th cent. B.C.)*

Leuctr·a -ōrum *npl* small town in Boeotia where Epaminondas defeated the Spartans in 371 B.C.

levām·en -inis *n* alleviation, comfort, consolation
levāment·um -ī *n* alleviation, comfort, consolation
levāti·ō -ōnis *f* lightening, easing; relief, comfort; lessening, mitigation
levicul·us -a -um *adj* somewhat vain
levidēns·is -is -e *adj* poor, inferior
levifid·us -a -um *adj* untrustworthy
lev·is -is -e *adj* light, not heavy; light-armed; lightly dressed; easily digested; thin, poor *(soil);* nimble; flitting; slight, small; unimportant, trivial; unfounded *(rumor);* easy, simple; mild; gentle, easy-going; capricious, unreliable, fickle; lacking authority; lacking power; unsubstantial, thin; **in levī habēre** to make light of
lēv·is -is -e *adj* smooth; slippery; hairless, beardless; delicate, tender; effeminate; smooth *(style)*
levisomn·us -a -um *adj* light-sleeping
levit·ās -ātis *f* lightness; mobility, nimbleness; levity, frivolity; *(fig)* shallowness
lēvit·ās -ātis *f* smoothness; *(fig)* fluency
leviter *adv* lightly; slightly, a little, somewhat; easily, without difficulty; nimbly
lev·ō -āre -āvī -ātus *tr* to lift up, raise; to lighten, relieve, ease; to console, comfort; to lift off, remove; to lessen, weaken; to release, free; to take away; to avert; to restore, refresh
lēv·ō -āre -āvī -ātus *tr* to make smooth, polish; to soothe
lēv·or -ōris *m* smoothness
lēx lēgis *f* motion, bill; law, statute; rule, regulation; principle, precept; condition, stipulation; **ad lēgem** neatly; **eā lēge ut** with the stipulation that, on condition that; **lēge** *(or* **lēgibus)** legally; **lēge agere** to go to court, take legal action; **lēgem abrogāre** to repeal a law; **lēgem dērogāre** to amend a bill *or* law; **lēgem ferre** to propose a bill; **lēgem iubēre** *(of the assembly)* to sanction a law; **lēgem perferre** to get a bill *or* law passed; **lēgēs** constitution; **lēgēs pācis** terms of peace; **sine lēgibus** without restraint, without control
lībām·en -inis *n* libation; firstfruits
lībāment·um -ī *n* libation; firstfruits
lībāti·ō -ōnis *f* libation
lībell·a -ae *f* small silver coin, one tenth of a denarius *(c. 10¢);* small sum; *(carpenter's)* level; **ad lībellam** to a tee, exactly; **hērēs ex lībellā** heir to one tenth of the estate
libell·us -ī *m* booklet, pamphlet; notebook; journal, diary; program; handbill, advertisement; petition; answer to a petition; letter; written accusation, indictment; libel; satirical verse
lib·ēns -entis *adj* **(lub-)** willing, ready, glad; merry, cheerful; **libentī animō** willingly
libenter *adv* **(lub-)** willingly, gladly, with pleasure
li·ber -brī *m* book, work, treatise; catalog, list, register; letter, rescript; bark *(of a tree)*
līb·er -era -erum *adj* free; open, unoccupied; unrestricted; unprejudiced; outspoken, frank; uncontrolled, unrestricted; *(of states or municipalities)* independent, autonomous; exempt; free of charge; *(w. abl or* **ab)** free from, exempt from; *(w. gen)* free of **‖** *mpl see* **līberī**
Līb·er -erī *m* Italian fertility god, later identified with Bacchus; wine
Līber·a -ae *f* Proserpina **‖** Ariadne *(the wife of Bacchus)*
Līberāl·ia -ium *npl* festival of Liber *(held on March 17, at which young men received the toga virilis)*
līberāl·is -is -e *adj* relating to freedom, relating to civil status, of free citizens; worthy of a freeman, honorable, gentleman's; courteous; liberal, generous; handsome
līberālit·ās -ātis *f* courtesy, politeness; liberality, generosity; grant, gift
līberāliter *adv* like a freeman, nobly; liberally *(e.g., educated);* courteously; liberally, generously
līberāti·ō -ōnis *f* liberation, freeing; release *(from debt); (leg)* acquittal
līberāt·or -ōris *m* liberator
līberē *adv* freely; frankly; ungrudgingly; like a freeman, liberally
līber·ī -ōrum *or* **-um** *mpl* children; sons; **iūs trium līberōrum** a privileged status granted by the *Lex Papia Poppaea* of A.D. 9 to fathers of three or more children *(occasionally extended to others)*
līber·ō -āre -āvī -ātus *tr* to free, set free, release; to acquit; to cancel, get rid of *(e.g., debts);* to pay for, cover *(an expense);* to exempt; to manumit; to cross *(threshold);* to draw *(a sword);* to clear *(positions of hostile forces); (w. abl or w.* **ab** *or* **ex)** to free from, release from, acquit of; **fidem līberāre** to keep one's promise; **nōmina līberāre** to cancel debts; **prōmissa līberāre** to fulfill promises **‖** *refl* to pay up a debt
lībert·a -ae *f* freedwoman, ex-slave
lībert·ās -ātis *f* liberty, freedom; status of a freeman; political freedom; freedom of speech, freedom of thought; frankness
lībertīn·us -a -um *adj* of the status of a freedman **‖** *m* freedman, ex-slave **‖** *f* freedwoman, ex-slave
lībert·us -ī *m* freedman, ex-slave
lib·et -ēre -uit *or* **libitum est** *v impers* **(lub-)** *(w. dat)* it pleases, it is pleasant for,

is agreeable to, is nice for *(s.o.)*; *(w. inf)* it is nice, pleasant to *(do s.th.)*; **mihi libet** I feel like, want; **quī libet** any you like to mention; **sī lubet** if you please; **ut lubet** as you please
libīdin·or -ārī -ātus sum *intr* to gratify lust
libīdinōsē *adv* willfully; arbitrarily
libīdinōs·us -a -um *adj* **(lub-)** willful; arbitrary; lustful, lecherous
libīd·ō -inis *f* **(lub-)** desire, longing, inclination, pleasure; will, willfulness, arbitrariness, caprice, fancy; lust, sexual desire; rut, heat; **ad** *(or* **per)** **libīdinem** *(w. gen)* at the pleasure of; **ex libīdine** arbitrarily; **libīdinem habēre in** *(w. abl)* to be fond of, take pleasure in
libīt·a -ōrum *npl* will, pleasure
Libitīn·a -ae *f* burial goddess; implements for burial; grave; death
līb·ō -āre -āvī -ātus *tr* to taste, sip; to pour as a libation, offer, consecrate; to touch lightly, barely touch, graze; to spill, waste; to extract, collect, compile
lībr·a -ae *f* balance, scales; plummet, level; pound *(of 12 ounces)*
lībrāment·um -ī *n* weight; balance, ballast; level surface, horizontal plane; gravity
lībrāri·a -ae *f* forelady *(who weighed out wool for slaves to spin)*
librāriol·us -ī *m* copyist, scribe
librāri·us -a -um *adj* book, of books; **taberna librāria** bookstore **‖** *m* copyist, scribe, secretary; bookseller **‖** *n* bookcase
lībrāri·us -a -um *adj* weighing a pound
lībrāt·or -ōris *m* surveyor
lībrāt·us -a -um *adj* horizontal, level; poised; well-aimed
lībrīl·is -is -e *adj* one-pound
lībrit·or -ōris *m* artilleryman
lībr·ō -āre -āvī -ātus *tr* to balance; to poise, level, hurl, launch; to sway
līb·um -ī *n or* **līb·us -ī** *m* cake *(usu. used in sacrficial offerings)*; **lībum nātāle** birthday cake
Liburni·a -ae *f* district of Illyria between Istria and Dalmatia
Liburn·us -a -um *adj* Liburnian **‖** *mf* Liburnian **‖** *f* Liburnian galley
Liby·a -ae *or* **Liby·ē -ēs** *f* Libya *(general term for all of N. Africa)*
Libyc·us -a -um *adj* Libyan, N. African
Lib·ys -yos *adj* of N. Africa, N. African **‖** *m* N. African
Libyss·us -a -um *adj* N. African
Libystīn·us *or* **Liby·us -a -um** *adj* Libyan; N. African
Libyst·is -idis *adj (fem only)* N. African
lic·ēns -entis *adj* free, unrestrained; licentious; forward, pushy, bold
licenter *adv* freely, without restraint; licentiously; boldly
licenti·a -ae *f* license, freedom; unruly behavior, lawlessness; outspokenness; licentiousness; free imagination; *(w. gen of gerund)* freedom to *(do s.th.)*; **lūdendī licentia** (unrestricted) freedom to play
lic·eō -ēre -uī *intr* to be for sale; *(w. abl or gen of price)* to cost, fetch
lic·eor -ērī -itus sum *tr* to bid on, bid for, make an offer for **‖** *intr* to bid
lic·et -ēre -uit *or* **-itum est** *v impers* it is permitted, it is lawful; *(w. dat & inf)* it is all right for *(s.o.)* to; **licet** *(to express assent)* yes, O.K.; **mihi licet** I may, I can *(often w. neut. pron as subject)*: **sī tibi hoc licitum est** if you are allowed to do this; *(w. the force of a conjunction, w. subj)* although, granting that
Lich·ās -ae *m* companion of Hercules
līch·ēn -ēnos *m* lichen *(resin used to cure skin diseases)*; ringworm *(a skin disease)*
licitāti·ō -ōnis *f* bidding *(at auction)*; haggling
licitāt·or -ōris *m* bidder
licit·or -ārī -ātus sum *tr* to bid for
licit·us -a -um *adj* permissible, lawful, legitimate **‖** *n* lawful action
lict·or -ōris *m* lictor *(attendant and bodyguard of a magistrate)*
li·ēn -ēnis *m* spleen
liēnōs·us -a -um *adj* splenetic
ligām·en -inis *n* string, tie; bandage
ligāment·um -ī *n* bandage
lignār·ius -(i)ī *m* carpenter
lignāti·ō -ōnis *f* gathering of lumber
lignāt·or -ōris *m* woodcutter, lumberjack
ligneol·us -a -um *adj* wooden
ligne·us -a -um *adj* wooden; woody; tough, wiry *(person)*
lign·or -ārī -ātus sum *intr* to gather wood
lign·um -ī *n* wood; *(also pl)* firewood *(as opp. to* **māteria** = lumber for building); stump; log, plank; writing tablet; tree; stone *(of olive, fruit)*; *(various objects made of wood)*: spear-shaft, money box, writing tablet, wooden mask, boat; **in silvam ligna ferre** *(prov)* to carry coals to Newcastle *(literally, to carry logs into the woods)*; **mōbile lignum** puppet
lig·ō -āre -āvī -ātus *tr* to tie, tie up, bandage; to close *(a deal)*; to draw tight, knot; to cement *(an alliance)*; to unite in harmony; *(w. dat or* **ad)** to tie to
lig·ō -ōnis *m* mattock, hoe; farming
ligul·a *or* **lingul·a -ae** *f* shoe strap; flap; *(geog)* tongue of land
Lig·ur *or* **Lig·us -uris** *mf* Ligurian
ligū(r)rīti·ō -ōnis *f* constant hankering for food
Liguri·a -ae *f* Liguria *(district along the N.W. coast of Italy)*
ligūr(r)·iō -īre -īvī *or* **-iī -ītus** *tr* to lick; to pick at, eat daintily; *(fig)* to be dying for; *(fig)* to sponge on
Ligus *see* **Ligur**

Ligusc·us *or* **Ligustic·us** *or* **Ligustīn·us -a -um** *adj* Ligurian
ligustr·um -ī *n (bot)* privet *(widely used for hedges)*
līl·ium -(i)ī *n (bot)* lily; *(mil)* trench lined with sharp stakes
līm·a -ae *f* file; *(fig)* revision, polishing; **līmae labor** *(fig)* the work of polishing
līmātius *adv* in a more polished style
līmātul·us -a -um *adj* refined, sensitive *(judgment)*
līm·āx -ācis *mf* snail
limbulāri·us -a -um *adj* hem; **textōrēs limbulāriī** tassel makers, hemmers
limb·us -ī *m* fringe, hem, tassel
līm·en -inis *n* lintel, threshold; doorway, entrance; outset, beginning; starting gate *(at racetrack)*; house, home
līm·es -itis *m* country trail; path; road along a boundary; boundary, frontier; *(fig)* limit; boundary marker; channel *(of river)*; course *(of life)*; track, trail *(of a shooting star)*; line of color, streak
līm·ō -āre -āvī -ātus *tr* to file; *(fig)* to polish, refine; to file down, take away from, lessen; to get down to *(the truth)*
līmōs·us -a -um *adj* muddy; growing in mud
limpid·us -a -um *adj* limpid, clear
līmul·us -a -um *adj* squinting
līm·us -a -um *adj* squinting; sidelong
līm·us -ī *m* ceremonial apron *(trimmed with purple and worn by priests at sacrifice)*
līm·us -ī *m* mud; dirt, grime
līne·a -ae *f* line; string, thread; fishing line; plumb line; outline; boundary line, limit; **ad līneam** *(or* **rēctā līneā)** in a straight line; vertically; horizontally; **extrēmā līneā amāre** to love at a distance; **līneās trānsīre** to go out of bounds
līneāment·um -ī *n* line; characteristic, feature; outline ‖ *npl* lineaments, lines *(of the face)*
līne·ō -āre -āvī -ātus *tr* to make straight, make perpendicular
līne·us -a -um *adj* flaxen, linen
lingō lingere līnxī līnctus *tr* to lick; to lap up
lingu·a -ae *f* tongue; speech, language, dialect; eloquence; utterance; style *(of s.o.'s speech)*; *(of animals)* note, song, bark; *(geog)* tongue of land; **favēte linguīs**! observe a sacred silence!; **linguam comprimere** *(or* **tenēre)** to hold one's tongue; **linguā prōmptus** insolent, cheeky; **utraque lingua** both languages *(Greek and Latin)*
lingul·a -ae *f* shoe strap; flap; *(geog)* tongue of land
lingulāc·a -ae *mf* gossip, chatterbox
līnig·er -era -erum *adj* wearing linen
linō linere lēvī *or* **līvī litus** *tr* to smear; to erase; to cover, coat; *(fig)* to mess up
linquō linquere līquī *tr* to leave, forsake; to depart from; to leave alone; to leave in a pinch ‖ *pass* to faint; **animō linquī** to faint ‖ *v impers* **linquitur** *(w.* **ut)** it remains to *(do s.th.)*
linteātus -a -um *adj* canvas
linte·ō -ōnis *f* linen-weaver
linteol·um -ī *n* small linen cloth
lin·ter -tris *f* skiff; vat, tank
linte·us -a -um *adj* linen ‖ *n* linen; linen cloth; canvas, sail; kerchief
lintricul·us -ī *m* small boat
līn·um -ī *n* flax; linen; thread; rope, line; fishing line; net; linen dress
Lin·us *or* **Lin·os -ī** *m* son of Apollo and instructor of Orpheus and Hercules
Lipar·a -ae *or* **Lipar·ē -ēs** *f* Lipara *(island off the N. coast of Sicily)* ‖ *fpl* the Aeolian Islands (*modern Lipari Islands*)
Liparae·us -a -um *or* **Liparēns·is -is -e** *adj* of Lipara
lipp·iō -īre -īvī *or* **-iī -ītum** *intr* to have sore eyes; *(of eyes)* to burn
lippitūd·ō -inis *f* running eyes, inflammation of the eyes
lipp·us -a -um *adj* with sore eyes; burning *(eyes)*; *(fig)* half-blind
liquām·en -inis *n* fish sauce
lique·faciō -facere -fēcī -factus *(pass:* **lique·fīō -fierī -factus sum)** *tr* to melt, dissolve; to decompose; to waste, weaken
liqu·ēns -entis *adj* clear, limpid; flowing, gliding
liqueō liquēre liquī *or* **licuī** *intr* to be liquid; to be clear ‖ *v impers* it is clear, is apparent, is evident; **liquet mihi** *(w. inf)* I am free to; **nōn liquet** *(leg)* it is not clear *(legal formula used by a hung jury)*
liquēscō liquēscere licuī *intr* to melt; to decompose; to grow soft, grow effeminate; to become clear; *(fig)* to melt away
liquidē *adv* clearly
liquidiuscul·us -a -um *adj* gentler
liquidō *adv* clearly, plainly, certainly
liquid·us -a -um *adj* liquid, fluid, flowing; clear, transparent; evident; pure *(pleasure)*; clear *(voice)*; calm *(mind)* ‖ *n* liquid, water; clearness, certainty
liqu·ō -āre -āvī -ātus *tr* to melt, dissolve; to strain, filter
līqu·or -ī *intr* to flow; to melt; *(fig)* to waste away; **in lacrimās līquī** to dissolve into tears
liqu·or -ōris *m* fluidity; liquid, fluid; sea
Līr·is -is *m* river between Latium and Campania
līs lītis *f (old form:* **stlīs stlītis)** matter of dispute; quarrel, dispute; wrangling; *(leg)* lawsuit, litigation; *(leg)* charge, accusation; **līs capitis** criminal charge; **lītem aestimāre** *(or* **taxāre)** to assess damages; **lītem intendere** *(or* **lītem īnferre)** *(w. dat)* to bring a suit against, sue *(s.o.)*

litāti·ō -ōnis *f* successful sacrifice *(i.e., obtaining of favorable omens from a sacrifice)*

litātō *adv* with favorable omens

lītera *see* **littera**

Lītern·um -ī *n* town on the coast of Campania

litic·en -inis *m* trumpeter

lītigāt·or -ōris *m (leg)* litigant

lītigiōs·us -a -um *adj* litigious; quarrelsome; disputed

lītig·ium -(i)ī *n* quarrel, dispute

lītig·ō -āre -āvī -tum *intr* to squabble; *(leg)* to go to court

lit·ō -āre -āvī -ātus *tr* to propitiate; to offer by way of atonement; to atone for; **litandum est** atonement must be made ‖ *intr* to obtain favorable omens from a sacrifice; *(of a sacrifice)* to give favorable omens; *(w. dat)* to appease, propitiate

lītorāl·is -is -e *adj* shore, of the shore

lītore·us -a -um *adj* at *or* along the seashore

litter·a *or* **līter·a -ae** *f* letter *(of the alphabet);* handwriting; **ad litteram** verbatim; **littera salūtāris** *(leg) (i.e.,* **A** = **absolvō)** vote of acquittal; **littera tristis** *(leg) (i.e.,* **C** = **condemnō)** vote of guilty ‖ *fpl* epistle, letter, dispatch; edict, ordinance; literature, books, literary works; book learning, liberal education, scholarship; branch of learning; records, account; inscription; **in litterās dīgerere** to arrange in alphabetical order; **litterās discere** to learn to read and write; **litterās scīre** to know how to read and write, be literate

litterāri·us -a -um *adj* of reading and writing; **lūdus litterārius** elementary school

litterātē *adv* legibly, in a clear handwriting; literally; learnedly

litterāt·or -ōris *m* elementary-school teacher, schoolmaster

litterātūr·a -ae *f* writing; alphabet; grammar; writings, literature

litterāt·us -a -um *adj* learned, scholarly; liberally educated; devoted to literature; *(of time)* devoted to studies; marked *or* inscribed with letters ‖ *m* man of culture; teacher of literature; scholar

litterul·a -ae *f* small letter ‖ *fpl* short letter, note; slight literary endeavors; ABC's

litūr·a -ae *f* erasure; erased passage; correction; smudge, smear

līt·us -oris *n* seashore, beach, coast; riverbank; **lītus arāre** *(prov)* to waste effort *(literally, to plow the shore)*

litus *pp of* **linō**

litu·us -ī *m* cavalry trumpet, clarion; *(fig)* signal; augur's wand *(a crooked staff carried by an augur);* **lituus meae profectiōnis** signal for my departure

līv·ēns -entis *adj* livid; black-and-blue

līv·eō -ēre *intr* to be black-and-blue, be livid; to be envious; *(w. dat)* to be jealous of

līvēsc·ō -ere *intr* to turn black-and-blue

Līvi·a -ae *f* second wife of Augustus and mother of Tiberius and Drusus (58 B.C.–A.D. 29)

līvidul·us -a -um *adj* inclined to be jealous, somewhat envious

līvid·us -a -um *adj* leaden *(in color);* blue; black-and-blue; jealous, envious, spiteful

Līv·ius -(i)ī *m* Livy *(Titus Livius Patavinus, historian, 58 B.C.–A.D. 17)* ‖ Livius Andronicus *(a Greek who was the first to write Latin poetry, both tragedies and comedies; his first drama was staged in 240 B.C.; he also translated the Odyssey into Saturnian verse)*

līv·or -ōris *m* leaden color; bluish color; black-and-blue mark; jealousy, envy, spite

lix·a -ae *m* peddler *(around a camp),* camp follower

locār·ius -(i)ī *m* ticket broker, scalper *(one who buys up theater seats as an investment)*

locāti·ō -ōnis *f* arrangement, placement; renting out, contract, lease

locāt·or -ōris *m* lessor

locāt·um -ī *n* lease, contract

locell·us -ī *m* small box

locit·ō -āre *tr* to lease out

loc·ō -āre -āvī -ātus *tr* to place, put, set, lay; to establish, constitute, set; to lay *(foundations);* to station *(troops);* to rent out, lease; to contract for; to invest *(effort);* to lend at interest; to farm out *(taxes);* **locāre in mātrimōnium** *(or* **nūptiīs** *or* **nūptum)** *(w. dat)* to give in marriage *(to s.o.)*

locul·us -ī *m* little place, spot; pocket; drawer

locupl·ēs -ētis *adj* rich; *(w. abl)* rich in, well supplied with; reliable, responsible; **locuplēs ōrātiōne** *(or* **in dīcendō) esse** to be a polished speaker

locuplēt·ō -āre -āvī -ātus *tr* to make rich, enrich; to embellish *(a building)*

loc·us -ī *(pl:* **loc·ī -ōrum** *mpl* passages, verses; **loc·a -ōrum** *npl* physical places) *m* place; site; spot; locality, district; seat; town, village; period (of time); opportunity, room, occasion; situation, position; category; rank, degree, birth; office, post; passage *(in a book);* topic, subject, point, division; *(mil)* post, station; *(in astrology)* house; **adhūc locōrum** until now; **ad id locōrum** until then; **ex aequō locō dīcere** to speak in the Senate; to hold a conversation; **ex** *(or* **dē) locō superiōre dīcere** to speak from the Rostra; **ex locō īnferiōre dīcere** to speak before a judge, speak in court; **inde locī** since then; **in eō**

locī in such a condition; **in locum** *(w. gen)* in place of, as a substitute for, instead of; **intereā locī** meanwhile; **loca** *(vulg)* female genitals; **locī commūnēs** general topics; public places, parks; **locō** *(w. gen)* in stead of, in place of; **locō** *(or* **in locō)** at the right time; on the spot; **locō cēdere** to give way, yield; **locō movēre** to dislodge; to dislocate *(a limb);* **locum dare** to make way; **locum habēre** to be valid, be applicable, hold good; **locum facere** to clear the way; **locum mūtāre** to change one's residence, move; **locus pūblicus** public building, public square; **mentem (meam, tuam, ēius) locō movēre** *(or* **pellere)** to drive (me, you, him) out of (my, your, his) mind; **nullō locō** under no circumstances; **posteā locī** afterwards; **post id locōrum** afterwards; **stare locō** to stand still; **ubicumque locī** whenever

lōcust·a -ae *f* locust

Lōcust·a -ae *f* **(Lūc-)** woman notorious as poisoner in the time of Claudius and Nero

locūti·ō -ōnis *f* speech; way of speaking; expression; word; pronunciation

locūtus *pp of* **loquor**

lōd·īx -īcis *f* blanket

logic·us -a -um *adj* logical **||** *npl* logic

log·os *or* **log·us -ī** *m* word; witticism **||** *mpl* mere words, empty talk

lōlīgō *see* **lollīgō**

lol·ium -(i)ī *n* darnel *(type of grass)*

lollīg·ō -inis *f* **(lōl-)** squid

lollīguncul·a -ae *f* small squid

lōment·um -ī *n* a face cream *(for cleansing skin)*

Londīn·ium -(i)ī *n* London

longaev·us -a -um *adj* aged

longē *adv* far, far off, a long way off; away, distant; out of reach; long, for a long period; *(to speak)* at greater length; *(w. comparatives)* far, by far, much; **longē lātēque** far and wide

longinquit·ās -ātis *f* length, extent; remoteness, distance; length, duration

longinqu·us -a -um *adj* long, extensive; far off, distant, remote; from afar, foreign; long, prolonged, continued, tedious; **e(x) longinquō** from far away; **in longinquō** far away

longitūd·ō -inis *f* length; **in longitūdinem 1** lengthwise, in length; **2** to an immoderate length, too far; **3** for the distant future; **longitūdine** *(or* **per longitūdinem)** lengthwise

longiūscul·us -a -um *adj* pretty long

longur·ius -(i)ī *m* long pole

long·us -a -um *adj* long; spacious; tall *(person);* protracted; tedious; **longa nāvis** battleship; **longum est** *(w. inf)* it would take too long to **||** *n* length; **in** *(or* **per)** **longum** for a long while; **nē longum faciam** to make a long story short

loquācit·ās -ātis *f* talkativeness

loquāciter *adv* long-windedly; at length, in detail

loquācul·us -a -um *adj* rather talkative

loqu·āx -ācis *adj* loquacious, talkative

loquēl·a -ae *f* **(-quell-)** speech; word, expression

loqu·ēns -entis *adj* articulate

loquit·or -ārī -ātus sum *intr* to chatter away

loquor loquī locūtus sum *tr* to say; to talk of, speak about; to tell, tell of, mention; *(fig)* to declare, show, indicate **||** *intr* to speak; to rustle, murmur; **Latīnē loquī** to speak Latin; *(coll)* to talk turkey; **male loquī** to speak abusively

lōrār·ius -(i)ī *m* slave driver

lōrāt·us -a -um *adj* tied with thongs

lōre·us -a -um *adj* made of strips of leather; **vostra faciam latera lōrea** *(coll)* I'll cut your hide to ribbons

lōrīc·a -ae *f* breastplate; parapet; **librōs mūtāre lōrīcīs** to exchange books for arms

lōrīcāt·us -a -um *adj* wearing a breastplate, mail-clad

lōrip·ēs -edis *adj* bowlegged

lōr·um -ī *n* strip of leathter, thong, strap; dog's leash; whip, scourge; leather badge **||** *npl* reins

Lōt·is -idis *f* a nymph who changed into a lotus tree to escape the advances of Priapus

Lōtophag·ī -ōrum *mpl* Lotus-eaters

lōt·os *or* **lōt·us -ī** *f* lotus *(fabulous plant bringing forgetfulness to those who eat its fruit);* flute *(of lotus wood)*

lōtus *see* **lautus**

Lu·a -ae *f* cult partner of Saturn *(to whom captured arms were dedicated)*

lub- = lib-

lubenti·a -ae *f* pleasure

lūbric·ō -āre -āvī -ātus *tr* to oil, grease, make smooth

lūbric·us -a -um *adj* slippery; smooth; slimy; *(of streams)* gently flowing, gliding; deceitful, tricky; precarious, ticklish *(situations, undertakings)* **||** *n* precarious situation, critical period; unstable condition; **in lūbricō pōnī** to be placed in a dangerous situation; **in lūbrīcō versārī** to be in a precarious situation

Lūc·a bōs *(gen:* **Lūc·ae bovis)** *f* elephant

Lūcāni·a -ae *f* district in S.W. Italy

Lūcān·us -a -um *adj* Lucanian **||** *m* Lucanian **||** Lucan *(Marcus Annaeus Lucanus, epic poet, condemned to death by Nero,* A.D. *39–65)*

lūc·ar -āris *n* funds allocated for public games *(derived from a forest tax)*

lucell·um -ī *n* slight profit

lū·ceō -cēre -xī *intr* to shine, be light, glow, glitter, be clear; *(fig)* to be clear, be apparent, be conspicuous ‖ *v impers* it is light, day is dawning

Lūcer·ēs -um *mpl* **(Luc-)** one of the three original Roman tribes

lucern·a -ae *f* oil lamp; *(fig)* midnight oil; **ad lucernam** after dark; **ante lucernās** before nightfall; **vīnum et lucernae** wine and lamps *(i.e., evening festivities)*

lūcēscō lūcēscere lūxī *intr* **(-cīsc-)** to begin to shine ‖ *v impers* it is getting light

Lūci·a -ae *f* female name

lūcidē *adv* clearly, distinctly

lūcid·us -a -um *adj* shining, bright, clear; lucid

lūcif·er -era -erum *adj* shiny

Lūcif·er -erī *m (astr)* morning star ‖ *(astr)* planet Venus ‖ son of Aurora and Cephalus

lūcifug·us -a -um *adj* light-shunning; avoiding the public eye, sulking

Lūcil·ius -(i)ī *m* Gaius Lucilius *(first Roman satiric poet, c. 180–102 B.C.)*

Lūcīn·a -ae *f* goddess of childbirth; childbirth

lūcīscō *see* **lūcēscō**

Lūc·ius -(i)ī *m* Roman first name *(praenomen; abbr: L.)*

Lucmō *see* **Lucumō**

Lucrēti·a -ae *f* wife of Collatinus, who, having been raped by Sextus Tarquinius, committed suicide in 509 B.C.

Lucrēt·ius -(i)ī *m* Spurius Lucretius *(father of Lucretia and consul in 509 B.C.)* ‖ Lucretius *(Titus Lucretius Carus, philosophical poet, 94?–55? B.C.)*

lucrificābil·is -is -e *or* **lucrific·us -a -um** *adj* profitable

lucrifug·a -ae *m* person not interested in profit, spendthrift

Lucrīn·us -a -um *adj* Lucrine; **Lacus Lucrīnus** Lucrine Lake *(near Baiae, famous for its oysters)*

lucripet·a -ae *m* profiteer

lucr·or -ārī -ātus sum *tr* to gain, win *(as profit)* ‖ *intr (w.* **ex**) to profit from

lucrōs·us -a -um *adj* profitable

lucr·um -ī *n* profit, gain; wealth; greed, love of gain; **lucrī facere** to gain for oneself; to make profit; **lucrī fierī** to be gained; **lucrō esse** *(w. dat)* to be advantageous to *(s.o.)*; **pōnere in lucrō** *(or* **in lucrīs**) to regard as gain; **vīvere dē lucrō** to be lucky to be alive

luctām·en -inis *n* wrestling; struggle, effort

luct·āns -antis *adj* reluctant

luctāti·ō -ōnis *f* wrestling; struggle, effort

luctāt·or -ōris *m* wrestler

lūctific·us -a -um *adj* causing sorrow, calamitous

lūctison·us -a -um *adj* sad-sounding

luct·or -ārī -ātus sum *or* **luct·ō -āre** *intr* to wrestle; *(w.* **cum**) to struggle with, grapple with; *(w. inf)* to struggle to

lūctuōsē *adv* so as to cause sadness

lūctuōsius *adv* more pitifully

lūctuōs·us -a -um *adj* causing sorrow, sorrowful; sad, feeling sad

lūct·us -ūs *m* sorrow, mourning, grief, distress; signs of sorrow, mourning clothes; source of grief

Luc(u)m·ō -ōnis *m* Etruscan personal name

lūcubrāti·ō -ōnis *f* working by lamp light; evening gossip

lūcubr·ō -āre -āvī -ātus *tr* to compose at night ‖ *intr* to burn the midnight oil

lūculentē *adv* splendidly, well; *(to beat)* soundly; *(to sell)* at an excellent price

lūculenter *adv* brilliantly, smartly

lūculent·us -a -um *adj* bright, brilliant; excellent, fine; good-looking

Lūcull·us -ī *m* Lucius Licinius Lucullus *(Roman general and politician, 117–56 B.C.)*

lūc·us -ī *m* sacred grove; woods

lūdi·a -ae *f* actress; gladiator *(female)*

lūdibr·ium -(i)ī *n* toy, plaything; derision; object of derision, butt of ridicule; frivolous behavior; sham, pretense; *(fig)* sucker; **lūdibriō esse** *(w. dat)* to be made a fool of by *(s.o.)*, be taken in by *(s.o.)*; **lūdibriō habēre** to take *(s.o.)* for a sucker ‖ *npl* outrages, insults

lūdibund·us -a -um *adj* playful, playing around, having fun; without effort, without danger; carefree

lūdi·cer -cra -crum *adj* for sport, in sport; *(theat)* of the stage, dramatic, acting; **lūdicra ars et scaena tōta** dramatic art and the stage in general; **lūdicra exercitātiō** sports; **lūdicra rēs** drama; **lūdicrās partēs sustinēre** *(theat)* to play a dramatic role, act on the stage; **lūdicrum praemium** sports award; ‖ *n* sport, game; toy; show, public game; stage play

lūdificābil·is -is -e *adj* used in mockery

lūdificāti·ō -ōnis *f* ridiculing, mocking; fooling, tricking

lūdificāt·or -ōris *m* mocker

lūdificāt·us -ūs *m* mockery

lūdific·ō -āre -āvī -ātus *or* **lūdific·or -ārī -ātus sum** *tr* to make a fool of, take for a sucker; to fool, trick

lūdi·ō -ōnis *m or* **lūd·ius -(i)ī** *m* actor

lū·dō -dere -sī -sus *tr* to play; to spend *(time)* in play; to lose *(money)* in gambling; to amuse oneself with, do for amusement, practice as a pastime; to imitate, mimic, do a takeoff on, ridicule; to tease, tantalize; to deceive, delude; **operam lūdere** to waste one's efforts; ‖ *intr* to play; to have fun; to jest, joke; to frolic; *(sl)* to play around, make love; **aleā**

lūdere to play dice; **pilā lūdere** to play ball

lūd·us -ī *m* play, game, sport, pastime, diversion; mere child's play; joke, fun; *(sl)* playing around, fooling around, lovemaking; school; public show, public game; **āmōtō lūdō** all joking aside; **in lūdum īre** *and* **itāre** to go to school; **lūdum alicui dare** *(w. dat)* to allow s.o. to enjoy himself; **lūdum frequentāre** to attend school; **lūdus gladiātōrius** gladiatorial school; **lūdus (litterārius, litterārum)** (elementary) school; **per lūdum** as a joke, for fun ‖ *mpl* public games, public exhibition; games, tricks; **lūdōs facere** *(or* **lūdōs reddere)** *(w. dat)* **1** to play tricks on; **2** to put on a show for; **3** to make fun of; **lūdōs sibi facere** to amuse oneself; **lūdī circēnsēs** festival of public games, contests, *or* theatrical shows held at the racetrack; **lūdī magister** school teacher; **lūdī magnī** special votive games; **lūdī plēbēiī** games given annually by the plebeian aediles on Nov. 4-17; **lūdī Rōmānī** games given annually by the curule aediles on Sept. 4-19; **lūdī scaenicī** public events held in the theater, plays

luell·a -ae *f* expiation, atonement

lu·ēs -is *f* infection, contagion, plague, pestilence; calamity

Lugdūnēns·is -is -e *adj* of Lyons

Lugdūn·um -ī *n* Lyons *(town in E. Gaul)*

lū·geō -gēre -xī -ctus *tr* to mourn, lament, deplore ‖ *intr* to mourn, be in mourning; to be in mourning clothes

lūgubr·ia -ium *npl* mourning clothes

lūgubr·is -is -e *adj* mourning; doleful; disastrous

lumbifrag·ium -(i)ī *n* physical wreck

lumbrīc·us -ī *m* earthworm; *(as a term of reproach)* worm, creep

lumb·us -ī *m* loin ‖ *mpl* loins; genitals

lūm·en -inis *n* light; lamp, torch; brightness, sheen, gleam; daylight; light of the eye, eye; light of life, life; window, window light; luminary, celebrity; glory, pride; *(leg) (usu. pl)* the amount of light falling on a building to which the owner is entitled; *(rhet)* strong point *(of an argument)*; *(rhet)* brilliant phrase *or* expression; **ad lūmina prīma** until lamp-lighting time, until dusk; **lūmen adferre** *(w. dat)* to shed light on *(a subject)*; **lūmen vītāle** light enjoyed by living creatures, life; **lūmina āmittere** to go blind; **lūminibus captus** blind; **sub lūmina prīma** around dusk, just before dusk

lūminōs·us -a -um *adj* luminous, dazzling; *(fig)* bright, conspicuous

lūn·a -ae *f* moon; month; night; crescent *(worn as an ornament by senators on their shoes)*; **ad lūnam** by moonlight; **lūna labōrāns** moon in eclipse, eclipse of the moon; **lūna minor** waning moon; **nova lūna** new moon

Lūn·a -ae *f* town in N. Etruria near modern Carrara

lūnār·is -is -e *adj* lunar, of the moon

lūnāt·us -a -um *adj* crescent-shaped

lūn·ō -āre -āvī -ātus *tr* to make crescent-shaped, curve

lūnul·a -ae *f* little crescent *(ornament worn by women)*

lu·ō -ere -ī *tr* to wash; to cleanse, purge; to set free, let go; to pay *(debt, penalty)*; to pay as a fine; to suffer, undergo; to atone for, expiate; to satisfy, appease; to avert by expiation *or* punishment; **poenās luere** to suffer a punishment *(by way of expiation)*

lup·a -ae *f* she-wolf; flirt, prostitute

lupān·ar -āris *n* brothel

lupāt·us -a -um *adj* jagged *(like wolf's teeth)* ‖ *npl* jagged bit *(for spunky horses)*

Luperc·al -ālis *n* shrine on the Palatine Hill sacred to Pan

Lupercāl·ia -ium *npl* Lupercalia *(festival of Lycaean Pan, celebrated in February)*

Luperc·us -ī *m* Pan

lupill·us -ī *m (bot)* small lupine

lupīn·us -a -um *adj* wolf's, lupine ‖ *m & n (bot)* lupine *(plant having clusters of flowers of various colors*

lup·us -ī *m* wolf; *(fish)* pike; jagged bit *(for horse)*; grapnel

lurc(h)·ō -ōnis *m* glutton

lūrid·us -a -um *adj* pale-yellow, wan, ghastly, lurid; causing paleness

lūr·or -ōris *m* sallowness, sickly yellow color

-lus -la -lum *suf* forming diminutives, e.g., **lapillus** pebble, **agellus** little field, plot, **homunculus** little man

lūscini·a -ae *f* nightingale

lūsciniol·a -ae *f* little nightingale

lūscin·ius -(i)ī *m* nightingale

lūsciōs·us *or* **lūscitiōs·us -a -um** *adj* partly blind

lūsc·us -a -um *adj* one-eyed

lūsī *perf of* **lūdō**

lūsi·ō -ōnis *f* play, game

Lūsitān·ī -ōrum *mpl* Lusitanian

Lūsitāni·a -ae *f* Lusitania *(modern Portugal and W. part of Spain)*

lūsit·ō -āre *intr* to like to play

lūs·or -ōris *m* player; gambler; humorous writer; joker

lūstrāl·is -is -e *adj* lustral, propitiatory; quinquennial

lūstrāti·ō -ōnis *f* purification, lustration; wandering, traveling

lūstr·ō -āre -āvī -ātus *tr* to purify; to travel over, traverse; to check, examine; to go around, encircle; to light up, make bright, illuminate; to scan *(with the eyes)*; to consider, review; to survey; *(mil)* to review *(troops)*

lustr·or -ārī -ātus sum *intr* to frequent brothels

lustr·um -ī *n* haunt, den, lair; wilderness; brothel; sensuality

lūstr·um -ī *n* purificatory sacrifice, lustration; lustrum, period of five years; period of years; **ingēns lūstrum** a century

lūsus *pp of* **lūdō**

lūs·us -ūs *m* play, game, sport, amusement; playing around *(amorously);* **lūsum lūdere** to play a game

lūteol·us -a -um *adj* yellowish

lūte·us -a -um *adj* golden-yellow, yellow, orange

lute·us -a -um *adj* of mud, of clay; muddy; dirty, grimy; (morally) dirty, filthy

lutit·ō -āre *tr* to splatter with mud; *(fig)* to throw mud at

lut·ō -āre -āvī -ātus *tr* to cover with mud, daub; *(fig)* to smear

lutulent·us -a -um *adj* muddy; dirty; *(fig)* filthy; turbid *(style)*

lūt·um -ī *n* yellow pigment, yellow

lut·um -ī *n* mud, mire; clay; **in lutō esse** *(or* **haerēre)** *(fig)* to be in a pickle; **prō lutō esse** to be dirt-cheap

lūx lūcis *f* light; light of day, life; daylight; public view, publicity; the public, the world; light of hope, encouragement; glory; elucidation; **lūce** *(or* **lūcī)** by daylight, in the daytime; **lūx aestīva** summer; **lūx brūmālis** winter; **(cum) prīmā lūce** at daybreak

lux·ō -āre -āvī -ātus *tr* to dislocate *(a limb)*

lux·or -ārī -ātus sum *intr* to live riotously, have a ball

luxuri·a -ae *or* **luxuri·ēs -ēī** *f* luxuriance; luxury, extravagance, excess, sumptuousness

luxuri·ō -āre -āvī -ātum *or* **luxur·ior -ārī -ātus sum** *intr* to grow luxuriantly; to luxuriate; *(of the body)* to swell up; *(of animals)* to be frisky; to lead a wild life

luxuriōsē *adv* luxuriously, voluptuously

luxuriōs·us -a -um *adj* luxuriant; exuberant; extravagant; voluptuous; highly fertile *(land)*

lux·us -ūs *m* luxury, extravagance, excess; splendor, pomp, magnificence

Lyae·us -a -um *adj* Bacchic ‖ *m* Bacchus; wine

Lycae·us -a -um *adj* Lycaean *(esp. applied to Pan);* **Mōns Lycaeus** Mount Lycaeus *(mountain in Arcadia where Jupiter and Pan were worshiped)*

Lycā·ōn -onis *m* king of Arcadia, whose daughter Callisto was changed into a she-bear and transferred to the sky as the Great Bear

Lycāon·is -idis *f* daughter of Lycaon *(i.e., Callisto)*

Lycāoni·us -a -um *adj* descended from Lycaon of Arcadia; **axis Lycāonia** North Pole *(where Callisto as the Great Bear is located)*

lychnūch·us -ī *m* lamp stand; **lychnūchus pēnsilis** chandelier

lychn·us -ī *m* lamp, chandelier

Lyci·a -ae *f* country in S. Asia Minor

Lycī·um -ī *n* **(Lycē-)** the Lyceum *(gymnasium near Athens where Aristotle taught)* ‖ Lyceum *(name given by Cicero to the gymnasium in his Tusculan villa)*

Lyci·us -a -um *adj* of Lycia, Lycian ‖ *mpl* Lycians

Lycomēd·ēs -is *m* king of the Greek island of Scyros, father of Deidamia

Lycophr·ōn -onis *or* **-onos** *m* Alexandrine poet, noted for his obscure style *(born c. 320 B.C.)*

Lycōr·is -idis *or* **-idos** *f* name under which the poet Gallus wrote about his mistress Cytheris

Lycorm·ās -ae *m* old name for the Aetolian river Evenus

Lycti·us -a -um *adj* Cretan, of Lyctos *(a town in Crete)*

Lycurgē·us -a -um *adj* Lycurgan *(resembling the orator Lycurgus, noted for his relentlessness as prosecutor)*

Lycurgīd·ēs -ae *m* son of the Arcadian king Lycurgus *(i.e., Ancaeus, killed by the Calydonian boar)*

Lycurg·us -ī *m* traditional founder of the Spartan constitution ‖ Athenian orator, contemporary with Demosthenes *(born c. 396 B.C.)* ‖ son of Dryas and king of the Edones, who persecuted Bacchus and his worshipers

Lyc·us -ī *m* king of Thebes and husband of Dirce ‖ name of numerous rivers in Asia Minor, *esp.* a tributary of the Menander

Lȳdi·a -ae *f* country in W. Asia Minor

Lȳdi·us -a -um *adj* Lydian

Lȳd·us -a -um *adj* Lydian ‖ *mf* Lydian; Etruscan

lygd·os -ī *f* marble from Paros

lymph·a -ae *f* water nymph; *(poet)* water

lymphātic·us -a -um *adj* frenzied

lymphāt·us -a -um *adj* frenzied, frantic

lymph·ō -āre *tr* to drive crazy ‖ *pass* to be in a state of frenzy

Lyncest·is -idis *adj (fem only)* of the Lycestae, a people of W. Macedonia

Lync·eus -eī *m* Argonaut, famed for his sharp eyesight ‖ son of Aegyptus and husband of Hypermestra

Lyncē·us -a -um *adj* of Lynceus the Argonaut; keen-sighted, Lynceus-like

Lyncīd·ēs -ae *m* descendant of Lynceus, husband of Hypermestra *(esp. his great-grandson Perseus)*

lyn·x -cis *or* **-cos** *mf* lynx

lyr·a -ae *f* lyre; *(fig)* lyric poetry ‖ **Lyra** *(astr)* Lyra *(constellation)*

Lyrcē·us -a -um *adj* of Mt. Lyrceum on the borders of Arcadia and Argolis

lyric·us -a -um *adj* of the lyre; lyric ‖ *m* lyric poet ‖ *npl* lyric poetry

Lyrnēs·is -idis *or* -**idos** *f* Briseis *(Achilles' slave girl from Lyrnesos, a town in Phrygia)*

Lȳsan·der -drī *m* Spartan general and statesman *(d. 395 B.C.)*

Lȳsi·ās -ae *m* Athenian orator *(c. 459–c. 380 B.C.)*

Lȳsimach·us -ī *m* bodyguard of Alexander the Great, who later became King of Thrace

M

M, m *(supply* littera) *f* twelfth letter of the Latin alphabet; letter name: **em**

M *abbr* **mīlle** one thousand

M. *abbr* **Marcus** *(Roman first name, praenomen)*

M'. *abbr* **Manius** *(Roman first name, praenomen)*

Macarē·is -idos *f* daughter of Macareus *(i.e., Isse)*

Macar·ēus -eī *or* **-eos** *m* son of Aeolus *(who lived in incest with his sister Canace)*

macc·us -ī *m* clown *(in Atellan farces)*

Maced·ō -onis *m* Macedonian

Macedoni·a -ae *f* Macedonia

Macedonic·us -a -um *adj* Macedonian

Macedoniēns·is -is -e *adj* Macedonian

Macedoni·us -a -um *adj* Macedonian

macellār·ius -(i)ī *m* grocer

macell·um -ī *n* grocery store; *(fig)* groceries

mac·eō -ēre *intr* to be lean, be skinny

ma·cer -cra -crum *adj* lean; skinny; poor *(soil);* scraggly *(plants);* lean *(meat)*

Ma·cer -crī *m* Gaius Licinius Macer *(Roman historian and orator, d. 66 B.C.)* ‖ Gaius Licinius Macer Calvus *(son of the former, and orator and poet, 82–46 B.C.)* ‖ Marcus Aemilius Macer *(poet and friend of Vergil and Ovid)*

māceri·a -ae *f* brick *or* stone wall; garden wall

mācer·ō -āre -āvī -ātus *tr* to soften, tenderize; to weaken, wear down; to soak; to worry, annoy, torment ‖ *refl & pass* to fret, worry

macēsc·ō -ere *intr* to grow thin; *(of fruit)* to shrivel

machaer·a -ae *f* **(macch-)** (single-edged) sword

machaerophor·us -ī *m* soldier armed with a single-edged sword

Machā·ōn -onis *m* famous physician of the Greek army in the Trojan War and son of Aesculapius

Machāoni·us -a -um *adj* of Machaon; *(fig)* medical

māchin·a -ae *f* large mechanism, machine; crane, derrick; pulley, windlass, winch; revolving stage; siege engine; platform on which slaves were exhibited for sale (= **catasta);** cage, pen; *(fig)* scheme, stratagem

māchināment·um -ī *n* contrivance, device; *(mil)* siege engine;

māchinār·ius -(i)ī *m* crane operator

māchināti·ō -ōnis *f* mechanism; machine; trick; art of making machines; *(mil)* field piece

māchināt·or -ōris *m* engineer, machinist; *(fig)* contriver

māchin·or -ārī -ātus sum *tr* to engineer, design, contrive; to scheme

māchinōs·us -a -um *adj* containing a mechanism

maci·ēs -ēī *f* leanness, thinness; barrenness; poverty *(of soil; of style)*

macilent·us -a -um *adj* skinny

macrēsc·ō -ere *intr* to grow thin

macritūd·ō -inis *f* leanness

macrocoll·um -ī *n* large-size sheet of paper

mactābil·is -is -e *adj* deadly

mactāt·us -ūs *m* sacrifice

mactē *interj* well done!; good luck!; bravo!; *(w. gen, acc, or abl)* hurrah for; **mactē virtūte estō**! bless you for your excellence!; well done!

mact·ō -āre -āvī -ātus *tr* to glorify, honor; to slay *(sacrificially),* sacrifice; to kill, slaughter, put to death; to destroy, overthrow, ruin; to trouble; *(w. abl)* to afflict *or* punish with

mact·us -a -um *adj* glorified; struck, smitten

macul·a -ae *f* spot, stain; mesh *(of net); (fig)* blemish, defect

macul·ō -āre -āvī -ātus to spot, stain, pollute; *(fig)* defile, dishonor, disgrace

maculōs·us -a -um *adj* spotted; stained; *(fig)* defiled, dishonored, filthy; **maculōsī senātōrēs** rotten senators

made·faciō -facere -fēcī -factus *(pass:* **made·fīō -fierī -factus sum)** *tr* to wet, moisten, drench, soak

mad·ēns -entis *adj* wet, moist; flowing *(hair);* melting *(snow);* reeking *(w. blood)*

mad·eō -ēre -uī *intr* to be wet, be moist, be soaked, be drenched; to drip; to flow; *(coll)* to be soused; to be full, overflow

mad·ēscō -ēscere -uī *intr* to become wet, become moist; *(coll)* to get soused

madidē *adv* drunkenly

madid·us -a -um *adj* wet, moist, drenched; dyed, steeped; *(coll)* drunk, soused

mad·or -ōris *m* moisture
maduls·a -ae *m (coll)* souse, drunkard
Maean·der *or* **Maean·dros** *or* **Maean·drus -drī** *m* river in Asia Minor, famous for its winding course; winding; winding border; devious course
Maecēn·ās -ātis *m* Gaius Cilnius Maecenas *(adviser to Augustus and friend of Vergil and Horace, d. 8 B.C.)*
maen·a -ae *f* sprat *(fish)*
Maenal·is -idis *adj* of Mt. Maenalus, Arcadian; **Maenalis ursa** Callisto *(who was changed into the Great Bear)*
Maenal·us *or* **Maenal·os -ī** *m or* **Maenal·a -ōrum** *npl* Mt. Maenalus *(in Arcadia, sacred to Pan)*
Maen·as -adis *f* Bacchante; frenzied woman
Maeni·us -a -um *adj (name of a Roman clan)* Maenian; **Maenia Columna** pillar in the Forum at which the **triumvirī capitālēs** held court and at which thieves, slaves, and debtors were tried and flogged
Maeon·es -um *mpl* Maeonians *(ancient name of the Lydians)*
Maeoni·a -ae *f* E. part of Lydia; *(from the alleged ancestry of its people)* Etruria
Maeonid·ēs -ae *m* native of Maeonia; Homer *(believed to have been born in Lydia);* an Etruscan
Maeon·is -idis *adj (fem only)* Lydian ‖ *f* Maeonian woman *(esp. Arachne or Omphale)*
Maeoni·us -a -um *adj* Lydian; Homeric; Etruscan ‖ *f see* **Maeonia**
Maeōt·ae -ārum *mpl* a Scythian people on Lake Maeotis *(Sea of Azov)*
Maeōt·is -idis *adj* Maeotic; Scythian; **Maeōtis lacus** Sea of Azov
Maeōti·us -a -um *adj* Maeotian, of the Maeotae *(a Scythian people)*
maer·eō -ēre *tr* to mourn for, grieve for ‖ *intr* to mourn, grieve
maer·or -ōris *m* mourning, grief
maestē *adv* mournfully, sadly
maestiter *adv* mournfully, sadly
maestiti·a -ae *f* sadness, sorrow, grief; gloom; dullness *(of style)*
maestitūd·ō -inis *f* sadness
maest·us -a -um *adj* mourning, sad, gloomy
Maev·ius -(i)ī *m* poetaster often ridiculed by Vergil and Horace
māgāl·ia -ium *npl* huts
mag·ē -ēs *f* magic
mage *see* **magis**
magic·us -a -um *adj* magic; **artēs magicae** magic
magis *or* **mage** *adv* more, to a greater extent, in a higher degree, rather; **eō magis** (all) the more; **magis ... atque** rather ... than; **magis aut minus** more or less; **magis est ut, quod** it is more the case that; **magis magisque** more and more; **magis ... quam** rather ... than; **nōn magis ... quam** not so much ... as
magis·ter -trī *m* chief, master, director; teacher; adviser, guardian; ringleader, author; *(in apposition with noun in the gen)* expert; *(keeper of animals)* shepherd, herdsman; **magister equitum** *(title of dictator's second-in-command)* Master of the Cavalry; **magister mōrum** censor; **magister sacrōrum** chief priest; **magister vīcī** ward boss; **nāvis magister** ship's captain
magister·ium -(i)ī *n* directorship, presidency, superintendence; control, governance; instruction; **magisterium mōrum** censorship
magistr·a -ae *f* directress, mistress; instructress, teacher
magistrāt·us -ūs *m* magistracy; magistrate, official; military command
magmentār·ium -(i)ī *n* receptacle for a part of the sacrificial animal
magnanimit·ās -ātis *f* magnanimity; high ideals; bravery
magnanim·us -a -um *adj* magnanimous, noble, big-hearted; brave
magnāri·us -a -um *adj* wholesale; **magnārius negōtiātor** wholesale dealer
magn·ēs -ētis *adj* magnetic; **magnēs lapis** magnet
Magn·ēs -ētis *adj* of Magnesia, Magnesian
Magnēsi·a -ae *f* district in E. Thessaly on the Aegean Sea ‖ city in Caria near the Menander River ‖ city in Lydia near Mt. Sipylus
magnēsi·us -a -um *adj* magnetic; **saxum magnēsium** lodestone
magnidic·us -a -um *adj* talking big
magnificē *adv* magnificently, splendidly; pompously
magnificenti·a -ae *f* magnificence, grandeur, splendor; pompousness
magnific·ō -āre -āvī -ātus *tr* to make much of
magnific·us -a -um *adj* magnificent, splendid; sumptuous; proud
magniloquenti·a -ae *f* pompous language, braggadocio; *(rhet)* lofty style
magniloqu·us -a -um *adj* (**-loc-**) sublime; bragging
magnitūd·ō -inis *f* magnitude; size; large quantity, large number; vastness, extent; greatness; importance; power, might; high station, dignity, high rank; dignity of character; length *(of time);* intensity *(of storm, etc.);* strength, loudness *(of voice)*
magnopere *or* **magnō opere** *adv* greatly, very much; particularly; strongly, earnestly, heartily
magn·us -a -um *(comp:* **māior;** *superl:* **maximus)** *adj* big, large; important; great; distinguished; impressive; complete, utter, full, pure; high, powerful *(in*

rank); long *(time);* high *(price);* loud *(voice);* heavy *(rain);* advanced *(age);* noble *(character);* **magna itinera** forced marches; **Magna Māter** Cybele; **magnō cāsū occidere** to happen by pure chance; **mare magnum** the ocean; **vir magnō iam nātū** a man advanced in years **II** *n* great thing; great value; boast, proud claim; **magnī (pretiī) aestimāre** *(or* **magnī habēre)** to value highly, have a high regard for; **magnō emere (vēndere)** to buy (sell) at a high price; **magnum spīrāre** to be proud

Māg·ō -ōnis *m* brother of Hannibal

mag·us -a -um *adj* magic; **artēs magae** magic **II** *m* magician; learned man *(among the Persians)*

māiāl·is -is *m* castrated hog; *(as term of abuse)* swine

māiest·ās -ātis *f* majesty, dignity, grandeur; sovereign power, sovereignty; authority; *(as a crime of diminishing the majesty of the Roman people)* high treason; **māiestās laesa** *(or* **imminūta)** high treason

māi·or -or -us *(comp of* **magnus)** *adj* bigger, larger; greater; more important; **annōs nātū māior quadrāgintā** forty years older; **in māius ferre** to exaggerate; **māiōris (pretiī)** at a higher price; **māior nātū** older **II** *mpl see* **māiōrēs II** *npl* worse things, worse sufferings

māiōr·ēs -um *mpl* ancestors, forefathers

Māi·us -a -um *adj & m* May **II** *f* daughter of Atlas and Pleione and mother of Mercury by Jupiter

māiuscul·us -a -um *adj* somewhat greater; a little older

māl·a -ae *f* cheekbone, upper jaw **II** *fpl* cheeks; *(fig)* jaws *(e.g., of death)*

malaci·a -ae *f* calm at sea, dead calm

malaciss·ō -āre -āvī -ātus *tr* to soften (up)

malac·us -a -um *adj* soft; luxurious

male *adv (comp:* **pēius;** *superl:* **pessimē)** badly, wrongly; wickedly, cruelly, maliciously; unfortunately, unsuccessfully; awkwardly; excessively, extremely, very much; *(w. adjectives having a bad sense)* terribly, awfully; **male accipere** to treat roughly; **male audīre** to be ill spoken of; **male dīcere** *(w. dat)* to say nasty things to; **male existimāre dē** *(w. abl)* to have a bad opinion of; **male emere** to buy at a high price; **male facere** *(w. dat)* to treat badly, treat cruelly; **male factum**! *(coll)* too bad!; **male ferre** to take (it) hard; **male fīdus** unsafe; **male grātus** ungrateful; **male habēre** to harass; **male metuere** to be terribly afraid of; **male perdere** to ruin utterly; **male sānus** insane; **male vēndere** to sell at a loss; **male vīvere** to be a failure in life

mal(e)fact·um -ī *n* wrong, injury

maledic·āx -ācis *adj* abusive, foul-mouthed

maledicē *adv* abusively, slanderously

maledīc·ēns -entis *adj* abusive, foul-mouthed

male·dīcō -dīcere -dīxī -dictum *intr (w. dat)* **1** to speak ill of, abuse, slander; **2** to say nasty things to

maledicti·ō -ōnis *f* abusive language, abuse

maledictit·ō -āre -āvī *intr (w. dat)* to keep saying nasty things to

maledict·um -ī *n* insult, taunt

maledic·us -a -um *adj* abusive, foul-mouthed; slanderous

male·faciō -facere -fēcī -factum *intr* to do wrong; *(w. dat)* to injure, do wrong to

malefact·or -ōris *m* malefactor, trouble-maker

maleficē *adv* mischievously

maleficenti·a -ae *f* harm, wrong, mischief

malefic·ium -(i)ī *n* evil deed, crime, offense; harm, injury, wrong, mischief; **maleficium admittere** *(or* **committere)** to commit a crime

malefic·us -a -um *adj* wicked, vicious, criminal **II** *m* mischief-maker

malesuād·us -a -um *adj* seductive

malevol·ēns -entis *adj* malevolent, spiteful, malicious **II** *mf* spiteful person

malevolenti·a -ae *f* malevolence, spitefulness, ill will

malevol·us -a -um *adj* malevolent, spiteful, nasty

Māliac·us -a -um *adj* Malian, of Malis; **sinus Māliacus** Malian Gulf *(in S. Thessaly, modern Gulf of Zeitouni)*

Māliēns·is -is -e *adj* of Malis *(a district of S. Thessaly)*

mālifer -a -um apple-bearing

malignē *adv* spitefully; jealously; grudgingly; scantily, poorly

malignit·ās -ātis *f* spite, malice, jealously; stinginess

malign·us -a -um *adj* spiteful, malicious, jealous; stingy; *(fig)* unproductive *(soil);* scanty *(light)*

maliti·a -ae *f* malice, ill-will, bad behavior **II** *fpl* devilish tricks

malitiōsē *adv* wickedly; craftily

malitiōs·us -a -um *adj* malicious, crafty, wicked, devilish

malleol·us -ī *m* small hammer, small mallet; fiery arrow

malle·us -ī *m* hammer, mallet; **malleus ferreus** pole-ax *(for slaughtering sacrificial animals)*

mālō *or* **māvolō mālle māluī** *tr* to prefer; **pecūniam quam sapientiam mālle** to prefer money to wisdom; *(w. inf)* to prefer to *(do s.th.); (w. acc & inf, w.* **ut)** to prefer that **II** *intr (w. dat)* to incline toward, be more favorably disposed to

malobathr·um -ī *n* malobathrum oil *(used as perfume)*

māl·um -ī *n* apple; **aureum mālum** quince; **fēlīx mālum** lemon; **mālum Persicum** peach; **mālum Pūnicum** *(or* **mālum grānātum)** pomegranate; **mālum silvestre** crab apple

mal·um -ī *n* evil, ill; harm; punishment; disaster; hardship; trouble; *(as a term of abuse):* **quī, malum, istī sunt?** who the heck are they?

mal·us -a -um *adj* bad; ill, evil; ugly; unpatriotic; adverse, unfavorable; unsucessful; harmful; inappropriate, misplaced; insulting, abusive *(words);* humble *(birth);* **ī in malam rem**! *(sl)* go to hell!; **mala aetās** old age; **rēs mala** trouble **‖** *n see* **malum**

māl·us -ī *f* apple tree

māl·us -ī *m* mast *(of ship);* pole

malv·a -ae *f* mallow *(used as food or mild laxative)*

Mām·ers -ertis *m* Mars

Māmertīn·ī -ōrum *mpl* inhabitants of Messana who precipitated the First Punic war

mamill·a -ae *f* breast, teat

mamm·a -ae *f* breast *(of a woman);* dug *(of an animal); (baby talk)* mummy, mamma

mammeāt·us -a -um *adj* large-breasted

mammōs·us -a -um *adj* large-breasted, chesty

mānābil·is -is -e *adj* penetrating *(cold)*

manc·eps -ipis *m* purchaser; contractor

mancip·ium -(i)ī *n* **(-cup-)** formal purchase; possession, right of ownership; slave; **mancipiō accipere** to take possession of; **mancipiō dare** to turn over possession of; **rēs mancipī** possessions *(basic to running a farm e.g., land, slaves, livestock, farm implements);* **rēs nec mancipī** possessions *(other than those needed to run a farm)*

mancip·ō -āre -āvī -ātus *tr* **(-cup-)** to sell, transfer

manc·us -a -um *adj* crippled, maimed; *(fig)* defective, weak

mandāt·um -ī *n* command, order, commission **‖** *npl* instructions

mandāt·us -ūs *m* command, order

mand·ō -āre -āvī -ātus *tr* to hand over; to commit, entrust; to command, order, enjoin; to commission; to delegate *(authority);* to prescribe, specify; **humō aliquem mandare** to bury s.o.; **memoriae** *(or* **animō)** **mandāre** to commit to memory, record **‖** *refl* **sē fugae mandāre** to run away

man·dō -dere -dī -sus *tr* to chew; to champ; to eat, devour; **humum mandere** *(fig)* to bite the dust

mandr·a -ae *f* stable, stall; column of pack animals *or* cattle; checkerboard

mandūc·us -ī *m* mask representing a glutton

māne *indecl n* morning **‖** *adv* in the morning; **bene māne** early in the morning; **crās māne** tomorrow morning; **herī māne** yesterday morning; **hodiē māne** this morning; **postrīdiē ēius diēī māne** the following morning

man·eō -ēre -sī -sus *tr* to wait for, await **‖** *intr* to stay, remain; to stop off, pass the night; to last, endure, continue, persist; to be left over; **in condiciōne manēre** to stick to an agreement; **in sententiā manēre** to stick to an opinion

mān·ēs -ium *mpl* spirits of the dead; lower world; mortal remains

mang·ō -ōnis *m* slave dealer; pushy salesman

manic·ae -ārum *fpl* handcuffs; grappling hook; long sleeves; gloves

manicāt·us -a -um *adj* long-sleeved

manicul·a -ae *f* little hand

manifestē *adv* plainly, distinctly

manifestō *adv* red-handed; plainly, manifestly, evidently

manifest·ō -āre -āvī -ātus *tr* to reveal; to make known; to clarify

manifest·us -a -um *adj* manifest, plain, clear, distinct; exposed, brought to light, detected, caught; *(w. gen)* caught in, convicted of; *(w. inf)* known to

manipl = manipul-

manip(u)l·us -ī *m* handful *(esp. of hay); (coll)* gang; *(mil)* maniple, company *(three of which constituted a cohort)*

manipulār·is -is -e *adj (mil)* of a maniple *or* company; **mīles manipulāris** private

manipulātim *adv (mil)* by companies

Manl·ius -(i)ī *m* Marcus Manlius Capitolinus *(consul in 392* B.C.*, who, in 389* B.C. *saved the Capitoline from the invading Gauls)* **‖** Titus Manlius Torquatus *(consul in 340* B.C.*, famous for his military discipline)*

mannul·us -ī *m* little pony

mann·us -ī *m* pony

mān·ō -āre -āvī -ātus *tr* to pour out; to shed *(tears)* **‖** *intr* to drip, trickle; *(w. abl)* to drip with; to leak; to flow, pour; to stream; *(of rumors)* to spread, circulate; *(of secrets)* to leak out; *(fig)* to be derived, emanate

mānsi·ō -ōnis *f* staying; stopover

mānsit·ō -āre -āvī *intr* to stay on

mānsuē·faciō -facere -fēcī -factus *(pass:* **mānsuē·fīō -fierī -factus sum)** *tr* to tame; to civilize

mānsu·ēs -is *or* **-ētis** *adj* tame, mild

mānsu·ēscō -ēscere -ēvī -ētus *tr* to tame **‖** *intr* to become tame; *(fig)* to become gentle; to relent; to grow less harsh

mānsuētē *adv* gently, mildly

mānsuētūd·ō -inis *f* mildness, gentleness

mānsuēt·us -a -um *adj* tame; mild, gentle

mānsus *pp of* **mandō** *and* **maneō**

mantēl·e -is *n* hand towel; napkin; tablecloth
mantēl·ium -(i)ī *n* hand towel; napkin
mantell·um -ī *n* (**-tēl-**) mantle
mantic·a -ae *f* knapsack
Mantinē·a -ae *f* town in Arcadia, where the Spartans were defeated by the Thebans in 362 B.C.
manticin·or -ārī -ātus sum *intr* to prophesy
mant·ō -āre *tr* to wait for ‖ *intr* to stay, remain, wait
Mant·ō -ūs *f* prophetic daughter of Tiresias
Mantu·a -ae *f* town in N. Italy, birthplace of Vergil
manuāl·e -is *n* wooden case for a book
manuāl·is -is -e *adj* that can be held in hand, hand-sized *(e.g., rocks)*
manubi·ae -ārum *fpl* money derived from the sale of booty; *(coll)* proceeds from robbery, loot
manubiāl·is -is -e *adj* obtained from the sale of booty
manubiāri·us -a -um *adj (coll)* bringing in the loot
manūbr·ium -(i)ī *n* handle; hilt
manufestāri·us -a -um *adj* (**mani-**) plain, obvious
manule·a -ae *f* long sleeve
manuleār·ius -(i)ī *m* sleeve maker
manuleāt·us -a -um *adj* long-sleeved
manūmissi·ō -ōnis *f* manumission, freeing *(of a slave)*
manū·mittō -mittere -mīsī -missus *tr* to manumit, set free *(a slave)*
manupret·ium -(i)ī *n* workman's pay, wages; *(fig)* pay, reward
man·us -ūs *f* hand; band, gang, company; force, violence, close combat; finishing touch; handwriting; work; workmanship; trunk *(of elephant)*; twigs *(of a tree)*; *(leg)* power of a husband over his wife and children; *(med)* surgery; **ad manum** close at hand, within easy reach; **ad manum habēre** to have at hand, have in readiness; **ad manum venīre** to come within reach; **ad manūs pervenīre** to resort to fighting; **aequā manū** *(or* **aequīs manibus)** on even terms; **ā manū servus** secretary; **dē manū** personally; **ē manū** at a distance, from a distance; **in manibus esse** *(gen)* to be in the power of; be under the jurisdiction of; **inter manūs** under one's hand, in one's arms; **inter manūs habēre** to have in hand, be busied with; **manibus pedibusque** *(fig)* with might and main; **manū** by hand, artificially; in deed; by force; *(mil)* by force of arms; **manū (ē)mittere** to set *(a slave)* free; **manū factus** man-made; **manum committere** *(or* **cōnserere** *or* **cōnferre)** to begin to fight; **manum dare** to lend a hand; **manum inicere** *(w. dat)* to lay hands on, arrest; **manūs dare** *(or* **manūs dēdere)** to surrender; **manus extrēma** *(or* **summa** *or* **ultima)** finishing touches; **manus (ferrea)** grappling iron; **manū tenēre** to know for sure; **media manus** a go-between; **per manūs** by hand; by force; from hand to hand, from mouth to mouth, from father to son; **plēnā manū** generously; **prae manibus** *(or* **prae manū)** at hand, in readiness; **sub manū** *(or* **sub manum)** at hand, near; immediately, promptly; **suspēnsā manū** reluctantly
mapāl·ia -ium *npl* African huts; *(fig)* a mess
mapp·a -ae *f* napkin; flag *(used in starting races at the racetrack)*
Marath·ōn -ōnis *f* site in E. Attica of the victory of Miltiades over the Persians *(490 B.C.)*
Marathōni·us -a -um *adj* of Marathon
Marcell·us -ī *m* Roman family name *(cognomen)* in the gens Claudia; Marcus Claudius Marcellus *(nephew of Augustus, 43–23 B.C.)*
marc·eō -ēre *intr* to wither, droop, shrivel; to be weak, be feeble; be decrepit, be rundown; to slack off
marcēsc·ō -ere *intr* to begin to wither, begin to droop; to become weak, become run-down; to become lazy
marcid·us -a -um *adj* withered, droopy; groggy
Marc·ius -(i)ī *m* Ancus Marcius *(fourth king of Rome)*
marcul·us -ī *m* small hammer
Mārc·us -ī *m* Roman first name *(praenōmen)*
mar·e -is *n* sea; saltwater; **mare caelō mīscēre** to raise a huge storm; *(fig)* to have all hell break loose; **mare īnferum** Tyrrhenian Sea; **mare magnum** the ocean; **mare nostrum** Mediterranean Sea; **mare superum** Adriatic Sea; **trāns mare** overseas, abroad
Mareōt·a -ae *f* town and lake near Alexandria in Egypt
Mareōtic·us -a -um *adj* Mareotic; Egyptian
margarīt·a -ae *f or* **margarīt·um -ī** *n* pearl
margin·ō -āre -āvī -ātus *tr* to furnish with a border; to curb *(a street)*
marg·ō -inis *f* margin, edge, border; frontier; bank *(of a stream)*; **margō cēnae** side-dishes
Mariān·ī -ōrum *mpl* partisans of Marius
Marīc·a -ae *f* nymph of Minturnae, mother of Latinus
marīn·us -a -um *adj* sea, marine; seagoing
marisc·a -ae *f* a fig; **tumidae mariscae** the piles
marīt·a -ae *f* wife

marītāl·is -is -e *adj* marital, nuptial; matronly, of a married woman
maritim·us -a -um *adj* **(-tum-)** sea, of the sea; seafaring, maritime; *(fig)* changeable *(like the sea);* **ōra maritima** seacoast **II** *npl* seacoast
marīt·ō -āre -āvī -ātus *tr* to provide with a husband *or* wife, marry; to train *(a vine to a tree)* **II** *pass* to get married
marīt·us -a -um *adj* matrimonial, nuptial **II** *m* husband **II** *f* wife
Mar·ius -(i)ī *m* Gaius Marius *(conqueror of Jugurtha and of the Cimbri and Teutons, and seven times consul, 157–86* B.C.*)*
marm·or -oris *n* marble; marble statue, marble monument; marble vessel; milestone; smooth surface of the sea **II** *npl* marble pavement
marmore·us -a -um *adj* marble, made of marble; marble-like
Mar·ō -ōnis *m* cognomen of Vergil
marr·a -ae *f* hoe, weeding hook
Mārs Mārtis *m* god of war and father of Romulus and Remus; battle, war; engagement; *(astr)* Mars; **aequō Mārte** on an equal footing, in an even battle; **stella** *(or* **sīdus) Mārtis** *(astr)* the planet Mars; **suō Mārte** by his own exertions, independently
Mars·ī -ōrum *mpl* Marsians *(a people of S. central Italy, regarded as tough warriors)*
marsupp·ium -(i)ī *n* purse, pouch
Marsy·ās *or* **Marsy·a -ae** *m* satyr who challenged Apollo with the flute and was flayed alive upon his defeat **II** statue of Marsyas in the Roman Forum
Mārtiāl·ēs -ium *mpl* college of priests of Mars; troops of the **legiō Mārtia** *(Martian legion)*
Mārtiāl·is -is *m* Martial *(Marcus Valerius Martialis, famous for his epigrams, c.* A.D. *40–120)*
Mārticol·a -ae *m* worshiper of Mars
Mārti·us -a -um *adj* Martian, of Mars; sacred to Mars; descended from Mars; of March; **mēnsis Mārtius** March *(third month of the year after the year 153* B.C.*, originally the first month)* **II** *m* March
mās maris *adj* male, masculine; manly, brave **II** *m* male
māsculīn·us -a -um *adj* male, masculine
māscul·us -a -um *adj* male, masculine; manly, vigorous **II** *m* male
mass·a -ae *f* mass, lump; *(coll)* chunk of money; bulk, size; heavy weight *(used in exercising)*
Massaget·ae -ārum *mpl* a nomadic tribe of Scythia
Massic·us -a -um *adj* Massic **II** *m* Mt. Massicus *(between Latium and Campania, famous for its wine)* **II** *n* Massic wine
Massili·a -ae *f* Greek Colony on S. coast of Gaul *(modern Marseilles)*
Massyl·ī -ōrum *mpl* tribe of E. Numidia
mastīgi·a *or* **mastīgi·ās -ae** *m* rascal *(whip-needer)*
mastrūc·a -ae *f* sheepskin; *(pej)* ninny
mastrūcāt·us -a -um *adj* dressed in a sheepskin coat
masturbāt·or -ōris *m* masturbator
masturb·or -ārī -ātus sum *intr* to masturbate
matar·a -ae *or* **matar·is -is** *f* Celtic javelin
matell·a -ae *f* chamber pot
matelli·ō -ōnis *m* small pot
mā·ter -tris *f* mother; matron; foster mother; *(in addressing an old woman)* ma'am; *(of animals)* dam; cause, origin, source; motherland, native land; native city; **Magna Māter** Cybele; **māter familiās** lady of the house
mātercul·a -ae *f* little mother, poor mother
māt·erfamiliās -risfamiliās *f* lady of the house, mistress of the household
māteri·a -ae *or* **māteri·ēs -ēī** *f* matter, stuff, material; lumber *(for building);* fuel; subject, subject matter, theme, topic; cause, source; occasion, opportunity; capacity, natural ability; disposition
māteriār·ius -(i)ī *m* lumber merchant
māteriāt·us -a -um *adj* built with lumber; **male materiātus** built with poor lumber
māteriēs *see* **māteria**
māteri·or -ārī -ātus sum *intr* to gather wood
mātern·us -a -um *adj* maternal, mother's, of a mother
māterter·a -ae *f* aunt, mother's sister; **mātertera magna** grandaunt, grandmother's sister
mathēmatic·a -ae *or* **mathēmatic·ē -ēs** *f* mathematics; astrology
mathēmatic·us -a -um *adj* mathematical, of arithmetic, of geometry **II** *m* mathematician; astrologer
Matīn·us -ī *m* mountain in Apulia near Horace's birthplace, famous for honey
mātricīd·a -ae *m* murderer of one's mother
mātricīd·ium -(i)ī *n* murder of one's mother, matricide
mātrimōn·ium -(i)ī *n* matrimony, marriage; **in mātrimōnium accipere** to marry *(a man);* **in mātrimōnium dare** *(or* **collocāre)** to give in marriage; **in mātrimōnium dūcere** to marry *(a woman)*
mātrim·us -a -um *adj* having a mother still living
mātrōn·a -ae *f* married woman, matron, wife; lady
Mātrōnāl·ia -ium *npl* festival celebrated by married women on March 1 in honor of Mars
mātrōnāl·is -is -e *adj* matronly, wifely, womanly
matt·a -ae *f* straw mat

matul·a -ae *f* pot; chamber pot; *(pej)* blockhead
mātūrātē *adv* promptly
mātūrē *adv* at the right time; in good time, in time; at an early date; at an early age; quickly; prematurely
mātūr·ēscō -ēscere -uī *intr* to get ripe, ripen, mature
mātūrit·ās -ātis *f* ripeness, maturity; harvest season; the proper time; *(fig)* maturity, height, perfection
mātūr·ō -āre -āvī -ātus *tr* to ripen, bring to maturity; to speed up, hasten; *(w. inf)* to be too quick in doing ‖ *intr* to hurry; **mātūrātō opus est** there is no time to lose
mātūr·us -a -um *adj* ripe, mature, full-grown; opportune, at the right time; *(of winter, etc.)* early, coming early; advanced in years; marriageable; mellow
Mātūt·a -ae *f* goddess of the dawn
mātūtīn·us -a -um *adj* morning, early; **diēs mātūtīnus** early part of the day; **tempora mātūtīna** morning hours
Mauritāni·a -ae *f* country of N.W. Africa
Maur·us -a -um *adj* Moorish; African
Maurūsi·us -a -um *adj* Moorish, Mauretanian
Māvor·s -tis *m* Mars; warfare; *(astr)* Mars
Māvorti·us -a -um *adj* Martian, of Mars; warlike, martial ‖ *m* Meleager *(son of Mars)*
maxill·a -ae *f* jaw
maximē *adv* **(-xum-)** very, most, especially, particularly; just, precisely, exactly; *(in sequences)* in the first place, first of all; *(in affirmations)* by all means, certainly, yes; **immo maximē** certainly not; **nūper maximē** just recently; **quam maximē** as much as possible; **tum cum maximē** at the precise moment when; **tum maximē** just then; **ut maximē ... ita maximē** the more ... so much the more
maximit·ās -ātis *f* magnitude
maxim·us -a -um *(superl of* **magnus)** *adj* **(-xum-)** biggest, largest; tallest; most important, leading, chief; highest, utmost; greatest *(in amount, number, value, power, or reputation); (with or without* **nātū)** oldest; **maximā vōce** at the top of one's lungs
mazonom·um -ī *n* serving dish
meāmet = meā, *abl fem sing of* **meus,** *strengthened by* **-met**
meāpte = meā, *abl fem sing of* **meus,** *strengthened by* **-pte**
meāt·us -ūs *m* motion, movement; course, channel
mecastor *interj* by Castor! *(used by women)*
mēchanic·us -ī *m* mechanic, engineer
mēcum = cum mē
mēd = mē *(archaic form of acc and abl)*
medd·ix -icis *m* **(mēd-)** magistrate *(among the Oscans);* **meddix tuticus** chief magistrate
Mēdē·a -ae *f* daughter of Aeëtes, the king of Colchis, and wife of Jason
Mēdē·is -idos *adj* magical
med·ēns -entis *m* doctor
med·eor -ērī *tr* to heal ‖ *intr (w. dat)* to heal, cure; *(w.* **adversus** *or* **contrā** *+ acc)* to be good for *(e.g., a cold, headache)*
Mēd·ī -ōrum *mpl* Medes; Parthians; Persians
Mēdi·a -ae *f* country of the Medes S. of the Caspian Sea
mediān·us -a -um *adj* central ‖ *n* central part, middle
mediast(r)īn·us -ī *m* servant *(without any specific skill)*
mēdic·a -ae *f* alfalfa
medicābil·is -is -e *adj* curable
medicām·en -inis *n* medicine, medication; drug, antidote; remedy; tincture; cosmetic; *(fig)* remedy
medicāment·um -ī *n* medicine, medication; potion; *(fig)* relief, antidote; *(rhet)* embellishment
medicāt·us -a -um *adj* healing, having healing powers; imbued with magical substances
medicāt·us -ūs *m* magic charm
medicīn·a -ae *f* medicine *(medication; science of medicine);* remedy; doctor's office; *(w. gen) (fig)* cure for, remedy for; **medicīnam exercēre** *(or* **facere)** to practice medicine
medicīn·us -a -um *adj* of medicine
medic·ō -āre -āvī -ātus *tr* to medicate, cure; to dye; to poison
medic·or -ārī -ātus sum *tr* to cure ‖ *intr (w. dat)* to heal, cure
medic·us -a -um *adj* medical; healing ‖ *m* doctor, surgeon ‖ *f* physician *(female),* midwife
Mēdic·us -a -um *adj* Median, of the Medes
medīdi·ēs -ēī *f (early form of* **merīdiēs)** noon; south
mediē *adv* moderately
mediet·ās -ātis *f* the mean; middle
medimn·um -ī *n or* **medimn·us -ī** *m* bushel *(containing six modii or "pecks")*
mediocr·is -is -e *adj* of medium size, medium, average, ordinary; undistinguished; mediocre; narrow, small; intermediate
mediocrit·ās -ātis *f* moderate size *or* amount; middle course, mean; moderation; mediocrity ‖ *fpl* moderate passions
mediocriter *adv* moderately, fairly; not particularly, not very, not much; calmly; with moderation; *(w. neg.)* in no slight degree, considerably, extraordinarily
Mediolānēns·is -is -e *adj* of Milan
Mediolān·um -ī *n* Milan

medioxum·us -a -um *adj (coll)* in the middle, intermediate
meditāment·um -ī *n* practice, drill, exercise *(in school, in the army)*
meditātē *adv* intentionally
meditāti·ō -ōnis *f* reflection, contemplation; practice; rehearsal; *(w. gen)* reflection on
meditāt·us -a -um *adj* premeditated
mediterrāne·us -a -um *adj* inland ‖ *n* interior *(of a country)*
medit·or -ārī -ātus sum *tr* to think over, reflect on; to practice, rehearse; to have in mind, intend; to plan, design ‖ *refl* to practice, train ‖ *intr* to prepare one's speech, rehearse; *(w.* **dē** *+ abl)* to reflect on, think about;
meditull·ium -(i)ī *n* the interior *(of a country);* middle, center
medi·us -a -um *adj* middle, central, the middle of, in the middle; intermediate; moderate; intervening *(time);* middling, ordinary, common; undecided, neutral, ambiguous; **diēs medius** *(or* **lūx media, sōl medius)** midday; the south; **in mediā viā** in the middle of the road; **media pars** half; **medium mare** the high seas ‖ *n* the middle part, center; the general public; intervening space; intermediate stage; **dē** *(or* **ē) mediō** from the scene; **in mediō** in mid-course; within reach; **in mediō positus** made available to all; **in mediō pōnere** to disclose; **in medium** on behalf of the general public; for the common good; **in medium prōferre** to make public; **in medium** *(or* **in mediō) relinquere** to leave undecided; **mediō temporis** in the meanwhile
medius fidius *interj* so help me God!; honest to God!
mēd·ix -icis *see* **meddix**
medull·a -ae *f* marrow; *(fig)* middle ‖ *fpl (fig)* heart; **īmīs medullīs** in the innermost heart, deep within one's heart
medullitus *adv* with all one's heart
medullul·a -ae *f* **ānseris medullula** goose down
Mēd·us -a -um Mede, of the Medes ‖ *m* son of Aegeus and Medea, the eponymous hero of the Medes
Medūs·a -ae *f* one of the three Gorgons, whose look turned people to stone
Medūsae·us -a -um *adj* Medusan; **equus Medūsaeus** Pegasus
Megaer·a -ae *f* one of the three Furies
Megalēns·ia *or* **Megalēs·ia -ium** *npl* festival of Cybele, celebrated on the 4th of April
Megalēns·is -is -e *adj* of the Magna Mater *or* Cybele; **lūdī Megalēnsēs** games in honor of Cybele
Megar·a -ae *f or* **Megar·a -ōrum** *npl* town near Athens on the Saronic Gulf ‖ Greek town in Sicily
Megar·a -ae *f* wife of Hercules, whom he killed in a fit of madness
Megarē·us *or* **Megaric·us -a -um** *adj* of Megara, Megarean
megistān·es -um *mpl* grandees
meherc(u)le *or* **mehercules** *interj* by Hercules!
mēi·ō -ere *intr (coll)* to pee
mel mellis *n* honey; **meum mel** *(as term of endearment)* my honey ‖ *npl* drops of honey
melancholic·us -a -um *adj* melancholy
melandry·um -ī *n* piece of salted tuna
Melanipp·a -ae *f or* **Melanipp·ē -ēs** *f* Melanippe *(daughter of Aeolus or Desmon, the mother of two children by Neptune)*
Melanth·ius -(i)ī *m* goatherd of Ulysses
melcul·um -ī *n (term of endearment)* little honey
Melea·ger *or* **Melea·gros -grī** *m* Meleager *(son of King Oeneus of Calydon and participant in the famous Calydonian boar hunt)*
Meleagrid·es -um *fpl* sisters of Meleager who were changed into birds
mēl·ēs -is *f* badger
Melicert·a -ae *or* **Melicert·ēs -ae** *m* Melicertes *(son of Ino and Athamas, who was changed into a sea-god, called Palaemon by the Greeks and Portunus by the Romans)*
melic·us -a -um *adj* musical, melodious; lyric
melilōt·os -ī *m* clover-like plant
melimēl·a -ōrum *npl* honey apples
mēlīn·a -ae *f* **(mell-)** leather pouch
Mēlīn·um -ī *n* pigment; Melian white *(from Melos)*
meli·or -or -us *(comp of* **bonus)** *adj* better; kinder, more gracious; **melius est** *(w. inf, w. acc & inf)* it is (would be) preferable to, that
melisphyll·um -ī *n* balm *(herb of which bees are fond)*
Melit·a -ae *or* **Melit·ē -ēs** *f* Malta; a sea nymph
Melitēns·is -is -e *adj* Maltese
melius *(comp of* **bene)** *adv* better
meliusculē *adv* pretty well
meliuscul·us -a -um *adj* a little better
mell·a -ae *f* mead *(mixture of honey and water)*
mellicul·us -a -um *adj* sweet as honey
melli·fer -fera -ferum *adj* producing honey
mellific·ō -āre *intr* to make honey
mellill·a -ae *f (term of endearment)* little honey

mellīn·a -ae *f* **(mēlī-)** leather pouch *(made from the skin of a badger)*
mellin·a -ae *f* sweetness, delight
mellīt·us -a -um *adj* honeyed; sweet as honey
mel·os -eos *n or* **mel·um -ī** *n or* **mel·os -ī** *m* song, tune
Melpomen·ē -ēs *f* Muse of tragic poetry
membrān·a -ae *f* membrane, skin; slough *(of a snake);* parchment; film
membrānul·a -ae *f* small piece of parchment
membrātim *adv* limb by limb; singly, piecemeal; in short sentences
membr·um -ī *n* member, organ, limb, genital; part, division *(of a thing);* apartment, room; *(gram)* clause; *(rhet)* small section of a speech *or* literary work
mēmet *pron (emphatic form of* **mē)** me
memin·ī -isse *(imperative:* **mementō; mementōte)** *tr* to remember **II** *tr (w. gen)* to remember, be mindful of
Memn·ōn -onis *m* son of Tithonus and Aurora, king of the Ethiopians, killed by Achilles **II** statue in Egypt *(actually of Amenhotep III)*
Memnonid·es -um *fpl* birds that rose from the pyre of Memnon
Memnoni·us -a -um *adj* Memnonian; Oriental; Moorish; black
mem·or -oris *adj* mindful, remembering having a good memory; careful, thoughtful; observant; *(w. gen)* mindful of, remembering
memorābil·is -is -e *adj* memorable, remarkable
memorand·us -a -um *adj* worth mentioning, notable
memorāt·us -ūs *m* mention
memori·a -ae *f* memory; remembrance; period of recollection, time, lifetime; a memory, past event, history; historical account; **in memoriā habēre** to bear in mind; **in memoriā redīre** *(or* **regredī)** to recollect; **in memoriā indūcere** *(or* **redigere)** to call to mind; **in memoriam** *(w. gen)* in memory of; **memoriā** *(w. gen)* in the time of; **memoriā tenēre** to keep in mind; to remember; **memoriae causā** as a reminder; **memoriae mandāre** *(or* **trādere)** to commit to memory; **memoriae prōdere** to hand down to posterity; **paulō suprā hanc memoriam** not long ago; **post hominum memoriam** within the memory of man; **superiōre memoriā** in earlier times
memoriāl·is -is -e *adj* for memoranda
memoriol·a -ae *f* poor memory
memoriter *adv* from memory, by heart
memor·ō -āre -āvī -ātus *tr* to mention, bring up; to name, call **II** *intr (w.* **dē** *+ abl)* to speak of

Memph·is -is *or* **-idos** *f* capital city of Pharaonic Egypt
Memphītic·us -a -um *adj* Egyptian
Menan·der *or* **Menan·dros -drī** *m* Greek playwright of Attic New Comedy *(342–291 B.C.)*
Menandrē·us -a -um *adj* of Menander
mend·a -ae *f* fault, blemish; slip of the pen
mendāciloqui·or -or -us *adj* more false
mendāc·ium -(i)ī *n* lie
mendāciuncul·um -ī *n* white lie, fib
mend·āx -ācis *adj* mendacious, lying, false **II** *m* liar
mendīcit·ās -ātis *f* begging
mendīc·ō -āre -āvī -ātus *or* **mendīc·or -ārī -ātus sum** *tr* to beg, beg for **II** *intr* to beg, be a beggar
mendīcul·us -a -um *adj* beggarly
mendīc·us -a -um *adj* needy, poverty-stricken; paltry *(meal)* **II** *m* beggar
mendōsē *adv* faultily, carelessly
mendōs·us -a -um *adj* full of physical defects; full of faults, faulty, incorrect, erroneous; blundering
mend·um -ī *n* defect, fault; blunder *(esp. in writing)*
Menelā·us -ī *m* son of Atreus, brother of Agamemnon, and husband of Helen
Menēn·ius -(i)ī *m* Menenius Agrippa *(told the plebs the fable of the belly and the limbs, 494 B.C.)*
Menoec·eūs -eī *or* **-eos** *m* son of Theban king Creon, who hurled himself off the city walls to save the city
Menoetiad·ēs -ae *m* son of Menoetius *(i.e., Patroclus)*
Menoet·ius -(i)ī *m* one of the Argonauts and father of Patroclus
mēn·s -tis *f* mind, intellect; frame of mind, attitude; will, inclination; understanding, reason; thought, opinion, intention, plan; courage, boldness; passion, impulse; **addere mentem** to give courage; **captus mente** crazy; **dēmittere mentem** to lose heart; **in mentem venīre** to come to mind; **mentis suae esse** to be in one's right mind
mēns·a -ae *f* table; meal, course, dinner; guests at table; counter; bank; sacrificial table, altar; **mēnsa secunda** dessert
mēnsār·ius -(i)ī *m* banker; treasury official; **triumvirī mēnsāriī** board of three treasury officials
mēnsi·ō -ōnis *f* measure, measuring; *(pros)* quantity *(of a syllable)*
mēns·is -is *(gen pl:* **mēnsium** *or* **mēnsum)** *m* month; **prīmō mēnse** at the beginning of the month
mēns·or -ōris *m* surveyor
mēnstruāl·is -is -e *adj* for a month
mēnstru·us -a -um *adj* monthly; lasting for a month **II** *n* rations for a month; month's term of office; monthly payment

mēnsul·a -ae *f* small table
mēnsūr·a -ae *f* measuring, measurement; standard of measure; amount, size, proportion, capacity, extent, limit, degree; **mēnsūra duōrum digitōrum** a pinch *(e.g., of salt)*
mēnsus *pp of* **metior**
ment·a *or* **menth·a -ae** *f* mint
menti·ēns -entis *m (phil)* sophism, fallacy
menti·ō -ōnis *f* mention; **mentiōnem facere** *(w. gen or* **dē** *+ abl)* to make mention of; **mentiōnēs serere** *(w.* **ad)** to throw hints to
ment·ior -īrī -ītus sum *tr* to invent, fabricate; to feign, imitate, fake ‖ *intr* to lie; to act deceitfully
Ment·ōr -oris *m* friend of Ulysses ‖ Greek silversmith of 4th cent. B.C.; *(fig)* a work by Mentor
mentul·a -ae *f (vulg)* penis, dick
ment·um -ī *n* chin
me·ō -āre -āvī -ātum *intr* to go, pass
mēopte *pron (emphatic form of* **mē)** me, me myself
mephīt·is -is *f* sulfurous fumes
merāc(u)l·us -a -um *adj* pretty pure
merāc·us -a -um *adj* undiluted, pure
mercābil·is -is -e *adj* buyable
merc·āns -antis *m* merchant
mercāt·or -ōris *m* merchant, dealer
mercātōri·us -a -um *adj* mercantile, trading, business; **nāvis mercātōria** merchant ship
mercātūr·a -ae *f* commerce, trade, trading; purchase ‖ *fpl* goods, wares
mercāt·us -ūs *m* market, marketplace; fair; trade, traffic
mercēdul·a -ae *f* poor pay; low rent
mercennāri·us *or* **mercēnāri·us -a -um** *adj* hired, paid, mercenary ‖ *m* common laborer
merc·ēs -ēdis *f* pay, wages; bribe; reward, recompense; cost; price; payment *(esp. for effort, pain, misfortune);* injury, detriment; stipulation, condition; retribution, punishment; rent, income, interest; **ūnā mercēde duās rēs assequī** *(prov)* to kill two birds with one stone *(literally, to buy two things for the price of one)*
mercimōn·ium -(i)ī *n* merchandise, goods, wares
merc·or -ārī -ātus sum *tr* to purchase ‖ *intr* to trade, buy and sell
Mercuriāl·is -is -e *adj* of Mercury ‖ *mpl* corporation of merchants in Rome
Mercur·ius -(i)ī *m* Mercury *(son of Jupiter and Maia, messenger of the gods, patron of commerce, diplomacy, gambling, etc.); (astr)* Mercury; **sīdus** *(or* **stella) Mercuriī** the planet Mercury
merd·a -ae *f* droppings, excrement
merend·a -ae *f* lunch, snack
mer·eō -ēre -uī -itus *or* **mer·eor -ērī -itus sum** *tr* to deserve, merit, be entitled to; to win, gain *(glory, fame, reproach);* to earn *(money);* **merēre pecūniam ut** to accept money on condition that; **stipendia** *(or* **stipendium) merēre** *(mil)* to serve ‖ *intr* to serve; to serve in the army; *(w.* **dē** *+ abl)* to serve, render service to, do a favor for; **bene dē rē pūblicā merēre** *(or* **merērī)** to serve one's country well; **dē tē meruī** I have done you a favor, I have treated you well; **equō merēre** to serve in the cavalry
meretrīciē *adv* like a prostitute
meretrīci·us -a -um *adj* prostitute's
meretrīcul·a -ae *f* cute little wench; *(pej)* the little wench
meretr·īx -īcis *f* prostitute, hooker
merg·ae -ārum *fpl* pitchfork; device for reaping
merg·es -itis *f* sheaf of wheat
mer·gō -gere -sī -sus *tr* to dip, plunge, sink; to flood, inundate, engulf, swallow up; to swamp, overwhelm; to bury; to drown ‖ *refl* to dive ‖ *pass* to sink; *(of heavenly bodies)* to go down; to drown; to go bankrupt
merg·us -ī *m* seagull
merīdiān·us -a -um *adj* midday, noon; southern, southerly
merīdiāti·ō -ōnis *f* siesta
merīdi·ēs -ēī *m* midday, noon; south; **ab merīdiē** in the south; **spectāre ad merīdiem** to face south
merīdi·ō -āre -āvī *or* **merīdi·or -ārī -ātus sum** *intr* to take a siesta
Mērion·ēs -ae *m* charioteer of Idomeneus of Crete in the Trojan War
meritō *adv* deservedly, rightly
merit·ō -āre -āvī -ātus *tr* to earn regularly
meritōri·us -a -um *adj* rented, hired ‖ *npl* rented lodgings
merit·us -a -um *adj* deserved, just, right, proper, deserving; guilty ‖ *n* service, favor, kindness; merit, worth; blame, fault, offense; **meritum reddere** to return a favor
merobib·us -a -um *adj* drinking unmixed wine
Merop·ē -ēs *f* one of the Pleiades, daughter of Atlas and Pleione
Merop·s -is *m* king of Ethiopia, husband of Clymene, and reputed father of Phaëthon
mer·ops -opis *m* bee-eater *(bird)*
mers·ō -āre -āvī -ātus *tr* to keep dipping *or* plunging; to drown; *(fig)* to engulf ‖ *pass (w. dat)* to plunge into
mersus *pp of* **mergō**
merul·a -ae *f* blackbird
mer·us -a -um *adj* pure, unmixed, undiluted; *(fig)* nothing but, mere ‖ *n* (undiluted) wine

mer·x -cis *f* merchandise, wares; **mala merx** *(fig)* a bad lot

Messallīn·a -ae *f* Valeria Messallina *(wife of Claudius and mother of Britannicus)* ‖ Statilia Messalina *(wife of Nero)*

Messān·a -ae *f* town in N.E. Sicily (*modern Messina*)

Messāpi·us -a -um *adj* of Messapia, of Calabria ‖ *f* town and district of Messapia in S.E. Italy

mess·is -is *f (acc:* **messem** *or* **messim**) harvest; harvest time; **adhūc tua messis in herbā est** *(prov)* don't count your chickens before they are hatched *(literally, your harvest is still on the stalk, i.e., in early stages of growth)*

mess·or -ōris *m* reaper, mower

messōri·us -a -um *adj* reaper's

messuī *perf of* **metō**

messus *pp of* **metō**

mēt·a -ae *f* marker for measuring a lap at a racetrack; haystack; *(fig)* goal, end; *(fig)* turning point

metall·um -ī *n* metal ‖ *npl* mine

metamorphōs·is -is *f* transformation

metaphor·a -ae *f* metaphor

mētāt·or -ōris *m* planner; **mētātor urbis** city planner

Metaur·us -ī *m* river in Umbria

Metell·us -ī *m* Roman family name *(cognomen);* Quintus Caecilius Metellus Numidicus *(commander of the Roman forces against Jugurtha, 109–107 B.C.)*

Mēthymn·a -ae *f* town on the Island of Lesbos

metīculōsus *see* **metūculōsus**

mētior mētīrī mēnsus sum *tr* to measure; to traverse, travel; to judge, estimate; *(w. dat)* to measure *(s.th.)* out to, distribute *(s. th.)* among; *(w. abl)* to judge *(s.o.)* by the standard of

metō metere messuī messus *tr* to reap, mow, gather, harvest; *(fig)* to mow down *(e.g., with the sword);* **ut sementem fēceris, ita et metēs** *(prov)* as you sow, so shall you reap

mēt·or -ārī -ātus sum *tr* to measure off; to lay out *(e.g., a camp)*

metrēt·a -ae *f* liquid measure *(about nine gallons)*

metūculōs·us -a -um *adj* (**metīc-**) fearful; scary; awful

metu·ēns -entis *adj* afraid, anxious

met·uō -uere -uī -ūtus *tr* to fear, be afraid of ‖ *intr* to be afraid, be apprehensive

met·us -ūs *m* fear, anxiety; **in metū esse** to be in a state of alarm; to be an object of concern

me·us -a -um *adj* my ‖ *pron* mine; **meā interest** it is of importance to me; **meum est** *(w. inf)* it is my duty to; **meus est** *(coll)* I've got him, he's mine

Mezent·ius -(i)ī *m* Etruscan ruler of Caere, slain by Aeneas

mī = mihi

mīc·a -ae *f* crumb, morsel

Micips·a -ae *m* son of Masinissa and king of Numidia *(148–118 B.C.)* ‖ *mpl (fig)* Numidians, N. Africans

mic·ō -āre -uī *intr* to vibrate, quiver; to twinkle, sparkle, flash

mictur·iō -īre *intr* to have to urinate

Mid·ās -ae *m* king of Phrygia, at whose touch everything turned to gold *(8th cent. B.C.)*

migrāti·ō -ōnis *f* moving, changing residence; migration; *(fig)* metaphorical use

migrō -āre -āvī -ātus *tr* to move, transport; *(fig)* to violate *(a law)* ‖ *intr* to move, change residence; migrate; *(fig)* to change, turn

mīl·es -itis *m* soldier; infantryman; private; *(fig)* army

Mīlēsi·us -a -um *adj* Milesian, of Miletus

Mīlēt·us -ī *f* town on W. coast of Asia Minor ‖ *m* founder of the town of Miletus

mīl·ia -ium *npl* thousands; *see* **mīlle**

mīliār·ium -(i)ī *n* milestone

mīlitār·is -is -e *adj* military

mīlitāriter *adv* in a military manner, like a soldier

mīlitāri·us -a -um *adj* soldierly, military

mīliti·a -ae *f* army; war; the military; military discipline; **mīlitiae** in war, on the battlefield, in the army; **mīlitiae domīque** abroad and at home, on the war front and on the home front

mīlit·ō -āre -āvī -ātum *intr* to be a soldier, do military service

mīl·ium -(i)ī *n* millet *(a food grain)*

mīlle *(indecl) adj* thousand; **mīlle hominēs** a thousand people ‖ **mīlia** *npl (declinable noun) (gen:* **mīlium**) thousands; *(w. gen):* **duo mīlia hominum** two thousand people; **duo mīlia passuum** two miles *(literally, two thousands of paces)*

mīllēsim·us *or* **mīllēnsim·us -a -um** *adj* thousandth

mīlliār·ium -(i)ī *n* milestone; **mīlliārium aureum** golden milestone *(set up by Augustus in the forum to indicate distances to various places in the Empire)*

mīlliēns *or* **mīlliēs** *adv* a thousand times; innumerable times

Mil·ō -ōnis *m* Titus Annius Papinianus Milo *(defended by Cicero on a charge of having murdered Clodius in 52 B.C.)*

Miltiad·ēs -is *m* Athenian general victorious at Marathon *(490 B.C.)*

mīlvīn·us *or* **mīluīn·us -a -um** *adj* rapacious *(as a kite)*

mīlv·us *or* **mīlv·os** *or* **mīlu·us -ī** *m* kite *(bird of prey);* flying gurnard *(fish); (astr)* mistakenly taken by Ovid as a constellation

mīm·a -ae *f* actress *(of mimes)*
Mimallon·es -um *fpl* Bacchantes
Mimallon·is -idis *f* a Bacchante
Mim·ās -antis *m* one of the Giants
mīmicē *adv* like a mime actor
mīmic·us -a -um *adj* suitable for the mime, farcical
Mimnerm·us -ī *m* Greek elegiac poet of Colophon on the W. coast of Asia Minor *(fl 630 B.C.)*
mīmul·a -ae *f* miserable little actress
mīm·us -ī *m* mime, farce; actor *(of a mime); (fig)* farce
min·a -ae *f* Greek unit of weight, equal to 100 drachmas, or 100 Roman denarii; Greek coin *(about 100 denarii, i.e., about $100)*
mināci·ae -ārum *fpl* threats
mināciter *adv* threateningly
min·ae -ārum *fpl* threats; projecting points of a wall
minanter *adv* threateningly
mināti·ō -ōnis *f* a threatening
min·āx -ācis *adj* threatening, menacing; projecting, jutting out
min·eō -ēre *intr* to project, jut out
Minerv·a -ae *f* goddess of wisdom and of the arts and sciences, identified with Athena; *(fig)* skill, genius; spinning and weaving; **invītā Minervā** against one's better judgment
mingō mingere mīnxī *or* **mīxī mīnctum** *or* **mīctum** *intr* (coll) to urinate
miniān·us -a -um *adj* vermilion
miniātul·us -a -um *adj* reddish
minimē *or* **minumē** *adv* least of all, least, very little; by no means, certainly not, not in the least; *(w. numerals)* at least; **minimē gentium** *(coll)* by no means
minim·us *or* **minum·us -a -um** *(superl of* **parvus)** *adj* smallest, least, very small; slightest, very insignificant; least important; youngest; shortest *(time);* **minimus nātū** youngest ‖ *n* the least, minimum; lowest price; **minimō emere** to buy at a very low price; **minimō prōvocāre** to provoke on the flimsiest pretext
mini·ō -āre -āvī -ātus *tr* to color red, paint red
minis·ter -trī *m* servant, attendant, helper; waiter; agent, subordinate, tool
minister·ium -(i)ī *n* activity of a servant *or* attendant, service, attendance; task, duty; office, ministry; occupation, work; agency, instrumentality ‖ *npl* servants
ministr·a -ae *f* servant, attendant, helper; waitress; handmaid
ministrāt·or -ōris *m or* **ministrātr·īx -īcis** *f* assistant, helper
ministr·ō -āre -āvī -ātus *tr* to serve, wait on; to tend; to execute, carry out *(orders); (w. dat)* to hand out *(s.th.)* to; *(w. abl)* to supply *(s.o. or s.th.)* with
minitābund·us -a -um *adj* threatening, menacing
minit·ō -āre *or* **minit·or -ārī -ātus sum** *tr* to make threats of *(e.g., war); (w. acc of thing and dat of person)* to threaten to bring *(e.g., evil, harm)* upon, hold *(s.th.)* threateningly over *(s.o.)* ‖ *intr* to jut out, project; to be menacing, make threats; *(w. dat)* to threaten
min·or -or -us *(comp of* **parvus)** *adj* smaller, less; shorter *(time);* inferior; less important; *(w. abl)* **1** *(of time)* too short for; **2** inferior to; **3** unworthy of; *(w. inf)* unfit to, incapable of; **dīmidiō minor quam** half as small as; **minor capitis** deprived of civil rights; **minōrēs facere fīliōs quam** to think less of the sons than of; **minor nātū** younger ‖ *mpl* descendants, posterity ‖ *n* less; **minōris emere** to buy at a lower price; **minus praedae** less booty
mīn·or -ārī *intr* to jut, project; *(w. dat)* to threaten; *(w. dat of person and acc of thing)* to threaten *(s.o.)* with; *(w. acc & inf)* to threaten that …
Mīn·ōs -ōis *or* **-ōnis** *m* son of Zeus and Europa, king of Crete, husband of Pasiphaë, and, after his death, judge in the lower world
Mīnōtaur·us -ī *m* monstrous offspring of Pasiphaë, half man and half bull, kept in the Labyrinth
minum- = minim-
min·uō -uere -uī -ūtus *tr* to diminish, lessen, reduce; to weaken, lower; to modify *(plans);* to settle *(controversies);* to limit *(authority);* to offend against, try to cheapen *(e.g., the majesty of the Roman people)* ‖ *intr* to diminish, abate, ebb; **minuente aestū** at ebbtide
minus *adv* less; not; by no means, not at all
minuscul·us -a -um *adj* smallish
minūt·al -ālis *n* hash, hamburger
minūtātim *adv* piecemeal; bit by bit
minūtē *adv* in a small-minded way
minūtul·us -a -um *adj* tiny
minūt·us -a -um *adj* small, minute; petty, narrow-minded
Miny·ae -ārum *mpl* descendants of Minyas, *esp.* the Argonauts
Miny·ās -ae *m* king of Thessaly
mīrābil·is -is -e *adj* remarkable, extraordinary, amazing, wonderful
mīrābiliter *adv* amazingly
mīrābund·us -a -um *adj* astonished, wondering
mīrācul·um -ī *n* wonder, marvel; surprise, amazement; *(pej)* freak; **septem mīrācula** the seven wonders *(of the ancient world)*
mīrand·us -a -um *adj* fantastic
mīrāti·ō -ōnis *f* astonishment, wonder
mīrāt·or -ōris *m,* **mīrātr·īx -īcis** *f* admirer

mīrē *adv* surprisingly, strangely; uncommonly; wonderfully; **mīrē quam** it is strange how, strangely
mīrificē *adv* wonderfully
mīrific·us -a -um *adj* causing wonder, wonderful; fascinating
mīrimodīs *adv* in a strange way
mirmill·ō -ōnis *m* gladiator *(who fought with Gallic arms)*
mīr·or -ārī -ātus sum *tr* to be amazed at, be surprised at; to look at with wonder, admire
mīr·us -a -um *adj* amazing, surprising, astonishing; wonderful; **mīrum est** *(w. acc & inf)* it is surprising that; **est mīrum quam** *(or* **mīrum quantum)** it is amazing how, it is amazing to what extent
mīscellāne·a -ōrum *npl* **(mīscill-)** hash, hodgepodge
mīsceō mīscēre mīscuī mīxtus *tr* to mix, blend, mingle; to combine, associate, share; to give and take; to mix up, confuse, turn upside down; to mix, prepare, brew; to fill *(with confused noise, etc.);* to unite sexually; **arma** *(or* **manūs** *or* **proelium** *or* **proelia)** **mīscēre** to join battle
misell·us -a -um *adj* poor little
Mīsēn·um -ī *n* promontory and town on the northern end of the Bay of Naples
mis·er -era -erum *adj* poor, pitiful; wretched, miserable, unhappy; sorry, worthless
miserābil·is -is -e *adj* miserable, pitiable; piteous
miserābiliter *adv* pitiably; piteously
miserand·us -a -um *adj* pitiful; deplorable
miserāti·ō -ōnis *f* pity, compassion, sympathy; appeal for sympathy
miserē *adv* wretchedly, miserably, unhappily; pitifully; desperately
miser·eō -ēre -uī -itum *or* **miser·eor -ērī -itus sum** *intr (w. gen)* to pity, feel sorry for, sympathize with **||** *v impers (w. acc of person who feels pity and gen of object of pity), e.g.,* **miseret** *(or* **miserētur) mē aliōrum** I feel sorry for the others
miserēsc·ō -ere *intr* to feel pity, feel sympathetic; *(w. gen)* to pity, feel sorry for **||** *v impers (w. acc of person who feels pity and gen of object of pity), e.g.,* **mē miserēscit virī** I feel sorry for the man, I pity the man
miseri·a -ae *f* pitiful condition, misery, distress, trouble
misericordi·a -ae *f* pity, sympathy, compassion; mercy
misericor·s -dis *adj* sympathetic, merciful
miseriter *adv* sadly
miser·or -ārī -ātus sum *tr* to deplore; to pity **||** *intr* to feel pity
mīsī *perf of* **mittō**
missicul·ō -āre -āvī -ātus *tr* to keep sending
missil·is -is -e *adj* missile, flying **||** *npl* missiles
missi·ō -ōnis *f* release, liberation; sending off, dispatching; military discharge; dismissal from office; **missiō cum ignōminiā** dishonorable discharge; **sine missiōne** without letup, to the death
missit·ō -āre -āvī -ātus *tr* to keep sending
missus *pp of* **mittō**
miss·us -ūs *m* letting go, throwing, hurling; sending
mītēsc·ō -ere *intr* to grow mild; to grow mellow, become ripe; *(fig)* to get soft; *(fig)* to become gentle, become tame; *(of feelings)* to become less intense, abate, cool off
Mithr·ās -ae *m* Mithra(s) *(sun-god of the Persians)*
Mithridāt·ēs -is *m* Mithridates the Great *(king of Pontus from 120 to 63 B.C.)*
Mithridātē·us *or* **Mithridātic·us -a -um** *adj* Mithridatic
mītigāti·ō -ōnis *f* mitigation
mītig·ō -āre -āvī -ātus *tr* to mellow, ripen; to soften; to calm down, appease; to make more tolerable, alleviate; to tone down *(a statement);* to soothe, mollify *(feelings);* to civilize
mīt·is -is -e *adj* mellow, ripe, soft; calm, placid; mild, gentle
mitr·a -ae *f* miter, turban
mittō mittere mīsī missus *tr* to send; to let fly, throw, hurl, launch; to emit, shed; to let out, utter; to let go of, drop; to free, release; to discharge, dismiss; to pass over in silence; to send for, invite; to pass up, forego; to dedicate *(a book);* to yield, produce; to export; to forget, dismiss *(from the mind);* **sanguinem mittere** to bleed; **sanguinem prōvinciae mittere** *(fig)* to bleed a province dry; **sub lēgēs orbem mittere** to subject the world to laws; **vōcēs mittere** to utter words
mītul·us -ī *m* limpet *(kind of mussel)*
mīxtim *adv* promiscuously
mīxtūr·a -ae *f* mixing, blending
mīxtus *pp of* **mīsceō**
Mnēmosyn·ē -ēs *f* mother of the Muses
mnēmosyn·on -ī *n* souvenir
mōbil·is -is -e *adj* mobile, movable, portable; nimble, active; shifty, changing; impressionable, excitable
mōbilit·ās -ātis *f* mobility; agility, quickness; shiftiness, fickleness
mōbiliter *adv* quickly, rapidly
mōbilit·ō -āre -āvī -ātus *tr* to impart motion to, endow with motion
moderābil·is -is -e *adj* moderate
moderām·en -inis *n* control
moderanter *adv* under control
moderātē *adv* with moderation

moderātim *adv* gradually
moderāti·ō -ōnis *f* controlling, control, regulation; curbing, checking; guidance; moderation, self-control
moderāt·or -ōris *m or* **moderātr·īx -īcis** *f* controller, director, guide
moderāt·us -a -um *adj* controlled, well-regulated, orderly, restrained
moder·ō -āre -āvī -ātus *or* **moder·or -ārī -ātus sum** *tr* to control, direct, guide **‖** *intr (w. dat)* **1** to moderate, restrain; **2** to allay, mitigate
modestē *adv* with moderation, discreetly; modestly
modesti·a -ae *f* moderation, restraint; discretion; modesty, sense of shame, sense of honor, dignity; propriety; mildness *(of weather)*
modest·us -a -um *adj* moderate, restrained; modest, discreet; orderly, obedient
modiāl·is -is -e *adj* containing a *modius* or peck
modicē *adv* moderately, with restraint; in an orderly manner; only slightly
modic·us -a -um *adj* moderate; small; modest, unassuming; ordinary; puny, trifling
modificāt·us -a -um *adj* regulated *(in length),* measured
mod·ius -(i)ī *m* modius, peck *(one-sixth of a medimnus or bushel);* **plēnō modiō** in full measure
modo *adv* only, merely, simply; *(of time)* just now, just recently, lately; presently, in a moment; **modo . . . deinde** *(or* **tum, posteā, interdum)** first . . . then, at one time . . . next time; **modo . . . modo** now . . . now, sometimes . . . sometimes, at one moment . . . at another; **nōn modo . . . sed etiam** *(or* **vērum etiam)** not only . . . but also **‖** *conj* if only, provided that
modulātē *adv* according to measure, in time; melodiously
modulāt·or -ōris *m* director, musician
modul·or -ārī -ātus sum *tr* to regulate the time of, measure rhythmically; to modulate; to sing; to play
modul·us -ī *m* small measure; small stature; unit of measurement
mod·us -ī *m* measured amount, quantity; standard of measurement, unit of measurement, measure; time, rhythm; size, extent, length; due *or* proper measure, limit, boundary; rule, regulation; way, manner, style, mode; kind, form, type; *(gram)* voice *(of a verb); (mus)* measure, beat, note, tone; *(poet)* verse, poetry, meter; *(rhet)* rhythmic pattern; **ad modum** *(or* **in modum)** in time, rhythmically; **ad modum** *(w. gen) or* **in modum** *(w. gen)* in the manner of, like; **cūiusdam modī** of a certain kind, a certain kind of; **cūiusdam modī pugna** a certain kind of fight; **cum modō** with restraint, moderately; **ēius modī homō** that kind of person; **ex Tūscō modō** in the Etruscan manner *or* style; **hūius modī homō** this kind of person; **modō** moderately; **modum adhibēre** *(or* **cōnstituere** *or* **facere** *or* **impōnere** *or* **pōnere** *or* **statuere)** to impose a limit, set bounds; **nullō modō** in no way, not at all; **omnī modō** in every case; **praeter** *(or* **suprā)** **modum** excessively; **prō modō** *(w. gen)* in proportion to; **quem ad modum** how; **quemnam ad modum** just how; **quid modī?** what limit?; **quōnam modō** just how; **sine modō** without restraint **‖** *mpl* tune, melody, song; poetry, poems
moech·a -ae *f* adulteress
moechiss·ō -āre *tr* to commit adultery with
moech·or -ārī -ātus sum *intr* to have an affair, commit adultery
moech·us -ī *m* adulterer
moen·ia -ium *npl* town walls, ramparts, fortifications; fortified town; castle, stronghold; defenses
moeniō *see* **mūniō**
moerus *see* **mūrus**
Moes·ī -ōrum *mpl* people of the Lower Danube basin
Moesi·a -ae *f* Moesia *(Roman province S. of the Danube and extending to the Black Sea)*
mol·a -ae *f* millstone; mill; flour **‖** *fpl* mill
molār·is -is *m* millstone; molar *(tooth)*
mōl·ēs -is *f* mass, bulk, pile; massive structure; dam, mole, pier; mass *(of people, etc.);* burden, effort, trouble; calamity; might, greatness
molestē *adv* with annoyance; with difficulty, with trouble; **molestē ferre** to be annoyed at, be disgruntled at, barely stand *or* tolerate
molesti·a -ae *f* annoyance, nuisance, trouble; worry; affectation *(of style)*
molest·us -a -um *adj* annoying, troublesome, distressing; labored, affected *(style)*
mōlīm·en -inis *n* great exertion, great effort; attempt, undertaking
mōlīment·um -ī *n* great exertion, great effort
mōl·ior -īrī -ītus sum *tr* to do with great effort, strain at, exert oneself over; to get rid of; to wield, heave, hurl *(missiles);* to wield *(a weapon, an instrument);* to get *(a ship)* under way; to get *(a vehicle)* moving; to rouse *(bodies of men)* to action; to work hard at; to build, erect *(usu. huge constructions);* to displace, shift from its position; to undertake, attempt; to perform; to cause, occasion **‖** *intr* to exert oneself, struggle, take great

pains; to make one's way *(w. effort),* proceed

mōlīti·ō -ōnis *f* building, erection; (the action of) shifting *or* moving; **rērum mōlītiō** the creation

mōlīt·or -ōris *m* builder; contriver, schemer

mōlītr·īx -īcis *f* contriver *(female)*

mōlītus *pp of* **mōlior**

molitus *pp of* **molō** ‖ *adj* ground, milled

mollēsc·ō -ere *intr* to become soft; to become gentle; to become effeminate

mollicul·us -a -um *adj* tender, dainty

moll·iō -īre -īvī *or* **-iī -ītus** *tr* to make soft, soften; *(fig)* to soften, mitigate; to demoralize

mollip·ēs -edis *adj* tender-footed

moll·is -is -e *adj* soft; springy; flexible; flabby; mild, calm; easy; gentle *(slope);* sensitive, impressionable; tender, touching; weak, effeminate; amatory *(verses);* changeable, untrustworthy

molliter *adv* softly; gently, smoothly; effeminately; voluptuously; patiently, with fortitude

molliti·a -ae *or* **molliti·ēs -ēī** *f* softness; flexibility; tenderness; sensitivity; weakness, irresolution; effeminacy, voluptuousness

mollitūd·ō -inis *f* softness; flexibility; susceptibility

mol·ō -ere -uī -itus *tr* to grind

Moloss·us -a -um *adj* Molossian ‖ *m* Molossian hound ‖ *mpl* Molossians *(a people of Epirus)*

mōl·y -yos *n* magic herb

mōm·en -inis *n* movement, motion; momentum

mōment·um -ī *n* movement, motion; alteration; turn, critical time; moment; impulse; momentum; influence; importance; motive

Mon·a -ae *f* Isle of Anglesey

monēdul·a -ae *f* jackdaw *(bird)*

mon·eō -ēre -uī -itus *tr* to call to mind, remind, advise, point out; to warn; to foretell; to teach; to inform

monēr·is -is *f* galley

Monēt·a -ae *f* Juno Moneta *(in whose temple on the Capitoline Hill money was coined);* mint; coin, money; stamp, die *(for money)*

monētāl·is -is -e *adj* of the mint ‖ *m* superintendent of the mint

monīl·e -is *n* necklace

monim- = monum-

monit·a -ōrum *npl* warnings; prophecies; precepts

moniti·ō -ōnis *f* reminder; warning

monit·or -ōris *m* reminder; counselor; teacher; prompter

monit·us -ūs *m* reminder; warning ‖ *mpl* promptings, warnings

monogramm·us -a -um *adj* sketchy, shadowy; unsubstantial, hollow

monopod·ium -(i)ī *n* table with a single central leg

monotrop·us -a -um *adj* single, alone

mōn·s -tis *m* mountain; hill; mountain range; mass, heap; **montīs aurī pollicērī** *(prov)* to make wild promises *(literally, to promise mountains of gold);* **summus mōns** mountaintop ‖ *mpl* hill country, the hills

mōnstrāti·ō -ōnis *f* pointing out

mōnstrāt·or -ōris *m* displayer, demonstrator

mōnstr·ō -āre -āvī -ātus *tr* to show, point out; to make known; to demonstrate, teach; to indicate, suggest; to appoint, designate ‖ *intr* to show the way

mōnstr·um -ī *n* sign, portent, wonder; warning; monster, monstrosity; atrocity; monstrous event

mōnstruōsē *adv* unnaturally

mōnstruōs·us -a -um *adj* unnatural, monstrous, strange

montān·us -a -um *adj* mountain, of a mountain; mountainous ‖ *mpl* hill-dwellers *(esp. of the seven hills of Rome)* ‖ *npl* mountainous regions

monticol·a -ae *m* mountaineer

montivag·us -a -um *adj* wandering over the mountains

montōs·us *or* **montuōs·us -a -um** *adj* mountainous

monument·um -ī *n* reminder; monument, memorial; literary work, book; history; record *(written or oral);* token of identification ‖ *npl* recorded tradition; **annālium monumenta** annals; **litterārum monumenta** literary record, document

Mopsopi·us -a -um *adj* Athenian ‖ *f* Athens; *(ancient name for)* Attica

mor·a -ae *f* delay; pause; spell, period of time; stop-off; **haud morā** without hesitation; **in morā esse** to be a hindrance; **in morā habēre** to allow to be a hindrance; **mora est** it will take too long; **moram afferre** to present difficulties, waste time; **moram facere** to obstruct; to cause delay

mor·a -ae *f (mil)* division *(of the Spartan army of from 300 to 700 men)*

mōr·a -ae *f* fool

mōrāl·is -is -e *adj* moral

morāt·or -ōris *m* obstructionist; loiterer; *(in court)* lawyer who spoke only to gain time

mōrāt·us -a -um *adj* -mannered, -natured; in character; *(of a thing)* natured; **bene mōrātus** well-mannered, civilized; **male mōrātus** ill-mannered, rude; **mīrābiliter mōrātus est** he is a strange creature

morbid·us -a -um *adj* sickly; causing sickness, unwholesome

morbōs·us -a -um *adj* sickly; sex-crazy, horny; **morbōsus in** *(w. acc)* mad about
morb·us -ī *m* sickness, disease, ailment; fault, vice; distress; **in morbum cadere** *(or* **in morbum incidere)** to fall sick
mordācius *adv* more bitingly; *(fig)* more radically
mord·āx -ācis *adj* biting, snapping; *(fig)* sharp, stinging, caustic; snarling; pungent, tart
mordeō mordēre momordī morsus *tr* to bite; to eat, devour; to grip; *(of cold)* to nip; *(of words)* to cut, hurt
mordic·ēs -um *mpl* bites; incisor teeth
mordicus *adv* by biting, with the teeth; *(fig)* tightly, doggedly
mōrē *adv* foolishly
morēt·um -ī *n* salad
moribund·us -a -um *adj* dying, at the point of death; mortal; deadly
mōriger·ō -āre *or* **mōriger·or -ārī -ātus sum** *intr (w. dat)* **1** to humor, pamper; **2** to yield to; **3** to comply with
mor·ior -ī -tuus sum *intr* to die; *(fig)* to decay, pass away, die out; *(of fires)* to die out; *(of flowers)* to wither, die off; **moriar nisi** *(coll)* hope to die if ... not
morm·ȳr -ȳris *f* Pontic fish
mor·or -ārī -ātus sum *tr* to delay, detain; to entertain, hold the attention of; to hinder, prevent; **nihil morārī** *(w. acc)* **1** to disregard, care nothing for, not value; **2** to have nothing against, have nothing to say against **II** *intr* to delay, linger, loiter; to stay, remain; to wait; **quid moror?** *(or* **quid multīs morer?)** why should I drag out the point?; to make a long story short
mōrōsē *adv* morosely, crabbily
mōrōsit·ās -ātis *f* moroseness, crabbiness
mōrōs·us -a -um *adj* morose, crabby; fastidious, particular; *(fig)* stubborn *(disease)*
Morph·eūs -eos *(acc:* **-ea)** *m* god of dreams
mors mortis *f* death; destruction; corpse; bloodshed; **morte commūnī** of natural causes; **mortem obīre** *(or* **oppetere)** to meet death; **mortem** *(or* **mortī) occumbere** to die; **mortem sibi cōnscīscere** to commit suicide *(literally, to decide on death for oneself)*; **mortis honōs** burial; **mortis poena** death penalty
mors·a -ōrum *npl* bits, little pieces
morsiuncul·a -ae *f* peck, kiss
morsus *pp of* **mordeō**
mors·us -ūs *m* bite; pungency; grip; corrosion; gnawing pain; sting; vicious attack
mortāl·is -is -e *adj* mortal, subject to death; human; transient; man-made **II** *m* mortal, human being
mortālit·ās -ātis *f* mortality; mortals, mankind
morticīn·us -a -um *adj & m* carrion
mortif·er *or* **mortif·erus -era -erum** *adj* lethal, deadly, fatal
mortiferē *adv* mortally
mortuāl·ia -ium *npl* dirges
mortu·us -a -um *adj* dead, deceased; withered, decayed; scared to death; over and done with; half-hearted, feeble **II** *m* dead person **II** *mpl* the dead
mōrul·us -a -um *adj* dark, blackberry-colored
mōr·um -ī *n* black mulberry
mōr·us -a -um *adj* foolish **II** *mf* fool
mōr·us -ī *f* black mulberry tree
mōs mōris *m* custom, usage, practice; caprice, mood; nature; manner; fashion, style; rule, regulation, law; **dē mōre** *(or* **ex mōre)** according to custom; **mōre** in the customary manner; **mōre** *(or* **in mōrem** *or* **dē mōre)** *(w. gen)* in the manner of, like; **mōrem gerere** *(w. dat)* to humor *(s.o.)*, to indulge *(s.o. or one's feelings)*; **mōs māiōrum** tradition; **nullō mōre** *(or* **sine mōre)** without restraint, wildly; lawlessly; **suprā mōrem** more than is usual **II** *mpl* morals; character; behavior; customs; laws; **ex meīs mōribus** according to my wishes
Mōs·ēs *or* **Moys·ēs -is** *m* Moses
mōti·ō -ōnis *f* motion, movement
mōtiuncul·a -ae *f* slight attack of fever
mōt·ō -āre -āvī -ātus *tr* to keep moving
mōtus *pp of* **moveō**
mōt·us -ūs *m* motion, movement; gesture; dancing; change *(e.g., of fortune)*; impulse, inspiration; passion; revolt, riot; tactical move; *(rhet)* figure of speech; **in mōtū** active; **in mōtū esse** to be in a state of flux; **mōtus animī** emotion; **mōtūs mentis** thought process; **mōtus pedum** activity; **mōtus terrae** earthquake
mov·ēns -entis *adj* active; restless, shifting; **rēs moventēs** movable property *(e.g., clothes, furniture)* **II** *npl* motives
moveō movēre mōvī mōtus *tr* to move; to stir, shake, disturb; to cause, occasion, promote; to begin; to undertake; to trouble, torment; to touch, influence, affect; to throw into political turmoil; to eject, expel *(from office, post)*; to degrade; to remove, take away; to dislodge *(the enemy)*; to shake, cause to waver; to plow; to strum, play *(a musical instrument)*; to dissuade; to exert, exercise; to turn over in the mind, ponder; **aliquem locō movēre** to dislodge s.o.; **arma** *or* **bellum movēre** to bring on a war, begin a war; **senātū movēre** to remove from the Senate roll; **signa movēre** to begin a march; **ventrem movēre** to move the bowels; **vōcem movēre carmine** to raise the voice in song **II** *refl* to move; to dance; *(of heavenly bodies)* to rise; *(of riots)* to break out; **sē ex locō movēre** to budge

from the spot ‖ *pass & intr* to move; to shake, quake, throb ‖ *intr* to move off, depart; *(of buds)* to sprout, come out

mox *adv* soon, presently; hereafter; next, then; later on

Moys·ēs -is *m* Moses

mūcid·us -a -um *adj* sniveling, snotty; moldy, musty

Mūc·ius -(i)ī *m* Roman clan name *(nomen);* Gaius Mucius Cordus Scaevola *(tried to kill Porsenna and, when caught, deliberately burned his right hand)*

mucr·ō -ōnis *m* sharp point, sharp edge; tip; sword; edge, boundary; keenness

mūc·us -ī *m* **(mucc-)** mucus, snot

mūgient·ēs -ium *mpl* oxen

mūg·il *or* **mūg·ilis -ilis** *m* gray mullet *(a sea fish)*

mūgīn·or -ārī -ātus sum *intr* to dilly-dally

mūg·iō -īre -īvī *or* **-iī -ītum** *intr* to moo, bellow, low; to roar, rumble; *(of a bugle)* to blast, sound

mūgīt·us -ūs *m* mooing, bellowing; roaring, rumbling

mūl·a -ae *f* mule

mul·ceō -cēre -sī -sus *or* **mul(c)tus** *tr* to stroke, pet; to stir gently; to soothe, alleviate; to appease; to gladden, delight

Mulcib·er -erī *or* **-eris** *m* Vulcan; *(fig)* fire

mulc·ō -āre -āvī -ātus *tr* to beat up, cudgel; to mistreat, injure; to worst *(in battle)*

mulctr·a -ae *f* milk pail

mulctrār·ium -(i)ī *or* **mulctr·um -ī** *n* milk pail

mul·geō -gēre -sī -sus *or* **-ctus** *tr* to milk

muliebr·is -is -e *adj* woman's, womanly, feminine; womanish, effeminate; *(of deities)* presiding over the lives of women; *(gram)* feminine; **pars muliebris** *(or* **partēs muliebrēs)** female sexual organs ‖ *npl* female sexual organs; **virī muliebria patiuntur** men play the role of women *(i.e., let themselves be used as catamites)*

muliebriter *adv* like a woman; effeminately

muli·er -eris *f* woman; wife

mulierāri·us -a -um *adj* woman's ‖ *m* womanizer, wolf

muliercul·a -ae *f* little *(or* weak *or* foolish) woman; sissy

mulierōsit·ās -ātis *f* weakness for women

mulierōs·us -a -um *adj* woman-crazy

mūlīn·us -a -um *adj* mulish

mūli·ō -ōnis *m* mule driver

mūliōni·us -a -um *adj* mule driver's

mullul·us -ī *m* little mullet *(fish)*

mull·us -ī *m* red mullet *(fish)*

mulsī *perf of* **mulceō** *and* **mulgeō**

muls·us -a -um *pp of* **mulceō** *and of* **mulgeō** ‖ *adj* honeyed, sweet as honey ‖ *f (term of endearment)* honey ‖ *n* mead *(wine mixed with honey)*

multa *adv* much, very; earnestly

mult·a -ae *f* fine; penalty; loss of money; **multam certāre** to contest a fine; **multam committere** to incur a fine; **multam dīcere** *(w. dat of person and acc of the fine)* to fine *(s. o. a certain amount);* **multam subīre** to incur a fine, be fined

mult·a -ōrum *npl* many things; much; **nē multa** in short

multangul·us -a -um *adj* having many angles, many-angled

multātīci·us -a -um *adj* of a fine; **multātīcia pecūnia** fine

multāti·ō -ōnis *f* fine, penalty

multēsim·us -a -um *adj* trifling, negligible

mult·ī -ōrum *mpl* many men, many; multitude, mass, common people

multibib·us -a -um *adj* fond of drinking, heavy-drinking

multicav·us -a -um *adj* porous

multīci·a -ōrum *npl* diaphanous garments

multifāriam *adv* in many places

multifid·us -a -um *adj* divided into many parts; splintered *(wood); (of a river)* having many tributaries

multifōrm·is -is -e *adj* multiform, manifold

multifor·us -a -um *adj* many-holed; *(flute)* having many stops

multigen·er -eris *or* **multigen·us -a -um** *adj* of many kinds, various

multiiug·is -is -e *or* **multiiug·us -a -um** *adj* many yoked together; many tied together; *(fig)* various

multiloqu·āx -ācis *adj* talkative

multiloqu·ium -(i)ī *n* talkativeness

multiloqu·us -a -um *adj* talkative

multimodīs *adv* in many ways

multiplex -icis *adj* with many folds; winding, serpentine; manifold; many; *(in comparisons)* many times as great, far greater; varied, complicated; versatile, changeable, many-sided; sly, cunning ‖ *n* manifold return

multiplicābil·is -is -e *adj* manifold, many

multipliciter *adv* in various ways

multiplic·ō -āre -āvī -ātus *tr* to multiply, increase, enlarge; to have *(or* use *or* practice) on many occasions

multipot·ēns -entis *adj* mighty, powerful

multitūd·ō -inis *f* great number, multitude, crowd, throng; rabble, common people; population

multivol·us -a -um *adj* passionate

multō *adv (w. comparatives)* much, far, by far, a great deal; **multō aliter ac** much different from; **multō ante** long before; **multō post** long after; **nōn multō secus fierī** to turn out just about the same

mult·ō -āre -āvī -ātus *tr* to punish; to fine

multum *adv* much, a lot, greatly, very; often, frequently; *(w. comparatives)* much, far; **multum valēre** to have considerable influence

mult·us -a -um *(comp:* **(plūs) plūrēs, plūra;** *superl:* **plūrimus)** *adj* many a, much, great; abundant, considerable, extensive; tedious, long-winded; full, numerous, thick, loud, heavy; constant; **ad multum diēm** till late in the day; **multā nocte** late at night; **multō diē** late in the day; *(with plural nouns)* many **‖** *mpl see* **multī ‖** *n* much; **multī** of great value, highly; **multī facere** to think highly of, make much of; **multum est** it is of great importance; **multum temporis** a great deal of time, much time **‖** *npl see* **multa**

mūl·us -ī *m* mule

Mulvi·us -a -um *adj* Mulvian; **Mulvius pōns** Milvian bridge *(across the Tiber, above Rome on the Via Flaminia)*

Mumm·ius -(i)ī *m* Lucius Mummius Achaicus *(conqueror of Corinth, 146 B.C.)*

mundān·us -a -um *adj* of the world **‖** *m* world citizen

mundē *or* **munditer** *adv* neatly, cleanly

munditi·a -ae *or* **munditi·ēs -ēī** *f* neatness, cleanliness; elegance; politeness; refinement of language

mundul·us -a -um *adj* trim, neat

mund·us -a -um *adj* neat, clean, nice; fine, smart, sharp, elegant; choice *(words)* **‖** *m* neat person; world, earth, universe; heavens; mankind; beauty aids; **in mundō** ready, in store; **mundus caelī** firmament

mūnerār·ius -(i)ī *m* producer of gladiatorial shows

mūnerigerul·us -ī *m* bearer of presents

mūner·ō -āre -āvī -ātus *or* **mūner·or -ārī -ātus sum** *tr* to reward, honor, present; *(w. acc of thing and dat of person)* to present *(s.th.)* to

mūni·a -ōrum *npl* official duties *or* functions

mūnic·eps -ipis *mf* citizen of a municipality; fellow citizen, fellow countryman

mūnicipāl·is -is -e *adj* municipal; *(pej)* provincial

mūnicipātim *adv* by municipalities

mūnicip·ium -(i)ī *n* municipality, town *(whose people were Roman citizens, but otherwise autonomous)*

mūnificē *adv* generously

mūnificenti·a -ae *f* generosity

mūnific·ō -āre -āvī -ātus *tr* to treat generously

mūnific·us -a -um *adj* generous; splendid

mūnīm·en -inis *n* defense

mūnīment·um -ī *n* defense, protection, fortification, rampart; *(fig)* shelter, defense, safeguard

mūn·iō -īre -īvī *or* **-iī -ītus** *tr* **(moen-)** to defend with a wall, wall in; to fortify, strengthen, defend, protect, secure; to build *(road);* to provide with a road; *(fig)* to guard, shelter, protect, support

mūn·is -is -e *adj* obliging, ready to be of service

mūnīti·ō -ōnis *f* building, fortifying, defending; fortification, rampart, trenches, lines; **mūnītiō flūminum** bridging of rivers; **mūnītiō viae** road construction

mūnīt·ō -āre *tr* to open up *(a road)*

mūnīt·or -ōris *m* builder *(of fortifications)*

mūnīt·us -a -um *pp of* **mūniō ‖** *adj* well-fortified, well-protected; *(fig)* safe, protected

mūn·us -eris *n* **(moen-)** service, function, duty; gift; favor, kindness; tax, duty; public entertainment, gladiatorial show; tribute *(to the dead),* rite, sacrifice; public office; **in mūnere** *(or* **mūnere** *or* **prō mūnere)** as a gift

mūnūscul·um -ī *n* small gift

mūraen·a -ae *f* moray *(eel-like fish)*

mūrāl·is -is -e *adj* wall, of a wall; wall-destroying; wall-defending

mūr·ex -icis *m* murex, mollusk *(yielding purple dye);* purple dye, purple; jagged rock; spiked trap *(as defense against cavalry attack)*

muri·a -ae *or* **muri·ēs -ēī** *f* brine *(used for pickling)*

muriātic·um -ī *n* pickled fish

mūricīd·us -ī *m* **(murr-)** mouse killer; *(fig)* coward

murmill·ō -ōnis *m* gladiator *(with Gallic arms, who fought against an opponent who used a net)*

murm·ur -uris *n* murmur, murmuring; buzz, hum; roar, crash; growling, grumbling; rumbling; hubbub

murmurill·um -ī *n* low murmur

murmur·ō -āre -āvī -ātus *tr* to murmur against **‖** *intr* to mutter, grumble; to rumble, roar

murr·a -ae *f* fluorspar *(mineral from which expensive vases were made)*

murr·a *or* **murrh·a** *or* **myrrh·a -ae** *f* myrrh tree; myrrh

murre·us -a -um *adj* made of fluorspar

murre·us -a -um *adj* **(myrrh-)** myrrh-colored, reddish-brown

murt- = myrt-

mūr·us -ī *m* wall; city wall(s); dike; rim *(of dish or pot); (fig)* defender, champion

mūs mūris *m* mouse; rat

Mūs·a -ae *f* Muse *(patron goddess of poetry, song, dance, literature, etc.);* poem, song; talent; poetic inspiration

Mūsae·us -ī *m* pre-Homeric bard in the time of Orpheus

Mūsae·us *or* **Mūsē·us -a -um** *adj* of the Muses, musical, poetic **‖** *n* institute of philosophy and research at Alexandria

mūsc·a -ae *f* fly; *(fig)* nosey person

mūscār·ium -(i)ī *n* fly swatter

mūscipul·a -ae *f or* **mūscipul·um -ī** *n* mousetrap
mūscōs·us -a -um *adj* mossy
mūscul·us -ī *m* little mouse; muscle; *(mil)* mantelet
mūsc·us -ī *m* moss
mūsic·a -ae *or* **mūsic·ē -ēs** *f or* **mūsic·a -ōrum** *npl* music; art of music *(including poetry)*
mūsicē *adv* pleasantly, elegantly
mūsic·us -a -um *adj* relating to the Muses; musical; melodious, tuneful; poetic; *(of a person)* expert in music ‖ *mf* musician
mussit·ō -āre -āvī -ātus *tr* to bear in silence ‖ *intr* to be silent; to mutter, grumble
muss·ō -āre -āvī -ātus *tr* to bear in silence; to brood over ‖ *intr* to mutter, murmur; to hesitate; *(of bees)* to hum
mustāce·us -ī *m or* **mustāce·um -ī** *n* wedding cake *(baked with must and set on laurel leaves)*
mustēl·a -ae *f* **(-tell-)** weasel
mustēlīn·us -a -um *adj* **(-tell-)** of a weasel
muste·us -a -um *adj* fresh; *(of a book)* in the early stages
must·um -ī *n* fresh grape juice, must; vintage
mūtābil·is -is -e *adj* changeable; fickle
mūtābilit·ās -ātis *f* mutability; fickleness
mūtāti·ō -ōnis *f* mutation, change; exchange, interchange; translation; **mūtātiō animī** change of heart
mutil·ō -āre -āvī -ātus *tr* to chop off, lop off, crop; to mutilate; to reduce; to rob
mutil·us -a -um *adj* mutilated; maimed; having chopped-off horns
Mutin·a -ae *f* town of N. Central Italy, S. of the Po *(modern Modena),* where Decimus Brutus was besieged by Antony *(44–43 B.C.)*
Mutinēns·is -is -e *adj* of Mutina
mūtiō *see* **muttiō**
mūtitiō *see* **muttitiō**
mūt·ō -āre -āvī -ātus *tr* to change, shift; to alter; to exchange, interchange, barter, sell; to modify, transform; to vary; to change for the better; to change for the worse; *(w.* **in** *+ acc)* to change *(s.th. or s.o.)* into; *(w. abl or w.* **cum** *or* **prō** *+ abl)* to exchange *or* substitute *(s.th. or s.o.)* for; **mūtāre fidem** to change allegiance, change sides; **mūtāre latus** to roll over *(in bed); (of fish)* to flip over ‖ *pass* to change; *(w.* **in** *+ acc)* to change into; *(w. abl)* to change in respect to: **silvae foliīs mūtantur** the forests change their leaves ‖ *intr* to change; **mūtāre in melius** *(or* **pēius)** to change for the better *(or* for the worse) ‖ *v impers* **nōn mūtat** it makes no difference
mutt·iō -īre -īvī -ītus *tr* **(mūt-)** to mutter, mumble
muttiti·ō *f* **(mūt-)** muttering
mutt·ō *or* **mūt·ō -ōnis** *m (vulg)* penis
mūtuē *adv* mutually; in turn
mūtuit·or -ārī *tr* to wish to borrow
mutūniāt·us -a -um *adj (vulg)* having a large penis
mūtuō *adv* mutually, in return
mūtu·or -ārī -ātus sum *tr* to borrow; to obtain, get; to derive
mūt·us -a -um *adj* mute; dumb, speechless; silent, still, noiseless; **mūta persōna** non-speaking actor ‖ *npl* dumb animals
mūtu·us -a -um *adj* mutual, reciprocal, interchangeable; borrowed, lent ‖ *n* loan; reciprocity; **aliquid mūtuum accipere** *(or* **sūmere)** to borrow s.th.; **aliquid mūtuum dare** *(w.* **cum)** to lend s.th. to *(s.o.);* **mūtuās pecūniās sūmere ab** to borrow money from; **mūtuum argentum rogāre ab** to ask *(s.o.)* for a loan of cash; **mūtuum facere cum aliquō** to reciprocate s.o.'s feelings ‖ *npl (w. advl sense)* mutually, reciprocally; **in mūtua** toward each other; **per mūtua** with one another
Mycēn·ae -ārum *fpl or* **Mycēn·ē -ēs** *f* Mycenae *(city of King Agamemnon in Argolis)*
Mycēn·is -idis *f* Mycenaean girl *(i.e., Iphigenia)*
Mygdon·es -um *mpl* a people of Thrace, some of whom later migrated to Phrygia
Mygdoni·us -a -um *adj* Phrygian
myopar·ōn -ōnis *m* galley
myrīc·a -ae *or* **myrīc·ē -ēs** *f* tamarisk
Myrmidon·es -um *mpl* Myrmidons *(people of Thessaly whom Achilles led in battle)*
Myr·ōn -ōnis *m* famous Greek sculptor *(5th cent. B.C.)*
myropōl·a -ae *m* perfumer
myropōl·ium -(i)ī *n* perfume shop
myrrh- = murr-
myrtēt·um -ī *n* **(mur-)** myrtle grove
myrte·us -a -um *adj* **(mur-)** myrtle; crowned with myrtle
Myrtō·um Mar·e *(gen:* **Myrtōī Maris)** *n* Myrtoan Sea *(between the Peloponnesus and the Cyclades)*
myrt·um -ī *n* myrtle berry
myrt·us -ūs *or* **-ī** *f* myrtle tree
Mȳsi·us -a -um *adj* Mysian ‖ *f* Mysia *(country in N.W. Asia Minor)*
myst·a *or* **myst·ēs -ae** *m* priest of the mysteries of Ceres; an initiate
mystagōg·us -ī *n* initiator; tourist guide
mystēr·ium -(i)ī *n* **(mist-)** secret religion, secret service, secret rite; divine mystery; secret; **mystēria facere** to hold service; **mystēria Rōmāna** festival of Bona Dea
mystic·us -a -um mystic
Mytilēn·ae -ārum *fpl or* **Mytilēn·ē -ēs** *f* Mytilene *(chief city of the island of Lesbos)*

Mytilēnae·us -a -um *or* **Mytilēnēns·is -is -e** *adj* of Mytilene

N

N, n *(supply* littera) *f* thirteenth letter of the Latin alphabet; letter name: **en**

N. *abbr* **Numerius** *(Roman first name, praenomen);* **Nōnae** the Nones; **Nummus** coin

Nabatae·us -a -um *adj* Nabataean; Eastern ‖ *mpl* Nabataeans *(a people of N. Arabia)*

nabl·ia -ium *npl* Phoenician harp

nactus *pp of* **nancīscor**

Naeviān·us -a -um *adj* of Naevius

Naev·ius -(i)ī *m* Gnaeus Naevius *(early Roman dramatic and epic poet, c. 270–200 B.C.)*

Nāï·as -adis *or* **Nā·is -idis** *or* **-idos** *f* Naiad, water nymph,

nam *conj* for; for in that case; *(affirmative)* yes, to be sure; *(transitional)* now, but now, on the other hand

namque *conj* for in fact, for no doubt, for surely

nan·cīscor -cīscī nānctus sum *or* **nactus sum** *tr* to get, obtain; to come across, find; to arrive at; to experience, meet with; to contract *(a disease)*

nān·us -ī *m* dwarf, midget

Napae·ae -ārum *fpl* dell nymphs

nāp·us -ī *m* turnip

Narb·ō -ōnis *m* Narbonne *(city in S. Gaul, from which the province of Narbonese took its name)*

Narbōnēns·is -is -e *adj* Narbonese

narciss·us -ī *m (bot)* narcissus ‖ **Narcissus** son of Cephisus and the nymph Liriope, who was changed into a narcissus ‖ powerful freedman of Claudius

nard·um -ī *n or* **nard·us -ī** *f* nard, spikenard *(fragrant ointment)*

nār·is -is *f* nose; **homō acūtae nāris** *(or* **ēmūnctae nāris**) a man of keen perception; **homō nāris obēsae** dimwit *(literally, thick-nosed man)* ‖ *fpl* nostrils, nose; **nārēs corrūgāre** to cause *(s.o.)* to turn up his nose; **nāribus dūcere** to smell; **nāribus ūtī** *(w.* **ad**) to turn up the nose at, ridicule

Narni·a -ae *f* town in Umbria

Narniēns·is -is -e *adj* of Narnia

nārrābil·is -is -e *adj* to be told

nārrāti·ō -ōnis *f* narrative

nārrātiuncul·a -ae *f* anecdote

nārrāt·or -ōris *m* narrator

nārrāt·um -ī *n* account, narrative

nārrāt·us -ūs *m* narrative, tale

nārr·ō -āre -āvī -ātus *tr* to tell, relate, narrate, recount; to describe, tell about ‖ *intr* to speak, tell; **bene nārrāre** *(w.* **dē** + *abl)* to tell good news about *(s.o.);* **male nārrāre** *(w.* **dē** + *abl)* to tell bad news about *(s.o.);* **tibi nārrō** *(coll)* I'm telling you, I assure you; **quam tū mihi nunc nāvem nārrās?** *(coll)* now, what's this ship you're talking about?

narthēc·ium -(i)ī *n* medicine chest

nārus *see* **gnārus**

Nāryci·us -a -um *adj* of Narycum *(birthplace of Ajax, son of Oileus)*

nāscor nāscī nātus sum *intr* **(gn-)** to be born; to begin, originate, spring forth, proceed; to be produced; *(of plants)* to grow; *(of rocks, minerals)* to be found, occur; *(astr)* to rise

Nāsīc·a -ae *m* Roman honorary name *(agnomen)* Publius Cornelius Scipio Nasica *(consul in 191 B.C.)*

Nās·ō -ōnis *m* Ovid *(Publius Ovidius Naso, Roman poet, 43 B.C.–A.D. 17)*

nass·a -ae *f* wicker trap *(for catching fish); (fig)* trap

nassitern·a -ae *f* large watering pot

nāsturc·ium -(i)ī *n (bot)* watercress

nās·us -ī *m or* **nās·um -ī** *n* nose; sense of smell; sagacity; scorn; satirical wit; spout, nozzle

nāsūtē *adv* sarcastically

nāsūt·us -a -um *adj* big-nosed; sarcastic, satirical

nāt·a *or* **gnāt·a -ae** *f* daughter

nātālici·us -a -um *adj* birthday; natal, congenital; **diēs nātālicius** birthday ‖ *f* birthday party ‖ *n* birthday present

nātāl·is -is -e *adj* of birth, natal, congenital; **diēs nātālis** birthday ‖ *m* birthday; foundation day *(of city, temple, etc.)* ‖ *mpl* birth, origin, parentage; **nātālibus suīs restituere** *(or* **reddere**) to confer the status of a free-born citizen on *(one born into slavery)*

nat·āns -antis *adj* swimming; swimming in the sea, marine ‖ *mf* fish

natāti·ō -ōnis *f* swimming, swim

natāt·or -ōris *m* swimmer

nat·ēs -ium *fpl see* **natis**

nāti·ō -ōnis *f* tribe, nation, people; race, stock; *(pej)* breed

nat·is -is *f* buttock, rump ‖ *fpl* buttocks, rear end

nātīv·us -a -um *adj* born; inborn, innate, original; native, local; produced by nature, natural; primitive *(words)*

nat·ō -āre -āvī -ātus *tr* to swim (across) ‖ *intr* to swim, float; to flow; to overflow; *(of eyes)* to be glassy; *(of birds)* to fly, glide; to waver, fluctuate; to hover; to move to and fro

nātr·īx -īcis *f* water snake

nātūr·a -ae *f* nature, natural constitution; character, temperament; ability; distinctive feature *or* characteristic; naturalness *(in art);* order of the world, course of things; element, substance; sex organs; **in**

nātūrā *(or* **in rērum nātūrā)** **esse** to be the natural choices, to be the alternatives; **nātūrā** *(or* **per nātūram)** naturally; **nātūra flūminis** the natural course of the river; **nātūra rērum** (physical) nature; **suā nātūrā** of its own accord

nātūrāl·is -is -e *adj* natural; by birth, one's own *(father, son, etc.)*; produced by nature; according to nature

nātūrāliter *adv* naturally, by nature

nāt·us *or* **gnāt·us -a -um** *pp of* **nāscor ‖** *adj* born; *(w. dat or* **ad** *or* **in** *+ acc)* born for, made for, naturally suited to, fit for; *(w.* **annōs)** at the age of . . . , . . . years old, *e.g.*, **annōs vīgintī nātus** at the age of twenty, twenty years old; **nōn amplius nōvem annōs nātus** no more than nine years old; **prō rē nātā** *(or* **ē rē nātā)** under the existing circumstances, as matters stand; **rēs nāta** the situation, the way things are **‖** *m* son **‖** *mpl* children **‖** *f* daughter

nauarch·us -ī *m* ship's captain, skipper

nauclēric·us -a -um captain's **‖** *m* ship owner, captain

nauclēr·us -ī *m* ship's captain

naucul·or -ārī -ātus sum *intr* to go boating, go sailing

nauc·um -ī *n* trifle; *(mostly in gen. of value with a negative)* **nōn naucī esse** to be good for nothing; **nōn naucī habēre** to regard as worthless

naufrag·ium -(i)ī *n* shipwreck; wreck, ruin, destruction; wreckage; *(fig)* shattered remains; **naufragium facere** to be shipwrecked; *(of things)* to be lost **‖** *npl* remnants, shattered remains; **naufragia Caesaris amīcōrum** the remnants of Caesar's friends

naufrag·ō -āre -āvī *intr* to suffer shipwreck

naufrag·us -a -um *adj* shipwrecked, of the shipwrecked; causing shipwreck, dangerous to shipping; *(fig)* ruined **‖** *m* shipwrecked person

naul·um -ī *n* fare, passage money

naumachi·a -ae *f* simulated naval engagement *(staged as an exercise or for amusement)*

naumachiār·ius -(i)ī *m* person taking part in a mock sea fight

Naupact·us -ī *f* town on the N. shore of the Gulf of Corinth

Naupliad·ēs -ae *m* son of Nauplius *(Palamedes)*

Naupl·ius -(i)ī *m* king of Euboea who wrecked the Greek fleet to avenge the death of his son Palamedes

nause·a -ae *f* seasickness; vomiting, nausea; **nausea fluēns** vomiting

nause·ō -āre -āvī *tr* to make *(s.o.)* throw up; *(fig)* to belch forth, throw up, utter **‖** *intr* to be seasick; to vomit; to feel squeamish, feel disgust; to cause disgust

nauseol·a -ae *f* slight squeamishness

Nausica·a -ae *f* daughter of Alcinoüs, king of the Phaeacians

naut·a *or* **nāvit·a -ae** *m* sailor, seaman, mariner; captain

naute·a -ae *f* nausea; bilge water

nautic·us -a -um *adj* nautical, sailor's **‖** *mpl* sailors, seamen

nāvāl·is -is -e *adj* naval, of ships, of a ship; **castra nāvālia** camp for the protection of ships; **fōrma nāvālis** shape of a ship **‖** *n* tackle, rigging **‖** *npl* dock, dockyard, shipyard; rigging

nāvē *adv* industriously

nāvicul·a -ae *f* small ship

nāviculāri·us -a -um *adj* of a small ship **‖** *m* skipper; ship owner **‖** *f* shipping business

nāvifrag·us -a -um *adj* dangerous, treacherous, causing shipwreck

nāvigābil·is -is -e *adj* navigable

nāvigāti·ō -ōnis *f* sailing, navigation, voyage

nāvig·er -era -erum *adj* navigable

nāvig·ium -(i)ī *n* ship; boat

nāvig·ō -āre -āvī -ātus *tr* to sail across, navigate **‖** *intr* to sail, put to sea; *(fig)* to swim

nāv·is -is *f* ship; *(astr)* Argo *(constellation)*; **nāvem appellere** *(or* **nāvem terrae applicāre)** to land a ship; **nāvem dēdūcere** to launch a ship; **nāvem solvere** to set sail; **nāvem subdūcere** to beach a ship; **nāvī** *(or* **nāvibus)** by ship, by sea; **nāvis aperta** ship without a deck; **nāvis longa** battleship; **nāvis mercātōria** merchant vessel; **nāvis onerāria** transport, cargo ship; **nāvis praetōria** flagship; **nāvis tēcta** ship with a deck

nāvit·a -ae *m see* **nauta**

nāvit·ās -ātis *f* energy, zeal

nāviter *adv* energetically, zealously, actively, busily; utterly, completely

nāv·ō -āre *tr* to do *or* perform energetically, conduct *or* carry out with vigor; **operam nāvāre** to act energetically; **operam nāvāre** *(w. dat)* to render assistance to

nāv·us -a -um *adj* **(gn-)** energetic, busy

Nax·os -ī *f* largest island of the Cyclades in the Aegean Sea

-ne *enclitic (introducing a question and added to the first important word of a clause; it does not imply anything about the expected answer); (introducing an alternative in a question)* Or . . . ?; *(in indirect questions)* whether; *(introducing a double or multiple indirect question)* whether

nē *interj (nearly always with a personal or demonstrative pronoun)* indeed, certainly, surely; **nē ego homō īnfēlīx fuī** I was indeed an unhappy man ‖ *adv* not; **nē ... quidem** *(to negate emphatically the words placed between)* not even; **nē timēte**! do not fear! ‖ *conj* that not, lest; so as to prevent *(s.th. from happening);* much less, let alone; **nē dīcam** not to mention; **nē mentiar** to tell the truth; **nē multa** *(or* **nē multīs)** to make a long story short ‖ *conj (after verbs and nouns denoting fear)* that

nebul·a -ae *f* mist, fog, vapor; cloud *(of dust, smoke); (fig)* darkness, obscurity

nebul·ō -ōnis *m* loafer, good-for-nothing

nebulōs·us -a -um *adj* foggy

nec *or* **neque** *adv* not ‖ *conj* nor, and not; **nec ... et** not only ... but also; **nec ... nec** *(or* **neque ... neque)** neither ... nor; **nec nōn (et)** *(introducing an emphatic affirmative)* and certainly, and besides

necdum *or* **neque dum** *conj* and not yet, nor yet

necessāriē *or* **necessāriō** *adv* necessarily, of necessity

necessāri·us -a -um *adj* necessary, indispensable, needful, requisite; inevitable; pressing, urgent; connected by blood or friendship, related, closely connected ‖ *mf* relative, kinsman; friend ‖ *npl* necessities

necesse *indecl adj* necessary; unavoidable, inevitable; requisite; **necesse esse** to be necessary; **necesse habēre** to regard as necessary, regard as inevitable

necessit·ās -ātis *f* necessity, inevitability; compulsion, urgency; requirement; privation, want; relationship, connection, friendship

necessitūd·ō -inis *f* necessity, need, want, distress; relationship, bond, connection, friendship ‖ *fpl* ties of friendship; relatives, friends, personal connections

necessum *indecl adj* necessary, requisite; inevitable

necne *conj* or not

nec·ō -āre -āvī -ātus *tr* to kill, murder

necopīn·āns -antis *adj* unaware

necopīnātō *adv* unexpectedly, by surprise

necopīnāt·us -a -um *adj* unexpected; **ex necopīnātō** unexpectedly

necopīn·us -a -um *adj* unexpected; unsuspecting; careless, off-guard

nect·ar -aris *n* nectar *(drink of the gods);* nectar *(term for honey, milk, wine, poetry, sweetness)*

nectare·us -a -um *adj* of nectar, sweet *(or* delicious) as nectar

nectō nectere nexuī *or* **nexī nexus** *tr* to tie, connect, fasten together, join; to weave; to clasp; to imprison; to fetter; to devise, contrive; *(fig)* to attach

nēcubi *conj* lest anywhere, so that nowhere

nēcunde *conj* lest from anywhere

nēdum *conj (after an expressed or implied negative)* much less, still less; *(after an affirmative)* not to say, much more

nefand·us -a -um *adj* unspeakable, heinous

nefāriē *adv* wickedly, foully

nefāri·us -a -um *adj* nefarious, heinous, criminal ‖ *n* crime, foul deed

nefās *indecl n* crime, wrong, wickedness; act contrary to divine law, sin; criminal, monster; **fās atque nefās** right and wrong; **nefās est** *(w. inf)* it is a crime to; **per omne fās ac nefās** by hook or by crook ‖ *interj* shocking!, dreadful!

nefāst·us -a -um *adj* forbidden, unlawful; impious, irreligious; criminal; **diēs nefāstus** day unfit for business; legal holiday ‖ *n* outrage

negāti·ō -ōnis *f* denial

negit·ō -āre -āvī *tr* to keep denying; to turn down, refuse repeatedly

neglēcti·ō -ōnis *f* **(nec-)** neglect

neglēctus (nec-) *pp of* **neglegō** ‖ *adj* neglected, despised, slighted

neglēct·us -ūs *m* **(nec-)** neglect

negleg·ēns -entis *adj* **(nec-)** negligent, careless, indifferent

neglegenter *adv* **(nec-)** carelessly

neglegenti·a -ae *f* **(nec-)** negligence, carelessness, neglect; **epistulārum neglegentia** failure to write

neg·legō -legere -lēxī -lēctus *tr* **(nec-)** to be unconcerned about; to neglect, disregard, overlook; to do without; to slight; to make light of; *(w. inf)* to fail to

neg·ō -āre -āvī -ātus *tr* to deny; *(w. acc & inf)* to say that ... not ‖ *refl* to refuse one's services ‖ *intr* to say no; to refuse; *(w. dat)* to say no to, turn down *(regarding marriage or sexual favors, dinner invitation, etc.)*

negōtiāl·is -is -e *adj* business

negōti·āns -antis *m* business man

negōtiāti·ō -ōnis *f* business, trade; business deal; business establishment

negōtiāt·or -ōris *m* businessman; banker; salesman, dealer

negōtiol·um -ī *n* minor matter

negōti·or -ārī -ātus sum *intr* to conduct business; to do banking; to trade; **homō negōtiāns** businessman

negōtiōs·us -a -um *adj* business; busy; **diēs negōtiōsus** workday

negōt·ium -(i)ī *n* business; occupation, employment; matter, thing, affair; situation; difficulty; trouble; banking, money-lending; trade, commerce; **dare negōtium alicui ut** to give s.o. the job of; **in magnō negōtiō habēre** *(w. inf)* to make a point of; **negōtium gerere** to conduct business; **negōtium suum** private affairs; **nōn negōtium est quīn** there is nothing to do but; **quid negōtī est?** what's the matter?; **quid negōtī tibi est?**

what business is it of yours?; **suum negōtium agere** *or* **gerere** to mind one's own business ‖ *npl* commercial activities, business transactions; lawsuits

Nēl·eus -eī *or* **-eos** *m* king of Pylos and father of Nestor

Nēlīd·ēs -ae *m* descendant of Neleus

Neme·a -ae *or* **Neme·ē -ēs** *f* Nemea *(town in Argolis, where Hercules slew a lion and founded the Nemean games)*

Neme·a -ōrum *npl* Nemean games *(held every two years at Nemea)*

Nemeae·us -a -um *adj* Nemean

Nemes·is -eōs *f* goddess of vengeance

nēm·ō -inis *mf* no one, nobody; a person of no consequence, a nobody; **nēmō alius** no one else; **nēmō dum** no one yet; **nēmō nōn** every; **nēmō quisquam** nobody at all; **nēmō ūnus** no single person, no one by himself; **nōn nēmō** someone, many a one, a few

nemorāl·is -is -e *adj* sylvan

nemorēns·is -is -e *adj* of a grove; of Diana's grove

nemoricultr·īx -īcis *f* denizen *(female)* of the forest

nemorivag·us -a -um *adj* roaming the woods

nemorōs·us -a -um *adj* wooded; covered with foliage

nempe *adv (in confirmation or in sarcasm)* of course, naturally; *(in questions)* do you mean?

nem·us -oris *n* cluster of trees; grove; sacred grove

nēni·a -ae *f* **(naen-)** funeral song; doleful song; incantation; ditty

neō nēre nēvī nētus *tr* to spin; to weave

Neoptolem·us -ī *m* the son of Achilles *(also called Pyrrhus)*

nep·a -ae *f* scorpion; crab; *(astr)* Scorpio

Nephelē·is -idos *f* Helle *(daughter of Nephele and Athamas)*

nep·ōs -ōtis *m* grandson; nephew; descendant; spendthrift, playboy; **sērī nepōtēs** distant descendants ‖ **Nepōs** Cornelius Nepos *(Roman biographer and friend of Cicero, c. 100–25 B.C.)*

nepōtul·us -ī *m* little grandson

nept·is -is *f* granddaughter; descendant *(female)*

Neptūni·us -a -um *adj* of Neptune

Neptūn·us -ī *n* Neptune *(god of the sea and brother of Jupiter)*

nēquam *(comp:* **nēquior;** *superl:* **nēquissimus)** *indecl adj* worthless, bad, good for nothing; naughty; **nēquam facere** to be naughty

nēquāquam *adv* by no means, not at all

neque *see* **nec**

nequedum *see* **necdum**

nequ·eō -īre -īvī *or* **-iī -ītum** *intr (w. inf)* to be unable to, be incapable of; *(w.* **quīn)** to be unable to keep oneself from; **nequit** *(w.* **quīn)** it is impossible to

nēqui·or -or -us *(comp of* **nēquam)** *adj* worse, more worthless

nēquīquam *or* **nēquicquam** *adv* pointlessly, for nothing, to no purpose; without good reason; with impunity

nēquissim·us -a -um *(superl of* **nēquam)** *adj* worst, most worthless

nēquiter *adv* wickedly; wrongly, with poor results; worthlessly; *(in playful use)* naughtily

nēquiti·a -ae *or* **nēquiti·ēs -ēī** *f* worthlessness, vileness, wickedness; naughtiness

Nērē·is -idis *f* Nereid, sea nymph *(one of the fifty daughters of Nereus)*

Nēr·eus -eī *or* **-eos** *m* son of Oceanus and Tethys, and husband of Doris, and father of the Nereids; sea

Nērīnē -ēs *f* daughter of Nereus

Nēriti·us -a -um *adj* of Neritus; **dux Nēritius** Ulysses; **Nēritia ratis** ship of Ulysses

Nērit·os *or* **Nērit·us -ī** *m* island near Ithaca

Ner·ō -ōnis *m* Nero Claudius Caesar *(A.D. 38–68; reigned A.D. 54–68)*

Nerōniān·us -a -um *adj* Nero's, Neronian

Nerv·a -ae *m* Marcus Cocceius Nerva *(A.D. 30–98; reigned A.D. 96–98)*

nervōsē *adv* strongly, vigorously

nervōs·us -a -um *adj* sinewy, brawny, muscular

nerv·us *or* **nerv·os -ī** *m* sinew, tendon, muscle; string, wire; bowstring; thong; strap; leather covering of a shield; *(vulg)* penis; prison ‖ *mpl* power, vigor, strength, nerve, force, energy; **nervī bellī pecūnia** money, the sinews of war; **nervī coniūrātiōnis** the force *(i.e., the leaders)* behind the conspiracy

nēsc·iō -īre -īvī *or* **-iī -ītus** *tr* not to know, be ignorant of, be unacquainted with; *(w. inf)* not to know how to, be unable to; **nēsciō modo** somehow or other; **nēsciō quandō** sometime or other; **nēsciō quid** something or other; **nēsciō quis** someone or other

nēsci·us -a -um *adj* unaware, ignorant; unknown; *(w. gen or* **dē** *+ abl)* ignorant of, unaware of; *(w. inf)* not knowing how to, unable to, incapable of; *(w. acc & inf)* unaware that, not knowing that

Ness·us -ī *m* centaur who was slain by Hercules with a poisoned arrow for trying to molest his wife

Nest·or -oris *m* son of Neleus, king of Pylos, and wise counselor of the Greeks at Troy

Nestorid·ēs -ae *m* son of Nestor *(i.e., Antilochus)*

neu *see* **nēve**

neu·ter -tra -trum *adj* neither *(of two);* neuter; of neither sex ‖ *pron* neither one *(of two)*

neutiquam *or* **ne utiquam** *adv* on no account, in no way

neutrāl·is -is -e *adj (gram)* neuter

neutrō *adv* to neither side, in neither direction

neutrubi *adv* in neither the one place nor the other

nēve *or* **neu** *conj* or not, and not; **nēve . . . nēve** *(or* **neu . . . neu)** neither . . . nor

nex necis *f* death; violent death, murder, slaughter; **necem (sibi) cōnscīscere** to decide to commit suicide *(literally, to decide on death for oneself);* **necī** *(or* **ad necem) dare** *(or* **mittere**) to put to death

nexil·is -is -e *adj* plaited, intertwined

nex·um -ī *n* slavery for debt; voluntary servitude for debt

nex·us -a -um *pp of* **nectō** ‖ *m* bondman *(person who has pledged his person as security for a debt)*

nex·us -ūs *m* bond; tie *(of kinship, etc.);* legal obligation; grip *(in wrestling);* embrace; combination ‖ *mpl* coils *(of snake);* knotty problem

nī *adv* not; **quid nī?** why not? ‖ *conj (in prohibition or negative purpose)* that not; *(in negative condition)* if not, unless

nīcētēr·ium -(i)ī *n* prize (of victory)

nict·ō -āre -āvī -ātum *or* **nict·or -ārī -ātus sum** *intr* to blink; to wink; *(w. dat)* to wink at

nīdāment·um -ī *n* material for a nest

nīd·or -ōris *m* steam, vapor, smell

nīdul·us -ī *m* small nest

nīd·us -ī *m* nest; nestlings, brood; pigeonhole *(fig)* home ‖ *mpl* nestlings, brood

ni·ger -gra -grum *adj* black; dark; swarthy; dismal; unlucky, ill-omened; bad *(character);* malicious

nigr·āns -antis *adj* black, dusky

nigr·ēscō -ēscere -uī *intr* to grow black, grow dark

nigr·ō -āre -āvī -ātus *tr* to blacken ‖ *intr* to be black

nigr·or -ōris *m* blackness, darkness

nihil *or* **nīl** *indecl n* nothing; *(w. partitive gen)* no, not a bit of *(e.g.,* **nihil cibī** no food); **nihil agere** to do nothing, sit still; **nihil aliud** nothing else; **nihil bonī** no good, not a bit of good; **nīl est** *(in replies)* it is pointless, it's no good; **nihil dum** nothing so far; **nihil est** it doesn't matter; **nihil est mihi cum** I have nothing to do with; **nihil est quod** *(or* **cūr** *or* **quamobrem)** there is no reason why; **nihil est ubi** *(or* **quō**) there is no place where *(or* to which); **nihil quicquam** nothing whatever; **nōn nihil** a considerable amount, quite a lot; to a considerable extent

nihilōminus *adv* nevertheless, just the same; no less

nihil·um *or* **nīl·um -ī** *n* nothing; **ad nihilum venīre** to come to nothing; **dē nihilō** for nothing, for no reason; **nihilī facere** *(or* **pendere**) to consider as worthless; **nihil** *(w. comparatives or words expressing difference, e.g.:* **nihil cārius** nothing dearer); **nihilō minus** nonetheless, nevertheless; **prō nihilō putāre** *(or* **dūcere** *or* **habēre**) to regard as worthless, disregard

nīl *see* **nihil**

Nīliac·us -a -um *adj* Nile, of the Nile; Egyptian

nīlum *see* **nihilum**

Nīl·us -ī *m* Nile; god of the Nile; a type of conduit

nimbāt·us -a -um *adj* light, frivolous

nimbif·er -era -erum *adj* stormy

nimbōs·us -a -um stormy, rainy

nimb·us -ī *m* rain cloud, storm cloud; cloud; rainstorm, heavy shower; shower, spray; *(fig)* storm; *(fig)* dense crowd

nimiō *adv* far, much; **nimiō plūs** far more, much more

nīmīrum *adv* no doubt, certainly sure; *(ironically)* of course

nimis *adv* very, very much, too much; **nōn nimis** not particularly

nimium *adv* too, too much; very much; **nimium quam** *(or* **nimium quantum)** very much indeed, ever so much, very; **nimium quam es barbarus** you are as uncouth as can be; **nōn nimium** not particularly, not very much

nimi·us -a -um *adj* very much; very great; too great, extraordinary, excessive; extravagant, intemperate; over-eager; over-confident; *(w. gen or abl of respect)* intemperate in, going overboard about; *(w. dat)* too much for, too strong for; **nimiō opere** to excess ‖ *n* excess

ning(u)it ningere ninguit *or* **nīnxit** *v impers* it is snowing

ningu·ēs -ium *fpl* snow flakes; snow; snowdrifts

Nin·os *or* **Nin·us -ī** *m* king of Assyria, legendary founder of Nineveh; Nineveh

Niob·a -ae *or* **Niob·ē -ēs** *f* Niobe *(daughter of Tantalus and wife of Amphion; she was turned into a weeping mountain)*

Nīr·eus -eī *or* **-eos** *m* second-handsomest Greek at Troy *(after Achilles)*

Nīsē·is -idis *f* daughter of Nisus, Scylla

nisi *conj* unless, if not; except; **nisi sī** unless, if not; **nisi quia** *(or* **quod)** except that

Nīs·us -ī *m* king of Megara and father of Scylla ‖ friend of Euryalus *(in the Aeneid)*

nīsus *pp of* **nītor**

nīs·us *or* **nīx·us -ūs** *m* pressure, effort; labor pains; soaring, flight; posture; **nīsū immōtus eōdem** immobile in the same posture

nītēdul·a -ae *f* dormouse *(squirrel-like rodent)*

nit·ēns -entis *adj* shining, bright, sparkling; brilliant; beautiful, glamorous; sleek *(cattle);* prosperous, thriving; illustrious, outstanding

nit·eō -ēre -uī *intr* to shine, gleam, glisten; to be glamorous; to glow with health; *(of animals)* to be sleek; *(of style)* to be brilliant; *(of fields, plants)* to be luxuriant

nit·ēscō -ēscere -uī *intr* to become shiny, become bright; to begin to glow *(with health or beauty);* to grow sleek; *(of plants)* to begin to thrive

nitidē *adv* brightly

nitidiusculē *adv* somewhat more sprucely

nitidiuscul·us -a -um *adj* a little more shiny

nitid·us -a -um *adj* shining, bright; glowing, radiant, handsome *(with health or beauty);* spruce, well-groomed, glamorous; glossy, lustrous *(hair);* sleek *(animals);* luxuriant, lush *(plants, fields);* cultivated, refined; elegant *(style)*

nītor nītī nīxus sum *(usually in the literal sense) or* **nīsus sum** *(usually in the figurative sense) intr* to make an effort, struggle, strain, strive; to be in labor; to push forward, advance, climb, fly; to contend, insist; *(w. abl or* **in** *+ acc)* to lean on, support oneself on; *(w. abl or* **in** *+ abl)* to depend on, rely on, trust to; *(w.* **ad)** to aspire to; *(w. inf)* to try to, endeavor to, struggle to

nit·or -ōris *m* brightness, sheen; luster; glamour, beauty; healthy glow; elegance *(of style);* dignity *(of character)*

nitr·um -ī *n* soda, potash; cleanser

nivāl·is -is -e *adj* snowy; covered with snow; cold, wintry; *(fig)* cold, chilly

nive·us -a -um *adj* snowy, covered with snow; snow-white; cooled with snow

nivōs·us -a -um *adj* snowy

nix nivis *f* snow **||** *fpl (fig)* grey hair

nix·or -ārī -ātus sum *intr* to struggle hard; *(w. abl)* to lean on, rest on

nīxus *pp of* **nītor**

nīx·us -ūs *see* **nīsus**

nō nāre nāvī *intr* to swim, float; to sail; to fly; *(of eyes)* to be glazed

nōbil·is -is -e *adj* known, familiar; noted; notable, remarkable, noteworthy; famous; notorious; noble; thoroughbred; fine, excellent; *(w. abl of cause)* famous for, noted for; **nōbile est** *(w. acc & inf)* it is well-known that **||** *m* notable, nobleman, aristocrat

nōbilit·ās -ātis *f* fame, renown; noble birth; nobility; the nobility, the nobles; excellence

nōbiliter *adv* with distinction

nōbilit·ō -āre -āvī -ātus *tr* to make generally known, call attention to; to make famous; to make notorious

noc·ēns -entis *adj* harmful; *(w. abl)* guilty of **||** *m* guilty person, criminal

noc·eō -ēre -uī -itum *intr (w. dat)* to harm, injure; **haud ignārus nocendī** well aware of the mischief

nocīv·us -a -um *adj* harmful, injurious

noctif·er -erī *m* evening star *(night-bringer)*

noctilūc·a -ae *f* moon *(she who shines by night)*

noctivag·us -a -um *adj (esp. of heavenly bodies)* wandering at night

noctū *adv* by night, at night

noctu·a -ae *f* owl *(night bird)*

noctuābund·us -a -um *adj* traveling by night

noctuīn·us -a -um *adj* of owls

nocturn·us -a -um *adj* nocturnal, of night, at night, by night, night

noctuvigil·us -a -um *adj* awake at night

nocu·us -a -um *adj* harmful

nōd·ō -āre -āvī -ātus *tr* to tie in a knot, knot

nōdōs·us -a -um *adj* knotty

nōd·us -ī *m* knot; knot *(in wood);* node *(in stem of grass or plant);* bond, tie; obligation; knotty point, problem, difficulty; coil *(of serpent)*; check, restraint; **igneus nōdus** fireball

Nōl·a -ae *f* town of Campania E. of Naples *(where Augustus died)*

nōlō nōlle nōluī *tr (w. inf)* to be unwilling to, wish not to, refuse to **||** *intr* to be unwilling; *(2nd person imperative w. inf to form negative command)* do not … : **nōlī** *(pl:* **nōlīte) tangere** do not touch!

Nom·as -adis *or* **-ados** *mf* nomad; Numidian

nōm·en -inis *n* name; clan *(or* middle) name *(e.g., Julius, as distinct from the praenomen, or first name, e.g., Gaius, and the cognomen, or family name, e.g., Caesar);* good name, reputation; title; stock, race; bond, claim, debt; debtor; pretext, pretense, excuse; authority; sake, behalf; reason, cause; responsibility; heading, category; entry *(of a loan, etc., in a ledger); (gram)* noun; **aetātis nōmine** on the pretext of age; on account of age; **eō nōmine** on that account; **nōmen alicūius accipere** *(or* **recipere)** *(of a presiding judge)* to consent to hear the case against s.o.; **nōmen dare** *(or* **ēdere** *or* **profitērī)** to enlist *(in the army; as a colonist);* **nōmen dēferre** *(w. gen)* to bring an accusation against, accuse *(s.o.);* **nōmen dissolvere** *(or* **nōmen expedīre**

or **nōmen solvere)** *(com)* to liquidate an account, pay off a debt; **nōmen Latīnum** those with Latin rights; **nōmen Rōmānum** the Roman people; **nōmina facere** *(com)* to enter a business transaction in a ledger; **nōmina magna** big shots, celebrities; **nōmina sua exigere** to collect one's debt; **nōmine** *(w. gen)* by the authority of, in the name of; on the pretext of; in the guise of; **nōn rē sed nōmine** not in reality but in name only; **oppidum nōmine Nōla** a town named Nola; **per nōmen** *(w. gen)* on the pretext of; in the guise of; **sub nōmine** *(w. gen)* by the authority of, in the name of; **suō nōmine** on one's own responsibility, independently; **ūnō nōmine** in a word

nōmenclāt·or -ōris *m* name-caller *(slave who accompanied his master and discreetly identified those whom they met, esp. during a political campaign)*

Nōment·um -ī *n* town in Latium on the Sabine border

nōminātim *adv* by name, expressly

nōmināti·ō -ōnis *f* nomination for office; name, term

nōminātīv·us -a -um *adj & m (gram)* nominative

nōminit·ō -āre -āvī -ātus *tr* to name, call, term

nōmin·ō -āre -āvī -ātus *tr* to name, call by name; to mention by name; to make famous; to nominate for office; to denounce, arraign

nomism·a -atis *n* coin; coinage; voucher, token

nōn *adv* not; no; by no means; **nōn iam** no longer

Nōn. *abbr* **Nōnae**

Nōnacrīn·us -a -um *adj* of Nonacris; **virgō** *(i.e., Callisto)*

Nōnacr·is -is *f* mountain and town in Arcadia

Nōnacri·us -a -um *adj* of Nonacris; **hērōs Nōnacrius** *(i.e., Evander)*

Nōn·ae -ārum *fpl* Nones *(the ninth day before the Ides, and so the fifth day in all months, except March, May, July, and October, in which the Nones occurred on the seventh)*

nōnāgēnsim·us -a **-um** *adj* **(-gēs-)** ninetieth

nōnāgiēns *adv* **(-giēs)** ninety times

nōnāgintā *indecl adj* ninety

nōnān·us -a -um *adj* of the ninth legion **‖** *m* soldier of the ninth legion

nōnāri·a -ae *f* prostitute

nōndum *adv* not yet

nōngent·ī -ae -a *adj* nine hundred

nōnne *adv (interrog particle in questions expecting a positive answer)* is it not?; *(in indirect questions)* whether not; **nōnne vidēs?** you see, don't you?, don't you see?; **quaeritur nōnne īre statim velīs** the question is whether you do not wish to go at once

nōnnūll·us -a -um *adj* some, a certain amount of; many a **‖** *pl* some, not a few

nōnnumquam *adv* **(-nunq-)** sometimes

nōnnūsquam *adv* in some places

nōn·us -a -um *adj* ninth **‖** *f* ninth hour

nōn·us decim·us -a -um *adj* nineteenth

Nōric·us -a -um *adj* of Noricum **‖** *n* Noricum *(Roman province between the Danube and the Alps)*

nōrm·a -ae *f (carpenter's)* square; *(fig)* standard, norm of behavior

nōs *pron* we; us *(at times used in place of* **ego,** *esp. in letter writing)*

nōscit·ō -āre -āvī -ātus *tr* to examine closely, observe; to know, recognize

nōscō nōscere nōvī nōtus *tr* **(gn-)** to get to know, become acquainted with, learn; to recognize; to examine, inquire into; to approve of; **nōvisse** to have become acquainted with, *(and therefore)* to know

nōsmet *pron (emphatic form of* **nōs)** we ourselves; us ourselves

nos·ter -tra -trum *adj* our, our own **‖** *pron* ours; **noster** our friend; **nostrī** our men, our soldiers, our side, our friends

nostrās -ātis *adj* born *or* produced in our country, native, of our country, indigenous

not·a -ae *f* note; mark; sign; letter, character; punctuation mark; brand *(of wine);* marginal note, critical mark; tattoo marks, brand; distinctive mark, distinctive quality; stamp *(on coin);* stigma; nickname; black mark *(against one's name);* reproach, disgrace; nod, sign, beck; sign of the zodiac; **in notam alicūius** so as to humiliate s.o.; **per notās scrībere** to write in code **‖** *fpl* letters of the alphabet; shorthand notes; memoranda

notābil·is -is -e *adj* notable, noteworthy, memorable; conspicuous

notābiliter *adv* notably, remarkably; perceptibly

notār·ius -(i)ī *m* stenographer; secretary

notāti·ō -ōnis *f* notation, mark; black mark *(of censor);* choice; observation; etymology

notāt·us -a -um *adj* noted, distinguished

nōt·ēscō -ēscere -uī *intr* to become known

noth·us -a -um *adj* bastard, illegitimate; mongrel, crossbreed; spurious; *(of the moon's light)* reflected

nōti·ō -ōnis *f* acquaintance; *(fig)* notion, idea; *(leg)* investigation

nōtiti·a -ae *or* **nōtiti·ēs -ēī** *f* acquaintance, knowledge; awareness; fame; notion, conception; familiarity *(w. things);* **nōtitia eī cum Perseō est** he is familiar with Perseus; **nōtitiam fēminae habēre** to have sex with a woman

nōt·ō -āre -āvī -ātus *tr* to mark; to mark out; to note, observe; to write down; to record; to take down in shorthand; to mark critically; to brand; to indicate, denote; to reproach; to indicate by a sign; *(of things)* to be a sign of; to mention *(in a speech or writing)*

nōt·or -ōris *m* guarantor

nōt·us -a -um *pp of* **nōscō** ‖ *adj* known, well-known; notorious; familiar, customary; **nōtum est** *(w. acc & inf)* it is common knowledge that; **nōtum facere** *(w. acc & inf)* to make it known that; **nōtum habēre** *(w. acc & inf)* to be informed that ‖ *m* an acquaintance; one who knows

novācul·a -ae *f* razor

novāl·is -is *f or* **novāl·e -is** *n* field plowed for the first time, reclaimed land; cultivated field; fallow land; crops

novātr·īx -īcis *f* innovator *(female)*

novē *adv* newly, in an unusual manner

novell·us -a -um *adj* new, fresh, young; newly acquired

novem *indecl adj* nine

Novem·ber *or* **Novem·bris -bris -bre** *adj* November; **mēnsis November** *(9th month of the Roman calendar until 153 B.C.)* ‖ **Novem·ber -bris** *m* November

novemdecim *indecl adj* **(noven-)** nineteen

novendiāl·is -is -e *adj* **(novem-)** nine-day; occurring on the ninth day; **cinerēs novendiālēs** *(fig)* ashes not yet cold ‖ *n* nine-day festival *(to mark the appearance of an omen);* funeral feast *(held nine days after death)*

novēn·ī -ae -a *adj* in groups of nine, nine each, nine

novēnsil·ēs -ium *mpl* new gods *(introduced from abroad)*

noverc·a -ae *f* stepmother

novercāl·is -is -e *adj* stepmother's, of a stepmother; like a stepmother

novīci·us -a -um *adj* new, brand new; recently imported *(slaves);* recently discovered *(things); (pej)* new-fangled

noviēns *or* **noviēs** *adv* nine times

novissimē *adv* of late, very recently

novissim·us -a -um *adj* latest, last, final; most recent; most extreme, utmost; **novissimum agmen** *(mil)* the rear; **novissima verba** parting words ‖ *mpl (mil)* rear guard ‖ *npl* the worst

novit·ās -ātis *f* newness, novelty; innovation; rareness, strangeness, unusualness; unexpectedness; recently acquired rank *(condition of being a* **novus homō);** **novitās rērum** revolution

nov·ō -āre -āvī -ātus *tr* to make new, renew, renovate; to repair; to refresh; to change; to coin *(words);* **rēs renovāre** to bring about a revolution

nov·us -a -um *adj* new; young; fresh; novel; unexpected; strange, unusual, unheard-of; recent, modern; unused; inexperienced; renewed, revived, as good as new; newly recuited *(soldiers);* inexperienced; subversive *(plans, activities);* fallow *(field);* newly arrived *(in a place);* **novae tabernae** new shops *(on N. side of the Forum);* **novus homō** self-made man *(first man of a family to reach a curule office);* **rēs nova** a new development; **rēs novae** revolution

nox noctis *f* night; night activity; sleep; death; darkness, blindness; mental darkness, ignorance; gloom; **ad multam noctem** till late at night; **nocte** *(or* **dē nocte)** at night, by night; **noctem et diem** night and day; **sub noctem** at nightfall ‖ *fpl* **noctēs et diēs** night and day, continually

nox·a -ae *f* harm, injury; offense; fault, guilt, responsibility; **in noxā esse** to be guilty of wrongdoing; **noxae** *(or* **ad** *or* **in** *+ acc)* **dēdere** to hand *(s.o.)* over for punishment; **noxā** *(or* **noxīs) solūtus** *(of a slave in a formula of sale)* guilty of no prior injurious conduct

noxi·us -a -um *adj* harmful, noxious; guilty; *(w. gen)* guilty of ‖ *f* harm, damage, injury; blame, guilt; fault; offense; **in noxiā esse** to be at fault

nūbēcul·a -ae *f* little cloud; gloomy expression

nūb·ēs -is *f or* **nūb·is -is** *m* cloud; gloom; veil

nūbif·er -era -erum *adj* cloudy; cloud-capped; cloud-bringing *(wind)*

nūbigen·a -ae *adj (masc only) (of the Centaurs, whom Ixion fathered on a cloud-image of Hera; of Phrixus, son of the cloud-goddess Nephele)* born of clouds

nūbil·is -is -e *adj* marriageable

nūbil·us -a -um *adj* cloudy; cloud-bringing *(wind);* troubled; gloomy, melancholy

nūbō nūbere nūpsī -nūptum *intr (of a woman)* to marry; *(w. dat)* to marry *(a man);* to be married to *(a man)* ‖ *refl* to get married

Nūceri·a -ae *f* town in Campania

Nūcerīn·us -a - um *adj* of Nuceria

nucifrangibul·um -ī *n (coll)* nutcracker *(i.e., teeth)*

nucle·us -ī *m* nut; kernel, stone *(of fruit)*

nudius [*contraction for* **nunc dius (diēs)**] *adv* it is now the ... day since, *e.g.,* **nudius tertius** it is now the third day since *(by Roman reckoning, the day before yesterday);* **nudius diēs dedī ad tē epistulam** it is now the third day since I mailed you a letter; ago, *e.g.,* **nudius tertius decimus** thirteen days ago *(twelve days ago by our reckoning, since the Romans counted both the first and last day)*

nūd·ō -āre -āvī -ātus *tr* to strip, bare; to lay bare, uncover; to explain; to strip *(a person of office or rank);* to empty *(a building)* of all its occupants; *(mil)* to leave undefended; *(w. abl)* to divest of; **terga nūdāre** to expose their backs *(to attack)*

nūd·us -a -um *adj* nude, naked; lightly clothed; bare, empty; defenseless; poor, needy; mere, simple, sole, only; *(w. gen or abl or w.* **ab)** bare of, without, stripped of, deprived of

nūg·a -ae *m (sl)* a nut, joker

nūg·ae -ārum *fpl* nonsense, baloney; trivia; trash, junk; a good-for-nothing, a nobody; **nūgae** *(or* **nūgās**)! nonsense!; baloney!; **nūgae sunt** it's no use; **nūgās agere** to waste one's effort

nūgāt·or -ōris *m* joker; fibber; babbler; braggart

nūgātōri·us -a -um *adj* worthless, useless, nonsensical; frivolous

nūg·āx -ācis *adj* nonsensical; frivolous

nūgigerul·us -ī *m* dealer in women's apparel

nūg·or -ārī -ātus sum *intr* to talk nonsense; *(w. dat)* to tell tall stories to

nūll·us -a -um *adj* no; *(coll)* not, not at all; non-existent; of no account ‖ *pron* none

num *adv (of time, used only w.* **etiam)** now, *e.g.,* **etiam num** now, even, now, still ‖ *adv (interrog particle expecting negative answer)* surely not, really, actually, *e.g.,* **num ista est nostra culpa?** is that really our fault?; that isn't our fault, is it? ‖ *conj (in indirect questions)* whether

Num. *abbr* **Numerius** *(Roman first name, praenomen)*

Num·a -ae *m* Numa Pompilius *(second king of Rome)*

numcubi *interrog adv* at any time, ever?

numell·a -ae *f* shackle, restrainer

nūm·en -inis *n* nod; will, consent; divine will; divine power; divine majesty; divinity, deity, godhead

numerābil·is -is -e *adj* easily counted, few in number

numerāt·um -ī *n* cold cash

numerāt·us -a -um *adj* counted out, paid down; in cold cash

numerō *adv* at the right time, just now; too soon

numer·ō -āre -āvī -ātus *tr* to number; to count; to pay out, pay down *(money);* to consider; to enumerate, mention; to relate, recount; to reckon as one's own, possess, own; *(w.* **in** + *abl or* **inter** + *acc)* to count among, include in *(a category); (w.* **in** + *acc)* to allocate to; *(w. pred. adj)* to treat as, class as; **Senātum numerāre** to count the Senate *(to see whether a quorum is present)*

numerōsē *adv* rhythmically

numerōs·us -a -um *adj* numerous; rhythmical

numer·us -ī *m* number; mere cipher; class, category; rank, position; estimation, regard; portion *(of work),* part, function; *(often w.* **suus)** the proper number, the full number, full complement; *(gram)* number; *(mil)* division, troop; *(mus, rhet)* rhythm, meter, verse; *(mus)* tune; *(pros)* quantity, measure; **ad numerum** *(or* **in numerum)** *(mus, pros, rhet)* rhythmically, in time; **aliquō (nūllō) numerō esse** to be of some (no) account; **extrā numerum** *(mus)* off beat, out of time; **in numerō esse** to be included in a group; **in numerō habēre** *(w. gen)* to be regarded as, be ranked among; **nūllō numerō esse** to be of no account; **nūmerō** at the right time, just now; too soon, too early; **numerō hūc advenīs ad prandium** you are arriving here too early for lunch; **suum numerum nāvium habēre** to have one's full complement of ships; **super** *(or* **suprā) numerum** not attached to the regular staff ‖ *mpl* mathematics, arithmetic; astronomy; notes of the scale; melody; **ad numerōs** *(mus, pros)* rhythmically, in time; **in numerīs esse** to be on active duty; **omnibus numerīs perfectus** perfect in every detail

Numid·a -ae *m* Numidian

Numidi·a -ae *f* Numidia *(country of N. Africa; Roman province, extending W. and S. of Carthage)*

Numidic·us -a -um *adj* Numidian

Numit·or -ōris *m* king of Alba, brother of Amulius, father of Ilia *(or* Rhea Silvia), and grandfather of Romulus and Remus

nummāri·us -a -um *adj* financial; *(pej)* mercenary, venal

nummāt·us -a -um *adj* rich; **bene nummātus** well-to-do, well-off

nummulār·ius -(i)ī *m* money changer

nummul·ī -ōrum *mpl* petty cash, small change

numm·us -ī *m* coin; cash, money; sesterce *(small silver coin, worth about a dime);* small sum, trifle; **in nummīs habēre** to have in cash

numquam *adv* **(nun-)** never; **nōn numquam** sometimes

numquid *adv (to introduce direct question):* **numquid meministī?** do you remember?; *(to introduce an indirect question)* whether

nunc *adv* now; nowadays, today; now, in view of this, but as matters now stand; **nunc ipsum** at this very moment; **nunc . . . nunc** at one time . . . at another, once . . . once

nuncupāti·ō -ōnis *f* name, title; public pronouncing *(of vows);* nomination *(to some position)*

nuncup·ō -āre -āvī -ātus *tr* to name, call; to take *(a vow)* publicly; to appoint *(as heir);* to utter the name of, invoke; to address *(a person)*

nūndin·ae -ārum *fpl* market day *(occurring regularly at intervals of eight days, i.e., every ninth day by Roman reckoning);* marketplace; market town; mart

nūndināl·is -is -e *adj* market

nūndināti·ō -ōnis *f* marketing, trading

nūndin·or -ārī -ātus sum *tr* to traffic in; to buy ‖ *intr* to hold a market, attend a market; to trade; to gather in crowds

nūndin·um -ī *n* market time; **inter nūndinum** the time between two market periods; **trīnum nūndinum** a sequence of three market periods *(i.e., 24 days)*

nunq- = numq-

nūnti·a -ae *f* messenger *(female)*

nūntiāti·ō -ōnis *f* announcement *(by an augur)*

nūnti·ō -āre -āvī -ātus *tr* to bring word of; to announce, declare; to report *(omens);* to give warning of *(some future event);* **gaudium nūntiāre** to bring good news; **salūtem nūntiāre** to send greetings

nūnti·us -a -um *adj* bringing news, announcing ‖ *m* messenger, courier; message, news; order, injunction; **nūntium remittere** *(w. dat)* to send a letter of divorce to, to divorce *(a wife)* ‖ *n* message, communication

nūper *adv* recently, lately; in modern times

nūper·us -a -um *adj* recent

nūpt·a -ae *f* bride, wife

nūpti·ae -ārum *fpl* marriage, wedding

nūptiāl·is -is -e *adj* nuptial, wedding

nur·us -ūs *f* daughter-in-law; young lady, young married woman

nūsquam *adv* nowhere; on no occasion; for nothing, to nothing; **nūsquam alibi** nowhere else; **nūsquam esse** not to exist; **nūsquam gentium** nowhere in the world; **plēbs nūsquam aliō nāta, quam ad serviendum** the plebs, born for nothing else than to serve

nūt·ō -āre -āvī -ātus *intr* to keep nodding; to sway to and fro, totter; to waver

nūtrīcāt·us -ūs *m* breast-feeding

nūtrīc·ius -(i)ī *m (child's)* guardian

nūtrīc·ō -āre -āvī -ātus *or* **nūtrīc·or -ārī -ātus sum** *tr* to breast-feed, nurse; to nourish, promote the growth of *(plants, animals);* to rear, bring up, support; to take care of, attend to; to cherish, cultivate

nūtrīcul·a -ae *f* nanny; wet-nurse; *(of persons or things)* fosterer

nūtrīm·en -inis *n* nourishment

nūtrīment·um -ī *n* nourishment ‖ *npl* upbringing *(of a child)*

nūtr·iō -īre -īvī *or* **-iī -ītus** *or* **nūtrior nūtrīrī nūtrītus sum** *tr* to breast-feed, suckle; to support with food, nourish; to feed *(animals, plants, fire);* to build up *(resources);* to take care of, attend to *(the skin, hair);* to bring up *(a child);* to raise *(animals, crops);* to give rise to, foster, promote *(a condition, feeling);* to treat *(a wound, sick person);* to look after *(material things);* to deal gently with *(faults, people at fault)*

nūtrīt·or -ōris *m* one who feeds

nūtr·īx -īcis *f* nurse ‖ *fpl* the breasts

nūt·us -ūs *m* nod; hint, intimation; nod of assent; will, pleasure; command; gravitation, gravitational pull; **nūtus et renūtus** nod of assent and nod of dissent

nux nucis *f* nut; nut tree; almond tree; **nucēs relinquere** *(fig)* to put away childish things; **nux abellāna** *(or* **avellāna)** hazelnut; **nux castanea** chestnut; **nux Graeca** (sweet) almond; **nux iuglāns** walnut; **nux pīnea** pine cone

Nyctē·is -idis *f* Antiope *(daughter of Nycteus, wife of Lycus (king of Thebes) and mother of Amphion and Zethus)*

Nyct·eus -eī *or* **-eos** *m* father of Antiope

nymph·a -ae *or* **nymph·ē -ēs** *f* nymph; bride; mistress; *(fig)* water *(cf.* lympha)

Nȳs·a -ae *f* legendary mountain on which Bacchus was alleged to have been born *(usually located in India)*

Nȳsae·us *or* **Nȳsi·us -a -um** *adj* of Nysa, Nysaean

Nȳs·eus -eī *or* **-eos** *m* Bacchus

Nȳsigen·a -ae *m* native of Nysa

O

O, o *(supply* littera) *f* fourteenth letter of the Latin alphabet; letter name: **o**

ō *interj* oh!

Ōapet·us -ī *m* a Titan, father of Prometheus, Epimetheus, and Atlas

Ōari·ōn -ōnis *m* Orion

Ōas·ius -(i)ī *m* son of Jupiter and Electra and brother of Dardanus

Oax·ēs *or* **Oax·is -is** *m* river in Crete

ob- *pref (also* **oc-, of-, og-, op-;** the **b** is lost in **ōmittō** and **operiō)** conveying the sense of: **1** movement toward a meeting: **obeō** to go to meet; **2** covering a surface: **oblimō** to cover with mud; **obdūcō** to cover the surface of; **3** protecting: **obdūcō** to draw *or* place as a protection *or* obstacle; **4** of overwhelming: **opprimō** to oppress; **5** counterbalancing: **oppōnō** to set off against by way of balance; **6** confrontation: **obstō** *(w. dat)* to stand in the way of, obstruct; **7** surprise or the unexpected: **obveniō** *(w. dat)* to fall to the lot of; **8** pleasant effect: **oblectō** to delight, entertain; **9** hostility: **obtrectō** to mistreat, disparage; **10** assault: **occīdō** to kill

ob *prep (w. acc)* **1** before, in front of: **ob oculōs** *(or* **ob ōs)** before one's eyes, right in front of s.o., under s.o.'s very nose; **2** on account of, because of, for: **quam ob rem** for which reason, accordingly, wherefore; **quās ob causās** for what reasons, why; **3** for the sake of, in the interest of: **ob rem pūblicam** for the sake of the country; **4** as a reward *or* punishment for, in return for: **ob mendācium tuum** in punishment for your lie; **5** *(in connection with bribes)* in payment for: **ob tua ēdicta pecūniae dabantur** you were given money *(i.e., bribes)* in payment for your edicts; **6** in connection with: **ob rem** to the purpose, usefully, profitably; **ob suam partem** on one's own account

obaerāt·us -a -um *adj* deeply in debt **II** *m* debtor

obambul·ō -āre -āvī -ātus *tr* to prowl all over, prowl about *(e.g., the city)* **II** *intr* to walk about; to wander; to prowl about; *(w. dat)* to prowl about near; *(w.* **ante** + *acc)* to wander around in front of

obarm·ō -āre -āvī -ātus *tr* to arm (*against*)

obar·ō -āre -āvī -ātus *tr* to plow up, plow over

obb·a -ae *f* decanter, beaker

obbrūt·ēscō -ēscere -uī *intr* to grow dull

obc- = occ-

ob·dō -dere -didī -ditus *tr* to set before; to fasten *(a bolt);* to close, lock *(a door);* to expose

obdorm·iō -īre -īvī *or* **-iī -ītum** *intr* to fall asleep

obdorm·īscō -īscere *intr* to fall fast asleep

ob·dūcō -dūcere -dūxī -ductus *tr (w.* **ad)** to lead *(troops)* toward *or* against; to extend in front as a barrier *or* protection; to fasten *(bolt);* to obstruct, block; to screen, protect; to cover the surface of; to close *(the curtains)*; to veil, envelop; to swallow; to put on *(clothes);* to bring forward as an opposing candidate; to pass *(time);* to dig *(ditch); (w. dat of thing protected)* to draw *or* place *(s.th.)* over; *(w. dat or* **ad)** to pit *(s.o. or s.th.)* against; **tenebrās obdūcere** *(w. dat)* to cast darkness over

obducti·ō -ōnis *f* veiling, covering

obduct·ō -āre *tr* to introduce as a rival

obduct·us -a -um *pp of* **obdūcō II** *adj* cloudy; gloomy; **obductus cicātrīx** a closed scar

obdūr·ēscō -ēscere -uī *intr* to grow hard, harden; to become insensitive; **Gorgonis vultū obdūrēscere** to become petrified *(literally, to grow hard at the sight of the Gorgon)*

obdūr·ō -āre -āvī -ātum *intr* to stick it out

ob·eō -īre -īvī *or* **-iī -itus** *tr* to go to meet; to travel, travel to, travel across; to wander through, traverse, encircle; to visit; to run over, review, enumerate *(in a speech);* to undertake, engage in; **diem ēdictī** *(or* **diem** *or* **diem suum** *or* **diem extrēmum** *or* **mortem) obīre** to meet one's death **II** *intr* to go; to pass away, die; to fade, disappear; *(of heavenly bodies)* to set

obequit·ō -āre -āvī -ātum *intr* to ride up *(on horseback); (w. dat)* to ride up to

oberr·ō -āre -āvī -ātum *intr* to ramble about, wander around; *(w. abl)* **1** to wander among; **2** to make a mistake on *or* at

obēs·us -a -um *adj* obese; swollen; crude, coarse

ob·ex -icis *mf* bar, bolt; barrier, barricade

obf- = off-

obg- = ogg-

obhae·rēscō -rēscere -sī *intr* to get stuck

obiac·eō -ēre -uī *intr (w. dat)* to lie before, lie at

obiectāti·ō -ōnis *f* reproach

obiect·ō -āre -āvī -ātus *tr* to oppose; to expose, endanger; to throw in the way; to cause *(delay); (w. dat)* **1** to impute to, throw up *(faults)* to; **2** to bring a charge of *(e.g., madness)* against, fling *(charges, abuse)* at; *(w. dat & acc & inf)* to throw a hint to *(s.o.)* that

obiect·us -a -um *pp of* **obiciō II** *adj* lying in the way, lying in front; *(w. dat)* **1** opposite; **2** exposed to **II** *npl* charges

obiect·us -ūs *m* interposition; obstacles, hindrance; protection; *(w. gen)* protection afforded by

ob·iciō -icere -iēcī -iectus *tr* to hold up as an example; to bring up, cite *(before an opponent as a ground for disapproval or condemnation),* throw up in one's face; to set up as a defense, use as a barrier *or* defense; to bar, shut *(the gates to prevent entry by an enemy);* to throw in, use, deploy *(troops); (w. dat)* **1** to throw *or* set *(e.g., food, fodder)* before; **2** to expose *(people)* to *(the wild beasts);* **3** *(coll)* to toss *or* hand out *(money)* to; **4** to put *(a bandage)* on *(a part of the body);* **5** to turn *(a ship)* so as to face *(e.g., a hostile shore);* to set up as a defense against; **6** to hold out *(false hopes, incentives, temptations)* to; **7** to throw up *(faults, weaknesses, etc.)* to, lay *(faults)* to one's charge; **hī exercituī Caesaris luxuriem obiciēbant** they were charging Caesar's army with extravagance; **8** to subject *(s.o.)* to *(danger, misfortune);* **9** to bring up, throw in *(troops)* against; **exceptiōnem obicere** to raise an objection; **interdum metus animō obicitur** at times fear crosses my mind; **portās obicere** to bar the gates; **religiōnem obicere** to raise the matter of religious scruples *(as a hindrance to some action);* **signum obicere** to raise an omen as an objection *(to some action)* ‖ *refl (w. dat)* to expose oneself to; **turba oculīs meīs modo sē obiēcit** a crowd just came into view ‖ *pass (w. dat)* to happen to, befall, occur to; *(geog) (w. dat)* to be located near *or* opposite (to)

obīr·āscor -āscī -ātus sum *intr (w. dat)* to get angry with

obiter *adv* on the way, as one goes along; *(fig)* in passing, incidentally

obitus *pp of* **obeō**

obit·us -ūs *m* approach, visit; death, passing; ruin, downfall; *(astr)* setting

obiūrgāti·ō -ōnis *f* scolding, rebuke

obiūrgāt·or -ōris *m* critic

obiūrgātōri·us -a -um *adj* reproachful

obiūrgit·ō -āre -āvī -ātus *tr* to keep on scolding

obiūrg·ō -āre -āvī -ātus *tr* to scold, rebuke, reprimand; to correct; to deter

oblangu·ēscō -ēscere -ī *intr* to taper off

oblātrātr·īx -īcis *f* nagging woman

oblātus *pp of* **offerō**

oblectām·en -inis *n* delight

oblectāment·um -ī *n* delight, amusement, pastime

oblectāti·ō -ōnis *f* delight, amusement; attraction; *(w. gen)* diversion from

oblect·ō -āre -āvī -ātus *tr* to delight, amuse, entertain, attract; to spend *(time)* pleasantly ‖ *refl* to amuse oneself, enjoy oneself

oblēvī *perf of* **oblinō**

ob·līdō -līdere -līsī -līsus *tr* to rush; to squeeze *(the throat),* strangle

obligāti·ō -ōnis *f* binding, pledging; obligation

obligāt·us -a -um *adj* obliged, under obligation; *(w. dat)* owed by right to, due to

oblig·ō -āre -āvī -ātus *tr* to tie up, bandage; to bind, obligate, put under obligation, make liable; to hamper; to earmark; to embarrass; to mortgage *(property); (w dat)* to pledge to, devote to; **fidem obligāre** to pledge one's word, make a solemn promise; to guarantee one's loyalty ‖ *refl* to bind oneself, pledge oneself ‖ *pass* to be liable; *(w. abl)* **1** to be guilty of; **2** to be obliged to, compelled to

oblīm·ō -āre -āvī -ātus *tr* to cover with mud; to dissipate, squander

ob·linō -linere -lēvī *or* **līvī -itus** *tr* to smear, daub, coat; to seal up *(jar); (fig)* to sully, sully the reputation of; *(fig)* to overload

oblīquē *adv* sideways; zigzag; *(fig)* indirectly

oblīqu·ō -āre -āvī -ātus *tr* to turn aside, twist, shift, slant; to avert *(eyes)*

oblīqu·us -a -um *adj* slanting, crosswise, sideways; zigzag; from the side; indirect *(language);* sly; envious; downhill *(road);* **oblīquus oculus** disapproving look; envious look ‖ *n* side; **ab** *(or* **ex)** **oblīquō** from the side, at an angle, obliquely; **in oblīquum** at an angle, sideways; **per oblīquum** diagonally across

oblīsī *perf of* **oblīdō**

oblīsus *pp of* **oblīdō**

oblit·ēscō -ēscere -uī *intr* to hide, disappear

oblitter·ō -āre -āvī -ātus *tr* (**-līt-**) to erase; to cancel; *(fig)* to blot out; **nōmina oblitterāre** to cancel debts

oblituī *perf of* **oblitēscō**

oblitus *pp of* **oblinō**

oblītus *pp of* **oblīvīscor**

oblīvi·ō -ōnis *f* oblivion; forgetting; forgetfulness

oblīviōs·us -a -um *adj* forgetful, oblivious; *(wine)* causing forgetfulness

oblī·vīscor -vīscī -tus sum *tr* to forget ‖ *intr* to forget; *(w. gen)* to forget, neglect, disregard, be indifferent to

oblīv·ium -(i)ī *n* forgetfulness, oblivion

oblocūt·or -ōris *m* one who contradicts

oblong·us -a -um *adj* oblong

ob·loquor -loquī -locūtus sum *intr (w. dat)* **1** to interrupt; **2** to rail at; **3** to accompany *(musically)*

obluct·or -ārī -ātus sum *tr (w. dat)* to struggle with, fight against

oblūdi·ō -āre *intr* to make a fool of oneself

oblūd·ō -ere *tr* to play jokes on

obmōl·ior -īrī -ītus sum *tr* to make a barricade of; to block up *(a gap)*

obmurmur·ō -āre -āvī -ātum *intr (w. dat)* to roar in answer to

obmūt·ēscō -ēscere -uī *intr* to become silent, hush up; to cease

obnāt·us -a -um *adj (w. dat)* growing on *(e.g., a river bank)*

ob·nītor -nītī -nīxus sum *intr* to strain, struggle, put on the pressure; *(w. dat)* **1** to press against, lean against; **2** to resist, oppose

obnīxē *adv* with all one's might; obstinately

obnīx·us -a -um *pp of* **obnītor** ‖ *adj* steadfast, firm, obstinate

obnoxiē *adv* guiltily; submissively

obnoxiōsius *adv* more slavishly

obnoxiōs·us -a -um *adj* submissive

obnoxi·us -a -um *adj* submissive, servile, obedient; weak, timid; *(w. dat)* **1** subservient to; **2** at the mercy of; **3** exposed to *(harm, danger, storms, etc.);* **4** indebted to, under obligation to; **5** legally liable to, answerable to; **obnoxium est** *(w. inf)* it is dangerous to

ob·nūbō -nūbere -nūpsī -nūptus *tr* to veil, cover *(the head)*

obnūntiāti·ō -ōnis *f* announcement *(of omens)*

obnūnti·ō -āre -āvī -ātum *intr* to make an announcement; to make an announcement that the omens are adverse; to announce bad news

oboedi·ēns -entis *adj* obedient; *(w. dat or* **ad)** obedient to; **dictō oboediēns** obedient to the command

oboedienter *adv* obediently

oboedienti·a -ae *f* (-**bēd-**) obedience

oboed·iō -īre -īvī *or* -**iī -ītum** *intr (w. dat)* **1** to obey, listen to; **2** *(of things)* to respond to

obol·eō -ēre -uī *tr* to smell of **||** *intr* to smell, stink

obor·ior -īrī -tus sum *intr* to rise. rise up, appear; *(fig) (of thoughts, sudden events)* occur, spring up

obp- = opp-

obrēp·ō -ere -sī -tus *tr* (**opr-**) to creep up on, sneak up on **||** *intr* to creep up; *(w. dat)* **1** to creep up on, sneak up on, take by surprise; **2** to trick, cheat; *(w.* **in** + *acc)* to steal over; **obrēpere ad honōrēs** to worm one's way into high positions

obrēpt·ō -āre -āvī -ātum *intr* (**opr-**) to sneak up

obrēt·iō -īre -īvī *or* -**iī -ītus** *tr* to entangle

obrig·ēscō -ēscere -uī *intr* to stiffen; to freeze

obrōd·ō -ere *tr* to gnaw at

obrog·ō -āre -āvī -ātum *intr (w. dat)* to supersede

obru·ō -ere -ī -tus *tr* to cover up, cover, hide, bury; to overwhelm, overthrow; to sink, cover with water, swamp; to overflow; to overpower, surpass, obscure, eclipse **||** *intr* to fall to ruin

obruss·a -ae *f* test, proof

obrutus *pp of* **obruō**

obsaep·iō -īre -**sī -tus** *tr* (-**sēp-**) to fence in; to block *(road); (fig)* to block

obsatur·ō -āre -āvī -ātus *tr* to cloy **||** *pass (w. gen)* to have more than enough of

obscaen- = obscēn-

obscaev·ō -āre -āvī -ātum *intr (w. dat)* to augur well for; to augur ill for

obscēnē *adv* (**-scaen-**) obscenely

obscēnit·ās -ātis *f* (**-scaen-**) obscenity

obscēn·us -a -um *adj* (**-scaen-**) obscene, indecent; dirty; filthy; ominous **||** *m* sexual pervert; foul-mouthed person **||** *npl* sexual *or* excretory parts *or* functions, private parts

obscūrāti·ō -ōnis *f* obscuring, darkening; disappearance

obscūrē *adv* indistinctly, dimly; in an underhand manner; cryptically; imperceptibly; **obscūrē ferre** to conceal, keep secret

obscūrit·ās -ātis *f* obscurity

obscūr·ō -āre -āvī -ātus *tr* (**ops-**) to obscure, darken; to cover, hide; to suppress; to veil *(words); (of love)* to blind

obscūr·us -a -um *adj* (**ops-**) obscure; dark, shady; dim, indistinct, dimly seen, shadowy; barely visible; not openly expressed, unpublicized; obscure, unintelligible; secret; reserved; vague, uncertain; gloomy **||** *n* the dark, darkness; obscurity; **in obscūrō est** it is not clear, it is doubtful

obsecrāti·ō -ōnis *f* (**ops-**) entreaty; public supplication of the gods

obsecr·ō -āre -āvī -ātus *tr* (**ops-**) to entreat, appeal to, implore; **fidem obsecrāre** to beg for protection *or* support; **tē obsecrō** I beseech you; please

obsecund·ō -āre -āvī -ātum *intr* (**ops-**) *(w. dat)* to comply with, humor

obsecūtus *pp of* **obsequor**

obsēp- = obsaep-

obsequ·ēns -entis *adj* (**ops-**) compliant, obedient; indulgent, gracious *(gods); (w. dat)* obedient to

obsequenter *adv* (**ops-**) compliantly

obsequenti·a -ae *f* (**ops-**) compliance, deference

obsequiōs·us -a -um *adj* (**ops-**) compliant, deferential

obsequ·ium -(i)ī *n* (**ops-**) compliance, indulgence; obedience, allegiance

ob·sequor -sequī -secūtus sum *intr* (**ops-**) *(w. dat)* **1** to comply with, yield to, give in to; **2** to gratify, humor; **3** to pay respect to

obser·ō -āre -āvī -ātus *tr* (**ops-**) to bolt, lock up

ob·serō -serere -sēvī -situs *tr* (**ops-**) to sow *or* plant thickly; to fill, cover

observābil·is -is -e *adj* perceptible; capable of being guarded against

observ·āns -antis *adj* attentive; *(w. gen)* **1** respectful of; **2** attentive to; **3** careful about

observanti·a -ae *f* regard, respect; *(w. gen or* **in** + *acc)* regard for, respect for

observāti·ō -ōnis *f* (**ops-**) observation; caution, care; observance, usage, practice; remark, observation; safeguarding, protection

observāt·or -ōris *m* observer

observit·ō -āre -āvī -ātus *tr* to watch carefully, note carefully

observ·ō -āre -āvī -ātus *tr* to watch; to watch out for *(dangers, opportunities);* to watch for *(to ensnare);* to take careful note of; to guard; to observe, keep, obey, comply with; to pay attention to, pay respect to; to regard as important *or* authoritative; to keep to *(a date); (w. predicate)* to regard as, accept as; to adopt *(a course of action); (w.* **ut)** to follow *(such a course of action)* that

obs·es -idis *mf* (**opses**) hostage; guarantee, pledge; bail

obsessi·ō -ōnis *f* blockade

obsess·or -ōris *m* **(ops-)** frequenter, regular visitor; blockader

ob·sideō -sidēre -sēdī -sessus *tr* **(ops-)** to sit near *or* at, remain by *or* near; to frequent; to block, choke; to occupy, fill; to look out for, watch closely; to keep guard over; *(mil)* to besiege, blockade

obsidiāl·is -is -e *adj (mil)* for breaking a blockade

obsidi·ō -ōnis *f (mil)* blockade, siege

obsid·ium -(i)ī *n* **(ops-)** *(mil)* blockade, siege; status of hostage

ob·sīdō -sīdere -sēdī -sessus *tr* to take possession of, occupy *(so as to bar passage); (mil)* to besiege, blockade

obsignāt·or -ōris *m* sealer; witness; **obsignātor testāmentī** witness to a will

obsign·ō -āre -āvī -ātus *tr* **(ops-)** to seal, to sign and seal; *(fig)* to stamp

ob·sistō -sistere -stitī -stitum *intr* **(ops-)** *(w. dat)* **1** to stand in the way of, block; **2** to resist, oppose; **3** to disapprove of, forbid

obsitus (ops-) *pp of* **obserō** (to sow) **||** *adj (w. abl)* overgrown with, covered with

obsole·faciō -facere -fēcī -factus *tr (pass:* **obsole·fīō -fierī -factus sum)** to degrade, lower the dignity of

obsol·ēscō -ēscere -ēvī -ētum *intr* to go out of style, become obsolete; to fade away; to suffer degradation; *(of reputation)* to become tarnished; *(of persons)* to sink into obscurity

obsolētē *adv* shabbily

obsolēt·us -a -um *adj* out of date, obsolete; worn out; shabby, threadbare; soiled, dirty; low, poor; *(of language)* hackneyed, trite

obsōnāt·or -ōris *m* **(ops-)** shopper *(for groceries)*

obsōnāt·us -ūs *m* **(ops-)** shopping *(for groceries)*

obsōn·ium -(i)ī *n* **(ops-)** shopping; groceries **||** *npl* groceries; pension

obson·ō -āre -āvī -ātum *intr (w. dat)* to drown out

obsōn·ō -āre -āvī -ātus *or* **obsōn·or -ārī -ātus sum** *tr* **(ops-)** to shop for *(groceries);* **famem obsōnāre** to work up an appetite **||** *intr* to go shopping; to provide food; *(w.* **dē** *+ abl)* to provide a feast for

obsorb·eō -ēre -uī *tr* **(ops-)** to gulp down

obstanti·a -ōrum *npl* obstacles, obstructions

obstetr·īx -īcis *f* **(ops-)** midwife

obstinātē *adv* resolutely, with determination; obstinately, stubbornly

obstinātī·ō -ōnis *f* determination; obstinacy, stubbornness

obstināt·us -a -um *adj* determined, fixed; obstinate, stubborn

obstin·ō -āre -āvī -ātus *tr* **(ops-)** to set one's mind on, persist in **||** *intr (w.* **ad)** to persist in

obstipēscō *see* **obstupēscō**

obstīp·us -a -um *adj* bent, bent forwards, bowed; **capite obstīpō stare** to stand with bowed head

obstit·us -a -um *adj* slanting, oblique

ob·stō -stāre -stitī -stātum *intr* **(ops-)** to stand in the way, raise opposition; *(w. dat)* **1** to stand in the way of, block the path of; **2** to block the view of, stand in front of; **3** to oppose, object to, resist, obstruct; **4** to constitute a boundary to; *(w.* **nē** *or* **quīn** *or* **quōminus** *or* **cūr nōn)** to prevent *(s.o.)* from

obstrep·ō -ere -uī -itus *tr* **(ops-)** to fill with noise, drown out **||** *intr* to make a racket, make noise; *(w. dat)* **1** to shout at, drown out, interrupt with shouts; **2** *(of the sea)* to resound against

ob·stringō -stringere strīnxī obstrictus *tr* **(ops-)** to tie a rope tightly around *(a neck); (w.* **ob** *+ acc)* to tie onto; to tie up, shut in, confine; *(fig)* to involve, put under obligation *(by an agreement, oath);* to pledge, promise *(s.th.);* **fidem obstringere** *(w. dat)* to pledge one's word to; **in verba alicūius obstringere** to have *(s.o.)* swear loyalty to s.o. **||** *refl & pass (w. abl)* **1** to get involved in; **2** to be guilty of

obstructi·ō -ōnis *f* obstruction

obstructus *pp of* **obstruō**

obstrū·do -dere -sī -sus *tr* **(obt-)** to gulp down; *(w. dat)* to force *(s.th.)* upon, thrust *(s.th.)* upon

obstru·ō -ere -xī -ctus *tr* **(ops-)** to pile up, block up, stop up; *(w. dat)* to block *or* close *(e.g., a road)* against

obstrūsus *pp of* **obstrūdō**

obstupe·faciō -facere -fēcī -factus *tr* to stun, astonish, strike dumb, daze; *(of drinks)* to stupefy; to paralyze *(emotions, etc.)*

obstup·ēscō -ēscere -uī *intr* **(-stip-)** to be astounded, be stunned, be paralyzed; to be struck with awe *or* wonder; *(of the body)* to become numb

obstupid·us -a -um *adj* **(ops-)** struck dumb, stunned, dazed, astounded

ob·sum -esse -fui *or* **offuī -futūrus** *intr (w. dat)* **1** to be opposed to, be against; **2** to be prejudicial to; **3** to be harmful to; **nihil obest dīcere** there is no harm in saying

ob·suō -suere -suī -sūtus *tr* to sew on; to sew up

obsurd·ēscō -ēscere -uī *intr* to become deaf; *(fig)* to turn a deaf ear

ob·tegō -tegere -tēxī -tēctus *tr* **(opt-)** to cover up *(w. clothing);* to protect; to conceal, screen; to keep secret

obtemperātī·ō -ōnis *f (w. dat)* obedience to, submissiveness to

obtemper·ō -āre -āvī -ātum *intr* **(opt-)** *(w. dat)* to comply with, be submissive to, obey, follow

obten·dō -dere -dī -tus *tr* **(opt-)** to spread, stretch out; to offer as an excuse; to envelop; to conceal; to allege **II** *pass (w. dat)* to lie opposite; **obtentā nocte** under cover of darkness

obtent·us -ūs *m* **(opt-)** screen, cover; pretext, pretense

ob·terō -terere -trīvī -trītus *tr* to trample on, trample down, crush; *(fig)* to trample on, degrade, destroy, crush

obtestāti·ō -ōnis *f* calling to witness; solemn invocation; solemn appeal

obtest·or -ārī -ātus sum *tr* **(opt-)** to call as witness; to make an appeal to, implore, entreat

obtex·ō -ere -uī -tus *tr* to cover, veil

obtic·eō -ēre -uī *intr* **(opt-)** to be silent

obtic·ēscō -ēscere -uī *intr* **(opt-)** to fall silent; to be dumbstruck

ob·tineō -tinēre -tinuī -tentus *tr* **(opt-)** to hold on to, keep up, persist in; to possess; to maintain, preserve, uphold; to remain in charge of; to retain military control of; to achieve *(a goal)*, gain *(one's point);* to secure *(rights);* to win *(one's case);* to secure *(one's rights);* to cover, extend over; to constitute; to comprise; *(of conditions)* to prevail over; to hold *(a rank, position; an opinion);* **auctōritātem obtinēre** *(w. gen)* to have the authority of; **locum obtinēre** *(w. gen)* to fulfill the function of; **rem obtinēre** to be successful, be victorious; **vim obtinēre** *(w. gen)* to have the force of **II** *intr* to carry the day, get one's way, succeed; *(of an opinion, report)* to be generally accepted

ob·tingō -tingere -tigī *intr* **(opt-)** to happen, occur; *(w. dat)* to happen to, befall

obtorp·ēscō -ēscere -uī *intr* **(opt-)** to become numb, become stiff; to become insensible

obtor·queō -quēre -sī -tus *tr* **(opt-)** to twist; to restrain with a noose

obtrectāti·ō -ōnis *f* **(opt-)** detraction, disparagement

obtrectāt·or -ōris *m* **(opt-)** detractor

obtrect·ō -āre -āvī -ātus *tr* **(opt-)** to treat spitefully, mistreat, disparage; to carp at **II** *intr (w. dat)* to detract from, disparage

obtrītus *pp of* **obterō**

obtrīvī *perf of* **obterō**

obtrūdō *see* **obstrūdō**

obtrunc·ō -āre -āvī -ātus *tr* **(opt-)** to cut off, cut down; *(in battle)* to cut down, kill

ob·tueor -tuērī -tuitus sum *or* **optu·or -ī** *tr* **(opt-)** to gaze at, gaze upon; to see clearly

ob·tundō -tundere -tudī -tūsus *or* **-tūnsus** *tr* **(opt-)** to beat, beat on, thump on; to blunt; *(fig)* to pound away at, stun; to deafen; to annoy

obturb·ō -āre -āvī -ātus *tr* **(opt-)** to throw into disorder; *(fig)* to disturb, confuse, distract

ob·turgēscō -turgēscere -tursī *intr* to begin to swell

obtūr·ō -āre -āvī -ātus *tr* **(opt-)** to block up, plug up; **aurēs obtūrāre** to refuse to listen; **ōs alicūius obtūrāre** to shut s.o. up

obtūs·us *or* **obtūns·us -a -um** *pp of* **obtundō II** *adj* dull; blunt; husky, coarse *(voice); (of utterances)* obtuse; *(of actions)* blunt, lacking in refinement

obtūt·us -ūs *m* **(opt-)** stare, gaze

obumbr·ō -āre -āvī -ātus *tr* to overshadow, shade; to darken, obscure; to cover, screen

obunc·us -a -um *adj* hooked

obūst·us -a -um *adj (of a stake)* having an end burned to a point; hardened in the fire; nipped *(by cold)*

obvāg·iō -īre *intr* to bawl

obvall·ō -āre -āvī -ātus *tr* to fortify *(with a rampart)*

ob·veniō -venīre -vēnī -ventum *intr* to come up, happen, come one's way; *(w. dat)* **1** to fall to *(s.o.'s)* lot; **2** to come to *(s.o.'s)* notice

obvers·or -ārī -ātus sum *intr* to make an appearance, show oneself; *(fig)* to appear *(before one's eyes, mind)*

obvers·us -a -um *adj (w.* **ad) 1** turned toward, facing; **2** inclined to; *(w. dat)* engaged in **II** *m* opponent

ob·vertō -vertere -vertī -versus *tr* **(-vor-)** *(w. dat or* **ad)** to turn *(s.th.)* toward *or* in the direction of; *(w.* **in** *+ acc)* to turn *(e.g., soldiers)* to face *(e.g., the enemy)* **II** *pass (w.* **ad)** to turn toward

obviam *or* **ob viam** *adv (w. dat)* **1** to meet, in order to meet, in the way of; **2** *(fig)* opposed to; **effundī obviam** *(w. dat)* to pour *or* rush out to meet; **obviam esse** *(w. dat)* **1** to meet; **2** to oppose, resist; **3** to be at hand, be handy; **obviam īre** *(or* **obviam prōcēdere)** *(w. dat)* **1** to go to meet; **2** to face up to *(dangers);* **obviam obsistere** *(w. dat)* to stand in the way of; **obviam prōdīre** *(or* **proficīscī** *or* **prōgredī)** *(w. dat)* to go to meet; **obviam venīre** *(w. dat)* to come *or* go to meet

obvigilāt·um -ī *n* vigilance

obvi·us -a -um *adj* in the way; exposed, open; accessible *(person);* ready, at hand; *(w. dat)* **1** to meet, so as to meet; **2** opposed to; **3** exposed to, open to; **obvius esse** *(w. dat)* to meet, encounter

obvol·vō -vere -vī -ūtus *tr* to wrap up, cover up

occaec·ō -āre -āvī -ātus *tr* **(obc-)** to blind; to darken, obscure; to hide; *(of fear)* to numb
occall·ēscō -ēscere -uī *intr* **(obc-)** to become thick-skinned, become callused; *(fig)* to become callous, become insensitive
occan·ō -ere -uī *intr (mil)* to sound the charge
occāsi·ō -ōnis *f* opportunity, good time, right moment, chance; pretext; *(mil)* surprise, raid; **ex occāsiōne** at the right time; **occāsiōnem āmittere** to lose the opportunity; **occāsiōnem arripere** to seize the opportunity; **per occāsiōnem** *(or* **occāsiōnēs)** at the right time
occāsiuncul·a -ae *f* nice little opportunity
occās·us -ūs *m* setting; sunset; the West; *(fig)* downfall, ruin, death
occāti·ō -ōnis *f* harrowing, breaking up of the soil
occāt·or -ōris *m* harrower
oc·cēdō -cēdere -cessī -cessum *intr* to go up; **obviam occēdere** *(w. dat)* to go to meet
occent·ō *or* **occant·ō -āre -āvī -ātus** *tr* **(obc-)** to serenade; to satirize in verse
occept·ō -āre -āvī -ātus *tr* to begin
occid·ēns -entis *m* the setting sun; the West; **vīta occidēns** the twilight of life
occīdi·ō -ōnis *f* massacre, annihilation; **occīdiōne occīdere** to massacre
oc·cidō -cidere -cidī -cāsum *intr* to fall, fall down; *(of the sun)* to set; to fall, be slain; *(of hope, etc.)* to fade; *(of species)* to become extinct, die out; *(fig)* to be ruined, be done for; **occidī**! *(coll)* I'm done for!
oc·cīdō -cīdere -cīdī -cīsus *tr* to kill; to murder; to knock down; to bring about the ruin of; *(fig)* to be the death of; to pester to death
occidu·us -a -um *adj* setting; western; *(fig)* sinking, fading, dying
occill·ō -āre -āvī -ātus *tr* to smash
oc·cinō -cinere -cecinī *or* **-cinuī** *or* **occan·ō -ere -uī** *intr* to sing inauspiciously, sound ominous
oc·cipiō -cipere -cēpī -ceptus *tr & intr* **(-cup-)** to begin
occipit·ium -(i)ī *or* **occip·ut -itis** *n* back of the head
occīsi·ō -ōnis *f* murder, killing
occīs·or -ōris *m* murderer, killer
occīsus *pp of* **occīdō**
occlāmit·ō -āre -āvī -ātus *tr* to shout at ‖ *intr* to shout, yell
occlū·dō -dere -sī -sus *tr* **(obc-)** to close up, shut up, lock up; to close access to *(buildings);* to restrain
occ·ō -āre -āvī -ātus *tr* to harrow, break up *(the soil)*
occub·ō -āre *intr* to lie; to rest; **crūdēlibus umbrīs occubāre** to lie dead in the cruel lower world
occulc·ō -āre -āvī -ātus *tr* to trample down
occul·ō -ere -uī -tus *tr* to cover; to cover up, hide
occultāti·ō -ōnis *f* concealment, hiding
occultāt·or -ōris *m* one who conceals
occultē *adv* secretly, in secret
occult·ō -āre -āvī -ātus *tr* to hide, conceal; to suppress, keep *(facts, information)* secret ‖ *refl & pass* to hide
occult·us -a -um *pp of* **occulō** ‖ *adj* hidden, secret; clandestine; recondite *(expressions);* invisible *(forces of nature);* reserved *(person)* ‖ *n* concealment; secret; **ex occultō** from a concealed position; **in occultō** in hiding; **per occultum** without being observed, secretly
oc·cumbō occumbere occubuī occubitus *tr* to meet *(death)* ‖ *intr* to fall dying; *(w. dat or abl)* to meet *(death);* **occumbere per** *(w. acc)* to die at the hands of
occupāti·ō -ōnis *f* occupation, employment, business; business engagement, task, job; occupying *(of a town);* preoccupation, concentration, close attention
occupāt·us -a -um *adj* occupied, busy, engaged
occup·ō -āre -āvī -ātus *tr* to occupy; to seize; to grasp, grab; to win, gain; to attack, strike down; to outstrip, overtake; to fill up, occupy *(a space);* to assume *(title, position);* to invest; to loan, lend, invest *(money);* to head for, reach; to forestall; to take by surprise; to take the lead over *(competitor); (w. inf)* to be the first to
oc·currō -currere -currī *or* **-cucurrī -cursum** *intr* **(obc-)** to run up; *(w. dat)* **1** to run up to, run to meet, hurry to meet; **2** to rush against, attack; **3** to resist, oppose, counteract; **4** to meet, answer, reply to, object to; **5** to relieve, remedy; **6** to occur to, suggest itself to, present itself to; **7** run into, run up against, get involved in; **8** to encounter
occursāti·ō -ōnis *f* hustle and bustle; excited welcome; officiousness
occurs·ō -āre -āvī -ātus *tr* **(obc-)** to run to meet ‖ *intr (w dat)* **1** to run to meet, come to meet, meet; **2** to attack, charge, oppose; **3** *(of thoughts)* to occur to
occurs·us -ūs *m* meeting; *(w. gen)* running into *(s.o. or s.th.)*
Ōceanīt·is -idis *or* **-idos** *f* ocean nymph, daughter of Oceanus
ōcean·us -ī *m* ocean ‖ **Ōceanus** Oceanus *(son of Uranus and Ge and father of the river gods and ocean nymphs)*
ocell·us -ī *m* eye; gem; darling
ōcim·um -ī *n* basil *(seasoning)*
ōcin·um -ī *n* fodder *(possibly clover)*

ōci·or -or -us *adj* swifter, quicker

ōcius *adv (superl:* **ōcissimē)** more swiftly, more quickly; sooner; more easily; immediately, on the spot; *(w. abl)* rather than; **ōcius sērius** sooner or later; **quam ōcissime** as quickly as possible

ocre·a -ae *f* greave, shin guard

ocreāt·us -a -um *adj* wearing shin guards

octaphoros *see* **octōphoros**

octāv·a -ae *f* one-eighth; eighth hour of the day *(i.e., 2:00 p.m.)*

Octāvi·a -ae *f* sister of Augustus, wife of Gaius Marcellus, and later of Marc Antony *(64–11 B.C.)* **||** daughter of Claudius and wife of Nero *(murdered in A.D. 62)*

Octāv·ius -(i)ī *m* Gaius Octavius *(Augustus, who, upon adoption by Julius Caesar, became Gaius Julius Caesar Octavianus, 63 B.C.–A.D. 14)*

octāvum *adv* for the eighth time

octāv·us -a -um *adj* eighth; **octāva pars** one-eighth **||** *f see* **octāva ||** *n* **cum octāvō efficere** to produce an eightfold yield

octāv·us decim·us -a -um *adj* eighteenth

octiēns *or* **octiēs** *adv* eight times

octingentēsim·us -a -um *adj* eight hundreth

octingent·ī -ae -a *adj* eight hundred

octip·ēs -edis *adj* eight-footed

octiplicāt·us -a -um *adj* eightfold

octō *indecl adj* eighteen

Octō·ber -bris -bre *adj* October, of October; **mēnsis Octōber** October *(8th month of the Roman calendar until 153 B.C.)* **|| Octō·ber -bris** *m* October

octōdecim *indecl adj* eighteen

octōgē(n)sim·us -a -um *adj* eightieth

octōgēnāri·us -a -um *adj & m* octogenarian

octōgēn·ī -ae -a *adj* eighty each

octōgiē(n)s *adv* eighty times

octōiug·is -is -e *adj* eight-horse

octōn·ī -ae -a *adj* eight at a time, eight each

octōphor·os -os -on *adj* **(octa-)** carried by eight men **||** *n* litter carried by eight men

octupl·us -a -um *adj* eightfold **||** *n* eightfold fine

octuss·is -is *m* copper coin, worth about eight cents

oculāt·us -a -um *adj* having eyes; exposed to view, conspicuous; **oculātus testis** eyewitness

ocule·us -a -um *adj* many-eyed

oculissim·us -a -um *adj (hum)* dearest

oculitus *adv (to love s.o.)* like one's own eyes, dearly

ocul·us -ī *m* eye; eyeball; eye, bud *(in plants);* sight, vision; mind's eye; **aequīs oculīs** contentedly; **alterō oculō captus** blind in one eye; **ante oculōs** in full view; *(fig)* obvious; **ante oculōs pōnere** to imagine; **ex oculīs abīre** to go out of sight, disappear; **in oculīs** in view, in public, in the limelight; **in oculīs ferre** *(or* **gestāre)** to hold dear, value; **oculōs adicere** *(w.* **ad)** to eye; to covet; **oculōs dēicere ab** to take one's eyes off; *(fig)* to lose sight of; **oculōs pāscere** *(w. abl)* to feast one's eyes on; **sub oculīs** *(w. gen)* in the presence of, under the very nose of

ōdī odisse ōsus sum *tr* to have taken a dislike to, dislike, hate, be disgusted with

odiōsē *adv* hatefully; unpleasantly

odiōsic·us -a -um *adj (hum)* odious, unpleasant, annoying

odiōs·us -a -um *adj* odious, unpleasant, annoying

od·ium -(i)ī *n* dislike, aversion, hatred; object of hatred, nuisance; dissatisfaction, disgust; offensive conduct, insolence; **odiō esse** *(w. dat)* to be hateful to, be disliked by, be hated by **||** *npl* feelings of hatred

od·or *or* **od·ōs -ōris** *m* odor, smell, scent; stench; pleasant smell, fragrance; perfume; inkling, suggestion, hint **||** *mpl* perfume

odōrāti·ō -ōnis *f* smell, smelling

odōrāt·us -a -um *adj* fragrant, scented

odōrāt·us -ūs *m* smell, smelling; sense of smell

odōrif·er -era -erum *adj* fragrant

odōr·ō -āre -āvī -ātus *tr* to make fragrant

odōr·or -ārī -ātus sum *tr* to sniff at, scent; to aspire to, aim at; to be sniffing after, search for, investigate; to get a smattering of

odōr·us -a -um *adj* smelly; fragrant; keen-scented

odōs *see* **odor**

Odrys·ae -ārum *mpl* a people of the Thracian interior

Odrysi·us -a -um *adj & m* Thracian

Odyssē·a *or* **Odyssī·a -ae** *f* the *Odyssey*

Oea·ger *or* **Oea·grus -grī** *m* Oeager *(king of Thrace and father of Orpheus)*

Oeagri·us -a -um *adj* Thracian

Oea·gus -grī *m* king of Thrace and father of Orpheus

Oebalid·ēs -ae *m* male descendant of Oebalus *(see* **Oebalus) ||** *mpl* Castor and Pollux

Oebali·us -a -um *adj* Spartan; Tarentine; Sabine **||** *f* Tarentum *(Spartan colony in S. Italy, modern Taranto)*

Oebal·us -ī *m* king of Sparta, father of Tyndareus, and grandfather of Helen, Clytemnestra, Castor, and Pollux

Oedip·ūs -odis *or* -ī *m* Oedipus

Oen·eus -eī *or* **-eos** *m* king of Calydon, husband of Althaea, and father of Meleager and Dejanira

Oenīd·ēs -ae *m* descendant of Oeneus; Meleager; Diomedes

Oenoma·üs -ī *m* king of Pisa in the Peloponnesus and father of Hippodamia
oenophor·um -ī *n* wine-bottle basket
Oenopi·a -ae *f* ancient name of Aegina
oenopōl·ium -(i)ī *n* wine shop
Oenōtri·us -a -um *adj* Oenotrian, Italic **II** *f* ancient name of S.E. Italy; Italy
oestr·us -ī *m* horsefly, gadfly; fancy, inspiration
oesyp·um -ī *n* **(-sop-)** lanolin
Oet·a -ae *or* **Oet·ē -ēs** *f* Mt. Oeta *(in S. Thessaly, on which Hercules died)*
Oetae·us -a -um *adj* Oetean **II** *m* Hercules
ofell·a -ae *f* small chunk of meat
off·a -ae *f* lump; dumpling; lump, swelling
offectus *pp of* **officiō**
offen·dō -dere -dī -sus *tr* to bump, bump against, stub, strike, hit; to hit upon, come upon, meet with, bump into, stumble upon, find; to offend, shock; to annoy, disgust; to hurt *(feelings);* to injure *(reputation);* **nihil offendere** to suffer no damage, receive no injury **II** *intr* to blunder, make a mistake; to give offense, be offensive; to fail, take a loss, be defeated, come to grief; to run aground; *(w. dat or* **in** *+ abl)* to hit against, bump against; *(w. dat)* to give offense to; *(w.* **in** *+ acc)* to take offense at; **terrae offendere** to run aground
offēns·a -ae *f* offense, affront; displeasure, resentment, hatred; crime; **offēnsā** *(w. gen)* out of hatred for
offēnsi·ō -ōnis *f* stubbing; tripping, stumbling; obstacle; setback, mishap; detriment; affront, outrage **II** *fpl* offensive acts; feelings of displeasure
offēnsiuncul·a -ae *f* slight mishap
offēns·ō -āre -āvī -ātus *tr & intr* to bump
offēns·us -a -um *pp of* **offendō II** *adj* offensive, odious; *(w. dat)* offended at, displeased with
offēns·us -ūs *m* bump; shock; offense
offerō offerre obtulī oblātus *tr* to offer, bring forward, present, show; to cause; to confer, bestow; to inflict; to deliver, hand over **II** *refl (w. adj)* to show oneself to be; *(w. dat)* **1** to meet, encounter; **2** to expose oneself to *(e.g., danger);* **3** to give oneself up to *(an authority);* **4** to offer one's services to, volunteer for **II** *refl & pass (esp. of an apparition)* to appear; *(of an idea)* to suggest itself
offerūment·a -ae *f (said humorously of a blow or welt)* present
officīn·a *or* **opificīn·a -ae** *f* shop, workshop, factory; office; artist's studio; training school
of·ficiō -ficere -fēcī -fectum *intr (w. dat)* **1** to get in the way of, interfere with, oppose; **2** to obstruct, hinder; **3** to be detrimental to
officiōsē *adv* obligingly, courteously
officiōs·us -a -um *adj* ready to serve, obliging; dutiful; officious
offic·ium -(i)ī *n* service, favor, kindness, courtesy; obligation, duty; function, part; social obligation, social call, social visit; ceremony; ceremonial observance, attendance; official duty; employment, business, job; sense of duty, conscience; allegiance; **officiō togae virīlis interesse** to attend the ceremony of the assuming of the manly toga
of·fīgō -fīgere -fīxī -fīxus *tr* to fasten down, nail down, drive in
offirmāt·us -a -um *adj* determined
offirm·ō -āre -āvī -ātus *refl & intr* to steel oneself, be determined
offlect·ō -ere *tr* to turn *(s.th.)* around
offrēnāt·us -a -um *adj* curbed
offrēn·ō -āre -āvī -ātus *tr (fig)* to curb
offūci·a -ae *f* cosmetic; *(fig)* trick, deception
offul·geō -gēre -sī *intr (w. dat)* to shine on
of·fundō -fundere -fūdī -fūsus *tr* to pour out; to cover; to fill; to eclipse **II** *pass (w. dat)* to pour out over, spread over
oggann·iō -īre -īvī *or* **-iī -ītus** *tr or intr* to growl
ogger·ō -ere *tr* to bring, offer
Ogyg·ēs -is *or* **Ogyg·us -ī** *m* mythical king of Thebes, in whose reign the Deluge allegedly occurred
Ogygi·us -a -um *adj* Theban; **Ogygius deus** Theban god *(i.e., Bacchus)*
oh *interj* oh!
ōhē *or* **ohē** *interj* whoa!
Oīl·eūs -eī *or* **-eos** *m* king of Locris in N. Greece and father of Ajax the archer
ole·a -ae *f* olive; olive tree
oleāgin·us -a -um *adj* olive, of an olive tree
oleāri·us -a -um *adj* oil, of oil **II** *m* oil merchant
oleas·ter -trī *m* oleaster, wild olive tree
Ōleni·us -a -um *adj* of Olenus *(town in Achaia and Aetolia);* Achaian, Aetolian
ol·ēns -entis *adj* smelling; fragrant; smelly, stinking; musty
ol·eō -ēre -uī *tr* to smell of, smell like; *(fig)* to betray **II** *intr* to smell; *(w. abl)* to smell of
ole·um -ī *n* olive oil, oil; *(fig)* palestra; **oleum addere camīnō** *(prov)* to pour oil on the fire; **oleum et operam perdere** to waste time and effort
ol·faciō -facere -fēcī -factus *tr* to smell
olfact·ō -āre -āvī -ātus *tr* to sniff at
olid·us -a -um *adj* smelly
ōlim *adv* once, once upon a time; at the time; for a good while; someday *(in the future),* hereafter; now and then, at times; ever, at any time
olit- = holit-
olīv·a -ae *f* olive; olive tree; olive wreath; olive branch; olive staff

olīvēt·um -ī *n* olive grove
olīvi·fer -fera -ferum *adj* producing olives, olive-growing
olīv·um -ī *n* olive oil; ointment; *(fig)* palestra
oll·a -ae *f* pot, jar
olle *or* **ollus = ille**
ol·or -ōris *m* swan
olōrīn·us -a -um *adj* swan
olus *see* **holus**
Olympi·a -ae *f* Olympia *(region in Elis, in the Peloponnesus, where the Olympic games were held)*
Olympi·a -ōrum *npl* Olympic games
Olympiac·us -a -um *adj* Olympic
Olympi·as -adis *or* **-ados** *f* Olympiad *(period of 4 years between Olympic games, starting in 776* B.C.*, according to which the Greeks reckoned time)* **II** Olympias (*wife of Philip V of Macedon and mother of Alexander the Great*)
Olympic·us -a -um *adj* Olympic, of the games held at Olympia
Olympionīc·ēs -ae *m* Olympic victor
Olympi·us -a -um *adj* Olympian *(cult title of Zeus); (of games)* Olympic, held at Olympia; *(of temple)* dedicated to Olympian Zeus
Olymp·us -ī *m* Mt. Olympus *(on the boundary of Macedonia and Thessaly, regarded as the home of the gods)*
omās·um -ī *n* tripe
ōm·en -inis *n* omen *(good or bad);* foreboding; **ōmen accipere** to believe an event to be an omen; **prīma ōmina** first marriage; **(procul) ōmen abestō**! *(or* **quod ōmen dī āvertant**!) God forbid!
ōment·um -ī *n* fatty membrane covering the bowels; the bowels
ōmināt·or -ōris *m* diviner
ōmin·or -ārī -ātus sum *tr* to foretell, predict, forebode
ōminōs·us -a -um *adj* ominous
ōmīsī *perf of* **ōmittō**
ōmiss·us -a -um *pp of* **ōmittō II** *adj* remiss, negligent, heedless
ōmittō ōmittere ōmīsī ōmissus *tr* to let go; to let go of, let fall, drop; to give up, abandon; to omit, pass over; to overlook, disregard; to release from custody; to allow to escape; to discard
omnigen·us -a -um *adj (also indecl)* every kind of
omnimodīs *or* **omnimodō** *adv* by all means, wholly
omnīnō *adv* altogether, entirely, wholly; *(w. numerals)* in all; *(in generalizations)* in general; *(in concessions)* no doubt, to be sure, yes, by all means; **haud omnīnō** *(or* **nōn omnīnō)** not quite, not entirely; absolutely not, not at all; not expressly; **omnīnō nēmō** absolutely no one
omnipar·ēns -entis *adj* all-producing *(earth)*
omnipot·ēns -entis *adj* omnipotent
omn·is -is -e *adj* all, every; every kind of; the whole **II** *mpl* all, everybody **II** *n* the universe **II** *npl* all things, everything; all nature; all the world
omnitu·ēns -entis *adj* all-seeing
omnivag·us -a -um *adj* roaming everywhere
omnivol·us -a -um *adj* all-craving
Omphal·ē -ēs *f* Lydian queen who bought Hercules as a slave for a year
ona·ger *or* **ona·grus -grī** *m* wild ass
onāg·os -ī *m* ass-driver
Onchēsmīt·ēs -ae *m* wind blowing from Onchesmus *(harbor in Epirus)*
onerāri·us -a -um *adj* carrying freight; **iūmenta onerāria** beasts of burden; **onerāria** *(or* **nāvis onerāria)** freighter, transport
oner·ō -āre -āvī -ātus *tr* to load, load down, burden; *(fig)* to overload, oppress; *(fig)* to pile on, aggravate
onerōs·us -a -um *adj* onerous, burdensome, oppressive; heavy
on·us -eris *n* burden; load; freight, cargo; trouble; tax burden; fetus, embryo; **onerī esse** *(w. dat)* to be a burden to
onust·us -a -um *adj* loaded down, burdened; filled, full
on·yx -ychis *mf* onyx; onyx box
opācit·ās -ātis *f* shade, shadiness
opāc·ō -āre -āvī -ātus *tr* to shade, make shady
opāc·us -a -um *adj* shady; dark, obscure **II** *npl* **opāca locōrum** shady places; **opāca viārum** dark streets
opell·a -ae *f* light work; small effort
oper·a -ae *f* effort, pains, exertion; work; care, attention; service, assistance; leisure, spare time; laborer, workman, artisan; a day's work *(by one person);* **operae esse** *(or* **operae pretium esse)** to be worthwhile; **operam dare** to take pains, exert oneself, be busied, pay attention, give attention, apply oneself; **operam fūnerī dare** to attend a funeral; **operam magistrō dare** *(or* **reddere)** to attend a teacher's lectures, study under a teacher; **operam lūdere** *(or* **perdere)** to waste one's time and effort; **operam sermōnī dare** to listen to a conversation; **operam tōnsōrī dare** to go see a barber, get a haircut; **operā meā (tuā,** *etc.)* through my (your, *etc.)* agency, thanks to me (you, *etc.)*
operāri·us -a -um *adj* working; working for hire **II** *m* workman **II** *f* working woman
opercul·um -i *n* lid, cover
operīment·um -ī *n* lid, cover

oper·iō -īre -uī -tus *tr* to cover, cover up; to shut; to hide; to clothe; to bury; to bury with a shower of missiles
oper·or -ārī -ātus sum *intr* to work hard, take pains; *(w. dat)* **1** to work hard at, be busied with, be engaged in; **2** to perform *(religious services);* **3** to attend; **4** to worship
operōsē *adv* with great effort, at great pains
operōs·us -a -um *adj* active, busy, painstaking; troublesome, difficult, elaborate; efficacious, powerful *(drugs)*
opertus *pp of* **operiō ‖** *adj* closed; hidden; secret **‖** *n* secret; secret place; **in opertō** inside, in secret **‖** *npl* depth; veiled oracles
operuī *perf of* **operiō**
opēs *see* **ops**
ophīt·ēs -ae *m* serpentine *(type of marble)*
Ophiūsi·us -a -um *adj* Cyprian **‖** *f* old name of Cyprus
ophthalmi·ās -ae *m* a type of fish
ophthalmic·us -ī *m* eye-doctor
Opic·us -a -um *adj* Oscan; boorish; ignorant *(esp. of Latin),* uncultured
opif·er -era -erum *adj* helpful
opif·ex -icis *m* maker, creator; craftsman, mechanic
opificīn·a -ae *f* workshop
opific·ium -(i)ī *n* work
ōpili·ō -ōnis *m* shepherd
opīmē *adv* splendidly; richly
opīmit·ās -ātis *f* prosperity
opīm·us -a -um *adj* fat, plump; fertile, fruitful; rich, enriched; abundant, plentiful; sumptuous, splendid; lucrative; noble; **spolia opīma** armor stripped from one general by another on the field of battle
opīnābil·is -is -e *adj* conjectural, imaginary
opīnāti·ō -ōnis *f* mere opinion, conjecture, supposition, hunch
opīnāt·us -a -um *adj* supposed, imagined
opīnāt·us -ūs *m* supposition
opīni·ō -ōnis *f* opinion; conjecture, guess, supposition; expectation; general impression; estimation; rumor; reputation, bad reputation; **amplius opīniōne** beyond expectation, beyond all hopes; **celerius opīniōne** sooner than expected; **hāc opīniōne ut** under the impression that; **in opīniōne esse** *(w. acc & inf)* to be of the opinion that; **praebēre opīniōnem timōris** to convey the impression of fear; **praeter opīniōnem** contrary to expectation, sooner than expected; **ut opīniō mea est** as I suppose
opīn·ō -āre *or* **opīn·or -ārī -ātus sum** *tr* to suppose, imagine, conjecture **‖** *intr (parenthetical)* to suppose, imagine
opiparē *adv* splendidly, sumptuously
opipar·us -a -um *adj* splendid, sumptuous, ritzy
opisthograph·us -a -um *adj* written on the back; **in opisthographō** on the reverse side of a document
opitul·or -ārī -ātus sum *intr (w. dat)* to bring help to, assist
oport·et -ēre -uit *v impers* it is right, it is proper; **mē abīre oportet** I ought to go, I should go
op·pangō -pangere -ēgī -pāctus *tr* to affix, imprint
oppect·ō -ere *tr* to comb off; *(coll)* to pluck, pick at, eat
oppēdō -ere *intr (vulg) (w. dat)* **1** to fart at; **2** *(fig)* to deride, mock
opper·ior -īrī -tus sum *tr* to wait for; *(w.* **num**) to wait and see whether **‖** *intr* to wait
oppet·ō -ere -īvī *or* **-iī -ītus** *tr* to meet, encounter *(prematurely)* **‖** *intr* to meet death, die
oppidān·us -a -um *adj* of a town, in a town; *(pej)* provincial **‖** *mpl* townspeople
oppidō *adv* absolutely, quite; *(as affirmative answer)* exactly, extremely; **oppidō quam breve intervallum** an extremely short distance
oppidul·um -ī *n* small town
oppid·um -ī *n* town
oppigner·ō -āre -āvī -ātus *tr* to pledge
oppīl·ō -āre -āvī -ātus *tr* to shut up, shut off
oppl·eō -ēre -ēvī -ētus *tr* to fill up, fill completely
op·pōnō -pōnere -posuī -positus *tr* to put, place, station; to oppose; to expose, lay bare, open; to wager; to mortgage; to bring forward, adduce, allege; to reply, object; to compare; **currum oppōnere** to block a rival's chariot
opportūnē *adv* at the right time
opportūnit·ās -ātis *f* opportunity, chance *(to do s.th.);* right time, opportuneness; advantage; suitability, fitness, convenience
opportūn·us -a -um *adj* opportune, suitable, convenient; advantageous, useful; exposed; **tempore opportūnissimō** in the nick of time
oppositi·ō -ōnis *f* opposition
opposit·us -a -um *pp of* **oppōnō ‖** *adj* opposite; *(w. dat)* opposite, across from
oppressi·ō -ōnis *f* force, violence, violent seizure; suppression, overthrow
oppressiuncul·a -ae *f* slight pressure
oppressus *pp of* **opprimō**
oppress·us -ūs *m* pressure
op·primō -primere -pressī -pressus *tr* **(obp-)** to press down, weigh down; to pressure, put pressure on; to shut; to overwhelm; to put down, quell; to sink *(ship);* to subvert, overthrow, crush, overpower; to conceal, suppress; to catch
opprobrāment·um -ī *n* disgrace, scandal

opprobr·ium -(i)ī *n* **(obp-)** disgrace, scandal, reproach; cause of disgrace; taunt, abuse, abusive word

opprobr·ō -āre -āvī -ātus *tr* **(obp-)** to throw up *(s.th.)* to *(s.o. as a reproach)*

oppugnāti·ō -ōnis *f* **(opr-)** assault; *(fig)* attack, accusation

oppugnāt·or -ōris *m* **(obp-)** assailant

oppugn·ō -āre -āvī -ātus *tr* to assault, attack, storm; *(fig)* to attack, assail

ops- = obs-

ops opis *f* power, might; help, aid; influence, weight; **nōn opis est nostrae** it is not in our power; **ope meā** with my help; **opem ferre** *(w. dat)* to bring help to, help ‖ *fpl* wealth, resources, means; military *or* political resources; **(ex) summīs opibus** with all one's might ‖ **Ops** *(goddess of abundance (sister and wife of Saturn and mother of Jupiter)*

optābil·is -is -e *adj* desirable

optāti·ō -ōnis *f* wishing, wish

optātō *adv* according to one's wish

optāt·us -a -um *adj* longed-for, desired, welcome ‖ *n* wish, desire

optigō *see* **obtegō**

optim·ās -ātis *m* **(-tum-)** aristocrat ‖ *mpl* aristocracy, aristocratic party

optimē *(superl of* **bene)** *adv* **(-tum-)** very well; thoroughly; best; most opportunely, just in time

optim·us -a -um *(superl of* **bonus)** *adj* **(-tum-)** very good, best; excellent; most beneficial, most advantageous; *(of a legal title)* most valid, having the soundest basis; **in optimam partem** most favorably; **optimā fide** with the utmost honesty; **optimum est** *(w. inf)* it is best to; **optimum factū est** *(w. inf)* the best thing to do is to; **ut optimus maximusque** *(leg) (of property)* in its optimum condition *(i.e., free from all encumbrances)*

opti·ō -ōnis *f* option, choice ‖ *m* helper, assistant; *(mil)* adjutant

optīv·us -a -um *adj* chosen

opt·ō -āre -āvī -ātus *tr* to choose, select; to pray for; to wish for, desire

optum- = optim-

opul·ēns -entis *adj* opulent, rich

opulentē *or* **opulenter** *adv* richly

opulenti·a -ae *f* opulence, wealth; resources; power

opulentit·ās -ātis *f* opulence; power

opulent·ō -āre -āvī -ātus *tr* to make rich, enrich

opulent·us -a -um *adj* opulent, rich; sumptuous; powerful

op·us -eris *n* work; product of work: structure, building; literary work, composition, book; work of art, workmanship; deed, achievement; literary genre; occupation, employment; what a person is expected to do, function, business; *(w. gen) (poet)* a thing the size of; *(mil)* offensive works, siege works; *(mil)* defensive works, fortifications; **dulce opus peragere** to perform one's pleasant business *(i.e., sexual intercourse)*; **in opere** at work; **magnō opere** greatly, to a great extent; **māiōre (summō) opere** to a greater (the greatest) extent; **opere** *(w. gen)* through the agency of; **quantō opere** how much, how greatly; **tantō opere** so much, so greatly; **operis alicūius esse** to be s.o.'s doing; **opus est** *(w. dat of person in need and abl of person or thing needed)* to need, *e.g.*, **opus est mihi duce** I need a leader; **suī operis esse** to be part of one's business

opuscul·um -ī *n* little work, minor work, small job

-or -ōris *m suf* forms nouns denoting **1** abstracts, *e.g.:* **candor** whiteness; **amor** love; **2** doer of the action of the verb, *e.g.*, **amātor** lover

ōr·a -ae *f* boundary, border, edge; coastline, coast; region, district; cable, hawser; *(fig)* people of the coast, people of the region; division of the world; **ōra maritima** seacoast ‖ *fpl* region, land; **ōrae extremae** the most distant lands, farthest shores; **ōrae lūminis** *(or* **ōrae superae)** the upper world

ōrāc(u)l·um -ī *n* oracle; prophesy

ōrāri·us -a -um *adj* coasting; **nāvis ōrāria** coasting vessel, coaster

ōrāt·a -ōrum *npl* prayer, requests

ōrāti·ō -ōnis *f* faculty of speech; speech, language; style of speech, manner of speaking, style, expression; oration, speech; theme, subject; prose; eloquence; dialect; imperial rescript; **ōrātiōnem habēre** to give a speech; **ōrātiō solūta** *(or* **ōrātiō prōsa)** prose; **pars ōrātiōnis** part of speech

ōrātiuncul·a -ae *f* short speech, insignificant speech

ōrāt·or -ōris *m* orator, speaker; suppliant; spokesman

ōrātōriē *adv* oratorically

ōrātōri·us -a -um *adj* orator's, oratorical

ōrātr·īx -īcis *f* suppliant *(female)*

ōrāt·us -ūs *m* request

orb·a -ae *f* orphan

orbāt·or -ōris *m* murderer *(of s.o.'s children or parents)*

Orbil·ius -(i)ī *m* Lucius Orbilius Pupillus *(Horace's teacher in Venusia)*

orb·is -is *m* circle; disk, ring; orbit *(of heavenly bodies)*; quoit; hoop; wheel; spinning wheel; potter's wheel; round shield; eye socket, eye; globe, earth, world, universe; region, territory, country; circuit, round; rotation; cycle, period; zodiac; *(rhet)* balance; **magnus orbis** a year; **orbis caelī** vault of heaven; **Orbis Lacteus** Milky Way; **orbis lūminis** eye;

orbis noster our section of the world; **orbis oculī** eyeball; **orbis terrae** *(or* **terrārum)** earth, world, universe
orbit·a -ae *f* rut; *(astr)* orbit; *(fig)* routine
orbit·ās -ātis *f* childlessness, widowhood, orphanhood
orbitōs·us -a -um *adj* full of ruts
orb·ō -āre -āvī -ātus *tr* to bereave of parents, father, mother, children, husband, *or* wife; to strip, rob, deprive; to make destitute
orb·us -a -um *adj* bereaved, bereft; destitute; orphaned, fatherless; childless; widowed; *(w. gen or abl or* **ab)** bereft of, without ‖ *mf* orphan
orc·a -ae *f* vat
Orcad·es -um *fpl* islands N. of Scotland *(modern Orkneys)*
orch·as -adis *f* a kind of olive
orchestr·a -ae *f* senatorial seats *(in the theater);* orchestra *(area in front of the Greek stage where the chorus sang and danced)*
Orc·us -ī *m* lower world; Pluto *(king of the lower world);* death
orde- = **horde-**
ōrdināri·us -a -um *adj* ordinary, usual, regular; normally elected *(consul)*
ōrdinātim *adv* in order, in good order; in sucession; regularly
ōrdināti·ō -ōnis *f* orderly arrangement; orderly government
ōrdināt·us -a -um *adj* regular; appointed
ōrdin·ō -āre -āvī -ātus *tr* to set in order, arrange, regulate; to govern, rule; to record chronologically
ōrdior ōrdīrī ōrsus sum *tr* to begin, undertake; to describe ‖ *intr* to begin; to begin to speak
ōrd·ō -inis *m* line, row; series; row of seats *(in theater);* order, methodical arrangement; order, class; social standing, rank, position; *(mil)* line, file *(of soldiers),* company, century, command of a company *or* century; **amplissimus ōrdō** senatorial order; **ex ōrdine** in succession, without a break; **extrā ōrdinem** extraordinarily, especially, uncommonly; **in ōrdine** *(mil)* in regular order, in battle array; **in ōrdinem cōgere** *(or* **redigere)** to put *(s.o.)* in his place, tell *(s.o.)* off; **ōrdine** *(or* **in ōrdine** *or* **per ōrdinem)** in order, in sequence; in a straight line; in detail; with regularity, regularly ‖ *mpl* officers of a company; promotions
Orē·as -adis *or* **-ados** *f* Oread *(mountain nymph)*
Orest·ae -ārum *mpl* tribe on the borders of Macedonia and Epirus
Orest·ēs -is *or* **-ae** *m* son of Agamemnon and Clytemnestra
Orestē·us -a -um of Orestes
orex·is -is *f* craving, appetite
organic·us -ī *m* organist
organ·um -ī *n* instrument, implement; musical instrument; water organ; organ pipe; **organum hydraulicum** water organ
orgi·a -ōrum *npl* Bacchic revels; orgies
orichalc·um -ī *n* copper ore; brass
ōricill·a -ae *f* little ear; lobe
ori·ēns -entis *m* rising sun, morning sun; morning; day; land of the rising sun, Orient, the East; **ab oriente** in the East
orīg·ō -inis *f* origin, source, beginning, start; birth, lineage, descent; race, stock, family; founder, progenitor; derivation *(of a word)*
Ōrī·ōn -ōnis *or* **-ōnos** *m* giant hunter, killed by Diana and turned into a constellation; *(astr)* Orion
orior orīrī ortus sum *intr* to rise; to get up; to become visible, appear; to be born, originate, be descended; to proceed, begin, start; *(of a spring, river)* to rise; *(of living creatures)* to come into existence, be born; *(of plants)* to come up, sprout; *(of events)* to arise, crop up; **homō ā sē ortus** a self-made man
Ōrīthȳi·a -ae *f* daughter of Erechtheus, king of Athens
oriund·us -a -um *adj* descended; *(w. abl)* originating from, originally from *(a place)*
ōrnāment·um -ī *n* equipment, trappings, apparatus; ornament, decoration; trinket, jewel; *(fig)* distinction; pride and joy; *(rhet)* rhetorical device
ōrnātē *adv* ornately, elegantly
ōrnātr·īx -īcis *f* hairdresser *(female)*
ōrnāt·us -ūs *m* equipment; apparel, outfit; furniture; decoration, ornament; preparation; *(rhet)* rhetorical embellishment
ōrn·ō -āre -āvī -ātus *tr* to equip, fit out, furnish; to outfit, dress; to set off, decorate, adorn; to show *(s.o.)* respect; *(w. abl)* **1** to honor with; **2** *(of things)* to give distinction to, enhance
orn·us -ī *f (bot)* mountain ash
ōr·ō -āre -āvī -ātus *tr* to beg, entreat, implore, plead with; to ask for; *(w. double acc)* to ask *(s.o.)* for; *(leg)* to plead *(a case)* ‖ *intr* to plead, beg, pray; *(w.* **cum)** to plead with, argue with
Orōd·ēs -is *m* name of several eastern kings, *esp.* Orodes II of Parthia, whose general defeated Crassus at Carrhae *(53 B.C.)*
Oront·ēs -is *or* **-ae** *m* chief river of Syria ‖ companion of Aeneas
Orontē·us -a -um *adj* from the River Orontes, Syrian
Orph·ēus -eī *or* **-eos** *m* famous musician and poet, husband of Eurydice
Orphē·us *or* **Orphic·us -a -um** *adj* Orphic

ōrs·us -a -um *pp of* **ōrdior** ‖ *npl* beginnings; utterance, words; attempt
ōrs·us -ūs *m* beginning; attempt, undertaking
orthographi·a -ae *f* spelling
ortus *pp of* **orior**
ort·us -ūs *m* rising; sunrise, daybreak; the East; birth *(of living creatures);* origin; source; **sōlis ortus** sunrise; the East; beginning, dawning *(of a period)*
Ortygi·a -ae *or* **Ortygi·ē -ēs** *f* Ortygia *(old name of Delos)* ‖ Ortygia *(island in the port of Syracuse in Sicily)* ‖ Ortygia *(old name of Ephesus)*
Ortygi·us -a -um *adj* of Ortygia, Delian; Syracusan
or·yx -ygis *m* gazelle
oryz·a -ae *f* rice
ōs ōris *n* mouth; beak; voice, speech; expression; lip, face, countenance, look; sight, presence *(of a person);* impudence; mask; opening, orifice, front; **favēte ōre**! observe a respectful silence!; **habēre aliquid in ōre** to be talking about s.th. continually; **in ōra hominum venīre** to become a household name; **in ōre omnium esse** to be on the lips of all; **in ōs aliquem laudāre** to praise s.o. to his face; **ōs amnis** mouth of a river; **ōs dūrum** hardened look *or* expression, big mouth; **ōs laedere** *(w. dat)* to insult s.o. to his, her face; **ōs oblinere** *(w. dat)* to hoodwink *(s.o.);* **ōs ostendere** to show one's face; **ōs timidum** expression of fear; **ōs vēnae** opening in a blood vessel; **per ōra ferrī** to go from mouth to mouth; **per** *(or* **praeter)** **ōra nostra** before our eyes; **summō ōre** just with the lips; **tria Dianae ōra** the three forms of Diana; **ūnō ōre** unanimously
os ossis *n* bone; marrow, innermost parts; kernel *(of a nut);* stone *(of fruit)* ‖ *npl* bones; skeleton; **ossa legere** to collect the bones *(from a pyre)*
ōsc·en -inis *mf* foreboding bird *(a bird of augury from whose note auguries were taken, e.g., crow, raven, owl)*
ōscill·um -ī *n* small mask
ōscit·āns -antis *adj* yawning; *(fig)* indifferent, bored
ōscit·ō -āre -āvī -ātus *or* **ōscit·or -ārī -ātus sum** *intr* to gape; to yawn
ōsculāti·ō -ōnis *f* kissing
ōscul·or -ārī -ātus sum *tr* to kiss; *(fig)* to make a fuss over
ōscul·um -ī *n* kiss; mouth, lips *(usually, puckered for a kiss);* **breve ōsculum** peck
Ōsc·us -a -um *adj* Oscan ‖ *mpl* Oscans *(ancient people of Campania and Samnium)*
Ōs·ī -ōrum *mpl* people of Germany on the Danube
Osīr·is -is *or* **-idis** *m* Egyptian god, husband of Isis
ōs·or -ōris *m* hater
Oss·a -ae *f* mountain in N.E. Thessaly
osse·us -a -um *adj* bony
osten·dō -dere -dī -tus *or* **-sus** *tr* to hold out for inspection; to show, exhibit, display, expose; to stretch out, stretch forth; to bring to one's attention; to expose; to reveal, disclose; to declare, make known; to represent in art; **ōs ostendere** to show one's face ‖ *refl* to show oneself, appear; **sē optimē ostendere** to appear very friendly
ostentāti·ō -ōnis *f* display; ostentation, showing off; mere show, pretense
ostentāt·or -ōris *m* show-off
ostent·ō -āre -āvī -ātus *tr* to show, exhibit; to show off, display, parade, boast of; to declare, point out, set forth
ostent·um -ī *n* portent, prodigy
ostent·us -ūs *m* display, show; **ostentuī** for appearances
Ōsti·a -ae *f or* **Ōsti·a -ōrum** *npl* Ostia *(port town at mouth of Tiber)*
ōstiār·ium -(i)ī *n* tax on doors
ōstiār·ius -(i)ī *m* doorman
ōstiātim *adv* from door to door
ōst·ium -(i)ī *n* door; entranceway; entrance, mouth
ostre·a -ae *f or* **ostre·um -ī** *n* oyster
ostreāt·us -a -um *adj* covered with oyster shells; *(fig)* black-and-blue
ostreōs·us -a -um *adj* abounding in oysters
ostri·fer -fera -ferum *adj* producing oysters, oyster-bearing
ostrīn·us -a -um *adj* purple
ostr·um -ī *n* purple dye; purple; purple garment, purple coverlet
-ōs·us -a -um *adjl suf (formed chiefly from nouns)* abounding in, rich in, full of: **ostreōsus** abounding in oysters
ōsus *pp of* **ōdī**
ōsūrus *fut p of* **ōdī**
Oth·ō -ōnis *m* Marcus Salvius Otho *(Roman emperor in* A.D. *69)* ‖ Lucius Roscius Otho *(author of the law of 67* B.C. *reserving 14 rows in theaters for the equestrian order)*
Othr·ys -yos *m* mountain range in S. Thessaly
ōtiol·um -ī *n* bit of leisure
ōti·or -ārī -ātus sum *intr* to take it easy
ōtiōsē *adv* at leisure; leisurely, without haste; calmly, fearlessly
ōtiōs·us -a -um *adj* at leisure, relaxing, having nothing to do; free from official obligations; quiet, calm; undisturbed; unconcerned, indifferent, neutral; passionless; having no practical use, useless; superfluous, unnecessary; leading a peaceful existence; *(of land)* unoccupied,

vacant ‖ *m* private person *(not holding public office);* civilian, non-combatant
ōt·ium -(i)ī *n* leisure, free time, relaxation; freedom from public affairs, retirement; peace, quiet; peaceful relations *(with another country);* ease, idleness, inactivity; calm weather; respite, lull; **(in) ōtiō** *(or* **per otium**) at leisure, undisturbed; **in ōtium venīre** to retire, go into retirement
ov·āns -antis *adj* joyful, jubilant
ovāti·ō -ōnis *f* ovation, minor triumph *(in which the victor went on foot rather than driving a chariot)*
ovāt·us -a -um *adj* triumphal, of an ovation
Ovid·ius -(i)ī *m* Ovid *(Publius Ovidius Naso, Latin poet, born at Sulmo, 43 B.C.–A.D. 17)*
ovīl·e -is *n* sheepfold; voting enclosures in the Campus Martius
ovīlis -is -e *adj* sheep, of sheep
ovill·a -ae *f* mutton, lamb
ovill·us -a -um *adj* sheep, of sheep
ov·is -is *f* sheep; wool; simpleton, ninny
ov·ō -āre -āvī -ātum *intr* to rejoice; to hold a celebration; to celebrate a minor triumph
ōv·um -ī *n* egg ‖ *npl* wooden balls used to mark the laps at the racetrack
oxycomin·a -ōrum *npl* pickled olives
oxygar·um -ī *n* fish sauce containing vinegar

P

P, p *(supply* littera) *f* fifteenth letter of the Latin alphabet; letter name: **pe**
P. *abbr* **Pūblius** *(Roman first name, praenomen)*
pābulāti·ō -ōnis *f* foraging
pābulāt·or -ōris *m* forager
pābul·or -ārī -ātus sum *intr* to forage; to feed, graze; *(coll)* to make a living
pābul·um -ī *n* feed, fodder; pasturage, grass; *(fig)* nourishment, fuel
pācāl·is -is -e *adj* of peace, peaceful
pācāt·us -a -um *adj* peaceful, quiet, calm; *(of people)* living in peace; of peacetime; pacified *(euphemism for conquered);* **pācātae rāmus olīvae** the olive branch, symbolic of peace; **vīcī male pācātī** villages not completely pacified ‖ *n* peaceful countryside
Pachȳn·um -ī *n or* **Pachȳn·os -ī** *f* S.E. point of Sicily
pācif·er -era -erum *adj* peace-bringing, peaceful; *(of olive and laurel)* symbolizing peace
pācificāti·ō -ōnis *f* pacification
pācificāt·or -ōris *m* peacemaker
pācificātōri·us -a -um *adj* peace-making
pācific·ō -āre -āvī -ātus *tr* to pacify, appease ‖ *intr* to make peace, conclude peace
pācific·us -a -um *adj* peace-making; peaceable
pac·īscor -īscī -tus sum *tr* to bargain for, agree upon; to stipulate; to barter; to become engaged to ‖ *intr* to come to an agreement, strike a bargain, make a contract; *(w. inf)* to agree to, pledge oneself to
pāc·ō -āre -āvī -ātus *tr* to pacify, soothe; to reclaim *(land by war)*
pact·a -ae *f* fiancée; bride
pacti·ō -ōnis *f* pact, contract, agreement; treaty, terms; condition, stipulation; collusion; *(leg)* settlement *(in a dispute);* **pactiō nūptiālis** marriage contract
Pactōl·us *or* **Pactōl·os -ī** *m* river in Lydia famous for its gold
pact·or -ōris *m* contractor, party *(in a contract);* negotiator
pact·um -ī *n* pact, contract, agreement; way, manner; **aliquō pactō** somehow; **ex pactō** according to the contract; **hōc pactō** in this way; **in pactō manēre** to stick to an agreement; **quō pactō** how, in what way
pact·us -a -um *pp of* **pacīscor** *and* **pangō** ‖ *adj* agreed, settled, determined, stipulated; **coniunx pacta** the betrothed, fiancée
Pācuv·ius -(i)ī *m* Marcus Pacuvius *(c. 220–133 B.C., Roman tragic poet, native of Brundisium and nephew of Ennius)*
Pad·us -ī *m* Po River *(in N. Italy)*
Padūs·a -ae *f* one of the mouths of the Po River
pae·ān -ānis *m* hymn to Apollo; paean, hymn of praise, victory song ‖ **Paeān** epithet of Apollo as god of healing
paedagōg·ium -iī *n* **(pēd-)** training school for pages
paedagōg·us -ī *m* **(pēd-)** slave in charge of school children; *(fig)* guide, leader
paedīc·ō -āre -āvī -ātus *tr* **(pēd-)** to have homosexual relations with *(boys)*
paedīc·ō -ōnis *m* **(pēd-)** homosexual, pedophile
paed·or -ōris *m* **(ped-)** filth
pael·ex -icis *f* **(pēl-, pell-)** concubine, mistress
paelicāt·us -ūs *m* **(pēl-)** concubinage
Paelign·ī -ōrum *mpl* **(Pēl-)** a people of central Italy
paene *adv* nearly, almost
paenīnsul·a -ae *f* peninsula
paenitend·us -a -um *adj* regrettable
paenitenti·a -ae *f* **(poen-)** repentance, regret
paenit·eō -ēre -uī paenitūrus *tr* **(poen-)** to cause to regret; to displease ‖ *intr (w. gen)* to regret ‖ *v impers (w. acc of person), e.g.,* **mē paenitet** I am sorry; *(w. acc*

of person and gen of thing), e.g., **mē paenitet cōnsilī** I regret the idea, am dissatisfied with the plan; *(w. acc of person and inf or* **quod**)*, e.g.,* **eōs paenitet animum tuum offendisse** *(or* **eōs paenitet quod animum tuum offenderint**) they regret having offended your feelings

paenul·a -ae *f* travel coat; raincoat

paenulāt·us -a -um *adj* wearing a traveling coat *or* raincoat

pae·ōn -ōnis *m (pros)* metrical foot containing one long and three short syllables *(first paeonic:* — ◡ ◡ ◡; *second paeonic:* ◡ — ◡ ◡; *third paeonic:* ◡ ◡ — ◡; *fourth paeonic:* ◡ ◡ ◡ —)

Paeon·es -um *mpl* a people inhabiting Paeonia

Paeoni·a -ae *f* Paeonia *(the country N. of Macedonia)*

paeōni·us -a -um *adj* healing, medicinal; **herba paeōnia** peony

Paestān·us -a -um *adj* of Paestum

Paest·um -ī *n* town in Lucania in S. Italy, famous for its roses

paetul·us -a -um *adj* slightly squint-eyed

paet·us -a -um *adj* squinting, squint-eyed; leering **‖ Paetus** *m* Roman family name *(cognomen)*

pāgān·us -a -um *adj* of a village, rustic; ignorant **‖** *m* villager, peasant; *(pej)* yokel

Pagas·a -ae *f or* **Pagas·ae -ārum** *fpl* town on the E. coast of Thessaly from which the *Argo* set sail

Pagasae·us -a -um *adj* Pagasean **‖** *m* Jason

pāgātim *adv* by villages, village by village, in every village

pāgell·a -ae *f* small page *or* sheet

pāgin·a -ae *f* page; *(poet)* piece of writing; **in īmā pāginā** at the bottom of the page

pāginul·a -ae *f* small page *or* sheet

pāg·us -ī *m* village; canton, province; country people, villagers

pāl·a -ae *f* spade

palaestr·a -ae *f* palaestra, wrestling school, gymnasium; school of rhetoric; rhetorical training; school; wrestling; exercise; brothel

palaestricē *adv* as at the palaestra

palaestric·us -a -um *adj* of the palaestra, gymnastic **‖** *f* gymnastics

palaestrīt·a -ae *m* wrestling coach; director of a palaestra

palam *adv* openly, publicly, plainly; **palam esse** to be public, be well known; **palam facere** to make public, disclose **‖** *prep (w. abl)* before, in the presence of, face to face with

Palātīn·us -a -um *adj* Palatine; imperial

Palāt·ium -(i)ī *n* Palatine Hill; palace; a temple on the Palatine

palāt·um -ī *n or* **palāt·us -ī** *m (anat)* palate; *(fig)* taste; *(fig)* literary taste

pale·a -ae *f* chaff

paleār·ia -ium *npl* dewlap *(fold of skin that hangs from the neck of a bovine animal)*

Pal·ēs -is *f* Italic goddess of shepherds and flocks

Palīc·ī -ōrum *mpl* twin sons of Jupiter and the nymph Thalia

Palīl·is -is -e *adj* of Pales **‖** *npl* feast of Pales *(celebrated April 21)*

palimpsest·um -ī *n* palimpsest *(parchment from which writing has been erased and new writing put on)*

Palinūr·us -ī *m* pilot of Aeneas who fell overboard and drowned **‖** promontory named after Palinurus

paliūr·us *or* **paliūr·os -ī** *mf (bot)* Christ's thorn *(a plant)*

pall·a -ae *f* ladies' long outdoor dress *(counterpart of the male's toga);* male outer garment *(restricted to non-Romans);* tragic actor's costume

pallac·a -ae *f* concubine

Pallacīn·a -ae *f* section of Rome near the Circus Flaminius

Palladi·us -a -um *adj* of Pallas, associated with Pallas Athene *(Minerva)* **‖** *n* statue of Pallas; Palladium *(Trojan statue of Pallas allegedly stolen by Odysseus and said subsequently to have been brought to Rome, since the safety of the city depended on it)*

Pallantē·um -ī *n* city in Arcadia, the home of Pallas **‖** city founded by Evander in Italy where Rome later stood

Pallantē·us -a -um *adj* of Pallas *(great-grandfather of Evander)*

Pall·as -adis *or* **-ados** *f* Athene; olive oil, oil; olive tree; Palladium *(Trojan statue of Pallas)*

Pall·ās -antis *m* great-grandfather of Evander **‖** son of Evander **‖** son of Pandion and brother of Aegeus **‖** father of Minerva

pall·ēns -entis *adj* pale; chartreuse, yellowish; sick-looking; dim *(light)*

pall·eō -ēre -uī *intr* to be pale, look pale; to have a pale *(greenish or yellowish)* color; to fade; to be dim; *(w. dat)* to grow pale over, worry about

pall·ēscō -ēscere -uī *tr* to turn pale at **‖** *intr* to turn pale; to turn yellow; to fade, grow dim

palliāt·us -a -um *adj* wearing a Greek cloak; **fābula palliāta** Latin play with Greek setting and characters

pallidul·us -a -um *adj* somewhat pale

pallid·us -a -um *adj* pallid, pale; grey-green, yellow-green, chartreuse

palliolātim *adv* in a mantle

palliolāt·us -a -um *adj* wearing a pallium

palliol·um -ī *n* short cloak; hood

pall·ium -(i)ī *n* pallium *(rectangular material worn mainly by men, esp. Greek men,* *as an outer garment);* bed cover, couch cover

pall·or -ōris *m* pallor, pale complexion; **pallōrem dūcere** to turn pale

pallul·a -ae *f* small outer garment *(see* **palla)**

palm·a -ae *f* palm of the hand, hand; palm tree, date; palm branch; palm wreath; palm of victory, first prize; victory; victor *(carrying a palm);* oar, oar blade

palmār·is -is -e *adj* excellent, deserving of the palm *or* prize ‖ *n* masterpiece

palmāri·us -a -um *adj* prize-winning, excellent ‖ *n* masterpiece

palmāt·us -a -um *adj* embroidered with palm-branch design; **tunica palmāta** embroidered tunic *(with palm-branch design, worn by a general)*

palm·es -itis *m* vine shoot, vine branch, vine; branch, twig *(of any tree)*

palmēt·um -ī *n* palm grove

palmi·fer -fera -ferum *adj* producing palms, palm-bearing

palmōs·us -a -um *adj* full of palm trees

palmul·a -ae *f* oar blade; date *(fruit of the palm tree)*

pāl·or -ārī -ātus sum *intr* to roam about, wander aimlessly

palpāti·ō -ōnis *f* stroking ‖ *fpl* flatteries

palpāt·or -ōris *m* flatterer

palpebr·a -ae *f* eyelid

palpit·ō -āre -āvī *intr* to throb, palpitate, quiver

palp·ō -āre -āvī -ātus *or* **palp·or -ārī -ātus sum** *tr* to stroke, pat; to wheedle, coax; to flatter ‖ *intr (w. dat)* **1** to coax; **2** to flatter

palp·us -ī *m* palm of the hand; coaxing, flattery

palūdāment·um -ī *n* general's cloak

palūdāt·us -a -um *adj* wearing a general's cloak

palūdōs·us -a -um *adj* swampy

palumb·ēs -is *mf* pigeon, dove

pāl·us -ī *m* stake, post; wooden sword *(used in practice)*

pal·ūs -ūdis *f* swamp, marsh; sedge

palus·ter *(or* **-tris) -tris -tre** *adj* swampy, marshy; growing in a swamp; used *or* located in a swamp ‖ *npl* swamp, marshland

pampine·us -a -um *adj* of vine tendrils, made of vine leaves; **odor pampineus** bouquet of wines

pampin·us -ī *m (f)* vine shoot, tendril; vine leaf; tendril *(of any kind)*

Pān Pānos *(acc:* **Pāna)** *m* Pan *(Greek god of flocks, shepherds, and woods, often identified with Faunus)*

panacē·a -ae *f or* **pan·ax -acis** *m or* **panac·ēs -is** *n* panacea, cure-all

Panaetōlic·us -a -um *adj* Pan-Aetolian

pānār·ium -(i)ī *n* breadbox; breadbasket; food basket; picnic basket

Panchāï·a -ae *f* region in Arabia famous for its frankincense

panchrest·os -os -on *adj* good for everything, universally useful; **panchreston medicāmentum** *(hum)* bribery *(the cure-all medication)*

pancraticē *adv (coll)* fine, splendidly; **pancraticē valēre** to get along splendidly

pancrat·ium *or* **pancrat·ion -iī** *n* contest which included the skills of boxing and wrestling

Pandar·us -ī *m* famous Lycian archer in the Trojan army ‖ companion of Aeneas, killed by Turnus

pandicul·or -ārī -ātus sum *intr (of a person while yawning)* to stretch

Pandī·ōn -onis *or* **-onos** *m* king of Athens and father of Procne and Philomela

Pandīoni·us -a -um *adj* of Pandion

pan·dō -dere -dī pānsus *or* **pāssus** *tr* to spread out, extend, expand, unfold; to open, lay open, throw open; to open up *(a road);* to make *(a place)* accessible, open *(a building);* to reveal, make known, publish; *(mil)* to deploy

pand·us -a -um *adj* curved

pangō pangere pānxī, *or* **pepegī** *or* **pēgī pāctus** *tr* to fasten, fix, drive in; to fix, set *(boundaries);* to settle *(a matter);* to agree upon, determine; to write, compose, celebrate, record; to promise in marriage; to provide; **indūtiās pangere cum** to conclude an armistice with

pānice·us -a -um *adj* made of bread; **mīlitēs pāniceī** *(coll)* Breadville brigade *(humorous coinage applied to bakers)*

pānicul·a -ae *f* tuft

pānic·um -ī *n* Italian millet *(cereal grass, raised for its seed or small grains to be used as food)*

pān·is -is *m* bread; loaf of bread; **pānem coquere** to bake bread; **pānis cibārius** coarse bread; **pānis secundus** stale bread

Pānīsc·us -ī *m* little Pan

pannicul·us -ī *m* rag

Pannoni·a -ae *f* Pannonia *(country of Lower Danube in the area of modern Austria)*

Pannoni·us -a -um *adj* Pannonian

pannōs·us -a -um *adj* tattered, threadbare; dressed in rags

pannūce·us *or* **pannūci·us -a -um** *adj* ragged; shriveled, wrinkled

pann·us -ī *m* patch; rag

Panop·ē -ēs *or* **Panopē·a -ae** *f* a sea nymph

pāns·a -ae *adj (masc & fem only)* flatfooted ‖ **Pānsa** *m* Roman family name *(cognomen, esp.* Gaius Vibius Pansa *(cos. 43 B.C.)*

pānsus *pp of* **pandō**

panthēr·a -ae *f* panther

Panthoid·ēs -ae *m* son of Panthus, *(i.e., Euphorbus, a Trojan warrior)*
Panth·us -ī *m* priest of Apollo at Troy and father of Euphorbus
pantic·ēs -um *mpl* guts; sausages
papae *interj (in delight)* great!, wonderful!; *(in pain)* ouch!; *(in astonishment)* wow!
pāp·as -ae *or* **-atis** *m* papa *(baby-talk for pedagogue)*
papāv·er -eris *n (m)* poppy; poppyseed
papāvere·us -a -um *adj* of poppies
Paphi·ē -ēs *f* Paphian goddess (*Venus*); *(poet)* heterosexual love
Paphi·us -a -um *adj* of Paphos
Paph·os -ī *f* town in S.W. Cyprus sacred to Venus ‖ *mf* child of Pygmalion
pāpili·ō -ōnis *m* butterfly; moth
papill·a -ae *f* nipple, teat; breast
papp·ō -āre *tr* to eat *(soft food)*
papp·us -ī *m* hairy seed *(of certain plants)*
papul·a -ae *f* pimple
papȳrif·er -era -erum *adj* papyrus-producing
papȳr·us -ī *f or* **papȳr·um -ī** *n* papyrus
pār paris *adj* equal, like, on a par, equally matched, well-matched; suitable, adequate; of equal size; *(w. dat or* **cum**) equal to, comparable to, similar to, as large as; *(w. limiting abl, w.* **ad** *or* **in** + *acc)* equal, similar, alike in; **pār est** it is right, it is proper; **pār proelium** even *or* indecisive battle; **ut pār est** *(used parenthetically)* as is only right ‖ *m* companion; equal, mate, spouse; **parēs cum paribus facillimē congregantur** *(prov)* birds of a feather flock together ‖ *n* pair, couple, the like; **pār parī** tit for tat
parābil·is -is -e *adj* available
parasīt·a -ae *f* parasite *(female)*
parasītas·ter -trī *m* poor parasite
parasītāti·ō -ōnis *f* sponging
parasītic·us -a -um *adj* parasitical
parasīt·or -ārī -ātus sum *intr* to be a parasite, sponge, freeload
parasīt·us -ī *m* parasite, sponger, freeloader
parātē *adv* with preparation; carefully; readily, promptly
parāti·ō -ōnis *f* preparing; procuring, acquisition
paratragoed·ō -āre *intr* to talk in the tragic style, be melodramatic, ham it up
parāt·us -a -um *adj* prepared, ready; ready at hand, available; furnished, equipped; learned, well-versed, skilled; *(w. dat or* **ad**) **1** ready for; **2** equipped for; *(w. inf)* prepared to, ready to; *(w. abl or* **in** + *abl)* versed in, experienced in
parāt·us -ūs *m* preparation; equipment, outfit; clothing, apparel; *(food at dinner table)* spread
Parc·a -ae *f* goddess of Fate, Fate
parcē *adv* sparingly, thriftily; moderately, with restraint; stingily; rarely
parcēprōm·us -ī *m* stingy person
parcō parcere pepercī parsūrus *tr* to spare, use sparingly ‖ *intr* to be sparing, economize; *(w. dat)* **1** to spare, use carefully; **2** to show mercy to, take it easy on; **3** to show consideration for; **4** to abstain from, refrain from; *(w. inf)* to cease to
parc·us -a -um *adj* thrifty, economical, frugal; stingy; moderate, conservative; slight, little, scanty, paltry *(thing given)*
pard·us -ī *m* leopard
pār·ēns -entis *adj* obedient, submissive ‖ *mpl* subjects
par·ēns -entis *m* parent, father; ancestor, grandparent; founder; inventor; **parēns patriae** father of one's country ‖ *mpl* ancestors ‖ *f* parent, mother; mother country; mother city
parentāl·is -is -e *adj* parental; **diēs parentālis** memorial day ‖ *npl* festival in honor of dead ancestors and relatives
parent·ō -āre -āvī -ātum *intr* to hold a memorial service in honor of dead parents *or* relatives; *(w. dat)* **1** to offer sacrifice to *(the dead)*; **2** to avenge *(dead person with the death of another person)*; **3** to appease, satisfy
pār·eō -ēre -uī -itum *intr* to appear, be visible, be evident, be at hand; *(w. dat)* **1** to obey, be obedient to; **2** to comply with; **3** to be subject to, be subservient to; **4** to yield to, gratify, satisfy *(pleasures, etc.)*; **5** to fulfill *(promises)*
pari·ēs -etis *m* wall *(inner or outer wall of house or other building)*; **intrā parietēs** in private, at home, under one's own roof
parietin·ae -ārum *fpl* tumble-down walls; *(lit & fig)* ruins
Parīl·ia -ium *npl* (**Palīl-**) festival of Pales *(April 21)*
paril·is -is -e *adj* equal, like; **aetās parilis** same age, like age
Parīl·is -is -e *adj* (**Palīl-**) connected with Pales *or* her festival
pariō parere peperī partus *tr* to bear, bring forth, give birth to; *(of animals)* to produce, spawn, lay *(eggs)*; *(of countries, of the earth)* to produce, be a source of; *(of things)* to give rise to; *(fig)* to create, devise, cause, accomplish; to acquire
Par·is -idis *m* son of Priam and Hecuba ‖ pantomime actor in the reign of Nero ‖ pantomime actor in the reign of Domitian
pariter *adv* equally, in like manner, as well, alike; at the same time, at one and the same time, together; side by side; evenly, uniformly; in equal quantity *or* degree; at once; **pariter ac** *(or* **atque** *or* **ut**) as well as; **pariter ac sī** just as if; **pariter cum** together with, at the same time as
parit·ō -āre *tr (w. inf)* to get ready to

Par·ium *or* **Par·ion -iī** *n* town of the Troad near the entrance to the Propontis *(modern Kemer)*

Pari·us -a -um *adj* Parian, of Paros

parm·a -ae *f* small round shield

parmāt·us -a -um *adj* armed with a small, round shield, light-armed

parmul·a -ae *f* small round shield

Parnās·is -idis *or* **Parnāsi·us -a -um** *adj* of Parnassus, Parnassian

Parnās·us *or* **Parnās·os -ī** *m* mountain forming the backdrop to Apollo's shrine at Delphi

par·ō -āre -āvī -ātus *tr* to prepare, make ready, provide, furnish; to get, procure; to purchase; to acquire, gather **II** *refl* to get ready **II** *intr* to get ready, make preparations, make arrangements; *(w. dat or* **ad)** to get ready for

paroch·a -ae *f* room and board *(which provincials had to provide for traveling Roman officials)*

paroch·us -ī *m* official host *(provided accommodations for traveling Roman dignitaries)*

parops·is -idis *f* dish; dessert dish

Par·os *or* **Par·us -ī** *f* Greek island of the Cyclades, famous for its white marble

parr·a -ae *f* owl

Parrhas·is -idis *or* **-idos** *f* Arcadian woman; Callisto *(as Ursa Major)*

Parrhasi·us -a -um *adj* Arcadian; **Parrhasia virgō** Callisto *(as Ursa Major)* **II** *f* district in Arcadia

parricīd·a -ae *mf* parricide *(murderer of one's parent or close relative);* assassin of a high magistrate; murderer; traitor, outlaw

parricīd·ium -(i)ī *n* parricide *(murder of a parent or close relative);* murder; assassination; high treason

par·s -tis *f* part, portion, share, section; fraction; side, direction, region; part, function, duty; part of body, member *(esp. genital organs);* **ab omnī parte** in every respect; **ā parte** partly; **exiguā parte** in a slight degree; **ex alterā parte** on the other hand; **ex parte** partly; **ex eā parte** *(or* **in eam partem) quātenus** to the extent that; **in eam partem** in that direction; in that sense; **in parte** *(or* **in partem)** partly, in part; in such a manner; **in parte alicūius reī esse** to form part of s.th., be included in s.th.; **in pēiōrem partem rapere** to put a worse construction on; **in utramque partem** in both directions; **magnā ex parte** to a great degree; **māior pars populī** the majority; **maximam partem** for the most part; **minor pars populī** a minority; **pars dīmidia (tertia, quārta,** *etc.)* one half (one-third, one-fourth, *etc.);* **pars . . . pars, pars** ... **aliī** some ... others; **pars ōrātiōnis** *(gram)* part of speech; **parte** in part, partly; **prō meā parte** to the best of my ability; **prō parte** in part, partially; **prō parte sēmisse** half and half; **prō ratā parte** in a fixed proportion; **prō suā parte** *(or* **prō virīlī parte)** to the best of one's ability **II** *fpl* part, role; task, function; character; political party; pieces, fragments; scraps *(esp. of food);* **omnibus partibus** in all respects; **partēs obscēnae** privates, private parts; **per partēs** *(or* **partibus)** (so much) at a time, in stages; **trēs partēs** three-fourths; **tuae partēs sunt** the task *(or* decision) devolves on you

parsimōni·a -ae *f* parsimony, thrift

Parthā·ōn -onis *m* king of Calydon, the son of Agenor and Epicaste and father of Oeneus

Parthāoni·us -a -um *adj* of Parthaon; Calydonian

parthenic·ē -ēs *f (bot)* chamomile *(plant with white flowers, used medicinally and as tea)*

Parthenopae·us -ī *m* one of the Seven against Thebes, the son of Meleager and Atalanta

Parthenop·ē -ēs *f* ancient name of Naples *(named after the Siren Parthenope who was supposedly buried there)*

Parthi·a -ae *f* Parthia *(country located S.E. of the Caspian Sea)*

Parthic·us -a -um *adj* Parthian; honorary title of several Roman Emperors

Parth·us -a -um *adj & m* Parthian

partic·eps -ipis *adj (w. gen)* sharing in, taking part in **II** *m* partner, confederate; *(w. gen)* partner in

particip·ō -āre -āvī -ātus *tr* to make *(s.o.)* a partner; to share *(s.th.)*

particul·a -ae *f* bit, particle, grain

partim *adv* partly, in part, to some extent; for the most part; *(w. gen or* **ex)** some of; **partim** ... **partim** some ... others, partly ... partly

part·iō -īre -īvī -ītus *or* **part·ior -īrī -ītus sum** *tr* to share; to distribute, apportion, divide

parti·ō -ōnis *f* bringing forth, producing

partītē *adv* with proper divisions

partīti·ō -ōnis *f* division, distribution, sharing; classification; *(rhet)* division of a speech

partitūd·ō -inis *f* bearing *(of young)*

partur·iō -īre -īvī *tr* to teem with; to be ready to produce; to bring forth, yield; *(fig)* to brood over **II** *intr* to be in labor

part·us -a -um *pp of* **pariō II** *adj* acquired **II** *n* acquisition; gain; store

part·us -ūs *m* giving birth; birth; young, offspring; embryo; *(fig)* beginnings

parum *adv & indecl n* a little, too little, insufficiently; **parum est** it is not enough; **parum habēre** to regard as unsatisfactory; **satis ēloquentiae sapientiae parum** enough eloquence but too little wisdom

parumper *adv* for a little while, just for a moment

parvit·ās -ātis *f* smallness

parvul·us -a -um *adj* **(-vol-)** tiny; slight, petty; young **II** *n* childhood, infancy; **ā parvulīs** from childhood, from infancy; **ā parvulō** from childhood on

parv·us -a -um *(comp:* **minor;** *superl:* **minimus)** *adj* small, little, puny; short; young; brief, short *(time);* slight; insignificant, unimportant; low, cheap *(price)* **II** *n* a little, trifle; childhood, infancy; **ā parvīs** *(or* **ā parvō)** from childhood, from infancy; **parvī esse** to be of little importance; **parvī facere** *(or* **aestimāre** *or* **habēre** *or* **dūcere)** to think little of, care little for; **parvī pretiī** of little worth; **parvī rēfert** it makes little difference, it matters little; **parvō** at a low price; **parvō animō esse** to be small-minded

pāsceol·us -ī *m* moneybag

pāscō pāscere pāvī pāstus *tr* to feed; to be food for; to pasture, keep, raise *(animals); (of land)* to provide food for; to cultivate, cherish; to feed *(fire; flames of passion);* to pile up *(debts);* to grow *(beard);* to lay waste, ravage *(fields);* to use *(land)* as pasturage; to feast *(the eyes, the mind)* **II** *refl & pass* to support oneself; *(w. abl)* to get rich on, grow fat on **II** *pass (of animals)* to graze; to feed; *(w. abl)* **1** to feast on, thrive on; **2** to gloat over **II** *intr* to feed, graze

pāscu·us -a -um *adj* grazing, pasture **II** *n* pasture

Pāsipha·ē -ēs *or* **Pāsipha·a -ae** *f* Pasiphaë *(daughter of Helios, sister of Circe, wife of Minos, and mother of Phaedra, Ariadne, and the Minotaur)*

pass·er -eris *m* sparrow; flounder; **passer marīnus** ostrich *(because imported from overseas)*

passercul·us -ī *m* little sparrow

passim *adv* here and there; all over the place; at random, without order, indiscriminately

passit·ō -āre *intr (of a starling)* to sing

passīv·us -a -um *adj (gram)* passive

pāssus *pp of* **pandō II** *adj* spread out, extended, open; disheveled; *(of grapes and other fruits spread out in the sun)* dried, dry **II** *f* raisin **II** *n* raisin wine

passus *pp of* **patior**

pāss·us -ūs *m* step, pace; footstep, track; **mīlle pāssūs** thousand paces, a mile; **tria mīlia pāssuum** three miles

pastill·us -ī *m* lozenge

pāsti·ō -ōnis *f* pasture, grazing

pāst·or -ōris *m* shepherd

pāstōrāl·is -is -e *adj* pastoral

pāstōrici·us -a -um *or* **pāstōri·us -a -um** *adj* shepherd's, pastoral

pāstus *pp of* **pāscō**

pāst·us -ūs *m* the feeding of animals; pasture; fodder, feed

patagiār·ius -(i)ī *m* fringe maker

patagiāt·us -a -um *adj (tunic)* with fringes

Patar·a -ae *f or* **Patar·a -ōrum** *npl* town in Lycia with an oracle of Apollo

Patar·ēus -eī *or* **-eos** *m* Apollo

Patavīn·us -a -um *adj* of Patavium

Patav·ium -(i)ī *n* city in N. Italy, birthplace of Livy *(modern Padua)*

pate·faciō -facere -fēcī -factus *(pass:* **pate·fīō -fierī)** *tr* to uncover, reveal; to open *(gates, windows, buildings, containers, etc.);* to throw open; to open up, make accessible; to bring to light; to disclose; *(mil)* to deploy; *(mil) (w. dat)* to expose to *(attack)*

patefacti·ō -ōnis *f* disclosure

patell·a -ae *f* pan, dish, plate

pat·ēns -entis *adj* open, accessible; extensive; exposed; evident

patentius *adv* more openly; more clearly

pat·eō -ēre -uī *intr* to stand open, be open; to be accessible; to be exposed; to open, stretch out, extend; to be clear, be plain, be well-known; to be attainable, be free; *(of the mind)* to be open, be receptive; *(of wounds)* to gape; **lātē patēre** to have wide application, cover a wide field

pa·ter -tris *m* father; **pater cēnae** host; **pater familiās** head of the family; **quārtus pater** great-great-grandfather **II** *mpl* forefathers; patricians; senators; **patrēs cōnscrīptī** gentlemen of the Senate

pater·a -ae *f* flat dish, saucer *(used esp. in making libations)*

paterfamiliās, *gen:* **patrisfamiliās** *m* head of the family

patern·us -a -um *adj* father's, paternal, fatherly; ancestral; of a native country, native

pat·ēscō -ēscere -uī *intr* to be opened, be open; to stretch out, extend; to be disclosed, be divulged, become evident; *(mil)* to be deployed

pathic·us -a -um *adj* lustful

patibil·is -is -e *adj* tolerable; sensitive

patibulāt·us -a -um *adj* fastened to a yoke *or* gibbet, pilloried

patibul·um -ī *n* pillory *(fork-shaped yoke to which criminals were fastened);* fork-shaped gibbet

pati·ēns -entis *adj* hardy, tough; hard; stubborn, unyielding; patient, tolerant; *(w. gen or* **ad)** able to endure, inured to, able to take; **amnis patiēns nāvium** navigable river

patienter *adv* patiently

patienti·a -ae *f* patience, endurance; resignation; submissiveness; sexual submission
patin·a -ae *f* dish, pan
patinări·us -a -um *adj* of pans; in a pan; **struēs patināria** pile of dishes
patior patī passus sum *tr* to experience, undergo, suffer; to put up with, allow; to submit to *(sexually);* **aegrē patī** to resent, be displeased with
patrāt·or -ōris *m* perpetrator
patrāt·us -ī *adj (masc only)* **pater patrātus** plenipotentiary senator *(sent on a foreign mission)*
patri·a -ae *f* native land, native city, home
patricē *adv* like a patrician
patriciāt·us -ūs *m* status of patrician
patrici·us -a -um *adj & m* patrician
patrimōn·ium -(i)ī *n* patrimony, inheritance
patrim·us -a -um *adj* having a father still living
patriss·ō -āre *intr* to take after one's father
patrīt·us -a -um *adj* father's, inherited from one's father
patri·us -a -um *adj* father's, of a father, fatherly; ancestral; traditional, hereditary; native ‖ *f see* **patria**
patrō -āre *tr* to bring about, effect, achieve, perform; to finish, conclude; **bellum patrāre** to bring a war to an end; **iūs iūrandum patrāre** to take an oath *(confirming a treaty);* **pācem patrāre** to conclude a peace; **prōmissa patrāre** to fulfill promises ‖ *intr* to reach a sexual climax
patrōcin·ium -(i)ī *n* patronage, protection; legal defense, legal representation
Patrocl·us -ī *m* son of Menoetius and friend of Achilles, killed by Hector
patrōn·a -ae *f* legal protectress, patroness; defender; safeguard
patrōncin·or -ārī -ātus sum *intr* to be a patron, afford protection; *(w. dat)* to serve *(s.o.)* as patron, protect, defend
patrōn·us -ī *m* legal protector, patron; advocate *(in court);* defender
patruēl·is -is -e *adj* on the father's side, cousin's; **frāter patruēlis** cousin; **soror patruēlis** cousin *(female)* ‖ *m* cousin
patru·us -a -um *adj* of a *(paternal)* uncle ‖ *m* father's brother, paternal uncle; **patruus magnus** great-uncle, granduncle
patul·us -a -um *adj* open, standing open; spreading, spread out, broad
pauc·ī -ae -a *adj* few ‖ *pron masc pl* few, a few; the select, elite; **inter paucōs** *(or* **in paucās** *or* **in pauca** *or* **in paucīs)** *(in connection with an adj)* among a few, especially, unusually, uncommonly ‖ *pron neut pl* a few things, a few words; **paucīs** in a few words, briefly
pauciloqu·ium -(i)ī *n* reticence
paucit·ās -ātis *f* paucity, scarcity, small number
paucul·ī -ae -a *adj* just a few, very few ‖ *npl* few words
paul(l)ātim *adv* little by little, gradually, by degrees; a few at a time
paul(l)isper *adv* for a little while
paul(l)ō *adv (as abl of degree of difference in comparisons)* a little, somewhat; **paulō ante** a little earlier; **paulō post** a little later
paul(l)ulō *adv* somewhat, a little; cheaply, at a low price
paul(l)ulum *adv* somewhat, a little
paul(l)ul·us -a -um *adj* very little ‖ *n* very little, a bit; **paullulum pecūniae** a bit of money, very little money
paul(l)um *adv* a little, to some extent
paul(l)·us -a -um *adj* small, little ‖ *n* a bit, trifle; **post paulum** after a bit
Paul·us -ī *m* Lucius Aemilius Paulus Macedonicus *(conqueror of Macedonia at Pydna in 168 B.C.)*
paup·er -eris *adj* poor *(financially);* scanty, meager; *(w. gen)* poor in ‖ *mf* pauper
paupercul·us -a -um *adj* poor little
pauperi·ēs -ēī *f* poverty
pauper·ō -āre -āvī -ātus *tr* to impoverish; *(w. abl)* to rob *(s.o.)* of
paupert·ās -ātis *f* poverty
paus·a -ae *f* pause, intermission, stop, end; **pausam dare** *(or* **facere)** to make a pause, take a break; **pausam facere** *(w. dat)* put an end to
pauxillātim *adv* little by little
pauxillisper *adv* bit by bit
pauxillulum *adv* a little, a bit ‖ *n (w. gen)* a bit of
pauxillul·us -a -um *adj* tiny
pauxill·us -a -um *adj* very little, tiny ‖ *n* small amount
pavefact·us -a -um *adj* frightened
paveō pavēre pāvī *tr* to be scared of, be terrified at ‖ *intr* to be terrified, tremble with fear
pavēsc·ō -ere *tr* to get scared of ‖ *intr* to begin to be alarmed
pāvī *perf of* **pāscō** *and of* **paveō**
pavidē *adv* in panic
pavid·us -a -um panicky, alarmed, trembling with fear, startled; with beating heart, nervous; causing alarm
pavīment·ō -āre *tr* to pave
pavīment·um -ī *n* pavement; floor
pav·iō -īre -īvī *or* **-iī -ītus** *tr* to strike, beat
pavit·ō -āre *tr* to be panicky over ‖ *intr* to quake with fear, be scared to death; to shiver *(w. fever)*
pāv·ō -ōnis *or* **pāv·us -ī** *m* peacock
pav·or -ōris *m* panic, terror, dread; dismay; quaking, shivering; **pavōrem inicere** *(w. dat)* to strike terror into

pāx *interj* quiet, enough!

pāx pācis *f* peace; peace treaty; reconciliation; compact, agreement; harmony, tranquility; favor, pardon *(from the gods);* **cum bonā pācē** with full consent; **pāce tuā** with your leave, with your permission

pecc·āns -antis *m* offender, sinner

peccāt·um -ī *n* fault, mistake, slip; moral offense, sin

pecc·ō -āre -āvī -ātum *intr* to make a mistake, blunder; to make a slip in speaking; to be wrong; to sin

pecorōs·us -a -um *adj* rich in cattle

pect·en -inis *m* comb; plectrum; rake; pubic bone; pubic region; scallop *(as seafood)*

pectō pectere pex(u)ī pexus *or* **pexitus** *tr* to comb; to card *(wool); (hum)* to thrash

pect·us -oris *n* breast, chest; heart, feeling; soul, conscience; mind, understanding; person, character; **dē summō pectore dīcere** to say off-hand; **tōtō pectore** heart and soul

pecū *(gen not in use; pl:* **pecua)** *n* flock, herd; **squamōsum pecū** *(hum)* school of fish ‖ *npl* farm animals; cattle; pastures

pecuāri·us -a -um *adj* **(pequ-)** of sheep, of cattle; **rēs pecuāria** livestock ‖ *m* cattleman, cattle breeder, rancher ‖ *f* livestock ‖ *npl* herds of cattle, herds of sheep

pecūlāt·or -ōris *m* embezzler

pecūlāt·us -ūs *m* **(peq-)** embezzlement

pecūliār·is -is -e one's own, as one's own private property; special; exceptional, singular

pecūliāriter *adv* especially

pecūliāt·us -a -um *adj* well off

pecūli·ō -āre -āvī -ātus *tr* to provide with personal property

pecūl·ium -(i)ī *n* personal property *or* savings *(of a slave or a son under his father's control)*

pecūni·a -ae *f* money; property, possessions

pecūniāri·us -a -um *adj* pecuniary, financial, money

pecūniōs·us -a -um *adj* rich, well-off; profitable

pec·us -oris *n* cattle, herd, flock; sheep; head of cattle; livestock; **pecus equīnum** stud; *(pej)* cattle

pec·us -udis *f* head of cattle; beast; sheep; domestic animal; land animal *(as opposed to birds and fish); (pej)* brute, beast, swine

pedāl·is -is -e *adj* one-foot-long

pedār·ius -(i)ī *m* senator of lower standing *(who lets others step all over him)*

pedāt·us -ūs *m* one of the three formal stages in issuing an ultimatum

ped·es -itis *m* infantryman, footsoldier; pedestrian; **equitēs peditēsque** all Roman citizens

pedes·ter *or* **pedes·tris -tris -tre** *adj* infantry; pedestrian; on land, by land; written in prose; prosaic, plain

pedetem(p)tim *adv* by feeling one's way, step by step, slowly, cautiously

pedic·a -ae *f* foot chain, fetter; trap, snare

pedīculōs·us -a -um *adj* lousy, full of lice

pēd·is -is *mf* louse

pedisequ·a -ae *f* attendant, handmaid

pedisequ·us -ī *m* attendant

peditastell·us -ī *m* poor infantryman

peditāt·us -ūs *m* infantry

pēdit·um -ī *n (vulg)* fart

Pedi·us -a -um *adj* name of a Roman clan *(nomen) (esp. Quintus Pedius, Caesar's nephew);* **lēx Pedia** law providing a trial for Caesar's murderers

Ped·ō -ōnis *m* Roman family name *(cognomen), esp.* Albinovanus Pedo, a poet and friend of Ovid

pēdō pēdere pepēdī pēditum *intr (vulg)* to fart

ped·um -ī *n* shepherd's crook

Pēgase·us *or* **Pēgasēï·us -a -um** *adj* of Pegasus, Pegasean

Pēgas·is -idis *or* **-idos** *adj (fem only)* of Pegasus *(with reference to Hippocrene)* ‖ *f* fountain nymph ‖ *fpl* Muses

Pēgas·us *or* **Pēgas·os -ī** *m* winged horse that sprang from the blood of Medusa

pegm·a -atis *n* bookcase; scaffold

pēierātiuncul·a -ae *f* petty oath

pēierāt·us -a -um *adj* **(-iūr-)** offended by false oaths; **iūs pēierātum** false oath

pēier·ō -āre -āvī -ātus *tr* **(-iūr-)** to swear falsely by ‖ *intr* to swear a false oath; *(coll)* to lie

pēierōs·us -a -um *adj* **(-iūr-)** perjured

pēi·or -or -us *(comp of* **malus)** *adj* worse

pēius *(comp of* **male)** *adv* worse

pelagi·us -a -um *adj* of the sea

pelag·us -ī *n* sea, open sea

pēlam·is -idis *or* **pēlam·ys -ydis** *f* young tuna

Pelasg·ī -ōrum *mpl* aborigines of Greece; *(poet)* certain early inhabitants of Italy; *(poet)* Greeks *(opp:* Trojans); *(poet)* Argives *(opp:* Thebans)

Pēl·eus -eī *or* **-eos** *m* king of Thessaly, son of Aeacus, husband of Thetis, and father of Achilles

Pēli·a -adis *adj (fem only)* of Mt. Pelion

Pēli·as -adis *adj (fem only)* of Mt. Pelion, from Mt. Pelion

Peli·ās -ae *m* king of Iolcos in Thessaly and uncle of Jason

Pēlīd·ēs -ae *m* descendant of Peleus; Achilles; Neoptolemus

Pēl·ion -(i)ī *n* mountain in E. Thessaly

Pēli·us *or* **Pēliac·us -a -um** *adj* of Mt. Pelion

Pell·a -ae *or* **Pell·ē -ēs** *f* Pella *(city in Macedonia, birthplace of Alexander the Great)*

pellāci·a -ae *f* charm, allurement

Pellae·us -a -um *adj* of *or* from Pella; **Pellaeus iuvenis** Alexander

pell·āx -ācis *adj* seductive, alluring

pellecti·ō -ōnis *f* perusal

pel·liciō -licere -lexī *or* **licuī -lectus (per-)** *tr* to captivate, allure, entice, coax

pellicul·a -ae *f* small *or* thin hide, skin

pelli·ō -ōnis *m* furrier

pell·is -is *f* skin, hide; leather; felt; tent; shield cover; **dētrahere pellem** to expose one's true character *(literally, to take off one's hide)*; **ossa ac pellis** mere skin and bones

pellīt·us -a -um *adj* clothed in skins; wearing a leather coat

pellō pellere pepulī pulsus *tr* to push, beat, strike, knock; to beat *(drum, chest);* to knock at *(door);* thrust; to drive, impel; to rouse, stimulate; to drive away, eject, expel; to banish; to repel, drive back, rout; to strum *(lyre, etc.);* to affect, impress, strike; to stomp *(the earth)*

pellūc- = perlūc-

Pelopēï·as -ados *or* **Pelopē·us -a -um** *adj* Pelopian, of Pelops; Mycenaean; Phrygian

Pelopē·is -idos *f* descendant of Pelops *(female)*

Pelopid·ae -ārum *mpl* descendants of Pelops

Peloponnēns·is -is -e *adj* **(-nnēs-)** Peloponnesian

Peloponnēsiac·us *or* **Peloponnēsi·us -a -um** *adj* Peloponnesian

Peloponnēs·us *or* **Peloponnēs·os -ī** *f* Peloponnesus *(modern Morea)*

Pel·ops -opis *m* son of Tantalus, father of Atreüs and Thyestes, and grandfather of Agamemnon and Menelaüs

pelōr·is -idos *m* large mussel

Pelōr·us *or* **Pelōr·os -ī** *m* N.E. promontory of Sicily *(modern Cape Faro)*

pelt·a -ae *f* small leather shield

peltast·a (·ēs) -ae *m* soldier armed with a small leather shield

peltāt·us -a -um *adj* armed with a small leather shield

Pēlūs·ium -(i)ī *n* city on the E. mouth of the Nile

pelv·is -is *f* basin, shallow bowl

penāri·us -a -um *adj* for storing food; **cella penāria** pantry

Penāt·ēs -ium *mpl* Penates, household gods; Penates of the State; hearth; house; home *(also applied to a nest, a hive, a temple)*

penātig·er -era -erum *adj* carrying the household gods

pendeō pendēre pependī *intr* to hang (down), be suspended; to hang loose; to be flabby; to be weak; to be in suspense, be uncertain, hesitate; to hang around, loiter; to hang in the air, hover, float; to overhang; *(of plants)* to droop; *(w. abl or* **ab, dē,** *or* **ex** *+ abl)* **1** to hang down from, hang by; **2** to depend on, be dependent upon; **3** to be based on, hinge on; **4** to result from; **5** to hang onto; *(w.* **in** *+ abl)* to be poised on, hover in, hover over; **animī pendēre** to be in suspense, be perplexed; **pendēre ab ōre** *(w. gen)* to hang on *(s.o.'s)* words, listen with rapt attention to; **pendēre ex vultū** *(w. gen)* to gaze intently at *(s.o.'s)* face

pendō pendere pependī pēnsus *tr* to weigh, weigh out; to pay, pay out; to ponder, consider, value, esteem; **floccī pendere** to think little of; **magnī (parvī) pendere** to think much (little) of; **poenās pendere** to pay the penalty; **supplicia pendere** to suffer punishment

pendul·us -a -um *adj* hanging, hanging down; doubtful, uncertain

Pēnē·is -idos *or* **Pēnēi·us -a -um** *adj* of the Peneus River *(in Thessaly)*

Pēnelop·a -ae *or* **Pēnelop·ē -ēs** *f* Penelope *(daughter of Icarius and Periboea and wife of Odysseus)*

penes *prep (w. acc of person only)* in the possession of, in the power of, belonging to, resting with; at the house of, with; **penes sē esse** to be in one's senses, be in one's right mind

penetrābil·is -is -e *adj* penetrating, piercing; penetrable

penetr·āl·e -is *n see* **penetrālis**

penetrāl·is -is -e *adj* penetrating, piercing; inner, internal, interior **||** *n* inner part, innermost recess *(of a building);* inner shrine *(of a temple);* shrine of the Penates; house, home **||** *npl* the interior, center; inner chambers; sanctuary; *(geog)* the interior, hinterlands

penetr·ō -āre -āvī -ātus *tr* to penetrate, enter; to cross *(river);* **pedem penetrāre intrā** *(w. acc)* to set foot inside **||** *refl* to go; **forās sē penetrāre** to go outside **||** *intr* to penetrate, enter; *(w. ad)* to go as far as, go all the way to, reach, gain entrance to; *(w.* **in** *+ acc)* to enter, penetrate

Pēnē·us *or* **Pēnī·os -ī** *m* the Peneüs River *(largest river in Thessaly)* **||** river god, the father of Cyrene and Daphne

pēnicill·us -ī *m or* **pēnicill·um -ī** *n* paint brush; sponge

pēnicul·us -ī *m* brush; sponge; little penis

pēn·is -is *m* tail; penis; *(fig)* lechery

penitē *adv* deep down inside

penit·us -a -um *adj* inner, inward

penitus *adv* internally, inside, deep within, deeply; from within; thoroughly, through and through; heartily

penn·a -ae *f* feather; wing; flight

pennāt·us -a -um *adj* feathered
pennig·er -era -erum *adj* winged, feathered
pennipot·ēns -entis *adj* able to fly
pennul·a -ae *f* little wing
pēnsil·is -is -e *adj* hanging; supported on arches; suspended in mid-air
pēnsi·ō -ōnis *f* payment *(esp. by installments),* installment; rent money; compensation
pēnsit·ō -āre -āvī -ātus *tr* to pay; to weigh, ponder, consider ‖ *intr* to be taxable
pēns·ō -āre -āvī -ātus *tr* to weigh out; to weigh, ponder, consider, examine; to compare, contrast; to pay; to atone for; to repay, compensate, requite
pēns·um -ī *n* work quota; duty, task; consideration, scruple; **nihil pēnsī habēre** *(or* **dūcere)** to have no scruples; **pēnsī esse** *(w. dat)* to be of value to, be of importance to; **pēnsī habēre** *(or* **dūcere)** to value, consider of importance
pēnsus *pp of* **pendō**
pentēr·is -is *f* galley, quinquereme
Penthesilē·a -ae *f* Amazon warrior queen, killed by Achilles at Troy
Penth·eūs -eī *or* **-eos** *m* king of Thebes, son of Echion and Agave, grandson of Cadmus
pen·um -ī *n or* **pen·us -ūs** *f (m) or* **pen·us -oris** *n* food, provisions *(in the pantry)*
pēnūri·a -ae *f* want, need, dearth
pen·us -ūs *f (m) see* **penum**
pependī *perf of* **pendeō** *and of* **pendō**
pepercī *perf of* **parcō**
peperī *perf of* **pariō**
pepl·um -ī *n or* **pepl·us -ī** *m* robe for the statue of Athena
pepulī *perf of* **pellō**
-per *advl suf* denoting the duration or the number of times, *e.g.:* **paulisper** for a little while
per- *pref* conveying the idea of: **1** through: **perfringere** to break through; **2** intensive force: **perfacile** very easy; **3** throughly, to the end: **perficere** to complete; **perlegere** to read through to the end; **perdomāre** to tame thoroughly; **4** of going in the wrong direction: **pervertere** to turn the wrong way; **perfidia** treachery *(a trust, gone in the wrong direction)*
per *prep (w. acc) (of space)* through; all over *(an area, space),* throughout; along *(a linear direction); (of time)* through, during, for, in the course of, over a period of; *(of agency)* through, by, by means of, at the hands of; *(of means or manner)* through, by, under pretense of; *(w. refl pron)* for one's *or* its own sake, on its own account, by: **multiplicāre VI per IIII fit XXIIII** multiplying 6 by 4 gives 24; **per causam** on the grounds *(that);* **per manūs trādere** to pass from hand to hand; **per mē** as far as I am concerned; **per mē stat** it is due to me *(that),* it is my fault *(that);* **per omnia** in all respects, throughout; **per speciem** on the pretext *(of);* **per omnēs deōs iūrāre** to swear by all the gods; **per sē** in itself, by itself *(or* himself, herself, *etc.);* **per tempus** at the right time; **per Tiberim** along the Tiber
pēr·a -ae *f* pouch *(bag slung over the shoulder for carrying the day's provisions)*
perabsurd·us -a -um *adj* completely absurd
peraccommodāt·us -a -um *adj* very convenient
perā·cer -cris -cre *adj* very sharp
peracerb·us -a -um *adj* very harsh, very sour
peracēsc·ō -ere *intr* to turn completely sour
perācti·ō -ōnis *f* conclusion; last act *(of a play)*
perāctus *pp of* **peragō**
peracūtē *adv* very acutely
peracūt·us -a -um *adj* very sharp; very clear *(voice, intellect)*
peradulēsc·ēns -entis *adj* very young
peradulēscentul·us -ī *m* very young man
peraequē *adv* quite equally, uniformly; in all cases, invariably; **omnēs peraequē** all alike
peragit·ō -āre -āvī -ātus *tr* to harass
per·agō -agere -ēgī -āctus *tr* to carry through to the end, complete, accomplish; to pierce; to travel through; to harass, disturb, trouble; to describe, relate, go over; to work, till, cultivate *(the soil);* to fulfill *(hopes, promises);* to live out *(a period of time);* to come to the end of *(of period of time);* to treat *(a subject)* thoroughly; to use up *(resources);* to deliver *(a speech); (leg)* to prosecute to a conviction; **partēs peragere** to play the part
peragrāti·ō -ōnis *f* traveling
peragr·ō -āre -āvī -ātus *tr* to travel through, travel, traverse ‖ *intr (fig)* to spread, penetrate
peram·āns -antis *adj (w. gen)* very fond of
peramanter *adv* very lovingly
perambul·ō -āre -āvī -ātus *tr* to walk through; to walk about in; to travel about in, tour
peramīcē *adv* in a very friendly way
peram·ō -āre -āvī -ātus *tr* to show a great liking for
peramoen·us -a -um *adj* very pleasant, very charming
perampl·us -a -um *adj* very large; very spacious
perangustē *adv* very narrowly
perangust·us -a -um *adj* very narrow
perantīqu·us -a -um *adj* very ancient, very old
perapposit·us -a -um *adj* very suitable, very appropriate

perardu·us -a -um *adj* very difficult
perargūt·us -a -um *adj* very clear; very sharp, very witty
perarmāt·us -a -um *adj* heavily armed
perar·ō -āre -āvī -ātus *tr* to plow through; to furrow; to write on *(a wax tablet);* to inscribe
pērātim *adv* bag by bag, bag after bag
perattentē *adv* very attentively
peraudiend·us -a -um *adj* that must be heard to the end
perbacch·or -ārī -ātus sum *tr* to carouse through *(e.g., the night)*
perbeāt·us -a -um *adj* very happy
perbellē *adv* very prettily
perbene *adv* very well
perbenevol·us -a -um *adj* very friendly, very well-disposed
perbenīgnē *adv* very kindly
perbib·ō -ere -ī *tr* to drink up, drink in, imbibe; *(of plants)* to be well watered
perbīt·ō -ere *intr* to perish, die
perbland·us -a -um *adj* very attractive, very charming
perbon·us -a -um *adj* very good, excellent
perbrev·is -is -e *adj* very short, very brief; **perbrevī** *(or* **perbrevī tempore)** in a very short time
perbreviter *adv* very briefly
perc·a -ae *f* perch *(fish)*
percalefact·us -a -um *adj* warmed through and through
percal·ēscō -ēscere -uī *intr* to become quite hot
percall·ēscō -ēscere -uī *tr* to become thoroughly versed in **II** *intr* to become very hardened
percār·us -a -um *adj* very dear; very costly
percaut·us -a -um *adj* very cautious
percelebr·ō -āre -āvī -ātus *tr* to make widely known **II** *pass* to be quite famous
percel·er -eris -ere *adj* very rapid
perceleriter *adv* very rapidly
per·cellō -cellere -culī -culsus *tr* to knock down, beat down, overthrow; to scare to death; to ruin; to send scurrying; *(lit & mil)* to hit hard
percēns·eō -ēre -uī *tr* to count up; to review, survey; to travel all through *(a country)*
percepti·ō -ōnis *f* comprehension; reaping, harvesting **II** *fpl* concepts
percept·us -a -um *pp of* **percipiō II** *n* rule, principle
percī·dō -dere -dī -sus *tr* to smash to pieces
perci·eō -ēre *or* **perc·iō -īre -īvī** *or* **-iī -ītus** *tr* to stir up, set in motion; to excite
per·cipiō -cipere -cēpī -ceptus *tr* to get a good hold of; to catch; to occupy, seize; to gather in, harvest, reap; *(of the senses)* to take in, perceive, feel; *(of feelings)* to get hold of, get the better of, come over *(s.o.)*; to learn, know, comprehend, perceive
percit·us -a -um *pp of* **percieō** *and of* **perciō II** *adj* aroused, provoked; impetuous, excitable
percoctus *pp of* **percoquō**
percol·ō -āre -āvī -ātus *tr* to strain, filter
percolō -colere -coluī -cultus *tr* to reverence, revere, worship; to beautify; to crown, complete
percōm·is -is -e *adj* very courteous
percommodē *adv* very conveniently; very well; very suitably
percommod·us -a -um *adj* very convenient, very comfortable; very suitable
percontāti·ō -ōnis *f* thorough investigation
percontāt·or -ōris *m* inquisitive fellow; interrogator
percont·or -ārī -ātus sum *tr* to question, investigate, interrogate; *(w. double acc)* to ask *(s.o. s.th.)*
percontum·āx -ācis *adj* very defiant
per·coquō -quere -xī -ctus *tr* to cook thoroughly; to heat thoroughly; to ripen; to scorch, blacken
percrēb(r)·ēscō -ēscere -uī *tr* to become widespread; to get to be widely believed
percrep·ō -āre -uī *intr* to resound, ring
percruci·or -ārī -ātus sum *intr* to be tormented
perculsus *pp of* **percellō**
percult·us -a -um *pp of* **percolō II** *adj* decked out; *(coll)* all dolled up
percupid·us -a -um *adj (w. gen)* very fond of
percup·iō -ere -iī -ītūs *tr* to desire greatly; *(w. inf)* to be very eager to, be dying to
percūriōs·us -a -um *adj* very curious
percūr·ō -āre -āvī -ātus *tr* to treat successfully, heal
percurrō percurrere per(cu)currī percursus *tr* to run through, run along, run over, pass over, speed over; *(fig)* to scan briefly, look over; *(in a speech)* to treat in succession, go over, run over; *(of feelings)* to run through, penetrate, pierce **II** *intr* to run fast, hurry along; *(w.* **ad)** to dash to; *(w.* **per** *+ acc)* **1** to run through *or* across, travel through; **2** *(fig)* to run through, mention quickly, treat in succession
percursāti·ō -ōnis *f* traveling; a tour
percursi·ō -ōnis *f* quick survey
percurs·ō -āre -āvī -ātum *tr & intr* to roam about
percussi·ō -ōnis *f* hitting, striking; snapping *(of fingers); (mus)* beat, time
percuss·or -ōris *m* assassin
percussus *pp of* **percutiō**
percuss·us -ūs *m* impact; striking
percu·tiō -tere -ssī -ssus *tr* to beat *or* hit hard; to strike *(w. lightning, sword, etc.);*

(of snakes) to bite; to knock at *(door);* to strum *(lyre, etc.);* to smash; to pierce, stab, run through; to shoot; to kill; to shock, make a deep impression on; to astound; to dig *(ditch);* to coin *(money);* to trick, cheat; **fustī percutere** to beat to death; **secūrī percutere** to behead

perdecōr·us -a -um *adj* very pretty

perdēlīr·us -a -um *adj* very silly, quite irrational; quite crazy

perdeps·ō -ere -uī *tr* to knead thoroughly; *(sl)* to feel up *(sexually)*

Perdicc·ās -ae *m* founder of the Macedonian monarchy **II** Perdiccas II, King of Macedonia from 454 to 413 B.C. **II** Perdiccas III *(d. 359 B.C.)* **II** distinguished general of Alexander the Great *(d. 321 B.C.)*

perdifficil·is -is -e *adj* very difficult

perdifficiliter *adv* with great difficulty

perdign·us -a -um *adj (w. abl)* quite worthy of

perdīlig·ēns -entis *adj* very diligent, very conscientious

perdīligenter *adv* very diligently, very conscientiously

per·discō -discere -didicī *tr* to learn thoroughly, learn by heart

perdisertē *adv* very eloquently

perditē *adv* recklessly, desperately

perdit·or -ōris *m* destroyer

perdit·us -a -um *adj* ruined, done-for; degenerate; infamous; reckless, incorrigible, hopeless; lost

perdit·us -ūs *m* ruination

perdiū *adv* for a very long time

perdiūturn·us -a -um *adj* protracted, long-lasting

perdīv·es -itis *adj* very rich

perd·īx -īcis *mf* partridge **II Perdīx** Perdix *(nephew of Daedalus; Perdix was changed into a partridge)*

per·dō -dere -didī -ditus *tr* to wreck, ruin, destroy; to waste, squander; to lose; **perdere operam** to waste one's efforts

perdoc·eō -ēre -uī -tus *tr* to teach thoroughly

perdoctē *adv* very skillfully

perdoct·us -a -um *pp of* **perdoceō II** *adj* very learned, very skillful

perdol·eō -ēre -uī -itum *intr* to be annoyed; to be a cause of annoyance

perdolēsc·ō -ere *intr* to become hurt, become annoyed

perdom·ō -āre -uī -itus *tr* to tame completely, subdue, subjugate

perdormīsc·ō -ere *intr* to sleep on, keep on sleeping

per·dūcō -dūcere -dūxī -ductus *tr* to lead, guide *(to a destination);* to bring *(to court); (of roads)* to lead *(to); (of a pimp)* to take *(s.o.)* to *(s.o. else's bed);* to cover, spread; to prolong, drag out; to induce; to seduce; *(w.* **ad)** **1** to lead, guide, escort to; **2** to build, run *(wall, ditch, road, etc.)* to; **3** to prolong, drag out, continue *(s.th.)* to *or* until; **4** to win over to, convince of

perduct·ō -āre -āvī -ātus *tr* to lead, guide

perduct·or -ōris *m* guide; pimp

perdūdum *adv* long long ago

perduelli·ō -ōnis *f* treason

perduell·is -is *m* enemy

perdūr·ō -āre -āvī -ātum *intr* to last, hold out

per·edō -edere *or* **-ēsse -ēdī -ēsus** *tr* to eat up, devour; *(of things)* to eat away

perēgī *perf of* **peragō**

peregrē *adv* abroad, away from home; from abroad; **peregrē abīre** *(or* **peregrē exīre)** to go abroad

peregrīn·a -ae *f* foreign woman

peregrīnābund·us -a -um *adj* traveling around, touring

peregrīnāti·ō -ōnis *f* living abroad; foreign travel, touring; *(of animals)* roaming, ranging

peregrīnāt·or -ōris *m* traveler *(abroad),* tourist

peregrīnit·ās -ātis *f* foreign manners, outlandish ways; alien status

peregrīn·or -ārī -ātus sum *intr* to live abroad; to travel abroad; *(fig)* to be a stranger

peregrīn·us -a -um *adj* foreign; strange; alien, exotic; outlandish; *(fig)* strange; *(fig)* inexperienced; **amōrēs peregrīnī** love affairs with foreign women; **praetor peregrīnus** praetor who tried cases involving disputes between foreigners and Roman citizens; **terror peregrīnus** fear of a foreign enemy **II** *mf* foreigner, alien

perēleg·āns -antis *adj* very elegant

perēleganter *adv* very elegantly

perēloqu·ēns -entis *adv* very eloquent

peremn·is -is -e *adj* **auspicia peremnia** auspices taken before crossing a river

peremptus *pp of* **perimō**

perendiē *adv* the day after tomorrow

perendin·us -a -um *adj* **diēs perendinus** the day after tomorrow

perenn·is -is -e *adj* perennial, continual, everlasting

perenniserv·os -ī *m* slave for life

perennit·ās -ātis *f* continuance, perpetuity

perenn·ō -āre *intr* to last

pērenticīd·a -ae *m (hum)* purse snatcher

per·eō -īre -iī -itum *intr* to pass away, pass on, die; to go to waste, perish, be destroyed; to be lost, be ruined, be undone; to be desperately in love, pine away; *(of snow)* to melt away; *(of iron)* to rust away; **periī**! *(coll)* I'm finished!, I'm washed up!

perequit·ō -āre -āvī -ātus *tr* to ride through *(on horseback)* ‖ *intr* to ride around *(on horseback)*
pererr·ō -āre -āvī -ātus *tr* to roam around, wander through; to survey, look *(s.o.)* over ‖ *intr* to roam all around
perērudīt·us -a -um *adj* very learned, erudite
perēsus *pp of* **peredō**
perexcels·us -a -um *adj* very high up
perexiguē *adv* very sparingly
perexigu·us -a -um *adj* tiny; insignificant; very short *(day)*
perexpedīt·us -a -um *adj* readily available
perfacētē *adv* very wittily
perfacēt·us -a -um *adj* very witty
perfacile *adv* very easily
perfacil·is -is -e *adj* very easy
perfamiliār·is -is -e *adj* very close, intimate ‖ *mf* very close friend
perfectē *adv* completely; perfectly
perfecti·ō -ōnis *f* completion; perfection
perfect·or -ōris *m* finisher, perfecter; **dīcendī perfector** stylist
perfect·us -a -um *pp of* **perficiō** ‖ *adj* complete, finished; perfect; *(gram)* perfect; **praeteritum perfectum** perfect tense
per·ferō -ferre -tulī -lātus *tr* to carry through; to endure to the end, bear with patience, put up with; to drive home *(a weapon);* to deliver *(message),* bring news of; to cause *(news)* to reach; to keep up *(an attitude, activity)* to the end; *(of things)* to be capable of accommodating; *(pol)* to get *(a law)* passed
per·ficiō -ficere -fēcī -fectus *tr* to complete, finish, bring to an end; to accomplish, carry out, execute; to perfect; to cause; *(w.* **ut, nē)** to bring it about (that, that not)
perfic·us -a -um *adj* that completes *or* perfects
perfidē *adv* dishonestly
perfidēl·is -is -e *adj* completely trustworthy
perfidi·a -ae *f* treachery, perfidy
perfidiōsē *adv* treacherously
perfidiōs·us -a -um *adj* treacherous, false
perfid·us -a -um *adj* treacherous, false; untrustworthy, dishonest, sneaky ‖ *m* a sneak
perfī·gō -gere -xī -xus *tr* to pierce
perflābil·is -is -e *adj* airy; invisible
perflāgitiōs·us -a -um *adj* utterly disgraceful, utterly scandalous
perflāt·us -ūs *m* draft
perfl·ō -āre -āvī -ātus *tr* to blow across, blow through; to blow throughout *(a period)* ‖ *intr* to blow hard, blow continuously
perfluctu·ō -āre -āvī -ātus *tr* to surge through
perflu·ō -ere -xī *intr* to flow along; to leak all over; *(w.* **per)** to flow through
per·fodiō -fodere -fōdī -fossus *tr* to dig through; to pierce, stab
perfor·ō -āre -āvī -ātus *tr* to bore through, pierce; to make by boring
perfortiter *adv* very bravely
perfoss·or -ōris *m* borer; **parietum perfossor** burglar *(literally, one who bores through walls)*
perfossus *pp of* **perfodiō**
perfrāctus *pp of* **perfringō**
perfrem·ō -ere *intr* to snort loud
perfrequ·ēns -entis *adj* very crowded, overcrowded
perfric·ō -āre -uī -tus *and* **-ātus** *tr* to rub hard, rub all over; **ōs perfricāre** to rub away blushes, put on a bold front
perfrīgefac·iō -ere *tr (fig)* to send a chill over, make shudder
per·frīgēscō perfrīgēscere perfrīxī *intr* to become chilled; to catch a bad cold
perfrīgid·us -a -um *adj* ice-cold
per·fringō -fringere -frēgī -frāctus *tr* to break through; to break into; to break to pieces, smash; to break down *(a door); (fig)* to break up *(conspiracy); (fig)* to break *(the law); (med)* to fracture
per·fruor -fruī -frūctus sum *intr (w. abl)* **1** to enjoy fully; **2** to perform gladly
perfug·a -ae *m* military deserter; political turncoat; refugee
per·fugiō -fugere -fūgī *intr (w.* **ad** *or* **in** + *acc)* **1** to flee to for refuge; **2** to desert to; **3** to have recourse to
perfug·ium -(i)ī *n* place of refuge, shelter, sanctuary; way of escape; *(fig)* an escape; excuse, defense; means of protection *or* safety
perfūncti·ō -ōnis *f* performance, performing, discharge
perfūnctus *pp of* **perfungor**
per·fundō -fundere -fūdī -fūsus *tr* to drench, bathe; to flood; to sprinkle; to dye; *(of river)* to flow through; *(of sun)* to drench *(w. light, color); (fig)* to fill, steep, inspire ‖ *refl & pass* to bathe, take a bath
per·fun·gor -fungī -fūnctus sum *tr* to enjoy ‖ *intr (w. abl)* **1** to perform, discharge, fulfill; **2** to endure, undergo; **3** to get rid of; **4** to be finished with, be done with; **5** to enjoy
perfur·ō -ere *intr* to rage wildly, rage on and on
perfūsus *pp of* **perfundō**
Pergam·a -ōrum *npl or* **Pergam·um -ī** *n* Pergamum *(citadel of Troy),* Troy
Pergame·us -a -um *adj* Trojan ‖ *f* **Pergamea** *(name given by Aeneas to his city on Crete)* ‖ *mpl* Trojans
Pergam·os -ī *f or* **Pergam·um -ī** *n or* **Pergam·on -ī** *n* Pergamum *(city of Mysia*

famous for its library and temple of Aesculapius)
pergaud·eō -ēre *intr* to be very glad
pergn·ōscō -ōscere -ōvī *tr* to be well-acquainted with
per·gō -gere -rēxī -rēctus *tr* to go on interruptedly with, continue; *(w. inf)* to continue to; **iter pergere** to go on one's way **||** *intr* to go straight on, continue, proceed; *(w.* **ad)** **1** to make one's way toward; **2** to pass on to, proceed to *(esp. a topic);* **perge modo**! go on now!, now get going!
pergraec·or -ārī *intr (coll)* to go completely Greek, have a ball
pergrand·is -is -e *adj* very large, huge; **pergrandis nātū** very old
pergraphic·us -a -um *adj* perfectly drawn
pergrāt·us -a -um *adj* very pleasant **||** *n* distinct pleasure; **pergrātum mihi fēceris sī** you would be doing me a very great favor if
pergrav·is -is -e *adj* very heavy; very important; very impressive
pergraviter *adv* very seriously
pergul·a -ae *f* open porch *(used for business, as a school, as a brothel)*
perhib·eō -ēre -uī -itus *tr* to present; to assert, regard, maintain; to call, name; to adduce, cite; **testimōnium perhibēre** to bear witness
perhīlum *adv* very little
perhonōrificē *adv* with all due respect, very respectfully
perhonōrific·us -a -um *adj* very complimentary; very respectful
perhorr·ēscō -ēscere -uī *tr* to begin to shudder at; to develop a terror of **||** *intr* to begin to tremble violently
perhūmāniter *adv* very kindly
perhūmān·us -a -um *adj* very kind
Pericl·ēs -is *m* famous Athenian statesman *(495–429 B.C.)*
perīclitāti·ō -ōnis *f* test, experiment
perīclit·or -ārī -ātus sum *tr* to test, put to the test, try; to jeopardize; to risk **||** *intr* to be in danger, be in jeopardy; to run a risk; *(w. abl)* to be in danger of losing *(life, reputation, etc.);* **capite perīclitārī** to risk one's life
perīc(u)l·um -ī *n* danger, peril, risk; trial, attempt; experiment, test; literary venture; *(leg)* case, trial, lawsuit, legal record, sentence; **perīculum facere** to run the risk; try it out; *(w. gen)* to test, put to the test *(e.g., s.o.'s loyalty);* **perīculum facere ex aliīs** to learn from the mistakes of others; **perīculum intendere** *(w. dat)* to expose *(s.o.)* to danger, endanger *(s.o.);* **volō perīculum facere an** I want to see whether
perīculōsē *adv* dangerously
perīculōs·us -a -um *adj* dangerous, risky, perilous
peridōne·us -a -um *adj* very suitable; *(w. dat or* **ad)** well-adapted to, well-suited to
Perillē·us -a - um *adj* of Perillus
Perill·us -ī *m* Athenian sculptor who made for the tyrant Phalaris a bronze bull in which to roast people alive
perillūstr·is -is -e *adj* very clear; very illustrious, very distinguished
perimbēcill·us -a -um *adj* very weak, very feeble
per·imō -imere -ēmī -emptus *tr* to take away completely; to destroy; to kill
perimpedīt·us -a -um *adj* rough *(terrain);* full of obstacles
perincommodē *adv* very inconveniently
perincommod·us -a -um *adj* very inconvenient
perinde *adv* in the same manner, equally, just as, quite as; *(w.* **ac, atque, ut, prout,** *or* **quam)** just as; *(w.* **ac sī, quasi, tamquam,** *or* **quamsi)** just as if; **nōn perinde** not particularly, not as much as one would expect
perindulg·ēns -entis *adj* very tender; *(w.* **ad)** very tender toward
perīnfirm·us -a -um *adj* very weak
peringeniōs·us -a -um *adj* very gifted
perinīqu·us -a -um *adj* very unfair; very upset, very annoyed; very impatient; very reluctant; **perinīquō animō patī** *(or* **ferre)** to be quite upset at, be very reluctant about
perīnsign·is -is -e *adj* very remarkable
perinvīt·us -a -um *adj* very unwilling
period·us -ī *f (rhet)* complete sentence, period *(a group of words organically related in grammar and sense)*
peripatētic·us -a -um *adj* Peripatetic, Aristotelian **||** *mpl* Peripatetics, Aristotelians
peripetasmat·a -um *npl* curtains, drapes
Periph·ās -antis *m* king of Attica, changed into an eagle by Zeus
periphras·is -is *f (acc:* **-in)** circumlocution
perīrāt·us -a -um *adj* very angry; *(w. dat)* very angry with
periscel·is -idis *f* anklet
peristrōm·a -atis *n* carpet; bedspread
peristȳl·ium -(i)ī *or* **peristȳl·um** *or* **peristȳl·on -ī** *n* peristyle *(inner court surrounded by a colonnade)*
perītē *adv* skillfully, expertly
perīti·a -ae *f* experience, practical knowledge, skill; *(w. gen)* experience in, familiarity with, knowledge of
perīt·us -a -um *adj (w. gen or abl, w.* **in** + *abl or* **ad)** experienced in, skillful in, expert in *or* at, familiar with; *(w. inf)* skilled in, expert at, *e.g.,* **perītus cantāre** skilled in singing; **iūris perītus** expert in the law, legal adviser, lawyer
periūcundē *adv* very pleasantly
periūcund·us -a -um *adj* very pleasant

periūr·ium -(i)ī *n* perjury; false oath; false promise

periūrō -āre *tr* **(-ier-)** to swear falsely by **‖** *intr* to swear a false oath, commit perjury; *(coll)* to lie

periūr·us -a -um *adj* **(-ier-)** perjured, oath-breaking; *(coll)* lying

per·lābor -lābī -lāpsus sum *intr* to glide along, skim across *or* over; *(w.* **per** *+ acc)* **1** to slip through; **2** to slip along, glide along; *(w.* **ad)** to come, move, glide, *or* slip toward; *(w.* **in** *+ acc)* to glide into, slip into

perlaet·us -a -um *adj* very glad, most joyful

perlāpsus *pp of* **perlābor**

perlātē *adv* very extensively

perlat·eō -ēre -uī *intr* to be completely hidden

perlātus *pp of* **perferō**

perlecebr·ae -ārum *fpl* enticement

perlēcti·ō -ōnis *f* thorough perusal

per·legō -legere -lēgī -lēctus *tr* to scan, survey thoroughly, to read through; to recount *(in a speech)*

perlepidē *adv* very nicely

perlev·is -is -e *adj* very light; very slight

perleviter *adv* very lightly; very slightly

perlib·ēns -entis *adj* **(-lub-)** very willing

perlibenter *adv* **(-lub-)** very gladly, very willingly

perlīberāl·is -is -e *adj* very well-bred, very genteel

perlīberāliter *adv* very generously

perlib·et -ēre *v impers* **(lub-) perlibet mē** *(w. inf)* I should very much like to

perliciō *see* **pelliciō**

perlit·ō -āre -āvī -ātus *tr* to sacrifice *(in order to get a favorable omen);* **‖** *intr* **bove perlitāre** to sacrifice an ox *(to obtain a favorable omen)*

perlongē *adv* a long way off

perlonginqu·us -a -um *adj* **(-os -a -om)** very long; very tedious

perlong·us -a -um *adj* very long; very tedious

perlub- = perlib-

per·lūceō -lūcēre *intr* **(pell-)** to shine clearly, be bright; to be clearly visible; to be transparent; to be clear, be intelligible

perlūcidul·us -a -um *adj* transparent

perlūcid·us -a -um *adj* **(pell-)** very bright; transparent

perlūctuōs·us -a -um *adj* very sad

per·luō -luere -luī -lūtus *tr* to wash thoroughly; to wash off; to bathe

perlūstr·ō -āre -āvī -ātus *tr* to traverse; to scan, survey, review

permade·faciō -facere -fēcī -factus *tr* to soak through and through, drench

permad·ēscō -ēscere -uī *intr* to become drenched

permagn·us -a -um *adj* very big; very great; very important **‖** *n* great thing; **permagnō** at a very high price, very dearly; **permagnum aestimāre** *(w. inf)* to think it quite something to

permānanter *adv* pervasively

permānāsc·ō -ere *intr (of a report)* to leak out

perman·eō -ēre -sī -sum *intr* to last, continue, hold out, remain, persist; *(of the voice)* to remain steady; **permanēre esse** to continue to be

permān·ō -āre -āvī -ātus *tr* to seep through, penetrate **‖** *intr* to penetrate; *(w.* **ad** *or* **in** *+ acc)* **1** to seep through to; **2** to seep into, penetrate; **3** *(fig)* to reach, extend to, penetrate

permānsi·ō -ōnis *f* persistence, continuance

permarīn·us -a -um *adj* seagoing

permātūr·ēscō -ēscere -uī *intr* to become fully ripe

permediocr·is -is -e *adj* completely normal, very moderate

permeditāt·us -a -um *adj* well-rehearsed, well-trained

permēiō -mēiere -mī(n)xī -ī(n)ctus *tr (sl)* to soak with urine, urinate all over

permēnsus *pp of* **permētior**

perme·ō -āre -āvī -ātus *tr* to go through, cross over, cross **‖** *intr (w.* **in** *+ acc)* to penetrate; *(w.* **per** *+ acc)* to penetrate, permeate

Permēss·us -ī *m* river in Boeotia sacred to Apollo and the Muses

per·mētior -mētīrī -mēnsus sum *tr* to measure exactly; to travel over, traverse; to pass right through *(a period of time);* **permētīrī oculīs** to take stock of, eye appraisingly

per·mingō -mingere -mīnxī -mī(n)ctus *tr (sl)* to soak with urine, urinate all over

permīr·us -a -um *adj* very surprising, truly amazing

per·mīsceō -mīscēre -mīscuī mīxtus *tr* to mix together, blend thoroughly, intermingle; to unite *(by marriage); (fig)* to involve, embroil; *(fig)* to mix up, confuse, treat as identical; to throw into confusion **‖** *pass (w.* **cum)** to combine with; *(w. abl or* **ex)** to consist of, be made up of

permissi·ō -ōnis *f* permission; unconditional surrender; *(as rhetorical device)* concession

permiss·us -a -um *pp of* **permittō** **‖** *n* permission

permiss·us -ūs *m* permission, leave

permitiāl·is -is -e *adj* destructive

permiti·ēs -ēī *f* wasting away; ruin; *(of persons)* source of ruin, ruination

per·mittō -mittere -mīsī -missus *tr* to let through, let go through; to hurl; to give up, surrender; to concede, relinquish; to let loose, let go; to let, permit, allow, grant; *(w. dat)* to surrender *(s.th.)* to, entrust *(s.th.)* to, grant *(s.th.)* to; *(w.* **in** + *acc)* to send flying at, hurl at

permīxtē *or* **permīxtim** *adv* confusedly; indiscriminately

permīxti·ō -ōnis *f* mixture; confusion, bedlam

permīxt·us -a -um *pp of* **permīsceō** ‖ *adj* confused; promiscuous; composite

permodest·us -a -um *adj* very modest, very moderate

permolestē *adv* with much trouble; **permolestē ferre** to be quite annoyed at

permolest·us -a -um *adj* very troublesome, very annoying

permol·ō -ere *tr* to grind up; **aliēnās uxōrēs permolere** *(sl)* to have sex with other men's wives

permōti·ō -ōnis *f* excitement; **animī permōtiō** *(or* **mentis permōtiō)** deep emotion

per·moveō -movēre -mōvī -mōtus *tr* to stir up, churn up *(the sea);* to move deeply, make a deep impression on; to excite, agitate, upset; to influence, induce

permul·ceō -cēre -sī -sus *tr* to stroke, pet; to soothe, calm down, relax; to smoothe out *(one's hair);* to charm, delight; to appease

permultō *adv* by far, much, far

permultum *adv* very much; **permultum ante** very often before; **permultum interest** it makes a world of difference

permult·us -a -um *adj* very much; *(w. pl nouns)* very many ‖ *n* a lot, much

permūn·iō -īre -īvī *or* **-iī -ītus** *tr* to fortify thoroughly; to finish fortifying

permūtāti·ō -ōnis *f* interchange; exchange; bartering; substitution, switch; reversal *(of an arrangment);* turning upside down, revolution; alternation, transformation

permūt·ō -āre -āvī -ātus *tr* to change *or* alter completely, transform; to interchange; to remit by bill of exchange; to reverse *(an order, arrangement);* to turn topsy-turvy *(w. abl or* **cum** *or* **prō** + *abl)* **1** to exchange for, replace with; **2** to receive in exchange for; **3** to acquire at the price of; **4** to substitute for

pern·a -ae *f* ham

pernecessāri·us -a -um *adj* very necessary; very closely related ‖ *m* close friend; close relative

pernecesse *indecl neut adj* very necessary, indispensable

perneg·ō -āre -āvī -ātus *tr* to deny flatly; to turn down flat

per·neō -nēre -nēvī -nētus *tr (of the Fates)* to spin out

perniciābil·is -is -e *adj* ruinous

pernici·ēs -ēī *f* ruin, destruction, disaster; pest, curse; cause of ruin

perniciōsē *adv* perniciously, ruinously

perniciōs·us -a -um *adj* pernicious, ruinous

pernīcit·ās -ātis *f* agility, nimbleness, swiftness

pernīciter *adv* nimbly, swiftly

perni·ger -gra -grum *adj* jet black; very dark *(eyes)*

pernimium *adv* much too much

pern·īx -īcis *adj* agile, nimble, swift, quick, speedy

pernōbil·is -is -e *adj* very famous

pernoct·ō -āre -āvī -ātum *intr* to spend the night

per·nōscō -nōscere -nōvī -nōtus *tr* to examine thoroughly; to become fully acquainted with, get accurate knowledge of

pernōt·ēscō -ēscere -uī *intr* to become generally known

per·nox -noctis *adj* all-night; **lūna pernox** full moon

pernumer·ō -āre -āvī -ātus *tr* to count up

pēr·ō -ōnis *m* clodhopper *(worn by peasants and soldiers)*

perobscūr·us -a -um *adj* very obscure; very vague

perō·dī -disse -sus *tr* to detest, loathe

perodiōs·us -a -um *adj* very annoying

perofficiōsē *adv* with attention, with great devotion; very politely

pērōnāt·us -a -um *adj* wearing clodhoppers

peropportūnē *adv* very conveniently, most opportunely

peropportūn·us -a -um *adj* most opportune, very convenient, well-timed

peroptātō *adv* very much in accordance with one's wishes

peroptāt·us -a -um *adj* greatly desired, longed-for

peropus *indecl n* great need; **peropus est** *(w. acc & inf)* it is essential that

perōrāti·ō -ōnis *f* peroration, summation

perōrnāt·us -a -um *adj* very flowery *(speech)*

perōrn·ō -āre -āvī -ātus *tr* to enhance the prestige of

perōr·ō -āre -āvī -ātus *tr* to bring *(a case, discussion)* to a close ‖ *intr* to bring a speech to a close; *(leg)* to wind up a case, give the summation

perōs·us -a -um *adj* hating, detesting; hated, hateful

perpāc·ō -āre -āvī -ātus *tr* to silence completely; to pacify thoroughly

perparcē *adv* most stingily

perparvul·us -a -um *adj* tiny

perparv·us -a -um *adj* very small

perpāst·us -a -um *adj* well-fed

perpauc·ī -ae -a *adj* very few ‖ *npl* very few words

perpaucul·ī -ae -a *adj* very few

perpaulum *adv* somewhat, slightly

perpaul·um -ī *n* small bit

perpaup·er -eris *adj* very poor
perpauxill·um -ī *n* little bit
perpave·faciō -facere -fēcī -factus *tr* to frighten the daylights out of
per·pellō -pellere -pulī -pulsus *tr* to push hard; to urge strongly, force; to drive all the way
perpendicul·um -ī *n* plumb line; **ad perpendiculum** perpendicularly
perpen·dō -dere -dī -sus *tr* to weigh carefully, consider; to value, judge
perperam *adv* incorrectly, wrongly; by mistake
Perpern·a *or* **Perpenn·a -ae** *m* Roman family name *(cognomen), esp.* Marcus Perperna Vento, partisan and later murderer of Sertorius
perp·es -etis *adj* continuous, uninterrupted
perpessi·ō -ōnis *f* endurance
per·petior -petī -pessus sum *tr* to endure, put up with, stand; to allow, permit
perpetr·ō -āre -āvī -ātus *tr* to accomplish, go through with, carry out, perform; to perpetrate, commit; to fulfill *(a promise); (w.* **ut)** to bring it about that
perpetuē *adv* constantly
perpetuit·ās -ātis *f* perpetuity
perpetuō *adv* constantly; forever
perpetu·ō -āre -āvī -ātus *tr* to perpetuate
perpetu·us -a -um *adj* perpetual, continuous; general, universal; whole; **quaestiōnēs perpetuae** standing courts; permanent committees **||** *n* **in perpetuum** continuously; forever
perplac·eō -ēre *intr (w. dat)* to please immensely
perplexābil·is -is -e *adj* perplexing, puzzling
perplexābiliter *adv* perplexingly
perplexē *or* **perplexim** *adv* confusedly, unintelligibly
perplex·or -ārī *intr* to cause confusion
perplex·us -a -um *adj* intricate, complicated; ambiguous; muddled, mistaken; baffling *(words)*
perplicāt·us -a -um *adj* entangled
perplu·ō -ere *intr (of roof, etc.)* to let the rain in; *(of rain)* to come in
perpol·iō -īre -īvī *or* **-iī -ītus** *tr* to bring to a high polish; *(fig)* to polish up, perfect
perpolīt·us -a -um *adj* highly polished, refined
perpopul·or -ārī -ātus sum *tr* to ravage, devastate
perpōtāti·ō -ōnis *f* heavy drinking; drinking party
perpōt·ō -āre -āvī -ātus *tr* to drink up **||** *intr* to drink heavily, carouse
per·primō -primere -pressī -pressus *tr* to press hard, squeeze hard
perpropinqu·us -a -um *adj* very near **||** *m* close relative
perprūrīsc·ō -ere *intr* to begin to itch all over
perpugn·āx -ācis *adj* very belligerent
perpul·c(h)er -c(h)ra -c(h)rum *adj* very beautiful, very handsome
perpulsus *pp of* **perpellō**
perpurg·ō -āre -āvī -ātus *tr* to cleanse thoroughly, clean up; *(fig)* to clear up
perpusill·us -a -um *adj* puny
perput·ō -āre -āvī -ātus *tr* to prune back hard; to explain in detail
perquam *adv* very, extremely
per·quīrō -quīrere -quīsīvī *or* **-quīsiī -quīsītus** *tr* to search carefully for; to examine carefully
perquīsītius *adv* more accurately, more critically
perquīsīt·or -ōris *m* enthusiast
perrārō *adv* very rarely
perrār·us -a -um *adj* very rare
perrecondit·us -a -um *adj* recondite
perrēctus *pp of* **pergō**
perrēp·ō -ere -sī *tr* to creep through; to crawl along *(the ground)*
perrept·ō -āre -āvī *tr* to creep through, sneak through **||** *intr* to creep around
perrēxī *perf of* **pergō**
Perrhaeb·us -a -um *adj* of Perrhaebia *(a mountainous region of N. Thessaly)* **||** *m* inhabitant of Perrhaebia
perrīdiculē *adv* most absurdly
perrīdicul·us -a -um *adj* utterly absurd
perrogāti·ō -ōnis *f* passage *(of a law)*
perrog·ō -āre *tr* to ask for in turn; to question in turn; **sententiās perrogāre** to poll the opinions *(in the senate)*
per·rumpō -rumpere -rūpī -ruptus *tr* to break through, force one's way through; to break in two, shatter, smash; to offend against, violate **||** *intr* to break through, make a breakthrough
Pers·a -ae *or* **Pers·ē -ēs** *f* Perse, a daughter of Oceanus, wife of the sun, and mother of Circe, Perses *(father of Hecate),* Aeëtes, and Pasiphaë *(wife of King Minos)*
Pers·a *or* **Pers·ēs -ae** *m* Persian
persaepe *adv* very often
persalsē *adv* very wittily
persals·us -a -um *adj* very witty
persalūtāti·ō -ōnis *f* round of greetings, greeting all in turn
persalūt·ō -āre -āvī -ātus *tr* to salute one after another
persanctē *adv* very solemnly
persapi·ēns -entis *adj* very wise
persapienter *adv* very wisely
perscienter *adv* very skillfully
per·scindō -scindere -scidī -scissus *tr* to tear to pieces; to split
perscīt·us -a -um *adj* very clever, very smart

per·scrībō -scrībere -scrīpsī -scrīptus *tr* to write out; to describe fully, give in detail; to finish writing; to record, register; to enter *(into an account book);* to write out in full *(as opposed to abbreviating);* **pecūniam perscrībere** to write a check for *(a certain sum of money)*

perscrīpti·ō -ōnis *f* entry, official record; check, payment by check

perscrīpt·or -ōris *m* bookkeeper, accountant

perscrīptus *pp of* **perscrībō**

perscrūt·or -ārī -ātus sum *tr* to search *or* examine thoroughly, scrutinize

Pers·ē -ēs *f see* **Persa** *f*

persec·ō -āre -uī -tus *tr* to dissect; to cut through; to lance *(a boil)*

persect·or -ārī -ātus sum *tr* to follow eagerly, investigate

persecūti·ō -ōnis *f* pursuit; *(leg)* right to sue; *(leg)* prosecution, suing

persecūtus *pp of* **persequor**

per·sedeō -sedēre -sēdī -sessum *intr* to remain seated

persēgn·is -is -e *adj* very slow-moving, very sluggish

Persē·is -idis *or* **-idos** *adj (fem only)* of Persa; of Perseus ‖ *f* daughter of Persa *(Hecate, Circe)* ‖ Persa

persen·tiō -tīre -sī -sus *tr* to perceive clearly, to feel deeply

persentīsc·ō -ere *tr* to become fully conscious of; to begin to feel deeply

Persephon·ē -ēs *f* daughter of Demeter and Zeus and queen of the lower world *(named Proserpina by the Romans)*

persequ·ēns -entis *adj* pursuing; *(w. gen)* given to the pursuit *or* practice of

perse·quor -quī -cūtus sum *tr* to follow persistently, follow up; to be in hot pursuit of, be on the heels of; to chase after, catch up to; to follow verbatim; to imitate, copy; to take vengeance on; to follow out, execute; to describe, explain; *(leg)* to prosecute

Pers·ēs *or* **Pers·a -ae** *or* **Pers·eūs -eī** *or* **-eos** *m* Perseus *(last king of Macedonia, conquered by Aemilius Paulus at Pydna in 169 B.C.)*

Pers·eūs -eī *or* **-eos** *m* son of Jupiter and Danaë, and slayer of Medusa ‖ *see* **Persēs**

Persē·us *or* **Persēī·us -a -um** *adj* of Perseus *(son of Jupiter and Danaë)*

persevēr·āns -antis *adj* persevering, persistent, relentless

persevēranter *adv* persistently

persevēranti·a -ae *f* perseverance

persevēr·ō -āre -āvī -ātus *tr* to persist in ‖ *intr* to persevere

persevēr·us -a -um *adj* very strict

Persi·a -ae *or* **Pers·is -idis** *or* **-idos** *f* Persia

Persic·us -a -um *adj* Persian; *(fig)* luxurious, soft; of Perseus *(king of Macedonia);* **mālum Persicum** peach ‖ *mpl* Persians ‖ *f* peach tree ‖ *n* peach ‖ *npl* Persian history

per·sīdō -sīdere -sēdī *intr* to sink down; *(w.* **ad** *or* **in** *+ acc)* to penetrate

persign·ō -āre -āvī -ātus *tr* to record in detail *(articles in an inventory)*

persimil·is -is -e *adj* very similar; *(w. gen or dat)* very similar to

persimpl·ex -icis *adj* very simple

Pers·is -idis *or* **-idos** *adj (fem only)* Persian ‖ *f* Persia; Persian woman

Pers·ius -(i)ī *m* Persius *(Aulus Persius Flaccus, satirist in the reign of Nero, A.D. 34–62)*

persōll·a -ae *f* little mask; *(pej)* you ugly little thing!

persōl·us -a -um *adj* all alone

per·solvō -solvere solvī -solūtus *tr* to solve; to explain; to pay up, pay in full; to pay *(a penalty);* to fulfill *(a vow);* to carry out *(a duty);* to render *(thanks);* to offer *(sacrifice); (w. gen)* to pay the penalty for *(a crime); (w. dat)* to pay *(the penalty)* at the hands of; to solve *(a problem, riddle);* **ab omnibus eī poenae persolūtae sunt** punishment was inflicted on him by all; **dēbitum nātūrae persolvere** to pay one's debt to nature *(i.e., to die);* **honōrem dīs persolvere** to offer sacrifices to the gods; **grātēs dīs persolvere** to render thanksgiving to the gods; **grātiam dīs persolvere** to render thanks to the gods; **iūsta persolvere** to pay honors to the dead; **poenās dīs hominibusque persolvere** to suffer punishment at the hands of gods and men; **vectīgālia persolvere** to pay taxes; **vōta persolvere** to fulfill vows

persōn·a -ae *f* mask; part, character; pretense; personality; person; *(gram)* person; *(leg)* the person involved in a case; **ab** *(or* **ex** *or* **in)** **suā persōnā** *(acting, speaking)* in one's own name, on one's own behalf; **in persōnā** *(w. gen)* in the case of, in the instance of; **mea persōna** my personality *or* character; **persōnae fictiō** personification; **persōna mūta** a character with no speaking part

persōnāl·is -is -e *adj* personal

persōnāliter *adv* personally

persōnāt·us -a -um *adj* wearing a mask, masked; *(fig)* under false pretenses, putting on a front; **pater persōnātus** the father in the play; **persōnāta fābula** a play in which actors wear masks; **persōnātus histriō** an actor wearing a mask

person·ō -āre -uī -ātus *tr* to make *(a place)* resound; to shout out; to sing loudly, belt out *(a song);* **aurem personāre** to make the ear ring ‖ *intr* to resound, reecho; *(of a musician w. abl. of instrument)* to play loudly on *(e.g., the lyre); (of a singer)* to sing loudly; **citharā personāre** to produce loud music on the lyre

perspargō *see* **perspergō**

perspectē *adv* intelligently

perspect·ō -āre -āvī -ātus *tr* to examine carefully; to watch steadily ‖ *intr* to look all around, have a look around

perspect·us -a -um *pp of* **perspiciō** ‖ *adj* well-known, clear, evident; **rēs penitus perspectae** matters clearly understood

perspecul·or -ārī -ātus sum *tr* to explore thoroughly; *(mil)* to reconnoiter

persper·gō -gere -sī -sus *tr* **(-spar-)** to sprinkle; to strew *(w. flowers)*

perspexī *perf of* **perspiciō**

perspic·āx -ācis *adj* sharp-sighted; keen, penetrating, perspicacious

perspicienti·a -ae *f* clear perception

per·spiciō -spicere -spexī -spectus *tr* to see through; to look through; to look closely at, look over, examine, inspect, observe; to discern, ascertain; to prove

perspicuē *adv* clearly

perspicuit·ās -ātis *f* clarity

perspicu·us -a -um *adj* clear; transparent; clearly visible, conspicuous; plain, evident; lucid *(expression)*

perspīr·ō -āre *intr* to blow steadily

perspissō *adv* very slowly

persternō -sternere -strāvī -strātus *tr* to pave *(a road)* along its full length

perstimul·ō -āre -āvī -ātus *tr* to stimulate; to continue to stir up

per·stō stāre -stitī -stātum *intr* to stand firm, hold one's ground; to remain standing; to remain unchanged, last; to be firm, persevere, hold out; *(of soldiers)* to continue under arms; *(of things)* to remain stationary; *(w. inf)* to continue obstinately to *(do s.th.)*

perstrātus *pp of* **persternō**

perstrep·ō -ere -uī *intr* to make a loud noise, make a lot of noise

perstringō perstringere perstrīnxī perstrictum *tr* to tie, tie up; to make unfavorable mention of; *(of sounds)* to grate on; to blunt, deaden *(the senses);* to dazzle *(the eyes);* to deafen *(the ears); (of a weapon)* to graze; to glance over; to touch lightly on; to wound *(s.o.'s)* feelings, offend; **Crassus meīs litterīs perstrictus est** Crassus was offended by *(or* took offense at) my letter; **horror ingēns spectantēs perstrīnxit** a deep shudder came over the onlookers

perstudiōsē *adv* enthusiastically

perstudiōs·us -a -um *adj (w. gen)* very fond of, enthusiastic about, very interested in

persuā·deō -dēre -sī -sum *intr (w. dat)* to persuade, convince; **sibi persuāsum habēre** to have oneself convinced

persuāsi·ō -ōnis *f* convincing; conviction, belief

persuāstr·īx -īcis *f* seductress

persuāsum *pp of* **persuādeō**

persuās·us -ūs *m* persuasion

persubtīl·is -is -e *adj* of very fine texture; very subtle, very ingenious

persult·ō -āre -āvī -ātus *tr* to prance about; to scour *(woods)* ‖ *intr* to gambol, prance, run around

per·taedet -taedēre -taesum est *v impers (w. acc of person = subject in English and gen. of thing = object in English)* to be weary of, be sick and tired of, be bored with, *e.g.,* **mē hūius negōtiī pertaedet** I am sick and tired of this business

per·tegō -tegere -tēxī -tēctus *tr* to cover up, cover completely; to roof over

pertempt·ō -āre -āvī -ātus *tr* **(-tent-)** to test thoroughly; to sound *(s.o.)* out; to consider well; *(fig)* to fill, pervade; **gaudia pertemptant pectus** joy fills *(their)* hearts

perten·dō -dere -dī -sus *or* **-tus** *tr* to press on with, continue, carry out ‖ *intr* to press on, continue, persevere, keep going

pertenu·is -is -e *adj* very thin, very slight, very small, very fine

perterebr·ō -āre -āvī -ātus *tr* to bore through

perter·geō -ēre -sī -sus *tr* to wipe off; *(of air)* to brush lightly against

perterre·faciō -facere -fēcī -factus *tr* to scare the life out of

perterr·eō -ēre -uī -itus *tr* to frighten, terrify; *(w.* **ab)** to frighten *(s.o.)* away from

perterricrep·us -a -um *adj* terrible-sounding, rattling frightfully

pertex·ō -ere -uī -tus *tr* to bring to an end, go through with, accomplish; to complete the composition of *(a speech, writing)*

pertic·a -ae *f* pole; rod, staff; ten-foot measuring pole; *(fig)* measure

pertimefact·us -a -um *adj* thoroughly frightened

pertim·ēscō -ēscere -uī *tr* to be alarmed at, become afraid of ‖ *intr* to become very frightened *or* alarmed

pertināci·a -ae *f* stubbornness; perseverance, determination

pertināciter *adv* stubbornly, tenaciously; through thick and thin

pertin·āx -ācis *adj* very tenacious; persevering, steadfast; stubborn

pertin·eō -ēre -uī *intr* to reach, extend; *(w.* **per** + *acc)* **1** to pervade; **2** reach; *(w.* **ad) 1** to extend to, reach; **2** to pertain to, relate to, concern; **3** to apply to, be applicable to, suit, be suitable to; **4** to be conducive to; **5** to belong to; **quod pertinet** *(w.* **ad)** as regards

perting·ō -ere *tr* to get as far as, reach **II** *intr* to extend; **collis in inmēnsum pertingēns** a hill extending a very long distance

pertoler·ō -āre -āvī -ātus *tr* to put up with, endure to the end

pertorqu·eō -ēre *tr* to twist, distort

pertractātē *adv* in a trite manner

pertractāti·ō -ōnis *f* handling, treatment

pertract·ō -āre -āvī -ātus *tr* to handle; *(fig)* to treat systematically; to examine in detail

per·trahō -trahere -trāxī -tractus *tr* to drag along; to drag by force *(to s.th. unpleasant);* to lure, lead on *(an enemy);* to tow

pertrect- = pertract-

pertrīst·is -is -e *adj* very sad; very stern

pertulī *perf of* **perferō**

pertumultuōsē *adv* very excitedly, hysterically

per·tundō -tundere -tudī -tūsus *tr* to punch a hole through, perforate

perturbātē *adv* in confusion

perturbāti·ō -ōnis *f* confusion, disorder; riot; distress, agitation; strong emotion

perturbātr·īx -īcis *f* disturbing element

perturbāt·us -a -um *adj* disturbed, troubled; excited, alarmed; embarrassed

perturb·ō -āre -āvī -ātus *tr* to throw into confusion, confuse; to disturb; to embarrass; to upset; to alarm

perturp·is -is -e *adj* downright shameful

pertūs·us -a -um *pp of* **pertundō II** *adj* perforated; tattered *(clothes)*

pērul·a -ae *f* small satchel

per·ung(u)ō -ung(u)ere -ūnxī -ūnctus *tr* to anoint thoroughly

perurbān·us -a -um *adj* very polite; very sophisticated **II** *m* snob

per·ūrō -ūrere -ūssī -ūstus *tr* to burn up; to consume; to inflame, rub sore; to scorch; *(of cold)* to nip, bite; *(fig)* to fire, inflame

Perusi·a -ae *f* town in Etruria *(modern Perugia)*

Perusīn·us -a -um *adj* of Perusia **II** *mpl* inhabitants of Perusia **II** *n* an estate in Perusia

perūssī *perf of* **perūrō**

perūstus *pp of* **perūrō**

perūtil·is -is -e *adj* very useful

per·vādō -vādere -vāsī -vāsus *tr* to pass through, go through; to pervade **II** *intr* to spread; to penetrate; *(w.* **ad** *or* **in** + *acc)* **1** to go as far as, spread to; **2** to reach, arrive at; **3** to penetrate; *(w.* **per** + *acc)* to spread through *or* over

pervagāt·us -a -um *adj* widespread, prevalent, well-known; general, common; of widespread application

pervag·or -ārī -ātus sum *tr* to spread through *or* over, pervade **II** *intr* to wander all over, range about; *(w.* **ad) 1** to spread to, extend to; **2** to be known as far as

pervag·us -a -um *adj* wandering about

perval·eō -ēre *intr (of a magnet)* to retain (its) power

pervariē *adv* in various versions

pervast·ō -āre -āvī -ātus *tr* to devastate

pervāsus *pp of* **pervādō**

perve·hō -here -xī -ctus *tr* to bring, carry, convey; to bring *(e.g, supplies)* through **II** *pass* to ride, drive, sail; **in portum pervehī** to sail into port, reach port

pervell·ō -ere -ī *tr* to pull hard; to pinch hard; to excite, arouse; to cause to twinge; *(fig)* to disparage; **aurem alicui pervellere** to pull s.o.'s ear *(as a reminder)*

per·veniō -venīre -vēnī -ventus *tr* to come to, reach **II** *intr* to come up; to arrive; *(w.* **ad** *or* **in** + *acc)* **1** to arrive at, reach; **2** *(fig)* to attain to

pervēn·or -ārī *tr* to search through, scour *(e.g., all the city)*

perversāriō *adv* **(-vors-)** in a wrong-headed way, wrongly

perversē *adv* **(-vors-)** wrongly, perversely

perversit·ās -ātis *f* perversity, unreasonableness; distortion

pervers·us -a -um *adj* **(-vors-)** turned the wrong way, awry, crooked; cross-eyed; *(fig)* crooked, wrong, perverse; *(fig)* spiteful, malicious

per·vertō -vertere -vertī -versus *tr* **(-vort-)** to overturn, upset, knock down; to invert the order of; to cause to face in the opposite direction; to bend out of shape, distort; to misrepresent, falsify *(statements);* to divert to an improper use, misuse, abuse; to undo, destroy; to pervert, spoil

pervesperī *adv* late in the evening

pervestīgāti·ō -ōnis *f* thorough search, examining, investigation

pervestīg·ō -āre -āvī -ātus *tr* to track down; to examine in detail; *(fig)* to trace, detect

pervet·us -eris *adj* very old, ancient

pervetust·us -a -um *adj* very ancient

pervexī *perf of* **pervehō**

perviam *adv* **perviam facere** to make accessible

pervicāci·a -ae *f* persistence; *(pej)* stubbornness; **pervicācia in hostem** obstinate resistance to the enemy

pervicācius *adv* more stubbornly

pervic·āx -ācis *adj* persistent, determined; *(pej)* headstrong, stubborn

pervīcī *perf of* **pervincō**

pervictus *pp of* **pervincō**

per·videō -vidēre -vīdī -vīsus *tr* to look over, survey; to see through; to examine, investigate; to realize, perceive fully

pervig·eō -ēre -uī *intr* to continue to thrive
pervig·il -ilis *adj* wide-awake, ever watchful
pervigilāti·ō -ōnis *f* religious vigil
pervigil·ium -(i)ī *n* all-night vigil
pervigil·ō -āre -āvī -ātus *tr* to spend *or* pass *(nights, days)* without sleep ‖ *intr* to stay awake all night, keep an all-night vigil
pervīl·is -is -e *adj* very cheap
per·vincō -vincere -vīcī -victus *tr* to defeat completely, completely get the better of; to outdo; to outbid; to convince; to prove ‖ *intr* to win, succeed; to carry a point; *(w.* **ut)** to succeed in, bring it about that; **nōn pervīcit ut referrent cōnsulēs** he did not succeed in having the consuls make a formal proposal
pervīsus *pp of* **pervideō**
pervi·us -a -um *adj* crossable, passable; open at both ends; perforated; accessible; open to entreaty ‖ *n* passage
per·vīvō -vīvere -vīxī *intr* to live on, go on living
pervolgō *see* **pervulgō**
pervolit·ō -āre -āvī -ātus *tr & intr* to fly about, flit about
pervol·ō -āre -āvī -ātus *tr* to fly through, fly about, flit about; to dart through, pass quickly over ‖ *intr* to fly about, flit about; *(w.* **in** + *acc)* to fly through to, arrive at, reach
per·volō -velle -voluī *tr* to wish very much; **tē quam prīmum pervelim vidēre** I'd like very much to see you as soon as possible
pervolūt·ō -āre -āvī -ātus *tr* to turn over often, read through *(a scroll)*
per·volvō -volvere -volvī -volūtus *tr* to roll *(s.o.)* over; to keep reading, read through *(a scroll)* ‖ *refl* to roll around ‖ *pass* to be busy
pervor- = perver-
pervulgāt·us -a -um *adj* **(-vol-)** widely known, very common
pervulg·ō -āre -āvī -ātus *tr* **(-vol-)** to make known, make public, publicize; to frequent ‖ *refl* to prostitute oneself
pēs pedis *m* foot *(of body, of table, of couch; in verse);* rope at lower part of a sail, sheet; **ad pedēs dēscendere** to dismount *(in order to fight on foot);* **ad pedēs pugna** an infantry fight; **aequīs pedibus lābī** to sail on an even keel; **ante pedēs** in plain view; **in pedēs** feet first; **pede dextrō** *(or* **fēlīce** *or* **secundō)** auspiciously *(the right foot being associated with good omens);* **pedem cōnferre** to come to close quarters; **pedem ferre** to come; to go; **pedem pōnere** *(w.* **in** + *abl)* to set foot in; **pedem referre** to step back, retreat; **pedēs tollere** to lift the legs *(for sexual intercourse);* **pedibus** on foot; **pedibus claudere** to set to verse, put in meter; **pedibus īre in sententiam** *(w. gen)* to vote in favor of the proposal of; **pedibus itur in sententiam** the proposal is put to a vote; **pedibus merēre** *(or* **pedibus merērī)** to serve in the infantry; **pedibus vincere** to win a footrace; **plānō pede** on level ground; **pugna ad pedēs** infantry battle; **sē in pedēs conicere** *(or* **sē in pedēs cōnferre** *or* **sē in pedēs dare** *or* **sē pedibus dare)** to take to one's heels; **servus ā pedibus** footman; **sub pedibus** under one's sway
pessimē *(superl of* **male)** *adv* **(-sum-)** worst; most wickedly; most unfortunately; by a stroke of bad luck
pessim·us -a -um *(superl of* **malus)** *adj* **(-sum-)** worst; most villainous; most distressing
Pessin·ūs -ūntis *m* Galatian town on the borders of Phrygia, famous for its cult of Cybele
pessul·us -ī *m* bolt *(of a door)*
pessum *adv* down, to the ground, to the bottom; **pessum dare** *(or* **pessumdare** *as one word)* to send to the bottom, sink, drown, ruin, destroy; **pessum īre** to go down, sink, go to pot, go to the dogs
pestif·er -era -erum *adj* pestilential; destructive, pernicious, disastrous ‖ *m* troublemaker
pestiferē *adv* disastrously
pestil·ēns -entis *adj* pestilential, unhealthful; *(fig)* disastrous
pestilenti·a -ae *f* pestilence, plague; unhealthful atmosphere *or* climate
pestilit·ās -ātis *f* pestilence, plague
pest·is -is *f* contagious disease; plague; death, destruction; instrument of death *or* destruction; *(of persons)* troublemaker, anarchist, subversive
petasāt·us -a -um *adj* wearing a hat; *(fig)* ready to travel
petas·ō -ōnis *m* ham, leg of pork
petasuncul·us -ī *m* little ham
petas·us -ī *m* broad-rimmed hat
petaur·um -ī *n* springboard
Petēli·a -ae *f* town in Bruttium, besieged by Hannibal
petess·ō -ere *tr* **(-tiss-)** to be eager for, pursue; **pugnam petessere** to be spoiling for a fight
petīti·ō -ōnis *f* attack, blow, thrust, aim; petition, request, application; *(leg)* claim, suit, suing, right to sue; *(pol)* candidacy, political campaign; **petītiōnī sē dare** to become a candidate
petīt·or -ōris *m* applicant; *(leg)* plaintiff; *(pol)* political candidate
petītr·īx -īcis *f (leg)* plaintiff *(female)*
petītur·iō -īre *intr (pol)* to be eager for office

petīt·us -a -um *pp of* **petō** ‖ *adj* **longē petītus** far-fetched ‖ *n* request

pet·ō -ere -īvī *or* **-iī -ītus** *tr* to make for, head for; to attack; to strive after; to aim at; to demand, require, exact; to ask for; to claim, lay claim to, sue for; to beg, entreat; to look for, go in search of, search for; to run after, chase *(girls);* to go and fetch; to obtain; to draw *(a sigh);* to run for *(office);* to refer to, relate to; *(w. dat or* **ad** *or* **in** + *acc)* to demand *(s.o. or s.th.) (for a specific purpose), e.g.,* **custōdem in vincula petere** to demand that the watchdog be chained; **astra petere** to mount to the stars; **terram petere** to fall to the earth

petorrit·um -ī *n* **(-tōri-)** open four-wheeled carriage *(of Celtic origin)*

Petosīr·is -idis *m* Egyptian astrologer; *(fig)* a great astrologer, mathemtician

Petr·a -ae *f* Petra *(name of several towns, esp. the chief town of Arabia Petraea)*

petr·a -ae *f* rock, crag

Petrēi·us -ī *m* Roman clan name *(nomen), esp.* Marcus Petreius *(legate of Gaius Antonius against Catiline and later of Pompey in the Civil War)*

Petrīn·um -ī *n* place near Sinuessa on the border between Latium and Campania ‖ estate in this area

petr·ō -ōnis *m* castrated ram; *(pej)* yokel

Petrōn·ius -(i)ī *m* Petronius Arbiter *(author and master of cermonies at the court of Nero)*

petul·āns -antis *adj* petulant, brash, smart-alecky; *(of sexual behavior)* horny

petulanter *adv* brashly, rudely

petulanti·a -ae *f* petulance, brashness; *(of speech)* rudeness; *(of sexual behavior)* horniness

petulc·us -a -um *adj* butting, apt to butt

Peuceti·a -ae *f* Peucetia *(S. section of Apulia)*

Peuceti·us -a -um *adj* of Peucetia

pexī *perf of* **pectō**

pex·us -a -um *pp of* **pectō** ‖ *adj* neatly combed; new, still having the nap on

P(h)thīōtic·us -a -um *adj* of Phthia *(native country of Achilles in Thessaly)*

Phaeāc·es -um *mpl* Phaeacians *(people living on a utopian island, according to the Odyssey)*

Phaeāci·us -a -um *adj* Phaeacian ‖ *f* Phaeacia *(sometimes identified with Corcyra and ruled by King Alcinoüs)*

Phaeāc·us -a -um *adj* Phaeacian

Phae·āx -ācis *m* Phaeacian ‖ *m* Phaeacian; well-fed man

Phaedr·a -ae *f* daughter of Minos and wife of Theseus

Phaedr·us -ī *m* one of the Socratic circle, who gave his name to a dialogue of Plato ‖ Epicurean philosopher of Athens, who taught Cicero ‖ writer of fables, freedman of Augustus

Phaesti·as -adis *or* **-ados** *adj (fem only)* a woman of Phestum

Phaesti·us -a -um *adj* of Phestum

Phaest·um -ī *n* town in S. Crete

Phaët(h)·ōn -ontis *or* **-ontos** *m* son of Helios, who was killed by Zeus while driving his father's chariot

Phaët(h)ontiad·es -um *fpl* sisters of Phaëthon, who were turned into trees

Phaëthonte·us -a -um *adj* of Phaëthon

Phaëthont·is -idis *or* **-dos** *adj (fem only)* of Phaëthon ‖ *fpl* sisters of Phaëthon

Phaëthūs·a -ae *f* the eldest sister of Phaëthon

pha·ger -grī *m* fish *(sea-bream?)*

phalang·a -ae *f* wooden roller *(for moving ships and siege engines)*

phalangīt·ae -ārum *mpl* soldiers belonging to a Macedonian phalanx

phal·anx -angis *f* phalanx *(compact body of heavy-armed men in battle formation first developed by the Macedonians)*

phalāric·a -ae *f* **(fal-)** firebrand, fiery missile *(shot by a catapult or thrown by hand)*

Phalar·is -idis *m* a tyrant of Agrigentum on S. coast of Sicily, notorious for the bronze bull in which he roasted his victims *(c. 570–554 B.C.)*

phaler·ae -ārum *fpl* military medals; medallions *(worn by horses on the forehead and chest)*

phalerāt·us -a -um *adj* wearing medals, decorated; ornamental

Phalēr·eus -eī *or* **-eos** *m* Demetrius of Phalerum *(Athenian statesman)*

Phalēric·us -a -um *adj* of Phaleron

Phalēr·um -ī *n* Athenian harbor

phantasm·a -atis *n* phantom, ghost

Pha·ōn -ōnis *f* legendary Lesbian, reputed lover of Sappho

pharetr·a -ae *f* quiver

pharetrāt·us -a -um *adj* carrrying a quiver

Phari·us -a -um *adj* of Pharos, Pharian; *(poet)* Egyptian

pharmaceutri·a -ae *f* witch, sorceress

pharmacopōl·a -ae *m* druggist; *(pej)* quack

Pharnac·ēs -is *m* Pharnaces I *(king of Pontus and grandfather of Mithridates, died c. 169 B.C.)* ‖ Pharnaces II *(son of Mithridates the Great, easily defeated by Caesar at Zela in 47 B.C.)*

Phar·os *or* **Phar·us -ī** *f (m)* Pharos *(island lying off Alexandria);* lighthouse *(built on the E. tip of Pharos by Ptolemy II Philadelphus);* a lighthouse *(in general); (poet)* Egypt

Pharsālic·us -a -um *adj* of Pharsalus

Pharsāli·us -a -um *adj* Pharsalian ‖ *f* Pharsalia *(district of Thessaly)*

Pharsāl·os *or* **Pharsāl·us -ī** *f* town in Thessaly near which Caesar defeated Pompey *(48 B.C.)*

phasēl·us *or* **phasēl·os -ī** *mf* kidney bean; light passenger ship

Phāsiac·us -a -um *adj* of the River Phasis in Colchis; Colchian

phāsiān·a -ae *f* pheasant *(female)*

phāsiān·us -ī *m* pheasant *(male)*

Phāsi·as -ados *adj (fem only)* Colchian **II** *f* Medea

Phās·is -idis *or* **-idos** *m* river in Colchis

phasm·a -atis *n* specter, ghost

Phēgēi·us -a -um *adj* of Phegeus, king of Psophis in Arcadia, the father of Alphesiboea

Phēm·ius -(i)ī *m* minstrel of Ithaca

Phene·us *or* **Phene·os -ī** *m or* **Phene·on -ī** *n* a town and stream with subterranean channels in Arcadia

Pher·ae -ārum *fpl* city in Thessaly, home of Admetus

Pherae·us -a -um *adj* of Pherae

Phereclē·us -a -um *adj* of Phereclus *(the builder of Paris' ship)*

phial·a -ae *f* saucer

Phīdiac·us -a -um *adj* of Phidias

Phīdi·ās -ae *m* Greek sculptor and friend of Pericles *(fl 440 B.C.)*

Philaen·ī -ōrum *mpl* two Carthaginian brothers who agreed to be buried alive to establish the frontier between Carthage and Cyrene

Philamm·ōn -ōnis *m* legendary musician, son of Apollo

philēm·a -atis *n* kiss

Philēm·ō(n) -onis *m* Philemon *(pious rustic who was changed into an oak tree while his wife Baucis was changed into a linden tree)*

Philippēns·is -is -e *adj* of Philippi **II** *mpl* the people of Philippi

Philippē·us -a -um *adj* of Philip II of Macedon *(esp. as epithet of gold coins minted by Philip)*

Philipp·ī -ōrum *mpl* city in Macedonia where Octavian and Antony defeated Brutus and Cassius *(42 B.C.)*

Philippic·ae -ārum *fpl* Philippics *(series of vitriolic speeches directed at Antony by Cicero)*

Philippopol·is -eos *f* city in Thessaly on the right bank of the Hebrus River

Philipp·us -ī *m* name of several kings of Macedon *(esp. Philip II, father of Alexander, c. 382–336 B.C.)*

Philist·us -ī *m* historian, from Syracuse *(d. 356 B.C.)*

philiti·a *or* **phīditi·a -ōrum** *npl* public meals at Sparta

Philoctēt·ēs -ae *m* Greek warrior who was abandoned by the Greek army on the island of Lemnos

philologi·a -ae *f* love of study; study of literature

philolog·us -a -um *adj* learned, scholarly **II** *m* scholar

Philomēl·a -ae *f* daughter of Pandion; she and her sister Procne were changed into nightingales

Phil·ō(n) -ōnis *m* Philo *(Academic philosopher and teacher of Cicero)*

philosoph·a -ae *f* philosopher *(female)*

philosophē *adv* philosophically

philosophi·a -ae *f* philosophy

philosoph·or -ārī -ātus sum *intr* to pursue philosophy; to philosophize, moralize

philosoph·us -a -um *adj* philosophical **II** *m* philosopher

philtr·um -ī *n* love potion

philyr·a -ae *f* inner bark of the lime tree *(from which bands for chaplets were made)*

Philyr·a -ae *f* nymph, the mother of Chiron by Saturn

Philyrēi·us -a -um *adj* of Philyra; of Chiron; **hērōs Philyrēius** Chiron

Philyrid·ēs -is *m* son of Philyra *(i.e., Chiron)*

phīm·us -ī *m* dice box

Phīnēi·us -a -um *adj* of Phineus

Phīn·eūs -ēī *or* **-eos** *m* king of Thrace, plagued by the Harpies

Phīnid·ēs -ae *m* descendant of Phineus

Phlegeth·ōn -ontis *m* river of fire in the lower world

Phlegethont·is -idis *adj (fem only)* of Phlegethon

Phlegr·a -ae *f* a country of Macedonia, later called Pelle *(where the Giants were said to have been struck by lightning in battle with the gods)*

Phlegrae·us -a -um *adj* of Phlegra

Phlegy·ae -ārum *mpl* a people of Thessaly

Phlegy·ās -ae *m* king of the Lapiths, son of Ares, and father of Ixion

Phlī·ūs -ūntis *f* city of N.E. Peloponnesus

phōc·a -ae *or* **phōc·ē -ēs** *f* seal

Phōcae·a -ae *f* Ionian city on the coast of Asia Minor

Phōcaeēns·is -is -e *adj* of Phocaea **II** *mpl* the people of Phocaea

Phōcae·us -a -um *adj* of Phocaea **II** *mpl* the people of Phocaea

Phōcaïc·us *or* **Phōci·us -a -um** *adj* Phocian

Phōc·is -idis *or* **-idos** *f* region of central Greece containing the oracle of Delphi

Phoeb·as -adis *f* prophetess, priestess of Apollo

Phoeb·ē -ēs *f* Phoebe *(moon goddess, the sister of Phoebus, identified with Diana)*; night

Phoebēi·us -a -um *adj* of Phoebus *(as sun-god and as god of prophecy, music, and healing)*; of Aesculapius; **āles Phoebēius**

the raven; **anguis Phoebēius** the snake of Aesculapius
Phoebē·us -a -um *adj* of Phoebus
Phoebigen·a -ae *m* son of Phoebus *(i.e., Aesculapius)*
Phoeb·us -ī *m* Apollo as sun-god; sun
Phoenīc·a -ae *or* **Phoenīc·ē -ēs** *f* Phoenicia
Phoenīc·es -um *mpl* Phoenicians
phoenīcopter·us -ī *m* flamingo
Phoeniss·a -ae *f* Phoenician woman *(esp. Dido)*
Phoen·īx -īcis *or* **-īcos** *m* Phoenician **II** son of Amyntor and companion of Achilles **II** son of Agenor and brother of Cadmus
phoen·ix -icis *or* **-īcos** *m* phoenix *(a bird said to live 500 years and from whose ashes a young phoenix would be born)*
Phol·us -ī *m* name of a Centaur
phōnasc·us -ī *m* voice teacher
Phorc·is -idos *f* daughter of Phorcus; Medusa **II** *fpl* the Graeae
Phorc·us -ī *m* son of Neptune and father of Medusa and the other Gorgons and the Graeae
Phorcȳn·is -idis *or* **-idos** *f* Medusa
Phormi·ō -ōnis *m* Athenian admiral *(died c. 428 B.C.)* **II** Peripatetic philosopher who lectured Hannibal on military science
Phraāt·ēs -ae *m* king of Parthia
phrenēs·is -is *f* frenzy, delirium
phrenētic·us -a -um *adj* frenetic, frantic, delirious
Phrix·us *or* **Phrix·os -ī** *m* Phrixus *(son of Athamas and Nephele and brother of Helle, with whom he fled to Colchis, riding the ram with a golden fleece)*
phronēs·is -is *f* wisdom
Phryg·es -um *mpl* Phrygians
Phrygi·a -ae *f* a country comprising part of the central and W. Asia; *(poet)* Troy
phrygi·ō -ōnis *m* **(fryg-)** embroiderer
Phrygi·us -a -um *adj & mf* Phrygian; Trojan
Phrȳn·ē -ēs *f* Athenian courtesan who offered to rebuild Thebes when it was destroyed by Alexander the Great
Phry·x -gis *or* **-gos** *adj* Phrygian *(often w. reference to Troy or the Trojans)*
Phthī·a -ae *f* home of Achilles in Thessaly
Phthī·as -adis *f* woman from Phthia
Phthīōt·a *or* **Phthīōt·ēs -ae** *m* native of Phthia
phthis·is -is *f* tuberculosis
Phthī·us -a -um *adj* of Phthia
phȳ *interj (to express disdain)* bah!
phylac·a -ae *f* prison
Phylac·ē -ēs *f* city of Thessaly, where Protesilaus was king
Phylacē·is -idos *adj (fem only)* of Phylace, *or* of Phylacus, the founder of Phylace
Phylacēi·us -a -um *adj* of Phylace *or* Phylacus; **coniūnx Phylacēia** Laodamia *(wife of Protesilaus)*
Phylacid·ēs -ae *m* descendant of Phylacus, son of Diomede *(esp. Protesilaus)*
phylarch·us -ī *m* tribal chief, emir
Phyllēi·us -a -um *adj* of the city of Phyllus in Thessaly; **Phyllēius iuvenis** Caeneus
Phyll·is -idis *or* **-idos** *f* daughter of King Sithon of Thrace, who was changed into an almond tree **II** stock female name in poetry
physic·a -ae *or* **physic·ē -ēs** *f* natural science
physicē *adv* scientifically
physic·us -a -um *adj* natural, physical, belonging to natural philosophy *or* physics **II** *m* natural philosopher, physicist **II** *npl* natural science
physiognōm·ōn -onis *m* physiognomist *(one who judges people's character by their appearance)*
physiologi·a -ae *f* natural science
piābil·is -is -e *adj* expiable
piāculār·is -is -e *adj* expiatory; demanding expiatory rites **II** *npl* expiatory sacrifices
piācul·um -ī *n* propitiatory sacrifice, victim; atonement, expiation; remedy; crime, sacrilege; punishment
piām·en -inis *n* atonement
pīc·a -ae *f* magpie, jay
picāri·a -ae *f* place where pitch is made
pice·a -ae *f* pine tree, spruce
Pīc·ēns -entis *adj* Picene, of Picenum
Pīcentīn·us -a -um *adj* of Picenum; of Picentia *(town in S. Campania)*
Pīcēn·um -ī *n* distinct on the Adriatic coast of central Italy
Pīcēn·us -a -um *adj & m* Picene **II** *n see* **Pīcēnum**
pice·us -a -um *adj* made of pitch; pitch-black
pic·ō -āre -āvī -ātus *tr* to tar, coat with pitch
pict·or -ōris *m* painter **II Pictor** Quintus Fabius Pictor *(earliest Roman historian, who wrote a history of Rome in Greek, fl 225 B.C.)*
pictūr·a -ae *f* painting; (art of) painting; embroidery
pictūrāt·us -a -um *adj* painted; embroidered
pict·us -a -um *pp of* **pingō II** *adj* painted; embroidered *(in color);* **tābula picta** a painting
pīc·us -ī *m* woodpecker; griffin **II Pīcus** *(son of Saturn and grandfather of Latinus; Picus was changed by Circe into a woodpecker)*
piē *adv* dutifully; affectionately
Pīeri·a -ae *f* district of S. E. Macedonia
Pīeri·ae -ārum *fpl* the Muses
Pīer·is -idos *f* daughter of Pieros; Muse **II** *fpl* the nine Muses
Pīeri·us -a -um *adj* Pierian; poetic; musical **II** *f see* **Pīeria II** *fpl* the Muses

Pier·os *or* **Pier·us -ī** *m* Pieros *(King of Emathia, or Macedonia, who named his nine daughters after the Muses; they were defeated in a contest with the Muses and were changed into birds)*

piet·ās -ātis *f* sense of responsibility, sense of duty; devotion, piety; *(of gods)* due regard *(for human beings);* kindness, tenderness; loyalty to the gods and country; *(w dat or* **adversus** *or* **ergā** *or* **in** *+ acc)* respect for, devotion to, loyalty to

pi·ger -gra -grum *adj* apathetic, slow, lazy; reluctant, unwilling; numbing *(cold);* slow-moving, tedious *(war, etc.);* backward, slow, dull

pig·et -ēre -uit *or* **-itum est** *v impers* it irks, pains, annoys; *(w. gen of cause of feeling), e.g.:* **piget stultitiae meae** I am irked by my own foolishness; *(w. inf), e.g.:* **illa mē composuisse piget** I regret having written those verses

pigmentār·ius -(i)ī *m* paint dealer

pigment·um -ī *n* pigment, paint, color; coloring *(of style)*

pignerāt·or -ōris *m* mortgagee

pigner·ō -āre -āvī -ātus *tr* to mortgage; to pawn; *(fig)* to pledge

pigner·or -ārī -ātus sum *tr* to take as a pledge, accept in good faith; to lay claim to; to assure

pign·us -eris *or* **-oris** *n* pledge, security, guarantee; hostage; mortgage; income from mortgages; wager, stake; *(fig)* pledge, assurance ‖ *npl* children

pigrē *adv* slowly, sluggishly

pigriti·a -ae *or* **pigriti·ēs -ēī** *f* sluggishness, laziness

pigr·ō -āre -āvī *or* **pigr·ōr -ārī** *intr* to be slow, be sluggish, be lazy

pīl·a -ae *f (vessel for pounding)* mortar; pillar; pier; funerary monument *(w. cavity for mortal remains)*

pil·a -ae *f* ball; ball game; globe; ballot *(used by jury);* **mea pila est** the ball is mine, I've won; **pilā lūdere** to play ball

pīlān·us -ī *m* soldier in the third rank in battle

pīlāt·us -a -um *adj* armed with javelin

Pīlāt·us -ī *m* Pontius Pilate *(prefect of Judea, A.D. 26–36)*

pīlent·um -ī *n* ladies' carriage

pilleāt·us -a -um *adj* **(pīl-)** wearing a felt skullcap *(as a symbol of freed status)*

pilleol·us -ī *m* (small felt) skullcap

pille·um -ī *n or* **pille·us -ī** *m or* **pīle·um -ī** *n* felt cap *or* hat *(worn by Romans at festivals, esp. at the Saturnalia, and given to a slave when freed as a symbol of his freedom);* freedom

pilōs·us -a -um *adj* hairy

pīl·um -ī *n* javelin

Pīlumn·us -ī *m* primitive Italic deity

pīl·us -ī *m* maniple *or* company of the triarii; company of veteran reserves; **prīmī pīlī centuriō** chief centurion of a legion; **prīmus pīlus** chief centurion *(of the triarii and therefore of the legion)*

pil·us -ī *n* hair; **nōn pilī facere** to not care a whit for

Pi(m)plē(i)·us -a -um *adj* of Pimpla ‖ *f* the spring at Pimpla

Pimpl·a -ae *f* town and spring in Pieria sacred to the Muses

Pimplē·a -ae *or* **Pi(m)plē·is -idis** *or* **idos** *f* Muse

pīn·a -ae *f* a bivalve shellfish

pinacothēc·a -ae *f* art gallery

Pīnāri·us -a -um *adj* name of a patrician clan at Rome, concerned with the cult of Hercules

Pindaric·us -a -um *adj* Pindaric

Pindar·us -ī *m* Pindar *(Greek lyric poet from Thebes in Boeotia, 519–438 B.C.)*

Pind·us -ī *m* mountain range separating Thessaly from Macedonia, connected with the Muses

pīnēt·um -ī *n* pine forest

pīne·us -a -um *adj* pine, of pine

pingō pingere pīnxī pictus *tr* to draw, paint; to embroider; to depict, represent, portray; to stain, color; to decorate; *(rhet)* to embellish

pingu·e -is *n* fat

pinguēsc·ō -ere *intr* to get fat; to become fertile

pingu·is -is -e *adj* fat; fatty, greasy; *(of lamps)* full of oil; *(of torches)* full of pitch; juicy; full-bodied *(wine);* rich, full *(sound);* rich, fertile *(land);* fat, sleek *(cattle);* thick *(in dimension);* strong *(words); (of altars)* caked with fat and blood; dense; stupid, dull; clumsy *(writing);* quiet, comfortable *(life, home, retreat);* **crūra lutō pinguia** legs caked with mud

pīnif·er *or* **pīnig·er -era -erum** *adj* pine-producing, pine-covered

pinn·a -ae *f* feather; wing; flight; fin; feathered arrow; pinnacle, battlement

pinnāt·us -a -um *adj* feathered, winged

pinnig·er -era -erum *adj* winged; feathered; having fins

pinnip·ēs -edis *adj* wing-footed

pinnipot·ēns -entis *adj* able to fly

pinnirap·us -ī *m* crest-snatcher *(gladiator who tried to get the crest of his opponent's helmet)*

pinnul·a -ae *f* little wing

pīnotēr·ēs -ae *m* hermit crab

pīnsit·ō -āre *tr* to pound (continually)

pīns·ō -ere pīnsī *or* **pīnsuī pīnsitus (pīs-)** to beat; to pound; **flāgrō pīnsere** to scourge, whip

pīn·us -ūs *or* **-ī** *f* pine tree, fir tree; pine forest; ship; torch; wreath of pine

pi·ō -āre -āvī -ātus *tr* to appease by sacrifice, propitiate; to honor with religious rites, worship; to purify with religious rites; to atone for, expiate; to avert
pip·er -eris *n* pepper
pīpil·ō -āre *intr* to chirp
pipinn·a -ae *f* childish term for the penis
pīpi·ō -āre *intr* to chirp
pīpul·um -ī *n or* **pīpul·us -ī** *m* shrieking, yelling
Pīrae·eus *or* **Pīrae·us -ī** *m or* **Pīrae·a -ōrum** *npl* Piraeus *(principal harbor of Athens)*
Pīrae·us -a -um *adj* of Piraeus ‖ *mpl* inhabitants of Piraeus
pīrāt·a -ae *m* pirate
pīrātic·us -a -um *adj* pirate ‖ *f* piracy; **pīrāticam facere** to practice piracy
Pīrēn·ē -ēs *or* **Pīrēn·a -ae** *f* Pirene *(spring on the citadel of Corinth near which Bellerophon caught Pegasus)*
Pīrēn·is -idos *adj (fem only)* of the spring of Pirene
Pīritho·üs -ī *m* son of Ixion and king of the Lapiths
pir·um -ī *n* pear
pir·us -ī *f* pear tree
Pīs·a -ae *f or* **Pīs·ae -ārum** *fpl* Pisa *(capital of Pisatis in Elis on the Alpheus River)*
Pīs·ae -ārum *fpl* Pisa *(ancient city of N. Etruria, alleged to have been founded by the people of Greek Pisa)*
Pīsae·us -a -um *adj* of Pisa ‖ *f* Hippodamia
Pīsān·us -a -um *adj* of Pisa *(in Etruria)*
Pisaur·um -ī *n* city in Umbria on the Adriatic coast *(modern Pisaro)*
piscāri·us -a -um *adj* fish; of fishing; **forum piscārium** fish market
piscāt·or -ōris *m* fisherman; fishmonger
piscātōri·us -a -um *adj* fishing; fish
piscāt·us -ūs *m* fishing; fish *(as food; (fig)* good haul
piscicul·us -ī *m (lit & fig)* little fish
piscīn·a -ae *f* fish pond; swimming pool
piscīnār·ius -(i)ī *m* person fond of swimming pools *or* of fish ponds
pisc·is -is *m* fish ‖ **Piscēs** *mpl (astr)* Pisces *(constellation)*
pisc·or -ārī -ātus sum *intr* to fish
piscōs·us -a -um *adj* full of fish
pisculent·us -a -um *adj* well-stocked with fish
Pisid·a -ae *m* Pisidian *(inhabitant of Pisidia, referred to in contempt for the alleged addiction of the Pisidians to augury)*
Pisidi·a -ae *f* region in S. Asia Minor
Pīsistratid·ae -ārum *mpl* sons of Pisistratus *(Hippias & Hipparchus)*
Pīsistrat·us -ī *m* enlightened tyrant of Athens *(560–527 B.C.)*
Pīs·ō -ōnis *m* Roman family name *(cognomen)* of the Calpurnian clan ‖ Gnaeus Calpurnius Piso *(consul 7 B.C., accused of the murder of Germanicus in A.D. 19)* ‖ Gaius Calpurnius Piso *(alleged leader of the conspiracy against Nero in A.D. 65)*
pīsō *see* **pīnsō**
pīstill·um -ī *n or* **pīstill·us -ī** *m* pestle
pīst·or -ōris *m* miller; baker
Pistōriēns·is -is -e *adj* of Pistorium *(town in Etruria)*
pīstōri·us -a -um *adj* baker's; **opus pīstōrium** pastry
pīstrill·a -ae *f* small mill; small bakery
pīstrīn·a -ae *f* flour mill; bakery
pīstrīnēns·is -is -e *adj* of *or* belonging to a bakery
pīstrīn·um -ī *n* flour mill; bakery; drudgery
pistr·is -is *or* **pistr·īx -īcis** *f* sea monster; whale, shark; swift ship; *(astr)* the Whale *(constellation)*
pīs·um -ī *n* pea
pithēc·ium -(i)ī *n* little monkey
Pitthē·is -idos *f* daughter of Pittheus *(i.e., Aethra)*
Pitth·eus -eī *or* **-eos** *m* king of Troezen and father of Aethra, the mother of Theseus
Pitthē·us *or* **Pitthēi·us -a -um** *adj* of Pittheus
pītuīt·a -ae *f* phlegm; rheum; head cold
pītuītōs·us -a -um *adj* full of phlegm, phlegmatic
pity·ōn -ōnis *m* woods of pine trees
pi·us -a -um *adj* conscientious, dutiful; god-fearing, godly, holy; fatherly, motherly, brotherly, sisterly; affectionate; patriotic; good; sacred, holy *(objects connected with religion)*
pix picis *f* pitch, tar ‖ *fpl* chunks of pitch
plācābil·is -is -e *adj* easily appeased; pacifying, appeasing
plācābilit·ās -ātis *f* readiness to forgive, conciliatory disposition
plācām·en -inis *n* means of appeasing, peace-offering
plācāment·um -ī *n* means of appeasing, peace-offering
plācātē *adv* calmly, quietly
plācāti·ō -ōnis *f* pacifying, propitiating
plācāt·us -a -um *adj* calm, quiet; appeased, reconciled
plac·ēns -entis *adj* pleasing
placent·a -ae *f* flat cake
placenti·a -ae *f* agreeableness
Placenti·a -ae *f* town on the river Po *(modern Piacenza)*
plac·eō -ēre -uī -itum *intr (w. dat)* to please, satisfy, give pleasure to, be acceptable to; **sibi placēre** to be pleased with oneself ‖ *v impers* it seems right, seems proper; it is settled, is agreed; it is resolved, is decided; **eīs placitum est ut cōnsīderārent** they decided to consider; **senātuī placuit** the senate decided
placidē *adv* calmly, gently, quietly

placid·us -a -um *adj* calm; gentle; quiet, peaceful; tame *(animal)*
placit·ō -āre *intr* to be very pleasing
placit·us -a -um *adj* pleasing, acceptable; agreed upon ‖ *n* principle, belief, tenet; **ultrā placitum laudāre** to praise excessively
plāc·ō -āre -āvī -ātus *tr* to calm, quiet; to appease; to reconcile
plāg·a -ae *f* blow; wound, gash, welt; *(fig)* blow
plag·a -ae *f* region, tract, zone; hunting net; mesh of a net; curtain; *(fig)* trap
plagiār·ius -(i)ī *m* plunderer; kidnapper; plagiarist
plāgig·er -era -erum *adj* covered with welts
plāgigerul·us -a -um *adj* covered with welts
plāgipatid·ēs -ae *m* whipping boy
plāgōs·us -a -um *adj* quick to use the rod
plagul·a -ae *f* curtain
plagūsi·a -ae *f* a kind of shellfish
plānctus *pp of* **plangō**
plānct·us -ūs *m* beating
plānē *adv* clearly, distinctly; legibly; completely, quite; certainly, to be sure
plan·gō -gere plānxī plānctus *tr* to strike, beat; to beat *(head, breast as sign of grief);* to lament, bewail; *(fig)* to wring the hands ‖ *pass* to beat one's breast; *(of bird)* to flap its wings ‖ *intr* to wail
plang·or -ōris *m* striking, beating; beating of the breast, wailing
plāniloqu·us -a -um *adj* outspoken
plānip·ēs -edis *m* barefooted actor *(in the role of a slave)*
plānit·ās -ātis *f* distinctness
plāniti·ēs -ēī *or* **plāniti·a -ae** *f* flat surface, level ground, plain
plant·a -ae *f* sprout, shoot, young plant, seedling; *(anat)* sole
plantār·ia -ium *npl* cuttings, slips
plantār·ium -(i)ī *n* seedbed *(for starting seedlings)*
plān·us -a -um *adj* flat, level, even; plain, clear ‖ *n* level ground; plain; **dē plānō** easily; **ē plānō** out of court
plan·us -ī *m* tramp; con man
plasm·a -atis *n* phoney accent
Platae·ae -ārum *fpl* Plataea *(town in Boeotia where the Greeks defeated the Persians in 479 B.C.)*
Plataeēns·is -is -e *adj* of Plataea ‖ *mpl* Plataeans
platale·a -ae *f* spoonbill *(waterfowl)*
platan·ōn -ōnis *m* grove of plane trees
platan·us -ī *or* **-ūs** *f* plane tree
plate·a *or* **platē·a -ae** *f* street
Plat·ō(n) -ōnis *m* Plato *(Greek philosopher, 429–348 B.C.)*
Platōnic·us -a -um *adj* Platonic ‖ *mpl* Platonists
plau·dō -dere -sī -sus *tr* **(plōd-)** to slap, clap, beat ‖ *intr* to clap, beat, flap; applaud; *(w. dat)* to applaud, approve of; **ālīs plaudere** to flap the wings; **manibus plaudere** to clap the hands
plausibil·is -is -e *adj* deserving of applause
plaus·or *or* **plōs·or -ōris** *m* applauder
plaustr·um -ī *n* **(plos-)** wagon, cart; **plaustrum percellere** *(fig)* to upset the applecart ‖ **Plaustrum** *(astr)* the Great Bear *(constellation)*
plausus *pp of* **plaudō**
plaus·us -ūs *m* clapping, flapping; applause
Plautīn·us -a -um *adj* of Plautus
Plauti·us -a -um *adj* of Plautus
Plaut·us -ī *m* Plautus *(Titus Maccius Plautus, Roman writer of comedies, born in Umbria, c. 254–184 B.C.)*
plēbēcul·a -ae *f* rabble
plēbēi·us -a -um *adj* plebeian, of the common people; common, low, vulgar ‖ *m* plebeian
plēbicol·a -ae *m* democrat; demagogue
plēbis(s)cīt·um -ī *n* decree of the assembly of the plebeians
plēbs *or* **plēps plēbis** *or* **plēb·ēs -ēī** *f* the plebeians, common people; the masses, proletariat
plectil·is -is -e *adj* plaited, braided
plēct·ō -ere *tr* to beat; to punish
plectō plectere plexī *or* **plexuī plexus** *tr* to plait, braid
plēctr·um -ī *n* plectrum; *(fig)* lyre
Plēï·as -adis *or* **-ados** *f* Pleiad ‖ *fpl* Pleiades *(seven daughters of Atlas and Pleione, who were placed among the stars)*
Plēïon·ē -ēs *f* daughter of Oceanus and Tethys, wife of Atlas, and mother of the Pleiades
Plēmyr·ium -(i)ī *n* headland at the S. end of the Bay of Syracuse
plēnē *adv* fully, completely
plēn·us -a -um *adj* full; stout, plump; pregnant; filled, satisfied, full; packed *(street, theater, etc.);* strong, loud *(voice);* full-length, unabridged, uncontracted; complete, entire; plentiful; advanced *(years);* complete; *(w. abl or gen)* full of
ple·ō -ēre *tr* to fill
plērumque *adv* generally, mostly, for the most part; often, frequently
plēr·usque -aque -umque *adj* a very great part of, the greater part of, most; a good many; **plērīque omnēs** nearly all ‖ *mpl* most people, the majority ‖ *n* the greatest part
Pleur·ōn -ōnis *f* a city in Aetolia
-pl·ex -icis *adj suf usu., formed from numerals, equivalent to the English "-fold," e.g.:* **centumplex** hundredfold
plex·us -a -um *pp of* **plectō** ‖ *adj* plaited

plicātr·īx -īcis *f* woman who folds clothes, folder

plic·ō -āre -āvī *or* **-uī -ātus** *or* **-itus** *tr* to fold, wind, coil up

Plīn·ius -(i)ī *m* Pliny the Elder *(Gaius Plinius Secundus, author of a work on natural history, d.* A.D. *79)* ‖ Pliny the Younger *(Gaius Plinius Caecilius Secundus (his nephew), author of Letters and Panegyric to Trajan,* A.D. *61–114)*

plīpi·ō -āre *intr (of a hawk)* to caw

plōdō *see* **plaudō**

plōrābil·is -is -e *adj* dismal

plōrātill·us -a -um *adj* tearful

plōrāt·or -ōris *m* mourner

plōrāt·us -ūs *m* wailing, crying

plōr·ō -āre -āvī -ātus *tr* to cry over ‖ *intr* to cry aloud, wail

plōstell·um -ī *n* small cart

plōstr·um -ī *n* wagon

ploxen·um -ī *n* **(-xin-)** wagon body

pluit pluere pluit *v impers (tr)* it is raining *(stones, blood, etc.)* ‖ *v impers (intr)* it is raining; *(w. abl)* it is raining *(stones, etc.);* **sanguine pluit** it rained blood

plūm·a -ae *f* down, soft feather; *(collectively)* down, feathers

plūmātil·e -is *n* dress embroidered with feathers

plūmāt·us -a -um *adj* covered with feathers

plumbe·us -a -um *adj* lead, of lead, leaden; oppressive *(weather);* dull *(blade);* cheap *(wine);* stupid

plumb·um -ī *n* lead; pellet *(for a sling);* pipe; ruler *(for drawing lines);* **plumbum album** *(or* **candidum)** tin

plūme·us -a -um *adj* downy; filled with down; like feathers

plūmip·ēs -edis *adj* with feathered feet

plūm·ō -āre -āvī -ātum *tr* to cause to be covered with feathers

plūmōs·us -a -um *adj* feathered, covered with feathers; *(fig)* feathery

plūrāl·is -is -e *adj (gram)* plural

plūrāliter *adv (gram)* in the plural

plūr·ēs -ēs -a *adj* more; several; too many; **plūribus (verbīs)** at great length, in greater detail ‖ *mpl* most people, the majority; the dead, "the majority" ‖ *npl* more things

plūrifāriam *adv* extensively, in many places

plūrimum *adv* **(-rum-)** very much, especially, commonly, generally, mostly; **plūrimum valēre** to be most powerful, have the greatest influence

plūrim·us -a -um *(superl of* **multus)** *adj* **(-rum-)** many a; most; very much; very many; very great, very intense; very powerful, very violent; **plūrimam salūtem dare** to send warmest greetings ‖ *mpl* most people, a very great number of people ‖ *n* a great deal; **plūrimī facere** to think very highly of, think a great deal of; **plūrimī vēndere** to sell at a very high price; **quam plūrimō vēndere** to sell at the highest possible price; **quam plūrimum** as much as possible

plūs *adv* more; **multō plūs** much more; **plūs minus** more or less; **paulō plūs** a little more

plūs plūris *(comp of* **multus)** *adj* more ‖ *n* more, too much; **plūs animī** more courage; **plūs nimiō** much too much; **plūs plūsque** more and more; **plūris esse** *(gen of value)* to be of more value, be worth more, be higher, be dearer; **plūris aestimāre** *(or* **facere** *of* **putāre** *or* **habēre)** to regard more highly, think more highly of ‖ *npl* more things; **quid plūra?** why say more?, in short, needless to say

plūscul·us -a -um *adj* a little more, somewhat more ‖ *n* a little more

plute·us -ī *m or* **plute·um -ī** *n* barrier, screen; low wall; parapet; headboard *or* footboard of bed *or* couch; *(fig)* couch; *(fig)* dining couch; bier; lectern; bookcase; *(mil)* movable mantlet *or* shed used to protect soldiers in siege works

Plūt·ō(n) -ōnis *m* Pluto *(king of the lower world, husband of Proserpina, and brother of Jupiter and Neptune)*

Plūtōni·us -a -um *adj* of Pluto

pluvi·a -ae *f* rain

pluviāl·is -is -e *adj* rain, of rain, rainy

pluvi·us -a -um *adj* rain, of rain, rainy; **pluvia aqua** rain water; **pluvius arcus** rainbow ‖ *f* rain

pōcill·um -ī *n* small drinking cup

pōc(u)l·um -ī *n* drinking cup; drink, draft; **pōculum (dūcere** *or* **exhaurīre)** to drain a cup

poda·ger -gra -grum *adj* suffering from sore feet

podagr·a -ae *f* arthritis

podagrōs·us -a -um *adj* arthritic

Podalīri·us -ī *m* legendary physician, son of Aesculapius

pōd·ex -icis *m (sl)* ass, behind

pod·ium -(i)ī *n* balcony; box seat *(for the emperor)*

Poeantiad·ēs -is *m* son of Poeas, Philoctetes

Poeanti·us -a -um *adj* of Poeas ‖ *m* Philoctetes

Poe·ās *or* **Poe·āns -antis** *m* father of

poēm·a -atis *n (dat & abl pl:* **poēmātibus** *or* **poēmatīs)** poem; poetry

poēmat·ium -(i)ī *n* short poem

poen·a -ae *f* punishment; penalty, fine; compensation, recompense, retribution, satisfaction; hardship, loss, pain; *(in games)* penalty; **poenam** *(or* **poenās)** **dare** *(or* **dēpendere, pendere, persol-**

vere, reddere, solvere, suscipere, sufferre) to pay the penalty; **poenam** *(or* **poenās) capere** *(or* **exigere, persequī, petere, repetere, repōscere)** to exact a penalty, demand satisfaction; **poena mortis** death penalty
Poenici·us -a -um *adj* Punic, Carthaginian
Poenīn·ī -ōrum *mpl* the Pennine Alps *(from Mont Blanc to Monte Rosa)*
poeniō *see* **pūniō**
Poenul·us -ī *m* little Phoenician *(i.e., Zeno the Stoic)*
Poen·us -a -um *adj* Phoenician; Carthaginian **II** *m* Carthaginian *(esp. Hannibal)*
poēs·is -is *f* art of poetry; poetry, poems
poēt·a -ae *m* poet; playwright; *(fig)* person of great skill, artist
poētic·a -ae *or* **poētic·ē -ēs** *f* art of poetry; poetics
poēticē *adv* poetically
poētic·us -a -um *adj* poetic
poētri·a -ae *f* poetess
poētr·is -idis *or* **-idos** *f* poetess
pol *interj* by Pollux!; Gads!; really, indeed; **certō pol** most assuredly
Polem·ōn -ōnis *m* Platonic philosopher, disciple of Xenocrates and teacher of Zeno
Polemōnē·us -a -um *adj* professing the philosophy of Polemon
polent·a -ae *f* pearl barley
polentāri·us -a -um *adj* caused by eating barley
pol·iō -īre -īvī *or* **-iī -ītus** *tr* to polish; to smooth; *(fig)* to polish
polītē *adv* in a polished manner, with taste, smoothly, elegantly
polītic·us -a -um *adj* political
polīt·us -a -um *adj (lit & fig)* polished, smooth
poll·en -inis *n or* **poll·is -inis** *mf* flour
poll·ēns -entis *adj* strong, powerful
pollenti·a -ae *f* might, power
poll·eō -ēre *intr* to be strong, be powerful; to be capable, be able; to have influence; *(of medicines)* to be efficacious; **in rē pūblicā plūrimum pollēre** to have tremendous influence in politics
poll·ex -icis *m* thumb; big toe; **pollicem premere** to press the thumb *(against the index finger to indicate approval);* **pollicem vertere** to turn the thumb down *(to indicate disapproval)*
pollic·eor -ērī -itus sum *tr* to promise
pollicitāti·ō -ōnis *f* promise
pollicit·or -ārī -ātus sum *tr* to keep promising
pollicit·us -a -um *pp of* **polliceor II** *n* promise
pollināri·us -a -um *adj* flour
pollīnct·or -ōris *m* mortician, undertaker
pol·lingō -lingere -līnxī -līnctus *tr* to prepare *(a corpse),* lay out
Polli·ō -ōnis *m* Gaius Asinius Pollio *(orator, poet, historian, and patron of literature, 76 B.C.–A.D. 4)*
poll·is -inis *mf* (fine) flour
pol·lūceō -lūcēre -lūxī -lūctus *tr* to offer up *(as a sacrifice);* to serve *(food, a meal)*
pollūcibiliter *adv* sumptuously
pollūctūr·a -ae *f* sumptuous dinner
pol·luō -luere -luī -lūtus *tr* to pollute; to violate; to dirty, soil
Poll·ūx *or rarely* **Poll·ūcēs -ūcis** *m* Pollux *(son of Tyndareus and Leda, twin brother of Castor, and patron of boxers)*
pol·us -ī *m* pole *(either end of the axis on which the heavenly spheres were believed to revolve);* star; sky; heaven; **polus austrālis** South Pole; **polus superior** North Pole
Polyb·ius -iī *m* Greek historian and friend of Scipio Aemilianus *(c. 203–120 B.C.)*
Polyclīt·us -ī *m* **(-clēt-)** Polycletus *(Greek sculptor of Argos, fl c. 452–412 B.C.)*
Polycrat·ēs -is *m* ruler of Samos in the 6th cent. B.C., patron of the arts and close friend of Anacreon
Polydam·ās -antos *m* **(Pōl-)** Trojan warrior, son of Panthus and friend of Hector
Polydōrē·us -a -um *adj* of Polydorus
Polydōr·us -ī *m* youngest son of Priam and Hecuba, murdered by Polymester, king of Thrace
Polyhymni·a -ae *f* one of the Muses; Muse of lyric poetry
Polymēst·ōr -oris *m* king of Thracian Chersonese, husband of Ilione (the daughter of Priam), and murderer of Polydorus
Polynīc·ēs -is *m* son of Oedipus and Jocasta, and brother of Eteocles, Antigone, and Ismene, and leader of the Seven against Thebes
Polyphēm·us -ī *m* son of Neptune and one of the Cyclopes
pōlyp·us -ī *m* polyp *(sea animal; tumor)*
Polyxen·a -ae *or* **Polyxen·ē -ēs** *f* Polyxena *(daughter of Priam and Hecuba whom Pyrrhus, son of Achilles, sacrificed at his father's tomb)*
Polyxeni·us -a -um *adj* of Polyxena
pōmāri·us -a -um *adj* fruit, of fruit trees **II** *m* fruit vendor **II** *n* orchard
pōmēr·ium -(i)ī *n* **(-moer-)** space kept free of buildings inside and outside a city wall
pōmif·er -era -erum *adj* fruit-bearing
Pōmōn·a -ae *f* Roman goddess of fruit
pōmōs·us -a -um *adj* loaded with fruit
pomp·a -ae *f* solemn procession; parade; retinue; pomp, ostentation
Pompēï·a *or* **Pompēi·a -ae** *f* Julius Caesar's second wife, the daughter of Quintus Pompeius Rufus *(consul in 88 B.C.)* **II** a daughter of Pompey, who married Faustus Cornelius Sulla

Pompēiān·us -a -um *adj* Pompeian ‖ *mpl* inhabitants of Pompeii ‖ soldiers *or* followers of Pompey

Pompēi·i -ōrum *mpl* city about 10 miles S. of Naples, destroyed by Vesuvius in A.D. 79

Pompēĭ·us -ī *m* Gnaeus Pompeius Strabo *(father of the the triumvir)* ‖ Pompey the Great *(Gnaeus Pompeius Magnus, Roman general and politician, 106–48 B.C.)* ‖ Sextus Pompeius Magnus *(his younger son, killed in 35 B.C.)*

Pompil·ius -(i)ī *m* Numa Pompilius *(second king of Rome and traditional founder of Roman state religion)*

pompil·us -ī *m* pilot-fish

Pompōniān·us -a -um *adj* of a member of the Pomponian clan

Pompōn·ius -(i)ī *m* Lucius Pomponius *(of Bononia, a writer of Atellan farces (c. 109–32 B.C.)* ‖ Titus Pomponius Atticus *(the friend and correspondent of Cicero (109–32 B.C.)* ‖ Publius Pomponius Secundus *(writer of dramatic verse)*

Pomptīn·us -a -um *adj* Pomptine; **Pomptīnae palūdēs** Pomptine Marshes *(in Latium near the seacoast)*

pōm·um -ī *n* fruit; fruit tree

pōm·us -ī *f* fruit tree

ponder·ō -āre -āvī -ātus *tr (lit & fig)* to weigh; to ponder, consider

ponderōs·us -a -um *adj* weighty, massive; *(fig)* dignified

pondō *indecl n* pound, pounds; *(in advl sense)* in weight; *(where specific number of pounds is given, the numeral is usually expressed in the neuter:* **argentī pondō bīna sēlībrās in mīlitem praestāre** to offer two and a half pounds of silver per soldier); **aurī quīnque pondō** five pounds of gold; **duo pondō saxum** a two-pound rock; **quot pondō tēd esse cēnsēs nūdum?** how many pounds do you think you weigh nude?

pond·us -eris *n* weight; mass; burden; importance; stability of character ‖ *npl* balance, equilibrium

pōne *adv* behind, after, back ‖ *prep (w. acc)* behind; **ī tū pōne mē** walk behind me

pōnō pōnere posuī pos(i)tus *tr* to put, set, place; to put down, put aside; to pitch *(camp);* to station, post *(troops);* to lay *(foundation, keel);* to build, found *(town, colony, building);* to plant *(tree); (of trees)* to shed leaves; to serve *(food);* to stage *(a play);* to lay down *(arms);* to take off *(clothes, ornaments);* to cut *(beard, hair, fingernails);* to arrange, smooth *(the hair);* to take *(steps);* to deposit *(money);* to bet *(money);* to lend *(money)* at interest; to set aside, store; to lay out, spend *(time, effort, etc.);* to file *(legal claim);* to lay down *(rule, law);* to stage *(a play);* to yield up *(life, breath);* to get rid of, drop; to esteem, value; to classify; to appoint *(to specific position);* to calm *(sea);* to lay *(egg);* to fix *(penalty, price);* to offer *(award);* to depict *(in art);* to assume, suppose; to quote, cite; to state *(in writing or speech);* to pose, ask *(question);* to spend *(time, money, energy);* to give as security; to give *(a name);* to lay out for burial; *(w.* **in** + *abl)* to base *or* stake *(upon);* **fīnem pōnere** *(w. dat)* to put an end to; **genū pōnere** to kneel down; **in locō** *(or* **locō** *or* **in numerō) pōnere** to place in a class *or* category; **in mediō pōnere** to make accessible to all; **modum pōnere** *(w. dat)* to limit, set bounds to ‖ *intr (of snow)* to fall; *(of wind)* to drop, stop; to be neutral

pōn·s -tis *m* bridge; gangway; drawbridge; deck; **pōns in flūmine** a bridge over the river

Ponti·ae -ārum *fpl* island in the Tuscan Sea S. of Circeii

ponticul·us -ī *m* small bridge

Pontic·us -a -um *adj* Pontic, of Pontus *(region around the Black Sea);* **mare Ponticum** Black Sea; **nux Pontica** hazelnut; **rādīx Pontica** rhubarb

pontif·ex -icis *m* **(-tuf-)** pontiff, pontifex, priest *(one of a board of 15);* **pontifex maximus** chief pontiff

pontificāl·is -is -e *adj* pontifical

pontificāt·us -ūs *m* pontificate

pontific·us -a -um *adj* pontifical

pont·ō -ōnis *m* ferry

Pont·us -ī *m* Euxine *or* Black Sea; region around the Black Sea ‖ Pontus *(kingdom of Mithridates, between Bithynia and Armenia, after 63 B.C. a Roman province)*

pont·us -ī *m* sea; sea water

pop·a -ae *m* priest's assistant *(who slew the victim)*

popan·um -ī *n* sacrificial cake

popell·us -ī *m* rabble, mob

popīn·a -ae *f* low-class restaurant, dive; food sold at a low-class restaurant

popīn·ō -ōnis *m* diner at a low-class restaurant

popl·es -itis *m* hollow of the knee; knee; **duplicātō poplite** on bended knee; **contentō poplite** with a stiff knee

Pōplicola *see* **Pūblicola**

popōscī *perf of* **pōscō**

poppysm·a -atis *n* smacking of the lips *(to indicate satisfaction)*

populābil·is -is -e *adj* destructible

populābund·us -a -um *adj* ravaging

populār·is -is -e *adj* of the people, people's; approved by the people, popular; favoring the people, democratic; demagogic; of the same country, native; common, coarse ‖ *mf* fellow countryman; party member; fellow member, associate;

(w. gen) partner *or* associate in ‖ *mpl* people's party, democrats ‖ *npl* general-admission seats

populārit·ās -ātis *f* courting popular favor; fellow citizenship

populāriter *adv* like the people; like a demagogue, to win popular favor; **populāriter loquī** to use slang

populāti·ō -ōnis *f* ravaging

populāt·or -ōris *m,* **populātr·īx -īcis** *f* ravager, destroyer

populāt·us -ūs *m* devastation

pōpule·us -a -um *adj* of poplars, poplar

pōpulif·er -era -erum *adj* poplar-bearing

pōpuln(e)us -a -um *adj* of poplar

popul·ō -āre -āvī -ātus *or* **popul·or -ārī -ātus sum** *tr* to ravage, devastate, lay waste; *(fig)* to pillage, ruin, spoil

pōpul·us -ī *f* poplar tree

popul·us -ī *m* the people *(as political community);* nation; public, crowd; citizens *(as opposed to soldiers),* civilians; region, district

por- *pref* giving the sense of "forth," *e.g.:* **portendō** to stretch forth

porc·a -ae *f* sow

porcell·a -ae *f* little sow, suckling pig

porcell·us -ī *m* little hog, suckling pig

Porci·a -ae *f* daughter of Cato Uticensis, married first to Marcus Bibulus, consul in 59 B.C., and afterwards to Marcus Brutus, the assassin of Julius Caesar

porcīnār·ius -(i)ī *m* pork seller

porcīn·us -a -um *adj* hog's, pig's ‖ *f* pork

Porc·ius -(i)ī *m* Cato *(Marcus Porcius Cato the Censor 235–149 B.C.)* ‖ Cato Uticensis *(Marcus Porcius Cato Uticensis (95–46 B.C.)*

porcul·a *or* **porculēn·a -ae** *f* little sow

porcul·us -ī *m* little pig

porc·us -ī *m* pig, hog

porgō *see* **porrigō**

porphyrētic·us -a -um *adj* made of porphyry *(a purple-streaked marble)*

porphyri·ō -ōnis *f* type of waterfowl

Porphyri·ōn -ōnis *m* one of the Giants who fought against the gods

Porphyr·ius -(i)i *m* Porphyry *(Neo-Platonic philosopher, born A.D. 233, who edited the works of Plotinus)*

porrēcti·ō -ōnis *f* extending, stretching out

porrēct·us -a -um *pp of* **porrigō** *and* **porriciō** ‖ *adj* stretched out, extended, extensive, long; protracted; laid out, dead; *(fig)* wide-spread ‖ *npl* offerings

por·riciō -ricere -rēxī -rēctus *tr* to offer up; **inter caesa et porrēcta** *(prov)* at the last moment, at the eleventh hour *(literally, between the slaughtering and the offering)*

porrīg·ō -inis *f* dandruff

por·rigō -rigere -rēxī -rēctus *tr* to reach out, stretch out, extend; to stretch out *(in sleep or death);* to offer, present, hand; to lengthen *(a syllable)* ‖ *refl & pass* to extend

Porrim·a -ae *f* cult name of the birth-goddess Antevorta

porrō *adv* forwards; farther on, on; far off, at a distance; long ago; in the future, hereafter; again, in turn; next, furthermore, moreover, on the other hand

porr·um -ī *n or* **porr·us -ī** *m* leek; chive

Porsenn·a *or* **Porsēn·a** *or* **Porsinn·a -ae** *m* Lars Porsen(n)a *(king of Clusium in Etruria who sided with Tarquin in a war against Rome)*

port·a -ae *f* city-gate; gate; entrance; outlet; camp-gate *(of which there were always four:* **praetōria, prīncipālis, decumānus, quaestōria)**

portāti·ō -ōnis *f* carrying

porten·dō -dere -dī -tus *tr* to indicate, foretell, portend, predict

portentific·us -a -um *adj* abnormal

portentōs·us -a -um *adj* abnormal, unnatural; monstrous

portent·um -ī *n* portent, omen, sign; monstrosity, monster; fantasy, far-fetched fiction; *(as term of contempt)* monster

portentus *pp of* **portendō**

porthm·eūs -eī *or* **-eōs** *m* ferryman *(i.e., Charon)*

porticul·a -ae *f* small portico

portic·us -ūs *f* portico, colonnade; *(mil)* gallery *(formed by placing vineae end to end);* Stoicism

porti·ō -ōnis *f* portion, share; ratio, proportion; installment, payment; **prō portiōne** proportionately, relatively

portīscul·us -ī *m* gavel *(used to keeping time for rowers)*

portit·or -ōris *m* customs officer; ferryman, boatman

port·ō -āre -āvī -ātus *tr* to carry; to bring

portōr·ium -(i)ī *n* port-duty, customs duty; tax *(on peddlers)*

portul·a -ae *f* small gate

Portūn·us -ī *m* tutelary deity of harbors

portuōs·us -a -um *adj* having good harbors

port·us -ūs *m* port, harbor; haven, refuge; mouth of a river

pōsc·a -ae *f* sour drink

pōscō pōscere popōscī *tr (weaker than* **flāgitō)** to ask, request, beg, demand; to ask for in marriage; *(at auction)* to bid for; *(of things)* to require, demand, need, call for, make necessary; *(w.* **ab)** to ask for *(s.th.)* from, demand *(s.th.)* of; *(w. double acc)* to demand *(s.th.)* of *(s.o.),* ask *(s.o.)* for *(s.th.)*

pōsi·a -ae *f* **(paus-)** unripe olive

Posīd·ēs -ae *m* favorite freedman of the Emperor Claudius

Posīdōn·ius -(i)ī *m* Stoic philosopher at Rhodes, teacher of Cicero *(135–51 B.C.)*

positi·ō -ōnis *f* putting, placing, setting; position, posture; situation

posit·or -ōris *m* builder

positūr·a -ae *f* posture; formation

posit·us -a -um *pp of* **pōnō** ‖ *adj* situated, located; stretched out, lying down

posit·us -ūs *m* position, site; arrangement; *(gram)* position *(of a syllable)*

possessi·ō -ōnis *f* possession; getting possession, occupation; estate

possessiuncul·a -ae *f* small estate

possess·or -ōris *m* possessor, occupant; *(leg)* defendant

possibil·is -is -e *adj* possible

pos·sideō -sidēre -sēdī -sessus *tr* to possess, occupy; to have, own; to dwell in, live in; *(fig)* to take hold of; *(poet)* to take up *(space)* with one's bulk

pos·sīdō -sīdere *tr* to take possession of, occupy, seize

possum posse potuī *intr* to be able; **multum (plūs, plūrimum) posse** to have much (more, very great) influence; **nōn possum quīn exclāmem** I can't help shouting out; **quantum** *(or* **ut) fierī potest** as far as is possible

post *older* **poste** *adv (of place)* behind, back, backwards; *(of time)* later, afterwards; *(of order)* next; **aliquantō post** somewhat later; **multīs post annīs** many years later ‖ *prep (w. acc) (of place)* behind; *(of time)* after, since

post- *pref used in the senses of the adverb*

posteā *adv* afterwards, after this, after that, hereafter, thereafter

posteāquam *conj (also as two words)* after; ever since, from the time that

posteri·or -or -us *adj* later, next, following; latter, posterior; inferior; hind *(e.g., legs)*

posterit·ās -ātis *f* the future, afterages, posterity, later generations; offspring *(of animals)*; **in posteritātem** in the future

posterius *adv* later, at a later date

poster·us -a -um *adj* following, ensuing, next, subsequent, future ‖ *mpl* future generations, posterity, descendants ‖ *n* future time; next day; consequence; **in posterum** until the next day; for the future

post·ferō -ferre *tr* to treat as less important, esteem less; to sacrifice

postgenit·us -a -um *adj* born later ‖ *mpl* later generations

posthab·eō -ēre -uī -itus *tr* to consider of secondary importance; to slight, neglect; *(w. dat)* to think *(s.th.)* less important than

posthāc *adv* hereafter, in the future

posthinc *or* **post hinc** *adv* from here, next

posthōc *or* **post hōc** *adv* after this, afterwards

postibi *adv* afterwards, then

postīcul·um -ī *n* small building in the rear, outhouse

postīc·us -a -um *adj* rear, back ‖ *n* back door; *(coll)* rear, rear end

postid *adv* then, afterwards

posteā *adv* afterwards, after that

postilēn·a -ae *f* rump; buttocks

postili·ō -ōnis *f* sacrifice demanded by the gods to make up for a previous omission in sacrifice

postillā(c) *adv* afterwards

post·is -is *m* doorpost; door ‖ *mpl* double doors

postlīmin·ium -(i)ī *n* right to return home and resume one's former rank and privileges after exile or capture; recovery, restoration

pos(t)merīdiān·us -a -um *adj* afternoon

postmerīdiē *adv* in the afternoon

postmodo *or* **postmodum** *adv* after a bit, a little later, afterwards

postpart·or -ōris *m* successor, heir

post·pōnō -pōnere -posuī -positus *tr* to consider of secondary importance; to postpone; *(w. dat)* to consider *(s.th.)* of less importance than, set *(s.th.)* aside in favor of; **omnibus rēbus postpositīs** laying aside everything

postprīncip·ium -(i)ī *n (also written as two words)* sequel; **postprīncipia** *(mil)* second line of battle

postput·ō -āre -āvī -ātus *tr (also written as two words)* to consider of secondary importance; *(w.* **prae** *+ abl)* to consider *(s.th.)* less important than

postquam *conj* after, when

postrēmō *adv* at last; finally

postrēmum *adv* for the last time, last of all

postrēm·us -a -um *(superl of* **posterus)** *adj* last; latest, most recent; last in line, rear; least important; lowest, worst ‖ *n* the end; **ad postrēmum** in the end, finally; in the last place

postrīdiē *adv* on the day after, on the following day; **postrīdiē māne** the next morning ‖ *prep (w. gen), e.g.,* **postrīdiē ēius diēī** on the day after that; *(w. acc), e.g.,* **postrīdiē lūdōs** on the day after the games

postrīduō *adv* on the day after

postscaen·ium -(i)ī *n* backstage

post·scrībō -scrībere -scrīpsī -scrīptus *tr (w. dat)* to add *(e.g., a name)* to; **Tiberī nōmen suō postscrībere** to add the name of Tiberius to his own

postulāti·ō -ōnis *f* demand, request, desire; complaint; *(leg)* application for permission to present a claim

postulāt·or -ōris *m* one who makes demands; plaintiff

postulāt·um -ī *n* demand; request; claim

postulāt·us -ūs *m* petition, request

postul·ō -āre -āvī -ātus *tr* to demand, claim; to look for as due, expect; *(of things)* to require; *(leg)* to arraign, prosecute; *(leg)* to apply for *(a writ from the praetor to prosecute)*

Postumi·us -a -um *adj* Roman clan name *(nomen), esp.* Aulus Postumius Tubertus *(father-in-law of Cincinnatus)* ‖ Gaius Postumius *(a soothsayer consulted by Sulla)*

postum·us -a -um *adj* last, latest-born; born after the father's death

Postum·us -ī *m* Roman first name *(praenomen),* subsequently in use as a family name *(cognomen)*

postus *pp of* **pōnō**

Postvert·a -ae *f* goddess presiding over breech births

posuī *perf of* **pōnō**

pōtāti·ō -ōnis *f* drinking; drinking party

pōtāt·or -ōris *m* drinker; a drunk

pot·ēns -entis *adj* capable; mighty, powerful, strong; efficacious, potent; influential; *(w. gen)* **1** capable of, equal to, fit for; **2** having power over; **3** presiding over; **4** having obtained *(one's wish);* **5** having carried out *(an order)*

potentāt·us -ūs *m* political power, rule, dominion

potenter *adv* powerfully, mightily, effectually, vigorously; according to one's ability

potenti·a -ae *f* force, power; political power *(esp. unconstitutional power in contrast to* **potestās)**

potēr·ium -iī *n* goblet

potest·ās -ātis *f* power, ability, capacity; efficacy, force; public authority, rule, power, sway, dominion, sovereignty, empire; magisterial power, magistracy, office; possibility, opportunity *(to choose, decide),* discretion, power of choice; permission; person in office, magistrate, ruler; property, quality

Pothīn·us -i *m* minister of Ptolemy XIII of Egypt, who ordered the assassination of Pompey the Great

potin *or* **potin'** = **potisne** can you?

pot·iō -īre -īvī -ītus *tr (w. acc and gen)* to put *(s.o.)* under the power of

pōti·ō -ōnis *f* drinking; drink, draught; magic potion

pōtiōnāt·us -a -um *adj (w. abl)* having been given a drink of

pot·ior -īrī -ītus sum *tr* to acquire, get possession of ‖ *intr (w. abl)* to acquire, get possession of, become master of, get hold of

poti·or -or -us *(comp of* **potis)** *adj* more powerful; more precious; better, preferable, superior; more important; *(w. gen)* having greater control over

potis *or* **pote** *indecl adj* able, capable; possible

potissimum *adv* chiefly, especially

potissim·us -a -um *adj* chief, principal, most important

pōtit·ō -āre -āvī -ātus *tr* to drink (habitually)

pōtiuncul·a -ae *f* a little drink

potius *adv* rather, more, by preference; **potius quam** more than, rather than

Potni·as -ados *adj (fem only)* of Potniae *(a Boeotian village)*

pōt·ō -āre -āvī -ātus *or* **-us** *tr* to drink; to absorb ‖ *intr* to drink

pōt·or -ōris *m* drinker; a drunk

pōtr·īx -īcis *f* drinker *(female)*

pōtulent·us -a -um *adj* drinkable; tipsy ‖ *npl* drinks

pōt·us -a -um *pp of* **pōtō** ‖ *adj* having drunk; drunken, intoxicated

pōt·us -ūs *m* drinking; a drink

prae *adv* before, in front; in preference ‖ *prep (w. abl)* **1** *(in its literal sense, usu. w. refl pron, in certain phrases)* before, in front of: **prae sē** in front of oneself, publicly, openly, plainly; **prae sē ferre** to display, manifest, profess; **prae manū** at hand; **2** compared with, in comparison with: **Gallīs prae magnitūdine corporum suōrum brevitās nostra contemptuī est** in comparison with the size of their own bodies the Gauls hold our shortness of stature in contempt; **3** by reason of, in consequence of, because of, for: **prae laetitiā lacrimāre** to weep for joy; **nec loquī prae maerōre potuit** he could not speak because of his grief; **4** in consequence of, out of: **prae pudōre** out of shame; **prae timōre** out of fear

prae- *pref* indicating **1** position in front, ahead: **praecēdere** to go in front, go ahead; **2** position in the end: **praeūrere** to burn at the extremity; **praeacuere** to sharpen to a point; **3** temporal precedence: **praedīcere** to tell in advance; **4** with adjectives, pre-eminence in the quality concerned: **praeacūtus** very sharp; **5** rank: **praeesse** to be in charge; **praetor** one in charge; **6** protection: **praesidium** defense, protection

praeac·uō -uere -uī -ūtus *tr* to sharpen to the point

praeacūt·us -a -um *adj* very sharp; pointed

praealt·us -a -um *adj* very high; very deep

praeb·eō -ēre -uī -itus *tr* to hold out, offer, present; to supply, give; to exhibit, represent, show; to give up, yield, surrender; to cause, occasion; to permit, allow; **praebēre aurem** *(or* **aurēs)** *(w. dat)* to listen to; **praebēre exemplum** to set an example; **praebēre suspiciōnem** to cause suspicion ‖ *refl* to show oneself, behave; to offer oneself as

praebib·ō -ere -ī -itus *tr (w. dat)* to drink *(e.g., a toast)* to
praebit·or -ōris *m* supplier
praecalid·us -a -um *adj* very hot
praecalv·us -a -um *adj* very bald
praecant·ō -āre -āvī -ātus *tr* **(-cen-)** to cast a spell over **||** *intr (w. dat)* to recite a spell over
praecantr·īx -īcis *f* witch, enchantress
praecān·us -a -um *adj* prematurely gray
prae·caveō -cavēre -cāvī -cautus *tr* to take precautions against, guard against, try to avoid **||** *intr* to take precautions, be on one's guard; *(w. dat)* to look out for, look after; *(w. abl)* to guard against, be on one's quard against
prae·cēdō -cēdere -cessī -cessus *tr* to precede, go out before, lead; to surpass **||** *intr* to excel; *(w. dat)* to be superior to
praecell·ēns -entis *adj* excellent, outstanding, preeminent
praecell·ō -ere *tr* to surpass, outdo **||** *intr* to distinguish oneself, excel; to take precedence; *(w. dat)* **1** to rule over; **2** to surpass
praecels·us -a -um *adj* towering
praecenti·ō -ōnis *f* singing before a sacrifice; prelude
praecentō *see* **praecantō**
praecentus *pp of* **praecinō**
praecēpī *perf of* **praecipiō**
praeceps *adv* headfirst
praec·eps -ipitis *adj* headfirst; downhill, steep, precipitous; sinking *(sun);* swift, rushing, violent; hasty, rash, inconsiderate; dangerous **||** *n* edge of a cliff, cliff; *(fig)* brink; danger; **in praeceps** *(or* **per praeceps)** headlong, straight downward; **in praecipitī** on the edge; *(fig)* on the brink of disaster
praecepti·ō -ōnis *f* preconception; precept, rule; instruction; *(leg)* receiving *(of an inheritance)* in advance *(of the general partition of an estate)*
praecept·or -ōris *m,* **praceptr·īx -īcis** *f* teacher, tutor
praecept·um -ī *n* instruction, bit of advice; rule; maxim; order, direction
praecerp·ō -ere -sī -tus *tr* to pick beforetime; *(w. dat) (fig)* to snatch away from
praecī·dō -dere -dī -sus *tr* to lop off, cut off; to cut short; to cut, cut through; to damage, mutilate; to break off, end suddenly *(a speech, etc.);* to end, destroy *(hopes, etc.);* to refuse, decline
prae·cingō -cingere cīnxī -cīnctus *tr* to gird; to surround, ring; to dress **||** *pass* to be surrounded, be ringed; **altius praecīnctus** with tunic tucked up higher; *(fig)* more energetic(ally); **ēnse cingī** to wear a sword; **male cīnctus** improperly dressed; **rēcte cinctus** properly dressed
prae·cinō -cinere -cinuī -centus *tr* to predict; *(w. dat)* to predict *(s.th.)* to **||** *intr* to make predictions; *(w. dat)* to sing *or* play before *or* at *(e.g., sacrifice, dinner, etc.)*
prae·cipiō -cipere -cēpī -ceptus *tr* to take in advance, occupy in advance; to receive in advance; to grasp beforehand, anticipate; to teach, instruct, direct, advise, order, bid, warn; to prescribe; **aliquantulum viae** *(or* **temporis) praecipere** *(or* **iter praecipere)** to get a headstart; **animō** *(or* **cogitātiōne) praecipere** to imagine beforehand, reckon on, anticipate, expect; **artem nandī praecipere** to give swimming instructions; **gaudium praecipere** to rejoice in advance; **oculīs praecipere** to see beforehand, get a preview of; **opīniōne praecipere** to suspect; **pecūniam mūtuam praecipere** to get an advance loan
praecipitanter *adv* at top speed
praecipit·ō -āre -āvī -ātus *tr* to throw down headfirst; to hasten, hurry, precipitate **||** *refl* to throw oneself down, throw oneself headfirst, jump down, dive; to sink **||** *intr* to rush headfirst, rush at top speed, rush thoughtlessly; to fall, sink; to be ruined
praecipuē *adv* especially, chiefly
praecipu·us -a -um *adj* special, peculiar, particular; chief, principal; distinguished, excellent, extraordinary **||** *n* excellence, superiority **||** *npl* outstanding *or* important elements; **praecipua rērum** highlights
praecīsē *adv* briefly, concisely; absolutely
praecīs·us -a -um *pp of* **praecīdō ||** *adj* abrupt, precipitous; rugged, rough; brief, shortened *(speech);* clipped *(words)*
praeclārē *adv* very clearly; excellently; *(to express agreement)* very good, excellent
praeclār·us -a -um *adj* very clear; very nice; splendid, noble, distinguished, excellent; famous; notorious
praeclū·dō -dere -sī -sus *tr* to shut, shut off, obstruct, bar the way of; to hinder, impede, stop; to preclude *(an action, event);* **portās cōnsulī praeclūdere** to shut the gates in the consul's face; **vōcem praeclūdere alicui** to shut s.o. up, hush s.o. up
praec·ō -ōnis *m* crier, herald; auctioneer; *(fig)* eulogist
praecōgit·ō -āre -āvī -ātus *tr* to premeditate
praecognit·us -a -um *adj* known beforehand, foreseen
prae·colō -colere -coluī -cultus *tr* to cultivate prematurely; *(fig)* to embrace prematurely
praecomposit·us -a -um *adj* arranged beforehand; studied, self-conscious
praecōni·us -a -um *adj* of a public crier; of an auctioneer **||** *n* crier's office; proclamation, announcement; praising, praise

praecōnsūm·ō -ere -psī -ptus *tr* to spend *or* use up beforehand
praecontrect·ō -āre *tr* to consider in advance
praecoqu·is -is -e *adj* premature; precocious
praecordi·a -ōrum *npl* midriff; lower chest; chest; diaphragm; insides, stomach; breast, heart *(as seat of emotions); (poet)* body
praecor·rumpō -rumpere -rūpī -ruptus *tr* to bribe in advance
prae·cox -cocis *adj* premature; early, precocious
praecupid·us -a -um *adj (w. gen)* very fond of
praecurrent·ia -ium *npl* antecedents
prae·currō -currere -(cu)currī cursus *tr* to precede, anticipate; to outdo, surpass **||** *intr* to run out ahead, take the lead; *(w.* **ante** + *acc)* to run out ahead of; *(w. dat)* to outdo
praecursi·ō -ōnis *f* previous occurrence; *(mil)* skirmish; *(rhet)* warmup *(of the audience)*
praecurs·or -ōris *m* forerunner; spy; *(mil)* scout; *(mil)* advance guard
praecursōri·us -a -um *adj* sent in advance
prae·cutiō -cutere *tr* to wave, brandish in front
praed·a -ae *f* booty, spoils, plunder; prey; *(of fish)* catch; *(in hunting)* the game; prize, profit; **praedae esse** *(w. dat)* to fall prey to; **vocāmus in partem praedamque Iovem** we invite Jupiter to share the game
praedābund·us -a -um *adj* pillaging, plundering, marauding
praedamn·ō -āre -āvī -ātus *tr* to condemn beforehand; **spem praedamnāre** to give up hope too soon
praedāti·ō -ōnis *f* plundering
praedātor -ōris *m* marauder, looter, vandal; hunter; greedy man
praedātōri·us -a -um *adj* marauding, looting; graspy, greedy
praedāt·us -ūs *m* robbery
praedēlass·ō -āre *tr* to tire out, weaken beforehand
praediāt·or -ōris *m* real-estate dealer
praediātōri·us -a -um *adj* concerned with real-estate; **iūs praediātōrium** *(leg)* mortgage law
praedicābil·is -is -e *adj* praiseworthy, laudable
praedicāti·ō -ōnis *f* announcement, publication; praise, commendation
praedicāt·or -ōris *m* eulogist
praedic·ō -āre -āvī -ātus *tr* to announce; to report; to assert, state; to praise, recommend
prae·dīcō -dīcere -dīxī -dictus *tr* to mention beforehand *or* earlier; to prearrange; to predict; to order beforehand, command beforehand
praedicti·ō -ōnis *f* prediction
praedict·um -ī *n* prediction, prophecy; command, order; **velut ex praedictō** as if by prearrangement
praediol·um -ī *n* small estate, small farm
praedisc·ō -ere *tr* to learn beforehand, find out in advance
praedisposit·us -a -um *adj* previously arranged
praedit·us -a -um *adj* gifted; *(w. abl)* endowed with, provided with, furnished with
praed·ium -iī *n* estate, farm; collateral *(consisting of land);* **praedium urbānum** *(whether in town or in the country)* building site
praedīv·es -itis *adj* very rich
praedīvīn·ō -āre -āvī -ātus *tr* to know in advance, have a presentiment of
praed·ō -ōnis *m* robber; pirate
praedoct·us -a -um *adj* instructed beforehand
praed·or -ārī -ātus sum *tr* to raid, plunder, loot, rob; *(fig)* to rob, ravish; **amōrēs alicūius praedārī** to steal s.o.'s sweetheart away **||** *intr* to plunder, loot, make a raid; *(w.* **ex)** to prey on, profit by, take advantage of, *e.g.,* **ex alterīus īnscientiā praedārī** to prey on *or* take advantage of another's ignorance
prae·dūcō -dūcere -dūxī -ductus *tr* to run *or* construct *(trench, wall)* out in front *(as a defense)*
praedulc·is -is -e *adj* very sweet; *(fig)* very satisfying *(honor, reward)*
praedūr·us -a -um *adj* very tough *(skin);* tough, brawny
praeēmin·eō *or* **praemin·eō -ēre** *tr* to surpass, excel **||** *intr* to project, stick out
prae·eō -īre -īvī *or* **-iī** *tr* to lead, precede; to read out, dictate, lead *(prayers)* **||** *intr* to go out ahead, take the lead; *(w. dat)* to walk in front of
praefāti·ō -ōnis *f* preface, introduction; formula
praefātus *pp of* **praefor**
praefectūr·a -ae *f* supervision, superintendence; office of prefect, superintendency; government of a district; prefecture *(Italian city governed by a Roman prefect);* territory of a prefecture, district
praefect·us -ī *m* prefect, supervisor, superintendent; commander; governor; *(w. gen or dat)* supervisor of, commander of, prefect *or* governor of; satrap; **praefectus classis** admiral; **praefectus praetōriō** commander of the imperial bodyguard
prae·ferō -ferre -tulī -lātus *tr* to hold out, carry in front; *(w. dat or* **quam)** to prefer *(one thing)* to *(another);* to anticipate; to display, reveal, betray; to offer, present;

to offer as a model ‖ *refl & pass (w. dat)* to surpass ‖ *pass* to ride past, ride by, march past; to outflank

praefer·ōx -ōcis *adj* very defiant; impetuous

praeferrāt·us -a -um *adj* iron-tipped; *(coll)* chained *(slave)*

praefervid·us -a -um *adj (lit & fig)* boiling

praefestīn·ō -āre -āvī -ātus *tr* to hurry past; *(w. inf)* to be in a big hurry to

praefic·a -ae *f* hired mourner *(female)*

prae·ficiō -ficere -fēcī -fectus *tr* to put *(s.o.)* in charge; *(w. double acc)* to appoint *(s.o.)* as; *(w. dat)* to put *(s.o.)* in charge of, set *(s.o.)* over, appoint *(s.o.)* to command

praefīd·ēns -entis *adj* too trustful; overconfident; *(w. dat)* too trustful of; **hominēs sibi praefīdentēs** overconfident people

praefī·gō -gere -xī -xus *tr* to fix, fasten, set up in front, fasten on the end; *(w. abl)* to tip with; *(w.* **in** *+ abl)* to impale on; **capistrīs praefīgere** to muzzle

praefīn·iō -īre -īvī *or* **-iī -ītus** *tr* to determine in advance; to prescribe, appoint; to limit

praefīnītō *adv* in the prescribed manner

praefiscinē *or* **praefiscinī** *or* **praefascinē** *adv* so as to avoid bad luck; meaning no offense

praefīxī *perf of* **praefīgō**

praefīx·us -a -um *pp of* **praefīgō** ‖ *adj* **cuspidibus praefīxus** pointed; **ferrō praefīxus** iron-tipped

praeflōr·ō -āre -āvī -ātus *tr* to deflower beforehand; *(fig)* to tarnish

praeflu·ō -ere *tr & intr* to flow by

praefōc·ō -āre -āvī -ātus *tr* to suffocate; to block *(windpipe, road)* ‖ *pass* to choke

prae·fodiō -fodere -fōdī -fossus *tr* to bury beforehand; to dig in front of; **portās praefodere** to dig trenches in front of the gates

prae·for -fārī -fātus sum *tr* to say beforehand, utter in advance, preface; to address in prayer beforehand; to fortell; to invoke ‖ *intr* to pray beforehand; *(w. dat)* to pray before

praefrāctē *adv* obstinately

praefrāct·us -a -um *pp of* **praefringō** ‖ *adj* determined reolute; abrupt

praefrīgid·us -a -um *adj* very cold

prae·fringō -fringere -frēgī -frāctus *tr* to break off at the tip; to break to pieces, smash

praeful·ciō -cīre -sī -tus *tr* to prop up, support in front; *(w. dat)* to use *(s.o.)* as a prop *or* support for

praeful·geō -gēre -sī *intr* to shine forth, glitter, sparkle

praegelid·us -a -um *adj* very cold

praegest·iō -īre *intr* to be very eager

praegn·āns -antis *or* **praegn·ās -ātis** *adj* pregnant; *(w. abl)* full of, swollen with

praegracil·is -is -e *adj* lanky

praegrand·is -is -e *adj* huge; very great; very powerful

praegrav·is -is -e *adj* very heavy; weighed down; very troublesome

praegrav·ō -āre -āvī -ātus *tr* to weigh down; to outweigh; *(fig)* to burden

prae·gredior -gredī -gressus sum *tr* to go in advance of, go ahead of; to go by, go past; *(fig)* to outstrip ‖ *intr* to walk out in front; *(w. dat)* to precede, lead

praegressi·ō -ōnis *f* procession; *(fig)* precedence

praegress·us -ūs *m* prior occurrence

praegustāt·or -ōris *m* taster, sampler

praegust·ō -āre -āvī -ātus *tr* to taste beforehand, sample, get a sample of

praehib·eō -ēre -uī -itus *tr* to offer, furnish, supply; to utter, speak; **operam praehibēre** to offer help

praeiac·eō -ēre *tr* to lie before, be located in front of ‖ *intr (w. dat)* to lie before

praeiūdicāt·us -a -um *adj* decided beforehand; prejudiced; **opīniō praeiūdicata** prejudice ‖ *n* prejudged matter; prejudice; **id prō praeiūdicātō ferre** to take it as a foregone conclusion

praeiūdic·ium -(i)ī *n* preliminary hearing; prejudice; presumption; precedent, example

praeiūdic·ō -āre -āvī -ātus *tr* to decide beforehand, prejudge ‖ *intr (w. dat of disadvantage)* to be prejudicial to

prae·iuvō -iuvāre -iūvī *tr* to help in advance

prae·lābor -lābī -lāpsus sum *tr & intr* to glide along, glide, by, float by

praelamb·ō -ere *tr* to lick beforehand

praelarg·us -a -um *adj* very ample

praelātus *pp of* **praeferō**

praelaut·us -a -um *adj* plush

praelēcti·ō -ōnis *f* lecture

prae·legō -legere -lēgī -lēctus *tr* to lecture on; to sail past

praelig·ō -āre -āvī -ātus *tr* to tie up; *(w. dat)* to tie *(s.th.)* to

praelong·us -a -um *adj* very long; very tall

prae·loquor -loquī -locūtus sum *tr* to make *(a speech)* before s.o. else; to say by way of preface; *(leg)* to present *(a case)* first; ‖ *intr* to speak first

prae·lūceō -lūcēre -lūxī *tr (fig)* to enkindle *(hope)* ‖ *intr (w. dat)* **1** to throw light on; **2** to outshine, outdo, surpass; **3** to light the way for

praelūsi·ō -ōnis *f* prelude

praelūstr·is -is -e *adj* magnificent

praemandāt·a -ōrum *npl (leg)* warrant for arrest

praemand·ō -āre -āvī -ātus *tr* to recommend beforehand; to order in advance

praemātūrē *adv* too soon, prematurely
praemātūr·us -a -um *adj* premature
praemedicāt·us -a -um *adj* protected by drugs *or* charms
praemeditāti·ō -ōnis *f* premeditation, prior consideration
praemedit·or -ārī -ātus sum *tr* to think over beforehand; to practice; to practice on *(e.g., a lyre);* **mala praemeditāta** premeditated crimes
praemerc·or -ārī -ātus sum *tr* to buy in advance
praemetu·ēns -entis *adj* apprehensive, anxious
praemetuenter *adv* anxiously; cautiously
praemetu·ō -ere *tr* to fear beforehand **‖** *intr (w. dat)* to be apprehensive about
praemin·eō -ēre *tr* to surpass, exceed **‖** *intr* to stand out prominently
prae·mittō -mittere -mīsī -missus *tr* to send out ahead, send in advance **‖** *intr* to send word
praem·ium -(i)ī *n* prize, reward, recompense; exploit *(worthy of reward);* gift, bribe
praemolesti·a -ae *f* apprehension, presentiment of trouble
praemōl·ior -īrī *tr* to prepare beforehand, work at in advance
praemon·eō -ēre -uī -itus *tr* to forewarn; to warn of; to foreshadow, presage, predict
praemonit·us -ūs *m* premonition, forewarning
praemōnstrāt·or -ōris *m* guide
praemōnstr·ō -āre -āvī -ātus *tr* to point out the way to, guide, direct; to predict
praemor·deō -dēre -dī *or* **-sī -sus** *tr* to bite the tip off *(s.th.); (fig)* to crib, pilfer
praemor·ior -ī -tuus sum *intr* to die too soon, die prematurely
praemūn·iō -īre -īvī -ītus *tr* to fortify in front; to protect, secure **‖** *intr (fig) (of a lawyer)* to prepare one's defenses
praemūnīti·ō -ōnis *f (rhet)* preparation, conditioning *(of the minds of the hearers)*
praenārr·ō -āre -āvī -ātus *tr* to relate beforehand
praenat·ō -āre -āvī *tr & intr* to float past, flow by
praenāvig·ō -āre -āvī -ātum *tr & intr* to sail by
Praenest·e -is *n (f)* ancient town in Latium *(c. 20 miles S.E. of Rome, modern Palestrina)*
Praenestīn·us -a -um *adj & m* Praenestine
praenit·eō -ēre -uī *intr (w. dat)* **1** to outshine; **2** to appear more attractive to
praenōm·en -inis *n* first name
prae·nōscō -nōscere -nōvī *tr* to find out beforehand
praenōti·ō -ōnis *f* innate idea, preconception
praenūbil·us -a -um *adj* heavily clouded; dark, gloomy
praenūnti·a -ae *f* harbinger, omen
praenūnti·ō -āre -āvī -ātus *tr* foretell
praenūnti·us -a-um *adj* foreboding **‖** *m* forecaster, harbinger, omen
praeoccupāti·ō -ōnis *f* seizing beforehand, advance occupation
praeoccup·ō -āre -āvī -ātus *tr* to occupy before another; to preoccupy; to anticipate, prevent
praeol·et -ēre *or* **praeol·it -ere** *v impers* a smell is emitted, there is a strong smell; **praeolit mihi quō tū velīs** I scent your wishes before you express them
praeopt·ō -āre -āvī -ātus *tr* to prefer
praepand·ō -ere *tr* to spread, extend; *(fig)* to reveal
praeparāti·ō -ōnis *f* preparation
praeparāt·us -a -um *adj* prepared, supplied, furnished, ready **‖** *n* stores; **ex ante preparātō** from the stores; *(fig)* by previous arrangement
praepar·ō -āre -āvī -ātus *tr* to get ready, prepare, prepare for; to gather together; to furnish beforehand; to plan in advance
praepedīment·um -ī *n* impediment
praeped·iō -īre -īvī *or* **-(i)ī -ītus** *tr* to shackle, chain; to hinder, obstruct, hamper; to embarrass
praepend·eō -ēre *intr* to hang down in front
praep·es -etis *adj (of birds of omen)* flying straight ahead, of good omen; winged, swift of flight **‖** *mf* bird of good omen; bird, large bird
praepilāt·us -a -um *adj* tipped with a ball; **missile praepilātum** blunted missile
praepingu·is -is -e *adj* very fertile
praepoll·eō -ēre -uī *intr* to be very powerful; to be superior; *(w. dat)* to surpass in power
praeponder·ō -āre -āvī -ātus *tr* to outweigh; to regard as superior **‖** *intr* to weigh more
prae·pōnō -pōnere -posuī -positus *tr (w. dat)* **1** to place, set, put *(s.th.)* in front of *or* before *(s.o.);* **2** to serve *(s.o. food);* **3** to entrust *(s.o.)* with; **4** to put *(s.o.)* in charge of *or* in command of; **5** to prefer *(s.o. or s.th.)* to, give priority to
praeport·ō -āre -āvī -ātus *tr* to carry before oneself
praepositi·ō -ōnis *f* preference; prefixing; *(gram)* preposition
praeposit·um -ī *n* preferable thing *(i.e., s.th. short of absolute good)*
praeposit·us -a -um *pp of* **praepōnō ‖** *adj* preferred, preferable **‖** *m* prefect, commander **‖** *n* that which is desirable, a desirable good
praeposterē *adv* out of the proper order

praeposter·us -a -um *adj* inverted, in the wrong order; badly timed; topsy-turvy; preposterous
praeposuī *pref of* **praepōnō**
praepot·ēns -entis *adj* very powerful; *(w. gen)* in full control of
praeproperanter *or* **praeproperē** *adv* very quickly, too fast
praeproper·us -a -um *adj* very quick; overhasty, sudden
praepūt·ium -(i)ī *n* foreskin
praequam *conj* in comparison to; **nihil hōc est, praequam aliōs sumptūs facit** this is nothing in comparison to the other expenses that he runs up
praequest·us -a -um *adj* complaining beforehand; **multa praequestus** having first voiced many complaints
praeradi·ō -āre *tr* to outshine
praerapid·us -a -um *adj* very swift
praereptus *pp of* **praeripiō**
praerig·ēscō -ēscere -uī *intr* to become very stiff
prae·ripiō -ripere -ripuī -reptus *tr* to snatch away, carry off; to anticipate, forestall; to count on too soon, presume upon; *(w. dat)* to snatch from
prae·rōdō -rōdere -rōsī -rōsus *tr* to bite the end of, nibble at; **digitōs praerōdere** to bite the fingernails
praerogātīv·us -a -um *adj* asked before others; *(pol)* voting first, privileged; **ōmen praerogātīvum** omen to vote first ‖ *f (pol)* first tribe *or* century to vote; *(pol)* vote of the first tribe *or* century to vote; *(pol)* previous election; sure sign, omen
praerōsī *perf of* **praerōdō**
praerōsus *pp of* **praerōdō**
prae·rumpō -rumpere -rūpī -ruptus *tr* to break off, tear away *(s.th.)* in front
praerupt·us -a -um *adj* broken off, broken up; rough *(terrain);* steep; hasty, impetuous; *(of an utterance)* cut short ‖ *n* precipice, steep place; *(fig)* dangerous undertaking
praes *adv* at hand, now
prae·s -dis *m* bondsman, surety; collateral
praesaep- = praesēp-
praesāgāti·ō -ōnis *f* power of knowing the future, presentiment
praesāg·iō -īre -īvī *or* **-iī** *or* **praesāg·ior -īrī** *tr* to have forebodings of, feel beforehand; to forebode, portend
praesāgīti·ō -ōnis *f* presentiment, strange feeling; prophetic power
praesāg·ium -(i)ī *n* presentiment, prophetic instinct; portent; prediction
praesāg·ō -āre -āvī *tr* to have a presentiment of
praesāg·us -a -um *adj* prophetic
praesc·iō -īre -īvī -ītus *tr* to know beforehand
praesc·īscō -īscere -(i)ī *tr* to find out *or* learn beforehand
praesci·us -a -um *adj* prescient, having foreknowledge; **praescius ventūrī** foreseeing the future
prae·scrībō -scrībere -scrīpsī -scrīptus *tr* to prefix in writing; to describe beforehand; to determine in advance, prescribe, ordain; to dictate; to outline, map out; to put forward as an excuse
praescrīpti·ō -ōnis *f* heading, title; preface; pretext; rule, law; limit, restriction
praescrīpt·um -ī *n* regulation, rule; boundary line; route
praesec·ō -āre -uī -tus *tr* to cut off; to cut away; to pare *(nails)*
praesegmin·a -um *npl* clippings
praes·ēns -entis *adj* present, in person, face to face; at hand; existing, contemporary; prompt, immediate, instant; impending; efficacious, powerful, effective; influential; resolute; *(of a god)* ready to help, propitious; *(of payment)* in cash; **in praesēns tempus** for the present; **in rem prasentem venīre** to come to the very spot; **(in) rē praesentī** on the spot; **praesēns pecūnia** cold cash; **praesentī diē** on the day in question; **sermō praesēns** a face-to-face talk ‖ *n* present time; **ad** *(or* **in)** **praesēns** for the present; **in praesentī** on the spot; in the present case; on the present occasion
praesēnsī *perf of* **praesentiō**
praesēnsi·ō -ōnis *f* presentiment; preconception
praesēnsus *pp of* **praesentiō**
praesentāne·us -a -um *adj (of a poison)* having an immediate effect
praesentāri·us -a -um *adj* paid in cash on the spot
praesenti·a -ae *f* presence; efficacy, effect; **animī praesentiā** presence of mind; resolution; **in praesentiā** at present, in the present state of affairs; **in praesentiā esse** to be present, be available; **in praesentiam** for the present
praesen·tiō -tīre -sī -sēnsus *tr* to feel beforehand, to realize in advance, have strange feelings about
praesēp·e -is *n or* **praesēp·ēs -is** *f* **(-saep-)** stall, stable; crib, manger; *(coll)* brothel; *(coll)* lodgings, room
praesēp·iō -īre -sī -tus *tr* **(-saep-)** to fence in, barricade
praesertim *adv* especially, particularly; **praesertim cum** especially because
praeserv·iō -īre *intr (w. dat)* to serve *(s.o.)* as a slave
praes·es -idis *m* guard, guardian, protector, defender; president, superintendent; captain, pilot; governor *(of a province)* ‖ *f* guardian, protectress
praesid·ēns -entis *m* president, ruler

prae·sideō -sidēre -sēdī *tr* to guard, protect, defend; to command, be in command of ‖ *intr* to be in charge, be in command; *(w. dat)* **1** to watch over, guard, protect; **2** to preside over, direct, manage; **3** to command

praesidiāri·us -a -um *adj* on garrison duty

praesid·ium -(i)ī *n* protection, defense; assistance; *(mil)* guard, garrison; *(mil)* garrison post, defensive position; *(naut)* convoy; **praesidium agitāre** to stand guard

praesignific·ō -āre -āvī -ātus *tr* to indicate in advance, foretoken

praesign·is -is -e *adj* outstanding

praeson·ō -āre -uī *tr & intr* to sound beforehand

praesparg·ō -ere *tr* to strew, scatter

praestābil·is -is -e *adj* excellent, outstanding; of outstanding importance

praest·āns -antis *adj* outstanding

praestanti·a -ae *f* excellence, preëminence, superiority

praestantissimē *adv* exceptionally well

praestern·ō -ere *tr* to strew in front

praest·es -itis *m* guardian, protecting deity

praestīgi·ae -ārum *fpl* sleight of hand; juggling; tricks; illusion

praestīgiāt·or -ōris *m,* **praestīgiātr·īx -īcis** *f* juggler; magician; imposter

praestin·ō -āre -āvī -ātus *tr* to buy, shop for, bargain for

praesti·tuō -tuere -tuī -tūtus *tr* to fix *or* set up beforehand; to prescribe

praestitus *pp of* **praestō**

praestō *adv* at hand, ready, present, here; **praestō esse** *(w. dat)* **1** to be on hand for, attend, serve, be helpful to, aid; **2** to be in the way of, resist, oppose

prae·stō -stāre -stitī -stitus *(fut participle:* **praestātūrus)** *tr* to be superior to, outdo; to show, exhibit, give evidence of, display; to answer for, be responsible for, take upon oneself; to perform, discharge, fulfill; to keep, maintain, retain; to present, offer, supply; **fidem praestāre** to keep one's word; **impetūs populī praestāre** to be responsible for popular outbreaks; **nihil praestāre** to be answerable for nothing; **officia praestāre** to perform duties; **sociōs salvōs praestāre** to keep the allies safe; **terga hostī praestāre** to show one's back to the enemy, retreat; **virtūtem praestāre** to display courage ‖ *refl* to show oneself, behave ‖ *intr* to stand out, be outstanding, be preëminent ‖ *v impers* it is preferable, it is better

praestōl·or -ārī -ātus sum *or* **praestōl·ō -āre** *tr* to wait for, expect ‖ *intr (w. dat)* to wait for, await

prae·stringō -stringere -strīnxī -strīctus *tr* to draw together, constrict, squeeze; to graze; *(fig)* to touch lightly on; to blunt *(an edge);* to blind, dazzle *(the eyes);* to dazzle, baffle; to throw into the shade

praestru·ō -ere -xī -ctus *tr* to build up, to block up, stop up; to build up *(e.g., confidence)* beforehand

praes·ul -ulis *or* **praesultāt·or -ōris** *m* dancer *(at the head of a religious procession)*

praesult·ō -āre -āvī -ātum *intr (w. dat)* to dance in front of, jump around in front of

prae·sum -esse -fuī -futūrus *intr* to preside; **in prōvinciā praeesse** to govern a province; *(w. dat)* **1** to preside over, be in charge of, be in command of; **2** to be preëminent in; **3** to govern *(a province)*

prae·sūmō -sūmere -sumpsī -sumptus *tr* to take in advance; to anticipate, presume, take for granted

praesumpti·ō -ōnis *f* anticipation; presumption; *(rhet)* anticipation *(of an opponent's objections)*

praesūt·us -a -um *adj* sewn up; covered

praetempt·ō -āre -āvī -ātus *tr* to try out in advance, test in advance; to grope for

praeten·dō -dere -dī -tus *tr* to hold *or* stretch in front of oneself; to present; to offer an an excuse, give as pretext, allege, pretend; *(w. dat)* to hold *(e.g., a toga)* in front of *(e.g., the eyes)* ‖ *pass (of places) (w. dat)* to lie to the front of *or* opposite

praetent·ō -āre *tr* to allege

praetep·ēscō -ēscere -uī *intr (of love)* to glow, grow warm

praeter *adv* by, past

praeter *conj* besides, other than ‖ *prep (w. acc)* **1** *(of place)* past, by, along, before, in front of: **praeter castra cōpiās suās dūcere** to lead his troops past *or* in front of the camp; **2** beyond in degree, surpassing: **praeter spem** beyond hope, unexpectedly; **3** despite, contrary to: **praeter speciem** despite appearances; **praeter cōnsuētūdinem** contrary to normal usage, contrary to custom; **4** in addition to, as well as, besides: **praeter haec** besides this, moreover; **praeter id quod** in addition to the fact that; **5** except, but, other than: **nunc quidem praeter nōs nēmō est** now there's really no one but us; **6** exclusive of, except for: **praetōrēs quotannīs praeter paucōs locuplētātī sunt** the praetors with few exceptions were getting rich every year

praeter- *pref* by, past

praeterag·ō -ere *tr (w. double acc)* to drive *(e.g., a horse)* past *(a place)*

praeterbīt·ō -ere *tr & intr* to go by *or* past

praeter·dūcō -dūcere -dūxī -ductus *tr* to lead by, conduct past

praetereā *adv (also written as two words)* besides, moreover; hereafter, thereafter

praeter·eō -īre -īvī *or* **-iī -itus** *tr* to go past, pass by; to skip, pass over in silence; to escape the notice of; to go beyond; to surpass ‖ *intr* to go by

praeterequit·āns -antis *adj* riding by *(on horseback)*

praeter·ferō -ferre -tulī -lātus *tr (w. double acc)* to carry *or* take *(s.o.)* past *(s.th.)* ‖ *pass* to move by *(a place)*

praeterflu·ō -ere *tr & intr* to flow by

praeter·gredior -gredī -gressus sum *tr* to march by, go past; to surpass ‖ *intr* to march by, go past

praeterhāc *adv* in addition

praeterit·us -a -um *pp of* **praetereō** ‖ *adj* past, bygone, former; *(gram)* **(tempus) praeteritum** past tense

praeter·lābor -lābī -lāpsus sum *tr & intr* to glide by, slip past

praeterlātus *pp of* **praeterferō**

praeterme·ō -āre *tr & intr* to go past

praetermissi·ō -ōnis *f* leaving out, omission; passing over, neglecting; *(w. gen)* omission of

praeter·mittō -mittere -mīsī -missus *tr* to let pass, let go by; to leave undone; to pass over, omit, disregard, overlook, neglect

praeternāvig·ō -āre *tr* to sail past

prae·terō -terere -trīvī *tr* to wear down in front *(by rubbing)*

praeterquam *or* **praeter quam** *conj* except that; **praeterquam quī** apart from a person who; **praeterquam quod** apart from the fact that; *(w. illipsis)* **num quō crīmine is esset accūsātus praeterquam venēnī?** had he ever been charged with any crime except that of poisoning?; **praeterquam bis** except on two occasions

praetertulī *perf of* **praeterferō**

praetervecti·ō -ōnis *f* passing by; sailing past; riding by

praeter·vehor -vehī -vectus sum *tr & intr* to pass by *or* past; to ride by; to sail by; to march by

praetervol·ō -āre *tr & intr* to fly by; *(of opportunity)* to slip by; to escape

praetex·ō -ere -uī -tus *tr* to border, edge, fringe; to adorn in front; *(fig)* to cloak, conceal, disguise; to use as a pretext, allege, pretend

praetext·a -ae *f* crimson-bordered toga *(worn by higher magistrates and by freeborn boys and possibly girls)*; tragedy; **praetextās docēre** to put on tragedies

praetextāt·us -a -um *adj* wearing the toga praetexta *(crimson-bordered toga)*; underage, juvenile; **mōrēs praetextātī** loose morals

praetext·um -ī *n* adornment, glory; pretext, cloak

praetext·us -a -um *pp of* **praetexō** ‖ *adj* bordered; wearing the crimson-bordered toga; **fābula praetexta** Roman tragic drama ‖ *f see* **praetexta** ‖ *n* pretext, pretense, excuse

praetext·us -ūs *m* show, appearance; pretext

praetim·eō -ēre *intr* to be apprehensive

praetīnct·us -a -um *adj* previously dipped

praet·or -ōris *m* praetor *(judicial magistrate, accompanied by six lictors)*; *(during early days of the Republic)* chief magistrate, chief executive; *(in Italian municipalities)* chief magistrate; **praetor peregrīnus** praetor who had jurisdiction over cases involving a Roman and a foreigner; **praetor urbānus** *(or* **urbis)** praetor with jurisdiction over cases involving Roman citizens; **prō praetōre** magistrate with extended governorship, or other persons ranked as such

praetōriān·us -a -um *adj* praetorian, belonging to the emperor's bodyguard; **mīles praetōriānus** a praetorian guard ‖ *mpl* praetorian guard

praetōrici·us -a -um *adj* received from the praetor *(at public games)*

praetōri·us -a -um *adj* of the commander in chief, of the commander *or* general; praetor's; propraetor's; **cohors praetōria** general's bodyguard; **comitia praetōria** praetorial elections; **nāvis praetōria** flagship; **porta praetōria** camp gate nearest the general's tent; **turba praetōria** crowd around the praetor ‖ *n* general's quarters, headquarters; official residence of the governor in a province; council of war; emperor's bodyguard; palace, mansion

praetor·queō -quēre -sī -tus *tr* to twist beforehand; to strangle first

praetract·ō -āre *tr* to consider in advance

praetrepid·ō -āre *intr* to tremble in anticipation

praetrepid·us -a -um *adj* very nervous, trembling

praetrīvī *perf of* **praeterō**

praetrunc·ō -āre -āvī -ātus *tr* to cut off; to lop off the tip of

praetulī *perf of* **praeferō**

praetūr·a -ae *f* praetorship; propraetorship

Praetūtiān·us -a -um *adj* of the Praetutii *(a people of Picenum)*

praeumbr·āns -antis *adj* casting a shadow; *(fig)* overshadowing

praeūst·us -a -um *adj* burnt at the tip, hardened by fire at the point; frostbitten

praeut *conj* as compared with, when compared with

praeval·ēns -entis *adj* exceptionally powerful, exceptionally strong

praeval·eō -ēre -uī *intr* to be stronger, have more power; to have greater influence; to have the upper hand

praevalid·us -a -um *adj* unusually strong, unusually powerful, imposing; too strong
praevāricāti·ō -ōnis *f (leg)* collusion
praevāricāt·or -ōris *m (leg)* prosecutor in collusion with the defense
praevāric·or -ārī -ātus sum *intr (leg) (of an attorney)* to act in collusion with his opposite to secure a particular outcome to a trial
praevār·us -a -um *adj* very crooked; very knock-kneed
prae·vehor -vehī -vectus sum *tr (of a river)* to flow by **ll** *intr* to ride in front, ride by; to sail by
prae·veniō -venīre -vēnī -ventus *tr* to come before, precede, get the jump on, anticipate; to prevent **ll** *intr* to come before, precede
praeverb·ium -(i)ī *n (gram)* prefix
praeverr·ō -ere *tr* to sweep *(the ground)* before
praever·tō -tere -tī -sus *or* **prae·vertor -vertī -versus sum** *tr* **(-vort-)** to go before, precede, outrun, outstrip; to turn to first, attend to first; to prefer; to come before, anticipate; to prevent; to preoccupy, surprise; *(w. dat or* **prae** *+ abl)* to prefer *(s.o. or s.th.)* to **ll** *intr (w. dat or* **ad**) to go first to, turn to first, attend to first
prae·videō -vidēre -vīdī -vīsus *tr* to foresee
praeviti·ō -āre -āvī -ātus *tr* to taint *or* pollute beforehand
praevi·us -a -um *adj* going before, leading the way
praevol·ō -āre -āvī *intr* to fly out in front
pragmatic·us -a -um *adj* experienced, worldly-wise **ll** *m* legal adviser
pran·deō -dēre -dī -sus *tr* to eat for breakfast, eat for lunch **ll** *intr* to have breakfast, have lunch
prand·ium -(i)ī *n* breakfast; lunch
prānsit·ō -āre *intr* to usually eat breakfast *or* lunch
prāns·or -ōris *m* guest at lunch
prānsōri·us -a -um *adj* suitable for lunch
prāns·us -a -um *pp of* **prandeō ll** *adj* having had breakfast *or* lunch, after eating; well-fed; **prānsus pōtus** having been wined and dined
prasināt·us -a -um *adj* wearing a green outfit
prasiniān·us -ī *m* fan of the green faction *(at the racetrack)*
prasin·us -a -um *adj* (bright) green; **factiō prasina** the Greens *(one of the stables of horses at the racetrack)*
prātēns·is -is -e *adj* meadow, growing in a meadow
prātul·um -ī *n* small meadow
prāt·um -ī *n* meadow; *(fig)* broad expanse of the sea **ll** *npl* meadow grass
prāvē *adv* crookedly; improperly, wrongly, badly, poorly; **prāvē factī versūs** poorly written verses
prāvit·ās -ātis *f* crookedness, distortion; impropriety, irregularity; perverseness, depravity
prāv·us -a -um *adj* crooked, distorted, deformed; irregular, improper, wrong, bad; perverse, vicious
Praxitel·ēs -ī *or* **-ūs** *or* **-ae** *m* Athenian sculptor *(4th cent.* B.C.*)*
Praxitelī·us -a -um *adj* of Praxiteles
precāriō *adv* upon request
precāri·us -a -um *adj* obtained by prayer; dependent on another's will, uncertain, precarious
precāti·ō -ōnis *f* prayer; **precātiōnēs facere** to say prayers
precāt·or -ōris *m* intercessor, suppliant
precēs = *pl of* **prex**
preci·ae -ārum *fpl* grapevine
prec·or -ārī -ātus sum *tr* to entreat, supplicate, pray to; to pray for; to wish for; *(w. double acc)* to pray to *(s.o.)* for; *(w. acc of thing and abl of person)* to request *(s.th.)* from; *(w.* **prō** *+ abl)* to entreat *(e.g., the gods)* on behalf of; *(w.* **ut, nē**) to pray that, pray that not; **longum Augustō diem precārī** to wish Augustus long life **ll** *intr* to pray; *(w.* **ad**) to pray to, *e.g.,* **dī ad quōs precantur** the gods to whom they pray; **male precārī** to curse, utter curses
prehen·dō *or* **pren·dō -dere -dī -sus** *tr* to take hold of, grasp, seize; to detain; to arrest; to catch, surprise; to reach, arrive at; to grasp, understand; *(w.* **in** *+ abl)* to catch a person in the act of; *(mil)* to occupy
prēl·um -ī *n* wine press, oil press; clothes press
premō premere pressī pressus *tr* to press, squeeze; to lie down on *(the ground); (of things)* to be on top of, rest on; to bury *(in the ground);* to trample on; to get on top of, have sex with *(a woman);* to hug *(the shore);* to suppress, hide; to cover, crown; to press hard, bear down on; to weigh down, burden; to put emphasis on *(a point of argument);* to chase, attack; to weigh down, load; to press together, close; to choke, throttle; to block *(an entranceway);* to keep shut up, prevent from escaping; to curb, stop *(movement, an action, a process);* to depress, lower; to submerge, sink; to drown out *(a noise); (of sleep, death)* to overcome, overpower; *(of darkness)* to cover, hide; to mark, impress; to prune; to pressure, urge, importune; to degrade, humble, disparage; to abridge, condense, compress *(words, thoughts);* to press *(wine, oil);* to subjugate; *(geog)* to hem in, surround;

forum premere to frequent the forum, walk about in the forum; **oculōs premere** to close the eyes *(of a dead person);* **pollicem premere** to give the good luck sign *(by pressing the thumb against the index finger);* **vestīgia premere** *(w. gen)* **1** to follow hard upon the tracks of; **2** *(fig)* to follow in *(s.o.'s)* tracks; **vōcem premere** to fall silent **||** *refl & pass* to lower oneself *(in dignity),* stoop **||** *refl* to huddle together

prēnsāti·ō -ōnis *f (pol)* campaign

prēns·ō *or* **prehēns·ō -āre -āvī -ātus** *tr* to take hold of, clutch at, grab; to buttonhole **||** *intr (pol)* to campaign

prēnsus *pp of* **prendō**

pressē *adv* distinctly, with articulation; concisely; accurately, simply

pressī *perf of* **premō**

pressi·ō -ōnis *f* pressure *(exerted by the fulcrum of a lever);* fulcrum

press·ō -āre -āvī -ātus *tr* to press, exert pressure on; to weigh down

pressūr·a -ae *f* pressure

press·us -a -um *pp of* **premō ||** *adj* closed, shut tight; compact, dense; low *(sound),* subdued *(voice);* tight *(embrace);* deliberate *(pace);* concise *(style);* **bāsia pressa** one kiss after another; **cōpia lactis pressī** a supply of cheese

press·us -ūs *m* pressure; expression *(of the face)*

pretiōsē *adv* at great cost, expensively

pretiōs·us -a -um *adj* precious, valuable; expensive; extravagant

pret·ium -(i)ī *n* price; value, worth; reward, return, recompense; bribe; pay, wages; ransom; **ad pretium redigere** to put a price on; **in pretiō esse** to be prized; to be held in high esteem; **in pretiō habēre** to prize, hold in high esteem; **pretiō meō (tuō)** at my (your) expense; **pretium cūrae esse** to be worth the trouble; **pretium facere** to set a price; **pretium habēre** to have value, be worth something; **pretium operae esse** to be worth the effort, be worthwhile

prex precis *f (usu. pl)* prayer; request; intercession; curse, imprecation

Priamē·is -idos *f* daughter of Priam *(Cassandra)*

Priameī·us -a -um *adj* of Priam

Priamid·ēs -ae *m* son of Priam

Priam·us -ī *m* Priam *(son of Laomedon, husband of Hecuba, father of Hector, Paris, Cassandra, etc., king of Troy)*

Priāp·us -ī *m* son of Dionysus and Aphrodite, god of gardens and vineyards, and protector of flocks

prīdem *adv* formerly, previously; once *(in the past);* long ago; **haud ita prīdem** not so long ago, not long before; **iam prīdem** long ago; **quam prīdem?** for how long?; how long ago?

prīdiān·us -a -um *adj* of the day before

prīdiē *adv* the day before

Priēn·ē -ēs *f* coastal town in Ionia, opposite Miletus

prīm·a -ōrum *npl* first part, beginning; first principles *or* elements; **cum prīmīs** among the first, especially; chiefly; first of all; **in prīmīs** above all, chiefly, particularly, especially

prīm·ae -ārum *fpl* lead, first rank, highest place, highest importance; **prīmās dare** *(w. dat)* to attach supreme importance to

prīmaev·us -a -um *adj* youthful

prīmān·ī -ōrum *mpl* soldiers of the first legion

prīmāri·us -a -um *adj* first in rank; first-rate

prīmē *adv* to the highest degree

prīmigen·us -a -um *adj* first-born

prīmipīlār·is -is *m* ranking centurion of a legion

prīmipīl·us -ī *m* ranking centurion of a legion

prīmiti·ae -ārum *fpl* first fruits; *(fig)* beginnings; **ā prīmitiīs** from the beginning, thoroughly

prīmitus *adv* originally, at first; for the first time

prīmō *adv* first, in the first place; at first, at the beginning

prīmord·ium -(i)ī *n* origin, beginning; commencement; beginning of a new reign

prīmōr·is -is -e *adj* first, leading; the front of, the beginning of; tip of; first, earliest; front *(teeth, battle line);* principal; basic; leading *(men);* **digitulī prīmōrēs** fingertips; **in labrīs prīmōribus** on the tip of one's tongue; **prīmoris manus** wrist **||** *mpl* leaders, chiefs, nobles; *(mil)* front ranks

prīmulum *adv* for the first time; at first, first of all

prīmul·us -a -um *adj* very first

prīmum *adv* first, in the first place, before all else; at first; for the first time; **cum prīmum** *(or* **ubi prīmum** *or* **ut prīmum)** as soon as; **prīmum dum** in the first place; **quam prīmum** as soon as possible

prīmumdum *adv* in the first place

prīm·us -a -um *adj* first; foremost; principal; distinguished; nearest; basic, fundamental; first-class; the earliest stages; the front of; front *(teeth);* the tip of, end of; **prīmā fronte** *(or* **faciē)** outwardly, at first glance; **prīmās partēs agere** to play the lead role; **prīmī pedēs** forefeet; **prīmīs digitīs** with *or* at the fingertips; **prīmō annō** at the beginning of the year *or* season; **prīmō quoque tempore** at the very earliest opportunity; **prīmus in**

prōvinciam introiit he was the first to enter the province; **prīmus quisque** the very first, the first possible; each in turn ‖ *mpl* leading citizens ‖ *fpl see* **prīmae** ‖ *n* beginning; front; **ā prīmō** from the first; **in prīmō** in the beginning; *(mil)* at the head of the column ‖ *npl see* **prīma**

prīnc·eps -ipis *adj* first; earliest; original; leading, in front; foremost, chief ‖ *m* leader, chief; emperor; *(mil)* maniple, company; *(mil)* captain, company commander, centurion; *(mil)* rank of centurion; **prīnceps prīmus** a centurion ranking second among the six centurions of a legion ‖ *mpl (mil)* soldiers of the second line *(between the* **hastātī** *and the* **triāriī**), second line

prīncipāl·is -is -e *adj* first, foremost; original, primitive; chief, principal; of the emperor; **via prīncipālis** *(mil)* main street *(of a camp)*; **porta prīncipālis** *(mil)* main gate *(of a camp)*

prīncipāt·us -ūs *m* first place; post of commander in chief; principate; rule, sovereignty; origin, beginning; **prīncipātum tenēre** to occupy first place, be in the lead

prīncipi·a -ōrum *npl* first principles; foundations; *(mil)* front line, front-line troops; *(mil)* headquarters

prīncipiāl·is -is -e *adj* initial

prīncipiō *adv* in the beginning, at first

prīncip·ium -(i)ī *n* beginning, start; starting point; origin; beginner, originator; basis; premise; *(pol)* first to vote; *(pol)* right to vote first; **ā prīncipiō** in the beginning, at first; **dē prīncipiō** right from the start; **prīncipium capere** *(or* **sūmere** *or* **exōrdīrī**) to begin; **prīncipium dūcere ab** to originate with ‖ *npl* foundations; *(mil)* headquarters; *(mil)* the second line in order of battle; *(phil)* rudimentary particles of matter, elements

pri·or -or -us *(gen:* **-ōris**) *comp; no positive exists) adj* previous, preceding, prior, former; more fundamental, basic; better, superior, preferable; *(of kings, rulers)* the elder; **in priōrem partem** in a forward direction; **priōrēs partēs agere** to play a more important role ‖ *mpl* forefathers, ancestors, ancients ‖ *fpl (only acc)* lead, preference ‖ *npl* earlier events

prīscē *adv* in the old-fashioned style

prīsc·us -a -um *adj* old, ancient; old-time, old-fashioned; former, previous

Prīsc·us -ī *m* Roman family name *(cognomen), esp.* Lucius Tarquinius Priscus *(the fifth king of Rome)* ‖ Quintus Servilius Priscus Fidenas *(conqueror of the Veientes and Fidenates in 435 B.C.)* ‖ Helvidius Priscus *(prominent Stoic under Nero and Vespasian)*

prīstin·us -a -um *adj* former, earlier; pristine, primitive, original; preceding, previous, yesterday's ‖ *n* **in prīstinum restituere** to restore to its former condition

pristr·is -is *(acc:* **-im** *or* **-in**) *f or* **pistr·īx -īcis** *f* sea monster; whale, shark; swift ship; *(astr)* the Whale *(constellation)*

prius *adv* earlier, before, previously, sooner, first; sooner, rather

priusquam *conj (also written as two words)* before

prīvātim *adv* privately, in private; as a private citizen; at home

prīvāti·ō -ōnis *f* removal, negation

prīvāt·us -a -um *adj* private; personal, individual, peculiar; isolated; ordinary *(language)* ‖ *m* private citizen; civilian; subject *(of a ruler)* ‖ *n* privacy, retirement; private property, private land; **ex prīvātō** out of one's own pocket; **in prīvātō** in private; **in prīvātum** for private use

Prīvern·ās -ātis *adj* of Privernum ‖ *mpl* the people of Privernum

Prīvern·um -ī *n* Latin town founded by the Volscians

prīvigna -ae *f* stepdaughter

prīvign·us -ī *m* stepson ‖ *mpl* stepchildren

prīvilēg·ium -(i)ī *n* privilege, special right; *(pol)* special bill directed against *or* in favor of an individual

prīv·ō -are *tr (w. abl)* **1** to deprive of, rob of; **2** to release from, relieve of, free from

prīv·us -a -um *adj* every, each, single; own, private; *(w. gen)* deprived of

prō *adv (w.* **quam** *or* **ut**) just as, according as ‖ *prep (w. abl)* before, in front of; in the presence of; for, on behalf of, in favor of, in the service of, on the side of; instead of, for, in lieu of; just as, the same as, for; in proportion to; according to; in comparison with; by virtue of; in name of; **esse prō** *(w. abl)* to be as good as, be the equivalent of; **esse** *(or* **stāre prō** + *abl)* to be on the side of *(s.o.)*; **prō certō habēre** to regard *(s.th.)* as certain; **prō eō** just the same; **prō eō atque** *(or* **ac**) just as, the same as; **prō eō quod** in view of the fact that; **prō eō quantum** in proportion to, according as; **prō eō ut** instead of being the case that; **prō hērēde** in his capactiy as heir; **prō occīsō relictus** left for dead; **prō rōstrō ōrātiōnem habēre** to speak from the rostrum; **prō sē quisque** each one for himself, individually; **prō sententiā dīcere** to state as his opinion; **prō testimōniō dīcere** to state by way of evidence; **prō vallō carrōs obiciunt** they put their wagons in the way to serve as a barricade; **utrum prō ancillā mē habēs an fīliā?** do you regard me as a maid or a daughter? ‖ *interj* oh!; **prō dī immortālēs**! oh, heavens above!

prō- **(pro-, prod-)** *pref* **1** forward movement: **prōgredī** to go forward; **2** downward movement: **prōclīvis** downhill; **3** action in front: **prōtegere** to cover in front; **4** bringing into the open: **prōdere** to bring out, publish; **5** priority in time: **prōvidēre** to see beforehand; **6** advantage: **prōdesse** *(w. dat)* to be advantageous to, be good for

proāgor·us -ī *m* mayor *(in some Greek provincial towns in Sicily)*

proauct·or -ōris *mf* early ancestor

proavi·a -ae *f* great-grandmother

proavīt·us -a -um *adj* great-grandfather's, ancestral

proav·us -ī *m* great-grandfather; ancestor, forefather

probābil·is -is -e *adj* worthy of approval, commendable, acceptable; pleasing, agreeable; probable, plausible, likely

probābilit·ās -ātis *f* probability

probābiliter *adv* probably

probāti·ō -ōnis *f* approval, approbation; criterion, test; proof

probāt·or -ōris *m* approver, supporter, backer

probāt·us -a -um *adj* approved, acceptable; tried, tested, good; esteemed

probē *adv* correctly, well, satisfactorily; thoroughly, very, very much; **haud probē** not really, no; **pereō probē** *(coll)* I'm absolutely a goner

probit·ās -ātis *f* probity, uprightness, honesty, goodness; sexual purity; good behavior

problēm·a -atis *m (rhet)* difficult question for debate, problem

prob·ō -āre -āvī -ātus *tr* to approve, commend, esteem; to make good, represent as good, make acceptable; to pronounce judgment on; to pronounce approval of; to make credible, prove, show, demonstrate; to test, try, inspect; **probāre prō** *(w. abl)* to pass *(s.o.)* off as **‖** *pass* **probārī prō** *(w. abl)* to pass for, be taken for

probosc·is -idis *f* snout; trunk *(of an elephant)*

probriperlecebr·ae -ārum *fpl* temptations

probrōs·us -a -um *adj* scandalous, shameful, abusive

probr·um -ī *n* abuse, invective, reproach; shameful act; lewdness, indecency; shame, disgrace; charge of disgraceful conduct

prob·us -a -um *adj* good, honest, upright, virtuous, decent; *(coll)* real, proper, downright

Prob·us -ī *m* Roman family name *(cognomen), esp.* Marcus Valerius Probus *(grammarian of the 1st cent.* A.D.*)*

Proc·a *or* **Proc·ās -ae** *m* Proca *(king of Alba Longa and father of Numitor and Amulius)*

procācit·ās -ātis *f* brashness

procāciter *adv* brashly

proc·āx -ācis *adj* brash

prō·cēdō -cēdere -cessī -cessum *intr* to proceed, go forward, advance; to make progress; to come out *(in public)*, show oneself, appear; to come forth, arise; *(of time)* to pass, elapse; to turn out, result, succeed; to continue

procell·a -ae *f* violent wind, squall, hurricane, storm; *(fig)* violence, commotion, storm; *(mil)* violent charge

prōcell·ō -ere *tr* to throw down **‖** *refl* **sē procellere in mēnsam** to flop down at the table

proc·er -eris *m* chief, noble

procellōs·us -a -um *adj* gusty, stormy

prōcērē *adv* far

procer·ēs -um *mpl* leading men *(of a society, etc.)*; leaders *(of a profession, art)*

prōcērit·ās -ātis *f* height, tallness; length **‖** *fpl* the different heights *(e.g., of trees)*

prōcērius *adv* farther, to a greater extent, more

prōcēr·us -a -um *adj* tall *(person, tree);* long *(neck, beak);* lofty *(idea); (pros)* long; **palmae prōcērae** open palms

prōcessī *perf of* **prōcēdō**

prōcessi·ō -ōnis *f* advance

prōcess·us -a -um *pp of* **prōcēdō** **‖** *adj* advanced *(age)*

prōcess·us -ūs *m* advance, progress

Prochyt·a -ae *or* **Prochyt·ē -ēs** *f* small island off the Campanian coast *(modern Procida)*

proc·ī -ōrum *mpl* class of leading citizens under the Servian constitution

prō·cidō -cidere -cidī *intr* to fall forwards, fall over, fall down, fall prostrate

prōcīnctū *(abl only) m* **in prōcīnctu** ready for combat, on red alert

prōclāmāt·or -ōris *m* loudmouth

prōclām·ō -āre -āvī -ātus *tr* to yell out; to exclaim; *(w. acc & inf)* to cry out that **‖** *intr* to yell; to practice public speaking

Procl·ēs -is *m* one of the first pair of kings to reign at Sparta, together with Eurysthenes

prōclīn·ō -āre -āvī -ātus *tr* to bend, bend forward; **rēs prōclīnāta** critical situation, crisis

prōclīv·e -is *n* slope, descent; **in prōclīvī esse** to be easy

prōclīvī *adv* downhill; effortlessly

prōclīv·is -is -e *or* **prōclīv·us -a -um** *adj* sloping down; sloping forward; downhill; easy; *(w.* **ad***)* inclined to, disposed to, ready for; *(of years, seasons)* declining; *(fig)* going downhill, insecure; *(w.* **ad***)* inclined to

prōclīvit·ās -ātis *f* proclivity, tendency, predisposition
prōclīviter *adv* readily; easily, effortlessly
prōclīvius *adv* more rapidly
prōclīv·us *see* **prōclīvis**
Procn·ē -ēs *f* **(Prog-)** Procne *(daughter of Pandion, sister of Philomela, wife of Tereus, and mother and murderess of Itys; she was changed into a swallow);* swallow
proc·ō -āre *or* **proc·or -ārī** *tr* to require, demand
prōcōns·ul *(and* **prō cōnsule) -ulis** *m* vice-consul, proconsul; governor of a province; military commander
prōcōnsulār·is -is -e *adj* proconsular
prōcōnsulāt·us -ūs *m* proconsulship, proconsulate
prōcrāstināti·ō -ōnis *f* procrastination
prōcrāstin·ō -āre -āvī -ātus *tr* to put off till the next day, postpone **II** *intr* to procrastinate
prōcreāti·ō -ōnis *f* procreation
prōcreāt·or -ōris *m* procreator; creator **II** *mpl* parents
prōcreātr·īx -īcis *f* mother
prōcre·ō -āre -āvī -ātus *tr* to procreate, beget; to produce
prōcrēsc·ō -ere *intr* to spring forth, be produced; to continue to grow, grow up
Procr·is -is *or* **-idis** *f* Procris *(wife of Cephalus, who mistook her for a wild beast and shot her with bow and arrow)*
Procrūst·ēs -ae *m* Procrustes (*notorious robber in Attica who stretched his victims to the length of his bed or mutilated them if they were too tall*)
prōcub·ō -āre -uī *intr* to lie stretched out
prō·cūdō -cūdere -cūsī -cūsus *tr (lit & fig)* to hammer out, forge
procul *adv* at a distance, in the distance; far away, a great way off; from a distance, from far; **haud procul āfuit quīn lēgātōs violārent** they came close to outraging the ambassadors; **nōn procul ab** not far from
prōculc·ō -āre -āvī -ātus *tr* to trample upon, trample down
Proculēi·us -ī *m* Roman clan name *(nomen), esp.* Gaius Proculeius *(friend of Augustus and literary patron)*
prōcumbō prōcumbere prōcubuī prōcubitum *intr* to fall down, sink down; to lean forward, bend over, be broken down; to lie down; *(fig)* to go to ruin; *(topog)* to extend, spread
prōcūrāti·ō -ōnis *f* attention; *(w. gen)* **1** concern for, care for; **2** responsibility for, charge over; **3** management of, administration of; **4** procuratorship of; **5** expiation of
prōcūrāt·or -ōris *m* procurator, manager, administrator; agent, deputy; governor of a (minor) province
prōcūrātr·īx -īcis *f* superintendent *(female)*
prōcūr·ō -āre -āvī -ātus *tr* to look after, attend to; to administer *(as procurator);* to have charge of; to avert by sacrifice; to expiate **II** *intr* to serve as procurator
prō·currō -currere -(cu)currī -cursum *intr* to run out ahead, dash forward; to jut out, project
prōcursāti·ō -ōnis *f* sally, charge
prōcursātōr·ēs -um *mpl* skirmishers
prōcurs·ō -āre *intr* to keep charging out; to continue to skirmish
prōcurs·us -ūs *m* sally, charge
prōcurv·us -a -um *adj* curving forwards; curving, winding *(shore)*
proc·us -ī *m* suitor; gigolo **II** *mpl* class of leading citizens in the Servian constitution; **impudentēs procī** shameless candidates
Procy·ōn -ōnis *m (astr)* Lesser Dog Star *(the constellation Canis Minor)*
prōdāctus *pp of* **prōdigō**
prōdeambul·ō -āre *intr* to go out for a walk
prōd·eō -īre -iī -itum *intr* to go out, come out, go forth, come forth; *(of plants)* to come out; to appear in public; to come forward *(in the assembly or court);* to appear *(on stage);* to go ahead, advance; **in proelium prōdīre** to go into battle; **obviam prōdīre** *(w. dat)* to go out to meet *(s.o.); (e.g., of a cliff)* to jut out, project
prō·dīcō -dīcere -dīxī -dictus *tr* to set *(a date)* beforehand *(for some activity);* **praetor reō atque accūsātōribus diem prōdīxit** *(leg)* the praetor announced the date of the trial to the defendant as well as the plaintiffs
prōdictāt·ōr -ōris *m* vice-dictator
Prodic·us -ī *m* sophist of Ceos, contemporary with Socrates
prōdigē *adv* lavishly
prōdigenti·a -ae *f* extravagance; **prōdigentia opum** wasting of resources
prōdigiāl·is -is -e *adj* marked with prodigies
prōdigiāliter *adv* to a fantastic degree
prōdigiōs·us -a -um prodigious; freakish
prōdig·ium -(i)ī *n* prodigy, portent; unnatural crime, monstrous crime; monster, freak
prōd·igō -igere -ēgī -āctus *tr* to squander, waste
prōdig·us -a -um *adj* wasteful; lavish, openhanded; *(w. gen)* free with; **animae prōdigus** free with *or* careless with one's life; **herbae prōdigus locus** spot with luxurious growth of grass

prōditi·ō -ōnis *f* betrayal, treason; **prōditiōnem agere** *(w. dat)* to commit treason against, betray
prōdit·or -ōris *m* betrayer, traitor
prō·dō -dere -didī -ditus *tr* to bring out, bring forth, produce; to reveal, disclose; *(of a writer, esp. w.* **memoriā** *or* **memoriae** *or* **ad memoriam)** to record, relate, report, hand down, transmit; to proclaim; to appoint; to give up, surrender; to forsake, betray; to prolong; *(w. dat)* **1** to betray to; **2** to reveal to
prōdoc·eō -ēre *tr* to teach publicly
prodrom·us -ī *m* forerunner; northerly winds *(that precede the Etesian winds)*
prō·dūcō -dūcere -dūxī ductus *tr* to bring out, bring forth; to produce; to promote, advance; to bring to light; to bring into the world; to raise, bring up; to educate; to drag out, protract; to lengthen *(a syllable);* to lead on, induce; to put off, adjourn; to put *(a slave)* up for sale; to produce, perform *(on the stage); (leg)* to bring to court
prōduct·a -ōrum *npl* preferable things, preferences
prōductē *adv* long; **prōductē litteram dīcere** to pronounce the letter *or* vowel long
prōducti·ō -ōnis *f* lengthening
prōduct·ō -āre *tr* to drag out
prōduct·us -a -um *pp of* **prōdūcō** ‖ *adj* lengthened, prolonged, long
proēgmen·on -ī *n* preference
proeliār·is -is -e *adj* battle, of battle
proeliāt·or -ōris *m* combatant
proeli·or -ārī -ātus sum *intr* to battle
proel·ium -(i)ī *n* battle, combat, fight; **proelium committere** *or* **facere** *or* **inīre** *or* **sūmere** to go into action, begin to battle ‖ *npl* fighting men, warriors
Proetid·es -um *fpl* daughters of Proetus, who were driven mad by Hera and imagined that they were cows
Proët·us -ī *m* Proëtus, king of Argos *or* Tiryns, twin-brother of Acrisius
profān·ō -āre -āvī -ātus *tr* to profane
profān·us -a -um *adj* unconsecrated, ordinary; impious; ill-omened
profātur *(3rd singl)* **profārī profātus est** *tr* to say, declare ‖ *intr* to speak out
prōfēcī *perf of* **prōficiō**
profecti·ō -ōnis *f* setting out, departure; source *(of money)*
profectō *adv* really, actually
prōfectus *pp of* **prōficiō**
profectus *pp of* **proficīscor**
prōfect·us -ūs *m* progress, advance; success; profit
prō·ferō -ferre -tulī -lātus *tr* to bring forward, advance, bring out; to extend, enlarge; to put off, postpone; to produce, discover, invent; to make known, publish; to express; to mention, cite, quote; **in medium** *(or* **in lūcem)** **prōferre** to publish, disclose; **pedem prōferre** to advance; **rēs prōferre** *(leg)* to declare a recess; **signa prōferre** *(mil)* to march forward
professi·ō -ōnis *f* public acknowledgment, profession, declaration; registration *(at which property, etc., was declared);* profession, business
profess·or -ōris *m* professor, teacher
professōri·us -a -um *adj* professorial; professional, expert
professus *pp of* **profiteor**
profēst·us -a -um *adj* non-holiday, ordinary; **diēs profēstus** workday
prō·ficiō -ficere -fēcī -fectum *intr* to make progress, make headway, advance; to have success; to be useful, do good, help, be conducive; **nihil prōficere** to do no good
pro·ficīscor -ficīscī -fectus sum *intr* to set out, start, go, depart; to originate, proceed, arise
pro·fiteor -fitērī -fessus sum *tr* to declare publicly, acknowledge, confess, profess; to offer freely, promise, volunteer; to follow as a profession, practice *(e.g., law);* to make a declaration of, register *(property, etc., before a public official);* **indicium profitērī** to volunteer evidence, testify freely; **nōmen profitērī** to put one's name in as a candidate; **sē adiūtōrem profitērī** *(w.* **ad)** to volunteer to help *(s.o.)* ‖ *intr* to make a confession, make an admission; to be a professor, be a teacher
prōflīgāt·or -ōris *m* big spender
prōflīgāt·us -a -um *adj* profligate
prōflīg·ō -āre -āvī -ātus *tr* to knock to the ground, knock down; to defeat; to bring to an end, do away with, finish off; to ruin, crush; to degrade, debase
prōfl·ō -āre -āvī -ātus *tr* to breathe out
prōflu·ēns -entis *adj* flowing along; fluent *(speech)* ‖ *f* running water
prōfluenter *adv* easily, effortlessly, fluently
prōfluenti·a -ae *f* fluency
prōflu·ō -ere -xī *intr* to flow out; to flow along; *(fig)* to proceed; **gravēdō prōfluit** the head cold results in a runny nose
prōfluv·ium -(i)ī *n* flow
pro·for -fārī -fātus sum *tr* to say, declare ‖ *intr* to speak out
prōfūdī *perf of* **prōfundō**
pro·fugiō -fugere -fūgī -fugitūrus *tr* to run away from, escape from ‖ *intr* to run away, escape; *(w.* **ad)** to take refuge with, take refuge at the house of
profug·us -a -um *adj* fugitive; banished, exiled; nomadic ‖ *m* refugee

pro·fundō -fundere -fūdī -fūsus *tr* to pour, pour out; to shed *(blood, tears)* freely; to utter; to give vent to; to spend freely, squander; **animam** *(or* **spīritum)** **prōfundere** to breathe one's last; **vītam prō patriā prōfundere** to give one's life for one's country **ll** *refl & pass* to come pouring out; to sprout

profund·us -a -um *adj* deep; boundless, vast; dense *(forest, cloud);* high; infernal; *(fig)* bottomless, boundless **ll** *n* depth; the deep, deep sea; abyss

profūsē *adv* in disorder, haphazardly, helter-skelter; extravagantly

profūsi·ō -ōnis *f* profusion

profūs·us -a -um *pp of* **prōfundō ll** *adj* extravagant, lavish, profuse; excessive, expensive

prōgen·er -erī *m* grandaughter's husband

prōgener·ō -āre -āvī -ātus *tr* to beget, give birth to; to produce

prōgeni·ēs -ēī *f* offspring, progeny; line, family; lineage, descent

prōgenit·or -ōris *m* progenitor

prō·gignō -gignere -genuī -genitus *tr* to beget, produce

prōgnāriter *adv* precisely, exactly

prōgnāt·us -a -um *adj (w. abl or* **ab** *or* **ex)** born of, descended from **ll** *m* child; grandson

Prognē *see* **Procnē**

prognōstic·on *or* **prognōstic·um -ī** *n* sign of the future, prognostic **ll** *npl* signs of the weather

prō·gredior -gredī -gressus sum *intr* to go forward, march forward; to advance; to go on, make headway, make progress; to go forth, go out

prōgressi·ō -ōnis *f* progress, advancement; increase, growth; *(rhet)* climax

prōgressus *pp of* **progredior**

prōgress·us -ūs *m* progress, advance; march *(of time or events)*

prōh *interj* oh!; **prōh dī immortālēs**! oh, heavens above!

pro(h)oemi·or -ārī *intr* to make an introduction *or* preface

pro(h)oem·ium *or* **pro(h)ēm·ium -(i)ī** *n* introduction, preface; prelude; *(fig)* prelude *(e.g., to a fight)*

prohib·eō -ēre -uī -itus *tr* to hold back, check, hinder, prevent, avert, keep off; to prohibit; to preclude; to keep away; to defend, protect; *(w.* **nē, quōminus,** *or in negative contexts* **quīn)** to keep *(s.o.)* from *(doing s.th.)*

prohibiti·ō -ōnis *f* prohibition

prōiēcī *perf of* **prōiciō**

prōiectīci·us -a -um *adj* exposed, abandoned *(child)*

prōiecti·ō -ōnis *f* stretching out; **prōiectiō bracchiī** stretching out of the arm

prōiect·us -a -um *pp of* **prōiciō ll** *adj* jutting out; prostrate, stretched out; abject, contemptible; downcast; *(w.* **ad)** prone to

prōiect·us -ūs *m* projection, extension

prō·iciō -icere -iēcī -iectus *tr* to throw down; to throw away, abandon, forsake; to fling from oneself as unwanted, discard; to hold out, extend; to banish, exile; to neglect, desert; to blurt out; to give up, sacrifice; to put off, delay; to throw overboard; *(w.* **in** + *acc or* **ad)** to abandon to *(a fate),* expose to; **prōicere in exilium** to drive out, banish **ll** *refl* to throw oneself, plunge; to rush; *(w.* **in** + *acc)* to give way to *(a feeling, tears, habit);* **sē prōicere ad pedēs** *(w. gen)* to throw oneself at the feet of; **sē prōicere ex nāve** to jump overboard; **sē prōicere in Forum** to rush into the Forum; **sē prōicere in muliebrēs flētūs** to give way to unmanly weeping **ll** *pass (geog)* to extend; *(of a promontory)* to jut out **ll** *intr* to jut out

proïnde *or* **proïn** *(or* **proin** *as monosyllable) adv* so then, consequently, accordingly; equally; likewise; **proïnde atque** *(or* **ac** *or* **ut** *or* **quam)** just as, exactly as; **proïnde atque sī** *(or* **ac sī** *or* **quasi)** just as if

prō·lābor -lābī -lāpsus sum *intr* to glide forward, slip *or* move forward; to fall forwards, fall on one's face; to slip out; *(of words)* to slip out, escape; to be led on, led astray *(by fear, greed, etc.); (fig)* to fail, go to ruin, collapse; **prōlābī per equī caput** to go flying over the head of the horse

prōlāpsi·ō -ōnis *f* slipping

prōlāpsus *pp of* **prōlābor**

prōlāti·ō -ōnis *f* extension *(of territory);* adducing, mentioning *(of precedents);* citing *(of examples);* delay, postponement

prōlāt·ō -āre *tr* to extend; to put off, delay

prōlātus *pp of* **prōferō**

prōlect·ō -āre -āvī -ātus *tr* to lure

prōl·ēs -is *f* offspring, progeny, children; descendants; race, stock; child; young man

prōlētār·ius -(i)ī *m* proletarian **ll** *mpl* proletariat

prōli·ciō -cere *tr* to entice, bring out, lead on; to incite

prōlixē *adv* freely, wildly, readily, cheerfully, willingly

prōlix·us -a -um *adj* long, freely growing, wild *(beard, hair, etc.);* favorable *(circumstances)*

prōlocūtus *pp of* **prōloquor**

prōlog·us -ī *m* prologue *(of a play);* actor who gives the prologue

prōlo·quor -quī -cūtus sum *tr & intr* to speak out

prōlub·ium -(i)ī *n* desire, inclination, yen

prōlū·dō -dere -sī -sum *tr* to be a prelude to ‖ *intr* to practice; *(of boxers)* to spar, shadowbox

prō·luō -luere -luī -lūtus *tr* to wash out, flush, wash off; *(of water)* to wash away; to wet, drench; to wash clean, wash out

prōlūsi·ō -ōnis *f* practice fight, dry run; sparring

prōlūtus *pp of* **prōluō**

prōluvi·ēs -ēī *f* flood; discharge, excrement

prōmercāl·is -is -e *adj* sold in the open market

prōmer·eō -ēre -uī -itus *or* **prōmer·eor -ērī -itus sum** *tr* to deserve, merit, earn ‖ *intr* to be deserving; *(w.* **dē** *+ abl)* to deserve the gratitude of; **bene dē multīs prōmerēre** *(or* **prōmerērī)** to deserve the full gratitude of many people

prōmerit·um -ī *n* favor; reward, due; merit; guilt; **bene (male) prōmeritum** a good (bad) turn

Promēth·eūs -eī *or* **-eos** *m* son of Iapetus and Clymene, brother of Epimetheus, and discoverer of use of fire, which he taught to men

Promēthē·us -a -um *adj* Promethean, of Prometheus

Promēthīd·ēs -ae *m* son of Prometheus, Deucalion *(who, with his wife Pyrrha, survived the Deluge)*

prōmin·ēns -entis *adj* prominent, projecting ‖ *n* headland

prōmin·eō -ēre -uī *intr* to jut out, stick out, stick up; *(of persons)* to lean out, bend forward; *(w.* **in** *+ acc)* to reach down to, reach out for

prōmīscam *or* **prōmīscē** *or* **prōmīscuē** *adv* in common; without distinction; all at the same time *or* in the same place

prōmīsc(u)·us -a -um *adj* promiscuous, haphazard, indiscriminate; in common, open to all; common

prōmissi·ō -ōnis *f* promise

prōmiss·or -ōris *m* one who promises *or* guarantees

prōmiss·us -a -um *adj* allowed to grow, long ‖ *n* promise; prediction

prō·mittō -mittere -mīsī -missus *tr* to send forth; to let *(e.g., hair)* grow; to promise, guarantee; to predict as certain; to give hope of; **ad cēnam** *(or* **ad aliquem)** **prōmittere** to accept an invitation to dinner *(or* to s.o.'s home); **damnī īnfectī prōmittere** to guarantee compensation for damage done; **prōmittere (in mātrimōniam)** to promise *(one's daughter)* in marriage ‖ *refl (w.* **ad)** to have expectations of attaining; **sibi prōmittere** to promise oneself, look forward to, count on

prōm·ō -ere -(p)sī -ptus *tr* to bring out, draw out; to produce *(arguments);* to bring to light, reveal; to bring out, express *(ideas, emotions)*

prōmon·eō -ēre *tr* to warn openly

prōmontōr·ium -(i)ī *n* promontory, cape

prōmōt·a -ōrum *npl* second choice

prō·moveō -movēre -mōvī -mōtus *tr* to move *(s.th.)* forward, cause to advance; to enlarge, extend; to effect, accomplish; to encourage, egg on; to promote *(to higher office);* to bring to light, reveal; to postpone; **gradum** *(or* **pedem)** **prōmovēre** to step forward; **nihil prōmovēre** to accomplish nothing, do no good, make no progress ‖ *intr* to make headway

promptārius *see* **promptuārius**

promptē *adv* readily; willingly; fluently

prompt·ō -āre *tr* to give out, distribute; to be treasurer of

promptuāri·us -a -um *adj* of a storehouse, storage; **cella promptuāria** *(coll)* jail, cooler ‖ *n* storeroom, cupboard

prompt·us -a -um *pp of* **prōmō** ‖ *adj* at hand, readily available; easy; glib *(tongue);* brought to light, evident; bold, enterprising; *(w. dat or* **ad** *or* **in** *+ acc)* **1** readily inclined to; **2** ready *or* prepared for; *(w.* **in** *+ abl)* quick at; *(w.* **adversus** *+ acc)* ready for, prepared against; *(w. inf)* ready to, quick to; **promptum est** *(w. inf)* it is an easy matter to

prompt·us -ūs *m* **in promptū 1** within easy reach, at one's disposal *or* command; **2** in full view, in a prominent position; **3** within one's powers *or* capabilities; **4** at one's command; **in promptū esse** to be obvious; **in promptū gerere** *(or* **habēre** *or* **ponere)** to display

prōmulgāti·ō -ōnis *f (pol)* promulgation, official publication *(of a proposed law)*

prōmulg·ō -āre -āvī -ātus *tr* to promulgate, to publish, publicize

prōmuls·is -idis *f* hors d'oeuvres

prōmuntur·ium *or* **prōmontōr·ium -(i)ī** *n* promontory, cape

prōm·us -ī *m* butler

prōmūtu·us -a -um *adj (fin)* on credit, advanced as a loan

prōnē *adv* downwards; slantwise

pronep·ōs -ōtis *m* great-grandson

pronept·is -is *f* great-grandaughter

pronoe·a -ae *f* divine providence

prōnōm·en -inis *n (gram)* pronoun; *(gram)* demonstrative pronoun

prōnub·a -ae *f* matron of honor *(who conducted the bride to the husband's home); (of Juno, Bellona, Tisiphone)* patroness of marriage

prōnūntiāti·ō -ōnis *f* proclamation, declaration; verdict; pronunciation *(of words);* proposition *(in logic); (rhet)* delivery

prōnūntiāt·or -ōris *m* narrator

prōnūntiāt·um -ī *n* proposition *(in logic)*

prōnūnti·ō -āre -āvī -ātus *tr* to proclaim, announce; to express *(opinion, judgment);* to pronounce *(words);* to hold out, promise *(rewards)* publicly; to recite, deliver; to narrate, relate; **sententiam prōnūntiāre** *(pol)* to announce a motion *(for discussion in the Senate),* to put a motion to a vote **II** *intr (theat) (of an actor)* speak one's lines

prōnūper *adv* quite recently

prōnur·us -ūs *f* grandson's wife

prōn·us -a -um *adj* leaning, inclined, bending, stooping, bent over, bent forwards; swift, rushing, dashing, moving swiftly along; sloping, steep *(hill, road);* sinking, setting *(sun, etc.);* downhill; easy; *(w. dat or* **ad** *or* **in** + *acc)* inclined toward, disposed toward, prone to; *(w. dat)* inclined to favor *(e.g., a winner)* **II** *n* downward tendency, gravity **II** *npl* slopes

propāgāti·ō -ōnis *f* propagation, reproduction; prolongation; transmission *(to posterity);* **nōminis propāgātiō** perpetuation of the name

propāgāt·or -ōris *m* one who extends *(s.th.)* in time; **propāgātor prōvinciae** grantor of an extended provincial command

propāg·ō -āre -āvī -ātus *tr* to produce *(plants)* from slips; to produce *(offspring);* to propagate *(race, religion);* to extend *(territory);* to prolong *(a period, life);* to cause *(a family name, tradition)* to endure, hand down *(to posterity)*

propāg·ō -inis *f* slip *(from which a plant is propagated);* offspring, progeny; race, line; descendants

prōpalam *adv* openly, publicly

prōpatul·us -a -um *adj* open **II** *n* open space; **in prōpatulō habēre** to display

prope *(comp:* **propius;** *superl:* **proximē)** *adv* near, nearby; *(of time)* near, at hand; *(of degree)* nearly, almost, practically, just about; *(w.* **ab** + *abl)* close by, near to; *(of time)* toward, about; **prope est cum** the time has come when **II** *prep (w. acc)* near, near to; **prope diem** very soon, any day now

propediem *adv* very soon, any day now

prō·pellō -pellere -pulī -pulsus *tr* to propel, drive forward; to push over, overturn, upset; to drive away, drive out; to banish, expel

propemodo *or* **propemodum** *adv* nearly, practically, almost

prōpen·deō -dēre -dī -sum *intr* to hang down; *(w.* **in** + *acc)* to be inclined to, be favorably disposed to

prōpēnsē *adv* readily, willingly

prōpēnsi·ō -ōnis *f* propensity, inclination

prōpēns·us -a -um *pp of* **prōpendeō II** *adj* weighty; approaching; inclined; ready, willing; *(w. dat, w.* **ad** *or* **in** + *acc)* favorably disposed to, partial to; **prōpēnsō animō** with ready mind, willingly; **prōpēnsus in alteram partem** inclined toward the other point of view

properanter *adv* hastily, quickly

properanti·a -ae *f* haste

properāti·ō -ōnis *f* haste

properātō *adv* hastily, speedily

properāt·us -a -um *adj* hurried, hasty, speedy **II** *n* speed; **properātō opus est** speed is required

properē *adv* hastily, in haste, quickly; without hesitation

properip·ēs -edis *adj* quick-moving, quick-footed

proper·ō -āre -āvī -ātus *tr* to speed up; to prepare hastily, do in haste **II** *intr* to be quick; to go *or* move quickly

Propert·ius -(i)ī *m* Sextus Aurelius Propertius *(Latin elegiac poet, native of Umbria, c. 50–15* B.C.*)*

proper·us -a -um *adj* quick, speedy

prōpex·us -a -um *adj* combed forward

prophēt·a -ae *m* prophet

propīn *n (only nom and acc in use)* apéritif

prōpīnāti·ō -ōnis *f* toast

prōpīn·ō -āre -āvī -ātus *tr* to drink *(e.g., a cup of wine)* as a toast; to drink a toast to *(s.o.); (w. dat)* **1** to drink *(e.g., a cup of wine as a toast)* to; **2** to pass on *(a cup)* to

propinqu·a -ae *f* relative *(female)*

propinquē *adv* near at hand

propinquit·ās -ātis *f* proximity, nearness, vicinity; relationship, affinity; friendship

propinqu·ō -āre -āvī -ātus *tr* to bring on; to hasten **II** *intr* to approach; *(w. dat)* to draw near to, approach

propinqu·us -a -um *adj* near, neighboring; *(of time)* near, at hand; closely related; *(w. dat)* akin to; **in spē propinquā missiōnis** in the hope of an early discharge; **nūlla propinqua spēs** no hope for the near future; **spēs propinquī reditūs** hope for an early return **II** *mf* relative **II** *n* neighborhood; **in propinquō** in the vicinity; *(of time, events)* near at hand, in the offing

propi·or -or -us *adj* nearer, closer; *(of time)* earlier; later, more recent; more closely related, more like, more nearly resembling; more imminent; more intimate, closer *(tie);* of more importance, of more concern; *(of battle)* fought at close range; shorter *(route); (w. dat)* **1** nearer to, closer to; **2** closer to *(in resemblance),* more like; **3** to be favorably disposed to; *(w. acc or w.* **ab** + *abl)* closer to **II** *npl* closer side *(e.g., of a river);* more recent events

propiti·ō -āre -āvī -ātus *tr* to propitiate, appease

propiti·us -a -um *adj (w. dat)* **1** propitious toward; **2** favorably disposed toward

propnigē·um *or* **propnigē·on -ī** *n* sweat room *(of a bath)*
Prōpoetid·es -um fpl Cyprian girls who denied the divinity of Venus, becoming the first prostitutes, subsequently turned to stone
propōl·a -ae *f* retailer, huckster
prōpollu·ō -ere *tr* to further pollute
prō·pōnō -pōnere -posuī -positus *tr* to put *or* place forward, expose to view, display; to propose, suggest; to imagine; to offer, propose; to say, report, relate, publish; to threaten; to denounce; to design, determine, intend
Propontiac·us -a -um *adj* of the Propontis
Propont·is -idis *or* **-idos** *f* Propontis, Sea of Marmora
prōporrō *adv* furthermore; wholly
prōporti·ō -ōnis *f* proportion, symmetry; *(gram)* analogy
prōport·ō -āre *tr* to cite
prōpositi·ō -ōnis *f* proposition; intention, purpose; theme; basic assumption *(in logic)*
prōposit·us -a -um *pp of* **prōpōnō** ‖ *adj* exposed, open; accessible; impending, at hand ‖ *n* intention, purpose; main point, theme; first premise *(in logic);* **mihi prōpositum** it is my intention, it is my plan; **prōpositum habēre** to have as one's object
prōpraet·or -ōris *m* propraetor *(ex-praetor as governor of a province)*
propriē *adv* in the strict sense; properly; strictly for oneself, personally; peculiarly, especially
propriet·ās -ātis *f* property, peculiarity, quality
proprītim *adv* specifically, properly
propri·us -a -um *adj* own, very own; special, peculiar, individual, particular, personal; lasting
propter *adv* near, near at hand
propter *prep (w. acc)* near, close, next to; on account of, because of, for the sake of; through, by means of; **propter quod** wherefore
propterea *or* **propter eā** *adv* for that reason, therefore, on that account; **propterea quod** for the very reason that
prōpudiōs·us -a -um *adj* shameful
prōpud·ium -(i)ī *n* shameful act; *(said of a person)* disgrace, vile wretch, skunk
prōpugnācul·um -ī *n* rampart, battlement; defense; *(fig)* safeguard
prōpugnāti·ō -ōnis *f* defense, vindication; protection
prōpugnāt·or -ōris *m* defender, champion
prōpugn·ō -āre -āvī -ātus *tr* to defend ‖ *intr* to come out and fight; to fight a defensive action, repel an assault; *(fig)* to put up a defense

prōpulsāti·ō -ōnis *f* repulse; warding off *(of danger)*
prōpuls·ō -āre -āvī -ātus *tr* to drive off, repel; *(fig)* to ward off, repel
prōpulsus *pp of* **prōpellō**
Propylae·a -ōrum *npl* Propylaea *(monumental gateway, esp. the entrance to the Athenian Acropolis)*
prōquaest·or -ōris *m* proquaestor *(magistrate who, after his quaestorship in Rome, was associated as a financial officer with a proconsul in the administration of a province)*
prōquam *or* **prō quam** *conj* just as, according as
prōr·a -ae *f* prow; *(fig)* ship; **mihi prōra et puppis est** my intention from first to last is *(literally, it is prow and stern to me)*
prōrēp·ō -ere -sī -ptum *intr* to creep ahead, crawl out
prōrēt·a -ae *m* lookout man at the prow
prōreus *m (nom only)* look-out man at the prow
prō·ripiō -ripere -ripuī -reptus *tr* to drag forth, drag out; to rush ‖ *refl* to rush, dash
prōrogāti·ō -ōnis *f* extension *(of a term of office);* putting off
prōrog·ō -āre -āvī -ātus *tr* to extend, prolong; to put off, postpone
prōrs·a *or* **prōs·a -ae** *f* prose
prōrsum *or* **prōsum** *adv* forwards, straight ahead; *(as an intensive)* altogether, absolutely; *(w. negatives)* absolutely, at all, *e.g.*, **prōrsum nihil** absolutely nothing, nothing at all
prōrsus *or* **prōsus** *adv* forward; straight *(to the destination); (intensifying a word, phrase, etc., which it may either precede or follow)* altogether, absolutely; *(w. a negative)* absolutely, at all; *(emphasizing the second and stronger of two related terms)* more than that, even; *(connecting a clause or sentence with what precedes)* in fact, all in all; *(in summing up)* in short, in a word; *(w. demonstrative pron or adv, emphasizing correspondence)* exactly, just
prō·rumpō -rumpere -rūpī -ruptus *tr* to make *(s.th.)* burst forth; to give vent to; to emit ‖ *pass* to rush forth, rush out ‖ *intr* to rush forth; *(of vapors, etc.)* to burst forth; *(of news)* to come out; *(mil)* to make an attack
prōru·ō -ere -ī -tus *tr* to overthrow, demolish ‖ *intr* to rush forth; to tumble
prōrupt·us -a -um *pp of* **prōrumpō** ‖ *adj* unrestrained
prōs·a -ae *(or* **prōsa ōrātiō)** *f* prose
prōsāpi·a -ae *f* stock, race, line
prōscaen·ium -(i)ī *n* **(-scēn-)** stage
prō·scindō -scindere -scidī -scissus *tr* to plow up, break up; *(fig)* to criticize harshly, cut to pieces

prōscrī·bō -bere -psī -ptus *tr* to publish in writing; to proclaim, announce; to advertise *(for sale, etc.);* to confiscate *(property);* to punish with confiscation; to proscribe, outlaw *(people)*

prōscrīpti·ō -ōnis *f* advertisement; proscription, political purge; notice of confiscation; notice of outlawry

prōscrīptur·iō -īre *intr* to be eager to hold a proscription *or* purge

prōscrīpt·us -a -um *pp of* **prōscrībō** ‖ *m* outlaw

prōsec·ō -āre -uī -tus *tr* to cut off *(esp. parts of a sacrificial victim)*

prōsecūtus *pp of* **prōsequor**

prōsed·a -ae *f* prostitute

prōsēmin·ō -āre -āvī -ātus *tr* to sow, scatter about, plant; to propagate, raise

prō·sentiō -sentīre -sēnsī *tr* to sense *or* realize beforehand, get wind of

prō·sequor -sequī -secūtus sum *tr* to escort, attend; to pursue *(enemy);* to chase, follow; to follow up *(actions, words);* to go on with, continue *(a topic);* to describe in detail; to follow, imitate; to honor, reward *(with)*; to send *(s.o.)* on his *or* her way with gifts; *(of events)* to occur after, succeed

prōser·ō -ere *tr* to stick out *(e.g., the tongue)*

Prōserpin·a -ae *f* daughter of Ceres and carried off by Pluto to become queen of the lower world

prōserp·ō -ere *intr* to creep *or* crawl forwards, creep along

proseuch·a -ae *f* synagogue

prōsil·iō -īre -uī *or* **-īvī** *or* **-iī** *intr* to jump forward, jump up; to jump to one's feet; *(of blood)* to spurt; *(of sparks)* to shoot out, fly; to dash

prōsoc·er -erī *m* wife's grandfather; husband's grandfather

prosōdi·a -ae *f* the tone *or* accent of a syllable, prosody

prosōpopoei·a -ae *f* impersonation

prōspect·ō -āre -āvī -ātus *tr* to view, look out at, gaze upon; *(of places)* to look toward, command a view of, face; to look for, hope for; *(w. indir. ques.)* to look to see *(what, whether)*

prōspectus *pp of* **prōspiciō**

prōspect·us -ūs *m* distant view; view; faculty of sight; a sight *(thing seen)*

prōspecul·or -ārī -ātus sum *tr* to look out for, watch for ‖ *intr* to look around, reconnoiter

prosper *see* **prosperus**

prosperē *adv* favorably, luckily, as desired, successfully

prosperit·ās -ātis *f* success, good fortune, prosperity; **prosperitās valētūdinis** good health

prosper·ō -āre *tr* to cause to succeed, make happy

prosp·erus *or* **prosp·er -era -erum** *adj* successful, fortunate, lucky, favorable, prosperous

prōspicienti·a -ae *f* foresight, precaution

prō·spiciō -spicere -spexī -spectus *tr* to see in the distance; to spot; to command a view of; to watch for; to look out for, provide for; to foresee ‖ *intr* to look forward; to look into the distance, have a view; to be on the lookout, exercise foresight; *(w.* **in** + *acc)* to command a view of, overlook; **ex superiōribus in urbem prōspicere** to have a view of the city from a vantage point; **parum prōspiciunt oculī** the eyes are nearsighted

prō·sternō -sternere -strāvī -strātus *tr* to throw to the ground, knock down; *(of sickness)* to strike down; to wreck, ruin, overthrow, subvert; to demean ‖ *refl* to debase oneself; **sē prōsternere ad pedēs** *(w. gen)* to throw oneself at the feet of, fall down before

prōstibil·is -is *f* prostitute

prōstibul·um -ī *n* prostitute

prōstit·uō -uere -uī -ūtus *tr* to expose for sale; to prostitute

prōstitūt·a -ae *f* prostitute

prō·stō -stāre -stitī -stitum *intr* to project, stick out; *(of wares)* to be set up for sale; to prostitute oneself, be a prostitute

prōstrātus *pp of* **prōsternō**

prōstrāvī *perf of* **prōsternō**

prōsubig·ō -ere *tr* to dig up in front

prōsum *adv see* **prōrsum**

prō·sum -desse -fuī -futūrus *intr* to be useful, do good, be profitable; *(w. dat)* to be good for, do *(s.o.)* good; **multum prōdesse** to do a lot of good

Prōtagor·ās -ae *m* Greek sophist, contemporary of Socrates, born at Abdera *(c. 485–415 B.C.)*

prō·tegō -tegere -tēxī -tēctus *tr* to cover in front, cover up; to cover with a roof; to shelter, protect; *(fig)* to cover, defend, protect

prōtēl·ō -āre -āvī -ātus *tr* to chase away

prōtēl·um -ī *n* team of oxen in tandem; row, series

prōten·dō -dere -dī -tus *tr* to stretch forth, stretch out, extend

prōtent·us -a -um *pp of* **prōtendō** ‖ *adj* extended

prōtenus *see* **prōtinus**

prō·terō -terere -trīvī -trītus *tr* to wear down; to rub out; to trample down, trample under foot; *(fig)* to trample upon, rub out, crush

prōterr·eō -ēre -uī -itus *tr* to scare away

protervē *adv* brashly, brazenly

protervit·ās -ātis *f* brashness

proterv·us -a -um *adj* brash, brazen

Prōtesilāē·us -a -um *adj* of Protesilaus
Prōtesilā·us -ī *m* first Greek casualty in the Trojan War, husband of Laodamia
Prōt·ēus -eī *or* **-eos** *m* a god of the sea with power to assume various forms
prothȳmē *adv* willingly, readily
prothȳmi·a -ae *f* willingness, readiness
prōtinam *adv* immediately
prōtinus *or* **prōtenus** *adv* straight on, forward, farther on; continuously, right on, without pause; on the spot
prōtoll·ō -ere *tr* to stretch out *(hand);* to put off, postpone
prōtoprāxi·a -ae *f (fin)* priority *(among creditors receiving payment)*
prō·trahō -trahere -trāxī -tractus *tr* to drag forward, drag out; to produce; to reveal, bring to light
prōtrītus *pp of* **prōterō**
prōtrīvī *perf of* **prōterō**
prōtrū·dō -dere -sī -sus *tr* to push forwards, push out; to postpone
prōturb·ō -āre -āvī -ātus *tr* to drive ahead, drive on in confusion; to drive away, repel; to knock down
proüt *(or* **prout,** *scanned as one syllable) conj* as, just as; in so far as, in as much as; *(introducing alternatives)* **prout** ... **ita** according to whether ... or
prōvect·us -a -um *adj* advanced; **aetāte prōvectus** advanced in years; **nox prōvecta erat** the night had been far advanced
prōve·hō -here -xī -ctus *tr* to carry forwards; to transport, convey; to lead, lead on; to promote, advance, raise ‖ *pass* to ride, drive, move, *or* sail ahead
prō·veniō -venīre -vēnī -ventum *intr* to go on, proceed; to succeed; to come out, appear; *(of plants, seeds)* to come out, come up, grow; to come about, happen
prōvent·us -ūs *m* result, outcome; success; yield, produce; harvest
prōverb·ium -iī *n* proverb
prōvexī *perf of* **prōvehō**
prōvid·ēns -entis *adj* prudent
prōvidenter *adv* prudently, with foresight
prōvidenti·a -ae *f* foresight, foreknowledge; precaution; **prōvidentia dēorum** divine providence
prō·videō -vidēre -vīdī -vīsus *tr* to see in the distance; to see coming; to foresee; to provide for; to provide against, guard against, avert, avoid; to look after, look out for, care for; to prepare, make ready; *(w.* **ut)** to see to it that ‖ *intr* to exercise forethought, take precautions; *(w. dat or* **dē** + *abl)* to look after, care for ‖ *v impers* **prōvīsum est** care was taken
prōvid·us -a -um *adj* foreseeing; prudent, cautious; provident; *(w. gen)* providing for
prōvinci·a -ae *f* province; sphere of administration *or* jurisdiction; office, duty, charge; public office, commission, command, administration; sphere of action
prōvinciāl·is -is -e *adj* provincial, of a province; in a province; **bellum prōvinciāle** war in a province; **molestia prōvinciālis** annoyance of administering a province ‖ *m* provincial
prōvinciātim *adv* province by province
prōvīsi·ō -ōnis *f* foresight; precaution; *(w. gen)* precaution against
prōvīsō *adv* with forethought
prōvīs·ō -ere *tr* to go out to see; to be on the lookout for
prōvīs·or -ōris *m* lookout *(person);* provider
prōvīsū *m (abl only)* by looking forward; *(w. objective gen)* **1** by foreseeing *(e.g., danger);* **2** by providing, providing for
prōvīsus *pp of* **prōvideō**
prō·vīvō -vīvere -vīxī *intr* to live on, go on living
prōvocāti·ō -ōnis *f* challenge; *(leg)* appeal
prōvocāt·or -ōris *m* challenger; a type of gladiator
prōvoc·ō -āre -āvī -ātus *tr* to challenge *(a person, a statement);* to provoke; to exasperate; to stir, stimulate; **bellum prōvocāre** to provoke a war; **beneficiō prōvocātus** touched *or* stirred by an act of kindness; **in aleam prōvocāre** to challenge to a game of dice; **prōvocāre maledictīs** to provoke *or* exasperate with nasty remarks ‖ *intr (leg)* to appeal; *(leg) (w.* **ab)** to appeal from the decision of *(a magistrate); (leg) (w.* **ad)** to appeal to *(a higher authority)*
prōvol·ō -āre -āvī *intr* to fly out, rush out, dash out
prōvol·vō -vere -vī -ūtus *tr* to roll forward, roll along; to roll over, overturn; to humble; to ruin ‖ *refl* to prostrate oneself, fall down, grovel
prōvom·ō -ere *tr* to vomit, throw up
prōvōrsus *adv* straight ahead
prōvulg·ō -āre -āvī -ātus *tr* to make publicly known
prox *interj (comic representation of a fart):* **dum ēnītor, prox! iam paene inquīnāvī pallium** as I struggle to my feet, bang! I darn near soiled my clothes
proxenēt·a -ae *m* business agent
proximē *adv* **(-umē)** *(superl of* **prope)** *(of place)* nearest, next; *(of time)* most recently, just recently; *(w. acc)* **1** close to, next to, at the side of; **2** very much like, resembling; *(w. dat) (of place)* next to; **proximē atque** almost as much as, nearly the same as; **proximē Pompēium sedēbam** I was sitting next to Pompey; **quam proximē** *(w. dat or acc)* as close as possible to

proximit·ās -ātis *f* proximity, vicinity; resemblance, similarity; close relationship
proximō *adv* very *(or* just) recently
proxim·us -a -um *adj* **(-xum-)** nearest, next; adjoining; living nearby, living next door; readiest at hand; *(of time)* immediately preceding, previous, most recent, following, latest, last; just mentioned; closely related; *(of affections)* closely devoted; *(of cause)* immediate, proximate; *(of an argument)* relevant; very like *(in character, resemblance);* nearest *(in degree);* next *(in rank, worth),* second-best; next in order; most direct *(route);* **proximum est ut** (+ *subj)* it is most likely that; the next point is that; the next thing is to **ll** *m* close relative, next of kin; heir next in succession; friend, intimate; next-door neighbor **ll** *n* neighborhood; the house next door; the recent past; **dē proximō** aptly, very closely; **ex proximō** from the readiest source; close by; **in proximō** within easy reach; close at hand; **in proximum** for the following day
prūd·ēns -entis *adj* foreseeing; conscious, aware; skilled, skillful, experienced; prudent, discreet, sensible, intelligent; *(w. gen or abl or w.* **in** + *abl)* **1** aware of, conscious of; **2** familiar with; **3** skilled in, experienced in, versed in **ll** *m* expert; *(leg)* jurist
prūdenter *adv* prudently, cautiously; skillfully
prūdenti·a -ae *f* foreseeing; prudence, discretion, good sense; **prūdentia iūris pūblicī** *(leg)* knowledge of *or* experience in constitutional law
pruīn·a -ae *f* frost; winter; **pruīnae** a covering of frozen snow
pruīnōs·us -a -um *adj* frosty
prūn·a -ae *f* live coal
prūnice·us -a -um *adj* made of plum-tree wood
prūniti·us -a -um *adj* of plum-tree wood
prūn·um -ī *n* plum
prūn·us -ī *f* plum tree
prūrīg·ō -inis *f* itch, tickle; yen
prūr·iō -īre *intr* to itch, tickle; to have an itch; to be sexually aroused; *(w.* **in** + *acc)* to be itching for
Prūsi·ās *or* **Prūsi·a -ae** *m* Prusias *(name of several kings of Bithynia, esp. Prusias Cholus, d. about 182 B.C., with whom Hannibal took refuge after his defeat)*
prytanē·um *or* **prytanī·um -ī** *n* town hall *(in some Greek cities where the Prytanes, or magistrates, held meetings and dined)*
prytan·is -is *m* magistrate *(in some Greek states)*
psall·ō -ere -ī *intr* to play the cithara
psaltēr·ium -(i)ī *n* cithara *(form of harp)*
psalt·ēs -ae *m* cithara-player, citharist
psaltri·a -ae *f* citharist *(female)*
Psamath·ē -ēs *f* a sea nymph, wife of Aeacus and mother of Phocus **ll** daughter of the Argive King Crotopus
psec·as -adis *f* female slave who perfumed her lady's hair; typical name of maidservants
psell·us -a -um *adj* faltering in speech
psēphism·a -atis *n (pol)* plebiscite of the Greek assembly
Pseudocat·ō -ōnis *m* a make-believe Cato
Pseudol·us -ī *m* "Little Liar" *(title of a play by Plautus)*
pseudomen·os *or* **pseudomen·us -ī** *m (phil)* fallacious syllogism
Pseudophilipp·us -ī *m* "False Philip" *(i.e., Andriscus, who claimed to be the son of Perseus of Macedon and was defeated by the Romans in 148 B.C.)*
pseudothyr·um -ī *n* hidden door
psīlocitharist·a -ae *m* one who plays the lyre without singing in accompaniment
psithi·us -a -um *adj* psithian (*the name of a type of vine*) **ll** *fpl* grapes
psittac·us -ī *m* parrot
Psōph·is -idos *f* town in Arcadia to the S. of Mt. Erymanthus
Psȳch·ē -ēs *f* girlfriend of Cupid, made immortal by Jupiter
psychomantī·um *or* **psychomantē·um -ī** *n* place of séance
-pte *enclitic (added to pronouns, usu. w. poss adj and esp. in abl)* self, own; **sonitū suōpte titinant aurēs** the ears are ringing (with their own sound)
ptisanār·ium -(i)ī *n* gruel
Ptolemae·us -ī *m* Ptolemy *(name of a series of thirteen Egyptian kings descended from Lagus, one of Alexander the Great's generals)*
Ptolomae·um -ī *n* name of a gymnasium **ll** tomb of the Ptolemies
pūb·ēns -entis *adj* full of sap, succulent, vigorous
pūber *see* **pūbēs**
pūbert·ās -ātis *f* puberty; manhood; sign of maturity, beard; physical signs of puberty
pūb·ēs -is *f* pubic hair; private parts; puberty; adult population, manpower; throng
pūb·ēs *or* **pūb·er -eris** *adj* grown up, adult; downy, covered with down **ll** *mpl* grown-ups, men
pūb·ēscō -ēscere *intr* to reach the age of puberty, arrive at maturity; *(of plants)* to grow up, ripen; *(of meadows, fields)* to be clothed, covered *(e.g., with flowers)*
pūblic·a -ae *f* prostitute
pūblicān·us -a -um *adj* of public revenues **ll** *m* revenue agent, publican, tax collector **ll** *f* public prostitute
pūblicāti·ō -ōnis *f* confiscation; disclosure
pūblicē *adv* publicly; officially, on behalf of the state, for the state; at public

expense; generally, universally; **pūblicē dīcere** to speak officially
pūblicitus *adv* at public expense, at the expense of the state; publicly
Pūblici·us -a -um *adj* Publician *(Roman clan name, nomen);* **Clīvus Pūblicius** Publician Slope *(road leading up to the Aventine Hill)*
pūblic·ō -āre -āvī -ātus *tr* to confiscate; to throw open to the general public; to prostitute
Pūblicol·a -ae *m* **(Popl-)** Publius Valerius Publicola *(regarded as one of the first consuls, fl 509 B.C.)*
pūblic·us -a -um *adj* public, of the people, common; of the state, state, national; ordinary, vulgar; general; **causa pūblica** affair of national importance; *(leg)* federal case *(i.e., criminal case);* **id bonō pūblicō facere** to do it for the public good; **pūblica ācta** the public record, the official gazette; **rēs pūblica** state, government, politics, public life, country; **rem pūblicam inīre** to enter politics **II** *m* public official **II** *n* public, publicity; public property; national treasury; federal revenue; **dē pūblicō** at public expense; **in pūblicō** in public, publicly; **in pūblicum prōdīre** to go out in public; **in pūblicum redigere** to hand over to the national treasury **II** *f* prostitute
pudend·us -a -um *adj* shameful, scandalous; **pars pudenda** genitals **II** *npl* genitals
pud·ēns -entis *adj* modest, bashful
pudenter *adv* modestly, bashfully
pud·eō -ēre -uī *or* **puditum est** *tr* to make ashamed, put to shame **II** *intr* to be ashamed **II** *v impers (w. acc of person and gen or abl of cause of feeling), e.g.,* **mē tuī pudet** I am ashamed of you
pudibund·us -a -um *adj* modest, bashful
pudīcē *adv* chastely, modestly, decently; in a subdued style
pudīciti·a -ae *f* chastity, purity
pudīc·us -a -um *adj* chaste, pure
pud·or -ōris *m* shame, sense of shame, decency, modesty; sense of honor, propriety; cause for shame, disgrace; blush
puell·a -ae *f* girl; girlfriend, sweetheart; young wife
puellār·is -is -e *adj* young girl's, girlish, youthful
puellāriter *adv* girlishly
puellul·a -ae *f* little girl; little sweetheart
puell·us -ī *m* little boy, lad; catamite
pu·er *also* **pu·erus -erī** *m* boy, lad; servant, slave *(regardless of age);* page; bachelor; **ā puerīs** *(or* **ā puerō)** from childhood on; **ex puerīs excēdere** to outgrow childhood
puerāsc·ō -ere *intr* to approach boyhood
puercul·us -ī *m* little son
puer(i)ti·a -ae *f* childhood; boyhood
puerīl·is -is -e *adj* boyish, childish, youthful, puerile
puerīliter *adv* like a child, childishly
puerper·a -ae *f* woman in labor; woman who has given birth
puerper·ium -(i)ī *n* childbirth, delivery, giving birth
puerper·us -a -um *adj* easing labor pains, helping childbirth
puertia *see* **pueritia**
puerul·us -ī *m* little boy; little slave
pūg·a *or* **pȳg·a -ae** *f* rear, buttocks
pug·il -ilis *m* boxer
pugilāti·ō -ōnis *f* boxing
pugilātōri·us -a -um *adj* boxing; **follis pugilātōrius** punching bag
pugilāt·us -ūs *m* boxing match
pugilicē *adv* like a boxer
pugillār·is -is -e *adj* hand-size **II** *mpl & npl* set of tablets; notebook
pūgi·ō -ōnis *m* dagger
pūgiuncul·us -ī *m* small dagger
pugn·a -ae *f* fistfight, brawl; fight, combat, battle
pugnācit·ās -ātis *f* pugnacity, aggressiveness
pugnāciter *adv* aggressively
pugnācul·um -ī *n* fortress
pugnant·ēs -ium *mpl* fighters, warriors
pugnant·ia -ium *npl* contradictions, inconsistencies
pugnāt·or -ōris *m* fighter, combatant
pugnātōri·us -a -um *adj* used in fighting; **arma pugnātōria** combat weapons
pugn·āx -ācis *adj* pugnacious, scrappy, aggressive; quarrelsome; dogged
pugne·us -a -um *adj* of the fist; **hospitiō pugneō accipere** *(hum)* to welcome s.o. with a reception of fists; **merga pugnea** *(hum)* punch reaper
pugn·ō -āre -āvī -ātus *tr* to fight; **clāra pugna ad Perusiam pugnāta est** a brilliant battle was fought at Perusia; **proelia, bella pugnāre** to fight battles, wars **II** *intr* to fight; to contend, dispute; *(w. dat or* **cum)** **1** to fight, fight against, struggle with, oppose; **2** to contradict
pugn·us -ī *m* fist
pul·c(h)er -c(h)ra -c(h)rum *adj* beautiful, fair, handsome
pulchell·us -a -um *adj* cute little
Pul·cher -chrī *m* Roman family name *(cognomen)* in the Claudian clan, *esp.* Publius Clodius Pulcher *(tribune of 58 B.C.)*
pulchrē *adv* beautifully, attractively; thoroughly; perfectly; *(in gloating or irony)* nicely; *(as exclamation)* fine!; **pulchrē mihi est** I am fine
pulchritūd·ō -inis *f* **(pulcr-)** beauty; excellence, attractiveness
pūlē·ium -(i)ī *n (bot)* pennyroyal, mint; *(fig)* fragrance, pleasantness

pūl·ex *or* **pūl·ix -icis** *m* flea
pullār·ius -(i)ī *m* keeper of the sacred chickens
pullāt·us -a -um *adj* wearing black, in black, in mourning
pullul·ō -āre -āvī -ātus *intr* to sprout; *(of animals)* to produce young
pull·us -a -um *adj* dark-grey, dark, blackish; mourning; **toga pulla** mourning toga ‖ *n* dark-grey garment
pull·us -ī *m* young *(of animals),* foal, offspring, chick; favorite boy, catamite; sprout, shoot ‖ *mpl* chickens *(used in divination)*
pulmentār·ium -(i)ī *n* relish, appetizer
pulment·um -ī *n* relish; appetizer; food
pulm·ō -ōnis *m* lung
pulmōne·us -a -um *adj* of the lungs, pulmonary
pulp·a -ae *f* lean meat; *(pej)* flesh *(man's carnal nature)*
pulpāment·um -ī *n* meat; game
pulpit·um -ī *n* platform; stage; podium
pulp·ō -āre *intr* to make the sound of a vulture
puls pultis *f* pulse, porridge, mush
pulsāti·ō -ōnis *f* knock
puls·ō -āre -āvī -ātus *tr* to batter, keep hitting; to knock at; to strum *(lyre);* to beat on, strike against; *(fig)* to jolt ‖ *intr* to throb
pulsus *pp of* **pellō**
puls·us -ūs *m* push, pushing; beat, beating, striking, stamping; blow, stroke; trampling; *(fig)* impression, influence
pultāti·ō -ōnis *f* knocking *(at door)*
Pultiphagōnid·ēs -ae *m (humorous patronymic)* son of Porridge-eater
pultiphag·us -ī *m* porridge eater
pult·ō -āre *tr* to knock at *(a door);* to beat
pulvere·us -a -um *adj* dust, of dust; dusty; fine as dust; raising dust
pulverulent·us -a -um *adj* dusty; raising dust; covered with dust
pulvill·us -ī *m* small cushion
pulvīn·ar -āris *n* cushioned couch; sacred couch for the images of the gods; seat of honor
pulvīnār·ium -(i)ī *n* cushioned seat of a god; *(naut)* dry dock
pulvīn·us -ī *m* pillow, cushion; seat of honor
pulv·is -eris *m (f)* dust, powder; scene of action, arena, field; effort, work
pulviscul·us -ī *m* fine dust; fine powder
pūm·ex -icis *m (f)* pumice *(esp. used to polish books and also used as a depilatory);* lava
pūmice·us -a -um *adj* pumice; lava
pūmic·ō -āre -āvī -ātus *tr* to polish with pumice
pūmili·ō -ōnis *m* midget, dwarf; pygmy
pūmil·ius -(i)ī *m* dwarf, pygmy
pūmil·us -a -um *adj* of short stature, dwarf
pūnctim *adv* with the point, with the pointed end
pūnct·um -ī *n* prick, puncture; point; spot, dot; moment; *(gram)* clause, phrase; *(math)* point; *(pol)* vote, ballot *(dot made on wax tablet to indicate vote);* **pūnctō temporis eōdem** at the same instant; **pūnctum temporis** moment, point in time, instant
pungō pungere pupugī *or* **pepugī pūnctus** *tr* to prick, puncture, dent; to sting, bite; to cause *(a wound);* to stab; *(fig)* to sting, annoy, disturb
Pūnicān·us -a -um *adj* Punic, Carthaginian, in the Carthaginian style
Pūnicē *adv* **(Poen-)** Punic, in the Punic language
pūnice·us -a -um *adj* **(poen-)** reddish, scarlet, crimson ‖ **Pūniceus (Poen-)** Punic, Carthaginian
Pūnic·us -a -um *adj* **(Poen-)** Punic, Carthaginian; red, crimson, reddish, pink; **Pūnicum mālum** *(or* **pōmum)** pomegranate ‖ *n* pomegranate
pūn·iō -īre -īvī *or* **-iī -ītus** *or* **pūn·ior -īrī -ītus -sum** *tr (older form:* **poen-)** to punish; to avenge ‖ *intr* to inflict punishment
pūnīti·ō -ōnis *f* punishment
pūnīt·or -ōris *m* avenger
pūp·a -ae *f* doll, puppet; girl, kid
pūpill·a -ae *f* orphan girl, ward; minor; *(anat)* pupil
pūpillār·is -is -e *adj* of an orphan, belonging to an orphan
pūpill·us -ī *m* orphan boy, ward
Pūpini·us -a -um *adj* **ager Pūpinius** a barren district between Rome and Tusculum
Pūpi·us -a -um *adj* Roman clan name *(nomen), esp.* Publius Pupius *(a tragedian)*
pupp·is -is *(acc sing usu.* **puppim)** *f* stern; ship; *(coll)* back; **ā puppī** astern
pūpul·a -ae *f* little girl, kid; *(anat)* pupil, eye
pūpul·us -ī *m* little boy, kid
pūp·us -ī *m* boy, child, kid
pūrē *adv* clearly, brightly; plainly, simply; chastely, purely
purgām·en -inis *n* dirt, filth; means of expiation, purification
purgāment·a -ōrum *npl* offscourings, dirt, filth, garbage; *(term of abuse)* trash, garbage
purgāti·ō -ōnis *f* cleansing, cleaning, cleanup; justification
purgāt·us -a -um *adj* cleansed, clean, pure
purg·ō -āre -āvī -ātus *tr* to cleanse, clean; to clear, clear away, remove; to clear of a charge; to excuse, justify; to refute; to purify ritually; to purge *(the body)* ‖ *refl & pass (of water, the sky)* to become clear
pūrific·ō -āre -āvī -ātus *tr* to purify

pūriter *adv* purely, cleanly; **vītam pūriter agere** to lead a clean life

purpur·a -ae *f* purple dye *(ranging in shade from blood-red to deep violet);* purple, deep-red, royal purple, crimson; royal-purple cloth; royal-purple robe; royalty; consular diginity; imperial dignity

purpurāri·us -a -um *adj* (royal) purple; relating to the purple dyeing *or* to the selling of purple cloth

purpurāsc·ō -ere *intr* to turn purple

purpurāt·us -a -um *adj* wearing royal purple **II** *m* courtier

purpure·us -a -um *adj* purple, crimson, royal purple *(and various shades as applied to roses, poppies, grapes, lips, flesh, blood, wine, dawn, sun at sunrise, hair)*

purpurissāt·us -a -um *adj* rouged

purpuriss·um -ī *n* rouge; red dye

pūr·us -a -um *adj* pure, clear, clean; cleared, cleansed; cleansing; purifying; chaste; plain, naked, unadorned, natural; plain *(toga),* without crimson border; faultless *(style); (leg)* unconditional, absolute; *(leg)* subject to no religious claims **II** *n* clear sky

pūs pūris *n* pus; *(fig)* venom, malice

pusill·us -a -um *adj* petty, puny **II** *n* bit, trifle

pūsi·ō -ōnis *m* little boy

pūsul·a *or* **pussul·a** *or* **pūstul·a -ae** *f* pimple; blister

pūsulāt·us *or* **pūstulāt·us -a -um** *adj* refined, purified *(silver)*

putām·en -inis *n* shell *(of nuts, eggs, turtles);* peel *(of fruit)*

putāti·ō -ōnis *f* pruning

putāt·or -ōris *m* pruner

pute·al -ālis *n* low wall *(around a well or sacred spot),* stone enclosure; **puteal Libōnis** stone enclosure in Roman Forum near which much business was transacted

puteāl·is -is -e *adj* of a well

pūtē·faciō -facere -fēcī -factus *tr* to cause to rot; to cause to crumble

pūt·eō -ēre -uī *intr* to stink; to be rotten

Puteolān·us -a -um *adj* of Puteoli

Puteol·ī -ōrum *mpl* Puteoli *(commercial city on the coast of the Bay of Naples, modern Pozzuoli)*

pu·ter *or* **pu·tris -tris -tre** *adj* putrid, rotting; crumbling; flabby

pūt·ēscō -ēscere -uī *intr* to become rotten

pute·us -ī *m* well; pit; dungeon

pūtidē *adv* disgustingly; affectedly

pūtidiūscul·us -a -um *adj* rather tedious

pūtid·us -a -um *adj* stinking, rotten; worn-out *(brain);* rotten *(person);* offensive *(words, actions);* unnatural, disgusting *(style)*

putill·us -a -um *adj* tiny

put·ō -āre -āvī -ātus *tr* to trim, prune; to think, ponder, consider, judge; to suppose, imagine; to reckon, estimate, value; to believe in, recognize *(gods);* to clear up, settle *(accounts);* **magnī putāre** to think highly of; **prō certō putāre** to regard as certain **II** *intr* to think, imagine, suppose

pūt·or -ōris *m* stench; rottenness

putre·faciō -facere -fēcī -factus *tr* to rot; to cause to crumble, soften

putrēsc·ō -ere *intr* to become rotten, get moldy

putrid·us -a -um *adj* rotten; flabby

putris *see* **puter**

put·us -a -um *adj (ancient word for* **pūrus** *and usu. used in combination with* **pūrus)** pure, bright, perfectly pure; splendid; unmixed; unmitigated; **certum pondus argentī pūrī putī** a certain weight of perfectly pure silver **II** *m* boy

pyct·a *or* **pyct·ēs -ae** *m* boxer

Pydn·a -ae *f* Pydna *(city in Macedonia near which Aemilius Paulus defeated Perseus, king of Macedonia, 169 B.C.)*

pyel·us -ī *m* bathtub

pȳg·a -ae *f* rear, buttocks

pȳgarg·us -ī *m* kind of antelope with white rump

Pygmae·ī -ōrum *mpl* Pygmies *(a dwarfish race, esp. in Africa, said to have been constantly at war with cranes, by whom they were always defeated)*

Pygmae·us -a -um *adj* of the Pygmies; **avis Pygmaeus** a crane

Pygmali·ōn -ōnis *or* **-ōnos** *m* son of Belus and brother of Dido **II** king of Cyprus who fell in love with a statue

Pylad·ēs -ae *or* **-is** *m* son of Strophius and friend of Orestes

Pyladē·us -a -um *adj* worthy of Pylades

Pyl·ae -ārum *fpl* Thermopylae

Pylaemen·ēs -is *m* king of the Paphlagonians and ally of Priam

Pylaïc·us -a -um of Thermopylae

Pyli·us -a -um *adj* of Pylos **II** *m* Nestor

Pyl·os -ī *f* Pylos *(home of Nestor in S.E. Peloponnesus)*

pyr·a -ae *f* pyre

pȳram·is -idis *or* **-idos** *f* pyramid; cone

Pȳram·us -ī *m* neighbor and boyfriend of Thisbe

Pȳrēnae·us -a -um *adj* of the Pyrenees

Pȳrēn·ē -ēs *f (geog)* the Pyrenees

Pyrēn·eūs -eī *m* king of Thrace who tried to rape the Muses

pyrethr·um -ī *n* Spanish camomile *(medicinal plant)*

Pyrgēns·is -is -e adj of (the town of) Pyrgi

Pyrg·ī -ōrum *mpl* town on the coast of Etruria

Pyriphlegeth·on -ontos *m* one of the rivers of the lower world *(= Phlegethon)*

pyrōp·us -ī *m* bronze
Pyrrh·a -ae *f* daughter of Epimetheus, wife of Deucalion, and survivor of the Deluge
Pyrrhi·as -adis *adj (fem only)* of (the town of) Pyrrha in Lesbos
Pyrrh·ō(n) -ōnis *m* Pyrrho *(philosopher of Elis, contemporary of Aristotle and founder of the school of Skepticism, c. 360–270 B.C.)*
Pyrrhōnē·us -a -um *adj* of the school founded by Pyrrho
Pyrrh·us -ī *m* son of Achilles and founder of Epirus *(also called Neoptolemus)* **||** king of Epirus who invaded Italy against the Romans in 280 B.C. *(319–272 B.C.)*
Pȳthagor·ās -ae *m* Greek philosopher and mathematician *(6th cent. B.C.)* **||** a servant of Nero
Pȳthagorē·us *or* **Pȳthagoric·us -a -um** *adj* Pythagorean
Pȳthi·a -ae *f* Pythia *(priestess of Apollo at Delphi)*
Pȳthi·as -adis *f* typical name for a slave girl in comedy
Pȳthic·us -a -um *adj* Pythian, Delphic
Pȳthi·us -a -um *adj* Pythian, Delphic **||** *m* Apollo **||** *f* Pythia *(priestess of Apollo at Delphi)* **||** *npl* Pythian games *(held in honor of Apollo every four years at Delphi)*
Pȳth·ō -ūs *f* ancient name of Delphi *or* its oracle
Pȳth·ōn -ōnis *or* **-ōnos** *m* dragon slain by Apollo near Delphi
pȳtism·a -atis *n* mouthful of wine *(spat out after tasting)*
pȳtiss·ō -āre *tr* to spit out *(wine after tasting it)*
pyx·is -idis *or* **-idos** *f* powder box, cosmetic box

Q

Q, q *(supply* littera) *f* sixteenth letter of the Latin alphabet; letter name: **qu**
Q. *abbr* **Quīntus** *(first name, praenomen)*
quā *adv (interrog)* by which road?, which way? in which direction?, by which route?, where?; by what means?, how? **||** *(rel)* where; to the extent that; in so far as; in as much as; in the manner in which, as **||** *(indef)* by any route, by any way; by any chance, in any way; **quā ... quā** partly ... partly, both ... and
quācumque *adv* **(-cunq-)** wherever; by whatever way, in whatever way; by whatever means, howsoever
quādam tenus *adv* to a certain point, only so far and no farther
quadr·a -ae *f* (square) dining table; square crust; square bit, cube *(of cheese, etc.);* (square) slice *(of bread, cake)*
quadrāgēn·ī -ae -a *adj* forty each
quadrāgēsim·us -a -um *adj* **(-gēnsi-)** fortieth **||** *f* one-fortieth; 2½% tax
quadrāgiēs *adv* **(-giēns)** forty times
quadrāgintā *indecl adj* forty
quadr·āns -antis *m* one-fourth, a quarter; penny *(smallest coin, worth one sixth of Roman* **as**); quarter of a pound; quarter pint *(quarter of a* **sextārius); quadrante lavātum īre** to take a bath for a penny *(usual price of a bath)*
quadrant·al -ālis *n* five-gallon jar
quadrantāri·us -a -um *adj* quarter; **mulier quadrantāria** two-bit wench *(woman who sells herself for a pittance);* **tabulae quadrantāriae** record of debts reduced to a fourth
quadrāt·us -a -um *adj* square; stocky *(build);* 90-degree *(angle);* compact *(style);* cube, cubic **||** *n* square; square object; cube
quadri- *pref* consisting of, having four of the things named
quadrīdu·um -ī *n* four-day period; **in quadrīduō** within four days; **quadrīduō** for a period of four days; within the next four days; **quadrīduō ante (post)** four days before (after)
quadrienn·ium -(i)ī *n* four-year period, four years
quadrifāriam *adv* in four directions; in four ways; in four places; in fours
quadrifid·us -a -um *adj* split into four parts
quadrīg·a -āe *f or* **quadrīg·ae -ārum** *fpl* four-horse team *(running four abreast);* four-horse chariot
quadrīgāri·us -a -um *adj* connected with chariot racing
quadrīgār·ius -(i)ī *m* chariot racer
quadrīgāt·us -a -um *adj (of a coin)* stamped with the image of a four-horse chariot
quadrīgul·ae -ārum *fpl (figurine of a)* four-horse chariot
quadriiug·is -is -e *or* **quadriiug·us -a -um** *adj* drawn by a four-horse team *(yoked abreast); (of horses)* yoked four abreast **||** *mpl* four-horse team
quadrilībr·is -is -e *adj* four-pound
quadrīmul·us -a -um *adj* only four years old
quadrīm·us -a -um *adj* four-year-old
quadringēnāri·us -a -um *adj* consisting of four hundred men each
quadringēn·ī -ae -a *adj* four hundred each
quadringentēsim·us -a -um *adj* four-hundredth
quadringent·ī -ae -a four hundred
quadringentiē(n)s *adv* four hundred times
quadripertītō *adv* in four parts, in four divisions
quadripertīt·us -a -um *adj* four-fold

quadrirēm·is -is -e *adj* having four banks of oars *(or possibly with four rowers to every bench)* ‖ *f* quadrireme
quadriv·ium -(i)ī *n* crossroads
quadr·ō -āre -āvī -ātus *tr* to make square; to complete; *(rhet)* to round out, give rhythmic finish to *(a speech)* ‖ *intr* to make a square; to be exact; *(of accounts)* to agree, come out right, tally; *(w. dat or* **in** *+ acc)* to suit, fit
quadr·um -ī *n* square; **in quadrum redigere sententiam** *(rhet)* to balance a sentence *(by changing word order)*
quadruped·āns -antis *adj* galloping ‖ *mpl* horses
quadruped·us -a -um *adj* galloping
quadrup·ēs -edis *adj* four-footed; on all fours ‖ *mf* quadruped
quadruplāt·or -ōris *m* informer *(who received ¼ of the forfeiture)*; corrupt judge
quadrupl·ex -icis *adj* quadruple, fourfold
quadruplic·ō -āre -āvī -ātus *tr* to quadruple, multiply by four
quadrupl·or -ārī -ātus sum *intr* to be an informer, be a whistleblower
quadrupl·us -a -um *adj* quadruple, fourfold ‖ *n* four times the amount
quaerit·ō -āre -āvī -ātus *tr* to keep looking for; to keep asking
quae·rō -rere -sīvī *or* **-siī -sītus** *tr* to look for, search for; to try to get; to get, obtain; to try to gain, earn, acquire; to miss, lack; to require, demand, call for; to ask, interrogate; to examine, investigate; to plan, devise, aim at; *(w. inf)* to try to, wish to; *(w.* **ab** *or* **dē** *or* **ex** *+ abl)* to ask *(s.th.)* of *or* from *(s.o.)* ‖ *intr* to hold an examination; *(w.* **dē** *+ abl)* to ask about; **quid quaeris?** *(introducing a short, clinching remark)* what more can I say?; **sī quaeris** *(or* **sī quaerimus)** to tell the truth
quaesīti·ō -ōnis *f (leg)* questioning under torture
quaesīt·or -ōris *m (leg)* judge *(praetor or other official who presided over a criminal trial)*
quaesīt·us -a -um *pp of* **quaerō** ‖ *adj* select, special; far-fetched; artificial, affected ‖ *npl* gains, earnings, acquisitions, store
quaes·ō -ere *tr* to try to obtain; to beg, ask for, request ‖ *intr* to carry out a search; **quaesō** *(usually parenthetical)* please; *(w. direct questions)* please tell me; *(in exclamations)* just look!; take note!
quaesticul·us -ī *m* slight profit
quaesti·ō -ōnis *f* inquiry, investigation, questioning, examination; *(leg)* judicial investigation, criminal trial, court of inquiry, court; *(leg)* questioning under torture, third degree; *(leg)* question, subject of investigation, case; *(leg)* court record; *(w.* **dē** *+ abl of the nature of the charge)* court investigating a charge of *(e.g., forgery)*; **in quaestiōne versārī** to be under investigation; **quaestiō extraōrdināria** investigation by a special board; **quaestiō inter sīcāriōs** murder trial, court investigating a murder; **quaestiō perpetua** standing court; **quaestiōnī pracesse** to preside over a case; **servōs in quaestiōnem dare** *(or* **ferre)** to hand over slaves for questioning under torture
quaestiuncul·a -ae *f* minor *or* trivial question; small problem, puzzle
quaest·or -ōris *m* quaestor *(serving, at various periods as: financial officer; treasury official; public prosecutor of criminal offenses; aide to a provincial governor; army paymaster; personal aide to the emperor)*; **prō quaestōre** acting quaestor, vice-quaestor
quaestōri·us -a -um *adj* quaestor's, of a quaestor; employed in a quaestor's office; qualified for the rank of quaestor; having quaestorian rank *(i.e., having held the office of quaestor)*; **ager quaestōria** conquered land sold on behalf of the state treasury; **porta quaestōria** the gate nearest the quaestor's tent *(perhaps* **porta decumāna)** ‖ *m* ex-quaestor ‖ *n* quaestor's tent in a camp; quaestor's residence in a province
quaestuōs·us -a -um *adj* profitable, productive; acquiring wealth; eager to make a profit, acquisitive; good at money-making; enriched, wealthy
quaestūr·a -ae *f* quaestorship; *(fig)* public funds
quaest·us -ūs *m* gain, profit; acquisition; way of gaining a livelihood, job, occupation, business, trade; income; *(fig)* benefit, advantage; **ad quaestum** for profit, to make a profit; **in quaestū esse** to be profitable; **in quaestū habēre** to derive profit from; **pecūniam in quaestū relinquere** to deposit money at interest; **quaestuī rem pūblicam habēre** to use public office for personal profit; **quaestum facere** to make money, make a living; **quaestūs facere** to make gains
quālibet *adv* **(-lub-)** anywhere, everywhere; in any way, as you please
quāl·is -is -e *adj* what sort of, what kind of; of such a kind, such as, as; *(w. quotations and citations)* as, as for example; **in hōc bellō, quāle** in this war, the likes of which; **quālis erat!** what a man he was!
quāl·iscumque -iscumque -ecumque (-cunque) *adj* of whatever kind; of any kind whatsoever, any at all; **hominēs, quālēscumque sunt** people, no matter what kind they are; **quāliscumque** *(or* **quālecumque)** **est** such as it is, for what it is worth

quāl·islibet -islibet -elibet *adj* of whatever kind, of whatever sort

quāl·isnam -isnam -enam *adj* just what kind of

quālit·ās -ātis *f* quality, nature; property, characteristic; high quality; *(gram)* mood *(of a verb)*

quāliter *adv* as, just as

quāl·us -ī *m or* **quāl·um -ī** *n* wicker basket, straw basket

quam *adv (in questions and exclamations)* how, how much; *(in comparisons)* as, than; *(with superlatives)* as ... as possible, *e.g.,* **quam celerrimē** as fast as possible; **quam plūrimō vēndere** to sell at the highest price possible; **quam prīmum** as soon as possible; *(indicating numerical proportion)* **dīmidium (duplex,** *etc.)* **quam** half as much as (twice as much as, *etc.*); *(as the correlative of* **tam**) the ... the: **quam magis id reputō, tam magis ūror** the more I think it over, the madder I get; *(after verbs of preferring)* than: **praestat nēminī imperāre quam alicui servīre** it is preferable to rule over no one than to be a slave to someone

quamdiū *or* **quam diū** *interrog & rel adv* how long ‖ *conj* as long as

quamlibet *adv* **(-lub-)** as much as you please

quamobrem *or* **quam ob rem** *adv* for what reason, why; for which reason, wherefore, why

quamquam *conj* although

quamvīs *adv (with adj or adv)* however, no matter how; ever so; **illa quamvīs rīdicula essent** no matter how funny they were ‖ *conj* although

quānam *adv* by what route *or* way

quandō *adv (in questions)* when, at what time; *(indefinite, after* **sī, nē, num**) ever, at any time ‖ *conj* when, because, since

quandōcumque *adv* **(-cunque)** at some time or other, someday ‖ *conj* whenever; as often as, no matter when

quandōque *adv* at some time, at one time or other, someday ‖ *conj* whenever; as often as; since

quandōquidem *conj* in as much as, whereas, seeing that

quantill·us -a -um *interrog adj* how much?, how little?

quantit·ās -ātis *f* quantity; size

quantō *adv* by how much, how much; **quantō ... tantō** the ... the: **quantō longior nox est, tantō brevior diēs fit** the longer night is, the shorter the day becomes

quantopere *or* **quantō opere** *adv* by how much, how much; with how great effort, how carefully

quantulum *adv* how little; **quantulum interest utrum** how little difference it makes whether

quantul·us -a -um *adj* how great, how much, how little, how small, how insignificant

quantuluscumque quantulacum quantulumcumque *adj* however small, however unimportant

quantum *adv* as much as, so much as, as great an extent; how much, how far, to what extent; *(w. comparatives)* the more, the greater; **quantum in mē fuit** as much as I could, to the best of my ability; **quantum maximā vōce potuit** at the top of his voice; **quantum potest** as much *(or* fast, quickly, soon, long, *etc.)* as possible

quantumcumque *adv* as much as; however much, however little; to whatever degree, as far as

quantumlibet *or* **quantum libet** *adv* however much

quantumvīs *adv (also written as two words)* however; **quantumvīs rūsticus** however unsophisticated, although unsophisticated

quant·us -a -um *adj (interrogative or exclamatory)* how great, how much, of what size, of what importance, of what worth ‖ *n* **in quantum** to whatever extent, as far as; **quantī** *(gen of price)* how much, how high, how dearly, at what price; **quantō** *(abl of price)* at what price, for how much; **quantum frūmentī** how much grain ‖ *pl* how many

quant·uscumque -acumque -umcumque *adj* however great; of whatever size; however small; however trifling; however important *(or* unimportant); **quantīcumque** at whatever price, at whatever cost

quant·uslibet -alibet -umlibet *adj* however great; ever so great

quantusquantus quantaquanta quantumquantum *adj (also written as two words)* however big, however great, of whatever degree ‖ *n* however much, whatever

quant·usvīs -avīs -umvīs *adj* of whatever size, amount, degree, *etc.,* you wish; however big, however great, no matter how great

quāpropter *adv* wherefore, why

quāquā *adv* by whatever route, in whatever way

quāquam *adv* in any way; anywhere

quārē *or* **quā rē** *adv* by what means, how; in what way, from what cause, why; whereby; wherefore; **nec quid nec quārē** without why or wherefore

quart·a -ae *f* a fourth, one quarter

Quart·a -ae *f* female first name *(praenomen)*

quartadecumān·ī -ōrum *mpl* **(-decim-)** *mpl* soldiers of the 14th legion

quartān·us -a -um *adj* occurring every fourth day **‖** *f* quartan fever **‖** *mpl* soldiers of the 4th legion

quartār·ius -(i)ī *m* quarter pint

quartō *adv* for the fourth time

quartum *adv* for the fourth time; in the fourth place, fourthly

quart·us -a -um *adj* fourth

quart·us decim·us -a -um *adj* fourteenth

quasi *adv* as it were, so to speak; about, nearly, almost; allegedly **‖** *conj* on the charge that; as would be the case if; *(expressing the supposed reason for an action)* on the grounds that; *(introducing a hypothetical situation after verbs of asserting or supposing)* saying that, believing that, to the effect that: **spārsit rūmōrem, quasi ... bellum gerere nōn possit** he spread a rumor to the effect that he could not fight a war

quasill·um -ī *n or* **quasill·us -ī** *m* small basket

quassāti·ō -ōnis *f* (violent) shaking

quass·ō -are *tr* to keep shaking, keep tossing, keep waving; to batter, shatter, smash to pieces; *(fig)* to shake, weaken **‖** *intr (of the head)* to keep on shaking

quass·us -a -um *pp of* **quatiō ‖** *adj* shattered, broken; quavering *(voice)*; chopped *(wood)*

quate·faciō -facere -fēcī -factus *tr* to shake; *(fig)* to weaken

quātenus *adv* how far, to what point; as far as, till when, how long; to what extent; **est quātenus** there is an extent to which **‖** *conj* as far as; insofar as, in as much as, seeing that, since, as

quater *adv* four times

quater deciē(n)s *adv* fourteen times

quatern·ī -ae -a *adj* four together, four in a group, four each

quatiō quatere *(no perf)* **quassus** *tr* to shake, cause to tremble, cause to vibrate; to brandish, wave about; to beat, strike, drive; to batter, crush; *(fig)* to touch, move, affect; *(fig)* to plague, harass

quattuor *indecl adj* four

quattuordecim *indecl adj* fourteen

quattuor·vir -virī *m* member of a board of four *(one of the four chief magistrates of a municipium; member of a committee of four at Rome)*

quattuorvirāt·us -ūs *m* membership on the board of four

quāvīs *adv* anyway you like, in any possible way

quax·ō -āre *intr (of frogs)* to croak

-que *enclitic conj* and; **-que ... -que** *(mostly poetical)* both ... and; **terrā marīque** on land and on sea

-que *suf used in the formation of certain adverbs and conjunctions, e.g.:* **itaque** and so, therefore; *esp. to give indefinite force to relative pronouns and adverbs, e.g.,* **quandōque** at some time or other, someday

quemadmodum *or* **quem ad modum** *adv* in what way, how **‖** *conj* just as, as

qu·eō -īre -īvī *or* **-iī -itum** *intr* to be able; *(w. inf)* to be able to

quercēt·um -ī *n* oak forest

querce·us -a -um *adj* oak, of oak

querc·us -ūs *f* oak tree; oak-leaf crown *(awarded to a soldier who saved a citizen in battle)*; acorns

querēl·a -ae *f* **(-ell-)** complaint; grievance, protest; difference of opinion

queribund·us -a -um *adj* full of complaints; whining *(voice)*

querimōni·a -ae *f* complaint, grievance; elegy

querit·or -ārī *intr* to keep complaining

quern·us -a -um *adj* oak, of oak

queror querī questus sum *tr* to complain of, complain about; to lament **‖** *intr* to complain; *(of birds)* to sing, warble, sing sadly, coo mournfully

querquētulān·us -a -um *adj (as name of various places and deities associated with oaks)* oak, covered with oak trees; **Mōns Querquētulānus** Oak Hill *(an old name for the Caelian Hill in Rome*; **Porta Querquētulāna** Oak Gate *(probably between the Caelian and the Esquiline Hills)*

querquēt·um -ī *n* oak forest

querul·us -a -um *adj* complaining, full of complaints, querulous; plaintive; warbling, cooing

questi·ō -ōnis *f* complaining

questus *pp of* **queror**

quest·us -ūs *m* complaint; plaintive note *(of the nightingale)*

quī *adv* how; why; at what price; whereby; in some way, somehow

quī quae *or* **qua quod** *adj (interrog)* which, what, what kind of; *(indef)* any **‖** *pron (rel)* who, that; *(indef, after* **sī, nisi, num, nē**) anyone

quia *conj* because

quianam *adv (interrog)* why in fact?, just why?

quicquam cūiusquam *pron* anything

quicque cūiusque *pron* each (one)

quīcum *(old abl of* **quī** *and* **cum)** *pron* with whom, with which

quīcumque quaecumque quodcumque *(also* **-cunque, -quomque)** *pron & adj (rel & indef)* whoever, whosoever, everyone who, whatever, whatsoever, everything ever

quid *adv* how?; why? **quid agis?** how do you do?; **quid plūra?** why say more?

quid cūius *pron (interrog)* what?; *(w. gen)* what kind of?: **quid mulieris uxōrem habēs?** what sort of woman do you have as your wife?; *(indef, after* **sī, nisi, num, nē**) anything

quīdam quaedam quiddam *pron* a certain one, a certain person, a certain thing

quīdam quaedam quoddam *adj* a certain; *(to soften an expression)* a kind of, what one might call

quidem *adv (emphasizing the word before it)* indeed, in fact; *(qualifying or limiting)* at least, at any rate; *(concessive)* it is true; of course; all right; *(exemplifying)* for example; **nē ... quidem** *(emphasizing the intervening word)* not even, *e.g.,* **nē tū quidem** not even you

quidnam *adv* why in the world

quidnam cūiusnam *pron (interrog)* just what?

quidnī *adv* why not?

quidpiam *adv* in some respect

quidpiam cūiuspiam *pron* anything, something

quidquid *adv* to whatever extent, the further

quidquid *or* **quicquid** *(gen and dat not in use; abl:* **quōquō**) *pron* whatever, whatsoever, everything which; **per quidquid deōrum** by all the gods

quīdum *adv* how so?

qui·ēs -ētis *f* quiet, rest, peace; calm, lull; neutrality; sleep; dream; sleep of death, death

qui·ēscō -ēscere -ēvī -ētum *intr (contracted forms:* **quiēsse = quiēvisse; quiērunt = quiēvērunt; quiēram = quiēveram)** to rest, keep quiet, be inactive; to fall asleep; to sleep, be asleep; to lie still, be still, be undisturbed; to say no more, be quiet; *(of the dead)* to find rest; to pause, make a pause; *(of a person)* to be calm, remain calm, be unruffled; *(of physical forces, of conditions)* to die down, subside, be still; *(of things)* to cease to operate; to be neutral, keep neutral, take no action; to refrain from violence, make no disturbance, remain peaceful; *(of troops)* to make no move; *(w. inf)* to cease to, stop; to take no steps to, omit to; *(w.* **ab** *+ abl)* to be free from

quiētē *adv* quietly, calmly

quiēt·us -a -um *adj* at rest, resting, free from exertion, inactive; quiet; peaceful, undisturbed; natural; calm; still, silent; idle ‖ *npl* period of peace

quīlibet quaelibet quidlibet (-lubet) *pron* anyone, any you wish, no matter who, anything, anything you wish, no matter what, everything

quīlibet quaelibet quodlibet (-lubet) *adj* any, any at all, any you wish

quīn *adv (interrog)* why not; *(corroborative)* in fact, as a matter of fact ‖ *conj* so that not, without; **facere nōn possum, quīn ad tē mittam librum** I can't help sending you the book; **nūllō modō introīre possem, quīn vidērent mē** I just couldn't walk in without their seeing me; *(after verbs of preventing, opposing)* from: **mīlitēs aegrē sunt retentī quīn oppidum oppugnārent** the soldiers could barely be kept from assaulting the town; *(after verbs of hesitation, doubt, suspicion):* **nōn dubitō quīn** I do not doubt that; *(esp. representing a nominative of a relative pronoun with a negative)* that ... not: **nēmō aspicere potest quīn dīcat** no one can look on without saying; **nēmō est quīn velit** there is no one who does not wish

quīnam quaenam quodnam *adj* which, what, just which, just what

quīnavīcēnāri·us -a -um *adj* of twenty-five; **lēx annōrum quīnavīcēnāria** the law prohibiting those under twenty-five years of age from making contracts

Quīnctili·us -a -um *adj* the name of a Roman gens *(nomen), esp.* Quinctilius Varus *(proconsul of Syria, later commander of the Romans in Germany, defeated by Armenius* A.D. *9)* ‖ Quinctilius Varus *(poet of Cremona, a friend of Horace and a relative of Vergil)*

Quīncti·us -a -um *adj* the name of a Roman gens *(nomen), esp.* Lucius Quinctius Cincinnatus *(called on his farm to become dictator in 458* B.C.*)* ‖ Titus Quinctius Flamininus *(consul in 198* B.C.*, who "liberated" Greece from Macedonia)* ‖ Publius Quinctius *(represented by Cicero in his first case, in 81* B.C.*)*

quīnc·ūnx -ūncis *m* five-twelfths; 5% *(interest);* the figure five *(as arranged on dice or cards)*

quīndeciē(n)s *adv* fifteen times

quīndecim *indecl adj* fifteen

quīndecimprīm·ī -ōrum *mpl* executive board of fifteen *(magistrates of a municipality)*

quīndecimvirāl·is -is -e *adj* of the board of fifteen

quīndecimvīr·ī -ōrum *mpl* board of fifteen; **quīndecimvīrī Sibyllīnī** board of fifteen in charge of the Sibylline Books

quīngēnāri·us -a -um *adj* of five hundred each, consisting of five hundred *(men, pounds, etc.)*

quīngēn·ī -ae -a *adj* five hundred each

quīngentēsim·us -a -um *adj* five-hundredth

quīngent·ī -ae -a *adj* five hundred

quīngentiē(n)s *adv* five hundred times

quīn·ī -ae -a *adj* five each; **quīnī dēnī** fifteen each; **quīnī vīcēnī** twenty-five each

quīnquāgēn·ī -ae -a *adj* fifty each
quīnquāgēsim·us -a -um *adj* fiftieth ‖ *f* 2% tax
quīnquāgintā *indecl adj* fifty
Quīnquātr·ūs -uum *fpl or* **Quīnquātr·ia -ium** *npl* festival in honor of Minerva *(celebrated from March 19 to 23 esp. by the trades and professions under her patronage);* **quīnquātrūs minōrēs** *(or* **minusculae)** festival of Minerva *(held on June 13)*
quīnque *indecl adj* five
quīnquennāl·is -is -e *adj* quinquennial, occurring every five years; five-year, lasting five years
quīnquenn·is -is -e *adj* five-year-old
quīnquenn·ium -(i)ī *n* five-year period, five years
quīnqueped·al -ālis *n* five-foot ruler
quīnquepertīt·us -a -um (-part-) *adj* fivefold, divided into five parts
quīnqueprīm·ī -ōrum *mpl* five-man board of magistrates
quīnquerēm·is -is -e *adj* having five banks of oars ‖ *f* quinquereme
quīnque·vir -virī *m* member of a five-man board *(created at various times for various purposes)*
quīnquevirāt·us -ūs *m* membership on a board of five
quīnquiē(n)s *adv* five times
quīnquipl·ex -icis *adj* fivefold; **cēra quīnquiplex** tablet consisting of five sheets
quīnquiplic·ō -āre -āvī -ātus *tr* to multiply by five
Quīnt·a -ae *f* woman's name *(praenomen)*
quīntadecimān·ī -ōrum *mpl* **(-decum-)** soldiers of the 15th legion
quīntān·us -a -um *adj* of the fifth ‖ *mpl* members of the fifth legion ‖ *f* camp street running between the 5th and 6th maniple and the 5th and 6th squadron of cavalry *(used as a market street of the camp)*
Quīntiliān·us -ī *m* Quintilian *(Marcus Fabius Quintilianus, orator and professor of rhetoric, A.D. c. 35–95)*
Quīntīl·is *or* **Quīnctīl·is -is -e** *adj & m* July *(fifth month of the old Roman calendar until 153 B.C.; renamed* **Iūlius** *after the Julian reform of the calendar)*
Quīnt·ius *or* **Quīnct·ius -(i)ī** *m* name of a Roman gens *(nomen)*
quīntō *or* **quīntum** *adv* for the fifth time
quīnt·us -a -um *adj* fifth ‖ **Quīntus** *m* Roman first name *(praenomen)*
quīnt·us decim·us -a -um *adj* fifteenth
quippe *adv* of course, naturally, obviously, by all means ‖ *conj* since, for; **quippe quī** since he *(is, was, will be one who),* inasmuch as he; **multa Caesar questus est quippe quī vīdisset ...** Caesar complained a lot since he had seen ...
quippiam = quidpiam
quippinī *adv* why not?; of course, to be sure
Quirīnāl·is -is -e *adj* of Quirinus *(i.e., Romulus);* **collis Quirīnālis** Quirinal Hill *(one of the seven hills of Rome)* ‖ *npl* festival in honor of Romulus *(celebrated on February 17)*
Quirīn·us -a -um *adj* of Quirinus ‖ *m* Quirinus *(epithet of Romulus after his deification, of Janus, of Augustus, and of Antony)*
Quir·īs -ītis *m* Roman citizen; inhabitant of Cures *(Sabine town) (after the union of the Sabines and Romans, the Romans called themselves* **Quirītēs** *in their peace-time capacity. They were styled on all solemn occasions* **Populus Rōmānus Quirītēs(que);** *in later times it was distorted into* **Populus Rōmānus Quirītēs)**
quirītāti·ō -ōnis *f* shrieking, shriek
quirītāt·us -ūs *m* shriek, scream
Quirītēs -ium *mpl (pl form of* **Quirīs)** *(see* **Quirīs)** Roman citizens; **iūs Quirītium** legal rights enjoyed by Roman citizens
quirīt·ō -āre *tr & intr* to shriek, scream
quīs = quibus
quis cūius *pron (interrog)* who, which one; *(indef)* anyone
quisnam quaenam *(see* **quidnam)** *pron (interrog)* who, just who
quispiam cūiuspiam *pron* someone
quispiam quaepiam quodpiam *adj* any
quisquam cūiusquam *pron* anyone
quisque cūiusque *pron* each, each one, everybody, everyone; **doctissimus quisque** everyone of great learning, all the most learned; **optimus quisque** all the best ones
quisque quaeque quodque *or* **quidque** *or* **quicque** *adj* each
quisquili·ae -ārum *fpl or* **quisquili·a -ōrum** *npl* refuse, scraps, trash, junk; **quisqiliae**! baloney!
quisquis *(gen and dat not in use; abl:* **quōquō)** *pron* whoever, whosoever; everyone who; everyone, each
quīvīs quaevīs quidvīs *pron* anyone at all, anyone you please; **quīvīs ūnus** any one person
quō *adv (interrog)* where?, to what place?; what for?, to what purpose?; *(after* **sī, nisi,** *or* **nē)** to any place, anywhere; **quō ... eō** the ... the; **quō magis ... eō magis** the more ... the more ‖ *conj* where, to which place; whereby, wherefore; *(replacing* **ut** *when the clause contains a comparative)* in order that, so that
quoad *adv* how far; to what extent; by what time, how soon; how long; **est modus quoad** there is a limit up to which ‖ *conj*

as long as; until, until such time as; as far as; *(w.* **ēius** *in the phrase:* **quoad ēius (facere) possum** as far as *(i.e.,* as well as) I can
quōcircā *adv* for which reason, wherefore, therefore, that's the reason
quōcumque (-cunque, -quomque) *adv* to whatever place, wherever
quod *conj* because; as for the fact that; the fact that; insofar as; as far as; **quod sī** *(or* **quodsī)** but if
quōdammodo *or* **quōdam modō** *adv* in a way
quoi = cui
quoiquoimodī *see* **cuicuimodī**
quōius = cūius
quoivīsmodī *see* **cuivīsmodī**
quōlibet *adv* anywhere you please, anywhere at all
quom *see* **cum**
quōminus *conj* that not; *(after verbs of hindering)* from, *e.g.,* **dēterrēre aliquem quōminus aliquid habeat** to keep s.o. from having s.th.
quōmodo *adv (interrog)* how, in what way; *(rel)* just as, as
quōmodocumque *adv* in whatever way, however
quōmodonam *interrog adv* where?, whereto?; to what purpose?, to what end?
quōnam *interrog adv* where on earth?, just where(to)? **quōnam ūsque** just how much longer? to what possible degree? to what conceivable end?
quondam *adv* once, at one time, formerly; at times, once in a while; someday, one day *(in the future)*
quoniam *conj* because, seeing that, now that
quōpiam *adv* at any place, anywhere
quōquam *adv* to any place; in any direction, anywhere
quoque *adv (always succeeds the word it emphasizes)* too
quōquō *adv* to whatever place, wherever
quōquōmodo *adv* in whatever way, however
quōquōversum *adv* **(-vōrsum, -sus)** in every direction, every way
quōrsum *interrog & rel adv* **(-sus)** in what direction, whereto; to what end, why
quot *indecl adj (interrog)* how many; *(correlative)* as many; **quot Kalendīs** every first of the month; **quot mēnsibus** every month
quotannīs *adv* every year
quotcumque *indecl adj* however many
quotēn·ī -ae -a *adj* how many each
quotīdiān·us -a -um *adj* **(cōt-, cott-)** daily
quotīdiē *adv* **(cōt-, cott-)** daily
quotiē(n)s *adv (interrog)* how many times; *(correlative)* as often as, whenever
quotīe(n)scumque *or* **quotiē(n)scunque** *adv* as often as, however often, whenever
quotquot *indecl adj* however many; **quotquot annīs** every year; **quotquot mēnsibus** every month
quotum·us -a -um *adj* which in number, which in order
quot·us -a -um *adj* which, what; what a small, what a trifling; **quota hōra est?** what time is it?; **quota pars** *(or* **portiō)** what part, what portion; **quotus quisque** how few?; **quotus quisque philosophōrum invenitur** how few of the philosophers are found *or* how rarely is one of the philosophers found?
quot·uscumque -acumque -umcumque *adj* just what, just which
quō ūsque *or* **quoūsque** *adv* how far, how long, till when; to what degree
quōvīs *adv* to any place whatsoever, anywhere; **quōvīs gentium** anywhere in the world
quum = cum *(conj)*
qūr *or* **quūr** *see* **cūr**

R

R, r *(supply* littera) *f* seventeenth letter of the Latin alphabet; letter name: **er**
rabidē *adv* rabidly, madly; furiously
rabid·us -a -um *adj* rabid, mad; furious, raving, uncontrolled
rabi·ēs *(gen not in use) f* madness; *(fig)* rage, anger, fury, wild passion; ferocity *(of animals);* rabies
rabiōsē *adv* furiously, madly
rabiōsul·us -a -um *adj* half-mad, rather rabid
rabiōs·us -a -um *adj* rabid *(animal);* mad; frenzied, furious, raving
rabō -ōnis *m (shortened form of* **arrabō)** token payment, down payment, deposit
rabul·a -ae *m* ranting lawyer
racēmif·er -era -erum *adj* clustered; covered with grape clusters
racēm·us -ī *m* cluster, bunch *(esp. of grapes); (fig)* wine
radi·āns -antis *adj* shining, beaming, radiant
radiāt·us -a -um *adj* spoked; having rays, radiant
rādīcitus *adv* by the roots, root and all; *(fig)* completely, utterly
rādīcul·a -ae *f* small root; radish
radi·ō -āre *or* **radi·or -ārī** *intr* to radiate, shine
radiōs·us -a -um *adj* radiant
rad·ius -(i)ī *m* stake, stick; spoke; ray, beam; *(in weaving)* shuttle; radius *(of a circle);* measuring rod; elongated olive
rād·īx -īcis *f* root; radish; foot *(of hill or mountain);* base, foundation; basis, origin

rā·dō -dere -sī -sus *tr* to scrape, scratch; to shave; to scratch out, erase; to graze, touch in passing; to strip off; *(of wind)* to lash

raed·a -ae *f* **(rēd-)** four-wheeled carriage, coach

raedār·ius -(i)ī *m* coach driver

Raetic·us -a -um *adj* **(Rhaet-)** Rhaetian

Raeti·us -a -um *adj* **(Rhaet-)** Rhaetian **II** *f* Rhaetia *(Alpine country between Germany and Italy)*

Raet·us -a -um *adj & m* **(Rhaet-)** Rhaetian

rall·us -a -um *adj* thin, threadbare

rāmāl·ia -ium *npl* brushwood, undergrowth

rāment·a -ae *f or* **rāment·um -ī** *n* chip, shaving

rāmes *see* **rāmex**

rāme·us -a -um *adj* of branches, of boughs

rām·ex -icis *m or* **ram·es -itis** *m* rupture; blood vessel of the lung **II** *mpl* lungs

Ramn·ēs *or* **Ramnēns·ēs -ium** *mpl* one of the three original Roman tribes; *(fig)* blue bloods

rāmōs·us -a -um *adj* having many branches, branching; branch-like

rāmul·us -ī *m* twig

rām·us -ī *m* branch, bough; branch *(of an antler);* genealogical branch

rān·a -ae *f* frog; **rāna quaxat** the frog croaks

ranc·ēns -entis *adj* putrid, stinking

rancidul·us -a -um *adj* stinky, rank; rather disgusting

rancid·us -a -um *adj* rancid, rank, stinking; disgusting

ranc·ō -āre *intr* (*of a tiger*) roar

rānuncul·us -ī *m* little frog, tadpole

rapācid·a -ae *m (humorous patronymic)* son of a thief

rapācit·ās -ātis *f* rapacity, greediness

rap·āx -ācis *adj* rapacious, grasping, greedy for plunder; insatiable

raphan·us -ī *m* radish

rapidē *adv* rapidly; *(to burn)* fiercely

rapidit·ās -ātis *f* rapidity, velocity, swiftness, rush

rapid·us -a -um *adj* tearing away, seizing; fierce, consuming, white-hot *(fire);* rapid, swift, rushing, impetuous

rapīn·a -ae *f* rapine, pillage; prey

rap·iō -ere -uī -tus *tr* to seize and carry off; to snatch, tear, pluck; to drag off; to hurry, drive, cause to rush; to carry off by force, ravish; to ravage, lay waste; to lead on hurriedly; **flammam rapere** to catch fire; **in iūs rapere** to haul off to court **II** *refl* to hurry, dash, take off

raptim *adv* hurriedly; suddenly

rapti·ō -ōnis *f* abduction, ravishing

rapt·ō -āre *tr* to seize and carry off; to abduct, kidnap; to drag away; to drag along; to plunder; **in iūs raptāre** to haul off to court

rapt·or -ōris *m* plunderer, robber; abductor

rapt·um -ī *n* plunder, loot

rapt·us -a -um *pp of* **rapiō II** *n* plunder, loot

rapt·us -ūs *m* snatching away; looting, robbery; abduction, kidnapping

rāpul·um -ī *n* little turnip

rāp·um -ī *n* turnip

rārē *adv* rarely; sparsely; loosely

rārē·faciō -facere -fēcī -factus *tr* to rarefy, thin out

rārē·fīō -fierī -factus sum *intr* to become less solid, rarefy

rārēsc·ō -ere *intr* to grow thin, lose density, become rarefied; to grow wider, widen out, open up; to become fewer; to disappear, die away

rārit·ās -ātis *f* looseness of texture; thinness; small number; sparseness; infrequency; rarity

rārō *adv* rarely, seldom

rār·us -a -um *adj* wide apart, of loose texture, thin; scattered, far apart; scarce, sparse; few; uncommon, rare; unusual; *(mil)* in open rank

rāsī *perf of* **rādō**

rāsil·is -is -e *adj* shaved smooth, scraped, polished

rāsit·ō -āre -āvī -ātus *tr* to shave (regularly)

rastell·us -ī *m* rake *(usu. of wood)*

rastr·um -ī *(pl:* **rastr·ī -ōrum** *mpl) n* rake; mattock

rāsus *pp of* **rādō**

rati·ō -ōnis *f* calculation, computation, reckoning, account; register; matter, affair, business, transaction; consideration, respect; grounds; guiding principle; scheme, system, method; procedure; theory, doctrine; science; relation, connection, reference; fashion, way, style; reasoning, reason, judgment, understanding; reasonableness; order, law, rule; view, opinion; *(w. gen)* a reason for; **(lībertus) ā ratiōnibus** bookkeeper, accountant; **fūgit tē ratiō** *(coll)* you're off your rocker; **nōn erat ratiō āmittere ēiusmodī occāsiōnem** there was no reason to pass up that kind of opportunity; **parēs ratiōnēs facere cum** to square accounts with; **populāris rātiō** popular cause; **prō ratiōne** proportionately; according to the rule, properly; **propter ratiōnem** *(w. gen)* out of regard for; **ratiō aerāria** rate of exchange; **ratiō atque ūsus** theory and practice; **ratiō cōnstat** the account tallies; **ratiō itineris** itinerary; **ratiōne** with good reason; according to the rules, properly; **ratiōnem cōnferre** *(or* **dēferre** *or* **referre)** *(w. gen)* to render *or* give an account of, account for; **ratiōnem**

(**dē**)**dūcere** to make a calculation, reckon; **ratiōnem habēre cum** to have to do with; **ratiōnem inīre** *(or* **reddere** *or* **tenēre**) to calculate, make a calculation; to embark on a scheme; **ratiō vītae** pattern of life, life style

ratiōcinātī·ō -ōnis *f* exercise of the reasoning powers, reasoning; theory, theorizing; deduction, inference

ratiōcinātīv·us -a -um *adj* concerned with reasoning, syllogistic

ratiōcināt·or -ōris *m* accountant

ratiōcin·or -ārī -ātus sum *tr & intr* to calculate, reckon; to reason, argue, conclude, infer

ratiōnāl·is -is -e *adj* rational; theoretical; dialectical

ratiōnār·ium -(i)ī *n* financial survey

rat·is -is *f* raft; *(poet)* ship, craft **||** *fpl* pontoons

ratiuncul·a -ae *f* small account; trifling reason; petty argumentation

rat·us -a -um *pp of* **reor ||** *adj* reckoned, calculated; fixed, established, settled, certain, sure; approved; **prō ratā parte** *(or* **prō ratā**) in proportion, proportionately; **ratum facere** *(or* **efficere**) to confirm, ratify, approve; **ratum habēre** *(or* **dūcere**) to consider valid, regard as certain *or* sure

raucison·us -a -um *adj* hoarse-sounding

rauc·us -a -um *adj* raucous, hoarse; screaming, strident; scraping; deep, deep-voiced

raud·us -eris *n* (**rōd-, rūd-**) copper coin; lump

rauduscul·um -ī *n* (**rōd-, rūd-**) bit of money

Ravenn·a -ae *f* Ravenna *(port and naval base)*

rāv·iō -īre *intr* to be hoarse

rāv·is -is *f* hoarseness

rāv·us -a -um *adj* greyish

re- *pref (also* **red-**) *denoting* **1** movement back, in reverse: **revocāre** to call back; **2** reversal of an action, un-: **retegere** to uncover; **3** restoration: **revalēscere** to recover again; **4** response: **respondēre** to respond; **rescrībere** to answer *(in writing);* **5** opposition: **rebellāre** to rebel; **6** separation: **removēre** to remove; **7** repeated action: **replēre** to refill; **reïterāre** repeat again and again

re·a -ae *f* defendant; guilty woman

Rēa *see* **Rhēa**

rēapse *adv* (**-abs-**) in fact, actually, really

Reāt·e -is *n* Sabine town

Reātīn·us -a -um *adj* of Reate

rebellāti·ō -ōnis *f* rebellion

rebellātr·īx -īcis *adj (fem only)* rebellious; **rebellātrīx Germānia** rebellious Germany

rebelli·ō -ōnis *f* rebellion

rebell·is -is -e *adj* rebellious **||** *mpl* rebels

rebell·ium -(i)ī *n* rebellion

rebell·ō -āre -āvī -ātum *intr* to rebel

rebell·us -a -um *adj* reddish

rebīt·ō -ere *intr* to go back

rebo·ō -āre *tr* to make reecho **||** *intr* to reecho, bellow back

recalcitr·ō -āre *intr* to kick back

recal·eō -ēre *intr* to get warm again; *(of a river)* to run warm *(e.g., w. blood)*

recal·ēscō -ēscere -uī *intr* to grow warm again

recal·faciō -facere -fēcī *tr* to warm up again

recalv·us -a -um *adj* bald in front, with receding hairline

recand·ēscō -ēscere -uī *intr* to grow white; *(w. dat)* to grow hot, glow in response to

recanō *see* **recinō**

recant·ō -āre -āvī -ātus *tr* to recant; to charm back, charm away **||** *intr* to reecho

reccidō *see* **recidō** *(to fall back)*

re·cēdō -cēdere -cessī -cessum *intr* to go back; to go away, withdraw, recede; to give ground, fall back; to depart; to vanish; to stand back, be distant

recell·ō -ere *intr* to recoil

recēns *adv* just, recently, lately

rec·ēns -entis *adj* recent, fresh, young; newly arrived, just arrived; modern; fresh; rested; **recentissimus** latest **||** *npl* recent events

recēns·eō -ēre -uī -sus *tr* to count, enumerate, number, survey; to recount, go over again, retell; *(mil)* to review; *(pol) (of a censor)* to revise the roll of, review, enroll

recēnsi·ō -ōnis *f* revision

recēnsus *pp of* **recēnseō**

recēns·us -ūs *m* review; census; valuation *(of property)*

recēpī *perf of* **recipiō**

receptācul·um -ī *n* receptacle, container; reservoir; place of refuge, shelter; hiding place

recepti·ō -ōnis *f* reception

recept·ō -āre *tr* to take back; to welcome frequently into the home, entertain; to tug at **||** *refl* to beat a hasty retreat

recept·or -ōris *m or* **receptr·īx -īcis** *f* shelterer; concealer

recept·us -a -um *pp of* **recipiō ||** *n* obligation

recept·us -ūs *m* taking back, recantation; way of escape; refuge; return; *(mil)* retreat; **(signum) receptuī canere** to sound the retreat

recessī *perf of* **recēdō**

recessim *adv* backwards

recess·us -ūs *m* retreat, withdrawal; departure; secluded spot, retreat; inner room, central chamber; recess; background

recharmid·ō -āre *ref* to stop being a Charmides *(character in Roman comedy)*

recidīv·us -a -um *adj* recurring, returning; rebuilt

re·cidō -cidere -cidī -cāsum *or* **reccid·ō -ere** *intr* to fall back; to jump back, recoil; to suffer a relapse; *(fig)* to fall back, sink, relapse; to turn out, result; *(w.* **ad** *or* **in** + *acc)* to pass to, be handed over to

recī·dō -dere -dī -sus *tr* to cut back, cut off, cut away, cut down; to abridge, cut short

re·cingō -cingere -cīnxī -cīnctus *tr* to loosen, undo, take off

recin·ō -ere *tr* to repeat, reecho **||** *intr* to sound a warning

reciper- = **recuper-**

re·cipiō -cipere -cēpī -ceptus *tr* to keep back, keep in reserve; to withdraw, bring back, carry back; to retake, recover, regain; to take in, accept, receive, welcome; to gain, collect, take in, make *(money);* to take up, assume, undertake; to guarantee, pledge; *(mil)* to retake, recapture, seize, take, occupy; **ad sē** *(or* **in sē) recipere** to take upon oneself, take the responsibility for, promise, guarantee **||** *refl* to get hold of oneself again, regain composure, recover, come to again; to retreat, escape; **sē recipere** *(w.* **ad** *or* **in** + *acc)* to retreat to, escape to, find refuge in

reciproc·ō -āre -āvī -ātus *tr* to move back and forth; to turn back; to back up *(e.g., a ship),* reverse the direction of; to reverse, convert *(a proposition)* **||** *intr (of the tide)* to ebb and flow, rise and fall

reciproc·us -a -um *adj* ebbing and flowing, going backwards and forwards

recīsus *pp of* **recīdō**

recitāti·ō -ōnis *f* reading aloud, recitation

recitāt·or -ōris *m* reader, reciter

recit·ō -āre -āvī -ātus *tr* to read out, read aloud, recite; to name in writing, appoint, constitute; **senātum recitāre** to take roll call in the Senate

reclāmāti·ō -ōnis *f* cry of disapproval; shout of protest

reclāmit·ō -āre *intr* to voice disapproval; *(w. dat)* to protest against

reclām·ō -āre -āvī -ātus *tr* to protest **||** *intr* to raise a protest, shout objections; to reverberate; *(w. dat)* to express disapproval to, contradict

reclīn·is -is -e *adj* reclining, leaning back

reclīn·ō -āre -āvī -ātus *tr* to bend back, lean back, rest; *(w.* **ab)** to distract *(s.o.)* from **||** *refl* to lean

reclū·dō -dere -sī -sus *tr* to open; to lay open, disclose; to draw *(sword);* to break up *(the soil)*

recoctus *pp of* **recoquō**

recōgit·ō -āre -āvī -ātum *tr* to consider, think over **||** *intr (w.* **dē** + *abl)* to think again about, reconsider

recogniti·ō -ōnis *f* formal inspection

reco·gnōscō -gnōscere -gnōvī -gnitus *tr* to call to mind again, review; to recognize; to look over, examine, inspect, investigate; to certify, authorize

recol·ligō -ligere -lēgī -lēctus *tr* to gather again, gather up, collect; **tē recollige**! get hold of yourself!; take heart! **||** *refl* to pull oneself together

re·colō -colere -coluī -cultus *tr* to till again, cultivate once more; to honor again; to call to mind, think over, consider; to practice again, resume

recomment·or -ārī -ātus sum *tr* to remember, recall

recomminīsc·or -ī *tr* to call to mind again, recall

recomposit·us -a -um *adj* rearranged

reconciliāti·ō -ōnis *f* winning back again, reestablishment, restoration; reconciliation

reconciliāt·or -ōris *m* reconciler; **pācis reconciliātor** restorer of peace

reconcili·ō -āre -āvī -ātus *tr* to bring back, regain, recover; to restore, reestablish; to win over again, conciliate; to bring together again, reconcile

reconcinn·ō -āre *tr* to set right again, repair

recondit·us -a -um *adj* hidden, concealed; recondite, abstruse, profound; reserved *(person)*

recon·dō -dere -didī -ditus *tr* to put back again; to put away, hoard; to hide, conceal; to plunge *(sword);* to close *(eyes)* again; to store up *(in the mind)*

recōnfl·ō -āre *tr* to rekindle

reco·quō -quere -xī -ctus *tr* to cook, boil, *or* bake again; to recast, remold

recordāti·ō -ōnis *f* recollection, remembrance

record·or -ārī -ātus sum *tr & intr* to recall, recollect, remember

recoxī *perf of* **recoquō**

recre·ō -āre -āvī -ātus *tr* to recreate, restore, renew; *(fig)* to revive, refresh

recrep·ō -āre *intr* to reecho

re·crēscō -crēscere -crēvī *intr* to grow again; to be renewed

recrūd·ēscō -ēscere -uī *intr (of a wound)* to open up again; *(of a revolt)* to break out again

rēctā *adv* by a direct route, straight

rēctē *adv* in a straight line; rightly, correctly; suitably, properly, well; quite; *(in answers)* good, very good; quite right; *(in evasive answers)* well, right, it's all right; *(in politely declining an offer, like* **benignē)** no, thank you.

rēcti·ō -ōnis *f* direction, controlling

rēct·or -ōris *m* guide, controller; rider, driver *(of an animal);* leader; master; pilot; tutor; *(mil)* commander; *(naut)* helmsman, pilot; *(pol)* ruler, governor

rēct·us -a -um *pp of* **regō ||** *adj* in a straight line, straight, direct; correct, right, proper, appropriate; just, upright, conscientious, virtuous; standing erect; *(impartial)* judge; straight-forward *(expression);* sheer *(cliff);* **aere rēctō cantāre** to play a reed pipe; **cāsus rēctus** *(gram)* nominative case; **fūnis rēctus** tightrope; **rēctīs oculīs** with eyes not lowered, without flinching **‖** *n* right; uprightness, rectitude, virtue; **in rēctum** in a straight line; in a vertical position *or* direction, vertically; straight forward

recub·ō -āre *intr* to lie on one's back, lie down, rest

rēcul·a -ae *f* little thing

recultus *pp of* **recolō**

re·cumbō -cumbere -cubuī *intr* to lie down (again); to recline *(esp. at table);* to sink down *(e.g., in a swamp);* to fall; *(of fog)* to settle down

recuperāti·ō -ōnis *f* recovery

recuperāt·or -ōris *m* **(-cip-)** recoverer; *(leg)* arbiter *(member of a bench of from 3 to 5 men who expedited cases needing speedy decisions)*

recuperātōri·us -a -um *adj* **(-cip-)** of the special court for summary civil suits

recuper·ō -āre -āvī -ātus *tr* **(-cip-)** to regain, recover, get back; to win over again

recūr·ō -āre -āvī -ātus *tr* to restore, refresh, restore to health

recur·rō -rere -rī -sum *intr* to run back, hurry back; to return *(to the starting point of a cycle);* to recur, come back *(to the mind); (of a process)* to run in the opposite direction; to revert *(to a former condition); (w.* **ad)** to have recourse to

recurs·ō -āre *intr* to keep running back; to keep recurring

recurs·us -ūs *m* return; retreat

recurv·ō -āre -āvī -ātus *tr* to curve, bend back

recurv·us -a -um *adj* curving, curved, bent, crooked

recūsāti·ō -ōnis *f* refusal; *(leg)* objection, protest; *(leg)* counterplea

recūs·ō -āre -āvī -ātus *tr* to raise objections to, reject, refuse; *(w. inf)* to be reluctant to, refuse to **‖** *intr* to raise an objection; to make a rebuttal

recuss·us -a -um *adj* reverberating

recu·tiō -tere -ssī -ssus *tr* to strike *(so as to cause to resound)*

recutīt·us -a -um *adj* raw *(skin, from being rubbed);* circumcised

red- *see* **re-**

redāctus *pp of* **redigō**

redambul·ō -āre *intr* to walk back

redam·ō -āre *tr* to love in return

redārdēsc·ō -ere *intr* to blaze up again

redargu·ō -ere -ī *tr* to disprove, refute, contradict; to disprove the existence of

redauspic·ō -āre *intr* to take the auspices again

red·dō -dere -didī -ditus *tr* to give back, return, restore, replace; to repay; to repeat *(words);* to recite, rehearse *(words);* to produce *(a sound);* to ascribe, attribute; to translate; to utter in response; to render, make; to give as due, pay, grant, deliver; to reflect, reproduce, imitate; **animam ā pulmōnibus reddere** to exhale *(lit: to give back a breath from the lungs);* **causam reddere** to give a reason *or* explanation; **conūbia reddere** to grant intermarriage rights; **iūdicium reddere** to administer justice; to grant a trial; **iūra reddere** to administer justice; **litterās reddere** to deliver a letter; **morbō nātūrae dēbitum reddere** to die of disease; **poenās reddere** to suffer punishment; **quī tē nōmine reddet** who will bear your name; **ratiōnem reddere** to render an account *(financial or other);* **reddere hostī clādem** to pay back the enemy for the massacre; **tālia eī reddere** to answer him in words such as this; **veniam reddere** *(w. dat)* to forgive; **verbum prō verbō reddere** to translate word for word; **vītam reddere** to die **‖** *refl* to return

redempti·ō -ōnis *f* ransoming; bribing; revenue collection

redempt·ō -āre *tr* to ransom (repeatedly)

redempt·or -ōris *m* contractor; revenue agent

redemptūr·a -ae *f* undertaking of public contracts

redemptus *pp of* **redimō**

red·eō -īre -iī -itum *intr* to go back, come back, return; *(of a speaker)* to return *(to the theme); (w.* **ad) 1** to return to, revert to; **2** to fall back on, have recourse to; **3** to be reduced to; **4** *(of power, inheritances, etc.)* to revert to, devolve upon; **ad sē redīre** to come to again, regain consciousness; to control oneself

redhāl·ō -āre *tr* to exhale

redhib·eō -ēre -uī -itus *tr (of a vendor)* to take back *(a defective purchase); (of a purchaser)* to return *(a defective purchase)*

red·igō -igere -ēgī -āctus *tr* to drive back, lead back, bring back; to call in, collect, raise, make *(money);* to gather in *(crops);* to repel *(the enemy);* to reduce *(in quantity, number, or to a condition);* to force, compel, subdue; *(w. double acc)* to render, make; *(w.* **in** *or* **sub** + *acc)* to bring under the power of; **ad vānum et irritum redigere** to make meaningless; to make null and void; **in memoriam redigere** to remember, recall; **in ōrdinem redigere** to bring into line; **in prōvinciam redigere** to reduce to the status of a province; **in potestātem redigere** *(w. gen)* to bring under the control of; **in pūblicum** *(or* **in**

aerārium) redigere to turn over *(money)* to the public treasury
redimīcul·um -ī *n* band, chaplet, fillet; chain, fetter
redim·iō -īre -iī -ītus *tr* to crown, wreathe; to surround, encircle
red·imō -imere -ēmī -emptus *tr* to buy back; to ransom, redeem; to buy off, ward off, avert; to pay for, compensate for, atone for; *(com)* to get by contract, collect under contract
redintegrāti·ō -ōnis *f* renewal; repetition
redintegr·ō -āre *tr* to make whole again, restore, revive, refresh; *(mil)* to bring to full strength
redipīsc·or -ī *tr* to get back
rediti·ō -ōnis *f* return
redit·us -ūs *m* return; *(fig)* restoration; *(astr)* orbit, revolution; *(fin)* revenue, proceeds, return; **(in) reditū esse** to yield a return
redivia *see* **reduvia**
redivīv·us -a -um *adj* second-hand
redol·eō -ēre -uī *tr* to smell of, smell like ‖ *intr* to smell, be redolent
redōn·ō -āre -āvī -ātus *tr* to restore, give back again; to give up, abandon
redorm·iō -īre *intr* to go back to sleep (again)
re·dūcō -dūcere -dūxī -ductus *tr* to lead back, bring back; to draw back; to revive *(a practice);* to escort *(an official, as mark of honor, to his home);* to remarry *(after a separation);* to restore to normal, restore to a previous condition; to withdraw *(troops); (leg)* to make retrospective; **gradum redūcere** to draw back; **in grātiam redūcere** to restore to favor; **in memoriam redūcere** to recall; **rem hūc redūcere ut** to make it possible that
reducti·ō -ōnis *f* restoration
reduct·or -ōris *m* restorer
reduct·us -a -um *pp of* **redūcō** ‖ *adj* remote, secluded, aloof
redunc·us -a -um *adj* bent backwards, curved backwards
redundanti·a -ae *f* excess; redundancy
redund·ō -āre -āvī -ātum *tr* to cause to overflow; **aqua redundāta** the overflow ‖ *intr* to overflow; to be too numerous, be too large; *(of writers)* to be excessive; to be soaked *(e.g., w. blood); (w. abl)* to abound in; *(w.* **ex** *or* **dē** *+ abl)* to stream from, overflow with
reduvi·a *or* **redivi·a -ae** *f* hangnail
red·ux -ucis *adj* **(redd-)** guiding back, rescuing; that brings back home *(esp. a soldier on a foreign mission);* brought back, restored
redūxī *perf of* **redūcō**
refecti·ō -ōnis *f* restoration, repairing; regaining one's strength; convalescence
refectus *pp of* **reficiō**
refell·ō -ere -ī *tr* to refute, disprove
refer·ciō -cīre -sī -tus *tr* **(refarc-)** to stuff, cram, choke, crowd
refer·iō -īre *tr* to strike back
referō referre rettulī relātus *tr* to bring back, carry back; to give back, return, restore; to pay back, repay; to (re)echo *(a sound);* to renew, revive, repeat; to direct, focus, turn *(mind, attention);* to present again, represent; to say in turn, reply; to announce, report, relate, tell; to note down, enter, register, record; to consider, regard; to refer, attribute, ascribe; to bring up, spit out, vomit; **gradum referre** to go back, retreat; **grātiam referre** to do a return favor; **grātiās referre** to return thanks, show gratitude; **pedem referre** to go back, retreat; **pedēs fertque refertque** he walks up and down; **ratiōnēs referre ad aerārium** to make an accounting to the treasury; **vestīgia referre** to retrace footsteps ‖ *refl* to go back, return ‖ *intr (pol)* to make a motion, make a proposal; **ad senātum referre** *(w.* **dē** *+ abl)* to bring before the Senate the matter of, make a proposal to the Senate about
rē·fert -ferre *v impers* it is of importance, it is of consequence, it concerns; **meā (tuā, nostrā) rēfert** it is of importance *or* of advantage to me (you, us); **nōn rēfert utrum** it makes no difference whether; **parvī rēfert** *(w. inf)* it is of little importance, of little advantage to; **quid rēfert?** what's the difference?; **quid rēfert ad mē?** what's the difference to me?
refert·us -a -um *pp of* **referciō** ‖ *adj* packed, crammed, stuffed; crowded; full, replete, chuck-full
referv·eō -ēre *intr* to boil over, bubble over
refervēsc·ō -ere *intr* to begin to boil *or* bubble
refībul·ō -āre *tr* to unpin
re·ficiō -ficere -fēcī -fectus *tr* to rebuild, repair, restore; to revive *(hope, etc.);* to refresh, invigorate; to get *(e.g., money)* back again; to reappoint, re-elect
refī·gō -gere -xī -xus *tr* to unfasten, undo; to take down *(posters, etc.);* to annul *(laws)*
refing·ō -ere *tr* to refashion
refīxus *pp of* **refīgō**
reflāgit·ō -āre *tr* to demand again, ask back
reflāt·us -ūs *m* headwind
re·flectō -flectere -flexī -flexus *tr* to bend back *or* backwards, turn around, turn away; *(fig)* to turn back, bring back, change
refl·ō -āre -āvī -ātus *tr* to breathe out again ‖ *intr* to blow in the wrong direction
reflu·ō -ere *intr* to flow back, run back; to overflow
reflu·us -a -um *adj* ebbing, receding

refocill·ō -āre -āvī -ātus *tr* to rewarm; to revive

refōrmāt·or -ōris *m* reformer

reformīdāti·ō -ōnis *f* dread

reformīd·ō -āre -āvī -ātus *tr* to dread, stand in awe of; to shrink from, shun

refōrm·ō -āre -āvī -ātus *tr* to reshape, remold, transform

re·foveō -fovēre -fōvī -fōtus *tr* to warm again; to restore, revive, refresh

refrāctāriol·us -a -um *adj* a bit refractory, somewhat stubborn

refrāctāri·us -a -um unruly

refrāctus *pp of* **refringō**

refrāg·or -ārī -ātus sum *or* **refrāg·ō -āre** *intr (w. dat)* to oppose, resist, thwart

refrēn·ō -āre -āvī -ātus *tr* to curb, restrain, keep down, control

refric·ō -āre -uī -ātus *tr* to rub open, scratch open; to irritate, reopen *(a wound); (fig)* to exasperate; *(fig)* to renew ‖ *intr* to break out again

refrīger·ō -āre -āvī -ātus *tr* to cool, cool off, chill; to refresh; to weary, exhaust ‖ *pass* to grow cool; to grow weary

re·frīgēscō -frīgēscere -frīxī *intr* to grow cool, become cool; *(fig)* to lose force, flag, abate, fail, grow dull, grow stale; *(fig)* to fall flat

re·fringō fringere -frēgī -frāctus *tr* to break open, break down; to tear off *(clothes); (fig)* to break, check, destroy, put an end to

re·fugiō -fugere -fūgī *tr* to run away from; to avoid ‖ *intr* to run away, escape; to disappear

refug·ium -(i)ī *n* place of refuge; recourse

refug·us -a -um *adj* receding, vanishing ‖ *m* fugitive, refugee

reful·geō -gēre -sī *intr* to gleam, reflect *(light),* glitter

re·fundō -fundere -fūdī -fūsus *tr* to pour back, pour out ‖ *pass* to flow back; to overflow

refūtāti·ō -ōnis *f* refutation

refūtāt·us -ūs *m* refutation

refūt·ō -āre -āvī -ātus *tr* to repress, suppress; to refute, disprove

rēgāliol·us -ī *m* wren

rēgāl·is -is -e *adj* regal, kingly; royal

rēgāliter *adv* royally; despotically

regel·ō -āre -āvī -ātus *tr* to cool off, air; to thaw, unfreeze, warm

re·gerō -gerere -gessī -gestus *tr* to carry back, throw back; *(fig)* to throw back *(remarks)*

rēgi·a -ae *f* palace; court *(royal or imperial establishment);* capital; *(in camp)* king's tent; regia *(originally the house of King Numa in the Roman Forum and later the residence of the Pontifex Maximus)*

rēgiē *adv* royally; despotically

Rēgiēns·is -is -e *or* **Rēgīn·us -a -um** *adj* **(Rhēg-)** of Rhegium ‖ *mpl* inhabitants of Rhegium *(in Bruttium in S. Italy)*

rēgific·us -a -um *adj* fit for a king

Rēgill·um -ī *n or* **Rēgill·ī -ōrum** *mpl* Sabine town from which the Fabian clan is said to have come

Rēgill·us -ī *m* family name *(cognomen)* in the Aemilian clan ‖ name of a small lake south of Gabii *(now dried up)* where the Romans defeated the Latins in 496 B.C.

regim·en -inis *n* steering *(of a ship);* steering oar; control *(of a horse);* direction, control *(of public and private affairs)*

rēgīn·a -ae *f* queen

Rēgīn·us -a -um (Rhēg-) of Rhegium *(in Bruttium)* ‖ *mpl* inhabitants of Rhegium

regi·ō -ōnis *f* straight line, line, direction; boundary, boundary line; region, area, quarter, neighborhood; ward *(of Rome);* district, province *(of a country);* department, sphere; geographical position; **ā rēctā regiōne** in a straight line; **dē rēctā regiōne dēflectere** to veer off the straight path; **ē regiōne** in a straight line, directly; *(w. gen or dat)* in the opposite direction to, exactly opposite; **rēctā regiōne** by a direct route

regiōnātim *adv* by districts

rēgi·us -a -um *adj* king's, royal, regal; like a king, worthy of a king, magnificent ‖ *mpl* king's troops ‖ *f see* **rēgia**

reglūtin·ō -āre *tr* to unglue

rēgnāt·or -ōris *m* ruler, sovereign

rēgnātr·īx -īcis *adj (fem only)* reigning, imperial

rēgn·ō -āre -āvī -ātum *intr* to reign; to be supreme, hold sway; to dominate; to rule the roost, play (the part of a) king; *(w. gen)* to be king of; *(w.* **in** *+ acc)* to rule over

rēgn·um -ī *n* monarchy, royal power, kingship; absolute power, despotism; supremacy, control, direction, sovereignty; kingdom, realm; domain, estate

regō regere rēxī rēctus *tr* to keep in a straight line; to keep on a proper course; to guide, conduct; to guide *(morally);* to manage, direct; *(mil)* to command; *(pol)* to rule, govern; **imperium regere** to exercise dominion, rule supreme; **regere fīnīs** *(leg)* to mark out the limits

re·gredior -gredī -gressus sum *intr* to step *or* go back; to come back, return; *(mil)* to march back, retreat

regressi·ō -ōnis *f (mil)* withdrawl; *(rhet)* repetition

regress·us -ūs *m* return; retreat

rēgul·a -ae *f* ruler *(for drawing straight lines or measuring);* rod, bar; rule, standard, model, principle *(in conduct, language)*

rēgul·us -ī *m* petty king; prince ‖ **Rēgulus** Marcus Atilius Regulus *(Roman general who refused to let himself be ransomed in the First Punic War)* ‖ Marcus Aquilius Regulus *(an informer under Nero, later a successful advocate)*

regust·ō -āre -āvī -ātus *tr* to taste again; *(fig)* to delve again into *(e.g., literature)*

re·iciō -icere -iēcī -iectus tr to throw back; to throw over one's shoulders; to beat back, repel; to reject; to refer, direct, assign; to postpone; *(leg) (of judges)* to challenge, overrule; **rem reicere** *(w.* **ad)** to refer the matter *(to s.o. for decision);* **potestās reiciendī** *(leg)* right to challenge

reiect·a -ōrum *npl (phil)* things which, while not absolutely bad, should be avoided

reiectāne·us -a -um *adj* to be rejected

reiecti·ō -ōnis *f* rejection; *(leg)* challenging; **reiectiō iūdicum** challenging potential jury members

reiectus *pp of* **reiciō**

re·lābor -lābī -lāpsus sum *intr* to slide *or* glide back; to sink down *(upon a couch); (of rivers)* to flow back; to sail back; *(fig)* to return

relangu·ēscō -ēscere -ī *intr* to faint; to be relaxed, relax; to weaken

relāti·ō -ōnis *f* report *(made by a magistrate to the Senate or the emperor);* repetition; **relātiō crīminis** *(leg)* responding to a charge

relāt·or -ōris *m (pol)* proposer of a motion in the Senate

relātus *pp of* **referō**

relāt·us -ūs *m* official report; narration; recital

relaxāti·ō -ōnis *f* relaxation; easing off, mitigation

relax·ō -āre -āvī -ātus *tr* to stretch out, widen, open; to loosen, open; to release, set free; to relax; to cheer up; to mitigate ‖ *pass* to relax

relēctus *pp of* **relegō**

relēgāti·ō -ōnis *f* banishment; sending into retirement

relēg·ō -āre -āvī -ātus *tr* to send away, remove; to send into retirement, retire; to banish; to relegate; to shift *(blame, responsibility);* to give back

re·legō -legere -lēgī -lēctus *tr* to collect again, gather up; to travel over, sail over again; to go over, review *(in thought, in a speech);* to reread

relentēsc·ō -ere *intr* to slack off, cool off

relev·ō -āre -āvī -ātus *tr* to lighten; to lift up *or* raise again; *(fig)* to relieve, ease the pain of; to lessen in force; to soothe

relicti·ō -ōnis *f* abandonment

relictus *pp of* **relinquō** ‖ *adj* abandoned, forsaken

relicuus *see* **reliquus**

relīd·ō -ere *tr* to dash back *(in the direction from which s.th. came)*

religāti·ō -ōnis *f* tying back *or* up

religi·ō -ōnis *f* religion; religious scruple, sense of right, conscience; misgivings; reverence, awe; sanctity, holiness; sect, cult; mode of worship; object of veneration, sacred object, sacred place; divine service, worship, ceremonies; religious practice, ritual; *(pej)* taboo; superstition; manifestation of divine sanction; *(w. gen)* scruple about, scrupulous regard for

religiōsē *adv* religiously, reverently, piously; scrupulously, conscientiously, carefully, exactly

religiōs·us -a -um *adj* religious, reverent, pious, devout; scrupulous, conscientious, exact, precise, accurate; superstitious; sacred, holy, consecrated; subject to religious claims, under religious liability

relig·ō -āre -āvī -ātus *tr* to tie back, tie up; to moor *(ship);* to untie, unfasten; to bind *(with a wreath, ribbon)*

re·linō -linere -lēvī *tr* to unseal, uncork

re·linquō -linquere -līquī -lictus *tr* to leave behind, not take along; to bequeath; to let remain; to leave alive; to forsake, abandon, leave in the lurch; to relinquish, resign; to leave unmentioned; **in mediō** *(or* **in medium)** **relinquere** to leave *(a question)* open; **locum integrum relinquere** to leave the place untouched

reliqu·ī -ōrum *mpl* the rest, the others; the survivors; posterity

reliqui·ae -ārum *fpl* remains, remnants, leftovers

reliqu·us -a -um *adj (also* **-cuus)** remaining, left over, left; subsequent, future *(time);* outstanding *(debt)* ‖ *mpl see* **reliquī** ‖ *n* remainder, rest, residue; **in reliquum** in the future, for the future; **nihil reliquī facere** to leave nothing undone, leave no stone unturned; **reliquum est** *(w. inf or* **ut)** it only remains to; **reliquum aliquid facere** *(or* **aliquid reliquī facere)** to leave s.th. behind, neglect s.th.

rellig- = relig-

relliq- = reliq-

relū·ceō -cēre -xī *intr* to reflect light, gleam, shine out, blaze

relū·cēscō -cēscere -xī *intr* to grow bright again, clear

reluct·or -ārī -ātus sum *intr* to fight back, put up a struggle, resist; to be reluctant

remacrēsc·ō -ere *intr* to shrink and become thin

remaledīc·ō -ere *intr* to return abuse

remand·ō -ere *tr* to chew again

reman·eō -ēre -sī -sum *intr* to stay behind; to remain, continue *(in a certain state)*

remān·ō -āre *intr* to flow back

remānsi·ō -ōnis *f* staying behind

remed·ium -(i)ī *n* remedy, cure
remēnsus *pp of* **remētior**
reme·ō -āre -āvī -ātus *tr* to retrace, relive **||** *intr* to go back, come back, return
re·mētior -mētīrī -mēnsus sum *tr* to remeasure; to retrace, go back over
rēm·ex -igis *m* rower, crew member; **rēmigēs -um** *mpl* crew
Rēm·ī -ōrum *mpl* a people of Gaul *(near modern Rheims)*
rēmigāti·ō -ōnis *f* rowing
rēmig·ium -(i)ī *n* rowing; oars; oarsmen, rowers; **rēmigium ālārum** *(poet)* flapping of wings
rēmig·ō -āre -āvī *intr* to row
remigr·ō -āre -āvī -ātum *intr* to move back; **domum remigrāre** to move back home
reminīsc·or -ī *tr* to call to mind, remember **||** *intr* to remember; *(w. gen)* to be mindful of, be conscious of, remember
re·mīsceō -mīscēre — -mixtus *tr* to mix up, intermingle; **vērīs falsa remīscēre** to mix in lies with the truth
remissē *adv* mildly, gently
remissi·ō -ōnis *f* release; easing, letting down, lowering; relaxing *(of muscles);* relaxation, recreation; mildness, gentleness; submissiveness; abating, diminishing; remission *(of debts)*
remiss·us -a -um *adj* relaxed, loose, slack; mild, gentle; remiss; easy-going, indulgent; gay, merry, light; low, cheap *(price);* **remissiōre ūtī genere dīcendī** to speak in a lighter vein
re·mittō -mittere -mīsī -missus *tr* to send back; to release; to slacken, loosen; to emit, produce, let out, give off; to return, restore; to reecho *(a voice);* to give up, reject, resign, concede; to relax, relieve *(the mind);* to pardon; to remit, *(penalty, debt, obligation); (w. inf)* to stop *(doing s.th.);* **frontem** *(or* **ōs** *or* **vultum) remittere** to relax the tense expression; **loquī remittere** to stop speaking; **nihil remittere** to spare no effort; **repudium remittere** to send a notice of divorce **||** *intr (of wind, rain)* to let up, slack off
remīxtus *pp of* **remīsceō**
remōl·ior -īrī -ītus sum *tr* to push *or* move back *or* away, heave back
remollēsc·ō -ere *intr* to soften again; to weaken
remoll·iō -īre -īvī -ītus *tr* to soften
remor·a -ae *f* hindrance, delay
remorāmin·a -um *npl* hindrances, delays
remor·deō -dēre -dī -sus *tr* to bite back; to attack in return; to worry, nag
remor·or -ārī -ātus sum *tr* to hinder, delay, hold back **||** *intr* to loiter, linger, delay, stay behind
remōtē *adv* at a distance, far away
remōti·ō -ōnis *f* withdrawal; removal, elimination *(of a condition);* **remōtiō crīminis** the shifting of a charge
remōt·us -a -um *adj* removed, out of the way, far off, remote, distant; *(fig)* remote, apart, separate; dead; *(w.* **ab) 1** removed from, separate from, apart from; **2** clear of, free from; **iocō remōtō** all joking aside
re·moveō -movēre -mōvī -mōtus *tr* to move back, withdraw; to put away; to remove; to shroud, veil; *(fig)* to put out of sight, set aside, abolish; **aliquem ā vītā removēre** to kill s.o. **||** *refl* to withdraw, retire
remūg·iō -īre *intr* to bellow back; *(fig)* to reecho, resound
remul·ceō -cēre -sī -sus *tr* to stroke, smooth back; **caudam remulcēre** to put the tail between the legs *(in fear)*
remulc·um -ī *n* towline, towrope
Remul·us -ī *m* a king of Alba Longa
remūnerāti·ō -ōnis *f* remuneration, recompense, reward
remūner·or -ārī -ātus sum *or* **remūner·ō -āre** *tr* to repay, remunerate
Remūri·a -ōrum *npl* **(Le-)** festival held in May to appease the spirits of the dead
remurmur·ō -āre *tr & intr* to murmur in reply
rēm·us -ī *m* oar; **ad rēmōs dare** to assign *(s.o.)* as rower; **rēmī corporis** *(fig)* hands and feet *(of a swimmer);* **rēmīs** by rowing; **rēmīs incumbere** to lean to the oars
Rem·us -ī *m* twin brother of Romulus, killed by him
renārr·ō -āre *tr* retell
re·nāscor -nāscī -nātus sum *intr* to be born again; to rise again; spring up again, be restored; to reappear; to recur
renāvig·ō -āre *intr* to sail back
ren·eō -ēre *tr* to unravel, undo
rēn·ēs -(i)um *mpl* kidneys
renīd·ēns -entis *adj* beaming, glad
renīd·eō -ēre *intr* to reflect (light), glitter, shine; to smile, grin all over; to beam with joy
renīdēsc·ō -ere *intr* to grow bright, gleam, begin to glitter
renī·tor -tī *intr* to fight back, put up a struggle, resist
ren·ō -āre -āvī *intr* to swim back, float back
rēn·ō -ōnis *m* **(rhē-)** reindeer skin *(used for clothing)*
renōd·ō -āre -āvī -ātus *tr* to tie back in a knot; to untie
renovām·en -inis *n* renewal, new form
renovāti·ō -ōnis *f* renovation, renewal; revision; *(fin)* compound interest
renov·ō -āre -āvī -ātus *tr* to make new again; to renovate, repair, restore; to plow up *(a fallow field);* to reopen *(a wound);*

to revive *(an old custom, etc.)*; to start *(a battle)* all over again; to refresh *(the memory)*; to repeat, keep repeating, reaffirm; **faenus renovāre in singulōs annōs** *(fin)* to compound the interest on a yearly basis
renumer·ō -āre -āvī -ātus *tr* to count over again, recount; to pay back, repay
renūntiāti·ō -ōnis *f* formal *or* official report, announcement
renūnti·ō -āre -āvī -ātus *tr* to report; to announce; to retract *(a promise, statement)*; to renounce *(an alliance, a friendship)*; to reject; to call off *(a previous engagement)*; *(w. dat)* to call off *(e.g., friendship, association, luncheon)* with *(s.o.)*; *(w. double acc)* to announce *or* declare *(s.o.)* elected as; *(w. acc & inf)* to bring back word that; **lēgātiōnem renūntiāre** *(of an ambassador)* to give an account of an embassy; **repudium renūntiāre** to break off an engagement, send a letter of divorce; **sibi renūntiāre** to say to oneself, remind oneself **||** *intr* to take back a message; *(w. dat)* to withdraw from, renounce, give up
renūnt·ius -(i)ī *m* reporter
renu·ō -ere -ī *tr* to nod refusal to, turn down, decline, say no to, reject **||** *intr* to shake the head in refusal; *(w. dat)* to say no to, deny *(a charge)*
renūt·ō -āre -āvī *intr* to refuse emphatically
reor rērī ratus sum *tr* to think, deem; to reckon, calculate; *(w. acc & inf)* to think that; *(w. acc & adj as objective complement)* to regard *(s.th.)* as **||** *intr* to think, suppose
repāgul·a -ōrum *npl* bolts, bars; *(fig)* restraints, regulations, rules, limits
repand·us -a -um *adj* curved backwards, concave; *(shoes)* with turned-up toes
reparābil·is -is -e *adj* capable of being repaired, reparable, retrievable
reparc·ō -ere repersī *intr (w. dat)* to be sparing with, take it easy on
repar·ō -āre -āvī -ātus *tr* to get again, acquire again; to recover, retrieve, make good; to restore, renew; to repair; to recruit *(a new army)*; **vīna merce reparāre** to get wine in exchange for wares, barter for wine
repastināti·ō -ōnis *f* the act of turning *(the ground)* over again for planting
repastin·ō -āre -āvī -ātus *tr* to turn *(the ground)* over again for planting
re·pectō -pectere -pexī -pexus *tr* to comb back; to comb again
repellō repellere reppulī repulsus *tr* to drive back, push back, repel; to reject; to remove; to refute
repen·dō -dere -pendī -pēnsus *tr* to repay, pay back; to ransom; *(fig)* to repay in kind, requite, recompense, reward; to compensate for; to balance, balance out; **magna rependere** to pay back in full
rēp·ēns -entis *pres p of* **rēpō**
rep·ēns -entis *adj* sudden, unexpected; completely new
repēnsus *pp of* **rependō**
repente *adv* suddenly, all of a sudden; unexpectedly
repentīnō *adv* suddenly; unexpectedly, without warning
repentīn·us -a -um *adj* sudden, unexpected; hasty, impetuous
reperc·ō -ere *intr (w. dat)* **1** to be sparing with; **2** to refrain from
repercussī *perf of* **repercutiō**
repercuss·us -a -um *pp of* **repercutiō ||** *adj* rebounding; reflected, reflecting; echoed, echoing
repercuss·us -ūs *m* reverberation, echo, repercussion; reflection
reper·cutiō -cutere -cussī -cussus *tr* to make *(s.th.)* rebound, make reverberate, make reflect
reperiō reperīre repperī repertus *tr* to find, discover; to find again; to get, procure, win; to find out, ascertain, realize; to invent, devise
repertīci·us -a -um *adj* newly discovered
repert·or -ōris *m* discoverer, inventor, author
repert·us -a -um *pp of* **reperiō ||** *npl* discoveries, inventions
repetīti·ō -ōnis *f* repetition; *(w.* **in** *+ acc)* going back to; *(rhet)* anaphora
repetīt·or -ōris *m* claimant
repet·ō -ere -īvī *or* **-iī -ītus** *tr* to head back to, try to reach again, return to; to aim at again; to fetch back; to attack again; to persecute again; to demand anew; to demand back, claim, demand in compensation, retake; to trace back, retrace; to trace in thought, think over, recall, recollect; to repeat, undertake again, resume, renew; **animō** *(or* **memoriā) repetere** to recall; **lēx dē pecūniīs** *(or* **rēbus) repetundīs** law on extortion *(literally, law concerning recovering money or property)*; **memoriam repetere** to recall the memory; **pecūniam repetere** to sue for the recovery of money; **poenam** *(or* **poenās) repetere** to demand satisfaction; **rēs repetere** to sue for the recovery of property; **reus pecūniārum repetundārum** guilty of extortion **||** *intr (w.* **ad)** to head back to
repetund·ae -ārum *fpl* money extorted; extortion; **repetundārum arguī** to be charged with extortion; **repetundārum tenērī** to be held on an extortion charge
repexus *pp of* **repectō**
repl·eō -ēre -ēvī -ētus *tr* **(reppl-)** to refill, replenish; to fill to the brim; to make up

for, replace, compensate for; *(mil)* to recruit, bring *(an army)* to full strength

replēt·us -a -um *pp of* **repleō** ‖ *adj* filled, full; *(of the body)* well-filled out; *(w. abl or gen)* **1** full of; **2** fully endowed with

replicāti·ō -ōnis *f* folding back, rolling back, rolling up; reflex action

replic·ō -āre -āvī -ātus *tr* to fold back, turn back; to unfold

rēp·ō -ere -sī *intr* to crawl, creep

re·pōnō -pōnere -posuī -positus *or* **-postus** *tr* to put back, set back, lay *(e.g., the head)* back; to replace; to restore; to substitute; to lay out, stretch out *(the body);* to lay aside, store, keep, preserve; to renew, repeat; to place, class; to repay, requite; **in scēptra repōnere** to reinstate in power; **membra repōnere** *(w. ab or* **in** *+ abl)* to stretch out on *(e.g., a bed);* **sē in cubitum repōnere** to rest on one's elbow; **spem repōnere** *(w.* **in** *+ abl)* to put one's hopes in *or* on, count on

report·ō -āre -āvī -ātus *tr* to bring back; to report; **victōriam reportāre** to win a victory

repōsc·ō -ere *tr* to demand back; to ask for, claim, require, demand

repos(i)t·us -a -um *pp of* **repōnō** ‖ *adj* out-of-the-way, remote

repositōr·ium -(i)ī *n* large serving dish

repost·or -ōris *m* restorer

repostus *pp of* **repōnō**

repōti·a -ōrum *npl* second round of drinks, seconds

repperī *perf of* **reperiō**

reppulī *perf of* **repellō**

repraesentāti·ō -ōnis *f* vivid presentation; *(fin)* cash payment

repraesent·ō -āre -āvī -ātus *tr* to present again, show, exhibit, display, depict; to do immediately, accomplish instantly; to rush, speed up *(e.g., plans);* to anticipate; to pay in cash; to apply *(medicines)* immediately

reprehen·dō *or* **repren·dō -dere -ī -sus** *tr* to hold back; to restrain, check; to blame, find fault with, criticize; to refute; *(leg)* to prosecute, convict, condemn

repre(hē)nsi·ō -ōnis *f* checking, check; finding fault, blame, criticism, rebuke; *(rhet)* refutation; *(rhet)* self-correction

reprehēns·ō -āre *tr* to hold back (continually *or* eagerly *or* strongly)

reprehēns·or -ōris *m* critic, censurer

reprendō *see* **reprehendō**

reprēnsō *see* **reprehēnsō**

repress·or -ōris *m* one who represses, restrainer

re·primō -primere -pressī -pressus *tr* to hold back, keep back; to restrain, limit, confine, curb, repress, suppress ‖ *refl* to control oneself; *(w.* **ab)** to refrain from

reprōmissi·ō -ōnis *f* counter-promise, promise in return

reprō·mittō -mittere -mīsī -missus *tr* to promise in return ‖ *intr (leg) (w. dat)* to make a counter-promise to *(s.o.)*

rept·ō -āre -āvī -ātum *intr* to crawl around

repudiāti·ō -ōnis *f* repudiation; refusal, rejection; refusal to approve a policy

repudi·ō -āre -āvī -ātus *tr* to repudiate, scorn; to refuse, reject; to jilt; to divorce

repudiōs·us -a -um *adj* objectionable, offensive

repud·ium -(i)ī *n* repudiation, separation, divorce; **repudium renūntiāre** *(or* **remittere)** *(w. dat)* to send a letter of divorce to

repuerāsc·ō -ere *intr* to become a child again; to behave childishly

repugn·āns -antis *adj* contradictory, inconsistent ‖ *npl* contradictions, inconsistencies

repugnanter *adv* reluctantly

repugnanti·a -ae *f* contradiction, inconsistency; conflicting demands; incompatibility

repugn·ō -āre -āvī -ātum *intr* to fight back; *(w. dat)* **1** to oppose, offer opposition to, fight against, be against; **2** to disagree with, be inconsistent with, be incompatible with; *(w.* **contrā** *+ acc)* to fight against

repuls·a -ae *f* defeat at the polls; rebuff, cold shoulder; **repulsa cōnsulātūs** defeat in running for the consulship; **repulsam ferre** to suffer a defeat, lose an election

repuls·āns -antis *adj* throbbing; reechoing

repuls·us -a -um *pp of* **repellō** ‖ *adj* rejected, spurned

repuls·us -ūs *m* reverberation, echo

repung·ō -ere *tr* to goad again

repurg·ō -āre -āvī -ātus *tr* to clean again; to purge away, remove

reputāti·ō -ōnis *f* rethinking, reconsideration, review; subject of thought, reflection

reput·ō -āre -āvī -ātus *tr* to think over, reflect upon, reconsider; to count back, calculate

requi·ēs -ētis *f* rest, relief; relaxation; break, pause, intermission; recreation, amusement, hobby; *(w. gen)* rest from

requi·ēscō -ēscere -ēvī -ētus *tr* to put to rest, quiet down, calm down ‖ *intr* to rest, take a rest; to come to rest, stop, end; to relax; to find peace, be consoled, find relief; to rest, lie quietly, sleep; *(of the dead)* to rest, sleep

requiēt·us -a -um *adj* rested up

requīrit·ō -āre *tr* to keep asking for; to be on a constant lookout for

re·quīrō -quīrere -quīsīvī *or* **-quīsiī -quīsītus** *tr* to look for, search for, hunt for; to miss; to ask; to ask for, demand, require; *(w.* **ab** *or* **dē** + *abl)* to ask *or* demand *(s.th.)* from *or* of

requīsītum -ī *n* a need

rēs reī *or* **rēī** *f* thing; matter, affair; object; cirumstance; event, occurrence; deed; condition, case; reality, truth, fact; property, possessions, wealth; estate, effects; benefit, advantage, interest, profit; business affair, transaction; cause, reason, motive, ground; historical event; theme, topic, subject matter; *(leg)* case, suit; *(mil)* operation, campaign, battle; *(pol)* state, government, politics; **ab rē** contrary to interests, disadvantageous, useless; **ad rem pertinēre** to be relevant to the matter at hand; **ex rē** according to circumstances, according to the situation; **ex rē istīus** for his good; **ex rē pūblicā** for the common good, in the public interest; **ex tuā rē** to your advantage; **in rē** *(or* **rē ipsā** *or* **rē vērā)** in fact, in reality; **in rē praesentī** on the spot; **in rem** for the good, useful, advantageous; **in rem praesentem** on the spot; **nīl ad rem est** *(frequently with ellipsis of* **est)** it is not to the point, it is irrelevant; **ob eam rem** for that reason; **ob rem** to the purpose, for the good, advantageous; **prō rē** according to circumstances; **quae rēs?** what's that? what are you talking about?; **rē** in fact, in practice, in reality, actually, really; **rem agere** *(leg)* to conduct a case; **rem gerere** *(mil)* to conduct a military operation; **rem solvere** to settle a matter; **rēs capitālis** *(or* **rēs capitis)** *(leg)* a case involving the death penalty *or* loss of civil rights; **rēs familiāris** private property; **rēs frūmentāria** grain situation; grain supply; foraging; **rēs iūdiciāria** administration of justice, department of justice; **rēs mihi tēcum est** I have some business with you; **rēs pecuāria et rūstica** livestock; **rēs rūstica** agriculture; **rēs pūblica** state, government, politics, public life, commonwealth, country; **rēs sit mihi cum hīs** let me handle them; **rēs solī** real property, real estate *(as contrasted with* **rēs mōbilis); rēs uxōria** marriage; dowry; **rēs Veneris** sexual intercourse, love making **||** *fpl* physical phenomena; property; affairs, public affairs; **rērum** *(w. superl adj)* the best in the world: **rērum facta est pulcherrima Rōma** Rome became the most beautiful city in the world; **rērum potīrī** to get control of the government; **rērum scrīptor** historian, annalist; **rēs gestae** exploits, accomplishments, military achievements; **rēs novae** revolution; **rēs Persicae** Persian history, Parthian history; **rēs populī Rōmānī perscrībere** to write (in full) a history of the Roman people; **rēs prōlātae** business adjourned *(for the holiday);* **rēs pūblicās inīre** to enter politics; **rēs secundae** prosperity; **summa rērum** world; universe; **tibi rēs tuās habē** *(formula for divorce)* take your things and go!

resacr·ō *or* **resecr·ō -āre** *tr* to ask again for; to free from a curse

resaevi·ō -īre *intr* to go wild again

resalūtāti·ō -ōnis *f* a greeting in return

resalūt·ō -āre -āvī -ātus *tr* to greet in return

resān·ēscō -ēscere -uī *intr* to heal again

resar·ciō -cīre -sī -tus *or* **-sus** *tr* to patch up; to repair; to make good *(a loss)*

re·scindō -scindere -scidī -scissus *tr* to tear off; to cut down; to tear open; to rescind, repeal; *(fig)* to expose

re·scīscō -scīscere -scīvī *or* **-sciī -scītus** *tr* to find out, learn, ascertain

re·scrībō -scrībere -scrīpsī -scrīptus *tr* to write back in reply; to rewrite, revise; to enlist, enroll; to pay back, repay **||** *intr* to write a reply

rēscrīpt·um -ī *n* imperial rescript

resec·ō -āre -uī -tus *tr* **(-sic-)** to cut back, cut short; to reap; *(fig)* to trim, curtail; **ad vīvum resecāre** to cut to the quick

resecr·ō *see* **resacrō**

resectus *pp of* **resecō**

resecūtus *pp of* **resequor**

resēmin·ō -āre *tr* to sow again; *(poet)* to reproduce

re·sequor -sequī -secūtus sum *tr* to reply to, answer

reser·ō -āre -āvī -ātus *tr* to unlock, unbar, open; to disclose; to begin *(a year)*

reserv·ō -āre -āvī -ātus *tr* to reserve, hold back; to spare; to hold on to; to store

res·es -idis *adj* remaining, left over; lazy, idle, inactive; slow, sluggish; calm

re·sideō -sidēre -sēdī *intr* to sit down, settle back; to sink down, settle, subside; to calm down

re·sīdō -sīdere -sēdī *or* **-sīdī** *intr* to sit down; *(of a person lying down)* to sit up; *(of birds)* to perch; *(after rising or climbing)* to fall back, sink back; *(of things)* to come to rest, lodge; *(of colonists)* to settle; *(of water)* to go down, subside; *(of swellings)* to go down, shrink; *(of natural features)* to dip (down); *(of wind, flame, rain)* to die down; *(of a person)* to quiet down; *(of activity, condition)* to diminish in intensity, abate; *(mil)* to encamp

residu·us -a -um *adj* remaining, left; in arrears, outstanding *(money)* **||** *n* the remainder, the rest

resign·ō -āre -āvī -ātus *tr* to unseal, open; to disclose; to give up, resign; to annul, cancel; to destroy *(confidence)*

resil·iō -īre -uī *or* **-iī** *intr* to spring back, jump back; to recoil; to contract

resīm·us -a -um *adj* turned-up, snub

rēsīn·a -ae *f* resin *(secreted by various trees, used to preserve and season wine, used as a depilatory, etc.)*
rēsināt·us -a -um *adj* rubbed with resin, resined
resip·iō -ere *tr* to taste of, taste like, have the flavor of
resip·īscō -īscere -īvī *or* **-iī** *or* **-uī** *intr* to come to one's senses
resist·ēns -entis *adj* firm, tough
re·sistō -sistere -stitī *intr* to stand still, stop, pause; to stay, stay behind, remain; to resist, put up resistance; to rise again; *(w. dat)* **1** to be opposed to, resist; **2** to reply to
resolūt·us -a -um *adj* loose, limp; effeminate
re·solvō -solvere -solvī -solūtus *tr* to untie, unfasten, undo; to open; to dissolve, melt, thaw; to relax *(the body);* to stretch out *(the limbs);* to unravel; to cancel; to dispel; to unnerve, enervate; to release, set free
resonābil·is -is -e *adj* resounding, answering *(echo)*
reson·āns -antis *adj* echoing
reson·ō -āre -āvī *tr* to repeat, reecho, resound with, make ring **II** *intr* to resound, ring, reecho; *(w.* **ad**) to resound in answer to
reson·us -a -um *adj* resounding, re-echoing
resorb·eō -ēre *tr* to suck in, swallow again
respargō *see* **respergō**
respect·ō -āre *tr* to look back on; to keep an eye on, care for; to have regard for, respect; to gaze at, look at **II** *intr* to look back; to look around
respectus *pp of* **respiciō**
respect·us -ūs *m* backward glance, looking back; looking around; refuge; respect, regard, consideration; **respectum habēre** *(w. dat or* **ad**) to have respect for
resper·gō -gere -sī -sus *tr* (**-spar-**) to sprinkle, splash, spray; to defile
respersi·ō -ōnis *f* sprinkling, splashing
respersus *pp of* **respergō**
re·spiciō -spicere -spexī -spectus *tr* to look back at, see behind oneself; to look around for; to look back upon *(the past, etc.);* to look at, gaze at; to regard, contemplate, consider; to notice; to look after, take care of, see to; to respect **II** *intr* to look back; to look around; *(w.* **ad**) to look at, gaze at
respīrām·en -inis *n* respiration, breathing; exhalation; letup, rest, pause *(to catch one's breath),* breathing space
respīrāti·ō -ōnis *f* respiration, breathing; breathing pause; *(fig)* exhalation, emission of vapor
respīrāt·us -ūs *m* respiration
respīr·ō -āre -āvī -ātus *tr* to breathe, breathe out, exhale **II** *intr* to breathe, take a breath, breathe again; to recover *(from fright, etc.); (of combat, passions, etc.)* to slack off, die down, subside; **ā continuīs clādibus respīrāre** to catch one's breath again after continuous disasters; **ā metū respīrāre** to recover from a shock
resplend·eō -ēre *intr* to glitter
respon·deō -dēre -dī -sus *tr* to answer; to say in reply; to say in refutation; **ficta respondēre** to make up answers; **hōc quod rogō respondē** answer my question; **multa respondēre** to give a lengthy reply; **pār parī respondēre** to give tit for tat; **verbum verbō respondēre** to answer word for word **II** *intr* to answer, reply; *(of officials, seers, priests)* to give an official *or* formal reply; to echo; to satisfy the claims *(of a creditor); (leg)* to answer a summons to appear in court; *(of lawyers)* to give an opinion, give legal advice; *(of priests)* to give a response *(from a god); (w. dat)* **1** to answer, reply to; **2** to match, balance, correspond to, be equal to; **3** to resemble; **4** to measure up to; **amōrī amōre respondēre** to return love for love; **nōminibus respondēre** to pay off debts
respōnsi·ō -ōnis *f* response, answer, reply; refutation; *(rhet)* **sibi ipsī respōnsiō** a reply to one's own arguments
respōnsit·ō -āre -āvī *intr* to give professional legal advice
respōns·ō -āre *intr* to answer, reply; to reecho; *(w. dat)* **1** to answer to, agree with; **2** to resist, defy; **3** to talk back to *(in disobedience)*
respōns·or -ōris *m* respondent
respōns·us -a -um *pp of* **respondeō II** *n* answer, response; oracular response; *(leg)* professional advice; **respōnsum auferre** *(or* **ferre**) *(w.* **ab**) to receive an answer from; **respōnsum referre** to deliver an answer
rēspūblica reīpūblicae *f* state, government, politics, public life, commonwealth, country; **rempūblicam inīre** to enter politics; *(see also* **rēs pūblica** *under* **rēs**)
respu·ō -ere -ī *tr* to spit out; to cast out, eject, expel; to refuse, to reject
restagn·ō -āre *intr* to form pools; to run over, overflow; to be inundated
restaur·ō -āre -āvī -ātus *tr* to restore, rebuild; to renew, take up again
resticul·a -ae *f* thin rope, cord
restīncti·ō -ōnis *f* quenching
restin·guō -guere -xī -ctus *tr* to quench, extinguish, put out; to snuff out; to exterminate, destroy
resti·ō -ōnis *f* rope dealer; *(hum)* roper *(person who is whipped with ropes)*
restipulāti·ō -ōnis *f* counterclaim
restipul·or -ārī -ātus sum *tr* to stipulate in return **II** *intr* to make a counterclaim
rest·is -is *f (acc:* **restem** *or* **restim**) rope

restit·ō -āre *intr* to stay behind, lag behind; to keep offering resistance
restitr·īx -īcis *f* a stay-at-home *(female)*
resti·tuō -tuere -tuī -tūtus *tr* to set up again; to restore, rebuild, reconstruct; to renew, reestablish, revive; to bring back, restore, reinstate; to give back, return, replace; to restore, repair, remedy; to reenact *(a law);* to reverse; to revoke, undo, cancel, make void; to make good, compensate for, repair
restitūti·ō -ōnis *f* restoration; reinstatement, pardon; recall *(from exile)*
restitūt·or -ōris *m* restorer, rebuilder
restitūtus *pp of* **restituō**
re·stō -stāre -stitī *intr* to stand firm, stand one's ground, resist; to stay behind, stay in reserve; to be left over ‖ *v impers (w. inf or* **ut)** it remains to *(do s.th.)*
restrictē *adv* sparingly; exactly, precisely
restrict·us -a -um *pp of* **restringō** ‖ *adj* tied back, tight; stingy; moderate, strict, stern
re·stringō -stringere -strīnxī -strictus *tr* to tie *(the hands, arms)* behind one; to draw tight, tie; to tighten; to draw back the cover from *(s.th. concealed); (of dogs)* to show *(the teeth); (fig)* to restrain; *(fig)* to restrict the activity of
resūd·ō -āre *intr* to sweat, ooze
result·ō -āre *intr* to rebound; to resound, reverberate
resūm·ō -ere -psī -ptus *tr* to resume; to recover *(strength)*
resu·ō -ere -uī -ūtus *tr* to undo the stitching of
resupīn·ō -āre -āvī -ātus *tr* to throw *(s.o.)* on his back, throw over, throw down; *(coll)* to knock for a loop; to break down *(door)*
resupīn·us -a -um *adj* lying on the back; bent back, thrown back; leaning backward; proud *(gait)*
resur·gō -gere -rēxī -rēctum *intr* to rise again; to appear again
resūscit·ō -āre *tr* to resuscitate
retardāti·ō -ōnis *f* retardation
retard·ō -āre -āvī -ātus *tr* to retard, slow down, hold back, delay; to keep back, check, hinder ‖ *intr* to lag behind
retax·ō -āre *tr* to rebuke
rēt·e -is *n* net; *(fig)* trap
re·tegō -tegere -tēxī -tēctus *tr* to uncover; to unclothe, expose; to open; to reveal, make visible; to disclose *(secrets)*
retempt·ō -āre -āvī -ātus *tr* to attempt again, try again; to test again
reten·dō -dere -dī -tus *or* **-sus** *tr* to release from tension, unbend, relax
retenti·ō -ōnis *f* holding back; slowing down; withholding *(assent)*
retent·ō -āre *tr* to hold back, hold tight; to attempt again; to retain the loyalty of; to keep *(feelings)* in check
retentus *pp of* **retendō** *and* **retineō**
retēxī *perf of* **retegō**
retex·ō -ere -uī -tus *tr* to unravel; to cancel, reverse, annul, undo; to weave anew; to renew, repeat; to correct, revise; to retract *(words)*
rēti·a -ae *f* net
rētiār·ius -(i)ī *m* net-man *(gladiator who tried to entangle his opponent in a net)*
reticenti·a -ae *f* reticence; *(rhet)* abrupt pause; **poena reticentiae** punishment for suppression of truth
retic·eō -ēre -uī *tr* to be silent about, suppress, keep secret ‖ *intr* to be silent, keep silent; *(w. dat)* to make no answer to
rēticulāt·us -a -um *adj* covered with a net; net-shaped, reticulate
rēticul·um -ī *n* small net; hair net; meshwork bag *(for protecting bottles);* racket *(for playing ball)*
retinācul·a -ōrum *npl* cable, rope
retin·ēns -entis *adj (w. gen)* clinging to, sticking to
retinenti·a -ae *f* retention
re·tineō -tinēre -tinuī -tentus *tr* to hold back, keep back; to restrain; to keep, retain; to hold in reserve; to preserve, maintain, uphold; to hold, engross *(attention);* to detain, delay
retinn·iō -īre *intr* to ring again, ring out, tinkle in response
reton·ō -āre *intr* to resound
retor·queō -quēre -sī -tus *tr* to twist *or* bend back; to hurl back *(weapons);* **mentem retorquēre** to change the mind; **oculōs retorquēre** *(w.* **ad)** to look back wistfully at
retorrid·us -a -um *adj* parched, dried out, withered; wily, shrewd
retortus *pp of* **retorqueō**
retractāti·ō -ōnis *f* holding back, hesitation; **sine retractātiōne** without hesitation
retractāt·us -a -um *adj* revised
retract·ō *or* **retrect·ō -āre** *tr* to rehandle, take in hand again, undertake once more, take up once more; to reexamine, review; to revise ‖ *intr* to refuse, decline; to be reluctant
retract·us -a -um *adj* remote, distant
retra·hō -here -xī -ctus *tr* to draw back, withdraw, pull back; to bring to light again, make known again; *(fig)* to drag away, remove
retrectō *see* **retractō**
retrib·uō -uere -uī -ūtus *tr* to hand back; to repay
retrō *adv* backwards, back; to the rear; behind, on the rear; in the past, formerly, back, past; in return; on the contrary, on

the other hand; in reverse order *(of words);* counting back to an earlier date, retrospectively; *(w. reference to reasoning)* back to first principles

retro·agō -agere -ēgī -āctus *tr* to drive backward; to reverse the order of, invert; to repeat backwards

retrō·cēdō -dere -cessī -cessum *intr* to move backward; to withdraw, retire

retrōrsum *adv* **(-sus)** back, backwards, in reverse; in reverse order

retrū·dō -dere — -sus *tr* to push back; to hide, conceal

retundō retundere retudī *(or* **rettudī)** **retūnsus** *(or* **retūsus)** *tr* to pound back; to dull, blunt; *(fig)* to deaden, weaken, repress, restrain

retūns·us *or* **retūs·us -a -um** *pp of* **retundō ‖** *adj* blunt, dull; *(fig)* dull

re·us -ī *m (either of the two parties involved in litigation)* defendant, the accused, plaintiff; convict, criminal, culprit; *(w. gen)* person charged with; **in reōs recipere** *(or* **referre)** to list among the accused; **reum agere** to try a defendant; **reum facere** to indict, bring a defendant to trial; **reum postulāre** to prosecute, force to face a trial

reval·ēscō -ēscere -uī *intr* to regain one's strength, recover; to become valid again

re·vehō -vehere -vexī -vectus *tr* to carry back, bring back **‖** *pass* to ride back, drive back; to sail back; *(fig)* to go back *(e.g., to an earlier period)*

re·vellō -vellere -vellī -vulsus *tr* to pull out, pull back, tear off, tear out; to tear up *(the ground),* dig up; *(fig)* to unmask *(deception)*

revēl·ō -āre -āvī -ātus *tr* to unveil, uncover

re·veniō -venīre -vēnī -ventum *intr* to come again, come back, return

rēvērā *adv* in fact, actually

reverber·ō -āre -āvī -ātus *tr* to beat back; to repel

reverend·us -a -um *adj* venerable, awe-inspiring; deserving respect

rever·ēns -entis *adj* reverent, respectful

reverenter *adv* respectfully

reverenti·a -ae *f* reverence, respect

rever·eor -ērī -itus sum *tr* to revere, respect, stand in awe of

reversi·ō -ōnis *f* **(-vor-)** turning back *(before reaching one's destination);* recurrence

revert·ō -ere -ī *or* **re·vertor -vertī -versus sum** *intr* **(-vor-)** to turn back, turn around, come back, return; *(in speaking)* to return, revert

revictus *pp of* **revincō**

revid·eō -ēre *tr* to go back to see

re·vinciō -vincīre -vīnxī -vīnctus *tr* to tie back, tie behind, tie up

re·vincō -vincere -vīcī -victus *tr* to conquer in turn; to refute, convict of falsehood; *(w. acc or gen of the charge)* to convict *(s.o.)* of

revīnctus *pp of* **revinciō**

revir·ēscō -ēscere -uī *intr* to become green again; to grow young again; to grow again, grow strong again, revive

revīs·ō -ere *tr* to revisit; to look back to see **‖** *intr* to come *or* go back; *(w.* **ad) 1** to look at again, look back at; **2** to return to, revisit

re·vīvīscō -vīvīscere -vīxī *intr* **(-ēscō)** to come back to life, be restored to life, revive; *(fig)* to recover, gain strength

revocābil·is -is -e *adj* capable of being recalled; **nōn revocābilis** irrevocable

revocām·en -inis *n* recall

revocāti·ō -ōnis *f* calling back, recall; calling away; retraction

revoc·ō -āre -āvī -ātus *tr* to call back, recall; to call off, withdraw *(troops);* to call back *(a performer)* for an encore; to bring back to life, revive; *(leg)* to arraign again; to regain *(strength, etc.);* to resume *(career, studies);* to revoke, retract; to check, control; to cancel; *(w.* **ad)** to refer, apply, subject, submit *(s.o. or s.th.)* to

revol·ō -āre -āvī *intr* to fly back

revolsus *see* **revulsus**

revolūbil·is -is -e *adj* able to be rolled back; **nōn revolūbilis** irrevocable *(fate)*

revol·vō -vere -vī -ūtus *tr* to roll back, unroll, unwind; to retravel; to unroll, read over, read again *(a scroll);* to reexperience; to go over, think over **‖** *pass* to revolve; to come around again, recur, return

revom·ō -ere -uī *tr* to throw up again, disgorge

revor- = rever-

revorr·ō -ere *tr* to sweep back

revulsus *pp of* **revellō**

rēx rēgis *m* king; patron; queen bee

Rhadamanth·us *or* **Rhadamanth·os -ī** *m* son of Jupiter, brother of Minos, and one of the three judges in the lower world

Rhaet·ī -ōrum *mpl* people of Rhaetia

Rhaeti·a -ae *f* Alpine country between Germany and Italy

Rhamn·ūs -untos *f* Attic deme famous for its statue of Nemesis

Rhamnūsi·us -a -um *adj* of the deme of Rhamnus; **Rhamnūsia virgō** the goddess worshiped at Rhamnus *(i.e., Nemesis)*

rhapsōdi·a -ae *f* Homeric lay, selection from Homer; **rhapsōdia secunda** second book *(of Homer)*

Rhe·a -ae *f* Cybele

Rhe·a Silvi·a -ae *f* daughter of Numitor and mother of Romulus and Remus by Mars, the god of war

rhēd- = raed-

Rhēg·ium -(i)ī *n (also* **Rēg-)** town at the toe of Italy
Rhēnān·us -a -um *adj* of *or* on the Rhine
rhēn·ō -ōnis *f* reindeer skin *(used as clothing)*
Rhēn·us -ī *m* the Rhine
Rhēs·us -ī *m* Thracian king who fought as an ally of Troy
rhēt·or -oris *m* rhetorician, teacher of rhetoric; orator
rhētoric·a -ae *or* **rhētoric·ē -ēs** *f* rhetoric, public speaking
rhētoric·a -ōrum *npl* treatise on rhetoric
rhētoricē *adv* rhetorically, in an oratorical manner
rhētoric·us -a -um *adj* rhetorician's, rhetorical; **doctōrēs rhētoricī** professors of rhetoric; **librī rhētoricī** textbooks on rhetoric
rhīnocer·ōs -ōtis *or* **-ōtos** *m* rhinoceros; vessel made of a rhinoceros's tusk; **puerī nāsum rhīnocerōtis habent** the children turn up their noses
rhō *indecl n* rho *(seventeenth letter of the Greek alphabet)*
Rhodan·us -ī *m* the Rhone River
Rhodiēns·is -is -e *or* **Rhodi·us -a -um** *adj* Rhodian, of Rhodes **||** *mpl* Rhodians
Rhodop·ē -ēs *f* mountain range in Thrace
Rhodopēi·us -a -um *adj* Thracian
Rhod·os *or* **Rhod·us -ī** *f* Rhodes *(island off the S.W. coast of Asia Minor)*
Rhoetē·us -a -um *adj* Trojan; of the promontory of Rhoeteum; **Rhoetēus ductor** Aeneas; **Rhoetēum profundum** sea near the promotory of Rhoeteum **||** *n* promontory on the Dardanelles near Troy
rhomb·us -ī *m* magic wheel; turbot *(fish)*
rhomphae·a -ae *f* long javelin
rhythmic·us -a -um *adj* rhythmical **||** *m* teacher of prose rhythm
rhythm·os *or* **rhythm·us -ī** *m* rhythm; symmetry
rhyt·ion -iī *n* conical cup *or* urn
rīc·a -ae *f* veil *(worn by Roman women at sacrifice)*
rīcīn·ium -(i)ī *n* short mantle with a cowl
rict·um -ī *n* snout; wide-open mouth
rict·us -ūs *m* snout; wide-open mouth; **rīsū rictum dīdūcere** to break into a broad grin **||** *mpl* jaws, gaping jaws
rīdeō rīdēre rīsī rīsus *tr* to laugh at, ridicule; to smile upon **||** *intr* to laugh; to smile, grin; *(w. dat or* **ad)** to smile at, laugh at
rīdibund·us -a -um *adj* laughing
rīdiculāri·us -a -um *adj* funny, laughable **||** *npl* jokes
rīdiculē *adv* jokingly, humorously; ridiculously
rīdiculōs·us -a -um *adj* funny, amusing; ridiculous
rīdicul·us -a -um *adj* funny, amusing, laughable; ridiculous, silly **||** *m* joker, clown **||** *n* joke
rig·ēns -entis *adj* rigid, stiff
rig·eō -ēre -uī *intr* to be stiff, be rigid; to be numb; to stand on end, stand erect; to stand stiff; to be unmoved by entreaties
rig·ēscō -ēscere -uī *intr* to grow stiff, become numbed; to stiffen, harden; to stand on end
rigid·a -ae *f (vulg)* penis in erect state
rigidē *adv* rigorously, severely
rigid·us -a -um *adj* rigid, stiff, hard, inflexible; stern, severe; rough, rude; erect *(penis)*
rig·ō -āre *tr* to wet, moisten, water; to conduct, convey *(water)*
rig·or -ōris *m* stiffness; numbness, cold; hardness; sternness
rigu·us -a -um *adj* constantly flowing, irrigating; well-watered, irrigated; **||** *npl* irrigated areas, flood plain; irrigation ditches
rīm·a -ae *f* crack; chap *(in the skin); (in a law)* loophole; **rīmās agere** to cause cracks to develop; **rīmās dūcere** to develop cracks
rīm·or -ārī -ātus sum *tr* to lay open, tear open; to pry into, search, examine; to search for *(facts);* to rummage about for; to ransack; **nāribus rīmārī** to sniff at; **oculīs rīmārī** to scrutinize
rīmōs·us -a -um *adj* full of cracks; leaky
ringor ringī *intr* to open the mouth wide; to show the teeth; to snarl; *(fig)* to be snappy
rīp·a -ae *f* river bank; **aequoris rīpa** seashore
Ripae·us -a -um *adj (also* **Rhip-)** of the Rhipean mountains; **mōns R(h)ipaeus** legendary mountain range in the extreme north
rīpul·a -ae *f* riverbank
rīsc·us -ī *m* chest, trunk
rīsiōn·ēs -um *fpl* laughs
rīs·or -ōris *m* scoffer; teaser
rīs·us -ūs *m* laugh, laughter, smile; laughingstock; **rīsum continēre** to keep from laughing; **rīsum movēre** *(w. dat)* to make *(s.o.)* laugh; **rīsūs captāre** to try to make people laugh, try to get a laugh
rīte *adv* according to religious usage; duly, justly, rightly, fitly; in the usual way, customarily
rīt·us -ūs *m* rite, ceremony; custom, habit, way, manner, style; **rītū** *(w. gen)* in the manner of, like; **pecudum rītū** like cattle
rīvāl·is -is *m* one who uses the same stream, neighbor; one who uses the same mistress, rival
rīvālit·ās -ātis *f* rivalry
rīvul·us *or* **rīvol·us -ī** *m* brook

rīv·us -ī *m* brook, stream; artificial watercourse, channel; flow *(of water in the aqueducts)*

rīx·a -ae *f* brawl, fight; squabble

rīx·or -ārī -ātus sum *intr* to brawl, come to blows, fight; to squabble

rōbīginōs·us -a -um *adj* **(rub-)** rusty; envious

rōbīg·ō -inis *f* rust; blight, mildew; film *(on teeth)*, tartar

rōbore·us -a -um *adj* **(-bur-)** oak

rōbor·ō -āre -āvī -ātus *tr* to strengthen

rōb·ur *or* **rōb·us -oris** *n* hardwood; oak; prison *(at Rome, also called Tullianum);* objects made of hardwood: lance, club, bench; physical strength, power, toughness; power *(of mind);* best part, flower, choice, cream, élite; stronghold

rōb·us -a -um *adj* red

rōbust·us -a -um *adj* hardwood; oak; robust, strong, tough *(body);* firm, solid *(character)*

rō·dō -dere -sī -sus *tr* to gnaw, gnaw at; to rust, corrode; to say nasty things about, slander, run down

rogāl·is -is -e *adj* of a funeral pyre

rogāti·ō -ōnis *f* proposal, bill *(in the Roman assembly);* request, invitation; *(rhet)* question; **rogātiōnem antiquāre** to reject a bill; **rogātiōnem ferre** to introduce a bill; **rogātiōnem perferre** to pass a bill; **rogātiōnem per vim perferre** to push through a bill; **rogātiōnem suādēre** to back, push, *or* speak in favor of a bill; **rogātiōnī intercēdere** to veto a bill

rogātiuncul·a -ae *f* inconsequential bill; minor question

rogāt·or -ōris *m* proposer *(of a bill to the Roman assembly);* poll clerk *(who collects and counts votes);* beggar

rogāt·us -ūs *m* request

rogitāti·ō -ōnis *f (pol)* bill

rogit·ō -āre -āvī -ātus *tr* to keep asking (for)

rog·ō -āre -āvī -ātus *tr* to ask, ask for, beg, request; to question; to invite; to nominate for election; to bring forward for approval, introduce, propose *(bill); (w. double acc)* to ask *(s.o. for s.th.);* **lēgem rogāre** to introduce a bill; **mīlitēs sacrāmentō rogāre** to swear in soldiers; **senātōrem sententiam rogāre** to ask a senator for his opinion, ask a senator how he votes; **sententiās rogāre** to call the roll *(in the Senate);* **populum rogāre** to ask the people about a bill, to propose *or* introduce a bill; **prīmus sententiam rogārī** to have the honor of being the first *(senator)* to be asked his view, be the first to vote

rog·us -ī *m or* **rog·um -ī** *n* funeral pyre; *(fig)* grave, destruction

Rōm·a -ae *f* Rome; Roma *(goddess of Rome)*

Rōmān·us -a -um *adj* Roman ‖ *mpl* Romans

Rōmule·us -a -um *adj* of Romulus; Roman

Rōmulid·ae -ārum *mpl* descendants of Romulus, Romans

Rōmul·us -a -um *adj* of Romulus; Roman ‖ *m* Romulus *(son of Rhea Silvia and Mars, twin brother of Remus, and founder as well as first king of Rome)*

rōrāri·ī -ōrum *mpl* skirmishers *(light-armed Roman troops who usually initiate an attack and then withdraw)*

rōrid·us -a -um *adj* dewy

rōrif·er -era -erum *adj* dewy, dew-bringing

rōr·ō -āre -āvī -ātus *tr* to drip, trickle, pour drop by drop; to moisten ‖ *intr* to drop dew, scatter dew

rōs rōris *m* dew; moisture; spray; water; teardrop; **rōs Arabus** perfume; **rōs marīnus** *(or* **maris)** rosemary *(see* **rōsmarīnum);** **rōrēs pluviī** drizzle; **rōrēs sanguineī** drops of blood

ros·a -ae *f* rose; rosebush; rose bed; wreath of roses

rosāce·us -a -um *adj (crown)* of roses; **oleum rosāceum** rose oil

rosār·ium -(i)ī *n* rose garden

rōscid·us -a -um *adj* wet with dew; consisting of dew; dewy *(conditions; as epithet of the moon, stars, associated with dew);* moistened, sprayed

Rōsc·ius -(i)ī *m* Lucius Roscius Otho *(Cicero's friend, whose law in 67 B.C. reserved 14 rows of seats in the theater for members of the equestrian order)* ‖ Quintus Roscius *(famous Roman actor and friend of Cicero, d. 62 B.C.)* ‖ Sextus Roscius *(of Ameria, defended by Cicero in a patricide trial in 80 B.C.)*

Rōse·a -ae *or* **Rōsi·a -ae** *f* fertile district between Reate and the Veline Lake

rosēt·um -ī *n* rose bed, rose garden

rose·us -a -um *adj* rose, made of roses; rose-colored *(covering a wide range of reds);* rosy, pink *(dawn, sunset, cheeks, skin)*

Rōse·us -a -um *adj* **(-si-)** of Rosea

rōsmarīn·um -ī *n* rosemary *(shrub used in medicines, in perfumes, and as a seasoning)*

rōstell·um -ī *n* little beak; pointed nose *(of a rodent)*

rōstrāt·us -a -um *adj* beaked; *(ship)* having a pointed bow; **columna rōstrāta** column adorned with the beaks of conquered vessels to commemorate a naval victory; **corōna rōstrāta** navy medal *(awarded to the first man to board an enemy ship)*

rōstr·um -ī *n* bill, beak; snout, muzzle; curved bow *(of ship)* ‖ *npl* rostrum *(in the Roman Forum, so called because it was adorned with the beaks of ships taken from the battle of Antium, 338 B.C.)*; **prō rōstrīs ōrātiōnem habēre** to give a speech from the rostrum

rōsus *pp of* **rōdō**

rot·a -ae *f* wheel; potter's wheel; torture wheel; mill wheel; magic wheel; child's hoop; disk *(of a heavenly body)*; chariot, car *(of sun, moon, time)*; **aquārum rota** water wheel

rot·ō -āre -āvī -ātus *tr* to turn, whirl about ‖ *pass* to roll around; to turn, revolve

rotul·a -ae *f* little wheel

rotundē *adv* smoothly, elegantly

rotundit·ās -ātis *f* roundness

rotund·ō -āre -āvī -ātus *tr* to make round; *(fig)* round off *(numbers)*

rotund·us -a -um *adj* rolling, revolving; round, circular, spherical; rounded, perfect; well-turned, smooth, polished *(style)*

rube·faciō -facere -fēcī -factus *tr* to make red, redden

rub·ēns -entis *adj* red; blushing

rub·eō -ēre *intr* to be red, be ruddy; to be bloody; to blush

ru·ber -bra -brum *adj* red *(including shades of orange)*; ruddy; **Saxa Rubra** town on the Via Flaminia N. of Rome; **Mare Rubrum** Red Sea

rub·ēscō -ēscere -uī *intr* to get red, redden; to blush

rubēt·a -ae *f* toad

rubēt·a -ōrum *npl* bramble bushes, thicket of brambles

rube·us -a -um *adj* bramble, of brambles

Rubic·ō(n) -ōnis *m* Rubicon *(small stream marking the boundary between Italy and Cisalpine Gaul)*

rubicundul·us -a -um *adj* reddish

rubicund·us -a -um *adj* red, reddish; ruddy, flushed *(complexion)*

rubid·us -a -um *adj* red; ruddy

rūbīg- = rōbīg-

rub·or -ōris *m* redness; blush; bashfulness, sense of shame; shame, disgrace

rubrīc·a -ae *f* red clay; red ochre; red chalk; chapter heading *(of book of law, painted red)*

rub·us -ī *m* bramble bush; blackberry bush; blackberry

rūctātr·īx -īcis *adj (fem only) (of foods)* that causes belching

rūct·ō -āre -āvī -ātus *or* **rūct·or -ārī -ātus sum** *tr & intr* to belch

rūct·us -ūs *m* belch, belching

rud·ēns -entis *m* rope ‖ *mpl* rigging

Rudi·ae -ārum *fpl* town in Calabria in S. Italy *(birthplace of Ennius)*

rudiār·ius -(i)ī *m* retired gladiator

rudīment·um -ī *n* first attempt, beginning; early training; **rudīmentum adulēscentiae pōnere** to pass the beginning of his youth; **rudīmentum mīlitāre** basic training ‖ *npl* first lessons; fruits of one's early training

Rudīn·us -ā -um *adj* of Rudiae *(a town in Calabria)*

rud·is -is -e *adj* in the natural state; raw, undeveloped, rough, wild, unformed; inexperienced, unskilled, ignorant; uncultured, uncivilized; unsophisticated; *(of land)* not yet cultivated, virgin; *(of wool)* uncombed; *(of artefacts)* crude, roughly fashioned; *(of movement)* awkward, clumsy; *(of fruit)* unripe; *(of animals)* unbroken; *(of recruits)* raw; *(of literary works)* crude, unpolished, rough; *(w. gen or abl, w.* **ad** *+ acc or* **in** *+ abl)* inexperienced in, ignorant of, awkward at

rud·is -is *f* stick; rod; practice sword; wooden sword *(presented to a retiring gladiator)*

rud·ō -ere -īvī -ītum *intr* **(rūd-)** to roar, bellow; *(of a donkey)* to bray; *(of inanimate things)* to creak loudly

rud·or -ōris *m* roar, bellow

rūd·us -eris *n* crushed stone; rubble; piece of brass

Rūful·ī -ōrum *mpl* military tribunes appointed by a general *(as opposed to military tribunes elected by the people)*

rūful·us -a -um *adj* reddish

rūf·us -a -um *adj* red; red-haired ‖ **Rūfus** *m* frequent Roman family name *(cognomen)*

rūg·a -ae *f* wrinkle; crease, small fold; shallow groove

rūg·iō -īre *intr* to bellow, roar

rūg·ō -āre *intr* to become wrinkled, become creased

rūgōs·us -a -um *adj* wrinkled, shriveled; corrugated

ruīn·a -ae *f* tumbling down, fall; collapse; debris, ruins; crash; catastrophe, disaster, destruction; defeat; wrecker, destroyer; *(fig)* downfall, ruin; *(fig)* source of ruin *or* destruction; **ruīnam dare** *(or* **trahere)** to fall with a crash

ruīnōs·us -a -um *adj* liable to ruin, going to ruin, tumbling; ruined, dilapidated

Rull·us -ī *m* Roman family name *(cognomen), esp.* Publius Servilius Rullus *(whose agrarian bill was defeated by Cicero in 63 B.C.)*

rum·ex -icis *mf* sorrel *(grown as a vegetable, used in salads)*

rūmifer·ō -āre *tr* to carry reports of

rūmific·ō -āre *tr* to report

Rūmīn·a -ae *f* Roman goddess who was worshiped near the fig tree under which the she-wolf had suckled Romulus and Remus

Rūmīnāl·is -is -e *adj* **fīcus Rūmīnālis** fig tree of Romulus and Remus
rūmināti·ō -ōnis *f* chewing the cud; *(fig)* rumination, thinking over
rūmin·ō -āre -āvī -ātus *tr* to chew again ‖ *intr* to chew the cud
rūm·or -ōris *m* rumor, hearsay; shouting, cheering, noise; popular opinion, current opinion; reputation, fame; notoriety; calumny; **adversō rūmōre esse** to be in bad repute, be unpopular
rumpi·a -ae *f* long Thracian javelin
rumpō rumpere rūpī ruptus *tr* to break, break down, break open; to burst, burst through; to tear, split; to cause to snap; to tear, rend *(hair, clothes);* to cause *(s.th.)* to break; to force, make *(e.g., a path)* by force; to break in on, interrupt, cut short; to break, violate *(a law, treaty);* to break out in, utter *(complaints, etc.);* **amōrēs rumpere** to break off a love affair; **nūptiās rumpere** to annul a marriage; **silentium** *(or* **silentia) rumpere** to break silence ‖ *refl & pass* to burst forth, erupt
rūmuscul·ī -ōrum *mpl* gossip
rūn·a -ae *f* dart
runc·ō -āre -āvī -ātus *tr* to weed, weed out
ru·ō -ere -ī -tus *tr* to throw down, hurl to the ground; to level *(e.g,, sand dunes);* to destroy, overthrow, lay waste; to sweep headlong; to upturn, churn up ‖ *intr* to dash, rush, hurry; *(of vehicles)* to go fast; *(of buildings)* to fall down, collapse; *(of fortunes)* to go to ruin; *(of rain)* to come pouring down; *(of the sun)* to set rapidly; *(w.* **in** + *acc)* **1** to charge, swoop down on; **2** to proceed with haste *or* impatience to *(an action);* **currū in bella ruere** to go into battle on the double
rūp·ēs -is *f* cliff
rupt·or -ōris *m* breaker, violator
ruptus *pp of* **rumpō**
rūricol·a -ae *mf* rustic, peasant ‖ *m* ox
rūrigen·a -ae *m* one born in the country, farmer
rūr·ō -āre *intr* to live in the country
rūrsus *or* **rūrsum** *or* **rūsum** *adv* back, backwards; on the contrary, on the other hand; in turn; again, a second time; *(in the direction from which one has come)* back again; once more; **rūrsus rūrsusque** again and again; **rūrsum prōrsum** *(or* **rūrsus (ac) prōrsus)** back and forth, backward and forward
rūs rūris *n* the country, countryside, lands, fields; farm, estate; **rūre** from the country; **rūre redīre** to return from the country; **rūrī** in the country, on the farm; **rūrī** *(or* **rūre) vītam agere** to live in the country; **rūs īre** to go into the country ‖ *npl* countryside
rūsc·um -ī *n or* **rūsc·us -ī** *m* broom *(of twigs)*
russāt·us -a -um *adj* red, ruddy; clothed in red
russ·us -a -um *adj* red, russet; red-haired
rūstic·a -ae *f* country girl
rūsticān·us -a -um *adj* rustic, country, rural
rūsticāti·ō -ōnis *f* country life
rūsticē *adv* like a farmer; plainly, simply; boorishly
rūsticit·ās -ātis *f* simple country ways, rusticity; boorishness, coarseness
rūstic·or -ārī -ātus sum *intr* to live *or* stay in the country
rūsticul·us -a -um *adj* of the country, in the country, rural; plain, simple, unspoiled, unsophisticated; coarse, boorish ‖ *m* farmer ‖ *f* country girl
rūstic·us -a -um *adj* of the country, rural, rustic, country; plain, simple, provincial, rough, gross, awkward, prudish ‖ *m* rustic; *(pej)* hick ‖ *f* country girl
rūsum *see* **rūrsus**
rūt·a -ae *f* rue *(bitter herb);* bitterness, unpleasantness
rūt·a -ōrum *npl* minerals; **rūta caesa** *(or* **rūta et caesa)** *(leg)* everything mined *or* cut down on an estate, timber and minerals
rutābul·um -ī *n* spatula; poker, fire shovel *(instrument with flattened end)*
rūtāt·us -a -um *adj* flavored with rue *(a bitter herb);* bitter
rutil·ō -āre -āvī -ātus *tr* to make red, color red, dye red ‖ *intr* to glow red
rutil·us -a -um *adj* red, reddish yellow; strawberry-blond
rutr·um -ī *n* shovel, spade
rūtul·a -ae *f* a bit of rue *(bitter herb)*
Rutul·ī -ōrum *mpl* ancient people of Latium whose capital was Ardea
rutus *pp of* **ruō**

S

S, s *(supply* littera) *f* eighteenth letter of the Latin alphabet; letter name: **es**
s. d. *abbr* **salūtem dīcere**
Sab·a -ae *f* town in Arabia Felix, famous for its incense
Sabae·a -ae *f (sc.* terra) *(country of the Sabaeans, modern Yemen)*
Sabae·us -a -um *adj* Arabian, Sabaean, of the Sabaeans ‖ *f see* **Sabaea** ‖ *mpl* the Sabaeans *(people of S.W. Arabia, modern Yemen)*
Sabāz·ius -(i)ī *m* Bacchus ‖ *npl* festival in honor of Bacchus
sabbat·a -ōrum *npl* Sabbath
sabbatāri·a -ae *f* Sabbath-keeper *(i.e., Jewish woman)*
Sabell·us -a -um *adj* Sabellian, Sabine ‖ *m* Sabine *(i.e., Horace)*

Sabīn·us -a -um *adj* Sabine; **herba Sabīna** *(bot)* savin *(a juniper, used to produce a drug);* **ōleum Sabīnum** oil derived from savin **II** *m* Roman family name *(cognomen) (e.g.,* Flavius Sabinus, the father of the Emperor Vespasian) **II** *mpl* an ancient people of central Italy **II** *f* Sabine woman **II** *n* Sabine wine; Horace's Sabine farm

sabul·um -ī *n or* **sabul·ō -ōnis** *m* gravel, coarse sand

saburr·a -ae *f* gravel; ballast

saburr·ō -āre -āvī -ātus *tr* to ballast; *(coll)* to gorge with food

Sac·ae -ārum *mpl* **(Sag-)** Scythian tribe

saccipēr·ium -(i)ī *n* pocket; purse

sacc·ō -āre -āvī -ātus *tr* to filter, strain

saccō -ōnis *m (pej) (of a rich person)* moneybags

saccul·us -ī *m* little bag; pouch

sacc·us -ī *m* sack, bag; pouch; bag for straining liquids, strainer

sacell·um -ī *n* chapel, shrine

sa·cer -cra -crum *adj* sacred, holy, consecrated; devoted to a deity for destruction, accursed; detestable; criminal, infamous **II** *n see* **sacrum**

sacerd·ōs -ōtis *m* priest **II** *f* priestess

sacerdōtāl·is -is -e *adj* priestly

sacerdōt·ium -(i)ī *n* priesthood

sacrāment·um -ī *n* guarantee, deposit *(sum of money which each of the parties to a lawsuit deposits and which is forfeited by the loser);* civil lawsuit; dispute; oath; voluntary oath of recruits; military oath; **eum obligāre mīlitiae sacrāmentō** to swear him into the army; **iūstīs sacrāmentīs contendere** to argue on equal terms; **omnēs sacrāmentō adigere** *(or* **rogāre)** *(mil)* to swear them all in; **sacrāmentum dīcere** *(mil)* to sign up; **sacrāmentum dīcere** *(w. dat)* to swear allegiance to

Sacrān·us -a -um *adj* of the Sacrani *(a people from Reate in Italy)*

sacrār·ium -(i)ī *n* shrine, chapel; sacristy

sacrāt·us -a -um *adj* hallowed, consecrated, holy, sacred

sacrif·er -era -erum *adj* carrying sacred objects

sacrificāl·is -is -e *adj* sacrificial

sacrificāti·ō -ōnis *f* sacrificing

sacrific·ium -(i)ī *n* sacrifice; **sacrificium facere** *(or* **perpetrāre)** *(w. dat)* to offer a sacrifice to

sacrific·ō -āre -āvī -ātus *tr & intr* to sacrifice

sacrificul·us -ī *m* sacrificing priest

sacrific·us -a -um *adj* sacrificial

sacrileg·ium -(i)ī *n* sacrilege; temple robbing; violation of sacred rites

sacrileg·us -a -um *adj* sacrilegious; profane, impious, wicked **II** *m* temple robber; wicked person **II** *f* impious woman

sacr·ō -āre -āvī -ātus *tr* to consecrate; to dedicate; to set apart, devote; give; to doom, curse; to hallow, declare inviolable; to hold sacred, worship; to immortalize

sacrōsānct·us -a -um *adj* sacred, inviolable, sacrosanct

sacr·um -ī *n* holy object, sacred vessel; holy place, temple, sanctuary; religious rite, act of worship, religious service; festival; sacrifice; victim **II** *npl* worship, religion; secret, mystery; inviolability; **sacra facere** to sacrifice; **sine sacrīs hērēditātis** *(fig)* godsend, windfall

saeclum *see* **saeculum**

saec(u)lār·is -is -e *adj* **(sēc-)** centennial

saec(u)l·um -ī *n* **(sēc-)** generation, lifetime; century; spirit of the age, fashion

saepe *adv* often

saepenumerō *or* **saepe numerō** *adv* oftentimes, on many occasions

saep·ēs -is *f* **(sēp-)** hedge, fence, enclosure

saepīment·um -ī *n* **(sēp-)** hedge, fence, enclosure

saep·iō -īre -sī -tus *tr* **(sēp-)** to fence in, hedge in, enclose; to surround, encircle; to guard, fortify, protect, strengthen

saepissimē *adv* very often

saepissim·us -a -um *adj* very frequent

saepius *adv* more frequently

saepsī *perf of* **saepiō**

saept·um -ī *n* **(sēp-)** fence, wall, enclosure; stake; sheepfold; voting booth **II** *npl* enclosure; voting booths, polls

saeptus *pp of* **saepiō**

saet·a -ae *f* **(sēt-)** bristle, stiff hair

saetig·er -era -erum *adj* **(sēt-)** bristly **II** *m* wild boar

saetōs·us -a -um *adj* **(sēt-)** shaggy, bristly

saevē *adv* savagely, fiercely

saevidic·us -a -um *adj* spoken in anger

saev·iō -īre -iī -ītum *intr* to be fierce, be savage, be furious; *(of persons)* to be brutal, be violent

saeviter *adv* savagely, cruelly

saeviti·a -ae *f* rage, fierceness; brutality, savageness *(of persons)*

saevitūd·ō -inis *f* savageness

saev·us -a -um *adj* raging, fierce, cruel; brutal, savage, barbarous

sāg·a -ae *f* fortuneteller; sorceress

sagācit·ās -ātis *f* sagacity, shrewdness; keenness

sagāciter *adv* keenly, with keen scent *or* sight; with insight

Sagan·a -ae *f* name of a witch

Sagar·is -is *m,* **Sangari·us -ī** *m* river flowing from Phyrgia into the Black Sea

Sagarīt·is -idis *f* a nymph, daughter of the river-god Sagaris, loved by Attis

sagāt·us -a -um *adj* wearing a military cloak
sag·āx -ācis *adj* keen-scented; sharp, perceptive *(mind)*
sagīn·a -ae *f* stuffing, fattening up; food, rations; rich food; fattened animal; fatness *(from overeating)*
sagīn·ō -āre -āvī -ātus *tr* to fatten
sāg·iō -īre *tr* to perceive quickly
sagitt·a -ae *f* arrow ‖ **Sagitta** *(astr)* Sagitta *(constellation)*; an arrow in the constellation Sagittarius
sagittāri·us -a -um *adj* of *or* for an arrow ‖ *m* archer ‖ **Sagittārius** *m (astr)* Sagittarius, the archer *(constellation)*
sagittāt·us -a -um *adj* barbed
sagittif·er -era -erum *adj* carrying an arrow
Sagittipot·ēns -entis *m (astr)* Sagittarius *(constellation)*
sagm·en -inis *n* tuft of sacred herbs *(plucked in the Capitol by the consul or praetor and worn by the Fetiales as a sign of inviolability)*
sagulāt·us -a -um *adj* wearing a military coat ‖ *m* soldier
sagul·um -ī *n* short military coat *(esp. that of general officers)*
sag·um -ī *n* coarse mantle; military uniform; **ad sagum īre** *(or* **sagum sūmere)** to get into uniform; **in sagīs esse** to be in uniform; to go to war
Saguntīn·us -a -um *adj & m* Saguntine
Sagunt·um -ī *n or* **Sagunt·us** *or* **Sagunt·os -ī** *f* Saguntum *(city on E. coast of Spain (modern Sagunto), which Hannibal attacked, thus bringing on the First Punic War)*
sāl salis *m (n)* salt; salt water, sea; seasoning; flavor; good taste, elegance; pungency *(of words)*; wit, humor, sarcasm ‖ *mpl* wisecracks
Salaci·a -ae *f* a sea goddess
salac·ō -ōnis *m* show-off, braggart
salamandr·a -ae *f* salamander
Salamīni·us -a -um *adj* of Salamis ‖ *mpl* people of Salamis
Salam·is -īnos *or* **-īnis** *(acc:* **Salamīna;** *abl:* **Salamīne)** *f* island in the Saronic Gulf near Athens, opposite Eleusis ‖ city in Cyprus
salapūt·ium -(i)ī *n* midget
Salāri·a -ae *f* Via Salaria *(from Porta Collina to the Sabine district)*
salāri·us -a -um *adj* salt, of salt; **annōna salāria** revenue from salt works; **Via Salāria** Salt Road *(from the Porta Collina to the Sabine district)* ‖ *m* salt-fish dealer ‖ *n* salary, allowance *(originally the allowance given to soldiers for salt)*; *(fig)* meal
sal·āx -ācis *adj* lustful; salacious, provocative
salebr·a -ae *f* a jolting; rut; roughness *(of speech)*
salebrōs·us -a -um *adj* rough, uneven
Sālentīn·ī -ōrum *mpl* **(Sall-)** a people who occupied the S.E. extremity of Italy
Salern·um -ī *n* town on the Campanian coast S.E. of Naples *(modern Salerno)*
Saliār·is -is -e *adj* Salian, of the Salii; sumptuous
Saliāt·us -ūs *m* Salian priesthood
salict·um -ī *n* willow grove
salient·ēs -ium *fpl* springs, fountains
salign·us -a -um *adj* willow
Sali·ī -ōrum *mpl* college of twelve priests dedicated to Mars who went in solemn procession through Rome on the Kalends of March
salīll·um -ī *n* small salt shaker
salīn·ae -ārum *fpl* salt pits, salt works; **salīnae Rōmānae** salt works at Ostia *(a state monopoly)*
salīn·um -ī *n* salt shaker
sal·iō -īre -uī *or* **-iī -tum** *tr (of an animal)* to mount ‖ *intr* to jump, leap, hop
Salisubsil(i)·ī -ōrum *mpl* dancing priests of Mars
saliunc·a -ae *f* wild nard *(aromatic plant)*
Sal·ius -(i)ī *m* priest of Mars *(see* **Saliī)**
salīv·a -ae *f* saliva; taste, flavor
sal·ix -icis *f* willow tree
Sallentīnī *see* **Sālentīnī**
Sallustiān·us -a -um *adj* of Sallust; **hortī Sallustiānī** park in the N. part of Rome owned by Sallust ‖ *m* imitator of Sallust's style ‖ *n* a Sallustian expression
Sallust·ius -(i)ī *m* Sallust *(Gaius Sallustius Crispus, Roman historian, 86–34 B.C.)* ‖ Gaius Sallustius Crispus *(his great-nephew and adopted son, an advisor to Augustus and Tiberius, d. A.D. 20)*
Salmac·is -idis *f* fountain at Halicarnassus on the W. coast of Asia Minor, which made all who drank from it soft and effeminate
Salmōn·eūs -ĕos *m* son of Aeolus who imitated lightning and was thrown by Jupiter into Tartarus
Salmōn·is -idis *or* **-idos** *f* Tyro *(daughter of Salmoneus)*
Sal·ō -ōnis *f* tributary of the River Ebro *(modern Jalon)*
Salōn·ae -ārum *fpl* city on the Illyrian coast *(near modern Split)*
salp·a -ae *f* saupe *(type of fish)*
salsāment·um -ī *n (usu. pl)* salted food *(esp. fish)*
salsē *adv* facetiously, humorously
salsipot·ēns -entis *adj* ruling the sea
salsūr·a -ae *f* (process of) pickling
sals·us -a -um *adj* salted; briny, salty; facetious, humorous, witty ‖ *npl* salty food; witty remarks, satirical writings
saltāti·ō -ōnis *f* dancing, dance

saltāt·or -ōris *m* dancer
saltātōri·us -a -um *adj* dance, for dancing
saltātr·īx -īcis *f* dancing girl
saltāt·us -ūs *m* dance
saltem *adv* at least, in any event, anyhow; **nōn** *(or* **neque) saltem** not even
salt·ō -āre -āvī -ātus *tr & intr* to dance
saltuōs·us -a -um *adj* wooded, covered with forest
salt·us -ūs *m* defile, pass; wooded pasture; opening in the woods, glade; forest; jungle; ravine; *(vulg)* female pudenda
salt·us -ūs *m* jump, leap; *(fig)* step, stage; **saltum dare** to leap
salū·ber *or* **salū·bris -bris -bre** *adj* healthful, healthy, wholesome; *(w. dat or* **ad)** good for, beneficial to
salūbrit·ās -ātis *f* healthiness, wholesomeness; health, soundness
salūbriter *adv* healthfully; healthily; beneficially; **emere salūbriter** to buy cheaply
saluī *perf of* **saliō**
sal·um -ī *n* billow; sea in motion; high seas; **aerumnōsō nāvigāre salō** *(poet)* to sail a sea of troubles; **tīrōnēs salō nauseāque cōnfectī** recruits, hit hard by seasickness
sal·ūs -ūtis *f* health; welfare; prosperity; safety; greeting, best regards; **salūtem dīcere** *(abbr:* **s.d.)** to send greetings; *(at end of letter)* to say goodbye; **salūtem magnam dīcere** *(w. dat)* to send warm greetings to, bid fond farewell to, say goodbye to; **salūtem plūrimam dīcere** *(abbr:* **s.p.d.)** to send warmest greetings; *(at end of letter)* to give best regards
salūtār·is -is -e *adj* salutary, healthful, wholesome; beneficial, advantageous, useful; *(w.* **ad)** good for, beneficial for; *(w. dat)* beneficial to; **ars salūtāris** art of healing; **salūtāris littera** vote of acquittal *(the letter* **A** *for* **Absolvō)**
salūtāriter *adv* beneficially
salūtāti·ō -ōnis *f* greeting, salutation; formal morning reception at the house of an important person; callers; **ubi salūtātiō dēfluxit** when morning callers have dispersed
salūtāt·or -ōris *m*, **salūtātr·īx -īcis** *f* morning caller
salūtif·er -era -erum *adj* health-giving
salūtigerul·us -a -um *adj* bringing greetings
salūt·ō -āre -āvī -ātus *tr* to greet, wish well; to send greetings to; to pay respects to, pay a morning call on; to pay reverence to *(gods);* to welcome; *(w. double acc)* to hail as
salvē *impv of* **salveō**
salvē *adv* well; in good health; **satine** *(or* **satisne) salvē?** *(supply* **agis** *or* **agit** *or* **agitur)** *(coll)* everything O.K.?
salv·eō -ēre *intr* to be well, be in good health; to be getting along well; **salvē, salvēte** *(or* **salvētō)**! hello!, good morning!, good day!; goodbye!; **salvēbis ā meō Cicerōne** my son Cicero wishes to be remembered to you; **tē salvēre iubeō** I bid you good day; **valē, salvē** goodbye
salv·us (salv·os) -a -um *adj* well, sound, safe, unharmed; living, alive; *(w. noun or pronoun in an abl absolute)* without violation of, without breaking, *e.g.,* **salvā lēge** without breaking the law; **salvos sum** *(coll)* I'm O.K.
Samae·ī -ōrum *mpl* inhabitants of Cephallenia
sambūc·a -ae *f* triangular stringed instrument, small harp
sambūcistri·a -ae *f* harpist *(female)*
Sam·ē -ēs *or (less frequently)* **Sam·os -ī** *f* ancient name of the island of Cephallenia
Samiol·us -a -um *adj* of Samian ware
Sami·us -a -um *adj* of Samos, Samian; **Iūnō Samia** Juno worshiped at Samos; **testa Samia** Samian potsherd *(noted for its thinness);* **vir Samius** Pythagoras **||** *mpl* Samians **||** *npl* delicate Samian pottery
Samn·īs -ītis *adj* Samnite **||** *m* gladiator armed with Samnite weapons **||** *mpl* the Samnites
Samn·ium -(i)ī *n* country of central Italy, whose inhabitants were the offshoot of the Sabines
Sam·os *or* **Sam·us -ī** *(acc:* **-on** *or* **-um)** *f* an island off the W. coast of Asia Minor, famous as the birthplace of Pythagoras **||** *see* **Samē**
Samothrāc·a -ae *f* Samothrace *(island off the Thracian coast)*
Samothrāc·es -um *mpl* Samothracians
Samothrāci·us -a -um *adj* Samothracian **||** *f* Samothrace *(island in N. Aegean Sea)*
sam(p)s·a -ae *f* crushed olive
sānābil·is -is -e *adj* curable
sānāti·ō -ōnis *f* healing, curing
sanciō sancīre sānxī sānctus *tr* to fulfill *(a threat, prophecy);* to ratify *(laws, agreements, treaties);* to enact *(a law);* to sanction *(a policy, practice);* to confirm the possession of *(property);* to condemn; *(w. abl of the penalty)* to make *(an offense, a person)* punishable by law with; **Solōn capite sānxit quī in seditiōne nōn alterīus utrīus partis fuisset** Solon condemned to death anyone who did not side with one party or the other in a revolution
sānctē *adv* solemnly, reverently, religiously, conscientiously, purely
sānctimōni·a -ae *f* sanctity, sacredness; chastity
sāncti·ō -ōnis *f* consecration; sanctioning; penalty clause *(that part of the law that provided for penalties against those breaking that law),* sanction

sānctit·ās -ātis *f* sanctity, sacredness, inviolability; integrity; purity
sānctitūd·ō -inis *f* sanctity
sānct·or -ōris *m* enactor *(of laws)*
sānct·us -a -um *adj* consecrated, hallowed, sacred, inviolable, holy; venerable, august, divine; chaste
Sanc·us -ī *m* epithet of Semo *(a god of Sabine origin)*
sandaliāri·us -a -um *adj* sandal-maker's; **Apollō Sandaliārius** Apollo of Shoemakers' Street
sandaligerul·ae -ārum *fpl* maids who brought slippers to their mistress
sandal·ium -iī *n* sandal, slipper *(one in which the toes were covered; cf.* **solea)**
sandapil·a -ae *f* simple coffin
sand·ȳx -ȳcis *f* vermilion, scarlet
sānē *adv* sanely, reasonably, sensibly; certainly, doubtless, truly, very; *(ironically)* of course, naturally; *(w. negatives)* really, at all; *(in concessions)* to be sure, however; *(in answers)* yes, of course; *(w. imperatives)* then; **haud** *(or* **nōn) sānē** not very; **nihil sānē** absolutely nothing; **sānē quam** extremely
sānēsc·ō -ere *intr* to get well; to heal
Sangari·us -a -um *adj* living near the Sagaris River *(in Phrygia)* **II** *m* Sagaris River
sangu·en -inis *m see* **sanguis**
sanguin·āns -antis *adj* bleeding; bloodthirsty
sanguināri·us -a -um *adj* bloodthirsty
sanguine·us -a -um *adj* bloody; bloodstained; blood-red; **sanguineus imber** a rain of blood
sanguinolent·us -a -um *adj* bloody, bloodstained; blood-red; vindictive
sangu·is -inis *m* blood; descent, parentage, family; descendant; murder, bloodshed; *(fig)* lifeblood, source of vitality, life, strength; forcefulness, life, vigor *(of a speech);* **sanguinem dare** to bleed; **sanguinem effundere** *(or* **profundere)** to bleed heavily; **sanguinem haurīre** to shed *(s.o.'s)* blood; **sanguinis missiō** *(med)* bloodletting; **sanguinem mittere** *(of a physician)* to let blood, bleed
sani·ēs -ēī *f* blood *(from a wound);* gore; foam, froth; venom
sānit·ās -ātis *f* health; sanity; common sense, discretion; solidity, healthy foundation *(for victory, etc.);* soundness, propriety *(of style)*
sann·a -ae *f* mocking grimace, sneer, face
sanni·ō -ōnis *m* clown
sān·ō -āre -āvī -ātus *tr* to cure, heal; to correct, repair; to allay, quiet, relieve
Sanquāl·is -is -e *adj* of Sancus *(Sabine deity);* **Sanquālis avis** osprey
Santon·ī -ōrum *mpl* Gallic tribe N. of the Geronne
Santonic·us -a -um *adj* of the Santoni; **herba** *(or* **virga) Santonica** wormwood *(bitter aromatic herb used as a tonic)*
Santr·a -ae *m* a grammarian of the time of Varro
sān·us -a -um *adj* sound, hale, healthy; sane, rational, sensible; sober; *(w.* **ab)** free from *(faults, etc.)*
sānxī *perf of* **sanciō**
sap·a -ae *f* (distilled) new wine
sāperd·a -ae *m* a fish *(from the Black Sea)*
sapi·ēns -entis *adj* wise, sensible, judicious, discreet **II** *m* sensible person; sage, philosopher; man of discriminating taste, connoisseur; title given to jurisconsults
sapienter *adv* wisely, sensibly
sapienti·a -ae *f* wisdom; common sense; philosophy; knowledge *(of principles, methods),* science
sap·iō -ere -īvī *or* **-iī** *tr* to have the flavor of, taste of; to smell like; to understand **II** *intr* to have the sense of taste; to have sense, be sensible, be discreet, be wise
sāp·ō -ōnis *m* pomade; soap
sap·or -ōris *m* taste, flavor; delicacy; refinement, sense of taste
Sapphic·us -a -um *adj* Sapphic; **Mūsa Sapphica** Sappho *(as a tenth Muse)*
Sapph·ō -ūs *f (acc:* **Sapphō)** Greek lyric poetess of Lesbos *(born c. 612 B.C.)*
sarcin·a -ae *f* package, bundle, pack; burden *(of a womb);* sorrow, trouble **II** *fpl* luggage, gear; movable goods, chattels, belongings
sarcināri·us -a -um *adj* luggage, of luggage; **iūmenta sarcināria** pack animals
sarcināt·or -ōris *m* patcher, repairer
sarcināt·us -a -um *adj* loaded down
sarcinul·ae -ārum *fpl* small bundles, little trousseau
sar·ciō -cīre -sī -tus *tr* to patch; to fix, repair
sarcophag·us -ī *m* stone coffin
sarcul·um -ī *n* garden hoe
Sardanapāl·us -ī *m* last king of the Assyrian empire of Nineveh *(c. 9th cent.)* whose decadence was legendary
Sard·ēs *or* **Sard·īs -ium** *fpl* Sardis *(capital of Lydia)*
Sardiān·us -a -um *adj* Sardian **II** *mpl* inhabitants of Sardis
Sardini·a -ae *f* Sardinia
Sardiniēns·is -is -e *adj* Sardinian
Sardīs *see* **Sardēs**
sardon·yx -ychis *or* **-ychos** *m (f)* sardonyx *(precious stone)*
Sardō·us *or* **Sard·us -a -um** *adj & m* Sardinian
sarg·us -ī *m* sar *(fish)*
sar·iō -īre -uī *intr* **(sarr-)** to hoe; to weed
sarīs(s)·a -ae *f* long Macedonian lance
sarīs(s)ophor·os -ī *m* Macedonian lancer

Sarmat·ae -ārum *mpl* Sarmatians *(barbarous people of S.E. Russia)*
Sarmati·a -ae *f* Sarmatia
Sarmaticē *adv* Sarmatian, in the Sarmatian language
Sarmatic·us -a -um *adj* Sarmatian
sarment·um -ī *n* brushwood **||** *npl* twigs, faggots
Sarn·us -ī *n* river in Campania near Paestum *(modern Sarno)*
Sarpēd·ōn -onis *or* **-onos** *m* king of Lycia who was killed by Patroclus at Troy
Sarr·a -ae *f* old name of Tyre
sarrāc·um -ī *n* **(serr-)** wagon
Sarrān·us -a -um *adj* Tyrian, Phoenician; dyed (Tyrian) purple
sarriō *see* **sariō**
sarsī *perf of* **sarciō**
sartāg·ō -inis *f* frying pan; hodgepodge
sart·us *or* **sarct·us -a -um** *pp of* **sarciō ||** *adj (occurring only with* **tēctus)** in good repair; **aedem Castoris sartam tēctam trādere** to hand over the temple of Castor in good repair **||** *npl* repairs; **sarta tēcta exigere** to complete the repairs
sat *adv* sufficiently, quite; **sat sciō** I am quite sure
sat *indecl adj* enough, sufficient, adequate **||** *n* enough; **sat agere** *(w. gen)* to have enough of, have one's hands full with
sat·a -ae *f* daughter; *(w. abl* begotten of)
sat·a -ōrum *npl* crops
sat·agō -agere -ēgī *intr* to have trouble enough, have one's hands full
satell·es -itis *mf* bodyguard, attendant, follower; *(pej)* lackey; partisan; *(w. gen)* accomplice in *(crime)*
sati·ās -ātis *f* sufficiency; overabundance, satiety, satisfied desire
Saticul·us -ī *m* inhabitant of Saticula *(Samnite town)*
satiet·ās -ātis *f* sufficiency, adequacy; satiety, weariness, disgust
satin' *or* **satine** (= **satisne)** *adv* quite, really
sati·ō -āre -āvī -ātus *tr* to satisfy, appease; to avenge; to fill, glut; to saturate; to cloy
sati·ō -ōnis *f* sowing, planting **||** *fpl* sown fields
satis *adv* enough, sufficiently, adequately; **satis bene** pretty well
satis *or* **sat** *indecl adj* enough, sufficient, adequate **||** *n* enough; *(leg)* satisfaction, security, guarantee; **satis accipere** to receive a guarantee; **satis dare** *(w. dat)* to give a guarantee to; **satis facere** *(w. dat)* to satisfy; to pay *(a creditor);* to make amends to *(by word or deed)*, apologize to; **satis facere** *(w. dat of person and acc & inf)* to satisfy *(s.o.)* with proof that, demonstrate sufficiently to *(s.o.)* that; **satis superque dictum est** more than enough has been said
satisdati·ō -ōnis *f* putting up bail, giving a guarantee
satis·dō -dare -dedī -datum *intr* (also written as two words) see **satis**
satis·faciō -facere -fēcī -factus *tr (also written as two words) see* **satis**
satisfacti·ō -ōnis *f* amends, satisfaction; apology, excuse
satius *(comp of* **satis)** *adj* (*neut only*) **satius est** *(w. inf)* it is better *or* preferable to
sat·or -ōris *m* sower, planter; father; promoter, author
satrapē·a *or* **satrapī·a -ae** *f* satrapy *(office or province of a satrap)*
satrap·ēs *or* **satrap·a -ae** *m* satrap *(provincial governor in the Persian empire)*
sat·ur -ura -urum *adj* full, well-fed, stuffed; plump; fertile; deep *(color)*
satur·a -ae *f* **(satir-)** dish of mixed ingredients; mixture, hodgepodge; medley, variety show; literary medley of prose and poetry; satire, satirical poem; **in** *(or* **per)** **saturam** at random; collectively, en block; **per saturam ferre** to propose as a rider to a bill
saturēi·a -ōrum *npl* savory *(seasoning)*
saturit·ās -ātis *f* satiety; plenty, overabundance
Sāturnāli·a -ium *npl* festival in honor of Saturn, beginning on the 17th of December and lasting several days; **iō Sāturnālia**! cry of merrymakers at this festival; **nōn semper Sāturnālia erunt** *(fig)* it won't be Christmas forever; **hilara Sāturnālia**! Merry Saturnalia!
Sāturni·a -ae *f* Juno *(daughter of Saturn)*
Sāturnīn·us -ī *m* Lucius Appuleius Saturninus *(demagogic tribune in 103 and 100 B.C.)*
Sāturni·us -a -um *adj* Saturnian; **Sāturnius numerus** Saturnian meter *(archaic Latin meter based on stress accent)* **||** *m* Jupiter; Pluto
Sāturn·us -ī *m* Saturn *(Italic god of agriculture, equated with the Greek god Cronos, ruler of the Golden Age, and father of Jupiter, Neptune, Juno, and Pluto)*
satur·ō -āre -āvī -ātus *tr* to fill, satisfy, glut, cloy, saturate; to satisfy, content
sat·us -a -um *pp of* **serō** (to plant) **||** *m* son *(w. abl:* begotten of); **satus Anchīsā** son of Achises *(i.e.,* Aeneas) **||** *f* daughter *(see* **sata) ||** *npl see* **sata**
sat·us -ūs *m* sowing, planting; begetting; race, stock; seed *(of knowledge)*
satyrisc·us -ī *m* little satyr
satyr·us -ī *m* satyr; satyr play *(in which chorus consisted of satyrs)*
sauciāti·ō -ōnis *f* wounding
sauci·ō -āre -āvī -ātus *tr* to wound

sauci·us -a -um *adj* wounded; *(fig)* smitten, offended, hurt; drunk, smashed; madly in love; melted *(snow)* **II** *mpl* the wounded
saurocton·os -ī *m (as title of a statue)* lizard killer
Sauromat·ae -ārum *mpl* Sarmatians *(barbaric tribe of S. Russia)*
sāviāti·ō -ōnis *f* **(suav-)** kissing
sāviol·um -ī *n* **(suav-)** little kiss, peck
sāvi·or -ārī -ātus sum *tr* **(suav-)** to kiss
sāv·ium -(i)ī *n* **(suav-)** puckered lips; kiss
saxātil·is -is -e *adj* rock, living among rocks **II** *m* saxatile *(fish)*
saxēt·um -ī *n* rocky place; stone quarry
saxe·us -a -um *adj* rocky, stony; **umbra saxea** shade of the rocks
saxific·us -a -um *adj* petrifying, changing objects into stone
saxifrag·us -a -um *adj* rock-breaking
saxōs·us -a -um *adj* rocky, stony
saxul·um -ī *n* small rock *or* crag
sax·um -ī *n* boulder, rock; Tarpeian Cliff *(W. side of the Capitoline Hill)*
s(c)irpe·us -a -um *adj* wicker, of wicker **II** *f* wickerwork
s(c)irpicul·a -ae *f* wicker basket
s(c)irpicul·us -ī *m* wicker basket
s(c)irp·us -ī *m* bulrush
scabellum *see* **scabillum**
sca·ber -bra -brum *adj* itchy; rough, scurfy
scābī *perf of* **scabō**
scabi·ēs -ēī *f* itch; eczema; *(fig)* itch
scabill·um -ī *n* **(-bell-)** stool, footstool; castanet tied to the ankle
scabiōs·us -a -um *adj* itchy, mangy; moldy
scabō scabere scābī *tr* to scratch
Scae·a port·a -ae *f* Scaean gate *(W. gate of Troy)*
scaen·a -ae *f* **(scēn-)** stage; backdrop, scenery; scene; *(fig)* public view, publicity; melodramatic behavior; pretense; pretext; canopy *(of forest acting like a backdrop)*; **tibi scenae serviendum est** you must keep yourself in the limelight
scaenicē *adv* **(scēn-)** like on the stage
scaenic·us -a -um *adj* **(scēn-)** of the stage, theatrical, scenic; **lūdi scaenicī** plays
scaev·a -ae *f* favorable omen
Scaevol·a -ae *m* Gaius Mucius Cordus Scaevola *(Roman hero who infiltrated Porsenna's camp to kill Porsenna, and on being discovered, burned off his own right hand)* **II** Quintus Mucius Scaevola *(consul in 95 B.C. and pontifex maximus)*
scaev·us -a -um *adj* left, on the left; perverse **II** *f* sign *or* omen appearing on the left *(hence, unfavorable)*
scāl·ae -ārum *fpl* ladder; flight of stairs, stairs
scalm·us -ī *m* oarlock; oar; boat
scalpell·um -ī *n* scalpel
scalp·ō -ere -sī -tus *tr* to carve; to scratch; to tickle, titillate
scalpr·um -ī *n* chisel; knife; penknife
scalpsī *perf of* **scalpō**
scalptōr·ium -(i)ī *n* back-scratcher
scalptūr·a -ae *f* engraving
scalpurr·iō -īre *intr* to scratch
Scaman·der -drī *m* river at Troy *(also called Xanthus)*
scamb·us -a -um *adj* bowlegged
scammōne·a -ae *f (bot)* scammony *(plant with trumpet-like flowers similar to the morning-glory, used as a laxative)*
scamn·um -ī *n* bench; stool; throne
scan·dō -dere -dī scānsus *tr* to climb, scale; to climb aboard; to mount **II** *intr* to climb; *(of buildings)* to rise, tower
scandul·a -ae *f* shingle *(of a roof)*
Scantīni·us -a -um *adj* Roman clan name *(nomen)*; **lēx Scantīnia** law against unnatural vice
scaph·a -ae *f* light boat, skiff
scaph·ium -iī *n* **(scaf-)** boat-shaped drinking cup; chamber pot
scapul·ae -ārum *fpl* shoulder blades; shoulders; back
scāp·us -ī *m* shaft *(of a column)*; stalk *(of a plant)*
scarīf·ō -āre *tr* to scratch open
scar·us -ī *m* scar *(fish)*
scatebr·a -ae *f* bubbling spring
scat·eō -ēre -uī *or* **scat·ō -ere** *intr* to bubble up, gush out; to teem
scatur(r)īgi·ō -inis *f* spring
scaturr·iō -īre *intr* to bubble, gush; to bubble over with enthusiasm
scaur·us -a -um *adj* clubfooted
scāz·ōn -ontis *m* scazon *(iambic trimeter with a spondee in the last foot)*
scelerātē *adv* criminally, wickedly
scelerāt·us -a -um *adj* profaned, desecrated; outlawed; criminal, wicked, infamous; **campus scelerātus** open field near the Colline gate where unchaste Vestals were buried alive; **vīcus scelerātus** street on Esquiline Hill where Tullia, daughter of Servius Tullius, drove over her father's corpse **II** *m* criminal; rascal
sceler·ō -āre -āvī -ātus *tr* to defile
scelerōs·us -a -um *adj* steeped in wickedness
scelestē *adv* wickedly, criminally
scelest·us -a -um *adj* wicked, villainous, criminal; unlucky **II** *m* rascal
scel·us -eris *n* wicked deed, crime, wickedness; calamity; *(pej)* rascal
scēn- = scaen-
scēptrif·er -era -erum *adj* sceptered
scēptr·um -ī *n* scepter **II** *npl* kingship, dominion, authority; kingdom; **scēptra Āsiae tenēre** to hold sway in Asia
scēptūch·us -ī *m* scepter-bearer *(high officer of state in the East)*

sc(h)ēm·a -ae *f*, **sc(h)ēm·a -atis** *or* **-atos** *n* figure, form; style; figure of speech
sched·a *or* **scid·a -ae** *f* sheet, page
schid·a -ae *f* **(scid-)** sheet *(of papyrus);* one of the strips forming a sheet of papyrus
Schoenē·is -idos *f* daughter of Schoeneus (*Atalanta*)
Schoenēi·us -a -um *adj* of Schoeneus **||** *f* Atalanta
Schoen·eus -eī *m* king of Boeotia and father of Atalanta
schoenobat·ēs -ae *m* tightrope-walker
schoen·us -ī *m* cheap perfume
schol·a -ae *f* school; lecture hall; lecture; learned debate; sect, followers
scholastic·us -a -um *adj* school, scholastic **||** *m* rhetoric teacher, rhetorician; grammarian
scida *see* **scheda**
scidī *perf of* **scindō**
sci·ēns -entis *adj* aware of a fact, cognizant; having full knowledge, with one's eyes wide open; *(w. gen)* cognizant of, familiar with, expert in; *(w. inf)* knowing how to
scienter *adv* wisely, expertly
scienti·a -ae *f* knowledge, skill, expertise; science; *(w.* **dē** *or* **in** *+ abl)* expertise in, skill in
sciī *perf of* **sciō**
scīlicet *adv* of course, evidently, certainly; *(ironically)* naturally, of course; *(as an explanatory particle)* namely, that is to say
scill·a -ae *f* **(squi-)** squill *(seaside plant of the lily family)*
scīn = scīsne, *i.e.,* **scīs + ne** do you know?
scindō scindere scidī scissus *tr* to cut, split, tear apart, tear open; to divide, separate; to interrupt
scintill·a -ae *f* spark; speck
scintill·ō -āre *intr* to sparkle, flash
scintillul·a -ae *f* little spark
sciō scīre scīvī *or* **sciī scītus** *tr* to know; to realize, understand; to have skill in; *(w. inf)* to know how to
Scīpiad·ās -ae *m* **(·ēs)** one of the Scipio family, a Scipio
scīpi·ō -ōnis *m* ceremonial staff *or* baton *(generally made of ivory and carried by persons of rank, such as a seer or a general at his triumph)* **|| Scīpiō** family name *(cognomen)* in the famous gens Cornelia **||** Publius Cornelius Scipio Africanus Maior *(victor in the Second Punic War, 236–184 B.C.)* **||** Publius Cornelius Scipio Aemilianus Africanus Minor *(victor in Third Punic War, c. 185–132 B.C.)*
Scīr·ōn -ōnis *or* **-ōnos** *m* robber who waylaid travelers on the road near Megara *(killed by Theseus)*
scīscitāt·or -ōris *m* interrogator
scīscit·ō -āre *or* **scīscit·or -ārī -ātus sum** *tr* to ask, question, interrogate; to consult; *(w. acc of thing asked and* **ex** *or* **ab** *of person asked)* to ask *(s.th.)* of *(s.o.),* check on *(s.th.)* with *(s.o.)* **||** *intr* (w. **dē** + *abl)* to ask about
scīscō scīscere scīvī scītus *tr (pol)* to approve, adopt, enact, decree; to learn, ascertain
sciss·or -ōris *m* carver *(person cutting meat at the table)*
scissūr·a -ae *f* crack, cleft
sciss·us -a -um *pp of* **scindō ||** *adj* split, rent; furrowed *(cheeks);* shrill *(voice)*
scītāment·a -ōrum *npl* delicacies, choice tidbits
scītē *adv* expertly, tastefully
scīt·or -ārī -ātus sum *tr* to ask; to consult *(oracle); (w. acc of thing and* **ab** *or* **ex)** to ask *(s.th.)* of *(s.o.)* **||** *intr* (w. **dē** + *abl)* to ask *or* inquire about
scītul·us -a -um *adj* neat, pretty
scīt·um -ī *n* statute, decree
scīt·us -a -um *adj* experienced, skillful; suitable, proper; judicious, sensible, witty; smart, sharp *(appearance); (w. gen)* skilled in, expert at
scīt·us -ūs *m* decree, enactment
sciūr·us -ī *m* squirrel
scīvī *perf of* **sciō** *and of* **scīscō**
-sc·ō -ere *vbl suf normally used only in the present system with inchoative force, e.g.,* **lūcēscō** to begin to shine
scob·is -is *f* sawdust, scrapings, filings
scom·ber -brī *m* mackerel
scōp·ae -ārum *fpl* broom; **ūnae scōpae** one broom
Scop·ās -ae *m* Greek sculptor from the island of Paros *(4th cent. B.C.)*
scopulōs·us -a -um *adj* rocky, craggy
scopul·us -ī *m* rock, cliff, crag; promontory; archery target
scop·us -ī *m* target
scorpi·ō -ōnis *or* **scorp·ius** *or* **scorp·ios -(i)ī** *m* scorpion; *(mil)* catapult **|| Scorpiō** *(astr)* Scorpion *(constellation)*
scortāt·or -ōris *m* a john *(prostitute's customer)*
scorte·us -a -um *adj* leather
scort·ōr -ārī *intr* to associate with prostitutes
scort·um -ī *n* prostitute; sex fiend *(of either sex)*
scort·um -i *n* skin, hide
screāt·or -ōris *m* hawker, hemmer *(one who constantly clears his throat)*
screāt·us -ūs *m* clearing of the throat
scre·ō -āre *intr* to clear the throat, hawk, hem
scrīb·a -ae *m* clerk, secretary
scrib(i)līt·a -ae *f* cheese cake
scrībō scrībere scrīpsī scrīptus *tr* to write, draw; to write down; to write out, com-

pose; to draw up, draft *(a law, treaty, decree);* to create *(characters, episodes in a play);* to lay down in writing, prescribe; to register *(a person);* to draft *(colonists to a place);* to name *(in a will);* to enlist *(soldiers); (w. double acc)* to appoint *(s.o.)* as ‖ *intr* to write

scrīn·ium -(i)ī *n* case for scrolls; letter case; portfolio

scrīpsī *perf of* **scrībō**

scrīpti·ō -ōnis *f* writing; composition; spelling; wording, text

scrīptit·ō -āre -āvī -ātus *tr & intr* to keep writing, write regularly

scrīpt·or -ōris *m* writer; scribe, secretary; author; **rērum scrīptor** historian

scrīptul·a -ōrum *npl* lines on a game board

scrīptūr·a -ae *f* writing; composing; written work, composition; tax paid on public pastures; testamentary provision

scrīpt·us -a -um *pp of* **scrībō** ‖ *n* composition, treatise, work, book; actual text *(of a law, document);* literal meaning, letter *(as opposed to spirit);* **duodecim scrīpta** a type of game board; **ōrātiōnem dē scrīptō dīcere** to read off a speech; **voluntās lēgis, nōn tantum scrīptum** the spirit of the law, not only the letter *(of the law)*

scrīpul·um -ī *n* **(scrīpt-)** small weight, smallest measure of weight, scruple *(one twenty-fourth of an uncia, or ounce)*

scrob·is -is *mf* ditch, trench; grave

scrōf·a -ae *f* breeding sow

scrōfipāsc·us -ī *m* pig breeder

scrūpe·us -a -um *adj* full of sharp rocks, made of jagged rocks, jagged

scrūpōs·us -a -um *adj* full of sharp rocks, jagged, rough

scrūpulōsē *adv* scrupulously, precisely, carefully

scrūpulōs·us -a -um *adj* full of sharp projections of rock, jagged; scrupulous, meticulous, precise

scrūpul·us -ī *m* uneasy feeling, scruple, worry, headache; thorny problem

scrūp·us -ī *m* rough *or* sharp stone; uneasiness

scrūt·a -ōrum *npl* trash, junk

scrūtāt·or -ōris *m* examiner

scrūt·or -ārī -ātus sum *tr* to scrutinize, examine

sculp·ō -ere -sī -tus *tr* to carve, chisel, engrave

sculpōne·ae -ārum *fpl* clogs, wooden shoes

sculpsī *perf of* **sculpō**

sculptil·is -is -e *adj* carved, engraved

sculpt·or -ōris *m* sculptor

sculptūr·a -ae *f* carving; sculpture

sculptus *pp of* **sculpō**

scurr·a -ae *m* jester, comedian; city slicker

scurrīl·is -is -e *adj* scurrilous, offensive

scurrīlit·ās -ātis *f* offensive humor, scurrility

scurrīliter *adv* with offensive humor, like a buffoon

scurr·or -ārī *intr* to clown around

scūtāl·e -is *n* thong of a sling

scūtār·ius -(i)ī *m* shield-maker

scūtāt·us -a -um *adj* carrying a shield ‖ *mpl* troops armed with shields

scutell·a -ae *f* saucer, shallow bowl

scutic·a -ae *f* whip

scūtigerul·us -a -um *m* shield-bearer

scutr·a -ae *f* pan, flat dish

scutul·a -**ae** *f* wooden roller

scutulāt·us -a -um *adj* diamond-shaped ‖ *npl* checkered clothing

scūtul·um -ī *n* small shield

scūt·um -ī *n* oblong shield; *(fig)* shield, defense, protection

Scyll·a -ae *f* female monster on Italian side of Strait of Messina, that snatched and devoured sailors from passing ships ‖ daughter of Nisus who betrayed her father by cutting off his purple lock of hair

Scyllae·us -a -um *adj* Scyllan

scymn·us -ī *m* cub, whelp

scyph·us -ī *m* goblet, cup

Scȳr·os *or* **Scȳr·us -ī** *f* island off Euboea

Scyth·a *or* **Scyth·ēs -ae** *m* Scythian *(member of nomadic tribe N. of the Black Sea)*

Scythi·a -ae *f* country N. of the Black Sea

Scythic·us -a -um *adj* Scythian

Scyth·is -idis *f* Scythian woman

sē *or* **sēsē** *(gen:* **suī;** *dat:* **sibi;** *acc & abl:* **sē** *or* **sēsē** *pron (refl)* himself, herself, itself, themselves; one another; **ad sē** *(or* **apud sē**) at home; **apud sē** in one's senses; **inter sē** each other, one another, mutually; **in sē** associated with each other, one another, together; **per sē** by himself *(herself, itself, etc.),* alone

sē- *pref (also* **sēd-, sō-)** *added to verbs, etc.:* **1** *in the sense of "apart," "aside," e.g.:* **sēdūcere** to take aside; **sēditiō** a going apart, mutiny; **2** *sometimes privative, e.g.:* **sōcors** lacking in vitality, inactive

sēb·um -ī *n* tallow, grease, suet

sē·cēdō -cēdere -cessī -cessum *intr* to withdraw; to depart; to rebel, go on a sit-down strike, secede; **in ōtium sēcēdere** to retire

sē·cernō -cernere -crēvī -crētus *tr* to separate; to dissociate; to distinguish; to reject, set aside

sēcessi·ō -ōnis *f* withdrawal; secession

sēcess·us -ūs *m* retirement, retreat; isolated spot; country retreat

sēclū·dō -dere -sī -sus *tr* to shut off, shut up; to shut out; to seclude, bar; to hide

sec·ō -āre -uī -tus *tr* to cut, cut off; to reap; to carve *(meat);* to split up *(in classification);* to cut through, traverse *(e.g., the* *sea);* to cut short; to settle, decide; to follow, chase; to castrate; *(med)* to operate on; *(med)* to cut out, excise, cut off, amputate; **viam secāre** to open up a path

sēcrēti·ō -ōnis *f* dividing, separating *(into constituent parts)*

sēcrētō *or* **sēcrētē** *adv* separately, individually, apart; secretly; in private; away from one's companions

sēcrēt·us -a -um *pp of* **sēcernō** ‖ *adj* separate; isolated, solitary; secret; *(w. gen or abl)* deprived of, in need of ‖ *n* secret, mystery; mystic rite, mystic emblem; secret nature *(of a business);* abstruseness *(of a subject);* private conversation *or* interview, audience; isolated spot; **ā sēcrētō** *(or* **in sēcrētō** *or* **in sēcrētum)** in private; **sēcrētō in occultō cum aliquō agere** to discuss *(s.th.)* with s.o. in a private conversation; **sēcrētum dare (petere)** to grant (ask for) a private conference

sect·a -ae *f* path; way, method, course; school of thought; political party; code of behavior; **secta (vītae)** way of life, occupation

sectāri·us -a -um *adj* followed (by the flock)

sectāt·or -ōris *m* follower, adherent

sectil·is -is -e *adj* cut, divided

secti·ō -ōnis *f* cutting; cut, division; section; dissection; auctioning off of confiscated property; a buying up of confiscated property in lots; right to confiscated property; things so to be sold, lots

sect·or -ārī -ātus sum *tr* to keep following, follow eagerly, run after; to hunt *(game);* to go about searching for; to imitate; to run after *(girls);* to avenge; to follow *(an example, practice);* to go regularly to, frequent; to aim continually at *(an objective)*

sect·or -ōris *m* speculator in confiscated estates *(one who buys up confiscated property with the intention of reselling);* **sector zōnārius** purse-snatcher

sectūr·a -ae *f* incision; stone quarry

sectus *pp of* **secō**

sēcubit·us -ūs *m* sleeping alone

sēcub·ō -āre -uī *intr* to sleep by oneself; to live alone

secuī *perf of* **secō**

sēcul- = **saecul-**

secund·a -ōrum *npl* success

secund·ae -ārum *fpl (theat)* secondary role in a play; *(fig)* second fiddle

secundān·ī -ōrum *mpl* soldiers of the second legion

secundāri·us -a -um *adj* secondary; second-rate, inferior

secundō *adv* secondly

secund·ō -āre -āvī -ātus *tr* to favor, further; to make *(conditions)* favorable for travel; **secundāns ventus** favorable wind, tail wind

secundum *adv* after, behind ‖ *prep (w. acc)* **1** *(of space)* beside, by, along, alongside: **īre secundum mē** to walk beside me; **legiōnēs secundum flūmen dūxit** he led the troops along the river; **2** *(of time)* immediately after: **secundum lūdōs** immediately after the games; **3** *(in rank or quality)* next to, after: **secundum deōs hominēs hominibus ūtilēs esse possunt** next to the gods, people can be helpful to people; **4** *(of agreement)* according to, in compliance with: **secundum nātūram vīvere** to live in accordance with nature; **5** *(leg)* in favor of, to the advantage of; **abscentibus secundum praesentēs facillimē dabat** when a party (to the suit) was absent, he would very readily decide in favor of the party present

secund·us -a -um *adj* following; next, second *(in time; in rank);* backing, favorable, supporting; secondary, subordinate, inferior, second-string; alternate *(heir);* *(w. dat or* **ab)** second only to; **annō secundō** the next year; **ā mēnsis fīne secunda diēs** the second-last day of the month; **in secundam aquam** with the current; **rēs secundae** success, prosperity; **secundae partēs** supporting role; **secunda mēnsa** dessert; **secundō flūmine** downstream, with the current; **secundō lūmine** on the following day; **secundō marī** with the tide; **secundō populō** with the backing of the people; **secundus pānis** stale bread; **secundus ventus** tailwind, fair wind ‖ **Secundus** *m* Roman first name *(praenomen)* ‖ *fpl see* **secundae** ‖ *npl see* **secunda**

sēcūrē *adv* securely, safely

secūricul·a -ae *f* hatchet

secūrif·er -era -erum *adj* carrying an ax, ax-carrying

secūrig·er -era -erum *adj* carrying an ax, ax-wielding

secūr·is -is *f (acc: usu.* **secūrim)** ax, hatchet; *(fig)* blow, mortal blow; *(fig) (from the ax in the fasces, usu. pl)* power of life and death, supreme authority, sovereignty; **graviōrem reī pūblicae īnflīgere secūrim** to inflict a more serious blow on the State

sēcūrit·ās -ātis *f* freedom from care, unconcern, composure; freedom from danger, security, safety; false sense of security; carelessness

sēcūr·us -a -um *adj* carefree; secure, safe; cheerful; careless; offhand

secus *adv* otherwise, differently; **haud** *(or* **haut** *or* **nōn) secus ac** *(or* **nōn secus quam)** not otherwise than, just as, exactly as; **haud** *(or* **haut** *or* **nōn) secus sī** exactly as if, just as though; **sī secus**

accidet if it turns out otherwise *(than expected),* if it turns out badly
secus *indecl n* sex; **secus muliebre** females; **secus virīle** males
secūt·or -ōris *m* chaser *(gladiator who fought against the net-man)*
secūtus *pp of* **sequor**
sed *or* **set** *conj* but; but also
sēdātē *adv* sedately, calmly
sēdāti·ō -ōnis *f* calming
sēdāt·us -a -um *adj* calm, composed
sēdecim *indecl adj* sixteen
sēdēcul·a -ae *f* little seat, low stool
sedentāri·us -a -um *adj* sedentary
sedeō sedēre sēdī sessum *intr* to sit, remain seated; *(of magistrates, esp. judge)* to sit, preside, hold court, be a judge; *(of an army)* to remain encamped; to keep the field; to settle down to a blockade; to be idle, be inactive; *(of clothes)* to fit; *(of buildings, towns)* to be located; *(of places)* to be low-lying; to sink, settle; to be firm, be fixed, be established; to stick fast, be stuck; to be determined
sēd·ēs -is *f* seat, chair, throne; residence, home; last home, burial place; base, foundation, bottom; **sēdēs bellī** theater of war
sēdī *perf of* **sedeō**
sedīl·e -is *n* seat, chair **||** *npl* seats in the theater; rowers' benches
sēditi·ō -ōnis *f* sedition, insurrection, mutiny; dissension, quarrel, disagreement; warring *(of elements)*
sēditiōsē *adv* seditiously, in mutiny
sēditiōs·us -a -um *adj* seditious, mutinous; quarrelsome; troubled
sēd·ō -āre -āvī -ātus *tr* to calm, settle, still
sē·dūcō -dūcere -dūxī -ductus *tr* to take aside, draw aside, lead off, withdraw; to carry off; to lead astray; to put aside; to divide, split
sēducti·ō -ōnis *f* taking aside
sēduct·us -a -um *pp of* **sēdūcō** **||** *adj* distant, remote
sēdulit·ās -ātis *f* application, earnestness; officiousness
sēdulō *adv* diligently; intentionally
sēdul·us -a -um *adj* diligent, busy; officious
sēdūxī *perf of* **sēdūcō**
seg·es -etis *f* grainfield; crop; arable land
Segest·a -ae *f* town in N.W. Sicily
Segestān·us -a -um *adj* of Segesta **||** *mpl* people of Segesta **||** *n* territory of Segesta
segmentāt·us -a -um *adj* trimmed with a flounce *(decorative border)*
segment·um -ī *n* section, segment; slice; trimming, flounce; zone *(of the earth)*
sēgnip·ēs -edis *adj* slow-footed
sēgn·is -is -e *adj* slow; inactive; sluggish, lazy
sēgniter *adv* slowly; lazily
sēgniti·a -ae *or* **sēgniti·ēs -ēī** *f* slowness; inactivity; laziness
sēgreg·ō -āre -āvī -ātus *tr* to segregate, separate; to dissociate; **ad sēsē sēgregandōs ā cēterīs** for the purpose of dissociating themselves from the rest; **sermōnem sēgregāre** to break off a conversation; **suspiciōnem ā sē sēgregāre** to ward off suspicion from oneself
Sēiāniān·us -a -um *adj* of Sejanus **||** *mpl* partisans of Sejanus
Sēiān·us -ī *m* Roman family name *(cognomen) (esp. Lucius Aelius Sejanus, the notorious praetorian prefect under the Emperor Tiberius)*
sēiugāt·us -a -um *adj* separated, detached
sēiug·is -is *m* six-horse chariot
sēiug·ō -āre -āvī -ātus *tr (w.* **ab**) to separate from, detach from
sēiūnctim *adv* separately
sēiūncti·ō -ōnis *f* separation, division
sē·iungō -iungere -iūnxī -iūnctus *tr* to separate, part, sever; *(fig)* to sever, part, disconnect; to distinguish
sēlēcti·ō -ōnis *f* choice, selection
sēlēctus *pp of* **sēligō**
sēlēgī *perf of* **sēligō**
Seleucī·a -ae *f* name of several towns in Asia
Seleuc·us -ī *m* name of a line of six kings of Syria, whose ancestor, Seleucus Nicator, was a general under Alexander the Great and founded the Syrian monarchy *(c. 358–280 B.C.)*
sēlībr·a -ae *f* half pound
sē·ligō -ligere -lēgī -lēctus *tr* to select
Selīn·ūs -untis *f* town on the S.W. coast of Sicily **||** town on the coast of Cilicia
sell·a -ae *f* chair, stool *(normally without back or armrests);* portable chair, sedan chair; **sella curūlis** magistrate's chair
sellāriol·us -a -um *adj (place)* for sitting *or* lounging
sellār·ius -(i)ī *m* lecher, lewd person
sellistern·ium -(i)ī *n* sacred banquet in honor of goddesses
sellul·a -ae *f* stool; sedan chair
sellulāri·us -a -um *adj* sedentary; **artifex sellulārius** craftsman who sits at his job **||** *mpl* sedentary craftsmen
sēmanimis *see* **sēmianimis**
semel *adv* once, one time; but once, once and for all; the first time; ever, at some time, at any time; **semel aut iterum** once or twice
Semel·ē -ēs *or* **Semel·a -ae** *f* Semele (*daughter of Cadmus and mother of Bacchus by Jupiter*)
Semelēi·us -a -um *adj* of Semele
sēm·en -inis *n* seed; seedling, young plant, shoot: offspring; race, stock; *(in physics)* particle; *(fig)* instigator, root: **sēmen omnium malōrum** root of all evils

sēmēnstris *see* **sēmēstris**
sēmentif·er -era -erum *adj* seed-bearing, fruitful
sēment·is -is *f* sowing, planting; young crops; **ut sēmentem fēceris, ita metēs** *(prov)* as you sow, so shall you reap
sēmentīv·us -a -um *adj* at seed time, of the sowing season
sēmerm·is -is -e *adj* half-armed
sēmēstr·is -is -e *adj* **(-mēns-)** for six months, half-yearly, semi-annual
sēmēs·us -a -um *adj* half-eaten
sēmet = *emphatic form of* **sē**
sēmi- *pref before nouns and adjectives with the sense of* "half-" *(sometimes* **sēm-** *before vowels, e.g.:* **sēmēsus** half-eaten; **sēm(i)animus** half-alive; *also reduced to* **sē-** *e.g.:* **sēlībra** half pound
sēm(i)erm·is -is -e *or* **sēm(i)erm·us -a -um** *adj* half-armed
sēm(i)ēs·us -a -um *adj* half-eaten
sēm(i)ūstilāt·us -a -um *adj* **(-tul-)** half-burned
sēmiadapert·us -a -um *adj* half-open
sēmianim·is -is -e *or* **sēm(i)anim·us -a -um** *adj* half-alive, half-dead
sēmiapert·us -a -um *adj* half-open
sēmib·ōs -ōvis *adj (masc only)* half-ox; **sēmibōs vir** the Minotaur
sēmica·per -prī *m (masc only)* half-goat *(i.e., Pan or Faunus)*
sēmicrem(āt)·us -a -um *adj* half-burned
sēmicubitāl·is -is -e *adj* half-cubit long *or* wide
sēmide·us -a -um *adj* semidivine ‖ *m* demigod
sēmidoctus -a -um *adj* half-educated
sēmifact·us -a -um *adj* half-finished
sēmifer·us -a -um *adj* half-beast; half-savage ‖ *m* centaur
sēmifult·us -a -um *adj* half-propped
sēmigermān·us -a -um *adj* half-German
semigraec·us -a -um *adj* half-Greek
sēmigrav·is -is -e *adj* half-drunk
sēmigr·ō -āre -āvī -ātum *intr* (w. **ab**) to go away from, move away from
sēmihi·āns -antis *adj* half-open
sēmihom·ō -inis *adj (masc only)* half-man, half-beast; subhuman
sēmihōr·a -ae *f* half hour
sēmi·lacer -lacera -lacerum *adj* half-mangled
sēmilaut·us -a -um *adj* half-washed
sēmilīb·er -era -erum *adj* half-free
sēmilix·a -ae *f (pej) (of a commander)* sad sack, little more than a camp follower
sēmimarīn·us -a -um *adj* half-submerged
sēmim·ās -aris *adj* half-male, gelded, castrated ‖ *m* hermaphrodite
sēmimortu·us -a -um *adj* half-dead
sēminār·ium -(i)ī *n* nursery garden; *(fig)* breeding ground
sēmināt·or -ōris *m* originator
sēmi·n(ex) -necis *adj* half-killed, half-dead
sēmin·ium -(i)ī *n* breeding; stock
sēmin·ō -āre *tr* to sow; to beget, procreate; to produce
sēminūd·us -a -um *adj* half-naked
sēmipāgān·us -ī *m* little clown
sēmiplēn·us -a -um *adj (forces)* at half-strength; *(ships)* half-manned
sēmiputāt·us -a -um *adj* half-pruned
Semīram·is -idis *f* famous queen of Assyria, builder of Babylon and consort and successor of King Ninus
Semīrami·us -a -um *adj* of Semiramis; Babylonian
sēmirās·us -a -um *adj* half-shaven
sēmireduct·us -a -um *adj* bent back halfway
sēmirefect·us -a -um *adj* half-repaired
sēm·is -issis *m* half; half an **as** *(small coin);* ½% per month *or* 6% per annum; **nōn semissis homō** worthless fellow
sēmisen·ex -is *m* elderly gent
sēmisepult·us -a -um *adj* half-buried
sēmisomn·is -is -e *or* **sēmisomn·us -a -um** *adj* half-asleep
sēmisupīn·us -a -um *adj* half-prone
sēmit·a -ae *f* path, lane, track
sēmitāl·is -is -e *adj* of byways, backroad
sēmitāri·us -a -um *adj* back-alley
sēmi·vir -virī *adj* half-man, half-beast; unmanned; unmanly ‖ *m* half-man; eunuch
sēmivīv·us -a -um *adj* half-alive, half-dead
sēmod·ius -iī *m* half a peck
sēmōt·us -a -um *adj* remote, distant; private, intimate ‖ *npl* faraway places
sē·moveō -movēre -mōvī -mōtus *tr* to separate, remove, exclude
semper *adv* always, ever
sempitern·us -a -um *adj* everlasting
Semprōnius *see* **Gracchus**
sēmūnci·a -ae *f* half ounce *(one twenty-fourth of a Roman pound);* trifle
sēmūnciāri·us -a -um *adj* half-ounce; **faenus sēmūnciārium** interest at the rate of one twenty-fourth of the capital *(i.e., about 5% per annum)*
sēmūst·us -a -um *adj* half-burned
senācul·um -ī *n* open-air meeting place of the Senate in the Forum
sēnāriol·us -ī *m (pros)* trifling trimeter
sēnāri·us -a -um *adj (pros)* six-foot *(verse)* ‖ *m (pros)* iambic trimeter
senāt·or -ōris *m* senator
senātōri·us -a -um *adj* senatorial; in the Senate; of a senator
senāt·us -ūs *m* Senate; Senate session; **senātūs cōnsultum** decree of the Senate; **senātum dare** *(or* **praebēre)** to grant an audience with the Senate; to give *(s.o.)* the floor

Senec·a -ae *m* Lucius Annaeus Seneca *(Stoic philosopher and instructor of Nero, 4 B.C.–A.D. 65)*

senect·us -a -um *adj* aged, old ‖ *f* old age, senility

senect·ūs -ūtis *f* old age; old person

sen·eō -ēre *intr* to be old

sen·ēscō -ēscere -uī *intr* to get old; to decline, become feeble, lose strength; to wane, draw to a close

sen·ex -is *adj* aged, old ‖ *m* old man

sēn·ī -ae -a *adj* six each, in groups of six, six at a time; *(used in multiplication):* **aspicē bis sēnōs cycnōs**! see those twelve swans!; **sēnī dēnī** sixteen each

senīl·is -is -e *adj* of old people, of an old man; aged; senile

sēni·ō -ōnis *m* a six *(on dice)*

seni·or -or (-us) *(comp of* **senex)** *adj* older, elder; more mature *(years)* ‖ *m* elderly person, an elder *(over 45 years of age)*

sen·ium -iī *n* feebleness of age, decline, senility; decay; grief, trouble; gloom; crabbiness; old man

sēns·a -ōrum *npl* thoughts, sentiments, ideas

sēnsī *perf of* **sentiō**

sēnsicul·us -ī *m* petty aphorism

sēnsif·er -era -erum *adj* producing a sensation

sēnsil·is -is -e *adj* capable of sensation, sentient

sēnsim *adv* gropingly; tentatively; carefully; gradually, gently

sēns·us -a -um *pp of* **sentiō** ‖ *npl see* **sēnsa**

sēns·us -ūs *m* capacity for feeling, sensation; sense *(of hearing, etc.);* self-awareness, consciousness; awareness *(of conditions, situations);* feeling, emotion, sentiment; attitude, frame of mind; idea, thought; understanding, judgment, viewpoint; meaning, sense *(of a word);* intent, plan of action; self-contained expression, sentence; **commūnēs sēnsūs** commonplaces, trite topics; **cum sēnsū** with taste; **sēnsus commūnis** civic pride, concern for the common good

sententi·a -ae *f* opinion, view, judgment; purpose, intention; *(in the Senate)* motion, proposal; meaning, sense; plan of action; sentence; maxim; *(leg)* verdict, sentence; **dē sententiā** *(w. gen)* in accordance with the wishes of; **ex animī (meī) sententiā** *(in an oath)* to the best of (my) knowledge; **ex meā sententiā** in my opinion; to my liking; **in sententiam alicūius pedibus īre** to vote in favor of s.o.'s proposal *(literally, to go on foot to s.o.'s proposal);* **sententiam dīcere** *(in the Senate)* to express a view; **sententia est** *(w. inf)* I intend to; **sententiam prōnūntiāre** *(or* **dīcere)** to pronounce *or* give the verdict

sententiol·a -ae *f* phrase; maxim

sententiōsē *adv* sententiously, in moralizing style

sententiōs·us -a -um *adj* full of meaning, pregnant, sententious

senticēt·um -ī *n* thorny bush

sentīn·a -ae *f* bilge water; cesspool; bilge; *(fig)* dregs, scum, rabble

sentiō sentīre sēnsī sēnsus *tr* to perceive with the senses, feel, hear, see, smell; to realize; to observe, notice; to experience; to think, judge ‖ *intr (leg)* to vote, decide

sent·is -is *m* thorny bush, briar

sentīsc·ō -ere *tr* to begin to realize; to begin to observe, perceive

sent·us -a -um *adj* rough, rugged; untidy *(person)*

seorsum *or* **seorsus** *or* **sōrsum** *or* **sōrsus** *adv* apart, separately; *(w. abl or* **ab)** apart from

sēparābil·is -is -e *adj* separable

sēparātim *adv* apart, separately

sēparāti·ō -ōnis *f* severing, separation

sēparātius *adv* less closely, more widely

sēparāt·us -a -um *adj* separate, distinct, different

sēpar·ō -āre -āvī -ātus *tr* to separate, divide, part; to distinguish

sepelībil·is -is -e *adj* that may be buried

sepel·iō -īre -īvī *or* **-iī sepultus** *tr* to bury; *(fig)* to overwhelm, ruin, destroy, suppress

sēpēs *see* **saepēs**

sēpi·a -ae *f* **(saep-)** cuttlefish

sēpīment·um *see* **saepīmentum**

sēpio *see* **saepiō**

sēpiol·a -ae *f* little cuttlefish

sē·pōnō -pōnere -posuī -positus *tr* to set aside, drop, discard; to banish; to disregard, forget; to separate, pick out, select; to reserve; to remove, take away, exclude; to distinguish

sēposit·us -a -um *adj* remote, distant; select; distinct; private

sēps sēpis *mf* a poisonous snake

sēpse = *emphatic* **sē**

septem *indecl adj* seven

Septem·ber -bris -bre *adj* September, of September; **mēnsis September** September *(seventh month of the old Roman calendar until 153 B.C.)* ‖ **Septem·ber -bris** *m* September

septemdecim *indecl adj* **(-ten-)** seventeen

septemflu·us -a -um *adj* seven-mouthed *(Nile)*

septemgemin·us -a -um *adj* sevenfold

septempedāl·is -is -e *adj* seven-foot, seven-foot-high

septempl·ex -icis *adj* sevenfold

septem·vir -virī *m* septemvir *(member of a board of seven, established in 44 B.C. to distribute land to veterans)* ‖ *mpl* board of seven officials; **septemvirī epulōnum**

college of priests responsible for sacred feasts

septemvirāl·is -is -e *adv* of the septemvirs, septemviral ‖ *mpl* septemvirs

septemvirāt·us -ūs *m* office of the septemvirs

septemvirī *see* **septemvir**

septēnār·ius -(i)ī *m (pros)* heptameter *(verse of seven feet)*

septendecim *indecl adj* **(septem-)** seventeen

septēn·ī -ae -a *adj* seven each, in groups of seven; **septēnī dēnī** seventeen each, seventeen in a group

septentri·ō -ōnis *m* the North; **ad** *or* **in septentriōnem** to the north, northward

septentriōnāl·is -is -e *adj* **(septem-)** northern; **Oceanus septentriōnālis** the North Sea ‖ *npl* northern regions, the North

septentriōn·ēs -um *mpl* **(septem-)** *(seven stars near the North Pole belonging to the Great Bear)* Great Bear; *(the seven stars of the Little Bear)* Little Bear; northern regions, the North; north wind

septiēns *or* **septiēs** *adv* seven times

septimān·us -a -um *adj* of *or* on the seventh ‖ *mpl* soldiers of the seventh legion

septimum *adv* for the seventh time

septim·us -a -um *adj* **(-tum-)** seventh

septim·us decim·us -a -um *adj* seventeenth

septingentēsim·us -a -um *adj* seven hundreth

septingent·ī -ae -a *adj* seven hundred

septuāgēsim·us -a -um *adj* seventieth

septuāgintā *indecl adj* seventy

septuenn·is -is -e *adj* seven-year-old

sēptum *see* **saeptum**

septūn·x -cis *m* seven ounces; seven-twelfths

sēptus *pp of* **sēpiō** *(see* **saepiō)**

sepulc(h)rāl·is -is -e *adj* of a tomb, sepulchral, funeral

sepulc(h)rēt·um -ī *n* grave, tomb

sepulc(h)r·um -ī *n* grave, tomb

sepultūr·a -ae *f* burial

sepultus *pp of* **sepeliō**

Sēquan·us -a -um *adj* of the Sequani ‖ *mf* the Seine River ‖ *mpl* the Sequani *(a tribe of E. Gaul)*

sequ·āx -ācis *adj* following, pursuing; penetrating *(fumes)*; eager

sequ·ēns -entis *adj* next, following

seques·ter -tra -trum *(or* **-ter -tris -tre)** *adj* intermediate; negotiating; **pāce sequestrā** under the protection of a truce ‖ *m* trustee *(with whom money or property is deposited)*; agent, go-between ‖ *n* **sequestrō dare** *(or* **pōnere)** to put in trust

sequius *or* **secius** *(comp of* **secus)** *adv* less; worse, more unfavorably; differently, otherwise; **nec eō secius** nonetheless; **nihilō** *(or* **nīlō)** **sequius** nevertheless

sequor sequī secūtus sum *tr* to follow; to escort, accompany, go with; to chase, pursue; to come after *(in time)*; to go after, aim at; to head for ‖ *intr* to go after, follow, come next; *(of words)* to come naturally

Ser. *abbr* **Servius** *(Roman first name, praenomen)*

ser·a -ae *f* bolt, bar *(of door)*

Serāp·is -is *or* **-idis** *m* **(Sar-)** Egyptian god of healing

serēnit·ās -ātis *f* fair weather; serenity; favorableness

serēn·ō -āre -āvī -ātus *tr* to make fair, clear up, brighten

serēn·us -a -um *adj* clear, bright, fair; cloudless; cheerful, serene ‖ *n* clear sky, fair weather

Sēr·es -um *mpl* Chinese

serēsc·ō -ere *intr* to dry off

Sergi·us -(i)ī *m* Roman clan name *(nomen)* *esp.* Lucius Sergius Catilina *(praetor in 68 B.C. and leader of the conspiracy put down by Cicero in 63 B.C.)*

sēri·a -ae *f* large jar

sēri·a -ōrum *npl* serious matters, serious business

Sēric·us -a -um *adj* Chinese ‖ *npl* silks

seri·ēs -ēī *f* series, row, succession; train, sequence, order, connection; lineage

sēriō *adv* seriously, in all sincerity

sēri·us -a -um *adj* serious, earnest ‖ *n* serious matter; seriousness, earnestness ‖ *npl* *see* **sēria**

sērius *adv* later; too late; **sērius ōcius** sooner or later

serm·ō -ōnis *m* conversation, talk; discussion, discourse; common talk, rumor, gossip; language; diction; prose, everyday language

sermōncin·or -ārī -ātus sum *intr* to talk, converse, chat, chitchat

sermuncul·us -ī *m* small talk, gossip, chitchat; brief talk, chat

sērō *adv (comp:* **sērius;** *superl:* **sērissimē)** late; too late

ser·ō -ere -uī -tus *tr* to join, connect; to entwine, wreathe; to compose, combine, contrive

serō serere sēvī satus *tr* to sow, plant; *(fig)* to sow the seed of

serp·ēns -entis *mf (large)* snake, serpent, dragon ‖ **Serpēns** *m (astr)* Draco *(constellation)*; Serpens *(constellation, in the hand of Ophiuchus)*

serpentigen·a -ae *m* dragon offspring

serpentip·ēs -edis *adj* dragon-footed

serperastr·um -ī *n* splint *(for straightening the crooked legs of children)*; *(mil)* officer who keeps his soldiers in check

serpillum *see* **serpyllum**

serp·ō -ere -sī *intr* to creep, crawl; to wind; to move along slowly, spread slowly

serpyll·um -ī *n* **(-pill-, -pull-)** wild thyme *(used for seasoning)*
serr·a -ae *f* saw
serrāc·um -ī *n* **(sarr-)** large wagon
serrāt·us -a -um *adj* serrated, toothed *(like a saw);* notched
serrul·a -ae *f* small saw
sert·a -ae *f* wreath
sert·a -ōrum *npl* wreathes; festoons
Sertōriān·ī -ōrum *mpl* partisans of Sertorius
Sertōr·ius -(i)ī *m* general of Marius, assassinated in Spain by Perperna *(c. 122–72 B.C.)*
sert·us -a -um *pp of* **serō** (to join) **‖** *f see* **serta ‖** *npl see* **serta**
seruī *perf of* **serō** (to join)
ser·um -ī *n* whey *(milk serum, the watery liquid separating from curds)*
sēr·us -a -um *adj* late; too late; occurring at a late hour; advanced, far gone; **annī sērī** ripe years; **ulmus sēra** slow-growing elm **‖** *n* late hour; **in sērum rem trahere** to drag out the matter until late
serv·a -ae *f* slave *(female)*
servābil·is -is -e *adj* retrievable
serv·āns -antis *adj* keeping; *(w. gen)* observant of
servāt·or -ōris *m,* **servātr·īx -īcis** *f* savior, preserver, deliverer
servīl·is -is -e *adj* slave, servile
servīliter *adv* slavishly
serv·iō -īre -īvī *or* **-iī -ītum** *intr* to be a servant *or* slave; to be obedient; *(of buildings, land)* to be mortgaged; *(w. dat)* **1** to be a slave to, be subservient to; **2** to serve; **3** to comply with, conform to; **4** to humor; **5** to be devoted to; **6** to work at; **7** to serve, be of use to
servit·ium -(i)ī *n* slavery; slaves
servitūd·ō -inis *f* servitude, slavery
servit·ūs -ūtis *f* slavery; slaves; property liability, easement
Serv·ius Tull·ius -(i)ī *m* sixth king of Rome *(credited with building the Servian Wall of tufa around Rome)*
serv·ō -āre -āvī -ātus *tr* to watch over, preserve, protect; to store, preserve; to keep, retain; to serve; to keep to, continue to dwell in
servol·a -ae *f* **(-ula)** young slave girl
servolicol·a -ae *f* slave of a slave *(female)*
servol·us -ī *m* **(-ulus)** young slave
serv·us *or* **serv·os -a -um** *adj* slave, servant **‖** *mf* slave, servant
sēscēnār·is -is -e *adj* **(sexc-)** a year and a half old
sēscēnāri·us -a -um *adj* six-hundred-man *(cohort)*
sēscēn·ī -ae -a *adj* six hundred each, in groups of six hundred
sēscentiēns *or* **sēscentiēs** *adv* **(sexc-)** six hundred times
sēsē *see* **sē**
sēsquī *adv* **(-que)** more by a half, one and a half times
sēsqui- *pref indicating that a quantity is multiplied by one and a half, e.g.,* **sēsquihōra** an hour and a half; **sēsquilībra** a pound and a half; *with ordinal numbers, it gives a number consisting of a unit and the fraction indicated by the numeral, e.g.,* **sēsquitertius** one and a third times as big; **sēsquioctāvus** one and an eighth times as big
sēsquialt·er -era -erum *adj* **(sēsque-)** one and a half times
sēsquihōr·a -ae *f* an hour and a half
sēsquilībr·a -ae *f* one and a half pounds
sēsquimod·ius -(i)ī *m* a peck and a half
sēsquioctāv·us -a -um *adj* **(sēsque-)** one and one-eighth times as big
sēsquiop·us -eris *n* the work of a day and a half
sēsquipedāl·is -is -e *adj* one and a half feet long *(or high, wide, thick, square, etc.)*
sēsqui·pēs -pedis *m* distance *or* length of one and a half feet
sēsquiplāg·a -ae *f* a stroke and a half
sēsquipl·ex -icis *adj* one and a half times as much
sēsquipl·us -a -um *adj* **(sēscupl·us)** one and a half times as big **‖** *n* one and a half times as much
sēsquiterti·us -a -um *adj* **(sēsque-)** one and a third times as big
sessibul·um -ī *n* seat, chair
sessil·is -is -e *adj (of the back of a centaur)* for sitting on; *(of plants)* low-growing
sessi·ō -ōnis *f* sitting; session; loafing
sessit·ō -āre -āvī -ātum *intr* to sit a lot, keep sitting, rest
sessiuncul·a -ae *f* small group *(sitting down together for a discussion)*
sess·or -ōris *m* spectator; resident
sessōr·ium -iī *n* sitting room
sēstertil·um -ī *n (coll)* a mere 100,000 sesterces
sēstert·ium -(i)ī *n (or declined as gen pl)* 100,000 sesterces
sēstert·ius -iī *(gen pl:* **sēstertium)** *(abbr:* **HS)** *m* sesterce *(small silver coin, equal to about one-fourth of a denarius, i.e., about 25¢, and used as the ordinary Roman unit in accounting; sums below 2000 sesterces are expressed by a cardinal number, e.g.,* **ducentī sēsteriī;** *sums from 2000 upwards are expressed by* **mīlia sēstertium** *(or* **sēstertia,** *with the distributives, or group-numbers (***bīna, quīnquāgēna,** *etc.); sums of 1,000,000 and upwards are expressed by the numeral adverb in* **-iēns (-iēs)** *with* **sēstertium** *(taken as a gen pl or declined as a neuter singular noun:* **deciēns** *(i.e.,* **deciēns**

centēna mīlia) sēstertium = *one million sesterces)*

Sest·os *or* **Sest·us -ī** *f* city on the Hellespont

sēt- = **saet-**

Sēti·a -ae *f* town in Latium famous for its wine *(modern Sezza)*

Sētīn·us -a -um *adj* Setine ‖ *n* Setine wine, wine from Setia

sētius *comp adv* **(sēc-)** later, more slowly; to a lesser degree, less readily; otherwise; **nihilō sētius** just the same, nonetheless; **quō sētius** *(w. subj)* so as to delay *or* prevent *(s.th. from happening):* **impedīmentō est Caepiō quō sētius lēx ferātur** Caepio is an impediment to having the law passed

seu *conj* or if; or; **seu** ... **seu** whether ... or

sevērē *adv* severely, sternly; seriously, in earnest; solemnly; **sevēre dīcere** to speak plainly

sevērit·ās -ātis *f* severity, sternness; self-discipline; seriousness

sevēritūd·ō -inis *f* severity, sternness; seriousness *(of expression)*

sevēr·us -a -um *adj* severe, strict, austere; serious, grave; ruthless, grim; plain, unadorned *(style of writing, architecture)*

sēvī *perf of* **serō** (to plant)

sēvoc·ō -āre -āvī -ātus *tr* to call aside, call away; to remove, withdraw; to separate; to appropriate *(from the common fund)*

sēv·um -ī *n* tallow, grease, suet

sex *indecl adj* six

Sex. *abbr* **Sextus** *(Roman first name, praenomen)*

sexāgē(n)sim·us -a -um *adj* sixtieth

sexāgēnāri·us -a -um *adj* sixty-year-old

sexāgēn·ī -ae -a *adj* sixty each; sixty at a time; sixty

sexāgiēns *or* **sexāgiēs** *adv* sixty times

sexāgintā *indecl adj* sixty

sexangul·us -a -um *adj* hexagonal

sexcēn- = **sēscen-**

sexcēnāri·us -a -um *adj* six-hundred-man *(cohort)*

sexenn·is -is -e *adj.* six-year-old; **sexennī diē** in a six-year period

sexenn·ium -(i)ī *n* six-year period, six years

sexiēns *or* **sexiēs** *adv* six times

sexprīm·ī *or* **sex prīm·ī -ōrum** *mpl* six-member council *(in provincial towns)*

sextadecimān·ī -ōrum *mpl* soldiers of the sixteenth legion

sext·āns -antis *m* one-sixth; small coin *(one-sixth of an* **as)**; one-sixth of a pint

sextār·ius -(i)ī *m* pint

Sextīl·is -is -e *adj* of Sixtilis *(the sixth month of the old Roman year, which began in March; Sextilis was afterwards called August in honor of Augustus)*

sextul·a -ae *f* sixth of an ounce

sextum *adv* for the sixth time

sext·us -a -um *adj* sixth

sext·us decim·us -a -um *adj* sixteenth

sex·us -ūs *m* sex; *(gram)* gender

sī *conj* if; **ō sī** *(expressing a wish)* if only!; **sī forte** if by any chance, in the hope that; **sī maximē** however much; **sī minus** if not; **sī modo** provided that; **sī vērō** *(expressing scepticism)* if really

sibī *see* **sē**

sībil·a -ōrum *npl* hisses, hissing

sībil·ō -āre -āvī -ātus *tr* to hiss at; to whistle at ‖ *intr* to hiss; to whistle

sībil·us -a -um *adj* hissing; whistling ‖ *m & n* hissing; whistling; rustling

Sibyll·a -ae *f* **(Sibu-)** Sibyl *(esp. the Sibyl at Cumae)*

Sibyllīn·us -a -um *adj* Sibylline

sīc *adv* thus, so, in this way; thus, as follows; in these circumstances; in such a way, to such a degree; *(in assent)* yes

sīc·a -ae *f* (curved) dagger

Sicān·ī -ōrum *mpl* ancient people of Italy who migrated to Sicily

Sicāni·a -ae *f* Sicily

Sicān·is -idis *adj* Sicilian

Sicāni·us -a -um *adj* Sicilian ‖ *f* Sicily

Sicān·us -a -um *adj* Sicilian ‖ *mpl see* **Sicānī**

sīcār·ius -(i)ī *m* murderer, assassin; **inter sīcāriōs accūsāre (dēfendere)** to prosecute (defend) on a murder charge

siccē *adv* dryly; *(fig)* firmly, *(rhet)* plainly

siccit·ās -ātis *f* dryness; drought; firmness, solidity; plainness *(of style)*

sicc·ō -āre *tr* to dry, dry up; to drain; **cruōrēs siccāre** to stanch the blood

siccocul·us -a -um *adj* dry-eyed

sicc·us -a -um *adj* dry; thirsty; sober; firm, solid *(body);* solid *(argument);* dry, insipid *(style)*

Sicili·a -ae *f* Sicily

sicilicissit·ō -āre *intr* to act like a Sicilian

sīcīlicul·a -ae *f* sickle

Siciliēns·is -is -e *adj* Sicilian

sīcine *adv* is this how ... ?

sīcubi *adv* if anywhere, wheresoever

sīcul·a -ae *f* little dagger; *(vulg)* penis

Sicul·ī -ōrum *mpl* ancient Italic people who migrated to Sicily; Sicilians

sīcunde *conj* if from some place

sīcut *or* **sīcutī** *conj* as, just as; *(in elliptical clauses)* just as, like; *(introducing a comparison)* as it were, so to speak; *(introducing an example)* as for instance; *(of condition)* as, in the same condition as; as if, just as if; **sīcut** ... **ita** although ... yet

sīcutī *adv (archaic form of* **sīcut)**

Sicy·ōn -ōnis *mf* town in the N. Peloponnesus

Sicyōni·us -a -um *adj* Sicyonian ‖ *mpl* Sicyonians

sīdere·us -a -um *adj* starry; star-spangled; heavenly, divine

sīdō sīdere sīdī *or* **sēdī sessum** *intr* to sit down; to settle; *(of birds)* to land; to sink; to settle down, subside; *(of ships)* to be grounded

Sīd·ōn -ōnis *f* city of Phoenicia

Sīdōn·is -idis *adj* Phoenician ‖ *f* Dido; Europa; Anna

Sīdōni·us -a -um *adj* Sidonian, Phoenician; Theban ‖ *mpl* Sidonians

sīd·us -eris *n* constellation; star, heavenly body; sky, heaven; light, glory, beauty, pride; season; climate, weather; *(in astrology)* star, destiny

Sigambr·ī -ōrum *mpl* German tribe

Sīgē(i)·us -a -um *adj* Sigean; Trojan

Sīgē·um *or* **Sīgē·on -ī** *n* promontory near Troy

sigillār·ia -ium *or* **-iōrum** *npl* small objects of pottery stamped in relief with figures *or* ornamentation ‖ art market in Rome ‖ festival forming the final day of the Saturnalia

sigillāt·us -a -um *adj* adorned with little figures *or* patterns in relief

sigill·um -ī *n* statuette, figurine; stamped *or* embossed figure, a relief; seal *(made by a seal ring);* figure woven in tapestry

sigm·a -atis *n* semicircular couch *(for reclining at table)*

signāt·or -ōris *m* sealer, signer; witness

signāt·us -a -um *adj* marked with a stamp, coined

signif·er -era -erum *adj* bearing the constellations, starry ‖ *m* standard-bearer; chief, leader

signific·āns -antis *adj* clear, distinct, expressive; significant, meaningful

significanter *adv* clearly, graphically; meaningfully, significantly

significāti·ō -ōnis *f* signal, indication, sign, mark; meaning, sense, signification; emphasis; expression of approval, applause

signific·ō -āre -āvī -ātus *tr* to show, indicate, express, point out; to intimate; to notify, publish; to portend; to mean, signify ‖ *intr* to make signs, indicate

Signīn·us -a -um *adj* of *or* from Signia *(town in Latium, modern Segni, famous for its astringent variety of wine)*

signipot·ēns -entis *adj* ruling over the constellations

sign·ō -āre -āvī -ātus *tr* to mark, stamp, impress, imprint; to seal, seal up; to coin; to signify, indicate, express; to adorn; to distinguish, note

sign·um -ī *n* sign; indication, proof; military standard, banner; password; cohort, maniple; omen; symptom; shop sign; statue; a figure *(in a relief, picture, or embroidery);* device on a seal, seal; heavenly sign, constellation; **ab signīs dīscēdere** to break ranks, disband; **signa cōnferre** to engage in close combat; to concentrate troops; **signa cōnstituere** to halt; **signa conversa ferre** to wheel around and attack; **signa ferre** to break camp; **signa movēre in hostem** to advance against the enemy; **signa prōferre** to march forward; **signa servāre** to keep the order of battle; **signa sequī** to march in rank; **signa subsequī** to keep the order of battle; **signa trānsferre** to desert, join the other side; **signīs collātīs** in regular battle formation

sīlān·us -ī *m* waterspout *(originally designed as a head of Silenus*

Silar·us -ī *m* **(Siler-)** Sele River *(forming the boundary between Lucania and Campania and flowing by the town of Paestum)*

sil·ēns -entis *adj* silent, calm, quiet ‖ *mpl* the dead

silent·ium -(i)ī *n* silence; inactivity; **silentium facere** to obtain silence; to keep silent; **silentium significāre** to call for silence

Sīlēn·us -ī *m* teacher and companion of Bacchus, usually drunk; a Silenus *(wood-spirit)*

sil·eō -ēre -uī *tr* to leave unmentioned, say nothing about ‖ *intr* to be silent, be still; to keep silent; to be hushed; to rest, cease

sil·er -eris *n* willow

silēsc·ō -ere *intr* to become silent, fall silent, become hushed

sil·ex -icis *mf* flint stone, lava stone *(used in road paving and other construction);* cliff, crag; *(fig)* hardheartedness

silicern·ium -(i)ī *n* funeral meal; *(coll)* old fossil

silīg·ō -inis *f* winter wheat; wheat flour

siliqu·a -ae *f* pod, husk ‖ *fpl* pulse *(the edible seeds of certain leguminous plants, as lentils, peas)*

sillyb·us -ī *m* label *(giving the title of the scroll and author's name)*

sīl·ō -ōnis *m* snub nose

silua *see* **silva**

siluī *perf of* **sileō**

silūr·us -ī *m* European catfish

sīl·us -a -um *adj* snub-nosed

silv·a *or* **silŭ·a -ae** *f* woods, forest; shrubbery, bush, foliage, crop, growth; mass, quantity; material, supply

Silvān·us -ī *m* god of woods ‖ *mpl* woodland gods

silvēsc·ō -ere *intr (of a vine)* to run wild

silvestr·is -is -e *adj* wooded, overgrown with woods; woodland, living in the woods; wild, growing wild; rural, pastoral ‖ *npl* woodlands

silvicol·a -ae *mf* denizen of the forest

silvicultr·īx -īcis *adj (fem only)* living in the woods
silvifrag·us -a -um *adj (of the wind)* forest-smashing
silvōs·us -a -um *adj* wooded
sīmi·a -ae *f* monkey, ape; *(pej)* monkey
simil·is -is -e *adj* similar; *(w. gen, mostly of persons, or dat, mostly of things)* similar to, resembling, like; **hominēs inter sē similēs** people resembling one another; **vērī similis** probable, likely, realistic ‖ *n* comparison, parallel
similiter *adv* similarly; **similiter atque** *(or* **ac)** just as; **similiter ut sī** just as if
similitūd·ō -inis *f* likeness, resemblance; imitation; analogy; comparison, simile; monotony; *(w. gen or dat)* similarity to; **est hominī cum deō similitūdō** there is a resemblance between man and a god
sīmiol·us -ī *m (also pej)* little monkey
simītū *adv* at the same time; *(w.* **cum** + *abl)* together with
sīm·ius -iī *m (also pej)* monkey, ape
Simo·īs -entis *m* stream at Troy
Simōnid·ēs -is *m* lyric poet of the Greek island of Ceos *(fl 500 B.C.)* ‖ iambic poet of the Greek island of Amorgos *(7th cent. B.C.)*
simpl·ex -icis *adj* single, simple; unmixed; plain, ordinary, natural, without elaboration; frank; naive; in single file
simplicit·ās -ātis *f* simplicity; candor, frankness
simpliciter *adv* simply, plainly; frankly, candidly
simpl·us -a -um *adj* simple ‖ *n* the simple sum *or* number *(opp:* **duplum)**
simpul·um -ī *n* small ladle
simpuv·ium -(i)ī *n* libation bowl
simul *adv* together, at the same time; likewise; *(w. abl or* **cum)** together with; **simul atque** *(or* **ac** *or* **et)** as soon as; **simul** ... **simul** both ... and ‖ *conj* as soon as
simulācr·um -ī *n* image, likeness; portrait; form, shape, phantom, ghost; conception; sign, emblem; mere shadow; portraiture, characterization; **simulācra cērea** dolls
simulām·en -inis *n* imitation, copy
simul·āns -antis *adj* imitating; *(w. gen)* imitative of, able to imitate
simulātē *adv* insincerely, deceitfully
simulāti·ō -ōnis *f* faking, bluffing, bluff, pretense; **simulātiōne** *(w. gen)* under the pretense of
simulāt·or -ōris *m* imitator; pretender, phoney
simul·ō -āre -āvī -ātus *tr* **(simil-)** to imitate, copy; to represent; to put on the appearance of, simulate
simult·ās -ātis *f* enmity, rivalry, feud; jealousy; grudge
sīmul·us -a -um *adj* rather snub-nosed
sīm·us -a -um *adj* snub-nosed
sīn *conj* if however, if on the other hand, but if; **sīn aliter** but if not
sināp·i *or* **sināp·e -is** *n,* **sināp·is -is** *f* (white) mustard
sincērē *adv* sincerely, honestly
sincērit·ās -ātis *f (physical)* soundness; purity; sincerity, integrity
sincēr·us -a -um *adj* sound, whole, clean; untainted; sincere, real, genuine
sincip·ut -itis *or* **sincipitāment·um -ī** *n* half a head *(as food);* cheek, jowl *(of a hog);* brain
sind·ōn -ōnis *f* fine cotton *or* linen fabric, muslin
sine *prep (w. abl)* without
singillātim *or* **singulātim** *adv* singly
singlāriter *see* **singulāriter**
singulār·is -is -e *adj* single, alone, one at a time; specific, peculiar, special; individual; unique; *(gram)* singular ‖ *mpl* crack troops
singulāriter *adv* singly; particularly; *(gram)* in the singular
singulāri·us -a -um *adj* single, separate; unique
singulātim *adv* singly, individually
singul·ī -ae -a *adj* single, one at a time, one by one, individual; one each, one apiece; **in singulōs diēs** on each successive day; every day, daily *(w. comp or words denoting increase or decrease):* **crēscit in diēs singulōs hostium numerus** the number of the enemy increases daily; **in singulōs hominēs** per man ‖ *mpl* individuals
singultim *adv* sobbingly, with sobs
singult·iō -īre *intr* to hiccup; to throb
singult·ō -āre -āvī -ātus *tr* to gasp out; to utter with sobs ‖ *intr* to gasp, sob
singult·us -ūs *m* sob, gasp; squirt *(of water, etc.);* death rattle
sinis·ter -tra -trum *adj* left, on the left; *(because in Roman augury the augur faced south, having the East on the left)* favorable, auspicious, lucky; *(because in Greek augury the augur faced north, having the East on his right)* unfavorable, inauspicious, unlucky; wrong, perverse, improper ‖ *mpl* soldiers on the left flank ‖ *f* left, left hand; left side; **a sinistrā** on the left ‖ *n* left side
sinisterit·ās -ātis *f* awkwardness
sinistrē *adv* badly, wrongly
sinistrōrsum *or* **sinistrōrsus** *adv* to the left
sinō sinere sīvī *or* **siī situs** *tr* to allow; **sine modo** only let, just let, if only
Sin·ōn -ōnis *m* Greek soldier who talked the Trojans into dragging the wooden horse into Troy
Sinōp·a -ae *or* **Sinōp·ē -ēs** *f* Sinope (*Greek colony on the S. coast of the Euxine or Black Sea*)

Sinuess·a -ae *f* **(Sino-)** city near the border between Latium and Campania

sīn·um -ī *n* large drinking cup

sinu·ō -āre -āvī -ātus *tr* to wind, curve; to fill out *(sails)*

sinuōs·us -a -um *adj* winding, sinuous, serpentine

sīn·us -ī *m* large drinking cup

sin·us -ūs *m* indentation, curve, fold, hollow; fold of the toga about the breast, pocket, purse; breast, bosom, lap; bay, gulf, lagoon; winding coast; valley, hollow; heart *(e.g., of a city),* interior; intimacy; **in sinū meō est** he *or* she is dear to me

sīpar·ium -(i)ī *n (theat)* curtain; **post sīparium** behind the scenes

sīp(h)·ō -ōnis *m* siphon; fire engine

sīphuncul·us -ī *m* small pipe

Sipyl·us *or* **Sipyl·os -ī** *m* mountain in Lydia on which Niobe was changed into a rock

sīquandō *or* **sī quandō** *conj* if ever

sīquidem *conj* if in fact

siremps *or* **sirempse = sī rem ipsam** *adj* the same; **sirempse lēgem iussit esse Iuppiter** Jupiter ordered the law to be the same

Sīr·ēn -ēnis *f* Siren *(sea nymph that had the power of charming sailors to their death with her song)*

Sīri·us -a -um *adj* of Sirius, of the Dog Star ‖ *m* Sirius, Dog Star *(in the constellation Canis Maior)*

sirp·e -is *n (bot)* silphium *(from which gum was extracted)*

sīr·us -ī *m* underground silo

sīs = sī vīs please, if you please

sistō sistere stitī *or* **stetī status** *tr* to cause to stand, make stand, put, place, set; to set up *(monument);* to establish; to stop, check, arrest; to put an end to; to produce in court; **pedem** *(or* **gradum)** **sistere** to halt, stop; **vadimōnium sistere** to answer bail, show up in court ‖ *refl* to present oneself, appear, come ‖ *pass* **sistī nōn potest** the crisis cannot be met, the case is hopeless ‖ *intr* to stand, rest; to stop, stay; to stand firm, last, endure; to show up in court; *(w. dat or* **contrā** *+ acc)* to stand firm against

sistrāt·us -a -um *adj* with a tambourine

sistr·um -ī *n* tambourine, rattle

Sīsyphid·ēs -ae *m* descendant of Sisyphus *(Ulysses)*

Sīsyphi·us -a -um *adj* of Sisyphus; **sanguine crētus Sīsyphiō** born of the stock of Sisyphys *(i.e., Ulysses)*

Sīsyph·us *or* **Sīsyph·os -ī** *m* Sisyphus *(son of Aeolus, king of Corinth, whose punishment in Hades was to roll a rock repeatedly up a hill)*

sitell·a -ae *f* lottery urn

Sīth·ōn -onis *adj* Thracian

Sīthon·is -idis *or* **-idos** *adj* Thracian ‖ *f* Thracian woman

Sīthoni·us -a -um *adj* Thracian ‖ *mpl* Thracians

sitīculōs·us -a -um *adj* thirsty, dry

siti·ēns -entis *adj* thirsting, thirsty; arid, parched; parching; *(w. gen)* thirsting for, eager for

sitienter *adv* thirstily, eagerly

sit·iō -īre *tr* to thirst for ‖ *intr* to be thirsty

sit·is -is *f* thirst; *(w. gen)* thirst for

sitīt·or -ōris *m* thirsty person; **sitītor aquae** one who thirsts for water

sittyb·us -ī *m* label *(giving the title of the scroll and author's name)*

situl·a -ae *f* bucket; basin, urn

sit·us -a -um *pp of* **sinō** ‖ *adj* situated, located, lying; founded; *(w.* **in** *+ abl)* resting on, dependent on

sit·us -ūs *m* position, situation, site, location; structure; neglect; mustiness; dust, dirt; idleness, inactivity, lack of use

sīve *or* **seu** *conj* or if; or; **sīve ... sīve** whether ... or

sīvī *perf of* **sinō**

smaragd·us *or* **smaragd·os -ī** *f (m)* emerald

smar·is -idis *f* a small sea fish

smīl·ax -acis *adj (bot)* smilax *(an evergreen climbing plant)*

Sminth·eūs -eī *m* epithet of Apollo

Smyrn·a -ae *f* town on W. coast of Asia Minor

sobol- = subol-

sōbriē *adv* soberly, moderately; sensibly

sōbriet·ās -ātis *f* sobriety

sobrīn·a -ae *f* cousin *(female, on the mother's side)*

sobrīn·us -ī *m* cousin *(on the mother's side)*

sōbri·us -a -um *adj* sober; temperate; sensible, reasonable

soccul·us -ī *m* small slipper

socc·us -ī *m* slipper; low shoe *(worn by actors in comedy); (fig)* comedy

soc·er *or* **soc·erus -erī** *m* father-in-law

soci·a -ae *f* associate, companion, ally, partner *(female)*

sociābil·is -is -e *adj* compatible, intimate

sociāl·is -is -e *adj* allied, confederate; nuptial, conjugal; sociable

sociāliter *adv* sociably

socienn·us -ī *m* buddy; partner

societ·ās -ātis *f* companionship, fellowship; association, society; partnership; alliance, confederacy

soci·ō -āre -āvī -ātus *tr* to unite, associate; to share

sociofraud·us -ī *m* double-crosser, heel

soci·us -a -um *adj* joint, allied, confederate; held in common, common ‖ *m* associate, companion, ally, partner ‖ *f see* **socia**

sōcordi·a -ae *f* silliness, stupidity; apathy, laziness
sōcordius *adv* too apathetically
sōc·ors -ordis *adj* silly, stupid; apathetic, lazy, inactive
Sōcrat·es -is *m* Athenian philosopher *(469–399 B.C.)*
Sōcratic·ī -ōrum *mpl* Socratics
socr·us -ūs *f* mother-in-law
sodālici·us -a -um *adj* of companionship **ll** *n* companionship, intimacy; society, secret society
sodāl·is -is *m* companion, fellow, buddy, crony; member *(of a society, priestly college, etc.);* accomplice; **sodālis Augustālis** member of a fraternity associated with the cult of Augustus
sodālit- = sodālic-
sodālit·ās -ātis *f* companionship, fellowship; society, club, association; secret society
sōdēs = sī audēs if you will, please
sōl sōlis *m* sun; sunlight, sunshine; day
sōlāciol·um -ī *n* a bit of comfort
sōlāc·ium -(i)ī *n* **(sōlāt-)** comfort, relief
sōlām·en -inis *n* comfort
sōlār·is -is -e *adj* sun; **lūmen sōlāre** sunlight, sunshine
sōlār·ium -(i)ī *n* sundial; clock; sunny spot, balcony
sōlāt- = sōlāc-
sōlāt·or -ōris *m* comforter
soldūri·ī -ōrum *mpl* retainers *(of a chieftain)*
soldus *see* **solidus**
sole·a -ae *f* sole; sandal *(with toes exposed; cf.* **sandalium);** fetter; sole *(flatfish)*
soleār·ius -(i)ī *m* sandal-maker
soleāt·us -a -um *adj* wearing sandals
soleō solēre solitus sum *intr (w. inf)* to be in the habit of, be used to; usually: *e.g.,* **solet cēnāre sērō** he usually eats late; *(w.* **cum** + *abl)* to have sex with
sol(i)d·us -a -um *adj* solid, firm, dense; whole, entire; genuine; trustworthy; resolute **ll** *n* entire sum, total; a solid; mass, substance; solid earth
solidē *adv* solidly; thoroughly, downright; firmly
solidit·ās -ātis *f* solidity
solid·ō -āre -āvī -ātus *tr* to make firm; to make dense; to strengthen
sōliferre·um -ī *n* all-iron spear
sōlistim·us -a -um *adj* **(-umus)** perfect, complete; **tripudium sōlistimum** perfectly auspicious omen
sōlitāri·us -a -um *adj* solitary, lonely
sōlitūd·ō -inis *f* loneliness; deprivation; solitude; wilderness; *(w. gen)* state of being forsaken by **ll** *fpl* desert, wilderness
solit·us -a -um *adj* usual, customary, characteristic **ll** *n* the usual, the customary; **formōsior solitō** more handsome than usual; **magis** *(or* **plūs) solitō** more than usual
sol·ium -(i)ī *n* seat, chair; throne; dominion, sway; bathtub; stone coffin
sōlivag·us -a -um *adj* roaming alone; single, solitary
sollemn·is -is -e *adj* annual, periodic; solemn, religious; usual **ll** *n* usage, practice; solemn rite, solemnity, ceremony; feat; sacrifice; festival, games *(in honor of Roman holy days)*
sollemniter *adv* solemnly, religiously
soll·ers -ertis *adj* **(sōl-)** skilled, skillful, expert, clever
sollerti·a -ae *f* **(sōl-)** skill, shrewdness; clever plan; *(w. gen)* skill in
sollicitāti·ō -ōnis *f* vexation; anxiety; incitement, instigation
sollicitē *adv* anxiously, with solicitude; diligently
sollicit·ō -āre -āvī -ātus *tr* to shake, disturb; to disquiet, annoy, molest; to worry, make anxious; to provoke, tempt; to stir up, incite to revolt
sollicitūd·ō -inis *f* anxiety, uneasiness; worry; solicitude; *(w. gen)* anxiety over
sollicit·us -a -um *adj* stirred up, stormy *(sea);* tossed *(by the waves);* troubled, disturbed, restless; solicitous, anxious, worried; incited to revolt
sollif- = sōlif-
sollist- = sōlist-
soloecism·us -ī *m* mistake in grammar, solecism
Sol·ō(n) -ōnis *m* Solon *(famous Athenian legislator c. 640–560 B.C.)*
sōl·or -ārī -ātus sum *tr* to console; to relieve, mitigate *(fear, etc.)*
sōlstiāl·is -is -e *adj* of the summer solstice; midsummer's; solar
sōlstit·ium -(i)ī *n* summer solstice, midsummer, summer heat
sōlum *adv* only, merely, barely; **nōn sōlum … sed etiam** not only … but also
sol·um -ī *n* bottom, ground, floor; soil, land, country; sole *(of foot, shoe)*
sōl·us -a -um *adj* only, single, sole, alone; lonely, solitary
solūtē *adv* loosely, freely, without hindrance; negligently; without vigor
solūti·ō -ōnis *f* loosening; payment
solūt·us -a -um *adj* loose, untied, unbandaged; negligent; free; fluent; unrhythmical; uncontrolled; exempt, free; unbiased; unbridled
sol·vō -vere -vī *or* **-uī -ūtus** *tr* to loosen, untie *(a cord);* to release, untie, free; to dissolve, break up; to detach, disengage; to unlock, open; to melt; to relax *(the body);* to smooth, soothe; to impair, weaken, destroy; to acquit; to accomplish, fulfill; to pay, pay off; to solve, explain; to break *(a siege);* to break down

(a barrier); to undergo *(punishment);* to get rid of *(feelings);* to loosen *(the bowels);* to remove *(surgical dressings);* to unharness, unyoke *(animals);* to disperse into the atmosphere, dissipate; to enervate, sap the strength of *(a person);* **crīnēs solvere** to let down the hair *(in mourning);* **nāvem** *(or* **rātem) solvere** to cast off, set sail; **ōra solvere** to open the mouth *(to speak)* **II** to melt, dissolve **II** *intr* to weigh anchor, set sail

Solym·a -ōrum *npl* Jerusalem

Solym·us -a -um *adj* of Jerusalem **II** *mpl* mountain tribe, supposed to have given its name to Jerusalem

somniculōsē *adv* sleepily, drowsily

somniculōs·us -a -um *adj* sleepy, drowsy

somnif·er -era -erum *adj* soporific, sleep-inducing; deadly *(poison)*

somni·ō -āre -āvī -ātus *tr* to dream of; to day-dream about, imagine; **somnium somniāre** to have a dream **II** *intr* to dream; to daydream

somn·ium -(i)ī *n* dream, vision; day-dream

somn·us -ī *m* sleep; night; sleep of death; indolence

sonābil·is -is -e *adj* noisy

sonip·ēs -edis *adj* loud-hoofed **II** *m* steed

sonit·us -ūs *m* sound, noise, clang

sonivi·us -a -um *adj* noisy

son·ō -āre -uī -itus *tr* to utter, say, sound, express; to denote, mean; to sound like **II** *intr* to sound; to ring, resound, make a noise; to be spoken of as

son·or -ōris *m* sound, noise, clang

sonōr·us -a -um *adj* sonorous, loud, noisy, clanging

sōns sontis *adj* guilty, criminal; *(w. abl of the crime)* guilty of **II** *m* guilty one, criminal

sontic·us -a -um *adj* serious, critical

sonuī *perf of* **sonō**

-son·us -a -um *adj/ suf denotes "sounding," e.g.:* **raucisonus** hoarse-sounding

son·us -ī *m* sound, noise; tone

sophi·a -ae *f* wisdom

sophist·ēs -ae *m* sophist

Sophocl·ēs -is *or* **-ī** Greek writer of tragedies *(c. 495–406 B.C.)*

Sophoclē·us -a -um *adj* Sophoclean

soph·us -a -um *adj* wise **II** *m* wise man, sage

sōp·iō -īre -īvī *or* **-iī -ītus** *tr* to put to sleep; to stun, knock unconscious; *(fig)* to calm, settle, lull

sop·or -ōris *m* deep sleep; stupor; apathy; sleeping potion

sopōrāt·us -a -um *adj* stupefied; unconscious; buried in sleep; allayed *(grief);* soporific

sopōrif·er -era -erum *adj* sleep-inducing

sopōr·us -a -um *adj* drowsy

Sōract·e -is *n* mountain in Etruria about 25 miles N.E. of Rome

sōrac·um -ī *n* chest, hamper

sorb·eō -ēre -uī -itus *tr* to suck in, gulp down; to absorb; *(fig)* to swallow

sorbil(l)·ō -āre -āvī -ātus *tr* to sip

sorbilō *adv* drop by drop, bit by bit

sorbiti·ō -ōnis *f* broth

sorb·um -ī *n* **(sorv-)** Juneberry

sorb·us -ī *f* **(sorv-)** Juneberry tree

sord·eō -ēre *intr* to be dirty, be shabby; to appear worthless

sord·ēs -is *f* dirt, filth; shabbiness, squalor; greed, stinginess; moral turpitude; meanness *(of behavior);* low rank, low condition; rabble, scum; **sordēs verbōrum** vulgarity **II** *fpl* rags, dark clothes *(often worn as a sign of mourning)*

sord·ēscō -ēscere -uī *intr* to become dirty, become soiled

sordidāt·us -a -um *adj* in shabby clothes *(esp. as sign of mourning)*

sordidē *adv* vilely; greedily

sordidul·us -a -um *adj* rather soiled, rather shabby; *(fig)* low

sordid·us -a -um *adj* dirty, filthy; shabby; soiled, stained; dressed in mourning clothes; low *(rank);* vulgar

sorditūd·ō -inis *f* dirt, filth

sōr·ex -icis *m* shrewmouse

sōricīn·us -a -um *adj* squealing like mice

sōrīt·ēs -ae *m* sorites *(logical conclusion drawn from cumulative arguments)*

sor·or -ōris *f* sister; cousin; companion, playmate; **sorōrēs doctae** Muses; **sorōrēs trēs** three Fates; **sorōrēs trīstēs** gloomy Fates

sorōricīd·a -ae *m* murderer of a sister

sorōri·us -a -um *adj* sister's, of a sister; sisterly; **stuprum sorōrium** incest with a sister

sors sortis *f* lot; casting of lots, decision by lot; prophecy; fate, destiny, lot in life; portion, share; sort, kind

sōrsum *see* **seōrsum**

sortileg·us -a -um *adj* prophetic **II** *m* soothsayer, fortuneteller

sort·iō -īre -īvī *or* **-iī -ītus** *or* **sort·ior -īrī -ītus sum** *tr* to cast lots for; to allot, assign by lot, appoint by lot; to obtain by lot; to choose, select; to share, divide; to receive, get by chance **II** *intr* to cast *or* draw lots

sortīti·ō -ōnis *f* drawing lots, determining by lots

sortītō *adv* by lot; by fate

sortīt·us -ūs *m* lottery

Sosi·ī -ōrum *mpl* the Sosii *(two brothers famous as booksellers in Rome at the time of Horace)*

sōsp·es -itis *adj* safe and sound; auspicious, lucky

sōspit·a -ae *f* preserver *(epithet of Juno)*

sōspitāl·is -is -e *adj* beneficial
sōspit·ō -āre *tr* to preserve, protect
sōt·ēr -ēris *m* savior, protector
sōtēri·a -ōrum *npl* party for a person recovering from an illness
Sp. *abbr* **Spurius** *(Roman first name, praenomen)*
spād·īx -īcis *m* chestnut-brown horse
spad·ō -ōnis *m* eunuch
spar·gō -gere -sī -sus *tr* to scatter, sprinkle, strew; to disperse; to disseminate; to spot, dapple
sparsi·ō -ōnis *f* sprinkling
spars·us -a -um *pp of* **spargō** ‖ *adj* freckled, spotty
Spart·a -ae *or* **Spart·ē -ēs** *f* Sparta *(capital of Laconia)*
Spartac·us -ī *m* Thracian gladiator who led a revolt of gladiators against Rome in 73–71 B.C.
Spartān·us -a -um *adj* Spartan ‖ *m* a Spartan
Spartiāt·ēs -ae *m* Spartan
Spartiātic·us *or* **Spartic·us -a -um** *adj* Spartan
spart·um *or* **spart·on -ī** *n* Spanish broom *(fibrous plant used in making ropes, nets, etc.)*
sparul·us -ī *m* bream *(fish)*
spar·us *m or* **spar·um -ī** *n* hunting spear
spath·a -ae *f* spatula; broad two-edged sword
spati·or -ārī -ātus sum *intr* to stroll, take a walk; to walk solemnly; to spread out
spatiōsē *adv* extensively; long
spatiōs·us -a -um *adj* extensive; spacious; wide; *(of time)* long, lengthy; *(of vowel)* long; *(w. advl force)* with its *(his, etc.)* great size
spat·ium -(i)ī *n* space, room, extent; open space, public square; distance *(between two points)*; walk, promenade *(place)*; lap *(of a race)*; racetrack; interval, period; time, opportunity; *(pros)* measure, quantity
speci·ēs -ēī *f* sight, view; outward appearance; outline, shape; fine appearance, beauty; deceptive appearance, show, semblance, pretense, pretext; resemblance; display, splendor; apparition; image, statue; idea, notion; reputation; species, sort; *(leg)* specific legal situation *or* case; **ad** *(or* **in)** **speciem** for show; **in speciem** *(or* **per speciem)** as a pretext, for the sake of appearances; **prīmā speciē** at first sight; **speciē** outwardly, to all appearances; **speciē** *(w. gen)* **1** in the guise of; **2** on the pretext of
specill·um -ī *n* probe *(surgical instrument)*
specim·en -inis *n* mark, sign, proof; example; model, ideal
speciō specere spexī spectus *tr* to look at
speciōsē *adv* splendidly
speciōs·us -a -um *adj* handsome, good-looking, beautiful; plausible; specious
spectābil·is -is -e *adj* visible; remarkable
spectāc(u)l·um -ī *n* sight, spectacle; public performance, show; stage play; theater
spectām·en -inis *n* sign, proof
spectāti·ō -ōnis *f* observation, view; examining, testing
spectāt·or -ōris *m* observer; spectator; critic, judge ‖ *mpl* audience
spectātr·īx -īcis *f* onlooker, observer; spectator *(female)*
spectāt·us -a -um *adj* tried, tested, proved; esteemed, distinguished
specti·ō -ōnis *f* observing the auspices; right to take the auspices
spect·ō -āre -āvī -ātus *tr* to observe, watch; to face in the direction of; to consider; to bear in mind; to aim at, tend toward; to examine, test
spectr·um -ī *n* specter, apparition
specul·a -ae *f* lookout, watchtower; summit; **in speculīs** on the lookout
spēcul·a -ae *f* slight hope; glimmer of hope
speculābund·us -a -um *adj* on the lookout
speculār·is -is -e *adj* transparent ‖ *n* windowpane *(of mica)*, window
speculāt·or -ōris *m* spy; explorer
speculātōri·us -a -um *adj* for spying, for reconnaissance ‖ *f* reconnaissance ship
speculātr·īx -īcis *f* spy *(female)*
specul·or -ārī -ātus sum *tr* to reconnoiter, observe, watch for
specul·um -ī *n* mirror *(made of polished metal)*
spec·us -ūs *m (n)* cave, cavern; grotto; *(any artificial excavation)* hole, pit, tunnel, ditch; cavity *(of a wound, etc.)*
spēlae·um -ī *n* **(-lē-)** den, cave
spēlunc·a -ae *f* cave
spērābil·is -is -e *adj* to be hoped for
spērāt·us -a -um *adj* hoped for, desired ‖ *f* fiancée
Sperchē·is -idos *adj (fem only)* of the Spercheus River
Sperchē·us -ī *m* **(-chi-)** Spercheus *(large river in Thessaly)*
spernō spernere sprēvī sprētus *tr* to spurn, scorn, reject; to speak disdainfully of; to separate, dissociate
spēr·ō -āre -āvī -ātus *tr* to hope for, expect, look forward to; to trust, trust in; to anticipate, await in fear; *(w. acc & inf; also w. nom & inf in imitation of the Greek; also w.* **ut** + *subj)* I hope that; **id quod nōn spērō** I hope that is not the case, I hope not ‖ *intr* to hope; **bene spērāre** to be optimistic; **nōn spērō** I hope not; **ut spērō** hopefully
spēs speī *f* hope; expectation; anticipation, apprehension *(of evil)*; person *or* thing on which hopes are based, *e.g.:* **Gāius Marius spēs subsidium patriae** Gaius

Marius, the hope and safeguard of our country; *(applied to one's offspring)* one's hopes for the future, *e.g.:* **mea cārissima fīliola et spēs reliqua nostra** my dearest little daughter and our only remaining hope; **in spē** in prospect; **in spē** *(w. gen)* with the prospect of; **in spem** *(w. gen)* so as to give the promise of; **praeter spem** beyond all expectation

sp(h)aer·a -ae *f* sphere, globe; ball; one of the imaginary spheres in which the heavenly bodies were supposed to travel around the earth; working model of the universe

sphaeristēr·ium -iī *n* ball field, ball court, tennis court

Sphin·x -gis *or* **-gos** *f* sphinx *(esp. the Sphinx of Boeotia whose riddle Oedipus was able to solve);* the Sphinx of Egypt at Giza

spīc·a -ae *f* point; ear *(of grain);* tuft, top, head *(of plants)*

spīce·us -a -um *adj* made of ears of grain

spīcul·um -ī *n* point; sting; dart, arrow

spīc·um -ī *n* ear *(of grain)*

spīn·a -ae *f* thorn; thornbush; prickle *(of animals);* spike *(of asparagus);* backbone, spine; *(fig)* thorny question

spīnēt·um -ī *n* thorn hedge, thorny thicket

spīne·us -a -um *adj* made of thorns

spīnif·er *or* **spīnig·er -era -erum** *adj* prickly, thorny

spīnōs·us -a -um *adj* thorny, prickly; *(fig)* thorny, difficult; obscure *(style)*

spint·ēr -ēris *m* bracelet

Spinth·ēr -ēris *m* Roman family name *(cognomen)*

spintri·a -ae *m* male prostitute *(given to particularly perverted acts)*

spinturnīc·ium -iī *n* bird of ill omen

spīn·us -ī *or* -ūs *f* thornbush

spīr·a -ae *f* coil *(of serpent);* chin strap

spīrābil·is -is -e *adj* good to breathe, life-giving *(air)*

spīrācul·um -ī *n* pore; vent

spīrāment·um -ī *n* vent; air hole; windpipe; breathing space, pause; **animae spīrāmenta** lungs

spīrit·us -ūs *m* breathing, breath; breeze, wind; air, air current; wind of the bowels; breath of life, life; inspiration; spirit, soul; character, courage; enthusiasm, vigor; pride, arrogance; morale; *(gram)* aspiration; **extrēmus** *(or* **ultimus)** **spīritus** one's last breath; **spīritum dūcere** to take a breath

spīr·ō -āre -āvī -ātus *tr* to breathe, blow; to exhale; to give off the odor of, smell of; to aspire to, aim at **‖** *intr* to breathe; to be alive; to breathe after exertion, recover one's breath; *(of the wind)* to blow, blow auspiciously, be favorable; *(of things)* to give off an odor; *(of a quality)* to emanate; to have poetic inspiration

spissāment·um -ī *n* stopper, plug

spissāt·us -a -um *adj* condensed, concentrated

spissē *adv* thickly, closely, tightly; with effort, slowly

spissēsc·ō -ere *intr* to condense, become thick, become more compact

spissigrad·us -a -um *adj* slow-paced

spiss·ō -āre -āvī -ātus *tr* to condense, concentrate; to pack tightly; to intensify *(efforts)*

spiss·us -a -um *adj* thick; tight; dense; solid, compact; slow, sluggish; late; closely-woven, thick; packed, crowded; *(of blows, kisses)* coming thick and fast

splēn splēnis *m* spleen

splend·eō -ēre *intr* to be clear and bright; to shine, gleam; to become glossy; to be illustrious, be glorious; to be resplendent

splendēsc·ō -ere *intr* to become bright, begin to shine; *(w. abl)* to take on luster from

splendidē *adv* splendidly, brilliantly

splendid·us -a -um *adj* clear and bright, gleaming, glistening, sparkling; spotless, noble *(character);* splendid; sumptuous; showy; illustrious

splend·or -ōris *m* splendor; brightness, brilliance; clearness

splēniāt·us -a -um *adj* wearing a patch

splēn·ium -iī *n* patch

spoliāti·ō -ōnis *f* stripping, plundering; unjust deprivation *(of honor, dignity);* ousting *(from office)*

spoliāt·or -ōris *m,* **spoliātr·īx -īcis** *f* despoiler, robber

spoliāt·us -a -um *adj* stripped, robbed

spoli·ō -āre -āvī -ātus *tr* to strip; to pillage, plunder, rob; to take away *(possessions)*

spol·ium -iī *n* hide, skin; spoils, booty, loot **‖** *npl* arms, equipment, etc., stripped from an enemy; **spolia opīma** the spoils taken by a Roman general from the enemy leader he had killed in single combat; **spolia secunda** lesser spoils

spond·a -ae *f* bedframe, sofa frame; bed, sofa

spondā(u)l·ium -(i)ī *n* ritual hymn accompanied by a flute

spondeō spondēre spopondī spōnsus *tr* to promise solemnly, pledge, vow; to promise in marriage; to vouch for, back up **‖** *intr (leg)* to give a guarantee, put up bail; *(w.* **prō** *+ abl)* to vouch for

spondē·us -ī *m (pros)* spondee *(foot consisting of two long syllables)*

spondyl·us -ī *m* a kind of shellfish, mussel

spongi·a -ae *f* **(-ge-)** sponge; sponge eraser; quilted corslet

spōns·a -ae *f* fiancée

spōnsāl·ia -ium *npl* engagement; engagement party

spōnsi·ō -ōnis *f* solemn promise; guarantee; bet; *(leg)* agreement between two parties that the loser pay a certain sum to the winner

spōns·or -ōris *m* guarantor, surety; **Ammonius spōnsor prōmissōrum Cleopatrae** Ammon, who backs up the promises of Cleopatra

spōns·us -a -um *pp of* **spondeō** ‖ *m* fiancé, bridegroom ‖ *f* fiancée ‖ *n* agreement, engagement

spōns·us -ūs *m* contract

sponte *(abl only) f (of persons, mostly with poss adj)* of one's own accord, voluntarily, deliberately, purposely; by oneself, unaided; *(of things)* of itself, spontaneously; on its own account, for its own sake; **meā (suā,** *etc.***) sponte** of my own *(his own, her own, etc.)* accord; **sponte aetātis** as a consequence of one's years; **sponte nātūrae (suae)** of its own nature, naturally, spontaneously; **suā sponte** considered in itself, inherently, essentially

spopondī *perf of* **spondeō**

sport·a -ae *f* plaited basket

sportell·a -ae *f* little basket

sportul·a -ae *f* little basket *(in which gifts of food were given by the patron to his clients);* dole, present *(of food or money);* gift

sprēt·or -ōris *m* despiser, scorner

sprētus *pp of* **spernō**

sprēvī *perf of* **spernō**

spūm·a -ae *f* foam, froth; hair dye; **spūmās agere ōre** to froth at the mouth

spūmāt·us -a -um *adj* covered with foam

spūmēsc·ō -ere *intr* to grow foamy

spūme·us -a -um *adj* foaming

spūmif·er *or* **spūmig·er -era -erum** *adj* foaming

spūm·ō -āre -āvī -ātum *intr* to foam, froth; *(of places, things)* to be covered with foam; **equī terga spūmantia** the back of the horse soaked with sweat

spūmōs·us -a -um *adj* full of foam, foaming; bombastic

spuō spuere spuī spūtus *tr* to spit, spit out ‖ *intr* to spit

spurcāt·us -a -um *adj* foul, filthy

spurcē *adv* filthily; offensively; in filthy language

spurcidic·us -a -um *adj* foul-mouthed, smutty, obscene

spurcific·us -a -um *adj* smutty

spurciti·a -ae *or* **spurciti·ēs -ēī** *f* filth, smut

spurc·ō -āre -āvī -ātus *tr* to make filthy, foul up; to defile

spurc·us -a -um *adj* filthy, nasty, impure, unclean; foul *(weather)*

spūtātilic·us -a -um *adj* deserving to be spit on, contemptible, disgusting

spūtāt·or -ōris *m* spitter

spūt·ō -āre -āvī -ātus *tr* to spit, spit out; to avert *(by spitting)*

spūt·um -ī *n* spit, sputum

squāl·eō -ēre -uī *intr* to be rough, be scaly; to be coated, be clotted, be stiff; to be covered with filth, be caked with mud; *(of clouds, shade)* to be dark, be murky; *(of places)* to be covered with weeds, be overgrown; *(of land)* to lie waste *(from neglect, barrenness); (of persons)* to wear mourning clothes

squālidē *adv* harshly, roughly

squālid·us -a -um *adj* rough, scaly; stiff, caked with dirt; squalid; in mourning; coarse *(speech);* barren, waste *(land)*

squāl·or -ōris *m* squalor, dirtiness; desolation; uncouthness *(of style);* squalid clothes *(as a sign of mourning)*

squal·us -ī *m* a type of sea fish

squām·a -ae *f* scale *(of fish, serpent, etc.);* scale armor; scale-like yellow band on the abdomen of a bee

squāme·us -a -um *adj* scaly

squāmif·er *or* **squāmig·er -era -erum** *adj* scaly ‖ *mpl* fish

squāmōs·us -a -um *adj* covered with scales, scaly

squill·a -ae *f* **(scill-)** shrimp, crayfish

st *interj* shhh!, ssst!

stabilīment·um -ī *n* support, prop; *(fig)* mainstay

stabil·iō -īre -īvī -ītus *tr* to stabilize; to establish firmly

stabil·is -is -e *adj* stable, firm, steady; steadfast, unwavering, immutable

stabilit·ās -ātis *f* stability, firmness, steadiness, durability

stabiliter *adv* firmly; steadfastly

stabul·ō -āre -āvī -ātus *tr* to stable *or* house *(animals)* ‖ *intr* to have a stall

stabul·um -ī *n* stable, stall; lair; hut; brothel; *(coll)* flea bag, cheap lodgings

stact·a -ae *or* **stact·ē -ēs** *f* myrrh oil

stad·ium -iī *n* furlong; running track, stadium; stade *(= 625 feet)*

Stagīr·a -ōrum *npl* town in Macedonia, birthplace of Aristotle

Stagīrīt·ēs -ae *m* Aristotle

stāgn·ō -āre -āvī -ātus *tr* to overflow, inundate ‖ *intr* to form a pool; to be inundated

stāgn·um -ī *n (expanse of water, natural or artificial)* pool, lake, lagoon, swamp, straits; alloy of silver and lead ‖ *npl* the depths

stalagm·ium -(i)ī *n* eardrop, earring *(w. pendant)*

stām·en -inis *n* vertical threads of a loom, warp; thread; string *(of an instrument);* fillet *(worn by priests)*

stāmine·us -a -um *adj* consisting of threads; wrapped in threads
stann·um -ī *n* tin
Stat·a -ae *f* a goddess who gave protection against fire
statāri·us -a -um *adj* standing, stationary; *(of plays, actors, speakers)* free from violent action, calm, quiet ‖ *mpl* actors in a refined type of comedy ‖ *f* refined comedy
statēr·a -ae *f* scales; **statēra aurificis** goldsmith's scales
staticul·us -ī *m* pose
statim *adv* at once, on the spot
stati·ō -ōnis *f* standing still, stationary position; station, post; position; residence; anchorage; **in statiōne** at one's post, on guard ‖ *fpl* sentries
Stāt·ius -(i)ī *m* Publius Papinius Statius *(poet of the Silver Age of Latin literature, c.* A.D. *40–96)*
statīv·us -a -um *adj* stationary; **castra statīva** bivouac ‖ *npl* bivouac; **cum diē statīvōrum** with a rest-day *(on the march)*
stat·or -ōris *m* attendant *(of provincial governor, later of the emperor)* ‖ **Stator** *m* cult title of Jupiter *(the Stayer from flight)*
statu·a -ae *f* statue
statūm·en -inis *n* rib *(of a hull)*
stat·uō -uere -uī -ūtus *tr* to cause to stand; to bring to a stop; to fix in the ground, plant; to erect, build; to set up *(a statue),* set up a statue of; to found *(a city);* to establish *(a practice, precedent, principle, state of affairs);* to decide, settle *(matters);* to decree; to strengthen, support; to appoint *(a time, place); (w. double acc)* to appoint *(s.o.)* as; to determine, fix, set *(a price, payment; penalty, punishment);* to draw up, arrange *(a battle line); (w.* **utrum)** to make up one's mind whether, decide whether; *(w. inf)* to decide to, resolve to; *(w.* **ut** + *subj)* to decide that; *(w. pred. noun or adj)* to judge, deem; **statuere fīnem** *(w. dat)* set a limit to
statūr·a -ae *f* stature, height; **brevis (longae) statūrae homō** a person of short (tall) stature
stat·us -a -um *pp of* **sistō** ‖ *adj* fixed, set *(times, places, seasons);* regular, average, normal
stat·us -ūs *m* position; posture; social standing, rank, prestige; state of affairs, situation, condition, status; *(gram)* mood of the verb; *(leg)* legal position *(in regard to rights, obligations); (mil)* position; *(rhet)* point at issue; **status reī pūblicae** type of government, form of constitution
statūt·us -a -um *adj* upstanding
steg·a -ae *f (naut)* deck
stel(l)i·ō -ōnis *m* newt, lizard *(with spotted back)*
stell·a -ae *f* star; constellation; starfish; **stella comāns** *(or* **crīnīta)** comet; **stella diurna** Lucifer; **stella errāns** planet; **stella dē caelō lāpsa** shooting star; **stella marīna** starfish; **stellae quīnque** the five *(recognized)* planets *(i.e., Mars, Mercury, Venus, Jupiter, Saturn)*
stell·āns -antis *adj* starry; star-shaped, starlike
stellāt·us -a -um *adj* set with stars, starry; made into a star; **stellātus Argus** *(fig)* Argus with bright eyes
stellif·er *or* **stellig·er -era -erum** *adj* starbearing, starry
stemm·a -atis *n* genealogical tree, family tree, lineage ‖ *npl* antiquity, history
stercore·us -a -um *adj (vulg)* full of shit
stercor·ō -āre -āvī -ātus *tr* to fertilize, manure
sterculīnum *see* **sterquilīnium**
sterc·us -oris *n* manure, dung
steril·is -is -e *adj* sterile, barren; causing barrenness, blighting; empty, bare; unprofitable; unrequited; wild *(tree)*
sterilit·ās -ātis *f* sterility
stern·āx -ācis *adj* bucking *(horse)*
sternō sternere strāvī strātus *tr* to strew, spread; to cover *(couch, horse)* with a cloth; to pave *(a road, floor);* to strike down, lay low, slay; to raze; to overwhelm, defeat utterly; to flatten, smooth; to calm, calm down; **trīclīnium sternere** to set the table; ‖ *pass* to stretch out *(on the ground)*
sternūment·um -ī *n* sneeze
sternu·ō -ere -ī *tr* to give *(an omen)* by sneezing ‖ *intr* to sneeze
Sterop·ē -ēs *f* one of the Pleiades
Sterop·ēs -ae *m* a Cyclops working in Vulcan's blacksmith shop
sterquilīn·ium -(i)ī *or* **sterquilīn·um -ī** *or* **sterculīn·um -ī** *n* manure pile
stert·ō -ere *intr* to snore
Stēsichor·us -ī *m* Greek lyric poet of Himera in Sicily *(c. 640–555* B.C.*)*
stetī *perf of* **stō**
Sthenel·us -ī *m* king of Mycenae, son of Perseus, and father of Eurystheus ‖ king of the Ligurians and father of Cycnus, who was changed into a swan
stibad·ium -(i)ī *n* semicircular seat *or* couch
stigm·a -atis *n* mark, brand; stigma *(of disgrace)*
stigmati·ās -ae *m* branded runaway slave
stigmōs·us -a -um *adj* branded
still·a -ae *f* drop; mere drop
stillicid·ium -(i)ī *n* drip, dripping
still·ō -āre -āvī -ātus *tr & intr* to drip
stil·us -ī *m* stylus *(pointed instrument for writing);* composition; style

stimulāti·ō -ōnis *f* stimulation, incitement
stimulātr·īx -īcis *f* a tease *(female)*
stimule·us -a -um *adj* of goads
stimul·ō -āre -āvī -ātus *tr* to goad, torment; to spur on, incite, excite
stimul·us -ī *m* goad, prick; *(fig)* stimulus, incentive, spur; *(mil)* pointed stake concealed below the ground
stingu·ō -ere *tr* to extinguish
stīpāti·ō -ōnis *f* crowd, throng
stīpāt·or -ōris *m* attendant, bodyguard ‖ *mpl* retinue
stīpendiāri·us -a -um *adj* liable to taxes, tributary ‖ *mpl* tributary peoples; mercenary troops
stīpend·ium -(i)ī *n* tax, tribute, tariff; *(mil)* pay; military service; year's service; campaign; **ēmererī stīpendia** to have served out one's term; **ēmeritīs stīpendiīs** at the end of one's military service, at discharge; **merēre** *(or* **merērī)** **stīpendia** to serve in the army
stīp·es -itis *m* log; trunk; branch, tree; *(pej)* blockhead
stīp·ō -āre -āvī -ātus *tr* to pack, cram, crowd; to crowd around, accompany in a groups
stips stipis *f* donation, gift; alms
stipul·a -ae *f* stalk, blade; stubble; *(mus)* reed pipe
stipulāti·ō -ōnis *f* agreement, bargain; *(leg)* formal promise
stipulātiuncul·a -ae *f* insignificant promise
stipulāt·us -a -um *adj* promised
stipul·or -ārī -ātus sum *tr (of a buyer)* to demand a guarantee from *(the seller that the purchase is fair by asking the formal question "spondēsne? dabisne?," i.e., "do you promise? will you give?")* ‖ *intr (leg)* to make a solemn promise *(by answering "spondeō, dabō," i.e., "I promise, I shall give")*
stīri·a -ae *f* icicle
stirpitus *adv* by the roots
stirp·s *or* **stirp·ēs** *or* **stirp·is -is** *f (m)* stock, stem, stalk; root; plant, shrub; race, lineage; offspring, descendant; character, nature; source, origin, beginning, foundation
stīv·a -ae *f* plow handle
stlattāri·us -a -um *adj* imported
stō stāre stetī statum *intr* to stand; *(of buildings, cities)* to remain standing; to last, endure; to stand firm; to stand upright; *(of hair)* to stand on end; *(of eyes)* to remain fixed; *(of battle)* to continue; *(of a ship)* to be moored, ride at anchor; to be motionless; to be stuck; *(w.* **ex)** to consist of; *(w. abl or* **in** *+ abl)* to depend on, rest with; *(w.* **per** *+ acc of person)* to depend on, be due to, be the fault of, thanks to; **per mē stetit quīn** *(or* **nē** *or* **quōminus)** **proeliō dīmicārētur** it was due to me that there was no battle; thanks to me, there was no battle; **per mē stetit ut** it was due to me that ‖ *v impers (w. inf)* it is a fixed resolve; **mihi stat** *(w. inf)* it is my fixed resolve to, I have made up my mind to
Stōic·a -ae *f* Stoic philosophy
Stōicē *adv* stoically, like a Stoic
Stōic·us -a -um *adj & m* Stoic
stol·a -ae *f* dress *(female outer garment, counterpart of the male toga);* ceremonial gown *(worn by musicians)*
stolāt·us -a -um *adj* wearing a **stola;** *(fig)* ladylike
stolidē *adv* stupidly, brutishly
stolid·us -a -um *adj* dull, stupid, slow, insensitive; *(of things)* inert
stomach·or -ārī -ātus sum *tr* to be indignant at ‖ *intr* to be angry, fume
stomachōsē *adv* irritably
stomachōsius *adv* rather angrily
stomachōs·us -a -um *adj* irritable
stomach·us -ī *m* stomach; esophagus, gullet; taste; appetite; irritation, annoyance; **stomachum movēre** *(or* **facere)** to cause annoyance; **stomachus bonus** good appetite; good humor, patience
store·a *or* **stori·a -ae** *f* straw mat
strab·ō -ōnis *m* squinter ‖ **Strabō** *see* **Pompēius**
strāg·ēs -is *f* devastation; heap; pile of debris; havoc; massacre
strāgul·us -a -um *adj* covering, serving as a covering ‖ *n* rug, carpet; bedspread; horse blanket
strām·en -inis *n* straw
strāment·um -ī *n* straw; covering; saddlecloth; **strāmentum agreste** straw bed
strāmine·us -a -um *adj* straw, made of straw
strangul·ō -āre -āvī -ātus *tr* to strangle; to suffocate; to constrict; to stifle
strangūri·a -ae *f* strangury *(difficulty with urinating)*
stratēgēm·a -atis *n* stratagem; ruse
strateg·us -ī *m* commander, general
stratiōtic·us -a -um *adj* soldierly
strāt·um -ī *n* quilt, blanket; bed, couch; horse blanket, saddlecloth; pavement; **strāta viārum** paved streets
strātūr·a -ae *f* paving *(of roads)*
strāt·us -a -um *pp of* **sternō** ‖ *n see* **strātum**
strāvī *perf of* **sternō**
strēn(u)·a -ae *f* good-luck omen; lucky gift sent at the New Year; **strēnuārum commercium** exchange of gifts
strēnuē *adv* briskly, quickly, actively, strenuously
strēnuit·ās -ātis *f* briskness, vigor, liveliness
strēnu·us -a -um *adj* brisk, vigorous, active; fast *(ship);* restless

strepit·ō -āre *intr* to be noisy; to clatter; to rustle

strepit·us -ūs *m* noise, din, racket; crash, bang, clank; rumble; rustle; creak, squeak

strep·ō -ere -uī -itus *tr* to shout ‖ *intr* to make a noise *(of any kind);* to rattle, clatter, clang; to rumble; to rustle; to creak, squeak; to roar; to hum; to murmur; *(of muscial instruments)* to sound, blare; *(of places)* to ring, resound, be filled

stri·a -ae *f* groove, channel, furrow

striāt·us -a -um *adj* grooved, fluted, furrowed ‖ *f* scallop *(marine mollusk)*

strictim *adv* superficially, cursorily

strictūr·a -ae *f* mass of hardened iron

strict·us -a -um *pp of* **stringō** ‖ *adj* close, tight, narrow

strīd·eō -ēre -ī *or* **strīd·ō -ere -ī** *intr* to make a high-pitched noise; to hiss, whistle; to whizz; to shriek, scream; to grate; to buzz; *(of a wound)* to gurgle; *(of wings)* to whirr

strīd·or -ōris *m* shrill *or* high-pitched sound (*e.g. of elephants, apes, monkeys, witches, rigging*); hiss *(of a snake, roasting meat);* whizzing; shriek, scream; whine *(of a saw);* harsh noise, grating *(of teeth, chain, etc.);* creak, squeak *(of door);* whirring *(of wings);* whistle *(of wind);* chirping *(of locusts, crickets, cicadas)*

strīdul·us -a -um *adj* shrill, strident; hissing, whistling; creaking

strigil·is -is *f* scraper, strigil *(used by athletes to scrape off oil, mud, etc.)*

strig·ō -āre *intr* to stop *(in ploughing);* to give out

strigōs·us -a -um *adj* lean, shriveled; bald *(style)*

stringō stringere strīnxī strictus *tr* to strip, clip; to draw *(a sword);* to draw tight, tie tight; to string *(a bow);* to pick *(fruit);* to strip off *(leaves);* to press together, compress; to graze, scratch; to border on; to touch lightly on *(a subject); (of a river)* to erode

string·or -ōris *m* **(strīg-)** twinge, shock

strix strigis *f* owl, screech owl

stroph·a -ae *f* **(strof-)** trick, feat of skill

Strophad·es -um *fpl* island home of the Harpies

strophiār·ius -(i)ī *m* bra-maker

stroph·ium -iī *n* brassiere, bra; head band

Stroph·ius -(i)ī *m* king of Phocis and father of Pylades

structil·is -is -e *adj* for building; **caementum structile** concrete

struct·or -ōris *m* builder, mason, carpenter; carver *(at table)*

structūr·a -ae *f* construction; structure

structus *pp of* **struō**

stru·ēs -is *f* pile, heap; row of sacrificial cakes

stru·īx -īcis *f* heap, pile

strūm·a -ae *f* tumor, swollen gland

strūmōs·us -a -um *adj (med)* scrofulous

stru·ō -ere -xī -ctus *tr* to build, erect; to deploy *(troops);* to arrange, regulate; to occasion; to compose; to construct *(words);* to plot, design, aim at; to load with

strūt(h)e·us -a -um *adj* **mālum strūtheum** *n (a small variety of)* quince

strūthocamēl·us -ī *m* ostrich

struxī *perf of* **struō**

Strȳm·ōn -onis *or* **-onos** *m* river on the Macedonian-Thracian border

Strȳmon·is -idis *f* Thracian woman

Strȳmoni·us -a -um *adj* of the Strymon, Thracian

stud·eō -ēre -uī *tr* to desire, be eager for; to make *(s.th.)* one's concern ‖ *intr (w. dat)* **1** to be eager for, be keen on, be interested in, be enthusiastic about; **2** to take pains with, busy oneself with, apply oneself to; **3** to pursue; **4** to study; **5** to be a partisan of

studiōsē *adv* eagerly, enthusiastically, diligently

studiōs·us -a -um *adj* eager, keen, enthusiastic; studious; *(w. gen)* partial to *(a person or cause); (w. gen or dat)* eager for, keen on, interested in, enthusiastic about, devoted to, fond of, desirous of; **litterārum studiōsus** studious

stud·ium -(i)ī *n* eagerness, keenness, enthusiasm; devotion *(to a person);* support, goodwill *(esp. in a political sense),* party spirit; study; *(w. gen)* eagerness for, enthusiasm for; *(w.* **ad** *or* **in** *+ acc)* enthusiasm for ‖ *npl* studies; **studia contrāria** opposite parties

stultē *adv* foolishly

stultiloquenti·a -ae *f or* **stultiloqu·ium -(i)ī** *n* silly talk

stultiloqu·us -a -um *adj* talking foolishly

stultiti·a -ae *f* foolishness, silliness

stultivid·us -a -um *adj (foolishly)* seeing things that are not there

stult·us -a -um *adj* foolish, silly

stūp·a -ae *f* tow, coarse flax, hemp

stupe·faciō -facere -fēcī -factus *(pass:* **stupe·fīō -fierī -factus sum)** *tr* to stupefy, stun, shock

stup·eō -ēre -uī *tr* to be amazed at, marvel at ‖ *intr* to be knocked senseless, be stunned, be astounded, be amazed; to be stopped in one's tracks

stup·ēscō -ēscere -uī *intr* to become amazed, become bewildered

stūpe·us -a -um *adj* of tow, hempen

stupidit·ās -ātis *f* stupidity

stupid·us -a -um *adj* amazed, astounded; stupid

stup·or -ōris *m* numbness; stupor; bewilderment, confusion; dullness, stupidity

stupp·a -ae *f* hemp, coarse flax
stuppe·us -a -um *adj* hempen
stupr·ō -āre -āvī -ātus *tr* to have illicit sex with; to ravish, rape; to defile; **struprum īnferre** *(w. dat)* to have sex with; to violate
stupr·um -ī *n* immorality; illicit sex; fornication *(as distinct from adultery);* rape
stupuī *perf of* **stupeō**
sturn·us -ī *m* starling
Stygi·us -a -um *adj* Stygian; hellish; deadly; dismal, melancholy
Stymphāli(c)·us -a -um *adj* Stymphalian
Stymphāl·um -ī *n or* **Stymphāl·us** *or* **Stymphāl·os -ī** *m* district in Arcadia famous for its vicious birds of prey which were killed by Hercules as one his Twelve Labors
Sty·x -gis *or* **-gos** *f* chief river in the lower world; river in Arcadia
suādēl·a -ae *f* persuasion
suā·deō -dēre -sī -sus *tr* to recommend, suggest, propose; to urge, impel, induce ‖ *intr (w. dat)* to advise, urge, suggest to, propose to; **sibi suādēre** *(w. acc & inf)* to satisfy *or* convince oneself that
suāsi·ō -ōnis *f* recommendation; support, backing *(a proposal);* persuasive eloquence
suās·or -ōris *m* adviser; advocate, supporter
suāsōri·a -ae *f* rhetorical exercise *(giving of advice based on historical situations)*
suāsōri·us -a -um *adj* concerned with advice
suās·um -ī *n* dirty grey color
suāsus *pp of* **suādeō**
suās·us -ūs *m* advice
suāveol·ēns -entis *adj* sweet-smelling, fragrant
suāviātiō *see* **sāviātiō**
suāvidic·us -a -um *adj* smooth *(verses);* smooth-talking
suāviloqu·ēns -entis *adj* smooth-talking, charming
suāviloquenti·a -ae *f* charming way of talking, smooth talk
suāviolum *see* **sāviolum**
suāvior *see* **sāvior**
suāv·is -is -e *adj* charming, pleasant, agreeable, attractive, nice
suāvit·ās -ātis *f* charm, pleasantness, attractiveness
suāviter *adv* charmingly, pleasantly, attractively, sweetly
suāvitūd·ō -inis *f (term of endearment)* honey, sweetie
suāvium *see* **sāvium**
sub *(prep) (w. abl)* **1** under, beneath, underneath: **sub sōle ārdente** under the blazing sun; **sub dīvō** under the sky, in the open; **2** under the surface of *(the earth, water):* **sub terrā** below ground; **3** down in *(a depression, valley):* **urbs sub vallibus sita est** the city is located down in the valley; **4** close behind: **sub ipsō ecce volat Diores** look, Diores comes flying close behind him; **5** close (up) to: **ager noster sub urbe** our land close to town; **6** close by: **sub dextrā (sinistrā)** on the right (left); **sub manū** close at hand; **7** at the foot of, close to, near, right under *(mountain, wall):* **sub rādīcibus montium** at the foothills of the mountains; **sub mūrō stāre** to stand close to the wall; **8** immediately before, at the approach of: **sub vespere** at the approach of evening; **9** in the reign of, during the term of office of, under: **sub Tiberiō Caesare** in the reign of Tiberius Caesar; **10** at the hands of: **māiōre sub hoste** at the hands of a greater enemy; **11** under the name *or* title of: **quī Caesareō iuvenēs sub nōmine crēscunt** these young men are growing up under Caesar's name; **12** on the pretext of: **sub excūsātiōne valitūdinis** on the pretext of poor health ‖ *(w. acc)* **1** to a position below, under, beneath: **ēius exercitum sub iugum mīserat** he had sent his army under the yoke; **sub lectum rēpere** to crawl under the bed; **2** to a point at the foot of: **succēdunt sub montem in quō** they advance to the foot of the mountain on which; **3** up *(walls, mountains):* **subīre sub montem** to go up the mountain; **4** just before *(a point of time, event),* on the eve of: **sub idem tempus** at almost the same time; **sub ipsum spectāculum gladiātōrium** on the eve of the gladiatorial show; **sub occāsum sōlis** just before sunset; **5** directly after: **sub eās litterās statim recitātae sunt tuae** your letter was read aloud right after that letter; **6** in response to: **sub hanc vōcem fremitus multitūdinis fuit** at this statement a roar went up in the crowd; **7** into a state of subjection: **Nīnus tōtam Asiam sub sē redēgit** Ninus subjected all of Asia to his control
sub- *pref* **1** *(before adjectives and verbs, giving the sense of reduced intensity):* **subamārus** somewhat bitter; **subrīdēre** to smile; **2** *(compounded with verbs it gives the senses of the preposition):* **2a** *(position underneath):* **subscrībere** to write underneath *or* below; **2b** *(movement up from below):* **subīre** to go up, climb; **2c** *(movement down):* **succīdere** to cut down; **2d** *(movement close to):* **subsequī** to follow close behind; **2e** *(substitution):* **sublegere** to substitute; **2f** *(secret activity and removal):* **subnotāre** to observe secretly; **subdūcere** to remove, steal; **3** *(before nouns, indicating lower rank):* **subcenturiō** assistant centurion
subabsurdē *adv* a bit absurdly

subabsurd·us -a -um *adj* a bit absurd
subaccūs·ō -āre *tr* to blame, find some fault with
subācti·ō -ōnis *f* working *(of the soil);* development *(of the mind)*
subāctus *pp of* **subigō**
subaerāt·us -a -um *adj (of gold)* having an inner layer of bronze
subagrest·is -is -e *adj* rather uncouth
subālār·is -is -e *adj* carried under the arms
subalb·us -a -um *adj* whitish, off-white
subamār·us -a -um *adj* somewhat bitter
subaquil·us -a -um *adj* somewhat dark *(complexion)*
subarroganter *adv* **(subadro-)** rather arrogantly
subauscult·ō -āre *tr* to eavesdrop on **II** *intr* to eavesdrop
subbasilicān·us -ī *m* loafer *(hanging around the basilicas)*
subbib·ō -ere -ī *tr* to drink a little
subbland·ior -īrī *intr (w. dat)* to flirt with
subc- = succ-
subcoll·ō -āre -āvī -ātus *tr* to carry on one's shoulders
subdifficil·is -is -e *adj* rather difficult, a bit difficult
subdiffīd·ō -ere *intr* to be a little distrustful
subditīci·us -a -um *adj* phoney
subditīv·us -a -um *adj* substituted, spurious
subditus *pp of* **subdō**
subdiū *adv* by day
sub·dō -dere -didī -ditus *tr* to put under; to subdue; to substitute; to forge, make up; to spread *(a rumor); (w. dat)* **1** to put *or* apply *(s.th.)* to, add *(s.th.)* to; **2** to subject *(s.o.)* to **II** *refl* **sē aquīs subdere** to plunge into the water
subdoc·eō -ēre *tr* to instruct *(as an assistant instructor)*
subdolē *adv* rather cunningly
subdol·us -a -um *adj* underhand, sly, cunning
subdom·ō -āre *tr* to tame somewhat
subdubit·ō -āre *intr* to be rather undecided
sub·dūcō -dūcere -dūxī -ductus *tr* to draw up from below; to pull up, raise; to remove, take away, steal; to haul up, beach *(a ship);* to withdraw *(troops);* to balance *(accounts)*
subducti·ō -ōnis *f* drydocking, beaching; calculation, computation
sub·edō -edere *or* **-ēsse -ēdī -ēsus** *tr* to eat away below *or* eat away at the bottom of; **scopulum unda subēdit** water wore away the bottom of the cliff
sub·eō -īre -īvī *or* **-iī -itus** *tr* to enter *(a place; the mind);* to approach, attack; to undergo *(danger, punishment, etc.);* to help, support; to climb; to slip under; to dodge *(a blow)* **II** *intr* to come *or* go up, climb; to follow; to advance, press forward; *(w.* **ad** *or* **in** + *acc)* **1** to come up against, attack; **2** to climb *(a mountain);* **3** to approach, enter
sūb·er -eris *n* cork tree, cork
subf- = suff-
subg- = sugg-
subhorrid·us -a -um *adj* rather coarse, rather uncouth
subiac·eō -ēre -uī *intr* to lie nearby; *(w. dat)* to lie under, lie close to; **montī subiacēre** to lie at the foot of the mountain
sub·iciō -icere -iēcī -iectus *tr* to throw up, fling up; to bring up; to bring up close, expose; to suggest; to add, append; to suborn; to substitute; to forge; *(w. dat or* **sub** + *acc)* **1** to put, place *(s.th.)* under; **2** to subject *(s.o.)* to; **3** to classify *(s.th.)* under; **4** to submit *(s.th.)* to *(one's judgment)*
subiecti·ō -ōnis *f* subjection; substitution; forgery
subiectissimē *adv* most humbly
subiect·ō -āre -āvī -ātus *tr* to toss up *(from below);* **stimulōs subiectāre** *(w. dat)* to prod s.o. on
subiect·or -ōris *m* forger
subiect·us -a -um *pp of* **subiciō II** *adj (w. dat)* **1** located near, bordering (on); **2** subject to; **subiecta māteria** subject matter **II** *m* subject, subordinate, underling
subigitāti·ō -ōnis *f (sl) (sexually)* fondling, feeling up
subigitātr·īx -īcis *f (sl)* a tease
subigit·ō -āre -āvī -ātus *tr (sl)* to arouse sexually by fondling, feel up
sub·igō -igere -ēgī -āctus *tr* to turn up, till, plow *(the soil);* to knead *(dough);* to grind, reduce to a powder: **farīna in pollinem subācta** flour reduced to a fine powder; to work *(wool into a smooth thread);* to rub down, massage *(the body, also in the erotic sense);* to tame, break in *(an animal);* to train, discipline *(the mind);* to conquer, subdue *(a country);* to row, propel *(a boat);* to make smooth *(by rubbing, polishing);* to lubricate; to whet, sharpen: **subigunt in cōte secūrīs** they sharpen their axes on a whetstone; to suppress, quell *(hostilities);* to subdue the spirit of, break the spirits of *(people); (w. inf or* **ut** + *subj)* to force, constrain *(s.o.)* to; *(w.* **ad)** to drive to: **subēgit nōs ad necessitūdinem dēdendī rēs** he drove us to the necessity of giving up our property
subimpud·ēns -entis *adj* rather shameless
subinān·is -is -e *adj* rather empty, rather pointless
subinde *adv* immediately afterwards; promptly; from then on; from time to time, now and then
subīnsuls·us -a -um *adj* rather insipid
subinvid·eō -ēre *intr (w. dat)* to envy *(s.o.)* a little

subinvīs·us -a -um *adj* rather disliked, somewhat unpopular
subinvīt·ō -āre *tr* to invite unenthusiastically
subīr·āscor -āscī -ātus sum *intr* to be annoyed; *(w. dat)* to be peeved at
subitāri·us -a -um *adj* requiring prompt action; *(of troops)* hastily called up *(to meet an emergency); (of buildings)* hastily erected; **rēs subitāria** emergency
subitō *adv* suddenly, unexpectedly, at once; **subitō dīcere** to speak extempore
subit·us -a -um *adj* coming on suddenly, sudden, unexpected; rash *(person);* emergency *(troops)* **II** *n* emergency; **dē subitō** *(or* **per subitum)** suddenly
sub·iungō -iungere -iūnxī -iūnctus *tr (w. dat)* **1** to yoke *or* harness to; **2** to join to, connect with, add to; **3** to make subject to
sub·lābor -lābī -lāpsus sum *intr* to sink, fall down, collapse; to glide imperceptibly; to fall back, fail
sublātē *adv* loftily, in lofty tones
sublāti·ō -ōnis *f* elevation, raising
sublāt·us -a -um *pp of* **sufferō** *and of* **tollō** **II** *adj* elated
sublect·ō -āre *tr* to coax, cajole
sub·legō -legere -lēgī -lēctus *tr* to gather up, pick up; to steal; to kidnap; to substitute; to overhear, pick up
sublest·us -a -um *adj* weak; trifling
sublevāti·ō -ōnis *f* alleviation
sublev·ō -āre -āvī -ātus *tr* to lift up, raise, support; to assist; to encourage; to promote, further *(an activity);* to lighten, alleviate; to make up for *(a fault)* **II** *refl* to get up
sublic·a -ae *f* stake, pile *(esp. for a bridge)*
sublici·us -a -um *adj* resting on piles; **pōns sublicius** wooden bridge *(across the Tiber, built by Ancus Marcius, third king of Rome)*
subligācul·um -ī *n* loincloth, shorts; apron
sublig·ar -āris *n* loincloth, shorts; apron
sublig·ō -āre -āvī -ātus *tr (w. dat)* to tie *or* fasten *(e.g., a sword)* to *or* below
sublīmē *adv* aloft, on high
sublīmen *adv* upwards, on high
sublīm·is -is -e *adj* high, raised up, lifted high; *(of ideas)* lofty, grand, exalted; borne aloft, through the sky; aspiring; having lofty ideals; exalted in rank, eminent, distinguished; lofty, majestic *(style)* **II** *npl* the heights
sublīmit·ās -ātis *f* loftiness, sublimity
sublīmius *comp adv of* **sublīmē**
sublingi·o -ōnis *m (hum)* dish-licker
sublingul·ō -ōnis *m (hum)* dish-licker, dishwasher
sub·linō -linere -lēvī -litus *tr* to smear over, coat *(a surface);* to smear the underside of; **ōs sublinere** *(w. dat)* to pull a practical joke on
sublūc·eō -ēre *intr* to shine faintly; *(w. dat)* to shine through
sub·luō -luere -luī -lūtus *tr* to wash underneath; to flow at the foot of *(a mountain);* to wash *(the underside of the body);* **quid solium sublūtō pōdice perdis?** why do you ruin the bathtub with washing your behind?
sublūstr·is -is -e *adj* dimly lighted; throwing some light, glimmering, flickering
subm- = summ-
sub·nāscor -nāscī -nātus sum *intr (w. dat)* to grow up underneath
sub·nectō -nectere -nexuī -nexus *tr* to fasten, tie *(s.th.)* underneath; to confine; *(w. dat)* to fasten *or* tie *(s.th.)* below *(s.th. else)*
subneg·ō -āre -āvī -ātus *tr* to half-refuse
subni·ger -gra -grum *adj* blackish
subnīsus -a -um *adj* **(-nix-)** propped up; *(w. dat)* **1** propped up on, resting on, leaning on; **2** relying on, confiding in; **3** elated by
subnot·ō -āre -āvī -ātus *tr* to note down, record, register; to observe secretly
subnub·a -ae *f* rival *(female)*
subnūbil·us -a -um *adj* somewhat cloudy, overcast
sub·ō -āre *intr* to be in heat
subobscēn·us -a -um *adj* somewhat obscene, shady, off-color
subobscūr·us -a -um *adj* somewhat obscure
subodiōs·us -a -um *adj* rather tiresome, rather annoying
suboffend·ō -ere *intr* to give some offense
subol·ēs -is *f* offspring; children; the young *(of animals)*; race, stock
subolēsc·ō -ere *intr* to grow up
subol·et -ēre *v impers* there is a faint smell; **mihi subolet** I have an inkling, I have a sneaking suspicion
subor·ior -īrī -tus sum *intr* to rise up in succession, arise, proceed
subōrn·ō -āre *tr* to equip, supply, provide; to employ as a secret agent, induce secretly, suborn; to dress up *(in a costume, disguise);* to prepare, instruct *(for some underhand purpose)*
subp- = supp-
subr- = surr-
sub·scrībō -scrībere -scrīpsī -scrīptus *tr* to write underneath; to sign; to write down, record, register **II** *intr (leg)* to sign an accusation, act as prosecutor; *(w. dat)* **1** to add in writing to; **2** to agree to; *(leg) (w.* **in** *+ acc)* to sign an accusation against, indict
subscrīpti·ō -ōnis *f* inscription underneath; signature; s.th. written under a heading; recording *(of an offense by the censor);* record, register; *(leg)* specification *(of crimes)* in an indictment, a count, charge

subscrīpt·or -ōris *m (leg)* signer, co-signer *(of an accusation)*
subscrīptus *pp of* **subscrībō**
subsc·ūs -ūdis *f* **(sups-)** tenon of a dovetail
subsecīvus *see* **subsicīvus**
subsec·ō -āre -uī -tus *tr* to clip, trim, cut off; to pare, clip *(nails)*
subsecūtus *pp of* **subsequor**
subsell·ium -(i)ī *n* seat, bench; stool; seat *or* bench on a lower level; seat in the Senate; *(leg)* seat in the court *(usu. where the judge, prosecution, or the defense and their witnesses sat)*; *(fig)* the bench, tribunal, court; seat *(in the theater)*; **versātus in utrīsque subsellīs** experienced as lawyer and judge **II** *npl* the courts; bleachers *(where the poor people sat)*; *(fig)* occupants of the bleachers
subsen·tiō -tīre -sī -sus *tr* to have some inkling of
sub·sequor -sequī -secūtus sum *tr* to follow close after; to pursue; to back up, support; to imitate; to adhere to, conform to; to come after, succeed *(in time or order)* **II** *intr* to ensue
subserv·iō -īre *intr (w. dat)* **1** to be subject to; **2** to accommodate oneself to, humor; **3** to support, aid
subsicīv·us *or* **subsecīv·us -a -um** *adj* **(sup-)** *(of land)* left over *(after an allotment)*; extra, spare *(time)*; extra, overtime *(work)*
subsidiāri·us -a -um *adj* in reserve; *(mil)* reserve **II** *mpl (mil)* reserves
subsid·ium -(i)ī *n* aid, support; mainstay; place of refuge; protection; *(mil)* reserves; military support, relief; **ad** *(or* **in)** **subsidium** for support; **subsidiō esse** *(w. dat)* to be of help to **II** *npl (mil)* reserves, reinforcements
sub·sīdō -sīdere -sēdī *tr* to lie in wait for **II** *intr* to sit down, crouch down, settle down; to sink, subside, settle; to settle down, establish residence; *(of female animals) (w. dat)* to crouch under
subsignān·us -a -um *adj (mil)* special reserve *(troops)*
subsign·ō -āre -āvī -ātus *tr* to endorse, subscribe to *(an opinion)*; to register, enter, record; to guarantee
subsil·iō -īre -uī *intr* **(suss-)** **(sups-)** to jump up
sub·sistō -sistere -stitī *tr* **(sups-)** to hold out against **II** *intr* to stand up; to take a firm stand; to come to a standstill, stop; to stay behind; *(w. dat)* **1** to take a stand against, oppose, fight; **2** to meet *(an expense)*
subsort·ior -īrī -ītus sum *tr* to choose as a substitute by lot **II** *intr* to choose a substitute by lot; *(in a passive sense)* to be chosen as a substitute
subsortīti·ō -ōnis *f* substitution by lot
substanti·a -ae *f* substance, essence; means, wealth, property
sub·sternō -sternere -strāvī -strātus *tr* to spread underneath; to cover; *(w. dat)* to put at the disposal of, make subservient to; **rem pūblicam libīdinī suae substernere** to misuse high office to serve one's lust
substit·uō -uere -uī -ūtus *tr* to submit, present; to substitute; *(w. dat or* **in locum** *w. gen)* to substitute for *or* in place of; **animō** *(or* **oculīs)** **substituere** to imagine
subst·ō -āre *intr* to stand firm, hold out; *(w. dat)* to stand up to
substrātus *pp of* **substernō**
substrāvī *perf of* **substernō**
substrict·us -a -um *adj* tight, narrow, small
sub·stringō -stringere -strīnxī -strictus *tr* to tie up, draw up; to restrain, control; *(w. dat)* to press *(s.th.)* close to
substructi·ō -ōnis *f* substructure, foundation
substru·ō -ere -xī -ctus *tr* to lay *(a foundation)*; **viās glareā substruere** to lay a foundation of gravel on the roads
subsult·ō -āre *intr* to jump up and down
sub·sum -esse *intr* **(sup-)** to be near, be at hand; *(w. gen) (of feelings, qualities, underlying cause or meaning)* to form the foundation for, be at the bottom of; *(w. dat)* **1** to be below *or* underneath, be under; **2** to be at the foot of; **3** to be (located) at the edge of *(the sea)*; **4** to be concealed in; **5** to be (worn) under *(e.g., a tunic)*; **6** to be attached to *(a document)*; **7** to be subject to, be subservient to
subsūt·us -a -um *adj* trimmed at the bottom
subtē(g)m·en -inis *n* weft, woof *(horizontal threads woven in between the warp threads in a loom)*; yarn
subter *adv* **(sup-)** below, underneath **II** *prep (w. abl)* beneath, below, underneath, under **II** *(w. acc)* underneath, beneath; up to, close to, close beneath
subter·dūcō -dūcere -dūxī -ductus *tr* **(sup-)** to remove secretly **II** *refl* to steal away, sneak away
subter·fugiō -fugere -fūgī *tr* **(sup-)** to evade, avoid **II** *intr* to run off secretly
subter·lābor -lābī *tr* to glide *or* flow under **II** *intr* to slip away
sub·terō -terere -trīvī -trītus *tr* **(sup-)** to wear away underneath
subterrāne·us -a -um *adj* subterranean, underground
subtex·ō -ere -uī -tus *tr* to sew on; to veil, cover; *(fig)* to work up, compose; *(w. dat)* **1** to sew onto; **2** to throw *(a covering)* over; **3** to work *(s.th.)* into *(a story or plot)*
subtīl·is -is -e *adj* **(sup-)** finely woven; delicate; subtle; discriminating, refined; pre-

cise, matter-of-fact; simple, unadorned *(style)*
subtīlit·ās -ātis *f* **(sup-)** fineness, minuteness; slenderness; exactness, precision; simplicity *(of style)*
subtīliter *adv* **(sup-)** finely, delicately; accurately; plainly, simply
subtim·eō -ēre *intr* to be a bit afraid
sub·trahō -trahere -trāxī -tractus *tr* **(sup-)** to drag up from beneath, drag out, draw off; to withdraw, remove; to withhold; to misappropriate, steal; to undermine; to avert *(eyes)*; *(w. dat)* to drag *(s.th.)* away from; *(w. abl)* to rescue *(s.o.)* from the threat of, snatch *(s.o.)* from *(impending danger, ruin)*; **oculīs subtrahere** to remove from sight ‖ *refl (w.* **ab)** to withdraw from, dissociate oneself from *(an activity, responsibility)*
subtrīst·is -is -e *adj* rather sad
subtrītus *pp of* **subterō**
subtrīvī *perf of* **subterō**
subturpicul·us -a -um *adj* somewhat disgraceful
subturp·is -is -e *adj* rather disgraceful, somewhat scandalous
subtus *adv* below, underneath
subtūs·us -a -um *adj* somewhat bruised
subūcul·a -ae *f* undertunic *(worn by both sexes)*
subulc·us -ī *m* swineherd
Subūr·a -ae *f* noisy business and nightlife district in Rome, N.E. of the Forum between the Esquiline and Quirinal Hills
Subūrān·us -a -um *adj* of the Subura
suburbānit·ās -ātis *f* proximity to Rome
suburbān·us -a -um *adj* suburban, near Rome ‖ *m* suburbanite ‖ *n* suburban Rome
suburb·ium -(i)ī *n* suburb
suburg·eō -ēre *tr (w.* **ad)** to keep *or* turn *(a ship)* close to
subvecti·ō -ōnis *f* transportation
subvect·ō -āre -āvī -ātus *tr* to bring up regularly; to transport regularly
subvect·us -ūs *m* bringing up; transportation
sub·vehō -vehere -vexī -vectus *tr* to carry *or* bring up; to transport
sub·veniō -venīre -vēnī -ventum *intr (w. dat)* to come up to aid, reinforce
subvent·ō -āre *intr (w. dat)* to rush to the aid of
subver·eor -ērī *intr* to be a bit apprehensive
subvers·ō -āre *tr* **(-vors-)** to ruin completely
subvers·or -ōris *m* one who overthrows *(a law)*
subver·tō -tere -tī -sus *tr* **(-vort-)** to turn upside down, upset, overthrow, subvert
subvex·us -a -um *adj* sloping upward
subvol·ō -āre *intr* to fly up
subvolturi·us -a -um *adj* vulture-like
subvolv·ō -ere *tr* to roll up(hill)
subvor- = subver-
suc(c)īdi·a -ae *f* leg *or* side of meat; *(fig)* extra income
succav·us -a -um *adj* hollow underneath
succēdāne·us -a -um *adj* **(succī-)** killed as a substitute
suc·cēdo -cēdere -cessī -cessus *tr* to climb; to march on *or* against, advance as far as ‖ *intr* to come up, climb; to come next, follow in succession; to turn out well, turn out successfully; *(w.* **ad, in,** *or* **sub** + *acc)* to climb, climb up; *(w. dat)* **1** to succeed, follow; **2** become a successor to; **3** to succeed in *(an undertaking)*; **4** to yield to, submit to; **5** to relieve *(e.g., tired troops)*; **6** to enter, go below to *(e.g., a shelter, a tomb)*; *(w.* **ad** *or* **in** + *acc) (fig)* to attain *(e.g., high honors)*, enter upon *(an inheritance)*; **bene succēdere** to turn out well
succen·dō -dere -dī -sus *tr* to set on fire, set fire to; to light *(a fire)*; *(fig)* to inflame, enkindle
succēns·eō -ēre -uī *intr* **(sūsc-)** *(w. dat)* to be enraged at
succēnsus *pp of* **succendō**
succenturiāt·us -a -um *adj* **(subc-)** in reserve
succenturi·ō -āre -āvī -ātus *tr* **(subc-)** to receive *(s.o.)* as a substitute into a *centuria*
succenturi·ō -ōnis *m* **(subc-)** assistant centurion, substitute for a centurion
successi·ō -ōnis *f* succession
success·or -ōris *m* successor
success·us -ūs *m* approach, advance uphill; outcome; success
succīdāneus *see* **succēdāneus**
suc·cīdō -cīdere -cīdī -cīsus *tr* **(subc-)** to cut down, cut off, mow down
suc·cidō -cidere -cidī *intr* **(subc-)** to sink, give way; to collapse, fail
succid·us -a -um *adj* **(sūci-)** juicy; *(coll)* plump *(girl)*
succidu·us -a -um *adj* sinking, falling, collapsing, giving way
succīnct·us -a -um *adj (of a person)* with clothes tucked up; *(of a statement)* concise; *(of a book)* compact; *(fig)* in a state of readiness; *(fig) (w. abl)* equipped with *(a means of defense, military strength)*; **cultrō succīnctus** carrying a knife in his belt
suc·cingō -cingere -cīnxī -cīnctus *tr* to tuck up; to put on *(a sword)*; to equip, arm; to surround closely ‖ *refl & pass (w. abl)* to gather up one's clothes with
succingul·um -ī *n* belt
succin·ō -ere *tr* to recite in a droning voice ‖ *intr* to chime in *(in conversation)*; *(w. dat)* to accompany *(in singing or playing)*

succīsus *pp of* **succīdō**
succlāmāti·ō -ōnis *f* shouting in reply
succlām·ō -āre -āvī -ātus *tr* **(subc-)** to shout out after; to interrupt with shouts, heckle; *(w. dat)* to shout out *(words)* at
succontumēliōsē *adv* **(subc-)** rather insolently
suc·crēscō -crēscere -crēvī *intr* **(subc-)** to grow up; to be replenished; *(w. dat)* to attain to
succrētus *pp of* **succernō**
succrīsp·us -a -um *adj* **(subc-)** rather curly
succulent·us -a -um *adj* **(subc-)** succulent
suc·cumbō -cumbere -cubuī -cubitum *intr* **(subc-)** to fall back, sink back; to succumb, yield, submit
suc·currō -currere -currī -cursum *intr (w. dat)* **1** to run up to; **2** to run to help; **3** to occur to, enter the mind of; **4** *(topog)* to extend to the foot of **II** *v impers* the thought occurs
succ·us *or* **sūc·us -ī** *m* sap, juice; taste, flavor; *(fig)* vitality
succuss·us -ūs *m* shaking, jolt
succust·ōs -ōdis *m* **(subc-)** assistant guard
suc·cutiō -cutere -cussī -cussus *tr* to toss up; to jolt *(a rider, vehicle)*
sūcidus *see* **succidus**
sūcin·us -a -um *adj & n* amber
sūctus *pp of* **sūgō**
sucul·a -ae *f* little pig
sucul·a -ae *f* winch, windlass
Sūcul·ae -ārum *fpl (astr)* Hyades
sūculent·us -a -um *adj* juicy, succulent
sūc·us -ī *m* juice; *(of the soil)* moisture; *(fig)* sap, vitality
sūdār·ium -(i)ī *n* handkerchief; towel
sūdātōri·us -a -um *adj* sweat, for sweating **II** *n* sweat room, sauna
sūdātr·īx -īcis *adj* causing sweat
sud·is -is *f* stake, pile; pike *(weapon);* sharp projection, spike
sūd·ō -āre -āvī -ātus *tr* to sweat, exude; to soak with sweat; *(fig)* to sweat at, sweat over **II** *intr* to sweat; to drip
sūd·or -ōris *m* sweat; moisture; *(fig)* hard work
sūducul·um -ī *n (hum)* sweat-maker *(i.e., a whipping post)*
sūd·us -a -um *adj* dry; clear, cloudless **II** *n* clear weather, bright sky
Suēb·ī -ōrum *mpl* **(Suēv-)** generic name of a group of German tribes
Suēbi·a -ae *f* district E. of the Elbe
suēscō suēscere suēvī suētus *tr* to accustom, familiarize **II** *intr (w. dat or inf)* to become accustomed to
Suētōn·ius -(i)ī *m* Roman clan name *(nomen) (esp. that of Gaius Suetonius Tranquillus, biographer, born c.* A.D. *69)*
suēt·us -a -um *pp of* **suēscō II** *adj* usual, familiar
Suēvī *see* **Suēbī**
sūf·es *or* **suff·es -etis** *m* chief magistrate in Carthage
suffarcināt·us -a -um *adj* **(subf-)** stuffed, padded
suffarcin·ō -āre -āvī -ātus *tr* **(subf-)** to stuff, cram
suffect·us -a -um *pp of* **sufficiō II** *adj* substitute; **cōnsul suffectus** substitute consul *(appointed to complete an unexpired term of another consul)*
sufferō sufferre sustulī sublātus *tr* **(subf-)** to suffer, bear, endure; to place at s.o.'s disposal, offer
suf·ficiō -ficere -fēcī -fectus *tr* to lay the foundation for; to dip, tinge, dye; to appoint to a vacancy; to yield, supply, afford **II** *intr* to be sufficient; *(w. dat)* to suffice for
suf·fīgō -fīgere -fīxī -fīxus *tr* to nail up, fasten
suffīm·en -inis *n* incense
suffīment·um -ī *n* incense
suff·iō -īre -īvī *or* **-(i)ī -ītus** *tr* to fumigate; to perfume
suffīxus *pp of* **suffīgō**
sufflām·en -inis *n* brake *(on a vehicle)*
sufflāmin·ō -āre -āvī -ātus *tr* to apply the brakes to
sufflāt·us -a -um *adj* puffed up, bloated; *(fig)* bombastic; *(fig)* fuming *(w. anger)*
suffl·ō -āre -āvī -ātus *tr* to blow up, inflate **II** *intr* to blow, puff
suffōc·ō -āre -āvī -ātus *tr* to choke, suffocate
suf·fodiō -fodere -fōdī -fossus *tr* **(subf-)** to stab, pierce; to dig under *(walls)*
suffrāgāti·ō -ōnis *f* **(subf-)** voting *(in s.o.'s favor),* support
suffrāgāt·or -ōris *m* **(subf-)** voter; supporter *(at the polls),* partisan
suffrāgātōri·us -a -um *adj* **(subf-)** partisan
suffrāg·ium -(i)ī *n* **(subf-)** ballot, vote; right to vote, franchise; decision, judgment; applause, approbation; **suffrāgium ferre** to cast a ballot; **suffrāgium ferre** *(w.* **dē** *or* **in** *+ abl)* to vote on
suffrāg·or -ārī -ātus sum *intr* to cast a favorable vote; *(w. dat)* to vote in favor of, support, vote for; **fortūnā suffrāgante** with luck on our side
suffring·ō -ere *tr* **(subf-)** to break
suffug·ium -(i)ī *n* shelter, cover
sufful·ciō -cīre -sī -tus *tr* to prop up, underpin, support
suf·fundō -fundere -fūdī -fūsus *tr* **(subf-)** to pour in, fill; to suffuse, spread; to tinge, color; to infuse; **virgineum ōre rubōrem suffundere** *(w. dat)* to make *(s.o.)* blush like a girl
suffūr·or -ārī *tr* to filch, snitch
suffūsc·us -a -um *adj* **(subf-)** darkish
suffūsus *pp of* **suffundō**

Sugambr·ī -ōrum *mpl* a German tribe living to the E. of the Lower Rhine, above the Ubii
sug·gerō -gerere -gessī -gestus *tr* **(subg-)** to supply, add; to suggest
suggest·um -ī *n* platform; stage
suggestus *pp of* **suggerō**
suggest·us -ūs *m* platform; stage
suggrand·is -is -e *adj* **(subg-)** rather huge
sug·gredior -gredī -gressus sum *tr & intr* **(subg-)** to approach
sūgillāti·ō -ōnis *f* **(suggill-, subgill-)** bruise; affront
sūgill·ō -āre -āvī -ātus *tr* to beat black-and-blue; to affront, insult
sūgō sūgere sūxī sūctus *tr* to suck
suī *perf of* **suō**
suī *see* **sē**
suill·us -a -um *adj* of swine; **carō suilla** pork; **grex suillus** herd of swine **II** *f* pork
sulc·ō -āre -āvī -ātus *tr* to furrow; to plow; to score, make a line in
sulc·us -ī *m* furrow; ditch, trench *(for plants);* track *(of a wheel or meteor);* wrinkle; plowing; wake *(of a ship)*
sulf·ur -uris *n* sulfur
Sull·a -ae *m* **(Syll-)** Sulla *(Cornelius Sulla Felix, Roman general, dictator, and political reformer, 138–78 B.C.)*
Sullān·ī -ōrum *mpl* **(Syll-)** partisans of Sulla
sullātur·iō -īre *intr* to wish to be a Sulla
Sulm·ō -ōnis *m* town c. 90 miles E. of Rome, and birthplace of Ovid
Sulmōnēns·is -is -e *adj* of Sulmo
sulp(h)·ur *or* **sulf·ur -uris** *n* sulfur
sulp(h)urāt·us -a -um *adj* saturated with sulfur
sulp(h)ure·us -a -um *adj* sulfurous
sultis = sī vultis if you please
sum esse fuī futūrus *intr* to be; to exist; *(w. gen of possession)* to belong to, pertain to, be characteristic of, be the duty of; *(w. gen or abl of quality)* to be of, be possessed of, have; *(w. gen or abl of value)* to be valued at, cost; *(w. dat)* to belong to; *(w.* **ab)** to belong to; *(w.* **ad)** to be designed for; *(w.* **ex)** to consist of; **est** *(w. inf)* it is possible to, it is permissible to; **est** *(w.* **ut)** it is possible that; **sunt quī** there are those who, there are people who, they are of the type that
sumbolus *see* **symbolus**
sūm·en -inis *n* breast; teat, udder; breeding sow
summ- = subm-
summ·a -ae *f* main thing; chief point, gist, summary; sum, amount; contents, substance; sum of money; sum-total *(of hopes, etc.);* the whole issue, the whole case; *(phil)* totality of matter, the universe; **ad summam** in short; generally, on the whole; as the crowning touch, to complete it all; **in summā** in all; **in summam** taken as a whole; **ad** *(or* **in) summam prōdesse** *(or* **prōficere)** to be of general good; **summa honōrāria** honorarium, voluntary payment to a lawyer; **summa rērum** the world; supreme power; general welfare; **summa summārum** the whole universe
summān·ō -āre *intr* **(subm-)** to drip a bit
Summān·us -ī *m* Roman god of night lightning
summ·ās -ātis *adj* aristocratic, first-class
summātim *adv* on the surface; generally, summarily
summē *adv* very, extremely, intensely
summer·gō -gere -sī -sus *tr* **(subm-)** to sink, submerge, drown
summers·us -a -um *adj* **(subm-)** sunken; living underwater; *(sunk)* below the horizon
summer·us -a -um *adj* **(subm-)** nearly straight, nearly pure
sumministr·ō -āre -āvī -ātus *tr* **(subm-)** to furnish
summissē *or* **summissim** *adv* **(subm-)** in a low voice, softly; modestly, humbly
summissi·ō -ōnis *f* lowering, dropping
summiss·us -a -um *adj* lowered, stooping; lowered, soft *(voice);* humble, unassuming; submissive; too submissive, abject; *(of hair)* worn long, let down
sum·mittō -mittere -mīsī -missus *tr* **(subm-)** to let down, lower, sink, drop; to let *(hair)* grow long; to lower, reduce, moderate, relax, lessen; to humble; to rear, produce, put forth; to send secretly; to send as a reinforcement; to send as a substitute; **animum summittere** *(w. dat)* to yield to **II** *refl* to bend down, stoop over; to condescend; *(w. dat)* to give in to
summolestē *adv* **(subm-)** with some annoyance
summolest·us -a -um *adj* **(subm-)** rather annoying
summon·eō -ēre -uī -itus *tr* to give *(s.o.)* a gentle reminder, remind privately; **patrēs salūtāvit nōminātim nūllō summonente** he greeted senators by name, with no one prompting him
summopere *or* **summō opere** *adv* with the greatest diligence, with utmost effort
summōt·us -a -um *adj* secluded, distant
sum·moveō -movēre -mōvī -mōtus *tr* **(subm-)** to move up, advance; to clear *(e.g., the court);* to remove; to expel, banish; to deny admission to, keep off; to clear from the path of a magistrate; to dispense with *(a procedure);* to ward off *(heat, cold); (fig)* to drive away, forget about *(e.g., worries); (mil)* dislodge
summul·a -ae *f* small sum of money

summum *adv (w. numbers)* at most; at latest; **ūnō aut summum alterō proeliō** in one or at most two battles

summ·us -a -um *adj* highest, uppermost; the top of, the surface of; last, latest, the end of; greatest, best, top, consummate; finest, first-rate; at the height of *(a season);* perfect *(peace, tranquility);* closest, best *(friend);* most distinguished; middle *(finger); (of affairs, concerns)* most important, of highest importance; *(of a diner)* farthest to the left on the couch *(from the viewpoint of those dining); (of a couch)* to the left of the middle couch; **omnia summa facere** to do one's utmost; **rēs summa** *(or* **rēs summae)** critical situation; **rēs summa** *(or* **rēspūblica summa)** the welfare of the state, the general welfare; **summa cēna** main course; **summa manus** finishing touches; **summa mēnsa** main course; **summa rudis** head instructor in a gladiatorial school *(literally, top practice-sword);* **summō iūre** with the full force of the law ‖ *m* head of the table; ‖ *f see* **summa** ‖ *n* top, surface; highest place, head of the table; **ab summō aut ab īmō** at the top or the bottom of the page ‖ *npl* extremities *(of the body or its parts);* general purport *(of a writing)*

sūmō sūmere sūmpsī sūmptus *tr* to take up; to put on, dress oneself in, wear; to exact, inflict *(penalty);* to take up, begin, enter upon; to eat, consume; to assume, suppose, take for granted; to cite, adduce, mention; to assume, appropriate *(a title, name);* to embrace *(a practice, way of life);* to borrow *(words, ideas from other people);* to select; to purchase, buy; to adopt *(a child);* **aliquid mūtuum sūmere** to borrow s.th.; **arma sūmere** to take up arms; **in manūs sūmere** to take in hand, take up *(for reading);* **in sē sūmere** to take upon oneself, assume; **mortem** *(or* **exitium)** *(usu. w.* **sponte)** **sūmere** to commit suicide; **supplicium sūmere** to exact punishment

sūmpti·ō -ōnis *f* assumption, premise

sūmptuāri·us -a -um *adj* expense, relating to expenses; *(of laws)* sumptuary, against extravagance

sūmptuōsē *adv* sumptuously, expensively

sūmptuōs·us -a -um *adj* costly, expensive; lavish, wasteful

sūmptus *pp of* **sūmō**

sūmpt·us -ūs *m* cost, expense; **sūmptui esse** *(w. dat)* to be expensive for; **sūmptum suum exercēre** to earn one's keep; **sūmptū tuō** at your expense

Sūn·ium *or* **Sūn·ion -iī** *n* S.E. promontory of Attica

suō suere suī sūtus *tr* to sew, stitch, tack together

suōmet = *emphatic form of* **suō**

suōpte = *emphatic form of* **suō**

suovetaurīl·ia -ium *npl* **(suovi-)** sacrifice of a pig, sheep, and bull

supell·ex -ectilis *f* furniture, household utensils; tableware; outfit, equipment

super *adv* on the top, on the surface, above; besides, moreover; in addition to what has been said; **satis superque** enough and to spare; **super esse** to be left over ‖ *prep (w. acc)* over, above; upon, on top of; *(w. numbers)* over, more than; besides, over and above; **alius super alium** one on top of another, one after another; **super cēnam** *(or* **mēnsam)** over dinner, at table *(i.e., during the meal);* **super omnia** *(or* **cūncta)** above all, more than anything ‖ *(w. abl)* above, over, upon, on; concerning, about, in the matter of; besides, in addition to; at *(e.g., midnight)*

sup·er -era -erum *adj see* **superus**

superā *adv* above

super·a -ōrum *npl* upper world, sky; heaven; heavenly bodies

superābil·is -is -e *adj* surmountable, climbable; conquerable

superad·dō -dere -didī -ditus *tr* to add besides, add to boot

super·āns -antis *adj* predominant; outstanding, remarkable

superāt·or -ōris *m* conqueror

superbē *adv* arrogantly, haughtily, snobbishly

superbi·a -ae *f* arrogance, haughtiness, snobbishness; pride

superbiloquenti·a -ae *f* haughty tone, arrogant speech

superb·iō -īre *intr* to be haughty; to be proud; to be superb, be magnificent; *(w. abl)* to take pride in

superb·us -a -um *adj* arrogant, haughty, snobbish; proud; overbearing, tyrannical; fastidious, disdainful; superb, magnificent; *(of an honor)* that is a source of pride; *(w. abl)* proud of; **āles superba** the phoenix

supercil·ium -(i)ī *n* eyebrow; frown, will *(of Jupiter);* stern looks; summit, brow *(of a hill);* arrogance, superciliousness; artificial eyebrow

superēmin·eō -ēre *tr* to tower over, top

superfici·ēs -ēī *f* top, surface; *(leg)* fixtures, improvements, buildings *(i.e., anything upon the property but not the land itself)*

super·fīō -fierī *intr* to be over and above; to be left over

superfīx·us -a -um *adj* stuck *or* impaled on top of; **rumpiīs superfīxa capita** heads stuck on top of long spears

superflu·ō -ere -xī *intr* to overflow; to be superfluous
superfuī *perf of* **supersum**
super·fundō -fundere -fūdī -fūsus *tr (w. abl)* to shower *(s.th.)* with; *(w. dat)* to pour *(s.th.)* upon **||** *refl & pass* to spread, spread out, extend
super·gredior -gredī -gressus sum *tr* to walk *or* step over; to surpass
super·ī -ōrum *mpl* the gods above; men on earth; mortals; upper world
super·iaciō -iacere -iēcī -iectus *or* -**iactus** *tr* to throw on top; to overshoot *(a target);* **fidem superiacere** to exceed the bounds of credibility; **natāre superiectō aequore** to swim in the flood waters
superimmin·eō -ēre *intr (w. dat)* to stand over *(s.o. in a threatening manner)*
superimpend·ēns -entis *adj* overhanging, towering overhead
superim·pōnō -pōnere -posuī -positus *tr* to place on top, place overhead
superimposit·us -a -um *adj* superimposed
superincid·ēns -entis *adj* falling from above
superincub·āns -antis *adj* lying above *or* on top
superin·cumbō -cumbere -cubuī *intr* to lean over; *(w. dat)* to lay oneself down on
superindu·ō -ere -ī *tr* to put on over one's other clothes
superin·iciō -icere -iēcī -iectus *tr* to throw on top
superin·sternō -sternere -strāvī -strātus *tr (w. abl)* to cover *(w. s.th.)*
superi·or -or -us *(comp of* **superus)** *adj* higher, upper; the upper part of; past, previous, preceding; older, elder, more advanced; superior, stronger; victorious, conquering; greater; **dē locō superiōre dīcere** to speak from the tribunal, handle a case in court; to speak from the rostra; **ex locō superiōre pugnāre** to fight from a vantage point
superiūmentār·ius -(i)ī *m* one charged with looking after the beasts of burden
superius *adv (e.g., mentioned)* above
superlāt·us -a -um *adj* exaggerated
supernē *adv* above, from above; on top; **dē supernē** from above
supern·us -a -um *adj* upper; situated high up; supernal, celestial
super·ō -āre -āvī -ātus *tr* to go over, pass over, rise above; to pass, go past, go beyond; to sail past, double; to outdo, surpass; to surmount *(difficulties);* to live past, live beyond; to overcome, vanquish; to arrive before *or* ahead of; **vītā superāre** to survive, outlive **||** *intr* to mount, ascend; to be superior, have the advantage; to be left over, survive; to be superfluous; to be abundant; to remain to be done; *(w. dat)* to pass over, pass above
superobru·ō -ere *tr (also written as two words)* to cover completely, smother
superoccup·ō -āre *tr* to pounce on
superpend·ēns -entis *adj* towering overhead
super·pōnō -pōnere -posuī -positus *tr (w. dat)* to put *(s.th.)* upon; *(w.* **in** *+ acc)* to put *(s.o.)* in charge of
superquam quod *conj* in addition to the fact that
superscand·ō -ere *tr* to step over, climb over
superscrībō -scrībere -scrīpsī -scrīptus *tr* to write over *or* on top of
super·sedeō -sedēre -sēdī -sessum *tr* **(-sid-)** to sit on top of **||** *intr* to sit on top; *(w. dat)* **1** to sit on *(e.g., an elephant);* **2** to preside over; **3** to refrain from, desist from; *(w. abl)* to refrain from, give up, steer clear of; *(w. inf)* to stop *(doing s.th.)*
superstagn·ō -āre -āvī *intr (of a river)* to overflow and form swamps
superst·es -itis *adj* standing by as a witness; surviving; posthumous; *(w. gen or dat)* outliving, surviving *(s.o.);* **superstes esse** to live on; **superstes esse** *(w. gen or dat)* to outlive *(s.o.)*
superstiti·ō -ōnis *f* superstition; blind adherence to rules
superstitiōsē *adv* superstitiously
superstitiōs·us -a -um *adj* superstitious; ecstatic; blindly adhering to rules
superstit·ō -āre *intr* to be left
superst·ō -āre -stetī *tr* to stand over **||** *intr (w. dat)* to stand on, stand over
superstrāt·us -a -um *adj* spread over *(as a covering)*
superstru·ō -ere -xī -ctus *tr* to build upon
super·sum -esse -fuī -futūrus *intr* to be left over, still exist, survive; to abound; to overflow; to be excessive; to be superfluous; to be adequate, suffice; *(w. dat)* to outlive, survive *(s.o.)*
super·tegō -tegere -tēxī -tēctus *tr* to cover over
superurg·ēns -entis *adj* putting on pressure, adding pressure
super·us *or* **super -a -um** *adj* upper; of this world, of this life; northern; **ad aurās superās redīre** to come back to life; **mare superum** Adriatic Sea **||** *mpl see* **superī ||** *npl see* **supera**
supervac(u)āne·us -a -um *adj* superfluous
supervacu·us -a -um *adj* superfluous
supervād·ō -ere *tr* to go over, climb over
super·vehor -vehī -vectus sum *tr* to sail, ride, *or* drive by *or* past
super·veniō -venīre -vēnī -ventus *tr* to come upon, come on top of; to overtake;

to come over, close over, cover; to surprise ‖ *intr* to arrive suddenly; *(w. dat)* to come upon by surprise
supervent·us -ūs *m* sudden arrival, unexpected arrival
super·vīvō -vīvere -vixī *intr (w. dat)* to outlive
supervolit·ō -āre -āvī *tr* to hover over
supervol·ō -āre -āvī *tr* to fly over ‖ *intr* to fly across
supīn·ō -āre -āvī -ātus *tr* to turn over *(by plowing)*
supīn·us -a -um *adj* face-up; lying on one's back; turned upwards; sloping, sloping upwards; *(of streams)* flowing upwards *(to their source);* on one's back; lazy, careless, indifferent
supp- = subp-
suppāctus *pp of* **suppingō (subp-)**
suppaenitet -ēre *v impers* **(subp-)** *(w. acc of person and gen of thing regretted), e.g.,* **illum furōris suppaenitet** he somewhat regrets the outburst
suppalp·or -ārī *intr* **(subp-)** *(w. dat)* to coax *(s.o.)* a little
supp·ār -aris *adj* nearly equal
supparasīt·or -ārī *intr (w. dat)* to flatter *(s.o.)* a little like a parasite
suppar·um -ī *n or* **suppar·us -ī** *m* linen dress; small sail
suppeditāti·ō -ōnis *f* **(subp-)** good supply
suppedit·ō -āre -āvī -ātus *tr* **(subp-)** to supply, furnish ‖ *intr* to stand by; to be on hand, be in stock, be available; *(w. dat)* to be at hand for; *(w.* **ad** *or* **in** *+ acc)* to be adequate for
suppēd·ō -ere *intr (vulg)* to fart quietly
suppernāt·us -a -um *adj* hamstrung
suppeti·ae -ārum *fpl* assistance
suppeti·or -ārī -ātus sum *intr* **(subp-)** *(w. dat)* to help, assist
suppet·ō -ere -īvī *or* **-iī -ītum** *intr* to be at hand, be in stock, be available; *(w. dat)* **1** to be at hand for, be available to; **2** to be equal to, suffice for; **3** to correspond to
suppīl·ō -āre -āvī -ātus *tr* **(subp-)** to filch, snitch
sup·pingō -pingere -pēgī -pāctus *tr* **(subp-)** to fasten underneath
supplant·ō -āre -āvī -ātus *tr* **(subp-)** to trip up, cause to stumble
supplēment·um -ī *n* **(subp-)** *(mil)* reinforcement(s)
suppl·eō -ēre -ēvī -ētus *tr* **(subp-)** to fill up; to make good *(losses, damage, etc.); (mil)* to bring to full strength
suppl·ex -icis *adj* kneeling, on one's knees, in entreaty; humble, submissive ‖ *mf* suppliant
supplicāti·ō -ōnis *f* public thanksgiving, day of prayer; thanksgiving for victory; day of humiliation
suppliciter *adv* suppliantly, humbly
supplic·ium -(i)ī *n* **(subp-)** kneeling down, bowing down, humble entreaty; public prayer, supplication; *(because criminals were beheaded kneeling)* execution, death penalty; punishment, torture; suffering, pain; **supplicium dare** to atone; **supplicium dare** *(or* **pendere,** *or* **expendere,** *or* **luere)** to pay the penalty, suffer punishment; **supplicium sūmere** *(or* **exigere)** to exact punishment; to accept reparation; *(w.* **ab, ex, ex** *+ abl)* to exact punishment from, put *(s.o.)* to death
supplic·ō -āre -āvī -ātum *intr* **(subpl)** *(w. dat)* to go on one's knees to, entreat, beg
supplō·dō -dere -sī -sus *tr* **(subp-)** to stamp *(the foot)*
supplōsi·ō -ōnis *f* **(subp-)** stamping *(one's foot)*
sup·pōnō -pōnere -posuī -positus *tr* **(subp-)** *(w. dat)* **1** to put, place, set *(s.th.)* under; **2** to put *(s.th.)* next to, add *(s.th.)* to; **3** to substitute *(s.th.)* for; **potentiam in grātiae locum suppōnere** to substitute power for influence
support·ō -āre -āvī -ātus *tr* **(subp-)** to bring up, transport
suppositīci·us -a -um *adj* **(subp-)** spurious
suppositi·ō -ōnis *f* substitution
suppositus *pp of* **suppōnō**
suppostr·īx -īcis *f* unfair substituter *(female)*
suppressi·ō -ōnis *f* holding back *(of money),* embezzlement
suppress·us -a -um *adj* soft *(voice);* soft-spoken *(person)*
sup·primō -primere -pressī -pressus *tr* **(subp-)** to press down *or* under; to sink; to repress, stop; to suppress, keep secret; to stifle *(an utterance);* to detain in one's private custody; to retain *(another's money)* in one's possession; to suppress *(feelings)*
supprōm·us -ī *m* **(subp-)** assistant butler
suppud·et -ēre *v impers* **(subp-)** to cause *(s.o.)* a slight feeling of shame; *(w. acc of person and gen of cause), e.g.:* **eōrum mē suppudet** I am a bit ashamed of them
suppūr·ō -āre -āvī -ātum *intr* to fester
supp·us -a -um *adj* lying on one's back, supine; upside down
supput·ō -āre -āvī -ātus *tr* to trim off the lower branches of; to count, compute
suprā *adv* on top, above; up above; earlier; beyond, more; **suprā quam** more than ‖ *prep (usu. w. acc; also w. abl) (sometimes following its object or separated from it by intervening words)* on, on top of; over, above; beyond; *(of time)* before, earlier

than; north of; to the far side of; *(of amount)* over, beyond; in charge of; *(w. reference to position at the dining table, from the standpoint of those eating)* on the left of; **Atticus suprā mē, īnfrā Verrius accubēbat** Atticus sat to the left of me, Verrius to the right of me; **gallīnāceus suprā virī umerum deinde in capite astitit** the rooster stood on the man's shoulder and then on his head; **suprā caput** *(in a threatening way)* (hanging) over one's head; **suprā terram** above ground

suprālāti·ō -ōnis *f* exaggeration

suprālāt·us -a -um *adj* exaggerated

suprāscand·ō -ere *tr* to climb over

suprāscrīpt·us -a -um *adj* written above *(as a correction)*

suprēmum *adv* for the last time; as a final tribute

suprēm·us -a -um *(superl of* **superus)** *adj* last, latest, final; highest; greatest, supreme, extreme; critical, desperate *(time);* closing, dying, final; **suprēma manus** finishing touches; **suprēma multa** maximum fine; **suprēmum iūdicium** last will and testament; **suprēmum supplicium** death penalty; **suprēmus mōns** mountain top **‖** *n* last moment **‖** *npl* moment of death; funeral rites

supt- = subt-

Sur- = Syr-

sūr·a -ae *f (anat)* calf

surcul·us -ī *m* shoot, sprout, twig; slip, graft

surdas·ter -tra -trum *adj* somewhat deaf

surdit·ās -ātis *f* deafness

surd·us -a -um *adj* deaf; silent, noiseless; unheeding; dull, faint

Sūrēn·a -ae *m* grand vizier *(in Parthia)*

surgō surgere surrēxī surrēctum *intr* to get up; to stand up; to rise; to spring up and grow tall

surr- = subr-

surrancid·us -a -um *adj* **(subr-)** somewhat rancid *or* spoiled

surrauc·us -a -um *adj* **(subr-)** somewhat hoarse

surrēctus *pp of* **surgō** *and* **surrigō**

surrēmig·ō -āre *intr* to row along

Surrentīn·us -a -um *adj* of Surrentum *(modern Sorrento)*

sur·rēpō -rēpere -rēpsī -rēptum *tr* **(subr-)** to creep under, crawl under **‖** *intr* to creep up; *(w. dat)* to creep up on

surreptīci·us -a -um *adj* **(subr-)** surreptitious; secretive

surreptus *pp of* **surripiō**

surrēptus *pp of* **surrēpō**

sur·rīdeō -rīdēre -rīsī *intr* **(subr-)** to smile

surrīdiculē *adv* **(subr-)** rather humorously

sur·rigō -rigere -rēxī -rēctus *tr* **(subr-)** to raise, lift up, erect

surring·or -ī *intr* **(subr-)** to grimace, make a face; to be somewhat annoyed

sur·ripiō -ripere -ripuī -reptus *tr* **(subr-)** to snatch secretly, pilfer; *(w. dat)* to pilfer *(s.th.)* from

surrīsī *perf of* **surrīdeō**

surrog·ō -āre -āvī -ātus *tr* **(subr-)** to propose as a substitute

surrostrān·ī -ōrum *mpl* **(subr-)** loafers around the Rostra *(in the Forum)*

surrub·eō -ēre *intr* **(subr-)** to blush slightly

surrūf·us -a -um *adj* **(subr-)** reddish

sur·ruō -ruere -ruī -rutus *tr* **(subr-)** to dig under; to loosen at the base; to tear down, demolish; *(fig)* to undermine, subvert

surrūstic·us -a -um *adj* **(subr-)** rather unsophisticated

surrutil·us -a -um *adj* **(subr-)** reddish

surrūtus *pp of* **surruō**

sūrsum *adv* **(sūrsus, sūsum, sūsus)** upwards, high up; **sūrsum deorsum** up and down

sūs suis *m* pig, hog; boar **‖** *f* sow

Sūs·a -ōrum *npl* capital of Persia

sūscēnseō *see* **succēnseō**

sūscepti·ō -ōnis *f* undertaking

sūscept·um -ī *n* enterprise, undertaking

sus·cipiō -cipere -cēpī -ceptus *tr* to catch *(s.th. before it falls);* to support; to pick up, resume *(conversation);* to bear *(children);* to accept, receive *(under one's protection);* to take up, undertake; to acknowledge, recognize *(a child)* as one's own

sūscit·ō -āre -āvī -ātus *tr* to stir up, shake up; to build, erect; to cause *(s.th.)* to rise; to wake *(s.o.)* up; to encourage; to stir up *(rebellion, love, etc.);* to rouse *(from inactivity);* to have *(s.o.)* stand up in court *(as witness)*

suspect·ō -āre -āvī -ātus *tr* to gaze up at; to suspect

suspect·us -a -um *pp of* **suspiciō ‖** *adj* suspect, suspected, mistrusted

suspect·us -ūs *m* view from below; respect, esteem

suspend·ium -(i)ī *n* hanging; hanging oneself

suspen·dō -dere -dī -sus *tr* to hang up, hang; to prop up, support; to keep in suspense; to check *(temporarily);* to interrupt **‖** *pass (w.* **ex)** to depend on

suspēns·us -a -um *adj* hanging, balanced; raised, poised; in suspense, uncertain, hesitant; marked by uncertainty; vague *(language); (w.* **ex)** dependent upon; **in suspēnsō** in suspense, on tenterhooks; undecided

suspic·āx -ācis *adj* suspicious; mistrustful

suspici·ō -ōnis *f* suspicion, mistrust; inkling; faint indication, trace, suggestion; *(w. gen)* suspicion *(of)*; *(w. acc & inf or* **quasi**) suspicion that; **in suspiciōnem cadere** to fall under suspicion; **in suspiciōnem venīre** to come under suspicion; **Tarentīnōrum dēfectiō iam diū in suspiciōne Rōmānīs fuerat** the revolt of the Tarentines long been suspected by the Romans

suspiciō suspicere suspexī suspectus *tr* to look up at; to look up to, admire; to mistrust, suspect ‖ *intr* to look up; *(w.* **in** + *acc)* to look up at *or* into

suspīciōsē *adv* suspiciously

suspīciōs·us -a -um *adj* mistrustful, suspicious; suspicious-looking; *(w.* **in** + *acc)* suspicious of

suspic·ō -āre *or* **suspic·or -ārī -ātus sum** *tr* to mistrust, suspect; to suppose, surmise, believe

suspīrāt·us -ūs *m* deep breath, sigh; labored breathing

suspīr·ium -(i)ī *n* deep breath, sigh; **suspīrium dūcere** *(or* **repetere** *or* **trahere**) to take a deep breath, sigh

suspīr·ō -āre -āvī -ātus *tr* to sigh for ‖ *intr* to sigh, heave a sigh

susque dēque *adv* up and down; **dē Octāviō susque dēque est** it's all one *(i.e., of no consequence)* as far as Octavian is concerned

suss- = **subs-**

sustentāti·ō -ōnis *f* delay

sustent·ō -āre -āvī -ātus *tr* to build up; to hold upright; to support; to sustain *(w. food)*; to maintain; to provide *(s.o. w. food, money, etc.)*, support, maintain; to uphold *(the law)*; to endure, hold up against; to hold back, keep in check; to delay, put off

sus·tineō -tinēre -tinuī *tr* to hold up, support; to hold back, hold in check; to uphold *(the law)*; to sustain, support *(w. food, etc.)*; to bear, endure *(trouble)*; to hold up, delay, put off

sustoll·ō -ere *tr* to lift up, raise; to kidnap

sustulī *perf of* **tollō**

sūsum *see* **sūrsum**

susurrāt·or -ōris *m* mutterer, whisperer

susurr·ō -āre *tr & intr* to mutter, murmur, whisper

susurr·us -a -um *adj* whispering

susurr·us -ī *m* low, gentle noise; murmur, whisper, buzz, hum

sūt·a -ōrum *npl* coat of mail; joints

sūtēl·ae -ārum *fpl* patches; tricks

sūtil·is -is -e *adj* sewn together; **cumba sūtilis** boat made of skins; **rosae sūtilēs** a wreath of roses

sūt·or -ōris *m* shoemaker

sūtōri·us -a -um *adj* shoemaker's ‖ *m (hum)* Shoemaker Emeritus

sūtrīn·us -a -um *adj* shoemaker's ‖ *f* shoemaker's shop

Sūtr·ium -(i)ī *n* town in Etruria

sūtūr·a -ae *f* stitch; seam

sūt·us -a -um *pp of* **suō** ‖ *npl* joints

su·us -a -um *or* **su·os -a -om** *adj* his own, her own, its own, their own, one's own; due, proper, peculiar ‖ *pron masc pl* one's own people, one's own family, one's own friends ‖ *pron neut pl* one's own property

Sybar·is -is *f* town in S. Italy noted for its luxurious living ‖ *m* Sybaris *(boy's name, suggestive of decadence)*

Sybarīt·a -ae *m* Sybarite

Sybarītic·us -a -um *adj* Sybarite; *(fig)* erotic

Sȳchae·us -ī *m* husband of Dido

sȳcophant·a -ae *m* swindler; slanderer; cunning parasite

sȳcophanti·a -ae *f* deceptive trickery

sȳcophantiōsē *adv* deceitfully

sȳcophant·or -ārī -ātus sum *intr* to cheat; *(w. dat)* to pull a fast one on

Syēn·e -ēs *f* town in Egypt *(modern Aswan)*

Sylla *see* **Sulla**

syllab·a -ae *f* syllable

syllabātim *adv* syllable by syllable

Symaethē·us -a -um *adj* of the River Symaethus

Symaeth·is -idis *f* daughter of the river-god Symaethus

Symaeth·us -ī *m* River Symaethus in Sicily near Catana

symbol·a -ae *or* **symbol·ē -ēs** *f* contribution *(of money to a feast)*; *(coll)* blows

symbol·us -ī *m* **(sumb-)** symbol, mark, token

symphōni·a -ae *f* harmony; symphony, band *(of singers or musicians)*

symphōniac·us -a -um *adj* concert, musical; **puerī symphōniacī** choristers ‖ *mpl* musicians

Symplēgad·es -um *fpl* two islands in the Black Sea which floated about and dashed against each other until they were fixed in place a split second after the *Argo* sailed by them

symplegm·a -atis *n* tangled group *(of persons embracing or wrestling)*

syngraph·a -ae *f* promissory note, I.O.U.

syngraph·us -ī *m* written contract; pass *(for safe-conduct)*

syn(h)od·ūs -ontos *m* bream *(fish)*

synhedr·us -ī *m* senator *(in Macedonia)*

Synnad·a -ōrum *npl or* **Synn·as -adis** *f* town in Phrygia, famous for its colored marble

synthesin·a -ae *f* dinner shirt
synthes·is -is *f* a set of matching articles; dinner service; (matching) dinner clothes
Syph·āx -ācis *m* **(Syf-)** king of Numidia at the time of the Second Punic War, siding with Carthage *(d. 203 B.C.)*
Syrācosi·us -a -um *adj* **(-cūs)** Syracusan ‖ *mpl* Syracusans
Syrācūs·ae -ārum *fpl* Syracuse *(chief city of Sicily)*
Syrācūsān·us *or* **Syrācūsi·us -a -um** *adj* Syracusan
Syri·a -ae *f* **(Sur-)** Syria *(usu. including Phoenicia and Palestine)*
Syriac·us -a -um *adj* Syrian; from Syria; produced in Syria
Syriātic·us -a -um *adj* Syrian
Sȳr·inx -ingos *f* nymph who was pursued by Pan and changed into a reed
Syri·us -a -um *adj* Syrian; of Syros in the Cyclades ‖ *m* Syrian
syrm·a -atis *n* robe with a train *(worn esp. by actors in tragedies);* tragedy
Syrophoen·īx -īcis *m* Syrophoenician *(Phoenicia was regarded as part of Syria)*
Sȳr·os -ī *f* Syros *(island in the Cyclades between Delos and Paros, modern Syria)*
syrt·is -is *f* sand bank, sand dune, quicksand ‖ **Syrtis** *f* Gulf of Sidra in N. Africa ‖ Gulf of Gabes ‖ *fpl* name of an area of sand dunes on the coast between Carthage and Cyrene
Syr·us -a -um *adj* **(Sur-)** Syrian ‖ *mf* Syrian; proper name of a slave

T

T, t *(supply* littera) *f* nineteenth letter of the Latin alphabet; letter name: **te**
*(***T.** *abbr* **Titus** *(Roman first name, praenomen)*
tabān·us -ī *m* horsefly
tabell·a -ae *f* small board, panel; plaque; writing tablet; page *(of a bound notebook);* ballot; picture, painting; votive tablet; game board; placard, notice; door panel ‖ *fpl* notebook
tabellāri·us -a -um *adj (leg)* regulating voting by secret ballot ‖ *m* mail carrier, courier
tāb·eō -ēre *intr* to waste away; to melt; to decay; to drip; **tābentēs genae** sunken cheeks
tabern·a -ae *f* hut; booth, stall, shop; inn; **taberna dīversōria** *(or* **meritōria)** inn
tabernācul·um -ī *n* tent; **tabernāculum capere** *(of an augur)* to set up a tent in which to take the auspices
tabernār·ius -(i)ī *m* shopkeeper
tāb·ēs -is *f* melting; wasting, decay; dwindling, shrinking; decaying matter, rot; disease; moral corruption; means of corruption
tāb·ēscō -ēscere -uī *intr* to begin to decay; to begin to melt; to rot
tābidul·us -a -um *adj* rotting; wasting
tābid·us -a -um *adj* wasting, decaying; melting; corrupting; infectious
tābific·us -a -um *adj* wasting; melting; *(fig)* gnawing
tabul·a -ae *f* plank, board; writing tablet; painting *(on a panel of wood);* game board; votive tablet; door panel; placard, advertisement; auction notice; will; record; counting board ‖ *fpl* account books, records, register, lists; **tabulae novae** clean slate *(i.e., cancellation of debts)*
tabulār·ium -(i)ī *n* archives; archives building
tabulār·ius -(i)ī *m* accountant, bookkeeper
tabulāti·ō -ōnis *f* flooring; floor, story
tabulāt·us -a -um *adj* boarded ‖ *n* floor, story; layer; deck *(of a ship);* row *(of trees)*
tāb·um -ī *n* rot, putrid matter; infectious disease, plague
tac·eō -ēre -uī -itus *tr* to be silent about, pass over in silence ‖ *intr* to be silent, be still
tacitē *adv* silently; secretly, privately; without publicity; tacitly, without express statement; imperceptibly, quietly
taciturnit·ās -ātis *f* taciturnity; silence; failure to communicate
taciturn·us -a -um *adj* taciturn, silent; noiseless, hushed, quiet
tacit·us -a -um *adj* silent; mute; unmentioned; secret; *(leg)* tacit; **per tacitum** in silence
Tacit·us -ī *m* Gaius(?) Cornelius Tacitus *(Roman historian, c. A.D. 55–115)*
tāctil·is -is -e *adj* tangible
tācti·ō -ōnis *f* touch, touching; feeling, sense of touch
tāctus *pp of* **tangō**
tāct·us -ūs *m* touch; handling; *(fig)* contact, influence
taed·a -ae *f* pine wood; pitch; pine board; pine tree; torch; wedding torch; *(fig)* wedding
tae·det -dēre -sum est *v impers* it irks; *(w. acc of person and gen of the cause), e.g.,* **mē taedet sermōnis tuī** I am sick of your talk, your talk irks me
taedi·fer -fera -ferum *adj* carrying a torch, torch-bearing
taed·ium -(i)ī *n* tediousness; weariness, boredom; feeling of disgust; object of disgust; nuisance

Taenarid·ēs -ae *m* man from Taenarus, Spartan *(esp. Hyacinthus)*
Taenar·is -idis *adj (fem only)* Spartan ‖ *f* Spartan woman
Taenari·us *or* **Taenare·us -a -um** *adj* of Taenarus, Taenarian; *(poet)* Spartan, Laconian
Taenar·um *or* **Taenar·on -ī** *n, or* **Taenar·os** *or* **Taenar·us -ī** *mf* Taenarus *(promontory at the S. tip of the Peloponnesus, near which a cavern was thought to lead to the lower world);* Hades
taeni·a -ae *f* band, ribbon; string
taesum est *see* **taedet**
tae·ter -tra -trum *adj* **(tet-)** offensive, revolting, loathsome; hideous; *(of actions)* monstrous, horrible
taetrē *adv* foully, hideously
taetricus *see* **tētricus**
tag·āx -ācis *adj* light-fingered *(thief)*
Tag·ēs -is *m* Etruscan god, originator of divination and grandson of Jupiter
tālār·is -is -e *adj* ankle-length ‖ *npl* ankle-length clothes; sandals; winged sandals; *(fig)* means of getting away
tālāri·us -a -um *adj* of dice; **lūdus tālārius** game of dice
talāsiō *interj* **(-lass-)** wedding cry
tāle·a -ae *f* rod, bar, stake
talent·um -ī *n* talent *(Greek weight, varying from state to state, but equal to about 50 lbs.; also a unit of currency, consisting of 60 minae, or about 600 denarii, or about $600);* **talentum magnum** Attic talent *(so called to distinguish it from talents from other cities of lower value)*
tāli·ō -ōnis *f (leg)* punishment in kind, exaction of compensation in kind
tāl·is -is -e *adj* such, of that kind; so great, so excellent; **tālis … quālis** such … as
tāliter *adv* in such a way
tālitr·um -ī *n* fillip *(flick with the tip of the middle finger and the thumb)*
talp·a -ae *mf* mole *(animal)*
Talthyb·ius -(i)ī *m* herald of Agamemnon
tāl·us -ī *m* ankle; anklebone; foot; knucklebone *(used in playing dice);* **tālīs lūdere** to play dice; **tālōs iacere** to roll the dice
tam *adv* to such an extent, to such a degree, so, so much; **tam … quam** the … the; **tam magis … quam magis** the more … the more
tamar·īx -īcis *f* tamarisk *(ornamental shrub or short tree)*
tamdiū *or* **tam diū** *adv* so long, how long; **tamdiū quam** *(or* **tamdiū dum)** as long as
tamen *adv* yet, nevertheless, still, just the same
tamendem *adv* all the same
tamenetsī *conj* even though ‖ *adv* all the same, nevertheless
Tames·is -is *m or* **Tames·a -ae** *f* Thames River
tametsī *conj* even if, although
tamquam *conj* **(tan-)** as, just as, as much as; just as if; **tamquam sī** just as if
Tana·ger -grī *m* river in Lucania
Tanagr·a -ae *f* town in Boeotia
Tana·is -is *m* river of Sarmatia *(modern River Don)*
Tanaqu·il -ilis *f* wife of the elder Tarquin
tandem *adv* at last, in the end, finally; *(expressing urgency or impatience)* now, tell me, please, just; **quoūsque tandem** just how long?
tangō tangere tetigī tāctus *tr* to touch; to handle, meddle with; to taste; to come to, reach; to border on; to hit, beat; to wash; to anoint; to gall; to move to pity; to dupe; to touch upon, mention; to touch, be related to; to undertake; **dē caelō** *(or* **fulmine)** **tangere** to strike with lightning
tanquam *see* **tamquam**
Tantale·us -a -um *adj* of Tantalus
Tantalid·ēs -ae *m* descendant of Tantalus *(e.g., Atreus, Aegisthus, Agamemnon, Menelaus)*
Tantal·is -idos *f* female descendant of Tantalus *(e.g., Niobe, Hermione)*
Tantal·us -ī *m* son of Jupiter and father of Pelops and Niobe; he was punished in Hades with constant hunger and thirst
tantill·us -a -um *adj* so small, so little ‖ *n* a bit; **tantillō minus** a little less
tantisper *adv* just so long *(and no longer);* just for the moment
tantopere *or* **tantō opere** *adv* so much, so greatly, to such a degree, so earnestly, so hard
tantulum *adv* so little, in the least
tantul·us -a -um *adj* so little, so small ‖ *n* so little, such a trifle; **tantulō vēndere** to sell for such a trifling amount
tantum *adv (see also the neut of* **tantus)** so much, so greatly, to such a degree, so far, so long, so; only, just, but just; hardly, scarcely; **nōn tantum** all but, almost; **nōn tantum omnēs opitulārī voluērunt** almost all wished to be of assistance; **nōn tantum … sed etiam** not only … but also; **tantum modo** only
tantummodo *adv* only
tantundem *adv* just as much, just as far, to the same extent
tant·us -a -um *adj* of such size, so big, so great; so much; so little; so important ‖ *pron neut* so much; so little; so small an amount, so small a number; to such an extent *or* degree; **alterum tantum** twice the amount; **in tantum** to such an extent;

tantī of such value, worth so much, at so high a price; of little account, of such small importance; **tantō** *(as abl of price)* at such a price, for so much; *(w. comparatives)* by so much, so much the; **tantō ante (post)** so much earlier (later); **tantō melior**! so much the better!; **tantō nequior**! so much the worse!; **tantum est** that is all; **tantum abesse ut** to be so far (from being the case) that; **tantum āfuit ut perīculōsum reī pūblicae putāret exercitum ut** (+ *subj)* so far was he from thinking that the army was a threat to the country that ... ; **ter (quater) tantum** three (four) times as much

tant·usdem -adem -undem *adj* just as big, just as large, just as great **||** *n* the same quantity, just as much; *(w. advl force)* to the same degree, just as much; **tantīdem** at the same price; **tantundem est** it comes to the same thing

tap·ēs -ētis *m,* **tapēt·e -is** *n,* **tapēt·um -ī** *n* carpet; tapestry; coverlet

tapēt·ia -ium *npl* tapestry

taratantara *n* sound produced by the trumpet; **at tuba taratantara dīxit** but the trumpet went "taratantara"

tardē *adv* slowly; with difficulty; late; **cum tardissimē** at the latest

tardēsc·ō -ere *intr* to become slow; to falter

tardip·ēs -edis *adj* limping

tardit·ās -ātis *f* tardiness; slowness; procrastination; dullness, stupidity

tarditūd·ō -inis *f* tardiness; slowness

tardiuscul·us -a -um *adj* rather slow, slowish, dragging

tard·ō -āre -āvī -ātus *tr* to slow down, delay, hinder; to check *(emotions);* to dull *(the senses)* **||** *intr* to go slow, take it easy; to hold back

tard·us -a -um *adj* tardy, slow; lingering; mentally slow, mentally retarded; deliberate; crippling; *(of events)* long drawn out, making slow progress

Tarentīn·us -a -um *adj* Tarentine **||** *mpl* Tarentines

Tarent·um -ī *n* Tarentum *(town on S. coast of Italy, modern Taranto)* **||** a section on the west side of the Campus Martius

tarm·es -itis *m* termite

Tarpēi·us -a -um *adj* Tarpeian; **mōns Tarpēius** *(or* **Tarpēia rūpēs** *(or* **Tarpēium saxum)** Tarpeian cliff *(on the Capitoline Hill from which criminals were thrown)* **||** *f* Roman girl who treacherously opened the citadel to the Sabine attackers

tarpezīt·a -ae *m* **(trap-)** banker, money-changer

Tarquiniān·us -a -um *adj* of the Tarquins

Tarquiniēns·is -is -e *adj* of the town of Tarquinii **||** *mpl* inhabitants of Tarquinii

Tarquini·ī -ōrum *mpl* Tarquinii *(important Etruscan city on the W. coast of Italy, about seventy miles N. of Rome, modern Tarquinia)*

Tarquini·us -a -um *adj* Tarquinian **||** *m* Tarquinius Priscus *(fifth king of Rome, c. 616–579 B.C.)* **||** Tarquinius Superbus *(seventh and last king of Rome, c. 534–510 B.C.)*

Tarracīn·a -ae *f or* **Terracīn·ae -ārum** *fpl* Terracina *(town in Latium)*

Tarrac·o -ōnis *f* Tarraco *(now Terragona, ancient town on the East coast of Spain, which Augustus made the capital of one of the three Spanish provinces)*

Tarracōnēns·is -is -e *adj* of Terragona, Tarragonian; **Hispānia Tarracōnēnsis** Tarragonian Spain

Tartar·a -ōrum *npl or* **Tartar·us** *or* **Tartar·os -ī** *m* Tartarus *(lower level of Hades reserved for notorious criminals)*

Tartare·us -a -um *adj* of Tartarus, infernal

tat *or* **tatae** *interj* uhoh! *(expression of surprise)*

tat·a -ae *m (coll)* daddy; grandpa

Tat·ius -(i)ī *m* Titus Tatius *(king of the Sabines who later ruled jointly with Romulus until the latter had him killed)*

tau *indecl n* the Greek letter tau

taure·us -a -um *adj* bull's, of a bull; **terga taurea** bulls' hides; drums **||** *f* rawhide, whip

Taur·ī -ōrum *mpl* inhabitants of Chersonesus Tauricus *(modern Crimea)*

Tauric·us -a -um *adj* Tauric **||** *mpl* the Tauri

taurif·er -era -erum *adj (of regions)* bull-producing

tauriform·is -is -e *adj* bull-shaped

taurīn·us -a -um *adj* bull's; made of bull's hide; bull-like **|| Taurīn·us -a -um** of the Taurini *(a Ligurian tribe)* **||** *mpl* the Taurini

Tauri·us -a -um *adj* Roman clan name *(nomen);* **lūdī Tauriī** games held in the Circus Flaminius in honor of the gods of the lower world

taur·us -ī *m* bull; bronze bull made as an instrument of torture **|| Taurus** *(astr)* Taurus *(constellation)* **|| Taurus** the Taurus mountain range in S.E. Asia Minor

taxāti·ō -ōnis *f* evaluation, assessment; *(leg)* maximum sum

taxill·us -ī *m* small die *(for playing dice)*

tax·ō -āre -āvī -ātus *tr* to touch repeatedly, handle; to appraise, assess the value of; to reproach; to tease

tax·us -ī *f* yew tree

Tāyget·ē -ēs *f (astr)* one of the seven Pleiads forming the constellation of the Pleiades

Tāyget·us -ī *m* mountain range in Laconia, separating it from Messenia to the W.

-te = *suf for* **tū** *and* **tē**

tē *pron, acc & abl of* **tū**

Teān·um -ī *n* town in Campania *(modern Teano)* **ll** town in Apulia *(modern Civitate)*

techn·a *or* **techin·a -ae** *f* trick

technyph·ion -iī *n* a little workroom

Tecmess·a -ae *f* mistress of Ajax son of Telamon

tēctē *adv* cautiously, guardedly

tēct·or -ōris *m* plasterer

tēctōriol·um -ī *n* bit of plasterwork

tēctōri·us -a -um *adj* plaster, of plaster; **opus tēctōrium** plasterwork, stucco **ll** *n* plaster, stucco; fresco painting; beauty preparation

tēct·um -ī *n* roof; ceiling; canopy; cover, shelter; house

tēct·us -a -um *pp of* **tegō ll** *adj* concealed; secret; guarded *(words);* reserved, secretive *(person)* **ll** *n see* **tēctum**

tēcum = cum tē

tēd- = taed-

Tege·a -ae *f* town in S.E. Arcadia

Tegeae·us -a -um *adj* Tegean, Arcadian **ll** *m* Pan **ll** *f* Arcadian maiden *(esp. Atalanta and Callisto)*

Tegeāt·ēs -ae *m* inhabitant of Tegea

teg·es -etis *f* mat *(used for lying on or as a covering)*

tegetīcul·a -ae *f* small mat

tegill·um -ī *n* hood, cowl

tegim·en *or* **teg(u)m·en** -**inis** *n (applied to clothing, armor, skin of an animal or of fruit)* cover, covering; vault *(of heaven)*

tegiment·um *or* **teg(u)ment·um -ī** *n (applied to clothing, armor, skins, shells)* cover, covering

tegō tegere tēxī tēctus *tr* to cover; to protect, shelter; to hide; to bury; **tegere lātus** *(w. gen)* to escort *(s.o.)*

tēgul·a -ae *f* tile **ll** *fpl* roof tiles, tiled roof; siding for walls

tegumen *see* **tegimen**

tegumentum *see* **tegimentum**

tēl·a -ae *f* web; warp *(horizontal threads of a loom);* yarn beam; loom; *(fig)* design, plan

Telam·ōn -ōnis *m* son of Aeacus, brother of Peleus, king of Salamis, and father of Ajax and Teucer

Telamōniad·ēs -ae *m* son of Telamon *(esp. Ajax)*

Telamōn·ius -(i)ī *m* Ajax *(son of Telamon)*

Tēlegon·us -ī *m* son of Ulysses and Circe

Telemach·us -ī *m* son of Ulysses and Penelope

Tēleph·us -ī *m* king of Mysia, wounded by the spear of Achilles and later cured by its rust

tēlin·um -ī *n* perfume made of fenugreek

tell·ūs -ūris *f* the earth; ground, earth; land, country; dry land

tēl·um -ī *n* missile, weapon; spear, javelin, dart; sword, dagger; ax; shaft *(of light);* **cum tēlis** *(or* **tēlō)** armed

temerāri·us -a -um *adj* casual, accidental; rash, thoughtless

temere *adv* by chance, without cause; at random; rashly, thoughtlessly; **nōn temere** not lightly; not easily; hardly ever; **nūllus diēs temere intercessit quō nōn scrīberet** hardly a day ever went by without his writing

temerit·ās -ātis *f* chance, accident; rashness, thoughtlessness **ll** *fpl* foolhardy acts

temer·ō -āre -āvī -ātus *tr* to darken, blacken; to violate, disgrace, defile

Temes·ē -ēs *f or* **Temes·a -ae** *f* town in Bruttium noted for its copper mines

tēmēt·um -ī *n* (intoxicating) liquor

temn·ō -ere *tr* to slight

tēm·ō -ōnis *m* pole, tongue *(of a carriage or plow);* wagon

Tempē *indecl npl* scenic valley between Mt. Olympus and Mt. Ossa in Thessaly

temperāment·um -ī *n* blend; moderation; temperate heat; restraint, balance

temper·āns -antis *adj* self-controlled

temperanter *adv* moderately

temperanti·a -ae *f* self-control, moderation

temperātē *adv* moderately

temperāti·ō -ōnis *f* blending; composition; proportion, symmetry; temperament; organization, constitution; control, controlling power

temperāt·or -ōris *m* controller; moderator; governor

temperāt·us -a -um *adj* tempered; self-controlled; moderate

temperī *or* **temporī** *adv* in time, on time; in due time, at the right time

temperi·ēs -ēī *f* blending; climate; mild climate, moderate temperature

temper·ō -āre -āvī -ātus *tr* to compound, combine, blend, temper; to regulate, modify *(in regard to temperature);* to adjust; to tune; to govern, control, rule; to control *(by steering)* **ll** *intr* to be moderate, exercise restraint; *(w. dat)* to exercise control over; *(w. abl or* **ab** + *abl, w.* **quīn, quōminus, nē,** *w. inf)* to refrain from

tempest·ās -ātis *f* time, period, season, occasion; stormy weather, storm; misfortune, disaster; hail *(of weapons)*

tempestīvē *adv* at the right time

tempestīvit·ās -ātis *f* right time, timeliness
tempestīvō *adv* at the right time
tempestīv·us -a -um *adj* timely, seasonable, fit; ripe, mature; in good time, early
templ·um -ī *n* temple, shrine, sanctuary; space marked off in the sky *or* on the earth for the observation of omens; open space, quarter; site for a temple
temporāl·is -is -e *adj* temporary; temporal
temporāri·us -a -um *adj* temporary; changeable *(character)*
tempore *or* **temporī** *adv* in time, on time; in due time, at the right time
temptābund·us -a -um *adj* making constant attempts, trying
temptām·en -inis *n* attempt, effort; *(w. gen)* test of
temptāment·um -ī *n* attempt, effort; temptation, trial
temptāti·ō -ōnis *f* trial; attack *(of sickness, of an enemy); (w. gen)* attack on
temptāt·or -ōris *m* assailant, attacker
tempt·ō -āre -āvī -ātus *tr* **(tent-)** to test, feel, probe; to attempt; to attack; to try to influence, tamper with, tempt, try to induce; to urge, incite, sound out; to worry, distress
temptus *pp of* **temnō**
temp·us -oris *n* time; period, season; occasion, opportunity; right time, good time, proper period; times, condition, state, position; need, emergency; *(anat)* temple; *(pros)* measure, quantity, cadence; **ad tempus** *(or* **temporis causā)** to suit the occasion; **ante tempus** before time, too soon; **ex tempore** on the spur of the moment; **idem temporis** at the same time; **id temporis** at that time; **in ipsō tempore** in the nick of time; **in tempore** at the right moment; just in time; as occasion offers; **in tempus** temporarily, for a time; **per tempus** just in time; **prīmum tempus** spring; **prō tempore** as time permits; according to circumstances; to suit the occasion; **tempore** at an opportune time; **temporī cēdere** to yield to circumstances; **tempus in ultimum** to the last extremity; **tunc tempus** for the time, at the time
tēmulent·us -a -um *adj* intoxicated
tenācit·ās -ātis *f* tenacity; miserliness
tenāciter *adv* tightly, firmly
ten·āx -ācis *adj* holding tight, gripping, clinging; sticky; firm; obstinate; stingy; *(w. gen)* clinging to
tendicul·ae -ārum *fpl* little snare, little noose, little trap
tendō tendere tetendī tentus *or* **tēnsus** *tr* to stretch, stretch out, hold out, spread; to strain; to head for; to aim, shoot *(an arrow);* to bend *(a bow);* to tune *(an instrument);* to pitch *(a tent)* **II** *intr* to pitch tents, be encamped; to travel, sail, move, march; to endeavor; to contend, fight; to exert oneself; *(w. inf)* to try to; *(w.* **ad) 1** to tend toward, be inclined toward; **2** to move toward, travel to, aim for; *(w.* **contrā** + *acc)* to fight against
tenebr·ae -ārum *fpl* darkness; night; blindness; dark place, haunts; unconsciousness; death; lower world; obscurity, low station; ignorance; gloomy state of affairs
tenebricōs·us -a -um *adj* dark, gloomy; hidden, concealed *(lust)*
tenebric·us -a -um *adj* dark, gloomy
tenebrōs·us -a -um *adj* dark, gloomy
Tened·os *or* **Tened·us -ī** *f* Tenedos *(island off the coast of Troy)*
tenellul·us -a -um *adj* tender little, dainty little
tenell·us -a -um *adj* dainty
ten·eō -ēre -uī -tus *tr* to hold, hold tight; to keep; to grasp, comprehend; to comprise; to possess, occupy, be master of; to hold back, restrain, repress; to charm, amuse; to have control of, get the better of; to interest; to keep, detain; to hold to, stick to, insist on *(an opinion); (w. inf)* to know how to; **cursum** *(or* **iter** *or* **viam) tenēre** to continue on a course; **II** *refl* to remain *(in a place),* stay put **II** *intr* to hold out, last, keep on; to continue, persist; to continue on a course; *(w.* **quīn, quōminus, nē** *or inf)* to refrain from; *(w.* **ut, nē)** to make good one's point (that, that not)
ten·er -era -erum *adj* tender, soft, delicate; young, youthful; impressionable; weak; effeminate; voluptuous
tenerāsc·ō *or* **tenerēsc·ō -ere** *intr* to grow weak; to become flabby
tenerē *adv* softly
tenerit·ās -ātis *f* weakness
teneritūd·ō -inis *f* tender age
tēnesm·os -ī *m* straining to defecate
ten·or -ōris *m* uninterrupted course; continuity; **ūnō tenōre** uninterruptedly
Tēn·os -ī *f* island of the Cyclades
tēns·a -ae *f* car carrying images of the gods in procession, float
tēns·us -a -um *pp of* **tendō II** *adj* stretched, drawn tight; stretched out
tentīg·ō -inis *f* lust
tentō *see* **temptō**
tentōr·ium -iī *n* tent
tent·us -a -um *pp of* **tendō** *and* **teneō II** *adj* stretched, drawn tight
Tentyr·a -ōrum *npl* town in Upper Egypt
tenuī *perf of* **teneō**
tenuicul·us -a -um *adj* poor, paltry
tenu·is -is -e *adj* thin; fine; delicate; precise; shallow *(groove, etc.);* slight, puny,

poor, insignificant; plain, simple; small, narrow; shallow *(water)*

tenuit·ās -ātis *f* thinness, fineness; leanness; simplicity; precision; poverty; simpleness *(of style)*

tenuiter *adv* thinly; slightly; poorly, indifferently; exactly, minutely; superficially

tenu·ō -āre -āvī -ātus *tr* to make thin; to contract; to dissolve; to lessen; to weaken; to rarefy; to make *(the voice)* shrill; to emaciate *(the body)*

ten·us -oris *n* trap, snare

tenus *prep (w. gen; more frequently, w. abl, always placed after the noun)* as far as, up to, down to; **nōmine** *(or* **verbō)** **tenus** as far as the name goes, nominally

Te·os *or* **Te·us -ī** *f* town on the coast of Asia Minor, the birthplace of Anacreon

tepe·faciō -facere -fēcī -factus *tr* to warm up

tepefact·ō -āre *tr* to be in the habit of warming

tep·eō -ēre -uī *intr* to get warm; to grow lukewarm; to glow with love; to be cool, be indifferent; **tepēre puellā** to be in love with the girl

tep·ēscō -ēscere -uī *intr* to grow warm; to grow lukewarm, grow indifferent

tepid·us -a -um *adj* warm, lukewarm, tepid

tep·or -ōris *m* warmth; coolness, lack of heat *(in a bath);* lack of fire *(in a speech)*

tepuī *perf of* **tepeō** *and* **tepēscō**

ter *adv* three times

-ter *advl suf of third-declension adjectives:* **audācter** boldly; *stems in* **-nt-** *drop* **-t-**: **prūdenter** prudently; *also of second-declension adjectives:* **hūmāniter** kindly

-ter -terī *or* **-trī** *m* **-tera -terum** *or* **-tra -trum** *adjl suf* often *used to forming pairs:* **magister** master, **minister** servant; **noster** our, **vester** your

terdeciēns *or* **terdeciēs** *adv* thirteen times

terebinth·us -ī *f* terebinth, turpentine tree

terebr·a -ae *f* drill

terebr·ō -āre -āvī -ātus *tr* to bore, drill a hole in, pierce

terēd·ō -inis *f* grubworm

Tēreid·ēs -ae *m* Itys *(son of Tereus)*

Terentiān·us -a -um *adj* of the Terentian clan; *esp.* written, portrayed, *etc.*, by the poet Terence

Terent·ius -(i)ī *m* Terence *(Marcus Terentius Afer, Roman comic poet, c. 190–159 B.C.)*

ter·es -etis *adj* smooth, well-rounded; polished, shapely; round, cylindrical; *(fig)* fine, elegant

Tēr·eūs -eī *or* **-eos** *m* evil king of Thrace, husband of Procne, and father of Itys

tergemin·us -a -um *adj* triplet, triple

ter·geō -gēre -sī -sus *or* **terg·ō -ere** *tr* to wipe off, wipe dry; to scour; to clean, cleanse

tergīn·um -ī *n* rawhide; scourge

tergiversāti·ō -ōnis *f* refusal; evasion, subterfuge

tergivers·or -ārī -ātus sum *intr* to turn one's back; to be shifty

tergō *see* **tergeō**

terg·um -ī *n or* **terg·us -oris** *n* back; back part, rear; ridge; hide; leather; leather objects: bag, shield, drum; *(mil)* rear; **ā tergō** in the rear, from behind; **in tergum** backward; **tergum dare** *or* **vertere** to turn tail, run away, flee

terment·um -ī *n* sore caused by friction

term·es -itis *m* branch, bough

Termindruāl·ia -ium *or* **-iōrum** *npl* festival in honor of Terminus *(god of boundaries, celebrated on February 23)*

termināti·ō -ōnis *f* the marking of the boundaries of a territory *(esp. w. boundary stones or posts);* boundary; tract of land along a boundary; end, goal *(of an activity);* decision, determining; *(rhet)* arrangement, ending *(of a sentence)*

termin·ō -āre -āvī -ātus *tr* to mark off with boundaries, bound, limit; to fix, determine, define; to terminate, conclude; to settle *(an issue); (rhet)* to round out *(a sentence)*

termin·us -ī *m* boundary, limit, bound ‖ **Terminus** god of boundaries

tern·ī -ae -a *adj* three apiece, three each, three at a time; three in a row

terō terere trīvī trītus *tr* to rub; to wear down; to wear out *(by constant handling);* to make *(words, expressions)* trite *(by repetition),* run into the ground; to travel *(a road)* repeatedly; to trample, crush; to spend, waste *(time);* to smooth, polish; to sharpen; to thresh *(grain);* to grind *(grain);* **ōtium terere** to waste time in idleness

Terpsichor·ē -ēs *f* Muse of dancing, of lyric poetry; *(fig)* poetry

ter(r)ūnc·ius -(i)ī *m* copper coin *(weighing three* **ūnciae** *= three-twelfths of an* **as** *or one-fortieth of a* **dēnārius,** *i.e., less than 1¢);* **hērēs ex terūnciō** heir to one fourth of an estate

terr·a -ae *f* the earth; land; earth, ground, soil; country, region, territory; **in terrā** *(or* **terrīs)** in the world, in existence; *(as contrasted with heaven)* on earth; *(astr)* the planet earth; **terrā ortus** sprung from the earth, indigenous; **terrae fīlius** a nobody; **terrae** *(or* **terrārum)** **mōtus** earthquake; **ubi terrārum** where in the world

terrāneol·a -ae *f* crested lark

terrēn·us -a -um *adj* earthly, terrestrial; earthen ‖ *n* land, ground
terr·eō -ēre -uī -itus *tr* to frighten, scare, terrify; to deter
terrestr·is -is -e *adj* of the earth, on the earth; land, earth; terrestrial; **proelium terrestre** land battle
terre·us -a -um *adj* earth-born
terribil·is -is -e *adj* terrible, frightful
terricul·a -ae *f* bogey; scary thing
terrific·ō -āre *tr* to terrify
terrific·us -a -um *adj* terrifying, awe-inspiring, alarming
terrigen·a -ae *m* earth-born creature
terriloqu·us -a -um *adj* ominous, alarming
terripav·ium -(i)ī *n* **(-pud·ium, -puv·ium)** *(etymologizing forms of* **tripudium)** *see* **tripudium**
territ·ō -āre -āvī *tr* to keep frightening; to try to scare, intimidate
territōr·ium -(i)ī *n* land around a town, territory, suburbs
terr·or -ōris *m* terror, alarm, dread
terruī *perf of* **terreō**
ters·us -a -um *pp of* **tergeō** ‖ *adj* clean, neat; terse; polished *(writing)*
tertiadecimān·ī -ōrum *mpl* soldiers of the thirteenth legion
tertiān·us -a -um *adj* recurring every three days, *(in our system: every other day)*, tertian *(fever)* ‖ *mpl* soldiers of the third legion
tertiō *adv* in the third place, thirdly; the third time
tertium *adv* for the third time
terti·us -a -um *adj* third
terti·us decim·us -a -um *adj* thirteenth
terūnci·us -ī *m* three-fifth of an **as**, a quarter-as; *(fig)* a mere trifle; **hērēs ex terūnciō** heir to one-fourth
tervenēfic·us -ī *m (term of abuse)* three-time killer, absolute villain
tesqu·a -ōrum *npl* wilderness, wilds
tesselāt·us -a -um *adj* tessellated, mosaic
tessell·a -ae *f* cubed mosaic stone
tesser·a -ae *f* cube; die; watchword, countersign; tally, token; ticket *(for the distribution of money or grain)*
tesserār·ius -(i)ī *m (mil)* officer of the day
tesserul·a -ae *f* small cube; ticket
test·a -ae *f* brick, tile; jug, crock; potsherd; shellfish; shell *(of a crustacean, snail, etc.)*; fragment, splinter *(esp. of a broken tooth or bone)*
testāmentāri·us -a -um *adj* pertaining to a will, testamentary ‖ *m* forger of wills
testāment·um -ī *n* testament, will
testāti·ō -ōnis *f* testifying to a fact; *(leg)* deposition
testāt·or -ōris *m* testator *(one who makes a will)*
testāt·us -a -um *adj* well-attested; witnessed
testicul·us -ī *m* testicle
testificāti·ō -ōnis *f* testifying; proof, evidence
testific·or -ārī -ātus sum *tr* to give as evidence, give proof of; to testify to; to vouch for; to invoke *(e.g., a god)* as one's witness; *(fig)* to give proof of
testimōn·ium -(i)ī *n* testimony
test·is -is *mf* witness ‖ *m* testicle
test·or -ārī -ātus sum *tr* to give as evidence; to show, prove, vouch for; to call to witness, appeal to ‖ *intr* to be a witness, testify; to make a will
test·ū -ūs *n see* **testum**
testūdine·us -a -um *adj* of a tortoise; made of tortoise shell
testūd·ō -inis *f* tortoise; tortoise shell; lyre, lute; arch, vault; *(mil)* protective shed *(for besiegers)*
testul·a -ae *f* potsherd
test·um -ī *n* earthenware lid; pot with a lid
tēte = *emphatic form of* **tē**
tetendī *perf of* **tendō**
Tēth·ys -yos *f* wife of Oceanus and mother of the sea nymphs; ocean, sea
tetigī *perf of* **tangō**
tetradrachm·um -ī *n* **(-trach-)** Greek silver coin *(worth four drachmas or four denarii or $4)*
tetra·ō -ōnis *m* game bird *(black grouse?)*
tetrarch·ēs -ae *m* tetrarch *(ruler of one fourth of a country)*; petty prince
tetrarchi·a -ae *f* tetrarchy
tetrastich·on -ī *n* four-line poem
tetric·us -a -um *adj* stern, gloomy, crabby; harsh, rough
tetrissit·ō -āre *intr* to quack
Teu·cer *or* **Teu·crus -crī** *m* son of Telamon and half-brother of Ajax ‖ son of Scamander of Crete, father-in-law of Dardanus, and later king of Troy
Teucri·a -ae *f* Troy, land of the Teucrians
Teucr·us -a -um *adj* Teucrian, Trojan ‖ *mpl* Trojans
Teuthrantē·us -a -um *adj* Mysian
Teuthranti·us -a -um *adj* of Teuthras; **turba Teuthrantia** fifty daughters of Thespius
Teuthr·ās -antis *m* ancient king of Mysia, father of Thespius
Teuton·ēs -um *or* **Teuton·ī -ōrum** *mpl* Teutons
Teutonic·us -a -um *adj* Teutonic
tex·ō -ere -uī -tus *tr* to weave; to plait; to build; to compose
textil·is -is -e *adj* woven; brocaded ‖ *n* fabric
text·or -ōris *m* weaver
textrīn·um -ī *n* weaving; weaving room

textr·īx -īcis *f* weaver *(female)*
textūr·a -ae *f* texture; web; fabric
text·us -a -um *pp of* **texō** ‖ *n* woven cloth, fabric; web
text·us -ūs *m* texture
texuī *perf of* **texō**
Thā·is -idis *or* **-idos** *f* notorious Athenian prostitute
thalam·us -ī *m* woman's room; bedroom; marriage bed; marriage
thalassic·us *or* **thalassin·us -a -um** *adj* sea-green, aquamarine
Thal·ēs -ae *m* Thales *(early Ionian philosopher of Miletus, regarded as one of the Seven Sages, fl 575 B.C.)*
Thalī·a *or* **Thalē·a -ae** *f* Muse of comedy and light verse ‖ one of the Graces ‖ a Nereid, sea nymph
thall·us -ī *m* green bough; green stem
Thaps·os -ī *f* city of N. Africa where Caesar defeated the Pompeians *(46 B.C.)*
Thasi·us -a -um *adj* of Thasos; **Thasius lapis** Thasian marble
Thas·os -ī *f* island in the Aegean Sea, off the coast of Thrace
Thaumantē·us -a -um *adj* descended from Thaumas *(a Titan)*
Thaumanti·as -adis *or* **Thaumant·is -idis** *f* Iris *(daughter of the Titan Thaumas)*
theātrāl·is -is -e *adj* theatrical
theātr·um -ī *n* theater
Thēb·ae -ārum *fpl* Thebes *(capital of Boeotia, founded by Cadmus)* ‖ Thebes *(city of Upper Egypt)* ‖ Thebes *(city in Mysia, home of Eetion, destroyed by Achilles)*
Thēba·is -idis *or* **-idos** *adj (fem only)* of Boeotian Thebes; of Thebes in Mysia; of Egyptian Thebes; **Thēbais nūpta** Theban bride *(i.e., Andromache)* ‖ *f* Theban woman; district around Egyptian Thebes, the Thebaid
Thēbān·us -a -um *adj & mf* Theban *(of Boeotia, Egypt, or Mysia)*
thēc·a -ae *f* case, box
them·a -atis *n* position of the planets *or* stars at one's birth, horoscope; *(rhet)* theme, topic proposed for debate in a school of rhetoric
Them·is -is *f* goddess of justice and of prophecy
Themistocl·ēs -is *m* Themistocles *(Athenian admiral and statesman, c. 528–459 B.C.)*
Themistoclē·us -a -um *adj* Themistoclean
thēnsaurāri·us -a -um *adj* of treasure
thēnsaurus *see* **thēsaurus**
Theocrit·us -ī *m* founder of Greek pastoral poetry, born at Syracuse *(3rd cent. B.C.)*
theologūmen·a -ōn *npl* essays on the gods
theolog·us -ī *m* theologian
therm·ae -ārum *fpl* hot baths, public baths *(which included rooms for social activities, lecture halls, theater, restaurants, workout rooms)*
Thermōd·ōn -ontis *m* river in Pontus, around which the Amazons were said to have lived
Thermōdontiac·us -a -um *adj* of the River Thermodon *(often applied to Amazons, esp. Hippolyta and Penthesilea, or to things connected with them)*
thermopōl·ium -(i)ī *n* hot-drink shop
thermopot·ō -āre *tr* to supply with warm drinks
Thermopyl·ae -ārum *fpl* **(-pul-)** Thermopylae *(famous pass in Thessaly, defended by Leonidas and his 400 Spartans in 480 B.C.)*
thermul·ae -ārum *fpl* small hot bath
Thersīt·ēs -ae *m* Greek soldier at Troy notorious for his ugliness
thēsaur·us -ī *m* **(thēns-)** storehouse; store, treasure, hoard
Thēs·eus -eī *or* **-eos** *m* king of Athens, son of Aegeus and husband *(or* lover) first of Ariadne and later of Phaedra
Thēsē·us -a -um *adj* of Theseus
Thēsīd·ae -ārum *mpl* Athenians
Thēsīd·ēs -ae *m* Hippolytus *(son of Theseus)* ‖ *mpl* Athenians
thes·is -is *f (rhet)* general question *(opp:* a particular case)
Thespiad·es -um *fpl* descendants of Thespius *(fifty sons of Thespius's fifty daughters)*
Thespi·ae -ārum *fpl* town in Boeotia near Mt. Helicon
Thesp·is -is *m* traditional founder of Greek tragedy *(his first presentation was in 535 B.C.)*
Thespi·us -a -um *adj* Thespian ‖ *m* a king of Mysia who had fifty daughters; *see* **Thespiades** ‖ *fpl* town in Boeotia near Mt. Helicon
Thessali·a -ae *f* Thessaly *(most northerly district of Greece)*
Thessalic·us -a -um *adj* Thessalian
Thessal·is -idis *or* **-idos** *adj (fem only)* Thessalian ‖ *f* Thessalian woman *(esp. a witch)*
Thessal·us -a -um *adj* Thessalian ‖ *mpl* people of Thessaly
Thestorid·ēs -ae *m* Calchas *(son of Thestor and famous Greek seer in the Trojan War)*
thēta *indecl n* the Greek letter theta *(written on tablets by jurors voting for the death sentence)*
Thet·is -idis *or* **-idos** *f* sea nymph, daughter of Nereus and Doris, wife of Peleus, and mother of Achilles

thias·us -ī *m* Bacchic dance; troupe of Bacchic dancers
Thisb·ē -ēs *f* girl in Bablyon, loved by Pyramus ‖ small town in Boeotia
Thoantē·us -a -um *adj* of Thoas
Tho·ās -antis *m* king of the Taurians, slain by Orestes ‖ king of Lemnos and father of Hypsipyle
thol·us -ī *m* rotunda
thōr·āx -ācis *m* breastplate
Thrāc·a -ae *or* **Thrāc·ē -ēs** *f* Thrace *(country N. of the Aegean)*
Thrāci·us -a -um *adj* Thracian ‖ *f* Thrace
Thraex *see* **Thrēx**
Thr·āx -ācis *m* Thracian
Thre(i)ss·a -ae *f* Thracian woman
Thr·ēx -ēcis *or* **Thr·aex -aecis** *m* Thracian gladiator *(i.e., armed like a Thracian with saber and small shield)*
thron·us -ī *m* throne
Thūcȳdid·ēs -is *or* **-ī** *m* Thucydides *(Greek historian of the Peloponnesian War, c. 456–400 B.C.)*
Thūl·ē *or* **T(h)ȳl·ē -ēs** *f* island located in the far north, perhaps Iceland or part of Scandinavia
thunn·us -ī *m* tuna
thūr- = tur-
Thūri·ī -ōrum *mpl* Thurii *(Greek city on the Tarentine Gulf in S. Italy)*
Thūrīn·us -a -um *adj & m* Thurian
thū·s -ris *n* incense, frankincense
Thybris *see* **Tiberis**
Thyēn·ē -ēs *f* nymph who nursed Bacchus
Thyest·ēs -ae *or* **-is** *m* son of Pelops, brother of Atreus, and father of Aegisthus
thymbr·a -ae *f (bot)* savory *(used as a spice in cooking)*
thym·um -ī *n (bot)* thyme *(common garden herb used as seasoning)*
Thȳni·a -ae *f* Bithynia *(country of Asia Minor on the S. coast of the Black Sea)*
Thȳniac·us -a -um *adj* Bithynian
thynn·us -ī *m* tuna
Thȳn·us -a -um *adj & m* Bithynian
Thyōn·eūs -eī *m* Bacchus
thyrs·us -ī *m* Bacchic wand twined with vine leaves and ivy, and crowned with a pine cone
Ti. *abbr* **Tiberius** *(Roman first name, praenomen)*
tiār·a -ae *f or* **tiār·ās -ae** *m* tiara
Tiberīn·is -idis *or* **-idos** *adj (fem only)* of the Tiber
Tiberīn·us -a -um *adj* of the Tiber River ‖ *m* eponymous hero of the Tiber River
Tiber·is *or* **Tibr·is** *or* **Thybr·is -is** *m* Tiber River
Tiber·ius -(i)ī *m* Tiberius *(Roman first name, praenomen); esp.* Tiberius Claudius Nero Caesar *(successor of Augustus, 42 B.C.–A.D. 37, ruling from A.D. 14–37)* ‖ Tiberius Sempronius Gracchus *(socialist reformer, killed in 133 B.C.)*
tībi·a -ae *f* shinbone, tibia; flute
tībiāl·e -is *n* stocking
tībīc·en -inis *m* flutist; prop; pillar
tībīcin·a -ae *f* flutist *(female)*
Tibull·us -ī *m* Albius Tibullus *(Roman elegiac poet, c. 54–19 B.C.)*
Tīb·ur -uris *n* town of Latium on the Anio *(modern Tivoli)*
Tīburn·us -a -um *adj* of Tibur ‖ *m* legendary founder of Tibur
Tībur·s -tis *adj* of Tibur ‖ *mpl* inhabitants of Tibur ‖ *n* estate at Tibur
Tīburtīn·us -a -um *adj* of Tibur; travertine *(stone)* ‖ *n* estate at Tibur
Tīburt·us -ī *m* legendary founder of Tibur *(see* **Tiburnus)**
Tīcīn·us -ī *m* tributary of the Po
Tigellīn·us -ī *m* notorious favorite of Nero
tigill·um -ī *n* beam; log
tignāri·us -a -um *adj* carpenter's; **faber tignārius** carpenter; **officīna tignāria** carpenter's shop
tign·um -ī *n* beam, plank; lumber
tigr·is -is *mf* tiger
tigr·is -is *or* **-idis** *f* tigress
Tigr·is -is *or* **-idis** *m* Tigris River
tīli·a -ae *f* linden tree, lime tree
Tīmae·us -ī *m* Greek historian of Sicily *(c. 346–250 B.C.)* ‖ Pythagorean philosopher of Locri in S. Italy *(after whom Plato named one of his dialogues, 5th cent. B.C.)*
Tīmāgen·ēs -is *m* brilliant rhetorician in the time of Augustus
Timāv·us -ī *m* river which flows into the gulf of Trieste
timefact·us -a -um *adj* frightened
tim·eō -ēre -uī *tr* to fear, be afraid of ‖ *intr* to be afraid; *(w. dat or* **dē** *or* **prō** *+ abl)* to fear for; *(w.* **ab** *+ abl of source of fear)* to fear harm from
timidē *adv* timidly, fearfully
timidit·ās -ātis *f* timidity, fearfulness, cowardice
timid·us -a -um *adj* timid, fearful, cowardly; *(w. gen)* afraid of
tim·or -ōris *m* fear; alarm, dread
tīnctil·is -is -e *adj* obtained by dipping
tīnctus *pp of* **tingō**
tine·a -ae *f* moth *(destructive of clothes, books),* bookworm
tingō (tinguō) tingere tīnxī tīnctus *tr* to dip, soak; to dye, color; to tinge; to imbue
tinnīment·um -ī *n* ringing
tinn·iō -īre -īvī *or* **-iī -ītus** *tr & intr* to ring
tinnīt·us -ūs *m* ring, ringing; tinkling, jingling

tinnul·us -a -um *adj* ringing, tinkling; shrill

tintin(n)ābul·um -ī *n* bell; doorbell; cowbell

tintin(n)·ō -āre *or* **tintin(n)·iō -īre** *intr* to ring

tintinnācul·us -a -um *adj* jingling **||** *mpl* chain gang

-tin·us -a -um *adjl suf forms adjectives from adverbs denoting time, e.g.:* **crāstinus** tomorrow's; **prīstinus** antique, ancient

tīn·us -ī *f* laurustinus *(evergreen shrub having white or pinkish flowers)*

-ti·ō -ōnis *fem suf forms verbal nouns to denote the action of the verb, e.g.:* **āctiō** act, action; *appears as* **-siō** *from verbs which form the supine in* **-sum,** *e.g.:* **cursiō** running

Tīph·ys -yos *m* pilot of the *Argo*

tippūl·a -ae *f* water spider

Tīresi·ās -ae *m* famous blind seer at Thebes at the time of Oedipus

Tīridāt·ēs -ae *m* name of three kings of Parthia

tīr·ō -ōnis *m* novice, beginner; young man who has just come of age; *(mil)* recruit **||** **Tīrō** Marcus Tullius Tiro *(Cicero's secretary)*

tīrōcin·ium -(i)ī *n* apprenticeship; beginning, first try; *(mil)* first campaign; *(mil)* military inexperience; *(mil)* body of raw recruits

tīruncul·us -ī *m* beginner, recruit

Tīryn·s -thos *f* town in the Argolid where Hercules was raised

Tīrynthi·us -a -um *adj* Tirynthian **||** *m* Hercules **||** *mpl* the people of Tiryns **||** *f* Alcmena

Tīsamen·us -ī *m* son of Orestes and king of Argos

tisan·a -ae *f* pearl barley

tisanār·ium -(i)ī *n* **(pti-)** gruel; **tisanārium oryzae** rice gruel

Tīsiphon·ē -ēs *f* one of the three Furies who haunted murderers

Tīsiphonē·us -a -um *adj* belonging to Tisiphone; *(fig)* deserving of punishment by the Furies, guilty

Tīt·ān -ānos *or* **Tītān·us -ī** *m* Titan; sun; Prometheus **||** *mpl* Titans *(giant sons of Uranus and Ge who rebelled against Uranus and put Cronus on the throne)*

Tītāni·us -a -um *adj* of the Titans, Titanic *(esp. of the sun, moon, or Prometheus)* **||** *m* sun-god **||** *f* Latona *(mother of Apollo and Diana)* **||** Diana **||** Pyrrha *(as descendant of Prometheus)* **||** Circe *(as daughter of Sol or Helios)*

Tīthōni·us -a -um *adj* Tithonian **||** *f* Aurora *(wife of Tithonus)*

Tīthōn·us -ī *m* son of Laomedon and husband of Aurora from whom he received the gift of immortality without eternal youth

Titiēns·is -is -e *adj* of the Tities tribe

Tit·iēs -ium *mpl* one of the three original Roman tribes

tītillāti·ō -ōnis *f* tickling, titillation;

tītill·ō -āre *tr* tickle, titillate

Titi·us -a -um *adj* Roman clan name *(nomen)*

tittibilīc·ium -(i)ī *n* trifle

titubanter *adv* falteringly

titubanti·a -ae *f* stumbling *(in speech)*

titubāti·ō -ōnis *f (lit & fig)* stumbling

titub·ō -āre -āvī -ātum *intr* to stagger, reel, totter; to falter, waver; to stumble, slip up *(in speech)*

titul·us -ī *m* inscription; label; title, heading *(of a book, chapter);* chapter *(of a book);* personal title; identification tag; notice, advertisement; pretext, ostensible motive; claim to fame; title of honor; renown; *(w. gen)* **1** honor *or* distinction arising from; **2** reputation for

Tit·us -ī *m* Roman first name *(praenomen); esp.* Titus Tatius *(a Sabine king who is said to have ruled with Romulus until the latter had him killed)* **||** the Emperor Titus *(Titus Flavius Vespasianus, son of Vespasian; ruled A.D. 79–81)*

Tity·os *or* **Tity·us -ī** *m* Tityus *(giant slain by Apollo for attempting to rape Latona and thrown into Tartarus)*

Tītyr·us -ī *m* shepherd in Vergil's pastorals, sometimes identified with Vergil himself

Tlēpolem·us -ī *m* son of Hercules

Tmar·os -ī *m* mountain in Epirus

Tmōlīt·ēs -is *adj (masc only)* of Mt. Tmolus **||** *m* wine from Mt. Tmolus

Tmōli·us -a -um *adj* of Mt. Tmolus

Tmōl·us -ī *m* **(Tim-)** Tmolus *(mountain in Lydia famous for its wines)*

toculli·ō -ōnis *m* loan shark

todill·us -ī *m* type of small bird

tōfīn·us -a -um *adj* made of tufa

tōf·us -ī *m* **(toph-)** tufa *(porous volcanic rock, used extensively in Republican Rome as building stone)*

tog·a -ae *f* toga *(outer garment of a Roman citizen);* **toga ātra** dark toga *(unwhitened toga worn as sign of mourning);* **toga candida** white toga *(treated with chalk and worn by candidates for office);* **toga picta** brocaded toga *(worn by triumphant generals);* **toga praetexta** crimson-bordered toga *(worn by magistrates and freeborn children);* **toga pulla** dark-gray toga *(worn by mourners);* **toga pūra** *(or* **virīlis** *or* **lībera)** toga of manhood *(worn*

by young men from about the age of sixteen); **ā togā pūrā** from boyhood
togāt·a -ae *f* Latin comedy *(on Roman themes and in Roman dress)*
togātār·ius -(i)ī *m* actor in a *fabula togata*
togātul·us -ī *m (pej)* miserable Roman *(of clients paying duty calls)*
togāt·us -a -um *adj* wearing a toga, true Roman; having a civilian occupation *or* status, civilian; peacetime; **fābula togāta** *(theat)* Latin comedy *(written on a native theme and presented in Roman dress);* **Gallia Togāta** Cisalpine Gaul *(between the Alps and the Po River)* ‖ *m* Roman citizen; civilian; humble client ‖ *f* prostitute; *see* **togāta**
togul·a -ae *f (pej)* little toga
tolerābil·is -is -e *adj* tolerable; patient
tolerābiliter *adv* without stress
toler·āns -antis *adj* tolerant; *(w. gen)* tolerant of, enduring
toleranter *adv* patiently
toleranti·a -ae *f* toleration, endurance
tolerāti·ō -ōnis *f* toleration, endurance
tolerāt·us -a -um *adj* tolerable, endurable
toler·ō -āre -āvī -ātus *tr* to tolerate, endure; to support, maintain, sustain
tollēn·ō -ōnis *m* crane, lift, derrick
tollō tollere sustulī sublātus *tr* to lift, raise; to raise *(the voice);* to draw *(lots);* to have *(a child);* to acknowledge *(a child);* to raise, educate; to weigh *(anchor); (of a ship)* to take on board; *(of a ship)* to have the capacity of; *(of a vehicle)* to pick up, take as a passenger; to win, carry off *(a prize);* to reap *(a profit);* to remove; to do away with, destroy; to cancel, abolish, abrogate; to lift, steal; to uplift, cheer up, excite; to erect, build up; to waste *(time);* **amīcum tollere** to cheer up a friend; **animōs tollere** to boost morale; **deōs tollere** to deny the existence of the gods; **dē mediō tollere** to kill; **diēm tollere** to take a day off *(from work);* **in crucem** *(or* **in furcam)** **tollere** to crucify ‖ *refl (of plants)* to grow high; **in caelum sē tollere** to ascend *or* climb into the sky ‖ *pass* to climb up, rise
Tolōs·a -ae *f* city in Narbonese Gaul *(modern Toulouse)*
Tolōsān·us -a -um *adj* **(Toloss-)** of Tolosa ‖ *mpl* people of Tolosa
Tolōs·ās -ātis *adj* produced in Tolosa ‖ *mpl* people of Tolosa
tolūtim *adv* at a trot, jogging
tomāc(u)l·um -ī *n* sausage
tōment·um -ī *n* pillow stuffing
Tom·ī -ōrum *mpl or* **Tom·is -is** *f* Tomi *(town on the Black Sea in modern Romania, where Ovid spent his years in exile)*
Tomīt·ae -ārum *mpl* people of Tomi
Tomītān·us -a -um *adj* of Tomi
tom·us -ī *m* a length of papyrus, sheet
Ton·āns -antis *m* Thunderer *(epithet of several gods, esp. Jupiter)*
tondeō tondēre totondī tōnsus *tr* to clip, shear, shave; to prune; to reap, mow; to crop, browse on; *(fig)* to fleece, rob; **ūsque ad cutem tondēre** *(fig)* to swindle, fleece *(literally, the clip right down to the skin)*
tonitrāl·is -is -e *adj* thunderous
tonitr·us -ūs *m or* **tonitr·um -ī** *n* thunder ‖ *mpl or npl* claps of thunder
ton·ō -āre -uī -itūrus *tr* to thunder forth *(words)* ‖ *intr* to thunder
tōns·a -ae *f* oar
tōnsil·is -is -e *adj* clipped
tōnsill·a -ae *f* **(tōs-)** tonsil
tōnsit·ō -āre *tr* to shear regularly
tōns·or -ōris *m* **(tōs-)** shearer; barber
tōnsōri·us -a -um *adj* shaving; barber's
tōnstrīcul·a -ae *f* little hairdresser, little barber *(female)*
tōnstrīn·a -ae f barbershop
tōnstrīn·um -ī *n* trade of a barber, barbering
tōnstr·īx -īcis *f* hairdresser, barber *(female)*
tōnsūr·a -ae *f* clipping, shearing; **capillōrum tōnsūra** haircut
tōns·us -a -um *pp of* **tondeō** ‖ *f* oar
tōns·us -ūs *m* haircut; hairdo
tonuī *perf of* **tonō**
tōph·us -ī *m* **(tōf-)** tufa *(porous volcanic rock, used as building material esp. in the Republican period)*
topiāri·us -a -um *adj* garden, landscape ‖ *m* gardener, landscaper ‖ *f* landscaping
topic·a -ōrum *npl* "commonplaces" *(title of work by Aristotle on which Cicero based his work on this topic)*
topic·ē -ēs *f (rhet)* resourcefulness in finding topics for speeches
-t·or -ōris *masc suf, formed from verbs to denote the doer of the action of the verb, e.g.:* **amātor** lover; *becomes* **-sor** *from verbs which form the past participle in* **-sus,** *e.g.:* **tōnsor** shearer, barber
tor·al -ālis *n* valance; coverlet
torcul·ar -āris *or* **torcul·um -ī** *n* wine press, oil press
toreum·a -atis *n* embossed work, relief
-tōr·ium -(i)ī *neut suf often denoting places, e.g.,* **praetōrium** headquarters of the praetor *or* commander
torment·um -ī *n* windlass; catapult, artillery piece; shot; torture rack; *(lit & fig)* torture ‖ *npl* artillery
tormin·a -um *npl* colic, bowel trouble
torminōs·us -a -um *adj* suffering from colic, colicky

torn·ō -āre -āvī -ātus *tr* to turn on a lathe
torn·us -ī *m* lathe
torōs·us -a -um *adj* brawny, muscular
torpēd·ō -inis *f* numbness, lethargy, listlessness; stingray *(fish)*
torp·eō -ēre -uī *intr* to numb; to be stiff; to be stupefied; to be groggy
torp·ēscō -ēscere -uī *intr* to grow numb; to grow listless
torpid·us -a -um *adj* numbed, paralyzed; groggy
torp·or -ōris *m* torpor, numbness; grogginess
torpuī *perf of* **torpeō** *and* **torpēscō**
torquāt·us -a -um *adj* wearing a collar *or* necklace ‖ **Torquātus** *m* Titus Manlius Torquatus *(legendary Roman hero who wore a necklace taken from a gigantic Gaul he had slain)*
tor·queō -quēre -sī -tus *tr* to twist, turn, wind; to bend out of shape; to hurl; to wind up *(catapult);* to turn *(so as to face in the opposite direction);* to roll *(eyes);* to crane *(neck);* to divert the course of; to spin; to curl *(hair);* to wreathe *(the head); (fig)* to torment; **aliquem torquēre** *(w.* **in** *or* **adversus, contrā** *+ acc)* to torture s.o. to give evidence against *(s.o.)*
torqu·ēs *or* **torqu·is -is** *m(f)* necklace; collar *(of twisted metal, as military decoration)*
torr·ēns -entis *adj* burning, seething; rushing, roaring *(stream);* fiery *(speech)* ‖ *m* torrent; current
torr·eō -ēre -uī tostus *tr* to roast, bake; to burn, scorch; to parch
torr·ēscō -ēscere -uī *intr* to become burned; to become parched
torrid·us -a -um *adj* baked, parched; dried up; frostbitten
torr·is -is *or* **torr·us -ī** *m* firebrand
torruī *perf of* **torreō**
torsī *perf of* **torqueō**
tortē *adv* crookedly
tortil·is -is -e *adj* twisted, winding, spiral, coiled
tort·ō -āre *tr* to twist, coil ‖ *pass* to writhe
tort·or -ōris *m* torturer
tortuōs·us -a -um *adj* tortuous, winding; *(fig)* complicated
tort·us -a -um *adj* bent, crooked, curved; coiled, twisted; curly *(hair);* winding *(road, labyrinth)*
tort·us -ūs *m* twist, coil; **tortūs dare** *(of a serpent)* to form loops
torul·us -ī *m* headband; tuft *(of hair)*
tor·us -ī *m* knot; bulge; muscle, brawn; bed, couch; mattress; cushion; mound; boss; flowery expression; **torus geniālis** conjugal bed
torvit·ās -ātis *f* grimness
torv·us -a -um *adj* grim
tostus *pp of* **torreō**
tot *indecl adj* so many, as many; **tot … quot** as many ... as
totiēns *or* **totiēs** *adv* so often, so many times
totondī *perf of* **tondeō**
tōt·us -a -um *adj* the whole, all, entire; **totūs in illīs** totally absorbed in those matters ‖ *n* the whole matter, all; **ex tōtō** totally; **in tōtō** on the whole, in general; **in tōtum** totally
toxic·um -ī *n* poison *(originally, a poison in which arrowheads were dipped)*
trabāl·is -is -e *adj* of *or* for beams; **clāvus trabālis** spike; **tēlum trabāle** beam-like shaft
trabe·a -ae *f* ceremonial robe *(with purple stripes and worn by magistrates, augurs, and as dress uniform of the equites)*
trabeāt·us -a -um *adj* wearing a *trabea*
trab·s -is *f* beam, plank; timber; tree; object made of beams: roof, shaft, table, battering ram
Trāch·īn -īnis *or* **Trāch·ȳn -ȳnos** *f* Trachis *(town in Thessaly on Mount Oeta, where Hercules had himself cremated)*
Trāchīni·us -a -um *adj* of Trachin (Trachis) ‖ *m* Ceyx *(king of Trachin)* ‖ *fpl* "Women of Trachis" *(title of a play by Sophocles)*
tractābil·is -is -e *adj* tractable, manageable; *(of weather)* fit for navigation
tractāti·ō -ōnis *f* handling, management; discussion, treatment *(of a subject);* lesson *(in a class)*
tractātr·īx -īcis *f* masseuse
tractāt·us -ūs *m* touching, handling; management; treatise
tractim *adv* little by little, slowly; in a drawn-out manner
tract·ō -āre -āvī -ātus *tr* to drag around, haul, pull; to touch, handle; to deal with, treat; to manage, control; to wield; to conduct, carry on, transact; to practice; to discuss; *(of an actor)* to play the role of; to examine, consider; **male tractāre** to mistreat ‖ *refl* to behave, conduct oneself ‖ *intr* to carry on a discussion
tract·us -a -um *pp of* **trahō** ‖ *adj* fluent; lengthy, continuous *(discourse)*
tract·us -ūs *m* dragging; dragging out, extension *(e.g., of a war);* track, trail; tract, expanse, extent, distance; region, district
trādidī *perf of* **trādō**
trāditi·ō -ōnis *f* handing over, surrender; transmission; item of traditional belief, custom, tradition
trādit·or -ōris *m* betrayer, traitor

trā·dō -dere -didī -ditus *tr* to hand over, surrender, deliver; to betray; to hand down, bequeath, transmit, pass on; to relate, recount; to teach; to introduce *(a person)* ‖ *refl (w. dat)* **1** to surrender to; **2** to devote oneself to

trā·dūcō -dūcere -dūxī -ductus *tr* to bring across *or* over, transfer; to convert, bring over; *(w.* **ad** *or* **in** *+ acc)* to cause *(s.o.)* to change *(from one attitude, habit, etc.)* to *(another);* to exhibit, display; to disgrace; to pass, spend; *(gram)* to derive; **trādūcere equum** *(of a member of the equestrian order who passed the censor's inspection)* to lead one's horse in the parade

trāducti·ō -ōnis *f* transference; passage *(of time);* metonymy; use of homonyms *or* homophones

trāduct·or -ōris *m* conveyor

trāductus *pp of* **trādūcō**

trād·ux -ucis *mf* vine branch *(trained across the space between trees in a vineyard)*

trādūxī *perf of* **trādūcō**

tragicē *adv* as in tragedy

tragicocōmoedi·a -ae *f* melodrama

tragic·us -a -um *adj* of tragedy, tragic; in the tragic style, grand, solemn; of a tragic nature, tragic ‖ *m* writer of tragedies

tragoedi·a -ae *f* tragedy

tragoed·us -ī *m* tragic actor

trāgul·a -ae *f* javelin

trag·us *or* **trag·os -ī** *m* body odor of the armpits; a fish *(of unknown type)*

trah·āx -ācis *adj* greedy

trahe·a -ae *f* sledge, drag *(used as a threshing device)*

tra·hō -here -xī -ctus *tr* to draw, drag, trail; *(in a temporal sense)* to bring in its wake; to draw out, pull out, extract; to drag out, protract; to lead, to come leading *(an animal); (of a river)* to carry along; to carry off *(as plunder);* to rob *(persons);* to take along *(on a trip);* to contract, wrinkle *(the brow);* to pull toward one; *(of physical forces)* to attract; to attract, lure, fascinate *(persons);* to draw *(water);* to draw *(conclusions);* to take on, assume; to acquire, get; to spin, manufacture; to win over *(to the other side);* to refer, ascribe; to distract; to keep on considering, ponder; **animam** *(or* **spīritum)** **trahere** to draw in breath; **pedem trahere** *(of a lame person)* to drag one foot

Trāiān·us -ī *m* Trajan *(Marcus Ulpius Trāiānus, Roman emperor,* A.D. *98–117)*

trā·iciō -icere -iēcī -iectus tr to throw *(a weapon)* across; *(of a weapon)* to pierce, pass through; to place *(a bridge, a bar)* across; to pass through, break through; to move, shift *(s.th. from one place to another); (w. double acc)* to bring *(e.g., troops)* across *(e.g., a river, mountain); (w.* **trāns** *+ acc)* to lead across; *(w.* **in** *+ acc)* to lead over into; to shift *(words from one part of the sentence to another)* ‖ *intr* to cross over

trāiecti·ō -ōnis *f* crossing, passage; transposition *(of words);* shift of meaning; exaggeration

trāiectus *pp of* **trāiciō**

trāiect·us -ūs *m* crossing over, passage

trālāt- = trānslāt-

Trall·ēs -ium *fpl* Tralles *(town in Lydia on the Menander River, variously set in Caria and Lydia)*

Tralliān·us -a -um *adj* of Tralles

trāloqu·or -ī *tr* to talk over, enumerate, recount

trālūceō *see* **trānslūceō**

trām·a -ae *f* woof, warp *(in some form of weaving)*

trām·es -itis *m* path, track, trail

trāmi- = trānsmi-

trānatō = trānsnatō

trān·ō *or* **trānsn·ō -āre -āvī -ātus** *tr* to swim across; to pass through, permeate ‖ *intr* to swim across; to pass through

tranquillē *adv* quietly, calmly

tranquillit·ās -ātis *f* tranquillity, stillness, calmness

tranquill·ō -āre -āvī -ātus *tr* to calm, quiet, compose

tranquill·us -a -um *adj* tranquil, calm, quiet ‖ *n* calm, quiet, tranquillity; calm sea

Tranquill·us -ī *m* Gaius Suetonius Tranquillus *(biographer of the emperors, born c.* A.D. *69)*

trāns- *pref (used with verbs or verbal derivatives in the sense of the preposition)*

trāns *prep (w. acc)* across, over, beyond

trānsab·eō -īre -īvī *or* **-iī** *tr* to pierce, pass right through *(and go some distance beyond)*

trānsācti·ō -ōnis *f* business transaction, business deal

trānsāct·or -ōris *m* manager, negotiator

trānsāctus *pp of* **trānsigō**

trānsad·igō -igere -ēgī -āctus *tr* to pierce; to run *(s.o.)* through; *(w. double acc)* to run *(e.g., a sword)* through *(s.o.)*

Trānsalpīn·us -a -um *adj* Transalpine

trānsbīt·ō -ere *intr* to come *or* go across

trānscen·dō *or* **trānsscen·do -dere -dī -sus** *tr* to climb *or* step over, surmount; to overstep, transgress ‖ *intr* to climb *or* step across

trāns·cīdō -cīdere -cīdī -cīsus *tr* to flog thoroughly

trāns·currō -currere -(cu)currī -cursum *tr & intr* to hurry, run *or* dash over; to run through; to run past; *(in writing)* to pass over quickly; to skim *(in reading)*

trānscurs·us -ūs *m* running through, passage; cursory mention, cursory treatment *(of a subject)*

trānsd- = trād-

trānsenn·a -ae *f* **(trās-)** lattice work; lattice window; fowler's net

trāns·eō -īre -īvī *or* **-iī -itus** *tr* to cross; to desert; to pass *(in a race);* to pass over, make no mention of; to treat cursorily; to overstep; to surpass **||** *intr* to go over, go across, pass over; to pass by, go by; to shift *(to another opinion, topic, etc.); (of time)* to pass by; to pass away; *(w.* **ad** + *acc)* **1** to cross over to *(a place);* **2** to desert to; *(w.* **in** + *acc)* to change into; *(w.* **per** + *acc)* to penetrate, permeate

trāns·ferō -ferre -tulī -lātus *(or* **trālātus)** *tr* **(trāf-)** to carry *or* bring across; to transfer *(by writing);* to copy; to shift; to transform; to postpone; to translate; to use figuratively

trāns·fīgō -fīgere -fīxī -fīxus *tr* to pierce; to run *(s.o.)* through

trānsfigūr·ō -āre -āvī -ātus *tr* to transform

trānsfīxus *pp of* **trānsfīgō**

trāns·fodiō -fodere -fōdī -fossus *tr* to stab, pierce, run through

trānsfōrm·is -is -e *adj* transformed

trānsfōrm·ō -āre -āvī -ātus *tr* to transform

trānsfossus *pp of* **trānsfodiō**

trānsfret·ō -āre -āvī -ātum *intr* to cross the sea

trānsfug·a -ae *m* deserter, turncoat

trāns·fugiō -fugere -fūgī *intr* to go over to the enemy, desert

trānsfug·ium -(i)ī *n* desertion

trāns·fundō -fundere -fūdī -fūsus *tr* to transfuse; to pour; *(w.* **in** + *acc)* to pour *(a liquid)* into; *(w.* **ad** + *acc) (fig)* to shift *(affection, allegiance)* to

trānsfūsi·ō -ōnis *f* pouring from one vessel into another; *(fig)* intermarriage

trānsfūsus *pp of* **trānsfundō**

trāns·gredior -gredī -gressus sum *tr* to cross, pass over; to exceed **||** *intr* to go across; to cross over *(to another party)*

trānsgressi·ō -ōnis *f* crossing; transition; transposition *(of words)*

trānsgressus *pp of* **trānsgredior**

trānsgress·us -ūs *m* crossing

trānsiciō *see* **trāiciō**

trānsiect- = trāiect-

trāns·igō -igere -ēgī -āctus *tr* to pierce, run through; to finish; to settle, transact; to accomplish, perform, conclude; to pass, spend **||** *intr* to come to an agreement, reach an understanding

trānsil·iō *or* **trānssil·iō -īre -uī** *tr* to jump over, jump across; to overstep; to skip, omit **||** *intr* to jump across

trānsit·āns -antis *adj* passing through

trānsiti·ō -ōnis *f* crossing, passage; switching *(to another party);* contagion, infection; passageway

trānsitōri·us -a -um *adj* affording a passage *(from one place to another)*

trānsitus *pp of* **trānseō**

trānsit·us -ūs *m* crossing, passage; passing; traffic; crossing over, desertion; change, period of change, transition; transference of possession *(of); fading (of colors);* **in trānsitū** in passing; **per trānsitum** by way of transition

trānslātīci·us -a -um *adj* **(trāl-)** transmitted, traditional, customary; usual, common

trānslāti·ō -ōnis *f* **(trāl-)** transfer, shift; transporting; translation; metaphor, figure

trānslātīv·us -a -um *adj* **(trāl-)** transferable

trānslāt·or -ōris *m* middleman *(in a transfer)*

trānslātus *pp of* **trānsferō**

trānsleg·ō -ere *tr (w. dat)* to read out to *(s.o.)*

trānsloqu·or -ī *tr* **(trāl-)** to recount from the beginning

trānslūc·eō -ēre *intr* **(trāl-)** to shine through; to be reflected

trānsmarīn·us -a -um *adj* from beyond the seas, foreign, overseas

trānsme·ō -āre *tr & intr* **(trām-)** to cross, pass through

trānsmigr·ō -āre -āvī -ātum *intr* **(trām-)** to move, change residence; to migrate, emigrate

trānsmin·eō -ēre *intr* to stick out on the other side

trānsmissi·ō -ōnis *f* crossing, passage

trānsmissus *pp of* **trānsmittō**

trānsmiss·us -ūs *m* passing over, crossing, passage

trāns·mittō -mittere -mīsī -missus *tr* **(trām-)** to send across; to transmit; to let pass; to hand over, entrust; to pass over, leave unmentioned; to endure; *(w.* **in** + *acc)* to send *(s.o.)* across to *or* into; *(w.* **per** + *acc)* to let *(s.o.)* pass through **||** *intr* to cross over, cross, pass *(from one place to another)*

trānsmontān·ī -ōrum *mpl* people living across the mountains

trāns·moveō -movēre -mōvī -mōtus *tr* to move, transfer

trānsmūt·ō -āre -āvī -ātus *tr* to change, shift

trānsnat·ō -āre -āvī -ātus *tr* **(trān-)** to swim (across) ‖ *intr* to swim across
trānsnō *see* **trānō**
trānsnōmin·ō -āre -āvī -ātus *tr (w. double acc)* to rename as
Trānspadān·us -a -um *adj* beyond *or* N. of the Po River
trānspect·us -ūs *m* view, prospect
trāns·pōnō -pōnere -posuī -positus *tr* to transfer, move across
trānsport·ō -āre -āvī -ātus *tr* to transport
trānspositus *pp of* **trānspōnō**
trānsrhenān·us -a -um *adj* beyond the Rhine, E. of the Rhine
trānss- = trāns-
trāns(s)pic·iō -ere *tr* to look through
trān(s)·scrībō -scrībere -scrīpsī -scrīptus *tr* to transcribe, copy off; *(leg)* to transfer, convey
trānstiberīn·us -a -um *adj* across the Tiber
trānstin·eō -ēre *intr* to provide a link *(from one side to the other)*
trānstr·um -ī *n* crossbeam; rower's seat, thwart
trānsult·ō -āre *intr* to jump across
trānsūt·us -a -um *adj* pierced through *(w. a pointed object)*
trānsvecti·ō -ōnis *f* **(trāv-)** transportation; riding past *(in review)*
trāns·vehō -vehere -vexī -vectus *tr* **(trāv-)** to transport; to carry past *(in a parade)* ‖ *pass* to ride by *(in a parade); (of time)* to elapse
trānsverber·ō -āre *tr* to pierce through and through, transfix
trānsversāri·us -a -um *adj* lying crosswise ‖ *n* crosspiece
trānsversē *adv* crosswise; across one's course
trānsvers·us *or* **trānsvors·us -a -um** *adj* **(trāv-)** lying across, lying crosswise; inopportune; astray; in the wrong direction ‖ *n* wrong direction; **dē trānsversō** unexpectedly; **ex trānsversō** unexpectedly; sideways
trānsvolit·ō -āre *tr* to flit through, fly through
trānsvol·ō -āre -āvī -ātus *tr & intr* **(trāv-)** to fly over, fly across, fly by
trānsvorsus *see* **trānsversus**
trapēt·um -ī *n or* **trapēt·us -ī** *m* oil press
trapezīt·a -ae *m* banker, money-changer
trapezophor·um -ī *n* ornate table
Trapez·os -untis *or* **-untos** *f* city in Pontus on the Black Sea
Trasimēn·us -ī *m* **(-menn-)** Lake Trasimene *(lake in Etruria, modern Trasimeno, where Hannibal defeated the Romans in 217 B.C.)*
trāv- = trānsv-
trāxī *perf of* **trahō**
Trebi·a -ae *f* river which flows into the Po near Placentia *(modern Trebbia River, near which Hannibal defeated the Romans in 218 B.C.)*
Trebulān·us -a -um *adj* of Trebula *(town in central Campania);* **ager Trebulānus** district of Trebula
trecēn·ī -ae -a *adj* three hundred each; three hundred each time ‖ *mpl* lots of three hundred *(men)*
trecentēsim·us -a -um *adj* three-hundredth
trecent·ī -ae -a *adj* three hundred
trecentiē(n)s *adv* three hundred times
trechedīpn·um -ī *n* light garment worn to dinner (by parasites)
tredecim *indecl adj* thirteen
tremebund·us -a -um *adj* trembling, shivering
treme·faciō -facere -fēcī -factus *tr* to shake, cause to shake
tremend·us -a -um *adj* **(-mi-)** awe-inspiring, terrible
trem·ēscō -ēscere -uī *tr* to (begin) tremble at ‖ *intr* to (begin) tremble
trem·ō -ere -uī *tr* to tremble at ‖ *intr* to tremble, shiver, quake
trem·or -ōris *m* trembling, shivering; dread; cause of fright, terror
tremuī *perf of* **tremō** *and* **tremēscō**
tremul·us -a -um *adj* trembling, quivering, tremulous, shivering
trepidanter *adv* tremblingly, nervously
trepidāti·ō -ōnis *f* nervousness, alarm; trembling
trepidē *adv* nervously, in alarm
trepid·ō -āre -āvī -ātus *tr* to start at, be startled by ‖ *intr* to be nervous, be jumpy, be alarmed; *(of a flame)* to flicker; *(of streams)* to rush along
trepid·us -a -um *adj* nervous, jumpy; restless; bubbling; perilous, critical, alarming; **in rē trepidā** in a ticklish situation
trēs trēs tria *adj* three; *(denoting a small number)* a couple of
tress·is -is *m* sum of three *"pennies";* mere trifle
trēsvirī *(gen:* **triumvirōrum)** *mpl* triumvirs, board of three commissioners; commissioners for distributing land among colonists; **trēsvirī Epulōnēs** superintendents of sacrifices and banquets of the gods
Trēver·ī *or* **Trēvir·ī -ōrum** *mpl* people E. of Gaul
tri- *pref* consisting of three of the things named, *e.g.,* **tricuspis** having three prongs
triangul·us -a -um *adj* triangular ‖ *n* triangle
triāri·ī -ōrum *mpl* soldiers of the third rank in a battle line, reserves

trib·as -adis *f* female sexual pervert
Triboc·ī -ōrum *mpl* tribe which settled on the Rhine in the region of modern Alsace
tribuāri·us -a -um *adj* tribal
tribuī *perf of* **tribuō**
tribūl·is -is *m* fellow tribesman
trībul·um -ī *n* threshing sledge *(wooden platform with iron teeth underneath)*
tribul·us -ī *m* caltrop *(thistle)*
tribūn·al -ālis *n* platform; tribunal, judgment seat; *(in camp)* general's platform; cenotaph; **prō tribūnālī** *(or* **in** *or* **ē tribūnālī)** officially
tribūnāt·us -ūs *m* tribuneship
tribūnici·us -a -um *adj* tribunician, tribune's **II** *m* ex-tribune
tribūn·us -ī *m* tribune; **tribūnus aerārius** paymaster; **tribūnus mīlitāris** *(or* **mīlitum)** military tribune *(six in each legion, serving under the legatus, and elected by the people or at times appointed by the commander);* **tribūnus plēbis** tribune of the people *(initially two, eventually ten in number, serving in the interests of the plebeians)*
trib·uō -uere -uī -ūtus *tr* to divide; to distribute, bestow, confer, assign; to give, present; to concede, grant, allow; to ascribe, impute; to devote, spend
trib·us -ūs *f* tribe *(orginally three in number and eventually increased to thirty-five)*
tribūtāri·us -a -um *adj* tributary, subject to tribute; **tribūtāriae tabellae** letters of credit
tribūtim *adv* by tribes, tribe by tribe
tribūti·ō -ōnis *f* distribution
tribūt·um -ī *n or* **tribūt·us -ī** *m* tribute, tax; contribution
tribūt·us -a -um *pp of* **tribuō** **II** *adj* arranged by tribes
trīc·ae -ārum *fpl* tricks; nonsense
trīcēn·ī -ae -a *adj* thirty each; thirty at a time, in groups of thirty
tric·eps -ipitis *adj* three-headed
trīcēsim·us -a -um *adj* **(-cēns-)** thirtieth
trichil·a *or* **tricli·a** *or* **tricle·a -ae** *f* bower, arbor; summer house
trīciēns *or* **trīciēs** *adv* thirty times
triclea *see* **trichila**
triclia *see* **trichila**
trīclīn·ium -(i)ī *n* dining couch *(running around three sides of a table);* dining room
trīc·ō -ōnis *m* schemer
trīc·or -ārī *intr* to cause trouble; to pull tricks
tricorp·or -oris *adj* triple-bodied
tricusp·is -idis *adj* three-pronged
trid·ēns -entis *adj* three-pronged **II** *m* trident
Tridentif·er *or* **Tridentig·er -erī** *m* Trident Bearer *(epithet of Neptune)*
tridu·um -ī *n* three-day period, three days
trienn·ia -ium *npl* triennial festival *(celebrated every three years)*
trienn·ium -(i)ī *n* three-year period, three years
tri·ēns -entis *m* one third; coin *(one third of a "penny");* third of a pint
trientābul·um -ī *n* land given by the State to those from whom the State had borrowed, equivalent to one third of the sum which the state owed
trienti·us -a -um *adj* sold for a third
triērarch·us -ī *m* captain of a trireme
triēr·is -is -e *adj* having oars *or* rowers arranged in threes **II** *f* trireme
trietēric·us -a -um *adj* triennial, recurring every three years **II** *npl* festival of Bacchus
trietēr·is -idis *or* **-idos** *f* three-year period; triennial festival in honor of Bacchus
trifāriam *adv* in three places, on three sides; under three headings
tri·faux -faucis *adj* triple-throated
trifid·us -a -um *adj* three-forked; split into three parts
trifīl·is -is -e *adj* having three threads *or* strands of hair
Trifolīn·us -a -um *adj* belonging to the district of Trifolium near Naples
trifol·ium -(i)ī *n* clover
trifōrm·is -is -e *adj* triple-form *(of the goddess having the three aspects of Luna, Diana, and Hecate; of three-headed Geryon; of the Chimera as composed of a lion, snake, and goat)*
tri·fūr -fūris *m* archthief
trifurcif·er -erī *m* archvillain, hardened criminal
trigemin·us -a -um *adj* **(terg-)** threefold, triple **II** *mpl* triplets
trīgintā *indecl adj* thirty
trig·ō(n) -ōnis *or* **-ōnos** *m* game of catch *(played with three players standing to form a triangle);* ball *(used in this game)*
trigōnāl·is -is -e *adj* **pila trigōnālis** ball used in the game of catch
trilībr·is -is -e *adj* three-pound
trilingu·is -is -e *adj* three-tongued
tril·īx -īcis *adj* three-ply, triple-stranded
trimē(n)str·is -is -e *adj* of three months
trimetr·us -ī *m (pros)* trimeter *(metric line consisting of three double feet, e.g., iambic trimeter, or a line consisting of six iambic feet)*
trimod·ius -iī *m* measure of three pecks
trīmul·us -a -um *adj* three-year-old
trīm·us -a -um *adj* three-year-old

-trīn·a -ae *f suf* denoting the place where an activity is conducted: **tōnstrīna** barbershop *(from* **tondēre** to cut, shear, clip)
Trīnacr·is -idis *fem adj* Sicilian
Trīnacri·us -a -um *adj* Sicilian ‖ *m* Empedocles ‖ *f* Sicily
trīn·ī -ae -a *adj* threefold, triple; three each, three at a time; *(w. nouns occurring only in pl)* three: **trīnae litterae** three letters, three epistles
Trinobant·ēs -um *mpl* a British tribe near Essex
trinoctiāl·is -is -e *adj* occurring on three successive nights
trinōd·is -is -e *adj* triple-knotted
trinumm·us -ī *m* popular name for a newly introduced coin of high value ‖ **Trinummus** title of a play by Plautus
triōbol·us -ī *m* three-obol coin, half-dramcha *or* half-denarius piece *(c. 50¢)*
triōn·ēs -um *mpl* team of three oxen used in plowing ‖ **Triōnēs** Great and Little Bear *(constellations)*
Triop·ās -ae *adj (masc & fem only)* of Erysichthon
Triopē·is -idos *f* Mestra *(daughter of Erysichthon and granddaughter of Triopas, king of Thessaly)*
Triopē·ius -(i)ī *m* Erysichthon *(son of Triopas, king of Thessaly)*
triparc·us -a -um *adj* extremely stingy, triply stingy
tripartītō *adv* **(-pert-)** in three parts, into three parts
tripartīt·us -a -um *adj* **(-pert-)** divided into three parts, threefold
tripector·us -a -um *adj* triple-bodied, triple-chested
tripedāl·is -is -e *adj* three-foot
tripertītus *see* **tripartītus**
trip·ēs -edis *adj* three-legged, three-footed
tripl·ex -icis *adj* threefold, triple ‖ *n* three times as much, triple portion
tripl·us -a -um *adj* triple, threefold
Triptolem·us -ī *m* son of Celeus the king of Eleusis, favorite of Ceres, inventor of agriculture and one of the judges in the lower world
tripudi·ō -āre -āvī -ātum *intr* to perform a ritual dance *(tripudium)*
tripud·ium -(i)ī *n* war dance *(ritual dance in triple time, originally performed by priests in honor of Mars);* favorable omen *(when the sacred chickens ate hungrily, letting some grains fall to the ground in the process)*
trip·ūs -odis *or* **-odos** *m* tripod *(three-footed caldron);* oracle, Delphic oracle
triquetr·us -a -um *adj* triangular; Sicilian
trirēm·is -is -e *adj* having three banks of oars ‖ *f* trireme
trīs *see* **trēs**
trīscel·um -ī *n* triangle
trīscurri·a -ōrum *npl* fantastic nonsense
trīsticul·us -a -um *adj* somewhat sad
trīstific·us -a -um *adj* saddening
trīstimōni·a -ae *f or* **trīstimōn·ium -(i)ī** *n* sadness
trīst·is -is -e *adj* sad, sorrowful; bringing sorrow, saddening; gloomy, sullen; stern, harsh; disagreeable, offensive *(odor);* bitter, sour *(taste);* unpleasant *(sound)*
trīstiter *adv (to cry)* bitterly; distressingly
trīstiti·a -ae *or* **trīstiti·ēs -ēī** *f* sadness, gloom, gloominess, depression; severity, sternness
trisulc·us -a -um *adj* with three furrows *or* grooves; three-pronged; three-fold, triple; three-forked
tritavi·a-ae *f* great-great-great-great-grandmother
tritav·us -ī *m* great-great-great-great-grandfather
trīticei·a -ae *f* facetious name of a fish invented to make a pun with *hordeia*
trītice·us -a -um *adj* wheat
trītic·um -ī *n* wheat
Trīt·ōn -ōnis *m* son of Neptune who blows through a shell to calm the seas ‖ river flowing through Lake Tritonis in N. Africa where Minerva was said to be born
Trītōniac·us -a -um *adj* Tritonian, associated with Minerva
Trītōn·is -idis *or* **-idos** *f* Minerva
Trītōni·us -a -um *adj* Tritonian ‖ *f* Tritonia *(i.e., Minerva)*
trīt·or -ōris *m* grinder
trītūr·a -ae *f* threshing; kneading
trīt·us -a -um *pp of* **terō** ‖ *adj* worn, well-worn; beaten *(path);* experienced, expert; common, trite
trīt·us -ūs *m* rubbing, friction
triump(h)e *interj* a cheer shouted in the parade of triumphing generals *or* in the procession of the Arval Brothers
triumphāl·is -is -e *adj* triumphal; having had a triumph ‖ *npl* triumphal insignia *(without the actual triumph)*
triumph·ō -āre -āvī -ātus *tr* to triumph over, vanquish ‖ *intr (w.* **dē** *or* **ex** *+ abl)* to celebrate a triumph *(over a people)*
triumph·us -ī *m* triumph, victory parade; victory; **triumphum agere** *(w.* **dē** *or* **ex** *+ abl)* to celebrate a triumph over *(a conquered people)*
trium·vir -virī *m* triumvir, commissioner; mayor *(of a provincial town)* ‖ *mpl* triumvirs; **triumvirī capitālēs** superintendents of prisons and executions
triumvirāl·is -is -e *adj* triumviral, of the triumvirs

triumvirāt·us -ūs *m* triumvirate *(appointed at various times to serve various purposes)*
triveneſic·a -ae *f* nasty old witch
trīvī *perf of* **terō**
Trivi·a -ae *f* epithet of Diana
triviāl·is -is -e *adj* appropriate for the street corners, common, vulgar
triv·ium -(i)ī *n* crossroads, intersection; public street; the "gutter"
trivi·us -a -um *adj* of *or* at the crossroads; worshiped at the crossroads **II** *f see* **Trivia**
-tr·īx -īcis *fem suf corresponding to the masc suf* **-tor** *and denoting female agents, e.g.,* **tōnstrīx** hairdresser, barber
Trō·as *or* **Trō·ias -adis** *or* **-ados** *adj (fem only)* Trojan **II** *f* Troad, district of Troy; Trojan woman
trochae·us -ī *m (pros)* trochee *(metrical foot)* (— ⏑), tribrach *(metrical foot)* (⏑ ⏑ ⏑)
trochle·a *f* block and tackle
troch·us *or* **troch·os -ī** *m* hoop
Troez·ēn -ēnis *or* **-ēnos** *f* town in the Argolid on the E. shore of the Peloponnesus
Troezēni·us -a -um *adj* of Troezen
Trōi·a -ae *f* Troy
Trōiān·us -a -um *adj & m* Trojan
Trōic·us -a -um *adj* Trojan
Trōil·us -ī *m* son of Priam, killed by Achilles
Trōiugen·a *adj (masc & fem only)* Trojan-born, born at Troy, of Trojan descent, Trojan **II** *m* Trojan
Trōi·us -a -um *adj* Trojan **II** *f see* **Trōia**
Tromentīn·us -a -um *adj* name of one of the rustic tribes of early Rome
tropae·um -ī *n* trophy, war memorial *(originally armor taken from the enemy and hung on a stake, but later a permanent war monument, set up to mark the defeat of an enemy)*
Trophōn·ius -(i)ī *m* Boeotian oracular god with a shrine at Lebadea
Trōs Trōis *m* Tros *(son of Erichthonius and grandson of Dardanus and king of Phrygia after whom Troy was named)* **II** a Trojan
trucīdāti·ō -ōnis *f* slaughter, massacre, butchery
trucīd·ō -āre *tr* to slaughter, massacre, cut down
trucil·ō -āre *intr (of a thrush)* to chirp
truculentē *or* **truculenter** *adv* grimly, fiercely
truculenti·a -ae *f* ferocity, savagery; harshness; **truculentia caelī** harsh weather
truculent·us -a -um *adj* grim, fierce
trud·is -is *f* pointed pole, pike
trū·dō -dere -sī -sus *tr* to push, shove; to thrust; to force, drive; to put forth *(buds)*
trull·a -ae *f* dipper, ladle, scoop, trowel; brazier; wash basin
-tr·um -ī *neut suf denoting instrument, e.g.:* **arātrum** plow
trunc·ō -āre -āvī -ātus *tr* to lop off, maim; to amputate
trunc·us -a -um *adj* lopped; stripped *(of branches and leaves),* trimmed; maimed, mutilated; imperfect, undeveloped **II** *m* tree trunk; trunk, body *(of a human being);* chunk of meat; blockhead
trūsī *perf of* **trūdō**
trūs·ō -āre *intr (w. dat)* to keep ramming *(s.o.) (i.e., have sexual intercourse with a girl)*
trūsus *pp of* **trūdō**
trutin·a -ae *f* pair of scales; criterion
trutin·or -ārī -ātus sum *tr* to weigh, balance
tru·x -cis *adj* savage, grim, fierce
trybl·ium -(i)ī *n* plate, bowl
trȳgōn·us ī *m* stingray
tū *pron* you *(singl)*
tuātim *adv* in your manner, as is typical of you
tub·a -ae *f* trumpet *(with a straight tube, as opposed to the* **cornū***) used in war, at religious ceremonies, at the start of public shows, at weddings, funerals, etc.)*
tub·er -eris *f* exotic type of fruit tree **II** *m* exotic kind of fruit
tūb·er -eris *n* lump, hump, swelling; **tūber terrae** *(bot)* truffle *(underground fungus used as food)*
Tūbert·us -ī *m* Roman family name *(cognomen), esp.* Aulus Postumius Tubertus *(dictator in 431* B.C. *and conqueror of the Aequi at Algidus)*
tubic·en -inis *m* trumpeter
tubilūstr·ium -(i)ī *n* festival of trumpets *(celebrated on March 23 and May 23 and including a ritual cleaning of the trumpets)*
tuburcin·or -ārī -ātus sum *tr (coll)* to gobble up
tub·us -ī *m* tube, pipe
tuccēt·um *or* **tūcēt·um -ī** *n* sausage
Tucci·us -a -um *adj* Roman clan name *(nomen), esp.* Tuccia *(a Vestal Virgin who vindicated her chastity by carrying water in a sieve)*
tudit·ō -āre *tr* to keep hitting
-tūd·ō -inis *fem suf forms abstract nouns, chiefly from adjectives, e.g.:* **fortitūdō** bravery, *from* **fortis** brave
tueor *or* **tuor tuērī tuitus sum** *or* **tūtus sum** *tr* to look at, gaze at, watch, observe; to took after, take care of; to guard, defend, protect; to keep in good order,

maintain; to keep up *(practice);* to preserve the memory of

tugur·ium -(i)ī *n* hut, hovel

tuiti·ō -ōnis *f* protection, support; upkeep, maintenance; **tuitiō suī** self-defense

tulī *perf of* **ferō**

Tulli·a -ae *f* Roman female name

Tulliān·um -ī *n* state dungeon at the foot of the Capitoline Hill, said to have been added by Servius Tullius to the *Carcer Mamertinus*

Tulliol·a -ae *f* little Tullia

Tull·ius -(i)ī *m* Roman clan name *(nomen), esp.* Marcus Tullius Cicero *(Roman orator and politician, 106-43 B.C.)* **||** Servius Tullius *(6th king of Rome)*

Tull·us -ī *m* early first name *(praenomen), esp.* Tullus Hostilius *(the third king of Rome)*

tum *adv* then, at that time; at that moment; in those days; next; moreover, besides; **cum ... tum** both ... and especially, not only ... but also, if ... then surely; **tum cum** at the point when, at the time when, just then when; **tum ... tum** first ... then, at one time ... at another, now ... now, both ... and, partly ... partly

tume·faciō -facere -fēcī -factus *tr* to cause to swell; *(fig)* to puff up *(with pride)*

tum·eō -ēre -uī *intr* to be swollen, swell up; to be inflated; *(of language or speaker)* to be bombastic; *(of a person)* to be excited, be in a dither, be in a rage; to be proud

tum·ēscō -ēscere -uī *intr* to begin to swell (up); *(of wars)* to brew; to grow excited; to become enraged; to become inflated

tumid·us -a -um *adj* swollen, swelling; bloated; rising high; proud, puffed up; arrogant; incensed, enraged, exasperated; bombastic

tum·or -ōris *m* tumor, swelling; protuberance, bulging; elevation *(of the ground);* commotion, excitement; anger, rage; vanity, pride

tumuī *perf of* **tumeō** *and* **tumēscō**

tumul·ō -āre -āvī -ātus *tr* to bury

tumulōs·us -a -um *adj* hilly, rolling

tumultuāri·us -a -um *adj* confused, disorderly; makeshift; *(mil)* emergency, drafted hurriedly to meet an emergency; **exercitus tumultuārius** emergency army; **pugna tumultuāria** irregular battle *(i.e., not fought in regular battle formation)*

tumultuāti·ō -ōnis *f* commotion

tumultu·ō -āre *or* **tumultu·or -ārī -ātus sum** *intr* to make a disturbance; to be in an uproar; *(mil)* to fight in a disorganized way

tumultuōsē *adv* disorderly, in confusion; in panic

tumultuōs·us -a -um *adj* boisterous, turbulent; panicky; **somnium tumultuōsum** nightmare

tumult·us -ūs *m* commotion, uproar; insurrection, rebellion, civil war; confusion *(of the mind);* outbreak *(of crime); (mil)* sudden attack

tumul·us -ī *m* mound; rising; ground swell; burial mound; **tumulus inānis** cenotaph

tūn = tūne (tū + ne) do you?

tunc *adv (of time past)* then, at that time; *(of future time)* then, in that event; *(of succession in time)* thereupon; *(in conclusion)* consequently, in that case; **tunc cum** then when, just when; only when; **tunc dēmum** not until then, then finally; **tunc maximē** just then; **tunc prīmum** then for the first time; **tunc quandō** whenever; **tunc quoque** then too; **tunc vērō** then to be sure, exactly then

tundō tundere tutudī tūnsus *or* **tūsus** *tr* to beat, pound, hammer, thump; to buffet; to thresh; *(fig)* to harp on

tunic·a -ae *f* tunic *(ordinary half-sleeved knee-length garment worn by both sexes);* military tunic *(made of mail or hides as armor);* skin, peel, husk, coating; *(anat, bot)* tunic; **tunica molesta** tunic with inflammable material, in which criminals were burned alive; **tunica rēcta** *(woven on a warp-weighted loom)* bridal tunic; **tunica palmāta** tunic embroidered with palm-leaf design, worn by triumphing generals and by magistrates presiding over games

tunicāt·us -a -um *adj* wearing a tunic; in shirt sleeves; coated; covered with (hard) skin, tunicate

tunic(u)l·a -ae *f* short tunic; thin skin; thin coating

tūnsus *pp of* **tundō**

tuor *see* **tueor**

turb·a -ae *f* turmoil, disorder, uproar, commotion; brawl; crowd, mob, gang; multitude; common crowd, masses; a large number; *(coll)* rumpus, to-do

turbāment·a -ōrum *npl* means of disturbance

turbātē *adv* in confusion

turbāti·ō -ōnis *f* confusion, disorder

turbāt·or -ōris *m* ringleader, rabble-rouser, demagogue

turbāt·us -a -um *adj* confused, disorderly; disturbed, annoyed

turbell·ae -ārum *fpl* stir, row; **turbellās facere** to cause quite a row

turben *see* **turbō** *m*

turbidē *adv* confusedly, in disorder

turbid·us -a -um *adj* confused, wild, boisterous; muddy, turbid; troubled, perplexed; vehement; disheveled *(hair)*; stormy *(weather, sky)*

turbine·us -a -um *adj* cone-shaped; gyrating like a spinning-top

turb·ō -āre -āvī -ātus *tr* to throw into confusion, disturb, agitate; to break, disorganize *(ranks in battle)*, cause to break ranks; to confuse; to alarm; to muddy; to stir *(a liquid in order to thicken it)*; to stir up *(ingredients; emotions)*; to jumble up *(sounds)*; to wipe out *(tracks, clues)*; to tamper with *(documents)*; to squander *(a fortune)* ‖ *intr* to behave in a disorderly manner, go wild; to be in a state of commotion; to riot, revolt

turb·ō -inis *m or* **turb·en -inis** *n* whirl, twirl; eddy; spinning, revolution; coil; spinning top; reel; spindle; wheel; tornado, whirlwind; wheel of fortune; *(fig)* whirlwind, storm

turbulentē *or* **turbulenter** *adv* boisterously, tumultuously, confusedly

turbulent·us -a -um *adj* turbulent, wild, stormy; disturbed, confused; seditious, trouble-making

turd·a -ae *f or* **turd·us -ī** *m* thrush

tūre·us -a -um *adj* of frankincense

tur·geō -gēre -sī *intr* to be swollen, be puffed up; to be bombastic

turgēsc·ō -ere *intr* to begin to swell (up); to begin to blow up *(in anger)*

turgidul·us -a -um *adj* poor swollen *(eyes)*

turgid·us -a -um *adj* swollen, puffed up; inflated; turgid, bombastic

tūribul·um -ī *n* censer

tūricrem·us -a -um *adj* incense-burning

tūrif·er -era -erum *adj* producing incense

tūrileg·us -a -um *adj* incense-gathering

turm·a -ae *f* troop, squadron *(of cavalry, originally consisting of 30 men)*; crowd, group

turmāl·is -is -e *adj* of a squadron; equestrian ‖ *mpl* troopers

turmātim *adv* by troops, by squadrons, squadron by squadron

Turn·us -ī *m* king of the Rutuli, killed by Aeneas

turpicul·us -a -um *adj* ugly little; somewhat indecent

turpificāt·us -a -um *adj* corrupted, degenerate

turpilucricupid·us -a -um *adj (coll)* eager to make a fast buck

turp·is -is -e *adj* ugly, deformed; foul, filthy, nasty; disgraceful, shameless; dirty, obscene, indecent

turpiter *adv* repulsively; disgracefully, scandalously, shamelessly

turpitūd·ō -inis *f* ugliness, deformity; foulness; disgrace; moral turpitude

turp·ō -āre -āvī -ātus *tr* to disfigure; to soil, defile, pollute; to disgrace

turrif·er -era -erum *adj see* **turriger**

turrig·er -era -erum *adj* turreted; *(of Cybele)* wearing a turreted crown *(representing earth with its cities)*

turr·is -is *f* turret, tower; howdah *(on an elephant)*; *(fig)* castle, mansion

turrīt·us -a -um *adj* turreted; fortified with turrets; crowned with turrets, adorned with a turret crown

turt·ur -uris *m* turtledove

tūs tūris *n* incense, frankincense

Tūsculānēns·is -is -e *adj* Tusculan

Tūsculān·us -a -um *adj* Tusculan ‖ *n* Tusculan estate *(esp. Cicero's)*

tūscul·um -ī *n* a little incense

Tūscul·us -a -um *adj* Tusculan ‖ *n* Tusculum *(town in Latium near Alba Longa, about 12 miles S. of Rome)*

Tūsc·us -a -um *adj* Etruscan

tussicul·a -ae *f* slight cough

tuss·iō -īre *intr* to cough, have a cough

tuss·is -is *(acc:* **tussim;** *abl singl:* **tussī)** *f* cough

tūsus *pp of* **tundō**

tūtām·en -inis *or* **tūtāment·um -ī** *n* means of protection; protector

tūte = tū + te *emphatic form of* **tū**

tūtē *adv* safely

tūtēl·a -ae *f* care, charge, protection, defense; guardianship; charge, thing protected; support, maintenance *(of persons)*; upkeep *(of buildings)*; guardian, keeper; **in suam tūtēlam (per)venīre** *(or* **tūtēlam accipere** *or* **suae tūtēlae fierī)** *(of a minor)* to become capable of managing one's own affairs

tūtemet = tū + te + met *emphatic form of* **tū**

tūtō *adv* safely, securely, without risk of harm; **tūtō esse** to exist safely

tūt·ō -āre *or* **tūt·or -ārī -ātus sum** *tr* to guard, protect, defend; to keep safe, watch, preserve; to ward off, avert; *(w.* **ab** *+ abl or w.* **ad** *or* **adversus** *+ acc)* to protect *(s.o.)* from, guard *(s.o.)* against

tūt·or -ōris *m* protector; *(leg)* guardian *(of minors, of women of any age, etc.)*

tutudī *perf of* **tundō**

tūt·us -a -um *pp of* **tueor** ‖ *adj* safe, secure; cautious, prudent ‖ *n* safe place, shelter, security; **ex tūtō** from a safe place, in safety

tu·us -a -um *(also* **tu·os -a -om)** *adj* your; your dear *(friend, etc.)*, dear to you; typical of you; devoted to you; *(of circumstances)* favorable to you ‖ *pron* yours; **dē tuō** at your expense; **in tuō** on your land; **quid tua?** what business is it of yours?; **tua** your girlfriend, your sweetheart; **tuā interest** *(or* **tuā rēfert** it is of importance to you); **tuī** your friends, your people, your family, your soldiers; **tuum est** *(w. inf)* it is your duty to, it's up to you to; **tuum est quod** it is thanks to you that

tuxtax *adv (a word meant to imitate the sound of blows)* whack, wham; **tuxtax meō tergō erit** *(coll)* it's going to be wham, whack all over my back

Tȳd·eūs -eī *or* **-eos** *m* Tydeus *(son of Oeneus, one of the Seven against Thebes, and father of Diomedes)*

Tȳdīd·ēs -ae *m* Diomedes *(son of Tydeus)*

tympaniz·ō -āre *intr* to play the drum

tympanotrīb·a -ae *m* timbrel player, drummer

tympan·um *or* **typan·um -ī** *n* drum, revolving cylinder; solid circular wheel *(used on carts and wagons);* dentated wheel *(used as a waterwheel); (mus)* drum, timbrel *(esp. used in the worship of Cybele or Bacchus)*

Tyndar·eūs -eī *or* **Tyndar·us -ī** *m* king of Sparta, husband of Leda, father of Castor and Clytemnestra, and reputed father of Pollux and Helen

Tyndarid·ēs -ae *m* descendant of Tyndareus *(esp. Castor and Pollux)*

Tyndar·is -idis *f* descendant of Tyndareus *(esp. Helen and Clytemnestra)*

Typhō·eūs -eī *or* **-eos** *or* **Tȳph·ōn -ōnis** *m* giant who was struck by Jupiter with lightning and buried under Mt. Etna

Typhōe·us -a -um *adj* of the monster Typhoeus

Tȳph·ōn -ōnis *m see* **Typhōeus**

typ·us -ī *m* figure, image, bas-relief *(on the wall)*

tyrannicē *adv* tyrannically

tyrannicīd·a -ae *m* assassin of a tyrant

tyrannic·us -a -um *adj* tyrannical

tyrann·is -idis *or* **-idos** *f* tyranny, despotism

tyrannocton·us -ī *m* tyrannicide, assassin of a tyrant

tyrann·us -ī *m* monarch, sovereign; *(in a Greek city-state)* unconstitutional (absolute) ruler

Tyrianthin·a -ōrum *npl* clothes of a violet color

Tyri·us -a -um *adj* Tyrian, Phoenician; Carthaginian; Theban; crimson *(because of the famous dye produced at Tyre)* **||** *mpl* Tyrians; Carthaginians

Tȳr·ō -ūs *or* **-ōnis** *f* daughter of Salmoneus and mother of Pelias and Neleus by Poseidon

Tyr·os *or* **Tyr·us -ī** *f* Tyre *(commercial city of Phoenicia, famous for its crimson dye, or "Tyrian purple"; its dye works were active until destroyed by the Crusaders)*

tȳrotarīch·os -ī *m* dish of salted fish and cheese *(as an example of a plain diet)*

Tyrr(h)ēnic·us -a -um *adj* Etrurian, Etruscan

Tyrr(h)ēn·us -a -um *adj* Etrurian, Etruscan; **mare Tyrrhēnum** Tyrrhenian Sea *(lying between the W. coast of Italy, Sardinia, and Sicily);* **Tyrrhēnae volucrēs** the Sirens **||** *mpl* Etruscans *(Pelasgian people who migrated to Italy, perhaps from Lydia in Asia Minor)*

Tyrrhēni·a -ae *f* Etruria

Tyrtae·us -ī *m* Spartan poet *(7th cent. B.C.)*

Tyrus *see* **Tyros**

U

U, u *(supply* littera) *f* twentieth letter of the Latin alphabet; letter name: **u**

ūb·er -eris *adj* rich, fertile; fruitful, productive; plentiful; plenty of; valuable; copious *(tears); (of things)* rich in content; imaginative *(writer, style); (fig)* productive **||** *n* (woman's) breast, nipple; udder; bosom *(of the earth);* fertility; fertile soil, fruitful field

ūberius *adv* more fully, in greater abundance; more fruitfully; with greater exuberance

ūbert·ās -ātis *f* richness; fertility; productiveness; abundance; richness of content

ūbertim *adv* copiously; **ūbertim flēre** to cry bitterly

ubi *or* **ubī** *adv (interrog)* where; **ubi gentium** *(or* **terrārum)** *(coll)* where in the world **||** *conj* where, in which; whereby; with whom, by whom; when, whenever

ubicumque *conj* wherever, wheresoever **||** *adv* anywhere, everywhere

Ubi·ī -ōrum *mpl* German tribe on the Lower Rhine

ubinam *adv* just where?, wherever?; **ubinam gentium** where in the world

ubiquāque *adv* everywhere

ubīque *adv* everywhere, anywhere

ubiubi *conj* wherever

ubivīs *adv* anywhere, everywhere, wherever you please; **ubivīs gentium** *(coll)* anywhere in the world

ūd·ō -ōnis *m* felt slipper

ūd·us -a -um *adj* wet, moist; humid

Ūf·ēns -entis *m* river in Latium

-ūg·ō -inis *fem suf formed from names of materials to denote a superficial film, e.g.:* **ferrūgō** (iron) rust; *formed from nouns, e.g.:* **vesperūgō** the Evening Star

-ul·a -ae *fem suf forms diminutives, e.g.:* **arcula** small box *or* chest

ulcer·ō -āre -āvī -ātus *tr* to cause to fester; *(fig)* to wound

ulcerōs·us -a -um *adj* ulcerous
ulcīscor ulcīscī ultus sum *tr* to avenge oneself on, take revenge on, punish; to avenge, requite
ulc·us -eris *n* ulcer, sore
-ulent·us -a -um *adjl suf forms adjectives meaning "abounding in," "full of," e.g.:* **vīnulentus** full of wine, intoxicated
ūlīg·ō -inis *f* moisture, dampness
Ulix·ēs -is *or* **-eī** *or* **-ī** *m* Ulysses *(king of Ithaca, son of Laertes, husband of Penelope, and father of Telemachus and Telegonus)*
ūll·us -a -um *adj* any
ulme·us -a -um *adj* elm, made of elm; *(hum)* elm-whipped
ulmitrib·a -ae *m (coll)* slaphappy *(from being flogged with elm whips)*
ulm·us -ī *f* elm tree **‖** *fpl* elm whips
uln·a -ae *f* elbow; arm; *(as measure of length, span of the outstretched arms, c. 45 inches)* ell
ulpic·um -ī *n* type of garlic
ulteri·or -or -us *adj* farther, on the farther side, more remote; further, additional, more; longer; in a higher degree; worse; **Gallia Ulterior** Transalpine Gaul; **Hispānia Ulterior** the western of the two provinces of the Iberian peninsula **‖** *mpl* more remote people, those beyond **‖** *npl* things beyond
ulterius *adv* to a more distant place, farther away; to a further extent, further, more than that; **ulterius quam** further than
ulterius *prep (w. acc)* beyond
ultimō *adv* finally, last of all
ultimum *adv* finally; for the last time
ultim·us -a -um *adj* **(-tum-)** farthest, most distant, extreme; earliest; latest, final, last; greatest; lowest; meanest **‖** *n* last thing, end; **ad ultimum** to the end; to the extreme; in the highest degree; to the last degree, utterly; *(in an enumeration)* finally; **in ultimō** finally **‖** *npl* extremes; the worst
ulti·ō -ōnis *f* vengeance, revenge
ult·or -ōris *m* avenger, punisher
ultrā *adv* beyond, farther, besides **‖** *prep* **1** *(w. acc) (in a physical sense)* on the farther side of, beyond, past: **nihil est ultrā altitūdinem montium quō pertimendum est** there is nothing beyond *(i.e., except)* the heights of the mountains that needs to be feared; **2** *(in the temporal sense)* to a point later than, at a later time than, after, past; to a time further back than, earlier than: **ultrā mediam noctem** till past midnight; **3** *(of number, measure, degree)* over, beyond, more than, over and above: **nōn ultrā trēs versūs** not more than three verses; **4** *(in negative sentences, indicating the limit of an activity)* **nihil ultrā nervōs atque cutem mortī concēderat ātrae** he had conceded to dark death nothing but sinews and skin *(i.e., his body)*
ultr·īx -īcis *adj (fem only)* avenging *(esp. of the Furies and other agents of retribution)* **‖** *f* avenger
ultrō *adv* to the farther side, beyond; on the other side; on both sides, in both directions; at the opposite end of the scale, conversely; besides, moreover, too; into the bargain, to boot; of one's own accord, without being asked; without being spoken to; unprovoked; **bella īnferre ultrō** to go to war (although) unprovoked; **ultrō et citrō** back and forth; **ultrō tribūta** expenditure incurred by the government for public works
ultus *pp of* **ulcīscor**
ulul·a -ae *f* owl
ululāt·us -ūs *m* howling *(esp. of dogs and wolves);* ulutation, wailing *(esp. of mourners);* war cry
ulul·ō -āre -āvī -ātus *tr* to howl out, howl at **‖** *intr* to howl; to ululate, wail; *(of places)* to resound
-ul·um -ī *neut suf forming diminutive neuter nouns:* **speculum** mirror
-ul·us *m and* **-ul·a** *f suf* **1** *forming diminutives:* **calculus** little stone; **2** *adjectives denoting repeated action:* **crēdulus** regularly believing, credulous; **3** *adjectives denoting diminished intensity:* **ūmidulus** dampish; **4** *nouns denoting instruments:* **furculus** pitchfork; **5** *nouns denoting endearment:* **uxorcula** dear wife
ulv·a -ae *f (bot)* sedge, rush
umbell·a -ae *f* umbrella, parasol
Um·ber -bra -brum *adj* Umbrian, of Umbria **‖** *m* Umbrian
umbilīc·us -ī *m* navel, bellybutton; midriff; middle, center; projecting end of dowels *or* cylinders on which scrolls were rolled; cockle, sea snail; **ad umbilīcum** *(or* **ad umbilīcōs)** to the end of the scroll *or* book
umb·ō -ōnis *m* boss *(of a shield);* shield; elbow
umbr·a -ae *f* shade; shadow; phantom, ghost; mere shadow *(of one's former self);* semblance; darkness, gloom; shelter, cover; privacy, retirement; umber *(fish);* **rhētorica umbra** rhetorician's school **‖** *fpl* darkness of night; lower world
umbrāc(u)l·um -ī *n* shade; bower, arbor; school; umbrella, parasol
umbrāticol·a -ae *mf* lounger *(in the shade)*

umbrātic·us -a -um *adj* too fond of the shade, lazy, inactive; secluded; private; **umbrāticus doctor** private tutor; pedant

umbrātil·is -is -e *adj* carried out in the shade, private, retired; academic

Umbri·a -ae *f* Umbria *(district in central Italy)*

umbrif·er -era -erum *adj* shady

umbr·ō -āre -āvī -ātus *tr* to shade, cast a shadow on; to overshadow

umbrōs·us -a -um *adj* shady

ūmect·ō -āre -āvī -ātus *tr* **(hūm-)** to wet, moisten

ūmect·us -a -um *adj* **(hūm-)** moist, damp

ūm·eō -ēre *intr* to be moist, be damp, be wet

umer·us -ī *m* **(hum-)** shoulder

ūmēsc·ō -ere *intr* to become moist, become wet

ūmidul·us -a -um *adj* dampish

ūmid·us -a -um *adj* **(hūm-)** moist, damp, wet; green, unseasoned *(lumber)* **‖** *n* wet place

ūmif·er -era -erum *adj* laden with moisture

ūm·or -ōris *m* **(hūm-)** moisture; liquid, fluid

umquam *or* **unquam** *adv* ever, at any time

ūnā *adv* together; **ūnā cum** together with; **ūnā venīre** to come along

ūnanim·āns -antis *adj* of one mind, of one accord

ūnanimit·ās -ātis *f* unanimity

ūnanim·us -a -um *adj* **(ūnian-)** unanimous; of one mind, of one heart

ūnci·a -ae *f* one-twelfth; ounce *(one-twelfth of a pound or* **lībra)**; *(of interest rate)* 1% a year; *(in length)* inch *(25 mm, one twelfth of a foot or* **pēs)**

ūnciāri·us -a -um *adj* containing one-twelfth; one-ounce; one-inch

ūnciātim *adv* ounce by ounce, little by little

uncīnāt·us -a -um *adj* hooked, barbed

uncīn·us -ī *m* hook

ūnciol·a -ae *f* a mere twelfth

unc·ō -āre *intr (of a bear)* to grunt

ūncti·ō -ōnis *f* rubdown with oil; *(fig)* wrestling

ūnctit·ō -āre *tr* to keep rubbing with oil, keep oiling

ūnctiuscul·us -a -um *adj* somewhat too oily; unctuous

ūnct·or -ōris *m* anointer, rubdown man, masseur

ūnct·um -ī *n* sumptuous dinner

ūnctūr·a -ae *f* anointing

ūnct·us -a -um *pp of* **ung(u)ō ‖** *adj* greasy; resinous; sumptuous

ūncul·us -a -um *adj* any at all

unc·us -a -um *adj* hooked, barbed; crooked **‖** *m* hook, clamp; grappling iron

und·a -ae *f* water; stream, river; wave; sea, seawater; current *(of air); (fig)* stream, tide, agitated mass

unde *adv* from where, whence; from whom; **unde unde** *(or* **undeunde)** by hook or by crook

ūndeciēns *or* **ūndeciēs** *adv* eleven times

ūndecim *indecl adj* eleven

ūndecim·us -a -um *adj* **(-decum-)** eleventh

undecumque *adv* **(-cun-)** from whatever place, from whatever source

ūndēn·ī -ae -a *adj* eleven in a group, eleven each, eleven

ūndēnōnāgintā *indecl adj* eighty-nine

ūndēoctōgintā *indecl adj* seventy-nine

ūndēquadrāgēsim·us -a -um *adj* thirty-ninth

ūndēquadrāgintā *indecl adj* thirty-nine

ūndēquīnquāgēsim·us -a -um *adj* forty-ninth

ūndēquīnquāgintā *indecl adj* forty-nine

ūndēsexāgintā *indecl adj* fifty-nine

undētrīcēsim·us -a -um *adj* twenty-ninth

ūndētrīgintā *indecl adj* twenty-nine

ūndēvīcēsimān·ī -ōrum *mpl* soldiers of the nineteenth legion

ūndēvicēsim·us -a -um *adj* nineteenth

ūndēvīgintī *indecl adj* nineteen

undique *adv* from all directions, on all sides, everywhere; in all respects, completely

undison·us -a -um *adj* of roaring waves; **undisonī deī** gods of the roaring waves

und·ō -āre -āvī -ātum *intr* to move in waves, undulate; to billow; to overflow

undōs·us -a -um *adj* full of waves, billowy; wave-washed *(shore)*

ūnetvīcē(n)sim·us -a -um *adj* twenty-first

ūnetvīcēsimān·ī -ōrum *mpl* soldiers of the twenty-first legion

ungō *or* **unguō ung(u)ere ūnxī ūnctus** *tr* to oil, grease, anoint

ungu·en -inis *n* fat, grease; ointment

unguentāri·us -(i)ī *m* perfumer

unguentāt·us -a -um *adj* anointed; perfumed, wearing perfume

unguent·um -ī *n* ointment; perfume

unguicul·us -i *m* fingernail; toenail; **ā tenerīs unguiculīs** from earliest childhood

ungu·is -is *m* fingernail; toenail; claw, talon; hoof; **ad unguem** to a tee, complete, perfect; **dē tenerō unguī** from earliest childhood

ungul·a -ae *f* hoof; claw, talon; *(fig)* horse

unguō *see* **ungō**

ūnicē *adv* singularly; particularly; **ūnicē ūnus** one and only

ūnicol·or -ōris *adj* of one and the same color, monochrome

ūnicorn·is -is -e *adj* one-horned

ūnic·us -a -um *adj* one and only, sole; singular, unique; uncommon
ūnifōrm·is -is -e *adj* uniform, having only one shape
ūnigen·a -ae *adj (masc & fem only)* only-begotten, only; of the same parentage
ūniman·us -a -um *adj* one-handed
ūni·ō -ōnis *f* single large pearl
ūnisubsell·ium -(i)ī *n* seat for one
ūniter *adv* jointly
ūniversāl·is -is -e *adj* universal
ūniversē *adv* generally, in general
ūniversit·ās -ātis *f* aggregate, whole; whole world, universe
ūnivers·us -a -um *adj* **(-vors-)** all, all together; all taken collectively; whole, entire **II** *n* the whole; whole world, universe; **in ūniversum** on the whole, in general
ūnocul·us -ī *m* one-eyed person
ūnomammi·a -ae *adj (fem)* single-breasted *(Amazon)*
unquam *or* **umquam** *adv* ever, at any time
ūnumquicquid *pron* every little thing
ūn·us -a -um *adj* one, single, only, sole; one and the same; *(indefinite)* one, some; **ūnae scōpae** one broom; **ūnus et alter** one or two; **ūnus quisque** each one, every single one **II** *pron* someone, a mere individual; **ad ūnum** to a man
ūnxī *perf of* **ung(u)ō**
ūpili·ō -ōnis *m* shepherd
upup·a -ae *f* hoopoe *(bird with fan-like crest and downward-curving bill);* hoe, mattock
-ūr·a -ae *fem suf forms nouns from nouns ending in* **-tor** *to denote office:* **praetūra** praetorship *(from* **praetor);** *forms nouns mainly from verbal derivatives in* **-tus: nātūra** nature *(from* **nātus)**
Ūrani·a -ae *or* **Ūrani·ē -ēs** *f* Muse of astronomy
urbānē *adv* politely, courteously; with sophistication; wittily
urbānit·ās -ātis *f* living in the city, city life; refinement; politeness; sophistication; wit; raillery
urbān·us -a -um *adj* of the city, city; courteous; sophisticated; witty; brash, forward **II** *m* city dweller; *(pej)* city slicker
urbicap·us -ī *m* conqueror of cities
urbic·us -a -um *adj* city, of the city
urbi·us -a -um *adj* **urbius clīvus** slope on the Esquiline Hill
ur·bs *or* **ur·ps -bis** *f* city; the city of Rome
urceol·us -ī *m* little pitcher, little pot
urce·us -ī *m* pitcher, water pot
urc·ō -āre *intr (of a lynx)* to snarl
ūrēd·ō -inis *f* blight *(on plants)*
urgeō urgēre ūrsī *tr* to prod on, urge forward; to pressure, put pressure on *(s.o.);* to crowd, hem in; to follow up, keep at, stick by **II** *intr* to be urgent; to be insistent
ūrīn·a -ae *f* urine
ūrīnāt·or -ōris *m* diver
ūrīn·ō -āre *or* **ūrīn·or -ārī** *intr* to dive
-ur·iō -īre -īvī *or* **-iī** *suf forming desideratives:* **cēnāturīre** to wish to eat
Ūrī·ōn -ōnis *m* Orion
Ūr·ios -iī *m* cult title of Zeus, as the sender of favorable winds
urn·a -ae *f* pot, jar; water pot; voting urn; urn of fate; cinerary urn; money jar; liquid measure *(= one half of an amphora)*
urnul·a -ae *f* small urn
ūrō ūrere ūssī ūstus *tr* to burn; to burn up, reduce to ashes, consume; to scorch, parch, dry up; to sting, pain; to nip, frostbite; to rub sore; to corrode; to annoy, gall, burn up, make angry; to inflame *(w. love)*
urps *see* **urbs**
urs·a -ae *f* she-bear **II Ursa Māior** *(astr)* Great Bear *(constellation);* **Ursa Minor** *(astr)* Little Bear *(constellation)*
ūrsī *perf of* **urgeō**
ursīn·us -a -um *adj* bear, bear's
urs·us -ī *m* bear
urtīc·a -ae *f (bot)* stinging nettle *(causing a burning rash upon contact)*; desire, itch
ūrūc·a *or* **ūrīc·a -ae** *f* caterpillar
ūr·us -ī *m* wild ox
Ūsīpet·ēs -um *mpl* German tribe on the Rhine
ūsitātē *adv* in the usual way, as usual
ūsitāt·us -a -um *adj* usual, customary, familiar; **ūsitātum est** *(w. inf)* it is customary to
ūspiam *adv* anywhere, somewhere, in some place or other
ūsquam *adv* anywhere *(in any place or to any place)*
ūsque *adv* all the way, right on; all the time, continuously; even, as much as; *(without addition of an adv or prep)* to the fullest extent, completely; **ūsque ab** *(w. abl)* all the way from; ever since; **ūsque ad** *(w. acc)* all the way to; all the way back in time to; **ūsque adeō** *(or* **ūsque eō) ut** to such an extent that; **ūsque quāque** every moment, continually; on all occasions, in everything **II** *prep (w. acc)* up to, as far as, right until
ūsquequāque *or* **ūsque quāque** *adv* everywhere, as far as one can go in either direction; *(fig)* in every conceivable situation; in every possible respect, wholly
ūssī *perf of* **ūrō**
ūsti·ō -ōnis *f* burning
ūst·or -ōris *m* cremator
ūstul·ō -āre -āvī -ātus *tr* to scorch, singe
ūstus *pp of* **ūrō**

ūsū·capiō -capere -cēpī -captus *tr (leg)* to acquire ownership of *(by long use)*

ūsūcapi·ō -ōnis *f (leg)* acquisition of ownership *(through long use)*

ūsūr·a -ae *f* use, enjoyment; interest *(on capital)*

ūsūrāri·us -a -um *adj* for use and enjoyment; paying interest, interest-bearing

ūsurpāti·ō -ōnis *f* use; *(w. gen)* making use of, use of

ūsurp·ō -āre -āvī -ātus *tr* to use, make *(constant)* use of, employ; to exercise *(a right);* to put into practice *(a custom, operation);* to take possession of, acquire; to usurp; to name, call, speak of; to assume *(a title, honor, esp. arbitrarily);* to take up *(an inheritance);* to perceive *(with the senses),* observe, experience; **memoriam ūsurpāre** *(w. gen)* to invoke the memory of

ūsus *pp of* **ūtor**

ūs·us -ūs *m* use, enjoyment; practice, employment; experience, skill; usage, custom; familiarity; usefulness, advantage, benefit; occasion, need, necessity; **ex ūsū esse** *(or* **ūsuī esse)** *(w. dat)* to be useful to, be a good thing for; **in ūsū** in one's everyday experience; **in ūsū esse** to be in use; to be customary; **in ūsū (meō, tuō,** *etc.)* **est** it is to (my, your, *etc.)* advantage; **in ūsū habēre** *(or* **continēre)** to keep in use; **quis ūsus est?** *(w. gen)* what useful purpose is served by?; **scientia et ūsus** theory and practice; **sī ūsus veniat** if the need should arise, if the opportunity should present itself; **ūsus adest** a good opportunity comes along; **ūsus est** *(w. abl)* there is a need of; **ūsus et frūctus** use and enjoyment; **ūsū venit** it happens, it occurs; **ūsus venit** *(w. dat)* the need arises for

ūsusfrūctus *(gen:* **ūsūsfrūctūs)** *m* use and enjoyment, usufruct

ut *(or* **utī,** *an older form, increasingly rare after Cicero, but affected by archaizing authors) adv (in direct and indirect questions; in exclamations)* how; **ut miser est quī**! how pitiful is the man who! **||** *conj (comparative)* as; *(adversative)* although; *(temporal)* when, while; *(purpose)* in order that; *(result, after* **adeō, eō, sīc, tālis, tam, tantus)** (to such a degree, so, such, so great) that; *(concessive)* granted that; *(introducing examples)* as, as for example; *(after verbs of fearing)* lest, that not; *(introducing an explanation or reason)* as, as being, inasmuch as; *(introducing indirect commands)* that; **ut maximē** at most; **ut perinde** *(or* **proinde)** according to the degree to which; **ut quī** (= **quippe quī**) as is natural for one who; **ut putā** *(indicating an example)* as say, as for example

utcumque *or* **utcunque** *or* **utquomque** *adv* however; whenever; one way or another

ūt·ēns -entis *adj* well-off, well-to-do

ūtēnsil·is -is -e *adj* useful **||** *npl* utensils, materials, provisions, similar things

u·ter -tra -trum *(gen:* **utrīus,** *dat:* **utrī)** *adj* which *(of the two)* **||** *pron* which one *(of the two);* one or the other

ū·ter -tris *m* bag, skin, bottle; inflated bag to keep swimmers afloat

utercumque utracumque utrumcumque *adj* whichever *(of the two)* **||** *pron* whichever one *(of the two)*

uterlibet utralibet utrumlibet *adj* whichever *(of the two)* you please **||** *pron* whichever one *(of the two)* you please, either one *(of the two)*

uterque utraque utrumque *adj* each *(of the two),* both; **sermōnēs utrīusque linguae** conversations in both languages *(i.e., Greek and Latin)* **||** *pron* each one *(of the two),* both; **uterque īnsāniunt** both are insane

uter·us -ī *m or* **uter·um -ī** *n* belly, abdomen; womb; potbelly *(of a man);* **uterum gerere** to be pregnant

utervīs utravīs utrumvīs *adj* whichever *(of the two)* you please, either **||** *pron* whichever one *(of the two)* you please, either one

utī *see* **ut**

ūtibil·is -is -e *adj* useful, usable, practical

Utic·a -ae *f* city in Africa, N.W. of Carthage, where the younger Cato committed suicide in 46 B.C.

Uticēns·is -is -e *adj* of Utica **||** *m* posthumous title of Cato

ūtil·is -is -e *adj* useful, profitable, practical; *(w. dat or* **ad** + *acc)* fit for, useful for, practical in

ūtilit·ās -ātis *f* usefulness, advantage

ūtiliter *adv* usefully, profitably

utinam *conj (introducing a wish)* if only, would that

utique *adv* anyhow, at least, at any rate; in particular, especially; without condition, absolutely; *(after negatives)* on any account; *(in obeying instructions)* without fail; **cūr utique** exactly why

ūtor ūtī ūsus sum *intr (w. abl)* **1** to use, make use of: **coquī hīs condīmentīs ūtuntur** cooks use these seasonings; **2** to enjoy: **valetūdine prosperā ūtī** to enjoy good health; **3** to practice, experience: **portīs patefactīs eō diē pāce prīmum ūsī sunt** as the gates were thrown open they experienced peace for the first time on that day; **4** to enjoy the friendship *or* companionship of: **multōs iam annōs tē**

ūsī sumus for many years now we have enjoyed your friendship; **5** *(w. adv or abl of manner)* to treat: **omnibus sociīs clēmentiā ūtī** to treat all our allies with kindness; **familiāriter ūtēbar Caesare** I was on familiar terms with Caesar; **6** to hold *(office, military command):* **honōre ūtī** to hold office; **tribūnī mīlitēs et imperiō et īnsignibus cōnsulāribus ūsī sunt** the military tribunes held military commands and wore the consular insignia; **7** to handle, manage, control: **bene armīs, optimē equīs ūsus est** he managed arms well and horses very well; **8** to consume *(food or drink):* **quī vetere vīnō ūtuntur** who drink old wine; **9** to wear *(clothes):* **solūtīs vestibus ūtuntur Grātiae** the Graces wear loose dresses; **10** to live *or* spend one's time *(in a place):* **eō marī ūtī cōnsuērunt** they were used to living on (the coast of) that sea; **11** to play *(a musical instrument):* **quī fidibus aut tibiīs ūtī volunt** those who want to play the lyre or the flute

utpote *adv (reinforcing explanatory phrases or clauses)* as one might expect, as is natural, naturally, inasmuch as; **utpote cum** as you might expect since; **utpote quī** inasmuch as *(he is one)* who, inasmuch as he, because he

ūtrār·ius -(i)ī *m* water carrier, water boy

ūtric(u)lār·ius -(i)ī *m* bagpipe player

utrimque *or* **utrinque** *adv* from *or* on both sides, on either side; **utrimque cōnstitit fidēs** on both sides their word of honor held good

utrō *adv* to which of the two sides, in which direction

utrobīque *adv* on both sides, on either hand

utrōlibet *adv* to either side

utrōque *adv* to both sides, in both directions

utrōqueversum *adv* **(-vors-)** in both directions

utrubi *adv* at *or* on which of the two sides

utrubīque *adv* on both sides, on either hand

utrum *conj* whether

utut *adv* in whatever way, however

ūv·a -ae *f* grape; grapes; bunch of grapes; vine; swarm of bees; *(anat)* uvula; **ūva pāssa** raisin *(literally, grape spread out to dry)*

ūvēsc·ō -ere *intr* to become moist; *(fig)* to get drunk

ūvidul·us -a -um *adj* a little moist, dampish

ūvid·us -a -um *adj* wet, moist, damp; humid; drunk

ux·or -ōris *f* wife; mate *(of animals)*

uxorcul·a -ae *f* dear (little) wife

uxorcul·ō -āre -āvī *intr* to play the role of a wife

uxōri·us -a -um *adj* of a wife, wifely; very fond of a wife; henpecked

V

V, v *(supply* littera) *f* twenty-first letter of the Latin alphabet; letter name: **ve**

V, v is used in this dictionary to represent consonantal *u*

vac·āns -antis *adj* vacant, unoccupied; at leisure; unemployed; unattached, single; *(w. abl)* lacking, without; **puella vacāns** a single girl **||** *npl* unoccupied estates

vacāti·ō -ōnis *f* freedom, exemption *(from duty, service, etc.);* exemption from military service; payment for being exempted from military service; vacation, holiday, day off

vacc·a -ae *f* cow

vaccīn·ium -(i)ī *n (bot)* hyacinth

vaccul·a -ae *f* heifer

vacē·fīō -fierī *intr* to become empty, be emptied, be vacated

vacerr·a -ae *f* fence post

vacerrōs·us -a -um *adj (pej)* cracked, crazy

vacillāti·ō -ōnis *f* tottering

vacill·ō -āre -āvī -ātum *intr* **(vacc-)** to stagger, reel; to vacillate, waver; to be untrustworthy

vacīvē *adv* at leisure

vacīvit·ās -ātis *f* want, lack

vacīv·us -a -um *adj* **(voc-)** *(of a place)* unoccupied, vacant; *(w. gen)* free of, devoid of, free from

vac·ō -āre -āvī -ātum *intr* **(voc-)** to be empty, be vacant; to be unoccupied; to be ownerless; to be without, not to contain; to be free, be carefree; to be at leisure, have free time; *(of things)* to lie idle; to be *(romantically)* unattached; *(w. abl or* **ab)** **1** to be free from; **2** to be devoid of; **3** to abstain from; **4** to be exempt from *(duty, responsibility); (w. dat or w.* **ad** *or* **in** + *acc)* to be free for, have time for, have spare time for; *(w. inf)* to have leisure to, have time to; **populō vacāre** to remain aloof from the people; **rēs pūblica et mīlite et pecūniā vacat** the country is relieved from furnishing an army and money; **semper philosophiae vacō** I always have time for philosophy **||** *v impers (w. dat)* there is time for, there is room for; *(w. inf)* there is time to *or* for

vacuāt·us -a -um *adj* empty

vacuē·faciō -facere -fēcī -factus *tr* to empty, clear, free

vacuit·ās -ātis *f* freedom, exemption; emptiness; empty space; vacancy *(in an office); (w. gen or w.* **ab)** freedom from *(s.th. undesirable)*

Vacūn·a -ae *f* Sabine goddess, later identified with Victory
Vacūnāl·is -is -e *adj* of the goddess Vacuna
vacu·ō -āre -āvī -ātus *tr* to empty, clear, free; to strip *(a place of defenders, inhabitants)*
vacu·us -a -um *adj* empty, clear, free; vacant; worthless, useless; single, unmarried; widowed; at leisure; carefree; *(w. gen or abl or w.* **ab)** free from, devoid of, without; *(w. dat)* free for
vadimōn·ium -(i)ī *n (leg)* promise *(to appear in court),* bail *(given as a guarantee of one's appearance in court);* **vadimōnium dēserere** to default, jump bail; **vadimōnium differre** to postpone appearance in court, grant a continuance; **vadimōnium facere** to put up bail; **vadimōnium sistere** to appear in court
vadis *genit of* **vas**
vādō vādere vāsī *intr* to go, make one's way, advance
vad·or -ārī -ātus sum *tr (of a plaintiff)* to demand that *(s.o.)* put up bail; to sue
vadōs·us -a -um *adj* shallow
vad·um -ī *n or* **vad·us -ī** *m* shallow place, shallow, ford; shallow part of the sea, shoal; bottom *(of the sea),* depths; sea, waters
vae *interj* woe!; *(w. acc or dat)* woe to
va·fer -fra -frum *adj* sly, cunning; subtle; ingenious
vafrē *adv* slyly, cunningly
vagē *adv* far and wide
vāgīn·a -ae *f* sheath, scabbard; hull *(of ear of grain); (anat)* vagina
vāg·iō -īre -īvī *or* **-iī** *intr (esp. of an infant)* to cry, bawl; *(of hares)* to squeal
vāgīt·us -ūs *m* cry
vag·or -ārī -ātus sum *or* **vag·ō -āre** *intr* to wander, range, roam
vāg·or -ōris *m* cry *(of a baby)*
vag·us -a -um *adj* wandering, roaming; shifting, inconstant; rambling *(speech);* roundabout *(explanation);* haphazard, erratic; fickle; *(of lovers)* changing from one partner to another; **stella vaga** planet
vāh *interj (expressing dismay, pain, annoyance, contempt, or surpise)* ah!, oh!; *(expressing unexpected admiration or surprise)* wow!
vaha *interj (expressing pleasant surprise)* aha!, wow!
valdē *adv* greatly, intensely; *(w. adj or adv)* very; *(as affirmative reply)* yes, certainly, to be sure
valē *interj* goodbye!
val·ēns -entis *adj* strong, powerful; healthy, well; coarse *(fabrics);* strong *(medicine);* vigorous *(plants);* potent, effective *(remedies; arguments)*
valenter *adv* strongly; energetically
valentul·us -a -um *adj* sturdy, robust
val·eō -ēre -uī valitūrus *intr* to be strong; to be vigorous; to be powerful; to be effective; to prevail, succeed; to be influential; to be valid; to be strong enough, be adequate, be capable, be able; to be of value, be of worth; to mean, signify; **tē valēre iubeō** I bid you farewell, goodbye to you; **valē** *(pl:* **valēte)** goodbye; **valē dīcere** to say goodbye, take leave
Valeriān·us -a -um *adj* belonging to Valerius
Valeri·us -a -um *adj* Roman clan name *(nomen), esp.* Publius Valerius Publicola *(recorded as one of the first two consuls in 509 B.C.)*
valēsc·ō -ere *intr* to grow strong, thrive; to grow powerful
valētūdinār·ium -(i)ī *n* hospital
valētūd·ō -inis *f* state of health; good health; ill health, illness; **bona** *(or* **commoda** *or* **firma** *or* **prospera** *or* **secunda)** **valētūdō** good health; **adversa** *(or* **īnfirma** *or* **mala)** poor health; **valētūdinis causā** for reasons of (poor) health
Valgi·us -a -um *adj* Roman clan name *(nomen), esp.* Gaius Valgius Rufus *(an Augustan poet and grammarian)*
valg·us -a -um *adj* knock-kneed
validē *adv* strongly, vehemently; *(in replies)* of course, certainly, definitely
valid·us -a -um *adj* strong, powerful, able; healthy; robust; fortified; influential; efficacious
vallār·is -is -e *adj* of a rampart; **corōna vallāris** crown awarded to the first soldier to scale the enemy's rampart
vall·ēs *or* **vall·is -is** *f* valley
vall·ō -āre -āvī -ātus *tr* to fortify with a rampart, wall in; to protect, defend
vall·um -ī *n* palisade of stakes on top of an embankment; rampart
vall·us -ī *m* stake, pale; rampart with palisades, stockade; tooth *(of a comb)*
valv·ae -ārum *fpl* folding doors, double doors
vānēsc·ō -ere *intr* to vanish, fade
vānidic·us -a -um *adj* lying; boasting ‖ *m* liar; boaster
vāniloquenti·a -ae *f* empty talk, mere talk
vāniloquidōr·us -ī *m* liar, windbag
vāniloqu·us -a -um *adj* talking nonsense; lying; bragging
vānit·ās -ātis *f* falsity, unreality, deception, untruth; bragging; lying; vanity; worthlessness; frivolity
vānitūd·ō -inis *f* falsehood
vann·us -ī *f* winnowing fan
vān·us -a -um *adj* empty, vacant; groundless; pointless; hollow, unreal; lying,

false; boastful; conceited, vain ‖ *n* emptiness; uselessness; deceptive appearance
vapidē *adv* poorly, badly
vapid·us -a -um *adj* flat, vapid, spoiled, bad; morally corrupt
vap·or -ōris *m* vapor, steam; warmth *(of the sun)*
vapōrār·ium -(i)ī *n* steam room
vapōr·ō -āre -āvī -ātus *tr* to steam up; to warm, heat ‖ *intr* to steam
vapp·a -ae *f* sour wine; *(pej)* brat, good-for-nothing
vāpulār·is -is -e *adj* in for a flogging
vapul·ō -āre *intr* to get a beating; *(of savings, etc.)* to take a beating
vārē *adv* in a straddling manner
varianti·a -ae *f* diversity, variety
Vāriān·us -a -um *adj* of Varus *(i.e., Publius Quintilius Varus, whose legions were cut to pieces in Germany)*
variāti·ō -ōnis *f* diversification; variation; divergence
vāric·ō -āre -āvī -ātus *intr* to spread the legs, stand with legs spread apart
varicōs·us -a -um *adj* varicose
vāric·us -a -um *adj* with legs wide apart
variē *adv* variously; in different degrees; differently; severally, respectively; in a varied style; with changing colors
variet·ās -ātis *f* variety, difference, diversity; vicissitudes; inconstancy
vari·ō -āre -āvī -ātus *tr* to vary, diversify, change, make different; to give variety to; to variegate ‖ *intr* to change color; to vary, differ, change; to be diversified; to differ in opinion; to waver; **bellum variante fortūnā** a war with varying success, a war with ups and downs ‖ *v impers* **sī variāret** if there were a difference of opinion
vari·us -a -um *adj* variegated, of different colors; varied; composed of different elements, motley; many-sided *(personality)*; conflicting *(opinions, reports)*; changing, fluctuating *(conditions, fortunes)*; versatile; inconstant, unsteady; untrustworthy, fickle *(character)*
Var·ius -(i)ī *m* Lucius Varius Rufus *(epic and tragic poet and friend of Vergil and Horace, died c. 12 B.C.)*
var·ix -icis *mf* varicose vein
Varr·ō -ōnis *m* Roman family name, *(cognomen), esp.* Gaius Terentius Varro *(consul in 216 B.C. and joint commander at Cannae)* ‖ Marcus Terentius Varro *(antiquarian, philologist, and librarian, 116–27 B.C.)* ‖ Publius Terentius Varro Atacinus *(born 82 B.C., poet, translator of Apollonius Rhodius' "Argonautica")*
vār·us -a -um *adj* knock-kneed; bent, crooked; opposed, contrary
vas vadis *m (leg)* bondsman *(person who provides surety or bail)*
vās vāsis *or* **vās·um -ī** *(pl:* **vās·a -ōrum)** *n* vessel, dish; utensil, implement ‖ *npl* equipment, gear; **vāsa colligere** *(mil)* to pack up one's gear; **vāsa conclāmare** *(mil)* to give the signal to pack the gear; **vāsa coquitātōria** pots and pans
vāsār·ium -(i)ī *n* allowance for furnishings *(given to a provincial governor)*
vāsculār·ius -(i)ī *m* metal worker; seller of housewear items
vāscul·um -ī *n* small vessel
vastāti·ō -ōnis *f* devastation
vastāt·or -ōris *m* devastator
vastē *adv* vastly, widely; coarsely, harshly; violently
vastific·us -a -um *adj* devastating
vastit·ās -ātis *f* wasteland, desert; state of desolation, emptiness; devastation, destruction; vastness, immensity; great open spaces
vastiti·ēs -ēī *f* ruin, destruction
vast·ō -āre -āvī -ātus *tr* to leave desolate; to lay waste; to cut *(troops)* to pieces
vast·us -a -um *adj* desolate; devastated; vast, enormous; uncouth; clumsy; unrefined *(pronunciation)*
vāt·ēs *or* **vāt·is -is** *m* seer, prophet; bard, poet ‖ *f* prophetess; poetess
Vāticān·us -a -um *adj* Vatican; **mōns** *(or* **collis)** **Vāticānus** hill in Rome on the right bank of the Tiber
vāticināti·ō -ōnis *f* prophesying, soothsaying, prophecy
vāticināt·or -ōris *m* prophet, seer
vāticin·ium -(i)ī *n* prophecy
vāticin·or -ārī -ātus sum *tr* to foretell, prophesy; to keep harping on ‖ *intr* to prophesy; to rant and rave, talk wildly
vāticin·us -a -um *adj* prophetic
vatill·um -ī *n* brazier
vātis *see* **vātēs**
vati·us -a -um *adj* knock-kneed
-ve *conj (enclitic)* or; **-ve … -ve** either … or
vēcordi·a -ae *f* **(vae-)** senselessness; madness
vēc·ors -ordis *adj* **(vae-)** senseless; insane
vectāti·ō -ōnis *f* riding *(on horseback or in a carriage)*
vectīg·al -ālis *n* tax; revenue; duty; tariff; private income; produce providing personal income; payment given to a magistrate *or* provincial governor; private income *or* revenue; **vectīgal aedīlicium** payment exacted by an aedile to finance games
vectīgāl·is -is -e *adj (of persons, cities, etc.)* subject to taxation, taxed, taxable; *(of land, etc.)* yielding taxes; **pecūnia vectīgālis** money raised by taxes

vecti·ō -ōnis *f* conveyance, transporting

Vect·is -is *f* Isle of Wight

vect·is -is *m* crowbar, lever; bar, bolt *(on a door or gate)*

vect·ō -āre -āvī -ātus *tr* to carry, transport *(by an habitual agent or means of conveyance)* **‖** *pass* to ride, drive, travel; **equō vectārī** to ride a horse; **nāve vectārī** to sail

vect·or -ōris *m* bearer, carrier; rider; passenger

vectōri·us -a -um *adj* of transportation; **nāvigia vectōria** cargo ships

vectūr·a -ae *f* transportation, conveyance; freight costs; fare

vectus *pp of* **vehō**

Vēdiov·is *or* **Vēiov·is -is** *m* Anti-Jove *(Etruscan divinity of the lower world, identified with the Jupiter of the lower world)* **‖** Little Jove *(identified with the infant Jupiter)*

veget·ō -āre *tr* to invigorate

veget·us -a -um *adj* vigorous; lively *(rhythm, time, mind, thoughts)* vivacious, energetic; bright *(eyes);* invigorating; vivid *(colors);* **intervallum temporis vegetissimum agricolīs** a period of time extremely busy for the farmers

vēgrand·is -is -e *adj* not huge, puny

vehem·ēns -entis *adj* **(vēm-)** vehement; intense *(heat, cold);* strong, powerful *(force);* strong *(taste, flavor);* potent *(drink, medicine);* severe *(pain);* serious *(illness);* drastic *(actions);* forceful, strongly expressive, tremendous *(writing, speech);* imperious, overmastering; forceful *(arguments);* violent *(men, animals, natural phenomena);* vigorous, active *(person);* ardent, great *(love)*

vehementer *adv* **(vēm-)** vehemently, impetuously; with great force, violently; firmly, strongly; energetically; in an impassioned manner; *(w. reference to feelings)* strongly, overpoweringly; *(modifying adjectives)* immensely, tremendously

vehic(u)l·um -ī *n* vehicle, wagon, cart; means of transportation; **praefectus vehiculōrum** director of the imperial post

veh·is -is *m (f)* wagonload

vehō vehere vexī vectus *tr* to carry, convey, transport **‖** *pass* to travel, ride, sail, be borne along

Vēi·ēns -entis *or* **Vēientān·us -a -um** *adj* of Veii

Vēi·ī -ōrum *mpl* old Etrurian city about 12 miles from Rome, captured by Camillus *(396 B.C.)*

Vēiov·is -is *or* **Vēdiovis -is** *m* ancient deity worshiped on the Capitoline Hill in Rome, considered to be the lower-world counterpart of Jupiter

vel *adv* even, actually; perhaps; for instance; *(with superlatives)* to the utmost **‖** *conj* either, or, as you wish, take your pick; **vel ... vel** either ... or

Vēlābrēns·is -is -e *adj* of the Velabrum

Vēlābr·um -ī *n* Velabrum *(low ground between the Capitoline and Palatine where a market was located)*

vēlām·en -inis *n* drape, covering, veil; clothing; robe; olive branch wrapped in wool *(symbol carried by a suppliant)*

vēlāment·um -ī *n* covering, wrapping; a wrap; olive branch wrapped in wool *(symbol carried by a suppliant); (fig)* screen, cover-up

vēlār·ium -(i)ī *n* awning *(over the open-air theater)*

vēlāt·ī -ōrum *mpl (mil)* reserves

vēl·es -itis *m* light-armed soldier, skirmisher

Veli·a -ae *f* the Velia *(elevated portion of the Palatine Hill in Rome)* **‖** town and port in Lucania

Veliēns·is -is -e *adj* of the Velia in Rome **‖** of Velia *(Lucanian town)*

vēlif·er -era -erum *adj* sail, sailing; **carīna vēlifera** sailboat, sailing ship

vēlificāti·ō -ōnis *f* sailing

vēlific·ō -āre -āvī -ātus *or* **vēlific·or -ārī -ātus sum** *tr* to sail through **‖** *intr* to sail; *(w. dat)* **1** to be under full sail toward, set one's course for; **2** to be hell-bent on *(e.g., high office)*

Velīn·us -a -um *adj* of Velia *(Lucanian town and port);* of the River Velinus; **lacus Valīnus** Valine Lake *(fed by the Veline river);* **tribus Velīna** one of the 35 Roman tribes, belonging to that region

Velīn·us -ī *m* river and lake in the Sabine territory

vēlitār·is -is -e *adj* of light-armed troops

vēlitāti·ō -ōnis *f* skirmishing

Velitern·us -a -um *adj* of Velitrae

vēlitēs = *pl of* **vēles**

vēlit·or -ārī -ātus sum *or* **vēlit·ō -āre** *intr* to make an irregular attack, skirmish; *(fig)* to indulge in a verbal skirmish

Velitr·ae -ārum *fpl* Volscian town in Latium on the S. side of the Alban Hills

Vēli·us -a -um *adj* Roman clan name, *(nomen), esp.* Velius Longus *(a grammarian of the age of Trajan)*

vēlivol·us -a -um *adj* speeding along under sail; sail-covered *(sea)*

velle *inf of* **vōlō**

vellic·ō -are *tr* to pluck, pinch, nip; to carp at, rail at

vellō vellere vellī *or* **vulsī** *or* **volsī vulsus** *or* **volsus** *tr* to pluck, pull, tear at, tear away, tear out; to tear up, tear down, destroy

vell·us -eris *n* fleece, skin, pelt; wool **||** *npl* fleecy clouds

vēl·ō -āre -āvī -ātus *tr* to veil, wrap, envelop; to cover, clothe; to encircle, crown; to cover up, hide; to adorn *(temples, etc., ritually);* **vēlātus** sail-clad, fitted with sails

vēlōcit·ās -ātis *f* velocity, speed

vēlōciter *adv* speedily, swiftly

vēl·ōx -ōcis *adj* speedy, swift

vēl·um -ī *n* sail; veil; curtain, awning, covering; **plēnīs vēlīs** full speed ahead; **rēmīs vēlīsque** *(fig)* with might and main; **(ventīs) vēla dare** to set sail; **vēla facere** to spread one's sails

velut *or* **velutī** *adv* as, just as, even as; as for example; *(to introduce a simile)* as, as it were; *(in elliptical clauses)* like; **velut** *(or* **velut sī)** just as if, just as though, as if, as though

vēmēns *see* **vehemēns**

vēn·a -ae *f* blood vessel *(whether vein or artery); (contrasted with* **artēria)** vein; artery *(believed to conduct air or food and drink to the body);* duct *(in the body);* penis; vein, streak *(in wood, stone, minerals);* vein *(of ore);* channel, trench; watercourse; store of talent *or* ability; natural disposition; strength; **vēna aquae** streamlet **||** *fpl (fig)* heart, core

vēnābul·um -ī *n* hunting spear

Venā·fer -fra -frum *or* **Venāfrān·us -a -um** *adj* of Venafrum

Venāfr·um -ī *n* Samnite town in S. central Italy

vēnālici·us -a -um *adj* for sale **||** *m* slave dealer **||** *npl* merchandise, imports and exports

vēnāl·is -is -e *adj* for sale; open to bribe **||** *mf* slave offered for sale

vēnātic·us -a -um *adj* hunting

vēnāti·ō -ōnis *f* hunt, hunting; wild-beast show; game

vēnāt·or -ōris *m* hunter

vēnātōri·us -a -um *adj* hunter's

vēnātr·īx -īcis *f* huntress

vēnātūr·a -ae *f* hunting

vēnāt·us -ūs *m* hunting; *(fig)* game, bag

vēndibil·is -is -e *adj* marketable; on sale; attractive, popular, acceptable

vēnditāti·ō -ōnis *f* advertising; showing off

vēnditāt·or -ōris *m* hawker, self-advertiser

vēnditi·ō -ōnis *f* sale

vēndit·ō -āre -āvī -ātus *tr* to try to sell; to sell *(regularly);* to advertise; to give as a bribe **||** *refl (w. dat)* to ingratiate oneself with

vēndit·or -ōris *m* vendor, seller; recipient of a bribe

vēnd·ō -ere -idī -itus *tr* to put up for sale; to sell, vend; to sell *(s.o.)* out, betray; to advertise; to praise, recommend

venēfic·a -ae *f* poisoner; sorceress, witch; *(term of abuse)* hag, witch

venēfic·ium -(i)ī *n* poisoning; poison; magical herb; magic, supernatural influence; dye; *(fig)* pernicious moral influence, malicious speech

venēfic·us -a -um *adj* poisoning, poisonous; magic **||** *m* poisoner; sorcerer, magician

venēnāt·us -a -um *adj* poisonous, venomous; filled with poison; magic; bewitched, enchanted; *(fig)* venomous, bitter

venēnif·er -era -erum *adj* poisonous, venomous

venēn·ō -āre -āvī -ātus *tr (lit & fig)* to poison

venēn·um -ī *n* poison; drug, potion; magic charm; sorcery; ruin; dye; virulence *(of speech)*

vēn·eō -īre -iī -itūrus *intr* to go up for sale, be sold

venerābil·is -is -e *adj* venerable, revered

venerābund·us -a -um *adj* reverend; reverential, worshiping

venerand·us -a -um *adj* venerable, august

venerāti·ō -ōnis *f* veneration, reverence, deep respect

venerāt·or -ōris *m* respecter, adorer; admirer

Venere·us *or* **Veneri·us -a -um** *adj* of Venus; of sexual love, erotic; **rēs Veneriae** sexual intercourse **||** *m* Venus throw *(best throw of the dice, when each of the four dice turns up a different number)* **||** *mpl* attendants in Venus' temple

vener·or -ārī -ātus sum *or* **vener·ō -āre** *tr* to venerate, revere, worship, pray to; to implore, beg; to pray for

Venet·ī -ōrum *mpl* a people in N.E. Italy in the region of modern Venice **||** a tribe in Gallia Lugdunensis

Veneti·a -ae *f* district of the Veneti in W. Gaul

Venetic·us -a -um *adj* of the Veneti *(of Gallia Lugdunensis)*

Venet·us -a -um *adj* Venetian; bluish **||** *m* Venetian; a Blue *(i.e., a member of one of the racing factions in Rome)*

veni·a -ae *f* kindness, favor, goodwill; permission; pardon, forgiveness; **veniam dare** *(w. dat)* **1** to grant forgiveness to; **2** to do a favor to; **3** to grant permission to; **veniam petere** to ask permission; **veniā vestrā** with your leave

Venīli·a -ae *f* Italian nymph *(wife of Faunus or of Janus)*

veniō venīre vēnī ventum *intr* to come; to be coming, be on the way; to appear in court; to come to dinner; *(of plants)* to come up; *(w.* **in** + *acc)* **1** to come into; **2** to enter into *(an agreement, friendship, etc.)*; **3** to fall into *(e.g., trouble, disgrace, etc.)*; **in buccam venīre** to be on the tip of the tongue; **in mentem venīre** to come to mind

vēn·or -ārī -ātus sum *tr & intr* to hunt

vent·er -ris *m* stomach, belly; womb; embryo, fetus, unborn child; belly, protuberance; appetite, gluttony

ventil·ō -āre -āvī -ātus *tr* to fan, wave; to display, show off

venti·ō -ōnis *f* coming

ventit·ō -āre -āvī -ātum *intr* to keep coming, come regularly

ventōs·us -a -um *adj* windy, full of wind; of the wind; wind-like, swift as the wind; conceited; fickle

ventricul·us -ī *m* belly; ventricle *(of the heart)*

ventriōs·us -a -um *adj* pot-bellied

ventul·us -ī *m* breeze

vent·us -ī *m* wind; intestinal wind; *(fig)* storm; **ventum ēmittere** to break wind

vēnūcul·a -ae *f* grape *(of the type well suited for preserving)*

vēn·um *(gen not in use; dat:* **vēnō)** *n* sale, that which is for sale; for sale; **vēnum** *(or* **vēnō) dare** to put up for sale, sell; to sell as a slave; **vēnum** *(or* **vēnō) darī** to be sold; **vēnum** *(or* **vēnō) īre** to go up for sale, be sold

vēnum·dō -dare -dedī -datus *tr* **(-und-)** to put up for sale, sell

ven·us -eris *f* beauty, charm; sexual intercourse, sex; mating; beloved, love ‖ **Venus** Venus *(goddess of love and beauty; planet)*; Venus-throw *(see* **Venereus)**

Venusi·a -ae *f* town in Apulia *(birthplace of Horace, modern Venosa)*

Venusīn·us -a -um *adj* of Venusia

venust·ās -ātis *f* beauty, charm, attraction

venustē *adv* prettily, charmingly

venustul·us -a -um *adj* cute, pretty

venust·us -a -um *adj* charming, attractive; interesting *(writing, writer)*

vēpallid·us -a -um *adj* very pale

veprēcul·a -ae *f* little brier bush

vepr·ēs -is *m (f)* brier, bramble bush

vēr vēris *n* spring, springtime; youth

vērātr·um -ī *n (bot)* hellebore *(used as a drug to treat insanity)*

vēr·āx -ācis *adj* truthful

verbēn·a -ae *f (bot)* verbena *(plant with clusters of flowers of various colors)* ‖ *fpl* sacred branches worn by heralds and priests

verb·er -eris *n* scourge, rod, whip; flogging, scourging; thong *(of a sling and similar weapon)* ‖ *npl* strokes, flogging

verberābilissum·us -a -um *adj* altogether deserving of a flogging

verberābund·us -a -um *adj* flogging all the way

verberāti·ō -ōnis *f* flogging

verberetill·us -a -um *adj* deserving of a flogging

verbere·us -a -um *adj* deserving of a flogging

verber·ō -āre -āvī -ātus *tr* to flog, scourge, whip; to batter, beat

verber·ō -ōnis *m* rascal *(deserving of flogging)*

verbivēlitāti·ō -ōnis *f* verbal skirmish

verbōsē *adv* verbosely

verbōs·us -a -um *adj* verbose

verb·um -ī *n* word; verb; saying, expression; proverb; mere talk, mere words; formula; **ad verbum** word for word, verbatim; literally, actually; **verba dare** *(w. dat)* to cheat *(s.o.)*, feed *(s.o.)* a line; **verba facere** to speak, make a speech; **verbī causā** *(or* **verbī grātiā)** for instance; **verbō** orally; in a word, briefly; nominally, in name only; in theory; **verbō dē verbō** *(or* **verbum prō verbō** *or* **verbum verbō)** word for word

Vercell·ae -ārum *fpl* town in N.W. Gaul *(modern Vercelli)*

Vercingetor·ix -igis *m* famous leader of the Arverni in the Gallic War

vērcul·um -ī *n (term of endearment)* sweet springtime

vērē *adv* really, truly

verēcundē *adv* bashfully, modestly

verēcundi·a -ae *f* bashfulness, shyness, modesty; respect, awe, reverence; sense of shame; feeling of disgrace, disgrace, shame

verēcund·or -ārī *intr* to be bashful, be shy, feel ashamed

verēcund·us -a -um *adj* bashful, shy, modest, reserved

verēd·us -ī *m* fast hunting horse

verend·us -a -um *adj* inspiring respect, venerable; awesome ‖ *npl* sexual organs

ver·eor -ērī -itus sum *tr* to revere, have respect for; to fear ‖ *intr* to feel uneasy, be anxious, be afraid; *(w. gen)* to stand in awe of, be afraid of; *(w. dat)* to be afraid for; *(w.* **dē** + *abl)* to be apprehensive about; *(w.* **ut)** to be afraid that not; *(w.* **nē)** to be afraid that

verētr·um -ī *n* male sexual organ

Vergili·ae -ārum *fpl (astr)* Pleiades *(constellation)*

Vergil·ius *or* **Virgil·ius -(i)ī** *m* Roman clan name *(nomen)*, *esp.* Vergil *(Publius*

Vergilius Maro, epic poet of the Augustan Age, 70–19 B.C.)

Vergīni·us -a -um *adj* Roman clan name *(nomen), esp.* Lucius Verginius *(said to have killed his daughter to save her from the lust of Appius Claudius and thus to have brought about the overthrow of the decemvirs in 449 B.C.)* **II** *f* his daughter

verg·ō -ere *tr* to cause to move in a downward direction, incline; to tilt down **II** *intr* to turn, incline; to slope back *or* away; to decline; to lie, be situated; *(w.* **ad)** **1** to verge toward; to extend to; **2** to face (toward); **3** to incline toward, tend toward *(usu. a worse condition); (w.* **in** + *acc)* to sink into, lapse into *(lethargy, old age)*

vēridic·us -a -um *adj* truthful, speaking the truth; truly spoken

vēriloqu·ium -(i)ī *n* argument based on the true meaning of a word

vērīsimil·is -is -e *adj* probable, likely; realistic

vērīsimilitūd·ō -inis *f* probability, likelihood

vērit·ās -ātis *f* truth, truthfulness; real life, reality; honesty, integrity; correctness *(in eytmology and grammar);* **ex vēritāte** in accordance with the truth

vēriverb·ium -(i)ī *n* truthfulness

vermiculāt·us -a -um *adj* inlaid with wavy lines, vermiculated

vermicul·us -ī *m* grubworm, maggot; **in vermiculō** in the larval state

vermin·a -um *npl* stomach cramps

verm·is -is *m* worm

vern·a -ae *mf* home-born slave *(born in the master's house);* native

vernācul·us -a -um *adj* of home-born slaves; home-grown, native, domestic; of the neighborhood; indigenous; proletarian; *(of troops)* levied locally; *(w. gen)* native to *(a place)* **II** *mf* home-born slave

vernīl·is -is -e *adj* servile; obsequious

vernīlit·ās -ātis *f* slavishness; rude behavior, impudence

vernīliter *adv* slavishly

vērn·ō -āre *intr* to show signs of spring; to burgeon, break into bloom; to be young

vernul·a -ae *mf* young slave *(born in the master's house);* native

vērn·us -a -um *adj* spring, of spring; **tempus vērnum** springtime

vērō *adv* in truth, in fact; certainly, to be sure; even; however

Vērōn·a -ae *f* city in N. Italy, birthplace of Catullus and Pliny the Elder

Vērōnēns·is -is -e *adj* Veronese **II** *mpl* the people of Verona

verp·a -ae *f* penis *(as protruded from the foreskin)*

verp·us -a -um *adj* circumsized; having the foreskin drawn back

verr·ēs -is *m* pig, boar **II Verrēs** Gaius Cornelius Verres *(notorious governor of Sicily in 73–70 B.C.)*

verrīn·us -a -um *adj* of a boar, of a pig, pork-

ver·rō -rere -rī -sus *tr* **(vor-)** to pull, drag, drag away, carry off; to sweep, scour, brush; *(of the wind)* to whip across, sweep *(the land)*

verrūc·a -ae *f* wart *(on the body);* small failing, minor blemish

verrūcōs·us -a -um *adj* full of warts; *(fig)* full of blemishes

verrunc·ō -āre *intr* to turn out well

versābil·is -is -e *adj* shifting, movable

versābund·us -a -um *adj* revolving

versātil·is -is -e *adj* capable of turning, revolving, movable; versatile

versicapill·us -a -um *adj* having hair that has turned grey, greying

versicol·or -ōris *adj* changing colors, of various colors

versicul·us -ī *m* short line, single line *(of verse or prose),* versicle **II** *mpl* poor little verses

versificāti·ō -ōnis *f* versification

versificāt·or -ōris *m* versifier

versific·ō -āre *tr* to put into verse **II** *intr* to write verse

versipell·is -is -e *adj* **(vors-)** changing appearance at will; sly **II** *m* werewolf

vers·ō -āre -āvī -ātus *tr* **(vor-)** to keep turning, spin, whirl; to twist, bend, wind *(material in order to change its shape);* to turn *(the eyes)* this way and that *(in uncertainty);* to keep shifting *(the limbs in restlessness);* to keep turning, maneuver *(a vehicle, a horse);* to swing *(a weapon)* in all directions; to stir *(the contents of a vessel, esp. the lots in an urn);* to keep turning over *(the ground, as in plowing); (fig)* to influence, sway *(a person in one direction or another); (fig)* to turn over in the mind, ponder, consider; *(pej)* to manipulate *(a person); (w.* **in** + *acc)* to focus *(the mind)* on; *(rhet)* to vary the expression *(of an idea)* **II** *refl* to keep going around, keep on revolving; to spin around *(so as to face in the opposite direction)*

vers·or -ārī -ātus sum *intr* **(vor-)** to come and go frequently; to live, stay; to be, be in operation, obtain; *(w. adverbs)* to behave *(in a certain way);* to revolve; to spin around *(so as to face in the opposite direction);* to toss, writhe; *(w.* **in** + *abl)* **1** to be involved in, be engaged in, be busy with; **2** to stay in, live in, pass one's time in *(a place, among persons, or in sur-*

roundings); **3** *(of things)* to be concerned with, have to do with; **4** to be subject to; **5** *(of an idea, mental image)* to be constantly present in *(the mind);* **6** *(of a speaker)* to dwell on; **in ōre vulgī versārī** to be constantly on people's lips
versōri·a -ae *f (naut)* rope used to set sail at an angle in order to tack
versum *adv* **(vor-)** *(usu. after another adv of direction)* back; **rūsum versum** backward; **sūrsum versum** up and down
versūr·a -ae *f* **(vor-)** rotation; loan *(of money to pay another debt);* **versūram facere** *(w.* **ab)** to get a loan from *(s.o. to pay another);* **versūrā solvere** to pay off *(another debt)* with borrowed money
versus *or* **versum** *adv* **(vor-)** *(w.* **ad)** toward, in the direction of; *(w.* **in** + *acc)* into, in toward; **sī in urbem versus ventūrī erunt** if they intend to come into the city; **sūrsum versus** upwards
versus *pp of* **verrō** *and* **vertō**
vers·us -ūs *m* **(vor-)** turning; furrow; line, row; turn, step *(in a dance); (in prose and poetry)* line, verse
versūtē *adv* **(vor-)** cunningly
versūti·ae -ārum *fpl* cunning, tricks
versūtiloqu·us -a -um *adj* smooth-talking, sly
versūt·us -a -um *adj* **(vors-)** clever, shrewd, ingenious; sly, cunning, deceitful
vert·ex -icis *m* **(vor-)** whirlpool, eddy, strong current; whirlwind, tornado; crown *or* top of the head; head; top, summit *(of mountain);* pole *(of the heavens);* **ex vertice** from above
verticōs·us -a -um *adj* swirling, full of whirlpools
vertīg·ō -inis *f* turning, whirling; dizziness
vert·ō -ere -ī versus *tr* **(vor-)** to turn, turn around, spin; to reverse; to invert, tilt; to change, alter, transform; to turn over, plow; to overturn, knock down; to destroy; to subvert, ruin; to ascribe, impute; to translate; *(w.* **ab)** to deflect from **||** *refl* to turn; *(w.* **in** + *acc)* to change into **||** *pass* to turn; *(w.* **in** + *acc)* to turn into; *(w.* **in** + *abl)* **1** to be in *(a place or condition);* **2** to be engaged in, be involved in **||** *intr* to turn; to change; to turn out; *(w.* **in** + *abl)* to center on, depend upon
vertrag·us -ī *m* Gallic greyhound
Vertumn·us -ī *m* **(Vor-)** god of the changing seasons
ver·ū -ūs *n* spit *(for roasting);* javelin, dart
veruīn·a -ae *f* spit; small javelin
vērum *adv* truly; yes; *(in responses)* true but, yes but; but in fact; but yet, but even; yet, still; **nōn sōlum** *(or* **modo** *or* **tantum)** ... **vērum** *(usu. followed by* **et, etiam** *or* **quoque)** not only ... but also
vērumtamen *adv* nevertheless
vēr·us -a -um *adj* true, actual, genuine, real; fair, reasonable **||** *n* truth, reality; honor, duty, right; **vērī similis** probable, likely; realistic; **vērī similitūdō** probability, likelihood
verūt·um -ī *n* dart, javelin
verūt·us -a -um *adj* armed with a javelin *or* dart
verv·ēx -ēcis *m* wether, castrated hog; *(term of abuse)* muttonhead
vēsāni·a -ae *f* **(vae-)** insanity, madness
vēsāni·ēns -entis *adj* raging
vēsān·us -a -um *adj* **(vae-)** insane; furious, savage, raging
vēsc·or -ī *intr (w. abl)* to feed on, eat; to feast on, enjoy
vēsc·us -a -um *adj* nibbled off; little, feeble; corroding, consuming
Veser·is -is *m* stream in Campania where Publius Decius Mus and Titus Manius Torquatus defeated the Latins in 340 B.C.
vēsīc·a -ae *f* bladder; bombast; objects made of bladder: purse, cap, football, lantern
vēsīcul·a -ae *f* little bladder; little bag
vesp·a -ae *f* wasp
Vespāsiān·us -ī *m* Vespasian *(Titus Flavius Vespasianus Sabinus, Roman Emperor, A.D. 70–79)*
Vespāsi·us -a -um *adj* Roman clan name *(nomen), esp.* Vespasia Polla *(mother of Emperor Vespasian)*
vesp·er -erī *or* **-eris** *(acc usu.* **vesperum)** *m* evening; supper; the West; **ad vesperum** toward evening; **prīmō vespere** early in the evening; **sub vespere** toward evening; **tam vesperī** so late in the evening; **vespere** *or* **vesperī** in the evening
vesper·a -ae *f* evening; **prīma vespera** twilight; **prīmā vesperā** at twilight, at dusk
vesper·āscō -āscere -āvī *intr* to grow toward evening; **vesperāscente diē** as the day was getting late **||** *v impers* evening is coming
vespertili·ō -ōnis *m* bat
vespertīn·us -a -um *adj* evening, in the evening; western
vesperūg·ō -inis *f* evening star
vespill·ō -ōnis *m* mortician
Vest·a -ae *f* Roman goddess of the hearth
Vestāl·is -is -e *adj* Vestal, of Vesta; **virgō Vestālis** Vestal virgin
ves·ter -tra -trum *adj* **(vos-)** your *(pl);* **||** *pron* yours; **vestrī** your friends, your relatives, your soldiers, your school, your party; **vestrum est** *(w. inf)* it is up to you to; **voster** your master

vēstibul·um -ī *n* entrance, forecourt; beginning
vestīg·ium -(i)ī *n* footstep, step; footprint, track; trace, vestige; moment, instant
vestīg·ō -āre *tr* to track, trace; to check, find out
vestīment·um -ī *n* clothing; garment; blanket
Vestīn·us -a -um *adj* of the Vestini **‖** *mpl* the Vestini *(Oscan-speaking tribe of the central Apennines)*
vest·iō -īre -īvī *or* **-iī -ītus** *tr* to dress, clothe; to adorn, array, attire; *(fig)* to dress, clothe
vestiplic·a -ae *f* laundress, folder *(employed in ironing and folding clothes)*
vest·is -is *f* garment, dress; clothing; coverlet; tapestry; blanket; slough, skin *(of a snake)*; **vestem mūtāre** to change one's clothes; to put on mourning clothes; **vestis longa** full dress including the full-length stola
vestispic·a -ae *f* female servant in charge of clothes
vestīt·us -ūs *m* clothing, clothes, dress, apparel; ornament *(of speech)*; **mūtāre vestītum** to put on mourning clothes; **redīre ad suum vestītum** to end the mourning period
Vesuvi·us -a -um *adj* of Mt. Vesuvius; **mōns Vesuvius** Mt. Vesuvius
veter·a -um *npl* tradition, antiquity
veterāmentāri·us -a -um *adj* dealing in second-hand clothes
veterān·us -a -um *adj & m* veteran
veter·āscō -āscere -āvī *intr* to grow old
veterāt·or -ōris *m* old hand, expert; sly old fox
veterātōriē *adv* cunningly, slyly
veterātōri·us -a -um *adj* cunning
veter·ēs -um *mpl* the ancients; ancient authors
veterīn·us -a -um *adj* of burden **‖** *fpl & npl* beasts of burden
veternōs·us -a -um *adj* lethargic; sleepy, drowsy
vetern·us -ī *m* lethargy; old age; drowsiness; listlessness *(of old age)*
vetit·um -ī *n* prohibition
vetitus *pp of* **vetō**
vet·ō -āre -uī -itus *tr* **(vot-)** to forbid, prohibit, oppose; to veto; *(w. inf, w.* **nē, quōminus)** to prevent from; *(w. inf, w. acc & inf, w.* **nē,** *w.* **quīn)** to forbid *(s.o. to do s.th.)*
vetul·us -a -um *adj* poor old
vet·us -eris *adj* old, aged; long-standing **‖** *mpl see* **veterēs ‖** *npl see* **vetera**
vetust·ās -ātis *f* age; ancient times, antiquity; long duration, great age
vetust·us -a -um *adj* old, ancient; old-time, old-fashioned, good old *(days, etc.)*; antiquated
vexām·en -inis *n* shaking, quaking
vexāti·ō -ōnis *f* shaking, jolting, tossing; distress
vexāt·or -ōris *m* jostler; harasser; troublemaker
vexī *perf of* **vehō**
vexillār·ius -(i)ī *m* standard-bearer **‖** *mpl* special reserves
vexillāti·ō -ōnis *f (mil)* detachment
vexill·um -ī *n* standard, flag, banner *(esp. the red flag hoisted above the general's tent as the signal for battle)*; replica of the military banner, awarded for distinguished service; detachment of troops; **vexillum praepōnere** to hoist the red flag *(as the signal for battle)*
vex·ō -āre *tr* to shake, toss; to vex, annoy; to harass *(troops)*
vi·a -ae *f* way, road, street, highway; march, journey; method; right way, right method; path *(of an arrow)*; **inter viās** on the road; **in viā** *(frontage)* on the road; **sēsē in viam dare** to hit the road, get on one's way; **trīduī via** a three-days' march; **viam mūnīre** to build a road; *(fig)* to pave the way; isle *(in the theater)*; **viā rēctā** by a direct route; **via vītae** pathway of life
viāl·is -is -e *adj* of the highway
viāri·us -a -um *adj* for highway maintenance
viāticāt·us -a -um *adj* provided with traveling money
viātic·us -a -um *adj* for the trip, for traveling, travel **‖** *n* travel allowance, provisions for the journey; *(mil)* soldier's saving fund
viāt·or -ōris *m* traveler; passenger; attendant *(of a magistrate)*; *(leg)* bailiff
vīb·īx -īcis *f* welt *(from a blow)*
vibr·ō -āre *tr* to brandish, wave around; to hurl **‖** *intr* to vibrate, quiver; *(of the tongue)* to flick
vīburn·um -ī *n (bot)* viburnum *(ornamental shrub, the bark of which was used in medicine)*
Vic·a Pot·a *(gen:* **Vic·ae Pot·ae)** *f* a goddess of victory
vīcān·us -a -um *adj* village **‖** *mpl* villagers
vicāri·us -a -um *adj* substitute **‖** *m* substitute, deputy, proxy; under-slave *(kept by another slave)*
vīcātim *adv* from street to street; from village to village; in hamlets
vice *prep (w. gen)* on account of; like, after the manner of
vicem *adv* in turn **‖** *prep (w. gen)* instead of, in place of; on account of; like, after the manner of

vīcēnāri·us -a -um *adj* of the number twenty
vīcēn·ī -ae -a *adj* twenty each, twenty apiece, twenty at a time, twenty in a group
vīcēsimān·ī -ōrum *mpl* soldiers of the twentieth legion
vīcēsimāri·us -a -um *adj* derived from the 5% tax
vīcēsim·us -a -um *adj* **(vīcēns-)** twentieth ‖ *f* 5% tax
vīcess·is -is *m* copper coin, worth about twenty cents
vici·a -ae *f* vetch *(grown for its edible seeds and used as fodder for animals)*
vīciē(n)s *adv* twenty times
vīcināl·is -is -e *adj* neighboring, nearby
vīcīni·a -ae *f* neighborhood; nearness, proximity
vīcīnit·ās -ātis *f* neighborhood, proximity; the neighborhood *(i. e., the neighbors)*
vīcīn·us -a -um *adj* neighboring, nearby, near; imminent ‖ *mf* neighbor ‖ *n* neighborhood; **ex vīcīnō** of a similar nature; **in vīcīnō** in close proximity
vicis *(gen; the nom singl and gen pl do not occur; acc singl:* **vicem;** *abl singl:* **vice)** *f* change, interchange, alternation; succession; exchange; interaction; return, recompense, retaliation; fortune, misfortune, condition; fate; plight, lot; changes of fate; duty, office, position; function, capacity, office; **ad vicem** *(w. gen)* after the manner of; **in vicem** *(or* **in vicēs** *or* **per vicēs)** in turn, alternately; **in vicem** *(or* **invicem)** *(w. gen)* instead of, in place of; **legendī vicem suscipere** to take one's turn in reading; **vice** in return; **vice** *(w. gen) or* **vicem** *(w. gen)* in place of, as a substitute for; **vice versā** *(or* **vicibus versīs)** vice-versa, conversely; **vicibus** in return
vicissim *or* **vicissātim** *adv* in turn, again
vicissitūd·ō -inis *f* change, interchange; regular succession, alternation; reversal, vicissitude; reciprocation
victim·a -ae *f* **(-tum-)** victim; sacrifice
victimār·ius -(i)ī *m* **(-tum-)** assistant at sacrifices
victit·ō -āre -āvī -ātum *intr* to live, subsist; *(w. abl)* to live on, subsist on
vict·or -ōris *m* victor; *(in apposition)* **victor exercitus** victorious army
victōri·a -ae *f* victory; **victōriam ferre** *or* **parere** *or* **reportāre dē** *or* **ex** to win a victory over
victōriāt·us -ī *m* victory coin *(of silver, stamped with the image of victory)*
Victōriol·a -ae *f* figurine of Victory
victr·īx -īcis *adj (fem & neut only)* victorious, triumphant
victus *pp of* **vincō**
vict·us -ūs *or* **-ī** *m* living, means of livelihood; way of life; food, sustenance
vīcul·us -ī *m* hamlet
vīc·us -ī *m* village, hamlet; ward, quarter *(in a city);* street, block
vidēlicet *adv* clearly, evidently; *(in irony)* of course, naturally; *(in explanations)* namely
vidēn = vidēsne? do you see?, do you get it?
videō vidēre vīdī vīsus *tr* to see, look at; to know; to consider; to understand, realize; *(w.* **ut)** to see to it that, take care that ‖ *pass* to seem, appear ‖ *v impers pass* it seems right, it seems good; **dīs vīsum est** the gods decided *(literally, it seemed (right) to the gods)*
vidu·a -ae *f* widow; spinster
viduit·ās -ātis *f* bereavement; want, lack; widowhood
vīdul·us -ī *m* leather travel bag, suitcase, knapsack
vidu·ō -āre -āvī -ātus *tr* to deprive, bereave; *(w. gen or abl)* to deprive of; **viduāta** left a widow
vidu·us -a -um *adj* bereft, destitute; unmarried; *(w. abl or* **ab)** bereft of, destitute of, without ‖ *f see* **vidua**
Vienn·a -ae *f* chief city of the Allobroges in Gallia Narbonensis *(modern Vienne)*
viēt·or -ōris *m* cooper
viēt·us -a -um *adj* shriveled
vig·eō -ēre -uī *intr* to thrive, be vigorous, flourish
vig·ēscō -ēscere -uī *intr* to become vigorous, gain strength, become lively
vīgēsim·us -a -um *adj* twentieth
vig·il -ilis *adj* awake, wakeful; alert, on one's toes ‖ *m* watchman, guard, sentinel; fireman, policeman
vigil·āns -antis *adj* watchful, alert; disquieting *(worries)*
vigilanter *adv* vigilantly, alertly
vigilanti·a -ae *f* wakefulness; vigilance, alertness
vigil·āx -ācis *adj* alert; disquieting, sleep-disturbing *(worries)*
vigili·a -ae *f* wakefulness, sleeplessness, insomnia; vigil; vigilance, alertness; watch *(one of the four divisions of the night for keeping watch); (mil)* standing guard; *(mil)* guards, sentinels; **vigiliās agere** *(or* **agitāre** *or* **servāre)** to keep watch
vigil·ō -āre -āvī -ātus *tr* to spend *(the night)* awake; to make, do, perform, write *(s.th.)* while awake at night ‖ *intr* to stay awake; to be watchful; to be alert; *(w. dat)* to be attentive to
vīgintī *indecl adj* twenty

vīgintī·vir -virī *m* member of a board of twenty *(appointed by Caesar in 59 B.C. to distribute parcels of land in Campania)* **‖** member of a board of twenty in municipal administration

vīgintīvirāt·us -ūs *m* membership on the board of twenty

vig·or -ōris *m* vigor, liveliness

vīlic·a -ae *f* **(vill-)** foreman's wife, manager's wife

vīlic·ō -āre -āvī -ātum *intr* **(vill-)** to be a foreman, be a manager *(of an estate);* to be an overseer *(in the state)*

vīlic·us -ī *m* **(vill-)** foreman, manager *(of an estate)*

vīl·is -is -e *adj* cheap, inexpensive; common, worthless, contemptible; **vīlī** at a cheap price, cheaply

vīlit·ās -ātis *f* lowness of price, cheapness, low price; worthlessness

vīliter *adv* cheaply, at a low price

vīll·a -ae *f* country home; farmhouse; **vīlla rūstica** farmhouse, homestead; **vīlla urbāna** *(also in the country, with no farm attached)* country villa

vīllic- = vīlic-

villōs·us -a -um *adj* hairy, shaggy, bushy

vīllul·a -ae *f* small farmhouse; small villa

vīll·um -ī *n* drop of wine

vill·us -ī *m* hair; fleece; nap *(of cloth)*

vīm·en -inis *n* osier; basket

vīment·um -ī *n* osier

Vīmināl·is -is -e *adj* Viminal; **Vīminālis Collis** Viminal Hill *(one of the seven hills of Rome)*

vīmine·us -a -um *adj* made of osiers

vīn *or* **vīn' = vīsne?** do you wish?, ya' wanna? *(fam)*

vīnāce·us -a -um *adj* grape, of grape **‖** *n* grape seed

Vīnāl·ia -ium *npl* wine festival; **Vīnālia priōra** earlier wine festival *(celebrated on April 23, when libations of wine from the previous year were poured to Jupiter);* **Vīnālia rūstica** country wine festival *(celebrated on August 19 and 20 in honor of Jupiter in thanksgiving for the successful harvest)*

vīnāri·us -a -um *adj* wine **‖** *m* wine dealer; vintner **‖** *npl* wine flasks

vincibil·is -is -e *adj* easily won

vinciō vincīre vīnxī vīnctus *tr* to bind, tie; to wrap; to encircle, surround; to restrain; *(med)* to bandage; *(med)* to ligature; *(rhet)* to link together, arrange rhythmically

vincō vincere vīcī victus *tr* to conquer; to get the better of, beat, defeat; to outdo; to convince, refute, persuade; to prove, demonstrate; to outlast, outlive **‖** *intr* to win, be victorious; to prevail; to succeed

vīnct·us -a -um *pp of* **vinciō ‖** *adj* fettered, in bonds

vincul·um *or* **vincl·um -ī** *n* chain; fetter, cord, band; sandal strap; thong, rope; mooring cable; tether **‖** *npl* bonds, fetters; imprisonment; prison; **vincula pūblica** chains worn by a state prisoner; **aliquem in vincula conicere** to put s.o. in chains

Vindelic·us -a -um *adj* of the Vindelici **‖** *mpl* people living between the Rhaetian Alps and the Danube

vīndēmi·a -ae *f* vintage

vīndēmiāt·or -ōris *m* grape picker

vīndēmiol·a -ae *f* small vintage; minor sources of income

Vindēmit·or -ōris *m (astr)* a star in Virgo

vind·ex -icis *adj* avenging **‖** *m (leg)* claimant; defender, protector, champion; liberator; avenger, punisher

Vind·ex -icis *m* Roman family name *(cognomen), esp.* Gaius Julius Vindex *(leader of a rebellion in Gaul against Nero in A.D. 69)*

vindicāti·ō -ōnis *f* avenging, punishment; *(leg)* claim

vindici·ae -ārum *fpl* legal claim; things *or* persons claimed; championship, protection; **vindiciās dare** *(or* **dīcere** *or* **dēcernere)** to hand over the things *or* persons claimed

vindic·ō -āre -āvī -ātus *tr* to lay legal claim to; to protect, defend; to appropriate; to demand; to demand unfairly; to claim as one's own; to avenge, punish; **in lībertātem vindicāre** to set free, liberate *(literally, to claim for freedom)*

vindict·a -ae *f* rod used in the ceremony of setting slaves free; defense, protection; vengeance, revenge, satisfaction

vīne·a *or* **vīni·a -ae** *f* vineyard; vine; *(mil)* shed *(used to defend besiegers against enemy missiles)*

vīnēt·um -ī *n* vineyard

vīnipoll·ēns -entis *adj* powerful through wine

vīnit·or -ōris *m* vine dresser

vinnul·us -a -um *adj* charming

vīnolenti·a -ae *f* **(vīnul-)** wine drinking, intoxication

vīnolent·us -a -um *adj* **(vīnul-)** drunk

vīnōs·us -a -um *adj* addicted to wine; tasting *or* smelling of wine

vīn·um -ī *n* wine

viol·a -ae *f* violet *(flower; color; dye)*

violābil·is -is -e *adj* vulnerable

violār·ium -(i)ī *n* bed of violets

violār·ius -(i)ī *m* dyer of violet

violāti·ō -ōnis *f* violation, profanation

violāt·or -ōris *m* violator, profaner

viol·ēns -entis *adj* violent, raging

violenter *adv* violently, vehemently

violenti·a -ae *f* violence
violent·us -a -um *adj* violent
viol·ō -āre -āvī -ātus *tr* to violate; to outrage, harm by violence
vīper·a -ae *f* viper; *(poisonous)* snake
vīpere·us -a -um *adj* viper's; snake's
vīperīn·us -a -um *adj* viper's, snake's
Vipsāni·us -a -um *adj* Roman clan name *(nomen);* **porticus Vipsānia** Vipsanian portico *(forming part of the Pantheon built by Agrippa in the Campus Martius)* **II** Agrippa *(Marcus Vipsanius Agrippa, Augustus' friend and successful admiral)* **II** *f* Vipsania *(esp. Vipsania Agrippina, daughter of Agrippa and the first wife of Emperor Tiberius)*
vir virī *m* man; he-man, hero; husband; lover; manhood, virility; *(mil)* infantryman
virāg·ō -inis *f* female warrior; heroine
Virb·ius -(i)ī *m* local deity, the reincarnation of Hippolytus, worshipped with Diana at Aricia **II** son of Hippolytus
virēct·um -ī stretch of green
vir·eō -ēre -uī *intr* to be green; to be fresh, be vigorous, flourish
vīrēs = *pl of* **vīs**
vir·ēscō -ēscere -uī *intr* to turn green
virg·a -ae *f* twig, sprout; graft; rod, switch *(for flogging);* wand; walking stick, cane; colored stripe in a garment; branch of a family tree
virgāt·or -ōris *m* flogger
virgāt·us -a -um *adj* made of twigs *or* osiers; striped
virgēt·um -ī *n* osier thicket
virge·us -a -um *adj* of twigs, of kindling wood
virgi(n)dēmi·a -ae *f (hum)* harvest of birch rods *(i.e., a sound flogging)*
virgināl·is -is -e *adj* maiden's, girl's, girlish **II** *n* female genitals
virgināri·us -a -um *adj* girl's
virgine·us *or* **virgini·us -a -um** *adj* virgin, of *or* for a virgin; proper to a virgin; of virgins
virginit·ās -ātis *f* girlhood; virginity
virg·ō -inis *f (marriageable)* girl, maiden; virgin **II Virgō** Virgo *(constellation; aqueduct constructed by Marcus Vipsanius Agrippa)*
virgul·a -ae *f* little twig; wand; **virgula dīvīna** divining rod
virgult·um -ī *n* thicket; shrub **II** *npl* brushwood; firewood; slips *(of trees)*
virgult·us -a -um *adj* covered with brushwood
virguncul·a -ae *f* lass, young girl
Vir(i)domar·us -ī *m* Insubrian leader killed in battle by Marcus Claudius Marcellus, 222 B.C., who thereby won the *spolia opima*
Viriāt(h)·us -ī *m* Lusitanian who led a guerrilla war against Rome *(147–140 B.C.)*
virid·āns -antis *adj* turning green; green
viridār·ium -(i)ī *n* garden
virid·is -is -e *adj* green; fresh, young **II** *npl* greenery
viridit·ās -ātis *f* greenness; freshness
virid·ō -āre *tr* to make green **II** *intr* to turn green
virīl·is -is -e *adj* male, masculine; adult; manly; *(gram)* masculine; **pars virīlis** male sexual organ; **prō virīlī parte** *(or* **portiōne)** to the best of one's ability **II** *npl* manly *or* heroic deeds; male sexual organs
virīlit·ās -ātis *f* manhood, virility
virīliter *adv* manfully, like a man
virīpot·ēns -entis *adj* almighty
virītim *adv* man by man; per man; individually
vīrōs·us -a -um *adj* slimy; strong-smelling, fetid, stinking
virt·ūs -ūtis *f* manliness, manhood, virility; strength; valor, gallantry; excellence, worth; special property; moral excellence, goodness, virtue; good quality, high quality *(of persons, animals, things);* potency, effectiveness *(of drugs, medications);* **virtūte** *(w. gen)* through the good services of, thanks to **II** *fpl* achievements; gallant deeds
vīr·us -ī *n* venom; slime; stench, pungency; saltiness
vīs *(gen not in use; dat & abl:* **vī;** *acc:* **vim;** *pl:* **vīr·ēs -ium)** *f* power, strength, force; influence; energy; hostile force, violence, attack; amount, quantity; meaning, force *(of words);* binding force *(of a law);* value, amount; **magna vīs** *(w. gen)* a large number of, a large amount of; **omnis vīs** *(w. gen)* the whole range of, the sum total of; **per vim** forcibly; **suā vī** in itself, intrinsically; **summā vī** with utmost energy; **vī** by force; **vim adferre** *(w. dat)* **1** to do violence to; **2** to rape; **3** to kill; **vim adferre sibī** *(or* **vītae suae)** to take one's own life; **vim facere** to make an assault; **vim habēre** *(w. gen)* to be equivalent *(in amount)* to **II vīrēs** *fpl* strength; resources; potency, power *(of herbs, drugs); (mil)* military strength, fighting power; control, influence; financial resources, assets; powers of intellect, capability; meaning *(of words);* value, amount; **prō vīribus** with all one's might
viscāt·us -a -um *adj* smeared with birdlime
viscer·a -um *npl* fleshy parts of the body *(as distinct from skin and bones);* viscera,

internal organs; womb; heart, vitals, bowels; *(fig)* innermost part, bowels, heart; center *(esp. of the earth); (fig)* bosom friend, favorite; *(fig)* person's flesh and blood *(family, offspring)*

viscerāti·ō -ōnis *f* public distribution of meat

visc·ō -āre -āvī -ātus *tr* to catch in birdlime

visc·um -ī *n or* **visc·us -ī** *m* mistletoe; birdlime

visc·us -eris *n (anat)* organ; entrails ‖ *npl see* **viscera**

vīsend·us -a -um *adj* worth going to see, worth visiting ‖ *npl* the sights

vīsī *perf of* **vīsō**

vīsi·ō -ōnis *f* appearance, apparition; notion, idea

vīsit·ō -āre -āvī -ātus *tr* to keep seeing; to visit, go to visit

vīs·ō -ere -ī *tr* to look at with attention, view; to come *or* go to look at; to find out; to go and see, visit; to look in on *(the sick)* ‖ *intr* to go and look; *(w.* **ad**) to go to visit, call on *(esp. an invalid)*

vispillō *see* **vespillō**

viss·iō -īre *intr (sl)* to fart softly

vīs·um -ī *n* sight, appearance

Visurg·is -is *m* river in N. Germany *(modern Weser)*

vīsus *pp of* **videō**

vīs·us -ūs *m* (faculty of) sight; thing seen, sight, vision

vīt·a -ae *f* life; way of life; means of living, livelihood; manner of life; course of life, career; biography

vītābil·is -is -e *adj* undesirable, deserving to be shunned

vītābund·us -a -um *adj* taking evasive action

vītāl·is -is -e *adj* of life, vital; life-giving; likely to live, staying alive; able to survive; living, alive ‖ *npl (anat)* vital parts

vītāliter *adv* vitally

vītāti·ō -ōnis *f* avoidance

Vitell·ius -(i)ī *m* Vitellius *(Aulus Vitellius, Roman Emperor, from January 2 to December 22, A.D. 69)*

vitell·us -ī *m* little calf; yolk *(of egg)*

vīte·us -a -um *adj* of the vine

vīticul·a -ae *f* little vine

vītif·er -era -erum *adj* producing vines, vine-producing

vītigen·us -a -um *adj* produced from the vine

viti·ō -āre -āvī -ātus *tr* to spoil, corrupt, violate, mar; to falsify

vitiōsē *adv* faultily, badly, corruptly; **vitiōsē sē habēre** to be defective

vitiōsit·ās -ātis *f* corrupt *or* bad condition

vitiōs·us -a -um *adj* faulty, defective; (morally) corrupt, bad, depraved

vīt·is -is *f* vine; vine branch; centurion's staff; centurionship

vītisāt·or -ōris *m* vine planter

vit·ium -(i)ī *n* fault, flaw; defect, disorder; sin, offense, vice; flaw in the auspices; injurious quality, disadvantage; augural impediment, unfavorable augury; *(leg)* legal defect, technicality; *(med)* lesion; **in vitiō esse** to be in a defective state, be defective; **meō vitiō pereō** I am ruined through my own fault; **vitiō** *(w. gen)* through the fault of; **vitiō dare** *(or* **vertere**) to regard as a fault; **vitium capere** *(or* **facere**) to develop a defect; **vitium dīcere** *(w. dat)* to insult s.o.

vīt·ō -āre -āvī -ātus *tr* to avoid, evade

vīt·or -ōris *m* basket-maker

vitre·us -a -um *adj* glass, of glass; glassy ‖ *npl* glassware

vītric·us -ī *m* stepfather

vitr·um -ī *n* glass; blue dye

vitt·a -ae *f* headband, fillet

vittāt·us -a -um *adj* wearing a fillet

vitul·a -ae *f* heifer

vitulīn·us -a -um *adj & f* veal

vītul·or -ārī *intr* to celebrate a festival; to be thankful and joyful; to shout for joy

vitul·us -ī *m* calf, young bull; foal; seal

vituperābil·is -is -e *adj* blameworthy

vituperāti·ō -ōnis *f* blaming, censuring; blame; scandalous conduct, blameworthiness

vituperāt·or -ōris *m* censurer

vituper·ō -āre -āvī -ātus *tr* to criticize, find fault with; to declare *(an omen)* invalid

vīvācit·ās -ātis *f* will to live; life-force; vitality

vīvār·ium -(i)ī *n* game preserve, zoo; fish pond

vīvāt·us -a -um *adj* animated, lively

vīv·āx -ācis *adj* long-lived; long-lasting, enduring; quick to learn

vīvē *adv* in a lively manner

vīverād·īx -īcis *f* rooted cutting *(i.e., having roots)*

vīvēscō *or* **vīvīscō vīvēscere** *intr* to become alive, come to life; to grow lively, get full of life

vīvid·us -a -um *adj* teeming with life, full of life; true to life, vivid, realistic; quick, lively *(mind);* vivid *(expression)*

vīvirād·īx -īcis *f see* **vīverādīx**

vīvīscō *see* **vīvēscō**

vīvō vīvere vixī victum *intr* to be alive, live; to be still alive, survive; to reside; *(w. abl or* **dē** *+ abl)* to live on, subsist on

vīv·us -a -um *adj* alive, living; lively; fresh; natural *(rock);* speaking *(voice);* **argentum vīvum** quicksilver; **calx vīva** lime; **mē vīvō** as long as I am alive ‖ *n* *(com)* capital; **ad vīvum resecāre** to cut to the quick

vix *adv* scarcely; hardly, with difficulty, barely

vixdum *adv* hardly then, scarcely yet

vocābul·um -ī *n* word, term; name, designation; noun; common noun

vōcāl·is -is -e *adj* having a voice, gifted with speech, speaking; gifted with song, singing; tuneful ‖ *f (gram)* vowel

vocām·en -inis *f* name, designation

vocāti·ō -ōnis *f* invitation *(to dinner); (leg)* summons

vocāt·or -ōris *m* inviter, host

vocāt·us -ūs *m* summons, call

vōciferāti·ō -ōnis *f* loud cry, yell

vōcifer·ō -āre *or* **vōcifer·or -ārī -ātus sum** *tr & intr* to shout, yell

vocit·ō -āre -āvī -ātus *tr* to call habitually, keep calling, usually call, name; to shout out again and again

voc·ō -āre -āvī -ātus *tr* to call, name; to summon; to call upon, invoke *(the gods);* to invite *(to dinner); (w. double acc)* to call *(s.o. s.th.);* to call for, require; *(w.* **dē** *+ abl)* to name *(s.o., s.th.)* after; *(mil)* to challenge; **ad sē vocāre** to summon; **aliquem ex iūre manum cōnsertum vocāre** *(leg)* to call out of court to settle the issue by physical combat; **in arma vocāre** to call to arms; **in dubium vocāre** to call into question; **in iūs vocāre** to summon to court; **in odium vocāre** to bring into disfavor; **in perīculum vocāre** to lead into danger

vōcul·a -ae *f* weak voice; soft note, soft tone; whisper, gossip

volaem·um -ī *n* **(volē-)** type of large pear

Volāterr·ae -ārum *fpl* old Etruscan hill town *(modern Volterra)*

Volāterrān·us -a -um *adj* of Volaterrae

volātic·us -a -um *adj* flying, winged; transitory, passing; inconstant

volātil·is -is -e *adj* able to fly; rapid; transitory

volāt·us -ūs *m* flight

Volcānāl·ia -ium *npl* **(Vulc-)** festival of Vulcan *(August 23)*

Volcāni·us -a -um *adj* **(Vulc-)** of Vulcan; **aciēs Vulcānia** Vulcan's battleline *(i.e., fire spreading in a line);* **arma Vulcānia** arms made by Vulcan *(for Achilles)*

Volcān·us -ī *m* **(Vul-)** Vulcan *(god of fire, son of Jupiter)*

vol·ēns -entis *adj* willing; permitting; ready; favorable ‖ *m* well-wisher

Voles·us -ī *m* Roman family name *(nomen), esp.* the father of Publius Valerius Publicola

volg- = vulg-

volit·āns -antis *m* winged insect

volit·ō -āre -āvī -ātum *intr* to flit about, fly about, flutter; to move quickly; to hover, soar

vol·ō -āre -āvī -ātum *intr* to fly

volō velle voluī *tr* to wish, want; to propose, determine; to hold, maintain; to mean; to prefer ‖ *intr* to be willing

Vologēs·us -ī *m* name of several Arsacid kings of Parthia

volōn·ēs -um *mpl* volunteers *(slaves who enlisted after the battle of Cannae, 216 B.C.)*

volpēs *see* **vulpēs**

Volsc·us -a -um *adj* Vulscan ‖ *mpl* Volscians *(ancient people in S. Latium, subjugated by the Romans in 5th & 4th cent. B.C.)*

volsell·a -ae *f* tweezers

Volsini·ī -ōrum *mpl* Etruscan city

volsus *pp of* **vellō**

volt = *older form of* **vult** he *(or* she *or* it) wishes

voltis = *older form of* **vultis** you wish

Voltumn·a -ae *f* Etruscan goddess in whose temple the twelve Etruscan states met

Volt·ur -uris *m* **(Vul-)** mountain of Apulia near the border of Samnium

Volturn·um -ī *n* town at the mouth of the Volturnus river ‖ old name of Capua

Volturn·us -ī *m* river flowing from the Apennines to the coast of Campania ‖ name for a S.E. wind

voltus *see* **vultus**

volūbil·is -is -e *adj* turning, spinning, revolving, swirling; voluble, rapid, fluent; changeable

volūbilit·ās -ātis *f* whirling motion; roundness; volubility; fluency; mutability

volūbiliter *adv* rapidly; fluently

volu·cer -cris -cre *adj* flying, winged; rapid, speedy

volu·cer -cris *m* bird

volucr·is -is *f* bird; fly. insect; **volucris Iūnōnis** the bird of Juno *(i.e., a peacock)*

voluī *perf of* **volō**

volūm·en -inis *n* roll, book; chapter; whirl, eddy; coil; fold

Volumni·us -a -um *adj* Roman clan name *(nomen)*

voluntāri·us -a -um *adj* voluntary ‖ *mpl* volunteers

volunt·ās -ātis *f* will, wish, desire, purpose, aim, intention; inclination; goodwill, sympathy; willingness, approval; choice, option; last will and testament; attitude *(good or bad);* meaning *(of words);* **ad voluntātem** *(w. gen)* according to the wishes of; **dē** *(or* **ex) voluntāte** *(w. gen)* at the desire of; **voluntāte** *(w. gen)* with the consent of

volup *adv* to one's satisfaction, with pleasure; **volup esse** to be a source of pleasure; **volup facere** *(w. dat)* to cause *(s.o.)* pleasure

voluptābil·is -is -e *adj* agreeable, pleasant

voluptāri·us -a -um *adj* pleasant, agreeable; voluptuous **||** *m* voluptuary

volupt·ās -ātis *f* pleasure, enjoyment, delight **||** *fpl* sensual pleasures; games, sports, public performances

voluptuōs·us -a -um *adj* pleasant, agreeable; giving pleasure

Volusi·us -a -um *adj* Roman clan name *(nomen), esp.* name of a Roman epic poet, mocked by Catullus

volūtābr·um -ī *n* wallow *(for swine)*

volūtābund·us -a -um *adj* wallowing about

volūtāti·ō -ōnis *f* rolling about, tossing about; wallowing; restlessness

volūt·ō -āre -āvī -ātus *tr* to roll about, turn over; to engross; to think over **||** *pass* to wallow, luxuriate

volūtus *pp of* **volvō**

volva *see* **vulva**

vol·vō -vere -vī -ūtus *tr* to roll, turn about, wind; *(of a river)* to roll *(e.g., rocks)* along; to breathe; to unroll, read *(books, scrolls);* to pour out, utter fluently; to consider, weigh; *(of time)* to bring on, bring around; to form *(a circle);* to undergo *(troubles)* **||** *pass* to roll, tumble; to revolve **||** *intr* to revolve; to roll on, elapse

vōm·er *or* **vōm·is -eris** *m* plowshare; *(vulg)* penis

vomic·a -ae *f* sore, boil, abscess, ulcer; annoyance

vōmis *see* **vōmer**

vomiti·ō -ōnis *f* vomiting

vomit·ō -āre *intr* to vomit *(frequently)*

vomit·us -ūs *m* vomiting; vomit

vom·ō -ere -uī -itus *tr & intr* to vomit, throw up

vorāg·ō -inis *f* deep hole, abyss, chasm, depth

vor·āx -ācis *adj* swallowing, devouring; greedy, ravenous

vor·ō -āre -āvī -ātus *tr* to swallow, devour; *(fig)* to devour *(by reading)*

vors- = **vers-**

vort- = **vert-**

vōs *pron* you *(pl); (refl)* yourselves

vōsmet *pron (emphatic form of* **vōs**) you yourselves

voster *see* **vester**

vōtīv·us -a -um *adj* votive, promised in a vow

vot·ō -āre *see* **vetō**

vōt·um -ī *n* solemn vow *(made to a deity);* votive offering *(made for a prayer answered);* prayer, wish; thing wished for, wish; **compos vōtī** *(or* **vōtō) esse** to have had one's prayer answered; **in vōtō est** *(w. inf)* it is *(my)* wish to; **in vōtō est** *(w.* **ut** *+ subj or w. acc & inf)* it is *(my)* wish that; **vōtī reus** obligated to fulfill a vow; **vōtō māior** surpassing one's fondest hopes; **vōtum est** *(w. inf)* it is *(my)* hope to; **vōtum est** *(w.* **ut** *+ subj or w. acc & inf)* it is *(my)* hope that

voveō vovēre vōvī vōtus *tr* to vow, promise solemnly, pledge, devote *(to a deity);* to wish, wish for

vōx vōcis *f* voice; sound, tone, cry, call; word *(written or spoken);* utterance, saying, expression; proverb; language; accent

Vulcānus *see* **Volcānus**

vulgār·is -is -e *adj* **(vol-)** common, general, usual, everyday; low-class; unimportant, routine *(business);* well-known, often repeated *(story)*

vulgāriter *adv* **(vol-)** in the usual way; commonly

vulgāt·or -ōris *m* **(vol-)** divulger

vulgāt·us -a -um *adj* **(vol-)** common, general; well-known; notorious

vulgivag·us -a -um *adj* roving; promiscuous

vulgō *adv* **(vol-)** generally, publicly, everywhere

vulg·ō -āre -āvī -ātus *tr* **(vol-)** to spread, publish, broadcast; to divulge; to prostitute; to level, make common

vulg·us -ī *n* **(vol-)** masses, public, people; crowd; herd, flock; rabble, populace; **in vulgus** *(or* **in vulgum**) to the general public, publicly

vulnerāti·ō -ōnis *f* **(vol-)** wounding, wound

vulner·ō -āre -āvī -ātus *tr* **(vol-)** to wound; to damage

vulnific·us -a -um *adj* inflicting wounds

vuln·us -eris *n* **(vol-)** wound; blow, stroke; blow, disaster

vulpēcul·a -ae *f* **(vol-)** little fox, sly little fox

vulp·ēs -is *f* **(vol-)** fox; craftiness, cunning

vuls·us *or* **vols·us -a -um** *pp of* **vellō ||** *adj* plucked, beardless, effeminate

vulticul·us -ī *m* **(vol-)** mere look

vult·um *see* **vultus**

vultuōs·us -a -um *adj* **(vol-)** full of airs, affected, stuck-up

vult·ur -uris *m* **(vol-)** vulture **|| Vultur** *m* mountain in Apulia

vulturīn·us -a -um *adj* **(vol-)** vulture-like, of a vulture

vultur·ius -(i)ī *m* **(vol-)** vulture

Vulturn·us -ī *m* **(Vol-)** principal river of Campania *(modern Volturno)*

vult·us -ūs *m* **(vol-)** face; looks, expression, features; look, appearance

vulv·a -ae *f* **(vol-)** wrapper, cover; womb; female genitalia, vulva; sow's womb *(as a delicacy)*

X

X, x *(supply* littera) *f* twenty-second letter of the Latin alphabet; letter name: **ix**

X = decem ten

Xanth·ō -ūs *f* a sea nymph *(daughter of Nereus and Doris)*

Xanthipp·e -ēs *f* wife of Socrates

Xanthipp·us -ī *m* father of Pericles **II** Spartan commander of the Carthaginians in the First Punic War

Xanth·us -ī *m* river at Troy, identified with the Scamander River **II** river and town of the same name in Lycia **II** name applied by Vergil to a river in Epirus

xen·ium -iī *n* gift, present *(given by a guest to a host or by a host to a guest)*

Xenocrat·ēs -is *m* Greek philosopher, a disciple of Plato

Xenophan·ēs -is *m* early Greek philosopher from Colophon *(c. 565–470 B.C.)*

Xenoph·ōn -ontis *m* Greek historian and pupil of Socrates *(c. 430–354 B.C.)*

xērampelin·ae -ārum *fpl* reddish-purple clothes

Xerx·ēs -is *m* Persian king, defeated at Salamis *(c. 519–465 B.C.)*

xylospong·ium -(i)ī *n* a sponge attached to a stick, used in the same way as toilet paper is used today

xiphi·ās -ae *m* swordfish

xyst·us -ī *m or* **xyst·um -ī** *n* open colonnade *or* portico, walk, planted with trees and shrubs

Y

Y, y *(supply* littera) *f* twenty-third letter of the Latin alphabet; letter name: **ipsilon**

Y, y letter adopted from Greek into the Latin alphabet for the transliteration of words containing an upsilon *(for which u was used earlier),* and pronounced approximately as German ü. It appears to have been in use by the time of Cicero; but its use was restricted to foreign words.

Z

Z, z *(supply* littera) *f* twenty-fourth letter of the Latin alphabet; letter name: **zeta**

Zacynth·us *or* **Zacynth·os -ī** *f* island off W. Greece **II** name for Saguntum, supposed to have been colonized by people from Zacynthus

Zaleuc·us -ī *m* traditional lawgiver of the Locrians

Zam·a -ae *f* town in Numidia where Scipio defeated Hannibal and brought the Second Punic War to an end *(202 B.C.)*

zāmi·a -ae *f* harm, damage, loss

Zanclae·us -a -um *adj* of Zancle

Zancl·ē -ēs *f* old name of Messina in N. Sicily

Zanclēi·us -a -um *adj* of Zancle

zēlotypi·a -ae jealousy

zēlotyp·us -a -um *f* jealous

Zēn·ō(n) -ōnis *m* Zeno the Stoic *(founder of Stoic philosophy and native of Citium in Cyprus, 335–263 B.C.)* **II** Zeno *(Epicurean philosopher, the teacher of Cicero and Atticus, born c. 150 B.C.)*

Zephyr·us *or* **Zephyr·os -ī** *m* zephyr; west wind; wind

Zēt·ēs -ae *m* one of the two sons of Boreas *(Aquilo)*

Zēth·us *or* **Zēt·os -ī** *m* son of Jupiter and Antiope and brother of Amphion

Zeux·is -idis *m* Greek painter of Heraclea in Lucania *(fl c. 400 B.C.)*

zinzi·ō -āre *intr (of a blackbird)* to sing

zmaragd·us -ī *f (m)* emerald

zōdiac·us -a -um *adj* of the zodiac; **zōdiacus circulus** *(or* **orbis**) the zodiac **II** *m* zodiac

Zōil·us -ī *m* a native of Amphipolis, proverbially stern critic of Homer, Plato, and others *(called Homeromastix = scourge of Homer)*

zōn·a -ae *f* belt, sash, girdle; money belt; zone, region; (*med*) shingles

zōnāri·us -a -um *adj* of a belt *or* girdle **II** *m* belt maker, girdle maker

zōnul·a -ae *f* little belt *or* girdle

zōthēc·a -ae *f* niche, alcove

zōthēcul·a -ae *f* little alcove

ENGLISH – LATIN

A

a *indef article (when modifying a substantive, is unexpressed in Latin);* **— little carelessly** parum attente; **— little later** paulo post; **ten denari — pound** decem denarii per libras; **twice — year** bis in anno
aback *adv* **taken —** attonit·us -a -um
abandon *tr* (de)relinquere
abandonment *s* derelicti·o -onis *f*
abashed *adj* erubesc·ens -entis
abate *tr (to lower)* imminuere; *(to slacken)* laxare; *(price)* remittere **‖** *intr (to lessen)* imminuere; *(to decline)* decedere; *(of passion)* defervescere
abbey *s* abbati·a -ae *f*
abbot *s* abb·as -atis *m*
abbreviate *tr* breviare
abbreviation *s* not·a -ae *f*
ABC's *spl* primae litter·ae -arum *fpl;* **to know one's —** litteras scire
abdicate *tr* abdicare **‖** *intr* se abdicare
abdication *s* abdicati·o -onis *f*
abdomen *s* abdom·en -inis *n*
abduct *tr* abducere; *(a girl)* rapere
abduction *s* rapt·us -ūs *m*
aberration *s (departure from right)* err·or -oris *m; (deviation from straight line)* declinati·o -onis *f*
abet *tr* adiuvare; **to — a crime** minister in maleficio esse
abeyance *s* **to be in —** iacēre
abhor *tr* abhorrēre ab *(w. abl)*
abhorrence *s* detestati·o -onis *f*
abhorrent *adj* **(to)** alien·us -a -um *(abl or* ab *w. abl)*
abide *intr* manēre; **— by** stare in *(w. abl)*
abiding *adj* mansur·us -a -um
ability *s (power)* potest·as -atis *f; (mental capacity)* ingen·ium -(i)i *n;* **ability to read and write** legendi scribendique facultas; **to the best of one's —** pro suā parte
abject *adj* abiect·us -a -um
abjectly *adv* abiecte, humiliter
ablative *s* ablativ·us -i *m;* **in the — case** casu ablativo
able *adj (having the power)* pot·ens -entis; *(having mental ability)* ingenios·us -a -um; **not — to fight** non pugnae potēns; **not to be — to** nequire *(w. inf); **to be — to** posse (w. inf)*
able-bodied *adj* valid·us -a -um
ablution *s* abluti·o -onis *f*
ably *adv* ingeniose
abnormal *adj* enorm·is -is -e
aboard *adv* in nave: **to go — a ship** navem conscendere
abode *s* domicil·ium -(i)i *n*
abolish *tr* tollere, abolēre
abolition *s* aboliti·o -onis *f*
abominable *adj* detestabil·is -is -e
abominably *adv* execrabiliter, odiose
abominate *tr* abominari, detestari
abomination *s* detestati·o -onis *f; (terrible crime)* flagit·ium -(i)i *n*
aborigines *spl* aborigin·es -um *mfpl*
abortion *s* abort·us -ūs *m*; **to perform an —** partum abigere
abortive *adj* abortiv·us -a -um; *(unsuccessful)* irrit·us -a -um
abound *intr* abundare, superesse; **to — in** abundare *(w. abl)*
abounding *adj* **— in** abund·ans -antis *(w. abl)*
about *adv (almost)* fere, ferme; *(approximately)* circa, circiter; **in — ten days** decem circiter diebus
about *prep (of place)* circa, circum *(w. acc); (of number)* circa, ad *(w. acc); (of time)* circa, sub *(w. acc); (concerning)* de *(w. abl)*
above *adv* supra, insuper; **to be —** *(e.g., bribery)* indignari *(w. acc);* **from —** desuper, superne
above *prep* supra, super *(w. acc);* **— all** ante omnia; **— all others** praeter omnes ceteros; **to be —** *(e.g., bribery)* indignari *(w. acc)*
abrasion *s* attrit·us -ūs *m*
abreast *adv* pariter; **to walk — of s.o.** latus alicui tegere
abridge *tr* breviare, contrahere; **to — a book** in compendium redigere
abridgment *s* epitom·e -es *f*
abroad *adv (in a foreign land)* peregre; *(of motion, out of doors)* foras; *(of rest, out of doors)* foris; **from —** extrinsec·us -a -um; *(w. verbs)* peregre; **to be** *or* **go** *or* **live —** peregrinari; **to get —** *(of news)* divulgari
abrogate *tr* abrogare, rescindere
abrupt *adj (sudden)* subit·us -a -um; *(rugged)* praerupt·us -a -um
abruptly *adv* subito, repente
abruptness *s* rapidit·as -atis *f*
abscess *s* vomic·a -ae *f*
absence *s* absenti·a -ae *f;* **in my —** me absente
absent *adj* abs·ens -entis; **— without leave** *(mil)* infrequ·ens -entis
absent *tr* **to — oneself** se removēre; *(not show up)* non comparēre
absentee *s* abs·ens -entis *mf*
absolute *adj* absolut·us -a -um, summ·us -a -um; *(unlimited)* īnfinit·us -a -um; **— power** dominat·us -ūs *m,* tyrann·is -idis *f;* **— ruler** domin·us -i *m,* tyrann·us -i *m*
absolutely *adv (unconditionally)* praecise; *(completely)* utique, prorsus; **— nothing**

nihil prorsus; **to rule — over** dominari *(w.* in *w. acc)*

absolution *s* absoluti·o -onis *f*

absolve *tr* veniam dare *(w. dat);* **to — from** absolvere ab *(w. abl)*

absorb *tr* absorbēre, (com)bibere; *(fig)* tenēre

absorbent *adj* bibul·us -a -um

abstain *intr* **(from)** se abstinēre *(w. abl)*

abstemious *adj* abstemi·us -a -um

abstinence *s* abstinenti·a -ae *f; (from food)* inedi·a -ae *f*

abstract *tr* **(from)** abstrahere (ab *w. abl); (an idea)* separare

abstract *s* compend·ium -(i)i *n;* **in the —** in abstracto

abstract *adj (idea)* mente percept·us -a -um; *(quantity)* abstract·us -a -um; **— noun** appellati·ō -ōnis *f*

abstraction *s* separati·o -onis *f; (idea)* noti·o -onis *f*

abstruse *adj* abstrus·us -a -um

absurd *adj* absurd·us -a -um

absurdity *s* inepti·a -ae *f*

abundance *s* abundanti·a -ae *f,* copi·a -ae *f*

abundant *adj* abund·ans -antis, larg·us -a -um; **to be —** abundare

abundantly *adv* abundanter, copiose

abuse *s (wrong use)* abus·us -ūs *m; (insult)* iniuri·a -ae *f,* convic·ium -(i)i *n;* **to heap — on** contumeliosissime maledicere *(w. dat)*

abuse *tr (to misuse)* abuti *(w. abl); (sexually)* stuprare; *(w. words)* maledicere *(w. dat)*

abusive *adj* **(toward)** contumelios·us -a -um (in *w. acc); (person)* maledic·us -a -um; **to be — to** abuti *(w. abl)*

abusively *adv* contumeliose

abyss *s* profund·um -i *n; (fig)* barathr·um -i *n*

academic *adj* academic·us -a -um

academy *s* academi·a -ae *f*

accede *intr* **to — to** assentire *(w. dat)*

accelerate *tr & intr* accelerare

acceleration *s* accelerati·o -onis *f*

accent *s* accent·us -ūs *m,* vo·x -cis *f; (peculiar tone of a people)* son·us -i *m;* **a Greek —** son·us -i *m* linguae Graecae; **to place an acute (grave, circumflex) — on a word** acutam (gravem, circumflexam) vocem in verbo ponere

accent *tr (in speaking)* acuere; *(in writing)* fastigare

accent mark *s* fastig·ium -(i)i *n*

accentuation *s (in speaking)* accent·us -ūs *m; (in writing, expr. by gerundive):* **careful in the — of syllables** in syllabis acuendis diligens

accept *tr* accipere, recipere; *(to approve of)* probare

acceptable *adj* **(to)** accept·us -a -um, probabil·is -is -e *(w. dat);* **to be — to** placēre *(w. dat)*

acceptably *adv* apte

acceptance *s* accepti·o -onis *f; (approval)* probati·o -onis *f*

access *s* adit·us -ūs *m,* access·us -ūs *m;* **— to books** copi·a -ae *f* librorum; **to gain — to** penetrare ad *(w. acc);* **to have — to** admitti *(w. dat)*

accessible *adj (of places)* pat·ens -entis; *(of persons)* facil·is -is -e; **to be — to** patēre *(w. dat)*

accession *s (addition)* accessi·o -onis *f;* **— to the throne** regni princip·ium -(i)i *n*

accessory *adj* adiunct·us -a -um; *(to a crime)* consci·us -a -um

accessory *s* affin·is -is *mf;* **— to this crime** affinis *mf* huic facinori

accident *s* cas·us -ūs *m;* calamit·as -atis *f* (autocinetica); **by —** casu

accidental *adj* fortuit·us -a -um; *(nonessential)* adventici·us -a -um

accidentally *adv* casu, forte

acclamation *s (shouts of applause)* clam·or -oris *m,* acclamati·o -onis *f; (oral vote)* conclamati·o -onis *f*

accommodate *tr (adapt)* **(to)** accommodare *(w. dat); (w. lodgings)* hospitium parare *(w. dat); (of an auditorium, etc.)* capere

accommodation *s* accommodati·o -onis *f; (convenience)* commodit·as -atis *f;* **—s** deversor·ium -(i)i *n*

accompaniment *s* concinenti·a -ae *f;* **to sing to the — of the flute** ad tibiam concinere

accompany *tr* comitari; *(mus)* concinere *(w. dat)*

accomplice *s* **(in)** partic·eps -itis *m (w. gen or* in *w. abl)*

accomplish *tr* efficere, perficere

accomplished *adj (skilled)* erudit·us -a -um; *(of a speaker)* disert·us -a -um

accomplishment *s (completion)* peracti·o -onis *f;* **—s** re·s -rum *fpl* gestae

accord *s* consens·us -ūs *m;* **of one's own —** suā sponte, ultro; **to be in — with** convenire *(w. dat);* **with one —** unanimiter

accordance *s* **in — with** secundum *(w. acc),* pro *(w. abl),* ex *(w. abl)*

accordingly *adv* proinde, itaque

according to *prep* secundum *(w. acc)*

accordion *s* harmonic·a -ae *f* diductilis

accost *tr* appellare, compellare; *(sexually)* lenare

account *s (financial)* rati·o -onis *f; (statement)* memori·a -ae *f; (story)* narrati·o -onis *f; (esteem)* reputati·o -onis *f;* **of little —** parvi preti; **of no —** nullius preti; **on — of** ob, propter *(w. acc);* **on that —** propterea; **the — balances** ratio constat; **to audit accounts** rationes dispungere; **to balance accounts** rationes conferre; **to**

be entered into an — rationibus inferri; to call to — rationem poscere; to give an — rationem reddere; to take — of rationem habēre *(w. gen)*
account *tr (to consider)* ducere; *(to esteem)* aestimare; **to — for** rationem reddere *(w. gen);* **to — for his absence** rationem adferre cur absit
accountable *adj* **(for)** re•us -a -um *(w. gen)*
accountant *s* ratiocinat•or -oris *m,* ratiocinat•rix -ricis *f*
account books *spl* tabul•ae -arum *fpl* (accepti et expensi)
accounting *s* confecti•o -onis *f* tabularum; **to keep (accounting) books** tabulas conficere
accredited *adj* aestimat•us -a -um
accrue *intr* accrescere; **to — to** accedere *(w. dat),* redundare in *(w. acc)*
accumulate *tr* accumulare ‖ *intr* crescere, augēri
accumulation *s* congest•us -ūs *m; (pile)* cumul•us -i *m*
accuracy *s (pains bestowed)* cur•a -ae *f; (exactness)* subtilit•as -atis *f*
accurate *adj* exact•us -a -um; *(of a definition, observation)* subtil•is -is -e
accurately *adv* exacte; subtiliter
accusation *s* accusati•o -onis *f; (charge)* crim•en -inis *n;* **to bring an — against** accusare
accusative *s* accusativ•us -i *m;* **in the accusative (case)** casu accusativo
accuse *tr* **(of)** accusare *(w. gen or* de *w. abl);* **to — falsely** calumniari; **to — s.o. of a capital offense** aliquem rei capitalis re•um (-am) facere
accused *s* re•us -i *m,* re•a -ae *f*
accuser *s* accusat•or -oris *m,* accusatr•ix -icis *f*
accusingly *adv* accusatorie
accustom *tr* **(to)** assuefacere *(w. abl, dat or* ad *w. acc, or inf);* **to — oneself** *or* **become —ed to** assuescere *(w. dat),* ad, in *(w. acc);* **to be —ed to** solēre *(w. inf)*
ache *s* dol•or -oris *m*
ache *intr* dolēre; **I — all over** totus (-a) doleo; **my head —s** caput mihi dolet
achieve *tr* conficere; *(to win)* consequi
achievement *s* res, rei *f* gesta
acid *s* acid•um -i *n*
acid *adj* acid•us -a -um
acknowledge *tr* agnoscere; *(a child)* tollere
acknowledgement *s* confessi•o -onis *f; (money receipt)* apoch•a -ae *f*
acorn *s* glan•s -dis *f*
acoustics *spl* acustic•a -orum *npl*
acquaint *tr* **(with)** certiorem facere (de *w. abl);* **to — oneself with** cognoscere
acquaintance *s* familiarit•as -atis *f; (person)* familiar•is -is *mf*
acquainted *adj* not•us -a -um; **— with** gnar•us -a -um *(w. gen);* **to become — with** cognoscere
acquiesce *intr* **(in)** acquiescere (in *w. abl),* stare *(w. abl or* in *w. abl)*
acquiescence *s* assens•us -ūs *m*
acquire *tr* adipisci, nancisci
acquisition *s* quaest•us -ūs *m; (thing acquired)* quaesit•um -i *n*
acquit *tr* **(of)** absolvere (de *w. abl);* **to — oneself** se gerere
acquittal *s* absoluti•o -onis *f*
acre *s* iuger•um -i *n (actually .625 of an acre)*
acrid *adj* a•cer -cris -cre
acrobat *s* petauristari•us -i *m* (•a -ae *f);*
across *adv* in transversum
across *prep* trans *(w. acc)*
act *s (deed, action)* fact•um -i *n; (decree)* decret•um -i *n; (theat)* act•us -ūs *m;* **caught in the —** manifestari•us -a -um; **in the very —** in flagranti; **public —s** act•a -orum *npl*
act *tr (role)* agere ‖ *intr* agere; **to — as a friend** amicum agere; **to — as a servant** servile officium tueri; **to — badly** se turpiter gerere
acting *s* acti•o -onis *f*
action *s* acti•o -onis *f,* act•us -ūs *m; (deed)* fact•um -i *n; (leg)* acti•o -onis *f; (mil)* pugn•a -ae *f; (of speaker)* gest•us -ūs *m;* **to bring an — against** actionem intendere in *(w. acc)*
active *adj (life)* actuos•us -a -um; *(mind)* veget•us -a -um; *(busy)* impi•ger -gra -grum; *(gram)* activ•us -a -um; **— voice** gen•us -eris *n* activum; **be — in** versari in *(w. abl);* **be on active service** stipendia facere; **verb in the — voice** verbum agendi modi
actively *adv* impigre; *(energetically)* gnaviter
activity *s* agitati•o -onis *f; (energy)* industri•a -ae *f,* gnavit•as -atis *f*
actor *s* histri•o -onis *m,* act•or -oris *m; (in comedy)* comoed•us -i *m; (in tragedy)* tragoed•us -i *m*
actress *s* actr•ix -icis *f; (in Roman times)* mim•a -ae *f [Note: females did not normally act in regular Roman dramas]*
actual *adj* ver•us -a -um
actuality *s* verit•as -atis *f*
actually *adv* re verā
acumen *s* acum•en -inis *n*
acute *adj (angle, pain)* acut•us -a -um; *(vision, intellect)* a•cer -cris -cre
acutely *adv* acute, acriter
acuteness *s (of senses, intellect)* aci•es -ei *f*
adage *s* proverb•ium -(i)i *n*
ad *s* praeconium -(i)i *n*
adamant *adj* obstinat•us -a -um
Adam's apple *s* nod•us -ī *m* gutturis
adapt *tr* accommodare, aptare

adaptation *s* accommodati·o -onis *f*
adapted *adj* apt·us -a -um
add *tr* (**to**) addere, adicere *(w. dat or* ad *w. acc); (in speaking)* superdicere; *(in writing)* subscribere; **to — up** computare; **to be —ed to** accedere *(w. dat or* ad *w. acc)*
addict *tr* **to be —ed to** se tradere *(w. dat)*
addicted *adj* **— to** dedit·us -a -um *(w. dat)*
adding machine *s* machin·a -ae *f* additionalis
addition *s* accessi·o -onis *f,* adiecti·o -onis *f;* **in —** praeterea, insuper; **in — to** praeter *(w. acc),* super *(w. acc)*
additional *adj* additici·us -a -um
additionally *adv* accedit quod *(w. indic)*
address *s* alloqu·ium -(i)i *n; (on an envelope)* inscripti·o -onis *f* cursualis; *(comput)* inscripti·o -onis *f* electronica; *(speech)* conti·o -onis *f,* orati·o -onis *f*
address *tr (to speak to)* alloqui, compellare; *(a letter)* inscribere
address book *s (comput)* lib·er -ri *m* inscriptionum electronicarum
adduce *tr (witness, evidence)* producere; *(arguments)* afferre
adept *adj* (**in**) perit·us -a -um (*w. gen or abl or* in *w. abl)*
adequacy *s* sufficienti·a -ae *f*
adequate *adj* suffici·ens -entis; **to be —** sufficere
adequately *adv* satis, apte
adhere *intr* (**to**) haerēre, cohaerēre *(w. dat, abl, or* in *w. acc);* **to — to** *(fig)* stare in *(w. abl)*
adherence *s* adhaes·us -ūs *m*
adherent *s* assectat·or -oris *m*
adhesion *s* adhaesi·o -onis *f*
adhesive *adj* ten·ax -acis
adhesive *s* glut·en -inis *n*
adhesive tape *s* taeni·a -ae *f* adhaesiva
adjacent *adj* confin·is -is -e; **to be — to** adiacēre *(w. dat,* ad *w. acc),* contermin·us -a -um esse *(w. dat)*
adjective *s* adiectiv·um -i *n*
adjectival *adj* adiectival·is -is -e
adjectively *adv* pro apposito; **the word is used —** vocabulum pro apposito ponitur
adjoin *tr* adiacēre *(w. dat)*
adjoining *adj* coniunct·us -a -um, iunct·us -a -um; **— rooms** iuncta cubicula
adjourn *tr* differre; *(leg)* ampliare ‖ *intr* diferri
adjournment *s* dilati·o -onis *f*; *(leg)* amplificati·o -onis *f*
adjudicate *tr* addicere
adjunct *s* adiunct·um -i *n*
adjust *tr* (**to**) aptare, accommodare (*w. dat or* ad *w. acc); (to put in order)* componere ‖ *intr* (**to**) se accommodare (*w. dat or* ad *w. acc)*
adjustment *s* accommodati·o -onis *f; (of a robe)* structur·a -ae *f*
adjutant *s* opti·o -onis *m*
administer *tr (to manage)* administrare; *(medicines)* adhibēre; *(oath)* adigere; **to — justice** ius dicere
administration *s* administrati·o -onis *f;* **— of justice** iurisdicti·o -onis *f;* **— of public affairs** procurati·o -onis *f* reipublicae
administrative *adj* ad administrationem pertin·ens -entis
administrator *s* administrat·or -oris *m,* procurat·or -oris *m*
admirable *adj* admirabil·is -is -e
admiral *s* classis praefect·us -i *m*
admiration *s* admirati·o -onis *f*
admire *tr* admirari
admirer *s* admirat·or -oris *m; (lover)* am·ans -antis *mf*
admiringly *adv (use participle:)* admir·ans -antis
admissible *adj* accipiend·us -a -um
admission *s* confessi·o -onis *f; (being let in)* adit·us -ūs *m,* access·us -ūs *m;* **by his own —** confessione suā
admission ticket *s* tesser·a -ae *f* aditialis
admit *tr (to allow to enter)* admittere; *(e.g., into the senate)* asciscere; *(to grant as valid)* dare; *(to acknowledge)* agnoscere; **it is —ed** cōnstat; **to — flatly** profiteri palam
admittedly *adv* sane
admonish *tr* admonēre
admonition *s (act)* admoniti·o -onis *f; (words used)* monit·um -i *n*
adolescence *s* adulescenti·a -ae *f*
adolescent *adj* adulesc·ēns -entis
adolescent *s* adulescentul·us -i *m*
adopt *tr (a child)* adoptare; *(an adult)* arrogare; *(customs, laws)* asciscere; *(a plan)* capere, inire
adoption *s* adopti·o -onis *f; (of an adult)* arrogati·o -onis *f; (of a custom)* assumpti·o -onis *f*
adoptive *adj* adoptiv·us -a -um
adorable *adj* adorand·us -a -um
adoration *s* adorati·o -onis *f*
adore *tr* adorare; *(fig)* demirari
adorn *tr* decorare, ornare
adornment *s (act)* exornati·o -onis *f; (object)* ornament·um -i *n*
Adriatic *adj* Adriatic·us -a -um
adrift *adv* **to be —** fluctuare; **to set —** aperto mari committere
adroit *adj* callid·us -a -um; *(dexterous)* dex·ter -tra -trum
adroitness *s* callidit·as -atis *f;* dexterit·as -atis *f*
adulation *s* adulati·o -onis *f*
adult *adj* adult·us -a -um; **— population** *(not including the aged)* pub·es -is *f*
adult *s* adult·us -i *m;* pub·es -eris *m*
adulterate *tr* adulterare
adulteration *s* adulterati·o -onis *f*
adulterer *s* adult·er -eri *m*
adulteress *s* adulter·a -ae *f*

adulterous *adj* adulterin•us -a -um
adultery *s* adulter•ium -(i)i *n;* **to commit —** adulterare
advance *tr (to more forward)* promovēre; *(money)* in antecessum solvere; *(a cause)* fovēre; *(to promote)* provehere; *(an opinion)* praeferre ‖ *intr (to go forward)* procedere; *(of steady movement on foot)* incedere; *(in riding or sailing)* provehi; *(to progress)* proficere; *(mil)* gradum *(or* pedem) inferre; **as the day —ed** die procedente
advance *s* progress•us -ūs *m;* **in —** ante; **to pay in —** pecuniam nondum debitam solvere
advanced *adj* provect•us -a -um; **at an — age** provectā aetate; **— in years** grand•is -is -e natu *(or* aevo)
advance man *s* praecurs•or -oris *m*
advancement *s* promoti•o -onis *f*
advantage *s (benefit)* commod•um -i *n; (a real good)* bon•um -i *n; (profit)* emolument•um -i *n; (usefulness)* utilit•as -atis *f;* **to be of —** prodesse; **to have an — over** praestare *(w. dat);* **to take — of** uti *(w. abl); (pej)* sibi quaestui habēre; **to take — of an opportunity** occasionem nancisci
advantageous *adj* util•is -is -e
advantageously *adv* utiliter
advent *s* advent•us -ūs *m*
adventure *s* cas•us -ūs *m*
adventurer *s* periclitat•or -oris *m*
adventurous *adj* aud•ax -acis
adverb *s* adverb•ium -(i)i *n*
adverbial *adj* adverbial•is -is -e
adverbially *adv* adverbialiter
adversary *s* adversar•ius -(i)i *m,* adversatr•ix -icis *f*
adversative *adj* adversativ•us -a -um
adverse *adj (mostly winds)* advers•us -a -um; *(times)* asp•er -era -erum; **— circumstances** re•s -rum *fpl* asperae
adversely *adv* male, infeliciter
adversity *s* re•s -rum *fpl* adversae; *(fig)* re•s -rum *fpl* asperae
advertise *tr* proscribere, divulgare
advertisement *s* praeconi•um -ī *n; (poster)* proscripti•o -onis *f*
advice *s* consil•ium -(i)i *n;* **to ask s.o. for —** aliquem consulere, aliquem consilium rogare; **to give good — to** rectum consilium dare *(w. dat)*
advisable *adj* **it is — to** expedit *(w. inf)*
advise *tr* suadēre *(w. dat)*
advisedly *adv* consulto
adviser *s* consult•or -oris *m*
advocate *s (leg)* advocat•us -i *m; (fig)* patron•us -i *m*
advocate *tr* suadēre
aedile *s* aedil•is -is *m*
aedileship *s* aedilit•as -atis *f*
aegis *s* aeg•is -idis *f; (fig)* tutel•a -ae *f*
aerial *adj* aëri•us -a -um
affable *adj* affabil•is -is -e
affably *adv* affabiliter
affair *s* negot•ium -i(i) *n,* res, rei *f; (love)* am•or -oris *m;* **to have an — with** consuetudinem habēre cum
affect *tr (to influence)* afficere; *(to move)* movēre; *(to pretend)* simulare
affectation *s* affectati•o -onis *f*
affected *adj* simulat•us -a -um; *(style)* putid•us -a -um
affection *s* am•or -oris *m*
affectionate *adj* am•ans -antis
affectionately *adv* amanter
affidavit *s* per tabulas testimon•ium -(i)i *n*
affiliated *adj* **to be — with a college** in collegio cooptari
affinity *s* affinit•as -atis *f;* **to have no — with** longe remot•us -a -um esse ab *(w. abl)*
affirm *tr* affirmare
affirmative *adj* affirm•ans -antis; **I reply in the —** aio; **to give an — answer** fateri ita se rem habere
affix *tr* affigere
afflict *tr* affligere; **to be —ed with** conflictari *(w. abl)*
affliction *s (cause of distress)* mal•um -i *n; (state of distress)* miseri•a -ae *f*
affluence *s* diviti•ae -arum *fpl*
affluent *adj* div•es -itis
afford *tr (opportunity, etc.)* praebēre; **I cannot —** res mihi non suppetit ad *(w. acc)*
affront *s* contumeli•a -ae *f*
afield *adv* in agro; *(astray)* vag•us -a -um, err•ans -antis
afloat *adj* nat•ans -antis; **to get a ship —** navem deducere
afoot *adv* pedibus; **to be —** *(fig)* geri; **what is —?** quid geritur?
aforementioned *adj* supra dict•us -a -um
afraid *adj* timid•us -a -um; **to be — of** timēre *(w. acc),* metuere *(w. acc);* **to make —** terrēre; **what are you afraid of?** quid est quod metuis?
afresh *adv* de integro, de novo
Africa *s* Afric•a -ae *f*
African *adj* African•us -a -um
African *s* Af•er -ri *m*
after *prep* post *(w. acc),* ab, ex *(w. abl); (in rank or degree)* secundum *(w. acc);* **(and) — all** (et) re verā; **— an interval** interposito deinde spatio; **— that** deinde, subinde; **— this** post hac; **a little —** paulo post; **immediately —** statim ab *(w. abl);* **named — his father** a patre nominat•us -a -um: **right —** sub *(w. acc);* **the day —** postridie (quam); **to be — s.o.** *(romantically)* aliquem petere
after *conj* postquam

afternoon *s* postmeridian·um -i *n;* **in the —** post meridiem, postmeridie; **this —** hodie post meridiem
afternoon *adj* postmeridian·us -a -um
afterthought *s* posterior cogitati·o -onis *f*
afterwards *adv* postea
again *adv* iterum, rursus; *(hereafter)* posthac; *(in turn)* invicem; *(further)* porro; **— and —** identidem; **once —** denuo; **over —** denuo
against *prep* contra *(w. acc); (in a hostile manner)* adversus *(w. acc),* in *(w. acc);* **— the current** adverso flumine; **to lean — a tree** se ad arborem applicare; **to be —** adversari *(w. dat)*
age *s (time of life)* aet·as -atis *f; (era)* saecul·um -i *n,* aet·as -atis *f;* **don't ask me my —** noli me percontari meum aevum; **of the same —** aequaev·us -a -um; **old —** senect·us -utis *f;* **to be of —** sui iuris esse; **to be under twelve years of age** minor viginti annorum esse; **twelve years of —** duodecim annos nat·us -a -um; **under —** inpub·is -is -e
age *tr* aetate conficere **II** *intr* maturescere; *(to grow old)* senescere
aged *adj* annos·us -a -um, aetate provect·us -a -um; **a man — forty** vi·r -i *m* annos quadraginta natus
agency *s* acti·o -onis *f; (means)* oper·a -ae *f; (office)* procurati·o -onis *f;* **through the — of** per *(w. acc)*
agent *s (doer)* act·or -oris *m*; *(com)* procurat·or -oris *m,* negotiorum curat·or -oris *m;* **man is a free —** homo sui iuris est
aggravate *tr (to make worse)* aggravare; *(a wound)* ulcerare; *(to annoy)* vexare; **to become —d** ingravescere
aggravating *adj* molest·us -a -um
aggravation *s (annoyance)* vexati·o -onis *f*
aggregate *adj* tot·us -a -um; **in the —** in toto
aggression *s* incursi·o -onis *f;* **to commit — against** incursionem hostiliter facere in *(w. acc)*
aggressive *adj* hostil·is -is -e
aggressor *s* qui bellum ultro infert
aggrieved *adj* qui iniuriam accepit
aghast *adj* stupefact·us -a -um; **to stand —** obstupescere
agile *adj* agil·is -is -e; *(mind)* veget·us -a -um
agility *s* agilit·as -atis *f*
agitate *tr (to move rapidly to and fro)* agitare; *(to excite)* agitare; *(to disturb)* perturbare
agitated *adj (sea)* tumultuos·us -a -um; *(fig)* turbulent·us -a -um
agitation *s (violent movement)* agitati·o -onis *f; (mental or political disturbance)* commoti·o -onis *f*
agitator *s* vulgi turbat·or -oris *m*
ago *adv* abhinc; **a short time —** haud ita pridem; **a short while —** paulo ante; **how long —?** quam pridem; **long —** iamdudum, multo ante; **not so long ago** haud ita pridem; **some time —** pridem; **three years —** abhinc tres annos
agonize *intr* (ex)cruciari
agonizing *adj* cruciabil·is -is -e
agony *s* acerbissimus dol·or -oris *m;* **to be in —** dolore angi
agrarian *adj* agrari·us -a -um
agree *intr* **— with** consentire cum *(w. abl); (to make a bargain)* pacisci cum *(w. abl); (of facts)* constare, convenire; **it had been —ed** convenerat; **it is generally —ed** fere convenit; **to — with s.o. about** assentire alicui de *(w. abl)*
agreeable *adj (pleasing)* grat·us -a -um; *(of persons)* commod·us -a -um; *(acceptable)* accept·us -a -um
agreeably *adv* grate, accommodate
agreement *s* consens·us -ūs *m; (pact)* pacti·o -onis *f,* pact·um -i *n; (proportion)* symmetri·a -ae *f;* **according to the —** ex pacto: **there is general —** fere convenit
agricultural *adj* rustic·us -a -um; **the Latins were an — people** Latini agriculturae studebant
agriculture *s* agricultur·a -ae *f*
ah *interj* ah!; *(of grief, indignation)* vah!; *(of admiration)* eia!; **— me** eheu!
aha *interj* attat!
ahead *adv use verb with prefix* prae- *or* pro-; **— of time** ante tempus; **to get — of s.o.** aliquem praevenire; **go —, tell me!** agedum, dic mihi!; **to walk — of s.o.** aliquem praecedere
aid *s* auxil·ium -(i)i *n*
aid *tr* adiuvare
aide-de-camp *s* opti·o -onis *m*
ail *tr* dolēre *(w. dat);* **what —s you?** quid tibi est?
ailment *s* mal·um -i *n*
aim *s (mark)* scop·us -i *m; (fig)* fin·is -is *m,* proposit·um -i *n*
aim *tr* (in)tendere **II** *intr* **to — at** *(a target)* destinare; *(to try to hit)* petere; *(to try to attain)* affectare; *(virtue, renown)* spectare
aimless *adj* van·us -a -um
aimlessly *adv* sine ratione
air *s* a·ër -eris *(acc:* aëra) *m; (upper air)* aeth·er -eris *m; (air in motion)* aur·a -ae *f; (attitude)* habit·us -ūs *m;* **— shaft** aestuar·ium -(i)i *n;* **in the open —** sub divo; **to let in fresh —** auras admittere; **to put on —s** se iactare; **up in the —** *(fig)* in medio relict·us -a -um
air *tr* ventilare; *(to disclose)* patefacere
airbag *s* aërius foll·is -is *m*
air conditioner *s* instrument·um -ī *n* aëri temperando
aircraft carrier *s* nav·is -is *f* aëroplanigera

airhead *s (coll)* cucurbit·a -ae *f*
airily *adv* hilare
airing *s* ventilati·o -onis *f; (of an idea)* praedicati·o -onis *f*
airline *s* tram·es -itis *m* aërius
airplane *s* aëroplan·um -i *n*
air pressure *s* pressi·o -onis *f* aëria
aisle *s* al·a -ae *f*
ajar *adj* semiapert·us -a -um
akimbo *adv* **to stand with arms —** ansat·us -a -um stare
akin *adj* **(to)** finitim·us -a -um *(w. dat)*
alabaster *s* alabas·ter -tri *m*
alarm *s (loud notice of danger)* clam·or -oris *m; (sudden fright)* pav·or -oris *m; (on a clock)* suscitabul·um -i *n;* **the — went off** suscitabulum sonuit; **to set the alarm for (six o'clock)** obicem ad (horam sextam) infigere; **to sound the —** signum monitorium dare; *(mil)* classicum canere
alarm *tr* perturbare; **to become —ed** expavescere
alarm clock *s* horologi·um -i *n* suscitatorium
alas *interj* eheu!
albumen *s* album·en -inis *n*
alcohol *s* spirit·us -ūs *m* vini
alcoholic *adj* alcoholic·us -a -um
alcoholic *s* bibos·us -i *m,* (·a -ae *f)*
alcove *s* zothec·a -ae *f*
ale *s* cerevisi·a -ae *f*
alert *adj* intent·us -a -um; **— mind** erecta men·s -tis *f*
alert *s* monitorium sign·um -i *n;* **on the —** intent·us -a -um; **to sound the —** signum monitorium dare
alert *tr (to warn)* praemonēre; *(to rouse)* excitare
alertness *s* alacrit·as -atis *f*
alias *s* nom·en -inis *n* mentitum
alibi *s (excuse)* speci·es -ei *f;* **to have an —** dicere se alibi fuisse; *(fig)* se excusare
alien *adj* peregrin·us -a -um
alien *s* alienigen·a -ae *mf*
alienate *tr* alienare
alienation *s* alienati·o -onis *f*
alike *adj* simil·is -is -e
alike *adv* pariter
alimony *s* alimon·ium -(i)i *n*
alive *adj* viv·us -a -um; *(fig)* ala·cer -cris -cre
all *adj* omn·is -is -e, cunct·us -a -um; *(whole, entire)* tot·us -a -um; *(denoting a unity of parts in a body)* univers·us -a -um; **— the most learned** doctissimus quisque
all *pron* omn·es -ium *mpl & fpl,* omn·ia -ium *npl;* **in —** in summā; *(with numbers)* omnino; **not at —** haudquaquam; **nothing at —** nihil omnino; **one's —** propr·ium -(i)i *n;* **write — you can** scribe quantum potes
all *adv* **— over** undique; **— along** usque ab initio; **— but** tantum non; **— powerful** omnipot·ens -entis; **— the better** tanto melius; **— the more** eo magis; **— too late** immo iam sero
allay *tr* sedare; **to be —ed** temperari
allegation *s* affirmati·o -onis *f*
allege *tr* arguere; **—ing that** tamquam *(w. subj)*
allegiance *s* fid·es -ei *f;* **to pledge — to** fidem obligare *(w. dat);* **to swear —** sacramentum dicere
allegorical *adj* allegoric·us -a -um
allegory *s* allegori·a -ae *f*
allergic *adj* **(to)** obnoxi·us -a -um *(w. dat)*
allergy *s* allergi·a -ae *f*
alleviate *tr* levare
alleviation *s* levati·o -onis *f*
alley *s* angiport·us -ūs *m*
alliance *s (by marriage)* affinit·as -atis *f; (of states)* foed·us -eris *n,* societ·as -atis *f;* **to conclude an — with** foedus icere cum *(w. abl),* **societatem facere cum** *(w. abl)*
allied *adj (pol)* foederat·us -a -um, soci·us -a -um; *(related)* finitim·us -a -um
alligator *s* crocodil·us -i *m*
alliteration *s* alliterati·o -onis *f*
allocate *tr (funds)* attribuere; *(to assign)* distribuere
allocation *s (of funds)* attributi·o -onis *f; (money)* attribut·um -i *n*
allot *tr* assignare
allotment *s* assignati·o -onis *f;* **an — of land** ag·er -ri *m* assignatus
allow *tr* concedere *(w. dat),* sinere; **it is —ed** licet; **it is —ed by Caesar** licet per Caesarem; **to — for** indulgēre *(w. dat)*
allowable *adj* licit·us -a -um; **it is —** fas est
allowance *s (permission)* permissi·o -onis *f; (concession)* veni·a -ae *f; (portion)* porti·o -onis *f; (money)* stipend·ium -(i)i *n; (food)* diari·a -orum *npl*
alloy *s* mixtur·a -ae *f; (of metals)* temperati·o -onis *f*
all right *adv* licet; **it's all right** recte est; bene habet
all-seeing *adj* omnitu·ens -entis
all-time *adj* post hominum memoriam
allude *intr* **to — to** attingere
allure *tr* allicere
allurement *s* blandiment·um -i *n*
alluring *adj* bland·us -a -um
allusion *s* significati·o -onis *f*
allusive *adj* obliqu·us -a -um
allusively *adv* oblique
ally *s* soc·ius -(i)i *m,* soci·a -ae *f*
ally *tr* sociare
almanac *s* fast·i -orum *mpl*
almighty *adj* omnipot·ens -entis
almond *s* amygdal·a -ae *f*
almond tree *s* amygdal·us -i *f*
almost *adv* paene, fere

alms *spl* stip•s -is *f*
aloft *adv (motion & rest)* sublime
alone *adj* sol•us -a -um; *(only)* un•us -a -um; **all —** persol•us -a -um; **to leave —** deserere; **to let —** mittere
alone *adv* solum
along *adv* porro, protinus; **all —** iamdudum; iam inde a principio; **— with** unā cum *(w. abl)*; **to bring —** afferre; **to get — with** consentire cum *(w. abl)*
along *prep* per *(w. acc)*, praeter *(w. acc)* secundum *(w. acc)*
aloof *adv* procul; **to keep — from the senate** curiā abstinēre; **to stand —** abstare
aloud *adv* clare
alphabet *s* element•a -orum *npl*, alphabet•um -i *n*
alphabetical *adj* litterarum ordine
alphabetically *adv* **to arrange —** in litteram digere
Alpine *adj* Alpin•us -a -um
Alps *spl* Alp•es -ium *fpl*
already *adv* iam
also *adv* etiam, et, necnon
altar *s* ar•a -ae *f*
alter *tr* mutare, commutare
alterable *adj* mutabil•is -is -e
alteration *s* mutati•o -onis *f*
altercation *s* altercati•o -onis *f*
alternate *adj* altern•us -a -um
alternate *tr & intr* alternare
alternately *adv* invicem, per vices
alternation *s* vicissitud•o -inis *f*
alternative *adj* alt•er -era -erum, alternat•us -a -um
alternative *s* alternata condici•o -onis *f*, opti•o -onis *f*
although *conj* quamquam *(w. indic)*, quavis *(w. subj)*, cum *(w. subj)*
altitude *s* altitud•o -inis *f*
altogether *adv* omnino
altruism *s* beneficenti•a -ae *f*
always *adv* semper
amass *tr* cumulare
amateur *s* idiot•a -ae *m*
amatory *adj* amatori•us -a -um
amaze *tr* obstupefacere
amazed *adj* **(at)** stupefact•us -a -um (cum *w. abl)*
amazement *s* stup•or -oris *m*
amazing *adj* mir•us -a -um
amazingly *adv* mirabiliter
Amazon *s* Amaz•on -onis *f*
ambassador *s* legat•us -i *m*
amber *s* electr•um -i *n*
ambidextrous *adj* aequiman•us -a -um
ambiguity *s* ambiguit•as -atis *f*
ambiguous *adj* ambigu•us -a -um
ambition *s* ambiti•o -onis *f*
ambitious *adj* laudis *(or* gloriae) studios•us -a -um; *(worker)* assidu•us -a -um; *(self-seeking)* ambitios•us -a -um
amble *intr* ambulare
ambrosia *s* ambrosi•a -ae *f*
ambulance arcer•a -ae *f*
ambush *s* insidi•ae -arum *fpl*
ambush *tr* insidiari *(w. dat)*
ameliorate *tr* corrigere, meliorem *or* melius facere **||** *intr* melior *or* melius fieri
amenable *adj* **(to)** tractabil•is -is -e *(w. dat)*
amend *tr* emendare **||** *intr* proficere
amendment *s* emendati•o -onis *f*
amends *spl* satisfacti•o -onis *f*; **to make —** satisfacere
amenity *s* amoenit•as -atis *f*; *(comfort)* commod•um -i *n*
America *s* Americ•a -ae *f*; **Central —** America Media; **North —** America Septentrionalis; **South —** America Australis
American *adj* American•us -a -um
American *s* American•us -i *m* (•a -ae *f*)
amethyst *s* amethyst•us -i *f*
amiable *adj* amabil•is -is -e
amiably *adv* suaviter
amicable *adj* amic•us -a -um
amicably *adv* amice
amid *prep* inter *(w. acc)*
amiss *adv* perperam; **to take —** aegre ferre
ammunition *s* missilium copi•a -ae *f*
amnesty *s* veni•a -ae *f*
among *prep* inter *(w. acc)*, apud *(w. acc)*; **from —** ex *(w. abl)*
amorous *adj* amatori•us -a -um; *(sexual)* libidinos•us -a -um
amount *s* summ•a -ae *f*
amount *intr* **to — to** efficere ad *(w. acc)*, esse ad *(w. acc)*; **it —s to the same thing** tantundem est; **to — to something** bonum exitum umquam factur•us -a -um esse; **what does it — to?** quid istuc valet?
amphitheater *s* amphitheatr•um -i *n*
ample *adj* ampl•us -a -um
amplification *s* amplificati•o -onis *f*
amplify *tr* amplificare
amply *adv* ample
amputate *tr* amputare
amputation *s* amputati•o -onis *f*
amuck *adv* **to run —** delirare
amulet *s* amulet•um -i *n*
amuse *tr* oblectare; **to — oneself (with)** se oblectare *(w. abl)*
amusement *s* oblectati•o -onis *f*; *(that which amuses)* oblectament•um -i *n*
amusement park *s* hort•i -orum *mpl* publici oblectarii
amusing *adj* festiv•us -a -um
an *indef article, unexpressed in Latin*
anachronism *s* temporum inversi•o -onis *f*
analogous *adj* analog•us -a -um
analogy *s* analogi•a -ae *f*
analysis *s* enodati•o -onis *f*; **to make an — of a compound substance** compositum in principia redigere
analytical *adj* analytic•us -a -um
analytically *adv* per analysin

analyze *tr* in principia redigere; *(words)* subtiliter enodare
anapest *s* anapaestus pe•s -dis *m*
anapestic *adj* anapaestic•us -a -um
anarchy *s* effrenata licenti•a -ae *f;* **to cause —** turbare omnia et permiscēre; **to have —** nullum omnino imperium habēre
anatomical *adj* anatomic•us -a -um
anatomy *s* anatomi•a -ae *f*
ancestor *s* proav•us -i *m;* **—s** maior•es -um *mpl*
ancestry *s* gen•us -eris *n*
anchor *s* ancor•a -ae *f;* **to weigh —** ancoram tollere
anchor *tr* ad ancoram deligare ‖ *intr* in ancorā stare
anchorage *s* stati•o -onis *f*
ancient *adj* antiqu•us -a -um, vetust•us -a -um; **in — times** antiquitus; **the —s** veter•es -um *mpl; (authors)* antiqu•i -orum *mpl*
and *conj* et, ac, atque, -que; **— so forth** et perinde; **— then** deincepsque
anecdote *s* fabell•a -ae *f*
anemic *adj* exsangu•is -is -e
anew *adv* denuo
angel *s* angel•us -i *m* (•a -ae *f*)
angelic *adj* angelic•us -a -um
anger *s* ir•a -ae *f*
anger *tr* irritare
angle *s* angul•us -i *m*
angler *s* piscat•or -oris *m*
angrily *adv* irate
angry *adj* irat•us -a -um; **to be — (with)** succensere, irasci *(w. dat);* **to get — with** irascari *(w. dat);* **to make —** irritare
anguish *s* ang•or -oris *m*
angular *adj* angular•is -is -e
animal *s* anim•al -alis *n; (wild beast)* besti•a -ae *f,* fer•a -ae *f; (domestic)* pec•us -udis *f*
animate *adj* animal•is -is -e
animate *tr* animare; *(fig)* excitare
animated *adj* veget•us -a -um
animosity *s* acerbit•as -atis *f*
ankle *s* tal•us -i *m*
ankle-length *adj* talar•is -is -e
anklet *s* periscel•is -idis *f*
annalist *s* annalium script•or -oris *m*
annals *spl* annal•es -ium *mpl*
annex *tr (nations)* adicere, adiungere
annexation *s* adiecti•o -onis *f*
annihilate *tr* delēre, ex(s)tinguere
annihilation *s* exstincti•o -onis *f*
anniversary *adj* anniversari•us -a -um
anniversary *s* festus di•es -ei *m* anniversarius
annotate *tr* annotare
annotation *s* annotati•o -onis *f*
announce *tr* nuntiare, indicere; *(to report)* renuntiare; *(officially)* denuntiare; *(laws, etc.)* proscribere
announcement *s* denuntiati•o -onis *f; (report)* renuntiati•o -onis *f*
announcer *s* annuntia•tor -toris *m* (•trix -tricis *f*)
annoy *tr* vexare, male habēre; **to be —ed at** stomachari ob *(w. acc),* moleste ferre
annoyance *s* molesti•a -ae *f*
annoying *adj* molest•us -a -um
annual *adj* annu•us -a -um
annually *adv* quotannis
annuity *s* annua pecuni•a -ae *f*
annul *tr (contract, law)* infirmare; *(a law)* abrogare; **to — a marriage** dirimere nuptias
annulment *s* infirmati•o -onis *f;* abrogati•o -onis *f*
anoint *tr* ung(u)ere
anointing *s* uncti•o -onis *f*
anomalous *adj* enorm•is -is -e; *(gram)* anomal•us -a -um
anomaly *s* enormit•as -atis *f; (gram)* anomali•a -ae *f*
anonymous *adj* sine nomine
anonymously *adv* sine nomine
another *adj* ali•us -a -ud; **—'s** alien•us -a -um; **at — time** alias; **in — place** alibi; **one after —** alius ex alio; **one —** inter se; **one . . . —** ali•us -a -ud . . . ali•us -a -ud; **to — place** alio
answer *tr* respondēre *(w. dat); (by letter)* rescribere *(w. dat); (to correspond to)* congruere cum *(w. abl)* **to — a question** ad interrogatum respondēre ‖ *intr* **to — for** rationem reddere *(w. gen);* **to — to the name of** vocari
answer *s* respons•um -i *n; (solution)* explicati•o -onis *f;* **that's not an — to my question** aliud te rogo
answerable *adj* re•us -a -um; **to be — for** praestare *(acc)*
answering machine *s* responstr•um -ī *n* telephonicum
ant *s* formic•a -ae *f*
antagonism *s* adversit•as -atis *f*
antagonist *s* adversar•ius -(i)i *m,* adversatr•ix -icis *f*
antarctic *adj* antarctic•us -a -um
antecedent *adj* anteced•ens -entis
antecedent *s* anteced•ens -entis *n; (gram)* nom•en -inis *n* antecedens
antechamber *s* atriol•um -i *n*
antedate *tr* diem vero antiquiorem ascribere *(w. dat); (to precede in time)* aetate antecedere *(w. dat or acc)*
antelope *s* tarandr•us -i *m*
antenna *s* antenn•a -ae *f*
antepenult *s* syllab•a -ae *f* antepaenultima
anterior *adj* anter•ior -ior -ius
anteroom *s* atriol•um -i *n*
anthem *s* hymn•us -i *m* elatior; **national —** patrium carm•en -inis *n*
anthology *s* anthologi•a -ae *f*

anthropologist *s* anthropolog·us -i *m* (·a -ae *f*)
anthropology *s* anthropologi·a -ae *f*
anticipate *tr* anticipare; *(to expect)* spectare; *(mentally)* praesumere
anticipation *s* anticipati·o -onis *f*, praesumpti·o -onis *f*
anticlimax *s* clim·ax -acis *f* inversa
antics *spl* mot·us -uum *mpl* ridiculi
antidote *s* antidot·ium -(i)i *n*
antipathy *s* antipathi·a -ae *f*
antiquarian *adj* antiquari·us -a -um
antiquarian *s* antiquar·ius -(i)i *m* (·a -ae *f*)
antiquated *adj* antiquat·us -a -um
antique *adj* prisc·us -a -um; **— statues** sign·a -orum *npl* operis antiqui
antique *s* antiqui artificis op·us -eris *n*
antiquity *s* antiquit·as -atis *f;* **in —** antiquitus [*adv*]
anti-Semitic *adj* Iudaeis avers·us -a -um
anti-Semitism *s* Iudaeorum od·ium -(i) *n*
antithesis *s* contrar·ium -(i)i *n*
antler *s* corn·u -us *n*
anus *s* an·us -i *m*
anxiety *s* anxiet·as -atis *f*
anxious *adj* anxi·us -a -um; *(eager)* **(for)** studios·us -a -um *(w. gen)*
anxiously *adv* anxie; *(eagerly)* avide
any *adj* ull·us -a -um; *(after* si, ne, nisi, num) quis, quid; **at — time** aliquando
any *adv* **— longer** diutius; **— more** amplius
anybody *pron* aliquis; *(after* si, nisi, ne, num) quis; *(interrog)* ecquis, numquis; *(after negative)* quisquam; **— else?** ecquis alius?; **— you wish** quisvis, quislibet
anyhow *adv* quoquomodo; *(in any event)* utique; *(just the same)* nec eo setius
anyone *see* **anybody**
anything *pron* aliquid, quicquam; *(after* si, nisi, ne, num) quid; *(interrog)* ecquid, numquid; *(after negative)* quiquam; **— else?** aliquid amplius, quicquam aliud; **— you wish** quidlibet; **hardly —** nihil fere
anyway *adv* quoquomodo; *(at least, in any event)* utique
anywhere *adv (in any place)* alicubi; *(frequently after* si) uspiam; *(usu. w. negative)* usquam; *(anywhere you please)* ubivis; *(to any place, usu. w.* si, ne, num) quo
aorta *s* grandis ven·a -ae *f* cordis
apart *adv* seorsum, separatim; **— from** praeter *(w. acc);* **to be —** distare; **to fall —** dilabi; **to set —** seponere; **to stand —** distare
apartment *s* diaet·a -ae *f*
apartment building *s* insul·a -ae *f*
apathetic *adj* lent·us -a -um
apathy *s* lentitud·o -inis *f*
ape *s* sim·ius -(i)i *m,* simi·a -ae *f*
ape *tr* imitari
Apennines *spl* Apenninus mon·s -tis *m*
aperture *s* foram·en -inis *n*
apex *s* cacum·en -inis *n*
aphorism *s* sententi·a -ae *f*
aphrodisiac *s* sature·um -i *n*
apiece *adv no exact Latin equivalent, but its sense is expressed by distributive numerals, e.g.:* **they went out with two garments —** cum binis vestimentis exierunt; **he stationed one legion — at Brindisium and Tarentum** legiones singulas posuit Brindisi, Tarenti
apocalypse *s* apocalyps·is -is *f*
apocryphal *adj* apocryph·us -a -um
apologetic *adj* se excus·ans -antis
apologize *intr* satis facere, se excusare; **I — to you** me tibi excuso; **to — for s.o.** aliquem excusare
apology *s* excusati·o -onis *f;* **please accept my apologies** quaeso, accipe excusationes; **to make an — for** excusare
apoplectic *adj* apoplectic·us -a -um
apostle *s* apostol·us -i *m*
apostolic *adj* apostolic·us -a -um
apostrophe *s* apostroph·e -es *f; (gram)* apostroph·us -i *f*
apothecary *s (drugstore)* tabern·a -ae *f* medicina; *(druggist)* medicamentar·ius -(i)i *m* (·a -ae *f*)
appall *tr* exterrēre
apparatus *s* apparat·us -ūs *m*
apparel *s* vestit·us -ūs *m*
apparel *tr* vestire
apparent *adj* manifest·us -a -um; *(seeming)* fict·us -a -um
apparently *adv* specie, per speciem; ut videtur
apparition *s* speci·es -ei *f*
appeal *intr (leg) (to a magistrate)* appellare *(acc); (to the people)* provocare (ad *w. acc);* **to — to** *(to be attractive to)* allicere; *(to the gods)* obtestari
appeal *s (leg)* appellati·o -onis *f; (to the people)* provocati·o -onis *f; (entreaty)* obtestati·o -onis *f; (attractiveness)* suavit·as -atis *f*
appealing *adj* suav·is -is -e; *(imploring)* suppl·ex -icis
appear *intr (to be visible)* apparēre; *(to show up)* comparēre; *(to arise suddenly)* oriri; *(to seem)* vidēri; *(in public, on the stage)* prodire; **to begin to —** patescere
appearance *s (becoming visible)* aspect·us -ūs *m; (outward show)* speci·es -ei *f; (likelihood)* similitud·o -inis *f; (vision)* vis·um -i *n;* **for the sake of —s** ad speciem; **to all —s** ut videtur; **to keep up —s** speciem gerere; **to make one's — in public** in publicum prodire; **to make one's — on the stage** in proscaenium prodire
appease *tr* placare
appeasement *s* placati·o -onis *f*

append *tr* subscribere
appendage *s* append·ix -icis *f*
appendicitis *s* appendicit·is -idis *f*
appendix *s* append·ix -icis *f; (anat)* append·ix -icis *f* coli
appetite *s* appetit·us -ūs *m; (for food)* cibi appetenti·a -ae *f;* **lack of —** inedi·a -ae *f;* **to control the —s** appetitūs regere
appetizer *s* gustati·o -onis *f*
applaud *tr* applaudere *(w. acc or dat); (to praise)* approbare **||** *intr* plaudere
applause *s* plaus·us -ūs *m;* **to look for —** plausūs captare
apple *s* mal·um -i *n;* **— of my eye** meus ocell·us -i *m*
applecart *s* **to upset the —** plaustrum percellere
apple peel *s* malicor·ium -(i)i *n*
apple pie *s* mala *npl* in crusto cocta
apple tree *s* mal·us -i *f*
appliance *s* instrument·um -i *n*
applicable *adj* (**to**) commod·us -a -um *(w. dat)*
applicant *s* petit·or -oris *m*
application *s (act of requesting)* petiti·o -onis *f; (act of applying)* adhibiti·o -onis *f; (industry)* sedulit·as -atis *f; (med)* foment·um -i *n*
apply *tr (to put on or to)* (**to**) adhibēre *(w. dat or* ad *w. acc); (to wounds)* inponere *(w. dat or* in *w. acc);* **to — oneself to** se conferre ad *(w. acc);* **to — the mind to** animum adhibēre ad *(w. acc)* **||** *intr* **to — to** pertinēre ad *(w. acc),* cadere in *(w. acc);* **to — for** petere
appoint *tr* designare, creare, dicere
appointment *s* creati·o -onis *f; (agreement to meet)* constitut·um -i *n; (order)* mandat·um -i *n;* **I have an — with you** constitutum tecum habeo; **to keep an —** ad constitutum venire
apportion *tr* dividere
apportionment *s* divisi·o -onis *f*
apposition *s* appositi·o -onis *f;* **a noun in — with** vocabulum appositum *(w. dat)*
appraisal *s* aestimati·o -onis *f; (com, fin)* taxati·o -onis *f*
appraise *tr* aestimare; *(com, fin)* taxare
appraiser *s* aestimat·or -oris *m; (com, fin)* taxat·or -oris *m*
appreciable *adj* aestimabil·is -is -e, haud exigu·us -a -um
appreciate *tr (to esteem)* magni aestimare; *(to discern)* cognoscere
appreciation *s* aestimati·o -onis *f; (gratitude)* grati·a -ae *f;* **to show — to s.o. for** gratiam alicui referre ob *(w. acc)*
apprehend *tr (to arrest; to grasp)* apprehendere
apprehension *s (arrest; understanding)* apprehensi·o -onis *f; (fear)* tim·or -oris *m,* sollicitud·o -inis *f*
apprehensive *adj* sollicit·us -a -um
apprentice *s* tir·o -onis *m*
apprenticeship *s* tirocin·ium -(i)i *n*
approach *tr* appropinquare *(w. dat); (to approximate)* accedere *(w. dat or* ad *w. acc)* **||** *intr* appropinquare, accedere; *(of an event)* appetere
approach *s* access·us -ūs *m; (of time)* appropinquati·o -onis *f; (by sea)* appuls·us -ūs *m*
approachable *adj (person)* facil·is -is -e; *(place)* pat·ens -entis
approbation *s* approbati·o -onis *f*
appropriate *adj* conveni·ens -entis, apt·us -a -um, idone·us -a -um; **it is — to** convenit *(w. inf or acc & inf)*
appropriate *tr (to claim)* vindicare; *(to claim presumptuously)* arrogare; *(money)* (**to**) dicere *(w. dat)*
appropriately *adv* apte, congruenter
appropriateness *s* convenienti·a -ae *f,* congruenti·a -ae *f*
appropriation *s* vindicati·o -onis *f; (of money)* (**for**) destinati·o -onis *f* (in *w. acc)*
approval *s* approbati·o -onis *f*
approve *tr* approbare; *(a law)* sciscere **||** *intr* **to — of** probare
approved *adj* probat·us -a - um
approximate *adj* proxim·us -a -um
approximate *tr* accedere ad *(w. acc)*
approximately *adv* prope, propemodum; *(w. numbers)* ad *(w. acc)*
apricot *s* armeniac·um -i *n*
apricot tree *s* armeniac·a -ae *f*
April *s* April·is -is *m or* mens·is -is *m* Aprilis; **in —** mense Aprili; **on the first of —** Kalendis Aprilibus
apron *s* sublig·ar -aris *n*
apt *adj* apt·us -a -um; **to be — to** *(w. inf)* solēre *(w. inf)*
aptitude *s* (**for**) ingen·ium -(i)i *n* (ad *w. acc)*
aptly *adv* apte
aptness *s (fitness)* convenienti·a -ae *f; (talent)* ingen·ium -(i)i *n; (tendency)* proclivit·as -atis *f*
aqueduct *s* aquaeduct·us -ūs *m*
arable *adj* arabil·is -is -e; **— land** arv·um -i *n*
arbiter *s* arbit·er -ri *m*
arbitrarily *adv* ad arbitrium
arbitrary *s* libidinos·us -a -um; *(imperious)* imperios·us -a -um
arbitrate *tr & intr* disceptare
arbitration *s* arbitr·ium -(i)i *n*
arbitrator *s* arbi·ter -tri *m*
arbor *s* umbracul·um -i *n*
arc *s* arc·us -ūs *m*
arcade *s* portic·us -ūs *f*
arch *s* arc·us -ūs *m,* forn·ix -icis *f*
arch *tr* arcuare, fornicare
arch *adj (chief)* summ·us -a -um; **— enemy** summus (·a) adversar·ius -(i)i *m* (·a -ae *f*)

archaeological *adj* archaeologic•us -a -um
archaeologist *s* archaeolog•us -i *m* (•a -ae *f*); **—s excavated this site** achaeologi hunc situm excaverunt
archaeology *s* archaeologi•a -ae *f*
archaic *adj* prisc•us -a -um
archaism *s* locuti•o -onis *f* obsoleta
archbishop *s* archiepiscop•us -i *m*
archer *s* sagittar•ius -(i)i *m; (astr)* Arcite-n•ens -entis *m*
archery *s* ar•s -tis *f* sagittandi
architect *s* architect•us -i *m (•a -ae f)*
architectural *adj* architectonic•us -a -um
architecture *s* architectur•a -ae *f*
archives *spl* tabul•ae -arum *fpl; (place)* tabular•ium -(i)i *n*
arctic *adj* arctic•us -a -um
ardent *adj* ard•ens -entis
ardently *adv* ardenter
ardor *s* ard•or -oris *m*
arduous *adj* ardu•us -a -um
area *s (open space; in geometry)* are•a -ae *f; (region)* regi•o -onis *f*
area code (telephonicus) numer•us -i *m* pralectorius
arena *s* (h)aren•a -ae *f*
Argonaut *s* argonaut•a -ae *m*
argue *tr (to reason)* arguere; *(to discuss)* disceptare de *(w. abl)*; **to — a case** causam agere **||** *intr* disputare; *(to wrangle)* altercari; **stop arguing** desine *(pl:* desinite) altercari
argument *s (discussion)* disputati•o -onis *f; (heated)* altercati•o -onis *f; (reason in support of a position)* argument•um -i *n;* **the force of his —** vis *f* argumenti eius; **to get into an —** in litem ambiguam descendere; **to put up an —** recusare
argumentative *adj* litigios•us -a -um
arid *adj* arid•us -a -um; *(fig)* ieiun•us -a -um
aright *adv* recte
arise *intr* surgere; *(of a group)* consurgere; *(of a storm, etc.)* oriri, cooriri; *(suddenly)* exoriri; *(to come into existence)* exsistere; *(to originate)* (**from**) nasci (ex *w. abl)*
aristocracy *s (class)* optimat•es -ium *mpl; (government)* optimatium dominat•us -ūs *m*
aristocrat *s* optim•as -atis *m; f*
aristocratic *adj* patrici•us -a -um
arithmetic *s* arithmetic•a -ae *f*
ark *s* arc•a -ae *f*
arm *tr* armare
arm *s* bracch•ium -(i)i *n; (upper arm)* lacert•us -i *m; (of the sea)* sin•us -ūs *m; (of a chair)* anc•on -onis *m;* **at —'s length** eminus *[adv];* **to carry in one's —s** in manibus gestare; **to carry under one's —s** sub alā portare; **with —s akimbo** ansat•us -a -um; **with folded —s** compressis manibus; **with open —s** sinu complexuque **||** *spl* arm•a -orum *npl;* **by force of —** vi et armis; **to be under —** in armis esse; **to lay down —** ab armis discedere; **to take up —** arma sumere
armaments *spl* apparat•us -ūs *m* belli
armchair *s* anconibus fabrefacta sell•a -ae *f*
armed *adj* armat•us -a -um
armistice *s* induti•ae -arum *fpl;* **to break off an —** indutias tollere
armlet *s* bracchiol•um -i *n; (bracelet)* armill•a -ae *f*
armor *s* arm•a -orum *npl*
armory *s* armamentar•ium -(i)i *n*
armpit *s* al•a -ae *f*
arms *see* **arm**
army *s* exercit•us -ūs *m; (in battle)* aci•es -ei *f; (on the march)* agm•en -inis *n;* **to join the —** ad militiam ire; **to raise an —** exercitum comparare
aroma *s* arom•a -atis *n; (of wine)* flo•s -ris *m*
aromatic *adj* aromatic•us -a -um
around *adv* circum, circa; **all —** undique
around *prep* circum *(w. acc); (approximately)* circa, ad *(w. acc)*
arouse *tr (feelings)* suscitare, exagitare; *(to wake up)* e somno excitare; *(fig)* excitare; **to — suspicion** suspicionem movēre
arraign *tr* accusare
arraignment *s* accusati•o -onis *f*
arrange *tr (to set in order)* ordinare; *(the hair)* componere, comere; *(a plan, meeting)* constituere; *(matters, a cloak to hang properly)* collocare; *(to agree)* pacisci; *(to put each thing separately in its place)* digerere; **—ed in a circle** in orbe disposit•us -a -um
arrangement *s* ord•o -inis *m; (of the year, of elections)* ordinati•o -onis *f; (of matters, of a garment)* collocati•o -onis *f; (of a speech, of books)* context•us -ūs *m;* **the — was that** convenit ut
array *s* vestit•us -ūs *m; (mil)* aci•es -ei *f*
array *tr* vestire; *(mil)* instituere
arrears *spl* reliqu•a -orum *npl,* residuae pecuni•ae -arum *fpl;* **to be in —** relinqui
arrest *s* prehensi•o -onis *f*
arrest *tr* (ap)prehendere; *(movement)* tardare; **to — the attention of all** omnes in se convertere
arrival *s* advent•us -ūs *m; (by sea)* appuls•us -ūs *m*
arrive *intr* advenire; *(by ship or on horseback)* advehi; *(of a ship)* appelli; **to — at** pervenire ad *(w. acc);* **to — before the messengers** nuntios praevenire; **to — in** *(a place, country)* pervenire in *(w. acc)*
arrogance *s* arroganti•a -ae *f*
arrogant *adj* arrog•ans -antis
arrogantly *adv* arroganter
arrow *s* sagitt•a -ae *f*
arrowhead *s* spicul•um -i *n*
arsenal *s* armamentar•ium -(i)i *n; (naval)* naval•ia -ium *npl*

arsenic *s* arsenic·um -i *n*
arson *s* incend·ium -(i)i *n* malo dolo
arsonist *s* incendiar·ius -(i)i *m* (·a -ae *f*)
art *s* ar·s -tis *f; (practice of some craft)* artific·ium -(i)i *n;* **fine —s** art·es -ium *fpl* elegantes; **to study —** artis studēre
artery *s* arteri·a -ae *f*
artful *adj* callid·us -a -um
artfully *adv* callide
art gallery *s* pinacothec·a -ae *f*
arthritis arthrit·is -idis *f,* articulorum dol·or -oris *m*
artichoke cinar·a -ae *f*
article *s (object)* res rei *f; (ware)* mer·x -cis *f; (term)* condici·o -onis *f; (in newspaper or magazine)* commentariol·us -i *m,* commentati·o -onis *f; (clause in a law)* cap·ut -itis *n; (gram)* articul·us -i *m;* **— of faith** decretum -i *n* fidei; **definite (indefinite) —** finitus (infinitus) articulus
articulate *tr* articulatim dicere
articulate *adj* dilucid·us -a -um
articulately *adv* articulate
articulation *s (distinct utterance)* explanati·o -onis *f; (anat)* commissur·a -ae *f*
artifice *s* artific·ium -(i)i *n*
artificial *adj (produced by human hands)* artificios·us -a -um; *(not genuine)* factici·us -a -um
artificially *adv* arte; *(by human hands)* manu
artillery *s* torment·a -orum *npl*
artisan *s* opif·ex -icis *mf; (usu. in hard material)* fa·ber -bri *m*
artist *s (of any of the fine arts)* artif·ex -icis *mf; (painter)* pict·or -oris *m* (·rix -ricis *f*)
artistic *adj* artif·ex -icis
artistically *adv* artificiose
as *conj & adv* ut; *(while)* ut, dum, cum; *(as article of comparison, denoting equality)* atque, ac; *(for example)* velut, ut, sicut; *(because)* cum; **— … —** *(degree)* tam … quam, aeque … atque; **— far —** quo(a)d; **— far — I know** quod scio; **— for instance** ut puta; **— good —** aeque bonus atque; **— great —** tantus … quantus; **— if** quasi; **— is** ut est; **— it were** tamquam; **— long —** tamdiu, tantisper dum, quam diu; **— many —** totidem; **— much** tantum; **— often —** toties … quoties; **— soon —** cum primum: **— soon as possible** quam primum; **— though** quasi; **— well —** ac, atque; **— yet** adhuc; **just — if** perinde ac si; **not — yet** nondum
ascend *tr & intr* ascendere
ascendency *s (superior influence)* potenti·a -ae *f;* **to gain the —** superior fieri
ascension *s* ascensi·o -onis *f*
ascent *s* ascensi·o -onis *f,* ascens·us -ūs *m;* **during the — to the summit** dum in summum ascenditur
ascertain *tr* comperire
ascetic *adj* ascetic·us -a -um
ascribe *tr* ascribere
ash *s* cin·is -eris *m; (tree)* fraxin·us -i *f;* **—es** cin·is -eris *m; (esp. ashes of the dead)* ciner·es -um *mpl*
ashamed *adj* pudibund·us -a -um; **I am — of** pudet me *(w. gen);* **I am — to tell** pudet me referre; **there is nothing to be — of** non est quod pudeatur
ashen *adj* pallid·us -a -um
ashore *adv (motion)* in terram; *(rest)* in litore; **to go —** in terram egredi
Asia *s* Asi·a -ae *f*
Asian *adj* Asian·us -a -um
Asiatic *adj* Asiatic·us -a -um
aside *adv* seorsum; **to call —** evocare; **to set** *or* **put —** seponere; **to take —** seducere; **to turn —** deflectere
aside from *prep* praeter *(w. acc)*
asinine *adj* asinin·us -a -um
ask *tr* rogare; *(esp. to seek information)* quaerere; *(to beg, petition for, esp. of a request made to a superior)* petere; *(to demand)* poscere, postulare; quaerere; **he —ed me whether** quaesivit a me *(or* de me *or* ex me) num; **he —ed you a question** ille te interrogavit; **I — you this question** hoc te rogo; **to — a few questions** pauca quaerere; **to — further questions** quaerere ultra; **to — many questions** multa quaerere *or* rogare; **to — one question after another** aliud ex alio quaerere; **to — questions** interrogare; **to — s.o. for s.th.** aliquem aliquid rogare; **to — that (that not)** rogare *(w.* ut *or* ne *w. subj);* **to — this question** hoc quaerere; **to — why** requirere quamobrem **||** *intr* **to — about (s.o., s.th)** de aliquo rogare; **to — for** petere
askance *adv* **to look — (at)** limis oculis aspicere
asleep *adj* dormi·ens -entis; **half —** semisomn·us -a -um; **to be (sound) —** (arte) dormire; **to fall —** obdormiscere
asparagus *s* asparag·us -i *m*
aspect *s* aspect·us -ūs *m*
asphalt *s* bitum·en -inis *n*
asphyxiation *s* asphyxi·a -ae *f*
aspirant *s* **(to)** appetit·or -oris *m (w. gen)*
aspiration *s* affectati·o -onis *f;* **to have lofty —s** magna spectare
aspire *intr* **to — to** appetere, affectare
aspiring *adj* **(after)** appet·ens -entis *(w. gen)*
ass *s* asin·us -i *m,* asin·a -ae *f; (fool)* asin·us -i *m; (anat)* clun·es -ium *mpl*
assail *tr* appetere; *(mil)* oppugnare
assailable *adj* expugnabil·is -is -e
assailant *s* oppugnat·or -oris *m*
assassin *s* percuss·or -oris *m,* parricid·a -ae *m*
assassinate *tr* per insidias interficere
assassination *s* caed·es -is *f* per īnsidias

assault *s* oppugnati·o -onis *f;* **aggravated — *(leg)*** vis *f;* **— and battery** vis *f* inlata; **sexual —** stuprati·o -onis *f;* **to take by —** expugnare
assault *tr (a person)* manūs inferre *(w. dat); (sexually)* stuprum īnferre *(w. dat); (mil)* oppugnare
assemblage *s* congregati·o -onis *f*
assemble *tr* cogere; *(to call together)* convocare **‖** *intr* convenire
assembly *s* coet·us -ūs *m; (mil, pol)* conti·o -onis *f; (electoral)* comiti·a -orum *npl;* **in the —** pro contione; **to hold an —** comitia *(or* contionem) habēre
assent *s* assens·us -ūs *m*
assent *intr* **(to)** assentiri *(w. dat);* **to — to a request** petenti annuere
assert *tr* affirmare, confirmare; *(to maintain, claim)* asserere
assertion *s* affirmati·o -onis *f; (claim)* asserti·o -onis *f*
assess *tr* taxare; *(for tax purposes)* censēre
assessment *s* taxati·o -onis *f; (for tax purposes)* cens·us -ūs *m*
assessor *s* cens·or -oris *m*
assets *spl* bon·a -orum *npl*
assiduous *adj* assidu·us -a -um
assiduously *adv* assidue
assign *tr* attribuere; *(land, duties)* assignare; *(time)* praestituere; *(task)* delegare; *(to allege)* afferre; *(in writing)* praescribere
assignment *s* attributi·o -onis *f; (of land, duties)* assignati·o -onis *f; (in school)* pens·um -i *n;* **to do the —** pensum *(or* praescriptum) perigere
assimilate *tr* assimulare; *(food)* digerere; *(knowledge)* concipere
assimilation *s* digesti·o -onis *f*
assist *tr* adesse *(w. dat),* adiuvare
assistance *s* auxil·ium -(i)i *n;* **to be of — to** auxilio esse *(w. dat)*
assistant *s* adiut·or -oris *m,* adiutr·ix -icis *f*
associate *s* soc·ius -(i)i *m* (·a -ae *f*)
associate *adj* soci·us -a -um
associate *tr* consociare, adiungere **‖** *intr* **to — with** familiariter uti *(w. dat)*
association *s* societ·as -atis *f;* **— with s.o** consociati·o -onis *f (w. gen)*
assort *tr* digerere
assortment *s (arrangement)* digesti·o -onis *f;* **a large — of jewelry** gemm·ae -arum *fpl* plurimae et cuiusve generis
assuage *tr* allevare
assume *tr* assumere; *(a task)* suscipere; *(improperly)* arrogare; *(to take for granted in argument)* ponere; *(a role)* induere
assumption *s* assumpti·o -onis *f; (improper)* arroganti·a -ae *f; (hypothesis)* sumpti·o -onis *f*
assurance *s* fiduci·a -ae *f; (confidence)* confidenti·a -ae *f; (guarantee)* fid·es -ei *f*
assure *tr (to promise)* confirmare, affirmare; **to be** *or* **feel —ed** confidere
assured *adj (e.g, victory)* explorat·us -a -um
assuredly *adv* profecto
asterisk *s* asterīsc·us -i *m*
asthma *s* asthm·a -atis *n;* **to have —** suspirio laborare
asthmatic *adj* asthmatic·us -a -um
astonish *tr* stupefacere
astonished *adj* attonit·us -a -um; **to be — at** obstupescĕre *(w. dat)*
astonishing *adj* mir·us -a -um
astonishingly *adv* admirabiliter
astonishment *s* admirati·o -onis *f; (speechlessness)* stup·or -oris *m*
astound *tr* (ob)stupefacere; **to be —ed** stupēre
astray *adv* vag·us -a -um; **to go —** errare; **to lead s.o. —** aliquem transversum agere
astrologer *s* astrolog·us -i *m,* mathematic·us -i *m*
astrology *s* astrologi·a -ae *f*
astronaut *s* astronaut·a -ae *m,* astronautri·a -ae *f*
astronomer *s* astrolog·us -i *m* (·a -ae *f*)
astronomical *adj* astronomic·us -a -um
astronomy *s* astronomi·a -ae *f*
astute *adj* astut·us -a -um
asylum *s* asyl·um -i *n*
at *prep (of place)* ad *(w. acc); (strictly, near)* apud *(w. acc); (usu. with names of towns, harbors, villas)* in *(w. abl), or locative case; (at the house of)* apud *(w. acc); (of time) use abl case;* **— all** omnino, prorsum; **— first** primo, initio; **— home** domi; **— least** duxtaxat, utique; **— most** summum; **— once** momento, continuo; **— present** in praesentiā; **— the right time** in tempore
atheism *s* deos esse negare *(used as a neuter noun)*
atheist *s* athe·os -i *m* (·a -ae *f*)
Athenian *adj* Athenae·us -a -um
Athenian *s* Atheniens·is -is *mf*
Athens *s* Athen·ae -arum *fpl*
athlete *s* athlet·a -ae *mf*
athletic *adj* athletic·us -a -um
athletics *spl* ar·s -tis *f* athletica
atlas *s* orbis terrarum descripti·o -onis *f*
atmosphere *s* cael·um -i *n*
atmospheric *adj* caeli *(gen)*
atom *s* atom·us -i *f*
atomic *adj* atomic·us -a -um; **— bomb** pyrobol·um -i *n* atomicum; **— energy** vis *f* atomica; **— theory** atomorum doctrin·a -ae *f*
atone *intr* **to — for** (ex)piare
atonement *s* expiati·o -onis *f*
atrocious *adj* atro·x -ocis
atrocity *s (atrociousness)* atrocit·as -atis *f; (deed)* atrox facin·us -eris *n*
attach *tr (to fasten to)* annectere, adiungere; *(e.g., meaning)* subicere; **to — importance to s.th.** aliquid magni aestimare; **to**

— oneself to s.o. se alicui adiungere; **to be —ed to** adhaerēre *(w. dat)*
attachment *s (contact)* iunctur·a -ae *f; (devotion)* stud·ium -(i)i *n;* **my — to the Roman people** studium meum in populum Romanum
attack *s* impet·us -ūs *m; (usu. on a town)* oppugnati·o -onis *f; (by cavalry)* incurs·us -ūs *m; (of a disease)* tentati·o -onis *f; (verbal)* petiti·o -onis *f*
attack *tr* aggredi; *(esp. w. physical force)* adoriri, vim īnferre *(w. dat)*; *(towns)* oppugnare; *(of a disease)*, tentare, invadere; *(verbally)* petere; **—ed by a sudden illness** corrept·us -a -um subitā valetudine
attacker *s* aggress·or -oris *m; (mil)* oppugnat·or -oris *m*
attain *tr* adipisci, cōnsequi; **to — to** pervenire ad *(w. acc)*
attainable *adj (by request)* impetrabil·is -is -e; **to be —** patēre
attempt *s* conat·us -ūs *m*
attempt *tr* conari, temptare, moliri
attend *tr (to accompany)* comitari; *(to escort)* prosequi; *(school, wedding, senate session)* frequentare; *(to be present at, e.g., a meeting)* adesse *(w. dat)*, interesse *(w. dat)*; *(of a doctor)* assidēre *(w. dat)*; **to — to** procurare, animadvertere, operam dare *(w. dat)*
attendance *s (in great numbers)* frequenti·a -ae *f; (of a doctor)* assiduit·as -atis *f*
attendant *adj* adiunct·us -a -um; **— circumstances** adiunct·a -orum *npl*
attendant *s (to officials)* apparit·or -oris *m; (servant)* minist·er -ri *m*, ministr·a -ae *f; (of a temple)* aeditu·us -i *m*
attention *s* attentus anim·us -i *m*, animi attenti·o -onis *f;* **pay attention!** attende! *(pl:* attendite!) *or* animum attende! *(pl:* animos attendite!); **pay — to what I am saying!** dictis meis attende! *(pl:* attendite!) **to attract —** animos hominum ad se convertere; **to call — to** indicare; **to call for —** animadverti iubēre; **to hold our —** animos nostros tenēre; **to pay — to** operam dare *(w. dat)*
attentive *adj* attent·us -a -um
attentively *adv* attente
attest *tr* testificare
attestation *s* testificati·o -onis *f*
attic *s* cenacul·um -i *n*
Attic *adj* Attic·us -a -um
Attica *s* Attic·a -ae *f*
attire *s* vestit·us -ūs *m*
attitude *s* habit·us -ūs *m; (of the body)* stat·us -ūs *m*
attorney *s* cognit·or -oris *m* (·rix -ricis *f*)
attorney general *s* advocat·us -i *m* (·a -ae *f*) fīsci

attract *tr (lit & fig)* trahere; **to — a buyer** emptorem adducere; **to — the attention of all** oculos omnium in se convertere
attraction *s* vis *f* attractionis; *(fig)* illecebr·a -ae *f*
attractive *adj* illecebros·us -a -um; *(esp. in looks)* specios·us -a -um, venust·us -a -um
attractively *adv* blande
attractiveness *s* lep·os -oris *m*
attributable *adj* ascribend·us -a -um
attribute *s* propr·ium -(i)i *n*, qualit·as -atis *f*
attribute *tr* (at)tribuere; *(to attribute wrongly)* affingere
attrition *s* attrit·us -ūs *m*
attune *tr* modulari
auburn *adj* fulv·us -a -um
auction *s* aucti·o -onis *f; (by the state)* hast·a -ae *f;* **to hold an —** auctionem habēre
auction *tr* **to —off** auctione vendere; *(by the state)* sub hastā vendere
auctioneer *s* praec·o -onis *m*
audacious *adj* aud·ax -acis
audaciously *adv* audacter
audacity *s* audaci·a -ae *f*
audible *adj* clar·us -a -um
audibly *adv* clarā voce
audience *s* auditor·es -um *mpl*, spectator·es -um *mpl; (bystanders)* coron·a -ae *f;* **to ask for a private —** secretum petere
audiocasette *s* phonocaset·a -ae *f*
audiotape *s* phonotaeni·a -ae *f*
audiovisual aid *s* audivisificum subsid·ium -(i)i *n*
audit *s* rationum inspecti·o -onis *f*
audit *tr* īnspicere ; (*educ*) extra ordinem audire
auditory *adj* auditori·us -a -um
Augean *adj* Augiae *(gen)*
augment *tr* augēre, ampliare ‖ *intr* augēri
augmentation *s* increment·um -i *n*
augur *s* aug·ur -uris *m;* **—'s staff** litu·us -i *m*
augur *intr* augurari
augury *s* augur·ium -(i)i *n*
August *s* August·us -i *m or* mens·is -is *m* Augustus; **on the first of —** Kalendis Augustis
Augustan *adj* Augustal·is -is -e
aunt *s (pateral)* amit·a -ae *f; (maternal)* materter·a -ae *f*
auricle *s* auricul·a -ae *f*
auspices *spl* auspic·ium -(i)i *n;* **to take the —** auspicari; **under the — of** sub clientela *(w. gen);* **without taking the —** inauspicato
auspicious *adj* fel·ix -icis
auspiciously *adv* feliciter
austere *adj* auster·us -a -um
austerely *adv* austere
austerity *s* austerit·as -atis *f*

authentic *adj* genuin·us -a -um
authenticate *tr* recognoscere
authenticity *s* auctorit·as -atis *f*
author *s (originator)* auct·or -oris *mf; (writer)* script·or -oris *m* (·rix -ricis *f*); *(inventor)* condit·or -oris *m*
authoritative *adj* grav·is -is -e; *(reliable)* cert·us -a -um; *(imperious)* imperios·us -a -um
authority *s* auctorit·as -atis *f; (leave)* licenti·a -ae *f; (power of a magistrate)* imper·ium -(i)i *n; (expert)* auct·or -oris *m;* **on good —** gravi auctore; **the authorities** magistrat·ūs -uum *mpl*
authorization *s* auctorit·as -atis *f*
authorize *tr* **to — s.o. to** auct·or -oris *m* esse alicui *(w. gerundive)*
authorship *s (origin)* auct·or -oris *m*
autobiography *s* lib·er -ri *m* de vitā suā
autocracy *s* dominati·o -onis *f*
autocrat *s* domin·us -i *m*
autocratic *adj* tyrannic·us -a -um
autograph *s* chirograph·um -i *n*
autograph *tr* manu suā scribere
automatic *adj* automatari·us -a -um
automobile *s* autocinet·um -ī *n*
autumn *s* autumn·us -i *m*
autumn(al) *adj* autumnal·is -is -e
auxiliaries *spl* auxili·a -orum *npl*
auxiliary *adj* auxiliar·is -is -e
avail *tr* prodesse *(w. dat);* **to — oneself of** uti *(w. abl);* **what do laws —?** quid leges faciunt? ‖ *intr* valēre
avail *s* **but to no —** sed frustra; **to be of no —** usui non esse
available *adj* in promptu; **to be —** praesto [*indecl*] esse
avalanche *s* nivis ruin·a -ae *f*
avarice *s* avariti·a -ae *f*
avaricious *adj* avar·us -a -um
avariciously *adv* avare
avenge *tr* ulcisci, vindicare
avenger *s* ult·or -oris *m,* vind·ex -icis *mf*
avenging *adj* ultr·ix -icis
avenue *s* vi·a -ae *f*
average *s* med·ium -(i)i *n;* **on the —** peraeque
average *adj* peraeque duct·us -a -um, modic·us -a -um
average *tr (to calculate)* peraeque ducere; *(to amount to)* peraequare
aversion *s* fastid·ium -(i)i *n;* **to have an — for** fastidire
avert *tr* avertere
avid *adj* avid·us -a -um
avidly *adv* avide
avocation *s* stud·ium -(i)i *n*
avoid *tr* evitare; *(a blow)* declinare
avoidable *adj* evitabil·is -is -e
avoidance *s* vitati·o -onis *f*
await *tr* exspectare, manēre
awake *adj* vigil·ans -antis, desomn·is -is -e; **to be —** vigilare; **to be — all night** pervigilare
awaken *tr* somno excitare ‖ *intr* expergisci
award *s* praem·ium -(i)i *n*
award *tr* tribuere; *(leg)* addicere
aware *adj* gnar·us -a -um; **to be — of** scire
awareness *s* cōnscienti·a -ae *f*
away *adv use verbs with prefix* ab-; **— with you!** abi hinc!; **far —** procul; **to be —** abesse; **to fly —** avolare; **to go —** abire
awe *s* reverenti·a -ae *f;* **to stand in — of** verēri
awesome *adj* verend·us -a -um; *(coll)* mirific·us -a -um
awful *adj* terribil·is -is -e
awfully *adv* terribiliter
awhile *adv* paulisper, aliquamdiu
awkward *adj* inept·us -a -um; *(unwieldly)* inhabil·is -is -e
awkwardly *adv* inepte
awkwardness *s* inepti·a -ae *f*
awning *s* velar·ium -(i)i *n*
awry *adv* oblique; **to go —** perquam evenire
ax *s* secur·is -is *f*
axiom *s* proloqu·ium -(i)i *n*
axis *s* ax·is -is *m*
axle *s* ax·is -is *m*
azure *adj* caerule·us -a -um

B

babble *s* garrulit·as -atis *f*
babble *intr* blatire; **to — on about** effutire
babbler *s* blater·o -onis *m*
babbling *adj* garrul·us -a -um
babe *s* inf·ans -antis *mf*
baby *s* inf·ans -antis *mf*
baby *tr* indulgēre *(w. dat)*
babyish *adj* infantil·is -is -e
bacchanal *s* bacch·ans -antis *m,* bacch·a -ae *f*
Bacchanalia *spl* bacchanal·ia -ium *npl*
bacchanalian *adj* bacchanal·is -is -e
Bacchic *adj* bacchic·us -a -um
Bacchus *s* Bacch·us -i *m*
bachelor *s* caeleb·s -is *m; (degree)* bacchelaure·us -i *m*
bachelorhood *s* caelibat·us -ūs *m*
back *s* terg·um -i *n,* dors·um -i *n;* **at one's —** a tergo; **— of the classroom** posterior par·s -tis *f* scholae; **— of the head** occipit·ium -(i)i *n;* **get off my —!** apage te a dorso meo!; **lying on one's —** resupin·us -a -um; **to climb on his —** super dorsum eius ascendere; **to turn one's — on** contemnere
back *adv* retro, retrorsum; *or use verbs with prefix* re- *or* retro-
back *tr* favēre *(w. dat)* ‖ *intr* **to — away from** refugere; **to — down** recedere; **to**

— out se recipere; **to — up** retrogradi; *(of water)* refluere
backboard *s* plute·us -i *m*
backbone *s* spin·a -ae *f*
back door *s* postic·um -i *n*
backer *s* faut·or -oris *m; (pol)* suffragat·or -oris *m*
background *s (in paintings)* abscedent·ia -ium *npl; (causes)* ort·ūs -ūs *m; (of a person)* prior aet·as -atis *f*
backpack *s* manic·a -ae *f*
back seat *s* sed·es -is *f* posterior
backside *s (anat)* clun·es -ium *mpl*
backstairs *spl* posticae scal·ae -arum *fpl*
backstroke *s* natati·o -onis *f* resupina; **to do the —** natare resupin·us -a -um
backward *adv* retro, retrorsum
backward *adj (reversed)* supin·us -a -um; *(slow)* tard·us -a -um; **to be —** cunctari
backwardness *s* tardit·as -atis *f*
bacon *s* lard·us -i *m;* **to bring home the —** habēre panem
bad *adj* mal·us -a -um; *(usu. morally bad)* improb·us -a -um; *(health, weather)* advers·us -a -um; *(harmful)* noxi·us -a -um; *(road)* iniqu·us -a -um; *(rotten)* putid·us -a -um; **— news** acerbum nunt·ium -(i)i *n;* **it is — to** *(w. inf)* alienum est *(w. inf);* **to go —** corrumpi; **too bad about Cicero** male de Cicerone; **wine is — for you** alienum tibi vinum est
badge *s* insign·e -is *n*
badger *tr* vexare
badly *adv* male; improbe; **to want —** valde cupere
badminton *s* lud·us -i *m* pilae pinnatae; **to play —** pilā pinnatā ludere
badness *s* maliti·a -ae *f; (moral)* improbit·as -atis *f*
baffle *tr* eludere
bag *s* sacc·us -i *m; (dim.)* saccul·us -i *m; (handbag)* bulg·a -ae *f*
baggage *s* sarcin·ae -arum *fpl; (mil)* impediment·a -orum *npl*
bagpipes *s* utricular·ium -(i)i *n;* **to play the —** utriculario ludere
bail *s* vadimon·ium -(i)i *n;* **to be out on —** vadari; **to put up — for** spondēre pro *(w. abl)*
bail *tr* **to — s.o. out** *(leg)* aliquem vadari; *(fig)* aliquem e periculo servare; **to — out the boat** sentinam e navicula egerere; **to — out water** sentinam egerere
bailiff *s (in a courtroom)* viat·or -oris *m; (manager of an estate)* villic·us -i *m*
bait *s* esc·a -ae *f; (fig)* incitament·um -i *n;* **to put the — on the hook** escam hamo imponere
bait *tr* inescare; *(to tease)* lacessere
bake *tr* coquere
baker *s* pist·or -oris *m,* pistr·ix -icis *f*
bakery *s* pistrin·a -ae *f*
balance *s (pair of scales)* trutin·a -ae *f; (equilibrium)* aequilibr·ium -(i)i *n; (in bookkeeping)* reliqu·a -orum *npl; (fig)* compensati·o -onis *f*
balance *tr* librare; **to — accounts** rationes dispungere; **to — joy with grief** laetitiam cum doloribus compensare ‖ *intr* constare; **the account —s** ratio constat
balance sheet *s* rati·o -onis *f* accepti et expēnsi
balancing *s* **— of accounts** dispuncti·o -onis *f*
balcony *s* maenian·um -i *n*
bald *adj* calv·us -a -um; *(style)* arid·us -a -um; **— head** *(person)* calvit·ium -(i)i *n;* **to be —** calvēre
baldhead *s* calv·us -i *m*
baldness *s* calvit·ium -(i)i *n; (of style)* arid·it·as -atis *f*
bale *s* fasc·is -is *m*
bale *tr (hay)* in fasces colligere
balk *tr* frustrari
ball *s* globul·us -i *m; (for playing)* pil·a -ae *f, (inflated)* foll·is -is *f;* **—s** *(anat) (sl) (lit & fig)* cole·i -orum *mpl;* **to play —** pilā ludere **to throw the —** follem *or* pollem coniecere
ballad *s* carm·en -inis *n*
ballet *s* saltati·o -onis *f*
ballet dancer *s* pantomim·us -i *m,* (·a -ae *f*)
ball field *s* camp·us -i *m* lusorius
ball game *s* lus·us -us *m* pilae *or* follis
ballot *s* suffrag·ium -(i)i *n;* **to cast a —** suffragium ferre
ballot box *s* suffragiorum cist·a -ae *f*
ballpoint pen *s* stil·us -i *m* sphaeratus
balm *s* balsam·um -i *n*
baloney *s* farcim·en -inis *n*; **baloney!** fabulae!
bamboo *s* arund·o -inis *f* Indica
bamboozle *tr* verba dare *(w. dat)*
ban *s* interdict·um -i *n*
ban *tr* interdicere
banana *s* arien·a -ae *f*
band *s (group)* man·us -ūs *f; (gang)* caterv·a -ae *f; (for the head)* inful·a -ae *f; (of musicians)* symphoni·a -ae *f*
band *intr* **to — together** coniungi; *(pej)* coniurare
bandage *s* fasci·a -ae *f*
bandage *tr (a wound)* astringere; *(an arm, etc.)* deligare
bandit *s* latr·o -onis *m*
banditry *s* latrocin·ium -(i)i *n*
bang *s* sonit·us -ūs *m,* crepit·us -ūs *m*
bang *tr* verberare; **to — together** concrepare ‖ *intr* sonitum facere; **to — on the door** fores pulsare
bangs *(of hair)* anti·ae -arum *fpl*
banish *tr (from the confines of a state)* exterminare; *(usual formula in time of Cicero)* aquā et igni interdicere; *(tem-*

porarily) relegare; *(to some island)* deportare; *(cares, etc.)* pellere, eximere
banishment *s (act)* relegati·o -onis *f,* interdicti·o -onis *f* aquā et igni; *(state)* exil·ium -(i)i *n*
banister *s* epimed·ion -(i)i *n*
bank *intr* **to — on** niti *(w. abl)*
bank *s (of river)* rip·a -ae *f; (of earth)* agg·er -eris *m; (com)* argentari·a -ae *f*
bank account *s* rati·o -onis *f* argentaria
bank book *s* libell·us -i *m* comparsorum
banker *s* argentar·ius -(i)i *m* (·a -ae *f*)
banking *s* argentaria negotiati·o -onis *f;* **to be engaged in —** argentariam facere
bank manager *s* argentariae modera·tor -toris *m* (·trix -tricis *f*)
bankrupt *adj* (creditoribus) decoct·us -a -um; *(fig)* in·ops -opis; **to be —** decoquere; **to go —** foro cedere, conturbare
bankruptcy *s* decocti·o -onis *f;* **to declare —** bonam copiam eiurare
bank teller *s* argentari·us -i *m* (·a -ae *f*)
bank window *s* ostiol·um -i *n* argentarium
banner *s* vexill·um -i *n*
banquet *s* conviv·ium -(i)i *n; (religious)* epul·ae -arum *fpl;* **to go to** *or* **attend a —** convivium inire
banter *s* cavillati·o -onis *f*
banter *intr* cavillari
bantering *s* cavillati·o -onis *f*
baptism *s* baptism·a -atis *n*
baptize *tr* baptizare
bar *s* vect·is -is *f; (of door)* ser·a -ae *f; (of gate)* ob·ex -icis *m; (ingot)* lat·er -eris *m; (legal profession)* for·um -i *n; (barroom)* oec·us -i *m* potorius; *(of chocolate or soap)* quadrul·a -ae *f;* **—s** *(of a cage)* clathr·i -orum *mpl;* **of the —** forens·is -is -e; **to practice at the —** causas agere
bar *tr (the door)* obserare; *(to keep away)* prohibēre; **to — s.o. from campaigning** submovēre aliquem petitione; **to — s.o.'s way** obstare alicui
barb *s* ham·us -i *m; (sting)* acule·us -i *m*
barbarian *adj* barbar·us -a -um
barbarian *s* barbar·us -i *m,* barbar·a -ae *f*
barbaric *adj* barbaric·us -a -um
barbarism *s* barbari·a -ae *f; (in speech)* barbarism·us -i *m*
barbarity *s* ferocit·as -atis *f*
barbarous *adj* barbar·us -a -um
barbed *adj* hamat·us -a -um
barbecue *tr* in craticulā assare
barbecue grill *s* craticul·a -ae *f*
barber *s* tons·or -oris *m,* tonstr·ix -icis *f*
barber chair *s* sell·a -ae *f* tonsoria
barbershop *s* tōnstrin·a -ae *f*
bard *s* vat·es -is *m*
bare *adj* nud·us -a -um; *(style)* press·us -a -um
bare *tr* nudare
barefaced *adj (shameless)* impud·ens -entis; *(unconcealed)* evidentissim·us -a -um
barefoot *adj & adv* nudis pedibus
bareheaded *adj* nudo capite
barely *adv* vix, aegre
bargain *s* pret·ium - (i)i *n* speciale; **a good —** empti·o -onis *f* secunda; **to buy at a —** bene emere; **to strike a —** pacisci
bargain *intr* pacisci; **to — for** depacisci
barge *s* lint·er -ris *f*
barge *intr* **to — in** *(coll)* intervenire
baritone *s* cant·or -oris *m* vocis gravis
bark *s (of tree)* cort·ex -icis *m; (of dog)* latrat·us -ūs *m; (ship)* rat·is -is *f*
bark *intr* latrare; **to — at** allatrare
barking *s* latrat·us -ūs *m*
barley *s* horde·um -i *n*
barley *adj* hordeac·us -a -um; **— flour** hordeaca farin·a -ae *f*
barmaid *s* cauponae ministr·a -ae *f*
barn *s* horre·um -i *n*
barnyard *s* cohor·s -tis *f*
barometer *s* barometr·um -i *n*
barometric *adj* barometric·us -a -um
baron *s* bar·o -onis *m*
barracks *spl* castr·a -orum *npl* stativa
barrel *s* cup·a -ae *f*
barren *adj* steril·is -is -e
barrenness *s* sterilit·as -atis *f*
barricade *s* claustr·a -orum *npl,* agg·er -eris *m; (of logs)* concaed·es -ium *fpl*
barricade *tr* obsaepire
barrier *s* sept·um -i *n; (fig)* claustr·a -orum *npl*
barrister *s* causidic·us -i *m* (·a -ae *f*)
bar stool *s* seliquastr·um -ī *n* praealtum
bartender *s* caup·o -onis *m,* inservit·or -oris *m*
barter *s* permutati·o -onis *f* mercium
barter *tr* mutare *(w. acc of thing given and abl of thing received);* **to — booty for wine** praedam vino mutare ‖ *intr* **(with)** merces mutare (cum *w. abl)*
base *adj* humil·is -is -e; *(morally)* turp·is -is -e; *(coinage)* adulterin·us -a -um
base *s (groundwork; of a column)* bas·is -is *f; (mil)* castr·a -orum *npl;* **first (second, third, home) —** basis prima (secunda, tertia, summa); **to play first (second, third) —** apud primam (secundam, tertiam) basim ludere
base *tr* fundare; **to — the country on laws** civitatem legibus fundare
baseball *s (the ball)* basipil·a -ae *f;* **— game** basipilae lus·us -us *m;* **to play —** basipilā lūdere
baseless *adj* van·us -a -um
basement *s* hypoge·um -i *n*
bash *tr (coll)* percutere; **to — in** perfringere; **to — in a man's head** alicui caput perfringere
bashful *adj* verecund·us -a -um

bashfully *adv* verecunde
bashfulness *s* verecundi·a -ae *f*
basic *adj* prim·us -a -um
basics *spl* element·a -orum *npl*
basic training *s* rudimenta *npl* militaria
basilica *s* basilic·a -ae *f*
basin *s* pelv·is -is *f; (reservoir)* lac·us -ūs *m*
basis *s* bas·is -is *f*
bask *intr* **to — in the sun** apricari
basket *s* corb·is -is *f; (money basket)* fisc·us -i *m; (for flowers, fruit)* calath·us -i *m; (small food basket)* sportell·a -ae *f*
basketball *s* corbifoll·is -is *m;* **to play —** corbifolle ludere
bas-relief *s* anaglypt·a -orum *npl; (on plates, vessels)* toreum·a -atis *n*
bass *s (fish)* perc·a -ae *f* fluvialis; *(mus)* son·us -i *m* gravissimus; **to sing —** voce imā cantare
bassinet *s* cun·ae -arum *fpl*
bass viol *s* contrabass·um -i *n*
bastard *adj* spuri·us -a -um
bastard *s* noth·us -i *m*
baste *tr* lardo perfundere; *(in sewing)* suturam *(w. gen)* solute suere
bat *s (bird)* vespertili·o -onis *m; (club)* clav·a -ae *f*
bat *tr & intr* clavo pulsare
batch *s* mass·a -ae *f; (pile)* cumul·us -i *m*
bath *s* balne·um -i *n; (public)* balne·a -orum *npl; (bath and community center)* therm·ae -arum *fpl;* **to take a cold (hot) —** frigidā (calidā) aquā lavari
bathe *tr* lavare; *(face, sore limb)* fovēre ‖ *intr* lavari
bather *s* qui (*or* quae) lavat; *(swimmer)* natat·or -oris *m* (·rix -ricis *f*); **—s** lavant·es -ium *mpl*
bathing *s* lavati·o -onis *f; (swimming)* natati·o -onis *f*
bathroom *s* balneol·um -i *n; (toilet)* loc·us -i *m* secretus; *(public toilet)* foric·a -ae *f*
bath towel *s* gausapin·a -ae *f*
bathtub *s* sol·ium -(i)i *n*
baton *s* virg·a -ae *f*
battalion *s* cohor·s -tis *f*
batter *s* farin·a -ae *f* lacte ovisque mixta
batter *s (in baseball)* clava·tor -toris *m* (·trix -tricis *f*)
batter *tr* verberare; *(to shake by battering)* percutere; **to — down** ariete deicere
battering ram *s* ari·es -etis *m*
battery *s* accumulatr·um -i *n*
battle *s (general & mil)* pugn·a -ae *f; (mil)* proel·ium -(i)i *n;* **naval — off** pugna navalis ante *(w. acc);* **the — of** *(at or near a town)* proelium apud *or* ad *(w. acc);* **to fight a —** proelium facere
battle *tr* certare ‖ *intr* proeliari
battle-ax *s* bipenn·is -is *f*
battle-cry *s* clam·or -oris *m* militum; *(of barbarians)* barit·us -ūs *m*
battlefield *s* aci·es -ei *f*
battle formation *s* aci·es -ei *f*
battlement *s* pinn·a -ae *f*
baubles *spl* tric·ae -arum *fpl*
bawl *intr* clamitare; *(to cry)* flēre; *(of babies)* vagire
bawling *s* vociferati·o -onis *f; (crying)* flet·us -ūs *m; (by a baby)* vagit·us -ūs *m*
bay *s (of the sea)* sin·us -ūs *m; (tree)* laur·us -i *f;* **at —** obsess·us -a -um; **to keep at —** arcēre
bay *adj (light-colored)* helv·us -a -um; *(horse)* spad·ix -icis; *(of bay tree)* laure·us -a -um
bay *intr* ululare
bayonet *s* pugi·o -onis *m*
bayonet *tr* pugione fodere
bazaar *s* for·um -i *n* rerum venalium
be *intr* esse; *(of a situation)* se habēre, versari; **— gone!** apage!; **that is the situation** sic res se habent; **to — absent** abesse; **to — against** adversari; **to — among** interesse *(w. dat);* **to — fine** bene se habēre; valēre; **to — for** favēre *(w. dat),* stare cum *(w. abl);* **to — present** adesse, interesse; **to — up for sale** vēnire; **to — up in years** aetate provect·us -a -um esse; **to — up to a task** operi par esse
beach *s* act·a -ae *f,* lit·us -oris *n*
beach *tr (a ship)* subducere
beach chair *s* sell·a -ae *f* litoralis *(or* cubitoria)
beacon *s* ign·is -is *m* in specula; *(lighthouse)* phar·us -i *f*
bead *s* bac·a -ae *f*
beagle *s* parvus can·is -is *m* venaticus
beak *s* rostr·um -i *n*
beaked *adj* rostrat·us -a -um
beaker *s (cup)* pocul·um -i *n; (decanter)* obb·a -ae *f*
beam *s (of wood)* trab·s -is *f; (of light)* iub·ar -aris *n; (ray)* rad·ius -(i)i *m*
beaming *adj* nit·ens -entis
bean *s* fab·a -ae *f; (kidney bean)* phasel·us -i *mf*
bear *tr (to carry)* portare, ferre; *(to endure)* ferre, pati; *(to produce)* ferre; *(to beget)* parere; **to — away** auferre; **to — in mind** recordari; **to — out** *(to confirm)* arguere; **to — witness** testari ‖ *intr* **to — down on** *(to approach)* appropinquare *(w. dat); (to press)* inniti in *(w. acc); (to oppress)* opprimere; **to — with** indulgēre *(w. dat)*
bear *s* urs·us -i *m,* urs·a -ae *f;* **—s grunt** ursi grunniunt
bearable *adj* tolerabil·is -is -e
bear cub *s* ursae catull·us -i *m*
beard *s* barb·a -ae *f; (of grain)* arist·a -ae *f;* **to cut his first —** barbatorium facere; **to grow a —** barbam summittere
bearded *adj* barbat·us -a -um
beardless *adj* inberb·is -is -e

bearer *s (porter)* baiul•us -i *m; (of litter)* lecticar•ius -(i)i *m; (of letter)* tabellar•ius -(i)i *m; (of news)* nunt•ius -(i)i *m*
bearing *s (posture)* gest•us -ūs *m; (direction)* regi•o -onis *f;* **to get one's —s** regionem reperire; **to have a — on** pertinēre ad *(w. acc)*
beast *s* besti•a -ae *f,* belu•a -ae *f; (brutish person)* belu•a -ae *f*
beastly *adj* beluin•us -a -um
beast of burden *s* iument•um -i *n*
beat *tr (to punish)* verberare; *(to knock on)* pulsare; *(to conquer)* vincere; *(the breast, drum)* plangere; **to — back** repellere; **to — down** demoliri; **to — in** perfringere; **to — the daylights out of** pulchre percopolare ‖ *intr* palpitare; **to — upon** *(of rain)* impluere in *(w. acc); (of waves)* illidere; **to — around the bush** circuitu uti, schemas loqui
beat *s (blow)* plag•a -ae *f,* ict•us -ūs *m; (of the heart)* palpitati•o -onis *f; (mus)* ict•us -ūs *m; (patrol area)* circuiti•o -onis *f*
beaten *adj (defeated)* vict•us -a -um; *(worn)* trit•us -a -um
beating *s* verberati•o -onis *f; (defeat)* repuls•a -ae *f; (of the heart)* palpitati•o -onis *f;* **to get a —** vapulare
beautician *s* orna•trix -tricis *f*
beautiful *adj* pul•cher -chra -chrum; *(shapely)* formos•us -a -um
beautifully *adv* pulchre
beautify *tr* ornare
beauty *s* pulchritud•o -inis *f*
beaver *s* fi•ber -bri *m*
because *conj* quod, quia, quoniam
because of *prep* ob, propter *(w. acc)*
beck *s* nut•us -ūs *m;* **at the — and call** ad arbitrium
beckon *tr* nutu vocare
become *tr* decēre ‖ *intr* fieri; **to — friends with me once again** in gratiam mecum redire
becoming *adj* dec•ens -entis
becomingly *adv* decenter
bed *s* lect•us -i *m; (small)* lectul•us -i *m; (in the garden)* areol•a -ae *f; (of a river)* alve•us -i *m;* **— of roses** rosar•ium -(i)i *n;* **to be confined to —** lecto teneri; **to get out of —** e lecto surgere; **to go to —** cubitum ire; **to make the —** lectum sternere
bedbug *s* sciniph•is -is *m*
bedding *s* stragul•um -i *n*
bed frame *s* spond•a -ae *f*
bedlam *s* tumult•us -ūs *m*
bedpost *s* fulcr•um -i *n*
bedraggled *adj* sordid•us -a -um
bedridden *adj* valetudinari•us -a -um; **to be — lecto** tenēri
bedroom *s* (dormitorium) cubicul•um -i *n*
bedspread *s* opertor•ium -(i)i *n*
bedstead *s* spond•a -ae *f*
bedtime *s* hor•a -ae *f* somni
bee *s* ap•is -is *f;* **—s buzz** apes bombilant
beech tree *s* fag•us -i *f*
beef *s* bubul•a *f;* **roast —** bubula assa
beefsteak *s* frust•um -i *n* bubulum
beehive *s* alve•us -i *m*
beeline *s* **to make a — for** directā viā contendere ad *(w. acc)*
beer *s* cer(e)visi•a -ae *f*
beer glass *s* hyal•us -i *m* cervisarius
beer mug *s* urce•us -i *m* cervisarius
beet *s* bet•a -ae *f*
beetle *s* scarabae•us -i *m*
befall *tr* contingere *(w. dat)* ‖ *intr* accidere, contingere
befit *tr* decēre
befitting *adj* dec•ens -entis; **it is —** decet
before *prep (in front of)* ante *(w. acc),* pro *(w. abl); (in time)* ante *(w. acc); (in the presence of)* coram *(w. abl); (leg)* apud *(w. acc);* **— all things** imprimis; **— long** propediem, iamdudum; **— now** antehac
before *conj* antequam, priusquam
beforehand *adv* antea
befriend *tr* in amicitiam recipere
beg *tr* petere, orare ‖ *intr* mendicare; **to — for** deprecari; *(alms)* mendicare; **to — s.o. to** aliquem deprecari ut *(w. subj);* **to — from door to door** ostiatim mendicare
beget *tr* gignere
beggar *s* mendic•us -i *m* (•a -ae *f*)
begging *s* mendicit•as -atis *f;* **to go —** mendicare
begin *tr & intr* incipere; *(without finishing)* inchoare; *(to initiate)* instituere; **to — at** incipere ab *(w. abl);* **to — to bloom** florescere; **to — with** primum (omnium)
beginner *s* tir•o -onis *mf*
beginning *s (the act of starting)* incepti•o -onis *f; (the start itself)* init•ium -(i)i *n; (origin)* orig•o -inis *f;* **at the — of winter** ineunte *or* primā hieme; **at the — of the year** ineunte anno, principio anni; **from the very —** iam inde a principio; **in the —** inter initia; **—s** principi•a -orum *npl*
begrudge *tr* **to — my enemy his victory** amici victoriae invidēre
beguile *tr* fraudare
behalf *s* **on — of** pro *(w. abl)*
behave *intr* se gerere; **to — oneself** se probe gerere; **to — toward** uti *(w. abl);* **well-behaved** bene morat•us -a -um
behavior *s* mor•es -um *mpl;* **your — towards me was unfriendly** inimice te in me gessisti
behead *tr* decollare
beheading *s* decollati•o -onis *f*
behind *adv* pone, a tergo; **to be left —** relinqui
behind *prep* post *(w. acc); (esp. w. verbs of motion)* pone *(w. acc); (in support)* pro *(w. abl);* **from —** a tergo; **to talk about a**

friend — his back absentem amicum rodere

behind *s (coll)* clun·es -ium *mpl,* postic·um -i *n*

behold *tr* conspicere

behold *interj* ecce!, en!

behoove *tr* **it behooves you to** *(w. inf)* oportet te *(w. inf)*

beige *adj* rav·us -a -um

being *s* en·s -tis *n;* **human —** hom·o -inis *m*

belabor *tr (to thrash)* verberare; *(to harp on)* cantare

belch *s* ruct·us -ūs *m*

belch *tr* **to — forth** eructare ‖ *intr* ructare

belfry *s* turr·is -is *f* campanis instructa

belie *tr (to prove false)* refellere; *(to disappoint)* frustrari; *(to disguise)* dissimulare

belief *s* fid·es -ei *f; (conviction) (in)* opini·o -onis *f (w. gen or* de *w. abl)*

believe *tr (thing)* credere; *(person)* credere *(w. dat); (to suppose)* existimare; **to make —** simulare

believer *s* cred·ens -entis *mf*

bell *s (large)* campan·a -ae *f; (small)* tintinnabul·um -i *n*

belle *s* bella puell·a -ae *f*

belligerent *adj (at war)* belliger·ans -antis; *(scrappy)* pugn·ax -acis

bellow *intr* mugire, boare

bell pepper *s* pip·er -eris *n* rotundum

bell tower *s* campanil·e -is *n*

belly *s* ven·ter -tris *m; (womb)* uter·us -i *m*

bellyache *s* tormin·a -um *npl;* **to have a —** dolēre a torminibus

belong *intr* **to — to** esse *(w. dat); (to be related)* pertinēre ad *(w. acc); (to be a member of)* in numero *(w. gen)* esse

belongings *spl* bon·a -orum *npl*

below *adj* infer·us -a -um

below *adv* infra

below *prep* infra *(w. acc)*

belt *s* cingul·um -i *n; (of women's clothes)* zon·a -ae *f; (sword belt)* balte·us -i *m; (area)* zon·a -ae *f;* **to tighten one's —** sumptui parcere

bemoan *tr* deplorare

bench *s* scamn·um -i *n; (esp. for senators and judges)* subsell·ium -(i)i *n; (for rowers)* transtr·um -i *n*

bend *tr* flectere, curvare; *(to cause to lean)* inclināre; *(the bow)* intendere, flectere; *(to persuade)* īnflectere; **to — back** reflectere; **to — down** deflectere ‖ *intr (e.g., of iron)* se inflectere; *(to give in)* cedere; **to — down** *or* **over** *(to stoop)* se inclinare, se demittere

bend *s* curvam·en -inis *n;* **— of the river** flex·us -ūs *m* fluminis; **— in the road** flex·us -ūs *m* viae infract·us -ūs *m*

bending *s* inclinati·o -onis *f*

beneath *adv* subter

beneath *prep* sub *(w. acc or abl);* **he thinks these matters are — him** arbitratur has res infra se positas

benefactor *s* largit·or -oris *m,* patron·us -i *m*

benefactress *s* patron·a -ae *f*

beneficence *s* beneficenti·a -ae *f*

beneficent *adj* benefi·cus -a -um

beneficial *adj* util·is -is -e, commod·us -a -um; **to be —** prodesse

benefit *s (deed)* benefic·ium -(i)i *n; (advantage)* commod·um -i *n;* **to have the — of** frui *(w. abl);* **to whose — is it?** cui bono est?

benefit *tr* prodesse *(w. dat),* iuvare ‖ *intr* proficere; *(financially)* lucrari; **to — from** utilitatem capere ex *(w. abl)*

benevolence *s* benevolenti·a -ae *f*

benevolent *adj* benevol·us -a -um

benevolently *adv* benevole

benign *adj* benign·us -a -um

bent *adj* flex·us -a -um, curv·us -a -um; **— backwards** recurv·us -a -um; **— forwards** pron·us -a -um; **— inwards** camur·us -a -um; **— on** *(fig)* attent·us -a -um ad *(w. acc)*

bent *s* curvatur·a -ae *f; (inclination)* inclinati·o -onis *f*

bequeath *tr* legare

bequest *s* legat·um -i *n*

bereave *tr* orbare

bereavement *s* orbit·as -atis *f*

bereft *adj* **— of** orbat·us -a -um *(w. abl or gen)*

berry *s* bac·a -ae *f*

berth *s (cabin)* diaet·a -ae *f; (space for ship at anchor)* stati·o -onis *f;* **to give wide — to** devitare

beseech *tr* obsecrare

beset *tr* urgēre; *(mil)* obsidēre

beside *prep* ad *(w. acc),* iuxta *(w. acc);* **— the point** nihil ad rem; **to be — oneself** delirare; **to sit — s.o.** assidēre alicui; **to walk — s.o.** alicui latus tegere

besides *adv* praeterea, ultro

besides *prep* praeter *(w. acc)*

besiege *tr* obsidēre; *(fig)* circumsedēre

best *adj* optim·us -a -um; *(most advantageous)* commodissim·us -a -um; *(friend)* summ·us -a -um; **it is — to** optimum est *(w. inf),* maxime prodest *(w. inf)*

best *s* flo·s -ris *m;* **to do one's —** pro virili parte agere; **to have the — of it** praevalēre; **to make the — of it** aequo animo ferre; **to the — of one's ability** pro viribus

best *tr* exsuperare

bestir *tr (to move)* ciēre; **to — oneself** *(to wake up)* expergisci

best man *s* pronub·us -i *m*

bestow *tr* **(on)** tribuere, deferre *(w. dat)*

bestowal *s* largiti·o -onis *f*

bet *s* sponsi•o -onis *f; (the stake)* pign•us -eris *n;* **to lose a —** sponsionis condemnari; **to win a —** sponsione vincere

bet *tr* ponere; **I — he has taken off** pono eum abivisse; **I — you he doesn't win** te sponsione provoco illum non esse victurum; **to — that . . .** spōnsionem facere *(w. acc & inf)*

betray *tr* prodere; *(feelings)* arguere

betrayer *s* prodit•or -oris *m*

betroth *tr* despondēre

betrothal *s* sponsal•ia -ium *npl*

betrothed *adj* spons•us -a -um

better *adj* mel•ior -ior -ius; *(preferable)* praestant•ior -ior -ius; **— half** *(fig)* alter•a -ae *f;* **for the —** in melius; **it is — to** *(w. inf)* commodius est *(w. inf);* **there, that's —** em istuc rectius; **to be —** *(in health)* melius esse; **to get —** convalescere; **to get the — of** praevalēre *(w. abl);* **where is your — half?** ubinam est tua altera?

better *adv* melius, potius

better *tr* meliorem *(or* melius) facere, corrigere; **to — oneself** proficere

betterment *s* correcti•o -onis *f*

betters *spl* melior•es -um *mpl*

between *prep* inter *(w. acc)*

bevel *tr* obliquare

beverage *s* pot•us -ūs *m*

bewail *tr* deplorare

beware *intr* cavēre; **to — of** cavēre

bewilder *tr* confundere

bewildered *adj* confus•us -a -um

bewilderment *s* confusi•o -onis *f*

bewitch *tr* fascinare; *(to charm)* demulcēre

beyond *adv* ultra

beyond *prep* ultra *(w. acc),* extra *(w. acc); (motion)* trans *(w. acc);* **to go — the limits** egredi extra terminos

bias *s (prejudice)* inclinati•o -onis *f; (line)* line•a -ae *f* obliqua

bias *tr* inclinare

Bible *s* Bibli•a -orum *npl*

Biblical *adj* Biblic•us -a -um

bibliography *s* bibliographi•a -ae *f*

bicker *intr* altercari

bickering *s* altercati•o -onis *f*

bicycle *s* birot•a -ae *f;* **to ride a —** birotā vehi

bicyclist *s* birotari•us -i *m* (•a -ae *f*)

bid *tr (to order)* iubēre; *(to invite)* invitare; *(at auction)* licitari; **to — farewell** valedicere

bid *s* licitati•o -onis *f;* **to make a —** licitationem facere

bidder *s* licitat•or -oris *m* (•rix -ricis *f*)

bidding *s (command)* iuss•um -i *n; (at auction)* licitati•o -onis *f;* **at his —** iussu eius; **to do s.o.'s —** iussum alicuius exsequi

bide *tr* **to — one's time** tempus idoneum opperiri

biennial *adj* biennial•is -is -e

bier *s* feretr•um -i *n; (euphem)* vitalis lect•us -i *m*

big *adj* magn•us -a -um, ing•ens -entis; **— with child** gravida; **— with young** praegn•ans -antis; **to talk —** ampullari

bigamist *s* bimarit•us -i *m*

bigamy *s* bigami•a -ae *f*

big-hearted magnanim•us -a -um

bigmouth *s* **bigmouth!** os durum!; **to be a —** *(coll)* durae buccae esse

bigot *s* qui suae opinioni nimium fidit

bigoted *adj* obstinate suae opinioni de partibus *(or* de religione *or* de genere) dedit•us -a -um

bigotry *s* nimia suae de partibus *(or* de religione *or* de genere) opinioni fiduci•a -ae *f*

big toe *s* poll•ex icis *m*

bile *s* bil•is -is *f*

bilk *tr* fraudare

bill *s (of bird)* rostr•um -i *n; (proposed law)* rogati•o -onis *f; (of money owed)* rati•o -onis *f* debiti; *(paper money)* numm•us -i *m* chartarius; **ten-dollar —** nummus chartarius decem dollarorum; **— of indictment** subscripti•o -onis *f;* **to introduce a —** legem ferre; **to pass a —** legem perferre; **to turn down a —** legem *or* rogationem antiquare

bill collector *s* flagitat•or -oris *m* (•rix -ricis *f*)

billion *s* billi•o -onis *f*

billow *s* fluct•us -ūs *m*

bin *s (in wine cellar)* locul•us -i *m; (for grain)* lac•us -ūs *m*

bind *tr* ligare; *(wounds)* stringere; *(to obligate)* obligare; *(books)* conglutinare; **to — fast** devincere; **to — together** colligare; **to — up** alligare; *(med)* astringere

binding *adj* obligatori•us -a -um; *(law)* rat•us -a -um

binding *s* religati•o -onis *f*

binoculars *spl* binocular•es -um *mpl*

biographer *s* vitae scrip•tor -toris *m* (•trix -tricis *f*), biograph•us -i *m* (-a -ae *f*)

biographical *adj* ad memoriam vitae pertinens

biography *s* vit•a -ae *f*

biological *adj* biologic•us -a -um; **— warfare** bellum biologicum

biology *s* biologi•a -ae *f*

biologist *s* biologic•us -i *m*

birch *adj* betulin•us -a -um

birch tree *s* betul•a -ae *f*

bird *s* av•is -is *f;* **—s of a feather flock together** pares cum paribus facillime congregantur

birdcage *s* cave•a -ae *f*

bird's nest *s* nid•us -i *m*

birth *s* part•us -ūs *m; (lineage)* gen•us -eris *n*

birthday *s* di•es -ei *m* natalis *(or simply* natalis); **Happy —!** Felicem Natalem (tibi exopto)!
birthday cake *s* lib•um -i *n* (natalicium)
birthday party *s* natalici•a -ae *f;* **to throw a —** nataliciam agitare
birthday present *s* natalic•ium -(i)i *n*
birthplace *s* patri•a -ae *f*
birthright *s* iu•s -ris *n* e genere ortum
biscuit *s* crustul•um -i *n*
bisect *tr* in duas partes aequales secare
bishop *s* episcop•us -i *m*
bison *s* bis•on -ontis *m*
bit *s (for horse)* fren•um -i *n; (small amount)* aliquantul•um -i *n; (of food)* off•a -ae *f;* **a — of peace** aliquid quietis; **— by —** minutatim; **to cut (chop) to —s** minutatim secare (concidere)
bitch *s* can•is -is *f*
bite *s* mors•us -ūs *m; (by an insect, snake)* ict•us -ūs *m*
bite *tr* mordēre; *(of pepper, frost)* urere; *(of an insect)* icere
biting *adj (apt to bite)* mord•ax -acis; *(cutting)* asp•er -era -erum
bitter *adj (lit & fig)* amar•us -a -um; *(hatred)* asp•er -era -erum *(painful, sharp)* acerb•us -a -um; **— taste in the mouth** amarum o•s -ris *n*
bitterly *adv (denoting wounded feeling)* amare; *(implying anger or harshness)* aspere; *(implying hostility)* infense; **to complain —** graviter queri; **to cry —** ubertim flēre, graviter lacrimare
bitterness *s (esp. of taste)* amarit•as -atis *f; (fig)* acerbit•as -atis *f; (wounded feeling)* amaritud•o -inis *f*
bitters *spl* absinth•ium -(i)i *n*
bivouac *s* excubi•ae -arum *fpl*
bivouac *intr* excubare
blab *tr* blaterare; **to — out** effutire ‖ *intr* deblaterare
black *adj (shiny black)* ni•ger -gra -grum; *(dull black)* a•ter -tra -trum; *(looks)* tru•x -cis
black *s (color)* nigr•um -i *n; (person)* Aethi•ops -opis *m;* **dressed in —** pullat•us -a -um
black-and-blue *adj* livid•us -a -um; **— mark** liv•or -oris *m*
blackberry *s* mor•um -i *n*
blackbird *s* merul•a -ae *f*
blackboard *s* tabul•a -ae *f* atra, tabula scriptoria
blacken *tr* nigrare
black eye *s* ocul•us -i *m* sugillatus
blacklist *s* proscripti•o -onis *f*
blacklist *tr* proscribere
black magic *s* magicae art•es -ium *fpl*
blackness *s* nigriti•a -ae *f*
blacksmith *s* ferrarius fa•ber -bri *m*
bladder *s* vesic•a -ae *f*
blade *s (edge)* lamin•a -ae *f; (of grass)* herb•a -ae *f; (of oar)* palm•a -ae *f*
blamable *adj* culpabil•is -is -e
blame *tr* culpare; **to — s.o. for** aliquem culpare ob *(w. acc);* **I am to —** ego in culpā sum; **you are to —** in culpā es
blame *s* culp•a -ae *f;* **to push the — on s.o.** culpam conferre in *(w. acc)*
blameless *adj* inte•ger -gra -grum
blame-worthy *adj* vituperabil•is -is -e
bland *adj (food)* len•is -is -e
blank *adj* inan•is -is -e; *(expression)* stolid•us -a -um
blanket *s* lod•ix -icis *f; (dim.)* lodicul•a -ae *f;* **— of snow** tegim•en -inis *n* niveum
blare *s* strepit•us -ūs *m*
blare *intr* strepare
blaspheme *tr* blasphemare
blasphemous *adj* blasphem•us -a -um
blasphemy *s* blasphemi•a -ae *f*
blast *s (of wind)* flam•en -inis *n; (of musical instrument)* flat•us -ūs *m;* **— of wind** flat•us -ūs *m*
blast *tr* discutere
blaze *s (glare)* fulg•or -oris *m; (fire)* incend•ium -(i)i *n;* **go to —s** *(coll)* i in malam rem!
blaze *tr* **to — a trail** semitam notare ‖ *intr* ardēre; **fires were —ing** ignes flagrabant; **to — up** exardescere
bleach *tr* dealbare
bleachers *spl* for•i -orum *mpl*
bleak *adj* immit•is -is -e; *(outlook, hope)* incommod•us -a -um
bleary-eyed *adj* lipp•us -a -um; **to be —** lippire
bleed *intr* sanguinem fundere
bleeding *adj* crud•us -a -um
bleeding *s* sanguinis profusi•o -onis *f; (bloodletting)* sanguinis missi•o -onis *f*
blemish *s (flaw)* vit•ium -(i)i *n; (on the body)* mend•um -i *n; (moral)* macul•a -ae *f*
blemish *tr* maculare
blend *tr* commiscēre; **to — in** immiscēre ‖ *intr* **to — in with** se immiscēre *(w. dat)*.
blend *s* mixtur•a -ae *f; (proportionate)* temperi•es -ei *f*
blender machin•a -ae *f* concisoria
bless *tr* beare; *(consecrate)* consecrare; *(w. success)* secundare; *(eccl)* benedicere; **— you!** *(after s.o. has sneezed)* salve! *or* salutem!; **— you!** *or* **— your little heart!** di te ament!
blessed *adj* beat•us -a -um; *(of dead emperors)* div•us -a -um
blessing *s (thing)* bon•um -i *n; (eccl)* benedicti•o -onis *f*
blight *s* robig•o -inis *f; (fig)* tab•es -is *f*
blight *tr* robigine afficere; *(fig)* nocēre *(w. dat)*
blind *adj (lit & fig)* caec•us -a -um
blind *tr (lit & fig)* occaecare

blind alley *s* fundul•a -ae *f*
blindfold *tr* oculos obligare *(w. dat)*
blindfolded *adj* oculis obligatis
blindly *adv* temere
blindness *s* caecit•as -atis *f*
blinds *spl (on window)* transenn•a -ae *f;* **to close (open) the —** transennam aperire (demittere)
blink *intr* connivēre
bliss *s* beatitud•o -inis *f*
blissful *adj* beat•us -a -um
blissfully *adv* beate
blister *s* pustul•a -ae *f*
blister *intr* pustulare
bloated *adj* sufflat•us -a -um
block *s (of wood)* stip•es -itis *f; (of marble, stone)* mass•a -ae *f; (in a city)* vic•us -i *m; (obstruction)* impediment•um -i *n;* **— by —** vicatim
block *tr (e.g., the road)* obstruere; *(to choke up)* opplēre; **to — s.o.'s way** obstare alicui; **to — up** *(e.g. a window)* obstruere
blockade *s* obsidi•o -onis *f;* **to lift a —** obsidionem solvere; **to undergo a —** in obsidione teneri
blockade *tr* obsidēre
block and tackle *spl* trochle•a -ae *f*
blockhead *s* caud•ex -icis *m*
blond *adj* flav•us -a -um
blonde *s* flava femin•a -ae *f*
blood *s* sangu•is -inis *m; (outside the body)* cru•or -oris *m; (lineage)* gen•us -eris *n;* **there was bad — between him and Caesar** huic simultas cum Caesare intercedebat; **to stain with —** cruentare
bloodless *adj* exsangu•is -is -e; *(without bloodshed)* incruent•us -a -um
blood pressure *s* pressur•a -ae *f* sanguinis; **high —** hypertoni•a -ae *f*
blood-red *adj* sanguine•us -a -um
blood relative *s* consanguine•us -i *m* (•a -ae *f*)
bloodshed *s* caed•es -is *f*
bloodshot *adj* **— eyes** cruore suffusi ocul•i -orum *mpl*
bloodstained *adj* cruent•us -a -um
bloodthirsty *adj* sanguinari•us -a -um
blood vessel *s* ven•a -ae *f*
bloody *adj* sanguine•us -a -um
bloom *s* flo•s -ris *m;* **to be in —** florid•us -a -um esse
bloom *intr* florēre; **to begin to —** florescere
blooming *adj* flor•ens -entis
blossom *s* flo•s -ris *m;* **to shed its —s** deflorēre
blossom *intr* florēre
blot *s* macul•a -ae *f*
blot *tr* maculare; **to — out** delēre; *(to erase)* oblit(t)erare
blotch *s (stain)* macul•a -ae *f; (on the skin)* var•us -i *m*
blotchy *adj* maculos•us -a -um
blouse *s* pelusi•a -ae *f*
blow *s (stroke)* plag•a -ae *f; (blow which wounds)* ict•us -ūs *m; (w. the fist)* colaph•us -i *m; (fig)* plag•a -ae *f*
blow *tr* flare; *(a horn)* inflare; **to — out** *(candle)* ex(s)tinguere; **to — the nose** se emungere; **to — up** pulvere nitrato destruere **II** *intr* flare; **to — hard** perflare; **to — over** *(of a storm)* cadere; **to — up** *(to get angry)* irasci
blowing *s* sufflati•o -onis *f*
blue *adj* caerule•us -a -um; *(dark blue)* cyane•us -a -um; *(pale blue)* subcaerule•us -a -um; *(melancholy)* melancholic•us -a -um
blue *s* caeruleus col•or -oris *m; (concrete)* caerule•um -i *n;* **—s** melancholi•a -ae *f;* **to have the —s** melancholic•us -a -um esse
blue-grey *adj (eyes)* caesi•us -a -um
blueprint *s* form•a -ae *f*
bluff *s* rup•es -is *f; (false threat)* simulata audaci•a -ae *f*
bluff *tr* decipere **II** *intr* simulatā audaciā uti
blunder *s* err•or -oris *m; (in writing)* mend•um -i *n*
blunder *intr* errare
blunderer *s* hom•o -inis *mf* ineptus (-a)
blunt *adj (dull)* heb•es -itis; *(person)* inurban•us -a -um; *(speech)* impolit•us -a -um
blunt *tr* hebetare
bluntly *adv* liberius
bluntness *s* hebetud•o -inis *f; (fig)* rusticit•as -atis *f*
blur *s* macul•a -ae *f*
blur *tr* obscurare
blurred *adj* **the eyes are —** oculi caligant; **to have — vision** quasi per caliginem vidēre
blurt *tr* **to — out** effutire
blush *s* rub•or -oris *m*
blush *intr* erubescere
bluster *intr (to swagger)* declamare, se iactare; *(of the wind)* saevire
bluster *s (boasting)* iactati•o -onis *f; (din)* strepit•us -ūs *m*
blustery *adj* ventos•us -a -um
boar *s* a•per -pri *m*
board *s (of wood)* tabul•a -ae *f; (food)* vict•us -ūs *m; (council)* colleg•ium -(i)i *n; (judicial)* quaesti•o -onis *f; (for games)* alve•us -i *m*
board *tr (vehicle, plane)* inscendere; *(ship)* conscendere; **to — up** contabulare **II** *intr (to be a boarder)* victitare; **to — with** devertere apud *(w. acc)*
boarder *s* deversit•or -oris *m*
boarding house *s* deversor•ium -(i)i *n*
boarding school *s* oecotrophe•um -i *n*
boardwalk *s* ambulacr•um -i *n* in litore
boast *intr* gloriari, se iactare
boast *s* iactanti•a -ae *f*
boastful *adj* glorios•us -a -um
boasting *s* gloriati•o -onis *f*

boat *s* navicul·a -ae *f*
boatman *s* naviculari·us -i *m,* lintrari·us -i *m*
bode *tr* portendere
bodiless *adj* incorporal·is -is -e
bodily *adj* corporis [*gen*]
body *s* corp·us -oris *n; (corpse)* cadav·er -eris *n; (person)* hom·o -inis *m; (of troops)* man·us -ūs *f; (of cavalry)* turm·a -ae *f; (frame)* compag·es -ium *fpl;* **to come in a —** agmine facto occurrere
bodyguard *s (single)* satell·es -itis *mf* satellit·es -um *mpl; (of the emperor)* cohor·s -tis *f* praetoria
bog *s* pal·us -udis *f*
bog *tr* **to — down** mergere; **to get —ed down** in luto haesitare; *(fig)* haesitare
bogus *adj (counterfeit)* adulterin·us -a -um; *(sham)* simulat·us -a -um; *(fictitious)* commentici·us -a -um
boil *tr (to cause to boil)* fervefacere; *(to cook)* coquere; **to — down** *(food)* decoquere; *(facts)* coartare **||** *intr* fervēre; *(fig)* bullire; **it makes my blood —** facit ut sanguis ab irā fervescit; **to — over** effervescere; **to — with indignation** indignatione bullire
boil *s (med)* furuncul·us -i *m*
boisterous *adj (noisy)* turbid·us -a -um; *(stormy)* procellos·us -a -um
bold *adj* aud·ax -acis
bold-faced *adj* impud·ens -entis
boldly *adv* audacter
boldness *s* audaci·a -ae *f*
bolster *tr* fulcire
bolt *s (of a door)* pessul·us -i *m,* ser·a -ae *f; (of lightning)* ful·men -inis *n; (pin)* clav·us -i *m; (screw)* cochle·a -ae *f*
bolt *tr* obserare; **—ed doors** oppessulatae for·es -ium *fpl;* **to — down** *(food)* devorare **||** *intr (of a horse)* se proripere; *(pol)* a factione deficere
bomb *s* missil·e -is *n* dirumpens, bomb·a -ae *f;* **atomic —** bomba atomica; **nuclear —** bomba nuclearis
bomb *tr* missilibus dirumpentibus concutere
bombard *tr* tormentis verberare; *(fig)* lacessere
bombardment *s* tormentis verberati·o -onis *f*
bombastic *adj* tumid·us -a -um; **to be —** ampullari
bomber aëroplan·um -i *n* bombiferum
bond *s* vincul·um -i *n; (legal document)* syngraph·a -ae *f; (of love)* copul·a -ae *f*
bondage *s* servit·us -utis *f; (captivity)* captivit·as -atis *f*
bondsman *s (slave)* famul·us -i *m; (leg)* spōns·or -oris *m*
bone *s* os, ossis *n; (of fish)* spin·a -ae *f*
bone *adj (of bone)* osse·us -a -um
bone *tr (to remove bones from)* exossare
boneless *adj* ex·os -ossis
bonfire *s* ign·es -ium *mpl* festi
bonnet *s* redimicul·um -i *n*
bonus *s* praem·ium -(i)i *n, (mil)* donativ·um -i *n*
bony *adj* osse·us -a -um
boogieman *s* larv·a -ae *f*
book *s* li·ber -bri *m;* **by the —** *(fig)* pro modo; **to write a —** librum componere
book bag *s* manic·a -ae *f* libraria
bookbinder *s* glutinat·or -oris *m*
bookcase *s* forul·i -orum *mpl*
bookish *adj* libris dedit·us -a -um
bookkeeper *s* tabular·ius -(i)i *m* (·a -ae *f*), dispēnsat·or -oris *m* (·rix -ricis *f*)
bookshelf *s* plute·us -i *m,* pegm·a -atis *n* librarium
bookstore *s* librari·a -ae *f*
bookworm *s* tine·a -ae *f; (fig)* librorum hellu·o -onis *m*
boom *s (of ship)* longur·ius -(i)i *m; (of harbor)* repagul·um -i *n; (sound)* sonit·us -ūs *m; (of waves)* frag·or -oris *m*
boor *s* rustic·us -i *m* (·a -ae *f*)
boorish *adj* rustic·us -a -um
boorishness *s* rusticit·as -atis *f*
boost *tr* efferre
boot *s* calce·us -i *m; (soldier's)* calig·a -ae *f; (of rawhide, reaching to the calf)* per·o -onis *m; (tragic)* cothurn·us -i *m*
boot *tr (coll)* calce petere **||** *intr* prodesse; **to —** insuper
booth *s* tabern·a -ae *f*
booting up *s (comput)* initiati·o -onis *f* systematis
boot up *intr (comput)* initiare systema
booze *s* temet·um -i *n*
border *s (edge)* marg·o -inis *mf; (seam)* fimbri·a -ae *f; (boundary)* fin·is -is *m; (frontier)* lim·es -tis *m;* **to mark the —** finem discernere
border *tr* attingere **||** *intr* **to — on** attingere
bordering *adj* finitim·us -a -um
bore *tr* terebrare; *(a person)* obtundere; **to — a hole in** excavare; **to — a hole through s.th.** aliquid perforare
bore *s (tool)* terebr·a -ae *f; (fig)* molest·us -i *m* (·a -ae *f*); **don't be a —** ne sis odios·us -a
born *adj* nat·us -a -um; **to be —** nasci; *(fig)* oriri
borough *s* municip·ium -(i)i *n*
borrow *tr* mutuari; *(fig)* imitari
borrowed *adj* mutu·us -a -um
bosom *s* sin·us -ūs *m; (of female)* mammill·ae -arum *fpl*
bosom friend *s* intimus(-a) familiar·is -is *mf*
boss *s (owner)* domin·us -i *m* (·a -ae *f*); *(coll)* ipsim·us -i *m; (ornamental fixture)* bull·a -ae *f; (on a shield)* umb·o -onis *m*
boss *tr* dominari in *(w. acc)*
botanical *adj* herbari·us -a -um
botanist *s* herbar·ius -(i)i *m* (·a -ae *f*)

botany *s* ar·s -tis *f* herbaria
botch *tr* male gerere
both *adj* amb·o -ae -o; *(of pairs)* gemin·us -a -um; *(each of two)* ut·erque, -raque, -rumque; **— parents** uterque par·ēns -entis *m;* **in — directions** utroque; **on — sides** utrimque
both *pron* amb·o -ae -o; *(w. singular verb)* ut·erque, -raque, -rumque
both *conj* **— … and** et … et
bother *tr* vexare ‖ *intr* **to — about** operam dare *(w. dat)*
bother *s* negot·ium -(i)i *n*
bothersome *adj* molest·us -a -um
bottle *s* ampull·a -ae *f; (large)* lagoen·a -ae *f*
bottle *tr* in ampullas infundere
bottom *s* fund·us -i *m; (of a ship)* carin·a -ae *f; (of a mountain)* rad·ix -icis *m;* **the — of** im·us -a -um; **the — of the sea** imum mar·e -is *n*
bottom *adj* im·us -a -um
bottomless *adj* profund·us -a -um
bough *s* ram·us -i *m*
boulder *s* sax·um -i *n*
bounce *tr* repercutere; *(coll)* eicere ‖ *intr* resilire
bounce *s (leap)* salt·us -ūs *m; (energy)* vig·or -oris *m*
bound *adj* alligat·us -a -um; **it is — to happen** necesse est accidat; **to be — for** tendere ad *or* in *(w. acc)*
bound *s (leap)* salt·us -ūs *m;* **to set —s** modum facere
bound *tr* terminare, continēre; **they are —ed on one side by the Rhine** unā ex parte flumine Rheno continentur ‖ *intr (to leap)* salire
boundary *s* fin·is -is *m; (esp. fortified)* lim·es -itis *m*
boundless *adj* infinit·us -a -um
bountiful *adj* larg·us -a -um
bounty *s* largit·as -atis *f*
bouquet *s* corollar·ium -(i)i *n; (of wine)* flo·s -ris *m*
bout *s* certam·en -inis *n*
bow *s* arc·us -ūs *m; (in a ribbon)* plex·us -ūs *m*
bow *s (of ship)* pror·a -ae *f; (bending)* capitis summissi·o -onis *f;* **to take a —** caput summittere
bow *tr* flectere; *(one's head)* demittere ‖ *intr* se demittere; **to — to** *(to accede to)* obtemperare *(w. dat)*
bowels *spl* alv·us -i *f*
bower *s* umbracul·um -i *n*
bowl *s* crater·a -ae *f; (large with handles)* catin·us -i *m; (smaller)* catill·us -i *mf (for libations)* pater·a -ae *f*
bowl *intr* conis ludere
bowling *s* conorum lus·us -us *m*
bowling alley *s* oec·us -i *m* conorum lusūs
bowling ball *s* glob·us -i *m* lusorius
bowling pin *s* con·us -i *m* lusorius
bowlegged *adj* valg·us -a -um
bowstring *s* nerv·us -i *m*
box *s (chest)* arc·a -ae *f; (for books)* caps·a -ae *f; (for clothes, etc.)* cist·a -ae *f; (for perfume, medicine)* pyx·is -idis *f*
box *tr (to enclose in a box)* includere; *(an opponent)* pugillare cum *(w. abl);* **to — s.o. on the ear** alicui alapam adhibēre ‖ *intr* pugillare
boxer *s* pug·il -ilis *mf*
boxing *s* pugillat·us -ūs *m*
boxing glove *s* caest·us -ūs *m*
boxing match *s* pugillat·us -ūs *m*
boy *s* pu·er -eri *m; (dim.)* puerul·us -i *m*
boyfriend *s* am·ans -antis *m*
boyhood *s* pueriti·a -ae *f;* **from —** a puero
boyish *adj* pueril·is -is -e
bra *s* stroph·ium -(i)i *n*
brace *s (strap)* fasci·a -ae *f; (pair)* pa·r -ris *n; (prop)* fulment·um -i *n*
brace *tr (to bind)* ligare; *(to strengthen)* firmare; *(to prop)* fulcire; **to — oneself for** se comparare ad *(w. acc)*
bracelet *s* armill·a -ae *f*
bracket *s* mutul·us -i *m;* **—s** *(in writing)* unc·i -orum *mpl*
brag *intr* se iactare; **to — about** iactare
braggart *s* iactat·or -oris *m* (·rix -ricis *f*)
bragging *s* iactanti·a -ae *f*
braid *s* limb·us -i *m; (of hair)* spir·a -ae *f*
braid *tr* plectere
brain *s* cerebr·um -i *n;* **—s** *(talent)* ingen·ium -(i)i *n;* **to have (no) —s** cor (non) habēre
brain *tr (sl)* caput elidere *(w. dat)*
brainless *adj* soc·ors -ordis
brainstorm *s* inflat·us -ūs *m* spiritūs
brain trust *s* consil·ium -(i)i *n* sapientium
brake *s (on wagon)* sufflam·en -inis *n; (thicket)* dumet·um -i *n;* **to apply (step on) the —** rotam sufflaminare
brake pedal pedal·e -is *n* sufflaminis
bramble *s* dum·us -i *m; (thorny bush)* sent·is -is *m*
branch *s (of tree)* ram·us -i *m; (of pedigree)* stemm·a -atis *n; (of knowledge)* disciplin·a -ae *f; (of medicine, etc.)* par·s -tis *f*
branch *intr* **to — out** ramos porrigere; *(fig)* scindi, diffundi
branch office *s* officin·a -ae *f* auxiliaria
brand *s (mark)* stigm·a -atis *n; (com)* not·a -ae *f; (type)* gen·us -eris *n; (of fire)* fa·x -cis *f*
branding iron *s* caut·er -eris *m*
brandish *tr* vibrare
brandy *s* vini spirit·us -ūs *m*
brash *adj* temerari·us -a -um
brass *s* orichalc·um -i *n*
brassiere *s* stroph·ium -(i)i *n*
brat *s* procax pusi·o -onis *mf*
brave *adj* fort·is -is -e

brave *tr* sustinēre
bravely *adv* fortiter
bravery *s* fortitud·o -inis *f*
bravo *interj* macte!
brawl *s* rix·a -ae *f*
brawl *intr* rixari
brawler *s* rixat·or -oris *m* (·rix -ricis *f*)
brawling *adj* iurg·ans -antis
brawn *s* lacert·us -i *m*
brawny *adj* lacertos·us -a -um
bray *intr* rudere
braying *s* rudit·us -ūs *m*
brazen *adj* aëne·us -a -um; *(fig)* impud·ens -entis
breach *s* ruin·a -ae *f; (of treaty)* dissid·ium -(i)i *n;* **— in the wall** ruin·a -ae *f* muri; **to commit a — of promise** fidem frangere; **to make a small — in the wall** aliquantulum muri discutere
bread *s* pan·is -is *m; (fig)* vict·us -ūs *m;* **loaf of —** panis *m;* **to earn one's —** sibi victum quaerere
bread basket *s* panar·ium -(i)i *n*
breadcrumb *s* mic·a -ae *f* panis
breaded *adj* saligne·us -a -um
breadth *s* latitud·o -inis *f;* **in —** in latitudinem
break *tr (arm, dish, treaty, one's word)* frangere; *(the law)* violare; *(leg, ankle)* suffringere; *(silence)* rumpere; *(camp)* movēre; *(in several places)* diffringere; **to — a fall** casum mitigare; **to — apart** diffringere; **to — a treaty** foedus frangere; **to — down** *(to demolish)* demoliri; **to — down into** *(categories)* deducere in *(w. acc);* **to — formation** ordinem solvere; **to — in** *(a horse)* domare; **to — in pieces** confringere; **to — off** *(e.g., a branch)* praefringere; *(friendship or action)* dirumpere; *(a meeting, conversation)* interrumpere; **to — one's word** fidem frangere; **to — open** effringere; **to — up** dissolvere ‖ *intr* frangi, rumpi; *(of day)* illucescere; *(of strength)* deficere; **to — forth** erumpere; **to —into** *(e.g., a house)* irrumpere *(w. acc or* intra *w. acc); (e.g., a city)* invadere *(w. acc or* in *w. acc);* **to — loose from** se eripere ex *(w. abl);* **to — off** *(to stop short)* repente desinere; **to — out** erumpere; *(of trouble)* exardescere; *(of war)* exoriri; *(of fire)* grassari; **to — up** dissolvi, dilabi; *(of a meeting)* dimitti; **to — with** dissidēre ab *(w. abl)*
break *s (of a limb)* ruptur·a -ae *f;* (*interruption*) intercaped·o -inis *f; (for rest)* intervall·um -i *n,* vacati·o -onis *f; (escape)* effug·ium -(i)i *n;* **— of day** prima lu·x -cis *f*
breakage *s* fractur·a -ae *f*
breakdown *s (of health)* debilit·as -atis *f; (mechanical)* defect·us -ūs *m; (division)* deducti·o -onis *f*
breaker *s* fluct·us -ūs *m* a saxo fractus
breakfast *s* ientacul·um -i *n;* **for —** in ientaculum; **to eat —** ientare
breakfast *intr* ientare
breakneck *adj* praec·eps -ipitis
breakup *s* dissoluti·o -onis *f*
breakwater *s* mol·es -is *f* lapidum in mari structa
breast *s* pect·us -oris *n; (of a woman)* mamm·a -ae *f; (when filled with milk)* ub·er -eris *n; (fig)* praecord·ia -ium *npl;* **to make a clean — of it** confiteri omnia
breast-feed *tr* uberibus alere
breastplate *s* loric·a -ae *f*
breath *s* spirit·us -ūs *m,* anim·a -ae *f;* **— of air** aur·a -ae *f;* **deep —** anhelit·us -ūs *m;* **out of —** anhel·us -a -um; **to catch one's —** respirare; **to draw a —** spiritum trahere; **to hold one's —** animam continēre; **to take a —** animam *or* spiritum ducere; **to take one's — away** exanimare; **to waste one's —** operam perdere
breathe *tr* ducere, spirare; *(to whisper)* susurrare; **to — fire** flammas exspirare; **to — one's last** animam exspirare ‖ *intr* spirare, respirare; **to — upon** inspirare *(w. dat)*
breather *s (breathing space)* spat·ium -(i)i *n*
breathing *s* respirati·o -onis *f*
breathless *adj* exanim·is -is -e
breeches *spl* brac·ae -arum *fpl*
breed *s* gen·us -eris *n*
breed *tr* parere, gignere; *(to cause)* producere; *(to raise)* educare, alere; **familiarity —s contempt** conversatio parit contemptum
breeder *s (man)* generat·or -oris *m; (animal)* matr·ix -icis *f; (fig)* nutr·ix -icis *f*
breeding *s* fetur·a -ae *f;* **good —** humanit·as -atis *f*
breeze *s* aur·a -ae *f*
breezy *adj* ventos·us -a -um
brethren *spl* fratr·es -um *mpl*
brevity *s* brevit·as -atis *f*
brew *s* cerevisiae ferment·um -i *n*
brew *tr* concoquere ‖ *intr* excitari
brewer *s* cerevisiae coct·or -oris *m*
brewery *s* officin·a -ae *f* ad cerevisiam concoquendam
bribe *s* pret·ium -(i)i *n,* praem·ium -(i)i *n,* pecuni·a -ae *f*
bribe *tr* (pecuniā) corrumpere
briber *s* corrupt·or -oris *m* (·rix -ricis *f*)
bribery *s* corrupti·o -onis *f; (pol)* ambit·us -ūs *m*
brick *s* lat·er -eris *m*
brick *adj* laterici·us -a -um
bricklayer *s* laterum struct·or -oris *m*
bridal *adj* nuptial·is -is -e; **— bed** genialis tor·us -i *m;* **— suite** thalam·us -i *m;* **— veil** flamme·um -i *n*
bride *s* nupt·a -ae *f*
bridegroom *s* marit·us -i *m*

bridesmaid *s* pronub•a -ae *f*
bridge *s* pon•s -tis *m*
bridge *tr* pontem imponere *(w. dat)*
brief *adj* brev•is -is -e; **make it —!** in pauca confer!
brief *tr* edocēre
brief *s (leg)* commentar•ius -(i)i *m*
briefing *s* mandat•a -orum *npl*
briefly *adv* breviter, paucis (verbis); **to put if —** ut breviter dicam
brigade *s (infantry)* legi•o -onis *f; (cavalry)* turm•a -ae *f*
brigadier *s* tribun•us -i *m* militum
brigand *s* latr•o -onis *m*
bright *adj* clar•us -a -um; *(day, sky)* seren•us -a -um; *(stars, gems)* lucid•us -a -um; *(beaming)* nitid•us -a -um; *(smart)* a•cer -cris -cre; **— eyes** oculi vegeti
brighten *tr* illuminare ‖ *intr* lucescere, clarēscere; **his face —ed up** vultus eius in hilaritatem solutus est
brightly *adv* clare, lucide
brightness *s* nit•or -oris *m,* cand•or -oris *m; (of sky)* serenit•as -atis *f*
brilliance *s* splend•or -oris *m; (ability)* lu•x -cis *f;* **— of style** nit•or -oris *m* orationis
brilliant *adj* splendid•us -a -um; *(esp. fig: achievement, speech, battle, etc.)* lucu-lent•us -a -um
brilliantly *adv* splendide, luculente
brim *s (rim)* or•a -ae *f; (border)* marg•o -inis *mf;* **to fill to the —** ad summam oram implēre
brimful *adj* ad summum plen•us -a -um
brimstone *s* sulf•ur -uris *n*
bring *tr* **(to)** afferre (ad *w. acc); (by carriage, etc.)* advehere; *(letters, report, news)* perferre; **to — about** efficere, perficere; **to — along** afferre; **to — (s.o.) around** circumagere (aliquem); **to — back** referre, reducere; *(to recall)* revocare; *(by force, authority)* redigere; **to — before a court of law** producere in iudicium; **to —** *(a matter)* **before the senate** ad senatum referre de *(w. abl);* **to — credit to** fidem ferre *(w. dat);* **to — down** deferre; *(e.g., a tower)* deicere; **to — forth** prodere, depromere; *(to yield)* ferre; **to — forward** proferre; **to — in** inferre; *(on a vehicle)* invehere; *(money, profit)* efficere; **to — it about that** efficere ut; **to — on** afferre; *(illness, fever)* adducere; *(fig)* obicere; **to — oneself to** animum inducere ut *(w. subj);* **to — out** *(to reveal)* proferre; *(to elicit)* elicere; *(the wine)* (ex)promere; *(a book)* prodere; **to — over** perducere; *(fig)* perducere, conciliare; **to — to** adducere; **to — together** cōnferre; *(to assemble)* cogere, contrahere; *(esp. forces)* comparare; *(estranged persons)* conciliare; **to — to order** in ordinem cogere; **to — to pass** efficere; **to — under one's control** subigere; **to — up** subducere; *(children)* educare; *(to vomit)* evomere; *(a topic)* mentionem facere de *(w. abl)*
brink *s* marg•o -inis *mf;* **on the — of death** morti vicin•us -a -um; **to be on the — of disaster** in summo discrimine versari
brisk *adj (lively)* ala•cer -cris -cre; *(wind)* vehement•ior -ior -ius; *(weather)* frigid•us -a -um; **to be —** vigēre
briskly *adv* alacriter
briskness *s* alacrit•as -atis *f,* vig•or -oris *m*
bristle *s* saet•a -ae *f*
bristle *intr* horrēre
Britain *s* Britanni•a -ae *f*
British *adj* Britannic•us -a -um
brittle *adj* fragil•is -is -e
broach *tr* in medium proferre
broad *adj* lat•us -a -um; *(grin)* solut•us -a -um; *(general)* commun•is -is -e; **in — daylight** *(fig)* propalam; **to sleep till — daylight** ad multum diem dormire
broadcast *s* emissi•o -onis *f*
broadcast *tr* divulgare; *(a program)* emittere
broadcast station *s* emistr•um -i *n*
broaden *tr (to widen)* dilatare; *(to enlarge)* ampliare ‖ *intr* in latitudinem crescere, latescere
brocade *s* seric•um -i *n* aureo *(or* argento) filo intertextum
broccoli *s* brassic•a -ae *f* oleracea Botyrtis
brochure *s* libell•us -i *m*
broil *s* rix•a -ae *f*
broil *tr* torrēre ‖ *intr* torrēri
broke *adj* **to be —** solvendo non esse
broken *adj* fract•us -a -um; *(by age, hard times)* confect•us -a -um; *(faltering)* infract•us -a -um; **— in** domit•us -a -um
broken-hearted *adj* deiect•us -a -um
broker *s* arillat•or -oris *mf*
bronze *s* ae•s -ris *n*
bronze *adj* aëne•us -a -um
brooch *s* fibul•a -ae *f*
brood *s* prol•es -is *f; (of birds, etc. hatched together)* fetur•a -ae *f*
brood *intr* **to — over** *(lit & fig)* incubare *(w. dat),* parturire
brook *s* rivul•us -i *m*
brook *tr* tolerare, pati
broom *s* scop•ae -arum *fpl*
broth *s* iu•s -ris *n*
brothel *s* lupan•ar -aris *n*
brother *s* fra•ter -tris *m*
brotherhood *s* fraternit•as -atis *f; (organization)* sodalit•as -atis *f*
brother-in-law *s* lev•ir -iri *m*
brotherly *adj* fratern•us -a -um
brow *s* fron•s -tis *f; (of a hill)* dors•um -i *n;* **to knit the —** frontem contrahere
browbeat *tr* minis et terrore commovēre
brown *adj (w. a dash of yellow)* fulv•us -a -um; *(chestnut color)* spad•ix -icis; *(of skin)* adust•us -a -um

browse *intr* depasci; *(comput) (the Web)* navigare; *(text documents)* perlustrare
browser *s (comput) (Web viewer)* navigatr·um -i *n; (viewer of text documents)* perlustratr·um -i *n*
bruise *tr* contundere; *(to make black-and-blue)* sugillare
bruise *s* contusi·o -onis *f; (black-and- blue)* suggillati·o -onis *f*
bruise mark *s* liv·or -oris *m*
brunette *s* puell·a -ae *f* subfusca
brunt *s* tota vis *f*
brush *s (scrub brush)* penicul·us -i *m; (painter's)* penicill·us -i *m; (skirmish)* aggressi·o -onis *f; (bushes)* vigult·a -orum *npl*
brush *tr (lightly)* verrere; *(teeth)* purgare; *(shoes)* detergēre; **to — aside** spernere; **to — away** or **out** detergēre ‖ *intr* **to — past s.o.** aliquem praetereundo leviter terere
brutal *adj* imman·is -is -e
brutality *s* immanit·as -atis *f*
brutally *adv* immaniter
brute *adj* brut·us -a -um
brute *s* belu·a -ae *f*
brutish *adj* imman·is -is -e
bubble *s* bull·a -ae *f*
bubble *intr* bullire, bullare; *(of a spring)* scatēre
bubbling *s* bullit·us -ūs *m; (of a spring)* scatebr·a -ae *f*
bubbly *adj (person)* argutis scat·ens -entis
buck *s* cerv·us -i *m; (he-goat)* hirc·us -i *m*
bucket *s* situl·a -ae *f;* **to kick the —** *(coll)* animam ebullire
buckle *s* fibul·a -ae *f*
buckle *tr* fibulā nectere ‖ *intr (to bend)* flecti; *(to collapse)* collabi; **to — down** se applicare; **to — up** se fibulā nectere, se accingere
buckler *s* parm·a -ae *f*
bucolic *adj* bucolic·us -a -um
bud *s* gemm·a -ae *f; (of a flower)* cal·yx -ycis *m;* **to nip s.th. in the —** aliquid maturum occupare
bud *intr* gemmare
buddy *s* conger·o -onis *m*
budge *tr* ciēre, movēre ‖ *intr* se movēre, loco cedere
budget *s* pecuniae rati·o -onis *f*
buffalo *s* ur·us -i *m*
buffet *s (sideboard)* abac·us -i *m; (slap)* alap·a -ae *f*
buffoon *s* scurr·a -ae *f;* **to play the —** scurrari
bug *s* cim·ex -icis *mf*
buggy *s (two-wheeled)* carpent·um -i *n; (four-wheeled)* pertorrit·um -i *n*
bugle *s* bucin·a -ae *f,* corn·u -ūs *n*
bugle call *s* classic·um -i *n*
bugler *s* bucinat·or -oris *m*
build *tr (house, ship)* aedificare; *(house, walls)* (ex)struere; *(bridge)* fabricare; *(wall, rampart)* ducere; *(road)* munire; *(hopes)* ponere; **to — up** exstruere
builder *s* aedificat·or -oris *m,* struct·or -oris *m*
building *s (act)* aedificati·o -onis *f,* exstructi·o -onis *f; (structure)* aedific·ium -(i)i *n*
building site *s* are·a -ae *f*
bulb *s* bulb·us -i *m*
bulge *intr (swell)* tumēre; *(to stand out)* prominēre
bulge *s* tub·er -eris *n*
bulk *s* amplitud·o -inis *f; (mass)* mol·es -is *f; (greater part)* maior par·s -tis *f*
bulkiness *s* magnitud·o -inis *f*
bulky *adj (huge)* ing·ens -entis; *(difficulty to handle)* inhabil·is -is -e
bull *s* taur·us -i *m; (sl)* fabul·ae -arum *fpl;* **to sling the —** *(sl)* confabulari
bulldog *s* can·is -is *m* Moloss·us
bulldozer *s* machin·a -ae *f* aggerandi
bullet *s* glan·s -dis *f* plumbea
bulletin *s* libell·us -i *m; (news)* nunt·ius -(i)i *m*
bulletin board *s* tabul·a -ae *f* publica
bullfrog *s* ran·a -ae *f* ocellata
bullock *s* iuvenc·us -i *m*
bull's eye *s* scop·us -i *m* medius; **hit the —** scopum medium ferire
bully *s* scordal·us -i *m*
bully *tr* procaciter lacessere
bulwark *s (wall)* moen·ia -ium *npl; (any means of defense)* propugnacul·um -i *n; (fig)* ar·x -cis *f*
bump *s (swelling)* tub·er -eris *n; (thump)* plag·a -ae *f,* sonit·us -ūs *m*
bump *tr* pulsare, pellere ‖ *intr* **to — against** offendere; **to — into s.o.** *(meet accidentally)* alicui occurrere
bumper *s* cont·us -i *m* tutorius
bumpy *adj* tuberos·us -a -um; *(road, ground)* iniqu·us -a -um
bun *s (roll)* lib·um -i *n,* collyr·is -idis *f*
bunch *s* fascicul·us -i *m; (of grapes)* racem·us -i *m; (group)* glob·us -i *m*
bunch *intr* **to — together** glomerari
bundle *s* fasc·is -is *m; (of straw)* manipul·us -i *m*
bundle *tr* **to — up** *(with clothes)* coöperire
bungle *tr (a job)* inscite gerere, inscite agere ‖ *intr* errare
bungler *s* imperit·us -i *m* (·a -ae *f*)
burden *s* on·us -eris *n*
burden *tr* onerare
burdensome *adj* oneros·us -a -um
bureau *s* minister·ium -(i)i *n; (chest)* armar·ium -(i)i *n; (for clothes)* vestiar·ium -(i)i *n*
burglar *s* effractar·ius -(i)i *m* (·a -ae *f*)
burglary *s* (domūs) effractur·a -ae *f*
burial *s (act)* sepultur·a -ae *f; (ceremony)* fun·us -eris *n*

burlesque *s* ridicula imitati•o -onis *f*
burly *adj* corpulent•us -a -um
burn *tr* urere, cremare; **to — down** deurere; **to — out** exurere; **to — up** comburere **ll** *intr* flagrare, ardēre; **to — down** deflagrare; **to — out** exstingui; **to — up** conflagrare
burn *s* adusti•o -onis *f; (injury)* ambust•um -i *n*
burner *s* disc•us -i *m* coctorius
burning *adj* ard•ens -entis
burn-out *s* defecti•o -onis *f* virium
burrow *intr* defodere
bursar *s* dispensat•or -oris *m* (•rix -ricis *f*)
burst *s (spurt)* impet•us -ūs *m; (noise)* frag•or -oris *m;* **— of anger** iracundiae impet•us -ūs *m;* **— of applause** clamor•es -um *mpl*
burst *tr* rumpere; *(with noise)* displodere; **to — asunder** dirumpere; **to — open** effrangere **ll** *intr* rumpi; **to — forth** prorumpere; **to — in** irrumpere; **to — out** erumpere; **to — out laughing** risum effundere
bury *tr* sepelire; *(to hide)* abdere; **to — the sword in his side** lateri abdere ensem
bus *s* raed•a -ae *f* longa
bus driver *s* raeda longae gubernat•or -oris *m* (•rix -ricis *f*)
bush *s* frut•ex -icis *m; (thorny bush)* dum•us -i *m;* **to beat around the —** circuitione uti
bushel *s* medimn•us -i *m*
bushy *adj (full of bushes)* dumos•us -a -um; *(full of branches)* ramos•us -a -um; *(tail)* villos•us -a -um
busily *adv* impigre, sedulo
business *s* negot•ium -(i)i *n; (trade, calling)* ar•s -tis *f; (matter)* res, rei *f; (establishment)* officin•a -ae *f;* **I always made it my — to be present** ego id semper egi ut adessem; **to mind one's own —** negotium suum agere; **what — do you have here?** quid negoti tibi hic est?; **what — is it of his?** quid illius interest?
business agent *s* negotiorum curat•or -oris *m* (•rix -ricis *f*)
business card *s* chartul•a -ae *f* negotialis
business district *s* empori•um -i *n*
business establishment *s (w. its premises)* negotiati•o -onis *f*
businessman *s* negotiat•or -oris *m*
businesswoman *s* negotiat•rix -ricis *f*
buskin *s* cothurn•us -i *m*
bust *s* imag•o -inis *f; (bosom)* pect•us -oris *n; (woman's)* mammill•ae -arum *fpl*
bustle *s (hurry)* festinati•o -onis *f; (running to and fro)* discurs•us -ūs *m*
bustle *intr* festinare; **to — about** discurrere
busy *adj* occupat•us -a -um; *(time)* operos•us -a -um; *(w. business matters)* negotios•us -a -um; **be — with** versari in *(w. abl)*
busy *tr* **to — oneself with** versari in *(w. abl)*
busybody *s* ardali•o -onis *mf*
but *prep* praeter *(w. acc)*
but *adv* modo, tantum
but *conj* sed; *(stronger)* at; **— if** quodsi; sin; **— if not** sin aliter
butcher *s* lan•ius -(i)i *m; (fig)* carnif•ex -icis *m*
butcher *tr (animals)* caedere; *(people)* contrucidare
butcher shop *s* lanien•a -ae *f*
butchery *s* trucidati•o -onis *f*
butler *s* prom•us -i *m*
butt *s (mark)* met•a -ae *f; (backside)* clun•es -ium *mpl;* **— of ridicule** ludibr•ium -(i)i *n*
butt *tr* arietare **ll** *intr* **to — in** interpellare
butter *s* butyr•um -i *n*
butter *tr* butyrum adhibēre ad *(w. acc);* **to — s.o. up** blandiri *(w. dat)*
butterfly *s* papili•o -onis *m*
buttermilk *s* lactis ser•um -i *n*
buttock *s* clun•is -is *mf*
button *s* globul•us -i *m* vestiarius; *(comput)* plectr•um -i *n*
button *tr* globulo *(or* globulis) stringere
buttress *s* anter•is -idis *f*
buttress *tr* suffulcire
buxom *adj* ampl•us -a -um
buy *tr* **(from)** emere, mercari de (w *abl*); **to — back** *or* **off** redimere; **to — up** coëmere
buyer *s* empt•or -oris *m* (•rix -ricis *f*)
buying *s* empti•o -onis *f*
buzz *s* bomb•us -i *m*
buzz *intr* bombilare
by *prep (agency)* a, ab *(w. abl); (of place) (near)* apud *(w. acc); (along)* secundum *(w. acc); (past)* praeter *(w. acc); (in oaths)* per *(w. acc);* **— and —** mox; **— means of** per *(w. acc);* **— oneself** per se; *(alone)* sol•us -a -um
bye vale! *(pl:* valete!)
bygone *adj* praeterit•us -a -um; *(olden)* prisc•us -a -um
bylaw *s* praescript•um -i *n*
bypass *s* circuit•us -ūs *m*
bypass *tr* ambire
bystander *s* spectat•or -oris *m* (•rix -ricis *f*)
byway *s* deverticul•um -i *n*
byword *s* proverb•ium -(i)i *n*

C

cab *s (for hire)* raed•a -ae *n* meritoria
cabbage *s* brassic•a -ae *f; (head of cabbage)* caul•is -is *m*
cabin *s (cottage)* cas•a -ae *f; (on a ship)* daiet•a -ae *f*
cabinet *s* armar•ium -(i)i *n; (pol)* consil•ium -(i)i *n* principis

cabinet member *s* consilia·tor -toris *m* (·trix -tricis *f*)
cable *s* rud·ens -entis *m; (for anchor)* ancoral·e -is *n*
cablecar *s* curr·us -i *m* funalis
cackle *intr (of hens)* gracillare; *(of geese)* gingrire
cackle *s* gingrit·us -ūs *m*
cactus *s* cact·us -i *m*
cad *s* hom·o -inis *mf* rudis
cadaver *s* cadav·er -eris *n*
cadaverous *adj* cadaveros·us -a -um
cadence *s* numer·us -i *m*
cadet *s* discipul·us -i *m* (·a -ae *f*) militaris
cafe *s* cafe·um -i *n*
cafeteria *s* refector·ium -(i)i *n*
cage *s* cave·a -ae *f*
cage *tr* in caveā includere
caged *adj* caveat·us -a -um
cagey *adj* callid·us -a -um
cahoots *spl* **be in — with** colludere cum *(w. abl)*
cajole *tr* lactare
cake *s* placent·a -ae *f; (birthday cake)* lib·um -i *n; (wedding cake)* mustace·us -i *m*
calamitous *adj* calamitos·us -a -um
calamity *s* calamit·as -atis *f;* **to suffer —** calamitatem perferre
calcium *s* calc·ium -(i)i *n*
calculate *tr* computare; *(fig)* existimare
calculated *adj* subduct·us -a -um
calculation *s* computati·o -onis *f; (fig)* ratiocinati·o -onis *f*
calculating *adj (pej)* versut·us -a -um
calculator *s* machinul·a -ae *f* calculatoria
caldron *s* cortin·a -ae *f; (of copper)* ahen·um -i *n*
calendar *s* calendar·ium -(i)i *n; (in Roman period)* fast·i -orum *mpl*
calends *spl* Kalend·ae -arum *fpl*
calf *s* vitul·us -i *m* (·a -ae *f*)*; (anat)* sur·a -ae *f*
caliber *s (fig)* ingen·ium -(i)i *n*
call *s* vocati·o -onis *f; (shout)* clam·or -oris *m; (visit)* salutati·o -onis *f; (summons)* accit·us -ūs *m;* **social —** offic·ium -(i)i *n;* **to make** *or* **pay a social —** officium peragere
call *tr (to summon)* ad se vocare; *(to name)* appellare, vocare; **to — aside** sevocare; **to — away** avocare; **to — back** revocare; **to — down** devocare; **to — forth** evocare; *(to cause)* provocare; *(fig)* elicere; **to — in** *(money)* cogere; *(for advice)* advocare; *(a doctor)* arcessere; **to — off** *(to cancel)* revocare, tollere; *(to read)* citare; **to — out** *(to call forth)* evocare; *(to shout)* exclamare; **to — to account** *(to upraid)* compellere; **to — together** convocare; **to — to mind** recordari; **to — to witness** testari; **to — up** *(mil)* evocare ‖ *intr* **to — for** *(to demand)* poscere; *(to require)* requirere; **to — on** *(to invoke)* invocare; *(for help)* implorare; *(to visit)* visere
caller *s* saluta·tor -toris *m* (·trix -tricis *f*)
calling *s (profession)* ar·s -tis *f; (station)* stat·us -ūs *m*
callous *adj* callos·us -a -um; *(fig)* dur·us -a -um; **to become —** occallescere; *(fig)* obdurescere
callus *s* call·um -i *n*
calm *adj (unruffled)* tranquill·us -a -um; *(sleep, sea, speech, old age)* placid·us -a -um; *(mentally)* aequ·us -a -um
calm *tr* sedare, tranquillare
calming *s* sedati·o -onis *f*
calmly *adv* tranquille, placide; *(of a person)* aequo animo
calmness *s (lit & fig)* tranquillit·as -atis *f;* **with —** aequo animo
calumny *s (abuse)* maledict·um -i *n; (slander)* calumni·a -ae *f*
camel *s* camel·us -i *m*
cameo *s* imag·o -inis *f* ectypa
camera *s* photomachinul·a -ae *f*
camouflage *s* dissimulati·o -onis *f*
camouflage *tr* dissimulare
camp *s* castr·a -orum *npl;* **summer —** aestiv·a -orum; *npl* **winter —** hibern·a -orum *npl*
camp *adj* castrens·is -is -e
camp *intr* castra ponere
campaign *s (mil)* expediti·o -onis *f,* stipend·ium -(i)i *n; (pol)* (**for**) petiti·o -onis *f (w. gen)*
campaign *intr (mil)* stipendium merēre; *(pol)* ambire, prensare
campaigning *s (pol)* ambiti·o -onis *f; (corruptly)* ambit·us -ūs *m*
camp follower *s* cal·o -onis *m*
can *s* vascul·um -i *n* stanneum
can *tr (to store)* condere ‖ *intr* posse; *(to have the power)* pollēre; **I — not** nequeo, non possum
canal *s* foss·a -ae *f* navigabilis
canary *s* fringill·a -ae *f* Canaria
cancel *tr* tollere; *(to cross out)* cancellare, delēre
cancellation *s* deleti·o -onis *f; (fig)* aboliti·o -onis *f*
cancer *s* can·cer -cri *m,* carcinom·a -atis *n*
cancerous *adj* canceros·us -a -um
candid *adj* apert·us -a -um
candidate *s (for)* candidat·us -i *m* (·a -ae *f*) *(w. gen);* **to announce oneself as —** profiteri
candidly *adv* aperte, libere
candied *adj* succharo condit·us -a -um
candle *s* candel·a -ae *f*
candlestick *s* candelabr·um -i *n*
candor *s* cand·or -oris *m*
candy *s* cuppedi·ae -arum *fpl;* **piece of —** dulciol·um -i *n*
cane *s (walking stick)* bacul·us -i *m; (reed)* harund·o -inis *f*

cane *tr* baculo verberare
canine *adj* canin·us -a -um
canister *s* pyx·is -idis *f*
cannibal *s* anthropophag·us -i *m*
cannon *s* torment·um -i *n*
cannonball *s* glob·us -i *m* missilis
canoe *s* scaph·a -ae *f*
canoe *intr* scapham impellere; **to go —ing** scaphā gestari
cannon *s* torment·um -i *n*
cannon ball *s* glob·us -i *m* tormenti
canon *s (eccl)* can·on -onis *m*
canonical *adj* canonic·us -a -um
canonize *tr* in numerum sanctorum referre
canon law *s* ius, iuris *n* canonicum
canopy *s* aulae·um -i *n*
canteen *s (flask)* laguncul·a -ae *f; (mil)* caupon·a -ae *f* castrensis
canter *s* lenis quadrupedans grad·us -ūs *m*
canter *intr* leniter currere
canton *s* pag·us -i *m*
canvas *s* linte·um -i *n* crassum; *(for painting)* textil·e -is *n*
cap *s* pille·us -i *m; (worn by certain priests)* galer·us -i *m*
capability *s* facult·as -atis *f*
capable *adj (skilled)* soller·s -tis, perit·us -a -um; (**of**) cap·ax -acis *(w. gen); —* **of enduring** *(cold, hunger, etc.)* pati·ens -entis *(w. gen);* **— of holding 500 spectators** cap·ax -acis quingentorum spectatorum
capably *adv* scite
capacity *s (extent of space)* capacit·as -atis *f; (extent of mental power)* mensur·a -ae *f; (ability)* ingen·ium -(i)i *n*
cape *s* promontor·ium -(i)i *n; (garment)* humeral·e -is *n*
caper *s (leap)* exsultati·o -onis *f; (prank)* ludibr·ium -(i)i *n; (bold criminal act)* scel·us -eris *n;* **to pull a —** scelus patrare
capital *adj (chief)* praecipu·us -a -um; *(offense, punishment)* capital·is -is -e; *(letters)* uncial·is -is -e
capital *s (chief city)* cap·ut -itis *n; (archit)* capitul·um -i *n; (com)* cap·ut -itis *n,* sor·s -tis *f*
capital punishment *s* supplic·ium -(i)i *n* capitis; **to suffer —** supplicio capitis affici
capitol *s* capitol·ium -(i)i *n*
capitulate *intr* se dedere
capitulation *s* dediti·o -onis *f*
capon *s* cap·o -onis *m*
caprice *s* libid·o -inis *f*
capricious *adj* inconst·ans -antis
capriciously *adv* inconstanter
Capricorn *s* Capricorn·us -i *m*
capsize *tr* evertere **||** *intr* everti
capsule *s* capsul·a -ae *f; (bot)* vascul·um -i *n*
captain *s (in infantry)* centuri·o -onis *m; (in cavalry)* praefect·us -i *m; (in navy)* navarch·us -i *m; (of merchant ship)* navis magis·ter -tri *m*
caption *s* capitul·um -i *n; (leg)* praescripti·o -onis *f*
captious *adj (tricky)* captios·us -a -um; *(carping)* moros·us -a -um
captivate *tr* capere
captive *adj* captiv·us -a -um
captive *s* captiv·us -i *m* (·a -ae *f*)
captor *s* capt·or -oris *m; (of a city)* expugnat·or -oris *m*
capture *s* comprehensi·o -onis *f; (of a city)* expugnati·o -onis *f; (of animals)* captur·a -ae *f*
capture *tr* capere, excipere; *(city)* expugnare; *(by surprise)* opprimere
car *s (chariot)* curr·us -ūs *m; (carriage)* raed·a -ae *f,* carr·us -i *m; (modern)* autocinet·um -i *n,* raed·a-ae *f;* **to drive a —** raedam gubernare *or* agere; **to go by —** raedā ire; **to go for a ride in a —** gestationem raedā facere; **to stop the —** raedam sistere; **to take s.o. by —** aliquem raedā ducere
caravan *s* commeat·us -ūs *m*
carbon *s* carbon·ium -(i)i *n*
carcass *s* cadav·er -eris *n*
card *s* chart·a -ae *f; (playing card)* chartul·a -ae *f* lusoria; **birthday —** charta natalicia; **calling —** charta salutatoria; **to cut (deal, shuffle) the —s** chartulas seponere (distribuere, miscēre); **to play —s** chartulis (lusoriis) ludere;
cardboard *s* chart·a -ae *f* crassior
cardinal *adj* principal·is -is -e; *(color)* ru·ber -bra -brum; *(numbers)* cardinal·is -is -e
cardinal *s (eccl)* cardinal·is -is *m*
car door *s* raedae ostiol·um -i *n*
card table *s* mens·a -ae *f* lusoria
care *s (anxiety, oversight, attention)* cur·a -ae *f,* oper·a -ae *f; (diligence)* diligenti·a -ae *f; (charge)* tutel·a -ae *f; (watching over)* custodi·a -ae *f;* **— was taken by the senate to** *(w.inf)* opera a senatu data est ut; **take — of yourself!** cura ut valeas!; **to take — not to** cavēre ne; **to take (good) — of** (diligenter) curare
care *intr* curare; **for all I —** meā causā; **I don't —** nil moror; **I don't — for wine** ego vinum nihil moror; **to — for** *(to look after)* curare; *(to like)* amare, diligere; *(to be fond of, with negatives)* morari; **what do I — ?** quid mihi est?
career *s* curricul·um -i *n; (pol)* curs·us -ūs *m* honorum
carefree *adj* secur·us -a -um
careful *adj (attentive)* dilig·ens -entis, curios·us -a -um; *(cautious)* caut·us -a -um; *(watchful)* vigil·ans -antis; *(of work)* accurat·us -a -um; **careful!** cave!
carefully *adv* diligenter; caute

carefulness *s* cur·a -ae *f,* diligenti·a -ae *f,* cauti·o -onis *f*
careless *adj* negleg·ens -entis, incurios·us -a -um
carelessly *adv* neglegenter
carelessness *s* incuri·a -ae *f; (stronger)* neglegenti·a -ae *f*
caress *s* amplex·us -ūs *m*
caress *tr* fovēre, palpare; *(to embrace)* amplecti
caretaker *s* cust·os -odis *mf*
carfare *s* vectur·a -ae *f* currūs
cargo *s* on·us -eris *n;* **to put a ship's — aboard** navem onerare
cargo plane *s* aëroplan·um -i *n* onerarium
cargo ship *s* nav·is -is *f* oneraria
caricature *s (picture)* gryll·us -i *m; (fig)* ridicula imitati·o -onis *f*
caricature *tr* imaginem *(w. gen)* in peius fingere; *(fig),* detorquēre
car key *s* clav·is -is *f* accensiva
carnage *s* strag·es -is *f*
carnal *adj* carnal·is -is -e; **— pleasure** volupt·as -atis *f* libidinosa
carnival *s* feri·ae -arum *fpl* ante quadragesimam
carnivorous *adj* carnivor·us -a -um
carol *s* cant·us -ūs *m*
carouse *intr* comissari
carp *s* cyprin·us -i *m*
carp *intr* **to — at** carpere
carpenter *s* fa·ber -bri *m* tignarius
carpentry *s* materiatur·a -ae *f* fabrilis
carpet *s* tapet·e -is *n*
carriage *s* vehicul·um -i *n,* raed·a -ae *f; (esp. women's)* carpent·um -i *n*
carrier *s* baiul·us -i *m*
carrot *s* carot·a -ae *f*
carry *tr* ferre; *(of heavier things)* portare; *(by vehicle)* vehere; *(a law)* perferre; **to get carried away with enthusiasm** studio efferri; **to — away** auferre; evehere; **to — in** importare; invehere; **to — off** auferre; *(by force)* rapere; **to — on** *(to conduct)* exercēre: *(war)* gerere; **to — out** efferre; evehere; *(to perform)* exsequi; **to — through** perferre; **to — weight** auctoritatem habēre **||** *intr (of sound)* audiri; **to — on** pergere; *(to behave)* se gerere
cart *s* plaustr·um -i *n; (dim.)* plostell·um -i *n; (two-wheeled, drawn by oxen)* carr·us -i *m;* **putting the — before the horse** praeposteris consiliis
cart *tr* plaustro vehere; **to — off** plaustro evehere
carve *tr* sculpere; *(to engrave)* caelare; *(at table)* secare
carver *s (engraver)* caelat·or -oris *m; (at table)* sciss·or -oris *m*
carving *s* caelatur·a -ae *f*
carving knife *s* cultell·us -i *m*
case *s (leg)* caus·a -ae *f; (matter, circumstances, condition)* res, rei *f; (instance)* exempl·um -i *n; (container)* involucr·um -i *n; (patient)* aeg·er -ri *m,* aegr·a -ae *f; (gram)* cas·us -ūs *m;* **if that's the —** si res sic habet; **in any —** utcumque; **in no —** nequaquam; **in the — of Priam** in Priamo; **since that's the —** quae cum ita sint
cash *s* pecuni·a -ae *f* praesens *(or* numerata), numm·i -orum *mpl,* numerat·um -i *n;* **in —** numerato; **in cold —** calidis nummis; **in hard —** in nummis: **to pay —** praesenti *(or* numeratā) pecuniā solvere
cash box *s* arc·a -ae *f*
cashier *s* dispensa·tor -toris *m* (·trix -tricis *f*)
cash payment *s* repraesentati·o -onis *f*
cash register *s* machin·a -ae *f* accepto et expenso numerando
casing *s (cover)* tegim·en -inis *n*
casino *s* aleator·ium -(i)i *n*
cask *s* cad·us -i *m*
casket *s* capul·us -i *m*
Caspian Sea *s* Caspium mar·e -is *n*
casserole *s (dish)* coctor·ium -(i)i *n; (food)* miscellane·a -orum *npl*
cassette *s* caset·a -ae *f; (for video)* caseta magnetoscopica
cassette recorder *s* casetophon·um -i *n*
cast *s (throw)* iact·us -ūs *m; (mold)* typ·us -i *m;* **— of characters** distributi·o -onis *f* partium in singulos actores
cast *tr* iacere; *(metal)* fundere; *(a vote)* ferre; **to — aside** abicere; **to — a vote** suffragium ferre; **to — down** deicere; **to — in** inicere; **to — off** *(skin)* exuere; *(fig)* ponere; **to — out** eicere, expellere; **to — upon** superinicere; *(fig)* aspergere **||** *intr* **to — off** navem solvere
caste *s* ord·o -inis *m*
castigate *intr* castigare
cast iron *s* ferr·um -i *n* fusum
castle *s* castell·um -i *n; (chess)* turr·is -is *f*
castrate *tr* castrare
castration *s* castrati·o -onis *f*
casual *adj* fortuit·us -a -um; *(person)* negleg·ens -entis
casually *adv* fortuito, casu, forte
casualty *s* cas·us -ūs *m; (mil)* bello caduc·us -i *m* (·a -ae *f*)
cat *s* fel·es -is *f,* catt·a -ae *f,* catt·us -i *m*
cataclysm *s* cataclysm·os -i *m*
catacombs *spl* catacumb·ae -arum *fpl*
catalogue *s* catalog·us -i *m*
cataract *s* cataract·a -ae *f; (of the eyes)* glaucom·a -atis *n*
catastrophe *s* calamit·as -atis *f*
catcall *s* irrisi·o -onis *f*
catch *s (of fish)* praed·a -ae *f; (fastening)* fibul·a -ae *f;* **to think s.o. a great —** aliquem magni facere; **what's the — ?** quid est captio?

catch *tr* capere; *(unawares)* excipere; *(to surprise)* deprehendere; *(to hear)* exaudire; *(falling object)* excipere, suscipere; *(in a net)* illaquēre; *(fish)* captare; *(birds)* excipere; **to — a cold** gravedine affligi; **to — fire** ignem *or* flammam concipere; **to — hell** convicium habēre; **to — his eye** experimentum oculorum eius capere; **to — red-handed** deprehendere; **to — one's breath** respirare; **to — sight of** conspicere ‖ *intr* **to — at** arripere; **to — on** comprehendere; **to — up to** *(or* **with)** consequi

catcher *s* excep·tor -oris *m* (·trix -tricis *f)*

catching *adj (contagious)* contagios·us -a -um; *(fig)* grat·us -a -um

categorical *adj* categoric·us -a -um

categorically *adv* categorice

category *s* categori·a -ae *f*

cater *intr* cibum suppeditare; **to — to** indulgēre *(w. dat)*

caterer *s* obsona·tor -toris *m* (·trix -tricis *f)*

caterpillar *s* eruc·a -ae *f; (mech)* vehicul·um -i *n* catenarium

cathedral *s* ecclesi·a -ae *f* cathedralis

Catholic *adj* Catholic·us -a -um

catnap *s* lenis *(or* brevis) somn·us -i *m;* **to take a —** somno brevi uti

cattle *s* pec·us -oris *n,* bov·es -um *mpl*

cauliflower *s* brassic·a -ae *f* Pompeiana; *(plant)* brassica oleracea botryitis

causal *adj* causal·is -is -e

cause *s* caus·a -ae *f; (motive)* rati·o -onis *f*

cause *tr* facere, efficere; *(pain, swelling, war)* movēre; **to — a quarrel** litem facere; **to — him to leave** facere ut abeat; **to — trouble** malum facere

causeway *s* agg·er -eris *m*

caustic *adj* caustic·us -a -um; *(fig)* mord·ax -acis

cauterize *tr* adurere

caution *s* cauti·o -onis *f;* **to use great —** diligenter circumspicere; **with —** pedetemptim

caution *tr* (ad)monēre

cautious *adj* caut·us -a -um

cautiously *adv* caute

cavalcade *s* pomp·a -ae *f*

cavalry *s* equitat·us -ūs *m,* equit·es -um *mpl*

cave *s* spec·us -ūs *m*

cave *intr* **to — in** corruere, collabi

caveat *s* monit·um -i *n*

cavern *s* cavern·a -ae *f*

cavernous *adj* cavernos·us -a -um

caviar *s* ov·a -orum *npl* acipenseris

cavity *s* cav·um -i *n; (anat)* lacun·a -ae *f; (in tooth or bone)* cari·es -ei *f*

cavort *intr* exsultare

caw *intr* crocire, crocitare

CD *s* compactus disc·us -i *m*

CD player *s* discophon·um -i *n*

CD-ROM *s* orbicul·us -i *m* opticus

CD-ROM drive *s* instrument·um -i *n* orbiculis legendis

cease *tr & intr* desinere; *(temporarily)* intermittere

cease-fire *s* induti·ae -arum *fpl;* **to call for a —** indutias poscere

ceaseless *adj* perpetu·us -a -um

ceaselessly *adv* perpetuo

cedar *s* cedr·us -i *f*

cedar *adj* cedre·us -a -um

cede *tr & intr* (con)cedere

ceiling *s* tect·um -i *n; (arched or vaulted)* camer·a -ae *f; (panelled)* lacun·ar -aris *n*

celebrate *tr* celebrare; *(in song)* canere

celebrated *adj* cele·ber -bris -bre

celebration *s* celebrati·o -onis *f; (of rites)* sollemn·e -is *n*

celebrity *s* celebrit·as -atis *f; (person)* hom·o -inis *mf* illustris

celery *s* heleoselin·um -i *n*

celestial *adj* caelest·is -is -e

celibacy *s* caelibat·us -ūs *m*

celibate *adj* caeleb·s -is

cell *s (room)* cell·a -ae *f; (biol)* protoplasm·a -atis *n*

cellar *s* hypoge·um -i *n*

cell phone *s* telephon·ium -(i)i *n* portabile

cellophane *s* membran·a -ae *f* pellucida

cement *s (concrete)* ferrum·en -inis *n; (glue)* ferrumen

cement *tr* ferruminare; *(to glue)* conglutinare ‖ *intr* coalescere

cemetery *s* sepulcret·um -i *n*

censer *s* turibul·um -i *n*

censor *s* cens·or -oris *m*

censorship *s* censur·a -ae *f; (of literature)* literarum censur·a -ae *f*

censure *s* vituperati·o -onis *f*

censure *tr* animadvertere; *(officially)* notare

census *s* civium enumerati·o -onis *f; (in the Roman sense)* cens·us -ūs *m;* **to conduct a —** recensum populi agere

cent *s* centesim·a -ae *f;* **I don't owe anyone a red —** assem aerarium nemini debeo

centaur *s* centaur·us -i *m*

centennial *adj* centenari·us -a -um

centennial *s* centesimus ann·us -i *m*

center *s* med·ium -(i)i *n; (math)* centr·um -i *n;* **in the — of the town** in medio oppido

center *tr* in centrum ponere ‖ *intr* **to — on** niti *(w. abl)*

central *adj* medi·us -a -um, central·is -is -e

central heating *s* calefacti·o -onis *f* centralis

centralize *tr (authority)* ad unum deferre

centurion *s* centuri·o -onis *m*

century *s* saecul·um -i *n; (mil, pol)* centuri·a -ae *f;* **— old** saecular·is -is -e

ceramic *adj* fictil·is -is -e

ceramics *s* ar·s -tis *f* figlina; *(objects)* fictil·ia -ium *npl*

cereal *s* cere·al -alis *n*

cerebellum *s* cerebell·um -i *n*

cerebrum *s* cerebr·um -i *n*
ceremonial *adj* sollemn·is -is -e
ceremonial *s* sollemn·e -is *n; (religious)* rit·us -ūs *m*
ceremonious *adj* solemn·is -is -e; *(person)* officios·us -a -um
ceremoniously *adv* rite
ceremony *s* caerimoni·a -ae *f; (pomp)* apparat·us -ūs *m;* **religious ceremonies** religion·es -um *fpl*
certain *adj (sure)* cert·us -a -um; *(indefinite)* quidam quaedam quoddam; **for —** certe, pro certo; **it is certain that** constat *(w. acc & inf);* **to make —** explorare
certainly *adv* profecto; *(in answers)* sane
certainty *s* cert·um -i *n; (belief)* fid·es -ei *f*
certificate *s* testimon·ium -(i)i *n*
certification *s* testificati·o -onis *f*
certified *adj* affirmat·us -a -um; *(of credentials)* testimonium hab·ens -entis, testimonial·is -is -e
certify *tr* confirmare; *(to attest)* testificari
cessation *s* cessati·o -onis *f; (temporary)* intermissi·o -onis *f;* **— of hostilities** induti·ae -arum *fpl*
chafe *tr* urere; *(w. the hand)* fricare; *(to excoriate)* atterere; *(to vex)* irritare **||** *intr* stomachari
chagrin *s* stomach·us -i *m*
chagrined *adj* **to be —** stomachari
chain *s* caten·a -ae *f; (necklace)* torqu·es -is *mf; (fig)* seri·es -ei *f;* **dog on a —** can·is -is *m* catenis vinctus
chain *tr* catenas inicere *(w. dat)*
chain store *s* tabern·a -ae *f* societatis
chair *s* sell·a -ae *f; (w. rounded back)* arcisell·ium -(i)i *n; (of a teacher)* cathedr·a -ae *f; (of a Roman magistrate)* sella *f* curulis
chair *tr (a meeting)* praesidēre *(w. dat),* praeesse *(w. dat)*
chairperson *s* praes·es -idis *mf*
chalice *s* cal·ix -icis *m*
chalk *s* cret·a -ae *f*
chalk *tr* cretā notare; *(cover with chalk)* cretā illinere; **to — up** notare
chalky *adj (chalk-like)* cretace·us -a -um; *(full of chalk)* cretos·us -a -um
challenge *s* provocati·o -onis *f; (leg)* reiecti·o -onis *f,* recusati·o -onis *f*
challenge *tr* provocare; *(a claim)* vindicare; *(validity)* recusare; *(leg)* reicere
challenger *s* provoca·tor -toris *m* (·trix -tricis *f)*
challenging *adj* provoc·ans -antis
chamber *s (room)* conclav·e -is *n; (bedroom)* cubicul·um -i *n; (pol)* curi·a -ae *f*
chambermaid *s* ancill·a -ae *f* cubicularia
chamber pot *s* lasan·um -i *n*
champ *tr & intr* mandere; **to — on the bit** frena dente premere
champagne *s* vin·um -i *n* effervescens
champion *s (sports)* summ·us (-a) athlet·a -ae *mf; (defender)* propugna·tor -toris *m* (·trix -tricis *f)*
championship *s* titul·us -i *m* victoriae
chance *s (accident)* cas·us -ūs *m; (opportunity)* potest·as -atis *f; (risk)* pericul·um -i *n*; *(prospect)* sp·es -ei *f; (fig)* ale·a -ae *f;* **by —** casu, forte; **by some — or other** nescio quo casu; **game of —** ale·a -ae *f;* **to give s.o. a — to** potestatem alicui facere *(w. inf);* **to stand a —** potestatem habēre; **to take a —** periculum adire
chance *tr* periclitari **||** *intr* accidere; *often expressed by the adverb* forte: **I —ed to see the aedile** aedilem forte conspexi; **to — on** occurrere *(w. dat)*
chance *adj* fortuit·us -a -um
chancellor *s (pol)* princ·eps -ipis *mf* consilii
chandelier *s* lampadum corymb·us -i *m*
change *s* mutati·o -onis *f; (complete)* commutati·o -onis *f,* permutati·o -onis *f; (variety)* variet·as -atis *f; (of fortune)* vicissitud·o -inis *f; (coins)* numm·i -orum *mpl* minores; **— of clothes** mutati·o -onis *f* vestis; **— of heart** animi mutati·o -onis *f;* **for a —** varietatis causā
change *tr* mutare; *(completely)* commutare; **to — into** convertere in *(w. acc);* **to — one's mind** sententiam mutare **||** *intr* mutari, variare; *(of the moon)* renovari; **the wind changed** ventus se vertit; **to — for the better (worse)** in meliorem (peiorem) partem mutari; **to — into** verti in *(w. acc)*
changeable *adj* mutabil·is -is -e; *(fickle)* inconst·ans -antis
changeless *adj* immutabil·is -is -e
channel *s (TV)* televisorius canal·is -is *m; (of rivers)* alve·us -i *m; (arm of the sea)* fret·um -i *n; (groove)* stri·a -ae *f*
channel *tr* sulcare, excavare; *(to guide)* ducere
chant *s* cant·us -ūs *m*
chant *tr* cantare
chaos *s* cha·os -i *n; (confusion)* perturbati·o -onis *f*
chaotic *adj* confus·us -a -um
chap *s* fissur·a -ae *f; (person)* hom·o -inis *m; (boy)* pu·er -eri *m*
chap *tr* diffindere; **—ed lips** fissur·ae -arum *fpl* labrorum **||** *intr* scindi
chapel *s* sacell·um -i *n*
chapter *s* cap·ut -itis *n*
char *tr* amburere
character *s* mor·es -um *mpl; (inborn)* indol·es -is *f,* ingen·ium -(i)i *n; (repute)* existimati·o -onis *f; (type)* gen·us -eris *n; (letter)* litter·a -ae *f; (theat)* person·a -ae *f;* **to assume the — of a plaintiff** petitoris personam capere
characteristic *s* propr·ium -(i)i *n*

characteristic *adj* propri·us -a -um; **it is — of a father to protect his family** patris est familiam suam tegere
characteristically *adv* proprie
characterize *tr* describere, pingere
character witness *s* advocat·us -i *m* (·a -ae *f*)
charade *s* mim·us -i *m;* **—s** aenigm·a -atis *n* syllabicum
charcoal *s* carb·o -onis *m*
charge *s* accusati·o -onis *f; (leg)* lis, litis *f,* crim·en -inis *n; (mil)* impet·us -ūs *m; (into enemy territory)* incurs·us -ūs *m; (command)* mandat·um -i *n; (trust)* cur·a -ae *f,* custodi·a -ae *f; (office)* mun·us -eris *n; (cost)* impens·a -ae *f;* **capital —** lis capitis; **free of —** gratis; **to be in — of** praeesse *(w. dat);* **to bring —s against** litem intendere *(w. dat);* **to put in — of** praeficere *(w. dat);* **to take — of** curare
charge *tr* indicare *(with gen of indefinite price or abl of definite price), e.g.,* **to — a lot for the meal** cenam multi indicare; **to — ten dollars for the meal** cenam decem dollaris indicare; *(to attack)* incurrere *(w. dat or acc); (to enjoin upon)* mandare *(w. dat of person and* ut *w. subj);* **to — a certain price for goods** pretium statuere merci; **to — a fixed price** pretium certum constituere; **to — an expense to the citizens** sumptum civibus inferre; **to — s.o. with** *(a crime)* arguere aliquem *(w. gen or abl of the charge)* **||** *intr (to make a charge)* irruere
charger *s* bellat·or -oris *m*
chariot *s* curr·us -ūs *m; (for racing)* curricul·um -i *n; (for war)* essed·um -i *n*
charioteer *s* aurig·a -ae *m; (combatant in a chariot)* essedar·ius -(i)i *m*
charitable *adj* benign·us -a -um; *(lenient in judgment)* mit·is -is -e
charitably *adv* benigne
charity *s* liberalit·as -atis *f; (Christian love)* carit·as -atis *f*
charlatan *s* ostentat·or -oris *m* (·rix -ricis *f*)*; (quack doctor)* pharmacopol·a -ae *mf*
charm *s (attractiveness)* venust·as -atis *f,* lep·os -oris *m; (spell)* carm·en -inis *n; (amulet)* amulet·um -i *n*
charm *tr (to bewitch)* incantare; *(to delight)* capere; **to lead a —ed life** vitam divinitus munitam gerere
charmer *s (fig)* delici·ae -arum *fpl*
charming *adj (esp. to the eye)* amoen·us -a -um; *(in manner)* lepid·us -a -um; *(beautiful)* venust·us -a -um
chart *s* tabul·a -ae *f; (nautical)* nautica tabul·a -ae *f*
chart *tr* designare
charter *tr (to hire)* conducere; *(to grant a charter to)* diploma donare *(w. dat)*
charter *s (instrument conferring privileges)* diplom·a -atis *n*
chartreuse *adj* chlorin·us -a -um
chase *s (hunt)* venati·o -onis *f; (pursuit)* insectati·o -onis *f*
chase *tr (to hunt)* venari; *(to engrave)* caelare; *(romantically)* petere; **to — away** abigere **||** *intr* **to — after** petere
chasm *s* hiat·us -ūs *m*
chaste *adj* cast·us -a -um
chastely *adv* caste
chasten *tr (to chastise)* castigare
chastise *tr* castigare
chastisement *s* castigati·o -onis *f*
chastity *s* castit·as -atis *f*
chat *s* familiaris serm·o -onis *m;* **to have a —** fabulari
chat *intr* fabulari
chattel *s* res, rei *f* mancipi; **—s** bon·a -orum *npl*
chatter *s* clang·or -oris *m; (idle talk)* garrulit·as -atis *f; (of teeth)* crepit·us -ūs *m*
chatter *intr* balbutire; *(of birds)* canere; **my teeth —** dentibus crepito
chatty *adj* garul·us -a -um
cheap *adj* vil·is -is -e; **to be — as dirt** pro luto esse; **to sell —er** minoris vendere
cheaply *adv* bene, vili (pretio); **to live —** parvo sumptu vivere
cheapen *tr* pretium minuere *(w. gen)*
cheapness *s* vilit·as -atis *f*
cheat *tr* fraudare; **to — s.o. out of his money** aliquem pecuniā fraudare **||** *intr (in school)* furtim exscribere
cheat *s* plan·us -i *m,* frau·s -dis *f*
cheater *s* frauda·tor -toris *m* (·trix -tricis *f*)
check *tr (to restrain, e.g., an onset, flow of blood, eager horses)* inhibēre; *(to slow down)* retardare; *(accounts)* dispungere; *(to verify)* comprobare; *(to mark with a check mark)* virgulā notare; **to — luggage** sarcinas mandare; **to — off** *(to make a check mark at)* notare; **to — out** *(to inquire into)* inquirere in *(w. acc)* **||** *intr (to balance, be correct)* constare; **to — up on** exquirere
check *s* syngraph·a -ae *f,* perscripti·o -onis *f; (bill)* rati·o -onis *f* nummaria; *(restraint)* coërciti·o -onis *f;* **to cash a —** arcario syngrapham praebēre; **to hold in —** supprimere; **to write a — for** argentum perscribere *(w. dat)*
checkbook *s* cod·ex -icis *f* syngrapharum
checker *s* latruncul·us -i *m;* **—s** *(game)* latrunculorum lud·us -i *m;* **to play —s** latrunculis ludere
checkered *adj* vari·us -a -um
checklist *s* ind·ex -icis *m*
check mark *s* virgul·a -ae *f;* **to put a — at** annotare, virgulā notare
checkup *s* inspecti·o -onis *f*
cheek *s* gen·a -ae *f; (when puffed out by eating, blowing)* bucc·a -ae *f*
cheekbone *s* maxill·a -ae *f*

cheer *s* clam•or -oris *m;* **to be of good —** bono animo esse
cheer *tr* hortari; **to — up** exhilare; **— up!** bono animo es!
cheerful *adj* hilar•us -a -um
cheerfully *adv* hilariter
cheerfulness *s* hilarit•as -atis *f*
cheerless *adj* illaetabil•is -is -e
cheese *s* case•us -i *m*
cheese cake *s* savill•um -i *n*
chef *s* archimagir•us -i *m* (•a -ae *f*)
chemical *adj* chemic•us -a -um
chemical *s* chemic•um -i *n*
chemist *s* chemic•us -i *m* (•a -ae *f*)
chemistry *s* chemi•a -ae *f*
cherish *tr* fovēre; *(fig)* colere
cherry *s* ceras•um -i *n*
cherry pie *s* cerasa *npl* in crusto cocta
cherry-red *adj* cerasin•us -a -um
cherry tree *s* ceras•us -i *f*
chess *s* lud•us -i *m* scacorum, scacilud•ium -(i)i *n;* **to play —** scacis ludere
chessboard *s* scacar•ium -(i)i *n*
chest *s* *(anat)* pect•us -oris *n; (box)* arc•a -ae *f,* armar•ium -(i)i *n; (for clothes)* vestiar•ium -(i)i *n*
chestnut *s* castane•a -ae *f*
chestnut tree *s* castane•a -ae *f*
chew *tr* manducare; **to — the cud** ruminare; **to — out** *(coll)* pilare
chewing gum *s* cumm•is -is *f* masticabilis
chicanery *s* praevaricati•o -onis *f*
chick *s* pull•us -i *m; (term of endearment)* pull•a -ae *f*
chicken *s* pull•us -i *m* gallinaceus, gallin•a -ae *f; (meat)* gallinace•a -ae *f*
chicken-hearted *adj* muricid•us -a -um
chicory *s* cichore•um -i *n*
chide *tr* increpitare
chief *adj* princ•eps -ipis; *(first in rank)* primari•us -a -um; **— justice** summus iud•ex -icis *m*
chief *s* princ•eps -ipis *m; (ringleader)* cap•ut -itis *n*
chiefly *adv* praecipue, inprimis
chief of police *s* praefect•us -i *m* (•a -ae *f*) vigilum
chieftain *s* du•x -cis *m*
child *s* inf•ans -antis *mf,* fil•ius -(i)i *m;* **children** liber•i -orum *mpl;* **to bear a —** parturire; **with —** gravida
childbearing *s* part•us -ūs *m*
childbirth *s* part•us -ūs *m*
childhood *s* infanti•a -ae *f,* pueriti•a -ae *f;* **from —** a puero *or* a pueris
childish *adj* pueril•is -is -e; *(fig)* inept•us -a -um
childishly *adv* pueriliter; *(fig)* inepte
childless *adj* orb•us -a -um
childlike *adj* pueril•is -is -e
chill *s* frig•us -oris *n; (of the body)* horr•or -oris *m;* **to have the —s** algēre
chill *tr* refrigerare
chilly *adj* frigidul•us -a -um; *(susceptible to cold)* alsios•us -a -um; **it's getting —** aër frigescit
chime *s* son•us -i *m*
chime *intr* concinere; **to — in** succinere; *(to interrupt)* interpellare
chimera *s* chimaer•a -ae *f*
chimney *s* camin•us -i *m*
chimpanzee *s* satyr•us -i *m*
chin *s* ment•um -i *n;* **to drop the —** labrum demittere
China *s* Ser•es -um *mpl*
china *s* murrin•a *(or* myrrhin•a) -orum *npl*
Chinese *adj* Seric•us -a -um
chink *s* rim•a -ae *f; (sound)* tinnit•us -ūs *m*
chink *intr* tinnire
chip *s* assul•a -ae *f; (of pottery)* fragment•um -i *n*
chip *tr (wood)* ascio dedolare; *(to break off a piece of)* praecidere; **to — in** *(money)* conferre
chipper *adj* ala•cer -cris -cre
chirp *s (of birds)* pipat•us -ūs *m; (of crickets)* strid•or -oris *m*
chirp *intr (of birds)* pipilare; *(of crickets)* stridēre
chisel *s* scalpr•um -i *n*
chisel *tr* scalpro caedere; *(to cheat)* emungere; *(to borrow)* mutuare
chivalrous *adj* magnanim•us -a -um
chivalry *s (knighthood)* equestris dignit•as -atis *f; (spirit)* magnanimit•as -atis *f*
chocolate *s* socolat•a -ae *f: (drink)* pot•us -ūs *m* socolatae
chocolate *adj* socolate•us -a -um
chocolate bar *s* tabell•a -ae *f* socolatae
chocolate pudding *s* erne•um -i *n* socolateum
chock-full *adj* refert•us -a -um
choice *s* electi•o -onis *f; (power of choosing)* opti•o -onis *f; (diversity)* variet•as -atis *f*
choice *adj* elect•us -a -um
choir *s* chor•us -i *m*
choke *tr* strangulare ‖ *intr* strangulari
choking *s* strangulati•o -onis *f*
choose *tr* eligere; **to — to** *(to prefer to)* malle *(w. inf)*
chop *s* ofell•a -ae *f;* **pork —** ofella *f* porcina
chop *tr (wood)* dolabrā caedere; **to — off** praecidere; **to — up** minutatim concidere
choral *adj* symphoniac•us -a -um
chord *s* nerv•us -i *m*
chore *s* pens•um -i *n;* **to do —s** pensa facere
chorus *s* chor•us -i *m*
chorus girl *s* ambubai•a -ae *f*
Christ *s* Christ•us -i *m*
christen *tr* baptizare
Christendom *s* cuncti Christian•i -orum *mpl*
Christian *adj* Christian•us -a -um
Christian *s* Christian•us -i *m* (•a -ae *f*)

Christianity *s* Christianism·us -i *m*
Christmas *s* fest·um -i *n* nativitatis Christi; **it won't be — forever** *(fig)* non semper Saturnalia erunt; **Merry —!** Fausta Festa Natalicia Christi (tibi exopto!); **to celebrate — all year long** *(fig)* semper Saturnalia agere
Christmas carol *s* cantic·um -i *n* de Christi natali
Christmas day *s* Christi di·es -ei *m* natalis
Christmas Eve *s* vigili·a -ae *f* nativitatis Christi
Christmas gift *s* natalicium munuscul·um -i *n;* **to give (exchange, receive, wrap) —s** offerre (inter se dare, accipere, involvere) natalicia munuscula
Christmas Holidays *spl* feri·ae -arum *fpl* nataliciae; **to spend the —** ferias natalicias agere
Christmas tree *s* arb·or -oris *f* natalicia; **to decorate the — with lights, balls, and tinsel** arborem nataliciam igniculis et globulis et laminis ornare
chronic *adj* long·us -a - um
chronicle *s* annal·es -ium *mpl*
chronological *adj* **in — order** servato temporis ordine
chronology *s* temporum ord·o -inis *m*
chubby *adj* crass·us -a -um
chuckle *intr* pressā voce cachinnare
chum *s* familiar·is -is *mf,* sodal·is -is *mf*
chummy *adj* familiar·is -is -e
chunk *s* frust·um -i *n*
church *s* ecclesi·a -ae *f*
chute *s* decliv·e -is *n*
cicada *s* cicad·a -ae *f*
cider *s* hydromel·um -i *n*
cigar *s* sigar·um -i *n*
cigarette *s* sigarell·um -i *n;* **pack of —s** capsell·a -ae *f* sigarellorum; **to smoke a —** fumum sigarelli sugere
cigarette lighter *s* ignitabul·um -i *n*
cinch *s (coll)* res, rei *f* facilis factu
cinder *s* favill·a -ae *f*
cinema *s* cinemate·um -i *n*
cinnamon *s* cinnamom·um -i *n*
cipher *s (code)* not·a -ae *f; (a nobody)* numer·us -i *m; (zero)* nihil *n*
circle *s* circul·us -i *m; (social)* coet·us -ūs *m; (movement)* gyr·us -i *m; (anything round)* orb·is -is *m;* **family —** coron·a -ae *f* domi; **to form a —** *(to stand in a circle)* in orbem consistere
circle *tr* circumdare, cingere; *(to draw)* circumducere ‖ *intr* circumagi
circuit *s* circuit·us -ūs *m;* **short —** dissoluti·o -onis *f* vis eletricae; **to make a —** circumire, circumagi
circuit court *s* convent·us -ūs *m*
circuitous *adj* flexuos·us -a -um; **by a — route** circuitu; **to take a — route** circumagi
circular *adj* rotund·us -a -um
circular *s* litter·ae -arum *fpl* passim dimissae
circulate *tr (to spread)* in vulgum spargere ‖ *intr (of money)* in usum venire; *(to flow)* circumfluere; *(of news, rumors)* percrebescere
circulation *s (of blood)* circulati·o -onis *f;* **to be in —** *(e.g., of books)* in manibus esse
circumcise *tr* circumcidere
circumcised *adj* recutit·us -a -um, curt·us -a -um
circumcision *s* circumcisi·o -onis *f*
circumference *s* ambit·us -ūs *m; (geom)* peripheri·a -ae *f*
circumflex *s* circumflexus accent·us -ūs *m*
circumlocution *s* ambit·us -ūs *m*
circumscribe *tr* circumscribere
circumspect *adj* circumspect·us -a -um
circumspection *s* circumspecti·o -onis *f*
circumstance *s* res, rei *f; (circumstances collectively)* temp·us -oris *n;* **according to —s** pro re, pro tempore; **as —s arise** e re natā; **in humble —s** tenui re; **to yield to —** tempori cedere; **under no —s** nequaquam; **under the —s** quae cum ita sint
circumstantial *adj (incidental)* adventici·us -a -um; **to rest on — evidence** coniecturā contineri
circumvent *tr* circumscribere
circumvention *s* circumscripti·o -onis *f*
circus *s* circ·us -i *m; (performance)* circens·es -ium *mpl*
cistern *s* cistern·a -ae *f*
citadel *s* ar·x -cis *f*
citation *s (summons)* vocati·o -onis *f; (quotation)* loc·us -i *m* allatus; *(act of quoting)* prolati·o -onis *f*
cite *tr (leg)* evocare, citare; *(to quote)* proferre; *(in writing)* ponere
citizen *s* civ·is -is *mf; (of a municipality)* munic·eps -ipis *mf;* **private —** privat·us -i *m* (·a -ae *f*)
citizenship *s* civit·as -atis *f*
city *adj* urban·us -a -um
city *s* urb·s -is *f*
city council *s* decurion·es -um *mpl*
civic *adj* civil·is -is-e
civil *adj* civil·is -is -e; *(polite)* urban·us -a -um; **— rights** iu·s -ris *n* civile; **to deprive s.o. of — rights** aliquem capite deminuere; **loss (taking away) of — rights** diminuti·o -onis *f* capitis
civilian *s* togat·us -i *m,* privat·us -i *m* (·a -ae *f*)
civilian *adj* togat·us -a -um, privat·us -a -um
civility *s* comit·as -atis *f*
civilization *s* (humanus) cult·us -ūs *m*
civilize *tr* excolere
civilized *adj* human·us -a -um
clad *adj* indut·us -a -um

claim *s (demand)* postulati•o -onis *f; (leg)* vindici•ae -arum *fpl; (land)* a•ger -gri *m* assignatus; *(assertion)* affirmati•o -onis *f;* **to lay — to** vindicare
claim *tr (to demand)* postulare; *(esp. leg)* vindicare; *(to assert)* affirmare; **to — the thing as ours** rem nostram vindicare
claimant *s* peti•tor -toris *m* (•trix -tricis *f*)
clam *s* my•ax -acis *m*
clamber *intr* scandere; **to — down** descendere; **to — up** *(e.g., a mountain)* scandere
clammy *adj* umid•us -a -um
clamor *s* clam•or -oris *m*
clamor *intr* vociferari; **to — for** flagitare
clamp *s* confibul•a -ae *f*
clamp *tr* constringere; **to — down on** *(fig)* compescere
clam shell *s* nyacis test•a -ae *f*
clan *s* gen•s -tis *f*
clandestine *adj* clandestin•us -a -um
clandestinely *adv* clam, furtim
clang *s* clang•or -oris *m*
clang *intr* clangere
clank *s* crepit•us -ūs *m*
clank *intr* crepare
clap *s (of hands)* plaus•us -ūs *m; (of thunder)* frag•or -oris *m;* **a loud — of thunder** gravis fragor *m*
clap *tr* **to — the hands** manūs complodere **||** *intr* plaudere
claptrap *s* iactati•o -onis *f*
clarification *s* explicati•o -onis *f*
clarify *tr* deliquare; *(fig)* explicare
clarity *s* clarit•as -atis *f*
clash *s* concurs•us -ūs *m; (sound)* crepit•us -ūs *m; (fig)* dissonanti•a -ae *f; (of colors)* repugnanti•a -ae *f*
clash *intr (to collide)* concurrere; *(to make a noise by striking)* concrepare; *(disagree)* discrepare
clasp *s* fibul•a -ae *f; (embrace)* amplex•us -ūs *m*
clasp *tr (to embrace)* amplecti; *(to grasp)* comprehendere
class *s (pol)* class•is -is *f,* ord•o -inis *m; (of pupils)* class•is -is *f; (kind)* gen•us -eris *n;* **lower —** ordo inferior; **middle —** ordo medius; **upper —** ordo superior; **working —** ordo operarius
class *tr (e.g., according to wealth)* describere; **to — as** in numero *(w. gen)* habēre
classical *adj* classic•us -a -um
classics *spl* scriptor•es -um *mpl* classici
classification *s* descripti•o -onis *f*
classify *tr* describere
clatter *s* strepit•us -ūs *m*
clatter *intr* strepare, crepitare
clause *s (gram)* articul•us -i *m,* membr•um -i *n; (leg)* cap•ut -itis *n*
claw *s* ungu•is -is *m; (of birds)* ungul•a -ae *f; (of a crab)* bracch•ium -(i)i *n*
claw *tr* lacerare
clay *s* lut•um -i *n; (white potter's clay)* argill•a -ae *f*
clay *adj* fictil•is -is -e
clean *adj* mund•us -a -um; *(lit & fig)* pur•us -a -um
clean *tr* purgare; *(to make tidy)* mundare; **to — s.o. out** *(of money)* aliquem excatarissare
cleaning rag *s* drapp•us -i *m*
cleanliness *s* munditi•a -ae *f*
cleanly *adv* omnino, penitus
cleanse *tr* purgare; *(by washing)* abluere; *(by rubbing)* detergēre
clear *adj* clar•us -a -um; *(unclouded)* seren•us -a -um, sud•us -a -um; *(liquids)* limpid•us -a -um; *(transparent)* pellucid•us -a -um; *(voice)* liquid•us -a -um; *(style)* lucid•us -a -um; *(explanation)* illustr•is -is -e; *(manifest)* conspicu•us -a -um; *(conscience)* rect•us -a -um; *(mind)* sag•ax -acis; **— of** exper•s -tis *(w. gen);* **it is —** manifestum est; *(leg)* liquet; **to keep — of** evitare
clear *tr* purgare; *(to make open)* expedire; *(to acquit)* absolvere; *(land)* exstirpare; *(the table)* mundare; *(profit)* lucrari; **to — away** detergēre, amovēre; *(by force)* amoliri; **to — out** emundare; **to — up** enodare **||** *intr (of weather)* disserenare; **— out!** apage!
clearance *s* purgati•o -onis *f; (space)* intervall•um -i *n*
clearly *adv* clare; *(obviously)* aperte
clearness *s* clarit•as -atis *f; (of sky)* serenit•as -atis *f; (of style)* perspicuit•as -atis *f*
clear-sighted *adj* **to be —** clare decernere
cleave *tr* findere **||** *intr* **to — to** adhaerēre *(w. dat)*
cleaver *s* dolabr•a -ae *f*
cleft *s* rim•a -ae *f,* fissur•a -ae *f*
clemency *s* clementi•a -ae *f*
clement *adj* clem•ens -entis
clench *tr* comprimere; **to — the fist** manum comprimere
clergy *s* cler•us -i *m*
cleric *s* cleric•us -i *m*
clerk *s* scrib•a -ae *mf; (in a shop)* tabernari•us -i *m* (•a -ae *f*)
clever *adj* callid•us -a -um
cleverly *adv* callide
cleverness *s* callidit•as -atis *f*
cliché *s* verb•um -i *n* tritum
click *s* crepit•us -ūs *m*
click *tr (comput)* deprimere, pulsare; **double-click** bis deprimere *(or* pulsare); **left-click** sinistrorsum deprimere; **right-click** dextrorsum deprimere **||** *intr* crepitare; *(to succeed)* bene vertere
client *s* cli•ens -entis *mf*
cliff *s* rup•es -is *f*
climate *s* cael•um -i *n;* **cold (hot, temperate, warm) —** fervens (frigidum, temper-

atum, tepidum) caelum; **mild —** temperi·es -ei *f*

climax *s (fig)* culm·en -inis *n; (rhet)* gradati·o -onis *f*

climb *tr* ascendere; *(to the top)* conscendere; **to — (up) a tree** in arborem inscendere, *(to the top)* arborem conscendere; **to — the stairs** pers scalas ascendere **||** *intr* ascendere

climb *s* ascens·us -ūs *m*

clinch *vt (to settle)* confirmare **||** *intr (in boxing)* amplecti

cling *intr (to)* adhaerēre *(w. abl or dat or* ab *w. abl);* **to — together** cohaerēre

clip *s* fibul·a -ae *f*

clip *tr (to cut)* tondēre; *(words, tail)* mutilare

clipping *s* tonsur·a -ae *f;* **—s** resegmin·a -um *npl*

cloak *s* pall·ium -(i)i *n; (cape with hood for travel)* paenul·a -ae *f; (mil)* sag·um -i *n; (general's)* paludament·um -i *n;* **wearing a —** palliat·us -a -um

cloak *tr* dissimulare, tegere

clock *s* horolog·ium -(i)i *n;* **at three o'clock** tertiā horā; **the — keeps good time** horologium recte metitur; **to set (wind) the —** horologium temperare (intendere)

clock *tr* horologio metiri

clog *tr (to hinder, fetter)* impedire; *(to block up)* obstruere

clogs *spl* sole·ae -arum *fpl*

cloister *s* portic·us -ūs *f; (eccl)* monaster·ium -(i)i *n*

close *adj (near)* propinqu·us -a -um; *(dense)* dens·us -a -um; *(tight)* art·us -a -um; *(intimate)* intim·us -a -um; *(shut)* occlus·us -a -um; *(atmosphere)* crass·us -a -um; **at — quarters** comminus [*adv*]; **— attention** anim·us -i *m* attentissimus; **— friend** familiar·is -is *mf;* **to be on the —est possible terms with s.o.** aliquo familiarissime uti; **to be — at hand** adesse, instare; **to keep — to** adhaerēre *(w. dat)*

close *adv* prope, iuxta; **— to** *(near)* prope *(w. acc),* iuxta *(w. acc); (almost)* paene

close *tr* claudere; *(eyes, lips)* premere; *(to end)* finire; *(comput)* concludere; **in —ing** denique; **to — down** claudere; **to — a bargain** pacisci; **to — up** praecludere **||** *intr* coïre, claudi; **to — in on the enemy** undique fauces hostium premere

close *s* fin·is -is *m;* **at the — of the year** exeunte anno; **to bring to a —** finire; **to draw to a —** terminari

closely *adv* prope; *(attentively)* attente

closet *s* armar·ium -(i)i *n; (for clothes)* vestiar·ium -(i)i *n* (parieti insertum)

closing *adj* ultim·us -a -um

closing *s* conclusi·o -onis *f*

clot *s* concretus cru·or -oris *m*

clot *intr* concrescere

cloth *s* pann·us -i *m; (linen)* linte·um -i *n; (as fabric)* text·um -i *n*

clothe *tr* vestire, induere

clothes *spl* vestiment·a -orum *npl*

clothes hanger *s* fulcim·en -inis *n* vestiarium

clothes hook *s* unc·us -i *m* vestiarius

clothing *s* vestit·us -ūs *m;* **an article of —** vestiment·um -i *n*

clothing store *s* tabern·a -ae *f* vestiaria

cloud *s* nub·es -is *f; (dark storm cloud)* nimb·us -i *m;* **small —** nubecul·a -ae *f*

cloud *tr* nubibus velare; *(fig)* obscurare **||** *intr* **to — up** nubescere

cloudburst *s* maximus im·ber -bris *m;* **I arrived in Capua in a —** maximo imbri Capuam veni

cloud-capped *adj* nubif·er -era -erum

cloudless *adj* seren·us -a -um, sud·us -a -um

cloudy *adj* nubil·us -a -um; **somewhat —** subnubil·us -a -um; **to get —** nubilare

clout *s* ict·us -ūs *m;* **to have —** *(coll)* plurimum posse

clove *s (of garlic)* nucle·us -i *m*

cloven *adj* bisulc·us -a -um; **— hoofs** ungul·ae -arum *fpl* spissae

clover *s* trifol·ium -(i)i *n*

clown *s* scurr·a -ae *m*

clown *intr* **to — around** scurrari

clownish *adj* scurril·is -is -e

club *s (cudgel)* clav·a -ae *f; (society)* sodalit·as -atis *f,* sodalic·ium -(i)i *n*

club *tr* clavā dolare

cluck *intr* glocidare, singultire

cluck *s* singult·us -ūs *m*

clue *s* indic·ium -(i)i *n*

clump *s* mass·a -ae *f;* **— of trees** arbust·um -i *n*

clumsily *adv* inscite, rustice

clumsiness *s* insciti·a -ae *f,* rusticit·as -atis *f*

clumsy *adj* inscit·us -a -um, incomcinn·us -a -um; *(of things)* inhabil·is -is -e

cluster *s (of fruit, flowers, berries)* corymb·us -i *m; (of grapes)* uv·a -ae *f; (of people)* coron·a -ae *f*

cluster *intr* congregari; **to — around** stipare

clutch *s* ungul·a -ae *f;* **from one's —es** e manibus; **in one's —es** in suā potestate

clutch *tr* arrigere

clutch *s (of a car)* pedal·e -is *n* iunctionis

clutter *s* congeri·es -ei *f*

clutter *tr* **to — up** conturbare

coach *s (four-wheeled)* raed·a -ae *f; (two-wheeled, closed in, with arched top, for women)* carpent·um -i *n; (trainer)* exerci·tor -toris *m* (·trix -tricis *f*); *(of gladiators)* lanist·a -ae *m*

coach *tr* exercitare; *(a student)* admonēre, docēre

coagulate *intr* coïre

coal *s* carb·o -onis *m*; lapis gagas (*gen*: lapidis gagatis) *m*
coalesce *intr* coalescere
coalition *s* coniuncti·o -onis *f*
coal mine *s* fodin·a -ae *f* carbonaria
coal miner *s* carbonum foss·or -oris *m*
coarse *adj (materials)* crass·us -a -um; *(unfinished)* rud·is -is -e; *(manners)* incult·us -a -um
coarseness *s* crassitud·o -inis *f; (of manners)* rusticit·as -atis *f*
coast *s* or·a -ae *f* maritima; **the — is clear** nihil obstat
coast *intr* **to — along the shore** oram praetervehi
coastguard *s* custod·es -um *mpl* orae maritimae
coastal *adj* maritim·us -a -um
coastline *s* or·a -ae *f* maritima
coat *s* amicul·a -ae *f*, paenul·a -ae *f; (of animals)* pell·is -is *f; (of paint, plaster)* inducti·o -onis *f*
coat *tr* illinere, obducere; **—ed tongue** lingu·a -ae *f* fungosa
coating *s* inducti·o -onis *f*
coat of arms *s* insign·ia -ium *npl*
coat rack *s* sustentacul·um -i *n* vestium
coax *tr* blandiri
coaxing *s* blandiment·a -orum *npl*
coaxing *adj* bland·us -a -um
coaxingly *adv* blande
cobbler *s* sut·or -oris *m*
cobweb *s* arane·um -i *n*
cock *s* gall·us -i *m*
cock-a-doodle-do *interj* cocococo!
cockeyed *adj* **— person** strab·o -onis *m*
cock fight *s* rix·a -ae *f* gallorum
cockpit *s* cell·a -ae *f* aëroplani
cockroach *s* blatt·a -ae *f*
cocksure *adj* omnino confid·ens -entis
cocktail *s* propom·a -atis *n*
cocky *adj* iact·ans -antis
cocoa *s* coco·a -ae *f*
cocoanut *s* nu·x -cis *f* palmae Indicae
cocoon *s* globul·us -i *m*
coddle *tr* indulgēre *(w. dat)*
code *s (laws)* leg·es -um *fpl; (rules)* praecept·a -orum *npl; (system of symbols)* not·ae -arum *fpl;* **in —** per notas
co-ed *s (coll)* condiscipul·a -ae *f*
codicil *s* codicill·i -orum *mpl*
codify *tr* digerere; **to — the law** ius *(or* leges) digerere
coerce *tr* coercēre, cogere
coercion *s* coerciti·o -onis *f*
coexist *intr* simul exsistere
coffee *s* caffe·um -i *n;* **cup of —** pocill·um -i *n* caffei
coffee maker *s* machin·a -ae *f* caffearia
coffeepot *s* hinnul·a -ae *f* caffei
coffee set *s* synthes·is -is *f* caffearia
coffer *s* arc·a -ae *f*
coffin *s* capul·us -i *m*
cog *s* den·s -tis *m*
cogent *adj* grav·is -is -e
cognate *adj* cognat·us -a -um
cognition *s* cogniti·o -onis *f*
cognizance *s* cogniti·o -onis *f;* **to take — of** cognitionem tractare de *(w. abl)*
cognizant *adj* **(of)** consci·us -a -um *(w. gen)*
cohabit *intr* consuescere
cohabitation *s* consuetud·o -inis *f*
cohere *intr* cohaerēre
coherence *s* context·us -ūs *m*
coherent *adj* cohaer·ens -entis
coherently *adv* constanter
cohesion *s* cohaerenti·a -ae *f*
cohesive *adj* ten·ax -acis
cohort *s* cohor·s -tis *f*
coil *s* spir·a -ae *f*
coil *tr* glomerare ‖ *intr* glomerari
coin *s* numm·us -i *m;* **gold —** aure·us -i *m;* **silver —** argent·um -i *n*
coin *tr (to mint)* cudere; *(to stamp)* signare; *(words)* fingere, novare
coinage *s* monet·a -ae *f*
coincide *intr* **(with)** congruere (cum *w. abl)*
coincidence *s* concursati·o -onis *f*
coincidental *adj* fortuit·us -a -um
cold *adj* frigid·us -a -um; *(icy)* gelid·us -a -um; **to be —** frigēre; **to become —** frigescere; **to turn —** frigescere
cold *s* frig·us -oris *n; (med)* graved·o -inis *f;* **to catch a —** gravedinem contrahere; **to have a —** gravedine laborare
cold-blooded *adj (fig)* crudel·is -ie -e
cold spell *s* frigor·a -um *npl*
coldly *adv (fig)* frigide
coldness *s* frig·us -oris *n*
cold wave *s* frigor·a -um *npl*
coleslaw *s* acetari·a -um *npl* e brassica facta
colicky *adj* colic·us -a -um
coliseum *s* amphitheatr·um -i *n*
collaborate *intr* adiu·tor -toris *m* (·trix -tricis *f*) esse; **to — with the enemy** hostibus subvenire
collapse *s* ruin·a -ae *f*
collapse *intr* collabi
collar *s* collar·e -is *n*
collar *tr* collo comprehendere
collarbone *s* iugul·um -i *n*
collate *tr* conferre
collateral *adj (lines of descent)* transvers·us -a -um; *(effect)* adiunct·us -a -um
collateral *s (com)* sponsi·o -onis *f*
colleague *s* colleg·a -ae *mf*, consor·s -tis *mf*
collect *tr* conferre, colligere; *(to assemble)* convocare; *(money)* exigere; **to — oneself** mentem *or* animum colligere; **to — paintings and statues** tabulas signaque comparare ‖ *intr (of water)* colligi
collected *adj* **to be —** praesentis animi esse
collection *s (act)* collecti·o -onis *f; (pile or group collected)* congeri·es -ei *f; (literary)* corp·us -oris *n*

collective *adj* commun•is -is -e; *(gram)* collectiv•us -a -um
collectively *adv* communiter, unā
college *s* colleg•ium -(i)i *n*
collegiate *adj* collegial•is -is -e
collide *intr* confligere, collidi
collision *s* conflicti•o -onis *f,* concurs•us -ūs *m;* **a — of ships with one another** concurs•us -ūs *m* navium inter se
colloquial *adj* cotidian•us -a -um; **— language** serm•o -onis *m* cotidianus
collusion *s* collusi•o -onis *f;* **to be in — with** colludere cum *(w. abl)*
colon *s (anat)* col•um -i *n; (gram)* col•on -i *n*
colonel *s* tribun•us -i *m* militum
colonial *adj* colonic•us -a -um
colonist *s* colon•us -i *m* (•a -ae *f*)
colonize *tr* coloniam deducere in *(w. acc)*
colonnade *s* portic•us -ūs *f*
colony *s* coloni•a -ae *f*
color *s* col•or -oris *m;* **—s** vexill•um -i *n;* **with flying —s** magnā cum gloriā
color *tr* colorare; *(to dye)* tingere
colossal *adj* imman•is -is -e
colossus *s* coloss•us -i *m*
colt *s* equul(e)•us -i *m*
column *s* column•a -ae *f; (line)* agm•en -inis *n*
comb *tr* pectere; **to — back** repectere; **to — out** expectere
comb *s* pect•en -inis *m*
combat *s* pugn•a -ae *f,* dimicati•o -onis *f;* **in hand-to-hand combat** comminus [*adv*]; **— with wild beasts** venati•o -onis *f*
combat *tr* pugnare cum *(w. abl)*
combatant *s* pugnat•or -oris *m*
combative *adj* pugn•ax -acis
combination *s (act)* coniuncti•o -onis *f; (result)* iunctur•a -ae *f; (of various ingredients)* compositi•o -onis *f;* **a syllable is a — of letters** syllaba est comprehensi•o -onis *f* litterarum
combine *tr* coniungere, miscēre, componere; *(in due proportion)* temperare ‖ *intr* coïre, coniungi
combined *adj* coniunct•us -a -um, in unum coact•us -a -um
combustible *adj* igni obnoxi•us -a -um
combustion *s* combusti•o -onis *f;* **during —** dum comburitur
come *intr* venire; *(to arrive)* pervenire; *(to happen)* fieri; *(of sleep)* accedere; **— here!** huc accede!; **— on!** agedum!; **— what may** quod fors feret; **to — about** evenire, fieri; **to — across** occurrere *(w. dat);* **to — after** (sub)sequi; **to — again** revenire; **to — along** procedere; *(to accompany)* comitari; **to — apart** solvi; **to — at** *(in a hostile manner)* petere; **to — away** abscedere; **to — back** revenire, redire; **to — before** praevenire; **to — between** intervenire; **to — by** praeterire; *(to get)* acquirere; **to — down** *(to descend)* descendere; *(e.g., to the sea)* devenire; **to — down from antiquity** ex antiquitate tradi; **to — down with an illness** morbo corripi; **to — first** antevenire; **to — forth** exire; *(fig)* exoriri; **to — forward** prodire; **to — from** venire ab (*(w. abl),* derivari ab *(w. abl);* **to — in** introire; **to — into play** accedere; **to — near** appropinquare, accedere; **to — off** *(e.g., stem comes off the apple)* recedere ab *(w. abl);* **to — off victorious** victor discedere; **to — off without a loss** sine detrimento discedere; **to — on** pergere; *(to progress)* proficere; **to — on top of** *(s.th. else)* supervenire *(w. dat);* **to — out** (**of**) exire (ex *w. abl); (to be published)* edi, emitti; *(of teeth)* cadere; *(of evidence)* emergere; *(to end)* evenire; **to — over** supervenire; *(to a different part)* transgredi; *(of feelings, conditions)* obire, occupare; **to — round** *(fig)* transgredi; **to — to** advenire ad *or* in *(w. acc); (to cost)* vēnire *(w. gen of price); (after fainting)* resipiscere; **to — to a head** concoqui; **to — to one's senses** ad se redire; **to — to pass** evenire, fieri; **to — to the assistance of** subvenire *(w. dat);* **to — together** convenire; **to — up** subvenire; *(to occur)* provenire; **to — up to** *(to approach)* accedere ad *(w. acc);* **to — upon** *(to find)* invenire; (*to attack, as diseases)* ingruere *(w. dat)*; **whatever —s into s.o.'s head** quae cuique libuissent
comedian *s* scurr•a -ae *m; (theat)* comoed•us -i *m* (•a -ae *f*)
comedy *s* comoedi•a -ae *f*
comely *adj* venust•us -a -um
comet *s* comet•es -ae *m*
comfort *s* solat•ium -(i)i *n;* **—s** commod•a -orum *npl*
comfort *tr* consolari
comfortable *adj* commod•us -a -um; **make yourselves —** rogo ut vobis suaviter sit
comfortably *adv* commode
comforter *s* consolat•or -oris *m* (•rix -ricis *f*); *(for bed)* stragul•um -i *n*
comforting *adj* consol•ans -antis
comic *adj* comic•us -a -um
comical *adj* ridicul•us -a -um
comics *spl* libell•i -orum *mpl* pictographici
comic strip *s* gryli•i -orum *mpl*
coming *adj* ventur•us -a -um; **he's got what's coming to him** habet quod sibi debetur
coming *s* advent•us -ūs *m*
comma *s* comm•a -atis *n*
command *s (order; comput)* iuss•um -i *n; (mil)* imper•ium -(i)i *n; (jurisdiction)* provinci•a -ae *f;* **— of language** copi•a -ae *f* verborum; **to be in — of** praesse *(w. dat);* **to give a — to** imperare *(w. dat);* **to**

hold supreme military — summam imperi tenēre; **to put s.o. in — of** aliquem praeficere *(w. dat)*
command *tr (to order)* iubēre; *(to control)* imperare *(w. dat); (to require)* exigere
commander *s* du·x -cis *m,* praefect·us -i *m*
commander-in-chief *s* imperat·or -oris *m;* **to be —** imperii summam tenēre
commanding officer *s* dux, ducis *mf*
commandment *s* mandat·um -i *n;* **the Ten —s** decalog·us -i *m*
commemorate *tr* celebrare
commemoration *s* celebrati·o -onis *f,* memori·a -ae *f;* **in — of** in memoriam *(w. gen)*
commence *tr & intr* incipere; **to — hostilities** belli initium facere
commencement *s* init·ium -(i)i *n; (educ)* admissi·o -onis *f* ad gradum academicum
commend *tr* approbare; *(to recommend; to commit)* commendare
commendable *adj* probabil·is -is -e
commendation *s* commendati·o -onis *f,* lau·s -dis *f*
commensurate *adj* **(with)** par, adaequat·us -a -um *(w. dat);* **to be — with** congruere *(w. dat or* cum *w. abl)*
comment *intr* **(on)** sententiam dicere *(or* scribere) (de *w. abl)*
comment *s* commentar·ius -(i)i *m,* sententi·a -ae *f; (note)* annotati·o -onis *f*
commentary *s* commentari·i -orum *mpl*
commentator *s* interpr·es -etis *mf*
commerce *s* commerc·ium -(i)i *n;* **to engage in —** negotiari
commercial *adj* mercatori·us -a -um
commercial *s* praecon·ium -(i)i *n*
commiserate *intr* **to — with** misereri *(w. gen)*
commission *s* mandat·um -i *n; (group)* consil·ium -(i)i *n;* **out of —** ex usu; **to do business on —** ex mandato negotiari
commission *tr* delegare, mandare
commissioner *s* curat·or -oris *m* (·trix -tricis *f);* **highway —** viarum curator *m;* **police —** praefect·us -i *m* vigilum; **water —** aquarum curator *m*
commit *tr (crime)* admittere; *(to entrust)* committere; **to — an error** errare; **to — a sin** peccare; **to — to memory** memoriae mandare; **to — to prison** in carcerem conicere; **to — to writing** litteris mandare
commitment *s* pign·us -oris *n*
committee *s* consil·ium -(i)i *n*
commodity *s* mer·x -cis *f*
common *adj (shared)* commun·is -is -e, public·us -a -um; *(ordinary)* cotidian·us -a -um, vulgar·is -is -e; *(well-known)* vulgat·us -a -um; **— noun** nom·en -inis *n* appellativum; **— people** vulg·us -i *n;* **to have — sense** cor habēre
common *s* **in —** communiter; *(for all)* in medium
commoner *s* plebei·us -i *m* (·a -ae *f);* **—s** pleb·s -is *f*
commonly *adv* vulgo, fere
commonplace *adj* vulgar·is -is -e
commonwealth *s* res, rei *f* publica
commotion *s* tumult·us -ūs *m*
commune *s* pag·us -i *m; (people)* commun·e -is *n*
commune *intr* confabulari, colloqui
communicate *tr* communicare; *(information)* impertire ‖ *intr* **to — with** communicare *(w. dat)*
communication *s* commerc·ium -(i)i *n; (talk)* communicati·o -onis *f; (message)* litter·ae -arum *fpl,* nunt·ius -(i)i *m*
communicative *adj* affabil·is -is -e
communion *s* communi·o -onis *f*
community *s* civit·as -atis *f*
commutation *s* mutati·o -onis *f; (reduction)* remissi·o -onis *f*
commute *tr* commutare; **his death sentence was —d to exile** capitis damnato exilium ei permissum est ‖ *intr (travel)* ultro citroque commeare
commuter *s* commeat·or -oris *m* (·trix -tricis *f)*
compact *adj* spiss·us -a -um, dens·us -a -um
compact *s* pact·um -i *n; (esp. public)* foed·us -eris *n;* **to abide by the —** in pacto manēre; **to make a —** *(of two parties)* foedus inter se facere
compact *tr* densare
compact disk (CD) *s* compactus disc·us -i *m*
compactly *adv* spisse, confertim
companion *s* com·es -itis *mf; (mil)* contubernal·is -is *m*
companionship *s* sodalit·as -atis *f;* **to enjoy s.o.'s —** aliquo familiariter uti
company *s (com)* societ·as -atis *f; (guests)* conviv·ium -(i)i *n; (mil)* centuri·o -onis *f; (theat)* gre·x -gis *m;* **to keep each other —** inter se colere
company commander *s* centuri·o -onis *m*
comparable *adj* comparabil·is -is -e, aequiperabili·is -is -e
comparative *adj* comparativ·us -a -um, aliorum ratione habitā; *(gram)* comparativ·us -a -um
comparative *s (gram)* comparativ·um -i *n,* grad·us -ūs *m* comparativus; **in the —** comparative, in comparatione
comparatively *adv* comparative
compare *tr* **(with)** comparare, conferre (cum *w. abl);* **—ed with** adversus *(w. acc)* ‖ *intr* aequiparare; *(to be on a level with s.o.)* aliquem aequiperare
comparison *s* comparati·o -onis *f;* **in — with** adversus *(w. acc)*
compartment *s* locul·us -i *m; (in a train, plane)* diaet·a -ae *f*

compass *s (instrument)* circin·us -i *m; (magnetic)* ac·us -ūs *f* magnetica
compassion *s* misericordi·a -ae *f*
compassionate *adj* misericor·s -dis
compassionately *adv* misericorditer
compatibility *s* congruenti·a -ae *f*
compatible *adj* congru·us -a -um
compatriot *s* civ·is -is *mf*
compel *tr* compellere, cogere
compendium *s* summar·ium -(i)i *n*
compensate *tr* compensare ‖ *intr* **to — for** repensare, rependere
compensation *s (act)* compensati·o -onis *f; (pay)* merc·es -edis *f; (for damages)* poen·a -ae *f*
compete *intr* certare
competence *s* facult·as -atis *f; (legal capacity)* iu·s -ris *n*
competent *adj* perit·us -a -um; *(leg)* locupl·es -etis
competently *adv* satis idoneë
competition *s* certam·en -inis *n*
competitor *s* competi·tor -toris *m* (·trix -tricis *f*)
compilation *s (act)* collecti·o -onis *f; (result)* collectane·a -orum *npl*
compile *tr* componere
compiler *s* composi·tor -toris *m* (·trix -tricis *f*)
complacency *s* am·or -oris *m* sui
complacent *adj* sibi placens
complain *intr* **(about)** queri (de *w. abl)*
complaint *s* querel·a -ae *f; (leg)* crim·en -inis *n; (med)* vit·ium -(i)i *n;* **to raise —s** querelas facere
complement *s* complement·um -i *n; (mil)* numer·us -i *m;* **to give the legions their full — of men** complēre legiones
complete *adj (entire)* plen·us -a -um; *(untouched)* integ·er -ra -rum; *(finished)* perfect·us -a -um; *(set)* iust·us -a -um
complete *tr (to accomplish)* perficere, peragere, conficere; *(years)* explēre; *(to finish)* absolvere; *(to make whole)* complēre
completely *adv* plane, prorsus
completion *s* completi·o -onis *f; (accomplishment)* perfecti·o -onis *f,* confecti·o -onis *f*
complex *adj* multipl·ex -icis
complexion *s* col·or -oris *m;* **having a healthy complexion** colorat·us -a -um
complexity *s* multiplex natur·a -ae *f*
compliance *s* obtemperati·o -onis *f;* **in — with an agreement** ex pacto et convento
compliant *adj* obsequ·ens -entis
complicate *tr* implicare
complicated *adj* implicat·us -a -um
complication *s* implicati·o -onis *f*
complicity *s* conscienti·a -ae *f*
compliment *s* blandiment·um -i *n;* **as a —** honoris gratiā; **to pay s.o. a —** gratulari *(w. dat)*
compliment *tr* gratulari *(w. dat)*
complimentary *adj* honorific·us -a -um
comply *intr* **to — with** obsequi *(w. dat),* morem gerere *(w. dat)*
component *s* element·um -i *n*
compose *tr* componere; *(verses)* condere; *(to calm)* sedare; **to — oneself** se colligere
composed *adj* tranquill·us -a -um; **to be — of** constare ex *(w. abl)*
composer *s* scrip·tor -toris *m* (·trix -tricis *f*); *(mus)* musicorum modorum script·or -oris *m*
composite *adj* composit·us -a -um
composition *s (act)* compositi·o -onis *f; (in literature)* scripti·o -onis *f; (work composed)* script·um -i *n*
composure *s* tranquillit·as -atis *f;* **to bear with —** aequo animo ferre; **to lose one's —** perturbari
compound *adj* composit·us -a -um
compound *s* compositi·o -onis *f; (noun)* compositum verb·um -i *n*
compound *tr* componere, duplicare
compound interest *s* anatocism·us -i *m*
comprehend *tr* continēre; *(to understand)* comprehendere
comprehensible *adj* perspicu·us -a -um
comprehension *s (act of grasping)* comprehensi·o -onis *f; (power of understanding)* intellect·us -ūs *m*
comprehensive *adj* ampl·us -a -um
compress *tr* comprimere; *(to abridge)* coartare
compress *s (med)* foment·um -i *n*
compression *s* compressi·o -onis *f*
comprise *tr* continēre; **to be —d of** constare ex *(w. abl)*
compromise *s (bilateral)* compromiss·um -i *n; (unilateral)* accommodati·o -onis *f*
compromise *tr* compromittere; *(to imperil)* in periculum ac discrimen vocare ‖ *intr* pacisci
compulsion *s* vis *f,* necessit·as -atis *f;* **by —** per vim
compulsory *adj* necessari·us -a -um
computation *s* computati·o -onis *f*
compute *tr* computare
computer *s* ordinatr·um -i *n*
computer *adj* ordinatral·is -is -e
computer game *s* lus·us -us *m* ordinatralis; **to play a —** lusum ordinatralem ludere
comrade *s* sodal·is -is *m; (mil)* contubernal·is -is *m*
comradery *s* societ·as -atis *f*
con *tr (coll)* verba dare *(w. dat);* defraudare; **to — s.o out of his money** aliquem pecuniā defraudare
con artist *s (coll)* plan·us -i *m*
concave *adj* concav·us -a -um
conceal *tr* celare, occultare, abdere
concealed *adj* celat·us -a -um

concealment *s (act)* occultati·o -onis *f; (place)* latebr·ae -arum *fpl;* **to be in —** latebras agere
concede *tr* concedere
conceit *s* superbi·a -ae *f*
conceited *adj* superbiā tum·ens -entis
conceivable *adj* quod fingi potest
conceive *tr* concipere **||** *intr* **to — of** fingere
concentrate *tr* in unum locum contrahere **||** *intr* **to — on** animum intendere in *(w. acc)*
concentrate *s (by boiling)* decocti·o -onis *f*
concentration *s* in unum locum contracti·o -onis *f; (fig)* animi intenti·o -onis *f*
concentric *adj* concentric·us -a -um; **— circles** orb·es -ium *mpl* orbibus impeditae
concept *s* sententi·a -ae *f*
conception *s (in womb)* concept·us -ūs *m; (idea)* informati·o -onis *f*
concern *s (affair)* res, rei *f,* negot·ium -(i)i *n; (interest, worry)* cur·a -ae *f; (importance)* moment·um -i *n;* **it is of — to me** mihi curae est
concern *tr* attinēre *or* pertinēre ad *(w. acc); (to worry)* sollicitare; **as far as I'm —ed** per me; **how does that — you?** quid id ad te attinet?; **it —s me (you)** meā (tuā) rēfert; **to — oneself** animum agitare, curare
concerned *adj (about, for)* sollicit·us -a -um de (pro) *(w. abl);* **I am concerned** mihi curae est; **I'm not terribly — about** laboro non valde de *(w. abl)*
concerning *prep* de *(w. abl)*
concert *s (mus)* concent·us -ūs *m,* symphoni·a -ae *f; (fig)* consens·us -ūs *m;* **in —** ex composito; **to attend a —** concentui adesse
concession *s* concessi·o -onis *f; (thing)* concess·um -i *n; (com)* conducti·o -onis *f;* **to make a —** concedere
conch *s* conch·a -ae *f*
conciliate *tr* conciliare
conciliation *s* conciliati·o -onis *f*
conciliatory *adj* pacific·us -a -um
concise *adj* press·us -a -um, brev·is -is -e
concisely *adv* presse
conciseness *s* brevit·as -atis *f*
conclave *s* conclav·e -is *n*
conclude *tr (to end)* terminare; *(to infer)* colligere; **I must — my speech** mihi perorandum est; **to — a treaty** foedus icere
conclusion *s (end)* fin·is -is *m,* conclusi·o -onis *f; (of speech)* perorati·o -onis *f; (inference)* conclusi·o -onis *f;* **in —** ad ultimum; **they came to the — that** eis placuit ut; **to draw the —** colligere
conclusive *adj* firm·us -a -um, cert·us -a -um
concoct *tr* concoquere; *(to contrive)* fingere, conflare
concoction *s* pot·us -ūs *m; (fig)* machinati·o -onis *f*
concomitant *adj* adiunct·us -a -um
concord *s* concordi·a -ae *f*
concourse *s (act)* concurs·us -ūs *m; (crowd)* frequenti·a -ae *f*
concrete *adj* concret·us -a -um; **— noun** vocabul·um -i *n (opp:* appellatio); **in the —, not in the abstract** re, non cogitatione
concrete *s* concret·um -i *n*
concubine *s* concubin·a -ae *f*
concur *intr* consentire
concurrence *s* consensi·o -onis *f*
concussion *s (med)* quassatur·a -ae *f*
condemn *tr* damnare; **to — to death** capitis damnare
condemnation *s* damnati·o -onis *f*
condensation *s* densati·o -onis *f*
condense *tr* (con)densare **||** *intr* densari
condescend *intr* se summittere
condescending *adj* fastidios·us -a -um
condescendingly *adv* fastidiose
condescension *s* comit·as -atis *f*
condition *s (state)* stat·us -ūs *m,* condici·o -onis *f; (stipulation)* condici·o -onis *f,* le·x -gis *f;* **in bad (good) —** male (bene) habit·us -a -um; **in excellent —** habitissim·us -a -um; **on — that** eā lege ut; **physical —** corporis habit·us -ūs *m*
condition *tr* informare
conditional *adj* condicional·is -is -e
conditionally *adv* condicionaliter
condolence *s* consolati·o -onis *f;* **I gave him my —** doloris eius particeps factus sum; **letter of —** litter·ae -arum *fpl* consolatoriae
condone *tr* condonare
conducive *adj* util·is -is -e ad *(w. acc)*
conduct *s (behavior)* mor·es -um *mpl; (management)* administrati·o -onis *f*
conduct *tr (to lead)* adducere; *(to manage)* administrare
conductor *s* (symphoniacorum) magis·ter -tri *m; (on a train)* traminis curat·or -oris *m*
conduit *s* canal·is -is *m*
cone *s* con·us -i *m*
confederacy *s (treaty)* foed·us -eris *n; (allied states)* civitat·es -um *fpl* foederatae
confederate *adj* foederat·us -a -um
confederate *s* soci·us -i *m* (·a -ae *f*)
confederation *s* civitat·es -um *fpl* foederatae
confer *tr* deferre, tribuere **||** *intr* colloqui, conferre
conference *s* colloqu·ium -(i)i *n; (gathering)* congress·us -ūs *m*
confess *tr* confiteri; *(a fault)* fateri
confessedly *adv* ex confesso
confession *s* confessi·o -onis *f*
confidant *s* consci·us -i *m* (·a -ae *f*)
confide *tr* committere **||** *intr* **to — in** confidere *(w. dat)*

confidence *s* fid·es -ei *f; (assurance)* fiduci·a -ae *f; (esp. self-confidence)* confidenti·a -ae *f;* **to have — in** fidem habēre *(w. dat);* **to inspire — in** fidem facere *(w. dat)*
confident *adj* (con)fid·ens -entis; **to be —** confidere; **to be — that** pro certo scire *(w. acc w. inf)*
confidential *adj (worthy of confidence)* fid·us -a -um; *(secret)* secret·us -a -um
confidently *adv* fidenter
configuration *s* figur·a -ae *f*
confine *tr* includere; *(to restrain)* cohibēre; *(to limit)* circumscribere
confined *adj* art·us -a -um, angust·us -a -um; **to be — to bed** lecto teneri
confines *spl* confin·ium -(i)i *n; (boundary)* fin·es -ium *mpl;* **on the — of** finitim·us -a -um *(w. dat);* **within the — of** in confinio *(w. gen)*
confirm *tr* confirmare; *(to prove)* comprobare; *(to ratify)* sancire
confirmation *s* confirmati·o -onis *f*
confirmed *adj* (con)firmat·us -a -um; *(habitual)* inveterat·us -a -um; *(proved)* comprobat·us -a -um
confiscate *tr* publicare
confiscation *s* publicati·o -onis *f*
conflagration *s* incend·ium -(i)i *n*
conflict *s* pugn·a -ae *f;* **to be in —** *(fig)* inter se repugnare
conflict *intr* inter se repugnare
conflicting *adj* repugn·ans -antis
confluence *s* conflu·ens -entis *m;* **at the — of the Tiber and the Anio** inter confluentes Tiberim et Anionem
conform *intr (to)* obtemperare *(w. dat),* se accommodare ad *(w. acc)*
conformity *s* convenienti·a -ae *f;* **in — with** secundum *(w. acc)*
confound *tr (to confuse)* confundere; *(to disconcert)* exanimare
confounded *adj* nefand·us -a -um
confront *tr* obviam ire *(w. dat); (to oppose)* obstare *(w. dat)*
confrontation *s* obstanti·a -ae *f*
confuse *tr* confundere, turbare
confused *adj* confus·us -a -um, turbat·us -a -um
confusedly *adv* confuse
confusion *s* confusi·o -onis *f*
confutation *s* refutati·o -onis *f*
confute *tr* confutare
congeal *tr* congelare ‖ *intr* concrescere, se congelare
congenial *adj* consentane·us -a -um
congenital *adj* nativ·us -a -um
congested *adj* refert·us -a -um
congestion *s (traffic)* frequenti·a -ae *f,* concurs·us -ūs *m;* **nasal —** stillati·o -onis *f*
congratulate *tr* gratulari *(w. dat)*
congratulations *spl* gratulation·es -um *fpl;* **—!** gratulationes *or* macte virtute esto *(pl:* estote)!
congratulatory *adj* gratulabund·us -a -um
congregate *tr* congregare ‖ *intr* congregari
congregation *s* coët·us -ūs *m*
congress *s* congress·us -ūs *m*
conical *adj* conic·us -a -um
conjectural *adj* coniectural·is -is -e
conjecturally *adv* ex coniecturā
conjecture *s* coniectur·a -ae *f*
conjecture *tr* coniectare
conjugal *adj* coniugal·is -is -e
conjugate *tr* declinare
conjugation *s* declinati·o -onis *f*
conjunction *s* concurs·us -ūs *m; (gram)* coniuncti·o -onis *f*
conjure *tr (to beseech solemnly)* obtestari; **to — up** *(ghosts)* elicere; *(fig)* excogitare, effingere
con man *s* plan·us -i *m*
connect *tr* connectere; *(in a series)* serere
connected *adj* coniunct·us -a -um; *(by marriage)* affin·is -is -e; *(of buildings)* **(to)** adfict·us -a -um *(w. dat);* **to be closely — with** inhaerēre *(w. dat);* **to be — with s.o. by blood and race** aliquem sanguine ac genere contingere
connection *s* coniuncti·o -onis *f,* nex·us -ūs *m; (kin)* necessitud·o -inis *f; (by marriage)* affinit·as -atis *f*
connivance *s* indulgenti·a -ae *f*
connive *intr* connivēre
connoisseur *s* doct·us -a existima·tor -toris *m* (·trix -tricis *f*)
connotation *s* significati·o -onis *f* latens
conquer *tr* vincere; **— a country** terrā potiri
conqueror *s* vict·or -oris *m,* vict·r·ix -icis *f*
conquest *s* victor·ia -ae *f*
conscience *s* conscienti·a -ae *f;* **good conscience** mens conscia recti; **guilty —** mala conscientia *f;* **to have no —** nullam religionem habēre
conscientious *adj* pi·us -a -um, religios·us -a -um
conscientiously *adv* diligenter
conscious *adj* consci·us -a -um
consciously *adv* sciens, de industriā
consciousness *s (awareness)* conscienti·a -ae *f;* **to lose —** animum relinquere; **to regain —** resipiscere
conscript *s* tir·o -onis *mf*
consecrate *tr* consecrare
consecration *s* consecrati·o -onis *f*
consecutive *adj* continu·us -a -um
consecutively *adv* continenter
consent *intr* assentiri
consent *s* assens·us -ūs *m;* **to give one's —** permittere; **with the — of the people** secundo populo; **without my —** me invito

consequence *s* consecuti•o -onis *f*, event•us -ūs *m;* **a man of —** hom•o -inis *m* auctoritate praeditus; **as a —** ex eo; **it is of great —** magni interest; **it is of no —** nihil refert; **thing of no —** parva res, rei *f*
consequent *adj* consequ•ens -entis
consequently *adv* igitur, itaque
conservation *s* conservati•o -onis *f*
conservative *adj* a rebus novandis abhorr•ens -entis; *(pol)* reipublicae statūs conservandi studios•us -a -um; **— party** optimat•es -um *mpl*
conserve *tr* conservare
consider *tr* considerare; *(to deem)* aestimare, ducere; *(to respect)* respicere; **to — it already done** istuc iam pro facto habēre
considerable *adj* aliquantul•us -a -um; *(of persons)* illustr•is -is -e; *(of size)* ampl•us -a -um
considerably *adv* aliquantum; *(w. comp)* multo, aliquanto
considerate *adj* human•us -a -um
consideration *s* considerati•o -onis *f; (regard)* respect•us -ūs *m; (ground, motive)* rati•o -onis *f; (payment)* pret•ium -(i)i *n;* **out of — for** ob *(w. acc);* **to have — for the wounded**; sauciorum rationem habēre; **to show — for s.th.** alicuius rei respectum habēre
considering *prep* pro *(w. abl)*
consign *tr* mandare
consignment *s* **goods given** (*or* **sent) on —** merc•es -ium *fpl* ex perscriptione traditae (*or* missae)
consist *intr* **to — of** constare ex *(w. abl),* consistere ex *(w. abl)*
consistency *s* constanti•a -ae *f*
consistent *adj* const•ans -antis
consistently *adv* constanter
consolation *s* consolati•o -onis *f; (thing)* solac•ium -(i)i *n*
console *tr* consolari
consolidate *tr* solidare, stabilire
consonant *s* conson•ans -antis *f*
consort *s* coniu•x -gis *mf*
consort *intr* **to — with** familiariter uti *(w. abl),* se associare cum *(w. abl)*
conspicuous *adj* conspicu•us -a -um
conspicuously *adv* insigniter
conspiracy *s* coniurati•o -onis *f*
conspirator *s* coniurat•us -i *m* (•a -ae *f)*
conspire *intr* coniurare
constable *s* viat•or -oris *m*
constancy *s* constanti•a -ae *f*
constant *adj (fixed)* const•ans -antis; *(loyal)* fid•us -a -um; *(incessant)* perpetu•us -a -um
constantly *adv* assidue, perpetuo
constellation *s* sid•us -eris *n*
consternation *s* consternati•o -onis *f;* **to be in —** trepidare; **to throw into —** perterrēre
constipated *adj* **he is —** venter eius est astrictus
constipation *s* alv•us -i *f* astricta
constituent *s (part)* element•um -i *n;* **—s** *(pol)* suffragator•es -um *mpl*
constitute *tr* constituere
constitution *s (physical)* habit•us -ūs *m; (pol)* reipublicae leg•es -um *fpl*
constitutional *adj* legitim•us -a -um
constitutionally *adv* legitime
constrain *tr* cogere
constraint *s* vis *f;* **by —** per vim
construct *tr* construere; *(esp. things of mechanical kind)* fabricare
construction *s* constructi•o -onis *f,* fabricati•o -onis *f; (of a road)* muniti•o -onis *f; (interpretation)* interpretati•o -onis *f; (gram)* constructi•o -onis *f*
construe *tr* interpretari; *(gram)* construere
consul *s* cons•ul -ulis *m;* **— elect** consul *m* designatus
consular *adj* consular•is -is -e; **a man of — rank** consular•is -is *m*
consulship *s* consulat•us -ūs *m;* **during my —** me consule; **in the — of Caesar and Bibulus** Caesare et Bibulo consulibus; **to hold the —** consulatum gerere; **to run for the —** consulatum petere
consult *tr* consultare ‖ *intr* deliberare
consultation *s* consultati•o -onis *f*
consume *tr* consumere
consumer *s* emp•tor -toris *m* (•trix -tricis *f)*
consuming *adj* ed•ax -acis
consummate *adj* summ•us -a -um
consummate *tr* consummare
consummation *s* consummati•o -onis *f; (end)* exit•us -ūs *m*
consumption *s* consumpti•o -onis *f; (disease)* tab•es -is *f*
contact *s* contact•us -ūs *m; (connection)* necessitud•o -inis *f;* **to come in — with** contingere
contagious *adj* contagios•us -a -um
contain *tr* continēre; *(to hold, as a vessel)* capere
container *s* receptacul•um -i *n,* va•s -sis *n*
contaminate *tr* contaminare
contamination *s* contaminati•o -onis *f*
contemplate *tr* contemplari; *(some action)* considerare
contemplation *s* contemplati•o -onis *f; (of an action)* considerati•o -onis *f*
contemplative *adj* contemplativ•us -a -um
contemporaneous *adj* aequal•is -is -e
contemporaneously *adv* simul
contemporary *s* aequaev•us -i *m* (•a -ae *f)*
contempt *s* contempt•us -ūs *m;* **to feel — for** comtemnere; **to hold s.o. in —** aliquem despicatum habēre
contemptible *adj* contempt•us -a -um
contemptibly *adv* abiecte
contemptuous *adj* **— of** despici•ens -entis *(w. gen)*

contend *tr (to aver)* affirmare ‖ *intr* contendere; *(to dispute)* verbis certare; **to — against** adversari
contending *adj* avers·us -a -um
content *adj* **(with)** content·us -a -um *(w. abl)*
content *s* **to your heart's —** arbitratu tuo
content *tr* satisfacere *(w. dat)*
contented *adj* content·us -a -um
contentedly *adv* aequo animo
contention *s* contenti·o -onis *f*
contentious *adj* pugn·ax -acis; *(litigious)* litigios·us -a -um
contentment *s* aequus anim·us -i *m*
contents *spl* quod inest, quae insunt; *(of a book)* argument·um -i *n; (see* **table of contents)**
contest *s* certam·en -inis *n*
contest *tr (to dispute)* resistere *(w. dat); (leg)* lege agere de *(w. abl)*
contestant *s* peti·tor -toris *m* (·trix -tricis *f)*
context *s* context·us -ūs *m*
contiguous *adj* contigu·us -a -um
continence *s* continenti·a -ae *f*
continent *s* par·s -tis *f* mundi [*not* continens, *which means "mainland"*]
contingent *s* man·us -ūs *f*
contingent *adj* adventici·us -a -um; **to be — on** dependēre ex *(w. abl)*
continual *adj* continu·us -a -um; *(lasting)* perpetu·us -a -um
continually *adv* assidue, continenter
continuance *s* continuati·o -onis *f; (leg)* prolati·o -onis *f*
continuation *s* continuati·o -onis *f*
continue *tr* continuare; *(leg)* proferre ‖ *intr* pergere; *(to last)* persistere
continuity *s* continuit·as -atis *f*
continuous *adj* continu·us -a -um, perpetu·us -a -um
continuously *adv* continenter
contortion *s* contorti·o -onis *f*
contour *s* lineament·um -i *n*
contraband *s* interdict·a -orum *npl*
contraception *s* conceptionis inhibiti·o -onis *f*
contraceptive *adj* conceptionem inhibit·ens -entis
contraceptive *s* atoc·ium -(i)i *n*
contract *tr* contrahere ‖ *intr* contrahi; **to — for** pacisci, locare; *(of the party undertaking the work)* conducere; **to — for the making of a statue** statuam faciendam locare
contract *s* pact·um -i *n; (on the part of the hirer)* locati·o -onis *f; (on the part of the one hired)* redempti·o -onis *f*
contraction *s* contracti·o -onis *f; (of a word)* compend·ium -(i)i *n*
contractor *s* conduct·or -oris *m*
contradict *tr* contradicere; **to — oneself** pugnantia loqui
contradiction *s* contradicti·o -onis *f; (inconsistency)* repugnanti·a -ae *f*
contradictory *adj* contradictori·us -a -um, repugn·ans -antis
contraption *s* machin·a -ae *f*
contrary *adj (opposite)* contrari·us -a -um; *(fig)* repugn·ans -antis; **— to** contra *(w. acc)*
contrary *s* contrar·ium -(i)i *n;* **on the —** contra
contrast *s* comparati·o -onis *f,* oppositi·o -onis *f*
contrast *tr* comparare, opponere ‖ *intr* discrepare
contribute *tr* contribuere, conferre ‖ *intr* **to — towards** conferre ad *or* in *(w. acc)*
contribution *s* contributi·o -onis *f; (money)* stip·s -is *f; (gift)* don·um -i *n*
contributor *s* colla·tor -toris *m* (·trix -tricis *f)*
contributory *adj* contribu·ens -entis
contrite *adj* paenit·ens -entis
contrition *s* paenitenti·a -ae *f; (eccl)* contriti·o -onis *f*
contrivance *s (act)* machinati·o -onis *f; (thing)* machin·a -ae *f*
contrive *tr* excogitare, machinari
control *s (restraint)* continenti·a -ae *f; (power)* moderati·o -onis *f,* potest·as -atis *f*
control *tr* continēre; *(to govern)* imperare *(w. dat)*
controller *s* modera·tor -toris *m* (·trix -tricis *f)*
controversial *adj* controvers·us -a -um
controversy *s* controversi·a -ae *f*
convalesce *intr* convalescere
convalescent *adj* convalesc·ens -entis
convene *tr* convocare ‖ *intr* coïre
convenience *s* commodit·as -atis *f; (thing)* commod·um -i *n;* **at your —** commodo tuo; **at your earliest —** commodissime
convenient *adj* commod·us -a -um; *(time, occasion)* opportun·us -a -um
conveniently *adv* commode, opportune
convention *s* convent·us -ūs *m; (custom)* consuetud·o -inis *f*
conventional *adj* vulgat·us -a -um
converge *intr* in medium vergere, in unum locum coïre
conversant *adj* perit·us -a -um; **to be — with** versari in *(w. abl)*
conversation *s* colloqu·ium -(i)i *n;* **to engage in — with** sermones cum *(w. abl)* conferre
conversational *adj* in colloquio usitat·us -a -um
converse *intr* colloqui
converse *s* convers·us -ūs *m*
conversely *adv* e converso
conversion *s* conversi·o -onis *f*
convert *tr* convertere
convert *s* neophyt·us -i *m* (·a -ae *f)*
convertible *adj* commutabil·is -is -e

convertible *s* autoraed·a -ae *f* tecto plicatile
convex *adj* convex·us -a -um
convey *tr* convehere, advehere; *(to impart)* significare; *(leg)* abalienare
conveyance *s (act)* advecti·o -onis *f; (vehicle)* vehicul·um -i *n; (leg)* abalienati·o -onis *f*
convict *s* qui ad poenam damnatus est
convict *tr* (**of**) convincere *(w. acc of the person and gen of the offense);* **—ed of a lie** mendaci manifest·us -a -um
conviction *s (leg)* damnati·o -onis *f; (belief)* persuasi·o -onis *f;* **it is my firm —** mihi persuasissimum est
convince *tr* persuadēre *(w. dat)*
convinced *adj* **I am firmly — that** plen·us (-a) persuasionis sum *(w. acc & inf)*
convincing *adj* ad persuadendum apt·us -a -um; **there is — proof that** magno argumento est *(w. acc & inf)*
convivial *adj* hilar·is -is -e
conviviality *s* hilarit·as -atis *f*
convocation *s* convocati·o -onis *f*
convoke *tr* convocare
convoy *s (naut)* praesidiaria class·is -is *f*
convulse *tr* convellere
convulsions *spl* spasm·us -i *m;* **to have —** spasmo vexari
convulsive *adj* spastic·us -a -um
coo *intr* canere; *(of a pigeon)* gemere
cooing *s* cant·us -ūs *m;* gemit·us -ūs *m*
cook *s* coqu·us -i *m,* coqu·a -ae *f*
cook *tr* coquere; **to — up** *(fig)* excogitare ‖ *intr* coquere
cooked *adj* elix·us -a -um
cookie *s* crustul·um -i *n*
cool *adj* frigidul·us -a -um; *(fearless)* impavid·us -a -um; *(indifferent)* frigid·us -a -um
cool *s* **to keep one's —** mentem compescere
cool *tr* refrigerare ‖ *intr* refrigerari; *(fig)* defervescere; **to — off** intepescere
cooling *adj* frigoric·us -a -um
coolness *s* frig·us -oris *n; (indifference)* lentitud·o -inis *f; (calmness)* aequus anim·us -i *m*
coop *s (for chickens)* cave·a -ae *f*
coop *tr* **to — up** includere; **to be cooped up in the house** in aedibus coartat·us (-a) esse
cooperate *intr* unā agere
cooperation *s* adiument·um -i *n,* coöperati·o -onis *f*
coordinate conjunction *s* coniuncti·o -onis *f* copulativa
cope *intr* **to — with** certare cum *(w. abl);* **to be able to — with** par *(w. dat)* esse; **to be unable to — with** impar *(w. dat)* esse
copier *s* polygraph·um -i *n*
copious *adj* copios·us -a -um
copiously *adv* copiose
copper *s* cupr·um -i *n,* ae·s -ris *n*
copper *adj* cuprin·us -a -um
copulate *intr* coïre
copulation *s* coït·us -ūs *m*
copulative *s (gram)* copulativ·us -a -um
copy *s* exempl·ar -aris *n,* exempl·um -i *n*
copy *tr (to imitate)* imitari; *(in writing)* (**from**) exscribere (ex *w. abl)*
copycat *s* simi·a -ae *mf*
copyright *s* ius, iuris *n* proprium scriptoris
cord *s* funicul·us -i *m*
cordial *adj* benign·us -a -um; *(sincere)* sincer·us -a -um; **to give s.o. a — welcome** aliquem benigne excipere
cordiality *s* comit·as -atis *f*
cordially *adv* benigne, ex animo
cordon *s* coron·a -ae *f*
cordon *tr* **to — off** saepire
corduroy *s* textil·e -is *n* crassum et striatum
core *s (of fruit)* volv·a -ae *f; (fig)* nucle·us -i *m*
Corinth *s* Corinth·us -i *f;* **gulf of —** Sin·us -us *m* Corthiniacus
Corinthian *adj* Corinthi·us -a -um
cork *s* cort·ex -icis *m; (stopper)* obturament·um -i *n*
corkscrew *s* extracul·um -i *n*
corn *s* maiz·ium -(i)i *n; (on toe)* call·us -i *m;* **— on the cob** maizium in spicā
corned beef *s* bubul·a -ae *f* muriatica
corner *s* angul·us -i *m; (of street)* compit·um -i *n; (tight spot)* angusti·ae -arum *fpl*
corner *tr* impedire; *(com)* coëmere ad quaestum
cornice *s* coron·a -ae *f*
cornucopia *s* corn·u -ūs *n* copiae
corollary *s* corollar·ium -(i)i *n*
coronation *s* coronati·o -onis *f*
coronet *s* diadem·a -atis *n*
corporal *adj* corporal·is -is -e, corporis [*gen*]; **— punishment** verber·a -orum *npl*
corporal *s* decuri·o -onis *mf*
corporate *adj* corporat·us -a -um
corporation *s* colleg·ium -(i)i *n*
corporeal *adj* corporeal·is -is -e
corps *s* legi·o -onis *f*
corpse *s* cadav·er -eris *n*
corpulent *adj* corpulent·us -a -um
corpuscle *s* corpuscul·um -i *n*
correct *adj* rect·us -a -um *(opp:* pravus); *(in the sense of "corrected")* correct·us -a -um; *(free from faults)* emendat·us -a -um
correct *tr* corrigere; *(esp. mistakes in writing)* emendare; *(to chastise)* castigare
correction *s* correcti·o -onis *f;* emendati·o -onis *f;* castigati·o -onis *f*
corrective *adj* ad corrigendum apt·us -a -um
corrective *s* remed·ium -(i)i *n*
correctly *adv* recte *(opp:* prave); emendate; **to speak (spell) —** recte loqui (scribere)
correlation *s* mutua rati·o -onis *f*

correspond *intr* congruere; *(to each other)* inter se congruere; *(by letter)* epistularum commercium habēre
correspondence *s* congruenti·a -ae *f; (exchange of letters)* epistularum commerc·ium -(i)i *n*
correspondent *s* epistularum scrip·tor -toris *m* (·trix -tricis *f)*
corridor *s* andr·on -onis *m*
corroborate *tr* confirmare
corrode *tr* erodere
corrosion *s* rosi·o -onis *f; (rust)* robig·o -inis *f; (on iron)* ferrug·o -inis *f; (on copper)* aerug·o -inis *f*
corrosive *adj* corrosiv·us -a -um; *(fig)* mord·ax -acis
corrupt *tr* corrumpere
corrupt *adj* corrupt·us -a -um, putrid·us -a -um; *(accessible to bribery)* venal·is -is -e; *(text)* depravat·us -a -um
corrupter *s* corrup·tor -toris *m* (·trix -tricis *f)*
corruption *s* corrupti·o -onis *f*
corsage *s* fascicul·us -i *m* florum
corselet *s (mil)* loric·a -ae *f*
cortege *s* comitat·us -ūs *m*
cosily *adv* commode
cosmetic *s* offucin·a -ae *f,* medicam·en -inis *n; (rouge-like)* fuc·us -i *m*
cost *s (price)* pret·ium -(i)i *n; (expense)* impens·a -ae *f;* **— of living** anon·a -ae *f*
cost *intr* constare *(w. gen of indefinite price and abl of definite price or w. advs);* **how much does it —?** quanti constat?; **the victory — the lives of many** victoria morte multorum constitit; **to — 200 denari** ducentis denariis constare; **to — a lot (little, nothing, more, less)** multi (parvi, gratis, pluris, minoris) constare; **to — very much** carissime constare; **to — very little** vilissime constare
costliness *s* carit·as -atis *f*
costly *adj* pretios·us -a -um; *(extravagant)* sumptuos·us -a -um
costume *s* habit·us -ūs *m,* cult·us -ūs *m*
cosy *adj* commod·us -a -um
cot *s* grabat·us -i *m*
cottage *s* cas·a -ae *f*
cotton *s* gossyp·ium -(i)i *n*
cotton *adj* gossypin·us -a -um
couch *s* lectul·us -i *m* tomento fartus; *(esp. for dining)* lect·us -i *m*
cough *s* tuss·is -is *(acc:* tussim) *f;* **to have a bad —** male tussire
cough *tr* **to — up** extussire **||** *intr* tussire
council *s* concil·ium -(i)i *n*
councilor *s* consiliar·ius -(i)i *m*
counsel *tr* consulere
counselor *s* consilia·tor -toris *m* (·trix -tricis *f)*
count *s* com·es -itis *m; (leg)* crim·en -inis *n*
count *s* computati·o -onis *f; (total)* summ·a -ae *f; (of indictment)* cap·ut -itis *n*
count *tr* numerare, computare; *(to regard)* habēre, ducere; **to — out** *or* **up** enumerare; **to — out to** annumerare *(w. dat)* **||** *intr* aestimari, habēri; **to — upon** confidere *(w. dat);* **you can — on it that** erit tibi perspectum *(w. acc & inf)*; **you can — on me** potes niti me [*abl*]; **you don't —** extra numerum es mihi
countdown *s* denumerati·o -onis *f* inversa
countenance *s* vult·us -ūs *m*
countenance *tr* indulgēre *(w. dat)*
counter *s (of shop, kitchen)* abac·us -i *m; (in games)* calcul·us -i *m*
counteract *intr* obsistere *(w. dat); (a sickness)* mederi *(w. dat)*
counterattack *s* impet·us -ūs *m* contra hostium impetum
counterattack *intr* impetum contra hostium impetum facere
counterfeit *tr (to pretend)* simulare; *(money)* adulterare
counterfeit *s* monet·a -ae *f* adulterina
counterfeit *adj* simulat·us -a -um; *(money)* adulterin·us -a -um
counterfeiter *s* falsari·us -i *m* (·a -ae *f)*
counterpart *s (person)* pa·r -ris *n; (thing)* res, rei *f* gemella
countersign *tr* contrascribere
countless *adj* innumerabil·is -is -e
country *s* terr·a -ae *f; (territory)* fin·es -ium *mpl; (not city)* ru·s -ris *n; (native)* patri·a -ae *f; (pol)* res publica *(gen* rei publicae) *f;* **of what —** cui·as -atis; **of what — are you?** cuiates estis?
country *adj* rustic·us -a -um
country estate *s* suburban·um -i *n*
country-fresh *adj* agrest·is -is -e
country house *s* vill·a -ae *f* urbana
countryman *s* civ·is -is *m*
country road *s* vi·a -ae *f* regionalis
countryside *s* agr·i -orum *mpl*
couple *s* pa·r -ris *n; (married couple)* marit·i -orum *mpl;* **a couple of** aliquantul·i -ae -a
couple *tr* copulare **||** *intr (of animals)* coïre
courage *s* virt·us -utis *f,* anim·us -i *m;* **to lose —** animum demittere; **to take —** bono animo esse
courageous *adj* fort·is -is -e
courageously *adv* fortiter
courier *s* curs·or -oris *m,* cursr·ix -icis *f; (letter carrier)* tabellari·us -i *m* (·a -ae *f)*
course *s (movement, of ship, of river, of stars; in school)* curs·us -ūs *m; (of life)* rati·o -onis *f; (of water)* duct·us -ūs *m; (route)* it·er -ineris *n; (at table)* fercul·um -i *n; (order)* seri·es -ei *f; (for racing)* circ·us -i *m,* stad·ium -(i)i *n;* **in due —** mox; **in the — of** inter *(w. acc);* **in the — of time** procedente tempore; **of —** nempe, profecto; *(sarcastically)* scilicet; **to be driven off —** cursu excuti; **to change —** iter flectere

court *s (leg)* for·um -i *n,* iudic·ium -(i)i *n; (open area)* are·a -ae *f; (inner court of a house)* cavaed·ium -(i)i *n; (palace)* aul·a -ae *f; (retinue)* comitat·us -ūs *m;* **court of appeal** iudicium appellatorium; **to hold —** ius dicere; **to take to —** in iudicium vocare
court *tr* colere, ambire; *(a woman)* petere; *(danger)* se offerre *(w. dat)*
court costs *spl* litis impens·ae -arum *fpl*
courteous *adj* com·is -is -e
courteously *adv* comiter
courtesan *s* meretr·ix -cis *f*
courtesy *s* comit·as -atis *f;* **— of** beneficio *(w. gen)*
courtesy call *s* offic·ium -(i)i *n*
courthouse *s* basilic·a -ae *f*
courtier *s* aulic·us -i *m*
courtly *adj* aulic·us -a -um
court-martial *s* iudic·ium -(i)i *n* castrense
court-marshal *tr* in iudicium castrense vocare
courtroom *s* iudici·um -i *n*
courtship *s* procati·o -onis *f*
courtyard *s* are·a -ae *f; (in a Roman house)* peristyl·ium -(i)i *n*
cousin *s (on mother's side; used also for cousin in general)* consobrin·us -i *m* (·a -ae *f*); *(on father's side)* patruel·is -is *mf*
cove *s* sin·us -ūs *m*
covenant *s* pact·um -i *n*
covenant *intr* pacisci
cover *s (for concealment and shelter)* tegment·um -i *n; (lid)* opercul·um -i *n; (mil)* praesid·ium -(i)i *n; (pretense)* speci·es -ei *f;* **to take —** suffugere; **under — of darkness** nocte adiuvante
cover *tr* tegere, operire; *(to hide)* celare; **to — up** obtegere; *(against the cold)* bene operire
coverlet *s* stragul·um -i *n; (for bed or couch)* toral·e -is *n*
covet *tr* concupiscere
covetous *adj* appet·ens -entis
covey *s* gre·x -gis *m*
cow *tr* domare
coward *s* hom·o -inis *mf* ignav·us (-a)
cowardice *s* ignavi·a -ae *f*
cowardly *adj* ignav·us -a -um
cowboy *s* bubulc·us -i *m* (Americanus)
cower *intr* subsidere
coy *adj* verecund·us -a -um
coyly *adv* verecunde
coyness *s* verecundi·a -ae *f*
cozily *adv* commode
cozy *adj* commod·us -a -um
crab *s* can·cer -cri *m*
crabbiness *s* morosit·as -atis *f*
crabby *adj* moros·us -a -um
crack *s* rim·a -ae *f; (noise)* crepit·us -ūs *m;* **at the — of dawn** primā luce
crack *tr* findere; *(nuts, etc.)* perfringere; *(a code)* enodare; **to — jokes** ioca dicere **||** *intr* rimas agere; *(to sound)* crepitare; *(of the voice)* irraucescere; **to — down on** compescere
cracked *adj* rimos·us -a -um; *(crazy)* cerrit·us -a -um
cracker *s* crustul·um -i *n*
crackle *intr* crepitare
crackling *s* crepit·us -ūs *m*
crack troops *spl* copi·ae -arum *fpl* electissimae
cradle *s* cunabul·a -orum *npl*
cradle *tr* fovēre
craft *s (trade)* artific·ium -(i)i *n; (skill)* ar·s -tis *f; (cunning)* dol·us -i *m; (naut)* navig·ium -(i)i *n*
craftily *adv* callide
craftsman *s* artif·ex -icis *m*
craftsmanship *s* artific·ium -(i)i *n*
crafty *adj* callid·us -a -um
cram *tr* farcire; **to — together** constipare **||** *intr (for an examination)* cuncta confertim menti inculcare
cramp *s* spasm·us -i *m*
cramp *tr* comprimere; **to be —ed for space** in angusto sedēre
crane *s (bird)* gru·s -is *mf; (machine)* tollen·o -onis *m*
crank *s (mech)* unc·us -i *m; (person)* moros·us -i *m* (·a -ae *f*)
crank *tr* volvere
crash *s* frag·or -oris *m*
crash *intr* fragorem dare; *(comput)* corruere; **to come —ing down** corruere
crass *adj* crass·us -a -um
crate *s* cist·a -ae *f*
crater *s* crat·er -eris *m*
crave *tr* concupiscere
craven *adj* ignav·us atque abiect·us -a -um
craving *s* desider·ium -(i)i *n*
crawl *intr* repere; *(esp. of snakes)* serpere
crawl *s (of babies)* reptati·o -onis *f*
crayon *s* cerul·a -ae *f*
craze *s* fur·or -oris *m*
craziness *s* dementi·a -ae *f*
crazy *adj (person)* dem·ens -entis; *(idea)* insuls·us -a -um; **he's — about her** eam deperit; **he's — about sports** morbosus est in athleticas; **to drive s.o. —** mentem *(w. gen)* alienare
creak *s* strid·or -oris *m*
creak *intr* stridēre
creaking *s* strid·or -oris *m*
creaking *adj* stridul·us -a -um
cream *s* crem·um -i *n,* spum·a -ae *f* lactis; *(fig)* flo·s -ris *m*
crease *s* plicatur·a -ae *f*
crease *tr* plicare **||** *intr* plicari
create *tr* creare; *(in the mind)* fingere
creation *s (act)* creati·o -onis *f; (world)* summ·a -ae *f* rerum, mund·us -i *m; (fig)* op·us -eris *n*
creative *adj* creatr·ix -icis; *(able)* ingenios·us -a -um

creator *s* creat·or -oris *m; (originator)* auc·tor -toris *m* (·trix -tricis *f*)
creature *s (living)* anim·al -alis *n; (tool)* minis·ter -tri *m*
credence *s* fid·es -ei *f;* **to gain —** fidem habēre; **to give — to** credere *(w. dat)*
credentials *spl* testimoni·a -orum *npl*
credibility *s* fid·es -ei *f*
credible *adj* credibil·is -is -e; *(of persons)* locupl·es -etis
credit *s (faith)* fid·es -ei *f; (authority)* auctorit·as -atis *f; (reputation)* existimati·o -onis *f; (com)* fid·es -ei *f; (recognition)* lau·s -dis *f;* **to buy on —** in diem emere; **to have —** fide stare
credit *tr* credere *(w. dat); (com)* acceptum referre *(w. dat);* **to — my teacher with my success** successum meum magistro ascribere
creditable *adj* honest·us -a -um
credit card *s* tabell·a -ae *f* tributaria
creditor *s* credit·or -oris *m*
credulity *s* credulit·as -atis *f*
credulous *adj* credul·us -a -um
creed *s* fid·es -ei *f*
creek *s* riv·us -i *m*
creep *s (pej)* larv·a -ae *f*
creep *intr* repere; **it makes my skin —** facit ut horream
crescent *s* lun·a -ae *f* crescens
crescent-shaped *adj* lunat·us -a -um
crest *s (of a hill)* iug·um -i *n; (of an animal or helmet)* crist·a -ae *f*
crew *s* gre·x -gis *m; (naut)* naut·ae -arum *mpl; (rowers)* remig·es -um *mpl*
crib *s (manger)* praesep·e -is *n; (for a baby)* lectul·us -i *m*
cricket *s* gryll·us -i *m;* **—s chirp** grylli strident
crime *s* scel·us -eris *n,* facin·us -eris *n*
criminal *adj* scelest·us -a -um, facineros·us -a -um
criminal *s* sons, sontis *mf*
criminally *adv* nefarie
crimp *tr* crispare
crimson *adj* coccine·us -a -um
crimson *s* cocc·um -i *n*
cringe *intr* abhorrēre; *(to behave servilely)* se demittere, adulari
cripple *s* claud·us -i *m* (·a -ae *f*)
cripple *tr* debilitare; *(fig)* frangere
crippled *adj (in the hands)* manc·us -a -um; *(lame)* claud·us -a -um
crisis *s* discrim·en -inis *n*
criterion *s* norm·a -ae *f*
critic *s* reprehens·or -oris *m* (·rix -ricis *f*); *(literary)* cens·or -oris *m* (·rix -ricis *f*)
critical *adj (relating to criticism; crucial)* critic·us -a -um; *(blaming)* censori·us -a -um; **the situation is —** res est in summo discrimine
criticism *s* reprehensi·o -onis *f; (literary)* iudic·ium -(i)i *n,* ar·s -tis *f* critica
criticize *tr* reprehendere; *(literature)* iudicare
croak *intr* coaxare; *(of ravens)* crocitare; *(to die) (coll)* animam ebullire
croaking *s* vox, vocis *f* rauca
crock *s* oll·a -ae *f*
crocodile *s* crocodil·us -i *m*
crook *s (shepherd's)* ped·um -i *n; (thief)* fur, furis *mf*
crook *tr* curvare
crooked *adj* curvat·us -a -um; *(fig)* dolos·us -a -um
crop *s (of grain)* seg·es -itis *f; (of a bird)* ingluvi·es -ei *f*
crop *tr (to cut)* tondēre; *(to harvest)* metere ‖ *intr* **to — up** exsistere, surgere
cross *s (structure)* cru·x -cis *f; (mark)* decuss·is -is *m; (fig)* cruciat·us -ūs *m*
cross *adj (across)* transvers·us -a -um; *(contrary)* contrari·us -a -um; *(peevish)* acerb·us -a -um; *(hybrid)* mixt·us -a -um
cross *tr* transire; *(a river)* traicere; *(a mountain)* transcendere; *(to thwart)* frustrari, adversari; *(hybrids)* miscēre; **to — one's mind** alicui in mentem venire; **to — one's path** alicui obviam venire; **to — the legs** poplites alternis genibus imponere; **to — out** expungere
crossbar *s* tign·um -i *n* transversum
crossbreed *s* hibrid·a -ae *mf*
crossbreed *tr* miscēre
cross-examination *f* interrogati·o -onis *f*
cross-examine *tr* interrogare
cross-eyed *adj* strab·us -a -um
crossing *s* transit·us -ūs *m; (of a river)* traiect·us -ūs *m; (of roads)* biv·ium -(i)i *n; (of three roads)* triv·ium -(i)i *n; (of four roads)* quadriv·ium -(i)i *n*
cross reference *s* indic·ium -(i)i *n* translatum
crossroads *spl* quadriv·ium -(i)i *n; (esp. in the country)* compit·um -i *n*
crosswise *adv* in transversum
crotch *s (anat)* bifurc·um -i *n*
crouch *intr* subsidere
crouch *s* **in a —** subsid·ens -entis
crow *s (bird)* corn·ix -icis *f; (of rooster)* gallicin·ium -(i)i *n;* **as the — flies** mensurā currente [*lit: in a running measurement*]; **—s craw** cornices crocitant
crow *intr (of roosters)* cucurire, canere; *(to boast)* gloriari
crowbar *s* vect·is -is *m*
crowd *s* frequenti·a -ae *f; (mob)* turb·a -ae *f; (of people flocking together)* concurs·us -ūs *m; (common people)* vulg·us -i *n*
crowd *tr* frequentare ‖ *intr* **to — around** stipare, circumfundi *(w. dat);* **to — together** congregari
crowded *adj* frequ·ens -entis; **— together** confert·us -a -um
crowing *s* cant·us -ūs *m*

crown *s (of king)* insign·e -is *n* regium; *(wreath)* coron·a -ae *f; (power)* regn·um -i *n; (top)* vert·ex -icis *m; (fig)* ap·ex -icis *m*
crown *tr* coronare; insigne regium capiti *(w. gen)* imponere
crucifix *s* imag·o -inis *f* Christi crucifixi
crucifixion *s* crucis supplic·ium -(i)i *n*
crucify *tr* crucifigere
crude *adj* rud·is -is -e, incult·us -a -um
crudely *adv* inculte
cruel *adj* crudel·is -is -e
cruelly *adv* crudeliter
cruelty *s* crudelit·as -atis *f*
cruise *intr* circumvectari, navigare
cruise *s* navigati·o -onis *f*
cruiser *s* nav·is -is *f* longa
crumb *s* mic·a -ae *f*
crumble *tr* friare **||** *intr* friari; *(to fall down)* corruere
crumbling *adj* friabil·is -is -e
crumple *tr* corrugare
crumpled *adj* corrugat·us -a -um
crunch *tr* dentibus frangere
crush *tr* contundere; *(fig)* opprimere
crush *s* contusi·o -onis *f; (crowd)* frequenti·a -ae *f* densissima
crust *s* crust·um -i *n*
crusty *adj* crustos·us -a -um; *(fig)* cerebros·us -a -um
crutch *s* bacul·um -i *n; (fig)* fultur·a -ae *f*
cry *s (shout)* clam·or -oris *m; (of a baby)* vagit·us -ūs *m*
cry *tr* clamare; **to — out** exclamare **||** *intr (to shout)* clamare; *(to shout repeatedly)* clamitare; *(to weep)* lacrimare, flēre; *(of infants)* vagire; **to — over** flere
crying *s* flet·us -ūs *m; (of a baby)* vagit·us -ūs *m*
crypt *s* crypt·a -ae *f*
cryptic *adj* occult·us -a -um
crystal *adj* crystallin·us -a -um
crystal *s* crystall·um -i *n*
crystal-clear *adj* pellucid·us -a -um
cub *s* catul·us -i *m*
cube *s* cub·us -i *m*
cubic *adj* cubic·us -a -um
cubit *s* cubit·um -i *n*
cuckoo *s* cucul·us -i *m*
cucumber *s* cucum·is -eris *m*
cud *s* rum·en -inis *n;* **to chew the —** ruminare
cudgel *s* fust·is -is *m*
cue *s (hint)* nut·us -ūs *m,* indic·ium -(i)i *n; (theat)* verb·um -i *n* monitorium
cuff *s (of sleeve)* extrema manic·a -ae *f; (blow)* colaph·us -i *m*
culminate *intr* ad summum venire
culmination *s* fastig·ium -(i)i *n*
culpable *adj* culpand·us -a -um
culprit *s* re·us -i *m,* re·a -ae *f*
cultivate *tr (land, mind, friendship)* colere
cultivation *s* cultur·a -ae *f*
cultivator *s* cult·or -oris *m*
culture *s* cultur·a -ae *f*
culvert *s* cloac·a -ae *f*
cumbersome *adj* inhabil·is -is -e
cunning *adj (clever)* callid·us -a -um; *(sly)* astut·us -a -um
cup *s* pocul·um -i *n*
cupboard *s* armar·ium -(i)i *n* in parieti insertum
Cupid *s* Cupid·o -inis *m*
cupidity *s* cupidit·as -atis *f*
cupola *s* thol·us -i *m*
cur *s (coll)* can·is -is *m* nothus; *(fig)* scelest·us -i *m*
curable *adj* sanabil·is -is -e
curative *adj* medicabil·is -is -e
curator *s* cura·tor -toris *m* (·trix -tricis *f)*
curb *s (& fig)* fren·um -i *n; (of the road)* crepid·o -inis *f*
curb *tr* frenare; *(fig)* refrenare
curbstone *s* crepid·o -inis *m*
curdle *tr* coagulare **||** *intr* coïre
cure *s (remedy)* remd·ium -(i)i *n; (process)* sanati·o -onis *f*
cure *tr* sanare; *(to pickle)* salire
curiosity *s* curiosit·as -atis *f; (thing)* miracul·um -i *n*
curious *adj* curios·us -a -um; *(strange)* mirabil·is -is -e
curiously *adv* curiose
curl *s (natural)* cirr·us -i *m; (artificial)* cincinn·us -i *m*
curl *tr* crispare **||** *intr* crispari; *(of smoke)* volvi
curler, curling iron *s* calamistr·um -i *n*
curly *adj* crisp·us -a -um, cirrat·us -a -um
currency *s* monet·a -ae *f; (use)* us·us -ūs *m;* **to gain —** percrebrescere
current *adj (opinion)* vulgar·is -is -e; *(in general use)* usitat·us -a -um
current *s* vis *f* fluminis *n; (of air)* afflat·us -ūs *m; (electrical)* electricum fluent·um -i *n;* **against the —** adverso flumine; **with the —** secundo flumine
curriculum *s* studiorum curricul·um -i *n*
curse *s* maledict·um -i *n; (fig)* pest·is -is *f*
curse *tr* maledicere *(w. dat)* **||** *intr* maledicere
cursed *adj* exsecrabil·is -is -e
cursing *s* convic·ium -(i)i *n*
cursor *s (comput)* curs·or -oris *m*
cursorily *adv* strictim
cursory *adj* lev·is -is -e, brev·is -is -e
curt *adj* abrupt·us -a -um
curtail *tr (to cut off a part of)* praecidere; *(to diminish)* minuere
curtain *s (on a window or shower)* vel·um -i *n; (theat)* aulae·um -i *n;* **to draw the —s** vela obducere
curvature *s* curvatur·a -ae *f*
curve *s (of road)* anfract·us -ūs *m; (of river)* flex·us -ūs *m*
curve *tr* incurvare, flectere **||** *intr* incurvari

curved *adj* curv·us -a -um; *(as a sickle)* falcat·us -a -um
cushion *s* pulvin·us -i *m; (fig)* levam·en -inis *n*
custard *s* artolagan·us -i *m*
custodian *s* cust·os -odis *mf*
custody *s* tutel·a -ae *f,* custodi·a -ae *f;* **to keep in —** custodire; **to take into —** in vincula conicere
custom *s* mo·s -ris *m,* consuetud·o -inis *f;* **according to the — of the Roman people** more populi Romani
customary *adj* consuet·us -a -um; *(regularly occurring)* sollemn·is -is -e
customer *s* cli·ens -entis *mf; (buyer)* emp·tor -toris *m* (·trix -tricis *f*)
customs *spl (tax)* portor·ium -(i)i *n*
customs officer *s* porti·tor -toris *m* (·trix -tricis *f*)
cut *tr* secare; *(hair)* tondēre; *(to fell)* caedere; *(to mow)* resecare; **cut it out!** desiste! *(pl:* desistite!); **cut the talk!** segrega sermonem!; **to — and paste** *(comput)* secare et glutinare; **to — apart** dissecare; **to — away** recidere, abscindere; **to — down** caedere; *(to kill)* occidere; **to — in pieces** concidere; **to — off** praecidere; *(to intercept)* intercludere; **to — open** incidere; **to — out** exsecare; *(out of a rock, etc.)* excidere; **to — short** intercidere; *(to abridge)* praecidere; *(to interrupt)* interpellare; **to — short the school day** ludum artare; **to — to pieces** concidere; **to — up** minutatim concidere; *(the enemy)* trucidare
cute *adj* bell·us -a -um, bellul·us -a -um
cutlery *s* instrument·a -orum *npl* escaria
cutlet *s* frust·um -i *n*
cutthroat *s* sicar·ius -(i)i *m*
cutting *adj (sharp)* acut·us -a -um; *(fig)* acerb·us -a -um
cutting *s (act)* secti·o -onis *f; (thing)* segm·en -inis *n; (for planting)* taleol·a -ae *f*
cyberspace *s* cyberspat·ium -(i) *n*
cycle *s* orb·is -is *m; (of events)* ord·o -inis *m*
cylinder *s* cylindr·us -i *m*
cylindrical *adj* cylindrat·us -a -um
cymbal *s* cymbal·um -i *n*
cynic *adj* cynic·us -a -um
cynic *s* cynic·us -i *m* (·a -ae *f*)
cynical *adj* acerb·us -a -um
cynicism *s* acerbit·as -atis *f*
cypress *s* cypress·us -i *f*

D

dab *s* massul·a -ae *f*
dab *tr* **to — on** illinere
dabble *intr* **to — in** leviter attingere
dad, daddy *s* tat·a -ae *m*
dactyl *s* dactyl·us -i *m*
dactylic *adj* dactylic·us -a -um
daffodil *s* asphodel·us -i *m*
daffy *adj (coll)* delir·us -a -um
dagger *s* pugi·o -onis *m*
daily *adj* cotidian·us -a -um
daily *adv* cotidie
dainties *spl* cuppedi·a -orum *npl*
dainty *adj* delicat·us -a -um
daisy *s* bell·is -idis *f*
dale *s* vall·is -is *f*
dally *intr (to linger)* morari; *(to trifle)* nugari; *(amorously)* blandiri
dam *s* mol·es -is *f; (of animals)* mat·er -ris *f*
dam *tr* **to — up** (operibus) obstruere
damage *s (loss)* damn·um -i *n; (injury)* nox·a -ae *f*
damage *tr* laedere; *(a person)* fraudi esse *(w. dat);* **to — s.o.'s reputation** aestimationem alicuius violare
dame *s* domin·a -ae *f; (girl)* puell·a -ae *f*
damn *tr* damnare, exsecrari
damnable *adj* damnabil·is -is -e
damnably *adv* damnabiliter
damnation *s* damnati·o -onis *f*
damp *adj* (h)umid·us -a -um
dampen *tr* humectare; *(fig)* restringere
dampness *s* ulig·o -inis *f*
damsel *s* puell·a -ae *f*
dance *s* saltati·o -onis *f*
dance *tr* **to — a number** canticum desaltare ‖ *intr* saltare
dance band *s* symphonicac·i -orum *mpl* saltationis
dancer *s* salta·tor -toris *m* (·trix -tricis *f*)
dancing *s* saltati·o -onis *f*
dandelion *s* aphac·a -ae *f*
dandruff *s* porrig·o -inis *f*
dandy *adj* bell·us -a -um
dandy *s* hom·o -inis *m* bellus
danger *s* pericul·um -i *n;* **to be in — of** periclitari *(w. abl);* **to be in grave —** in praecipite esse
dangerous *adj* periculos·us -a -um
dangerously *adv* periculose; *(seriously)* graviter
dangle *tr* suspendere ‖ *intr* pendēre
dank *adj* (h)umid·us et frigid·us -a -um
Danube River *s* Davuvi·us -i amn·is -is *m*
dare *tr* provocare ‖ *intr* audēre
daredevil *s* parabol·us -i *m*
daring *adj* aud·ax -acis
daring *s* audaci·a -ae *f*
dark *adj* obscur·us -a -um; *(in color)* fusc·us -a -um; *(gloomy)* a·ter -tra -trum; *(stern)* atr·ox -ocis; **—est night** spississima no·x -ctis *f;* **— eyes** nigri ocul·i -orum *mpl;* **it is growing —** advesperascit
dark *s* tenebr·ae -arum *fpl;* **after —** de nocte; **in the —** *(i.e., secretly)* clam et occulte; **I am in the —** *(i.e., mentally)*

mihi tenebrae sunt; **to keep in the —** celare

darken *tr* obscurare; *(colors)* fuscare

dark horse *s* canditat·us -i *m* (·a -ae *f)* inopinat·us (-a)

darkness *s* tenebr·ae -arum *fpl;* **— fell** tenebrae factae sunt

darling *adj* suavissim·us -a -um

darling *s* delici·ae -arum *fpl,* ocell·us -i *m;* **my darling** *(in address)* mi ocelle

darn *tr* resarcire

darn *interj* (me) hercule!

darn *s* **I don't give a — about that (him, them)** id (eum, eos) non flocci facio

darned *adj* **I'll be — if ...** male mi sit, si ...

dart *s* spicul·um -i *n*

dart *intr (to move quickly)* provolare; *(of snake's tongue)* vibrare; **to — out** emicare

dash *tr (to splash)* aspergere; *(hopes)* frustrari; **to — against** allidere ad *(w. acc);* **to — off** *(letter)* scriptitare; **to — to pieces** discutere; **to — to the ground** affligere **||** *intr* ruere

dash *s* impet·us -ūs *m; (animation)* alacrit·as -atis *f; (small amount)* mensur·a -ae *f* duorum digitorum

dashboard *s* tabul·a -ae *f* indicatoria

dashing *adj* ala·cer -cris -cre; *(showy)* nitid·us -a -um

data *spl* dat·a -orum *npl*

database *s (comput)* datorum repositor·ium -(i)i *n*

date *s* di·es -ei *f; (appointment)* constitut·um -i *n; (fruit)* palmul·a -ae *f;* **by what —?** quam ad diem?; **out of —** obsolet·us -a -um; **to —** adhuc; **to have a — with** consitutum habere cum *(w. abl);* **up to —** rec·ens -entis

date *tr* diem ascribere *(w. dat); (a girl)* constitutum habere cum *(w. abl)* **||** *intr* **to — from** originem trahere ab *(w. abl)*

dative *s* dativ·us -i *m,* cas·us -ūs *m* dativus

daub *tr* oblinere

daughter *s* fili·a -ae *f*

daughter-in-law *s* nur·us -i *f*

daunt *tr* perterrēre

dauntless *adj* impavid·us -a -um

dauntlessly *adv* impavide

dawdle *intr* cessare

dawn *s* auror·a -ae *f;* **at —** primā luce; **before —** anteluculo

dawn *intr* dilucescere; **to — on** *(fig)* occurrere *(w. dat)*

day *s* di·es -ei *m;* **any —now** propediem; **by —** interdiu; **— after —** diem de die, in singulos dies; **— by —** in dies; **— and night** diem noctemque, et dies et noctes; **every —** cotidie; **from — to —** in dies; **from that — on** ex eo die; **just the other —** nuper quidem; **next —** postridie; **one — *(in the past)*** quodam die; **some —** olim; **the — after** postridie; **the — after that** postridie eius diei; **the — after tomorrow** perendie; **the — before** pridie; **the — before yesterday** nudiustertius [*adv*]; **the following —** postero die; **these —s** his temporibus; **till late in the —** ad multum diem; **three —s after that** post quartum eius diei

day *adj* diurn·us -a -um

daybreak *s* dilucul·um -i *n;* **at —** primā luce; **before —** antelucio; **till —** in primam lucem

daydream *s* hallucinati·o -onis *f*

daydream *intr* hallucinari

daydreamer *s* hallucina·tor -toris *m* (·trix -tricis *f)*

daylight *s* lu·x -cis *f,* dies, diei *m;* **to let in the —** diem admittere

daytime *s* temp·us -oris *n* diurnum; **in the —** interdiu

daze *s* stup·or -oris *m*

daze *tr* obstupefacere

dazzle *tr* praestringere

dazzling *adj* fulgid·us -a -um

DCD *s* digitalis compactus disc·us -i *m*

deacon *s* diacon·us -i *m*

dead *adj* mortu·us -a -um; *(without sensation)* sine sensu; **I'm —!** *(coll)* interii! *or* perii!

dead *s* **— of night** media no·x -ctis *f;* **— of winter** brum·a -ae *f;* **the —** man·es -ium, mortu·i -orum *mpl*

dead *adv* omnino, prorsus

deaden *tr* obtundere

dead end *s* fundul·a -ae *f; (fig)* cessati·o -onis *f*

dead-end street *s* fundul·a -ae *f*

deadline *s* praestituta di·es -ei *f;* **to meet the —** diem praestitutam obire; **to set the —** diem praestituere

deadly *adj* mortif·er -era -erum; *(hatred)* capital·is -is -e

deaf *adj* surd·us -a -um; **to be — to** non audire; **to go —** obsurdescere; **to turn a — ear** obsurdescere; **you're preaching to deaf ears** ad surdas aures cantas

deafen *tr* exsurdare

deaf-mute *adj* surd·us idemque mut·us -a -um

deafness *s* surdit·as -atis *f*

deal *s (quantity)* copi·a -ae *f,* vis *f; (pact)* pacti·o -onis *f; (com)* negot·ium -(i)i *n;* **a good — longer** multo diutius; **a good — of** aliquantum *(w. gen);* **it's a deal!** pactam rem habeto *(pl:* habetote)!

deal *tr* partiri; *(cards)* distribuere; **to — him a blow in the stomach** pugnos in ventrem ingerere **||** *intr (com)* negotiari; **easy to — with** tractabil·is -is -e; **I'll — with you later** tecum mihi res erit serius; **to — with** *(a topic)* agere *(w. abl),* tractare; **(a person)** uti *(w. abl)*

dealer *s* negotia•tor -toris *m* (•trix -tricis *f*); *(of cards)* distribu•tor -toris *m* (•trix -tricis *f*)
dealings *spl (com)* negotiati•o -onis *f*; *(relations)* commerc•ium -(i)i *n*; **to have —s with** commercium habēre cum *(w. abl)*
dean *s* decan•us -i *m* (•a -ae *f*)
dear *adj (highly valued; high-priced)* car•us -a -um; **my — friend!** mi amice!
dear *interj* **O —!** *(in dismay)* hei!; *(in embarrassment)* au au!
dearly *adv (intensely)* valde; *(at high cost)* magni
dearness *s* carit•as -atis *f*
dearth *s* inopi•a -ae *f*
death *s* mor•s -tis *f*; *(in violent form)* ne•x -cis *f*; **to condemn s.o. to —** aliquem capitis damnare; **to meet one's —** mortem obire; **to put s.o. to —** aliquem ad mortem dare, supplicium de aliquo sumere
deathbed *s* tor•us -i *m* extremus
deathless *adj* immortal•is -is -e
deathlike *adj* mortuos•us -a -um
deathly *adj* pallid•us -a -um
death penalty *s* supplic•ium -(i)i *n* capitis
death sentence *s* **to receive the —** capitis damnari
debase *tr* depravare; *(coinage)* adulterare; **to — oneself** se demittere
debasement *s* adulterati•o -onis *f*
debatable *adj* controversios•us -a -um, ambigu•us -a -um
debate *s* disceptati•o -onis *f*
debate *tr* disceptare de *(w. abl)* **||** *intr* disserere, disputare
debater *s* disputa•tor -toris *m* (•trix -tricis *f*)
debauchery *s* licenti•a -ae *f*
debilitate *tr* debilitare
debit *s* expens•um -i *n*
debit *tr* in expensum referre
debt *s* ae•s -ris *n* alienum; *(fig)* debit•um -i *n*; **to be in —** aere alieno esse; **to pay off a —** aes alienum persolvere; **to run up a —** aes alienum conflare
debtor *s* debi•tor -toris *m* (•trix -tricis *f*)
decade *s* dec•as -adis *f*
decadence *s* occas•us -ūs *m*
decadent *adj* degen•er -era -erum
decalogue *s* decalog•us -i *m*
decamp *intr* castra movēre
decapitate *tr* detruncare
decathlon *s* decathl•um -i *n*
decay *s* tab•es -is *f*; *(fig)* defecti•o -onis *f*
decay *intr* putrescere, tabescere
decease *s* decess•us -ūs *m*
deceased *adj* defunct•us -a -um
deceit *s* frau•s -dis *f*, dol•us -i *m*
deceitful *adj* fall•ax -acis
deceitfully *adv* fallaciter
deceive *tr* decipere, fallere
December *s* Decem•ber -bris *m or* mens•is -is *m* December; **in —** mense Decembri; **on the first of —** Kalendis Decembribus
decency *s* decor•um -i *n*
decent *adj* dec•ens -entis; *(adequate)* rect•us -a -um
decently *adv* decenter
deception *s* fallaci•a -ae *f*
deceptive *adj* fall•ax -acis
decide *tr & intr* decernere; **the Senate decided** senatui placuit; **to — to** constituere *(w. inf)*
decided *adj* cert•us -a -um
decimate *tr* decimare; *(fig)* depopulari
decipher *tr* enodare
decision *s* sententi•a -ae *f*; *(of deliberative body)* decret•um -i *n*; *(of Senate)* auctorit•as -atis *f*; *(leg)* iudic•ium -(i)i *n*; *(a win in sports)* praevalenti•a -ae *f* punctorum; **to make a (wise) —** (sapienter) decernere
decisive *adj* cert•us -a -um; **— battle** decretoria pugn•a -ae *f*
deck *s (naut)* pon•s -tis *m*; **ship with a —** nav•is -is *f* constrata
deck *tr* ornare; *(tables)* sternere
deck chair *s* sell•a -ae *f* cubitoria
decked out *adj* **(in)** subornat•us -a -um *(w. abl)*
declaim *intr* declamare
declamation *s* declamati•o -onis *f*
declamatory *adj* declamatori•us -a -um
declaration *s* declarati•o -onis *f*; *(of war)* denuniati•o -onis *f*
declarative *adj* declarativ•us -a -um
declare *tr* declarare; *(to say out plainly)* edicere; *(war)* indicere **||** *intr* **to — for** favēre *(w. dat)*
declension *s* declinati•o -onis *f*
declinable *adj* declinabil•is -is -e
decline *s (slope)* decliv•e -is *n*; *(of strength, etc.)* deminuti•o -onis *f*; **to cause a — in prices** pretia levare
decline *tr (to refuse)* recusare; *(gram)* declinare, flectere; **to — battle** pugnam detrectare **||** *intr* inclinare; *(to decay, fail)* deficere, decrescere; *(of prices)* laxare
decode *tr* enodare
decompose *tr* resolvere **||** *intr* putrescere, dissolvi
decomposition *s* dissoluti•o -onis *f*
decorate *tr* ornare
decoration *s (act)* ornati•o -onis *f*; *(ornament)* ornament•um -i *n*; *(distinction)* dec•us -oris *n*
decorator *s* exorn•ator -toris *m* (•trix -tricis *f*)
decorum *s* decor•um -i *n*
decoy *s* ill•ex -icis *mf*
decoy *tr* allicere
decrease *s* imminuti•o -onis *f*
decrease *tr* imminuere **||** *intr* decrescere; *(of prices)* retro abire

decreasingly *adv* in minus
decree *s* decret·um -i *n; (of the Senate)* senatūs consult·um -i *n; (of the assembly)* scit·um -i *n;* **to pass a — of the senate** senatūs consultum facere
decree *tr* decernere; **the people —d** populus iussit
decrepit *adj* decrepit·us -a -um
decry *tr* vituperare
dedicate *tr (book, etc.)* dedicare; **to — oneself to** se dedere *(w. dat)*
dedication *s* dedicati·o -onis *f; (of a book)* nuncupati·o -onis *f; (devotion)* stud·ium -(i)i *n*
deduce *tr (to infer)* colligere
deduct *tr* deducere; **to — from the capital what has been paid in interest** de capite deducere quod usuris pernumeratum est
deduction *s* deducti·o -onis *f; (inference)* conclusi·o -onis *f*
deed *s* fact·um -i *n; (pej)* facin·us -oris *n; (leg)* instrument·um -i *n;* **good —** benefic·ium -(i)i *n*
deem *tr* ducere, habēre
deep *adj* alt·us -a -um; *(very deep)* profund·us -a -um; *(of sounds)* grav·is -is -e; *(of color)* satur -a -um; *(sleep)* art·us -a -um; *(recondite)* recondit·us -a -um; **— silence fell** ingens silentium factum est; **in — thought** cogitabund·us -a -um
deep *s* alt·um -i *n*
deepen *tr* defodere; *(e.g., affection)* augēre ‖ *intr* alt·ior -ior -ius fieri
deepfreezer *s* arc·a -ae *f* gelatoria
deeply *adv* alte; *(inwardly)* penitus; *(fig)* graviter, valde; **to be — grieved** graviter dolēre; **to be — in love** graviter amare
deep red *adj* coccine·us -a -um
deep-seated *adj* insit·us -a -um
deep-sunk *adj (eyes)* concav·us -a -um
deer *s* cerv·us -i *m,* cerv·a -ae *f*
deface *tr* deformare
defaced *adj* deform·is -is -e
defacement *s* deformit·as -atis *f*
defamation *s* obtrectati·o -onis *f*
defamatory *adj* probros·us -a -um
defame *tr* diffamare, infamare
default *s* delict·um -i *n*
defeat *s (pol)* repuls·a -ae *f; (mil)* clad·es -is *f; (sports)* adversum certam·en -inis *n;* **a — at the polls** comitiis repulsa; **— in running for the consulship** consulatūs repulsa; **to suffer a —** *(pol)* repulsam ferre; *(mil)* cladem accipere
defeat *tr* vincere, superare; *(to baffle)* frustrari; **to — a bill** rogationem antiquare
defect *s* vit·ium -(i)i *n*
defect *intr (to desert)* deficere
defection *s* defecti·o -onis *f; (to the enemy)* transfug·ium -(i)i *n*
defective *adj* vitios·us -a -um; *(gram)* defectiv·us -a -um
defend *tr* defendere; *(leg)* patrocinari *(w. dat)*
defendant *s* re·us -i *m,* re·a -ae *f*
defender *s* defens·or -oris *m* (·trix -tricis *f*); *(leg)* patron·us -i *m* (·a -ae *f*)
defense *s (act)* defensi·o -onis *f; (means)* praesid·ium -(i)i *n; (leg)* patrocin·ium -(i)i *n; (speech)* defensi·o -onis *f*
defense lawyer *s* defens·or -oris *m* (·trix -tricis *f*)
defenseless *adj* infens·us -a -um; *(unarmed)* inerm·is -is -e
defensible *adj* defensibil·is -is -e
defensive *adj* **— and offensive alliance** societ·as -atis *f* ad bellum defendendum atque inferendum facta; **— and offensive weapons** tela ad tegendum et ad nocendum; **to put s.o. on the —** aliquem ad sua defendenda cogere
defer *tr* differre ‖ *intr* **to — to** obsequi *(w. dat)*
deference *s* observanti·a -ae *f;* **out of —** reverenter
deferential *adj* **(to)** observ·ans -antis *(w. gen)*
defiance *s* contempti·o -onis *f;* **in — of the law** invitis legibus
defiant *adj* insol·ens -entis
deficiency *s* defect·us -ūs *m; (of supplies, water, money)* penuri·a -ae *f*
deficient *adj* **(in)** in·ops -opis *(w. gen);* **to be —** deesse
deficit *s* lacun·a -ae *f;* **there is a —** deficit; **to make up the —** lacunam explēre
defile *s* fauc·es -ium *fpl*
defile *tr* inquinare; *(usu. fig)* contaminare
defilement *s* contaminati·o -onis *f*
define *tr* definire
definite *adj* definit·us -a -um *(opp:* infinitus)
definitely *adv* certe
definition *s* definiti·o -onis *f*
definitive *adj* definitiv·us -a -um
definitively *adv* definite
deflect *tr* deflectere
deflection *s* deflecti·o -onis *f*
deflower *tr* devirginare
deform *tr* deformare
deformed *adj* deform·is -is -e
deformity *s* deformit·as -atis *f*
defraud *tr* fraudare
defray *tr* suppeditare; **to — the costs** sumptūs suppeditare
deft *adj* agil·is -is -e, habil·is -is -e
deftly *adv* scite
defunct *adj* defunct·us -a -um
defy *tr* contemnere
degeneracy *s* mor·es -um *mpl* deteriores
degenerate *adj* degen·er -eris
degenerate *s* hom·o -inis *mf* degen·er (-eris)
degradation *s* ignomini·a -ae *f*

degrade *tr (to lower rank)* in ordinem redigere; *(fig)* dehonestare
degrading *adj* indign·us -a -um
degree *s* grad·us -ūs *m; (diploma)* studiorum diplom·a -atis *n;* **by —s** gradatim; **in some —** aliquatenus; **positive (comparative, superlative) —** gradus positivus (comparativus, superlativus); **third —** quaesti·o -onis *f* severissia; **to such a — that** adeo ut
deification *s* consecrati·o -onis *f*
deify *tr* inter deos referre
deign *tr* dignari, curare
deism *s* deism·us -i *m*
deity *s* num·en -inis *n*
dejected *adj* demiss·us -a -um
dejection *s* animi abiecti·o -onis *f*
delay *s* mor·a -ae *f*
delay *tr* demorari ‖ *intr* morari
delectable *adj* delectabil·is -is -e
delegate *s* legat·us -i *m* (·a -ae *f*)
delegate *tr (to depute)* delegare; *(to entrust)* demandare
delegation *s (act)* mandat·us -ūs *m; (group)* legati·o -onis *f*
delete *tr* eradere; *(comput)* delēre
deleterious *adj* noxi·us -a -um
deliberate *adj* deliberat·us -a -um
deliberate *intr* deliberare, consulere
deliberately *adv* de industriā
deliberation *s* deliberati·o -onis *f*
delicacy *s* subtilit·as -atis *f; (food)* matte·a -ae *f;* **delicacies** cuppedi·a -orum *npl*
delicate *adj (of fine texture)* subtil·is -is -e; *(e.g., girl)* delicat·us -a -um; *(taste, work of art)* eleg·ans -antis; *(health)* infirm·us -a -um; *(matter)* lubric·us -a -um
delicious *adj* sapid·us -a -um
delight *s* delectati·o -onis *f; (cause of delight)* delici·ae -arum *fpl*
delight *tr* delectare ‖ *intr* **to — in** delectari *(w. abl)*
delighted *adj* (**with**) delectat·us -a -um *(w. abl)*
delightful *adj* suav·is -is -e
delightfully *adv* suaviter
delineate *tr* delineare, describere
delineation *s* descripti·o -onis *f*
delinquency *s* delict·um -i *n*
delinquent *adj* noxi·us -a -um
delinquent *s* noxi·us -i *m* (·a -ae *f*)
delirious *adj* delir·us -a -um
delirium *s* delir·ium -(i)i *n*
deliver *tr (to hand over)* tradere; *(to free)* liberare; *(to surrender)* prodere; *(a speech)* habēre, dicere; *(sentence)* dicere; *(message)* referre; *(blow)* intendere; *(child)* obstetricari; *(a letter)* reddere
deliverance *s* liberati·o -onis *f*
deliverer *s* libera·tor -toris *m* (·trix -tricis *f*)
delivery *s (freedom)* liberati·o -onis *f; (of goods)* traditi·o -onis *f; (of a speech)* acti·o -onis *f; (childbirth)* part·us -ūs *m*
delude *tr* deludere
deluge *s* diluv·ium -(i)i *n*
deluge *tr* obruere, inundare
delusion *s* delusi·o -onis *f*
demagogue *s* publicol·a -ae *m*
demand *s* postulati·o -onis *f,* postulat·um -i *n*
demand *tr* postulare, flagitare
demanding *adj* **to be —** multa exigere
demarcation *s* confin·ium -(i)i *n*
demean *tr* **to — oneself** se demittere
demeanor *s* gest·us -ūs *m*
demented *adj* dem·ens -entis
demerit *s* vit·ium -(i)i *n; (mark)* vitii not·a -ae *f*
demigod *s* her·os -oïs *m*
demise *s* decess·us -ūs *m*
democracy *s* civit·as -atis *f* popularis
democrat *s* civ·is -is *m* popularis
democratic *adj* popular·is -is -e; **— party** part·es -ium *fpl* populares
democratically *adv* populi voluntate
demolish *tr* demoliri
demolition *s* demoliti·o -onis *f*
demon *s* daem·on -onis *m*
demonstrable *adj* demonstrabil·is -is -e
demonstrably *adv* manifeste
demonstrate *tr (to show)* monstrare; *(to prove)* demonstrare
demonstration *s (proof)* demonstrati·o -onis *f; (display)* ostent·us -ūs *m; (popular display of opinion)* protestati·o -onis *f* popularis
demonstrative *adj* demonstrativ·us -a -um
demoralization *s* depravati·o -onis *f*
demoralize *tr (to corrupt)* depravare; *(to discourage)* percellere
demote *tr* loco movēre
demotion *s* a gradu moti·o -onis *f*
demure *adj* modest·us -a -um
demurely *adv* modeste
den *s* latibul·um -i *n*; *(in a home)* tablin·um -i *n*
denarius *s* denari·us -i *m (worth about one dollar)*
deniable *adj* infitiand·us -a -um
denial *s* negati·o -onis *f; (refusal)* repudiati·o -onis *f;* **to give s.o. a flat —** praecise alicui negare
denomination *s (name)* denominati·o -onis *f; (sect)* sect·a -ae *f*
denominator *s* numer·us -i *m* dividens
denotation *s* denotati·o -onis *f*
denote *tr* significare
denounce *tr (to inform against)* deferre; *(to condemn)* reprehendere
dense *adj* dens·us -a -um; *(crowded)* spiss·us -a -um; *(stupid)* crass·us -a -um
densely *adv* dense, crebro; **— populated region** regi·o -onis *f* uberrimae multitudinis
density *s* densit·as -atis *f*
dent *s* not·a -ae *f*

dent *tr* imprimere, cavare
dented *adj* collis·us -a -um
dentist *s* medic·us -i *m* dentarius, medic·a -ae *f* dentaria
dentistry *s* dentium medicin·a -ae *f*
denture *s* prostes·is -is *f* dentalis
denude *tr* nudare
denunciation *s (by informer)* delati·o -onis *f; (condemnation)* reprehensi·o -onis *f*
deny *tr* negare, infitiari; *(to refuse)* (de)negare, abnuere
depart *intr* abire; *(to die)* obire; **to — for his province** abire in provinciam
departed *adj* defunct·us -a -um
department *s (of administration)* provinci·a -ae *f,* administrati·o -onis *f; (branch)* gen·us -eris *n*; *(academic)* facult·as -atis *f;* **— of classics** litterarum classicarum facultas
department store *s* pantopol·ium -(i)i *n*
departure *s* abit·us -ūs *m,* abscess·us -ūs *m; (death)* obit·us -ūs *m*
depend *tr* **to — on** dependēre de *(w. abl),* niti *(w. abl)*; **it —s on you** in te positum est; **it — a lot on whether** plurimum refert num
dependable *adj* fid·us -a -um
dependant *s* cli·ens -entis *mf*
dependence *s* fiduci·a -ae *f*
dependency *s* provinci·a -ae *f*
dependent *adj* obnoxi·us -a -um
depict *tr (to paint)* pingere; *(in words)* describere, depingere
deplete *tr* deminuere
depletion *s* deminuti·o -onis *f*
deplorable *adj* miserabil·is -is -e
deplore *tr* deplorare
deploy *tr (mil)* expedire, instruere
deponent *s* depon·ens -entis *n,* verb·um -i *n* deponens
depopulate *tr* vacuefacere
deportment *s* gest·us -ūs *m*
depose *tr* summovēre; *(leg)* testificari
deposit *s* deposit·um -i *n; (earnest money)* arrhab·o -onis *m; (of fluids)* sedim·en -inis *n;* **to put down 10 denari as a —** decem denarios arrhaboni dare
deposit *tr* **to — money in a bank** pecuniam in argentariā deponere
deposition *s (leg)* testimon·ium -(i)i *n*
depositor *s* deposi·tor -toris *m* (·trix -tricis *f)*
depot *s (com)* empor·ium -(i)i *n; (mil)* armamentar·ium -(i)i *n*
depraved *adj* prav·us -a -um
depravity *s* pravit·as -atis *f*
deprecate *tr* deprecari
deprecation *s* deprecati·o -onis *f*
depreciate *tr* detrectare
depreciation *s* detrectati·o -onis *f; (of price)* vilit·as -atis *f*
depredation *s* spoliati·o -onis *f*
depress *tr* deprimere; *(fig)* infringere
depressed *adj* abiect·us -a -um; **to be —** abiecto animo esse
depressing *adj* trist·is -is -e
depression *s (emotional)* anim·us -i *m* fractus; *(fin)* res adversae
deprivation *s (act)* privati·o -onis *f; (state)* inopi·a -ae *f*
deprive *tr* privare; **to — s.o. of** aliquem privare *(w. abl)*
depth *s* altitud·o -inis *f;* **a hundred feet in —** *(as opposed to frontage)* centum pedes in agrum; **the —s** profund·um -i *n*
deputation *s* legati·o -onis *f*
deputy *s* legat·us -i *m* (·a -ae *f)*
derange *tr* conturbare
deranged *adj* mente capt·us -a -um
derangement *s (of mind)* mentis alienati·o -onis *f*
dereliction *s* derelicti·o -onis *f*
deride *tr* irridēre
derision *s* irrisi·o -onis *f*
derisive *adj* irrid·ens -entis
derivation *s* derivati·o -onis *f*
derivative *adj* derivativ·us -a -um
derive *tr* (de)ducere; *(words)* derivare; **to — pleasure from** voluptatem capere ex *(w. abl)* **||** *intr* procedere
derogatory *adj* indign·us -a -um
descend *intr* descendere; **to — on** *(to attack)* irrumpere in *(w. acc)*
descendant *s* progeni·es -ei *f;* **the —s** poster·i -orum *mpl*
descent *s* descens·us -ūs *m; (slope)* cliv·us -i *m; (lineage)* gen·us -eris *n*
describe *tr* describere
description *s* descripti·o -onis *f*
desecrate *tr* profanare
desecration *f* violati·o -onis *f*
desert *s* desert·a -orum *npl*
desert *tr* deserere, relinquere **||** *intr* deserere; *(esp. mil)* transfugere
deserter *s* transfug·a -ae *mf*
desertion *s (abandonment)* deserti·o -onis *f; (esp. mil)* transfug·ium -(i)i *n*
deserts *spl* merit·a -orum *npl;* **he got his —** habet quod sibi debebatur
deserve *tr* merēre, merēri
deservedly *adv* merito, iure
deserving *adj* **(of)** dign·us -a -um *(w. abl)*
design *s (of a building, etc.)* descripti·o -onis *f; (drawing)* adumbrati·o -onis *f; (plan)* form·a -ae *f*
design *tr* designare; *(to draw in lines)* delineare; *(to sketch)* adumbrare; *(fig)* machinari
designate *tr* designare
designation *s (appointment)* designati·o -onis *f; (name)* nom·en -inis *n*
designer *s (of s.th. new)* invent·or -oris *m* (·trix -tricis *f); (as an architect)* designa·tor -toris *m* (·trix -tricis *f); (of a stratagem)* fabrica·tor -toris *m* (·trix -tricis *f)*

designing *adj* callid·us -a -um
desirable *adj* desiderabil·is -is -e
desire *s* cupidit·as -atis *f; (longing)* desider·ium -(i)i *n; (sexual)* libid·o -inis *f*
desire *tr* cupere, optare; *(to long for what is lacking)* desiderare
desirous *adj* **(of)** cupid·us -a -um *(w. gen)*
desist *intr* **(from)** desistere *(w. abl or* de *w. abl)*
desk *s* mens·a -ae *f* scriptoria; *(teacher's)* pulpit·um -i *n*
desolate *adj* desolat·us -a -um; *(of persons)* afflict·us -a -um
desolation *s* solitud·o -inis *f*
despair *s* desperati·o -onis *f*
despair *intr* desperare; **to — of** desperare *(w. acc or* de *w. abl)*
desperado *s* sicar·ius -(i)i *m*
desperate *adj (hopeless)* desperat·us -a -um; *(dangerous)* periculos·us -a -um; **in their — situation** in extremis rebus suis; **to take — measures** ad extrema descendere
desperately *adv* vehementer; **to be — in love** perdite amare
desperation *s* desperati·o -onis *f*
despicable *adj* despicat·us -a -um
despise *tr* despicere, spernere
despite *prep* contra *(w. acc)*
despoil *tr* spoliare
despondency *s* animi abiecti·o -onis *f*, tristiti·a -ae *f*
despondent *adj* abiect·us -a -um; **to be —** animo demisso esse
despondently *adv* animo demisso
despot *s* tyrann·us -i *m*
despotic *adj* tyrannic·us -a -um
despotically *adv* tyrannice
despotism *s* dominati·o -onis *f*
dessert *s* secunda mens·a -ae *f*, bellari·a -orum *npl*
destination *s* loc·us -i *m* destinationis
destine *tr* destinare
destiny *s* fat·um -i *n*, sor·s -tis *f*
destitute *adj* **(of)** inop·s -is *(w. gen or abl)*, eg·ens -entis *(w. gen)*
destitution *s* inopi·a -ae *f*
destroy *tr* destruere, delēre; **to be —ed** interire
destroyer *s* dele·tor -toris *m* (·trix -tricis *f*)
destruction *s* exit·ium -(i)i *n*
destructive *adj* exitial·is -is -e
desultory *adj* inconst·ans -antis
detach *tr* seiungere; *(by breaking)* abscindere; *(by pulling)* avellere
detached *adj* seiunct·us -a -um
detachment *s (act)* seiuncti·o -onis *f; (mil)* man·us -ūs *f; (aloofness)* secess·us -ūs *m*
detail *s* **—s** singul·a -orum *npl;* **in —** singulatim, diligenter; **to go into —** per singula ire
detail *tr* exsequi, enarrare
detain *tr* morari, retinēre
detect *tr* detegere, deprehendere
detection *s* deprehensi·o -onis *f*
detective *s* inquisi·tor -toris *m* (·trix -tricis *f*), indiga·tor -oris *m* (·trix -tricis *f*)
detention *s* retenti·o -onis *f*
deter *tr* deterrēre
detergent *s* smegm·a -atis *n*
deteriorate *tr* deteri·orem -orem -us facere ‖ *intr* deteri·or -or -us fieri
determination *s (resolution)* constanti·a -ae *f; (decision)* consil·ium -(i)i *n*
determine *tr (to fix)* determinare; *(to decide)* constituere
determined *adj (resolute)* firm·us -a -um; *(fixed)* cert·us -a -um
detest *tr* detestari
detestable *adj* detestabil·is -is -e
detestation *s* detestati·o -onis *f*
dethrone *tr* regno depellere
detonate *intr* crepare
detonation *s* frag·or -oris *m*
detour *s* circumit·us-ūs *m;* **to take a —** circumire
detract *tr* detrahere ‖ *intr* **to — from** obtrectare
detraction *s* obtrectati·o -onis *f*
detractor *s* obtrecta·tor -toris *m* (·trix -tricis *f*)
detriment *s* detriment·um -i *n*
detrimental *adj* damnos·us -a -um; **to be — to** detrimento esse *(w. dat)*
devastate *tr* vastare
devastating *adj* damnos·us -a -um
devastation *s (act)* vastati·o -onis *f; (state)* vastit·as -atis *f*
develop *tr (character, mind)* confirmare; *(to improve)* excolere; ‖ *intr* crescere; *(to advance)* progredi; **to — into** evadere in *(w. acc)*
development *s (unfolding)* explicati·o -onis *f; (advance)* progress·us -ūs *m;* **— of events** event·us -ūs *m;* **to attain full —** adolescere
deviate *intr* **(from)** se declinare (de *w. abl); (to act in violation of)* **(from)** discedere (ab *w. abl);* **not to — from the course** cursum tenēre
deviation *s* declinati·o -onis *f*
device *s* artific·ium -(i)i *n*, machin·a -ae *f; (plan)* consil·ium -(i)i *n; (emblem)* sign·um -i *n*
devil *s* diabol·us -i *m;* **go to the —!** abi in malam crucem!; **those —s!** istae larvae!
devilish *adj* diabolic·us -a -um; *(fig)* nefand·us -a -um
devious *adj* devi·us -a -um; *(person)* astut·us -a -um, versut·us -a -um
devise *tr* excogitare
devoid *adj* exper·s -tis *(w. gen or abl);* **to be — of** carēre *(w. abl)*
devolve *intr* **to — upon** cedere in *(w. acc); (by inheritance)* pervenire ad *(w. acc)*

devote *tr* devovēre, consecrare; **to — oneself to** se dedere *(w. gen)*
devoted *adj* **(to)** dedit•us -a -um *(w. dat),* studios•us -a -um *(w. gen)*
devotee *s* cul•tor -toris *m* (•trix -tricis *f)*
devotion *s* devoti•o -onis *f;* **—s** prec•es -um *fpl*
devour *tr* vorare; *(fig)* haurire
devout *adj* pi•us -a -um
devoutly *adv* pie
dew *s* ro•s -ris *m*
dewy *adj* roscid•us -a -um
dexterity *s* callidit•as -atis *f*
dexterous *adj* callid•us -a -um
dexterously *adv* callide
diabolical *adj* diabolic•us -a -um
diadem *s* diadem•a -atis *n*
diagnose *tr* discernere
diagnosis *s* diagnos•is -is *f*
diagonal *adj* diagonal•is -is -e
diagonally *adv* in transversum
diagram *s* form•a -ae *f,* descripti•o -onis *f*
diagram *tr* describere
dial *s (of clock)* tabul•a -ae *f* horaria; *(of a telephone)* tabula selectoria
dial *tr* seligere ‖ *intr* numerum seligere
dialect *s* dialect•us -i *f*
dialectic *adj* dialectic•us -a -um
dialectics *s* dialectic•a -ae *f*
dialogue *s* serm•o -onis *m; (written discussion)* dialog•us -i *m*
diameter *s* diametr•os -i *f*
diamond *s* adam•as -antis *m*
diaper *s* fasci•ae -arum *fpl*
diaphragm *s* sept•um -i *n* transversum, diaphragm•a -atis *n*
diarrhea *s* alvi defusi•o -onis *f*
diary *s* diar•ium -(i)i *n*
diatribe *s* convic•ium -(i)i *n*
dice *spl* ale•ae -arum *fpl; (the game)* ale•a -ae *f;* **to roll the —** aleas iactare; **to play —** aleā ludere
dictate *tr* dictare; *(to prescribe)* praescribere
dictate *s* praescript•um -i *n*
dictation *s* dictati•o -onis *f;* **to take —** dictata exscribere
dictator *s* dictat•or -oris *m*
dictatorial *adj* dictatori•us -a -um
dictatorship *s* dictatur•a -ae *f*
diction *s* dicti•o -onis *f*
dictionary *s* glossiar•ium -(i)i *n,* lexic•on -i *n*
didactic *adj* didascalic•us -a -um
die *s* ale•a -ae *f;* **the — is cast** alea iacta est
die *intr* mori; **to — laughing** risu emori; **to — off** demori; **to — out** emori
Diesel *adj* Diselian•us -a -um
diet *s (food)* victūs rati•o -onis *f; (dietary regime)* diaet•a -ae *f;* **to be on a —** victūs rationem observare
diet *intr* victūs rationem inire
dietary *adj* diatetic•us -a -um
differ *intr* differre; *(in opinion)* dissentire; *(to disagree)* discrepare
difference *s* differenti•a -ae *f; (wide difference)* distanti•a -ae *f; (disagreement)* discrepanti•a -ae *f;* **— of opinion** dissensi•o -onis *f;* **how much — does it make?** quantum interest?; **it makes no (a lot of) — to me (you) whether … or** nil meā (tuā) interest *or* rēfert utrum … an; **there is no — between god and god** nihil inter deum et deum interest; **there isn't the slightest — between them** ne minimum quidem inter eos interest; **what — does it make whether … ?** quid refert utrum … ?
differentiate *tr* discernere
differently *adv* aliter; *(variously)* varie, diverse
differing *adj* disson•us -a -um
difficult *adj* difficil•is -is -e; *(blocked up, e.g., a road)* impedit•us -a -um; **it is a — thing to** magnum est *(w. inf)*
difficulty *s* difficult•as -atis *f;* **with —** aegre
diffidence *s (distrust)* diffidenti•a -ae *f; (modesty)* verecundi•a -ae *f*
diffident *adj* diffid•ens -entis; *(modest)* verecund•us -a -um
diffuse *adj* diffus•us -a -um; *(verbally)* verbos•us -a -um
diffuse *tr* diffundere
diffusely *adv* effuse
diffusion *s* diffusi•o -onis *f*
dig *tr (garden, well)* fodere; **to — a hole in the ground** terram excavare; **to — a hole in the wall (wood)** parietem (lignum) perfodere; **to — up** *(e.g., the garden, the earth)* confodere; **to — up s.th. about** *(fig)* quicquam eruere de *(w. abl)*
digest *s* summar•ium -(i)i *n*
digest *tr* concoquere
digestion *s* concocti•o -onis *f*
digestive *adj* peptic•us -a -um
digging *s* fossi•o -onis *f*
digit *s* numer•us -i *m*
digital *adj* digital•is -is -e; **— clock** horolog•ium -(i)i *n* digitale
dignified *adj* grav•is -is -e
dignify *tr* honestare
dignitary *s* vir -i *m* amplissimus, femina -ae amplissima
dignity *s* dignit•as -atis *f,* gravit•as -atis *f*
digress *intr* digredi
digression *s* digressi•o -onis *f*
dike *s* agg•er -eris *m*
dilapidated *adj* ruinos•us -a -um
dilate *tr* dilatare ‖ *intr* dilatari
dilatory *adj* cunctabund•us -a -um
dilemma *s (difficulty)* angusti•ae -arum *fpl; (logical)* dilemm•a -atis *n;* **to be in a —** haerēre in salebrā
diligence *s* diligenti•a -ae *f*
diligent *adj* dilig•ens -entis

diligently *adv* diligenter
dilute *tr* diluere
dilution *s* mixtur·a -ae *f*
dim *adj* heb·es -etis, obscur·us -a -um; **to be —** hebēre; **to become —** hebescere
dim *tr* hebetare **||** *intr* hebescere
dimensions *spl* mensur·a -ae *f;* **to take the —s of** mensuram *(w. gen)* agere
diminish *tr* minuere; *(weight, value, authority)* levare **||** *intr* minui
diminutive *adj* exigu·us -a -um; *(gram)* deminutiv·us -a -um
diminutive *s (gram)* deminutiv·um -i *n*
dimness *s* hebetud·o -inis *f*
dimple *s* gelasin·us -i *m*
din *s* strepit·us -ūs *m;* **to make a —** strepare
dine *intr* cenare; **to — out** foris cenare
diner *s* conviv·a -ae *mf*
dingy *adj* squalid·us -a -um
dining car *s* curr·us -ūs *m* cenatorius
dining couch *s* tor·us -i *m*
dining room *s* cenati·o -onis *f,* triclin·ium -(i)i *n*
dining table *s* mens·a -ae *f* escaria
dinner *s* cen·a -ae *f;* **over —** per cenam; **to eat —** cenare, cenam sumere; **what did you have for —** quid in cenā habuisti?
dinner clothes *spl* cenatori·a -orum *npl*
dinner guest *s* conviv·a -ae *mf*
dinner party *s* conviv·ium -(i)i *n*
dinner time *s* hor·a -ae *f* cenandi
dinosaur *s* dinosaur·us -i *m*
dint *s* **by — of** per *(w. acc)*
diocese *s* dioeces·is -is *f*
dip *tr* immergere; *(to wet by dipping)* ting(u)ere **||** *intr* mergi; **to — into** *(fig)* attingere
dip *s (decrease)* deminuti·o -onis *f; (slope)* declivit·as -atis *f; (food)* embamm·a -atis *n;* **to take a —** *(short swim)* natare
diphthong *s* diphthong·us -i *f*
diploma *s* studiorum diplom·a -atis *n;* **to get a —** studiorum diploma merere
diplomacy *s* **to settle matters by —** rem legationibus componere
diplomatic *adj (fig)* sag·ax -acis
dipper *s* trull·a -ae *f;* **Big Dipper** Urs·a -ae *f* Maior; **Little Dipper** Urs·a -ae *f* Minor
dire *adj* dir·us -a -um
direct *adj* (di)rect·us -a -um
direct *vt* dirigere; *(to manage)* administrare; *(to order)* iubēre; *(a weapon)* intendere; *(a letter)* inscribere; **to — attention to** animum attendere ad *(w. acc)*
direction *s (act)* directi·o -onis *f; (quarter)* par·s -tis *f; (management)* administrati·o -onis *f; (instruction)* mandat·um -i *n; (order)* praecept·um -i *n;* **in all —s** in omnes partes; **in a southerly —** in meridiem versus; **in both —** utroque; **in every —** quoquoversus; **in the — of Gaul** in Galliam versus; **in the — of Rome** Romam versus
directive *s* mandat·um -i *n*
directly *adv* directe, rectā; *(immediately)* **director** *s* rect·or -oris *m,* rec·trix -tricis *f*
director *s* rect·or -oris *m*
directory *s (office of director)* magister·ium -(i)i *n; (list, catalog)* ind·ex -icis *m; (comput)* plicarum ind·ex -icis *m*
dirge *s* neni·a -ae *f*
dirt *s* sord·es -is *f (usu. pl); (mud)* lut·um -i *n*
dirt-cheap *adj* pro luto
dirtiness *s* spurciti·a -ae *f*
dirty *adj* sordid·us -a -um, spurc·us -a -um; *(fig)* obscen·us -a -um; **— old man** salax sen·ex -is *m;* **— talk** serm·o -onis *m* obscenus; **to give s.o. a — look** aliquem minus familiari vultu respicere
dirty *tr* spurcare, foedare
disability *s* imbecillit·as -atis *f*
disable *tr (to weaken)* debilitare; *(to cripple)* mutilare; *(a ship)* afflictare
disabled *adj* invalid·us -a -um; *(maimed)* manc·us -a -um; **totally —** omnibus membris capt·us -a -um
disadvantage *s* incommod·um -i *n*
disadvantaged *adj* incommodat·us -a -um
disadvantageous *adj* incommod·us -a -um, iniqu·us -a -um
disagree *intr* **(with)** dissentire (ab *w. abl*); **the food —d with me** cibus stomachum offendit; **to strongly —** vehmenter dissentire
disagreeable *adj* iniucund·us -a -um; *(smell)* graveol·ens -entis; *(person)* importun·us -a -um
disagreement *s* dissensi·o -onis *f*
disallow *tr* vetare
disappear *intr* evanescere; **to — from sight** oculis subduci, abire ex oculis
disappearance *s* exit·us -ūs *m*
disapppoint *tr* fallere, frustrari; **I'll not — you** opinionem tuam non fallam
disappointment *s (act)* frustrati·o -onis *f; (result)* incommod·um -i *n*
disapproval *s* improbati·o -onis *f*
disapprove *tr* improbare **||** *intr* **to — of** improbare
disarm *tr* exarmare
disarrange *tr* turbare
disarray *s* perturbati·o -onis *f*
disaster *s* calamit·as -atis *f; (mil)* clad·es -is *f*
disastrous *adj* calamitos·us -a -um
disastrously *adv* calamitose
disavow *tr* diffiteri, infitieri
disavowal *s* infitiati·o -onis *f*
disband *tr* dimittere **||** *intr* dimitti
disbelief *s* incredulit·as -atis *f*
disbeliever *s* incredul·us -i *m* (·a -ae *f*)
disburse *tr* expendere, erogare

disbursement *s* erogati·o -onis *f,* impens·a -ae *f*
disc *s* orb·is -is *m*
discard *tr* abicere
discern *tr (to distinguish)* discernere; *(to see clearly)* perspicere
discernible *adj* dignoscend·us -a -um
discerning *adj* perspic·ax -acis
discernment *s (faculty)* discrim·en -inis *n; (act)* perspicienti·a -ae *f*
discharge *s (release)* liberati·o -onis *f; (mil)* missi·o -onis *f; (of missiles)* coniect·us -ūs *m,* emissi·o -onis *f; (of duty)* perfuncti·o -onis *f; (bodily)* defluxi·o -onis *f;* **dishonorable —** missio *f* cum ignominiā; **honorable —** missio honesta
discharge *tr (to perform)* perfungi *(w. abl); (mil)* dimittere; *(debt)* exsolvere; *(defendant)* absolvere; *(missiles)* immittere, conicere
disciple *s* discipul·us -i *m*
disciplinarian *s* **a strict —** exac·tor -toris *m* (·rix -ricis *f*) gravissimus (-a) disciplinae
discipline *s* disciplin·a -ae *f; (punishment)* castigati·o -onis *f*
discipline *tr* disciplinā instituere; *(to punish)* castigare
disclaim *tr* infitiari
disclaimer *s* infitiati·o -onis *f*
disclose *tr (to reveal)* patefacere, detegere; *(to tell)* promere; *(to divulge)* enuntiare
disclosure *s* patefacti·o -onis *f*
discolor *tr* decolorare ‖ *intr* decolorari; *(to fade)* pallescere
discomfit *tr* profligare
discomfort *s* incommod·um -i *n*
discomfort *tr* incommodare
disconcerting *adj* molest·us -a -um
disconnect *tr* disiungere
disconsolate *adj* maest·us -a -um
discontent *s* offensi·o -onis *f*
discontent *tr* offendere
discontented *adj* parum content·us -a -um
discontentedly *adv* animo iniquo
discontinue *tr* intermittere ‖ *intr* desinere
discord *s* discordi·a -ae *f; (mus)* dissonanti·a -ae *f*
discordant *adj* discor·s -dis; *(mus)* disson·us -a -um
discotheque *s* discothec·a -ae *f*
discount *tr* deducere; *(to disregard)* praetermittere
discount *s (com)* decessi·o -onis *f;* **a five- (ten-, twenty-) percent —** quinarum (denarum, vicesimarum) centesimarum decessio
discourage *tr* animum (animos) *(w. gen)* infringere; *(to dissuade)* dehortari; **to be —d** animo (animis) deficere, animum (animos) demittere
discouragement *s* animi infracti·o -onis *f*
discouraging *adj* advers·us -a -um
discourse *s* serm·o -onis *m; (written)* libell·us -i *m*
discourse *intr* **(on)** disserere *(w. abl)* de
discourteous *adj* inurban·us -a -um
discourteously *adv* inurbane
discourtesy *s* inurbanit·as -atis *f*
discover *tr* invenire; *(to explore)* explorare
discoverable *adj* indagabil·is -is -e
discoverer *s* inven·tor -toris *m* (·rix -ricis *f*)
discovery *s* inventi·o -onis *f; (thing discovered)* invent·um -i *n*
discredit *s* dedec·us -oris *n;* macul·a -ae *f;* **to be a — to one's family** familiae suae dedecori esse; **to bring — upon oneself** maculam suscipere *(w. abl of cause)*
discredit *tr (to disbelieve)* non credere *(w. dat); (to disgrace)* labem inferre *(w. dat)*
discreet *adj* caut·us -a -um, prud·ens -entis
discrepancy *s* discrepanti·a -ae *f*
discretion *s (tact)* iudic·ium -(i)i *n; (entire control)* arbitr·ium -(i)i *n;* **at one's —** ad arbitrium suum
discretionary *adj* lib·er -era -erum; **to give s.o. — power** liberum arbitrium alicui permittere
discriminate *tr* distinguere
discriminating *adj* discern·ens -entis
discrimination *s (act of distinguishing)* distincti·o -onis *f; (discernment)* discrim·en -inis *n; (prejudice)* opini·o -onis *f* praeiudicata
discuss *tr* disputare de *(w. abl),* disceptare de *(w. abl)*
discussion *s* disputati·o -onis *f;* **there was a long — about** diu disputatum est de *(w. abl)*
disdain *tr* fastidire
disdain *s* fastid·ium -(i)i *n;* **to treat with —** dedignari
disdainful *adj* fastidios·us -a -um
disdainfully *adv* fastidiose
disease *s* morb·us -i *m*
diseased *adj* aegrot·us -a -um
disembark *tr* e nave exponere ‖ *intr* e nave exire
disengage *tr* expedire, eximere
disentangle *tr* explicare
disfavor *s* invidi·a -ae *f,* offens·a -ae *f;* **to be in great — with s.o.** magnā in offensā esse apud aliquem; **to fall into — with s.o.** suscipere invidiam apud aliquem
disfigure *tr* deformare
disfranchise *tr* civitatem adimere *(w. dat)*
disgorge *tr* evomere
disgrace *s* dedec·us -oris *n,* ignomini·a -ae *f; (thing)* flagit·ium -(i)i *n; (public disgrace)* ignomin·ia -ae *f;* **that's a darn —!** edepol facinus improbum est!; **to become a —** to dedecori esse *(w. dat)*
disgrace *tr* dedecorare
disgraceful *adj* dedecor·us -a -um
disgracefully *adv* turpiter

disguise *s* vestit·us -ūs *m* alienus; *(fig)* person·a -ae *f;* **in —** mutatā veste
disguise *tr* dissimulare
disgust *s* taed·ium -(i)i *n*
disgust *tr* stomachum movēre *(w. dat);* **I am —ed with** me taedet *(w. gen),* me piget *(w. gen)*
disgusting *adj* foed·us -a -um
disgustingly *adv* foede
dish *s (open and flat)* patin·a -e *f; (small)* catill·us -i *m; (large)* lan·x -cis *f; (course)* fercul·um -i *n;* **to wash the —es** vasa coquinatoria eluere
dishearten *tr* animum (animos) *(w. gen)* infringere; **to be —ed** animum (animos) demittere
disheveled *adj (hair)* pass·us -a -um
dishonest *adj* fraudulent·us -a -um; *(lying)* mend·ax -acis
dishonestly *adv* dolo malo
dishonesty *s* frau·s -dis *f*
dishonor *s* dedec·us -oris *n*
dishonor *tr* dedecorare
dishonorable *adj* dedecor·us -a -um, inhonest·us -a -um; **— discharge** missi·o -onis *f* cum ignominiā
dishonorably *adv* inhoneste
dishpan *s* labr·um -i *n* (ad vasa coquin-atoria eluenda)
dishwasher *s* machin·a -ae *f* elutoria
disillusion *tr* errorem adimere *(w. dat)*
disinclination *s* declinati·o -onis *f*
disinfect *tr* contagia depellere de *(w. abl)*
disinfectant *s* remed·ium -(i)i *n* ad contagia depellenda aptum
disinherit *tr* exheredare
disintegrate *intr* dilabi
disinter *tr* effodere
disinterested *adj* inte·ger -gra -grum
disinterestedly *adv* integre
disjoin *tr* disiungere
disjointed *adj* incomposit·us -a -um
disjointedly *adv* incomposite
disk *s* orb·is -is *m; (comput)* disc·us -i *m;* **floppy —** discus flexibilis
disk drive *s (comput)* instrument·um -i *n* disculis legendis
diskette *s (comput)* discul·us -i *m*
dislike *s* od·ium -(i)i *n*
dislike *tr* aversari
dislocate *tr* luxare
dislocation *s* luxatur·a -ae *f*
dislodge *tr* depellere
disloyal *adj* perfid·us -a -um
disloyally *adv* perfide
disloyalty *s* perfidi·a -ae *f*
dismal *adj* maest·us -a -um
dismally *adv* maeste
dismantle *tr* diruere
dismay *s* consternati·o -onis *f*
dismay *tr* percellere
dismember *tr* membratim dividere
dismemberment *s* mutilati·o -onis *f*
dismiss *tr* dimittere; *(fear)* mittere
dismissal *s* dimissi·o -onis *f*
dismount *intr* ex equo desilire
disobedience *s* inobedienti·a -ae *f*
disobedient *adj* parum obedi·ens -entis
disobey *tr* non obedire *(w. dat)*
disorder *s* confusi·o -onis *f; (of mind)* perturbati·o -onis *f; (med)* mal·um -i *n; (pol)* tumult·us -ūs *m*
disordered *adj* turbat·us -a -um; *(of mind or body)* aegrot·us -a -um
disorderly *adj* inordinat·us -a -um; *(of troops)* effus·us -a -um; *(unruly)* turbulent·us -a -um
disorganization *s* dissoluti·o -onis *f*
disorganize *tr* conturbare
disorganized *adj* dissolut·us -a -um
disown *tr (statement)* infitiari; *(heir)* abdicare; *(thing)* repudiare
disparage *tr* obtrectare
disparagement *s* obtrectati·o -onis *f*
disparaging *adj* obtrect·ans -antis
disparity *s* discrepanti·a -ae *f*
dispassionate *adj* frigid·us -a -um
dispassionately *adv* frigide
dispatch *tr* mittere; *(to finish)* perficere; *(to kill)* interficere
dispel *tr* dispellere, depellere
dispensary *s* medicamentaria tabern·a -ae *f*
dispensation *s* distributi·o -onis *f; (exemption)* immunit·as -atis *f*
dispense *tr* distribuere; *(to release)* solvere ‖ *intr* **to — with** remittere
dispenser *s* dispensa·tor -toris *m* (·trix -tricis *f*)
disperse *tr* dispergere, dissipare ‖ *intr* diffugere; *(gradually)* dilabi
dispersion *s* dispersi·o -onis *f*
dispirited *adj* animo fract·us -a -um
displace *tr* summovēre; **—ed person** profug·us -i *m,* profug·a -ae *f*
displacement *s* amoti·o -onis *f*
display *s (exhibit)* ostent·us -ūs *m; (ostentation)* ostentati·o -onis *f*
display *tr* ostendere; *(to show off)* ostentare
displease *tr* displicēre *(w. dat)*
displeased *adj* offens·us -a -um; **to be — at** aegre ferre
displeasing *adj* ingrat·us -a -um
displeasure *s* offens·a -ae *f*
disposable *adj* in promptu
disposal *s* dispositi·o -onis *f;* **at your —** penes te
dispose *tr* disponere, ordinare; *(to incline)* inclinare ‖ *intr* **to — of** *(to settle)* componere; *(to sell)* abalienare; *(to get rid of)* tollere
disposed *adj* inclinat·us -a -um; *(pej)* pron·us -a -um
disposition *s (character)* indol·es -is *f; (arrangement)* dispositi·o -onis *f;*
dispossess *tr (of)* pellere *(w. abl)*
disproportion *s* inconcinnit·as -atis *f*

disproportionate *adj* inaequal·is -is -e
disproportionately *adv* inaequaliter
disprove *tr* refellere, redarguere
disputable *adj* disputabil·is -is -e
dispute *s (debate)* disputati·o -onis *f; (argument)* altercati·o -onis *f;* **beyond —** indisputabil·is -is -e; **that is a matter of —** id disputari potest
dispute *tr & intr* disputare
disputed *adj* controvers·us -a -um
disqualify *tr* excipere; **to — s.o. from** aliquem excipere ex *(w. abl) or* ne *or* quominus
disquiet *tr* inquietare
disquieted *adj* inquiet·us -a -um
disregard *s* **(for)** incuri·a -ae *f (w. gen),* neglegenti·a -ae *f (w. gen)*
disregard *tr* neglegere, omittere
disreputable *adj* infam·is -is -e
disrepute *s* infami·a -ae *f*
disrespect *s* neglegenti·a -ae *f*
disrespectful *adj* **(toward)** negleg·ens -entis (in *w. acc)*
disrespectfully *adv* parum honorifice
disrupt *tr* disturbare
disruption *s* discid·ium -(i)i *n*
dissatisfaction *s* displicenti·a -ae *f*
dissatisfied *adj* parum content·us -a -um
dissatisfy *tr* male satisfacere *(w. dat)*
dissect *tr* insecare
dissection *s* incisi·o -onis *f*
dissemble *tr & intr* dissimulare
disseminate *tr* disseminare
dissension *s* dissensi·o -onis *f*
dissent *s* dissensi·o -onis *f*
dissent *intr* dissentire
dissertation *s* commentati·o -onis *f*
dissimilar *adj* dissimil·is -is -e
dissimiliarity *s* dissimilitud·o -inis *f*
dissipate *tr* dissipare ‖ *intr* dissipari
dissipation *s* dissipati·o -onis *f*
dissolute *adj* dissolut·us -a -um
dissolution *s* dissoluti·o -onis *f*
dissolve *tr* dissolvere; *(to melt)* liquefacere; *(meeting)* dimittere ‖ *intr* liquescere; *(to break up)* dissolvi
dissonance *s* dissonanti·a -ae *f*
dissuade *tr* dissuadēre *(w. dat)*
distance *s* distanti·a -ae *f,* spat·ium -(i)i *n; (lŏng way)* longinquit·as -atis *f;* **at a —** procul, longe
distant *adj* dist·ans -antis; *(remote)* longinqu·us -a -um; *(fig)* parum familiar·is -is -e; **to be — from** abesse *or* distare ab *(w. abl)*
distaste *s* **(for)** fastid·ium -(i)i *n (w. gen)*
distasteful *adj (of food)* tet·er -ra -rum; *(fig)* odios·us -a -um
distend *tr* distendere; *(sails)* tendere
distil *tr & intr* stillare, destillare
distinct *adj (different)* divers·us -a -um; *(clear)* distinct·us -a -um
distinction *s (act of distinguishing)* distincti·o -onis *f; (the thing distinguished)* discrim·en -inis *n; (mark, badge)* insign·e -is *n; (honor)* hon·or -oris *m; (status)* amplitud·o -inis *f; (decoration)* praem·ium -(i)i *n*; **a man of —** vir -i *m* illustris; **without —** promiscue
distinctive *adj* propri·us -a -um
distinguish *tr* distinguere, discernere; **to — oneself** enitēre
distinguishable *adj* spectand·us -a -um
distinguished *adj* insign·is -is -e; *(of high rank)* ampl·us -a -um; **to be —** enitēre
distort *tr* distorquēre; *(words)* detorquēre; *(to misinterpret)* male interpretari
distortion *s* distorti·o -onis *f; (fig)* depravati·o -onis *f*
distract *tr* distrahere, vocare
distracted *adj* distract·us -a -um; *(distraught)* vecor·s -dis
distraction *s (cause)* avocament·um -i *n; (state)* distracti·o -onis *f* animi; *(w. verbs of loving, etc.)* **to —** efflictim
distraught *adj* vecor·s -dis
distress *s* miseri·a -ae *f,* dol·or -oris *m; (difficulty)* angusti·ae -arum *fpl*
distress *tr* angere, afflictare
distressed *adj* sollicit·us -a -um
distressing *adj* importun·us -a -um
distribute *tr* distribuere
distributer *s* distribu·tor -toris *m* (·trix -tricis *f*)
distribution *s* distributi·o -onis *f*
district *s (esp. in a city)* regi·o -onis *f; (an extent of country)* tract·us -ūs *m*
distrust *s* **(of)** diffidenti·a -ae *f (w. gen)*
distrust *tr* diffidere *(w. dat)*
distrustful *adj* **(of)** diffid·ens -entis *(w. dat)*
distrustfully *adv* diffidenter
disturb *tr* perturbare; *(to render anxious)* sollicitare; *(to upset)* commovēre; *(s.o.'s sleep)* inquietare
disturbance *s* perturbati·o -onis *f; (pol)* tumult·us -ūs *m*
disturber *s* **— of the peace** turbat·or -oris *m* oti
disuse *s* desuetud·o -inis *f*
ditch *s* foss·a -ae *f*
ditty *s* cantilen·a -ae *f*
divan *s* lectul·us -i *m*
dive *s (of a swimmer)* salt·us -ūs *m; (coll)* popin·a -ae *f*
dive *intr* praeceps desilire; *(e.g. of a submarine)* urinari
diver *s* urina·tor -toris *m* (·trix -tricis *f*)
diverge *intr* deflectere, declinare; *(of view)* discrepare
diverse *adj* divers·us -a -um
diversification *s* variati·o -onis *f*
diversify *tr* variare
diversion *s (recreation)* oblectament·um -i *n; (of a river)* derivati·o -onis *f; (pastime)* avocati·o -onis *f*

diversity *s* diversit·as -atis *f*
divert *tr (rivers)* avertere, divertere; *(attention)* avocare; **to — s.o.'s anger and turn it on oneself** iram alicuius in se derivare
divest *tr* exuere, nudare; **to — oneself of** exuere, ponere
divide *tr* dividere; *(to distribute)* partiri; **to — the year into 12 months** annum in duodecim menses discribere ‖ *intr* se scindere
divination *s* divinati·o -onis *f*
divine *adj* divin·us -a -um
divine *tr* divinare; *(to guess)* conicere
divinely *adv* divinitus
diviner *s* aug·ur -uris *m,* harusp·ex -icis *m*
diving board *s* tabul·a -ae *f* desultoria
divinity *s* divinit·as -atis *f; (god)* num·en -inis *n*
divisible *adj* dividu·us -a -um
division *s* divisi·o -onis *f; (part)* par·s -tis *f; (mil)* legi·o -onis *f;* **— of opinion** dissensi·o -onis *f*
divorce *s* divort·ium -(i)i *n*
divorce *tr* divortium facere cum *(w. abl)*
divulge *tr* vulgare, divulgare
dizziness *s* vertig·o -inis *f*
dizzy *adj* vertiginos·us -a -um
do *tr* agere, facere; *(to carry out, succeed in doing)* efficere; **to — a hitch in the army** stipendia facere; **to — a kindness** beneficium facere; **to — one's best to** *(w. inf)* operam dare ut *(w. subj);* **to — s.o. in** aliquem pessum dare; **to have enough to —** satagere; **what am I to —?** quid faciam?; **what have I to — with you?** quid mihi et tibi est? ‖ *intr* agere; *(for emphatic auxiliary, use* vero: **I — wish to go** cupio vero ire); *(when* **I —.** *is used to answer a question, repeat the verb in the question:* **— you believe? I —.** credisne? credo.); **how — you —?** quid agis?; **it will — you (a lot of, no) good** (multum, nihil) proderit tibi; **it won't — to** non satis est *(w. inf);* **that'll —!** satis est!; **to — away with** tollere, perdere; **to — well** *(to make out well)* recte facere; *(to have good health)* bene valēre; **to — without** carēre *(w. abl);* **what's doing?** quid agitur?; **will this —?** satin(e) est?
docile *adj* docil·is -is -e, tractabil·is -is -e
dock *s* naval·e -is *n; (leg)* cancell·i -orum *mpl*
docket *s* memnisc·us -i *m*
dockyard *s* naval·ia -ium *npl*
doctor *s* medic·us -i *m* (·a -ae *f*); *(academic title)* doc·tor -toris *m* (·trix -tricis *f*)
doctorate *s* doctoris grad·us -ūs *m*
doctrine *s* doctrin·a -ae *f,* dogm·a -atis *n*
document *s* instrument·um -i *n*
documentary *s* documentar·ium -(i)i *n*
dodge *s* dol·us -i *m*
dodge *tr* eludere; *(to shift aside and so avoid)* declinare; **to — the draft** sacramentum detrectare
doe *s* cerv·a -ae *f*
dog *s* can·is -is *mf;* **to go to the —s** *(coll)* pessum ire
dogged *adj* pervic·ax -acis
doggedness *s* pervicaci·a -ae *f*
doggerel *s* inepti versicul·i -orum *mpl*
dog house, dog kennel *s* canis cubil·e -is *n*
dogma *s* dogm·a -atis *n*
dogmatic *adj* dogmatic·us -a -um; *(pej)* arrog·ans -antis
dogmatism *s* arroganti·a -ae *f*
dog star *s* canicul·a -ae *f,* Siri·us -i *m*
doing *s* facin·us -eris *n;* **what's —?** quid agitur?
dole *s* sportul·a -ae *f*
dole *tr* **to — out** parce dare
doleful *adj* lugubr·is -is -e
dolefully *adv* maeste
doll *s* pup·a -ae *f*
dollar *s* dollar·us -i *m*
dolphin *s* delphin·us -i *m*
dolt *s* caud·ex -icis *m*
domain *s (kingdom)* regn·um -i *n;* **public —** ag·er -ri *m* publicus
dome *s* thol·us -i *m*
domestic *adj* domestic·us -a -um
domestic *s* famul·us -i *m,* famul·a -ae *f*
domesticate *tr* domare
domicile *s* domicil·ium -(i)i *n*
dominant *adj* praeval·ens -entis; **to be —** auctoritate pollēre; **to become —** potent·ior -ior -ius fieri
dominate *intr* **(over)** dominari (in *w. acc)*
domination *s* domin·ium -(i)i *n*
domineer *intr* dominari
domineering *adj* imperios·us -a -um
dominion *s* imper·ium -(i)i *n*
don *tr* induere
donation *s* donati·o -onis *f*
done *adj* **I'm — for!** nullus sum! *or* perii!; **have — with fear!** omitte timorem!; **no sooner said than —** dictum factum; **well done!** macte virtute!
donkey *s* asin·us -i *m,* asell·us -i *m*
donor *s* dona·tor -toris *m,* dona·trix -tricis *f*
doom *s* fat·um -i *n*
doom *tr* damnare
door *s* ianu·a -ae *f,* ost·ium -(i)i *n; (double doors)* for·es -ium *fpl; (folding doors)* valv·ae -arum *fpl;* **back —** postic·um -i *n;* **from — to ——** ostiatim; **out of doors** *(position)* foris; *(direction)* foras; **there's the —** *(turning a person out)* exeundum hinc foras
doorbell ostii tintinabul·um -i *n;* **the — is ringing** ostii tintinabulum tinnit; **to ring the —** pulsabulum comprimere
doorkeeper *s* ostiar·ius -(i)i *m*
doorknob *s* ianuae manubr·ium -(i)i *n*

doorpost *s* post·is -is *m*
doorstep *s* lim·en -inis *n*
doorway *s* ost·ium -(i)i *n*
Doric *adj* Doric·us -a -um
dormant *adj* res·es -idis; *(hidden)* lat·ens -entis; **to lie —** iacēre
dormitory *s* dormitor·ium -(i)i *n*
dorsal *adj* dorsal·is -is -e; **—** finn·a -ae *f* dorsalis
dose *s* porti·o -onis *f;* **small —** portiuncul·a -ae *f*
dot *s* punct·um -i *n*
dot *tr* punctum imponere *(w. dat)*
dotage *s* sen·ium -(i)i *n*
dote *tr* **to — on** deamare
doting *adj* deam·ans -antis
double *adj* dupl·ex -icis; *(of pairs)* gemin·us -a -um; *(as much again)* dupl·us -a -um; *(meaning)* ambigu·us -a -um; **— "i" as in "arm**arii" i littera geminata, ut armarii
double *s* dupl·um -i *n;* **—s** *(in tennis)* lud·us -i *m* bis binorum; **on the —** curriculo
double *tr* duplicare; *(a cape)* praetervehi **||** *intr* duplicari
double-dealing *s* frau·s -dis *f*
double-dealing *adj* versut·us -a -um
double-edged *adj* bipenn·is -is -e
double home *s* dom·us -ūs *f* duplex
double room *s* cubicul·um -i *n* duorum lectorum
double-talk *s* simulati·o -onis *f* et fallaci·a -ae *f*
doubly *adv* dupliciter
doubt *s* dub·ium -(i)i *n; (distrust)* suspici·o -onis *f;* **there is no — that** non dubium est quin *(w. subj);* **without —** sine dubio
doubt *tr* dubitare *(w. acc of neuter pronoun only; otherwise use* de *w. abl);* **I do not — that** non dubito quin *(w. subj)*
doubtful *adj (of persons)* dubi·us -a -um; *(of things)* incert·us -a - um, anc·eps -ipitis
doubtfully *adv* dubie; *(hesitatingly)* dubitanter
doubtless *adv* haud dubie, sine dubio
dough *s* farin·a -ae *f* ex aquā subacta
douse *tr (to put out)* exstinguere; *(to drench)* madefacere
dove *s* columb·us -i *m* (·a -ae *f*)
down *s* plum·a -ae *f; (of hair)* lanug·o -inis *f; (of plants)* papp·us -i *m*
down *adv* deorsum; *(often expressed by the prefix* de-: **to flow —** defluere); **to pay money —** repraesentare pecuniam; **to run —** decurrere; **— from** de *(w. abl);* **— to** usque ad *(w. acc)*
down *prep* de *(w. abl)*
down *adj* decliv·is -is -e; *(depressed)* demiss·us -a -um; *(financially)* ad inopiam redact·us -a -um; **to feel — and out** infractum animum gerere **to hit a man when he is —** iacentem ferire
downcast *adj (in low spirits)* demiss·us -a -um; **with — eyes** deiectis in terram oculis
downfall *s* occas·us -ūs *m*
downgrade *tr* in ordinem redigere
downhearted *adj* animo fract·us -a -um
downhill *adj* decliv·is -is -e, pron·us -a -um; **it was all — after that** proclivia omnia erant postilla; **the last part of the road is —** ultima via est prona
downhill *adv* per declive; **as his business went —** inclinatis rebus suis
download *tr (comput)* ex rete prehendere, ex rete expromere
downpour *s* im·ber -bris *m* maximus
down pat *adv* **you have the whole thing —** ordine omnem rem tenes
down payment *s* arrab·o -onis *f;* **to make a — of $100** centum dollaros arraboni dare
downright *adj* direct·us -a -um; *(unmixed)* mer·us -a -um
downright *adv* prorsus, plane
downstairs *adv (direction)* deorsum; *(position)* in imo tabulato; **to go —** per scalas descendere
downstream *adv* secundo flumine
downward *adj* decliv·us -a -um, pron·us -a -um
downwards *adv* deorsum
downy *adj* plume·us -a -um
dowry *s* do·s -tis *f*
doze *intr* dormitare; **to — off** in somnium delabi
dozen *adj & pron* duodecim *(indecl)*
drab *adj* cinere·us -a -um
draft *s (drink)* haust·us -ūs *m; (mil)* dilect·us -ūs *m; (breeze)* aur·a -ae *f; (first copy)* exempl·ar -aris *n; (money)* syngraph·a -ae *f; (of net)* iact·us -ūs *m; (of ship)* immersi·o -onis *f;* **to hold a —** *(mil)* dilectum habēre
draft *tr (mil)* conscribere
draft-dodger *s* qui militiam subterfugit
drag *s (fig)* impediment·um -i *n;* **to be a — on s. o.** aliquem retardare
drag *tr* trahere; *(w. suddenness or violence)* rapere; **to — away** abstrahere; **to — down** detrahere; **to — out** protrahere **||** *intr* trahi; **to — on** protrahi
dragnet *s* tragul·a -ae *f*
dragon *s* drac·o -onis *m*
drain *s* cloac·a -ae *f; (loss)* defecti·o -onis *f*
drain *tr (marshland)* siccare; *(a cup, the treasury, strength)* exhaurire
drainage *s* exsiccati·o-onis *f*
drainage ditch *s* incil·e -is *n*
drainpipe *s* canal·is -is *m*
drama *s (single play)* fabul·a -ae *f; (genre)* dram·a -atis *n*
dramatic *adj* scaenic·us -a -um; *(fig)* animum mov·ens -entis

dramatics *s* histrioni·a -ae *f*
dramatist *s* poet·a -ae *m* scaenicus
dramatize *tr* ad scaenam componere
drape *s* aulae·um -i *n*
drape *tr* *(to wrap)* amicire; *(to cover)* velare
drapery *s* aulae·a -orum *npl*
drastic *adj* ultim·us -a -um; severissim·us -a -um
draw *tr* *(to pull)* trahere; *(a picture)* delineare; *(a line)* ducere; *(inference)* colligere; *(bow)* adducere; *(sword)* educere; *(water)* haurire; *(breath)* ducere; *(geometrical figures)* describere; **to — aside** seducere; **to — apart** diducere; **to — away** avertere; **to — back** retrahere; **to — blood** cruorem ducere; **to — off** detrahere, abducere; *(wine)* depromere; **to — out** extrahere; *(fig)* elicere; **to — the conclusion** colligere; **to — together** contrahere; **to — up** subducere; *(to write)* componere; *(mil)* instituere ‖ *intr* **to — back** pedem referre; *(fig)* recedere; **to — near** appropinquare; **to — up to** *(of ships)* appetere
drawback *s* impediment·um -i *n*
drawbridge *s* pon·s -tis *m* versatilis
drawer *s* locul·us -i *m*
drawing *s* pictur·a -ae *f* linearis
drawl *s* lentior pronuntiati·o -onis *f*
drawl *intr* voces lentius pronuntiando trahere
dread *s* formid·o -inis *f*
dread *tr* formidare
dread *adj* dir·us -a -um
dreadful *adj* terribil·is -is -e
dreadfully *adv* horrendum in modum
dream *s* somn·ium -(i)i *n;* **in a —** in somnio
dream *tr & intr* somniare; **to — about** somniare de *(w. abl)*
dreamer *s* *(fig)* nuga·tor -toris *m* (·trix -tricis *f)*
dreamy *adj* somniculos·us -a -um
drearily *adv* triste
dreary *adj* *(place)* vast·us -a -um; *(person)* trist·is -is -e
dredge *tr* machinā alveum *(w. gen)* perfodere
dregs *spl* fae·x -cis *f; (fig)* sentin·a -ae *f*
drench *tr* madefacere
dress *s* vest·is -is *f* muliebris; *(ankle-length)* vestis talaris; *(Roman)* stol·a -ae *f*
dress *tr* vestire, induere; *(to deck out)* exornare; *(wounds)* curare; *(the hair)* comere; **—ed in a (fancy) coat** subornat·us -a -um aliculā; **—ed in white** amict·us -a -um veste albā; **to — down** *(to chew out)* pilare; **to get —ed** amiciri; *(in fancy clothes)* se exornare ‖ *intr* se induere; **to — up** se exornare
dresser *s* vestiar·ium -(i)i *n*
dressing *s* ornati·o -onis *f; (stuffing)* fart·um -i *n; (med)* foment·um -i *n; (on salad)* embamm·a -atis *n;* **Caesar (Blue Cheese, French, Italian, Russian, Thousand Island) —** embamma Caesarianum (Casei Caerulei, Gallicum, Italicum, Russicum, Mille Insularum)
dressing room *s* *(at a bath)* apodyter·ium -(i)i *n*
dressing table *s* mens·a -ae *f* comatoria
dressmaker *s* vestific·a -ae *f*
dress shoes *spl* socc·i -orum *mpl; (for women, of different colors)* soccul·i -orum *mpl*
dribble *tr* *(basketball)* repercutitare ‖ *intr* stillare
dribbling *s* *(basketball)* repercuti·o -onis *f*
drift *s* *(intent)* proposit·um -i *n*
drift *intr* fluitare
drifter *s* larifug·a -ae *mf*
drill *s* *(tool)* terebr·a -ae *f; (mil)* exercitati·o -onis *f; (school)* exercit·ium -(i) *n*
drill *tr* *(to bore)* terebrare; *(mil)* exercēre; *(students)* instituere
drink *tr* bibere, potare; **to — in** *(fig)* haurire; **to — up** epotare ‖ *intr* bibere; **to — to** propinare *(w. dat)*
drink *s* pot·us -ūs *m,* poti·o -onis *f*
drinkable *adj* potabil·is -is -e
drinker *s* pot·or -oris *m; (habitual)* potat·or -oris *m*
drinking *s* poti·o -onis *f*
drinking *adj* bibos·us -a -um
drinking cup *s* scyph·us -i *m*
drinking straw *s* siph·o -onis *m*
drip *s* stillicid·ium -(i)i *n*
drip *intr* destillare
drive *tr* agere, pellere; *(to force)* compellere; *(a vehicle)* agitare, gubernare; *(to convey)* vehere; **to — away** abigere; *(fig)* depellere; *(in confusion)* deturbare; **to — back** repellere; **to — home** *(in a car)* domum autoraedā adducere; *(fig)* animo infigere; **to — in** *(sheep, etc.)* cogere; *(nails)* infigere; **to — mad** dementem facere; **to — off** abigere; **to — on** impellere; **to — out** expellere; **to — out of one's mind** infuriare; **to — up** subigere ‖ *intr (in a carriage)* vehi; **to — off** *(in a carriage)* avehi; **to — on** *or* **past** praetervehi
drive *s* *(in carriage)* vectur·a -ae *f; (energy)* vis *f,* impigrit·as -atis *f*
drivel *s* saliv·a -ae *f; (fig)* inepti·ae -arum *fpl*
drivel *intr* *(fig)* delirare
driver *s* raedari·us -i *m* (·a -ae *f);* agita·tor -toris *m* (·trix -tricis *f); (of a chariot)* aurig·a -ae *m*
driver's license *s* raedarii diplom·a -atis *n*
drizzle *s* pluvi·a -ae *f* rara et minuta
drizzle *intr* leniter pluere

drone *s (bee)* fuc·us -i *m; (buzz)* bomb·us -i *m; (person)* cessat·or -oris *m*
drone *intr* murmurrare
droop *tr* demittere ‖ *intr* languēre
drooping *adj* languid·us -a -um
drop *s* gutt·a -ae *f; (a drop as falling)* still·a -ae *f; (fall)* cas·us -ūs *m,* laps·us -ūs *m; (decrease)* deminuti·o -onis *f; (a little bit)* paulul·um -i *n;* **— by —** stillatim
drop *tr (purposely)* demittere, deicere; *(to let slip)* omittere; *(to lay low)* sternere; *(a hint)* emittere; *(anchor)* iacere; *(work)* desistere ab *(w. abl);* **— it!** *(no more of that)* missa istaec fac!; **let's — the subject** missa haec faciamus ‖ *intr (to lessen)* cadere, concidere; *(to trickle)* (de)stillare; *(to fall)* decidere; *(esp. from the sky)* delabi, decidere; **to — behind** cessare; **to — down** decidere; **to — in on** visere; **to — off to sleep** obdormiscere; **to — out of** excidere de *(w. abl)*
drop-out *s* desti·tor -toris *m* (·trix -tricis *f*) de scholā
droppings *spl* merd·ae -arum *fpl*
drought *s* siccit·as -atis *f*
drove *s* gre·x -gis *m*
drown *tr* demergere; *(fig)* opprimere; **to — out** obscurare ‖ *intr* submergi
drowsily *adv* somniculose
drowsy *adj* somniculos·us -a -um
drub *tr* pulsare, verberare
drudge *s (slave)* mediastin·us -i *m* (·a -ae *f*)
drudgery *s* oper·a -ae *f* servilis
drug *s* medicam·en -inis *n; (narcotic)* medicament·um -i *n* psychotropicum
drug addict *s* medicamentis psychotropicis dedit·us -i *m* (·a -ae *f*)
druggist *s* medicamentar·ius -(i)i *m* (·ia -iae *f*)
drugstore *s* medicamentari·a -ae *f*
Druids *spl* Druid·ae -arum *mpl*
drum *s* tympan·um -i *n;* **to play the —** tympanum pulsare
drum *tr* **to — up** exquirere ‖ *intr* tympanum pulsare; **to — on the table** mensam digitis pulsare
drummer *s* tympanist·a -ae *m* (·ria -riae *f*)
drunk *adj* ebri·us -a -um; *(habitually)* ebrios·us -a -um
drunk, drunkard *s* ebrios·us -i *m* (·a -ae *f*)
drunken *adj* ebri·us -a -um
drunkenness *s* ebriet·as -atis *f; (habitual)* ebriosit·as -atis *f*
dry *adj* arid·us -a -um, sicc·us -a -um; *(thirsty)* sicc·us -a -um; *(wine)* auster·us -a -um; *(boring)* ieiun·us -a -um
dry *tr* siccare; **to — out** exsiccare; **to — up** arefacere ‖ *intr* arescere
dryad *s* dry·as -adis *f*
dry cleaner *s* full·o -onis *m; (shop)* fullonic·a -ae *f*
drydock *s* siccum naval·e -is *n*
dryer *s (for hair)* instrument·um -i *n* siccatorium; *(for clothes)* machin·a -ae *f* siccatoria
dry land *s* arid·um -i *n*
dryness *s* siccit·as -atis *f*
dry run *s* simulacr·um -i *n*
dual *adj* dual·is -is -e
dub *tr* appellare
dubious *adj* dubi·us -a -um; *(shady)* anc·eps -ipitis
duck *s* an·as -atis *f; (as food)* anatin·a -ae *f;* **—s quack** anates tetrinniunt
duck *tr (in the water)* deprimere; **to — the issue** rem evitare ‖ *intr* se inclinare
duckling *s* anaticul·a -ae *f*
duct *s* tub·us -i *m*
due *adj (owed)* debit·us -a -um; *(merited)* merit·us -a -um, iust·us -a -um; **— honors** meriti honor·es -um *mpl;* **— to** propter *(w. acc),* causā *(w. gen);* **to be — to** fieri ab *(w. abl);* **to fall — on the fifth day** in quintum diem cadere
due *s* debit·um -i *n;* **—s** stipendi·a -orum *npl;* **to give everyone his —** suum cuique tribuere
due *adv* rectā; **— east** rectā ad orientem
duel *s* singulare certam·en -inis *n*
duel *intr* viritim pugnare
duet *s* bicin·ium -(i)i *n*
duffel bag *s* sarcinul·a -ae *f*
duke *s* du·x -cis *m*
dull *adj* heb·es -itis; *(mind)* tard·us -a -um; *(uninteresting)* frigid·us -a -um
dull *tr* hebetare
dullness *s (of minds)* tardit·as -atis *f*
duly *adv* rite, recte
dumb *adj* mut·us -a -um; *(fig)* stupid·us -a -um
dumbfounded *adj* obstupefact·us -a -um; *(speechless)* elingu·is -is -e
dummy *s* effigi·es -ei *f; (stupid person)* bar·o -onis *m*
dumpling *s* farinae subactae globul·us -i *m*
dumpy *adj* brev·is -is -e et obes·us -a -um
dunce *s* bar·o -onis *m*
dung *s* sterc·us -oris *n; (of birds)* merd·ae -arum *fpl*
dungeon *s* rob·ur -oris *n*
dupe *tr* decipere
duplicate *adj* dupl·ex -icis
duplicate *s* exempl·ar -aris *n*
duplicate *tr* duplicare
duplicity *s* duplicit·as -atis *f*
durability *s* firmit·as -atis *f*
durable *adj* durabil·is -is -e
duration *s (period of time itself)* spat·ium -(i)i *n; (lastingness)* diurnit·as -atis *f;* **of long —** diuturn·us -a -um; **of short —** brev·is -is -e
during *prep* inter *(w. acc),* per *(w. acc)*
dusk *s* crepuscul·um -i *n*
dusky *adj* fusc·us -a -um

dust *s* pulv·is -eris *m*
dust *tr* detergēre
dustpan *s* vatill·um -i *n*
dusty *adj* pulverulent·us -a -um
dutiful *adj* pi·us -a -um, officios·us -a -um
duty *s (social or moral)* offic·ium -(i)i *n; (task)* mun·us -eris *n; (tax)* portor·ium -(i)i *n;* **to be on —** *(mil)* stationem agere; **when I do my —** *(coll)* cum mea facio
DVD *s* digitalis discul·us -i *m* magnetoscopicus
dwarf *s* pumili·o -onis *mf*
dwarfish *adj* pumil·us -a -um
dwell *intr* habitare; **to — upon** commorari in *(w. abl)*
dweller *s* incol·a -ae *mf*
dwelling place *s* sed·es -is *f*
dwindle *intr* imminui, decrescere
dye *s* tinctur·a -ae *f*
dye *tr* ting(u)ere, inficere
dying *adj* moribund·us -a -um; **I am — to know** valde aveo scire
dynamic *adj (fig)* vehem·ens -entis
dynamics *spl* dynamic·a -ae *f*
dynasty *s* dom·us -ūs *f* regnatrix; **under the Flavian —** potiente rerum Flaviā domu
dysentery *s* dysenteri·a -ae *f*
dyspepsia *s* dyspepsi·a -ae *f*

E

each *adj & pron* quisque, quidque; *(of two)* uterque, utraque utrumque; *(individually)* singul·i -ae -a; **— and every** unusquisque, unaquaeque, unumquodque; **— day** cotidie; **— other** inter se, invicem; **he stationed one legion — in Brundisium, Tarentum, and Sepontum** legiones singulas posuit Brindisi, Tarenti, Seponti
eager *adj* **(for)** cupid·us -a -um *(w. gen),* avid·us -a -um *(w. gen),* studios·us -a -um *(w. gen)*
eagerly *adv* cupide, avide
eagerness *s* avidit·as -atis *f*
eagle *s* aquil·a -ae *f;* **—s screech** aquilae strident
ear *s* aur·is -is *f; (outer ear)* auricul·a -ae *f; (of corn)* spic·a -ae *f;* **to give an — to** aurem praebēre *(w. dat)*
earache *s* auris dol·or -oris *m;* **to have an —** ab aure laborare
earl *s* com·es -itis *m*
earlobe *s* lann·a -ae *f* auris
early *adj (in the morning)* matutin·us -a -um; *(coming naturally early)* matur·us -a -um; *(before its time)* praematur·us -a -um, praec·ox -ocis; *(of early date)* antiqu·us -a -um; *(beginning)* prim·us -a -um; **from — youth** a primā adolescentiā; **in — spring** primo vere; **in — times** antiquitus
early *adv (in the morning)* (bene) mane; *(too soon)* praemature; *(in good time)* mature; **as — as possible** quam maturrime; **— enough** satis temperi; **— in life** ab ineunte aetate **— in the morning** bene mane; **his father died —** pater eius decessit mature
earmark *tr* destinare
earn *tr* merēre, merēri; **to — a living** quaestum facere
earnest *adj (eager)* intent·us -a -um; *(serious)* seri·us -a -um; **— money** arrab·o -onis *m*
earnest *s* **in —** ex bonā fide, serio
earnestly *adv* intente, valde
earnestness *s* gravit·as -atis *f*
earnings *spl* quaest·us -ūs *m*
earrings *spl* inaur·es -ium *fpl; (of several pearls)* crotali·a -orum *npl*
earth *s (land)* terr·a -ae *f; (planet)* tell·us -uris *f; (globe)* orb·is -is *m* terrarum; **of —, made of —** terren·us -a -um, terre·us -a -um; **why on —** quidnam
earthen *adj* terren·us -a -um; *(pottery)* fictil·is -is -e
earthenware *s* fictil·ia -ium *npl*
earthly *adj (made of earth)* terren·us -a -um; *(opposed to heavenly)* terrestr·is -is -e; **for what — reason** quare tandem
earthquake *s* terrae mot·us -ūs *m*
earthy *adj (humor)* terren·us -a -um
earthworm lubric·us -i *m*
ease *s (leisure)* ot·ium -(i)i *n; (easiness)* facilit·as -atis *f;* **at one's —** otios·us -a -um; **to live in —** in otio vivere; **to set s.o.'s mind at —** alicuius animum tranquillum reddere; **to speak with —** solute loqui
ease *tr* levare, laxare; *(to assuage)* mitigare
easily *adv* facile
east *adj* oriental·is -is -e
east *s* ori·ens -entis *m;* **from — to west** ab oriente ad occidentem; **on the —** ab oriente; **to sail —** ad *or* in orientem navigare; **to the —** in orientem versus [*versus is an adverb*]
Easter *s* Pasch·a -ae *f,* Pasch·a -atis *n*
Easter *adj* Paschal·is -is -e
easterly *adj* oriental·is -is -e
eastern *adj* oriental·is -is -e
Eastertime *s* temp·us -oris *n* Paschale
eastward *adv* ad orientem
east wind *s* Eur·us -i *m*
easy *adj* facil·is -is -e; *(graceful)* lepid·us -a -um; *(without obstacles, e.g., a road)* expedit·us -a -um; *(life)* otios·us -a -um; **— to understand** intellectu facil·is -is -e; **take it —!** *(farewell)* i *(or* ambula otiose!; **to take it —** otiari
easy chair *s* arcisell·ium -(i)i *n* tomento fartum
easy-going *adj* secur·us -a -um, facil·is -is -e

eat *tr* edō edere *or* ēsse; *(to live on)* vesci *(w. abl);* **to — away** corrodere; **to — breakfast** ientare, ientaculum sumere; **to — dinner** cenare; **to — lunch** prandēre; **to — up** comēsse ‖ *intr* ēsse, cenare; **to — and drink** cibum et potionem adsumere; **to — out** foris cenare
eatable *adj* esculent•us -a -um
eating *s* es•us -ūs *m*
eaves *spl* suggrund•a -ae *f*
eavesdrop *intr* subauscultare; **— on** subauscultare
eavesdropper *s* auc•eps -ipis *mf*
ebb *s* recess•us -ūs *m;* **— and flow** aestūs recess•us -ūs *m* et access•us -ūs *m;* **to be at a low —** *(fig)* iacēre
ebb *intr* recedere, refluere; *(fig)* decrescere
ebony *s* eben•um -i *n*
ebony *adj* ebenin•us -a -um
eccentric *adj* abnorm•is -is -e
ecclesiastic *adj* ecclesiastic•us -a -um
echo *s* repercuss•us -ūs *m,* ech•o -us *f; (poet)* imag•o -inis *f*
echo *tr* repercutere; *(to repeat what s.o. has said)* subsequi; **to — a sound** sonum referre ‖ *vi* resonare
echoing *adj* reson•us -a -um
eclectic *adj* eclectic•us -a -um
eclipse *s* defecti•o -onis *f*
eclipse *tr* obscurare
eclogue *s* eclog•a -ae *f*
economic *adj* economic•us -a -um, ad opes publicas pertin•ens -entis
economical *adj* frugi *(indecl),* parc•us -a -um
economically *adv* parce
economics *s* publicarum opum scienti•a -ae *f*
economist *s* qui *or* quae rei publicae opes exponit
economize *intr* (**on**) parcere *(w. dat); (of the state)* publicos sumptūs minuere
economy *s* frugalit•as -atis *f;* **public —** publicarum opum administrati•o -onis *f*
ecstasy *s (trance)* ecstas•is -is *f; (rapture)* elati•o -onis *f* voluptaria; **to be in —** laetitiā gestire
eddy *s* vort•ex -icis *m*
eddy *intr* (in se) volutari
edge *s (very often expressed by* extrem•us -a -um *modifying the substantive); (margin)* marg•o -inis *mf; (of knife, etc.)* aci•es -ei *f; (of forest)* or•a -ae *f;* **on —** anxi•us -a -um; **on the —** in praecipiti
edge *tr (garment)* praetexere; *(to sharpen)* acuere ‖ *intr* **to — away** sensim abscedere; **to — closer** sensim appropinquare
edgewise *adv* **to get in a word —** vocem in sermonem insinuare
edging *s (fringe)* limb•us -i *m; (gold border)* patag•ium -(i)i *n*
edible *adj* edul•is -is -e
edict *s* edict•um -i *n;* **to issue an —** edictum proponere
edification *s* humanit•as -atis *f*
edifice *s* aedific•ium -(i)i *n*
edify *tr* ad humanitatem excolere
edit *tr* edere; *(to correct)* emendare
edition *s* editi•o -onis *f*
editor *s* edi•tor -toris *m* (•trix -tricis *f*)
educate *tr* erudire, instituere
educated *adj* erudit•us -a -um
education *s* eruditi•o -onis *f*
educational *adj* scholastic•us -a -um; *(teaching)* praeceptiv•us -a -um
educator *s* praecep•tor -toris *m* (•trix -tricis *f*)
eel *s* anguill•a -ae *f*
eerie *adj* prodigios•us -a -um
efface *tr* delēre
effect *s* effect•um -i *n; (show)* iactati•o -onis *f;* **cause and —** caus•a -ae *f* et consecuti•o -onis *f;* **—s** bon•a -orum *npl;* **for mere —** ad iactationem; **in —** reapse; **to go into —** valēre; **to have an —** valēre; *(med)* pollēre; **to have a beneficial — on** prodesse *(w. dat);* **to have a harmful** *or* **negative — on** obesse *(w. dat);* **to put into —** efficacem reddere; **to take —** operari, efficax fieri; **to the same —** in eandem sententiam; **to this —** huiusmodi; **without —** frustra
effect *tr* conficere, efficere
effective *adj* profici•ens -entis, effic•ax -acis, habil•is -is -e
effectively *adv* efficienter; **to speak —** plurimum in dicendo valēre
effectual *adj* effic•ax -acis
effeminate *adj* effeminat•us -a -um
effeminately *adv* effeminate
effete *adj* effet•us -a -um
efficacious *adj* effic•ax -acis
efficaciously *adv* efficaciter
efficacy *s* virt•us -utis *f,* efficacit•as -atis *f*
efficiency *s* efficienti•a -ae *f*
efficient *adj (competent)* habil•is -is -e
efficiently *adv* diligenter, perite
effigy *s* effigi•es -ei *f*
effort *s* nis•us -ūs *m;* **to be worth the —** pretium operae esse; **to make an —** eniti; **with great —** enixe
effortless *adj* facil•is -is -e
effortlessly *adv* sine labore
effrontery *s* os oris *n;* **you have the — to** *(w. inf)* os tibi inest ut *(w. subj)*
effusion *s* effusi•o -onis *f*
effusive *adj* effus•us -a -um
effusively *adv* effuse
egg *s* ov•um -i *n;* **fried —s** ova *npl* fricta; **hard-boiled —** ovum *n* durum excoctum; **scrambled —s** ova *npl* permixta; **soft-boiled —** ovum molliter coctum *n;* **to lay an —** ovum parere
egg *tr* **to — on** incitare
egghead *s* hom•o -inis *mf* ingeniosus (-a)
eggplant *s* melongen•a -ae *f*

egg-shaped *adj* oval•is -is -e
eggshell *s* ovi putam•en -inis *n*
egg white *s* ovi alb•um -i *n*
egotism *s* am•or -oris *m* sui
egotist *s* sui ama•tor -toris *m* (•trix -tricis *f*)
egotistical *adj* sibi soli consul•ens -entis
egress *s* egress•us -ūs *m*
egress *intr* egredi
eight *adj* octo [*indecl*]; **— times** octies
eighteen *adj* duodeviginti [*indecl*]
eighteenth *adj* duodevicesim•us -a -um
eighth *adj* octav•us -a -um
eighth *s* octava par•s -tis *f*
eightieth *adj* octogesim•us -a -um
eighty *adj* octoginta [*indecl*]
either *adj & pron* u•ter -tra -trum
either *conj* **— … or** vel … vel; *(where the alternatives are mutually exclusive)* aut … aut
eject *tr* eicere
ejection *s* eiecti•o -onis *f*
eke *tr* **to — out a livelihood** victum aegre parare
elaborate *adj* elaborat•us -a -um, exquisit•us -a -um
elaborate *tr* elaborare **‖** *intr* (**on**) singillatim loqui (de *w. abl*)
elaboration *s* lim•a -ae *f*
elapse *intr* praeterire, intercedere
elastic *adj* elastic•us -a -um
elasticity *s* elasticit•as -atis *f*
elated *adj* **to be —** efferri
elation *s* anim•us -i *m* elatus
elbow *s* cubit•um -i *n;* **resting on one's —** in cubitum erect•us -a -um; **to lean one one's —** cubito inniti; **to rub —s with** conversari cum *(w. abl)*
elbow *tr* cubitis pulsare; **to — one's way through the crowd** cubitis turbam depulsare de viā
elbowroom *s* spat•ium -(i)i *n* satis laxum
elder *adj* mai•or -or -us natu
elderberry *s (bush)* sambuc•us -i *f; (berry)* sambuc•um -i *n;* **— wine** vin•um -i *n* sambuceum
elderly *adj* aetate provect•ior -ior -ius
eldest *adj* maxim•us -a -um natu
elect *tr* creare, eligere
elect *adj (office)* designat•us -a -um; *(elite)* lect•us -a -um
elect *npl* **the —** *(eccl)* elect•i -orum *mpl*
election *s (act of choosing)* electi•o -onis *f;* **—s** *(pol)* comiti•a -orum *npl;* **to hold —s** comitia habēre
election day *s* di•es -ei *m* comitialis
electioneering *s* ambiti•o -onis *f*
elective *adj (pol)* suffragiis creat•us -a -um; *(of choice)* elegend•us -a -um
elective *s* disciplin•a -ae *f* electa
electoral *adj* suffragatori•us -a -um
electorate *s* suffragator•es -um *mpl*
electric(al) *adj* electric•us -a -um
electrical appliances *spl* electrica instrument•a -orum *npl*
electrical engineer *s* machinat•or -oris *m* electricus
electrical engineering *s* machinati•o -onis *f* electrica
electric bulb *s* globul•us -i *m* electricus
electric chair *s* sell•a -ae *f* electrica interficiendi
electric cord *s* funicul•us -i *m* electricus
electric current *s* fluent•um -i *n* electricum
electric fan *s* machin•a -ae *f* ventigena
electrician *s* electridis opif•ex -icis *mf*
electricity *s* vis *f* electrica, electr•is -idis *f*
electric light lum•en -inis *n* electricum; **to turn on (turn off) the light** lumen accendere (extinguere)
electric razor *or* **shaver** *s* rasor•ium -(i)i *n* electricum
electric stove *s* focul•us -i *m* electricus
electric wire *s* fil•um -i *n* electricum
electrify *tr* electricā vi afficere; *(to thrill)* vehementer excitare
electrocute *tr* vi electricā interficere
electrocution *s* interit•us -ūs *m* electricus
electronic *adj* electronic•us -a -um
elegance *s* eleganti•a -ae *f*
elegant *adj* eleg•ans -antis
elegantly *adv* eleganter
elegiac *adj* elegiac•us -a -um; **— verse** eleg•i -orum *mpl*
elegy *s* elegi•a -ae *f*
element *s* element•um -i *n;* **—s** principi•a -orum *npl* rerum; *(fig)* rudiment•a -orum *npl;* **to be out of one's —** peregrin•us (•a) et hospes esse
elemental *adj* primordi•us -a -um
elementary *adj* simpl•ex -icis; **— instruction** element•a -orum *npl*
elementary school *s* lud•us -i *m* litterarius
elementary school teacher *s* litterari•us -i *m* (•a -ae *f*)
elephant *s* elephant•us -i *m;* **—s trumpet** elephanti barriunt
elevate *tr* levare, (at)tollere; *(fig)* efferre
elevated *adj* edit•us -a -um
elevation *s* elati•o -onis *f; (height)* altitud•o -inis *f; (hill)* loc•us -i *m* editus
elevator *s* cellul•a -ae *f* scansoria
eleven *adj* undecim [*indecl*]
eleventh *adj* undecim•us -a -um
elf *s* num•en -inis *n* pumilum
elicit *tr* elicere
elide *tr* elidere
eligible *adj (pol)* qui *or* quae per leges deligi potest; *(bachelor)* optabil•is -is -e
eliminate *tr* amovēre, tollere
elimination *s use a verbal paraphrase or* amoti•o -onis *f*
elision *s* elisi•o -onis *f*
elite *adj* elect•us -a -um
elite *s* flo•s -ris *m*
elk *s* alc•es -is *f*

ellipsis *s* ellips·is -is *f*
elliptical *adj* elliptic·us -a -um
elm *s* ulm·us -i *f*
elocution *s* pronuntiati·o -onis *f*
elongate *tr* producere, longius facere
elongated *adj* praelong·us -a -um
elope *intr* insciis atque invitis parentibus cum amatore *(or* amatrice) domo fugere
elopement *s* clandestina fug·a -ae *f* et nupti·ae -arum *fpl*
eloquence *s* eloquenti·a -ae *f; (natural)* facundi·a -ae *f*
eloquent *adj* eloquens, disert·us -a -um
eloquently *adv* eloquenter, diserte
else *adj* **anyone —** quivis alius; **anything —?** aliquid amplius?; **no one —** nem·o -inis *m* alius; **nothing —** nihil aliud; **who — ?** quis alius?
else *adv (besides)* praeterea; *(otherwise)* aliter; **or —** alioquin; **somewhere —** *(position)* alibi; *(direction)* alio
elsewhere *adv (position)* alibi; *(direction)* alio
elucidate *tr* illustrare, explicare
elucidation *s* explicati·o -onis *f*
elude *tr* eludere
elusive *adj (difficult to grasp)* fug·ax -acis; *(difficult to describe)* recondit·us -a -um
Elysian *adj* Elysi·us -a -um; **— Fields** Camp·i -orum *mpl* Elysii
emaciate *tr* macerare
emaciated *adj* ma·cer -cra -crum; **to become —** emacrescere
emaciation *s* maci·es -ei *f*
e-mail *s* litter·ae -arum *fpl* electronicae; *(the system)* curs·us -ūs *m* electronicus
e-mail *tr* litteras electronicas mittere ad *(w. acc)*
e-mail address *s* inscripti·o -onis *f* electronica
emanate *intr* emanare
emanation *s (gas)* exspirati·o -onis *f; (issue)* emissi·o -onis *f*
emancipate *tr (a son)* emancipare; *(a slave)* manumittere
emancipation *s (of a son)* emancipati·o -onis *f; (of a slave)* manumissi·o -onis *f*
emasculated *adj (lit & fig)* effeminat·us -a -um
embalm *tr* condire
embankment *s* agg·er -eris *m*
embargo *s (on goods)* prohibiti·ō -onis *f* commercii; *(on ships)* retenti·o -onis *f* navium; **to lay an — on ships** naves ab exitu prohibēre; **to lift the — on ships** naves dimittere
embark *tr* imponere ‖ *intr* (in navem) conscendere; **to — upon** *(fig)* ingredi
embarkation *s* conscensi·o -onis *f; (usu. expressed by the verb:* **after the — of the army** exercitu in naves imposito)
embarrass *tr* perturbare; **to be —ed** erubescere
embarrassing *adj* erubescund·us -a -um
embarrassment *s* conturbati·o -onis *f; (financial)* angusti·ae -arum *fpl*
embassy *s* legati·o -onis *f*
embellish *tr* exornare; **to — facts rather than report them accurately** res gestas magis exornare quam fideliter narrare
embellishment *s (act)* exornati·o -onis *f; (result)* ornament·um -i *n*
ember *s* favill·a -ae *f*
embezzle *tr* (pecuniam) avertere
embezzlement *s* peculat·us -ūs *m*
embezzler *s* pecula·tor -toris *m* (·trix -tricis *f*), avers·or -oris *m* (·rix -ricis *f*)
embitter *tr* exacerbare
embittered *adj* exacerbat·us -a -um
emblazon *tr* insignire
emblem *s* indic·ium -(i)i *n; (badge)* insign·e -is *n*
emblematic *adj* symbolic·us -a -um
embodiment *s* effigi·es -ei *f*, form·a -ae *f*
embody *tr* includere, informare, effingere
emboss *tr* caelare
embrace *s* amplex·us -ūs *m*
embrace *tr* amplect·or -ī amplexus sum
embroider *tr* acu pingere
embroidered *adj (w. colors)* pict·us -a -um
embroidery *s (art)* ar·s -tis *f* acu pingendi; *(product)* pictur·a -ae *f* in textili (facta); picta vest·is -is *f*
embroil *tr* implicare
embroilment *s* implicati·o -onis *f*
embryo *s* part·us -ūs *m* inchoatus
emend *tr* emendare
emendation *s* emendati·o -onis *f*
emerald *s* smaragd·us -i *f (m)*
emerald *adj* smaragdin·us -a -um
emerge *intr* emergere; *(to arise)* existere
emergency *s* discrim·en -inis *n*
emergency *adj* subitari·us -a -um
emigrant *s* emigr·ans -antis *mf*
emigrate *intr* (**to**) emigrare (in *w. acc)*
emigration *s* emigrati·o -onis *f*
eminence *s* praestanti·a -ae *f; (rise in the ground)* loc·us -i *m* editus
eminent *adj* emin·ens -entis, egregi·us -a -um, ornatissim·us -a -um
eminently *adv* insigniter
emissary *s* legat·us -i *m* (·a -ae *f*)
emission *s* emissi·o -onis *f*
emit *tr* emittere; *(to utter)* proferre; *(scent)* exhalare
emotion *s* animi mot·us -ūs *m;* affect·us -ūs *m;* **strong —** permoti·o -onis *f;* **to express —s** animi emotūs exprimere
emotional *adj* affectūs animi mov·ens -entis
emperor *s* imperat·or -oris *m; (title chosen by Augustus)* princ·eps -ipis *m*
emphasis *s* vis *f; (gram)* impressi·o -onis *f*
emphasize *tr (a word)* premere; *(idea)* exprimere
emphatic *adj* grav·is -is -e

emphatically *adv* graviter
empire *s* imper·ium -(i)i *n*
empirical *adj* empiric·us -a -um
empirically *adv* ex experimentis
empiricism *s* empiric·e -es *f*
employ *tr (to use)* uti *(w. abl)*, adhibēre; *(to hire)* conducere **to — precaution** uti observatione
employee *s* conduct·us -i *m* (·a -ae *f*)
employer *s* conduc·tor -toris *m* (·trix -tricis *f*)
employment *s (act)* us·us -ūs *m; (as a means of livelihood)* quaest·us -ūs *m; (hiring)* conducti·o -onis *f*
empower *tr* potestatem *(w. dat)* facere; *(to enable)* facultatem dare *(w.dat)*
empress *s* impera·trix -tricis *f*
emptiness *s* inanit·as -atis *f; (fig)* vanit·as -atis *f*
empty *adj* vacu·us -a -um, inan·is -is -e; *(street)* desert·us -a -um; *(fig)* van·us -a -um; *(stomach)* ieiun·us -a -um
empty *tr (contents)* vacuefacere; *(bottle, stomach)* exhaurire; *(to strip bare)* exinanire **||** *intr (of river)* se effundere
empty-handed *adj* inan·is -is -e; *(without a gift)* immun·is -is -e
empty-headed *adj* frivol·us -a -um
emulate *tr (to rival)* aemulari; *(to imitate)* imitari
emulation *s* aemulati·o -onis *f; (imitation)* imitati·o -onis *f*
emulous *adj* **(of)** aemul·us -a -um *(w. gen)*
enable *tr* facultatem *(w. dat)* dare
enact *tr* sancire; *(of the plebs)* sciscere; *(of the Roman people)* iubēre; *(of a absolute ruler)* imponere
enactment *s (of senate)* senatūs consult·um -i *n; (of the plebs)* plebis scit·um -i *n;* sancti·o -onis *f*
enamel *s* smalt·um -i *n*
enamel *adj* smaltin·us -a -um
enamored *adj* **to be — of** deamare
encamp *intr* castra ponere, (in castris) considere
encampment *s* castr·a -orum *npl*
encase *tr* includere
enchant *tr* fascinare; *(fig)* capere
enchanted *adj* incantat·us -a -um, capt·us -a -um
enchanting *adj (fig)* venust·us -a -um
enchantment *s* incantament·um -i *n; (fig)* illecebr·ae -arum *fpl*
enchantress *s* mag·a -ae *f*
encircle *tr* circumdare
enclictic *s* enclitic·um -i *n*
enclose *tr* includere; *(with a fence)* saepire; **to — a document in a letter** libellum litteris subicere
enclosure *s (fence)* saept·um -i *n; (mail)* res *f* epistulae subiecta
encompass *tr (to surround)* cingere; *(to include)* complecti
encore *s* revocati·o -onis *f;* **he received an —** revocatus est
encounter *s (meeting)* congress·us -ūs *m; (fight)* pugn·a -ae *f*
encounter *tr (unexpectedly)* occurrere *(w. dat),* offendere; *(the enemy)* obviam ire *(w. dat);* **to — death** mortem oppetere
encourage *tr* (ad)cohortari; *(of one cast down)* animum *or* animos *(w. gen)* confirmare
encouragement *s* hortat·us -ūs *m;* confirmati·o -onis *f*
encroach *intr* invadere; **to — upon** occupare; *(rights)* imminuere; **to — upon a neighbor's land** terminos agri proferre
encroachment *s* usurpati·o -onis *f; (on rights)* imminuti·o -onis *f*
encumber *tr* impedire
encumbrance *s* impediment·um -i *n*
encyclical *s* litter·ae -arum *fpl* publicae pontificales
encyclopedia *s* orb·is -is *m* doctrinae
end *s* fin·is -is *m,* termin·us -i *m; (termination of life)* exit·um -i *n; (aim)* proposit·um -i *n; (of a speech)* perorati·o -onis *f;* **at the — of the day** extremo die; **at the — of the letter** in extremis litteris; **at the — of the year** exeunte anno; **in the —** ad extremum, denique; **that's the — of me** actum est de me; **to come to an —** finem capere; **to make both —s meet** aegre intra modum nummorum vivere; **to put an — to** finem imponere *(w. dat);* **to the — of spring** ad ultimum ver; **toward the — of his life** tempore extremo; **to what — ?** quo?, quorsum?
end *tr* finire, terminare **||** *intr* desinere, finem capere; *(of time)* exire; **to — up** evenire, evadere
endanger *tr* in periculum vocare
endear *tr* carum (-am) reddere, devincire
endearing *adj* car·us -a -um, bland·us -a -um
endearment *s* blanditi·ae -arum *fpl*
endeavor *s* conat·us -ūs *m*
endeavor *intr* conari, niti
ending *s* fin·is -is *m,* exit·us -ūs *m*; *(gram)* terminati·o -onis *f*
endless *adj* infinit·us -a -um; *(time)* aetern·us -a -um
endlessly *adv* sine fine
endorse *tr* comprobare; *(a check)* chirographum a tergo *(w. gen)* inscribere
endorsement *s* fav·or -oris *m; (com)* subscripti·o -onis *f*
endow *tr* donare
endowed *adj* **(with)** praedit·us -a -um *(w. abl)*
endowment *s (of body or mind)* do·s -tis *f; (financial)* dotati·o -onis *f*
endurable *adj* tolerabil·is -is -e
endurance *s* patienti·a -ae *f; (duration)* durati·o -onis *f*

endure *tr* tolerare ‖ *intr* durare
enduring *adj* toler·ans -antis; *(lasting)* durabil·is -is -e
enemy *s (public)* host·is -is *m; (private)* inimic·us -i *m* (·a -ae *f*)
enemy *adj* hostic·us -a -um, infest·us -a -um; inimic·us -a -um
energetic *adj* impi·ger -gra -grum
energy *s* vis *f;* **atomic energy** vis atomica
enervate *tr* enervare
enforce *tr (the law)* exercēre, exsequi
enforcement *s* executi·o -onis *f*
enfranchise *tr* civitate donare; *(a slave)* manumittere; *(to vote)* suffragium dare *(w. dat)*
enfranchisment *s* civitatis donati·o -onis *f; (of a slave)* manumissi·o -onis *f; (right to vote)* suffragii ius, iuris *n*
engage *tr (to hire)* conducere; *(to employ)* adhibēre; *(attention)* occupare; *(to involve)* implicare; *(enemy)* proelium facere cum *(w. abl),* dimicare cum *(w. abl)* ‖ *intr* **to — in** suscipere, ingredi; **to — in battle** proeliari; **to — in conversation** sermonem instituere *(or* serere)
engaged *adj (to marry)* spons·us -a -um; **to be — in** versari in *(w. abl)*
engagement *s (to marry)* pacti·o -onis *f* nuptialis; *(business)* occupati·o -onis *f; (mil)* proel·ium -(i)i *n;* **to break off the —** sponsum repudiare
engagement party *s* sponsal·ia -ium *npl*
engaging *adj* suav·is -is -e
engender *tr* gignere
engine *s* machin·a -ae *f*
engineer *s* machina·tor -toris *m* (·trix -tricis *f*); *(mil)* fa·ber -bri *m*
engineering *s* machinalis scienti·a -ae *f*
England *s* Angli·a -ae *f,* Britanni·a -ae *f*
English *adj* Anglic·us -a -um
English *s* **to know —** Anglice scire; **to speak —** Anglice loqui; **to teach —** Anglice docēre
engrave *tr* caelare
engraver *s* caelat·or -oris *m*
engraving *s* caelatur·a -ae *f*
engross *tr* (**in**) animum occupare in *(w. abl);* **to be —ed in** tot·us -a -um esse in *(w. abl)*
engulf *tr* devorare, mergere
enhance *tr* amplificare
enhancement *s* amplificati·o -onis *f*
enigma *s* aenigm·a -atis *n*
enigmatic *adj* ambigu·us -a -um
enigmatically *adv* per aenigmata
enjoin *tr* iubēre
enjoy *tr* frui *(w. abl); (to have the benefit of, e.g., good health, friendship, company)* uti *(w. abl)*
enjoyment *s* fruct·us -ūs *m; (the sense of pleasure itself)* delectati·o -onis *f*
enlarge *tr* amplificare
enlargement *s* amplificati·o -onis *f*
enlighten *tr (physically)* illustrare; *(mentally)* illuminare; *(to instruct)* erudire
enlightened *adj* erudit·us -a -um
enlightenment *s* humanit·as -atis *f*
enlist *tr (support)* conciliare; *(mil)* conscribere; *(to swear in)* sacramento adigere ‖ *intr (mil)* sacramentum dicere, nomen dare
enlistment *s* conscripti·o -onis *f*
enliven *tr* excitare
enmity *s* simult·as -atis *f;* **to be at — with** in simultate esse cum *(w. abl);* **to feel — toward** simultatem habēre cum *(w. abl)*
ennoble *tr* honestare, nobilitare
ennui *s* taed·ium -(i)i *n*
enormity *s* immanit·as -atis *f*
enormous *adj* imman·is -is -e
enormously *adv* praeter modum
enough *adj* satis [*indecl*]; **— trouble** satis laboris; **time —** satis temporis
enough *adv* satis; **— of this!** haec hactenus!; **more than —** satis superque
enrage *tr* infuriare
enrapture *tr* oblectare; **to be —d** gaudio efferri
enrich *tr* locupletare, ditare
enroll *tr* ascribere; **to — s.o. in the patrician order** aliquem inter patricios asciscere ‖ *intr* ascribi, nomen dare
enshrine *tr* consecrare
ensign *s (banner)* sign·um -i *n; (officer)* signif·er -eri *m*
enslave *tr* in servitutem redigere
enslavement *s* servit·us -utis *f,* servit·ium -(i)i *n*
ensnare *tr* illaquēre; *(fig)* illicere
ensue *intr* insequi
ensuing *adj* insequ·ens -entis
entail *tr* adferre
entangle *tr* implicare
entanglement *s* implicati·o -onis *f*
enter *tr* intrare, ingredi, inire; *(office)* inire; *(to pierce)* penetrare in *(w. acc); (comput)* in ordinatrum referre; **to — in a memorandum** in libellum referre; **to — in an account book** in rationem inducere; **to — politics** rem publicam inire ‖ *intr* intrare, ingredi, inire; **to — into an alliance with s.o.** societatem cum aliquo facere; **to — upon** *(to undertake)* suscipere; *(a magistracy)* inire
enterprise *s (undertaking)* incept·um -i *n; (project)* op·us -eris *n; (venture)* aus·um -i *n; (enterprising disposition)* alacer ac promptus anim·us -i *m*
enterprising *adj* ala·cer -cris -cre et prompt·us -a -um
entertain *tr (a guest)* excipere; *(idea)* admittere; *(to amuse)* oblectare
entertainer *s* ludi·o -onis *m; (host)* hosp·es -itis *mf*
entertaining *adj* festiv·us -a -um

entertainment *s (amusement)* oblectati•o -onis *f; (cultural, esp. at a dinner party)* acroam•a -atis *n; (by the host)* hospit•ium -(i)i *n;* **public —s** spectacul•a -orum *npl*
enthrall *tr* captare
enthusiasm *s* stud•ium -(i)i *n*
enthusiastic *adj* **(about)** studios•us -a -um *(w. gen)*
enthusiastically *adv* studiose
entice *tr* allicere
enticement *s* illecebr•a -ae *f*
enticing *adj* illecebros•us -a -um
entire *adj* tot•us -a -um, univers•us -a -um
entirely *adv* omnino
entirety *s expressed by* univers•us -a -um: **to look at the matter in its —** rem universam contemplari
entitle *tr (a book, essay)* inscribere; *(to name)* appellare; *(to give title to)* potestatem dare *(w. dat);* **to be —d to do anything** ius aliquid faciendi habēre; dignus esse qui aliquid faciat
entity *s* en•s -tis *n*
entomb *tr* sepulchro condere
entomologist *s* entomologic•us -i *m* (•a -ae *f*)
entomology *s* entomologi•a -ae *f*
entourage *s* comitat•us -ūs *m*
entrails *spl* ext•a -orum *npl*
entrance *s* adit•us -ūs *m,* introit•us -ūs *m; (act)* ingressi•o -onis *f; (doorway)* osti•um -i *n;* **at the — to the theater** in aditu theatri
entrance *tr* rapere
entrance hall *s* vestibul•um -i *n*
entrance way *s* ost•ium -(i)i *n*
entreat *tr* obsecrare
entreaty *s* obsecrati•o -onis *f*
entree *s* cen•a -ae *f* altera
entrench *tr (lit & fig)* vallare; **to — oneself** subsidere
entrenchment *s* muniment•um -i *n*
entrepreneur *s* negotia•tor -toris *m* (•trix -tricis *f*)
entrust *tr* committere
entry *s (act)* ingressi•o -onis *f,* introït•us -ūs *m; (of house)* ost•ium -(i)i *n; (in accounts)* nom•en -inis *n*
entwine *tr* implicare, implectere
enumerate *tr* enumerare
enumeration *s* enumerati•o -onis *f*
enunciate *tr* exprimere
enunciation *s (of sounds)* explanati•o -onis *f; (setting forth)* enuntiati•o -onis *f*
envelop *tr* involvere
envelope *s* involucr•um -i *n* (epistulare)
enviable *adj* invidios•us -a -um
envious *adj* invid•us -a -um; **to be — of** invidēre *(w. dat)*
environment *s* circumiect•a -orum *npl*
environs *spl* vicinit•as -atis *f*
envision *tr* fingere
envoy *s* legat•us -i *m* (•a -ae *f*)
envy *s* invidi•a -ae *f*
envy *tr* invidēre *(w. dat)*
enzyme *s* enzym•a -ae *f*
eons *spl* plurima saecul•a -orum *npl*
ephemeral *adj (brief)* brev•is -is -e; *(perishable)* caduc•us -a -um
epic *adj* epic•us -a -um
epic *s* epos *n (only in nom & acc),* poem•a -atis *n* epicum
epicure *s* hellu•o -onis *m*
Epicurean *adj (of Epicurus)* Epicure•us -a -um; *(fig)* voluptari•us -a -um
Epicurean *s* Epicure•us -i *m; (hedonist)* voluptari•us -i *m* (•a -ae *f*)
epidemic *adj* epidem•us -a -um
epidemic *s* pestilenti•a -ae *f*
epidermis *s* epiderm•is -is *f,* summa cut•is -is *f*
epigram *s* epigramm•a -atis *n*
epilepsy *s* morb•us -i *m* comitialis
epilogue *s* epilog•us -i *m*
episcopal *adj* episcopal•is -is -e
episode *s* event•us -ūs *m,* cas•us -ūs *m*
epistle *s* epistul•a -ae *f*
epitaph *s* titul•us -i *m* (sepulchri)
epithet *s* epithet•on -i *n*
epitome *s* empitom•a -ae (•e -es) *f*
epoch *s* saecul•um -i *n*
equal *adj* aequ•us -a-um; *(matching)* pa•r -ris; **to be — to the task** muneri par esse
equal *s* pa•r -ris *mf & n;* **to be on an — with the gods** in aequo dis stare
equal *tr* aequare
equality *s* aequalit•as -atis *f;* **to be on — with** in aequo *(w. dat)* stare
equalization *s (act)* exaequati•o -onis *f; (state)* aequalit•as -atis *f*
equally *adv* aeque
equanimity *s* aequus anim•us -i *m*
equate *tr* **(with)** aequiparare (cum *or* ad *or dat)*
equation *s* aequati•o -onis *f*
equator *s* aequinoctialis circul•us -i *m*
equestrian *adj* equestr•is -is -e
equestrian *s* equ•es -itis *m*
equidistant *adj* **to be —** aequo intervallo inter se distare
equilibrium *s* aequilibr•ium -(i)i *n*
equinox *s* aequinoct•ium -(i)i *n*
equip *tr* ornare; *(with arms)* armare
equipment *s* instrument•um -i *n,* apparat•us -ūs *m*
equitable *adj* aequ•us -a -um
equitably *adv* aeque
equity *s* aequ•um -i *n*
equivalence *s* aequalit•as -atis *f*
equivalent *adj* pa•r -ris, aequ•us -a -um; **one gold coin is — to ten silver ones** pro decem argenteis aureus unus valet; **to be —** valēre
equivalent *s* quod idem valet
equivocal *adj* ambigu•us -a -um
equivocate *intr* tergiversari
era *s* temp•us -oris *n,* saecul•um -i *n*

eradicate *tr* eradicare, exstirpare
eradication *s* exstirpati·o -onis *f*
erase *tr* eradere, delēre
eraser *s* deletil·e -is *n,* cumm·is -is *f* deletilis
erasure *s* litur·a -ae *f*
ere *conj* priusquam
ere *prep* ante *(w. acc);* **— long** mox; **— now** ante hoc tempus, antehac
erect *adj* erect·us -a -um
erect *tr (to raise)* erigere; *(to build)* exstruere; *(statue)* ponere, statuere
erection *s (building)* exstructi·o -onis *f; (setting up)* erecti·o -onis *f*
erode *tr* erodere
erosive *adj* erod·ens -entis
erotic *adj* libidinos·us -a -um
err *intr* errare, peccare
errand *s* mandat·um -i *n,* mun·us -eris *n*
erratic *adj* inconst·ans -antis
erroneous *adj* fals·us -a -um; **to be —** in erratis esse
erroneously *adv* perperam
error *s (of opinion)* err·or -oris *m; (instance)* errat·um -i *n; (in writing, clerical)* mend·a -ae *f,* mend·um -i *n; (in grammar)* vit·ium -(i)i *n;* **to commit an —** mendum admittere; **to make many —s** multa errare
erudite *adj* erudit·us -a -um
erudition *s* eruditi·o -onis *f*
erupt *intr* erumpere
eruption *s* erupti·o -onis *f*
escalate *tr (to increase)* augēre; *(to intensify)* intendere ‖ *intr* (in)crescere, ingravescere
escalator *s* scal·ae -arum *fpl* mobiles
escapade *s* facin·us -oris *n* temerarium
escape *s* effug·ium -(i)i *n*
escape *tr* fugere; *(in a quiet way)* subterfugere; **to — the notice of** fallere ‖ *intr* effugere
escort *s* comitat·us -ūs *m; (protection)* praesid·ium -(i)i *n*
escort *tr* prosequi
esophagus *s* gul·a -ae *f*
especially *adv* praecipue, potissimum, maxime; *(w. clauses)* praesertim
espresso *s* caffe·a -ae *f* expressa
essay *s (treatise)* libell·us -i *m*
essence *s* essenti·a -ae *f*
essential *adj* necessari·us -a -um; *(basic)* prim·us -a -um
essentially *adv* necessario
establish *tr* constituere; *(to settle firmly)* stabilare; *(to prove)* probare
establishment *s (act)* constituti·o -onis *f; (com)* negot·ium -(i)i *n*
estate *s (landed property)* fund·us -i *m,* praed·ium -(i)i *n; (state)* stat·us -ūs *m*
esteem *s* aestimati·o -onis *f;* **to hold s.o in high (highest) —** aliquem magni (maximi) facere
esteem *tr* aestimare; **to — highly (more, very highly)** magni (pluris, maximi) facere
estimate *s (valuation)* aestimati·o -onis *f; (judgment)* iudic·ium -(i)i *n;* **to form an —** iudicium facere; **to give an —** modum impensarum explicare
estimation *s* aestimati·o -onis *f*
estrange *tr* alienare; **to become —ed from s.o.** aliquem a se alienare
estrangement *s* alienati·o -onis *f*
estuary *s* aestuar·ium -(i)i *n*
eternal *adj* aetern·us -a -um
eternally *adv* in aeternum
eternity *s* aeternit·as -atis *f*
ether *s* aeth·er -eris *m*
ethereal *adj* aethere·us -a -um
ethical *adj* moral·is -is -e
ethics *spl* ethic·e -es *f; (of an individual)* mor·es -ium *mpl*
Ethiopia *s* Aethiopi·a -ae *f*
Etruria *s* Etruri·a -ae *f*
etiquette *s* regim·en -inis *n* morum
etymological *adj* etymologic·us -a -um
etymology *s* etymologi·a -ae *f*
eulogist *s* lauda·tor -toris *m* (·trix -tricis *f*)
eulogize *tr* laudare
eulogy *s* laudati·o -onis *f*
eunuch *s* eunuch·us -i *m; (pej)* spad·o -onis *m*
euphemism *s* euphemism·us -i *m*
euphemistic *adj* **— expression** vo·x -cis *f* per euphemismum usurpata
euphony *s* vocalit·as -atis *f*
Europe *s* Europ·a -ae *f*
European *adj* Europae·us -a -um
evacuate *tr* vacuefacere; *(people)* deducere; *(bowels)* exonerare
evacuation *s (mil)* deducti·o -onis *f;* **— of the bowels** alvi purgati·o -onis *f*
evade *tr* eludere
evaluate *tr* aestimare
evaluation *s* aestimati·o -onis *f*
evangelical *adj* evangelic·us -a -um
evangelist *s* evangelist·a -ae *m* (·ria -riae *f*)
evangelize *tr* evangelizare
evaporate *tr* evaporare ‖ *intr* evaporari
evaporation *s* evaporati·o -onis *f*
evasion *s (avoidance)* fug·a -ae *f; (dodging)* tergiversati·o -onis *f; (round-about speech)* ambag·es -um *fpl;* **to practice —** tergiversari
evasive *adj* ambigu·us -a -um
evasively *adv* ambigue
eve *s* vesp·er -eri *m; (of a feastday)* vigili·ae -arum *fpl;* **on the — of** sub *(w. acc),* pridie (eius diei)
even *adj* aequal·is -is -e; *(level)* plan·us -a -um; *(of numbers)* pa·r -ris; **to get — with s.o.** aliquem ulcisci
even *adv* etiam; *(esp. to emphasize single words)* vel; **— if, — though** etsi, etiamsi; **— so** nihilominus; **not —** ne … quidem

evening *s* vesp·er -eri *m,* vesper·a -ae *f;* **all —** totā vesperā; **early in the —** primo vespere; **in the —** vespere, vesperi; **— falls** vesperascit; **good —!** salve!, *(pl:* salvete!); **last —** heri vesperi; **on Saturday —** die Saturni vesperi; **this —** hodie vesperi; **toward —** sub vesperum; **in the early —** primo vespere; **very late in the —** pervespere; **yesterday —** heri vesperi

evening *adj* vespertin·us -a -um

evening star *s* Hesper·us -i *m*

evenness *s* aequalit·as -atis *f*

event *s* res, rei *f; (adverse)* cas·us -ūs *m; (outcome)* event·us -ūs *m;* **at all —s** saltem; **in any —** utique; **in the — that** si forte

eventful *adj* memorabil·is -is -e

eventual *adj* ultim·us -a -um

eventuality *s* event·us -ūs *m*

eventually *adv* aliquando, denique

ever *adv (always)* semper; *(at any time)* umquam; *(after* si, nisi, num, ne) quando; **— since** ex quo (tempore); **for —** in aeternum; **greater than —** maior quam umquam; **more than —** magis quam umquam

evergreen *adj* semperviv·us -a -um; **— tree** arbor quae semper viret

everlasting *adj* sempitern·us -a -um

evermore *adv* **for —** in aeternum

every *adj* omn·is -is -e, quisque, quaeque, quodque; **— day** cotidie, in dies; **— night** per singulas noctes; **— now and then** interdum; **— other day** alternis diebus; **— year** quotannis

everybody *pron (each one)* quisque; *(all)* omn·es -ium *mpl; (stronger)* nem·o -inis *m* non; **— for himself** pro se quisque

everyday *adj* co(t)tidian·us -a -um; *(ordinary)* usitat·us -a -um

everyone *pron see* **everybody**

everything *pron* omn·ia -ium *npl,* nihil non

everywhere *adv* ubique

evict *tr* expellere, detrudere

eviction *s* expulsi·o -onis *f*

evidence *s* testimon·ium -(i)i *n; (information given)* indic·ium -(i)i *n;* **to give —** testari; **to give — against s.o.** testimonium dare in aliquem; **on what — will you convict me?** quo me teste convinces?; **to turn state's** indicium profiteri

evident *adj* manifest·us -a -um; **it is —** apparet, manifestum est, constat

evidently *adv* manifeste

evil *adj* mal·us -a -um

evil *s* mal·um -i *n*

evil-minded *adj* malevol·us -a -um

evince *tr* praestare

evoke *tr* evocare, excitare

evolution *s* progress·us -ūs *m,* evoluti·o -onis *f*

evolve *tr* evolvere per gradūs ‖ *intr* evolvi per gradūs

exact *adj* exact·us -a -um, accurat·us -a -um; *(persons)* dilig·ens -entis; **at the — time when** ipso tempore quo

exact *tr* exigere

exaction *s* exacti·o -onis *f*

exactly *adv* accurate; **— as** sic ut

exactness *s* accurati·o -onis *f*

exaggerate *tr* in maius extollere; *(numbers)* augēre; **to — the facts** excedere actae rei modum

exaggeration *s* superiecti·o -onis *f* veri; **falsehoods and —s** falsa et maiora vero; **he is given to —** omnia in maius extollere solet

exalt *tr* amplificare, efferre

exaltation *s* elati·o -onis *f*

exam *s* probati·o -onis *f;* **to flunk an —** probatione cadere; **to pass an —** probationem sustinere, e probatione feliciter evadere; **to take an —** probationem obire; **tough —** probatio rigorosa

examination *s* investigati·o -onis *f; (leg)* quaesti·o -onis *f; (in school)* probati·o -onis *f*

examine *tr* investigare, scrutari; *(witnesses)* interrogare; *(students)* probare

examiner *s* investiga·tor -toris *m* (·trix -tricis *f); (leg)* inquisi·tor -toris *m* (·trix -tricis *f)*

example *s (illustration)* exempl·um -i *n; (lesson)* document·um -i *n;* **for —** exempli gratiā; **to set an —** exemplum praebēre

exasperate *tr* exasperare

exasperated *adj* irat·us -a -um

exasperation *s* irritati·o -onis *f*

excavate *tr* excavare

excavator *s (person)* foss·or -oris *m; (machine)* machin·a -ae *f* fossoria

excavation *s* excavati·o -onis *f*

exceed *tr* excedere, superare

exceedingly *adv* magnopere, valde, nimium

excel *tr* superare ‖ *intr* excellere, praestare

excellence *s* excellenti·a -ae *f*

Excellency *s (eccl)* Eminentissim·us -i *m*

excellent *adj* optim·us -a -um, excell·ens -entis; *(excelling others)* praest·ans -antis

excellently *adv* egregie, optime

except *tr* excipere

except *prep* praeter *(w. acc);* **— that** nisi quod

exception *s* excepti·o -onis *f;* **with the — of** praeter *(w. acc);* **with this —** hoc excepto; **without a single —** ne uno quidem excepto; **without —** omnes ad un·um -am -um

exceptional *adj* praest·ans -antis

exceptionally *adv* praeter modum

excess *s* nim·ium -(i)i *n;* **to be in —** superesse; **to —** nimis; **to go to — in anything** nimium esse in aliqua re

excess *adj* nimi·us -a -um
excessive *adj* **(in)** immodic·us -a -um *(w. gen or abl)*
excessively *adv* immodice, nimis
exchange *s (of goods)* permutati·o -onis *f; (of money)* collyb·us -i *m;* **in — for** pro *(w. abl);* **rate of —** collyb·us -i *m*
exchange *tr* **(for)** permutare *(w. abl);* **to — greetings** consalutare; **to — letters** commercium epistulare habēre; **to — prisoners** capitivos inter se permutare
excise *tr* exsecare, excidere
excision *s* exsecti·o -onis *f*
excitable *adj* percit·us -a -um; *(irritable)* irritabil·is -is -e
excite *tr* excitare; *(to provoke)* incitare
excited *adj* commot·us -a -um, excitat·us -a -um
excitement *s* commoti·o -onis *f; (that which excites)* incitament·um -i *n;* **to feel —** excitari
exclaim *tr* exclamare; *(as a group)* conclamare; *(in reply)* succlamare
exclamation *s* exclamati·o -onis *f*
exclamation point *s* sign·um -i *n* exclamationis
exclude *tr* excludere
exclusion *s* exclusi·o -onis *f*
exclusive *adj* propri·us -a -um; **— of** praeter *(w. acc)*
exclusively *adv* solum
excommunicate *tr* excommunicare
excommunication *s* excommunicati·o -onis *f*
excrete *tr* emittere
excrement *s* excrement·um -i *n*
excretion *s (act)* excreti·o -onis *f; (result)* excrement·um -i *n*
excruciating *adj* cruci·ans -antis
excursion *s* it·er -ineris *n* voluptatis causā susceptum
excusable *adj* excusabil·is -is -e
excuse *s* excusati·o -onis *f; (pretext)* praetext·um -i *n*
excuse *tr* ignoscere *(w. dat);* **— me!** ignosce mihi!; **please excuse me** obsecro, mihi ignoscas; **to — oneself** se excusare
execute *tr (a criminal)* supplicio capitis afficere; *(to perform)* exsequi, efficere
execution *s* exsecuti·o -onis *f; (capital punishment)* supplic·ium -(i)i *n* capitis
executioner *s* carnif·ex -icis *m*
executive *adj* ad administrationem pertin·ens -entis
executive *s* administra·tor -toris *m* (·trix -tricis *f*)
executor *s* curat·or -oris *m* testamenti
executrix *s* cura·trix -tricis *f* testamenti
exemplary *adj* eximi·us -a -um
exemplify *tr* exemplum *(w. gen)* exponere
exempt *tr* eximere
exempt *adj* **(from)** vacu·us -a -um (ab *w. abl); (from tribute)* immun·is -is -e, lib·er -era -erum; **to be — from military service** militiae vacationem habēre
exemption *s* immunit·as -atis *f; (from military service)* vacati·o -onis *f* militiae
exercise *s (bodily)* exercitati·o -onis *f; (athletic)* palaestr·a -ae *f; (written; mil)* exercit·ium -(i)i *n; (literary)* them·a -atis *n; (use)* us·us -ūs *m*
exercise *tr* exercēre; *(to use)* uti, adhibēre **II** *intr* se exercēre
exert *tr* adhibēre; **to — oneself** viribus eniti
exertion *s* contenti·o -onis *f*, nis·us -ūs *m*
exhalation *s* exhalati·o -onis *f*
exhale *tr* exhalare **II** *intr* exspirare
exhaust *s* emissar·ium -(i)i *n*
exhaust *tr (to drain)* exhaurire; *(to tire out)* defatigare, conficere; **to — a subject** totam rem acuratissime plenissimeque tractare
exhausted *adj* fatigat·us -a -um, defess·us -a - um; **to be** *or* **become —** a viribus deficere
exhausting *adj* laborios·us -a -um
exhaustion *s* defecti·o -onis *f* virium
exhibit *tr* exhibēre; *(games)* ēdere
exhibition *s* exhibiti·o -onis *f; (display)* ostentati·o -onis *f; (public performance)* lud·i -orum *mpl; (gladiatorial show)* mun·us -eris *n*
exhilarate *tr* exhilare
exhilarating *adj* animum exhilar·ans -antis; **the morning air is —** exhilarant animos aurae matutinae
exhilaration *s* hilarit·as -atis *f*
exhort *tr* hortari
exhortation *s* hortam·en -inis *f; (act)* hortati·o -onis *f*
exhume *tr* exhumare
exigency *s* necessit·as -atis *f*
exile *s (temporary)* ex(s)il·ium -(i)i *n; (for life)* deportati·o -onis *f; (person)* exs·ul -ulis *mf*
exile *tr* exterminare; *(for a time)* relegare; *(for life)* deportare
exist *intr* esse, ex(s)istere; *(to be extant)* exstare; *(of human beings)* vivere
existence *s (of human beings)* vit·a -ae *f;* **he denies the — of gods** negat deos esse
exit *s* exit·us -ūs *m*
exonerate *tr* absolvere, culpā liberare
exorbitant *adj* immodic·us -a -um; **to make — demands** immodice postulare
exotic *adj* mirific·us -a -um
expand *tr* expandere, extendere **II** *intr* expandi, se extendere
expanse *s* spat·ium -(i)i *n*
expansion *s* prolati·o -onis *f; (fig)* auct·us -ūs *m*
expatriate *tr* exterminare
expatriate *s* exs·ul -ulis *mf*
expect *tr* exspectare; **not —ing** necopin·ans -antis; **sooner than —ed**

opinione celerius; **what do you —?** quid vis fieri?
expectancy *s* spe·s -i *f*
expectation *s* exspectati·o -onis *f;* **contrary to —** praeter opinionem
expectorate *tr & intr* exspuere
expediency *s* utilit·as -atis *f*
expedient *adj* util·is -is -e; **it is — that** expedit *(w. acc & inf)*
expedient *s* mod·us -i *m*
expedite *tr* expedire, maturare
expedition *s (mil)* expediti·o -onis *f; (speed)* celerit·as -atis *f;* **to lead troops on an —** copias educere in expeditionem
expeditious *adj* cel·er -eris -ere
expeditiously *adv* celeriter; **as — as possible** quam celerrime
expel *tr* expellere
expend *tr* impendere, expendere
expenditure *s* impens·a -ae *f*
expense *s (cost)* pret·ium -(i)i *n; (outlay)* impens·a -ae *f,* sumpt·us -ūs *m;* **at great —** magno sumptu; **at my own —** meo sumptu
expensive *adj* car·us -a -um, pretios·us -a -um, sumptuos·us -a -um
expensively *adv* sumptuose
experience *s* us·us -ūs *m,* experienti·a -ae *f;* **military —** usus *m* in re militari; **political —** usus *m* in republicā; **a man of long —** vi·r -ri *m* longā experientiā
experience *tr* experiri, cognoscere, subire
experienced *adj* **(in)** perit·us -a -um *(w. gen)*
experiment *s* experiment·um -i *n*
experimental *adj* usu comparat·us -a -um
expert *s* **(in)** peritissim·us -i *m* (·a -ae *f*) *(w. gen)*
expert *adj* **(in)** perit·us -a -um *(w. gen)*
expertly *adv* scienter, callide
expertness *s* callidit·as -atis *f*
expiate *tr* expiare, luere
expiation *s* expiati·o -onis *f*
expiration *s* exit·us -ūs *m;* **at the — of the fifth year** quinto anno exeunte
expire *intr (to die)* exspirare; *(of time)* exire
explain *tr* explanare, explicare
explainable *adj* explicabil·is -is -e
explanation *s* explanati·o -onis *f,* explicati·o -onis *f*
expletive *s* explement·um -i *n*
explicit *adj* apert·us -a -um
explicitly *adv* aperte, plane
explode *tr* displodere; *(fig)* explodere **||** *intr* displodi
exploit *s* facin·us -oris *n;* **—s** re·s -rum *fpl* gestae
exploit *tr* uti *(w. abl); (pej)* abuti *(w. abl)*
exploration *s* explorati·o -onis *f,* indagati·o -onis *f*
explore *tr* explorare, indagare
explorer *s* explorat·or -oris *m*
explosion *s* dirupti·o -onis *f; (sound)* frag·or -oris *m*
exponent *s* interpr·es -etis *mf*
export *tr* exportare, evehere
exporter *s* exportat·or -oris *m*
exports *spl* merc·es -ium *fpl* quae exportantur
expose *tr* exponere; *(to bare)* nudare; *(to uncover)* detegere; *(to danger)* obicere; **to be —ed to** patēre *(w. dat)*
exposition *s* expositi·o -onis *f*
exposure *s (to cold)* expositi·o -onis *f; (of guilt)* deprehensi·o -onis *f*
expound *tr* exponere, interpretari
express *adj* express·us -a -um
express *tr* exprimere; *(to show)* significare; **to — oneself** loqui, dicere
expression *s* verb·um -i *n; (of the face)* vult·us -ūs *m;* **joy beyond —** gaudia maiora quam quae verbis exprimi possint
expressive *adj* signific·ans -antis; *(eyes)* argut·us -a -um; *(fig)* loqu·ax -acis; **— of** ind·ex -icis *(w. gen)*
expressly *adv* plane
express train *s* tram·en -inis *n* citissimum
expressway *s* vi·a -ae *f* citissima
expulsion *s* expulsi·o -onis *f,* exacti·o -onis *f*
expunge *tr* oblitterare
expurgate *tr* expurgare
exquisite *adj* exquisit·us -a -um
exquisitely *adv* exquisite
extant *adj* superst·es -itis; **to be —** exstare
extempore *adv* ex tempore
extemporaneous *adj* extemporal·is -is -e
extemporaneously *adv* ex tempore
extemporize *intr* ex tempore dicere
extend *tr (time)* extendere, producere; *(a hand)* porrigere; **to — the empire** ampliare imperium; **to — the governor's term** prorogare imperium **||** *intr* extendi; *(of land, body of water)* tendere, patēre, pertinēre; **to — to** tendere ad *(w. acc);* **to extend over** *(to cover)* obtinēre
extension *s* extenti·o -onis *f; (lengthening)* producti·o -onis *f; (e.g., of the fingers)* porrigi·o -onis *f; (of size, of time)* prolati·o -onis *f;* **— of the term of office** prorogati·o -onis *f* imperii
extensive *adj* lat·us -a -um
extensively *adv* late
extent *s* spat·ium -(i)i *n; (of a country)* fin·es -ium *mpl;* **to a great —** magnā ex parte; **to some —** aliquā ex parte; **to this —** hactenus
extenuating *adj* **— circumstances** eae res quibus culpa minuitur
exterior *adj* exter·ior -ior -ius
exterior *s* speci·es -ei *f*
exterminate *tr* ad internecionem delēre
extermination *s* interneci·o -onis *f*
external *adj* extern·us -a -um
externally *adv* extrinsecus

extinct *adj* exstinct•us -a -um; **to become —** obsolescere
extinction *s* exstincti•o -onis *f*
extinguish *tr* exstinguere
extol *tr* laudibus efferre
extort *tr* extorquēre
extortion *s* res *fpl* repetundae
extortionist *s* extor•tor -toris *m* (•trix -tricis *f*)
extra *adj* addit•us -a -um; **— charge** additament•um -i *n* pretii
extra *adv* insuper, praeterea
extract *s (chemical)* expressi•o -onis *f; (literary)* excerpt•um -i *n; (synopsis)* compend•ium -(i)i *n*
extract *tr* extrahere; *(to squeeze out)* exprimere; *(teeth)* evellere; *(from a literary source)* excerpere
extraction *s (act)* evulsi•o -onis *f; (descent)* stirp•s -is *f;* **of German —** oriund•us -a -um a Germanis
extracurricular *adj* extraordinari•us -a -um
extraneous *adj* alien•us -a -um
extraordinarily *adv* praeter modum
extraordinary *adj* extraordinari•us -a -um, insolit•us -a -um; *(outstanding)* eximi•us -a -um
extravagance *s* sumpt•us -ūs *m*
extravagant *adj (exceeding bounds)* immodic•us -a -um; *(in expenditure)* sumptuos•us -a -um; *(spending)* prodig•us -a -um
extravagantly *adv* immodice; *(expensively)* sumptuose; *(lavishly)* profuse, prodige
extreme *adj* extrem•us -a -um
extreme *s* extrem•um -i *n;* **from one — to another** ab imo ad summum; **in the —** ad extremum; **to go to —s** descendere ad extrema
extremely *adv* summe, perquam
extremist *s* assecta•tor -toris *m* (•trix -tricis *f*) rerum novarum
extremity *s* extremit•as -atis *f,* extrem•um -i *n;* **extremities of the body** eminentes part•es -ium *fpl* corporis; **we have been reduced to extremities** ad extrema perventum est
extricate *tr* expedire, extrahere
extrinsic *adj* extrari•us -a -um
extrude *tr* extrudere ‖ *intr* extrudi
exuberance *s (of growth)* luxuri•es -ei *f; (of spirit)* redundanti•a -ae *f*
exuberant *adj (growth)* luxurios•us -a -um; *(unrestrained)* effus•us -a -um; **to be —** *(of style)* redundare
exude *tr* exudare ‖ *intr* emanare
exult *intr* exsultare, gestire
exultant *adj* laetabund•us -a -um
exultantly *adv* laete
exultation *s* exsultati•o -onis *f*
eye *s* ocul•us -i *m; (of needle)* foram•en -inis *n; (of plant)* gemm•a -ae *f;* **blind in one —** lusc•us -a -um; **keep your — on that guy!** adserva *(pl:* adservate) istum!; **keep your —s open!** cave circumspicias!; **look me in the —!** aspicedum contra me!; **to be in the public —** scaenae servire; **to keep an — on** cavēre, in oculis habēre; **to shut one's —s to** conivēre; **with —s wide open** hiantibus oculis
eye *tr* aspicere
eyeball *s* orb•is -is *m* oculi, ocul•us -i *m*
eyebrow *s* supercil•ium -(i)i *n*
eyeglasses *spl* perspicill•a -orum *npl;* **to wear —** perspicillis uti
eyelash *s* palpebrae pil•us -i *m;* **—s** palpebrarum pil•i -orum *mpl*
eyelid *s* palpebr•a -ae *f*
eyesight *s* aci•es -ei *f,* vis•us -ūs *m;* **to lose one's —** oculos perdere
eyesore *s (fig)* res, rei *f* taetra
eyewitness *s* oculat•us (-a) test•is -is *mf*

F

fable *s* fabul•a -ae *f*
fabled *adj* fabulos•us -a -um
fabric *s (pattern of weaving)* text•us -us *m; (framework)* fabric•a -ae *f;* **coarse (sheer, thin; thick) —** crassus (tenuis; pinguis) textus
fabricate *tr* fabricare; *(fig)* fingere
fabrication *s* fabricati•o -onis *f; (fig)* comment•um - *n*
fabulous *adj* mirabil•is -is -e
fabulously *adv* perquam
face *s* faci•es -ei *f,* o•s -ris *n; (forward part of anything)* fron•s -tis *f;* **— to —** coram; **— to — with** coram *(w. abl);* **on the — of it** primā facie; **to lose —** honestatem amittere; **to make a —** os ducere; **to one's —** coram; **to save —** dignitatem conservare
face *tr (to look towards)* aspicere; *(to withstand, e.g., danger)* obviam ire *(w. dat); (to confront)* se opponere *(w. dat)* ‖ *intr* spectare; **to — about** *(mil)* signa convertere; **to — north (south,** *etc.)* ad *or* in septentrionem (in meridiem, *etc.)* spectare
face powder *s* fuc•us -i *m*
facet *s* gemmae superfici•es -ei *f; (fig)* aspect•us -ūs *m*
facetious *adj* facet•us -a -um
facetiously *adv* facete
face value *s (com)* nom•en -inis *n; (fig)* speci•es -ei *f*
facilitate *tr* facilius reddere
facility *s (skill)* facult•as -atis *f; (ease)* facilit•as -atis *f;* **facilities** commod•a -orum *npl*
facing *s (archit)* tector•ium -(i)i *n*
facing *adj* adversus *(w. acc)*
facsimile *s* imag•o -inis *f*

fact *s* fact·um -i *n*, res, rei *f*; **as a matter of —** enimvero; **in —** vero, quidem; **the — that ...** quod (*w. indic*); **the —s speak for themselves** res ipsa indicat *or* res pro se loquitur

faction *s* facti·o -onis *f*; *(party)* part·es -ium *fpl*

factory *s* officin·a -ae *f*

faculty *s* facult·as -atis *f*; *(educ)* ord·o -inis *m* professorum

fade *intr (of colors)* pallēre; *(of strength, etc.)* marcescere; **to — away** evanescere

fag, faggot *s (sl)* cinaed·us -i *m*

fail *tr (to disappoint)* deficere; *(to desert)* deserere, destituere; **time, voice, lungs — me** me dies, vox, latera deficiunt; **to — a test** probatione cadere; **words — me** quid dicam non invenio ‖ *intr* deficere; *(educ)* cadere; *(com)* decoquere

fail *s* **without —** certo, omnino

failing *s (deficiency)* defect·us -ūs *m*; *(fault)* vit·ium -(i)i *n*; *(ceasing)* remissi·o -onis *f*

failure *s (of strength, breath, supplies)* defecti·o -onis *f*; *(lack of success)* offensi·o -onis *f*; *(com)* ruin·a -ae *f* fortunarum; *(person)* hom·o -inis *mf* perditus (-a); *(fault)* vit·ium -(i)i *n*

faint *adj (weary)* fess·us -a -um; *(drooping)* languid·us -a -um; *(sight, etc.)* heb·es -itis; *(sound)* surd·us -a -um; *(colors)* pallid·us -a -um; *(courage)* timid·us -a -um

faint *intr* collabi, animo linqui

faint-hearted *adj* ignav·us -a -um

faintness *s (of impression)* levit·as -atis *f*; *(of body)* langu·or -oris *m*

fair *adj (handsome)* pul·cher -chra -chrum; *(complexion)* candid·us -a -um; *(hair)* flav·us -a -um; *(weather)* seren·us -a -um; *(cloudless)* sud·us -a -um; *(wind)* secund·us -a -um; *(impartial)* aequ·us -a -um; *(ability)* mediocr·is -is -e; **— and square** sine fuco ac fallaciis; **I think that's —** id aequi facio; **that's not — of you** non aequum facis

fair *s* nundin·ae -arum *fpl*

fairground *s* prat·um -i *n* festivum

fairly *adv* aeque; *(somewhat)* aliquantulūm; *(moderately)* mediocriter

fair-minded *adj (just)* iust·us -a -um; *(impartial)* aequ·us -a -um

fairness *s (justice)* aequit·as -atis *f*; *(of complexion)* cand·or -oris *m*

fairy *s* num·en -inis *n*; *(water fairy)* nymph·a -ae *f*; *(wood fairy)* dry·as -adis *f*; *(homosexual) (sl)* cinaed·us -i *m*

fairytale *s* fabul·a -ae *f*

faith *s* fid·es -ei *f*; **in bad —** de fide malā; **in good —** ex bonā fide; **to have — in** credere *(w. dat)*

faithful *adj* fid·us -a -um, fidel·is -is -e

faithfully *adv* fideliter

faithfulness *s* fidelit·as -atis *f*

faithless *adj* infidel·is -is -e

faithlessly *adv* perfide

fake *s* simulati·o -onis *f*; *(person)* simula·tor -oris *m* (·trix -tricis *f*)

fake *adj* fucos·us -a -um, fall·ax -acis

fake *tr* simulare

falcon *s* falc·o -onis *m*

fall *s (drop)* cas·us -ūs *m*; *(by slipping)* laps·us -ūs *m*; *(autumn)* autumn·us -i *m*; *(e.g., of a tower)* ruin·a -ae *f*; *(of a town)* excid·ium -(i)i *n*; *(decrease)* deminuti·o -onis *f*; *(moral)* laps·us -ūs *m*; **the —s** desiliens aqu·a -ae *f*

fall *intr* cadere; *(several together)* concidere; *(to die)* occidere; *(to abate)* decrescere; *(violently)* corruere; *(to occur)* accidere, incidere; *(by lot)* contingere; **to — apart** dilabi; **to — at the feet of** procubare ad pedes *(w. gen)*; **to — asleep** in somnum decidere, obdormiscere; **to — away** desciscere; **to — back** recidere; *(to retreat)* pedem referre; **to — back on** recurrere ad *(w. acc)*; **to — down on** *(e.g., the bed)* decidere in *(w. acc)*; **to — due** cadere; **to — for** *(a person)* amore perdi in *(w. acc)*; *(a trick)* falli *(w. abl)*; **to — forwards** procidere, prolabi; **to — in love with** amare, coepisse amare; **to — into** incidere in *(w. acc)*; **to — in with** *(to meet)* incidere in *(w. acc)*; *(to agree)* congruere cum *(w. abl)*; **to — into a trap** in plagas incidere; **to — into the hands of** in manūs *(w. gen)* incidere, in potestatem *(w. gen)* devenire; **to — off** *(e.g., a wagon)* decidere de *or* ex *(w. abl)*; *(fig)* in deterius mutari; **to — on** *(a certain day)* incidere in *(w. acc)*; **to — on one's sword** in gladium incumbere; **to — on top of** incidere super *(w. acc)*; **to — out** *(mil)* ordine egredi; **to — out of** excidere de *(w. abl)*; **to — out with** *(in disagreement)* dissentire ab *(w. abl)*; **to — short of** non contingere; **to — over** *(to topple over)* cadere; *(to stumble over)* pedem offendere ad *(w. acc)*; **to — short** deficere; **to — short of the goal** metam non contingere; **to — sick** in morbum incidere; **to — to** *(of inheritances, etc.)* obvenire *(w. dat)*; **to — to the ground** in terram decidere; **to — under** *(to be listed under)* cadere sub *(w. acc)*; **to — under s.o.'s sway** in ditionem alicuius venire, in potestatem alicuius cadere; **to — upon** incidere ad *(w. acc)*; *(to assail)* incidere in *(w. acc)*; **to let —** demittere

fallacious *adj* fall·ax -acis

fallacy *s* capti·o -onis *f*

fallible *adj* errori obnoxi·us -a -um

fallow *adj (land)* noval·is -is -e; **to lie —** cessare

false *adj* fals·us -a -um; *(counterfeit)* adulterin·us -a -um

falsehood *s* comment·um -i *n*

falsely *adv* falso
falsify *tr (documents)* corrumpere; *(to tamper with)* vitiare
falsity *s* fals·um -i *n*
falter *intr (to stammer)* haesitare; *(to totter)* titubare
falteringly *adv* titubanter
fame *s* fam·a -ae *f,* clarit·as -atis *f*
famed *adj* clar·us -a -um
familiar *adj* **(with)** familiar·is -is -e *(w. dat); (well known)* not·us -a -um; **to be on — terms with** familiariter uti *(w. abl)*
familiarity *s* familiarit·as -atis *f;* **to be on terms of — with** familiariter uti *(w. abl)*
familiarize *tr* **(with)** assuefacere *(w. dat)*
family *s (parents and children)* dom·us -ūs *f; (household and domestics)* famili·a -ae *f;* **— on the father's (mother's) side** paternum (maternum) gen·us -eris *n;* **to come from a good —** honesto loco nat·us -a -um esse
family *adj* familiar·is -is -e; **— inheritance** heredit·as -atis *f* gentilicia; **— name** gentile nom·en -inis *n;* **— secrets** arcan·a -orum *npl* domūs; **— tree** gen·us -eris *n,* stemm·a -atis *n*
famine *s* fam·es -is *f*
famished *adj* famelic·us -a -um
famous *adj* (prae)clar·us -a -um; **— for** inclut·us -a -um *(w. abl)*
famously *adv* insigniter
fan *s* flabell·um -i *n; (admirer)* fau·tor -toris *m* (·trix -tricis *f*); *(winnowing)* vann·us -i *m*
fan *tr* ventilare; *(fire)* accendere; *(fig)* excitare
fanatic *adj* fanatic·us -a -um
fanaticism *s* fur·or -oris *m* (religiosus)
fancied *adj* fict·us -a -um
fanciful *adj* commentici·us -a -um
fancy *adj* sumptuos·us -a -um, pretios·us -a -um
fancy *s* imaginati·o -onis *f; (caprice)* libid·o -inis *f; (liking)* prolub·ium -(i)i *n*
fancy *tr* imaginari
fang *s* den·s -tis *m*
fantastic *adj (unreal)* van·us -a -um; *(wonderful)* mirific·us -a -um
far *adj* longinqu·us -a -um; **on the — side of the Po** ultra Padum
far *adv* procul; *(of degree)* longe; **as — as** quantum, quatenus; *(up to)* tenus *(always after the governed word) (w. abl or gen);* **as — as I'm concerned** per me; **as — as the neck** cervicibus tenus; **by —** longe, multo; **by — the wealthiest state** longe opulentissima civit·as -atis *f;* **— away** procul; **— and near** longe lateque; **— be it from me to say** equidem dicere nolim; **— from it!** minime!; **— off** procul; **— otherwise** longe aliter; **how —** quoad, quousque; **so —** hactenus; **so — so good** belle adhuc; **thus —** hactenus; **to be — away (from)** longe abesse (ab *w. abl);* **to be very — from the truth** longissime abesse a vero
faraway *adj (distant)* longuinqu·us -a -um
farce *s (lit & fig)* mim·us -i *m*
farcical *adj* mimic·us -a -um
fare *s (food)* vict·us -ūs *m; (money)* vectur·a -ae *f; (passenger)* vec·tor -toris *m* (·trix -tricis *f*)
fare *intr* agere, se habēre
farewell *interj* vale! *(pl:* valete!)
far-fetched *adj* arcessit·us -a -um, quaesit·us -a -um; **— idea** quisitum consil·ium -(i)i *n*
far-flung *adj* late pat·ens -entis
farm *s* fund·us -i *m,* rus, ruris *n;* **on the —** ruri
farm *tr (to till)* arare, colere; *(taxes)* redimere; **to — out** locare
farm animals *spl* pecor·a -um *npl*
farmer *s* agricol·a -ae *m*
farm house *s* vill·a -ae *f* (rustica)
farming *s* agricultur·a -ae *f*
farm worker *s* colon·us -i *m*
far-off *adj* longinqu·us -a -um
far-reaching *adj* grav·is -is -e
farsighted *adj* provid·us -a -um
fart *s (sl)* pedit·um -i *n*
fart *intr (sl)* pedere
farther *adj* ulter·ior -ior -ius
farther *adv* longius, ulterius; **no — than** non ultra quam; **to advance —** procedere ulterius
farthermost *adj* ultim·us -a -um
farthest *adj* ultim·us -a -um
fasces *spl* fasc·es -ium *fpl*
fascinate *tr* capere
fascinating *adj* mirific·us -a -um, bland·us -a -um
fascination *s* blanditi·a -ae *f*
fashion *s* mod·us -i *m,* mo·s -ris *m;* **to be in — more** fieri; **to come into —** in morem venire; **to go out of —** obsolescere
fashion *tr* fabricare; *(to form a figure of)* effingere
fashionable *adj* eleg·ans -antis; **it is — moris** est
fashionably *adv* ad morem
fast *adj (swift)* cel·er -eris -ere; *(firm)* firm·us -a -um; *(tight)* astrict·us -a -um; *(shut)* occlus·us -a -um; *(color)* stabil·is -is -e; *(talk)* expedit·us -a -um
fast *adv (swiftly)* celeriter; *(firmly)* firmiter; **to be — asleep** arte dormire
fast *s* ieiun·ium -(i)i *n;* **to break the —** ieiunium solvere; **to keep the —** ieiunium servare
fast *intr* ieiunare, cibo abstinēre
fasten *tr* affigere, astringere; *(to tie)* ligare; **to — down** defigere; **to — to** *(w. nails, rivets)* affigere *(w. dat or* ad *w. acc); (by tying)* annectere, illigare *(w. dat or* ad *w. acc);* **to — together** *(w. nails, etc.)* con-

figere; *(by tying)* connectere, colligare ‖ *intr* **to — upon** arripere
fastener *s (clip)* fibul·a -ae *f*
fastening *s (act)* colligati·o -onis *f; (device)* vincul·um -i *n*
fastidious *adj* fastidios·us -a -um
fastidiously *adv* fastidiose
fasting *s* ieiun·ium -(i)i *n*
fat *adj* pingu·is -is -e; **to get —** pinguescere
fat *s* ad·eps -ipis *mf*
fatal *adj* fatal·is -is -e, letal·is -is -e
fatality *s* cas·us -ūs *m* fatalis
fatally *adv* fataliter
fate *s* fat·um -i *n; (lot)* sor·s -tis *f*
fated *adj* fatal·is -is -e
fateful *adj* fatal·is -is -e
Fates *spl* Parc·ae -arum *fpl*
fathead *s (sl)* fatu·us -i *m* (·a -ae *f*)
father *s* pa·ter -tris *m;* **— of the family** paterfamilias *(gen:* patrisfamilias) *m;* **on the —'s side** patri·us -a -um
fatherhood *s* paternit·as -atis *f*
father-in-law *s* soc·er -eri *m*
fatherless *adj* orb·us -a -um
fatherly *adj* patern·us -a -um; *(kind)* patri·us -a -um
fathom *s* uln·a -ae *f*
fathom *tr* penitus cognoscere
fathomless *adj* profund·us -a -um
fatigue *s* (de)fatigati·o -onis *f*
fatigue *tr* (de)fatigare
fatigued *adj* (de)fatigat·us -a -um
fatten *tr* saginare ‖ *intr* **to — up** pinguescere
fatty *adj* pingu·is -is -e; **all — substances** omnia quae adipis naturam habent
fatuous *adj* fatu·us -a -um
faucet *s* epitom·ium -(i)i *n;* **to turn on (off) the —** epitomium versare (reversare)
fault *s* culp·a -ae *f,* delict·um -i *n;* **I am at —** in culpā sum, penes me culpa est; **not to be at —** extra culpam esse; **to be at —** *(leg)* in noxā esse; **to find — with** vituperare
faultless *adj* inte·ger -gra -grum; *(without blemish)* emendat·us -a -um
faultlessly *adv* emendate
faulty *adj* vitios·us -a -um; *(having errors)* mendos·us -a -um
faun *s* faun·us -i *m*
favor *s* fav·or -oris *m; (good will of a party or nation)* grati·a -ae *f; (good turn)* benefic·ium -(i)i *n,* grat·um -i *n,* grati·a -ae *f;* **to ask s.o. a —** gratiam ab aliquo petere; **to be in — of** favēre *(w. dat);* **to be in — with s.o.** cum aliquo in gratiā esse; **to do s.o. a —** gratum alicui facere; **to do s.o. a bigger —** gratius alicui facere; **to return s.o. a —** gratiam alicui referre; **to restore s.o. to —** aliquem in gratiam restituere; **to show —** gratiam facere
favor *tr* favēre *(w. dat),* secundare; **to — severer measures** asperiora suadēre
favorable *adj* prosper·us -a -um; *(wind, circumstances, auspices, gods)* secund·us -a -um; *(suitable)* idone·us -a -um
favorably *adv* benigne; **to be — disposed toward s.o.** bono animo esse in aliquem
favored *adj* grat·us -a -um
favorite *adj* dilect·us -a -um
favorite *s* delici·ae -arum *fpl*
favoritism *s* iniquit·as -atis *f*
fawn *s* hinnule·us -i *m*
fawn *intr* **to — on** adulari
fawning *adj* bland·us -a -um
fax *s* telecopi·a -ae *f*
fax *tr* per telecopiam mittere
fax machine telecopiatr·um -i *n*
fear *s* met·us -ūs *m; (timidity, as a variety of* metus) tim·or -oris *m;* **he put the — of God into them** curavit ut illis Iuppiter iratus esset; **out of —** prae metu; **to be in —** in metu esse; **to be in — of** metuere; **to be inspired with —** metum capere
fear *tr & intr* timēre; *(as a constant condition)* metuere
fearful *adj* **(of)** timid·us -a -um *(w. gen or* ad *w. acc); (dreadful)* terribil·is -is -e, dir·us -a -um
fearless *adj* impavid·us -a -um
fearlessly *adv* impavide, intrepide
feasibility *s* possibilit·as -atis *f*
feasible *adj* possibil·is -is -e
feast *s* epul·ae -arum *fpl; (religious)* di·es -ei *m* festus
feast *tr* pascere; **to — one's eyes on** oculos pascere *(w. abl)* ‖ *intr* epulari
feat *s* facin·us -oris *n;* **— of arms** facinus *n* militare; **—s** re·s -rum *fpl* gestae
feather *s* penn·a -ae *f; (downy)* plum·a -ae *f*
feather *tr* **to — one's nest** *(fig)* opes accumulare
feathered *adj* pennat·us -a -um
feathery *adj* plumos·us -a -um
feature *s* lineament·um -i *n; (fig)* propriet·as -atis *f*
February *s* Februar·ius -(i)i *m or* mens·is -is *m* Februarius; **in —** mense Februario; **on the first of —** Kalendis Februariis
federal *adj* foederat·us -a -um
federalize *tr* confoederare
federation *s* consociati·o -onis *f*
fee *s* merc·es -edis *f; (for tuition)* Minerv·al -alis *n; (for membership)* honorar·ium -(i)i *n*
feeble *adj (infirm)* imbecill·us -a -um; *(frail)* infirm·us -a -um; *(senses, impression made)* heb·es -etis; **to grow —** languescere
feebleness *s* imbecillit·as -atis *f*
feebly *adv* infirme
feed *tr* pascere; *(to nourish)* alere, nutrire; *(of streams, etc.)* servire *(w. dat)* ‖ *intr* **(on)** pasci *(w. abl),* vesci *(w. abl)*
feed *s* pabul·um -i *n*

feel *tr (hunger, pain, heat, cold, etc.)* sentire; *(with hands)* tentare; **to — compassion for** misereri *(w. gen);* **to — grief** dolēre; **to — one's way** viam tentare; *(fig)* caute et cogitate rem tractare; **to — pain** dolore affici; **to — pity for** misereri *(w. gen);* **to — the pulse** *(med)* pulsum venarum attingere, venas tentare ‖ *intr* **because I felt like it** quia mihi libitum est; **I wasn't —ing well** ego me non belle habebam; **to — annoyed** gravari; **to — bad (good)** *(physically)* se male (bene) habēre; **to — better** *(physically)* melius se habēre; **to — fine** se bene habere; **to feel glad** laetari; **to — happy** gaudēre; **to — really bad about** valde dolere; **to — sad** maest·us -a -um esse
feel *s* tact·us -ūs *m*
feeler *s* experiment·um -i *n;* **to send out —s to** tentare
feeling *s (touch, sensation)* tact·us -ūs *m; (sensibility)* sens·us -ūs *m; (emotion)* affect·us -ūs *m; (taste)* iudic·ium -(i)i *n; (compassion)* misericordi·a -ae *f;* **to hurt s.o.'s —s** aliquem offendere
feign *tr* fingere, dissimulare
feint *s* simulati·o -onis *f*
felicitous *adj* fel·ix -icis
feline *adj* felin·us -a -um
fell *tr (trees)* caedere; *(person)* sternere
fellow *s (companion)* soc·ius -(i)i *m; (coll)* hom·o -inis *m;* **my good —, what have you there?** mi homo, quid istuc est?; **young —** adulescentul·us -i *m*
fellow citizen *s* civ·is -is *mf*
fellow countryman *s* civ·is -is *m*
fellow creature *s* hom·o -inis *m*
fellow man *s* alt·er -erius *m*
fellow member *s* sodal·is -is *mf*
fellow passenger *s* convec·tor -toris *m* (·trix -tricis *f*)
fellow soldier *s* commilit·o -onis *m*
fellow student *s* condiscipul·us -i *m* (·a -ae *f*)
fellowship *s* sodalit·as -atis *f; (award)* stipend·ium -(i)i *n* in sumptūs studiosorum
fellow townsman *s* munic·eps -ipis *m*
fellow worker *s* soci·us -i *m* (·a -ae *f*) operum
felon *s* scelest·us -i *m* (·a -ae *f*)
felonious *adj* scelest·us -a -um
felony *s* scel·us -eris *n*
felt *adj* coact·us -a -um
felt *s* coact·a -orum *npl*
female *adj* muliebr·is -is -e
female *s* muli·er -eris *f*
feminine *adj* muliebr·is -is -e; *(gram)* feminin·us -a -um
fence *s* saep·es -is *f*
fence *tr* **to — in (off)** saepire ‖ *intr* batuere
fencing *s* gladii ar·s -tis *f*
fend *tr* **to — off** arcēre ‖ *intr* **to — for oneself** sibi consulere
fender *s* luticipul·um -i *n*
ferment *s* ferment·um -i *n; (fig)* aest·us -ūs *m*
ferment *tr* fermentare; *(fig)* excitare ‖ *intr* fermentari; *(fig)* fervēre
fermentation *s* fermentati·o -onis *f*
fern *s* fil·ix -icis *f*
ferocious *adj* saev·us -a -um
ferociously *adv* saeve
ferocity *s* saeviti·a -ae *f*
ferret *tr* **to — out** eruere
ferry *s* nav·is -is *f* traiectoria
ferry *tr* traicere
ferryboat *s* cymb·a -ae *f*
ferryman *s* portit·or -oris *m*
fertile *adj* fertil·is -is -e
fertility *s* fertilit·as -atis *f*
fertilize *tr* laetificare
fertilizer *s* laetam·en -inis *n*
fervent *adj* ard·ens -entis
fervently *adv* ardenter
fervid *adj* fervid·us -a -um
fervidly *adv* fervide
fervor *s* ferv·or -oris *m*
fester *intr* suppurare
festival *s* fest·um -i *n*
festive *adj* festiv·us -a -um
festivity *s (celebration)* solemn·ia -ium *npl; (gaiety)* festivit·as -atis *f*
fetch *tr (to summon)* arcessere; *(to go to get)* petere
fetid *adj* foetid·us -a -um
fetter *s* comp·es -edis *m*
fetter *tr* compedes inicere *(w. dat); (fig)* impedire
feud *s* simult·as -atis *f*
fever *s* febr·is -is *f;* **high —** ardens febris *f;* **slight —** febricul·a -ae *f;* **to have** *(or* **to run) a —** febricitare
feverish *adj* febriculos·us -a -um
few *adj* pauc·i -ae -a; **a —** aliquot [*indecl*]; **in a — words** paucis
fiasco *s* calamit·as -atis *f*
fiber *s* fibr·a -ae *f*
fickle *adj* mobil·is -is -e
fickleness *s* mobilit·as -atis *f*
fiction *s* ficti·o -onis *f;* narrati·o -onis *f* fabulosa
fictitious *adj* fict·us -a -um
fictitiously *adv* ficte
fiddle *s* fid·es -ium *fpl*
fiddle *intr* fidibus canere
fiddler *s* fidic·en -inis *m,* fidicin·a -ae *f*
fiddlesticks *spl (coll)* nugae!
fidelity *s* fidelit·as -atis *f*
fidget *intr* trepidare
fidgety *adj* inquiet·us -a -um
field *s* ager, agri *m; (plowed)* arv·um -i *n; (undeveloped)* camp·us -i *m; (sports)* are·a -ae *f; (mil)* aci·es -ei *f; (of studies)* disciplin·a -ae *f*
fiend *s* diabol·us -i *m*
fiendish *adj* diabolic·us -a -um

fierce *adj* atr•ox -ocis; *(intensive)* fer•ox -ocis
fiercely *adv* atrociter; ferociter
fierceness *s* atrocit•as -atis *f;* ferocit•as -atis *f*
fiery *adj* igne•us -a -um; *(fig)* ard•ens -entis
fife *s* tibi•a -ae *f*
fifteen *adj* quindecim [*indecl*]; — **times** quindecies
fifteenth *adj* quint•us decim•us -a -um
fifth *adj* quint•us -a -um; **for the — time** quinto
fifth *s* quinta par•s -tis *f*
fiftieth *adj* quinquagesim•us -a -um
fifty *adj* quinquaginta [*indecl*]
fig *s (fruit, tree)* fic•us -i *f*
fight *s* pugn•a -ae *f; (battle)* proel•ium -(i)i *n; (brawl)* rix•a -ae *f; (boxing)* pugilati•o -onis *f*
fight *tr* pugnare cum *(w. abl)* ‖ *intr* pugnare; *(to brawl)* rixari; *(to box)* pugilari; *(w. sword)* digladiari; **to — it out** depugnare; **to — hand to hand** cominus pugnare
figment *s* **— of the imagination** figment•um -i *n*
figurative *adj* translat•us -a -um
figuratively *adv* per translationem
figure *s* figur•a -ae *f; (any form)* form•a -ae *f; (in a painting)* imag•o -inis *f;* **female** — forma muliebris
figure *tr (to think)* putare; **to — out** excogitare ‖ *intr* **to — on** niti *(w. abl)*
figured *adj (adorned w. figures)* sigillat•us -a -um
figure of speech *s* figur•a -ae *f* orationis
figure skating *s* patinati•o -onis *f* artificiosa
filament *s* fil•um -i *n*
filbert *s* nu•x -cis *f* avellana
file *s (for iron)* lim•a -ae *f; (for woodwork)* scobin•a -ae *f; (for papers)* scap•us -i *m; (cabinet)* scrin•ium -(i)i *n; (row)* ord•o -inis *m; (comput)* document•um -i *n;* **—s** document•a -orum *npl,* act•a -orum *npl;* **in single** — singul•i -ae -a per ordinem
filial *adj* pi•us -a -um
filibuster *intr* legem latam orationibus protractis retardare
filings *spl* scob•is -is *f*
fill *s* **to have one's** — se replēre
fill *tr* implēre; *(office)* fungi *(w. abl)*; **to — up** complēre, explēre ‖ *intr* **to — up on** se implēre *(w. abl)*
filly *s* equul•a -ae *f*
film *s (haze)* calig•o -inis *f; (for camera)* taeniol•a -ae *f,* pellicul•a -ae *f;* **documentary** — taeniola documentaria; **movie** — taeniola cinematographica; **photographic** — taeniola photographica; **to show a** — taeniolam (cinematographicam) exhibēre
filter *s* col•um -i *n*
filter *tr* percolare ‖ *intr* percolari
filtering *s* percolati•o -onis *f*
filth *s* sord•es -ium *fpl*
filthiness *s* squal•or -oris *m; (fig)* obscenit•as -atis *f*
filthy *adj* sordid•us -a -um; *(fig)* obscen•us -a -um
filtration *s* percolati•o -onis *f*
fin *s* pinn•a -ae *f*
final *adj* ultim•us -a -um
finally *adv* denique, postremo
finance *s (private)* res, rei *f* familiaris; *(public)* rati•o -onis *f* aeraria
finance *tr* faenerare
financial *adj* pecuniari•us -a -um
find *tr* invenire, reperire; *(to hit upon)* offendere; **to — out** cognoscere
finder *s* reper•tor -toris *m* (•trix -tricis *f*)
findings *spl* compert•a -orum *npl*
fine *adj (thin)* tenu•is -is -e; *(opp. of coarse)* subtil•is -is -e; *(superior)* perbon•us -a -um; *(nice)* bell•us -a -um; *(weather)* seren•us -a -um; — **arts** art•es -ium *fpl* elegantiores *(or* ingenuae); **that's** — bene hoc est; **to feel** — se bene habēre; **you did** — probe fecisti
fine *s* mul(c)t•a -ae *f*
fine *tr* mul(c)tare *(w. abl of the fine)*
finery *s* munditi•ae -arum *fpl*
finesse *s* arguti•ae -arum *fpl;* **with** — argute
finger *s* digit•us -i *m; (of glove)* digital•e -is *n;* **index** — index digitus *m;* **little** — minimus digitus *m;* **middle** — medius digitus *m; (as an obscene gesture)* digitus inpudicus *or* infamis *or* obscenus; **not lift a** — pressis manibus sedēre; **ring** — minimo proximus digitus; **to point the — at** digitum intendere ad *(w. acc);* **to snap the —s** digitis concrepare
finger *tr (to handle)* attrectare; *(to inform on)* deferre; *(mus)* pulsare
fingernail *s* ungu•is -is *m*
fingertip *s* digit•us -i *m* primoris
finicky *adj* fastidios•us -a -um; — **appetite** fastid•ium -(i)i *n*
finish *s* fin•is -is *m; (in art)* perfecti•o -onis *f; (polish)* politur•a -ae *f*
finish *tr* conficere; *(to put an end to)* terminare; **to — off** conficere; *(to use up)* consumere; *(to destroy)* perdere; *(to kill)* occidere; **to add the —ing touch to** ultimam manum afferre *(w. dat)*; **to — speaking** sermonem finire; **to — writing** *(a book, etc.)* absolvere ‖ *intr* desinere
finish line *s (sports)* calx, calcis *f,* cret•a -ae *f*
finite *adj* finit•us -a -um
fire *s* ign•is -is *m; (conflagration)* incend•ium -(i)i *n; (of artillery)* coniect•us -ūs *m; (fig)* ard•or -oris *m;* **by — and sword** ferro ignique; **on** — flagr•ans -antis; **to be on** — ardēre; **to catch** — ignem concipere; **to put out a** — incendium exstinguere; **to set on** — incendere, inflammare

fire *tr* accendere; *(missile)* conicere; *(to dismiss)* amovēre
fire alarm *s* sign·um -i *n* monitorium incendii
fire chief *s* praefect·us -i *m* vigilum
fire engine *s* siph·o -onis *m*
firefighter *s* vig·il -is *mf*
fireplace *s* foc·us -i *m*
fireproof *adj* ignibus impervi·us -a -um
fireside *s* foc·us -i *m*
fire station *s* stati·o -onis *f* vigilum
firewood *s* lign·a -orum *npl*
fireworks spectacul·um -i *n* pyrotechnicum
firm *adj* firm·us -a -um; *(foundation)* stabil·is -is -e; **to stand —** perstare
firm *s (com)* societ·as -atis *f*
firmament *s* cael·um -i *n*
firmly *adv* firme; *(w. firm hold)* tenaciter
firmness *s* firmit·as -atis *f*
first *adj* prim·us -a -um; *(of two)* pri·or -or -us; **among the —** in primis; **for the — time** primum; **he was the — to enter** primus intravit
first *adv* primum; **at —** primo; **— of all** imprimis
first aid *s* prima curati·o -onis *f*
firstborn *adj* primogenit·us -a -um
first-class *adj* eximi·us -a -um; *(masterly)* graphic·us -a -um; **— seat** sed·es -is *f* primae classis
first fruits *spl* primiti·ae -arum *fpl*
fiscal *adj* aerari·us -a -um; *(belonging to the emperor's finances)* fiscal·is -is -e
fish *s* pisc·is -is *m; (as food)* piscat·us -ūs *m;* **little —** *(lit & fig)* piscicul·us -i *m;* **to catch —** pisces captare
fish *tr* piscari; **to — for** *(fig)* expiscari; **to go fishing** piscatum ire
fisher *s* pisc·ator -toris *m* (·trix -tricis *f*)
fishhook *s* ham·us -i *m*
fishing *s* piscat·us -ūs *m*
fishing line *s* lin·um -i *n*
fishing rod *s* (h)arund·o -inis *f* (piscatoria)
fishing tackle *s* instrument·um -i *n* piscatorium
fish market *s* for·um -i *n* piscarium
fish pond *s* piscin·a -ae *f*
fishy *adj* pisculent·us -a -um; *(fig)* suspicios·us -a -um
fissure *s* fissur·a -ae *f*
fist *s* pugn·us -i *m;* **to make a —** pugnum facere
fistfight *s* **to have a —** pugnis certare
fistula *s* fistul·a -ae *f*
fit *s (of anger, etc.)* impet·us -ūs *m;* **a good —** vestiment·um -i *n* bene factum; **by —s and starts** carptim; **fainting —** defecti·o -onis *f;* **—s** morb·us -i *m* comitialis; **to have the —s** *(fig)* delirare; *(in anger)* furere
fit *adj* **(for)** apt·us -a -um, idone·us -a -um *(w. dat); (healthy)* san·us -a -um
fit *tr* accommodare; *(to apply)* applicare; **to — out** instruere, ornare ‖ *intr* convenire; **to — in with** congruere cum *(w. abl);* **to — together** inter se cohaerēre
fitful *adj (sleep)* inquiet·us -a -um
fitly *adv* apte
fitness *s* convenienti·a -ae *f; (of persons)* habilit·as -atis *f*
fitting *adj* dec·ens -entis; **it is —** convenit, decet
five *adj* quinque [*indecl*]; *(distributives)* quin·i -ae -a, *modifying nouns which have no singular, e.g.,* **five camps** quina castr·a -orum *npl;* **— times** quinquies; **— years** quinquenn·ium -(i)i *n*
fix *s* **a quick —** praesens remed·ium -(i)i *n;* **to be in a —** *(coll)* in angustiis versari
fix *tr (to repair)* reficere, corrigere; *(to patch)* resarcire; *(to arrange)* disponere; *(to adjust)* accommodare; *(meals)* parare; *(to fasten)* figere; *(the eyes)* intendere; *(time, place, limits)* statuere; *(to avenge)* ulcisci ‖ *intr* **to — upon** inhaerēre *(w. dat)*
fixed *adj (day, boundaries)* cert·us -a -um; **— resolve** men·s -tis *f* solida; **— stars** stell·ae -arum *fpl* inerrantes; **— upon** *(intent upon)* intent·us -a -um *(w. dat)*
fixture *s* affix·um -i *n*
fizz *intr* sibilare
fizzle *intr* sibilare; *(coll)* deficere, cadere
flabbergast *tr* conturbare
flabbiness *s* molliti·a -ae *f*
flabby *adj* flacc·us -a -um
flaccid *adj* flaccid·us -a -um
flag *s* vexill·um -i *n;* **to wave the —** vexillum quassare
flag *tr* signo indicare ‖ *intr* languescere; *(to lose interest)* refrigescere
flagrant *adj* nefari·us -a -um
flagship *s* nav·is -is *f* praetoria
flail *s* pertic·a -ae *f*
flail *tr* fustibus cudere
flake *s* squam·a -ae *f;* **snow —s** plumeae niv·es -ium *fpl*
flaky *adj (sl)* delir·us -a -um
flame *s (of fire; sweetheart)* flamm·a -ae *f*
flame *intr* flammare; **to — up** scintillare; *(fig)* exardescere
flank *s (of animal)* il·ia -ium *npl; (mil)* lat·us -eris *n;* **on the —** a latere
flank *tr* tegere latus *(w. gen)*
flap *s (of dress)* lacini·a -ae *f*
flap *tr* plaudere *(w. abl);* **to — the wings** alis plaudere ‖ *intr (to hang loosely)* fluitare
flare *s* fulg·or -oris *m; (torch)* fa·x -cis *f*
flare *intr (to blaze)* coruscare; **to — up** *(of diseases)* urgēre; *(of anger, passions)* exardescere
flash *s* fulg·or -oris *m;* **— of lightning** fulg·ur -uris *n;* **in a —** ictu temporis
flash *tr* ostentare ‖ *intr* fulgēre, coruscare

flashback *s* veteris memoriae recordati·o -onis
flashlight *s* instrument·um -i *n* micans
flashy *adj* specios·us -a -um
flask *s* laguncul·a -ae *f*
flat *adj (level)* plan·us -a -um; *(not mountainous)* campes·ter -tris -tre; *(on one's back)* supin·us -a -um; *(on one's face)* pron·us -a -um; *(insipid)* vapid·us -a -um; **to fall —** *(e.g., of a play, speech)* frigēre
flatfooted *adj* plaut·us -a -um
flatly *adv* palam
flatness *s* planiti·es -ei *f*
flatten *tr* complanare; *(to prostrate)* prosternere
flatter *tr* blandiri
flatterer *s* adula·tor -toris *m* (·trix -tricis *f*)
flattering *adj* bland·us -a -um
flattery *s* blanditi·a -ae *f*
flatulence *s* inflati·o -onis *f*
flatware *s* instrument·a -orum *npl* escaria
flaunt *tr* iactare
flaunting *adj* glorios·us -a -um
flaunting *s* iactati·o -onis *f*
flavor *s* sap·or -oris *m; (substance)* condiment·um -i *n*
flavor *tr* condire
flaw *s (defect)* vit·ium -(i)i *n; (chink)* rimul·a -ae *f*
flawless *adj* sine vitio
flax *s* lin·um -i *n*
flea *s* pul·ex -icis *m*
flea market *s* for·um -i *n* rerum venalium
fleck *s* macul·a -ae *f*
fledgling *s* pull·us -i *m*
flee *tr* effugere ‖ *intr* fugere; **to — to** confugere ad *or* in *(w. acc)*
fleece *s* vell·us -eris *n*
fleece *tr (fig)* spoliare
fleecy *adj* lanig·er -era -erum
fleet *s* class·is -is *f*
fleet *adj* cel·er -eris -ere
fleet-footed *adj* celerip·es -edis
fleeting *adj* fug·ax -acis
flesh *s* car·o -nis *f;* **in the —** viv·us -a -um
flesh wound *s* car·o -nis *f* vulnerata
fleshy *adj* corpore·us -a -um; *(fat)* corpulent·us -a -um
flexibility *s* flexibilit·as -atis *f; (fig)* molliti·es -ei *f*
flexible *adj (lit & fig)* flexibil·is -is -e
flick *s* crepit·us -ūs *m; (of the finger)* talitr·um -i *n*
flick *tr* **to — away** excutere
flicker *intr (of a flame)* trepidare
flickering *adj* tremul·us -a -um; **— lamps** occidentes lucern·ae -arum *fpl*
flier *s (circular)* libell·us -i *m*
flight *s (flying)* volat·us -ūs *m; (escape)* effug·ium -(i)i *n; (covey)* gre·x -gis *m;* **— of steps** gradati·o -onis *f;* **to put to —** fugare; **to take to —** terga vertere
flighty *adj* lev·is -is -e
flimsy *adj* praetenu·is -is -e; *(trivial)* frivol·us -a -um
flinch *intr* tergiversari; *(to start)* absilire
fling *s* iact·us -ūs *m;* **to have a —** ingenio indulgēre
fling *tr* conicere; **to — away** abicere; **to — down** deicere; **to — open** reicere, patefacere
flint *s* sil·ex -icis *mf*
flinty *adj* silice·us -a -um
flippancy *s* protervit·as -atis *f*
flippant *adj* prompt·us -a -um atque lev·is -is -e
flippantly *adv* temere ac leviter
flirt *s* lup·us -i *m,* lup·a -ae *f*
flirt *intr* **to — with** *(a person)* subblandiri *(w. dat); (an idea)* ludere cum *(w. abl)*
flirtation *s* leves amor·es -um *mpl*
flit *intr* volitare
float *s (raft)* rat·es -is *f; (on fishing line)* cort·ex -icis *m;* **a — in a parade** fercul·um -i *n* in pompā
float *tr (to launch)* deducere ‖ *intr* fluitare; *(in the air)* volitare
flock *s (of birds, goats, sheep)* gre·x -gis *m;* **in —s** gregatim
flock *intr* **to — around** circumfluere *(w. acc);* **to — to** affluere ad *(w. acc);* **to — together** congregari
floe *s* fragment·um -i *n* glaciei natans
flog *tr* verberare
flogging *s* verberati·o -onis *f;* **to get a —** vapulare
flood *s (deluge)* diluv·ium -(i)i *n; (of tears, words)* flum·en -inis *n;* **the Flood** inundanti·a -ae *f* terrarum
flood *tr (lit & fig)* inundare ‖ *intr* inundare
floodgates *spl* cataract·ae -arum *fpl;* **to open the — of** *(fig)* effundere habenas *(w. gen)*
floodtide *s* access·us -ūs *m*
floor *s (ground)* sol·um -i *n; (paved)* paviment·um -i *n; (story)* tabulat·um -i *n;* **to have the —** veniam dicendi habēre; **to lay the —** pavimentum facere; *(on an upper story)* contabulare; **to throw on the —** in pavimentum proicere
floor *tr (to knock down)* sternere; *(to shock, make a deep impression on)* percutere
flooring *s* contabulati·o -onis *f*
flop *s (failure)* naufrag·ium -(i)i *n*
flop *intr* deficere; *(business)* decoquere; *(theat)* frigēre; **to — down** corruere
floppy disk *s (comput)* discul·us -i *m* flexibilis
floral *adj* flore·us -a -um
florist *s* vendi·tor -toris *m* (·trix -tricis *f*) florum
flotilla *s* classicul·a -ae *f*
flounce *s* instit·a -ae *f*
flounder *s (fish)* pass·er -eris *m*
flounder *intr* volutari; *(in speech)* haesitare
flour *s* farin·a -ae *f; (finest)* poll·en -inis *m*

flourish *s (mus)* taratantara *n* [*indecl*]
flourish *tr* vibrare; *(to sound)* canere **II** *intr* florēre; *(mus)* praeludere
flour mill *s* pistrin·um -i *n*
flout *tr (to scorn)* spernere; *(to mock)* deridēre
flow *s* fluxi·o -onis *f; (of the tide)* access·us -ūs *m; (of words)* flum·en -inis *n*
flow *intr* fluere; **to — by** adluere; **to — down from** defluere de *(w. abl)*; **to — into** influere in *(w. acc)*; **to — past** praeterfluere
flower *s (lit & fig)* flo·s -ris *m*
flower *intr* florescere
flower bed *s* are·a -ae *f* floribus consita
flowery *adj* florid·us -a -um
flower shop *s* tabern·a -ae *f* floralis
flu *s* graved·o -inis *f;* **to suffer from the —** gravedine loborare
fluctuate *intr* fluctuare; *(fin)* iactari, se iactare
fluctuation *s* fluctuati·o -onis *f; (variation)* mutati·o -onis *f*
flue *s* cunicul·us -i *m* fornacis
fluency *s* volubilit·as -atis *f*
fluent *adj* volubil·is -is -e, perflu·ens -entis
fluently *adv* volubiliter
fluid *adj* fluid·us -a -um
fluid *s* um·or -oris *m*
fluke *s (of anchor)* den·s -tis *m; (luck)* fortuit·um -i *n*
flunk: to — a test in probatione cadere
fluorescent light tubul·us -i *m* florescens
flurry *s* commoti·o -onis *f;* **— of activity** festinati·o -onis *f*
flush *s (blush)* rub·or -oris *m; (onrush)* impet·us -ūs *m*
flush *tr (to purge)* proluere; **to — out** *(game)* excitare **II** *intr* erubescere
fluster *tr* turbare, inquietare
flute *s* tibi·a -ae *f; (archit)* stri·a -ae *f*
fluting *s (archit)* striatur·a -ae *f*
flutist *s* tibic·en -inis *m; (female)* tibicin·a -ae *f*
flutter *s (of wings)* plaus·us -ūs *m; (bustle)* festinati·o -onis *f; (vibration)* trem·or -oris *m; (of the heart)* palpitati·o -onis *f*
flutter *intr (of a heart)* palpitare; *(of a bird)* volitare; *(of a flag)* fluitare; *(w. alarm)* trepidare
flux *s* flux·us -ūs *m;* **to be in a state of —** fluere
fly *s* musc·a -ae *f;* **a — buzzes** musca bombilat
fly *tr* **to — a plane** aëroplanum gubernare **II** *intr* volare; *(to flee)* fugere; **to — apart** dissilire; **to — away** *or* **off** avolare; **to — in the face of** lacessere; **to — off the handle** exardescere; **to — open** dissilire, patēre; **to — out** evolare, provolare; **to — under** subtervolare; **to — up** subvolare
flyer *s see* **flier**
flying *adj* volatil·is -is -e
flying *s* volat·us -ūs *m*
foal *s* pull·us -i *m; (of horse)* equul·us -i *m; (of asses)* asell·us -i *m*
foal *tr & intr* pario parere peperi
foam *s* spum·a -ae *f*
foam *intr* spumare; *(of sea)* aestuare
foaming *adj* spum·ans -antis
foamy *adj* spume·us -a -um
focus *tr* **to — attention** *(or* **mind)** **on** animum attendere ad *(w. acc)*
fodder *s* pabul·um -i *n*
foe *s (public)* host·is -is *m; (private)* inimic·us -i *m* (·a -ae *f*)
fog *s* nebul·a -ae *f*
foggy *adj* nebulos·us -a -um
foible *s* vit·ium -(i)i *n*
foil *s (for fencing)* rud·is -is *f; (leaf of metal)* lamin·a -ae *f; (very thin)* bracte·a -ae *f; (fig)* umbr·a -ae *f*
foil *tr* eludere, frustrari
fold *s* sin·us -ūs *m; (wrinkle)* rug·a -ae *f; (for sheep; the Church)* ovil·e -is *n*
fold *tr* plicare; **to — up** complicare
folder *s* integument·um -i *n* astrictorium; *(comput)* coöpercul·um -i *n*
foliage *s* fron·s -dis *f*
folio *s* li·ber -bri *m* maximae formae
folk *s* homin·es -um *mpl;* **common —** vulg·us -i *n*, pleb·s -is *f*
folk music *s* music·a -ae *f* vulgaris
folk song *s* carm·en -inis *n* vulgare
follow *tr* sequi; *(closely)* instare *(w. dat)*, assequi; *(immediately after)* subsequi; *(instructions)* parēre *(w. dat)*; *(to understand)* intellegere; **to — up** *(to the end)* persequi **II** *intr* insequi; **it —s that** sequitur ut; **to — up on** persequi; **to — upon** supervenire *(w. dat)*
follower *s* secta·tor -toris *m* (·trix -tricis *f*); *(hanger-on)* assec(u)l·a -ae *mf*
following *s (attendants)* comitat·us -ūs *m; (pol)* facti·o -onis *f*
following *adj* sequ·ens -entis, proxim·us -a -um, poster·us -a -um
folly *s* stultiti·a -ae *f*
foment *tr* fovēre
fond *adj* **(of)** am·ans -antis *(w. gen)*, studios·us -a -um *(w. gen)*; **to be — of** amare
fondle *tr* mulcēre, fovēre
fondly *adv* amanter
fondness *s* **(for)** *(persons, country)* carit·as -atis *f* (erga *w. acc*); **(for)** *(things)* stud·ium -(i)i *n (w. gen)*
food *s* cib·us -i *m*
food processor *s* machin·a -ae *f* coquinaria
fool *s* stult·us -i *m* (·a -ae *f*); *(idiot)* fatu·us -i *m* (·a -ae *f*); **to make a — of** ludificare; **to make a — of oneself** fatuari, ineptire
fool *tr* fallere
foolhardily *adv* temere
foolhardy *adj* temerari·us -a -um
foolish *adj* stult·us -a -um

foolishly *adv* stulte; **to act —** ineptire
foolishness *s* stultiti•a -ae *f*
foot *s (of men, animals, tables, chairs)* pe•s -dis *m; (of mountain)* rad•ix -icis *m; (of pillar)* bas•is -is *f;* **on —** pedibus; **to set — in** pedem ponere in *(w. abl);* **to tread under —** calcare
foot *tr* **to — a bill** impensam sumere
football *s (ball)* pedifoll•is -is *m; (game)* pedifoll•ium -i *n,* pedilud•ium -(i)i *n;* **to kick (pass) the —** pedifollem pulsare (transmittere); **to play —** pedifolle ludere
football player *s* pedilus•or -oris *m*
foothills *spl* radic•es -um *mpl* montis
foothold *s* grad•us -ūs *m* stabilis
footing *s* grad•us -ūs *m;* **on an equal —** ex aequo; **to be on an equal — with** in aequo stare *(w. dat);* **to get one's —** locum capere; **to lose one's —** de gradu labi
footnote *s* annotati•o -onis *f* imae paginae
footpath *s* semit•a -ae *f*
footprint *s* vestig•ium -(i)i *n*
footrace *s* curs•us -ūs *m*
foot soldier *s* ped•es -itis *m*
footstool *s* scabell•um -i *n*
footwear *s* calceament•um -i *n*
for *prep (extent of time or space) render by acc; (price) render by gen or abl; (on behalf of; in place of; instead of; in proportion to, in consideration of)* pro *(w. abl); (purpose)* ad *(w. acc); (cause)* causā *(w. gen) (always after the governed word),* ob *(w. acc); (after negatives)* prae *(w. abl); (toward)* erga *(w. acc); (out of, for, e.g., joy, fear)* prae *(w. abl); (to denote the appointment of a definite time)* in *(w. acc);* **as for** quod attinet ad *(w. acc);* **— all that** nec eo setius; **— nothing** gratis, gratuito; *(in vain)* frustra; **— the last three months** in ternos novissimos menses; **— the rest of the year** in reliquum anni tempus; **— these reasons** his de causis; **good — nothing** ad nullam rem util•is -is -e; **to be —** *(to be in favor of)* studēre *(w. dat),* favēre *(w. dat);* **to live — the day** in diem vivere; **what —?** quare?
for *conj (generally first in a clause)* nam, siquidem, *(never first)* enim
forage *s* pabul•um -i *n*
forage *intr* pabulari
foray *s* incursi•o -onis *f*
forbear *intr* desistere
forbearance *s* patienti•a -ae *f*
forbid *tr* vetare, prohibēre
forbidding *adj* odios•us -a -um
force *s* vis *(acc:* vim; *abl:* vi; *pl:* vires) *f;* **by —** vi; **large (small) force** magnae (exiguae) copi•ae -arum *fpl;* **—s** *(mil)* vir•es -ium *fpl,* copiae *fpl;* **to be in —** *(of laws)* valēre; **to use —** vim adhibēre
force *tr* cogere, impellere; *(a door)* rumpere; **to — back** repellere; **to — down** detrudere; **to — out** extrudere, extorquēre; **to — s.o. to surrender** aliquem in dicionem redigere
forced *adj (unnatural)* quaesit•us -a -um; **— march** magnum *or* maximum it•er -ineris *n*
forceful *adj* valid•us -a -um, val•ens -entis
forceps *spl* forc•eps -ipis *mf*
forcible *adj* per vim fact•us -a -um
forcibly *adv* per vim, vi
ford *s* vad•um -i *n*
ford *tr* vado transire
fore *adj* pr•ior -ior -ius
forearm *s* bracch•ium -(i)i *n*
forearm *tr* praemunire; **to be —ed** praecavēre
forebears *spl* maior•es -um *mpl*
forebode *tr* portendere
foreboding *s* portent•um -i *n; (feeling)* praesensi•o -onis *f*
foreboding *adj* presag•us -a -um
forecast *s* coniectur•a -ae *f,* praedicti•o -onis *f; (of weather)* (caeli) praenuntiati•o -onis *f*
forecast *tr* praedicere, praenuntiare
forecastle *s* pror•a -ae *f*
foredoom *tr* praedestinare
forefather *s* atav•us -i *m;* **—s** maior•es -um *mpl*
forefinger *s* index digit•us -i *m*
forego *tr* dimittere
foregone conclusion *s* praeiudicat•um -i *n;* **to take it as a —** id pro praeiudicato ferre
foregoing *adj* pr•ior -ior -ius
forehead *s* fron•s -tis *f*
foreign *adj (of another country)* extern•us -a -um; *(opposite of home-produced)* adventici•us -a -um; *(coming from abroad)* peregrin•us -a -um; *(not pertaining to)* alien•us -a -um; **to live (travel) in a — country** peregrinari
foreigner *s* peregrin•us -i *m* (•a -ae *f*)
foreknowledge *s* providenti•a -ae *f*
forelady *s* procura•trix -tricis *f*
foreman *s* procura•tor -toris *m; (on an estate)* villic•us -i *m*
foremost *adj* prim•us -a -um; *(of chief importance)* princ•eps -ipis
forenoon *s* antemeridianum temp•us -oris *n;* **in the —** ante meridiem
forensic *adj* forens•is -is -e
foreground *s* prior par•s -tis *f*
forerunner *s* praenunt•ius -(i)i *m,* praecurs•or -oris *m*
foresee *tr* providēre
foreseeing *adj* provid•us -a -um
foresight *s* providenti•a -ae *f; (precaution)* provisi•o -onis *f*
forest *adj* silvestr•is -is -e
forest *s* silv•a -ae *f*
forestall *tr* praeoccupare

foretell *tr* praedicere
forethought *s* providenti·a -ae *f*
forever *adv* in perpetuum
forewarn *tr* praemonēre
forfeit *s* mult·a -ae *f*
forfeit *tr* multari *(w. abl)*
forfeiture *s* amissi·o -onis *f*
forge *s* forn·ax -acis *f* ferraria
forge *tr* excudere; *(a document)* corrumpere; **to — a signature on** *(a document)* signo adulterino obsignare
forged *adj* fals·us -a -um
forger *s (of wills)* subiec·tor -toris *m* (·trix -tricis *f); (***of any document***)* falsari·us -i *m* (·a -ae *f*)
forgery *s* fals·um -i *n*
forget *tr* **(about)** oblivisci *(w. gen);* **— about it!** eice id ex animo!
forgetful *adj* oblivios·us -a -um
forgetfulness *s* oblivi·o -onis *f*
forgive *tr* ignoscere *(w. dat)*
forgiveness *s* veni·a -ae *f*
forgiving *adj* ignosc·ens -entis
forgo *tr* dimittere; **to — a triumph** triumphum dimittere
fork *s* furc·a -ae *f; (small fork)* furcill·a -ae *f; (in the road)* biv·ium -(i)i *n*
fork *tr* **to — over** *(coll)* persolvere; **— over!** cedo! *(pl)* **cette!**
forlorn *adj* destitut·us -a -um
form *s* form·a -ae *f; (document)* formul·a -ae *f; (gram)* figur·a -ae *f;* **in due —** rite
form *tr* formare; *(to produce)* efficere; *(a plan, partnership, alliance)* inire; **to — a long line** agmen longum facere; **to — an opinion** iudicium facere; **to — such bitter enmities** tam graves simultates excipere; **to — the imperative** imperativum facere ‖ *intr* nasci, fieri
formal *adj* iust·us -a -um; *(stiff)* composit·us -a -um
formality *s* rit·us -ūs *m;* **formalities** iust·a -orum *npl;* **with due —** rite
formation *s* conformati·o -onis *f;* **in —** instruct·us -a -um
former *adj* pr·ior -ior -ius; *(immediately preceding)* super·ior -ior -ius; *(original, olden)* pristin·us -a -um; **the — ... the latter** ille ... hic
formerly *adv* antehac, antea
formidable *adj* formidabil·is -is -e
formless *adj* inform·is -is -e
formula *s* formul·a -ae *f; (leg)* acti·o -onis *f*
forsake *tr* deserere
forswear *tr* adiurare
fort *s* castell·um -i *n*
forth *adv (often expressed in Latin by a prefix, e.g.,* **to go —** exire); **and so —** et cetera; **from that day —** inde, ex eo (die)
forthcoming *adj* futur·us -a -um; **to be —** praesto esse
forthright *adj* apert·us -a -um
forthwith *adv* protinus, extemplo
fortieth *adj* quadragesim·us -a -um
fortification *s* muniment·um -i *n*
fortify *tr* munire
fortitude *s* fortitud·o -inis *f*
fortress *s* castell·um -i *n*
fortuitous *adj* fortuit·us -a -um
fortuitously *adv* fortuito
fortunate *adj* fortunat·us -a -um
fortunately *adv* feliciter
fortune *s* fortun·a -ae *f; (estate)* op·es -ium *fpl,* res, rei *f;* **bad —** fortuna *f* adversa; **good —** fortuna *f* prospera; **to make a —** rem facere; **to squander one's —** rem dissipare; **to tell —s** hariolari
fortuneteller *s* hariol·us *m* (·a -ae *f*)
fortunetelling *s* hariolati·o -onis *f*
forty *adj* quadraginta [*indecl*]
forum *s* for·um -i *n*
forward *s (sports)* oppugna·tor -toris *m* (·trix -tricis *f*)
foreward *tr (mail, e-mail)* deferre
forward *adv* prorsus, prorsum; *(often expressed by the prefix* pro-, *e.g.,* **to move —** promovēre)
forward *adj (cocky)* proterv·us -a -um; **— motion** progress·us -ūs *m*
foster *tr* alere, fovēre
foster brother *s* collacte·us -i *m*
foster child *s* alumn·us -i *m* (·a -ae *f*)
foster father *s* alt·or -oris *m*
foster mother *s* altr·ix -icis *f*
foster sister *s* collacte·a -ae *f*
foul *s* **to commit a —** *(sports)* poenaliter agere
foul *adj (dirty)* foed·us -a -um; *(language)* obscen·us -a -um; *(weather)* turbid·us -a -um; *(deed)* foed·us -a -um; *(smell)* te·ter -tra -trum; **— play** dol·us -i *m* malus; **to run — of** inruere in *(w. acc)*
foul *tr* inquinare; *(morally)* contaminare; **to — up** *(coll)* conturbare
foully *adv* foede
foul-mouthed *adj* maledic·us -a -um
found *tr* fundare, condere
foundation *s* fundament·um -i *n;* **to lay the — for** *(lit & fig)* fundamenta iacere *(w. gen)*
founder *s* condi·tor -toris *m* (·trix -tricis *f*)
founder *intr (lit & fig)* pessum ire
foundling *s* expositici·us -i *m* (·a -ae *f*)
fountain *s* fon·s -tis *m*
fountainhead *s* cap·ut -itis *n* fontis
fountain pen *s* graph·ium -(i)i *n* replebile
four *adj* quattuor [*indecl*] **— each** quatern·i -ae -a; **— times** quater; **— years** quadrenn·ium -(i)i *n;* **on all —** rep·ens -entis
fourfold *adj* quadrupl·us -a -um
four-footed *adj* quadrup·es -edis
fourscore *adj* octoginta [*indecl*]
fourteen *adj* quattuordecim [*indecl*]
fourteenth *adj* quart·us decim·us -a -um
fourth *adj* quart·us -a -um; **for the — time** quartum

fourth *s* quarta par·s -tis *f;* **three —s** tres part·es -ium *fpl*
fourthly *adv* quarto
fowl *s* av·is -is *f; (domestic)* gallin·a -ae *f*
fox *s* vulp·es -is *f;* **an old —** *(coll)* veterat·or -oris *m;* **foxes yelp** vulpes genniunt
foyer *s* vestibul·um -i *n*
fracas *s (brawl)* rix·a -ae *f; (quarrel)* iurg·ium -(i)i *n*
fraction *s* par·s -tis *f* exigua; *(math)* fracti·o -onis *f*
fracture *s* fractur·a -ae *f*
fracture *tr* frangere
fragile *adj* fragil·is -is -e
fragility *s* fragilit·as -atis *f*
fragment *s* fragment·um -i *n*
fragrance *s* suavis od·or -oris *m*
fragrant *adj* suaveol·ens -entis
frail *adj* infirm·us -a -um
frailty *s* infirmit·as -atis *f*
frame *s (of a picture)* form·a -ae *f; (of the body* figur·a -ae *f; (of buildings, etc.)* compag·es -is *f; (of bed)* spond·a -ae *f;* **— of mind** anim·us -i *m;* **to be in a good — of mind** bono animo esse
frame *tr* fabricari; *(to contrive)* moliri; *(a picture)* in formā includere; *(a person)* falso insimulare; *(to draw up a form of words)* concipere
framework *s* compag·es -is *f; (of wood)* contignati·o -onis *f*
France *s* Galli·a -ae *f*
franchise *s* iu·s -ris *n* suffragii
frank *adj* lib·er -era -erum, simpl·ex -icis
frankincense *s* tus, turis *n*
frankly *adv* aperte, candide
frankness *s* libert·as -atis *f*
frantic *adj* fur·ens -entis
frantically *adv* furenter
fraternal *adj* fratern·us -a -um
fraternally *adv* fraterne
fraternity *s* sodalit·as -atis *f*
fraternize *intr* conversari
fratricide *s (doer)* fratricid·a -ae *mf; (deed)* fratris parricid·ium -(i)i *n*
fraud *s* frau·s -dis *f; (leg)* dol·us -i *m* malus
fraudulent *adj* fraudulent·us -a -um
fraudulently *adv* fraudulenter
fraught *adj (with)* plen·us -a -um *(w. abl)*
fray *s* rix·a -ae *f; (contest)* certam·en -inis *n*
freak *s* monstr·um -i *n; (whim)* libid·o -inis *f;* **— of nature** lus·us -ūs *m* naturae
freakish *adj* monstruos·us -a -um
freckle *s* lentig·o -inis *f*
freckled *adj* lentiginos·us -a -um
free *adj* lib·er -era -erum; *(disengaged) (from)* vacu·us -a -um *(w. abl); (generous)* liberal·is -is -e; *(from duty, taxes)* immun·is -is -e; *(unencumbered)* exped·it·us -a -um; **— of charge** gratuito; **for —** gratis; **if you are —** si vacabis; **to be — from** vacare *(w. abl)*
free *tr* liberare; *(slave)* manumittere; *(son)* emancipare
freeborn *adj* ingenu·us -a -um
freely *adv* libere; *(of one's own accord)* sponte, ultro; *(frankly)* aperte; *(generously)* large
freedman *s* libert·us -i *m*
freedom *s* libert·as -atis *f*
freedwoman *s* libert·a -ae *f*
free-style swimming *s* natati·o -onis *f* libera
free will *s* volunt·as -atis *f;* **of one's own —** suā sponte
freeze *tr & intr* gelare; **to — up** congelare
freezer *s* caps·a -ae *f* frigorifica
freezing *adj* gelid·us -a -um
freezing, freezing mark *s* punct·um -i *n* glaciale; **three degrees above —** tres gradūs supra punctum glaciale
freight *s (cargo)* on·us -eris *n; (cost)* vectur·a -ae *f*
freighter *s* nav·is -is *f* oneraria
freight train *s* tram·en -inis *n* onerarium
French *adj* Gallic·us -a -um; **in —** Gallice; **to speak —** Gallice loqui
French fries *spl* pom·a -orum *npl* (terrestria) fricta
frenzied *adj* fur·ens -entis
frenzy *s* fur·or -oris *m*
frequency *s* crebrit·as -atis *f*
frequent *adj* cre·ber -bra -brum; **to become —** crebrescere
frequent *tr* frequentare
frequenter *s* frequenta·tor -toris *m* (·trix -tricis *f*)
frequently *adv* crebro; **more —** crebrius; **most —** creberrime
fresco *s* op·us -eris *n* tectorium
fresh *adj (food, flowers, etc.)* rec·ens -entis; *(cool)* frigidul·us -a -um; *(not tired)* inte·ger -gra -grum; *(forward)* proterv·us -a -um; *(green)* virid·is -is -e; *(water)* dulc·is -is -e; **— air** aur·a -ae *f*
freshen *tr* recreare, renovare ‖ *intr (of wind)* increbrescere; **to — up** se recreare
freshly *adv* recenter
freshman *s* tir·o -onis *mf*
freshness *s* viridit·as -atis *f*
fret *intr* angi, stomachari
fretful *adj* stomachos·us -a -um
fretting *s* sollicitud·o -inis *f*
friction *s* fricti·o -onis *f*
Friday *s* di·es -ei *m* Veneris
fried *adj* frict·us -a -um; **— eggs** ov·a -orum *npl* in oleo fricta
friend *s* amic·us -i *m* (·a -ae *f*), familiar·is -is *mf; (of a thing)* ama·tor -toris *m* (·trix -tricis *f*); **best —** summus amicus, summa amica
friendless *adj* amicorum in·ops -opis
friendliness *s* benevolenti·a -ae *f*
friendly *adj* amic·us -a -um; **in a — manner** amice

friendship *s* amiciti•a -ae *f*
frieze *s* zoöphor•us -i *m*
fright *s* terr•or -oris *m*
frighten *tr* terrēre; **to — away** absterrēre
frightening *adj* terrific•us -a -um
frightful *adj* terribil•is -is -e
frightfully *adv* foede
frigid *adj* frigid•us -a -um
frigidity *s* frig•us -oris *n*
frigidly *adv* frigide
frill *s (plaited border)* instit•a -ae *f;* **—s** *(fig)* tric•ae -arum *fpl*
fringe *s (trim)* fimbri•ae -arum *fpl; (border)* marg•o -inis *m*
fringe *adj (outer)* ultimus -a -um; *(secondary)* secundari•us -a -um
fringed *adj* fimbriat•us -a -um
frisk *tr* scrutari **||** *intr* lascivire
fritter *s* lagan•um -i *n*
fritter *tr* **to — away** terere
frivolity *s* levit•as -atis *f; (thing)* nug•ae -arum *fpl*
frivolous *adj* frivol•us -a -um
frivolously *adv* nugatorie
frizzle *tr* crispare
frizzled *adj* calamistrat•us -a -um
fro *adv* **to and —** huc (et) illuc
frog *s* ran•a -ae *f;* **—s croak** ranae coaxant
frolic *intr* lascivire
from *prep* a(b) *(w. abl); (denoting strictly descent from above, but used in other senses; subtraction; source)* de *(w. abl); (from within, out of)* e(x) *(w. abl); (cause)* ob *(w. acc)*; **— above** desuper; **— a to z** *(fig)* ab acia et acu; **— day to day** diem de die; **— here** hinc; **— there** illinc; **— where** unde; **— within** intrinsecus; **— without** extrinsecus
front *s* fron•s -tis *f; (on the march)* primum agm•en -inis *n; (appearance)* speci•es -ei *f;* **in —** a fronte, adversus; **in — of** *(in the presence of)* coram *(w. abl); (position)* pro *(w. abl);* **the — of the classroom** prior par•s -tis *f* conclavis scholaris; **the — of the house** frons aedium
front *adj* pr•ior -ior -ius; *(feet)* prim•us -a -um; **— door** antic•um -i *n;* **— hall** vestibul•um -i *n,* fauc•es -ium *fpl;* **— seat** sed•es -is *f* anterior; **— teeth** dent•es -ium *mpl* primores
frontage *s* fron•s -tis *f;* **a hundred feet of —** centum pedes in fronte
frontal *adj* advers•us -a -um; **— attack** impet•us -ūs *m* ex adverso
frontier *s* lim•es -itis *m; (fig)* termin•us -i *m*
frontline *s (mil)* aci•es -ei *f*
frost *s* pruin•a -ae *f*
frostbitten *adj* frigore ambust•us -a -um
frosty *adj* pruinos•us -a -um
froth *s* spum•a -ae *f*
froth *intr* spumare
frothy *adj* spume•us -a -um
frown *s* contracti•o -onis *f* frontis
frown *intr* frontem contrahere; **to — on** improbare
frozen *adj* frigore *(or* glacie) concret•us -a -um
frugal *adj* frugi [*indecl*]
frugality *s* frugalit•as -atis *f*
frugally *adv* frugaliter
fruit *s* fruct•us -ūs *m; (esp. orchard fruit)* pom•um -i *n; (of tree)* mal•a -orum *npl;* **—s of the earth** frug•es -ium *fpl*
fruitful *adj* fecund•us -a -um; *(actually yielding fruit)* frugif•er -era -erum
fruitfully *adv* fecunde
fruitfulness *s* fecundit•as -atis *f*
fruit juice suc•us -i *m* pomarius
fruitless *adj* steril•is -is -e; *(fig)* irrit•us -a -um
fruitlessly *adv* frustra
fruit stand *s* tabern•a -ae *f* pomaria
fruit tree *s* pom•us -i *f*
frustrate *tr (to break off, e.g., an undertaking)* dirimere, ad irritum redigere; *(to baffle)* frustrari
frustrating *adj* incommod•us -a -um
frustration *s* frustrati•o -onis *f*
fry *s (dish of things fried)* frix•a -ae *f*
fry *tr* frigere
frying pan *s* sartag•o -inis *f*
fuel *s* aliment•um -i *n,* materi•a -ae *f* propulsoria; **to add — to the flames** *(fig)* oleum addere camino
fuel oil *s* ole•um -i *n* incendiarium
fuel tank *s* olei receptacul•um -i *n*
fugitive *s (from country or home)* profug•a -ae *mf; (pej)* fugitiv•us -i *m* (•a -ae *f)*
fugitive *adj* fugitiv•us -a -um
fulcrum *s (of lever)* pressi•o -onis *f*
fulfill *tr (a duty)* explēre, praestare; *(prophecy)* implēre; **to — a promise** promissum exsolvere
fulfilled *adj (prayer, hope)* rat•us -a -um
fulfillment *s (carrying out)* exsecuti•o -onis *f; (of a prophecy, etc.)* perfecti•o -onis *f*
full *adj (of)* plen•us -a -um *(w. gen or abl); (filled up)* explet•us -a -um; *(entire)* solid•us -a -um; *(satisfied)* sat•ur -ura -urum; *(dress)* fus•us -a -um; **at — speed** citato gradu; **in — swing** in mediis rebus
full-blown *adj (flowers)* apert•us -a -um; *(mature)* adult•us -a -um
full-grown *adj* adult•us -a -um
full-length *(dress)* talar•is -is -e
fully *adv (completely)* plene, funditus; *(quite)* penitus, prorsus
full moon *s* plenilun•ium -(i)i *n*
fumble *tr (the ball)* demittere **||** *intr* haesitare; **to — for** explorare
fume *s* halit•us -ūs *m*
fume *intr* exaestuare
fumigate *tr* fumigare, suffire
fumigation *s* suffit•us -ūs *m*
fun *s* ioc•us -i *m;* **pure —** mera hilar•ia -ium *npl;* **to have —** se oblectare; **to**

make — of *(or* **poke —at)** eludere; **to say it for** — id per iocum dicere
function *s* mun•us -eris *n,* offic•ium -(i)i *n; (gram)* potenti•a -ae *f*
function *intr* fungi, munus implēre
functionary *s* magistrat•us -ūs *m*
fund *s* pecuni•a -ae *f* collecta; *(store of anything)* copi•a -ae *f;* **—s** pecunia *f,* op•es -um *fpl*
fundamental *adj* prim•us -a -um
fundamentally *adv* funditus, penitus
funeral *s* fun•us -eris *n; (funeral procession and obsequies)* exsequi•ae -arum *fpl;* **to attend a —** (con)venire in funus
funeral *adj* funere•us -a -um; **to perform the — rites** parentare
funereal *adj* funebr•is -is -e
fungus *s* fung•us -i *m*
funnel *s* infundibul•um -i *n*
funny *adj* ridicul•us -a -um; *(humorous)* festiv•us -a um
fur *s* pell•is -is *f*
furious *adj* furios•us -a -um
furiously *adv* furiose
furl *tr* complicare; *(sail)* legere
furlough *s* commeat•us -ūs *m;* **on —** in commeatu; **to get a —** commeatum impetrare; **to grant a —** commeatum dare
furnace *s* forn•ax -acis *f*
furnish *tr* suppeditare; *(to fit out)* ornare, instruere; **to — a home (an apartment)** supellectile instruere
furnished *adj* (supellectile) instruct•us -a -um
furniture *s* supell•ex -ectilis *f;* **piece of —** par•s -tis *f* supellectilis
furrow *s* sulc•us -i *m*
furry *adj* villos•us -a -um
further *adj* ulter•ior -ior -ius; **without — ado** sine morā; sine ullo tumultu
further *adv* ultra, longius
further *tr (to serve)* servire *(w. dat); (to promote)* promovēre; *(to aid)* adiuvare; **to — our own interests** nostris commodis servire
furtherance *s* progress•us -ūs *m*
furthermore *adv* porro, praeterea
furthest *adj* ultim•us -a -um
furthest *adv* longissime
furtive *adj* furtiv•us -a -um
furtively *adv* furtim, furtive
fury *s* fur•or -oris *m*
fuse *tr* fundere **||** *intr* coalescere
fusion *s* fusur•a -ae *f*
fuss *s* perturbati•o -onis *f;* **to make a great — over nothing** laborare in angusto, *(coll)* de lanā caprinā rixari
fuss *intr* satagere, tumultuari
fussy *adj* fastidios•us -a -um
futile *adj* futil•is -is -e
futility *s* futilit•as -atis *f*
future *adj* futur•us -a -um; **for all — time** in posterum; **— perfect tense** temp•us -oris *n* futurum perfectum; **— tense** tempus futurum
future *s* futur•a -orum *npl,* posterum temp•us -oris *n;* **in the —** posthac; **for the —** in posterum

G

gab *s* garrulit•as -atis *f*
gab *intr* garrire
gabby *adj* garrul•us -a -um
gable *s* fastig•ium -(i)i *n*
gadfly *s* taban•us -i *m*
gag *s (joke)* ioc•us -i *m*
gag *tr* os obstruere *(w. dat)* **||** *intr* nauseare
gaiety *s* hilarit•as -atis *f*
gaily *adv* hilare
gain *s* lucr•um -i *n*
gain *tr* consequi, acquirere; *(victory)* consequi, adipisci; *(by asking)* impetrare; *(office, military command)* capere; **to — access to a person** penetrare ad aliquem; **to — ground** *(fig)* increbrescere; **to — possession of** potiri *(w. abl)*
gainful *adj* lucros•us -a -um
gainsay *tr* contradicere *(w. dat)*
gait *s* incess•us -ūs *m*
gala *adj* festiv•us -a -um
gala *s* festivit•as -atis *f*
galaxy *s* ingens coët•us -ūs *m* stellarum; vi•a -ae *f* lactea
gale *s* procell•a -ae *f*
gall *s* bil•is -is *f; (insolence)* insolenti•a -ae *f*
gall *tr* urere, mordēre
gallant *adj* fort•is -is -e; *(polite)* officios•us -a -um
gallantly *adv* fortiter
gallantry *s* fortitud•o -inis *f*
gall bladder *s* fel, fellis *n*
gallery *s* portic•us -ūs *f; (open)* peristyl•ium -(i)i *n; (for paintings)* pinacothec•a -ae *f*
galley *s* nav•is -is *f* longa; *(two banks of oars)* birem•is -is *f; (three banks of oars)* trirem•is -is *f; (kitchen)* culin•a -ae *f*
Gallic *adj* Gallic•us -a -um
galling *adj* mord•ax -acis
gallon *s* cong•ius -(i)i *m*
gallop *s* citissimus curs•us -ūs *m;* **at a —** citato equo
gallop *intr (of a horse)* quadrupedare; *(of the rider)* citato equo contendere
gallows *s* patibul•um -i *n*
gallstone *s* calcul•us -i *m*
galore *adv* satis superque
galvanize *tr* incitare
gamble *tr* **to — away** in aleā perdere **||** *intr* aleā ludere
gambler *s* alea•tor -toris *m* (•trix -tricis *f)*
gambling *s* ale•a -ae *f*
game *s* lud•us -i *m; (w. dice)* ale•a -ae *f; (venison)* praed•a -ae *f;* **to make — of** ludificari; **to play a —** lusum ludere

gamecock *s* gall·us -i *m* rixosus
game show *s* spectacul·um -i *n* lusorium
gamut *s* tota rerum seri·es -ei *f;* **to run the —** omnia amplecti
gander *s* ans·er -eris *m;* **to take a — at** *(coll)* strictim aspicere
gang *s* gre·x -gis *m,* man·us -ūs *f; (of ruffians)* grex grassatorum
gang *intr* **to — together** coniurare; **to — up on** conspirare in *(w. acc)*
gang member *s* praed·o -onis *m* gregalis
gangplank *s (naut)* pon·s -tis *m*
gangrene *s* gangren·a -a *f*
gangster *s* grassat·or -oris *m*
gangway *s (naut)* for·us -i *m*
gap *s* hiat·us -ūs *m*
gape *intr* hiare; **to — at** attonito animo inhiare *(w. dat)*
gaping *adj* hi·ans -antis
garage *s* autocineti *(or* autocinetorum) receptacul·um -i *n*
garb *s* vestit·us -ūs *m,* cult·us -ūs *m*
garbage *s* quisquili·ae -arum *fpl*; **— in, — out** ex quisquiliis fiunt quisqiliae
garble *tr* corrumpere, detorquēre
garden *s* hort·us -i *m*
gardener *s* hortulan·us -i *m; (ornamental)* topiar·ius -(i)i *m*
gardening *s* hortorum cult·us -ūs *m; (ornamental)* topiaria ar·s -tis *f*
gargle *intr* gargarizare
gargling *s* gargarizati·o -onis *f*
garland *s* coron·a -ae *f,* sert·a -ae *f*
garlic *s* al(l)·ium -(i)i *n*
garment *s* vestiment·um -i *n*
garner *tr* colligere
garnish *tr* ornare
garret *s* cenacul·um -i *n*
garrison *s* praesid·ium -(i)i *n*
garrison *tr (a post w. troops)* praesidium collocare in *(w. abl)*
garter *s* periscel·is -idis *f*
gas *s (anat)* inflati·o -onis *f; (gasoline)* benzin·um -i *n;* **step on the — !** *(coll)* matura *(pl:* maturate)!; **to step on the —** pedale benzinarium deprimere
gash *s* patens plag·a -ae *f*
gash *tr* caesim ferire
gasp *s* anhelit·us -ūs *m*
gasp *intr* anhelare; **to — for breath** singultare animam
gas pedal *s* pedal·e -is *n* benzinarium
gas pump *s* antli·a -ae *f* benzinaria
gas station *s* stati·o -onis *f* benzinaria
gas stove *s* focul·us -i *n* gaseus
gas tank *s* immissar·ium -(i)i *n* benzinarium
gastric *adj* stomachi [*gen*]
gastronomy *s* ars, artis *f* coquinaria
gate *s* port·a -ae *f*
gateway *s* adit·us -ūs *m*
gather *tr (to assemble)* colligere; *(fruit, nuts, flowers)* legere; *(to infer)* colligere, conicere; *(to suspect)* suspicari; **to — up** colligere ‖ *intr* convenire
gathering *s* convent·us -ūs *m; (collecting)* collecti·o -onis *f*
gaudily *adv* laute
gaudiness *s* lautiti·a -ae *f*
gaudy *adj* laut·us -a -um
gauge *s* modul·us -i *m*
gauge *tr* metiri
gaunt *adj* ma·cer -cra -crum
gauntlet *s* digital·ia -ium *npl;* **to throw down the —** provocare
gauze *s* co·a -orum *npl*
gawk *intr* **(at)** stupide spectare
gawky *adj* inept·us -a -um
gay *adj* hilar·is -is -e; *(homosexual)* cinaed·us -a -um
gay *s* cinaed·us -i *m*
gaze *s* conspect·us -ūs *m; (fixed look)* obtut·us -ūs *m*
gaze *intr* tueri; **to — at** intueri
gazelle *s* dorc·as -adis *f*
gear *s* apparat·us -ūs *m*
gearshift *s* iuncti·o -onis *f* velocitatum
gee *interj* hercle!; edepol!
geez *interj* eu hercle!; eu edepol!
gem *s* gemm·a -ae *f*
gender *s* gen·us -eris *n*
genealogy *s* propagin·es -um *fpl*
general *adj (as opposed to specific)* general·is -is -e; *(wide-spread)* vulgar·is -is -e; *(shared by all)* commun·is -is -e, public·us -a -um; **in —** ad summum, generatim
general *s* du·x -cis *mf,* impera·tor -toris *m* (·trix -tricis *f*)
generalize *intr* in summam loqui
generally *adv (opp: specifically:* membratim) generatim; *(for the most part)* plerumque, fere
generalship *s* duct·us -ūs *m*
general store *s* pantopol·ium -(i)i *n*
generate *tr* generare
generation *s (act of producing)* generati·o -onis *f; (age)* aet·as -atis *f*
generic *adj* general·is -is -e
generosity *s* liberalit·as -atis *f*
generous *adj* liberal·is -is -e
generously *adv* liberaliter
genesis *s* orig·o -inis *f*
genial *adj* com·is -is -e
geniality *s* comit·as -atis *f*
genially *adv* comiter
genitals *spl* genital·ia -ium *npl; (female)* muliebr·ia -ium *npl*
genitive *s* genitiv·us -i *m,* cas·us -ūs *m* genitivus
genius *s* ingen·ium -(i)i *n*
genteel *adj* urban·us -a -um
gentile *adj* gentil·is -is -e
gentile *s* gentil·is -is *mf*
gentility *s* nobilit·as -atis *f*

gentle *adj* clem•ens -entis, mit•is -is -e; *(gradual)* moll•is -is -e; *(wind, etc.)* len•is -is -e; *(tame)* mansuet•us -a -um
gentleman *s* vi•r -ri *m* honestus
gentleness *s* clementi•a -ae *f; (gradualness)* lenit•as -atis *f; (tameness)* mansuetud•o -inis *f*
gently *adv* leniter, clementer; *(gradually)* sensim
gentry *s* optimat•es -um *mpl*
genuine *adj* sincer•us -a -um
genuinely *adv* sincere
genus *s* gen•us -eris *n*
geographer *s* geograph•us -i *m* (•a -ae *f*)
geographical *adj* geographic•us -a -um
geography *s* geographi•a -ae *f*
geological *adj* geologic•us -a -um
geologist *s* geolog•us -i *m* (•a -ae *f*)
geology *s* geologi•a -ae *f*
geometric(al) *adj* geometric•us -a -um
geometry *s* geometri•a -ae *f*
germ *s* germ•en -inis *n*
German *adj* Germanic•us -a -um
German *s* German•us -i *m* (•a -ae *f*); **to speak —** Germanice loqui
germane *adj* affin•is -is -e
Germany *s* Germani•a -ae *f*
germinate *intr* germinare
germination *s* germinat•us -ūs *m*
gerund *s* gerund•ium -(i)i *n*
gesticulate *intr* gesticulari
gesture *s* gest•us -ūs *m*
gesture *intr* gestu indicare
get *tr (to acquire)* nancisci; *(to receive)* accipere; *(by purchase)* parare, comparare; *(by entreaty)* impetrare; *(to fetch)* afferre; *(to understand)* tenēre, comprehendere; *(a cold)* incidere in *(w. acc)*; **I can't — him to talk** non queo orare ut loquatur; **now — this** nunc cognosce rem; **to — back** recuperare, repetere; **to — down** depromere; **to — hold of** prehendere; **to — in** *(crops)* condere; **to —** *(a defendant)* **off** expedire, servare; **to — out** *(a spot)* oblitterare; *(to extort)* extorquēre; **to — ready** parare; **to — rid of** tollere; *(a person)* amoliri; **to — the better of** superare; **to — together** cogere ‖ *intr (to become)* fieri; **— out of my way!** de via mea decede *(pl:* decedite)!; **to — abroad** palam fieri; **to — along well** bene se habēre; **to — along with** concorditer congruere cum *(w. abl)*; **to — away** aufugere, evadere; **to — at** ulcisci; **to — back** reverti; **to — down** descendere; **to — dressed** amiciri; **to — even with** malum vicissim dare *(w. dat)*; **to — in** pervenire; **to — off** aufugere; *(a bus, plane, ship, train)* egredi de *(w. abl)*; **to — on** procedere; *(a horse)* conscendere; *(a bus, plane, ship, train)* inscendere in *(w. acc)*; **to — on well** bene se habēre; *(to succeed)* bene succedere; **to — out** exire; (e curru) descendere; **to — out of** *(a situation)* evadere; **to — over** *(a wall)* transcendere; *(difficulty)* superare; *(a sickness)* convalescere ex *(w. abl)*; **to — ready** sese parare; **to — rid of (that pest)** (istum molestum) amoliri; **to — somewhere** aliquid consequi; **to — through** *(to complete)* conficere; **to — to** *(a place)* prevenire; **to — together** congregari, convenire; **to — up** surgere; *(as a group)* consurgere; *(from sleep)* expergisci; *(out of respect due s.o.)* assurgere
ghastly *adj (deadly pale)* lurid•us -a -um; *(shocking)* foed•us -a -um
ghost *s* umbr•a -ae *f; (haunting spirit)* larv•a -ae *f*; **to give up the —** animam ebullire
ghost town *s* urb•s -is *f* deserta
giant *s* gig•as -antis *m*
gibberish *s* nug•ae -arum *fpl*
gibbet *s* patibul•um -i *n*
gibe *s* irrisi•o -onis *f*
gibe *tr & intr* irridēre
giblets *spl* gingeri•a -orum *npl*
Gibraltar *s* Calp•e -es *f*; **strait of —** fret•um -i *n* Gaditanum
giddiness *s* vertig•o -inis *f*
giddy *adj* vertiginos•us -a -um; *(light-minded)* lev•is -is -e
gift *s* don•um -i *n*, mun•us -eris *n; (e.g., of beauty)* do•s -tis *f*
gifted *adj* ingenios•us -a -um; *(endowed)* praedit•us -a -um
gig *s (carriage)* cis•ium -(i)i *n*
gigantic *adj* praegrand•is -is -e
giggle *intr* summissim cachinnare
gild *tr* inaurare
gilded *adj* inaurat•us -a -um
gilding *s (art)* auratur•a -ae *f; (gilded work)* aur•um -i *n* inductum
gills *spl* branchi•ae -arum *fpl*
gilt *adj* inaurat•us -a -um
gin *s* iunipero infectus spirit•us -ūs *m*
ginger *s* zingi•ber -beris *n*
gingerly *adv* pedetemptim
giraffe *s* camelopardal•is -is *f*
gird *tr* cingere; **to — oneself** cingi
girder *s* tign•um -i *n*
girdle *s* stropp•i -orum *mpl*
girdle *tr* cingere
girl *s* puell•a -ae *f; (unmarried girl)* virg•o -inis *f*
girlfriend *s* amicul•a -ae *f*
girlhood *s* puellaris aet•as -atis *f*
girlish *adj* puellar•is -is -e
girth *s (measure around)* ambit•us -ūs *m; (of a horse)* cingul•a -ae *f*
gist *s* summ•a -ae *f*
give *tr* dare; *(as a gift)* donare; *(to deliver)* tradere; **give it here!** cedo *(pl:* cette)! [*an old imperative; can take a direct object*]; **— it to 'em!** adhibe! *(pl:* adhibite!); **not — a hoot about s.o.** aliquem dupundi

non facere; **to — in marriage** in matrimonium dare; **to — away** donare; *(to betray)* prodere; **to — back** reddere; **to — forth** emittere; **to — oneself up to** se addicere *(w. dat)*; **to — off** emittere; **to — out** ēdere; **to — s.o. a dirty look** respicere aliquem minus familiari vultu; **to — s.o. the slip** alicui subterfugere; **to — up** *(hope, power)* deponere; *(to abandon)* dimittere; **to — up the ghost** animam ebullire; **to — way** *(to yield)* cedere; *(to comply)* obsequi; *(mil)* pedem referre ‖ *intr* **to — in to** cedere *(w. dat)*; **to — up** *(to surrender)* se dedere; *(to stop)* desistere

giver *s* da·tor -toris *m* (·trix -tricis *f*)

giving *s* dati·o -onis *f*

glacial *adj* glacial·is -is -e

glacier *s* mol·es -is *f* conglaciata

glad *adj* laet·us -a -um; **I am — to hear that** libenter audio *(w. acc & inf)*; **to be —** gaudēre

gladden *tr* laetificare

glade *s* nem·us -oris *n*

gladiator *s* gladiat·or -oris *m*

gladiatorial *adj* gladiatori·us -a -um; **— show** mun·us -eris *n*

gladiola *s* gladiol·us -i *m*

gladly *adv* libenter

gladness *s* gaud·ium -(i)i *n*

glamor *s* nit·or -oris *m*

glamorous *adj* nitid·us -a -um; **to be —** nitēre

glance *s* aspect·us -ūs *m*; **at a —** primo aspectu; **to cast a — at** strictim aspicere

glance *intr* **to — at** strictim aspicere; *(in reading)* strictim legere; **to — off** stringere

gland *s* glandul·a -ae *f*

glare *s* fulg·or -oris *m*

glare *intr* fulgēre; **to — at** torvis oculis tueri

glaring *adj* fulg·ens -entis; *(striking)* manifest·us -a -um

glass *s (material)* vitr·um -i *n*; *(for drinking)* cal·ix -icis *m* vitreus, pocill·um -i *n* vitreum; **—es** perspicill·a -orum *npl*; **to wear —es** perspicillis uti

glass *adj* vitre·us -a -um

glassware *s* vitre·a -orum *npl*

glaze *tr* vitrum illinere *(w. dat)*

gleam *s* fulg·or -oris *m*; *(fig)* aur·a -ae *f*; **slight — of hope** levis aur·a -ae *f* spei

gleam *intr* coruscare

gleaming *adj* corusc·us -a -um

glean *tr* colligere

gleaning *s* spicileg·ium -(i)i *n*

glee *s* laetiti·a -ae *f*

gleeful *adj* laet·us -a -um

gleefully *adv* laete

glib *adj* volubil·is -is -e

glibly *adv* volubiliter

glide *intr* labi

glider *s* anemoplan·um -i *n*

glimmer *s* lu·x -cis *f* dubia; **— of hope** specul·a -ae *f*

glimmer *intr* sublucēre

glimpse *s* aspect·us -ūs *m* brevis; **to have a — of** dispicere

glisten *tr* nitēre

glistening *adj* nitid·us -a -um

glitter *s* fulg·or -oris *m*

glitter *intr* fulgēre

gloat *intr* oculos pascere; **to — over** oculos pascere *(w. abl)*, exsultare *(w. abl)*

globe *s* glob·us -i *m*; *(earth)* orb·is -is *m* terrarum

globule *s* globul·us -i *m*

gloom *s* tenebr·ae -arum *fpl*; *(fig)* maestiti·a -ae *f*

gloomily *adv* maeste

gloomy *adj* tenebros·us -a -um; *(fig)* maest·us -a -um

glorification *s* glorificati·o -onis *f*

glorify *tr* glorificare

glorious *adj* glorios·us -a -um

gloriously *adv* gloriose

glory *s* glori·a -ae *f*

glory *intr* **(in)** gloriari (in *w. abl)*

gloss *s (on a word)* interpretati·o -onis *f*; *(sheen)* nit·or -oris *m*

gloss *tr* annotare; **to — over** colorare

glossary *s* glossar·ium -(i)i *n*

glossy *adj* nitid·us -a -um

glove *s* chirothec·a -ae *f*; *(for work)* digitabul·um -i *n*

glow *s* ard·or -oris *m*

glow *intr* ardēre

glowing *adj* ard·ens -entis; *(w. heat)* cand·ens -entis; **to speak in — terms about** ornatissime loqui de *(w. abl)*

glowingly *adv* ferventer

glue *s* glut·en -inis *n*

glue *tr* glutinare; **to — together** conglutinare

glum *adj* maest·us -a -um, trist·is -is -e

glut *tr* satiare

glutton *s* hellu·o -onis *m*; **to be a —** helluari

gluttonous *adj* gulos·us -a -um

gnarled *adj* nodos·us -a -um

gnash *tr* **to — the teeth** dentibus frendere

gnat *s* cul·ex -icis *m*

gnaw *tr & intr* rod·o -ere rosi rosus; **to — at** arrodere

gnawing *adj* mord·ax -acis

go *s (try)* conat·us -ūs *m*; **to have a — at** tentare; **to make a — of it** rem bene gerere; **on the —** nav·us -a -um

go *intr* eo ire ii *or* ivi iturus; **to — about** *(work)* aggredi; **to — abroad** peregre exire; **to — after** petere; **to — against** obstare, adversari *(w. dat)*; **to — along with** assentire *(w. dat)*; **to — around** circumire; **to — aside** discedere; **to — astray** errare; **to — back** reverti; **to —**

back on one's word fidem fallere; **to — before** praeire *(w. dat)*; **to — between** intervenire; **to — beyond** egredi; *(fig)* excedere; **to — by** *(to pass)* praeterire; *(the rules)* servare; *(promises)* stare *(w. abl)*; **to — down** descendere; *(of sun)* occidere; *(of ship)* mergi; *(of price)* laxari; *(of swelling)* se summittere; **to — for** petere; *(to fetch a person)* adducere; *(a thing)* adferre; *(the bait)* appetere; **to — forth** exire; **to — in** introire; **to — into** inire; **to — off** abire; *(as gun)* displodere; **to — on** *(to continue)* pergere; *(to happen)* fieri, agi; **to — out** exire; *(of fire)* exstingui; **to — out ahead** antecedere; **to — out of doors** prodire; **to — over** *(to cross)* transire; *(a subject)* percurrere; *(to examine)* perscrutari; *(to repeat)* repetere; **to — straight** rectum iter vitae insistere; **to — through** *(to travel through)* obire; *(to suffer)* perferre; **to — through with** pertendere; **to — to** adire, accedere ad; **to — to and fro** commeare; **to — to the aid of** succurrere *(w. dat)*; **to — towards** petere; **to — under** submergi; **to — up** subire *(w. acc)*; *(of prices)* ingravescere; **to — with** comitari; **what's going on?** quid agitur?; **what's going on here?** quid rei hic est?

goad *s* stimul·us -i *m*

goad *tr* instigare; *(fig)* stimulare; *(to exasperate)* exasperare

goal *s* fin·is -is *m; (at the racetrack)* cal·x -cis *f; (sports)* port·a -ae *f*; **to score a —** *(in soccer)* follem in portam pede pulsare

goal keeper *s* portari·us -i *m* (·a -ae *f*)

goal line *s* calx, calcis *f*, cret·a -ae *f*

goal post *s* pal·us -i *m* portae

goat *s* ca·per -pri *m*, capr·a -ae *f*; **—s bleat** capri balant

gobble *tr* devorare

gobbler *s* hellu·o -onis *m*

go-between *s* internunti·us -i *m* (·a -ae *f*)

goblet *s* pocul·um -i *n*

goblin *s* larv·a -ae *f*

god *s* de·us -i *m*; **God** De·us -i *m*; **God bless you!** tibi di bene faciunt!; *(to s.o. sneezing)* salve! *or* salutem!; **— forbid!** Deus averruncet!; **— willing** Deo volente; **thank —** Deo gratias!; **ye —s!** di superi!

god-awful *adj* taeterrim·us -a -um

goddess *s* de·a -ae *f*

godfather *s* spons·or -oris *m* loco infantis, patrin·us -i *m*

godhead *s* deit·as -atis *f*

godless *adj* impi·us -a -um

godlike *adj* divin·us -a -um

godliness *s* piet·as -atis *f*

godmother *s* spons·trix -tricis *f* loco infantis, matrin·a -ae *f*

going *s* iti·o -onis *f*; **good —!** bene factum!

gold *adj* aure·us -a -um

gold *s* aur·um -i *n*

golden *adj* aure·us -a -um

goldfinch *s* cardel·is -is *f*

goldfish *s* hippur·us -i *m*

gold leaf *s* auri bracte·a -ae *f*

gold mine *s* aurifodin·a -ae *f*

gold-plated *adj* aurat·us -a -um

goldsmith *s* aurif·ex -icis *m*

good *adj* bon·us -a -um; *(morally)* prob·us -a -um; *(useful)* util·is -is -e; *(beneficial)* salutar·is -is -e; *(kindhearted)* benevol·us -a -um; *(fit)* idone·us -a -um; **— and proper** plane et probe; **— for you!** *(said in praise)* macte virtute esto! *(pl:* estote!); **— going!** bene factum!; **— —!** euge, euge!; **— job!** bene *(or* recte) factum!; **— thinking!** bene putas!; **— turn** benefic·ium -(i)i *n*; **I am having a — time** mihi pulchre est; **it is — to** *(w. inf)* commodum est *(w. inf)*; **it is not — to** *(w. inf)* non convenit *(w. inf)*; **to be — for** prodesse *(w. dat)*; *(to be valid)* valēre; **to do s.o. —** alicui prodesse; **to have a — time** *(to celebrate)* genio indulgēre; **to make —** compensare; **to seem —** videri

good *n* bon·um -i *n*; *(profit)* lucr·um -i *n*; **for —** in perpetuum; **—s** bon·a -orum *npl*; *(for sale)* merc·es -cium *fpl*; **it does no —** non prodest; **to do s.o. —** alicui prodesse

good *interj* bene!; **very —** bene sane!

goodbye *interj* vale! *(pl:* valete!); **to say —** vale iubēre

good-for-nothing *s* **to be a —** nihil hominis esse

good-for-nothing *adj* nequam [*indecl*]

good-hearted *adj* benevol·us -a -um

goodly *adj (amount)* ampl·us -a -um; **a — number of** nonnull·i -ae -a

good-natured *adj* facil·is -is -e

goodness *s* bonit·as -atis *f*; *(moral)* probit·as -atis *f*; *(generosity)* benignit·as -atis *f*

goodwill *s* **(toward)** benevolenti·a -ae *f* (in *w. acc)*

goose *s* ans·er -eris *m*; **geese cackle** anseres gingriunt

gooseberry *s* acin·us -i *m* grossulae

gore *s* cru·or -oris *m*

gore *tr* cornibus confodere

gorge *s* angusti·ae -arum *fpl*

gorge *tr* **to — oneself** se ingurgitare

gorgeous *adj* laut·us -a -um

gorgeously *adv* laute

Gorgon *s* Gorg·o -onis *f*

gory *adj* cruent·us -a -um

gospel *s* evangel·ium -(i)i *n*

gossamer *s* arane·a -ae *f*

gossip *s (talk)* gerr·ae -arum *fpl*, fam·a -ae *f; (person)* garrul·us -i *m* (·a -ae *f*)

gossip *intr* garrire

gouge *tr* **to — out s.o.'s eye** oculum alicui eruere; *(to swindle)* fraudare

gourd *s* cucurbit·a -ae *f*
gout *s* arthrit·is -idis *f; (in the feet)* podagr·a -ae *f; (in the hands)* chiragr·a -ae *f*
govern *tr* imperare *(w. dat),* gubernare; *(to control)* moderari; *(a province)* praeesse *(w. dat); (gram)* iungi *(w. dat)*
governess *s* magistr·a -ae *f*
government *s* res *f* publica *(gen:* rei publicae) [*also written as one word*]
governor *s (of a province)* praes·es -idis *m; (of an imperial province)* legat·us -i *m; (of a Roman province)* procons·ul -ulis *m; (of a smaller province)* procurat·or -oris *m*
governorship *s* praefectur·a -ae *f*
gown *s* vest·is -is *f* talaris; *(of a Roman woman)* stol·a -ae *f*
grab *tr* rapere; **to — hold of** invadere; **to — with both hands** inicere utramque manum *(w. dat)*
grace *s* grati·a -ae *f; (pardon)* veni·a -ae *f;* to say — *(before meals)* consecrationem recitare; *(after meals)* gratias agere
grace *tr (to adorn)* decorare; *(to add honor and distinction)* honestare
graceful *adj* decor·us -a -um
gracefully *adv* decore
graceless *adj* illepid·us -a -um
Graces *spl* Grati·ae -arum *fpl*
gracious *adj* benign·us -a -um
graciously *adv* benigne
gradation *s* grad·us -ūs *m; (rhet)* gradati·o -onis *f*
grade *s* grad·us -ūs *m; (mark or letter for performance)* not·a -ae *f*
grade *tr (papers)* notare; *(to evaluate students' work)* aestimare
gradient *s* proclivit·as -atis *f*
gradual *adj* per gradus
gradually *adv* gradatim, sensim
graduate *tr* ad gradum admittere ‖ *intr* gradūs suscipere, diploma studiorum adipisci
graduate *s* graduat·us -i *m* (·a -ae *f*)
graft *s* surcul·us -i *m; (pol)* ambit·us -ūs *m*
graft *tr* inserere
grain *s (single)* gran·um -i *n;* frument·um -i *n; (in wood)* fibr·a -ae *f;* **against the —** transversis fibris; *(fig)* invitā Minervā; **with a — of salt** cum grano salis
grammar *s* grammatic·a -ae *f; (book)* ars, artis *f*
grammarian *s* grammatic·us -i *m*
grammatical *adj* grammatic·us -a -um
granary *s* horre·um -i *n*
grand *adj* grand·is -is -e; **— old style of oratory** grandis orati·o -onis *f*
grandchild *s* nep·os -otis *m,* nept·is -is *f*
granddaughter *s* nept·is -is *f*
grandeur *s* maiest·as -atis *f*
grandfather *s* av·us -i *m*
grandiloquent *adj* grandiloqu·us -a -um
grandmother *s* avi·a -ae *f*
grand piano *s* clavicord·ium -(i)i *n* aliforme
grandson *s* nep·os -otis *m*
grant *tr (to bestow)* concedere; *(usu. s.th. that is due)* tribuere; *(to acknowledge)* fatēri; *(in geometry)* dare; **—ed, he himself is nothing** esto, ipse nihil est; **— that** sit quidem ut; **to take for —ed** sumere
grant *s* concessi·o -onis *f;* **to make anyone a — of anything** aliquid alicui concedere
granular *adj* granos·us -a -um
grape *s* uv·a -ae *f,* acin·us -i *m;* **bunch of —s** uva
grape picker *s* vindemit·or -oris *m*
grapevine *s* vit·is -is *f; (fig)* fam·a -ae *f*
graphic *adj (fig)* express·us -a -um
graphically *adv (fig)* expresse
grapnel *s* unc·us -i *m*
grapple *intr* luctari
grasp *s (act of grasping; comprehension)* comprehensi·o -onis *f;* **he escaped my —** manus meas effugit; **to wrest from one's —** de manibus extorquēre; **within one's —** inter manūs
grasp *tr* prehendere; *(mentally)* comprehendere ‖ *intr* **to — at** *(lit & fig)* captare
grasping *adj* avar·us -a -um
grass *s* gram·en -inis *n,* herb·a -ae *f*
grasshopper *s* grill·us -i *m;* **—s chirp** grilli fritinniunt
grassy *adj* graminos·us -a -um
grate *s* clathr·i -orum *mpl; (hearth)* camin·us -i *m*
grate *tr* conterere ‖ *intr* stridēre; **to — upon s.o.** alicuius animum offendere
grateful *adj* grat·us -a -um; **I am deeply — to you for** tibi gratiam habeo maximam quod *(w. indic)*
gratefully *adv* grate
gratification *s* gratificati·o -onis *f; (pleasure, delight)* volupt·as -atis *f,* delectati·o -onis *f;* **— of natural desires** expleti·o -onis *f* naturae
gratify *tr* gratificari *(w. dat)*
gratifying *adj* grat·us -a -um
grating *s* cancell·i -orum *mpl; (sound)* strid·or -oris *m*
gratis *adv* gratis
gratitude *s* grati·a -ae *f;* **to feel —** gratiam habēre; **to show —** gratiam referre
gratuitous *adj* gratuit·us -a -um
gratuitously *adv* gratuito
gratuity *s* stip·s -is *f*
grave *adj* grav·is -is -e; *(stern)* sever·us -a -um
grave *s* sepulcr·um -i *n*
gravel *s* glare·a -ae *f*
gravely *adv* graviter
gravestone *s* monument·um -i *n,* cipp·us -i *m*
graveyard *s* sepulcret·um -i *n*
gravitate *intr* vergere
gravitation *s* ponderati·o -onis *f*

gravity *s (importance; gravitational pull)* gravit•as -atis *f; (personal)* severit•as -atis *f*
gravy *s* iu•s -ris *n*
gravy bowl *s* vascul•um -i *n* iuris
gray *adj* can•us -a -um; **to become —** canescere
gray-eyed *adj* caesi•us -a -um
gray-headed *adj* can•us -a -um
grayish *adj* canesc•ens -entis
grayness *s* caniti•es -ei *f*
graze *tr (cattle)* pascere; *(to touch lightly)* perstingere ‖ *intr* pasci
grease *s* ad•eps -ipis *m; (lubricant)* axungi•a -ae *f*
grease *tr* ungere, illinere
grease job *s* uncti•o -onis *f* autocineti
greasy *adj* unct•us -a -um
great *adj* magn•us -a -um; *(thirst)* ing•ens -entis; **as — as** tant•us ... quant•us -a -um; **— amount of money** ingens pecuni•a -ae *f;* **— big** grand•is -is -e; **it was really —!** bene fuit mehercule!; **how —** quant•us -a -um; **so —** tant•us -a -um; **very —** permagn•us -a -um, maxim•us -a -um
great *interj* eu!; papae! *(expression of surprise and delight)*
great-aunt *s (on father's side)* proamit•a -ae *f; (on mother's side)* promaterter•a -ae *f*
great-granddaughter *s* pronept•is -is *f*
greater *adj* mai•or -or -us *(gen:* maioris)
greatest *adj* maxim•us -a -um
great-grandfather *s* prova•us -i *m*
great-grandmother *s* proavi•a -ae *f*
great-grandson *s* pronep•os -otis *m*
great-great-grandfather *s* abav•us -i *m*
great-great-great-grandfather *s* atav•us -i *m*
greatness *s* magnitud•o -inis *f*
great-uncle *s* avuncul•us -i *m* maior
greaves *spl* ocre•ae -arum *fpl*
Grecian *adj* Graec•us -a -um
Greece *s* Graeci•a -ae *f*
greed *s* avariti•a -ae *f*
greedily *adv* avide
greediness *s* avariti•a -ae *f*
greedy *adj* avid•us -a -um
Greek *adj* Graec•us -a -um
Greek *s* Graec•us -i *m;* **to know (read, speak, teach) —** Graece scire (legere, loqui, docēre)
green *adj* virid•is -is -e; *(dark-green)* prasin•us -a -um; *(fresh)* rec•ens -entis; *(unripe, e.g., apples)* crud•us -a -um; **to become —** virescere
green *s* col•or -oris *m* viridis; *(lawn)* loc•us -i *m* herbidus; **—s** holer•a -um *npl*
greenhouse *s* viridar•ium -(i)i *n* hibernum
greenish *adj* subvirid•is -is -e
greenness *s* viridit•as -atis *f; (fig)* crudit•as -atis *f*
green pepper *s* piperit•is -idis *f*
greet *tr* salutare, salutem dicere *(w. dat)*
greeting *s* salutati•o -onis *f;* **to return a —** resalutare
gregarious *adj* gregal•is -is -e; *(person)* social•is -is -e
grenade *s* pyrobol•us -i *m*
grey *see* **gray**
greyhound *s* vertag•us -i *m* (•a -ae *f)*
gridiron *s* craticul•a -ae *f*
grief *s* dol•or -oris *m,* maer•or -oris *m;* **good —!** mehercules!; **to come to —** perire; **to be overwhelmed with —** in maerore iacēre; **to feel — (over)** dolorem capere (ex *w. abl)*
grievance *s* querell•a -ae *f*
grieve *tr* dolore afficere ‖ *intr* maerēre, dolēre
grievous *adj* grav•is -is -e
grievously *adv* graviter
griffin *s* gryp•s -is *m*
grill *s* craticul•a -ae *f*
grill *tr* super craticulum assare; *(w. questions)* percontari
grim *adj* torv•us -a -um; *(e.g., winter)* deform•is -is -e
grimace *s* vult•us -ūs *m* distortus
grimly *adv* torve
grin *s* subris•us -ūs *m* distortus
grin *intr* distorto vultu subridēre
grind *tr (grain)* molere; *(in mortar)* contundere; *(on whetstone)* exacuere; **to — out a song** canticum extorquēre; **to — the teeth** dentibus frendere
grindstone *s* co•s -tis *f*
grip *s* comprehensi•o -onis *f*
grip *tr* comprehendere
gripping *adj* mov•ens -entis
grisly *adj* horrend•us -a -um
gristle *s* cartilag•o -inis *f*
gristly *adj* cartilaginos•us -a -um
grit *s* haren•a -ae *f*
gritty *adj* harenos•us -a -um
grizzly *adj* can•us -a -um
grizzly bear *s* urs•us -i *m* horridus
groan *s* gemit•us -ūs *m*
groan *intr* gemere
grocer *s* olitari•us -i *m* (•a -ae *f)*
groceries *spl* obsoni•a -orum *npl;* **to shop for —** obsonare
grocery store *s* tabern•a -ae *f* cibaria
groggy *adj* titub•ans -antis
groin *s* ingu•en -inis *n*
groom *s* novus marit•us -i *m*
groom *tr* curare
groove *s* stri•a -ae *f*
groove *tr* striare
grope *intr* praetentare
gropingly *adv* pedetentim
gross *adj (corpulent)* crass•us -a -um; *(indelicate)* indecor•us -a -um; *(coarse)* rud•is -is -e; *(inordinate)* nimi•us -a -um; *(ignorance, folly)* ing•ens -entis
grossly *adv* nimium

grotesque *adj* distort·us -a -um
grotto *s* antr·um -i *n*
ground *s* sol·um -i *n,* hum·us -i *m,* terr·a -ae *f; (level ground)* sol·um -i *n; (reason)* rati·o -onis *f; (place)* loc·us -i *m;* **on the —** humi; **to be burnt to the —** ad solum exuri; **to fall to the —** ad terram decidere; **to gain —** proficere; **to level with the —** solo adaequare; **to lose —** recedere; *(mil)* pedem referre
ground *tr* fundare; *(to teach)* imbuere; *(a ship)* subducere; **||** *intr (naut)* haerēre
ground beef *s* bubul·a -ae *f* concisa
ground floor *s* pedeplan·a -orum *npl*
groundless *adj* van·us -a -um; *(false)* fals·us -a -um
groundwork *s* substructi·o -onis *f; (fig)* fundament·um -i *n;* **to lay the —** fundamentum iacēre *(or* agere)
group *s (band)* man·us -ūs *f; (class)* gen·us -eris *n; (crowd)* glob·us -i *m*
group *tr* disponere **||** *intr* **to — around** circulari, stipari
grouping *s* dispositi·o -onis *f*
grouse *s (bird)* tetra·o -onis *m*
grove *s* nem·us -oris *n; (sacred grove)* luc·us -i *m*
grovel *intr* repere, se prosternere
grow *tr* colere, serere **||** *intr* crescere; *(to become)* fieri; *(of vegetables)* nasci; *(to shoot up)* se promittere; **to let the hair, beard — long** capillam, barbam promittere; **to — back** renasci; **to — old** senescere; **to — out** excrescere; **to — out of** *(e.g., a wall)* innasci *(w. dat or* in *w. abl); (fig)* oriri ex *(w. abl);* **to — over** *(e.g., of a skin over a wound)* induci *(w. dat);* **to — silent** tacēre; **to — up** adolescere; *(to arrive at puberty)* pubescere
grower *s* cult·or -oris *m*
growl *s* fremit·us -ūs *m*
growl *intr* fremere; **to — at** ogganire
grown-up *adj* adult·us -a -um
growth *s* increment·um -i *n;* **full —** maturit·as -atis *f*
grub *s* vermicul·us -i *m; (food)* vict·us -ūs *m*
grub *intr* effodere
grudge *s* invidi·a -ae *f;* **to hold a — against** succensēre *(w. dat)*
grudgingly *adv* invit·us -a -um *(adj in agreement with the subject)*
gruelling *adj* (de)fatig·ans -antis
gruesome *adj* tae·ter -tra -trum
gruff *adj* asp·er -era -erum
gruffly *adv* aspere
gruffness *s* asperit·as -atis *f*
grumble *intr* murmurare; *(in a suppressed tone)* mussare; **to — about** queri de *(w. abl)*
grumbling *s* increpati·o -onis *f*
grumpy *adj* stomachos·us -a -um
grunt *s (of a bear, pig)* grunnit·us -ūs *m*
grunt *intr (of a bear, pig)* grunnire
guarantee *s* fid·es -ei *f; (money)* sponsi·o -onis *f; (person who guarantees)* va·s -dis *m; (in legal contracts)* satisdati·o -onis *f;* **to give, receive a —** fidem dare, accipere
guarantee *tr* fidem dare *(w. dat),* spondēre
guaranteed *adj* spons·us -a -um
guarantor *s* spons·or -oris *m* (·rix -ricis *f)*
guard *s* custodi·a -ae *f; (mil)* praesid·ium -(i)i *n; (person)* cust·os -odis *mf;* **to be on one's — against** praecavēre; **to mount —** custodiam agere
guard *tr* custodire **||** *intr* **to — against** cavēre
guarded *adj* caut·us -a -um
guardedly *adv* caute
guardhouse *s* carc·er -eris *m* militaris
guardian *s* cust·os -odis *mf; (of minor or orphan)* tut·or -oris *m*
guardianship *s* custodi·a -ae *f; (of minor or woman)* tutel·a -ae *f*
guess *s* coniecti·o -onis *f*
guess *tr & intr* conicere, divinare
guest *s* hosp·es -itis *mf; (at dinner)* conviv·a -ae *mf*
guest room *s* hospit·ium -(i)i *n*
guidance *s* duct·us -ūs *m; (advice)* consil·ium -(i)i *n;* **under the — of the deity** deo ducente
guidance counselor *s* consiliat·or -oris *m* academicus, consiliatr·ix -icis *f* academica
guide *s* dux, ducis *mf;* itineris dux *mf*
guide *tr (as a local guide)* ducere; *(to manage, control)* regere
guidebook *s* itinerar·ium -(i)i *n*
guided missile *s* missil·e -is *n* directum
guild *s* colleg·ium -(i)i *n*
guile *s* dol·us -i *m*
guileful *adj* dolos·us -a -um
guileless *adj* simpl·ex -icis
guilt *s* culp·a -ae *f*
guilty *adj* son·s -tis; **— of** noc·ens -entis *(w. gen or abl);* **the — one** sons, sontis *mf;* **to be found — of** noxi·us -a diiudicari *(w. gen or abl);* **to be —** in culpā esse; **to punish the —** sontes punire
guise *s* speci·es -ei *f; (features, dress)* habit·us -ūs *m;* **under the — of** sub specie *(w. gen)*
guitar *s* cithar·a -ae *f* Hispanica
gulf *s* sin·us -ūs *m*
gull *s* merg·us -i *m*
gullet *s* gul·a -ae *f*
gullibility *s* credulit·as -atis *f*
gullible *adj* credul·us -a -um
gulp *s* singult·us -ūs *m*
gulp *tr* **to — down** absorbēre **||** *intr* singultare
gum *s* gummi *n* [*indecl*], gumm·is -is *f; (anat)* gingiv·a -ae *f*
gumption *s* alacrit·as -atis *f*
gun *s* sclopet·um -i *n;* **to fire the —** sclopetare; **to jump the —** signum praev-

ertere; **to stick to one's —s** in sententiā stare
gurgle *intr* singultare; *(of a stream)* murmurare
gurgling *s* singult•us -ūs *m; (of a stream)* murmurati•o -onis *f*
gush *s* effusi•o -onis *f,* erupti•o -onis *f; (of water)* scatebr•a -ae *f;* **with a — of tears** profusis lacrimis
gush *intr* scaturire; **to — out** prorumpere; *(of blood from a wound)* emicare
gust *s* flam•en -inis *n,* flat•us -ūs *m*
gusto *s* stud•ium -(i)i *n*
gusty *adj* procellos•us -a -um
gut *s* intestin•um -i *n*
gut *tr* exenterare; *(a building)* amburere
gutted *adj (by fire)* ambust•us -a -um
gutter *s* canal•is -is *m,* riv•us -i *m;* **to clean out the —** rivos deducere
guttural *adj* guttural•is -is -e
guy *s* **poor —** homuncul•us -i *m;* **that —** iste
guzzle *tr & intr* potare gulose
guzzler *s* po•tor -toris *m,* (•trix -ricis) *f*
gym *s* gymnas•ium -(i)i *n*
gym instructor exercita•tor -oris *m* (•trix -tricis *f*)
gym shoes *spl* calce•i -orum *mpl* gymnici
gymnasium *s* gymnas•ium -(i)i *n*
gymnastic *adj* gymnastic•us -a -um
gymnastics *spl* palaestric•a -ae *f*
gynecology *s* gynaecologi•a -ae *f*
gypsum *s* gyps•um -i *n*
gyrate *intr* gyrare

H

habit *s* consuetud•o -inis *f; (dress)* habit•us -ūs *m;* **to be in the — of** consuescere *(w. inf);* **to break the —** abscedere ab usu; **to get into the — of** se assuefacere *(w. inf)*
habitation *s* habitati•o -onis *f*
habitual *adj* usitat•us -a -um
habitually *adv* de more, ex more
habituate *tr* assuefacere
hack *s (cut)* plag•a -ae *f; (taxicab) (coll)* raed•a -ae *f* meritoria
hack *tr* caedere; **to — to pieces** concidere
hacker *s (comput)* effractar•ius -(i)i *m* electronicus, effractari•a -ae *f* electronica
hackneyed *adj* trit•us -a -um
haddock *s* gad•us -i *m*
hag *s* an•us -ūs *f*
haggard *adj* ma•cer -cra -crum
haggle *intr (to bargain)* licitari; *(to wrangle)* altercari
ha-ha-ha *interj* hahhahae!
hail *s* grand•o -inis *f*
hail *intr* **it is —ing** grandinat
hail *tr* appellare
hail *interj* salve! *(pl:* salvēte!)
hailstone *s* grandinis gran•um -i *n*
hailstorm *s* grandin•es -um *fpl*
hair *s (of head or beard)* capill•us -i *m, (or* capill•i -orum *mpl); (in locks or dressed)* crin•is -is *m; (hair as an ornament, of men or women)* com•a -ae *f; (single)* pil•us -i *m; (of an animal)* saet•a -ae *f;* **he was within a —'s breadth of** nil propius est factum quam ut; **long —** *(left uncut)* capilli promissi; **to split —s** cavillari
hairbrush *s* penicul•us -i *m* comatorius
haircut *s* tons•us -ūs *m;* **to get a —** facere ut capilli tondeantur
hairdo *s* compt•us -ūs *m*
hairdresser *s* tons•trix -tricis *f*
hair dryer *s* favoni•us -i *m*
hairless *adj (of head)* calv•us -a -um; *(of body)* gla•ber -bra -brum
hairnet *s* reticul•um -i *n*
hair oil *s* capillar•e -is *n*
hairpin *s* crinal•e -is *n*
hairstyle *s* compt•us -ūs *m*
hairy *adj* pilos•us -a -um; *(chest)* saetos•us -a -um, hirsut•us -a -um
hale *adj* **— and hardy** salv•us et valid•us -a -um
half *s* dimidia par•s -tis *f*
half *adv* dimidio; *(partly)* partim; **— and —** pro parte semissā
half *adj* dimidiat•us -a -um, dimidi•us -a -um; **— the drinks** dimidiae potion•es -um *fpl*
half alive *adj* semiviv•us -a -um
half asleep *adj* semisomn•us -a -um
halfbreed *s* hybrid•a -ae *mf*
half brother *s (on mother's side)* fra•ter -tris *m* uterin•us; *(on father's side)* fra•ter -tris *m* consanguineus
half-burnt *adj* semiust•us -a -um
half-cooked *adj* semicoct•us -a -um
half-dead *adj* semianim•us -a -um
half-eaten *adj* semes•us -a -um
half-finished *adj* semiperfect•us -a -um
half-full *adj* semiplen•us -a -um
half-hour *s* semihor•a -ae *f*
half-moon *s* lun•a -ae *f* dimidiata; *(shape)* lunul•a -ae *f*
half-open *adj* semiapert•us -a -um
half pint *s (sl)* homuncul•us -i *m*
half pound *s* selibr•a -ae *f*
half sister *s (on mother's side)* sor•or -oris *f* uterina; *(on father's side)* sor•or -oris *f* consanguinea
halftime *s (sports)* dimidium temp•us -oris *n*
halfway *adj* medi•us -a -um
half-year *adj* semestr•is -is -e
hall *s (large room)* atr•ium -(i)i *n,* aul•a -ae *f; (corridor)* andr•on -onis *m; (building for meetings)* curi•a -ae *f,* basilic•a -ae *f*
hallo *interj* heus!
hallucinate *intr* alucinari
hallucination *s* alucinati•o -onis *f*

hallway *s* andr·on -onis *m; (at front of house)* fauc·es -ium *fpl*
halo *s* coron·a -ae *f*
halt *s* paus·a -ae *f,* mor·a -ae *f;* **to come to a —** consistere
halt *tr* sistere ‖ *intr* consistere; *(to limp)* claudicare
halter *s* capistr·um -i *n*
halting *adj* claud·us -a -um; *(fig)* haesitabund·us -a -um
halve *tr* ex aequo dividere
ham *s* pern·a -ae *f; (back of the knee)* popl·es -itis *m;* **smoked —** perna fumosa
hamburger *s* bubul·a -ae *f* concisa
hamlet *s* vic·us -i *m*
hammer *s* malle·us -i *m*
hammer *tr* malleo tundere
hamper *s* corb·is -is *m*
hamper *tr* impedire
ham sandwich *s* pastill·um -i *n* pernā fartum
hamstring *s* poplitis nerv·us -i *m*
hamstring *tr* poplitem succidere *(w. dat); (fig)* impedire
hand *s* man·us -ūs *f; (handwriting)* chirograph·um -i *n; (of dial)* gnom·on -onis *n; (worker)* operar·ius -(i)i *m;* **at —** praesto, ad manum; **by —** manu; **from — to —** de manu in manum; **— in —** iunctis manibus; **—s off!** noli *(pl:* nolite) tangere!; aufer(te) manūs!; **—s up!** tolle *(pl:* tollite) manus!; **left —** laev·a -ae *f,* sinistr·a -ae *f;* **old —** veterat·or -oris *mf;* **on the one —, on the other** unā ex parte ... alterā ex parte; *or use* hic ... ille; **on the other —** contra; **right —** dext(e)r·a -ae *f;* **these things are not in our —s** haec non sunt in nostra manu; **to be near at —** subesse; **to have a — in s.th.** interesse alicui rei; **to have clean —s** manūs pecuniae abstinentes habēre; **to have in —** in manibus habēre; **to have one's —s full** satagere; **to lay —s on** manum inicere *(w. dat);* **to live from — to mouth** in horam vivere; **to pass a thing from — to —** aliquid de manu in manum tradere; **to shake —s** dextram dextrae iungere; **to sit on one's —s** *(fig)* compressis manibus sedēre; **to take in —** suscipere
hand *tr* tradere, porrigere; **to be —ed over to** *(by a judge)* adiudicari *(w. dat);* **to — around** circumferre; **to — down** tradere; **to — in** reddere; **to — over** tradere; *(to betray)* prodere
handbag *s* bulg·a -ae *f; (for traveling)* vidul·a -ae *f*
handbook *s* enchirid·ion -(i)i *n,* manual·e -is *n*
handbrake *s* sufflam·en -inis *n* manuale
handcuff *tr* manicas inicere *(w. dat)*
handcuffs *spl* manic·ae -arum *fpl*
handful *s* manipul·us -i *m*
handicraft *s* artific·ium -(i)i *n*
handiwork *s* opific·ium -(i)i *n*
handkerchief *s* sudar·ium -(i)i *n,* mucinn·ium -(i)i *n*
handle *s* manubr·ium -(i)i *n; (of a cup)* ansul·a -ae *f*
handle *tr* tractare
handlebars *spl* manubr·ium -(i)i *n*
handling *s* tractati·o -onis *f*
hand luggage *s* sarcinul·ae -arum *fpl* manuales
handsome *adj* pul·cher -chra -chrum
handsomely *adv* pulchre; *(liberally)* liberaliter
handsomeness *s* pulchritud·o -inis *f*
handwriting *s* chirograph·um -i *n*
handy *adj (of things)* habil·is -is -e; *(of persons)* soller·s -tis; *(at hand)* praesto
hang *tr* suspendere; *(by a line)* appendere; *(the head)* demittere; **go — yourself!** abi in malam crucem! ‖ *intr* pendēre; **—ing down** demiss·us -a -um; **to — around with** frequens adesse cum *(w. abl);* **to — down** dependēre; **to — on to** haerēre *(w. dat);* **to — out with** *(coll)* morari cum *(w. abl);* **to — over** imminēre *(w. dat)*
hangar *s* receptacul·um -i *n* aëroplani *(or* aëroplanorum)
hanger-on *s* assecl·a -ae *mf*
hanging *adj* pensil·is -is -e
hanging *s (execution)* suspend·ium -(i)i *n;* **—s** aulae·a -orum *npl*
hangman *s* carnif·ex -icis *m*
hangout *s* desidiabul·um -i *n*
hangover *s* crapul·a -ae *f;* **to sleep off a —** crapulam obdormire
hanker *intr* **— for** desiderare
haphazard *adj* fortuit·us -a -um
happen *intr* accidere, fieri, contingere; **I happened to spot** forte conspexi; **it happens that** contingit ut; **to — to s.o.** alicui contingere; **to — upon** incidere in *(w. acc);* **what happened?** quid factum est?
happily *adv* feliciter, beate
happiness *s* felicit·as -atis *f*
happy *adj* felix, beat·us -a -um
harangue *s* conti·o -onis *f;* **to give a —** contionem habēre
harangue *tr & intr* contionari
harass *tr* vexare
harassment *s* vexati·o -onis *f*
harbinger *s* praenunti·us -i *m* (·a -ae *f)*
harbor *s* port·us -ūs *m*
harbor *tr* excipere; **to — hopes, thoughts** portare spes, cogitationes
hard *adj* dur·us -a -um; *(difficult)* difficil·is -is -e; *(severe)* a·cer -cris -cre; **— on** dur·us -a -um in *(w. acc);* **— to please** difficil·is -is -e; **— work** op·us -eris *n* arduum; **it is — to do** est difficile factu; **to become —** durescere
hard *adv* valde, sedulo, summā vi; **to take s.th. —** aliquid aegre ferre

hardback *or* **hardcover book** li·ber -bri *m* lino contectus
hard drive *s (comput)* stati·o -onis *f* dura
harden *tr* durare; *(fig)* indurare ‖ *intr* durescere; *(fig)* obdurescere
hardhearted *adj* dur·us -a -um
hardiness *s* rob·ur -oris *n*
hardly *adv* vix, aegre; — **any** null·us -a -um fere
hardness *s* duriti·a -ae *f; (fig)* acerbit·as -atis *f*
hardship *s* lab·or -oris *m*
hardware *s* ferrament·a -orum *npl; (comput)* apparat·us -ūs *m* ordinatralis *(or* computatralis)
hardware store *s* tabern·a -ae *f* ferraria
hardworking *adj* laborios·us -a -um
hardy *adj* robust·us -a -um
hare *s* lep·us -oris *m*
harem *s* gynaece·um -i *n*
hark *interj* heus!
harken *intr* audire; **to — to** auscultare *(w. dat)*
harlot *s* meretr·ix -icis *f*
harm *s* iniuri·a -ae *f,* noxi·a -ae *f;* **to come to —** detrimentum accipere
harm *intr* nocēre *(w. dat),* laedere
harmful *adj* noxi·us -a -um
harmless *adj* innocu·us -a -um
harmonica *s* homonic·a -ae *f* inflatilis
harmonious *adj* canor·us -a -um; *(fig)* concor·s -dis
harmoniously *adv* consonanter; *(fig)* concorditer
harmonize *tr* componere ‖ *intr* concinere; *(fig)* consentire
harmony *s* harmoni·a -ae *f; (fig)* concordi·a -ae *f*
harness *s* equi ornament·a -orum *npl*
harp *s* lyr·a -ae *f;* **to play the —** lyrā ludere
harp *intr* **(on)** cantare; **to — on the same theme** cantilenam eandem canere
harpist *s* psalt·es -ae *m*
harpoon *s* iacul·um -i *n* hamatum
harpoon *tr* iaculo hamato transfigere
Harpy *s* Harpyi·a -ae *f*
harrow *s* irp·ex -icis *m*
harrow *tr* occare
harsh *adj* asp·er -era -erum; *(sound)* rauc·us -a -um; *(fig)* dur·us -a -um, sever·us -a -um; **— towards** dur·us -a -um in *(w. acc)*
harshly *adv* aspere, severe
harshness *s* asperit·as -atis *f,* duriti·a -ae *f*
harvest *s (reaping)* mess·is -is *f; (the crops)* provent·us -ūs *m*
harvest *tr* met·o -ere messui messus
hash *s* minut·al -alis *n*
hash *tr* comminu·o -ere -i -tus
haste *s* festinati·o -onis *f;* **in —** propere, festinanter; **to make —** properare
hasten *tr & intr* properare
hastily *adv* propere, raptim; *(without reflection)* temere
hastiness *s* celerit·as -atis *f; (without reflection)* temerit·as -atis *f*
hasty *adj* temerari·us -a -um
hat *s* petas·us -i *m*
hatch *s (naut)* foram·en -inis *n*
hatch *tr (fig)* coquere; *(of chickens)* ex ovis excludere
hatchet *s* asci·a -ae *f*
hate *s* od·ium -(i)i *n*
hate *tr* od·i -isse [*v defect*]
hateful *adj* odios·us -a -um, invis·us -a -um; **to be — to** odio esse *(w. dat)*
hatefully *adv* odiose
hatred *s* **(of, toward)** od·ium -(i)i *n* (in *w. acc)*
haughtily *adv* superbe
haughtiness *s* superbi·a -ae *f*
haughty *adj* superb·us -a -um
haul *s (catch)* captur·a -ae *f; (transport)* vectur·a -ae *f*
haul *tr* trahere, vehere; **to — off to prison** rapere in carcerem; **to — up** *(a boat)* subducere
haunch *s* clun·is -is *f* et cox·a -ae *f*
haunt *s* loc·us -i *m* frequentatus; *(of animals)* latebr·ae -arum *fpl*
haunt *tr* frequentare; *(to disturb)* inquietare
haunted *adj* a larvis frequentat·us -a -um
have *tr* habēre; *(to be obliged)* debēre; **— it your way!** esto ut libet; **I — confidence** fiducia est mihi; **to — a tough time of it** valde laborare; **to — it in for s.o.** alicui periculum denuntiare; **what do you — to do with her?** quid rei tibi est cum illā?
haven *s* port·us -ūs *m*
have-not *s* paup·er -eris *mf*
havoc *s* strag·es -is *f;* **to wreak —** stragem dare
hawk *s* accipi·ter -tris *mf;* **—s caw** accipitres crocitant
hawk *tr* venditare; **to — up phlegm** pituitam exsecrare per tussim
hawker *s* circulat·or -oris *m*
hawk-eyed *adj* lynce·us -a -um
hawser *s* retinacul·um -i *n*
hay *s* faen·um -i *n;* **make — while the sun shines!** occasionem amplectere!; carpe diem!; **to make —** faenum secare
hayloft *s* faenil·ia -ium *npl*
haystack *s* faeni met·a -ae *f*
hazard *s* pericul·um -i *n*
hazard *tr* **to — a guess** coniecturam tentare
hazardous *adj* periculos·us -a -um
haze *s* nebul·a -ae *f*
hazelnut *s* nu·x -cis *f* avellana
hazy *adj* nebulos·us -a -um; *(fig)* obscur·us -a -um
he *pron* hic, is; *(male)* ma·s -ris *m*
head *s* cap·ut -itis *n; (mental faculty)* ingen·ium -(i)i *n; (fig)* princ·eps -ipis *m;* **back of the —** occipit·um -i *n;* **from —**

to foot ab imis unguibus usque ad verticem summum; — **first** praec·eps -cipitis; — **of state** rec·tor -toris *m* (·trix -tricis *f*) civitatis; — **over heels in love** tot·us -a -um in amore; **it all came to a —** in discrimen summa rerum adducta est; **to be a — taller than** toto vertice supra *(w. acc)* esse; **to come into s.o.'s —** alicui in buccam venire; **to come to a —** *(of a boil)* caput facere; **to have a good —** cor habēre; **to put —s together** capita conferre; **use your — !** cogita! *(pl:* cogitate!); **wine goes to my —** vinum in cerebrum mihi abit
head *adj* prim·us -a -um
head *tr* praesse *(w. dat),* ducere ‖ *intr* **to — for** tendere ad *(w. acc)*
headache *s* capitis dol·or -oris *m*
headband *s* inful·a -ae *f*
headfirst *adv* prae·ceps -cipitis
headgear *s* capitis tegm·en -inis *n*
heading *s* titul·us -i *m*
headland *s* promuntur·ium -(i)i *n*
headless *adj* trunc·us -a -um
headlight *s* (autocineti) luminar·e -is *n;* **to turn on (turn off) the (bright) —s** luminaria (praecandentia) accendere (exstinguere)
headlong *adv* praec·eps -itis
headmaster *s* scholae rect·or -oris *m*
headmistress *s* scholae rec·trix -tricis *f*
headquarters *spl* sed·es -is *f; (mil)* praetor·ium -(i)i *n*
head start *s* **to get a —** iter praecipere; *(fig)* aliquantum temporis praecipere
headstrong *adj* contum·ax -acis
headway *s* **to make —** proficere; **to make no —** nihil proficere; **we are making some —** proficimus aliquantum
headwind *s* vent·us -i *m* adversus
heady *adj (of wine)* fervid·us -a -um
heal *tr* mederi *(w. dat),* sanare ‖ *intr* sanescere; *(of wounds)* coalescere
healer *s* medic·us -i *m* (·a -ae *f*)
healing *adj* salutar·is -is -e
healing *s* sanati·o -onis *f*
health *s (good or bad)* valetud·o -inis *f;* **bad (delicate, good, ill) —** adversa (infirma, secunda, incommoda) valetudo; **for reasons of (bad) —** valetudinis causā; **to be in good —** bene valēre; **to drink to the — of** propinare *(w. dat);* **to enjoy excellent —** optima valitudine uti
healthful *adj* salubr·is -is -e
healthily *adv* salubriter
healthy *adj* san·us -a -um; *(places)* salubr·is -is -e
heap *s* cumul·us -i *m,* acerv·us -i *m*
heap *tr* acervare; **to — up** accumulare, exstruere; **to — *(blows, favors, abuse)* upon** congerere (plagas, beneficia, maledicta) *(w. dat or* in *w. acc)*
hear *tr* **(from)** audire (ex *w. abl); (to learn)* **(from)** cognoscere, accipere (ex *w. abl)*
hearing *s (act)* auditi·o -onis *f; (sense)* audit·us -ūs *m; (leg)* cogniti·o -onis *f;* **hard of —** surdas·ter -tra -trum; **to hold a —** cognitionem habēre
hearken *intr* auscultare; **to — to** auscultare *(dat)*
hearsay *s* auditi·o -onis *f*
heart *s* cor, cordis *n; (fig)* anim·us -i *m;* **by —** ex memoria; **from the —** ex animo; **— and soul** toto pectore; **my — was in my throat** anima mihi in naso erat; **to learn by —** ediscere; **to love with all one's —** toto pectore amare; **to take to —** cordi habēre
heartache *s (fig)* cur·a -ae *f,* cordol·ium -(i)i *n*
heart attack *s* impet·us -ūs *m* cordiacus
heartbreak *s* ang·or -oris *m*
heartbroken *adj* ae·ger -gra -grum animo
heartburn *s* praecordiorum dol·or -oris *m*
heart failure *s* defecti·o -onis *f* cardiaca
heart-felt *adj* haud simulat·us -a -um
hearth *s* foc·us -i *m*
heartily *adv* cum summo studio
heartiness *s* alacrit·as -atis *f*
heartless *adj* inhuman·us -a -um
heartlessly *adv* inhumane
heartsick *adj* animo ae·ger -gra -graum
heart-to-heart *adj* intim·us -a -um
hearty *adj* sincer·us -a -um; *(meal)* laut·us -a -um
heat *s* cal·or -oris *m,* ard·or -oris *m; (fig)* ferv·or -oris *m;* **— of the day** aest·us -ūs *m*
heat *tr* cal(e)facere ‖ *intr* calescere
heathen *adj* pagan·us -a -um
heathen *s* pagan·us -i *m* (·a -ae *f*)
heating *s* calefacti·o -onis *f*
heave *tr* attollere; **to — a sigh (of relief)** gemitum (levationis) ducere ‖ *intr (to swell)* fluctuare; *(of the chest)* anhelare
heaven *s* cael·um -i *n;* **for —'s sake** obsecro [*lit: I pray*]; **good —s!** pro divum fidem!; **—s above!** O di immortales!; **— forbid!** di melius faxint!; **I'm in seventh —** digito caelum attingo; **in —'s name** pro deum fidem; **thank —** dis gratia; **to move — and earth** caelum ac terras miscēre
heavenly *adj* caelest·is -is -e
heavily *adv* graviter; *(slowly)* tarde
heaviness *s* gravit·as -atis *f*
heavy *adj* grav·is -is -e; *(sad)* maest·us -a -um; *(rain)* magn·us -a -um
Hebraic *adj* Hebraic·us -a -um
Hebrew *adj* Hebrae·us -a -um
Hebrew *s* Hebrae·us -i *m* (·a -ae *f*); *(language)* lingu·a -ae *f* Hebraea; **to know (read, speak) —** Hebraice scire (legere, loqui)
hecatomb *s* hecatomb·e -es *f*

heck *s & interj* — **no!** minine vero!; **to give s.o.** — aliquem verbis malis obiurgare; **who the heck are they?** qui, malum, isti sunt?
heckle *tr* interpellare
heckler *s* convicia·tor -toris *m* (·trix -tricis *f*)
hectic *adj* febriculos·us -a -um
hedge *s* saep·es -is *f*
hedge *tr* **to — in** saepire; **to — off** intersaepire **||** *intr* tergiversari
heed *s* cur·a -ae *f;* **to take —** curare
heed *tr* curare, observare; *(to obey)* parēre *(w. dat)*
heedless *adj* incaut·us -a -um; **— of** immem·or -oris *(w. gen)*
heedlessness *s* neglegenti·a -ae *f*
heel *s* cal·x -cis *mf; (of a shoe)* fulment·um -i *n; (sl)* nequam hom·o -inis *mf;* **to take to one's —s** se in pedes conicere
hefty *adj* robust·us -a -um; *(thing)* ing·ens -entis
heifer *s* iuvenc·a -ae *f*
height *s* altitud·o -inis *f; (of person)* procerit·as -atis *f; (top)* culm·en -inis *n; (fig)* fastig·ium -(i)i *n*
heighten *tr* amplificare, augēre
heinous *adj* atr·ox -ocis
heir *s* her·es -edis *mf*
heir apparent *s* her·es -edis *mf* legitim·us (-a)
heiress *s* her·es -edis *f*
heirloom *s* res, rei *f* hereditaria
helicopter *s* helicopter·um -i *n*; **to fly a —** helicopterum gubernare; **to fly in a —** helcoptero vehi
hell *s* infer·i -orum *mpl,* Orc·us -i *m; (eccl)* Gehenn·a -ae *f;* **go to —!** *(sl)* i *(pl:* ite) in malam crucem!; **to catch —** *(sl)* convicium habēre
Hellenic *adj* Hellenic·us -a -um
Hellenism *s* Hellenism·us -i *m*
hellish *adj* infern·us -a -um
hello *interj* salve *(pl:* salvete)!; **— there!** eho istic!; **Terentia says — to you** Terentia tibi salutem dicit
helm *s* gubernacul·um -i *n*
helmet *s (of leather)* gale·a -ae *f; (of metal)* cass·is -idis *f*
helmsman *s* gubernat·or -oris *m*
help *s* auxil·ium -(i)i *n*
help *tr* opem ferre *(w. dat)*, iuvare, adiuvare
helper *s* adiu·tor -toris *m* (·tr·ix -icis *f*)
helpful *adj* util·is -is -e
helpless *adj* inop·s -is
helplessness *s* inopi·a -ae *f*
hem *interj* hem!, ehem!
hem *s* or·a -ae *f,* limb·us -i *m*
hem *tr* circumsuere; **to — in** *(to surround)* circumdare; *(by entrenchments)* circumvallare; *(to restrain)* cohibēre
hemisphere *s* hemisphaer·ium -(i)i *n*
hemlock *s* cicut·a -ae *f*
hemorrhage *s* sanguinis profluv·ium -(i)i *n*
hemorrhoids *spl* haemorrhoid·a -ae *f*
hemp *s* cannab·is -is *f*
hempen *adj* cannabin·us -a -um
hen *s* gallin·a -ae *f*
hence *adv* hinc; *(consequently)* igitur
henceforth *adv* posthac, dehinc
henchman *s* adiut·or -oris *m*
henpecked *adj* uxori·us -a -um
her *pron* eam, illam, hanc
her *adj* eius, illius, huius; **— own** su·us -a -um
herald *s (pol)* fetial·is -is *m; (crier)* praec·o -onis *m*
herald *tr* (prae)nuntiare
herb *s* herb·a -ae *f*
herd *s (of animals)* gre·x -gis *m; (of oxen and large animals)* arment·um -i *n; (pej)* vulg·us -i *n*
herd *tr* **to — together** congregare **||** *intr* **to — together** congregari
herdsman *s* armentar·ius -(i)i *m*
here *adv* hic; **— and now** depraesentiarium [*adv*]; **— and there** passim; **— I am!** ecce me!; **— with it!** cedo *(pl:* cette)! [*can take an object, e.g.,* **— with that book!** cedo illum librum!]
hereabouts *adv* hic alicubi
hereafter *adv* posthac
hereafter *s* vit·a -ae *f* post mortem
hereby *adv* ex hoc, hinc
hereditary *adj* hereditari·us -a -um
heredity *s* gen·us -eris *n;* **by —** iure hereditario, per successiones
herein *adv* in hoc, in hac re, hic
heresy *s* haeres·is -is *f*
heretical *adj* haeretic·us -a -um
hereupon *adv* hic
herewith *adv* ūnā cum hac re
heritage *s* heredit·as -atis *f*
hermaphrodite *s* androgyn·us -i *m*
hermit *s* eremit·a -ae *m*
hermitage *s* eremitae cell·a -ae *f*
hernia *s* herni·a -ae *f*
hero *s* vi·r -ri *m; (demigod)* her·os -oïs *m*
heroic *adj (age)* heroïc·us -a -um; fortissim·us -a -um
heroically *adv* fortissime
heroin *s* heroin·um -i *n;* **to use —** heroino uti
heroine *s* virag·o -inis *f; (myth)* heroïn·a -ae *f*
heroism *s* virt·us -utis *f*
heron *s* arde·a -ae *f*
herring *s* hareng·a -ae *f*
hers *pron* eius, illius
herself *pron (refl)* se; *(intensive)* ipsa; **by — per se; to — sibi; with —** secum
hesitant *adj* dubi·us -a -um
hesitantly *adv* cunctanter
hesitate *intr* dubitare
hesitation *s* dubitati·o -onis *f; (in speaking)* haesitati·o -onis *f*
heterogeneous *adj* divers·us -a -um

hew *tr* dolare, caedere
hey *interj* ohe!; — **you!** heus tu!
hi *interj* salve *(pl:* salvete)!
hiatus *s* hiat•us -ūs *m*
hiccup *s* singult•us -ūs *m*
hiccup *intr* singultire
hidden *adj* occult•us -a -um; **to lie** — latēre
hide *s* cor•ium -(i)i *n; (pelt)* pell•is -is *f;* **to be after s.o.'s** — corium alicuius petere; **to risk one's own** — corio suo ludere; **to save one's own** — corium servare
hide *tr* abdere, celare ‖ *intr* latēre
hide and seek *s* **to play** — per lusum latitare et quaeritare
hideous *adj* foed•us -a -um
hideously *adv* foede
hideousness *s* foedit•as -atis *f*
hiding *s* occultati•o -onis *f; (whipping)* verberati•o -onis *f*
hiding place *s* latebr•a -ae *f*
hierarchy *s* hierarchi•a -ae *f*
high *adj* alt•us -a -um; *(rank)* ampl•us -a -um; *(price)* magn•us -a -um; *(wind)* vehem•ens -entis; *(fever)* ard•ens -entis; *(note)* acut•us -a -um; *(expensive)* car•us -a -um; *(ground)* edit•us -a -um; *(virtue, good, etc.)* summ•us -a -um; **at a — price** magni (pretii) *or* magno pretio; — **and dry** auxilii exper•s -tis; — **and low** ubique; — **and mighty** superb•us -a -um; — **noon** meridi•es -ei *m;* — **blood pressure** hypertoni•a -ae *f;* — **opinion** magna opini•o -onis *f;* — **seas** alt•um -i *n;* — **tide** maximus aest•us -ūs *m;* **to be — on drugs** a medicamentis psychotropicis inebriare
high *adv* alte; **to aim** — magnas res appetere; **from on** — desuper; **on** — sursum versum
highball *s* aqu•a -ae *f* vitae aquā effervescenti commixta
highborn *adj* generos•us -a -um
high-class *adj* praest•ans -antis; *(goods)* laut•us -a -um
high-flown *adj* inflat•us -a -um
highhanded *adj* insol•ens -entis
highhandedly *adv* insolenter
high jump *s* salt•us -ūs *m* in altum
highlander *s* montan•us -i *m* (•a -ae *f*)
highlands *spl* regi•o -onis *f* montuosa
highlights *spl* praecipu•a -orum *npl* rerum
highly *adv (value)* magni; *(intensity)* vehementer, valde
high-minded *adj (noble)* magnanim•us -a -um
high-pitched *adj* acut•us -a -um
high priest *s* pontif•ex -icis *m,* sacerd•os -otis *m* maximus
highrise (building) *s* multizon•ium -(i)i *n*
high school *s* schol•a -ae *f* superior
high treason *s* maiest•as -atis *f* (laesa); **convicted of** — de maiestate damnat•us -a -um
highway *s* strat•a -ae *f* autocinetica
hijack *tr* vi abducere
hijacker *s* latr•o -onis *m*
hike *s* ambulati•o -onis *f;* **to go for a** — ambulatum ire
hike *tr (to increase)* augēre, efferre ‖ *intr* ambulare
hilarious *adj* hilar•us -a -um
hilariously *adv* hilare
hilarity *s* hilarit•as -atis *f*
hill *s* coll•is -is *m*
hillock *s* tumul•us -i *m*
hillside *s* cliv•us -i *m*
hilly *adj* clivos•us -a -um
hilt *s* capul•us -i *m*
him *pron* eum, illum, hunc; **of** — eius, illius huius
himself *pron (refl)* se; *(intensive)* ipse; **to** — sibi; **with** — secum
hind *s* cerv•a -ae *f*
hind *adj* poster•ior -ior -ius; — **end** *(coll)* postic•um -i *n*
hinder *tr* impedire, prohibēre; *(to block)* obstare *(w. dat)*
hindmost *adj* postrem•us -a -um
hindrance *s* impediment•um -i *n*
hindsight *s* posteriores cogitation•es -um *fpl*
hinge *s* card•o -inis *m*
hinge *intr* **to — on** *(fig)* niti *(w. abl)*
hint *s* significati•o -onis *f,* indic•ium -(i)i *n;* **to throw clear —s** nec dubias significationes iacere
hint *tr* suggerere, innuere
hip *s* cox•a -ae *f*
hippie *s* anticonformist•a -ae *m* (•ria -riae *f*)
hippodrome *s* hippodrom•os -i *m*
hippopotamus *s* hippopotam•us -i *m*
hire *s* merc•es -edis *f; (act)* conducti•o -onis *f*
hire *tr* conducere; **to — oneself out** auctorari; **to — out** locare
hired *adj* conduct•us -a -um, mercenari•us -a -um
hireling *s* mercenari•us -i *m* (•a -ae *f*)
his *adj* eius, illius, huius; — **own** su•us -a -um, propri•us -a -um
hiss *s* sibil•us -i *m*
hiss *tr & intr* sibilare
historian *s* historic•us -i *m* (•a -ae *f*)
historical *adj* historic•us -a -um
history *s* histori•a -ae *f;* **ancient** — antiqua historia *f;* **modern** — recentioris aetatis historia *f;* **to write a — of the Roman people** res (gestas) populi Romani perscribere
histrionic *adj* histrional•is -is -e
hit *s* plag•a -ae *f,* ict•us -ūs *m; (success)* success•us -ūs *m*
hit *tr* icere, ferire; *(a baseball)* pulsare; *(of an illness)* affligere, occupare; **to — it off with** concordare cum *(w. abl);* **to — s.o. for a loan** ferire aliquem mutuo argento;

you've — the nail on the head acu rem tetigisti ‖ *intr* **to — upon** offendere
hitch *s* nod·us -i *m;* **there is a —** haeret res (in salebrā); **without a —** sine difficultate
hitch *tr* coniungere
hitchhike *intr* alienis vect·us (-a) iter facere
hither *adv* huc
hither *adj* citer·ior -ior -ius
hitherto *adv (of time)* adhuc; *(of place)* huc usque
hive *s* alve·us -i *m*
hmmm *interj* hem!
hoard *s* acerv·us -i *m*
hoard *tr* coacervare, recondere
hoarder *s* accumula·tor -toris *m* (·trix -tricis *f)*
hoarse *adj* rauc·us -a -um; **to get —** irraucescere
hoarsely *adv* raucā voce
hoary *adj* can·us -a -um
hoax *s* frau·s -dis *f*
hobble *intr* claudicare
hobby *s* avocament·um -i *n*
hobnob *intr* **(with)** conversari (cum *w. abl)*
hock *tr (to pawn) (coll)* pignernare
hock *s* **in —** pignerat·us -a -um
hockey *s* lud·us -i *m* hocceius; **field —** ludus hocceius campestris; **ice —** ludus hocceius glacialis; **to play —** hocceio ludere
hockey puck *s* discul·us -i *m*
hockey stick *s* ferul·a -ae *f* repanda
hoe *s* sarcul·um -i *n*
hoe *tr* sarculare
hog *s* porc·us -i *m,* sus suis *mf;* **—s oink** sues grunniunt
hogwash *s* **that's —** quisquiliae!
hoist *tr* sublevare
hold *s (of ship)* cavern·a -ae *f;* **to get** *or* **take — of** prehendere; *(with both hands)* comprehendere
hold *tr* tenēre; *(to contain)* capere; *(to think)* habēre; *(elections, meeting, discussions)* habēre; *(office, consulship, etc.)* gerere; **able to —** *(e.g., of a theater)* cap·ax -acis *(w. gen);* **— it!** *(stop!)* asta!; **— it please!** mane obsecro!; **to — back** retinēre; *(laughter, tears)* tenēre; **to — court** *(leg)* quaerere; **to — forth** *(e.g., hands)* porrigere; *(to offer)* praebēre; **to — in** inhibēre, cohibēre; **to — in high (highest) esteem** magni (maximi) facere; **to — in honor** in honore habēre; **to — off** arcēre; **to — one's breath** animam comprimere; **to — one's tongue** tacēre; **to — out** *(e.g., hands)* protendere; **to —** *(e.g., a compress)* **to** *(e.g., one's cheek)* admovēre (fomentum) ad (malam); **to — up** attollere; *(to detain)* detinēre, impedire; **to — up one's head** mentum tollere ‖ *intr* **to — back** cunctari; **to — forth** *(to speak)* contionari; **to — on to** tenēre; **to — out** *(to last)* durare, permanēre; **to — together** cohaerēre
holder *s* possess·or -oris *m; (instrument)* receptacul·um -i *n*
holding *s* possessi·o -onis *f*
hole *s* foram·en -inis *n; (of mice, etc.)* cav·um -i *n;* **to dig a — in the ground** locum in terra excavare; **to dig a — in the wall** parietem perfodere
hole-in-the-wall *s (cheap lodgings)* stabul·um -i *n*
holiday *s* di·es -ei *m* festus; fest·um -i *n; (from school)* dies feriatus; **—s** feri·ae -arum *fpl;* **public —** di·es -ei *m* sollemnis
holiness *s* sanctit·as -atis *f*
hollow *adj* cav·us -a -um; *(fig)* inan·is -is -e
hollow *s* cav·um -i *n; (depression)* lacun·a -ae *f;* **— of the hand** cava man·us -ūs *f*
hollow *tr* **to — out** excavare
holly *s* il·ex -icis *n* aquifolium
holocaust *s* holocaust·um -i *n*
holy *adj* sanct·us -a -um
homage *s* cult·us -ūs *m;* **to pay — to** colere
home *s* aed·es -ium *fpl,* dom·us -ūs *f;* **at —** domi; **at my —** domi meae, apud me; **at your —** domi tuae, apud te; **from —** domo; **to make oneself at —** se intimum facere; **to my —** ad me
home *adv (motion)* domum; *(place where)* domi
home *adj* domestic·us -a -um
home appliance *s* electricum instrument·um -i *n* domesticum; **—s** electrica utensil·ia -ium *npl* domestica
homebody *s* hom·o -inis *mf* umbratilis
home front *s* **on the — and on the war front** domi et militiae
home invader *s* effractari·us -i *m* (·a -ae *f)*
home invasion *s* effractur·a -ae *f*
homeland *s* patri·a -ae *f*
homeless *adj* tecto car·ens -entis
homelike *adj* familiar·is -is -e
homeliness *s* rusticit·as -atis *f*
homely *adj* inspecios·us -a -um
homemade *adj* domestic·us -a -um
homemaker *s* materfamilias *(gen:* matrisfamilias) *f*
home page *(comput)* pagin·a -ae *f* domestica
home plate *s* bas·is -is *m* summa
home run *s* circuit·us -ūs *m* basium; **to hit a —** circuitum basium facere
homesick *adj* appet·ens -entis tecti sui; **to be —** ex desiderio tecti sui laborare
homesickness *s* tecti sui desider·ium -(i)i *n*
homestead *s* fund·us -i *m*
hometown *s* patri·a -ae *f*
homeward *adv* domum
homework *s* pens·um -i *n* domesticum; *(written)* praescript·um -i *n* domesticum
homicidal *adj* cruent·us -a -um
homicide *s (person)* homicid·a -ae *mf; (deed)* homicid·ium -(i)i *n*
homily *s* tractat·us -ūs *m* moralis

homogeneous *adj* pari naturā praedit·us -a -um
homosexual *adj* cinaed·us -a -um; **— partner** *(euphem)* fra·ter -tris *m*
homosexual *s* cinaed·us -i *m*
hone *tr* acuere
honest *adj* prob·us -a -um; *(truthful)* ver·ax -acis; **— to God, — to goodness** mediusfidius
honestly *adv* **tell me —** dic bonā fide
honesty *s* probit·as -atis *f*
honey *s* mel, mellis *n; (term of endearment)* melill·a -ae *f,* mel, mellis *n,* melcul·um -i *n*
honeycomb *s* fav·us -i *m*
honeysuckle *s* clymen·us -i *m*
honor *s* hon·or -oris *m; (mark of distinction)* dignit·as -atis *f;* **on my —** meā fide; **on your —** per fidem; **sense of —** pud·or -oris *m;* **word of —** fid·es -ei *f*
honor *tr* honorare; *(to respect)* colere
honorable *adj* honest·us -a -um
honorably *adv* honeste
honorary *adj* honorari·us -a -um, honoris causā
hood *s* cucull·us -i *m; (of a car)* ploxen·um -i *n*
hoodlum *s* grassat·or -oris *m*
hoof *s* ungul·a -ae *f*
hook *s* unc·us -i *m; (esp. for fishing)* ham·us -i *m;* **by — or by crook** quocumque modo
hook *tr (to catch w. a hook)* inuncare; *(fig)* capere
hooked *adj* hamat·us -a -um; *(crooked)* adunc·us -a -um
hookey *s* **to play —** insciis parentibus a scholā abesse
hoop *s* circul·us -i *m; (toy)* troch·us -i *m; (shout)* clam·or -oris *m*
hoot *s* cant·us -ūs *m;* **not give a — about** pili facere *(w. acc),* flocci non facere *(w. acc)*
hoot *tr* explodere ‖ *intr* obstrepere; *(of owls)* bubulare
hop *s* salt·us -ūs *m*
hop *intr* salire, subsaltare
hope *s* spes spei *f;* **glimmer of —** specul·a -ae *f;* **to give up all —** desperare
hope *intr* sperare; **to — for** exspectare; **to — that** sperare *(w. acc & inf)*
hopeful *adj* bonae spei
hopefully *adv* ut spero [*as I hope*]
hopefuls *spl (persons)* spe·s -rum *fpl*
hopeless *adj* desperat·us -a -um
hopelessly *adv* desperanter
hopelessness *s* desperati·o -onis *f*
hopper *s (in a restroom)* sell·a -ae *f* familiarica; *(funnel-shaped container)* infundibul·um -i *n*
horde *s* turb·a -ae *f; (wandering)* vaga multitud·o -inis *f*
horizon *s* fini·ens -entis *m*
horizontal *adj* librat·us -a -um
horizontal bar *s* ferr·um -i *n* transversum
horizontally *adv* per libram
hormone *s* hormon·um -i *n*
horn *s (of an animal)* corn·u -ūs *n; (mus)* bucin·a -ae *f;* **to blow the —** bucinā clangere
horned *adj* cornig·er -era -erum
hornet *s* crab·o -onis *m*
horny *adj* sal·ax -acis
horoscope *s* horoscop·us -i *m;* **to cast a —** horoscopare; **to have the same —** uno astro esse
horrible *adj* horribil·is -is -e
horribly *adv* horribili modo
horrid *adj* horrid·us -a -um
horrify *tr* horrificare
horror *s* horr·or -oris *m; (strong aversion)* od·ium -(i)i *n*
hors d'oeuvres *spl* promuls·is -idis *f*
horse *s* equ·us -i *m,* equ·a -ae *f;* **to beat a dead —** asellum currere docēre
horseback *s* **on —** in equo; **to fight on —** ex equo pugnare; **to ride —** in equo vehi
horsehair *s* pil·us -i *m* equinus
horsefly *s* taban·us -i *m;* **—s buzz** tabani bombilant
horseman *s* equ·es -itis *m*
horserace *s* curricul·um -i *n* equorum; **—s** equirri·a -orum *npl*
horseradish *s* armoraci·a -ae *f*
horseshoe *s* sole·a -ae *f* (equi)
horsewhip *s* scutic·a -ae *f*
horsewhip *tr* scuticā verberare
horticultural *adj* ad hortorum cultum pertin·ens -entis
horticulture *s* hortorum cult·us -ūs *m*
hose *s (tube)* tubul·us -i *m; (stocking)* tibial·e -is *n;* **rubber —** tubulus cummeus
hosiery *s* feminal·ia -ium *npl*
hospitable *adj* hospital·is -is -e
hospitably *adv* hospitaliter
hospital *s* valetudinar·ium -(i)i *n*
hospitality *s* hospitalit·as -atis *f*
host *s (entertainer)* hosp·es -itis *m; (army)* copi·ae -arum *fpl; (immense number)* multitud·o -inis *f; (wafer)* hosti·a -ae *f*
hostage *s* obs·es -idis *mf;* **to exchange —s** obsides inter se permutare
hostess *s* hospit·a -ae *f; (at an inn)* cop·a -ae *f*
hostile *adj* infens·us -a -um; *(forces, soil)* hostil·is -is -e; **in a — manner** hostiliter, infense
hot *adj* calid·us -a -um; *(boiling)* ferv·ens -entis; *(seething, sultry)* aestuos·us -a -um; *(of spices)* a·cer -cris -cre; *(fig)* ard·ens -entis; **— weather** aest·us -ūs *m;* **it is (very) — today** hodie (maxime) caletur; **to be —** calēre; **to become —** calescere; **to be in — water** *(coll)* in angustiis versari
hotbed *s* seminar·ium -(i)i *n*

hotdog *s* hill·a -ae calens *(gen:* hillae calentis) *f*
hotel *s* deversor·ium -(i)i *n;* **to stay at a —** in deversorio morari
hot-headed *adj* cerebros·us -a -um
hotel manager *s* deversorii direc·tor -toris *m* (·trix -tricis *f)*
hot pants *spl* brac·ae -arum *fpl* brevissimae
hot plate *s* disc·us -i *m* coctorius
hot-tempered *adj* stomachos·us -a -um
hound *s* catul·us -i *m*
hound *tr* instare *(w. dat)*
hour *s* hor·a -ae *f;* **a half —** semihora; **an — and a half** sesquihora; **a quarter of an —** quadr·ans -antis *m* horae; **at all —s** omnibus horis; **every —** singulis horis; **from — to —** in horas; **three quarters of an —** dodr·ans -antis *m* horae
hourly *adv* in horas
hourly *adj* in horas; *(output)* in horā
house *s* dom·us -ūs *m,* aed·es -ium *fpl; (family)* dom·us -ūs *m,* gen·s -tis *f;* **at the — of** apud *(w. acc)*
house *tr* domo excipere; *(things)* condere
house arrest *s* custodi·a -ae *f* libera
housebreaker *s* effractari·us -i *m* (·a -ae *f)*
housebroken *adj* domit·us -a -um
household *adj* familiar·is -is -e
household *s* famili·a -ae *f*
household gods *spl* Lar·es et Penat·es -um *mpl*
housekeeper *s* dispensa·tor -toris *m* (·trix -tricis *f)*
housekeeping *s* rei familiaris cur·a -ae *f*
housemaid *s* ancill·a -ae *f*
housewife *s* materfamilias *(gen:* matrisfamilias) *f*
hovel *s* tugur·ium -(i)i *n*
hover *intr* pendēre; **to — over** impendēre *(w. dat)*
how *adv* quomodo, quo pacto; *(chiefly after verbs of hearing, telling, etc.)* ut *w. subj); (to what degree)* quam; **— are you? (— are you doing?)** quid agis? *(pl:* quid agitis?); **— come?** qui fit? *or* qui istuc?; **— far is ... from ... ?** quantum distat *(or* abest) ... ab *(w. abl)?;* **— goes it?** qui fit?; **— long** quamdiu, quousque; **— long ago** quam pridem, quam dudum; **— many** quot [*indecl*]; **— many times** quotiens, quoties; **— much** quantus -a -um; **— much** *(at what price)* quanti; **how much did this sell for?** quanti hoc venit? **— much does this cost?** quanti hoc constat? **— much is this?** hoc quanti constat? **— often** quotiens; **— old are you?** quot annos nat·us (-a) es? **— so?** quid ita?; **— soon** quam dudum; **—'s that?** *(what did you say?)* quidum? *or* qui iam?
however *adv (nevertheless)* tamen, autem; *(in whatever way)* quoquomodo; *(to whatever degree)* quamvis *(esp. w. adj or adv; followed by subj);* **— great** quant·uscumque -acumque -umcumque; **— many** quotquot; **— often** quotiescumque
howl *s* ululat·us -ūs *m*
howl *intr (lit & fig)* ululare
hub *s* ax·is -is *m*
hubbub *s* tumult·us -ūs *m; (noise of brawling)* convic·ium -(i)i *n*
huckster *s* instit·or -oris *m*
huddle *intr* coacervari, stipari; **—ed together** confert·i -ae -a
huddle *s* coron·a -ae *f; (sports)* symplegm·a -atis *n*
hue *s* col·or -oris *m;* **to raise a — and cry** conclamare; *(to complain)* conqueri
huff *s* offensi·o -onis *f;* **to be in a —** stomachari
huff *intr* stomachari
hug *s* complex·us -ūs *m*
hug *tr* complecti, amplecti; **to — each other** inter se amplecti
huge *adj* ing·ens -entis; *(of monstrous size)* imman·is -is -e; **— sum of money** ingens pecuni·a -ae *f*
hugeness *s* immanit·as -atis *f*
hulk *s (hull of unseaworthy ship)* alve·us -i *m* desertus; *(heavy ship)* nav·is -is *f* oneraria
hulking, hulky *adj* grav·is -is -e
hull *s* alve·us -i *m*
hum *s* murm·ur -uris *m; (of bees)* bomb·us -i *m*
hum *intr* murmurare; *(of bees)* bombilare
human *adj* human·us -a -um; **— feelings** humanit·as -atis *f;* **— race** gen·us -eris *n* humanum
human being *s* hom·o -inis *mf*
humane *adj* human·us -a -um
humanely *adv* humane
humanity *s* humanit·as -atis *f; (people)* homin·es -um *mpl*
humanize *tr* excolere
humble *adj (modest)* summiss·us -a -um; *(obscure)* humil·is -is -e
humble *tr* deprimere; **to — oneself before s.o.** se summittere alicui
humbly *adv* summisse
humdrum *adj (dull)* molest·us -a -um; *(banal)* trit·us -a -um
humid *adj* umid·us -a -um
humidity *s* um·or -oris *m*
humiliate *tr* deprimere
humiliating *adj* humil·is -is -e
humiliation *s* dedec·us -oris *n*
humility *s* humilit·as -atis *f*
humor *s* festivit·as -atis *f; (mood)* anim·us -i *m;* **he is in bad —** stomachosus est; **he is in good —** festivus est; **sense of —** festivit·as -atis *f*
humor *tr* indulgēre *(w. dat),* morem gerere *(w. dat)*
humorous *adj* festiv·us -a -um
humorously *adv* festive

hump *s* gibb·er -eris *m*
humpbacked *adj* gibb·er -era -erum
hunch *s* opini·o -onis *f;* **to have a —** opinari
hundred *adj* centum [*indecl*]; **— times** centie(n)s
hundredfold *adj* centupl·ex -icis
hundredfold *s* centupl·um -i *n*
hundredth *adj* centesim·us -a -um
hunger *s* fam·es -is *f; (voluntary)* inedi·a -ae *f*
hunger *intr* esurire; **to — for** cupere
hung jury *s* **to be acquitted by a —** sententiis paribus absolvi
hungrily *adv* avide, voraciter
hungry *adj* esuri·ens -entis; **to be —** esurire
hunt *s* venati·o -onis *f*
hunt *tr* venari **||** *intr* **to — for** quaerere
hunter *s* vena·tor -toris *m* (·trix -tricis *f*); *(horse)* equ·us -i *m* venaticus
hunting *s* venat·us -ūs *m;* **to go —** venari
hunting *adj* venatic·us -a -um; **— dog** can·is -is *m* venaticus; **— gear** instrument·um -i *n* venatorium; **— spear** venabul·um -i *n*
huntress *s* venatr·ix -icis *f*
hurdle *s (obstacle)* ob·ex -icis *mf*
hurl *tr* conicere
hurray *interj* euax!, io!
hurricane *s* ingens procell·a -ae *f*
hurried *adj* praeproper·us -a -um; *(too hasty)* praec·eps -ipitis
hurriedly *adv* raptim; *(carelessly)* neglìgenter
hurry *tr* rapere; **to — away** abripere **||** *intr* properare, festinare; *(to rush hurriedly)* ruere; **to — along** se agere; **— up!** matura! *(pl:* maturate!)
hurry *s* festinati·o -onis *f;* **in a —** festinanter; **to be in a —** festinare, properare
hurt *s* iniuri·a -ae *f*
hurt *adj* sauci·us -a -um; *(emotionally)* sauci·us -a -um, offens·us -a -um
hurt *tr* nocēre *(w. dat),* laedere; *(fig)* offendere **||** *intr* dolēre; **to — a lot** vehementer dolēre
husband *s* marit·us -i *m*
husbandry *s* agricultur·a -ae *f*
hush *s* silent·ium -(i)i *n*
hush *tr* comprimere; *(a secret)* celare **||** *intr* tacēre
hush *interj* st!
husk *s* follicul·us -i *m; (of beans, etc.)* siliqu·a -ae *f; (of grain)* glum·a -ae *f*
husky *adj* robust·us -a -um; *(of voice)* rauc·us -a -um
hustle *tr* trudere **||** *intr* inter se trudere
hustler *s* hom·o -inis *mf* strenu·us (-a)
hut *s* tugur·ium -(i)i *n*
hyacinth *s* hyacinth·us -i *m*
hybrid *s* hybrid·a -ae *f*
Hydra *s* Hydr·a -ae *f*
hydraulic *adj* hydraulic·us -a -um
hydrophobia *s* hydrophobi·a -ae *f*
hyena *s* hyaen·a -ae *f*
hygiene *s* salubrit·as -atis *f,* hygien·e -es *f;* **to practice —** hygienen exercēre
hygienic *adj* salubr·is -is -e, hygienic·us -a -um
hymn *s* hymn·us -i *m*
hyperbole *s* hyperbol·e -es *f*
hypercritical *adj* nimis sever·us -a -um
hypertext *s* hypertext·us -ūs *m*
hypertext *adj* hypertextual·is -is -e
hyphen *s* hyphen [*indecl*] *n*
hypenate *tr* hypen ponere
hypochondriac *s* melancholic·us -i *m* (·a -ae *f*)
hypocrisy *s* simulati·o -onis *f*
hypocrite *s* simula·tor -toris *m* (·trix -tricis *f*)
hypocritical *adj* simulat·us -a -um
hypothesis *s* hypothes·is -is *m*
hypothetical *adj* hypothetic·us -a -um
hysteria *s* delirati·o -onis *f*
hysterical *adj* delir·us -a -um

I

I *pron* ego; **— myself** egomet
iamb *s (pros)* iamb·us -i *m*
iambic *adj (pros)* iambe·us -a -um
ice *s* glaci·es -ei *f*
iceberg *s* glaciei niviumque concreta mol·es -is *f*
icebound *adj* glacie consaept·us -a -um
ice cream *s* gelidum crem·um -i *n*
ice hockey *s see* **hockey**
ice rink *s* stad·ion -(i)i *n* glaciale
ice skate *s* patin·us -i *m*
ice skate *intr* patinare
ice skater *s* patina·tor -toris *m* (·trix -tricis *f*)
ice skating *s* patinati·o -onis *f*
ice water *s* nivata aqu·a -ae *f*
icicle *s* stiri·a -ae *f*
icon *s (comput)* ic·on -onis *f*
icy *adj* glacial·is -is -e
idea *s (notion)* consil·ium -(i)i *n*; *(thought)* sententi·a -ae *f;* **it's a good — to** expedit *(w. inf)*
ideal *adj* perfect·us -a -um
ideal *s* exempl·ar -aris *n*
idealist *s* hom·o -inis *mf* summae virtutis
idealistic *adj* omnibus virtutibus ornat·us -a -um
identical *adj* idem eadem idem, unus atque idem
identify *tr* agnoscere
identity *s* identit·as -atis *f*
idiocy *s* fatuit·as -atis *f*
idiom *s* propriet·as -atis *f* linguae (Latinae *or* Anglicae)
idiomatic expression *s* vox quae linguae (Latinae *or* Anglicae) propria est
idiosyncrasy *s* propr·ium -(i)i *n*

idiot *s* fatu·us -i *m* (·a -ae *f)*
idiotic *adj* fatu·us -a -um
idle *adj* vacu·us -a -um; *(pointless)* van·us -a -um; *(lazy)* ignav·us -a -um; **to be —** cessare
idle *tr* **to — away** terere ‖ *intr* cessare, vacare
idleness *s* cessati·o -onis *f*
idler *s* cessa·tor -toris *m* (·trix -tricis *f)*
idle talk *s* nug·ae -arum *fpl*
idly *adv* segniter
idol *s* simulacr·um -i *n; (eccl)* idol·um -i *n; (fig)* delici·ae -arum *fpl*
idolater *s* idololatr·es -ae *mf*
idolatrous *adj* idololatric·us -a -um
idolatry *s* idololatri·a -ae *f*
idolize *tr* venerari
idyl *s* idyll·ium -(i)i *n*
if *conj* si; **as —** quasi, tamquam; **and —, but —** quodsi; **even —** etiamsi; **— not** ni, si minus; **— only** si modo; *(to express a wish)* utinam *(w. subj)*
iffy *adj (coll)* dubi·us -a -um
igneous *adj* igne·us -a -um
ignite *tr* accendere ‖ *intr* flammam concipere, exardescere
ignoble *adj* ignobil·is -is -e; *(base)* turp·is -is -e
ignobly *adv* turpiter
ignominious *adj* ignominios·us -a -um
ignominiously *adv* ignominiose
ignominy *s* ignomini·a -ae *f*
ignoramus *s* nesapi·us -i *m* (·a -ae *f)*
ignorance *s* ignoranti·a -ae *f*, insciti·a -ae *f*
ignorant *adj* ignar·us -a -um, inscit·us -a -um; *(unlearned)* indoct·us -a -um; **to be — of** ignorare
ignorantly *adv* inscienter
ignore *tr* praeterire; *(to omit)* neglegere
Iliad *s* Ili·as -adis *f*
ill *adj (used of body or mind)* ae·ger -gra -grum; *(used of body)* aegrot·us -a -um; *(evil)* mal·us -a -um; **to be —** aegrotare; **to fall —** in morbum incidere
ill *adv* male; **to be — at ease** sollict·us -a -um esse
ill *s* mal·um -i *n*
ill-advised *adj* inconsult·us -a -um
ill-boding *adj* infaust·us -a -um
ill-bred *adj* inurban·us -a -um
ill-disposed *adj* **(toward)** malevol·us -a -um *(w. dat)*
illegal *adj* illicit·us -a -um
illegitimate *adj* haud legitim·us -a -um; *(of birth)* noth·us -a -um
illegitimately *adv* contra legem
ill-fated *adj* infel·ix -icis
ill-gotten *adj* male part·us -a -um
ill health *s* valetud·o -inis *f* adversa; **for reasons of —** valetudinis causā
illiberal *adj* illiberal·is -is -e
illicit *adj* illicit·us -a -um
illicitly *adv* illicite
illiteracy *s* ignorati·o -onis *f* legendi scribendique
illiterate *adj* illiterat·us -a -um
ill-mannered *adj* male morat·us -a -um
illness *s* morb·us -i *m*
illogical *adj* absurd·us -a -um
illogically *adv* absurde
ill-omened *adj* infel·ix -icis
ills *spl* mal·a -orum *npl*
ill-starred *adj* infel·ix -icis
ill-tempered *adj* iracund·us -a -um
ill-timed *adj* intempestiv·us -a -um
illuminate *tr* illuminare; *(to enlighten)* excolere
illumination *s* illuminati·o -onis *f*
illusion *s* err·or -oris *m;* **optical —** oculorum ludibr·ium -(i)i *n*
illusive *adj* van·us -a -um
illusory *adj* fall·ax -acis
illustrate *tr (to shed light on)* illustrare; *(to exemplify)* exempla *(w. gen)* adducere; *(to draw)* delineare; *(to picture)* in tabulis depingere
illustration *s (example)* exempl·um -i *n; (picture)* tabul·a -ae *f*
illustrious *adj* illustr·is -is -e
ill will *s* malevolenti·a -ae *f*
image *s* sign·um -i *n; (esp. a portrait or bust)* imag·o -inis *f; (esp. a figure of a god)* simulacr·um -i *n*
imagery *s* imagin·es -um *fpl*
imaginary *adj* commentici·us -a -um, imaginari·us -a -um
imagination *s (faculty)* imaginati·o -onis *f;* cogitati·o -onis *f*
imaginative *adj* ingenios·us -a -um
imagine *tr* (animo) fingere, imaginari
imbecile *s* fatu·us -i *m* (·a -ae *f)*
imbecile *adj* fatu·us -a -um
imbedded *adj* **(in)** infix·us -a -um (in *w abl)*
imbibe *tr* imbibere
imbue *tr* imbuere
imitate *tr* imitari
imitation *s (act)* imitati·o -onis *f; (thing)* imag·o -inis *f*
imitator *s* imita·tor -toris *m* (·trix -tricis *f)*
immaculate *adj* immaculat·us -a -um
immaterial *adj* incorporal·is -is -e; *(unimportant)* nullius momenti
immature *adj* immatur·us -a -um
immaturity *s* immaturit·as -atis *f*
immeasurable *adj* immens·us -a -um
immediate *adj* proxim·us ·a -um
immediately *adv* statim, confestim; **— after** sub *(w. acc)*
immemorial *adj* antiquissim·us -a -um; **from time —** ex omni memoriā aetatum
immense *adj* immens·us -a -um
immensely *adv* vehementer
immensity *s* immensit·as -atis *f*
immerse *tr* (im)mergere
immersion *s* immersi·o -onis *f*

imminent *adj* immin•ens -entis; **to be —** instare
immobile *adj* immobil•is -is -e
immobility *s* immobilit•as -atis *f*
immoderate *adj* immodic•us -a -um
immoderately *adv* immodice
immodest *adj* impudic•us -a -um
immodesty *s* immodesti•a -ae *f*
immolate *tr* immolare
immolation *s* immolati•o -onis *f*
immoral *adj* prav•us -a -um
immorality *s* perditi mor•es -um *mpl*
immortal *adj* immortal•is -is -e
immortality *s* immortalit•as -atis *f*
immortalize *tr* immortalitati tradere
immovable *adj (lit & fig)* immobil•is -is -e
immune *adj* immun•is -is -e
immunity *s* immunit•as -atis *f,* vacati•o -onis *f;* **promise of —** fid•es -ei *f* publica
immutability *s* immutabilit•as -atis *f*
immutable *adj* immutabil•is -is -e
imp *s* pu•er -eri *m* protervus
impact *s* impuls•us -ūs *m*
impair *tr* imminuere
impale *tr* palo infigere
impart *tr* impertire, communicare
impartial *adj* aequ•us -a -um
impartiality *s* aequit•as -atis *f*
impartially *adv* aequabiliter; **to judge —** aequo (animo) iudicare
impassable *adj* impervi•us -a -um
impassioned *adj* vehem•ens -entis; **with — gestures** ardenti motu gestuque
impassive *adj* sensu car•ens -entis
impatience *s* impatienti•a -ae *f*
impatient *adj* impati•ens -entis; iniquo animo; **to be — with** iniquo animo ferre
impatiently *adv* iniquo animo
impeach *tr* criminari, accusare
impeachment *s* accusati•o -onis *f*
impede *tr* impedire
impediment *s* impediment•um -i *n; (in speech)* haesitati•o -onis *f*
impel *tr* impellere
impending *adj* immin•ens -entis
impenetrable *adj* impenetrabil•is -is -e; *(fig)* occult•us -a -um
impenitence *s* impaenitenti•a -ae *f*
imperative *adj* inst•ans -antis; *(gram)* imperativ•us -a -um; **— mood** mod•us -i *m* imperativus
imperceptible *adj* tenuissim•us -a -um
imperceptibly *adv* sensim
imperfect *adj (not completed)* imperfect•us -a -um; *(faulty)* vitios•us -a -um; **— tense** temp•us -oris *n* praeteritum
imperfection *s* vit•ium -(i)i *n*
imperfectly *adv* vitiose
imperial *adj* imperiatori•us -a -um; *(of an emperor)* principal•is -is -e
imperil *tr* in periculum adducere
imperious *adj* imperios•us -a -um
imperiously *adv* imperiose
imperishable *adj* incorrupt•us -a -um
impermeable *adj* impervi•us -a -um
impersonal *adj (detached)* incurios•us -a -um; *(gram)* impersonal•is -is -e
impersonally *adv (gram)* impersonaliter
impersonate *tr* sustinēre partes *(w. gen),* simulare
impersonation *s* simulati•o -onis *f*
impertinence *s* protervit•as -atis *f*
impertinent *adj* proterv•us -a -um; *(not to the point)* nihil ad rem
impertinently *adv* proterve
impervious *adj* impervi•us -a -um
impetuosity *s* violenti•a -ae *f*
impetuous *adj* viol•ens -entis
impetus *s* impet•us -ūs *m*
impiety *s* impiet•as -atis *f*
impinge *intr* **— on** incidere *(w. dat)*
impious *adj* impi•us -a -um; *(stronger)* nefari•us -a -um
impiously *adv* impie; *(stronger)* nefarie
impish *adj* proterv•us -a -um
implacable *adj* implacabil•is -is -e
implacably *adv* implacabiliter
implant *tr* inserere, ingenerare
implement *s* instrument•um -i *n; (iron tool)* ferrament•um -i *n*
implement *tr* exsequi
implicate *tr* implicare
implication *s* indic•ium -(i)i *n; (act)* implicati•o -onis *f;* **by —** tacite
implicit *adj* tacit•us -a -um; *(absolute)* summ•us -a -um
implicitly *adv* tacite
implied *adj* tacit•us -a -um; **to be — in** inesse in *(w. abl)*
implore *tr* implorare
imply *tr* innuere, indicare; *(to mean)* significare
impolite *adj* inurban•us -a -um
impolitely *adv* inurbane
impoliteness *s* inurbanit•as -atis *f*
impolitic *adj* inconsult•us -a -um
import *tr* importare, invehere
import *s (meaning)* significati•o -onis *f;* **—s** importatici•a -orum *npl*
importance *s* moment•um -i *n;* nostrā) refert; **it is of the greatest — to me** permagni meā interest; **of —** grav•is -is -e; **to be a person of great —** plurimum pollēre; **to be of great —** magni esse
important *adj* magn•us -a -um; *(weighty)* grav•is -is -e; **an — and wealthy city** gravis atque opulenta civit•as -atis *f;* **it is — to me (to you, to us)** meā (tuā, vestrā, nostrā) refert; **it's not all that — to me** mihi tanti non est; **to be —** magni (momenti *or* negoti) esse; **to be very —** maximi (momenti *or* negoti) esse
importune *tr* flagitare, sollicitare
impose *tr* imponere; *(to enjoin)* iniungere; **to — a fine (a punishment) on s.o.** alicui

multam (poenam) irrogare ‖ *intr* **to — upon** abuti *(w. abl)*

imposition *s (excessive burden)* importunit·as -atis *f; (act) use* imponere

impossibility *s* impossibilit·as -atis *f*

impossible *adj* impossibil·is -is -e; **it is —** non fieri potest

imposter *s* frauda·tor -toris *m* (·trix -tricis *f)*

impotence *s* infirmit·as -atis *f; (sexual)* sterilit·as -atis *f*

impotent *adj* infirm·us -a -um; *(sexually)* steril·is -is -e

impound *tr* publicare; *(animals)* includere

impoverish *tr* in egestatem redigere

impoverished *adj* eg·ens -entis

impractical *adj* inutil·is -is -e

impregnable *adj* inexpugnabil·is -is -e

impregnate *tr* gravidam facere

impregnation *s* fecundati·o -onis *f*

impress *tr (on the mind; to imprint)* imprimere; *(a person)* commovēre; **to — s.th. on s.o.** aliquid alicui inculcare

impression *s (on a person)* animi mot·us -ūs *m; (print)* impressi·o -onis *f; (copy)* exempl·ar -aris *n; (idea)* opini·o -onis *f;* **to make a (deep) — on** (maxime) commovēre *(w. acc)*

impressive *adj* grav·is -is -e

impressively *adv* graviter

imprint *s* impressi·o -onis *f*

imprint *tr* imprimere; **to be —ed on the mind** in animum imprimi

imprison *tr* in vincula conicere

imprisonment *s* custodi·a -ae *f*

improbable *adj* haud credibil·is -is -e, haud probabil·is -is -e

impromptu *adj* subit(ari)·us -a -um

impromptu *adv* ex tempore

improper *adj* indecor·us -a -um

improperly *adv* indecore

improve *tr* mel·iorem -iorem -ius facere; *(where a fault exists)* emendare; *(soil)* laetificare ‖ *intr* mel·ior -ior -ius fieri; *(med)* convalescere

improvement *s* emendati·o -onis *f; (condition)* mutati·o -onis *f* in meliorem statum; *(progress made)* profect·us -ūs *m;* **to make —** proficere

improvise *tr* ex tempore dicere *or* componere

imprudence *s* imprudenti·a -ae *f*

imprudent *adj* imprud·ens -entis

imprudently *adv* imprudenter

impudent *adj* impud·ens -entis

impugn *tr* inpugnare, in dubium vocare

impulse *s* animi impet·us -ūs *m*

impulsive *adj* temerari·us -a -um

impulsively *adv* impetu quodam animi

impunity *s* impunit·as -atis *f;* **with —** impune

impure *adj* immund·us -a -um; *(morally)* impur·us -a -um

impurely *adv* impure

impurity *s* immunditi·a -ae *f; (moral)* impurit·as -atis *f*

impute *tr* imputare

in *prep* in *(w. abl); (in cities, use locative); (in the writings of)* apud *(w. acc); (of time) render by abl; (denoting rule, standard or manner)* in *(w. acc), e.g.,* **— the manner of slaves** servilem in modum; **— all** ex toto; **— that** quod; **— the course of the night** de nocte; **— the course of the third watch** de tertiā vigiliā; **— the likeness of** ad similitudinem *(w. gen);* **— the month of September** (de) mense Septembri; **— the same manner** ad eundem modum, eodem modo

in *adv (motion)* intro; *(rest)* intra, intus; **is your father —** estne pater intus?

inability *s* impotenti·a -ae *f,* nulla facult·as -atis *f*

inaccessible *adj* inacess·us -a -um; **to be —** *(of a person)* rari aditūs esse

inaccuracy *s* indiligenti·a -ae *f,* incuri·a -ae *f; (error)* err·or -oris *m*

inaccurate *adj* parum accurat·us -a -um; *(in error)* vitios·us -a -um

inaccurately *adv* parum accurate

inactive *adj* iner·s -tis

inactivity *s* inerti·a -ae *f*

inadequate *adj* im·par -paris

inadequately *adv* parum, haud satis

inadmissible *adj* illicit·us -a -um

inadvertent *adj* imprud·ens -entis

inadvertently *adv* imprudenter; *more frequently expressed by the adjective* imprud·ens -entis

inalienable *adj* quod alienari non potest

inane *adj* inan·is -is -e

inanimate *adj* inanim·us -a -um

inapplicable *adj* **to be —** non valēre

inappropriate *adj* haud apt·us -a -um

inappropriately *adv* parum apte

inarticulate *adj* indistinct·us -a -um

inasmuch as *conj* quandoquidem

inattention *s* indiligenti·a -ae *f*

inattentive *adj* haud attent·us -a -um

inattentively *adv* neglegenter

inaudible *adj* **to be —** audiri non posse

inaugurate *tr (an official)* inaugurare; *(to begin)* incipere

inauguration *s* inaugurati·o -onis *f;* init·ium -(i)i *n*

inauspicious *adj* infaust·us -a -um

inauspiciously *adv* malo omine

inborn, inbred *adj* innat·us -a -um

incalculable *adj* inaestimabil·is -is -e; *(fig)* immens·us -a -um

incantation *s* incantament·um -i *n*

incapable *adj* incap·ax -acis; **to be — of** non posse *(w. inf)*

incapacitate *tr* debilitare

incarcerate *tr* in carcerem conicere

incarnate *adj* incarnat·us -a -um

incarnation *s* incarnati·o -onis *f*

incautious *adj* incaut·us -a -um
incautiously *adv* incaute
incendiary *adj* incendiari·us -a -um
incense *s* tus, turis *n*
incense *tr* ture fumigare; *(to anger)* incendere
incentive *s* incitament·um -i *n*
incessant *adj* assidu·us -a -um
incessantly *adv* assidue
incest *s* incest·us -ūs *m*
incestuous *adj* incest·us -a -um
inch *s* unci·a -ae *f;* **— by —** unciatim; **not to yield an —** non tranversum digitum discedere
incident *s* cas·us -ūs *m,* res, rei *f*
incidental *adj* fortuit·us -a -um
incidentally *adv* casu, inter alias res
incinerate *tr* cremare
incinerator *s* receptacul·um -i *n* cremandi
incipient *adj* incipi·ens -entis
incision *s* incisur·a -ae *f*
incisive *adj* a·cer -cris -cre
incisors *spl* dent·es -ium *mpl* primores
incite *tr* incitare
incitement *s* incitament·um -i *n*
incivility *s* rusticit·as -atis *f*
inclemency *s* inclementi·a -ae *f; (of weather)* asperit·as -atis *f*
inclement *adj* asp·er -era -erum
inclination *s (act, propensity)* inclinati·o -onis *f; (slope)* proclivit·as -atis *f*
incline *s* acclivit·as -atis *f*
incline *tr & intr* inclinare
inclined *adj* propens·us -a -um; **I am — to believe** crediderim
include *tr (to contain)* continēre; *(to enclose)* includere; *(to comprise)* comprehendere; **—ing me** me haud excepto; **—ing your brother** in his frater tuus
inclusive *adj expressed by* adnumerare: **from the 1st to the 10th —** a primo die ad decimum adnumeratum *(or* ipso decimo adnumerato)
incognito *adv* alienā indutā personā
incoherent *adj* perturbat·us -a -um; **to be —** non cohaerēre
incoherently *adv* **to speak —** male cohaerentia loqui
income *s* quaest·us -ūs *m,* merc·es -edis *f*
incomparable *adj* incomparabil·is -is -e
incomparably *adv* unice
incompatibility *s* repugnanti·a -ae *f*
incompatible *adj* repugn·ans -antis
incompetence *s* insciti·a -ae *f*
incompetent *adj* inscit·us -a -um
incomplete *adj* imperfect·us -a -um
incomprehensible *adj* quod mente non comprehendi potest
inconceivable *adj* incredibil·is -is -e
inconclusive *adj* anc·eps -ipitis
incongruous *adj* male congru·ens -entis, inconveni·ens -entis
inconsiderable *adj* exigu·us -a -um
inconsiderate *adj* inconsiderat·us -a -um
inconsistency *s* discrepanti·a -ae *f*
inconsistent *adj* inconst·ans -antis; **to be — with** abhorrēre ab *(w. abl)*
inconsistently *adv* inconstanter
inconsolable *adj* inconsolabil·is -is -e
inconstancy *s* inconstanti·a -ae *f*
inconstant *adj* inconst·ans -antis
incontestible *adj* non contentend·us -a -um
incontinence *s* incontinenti·a -ae *f; (of sex)* licenti·a -ae *f*
incontinent *adj* incontin·ens -entis; *(sexually)* libidinos·us -a -um
incontrovertible *adj* quod refutari non potest
inconvenience *s* incommod·um -i *n*
inconvenience *tr* incommodare
inconvenient *adj* incommod·us -a -um
inconveniently *adv* incommode
incorporate *tr* adicere; *(to unite, esp. politically)* contribuere; *(to form into a corporation)* constituere
incorporeal *adj* incorporal·is -is -e
incorrect *adj* mendos·us -a -um, vitios·us -a -um
incorrectly *adv* perperam
incorrigible *adj* perdit·us -a -um
incorrupt *adj* incorrupt·us -a -um
incorruptible *adj* incorruptibil·is -is -e; *(upright)* inte·ger -gra -grum
increase *s* increment·um -i *n; (act)* accreti·o -onis *f*
increase *tr* augēre, ampliare **||** *intr* augeri, crescere
incredible *adj* incredibil·is -is -e
incredibly *adv* incredibiliter
incredulity *s* incredulit·as -atis *f*
incredulous *adj* incredul·us -a -um
increment *s* increment·um -i *n*
incriminate *tr* criminari
incubate *tr* incubare
incubation *s* incubati·o -onis *f*
inculcate *tr* inculcare
inculcation *s* inculcati·o -onis *f*
incumbent *adj* **it is — on** oportet *(w. acc)*
incumbent *s* qui *(or* quae) honorem gerit
incur *tr* subire; *(guilt)* admittere
incurable *adj* insanabil·is -is -e
incursion *s* incursi·o -onis *f*
indebted *adj* obaerat·us -a -um; *(obliged)* obnoxi·us -a -um; **to be — to s.o. for a sum of money** pecuniam alicui debēre
indecency *s* impudiciti·a -ae *f*
indecent *adj* impudic·us -a -um
indecently *adv* impudice
indecision *s* haesitati·o -onis *f*
indecisive *adj (battle)* anc·eps -ipitis; *(person)* dubi·us -a -um
indeclinable *adj* indeclinabil·is -is -e
indeed *adv* vere, profecto; *(concessive)* quidem; *(reply)* certe, vero; *(interrog)* itane?
indefatigable *adj* indefatigabil·is -is -e

indefensible *adj (an action)* non excusand·us -a -um; *(mil)* parum firm·us -a -um; **to be —** defendi non posse
indefinite *adj* incert·us -a -um; *(vague)* anc·eps -ipitis; *(gram)* infinit·us -a -um *(opp:* finitus)
indelible *adj* indelibil·is -is -e
indelicate *adj* inurban·us -a -um
indemnify *tr* damnum restitutere *(w. dat)*, compensare
indemnity *s* indemnit·as -atis *f*, damni restituti·o -onis *f*
indent *tr (to notch)* incisuris signare; *(a line)* a margine movēre
indentation *s* incisur·a -ae *f*
indented *adj* incis·us -a -um; *(serrated)* serrat·us -a -um
independence *s* libert·as -atis *f*
independent *adj* lib·er -era -erum; *(one's own master)* sui pot·ens -entis; *(leg)* sui iuris
independently *adv* libere, suo arbitrio
indescribable *adj* inenarrabil·is -is -e
indescribably *adv* inenarrabiliter
indestructible *adj* indelebil·is -is -e
indeterminate *adj* indefinit·us -a -um
index *s* ind·ex -icis *m*
Indian *adj* Indic·us -a -um
Indian *s* Ind·us -i *m* (·a -ae *f*)
indicate *tr* indicare, significare; **to — that** docēre *(w. acc & inf)*
indication *s* indic·ium -(i)i *n*
indicative *s (gram)* indicativus mod·us -i *m*
indict *tr* nomen *(w. gen)* deferre
indictment *s* nominis delati·o -onis *f;* **bill of —** libell·us -i *m*
indifference *s* aequus anim·us -i *m; (apathy)* lentitud·o -inis *f*, neglegenti·a -ae *f*
indifferent *adj (apathetic)* indiffer·ens -entis; *(mediocre)* mediocr·is -is -e; **to be — to s.th.** aliquid nil morari
indifferently *adv* indifferenter
indigenous *adj (home-grown)* vernacul·us -a -um; *(of people)* indigen·a -ae; **the — Latins** indigenae Latini
indigent *adj* eg·ens -entis
indigestible *adj* crud·us -a -um
indigestion *s* crudit·as -atis *f*
indignant *adj* indignabund·us -a -um; **— at** indign·ans -antis *(w. gen);* **to be —** indignari
indignantly *adv* indignanter
indignation *s* indignati·o -onis *f*
indignity *s* indignit·as -atis *f*
indirect *adj* indirect·us -a -um; **— discourse** obliqua orati·o -onis *f*
indirectly *adv* indirecte
indiscreet *adj* inconsult·us -a -um
indiscreetly *adv* inconsulte
indiscretion *s* imprudenti·a -ae *f;* **driven by youthful —** licentiā iuvenali impuls·us -a -um
indiscriminate *adj* promiscu·us -a -um
indiscriminately *adv* sine discrimine
indispensable *adj* omnino necessari·us -a -um
indisposed *adj* (**to**) avers·us -a -um (ab *w. abl); (sick)* aegrot·us -a -um
indisputable *adj* cert·us -a -um, haud dubi·us -a -um
indissoluble *adj* indissolubil·is -is -e
indistinct *adj* parum clar·us -a -um
indistinctly *adv* parum clare
individual *adj (of one only)* singular·is -is -e; *(of more than one)* singul·i -ae -a; *(particular)* quidam quaedam, quoddam; *(peculiar)* propri·us -a -um
individual *s* hom·o -inis *mf;* **—s** singul·i -ae -a; **to benefit the country or —s** civitati aut singulis civibus prodesse
individually *adv* singulatim
individuality *s* proprium ingen·ium -(i)i *n*
indivisible *adj* indivisibil·is -is -e
indolence *s* inerti·a -ae *f*
indolent *adj* in·ers -ertis
indomitable *adj* indomit·us -a -um
indorse *tr* ratum facere
indubitable *adj* indubitabil·is -is -e
indubitably *adv* sine dubio
induce *tr* adducere
inducement *s* incitament·um -i *n*
indulge *tr* indulgēre *(w. dat)*
indulgent *adj* indulg·ens -entis
indulgently *adv* indulgenter
industrial *adj* ad frabricationem et venditionem mercium pertin·ens -entis
industrialist *s* magis·ter -tri *m* officinarum
industrious *adj* industri·us -a -um
industriously *adv* industrie
industry *s (effort)* industri·a -ae *f; (com)* fabricati·o -onis *f* et venditi·o -onis *f* mercium
inebriated *adj* ebri·us -a -um
ineffable *adj* ineffabil·is -is -e
ineffective *adj* irrit·us -a -um, ineffic·ax -acis; **to be —** effectu carēre
ineffectual *adj* ineffic·ax -acis
ineffectually *adv* frustra
inefficient *adj* ineffic·ax -acis
inelegant *adj* ineleg·ans -antis
ineligible *adj* non eligend·us -a -um
inept *adj* inept·us -a -um
ineptitude *s* inepti·ae -arum *fpl*
inequality *s* inaequalit·as -atis *f; (social)* iniquit·as -atis *f*
inequitable *adj* iniqu·us -a -um
inert *adj* in·ers -ertis
inertia *s* inerti·a -ae *f*
inevitable *adj* inevitabil·is -is -e
inevitably *adv* necessario
inexact *adj* haud accurat·us -a -um; *(of persons)* indilig·ens -entis
inexcusable *adj* inexcusabil·is -is -e
inexhaustible *adj* infinit·us -a -um, copios·us -a -um
inexorable *adj* inexorabil·is -is -e

inexpensive *adj* vil·is -is -e
inexperience *s* imperiti·a -ae *f*
inexperienced *adj* **(in)** imperit·us -a -um *(w. gen)*
inexplicable *adj* inexplicabil·is -is -e
inexpressible *adj* inenarrabil·is -is -e
inextricable *adj* inextricabil·is -is -e
infallibility *s* erroris immunit·as -atis *f*
infallible *adj* qui *or* quae errare non potest
infamous *adj (ill-famed)* infam·is -is -e; *(wicked)* nefand·us -a -um, nefari·us -a -um
infamously *adv* cum infamiā
infancy *s* infanti·a -ae *f*
infant *s* inf·ans -antis *mf*
infanticide *s (deed)* infanticid·ium -(i)i *n; (person)* infanticid·a -ae *mf*
infantile *adj* infantil·is -is -e
infantry *s* peditat·us -ūs *m,* pedit·es -um *mpl*
infantry man *s* ped·es -itis *m*
infatuated *adj* mente capt·us -a -um; **to be — with s.o.** aliquem afflictim amare
infatuation *s* dementi·a -ae *f*
infect *tr* inficere; *(fig)* contaminare
infection *s* contagi·o -onis *f*
infectious *adj* contagios·us -a -um
infer *tr* colligere, conicere; **I — from what you say that ...** ex verbis tuis colligo *(w. acc & inf)*
inference *s* coniectur·a -ae *f,* deducti·o -onis *f; (logic)* conclusi·o -onis *f*
inferior *adj* deter·ior -ior -ius
infernal *adj* infern·us -a -um; *(fig)* nefand·us -a -um
infertile *adj* steril·is -is -e
infertility *s* sterilit·as -atis *f*
infest *tr* infestare
infidel *s* infidel·is -is *mf*
infidelity *s* infidelit·as -atis *f*
infiltrate *tr* se insinuare in *(w. acc)*
infinite *adj* infinit·us -a -um
infinitely *adv* infinite; *(coll)* infinito
infinitive *s* infinitiv·um -i *n*
infinity *s* infinit·as -atis *f*
infirm *adj* infirm·us -a -um
infirmary *s* valetudinar·ium -(i)i *n*
infirmity *s* infirmit·as -atis *f*
inflame *tr (lit & fig)* inflammare; *(fig)* incendere
inflammable *adj* ad exardescendum facil·is -is -e
inflammation *s* inflammati·o -onis *f*
inflammatory *adj* turbulent·us -a -um
inflate *tr* inflare
inflated *adj* inflat·us -a -um
inflation *s* inflati·o -onis *f*
inflect *tr (gram)* declinare
inflection *s* declinati·o -onis *f*
inflexible *adj* inflexibil·is -is -e; *(fig)* obstinat·us -a -um
inflexibly *adv* obstinate
inflict *tr* infligere, inferre; **to — a deadly blow** mortiferam plagam infligere; **to — punishment on s.o.** aliquem supplicio afficere; **to — wounds on** vulnera inferre *(w. dat)*
influence *s* grati·a -ae *f;* **to have — on** valēre apud *(w. acc);* **to have (great, more, very great, little, no) influence on** magnum (plus, plurimum. paulum, nihil) posse apud *(w. acc)*
influence *tr* movēre
influential *adj* auctoritate grav·is -is -e, gratios·us -a -um
influenza *s* catarrh·us -i *m*
influx *s* influxi·o -onis *f*
inform *tr* certiorem facere, docēre; **having been —ed about this** his rebus cognitis **||** *intr* **to — against** deferre de *(w. abl)*
informal *adj (casual)* familiar·is -is -e, facil·is -is -e; *(unofficial)* privat·us -a -um
informality *s* familiarit·as -atis *f*
informant *s* ind·ex -icis *mf*
information *s* re·s -rum *fpl,* nunt·ius -(i)i *m; (leg)* indic·ium -(i)i *n;* **having received this —** his rebus cognitis
informer *s* dela·tor -toris *m* (·trix -tricis *f)*
infraction *s* infracti·o -onis *f*
infrequency *s* rarit·as -atis *f*
infrequent *adj* rar·us -a -um
infrequently *adv* raro
infringe *tr* violare **||** *intr* **to — upon** usurpare
infringement *s* violati·o -onis *f; (of rights)* imminuti·o -onis *f*
infuriate *tr* efferre, exasperare
infuse *tr* infundere; *(fig)* inicere
infusion *s* infusi·o -onis *f*
ingenious *adj* ingenios·us -a -um, soll·ers -ertis
ingeniously *adv* sollerter
ingenuity *s* sollerti·a -ae *f*
ingest *tr* ingerere
inglorious *adj* inglori·us -a -um
ingloriously *adv* sine gloriā
ingot *s* lat·er -eris *m*
ingrained *adj* insit·us -a -um
ingratiate *tr* **to — oneself with** gratiam inire ab *(w. abl)*
ingratitude *s* ingratus anim·us -i *m*
ingredient *s (generally not expressed by a noun)* element·um -i *n;* **a composition, the —s of which** compositio quae habet; **the medication consists of the following —s** medicamentum constat ex his
inhabit *tr* incolere
inhabitable *adj* habitabil·is -is -e
inhabitant *s* incol·a -ae *mf*
inhale *tr* haurire, ducere **||** *intr* spiritum ducere
inharmonious *adj* disson·us -a -um
inherent *adj* inhaer·ens -entis; **to be — in** inhaerēre in *(w. abl),* inesse in *(w. abl)*
inherit *tr* hereditate excipere

inheritance *s* heredit·as -atis *f;* **to come into an —** hereditatem adire
inhospitable *adj* inhospital·is -is -e
inhuman *adj* inhuman·us -a -um
inhumanly *adv* inhumane
inhumanity *s* inhumanit·as -atis *f*
inimical *adj* inimic·us -a -um
inimitable *adj* inimitabil·is -is -e
iniquitous *adj* improb·us -a -um
iniquity *s* improbit·as -atis *f*
initial *adj* prim·us -a -um
initial *s* prima nominis litter·a -ae *f*
initial *tr* primis litteris nominis signare
initiate *tr* initiare
initiation *s* initiati·o -onis *f*
initiative *s* vis *f;* **on my own —** meā sponte
inject *tr* inicere, immittere
injection *s* iniecti·o -onis *f*
injudicious *adj* inconsult·us -a -um
injudiciously *adv* inconsulte
injunction *s* mandat·um -i *n;* **to get an —** ad interdictum venire
injure *tr* nocēre *(w. dat),* laedere
injurious *adj* noxi·us -a -um
injury *s* nox·a -ae *f,* iniuri·a -ae *f*
injustice *s* iniustiti·a -ae *f; (act of injustice)* iniuri·a -ae *f*
ink *s* atrament·um -i *n*
inkling *s* obscura significati·o -onis *f;* **to have an —** suspicari
inland *adj* mediterrane·us -a -um
inland *adv* intus; **towns — from Tarentum** oppida per continentem a Tarento
in-law *s* affin·is -is *mf*
inlay *tr* inserere; *(with mosaic)* tessellare
inlay *s* caelatur·a -ae *f*
inlet *s* aestuar·ium -(i)i *n*
inmate *s* (carceris) inquilin·us -i *m* (·a -ae *f*)
inmost *adj* intim·us -a -um
inn *s* deversor·ium -(i)i *n, (esp. of an inferior type)* caupon·a -ae *f*
innate *adj* innat·us -a -um
inner *adj* inter·ior -ior -ius
innermost *adj* intim·us -a -um
inning *s (of baseball)* miss·us -ūs *m*
innkeeper *s* caup·o -onis *m; (female)* caupon·a -ae *f,* cop·a -ae *f*
innocence *s* innocenti·a -ae *f*
innocent *adj* **(of)** innoc·ens -entis *(w. gen)*
innocently *adv* innocenter
innocuous *adj* innocu·us -a -um
innocuously *adv* innocue
innovate *tr* novare
innovation *s* novit·as -atis *f,* re·s -ei *f* nova
innovative *adj* multa nov·ans -antis
innovator *s* qui *(or* quae) multa novat
innumerable *adj* innumer·us -a -um
inoculate *tr* serum inserere *(w. dat)*
innoculation *s* seri insiti·o -onis *f*
inoffensive *adj* innoxi·us -a -um
inopportune *adj* intempestiv·us -a -um
inopportunely *adv* parum in tempore
inordinate *adj* immoderat·us -a -um
inordinately *adv* immoderate
input *s (comput)* (datorum) init·us -ūs *m;* **— and output** (datorum) initus exitusque
inquest *s* inquisiti·o -onis *f; (leg)* quaesti·o -onis *f;* **an — was held on the cause of death** quaesitum est quae mortis causa fuisset
inquire *intr* **(into)** inquirere (in *w. acc)*
inquiry *s* quaesti·o -onis *f*
inquisition *s* inquisiti·o -onis *f*
inquisitive *adj* curios·us -a -um
inquisitor *s* quaesit·or -oris *m*
inroad *s* incursi·o -onis *f;* **to make —s into territory** incursiones in fines facere
insane *adj* insan·us -a -um
insanely *adv* insane
insanity *s* insanit·as -atis *f*
insatiable *adj* insatiabil·is -is -e
inscribe *tr* inscribere
inscription *s* inscripti·o -onis *f*
inscrutable *adj* occult·us -a -um
insect *s* insect·um -i *n*
insecure *adj* haud tut·us -a -um
insecurity *s* **feeling of —** sollicitud·o -inis *f*
insensible *adj* insensil·is -is -e; *(fig)* dur·us -a -um
insensitive *adj* dur·us -a -um
insensitivity *s* duriti·a -ae *f*
inseparable *adj* inseparabil·is -is -e
insert *tr* inserere, interponere; *(in writing)* ascribere
insertion *s* interpositi·o -onis *f*
inside *adj* inter·ior -ior -ius; **— of** *(time)* intra *(w. acc);* **— out** inversus
inside *adv* intus; **go —!** i *(pl:* ite) intus!
inside *prep* intro *(w. acc)*
inside *s* interior par·s -tis *f;* **—s** viscer·a -um *npl*
inside of *prep* intra *(w. acc)*
insidious *adj* insidios·us -a -um
insidiously *adv* insidiose
insight *s* cogniti·o -onis *f;* **to have a profound — into human character** mores hominum atque ingenia penitus perspecta habēre
insignia *spl* insign·ia -ium *npl*
insignificance *s* exiguit·as -atis *f*
insignificant *adj* exigu·us -a -um, nullius momenti, parv·us -a -um
insincere *adj* insincer·us -a -um
insincerely *adv* haud sincere
insincerity *s* ingen·ium -(i)i *n* haud sincerum
insinuate *tr (to hint)* operte significare
insinuation *s* significati·o -onis *f*
insipid *adj* insuls·us -a -um
insipidly *adv* insulse
insist *intr* instare; **I — that** certum est mihi *(w. acc & inf);* **to — on** urgēre, postulare
insistence *s* pertinaci·a -ae *f*
insistent *adj* pertin·ax -acis; *(urgent)* urg·ens -entis

insolence *s* insolenti·a -ae *f*
insolent *adj* insol·ens -entis
insoluble *adj* insolubil·is -is -e; *(fig)* inexplicabil·is -is -e
insolvent *adj* decoct·us -a -um; **I am insolvent** solvendo non sum
inspect *tr* inspicere; *(mil)* recensēre
inspection *s* inspecti·o -onis *f; (mil)* recensi·o -onis *f*
inspector *s* cura·tor -toris *m* (·trix -tricis *f*)
inspiration *s (divine)* afflat·us -ūs *m; (prophetic)* fur·or -oris *m; (idea)* noti·o -onis *f*
inspire *tr* inspirare; **divinely —d** divino spiritu instinct·us -a -um; **to — s.o. with courage** animos alicui addere; **to — s.o. with fear** alicui formidinem inicere
instability *s* instabilit·as -atis *f*
install *tr (mechanically)* instruere; *(w. augural solemnity)* inaugurare
installation *s* inaugurati·o -onis *f; (mechanical)* constructi·o -onis *f; (mil)* castr·a -orum *npl* stativa
installment *s (com)* pensi·o -onis *f;* **to pay in five —s** quinque pensionibus solvere
instance *s* exempl·um -i *n;* **for —** exempli gratiā; **for — when** ut enim cum; **in this —** in hac re
instant *adj* praes·ens -entis; **this —** statim
instantaneous *adj* praes·ens -entis
instantaneously *adv* continuo
instantly *adv* confestim, statim
instead *adv* potius, magis
instead of *prep* pro *(w. abl); (w. verb)* non ... sed
instigate *tr* instigare, concitare
instigation *s* instigati·o -onis *f;* **at your —** te auctore
instigator *s* auct·or -oris *mf,* instiga·tor -toris *m* (·trix -tricis *f*)
instill *tr* instillare
instinct *s* natur·a -ae *f*
instinctive *adj* natural·is -is -e
instinctively *adv* naturā
institute *tr* instituere
institute *s* institut·um -i *n*
institution *s (act)* instituti·o -onis *f; (thing instituted)* institut·um -i *n*
instruct *tr (to teach)* instituere, docēre; *(to order)* mandare *(w. dat or* ut, ne); **to — s.o. in s.th.** aliquem aliquo instruere
instruction *s* instituti·o -onis *f,* doctrin·a -ae *f;* **—s** praecept·a -orum *npl; (orders to do s.th.)* mandat·a -orum *npl;* **to give —s to** mandare *(w. dat)*
instructive *adj* ad docendum apt·us -a -um
instructor *s* doc·ens -entis *mf,* praecep·tor -toris *m* (·trix -tricis *f*)
instrument *s* instrument·um -i *n; (mus)* organ·um -i *n; (leg)* syngraph·a -ae *f*
instrumental *s* util·is -is -e; **you were — in bringing s.th. to pass** tuā operā factum est; *(in negative sentences)* **you were instrumental in not ...** per te stetit quominus ...
instrumentality *s* oper·a -ae *f*
insubordinate *adj (mutinous)* seditios·us -a -um; *(disobedient)* male par·ens -entis
insubordination *s (mutiny)* sediti·o -onis *f;* **to be guilty of —** per licentiam ducibus non parēre
insufferable *adj* intolerand·us -a -um
insufficiency *s* inop·ia -ae *f*
insufficient *adj* haud suffici·ens -entis
insufficiently *adv* haud satis
insular *adj* insulan·us -a -um
insulate *tr* segregare
insult *s* contumeli·a -ae *f*
insult *tr* contumeliā afficere
insulting *adj* contumelios·us -a -um
insultingly *adv* contumeliose
insuperable *adj* insuperabil·is -is -e
insurance *s* cauti·o -onis *f* indemnitatis, assecurati·o -onis *f;* **car —** assecuratio vehicularia; **casualty —** assecuratio indemnitatis; **health —** assecuratio valetudinaria; **life —** vitae assecuratio, pro vita cautio
insurance company *s* eran·us -i *m*
insurance policy *s* cauti·o -onis *f* indemnitatis
insure *tr* praecavēre de damnis
insurgent *adj* rebell·is -is -e
insurgent *s* rebell·is -is *mf*
insurmountable *adj* inexsuperabil·is -is -e
insurrection *s* rebelli·o -onis *f; (civil strife)* sediti·o -onis *f*
intact *adj* incolum·is -is -e
intangible *adj* intactil·is -is -e
integer *s* numer·us -i *m* integer
integral *adj* ad totum necessari·us -a -um; *(entire)* integ·er -ra -rum
integrity *s* integrit·as -atis *f*
intellect *s* intellect·us -ūs *m*
intellectual *adj* intelleg·ens -entis
intelligence *s* intellegenti·a -ae *f; (information)* nunt·ius -(i)i *m*
intelligent *adj* intelleg·ens -entis
intelligently *adv* intellegenter
intelligible *adj* intellegibil·is -is -e
intelligibly *adv* intellegibiliter
intemperance *s* intemperanti·a -ae *f*
intemperately *adv* intemperanter
intend *tr* in animo habēre, destinare, in animo esse *(w. dat of the subject)*
intended *adj* destinat·us -a -um; *(of future spouse)* spons·us -a
intense *adj* extrem·us -a -um, summ·us -a -um; *(vigorous)* a·cer -cris -cre; *(emotions)* grand·is -is -e; *(heat, cold)* magn·us -a -um; *(excessive)* nimi·us -a -um
intensely *adv* valde, vehementer
intensify *tr* intendere
intensity *s* vehementi·a -ae *f,* vis *f*
intensively *adv* vehementer

intensive pronoun *s* pronom·en -inis *n* intentionis
intent *adj* intent·us -a -um; **to be — on** animum intendere in *(w. acc)*
intently *adv* intente
intention *s* consil·ium -(i)i *n; (meaning)* significati·o -onis *f;* **with the best —s** optimo animo utens
intentionally *adv* de industriā
inter *tr* inhumare
intercede *intr (on behalf of)* deprecari (pro *w. abl)*
intercept *tr* intercipere
interception *s* intercepti·o -onis *f*
intercession *s* deprecati·o -onis *f; (of a tribune)* intercessi·o -onis *f*
intercessor *s* depreca·tor -toris *m* (·trix -tricis *f)*
interchange *s* permutati·o -onis *f; (of a highway)* coniuncti·o -onis *f* viarum
interchange *tr* permutare
intercourse *s (sexual)* coït·us -ūs *m; (social; sexual)* consuetud·o -inis *f*
interdict *tr* interdicere *(w. acc of person and abl of thing; dat of person and acc of thing)*
interdiction *s* interdicti·o -onis *f*
interest *s (attention)* **(in)** stud·ium -(i)i *n (w. gen); (advantage)* us·us -ūs *m; (fin)* faen·us -oris *n,* usur·a -ae *f;* **compund —** anatocism·us -i *m;* **it is in my —** meā interest; **rate of —** usur·ae -arum *fpl;* **simple —** perpetuum faenus; **to have an — in painting** studium pinguendi habere; **to lend money at —** pecuniam faenori dare; **to take an — in s.th.** studio alicuius teneri
interest *tr (to affect the mind)* tenēre; *(to delight)* delectare; **sports don't — me** athleticae me non tenent
interested *adj* **— in** studios·us -a -um *(w. gen),* attent·us -a -um *(w. dat);* **children are —ed in games** liberi ludis tenentur; **I am — in music** musicae [*dat*] studeo; **I am not the least bit — in races** circensibus ne levissime quidem teneor
interesting *adj* iucund·us -a -um; **this books is —** hic liber me tenet
interfere *intr* se interponere *(w. dat); (to prevent s.th.)* intercedere; **the tribunes will not — with the praetor's making a motion** tribuni non praetori intercessuri sunt, quominus referat
interference *s* intercessi·o -onis *f*
interim *s* intervall·um -i *n;* **in the —** interim
interior *adj (inner)* inter·ior -ior -ius; *(inland)* mediterrane·us -a -um
interior *s* interior par·s -tis *f; (region)* mediterrane·a -orum *npl;* **in the —** in mediterraneo, intus; **toward the —** intus
interjection *s* interiecti·o -onis *f*
interlinear *adj* interscript·us -a -um
interlude *s (pause, break, intermission)* dilud·ium -(i)i *n,* intercaped·o -inis *f; (theat)* embol·ium -(i)i *n*
intermarriage *s* co(n)nub·ium -(i)i *n*
intermarry *intr* matrimonio inter se coniungi
intermediary *s* internunti·us -i *m* (·a -ae *f)*
intermediate *adj* medi·us -a -um
interment *s* sepultur·a -ae *f*
interminable *adj* infinit·us -a -um
intermission *s* intercaped·o -inis *f*
intermittent *adj* intermitt·ens -entis
intermittently *adv* interdum
internal *adj* intestin·us -a -um, intern·us -a -um
internally *adv* intus, interne
international *adj* inter gentes; **— law** ius, iuris *n* gentium
internet *s* interret·e -is *n*
internet *adj* interretial·is -a -um
interpolate *tr* interpolare
interpolation *s* interpolati·o -onis *f*
interpret *tr* interpretari
interpretation *s* interpretati·o -onis *f*
interpreter *s* interpr·es -etis *mf*
interrogate *tr* interrogare
interrogation *s* interrogati·o -onis *f*
interrogative *adj* interrogativ·us -a -um
interrupt *tr* interrumpere; *(speech)* interpellare
interruption *s* interrupti·o -onis *f; (of a speaker)* interpellati·o -onis *f*
intersect *tr* intersecare
intersection *s* intersecti·o -onis *f; (of roads)* compit·um -i *n,* quadriv·ium -(i)i *n*
intersperse *tr* immiscēre
interstate *adj* inter civitates
intertwine *tr* intertexere
interval *s* intervall·um -i *n*
intervene *intr (to be between)* interiacēre, interesse; *(to come between)* intercedere, intervenire
intervening *adj* medi·us -a -um
intervention *s* intervent·us -ūs *m*
interview *s* colloqu·ium -(i)i *n* interrogatorium
interview *tr* percontari
interviewer *s* perconta·tor -toris *m* (·trix -tricis *f)*
interweave *tr* intertexere
intestinal *adj* ad intestina pertin·ens -entis
intestine *adj* intestin·us -a -um
intestine *s* intestin·um -i *n;* **the large —** intestinum crassius; **the small —** intestinum tenue
intimacy *s* familiarit·as -atis *f,* consuetud·o -inis *f,* nessitud·o -inis *f; (sexual)* consuetudo
intimate *adj* familiar·is -is -e; *(stronger than preced.)* intim·us -a -um
intimately *adv* familiariter, intime
intimate *tr* indicare, innuere
intimation *s* indic·ium -(i)i *n*

intimidate *tr* (per)terrēre
intimidation *s* min•ae -arum *fpl*
into *prep* in *(w. acc)*
intolerable *adj* intolerabil•is -is -e
intolerably *adv* intoleranter
intolerance *s* intoleranti•a -ae *f*
intolerant *adj* intoler•ans -antis
intonation *s (chant)* cant•us -ūs *m; (stress)* accent•us -ūs *m*
intone *tr* cantare
intoxicate *tr* ebrium *(or* ebriam) reddere
intoxicated *adj* ebri•us -a -um
intoxication *s* ebriet•as -atis *f*
intractable *adj* intractabil•is -is -e
intramural *adj* intramuran•us -a -um
intransigence *s* obstinati•o -onis *f*
intransigent *adj* obstinat•us -a -um
intransitive *adj (gram)* intransitiv•us -a -um
intrepid *adj* intrepid•us -a -um
intrepidly *adv* intrepide
intricate *adj* contort•us -a -um
intricately *adv* contorte
intrigue *s* consil•ium -(i)i *n* clandestinum
intrigue *tr* tenēre, capere
intriguing *adj (engaging)* illecebros•us -a -um; *(baffling)* nodos•us -a -um
intrinsic *adj* ver•us -a -um, per se; **it has no — worth** res ipsa per se nullius pretii est
intrinsically *adv* vere
introduce *tr (e.g., a custom, theory)* introducere; *(a person)* tradere
introduction *s (preamble)* praefati•o -onis *f; (of a speech, book)* exord•ium -(i)i *n; (a bringing in)* introducti•o -onis *f*
instrospection *s* sui contemplati•o -onis *f*
introspective *adj* se ipsum inspici•ens -entis
introvert *s* hom•o -inis *mf* umbratic•us (-a)
intrude *intr* se interponere; **to — on** se imponere *(w. dat)*
intruder *s* intervent•or -oris *m; (into a home)* effrac•tor -toris *m* (•trix -tricis *f)*
intrusion *s* irrupti•o -onis *f*
intuition *s* intuit•us -ūs *m*
intuitive *adj* intuitiv•us -a -um
intuitively *adv* mentis propriā vi ac naturā
inundate *tr* inundare
inundation *s* inundati•o -onis *f*
invade *tr* invadere in *(w. acc)*
invader *s* invas•or -oris *m*
invalid *adj* irrit•us -a -um
invalid *s* aegrot•us -i *m* (•a -ae *f)*
invalidate *tr* irrit•um -am -um facere
invaluable *adj* inaestimabil•is -is -e
invariable *adj* immutabil•is -is -e
invariably *adv* semper
invasion *s* incursi•o -onis *f; (fig)* violati•o -onis *f*
invective *s* convic•ium -(i)i *n*
inveigh *intr* **to — against** invehi in *(w. acc),* insectari
invent *tr* invenire; *(to contrive)* excogitare, fingere
inventive *adj* ingenios•us -a -um
invention *s (act)* inventi•o -onis *f; (thing invented)* invent•um -i *n*
inventor *s* inven•tor -toris *m* (•trix -tricis *f)*
inventory *s* bonorum ind•ex -icis *m,* inventar•ium -(i)i *n*
inverse *adj* invers•us -a -um
inversely *adv* inverso ordine
inversion *s* inversi•o -onis *f*
invert *tr* invertere
invest *tr (money)* collocare; *(to besiege)* obsidēre
investigate *tr* investigare; *(leg)* quaerere, cognoscere
investigation *s* investigati•o -onis *f; (leg)* cogniti•o -onis *f*
investigator *s* investiga•tor -toris *m* (•trix -tricis *f) (leg)* quaesi•tor -toris *m* (•trix -tricis *f)*
investment *s (of money)* collocati•o -onis *f; (money invested)* locata pecuni•a -ae *f; (mil)* obsessi•o -onis *f*
inveterate *adj* inveterat•us -a -um
invigorate *tr* corroborare
invigorating *adj* apt•us -a -um ad corpus firmandum
invincible *adj* insuperabil•is -is -e, invict•us -a -um
inviolable *adj* sacrosanct•us -a -um
inviolate *adj* inviolat•us -a -um
invisible *adj* invisibil•is -is -e
invitation *s* invitati•o -onis *f*
invite *tr* invitare; **to — to dinner** ad cenam vocare
inviting *adj* suav•is -is -e
invitingly *adv* suaviter
invocation *s* invocati•o -onis *f*
invoice *s* tabul•a -ae *f* mercium
invoke *tr* invocare
involuntarily *adv* sine voluntate
involuntary *adj* haud voluntari•us -a -um; **— bodily action** naturalis acti•o -onis *f* corporis
involve *tr* implicare, *(to comprise)* continēre
involved *adj (intricate)* involut•us -a -um; *(occupied)* implicat•us -a -um; **to be — in debt** aere alieno laborare; **to be — in many errors** multis erroribus implicari; **to be — in war** illigari bello
invulnerable *adj* invulnerabil•is -is -e
inward *adj* inter•ior -ior -ius
inwardly *adv* intus, intrinsecus
inwards *adv* introrsus
Ionian *adj* Ionic•us -a -um
irascible *adj* iracund•us -a -um
Ireland *s* Hiberni•a -ae *f*
iris *s* ir•is -idis *f*
Irish *adj* Hibernic•us -a -um
irk *tr* incommodare; **I am —ed, it —s me** me taedet

irksome *adj* molest·us -a -um
iron *s (metal; for clothes)* ferr·um -i *n*
iron *adj* ferre·us -a -um
iron *tr (clothes)* premere, (ferro) levigare
ironical *adj* ironic·us -a -um
ironically *adv* per ironiam
irony *s* ironi·a -ae *f*
irradiate *tr* illustrare ‖ *intr* effulgēre
irrational *adj* irrational·is -is -e
irrationally *adv* absurde
irreconcilable *adj* implacabil·is -is -e; *(incompatible)* omnino inter se contrari·i -ae -a
irrecoverable *adj* irreparabil·is -is -e
irrefutable *adj* certissim·us -a -um
irregular *adj (having no regular form)* enorm·is -is -e; *(not uniform)* inaequal·is -is -e; *(fever)* incert·us -a -um; *(gram)* anomal·us -a -um; **— army** exercit·us -ūs *m* tumultuarius; **— verb** verb·um -i *n* inaequale
irregularity *s* enormit·as -atis *f; (gram)* anomali·a -ae *f;* **to be guilty of some —** peccare aliquid
irregularly *adv* inaequaliter; **"duo" is — declined** "duo" inaequaliter declinatur
irrelevant *adj* alien·us -a -um; **it is —** nil ad rem pertinet
irreligious *adj* impi·us -a -um erga deos; *(actions)* irreligios·us -a -um
irremediable *adj* insanabil·is -is -e
irreparable *adj* irreparabil·is -is -e
irreproachable *adj* inte·ger -gra -grum
irresistible *adj* invict·us -a -um; *(enticing)* blandissim·us -a -um
irresolute *adj* incert·us -a -um (sententiae); *(permanent characteristic)* parum firm·us -a -um
irresolutely *adv* dubitanter
irresolution *s* dubitati·o -onis *f*, anim·us -i *m* parum firmus
irresponsibility *s* incuri·a -ae *f*
irresponsible *adj* incurios·us -a -um
irretrievable *adj* irreparabil·is -is -e
irreverence *s* irreverenti·a -ae *f*
irreverent *adj* irrever·ens -entis (deorum)
irrevocable *adj* irrevocabil·is -is -e
irrigate *tr* irrigare
irrigation *s* irrigati·o -onis *f*
irritability *s* iracundi·a -ae *f*
irritable *adj* iracund·us -a -um
irritate *tr* irritare; *(a wound)* inflammare
irritation *s* irritati·o -onis *f*
island *s* insul·a -ae *f*
islander *s* insulan·us -i *m* (·a -ae *f*)
islet *s* parva insul·a -ae *f*
isolate *tr* secernere
issue *s (result)* event·us -ūs *m; (question)* res, rei *f; (offspring)* prol·es -is *f; (of a book)* editi·o -onis *f; (of money)* emissi·o -onis *f*
issue *tr (to distribute)* distribuere; *(orders)* edere, promulgare; *(money)* erogare; *(book)* edere ‖ *intr* emanare, egredi; *(to turn out, result)* evenire
isthmus *s* isthm·us -i *m*
it *pron* id
Italian *adj* Italic·us -a -um, Ital·us -a -um
italics *spl* litter·ae -arum *fpl* inclinatae
Italy *s* Itali·a -ae *f*
itch *s* prurig·o -inis *f*
itch *intr* prurire; *(fig)* gestire; **to have —ing ears** auribus prurire
itchy *adj* pruriginos·us -a -um
item *s* res, rei *f; (news)* nunt·ius -(i)i *m;* **— of merchandise** merx, mercis *f*
itinerant *adj* circumforane·us -a -um
itinerary *s* itinerar·ium -(i)i *n*
its *pron* eius; **— own** su·us -a -um
itself *pron (refl)* se, sese; *(intensive)* ipsum
ivory *s* eb·ur -oris *n*
ivory *adj* eburne·us -a -um
ivy *s* heder·a -ae *f*

J

jab *s* puls·us -ūs *m*
jab *tr* fodicare
jabber *intr* blaterare, garrire
jabbering *s* garrulit·as -atis *f*
jack *s* machin·a -ae *f* ad levandum; *(cards)* scurr·a -ae *m*
jackass *s* asin·us -i *m*
jacket *s* iacc·a -ae *f;* **leather —** iacca scortea
jack-of-all-trades *s* hom·o -inis *m* omnis Minervae
jackpot *s* **to hit the —** Venerem iacere; *(fig)* magnum lucrum facere
jaded *adj* defess·us -a -um
jagged *adj* serrat·us -a -um; *(of rocks)* praerupt·us -a -um
jail *s* carc·er -eris *m*
jail *tr* in carcere includere
jailbird *s* furcif·er -eri *m*
jailer *s* carcerari·us -i *m* (·a -ae *f*)
jam *s* baccarum conditur·a -ae *f;* **to be in a —** *(fig)* in angustiis versari
jam *tr* frequentare; *(to obsbruct)* obstruere
jamb *s* post·is -is *m*
jangle *tr & intr* crepitare
janitor *s* ianit·or -oris *m*
January *s* Ianuar·ius -(i)i *m or* mens·is -is *m* Ianuarius; **in —** mense Ianuario; **on the first of —** Kalendis Ianuariis
jar *s* oll·a -ae *f; (large, with two handles)* amphor·a -ae *f*
jar *tr (to shock)* offendere; *(of sound)* strepere ‖ *intr* discrepare
jargon *s* confusae voc·es -ium *fpl*
jarring *adj* disson·us -a -um
jaundice *s* morb·us -i *m* regius
jaundiced *adj* icterici·us -a -um; **to see things with — eyes** omnia in deteriorem partem interpretari

jaunt *s* excursi·o -onis *f;* **to take a —** excurrere
jaunty *adj* veget·us -a -um
javelin *s* iacul·um -i *n;* **to hurl a —** iaculari
jaw *s (upper)* mal·a -a *f; (lower)* maxill·a -ae *f;* **—s** fauc·es -ium *fpl*
jawbone *s* maxill·a -ae *f*
jay *s* gracul·us -i *m*
jealous *adj* zelotyp·us -a -um
jealousy *s* zel·us -i *m,* zelotypi·a -ae *f*
jeans *spl* bracc·ae -arum *fpl* Genuenses
jeer *s* irris·us -ūs *m*
jeer *tr* deridēre ‖ *intr* deridēre; **to —at** irridēre
jello *s* sorbill·um -i *n* concretum
jelly *s* cyl·on *(also* quil·on) -i *n*
jellyfish *s* pulm·o -onis *m*
jeopardize *tr* periclitari
jeopardy *s* pericul·um -i *n*
jerk *s* mot·us -ūs *m* subitus; *(person)* hom·o -inis *mf* nequam
jerk *tr (to push)* subito trudere; *(to pull)* subito revellere
jerky *adj* salebros·us -a -um
jest *s* ioc·us -i *m;* **in —** iocose
jest *intr* iocari
jester *s* ioculat·or -oris *m; (buffoon)* scurr·a -ae *m*
jestingly *adv* per iocum
Jesus *s* Ies·us -u *(dat, abl, voc:* Iesu; *acc:* Iesum) *m*
jet *s* scatebr·a -ae *f*
jet-black *adj* nigerrim·us -a -um
jet engine *s* machin·a -ae *f* pyraulocinetica
jet plane *s* aëroplan·um -i *n* pyraulocineticum
jetty *s* mol·es -is *f*
Jew *s* Iudae·us -i *m*
jewel *s* gemm·a -ae *f*
jeweler *s* gemmari·us -i *m* (·a -ae *f)*
jewelry *s* gemm·ae -arum *fpl*
jewelry store *s* gemmari·a -ae *f*
Jewess *s* Iudae·a -ae *f*
Jewish *adj* Iudae·us -a -um
jilt *tr* repudiare
jingle *s* tinnit·us -ūs *m*
jingle *intr* tinnire
jitters *spl* scrupul·us -i *n;* **to give s.o. the —** scrupulum alicui inicere
jittery *adj* scrupulos·us -a -um
job *s (piece of work)* op·us -eris *n; (as a means of livelihood)* quaest·us -ūs *m; (task)* pens·um -i *n,* mun·us -eris *n;* **a tough —** spissum opus et operosum; **good —!** recte factum!; **to get a —** quaestum impetrare
jobless *adj* quaestūs exper·s -tis
jockey *s* agas·o -onis *m*
jocular *adj* iocular·is -is -e
jog *intr* tolutim currere
join *tr (to connect)* coniungere, connectere; *(to come into the company of)* se iungere *(w. dat); (to join as a companion)* supervenire *(w. dat); (to go over to)* transire; **—ing hands** manibus nex·i -ae -a ‖ *intr* coniungi; **to — in** particeps esse *(w. gen);* **to — together** inter se coniungi
joint *adj* commun·is -is -e
joint *s (anat)* articul·us -i *m; (of a plant)* genicul·um -i *n,* nod·us -i *m; (of a structure)* compag·es -inis *f;* **to smoke a —** fumum cannabis sugere
jointly *adv* unā, communiter
joist *s* tign·um -i *n*
joke *s* ioc·us -i *m;* **as a —** per iocum; **to make a — of** iocum risumque facere de *(w abl)*; **to play a — on** ludibrio habēre
joke *intr* iocari; **now you're —ing** iocaris nunc tu; **to be —ing** iocari
joker *s* iocula·tor -toris *m* (·trix -tricis *f); (cards)* chartul·a -ae *f* fortunans
joking *s* iocati·o -onis *f;* **all — aside** ioco remoto
jokingly *adv* per iocum
jolly *adj* hilar·is -is -e, hillar·us -a -um
jolt *s* (im)puls·us -ūs *m*
jolt *tr* iactare; *(fig)* percellere ‖ *intr* iactari
jolting *s* iactati·o -onis *f*
jostle *tr* pulsare
jot *s* hil·um -i *n;* **not a —** minime; **to care not a — for** non flocci facere
jot down *tr* breviter scribere *(or* notare)
journal *s (magazine)* ephemer·is -idis *f; (diary)* diar·ium -(i)i *n*
journalist *s* scrip·tor -toris *m* (·trix -tricis *f)* actorum
journey *s* it·er -ineris *n;* **to take a —** iter facere
journey *intr* iter facere; **to — abroad** peregrinari
journeyman *s* opif·ex -icis *m*
Jove *s* Iuppiter, Iovis *m*
jovial *adj* hilar·is -is -e
jowl *s* bucc·a -ae *f*
joy *s* gaud·ium -(i)i *n;* **to feel —** gaudēre
joyful *adj* laet·us -a -um
joyfully *adv* laete
joyless *adj* illaetabil·is -is -e
joystick *s (comput)* vectul·us -i *m*
jubilant *adj* laetitiā exsult·ans -antis
jubilation *s* exsultati·o -onis *f*
jubilee *s* ann·us -i *m* anniversarius
Judaic *adj* Iudaïc·us -a -um
Judaism *s* Iudaïsm·us -i *m*
judge *s* iud·ex -icis *mf; (in criminal cases)* quaesi·tor -toris *m* (·trix -tricis *f);* **to sit as —** *(to hold court)* ius dicere
judge *tr* iudicare; *(to think)* existimare; *(to value)* aestimare; *(to decide between)* diiudicare
judgment *s* iudic·ium -(i)i *n,* sententi·a -ae *f;* **against my better —** adversum ingenium meum; **in my —** iudicio meo; **to pronounce —** ius dicere; **to sit in — over** ius dicere inter *(w. acc)*
judgment seat *s* tribun·al -alis *n*

judicial *adj* iudicial·is -is -e; **— proceedings** iudici·a -orum *npl;* **— system** rati·o -onis *f* iudicialis
judicially *adv* iure
judicious *adj* sapi·ens -entis
judiciously *adv* sapienter
judo *s* luct·a -ae *f* iudoïca
jug *s* urce·us -i *m*
juggle *tr (figures)* vitiare, interpolare **||** *intr* praestigias agere
juggler *s* praestigiat·or -oris *mf*
juice *s* suc·us -i *m*
juicy *adj* sucos·us -a -um
July *s* Iul·ius -(i)i *or* mens·is -is *m* Iulius; **in —** mense Iulio; **on the first of —** Kalendis Iuliis
jumble *s* congeri·es -ei *f*
jumble *tr* permiscēre
jump *s* salt·us -ūs *m*
jump *tr* transalire; **to — rope** ad funem salire **||** *intr* salire; **to —at** *(opportunity)* captare; **to — for joy** dissilire gaudimonio, exsultare; **to — up** exsurrigere
junction *s* coniuncti·o -onis *f; (roads)* compit·um -i *n*
juncture *s* temp·us -oris *n;* **at this —** hic
June *s* Iun·ius -(i)i *m or* mens·is -is *m* Iunius; **on the first of —** Kalendis Iuniis
jungle *s* silv·a -ae *f* densa
junior *adj* min·or -or -us natu
junior *s* iuni·or -oris *m*
juniper *s* iuniper·us -i *f*
junk *s* scrut·a -orum *npl*
jurisdiction *s* iurisdicti·o -onis *f*
jurisprudence *s* iurisprudenti·a -ae *f*
jurist *s* iurisconsult·us -i *m* (·a -ae *f*)
juror *s* iud·ex -icis *m,* iudiatr·ix -icis *f*
jury *s* iudic·es -um *mpl*
just *adj* iust·us -a -um; *(fair)* aequ·us -a -um; *(deserved)* merit·us -a -um
just *adv (only)* modo; *(exactly)* prorsus; *(w. adv)* demum, denique; **— about** *(pretty well, virtually)* propemodum; **— after** sub *(w. acc);* **— a moment ago** modo; **— as** *(comparison)* perinde ac, sic ut; *(temporal)* cum maxime; **— before** sub *(w. acc);* **— in time** tempori; **— now** modo; **— so** ita prorsus; **— then** tunc maxime; **— what?** quidnam?; **— when** cum proxime **— who?** quisnam?
justice *s* iustiti·a -ae *f; (just treatment)* ius iuris *n; (person)* praet·or -oris *m*
justifiable *adj* excusat·us -a -um
justifiably *adv* iure
justification *s* excusati·o -onis *f*
justify *tr* excusare, expurgare
jut *intr* prominēre; **to — out** procurrere; **to — out into the sea** in aequor procurrere
juvenile *adj* iuvenil·is -is -e; **— delinquent** adulesc·ens -entis *mf* noxi·us (-a)
juvenile *s* adulesc·ens -entis *mf*
juxtaposition *s* propinquit·as -atis *f;* **to put in —** apponere

K

kale *s* cramb·e -es *f*
kangaroo *s* halmatur·us -i *m*
karate *s* luct·a -ae *f* caratica
keel *s* carin·a -ae *f*
keel *intr* **to — over** collabi
keen *adj* a·cer -cris -cre
keenly *adv* acriter
keenness *s (of scent)* sagacit·as -atis *f; (of sight)* aci·es -ei *f; (of pain)* acerbit·as -atis *f; (enthusiasm)* stud·ium -(i)i *n*
keen-scented *adj* sagacissim·us -a -um
keep *tr* tenēre; *(to preserve)* servare; *(to celebrate)* agere; *(to guard)* custodire; *(to obey)* observare; *(to support)* alere; *(animals)* alere, pascere; *(to store)* condere; *(to detain, hold back)* detinēre; **— a stiff upper lip!** fac ut animo forti sis!; **— your cool!** compesce mentem!; **to — annoying** subinde molestare; **to — apart** distinēre; **to — at bay** sustinēre; **to — away** arcēre; **to — back** retinēre, cohibēre; *(to conceal)* celare; **to — back nothing** nihil reticēre; **to — back tears** lacrimas tenēre; **to — company** comitari; **to — down** reprimere; **to — from** prohibēre; **to — hands off** manum abstinēre; **to — in** cohibēre; **to — in custody** asservare; **to — in line the wavering Senate** confirmare labantem ordinem; **to — in mind** in memoriā habēre *or* tenēre; **to — off** arcēre, defendere; **to — to oneself** secum habēre; **to — pace with** pariter ire cum *(w. abl);* **to — secret** celare; **to — the company waiting** convivas morari; **to — together** continēre; **to — under control** compescere; **to — under lock and key** clavi servare; **to — up** sustinēre; **to — up one's courage** animo erecto esse; **to —** *(a person)* **waiting** detinēre, demorari; **to — your eyes on** oculos intentare in *(w. acc);* **what kept you?** quid tenuit quominus venires? **||** *intr (to last)* durare; **to — away from** abstinēre ab *(w. abl);* **to — up with** *(to keep pace with)* subsequi; *(to equal)* aequare, aemulari
keep *s* custodi·a -ae *f; (support)* aliment·um -i *n*
keeper *s* cust·os -odis *mf*
keeping *s* tutel·a -ae *f;* **in — with** pro *(w. abl)*
keepsake *s* monument·m -i *n*
keg *s* cad·us -i *m*
kennel *s* stabul·um -i *n* caninum
kerchief *s* sudar·ium -(i)i *n*
kernel *s* nucle·us -i *m; (fig)* medull·um -i *n*
ketchup *s* ketsup·um -i *n*
kettle *s* leb·es -etis *f*
kettledrum *s* tympan·um -i *n* aeneum
key *s* clav·is -is *f; (pitch)* voculati·o -onis *f; (clue)* ans·a -ae *f; (on a piano)* plectr·um

-i *n; (on the keyboard)* malleol·us -i *m;* **to hit the —** malleolum pulsare
keyboard *s (of a computer or typewriter)* plectrolog·ium -(i)i *n; (on a piano or organ)* clavitur·a -ae *f*
keyhole *s* claustell·um -i *n*
kid *s (coll)* frust·um -i *n* pueri *or* puellae
kid *tr* ludere, ludificare, jocari
kick *s* cal·x -cis *mf*
kick *tr* calce ferire; *(a ball)* pede pulsare; **to — the bucket** *(coll)* animam ebullire **||** *intr* calcitrare
kid *s* haed·us -i *m; (child)* parvul·us -i *m* (·a -ae *f)*
kid *tr & intr* ludificari
kidnap *tr* surripere
kidnapper *s* plagiar·ius -(i)i *m* (·a -ae *f)*
kidnapping *s* plag·ium -(i)i *n*
kidney *s* ren, renis *m*
kidney bean *s* phasel·us -i *m*
kill *s* nex, necis *f; (prey)* praed·a -ae *f*
kill *tr* interficere; *(by cruel means)* necare; *(by wounds or blows)* caedere; **to — time** tempus perdere *(or)* fallere; **you're —ing me!** me enicas!
killer *s* interfec·tor -toris *m* (·trix -tricis *f)*
kiln *s* forn·ax -acis *f*
kilogram *s* chilogramm·a -atis *n*
kilometer *s* chilometr·um -i *n*
kin *s* cognat·i -orum *mpl;* **next of —** proxim·i -orum *mpl*
kind *adj* benign·us -a -um; **— to** *or* **toward** benevol·us -a -um erga *(w. acc)*
kind *s* gen·us -eris *n;* **that — of war** eius modi bell·um -i *n;* **what — of** qual·is -is -e, qui quae quod
kindergarten *s* paedotrophe·um -i *n*
kindhearted *adj* benign·us -a -um, benevol·us -a -um
kindle *tr* incendere, accendere
kindly *adj* human·us -a -um
kindly *adv* benigne
kindness *s* benignit·as -atis *f; (deed)* benefic·ium -(i)i *n;* **to bestow a — on s.o.** beneficium apud aliquem collocare; **to do (return) an act of —** beneficium dare (reddere)
kindred *adj* consanguine·us -a -um
kindred *s* consanguinit·as -atis *f; (relatives)* consanguine·i -orum *mpl* (·ae -arum *fpl)*
king *s* re·x -gis *m*
kingdom *s* regn·um -i *n*
kingfisher *s* alced·o -inis *f*
kingly *adj* regi·us -a -um; *(worthy of a king)* regal·is -is -e
king-sized *adj* imman·is -is -e
kinsman *s* necessar·ius -(i)i *m*
kinswoman *s* necessari·a -ae *f*
kiss *s* oscul·um -i *n; (passionate)* bas·ium -(i)i *n*
kiss *tr* osculari; *(passionately)* basiare
kissing *s* osculati·o -onis *f,* basiati·o -onis *f*
kit *s* apparat·us -ūs *m*
kitchen *s* culin·a -ae *f*
kitchen knife *s* cul·ter -tri *m* coquinaris
kitchen utensils *spl* instrument·a -orum *npl* coquinatoria
kite *s (bird)* milv·us -i *m; (toy)* milvus papyraceus; **to fly a —** facere ut milvus papyraceus volet
kith and kin *spl* propinqu·i -orum et adfin·es -ium *mpl*
kitten *s* catul·us -i *m* felinus
knack *s* sollerti·a -ae *f*
knapsack *s* sacciper·ium -(i)i *n* dorsuale
knave *s* scelest·us -i *m*
knead *tr* subigere
knee *s* gen·u -us *n;* **on bended —** duplicato poplite; **to fall at s.o.'s —s** *(in entreaty)* se ad genua alicuius proicere; **to fall on one's —s to** genua ponere *(w. dat of person so honored)*
kneecap *s* patell·a -ae *f*
knee-deep *adj* genibus tenus alt·us -a -um
kneel *intr* genibus niti; **to — down** ad genua procumbere
knell *s* campan·a -ae *f* funebris
knife *s* cul·ter -tri *m; (small)* cultell·us -i *m; (for surgery)* scalpell·um -i *n*
knight *s* equ·es -itis *m*
knighthood *s* equestris dignit·as -atis *f*
knightly *adj* eques·ter -tris -tre
knit *tr* texere; **to — the brow** frontem contrahere
knob *s* tub·er -eris *n; (on door)* bull·a -ae *f*
knock *s* puls·us -ūs *m*
knock *tr* **knock it off!** *(coll)* parce! *(pl:* parcite!); **to — down** deicere; *(in boxing)* sternere; *(fig) (at auction)* addicere; **to — in** impellere; **to — one's head against the wall** caput ad parietem offendere; **to — out** *(in boxing)* consternere; **to — out s.o.'s brains** cerebrum alicui excutere **||** *intr* **to — about** *(to ramble)* vagari; **to — at** pulsare, percutere
knocking *s* pulsati·o- onis *f*
knock-kneed *adj* var·us -a -um
knoll *s* tumul·us -i *m*
knot *s* nod·us -i *m; (of people)* turbul·a -ae *f;* **to tie a —** nodum facere; **to untie a —** nodum expedire
knot *tr* nodare
knotty *adj* nodos·us -a -um; *(fig)* spinos·us -a -um
know *tr* scire; *(a person, place)* novisse; **let me — how you are doing** fac ut sciam *(or* fac me certiorem) quid agas; **to get to —** noscere; **not to —** ignorare, nescire; **to — for sure** certum *(or* certo) scire; **to — how to** scire *(w. inf)*
know-how *s* sollerti·a -ae *f*
knowing *adj* callid·us -a -um
knowingly *adv* scienter, prudens

knowledge *s* scienti·a -ae *f; (of s.th.)* cogniti·o -onis *f;* **without the — of** clam *(w. abl);* **without your —** clam vobis

known *adj* not·us -a -um; **it is well — that** nobile est *(w. acc & inf);* **— to me by sight** familiar·is -is -e oculis meis; **to become —** enotescere; **to make —** divulgare, palam facere; **well —** notissim·us -a -um

knuckle *s* articul·us -i *m* digiti

knuckle *intr* **to — down to** incumbere in *(w. acc);* **to — under to** cedere *(w. dat)*

knucklehead *s (coll)* bar·o -onis *m*

kowtow *intr* **(to)** adulari *(w. dat)*

kudos *s* laus, laudis *f*

L

label *s* pittac·ium -(i)i *n*

label *tr* pittacium affigere *(w. dat); (fig)* notare

labor *s* lab·or -oris *m; (manual work)* oper·a -ae *f; (work done)* op·us -eris *n;* **to be in —** laborare in utero; **woman in —** puerper·a -ae *f*

labor *intr* laborare, eniti; **to — under** laborare *(w. abl)*

laboratory *s* officin·a -ae *f* experimentis agendis

labored *adj* affectat·us -a -um

laborer *s* operar·ius -(i)i *m,* oper·a -ae *f*

labor union *s* colleg·ium -(i)i *n*

labyrinth *s* labyrinth·us -i *m*

lace *s* op·us -eris *n* reticulatum

lace *tr (to tie)* nectere; *(to tighten)* astringere

lacerate *tr* lacerare

laceration *s* lacerati·o -onis *f*

lack *s* inopi·a -ae *f;* **for — of** inopiā *(w. gen)*

lack *tr* carēre *(w. abl)* ‖ *intr* **to be —** deficere; *(to be missing)* deesse

lackadaisical *adj* remiss·us -a - um

lackey *s* pedisequ·us -i *m; (fig)* assecl·a -ae *mf*

laconic *adj* brev·is -is -e

lacrosse *s* lud·us -i *m* lacrossensis; **to play —** ludo lacrossensi ludere

lacrosse stick *s* coroci·a -ae *f;* **to cradle the —** corociam agitare

lad *s* pu·er -eri *m*

ladder *s* scal·ae -arum *fpl; (fig)* grad·us -ūs *m;* **one —** unae scalae

laden *adj* onust·us -a -um

ladle *s* ligul·a -ae *f; (for wine)* trull·a -ae *f*

ladle *tr* ligulā fundere

lady *s* domin·a -ae *f*

lady-like *adj* liberal·is -is -e

lag *intr* morari; **to — behind** cessare

laggard *s* cessa·tor -toris *m* (·trix -tricis *f*)

lagoon *s* lacun·a -ae *f*

laid up *adj (sick)* lecto affix·us -a -um

lair *s* cubil·e -is *n*

laity *spl* laïc·i -orum *mpl*

lake *s* lac·us -ūs *m*

lamb *s* agn·us -i *m,* agn·a -ae *f; (meat)* agnin·a -ae *f*

lame *adj* claud·us -a -um; **— in one leg** claud·us -a -um altero pede; **to be —** claudicare

lamely *adv (fig)* inconcinne

lameness *s* claudit·as -atis *f*

lament *s* lament·um -i *n; (complaint)* querel(l)·a -ae *f*

lament *tr* lamentari ‖ *intr* deplorare

lamentable *adj* lamentabil·is -is -e

lamentation *s* lamentati·o -onis *f*

lamp *s* lucern·a -ae *f,* lamp·as -adis *f*

lampoon *s* libell·us -i *m* ad infamiam

lampoon *tr* diffamare

lamppost *s* pil·a -ae *f* lanternā affixa

lamprey *s* muren·e -es *f*

lance *s* lance·a -ae *f*

lance *tr* incidere, pungere

land *s* terr·a -ae *f; (soil)* sol·um -i *n; (territory)* fin·es -ium *fpl; (as a possession)* a·ger -gri *m;* **on — and sea** terrā marique; **piece of —** ager; **public —** ager publicus *(or* agri publici)

land *tr* in terram exponere; *(to get) (coll)* adipisci ‖ *intr (of a person)* in terram egredi; *(of a ship)* (ad terram) appellere; *(of a plane)* deorsum appellere; *(of flying creatures)* **(on)** considere in *(w. abl),* insidere *(w. dat)*

land *adj (animals, route)* terren·us -a -um; *(animals, route, troops)* terrestr·is -is -e; *(battle)* pedes·ter -tris -tre

landholder *s* agrorum possess·or -oris *m* (·rix -ricis *f*)

landing *s* egress·us -ūs *m; (of a plane)* appuls·us -ūs *m; (on stairs)* scalar·ium -(i)i *n*

landing place *s* appuls·us -ūs *m*

landlady *s* (insulae) domin·a -ae *f*

landlord *s* (insulae) domin·us -i *m*

landmark *s* lap·is -idis *m* terminalis

landscape *s* regionis sit·us -ūs *m*

landslide *s* terrae laps·us -ūs *m*

land tax *s* vectig·al -alis *n*

lane *s* semit·a -ae *f; (for planes)* aëria vi·a -ae *f*

language *s* lingu·a -ae *f,* serm·o -onis *m; (diction)* orati·o -onis *f;* **abusive and insulting — against s.o.** maledice contumelioseque dict·a -orum *npl* in aliquem; **the Latin —** lingua Latina, sermo Latinus

language lab *s* officin·a -ae *f* loquelaris

languid *adj* languid·us -a -um

languish *intr* languēre

languishing *adj* languid·us -a -um

languor *s* langu·or -oris *m*

lanky *adj* prolix·us -a -um

lantern *s* la(n)tern·a -ae *f*

lap *s* sin·us -ūs *m; (fig)* grem·ium -(i)i *n; (in a race)* spat·ium -(i)i *n*
lap *tr* lambere; **to — up** haurire, absorbēre
lapse *s* laps·us -ūs *m; (error)* peccat·um -i *n;* **after a — of one year** interiecto anno; **the — of time** lapsus temporum
lapse *intr* labi; **to — into** recidere in *(w. acc)*
laptop computer *s* ordinatrul·um -i *n* portabile
laquer *s* resin·a -ae *f* temeto soluta
laquer *tr* resinā obducere
larceny *s* furt·um -i *n*
lard *s* ad·eps -ipis *mf; (from bacon)* lar(i)d·um -i *n*
large *adj* magn·us -a -um; **to a — extent** magnā ex parte
largely *adv* plerumque
largess *s* largiti·o -onis *f;* **to give a — to** largiri *(w dat)*
lark *s* alaud·a -ae *f*
larynx *s* gutt·ur -uris *n*
lascivious *adj* lasciv·us -a -um
lasciviously *adv* lascive
lash *s (blow)* verb·er -eris *n; (whip)* flagell·um -i *n*
lash *tr* verberare, flagellare; *(to censure severely)* castigare; *(to fasten)* annectere, alligare ‖ *intr* **to — out at** castigare
lashing *s* verberati·o -onis *f*
lass *s* puell·a -ae *f*
lassitude *s* lassitud·o -inis *f*
last *adj* postrem·us -a -um, ultim·us -a -um; *(immediately preceding)* proxim·us -a -um; *(in line)* novissim·us -a -um; **at —** demum; **for the — time** postremo; **— but one** paenultim·us -a -um; **— night** heri vesperi, proximā nocte; **the night before —** superiore nocte; *(adj used where English uses an adv, e.g.,* **Cicero spoke last** Cicero novissimus locutus est)
last *intr* durare; **to — for some time** aliquod tempus habēre; **to — long** *(of a fever, etc.)* diu permanēre
lasting *adj* diuturn·us -a -um
lastly *adv* denique, postremo
latch *s* pessul·us -i *m*
latch *tr* oppessulare
late *adj* ser·us -a -um; *(loitering behind time)* tard·us -a -um; *(far advanced)* mult·us -a -um; *(recent in date)* rec·ens -entis; *(deceased)* demortu·us -a -um; *(of an emperor)* divus; **Homer was not —r than Lycurgus** Homerus non infra Lycurgum fuit; **it was — in the day** serum erat diei; **till — at night** ad multam noctem
late *adv* sero; **all too —** immo iam sero; **— at night** multā nocte; **— in life** seri anni; **not till — in the day** multo denique die; **too —** serius; **very —** serissime
lately *adv* nuper
latent *adj* lat·ens -entis, occult·us -a -um
later *adv* postea; **a little —** postea aliquanto; **many years —** multis post annis; **sooner or —** ocius serius; **to postpone till —** differre in aliud tempus
lateral *adj* lateral·is -is -e
latest *adv* **at —** summum; **perhaps tomorrow, at latest, the day after that** fortasse cras, summum perendie
Latin *adj* Latin·us -a -um; **the Latin people** Latin·i -orum *mpl* ‖ *s* lingu·a -ae *f,* Latina, serm·o -onis *m* Latinus; **in first year Latin** primo anno Latinitatis; **to learn —** Latine discere; **to know (understand) —** Latine scire; **to speak —** Latine (loqui); **to teach —** Latine docēre; **to translate into —** Latine reddere; **to translate from Greek into Latin** ex Graeco in Latinum (con)vertere *(or* transferre); **to understand —** Latine scire; **to write —** Latine scribere
Latinity *s* Latinit·as -atis *f*
Latin teacher *s* Latinitatis magis·ter -tri *m* (·tra -trae *f*)
latitude *s* latitud·o -inis *f; (fig)* libert·as -atis *f*
Latium *s* Lat·ium -(i)i *n*
latter *adj* poster·ior -ior -ius; **the —** hic
lattice *s* cancell·i -orum *mpl*
laudable *adj* laudabil·is -is -e
laudably *adv* laudabiliter
laudatory *adj* laudativ·us -a -um
laugh *s* ris·us -ūs *m*
laugh *intr* ridēre; **to — at** ridēre; *(to mock)* irridēre
laughable *adj* ridicul·us -a -um
laughingstock *s* ludibr·ium -(i)i *n*
laughter *s* ris·us -ūs *m; (loud, indecorous)* cachinnati·o -onis *f*
launch *tr* deducere; *(to hurl)* iaculari ‖ *intr* **to — out** proficisci
launder *tr* lavare
laundress *s* lotr·ix -icis *f*
laundry *s* lavator·ium -(i)i *n; (Roman)* fullonic·a -ae *f; (dirty clothes)* lavandari·a -orum *npl*
laureate *adj* laureat·us -a -um
laurel *adj* laure·us -a -um
laurel tree *s* laur·us -i *f*
lava *s* liquefacta mass·a -ae *f*
lavender *s* lavandulace·us -a -um
lavish *adj* prodig·us -a -um
lavish *tr* prodigere, profundere
lavishly *adv* prodige
law *s* lex, legis *f; (right; the entire body of law)* ius, iuris *n; (divine)* fas *n* [*indecl*]; **against the law** contra ius; *(against a specific law)* contra legem; **by —** lege; **in accordance with the —** lege; **to break a —** legem violare; **to lay down the —** *(to scold)* vehementer obiurgare; **to introduce a —** legem ferre; **to pass a —** legem perferre; **unwritten —** mos moris *m*

law-abiding *adj* bene morat•us -a -um, legi obsequ•ens -entis
law court *s* iudic•ium -(i)i *n; (building)* basilic•a -ae *f*
lawful *adj* legitim•us -a -um; **it is —** fas est
lawfully *adv* legitime
lawless *adj* ex•lex -legis
lawlessness *s* licenti•a -ae *f*
lawmaker *s* legisla•tor -toris *m* (•trix -tricis *f*)
lawn *s* pratul•um -i *n;* **to mow the —** pratulum resecare
lawnmower *s* herbisectr•um -i *n*
lawsuit *s* lis, litis *f,* caus•a -ae *f;* **to bring** *or* **file a — against s.o.** litem alicui intendere
lawyer *s* iurisconsult•us -i *m* (•a -ae *f*); **defense —** advocat•us -i *m* (•a -ae *f*); **trial —** causidic•us -i *m* (•a -ae *f*)
lax *adj (person)* remiss•us -a -um; *(discipline)* lax•us -a -um
laxity *s* remissi•o -onis *f*
lay *tr (to put)* ponere; *(eggs)* parere; *(foundations)* iacere; *(bricks)* struere; *(hands)* inicere; **to — a finger on s.o.** aliquem uno digito attingere; **to — an ambush** insidiari; **to be laid up** cubare; **to — aside** ponere; *(cares, fear)* amovēre; **to — before** proponere; **to — claim to** arrogare, vindicare; **to — down** deponere; *(rules)* statuere; **to — down arms** ab armis discedere; **to — hands on s.th.** aliquid invadere; **to — hold of** prehendere; **to — it on the line** *(coll)* directum loqui; **to — out** *(money)* expendere; *(plans)* designare; **to — siege to** obsidēre; **to — the blame on** culpam conferre in *(w. acc);* **to — up** condere; **to — waste** vastare **‖** *intr* **— off!** *(coll)* desine! *(pl:* desinite!); **to — for** insidiari; **to — over** *(on a trip)* commorari
lay *s (mus)* cantilen•a -ae *f*
layer *s* lamin•a -ae *f; (stratum)* cor•ium -(i)i *n*
layer *tr* **to — the hair** comam in gradūs frangere
layover *s* commorati•o -onis *f*
lazily *adv* ignave, pigre
laziness *s* pigriti•a -ae *f*
lazy *adj* ignav•us -a -um, pi•ger -gra -grum
lead *s (metal)* plumb•um -i *n*
lead *adj* plumbe•us -a -um
lead *s* primus loc•us -i *m; (theat)* primae part•es -ium *fpl;* **to take the —** praeesse; *(theat)* primas partes suscipere
lead *tr* ducere; *(life)* agere; **to — about** circumducere; **to — astray** in errorem inducere; **to — away** abducere; **to — off** divertere; **to — on** conducere, illicere **‖** *intr (of a road)* **to — to** ducere ad *(w. acc);* **to — up to** tendere ad *(w. acc)*
leaden *adj* plumbe•us -a -um
leader *s* du•x -cis *mf,* princ•eps -ipis *mf*
leadership *s* duct•us -ūs *m;* **under my —** me duce
leading *adj* princ•eps -cipis, primari•us -a -um; **— man (lady)** *(theat)* histri•o -onis *mf* primarum partium
leaf *s* fol•ium -(i)i *n; (of vine)* pampin•us -i *m; (of paper)* sched•a -ae *f; (of metal)* bracte•a -ae *f;* **to turn over a new —** ad bonam frugem se recipere
leafless *adj* fronde nudat•us -a -um
leafy *adj* frondos•us -a -um
league *s* foed•us -eris *n*
leak *s* rim•a -ae *f*
leak *tr (information)* divulgare; **‖** *intr* rimas agere, perfluere
leaky *adj* rimos•us -a -um
lean *adj (meat, person)* ma•cer -cra -crum
lean *tr* inclinare **‖** *intr* inclinare, niti; **—ing forward** inclinat•us -a -um; **to — against** se applicare *(w. dat);* **to — back** se inclinare, reclinare; **to — on** inniti in *(w. abl)*
leap *s* salt•us -ūs *m*
leap *intr* salire; **to — for joy** exsultare
leap year *s* bisextilis ann•us -i *m,* intercalaris annus
learn *tr* discere; *(from elders)* accipere; **to — by heart** ediscere; **to — thoroughly** perdiscere **‖** *intr* **to — about** cognoscere; *(to be informed about)* certior fieri de *(w. abl)*
learned *adj* doct•us -a -um, erudit•us -a -um
learnedly *adv* docte
learner *s* disc•ens -entis *mf*
learning *s* doctrin•a -ae *f,* eruditi•o -onis *f*
lease *s* conducti•o -onis *f; (act on part of proprietor)* locati•o -onis *f*
lease *tr* conducere; **to — out** locare
leash *s* cingul•um -i *n*
leash *tr* cingulo alligare
least *adj* minim•us -a -um
least *adv* minime; **at —** utique; *(emphasizing a particular word)* saltem
least *n* minim•um -i *n;* **not in the —** ne minimum quidem
leather *s (tanned or untanned)* cor•ium -(i)i *n; (tanned)* alut•a -ae *f*
leather *adj* ex corio, scorte•us -a -um; **— raincoat** scortea paenul•a -ae *f*
leathery *adj* lent•us -a -um
leave *tr* relinquere; *(to entrust)* mandare, tradere; *(legacy)* legare; **— me alone!** omitte *(pl:* omittite) me!; **to — behind** relinquere; **to — it up to s.o. to** alicui mandare ut *(w. subj);* **to — no stone unturned** nullo loco deesse; **to — out** omittere **‖** *intr (to depart)* discedere, abire; **to — off** desinere
leave *s* permissi•o -onis *f;* **— of absence** commeat•us -ūs *m;* **to ask —** veniam petere; **to obtain —** veniam impetrare; **to**

take — of valēre iubēre; **with your —** pace tuā (vestrā)
leaven *s* ferment·um -i *n*
lecherous *adj* libidinos·us -a -um
lectern *s* lector·ium -(i)i *n*
lector *s* lec·tor -toris *m* (·trix -tricis *f*)
lecture *s* lecti·o -onis *f; (public)* acroas·is -is *f; (less formal)* schol·a -ae *f; (explaining an author)* praelecti·o -onis *f;* **to give a — on** acroasin facere de *(w. abl); (less formally)* scholam habēre de *(w. abl)*
lecture *tr (to reprove)* obiurgare **||** *intr* acroases facere; *(less formally)* scholas habēre
lecture hall *s* auditor·ium -(i)i *n*
lecturer *s* lec·tor -toris *m* (·trix -tricis *f*)
ledge *s* proiectur·a -ae *f; (of a cliff)* dors·um -i *n*
ledger *s* cod·ex -icis *m* (accepti et expensi)
leech *s* sanguisug·a -ae *f*
leer *intr* limis oculis spectare
leering *adj* lim·us -a -um
left *adj* laev·us -a -um, sinis·ter -tra -trum; **on the —** a sinistrā; **to the —** sinistrorsum
left-handed *adj* laev·us -a -um
leftover *adj* reliqu·us -a -um
leftovers *spl* reliqui·ae -arum *fpl*
leg *s* cru·s -ris *n; (of table, etc.)* pes pedis *m*
legacy *s* legat·um -i *n*
legal *adj* legitim·us -a -um
legally *adv* legitime, lege *or* legibus
legalize *tr* sancire
legate *s* legat·us -i *m* (·a -ae *f*)
legation *s* legati·o -onis *f*
legend *s* fabul·a -ae *f; (inscription)* titul·us -i *m*
legendary *adj* fabulos·us -a -um, commentici·us -a -um,
legging *s* ocre·a -ae *f*
legible *adj* legibil·is -is -e
legion *s* legi·o -onis *f*
legionary *s* mil·es -itis *m* legionarius
legislate *intr* leges dare *or* ferre
legislation *s (act)* legum dati·o -onis *f; (the laws)* leg·es -um *fpl*
legislator *s* legum la·tor -toris *m* (·trix -tricis *f*)
legitimate *adj* legitim·us -a -um
legitimately *adv* legitime
leisure *s* ot·ium -(i)i *n;* **at —** otios·us -a -um; **to be at —** vacare, otiari
leisure *adj* otios·us -a -um, vacu·us -a -um; **— activity** op·us -eris *n* subsicivum
leisure time *s* temp·us -oris *n* vacuum
leisurely *adj* lent·us -a -um
lemon *s* pom·um -i *n* citreum
lemonade *s* aqu·a -ae *f* limonata
lend *tr* **to — money** pecuniam mutuam dare *or* commodare; *(at interest)* pecuniam faenerare; **to — one's ear to** aures praebēre *(w. dat)*
length *s* longitud·o -inis *f; (of time)* longinquit·as -atis *f;* **at —** tandem; **in —** in longitudinem
lengthen *tr (space)* extendere; *(vowels)* producere *(opp:* corripere); *(time)* protrahere **||** *intr* longior fieri
lengthwise *adv* in longitudinem
lengthy *adj* long·us -a -um
leniency *s* lenit·as -atis *f*
lenient *adj* len·is -is -e
leniently *adv* leniter
lens *s* len·s -tis *f* optica
lentil *s* len·s -tis *f*
leopard *s* (leo)pard·us -i *m*
leper *s* lepros·us -i *m* (·a -ae *f*)
leprosy *s* lepr·ae -arum *fpl*
less *adj* min·or -or -us
less *adv* minus
lessee *s* conduc·t·or -toris *m* (·trix -tricis *f*)
lessen *tr* (im)minuere **||** *intr* decrescere
lesson *s* document·um -i *n; (in school)* lecti·o -onis *f,* praecept·um -i *n;* **to be a — to** documento esse *(w. dat);* **to give —s in** docēre; **to give —s in grammar** grammaticam docēre
lessor *s* loca·tor -toris *m* (·trix -tricis *f*)
lest *conj* ne
let *tr (to allow)* sinere, permittere; *(to lease)* locare; **— me see** licet (ut) videam; **let's go** eamus; **to — alone** omittere; **to — down** *(to disappoint)* deësse *(w. dat);* **to — fall** a manibus mittere; **to — fly** emittere; **to — go** (di)mittere; **to — in** admittere; **to — off** absolvere; **to — out** emittere; **to — pass** omittere; **to — slip an opportunity** occasionem amittere **||** *intr* **to — up** residēre; **the rain is letting up** imber detumescit
lethal *adj* morti·fer(us) -fera -ferum
lethargic *adj* lethargic·us -a -um
lethargy *s* letharg·us -i *m*
letter *s (of alphabet)* litter·a -ae *f; (epistle)* litter·ae -arum *fpl,* epistul·a -ae *f;* **by —** per litteras; **capital —** littera grandis; **—s form syllables** litterae faciunt syllabas; **to the —** ad verbum
letter carrier *s* tabellari·us -i *m* (·a -ae *f*)
lettered *adj* litterat·us -a -um
letterhead *s* titul·us -i *m*
lettering *s* titul·us -i *m,* litter·ae -arum *fpl*
letter opener *s* ensicul·us -i *m* epistularis
lettuce *s* lactuc·a -ae *f*
leukemia *s* leukaemi·a -ae *f*
levee *s* agg·er -eris *m*
level *adj* plan·us -a -um
level *s* planiti·es -ei *f; (tool)* libr·a -ae *f;* **to be on a — with** par esse *(w. dat)*
level *tr* (ad)aequare; *(to destroy)* diruere; **to — to the ground** solo aequare
lever *s* vect·is -is *m*
levity *s* levit·as -atis *f*
levy *s* delect·us -ūs *m*
levy *tr (troops)* conscribere; *(tax)* exigere

lewd *adj* incest·us -a -um
lewdly *adv* inceste
lewdness *s* impudiciti·a -ae *f*
liable *adj* obnoxi·us -a -um; *(inclined)* inclinat·us -a -um
liar *s* mend·ax -acis *mf*
libation *s* libati·o -onis *f;* **to pour a —** libare
libel *s* calumni·a -ae *f*
libel *tr* calumniari
libelous *adj* famos·us -a -um
liberal *adj* liberal·is -is -e; *(free)* lib·er -era -erum; *(in giving)* larg·us -a -um; **— arts** art·es -ium *fpl* liberales, artes bonae, artes ingenuae
liberality *s* liberalit·as -atis *f*
liberally *adv* liberaliter, large
liberate *tr* liberare; *(a slave)* manumittere
liberation *s* liberati·o -onis *f*
liberator *s* libera·tor -toris *m* (·trix -tricis *f*)
libertine *s* hom·o -inis *mf* dissolutus (-a)
liberty *s* libert·as -atis *f;* **at —** lib·er -era -erum; **to be at —** licet *(w. dat of English subject);* **to take liberties with s.o.** liberius se in aliquem gerere
librarian *s* bibliothecari·us -i *m* (·a -ae *f*)
library *s* bibliothec·a -ae *f*
license *s (permission)* copi·a -ae *f,* potest·as -atis *f; (freedom)* licenti·a -ae *f; (to drive)* diplom·a -atis *n* gubernationis
license *tr* potestatem dare *(w. dat)*
license plate *s* notacul·um -i *n* autocineti
licentious *adj* dissolut·us -a -um
licentiously *adv* dissolute
lick *tr* lambere; *(daintily)* ligurrire; *(to thrash)* verberare; *(to defeat)* (de)vincere **to — the plate** catillare; **to — out** elingere; **to — up** delingere
licking *s (spanking)* verberati·o -onis *f;* **to get a —** vapulare
lictor *s* lict·or -oris *m*
lid *s* operiment·um -i *n*
lie *s* mendac·ium -(i)i *n;* **to give the — to** redarguere; **to tell a —** mendacium dicere
lie *intr (to tell a lie or lies)* mentiri; *(to be lying down)* iacēre; *(in bed)* cubare; *(to be situated)* sit·us -a -um esse; **to — down** iacēre; *(to rest)* decumbere; **to — in the direction of** vergere ad *(w. acc);* **to — in wait for** insidiari *(w. dat);* **to — on** *or* **upon** incubare *(w. dat);* **to — on one's back** resupin·us -a -um iacēre; **to — on one's left (right) side** in latus sinistrum (dextrum) cubare; **to — on one's stomach** pron·us -a -um iacēre
lieu *s* **in — of** loco *(w. gen)*
lieutenant *s* legat·us -i *m; (mil)* centuri·o -onis *m; (modern)* locumten·ens -entis *mf*
life *s* vit·a -ae *f; (age)* aet·as -atis *f; (fig)* alacrit·as -atis *f;* **but such is —** sed vita fert; **it's not a question of — or death** non capitis res agitur; **on my —!** ita vivam!; **spark of —** animul·a -ae *f;* **to come to —** reviviscere; **to lead the — of Riley** vitam Chiam gerere; **to lose one's —** animam amittere; **true to —** veri simil·is -is -e
life blood *s* suc·us -i *m* et sangu·is -inis *m*
lifeboat *s* navicul·a -ae *f* ad servandum
life-giving *adj* alm·us -a -um
lifeguard *s* cust·os -odis *mf* nantium
life imprisonment *s* **he was given —** carceri quoad vivat damnatus est; **to give s.o. —** aliquem damnare carceri quoad vivat
life insurance *s* vitae assecurati·o -onis *f*
lifeless *adj* inanim·us -a -um, exanim·is -is -e; *(fig)* exsangu·is -is -e, frigid·us -a -um
lifelessly *adv* frigide
life style *s* vitae proposit·um -i *n*
lifetime *s* aet·as -atis *f;* **once in a —** singulis aetatibus
lift *tr* tollere; **to — her hand to her face** manum ad faciem suam admovēre; **to — up** attollere; **to — weights** libramenta tollere
ligament *s* ligament·um -i *n*
ligature *s* ligatur·a -ae *f*
light *s* lu·x -cis *f,* lum·en -inis *n* (electricum); *(lamp)* lucern·a -ae *f;* **— and shade** *(in painting)* lum·en -inis *n* et umbr·ae -arum *fpl;* **to bring to —** in lucem proferre; **to come to —** apparēre; **to throw — on** lumen adhibēre *(w. dat);* **to turn on (off) the —** lumen (electricum) accendere (expedlre)
light *adj (in weight)* lev·is -is -e; *(bright)* lucid·us -a -um; *(of colors)* candid·us -a -um; *(easy)* facil·is -is -e; *(nimble)* agil·is -is -e; *(wine)* tenu·is -is -e, len·is -is -e; *(food)* lev·is -is -e; **to grow —** lucescere; **to make — of** in levi habēre
light *tr* accendere; *(to illuminate)* illuminare **II** *intr* flammam concipere; **to — up** *(fig)* hilar·is -is -e fieri; **to — upon** offendere
light bulb *s* globul·us -i *m* electricus
lighten *tr (to illumintate)* illustrare; *(weight)* allevare, exonerare **II** *intr (in the sky)* fulgurare
lighter *s* ignitabul·um -i *n*
light-hearted *adj* hilar·is -is -e
lighthouse *s* phar·us -i *f (m)*
lightness *s* levit·as -atis *f*
lightning *s* fulg·ur -uris *n; (in its destructive effects)* fulm·en -inis *n;* **struck by —** fulmine ict·us -a -um
likable *adj* amabil·is -is -e, grat·us -a -um
like *adj* simil·is -is -e *(w. dat); (equal)* par *(w. dat),* aequ·us -a -um *(w. dat);* **in — manner** similiter
like *prep* instar *(w. gen);* tamquam, ut; **he said s.th. — this** haec fere dixit; **that's more — it** propemodum est
like *tr* amare, curare; **he —s to paint** libentissime pingit; **I — this (best)** hoc mihi

(potissimum) placet; **I'd like to** velim *(w. inf);* **I — to do this** me iuvat hoc facere; **I — to watch the races** libenter circenses specto; **stay if you —** mane *(pl:* menēte) si libet
likeable *adj see* **likable**
likelihood *s* verisimilitud·o -inis *f*
likely *adj* verisimil·is -is -e, probabil·is -is -e; **it is more — that** verisimilius est *(w. acc & inf);* **it is most — that** proximum est *(w. acc & inf)*
likely *adv* probabiliter; **more —** probabilius
liken *tr* comparare
likeness *s* similitud·o -inis *f; (portrait)* effigi·es -ei *f,* simulacr·um -i *n*
likewise *adv* pariter, similiter, item
liking *s* am·or -oris *m; (fancy)* libid·o -inis *f;* **according to one's —** ex libidine; **to my —** ex meā sententiā; **to their —** ad arbitrium
lilac *s* syring·a -ae *f* vulgaris
lily *s* lil·ium -(i)i *n*
lily of the valley *s* convallaria maial·is -is *f*
limb *s* art·us -ūs *m,* membr·um -i *n; (of tree)* ram·us -i *m*
limber *adj* flexil·is -is -e
limbo *s (eccl)* limb·us -i *m*
lime *s* cal·x -cis *f; (fruit)* mal·um -i *n* citreum
limestone *s* cal·x -cis *f*
lime tree *s* tili·a -ae *f*
limit *s* fin·is -is *m,* mod·us -i *m;* **to set —s to** finire
limit *tr* finire, terminare; *(to restrict)* circumscribere
limitation *s* circumscripti·o -onis *f*
limited *adj* finit·us -a -um; *(time)* brev·is -is -e; *(resources)* exigu·us -a -um
limp *s* claudicati·o -onis *f*
limp *intr* claudicare
limp *adj* flaccid·us -a -um
linden tree *s* tili·a -ae *f*
line *s (drawn)* line·a -ae *f; (row)* seri·es -ei *f,* agm·en -inis *n; (lineage)* stirp·s -is *f,* gen·us -eris *n; (mil)* aci·es -ei *f; (of poetry or prose)* vers·us -ūs *m; (cord)* fun·is -is *m;* **drop me a — when you have time** scribe aliquid litterarum quando vacas; **he's feeding you a —** verba tibi iste dat; **in a straight —** rectā lineā; **I will write a few —s in answer to your letter** pauca ad tuas litteras rescribam; **— of work** *or* **business** quaest·us -ūs *m;* **the front —** *(mil)* principi·a -orum *npl;* **to draw a —** lineam ducere; **to form a long —** agmen longum facere; **to keep s.o. in —** imperare *(w. dat);* **to lay it on the —** *(fig)* directum loqui
line *tr (the streets)* saepire; **to — a garment with wool** vestem introrsum lanā obducere
lineage *s* gen·us -eris *n*
lineal *adj* linear·is -is -e
lineally *adv* rectā lineā
lineament *s* lineament·um -i *n*
linear *adj* linear·is -is -e
linen *s* linte·um -i *n,* lin·um -i *n*
linen *adj* linte·us -a -um; **— cloth** linteol·um -i *n*
linesman *s (sports)* iud·ex icis *m* linearius
linger *intr* morari, cunctari
lingering *adj* cunctabund·us -a -um
lingering *s* cunctati·o -onis *f*
linguist *s* linguarum perit·us -i *m* (·a -ae *f*)
linguistics *s* linguistic·a -ae *f*
liniment *s* leniment·um -i *n*
link *s (of chain)* anul·us -i *m; (bond)* vincul·um -i *n; (comput)* conex·us -ūs *m*
link *tr* coniungere; *(comput)* conectere
linking *s (comput)* conecti·o -onis *f*
linseed oil *s* ex lini semine ole·um -i *n*
lint *s* linament·um -i *n*
lintel *s* lim·en -inis *n* superum
lion *s* le·o -onis *m;* **—s roar** leones rugiunt
lioness *s* leaen·a -ae *f*
lip *s* labr·um -i *n; (edge)* or·a -ae *f;* **keep a stiff upper —** fac ut animo forti sis; **lower (upper) —** interius (superius) labrum; **to be on everyone's —s** in ore esse omni populo
lip service *s* obseq·ium -(i)i *n* falsum
liquefy *tr* liquefacere
liquid *adj* liquid·us -a -um
liquid *s* um·or -oris *m*
liquidate *tr* removēre, dimittere; *(accounts)* persolvere; *(convert into cash)* in pecuniam vertere
liquor *s* temet·um -i *n*
lisp *s* balbutire
lisping *adj* blaes·us -a -um
list *s* numer·us -i *m; (naut)* inclinati·o -onis *f;* **— of charges** subscripti·o -onis *f; (e-mail list)* grex, gregis *m* (interretialis)
list *tr* enumerare; **to — among the murderers** habēre sicariorum numero ‖ *intr (naut)* inclinare
listen *intr* auscultare; **to — to** auscultare *(w. dat);* **— to me!** ausculta mihi!
listless *adj* languid·us -a -um; des·es -idis
listlessly *adv* languide
list owner *s (comput)* gregis modera·tor -toris *m* (·trix -tricis *f*)
litany *s* litani·a -ae *f*
liter *s* litr·a -ae *f*
literal *adj* propri·us -a um *(opp:* translativus)
literally *adv* ad verbum, proprie *(opp:* figurate)
literary *adj (person)* litterat·us -a -um; **— pursuits** studi·a -orum *npl* litterarum; **— style** scribendi gen·us -eris *n,* stil·us -i *m*
literature *s* litter·ae -arum *fpl; (printed matter)* libr·i -orum *mpl* editi
litigant *s* litig·ans -antis *mf*
litigate *intr* litigare
litigation *s* li·s -tis *f*

litter *s (vehicle)* lectic·a -ae *f; (of straw, etc.)* strament·um -i *n; (brood)* fet·us -ūs *m; (refuse)* reiect·a -orum *npl*
litter *tr* spargere; **to — the streets** scruta viis spargere ‖ *intr* reiecta dispergere
little *adj* parv·us -a -um; **for a — while** paulisper; **— brother** fratercul·us -i *m;* **— sister** sororcul·a -ae *f*
little *adv* parum, paulum; **a —** paululum, pusillum; **a — bigger** paulo amplior; **— by —** paulatim
little *s* aliquantul·um -i *n*
little people *spl (coll)* popul·us -i *m* minutus
live *tr* **to — a good life** vitam bonum agere; **to — it up** ferias agere ‖ *intr* vivere, vitam agere; *(to reside)* habitare, incolere; **to — near** accolere; **to — in the city** urbem incolere; **to — in the Subura** habitare in Suburā; **to — on** *(food)* vesci *(w. abl);* **to — on borrowed time** de lucro vivere; **to — up to** aequiparare
live *adj* viv·us -a -um
livelihood *s* vict·us -ūs *m;* **to gain a —** victum quaeritare
liveliness *s* alacrit·as -atis *f*
lively *adj* veget·us -a -um
liver *s* iec·ur -oris *n*
livestock *s* pec·us -oris *n*
livid *adj* livid·us -a -um; **to be —** livēre
living *adj* viv·us -a -um; **as long as Hannibal was —** Hannibale vivo
living *s (livelihood)* vict·us -ūs *m,* quaest·us -ūs *m;* **to make a —** quaestum facere *or* victum quaeritare
living room *s* sessor·ium -(i)i *n*
lizard *s* lacert·us -i *m* (·a -ae *f*)
load *s* on·us -eris *n*
load *tr* onerare
loaded *adj (rich)* bene nummat·us -a -um, pecuniosissim·us -a -um; *(drunk)* uvid·us -a -um
loaf *s* **(of bread)** pan·is -is *m*
loaf *intr* cessare
loafer *s* cessa·tor -toris *m* (trix -tricis *f*)
loafing *s* cessati·o -onis *f*
loam *s* lut·um -i *n*
loan *s* (argenti) mutu·um -i *n;* **to hit s.o. for a —** aliquem mutuo ferire
loan *tr* faenerari
loathe *tr* fastidire
loathing *s* fastid·ium -(i)i *n*
loathsome *adj* tae·ter -tra -trum
lobby *s* vestibul·um -i *n*
lobe *s* lob·us -i *m*
lobster *s* astac·us -i *m*
local *adj* loci [*gen*], regionis [*gen*]
locality *s* loc·us -i *m*
local number *s* numer·us -i *m* localis
local train *s* tram·en -inis *n* commune
located *adj* sit·us -a -um
lock *s (of door)* ser·a -ae *f; (of hair)* crin·is -is *m;* **—, stock, and barrel** cum porcis, cum fiscinā; **to be kept under — and key** esse sub clavi
lock *tr* obserare, oppessulare; **to — in** includere; **to — out** excludere; **to — up** occludere; *(in prison)* in carcerem compingere
locker *s* loculament·um -i *n*
locket *s* capsell·a -a *f; (worn by boys, of leather, silver, or gold)* bull·a -ae *f;* **to wear a — around the neck** capsellam de cervice gerere; **wearing a —** bullat·us -a -um
lockjaw *s* tetan·us -i *m*
locomotive *s* (vaporaria) machin·a -ae *f* tractoria
locust *s* locust·a -ae *f;* **—s chirp** locustae strident
lodge *tr* **to — a complaint against s.o.** nomen alicuius deferre ‖ *intr* **(with)** deversari (apud *w. acc); (to stick)* inhaerēre
lodger *s* hosp·es -itis *mf; (in a tenement)* insulari·us -i *m* (·a -ae *f*)
lodging *s* hospit·ium -(i)i *n;* **to take up —** hospitium accipere
loft *s* tabulat·um -i *n*
lofty *adj* (ex)cels·us -a -um; *(fig)* sublim·is -is -e
log *s* stip·es -itis *m*
loggerheads *spl* **to be at —** rixari
logic *s* dialectic·a -orum *npl*
logical *adj* logic·us -a -um; *(reasonable)* rational·is -is -e
logically *adv* ex ratione
log in *intr (comput)* inire
log out *intr (comput)* exire
loin *s* lumb·us -i *m*
loiter *intr* cessare
loiterer *s* cessa·tor -toris *m* (·trix -tricis *f*)
loll *intr* recumbere
lone *adj* sol·us -a -um
loneliness *s* solitud·o -inis *f*
lonely *adj* solitari·us -a -um
lonesome *adj* solitari·us -a -um
long *adj* long·us -a -um; *(of time)* diuturn·us -a -um; *(lengthened; syllable)* product·us -a -um; *(opp:* brevis, correptus); **a — way off** longinqu·us -a -um; **for a — time** iam diu; **ten miles long** decem milia passuum in longitudinem
long *adv* diu; **a little —er** paulo longius; **— how long?** quamdiu?; **how much —er?** quamdiu etiam; **— after** multo post; **— ago** iamdudum, iampridem; **— before** multo ante; **it would take too — to ...** longum erat *(w. inf);* **—er** diutius; **too —** nimium diu
long *intr* avēre; **to — for** desiderare
long-distance number *s* numer·us -i *m* longinquus
longed-for *adj* expectat·us -a -um
longevity *s* longaevit·as -atis *f*
longing *s* desider·ium -(i)i *n*
longing *adj* avid·us -a -um

longingly *adv* avide
longitude *s* longitud·o -inis *f*
long jump *s (sports)* salt·us -ūs *m* in longum
long-lasting *adj* diutin·us -a -um
long-lived *adj* viv·ax -acis, longaev·us -a -um
long-sleeved *adj* manicat·us -a -um
long-standing *adj* vetustissim·us -a -um
long-suffering *adj* pati·ens -entis
long-winded *adj* long·us -a -um
look *s (act of looking)* aspect·us -ūs *m; (facial expression)* vult·us -ūs *m; (appearance)* speci·es -ei *f;* **—s** *(general appearance)* habit·us -ūs *m*
look *intr* aspicere; *(to seem)* videri; **he —s stern** severitas inest in vultu eius; **I don't know what he (she) —s like** quā sit facie nescio; **it —s that way to me** ita mihi videtur; **— !** aspice!; **— here, you!** eho, tu! **to — about** circumspicere; **to — after** curare; **to — after oneself** sibi consulere; **to — around** respicere, circumspicere; **to — around for** prospicere; **to — at** intuēri, aspicere; *(to study)* considerare; **to — back** respicere; **to — down** despicere; **to — down on** despicere *(w. acc);* **to — for** quaerere; **to — forward to** exspectare; **to — glad** laetitiam vultu aperte ferre; **to look into** *(lit & fig)* inspicere; *(to examine)* perscrutari; **to — into one's own mind** introspicere in mentem suam; **to — on** intueri, observare; **to — out** prospicere; **to — out for** quaerere; **to — out of the window** ex fenestrā prospicere; **to — s.o. in the face** rectis oculis aliquem aspicere; **to — towards** spectare; **to — up** suspicere, oculos erigere; *(to research)* inquirere in *(w. acc);* **to — up at** suspicere; **to — up to** *(implying respect)* suspicere; **to — up to heaven** in caelum suspicere; **to — upon** *(to regard)* habēre
looker-on *s* specta·tor -toris *m* (·trix -tricis *f*)
look-out *s (person)* specula·tor -toris *m* (·trix -tricis *f*)*;* **to keep a careful —** omnia circumspectare
loom *s* tel·a -ae *f*
loom *intr* in conspectum prodire
loop *s* sin·us -ūs *m*
loophole *s (in a law)* rim·a -ae *f*
loose *adj* lax·us -a -um; *(flowing, slack)* flux·us -a -um; *(not chaste)* dissolut·us -a -um; **— bowels** fusa alv·us -i *f*
loose-leaf folder *s* collector·ium -(i)i *n*
loose-leaf tablet *s* codicill·us -i *m* chartarum
loosely *adv* laxe; *(dissolutely)* dissolute
loosen *tr* solvere, laxare ‖ *intr* solvi
lop *tr* **to — off** praecidere; *(in pruning)* amputare
lop-sided *adj* inaequal·is -is -e
loquacious *adj* loqu·ax -acis
lord *s* domin·us -i *m*
Lord *s* Domin·us -i *m*
lord *intr* **to — it over** dominari in *(w. acc)*
lordly *adj* imperios·us -a -um
lordship *s* dominati·o -onis *f*
lore *s* doctrin·a -ae *f*
lose *tr (mostly unintentionally)* amittere, *(mostly blamably)* perdere; **to — one eye** altero oculo capi; **to — heart** deficere; **to — one's way** (ab)errare, viā decedere
loss *s (act)* amissi·o -onis *f; (damage sustained)* damn·um -i *n; (com, fin)* iactur·a -ae *f; (mil)* adversa pugn·a -ae *f; (pol)* repuls·a -ae *f;* **to incur some —** aliquid damni contrahere; **to suffer a —** damnum *(or* repulsam) ferre, iacturam facere
lost *adj* perdit·us -a -um; **to be —** perire; **to get —** aberrare
lot *s* sor·s -tis *f; (destiny)* fat·um -i *n; (piece of land)* agell·us -i *m;* **a —** *(coll)* multum; **a — better** *(coll)* multo melior; **casting of —s** sortiti·o -onis *f;* **—s of people** mult·i -orum *mpl;* **to draw —s for** sortiri
lotion *s* liniment·um -i *n*
lottery *s* sortiti·o -onis *f*
loud *adj* magn·us -a -um ‖ *adv* magnā voce, clare
loudmouth *s* clama·tor -toris *m* (·trix -tricis *f*)
loudspeaker *s* magaphon·um -i *n*
lounge *s (room)* exedr·ium -(i)i *n; (couch)* lectul·us -i *m*
lounge *intr* otiari
louse *s* pedicul·us -i *m; (pej)* lubric·us -i *m*
lousy *adj* pediculos·us -a -um; *(coll)* foed·us -a -um
lout *s* rustic·us -i *m*
loutish *adj* rustic·us -a -um
lovable *adj* amabil·is -is -e
love *s* am·or -oris *m;* **to be in love with** amare; **to fall in — with** in amorem *(w. gen)* incidere
love *tr* amare, diligere
love affair *s* am·or -oris *m*
loveliness *s* venust·as -atis *f*
lovely *adj* venust·us -a -um
love potion *s* philtr·um -i *n*
lover *s* am·ans -antis *mf; (homosexual partner)* fra·ter -tris *m*
loveseat *s* bisell·ium -(i)i *n* (tomento fartum)
lovesick *adj* amore ae·ger -gra -grum
loving *adj* am·ans -antis
low *adj (close to the ground; in status)* humil·is -is -e; *(of price)* vil·is -is -e; *(of birth)* obscur·us -a -um; *(low-pitched)* grav·is -is -e; *(not loud)* summiss·us -a -um; *(depressed)* trist·is -is -e; *(vile)* turp·is -is -e; **at — tide** ubi aestus recessit; **— interest** leve faen·us -oris *n*
low *adv* humiliter; summissā voce
low *intr* mugire
lowborn *adj* degen·er -eris

lower *tr* demittere, deprimere; *(price)* imminuere
lower *adj* infer·ior -ior -ius; **— jaw** mandibul·a -ae *f;* **of the — world** infer·us -a -um; **the — world** infer·i -orum *mpl*
lowermost *adj* infim·us -a -um
lowing *s* mugit·us -ūs *m*
lowlands *spl* campestr·ia -ium *npl*
lowly *adj* humil·is -is -e
loyal *adj* fidel·is -is -e, fid·us -a -um; **to remain —** in fide manēre
loyally *adv* fideliter
loyalty *s* fidelit·as -atis *f*
lube job *s* uncti·o -onis *f* autocineti
lubricate *tr* unguere
lucid *adj* lucid·us -a -um
Lucifer *s* Lucif·er -eri *m*
luck *s* fortun·a -ae *f;* **bad —** fortun·a -ae *f,* infortun·ium -(i)i *n;* **good —** fortun·a -ae *f;* **good —!** feliciter!
luckily *adv* feliciter
luckless *adj* infel·ix -icis
lucky *adj* fel·ix -icis; **— stiff** Fortunae fil·ius -(i)i *m*
lucrative *adj* lucrativ·us -a -um
lucre *s* lucr·um -i *n*
ludicrous *adj* ridicul·us -a -um
ludicrously *adv* ridicule
lug *tr* trahere
luggage *s* sarcin·ae -arum *fpl*
luggage rack *s* retinacul·um -i *n* sarcinale
luggage tag *s* pittac·ium -(i)i *n* sarcinale
lukewarm *adj* tepid·us -a -um; *(fig)* segn·is -is -e, frigid·us -a -um
lukewarmly *adv* segniter
lull *s* qui·es -etis *f*
lull *tr* sopire; *(to calm, as a storm)* sedare; *(fig)* demulcēre
lullaby *s* lall·um -i *n*
lumber *s* materi·a -ae *f*
luminary *s* lum·en -inis *n*
luminous *adj* lucid·us -a -um; *(fig)* dilucid·us -a -um
lump *s* glaeb·a -ae *f,* mass·a -ae *f;* *(on the body)* tub·er -eris *n*
lump *tr* **to — together** coacervare; **to — s.o. together with** aliquem accudere *(w. dat)*
lumpy *adj* glaebos·us -a -um
lunacy *s* alienati·o -onis *f* mentis
lunar *adj* lunar·is -is -e
lunatic *s* insan·us -i *m* (·a -ae *f*)
lunch *s* prand·ium -(i)i *n;* **to eat (have) —** prandium sumere; **to have for —** in prandium habēre
lunch *intr* prandēre
luncheon *s* prand·ium -(i)i *n*
lung *s* pulm·o -onis *m*
lunge *s* ict·us -ūs *m*
lunge *intr* prosalire
lurch *s* propuls·us -ūs *m;* **to leave in a —** derelinquere
lurch *intr* titubare
lure *s* illecebr·a -ae *f;* *(bait)* esc·a -ae *f*
lure *tr* allicere; *(an animal)* inescare
lurid *adj* horrend·us -a -um
lurk *intr* latēre, latitare
luscious *adj* praedulc·is -is -e, suav·is -is -e
lush *adj* luxurios·us -a -um
lust *s* libid·o -inis *f;* *(for power, etc.)* cupidit·as -atis *f*
lust *intr* **to — after** concupiscere
luster *s* splend·or -oris *m*
lustful *adj* libidinos·us -a -um
lustfully *adv* libidinose, lascive
lustily *adv* valide
lusty *adj* valid·us -a -um
luxuriance *s* luxuri·es -ei *f*
luxuriant *adj* luxurios·us -a -um; *(fertile, rich)* laet·us -a -um
luxuriate *intr* luxuriare
luxurious *adj* sumptuos·us -a -um
luxuriously *adv* sumptuose
luxury *s* luxuri·a -ae *f*
lye *s* lixivi·a -ae *f*
lying *adj* mend·ax -acis, falsiloqu·us -a -um
lying *s* mendacit·as -atis *f*
lymph *s* lymph·a -ae *f*
lynx *s* lyn·x -cis *mf*
lyre *s* lyr·a -ae *f*
lyric *adj* lyric·us -a -um
lyric *s* (lyricum) carm·en -inis *n*

M

macaroni *s* collyr·a -ae *f,* past·a -ae *f* tubulata
mace *s* virg·a -ae *f*
machination *s* dol·us -i *m*
machine *s* machin·a -ae *f*
machinery *s* machinament·um -i *n*
machinist *s* machinat·or -oris *m*
mackerel *s* scom·ber -bri *m*
mad *adj* insan·us -a -um, furios·us -a -um; *(angry)* irat·us -a -um; **to be —** furere; **to be — about s.o.** *(to be madly in love with)* aliquem deperire; **to be — at s.o.** suscensēre *(w. dat);* **to go —** mente alienari
madam *s* domin·a -ae *f*
madden *tr* mentem alienare *(w. dat); (fig)* furiare
maddening *adj* molest·us -a -um, exacerb·ans -antis
madly *adv* furiose; **to be — in love** insane amare
madman *s* hom·o -inis *m* furiosus
madness *s* fur·or -oris *m*
magazine *s (journal)* commentari·i -orum *mpl* periodici imaginei; *(storehouse)* horre·um -i *n*
maggot *s* verm·is -is *m*
magic *adj* magic·us -a -um; **to perform — tricks** praestigiari

magic *s* magica ar·s -tis *f*
magically *adv* velut magicā quādam arte et vi
magician *s* mag·us -i *m*, mag·a -ae *f*
magisterial *adj* ad magistratum pertin·ens -entis
magistracy *s* magistrat·us -ūs *m*
magistrate *s* magistrat·us -ūs *m*
magnanimity *s* magnanimit·as -atis *f*
magnanimous *adj* magnanim·us -a -um
magnet *s* magn·es -etis *m*
magnetic *adj* magnetic·us -a -um
magnificence *s* magnificenti·a -ae *f*
magnificent *adj* magnific·us -a -um
magnificently *adv* magnifice
magnify *tr* amplificare
magnitude *s* magnitud·o -inis *f*
maid *s* ancill·a -ae *f*
maiden *s* virg·o -inis *f*
maidenhood *s* virginit·as -atis *f*
maidenly *adj* virginal·is -is -e
mail *s* res, rerum *fpl* cursuales; *(letters)* epistul·ae -arum *fpl; (postal system)* curs·us -ūs *m* publicus; *(armor)* loric·a -ae *f*; **to deliver (forward) the —** res cursuales reddere (deferre); **stack of —** multiiugae litterae *fpl*
mail *tr* dare
mailbox *s* capsul·a -ae *f* tabellaria
mailman *s* tabellar·ius -(i)i *m*
maim *tr* mutilare
maimed *adj* manc·us -a -um
main *adj* praecipu·us -a -um; **the — point** cap·ut -itis *n;* **in the —** magnā ex parte
main *s* pelag·us -i *m*
mainland *s* contin·ens -entis *f*
mainly *adv* praecipue
main road *s* vi·a -ae *f* principalis
maintain *tr (to keep)* tenēre; *(to keep alive)* alere; *(to defend)* sustinēre; *(to argue)* affirmare
maintenance *s (support)* sustentati·o -onis *f; (means of living)* vict·us -ūs *m*
majestic *adj* august·us -a -um; **how — was his address!** quanta fuit in oratione maiestas!
majesty *s* maiest·as -atis *f*
major *adj* ma·ior -ior -ius
major *s (mil)* tribun·us -i *m* militaris; *(in logic)* maior praemiss·a -ae *f; (educ)* disciplin·a -ae *f* primaria
major in *intr* operam primariam *(cuidam disciplinae)* dare
majority *s* maior par·s -tis *f*
make *s* form·a -ae *f*, figur·a -ae *f*
make *tr* facere; *(to render by molding, shaping)* fingere; *(to render)* reddere; *(to construct)* fabricare; *(to appoint)* creare; *(to force)* cogere; **to — amends for** corrigere; **to — believe (that)** assimulare quasi *(w. subj)*, simulare *(w. acc & inf)*; **to — fun of** eludere; **to — haste** festinare; **to — light of** parvi facere; **to — money** pecuniam facere; **to — much of** magni facere; **to — over** transferre; **to — peace** pacem parere; **to — public** publicare; **to — the bed** lectum sternere; **to — up** *(story)* fingere; **to — up for lost time** cessata tempora corrigere; **to — up with (s.o)** reverti in gratiam cum *(w. abl)*; **to — use of** uti *(w. abl)*; **to — way for** cedere *(w. dat)*, viam dare *(dat)* ‖ *intr* **to — away with** amovēre; **to — do** suppetere; **to — for** petere
make-believe *adj* fict·us -a -um
maker *s* fabrica·tor -toris *m* (·trix -tricis f)
make-up *s* compositi·o -onis *f; (disposition)* indol·es -is *f; (cosmetics)* fuc·us -i *m*
maladministration *s* mala administrati·o -onis *f*
malady *s* morb·us -i *m*
malaria *f* malari·a -ae *f*
malcontent *adj* dissid·ens -entis
male *adj* masculin·us -a -um
male *s* ma·s -ris *m*
malevolence *s* malevolenti·a -ae *f*
malevolent *adj* malevol·us -a -um
malice *s* malevolenti·a -ae *f*
malicious *adj* malevol·us -a -um
maliciously *adv* malevolo animo
malign *tr* obtrectare
malignant *adj* malevol·us -a -um; *(med)* malign·us -a -um
mall *s* for·um -i *n*
mallet *s* malle·us -i *m*
malnutrition *s* aliment·um -i *n* tenue
malpractice *s* delict·a -orum *npl*
maltreat *tr* vexare, abuti *(w. abl); (w. blows, etc.)* mulcare
mama *s* mamm·a -ae *f*
man *s (human being)* hom·o -inis *m; (male)* vir, viri *m*
man *tr (ships)* complēre; *(the walls)* praesidio firmare
manage *tr* curare; *(a bank)* moderari; *(esp. on large scale)* administrare, gerere; **if you can — it** si id conficere poteris
manageable *adj* tractabil·is -is -e
management *s* cur·a -ae *f*, administrati·o -onis *f*
manager *s* cura·tor -toris *m* (·trix -tricis *f*); *(steward)* procurat·or -oris *m; (of an estate)* villic·us -i *m; (of a bank)* modera·tor -toris *m* (·trix -tricis *f*)
mandate *s* mandat·um -i *n*
mane *s* iub·a -ae *f*
maneuver *s (mil)* decurs·us -ūs *m; (trick)* dol·us -i *m*
maneuver *intr (mil)* decurrere; *(fig)* machinari, tractare
manger *s* praesep·e -is *n*
mangle *tr* lacerare, dilaniare
manhood *s* virilit·as -atis *f; (period of puberty)* pubert·as -atis *f*
mania *s* insani·a -ae *f*
maniac *s* furios·us -i *m* (·a -ae *f*)

manifest *adj* manifest·us -a -um
manifest *tr* manifestare, declarare
manifestation *s* patefacti·o -onis *f*
manifestly *adv* manifeste
manifesto *s* edict·um -i *n*
manifold *adj* vari·us -a -um
maniple *s* manipul·us -i *m*
manipulate *intr* tractare
manipulation *s* tractati·o -onis *f*
mankind *s* gen·us -eris *n* humanum
manliness *s* virt·us -utis *f;* **to act with —** viriliter agere
manly *adj* viril·is -is -e
manner *s* mod·us -i *m; (custom)* consuetud·o -inis *f;* **after the — of** ritu *(w. gen),* more *(w. gen);* **bad —s** rusticit·as -atis *f;* **good —s** urbanit·as -atis *f;* **in a cruel —** crudelem in modum
mannerism *s* mala affectati·o -onis *f*
mannerly *adj* urban·us -a -um
mannikin *s* homuncul·us -i *m* (·a -ae *f*)
man-of-war *s* nav·is -is *f* longa
manor *s* praed·ium -(i)i *n*
man servant *s* serv·us -i *m*
mansion *s* dom·us -ūs *f*
manslaughter *s* homicid·ium -(i)i *n*
mantel *s* plute·us -i *m* fornacis
mantle *s (women's outdoor wear)* pall·a -ae *f; (fig)* velament·um -i *n*
mantle *tr* tegere, dissimulare
manual *adj* manual·is -is -e; **— labor** oper·a -ae *f* quae manibus exercetur
manual *s* enchiridi·on -onis *n,* ars, artis *f*
manufacture *s* fabric·a -ae *f*
manufacture *tr* fabricari
manufacturer *s* fabrica·tor -toris *m* (·rix -ricis *f*)
manure *s* sterc·us -oris *n*
manure *tr* stercorare
manuscript *s* cod·ex -icis *m*
many *adj* mult·i -ae -a; **a good —** nonnull·i -ae -a; **as — … as** quot … tot; **how —** quot [*indecl*]; **in — ways** multifariam; **so —** tot [*indecl*]
many-colored *adj* multicol·or -oris
many-sided *adj* multipl·ex -icis; *(fig)* versatil·is -is -e
map *s* tabul·a -ae *f* geographica; **— of the world** orb·is -is *m* terrarum pictus
map *tr* **to — out** designare
maple *adj* acern·us -a -um
maple tree *s* ac·er -eris *n*
mar *tr* foedare; *(esp. fig)* deformare
marauder *s* praedat·or -oris *m*
marauding *s* praedati·o -onis *f*
marble *adj* marmore·us -a -um
marble *s* marm·or -oris *n*
March *s* Mart·ius -(i)i *m or* mens·is -is *m* Martius; **in —** mense Martio; **on the first of —** Kalendis Martiis
march *s* iter, itineris *n*
march *tr* ducere ‖ *intr* iter facere, incedere; **to — on** signa proferre
mare *s* equ·a -ae *f*
margarine *s* margarin·um -i *n*
margin *s* marg·o -inis *mf*
marginal *adj* margini ascript·us -a -um
marigold *s* calth·a -ae *f*
marijuana *s* cannab·is -is *f;* **to smoke —** fumum cannabis sugere
marine *adj* marin·us -a -um
marine *s* mil·es -itis *mf* classic·us (-a); **the —s** classiari·i -orum *mpl*
mariner *s* naut·a -ae *m*
maritime *adj* maritim·us -a -um
mark *s* not·a -ae *f; (sign, token)* indic·ium -(i)i *n; (brand)* stigm·a -atis *n; (blemish)* macul·a -ae *f; (target)* scop·us -i *m; (of wound)* cicatr·ix -icis *f; (characteristic) expressed with gen after verb* esse, *e.g.,* **it is the — of a small mind** pusilli animi est
mark *tr (to draw or make a mark on anything)* notare; *(to observe)* animadvertere; *(with pencil, etc.)* designare; **— my words!** animum intende *(pl:* animos intendite) in mea dicta!; **to — down** scribere; **to — down the price** pretium circumcidere; **to — off** metiri
marked *adj* distinct·us -a -um, manifest·us -a -um
markdown *s* pretii deminuti·o -onis *f*
marker *s* ind·ex -icis *m; (tombstone)* monument·um -i *n*
market *s* macell·um -i *n; (demand)* desider·ium -(i)i *n;* **on the open —** promercal·is -is -e
marketable *adj* venal·is -is -e
market day *s* nundin·ae -arum *fpl*
marketplace *s* for·um -i *n*
market town *s* empor·ium -(i)i *n*
marmalade *s* quil·on -onis *n* ex aurantis confectum
maroon *tr* derelinquere
marriage *s* matrimon·ium -(i)i *n;* **to give a daughter in —** filiam in matrimonio collocare
marriageable *adj (girl)* nubil·is -is -e
marriage alliance *s* affinit·as -atis *f*
marriage contract *s* pacti·o -onis *f* nuptialis
married *adj (of a woman)* nupta; *(of a man)* maritus; **to get —** matrimonio coniungi
marrow *s* medull·a -ae *f*
marry *tr (said of a man)* in matrimonium ducere, uxorem ducere; *(said of a woman)* nubere *(w. dat)*
marsh *s* pal·us -udis *f*
marshal *s* du·x -cis *m*
marshal *tr* disponere
marshy *adj* palus·ter -tris -tre
mart *s* empor·ium -(i)i *n*
martial *adj* bellicos·us -a -um
martyr *s* mart·yr -yris *mf*
martyrdom *s* martyr·ium -(i)i *n*
marvel *s* miracul·um -i *n*
marvel *intr* **to — at** mirari

marvelous *adj* mir·us -a -um
marvelously *adv* mire
masculine *adj* mascul·us -a -um; *(gram)* masculin·us -a -um
mash *s* mixtur·a -ae *f; (for cattle)* forag·o -inis *f*
mash *tr* commiscēre; *(to bruise)* contundere
mask *s* person·a -ae *f*
mask *tr (fig)* dissimulare
mason *s* lapidar·ius -(i)i *m*
masonry *s* op·us -eris *n* caementicium
mass *adj* tot·us -a -um; *(large-scale)* magnari·us -a -um
mass *s* mol·es -is *f; (large amount)* copi·a -ae *f; (of people)* turb·a -ae *f; (eccl)* miss·a -ae *f;* **the —es** vulg·us -i *n*
mass *tr* congerere, coacervare ‖ *intr* congeri, coacervari
massacre *s* trucidati·o -onis *f*
massacre *tr* trucidare
massage *s* iatraliptic·e -es *f*
massage *tr* fricare
masseur *s* iatralipt·es -ae *m*
masseuse *s* iatralipt·es -ae *f*
massive *adj* solid·us -a -um, ing·ens -entis
mast *s (of ship)* mal·us -i *m; (for cattle)* glan·s -dis *f*
master *s* domin·us -i *m; (teacher)* magis·ter -tri *m; (controller)* arbi·ter -tri *m;* **to be — of** potens esse *(w. gen),* compos esse *(w. gen);* **not be — of** impotens esse *(w. gen)*
master *tr* superare; *(to learn)* perdiscere; *(passion)* continēre
masterful *adj* pot·ens -entis, imperios·us -a -um
master key *s* clav·is -is *m* complures ianuas aperiens
masterly *adj* perit·us -a -um
master of ceremony *s* magis·ter -tri *m* convivii
masterpiece *s* magnum op·us -eris *n*
master's degree *s* grad·us -us *m* magistralis
mastery *s* dominati·o -onis *f;* **having — of** pot·ens -entis *(w. gen)*
masticate *tr* mandere
mastiff *s* Moloss·us -i *m*
mat *s* teg·es -etis *f*
match *s (marriage)* nupti·ae -arum *fpl; (contest)* certam·en -inis *n; (an equal)* par paris *mf; (to light)* rament·um -i *n* flammiferum; **a — for** par *(w. dat);* **not a — for** impar *(w. dat)*
match *tr* adaequare ‖ *intr* quadrare
matchless *adj* incomparabil·is -is -e
match maker *s* nuptiarum concilia·tor -toris *m* (·trix -tricis *f*)
mate *s* soc·ius -(i)i *m* (·a -ae *f*); *(spouse)* coniu·(n)x -gis *mf*
mate *intr* coïre
material *adj* corpore·us -a -um; *(significant)* haud lev·is -is -e
material *s* materi·a -ae *f; (cloth)* textil·e -is *n*
materially *adv* magnopere
maternal *adj* matern·us -a -um; **— aunt** materter·a -ae *f;* **— uncle** avuncul·us -i *m*
maternity dress *s* puerperae vest·is -is *f*
mathematical *adj* mathematic·us -a -um
mathematician *s* mathematic·us -i *m* (·a -ae *f*)
mathematics *s* mathematic·a -ae *f*
matrimony *s* matrimon·ium -(i)i *n*
matrix *s* form·a -ae *f*
matron *s* matron·a -ae *f*
matronly *adj* matronal·is -is -e
matter *s (substance)* materi·a -ae *f; (affair)* res, rei *f; (med)* pus, puris *n;* **for that —** adeo; **no —** nihil interest; **no — how ...** quamvis *(w. subj);* **what on earth's the —?** quidnam est?; **what's the — with you?** quid est tibi *(or* tecum)?
matter *intr impers* refert; **it does not —** nihil interest; nihil refert; **it —s a lot** multum *or* magnopere refert; **what does that — to me (to you)?** quid refert meā (tuā)?
matting *s* teget·es -um *fpl*
mattress *s* culcit·a -ae *f;* **air —** culcita inflatilis
mature *adj* matur·us -a -um
mature *intr* maturare
maturely *adv* mature
maturity *s* maturit·as -atis *f*
maul *tr* mulcare
mausoleum *s* mausole·um -i *n*
maw *s* ingluvi·es -ei *f*
mawkish *adj* putid·us -a -um
mawkishly *adv* putide
maxim *s* axiom·a -atis *n; (rule, precept)* praecept·um -i *n*
maximum *adj* quam maxim·us -a -um
maximum *s* maxim·um -i *n,* summ·um -i *n*
May *s* Mai·us -i *m or* mens·is -is *m* Maius; **in —** mense Maio; **on the first of —** Kalendis Maiis
may *intr* posse; **— I leave?** licetne mihi abire? *or* licetne mihi (ut) abeam?; *(possibility, expressed by subj):* **I — go** eam; **perhaps s.o. may say** fortasse quispiam dixerit
maybe *adv* forsitan, fortasse
mayhem *s* iniuri·a -ae *f* violenta corporis; *(havoc)* strag·es -is *f*
mayonnaise *s* liquam·en -inis *n* Nagonicum
mayor *s* praefect·us -i *m* (·a -ae *f*) urbi
mayoralty *s* praefectur·a -ae *f* urbi
maze *s* labyrinth·us -i *m*
me *pron* me; **by —** a me; **to —** mihi; **with —** mecum
mead *s (drink)* muls·um -i *n*
meadow *s* prat·um -i *n*
meager *adj* exil·is -is -e; *(insufficient)* exigu·us -a -um
meagerly *adv* exiliter

meagerness *s* exilit·as -atis *f*
meal *s* cib·us -i *m; (flour)* farin·a -ae *f;* **to eat a —** cibum sumere
mealymouthed *adj* blandiloqu·us -a -um
mean *adj (middle)* medi·us -a -um; *(low)* humil·is -is -e; *(cruel)* vil·is -is -e
mean *s* med·ium -(i)i *n*
mean *tr* significare; *(after s.th. has been mentioned)* dicere, *e.g.,* **of course, you — Plato** Platonem videlicet dicis; *(to intend)* velle, in animo habēre; **do you — me?** mene vis?; **Yes, I do** aio; **how do you — that?** qui istuc vis?; **now you know what I —** scis iam quid loquar; **what does this —** quid hoc sibi vult?; **what do you — by that?** quid istuc est verbi?; **what I — is** *(in correcting a misunderstanding)* at enim; **what does my father —?** quid sibi vult pater?
meander *intr* sinuoso cursu labi
meaning *s* sens·us -ūs *m,* significati·o -onis *f;* **basic —** princeps significatio
meaningful *adj* signific·ans -antis
meanness *s (lowliness)* humilit·as -atis *f; (cruelty)* crudelit·as -atis *f*
means *spl (way, method)* rati·o -onis *f,* mod·us -i *m;* **by all —** maxime, omnino; **by fair —** recte; **by — of** *render by abl or* per *(w. acc);* **by no —** haudquaquam
meantime *adv see* **meanwhile**
meanwhile *adv* **in the —** interea, interim
measles *spl* morbill·i -orum *mpl*
measurable *adj* mensurabil·is -is -e
measure *s* mensur·a -ae *f; (proper measure)* mod·us -i *m; (course of action)* rati·o -onis *f; (leg)* rogati·o -onis *f;* **beyond —** supra modum; **in some —** aliquā ex parte; **to take —s** consulere *(w. dat of that on behalf of which;* in *w. acc of person against whom)*
measure *tr* metiri; **to — off** metari **II** *intr* patēre, colligere; **measuring ten miles in circumference** patens *(or* colligens) decem milia passuum circuitu
measurement *s* mensur·a -ae *f*
meat *s* car·o -nis *f*
meatball *s* globul·us -i *m* carneus
meat grinder *s* machin·a -ae *f* carnaria
meat tray *s* carnar·ium -(i)i *n*
meaty *adj (fig)* sententios·us -a -um
mechanic *s* opif·ex -icis *m*
mechanical *adj* mechanic·us -a -um; **— engineer** mechinat·or -oris *m*
mechanics *s* mechanica ar·s -tis *f*
mechanism *s* mechinati·o -onis *f,* instrument·um -i *n*
medal *s* **(gold, silver, bronze)** insign·e -is *n* (aureum, argenteum, aereum)
medallion *s* nomism·a -atis *n* sollemne
meddle *intr* **(in)** se interponere (in *w. acc)*
meddler *s* ardali·o -onis *mf*
meddlesome *adj* curios·us -a -um
medial *adj* medi·us -a -um
median *adj* dimidi·us -a -um
median *s* mediocrit·as -atis *f*
mediate *tr* conciliare **II** *intr* se interponere ad componendam litem; **to — between estranged friends** aversos amicos componere
mediation *s* intercessi·o -onis *f*
mediator *s* interces·sor -soris *m* (·rix -ricis *f)*
medical *adj* medic·us -a -um; **— practice** medicin·a -ae *f*
medicate *tr* medicare
medication *s* medicament·um -i *n*
medicinal *adj* medicat·us -a -um
medicine *s (science)* medicin·a -ae *f; (remedy)* medicament·um -i *n;* **to practice —** medicinam exercēre
medieval *adj* medii aevi *(gen used as adj)*
mediocre *adj* mediocr·is -is -e
mediocrity *s* mediocrit·as -atis *f*
meditate *intr* cogitare, meditari
meditation *s* cogitati·o -onis *f,* meditati·o -onis *f*
meditative *adj* cogitabund·us -a -um
Mediterranean *s* mar·e -is *n* internum, mar·e -is *n* nostrum
medium *s (middle)* med·ium -(i)i *n; (expedient)* mod·us -i *m; (agency)* concilia·tor -toris *m* (·trix -tricis *f)*
medium *adj* mediocr·is -is -e
medley *s* farrag·o -inis *f*
meek *adj* mit·is -is -e; *(unassuming)* summiss·us -a -um
meekly *adv* summisse
meekness *s* anim·us -i *m* summissus
meet *tr* convenire, obviam ire *(w. dat); (danger, death, etc.)* obire **II** *intr* convenire; *(to converge)* confluere; *(to cross)* intersecare; **to — half way** compromittere; **to — with** offendere, subire
meet *s (contest)* certam·en -inis *n*
meeting *s (of two or many individuals)* congress·us -ūs *m; (assembly)* convent·us -ūs *m; (for consultation)* consil·ium -(i)i *n;* **to hold a —** conventum habēre; consilium habēre
megaphone *s* megaphon·um -i *n*
melancholy *s* maestiti·a -ae *f*
melancholy *adj* maest·us -a -um
melee *s* turb·a -ae *f,* tumult·us -ūs *m*
mellow *adj* matur·us -a -um; *(from drinking)* temulent·us -a -um
melodious *adj* canor·us -a -um
melodiously *adv* canore, modulate
melodramatic *adj* **to be —** paratragoedare
melody *s* mel·os -i *n,* melodi·a -ae *f,* cant·us -ūs *m*
melt *tr* liquefacere, dissolvere; **to — down** conflare **II** *intr* liquescere
melting *s* liquati·o -onis *f*
melting pot *s* mixtur·a -ae *f* multarum gentium

member *s (of the body)* membr·um -i *n; (part)* pars, partis *f; (of an organization)* sodal·is -is *mf*
membership *s (the members)* sodal·es -ium *mpl;* **to be admittted to —** sodalis ascribi *or* cooptari
membrane *s* membran·a -ae *f*
memento *s* monument·um -i *n*
memoirs *spl* commentari·i -orum *mpl*
memorable *adj* memorabil·is -is -e
memorandum *s* not·a -ae *f*
memorial *adj* memoral·is -is -e; **— service** rit·us -ūs *m* memoralis
memorial *s* monument·um -i *n*
memorize *tr* memoriae mandare, ediscere
memory *s* memori·a -ae *f;* **from —** ex memoriā, memoriter; **if — serves me right** si ego satis commemini; **in — of** in memoriam *(w. gen);* **to commit to —** memoriae mandare; **to have a good —** esse memoriā bonā; **within the — of man** post hominum memoriam
menace *s* min·ae -arum *fpl*
menace *tr* minari, minitari; *(of things)* imminēre *(w. dat)*
menacing *adj* min·ax -acis; *(only of persons)* minitabund·us -a -um
mend *tr* emendare; *(clothes)* sarcire ‖ *intr (to improve in health)* melior fieri
mendicant *s* mendic·us -i *m* (·a -ae *f*)
menial *adj* servil·is -is -e
menial *s* serv·us -i *m,* serv·a -ae *f*
menses *spl* menstru·a -orum *npl*
mental *adj* mente concept·us -a -um
mentally *adv* mente, animo
mention *s* menti·o -onis *f;* **to make — of** mentionem facere *(w. gen)*
mention *tr* commemorare; *(by name)* nominare; **not to —** silentio praeterire; **not to — the fact that ...** ut mittam quod *(w. indic);* **not to — the others** ne de alteris referam
menu *s* ciborum tabell·a -ae *f; (comput)* iussorum tabella *f*
mercantile *adj* mercatori·us -a -um
mercenary *adj* mercenari·us -a -um
mercenary *s* mil·es -itis *m* mercenarius
merchandise *s* merc·es -ium *fpl*
merchant *s* mercat·or -oris *m; (in a market)* macellari·us -i *m* (·a -ae *f*)
merchant ship *s* nav·is -is *f* mercatoria
merciful *adj* misericor·s -dis
mercifully *adv* misericorditer
merciless *adj* immisericor·s -dis
mercilessly *adv* immisericorditer
mercurial *adj* a·cer -cris -cre
Mercury *s* Mercur·ius -(i)i *m*
mercury *s* argent·um -i *n* vivum
mercy *s* misericordi·a -ae *f*
mere *adj* mer·us -a -um
merely *adv* tantummodo, solum
meretricious *adj* meretrici·us -a -um
merge *tr* confundere ‖ *intr* confundi
meridian *s* meridianus circul·us -i *m*
merit *s* merit·um -i *n*
merit *tr* merēre, merēri
meritorious *adj* laudabil·is -is -e
mermaid *s* nymph·a -ae *f* marina
merrily *adv* festive, hilare
merry *adj* hilar·us -a -um, festiv·us -a -um, fest·us -a -um; **Merry Christmas** fausta festa Natalici·a -ae *f* Christi
merry-go-round *s* orb·is -is *m* volubilis lusorius
merrymaking *s* festivit·as -atis *f*
mesh *s (of net)* macul·a -ae *f*
mess *s (dirt)* squal·or -oris *m; (confusion)* rerum perturbati·o -onis *f;* **geez, what a —!** eu edepol res turbulentas!; **to make a —** turbas conciēre
mess *tr* inquinare, foedare; **to — up** *(to upset)* conturbare, confundere
message *s* nunt·ius -(i)i *m*
messenger *s* nunti·us -i *m* (·a -ae *f*)
mess hall *s* cenati·o -onis *f*
metal *adj* metallic·us -a -um
metal *s* metall·um -i *n*
metallurgy *s* metallurgi·a -ae *f*
metamorphosis *s* metamorphos·is -is *f,* transfigurati·o -onis *f*
metaphor *s* translati·o -onis *f*
metaphorical *adj* translat·us -a -um
metaphorically *adv* per translationem
metaphysical *adj* metaphysic·us -a -um
metaphysics *s* metaphysic·a -ae *f; (as a title)* metaphysic·a -orum *npl*
meteor *s* fa·x -cis *f* caelestis
meteorology *s* meteorologi·a -ae *f*
mete out *tr* emetiri
meter *s (unit of measure; verse)* metr·um -i *n*
method *s* rati·o -onis *f*
methodical *adj* disposit·us -a -um
methodically *adv* disposite
meticulous *adj* accurat·us -a -um
meticulously *adv* accurate
metonymy *s* metonymi·a -ae *f*
metrical *adj* metric·us -a -um
metropolis *s* cap·ut -itis *n,* metropol·is -is *f*
metropolitan *adj* metropolitan·us -a -um
mettle *s* anim·us -i *m*
miasma *s* noxius halit·us -ūs *m*
microphone *s* microphon·um -i *n*
microscope *s* microscop·ium -(i)i *n*
microwave oven *s* furnul·us -i *m* undarum brevium
mid *adj* medi·us -a -um
midday *adj* meridian·us -a -um
midday *s* meridi·es -ei *f*
middle *adj* medi·us -a -um; **— age** aet·as -atis *f* media
middle *s* med·ium -(i)i *n;* **in the middle of the road** in mediā viā
middle class *s* ord·o -inis *m* medius; *(Roman)* equit·es -um *mpl*
middle school *s* schol·a -ae *f* media
midget *s* pumili·o -onis *mf*

midnight *s* media no•x -ctis *f;* **around —** mediā circiter nocte; **at —** (de) media nocte
midriff *s* diaphragm•a -atis *n*
midst *s* med•ium -(i)i *n;* **in the — of** inter *(w. acc)*
midsummer *s* summa aest•as -atis *f*
midway *adv* medi•us -a -um; **he stood — between the lines** stabat medius inter acies
midwife *s* obstetr•ix -icis *f*
midwinter *s* brum•a -ae *f*
midwinter *adj* brumal•is -is -e
might *s* vis *f;* **with all one's —** summā ope; **with — and main** manibus pedibusque
might *intr render by imperfect subjunctive*: **he might say** diceret
mightily *adv* valde
mighty *adj* validissim•us -a -um
migraine *s* hemicrani•a -ae *f;* **to have a — headache** dolere ab hemicraniā
migrate *intr* migrare
migration *s* migrati•o -onis *f*
migratory *adj* migr•ans -antis; **— birds** volucr•es -um *fpl* advenae
mild *adj* mit•is -is -e; *(esp. of weather)* clem•ens -entis; **to grow —** mitescere
mildew *s* muc•or -oris *m*
mildewed *adj* **to become —** mucorem contrahere
mildness *s* lenit•as -atis *f; (of weather)* clementi•a -ae *f*
mile *s* mille *n* passūs; **three —s** tria milia *npl* passuum
milestone *s* milliar•ium -i(i) *n; (fig)* gradati•o -onis *f*
militant *adj* milit•ans -antis
military *adj* militar•is -is -e; **— age** aet•as -atis *f* militaris; **— command** imper•ium -(i)i *n;* **— service** militi•a -ae *f;* **to perform — service** militare
military *s* militi•a -ae *f*
militia *s* militi•a -ae *f* domestica
milk *s* lac, lactis *n*
milk *tr* mulgēre
milky *adj* lacte•us -a -um
Milky Way *s* Vi•a -ae *f* Lactea
mill *s* mol•a -ae *f; (factory)* fabric•a -ae *f*
mill *intr* **— around** circumfundi, tumultuari
millennium *s* mille ann•i -orum *mpl*
miller *s* pist•or -oris *m*
million *adj* decies centena milia *(w. gen)*
millionaire *s* hom•o -inis *mf* praedives
millstone *s* mol•a -ae *f*
mime *s* mim•us -i *m*
mimic *s* imita•tor -toris *m* (•trix -tricis *f)*
mimic *tr* imitari
mimicry *s* imitati•o -onis *f*
mince *tr* concidere; **not to — words** Latine loqui; **without mincing words** sine fuco ac fallaciis
mind *s (most general)* anim•us -i *m; (strictly intellectual)* men•s -tis *f;* **it slipped my — to write to you** fugit me ad te scribere; **I was out of my — when ...** desipiebam mentis cum ... ; **set your — at ease** habe animum lenem et tranquillum; **to bear in —** meminisse *(w. gen)*; **to be in one's right —** compo•s -tis mentis suae esse; **to be of sound —** comp•os -otis mentis esse; **to be out of one's —** a se alienat•us -a esse; **to call to —** cum animo suo recordari; **to change one's —** mentem *(or* sententiam) mutare; **to come to —** in mentem venire, *(coll)* in buccam venire; **to have in —** in animo habēre; **to make up one's — to ...** constituere *(w. inf);* **to show presence of —** schemas non loqui; **what's on your —?** quid tibi in animo est
mind *tr (to look after)* curare; *(to regard)* respicere; *(to object to)* aegre ferre; **— your manners!** mores tuos respice!; **never — what he says** mitte *(pl:* mittite) quod dicit; **to — one's own business** suum negotium agere ‖ *intr* gravari; **I don't —** nil moror; **never —!** sine!
mindful *adj* mem•or -oris
mine *s* fodin•a -ae *f,* metall•um -i *n; (fig)* thesaur•us -i *m*
mine *tr* effodere
mine *adj* me•us -a -um
miner *s* foss•or -oris *m,* metallic•us -i *m*
mineral *s* metall•um -i *n*
mineral *adj* metallic•us -a -um
mineralogist *s* metallorum perit•us -i *m*
mineralogy *s* metallorum scienti•a -ae *f*
mineral water *s* aqu•a -ae *f* mineralis
mingle *tr* commiscēre ‖ *intr* se immiscēre
miniature *s* minuta tabul•a -ae *f*
miniature *adj* minut•us -a -um
minimum *adj* quam minim•us -a -um
minimum *s* minim•um -i *n*
minion *s* clien•s -tis *mf*
miniskirt *s* castul•a -ae *f* brevissima *(or* decurtata)
minister *s* adminis•ter -tri *m; (eccl)* minis•ter -tri *mf,* sacerd•os -otis *mf*
minister *intr* ministrare
ministry *s* ministrati•o -onis *f*
minor *s* pupill•us -i *m,* pupill•a -ae *f*
minor *adj* min•or -or -us
minority *s* minor par•s -tis *f*
minstrel *s* (vagus) fidic•en -inis *m*
mint *s (for making money)* monet•a -ae *f; (bot)* menth•a -ae *f*
mint *tr* cudere
minute *s* temporis moment•um -i *n,* minut•a -ae *f;* **any — now** iam iamque; **in a —** momento temporis; **the — I saw you** extemplo ubi ego te vidi; **this —** *(right now)* iam; *(immediately)* actutum; **to keep —s** acta diurna conficere; **wait a —!** mane dum!

minute *adj (small)* minut•us -a -um; *(exact)* accurat•us -a -um
minutely *adv* minute, subtiliter
miracle *s* miracul•um -i *n*
miraculous *adj* miraculos•us -a -um
miraculously *adv* miraculose
mirage *s* imag•o -inis *f* ficta
mire *s* lut•um -i *n*
mirror *s* specul•um -i *n;* **to look at oneself in the —** se in spectaculo tueri; **to look into the —** in speculum inspicere
mirth *s* hilarit•as -atis *f*
mirthful *adj* hilar•is -is -e
misadventure *s* infortun•ium -i(i) *n*
misapply *tr* abuti *(w. abl)*
misapprehend *tr* male intellegere
misapprehension *s* falsa concepti•o -onis *f*
misbehave *intr* indecore *(or* male) se gerere
misbehavior *s* morum pravit•as -atis *f*
miscalculate *tr* male iudicare ‖ *intr* errare
miscalculation *s* err•or -oris *m*
miscarriage *s* abort•us -ūs *m; (fig)* malus success•us -ūs *m*
miscarry *intr* abortum facere; *(fig)* male succedere
miscellaneous *adj* miscellane•us -a -um
mischance *s* infortun•ium -(i)i *n*
mischief *s* malefic•ium -(i)i *n; (of children)* lascivi•a -ae *f;* **to refrain from doing any —** ab iniuria et maleficio temperare
mischievous *adj* malefic•us -a -um; *(playful)* lasciv•us -a -um
misconceive *tr* perperam intellegere
misconception *s* falsa opini•o -onis *f*
misconduct *s* delict•um -i *n;* **to be guilty of —** delictum in se admittere
misconstrue *tr* perperam interpretari
misdeed *s* delict•um -i *n*
misdemeanor *s* levius delict•um -i *n*
misdirect *tr* fallere
miser *s* avar•us -i *m* (•a -ae *f*)
miserable *adj* mis•er -era -erum
miserably *adv* misere
miserly *adj* avar•us -a -um
misery *s* miseri•a -ae *f*
misfortune *s* infortun•ium -(i)i *n*
misgiving *s* sollicitud•o -inis *f;* **to have —s about** diffidere *(w. dat)*
misgovern *tr* male administrare, male regere
misguide *tr* seducere
misguided *adj (fig)* dem•ens -entis
mishap *s* incommod•um -i *n*
misinform *tr* falsa docēre *(w. acc)*
misinterpret *tr* perperam interpretari
misinterpretation *s* prava interpretati•o -onis *f*
misjudge *tr & intr* male iudicare
mislay *tr* amittere, alieno loco ponere
mislead *tr* seducere, decipere
mismanage *tr* male gerere
mismanagement *s* mala administrati•o -onis *f*
misnomer *s* falsum nom•en -inis *n*
misplace *tr* alieno loco ponere; **confidence in such persons is —ed** is male creditur
misprint *s* errat•um -i *n* typographicum, mend•um -i *n*
misquote *tr* aliis verbis ponere
misquotation *s* falsa prolati•o -onis *f*
misrepresent *tr* detorquēre
misrepresentation *s* sinistra interpretati•o -onis *f*
misrule *s* prava administrati•o -onis *f*
miss *s* err•or -oris *m; (term of respect)* domin•a -ae *f*
miss *tr (to overlook)* omittere; *(one's aim)* aberrare *(w. abl),* non attingere; *(to feel the want of)* desiderare; **to — the mark** destinato aberrare ‖ *intr (to fall short)* errare
misshapen *adj* deform•is -is -e
missile *s* missil•e -is *n*
missing *adj* abs•ens -entis; *(lost)* amiss•us -a -um; **to be —** deësse
mission *s (delegation, sending)* missi•o -onis *f; (goal)* fin•is -is *m*
misspell *tr* perperam scribere
misspend *tr* prodigere
misstate *tr* parum accurate memorare
misstatement *s* fals•um -i *n*
mist *s* nebul•a -ae *f*
mistake *s* err•or -oris *m,* errat•um -i *n; (esp. in writing)* mend•um -i *n;* **by —** perperam; **full of —s** mendos•us -a -um; **to make a —** errare; **you're making a big —** erras perverse
mistake *tr* **to —** *(s.o. or s.th.)* **for** habēre pro *(w. abl)*
mistaken *adj* fals•us -a -um; **to be —** falli; **unless I am —** ni fallor
mistletoe *s* visc•um -i *n*
mistress *s* domin•a -ae *f,* her•a -ae *f; (paramour)* concubin•a -ae *f; (teacher)* magistr•a -ae *f*
mistrust *s* diffidenti•a -ae *f*
mistrust *tr* diffidere *(w. dat)*
mistrustful *adj* diffid•ens -entis
mistrustfully *adv* diffidenter
misty *adj* nebulos•us -a -um
misunderstand *tr* perperam intellegere
misunderstanding *s* falsa opini•o -onis *f; (disagreement)* dissid•ium -(i)i *n*
misuse *s* abus•us -ūs *m;* **that is a — of the term** id est verbum alieno loco adhibēre
misuse *tr* abuti *(w. abl); (to revile)* conviciari
mite *s (bit)* parvul•us -i *m; (coin)* sext•ans -antis *m*
miter *s* mitr•a -ae *f*
mitigate *tr* mitigare
mitigation *s* mitigati•o -onis *f*
mix *tr* miscēre; **to — in** admiscēre; **to — up** commiscēre; *(fig)* confundere

mixed *adj* mixt·us -a -um; *(undistinguished)* promiscu·us -a -um; **— salad** commixta acetari·a -orum *npl*
mixer *s* machin·a -ae *f* mixtoria
mixture *s* mixtur·a -ae *f*
moan *s* gemit·us -ūs *m*
moan *intr* gemere
moat *s* foss·a -ae *f*
mob *s* turb·a -ae *f,* vulg·us -i *n*
mob *tr* stipare
mobile *adj* mobil·is -is -e
mobile home *s* domuncul·a -ae *f* subrotata
mobility *s* mobilit·as -atis *f*
mock *tr* irridēre
mock *adj* mimic·us -a -um; **— death** mimica mor·s -tis *f;* **— sea battle show** naumachiae spectacul·um -i *n*
mockery *s* irrisi·o -onis *f*
mode *s* mod·us -i *m,* rati·o -onis *f; (fashion)* us·us -ūs *m;* **— of life** vitae rati·o -onis *f*
model *s* exempl·ar -aris *n; (of clothes)* vestimentorum monstra·trix -tricis *f (or* monstra·tor -toris *m);* **on the — of** ad simulacrum *(w. gen)*
model *tr* formare; *(e.g., a statue)* fingere; **to — oneself after** imitari
modem *s (comput)* transmodulatr·um -i *n*
moderate *adj (of persons)* moderat·us -a -um; *(of things)* modic·us -a -um; **of — size** modic·us -a -um
moderate *tr* moderari, temperare
moderately *adv* moderate
moderation *s* moderati·o -onis *f*
moderator *s* praes·es -idis *mf*
modern *adj* rec·ens -entis
modest *adj (restricted)* modest·us -a -um, verecund·us -a -um; *(slight)* modic·us -a -um
modestly *adv* verecunde
modesty *s* modesti·a -ae *f,* verecundi·a -ae *f*
modification *s* mutati·o -onis *f*
modify *tr* (im)mutare; *(gram)* adici *(w. dat);* **which noun does "bonus" —?** cui nomini "bonus" adicitur?
modulate *tr* flectere
modulation *s* flexi·o -onis *f*
moist *adj* (h)umid·us -a -um
moisten *tr* (h)umectare
moisture *s* hum·or -oris *m*
molar *s* den·s -tis *m* molaris
molasses *s* sacchari fae·x -cis *f*
mold *s* form·a -ae *f; (mustiness)* muc·or -oris *m*
mold *tr* formare, fingere ‖ *intr* mucescere
molder *intr* putrescere
moldiness *s* muc·or -oris *m*
moldy *adj* mucid·us -a -um
mole *s (animal)* talp·a -ae *f; (sea wall)* mol·es -is *f; (on skin)* naev·us -i *m*
molecule *s* particul·a -ae *f*
molehill *s* **to make mountains out of —s** e rivo flumina magna facere
molest *tr* vexare
molt *intr* plumas ponere
molten *adj* liquefact·us -a -um
mom *s* mamm·a -ae *f*
moment *s* temporis moment·um -i *n;* **at any —** omnibus momentis; **at the —** nunc, isto tempore; **at the very —** ipso tempore; **at the very same —** puncto temporis eodem; **for a —** paulisper; **in a —** momento temporis; *(presently)* statim;; **just a — ago** modo
momentarily *adv* statim
momentary *adj* brev·is -is -e
momentous *adj* magni momenti *(gen, used adjectively)*
monarch *s* rex, regis *m*
monarchical *adj* regi·us -a -um
monarchy *s* regn·um -i *n*
monastery *s* monaster·ium -(i)i *n*
Monday *s* di·es -ei *m* Lunae; **every —** singulis diebus Lunae
monetary *adj* pecuniari·us -a -um
money *s* pecuni·a -ae *f,* argent·um -i *n; (of paper)* monet·a -ae *f* chartacea
money belt *s* ventral·e -is *n; (of cloth)* zon·a -ae *f*
moneychanger *s* numular·ius -(i)i *m*
moneylender *s* faenerat·or -oris *m*
money order *s* (nummorum) mandat·um -i *n* cursuale
mongrel *s* hybrid·a -ae *m*
monitor *m* admoni·tor -toris *m* (·trix -tricis *f); (comput)* monitor·ium -(i)i *n*
monk *s* monach·us -i *m*
monkey *s (also as term of abuse)* sim·ius -(i)i *m,* simi·a -ae *f;* **—s chatter** simii strident
monogram *s* monogramm·a -atis *n*
monologue *s* monologi·a -ae *f*
monopolize *tr* monopolium exercēre in *(w. acc)*
monopoly *s* monopol·ium -(i)i *n*
monosyllabic *adj* monosyllab·us -a -um
monosyllable *s* monosyllab·um -i *n*
monotonous *adj* semper idem (eadem, idem); *(sing-song)* canor·us -a -um
monotony *s* taed·ium -(i)i *n*
monster *s* monstr·um -i *n*
monstrosity *s* monstr·um -i *n*
monstrous *adj* monstros·us -a -um
monstrously *adv* monstrose
month *s* mens·is -is *m;* **on the first of the —** Kalendis
monthly *adj* menstru·us -a -um
monthly *adv* singulis mensibus
monument *s* monument·um -i *n*
monumental *adj (huge)* ing·ens -entis; *(important)* grav·is -is -e
moo *intr* mugire
mood *s* animi habit·us -i *m; (gram)* mod·us -i *m;* **imperative (indicative, subjunctive) —** modus imperativus (indicativus, subiunctivus); **to be in a good —** bonum

animum habēre; **to get over one's —** animum superare
moodiness *s* morosit·as -atis *f*
moody *adj* moros·us -a -um
moon *s* lun·a -ae *f;* **full —** luna plena; **new —** luna nova; **the — is shining** luna nitescit; **time of full —** plenilun·ium -(i)i *n;* **time of new —** novilun·ium -(i)i *n*
moonlight *s* lunae lum·en -inis *n;* **by —** per lunam
moonshine *s (coll)* temet·um -i *n* illicitum
moonstruck *adj* lunatic·us -a -um
Moor *s* Maur·us -i *m*
moor *tr* religare, ancoris retinēre
moor *s* tesc·a -orum *npl*
moose *s* alc·es -is *f*
mop *s* penicul·us -i *m*
mop *tr* detergēre; **to — up** *(mil)* vestigia hostium amoliri
mope *intr* languescere; *(to be in a gloomy mood)* maerēre
moped *s* autobirot·a -ae *f*
moral *adj (relating to morals)* moral·is -is -e; *(morally proper)* honest·us -a -um, prob·us -a -um
moral *s (of story)* document·um -i *n*
morale *s* anim·us -i *m; (of several)* anim·i -orum *mpl;* **— is low** animi deficiunt
morality *s* boni mor·es -um *mpl,* integrit·as -atis *f*
moralize *intr* de moribus disserere
morals *spl* mor·es -um *mpl*
morass *s* pal·us -udis *f*
morbid *adj* morbid·us -a -um
more *adj* plus *(w. gen); (pl)* plur·es -es -ia; *(denoting greater extent of space or time)* amplius: **for — than four hours** amplius quattuor horis; **— money, strength, power** plus pecuniae, virium, potentiae; **— of this at another time** de hoc alias pluribus; **— than** plus quam; **— than enough** ultra quam satis; **and what's —, he even comes into the senate** immo vero etiam in senatum venit
more *adv* magis; **— and —** magis magisque; **— or less** plus minus; **no —** non diutius; **once —** iterum, denuo
moreover *adv* praeterea
morning *s* mane *n (indecl),* temp·us -oris *n* matutinum; **early in the —** bene mane; **from — till evening** a mane usque ad vesperam; **good —!** salve!; **in the —** mane; **the next —** mane postridie; **this —** hodie mane; **to sleep all —** totum mane dormire
morning *adj* matutin·us -a -um
morning star *s* Lucif·er -eri *m*
morose *adj* moros·us -a -um
morosely *adv* morose
moroseness *s* morosit·as -atis *f*
morsel *s* off·a -ae *f*
mortal *adj* mortal·is -is -e; *(deadly)* mórtif·er -era -erum
mortal *s* mortal·is -is *mf*
mortality *s* mortalit·as -atis *f*
mortally *adv* mortifere; **to be — wounded** mortiferum vulnus accipere
mortar *s* mortar·ium -(i)i *n*
mortgage *s* hypothec·a -ae *f;* **to pay off a —** hypothecam liberare; **to take out a —** hypothecam obligare
mortgage *tr* obligare
mortify *tr (to vex)* offendere
mosaic *s* tessellatum op·us -eris *n*
mosaic floor *s* tesselatum et sectile paviment·um -i *n*
mosquito *s* cul·ex -icis *m*
moss *s* musc·us -i *m*
mossy *adj* muscos·us -a -um
most *adj* plurim·us -a -um, plerusque, -aque, -umque; **for the — part** maximā ex parte; **— people** plerique
most *adv (w. verbs)* maxime; *(w. adjectives and adverbs, expressed by superl., or w. adjectives ending in* -ius, *expressed w.* maxime *w. positive);* **— enthusiastically** animosissime
mostly *adv (principally, for the most part)* maximam partem; *(generally)* plerumque
motel *s* deversor·ium -(i)i *n* vehicularium
moth *s* blatt·a -ae *f*
moth-eaten *adj* blattis peres·us -a -um
mother *s* ma·ter -tris *f*
motherhood *s* matris stat·us -ūs *m*
mother-in-law *s* socr·us -ūs *f*
motherless *adj* matre orb·us -a -um
motherly *adj* matern·us -a -um
motion *s* mot·us -ūs *m; (proposal of a bill)* rogati·o -onis *f;* **to make a — regarding** referre (de *w. abl);* **to oppose a —** rogationi obsistere; **to set in —** ciēre, movēre
motion *intr* significare; *(to nod)* innuere
motionless *adj* immot·us -a -um
motivate *tr* concitare
motivation *s* **(for)** rati·o -onis *f (w. gen),* incitament·um -i *n (w. gen);* **— to study** incitamentum studiendi
motive *s* rati·o -onis *f;* **he had a strong —** ratio magna ei erat
motive *adj* mov·ens -entis
motley *adj* vari·us -a -um
motor *s* motor·ium -(i)i *n,* motr·um -i *n*
motor boat *s* scaph·a -ae *f* automaria
motor oil *s* ole·um -i *n* motorii
motorcycle *s* autobirot·a -ae *f*
motorcyclist *s* autobirotari·us -i *m* (·a -ae *f*)
motorist *s* autoraedari·us -i *m* (·a -ae *f*), autocinetist·es -ae *mf*
mottled *adj* maculos·us -a -um
motto *s* sententi·a -ae *f,* dict·um -i *n*
mound *s (round)* tumul·us -i *m; (reaching lengthwise)* agg·er -eris *m*
mount *s* mon·s -tis *m*
mount *tr* conscendere ‖ *intr* ascendere
mountain *s* mon·s -tis *m*

mountain chain *s* mont·es -ium *mpl* perpetui
mountaineer *s* montan·us -i *m* (·a -ae *f*)
mountainous *adj* montan·us -a -um
mountain top *s* culm·en -inis *n* summi montis
mounted *adj (on horse)* equestr·is -is -e
mourn *tr & intr* lugēre
mourner *s* plora·tor -toris *m* (·trix -tricis *f*)
mournful *adj* lugubr·is -is -e
mournfully *adv* maeste
mourning *s* maer·or -oris *m; (outward expression)* luct·us -ūs *m; (dress)* vest·is -is *f* lugubris; **in —** pullat·us -a -um; **to go into —** vestitum mutare
mouse *s (animal & comput)* mu·s -ris *m;* **mice squeak** mures mintriunt
mouse clicker *s (comput)* muris pulsabul·um -i *n*
mousetrap *s* muscipul·um -i *n*
mouth *s* os, oris *n; (of beast)* fau·x -cis *f; (of river)* ost·ium -(i)i *n; (of bottle)* lur·a -ae *f;* **shut your —!** obsera os tuum!
mouthful *s* bucc·a -ae *f*
mouthpiece *s* interpr·es -etis *mf*
movable *adj* mobil·is -is -e
movables *spl* mobil·ia -ium *npl*
move *tr* movēre; *(emotionally)* commovēre; *(to propose)* ferre ‖ *intr* movēri, se movēre; *(to change residence)* migrare; **to — on** progredi
movement *s* mot·us -ūs *m*
movie *s* taeniol·a -ae *f* cinematographica, fabul·a -ae *f* cinematographica; **to go to see a —** ludum cinematographicum visere; **to show a —** taeniolam cinematographicam exhibēre
movie camera *s* machinul·a -ae *f* cinematographica
movie projector *s* proiectr·um -i *n* cinematographicum
movie screen *s* linte·um -i *n* late extentum
movie theater *s* cinemate·um -i *n;* **to go to the —** *(or* **to the movies)** in cinemateum ire
moving *adj* flebil·is -is -e, flexanim·us -a -um
mow *tr* resecare; **to — the lawn** pratulum resecare
mower *s* herbisectr·um -i *n*
mowing *s* herbisic·ium -(i)i *n*
much *adj* mult·us -a -um; **as — … as** tantus … quantus; **how —** quant·us -a -um; **how — does this cost?** quanti hoc constat?; **— less** nedum; **so —** tant·us -a -um; **too —** nimi·us -a -um; **very —** plurim·us -a -um
much *adv* multum; *(w. comparatives)* multo; **very —** plurimum
muck *s* sterc·us -oris *n*
mucous *adj* mucos·us -a -um
mucus *s* muc·us -i *m*
mud *s* lut·um -i *n,* lim·us -i *m*
muddle *tr* turbare; *(fig)* perturbare
muddle *s* turb·a -ae *f*
muddy *adj* lutulent·us -a -um; *(troubled)* turbid·us -a -um
muffin *s* scriblit·a -ae *f*
muffle *tr (to wrap up)* involvere; *(to weaken)* hebetare, diluere; **to — up** obvolvere
muffled *adj* surd·us -a -um
mug *s (cup)* pocul·um -i *n; (face)* vult·us -ūs *m*
mug *tr* mulcare
mugger *s* percuss·or -oris *m*
muggy *adj* humid·us -a -um
mulberry *s* mor·um -i *n*
mulberry tree *s* mor·us -i *f*
mule *s* mul·us -i *m;* **—s bray** muli rudiunt
mulish *adj* obstinat·us -a -um
mull *intr* **to — over** aestuare in *(w. abl)*
multifarious *adj* vari·us -a -um
multiplication *s* multiplicati·o -onis *f*
multiply *tr* multiplicare ‖ *intr* augēri
multitude *s* multitud·o -inis *f; (crowd)* turb·a -ae *f*
mumble *tr & intr* murmurare
mumps *spl* parotit·is -idis *f*
munch *tr* manducare
mundane *adj* mundan·us -a -um
municipal *adj* municipal·is -is -e
municipality *s* municip·ium -(i)i *n*
munificence *s* munificenti·a -ae *f*
munificent *adj* munific·us -a -um
munificently *adv* munifice
munitions *spl* apparat·us -ūs *m* belli
mural *adj* mural·is -is -e
mural *s* pictur·a -ae *f* muralis
murder *s (active in sense)* caed·es -is *f; (passive in sense)* nex, necis *f*
murder *tr* caedere, necare, interficere; **to — a song** lacerare canticum
murderer *s* homicid·a -ae *mf; (of father, mother, or near relative)* parricid·a -ae *mf*
murderous *adj* cruent·us -a -um
murky *adj* caliginos·us -a -um
murmur *s* murm·ur -uris *n*
murmur *tr & intr* murmurare
murmuring *s* admurmurati·o -onis *f*
muscle *s* muscul·us -i *m;* **to pull a —** musculum distorquēre
muscular *adj* musculos·us -a -um
Muse *s* Mus·a -ae *f*
muse *intr* secum agitare
museum *s* muse·um -i *n*
mushroom *s* bolet·us -i *m*
music *s* music·a -ae *f; (of instruments and voices)* cant·us -ūs *m*
musical *adj (of persons, things)* music·us -a -um; *(of sound)* canor·us -a -um; **— instrument** instrument·um -i *n* musicum
musician *s* music·us -i *m* (·a -ae *f*); *(of stringed instrument)* fidic·en -inis *m; (female)* fidicin·a -ae *f; (of wind instruments)* tibic·en -inis *m; (female)* tibicin·a -ae *f*

musket *s* scoplet·um -i *n*
must *s* must·um -i *n*
must *intr* **I — go** mihi eundum est, me oportet ire, debeo ire, necesse est (ut) eam
mustache *s* sub·ium -(i)i *n*
mustard *s* sinap·is -is *f*
muster *tr (mil)* lustrare; *(fig)* cogere; **to — up courage** animum sumere ‖ *intr* coïre
muster *s (mil)* copiarum lustrati·o -onis *f*
musty *adj* mucid·us -a -um
mutable *adj* mutabil·is -is -e
mute *adj* mut·us -a -um
mutilate *tr* mutilare, truncare
mutilated *adj* mutil·us -a -um
mutilation *s* mutilati·o -onis *f*
mutineer *s* seditios·us -i *m* (·a -ae *f*)
mutinous *adj* seditios·us -a -um
mutiny *s* sediti·o -onis *f*
mutiny *intr* seditionem facere
mutter *s* murmurati·o -onis *f*
mutter *tr & intr* mussare
mutton *s* ovillin·a -ae *f*
mutual *adj* mutu·us -a -um
mutually *adv* mutuo, inter se
muzzle *s* capistr·um -i *n*
muzzle *tr* capistrare
my *adj* me·us -a -um; **— own** propri·us -a -um
myriad *adj (innumerable)* sescent·i -ae -a
myrrh *s* myrrh·a -ae *f*
myrtle *s* myrt·us -i *f*
myself *pron (refl)* me; *(intensive)* ipse, egomet; **by —** sol·us -a; **to —** mihi
mysterious *adj* arcan·us -a -um
mysteriously *adv* arcane
mystery *s* myster·ium -(i)i *n; (fig)* res, rei *f* occultissima
mystical *adj* mystic·us -a -um
mystically *adv* mystice
mystify *tr* confundere
myth *s* myth·os -i *m,* fabul·a -ae *f*
mythical *adj* fabulos·us -a -um, fabular·is -is -e
mythological *adj* fabulos·us -a -um
mythology *s* histori·a -ae *f* fabularis, mythologi·a -ae *f*

N

nab *tr* prehendere
nadir *s* fund·us -i *m*
nag *s (horse)* caball·us -i *m; (woman)* oblatra·trix -tricis *f*
nag *tr* obiurgitare
nagging *adj* obiurgatori·us -a -um; *(annoying)* molest·us -a -um
naiad *s* naï·as -adis *f*
nail *s* clav·us -i *m; (of finger, toe)* ungu·is -is *m;* **to cut the —s** ungues resecare; **to drive in a —** clavum figere; **you hit the — on the head** tu rem acu tetigisti
nail *tr* clavīs (con)figere *(w. dat of that to which);* **to — (boards) together** (tabulas) inter se clavīs configere; **to — to the cross** cruci figere
naive *adj* simpl·ex -icis
naively *adv* simpliciter
naiveté *s* simplicit·as -atis *f*
naked *adj* nud·us -a -um; **the — truth** verit·as -atis *f* plana; **with the — eye** sine amplificatione visus
nakedly *adv (fig)* aperte
name *s* nom·en -inis *n; (a significant designation)* appellati·o -onis *f; (good name, reputation)* fam·a -ae *f; (term)* vocabul·um -i *n;* **by —** nominatim; **her — is Maria** Maria appellatur *or* illi nomen est Maria *or* illi nomen est Mariae; **in — only** sub nomine; **family —** cognom·en -inis *n;* **first —** praenom·en -inis *n;* **middle —** nomen; **to have a bad —** male audire; **to have a good —** bene audire
name *tr (to call by a name; to mention by name)* nominare; *(to enumerate)* nuncupare; *(to appoint)* dicere; **named Tiberius** nomine Tiberius; **to be named after one's father** nominari a patre
nameless *adj* nominis exper·s -tis
namely *adv* scilicet
namesake *s* person·a -ae *f* cognominis
nap *s* brevis somn·us -i *m; (of cloth)* vill·us -i *m;* **to take a —** brevi somno uti
nap *intr* breviter obdormiscere; meridiare
nape *s* **— of the neck** cerv·ix -icis *f*
napkin *s* mapp·a -ae *f*
Naples *s* Neapol·is -is *f*
narcissus *s* narciss·us -i *m*
narcotic *s* medicament·um -i *n* psychotropicum
nard *s* nard·um -i *n*
narrate *tr* narrare
narration *s* narrati·o -onis *f*
narrative *s* narrati·o *f,* fabul·a -ae *f,* histori·a -ae *f*
narrator *s* narra·tor -toris *m* (·trix -tricis *f*)
narrow *adj* angust·us -a -um; *(fig)* art·us -a -um; **to have a — escape** aegre periculum effugere
narrow *tr* coar(c)tare ‖ *intr* coar(c)tari
narrowly *adv* vix, aegre
narrow-minded *adj* animi angusti *or* parvi *(gen used adjectively);* **to be —** angusti animi esse
narrowness *s* angusti·ae -arum *fpl*
narrows *spl* angusti·ae -arum *fpl,* fauc·es -ium *fpl*
nasal *adj* ad nares pertin·ens -entis; **to have a — voice** de naribus loqui
nasty *adj (foul)* foed·us -a -um; *(mean)* turp·is -is -e, taetric·us -a -um
natal *adj* natal·is -is -e
nation *s* gen·s -tis *f,* nati·o -onis *f; (organized political community)* popul·us -i *m*

national *adj (expr. by gen of* gens *or* natio *or* populus): **— customs** gentis mor·es -um *mpl;* **— assembly** concil·ium -(i)i *n* populi
nationality *s* civit·as -atis *f*
nationalize *tr* publicare, in usum publicum vertere
native *adj* indigen·a -ae *mf;* **— land** patri·a -ae *f;* **— language** patrius serm·o -onis *m*
native *s* indigen·a -ae *mf;* **he is a — of Athens** Athenis natus est
nativity *s* ort·us -ūs *m,* genitur·a -ae *f*
natural *adj (history, law, daughter, death)* natural·is -is -e; *(not man-made)* nativ·us -a -um; *(innate; opp:* traditus) innat·us -a -um; *(unaffected)* incomposit·us -a -um, simplex
natural disposition *s* indol·es -is *f*
naturalization *s* civitatis donati·o -onis *f*
naturalize *tr* civitate donare
naturally *adv* naturā, naturaliter; *(unaffectedly)* simpliciter; *(of its own accord)* sponte; *(of course)* nempe, utpote
natural science *s* physic·a -ae *f*
nature *s (of a specific thing)* natur·a -ae *f; (universal nature)* rerum natur·a -ae *f; (mostly of persons)* ingen·ium -(i)i *n;* **second —** altera natur·a -ae *f;* **beauties of —** amoenitat·es -um *fpl* locorum
naught *s* nihil; **to come to —** deficere; **to set at —** nihili facere
naughty *adj* improbul·us -a -um; *(saucy)* petul·ans -antis
nausea *s* nause·a -ae *f; (fig)* fastid·ium -(i)i *n*
nauseate *tr (fig)* fastidium movēre *(w. dat);* **to be —ed** fastidire
nautical *adj* nautic·us -a -um
naval *adj* naval·is -is -e
nave *s (archit)* nav·is -is *f*
navel *s* umbilic·us -i *m*
navigable *adj* navigabil·is -is -e
navigate *tr* gubernare **‖** *intr* navigare
navigation *s* navigati·o -onis *f; (as a field)* re·s -rum *fpl* nauticae
navigator *s* guberna·tor -toris *m* (·trix -tricis *f*)
navy *s* copi·ae -arum *fpl* navales; **to have a powerful —** navibus plurimum posse
navy yard *s* naval·ia -ium *npl*
nay *adv* non ita, immo
near *prep* prope *(w. acc); (esp. to denote a battle site)* ad *(w. acc),* apud *(w. acc); (in the vicinity, e.g., of a city)* apud *(w. acc)*
near *adj* propinqu·us -a -um; *(of relation)* proxim·us -a -um; *(neighboring)* vicin·us -a -um *(w. dat),* prope *(w. acc);* **— at hand** in promptu, praesto; **nearer** propr·ior -ior -ius; **nearest** proxim·us -a -um
near *adv* prope, iuxta
near *tr* accedere *(w. acc or* ad *w. acc),* appropinquare *(w. dat or* ad *w. acc)*
nearby *adv* in proximo
nearly *adv* prope, fere, ferme
nearness *s* propinquit·as -atis *f*
nearsighted *adj* myop·s -is
neat *adj (clean, elegant)* mund·us -a -um; *(properly groomed)* compt·us -a -um; *(in good taste)* concinn·us -a -um
neat *interj* optime!
neatly *adv* munde; concinne
neatness *s* munditi·a -ae *f*
necessarily *adv* necessario
necessary *adj* necessari·us -a -um; **consultation is —** consulto opus est; **if it is — for your health** si opus est ad tuam validtudinem; **if it is — for you to stay** si opus est te commorari; **it is —** necesse est
necessitate *tr* cogere
necessity *s* necessit·as -atis *f; (want)* egest·as -atis *f; (thing)* res necessaria *f;* **— is the mother of invention** ingeniosa est rerum egestas
neck *s (of body or bottle)* cerv·ix -icis *f (often pl. without change of meaning); (of animal)* coll·um -i *n;* **— and —** cursu aequo
necklace *s* monil·e -is *n; (of precious stones)* monile gemmatum
necktie *s* focal·e -is *n*
nectar *s* nect·ar -aris *n*
need *s (necessity)* necessit·as -atis *f; (want)* inopi·a -ae *f;* **there is — of** opus est *(w. abl)*
need *tr* egēre *(w. abl, more rarely w. gen),* indigēre *(w. abl); (to require)* requirere; **I (you, we) — money** opus est mihi (tibi, nobis) argento [*abl*]
needle *s* ac·us -ūs *f*
needle *tr* instigare, stimulare
needless *adj* minime necessari·us -a -um; **— to say** quid multa?, quid quaeris?
needlessly *adv* sine causā
needy *adj* egen·s -tis, in·ops -opis
nefarious *adj* nefari·us -a -um
negation *s* negati·o -onis *f*
negative *adj* negativ·us -a -um
negative *s* negati·o -onis *f;* **to answer in the —** negare
neglect *tr* neglegere
neglect *s* neglect·us -ūs *m*
neglectful *adj* neglegen·s -tis
negligence *s* negligenti·a -ae *f,* incuri·a -ae *f*
negligent *adj* neglig·ens -entis
negligible *adj* tenu·is -is -e, lev·is -is -e
negotiable *adj* mercabil·is -is -e
negotiate *tr* agere de *(w. abl);* **to — a peace** de pacis condicionibus agere **‖** *intr* negotiari
negotiation *s* transacti·o -onis *f;* **to settle disputes by —** controversias per colloquia componere
negotiator *s* concilia·tor -toris *m* (·trix -tricis *f*)
Negro *s* Aethiop·s -is *mf*

neigh *intr* hinnire; **to — at** adhinnire
neigh *s* hinnit·us -ūs *m*
neighbor *s (in the neighborhood)* vicin·us -i *m* (·a -ae *f*); *(next door)* proxim·us -i *m* (·a -ae *f*). *(on the border)* finitim·us -i *m* (·a -ae *f*)
neighborhood *s* vicini·a -ae *f*
neighboring *adj* vicin·us -a -um; *(next-door)* proxim·us -a -um
neighborly *adj* benign·us -a -um
neither *pron* neu·ter -tra -trum
neither *conj* nec, neque; **— … nor** neque … neque; **that's — here nor there** *(matter of indifference)* susque deque est
neophyte *s* tir·o -onis *mf*
nephew *s* fratris *(or* sororis) fil·ius -(i)i *m*
nepotism *s* nimius in necessarios fav·or -oris *m*
nerd *s* inconcinn·us -i *m* (·a -ae *f*)
Nereid *s* Nere·is -idos *f*
nerve *s* nerv·us -i *m; (fig)* audaci·a -ae *f;* **to get on one's —s** irritare; **what nerve!** O audaciam!
nervous *adj* trepid·us -a -um
nervously *adv* trepide
nervousness *s* trepidati·o -onis *f*
nest *s* nid·us -i *m;* **to build a —** nidificare
nest *intr* nidificare
nestle *intr* recubare
net *s (also comput)* ret·e -is *n*
net *tr (to catch in a net)* irretire; *(com)* lucrari sumptibus deductis
netting *s* reticul·um -i *n*
nettle *tr* vexare
network *s* op·us -eris *n* reticulatum
neuter *adj (gram)* neu·ter -tra -trum, neutral·is -is -e; **in the —** neutraliter
neutral *adj* medi·us -a -um; **to be —** medium se gerere; neutri parti favēre
neutrality *s* nullam in partem propensi·o -onis *f*
neutralize *tr* aequare
never *adv* numquam; **— mind!** sine! *(pl:* sinite!); **— yet** nondum
nevermore *adv* numquam posthac
nevertheless *adv* nihilominus, tamen
new *adj* nov·us -a -um
newfangled *adj* novici·us -a -um
newly *adv* nuper, modo
newlyweds *spl* coniug·es -um *mpl* recentes
newcomer *s* adven·a -ae *mf*
news *s (no single Latin counterpart exists) (message)* nunt·ium -(i)i *n,* nunt·ius -(i)i *m;* **any — ?** num quidnam novi?; **good —** boni nuntii *mpl;* **I just got — that …** modo mihi nuntiatum est *(w. acc & inf);* **if you have to have any — about** si quid forte novi habes de *(w. abl);* **is there any — ?** numquid novi?; **— came** nuntiatum est; **no other —?** nihil praeterea novi?; **to bring good —** gaudium nuntiare; **when he heard this —** his auditis
news broadcast *s* nunti·i -orum *mpl* (radiophonici, televisifici)
newscast *s* telediar·ium -(i)i *n*
newscaster *s* radiophonic·us -a *or* televisific·us -a annuntia·tor -toris *m* (·trix -tricis *f*)
newspaper *s* act·a -orum *npl* diurna; **morning (evening, weekly) —** acta diurna matutina (vespertina, hebdomadalia)
newsstand *s* tabernul·a -ae *f* actorum diurnorum
New Testament *s* Testament·um -i *n* Novum
New Year *s* ann·us -i *m* novellus; **—'s Day** Kalend·ae -arum *fpl* Ianuariae; **—'s Eve** pridi·es -ei *m* Kalendarum Ianuariarum
next *adj* proxim·us -a -um; *(of time)* insequen·s -tis; **— best** secund·us -a -um; **— day** postridie; **— to** proxim·us -a -um *(w. dat),* iuxta *(w. acc)*
next *adv (place)* proxime; *(time)* deinde, mox
next of kin *spl* proxim·i -orum *mpl*
nibble *tr* arrodere; *(fig)* carpere **||** *intr* rodere; **to — at** arrodere
nice *adj (dainty)* delicat·us -a -um; *(pleasant)* suav·is -is -e; *(cute)* bell·us -a -um; *(exact)* accurat·us -a -um; *(weather)* seren·us -a -um; **it was — of you to invite me** bene me vocas; **to say s.th. nice** aliquid belli dicere
nicely *adv (well)* bene; *(exactly)* subtiliter; *(prettily)* belle
nicety *s* subtilit·as -atis *f*
niche *s* aedicul·a -ae *f; (fig)* loc·us -i *m* proprius
nick *s* incisur·a -ae *f;* **in the very — of time** in ipso articulo temporis
nick *tr* incidere
nickname *s* agnom·en -inis *n*
niece *s* fratris *(or* sororis) fili·a -ae *f*
niggardly *adj* parc·us -a -um
nigh *adj* propinqu·us -a -um
night *s* no·x -ctis *f;* **at —, by —** nocte, noctu; **every —** per singulas noctes; **good —!** bene valeas et quiescas!; **last —** proximā nocte; **late at —** multā de nocte; **— after —** per singulas noctes; **— and day** *(continually)* noctes et dies; **one —** quādem nocte; **on the following —** insequente nocte; **(on) the — before last** superiore nocte; **till late at —** ad multam noctem; **to spend the —** pernoctare
nightcap *s (drink)* embasiocoet·as -ae *m*
nightclub *s* discothec·a -ae *f*
nightfall *s* prim·ae tenebr·ae -arum *fpl;* **at —** sub noctem, primis tenebris; **till —** usque ad noctem
nightingale *s* luscini·a -ae *f*
nightly *adj* noctum·us -a -um
nightly *adv* de nocte

nightmare *s* tumultuosum somn·ium -(i)i *n;* **to have —s** per somnium exterrēri, somnium turbulentum pati
night owl *s (bird)* noctu·a -ae *f; (person)* noctis av·is is *mf*
night watch *s* vigili·a -ae *f; (guard)* vig·il -ilis *m*
night table *s* mensul·a -ae *f* cubicularis
nil *s* nihil *n* [*indecl*]
nimble *adj* agil·is -is -e
nine *adj* novem [*indecl*]; **— times** noviens
nineteen *adj* undeviginti [*indecl*]
nineteenth *adj* undevicesim·us -a -um
ninetieth *adj* nonagesim·us -a -um
ninety *adj* nonaginta [*indecl*]
ninth *adj* non·us -a -um
nip *tr* vellicare; *(of frost)* urere; **— the thing in the bud!** principiis obsta!; **to — off** desecare
nippers *spl* for·ceps -cipitis *m*
nipple *s* papill·a -ae *f*
nitwit *s (sl)* barcal·a -ae *mf*
no *adj* null·us -a -um; **by — means** nequaquam, haud; **he has — more money** non plus pecuniae habet; **— doubt** nempe; **— more than three times** ter nec amplius; **— parking!** cave statuas vehiculum!; **— passing!** cave praeveharis! **— stopping!** ne sistito!; **— trouble** nihil negotii; **— way!** nullo modo!, nequiquam!; **there is — news** nihil novi est
no *adv* non, minime; **— indeed** minime vero; **— longer** non iam; **no, thank you** benigne; **to say —** negare
nobility *s* nobilit·as -atis *f; (the nobles as a group)* nobil·es -ium *mpl*
noble *adj* nobil·is -is -e; *(morally)* honest·us -a -um
noble *s* hom·o -inis *mf* nobilis
nobleman *s* vir! -i *m* nobilis
nobly *adv* praeclare
nobody *pron* nem·o -inis *m;* **some — or other** nescio qui terrae filius
nocturnal *adj* noctum·us -a -um
nod *s* nut·us -ūs *m*
nod *intr* nutare; *(to doze)* dormitare; *(in assent)* annuere
noise *s* strepit·us -ūs *m; (high-pitched)* strid·or -oris *m; (crash)* frag·or -oris *m; (crackling, rattling)* crepit·us -ūs *m; (esp. of people talking loud)* convic·ium -(i)i *n;* **to make —** strepere, crepitare
noise *tr* **to — abroad** evulgare
noiseless *adj* tacit·us -a -um
noiselessly *adv* tacite
noisily *adv* cum strepitu
noisy *adj* strep·ens -entis; *(clamorous)* clamos·us -a -um, turbulent·us -a -um
nomad *s* nom·as -adis *mf*
nomadic *adj* vag·us -a -um
nominal *adj (not in fact)* simulat·us -a -um; *(slight)* exigu·us -a -um
nominally *adv* nomine, verbo
nominate *tr* nominare
nomination *s* nominati·o -onis *f*
nominative *adj* nominativ·us -a -um; **— case** cas·us -ūs *m* nominativus *or* rectus
nominee *s* hom·o -inis *mf* designat·us (-a)
nonchalant *adj* **to be —** aequo animo esse
nonchalantly *adv* aequo animo
noncomittal *adj* anc·eps -ipitis
nondescript *adj* non describend·us -a -um
none *pron* nem·o -inis *m*
nonentity *s* nihil·um -i *n*
nones *spl* Non·ae -arum *fpl (on the 7th day in March, May, July, and October; in all other months, on the 5th day)*
nonessential *adj* supervacane·us -a -um
nonplussed *adj* perplex·us -a -um
nonsense *s* nug·ae -arum *fpl;* **cut out the —!** omitte *(pl:* omittite) nugas!; **—!** nugas!; **no —!** ne nugare!; **that's a lot of —** nugae sunt istae magnae; **to talk —** (nugas) garrire, nugari
nonsensical *adj* inept·us -a -um
noodle *s* collyr·a -ae *f*
noodle soup *s* ius iuris *n* collyricum
nook *s* angul·us -i *m*
noon *s* meridi·es -ei *m;* **at —** meridie; **before —** ante meridiem
noonday *adj* meridian·us -a -um
no one *pron* nem·o -inis *m;* **— else** nemo alius
noose *s* laque·us -i *m; (knot)* nod·us -i *m*
nor *conj* nec, neque, neve
norm *s (rule, standard)* norm·a -ae *f; (average)* med·ium -(i)i *n; (pattern)* exempl·um -i *n*
normal *adj* solit·us -a -um
normally *adv* usitate, ex more; *(usually)* plerumque
north *s* septentrion·es -um *mpl;* **on the —** a septentrionibus; **to face —** in septentriones spectare
north *adv* ad septentriones; **— of** supra *(w. acc)*
north *adj* septentrional·is -is -e; **— of** supra *(w. acc)*
northeast *adj & adv* inter septentriones et orientem solem
northern *adj* septentrional·is -is -e
northern lights *spl* auror·a -ae *f* Borealis
north pole *s* arct·os -i *m*
northwards *adv* (ad) septentriones versus [versus *is an adverb*]
north wind *s* aquil·o -onis *m*
nose *s (as a feature of the face)* nas·us -ūs *m; (of animal)* rostr·um -i *n; (as a function of smell)* nar·es -ium *fpl;* **by a —** aegre, vix; **having a large —** nasut·us -a -um; **to blow the —** emungere; **to have a good — for** festive odorari; **to look down one's — at** contemnere; **to turn up one's — at** naso adunco suspendere *(w. acc);* **under his very —** ante oculos eius

nosebleed *s* sanguinis profluv·ium -(i)i *n* per nares
nostril *s* nar·is -is *f*
nosey *adj* curios·us -a -um; **I don't want to be — but ...** non libet curios·us (-a) esse sed ...
not *adv* non; *(more emphatic and used chiefly before adjs and advs)* haud, *e.g.,* **I do — quite understand** haud sane intellego; *(less than should be)* parum, minus, *e.g.,* **Terentia has not been feeling well** Terentia minus belle habuit; **and —** nec, neque; **— at all** non omnino, haudquaquam; **— bad** non male; **— even** ne ... quidem; **— including** sine *(w. abl),* praeter *(w. acc);* **— including you** te excepto; **— only ... but also** non solum ... sed etiam; **— that** non quod *(w. subj);* **— yet** nondum
notable *adj* notabil·is -is -e
notably *adv* insigniter
notary *s* scrib·a -ae *mf*
notation *s* notati·o -onis *f*
notch *s* incisur·a -ae *f*
notch *tr* incidere
note *s (mark)* not·a -ae *f; (comment)* annotati·o -onis *f; (brief letter)* litterul·ae -arum *fpl; (sound)* son·us -i *m,* vo·x -cis *f; (com)* chirograph·um -i *n;* **a brief —** scriptur·a -ae *f* brevis; **to make — of** in commentarios referre; **to take —s** enotare
note *tr* notare; *(to notice)* animadvertere
notebook *s* libell·us -i *m,* pugillar·es -ium *mpl*
noted *adj (well-known)* not·us -a -um; *(famous)* praeclar·us -a -um
notepad *s* pugillar·es -ium *mpl*
noteworthy *adj* notabil·is -is -e
nothing *pron* nihil, nil; **for —** *(free)* gratis, gratuito; *(in vain)* frustra; **good for —** nequam [*indecl*]; **— but** nihil nisi; **to think — of** nihili facere
notice *s (act of noticing)* notati·o -onis *f; (announcement)* denuntiati·o -onis *f; (sign)* proscripti·o -onis *f,* titul·us -i *m;* **to escape —** latēre; **to escape the — of** fallere; **to give — of** denuntiare
notice *tr* animadvertere
noticeable *adj* insign·is -is -e
noticeably *adv* insigniter
notification *s* denuntiati·o -onis *f*
notify *tr* certiorem facere, denuntiare
notion *s* noti·o -onis *f; (whim)* libid·o -inis *f*
notoriety *s* fam·a -ae *f; (bad)* infami·a -ae *f*
notorious *adj* infam·is -is -e
notwithstanding *adv* nihilominus
notwithstanding *prep expr. by various participles, e.g.,* **notwithstanding the auspices** neglectis auspiciis
nought *pron* nihil
noun *s* nom·en -inis *n;* **proper and common —s** nomina propria et appellativa
nourish *tr* alere, nutrire
nourishing *adj* frugi [*indecl*], salubr·is -is -e
nourishment *s* aliment·um -i *n*
novel *adj* novici·us -a -um, inaudit·us -a -um
novel *s* histori·a -ae *f* commenticia, op·us -eris *n* fabulosum
novelist *s* scrip·tor -toris *m* (·trix -tricis *f*) operis fabulosi
novelty *s* novit·as -atis *f*
November *s* Novem·ber -bris *m or* mens·is -is *m* November; **in —** mense Novembri; **on the first of —** Kalendis Novembribus
novice *s* tir·o -onis *mf; (eccl)* novici·us -i *m* (·a -ae *f*)
now *adv* nunc; *(denoting urgency and emphasis)* iam; *(transitional, esp. in argumentation; never the first word in the sentence)* autem; **even —** etiam nunc; **from — on** ab hoc tempore, iam inde; **just —** *(a moment ago)* modo; **— and then** iterdum; **— at last** nunc tandem; **— ... —** modo ... modo; **— that** posteaquam *(w. indic);* **— what?** quid nunc?; **right —** iam iam; **ten years from —** ad decem annos
nowadays *adv* his temporibus
nowhere *adv* nusquam
noxious *adj* noxi·us -a -um
nozzle *s* ans·a -ae *f*
nuclear *adj* nuclear·is -is -e; **— energy** vis *f* nuclearis
nude *adj* nud·us -a -um
nudge *tr* fodicare
nudity *s* nudati·o -onis *f*
nugget *s* mass·a -ae *f*
nuisance *s* molesti·a -ae *f;* **what a — it is!** quam molestum est!
null *adj* **— and void** irrit·us -a -um; **to be — and void** cessare; **to render —** infringere
nullification *s* abrogati·o -onis *f*
nullify *tr* irritum facere, abrogare
numb *adj* torpid·us -a -um; **to become —** torpescere; **to be —** torpēre
number *s (gram & math)* numer·us -i *m;* **a — of** aliquot; **relying on their superior —s** multitudine fret·us -a -um; **to assemble in large —s** frequentissimi convenire; **without —** innumerabil·is -is -e
number *tr* numerare; **a fleet —ing 1000 ships** classis mille numero navium; **to be —ed among** adnumerat·us -a -um *(w. dat)*
numberless *adj* innumer·us -a -um
numbness *s* torp·or -oris *m; (fig)* stup·or -oris *m*
numeral *s* nom·en -inis *s* numerale
numerator *s* numerat·or -oris *m*
numerical *adj* numeral·is -is -e

numerically *adv* numero
numerous *adj* cre•ber -bra -brum
numismatics *s* doctrin•a -ae *f* nummorum
numskull *s* bar•o -onis *mf*
nun *s* nonn•a -ae *f*
nuncio *s* nunt•ius -(i)i *m*
nuptial *adj* nuptial•is -is -e
nuptials *spl* nupti•ae -arum *fpl*
nurse *s* nutr•ix -icis *f; (med)* nosocom•a -ae *f; (male)* nosocom•us -i *m*
nurse *tr (a baby)* nutrire; *(the sick)* curare; *(fig)* fovēre
nursery *s (for children)* infantium diaet•a -ae *f; (for plants)* seminar•ium -(i)i *n*
nursing home *s* nosocom•ium -(i)i *n*
nurture *tr* nutrire, colere
nut *s* nu•x -cis *f;* **a hard — to crack** *(fig)* quaesti•o -onis *f* nodosa; **he is a —** *(pej)* nuga iste est; **to be —s** a se alienat•us -a esse; **to be —s about** (amore) deperire *(w. acc);* **you're —s** deliras
nutcracker *s* nucifrangibul•um -i *n*
nutriment *s* nutriment•um -i *n*
nutrition *s* nutriti•o -onis *f*
nutritious *adj* alibil•is -is -e
nutshell *s* nucis putam•en -inis *n;* **in a —** *(fig)* paucis verbis
nutty *adj (coll)* vecor•s -dis, baceol•us -a -um
nymph *s* nymph•a -ae *f*

O

oaf *s* stult•us -i *m* (•a -ae *f*)
oak *adj* querce•us -a -um
oak *s* querc•us -ūs *f; (esp. timber)* rob•ur -oris *n*
oar *s* rem•us -i *m;* **to pull the —s** remos ducere
oarsman *s* rem•ex -igis *m*
oasis *s* fertilis regi•o -onis *f* in desertis
oath *s* iusurandum *(gen:* iurisiurandi) *n; (mil)* sacrament•um -i *n;* **false —** periur•ium -(i)i *n;* **to take an —** iurare; *(mil)* sacramentum dicere
oats *spl* aven•a -ae *f*
obdurate *adj* obstinat•us -a -um
obdurately *adv* obstinate
obedience *s* oboedienti•a -ae *f*
obedient *adj* **(to)** oboedien•s -tis *(w. dat)*
obediently *adv* oboedienter
obeisance *s* **to make — to** *(fig)* venerari
obelisk *s* obelisc•us -i *m*
obese *adj* obes•us -a -um
obesity *s* obesit•as -atis *f*
obey *tr* parēre *(w. dat),* oboedire *(w. dat)*
obfuscate *tr* confundere; *(to darken)* obscurare
obituary *s* Libitinae rati•o -onis *f,* denuntiati•o -onis *f* mortis
object *s* obiect•um -i *n,* res, rei *f; (aim)* proposit•um -i *n; (gram) expressed by the verb* adiungi, *e.g.,* **"the man" is the object of the verb** "hic homo" verbo adiungitur
object *intr (to feel annoyance)* gravari; *(to make objections)* recusare; **to — to** aegre ferre; **I do not —, provided that ...** non repugno dummodo ... ; **I do not — to your leaving** non recuso quominus abeas
objection *s* oppositi•o -onis *f;* **if you have no —** si per te licet; **I have no —** per me licet; **to raise many —s** multa in contrariam partem afferre
objectionable *adj* improbabilis -is -e
objective *adj (real)* ver•us -a -um; *(unbiased)* aequ•us -a -um; *(gram)* accusativ•us -a -um
objective *s* proposit•um -i *n*
object lesson *s* document•um -i *n*
obligation *s* obligati•o -onis *f; (duty)* offic•ium -(i)i *n;* **be under —** debēre
obligatory *adj* necessari•us -a -um
oblige *tr (to force)* cogere; *(to put under obligation)* obligare; *(to do a favor for)* morigerari *(w. dat);* **to be —ed to** debēre *(w. inf); (to feel gratitude toward)* gratiam habēre *(w. dat)*
obliged *adj* **I am much — to you for sending me your book** fecisti mihi pergratum quod librum ad me misisti
obliging *adj* officios•us -a -um, commod•us -a -um
obligingly *adv* officiose
oblique *adj* obliqu•us -a -um
obliquely *adv* oblique
oblong *adj* oblong•us -a -um
obnoxious *adj* invis•us -a -um
obscene *adj* obscen•us -a -um
obscenely *adv* obscene
obscenity *s* obscenit•as -atis *f*
obscure *adj* obscur•us -a -um
obscure *tr* obscurare
obscurely *adv* obscure
obscurity *s* obscurit•as -atis *f; (of birth)* humilit•as -atis *f,* ignobilit•as -atis *f; (of speech)* ambiguit•as -atis *f*
obsequies *spl* exsequi•ae -arum *fpl*
obsequious *adj* nimis obsequ•ens -entis
obsequiousness *s* obsequ•ium -(i)i *n*
observable *adj* notabil•is -is -e
observance *s* observanti•a -ae *f; (rite)* rit•us -ūs *m*
observant *adj* attent•us -a -um; **— of** dilig•ens -entis *(w. gen)*
observation *s* observati•o -onis *f; (remark)* notati•o -onis *f*
observe *tr (to watch, keep, comply with)* observare; *(to remark)* dicere
observer *s* specta•tor -toris *m* (•trix -tricis *f*)
obsess *tr* occupare; **I am obsessed by** tot•us -a sum in *(w. abl)*
obsession *s* mentis prehensi•o -onis *f*
obsolescent *adj* obsolesc•ens -entis; **to be —** obsolescere

obsolete *adj* obsolet•us -a -um; **to become —** exsolescere
obstacle *s* impediment•um -i *n; (barrier)* ob•ex -icis *m*
obstinacy *s* obstinati•o -onis *f*
obstinate *adj* obstinat•us -a -um
obstinately *adv* obstinate
obstreperous *adj* tumultuos•us -a -um, clamos•us -a -um
obstruct *tr* obstare *(w. dat)*
obstruction *s* impediment•um -i *n*
obtain *tr* adipisci; *(by asking)* impetrare; **to — pardon** veniam impetrare
obtainable *adj* impetrabil•is -is -e
obtrude *intr* intervenire
obtrusive *adj* molest•us -a -um, importun•us -a -um
obtuse *adj* obtus•us -a -um
obviate *tr* praevertere
obvious *adj* apert•us -a -um; **it was — that** apparebat *(w. acc & inf)*
obviously *adv* aperte, manifeste
occasion *s* occasi•o -onis *f*, facult•as -atis *f; (reason)* caus•a -ae *f; (time)* temp•us -oris *n;* **if the — should arise** si occasio fuerit; **for the —** *(temporary)* ad tempus
occasion *tr* locum dare *(w. dat)*
occasional *adj* rar•us -a -um
occasionally *adv* interdum, per occasionem
occidental *adj* occidental•is -is -e
occult *adj* occult•us -a -um
occupant *s* habita•tor -toris *m* (•trix -tiricis *f*)
occupation *s* possessi•o -onis *f; (employment)* occupati•o -onis *f*, quaest•us -ūs *m;* **what is your —** quem quaestum facis?
occupy *tr* occupare; *(to possess)* possidēre; *(to take by force)* capere; *(space)* complēre; *(time)* uti *(w. abl)*
occur *intr (to take place)* accidere; *(to show up, appear)* nasci; *(to the mind)* in mentem venire; **it occurred to me** mihi in mentem venit; **to — at the right time** competere
occurrence *s* cas•us -ūs *m*, event•us -ūs *m*
ocean *s* ocean•us -i *m*
oceanic *adj* oceanens•is -is -e
ochre *adj* silace•us -a -um
octave *s (mus)* intervall•um -i *n* octavum
October *s* Octo•ber -bris *m or* mens•is -is *m* October; **in —** mense Octobri; **on the first of —** Kalendis Octobribus
ocular *adj* ocular•is -is -e
oculist *s* oculari•us (-a) medic•us -i *m* (•a -ae *f*)
odd *adj (of number)* im•par -paris; *(quaint)* insolit•us -a -um; *(remaining)* reliqu•us -a -um; **how —!** quam ridiculum!
oddity *s* rarit•as -atis *f; (thing)* mir•um -i *n*
oddly *adv* mirum in modum
odds *spl* **— and ends** quisquili•ae -arum *fpl;* **the — are against us** impares sumus; **the — are that** probabilitas est ut *(w. subj);* **to be at — with** dissidēre ab *(w. abl);* **to lay — that not** pignore certare ne *(w. subj)*
odious *adj* odios•us -a -um
odium *s* od•ium -(i)i *n*, invidi•a -ae *f*
odor *s* od•or -oris *m*
odorous *adj* odorat•us -a -um
Odyssey *s* Odysse•a -ae *f; (fig)* it•er -ineris *n* operosum
of *prep (possession) rendered by gen; (origin)* de *(w. abl)*, ex *(w. abl); (concerning)* de *(w. abl); (denoting description or quality) expr. by gen or abl:* **a man — of highest talents** vir summi ingeni *(or* summo ingenio); **one — them** unus de illis *(or* ex illis); **statue of bronze** statua ex aere facta
off *adv* procul, longe; **far —** procul; **to be a long way —** longe abesse; **to be — to** hinc abire ad *(w. acc)*, se hinc agere ad *(w. acc);* **— with you!** aufer te modo!; **well —** *(rich)* bene nummerat•us -a -um; **where are you — to?** quo te agis?
off *prep* de *(w. abl); (said of an island)* ante *(w. acc);* **— (the coast of) Italy** ante Italiam
offend *tr* offendere ‖ *intr* **to — against** violare
offender *s* re•us -i *m* (•a -ae *f*), sons sontis *mf*
offense *s (fault)* offens•a -ae *f*, delict•um -i *n; (insult)* iniuri•a -ae *f; (displeasure)* offensi•o -onis *f;* **to give — to** offendere
offensive *adj* iniurios•us -a -um; *(odors, etc.)* odios•us -a -um, foed•us -a -um; *(language)* malign•us -a -um; *(aggressive)* bellum inferens; **to go on the —** bellum inferre
offer *tr* offerre, praebēre; **to — help to** opem ferre *(w. dat);* **to — violent resistance to** vim afferre *(w. dat)*
offer *s* propositi•o -onis *f; (of marriage)* condici•o -onis *f*
offering *s* don•um -i *n*
offhand *adj* incurios•us -a -um; **— remark** dict•um -i *n* incuriosum; obiter dictum
offhand *adv* confestim, ex tempore; **to say —** de summo pectore dicere
office *s (place of work)* officin•a -ae *f; (pol)* hon•or -oris *m; (duty)* offic•ium -(i)i *n;* **through the good —s of** per *(w. acc);* **to reach high —** ad honorem pervenire
officer *s* magistrat•us -ūs *m; (mil)* sagat•us -i *m* (•a -ae *f*); *(police)* vig•il -ilis *mf*
official *adj* public•us -a -um; **— residence** dom•us -ūs *f* publica
official *s* magistrat•us -ūs *m*
officiate *intr* officio *(or* munere) fungi; *(of a clergyman)* rem divinam facere
officious *adj* importun•us -a -um
officiously *adv* importune
offing *s* **in the —** in promptu
offset *tr* compensare

offshoot *s* surcul·us -i *m; (fig)* consequ·ens -entis
offshore *adj* litore dist·ans -antis
offside *adj* **to be —** seorum stare
offspring *s* prol·es -is *f*
offstage *adj & adv* in postscaenio
often *adv* saepe; **very —** persaepe
ogle *tr* oculis amatoriis tuēri
ogre *s* larv·a -ae *f*
oh *interj* oh!, ohe!; **— boy!** eu!; **— my!** vae mihi!
oho *interj* eho!
oil *s* ole·um -i *n*
oil *tr* ung(u)ere
oil press *s* torcul·ar -aris *n*
oily *adj* oleos·us -a -um; *(like oil)* oleace·us -a -um; **to have an — taste** oleum sapere
ointment *s* unguent·um -i *n*
old *adj* vet·us -eris [*single ending*]; *(aged)* sen·ex -is, aetate provect·us -a -um; *(out of use)* obsolet·us -a -um; *(worn)* trit·us -a -um; *(ancient)* antiqu·us -a -um; **good — days** prisca tempor·a -um *npl;* **of —** olim, quondam; **—er** ma·ior -ior -ius (natu); *(among old people)* sen·ior -ior -ius; **—est** maxim·us -a -um (natu); **to be no more than ten years —** non plus quam decem annos habēre; **to be ten years —** decem annos nat·us -a -um esse; **to grow —** senescere
old age *s* senect·us -utis *f*
old-age home *s* gerontocom·ium -(i)i *n*
old-fashioned *adj* prisc·us -a -um
old lady *s* an·us -ūs *f;* **little —** anicul·a -ae *f*
old maid *s* an·us -ūs *f* innupta
old man *s* sen·ex -is *m*
old woman *s* an·us -ūs *f*
oldster *s* sen·ex -icis *mf*
oldtimer *s* sen·ex -icis *mf*
oligarchy *s* paucorum gubernati·o -onis *f* civitatis; *(members of the oligarchy)* opimat·es -um *mpl*
olive *s* ole·a -ae *f,* oliv·a -ae *f*
olive grove *s* olivet·um -i *n*
olive oil *s* ole·um -i *n*
olive tree *s* oliv·a -ae *f*
Olympia *s* Olympi·a -ae *f*
Olympiad *s* Olympi·as -adis *f*
Olympic *adj* Olympic·us -a -um
omelet *s* lagan·um -i *n* de ovis confectum
omen *s* om·en -inis *n;* **bad —** omen malum *(or* infaustum); **good —** bonum *(or* secundum) omen; **to announce unfavorable —s** obnuntiare; **to get favorable —s** litare
ominous *adj* ominos·us -a -um
omission *s* omissi·o -onis *f,* praetermissi·o -onis *f; (thing)* mend·um -i *n*
omit *tr* (o)mittere, praetermittere
omnipotence *s* omnipotenti·a -ae *f*
omnipotent *adj* omnipoten·s -tis
omniscient *adj* omnia sci·ens -entis
omnivorous *adj* omnivor·us -a -um

on *prep (place)* in *(w. abl); (about, concerning)* de *(w. abl); (ranged with)* ab *(w. abl); (depending, hanging on)* de *(w. abl); (close to, e.g., a river)* iuxta *(w. acc),* ad *(w. acc); (on the side of, in the direction of)* ab *(w. abl):* **— me** meā impensā; **— my side** cum me; **— the east** ab oriente; **— the west** ab occidente
on *adv* porro; *(continually)* usque; **and so —** et cetera; **from then —** ex eo (tempore); **— and —** continenter; **to drink — till daylight** potare usque ad primam lucem; **to go —** pergere; **to move—** procedere
once *adv (one time)* semel; *(formerly)* olim, quondam; **at —** statim, illico, continuo; **for —** demum; **— and for all** semel (et) in perpetuum; **— I get started, I can't stop** quando incipio, desinere non queo; **— more** iterum; **— or twice** semel iterumque; **— upon a time** olim
onceover *s* conspect·us -ūs *m* brevis
one *adj* un·us -a -um; **— day** *(in the past)* quodam die; *(in the future)* aliquando; **at — time** simul; **— ladder** unae scal·ae -arum *fpl;* **to have — and the same wish** idem velle
one *pron* un·us -a -um; *(a certain person)* quidam, quaedam, quoddam; **it is all —** perinde est; **— and the same** unus et idem; **— after another** ali·us -a -um ex alio; **— another** inter se, alius alium; **— by —** singulatim; **— house** unae aed·es -ium *fpl;* **— or the other** alterut·er alterut·ra alterut·rum; **— or two** un·us -a -um et alt·er -era -erum *(w. pl verb);* **—'s own** propri·us -a -um; **— would think that time stood still** putes stare tempus; **only —** unic·us -a -um
one-eyed *adj* lusc·us -a -um
onerous *adj* oneros·us -a -um; *(hard)* difficil·is -is -e
oneself *pron (refl)* se; **by —** per se; **to keep to —** se secludere; **to —** sibi; **with —** secum
one-sided *adj* inaequal·is -is -e
onetime *adj* prisc·us -a -um; *(outdated)* obsolet·us -a -um
one-track mind *s* anim·us -i *m* angustus
one-way street *s* vi·a -ae *f* unici cursūs
onion *s* caep·a -ae *f*
onlooker *s* specta·tor -toris *m* (·trix -tricis *f*)
only *adj* sol·us -a -um, unic·us -a -um, un·us -a -um
only *adv* solum, tantum, dumtaxat; **not — ... but also** non solum ... sed etiam
only-begotten *adj* unigenit·us -a -um
onrush *s* irrupti·o -onis *f*
onset *s* impet·us -ūs *m*
onslaught *s* oppungnati·o -onis *f,* incurs·us -ūs *m*
onward *adv* porro
onyx *s* on·yx -ychis *m*

ooze *intr* manare
opal *s* opal·us -i *m*
opaque *adj* haud translucid·us -a -um
open *adj (not shut)* apert·us -a -um, paten·s -tis; *(evident)* manifest·us -a -um; *(sincere)* candid·us -a -um; *(public)* public·us -a -um; *(of a question, undecided)* inte·ger -gra -grum; **in the — (air)** sub divo; **to be — to** *(e.g, bribery, disease)* patēre *(w. dat);* **to lie —** patēre
open *tr* aperire; *(to uncover)* retegere; *(letter)* resignare; *(book)* evolvere; *(conversation)* exordiri; *(w. ceremony)* inaugurare; *(mouth)* diducere; *(door)* recludere; **to — up a hole** foramen laxare ‖ *intr* patescere, se pandere; *(gape)* dehiscere; *(of a wound)* recrudescere
open-handed *adj* larg·us -a -um
open-hearted *adj* ingenu·us -a -um
opening *s (act)* aperti·o -onis *f; (aperture)* foram·en -inis *n; (e.g., of a cave)* os, oris *n; (opportunity)* loc·us -i *m*
opening night *s* prima nox *f*
openly *adv* (pro)palam
open-minded *adj* docil·is -is -e, liberal·is -is -e
opera *s* melodram·a -atis *n;* **to go to see an —** melodrama visere
opera house *s* theatr·um -i *n* melodramaticum
operate *tr* agere; *(to manage, e.g., a business)* exercēre ‖ *intr* operari; **to — on** *(surgically)* secare
operating system *s (comput)* system·a -atis *n* internum
operation *s (act of doing or working)* effecti·o -onis *f; (surgical)* secti·o -onis *f; (business)* negot·ium -(i)i *n;* **to conduct military —s** res gerere
operative *adj* effica·x -cis
operator *s* opif·ex -icis *mf*
operetta *s* melodramat·ium -(i)i *n*
opinion *s* opini·o -onis *f,* sententi·a -ae *f;* **good — of** aestimati·o -onis *f* de *(w. abl);* **in my —** meā sententiā, meo iudicio, meo animo; **public —** fam·a -ae *f;* **to ask s.o. for his —** aliquem sententiam rogare; **to be of the —** opinari; **to express an —** sententiam dicere; **to form an —** iudicium facere; **to hold the — that** opinionem habēre *(w. acc & inf)*; **to stick to one's —** in sententiā perstare; **what is your — about … ?** quid opinaris de *(w. abl)?*
opinion poll *s* interrogati·o -onis *f* publica, rogati·o -onis *f* sententiarum
opium *s* op·ium -(i)i *n*
opponent *s* adversari·us -i *m* (·a -ae *f*); *(pol)* competi·tor -toris *m* (·trix -tricis *f*)
opportune *adj* opportun·us -a -um
opportunist *s* indaga·tor -toris *m* (·trix -tricis *f*) occasionis
opportunity *s* occasi·o -onis *f,* potest·as -atis *f;* **as — offered** ex occasione; **to give s.o. the — to** alicui potestatem dare *(w. gen of gerundive);* **to take** *or* **get the —** occasionem nancisci
oppose *tr* adversari *(w. dat); (w. words)* contra dicere *(w. dat);* **to — the idea that** adversari ne *(w. subj)*
opposite *adj* advers·us -a -um, contrari·us -a -um
opposite *prep* contra *(w. acc);* versus *(w. acc)* [*often postpositive*]; **— of** exadverso *(w. gen)*
opposition *s* oppositi·o -onis *f; (obstacle)* impediment·um -i *n;* **— party** par·s -tis *f* diversa
oppress *tr* opprimere, gravare
oppression *s* oppressi·o -onis *f,* iniuri·a -ae *f; (harsh rule)* dominati·o -onis *f*
oppressive *adj* praegrav·is -is -e; **to become —** ingravescere
oppressor *s* oppress·or -oris *m,* tyrann·us -i *m*
opprobrium *s* ignomini·a -ae *f*
optic *adj* ocular·is -ie -e
optical *adj* opticus -a -um
optician *s* fab·er -ri *m* opticus
option *s* opti·o -onis *f;* **you have the — either to … or to** tibi optio datur utrum … an
or *conj* vel, aut, —ve; *(in questions)* an; **either … or** *(mutually exclusive)* aut … aut; *(optional)* vel … vel; *(in uncertainty)* sive … sive **— else** alioquin; **— not** annon; *(in indirect questions)* necne
oracle *s* oracul·um -i *n*
oracular *adj* fatidic·us -a -um
oral *adj* verbal·is -is -e, verbo tradit·us -a -um
orally *adv* voce, verbis
orange *s* mal·um -i *n* aurantium; *(color)* col·or -oris *m* luteus
orange *adj (color)* lute·us -a -um, auranti·us -a -um
orangeade *s* mali aurantii poti·o -onis *f*
orange juice *s* aurantii suc(c) ·us -i *m*
oration *s* orati·o -onis *f;* **to deliver an —** orationem habēre
orator *s* orat·or -oris *m* (·trix -tricis *f*)
oratorical *adj* oratori·us -a -um
oratory *s* oratoria ar·s -tis *f*
orb *s* orb·is -is *m*
orbit *tr* **to — the earth** orbem terrae circumagere
orbit *s (astr)* orbit·a -ae *f,* ambit·us -ūs *m;* **to go into —** in orbitam ire
orchard *s* pomar·ium -(i)i *n*
orchestra *s* symphoni·a -ae *f; (part of theater)* orchestr·a -ae *f*
orchid *s* orch·is -is *m*
ordain *tr* decernere, edicere; *(eccl)* ordinare
ordeal *s* discrim·en -inis *n*
order *s (class, arrangement, sequence)* ord·o -inis *m; (command)* iuss·um -i *n; (mil)* imperat·um -i *n;* **to call to —** con-

vocare; **in — to** ut *(w. subj);* **in — not to** ne *(w. subj);* **in short** — brevi; **made to —** proprie fact·us -a -um; **out of —** ex usu, inordinat·us -a -um; *(unruly)* effrenat·us -a -um; **out of the regular —** extra ordinem; **to arrange in —** ordinare; **to draw up an army in — of battle** aciem ordinare
order *tr (to command)* imperare *(w. dat),* iubēre; *(to arrange)* disponere, ordinare; *(to ask for)* postulare, poscere
orderly *adj* composit·us -a -um; *(well behaved)* modest·us -a -um
orderly *s* accens·us -ūs *m; (mil)* tessarari·us -i *m* (·a -ae *f*)
ordinal *adj* ordinal·is -is -e
ordinance *s* edict·um -i *n,* decret·um -i *n*
ordinarily *adv* plerumque, fere
ordinary *adj* usitat·us -a -um, solit·us -a -um; *(everyday)* cotidian·us -a -um; *(traditional, not novel)* tralatici·us -a -um
ordnance *s (mil)* apparat·us -ūs *m* belli; *(artillery)* torment·a -orum *npl*
ore *s* ae·s -ris *n;* **iron —** ferr·um -i *n* infectum
organ *s (anat)* par·s *f* corporis, visc·us -eris *n; (mus)* organ·um -i *n;* **the internal —s** viscer·a -um *npl;* **to play the —** organo canere
organic *adj* pertinen·s -tis ad partem corporis
organism *s* compag·es -is *f*
organist *s* organic·en -inis *m,* organicin·a -ae *f*
organize *tr* ordinare, instituere, componere
organizer *s* auc·tor -toris *m* (·trix -tricis *f*)
organization *s* structur·a -ae *f; (society)* sodalit·as -atis *f*
orgy *s* comissati·o -onis *f*
Orient *s* orien·s -tis *m*
oriental *adj* oriental·is -is -e
origin *s* orig·o -inis *f; (birth)* gen·us -eris *n; (source)* fon·s -tis *m*
original *adj* primitiv·us -a -um, prim·us -a -um; *(one's own)* propri·us -a -um; *(new)* inaudit·us -a -um
original *s* archetyp·um -i *n,* exempl·ar -aris *n; (writing)* autograph·um -i *n*
originality *s* propriet·as -atis *f* ingenii
originally *adv* initio, principio
originate *tr* instituere ‖ *intr* oriri
originator *s* auc·tor -toris *m* (·trix -tricis *f*)
ornament *s* ornament·um -i *n*
ornamental *adj* decor·us -a -um
ornate *adj* ornat·us -a -um
ornately *adv* ornate
orphan *s* orb·us -i *m* (·a -ae *f*)
orphaned *adj* orbat·us -a -um
orphanage *s* orphanotroph·ium -(i)i *n*
orthodox *adj* orthodox·us -a -um
orthodoxy *s* rati·o -onis *f* orthodoxa
orthography *s* orthographi·a -ae *f*
oscillate *intr* ultro citroque se inclinare; *(fig)* dubitare
oscillation *s* ultro citroque inclinati·o -onis *f; (fig)* dubitati·o -onis *f*
ostensible *adj* simulat·us -a -um
ostensibly *adv* per speciem
ostentation *s* ostentati·o -onis *f*
ostentatious *adj* specios·us -a -um
ostracism *s* relegati·o -onis *f; (Athenian custom)* testarum suffragi·a -orum *npl*
ostrich *s* struthiocamel·us -i *m*
other *adj (different)* ali·us -a -ud; *(remaining)* reliqu·us -a -um; *(additional)* ceter·us -a -um; **all the —s** omnes alii *(or* aliae); **every — day** tertio quoque die; **on the — hand** contra; **the —** alt·er -era -erum; **the — day** nuper; **to attend to — people's affairs** aliena curare
other *adv* aliter; **— than** praeter *(w. acc),* extra *(w. acc)*
otherwise *adv* aliter; *(in the contrary supposition)* alioquin; **to think —** aliter sentire; **you didn't do it yet; — you would have told me** nondum id fecisti; alioquin mihi narasses
otter *s* lutr·a -ae *f*
ouch *interj* au!; ei!; oeei!
ought *intr* **I — to** debeo *(w. inf),* oportet me *(w. inf)*
ounce *s* unci·a -ae *f*
our *adj* nos·ter -tra -trum; **— men** nostr·i -orum *mpl*
ours *pron* nos·ter -tra -trum
ourselves *pron refl* nos(met); **by —** per nos; **to —** nobis; **we —** *(intensive)* nosmet ips·i -ae
oust *tr* eicere
out *adv (outside)* foris; *(motion)* foras; **get —!** apage!; **— with it!** *(tell me!)* cedo! *(pl:* cette!) [*an old imperative*]; **the book is not yet —** liber nondum in manibus est; **the fire is —** incendium est extinctum; **the secret is —** arcanum est palam; **to dine —** foris cenare; **to go all —** se extendere
out of *prep (from)* ex *(w. abl); (esp. after verbs denoting material; also selection from a number)* de *(w. abl); (on account of)* ob *(w. acc),* propter *(w. acc); (beyond)* extra *(w. acc),* praeter *(w. acc);* **I am — money** argento expers sum; **if it is not — place** nisi alienum est; **— doors** foris; **— the way** devi·us -a -um; **— wood** de ligno; **to be — country** peregrinari
out-and-out *adv* tot·us -a -um
outbreak *s* erupti·o -onis *f; (disturbance)* sediti·o -onis *f*
outburst *s* erupti·o -onis *f;* **in an — of anger** impoten·s -tis irae
outcast *s* ex·sul -sulis *mf*
outcome *s* event·us -ūs *m*
outcry *s* clam·or -oris *m; (noisy shouting)* convic·ium -(i)i *n*

outdo *tr* superare
outdoors *adv* foris; *(motion)* foras
outer *adj* exter·ior -ior -ius; **— space** intermundi·a -orum *npl*
outermost *adj* extrem·us -a -um
outfielder *s* extern·us -a cust·os -odis *mf*
outfit *s* apparat·us -ūs *m; (dress)* habit·us -ūs *m,* synthes·is -is *f; (costume)* cult·us -ūs *m*
outfit *tr* ornare
outflank *tr* circumire
outflow *s* effluv·ium -(i)i *n*
outgrow *tr* excedere ex *(w. abl),* staturā superare
outing *s* excursi·o -onis *f*
outlandish *adj* absurd·us -a -um
outlast *tr* diutius durare *(w. abl),* durando superare
outlaw *s* proscript·us -i *m* (·a -ae *f*)
outlaw *tr* aquā et igni interdicere *(w. dat),* proscribere
outlay *s* impens·a -ae *f*
outlet *s* exit·us -ūs *m; (for water)* emissar·ium -(i)i *n; (com)* mercat·us -ūs *m;* **electrical —** electrica capsul·a -ae *f* contactūs
outline *s* adumbrati·o -onis *f,* delineati·o -onis *f;* **to draw the — of a thing** primas modo lineas alicuius rei ducere
outline *tr* delineare, adumbrare
outlive *tr* supervivere *(w. dat),* superst·es -itis esse *(w. dat)*
outlook *s* prospect·us -ūs *m; (prospect)* expectati·o -onis *f; (chance)* fortun·a -ae *f*
outlying *adj* extern·us -a -um; *(just outside)* circumiect·us -a -um; *(far out)* remot·us -a -um
outmoded *adj* obsolet·us -a -um, desuet·us -a -um
outnumber *tr* multitudine superare
out-of-date *adj* obsolet·us -a -um
out-of-doors *adj & adv* sub divo
out-of-the-way *adj* devi·us -a -um, remot·us -a -um
outpost *s* stati·o -onis *f*
outpouring *s* effusi·o -onis *f*
output *s* fruct·us -ūs *m; (comput)* exit·us -ūs *m*
outrage *s* iniuri·a -ae *f,* flagit·ium -(i)i *n*
outrage *tr* iniuriā afficere
outrageous *adj* flagitios·us -a -um
outrageously *adv* flagitiose
outrank *tr* dignitate antecedere *(w. dat)*
outright *adj* manifest·us -a -um
outright *adv* prorsus; *(at once)* statim
outrun *tr* cursu superare
outset *s* init·ium -(i)i *n;* **from the —** a principio
outshine *tr* praelucēre *(w. dat)*
outside *s* par·s -tis *f* exterior; *(appearance)* speci·es -ei *f;* **on the —** extrinsecus
outside *prep* extra *(acc)*
outside *adv (position)* foris; *(motion)* foras; **from —** extrinsecus
outside *adj* extern·us -a -um
outsider *s* advem·a -ae *mf; (from abroad)* peregrin·us -i *m* (·a -ae *f*)
outskirts *spl* circumiect·a -orum *npl,* suburb·ium -(i)i *n;* **just on the — of the province** fere ad extremum provinciae finem
outspoken *adj* liberius dic·ax -acis
outspread *adj* patul·us -a -um
outstanding *adj* praest·ans -antis; *(of debts)* residu·us -a -um
outstretched *adj* porrect·us -a -um
outstrip *tr (in running)* cursu superare; *(excel)* excellere *(w. dat of person outstripped)*
outward *adj* extern·us -a -um
outwardly *adv* extrinsecus
outweigh *tr* praeponderare; *(fig)* praevertere *(w. dat)*
outwit *tr* deludere, dolis vincere
oval *adj* ovat·us -a -um
oval *s* ovata form·a -ae *f*
ovation *s* plaus·us -ūs *m; (second-class triumph)* ovati·o -onis *f*
oven *s* furn·us -i *m*
over *adv (excess)* nimis; **all —** *(everywhere)* ubique; **it's all —!** *(coll)* actum est!; **— and —** identidem; **— there** illic, in illo loco; *(motion)* illuc; **when the battle was —** confecto proelio
over *prep (motion over, above)* super *(w. acc); (across)* trans *(w. acc); (in position above)* supra *(w. acc); (w. verbs of motion, denoting space traversed)* per *(w. acc); (w. numbers)* plus quam; **— and above** super *(w. acc);* **— sixty years old** maior (quam) annos sexaginta annos nat·us -a -um; **the water was — a man's head** humanā magnitudine maior erat fluminis altitudo
overabundant *adj* supervacane·us -a -um
overall *adj* tot·us -a -um
overall *adv* in toto
overalls *spl* encombom·a -atis *n*
overawe *tr* (de)terrēre
overbalance *tr* praeponderare
overbearing *adj* superb·us -a -um, insol·ens -entis
overboard *adv* ex nave (in mare); **to go — for** nimis studēre *(w. dat);* **to throw —** iacturam facere *(w. gen of person or thing thrown)*
overburden *tr* nimis onerare
overcast *adj* obnubil·us -a -um, nubilos·us -a -um
overcharge *tr* plus aequo exigere ab *(w. abl)*
overcoat *s* paenul·a -ae *f,* superindument·um -i *n*
overcome *tr* superare, vincere
overconfident *adj* nimis confid·ens -entis

overcooked *adj* percoct•us -a -um
overdo *tr* exaggerare, in maius extollere; **to — it** se supra vires extendere
overdose *s* medicament•um -i *n* supra modum
overdose *intr* medicamentum supra modum (con)sumere
overdraw *tr* **— one's account** amplius scribere quam apud argentariam pecuniae praesto sunt
overdue *adj (money)* residu•us -a -um
overeat *intr* immodice ēsse, heluari
overestimate *tr* maioris aestimare
overflow *s* inundati•o -onis *f*
overflow *tr* inundare ‖ *intr* abundare, redundare
overgrown *adj* obsit•us -a -um; *(too big)* praegrand•is -is -e
overhang *tr* impendēre *(w. dat)*
overhanging *adj* impend•ens -entis
overhasty *adj* praeproper•us -a -um
overhaul *tr* reficere; *(to pass)* consequi
overhead *adv* desuper, insuper
overhead *adj* super•us -a -um, immin•ens -entis
overhead *s (fin)* impens•a -ae *f* negotii
overhead projector *s* proiector•ium -(i)i *n* supracapitale
overhear *tr* auscultare, excipere
overheat *tr* percalefacere
overindulge *intr* immodice indulgēre
overjoyed *adj* **I am —!** *(coll)* immortaliter gaudeo!; **to be — at the sight of a son** ad conspectum filii laetitiā exsultare
overladen *adj* praegravat•us -a -um
overland *adj* per terram
overlap *tr* excedere ‖ *intr (to coincide)* convenire, congruere
overlay *tr* inducere, illinere
overlay *s* tegim•en -inis *n,* obducti•o -onis *f*
overload *tr* nimis onerare
overlook *tr (not to notice)* praetermittere; *(to pardon)* ignoscere *(w. dat),* omittere; *(a view)* prospicere, spectare
overlord *s* domin•us -i *m*
overnight *adv* nocte, per noctem; **to stay —** pernoctare
overpass *s* transit•us -ūs *m*
overpopulated *adj* confert•us -a -um
overpower *tr* opprimere, subigere
overpowering *adj* praeval•ens -entis
overrate *tr* nimis magni aestimare; **to be an —ed man** famā minor esse
overreach *tr* circumvenire
overriding *adj* praecipu•us -a -um
overripe *adj* permatur•us -a -um
overrun *tr* occupare
overseas *adj* transmarin•us -a -um
overseas *adv* trans mare
oversee *tr* praeesse *(w. dat),* procurare
overseer *s* cura•tor -toris *m* (•trix -tricis *f*)
overshadow *tr* obumbrare; *(fig)* obscurare
overshoot *tr* excedere; **to — the mark** ex orbitā ire; **don't — the mark** ne ultra quam est opus contendas
oversight *s (superintendence)* cur•a -ae *f; (carelessness)* incuri•a -ae *f*
oversleep *intr* diutius dormire
overspread *tr* obducere
overstate *tr* in maius extollere
overstep *tr* transgredi
overstock *tr* **to — a shop** tabernam super quam est opus rebus venalibus instruere
overt *adj* apert•us -a -um
overtake *tr* consequi
overtax *tr (fig)* abuti *(w. abl)*
overthrow *s* eversi•o -onis *f*
overthrow *tr* evertere, deicere
overtime *adj* **— work** oper•a -ae *f* subsiciva
overtime *s (in a game)* additicium temp•us -oris *n*
overtly *adv* palam
overture *s (proposal)* condici•o -onis *f; (mus)* exord•ium -(i)i *n* (melodramatis); **to make —s to** agere cum *(w. abl)*
overturn *tr* evertere; **—ed tables** eversae mens•ae -arum *fpl* ‖ *intr* everti
overwhelm *tr* obruere, opprimere; **to be —ed with work** obrui tamquam fluctu, sic opere
overwork *tr* immodico labore onerare; **to — oneself** plus aequo laborare
overwrought *adj* perturbat•us -a -um
owe *tr* debēre
owing to *prep* propter *(w. acc)*
owl *s* bub•o -onis *m;* **— hoot** bubones bubilant
own *adj* propri•us -a -um; **one's —** su•us -a -um, propri•us -a -um
own *tr* tenēre, possidēre; *(to acknowledge)* confitēri
owner *s* domin•us -i *m* (•a -ae *f*)
ownership *s* domin•ium -(i)i *n*
ox *s* bos, bovis *m;* **oxen bellow** boves boant
oyster *s* ostre•a -ae *f*
oyster bed *s* ostrear•ium -(i)i *n*
oyster shell *s* ostreae test•a -ae *f*

P

pace *s (step)* pass•us -ūs *m,* grad•us -ūs *m; (measure of length; five Roman feet)* pass•us -ūs *m; (speed)* velocit•as -atis *f;* **to keep — with** pariter ire cum *(w. abl)*
pace *tr* **to — off** passibus emetiri ‖ *intr* gradi; **to — up and down** inambulare
pacific *adj* pacific•us -a -um
pacification *s* pacificati•o -onis *f*
pacifist *s* imbell•is -is *mf*
pacify *tr* placare
pack *s (bundle)* sarcin•a -ae *f; (of animals, of people)* gre•x -gis *m; (throng)* turb•a

-ae *f;* **— of cigarettes** capsell•a -ae *f* sigarellorum
pack *tr (items of luggage)* colligere; *(a theater)* stipare; *(to fill completely)* frequentare, complēre; *(to compress)* stipare; **to — up the luggage** sarcinas (*or* vasa) colligere
package *s* sarcin•a -ae *f*
packet *s* fascicul•us -i *m*
pact *s* pact•um -i *n;* **to make a —** pacisci
pad *s* pulvill•us -i *m*
pad *tr* suffarcinare
padding *s* fartur•a -ae *f*
paddle *s* rem•us -i *m*
paddle *intr* remigare
paddock *s* saept•um -i *n*
pagan *adj* pagan•us -a -um
pagan *s* pagan•us -i *m* (•a -ae *f)*
paganism *s* paganit•as -atis *f*
page *s (of book)* pagin•a -ae *f; (boy)* pu•er -eri *m; (messenger)* nunt•ius -(i)i *m;* **at the top (bottom) of the —** in summā (imā) paginā
page *tr* arcessere
pageant *s* pomp•a -ae *f*
pail *s* situl•a -ae *f*
pain *s* dol•or -oris *m; (fig)* ang•or -oris *m;* **— in the neck** *(coll)* molest•us -i *m;* **severe —** ingens *or* vehemens dolor; **stop being a —in the neck** molest•us (-a) ne sis; **to be in —** dolēre; **to feel —** dolore affici; **to take —s to** operam dare (ut *w. subj or w. inf);* **to take great —s to** in magno negotio habēre *(w. inf)*
pain *tr* dolore afficere **||** *intr* dolēre
painful *adj* molest•us -a -um; *(bitter, distressful)* acerb•us -a -um; **to be extremely —** dolores magnos movēre
painfully *adv* magno cum dolore
painkiller *s* medicament•um -i *n* anodynum
painless *adj* doloris exper•s -tis
painstaking *adj* operos•us -a -um
paint *s* pigment•um -i *n*
paint *tr & intr* ping•o -ere pinxi pictus
paintbrush *s* penicill•us -i *m*
painter *s* pic•tor -toris *m* (•trix -tricis *f)*
pair *s* par, paris *n; (of oxen)* iug•um -i *n*
pair *tr* coniungere **||** *intr* coïre
pajamas *spl* synthes•is -is *f* dormitoria
palace *s* regi•a -ae *f,* aul•a -ae *f*
palatable *adj* sapid•us -a -um
palate *s* palat•um -i *n; (sense of taste)* gustat•us -ūs *m*
palatial *adj* regi•us -a -um
pale *adj* pallid•us -a -um; **to be —** pallēre; **to grow —** pallescere
pale *s* pal•us -i *m; (enclosure)* saept•um -i *n*
paleography *s* palaeographi•a -ae *f*
palette *s* pictoris tabul•a -ae *f*
palisade *s* vall•um -i *n*
palliative *s* leniment•um -i *n*
pallid *adj* pallid•us -a -um
pallor *s* pall•or -oris *m*
palm *s (of the hand; palm tree; palm branch, as token of victory)* palm•a -ae *f;* **to grease s.o.'s —** aliquem pecuniā corrumpere; **to win the —** palmam ferre
palm off *tr* **(on)** imponere *(w. dat)*
palpable *adj* tractabil•is -is -e; *(fig)* manifest•us -a -um
palpitate *intr* palpitare
palpitation *s* palpitati•o -onis *f*
palsy *s* paralys•is -is *f*
paltry *adj* vil•is -is -e
pamper *tr* indulgēre *(w. dat)*
pamphlet *s* libell•us -i *m*
pan *s* patin•a -ae *f; (for frying)* sartag•o -inis *f*
pan *intr* **to — out** *(coll)* bene evenire
panacea *s* panace•a -ae *f*
pancake *s* lagan•um -i *n*
pandemic *adj* evagat•us -a -um
pandemic *s* evagata pestilenti•a -ae *f*
pandemonium *s* tumult•us -ūs *m*
pander *intr* lenocinari; **to — to** indulgēre *(w. dat)*
panderer *s* len•o -onis *m*
pandering *s* lenocin•ium -(i)i *n*
panegyric *s* laudati•o -onis *f*
panel *s (of wall)* abac•us -i *m; (of ceiling)* lacun•ar -aris *n; (of door)* tympan•um -i *n; (of jury)* iudic•es -um *mpl; (discussion group)* colleg•ium -(i)i *n*
paneled *adj* laqueat•us -a -um
pang *s* dol•or -oris *m*
panic *s* pav•or -oris *m*
panicky, panic-stricken *adj* pavid•us -a -um
panoply *s* arm•a -orum *npl*
panorama *s* prospect•us -ūs *m*
pant *intr* anhelare; **to — after** *(fig)* gestire
pantheism *s* pantheism•us -i *m*
pantheist *s* pantheist•a -ae *m* (•ria -riae *f)*
Pantheon *s* Panthe•um -i *n*
panther *s* panther•a -ae *f*
panting *adj* anhel•us -a -um
panting *s* anhelit•us -ūs *m*
pantomime *s (play; actor)* mim•us -i *m; (actress)* mima -ae *f*
pantry *s* cell•a -ae *f* penaria
pants *spl* brac•ae -arum *fpl;* **hot —** perbreves bracae femineae
pantyhose *spl* tibial•ia -ium *npl* bracaria
papa *s* tat•a -ae *m*
paper *s (stationery)* chart•a -ae *f; (newspaper)* act•a -orum *npl* diurna; **packing —** charta emporetica; **—s** script•a -orum *npl*
paper *adj* chartace•us -a -um
paper clip *s* fibicul•a -ae *f* chartarum
paperback *s* lib•er -ri *m* chartā contectus
paperhanger *s* tapetar•ius -(i)i *m,* parietum exornat•or -oris *m*
paprika *s* capsic•um -i *n*
papyrus *s* papyr•us -i *f*
par *s* **to be on a — with** par esse *(w. dat)*
parable *s* parabol•a -ae *f*

parachute *s* decidicul·um -i *n*
parachute *intr* decidiculo descendere
parade *s* pomp·a -ae *f; (mil)* decurs·us -ūs *m*
parade *tr* ostentare ‖ *intr* in pompā incedere; *(mil)* decurrere
paradise *s* paradis·us -i *m*
paradox *s* paradox·um -i *n*
paragon *s* specim·en -inis *n*
paragraph *s* cap·ut -itis *n*
parallel *adj* parallel·us -a -um; *(fig)* consimil·is -is -e
parallel *tr* exaequare
paralysis *s* paralys·is -is *f*
paralytic *adj* paralytic·us -a -um
paralyze *tr* enervare; *(fig)* percellere
paralyzed *adj* per omnia membra resolut·us -a -um
paramount *adj* suprem·us -a -um
paramour *s (male)* moech·us -i *m; (female)* meretr·ix -icis *f*
parapet *s* plute·us -i *m*
paraphernalia *s* apparat·us -ūs *m*
paraphrase *s* paraphras·is -is *f*
paraphrase *tr* laxius liberiusque interpretari
parasite *s* parasit·us -i *m*
parasol *s* umbell·a -ae *f*
parcel *s* fascicul·us -i *m* (cursualis); *(plot of land)* agell·us -i *m*
parcel *tr* **to — out** dispertire
parch *tr* torrēre
parched *adj* torrid·us -a -um
parchment *s* membran·a -ae *f*
pardon *s* veni·a -ae *f;* **to obtain a —** veniam impetrare; **to grant a — to** *(leg)* absolvere
pardon *tr* ignoscere *(dat); condonare (w. acc of thing & dat of person); (leg)* absolvere; **after being —ed** post impetratam veniam; **— me for what I said** ignosce mihi, quod dixero
pardonable *adj* ignoscend·us -a -um
pare *tr (vegetables)* deglubere; *(the nails)* resecare
parent *s* paren·s -tis *mf*
parentage *s* gen·us -eris *n,* stirp·s -is *f*
parental *adj* parental·is -is -e
parenthesis *s* interclusi·o -onis *f*
pariah *s* sentin·a -ae *f* reipublicae
parity *s* parit·as -atis *f*
park *s* hort·i -orum *mpl* publici
park *tr (a car)* statuere ‖ *intr* vehiculum statuere
parking meter *s* statimetr·um -i *n;* **to put a coin into the —** nummum in statimetrum immittere
parking fee *s* tax·a -ae *f* stativa
parking garage *s* multizon·ium -(i)i *n* stativum
parking lot *s* are·a -e *f* stativa
parking-lot attendant *s* cust·os -odis *mf* areae stativae
parley *s* colloqu·ium -(i)i *n*
parley *intr* colloqui
parliament *s* parliament·um -i *n;* **member of —** parliamentari·us -i *m* (·a -ae *f)*
parlor *s* sessor·ium -(i)i *n*
parody *s* parodi·a -ae *f*
parole *s* fid·es -ei *f* data; **on —** custodiae immun·is -is -e (per bonos mores)
parole *tr* fide interpositā demittere
paroxysm *s* access·us -ūs *m*
parricide *s (murder)* parricid·ium -(i)i *n; (murderer)* parricid·a -ae *mf*
parrot *s* psittac·us -i *m*
parse *tr* proprietates *(w. gen)* describere
parsimonious *adj* parc·us -a -um
parsimoniously *adv* parce
parsley *s* petroselin·um -i *n*
part *s* par·s -tis *f; (role)* part·es -ium *fpl; (duty)* offic·ium -(i)i *n;* **for the most —** maximā ex parte; **in —** partim; **on the — of** ab *(w. abl);* **to act the — of** sustinēre partes *(w. gen);* **to take — in** interesse *(w. dat)*
part *tr* separare, dividere; **to — company** discedere ‖ *intr* discedere, abire; *(to go open)* dehiscere; **to — with** dimittere
partial *adj (unfair)* iniqu·us -a -um; *(incomplete)* manc·us -a -um, per partes
partiality *s* fav·or -oris *m; (unfairness)* iniquit·as -atis *f*
partially *adv* aliquā ex parte, partim
participant *s* parti·ceps -cipis *mf*
participate *intr* **to — in** interesse *(w. dat),* particeps esse *(w. gen)*
participation *s* societ·as -atis *f*
participial *adj (gram)* participial·is -is -e
participle *s* particip·ium -(i)i *n;* **future —** futuri temporis participium; **perfect —** praeteriti temporis participium; **present —** praesentis temporis participium
particle *s (faint trace)* vestig·ium -(i)i *n; (tibit)* particul·a -ae *f; (gram)* particul·a -ae *f*
particular *adj (special)* praecipu·us -a -um; *(fussy)* fastidios·us -a -um; **in —** potissimum
particularly *adv* praecipue, praesertim
particularize *tr* exsequi, enumerare
particulars *spl* singul·a -orum *npl*
parting *s* discess·us -ūs *m*
partisan *s* fau·tor -toris *m* (·trix -tricis *f; (guerilla)* factiosus armig·er -eri *m*
partition *s* partiti·o -onis *f; (between rooms)* pari·es -etis *m; (compartment)* loculament·um -i *n; (section)* pars, partis *f*
partition *tr* dividere
partitive *adj (gram)* partitiv·us -a -um
partly *adv* partim
partner *s* soc·ius -(i)i *m,* soci·a -ae *f,* partic·eps -ipis *mf; (in office)* colleg·a -ae *mf; (in marriage)* con·iu(n)x -iugis *mf*

partnership *s* societ·as -atis *f;* **to dissolve a —** dissociari; **to form a —** societatem inire
partridge *s* perd·ix -icis *mf*
party *s (for entertainment)* conviv·ium -(i)i *n; (side)* pars, partis *f; (pol)* facti·o -onis *f,* part·es -ium *fpl; (detachment)* man·us -ūs *f;* **opposite —** partes diversae; **to give a —** convivium dare; **to join a —** parti se adiugere; **to throw a —** convivium agitare
pass *s (defile)* angusti·ae -arum *fpl,* salt·us -ūs *m; (basketball, football)* follis transmiss·us -ūs *m; (free ticket)* tesser·a -ae *f* gratuita; **things have come to such a — that** eo rerum ventum erat ut *(w. subj)*
pass *tr (to go by)* praeterire; *(exceed)* excedere; *(to approve)* probare; *(time)* degere; *(a law)* perferre; *(by the assembly)* iubēre; *(basketball, football, lacrosse)* transmittere; **he tried to — himself off for Philip** se Philippum ferebat; **— me the vegetables** porrige mihi holera; **to — around** circumferre; **to — down** tradere; **to — a test** probationem sustinere; **to — out** distribuere; **to — sentence** ius dicere; **to — the test** approbari; **to — up** praetermittere ‖ *intr (of time)* transire; *(to walk by)* praeterire; *(to ride by)* praetervehi; **to come to —** fieri, evenire; **to let —** praetermittere; **to let an army — through the country** exercitum per fines transmittere; **to — away** *(to die)* perire, decedere; *(to come to an end)* transire; **to — by** *(e.g.,* **a park)** praeterire (hortos); *(in a carriage or ship)* praetervehi; **to — for** habēri; **to — on** *(to go forward)* pergere; *(to another subject)* transire; *(to die)* perire; **to — out** collabi, intermori; **to — over** *(e.g., of a storm)* transire; *(to make no mention of)* praeterire; **to — over the fact that** mittere quod *(w. subj);* **to — through** *(e.g.,* **a town)** transire; *(of an arrow, spear)* ire per *(w. acc);* **to — through enemy lines** per hostes vadere
passable *adj (of road)* pervi·us -a -um; *(tolerable)* tolerabil·is -is -e
passably *adv* tolerabiliter
passage *s (act)* transit·us -ūs *m; (by water)* traiecti·o -onis *f; (road)* it·er -ineris *n; (in a book)* loc·us -i *m (pl:* loc·i -orum); **to allow anyone a — through the province** alicui transitum dare per provinciam
passbook *s (bank book)* argentariae libell·us -i *m*
passenger *s* vec·tor -toris *m* (·trix -tricis *f)*
passenger train *s* tram·en -inis *n* commune
passer-by *s* praeter·iens -euntis *mf*
passing *s* obit·us -ūs *m;* **no —!** cave praeveharis!
passion *s (strong desire of any kind, esp. lust)* cupidit·as -atis *f; (strong emotion)* animi permoti·o -onis *f; (lust)* libid·o -inis *f; (violent anger)* iracundi·a -ae *f;* **to fly into a —** exardescere iracundiā et stomacho
passionate *adj* ard·ens -entis; *(given to bursts of anger)* iracund·us -a -um
passionately *adv* ardenter; iracunde
passive *adj* toler·ans -antis, iner·s -tis; *(gram)* passiv·us -a -um
passively *adv* toleranter; *(gram)* passive
Passover *s* Pascha [*indecl*], Pasch·a -atis *n*
passport *s* (commeatūs) diplom·a -atis *n*
password *s (also comput)* tesser·a -ae *f*
past *adj* praeterit·us -a -um; *(immediately preceding)* proxim·us -a -um, super·ior -ior -ius; **— participle** praeteriti temporis particip·ium -(i)i *n*
past *s* praeterit·um -i *n; (past tense)* praeteritum temp·us -oris *n*
past *prep* praeter *(w. acc)*
pasta *s* collyr·a -ae *f*
paste *s* glut·en -ineris *n*
paste *tr* glutinare; *(to strike)* ferire
pasteboard *s* chart·a -ae *f* crassa
pastime *s* oblectament·um -i *n;* **by way of —** oblectamenti causā
pastoral *adj (poetry)* bucolic·us -a -um; *(of shepherds)* pastoral·is -is -e
pastoral *s* bucolic·um -i *n*
pastry *s* crustul·a -orum *npl;* **pastries** cuppedi·a -orum *npl*
pastry shop *s* cuppedinari·a -ae *f*
pasture *s (grazing land)* pascu·um -i *n; (feeding of animals)* past·us -ūs *m*
pasture *tr* pascere ‖ *intr* pasci; **to go out to —** pastum ire
pat *s* plag·a -ae *f* lenis; **— on the back** *(fig)* approbati·o -onis *f*
pat *tr* demulcēre
patch *s* pann·us -i *m*
patch *tr* resarcire; **to — up** *(fig)* refovēre
patchwork *s* cent·o -onis *m;* **to make —** *(out of old clothes)* centones facere
patent *adj* manifest·us -a -um
patent *s* ius, iuris *n* praecipuum
patently *adv* manifesto
paternal *adj* patern·us -a -um; *(like a father)* patri·us -a -um
paternity *s* paternit·as -atis *f*
path *s* semit·a -ae *f,* call·is -is *m*
pathetic *adj* flebil·is -is -e
pathless *adj* invi·us -a -um
pathos *s* vis *f* ad misericordiam movendam
pathway *s* semit·a -ae *f;* **the — of life** vitae semita
patience *s* patienti·a -ae *f*
patient *adj* pati·ens -entis
patient *s* ae·ger -gri *m* (·gra -grae *f)*
patiently *adv* aequo animo, patienter
patriarch *s* patriarch·a -ae *m*
patriarchal *adj* patriarchic·us -a -um

patrician *adj* patrici·us -a -um
patrician *s* patric·ius -(i)i *m*
patrimony *s* patrimon·ium -(i)i *n*
patriot *s* am·ans -antis *mf* patriae
patriotic *adj* am·ans -antis patriae
patriotism *s* am·or -oris *m* patriae
patrol *s* circuitor·es -um *mpl*
patrol *tr & intr* circumire
patron *s* patron·us -i *m*
patronage *s* patrocin·ium -(i)i *n*
patroness *s* patron·a -ae *f*
patronize *tr* favēre *(w. dat); (a shop)* frequentare
patter *s* crepit·us -ūs *m;* **the — of feet** mollis puls·us -ū *m* pedum
pattern *s* exempl·ar -aris *n; (of weaving)* text·us -ūs *m;* **— of behavior** indol·es -is *f*
pattern *tr* **— after** imitari
paucity *s* paucit·as -atis *f*
paunch *s* ven·ter -tris *m* obesus; **to have a —** ventre obeso esse
pauper *s* pau·per -eris *mf*
pause *s* paus·a -ae *f; (break)* intercaped·o -inis *f,* intermissi·o -onis *f; (music)* caesur·a -ae *f*
pause *intr* subsistere; *(to halt)* insistere; **to — in speaking** in dicendo subsistere
pave *tr* sternere; **to — the way to** *(fig)* viam facere ad *(w. acc)*
pavement *s* paviment·um -i *n*
pavilion *s* tentor·ium -(i)i *n*
paving stone *s* sax·um -i *n* quadratum
paw *s* pe·s -dis *m*
paw *tr* pedibus pulsare
pawn *s* pign·us -oris *n*
pawn *tr* pignerare
pawnbroker *s* pignerna·tor -toris *m* (·trix -tricis *f*)
pay *s* merc·es -edis *f; (mil)* stipend·ium -(i)i *n*
pay *tr (money)* solvere; *(in full)* persolvere, pendere; *(a person)* pecuniam (mercedem) solvere *(dat); (mil)* stipendium numerare *(w. dat);* **to — back** restituere; *(to avenge)* vindicare; **to — in cash** numerare; **to — off a debt** nomen exsolvere, aes alienum persolvere; **to — on time** ad tempus *or* ad diem dictam solvere; **to — out (money) to** denumerare (nummos) *(w. dat);* **to — s.o. a compliment** aliquem laudare; **to — s.o. a visit** aliquem invisere; **to — (s.o.) for** solvere *(w. acc of thing and dat of person);* **to — respects to** salutare; **to — the penalty** poenam dare **‖** *intr* **it —s to ...** operae pretium est *(w. inf);* **to — for** *(merchandise)* emere; *(a misdeed)* poenas dare ob *(w. acc)*
payable *adj* solvend·us -a -um
payday *s* di·es -ei *f* pecuniae
paymaster *s* dispensat·or -oris *m*
payment *s (act)* soluti·o -onis *f; (sum of money)* pensi·o -onis *f*
pay phone *s* telephon·um -i *n* nummarium
pea *s* pis·um -i *n*
peace *s* pa·x -cis *f;* **in a state of —** pacat·us -a -um; **in — and in war** domi et militiae *(or* in militiā); **to break the —** pacem frangere; **to bring about — between** pacem conciliare inter *(w. acc);* **to conclude — on these terms** pacem his legibus constitŭere; **to conduct — negotiations with s.o.** cum aliquo de pace agere; **to hold one's —** tacēre; **to live in —** pacem agitare; **to make — with** pacificare cum *(w. abl)*
peaceably *adv* cum bonā pace
peaceful *adj* tranquill·us -a -um
peacefully *adv* tranquille, cum bonā pace
peace-loving *adj* pacis am·ans -antis
peacemaker *s* pacifica·tor -toris *m* (·trix -tricis *f*)
peace offering *s* placam·en -inis *n*
peacetime *s* ot·ium -(i)i *n*
peach *s* persic·um -i *n*
peach *adj (color)* punice·us -a -um
peacock *s* pav·o -onis *mf*
peak *s* vert·ex -icis *m; (of a mountain)* cacum·en -inis *n*
peal *s (of thunder)* frag·or -oris *m; (of bells)* concent·us -ūs *m*
peal *intr* resonare
peanut *s* arach·is -idis *f* hypogea
peanut butter *s* butyr·um -i *n* ex arachidibus
peanut butter sandwich *s* pastill·um -i *n* butyro ex arachidibus fartum
pear *s* pir·um -i *n*
pearl *s* margarit·a -ae *f*
pearl earrings *spl* inaur·es -ium *fpl* ex margaritis
pearl necklace *s* monil·e -is *n* ex margaritis
pearly *adj* gemme·us -a -um
pear tree *s* pir·us -i *f*
peasant *s* rustic·us -i *m* (·a -ae *f*)
peasantry *s* agrest·es -ium *mpl*
pea soup *s* ius, iuris *n* ex pisis
pebble *s* calcul·us -i *m*
peck *s* mod·ius -(i)i *m; (perfunctory kiss)* basiol·um -i *n*
peck *tr* vellicare
peculiar *adj* peculiar·is -is -e; *(belonging to one person or thing only)* propri·us -a -um; *(odd)* inusitat·us -a -um, absurd·us -a -um
peculiarity *s* propriet·as -atis *f*
pedagogue *s* paedagog·us -i *m*
pedal *s* pedal·e -is *n*
pedant *s* hom·o -inis *mf* moros·us (-a)
pedantic *adj* moros·us -a -um
pedantry *s* morosit·as -atis *f*
peddle *tr* venditare
peddler *s* instit·or -oris *m;* **door-to-door —** qui *(or* quae) merces suas ostiatim venditat

pedestal *s* bas·is -is *f*
pedestrian *adj* pedes·ter -tris -tre; **— crossing** transit·us -ūs *m* peditum
pedestrian *s* ped·es -itis *mf*
pedigree *s* stemm·a -atis *n*
pediment *s* fastig·ium -(i)i *n*
pedophile *s* pedica·tor -toris *m* (·a -ae *f*)
pee *intr (coll)* facere (*for* aquam facere)
peel *s* cut·is -is *f; (rind, thick skin)* cor·ium -(i)i *n;* **apple —** mali cutis; **orange peel** corium mali aurantii
peel *tr* resecare cutem *(w. gen)*
peep *s* conspect·us -ūs *m* fugax
peep *intr* furtim conspicere
peephole *s* conspicill·um -i *n*
peer *s* par, paris *mf*
peer *intr* **to — at** intuēri
peerless *adj* incomparabil·is -is -e
peevish *adj* stomachos·us -a -um
peevishly *adv* stomachose
peg *s* paxill·us -i *m*
pelican *s* pelican·us -i *m,* onocrotal·us -i *m*
pellet *s* globul·us -i *m*
pell-mell *adv* turbate
pelt *s* pell·is -is *f*
pelt *tr (to hurl)* conicere; **to — s.o. with stones** aliquem lapidare
pen *s* calam·us -i *m; (enclosure)* saept·um -i *n; (for pigs)* suil·e -is *n; (for sheep)* ovil·e -is *n*
pen *tr* scribere; **to — in** includere, saepire
penal *adj* poenal·is -is -e
penalize *tr* mul(c)tare
penalty *s* poen·a -ae *f; (fine)* mul(c)t·a -ae *f;* **to pay the —** poenas dare *or* (per)solvere
penance *s* satisfacti·o -onis *f; (eccl)* expiati·o -onis *f;* **to do — for** expiare
pencil *s* graph·is -idis *f*
pencil sharpener *s* instrument·um -i *n* cuspidarium
pendant *s* ornament·um -i *n* pensile
pending *adj* suspens·us -a -um; *(leg)* sub iudice
pending *prep* inter *(acc)*
pendulum *s* librament·um -i *n*; *(of clock)* oscill·ium -(i)i *n*
penetrate *tr* penetrare ad *(w. acc)* **||** *intr* penetrare
penetrating *adj (cold)* acut·us -a -um *(keen-sighted)* perspic·ax -acis
penetration *s* introit·us -ūs *m;* aci·es -ei *f* mentis
penguin *s* aptenodyt·es -is *f*
peninsula *s* paeninsul·a -ae *f*
penitence *s* paenitenti·a -ae *f*
penitent *adj* paenit·ens -entis
penitentiary *s* ergastul·um -i *n*
penknife *s* cultell·us -i *m*
penmanship *s* man·us -ūs *f*
pennant *s* vexill·um -i *n*
penniless *adj* in·ops -opis
penny *s* as, assis *m*
pension *s* annu·a -orum *npl*
pensive *adj* meditabund·us -a -um
pentathlon *s* pentathl·um -i *n;* **to win the —** pentathlo vincere
penult *s* paenultima syllab·a -ae *f*
penultimate *adj* paenultim·us -a -um
people *s* homin·es -um *mpl; (as political entity)* popul·us -i *m; (of a country)* gen·s -tis *f;* **common —** vulg·us -i *n;* **— say** aiunt; **— who say** qui aiunt, qui dicunt
people *tr* frequentare
pep *s* alacrit·as -atis *f*
pep rally *s* convent·us -ūs *m* hortatorius
pep talk *s* conti·o -onis *f;* **to give a —** contionem habēre
pepper *s* pip·er -eris *n*
pepper *tr* pipere condire; *(w. blows)* verberare
peppermint *s* menth·a -ae *f*
pepper shaker *s* piperin·um -i *n*
perceive *tr* percipere
percent *s* per centum, centesim·a -ae *f*
percentage *s* porti·o -onis *f*
perceptible *adj* percipiend·us -a -um
perceptibly *adv* sensim
perch *s (for birds)* pertic·a -ae *f; (fish)* perc·a -ae *f*
perch *intr* **(on)** insidēre *(w. dat)*
perchance *adv* forte
percolate *tr* percolare **||** *intr* permanare
percussion *s* percuss·us -ūs *m*
percussion instrument *s* percussionale instrument·um -i *n* musicum
perdition *s* interit·us -ūs *m*
peremptory *adj* arrogan·s -tis
perennial *adj* perenn·is -is -e
perfect *adj* perfect·us -a -um; *(utter, total)* tot·us -a -um; **the perfect tense** tempus praeteritum perfectum; **to enjoy almost — health** inlaesā prope valetudine uti
perfect *s (gram)* praeterit·um perfect·um -i *n*
perfect *tr* perficere
perfection *s (act)* perfecti·o -onis *f; (excellence)* summ·a -ae *f*
perfectly *adv* perfecte; *(totally)* plane
perfidious *adj* perfid·us -a -um
perfidy *s* perfidi·a -ae *f*
perforate *tr* perforare
perforation *s* foram·en -inis *n*
perform *tr* perficere, peragere; *(duty)* fungi *(w. abl),* praestare; *(theat)* agere
performance *s* perfuncti·o -onis *f; (work)* op·us -eris *n; (of a play)* acti·o -onis *f; (play)* fabul·a -ae *f*
performer *s* ac·tor -toris *m* (·trix -tricis *f*); *(theat)* histri·o -onis *mf*
perfume *s* od·or -oris *m,* ungent·um -i *n*
perfume *tr* odoribus imbuere
perfunctorily *adv* parum diligenter
perfunctory *adj* parum dilig·ens -entis
perhaps *adv* fortasse, forsitan
peril *s* pericul·um -i *n*

perilous *adj* periculos•us -a -um
perilously *adv* periculose
perimeter *s* circinati•o -onis *f; (geom)* perimetr•os -i *f*
period *s (span of time, class period)* spat•ium -(i)i *n; (chronological)* temp•us -oris *n; (punctuation mark)* punct•um -i *n; (complete phrase or sentence)* period•us -i *m,* ambit•us -ūs *m;* **I'm not going. period!** non ibo, dixi!; **— of life** aet•as -atis *f;* **over a long — of time** in diuturno spatio
periodic *adj* recurr•ens -entis
periodical *s* commentar•ium -(i)i *n*
periodically *adv* temporibus statis
periphery *s* peripheri•a -ae *f*
periphrastic *adj* periphrastic•us -a -um
perish *intr* interire, perire
perishable *adj* quae cito corrumpuntur
peristyle *s* peristyl•ium -(i)i *n*
perjure *tr* **to — oneself** periurare
perjured *adj* periur•us -a -um
perjury *s* periur•ium -(i)i *n;* **to commit —** periurare
perk up *tr* erigere; **to — the spirits** animum demissum erigere **||** *intr* **to —** reviviscere
perky *adj* ala•cer -cris -cre
permanence *s* stabilit•as -atis *f*
permanent *adj* perpetu•us -a -um
permanently *adv* perpetuo
permeable *adj* pervi•us -a -um
permeate *tr* permanare, permeare
permissible *adj* **it is — for me to** licet mihi ire *(or* licet eam)
permission *s* permiss•um -i *n;* **to grant — to** permittere *(w. dat);* **with your —** bonā tuā veniā; **without your father's —** invito patre; **you have my — to leave** per me licet ut abeas
permit *tr* permittere *(w. dat)*
permutation *s* permutati•o -onis *f*
pernicious *adj* pernicios•us -a -um; *(deadly)* letal•is -is -e
perniciously *adv* perniciose
peroration *s* perorati•o -onis *f*
perpendicular *adj* perpendicular•is -is -e
perpendicular *s* line•a -ae *f* perpendicularis
perpendicularly *adj* ad perpendiculuum
perpetrate *tr* perficere, peragere
perpetrator *s* auc•tor -toris *m* (•trix -tricis *f)*
perpetual *adj* perpetu•us -a -um
perpetually *adv* perpetuo
perpetuate *tr* perpetuare
perpetuity *s* perpetuit•as -atis *f*
perplex *tr* distrahere, turbare
perplexing *adj* perplex•us -a -um
perplexity *s* dubitati•o -onis *f,* perturbati•o -onis *m*
persecute *tr* insectari
persecution *s* insectati•o -onis *f*
persecutor *s* insecta•tor -toris *m* (•trix -tricis *f)*
perseverance *s* perseveranti•a -ae *f*
persevere *intr* perseverare, perstare
persevering *adj* persever•ans -antis
persist *intr* perseverare, perstare
persistence *s* perseveranti•a -ae *f*
persistent *adj* pertin•ax -acis
persistently *adv* pertinaciter
person *s* hom•o -inis *mf,* person•a -ae *f; (gram)* persona *f;* **in —** ips•e -a -um
personable *adj* com•is -is -e
personage *s* hom•o -inis *mf* praestabilis
personal *adj* privat•us -a -um; *(gram, leg)* personal•is -is -e; **— appearance** form•a -ae *f* et habit•us -ūs *m;* **— computer** ordinatr•um -i *n* domesticum; **— finances** res, rei *f* familiaris
personality *s* indol•es -is *f*
personally *adv rendered by* ips•e -a -um
personification *s* prosopopei•a -ae *f*
personify *tr (inanimate objects)* vitam sensumque tribuere *(dat);* **to — evil** malum in personam suam constituere
personnel *s* operari•i -orum *mpl;* soci•i -orum *mpl*
perspective *s (viewpoint)* conspect•us -ūs *m* animi; *(in drawing)* scaenographi•a -ae *f*
perspiration *s (sweating)* sudati•o -onis *f; (sweat)* sud•or -oris *m*
perspire *intr* sudare
persuade *tr* persuadēre *(w. dat)*
persuasion *s* persuasi•o -onis *f*
persuasive *adj* persuasibil•is -is -e
persuasively *adv* persuabiliter
pert *adj* proc•ax -acis
pertain *intr* **(to)** pertinēre (ad *w. acc)*
pertinence *s* congruenti•a -ae *f*
pertinent *adj* apposit•us -a -um; **to be —** ad rem pertinēre
perturb *tr* perturbare
perusal *s* perlecti-o -onis *f*
peruse *tr* perlegere
pervade *tr* permanare per *(w. acc)*
pervasive *adj* undique circumfus•us -a -um
perverse *adj* pervers•us -a -um
perversely *adv* perverse
perversion *s* perversit•as -atis *f*
perversity *s* perversit•as -atis *f*
pervert *s* hom•o -inis *mf* pervers•us (-a)
pervert *tr* depravare; *(words)* detorquēre
pessimist *s* hom•o -inis *mf* moros•us (-a)
pessimistic *adj* moros•us -a -um
pest *s* vexa•tor -toris *m* (•trix -tricis *f)*
pester *tr* vexare
pestilence *s* pestilenti•a -ae *f*
pestle *s* pistill•um -i *n*
pet *s* delici•ae -arum *fpl;* **to have a dog as a —** canem in deliciis habēre
pet *tr (to stroke)* permulcēre; *(to fondle)* subigitare **||** *intr* inter se subigitare
petal *s* floris fol•ium -(i)i *n*
petition *s* petiti•o -onis *f; (pol)* libell•us -i *m*
petition *tr* supplicare

petitioner *s* suppl•ex -icis *mf*
petrify *tr* in lapidem convertere; *(fig)* perterrēre **||** *intr* lapidescere
petticoat *s* inducul•a -ae *f*
pettiness *s* anim•us -i *m* angustus
petty *adj* minut•us et angust•us -a -um
petulance *s* petulanti•a -ae *f*
petulant *adj* petul•ans -antis
pew *s* subsell•ium -(i)i *n*
phantasy *s* phantasi•a -ae *f*
phantom *s* larv•a -ae *f,* spectr•um -i *n*
pharmacist *s* medicamentari•us -i *m* (•a -ae *f*)
pharmacy *s* tabern•a -ae *f* medicamentaria
phase *s* lunae faci•es -ei *f; (fig)* vic•es -ium *fpl*
pheasant *s* phasian•us -i *m* (•a -ae *f*)
phenomenal *adj* singular•is -is -e
phenomenon *s* res, rei *f; (s.th. remarkable)* miracul•um -i *n*
phew *interj (gratified surprise or relief)* ehem!; *(at a bad odor)* fi!
philanthropic *adj* human•us -a -um
philanthropy *s* humanit•as -atis *f*
philologist *s* philolog•us -i *m* (•a -ae *f*)
philology *s* philologi•a -ae *f*
philosopher *s* philosoph•us -i *m*
philosophical *adj* philosophic•us -a -um
philosophically *adv* philosophice; *(calmly)* aequo animo
philosophize *intr* philosophari
philosophy *s* philosophi•a -ae *f; (theory)* rati•o -onis *f*
phlegm *s* phlegm•a -atis *n*
phobia *s* formid•o -inis *f*
phone *s* telephon•um -i *n*
phone *tr* per telephonum loqui cum *(w. abl)*
phoney *adj* affectat•us -a -um
phosphorus *s* phosphor•us -i *m*
photo *s see* **photograph**
photo shop *s* officin•a -ae *f* photographica
photocopier *s* machin•a -ae *f* phototypica
photocopy *s* exempl•ar -aris *n* phototypicum
photograph *s* imag•o -inis *f* photographica; **to take —s** imagines luce exprimere
photograph *tr* photographice reddere
photographer *s* photograph•us -i *m* (•a -ae *f*)
photographic film *s* taeniol•a -ae *f* photographica
photography *s* photographi•a -ae *f*
phrase *s* locuti•o -onis *f*
phrase *tr* verbis exprimere
phraseology *s* loquendi rati•o -onis *f*
physical *adj (relating to nature)* physic•us -a -um; **— condition** corporis habit•us -ūs *m;* **— strength** corporis vir•es -ium *fpl*
physical therapist *s* iatralipt•es -ae *mf*
physical therapy *s* iatraliptic•e -es *f*
physician *s* medic•us -i *m* (•a -ae *f*)
physicist *s* physic•us -i *m* (•a -ae *f*)
physics *s* physic•a -orum *npl*
physiognomy *s* physiognomi•a -ae *f*
physiological *adj* physiologic•us -a -um
physiologist *s* physiolog•us -i *m* (•a -ae *f*)
physiology *s* physiologi•a -ae *f*
physique *s* corporis habit•us -ūs *m*
pianist *s* clavic•en -inis *m* (•ina -inae *f*)
piano *s* clavicord•ium -(i) i *n;* **to play the —** clavicordio canere
pick *tr (to choose)* eligere; *(to pluck)* carpere; *(to gather)* legere; **to — a quarrel** iurgi causam inferre; **to — out** eligere; **to — pockets** manticulari; **to — the teeth** dentes perfodere; **to — up** *(to raise)* tollere; *(a language)* perbibere **||** *intr* **to — on s.o.** aliquem carpere
pick *s (tool)* dolabr•a -ae *f; (the best)* flo•s -ris *m*
pickax *s* dolabr•a -ae *f*
picked *adj* elect•us -a -um
picket *s (mil)* stati•o -onis *f*
pickle *s (brine)* muri•a -ae *f; (vegetable)* oxycucum•er -eris *m;* **to be in a —** in angustiis versari
pickled *adj* muriā condit•us -a -um; *(drunk)* madid•us -a -um; **— olives** oxycomin•a -orum *npl*
pickpocket *s* sacculari•us -i *m* (•a -ae *f*)
picnic *s* conviv•ium -(i)i *n* sub divo
picnic basket *s* panar•ium -(i)i *n*
pictorial *adj* pictori•us -a -um
picture *s* tabul•a -ae *f* picta
picture *tr* effingere
picture gallery *s* pinacothec•a -ae *f*
picturesque *adj* amoen•us -a -um
pie *s* crust•um -i *n;* **apple —** mal•a -orum *npl* in crusto cocta; **cherry —** ceras•a -orum *npl* in crusto cocta
piece *s* par•s -tis *f; (of food)* frust•um -i *n; (broken off)* fragment•um -i *n; (drama)* fabul•a -ae *f; (very often not expressed by a separate word, e.g.,* **a — of bread** pan•is -is *m;* **a — of cheese** case•us -i *m;* **a — of ground** agell•us -i *m;* **a — of meat** car•o -nis *f;* **a — of paper** chart•a -ae *f*); **to break in —s** confringere; **to cut in —s** minute concidere; **to fall to —s** dilabi; **to tear to —s** dilaniare; *(e.g., paper)* conscindere
piece *tr* **to — together** fabricari *or* fabricare
piecemeal *adv* frustillatim, separatim
pier *s* mol•es -is *f*
pierce *tr* perforare; *(w. a sword)* perfodere; *(fig)* pungere
piercing *adj* acut•us -a -um
piety *s* piet•as -atis *f*
pig *s* porc•us -i *m;* **—s oink** porci grunniunt
pigeon *s* columb•a -ae *f;* **—s coo** columbae gemunt
pigeon coop *s* columbar•ium -(i)i *n*
pigheaded *adj* obstinat•us -a -um
pigment *s* pigment•um -i *n*
pigsty *s* suil•e -is *n*
pike *s* hast•a -ae *f; (fish)* lup•us -i *m*
pilaster *s* parastatic•a -ae *f*

pile *s* acerv·us -i *m; (nap of cloth)* vill·us -i *m; (for cremation)* rog·us -i *m*
pile *tr* **(on)** congerere *(w. dat);* **to — up** exstruere **||** *intr* **to — up** crescere
pilgrim *s* peregrina·tor -toris *m* (·trix -tricis *f*) religionis causā
pilgrimage *s* peregrinati·o -onis *f* religionis causā
piling *s* sublic·a -ae *f*
pill *s* pilul·a -ae *f*
pillage *s* rapin·a -ae *f*
pillage *tr* diripere **||** *intr* praedari
pillar *s* pil·a -ae *f*
pillow *s* cervic·al -alis *n*
pillowcase *s* cervicalis tegim·en -inis *n*
pilot *s* guberna·tor -toris *m* (·trix -tricis *f*)
pilot *tr* gubernare
pimp *s* len·o -onis *m*
pimp *tr & intr* lenocinari
pimple *s* pustul·a -ae *f*
pin *s* ac·us -ūs *f; (peg)* clav·us -i *m*
pin *tr* acu figere; **to — down** defigere; *(fig)* devincire
pincers *spl* forc·eps -ipis *mf*
pinch *tr* vellicare **||** *intr (of cold; of shoe)* (ad)urere
pinch *s (e.g., of salt)* mensur·a -ae *f* duorum *(or* trium) digitorum; **in a —** *(fig)* in angustiis; *(in a doubtful situation)* in re dubiā
pine *s* pin·us -i *f*
pine *intr* **to — away** tabescere; **to — for** desiderare
pineapple *s* pom·um -i *n* pineum
pink *adj* punice·us -a -um, rose·us -a -um; **to be in the — of health** optimā valetudine uti
pinnacle *s* fastig·ium -(i)i *n*
pint *s* sextar·ius -(i)i *m*
pioneer *s* praecurs·or -oris *m; (originator)* auc·tor -toris *m* (·trix tricis *f*)
pious *adj* pi·us -a -um, prob·us -a -um
piously *adv* pie, religiose, sancte
pipe *s* tub·us -i *m;* fistul·a -ae *f* aquaria; *(conduit)* canal·is -is *m; (mus)* fistul·a -ae *f*
pipe organ *s* organ·um -i *n* fistuli instructum
pique *tr* offendere
piracy *s* latrocin·ium -(i)i *n*
pirate *s* pirat·a -ae *m*
piratical *adj* piratic·us -a -um
pistachio *s* pistac·ium -(i)i *n*
pit *s* fove·a -ae *f; (quarry)* fodin·a -ae *f; (theat)* cave·a -ae *f*
pit *tr* **to — one against another** alium cum alio committere
pitch *s* pi·x -cis *f; (sound)* son·us -i *m; (degree)* grad·us -ūs *m; (slope)* fastig·ium -(i)i *n;* **to such a — of** eo *(w. gen)*
pitch *tr (to fling)* conicere; *(camp)* ponere; *(tent)* tendere
pitcher *s* urce·us -i *m; (baseball)* coniec·tor -toris *m* (·trix -tricis *f*)
pitcher's mound *s* coiectoris (coniectricis) grum·us -i *m*
pitchfork *s* furc·a -ae *f*
piteous *adj* miserabil·is -is -e
piteously *adv* miserabiliter
pitfall *s (& fig)* fove·a -ae *f*
pith *s* medull·a -ae *f*
pithy *adj* sententios·us -a -um
pitiable *adj* miserand·us -a -um
pitiful *adj* flebil·is -is -e; *(contemptible)* abiect·us -a -um
pitifully *adv* misere
pitiless *adj* immisericor·s -dis
pitilessly *adv* immisericorditer
pittance *s* mercedul·a -ae *f*
pity *s* misericordi·a -ae *f;* **it is a — that . . .** male accidit *(w. acc & inf);* **to feel — for** commiserescere *(w. gen)*
pity *tr* miserēre *(w. gen),* miserēri *(w. gen);* **I — him** miseret me eius.
pivot *s* ax·is -is *m; (fig)* card·o -inis *m*
placard *s* titul·us -i *m*
place *s* loc·us -i *m (pl:* loc·a -orum *npl);* **at your —** apud te; **from that —** illinc; **from this —** hinc; **in — of** *(in stead of)* pro *(w. abl);* **in — of parents** in locum parentum; **in the first —** primum; **in the last —** postremo; **in the same —** ibidem; **out of —** alien·us -a -um; **this is not the — to . . .** non est hic locus ut *(w. subj);* **to take —** fieri; **to take s.o.'s —** locum alicuius usurpare; **to that —** eo; **to the same —** eodem
place *tr* ponere, locare; *(pointing to the placing of an object in connection with other objects)* (col)locare; *(to identify)* (re)cognoscere
placement *s* collocati·o -onis *f*
placid *adj* placid·us -a -um
placidly *adv* placide
plagiarism *s* furt·um -i *n* litterarium
plagiarist *s* fu·r -ris *mf* litterari·us (-a)
plagiarize *tr* furari, compilare
plague *s* pestilenti·a -ae *f; (fig)* pest·is -is *f*
plague *tr* vexare
plain *s* planiti·es -ei *f,* camp·us -i *m;* **open —s** campi latentes
plain *adj (clear)* manifest·us -a -um; *(unadorned)* simpl·ex -icis; *(of one color)* unicol·or -oris; *(frank)* sincer·us -a -um; *(homely)* invenust·us -a -um
plainly *adv* plane; simpliciter
plaintiff *s* peti·tor -toris *m* (·trix -tricis *f*)
plaintive *adj* flebil·is -is -e
plaintively *adv* flebiliter
plan *s* consil·ium -(i)i *n; (for a building)* form·a -ae *f;* **to form a —** consilium inire; **to make —s for a trip** de itinere consilium facere

plan *tr* destinare, in animo habēre; *(to scheme)* meditari **||** *intr* **to — on** in animo habēre
plane *s (tool)* runcin•a -ae *f; (level surface)* planiti•es -ei *f; (airplane)* aëroplan•um -i *n*
plane *tr* runcinare
planet *s* planet•a -ae *f*
plank *s* tabul•a -ae *f; (builder's term)* ax•is -is *m*
plant *s* plant•a -ae *f; (industrial)* fabric•a -ae *f*
plant *tr* serere; **his feet are —ed on** pedes stipantur in *(w. abl);* **to — a field** agrum conserere; **to — one's feet on the ground** pedes in terram deferre
plantation *s* plantar•ium -(i)i *n*
planter *s* sat•or -oris *m*
planting *s* sat•us -ūs *m*
plaster *s* tector•ium -(i)i *n*
plaster *tr* tectorium inducere *(w. dat)*
plasterer *s* tect•or -oris *m*
plaster of Paris *s* gyps•um -i *n*
plastic *adj* plastic•us -a -um
plastic *s* materi•a -ae *f* plastica
plate *s* patin•a -ae *f,* catin•us -i *m; (small dish)* patell•a -ae *f,* catill•us -i *m; (sheet)* lamin•a -ae *f*
plate licker *s* catill•o -onis *m*
plateau *s* aequ•um -i *n*
platform *s* suggest•us -ūs *m; (in train station)* crepid•o -inis *f* (ferriviaria)
platitude *s* trita sententi•a -ae *f*
Platonic *adj* Platonic•us -a -um
platoon *s* manipul•us -i *m*
platter *s* lan•x -cis *f*
plaudits *spl* plaus•us -ūs *m*
plausible *adj* verisimil•is -is -e
play *s* lud•us -i *m; (theat)* fabul•a -ae *f;* **to be at —** ludere
play *tr* ludere; *(radio, television, records, tapes)* usūrpare; *(instrument)* canere *(w. abl);* **stop —ing games!** desiste ludos facere!; **to — ball** pilā ludere; **to — a trick on** ludificari; **to — the lead role** primas partes agere; **to — the role of a parasite** parasitum agere **||** *intr* **to — up to** adulari
player *s* lus•or -oris *m,* lus•rix -ricis *f; (theat)* histri•o -onis *mf; (on wind instrument)* tibic•en -inis *m,* tibicin•a -ae *f; (on stringed instrument)* fidic•en -inis *m,* fidicin•a -ae *f*
playful *adj* ludibund•us -a -um; *(frolicsome)* lasciv•us -a -um
playfully *adv* per ludum
playfulness *s* lascivi•a -ae *f*
playground *s* are•a -ae *f* lusoria
playing cards *spl* chartul•ae -arum *fpl* lusoriae
playing field *s* camp•us -i *m* lusorius
playmate *s* collus•or -oris *m* (•rix -ricis *f*)
plaything *s* ludibr•ium -(i)i *n*
playwright *s* fabularum scrip•tor -toris *m* (•trix -tricis *f*)
plea *s* supplicati•o -onis *f; (law)* excepti•o -onis *f;* **to enter a — against s.o.** exceptionem obicere alicui; **well-founded —** iusta exceptio *f*
plead *tr (ignorance)* causari; **to — a case before the court** causam pro tribunali agere **||** *intr* **to — for** petere; **to — with s.o.** aliquem supplicare
pleasant *adj* iucund•us -a -um; *(to sight)* amoen•us -a -um
pleasantly *adv* iucunde
pleasantry *s* iocosa dicacit•as -atis *f*
please *tr* placēre *(w. dat);* **anyone you —** quilibet, quaelibet; **anything you —** quidlibet; **if you —** si placet; si videtur; **—!** sis (= si vis); amabo te *(coll);* **pleased to meet you!** mihi pergratum est te convenire!; **— God!** Deo volente
pleasing *adj* grat•us -a -um
pleasurable *adj* iucund•us -a -um
pleasure *s* volupt•as -atis *f;* **at their own —** suo arbitrio; **it is my —** libet; **to derive (great) — from** (magnam) voluptatem capere de *(w. abl);* **with —** libemter
pleat *s* plicatur•a -ae *f*
pleat *tr* plicare
pleated *adj* plicat•us -a -um
plebeian *adj* plebei•us -a -um
plebeians *spl* pleb•s -is *f*
plebiscite *s* plebiscit•um -i *n*
plebs *spl* plebs, plebis *f*
pledge *s* pign•us -oris *n; (proof)* testimon•ium -(i)i *n*
pledge *tr* (op)pignerare, obligare; **to — one's word** fidem obligare
Pleiades *spl* Pleiad•es -um *fpl*
plenary *adj* plen•us -a -um
plentiful *adj* larg•us -a -um, copios•us -a -um
plenty *s* copi•a -ae *f;* **to have — of** abundare *(w. abl)*
plethora *s* redundanti•a -ae *f*
pleurisy *s* pleurit•is -idis *f*
pliable *adj* tractabil•is -is -e
pliant *adj* lent•us -a -um
pliers *spl* for•ceps -cipis *mf*
plight *s* discrim•en -inis *n;* **in a sorry —** male perdit•us -a -um; **what a sorry —!** O rem miseram!
plod *intr* assidue laborare
plodder *s* sedul•us (-a) hom•o -inis *mf*
plodding *adj* sedul•us -a -um
plot *s (conspiracy)* coniurati•o -onis *f; (of ground)* agell•us -i *m; (of a play)* argument•um -i *n*
plot *intr* coniurare, moliri
plow *s* aratr•um -i *n*
plow *tr* arare; **to — under** inarare; **to — up** exarare
plowing *s* arati•o -onis *f*
plowshare *s* vom•er -eris *m*

pluck *s* anim•us -i *m*
pluck *tr (flowers, fruit)* carpere; *(feathers)* vellere; **to — off** decerpere; **to — out** evellere; **to — up one's courage** animo esse
plug *s* obturament•um -i *n; (electrical)* spin•a -ae *f* contactūs electrici; *(a boost)* verb•a -orum *npl* suadentia
plug *tr* obturare; **to — in** adnectere, inserere ‖ *intr* **to — away at** assidue laborare
plum *s* prun•um -i *n*
plumage *s* plum•ae -arum *fpl*
plumber *s* plumbar•ius -(i)i *m*
plume *s* crist•a -ae *f*
plummet *s* perpendicul•um -i *n*
plummet *intr* praecipitare
plump *adj* pingu•is -is -e
plum tree *s* prun•us -i *f*
plunder *s (act)* rapin•a -ae *f; (booty)* praed•a -ae *f*
plunder *tr* praedari
plunderer *s* praedat•or -oris *m*
plundering *s* rapin•a -ae *f*
plundering *adj* praedatori•us -a -um
plunge *tr* mergere; *(sword, etc.)* condere ‖ *intr* se mergere; **to — into the midst of the enemy** inter mucrones hostium se immergere
pluperfect (tense) *s* plus quam perfectum temp•us -oris *n*
plural *adj* plural•is -is -e
plural *s* numer•us -i *m* multitudinis; **in the —** pluraliter
plurality *s* multitud•o -inis *f; (majority)* maior par•s -tis *f*
plush *adj* laut•us -a -um
plus *s* **consider it a —** id deputa esse in lucro
plus *conj* **2 plus 2 are 4** duo et duo sunt *(or* fiunt) quattuor
plus sign *s* crucicul•a -ae *f*
ply *tr* exercēre, urgēre
poach *tr (eggs)* frigere ‖ *intr* illicitā venatione uti
poacher *s* vena•tor -toris *m* (•trix -tricis *f*) illicit•us (-a)
pocket *s* saccul•us -i *m;* **to line one's —s** ditescere
pocket *tr* in sacculo condere
pocketbook *s (small book)* pugillar•es -ium *mpl; (purse)* marsup•ium -(i)i *n*
pocket knife *s* cultell•us -i *m* plicabilis
pockmark *s* cicatr•ix -icis *f*
pod *s* siliqu•a -ae *f*
podium *s* pod•ium -(i)i *n,* pulpit•um -i *n*
poem *s* poëm•a -atis *n;* **to write a —** poema condere
poet *s* poët•a -ae *m*
poetess *s* poëtri•a -ae *f*
poetic *adj* poëtic•us -a -um
poetically *adv* poëtice
poetics *s* ar•s -tis *f* poëtica
poetry *s (art)* poëtic•e -es *f; (poems)* poës•is -is *f,* carm•en -inis *n*
poignant *adj* acerb•us -a -um
poinsettia *s* euphorbi•a -ae *f*
point *s* punct•um -i *n; (pointed end)* acum•en -inis *n; (of sword, etc.)* mucr•o -onis *m; (of a spear)* cusp•is -idis *f; (point in dispute)* quaesti•o -onis *f; (gram, sports)* punct•um -i *n; (in time)* articul•a -ae *f* temporis; **at this very —** hoc ipso in loco; **beside the —** ab re, nihil ad rem; **but to return to the —** sed ad propositum; **from this — on** posthac, hinc; **get the —?** tenesne *(pl:* tenetisne) rem?; **get to the —!** veni ad rem!; **main —** cap•ut -itis *n;* **now here's the —** nunc cognosce rem; **on that —** hac de re; **— of view** sententi•a -ae *f,* opini•o -onis *f;* **to come to a —** acui; **to be on the — of** in eo esse ut, *e.g., he was on the point of being arrested* in eo erat *(or* haud abfuit) ut comprehenderetur; **the —is that I no longer care about such things** quod caput est, iam ista non curo; **to score a —** punctum ferre; **to such a — that** eo ut; **to the —** ad rem; **up to this —** hactenus; **what's your —?** *(what are you driving at?)* quo evadis?; **what was your — in writing to me?** quid retulit te mittere ad me litteras?; **you miss the —** nihil ad rem pertinet
point *tr (to sharpen)* acuere; **to — out** monstrare, indicare; **to — the finger at** digitum intendere ad (*w. acc*) ‖ *intr* **to — at** digito monstrare
point-blank *adv* **to turn down —** omnino repudiare
pointed *adj* acut•us -a -um; *(fig) (stinging)* aculeat•us -a -um
pointer *s* ind•ex -icis *mf; (comput)* (muris) index
pointless *adj* supervacu•us -a -um
poise *s* urbanit•as -atis *f*
poise *tr* librare
poison *s* venen•um -i *n*
poison *tr* venenare; *(fig)* vitiare
poisoning *s* venefic•ium -(i)i *n*
poke *tr (to jab)* fodicare, pungere; *(w. the elbow)* cubito pulsare; *(fire)* fodere; **to — fun at** eludere
poker *s* rutabul•um -i *n*
polar *adj* arctic•us -a -um
pole *s* ass•er -eris *m; (short pole)* asserul•us -i *m; (long pole)* longur•ius -(i)i *m; (of the earth)* pol•us -i *m;* **North (South) Pole** ax•is -is *m* septentrionalis (meridianus)
pole vaulting *s* salt•us -ūs *m* perticarius
police *s* vigil•es -um *mpl*
police officer *s* vig•il -ilis *mf*
policy *s* rati•o -onis *f; (document)* chirograph•um -i *n; (contract)* pact•um -i *n;* **insurance —** cauti•o -onis *f* indemnitatis

polish *s (shine)* nit·or -oris *m; (refined manners)* urbanit·as -atis *f; (for shoes)* cerom·a -atis *n*
polish *tr* polire; **to — up** expolire
polite *adj* urban·us -a -um; **(to)** com·is -is -e *(w. dat or* erga *w. acc)*
politely *adv* urbane, comiter
politeness *s* urbanit·as -atis *f*, comit·as -atis *f*
politic *adj* prud·ens -entis
political *adj* civil·is -is -e; **for — reasons** rei publicae causā; **from — motives** per ambitionem; **— affairs (matters)** res, rerum *fpl* civiles; **— career** curs·us -ūs *m* publicus; **— science** scienti·a -ae *f* civilis; **— supporter** suffraga·tor -toris *m* (·trix -tricis *f*)
politician *s* vir, viri *m*, (femin·a -ae *f*) civilium rerum perit·us (-a)
politics *s* respublica *(gen:* reipublicae) *f;* **to be (involved) in —** in republicā versari **to enter —** rempublicam inire; **to talk — at table** ad mensam res publicas crepare
polka *s* saltati·o -onis *f* Bohemica; **to dance the —** Bohemice saltare
poll *s* diribitor·ium -(i)i *n; (survey)* rogati·o -onis *f* sententiarum; **the —s** suffragi·a -orum *npl;* comiti·a -orum *npl*
polling booth *s* saept·um -i *n*
poll tax *s* capitum exacti·o -onis *f*
pollute *tr* polluere
pollution *s* polluti·o -onis *f*
polo *s* alsulegi·a -ae *f* equestris
polo shirt *s* subucul·a -ae *f* cum curtis manicis
polygamy *s* polygami·a -ae *f*
polysyllabic *adj* polysyllab·us -a -um
polytheism *s* multorum deorum cult·us -ūs *m*
pomegranate *s* mal·um -i *n* Punicum, mal·um -i *n* granatum
pommel *tr* pulsare, verberare
pomp *s* apparat·us -ūs *m*
pompous *adj* magnific·us -a -um, glorios·us -a -um
pompously *adv* magnifice
pond *s* stagn·um -i *n*
ponder *tr* animo volutare
ponderous *adj* ponderos·us -a -um
pontiff *s* pontif·ex -icis *m*
pontifical *adj* pontifical·is -is -e
pontificate *s* pontificat·us -ūs *m*
pontificate *intr* ex cathedrā loqui
pontoon *s* pont·o -onis *m*
pony *s* mannul·us -i *m*
pool *s (of water)* lacun·a -ae *f; (for swimming)* piscin·a -ae *f; (billiards)* lud·us -i *m* tudicularis; **to shoot —** globulos eburneos clavā tudiculari super mensam impellere
pool *tr* conferre
poor *adj (impoverished)* paup·er -eris: *(pitiable)* mis·er -era -erum; *(meager)* exil·is -is -e; *(soil)* ma·cer -cra -crum; **poor guy** mis·er -eri *m*
poorly *adv* parum, mediocriter
pop *s* crepit·us -ūs *m; (father)* pap·a -ae *m*, tat·a -ae *m*
pop *intr* crepare; **to — out** exsilire
popcorn *s* maiz·ium -(i)i *n* inflatum
pope *s* pap·a -ae *m*
poplar *s* popul·us -i *f*
pop music *s* music·a -ae *f* popularis
poppy, poppyseed *s* papav·er -eris *n*
populace *s* vulg·us -i *n*
popular *adj* popular·is -is -e; **be — with** gratios·us -a -um esse apud *(w. acc);* **— feeling** sens·us -ūs *m* populi
popularity *s* grati·a -ae *f*, fav·or -oris *m* populi; **to enjoy — among** gratiam habēre apud *(w. acc)*; **to seek —** favorem populi sectari
populate *tr* frequentare
population *s* multitud·o -inis *f*
populous *adj* frequ·ens -entis
porcelain *s* fictil·ia -ium *npl* elegantia
porch *s* pergul·a -ae *f*
porcupine *s* hystr·ix -icis *f*
pore *s* foram·en -inis *n*
pore *intr* **to — over** diligenter scrutari
pork *s* porcin·a -ae *f*
pork chop *s* off·a -ae *f* porcina
porpoise *s* porcul·us -i *m* marinus
porridge *s* pul·s -tis *f*
port *s (also comput)* port·us -ūs *m*
portal *s* port·a -ae *f*
portend *tr* portendere
portent *s* portent·um -i *n*
portentous *adj* prodigios·us -a -um
porter *s* atriens·is is *m; (carrier)* baiul·us -i *m*
portfolio *s* scrin·ium -(i)i *n*
portico *s* portic·us -ūs *f*
portion *s* porti·o -onis *f*
portion *tr* partire; **to — out** dispertire
portly *adj* **to be —** opimo corporis habitu esse
portrait *s* imag·o -inis *f*
portray *tr* depingere, exprimere
pose *s* stat·us -ūs *m*
pose *intr* statum sumere
position *s* positi·o -onis *f; (of the body)* gest·us -ūs *m; (office)* hon·or -oris *m; (rank)* dignit·as -atis *f; (state)* condici·o -onis *f; (sports)* loc·us -i *m;* **what — do you play?** quo loco ludis?
positive *adj* cert·us -a -um; *(opp: negative)* affirmativ·us -a -um; *(gram)* positiv·us -a -um; **are you — that ...** scisne pro certo *(w. acc & inf);* **— degree** grad·us -ūs *m* positivus
positively *adv* certo, praecise
possess *tr* possidēre
possession *s* possessi·o -onis *f;* **in the — of** penes *(w. acc);* **to gain — of** potiri *(w. abl)*

possessive *adj* quaestuos·us -a -um; *(gram)* possessiv·us -a -um
possessor *s* possess·or -oris *m,* possestr·ix -icis *f*
possibility *s* facult·as -atis *f*
possible *adj* possibil·is -is -e; **as quickly as —** quam celerrime; **is it really possible that you are telling the truth?** numquid vera dicis?; **it is —** fieri potest; **it is — for me to** possum *(w. inf)*
possibly *adv (perhaps)* fortasse; **as carefully as I — can** quam diligentissime possum; **I may — go to Sicily** fieri potest ut in Siciliam proficiscar
post *s (stake)* post·is -is *m,* pal·us -i *m; (station)* stati·o -onis *f; (in a race)* met·a -ae *f*
post *tr (a notice)* in publicum proponere; *(to station)* collocare: **to — a letter** litteras dare
postage *s* vectur·a -ae *f* litterarum; **to pay the —** pro vecturā epistulae solvere
postage stamp *s* pittac·ium -(i)i *n* cursuale
postal delivery *s* perlati·o -onis *f* cursualis
postcard *s* chartul·a -ae *f* cursualis; *(with a picture)* photochartul·a -ae *f* cursualis
postdate *tr* diem seriorem scribere *(w. dat)*
poster *s* fol·ium -(i)i *n* murale; **to put up a —** folium murale proponere
posterior *adj* poster·ior -ior -ius
posterity *s* posterit·as -atis *f; (descendants)* poster·i -orum *mpl*
posthaste *adv* quam celerrime
posthumous *adj* postum·us -a -um
postman *s* tabellar·ius -(i)i *m*
post office *s* diribitor·ium -(i)i *n* cursuale
post office window ostiol·um -i *n* cursuale
postpone *tr* differre
postponement *s* dilati·o -onis *f*
postscript *s* adiecti·o -onis *f* litterarum
posture *s* stat·us -ūs *m*
pot *s (of clay)* oll·a -ae *f; (of bronze)* ahen·um -i *n; (chamber pot)* matell·a -ae *f; (marijuana)* cannab·is -is *f;* **—s and pans** vas·a -orum *npl* coquinaria; **to go to —** *(fig)* pessum ire; **to smoke —** fumum cannabis sugere
potato *s* pom·um -i *n* terrestre; **baked —** pomum terrestre in furno coctum; **fried potatoes** poma terrestria fricta; **mashed potatoes** pulticul·a -ae *f* ex pomis terrestribus
potato chips *s* lamin·ae -ae *fpl* pomorum terrestrium
pot-bellied *adj* ventrios·us -a -um
pot belly *s* vent·er -ris *m* obesus *or* poriectus; **to have a —** ventre obeso esse
potentate *s* tyrann·us -i *m*
potential *adj* cap·ax -acis, futur·us -a -um
potential *s* potenti·a -ae *f* latens
potholder *s* bascaud·a -ae *f*
potion *s* poti·o -onis *f*
potroast *s* ass·a -ae *f*
potsherd *s* test·a -ae *f*
potshot *s* ict·us -ūs *m* reperticius
potter *s* figul·us -i *m;* **—'s wheel** rot·a -ae *f* figularis
pottery *s* fictil·ia -ium *npl*
potty *s* matell·a -ae *f*
pouch *s* saccul·us -i *m*
poultry *s* av·es -ium *fpl* cohortales
poultry *s* av·es -ium *fpl* cohortales
pounce *intr* **to — on** insilire *(w. dat or* **in** *w. acc)*
pound *s* libr·a -ae *f (w.* pondo *sometimes added);* **a half —** selibr·a -ae *f;* **a — and a half** sesquilibr·a -ae *f;* **a —** *(or* **per —)** in libras; **a quarter —** quadran·s -tis *f* pondo
pound *s (for animals)* saept·um -i *n*
pound *tr* contundere; **to — the pavement** *(fig)* vicatim ambulare
pour *tr* fundere; **to — into** infundere *(in w. acc);* **to — out** effundere; **to — water on his hands** aquam in eius manūs infundere; **to — water on his head** caput illi aquā perfundere **II** *intr* fundi, fluere; **to come —ing out** *(of people)* se effundere; **to — down** *(of rain)* ruere; **to — into** *(of people)* se infundere in *(w. acc)*
pouring *adj (rain)* effus·us -a -um
pout *intr* labellum extendere
poverty *s* paupert·as -atis *f; (inadequacy)* egest·as -atis *f*
poverty-stricken *adj* inop·s -is
powder *s* pulv·is -eris *m*
powder *tr* pulvere conspergere
powder puff *s* pulvill·us -i *m* ad fucandum
power *s (strength)* vis *f; (ability)* copi·a -ae *f; (control, dominium)* potest·as -atis *f; (excessive; non-constitutional)* potenti·a -ae *f; (mil, pol)* imper·ium -(i)i *n;* **as far as is in our —** quantum in nobis est; **— of the mind** vir·es -ium *fpl* ingenii; **to have great —** multum posse
power drill *s* terebr·a -ae *f* machinalis
powerful *adj (physically)* valid·us -a -um; *(kings, etc.)* pot·ens -entis; *(e.g., medicine)* effic·ax -acis
powerfully *adv* valde
powerless *adj* invalid·us -a -um, impot·ens -entis; **to be —** nil valēre
power saw *s* serr·a -ae *f* machinalis
practical *adj* util·is -is -e; *(sensible)* prud·ens -entis; *(philosophy)* effectiv·us -a -um
practically *adv* usu; *(almost)* fere
practice *s (actual employment or experience)* us·us -ūs *m; (repeated action)* exercitati·o -onis *f; (rehearsal)* meditati·o -onis *f; (custom)* consuetud·o -inis *f;* **to have a large — as a doctor** medicus praecipuae celebritatis esse; **to make a — of** factitare
practice *tr (medicine, patience)* exercēre; *(to rehearse)* meditari

practice session *s* spat·ium -(i)i *n* exercitationis *(or* meditationis)
practitioner *s* exercita·tor -toris *m* (·trix -tricis *f); (medical)* medic·us -i *m* (·a -ae *f)*
praetor *s* praet·or -oris *m*
praetorship *s* praetur·a -ae *f;* **to hold the —** praeturam gerere
pragmatic *adj* pragmatic·us -a -um
prairie *s* camp·us -i *m* latissime patens herbisque obsitus
praise *s* lau·s -dis *f*
praise *tr* laudare
praiseworthy *adj* laudabil·is -is -e
prance *intr* exsilire
prank *s* lud·us -i *m*
prankster *s* lus·or -oris *m* (·rix -ricis *f)*
pray *intr* precari, orare; **to — for** petere, precari; **to — to** adorare; **to — to the gods for peace** deos pacem precari
prayer *s* pre·x -cis *f*
preach *tr & intr* praedicare
preacher *s* praedica·tor -toris *m* (·trix -tricis *f)*
preamble *s* exord·ium -(i)i *n*
precarious *adj* precari·us -a -um; **in a most — position** in summo discrimine
precariously *adv* precario
precaution *s* cauti·o -onis *f;* **to take —s** praecavēre
precede *tr* antecedere *(w. acc or dat)*
precedence *s* prior loc·us -i *m;* **to take — over** antecedere
precedent *s* exempl·um -i *n*
preceding *adj* pr·ior -ior -ius
precept *s* praecept·um -i *n*
preceptor *s* praecep·tor -toris *m* (·trix -tricis *f)*
precinct *s* termin·i -orum *mpl; (pol)* regi·o -onis *f*
precious *adj* pretios·us -a -um; **— stone** gemm·a -ae *f*
precipice *s* praec·eps -ipitis *n;* **down a —** in praeceps; **over the —** per praecipitia
precipitate *tr* praecipitare
precipitious *adj* praec·eps -ipitis
precise *adj (exact)* exact·us -a -um; *(particular)* accurat·us -a -um
precisely *adv* subtiliter
precision *s* accurati·o -onis *f*
preclude *tr* praecludere
precocious *adj* praec·ox -ocis
preconceive *tr* praecipere; **—d idea** praeiudic·ium -(i)i *n*
preconception *s* praeiudicata opini·o -onis *f*
precursor *s* praenuntia·tor -toris *m* (·trix -tricis *f)*
predatory *adj* praedatori·us -a -um
predecessor *s* deces·sor -soris *m* (·rix -ricis *f)*
predestine *tr* praedestinare
predicament *s* discrim·en -inis *n*
predicate *s* praedicat·um -i *n*
predict *tr* praedicere
prediction *s* praedicti·o -onis *f*
predilection *s* **(for)** stud·ium -(i)i *n (w. gen)*
predispose *tr* inclinare
predisposed *adj* **(to)** obnoxi·us -a -um *(w. dat)*
predisposition *s* inclinati·o -onis *f*
predominant *adj* praeval·ens -entis
predominate *intr* praevalēre
preeminent *adj* praecipu·us -a -um, praest·ans -antis
preempt *tr* praeoccupare
preexist *intr* antea exsistere *or* esse
preexistent *adj* anteced·ens -entis
preface *s* praefati·o -onis *f*
prefatory *adj* **to make a few — remarks** pauca praefari
prefect *s* praefect·us -i *m*
prefecture *s* praefectur·a -ae *f*
prefer *tr* praeponere, praeferre, malle; *(charges)* deferre; **I — to** *(would rather)* malo *(w. inf)*
preferable *adj* pot·ior -ior -ius, praestant·ior -ior -ius; *(when more than two are compared)* potissim·us -a -um
preference *s* fav·or -oris *m;* **in — to** potius quam; **to give — to s.o. over** aliquem anteponere *(w. dat)*
prefix *s* praepositi·o -onis *f* (per compositionem)
prefix *tr* **(to)** praeponere *(dat)*
pregnancy *s* gravidit·as -atis *f*
pregnant *adj* gravid·us -a -um; *(of language)* press·us -a -um
prejudge *tr* praeiudicare
prejudice *s* praeiudicata opini·o -onis *f*
prejudice *tr* **to be —d against** praeiudicatam opinionem habēre in *(w. acc);* **to — the people against** studia hominum inclinare in *(w. acc)*
prejudicial *adj* noxi·us -a -um
preliminary *adj* pr·ior -ior -ius; **to make a few — remarks** pauca praefari
prelude *s (mus)* praecenti·o -onis *f; (fig)* praelusi·o -onis *f*
premature *adj* praematur·us -a -um
prematurely *adv* ante tempus
premeditate *tr* praemeditari
premeditated *adj* praemeditat·us -a -um
premeditation *s* praemeditati·o -onis *f*
premier *s* princ·eps -ipitis *mf*
premise *s (major)* propositi·o -onis *f; (minor)* assumpti·o -onis *f;* **—s** praed·ium -(i)i *n*
premium *s* praem·ium -(i)i *n;* **at a —** car·us -a -um
premonition *s* praemonit·us -ūs *m*
preoccupation *s* nescio qua de re sollicitati·o -onis *f*
preoccupied *adj* nescio qua de re sollicit·us -a -um
preoccupy *tr* distringere

preparation *s* praeparati·o -onis *f;* **to make careful —s** diligentem praeparationem adhibēre
prepare *tr (to make ready)* parare; *(to make ready beforehand)* praeparare; *(a medicine)* componere; *(a speech, case)* meditari; **to — to** parare *(w. inf)* ‖ *intr* **to — for** se (prae)parare ad *(w. acc)*
preponderance *s* praestanti·a -ae *f*
preposition *s* praepositi·o -onis *f;* **—s take either the accusative or the ablative** praepositiones aut accusativo aut ablativo casui serviunt
preposterous *adj* absurd·us -a -um
prerogative *s* iu·s -ris *n* praecipuum
presage *tr* praesagire
prescribe *tr* mandare; *(a medicine)* praescribere
prescription *s (med)* praescript·um -i *n;* **to write a —** medicinam praescribere
presence *s* praesenti·a -ae *f;* **in my —** me praesente; **in the — of** coram *(w. abl);* **— of mind** praesenti·a -ae *f* animi
present *adj* praesen·s -tis; **at —** hoc tempore; **for the —** in praesentiā; **— tense** praesens temp·us -oris *n;* **to be — (at)** adesse *(w. dat); (of fever, infection)* inesse
present *s* don·um -i *n*
present *tr (to give)* donare; *(to introduce)* introducere; *(to bring forward)* praebēre, offerre; **an opportunity —s itself** occasio obvenit; **to — evidence** testimonium dicere
presentable *adj* dec·ens -entis, idone·us -a -um, spectabil·is -is -e
presentation *s (of gifts)* donati·o -onis *f; (show)* spectacul·um -i *n; (introduction)* introducti·o -onis *f*
presentiment *s* praesensi·o -onis *f*
presently *adv* mox, statim
preservation *s* conservati·o -onis *f*
preserve *tr* conservare, tuēri; *(fruit)* condire
preserves *spl* conditur·a -ae *f*
preserver *s* conserva·tor -toris *m* (·trix -tricis *f*)
preside *intr* **(over)** praesidēre *(w. dat);* **to — at a trial** iudicio praeesse, ius dicere
presidency *s* praefectur·a -ae *f; (term of office)* magister·ium -(i)i *n*
president *s* praes·es -idis *mf*
presidential *adj* praesidial·is -is -e
press *s (for wine)* prel·um -i *n; (press)* prelum typographicum; *(the journalists)* diurnari·i -orum *mpl; (printed matter)* script·a -orum *npl* typis edita; **freedom of the —** licenti·a -ae *f* scribendi; **hot off the —** modo ex prelo typographico; **to send to the —** prelo subicere
press *tr* primere; *(clothes)* levigare; *(a typewriter key)* deprimere *(fig)* urgēre; **to — down** deprimere; **to — together** comprimere ‖ *intr* **to — forward** anniti; **to — on** pergere, instare
press conference *s* congress·us -ūs *m* diurnariis docendis
pressing *adj* urg·ens -entis, inst·ans -antis
pressure *s* pressur·a -ae *f; (strain)* ang·or -oris *m*
pressure *vt* urgēre
prestige *s* auctorit·as -atis *f*
presumably *adv* sane
presume *tr* inferre, sumere, conicere; *(to take liberties)* sibi arrogare
presumption *s* praesumpti·o -onis *f*
presumptuous *adj* praesumptios·us -a -um
presuppose *tr* praesumere
pretend *tr (to pretend what is not, followed by acc & inf)* simulare, fingere; *(to hide what is by pretending)* dissimulare; **I'll — I don't know him** dissimulabo me eum novisse; **I'll — I'm leaving** simulabo quasi abeam; **to — to be shocked** fingere se inhorrescere
pretender *s* simula·tor -toris *m* (·trix -tricis *f*); *(to the throne)* petit·or -oris *m*
pretense *s* simulati·o -onis *f;* **under false —s** dolo malo; **under the — of** per speciem *(w. gen);* **without —** sine fuco
pretension *s (claim)* postulati·o -onis *f; (display)* ostentati·o -onis *f;* **to make —s to** affectare, sibi arrogare
pretentious *adj* jact·ans -antis; *(showy)* specios·us -a -um
preterite *s* temp·us -oris *n* praeteritum
preternatural *adj* praeter naturam
pretext *s* praetext·um -i *n,* speci·es -ei *f;* **a — for war** praetextum belli; **he left under the pretext that …** hinc abiit quasi *(w. subj);* **under the — of** (sub) specie *(w. gen)*
pretor *see* **praetor**
prettily *adv* belle
pretty *adj* bell·us -a -um, bellul·us -a -um
pretty *adv* satis, admodum; **a — considerable quantity** aliquantul·um -i *n;* **— well** mediocriter; *(just about)* propemodum
pretzel *s* pretiol·a -ae *f*
prevail *intr (to be prevalent)* obtinēre, praevalēre; *(to win)* vincere; **to — upon** persuadēre *(w. dat)*
prevalent *adj* (per)vulgat·us -a -um; **to become —** increbrescere
prevaricate *intr* praevaricari
prevent *tr* prohibēre; **to — s.th. from happening** prohibēre ne *(or* quominus) quid fiat
prevention *s* impediti·o -onis *f*
preventive *adj* **to adopt all — measures** omnia providēre et curare
previous *adj* pri·or -or -us
previously *adv* antehac, antea, prius
prey *s* praed·a -ae *f*
prey *intr* **to — on** praedari

price *s* pret·ium -(i)i *n;* **at a high (low, very low, exorbitant) —** magni (parvi, minimi, nimii); **at any —** quanticumque pretii; **to set the —** pretium constituere
priceless *adj* inaestimabil·is -is -e
price list *s* pretiorum ind·ex -icis *m*
price tag *s* pretii pittac·ium -(i)i *n*
prick *tr* pungere; *(fig)* stimulare; **to — up the ears** aures arrigere
prick *s (puncture)* punct·um -i *n;* **— of conscience** ang·or -oris *m* conscientiae
prickle *s* acule·us -i *m*
prickly *adj* spinos·us -a -um
pride *s* superbi·a -ae *f; (source of pride)* dec·us -oris *n;* **to take — in** gloriari de *or* in *(w. abl)*
pride *tr* **to — oneself on** iactare
priest *s* sacerd·os -otis *mf; (of a particular god)* flam·en -inis *m*
priestess *s* sacerd·os -otis *f*
priesthood *s (office)* sacerdot·ium -(i)i *n*
priestly *adj* sacerdotal·is -is -e
prim *adj* (nimis) dilig·ens -entis
primacy *s* primat·us -ūs *m*
primarily *adv* praecipue, principio
primary *adj* principal·is -is -e; *(chief)* praecipu·us -a -um
prime *s* flo·s -ris *m;* **to be in one's —** aetate florēre
prime *adj* prim·us -a -um, optim·us -a -um
prime minister *s* minis·ter -tri *m* (·tra -trae *f*) primari·us (-a)
primer *s* libell·us -i *m* elementarius
primeval *adj* pristin·us -a -um
primitive *adj* primitiv·us -a -um
primordial *adj* primordi·us -a -um
primrose *s* primul·a -ae *f* vulgaris
prince *s* regis fil·ius -(i)i *m*
princely *adj* regi·us -a -um
princess *s* regis fili·a -ae *f*
principal *adj* principal·is -is -e, praecipu·us -a -um; **— parts** part·es -ium *fpl* principales
principal *s (of a school)* scholae rec·tor -toris *m* (·trix -tricis *f*); *(fin)* cap·ut -itis *n;* **assistant** *or* **vice —** scholae rec·tor -toris *m* vicarius, scholae rec·trix -tricis *f* vicaria; **—'s office** rectoris (rectricis) officin·a -ae *f*
principality *s* principat·us -ūs *m*
principally *adv* praecipue
principle *s* princip·ium -(i)i *n; (rule of conduct)* praecept·um -i *n;* **a man of —** vi·r -ri *m* gravis et severus
print *s* not·a -ae *f* impressa; *(cloth)* pann·us -i *m* imaginibus impressus
print *tr* imprimere; *(with type)* typis imprimere
printer *s (person)* typograph·us -i *m; (mechanical device)* machin·a -ae *f* typographica, impressor·ium -(i)i *n*
printing *s* typographi·a -ae *f*
printing press *s* prel·um -i *n* typographicum
print shop *s* officin·a -ae *f* typographica
prior *adj* pr·ior -ior -ius
priority *s* primat·us -ūs *m,* ius, iuris *n* praecipuum
prism *s* prism·a -atis *n*
prison *s* carc·er -eris *m;* **to throw into —** in carcerem conicere
prisoner *s (leg)* re·us -i *m,* re·a -ae *f; (of war)* captiv·us -i *m,* captiv·a -ae *f; (for debt)* nex·us -i *m;* **to exchange —s** captivos inter se permutare
pristine *adj* pristin·us -a -um; *(unspoiled)* inte·ger -gra -grum
privacy *s (seclusion)* secess·us -ūs *m; (secrecy)* secret·um -i *n*
private *adj (secluded)* secret·us -a -um; *(person)* privat·us -a -um; *(tutor)* domestic·us -a -um; *(one's own)* propri·us -a -um; *(mil)* gregari·us -a -um; **in —** in privato, secreto
private *s* mil·es -itis *mf* gregari·us (·a)
privately *adv* clam, secreto; *(in a private capacity)* privatim
privation *s* egest·as -atis *f; (loss)* privati·o -onis *f*
privilege *s* privileg·ium -(i)i *n*
privy *adj* privat·us -a -um; **— to** consci·us -a -um *(w. gen)*
privy *s* loc·us -i *m* secretus, latrin·a -ae *f*
prize *s (reward)* praem·ium -(i)i *n; (prey)* praed·a -ae *f;* **first —** primar·ium -(i)i *n;* **second —** secundar·ium -(i)i *n;* **to win a —** praemium auferre
prize *tr* magni aestimare
prize fighter *s* pug·il -ilis *m* mercenarius
pro *adj* affirmativ·us -a -um; *(professional)* veteran·us -a -um; **pro vote** confirmativ·um -i *n*
pro *s (professional)* veteran·us -i *m* (·a -ae *f*); **to weigh the —s and cons** dubitare (in) diversitate rationum
pro *prep* pro *(w. abl)*
probability *s* veri similitud·o -inis *f*
probable *adj* verisimil·is -is -e
probably *adv* probabiliter
probation *s* probati·o -onis *f;* **on —** in liberā custodiā
probe *s* indagati·o -onis *f; (med)* specill·um -i *n*
probe *tr* scrutari
problem *s* quaesti·o -onis *f,* aerumn·a -ae *f; (math)* problem·a -atis *n;* **to have stomach (heart, back) —s** stomacho (corde, tergo) dolēre; **the — is ...** quaeritur ... ; **what's the — ?** quid est negotii?
problematical *adj* anc·eps -ipitis
procedure *s* mod·us -i *m* operandi, rati·o -onis *f*
proceed *intr* procedere; *(to go on)* pergere; **to — against** persequi; **to — from** oriri ex *(w. abl)*
proceedings *spl* act·a -orum *npl; (leg)* acti·o -onis *f*

proceeds *spl* redit·us -ūs *m*
process *s* rati·o -onis *f; (leg)* acti·o -onis *f*
processor *s (comput)* editor·ium -(i)i *n*
proclaim *tr* pronuntiare
proclamation *s (act)* pronuntiati·o -onis *f;* pronunt·ium -(i)i *n*
proclivity *s* proclivit·as -atis *f*
proconsul *s* procons·ul -ulis *m*
proconsular *adj* proconsular·is -is -e
proconsulship *s* pronconsulat·us -ūs *m*
procrastinate *intr* procrastinare
procrastination *s* procrastinati·o -onis *f*
procreate *tr* procreare
procreation *s* procreati·o -onis *f*
proctor *s* procura·tor -toris *m* (·trix -tricis *f*)
procurable *adj* comparand·us -a -um
procure *tr* comparare
procurement *s* comparati·o -onis *f*
prodigal *adj* prodig·us -a -um
prodigality *s* dissipati·o -onis *f*
prodigious *adj* imman·is -is -e
prodigy *s* prodig·ium -(i)i *n; (fig)* miracul·um -i *n*
produce *s* fruct·us -ūs *m*
produce *tr (to bring forward)* producere, proferre; *(to bring into existence)* parere, gignere; *(to cause)* efficere, movēre; *(a play)* docēre; *(public games)* edere; *(crops)* ferre
producer *s* chorag·us -i *m*
product *s* op·us -eris *n; (result)* exit·us -ūs *m*
production *s (act)* fabricati·o -onis *f; (work)* op·us -eris *n*
productive *adj* efficien·s -tis; *(fertile)* fer·ax -acis, fertil·is -is -e
productivity *s (of fields, mines, etc.)* fertilit·as -atis *f*
profanation *s* violati·o -onis *f*
profane *adj* profan·us -a -um
profanity *s* verb·a -orum *npl* profana
profess *tr* profitēri
professed *adj* manifest·us -a -um
profession *s (learned occupation; declaration)* professi·o -onis *f*
professional *adj* ad professionem pertin·ens -entis; veteran·us -a -um; *(expert)* perit·us -a -um
professor *s* profess·or -oris *m,* profes·trix -tricis *f;* **to be a —** profiteri
proffer *tr* promittere
proficiency *s* progress·us -ūs *m,* periti·a -ae *f*
proficient (in) *adj* perit·us -a -um (*w. gen*)
profile *s* faci·es -ei *f* obliqua; *(portrait)* imag·o -inis *f* obliqua; *(description)* descripti·o -onis *f*
profit *s (financial)* lucr·um -i *n; (benefit)* emolument·um -i *n* bonum; **to make a —** lucrum facere
profit *tr* prodesse *(w. dat)* ‖ *intr* **to — by** uti *(w. abl);* **to — from** proficere *(w. abl)*
profitable *adj* fructuos·us -a -um; *(fin)* quaestuos·us -a -um; **to be — for s.o.** prodesse alicui
profitably *adv* utiliter
profitless *adj* inutil·is -is -e, van·us -a -um
profound *adj* alt·us -a -um; *(recondite)* abstrus·us -a -um
profoundly *adv* funditus
profundity *s* altitud·o -inis *f*
profuse *adj* profus·us -a -um
profusely *adv* profuse
profusion *s* profusi·o -onis *f*
progeny *s* progeni·es -ei *f*
prognosis *s* praedict·um -i *n* (medici *or* medicae)
prognosticate *tr* praedicere
prognostication *s* praedicti·o -onis *f*
program *s* institut·um -i *n,* rati·o -onis *f; (booklet)* libell·us -i *m; (comput)* programm·a -atis *n*
program *tr (comput)* programmare
programmer *s (comput)* programma·tor -toris *m* (·trix -tricis *f*)
progress *s* progress·us -ūs *m;* **in —** in motu, in progressu; **to make —** proficere
progress *intr* progredi
progression *s* progress·us -ūs *m*
progressive *adj* profici·ens -entis
progressively *adv* gradatim
prohibit *tr* vetare
prohibition *s* interdicti·o -onis *f*
project *s* proposit·um -i *n*
project *tr* proicere ‖ *intr* prominēre, exstare; *(of land)* excurrere
projectile *s* missil·e -is *n*
projecting *adj* emin·ens -entis
projection *s* proiectur·a -ae *f*
projector *s* proiector·ium -(i)i *n;* **overhead —** proiectorium supracapitale
proletarian *adj* proletari·us -a -um
proletariat *s* pleb·s -is *f*
prolific *adj* fecund·us -a -um
prologue *s* prolog·us -i *m*
prolong *tr* producere; *(term of office)* prorogare
prolongation *s* dilati·o -onis *f; (of term of office)* prorogati·o -onis *f*
promenade *s (walk)* ambulati·o -onis *f; (place)* ambulacr·um -i *n*
promenade *intr* spatiari
prominence *s* eminenti·a -ae *f*
prominent *adj* promin·ens -entis
promiscuous *adj* promiscu·us -a -um
promiscuously *adv* promiscue
promise *s* promiss·um -i *n;* **I am not making any definite —s** nihil certi polliceor; **— of immunity** fid·es -ei *f* publica; **to break a — (made to)** fidem (datam *w. dat)* fallere; **to keep a —** promissum servare; **to make a —** fidem dare, promissum facere; **to make many —s** multa promittere

promise *tr* promittere, pollicēri; *(in marriage)* despondēre
promising *adj* bonā (maximā, summā) spe *(abl used adjectively)*; **less —** min·or -or -us opinione
promissory note *s* chirograph·um -i *n*, syngraph·a -ae *f*
promontory *s* promuntur·ium -(i)i *n*, ligul·a -ae *f*
promote *tr (in rank)* promovēre; *(a cause, the arts, etc.)* favēre *(w. dat)*; *(in school)* in superiorem classem *(or* gradum) pronovēre; **to — to a higher rank** in ampliorem gradum promovēre
promoter *s* fau·tor -toris *m* (·trix -tricis *f)*
promotion *s (act)* promoti·o -onis *f*; *(result)* amplior grad·us -ūs *m*
prompt *s (comput)* monit·us -ūs *m*
prompt *adj* prompt·us -a -um
prompt *tr* subicere, suggerere; *(incite)* commovēre
promptly *adv* statim, extemplo
promulgate *tr* promulgare
promulgation *s* promulgati·o -onis *f*
prone *adj* **(to)** pron·us -a -um (ad *or* in *w. acc)*
prong *s* den·s -tis *m*
pronominal *adj* pronominal·is -is -e
pronoun *s* pronom·en -inis *n*
pronounce *tr (to declare)* pronuntiare; *(a word, judicial sentence)* dicere; **to — a vowel short or long** vocalem correpte aut pruducte pronuntiare
pronunciation *s* pronuntiati·o -onis *f*
proof *s* document·um -i *n*; *(indication)* indic·ium -(i)i *n*
proof *adj* **— against** impervi·us -a -um *(w. dat)*
proofread *tr* legere et emendare
proofs *spl (from the press)* plagul·ae -arum *fpl*; **to correct —s** plagulas corrigere
prop *s* fulcr·um -i *n*
prop *tr* fulcire; **to — oneself up on** se fulcire *(w. dat)*
propaganda *s* re·s -rum *fpl* ad animos hominum movendos
propagate *tr* propagare; *(information)* disseminare
propagation *s* propagati·o -onis *f*; disseminati·o -onis *f*
propel *tr* propellere
propeller *s* propulsr·um -i *n*
propensity *s* propensi·o -onis *f*
proper *adj (becoming)* decor·us -a -um, dec·ens -entis; *(suitable)* idone·us -a -um; **it is — for an orator to speak** decet oratorem loqui; **— noun** proprium nom·en -inis *n (opp:* appellativum nomen)
properly *adv (in the strict sense)* proprie; *(fitly)* apte, commode
property *s* bon·a -orum *npl; (characteristic)* virt·us -utis *f*, propriet·as -atis *f*; **private —** res, rei *f* familiaris
prophecy *s* vaticinati·o -onis *f*
prophesy *tr* vaticinari
prophet *s* vat·es -is *mf; (Biblical)* prophet·a -ae *m*
prophetess *s* vat·es -is *f*
propitiate *tr* propitiare
propitiation *s* propitiati·o -onis *f*
propitious *adj* propiti·us -a -um
proportion *s* proporti·o -onis *f*; **in —** pro ratā parte; **in — to** pro *(w. abl)*
proportionately *adv* pro portione
proposal *s* propositi·o -onis *f*, condici·o -onis *f*; **to accept a —** condicionem accipere; **to make a — that** condicionem ferre ut
propose *tr* proponere; *(esp. a law)* ferre; *(esp. of the tribunes)* rogare; **to — a toast to** propinare *(w. dat)*
proposition *s (offer)* condici·o -onis *f*; *(logic)* propositi·o -onis *f*
propound *tr* proponere, exponere
proprietor *s* domin·us -i *m*
proprietress *s* domin·a -ae *f*
propriety *s* decor·um -i *n*
propulsion *s* propulsi·o -onis *f*
prosaic *adj* ieiun·us -a -um, frigid·us -a -um
proscribe *tr* proscribere
proscription *s* proscripti·o -onis *f*
prose *s* pros·a -ae *f*
prosecute *tr (to carry out)* exsequi; *(leg)* litem intendere *(w. dat)*, iudicio persequi; **to — offenses** delicta exsequi
prosecution *s* exsecuti·o -onis *f*; *(leg)* accusati·o -onis *f*
prosecutor *s* accusa·tor -toris *m* (·trix -tricis *f)*
prospect *s* prospect·us -ūs *m*; *(hope)* spes, spei *f*; **his —s are good** is in bonā spe est
prospective *adj* futur·us -a -um
prosper *intr* vigēre
prosperity *s* re·s -rum *fpl* secundae
prosperous *adj* prosper·us -a -um
prosperously *adv* prospere
prostitute *s* meretr·ix -icis *f*, prostitut·a -ae *f*; **to be a —** prostare
prostitute *tr* prostituere
prostrate *tr* sternere; **to — oneself at the feet of** se proicere ad pedes *(w. gen)*
prostrate *adj* prostrat·us -a -um; *(fig)* fract·us -a -um; **to fall —** se proicere
prostration *s (act)* prostrati·o -onis *f*; *(state)* anim·us -i *m* fractus
protect *tr* (pro)tegere
protection *s* praesid·ium -(i)i *n*; *(protecting power)* tutel·a -ae *f*
protective *adj* proteg·ens -entis
protector *s* tu·tor -toris *m*, tu·trix -tricis *f*
protest *s* obtestati·o -onis *f*

protest *tr (to assert positively)* asseverare, declarare **||** *intr* contra dicere; **to — against** contra dicere *(w. dat)*
prototype *s* exempl·ar -aris *n*
protract *tr* producere
protracted *adj* product·us -a -um
protrude *intr* prominēre, eminēre
proud *adj* glorios·us -a -um; *(haughty)* superb·us -a -um; **to be — of** superbire *(w. abl)*, gloriari *(w. acc or* de *or* in *w. abl)*
proudly *adv* superbe
prove *tr (by evidence, argument)* probare; **this —s that ...** documento est *(w. acc & inf)* **||** *intr (of persons)* se praebēre, se praestare; *(of a thing, event)* evadere, fieri, exire
proverb *s* proverb·ium -(i)i *n*
proverbial *adj* proverbial·is -is -e
provide *tr (to get ready)* parare; *(to furnish)* suppeditare; *(to equip)* ornare; **to — by law that** sancire ut **||** *intr* **to — for** providēre *(w. dat)*; *(of laws)* iubēre
provided *adj* instruct·us -a -um; **well —** refert·us -a -um
provided (that) *conj* dummodo *(w. subj)*
providence *s* providenti·a -ae *f*
provident *adj* provid·us -a -um
providential *adj* divin·us -a -um
providentially *adv* divinitus
provider *s* provis·or -oris *m* (·(t)rix -(t)ricis *f*)
province *s* provinci·a -ae *f*
provincial *adj* provincial·is -is -e; *(pej)* rustic·us -a -um
provision *s (stipulation)* condici·o -onis *f*; **—s** vict·us -ūs *m*; *(mil)* commeat·us -ūs *m*; **with the added —** exceptione adiectā
provisional *adj* temporari·us -a -um
provisionally *adv* ad tempus
proviso *s* condici·o -onis *f*; **with the — that** eā condicione ut, hac lege ut
provocation *s* irritament·um -i *n*
provocative *adj (language)* molest·us -a -um; *(enticing)* ill·ex -icis
provoke *tr (to cause)* (com)movēre; *(to irritate)* irritare, movēre
provoking *adj* molest·us -a -um
provost *s* praeposit·us -i *m* (·a -ae *f*)
prow *s* pror·a -ae *f*
prowess *s* vir·es -ium *fpl*, virt·us -utis *f*
prowl *intr* vagari, grassari
prowler *s* praeda·tor -toris *m* (·trix -tricis *m*)
proximity *s* propinquit·as -atis *f*
proxy *s* vicari·us -i *m* (·a -ae *f*)
prude *s* tetric·a -ae *f*
prudence *s* prudenti·a -ae *f*
prudent *adj* prud·ens -entis
prudently *adv* prudenter
prudish *adj* tetric·us -a -um
prune *s* prun·um -i *n* passum
prune *tr* (am)putare
pruning *s* putati·o -onis *f*
pruning shears *spl* fal·x -cis *f*
pry *intr* perscrutari; **to — into** investigare
prying *adj* curios·us -a -um
pseudonym *s* falsum nom·en -inis *n*
psychiatric *adj* psychiatric·us -a -um
psychiatrist *s* psychiat·er -ri *m* (·ria -riae *f*)
psychiatry *s* psychiatri·a -ae *f*
psychic *adj* psychic·us -a -um
psychoanalysis *s* psychoanalys·is -is *f*
psychoanalyst *s* psycholanalyst·a -ae *m* (·ria -riae *f*)
psychological *adj* de animo, psychologic·us -a -um
psychologist *s* psycholog·us -i *m* (·a -ae *f*)
psychopath *s* psychopathic·us -i *m* (·a -ae *f*)
puberty *s* pubert·as -atis *f*
public *adj* public·us -a -um; *(known)* vulgat·us -a -um; **in a — capacity** publice; **— affairs** respublica *(gen:* reipublicae) *f*
public *s* public·um -i *n*, vulg·us -i *n*; **in —** propalam; *(outdoors)* foris; **to appear in —** prodire in publicum; **to open** *(e.g., a road)* **to the —** publicare
publican *s* publican·us -i *m*
publication *s* publicati·o -onis *f*; *(of a book)* editi·o -onis *f*; *(book)* li·ber -bri *m*
publicity *s* celebrit·as -atis *f*
publicly *adv* propalam
publish *tr* publicare, patefacere; *(book)* edere
publisher *s* edi·tor -toris *m* (·trix -tricis *f*; *(publishing house)* dom·us -ūs *f* editoria
pucker *intr* **to — up the lips** osculari
pudding *s* erne·um -i *n*
puddle *s* lacun·a -ae *f*
puerile *adj* pueril·is -is -e
puff *s* flat·us -ūs *m*
puff *tr* inflare; **to be —ed up** tumēre **||** *intr (to pant)* anhelare; **to — up** intumescere
puffy *adj* sufflat·us -a -um; *(swollen)* tum·ens -entis
pull *tr (to drag)* trahere, tractare; **to — a fast one on s.o.** os alicui sublinere; **to — apart** distrahere; **to — away** avellere; **to — down** detrahere; *(buildings)* demoliri, destruere; **to — oneself together** se colligere; **to — out** extrahere; *(hair)* evellere; *(e.g., a weapon, tooth)* eximere; **to — out by the roots** exstirpare; *(weeds)* eruncare; **to — the wool over s.o.'s eyes** sobdol·us (-a) esse adversus aliquem **||** *intr* **to — at** vellicare; **to — through** pervincere; *(from an illness)* convalescere
pull *s (act)* tract·us -ūs *m*; *(influence)* grati·a -ae *f*; **to have — with** gratiam habēre apud *(w. acc)*
pulley *s* trochle·a -ae *f*
pullman car *s* curr·us -ūs *m* dormitorius
pulmonary *adj* pulmone·us -a -um; *(disease)* pulmonari·us -a -um
pulp *s* pulp·a -ae *f*

pulpit *s* pulpit·um -i *n; (eccl)* cathedr·a -ae *f*
pulsate *intr* palpitare
pulse *s* puls·us -ūs (venarum) *m;* **fast (weak) —** venarum pulsus vegetus (languidior); **to feel s.o.'s —** venas *(or* pulsum venarum) alicuius tentare
pulverize *tr* pulverare, contundere
pump *s* antli·a -ae *f*
pump *tr* haurire; **to — out, — dry** exhaurire; **to — with questions** percontari
pumpkin *s* pep·o-onis *m*
pun *s* verborum lus·us -ūs *m*
punch *s (tool)* verucul·um -i *n; (blow)* pugn·us -i *m; (drink)* poti·o -onis *f* ex fructuum suco; **to give s.o. a —, land a — on s.o.** pugnum alicui ducere
punch *tr* pugnum ducere *(w. dat),* pugno *(or* pugnis) caedere; **to — a hole in** pungere
punch-drunk *adj* stupefact·us -a -um
punching bag *s* coryc·us -i *m*
punctual *adj* dilig·ens -entis, prompt·us -a -um; **to be —** ad tempus venire
punctually *adv* ad tempus, tempori
punctuate *tr* interpungere
punctuation *s* interpuncti·o -onis *f*
punctuation mark *s* interpunct·um -i *n*
puncture *s (act)* puncti·o -onis *f; (small hole)* punct·um -i *n*
puncture *tr* pungere
pungent *adj* acut·us -a -um
Punic *adj* Punic·us -a -um
punish *tr* punire, animadvertere in *(w. acc),* poenā afficere, supplicium sumere de *(w. abl);* **to — with loss of one half of one's property** multare dimidiā parte; **to — with loss of the priesthood and dowry** multare sacerdotio et uxoris dote
punishable *adj* puniend·us -a -um
punishment *s (act)* puniti·o -onis *f; (penalty)* poen·a -ae *f,* supplic·ium -(i)i *n;* **— for crimes** poena facinorum; **to inflict — on s.o.** aliquem poenā afficere; **without —** impune
puny *adj* pusill·us -a -um
pup *s* catul·us -i *m,* catell·a -ae *f;* **—s whimper** catuli ganniunt; **to have —s** catulos parere
pupil *s* discipul·us -i *m* (·a -ae *f); (of the eye)* pupill·a -ae *f*
puppet *s* pup·a -ae *f,* neuropast·um -i *n; (fig)* minist·er -tri *m*
puppy *s* catul·us -i *m,* catell·a -ae *f*
purchase *s (act)* empti·o -onis *f; (merchandise)* mer·x -cis *f*
purchase *tr* emere, comparare, mercari
purchase price *s* pret·ium -(i)i *n; (of grain)* annon·a -ae *f*
purchaser *s* emp·tor -toris *m* (·trix -tricis *f)*
pure *adj* pur·us -a -um; *(unmixed)* mer·us -a -um; *(morally)* cast·us -a -um
purely *adv* pure; *(quite)* omnino; *(solely)* solum
purge *tr* purgare, mundare
purge *s* purgati·o -onis *f; (pol)* proscripti·o -onis *f*
purification *s* purificati·o -onis *f*
purify *tr* purificare; *(fig)* expiare
purity *s* purit·as -atis *f; (moral)* castit·as -atis *f*
purple *s* purpur·a -ae *f;* **dressed in —** purpurat·us -a -um
purple *adj* purpure·us -a -um
purport *s* significati·o -onis *f,* sententi·a -ae *f;* **a communication to the same —** tabell·ae -arum *fpl* in eandem fere sententiam
purport *tr* significare
purpose *s (aim, end)* proposit·um -i *n,* fin·is -is *m; (wish)* men·s -tis *f;* **on —** consulto; **to no —** frustra, nequaquam; **to what —** quorsum
purpose *tr* in animo habēre
purposely *adv* consulto, de industriā
purr *intr* murmurare
purr *s (of a cat)* murm·ur -uris *n*
purring *s* murmurati·o -onis *f*
purse *s* marsupp·ium -(i)i *n*
purse *tr (to pucker up)* astringere
pursuance *s* executi·o -onis *f;* **in — of** secundum *(w. acc),* ex *(w. abl)*
pursuant to *prep* secundum *(w. acc)*
pursue *tr (an enemy)* insequi; *(a course, plan)* insistere *(w. acc or dat);* **I will not — this subject further** quod non prosequar longius; **to — one's studies** studiis insistere; **to — an advantage** utilitatem sequi; **to — wealth and power** opes et potentiam consectari
pursuit *s* insectati·o -onis *f; (striving after)* consectati·o -onis *f; (eager desire for and aiming at; occupation)* stud·ium -(i)i *n*
pus *s* pu·s -ris *n*
push *tr* trudere, impellere; **to — away** *or* **back** repellere ‖ *intr* **to — on** contendere, iter facere
push *s* puls·us -ūs *m; (strong effort)* nis·us -ūs *m; (mil)* impet·us -ūs *m*
pushy *adj* aud·ax -acis, proc·ax -acis
pussy *s* cat·us -i *m,* fel·es -is *f*
put *tr* ponere, collocare; **— yourself in my place** fac qui ego sum, te esse **to — an end to** finem facere *(w. dat);* **to — aside** ponere; **to — away** seponere, abdere; *(in safety)* recondere; **to — back** reponere; **to — down** deponere; *(to suppress)* supponere, sedare; *(in writing)* scribere; **to — his hand to his mouth** manum ad os apponere; **to — in** inserere; **to — in order** ordinare; **to — in prison** in custodiam tradere; **to — off (to another time)** differre (in aliud tempus); **to — on** imponere *(w. dat); (to add)* addere; *(clothes)* se induere *(w. abl); (a ring)*

(anulum) digito aptare; *(a cap)* (pilleum) capiti suo imponere; *(a sword)* cingere latus (gladio); **to — on the table** ponere super mensam; **to — out** *(the hand)* proferre; *(to remove, e.g., from office)* submovēre; *(a fire)* exstinguere; **to — out of one's mind** ex animo delēre; **to — out of the way** demovēre; *(to murder)* de medio tollere; **to — together** componere, conferre; **to — up** *(to erect)* statuere, erigere; *(to build)* aedificare; *(to raise, e.g., hands)* erigere; **to — up for sale** venum dare; ‖ *intr* **to — in** *(of ships)* appellere; **to — in to port** portum petere; **to — out to sea** solvere; **to — up with** tolerare

putrefy *intr* putrescere

putrid *adj* putrid•us -a -um

putty *s* glut•en -inis *n* vitrariorum

puzzle *s* aenigm•a -atis *n*

puzzle *tr* confundere

puzzled *adj* confus•us -a -um

puzzling *adj* perplex•us -a -um

pygmy *s* pygmae•us -i *m*

pyjamas *spl* synthes•is -is *f* dormitoria

pylon *s* colum•en -inis *n*

pyramid *s* pyram•is -idis *f*

pyre *s* rog•us -i *m*

pyrrhic *adj* pyrrhichi•us -a -um; **— foot** ped•es -is *m* pyrrhichius

Pythagorean *adj* Pythagorae•us -a -um

Pythian *adj* Pythi•us -a -um

Q

quack *s (phoney)* circulat•or -oris *m; (bad physician)* pharmacopol•a -ae *m; (of a duck)* tetrissitat•us -ūs *m*

quack *intr* tetrissitare

quadrangle *s* quadriangul•um -i *n; (of a college)* are•a -ae *f*

quadrangular *adj* quadriangul•us -a -um

quadruped *s* quadrup•es -edis *mf*

quadruple *tr* quadruplicare

quadruple *adj* quadrupl•us -a -um, quadrupl•ex -icis

quadruplets *spl* quattuor liber•i -orum *mpl* gemini

quaestor *s* quaest•or -oris *m*

quaestorship *s* quaestur•a -ae *f;* **to hold the —** quaesturam gerere

quagmire *s* pal•us -udis *f*

quail *s* coturn•ix -icis *f*

quaint *adj* insolit•us -a -um

quake *intr* tremere

quake *s* trem•or -oris *m*

qualification *s (endowment)* indol•es -is *f; (limitation)* excepti•o -onis *f*

qualified *adj (competent)* perit•us -a -um; *(limited)* modic•us -a -um; **— for** apt•us -a -um ad *(w. acc),* habil•is -is -e ad *(w. acc)*

qualify *tr* aptum *or* idoneum reddere; *(to limit)* temperare ‖ *intr* apt•us -a -um esse, idone•us -a -um esse

quality *s* qualit•as -atis *f; (excellence)* virt•us -utis *f*

qualm *s* fastid•ium -(i)i *n;* **— of conscience** scrupul•us -i *m*

quantity *s* numer•us -i *m,* quantit•as -atis *f;* **a large —** frequenti•a -ae *f*

quarantine *s* separati•o -onis *f* per pestilentiam

quarantine *tr* segregare, separare

quarrel *s* iurg•ium -(i)i *n; (stronger)* rix•a -ae *f;* **to pick a — with** iurgio contendere cum *(w. abl)*

quarrel *intr* iurgare, altercari; rixari; **to — with one another about** inter se iurgare de *(w. abl)*

quarrelsome *adj* iurgios•us -a -um

quarry *s* lapicidin•ae -arum *fpl; (prey)* praed•a -ae *f*

quart *s* duo sextari•i -orum *mpl*

quarter *s (fourth part)* quarta par•s -tis *f,* quadran•s -tis *m; (side, direction)* par•s -tis *f; (district)* regi•o -onis *f;* **at close —s** comminus [*adv*]; **—s** *(dwelling)* tect•um -i *n; (temporary abode)* hospit•ium -(i)i *n;* **neither giving nor asking for —** sine missione

quarter *tr* in quattuor partes dividere; *(to give lodgings to)* hospitium praebēre *(w. dat)*

quarterly *adj* trimestr•is -is -e

quarterly *adv* tertio quoque mense

quartermaster *s* castrorum praefect•us -i *m*

quash *tr (rebellion)* opprimere; *(a law)* rescindere

quatrain *s* tetrastich•on -i *n*

quavering *adj* tremul•us -a -um

queasy *adj* nauseabund•us -a -um; **to feel —** nauseare

queen *s* regin•a -ae *f*

queen bee *s* rex, regis *m* apium

queer *adj* insolit•us -a -um; *(strange)* inept•us -a -um; *(eccentric)* inconcinn•us -a -um; *(effeminate)* effeminatus

queer *s* effeminat•us -i *m*

quell *tr* sedare

quench *tr* exstinguere; **to — a thirst** sitim sedare

querulous *adj* querul•us -a -um

query *s* quaesti•o -onis *f*

query *tr & intr* quaerere

quest *s* inquisiti•o -onis *f;* **to be in — of** requirere; **to go in — of** investigare

question *s* quaesti•o -onis *f,* interrogati•o -onis *f;* **I ask you this —** hoc te rogo; **many —s are raised** multa quaeruntur; **no —, he's at fault** nempe in culpā est; **out of the —** haud licit•us -a -um; **that's a loaded —** captiosum interrogatum est; **there is no — that** non dubium est quin *(w. subj);* **to ask a —** interrogare, quaerere; **to answer the question** ad rogatum *(or* interrogatum) respondēre; **to ask a loaded —** captiose interrogare; **to ask many —s** multa interrogare; **to call into —** in dubium vocare; **to keep asking —s** rogitare; **why do you ask such —s?** cur ista quaeris? **without —** sine dubio

question *tr* interrogare, percontari; *(to doubt)* dubitare, in dubium vocare; *(to examine)* scrutari

questionable *adj* dubi•us -a -um

questioning *s* interrogati•o -onis *f,* indagati•o -onis *f*

question mark *s* not•a -ae *f* interrogativa

queue *s (line)* ord•o -inis *m*

queue up *intr* se in ordinem adducere

quibble *s* capti•o -onis *f*

quibble *intr* cavillari

quibbler *s* cavilla•tor -toris *m* (•trix -tricis *f)*

quibbling *s* cavillati•o -onis *f*

quick *adj* cel•er -eris -ere; *(agile)* agil•is -is -e; *(mentally)* astut•us -a -um; *(w. hands)* facil•is -is -e; *(w. wits)* argut•us -a -um

quicken *tr* accelerare

quick lime *s* calx, calcis *f* viva

quickly *adv* cito

quickness *s* celerit•as -atis *f; (of mind)* acum•en -inis *n; (agility)* agilit•as -atis *f*

quicksand *s* syrt•is -is *f*

quicksilver *s* argent•um -i *n* vivum

quick-tempered *adj* iracund•us -a -um

quiet *adj* quiet•us -a -um; *(silent)* tacit•us -a -um; **quiet!** fac *(pl:* facite) silentium!; **to keep —** quiescere; *(to refrain from talking)* silēre

quiet *s* qui•es -etis *f; (leisure)* ot•ium -(i)i *n; (silence)* silent•ium -(i)i *n*

quiet *tr* tranquillare, sedare

quill *s* penn•a -ae *f*

quilt *s* culcit•a -ae *f*

quince *s* cydon•ium -(i)i *n*

quintessence *s* medull•a -ae *f; (fig)* summ•a -ae *f*

quip *s* faceti•ae -arum *fpl*

quip *tr & intr* per iocum dicere

quirk *s* propr•ium -(i)i *n*

quit *tr (to leave)* relinquere, deserere; *(a position, job)* se abdicare *(w. abl); (to stop)* cessare, desinere; **— laughing!** noli *(pl:* nolite) ridēre! **||** *intr* cessare; *(to resign)* se abdicare

quite *adv* omnino, admodum; **not —** parum, aegre; *(not yet)* nondum

quiver *s* pharetr•a -ae *f;* **wearing a —** pharetrat•us -a -um

quiver *intr* tremere

quivering *s* trem•or -oris *m*

Quixotic *adj* ridicul•us -a -um

quizz *s* probatiuncul•a -ae *f (see* **exam)**

quoit *s* disc•us -i *m;* **to play —s** disco ludere

quota *s* rata par•s -tis *f*

quotation *s (act)* prolati•o -onis *f; (words quoted)* loc•us -i *m* allatus

quote *tr* ponere, afferre

R

rabbi *s* rabbi *m* [*indecl*]

rabbit *s* cunicul•us -i *m*

rabble *s* turb•a -ae *f,* vulg•us -i *n*

race *s (lineage)* gen•us -eris *n; (foot race)* certam•en -inis *n* cursūs; *(horse race)* curs•us -ūs *m* equorum; *(of chariots)* curricul•um -i *n; (of cars)* certamen autocinetorum

race *intr* certare; *(running)* pedibus certare; *(on horseback)* cursu equestri certare

race car *s* autocinet•um -i *n* currile

racecourse *s* stad•ium -(i)i *n*

racehorse *s* cel•es -etis *m*

racer *s* curs•or -oris *m*

racetrack *s* curricul•um -i *n; (for horses)* hippodrom•us -i *m*

rack *s (shelf)* plute•us -i *m; (for punishment)* equule•us -i *m;* **to put to the —** equuleo torquēre

rack *tr* **to be —ed with pain** dolore distinēri; **to — one's brains about s.th.** aliquā re scrutandā fatigari

racket *s (noise)* strepit•us -ūs *m; (shouting)* clam•or -oris *m; (for tennis)* reticul•um -i *n;* **to raise a —** clamorem tollere

racketeer *s* circula•tor -toris *m* (•trix -tricis *f)*

radiance *s* fulg•or -oris *m*

radiant *adj* fulgid•us -a -um

radiate *tr* emittere **||** *intr* radiare

radiation *s* radiati•o -onis *f*

radiator *s* caloris radiatr•um -i *n*

radical *adj* innat•us -a -um; *(thorough)* tot•us -a -um

radical *s* rerum novarum cupid•us -i *m* (•a -ae *f)*

radically *adv* penitus

radio *s* radiophon•um -i *n;* **to turn down (up) the —** vim radiophoni remittere (amplificare); **to turn on (turn off) the —** radiophonum excitare *or* accendere (expedire)

radio broadcast *s* emissi•o -onis *f* radiophonica

radio station *s* stati•o -onis *f* radiophonica

radish *s* raphan•us -i *m*

radius *s* rad•ius -(i)i *m*

raffle *s* ale•a -ae *f,* sortiti•o -onis *f*

raffle *tr* **to — off** aleā vendere, sortiri

raft *s* rat•is -is *f*

rafter *s* trab•s -is *f*

rag *s* pannicul•us -i *m*

rage *s* fur•or -oris *m,* ir•a -ae *f;* **to fly into a —** irā efferri

rage *intr* furere, saevire

ragged *adj* pannos•us -a -um

raid *s* incursi•o -onis *f*
raid *tr* praedari
raider *s* praedat•or -oris *m*
rail *s* longur•ius -(i)i *m*
rail *intr* **to — at** insectari
railing *s (fence)* saepiment•um -i *n; (abuse)* convic•ium -(i)i *n*
railroad *s* ferrivi•a -ae *f*
railroad car *s* curr•us -ūs *m* ferriviarius
railroad station *s* stati•o -onis *f* ferriviaria
raiment *s* vestit•us -ūs *m*
rain *s* pluvi•a -ae *f; (stormy)* imb•er -ris *m;* **heavy, steady —** magni et assidui imbres; **the — is letting up** *or* **tapering off** imber detumescit
rain *impers* pluit pluere pluit; **it is —ing** pluit; **to — buckets** urceatim pluere; **to — hard** vehementer pluere
rain basin *s (in the atrium)* impluv•ium -(i)i *n*
rainbow *s* arc•us -ūs *m* pluvius
rain cloud *s* nimb•us -i *m*
raincoat *s* scorte•a -ae *f; (hooded)* paenul•a -ae *f*
rainy *adj* pluvi•us -a -um
raise *tr (to lift up)* tollere; *(finger, ladder, eyes)* erigere; *(to build)* exstruere; *(money)* expedire; *(an army)* (con)scribere, comparare; *(siege)* solvere; *(children, crops, animals)* educare; *(to stir up)* excitare; *(to promote)* provehere; *(prices)* augēre; *(crops)* colere; *(beard)* demittere; **to — the curtain** aulaea premere; **to — the head (eyes)** caput (oculos) attollere
raisin *s* (uva) pass•a -ae *f*
rake *s* rastell•us -i *m*
rake *tr* radere; **to — in money** pecuniam corradere
rally *s* conti•o -onis *f*
rally *tr (mil)* in ordines revocare **‖** *intr* se colligere; *(after a retreat)* se ex fugā colligere; *(from sickness)* convalescere
ram *s* ari•es -etis *m;* **—s bleat** arietes balant
ram *tr* fistucare; *(to cram)* infercire
RAM *(comput)* memori•a -ae *f* volatilis
ramble *s* vagati•o -onis *f*
ramble *intr* vagari, errare; **to — on** *(in speech)* garrire
rambling *adj* err•ans -antis; *(fig)* vag•us -a -um
ramification *s* ramificati•o -onis *f*
ramp *s* agg•er -eris *m*
rampage *s* **to go on a —** ferocire
rampage *intr* furere
rampant *adj* effrenat•us -a -um; *(widespread)* divulgat•us -a -um
rampart *s* vall•um -i *n*
ranch *s* latifund•ium -(i)i *n*
rancher *s* pecuar•ius -(i)i *m*
rancid *adj* rancid•us -a -um
rancor *s* iracundi•a -ae *f*
random *adj* fortuit•us -a -um; **at —** temere
range *s (row)* ord•o -inis *m; (of mountain)* iug•um -i *n; (reach)* iact•us -ūs *m; (extent)* fin•es -ium *mpl;* **to be in —** intra teli iactum esse; **to be out of —** extra teli iactum abesse; **the enemy were just within —** non longius hostes aberant quam quo telum adici posset
range *tr* ordinare, disponere **‖** *intr (to rove at large)* pervagari; *(to vary)* discrepare
rank *s* ord•o -inis *m,* grad•us -ūs *m; (high rank)* dignit•as -atis *f;* **in close —** *(mil)* firmis ordinibus; **the — and file** *(i.e., ordinary soldiers)* manipular•es -ium *mpl*
rank *tr* in numero habēre **‖** *intr* in numero haberi; **to — first** primatum obtinēre
rank *adj (extreme)* summ•us -a -um; *(of smell)* foetid•us -a -um
ransack *tr* diripere; *(to search thoroughly)* exquirere
ransom *s (act)* redempti•o -onis *f; (money)* pret•ium -(i)i *n*
ransom *tr* redimere
rant *intr* ampullari; **to — and rave** debacchari
rap *s (slap)* alap•a -ae *f; (blow)* ict•us -ūs *m; (at door)* pulsati•o -onis *f; (w. knuckles)* talitr•um -i *n;* **not to give a — about** non flocci facere *(w. acc)*
rap *tr (to criticize)* exagitare **‖** *intr* **to — at** *(a door)* pulsare
rapacious *adj* rap•ax -acis
rape *s* stupr•um -i *n* per vim
rape *tr* per vim stuprare, stupro violare
rapid *adj* rapid•us -a -um
rapidity *s* rapidit•as -atis *f*
rapidly *adv* rapide
rapids *spl* vad•um -i *n* candicans
rapine *s* rapin•a -ae *f*
rapist *s* constuprat•or -oris *m*
rapture *s* exsultati•o -onis *f;* **to be in —s of delight** gaudio efferi
rapturous *adj* exsult•ans -antis
rare *adj* rar•us -a -um; *(meat)* semicoct•us -a -um *(opp:* percoctus)
rarefied *adj* rarefact•us -a -um
rarely *adv* raro
rarity *s* rarit•as -atis *f,* paucit•as -atis *f; (thing)* res, rei *f* rara
rascal *s* scelest•us -i *m* (•a -ae *f*)
rascally *adj* scelest•us -a -um
rash *adj* temerari•us -a -um
rash *s* impetig•o -inis *f*
rashly *adv* temere
rashness *s* temerit•as -atis *f*
raspberry *s* mor•um -i *n* Idaeum
raspberry bush *s* mor•a -ae *f* Idaea
rat *s* mus, muris *m; (person)* transfug•a -ae *m;* **I smell a —** aliquid mihi subolet; **like drowned —s** tamquam mures udi; **—s squeak** mures mintriunt
rat *intr* **to — on s.o.** aliquem deferre
rate *s* proporti•o -onis *f; (price)* pret•ium -(i)i *n; (scale)* norm•a -ae *f;* **at any —**

utique; **— of exchange** collyb·us -i *m;* **— of interest** faen·us -oris *n*
rate *tr* aestimare, taxare; **to — s.o. highly** aliquem magni facere
rather *adv* potius, prius; *(somewhat)* aliquanto, paulo, *or render by comparative of adjective or adverb*
ratification *s* sancti·o -onis *f*
ratify *tr* sancire, comprobare
rating *s* aestimati·o -onis *f*
ratio *s* proporti·o -onis *f*
ration *s (portion)* demens·um -i *n;* **—s** *(mil)* cibari·a -orum *npl*
ration *tr* demetiri
rational *adj* ratione praedit·us -a -um; sapi·ens -entis; *(sane)* san·us -a um; **to be —** sapere
rationalize *intr* ratiocinari, rationaliter explicare
rationally *adv* ratione, sapienter
rattle *s* crepit·us -ūs *m; (toy)* crepitacul·um -i *n*
rattle *tr* crepitare *(w. abl);* **to — off** cito volvere **II** *intr* crepare, crepitare; **to — on** garrire
rattlesnake *s* crotal·us -i *m* horridus
raucous *adj* rauc·us -a -um
ravage *tr* vastare, populari
ravages *spl* vastati·o -onis *f*
rave *intr* furere, saevire
raven *s* corv·us -i *m;* **—s croak** corvi crocitant
ravenous *adj* vor·ax -acis
ravenously *adv* voraciter
ravine *s* vall·is -is *f* praerupta
raving *adj* furios·us -a -um; **to be — mad** plane furere
ravish *tr* stuprare
ravishing *adj* suavissim·us -a -um
raw *adj* crud·us -a -um; *(weather)* asp·er -era -erum; *(jokes)* incondit·us -a -um
ray *s* rad·ius -(i)i *m;* **— of hope** specul·a -ae *f*
raze *tr* solo aequare
razor *s* novacul·a -ae *f;* **electric —** rasor·ium -(i)i *n* electricum
reach *s (grasp, capacity)* capt·us -ūs *m; (of weapon)* iact·us -ūs *m;* **out of my —** extra ictum meum; **within my —** sub meo ictu
reach *tr (e.g., a high branch)* contingere, attingere; *(of space)* pertinēre ad *(w. acc),* extendi ad *(w. acc); (to come up to)* assequi; *(to arrive at)* pervenire ad *or* in *(w. acc); (to hand)* porrigere; *(to attain to, e.g., old age)* adipisci; **to — out the hand** manum porrigere
react *intr* affici; **to — to** referre
reaction *s* affect·us -ūs *m;* **what was his — to … ?** quo animo tulit … ?
reactionary *s* qui *or* quae pristinum rerum statum revocare vult
read *tr & intr* legere; **to — aloud** recitare, clare legere; **to — over** translegere; **to — through** perlegere; **to — well** commode legere
readable *adj* lectu facil·is -is -e
reader *s* lec·tor -toris *m* (·trix -tricis *f); (book)* lib·er -ri *m*
readily *adv (willingly)* libenter; *(easily)* facile
readiness *s* facilit·as -atis *f;* **in —** in promptu
reading *s* lecti·o -onis *f; (public recital)* recitati·o -onis *f*
reading lamp *s* lamp·as -adis *f* lectoria
reading room *s* oec·us -i *m* lectorius
ready *adj* **(for)** parat·us -a -um, prompt·us -a -um (ad *w. acc)*
real *adj* ver·us -a -um
real estate *s* re·s -rum *fpl* soli *(opp:* re·s -rum *fpl* mobiles); **piece of —** praed·ium -(i)i *n*
real estate broker *s* praedia·tor -toris *mf*
realistic *adj* verisimil·is -is -e
reality *s* res, rei *f,* verit·as -atis *f;* **in —** re verā
realization *s (e.g., of plans)* effect·us -ūs *m; (of ideas)* comprehensi·o -onis *f*
realize *tr* sentire; *(to effect)* efficere, ad exitum perducere; **to — great profits from** magnas pecunias facere ex *(w. abl)*
really *adv* vero, profecto, re verā; *(surely)* sane, certe
realm *s* regn·um -i *n*
reap *tr* metere; *(fig)* percipere; **to — the reward for** fructum percipere ex *(w. abl)*
reaper *s* mess·or -oris *m;* machin·a -ae *f* messoria
reappear *intr* redire, revenire; *(from below)* resurgere
rear *tr* educare **II** *intr (of horses)* arrectum se tollere
rear *s* terg·um -i *n; (sl)* clun·es -ium *mpl or fpl; (mil)* novissimum agm·en -inis *n;* **on the —** a tergo; **to bring up the —** agmen cogere
rear (end) *s (sl)* postic·um -i *n*
rearing *s* educati·o -onis *f*
reason *s (faculty; reasonable ground)* rati·o -onis *f; (cause)* caus·a -ae *f; (moderation)* mod·us -i *m;* **for good —s** iustis de causis; **for that —** ideo, idcirco, eā de causā; **for this —** hāc de causā, itaque, quamobrem; **for —s of poor health** valetudinis causā; **for various —s** multis de causis; **there is no — why** nihil causae est, cur; **to give a — why** adferre rationem, quamobrem; **what's the — why** quid est enim, cur; **with —** cum causā
reasonable *adj (fair)* aequ·us -a -um; *(moderate)* modic·us -a -um; *(judicious)* prud·ens -entis
reasonably *adv* ratione, iuste; modice

reasoning *s* ratiocinati·o -onis *f; (discussing)* disceptati·o -onis *f*
reassemble *tr* recolligere, rursus cogere
reassert *tr* iterare
reassurance *s* confirmati·o -onis *f*
reassure *tr* confirmare, redintegrare
rebate *s* deminuti·o -onis *f*
rebel *s* rebell·is -is *mf*
rebel *intr* rebellare, desciscere
rebellion *s* rebelli·o -onis *f*
rebellious *adj* rebell·is -is -e; *(disobedient)* contum·ax -acis
rebirth *s* novus ort·us -ūs *m*
reboot *tr (comput)* redinitiare
rebound *s* result·us -ūs *m*
rebound *intr* resultare, resilire
rebuff *s* repuls·a -ae *f*, reici·o -onis *f*
rebuff *tr* repellere, reicere
rebuild *tr* reficere
rebuke *s* reprehensi·o -onis *f*
rebuke *tr* reprehendere, vituperare
rebut *tr* refutare, redarguere
rebuttal *s* refutati·o -onis *f*
recall *s* revocati·o -onis *f*
recall *tr* revocare; *(to remember)* recordari; **as I —** ut mea memoria est; **to — to mind** in memoriam redigere
recant *tr* recantare, retractare
recapitulate *tr* summatim colligere
recapitulation *s* repetiti·o -onis *f*, compend·ium -(i)i *n*
recapture *s* recuperati·o -onis *f*
recapture *tr* recuperare
recede *intr* recedere
receipt *s (act)* accepti·o -onis *f; (document)* apoch·a -ae *f;* **—s and expeditures** accept·a -orum *npl* et dat·a -orum *npl*
receive *tr* accipere
receiver *s* recep·tor -toris *m* (·trix -tricis *f*); *(of a telphone)* auscultabul·um -i *n*
recent *adj* rec·ens -entis
recently *adv* nuper
receptacle *s* receptacul·um -i *n*
reception *s (act)* accepti·o -onis *f; (social event)* hospit·ium -(i)i *n*
receptionist *s* salutatr·ix -icis *f*
receptive *adj* docil·is -is -e; **to be — to treatment** recipere curationem
recess *s (place)* recess·us -ūs *m; (in a wall)* adyt·um *-n; (intermission)* intermissi·o -onis *f*, paus·a -ae *f; (vacation)* feri·ae -arum *fpl; (leg)* iustit·ium -(i)i *n*
recipe *s* praescript·um -i *n*
recipient *s* accep·tor -toris *m* (·trix -tricis *f*)
reciprocal *adj* mutu·us -a -um
reciprocally *adv* mutuo, invicem
reciprocate *tr* reddere **II** *intr* reciprocare
recital *s* recitati·o -onis *f*
recitation *s* recitati·o -onis *f*
recite *tr* recitare
reckless *adj* temerari·us -a -um
recklessly *adv* temere
recklessness *s* temerit·as -atis *f*
reckon *tr* aestimare **II** *intr* **to — on** confidere *(w. dat)*
reckoning *s* numerati·o -onis *f; (account to be given)* rati·o -onis *f;* **— of time** ratio *f* temporis
reclaim *tr* reposcere, repetere
recline *intr* recubare; *(at table)* accumbere, recumbere; *(said of several guests)* discumbere
recluse *s* solitari·us -i *m* (·a -ae *f*)
recognition *s* agniti·o -onis *f*
recognizance *s* vadimon·ium -(i)i *n*
recognize *tr* agnoscere; *(to acknowledge)* noscere; *(to admit)* accipere
recoil *intr* resilire; *(in horror)* (**from**) refugere (ab *w. abl*); *(fig)* fastidire *(w. acc)*
recoil *s* recessi·o -onis *f*
recollect *tr* recordari
recollection *s* recordati·o -onis *f*
recommence *tr* redintegrare **II** *intr* redire
recommend *tr* commendare
recommendation *s* commendati·o -onis *f;* **letter of —** litter·ae -arum *fpl* commendaticiae
recompense *s* remunerati·o -onis *f*
recompense *tr* remunerare; *(to indemnify)* compensare
reconcilable *adj* placabil·is -is -e; *(of things)* conveni·ens -entis
reconcile *tr* reconciliare, componere; **to be —ed** in gratiam restitui
reconciliation *s* reconciliati·o -onis *f*
reconnaissance *s* speculati·o -onis *f*
reconnoiter *tr* perspeculari
reconquer *tr* revincere
reconsider *tr* reputare, revolvere
reconstruct *tr* restituere, renovare
reconstruction *s* restituti·o -onis *f*, renovati·o -onis *f*
record *s* monument·um -i *n;* orb·is -is *m* phonographicus; *(top performance)* palm·a -ae *f;* **—s** act·a -orum *npl*, annal·es -ium *mpl; (in bookkeeping)* tabul·ae -arum *fpl;* **to break the —** gradum praestitutum superare; **to play (listen to) —s** orbes phonographicos exhibēre (audire)
record *tr* referre *or* scribere in tabulas; *(sounds)* (voces, musicam) per machinam phonographice imprimere
recorder *s* procura·tor -toris *m* (·trix -tricis *f*) ab actis; *(machine)* machinul·a -ae *f* phonographica, discophon·um -i *n*
recording *s* impressi·o -onis *f (w. gen)* per discophonum
recording secretary *s* ab actīs *mf*
record player *s* machinul·a -ae *f* phonographica; discophon·um -i *n*
recount *tr* enarrare
recoup *tr* recuperare
recourse *s* refug·ium -(i)i *n;* **to have — to** fugere ad; *(to resort to)* descendere ad

recover *tr (to regain)* recuperare **||** *intr (from an illness)* convalescere; *(to come to one's senses)* ad se redire
recoverable *adj* reparabil•is -is -e; *(of persons)* sanabil•is -is -e
recovery *s* recuperati•o -onis *f; (from illness)* recreati•o -onis *f*
recreate *tr* recreare
recreation *s* oblectati•o -onis *f*
recriminate *tr* invicem accusare
recrimination *s* mutua accusati•o -onis *f*
recruit *s* tir•o -onis *mf;* **raw —** tiro rudis
recruit *tr (mil)* conscribere; *(one's strength)* reficere
recuiting *s* delect•us -ūs *m*
recruiting officer *s* conquisi•tor -toris *m* (•trix -tricis *f)*
recruitment *s* dilect•us -ūs *m*
rectify *tr* corrigere, emendare
rectitude *s* probit•as -atis *f*
rector *s* rect•or -oris *m*
rectum *s* an•us -i *m*
recur *intr* redire
recurrence *s* redit•us -ūs *m*
recurrent *adj* recurr•ens -entis, assidu•us -a -um
red *adj* ru•ber -bra -brum; *(hair)* ruf•us -a -um; *(ruddy)* rubicund•us -a -um; **to be —** rubēre; **to grow —** rubescere
red cent *s* **I don't owe anyone a —** assem aerarium nemini debeo; **I haven't a —** assem aerarium habeo nullum
redden *tr* rubefacere, rutilare **||** *intr* rubescere; *(to blush)* erubescere
reddish *adj* subru•ber -bra -brum; *(hair)* subruf•us -a -um
redeem *tr* redimere
redeemer *s* liberat•or -oris *m; (eccl)* Redempt•or -oris *m*
redemption *s* redempti•o -onis *f*
redhead *s* ruf•us -i *m* (•a -ae *f),* rutil•us -i *m* (•a -ae *f)*
red-hot *adj* cand•ens -entis
redness *s* rub•or -oris *m*
redouble *tr* ingeminare
redound *intr* redundare
redress *s* satisfacti•o -onis *f;* **to demand —** res repetere
redress *tr* restituere, emendare
reduce *tr* minuere; *(to a condition)* redigere; *(mil)* expugnare
reduction *s* deminuti•o -onis *f; (mil)* expugnati•o -onis *f*
redundancy *s* redundanti•a -ae *f*
redundant *adj* supervacu•us -a -um
reed *s* harund•o -inis *f*
reef *s* scopul•us -i *m*
reek *intr* fumare; **to — of** olēre
reeking *adj* putid•us -a -um
reel *s* fus•us -i *m*
reel *tr* **to — off** recitare volubiliter **||** *intr (to stagger)* titubare
reelect *tr* iterum eligere *or* creare
reenter *tr* iterum intrare in *(w. acc)*
reentry *s* redit•us -ūs *m; (of a missile)* reditus in aërem terrae
reestablish *tr* restituere
reestablishment *s* restituti•o -onis *f*
refashion *tr* renovare, restituere
refectory *s* cenati•o -onis *f*
refer *tr* referre, remittere **||** *intr* **to — to** attingere, alludere
referee *s* arbi•ter -tri *m* (•tra -trae *f)*
reference *s* rati•o -onis *f; (place in a book)* loc•us -i *m; (as to character)* commendati•o -onis *f;* **in — to s.th.** ex relatione ad aliquid; **letter of —** litterae commendaticiae; **with — to our annals** ad nostrorum annalium rationem
refine *tr* expolire; *(metals)* excoquere; *(manners)* excolere
refined *adj* urban•us -a -um, human•us -a -um
refinement *s (of liquids)* purgati•o -onis *f; (fig)* urbanit•as -atis *f,* humanit•as -atis *f*
reflect *tr* repercutere **||** *intr* **to — on** considerare, reputare
reflection *s* repercussi•o -onis *f; (thing reflected)* imag•o -inis *f; (thinking over)* considerati•o -onis *f;* **without —** inconsulte
reflective *adj* cogitabund•us -a -um
reflexive *adj* reciproc•us -a -um
reform *tr* reficere; *(to amend)* corrigere, emendare **||** *intr* se corrigere
reform *s* correcti•o -onis *f*
reformation *s* correcti•o -onis *f*
Reformation *s* Reformati•o -onis *f*
reformer *s* correc•tor -toris *m* (•trix -tricis *f)*
refract *tr* refringere
refraction *s* refracti•o -onis *f*
refractory *adj* contum•ax -acis
refrain *s* vers•us -ūs *m* intercularis
refrain *intr* **to — from** abstinēre ab *(w. abl);* **I — from speaking** abstineo quin dicam; **he will not — from boasting** non temperabit quin iactet
refresh *tr* recreare, reficere; *(the memory)* redintegrare
refreshing *adj* iucund•us -a -um
refreshment *s (food)* cib•us -i *m; (drink)* pot•us -ūs *m*
refrigerate *tr* refrigidare
refrigerator *s* frigidar•ium -(i)i *n*
refuge *s* refug•ium -(i)i *n;* **to take — with** confugere in *(w. acc)*
refugee *s* profug•us -i *m* (•a -ae *f),* ex(s)•ul -ulis *mf*
refulgent *adj* fulgid•us -a -um
refund *tr* restituere
refund *s* pecuni•a -ae *f* restituta
refusal *s* recusati•o -onis *f*
refuse *tr* recusare, negare
refutation *s* refutati•o -onis *f*
refute *tr* refutare, redarguere

regain *tr* recuperare
regal *adj* regal·is -is -e
regally *adv* regaliter
regard *s* rati·o -onis *f; (concern)* cur·a -ae *f; (esteem)* grati·a -ae *f;* **give him (her) my best —s** dicito ei plurimam meis verbis salutem; **give my —s to your brother** fratrem tuum iube salvēre; **to have — for** rationem *(w. gen)* habēre; **to send best —s to** salutem plurimam ascribere *(w. dat)*
regard *tr (to look at)* respicere, intueri; *(to concern)* spectare ad *(w. acc); (to esteem)* aestimare; *(to consider)* habēre; **to — his word as law** pro legibus habēre quae dicat
regarding *prep* de *(w. abl)*
regardless *adj* **— of** negleg·ens -entis *(w. acc);* **— of order of preference** omisso ordine
regardless *adv* quidquid accedat
regatta *s* curs·us -ūs *m* navium
regency *s* interregn·um -i *n*
regenerate *tr* regenerare
regeneration *s* regenerati·o -onis *f*
regent *s* inter·rex -regis *m*
regicide *s (murderer)* regis occis·or -oris *m; (deed)* caed·es -is *f* regis
regime *s* administrati·o -onis *f*
regimen *s* vict·us -ūs *m*
regiment *s* legi·o -onis *f*
regimental *adj* legionari·us -a -um
regimental commander *s* legat·us -i *m* legionis
region *s* regi·o -onis *f;* **in the — of** circa *(w. acc)*
regional *adj* regional·is -is -e; *(characteristic)* peculiar·is -is -e
register *s (list)* tabul·ae -arum *fpl; (public records)* act·a -orum *npl*
register *tr* perscribere, in tabulas referre; *(emotions)* ostendere ‖ *intr* nomen dare, nomen in tabulas referre
registrar *s* tabulari·us -i *m* (·a -ae *f*)
registration *s* in tabulas relati·o -onis *f,* perscripti·o -onis *f*
registry *s* tabular·ium -(i)i *n*
regret *s* paenitenti·a -ae *f*
regret *tr* **I —** me paenitet *(w. gen)*
regretful *adj* paenit·ens -entis
regrettable *adj* paenitend·us -a -um
regular *adj (common)* usitat·us -a -um; *(proper)* iust·us -a -um; *(consistent)* const·ans -antis; *(arranged, coming in order)* ordinari·us -a -um; **— army** exercit·us -ūs *m* permanens
regularity *s (orderly arrangement)* ord·o -inis *m; (evenness, unbroken succession)* constanti·a -ae *f*
regularly *adv* ordine, constanter, assidue
regulate *tr* ordinare, disponere; *(to control)* moderari *(w. dat); (to adjust)* temperare, accommodare
regulation *s (act)* ordinati·o -onis *f; (rule)* praecept·um -i *n,* iuss·um -i *n*
rehabilitate *tr* restituere
rehearsal *s* meditati·o -onis *f; (theat)* prolusi·o -onis *f*
rehearse *tr* meditari; *(theat)* proludere
reign *s* regn·um -i *n,* imper·ium -(i)i *n;* **during his —** eo rege; **— of terror** *(fig)* tempor·a -um *npl* violenta
reign *intr* regnare; **to — over** regnare in *(w. abl),* dominari in *(w. acc)*
reimburse *tr* rependere
reimbursement *s* pecuniae restituti·o -onis *f*
rein *s* haben·a -ae *f;* **to give free — to** frena dare *(w. dat);* **to give full — to** habenas immittere *(w. dat);* **to loosen the —s** frena dare; **to tighten the —s** habenas adducere
reindeer *s* tarandr·us -i *m*
reinforce *tr* firmare, supplēre
reinforcement *s* subsid·ium -(i)i *n;* **—s** *(mil)* supplement·um -i *n; (fresh troops)* subsidiari·i -orum *mpl*
reinstate *tr* restituere
reinstatement *s* restituti·o -onis *f*
reinvest *tr* iterum locare
reiterate *tr* iterare
reiteration *s* iterati·o -onis *f*
reject *tr* reicere; **to — a bill** regationem antiquare
rejection *s* reiecti·o -onis *f,* repuls·a -ae *f*
rejoice *intr* gaudēre
rejoin *tr* redire ad *(w. acc)* ‖ *intr* respondēre
rejoinder *s* respons·um -i *n*
rekindle *tr* resuscitare
relapse *s* recidiv·a -ae *f;* **to have a —** recidere
relapse *intr* recidere
relate *tr* referre, narrare ‖ *intr* **to — to** pertinēre ad
related *adj* propinqu·us -a -um; *(by birth)* (**to**) cognat·us -a -um *(w. dat); (by marriage)* (**to**) affin·is -is -e *(w. dat)*
relation *s* narrati·o -onis *f; (reference)* rati·o -onis *f; (relative)* cognat·us -i *m* (·a -ae *f*)*; (relationship)* cognati·o -onis *f*
relationship *s (by blood)* consanguinit·as -atis *f,* cognati·o -onis *f; (by marriage; connection)* affinit·as -atis *f*
relative *adj* cum ceteris comparat·us -a -um; *(gram)* relativ·us -a -um; **— to** de *(w. abl)*
relative *s* cognat·us -i *m* (·a -ae *f*)
relatively *adv* comparate; **not absolutely but —** non simpliciter sed comparatione
relax *tr* remittere, relaxare ‖ *intr* se remittere, se laxare
relaxation *s* relaxati·o -onis *f,* remissi·o -onis *f*
relaxing *adj* remissiv·us -a -um
release *s* liberati·o -onis *f*
release *tr* solvere; *(a prisoner)* liberare

relegate *tr* relegare
relent *intr* mitescere
relentless *adj* inexorabil•is -is -e, dir•us -a -um; *(unending)* continu•us -a -um
relentlessly *adv* sine missione
relevant *adj* **to be —** ad rem attinēre
reliable *adj* cert•us -a -um; *(person)* fid•us -a -um
reliance *s* fiduci•a -ae *f*
reliant *adj* **(on)** fret•us -a -um *(w. abl)*
relic *s* reliqui•ae -arum *fpl; (trace)* vestig•ium -(i)i *n*
relief *s (alleviation)* levati•o -onis *f; (comfort)* lenim•en -inis *n; (help)* auxil•ium -(i)i *n; (in sculpture)* toreum•a -atis *n; (of sentries)* mutati•o -onis *f;* **to be a —** levamento esse
relieve *tr* levare, mitigare; *(to aid)* succurrere *(w. dat); (a guard)* succedere *(w. dat),* excipere; **to — oneself** *(to urinate)* vesicam exonerare; *(coll)* facere; *(to have a bowel movement)* ventrem exonerare
religion *s* religi•o -onis *f;* **regard for —** religi•o -onis *f*
religious *adj* religios•us -a -um; **— ceremonies, — rites** religion•es -um *fpl*
relinquish *tr* relinquere; *(office)* se abdicare ab *(w. abl)*
relish *s (flavor)* sap•or -oris *m; (enthusiasm)* stud•ium -(i)i *n; (seasoning)* condiment•um -i *n*
relish *tr* gustare, non male appetere
reluctance *s* aversati•o -onis *f;* **with —** invite
reluctant *adj* invit•us -a -um, luct•ans -antis
reluctantly *adv* invite
rely *intr* **to — on** confidere *(w. dat),* niti *(w. abl);* **—ing on** fret•us -a -um *(w. dat or abl)*
remain *intr* manēre, permanēre; *(of things)* restare; *(to be left over)* superesse; **it —s that ...** restat ut *(w. subj);* **to — in that condition** subsistere in eo habitu
remainder *s* reliqu•um -i *n*
remaining *adj* reliqu•us -a -um
remains *spl* reliqui•ae -arum *fpl*
remark *tr* dicere
remark *s* dict•um -i *n*
remarkable *adj* notabil•is -is -e
remarkably *adv* mire, egregie
remedial *adj* remedial•is -is -e; *(med)* medicabil•is -is -e
remedy *s* **(for)** remed•ium -(i)i *n* (contra *w. acc); (a healing drug)* medicament•um -i *n;* **a quick (powerful, efficacious) —** praesentaneum (strenuum, praesentissimum) remedium; **to apply a — to** remedium adhibēre *(w. dat)*
remedy *tr* corrigere; *(med)* mederi *(w. dat)*
remember *tr* meminisse *(w. gen),* recordari, memoriā tenēre; **if I — right** si bene memini
remembrance *s* recordati•o -onis *f*
remind *tr* (ad)monēre
reminder *s* admoniti•o -onis *f;* **as a —** memoriae causā
reminisce *intr* meditari; **to — about** recordari
reminiscence *s* recordati•o -onis *f*
remiss *adj* negleg•ens -entis
remission *s* remissi•o -onis *f,* veni•a -ae *f*
remit *tr* remittere
remittance *s* remissi•o -onis *f,* pecuni•a -ae *f* transmissa
remnant *s* reliqu•um -i *n;* **—s** reliqui•ae -arum *fpl*
remodel *intr* reformare, transfigurare
remonstrate *intr* **to — with** obiurgare
remorse *s* paenitenti•a -ae *f*
remorseless *adj* immisericor•s -dis
remote *adj* remot•us -a -um
remote control *s* moderatr•um -i *n* remotum
remotely *adv* procul
remoteness *s* longinquit•as -atis *f*
removable *adj* mobil•is -is -e
removal *s* amoti•o -onis *f; (of fear, pain)* depulsi•o -onis *f*
remove *tr* amovēre, tollere
remunerate *tr* remunerari
remuneration *s* remunerati•o -onis *f*
rend *tr* lacerare, scindere; *(to split)* findere
render *tr* reddere; *(to translate)* vertere; **to — thanks** gratias reddere
rendezvous *s (meeting)* constitut•um -i *n; (meeting place)* loc•us -i *m* praestitutus
renegade *s* transfug•a -ae *mf*
renew *tr* renovare, redintegrare; **to — one's strength** recipere ex integro vires
renewal *s* renovati•o -onis *f*
renown *s* fam•a -ae *f*
renowned *adj* praeclar•us -a -um
rent *s* merc•es -edis *f; (tear)* scissur•a -ae *f;* **to pay the — for this room** mercedem huic cubiculo dare
rent *tr (to let out)* locare; *(to hire)* conducere; **to — out** locare
renunciation *s* repudiati•o -onis *f*
reopen *tr* iterum aperire; **the discussion was —ed** res retractata est
reorganize *tr* denuo constituere
repair *tr* reparare, reficere; *(clothes)* resarcire
repair *s* refecti•o -onis *f;* **in bad —** ruinos•us -a -um; **in good —** bene reparat•us -a -um
repairman *s* refect•or -oris *m*
repair shop *s* officin•a -ae *f* reparatoria
reparation *s* satisfacti•o -onis *f;* **to make —s** satisfacere
repay *tr* remunerari; *(money)* reponere, retribuere
repayment *s* remunerati•o -onis *f*
repeal *tr* abrogare, tollere
repeal *s* abrogati•o -onis *f*

repeat *tr* iterare, repetere; *(a ritual)* instaurare; — **after me** eisdem verbis mihi redde *(pl:* reddite)
repeatedly *adv* identidem
repel *tr* repellere; *(fig)* aspernari
repent *tr* **I** — me paenitet *(w. gen)* **II** *intr* **I** — me paenitet
repentance *s* paenitenti·a -ae *f*
repentant *adj* paenit·ens -entis
repercussion *s* repercuss·us -ūs *m*
repetition *s* iterati·o -onis *f*, repetiti·o -onis *f*
replace *tr* reponere
replant *tr* reserere
replenish *tr* replēre
replete *adj* replet·us -a -um
reply *s* respons·um -i *n*
reply *tr & intr* respondēre
report *s (rumor)* fam·a -ae *f; (official)* renuntiati·o -onis *f; (noise)* frag·or -oris *m;* **the — spread** fama percrebuit
report *tr* **(to)** referre, nuntiare, *(officially)* renuntiare *(w. dat);* **it is —ed** fama est; **to — for duty** in promptu operae se habēre
reporter *s* rela·tor -toris *m* (·tris -tricis *f*); *(for a newspaper)* diurnari·us -i *m* (·a -ae *f*)
repose *s* qui·es -etis *f*
repose *intr* quiescere
repository *s* receptacul·um -i *n*
reprehend *tr* reprehendere
reprehensible *adj* vituperabil·is -is -e, improb·us -a -um
represent *tr (to portray)* repraesentare; *(to stand in the place of another)* personam *(w. gen)* gerere; in loco *(w. gen)* stare; *(a character)* partes *(w. gen)* agere
representation *s (act)* repraesentati·o -onis *f; (likeness)* imag·o -inis *f*
representative *s* vicari·us -i *m* (·a -ae *f*)
repress *tr* reprimere, cohibēre
repression *s* cohibiti·o -onis *f*, continenti·a -ae *f*
reprieve *s* supplicii dilati·o -onis *f;* **to grant a —** supplicium differrè
reprimand *s* reprehensi·o -onis *f*
reprimand *tr* reprehendere
reprint *tr* denuo imprimere
reprint *s* altera editi·o -onis *f*
reprisal *s* ulti·o -onis *f;* **to make —s** retaliare
reproach *s* exprobrati·o -onis *f; (disgrace)* opprobr·ium -(i)i *n*
reproach *tr* opprobrare, vituperare
reproachful *adj* obiurgatori·us -a -um, contumelios·us -a -um
reprobate *s* perdit·us -i *m* (·a -ae *f*)
reproduce *tr* regenerare, propagare; **to — a play** iterum fabulam referre
reproduction *s* regenerati·o -onis *f; (likeness)* effigi·es -ei *f*
reproductive *adj* genital·is -is -e; **— organs** genital·ia -ium *npl*
reproof *s* obiurgati·o -onis *f*
reprove *tr* obiurgare
reptile *s* besti·a -ae *f* serpens
republic *s* respublica *(gen:* reipublicae) *f; (modern form)* civit·as -atis *f* popularis
republican *adj* optimatibus addict·us -a -um
republicans *spl* optimat·es -ium *mpl*
repudiate *tr* repudiare
repudiation *s* repudiati·o -onis *f*
repugnance *s* aversati·o -onis *f*
repugnant *adj* avers·us -a -um
repulse *s* depulsi·o -onis *f; (political defeat)* repuls·a -ae *f*
repulse *tr* repellere
repulsive *adj* odios·us -a -um, foed·us -a -um
reputable *adj* honest·us -a -um
reputation *s* fam·a -ae *f;* **bad —** infami·a -ae *f;* **good —** honest·as -atis *f*
repute *s* fam·a -ae *f*
request *s* petiti·o -onis *f;* **to deny a —** negare roganti; **to grant a —** satisfacere petenti
request *tr* petere, rogare
require *tr* poscere, postulare; *(to need)* egēre *(w. gen); (to call for)* requirere, desiderare
requirement *s* necessar·ium -(i)i *n*
requisite *adj* necessari·us -a -um
requisition *s* postulati·o -onis *f*
requital *s* retributi·o -onis *f*
requite *tr* compensare, retribuere; *(for a favor)* remunerari
rescind *tr* rescindere
rescue *s* liberati·o -onis *f;* **to come to s.o.'s —** subvenire alicui
rescue *tr (to snatch away)* **(from)** eripere *(dat or* ab, de, ex *w. abl); (to free)* liberare
research *s* investigati·o -onis *f*, indagati·o -onis *f*
research *tr* investigare, indagare
resemblance *s* similitud·o -inis *f*
resemble *tr* simil·is -is -e esse *(w. gen, esp. of persons, or w. dat)*
resembling *adj* simil·is -is -e *(w. gen, esp. of persons, or w. dat)*
resent *tr* aegre ferre, indignari
resentful *adj* iracund·us -a -um, indign·ans -antis
resentment *s* iracundi·a -ae *f*, indignati·o -onis *f*
reservation *s* reservati·o -onis *f*, retenti·o -onis *f;* **mental —s** exception·es -um *fpl* animo conceptae
reserve *s (restraint)* pud·or -oris *m; (stock)* copi·a -ae *f; (mil)* subsid·ium -(i)i *n;* **in —** seposit·us -a -um; **—s** *(mil)* subsidiari·i -orum *mpl*
reserve *adj (mil)* subsidiari·us -a -um
reserve *tr* reservare

reserved *adj (of seat)* assignat·us -a -um; *(of disposition)* taciturn·us -a -um; *(discreet)* modest·us -a -um
reservoir *s* lac·us -ūs *m; (of an aqueduct)* castell·um -i *n*
reset *tr* reponere
reside *intr* habitare, colere; **to — in** inhabitare, incolere
residence *s* sed·es -is *f,* domicili·ium -(i)i *n*
resident *s* incol·a -ae *mf*
residue *s* residu·um -i *n*
resign *tr (an office)* se abdicare ab *(w. abl);* **to — oneself to** animum summittere *(w. dat)* **‖** *intr* **(from)** se abdicare *(w. abl)*
resignation *s* abdicati·o -onis *f; (fig)* aequus anim·us -i *m*
resigned *adj* summiss·us -a -um; **to be —** aequo animo esse; **to be — to** aequo animo ferre
resilience *s* molliti·a -ae *f*
resilient *adj* resili·ens -entis
resin *s* resin·a -ae *f*
resist *tr* resistere *(w. dat),* obstare *(w. dat),* repugnare *(w. dat)*
resistance *s* repugnanti·a -ae *f;* **to offer — to** obsistere *(w. dat)*
resolute *adj* const·ans -antis, confirmat·us -a -um
resolutely *adv* constanter
resolution *s (determination)* constanti·a -ae *f; (decision, decree)* decret·um -i *n; (of Senate)* consult·um -i *n*
resolve *s* constanti·a -ae *f*
resolve *tr* constituere; *(to reduce, convert)* resolvere, dissolvere
resonance *s* resonanti·a -ae *f*
resonant *adj* reson·us -a -um
resort *s* loc·us -i *m* celeber; **last —** ultimum auxil·ium -(i)i *n*
resort *intr* **to — to** *(to frequent)* frequentare; *(to have recourse to)* confugere ad *(w acc.); (to lower oneself)* descendere ad *(w. acc.)*
resource *s* subsid·ium -(i)i *n;* **—s** op·es -ium *fpl*
respect *s (high esteem)* observanti·a -ae *f,* hon·or -oris *m; (regard)* respect·us -ūs *m; (religious awe)* religi·o -onis *f, e.g,* **— for an oath** religio iuris iurandi; **in every —** ex omni parte; **in other —s** ceterum; **in — to knowledge** scientiā; **to mention s.o. out of —** aliquem honoris causā nominare
respect *tr (to esteem highly)* observare; *(to esteem with fear)* verēri
respectability *s* honest·as -atis *f*
respectable *adj* honest·us -a -um
respectably *adv* honeste
respectful *adj* rever·ens -entis, observ·ans -antis
respectfully *adv* reverenter
respecting *prep* de *(w. abl)*
respective *adj* propri·us -a -um
respectively *adv* proprie
respiration *s* respirati·o -onis *f*
respite *s* intermissi·o -onis *f*
resplendent *adj* splendid·us -a -um
respond *tr & intr* respondēre
respondent *s (leg)* re·us -i *m* (·a -ae *f*)
response *s* respons·um -i *n*
responsibility *s* **(for)** cur·a -ae *f (w. gen);* **it is my — to** est mihi curae *(w. inf);* **it is the — of a father to say this** patris est haec dicere; **sense of —** piet·as -atis *f*
responsible *adj* obnoxi·us -a -um; *(reliable)* fid·us -a -um; **to be — for** praestare *(w. acc);* **to hold anyone —** rationem reposcere ab aliquo
rest *s* qui·es -etis *f; (support)* fulcr·um -i *n; (remainder)* reliqu·um -i *n;* **the — of the men** ceter·i -orum *mpl*
rest *tr (to lean)* reclinare **‖** *intr* (re)quiescere; *(to pause)* cessare; **to — on** inniti in *(w. abl),* niti *(w. abl);* **—ing on his elbow** reclinatus in cubitum
restaurant *s* caupon·a -ae *f*
restitution *s* restituti·o -onis *f;* **to demand —** res repetere; **to make —** restituere
restive *adj* contum·ax -acis
restless *adj* inquiet·us -a -um
restlessly *adv* inquiete
restlessness *s* sollicitud·o -inis *f*
restoration *s* restaurati·o -onis *f*
restore *tr* restituere, reddere; *(to rebuild)* restaurare, reficere; **to — to health** recurare; **to — to order** in integrum reducere
restrain *tr* coërcēre; *(tears, laughter)* tenēre; *(emotions)* cohibēre
restraint *s* fren·um -i *n; (moderation)* moderati·o -onis *f*
restrict *tr* restringere; *(to limit)* **(to)** definire *(w. dat)*
restriction *s* mod·us -i *m; (limitation)* excepti·o -onis *f*
restrictive *adj (gram)* restring·ens -entis
restroom *s* loc·us -i *m* secretus; *(public)* foric·a -ae *f*
result *s* exit·us -ūs *m,* event·us -ūs *m;* **without —** nequiquam
resume *tr* resumere
resumé *s* summar·ium -(i)i *n*
resumption *s* resumpti·o -onis *f*
resurrection *s* resurrecti·o -onis *f*
resuscitate *tr* resuscitare
retail *tr* (*sell retail*) divendere
retailer *s* propol·a -ae *mf*
retain *tr* retinēre
retainer *s (adherent)* assectat·or -oris *m; (fee)* arrab·o -onis *m*
retake *tr (e.g. a town)* recipere
retaliate *intr* ulcisci
retaliation *s* ulti·o -onis *f*
retard *s* heb·es -etis *mf*
retard *tr* tardare
retarded *adj* heb·es -etis
retch *intr* sine vomitu nauseare

retention *s* retenti·o -onis *f*
retentive *adj* ten·ax -acis
reticence *s* taciturnit·as -atis *f*
reticent *adj* taciturn·us -a -um
retinue *s* comitat·us -ūs *m*
retire *intr* recedere; *(from work)* in otium venire; *(from office)* abire; *(for the night)* dormitum ire
retired *adj* emerit·us -a -um
retirement *s (act)* recess·us -ūs *m; (state)* ot·ium -(i)i *n;* **to go into —** in otium venire
retiring *adj* modest·us -a -um
retort *s* respons·um -i *n*
retort *tr & intr* respondēre
retrace *tr* repetere
retract *tr (words)* retractare; *(a promise)* revocare
retraction *s* retractati·o -onis *f*
retreat *s (act; place)* recess·us -ūs *m; (mil)* recept·us -ūs *m;* **to sound the —** *(mil)* receptui canere
retreat *intr* recedere, se recipere
retribution *s* retributi·o -onis *f*
retrieve *tr* recuperare, recipere
retrievable *adj (loss)* pensabil·is -is -e
retrospect *s* **in —** respici·ens -entis
retrospective *adj* respici·ens -entis
return *s (coming back)* redit·us -ūs *m; (gain)* redit·us -ūs *m,* quaest·us -ūs *m; (profit)* fruct·us -ūs *m*
return *tr (to give back)* reddere; *(to send back)* remittere; **to — a favor** gratiam referre **II** *intr (to go back)* redire; *(to come back)* reverti
reunion *s* readunati·o -onis *f; (social)* comitum convent·us -ūs *m*
reunite *tr* iterum coniungere; *(to reconcile)* reconciliare **II** *intr* reconciliari
reveal *tr* retegere, recludere; *(to unveil)* revelare
revel *s* comissati·o -onis *f*
revel *intr* comissari, debacchari
revelation *s* patefacti·o -onis *f*
reveler *s* comissa·tor -toris *m* (·trix tricis *f*)
revelry *s* comissati·o -onis *f*
revenge *tr* ulcisci
revenge *s* ulti·o -onis *f,* vindict·a -ae *f;* **to seek —** ultionem petere; **to take — for s.th. small** vindictam parvae rei quaerere; **to take — on** se vindicare in *(w. acc)*
revengeful *adj* ulciscendi cupid·us -a -um
revenue *s (of both private and public income)* vectig·al -alis *n*
reverberate *intr* resonare
reverberation *s* resonanti·a -ae *f*
revere *tr* revereri, venerari
reverence *s* reverenti·a -ae *f;* **— due to the gods** deorum caerimoni·a -ae *f*
reverend *adj* reverend·us -a -um
reverent *adj* rever·ens -entis
reverential *adj* venerabund·us -a -um
reverently *adv* reverenter

reversal *s* reversi·o -onis *f*
reverse *s* contrar·ium -(i)i *n; (change)* conversi·o -onis *f; (defeat)* clad·es -is *f;* **to suffer a —** *(mil)* cladem accipere; *(pol)* repulsam ferre
reverse *tr* invertere, (com)mutare; *(decision)* rescindere, abrogare
revert *intr* reverti
review *s* recogniti·o -onis *f; (e.g., of a lesson)* retractati·o -onis *f; (of a book)* censur·a -ae *f; (mil)* recensi·o -onis *f*
review *tr* recensēre; *(a lesson)* retractare
reviewer *s* cens·or -oris *m* (·rix -ricis *f*)
revile *tr* maledicere *(w. dat)*
revise *tr* corrigere, emendare; *(laws)* retractare
revision *s* emendati·o -onis *f; (literary)* recensi·o -onis *f*
revisit *tr* revisere, revisitare
revival *s* redanimati·o -onis *f; (fig)* renovati·o -onis *f*
revive *tr* resuscitare; *(to renew)* renovare; *(strength)* refovēre **II** *intr* reviviscere
revocation *s* revocati·o -onis *f*
revoke *tr* revocare; *(a law)* rescindere, abrogare
revolt *s* rebelli·o -onis *f; (civil discord)* sediti·o -onis *f;* **to rise in — against s.o.** coöriri in aliquem
revolt *tr* offendere **II** *intr* deficere
revolting *adj* tae·ter -tra -trum
revolution *s (e.g., of a wheel)* conversi·o -onis *f; (change)* commutati·o -onis *f; (of planets)* ambit·us -ūs *m; (pol)* res novae *fpl*
revolutionary *adj* nov·us -a -um, inusitat·us -a -um; *(pol)* seditios·us -a -um
revolutionary *s* hom·o -inis *mf* rerum novarum cupidus (-a)
revolutionize *tr* novare
revolve *tr (in mind)* volutare **II** *intr* revolvi
revulsion *s* revulsi·o -onis *f*
reward *s* praem·ium -(i)i *n*
reward *tr* praemio afficere
rewrite *tr* rescribere
rhapsody *s* rhapsodi·a -ae *f*
rhetoric *s* rhetoric·a -ae *f;* **to practice —** declamare
rhetorical *adj* rhetoric·us -a -um; **— question** quaesti·o -onis *f* non respondenda
rhetorician *s* rhet·or -oris *m*
rheumatism *s* dol·or -oris *m* artuum, rheumatism·us -i *m*
rhinoceros *s* rhinocer·os -otis *m*
rhubarb *s* rad·ix -cis *f* Pontica
rhyme *s* homoeoteleut·on -i *n*
rhythm *s* numer·us -i *m*
rhythmical *adj* numeros·us -a -um
rib *s* cost·a -ae *f*
rib *tr (to taunt)* taxare
ribbon *s* taeni·a -ae *f; (as badge of honor)* inful·a -ae *f*
rice *s* oryz·a -ae *f*

rich *adj* div·es -itis; *(of soil)* opim·us -a -um; *(food)* pingu·is -is -e; *(costly)* laut·us -a -um
rich buck *s (sl)* sacc·o -onis *mf*
riches *spl* diviti·ae -arum *fpl*
richly *adv* copiose, laute
rickety *adj* instabil·is -is -e
rid *tr* liberare; **to get — of** *(worries)* diluere; *(persons)* amoliri
riddle *s* aenigm·a -atis *n*
riddle *tr* confodere
ride *tr* **to — a horse (bike)** equo (birotā) vehi ‖ *intr* equitare, equo vehi; **to — off** avehi
ride *s* vecti·o -onis *f;* **to go for a —** gestationem autocineto facere
rider *s (on horse)* rec·tor -toris *m* (·trix -tricis *f*); *(in carriage)* vec·tor -toris *m* (·trix -tricis *f*); *(attached to documents)* adiecti·o -onis *f*
ridge *s* iug·um -i *n,* dors·um -i *n*
ridicule *s* (de)ridicul·um -i *n*
ridicule *tr* irridēre
ridiculous *adj* ridicul·us -a -um
ridiculously *adv* ridicule
riding *s* equitati·o -onis *f; (in a carriage)* vectati·o -onis *f*
rife *adj* **(with)** frequ·ens -entis *(w. abl)*
riffraff *s* fae·x -cis *f* populi
rifle *tr* expilare
rifle *s* sclopet·um -i *n* striatum; **automatic —** sclopetum automatum; **to fire a —** sclopetare
rifleman *s* sclopetat·or -oris *m*
rig *tr* adornare; *(ship)* ornare
rigging *s* fun·es -ium *mpl*
right *adj (correct)* rect·us -a -um; *(opp. of left)* dex·ter -tra -trum; *(just)* iust·us -a -um; *(suitable)* idone·us -a -um, apt·us -a -um; *(true, reasonable)* ver·us -a -um; **all —** recte, probe; **on the —** a dextrā; **that's —** sic *(or* ita) est; **to do the — thing** frugem facere; **to the —** dextrorsum; **you're —** probe dicis, bene dixisti, vera dicis
right *adv (correctly)* recte; **— away** statim, continuo; **— from the start** in principio ilico; **— now** nunciam; **to turn —** dextrorsum se vertere
right *s (hand)* dextr·a -ae *f; (leg)* ius, iuris *n; (what is permitted by God or conscience)* fas *n* [indecl]; **by what —** quo iure; **on the — as you come in** dextrā introeunti; **the —** *(of knights and senators)* **to wear the gold ring** ius anuli; **to waive one's —s** iure suo decedere; **you have every — to ...** omne fas tibi est *(w. inf)*
right *tr (to correct)* emendare, corrigere; *(a fallen statue)* restituere; *(to avenge)* vindicare
righteous *adj* iust·us -a -um
righteousness *s* iustiti·a -ae *f*
rightful *adj* legitim·us -a -um
rightfully *adv* iuste
right-hand *adj* dex·ter -tra -trum; **— man** dextell·a -ae *f*
rigid *adj* rigid·us -a -um
rigidity *s* rigidit·as -atis *f*
rigidly *adv* rigide
rigor *s* rig·or -oris *m*
rigorous *adj* sever·us -a -um, dur·us -a -um
rim *s* or·a -ae *f,* marg·o -inis *f; (of a jar)* labr·um -i *n; (of a wheel)* canth·us -i *m*
rind *s (thick skin of fruit)* cor·ium -(i)i *n*
ring *s* anul·us -i *m; (of people)* coron·a -ae *f; (for fighting)* aren·a -ae *f; (for boxing)* suggest·us -ūs *m* pugilatorius; *(sound)* sonit·us -ūs *m; (of bells)* tinnit·us -ūs *m;* **engagement —** anulus pronubus; **to take off a —** anulum detrahere; **to wear a —** anulum gestare; **wedding —** anulus nuptialis
ring *tr* **to — a bell** tintinnabulum tractare ‖ *intr* tinnire, resonare
ringing *s* tinnit·us -ūs *m*
ringleader *s* instiga·tor -toris *m* (·trix -icis *f*)
rinse *tr* colluere; **to — out** eluere
rinsing *s* colluvi·es -ei *f*
riot *s* tumult·us -ūs *m;* **to run —** luxuriari
riot *intr* tumultuari, seditionem movēre
rioter *s* seditios·us -i *m* (·a -ae *f*)
riotous *adj* seditios·us -a -um; **— living** luxuri·a -ae *f*
rip *tr* scindere; **to — apart** discindere; *(fig)* discerpere
ripe *adj* matur·us -a -um
ripen *tr* maturare ‖ *intr* maturescere
ripple *intr* trepidare
ripple *s* flucticul·us -i *m,* undul·a -ae *f*
rise *intr (from a seat, from sleep; of the sun)* surgere; *(in a body)* consurgere; *(out of respect)* assurgere; *(of heavenly bodies)* oriri; *(of a river, have its source)* exoriri *(of the voice)* crescere; **to — again** resurgere; **to — up against** adoriri
rise *s* ort·us -ūs *m; (to higher office)* ascens·us -ūs *m; (slope)* cliv·us -i *m;* **— in the ground** loc·us -i *m* editus; **to give — to** parere, gignere, excitare
riser *s* **early —** tempestiv·us -i *m* (·a -ae *f*)
rising *s* ort·us -ūs *m*
rising *adj* ori·ens -entis; **gently — ground** loc·us -i *m* paulatim ab imo acclivis; **— star** *(fig)* adolescen·s -tis *mf* summā spe et animi et ingenii praedit·us (-a)
risk *s* pericul·um -i *n;* **at your own —** tuo periculo; **to be at —** periclitari; **to run the —** periculum subire, periculum facere; **to take a —** periculum adire
risk *tr* in periculum vocare, periclitari
risky *adj* an·ceps -cipitis, periculos·us -a -um
rite *s* rit·us -ūs *m,* caeremoni·a -ae *f*
ritual *adj* ritual·is -is -e
ritual *s* rit·us -ūs *m*

rival *s* rival·is -is *mf; (pol)* competi·tor -toris *m* (·trix -tricis *f*)
rival *adj* aemul·us -a -um
rival *tr* aemulari
rivalry *s* aemulati·o -onis *f; (among lovers)* rivalit·as -atis *f*
river *s* flum·en -inis *n,* amn·is -is *m*
rivet *s* clav·us -i *m*
river bed *s* alve·us -i *m*
rivet *tr (eyes, attention)* defigere
rivulet *s* rivul·us -i *m*
road *s* vi·a -ae *f; (route)* it·er -ineris *n;* **on the —** in itinere; **paved —** strat·a -ae *f;* **to build a —** viam munire
roadside *s* **by the —** secundum viam
roam *intr* errare, vagari
roar *s (of tigers)* fremit·us -ūs *m; (of lions)* rugit·us -ūs *m*; *(noise, as of a river)* strepit·us -ūs *m*
roar *intr (of lions)* fremere, rugire; *(of tigers)* fremere; *(to laugh hard)* cachinnare
roast *adj* ass·us -a -um
roast *s* ass·um -i *n*
roast *tr* torrēre; *(esp. meat)* assare
roast beef *s* bubul·a -ae *f* assa
roast chicken *s* gallinace·a -ae *f* assa
roast pork *s* porcin·a -ae *f* assa
roast veal *s* vitulin·a -ae *f* assa
rob *tr* rapere, eripere; *(to deprive)* privare; **to — s.o. of** spoliare aliquem *(w. abl)* ‖ *intr* latrocinari
robber *s* latr·o -onis *mf; (home invader)* perfoss·or -oris *m*
robbery *s* latrocin·ium -(i)i *n*
robe *s* vest·is -is *m; (of kings, augurs, knights)* trabe·a -ae *f; (of tragic actors)* pall·a -ae *f*
robe *tr* vestire
robin *s* rubecul·a -ae *f;* **—s chirp** rubeculae pipilant
robust *adj* robust·us -a -um
rock *s* sax·um -i *n; (cliff)* rup·es -is *f;* **between a — and a hard place** inter sacrum saxumque
rock *tr* movēre, motare; **to — the cradle** cunas agitare ‖ *intr* vibrare; **to — from side to side** in utramque partem toto corpore vacillare
rocket *s* missil·e -is *n,* rochet·a -ae *f*
rocking chair *s* sell·a -ae *f* oscillaris
rocky *adj* saxos·us -a -um
rod *s* virg·a -ae *f,* ferul·a -ae *f*
rodent *s* mus, muris *mf*
rogue *s* furcif·er -eri *m*
roguish *adj* nequam [*indecl*]
role *s* part·es -ium *fpl;* **to take the lead —** primas partes suscipere
role model *s* exempl·ar -aris *n*
roll *tr* volvere; **to — back** revolvere; **to — out** extendere, pandere; **to — over** evolvere; **to — over and over** pervolvere; **to — the dice** talos mittere; **to — together** *(to twist)* convolvere; **to — up** convolvere; *(from below)* subvolvere ‖ *intr* volvi
roll *s (book)* volum·en -inis *f; (of names)* catalog·us -i *m; (leg)* alb·um -i *n; (bun)* collyr·a -ae *f; (sweet roll)* pastill·us -i *m;* **to call —** nomina recitare
roll call *s* nominum recitati·o -onis *f*
roller *s* cylindr·us -i *m,* orbicul·us -i *m*
rollerblade *intr* pedirotis labi
rollerblades *spl* pedirot·ae -arum *fpl*
Roman *adj* Roman·us -a -um
Roman *s* Roman·us -i *m* (·a -ae *f*)
romance *s* fabul·a -ae *f* amatoria; *(affair)* amor·es -um *mpl*
romantic *adj* amatori·us -a -um
Romeo *s* agag·a -ae *m*
romp *intr* lascivire
roof *s* tect·um -i *n;* **— of the mouth** palat·um -i *n*
roof *tr* contegere
roof tile *s* tegul·a -ae *f*
room *s (of house)* conclav·e -is *n,* cubicul·um -i *n; (small room)* cell·a -ae *f; (tiny room)* cellul·a -ae *f; (space)* loc·us -i *m,* spat·ium -(i)i *n;* **— with bath** cubiculum balneo instructum
room *intr* manēre
roominess *s* laxit·as -atis *f*
roommate *s* soci·us -i *m* (·a -ae *f*) cubicularis
roomy *adj* lax·us -a -um
roost *s* pertic·a -ae *f*
roost *intr* cubitare, insistere
rooster *s* gall·us -i *m* gallinaceus; **—s crow** galli canunt, cucuriunt
root *s* rad·ix -icis *f; (fig)* fon·s -tis *m;* **to take —** coalescere
root *tr* **to become —ed** *(lit & fig)* radices agere; **to be —ed** inhaerēre; **to — out** eradicare ‖ *intr* **to — for** acclamare
rope *s* fun·is -is *m,* rest·is -is *f*
rosary *s* rosar·ium -(i)i *n*
rose *s* ros·a -ae *f*
rosebed *s* rosar·ium -(i)i *n*
rosebud *s* rosae cal·yx -ycis *m*
rosebush *s* frut·ex -icis *f* rosae
rose garden *s* roset·um -i *n*
rosemary *s* ro·s -ris *m* marinus
rosin *s* resin·a -ae *f*
rostrum *s* rostr·a -orum *npl;* **to speak from the —** pro rostris loqui
rosy *adj* rose·us -a -um; *(fig)* festiv·us -a -um
rot *intr* putrescere, tabescere
rot *s* putred·o -inis *f,* tab·es -is *f*
rotate *intr* volvi
rotation *s* rotati·o -onis *f;* **in —** per *or* in orbem; **— of command** vicissitud·o -inis *f* imperitandi
rote *s* **by —** memoriter
rotten *adj* putrid·us -a -um
rotunda *s* thol·us -i *m*

rouge *s* fuc·us -i *m*
rough *adj* asp·er -era -erum; *(of character)* dur·us -a -um; *(weather)* inclem·ens -entis, turbid·us -a -um; *(shaggy)* hirsut·us -a -um; *(masonry)* impolit·us -a -um; **— guess** informata cogitati·o -onis *f*
rough-and-ready *adj* prompt·us -a -um
roughen *tr* asperare
roughly *adv* aspere, duriter; *(approximately)* fere
roughneck *s (coll)* rup·ex -icis *m*
roughness *s* asperit·as -atis *f; (brutality)* ferit·as -atis *f*
round *adj* rotund·us -a -um
round *s (in boxing)* congress·us -ūs *m;* **to give a — of applause** plausum dare; **— of beef** fem·ur -oris *n* bubulum transverse sectum; **—s of applause** plaus·us -ūs *m* multiplex; **to make the —s** *(of a policeman)* vigilias circumire; **to go the —s of** circumire *(w. acc)*
round *tr (a corner)* circumire; *(a cape)* superare; **to — off** concludere; **to — out** complere; **to — up** cogere
roundabout *adj* **in a — way** per ambages, circuitu; **— route** circuit·us -ūs *m;* **to tell a — story to** ambages narrare *(w. dat)*
rouse *tr* excitare
rousing *adj* vehem·ens -entis; **a — harangue** incitata et vehemens conti·o -onis *f*
rout *s* fug·a -ae *f; (defeat)* clad·es -is *f; (rabble)* vulg·us -i *n;* **to put to —** in fugam convertere
rout *tr* fugare, fundere
route *s* it·er -ineris *n*
routine *s* ord·o -inis *m;* **daily —** cotidianus ordo *m*
routinely *adv* ex consuetudine
rove *intr* errare, vagari
rover *s* err·o -onis *m*
row *s* ord·o -inis *m,* seri·es -ei *f;* **in a row** continu·us -a -um; **for seven days in a —** per septem continuos dies; **— of seats** grad·us -ūs *m;* **— of trees** ordo arborum; **three days in a —** triennio continuo
row *tr* remis propellere ‖ *intr* remigare; **to — hard** remis contendere
rowboat *s* scaph·a -ae *f* remigera
rower *s* rem·ex -igis *mf*
row home *s* aed·es -ium *fpl* seriales
rowing *s* remig·ium -(i)i *n*
royal *adj* regi·us -a -um; *(worthy of a king)* regal·is -is -e; **— power** regn·um -i *n*
royally *adv* regie, regaliter
royalty *s* regn·um -i *n*
rub *tr* fricare; **to — away** detergēre; **to — down** defricare; **to — in** infricare
rub *s* fricat·us -ūs *m;* **and that's the —** hoc opus, hic labor est
rubbing *s* fricti·o -onis *f*
rubbish *s (lit & fig)* quisquili·ae -arum *fpl*
rubble *s* rud·us -eris *n*
rubric *s* rubric·a -ae *f*
ruby *s* carbuncul·us -i *m*
ruckus *s* clam·or -oris *m;* **why are you raising such a —?** quid istum clamorem tollis?
rudder *s* gubernacul·um -i *n*
ruddy *adj* rubicund·us -a -um
rude *adj* rud·is -is -e; *(impolite)* inurban·us -a -um; *(character)* asp·er -era -erum
rudeness *s* inhumanit·as -atis *f,* inurbanit·as -atis *f*
rudiment *s* element·um -i *n*
rudimentary *adj* elementari·us -a -um
rue *tr* **I rue** me paenitet *(w. gen)*
rueful *adj* maest·us -a -um
ruffian *s* rup·ex -icis *m*
ruffle *s* limb·us -i *m*
rug *s* stragul·um -i *n,* tapet·e -is *n*
rugby *s* harpast·um -i *n;* **to play —** harpasto ludere
rugged *adj* asp·er -era -erum, dur·us -a -um; *(terrain)* praerupt·us -a -um
ruin *s* exit·ium -(i)i *n;* **—s** rud·us -eris *n;* **to go to —** ruere, pessum ire, perire
ruin *tr* perdere, corrumpere; *(morally)* depravare
ruinous *adj* exitios·us -a -um
rule *s (instrument; regulation)* regul·a -ae *f; (government)* regim·en -inis *n;* **absolute —** dominati·o -onis *f;* **to break the —** regulam frangere; **to follow (observe) the —** regulam servare; **to lay down the —s** regulas instituere
rule *tr* regere ‖ *intr* regnare, dominari; **to — out** excludere, excipere; **to — over** imperare *(w. dat),* dominari in *(w. acc)*
ruler *s* rec·tor -toris *m* (·trix -tricis *f); (instrument)* regul·a -ae *f*
ruling *s* sententi·a -ae *f*
rum *s* sicer·a -ae *f,* vin·um -i *n* Indicum
rumble *s* murm·ur -uris *n*
rumble *intr* murmurare; **my stomach is rumbling** sonat mihi circum stomachum
rumbling *s* murm·ur -uris *n*
ruminate *intr* ruminare
rummage *intr* **to — through** perscrutari
rummage sale *s* venditi·o -onis *f* scrutaria
rumor *s* rum·or -oris *m;* **there's a — going around** rumor pervagatur
rump *s* clun·es -ium *fpl*
rumple *s (in garment)* rug·a -ae *f*
rumple *tr* corrugare
rump roast *s* ass·um -i *n* posterius
rumpus *s* **to raise a —** turbas dare
run *tr (to manage)* exercēre; **to — a fever** febricitare; **to — a program** programma administrare; **to — down** *(to disparage)* detrectare; *(w. vehicle)* obterere; **to — her hand over my hair** ducere capillos meos lentā manu; **to — up** *(increase)* augēre; **to — up bills** aes alienum conflare ‖ *intr* currere; *(to flow)* fluere; **the program is running** programma oper-

atur; **to — about** discurrere; **to — after** petere; **to — around** discurrere; **to — around the table** discurrere circa mensam; **to — away** aufugere; **to — aground** offendere; **to — down** decurrere; *(of water)* defluere; **to — for office** honorem petere; **to — foul of** impingere; **to — high** *(of a river, sea)* tumēre; **to — into** *(to meet)* occurrere *(w. dat)*, incidere in *(w. acc)*, offendere; **to — low** deficere; **to — off** aufugere; *(of water)* defluere; **to — on** percurrere, continuare; **to — out** excurrere; *(of time)* exire; *(of supplies)* deficere; **to — over** *(of fluids)* superfluere; *(details)* percurrere; **to — short** deficere; **to — through** *(to dissipate)* dissipare; **to — through a list of** exsequi; **to — together** concurrere; **to — up and down** modo huc modo illuc currere; **to — up to s.o.** accurrere ad aliquem

run *s* curs·us -ūs *m;* **in the long —** in exitu; **on the —** cursim; **to have the —s** citā alvo laborare

runaway *s* transfug·a -ae *mf*

rundown *s* compend·ium -(i)i *n*

run-down *adj* defatigat·us -a -um; *(dilapidated)* ruinos·us -a -um

rung *s (of ladder)* grad·us -ūs *m*

run-in *s* altercati·o -onis *f*

runner *s* curs·or -oris *m* (·rix -ricis *f*)

runner-up *s* competi·tor -toris *m* (·trix -tricis *f*) iuxta victorem *(or* victricem)

running *s* cursur·a -ae *f;* **— for office** petiti·o -onis *f* honoris; **— of the government** administrati·o -onis *f* rei publicae

runny nose *s* distillation·es -um *fpl*

run-off *s* certam·en -inis *n* ultimum

runt *s* pumili·o -onis *mf*

runway *s* aërdrom·os -i *m*

rupture *s (of relations)* discid·ium -(i)i *n; (med)* herni·a -ae *f*

rupture *tr* rumpere ‖ *intr* rumpi

rural *adj* rural·is -is -e

ruse *s* dol·us -i *m*

rush *s (plant)* iunc·us -i *m; (charge)* impet·us -ūs *m; (of people)* **(on)** concurs·us -ūs *m* (ad *w. acc.); (hurry)* festinati·o -onis *f*

rush *tr (to attack)* oppugnare; *(to do in a hurry)* festinare; *(to cause to hurry)* urgēre ‖ *intr* festinare, ruere; **to — away** avolare; **to — by** praeterlabi; **to — forth** se proripere; **to — in** irruere; **to — into** irruere in *(w. acc);* **to — out** evolare, erumpere

rust *s* rubig·o -inis *f; (of iron)* ferrug·o -inis *f*

rust *intr* rubiginem trahere

rustic *adj* rustic·us -a -um

rustic *s* rustic·us -i *m* (·a -ae *f*)

rustle *intr* crepitare

rustle *s* crepit·us -ūs *m*

rusty *adj* rubiginos·us -a -um; **to become —** rubigine obduci; *(fig)* desuescere

rut *s* orbit·a -ae *f*

ruthless *adj* immisericor·s -dis

ruthlessly *adv* immisericorditer

rye *s* secal·e -is *n*

S

Sabbath *s* sabbat·a -orum *npl;* **to keep the —** sabbatizare, sabbata observare; **to break the —** sabbata violare *(or* neglegere)

saber *s* acinac·es -is *m*

sabotage *s* eversi·o -onis *f (or* vastati·o -onis *f)* occulta

sabotage *tr* occulte evertere

saboteur *s* evers·or -oris *m* (·trix - tricis *f*)

saccharin *s* sacchar·on -i *n*

sack *s* sacc·us -i *m; (of leather)* culle·us -i *m; (mil)* direpti·o -onis *f*

sack *tr* in saccos condere; *(mil)* diripere; *(coll) (to fire)* amovēre

sackcloth *s* cilic·ium -(i)i *n;* **in — and ashes** sordidat·us -a -um

sacrament *s (eccl)* sacrament·um -i *n*

sacred *adj* sa·cer -cra -crum

sacrifice *s (act)* sacrific·ium -(i)i *n; (victim)* hosti·a -ae *f; (fig)* iactur·a -ae *f;* **to offer (perform) a —** sacrificium agere (facere), rem divinam facere

sacrifice *tr* sacrificare, immolare; **to — an eye for** oculum impendere pro *(w. abl);* **to — one's life for another** vitam pro aliquo profundere

sacrilege *s* sacrileg·ium -(i)i *n*

sacrilegious *adj* sacrileg·us -a -um

sacristan *s* neocor·us -i *m,* aeditu·us -i *m*

sad *adj* trist·is -is -e *(showing grief on one's face)* maest·us -a -um

sadden *tr* contristare

saddle *s* ephipp·ium -(i)i *n*

saddle *tr (fig)* imponere *(w. acc of thing and dat of person);* **to — a horse** equum sternere

sadly *adv* maeste

sadness *s* tristiti·a -ae *f; (outer display)* maestiti·a -ae *f*

safe *adj* tut·us -a -um; *(unharmed)* incolum·is -is -e; *(harmless)* innocu·us -a -um; *(sure)* cert·us -a -um; **— and sound** salv·us -a -um; **— from danger** tutus a periculo

safe *s* arc·a -ae *f*

safe-conduct *s* **under —** publicā fide interpositā

safe-deposit box *s* deposito r·ium -(i)i *n* syngrapharum

safeguard *tr* tueri

safeguard *s* cauti·o -onis *f;* **there is but one — against these troubles** horum

incommodorum cautio una est *(followed by* ut *or* ne)
safekeeping *s* **for —** in fidem
safely *adv* tute, tuto
safety *s* sal·us -utis *f;* **in —** tuto
safety pin *s* fibul·a -ae *f*
safety valve *s* spirament·um -i *n*
saffron *s* croc·us -i *m*
saffron *adj* croce·us -a -um
sag *intr* prave dependēre; *(to decline in value)* decrescere; *(to lose vigor)* languēre
sagacious *adj* sag·ax -acis
sagacity *s* sagacit·as -atis *f*
sage *s (wise person)* hom·o -inis *mf* sapi·ens -entis
sage *adj* sapi·ens -entis
sail *s* vel·um -i *n;* **to set —** vela dare
sail *intr* nave vehi, navigare; **to — down to** devehi ad *or* in *(w. acc);* **to — up to** subvehi ad *or* in *(w. acc)*
sail boat *s* scaph·a -ae *f* velifera
sailing *s* navigati·o -onis *f*
sailor *s* naut·a -ae *m,* nautri·a -ae *f*
saint *s* sanct·us -i *m* (·a -ae *f)*
saintly *adj* sanct·us -a -um
sake *s* **for heaven's — !** pro deum fidem! **for the — of** causā *or* gratiā *(w. gen);* **for the — of glory** gloriae causā *(or* gratiā); **for your —** tuā *(pl:* vestrā) causā
salable *adj* vendibil·is -is -e
salacious *adj* sal·ax -acis
salad *s* acetari·a -orum *npl*
salad dressing embamm·a -atis *n (see* **dressing)**
salamander *s* salamandr·a -ae *f*
salary *s* mer·ces -cedis *f,* salar·ium -(i)i *n;* **to pay s.o. a fair —** mercedem aequam alicui solvere
sale *s* venditi·o -onis *f;* **for —** venal·is -is -e; **this house is for —** haec aedes sunt venales; **to advertise a house for —** aedes venales inscribere; **to go up for —** venum ire; **to put up for —** venum dare, prostare
saleslady *s (in a shop)* tabernari·a -ae *f; (in a clothing store)* vestiari·a -ae *f*
salesman *s (in a shop)* tabernar·ius -(i)i *m;* **traveling —** instit·or -oris *m*
salient *adj* promin·ens -entis; *(chief)* prin·ceps -cipis
saline *adj* sals·us -a -um
saliva *s* saliv·a -ae *f*
sallow *adj* pallid·us -a -um
sally *intr* eruptionem facere
sally *s* procurs·us -ūs *m (or* erupti·o -onis *f)* (militum)
salmon *s* salm·o -onis *m*
saloon *s* caupon·a -ae *f,* tabern·a -ae *f* potoria
salt *s* sal, salis *m*
salt *tr* salire, sale condire; **to — away** *(coll)* seponere
saltless *adj* insals·us -a -um
salt mine *s* salin·ae -arum *fpl*
salt shaker *s* salin·um -i *n*
salt water *s* aqu·a -ae *f* marina *(or* salsa)
salty *adj* sals·us -a -um
salubrious *adj* salu·ber -bris -bre
salutary *adj* salutar·is -is -e
salutation *s* salutati·o -onis *f*
salute *s* sal·us -utis *f*
salute *tr* salutare
salvage *tr* (con)servare, redimere
salvage *s (act)* conservati·o -onis *f; (objects)* reliqu·um -i *n*
salvation *s* sal·us -utis *f*
salve *s* unguent·um -i *n*
same *adj* idem, eadem, idem *(gen:* eiusdem *for all genders);* **at the — place** ibidem; **at the — time** simul, eodem tempore; **in the — way** eodem modo; **it's all the — to me** meā nihil interest; **the — thing** idem; **the very —** ipsissim·us -a -um
sameness *s* similitud·o -inis *f*
sample *s* exempl·um -i *n*
sample *tr* tentare; *(food, drink)* libare
sanctify *tr* sanctificare
sanctimonious *adj* sanctitatem affect·ans -antis
sanction *s* auctorit·as -atis *f; (approval)* approbati·o -onis *f;* **with the — of the people** iussu populi; **without the — of the people** iniussu populi
sanction *tr* ratum facere
sanctity *s* sanctit·as -atis *f*
sanctuary *s* sanctuar·ium -(i)i *n; (refuge)* asyl·um -i *n*
sand *s* (h)aren·a -ae *f*
sandal *s (simplest form, with sole fastened to feet with thongs)* sole·a -ae *f; (w. covered toes)* sandal·ium -(i)i *n*
sandbag *s* sacc·us -i *m* harenae
sandbank *s* syrt·is -is *(or* -idis) *f*
sandpile *s* cumul·us -i *m* harenae
sandstone *s* lap·is -idis *m* (h)arenaceus
sand trap *s (golf)* harenari·a -ae *f*
sandwich *s* pastill·um -i *n* fartum; **ham —** pastillum pernā fartum
sandy *adj* (h)arenos·us -a -um
sandy-haired *adj* ruf·us -a -um
sane *adj* san·us -a -um
sanguine *adj* plen·us -a -um spei
sanitarium *s* valetudinar·ium -(i)i *n*
sanitary *adj* salubr·is -is -e
sanitation *s* purgati·o -onis *f*
sanity *s* sanit·as -atis *f*
sap *s* suc·us -i *m*
sap *tr* (ex)haurire
sapling *s* surcul·us -i *m*
Sapphic *adj* Sapphic·us -a -um
sapphire *s* sapphir·us -i *f*
sarcasm *s* dicacit·as -atis *f*
sarcastic *adj* dicacul·us -a -um, dic·ax -acis
sarcastically *adv* acerbe
sarcophagus *s* sarcophag·us -i *m*

sardine *s* sard·a -ae *f*
sardonic *adj* amar·us -a -um
sash *s* zon·a -ae *f*
Satan *s* Satan *m* [*indecl*]
Satanic *adj* Satanic·us -a -um, diabolic·us -a -um
satchel *s* per·a -ae *f*
satellite *s* satell·es -itis *mf; (astr)* stell·a -ae *f* minor
satiate *tr* satiare
satiated *adj* sat·ur -ura -urum
satire *s* satir·a, satur·a -ae *f*
satirical *adj* satiric·us -a -um; *(biting)* mord·ax -acis
satirist *s* script·or -oris *m* saturarum
satirize *tr* arripere
satisfaction *s* volupt·as -atis *f; (amends)* satisfacti·o -onis *f;* **my house gives me great —** domus mea mihi valde placet; **to derive the greatest — from** incredibilem voluptatem capere ex *(w. abl);* **to your —** ex tuā sententiā
satisfactorily *adv* satis bene
satisfactory *adj* idone·us -a -um
satisfied *adj* content·us -a -um; *(repaid)* compensat·us -a -um
satisfy *tr* satisfacere *(w. dat); (thirst, hunger, expectation)* explēre; *(creditors)* satisfacere *(w. dat)*
saturate *tr* saturare
Saturday *s* di·es -ei *m* Saturni
Saturn *s* Saturn·us -i *m;* **feast of —** Saturnal·ia -ium *npl (Dec. 17-23)*
satyr *s* satyr·us -i *m*
sauce *s* condiment·um -i *n,* ius, iuris *n*
saucepan *s* cacub·us -i *m,* sartag·o -inis *f*
saucer *s* patell·a -ae *f*
saucily *adv (fig)* petulanter
saucy *adj (fig)* petul·ans -antis
sauna *s* sudator·ium -(i)i *n*
saunter *intr* vagari
sausage *s* farcim·en -inis *n*
savage *adj (wild, untamed)* fer·us -a -um; *(cruel)* saev·us -a -um
savage *s* hom·o -inis *mf* ferox
savagely *adv* atrociter
save *tr* **(from)** servare (ex *w. abl); to* **— up** reservare
save *prep* praeter *(w. acc)*
saving *s* conservati·o -onis *f;* **—s** pecul·ium -(i)i *n*
savings account *s* comput·us -i *m* conditorius
savings bank *s* argentari·a -ae *f* peculiis asservandis
savior *s* serva·tor -toris *m* (·trix -tricis *f*)
Savior *s* Salvat·or -oris *m*
savor *s* sap·or -oris *m*
savor *tr* sapere
savory *adj* sapid·us -a -um
saw *s (tool)* serr·a -ae *f; (saying)* proverb·ium -(i)i *n*
saw *tr* serrā secare **||** *intr* serram ducere
sawdust *s* scob·is -is *f*
saxophone *s* saxophon·um -i *n*
say *tr* dicere; **as they say** ut aiunt; **needless to —** quid multa?; **no sooner said than done** dictum (ac) factum; **— hello to Rose** iube *(pl:* iubete) Rosam salvēre; **so they —** ita aiunt; **that is to —** scilicet; **they —** dicitur; **to — that … not** negare *(w. acc & inf)*
saying *s* dict·um -i *n;* **as the — goes** ut aiunt
say-so *s* auctorit·as -atis *f;* **on your —** te auctore
scab *s* crust·a -ae *f*
scabbard *s* vagin·a -ae *f*
scaffold *s* fal·a -ae *f*
scald *tr* urere
scale *s (for weighing)* trutin·a -ae *f; (of fish)* squam·a -ae *f; (gradation)* grad·us -ūs *m; (mus)* diagramm·a -atis *f;* **pair of —s** stater·a -ae *f*
scale *tr (fish)* desquamare; **to — a wall** murum per scalas ascendere
scallop *s (shellfish)* pect·en -inis *m; (curve)* sin·us -ūs *m*
scalp *s* pericran·ium -(i)i *n*
scaly *adj* squamos·us -a -um
scam *s* frau·s -dis *f*
scam artist *s* plan·us -i *m* (·a -ae *f*)
scammer *s* frauda·tor -toris *m* (·trix -tricis *f*)
scamp *s* furcif·er -eri *m*
scamper *intr* cursare; **to — about** cursitare, discurrere; **to — away** aufugere
scan *tr* examinare; *(to read over)* perlegere; *(verse; comput)* scandere
scandal *s* opprobr·ium -(i)i *n;* **to be a — to the community** opprobrio esse civitati
scandalize *tr* offendere
scandalous *adj* probros·us -a -um, flagitios·us -a -um
scanner *s (comput)* scansor·ium -(i)i *n*
scansion *s* syllabarum enarrati·o -onis *f*
scant *adj* exigu·us -a -um
scantily *adv* exigue
scantiness *s* exiguit·as -atis *f*
scanty *adj* exigu·us -a -um
scapegoat *s* piacul·um -i *n*
scar *s* cicatr·ix -icis *f*
scar *tr* cicatricibus foedare; *(fig)* maculare
scarce *adj* rar·us -a -um
scarcely *adv* vix; *(with effort)* aegre
scarcity *s* rarit·as -atis *f,* inopi·a -ae *f*
scare *tr* terrēre; **to — off** absterrēre
scarecrow *s* terricul·um -i *n*
scared *adj* territ·us -a -um; **I'm — to death** exanimat·us (-a) metu sum
scarf *s* amictor·ium -(i)i *n* (collare)
scarlet *adj* coccin·us -a -um
scarlet fever *s* febr·is -is *f* purpurea
scathing *adj* aculeat·us -a -um
scatter *tr* spargere, dispergere **||** *intr* dilabi, diffugere

scavenger *s* cloacar·ius -(i)i *m* (·a -ae *f*)

scene *s (vista)* prospect·us -ūs *m; (picture)* pictur·a -ae *f; (theat)* scaen·a -ae *f;* **behind the —s** post siparium; **Italy, the — of the civil war** Italia, arena belli civilis; **on the —** in re praesenti; **to make a —** convicium facere

scenery *s (theat)* scenae apparat·us -ūs *m; (of nature)* speci·es -ei *f* regionis

scent *s (sense)* odorat·us -ūs *m; (of dogs)* sagacit·as -atis *f; (fragrance)* od·or -oris *m*

scent *tr* odorari

scented *adj* odorat·us -a -um

scepter *s* sceptr·um -i *n*

sceptic *s* sceptic·us -i *m* (·a -ae *f*)

sceptical *adj* **to be —** dubitare

schedule *s* schedul·a -ae *f; (timetable)* horar·ium -(i)i *n;* **bus —** horarium autoraedarum longarum; **class —** horarium academicum; **flight -** horarium aëroplanorum; **train —** horarium traminum

schedule *tr* tempus *(w. gen)* constituere

scheme *s* consil·ium -(i)i *n; (pej)* dol·us -i *m*

scheme *intr* moliri

scholar *s* philolog·us -i *m* (·a -ae *f*), erudit·us -i *m* (·a -ae *f*)

scholarly *adj* erudit·us -a -um, doct·us -a -um

scholarship *s* eruditi·o -onis *f,* litter·ae -arum *fpl; (grant)* pecuni·ae -arum *fpl* quae scholari alendo praebentur

scholastic *adj* scholastic·us -a -um

school *s* lud·us -i *m; (advanced school)* schol·a -ae *f; (group holding like opinions)* sect·a -ae *f; (of fish)* grex, gregis *m;* **elementary —** lud·us -i *m* litterarius; **to attend —** scholam frequentare; **to go to —** in scholam itare; **to skip —** insciis parentibus a scholā abesse

school book li·ber -bri *m* scholaris

schoolboy *s* discipul·us -i *m*

school building *s* aedific·ium -(i)i *n* scholare

schoolgirl *s* discipul·a -ae *f*

schoolmaster *s* ludi magis·ter -tri *m*

schoolmate *s* condiscipul·us -i *m* (·a -ae *f*)

school mistress *s* ludi magistr·a -ae *f*

schoolroom *s* schol·a -ae *f*

school supplies *spl* instrument·um -i *n* scholare

science *s* scienti·a -ae *f,* disciplin·a -ae *f;* **natural —** rati·o -onis *f* physica

scientific *adj* physic·us -a -um

scientifically *adv* ratione

scientist *s* physic·us -i *m* (·a -ae *f*)

scion *s* edit·us -i *m*

scissors *spl* forf·ex -icis *f*

scoff *s* cavillati·o -onis *f*

scoff *intr* cavillari; **to — at** irridēre

scoffer *s* irris·or -oris *m* (·(t)rix -(t)ricis *f*)

scold *tr* obiurgare

scolding *s* obiurgati·o -onis *f;* **to get a —** obiurgari

scoop *s* trull·a -ae *f; (news)* nunti·us -i *m* proprius

scoop *tr* **to — out** excavare

scoot *intr* provolare; *(to run off)* celeriter fugere

scooter *s* birot·a -ae *f* pede pulsa; **motor —** motoria birota pede pulsa

scope *s (extent)* spat·ium -(i)i *n; (range)* aspect·us -ūs *m*

scorch *tr* adurere

scorching *adj (sun, day, etc.)* flagrantissim·us -a -um; **— heat** aest·us -ūs *m* flagrantissimus

score *s (total)* stat·us -ūs *m,* summ·a -ae *f; (twenty)* viginti [*indecl*]; **(reckoning)** rati·o -onis *f;* **final —** status finalis; **the — is tied** summae punctorum sunt pares; **to even the — with** *(fig)* ulcisci; **to keep —** rationem notare; **to know the —** *(fig)* scire quid agatur

score *tr* notare; **to — a goal** *(soccer)* follem per portam pede pulsare; *(lacrosse)* pilam per portam iacere; **to — a point** punctum ferre; **to — a touchdown** calcem *(or* cretam) attingere

scorn *s* contempti·o -onis *f*

scorn *tr* contemnere

scornful *adj* fastidios·us -a -um

scornfully *adv* contemptim

scorpion *s* scorpi·o -onis *m;* **—s sting** scorpiones icunt

Scot *adj* Scotic·us -a -um

Scot *s* Scot·us -i *m*

Scotch *adj* Scotic·us -a -um; *(tight with money) (sl)* sordid·us -a -um

scot-free *adj* **to get off —** impunit·us -a -um dimitti

Scotland *s* Scoti·a -ae *f*

scoundrel *s* furci·fer -feri *m,* propud·ium -(i)i *n*

scour *tr (to rub clean)* tergēre; *(to roam over)* pervagari

scourge *s* flagell·um -i *n; (fig)* pest·is -is *f*

scourge *tr* flagellare

scourging *s* flagellati·o -onis *f*

scout *s* explorat·or -oris *m*

scout *tr* explorare

scowl *s* contracti·o -onis *f* frontis

scowl *intr* frontem contrahere

scowlingly *adv* fronte contractā

scram *interj* apage!

scramble *s (hurried climbing)* ascens·us -ūs *m* rapidus; *(scuffle, struggle)* nix·us -ūs *m,* contenti·o -onis *f*

scramble *tr (eggs)* commiscēre **||** *intr (to climb hurriedly)* scandere operose; *(to scuffle)* eniti, turbare; **to — for** diripere, certatim captare; **to — up** scandere

scrap *s (small piece)* frust·um -i *n; (brawl)* rix·a -ae *f; (junk)* metall·um -i *n* scrutari-

um, scrut·a -orum *npl;* **to get into a — in** rixam iri
scrap *tr* reicere ‖ *intr (to brawl)* rixari
scrape *s (scratch)* rasur·a -ae *f,* levis inscisur·a -ae *f; (fig)* difficult·as -atis *f; (quarrel)* rix·a -ae *f*
scrape *tr* radere; **to — together** *(money, etc.)* corradere
scraping *s* rasur·a -ae *f*
scratch *tr* radere; *(the head)* scabere; **to — up** *(e.g., the earth)* scalpere
scratch *s* levis incisur·a -ae *f*
scrawl *s* mala scriptur·a -ae *f*
scrawl *tr & intr* male scribere
scrawny *adj* strigulos·us -a -um
scream *s* ululat·us -ūs *m,* clam·or -oris *m; (of child)* vagit·us -ūs *m*
scream *intr* ululare; *(of child)* vagire
screech *s* strid·or -oris *m*
screech *intr* stridēre
screen *s* umbracul·um -i *n; (on TV or comput)* quadr·um -i *n* visificum; *(movie screen)* linte·um -i *n* cinematicum; **the —** ars, artis *f* cinematica
screen *tr (to shelter)* (pro)tegere; *(to test)* probare
screen play *s* script·um -i *n* scaenarium
screw *s* cochle·a -ae *f*
screw *tr* torquēre; *(to defraud)* defraudare; *(sexually) (vulg)* debattuere
screwdriver *s* cochleatorstr·um -i *n*
scribble *tr & intr* conscribillare
scribe *s* scrib·a -ae *m*
script *s* script·um -i *n; (hand)* man·us -ūs *f*
scroll *s* volum·en -inis *n*
scroll *intr (comput)* volvere; **to — down** devolvere
scrub *tr* (de)tergēre
scruple *s* scrupul·us -i *m; (misgiving)* diffidenti·a -ae *f*
scrupulous *adj* scrupulos·us -a -um
scrupulously *adv* diligenter
scrutinize *tr* (per)scrutari
scrutiny *s* (per)scrutati·o -onis *f*
scuffle *s* rix·a -ae *f*
scuffle *intr* rixari
sculptor *s* sculpt·or -oris *m*
sculptress *s* sculptr·ix -icis *f*
sculpture *s (art)* sculptur·a -ae *f; (work)* sign·um -i *n* (marmoreum)
sculpture *tr* sculpere
scum *s (foam)* spum·a -ae *f; (fig)* sentin·a -ae *f*
scurrilous *adj* scurril·is -is -e
scurry *intr* volitare, properare
scuttle *tr* pertundere ac deprimere
scythe *s* fal·x -cis *f*
sea *s* mar·e -is *n;* **by —** mari, nave
seacoast *s* or·a -ae *f* maritima
seafaring *adj* maritim·us -a -um
seafood *s* vict·us -ūs *m* maritimus
sea gull *s* lar·us -i *m*
sea horse *s* hippocamp·us -i *m*

seal *s* sigill·um -i *n; (animal)* phoc·a -ae *f*
seal *tr* signare; **to — up** obsignare
seam *s* sutur·a -ae *f*
seaman *s* naut·a -ae *m*
seamanship *s* nauticarum rerum us·us -ūs *m*
seamstress *s* sarcinatr·ix -icis *f*
seaport *s* port·us -ūs *m*
sear *tr* adurere
search *s* investigati·o -onis *f,* indagati·o -onis *f*
search *tr* investigare; *(to shake down a person)* excutere; **to — out** exquirere ‖ *intr* quaerere; **to — for** quaerere
searchlight *s* luminar·e -is *n*
seashore *s* act·a -ae *f*
seasick *adj* nauseabund·us -a -um; **to be —** nauseare
seasickness *s* nause·a -ae *f*
season *s* anni temp·us -oris *n; (proper time)* opportunit·as -atis *f,* tempus *n;* **in due —** (in) tempore; **in —** tempestiv·us -a -um
season *tr* condire; *(fig)* assuefacere
seasonable *adj* temptestiv·us -a -um
seasoned *adj (spicy)* condit·us -a -um; *(inured)* inveterat·us -a -um
seasoning *s* condiment·um -i *n*
seat *s* sed·es -is *f,* sell·a -ae *f; (on a fixed bench or chair)* sedil·e -is *n; (in school)* subsell·ium -(i)i *n; (fixed abode)* domicil·ium -(i)i *n;* **back (front) —** sedes posterior (anterior); **reserved —** sedes reservata; **— of honor** *(in dining room)* loc·us -i *m* praetorius; **to take one's —** considere
seat *tr* sede locare; **to — oneself** considere
seatbelt *s* cinctur·a -ae *f* securitatis; **to fasten (unfasten) the —** cincturam securitatis accingere (laxare)
seawater *s* aqu·a -ae *f* marina
seaweed *s* alg·a -ae *f*
secede *intr* secedere
secession *s* secessi·o -onis *f*
seclude *tr* secludere
secluded *adj* seclus·us -a -um, secret·us -a -um
seclusion *s* secess·us -ūs *m,* solitud·o -inis *f*
second *adj* secund·us -a -um; **a —** alt·er -era -erum; **a — time** iterum; **in the — place** deinde; **ranking — to s.o.** alter ab aliquo; **— to Achilles** ab Achille secundus; **to play — fiddle** secundas partes agere
second *s (handler)* adiu·tor -toris *m* (·trix -tricis *f*)*; (of time)* moment·um -i *n* temporis, secund·a -ae *f*
second *tr* adesse *(w. dat),* favēre *(w. dat);* **to — a motion** in sententiam alicuius dicere
secondary *adj* secundari·us -a -um
secondhand *adj* trit·us -a -um
second nature *s* consuetud·o -inis *f*
second-rate *adj* secundari·us -a -um

secrecy *s* secret·um -i *n; (keeping secret)* silent·ium -(i)i *n*
secret *adj* secret·us -a -um; **to keep —** celare
secret *s* secret·um -i *n;* **and he makes no — of it** neque id occulte fert; **in —** clam; **keep this a —!** haec tu tecum habeto! **to keep a —** commissum celare; **to reveal a —** commissum enuntiare
secretary *s* scrib·a -ae *mf,* amanuens·is -is *mf; (corresponding)* ab epistulis; *(pol)* (ad)minist·er -ri *m* (·ra -ae *f*), praefect·us -i *m* (·a -ae *f*), e.g., **— of agriculture** agriculturae provehendae praefectus (-a); **— of commerce** commercii praefectus (-a); **— of education** eruditionis praefectus (-a); **— of the interior** rerum interiorum praefectus (-a); **— of state** *or* **of foreign affairs** rerum externarum praefectus; **— of the treasury** aerarii praefectus (-a)
secrete *tr (to hide)* abdere; *(med)* secernere, distillare
secretion *s* secreti·o -onis *f,* distillati·o -onis *f*
sect *s* sect·a -ae *f*
section *s* secti·o -onis *f,* pars, partis *f;* **(of a city)** regi·o -onis *f*
sector *s (math)* sect·or -oris *m; (mil)* par·s -tis *f* aciei
secular *adj* profan·us -a -um; *(laic)* laic·us -a -um, secular·is -is -e
secure *adj* tut·us -a -um
secure *tr (to make safe)* munire; *(to obtain)* comparare; *(to fasten)* religare, affigere; **to — oneself against fraud** muniri contra fraudes
securely *adv* tuto
security *s* securit·as -atis *f; (pledge)* satisdati·o -onis *f,* pign·us -oris *n*
sedate *adj* sedat·us -a -um
sedate *tr* sedare
sedentary *adj* sedentari·us -a -um
sedge *s* ulv·a -ae *f*
sediment *s* sediment·um -i *n*
sedition *s* sediti·o -onis *f*
seditious *adj* seditios·us -a -um
seduce *tr (to entice)* illicere, pellicere; *(to ravish)* stuprum inferre *(w. dat),* stuprare
seducer *s* corrupt·or -oris *m,* ill·ex -icis *mf*
seduction *s* corruptel·a -ae *f*
seductive *adj* illecebros·us -a -um
see *tr* vidēre; *(to distinguish w. the eyes)* cernere; *(to look at)* aspicere; *(to spot from afar)* prospicari; **I see** *(understand)* teneo; **to go to —** visere; **II** *intr* vidēre; **see to it that you ...** fac ut *(w. subj),* cura *(or* da curam) ut *(w. subj);* **to — about** investigare, inquirere; **to — after** curare; **to — eye to eye with** consentire cum *(w. abl);* **to — off** deducere, comitari usque ad profectum; **you see** [*parenthetical*] enim
see *interj* ecce!
see *s* sed·es -is *f*
seed *s* sem·en -inis *n; (offspring)* progeni·es -ei *f; (in fruit)* acin·um -i *n*
seedbed *s* seminar·ium -(i)i *n*
seedling *s* surcul·us -i *m*
seedy *adj (unkempt)* sordidat·us -a -um
seek *tr* quaerere, petere; *(to strive after)* consectari; **to — to** conari *(w. inf)*
seem *intr* videri; **as it —s** ut videtur; **it —s to me** meā sententiā
seeming *adj* specios·us -a -um
seemingly *adv* ut videtur
seemly *adj* decor·us -a -um
seep *intr* manare; **to — through** permanare
seer *s* vat·es -is *m*
seethe *intr* aestuare
segment *s* segment·um -i *n*
segregate *tr* segregare, separare
segregation *s* separati·o -onis *f*
seismograph *s* apparat·us -ūs *m* ad terrae motum observandum
seize *tr* prehendere, arripere; *(mil)* occupare; *(fig)* afficere
seizure *s* comprehensi·o -onis *f; (med)* accessi·o -onis *f*
seldom *adv* raro; **very —** perraro
select *tr* seligere, eligere
selection *s (act)* selecti·o -onis *f; (things chosen)* elect·a -orum *npl*
self *pron* ips·e -a -um; **he was never again his old —** coloris sui numquam fuit
self-appointed *adj* sibi arrog·ans -antis
self-assurance *s* confidenti·a -ae *f*
self-assured *adj* fid·ens -entis
self-centered *adj* sibi dedit·us -a -um
self-confidence *s* fiduci·a -ae *f*
self-confident *adj* sibi fid·ens -entis
self-conscious *adj* diffid·ens -entis
self-control *s* continenti·a -ae *f*
self-controlled *adj* comp·os -otis sui
self-defense *s* sui defensi·o -onis *f;* **in —** sui defendendi causā
self-denial *s* abstinenti·a -ae *f*
self-esteem *s* sui approbati·o -onis *f*
self-evident *adj* manifest·us -a -um
self-government *s* ius, iuris *n* sui gubernandi
self-indulgent *adj* intemper·ans -antis
self-interest *s* sui utilit·as -atis *f*
selfish *adj* avar·us -a -um
selfishness *s* avariti·a -ae *f*
self-made *adj* **he is a — man** de nihilo crevit
self-respect *s* pud·or -oris *m,* dignit·as -atis *f*
self-righteous *adj* prave sanct·us -a -um
self-sufficient *adj* per se suffici·ens -entis
sell *tr* vendere; *(as a practice)* venditare; **to — for 3000 sesterces per pound** vendere ternis milibus nummum in libras; **to — short** *(fig)* levi momento aestimare **II** *intr* venire, venum ire
seller *s* vendi·tor -toris *m* (·trix -tricis *f*)

semblance *s* speci•es -ei *f,* umbr•a -ae *f;* **under the — of a just treaty** sub umbrā *(or* sub specie) foederis aequi
semester *s* semestr•e -is *n*
semicircle *s* semicircul•us -i *m*
semicircular *adj* semicircul•us -a -um
semicolon *s* punct•um et caes•um -i *n*
seminar *s* seminar•ium -(i)i *n* academicum
seminary *s* seminar•ium -(i)i *n*
semivowel *s* semivocal•is -is *f (supply* littera)
senate *s* senat•us -ūs *m; (building)* curi•a -ae *f;* **— session** senatus *m;* **a — session was held on that very day** senatus eo ipso die agebatur
senatorial *adj* senatori•us -a -um
send *tr* mittere; *(on public business)* legare; **to — away** dimittere; **to — back** remittere; **to — forward** praemittere; **to — into** intromittere in *(w. acc);* **to — out** emittere **II** *intr* **to — for** arcessere
sender *s* qui (quae) mittit
senile *adj* senil•is -is -e
senility *s* sen•ium -(i)i *n*
senior *adj* (natu) mai•or -or -us; *(in school)* seni•or -oris *mf*
seniority *s* aetatis praerogativ•a -ae *f*
sensation *s* sens•us -ūs *m; (fig)* mir•um -i *n;* **a painful —** doloris sensus; **to make a —** conspici
sensational *adj* mirabil•is -is -e
sense *s (faculty; meaning)* sens•us -ūs *m; (understanding)* prudenti•a -ae *f; (meaning)* vis *f,* significati•o -onis *f;* **— of duty, of responsibility** piet•as -atis *f*
sense *tr* sentire
senseless *adj* absurd•us -a -um; *(unconscious)* omni sensu car•ens -entis
sensible *adj* prud•ens -entis; **to be —** sapere
sensibly *adv* prudenter
sensitive *adj* sensil•is -is -e; *(touchy, sore)* moll•is -is -e
sensual *adj* voluptari•us -a -um; **— pleasure** corporis volupt•as -atis *f*
sensuality *s* libid•o -inis *f*
sentence *s (gram)* sententi•a -ae *f,* orati•o -onis *f; (leg)* iudic•ium -(i)i *n; (decision of an arbiter)* arbitr•ium -(i)i *n;* **to pass — on s.o.** arbitrium de aliquo agere; *(leg)* iudicium facere de aliquo
sentence *tr* damnare, condemnare; **to — to death** capitis damnare
sententious *adj* sententios•us -a -um
sentiment *s (opinion)* sententi•a -e *f,* opini•o -onis *f; (feeling)* sens•us -ūs *m*
sentimental *adj* moll•is -is -e, sensu affect•us -a -um
sentimentality *s* animi molliti•es -ei *f*
sentinel, sentry *s* cust•os -odis *mf,* vig•il -is *mf; (collectively)* stati•o -onis *f;* **to be on sentry duty** in statione esse
separable *adj* separabil•is -is -e
separate *tr* separare, disiungere **II** *intr* separari, disiungi
separate *adj* separat•us -a -um
separately *adv* separatim
separation *s* separati•o -onis *f*
September *s* Septem•ber -bris *m or* mens•is -is *m* September; **in —** mense Septembri; **on the first of —** Kalendis Septembribus
sepulcher *s* sepulcr•um -i *n*
sequel *s* sequel•a -ae *f,* postprincip•ium -(i)i *n*
sequence *s* ord•o -inis *m*
serenade *tr* occentare
serenade *s* nocturnus concent•us -ūs *m*
serene *adj* seren•us -a -um
serenely *adv* serene
serenity *s* serenit•as -atis *f*
serf *s* serv•us -i *m*
serfdom *s* servit•ium -(i)i *n*
sergeant *s* opti•o -onis *mf*
series *s* seri•es -ei *f*
serious *adj* seri•us -a -um, grav•is -is -e; **are you —?** serione dicis tu?
seriously *adv* serio, graviter; **to take —** in serium convertere
seriousness *s* gravit•as -atis *f; (of things)* ser•ium -(i)i *n*
sermon *s* homili•a -ae *f;* **to give a —** homiliam habēre
serpent *s* angu•is -is *mf,* serp•ens -entis *mf;* **—s hiss** serpentes sibilant
servant *s* famul•us -i *m* (•a -ae *f*), serv•us -i *m* (•a -ae *f*)
serve *tr (to be a servant to)* servire *(w. dat); (food)* apponere; *(to be useful)* prodesse *(w. dat);* **to — a sentence** poenam subire; **to — a summons on** diem dare *(dat);* **to — one's country** de re publica merēre **II** *intr (mil)* (stipendia) merēre; *(to suffice)* sufficere; *(tennis)* deicere; **the trunk — the elephant as a hand** proboscis elephanto pro manu est; **to — as a soldier or sailor** (ut) miles aut nauta merēre
service *s (favor)* offic•ium -(i)i *n; (mil)* militi•a -ae *f,* stipendi•a -orum *npl; (work)* minister•ium -(i)i *n;* **to be at s.o.'s —** alicui praesto esse; **to be of — to** prodesse *(w. dat)*
serviceable *adj* util•is -is -e
serviceman *s* militar•is -is *m*
service station *s* stati•o -onis *f* benzinaria
servile *adj* servil•is -is -e
servitude *s* servit•us -utis *f*
sesame *s* sesam•um -i *n*
session *s* sessi•o -onis *f;* **to be in —** sedēre
sesterce *s* sestert•ius -(i)i *m (used in smaller sums; large sums are expressed by the collective form* sestertium = mille sesterti, *usually with the distributive numeral, e.g.,* **hundred thousand sesterces** centena sestertia, *but also with the cardinal, as,* septem sestertia **seven hundred thousand sesterces)**

set *tr (to place)* ponere; *(to make to stand)* sistere, statuere; *(diamonds, etc.)* includere; *(a broken limb)* collocare; *(course)* dirigere; *(date)* constituere; *(example)* praebēre; *(limit)* imponere; *(table)* instruere; *(plants)* serere; *(clock)* constituere; **to — apart** seponere; **to — a price** pretium statuere; **to — aside** ponere; *(to rescind)* rescindere; **to — a trap** insidias tendere; **to — bounds to** modum *(w. gen)* habēre; **to — down** deponere; *(in writing)* perscribere; **to — foot in** attingere; **to — forth** exponere, proponere; **to — free** liberare; **to — in motion** ciēre; **to — in order** componere; **to — off** *(to adorn)* adornare; **to — on fire** incendere; **to — one's hopes on** spem collocare in *(w. abl)*; **to — s.o. over** aliquem praeficere *(w. dat)*; **to — up** statuere ‖ *intr (of stars, sun)* occidere; **to — about waging wars** bella incipere; **to — in** *(to begin)* incipere; **to — out** proficisci

set *adj (fixed)* cert·us -a -um; *(prescribed, e.g., day, sacrifice)* stat·us -a -um; *(prepared)* parat·us -a -um; **in — terms** composite; **— speech** declamati·o -onis *f*

set *s (a set of two)* par, paris *n; (gear, set of tools)* instrument·um -i *n; (number of persons customarily associated)* glob·us -i *m;* **a — of tools for one's trade** artis instrumentum *n*

setback *s* **to suffer a —** *(mil)* adversum casum experiri; *(pol)* repulsam ferre

setting *s (of sun)* occas·us -ūs *m; (situation)* res, rerum *fpl*

settle *tr* statuere; *(business)* transigere; *(colony)* deducere; *(people, e.g., on public lands)* constituere; *(disagreement)* componere; *(debt)* expedire; **to — accounts with** rationes putare cum *(w. abl)* ‖ *intr (to the bottom)* subsidēre; *(to alight, land)* (**on**) insidere *(w. dat); (to fix one's home)* (**in**) considere *or* insidere (in *w. abl); **we —d among ourselves to** constituimus inter nos ut

settled *adj (sure, certain)* cert·us -a -um

settlement *s (of a colony)* deducti·o -onis *f; (the colony itself)* coloni·a -ae *f; (of an affair)* compositi·o -onis *f; (terms)* pact·um -i *n*

settler *s* colon·us -i *m,* adven·a -ae *mf*

seven *adj* septem [*indecl*]; **— times** septies

sevenfold *adj* septempl·ex -icis

seventeen *adj* septendecim [*indecl*]

seventeenth *adj* septim·us decim·us -a -um

seventh *adj* septim·us -a -um; **to be in — heaven** in caelo esse

seventieth *adj* septuagesim·us -a -um

seventy *adj* septuaginta [*indecl*]

sever *tr* separare ‖ *intr* disiungi

several *adj* aliquot [*indecl*]

severally *adv* singulatim

severe *adj (rigorous, strict)* sever·us -a -um; *(wound, punishment)* grav·is -is -e; *(winter)* a·cer -cris -cre; *(cold, pain)* dur·us -a -um

severely *adv* severe, graviter

severity *s* severit·as -atis *f,* gravit·as -atis *f*

sew *tr* suere; **to — up** consuere

sewer *s* cloac·a -ae *f*

sewing *s* sutur·a -ae *f*

sewing machine *s* machin·a -ae *f* sutoria

sex *s (gender)* sex·us -ūs *m; (intercourse)* Ven·us -eris *f,* coït·us -ūs *m;* **to have illicit — with** stuprum inferre *(w. dat)*

sextant *s* sext·ans -antis *m*

sexton *s* aeditu·us -i *m*

sexual *adj* sexual·is -is -e; **— desire** libid·o -inis *f;* **— intercourse** coït·us -ūs *m*

sh-h-h *interj* st! st!

shabbily *adv* sordide

shabbiness *s* sord·es -ium *fpl*

shabby *adj* sordid·us -a -um; *(worn out, torn)* obsolet·us -a -um

shackle *tr* compedibus constringere

shackles *spl* vincul·a -orum *npl; (on the legs)* comped·es -um *fpl*

shade *s* umbr·a -ae *f;* **—s** *(of the dead)* man·es -ium *mpl*

shade *tr* opacare, adumbrare

shadow *s* umbr·a -ae *f*

shadowy *adj* umbros·us -a -um; *(fig)* inan·is -is -e, exil·is -is -e

shady *adj* opac·us -a -um; *(pej)* infam·is -is -e

shaft *s (arrow)* sagitt·a -ae *f; (of spear)* hastil·e -is *n; (of a mine)* pute·us -i *m*

shaggy *adj* villos·us -a -um

shake *tr* quatere, concutere; *(violently)* quassare; *(head)* nutare; *(to get rid of)* amoliri; **to — hands (with)** dextram iungere (cum *w. abl); (when campaigning)* manus prensare; **to — off a bad reputation** infamiam discutere; **to — the head** nutare; *(in dissent)* abnutare; **to — up** *(fig)* commovēre, perturbare ‖ *intr* tremere; *(to totter)* vacillare; **her sides shook with laughter** eius latera commoverunt risu; **to begin to —** intremescere

shakedown *s* extorsi·o -onis *f*

shake-up *s* magna commutati·o -onis *f*

shaking *s* quassati·o -onis *f; (w. cold, fear)* trem·or -oris *m*

shaky *adj* tremul·us -a -um; *(weak)* debil·is -is -e; *(unreliable)* instabil·is -is -e

shallow *adj (river, sea)* tenu·is -is -e; *(trench)* humil·is -is -e; *(well)* brev·is -is -e; *(fig)* lev·is -is -e; **quite —** minime alt·us -a -um

shallows *spl* vad·a -orum *npl*

sham *s* dol·us -i *m*

sham *adj* simulat·us -a -um

shambles *spl* turb·a -ae *f,* confusi·o -onis *f*

shame *s* pud·or -oris *m; (disgrace)* dedec·us -oris *n;* **— on our Senate and morals!** pro senatu et moribus! **— on you!** sit pudor!; **that's a darn shame!** edepol facinus improbum!; **to have lost all sense of —** omnem pudorem exuisse; **to put s.o. to —** ruborem alicui incutere; **what a —!** facinus indignum!; O rem indignam!
shame *tr* ruborem incutere *(w. dat)*
shamefaced *adj* verecund·us -a -um
shameful *adj* probros·us -a -um, ignominios·us -a -um
shamefully *adv* probrose, turpiter
shameless *adj* impud·ens -entis
shamelessly *adv* impudenter
shampoo *s* loment·um -i *n* capillare
shamrock *s* trifol·ium -(i)i *n*
shank *s* cru·s -ris *n*
shanty *s* tugur·ium -(i)i *n*
shape *s* form·a -ae *f,* figur·a -ae *f;* **to be in good (bad) —** boni (mali) habitūs esse
shape *tr* figurare, formare
shapeless *adj* inform·is -is -e
shapely *adj* formos·us -a -um; *(limbs)* ter·es -etis
shard *s* test·a -ae *f*
share *s* par·s -tis *f,* porti·o -onis *f; (stock)* acti·a -ae *f*
share *tr* partire; *(to enjoy with, have in common with)* (**with**) communicare (cum *w. abl)* **‖** *intr* **to — in** particeps esse *(w. gen)*
shark *s* pistr·ix -icis *f,* pistr·is -is *f*
sharp *adj* acut·us -a -um; *(abrupt)* prae·ceps -cipis; *(mind)* ac·er -ris -re, sag·ax -acis; *(taste)* acerb·us -a -um
sharpen *tr* (ex)acuere
sharply *adv* acriter
sharpness *s* aci·es -ei *f;* **— of vision** oculorum acies; *(of mind)* acum·en -inis *n*
shatter *tr* quassare, confringere; *(to knock apart)* discutere
shave *tr* radere; **to — off** deradere **‖** *intr* barbam *(or* faciem) radere
shave *s* rasur·a -ae *f;* **to have a close —** *(fig)* aegre effugere
shaven *adj* adras·us -a -um
shavings *spl* rament·a -orum *npl*
shawl *s* amicul·um -i *n*
she *pron* ea, illa, haec
sheaf *s* fasc·is -is *m*
shear *tr* tondēre
shearing *s* tonsur·a -ae *f*
shears *spl* forf·ex -icis *f*
sheath *s* vagin·a -ae *f*
sheathe *tr* in vaginam recondere
shed *tr (tears, blood, etc.)* fundere, effundere; *(to cast off)* exuere, spargere; *(feathers, leaves)* ponere; **to — light on a subject** lumen alicui rei adhibēre **‖** *intr (of plants)* deflorescere
shed *s* tugur·ium -(i)i *n; (mil)* vine·a -ae *f*
sheep *s* ov·is -is *f*
sheepfold *s* ovil·e -is *n*
sheepish *adj* pudibund·us -a -um
sheepishly *adv* pudenter
sheepskin *s* pell·is -is *f* ovilla
sheer *adj (pure, utter)* mer·us -a -um; *(steep)* praerupt·us -a -um
sheet *s (for the bed)* stragul·um -i *n* linteum; *(of paper)* sched·a -ae *f; (of metal)* lamin·a -ae *f;* **— of papyrus** chart·a -ae *f*
shelf *s* plute·us -i *m*
shell *s (of clam or oyster)* conch·a -ae *f,* test·a -ae *f; (of a turtle)* testud·o -inis *f; (of nuts, eggs)* putam·en -inis *n*
shellac *s* malth·a -ae *f*
shellfish *s* conch·a -ae *f*
shelter *s* tegm·en -inis *n; (refuge)* refug·ium -(i)i *n; (lodgings)* hospit·ium -(i)i *n*
shelter *tr* tegere; *(refugees)* excipere
shepherd *s* past·or -oris *m*
sheriff *s* geraif·a -ae *mf*
shield *s (round)* parm·a -ae *f; (oblong)* scut·um -i *n*
shield *tr* protegere
shift *tr (to change)* mutare; *(transfer)* transferre **‖** *intr* mutari; **to — for oneself** sibi providēre
shift *s (change)* mutati·o -onis *f; (period of work)* laboris spat·ium -(i)i *n*
shifting *adj (wind, weather)* vari·us -a -um
shiftless *adj* pi·ger -gra -grum
shifty *adj* mobil·is -is -e; *(untrustworthy)* prav·us -a -um
shimmer *intr* micare, tremere
shimmer *s* lum·en -inis *n* tremulum
shin *s* tibi·a -ae *f*
shinbone *s* tibi·a -ae *f*
shine *s* nit·or -oris *m,* fulg·or -oris *m*
shine *intr* lucēre; *(with a bright light)* fulgēre; *(to excel)* praestare; **to — forth** elucēre, enitēre; **to — on** affulgēre *(w. dat)*
shingle *s* tegul·a -ae *f*
shiny *adj* fulgid·us -a -um, nitid·us -a -um
ship *s* nav·is -is *f;* **—'s captain** navarch·us -i *m*
ship *tr* navi invehere, devehere; *(to send)* mittere
shipbuilder *s* naupeg·us -i *m*
ship owner *s* navicular·ius -(i)i *m*
shipwreck *s* naufrag·ium -(i)i *n;* **to suffer —** naufragium facere
shipwrecked *adj* naufract·us -a -um
shipyard *s* naval·ia -ium *npl*
shirk *tr* abhorrēre ab *(w. abl),* evitare
shirt *s* subucul·a -ae *f,* camisi·a -ae *f*
shiver *intr* horrēre, tremere
shiver *s* horr·or -oris *m,* trem·or -oris *m*
shoal *s (of fish)* exam·en -inis *n; (shallow)* vad·um -i *n*
shock *s* offensi·o -onis *f;* electricus ict·us -ūs *m*

shock *tr (emotionally)* percutere, attonere; **to be —ed** inhorrescere
shocked *adj* attonit·us -a -um
shocking *adj* tae·ter -tra -trum, horrend·us -a -um
shoe *s (worn with toga)* calce·us -i *m; (oxfords)* calceus subtalaris; *(fancy low shoe, of different colors, decorated with pearls, etc.)* socc·us -i *m,* soccul·us -i *m; (red shoes of a senator)* calceus mulleus
shoe polish *s* cerom·a -atis *n* sutorium
shoemaker *s* sut·or -oris *m*
shoe store *s* tabern·a *f* sutrina
shook up *adj* consternat·us -a -um; **all —** vehmenter perturbat·us -a -um
shoot *tr (missile)* conicere; *(person)* sclopeto transfigere; **I shot myself in the foot** mihi asciam in crus impegi **||** *intr* volare; **to — up** crescere; *(to sprout)* germinare; *(sl)* medicamentum psychotropicum infundere
shoot *s* surcul·us -i *m*
shooting star *s* fae·x -cis *f* caelestis
shop *s* tabern·a -ae *f; (workshop)* officin·a -ae *f*
shop *intr* mercari; *(for groceries)* obsonare; **to — for** mercari; *(groceries)* obsonare; **to go shopping** emptum ire; **I shopped for clothes** per tabernas lustravi ut vestes emerem
shopkeeper *s* tabernari·us -i *m* (·a -ae *f*)
shopper *s* emp·tor -toris *m* (·trix -tricis *f*); *(for groceries)* obsona·tor -toris *m* (·trix -tricis *f*)
shopping *s* empti·o -onis *m; (for groceries)* obsonat·us -ūs *m*
shopping spree *s* emacit·as -atis *f*; **to go on a —** effundi in emacitate
shore *s* lit·us -oris *n,* or·a -ae *f*
shore *tr* **to — up** fulcire
short *adj* brev·is -is -e; **a — vowel** vocal·is -is *f* correpta; **in a — time** brevi; **in —** ad summam; **to make — shrift of** dimittere; **to run —** deficere
short *s (electrical)* defectus curs·us -ūs *m* electricus
shortage *s* inopi·a -ae *f,* exiguit·as -atis *f*
shortchange *tr* non satis pecuniae reddere; *(fig)* fraudare (*w. dat*)
shortcoming *s* defect·us -ūs *m*
shortcut *s* compendari·a -ae *f;* **to take a —** compendariā ire
shorten *tr* curtare, imminuere; contrahere; *(to limit)* coarctare; *(a syllable)* corripere **||** *intr* contrahi, minui
shorthand *s* not·ae -ārum *fpl;* **to take down in —** notis excipere
short-lived *adj* brev·is -is -e, fug·ax -acis
shortly *adv* brevi, mox
shortness *s* brevit·as -atis *f;* **— of breath** asthm·a -atis *n*
shorts *spl* breves brac·ae -arum *fpl; (underwear)* subligacul·um -i *n*
shortsighted *adj* my·ops -opis; *(fig)* improvid·us -a -um
shortstop *s* intermedius basiari·us -i *m,* intermedia basiari·a -ae *f*
shorttempered *adj* iracund·us -a -um
short-winded *adj* anhel·us -a -um
shorty *s* pumili·o -onis *mf*
shot *s (of a gun)* scopleti crepit·us -ī *m; (of liquor)* mera poti·o -onis *f; (guess)* coniectur·a -ae *f;* **long —** dubia ale·a -ae *f;* **— in the arm** *(fig)* instigati·o -onis *f;* **to take a — at it** *(fig)* id periclitari
shot *adj (worn out)* attrit·us -a -um
shotgun *s* focil·e -is *n* (bifistulatum)
should *intr (ought)* debēre; **I — go** mihi eundum est; **if I — say no** si negem
shoulder *s* umer·us -i *m; (of animals)* arm·us -i *m;* **to give s.o. the cold —** aliquem reicere; **to shrug the —s** umeros allevare
shoulder *tr* suscipere
shoulder bag *s* per·a -ae *f*
shoulder blade *s* scapul·a -ae *f*
shout *s* clam·or -oris *m; (of approval)* acclamati·o -onis *f*
shout *tr* clamare, acclamare; **to — s.o. down** alicui obstrepere; **to — out** exclamare **||** *intr* clamare; *(continuously)* clamitare
shove *tr* trudere, pulsare; **to — the book under the bed** mittere librum subter lectum **||** *intr* **to — off** *(to depart)* proficisci; *(naut)* terram repellere
shove *s* impulsi·o -onis *f,* impuls·us -ūs *m*
shovel *s* rutr·um -i *n*
shovel *tr* rutro tollere; **to — out** rutro eicere
show *tr* monstrare, ostendere; *(to display)* exhibēre; *(to explain)* docēre; **this —s that ...** indicio est *(w. acc & inf);* **to — off** ostentare **||** *intr* manifest·us -a -um esse; **to — off** se iactare; **to — up** apparēre
show *s (appearance)* speci·es -ei *f; (display)* ostentati·o -onis *f; (pretense)* simulati·o -onis *f; (public entertainment)* spectacul·um -i *n;* **for —** ad speciem; **to put on a public —** spectaculum edere
shower *s (rain)* im·ber -bris *m; (of stones, darts)* vis *f,* multitud·o -inis *f; (for bathing)* balne·um -i *n* pensile; **bridal —** conviv·ium -(i)i *n* nuptiale; **to take a —** balneo pensili uti
shower *tr* fundere; **to — down arrows on** infundere sagittas *(w. dat)*
showy *adj* specios·us -a -um
shred *s* segment·um -i *n* panni; **in —s** sciss·us -a -um, pannos·us -a -um; **not a — of evidence** nihil omnino testimonii; **to tear to —s** discindere
shred *tr* discindere, concidere
shrewd *adj* astut·us -a -um; *(calculating)* callid·us -a -um
shrewdly *adv* astute, callide

shrewdness *s* acum·en -inis *n;* callidit·as -atis *f*
shriek *s* strid·or -oris *m*
shriek *intr* stridēre
shrill *adj* peracut·us -a -um
shrimp *s* squill·a -ae *f; (person)* pumili·o -onis *mf*
shrine *s* delubr·um -i *n,* fan·um -i *n*
shrink *tr* contrahere ‖ *intr* contrahi; *(to withdraw)* refugere; **to — from** abhorrēre *or* refugere ab *(w. abl)*
shrink *s (coll)* pyschiat·er -ri *m* (·ria -riae *f*)
shrivel *tr* corrugare ‖ *intr* corrugari
shriveled *adj* rugos·us -a -um
shroud *s* vestiment·um -i *n* funebre; *(cover)* integument·um -i *n*
shroud *tr* involvere
shrub *s* frut·ex -icis *m*
shrubbery *s* fruticet·um -i *n*
shrug *tr* **to — the shoulders** umeros allevare
shrug *s* umerorum allevati·o -onis *f*
shudder *intr* horrēre; **to — at the sight** horrēre visu
shudder *s* horr·or -oris *m*
shuffle *tr (cards)* permiscēre ‖ *intr* claudicare
shun *tr* (de)vitare, evadere; **to — publicity** forum ac lucem fugere
shut *tr* claudere; **to — down** *(comput)* claudere; **to — in** includere; **to — off** occludere; **to — one's eyes to** connivēre in *(w. acc);* **to — out** excludere; **to — up** concludere ‖ *intr* **to — down** cessare **to — up** conticescere; **— up!** obsera os tuum!; **why don't you just — up?** quin tu taces modo?
shutdown *s* cessati·o -onis *f*
shutter *s* foricul·a -ae *f*
shy *adj* verecund·us -a -um; *(timid)* timid·us -a -um
shy *intr (of horses)* consternari; **to — away from** abhorrēre ab *(w. abl)*
shyly *adv* verecunde, timide
shyness *s* verecundi·a -ae *f*
shyster *s* legulei·us -i *m* (·a -ae *f*)
sibyl *s* sibyll·a -ae *f*
sibylline *adj* Sibyllin·us -a -um
sic *tr* **to — the dog on** instigare canem in *(w. acc)*
Sicily *s* Sicili·a -ae *f*
sick *adj (mentally or physically)* ae·ger -gra -grum; *(physically)* aegrot·us -a -um; **I am — and tired of** me valde pertaedet *(w. gen);* **to be —** aegrotare; **to fall —** in morbum incidere; **to feel —** nauseare
sickbed *s* lect·us -i *m* aegrotantis
sicken *tr* fastidium movēre *(w. dat)* ‖ *intr* in morbum incidere; *(to feel disgust)* fastidire
sickening *adj* tae·ter -tra -trum
sickle *s* fal·x -cis *f*
sickly *adj* morbos·us -a -um, infirm·us -a -um
sickness *s* morb·us -i *m,* aegritud·o -inis *f*
side *s (of a body, hill, camp, ship, etc.)* lat·us -eris *n; (quarter, direction)* par·s -tis *f; (faction)* part·es -ium *fpl; (kinship)* gen·us -eris *n;* **at the — of** a latere *(w. gen);* **from all —s** undique; **having heard only one —, he condemned her** alterā tantum parte auditā condemnavit eam; **on all —s** undique; **on both —s** utrimque; **one — of the island** unum latus insulae; **on one —** unā ex parte; **on that —** illinc; **on the one — ... on the other** hinc ... illinc; **on their —** pro illa parte; **on the right — of** latere dextro *(w. gen);* **on the mother's —** materno genere; **on this —** hinc; **on this — of** cis *(w. acc),* citra *(w. acc);* **— by —** alius alium iuxta, contigu·us -a -um; **to be on the — of** stare ab *(w. abl),* sentire cum *(w. abl);* **to leave s.o.'s —** a latere alicuius discedere; **to lie on his —** in latus cubare; **to take —s** favēre; **to walk at s.o.'s —** tegere latus alicui
side *adj* lateral·is -is -e
side *intr* **to — with** partes sequi *(w. gen),* stare ab *(w. abl),* sentire cum *(w. abl)*
sideboard *s* abac·us -i *m*
sided *adj* **many-sided** multilater·us -a -um; **one-sided** unilter·us -a -um
sidekick *s (coll)* contubernal·is -is *mf*
sideline *s (sports)* line·a -ae *f* lateralis; **on the —s** *(fig)* remot·us -a -um, non partic·eps -itis
sidelong *adj* obliqu·us -a -um
sidestep *tr* (e)vitare, effugere
side street *s* deverticul·um -i *n,* vi·a -ae *f* lateralis
sideswipe *tr* obliquo ictu concutere
sidetrack *tr* deflectere, divertere
sidewalk *s* crepid·o -inis *f*
sideways *adv* in obliquum, oblique
siege *s* obsidi·o -onis *f;* **to lay — to** obsidēre
siesta *s* meridiati·o -onis *f;* **to take a —** meridiare
sieve *s* cribr·um -i *n; (little sieve)* cribell·um -i *n*
sift *tr* cribrare; *(fig)* scrutari ‖ *intr* **to — through** (per)scrutari
sigh *s* suspir·ium -(i)i *n*
sigh *intr* suspirare; **to — for** desiderare
sight *s (sense)* vis·us -ūs *m; (act of seeing)* aspect·us -ūs *m; (range)* conspect·us -ūs *m; (appearance)* speci·es -ei *f; (show)* spectacul·um -i *n;* **at first —** *(on the first appearance of a person or thing)* primā specie; *(looking at it subjectively)* primo aspectu; **at —, by —** aspectu. **in —** in conspectu, ante oculos; **out of —** e conspectu; **to catch — of** conspicere; **to lose — of** e conspectu amittere

sight *tr* conspicari, conspicere
sightseeing *s* spectati·o -onis *f* visendorum
sightseer *s* specta·tor -toris *m* (·trix -tricis *f*) visendorum
sign *s* sign·um -i *n*, indic·ium -(i)i *n*; *(mark)* not·a -ae *f*; *(distinction)* insign·e -is *n*; *(omen)* portent·um -i *n*
sign *tr (document)* subscribere; *(to ratify by signature and seal)* signare; **to — one's name to a letter** nomen epistulae notare
signal *intr* signum dare; *(by a nod)* annuere
signal *s* sign·um -i *n*; *(mil)* classic·um -i *n*
signal *adj* insign·is -is -e
signature *s* subscriptum nom·en -inis *n*, subscripti·o -onis *f*
signer *s* signa·tor -toris *m* (·trix -tricis *f*)
signet *s* sigill·um -i *n*
signet ring *s* annul·us -i *m* signatorius
significance *s (meaning)* significati·o -onis *f*; *(importance)* moment·um -i *n*
significant *adj* signific·ans -antis, magni momenti
signify *tr* significare
silence *s* silent·ium -(i)i *n*; **—!** tace! *(pl:* tacete!); **to call for —** silentium facere; **to pass over in —** silentio praeterire
silence *tr* comprimere; *(by argument)* refutare
silent *adj* tacit·us -a -um; **be! —** tace! *(pl:* tacete!); **to become —** conticescere; **to be —** tacēre; **to keep s.th. —** aliquid tacēre; **to keep — about s.th.** de aliquo silēre
silently *adv* tacite
silk *s* seric·um -i *n*
silk *adj* seric·us -a -um
silkworm *s* bomb·yx -ycis *mf*
sill *s* lim·en -inis *n* inferum
silliness *s* inepti·a -ae *f*
silly *adj* desipi·ens -entis; **don't be —** noli ineptire; **to be —** desipere, ineptire
silver *s* argent·um -i *n*
silvermine *s* argentifodin·a -ae *f*
silversmith *s* fa·ber -bri *m* argentarius
silverware *s* argente·a -orum *npl*, vas·a -orum *npl* argentea
silvery *adj* argente·us -a -um; *(of hair)* can·us -a -um
similar *adj* simil·is -is -e
similarity *s* similitud·o -inis *f*
similarly *adv* similiter, pariter
simile *s* translat·um -i *n*
simmer *intr* leniter fervēre
simple *adj* simpl·ex -icis; *(easy)* facil·is -is -e; *(weak-minded)* inept·us -a -um; *(frank)* sincer·us -a -um
simpleton *s* inept·us -i *m* (·a -ae *f*), caud·ex -icis *m*
simplicity *s* simplicit·as -atis *f*
simplify *tr* facil·iorem -iorem -ius reddere
simply *adv (in a simple manner)* simpliciter; *(only)* tantummodo; **I — don't know what he is thinking of** plane quid cogitet nescio
simulate *tr* simulare
simulation *s* simulati·o -onis *f*
simultaneous *adj* eodem tempore
simultaneously *adv* simul, unā
sin *s* peccat·um -i *n*
sin *intr* peccare
since *prep* ex *(w. abl)*, ab *(w. abl)*, post *(w. acc)*; **ever —** usque ab *(w. abl)*, ex quo tempore
since *adv* abhinc; **long —** iamdudum
since *conj (temporal)* ex quo tempore, postquam, cum; *(causal)* quod, quia, quoniam, cum
sincere *adj* sincer·us -a -um
sincerely *adv* sincere
sincerity *s* sincerit·as -atis *f*
sinew *s* nerv·us -i *m*
sinful *adj* prav·us -a -um
sing *tr & intr* canere, cantare
singe *tr* adurere, amburere
singer *s* canta·tor -toris *m* (·tr·ix -icis *f*)
singing *s* cant·us -ūs *m*
single *adj* sol·us -a -um, unic·us -a -um; *(unmarried male)* caeleb·s -is; *(ummarried female)* innupta; **in — combat** vir unus cum viro congrediendo; **not a — one** ne un·us -a -um quidem; **— room** cubicul·um -i *n* unius lecti
single *tr* **to — out** eligere
singly *adv* singulatim
singsong *s* cantic·um -i *n*
singsong *adj* canor·us -a -um
singular *adj (only one; outstanding; gram)* singular·is -is -e; **in the —** singulariter
singularly *adv* singulariter, unice
sinister *adj* malevol·us -a -um
sink *tr* submergere; *(as a hostile act)* deprimere; *(money)* collocare ‖ *intr (to settle at the bottom)* (de)sidere; *(of ships)* mergi; *(of morale)* cadere; **to — in the mud** limo se immergere
sink *s (in kitchen)* fusor·ium -(i)i *n*; *(in bathroom)* labell·um -i *n*
sinless *adj* peccati exper·s -tis
sinner *s* pecca·tor -toris *m* (·trix -tricis *f*)
sip *tr* sorbillare
sip *s* sorbiti·o -onis *f*
siphon *s* siph·o -onis *m*
sir *interj (to a master)* ere! *(to an equal)* bone vir! *(to a superior)* domine!
sire *s* genit·or -oris *m*
siren *s* sir·en -enis *f*; *(alarm)* classic·um -i *n*
sister *s* sor·or -oris *f*; **little —** sororcul·a -ae *f*
sisterhood *s* sororum societ·as -atis *f*
sister-in-law *s* glo·s -ris *f*; *(sister of husband)* sor·or -oris *f* mariti; *(wife of brother)* ux·or -oris *f* fratris
sisterly *adj* sorori·us -a -um

sit *intr* sedēre; **to — as judge** ius dicere; **to — beside** assidēre *(w. dat)*; **to — down (on)** considere (super *w. acc)*; **to — on** insidēre *(w. dat)*; **to — up** *(to stay awake)* vigilare; *(straight)* recte sedēre; **to — up all night** pervigilare
site *s* sit·us -ūs *m*; *(for building)* are·a -ae *f*
sitting *s* sessi·o -onis *f*
sitting duck *s (coll)* facilis praed·a -ae *f*
sitting room *s* sessor·ium -(i)i *n*
situated *adj* sit·us -a -um; **— near, on** apposit·us -a -um *(w. dat)*
situation *s* sit·us -ūs *m*; *(circumstances)* res, rei *f*; **that's the —** res sic se habet; **you see what the — is** vides quo in loco haec res sit
situps *spl* **to do —** identidem residere
six *adj* sex [*indecl*]; **— times** sexies
sixfold *adj* sextupl·us -a -um
sixteen *adj* sedecim [*indecl*]
sixteenth *adj* sext·us decim·us -a -um
sixth *adj* sext·us -a -um
sixth *s* sexta par·s -tis *f*
sixtieth *adj* sexagesim·us -a -um
sixty *adj* sexaginta [*indecl*]
size *s* magnitud·o -inis *f*, amplitud·o -inis *f*; **of huge —** ing·ens -entis
skate *intr* (rotulis) patinare
skate *s* calce·us -i *m* subrotatus
skateboard *s* tabul·a -ae *f* subrotata
skater *s* patina·tor -toris *m* (·trix -tricis *f*)
skating *s* patinati·o -onis *f*
skein *s* glom·us -i *m*
skeleton *s* scelet·us -i *m*
skeleton key *s* adultera clav·is -is *f*
sketch *s* adumbrati·o -onis *f*
sketch *tr* adumbrare, delineare; *(in words)* describere
ski *intr* nartare
ski *s* nart·a -ae *f*; **— boot** *s* calig·a -ae *f* nartatoria; **— jump** *s* suggest·us -us *m* desultorius; **— jumping** *s* desultur·a -ae *f* nartatoria; **— lift** *s* anabathr·um -i *n* nartatorium; **— lodge** *s* deversor·ium -(i)i *n* nartatorium; **— pole** *s* bacul·um -i *n* nartatorium; **— slope** *s* cliv·us -i *m* nartatorius **to put on —** nartas pedibus aptare, nartas adstringere; **to take off the —s** nartas destringere
skier *s* narta·tor -toris *m* (·trix -tricis *f*)
skiing *s* nartati·o -onis *f*
skiff *s* scaph·a -ae *f*
skill *s* sollerti·a -ae *f*; *(derived from experience)* periti·a -ae *f*
skilled *adj* perit·us -a -um
skillful *adj* sol·ers -ertis, scit·us -a -um; *(w. hands)* habil·is -is -e
skillfully *adv* sollerter, scite
skillet *s* cucumell·a -ae *f*
skim *tr (milk)* despumare; *(glance through)* cursim legere, percurrere
skim milk *s* lac, lactis *n* despumatum
skimp *intr* parcere, sumptūs concidere; **to — on** parce uti *(w. abl)*
skimpy *adj* parc·us -a -um, exigu·us -a -um
skin *s (of man)* cut·is -is *f*; *(of animals)* pell·is -is *f*; (**pale** pallida; **dry** arida; **tough** dura; **wrinkled** rugosa)
skin *tr* pellem detrahere *(w. dat)*
skinny *adj* mac·er -era -erum
skip *tr* praeterire, praetermittere ‖ *intr* subsultare; **to — over** transilire
skipper *s* nauarch·us -i *m*
skirmish *s* leve certam·en -inis *n*
skirmish *intr* levia proelia conserere
skirt *s* gunn·a -ae *f*, castul·a -ae *f*
skirt *tr* tangere
skit *s* parodi·a -ae *f*
skittish *adj (restive)* contum·ax -acis; *(shy)* verecund·us -a -um
skull *s* calvari·a -ae *f*; **fractured —** cap·ut -itis *n* fractum; **to break s.o.'s —** *(coll)* caput dirumpere
skunk *s* viverr·a -ae *f* putoria; *(person) (sl)* propud·ium -(i)i *n*
sky *s* cael·um -i *n*; **under the open —** sub divo
sky-blue *adj* caerule·us -a -um
skylark *s* alaud·a -ae *f*
skylight *s* compluv·ium -(i)i *n*
skyscraper *s* multizon·ium -(i)i *n*
slab *s* tabul·a -ae *f*, quadr·a -ae *f*
slack *adj* lax·us -a -um
slacken *tr* remittere, laxare ‖ *intr* remitti, minui
slain *adj* occis·us -a -um
slake *tr (thirst)* exstinguere
slalom *s* decursi·o -onis *f* flexuosa
slam dunk *s* tuxtax-immissi·o -onis *f*
slander *s* calumni·a -ae *f*
slander *tr* calumniari
slanderer *s* obtrecta·tor -toris *m* (·trix -tricis *f*)
slanderous *adj* calumnios·us -a -um
slang *s* vulgaria verb·a -orum *npl*
slant *tr* acclinare; *(fig)* detorquēre ‖ *intr* proclinari
slanted *adj* transvers·us -a -um; *(news)* distort·us -a -um
slanting *adj* obliqu·us -a -um
slap *s* alap·a -ae *f*; **— in the face** *(fig)* repuls·a -ae *f*
slap *tr* alapam dare *(w. dat)*; **to — s.o. in the face** os alicuius palmā pulsare
slaphappy *adj (dazed from blows)* torpid·us -a -um; *(happy-go-lucky)* secur·us -a -um
slash *s (cut)* caesur·a -ae *f*; *(blow)* ict·us -ūs *m*; *(wound)* vuln·us -eris *n*
slash *tr* caedere, vulnerare; *(to reduce)* imminuere
slat *s* tigill·um -i *n*
slate *s* tegul·a -ae *f*; *(pol)* ind·ex -icis *m* candidatorum; **clean slate** tabul·a -ae *f* rasa
slaughter *s* trucidati·o -onis *f*

slaughter *tr* trucidare, mactare
slaughterhouse *s* carnar•ium -(i)i *n*
slave *s* serv•us -i *m* (•a -ae *f*)
slave *intr* sudare, laborare operose
slave dealer *s* mang•o -onis *m*
slavery *s* servitud•o -inis *f*
slave labor *s* op•us -eris *n* servile
slave trade *s* venalic•ium -(i)i *n*
slavish *adj* servil•is -is -e
slavishly *adv* serviliter
slay *tr* interficere
slayer *s* interfec•tor -toris *m* (•trix -tricis *f*)
sled *s* trahe•a -ae *f* (lusoria)
sledge *s* trahe•a -ae *f*
sledgehammer *s* marc•us -i *m*
sleek *adj* nitid•us -a -um
sleep *s* somn•us -i *m;* **deep —** sop•or -oris *m;* **sound —** somnus artus
sleep *tr* **to — off a hangover** crapulam edormire ‖ *intr* dormire, quiescere; **to go to —** dormitum ire; *(to doze off)* obdormiscere; **to put to —** in sumnum collocare, consopire; **to — over** indormire *(w. abl)*
sleepily *adv* somniculose
sleeping bag *s* sacc•us -i *m* dormitoriā
sleeping car *s* curr•us -ūs *m* dormitorius
sleeping pill *s* catapot•ium -(i)i *n* somniferum
sleepless *adj* insomn•is -is -e
sleeplessness *s* insomni•a -ae *f*
sleepwalk *intr* dormiens ambulare
sleepwalker *s* somnambul•us -i *m* (•a -ae *f*)
sleepy *adj* semisomn•is -is -e, somniculos•us -a -um
sleet *s* nivosa grand•o -inis *f*
sleeve *s* manic•a -ae *f*
sleeveless *adj* sine manicis
sleigh *s* trahe•a -ae *f;* **to go — riding** traheā vehi
sleight of hand *s* praestigi•ae -arum *fpl*
slender *adj (slim)* gracil•is -is -e; *(meager)* exigu•us -a -um
slice *s* segment•um -i *n*
slice *tr* secare; **to — off** desecare
slick *adj (smooth, slippery)* lubric•us -a -um; *(shrewd)* callid•us -a -um; *(wily)* cat•us -a -um
slide *intr* labor labi lapsus sum
slide *s* laps•us -ūs *m; (photo)* imag•o -inis *f* translucida; **to show —s** imagines translucidas exhibēre
slide projector *s* proiector•ium -(i)i *n* imaginum translucidarum
slight *adj* exigu•us -a -um; *(of small account)* lev•is -is -e
slight *s* neglegenti•a -ae *f*
slight *tr* neglegere; *(to offend)* aspernari
slightly *adv* parum
slily *adv* astute, callide
slim *adj* gracil•is -is -e; **— hope** specul•a -ae *f*
slime *s* lim•us -i *m*
slimy *adj* limos•us -a -um
sling *s* fund•a -ae *f; (med)* fasci•a -ae *f*
sling *tr* iaculari
slingshot *s* fund•a -ae *f*
slink *intr* **to — away** furtim se subducere
slip *s* laps•us -ūs *m; (of paper)* schedul•a -ae *f; (error)* peccat•um -i *n; (in grafting)* surcul•us -i *m; (underdress)* subucul•a -ae *f;* **— of the tongue** lapsus -ūs *m* linguae; **— of the pen** mend•um -i *n;* **to give s.o. the —** aliquem fallere
slip *tr (to give furtively)* furtim dare ‖ *intr* labi; **to let —** amittere, praetermittere; **to — away** elabi; *(to leave furtively)* furtim se subducere; **to — out of** elabi ex *(w. abl); (to escape from)* excidere ex *(w. abl)*
slipper *s* sole•a -ae *f;* **wearing —s** soleat•us -a -um
slippery *adj* lubric•us -a -um; *(deceitful)* subdol•us -a -um
slipshot *adj* negleg•ens -entis
slit *s* incisur•a -ae *f*
slit *tr* incidere, insecare
sliver *s* schidi•a -ae *f; (small piece)* frustul•um -i *n*
slobber *intr* **to — on** conspuere
slop *s* quisquili•ae -arum *fpl*
slope *s* cliv•us -i *m;* **steep (gentle) —** ardu•us (lenis) clivus
slope *intr* proclinari, vergere; **—ing toward the sea** vergens ad mare
sloping *adj* decliv•is -is -e; *(upwards)* accliv•is -is -e
sloppy *adj (roads)* lutulent•us -a -um; *(weather)* spurc•us -a -um; *(person, work)* negleg•ens -entis
slot *s* rim•a -ae *f*
sloth *s* pigriti•a -ae *f*
slothful *adj* pi•ger -gra -grum
slot machine *s* machin•a -ae *f* aleatoria; **to play a —** machinam aleatoriam impellere
slouch *intr* languide incedere; **to — down** *(in a chair)* parum erecte sedēre
slouch *s (loafer)* cessa•tor -toris *m* (•trix -tricis *f*)
slough *s (of snake)* exuvi•ae -arum *fpl*
slovenly *adj* incompt•us -a -um
slow *adj* tard•us -a -um; *(physically, mentally)* lent•us -a -um; **— to learn** segn•is -is -e
slow down *tr* retardare, impedire ‖ *intr (of rain)* detumescere; *(walk, run)* cursum reprimere
slowly *adv* tarde, lente
slowpoke *s* cuncta•tor -toris *m* (•trix -tricis *f*)
slug *s* lim•ax -acis *mf; (of a bullet)* glans, glandis *f* plumbea
slug *tr (to hit)* percut•io -ere percussi percussus
sluggish *adj* pi•ger -gra -grum, heb•es -etis; **to be —** hebēre
sluggishly *adv* pigre

sluggishness *s* pigriti·a -ae *f*
slumber *s* somn·us -i *m,* sop·or -oris *m*
slumber *intr* dormitare
slur *s* macul·a -ae *f*
slur *tr (words)* balbutire
slush *s* niv·es -ium *fpl* solutae
slush fund *s* largition·es -um *fpl*
slut *s* meretr·ix -icis *f*
sly *adj* astut·us -a -um; **on the —** clam
slyness *s* astuti·a -ae *f*
smack *s (flavor)* sap·or -oris *m; (blow)* alap·a -ae *f; (kiss)* bas·ium -(i)i *n*
smack *tr* ferire; *(to kiss)* basiare; **to — one's lips** labra claudere cum strepitu **||** *intr* **to — of** sapere *(w. acc)*
small *adj* parv·us -a -um
smaller *adj* min·or -or -us
smallest *adj* minim·us -a - um
small-minded *adj* pusilli animi, soc·ors -ordis; **to be —** angusti *(or* pusilli) animi esse
smallpox *s* variol·ae -arum *fpl;* **to have —** variolis laborare
small talk *s* sermuncul·us -i *m*
smart *adj (clever)* callid·us -a -um, soll·ers -ertis; *(talented)* ingenios·us -a -um; *(elegant)* eleg·ans -antis; *(stylish)* laut·us -a -um; *(impertinent)* insol·ens -entis; *(of pace)* vel·ox -ocis; **don't talk — to me** noli male mihi dicere
smart *s* dol·or -oris *m*
smart *intr* dolēre
smart aleck *s* hom·o -inis *mf* impudens
smart-ass *s (sl)* impud·ens -entis *mf*
smartly *adv* callide; eleganter
smash *s* concussi·o -onis *f*
smash *tr (also* **— up**) confringere
smashup *s* collisi·o -onis *f*
smattering *s* cogniti·o -onis *f* manca
smear *s* macul·a -ae *f*
smear *tr* oblinere, illinere; *(to vilify)* inquinare
smell *s (sense)* odorat·us -ūs *m; (odor)* od·or -oris *m;* **to have a keen sense of —** bene olēre
smell *tr* olfacere **||** *intr* olēre; **to — bad** male olēre, obolēre; **to — good** bene olēre, iucunde olēre; **to — like** *or* **of** olēre *(w. acc)*
smelly *adj* olid·us -a -um
smelt *tr* liquefacere, fundere
smile *s* subris·us -ūs *m;* **with a —** subrid·ens -entis
smile *intr* subridēre; **to — at** arridēre *(w. dat)*
smirk *s* molestus subris·us -ūs *m*
smirk *intr* moleste subridēre
smite *tr* ferire, percutere
smock *s* tunic·a -ae *f*
smoke *s* fum·us -i *m;* **where there's — there's fire** flamma fumo est proxima
smoke *tr (meat)* infumare; *(cigar, cigarette, marijuana)* fumum (sigari, sigarelli, cannabis) sugere **||** *intr* fumare
smoker *s* fuma·tor -toris *m* (·trix -tricis *f*
smoky *adj* fumos·us -a -um
smooth *adj* lēv·is -is -e; *(hairless)* gla·ber -bra -brum; *(polished)* ter·es -itis; *(calm)* placid·us -a -um; *(of talk)* bland·us -a -um
smoothly *adv* lēviter; blande
smooth *tr* lēvare; *(to file)* limare; **to — the path to** viam facere ad *(w. acc)*
smoothness *s* lev·or -oris *m*
smooth-talking *adj* blandiloqu·us -a -um
smother *tr (flames, tears, anger)* opprimere; *(to choke)* suffocare
smudge *s* lab·es -is *f,* macul·a -ae *f; (smear)* litur·a -ae *f*
smudge *tr* inquinare, maculare
smug *adj* sui content·us -a -um, confid·ens -entis
smuggle *tr f* furtim sine portorio exportare *or* importare
smuggler *s* vec·tor -toris *m* (·trix -tricis *f*) vetitae mercis
smugness *s* confidenti·a -ae *f*
smut *s (soot)* fulig·o -inis *f; (foul language, writing)* obscenit·as -atis *f*
smutty *adj* fumos·us -a -um; *(obscene)* obscen·us -a -um
snack *s* merend·a -ae *f;* **to have a —** merendam capere
snack *intr* adedere
snack bar *s* voratrin·a -ae *f*
snafu *adj* confus·us -a -um
snag *s (stumbling block)* impediment·um -i *n;* **to hit a —** impedimento occurrere
snail *s* cochle·a -ae *f; (without shell)* lim·ax -acis *f*
snake *s* angu·is -is *mf;* **— in the grass** *(fig)* amic·us -i *m* perfidus, amic·a -ae *f* perfida
snap *s (noise)* crepit·us -ūs *m; (bite)* mors·us -ūs *m; (easy task)* op·us -eris *n* facile; **cold —** frigor·a -um *npl*
snap *tr (to break off suddenly)* praefrangere; **to — the fingers** digitis concrepare; **to — up** corripere **||** *intr (to break with a sharp noise)* dissilire; *(to make a sharp sound)* crepare; *(to go mad)* subito furere; **to — at** *(w. teeth)* morsu petere; *(in speaking)* increpare; **to — out of it** repente resipiscere
snappy *adj (brisk)* ala·cer -cris -cre, veget·us -a -um; *(chic)* eleg·ans -antis; **make it —!** matura! *(pl:* maturate!)
snapshot *s* imag·o -inis *f* photographica
snare *s* laque·us -i *m;* **to lay —s for a rival** rivali laqueos disponere
snare *tr* illaquēre; **to — wild animals** feras laqueis captare
snarl *s (of a dog)* rict·us -ūs *m,* hirrit·us -ūs *m; (of a person)* gannit·us -ūs *m*

snarl *tr* increpare ‖ *intr (dog)* ringi, hirrire; *(person)* gannire
snatch *tr* rapere, arripere; *(to steal)* surripere; **to — away** eripere; **to — up** corripere
sneak *s* lucifug·us -i *m* (·a -ae *f*)
sneak *intr* correpere; **to — away** clam se seducere; **to — away from (s.o.)** clam se subducere *(w. dat)*; **to — into** correpere in *(w. acc)*; **to — off** clanculum abire; **to — out of** correpere ex *(w. abl)*; **to — up on** obrepere *(w. dat)*
sneakers *spl* calce·i -orum *mpl* gymnici
sneer *s* rhonch·us -i *m*
sneer *intr* irridēre; **to — at** irridēre, aspernari
sneeze *s* sternument·um -i *n*
sneeze *intr* sternuere
snicker *s* ris·us -ūs *m* insulsus
snicker *intr* ridēre inepte
snide *adj* maledic·us -a -um, mord·ax -acis; **to make a — remark** mordaciter dicere
sniff *s* **to get a — of** olfacere
sniff *tr* naribus captare; *(cocaine)* naribus ducere; *(e.g., trouble)* odorari
sniffle *intr* mucum inspirare; *(to weep lightly)* leviter flēre
sniffles *spl* **to have the —** gravedine laborare
snip *tr* **to — off** praecidere
snippy *adj* insol·ens -entis
snivel *s* muc·us -i *m*
snivel *intr* mucum resorbēre; *(to whine)* queri
snob *s* hom·o -inis *mf* fastidios·us (-a)
snobbish *adj* fastidios·us -a -um
snore *s* r(h)onch·us -i *m*
snore *intr* stertere, r(h)onchare
snort *s* fremit·us -ūs *m*
snort *intr* fremere
snout *s* rostr·um -i *n*
snow *s* nix, nivis *f*
snow *tr* **to — in** nive obruere ‖ *v impers* ningit ningere ninxit; **it is —ing** ningit
snowball *s* pil·a -ae *f* nivis
snowball *intr* percrebescere
snowbank *s* cumul·us -i *m* nivis
snowbound *adj* nivibus obrut·us -a -um
snowdrift *s* niveus agg·er -eris *m*
snowed under *adj* **I am — with** *(fig)* obruor, tamquam nive, sic ego *(w. abl)*
snowfall *s* nivis cas·us -ūs *m*
snowflakes *spl* ningu·es -um *fpl*
snowstorm *s* ning·or -oris *m*
snow-white *adj* nive·us -a -um
snowy *adj* nival·is -is -e
snub *tr* neglegere
snub *s* repuls·a -ae *f*
snuff *tr* inhalare; **to — out** exstinguere
snug *adj* commod·us -a -um
snugly *adv* commode
so *adv* sic, ita, *(before adjectives)* tam; **and — forth** et cetera; **— far** eatenus, adhuc; **— help me** mehercules; **how —** quid ita?; **is that —?** itane?; **— far — good** belle adhuc; **— many** tot [*indecl*]; **— much** tant·us -a -um; *(so greatly)* tantopere; **— much for that** eatenus; **— often** totiens; **— slight a** *(e.g., fever)* tantul·us -a -um; **— so** *(tolerably well)* sic tenuiter; **— that** ut; **— that not** ne; **— then** quapropter; **— to speak** ut ita dicam; **that's not —** haud ita est; **— what?** quid ergo?
so *pron* **— and —** ille et ille
soak *tr* madefacere; *(to soften while soaking)* macerare ‖ *intr* madēre
soap *s* sap·o -onis *m;* **bar of —** saponis quadrul·a -ae *f;* **liquid —** sapo liquidus
soar *intr* in sublime ferri; *(of birds)* subvolare
sob *s* singult·us -ūs *m*
sob *intr* singultare
sober *adj* sobri·us -a -um *(opp;* ebrius); *(fig)* moderat·us -a -um
soberly *adv* sobrie; moderate
sobriety *s* sobriet·as -atis *f*
so-called *adj* sub nomine, suppositici·us -a -um
soccer *s* pedifoll·ium -(i)i *n;* **to play —** pedifolle ludere
soccer ball *s* pedifoll·is -is *m*
soccer field *s* camp·us -i *m* pedifollii, camp·us -i *m* lusorius
soccer player *s* lus·or -oris *m* (lusr·ix -icis *f*) pedifollii
soccer shoes *spl* calceament·a -orum *npl* pedifollii
sociable *adj* sociabil·is -is -e; *(pleasant in society)* facil·is -is -e
social *adj (companionable)* social·is -is -e; *(life)* commun·is -is -e; *(institutions, laws, customs, duties)* civil·is -is -e; **— call** offic·ium -(i)i *n*
social security *s* assecurati·o -onis *f* socialis
social science *s* disciplin·a -ae *f* civilis
society *s* societ·as -atis *f;* **high —** optimat·es -ium *mpl;* **secret —** sodalit·as -atis *f;* **— as a whole** omnes homin·es -um *mpl*
sock *s* pedal·e -is *n*, ud·o -onis *m; (blow)* ict·us -ūs *m*
sock *tr (coll)* percutere, icere
socket *s* contact·um -i *n* electricum; *(anat)* cav·um -i *n*
sod *s* caesp·es -itis *m*
soda *s (soft drink)* aqu·a -ae *f* Selterana; *(in natural state)* nitr·um -i *n*
sofa *s* lectul·us -i *m* tomento fartus
soft *adj* moll·is -is -e; *(fruit)* mit·is -is -e; *(fig)* delicat·us -a -um
soften *tr* mollire; *(fig)* lenire ‖ *intr* mollescere; *(of fruit)* mitescere; *(fig)* mitescere
softhearted *adj* miseric·ors -ordis

softly *adv* molliter; *(noiselessly)* leniter; *(opp. of loudly)* summissā voce
software *s* *(comput)* part·es -ium *fpl* programmationis
soil *s* sol·um -i *n*, hum·us -i *f*
soil *tr* inquinare, spurcare
sojourn *s* commorati·o -onis *f*
sojourn *intr* commorari
solace *s* solat·ium -(i)i *n*
solace *tr* consolari
solar *adj* solar·is -is -e; **— eclipse** solis defecti·o -onis *f*
solder *s* ferrum·en -inis *n*
solder *tr* ferruminare
soldier *s* mil·es -itis *mf*
soldierly *adj* militar·is -is -e
sole *adj* sol·us -a -um, unic·us -a -um
sole *s* *(of shoe)* sol·um -i *n; (anat)* plant·a -ae *f; (fish)* sole·a -ae *f*
solely *adv* solum, tantummodo
solemn *adj* sollemn·is -is -e
solemnity *s* sollemnit·as -atis *f*
solemnly *adv* sollemniter; **to swear —** religiosissimis verbis iurare
solemnize *tr* celebrare
solicit *tr* flagitare; **to — sex from s.o.** aliquem stuprum rogare
solicitation *s* flagiti·o -onis *f*
solicitor *s* flagita·tor -toris *m* (·trix -tricis *f*); *(leg)* iurisperit·us -i *m* (·a -ae *f*)
solicitous *adj* anxi·us -a -um
solicitude *s* anxiet·as -atis *f*, sollicitud·o -inis *f*
solid *adj* solid·us -a -um; *(food)* plen·ior -ior -ius; *(real, true)* firm·us -a -um; **men of — character** homin·es -um *mpl* probati; **— gold** totum aur·um -i *n*
solidly *adv* solide, firme
soliloquize *intr* secum loqui
soliloquy *s* soliloqu·ium -(i)i *n*
solitary *adj* solitari·us -a -um
solitude *s* solitud·o -inis *f*
solstice *s* solstit·ium -(i)i *n*
soluble *adj* dissolubil·is -is -e
solution *s* dilut·um -i *n; (solving)* soluti·o -onis *f*, explicati·o -onis *f*
solve *tr* (dis)solvere
solvency *s* facult·as -atis *f* solvendi
some *adj* ali·qui -qua -quod; *(a certain)* quidam quaedam quoddam; *(several)* nonnull·i -ae -a; *(a few)* aliquot [*indecl*]; *(some amount of)* aliquid *(w. gen)*; **— twenty days later** aliquos viginti dies post; **— … or other** nescio qui, nescio quae, nescio quod; **— war or other** nescio quod bellum; **to drink — wine** aliquid vini bibere
some *pron* aliqu·i -ae -a; *(several)* nonnull·i -ae -a; *(certain people)* quidam, quaedam, quaedam; **— … others** alii … alii
somebody *pron* aliquis; **— or other** nescio quis
somebody *s* hom·o -inis *mf* (-a) amplissimus
someday *adv* olim, aliquando
somehow *adv* aliquā (viā); **— or other** nescio quomodo
someone *pron* aliquis; **— else** ali·us -a
somersault *s* **to do a —** cernuare
somersault *intr* cernuare
something *pron* aliquid; **— else** aliud ultra; **— or other** nescio quid
sometime *adv* aliquando; **— ago** dudum, pridem
sometimes *adv* interdum, nonnumquam; **— … —** modo … modo
somewhat *adv* aliquantum; *(w. comparatives)* aliquanto, paulo; **to feel — better** meliuscul·us -a -um esse
somewhere *adv* alicubi; *(w. motion)* aliquo; **— else** alibi; *(w. motion)* alio
somnolence *s* somnolenti·a -ae *f*
somnolent *adj* somnolent·us -a -um
son *s* fil·ius -(i)i *m*
song *s* cant·us -ūs *m*
son-in-law *s* gen·er -eri *m*
sonorous *adj* sonor·us -a -um
soon *adv* mox, brevi (tempore); *(in a minute)* iam; *(at any moment)* iam iam; **as — as** simulatque, cum primum; **as — as possible** quam primum; **how — ?** quam mox?; **— thereafter** mox deinde; **too —** nimium cito; **very —** perbrevi tempore
sooner *adv* prius; *(preference)* potius; **no — said than done** dicto citius *or* dictum factum; **— or later** serius ocius
soot *s* fulig·o -inis *f*
soothe *tr* mulcēre, lenire
soothsayer *s* vat·es -is *m*
soothsaying *s* vaticinati·o -onis *f*
sooty *adj* fuliginos·us -a -um
sop *s* offul·a -ae *f*
sop *tr* **to sop up** absorbēre
sophism *s* sophism·a -atis *n*
sophist *s* sophist·es -ae *m*
sophisticated *adj* urban·us -a -um
sophistry *s* capti·o -onis *f*
sophomore *s* sophomor·us -i *m* (·a -ae *f*)
soprano *s* supranist·a -ae *f*
sorcerer *s* mag·us -i *m*
sorceress *s* mag·a -ae *f*
sorcery *s* magae art·es -ium *fpl*
sordid *adj* sordid·us -a -um
sordidly *adv* sordide
sore *adj* *(aching)* dol·ens -entis; *(angry)* irat·us -a -um; **— throat** exasperatae fauc·es -ium *fpl*
sore *s* ulc·us -eris *n*
sorely *adv* vehementer
soreness *s* dol·or -oris *m*
sorority *s* sodalit·as -atis *f* alumnarum
sorrow *s* dol·or -oris *m*
sorrow *intr* dolēre
sorrowful *adj* maest·us -a -um
sorrowfully *adv* maeste

sorry *adj* mis•er -era -erum; **I am — about** me paenitet *(w. gen);* **I (you) feel — for** me (te) miseret *(w. gen)*
sort *s* gen•us -eris *n;* **that — of man** eius generis *(or* modi) vi•r -ri *m*
sort *tr* digerere; *(ballots, mail)* diribēre
sot *s* fatu•us -i *m; (drunkard)* potat•or -oris *m*
soul *s (principle of life)* anim•a -ae *f; (principle of intellection and sensation)* anim•us -i *m;* **not a —** nem•o -inis *m; (human being)* mortal•is -is *m*
sound *adj (healthy)* san•us -a -um; *(strong)* valid•us -a -um; *(unimpaired, e.g., apple)* inte•ger -gra -grum; *(true, genuine)* ver•us -a -um; *(sleep)* art•us -a -um; *(stomach)* firm•us -a -um; **a — mind in a —body** mens sana in corpore sano; **to be of — mind** comp•os -otis mentis esse
sound *s* son•us -i *m; (noise)* strepit•us -ūs *m; (of trumpet)* clang•or -oris *m; (strait)* fret•um -i *n;* **loud —** frag•or -oris *m*
sound *tr* **to — the alarm** classicum canere; **to — the signal for battle** bellicum canere; **to — the retreat** receptui canere; **to — the trumpet** bucinam inflare **||** *intr* sonare; *(to seem)* videri; **to — off** clamitare
soundly *adv (of beating)* egregie; *(of sleeping)* arte
soundness *s* sanit•as -atis *f; (firmness)* firmit•as -atis *f; (correctness)* integrit•as -atis *f*
soup *s* iu•s -ris *n;* **noodle —** ius collyricum
soup bowl *s* magid•a -ae *f*
soup ladle *s* trull•a -ae *f*
soup spoon *s* cochle•ar -aris *n*
sour *adj* acid•us -a -um, acerb•us -a -um; *(fig)* amar•us -a -um, moros•us -a -um; **I have a — stomach** cibus mihi acescit; **to turn —** acescere
source *s* fon•s -tis *m,* orig•o -inis *f*
souse *s (sl)* pota•tor -toris *m* (•trix -tricis *f*)
soused *adj (sl)* uvid•us -a -um
south *s* meridi•es -ei *m;* **in the —** a meridie; **to face —** in meridiem spectare
south *adv* ad *(or* in) meridiem
south *adj* meridian•us -a -um; **— of** infra *(w. acc)*
southeast *adv* inter meridiem et solis ortum
southern *adj* austral•is -is -e, meridional•is -is -e
southward *adv* in meridiem
southwest *adv* inter solis occasum et meridiem
south wind *s* aus•ter -tri *m*
souvenir *s* monument•um -i *n*
sovereign *adj* suprem•us -a -um
sovereign *s* princ•eps -ipis *m,* rex, regis *m*
sovereignty *s* principat•us -ūs *m*
sow *s* porc•a -ae *f,* sus, suis *f;* **—s oink** sues grunniunt
sow *tr* serere; *(a field)* conserere
sower *s* sat•or -oris *m*
space *s* spat•ium -(i)i *n; (of time)* intervall•um -i *n*
spacious *adj* ampl•us -a -um
spaciousness *s* amplitud•o -inis *f*
spade *s* pal•a -ae *f;* **to call a — a —** quamque rem suo nomine appellare
spaghetti *s* spacell•i -orum *mpl*
Spain *s* Hispani•a -ae *f*
spam *s (comput)* saginati•o -onis *f*
span *s (exent)* spat•ium -(i)i *n; (measure)* palm•us -i *m;* **brief — of life** exigua brevit•as -atis *f* vitae
Spaniard *s* Hispan•us -i *m* (•a -ae *f*)
Spanish *adj (esp. people)* Hispan•us -a -um; *(esp. things)* Hispanic•us -a -um; *(esp. foreign things connected with Spain)* Hispaniens•is -is -e; **to speak —** Hispanice loqui
spank *tr* ferire palmā
spanking *s* **to get a —** vapulare
spar *s* tign•um -i *n*
spar *intr* dimicare; *(fig)* digladiari
spare *tr* parcere *(w. dat)*
spare time *s* temp•us -oris *n* subsicivum
sparing *adj* parc•us -a -um
sparingly *adv* parce
spark *s* scintill•a -ae *f; (fig)* ignicul•us -i *m*
sparkle *intr* scintillare
sparkling *adj* corusc•us -a -um
spark plug *s* candel•a -ae *f* accensiva
sparrow *s* pass•er -eris *m*
sparse *adj* rar•us -a -um
Spartan *adj* Laconic•us -a -um
spasm *s* distenti•o -onis *f* nervorum; **to have a muscle —** a musculi spasmo laborare
spasmodically *adv* interdum
spatter *tr* aspergere; **—ed with rain and mud** imbre lutoque aspers•us -a -um
spatula *s* spath•a -ae *f*
spawn *s* ov•a -orum *npl*
spawn *intr* ova parere
speak *tr* loqui, dicere; **to — Latin** Latine loqui **||** *intr* loqui; **so to —** ut ita dicam; **— of the devil** lupus in fabulā; **to — of** dicere de *(w. abl);* **to — to** alloqui *(w. acc);* **to — up** eloqui; **to — with** colloqui cum *(w. abl);* **well, speak up!** quin tu eloquere!
speaker *s* dic•ens -entis *mf; (speech maker)* ora•tor -toris *m* (•trix -tricis *f*)*; (device)* megaphon•um -i *n*
spear *s* hast•a -ae *f*
spear *tr* hastā transfigere
special *adj* praecipu•us -a -um; **— delivery letter** epistul•a -ae *f* accelerata
speciality *s* propriet•as -atis *f*
specially *adv* praecipue
species *s* speci•es -ei *f*
specific *adj* cert•us -a -um
specify *tr* subtiliter enumerare

specimen *s* exempl·um -i *n,* speci·men -inis *n*
specious *adj* specios·us -a -um
speck *s* macul·a -ae *f*
speckled *adj* maculos·us -a -um
spectacle *s* spectacul·um -i *n*
spectator *s* specta·tor -toris *m* (·trix -tricis *f*)
specter *s* larv·a -ae *f*
spectral *adj* larval·is -is -e
spectrum *s* spectr·um -i *n*
speculate *intr* coniecturam facere; *(com)* foro uti
speculation *s (guess)* coniectur·a -ae *f; (com)* ale·a -ae *f*
speculative *adj* coniectural·is -is -e
speculator *s* contempla·tor -toris *m* (·trix -tricis *f*)*; (com)* dardanar·ius -(i)i *m* (·a -ae *f*)
speech *s (faculty of speech; address)* orati·o -onis *f;* **to make a —** verba facere, orationem habēre
speechless *adj* elingu·is -is -e; **he was struck —** mutus erat ilico, obstupefactus est
speed *s* celerit·as -atis *f*; *(haste)* festinati·o -onis *f;* **at full —** magno cursu
speed *tr* prosperare, secundare; **to — up** accelerare ‖ *intr* properare, festinare; *(in a car)* velociter gubernare
speedboat *s* nav·is -is *f* velox
speedily *adv* celeriter
speedy *adj* cit·us -a -um
spell *tr* scribere; **to — correctly** recte scribere; **to spell with** scribere per *(w. acc) e.g.:* **some — "cum" with a "q" if it signifies time** quidem scribunt "cum" per "q" litteram, si tempus significat
spell *s (charm)* incantament·um -i *n; (period)* spat·ium -(i)i *n* temporis
spellbound *adj* fascinat·us -a -um
spelling *s* orthographi·a -ae *f*
spend *tr (money, time, effort)* impendere; *(time)* agere, consumere; *(w. the idea of waste)* terere; **to — effort, money (on)** operam, pecuniam impendere (in *w. acc or w. dat);* **to — the night** pernoctare; **to — the summer** aestivare; **to — the winter** hiemare
spendthrift *s* nep·os -otis *mf,* prodig·us -i *m* (·a -ae *f*)
spent *adj (weary)* fess·us -a -um; *(worn out)* effet·us -a -um
sperm *s* sem·en -inis *n*
spew *tr* vomere
sphere *s* sphaer·a -ae *f; (fig)* provinci·a -ae *f*
spherical *adj* sphaeric·us -a -um
sphinx *s* sphin·x -gis *f*
spice *s* condiment·um -i *n*
spice *tr* condire
spicy *adj* condit·us -a -um, a·cer -cris -cre; *(racy)* sal·ax -acis
spider *s* arane·a -ae *f*
spider web *s* arane·um -i *n,* araneae tel·a -ae *f*
spigot *s* epistom·ium -(i)i *n*
spike *s* clav·us -i *m* trabalis
spike *tr* pungere; **to — a drink** potioni temetum adicere
spill *tr* effundere; **to — blood** sanguinem fundere ‖ *intr* effundi, effluere
spill *s ((coll)* laps·us -ūs *m,* cas·us -ūs *m;* **to take a —** labi, cadere
spin *tr* versare; *(thread)* nēre; **to — a top** turbinem versare; **to — a web** telam texere ‖ *intr* versari
spinach *s* spinace·a -ae *f* oleracea
spinal *adj* spinae [*gen*]
spine *s (anat)* spin·a -ae *f* dorsi
spineless *adj* enervat·us -a -um
spinster *s* innupt·a -ae *f*
spiral *adj* spiral·is -is -e
spiral *s* spir·a -ae *f*
spirit *s* spirit·us -ūs *m;* anim·us -i *m; (temper, disposition)* ingen·ium -(i)i *n; (ghost)* larv·a -ae *f,* umbr·a -ae *f;* **full of —** animos·us -a -um; **— of the law** volunt·as -atis *f* legis; **—s of the dead** man·es -ium *fpl;* **that's the right — now** nunc tu frugi bonae es; **to be in high —s** hilar·us -a -um esse; **to be in low —s** demiss·us -a -um esse; **to defend with such —** tam enixe defendere
spirited *adj* animos·us -a -um
spiritless *adj* ignav·us -a -um
spiritual *adj* animi [*gen*]; *(incorporeal)* incorporeal·is -is -e; *(devout)* religios·us -a -um
spit *s (for cooking)* ver·u -us *n; (spittle)* sput·um -i *n*
spit *tr* spuere; *(frequentative)* sputare; **to — out** exspuere ‖ *intr* spuere; **to — in s.o.'s face** in faciem *(w. gen)* inspuere
spite *tr* offendere
spite *s* malevolenti·a -ae *f;* **for —** consulto; **in — of** *(no exact Latin equivalent, sometimes expressed by an abl. absolute, e.g.,* **in — of all the arguments of his opponent, he stuck to this guns** contemptis omnibus adversari rationibus, in sententiā suā perseveravit
spiteful *adj* malevol·us -a -um
splash *tr* aspergere; **to — the face with warm water** faciem aquā tepidā fovēre
splash *s* sonit·us -ūs *m* undae; *(display)* ostentati·o -onis *f*
spleen *s* splen, splenis *m;* **to vent one's —** iram effundere
splendid *adj* splendid·us -a -um; **— !** euge!
splendidly *adv* splendide
splendor *s* splend·or -oris *m*
splint *s (med)* ferul·a -ae *f*
splinter *s* assul·a -ae *f*; **bone —** fragment·um -i *n* ossis
splinter *tr* assulatim findere

split *s* fissur•a -ae *f*
split *tr* findere; **to — one's sides laughing** ilia sua risu dissolvere ‖ *intr* findi; *(to depart) (sl)* abire, discedere
splotch *s* macul•a -ae *f*
splotch *tr* maculare
spoil *tr (to mar)* vitiare; *(to ruin)* perdere; *(a child)* depravare; *(food)* corrumpere ‖ *intr (of food)* corrumpi
spoils *spl* spoli•a -orum *npl*
spoke *s* rad•ius -(i)i *m*
spokesman *s* interpr•es -etis *m*
spondee *s* sponde•us -i *m*
sponge *s* spongi•a -ae *f*
sponge *tr* **to — a meal** cenam captare
sponge stick *s (used by Romans in place of toilet paper)* xilospong•ium -(i)i *n*
sponsor *s* auct•or -oris *m,* faut•or -oris *m; (godparent)* spons•or -oris *m* (•rix -ricis *f)*
sponsor *tr* favēre *(w. dat); (a law)* proponere, ferre; **to — games** ludos edere
sponsorship *s* auctorit•as -atis *m;* **under my —** me auctore
spontaneity *s* alacrit•as -atis *f*
spontaneous *adj* automat•us -a -um, subitari•us -a -um
spontaneously *adv* sponte, ultro
spool *s* fus•us -i *m*
spoon *s* cochle•ar -aris *n*
spoonful *s* cochlearis mensur•a -ae *f*
sporadic *adj* rar•us -a -um
sporadically *adv* dispersim
sport *s* lud•us -i *m,* athletic•a -ae *f,* disport•us -ūs *m; (person)* hom•o -inis *mf* genialis
sport *tr* ostentare
sportive *adj* iocos•us -a -um
sport shirt *s* camisi•a -ae *f* campestris
sportsman *s* venat•or -oris *m; (fig)* aequus lus•or -oris *m*
sportswear *s* vest•is -is *f* campestris
spot *s* macul•a -ae *f; (stain)* lab•es -is *f; (place)* loc•us -i *m;* **on the —** *(immediately)* ilico; *(in trouble)* in angustiis, in artibus rebus; **to hit the —** oblectare; **to the same —** eodem
spot *tr (to espy)* conspicere, conspicari; *(to stain)* maculare
spotless *adj* immaculat•us -a -um
spotlight *s* lumin•a -um *npl* scaenica; **be in the —** scaenae servire
spotted *adj* maculos•us -a -um
spouse *s* coniu(n)x, coniugis *mf*
spout *s (jet)* torr•ens -entis *m; (rain spout)* os, oris *n* canalis; *(of jug)* os, oris *n*
spout *tr* eiaculari; *(speeches)* declamare ‖ *intr* emicare
sprain *tr* luxare; **to — an ankle** talum luxare
sprain *s* luxatur•a -ae *f*
sprawl *intr* insulse recumbere; *(to extend)* late extendi
spray *s* asperg•o -inis *f*
spray *tr* aspergere
spread *tr (to unfold)* pandere; *(to stretch)* extendere; *(to smear on)* oblinere; *(to scatter)* dispergere; *(to make known)* divulgare; **to — a blanket on the floor** extendere lodiculam in pavimento ‖ *intr* patēre, patescere; *(of rumor)* percrebrescere; *(of disease)* serpere
spread *s (expanse)* spat•ium -(i)i *n; (dissemination)* divulgati•o -onis *f; (ranch)* latifund•ium -(i)i *n; (feast)* cen•a -ae *f* lautissima
spreading *adj (tree)* patul•us -a -um; *(epidemic)* evag•ans -antis
spread sheet *s (comput)* chart•a -ae *f* computativa
spree *s* **drinking —** commissati•o -onis *f;* **shopping —** effrenata empti•o -onis *f*
sprig *s* ramul•us -i *m,* surcul•us -i *m*
sprightliness *s* alacrit•as -atis *f*
sprightly *adj* veget•us -a -um, ala•cer -cris -cre
spring *s (season)* ve•r -ris *n; (leap)* salt•us -ūs *m; (of water)* scaturg•o -inis *f,* fon•s -tis *m*
spring *adj* vern•us -a -um
spring *tr* **to — a leak** rimas agere ‖ *intr (to come from)* oriri, enasci; *(of rivers, etc.)* exoriri; *(to leap)* salire; **to — down** desilire; **to — forth** *(to sprout)* pullulare; **to suddenly — open** subito se pandere; **to — up** subito crescere
springboard *s* petaur•us -i *m*
spring break *s* feri•ae -arum *fpl* vernae; **to spend the —** ferias vernas agere
springtime *s* vernum temp•us -oris *n*
sprinkle *tr* spargere; **to — s.th. on** inspergere aliquid *(w. dat or super w. acc)* ‖ *intr* leviter pluere
sprinkle *s* levis pluvi•a -ae *f*
sprinkling *s* aspersi•o -onis *f; (small number)* rarae personae
sprinkling can *s* nassitern•a -ae *f*
sprint *s* curs•us -ūs *m* brevis
sprint *intr* breviter currere
sprout *s* pull•us -i *m*
sprout *intr* pullulare, germinare
spruce *s (tree)* abi•es -etis *f*
spruce *adj* laut•us -a -um
spruce *tr* **to — up** mundare ‖ *intr* **to — up** se mundare
spry *adj* agil•is -is -e
spunk *s* alacrit•as -atis *f*
spunky *adj* ala•cer -cris -cre
spur *s* calc•ar -aris *n; (fig)* incitament•um -i *n;* **on the — of the moment** de improviso
spur *tr (a horse)* calcaribus concitare; *(fig)* urgēre, stimulare
spurious *adj* spuri•us -a -um
spurn *tr* spernere
spurt *intr* emicare
sputter *tr & intr (spit)* spuere; *(words, sounds)* balbutire

spy *s* specula·tor -toris *m* (·trix -tricis *f*)
spy *tr (to catch sight of)* conspicari **||** *intr* speculari; **to — on** speculari, explorare
squabble *s* rix·a -ae *f*
squabble *intr* rixari
squad *s* manipul·us -i *m,* turm·a -ae *f*
squadron *s (of cavalry)* turm·a -ae *f; (of ships)* class·is -is *f*
squalid *adj* squalid·us -a -um
squall *s* procell·a -ae *f*
squalor *s* squal·or -oris *m*
squander *tr* dissipare, prodigare
squanderer *s* prodig·us -i *m* (·a -ae *f*)
square *adj* quadrat·us -a -um; *(fig)* honest·us -a -um; **— foot** quadratus pe·s pedis *m;* **— meal** largior cib·us -i *m*
square *s* quadrat·um -i *n; (open, four-sided space)* are·a -ae *f; (tool)* norm·a -ae *f*
square *tr (math)* quadrare; **to — accounts** rationem habēre **||** *intr* convenire, congruere; **this simply does not —** non sane quadrat; **to — off** pugnis minitari
squash *tr* conterere
squash *s* cucurbit·a -ae *f*
squat *intr* subsidere
squat *adj* parv·us atque obes·us -a -um
squeak *intr* stridēre; *(of mice, rats)* mintrire
squeak *s* strid·or -oris *m*
squeamish *adj* fastidios·us -a -um; **to feel —** fastidire
squeeze *tr* comprimere; **to — out** exprimere; **to — the flesh** *(when campaigning)* prensare
squint *intr* limis oculis aspicere
squint-eyed *adj* strab·us -a -um
squirrel *s* sciur·us -i *m*
squirt *tr* proicere, effundere **||** *intr* emicare
squirt *s* coniect·us -ūs *m; (coll)* pu·er -eri *m* procax
stab *s* ict·us -ūs *m,* punct·a -ae *f*
stab *tr* pungere, fodere, perforare
stability *s* stabilit·as -atis *f*
stabilize *tr* stabilire, firmare
stable *adj* stabil·is -is -e
stable *s* stabul·um -i *n; (for horses)* equil·e -is *n; (for cows, oxen)* bubil·e -is *n; (of boxers, gladiators)* famili·a -ae *f*
stack *s* acerv·us -i *m,* stru·es -is *f*
stack *tr* coacervare
stadium *s* stadi·um -i *n*
staff *s (scepter)* scipi·o -onis *m; (personnel)* operari·i -ōrum *mpl; (mil)* contubernal·es -ium *mpl,* legat·i -orum *mpl*
staff member, staff officer *s* legat·us -i *m,* contubernal·is -is *mf*
stag *s* cerv·us -i *m*
stage *s (theat)* scaen·a -ae *f; (degree)* grad·us -ūs *m;* **during the early —s of** inter initia *(w. gen);* **— of life** par·s -tis *f* aetatis; **to go on the —** in scaenam prodire
stage play *s* lud·us -i *m* scaenicus
stagger *tr* obstupefacere **||** *intr* titubare
stagnant *adj* stagn·ans -antis; *(fig)* in·ers -ertis
stagnate *intr* stagnare; *(fig)* torpēre, cessare
stagnation *s (fig)* cessati·o -onis *f*
stag party *s* conviv·ium -(i)i *n* sine feminis
stain *s* lab·es -is *f,* macul·a -ae *f*
stain *tr* maculare; *(to dye)* tingere
stainless *adj* immaculat·us -a -um
stair *s* grad·us -ūs *m;* **—s** scal·ae -arum *fpl,* grad·ūs -uum *mpl;* **to climb the —** per gradūs ascendere
staircase *s* scal·ae -arum *fpl*
stairway *s* scal·ae -arum *fpl*
stairwell *s* scalar·ium -(i)i *n*
stake *s* pal·us -i *m; (wager)* deposit·um -i *n;* **to be at —** agi; **to burn at the —** ad palum igni interficere
stake *tr (to wager)* deponere
stale *adj* vet·us -eris; *(bread)* secund·us -a -um, hestern·us -a -um
stalk *s (of plant)* stirp·s -is *m,* caul·is -is *m; (of grain)* calam·us -i *m;* **— of asparagus** stirps asparagi
stalk *tr (game)* venari; *(a person)* insidiis persequi
stall *s* stabul·um -i *n; (small shop)* tabern·a -ae *f*
stall *tr* sistere, impedire **||** *intr* morari, cunctari
stallion *s* admissar·ius -(i)i *m*
stamina *s* vir·es -ium *fpl,* firmit·as -atis *f*
stammer *tr & intr* balbutire
stammering *adj* balb·us -a -um
stammering *s* balbuti·es -ei *f*
stamp *s (mark)* not·a -ae *f; (impression made)* impressi·o -onis *f; (on a letter)* pittac·ium -(i)i *n* cursuale; **— of the foot** supplosi·o -onis *f* pedis
stamp *tr* imprimere, notare; *(money)* cudere; *(feet)* supplodere; **to — out** conterere; *(fig)* supprimere, exstinguere
stampede *s (of animals)* erupti·o -onis *f,* fug·a -ae *f; (fig)* tumult·us -us *m*
stampede *intr* aufugere, discurrere
stance *s* stat·us -ūs *m;* **to take the — of a fighter** statum proeliantis componere
stand *s (halt)* stati·o -onis *f,* mor·a -ae *f; (platform)* suggest·us -ūs *m; (point of view)* sententi·a -ae *f;* **to make a — against** restare adversus *(w. acc);* **to take the —** testificari
stand *tr (to set upright)* statuere; *(to tolerate)* tolerare, ferre; **I can't — him** istum ferre non queo; **I can't — the cold** frigoris impatiens sum; **to — one's ground** perstare; **to — one's ground against** subsistere *(w. dat)* **||** *intr* stare; **how do matters — ?** quomodo res se habent?; **to keep —ing** perstare; **to — aloof** abstare; **to — at the door** adsistere ad fores; **to — by** adesse *(w. dat),* favēre *(w. dat);* **to — by one's promises** promissis manēre; **to — by one's word** in fide stare; **to —**

close to adsistere ad *(w. acc);* **to — fast** consistere; **to — for** significare, indicare; *(to put up with)* tolerare; **to — for office** honorem petere; **to — in awe of** in metu habēre; **to — in for** in loco *(w. gen)* esse; **to — in the way of** obstare *(w. dat);* **to — in need of** indigēre *(w. abl);* **to — on end** *(of hair)* inhorrescere; **to — out** exstare, eminēre; **to — still** consistere; **to — up** surgere; **to — up for s.o.** alicui adesse; **to — up to anyone** coram alicui resistere

standard *adj* solit·us -a -um; **— author** script·or -oris *m* classicus

standard *s* norm·a -ae *f,* mensur·a -ae *f;* *(mil)* vexill·um -i *n*

standard-bearer *s* vexillar·ius -(i)i *m*

standard of living *s* consuetud·o -inis *f* victūs

stand-in *s* vicar·ius -(i)i *m* (·a -ae *f*)

standing *s* stat·us -ūs *m;* **of long —** vet·us -eris

standing *adj* perpetu·us -a -um

standing ovation *s* **to give s.o. a —** alicui stantes plaudere

stands *spl (bleachers)* for·i -orum *mpl*

standstill *s* **to be at a —** haerēre; **to come to a —** consistere

stanza *s* vers·ūs -uum *mpl; (of four lines)* tetrastich·on -i *n*

staple *adj* necessari·us -a -um; *(chief)* praecipu·us -a -um; **—s** vict·us -ūs *m*

staple *s* uncinul·us -i *m* (metallicus)

staple *tr* consuere

stapler *s* uncinator·ium -(i)i *n,* consutor·ium -(i)i *n* (chartarum)

star *s* stell·a -ae *f,* sid·us -eris *n; (fig)* lum·en -inis *n*

star *intr (theat)* primas partes agere

starch *s* amyl·um -i *n*

starch *tr* amylare

stare *s* obtut·us -ūs *m*

stare *intr* stupēre; **to — at** intueri

starfish *s* stell·a -ae *f*

stark *adj* rigid·us -a -um

stark *adv* omnino, penitus

starlight *s* siderum lum·en -inis *n*

starling *s* sturn·us -i *m*

starry *adj* sidere·us -a -um, stellat·us -a -um

start *s (beginning)* init·ium -(i)i *n,* incip·ium -(i)i *n; (startled reaction)* trepidati·o -onis *f; (sudden movement)* salt·us -ūs *m; (of journey)* profecti·o -onis *f;* **at the — of the year** anno ineunte; **from the —** a principio; **to get a head — on** antecedere; **to get a — on s.o.** aliquem occupare; **to get off to a bad —** initia male ponere; **to have a two-day — on s.o.** biduo antecedere aliquem; **to make a —** initium capere; **you've made a good —** bene se habent tibi principia

start *tr* incipere, instituere ‖ *intr* incipere, (ex)ordiri; *(to take fright)* resilire; **to — out** proficisci; **to — with** incipere ab *(w. abl)*

starter *s (of a car)* incitatr·um -i *n;* **for —s** principio

starting gate *s* carcer·es -um *mpl*

startle *tr* terrēre

starvation *s* fam·es -is *f;* **to die of —** fame enecari *or* mori; **to go on a — diet** abstin·ax -acis esse

starve *tr* fame interficere ‖ *intr* fame confici, fame consumi

starved *adj* **I'm —** fame enectus sum

state *s* stat·us -ūs *m; (pol)* civit·as -atis *f,* respublica *(gen:* reipublicae) *f;* **— of affairs** re·s -rum *fpl;* **— of mind** affecti·o -onis *f* animi; **to be in a better —** in meliore loco esse; **to be in a worse —** deteriore statu esse; **to restore s.th. to its former —** in pristinum statum aliquid restituere

state *tr* declarare, affirmare; *(of writers)* auctor esse; *(in writing)* scribere

statement *s* dict·um -i *n,* affirmati·o -onis *f; (of a witness in court)* testimon·ium -(i)i *n;* **to make a —** profiteri

statesman *s* vir, viri *m* reipublicae administrandae peritus, vir civilis

statesmanship *s* ar·s -tis *f* reipublicae administrandae

station *s* stati·o -onis *f*

station *tr* locare, disponere

stationary *adj* stabil·is -is -e, immot·us -a -um

stationery *s* re·s -rum *fpl* scriptoriae, chart·a -ae *f* epistularis

stationery store *s* tabern·a -ae *f* chartaria

statistics *spl* cens·us -ūs *m,* breviar·ium -(i)i *n*

statue *s* statu·a -ae *f,* sign·um -i *n*

stature *s* statur·a -ae *f; (fig)* amplitud·o -inis *f*

status *s* stat·us -ūs *m;* **the — quo** praesens status

statute *s* constitut·um -i *n,* lex, legis *f* scripta

staunch *adj* fid·us -a -um, firm·us -a -um

staunch *tr* **to — the flow of blood** sanguinem cohibēre

stave *tr* **to — off** arcēre

stay *tr* detinēre; *(to curb)* coercēre ‖ *intr* manēre; *(temporarily)* morari, commorari; **to — at home** se continēre; **to — away from** abstinēre *(w. abl)*

stay *s (sojourn)* mansi·o -onis *f; (delay)* mor·a -ae *f; (prop)* fulcr·um -i *n;* **— of execution** prolati·o -onis *f* supplicii extremi

steadfast *adj* const·ans -antis

steadfastly *adv* constanter

steadily *adv* firme, constanter

steadiness *s* constanti·a -ae *f*

steady *adj* stabil·is -is -e, firm·us -a -um; *(fig)* const·ans -antis; **— weather** aequales tempestat·es -um *fpl*
steak *s* off·a -ae *f* bubula
steal *tr* furari, surripere ‖ *intr* furari; **to — away** se subducere, clam aufugere; **to — over** subrepere *(w. dat)*
stealth *s* furt·um -i *n;* **by —** furtim
stealthily *adv* furtim, clam
stealthy *adj* furtiv·us -a -um
steam *s* vap·or -oris *m (coll)* vis *f;* **to let off —** *(coll)* motūs animi effundere
steam *intr* vaporare, fumare
steam bath *s* sudator·ium -(i)i *n*
steamboat *s* nav·is -is *f* vapore acta
steam engine *s* vaporia machin·a -ae *f* vectoria
steed *s* equ·us -i *m* bellator
steel *s* chalyb·s -is *m*
steel *adj* chalybei·us -a -um
steel *tr* **to — oneself against** obdurescere contra *(w. acc)*
steel mill *s* fabric·a -ae *f* chalybeia
steep *adj* ardu·us -a -um
steep *tr* madefacere; **—ed in crime** inquinat·us -a -um sceleribus
steeple *s* turr·is -is *f* campanaria
steepness *s* arduit·as -atis *f*
steer *s* iuvenc·us -i *m*
steer *tr* gubernare, dirigere
steering *s* gubernati·o -onis *f*
steering wheel *s* gubernacul·um -i *n*
stem *s* stirp·s -is *f; (of a ship)* pror·a -ae *f*
stem *tr* obsistere *(w. dat)*
stench *s* put·or -oris *m,* foet·or -oris *m*
stenographer *s* notari·us -i *m* (·a -ae *f*)
stenography *s* scripti·o -onis *f* notaria
step *s* pass·us -ūs *m,* grad·us -ūs *m; (measure)* rati·o -onis *f;* **flight of —s** scal·ae -arum *fpl;* **— by —** gradatim; **—s** *(of stairs)* grad·ūs -uum *mpl;* **out of —** *(fig)* abson·us -a -um; **to keep in —** *(march)* presso gradu incedere; *(fig)* congruere; **to take —s** *(to take measures)* rationem inire; **to watch one's —** cavēre
step *intr* grad·ior -i gressus sum; **to — down** degredi; *(fig)* se abdicare; **to — in** ingredi; *(fig)* intervenire, intercedere; **to — on** calcare; **to — up** *(increase)* augēre, accelerare; **— on it!** matura! *(pl:* maturate!)
stepbrother *s (on father's side)* vitrici fil·ius -(i)i *m; (on mother's side)* novercae fil·ius -(i)i *m*
stepdaughter *s* privign·a -ae *f*
stepfather *s* vitric·us -i *m*
stepmother *s* noverc·a -ae *f*
stepping stone *s (fig)* facult·as -atis *f* procedendi
stepsister *s (on father's side)* vitrici fili·a -ae *f; (on mother's side)* novercae filia
stepson *s* privign·us -i *m*
stereo *s* stereophon·ium -(i)i *n*
stereophonic *adj* stereophonic·us -a -um
stereotype *s (fig)* res, rei *f* trita
stereotyped *adj* trit·us -a -um
sterile *adj* steril·is -is -e
sterility *s* sterilit·as -atis *f*
sterling *adj* argente·us -a -um; *(genuine)* ver·us -a -um; *(upright)* prob·us -a -um
stern *adj* sever·us -a -um
sternly *adv* severe
sternness *s* severit·as -atis *f*
stew *s* carn·es -ium *fpl* cum condimentis elixae; **to be in a —** turbid·us -a -um animi esse; **to be in a — over** aestuare *(w. causal abl or* in *w. abl)*
stew *tr* lento igne coquere ‖ *intr* **I —ed over it for a long time** in eo aestuavi diu
steward *s* procurat·or -oris *m; (of country estate)* villic·us -i *m; (in a plane)* hosp·es -itis *m* aërius
stewardess *s* hospit·a -ae *f* aëria
stewardship *s* procurati·o -onis *f*
stewed *adj* iurulent·us -a -um; *(drunk)* elix·us -a -um
stick *s (twig)* ramul·us -i *m; (for striking)* fust·is -is *m; (cane)* bacul·um -i *n*
stick *tr* figere; **to — one's neck in the noose** cervices nodo condere; **to — up** *(to rob)* latrocinari *(w. dat)* ‖ *intr* haerēre, haesitare; **to — out** eminēre, prominēre; **to — to the usual order** ordinem conservare; **to — to the truth** in veritate manēre; **to — to one's guns** in sententiā stare
sticky *adj* viscos·us -a -um
stiff *adj* rigid·us -a -um; *(knee)* content·us -a -um; *(formal)* frigid·us -a -um
stiffly *adv* rigide; frigide
stiffen *tr* durare, rigid·um -am -um facere; *(w. starch)* amylare ‖ *intr* obdurescere
stiffness *s* rig·or -oris *m; (of joints)* articulorum dol·or -oris *m*
stifle *tr* suffocare; *(fig)* opprimere
stigma *s* stigm·a -atis *n,* not·a -ae *f; (stain)* dedec·us -oris *n*
stigmatize *tr* notare
still *adj* quiet·us -a -um; immot·us -a -um; **to be —** silēre, tacēre; **to hold —** non movēre
still *adv (adversative)* tamen; *(till now)* adhuc, etiamnum; *(w. comparatives)* etiam, etiamnum
still *tr* pacare, sedare
stillborn *adj* abortiv·us -a -um
stillness *s (silence)* silent·ium -(i)i *n; (quiet)* qui·es -etis *f*
stilted *adj* arcessit·us -a -um
stilts *spl* grall·ae -arum *fpl;* **a walker on —** grallat·or -oris *mf*
stimulant *s* irritament·um -i *n*
stimulate *tr* stimulare
stimulus *s* stimul·us -i *m*

sting *s (on an insect)* acule·us -i *m; (bite)* ict·us -ūs *m; (of conscience)* ang·or -oris *m*

sting *tr (of a bee)* icere; *(fig)* mordēre ‖ *intr (to hurt)* dolēre

stinginess *s* sord·es -ium *fpl*

stingray *s* pastinac·a -ae *f*

stingy *adj* sordid·us -a -um

stink *s* put·or -oris *m*, fet·or -oris *m*

stink *intr* putēre, fetēre; **to — of garlic** obolēre allium

stinky *adj* fetid·us -a -um

stint *s* **without —** sine modo

stint *tr* coercēre ‖ *intr* parcere, frugi [*indecl*] esse

stipend *s* salar·ium -(i)i *n*

stipulate *tr* stipulari

stipulation *s* stipulati·o -onis *f*, condici·o -onis *f*; **with the — that** eā condicione ut *(w. subj)*

stir *s* tumult·us -ūs *m*

stir *tr* excitare ‖ *intr* se movēre

stirring *adj* ad movendos animos apt·us -a -um

stirrup *s* staped·ium -(i)i *n*

stitch *tr* suere

stitch *s* tract·us -ūs *m* acūs; **— in the side** subitus lateris dol·or -oris *m*; **to be in —es** in cachinnum effundere

stock *s (supply)* copi·a -ae *f*; *(race)* gen·us -eris *n*; *(handle)* lign·um -i *n*; *(fin)* acti·a -ae *f* **to take — of** permetiri

stock *tr (to provide with)* instruere; *(to store)* condere

stockade *s* vall·um *n*

stocking *s* tibial·e -is *n*

stock broker *s* collybist·a -ae *m* (·ria -riae *f*)

stock exchange *s* collyb·us -i *m*

stock market *s* chrematister·ium -(i)i *n*, burs·a -ae *f*

Stoic *adj* Stoic·us -a -um

Stoic *s* Stoic·us -i *m*

stoical *adj* dur·us -a -um, pati·ens -entis

Stoicism *s* Stoica disciplin·a -ae *f*

stole *s* amict·us -ūs *m*

stolen *adj* furtiv·us -a -um; **— goods** furt·a -orum *npl*

stomach *s* stomach·us -i *m*; **to have — trouble** a stomacho laborare

stomach *tr* tolerare

stomachache *s* stomachi dol·or -oris *m*

stone *s* lap·is -idis *m*, sax·um -i *n*; *(of olive, peach)* os, ossis *n*; **to leave no — unturned** nihil praetermittere

stone *tr* lapidare, lapidibus obruere

stoned *adj (drunk)* elix·us -a -um

stonecutter *s* lapicid·a -ae *m*

stone quarry *s* lapidicin·a -ae *f*

stony *adj (full of stones)* lapidos·us -a -um

stool *s (bench)* scabell·um -i *n*; *(for sitting or mounting)* scamn·um -i *n*; *(feces)* alv·us -i *f*; **when the — is not passed** ubi alvus non descendit

stoolpigeon *s* ind·ex -icis *mf*

stoop *s (posture)* inclinati·o -onis *f*, curvatur·a -ae *f*; *(of a house)* pergul·a -ae *f*

stoop *intr* se inclinare *or* proclinare; **to — to** descendere in *(w. acc)*

stop *tr* sistere; *(to desist from)* desinere *(w. inf)*; **to — up** obturare ‖ *intr* consistere; *(to cease)* desistere; **—!** asta!; **— right there!** sta ilico!; **— talking** desine *(pl:* desinite) loqui!; **they finally —ed talking** finem loquendi demum fecerunt; **to — off at** deversari apud *(w. acc)*

stop *s* mor·a -ae *f*; **to come to a —** consistere; **to put a — to** comprimere

stopgap *s* tibic·en -inis *m*

stop-over *s* commorati·o -onis *f*; **to make a —** commorari

stoppage *s* obstructi·o -onis *f*

stopper *s* obturament·um -i *n*; *(halt)* cessati·o -onis *f*

stop sign *s* sign·um -i *n* subsistendi

stop watch *s* chronoscop·ium -(i)i *n*

store *s (supply)* copi·a -ae *f*; *(shop)* tabern·a -ae *f*; **in —** prompt·us -a -um, in expedito; **to set great — by** magni facere

store *tr* condere, reponere; **to — away** recondere; **to — up** reponere

storehouse *s* promptuar·ium -(i)i *n*; *(for grain)* horre·um -i *n*; *(fig)* thesaur·us -i *m*

storekeeper *s* tabernari·us -i *m* (·a -ae *f*)

storeroom *s* cellar·ium -(i)i *n*

stork *s* ciconi·a -ae *f*

storm *s* tempest·as -atis *f*, procell·a -ae *f*; **a — arose** tempestas coörta est; **a — of protests** tempestas querelarum; **to take by —** expugnare

storm *tr* expugnare ‖ *intr* desaevire; **to come —ing in** se infundere

stormy *adj* turbid·us -a -um, procellos·us -a -um; *(fig)* tumultuos·us -a -um

story *s* fabul·a -ae *f*; *(rumor)* fam·a -ae *f*; *(of a building)* tabulat·um -i *n*, contignati·o -onis *f*; **to make a long — short** ne long·us -a sim *or* ne longam faciam

storyteller *s* fabula·tor -toris *m* (·trix -tricis *f*)

stout *adj* corpulent·us -a -um, plen·us -a -um; *(brave)* fort·is -is -e; *(strong)* valid·us -a -um

stoutly *adv* fortiter

stove *s* foc·us -i *m*, focul·us -i *m*; **electric (gas) —** focus electricus (gaseus)

stow *tr* condere ‖ *intr* **to — away** in navi delitescere

stowaway *s* vec·tor -toris *m* (·trix -tricis *f*) clandestin·us -a

straddle *tr* cruribus varicatis insistere super *(w. acc)*

straggle *intr* palari; **to — over the countryside** palari per agros

straggler *s* palat·us -i *m* (·a -ae *f*)

straggly *adj* **— beard** horrida barb·a -ae *f*

straight *adj* rect·us -a -um, direct·us -a -um; **— as a line** lineae modo rect·us -a -um

straight *adv* directo, rectā

straighten *tr* rect·um -am -um facere; **to — out** corrigere, explicare; **to — up** ordinare

straightforward *adj* apert·us -a -um, simpl·ex -icis

straightlaced *adj* sever·us -a -um

straightway *adv* statim, prorsus

strain *tr* contendere; *(muscle)* luxare; *(to filter)* percolare ‖ *intr* enit·or -i enixus sum

strain *s (tension)* contenti·o -onis *f; (effort)* lab·or -oris *m,* nis·us -ūs *m; (wrench)* lux·us -ūs *m; (mus)* mod·us -i *m*

strained *adj (style)* arcessit·us -a -um

strainer *s* col·um -i *n*

strait *s* fret·um -i *n;* **Strait of Messina** Fretum Siculum; **to be in dire —s** in angustiis esse

strand *s (of hair)* flocc·us -i *m; (of rope)* fil·um -i *n*

strand *tr* vadis illidere

stranded *adj (ship)* vadis illis·us -a -um; *(fig)* sol·us -a -um et in·ops -opis

strange *adj* mir·us -a -um, *(unfamiliar)* inusitat·us -a -um, insolit·us -a -um; *(incongruous)* abson·us -a -um; *(foreign)* peregrin·us -a -um; **— to say** mirabile dictu

strangely *adv* mirum in modum

strangeness *s* novit·as -atis *f*

stranger *s* peregrln·us -i *m* (·a -ae *f*)*;* **a perfect —** omnino ignot·us -i *m* (·a -ae *f*)

strangle *tr* strangulare

strap *s* lor·um -i *n; (for shoe or sandal)* obstragul·um -i *n*

strap *tr* ligare, astringere; **to be —ed for money** in artibus rebus esse

strapping *adj* robust·us -a - um

stratagem *s* stratagem·a -atis *n; (trick)* dol·us -i *m*

strategic *adj* bene ordinat·us -a -um; *(advantageous)* commod·us -a -um; *(mil)* apportun·us -a -um

strategy *s (artfulness)* astuti·a -ae *f; (mil)* rati·o -onis *f* militaris

straw *adj* stramentici·us -a -um

straw *s* strament·um -i *n; (a single stalk)* culm·us -i *m; (for drinking)* siph·o -onis *m;* **cottages thatched with —** cas·ae -arum *fpl* stramento tectae; **to clutch at —s** ultimam spem capere

strawberry *s* frag·um -i *n*

strawberry-blond(e) *adj* fulv·us -a -um

stray *intr* errare, aberrare

stray *adj* err·ans -antis; *(dog, cat)* extrari·us -a -um

streak *s* line·a -ae *f; (of character)* ven·a -ae *f; (tendency)* proclivit·as -atis *f; (spell)* curs·us -ūs *m* brevis; **— of lightning** fulg·or -oris *m;* **yellow —** ignavi·a -ae *f*

streak *tr* lineis distinguere; maculare ‖ *intr (to dash)* ruere

stream *s* riv·us -i *m;* **down the —** secundo flumine; **—s of sweat** rivi *mpl* sudoris; **up the —** adverso flumine

stream *intr* se effundere

streamer *s* vexill·um -i *n*

street *s* vi·a -ae *f; (in city)* vic·us -i *m; (with houses)* plate·a -ae *f; (very narrow)* tram·es -itis *m*

streetcar *s* curr·us -ūs *m* electricus

streetcleaner *s* purgat·or -oris *m* viarum

street clothes *spl* forens·ia -ium *npl*

street map *s* tabul·a -ae *f* viaria

streetwalker *s* muli·er -eris *f* secutuleia

strength *s* vir·es -ium *fpl*

strengthen *tr* confirmare

strenuous *adj (brisk)* strenu·us -a -um; *(unremitting)* sedul·us -a -um; *(arduous)* laborios·us -a -um

strenuously *adv* strenue

stress *s (accent)* ict·us -ūs *m; (emphasis)* vis *f,* pond·us -eris *n;* **(tension)** tensi·o -onis *f; (importance)* pond·us -eris *n;* **not to lay much — upon a matter** aliquid levi momento aestimare; **to lay — on trifles** addere pondus nugis

stress *tr* exprimere, in mentem imprimere

stretch *tr* tendere; *(to tighten what is already stretched)* contendere; *(in different directions)* distendere; *(to elongate, e.g., the skin)* producere; **to — or relax the muscles** nervos intendere aut remittere; **to — out the hand to** *(to help s.o.)* manum intendere *(w. dat);* **to — the legs** crura in longitudinem extendere ‖ *intr* extendi, distendi; *(geog)* tendere; *(of a person while yawning)* pandiculari; **to — out on the couch** se extendere super torum

stretch *s (expanse)* tract·us -ūs *m,* spat·ium -(i)i *n; (extension)* extensi·o -onis *f*

stretcher *s* lecticul·a -ae *f*

strew *tr* spargere, sternere

stricken *adj* afflict·us -a -um

strict *adj (severe)* sever·us -a -um; *(accurate)* dilig·ens -entis; *(person in authority)* acerb·us -a -um; **according to the — letter of the law** summo iure; **— meaning of the word** verbi sens·us -ūs *m* proprius; **— truth** verit·as -atis *f* ipsa

strictly *adv* severe; *(carefully)* diligenter; **— speaking** proprie, immo

strictness *s* severit·as -atis *f*

stricture *s* vituperati·o -onis *f*

stride *s* pass·us -ūs *m* grandis; **to make —s** procedere

stride *intr* procedere passibus grandibus

strife *s* iurg·ium -(i)i *n,* discordi·a -ae *f; (struggle)* contenti·o -onis *f*

strike *tr* ferire, percutere, icere; **I was struck by his boldness** miratus sum audaciam eius; **struck blind** oculis capt·us -a -um; **struck by lightning** de caelo percuss·us -a -um; **to — a bargain, deal** pacisci; **to — fear into s.o.** incutere timorem in *(w. acc)* ‖ *intr (of workers)* opere faciendo cessare

strike *s* cessati·o -onis *f* operis, operistit·ium -(i)i *n; (blow)* ict·us -ūs *m;* **to go on —** opus intermittere; **to make a —** *(in bowling)* omnes conos simul prosternere

striking *adj* insign·is -is -e

strikingly *adv* mirum in modum

string *s* funicul·us -i *m; (thread)* fil·um -i *n; (for bow)* nerv·us -i *m; (mus)* chord·a -ae *f; (comput)* seri·es -ei *f;* **— of pearls** line·a -ae *f* margaritarum

string *tr (a bow)* intendere; **to — together** colligare

stringent *adj* sever·us -a -um

stringy *adj* fibrat·us -a -um

strip *tr* (de)nudare, spoliare; **to — off** *(clothes)* exuere; *(e.g., a tribune of power)* privare; *(of rights)* nudare ‖ *intr* se exuere vestibus

strip *s (of cloth; of land)* lacini·a -ae *f; (of paper)* sched·a -ae *f; (e.g., of bacon)* segment·um -i *n*

stripe *s (streak)* lim·es -itis *m; (welt)* vib·ex -icis *m; (blow)* ict·us -ūs *m; (line)* lineament·um -i *n; (on toga)* clav·us -i *m*

strive *intr* **(after, for)** nit·or -i nisus *(or* nixus) sum (ad *or* in *w. acc)*

striving *s* contenti·o -onis *f,* nis·us -ūs *m*

stroke *s* ict·us -ūs *m,* plag·a -ae *f; (of oars)* verb·er -eris *m; (in swimming)* mot·us -ūs *m* bracchiorum; *(med)* apoplexi·a -ae *f;* **— of luck** lus·us -ūs *m* fortunae mirabilis; **— of the oars** verber remorum; **— of the pen** pennae duct·us -ūs *m*

stroke *tr* (per)mulcēre

stroll *s* ambulati·o -onis *f* otiosa; **to take a —** spatiari

stroll *intr* spatiari

stroller *s* lecticul·a -ae *f* rotalis infantium; *(person)* spatia·tor -toris *m* (·trix -tricis *f)*

strong *adj (body, remedy)* valid·us -a -um *(opp:* imbecillus); *(smell)* grav·is -is -e; *(powerful)* pot·ens -entis; *(feeling)* a·cer -cris -cre; *(language)* vehem·ens -entis

strongly *adv* valide, vehementer

strongbox *s* arc·a -ae *f*

stronghold *s* castell·um -i *n*

structure *s (disposition, arrangement, building)* structur·a -ae *f; (makeup)* compositi·o -onis *f,* natur·a -ae *f*

struggle *s* certam·en -inis *f,* pugn·a -ae *f; (fig)* luctati·o -onis *f*

struggle *intr* contendere, luctari

strum *tr* pulsare

strumpet *s* scort·um -i *n*

strut *s* incess·us -ūs *m* magnificus

strut *intr* magnifice incedere

stub *tr* offendere

stub *s* segment·um -i *n,* reliqu·um -i *n*

stubble *s* stipul·a -ae *f*

stubborn *adj* obstinat·us -a -um; *(defiant and unyielding)* contum·ax -acis

stubbornly *adv* obstinate, contumaciter

stubbornness *s* obstinati·o -onis *f,* contumaci·a -ae *f*

stucco *s* tector·ium -(i)i *n*

stuck *adj* **to be —** *(out of ideas)* haerēre; **to be — on someone** in amore haerēre erga aliquem

stuck-up *adj* vultuos·us -a -um, fastidios·us -a -um; **to be —** fastidire

stud *s* clav·us -i *m; (horse)* admissar·ius -(i)i *m*

student *s* discipul·us -i *m* (·a -ae *f); (at university)* scholastic·us -i *m* (·a -ae *f);* **a law —** iuris studios·us -a; **a medical —** medicinae studios·us -a

studied *adj* meditat·us -a -um

studies *spl* studi·a -orum *npl*

studio *s* officin·a -ae *f* artificis

studious *adj* studios·us -a -um discendi

study *s* stud·ium -(i)i *n; (room)* tablin·um -i *n*

study *tr* studēre *(w. dat); (to scrutinize)* perscrutari ‖ *intr* studēre; *(at night)* lucubrare; **to — under a teacher of rhetoric** operam dare dicendi magistro

study period *s* spat·ium -(i)i *n* ad studiendum

stuff *s* materi·a -ae *f; (goods)* bon·a -orum *npl,* res, rerum *fpl; (junk)* scrut·a -orum *npl*

stuff *tr* farcire; *(w. food)* saginare; **to — it down s.o.'s throat** saginare aliquem recusantem

stuffed *adj* fart·us -a -um, refert·us -a -um; *(gorged)* saturat·us -a -um

stuffed shirt *s (coll)* hom·o -inis *mf* tumid·us (-a)

stuffing *s (in cooking)* fart·um -i *n; (in pillow, upholstery)* toment·um -i *n*

stuffy *adj (air)* crass·us -a -um

stultify *tr* ad irritum redigere

stumble *intr* offendere; **to — over new words** nova verba offendere; **to — upon** incidere in *(w. acc)*

stumbling block *s* offensi·o -onis *f*

stump *s* caud·ex -icis *m*

stun *tr* stupefacere; *(fig)* obstupefacere

stunned *adj* attonit·us -a -um

stunt *s* aus·um -i *n*

stunted *adj* curt·us -a -um

stupefy *tr* obstupefacere

stupendous *adj* permir·us -a -um

stupid *adj* stupid·us -a -um

stupidity *s* stupidit·as -atis *f*

stupidly *adv* stupide

stupor *s* stup·or -oris *m*

sturdiness *s* firmit·as -atis *f*

sturdy *adj* firm•us -a -um
sturgeon *s* acipens•er -eris *m*
stutter *intr* balbutire
stutterer *s* balb•us -i *m* (•a -ae *f*)
stye *s* suil•e -is *n*
style *s (kind)* gen•us -eris *n; (manner)* mod•us -i *m; (fashion)* mos, moris *m,* consuetud•o -inis *f; (of writing)* stil•us -i *m; (literary)* scribendi genus *n; (rhetorical)* dicendi genus *n; (architectural)* structurae genus *n; (of dress)* habit•us -ūs *m;* **in the new —** novo more; **to go out of —** exolescere
style *tr* vocare, nominare
stylish *adj* specios•us -a -um
subdirectory *s (comput)* plicarum subind•ex -icis *m*
subdivide *tr* iterum dividere
subdivision *s* subdivisi•o -onis *f; (of land)* segment•um -i *n* agri
subdue *tr (to conquer)* subicere; *(to overcome)* superare; *(to soften)* domare, placare
subject *adj* subiect•us -a -um; **— to** subiectus *(w. dat); (to disease)* obnoxi•us -a -um *(w. dat)*
subject *tr* subicere, subigere; **to — to** *(to expose to)* obicere *(w. dat)*
subject *s (e.g., English, math)* disciplin•a -ae *f; (one under the rule of others)* subiect•us -i *m,* civ•is -is *m,* cli•ens -entis *mf; (topic)* res, rei *f,* argument•um -i *n; (gram)* subiect•um -i *n;* **to change the —** in aliā aquā navigare
subjection *s* servit•us -utis *f*
subjective *adj* propri•us -a -um
subject matter *s* materi•a -ae *f*
subjugate *tr* subigere
subjunctive *adj* subiunctiv•us -a -um; **— mood** mod•us -i *m* subiunctivus
subjunctive *s* subiunctiv•us -i *m*
sublime *s* sublimit•as -atis *f,* summ•a -ae *f*
sublime *adj* sublim•is -is -e
sublimely *adv* excelse
submarine *s* nav•is -is *f* submarina
submerge *tr* demergere, inundare **‖** *intr* se demergere
submission *s (yielding)* dediti•o -onis *f; (humbleness)* obsequ•ium -(i)i *n*
submissive *adj* summiss•us -a -um
submissively *adv* summisse
submit *tr (e.g., a proposal)* referre **‖** *intr* se submittere; **to — to** obtemperare *(w. dat)*
subordinate *tr* subicere, supponere
subordinate *adj* subiect•us -a -um; **— conjunction** coniuncti•o -onis *f* subiunctiva
subordinate *s* subiect•us -i *m* (•a -ae *f*), inferi•or -oris *mf*
suborn *tr* subornare
subscribe *intr* **to — to** *(to agree with)* assentiri *(w. dat); (a magazine)* praescribere
subscriber *s* subscrip•tor -toris *m* (•trix -tricis *f*
subscription *s* subscripti•o -onis *f; (magazine)* praescript•um -i *n*
subsequent *adj* sequ•ens -entis
subsequently *adv* deinde, postea
subservient *adj* obsequios•us -a -um
subside *intr (of panic, the sea, wind)* desidere; *(of passion)* defervescere
subsidiary *adj* subsidiari•us -a -um
subsidy *s* subsid•ium -(i)i *n*
subsist *intr* subsistere
subsistence *s* vict•us -ūs *m*
substance *s* substanti•a -ae *f; (wealth)* res, rei *f; (gist)* summ•a -ae *f*
substantial *adj* solid•us -a -um; *(real)* ver•us -a -um; *(rich)* opulent•us -a -um; *(important)* magn•us -a -um; *(meal)* plen•us -a -um
substantially *adv* magnā ex parte
substantiate *tr* confirmare
substantive *s* substantiv•um -i *n*
substitute *adj* vicari•us -a -um, suppositi•us -a -um
substitute *s* vicari•us -i *m* (•a -ae *f*); **as a —** in vicem; **I will go as a — for you** ibo pro te
substitute *tr* **(for)** substituere (pro *w. abl*), supponere (pro *w. abl*) **‖** *intr (for)* in locum *(w. gen)* succedere
substitution *s* substituti•o -onis *f*
subterfuge *s* perfug•ium -(i)i *n*
subterranean *adj* subterrane•us -a -um
subtle *adj (e.g., definition)* subtil•is -is -e; *(crafty)* astut•us -a -um; **a — distinction** tenuis et acuta distincti•o -onis *f;* **a — plan** rati•o -onis *f* astuta
subtlety *s* subtilit•as -atis *f*
subtract *tr* detrahere, **to — the interest paid from the capital** de capite deducere quod usuris pernumeratum est
subtraction *s* deducti•o -onis *f*
suburb *s* suburb•ium -(i)i *n*
suburban *adj* suburban•us -a -um
subversion *s* eversi•o -onis *f*
subversive *adj* seditios•us -a -um
subvert *tr* evertere
succeed *tr* succedere *(w. dat),* insequi **‖** *intr (of persons)* rem bene gerere; *(of activities)* prospere evenire
success *s* success•us -ūs *m; (person)* hom•o -inis *mf* beat•us (-a); *(thing)* bene res, rei *f* gesta
successful *adj (of persons)* fel•ix -icis; *(of things)* prosper•us -a -um
successfully *adv* prospere, fortunate
succession *s* successi•o -onis *f; (series)* seri•es -ei *f*
successive *adj* continu•us -a -um; **on five — nights** quinque continuis noctibus
successor *s* success•or -oris *m* (•rix -ricis *f*)
succinct *adj* press•us -a -um
succinctly *adv* presse

succulence *s* suc·us -i *m*
succulent *adj* suculent·us -a -um
succumb *intr* succumbere
such *adj* tal·is -is -e; **as —** per se; **in — a way** tali modo; **— a big** tant·us -a -um; **— ... as** talis ... qualis; **— is the case** res se ita habent
such *adv (coll)* tantopere
suck *tr* sugere; **to — dry** ebibere; **to — in** sorbēre; **to — up** exsorbēre
sucker *s (fool)* barcal·a -ae *mf; (bot)* surcul·us -i *m;* **to take s.o. for a —** alicui os sublinere
suckle *tr* alere, mammam dare *(w. dat)*
suction *s* suct·us -ūs *m*
suction cup *s* cucurbitul·a -ae *f*
sudden *adj* subit·us -a -um, repentin·us -a -um; **all of a —** de improviso
suddenly *adv* subito, repente
suddenness *s* impet·us -ūs *m*
suds *spl* aqu·a -ae *f* sapone infecta
sue *tr* litem intendere *(dat)* ‖ *intr (leg)* litem inferre; **to —for** petere, poscere
suffer *tr* pati, tolerare; **to — the punishment** poenam dare, supplicium dare ‖ *intr* pati; **to — from** laborare *(w. abl);* **—ing from** oppress·us -a -um *(w. abl)*
sufferable *adj* tolerabil·is -is -e
suffering *s* dol·or -oris *m,* ang·or -oris *m*
suffice *intr* sufficere, satis esse
sufficient *adj* satis *(w. gen)*
sufficiently *adv* satis, affatim
suffocate *tr* suffocare ‖ *intr* suffocari
suffocation *s* suffocati·o -onis *f*
suffrage *s* suffrag·ium -(i) *n*
sugar *s* sacchar·um -i *n*
sugar *tr* saccharo condire
sugar bowl *s* vascul·um -i *n* sacchari
sugar cane *s* arund·o -inis *f* sacchari
sugarcoat *tr (fig)* lenire
suggest *tr* suadere; *(to propose)* proponere; **as you —** quemadmodum suades
suggestion *s (act)* (ad)moniti·o -onis *f; (proposal)* monit·um -i *n; (inkling)* indicati·o -onis *f*
suggestive *adj* indic·ans -antis
suicide *s* mor·s -tis *f* voluntaria; **to commit —** sibi mortem consciscere
suit *s (of clothes)* synthes·is -is *f; (leg)* lis, litis *f,* acti·o -onis *f;* **to bring a — against** actionem intendere *(w. dat)*
suit *tr* accommodare, convenire *(w. dat);* **not —** displicēre *(w. dat)*
suitable *adj* apt·us -a -um, idone·us -a -um
suitcase *s* vidul·us -i *m*
suite *s (apartment)* diaet·a -ae *f; (retinue)* comitat·us -ūs *m*
suitor *s* proc·us -i *m*
sulfur *s* sulf·ur -uris *n*
sulk *intr* aegre ferre, moros·us -a -um esse
sulky *adj* moros·us -a -um
sullen *adj* contum·ax -acis
sullenly *adv best expressed by the adjective*
sully *tr* inquinare
sultry *adj* aestuos·us -a -um
sum *s* summ·a -ae *f;* **for a large —** magni *or* magno; **for a small —** parvi *or* parvo; **— and substance of a letter** cap·ut -itis *n* litterarum; **— total** summ·a -ae *f* summarum
sum *tr* **to — up** computare; *(to summarize)* summatim describere; **to — up** ad summum, in summā
summarily *adv* summatim
summarize *tr* summatim describere
summary *s* summar·ium -(i)i *n,* breviar·ium -(i)i *n*
summation *s* perorati·o -onis *f*
summer *s* aest·as -atis *f;* **to spend the —** aestivare
summer *adj* aestiv·us -a -um; **— resort** aestiv·a -orum *npl;* **— vacation** feri·ae -arum *fpl* aestivae; **to spend the — vacation** ferias aestivas agere
summit *s* culm·en -inis *n; (fig)* fastig·ium -(i)i *n;* **the — of the mountain** summus mon·s -tis *m*
summit conference *s* colloqu·ium -(i)i *n* primorum civitatum
summon *tr* arcessere; *(meeting)* convocare; **—ed as a witness** citat·us -a -um testis; **to — to an inquiry** vocare ad disquisitionem; **to — up courage** animum erigere
summons *s (leg)* vocati·o -onis *f;* **to issue s.o. a —** diem dicere *(w. dat)*
sumptuary *adj* sumptuari·us -a -um
sumptuous *adj* sumptuos·us -a -um
sumptuously *adv* sumptuose
sun *s* sol, solis *m*
sun *tr* **to — oneself** apricari
sunbathe *intr* apricari
sunbathing *s* aprication -onis *f*
sunbeam *s* rad·ius -(i)i *m* solis
sunburnt *adj* adust·us -a -um
Sunday *s* di·es -ei *m* solis; *(eccl)* Dominic·a -ae *f*
Sunday school *s* schol·a -ae *f* Dominicis habita
sundial *s* solar·ium -(i)i *n*
sundown *s* solis occas·us -ūs *m*
sundried *adj* pass·us -a -um
sundry *adj* divers·i -ae -a, aliquot [*indecl*]
sunflower *s* helianth·us -i *m*
sun glasses *spl* perspicill·a -orum *npl* solaria *(or* infuscata)
sunken *adj* depress·us -a -um
sunlight *s* sol, solis *m*
sunny *adj* apric·us -a -um
sunrise *s* solis ort·us -ūs *m;* **at —** sole orto
sunset *s* solis occas·us -ūs *m;* **at —** sole occidente
sunshine *s* sol, solis *m*
suntan *s* adustus col·or -oris *m;* **to get a —** colorare
suntanned *adj* colorat·us -a -um

superabundant *adj* nimi·us -a -um
superabundantly *adv* satis superque
superb *adj* magnific·us -a -um
superbly *adv* magnifice
superficial *adj (fig)* lev·is -is -e; **— wound** vuln·us -eris *n* quod in summa parte est
superfluous *adj* supervacane·us -a -um; **to be regarded as —** pro supervacuo haberi; **to be —** redundare
superhuman *adj* divin·us -a -um; *(fig)* incredibil·is -is -e; **— form** form·a -ae *f* maior humanā
superintend *tr* praeesse *(w. dat)*
superintendence *s* cur·a -ae *f*
superintendent *s* (pro)cura·tor -toris *m* (·trix -tricis *f*); *(of an apt. bldg.)* procurat·or -oris *m* insulae
superior *adj* super·ior -ior -ius; **to be — in cavalry** plus valēre equitatu
superior *s* praeposit·us -i *m* (·a -ae *f*)
superiority *s* praestanti·a -ae *f*
superlative *adj* eximi·us -a -um; *(gram)* superlativ·us -a -um
superlative *s* grad·us -ūs *m* superlativus; **in the** superlative; **give me "laetus" in the —** dic "laetus" superlative
supermarket *s* superinstitor·ium -(i)i *n*
supernatural *adj* divin·us -a -um; supra naturam
supersede *tr* succedere *(w. dat)*
superstition *s* superstiti·o -onis *f*
superstitious *adj* superstitios·us -a -um
supervise *tr* (pro)curare
supervision *s* cur·a -ae *f*
supine *adj* supin·us -a -um
supine *s* supin·um -i *n*
supper *s* cen·a -ae *f*; **after —** cenat·us -a -um; **for —** in cenam; **to eat —** cenare
supplant *tr* supponere, praevertere
supple *adj* flexibil·is -is -e, moll·is -is -e
supplement *s* supplement·um -i *n*
supplement *tr* amplificare
suppliant *s* suppl·ex -icis *mf*
supplicate *tr* supplicare
supplication *s* supplicati·o -onis *f*
supplied *adj* **well — with** copios·us -a -um *(w. abl)*
supply *s* copi·a -ae *f*; **supplies** *(mil)* commeat·us -ūs *m (used both as collective singular and in the plural)*; **to cut off the enemy's —** intercludere hostes commeatibus
supply *tr (to furnish)* praebēre, suppeditare; *(to fill up)* supplēre; **to be supplied with** suppeditare *(w. abl)*
support *s (prop)* fulcr·um -i *n*; *(help)* subsid·ium -(i)i *n*; *(maintenance)* aliment·um -i *n*; *(backing)* stud·ium -(i)i *n*
support *tr (to hold up)* fulcire, sustinēre; *(to maintain)* alere; *(children) (leg)* exhibēre; *(to help)* adiuvare; *(to back)* favēre *(w. dat)*
supportable *adj* tolerabil·is -is -e
supporter *s* fau·tor -toris *m* (·trix -tricis *f*)
suppose *tr & intr* opinari, putare; **I —** *(parenthetical)* ut opinor
supposition *s* opini·o -onis *f*
suppress *tr* comprimere; *(for a time)* reprimere; *(information)* opprimere
suppression *s* suppressi·o -onis *f*
supremacy *s* dominat·us -ūs *m*; *(supreme power)* imper·ium -(i)i *n*; **to exercise —** dominari
supreme *adj* suprem·us -a -um, summ·us -a -um
supremely *adv* unice, maxime
sure *adj* cert·us -a -um; *(faithful)* fid·us -a -um; **be — to come** facito *(or* fac) modo ut venias; **for —** pro certo; **I am —** mihi persuadeo; **I am — that …** certus (-a) sum *(w. acc & inf)*; **to be —** nempe; **to know for —** certum *(or* pro certo) scire
surely *adv* certe, profecto, quidem
surf *s* aest·us -ūs *m*
surf *tr (comput)* navigare ‖ *intr* tabulā fluctivagā per summas undas prolabi
surface *s* superfici·es -ei *f*; **— of the sea** summum mar·e -is *n*
surfboard *s* tabul·a -ae *f* fluctivaga
surge *s* aest·us -ūs *m*
surge *intr* surgere, tumescere; **to — forward** proruere
surgeon *s* chirurg·us -i *m* (·a -ae *f*); **the — operated on her** chirurgus eam secuit
surgery *s (the art)* chirurgi·a -ae *f*; *(practice)* man·us -ūs *f*; **to use — on** manum adhibēre *(w. dat)*
surgical *adj* chirurgic·us -a -um
surly *adj* moros·us -a -um et difficil·is -is -e
surmise *s* coniectur·a -ae *f*; **to make —s** opinari
surmise *tr* conicere, opinari
surmount *tr* superare
surmountable *adj* superabil·is -is -e
surname *s* cognom·en -inis *n*
surpass *tr* superare, excedere
surplus *s* residu·um -i *n*
surplus *adj* subsiciv·us -a -um
surprise *s (feeling)* mirati·o -onis *f*; *(thing)* mir·um -i *n*; **to catch by —** deprehendere; **to feel —** mirari; **to the — of all, he says …** cunctis improvisis ait … ; **to take s.o. by —** excipere aliquem incaut·um -am
surprise *tr* de improviso excipere; *(pleasantly)* admirationem movēre *(w. dat)*; *(mil)* opprimere; **to be —d at** mirari, admirari; **to be —d that …** mirari *(w. acc & inf)*
surprise attack *s* subita incursi·o -onis *f*
surprising *adj* mir·us -a -um
surprisingly *adv* mire, mirabiliter
surrender *s* traditi·o -onis *f*; *(leg)* cessi·o -onis *f*; *(mil)* dediti·o -onis *f*

surrender *tr* tradere, dedere ‖ *intr* se dedere, se tradere; **to force a people to —** populum in deditionem venire cogere
surreptitious *adj* furtiv·us -a -um
surreptitiously *adv* furtim
surround *tr* circumdare, cingere
surroundings *spl* vicini·a -ae *f*
survey *s* inspecti·o -onis *f; (of land)* mensur·a -ae *f*
survey *tr* oculis lustrare; *(land)* permetiri
surveyor *s* agrimens·or -oris *m*
survival *s* sal·us -utis *f*
survive *tr* supervivere *(w. dat),* superesse *(w. dat)* ‖ *intr* superst·es -itis esse
surviving *adj* superst·es -itis
survivor *s* superst·es -itis *mf*
susceptible *adj* moll·is -is -e; **— to** obnoxi·us -a -um *(w. dat)*
suspect *s* suspect·us -i *m* (·a -ae *f*)
suspect *tr* suspicari; *(to surmise)* opinari; **to be —ed of** in suspicionem venire quasi *(w. subj)*
suspend *tr* suspendere, differre; **to be — ed from office** summoveri administratione rei publicae
suspense *s* exspectati·o -onis *f;* **in —** suspens·us -a -um; **to end the —** exspectationem discutere
suspension *s* interrupti·o -onis *f,* intermissi·o -onis *f*
suspicion *s* suspici·o -onis *f;* **to come under —** in suspicionem venire; **to throw — on** suspicionem adiungere ad *(w. acc)*
suspicious *adj* suspic·ax -acis; *(suspected)* suspect·us -a -um
suspiciously *adv* suspiciose
sustain *tr* sustinēre; *(hardships, loss, injury, etc.)* ferre
sustenance *s* vict·us -ūs *m*
suture *s* sutur·a -ae *f*
swab *s* spongi·a -ae *f; (brush)* penicul·us -i *m*
swab *tr* detergēre
swaddling clothes *spl* incunabul·a -orum *npl*
swagger *intr* se iactare
swallow *s* haust·us -ūs *m; (bird)* hirund·o -inis *f*
swallow *tr* vorare; *(liquids)* sorbēre; **to — up** devorare, absorbēre
swamp *s* pal·us -udis *f*
swamp *tr* demergere
swampy *adj* paludos·us -a -um
swan *s* cycn·us -i *m*
swank *adj* laut·us -a -um
swap *tr* permutare; **to — places** loca inter se permutare
swap *s* permutati·o -onis *f*
swarm *s* exam·en -inis *n*
swarm *intr (of bees)* examinare; *(of people)* congregari, frequentare
swarthy *adj* fusc·us -a -um
swathe *s* fasci·a -ae *f*
sway *s* dici·o -onis *f,* imper·ium -(i)i *n;* **to hold —** regnare
sway *tr (to influence)* suadēre *(w. dat)* ‖ *intr* vacillare
swear *tr* iurare; **to — in** sacramento adigere ‖ *intr* iurare; **to — off** eiurare
sweat *s* sud·or -oris *m;* **no —!** non laboro!; **to break a —** insudare
sweat *intr* sudare
sweat suit *s* vest·is -is *f* gymnica
sweep *tr* verrere; **to — s.o. off his feet** aliquem captare; **to — out** everrere ‖ *intr* **to — by** *(to dash by)* praetervolare
sweeper *s (soccer)* lus·or -oris *m* liber, lusr·ix -icis *f* libera
sweet *adj* dulc·is -is -e; *(fig)* bland·us -a -um
sweeten *tr* dulcem *(or* dulce) reddere; *(fig)* lenire
sweetheart *s* delici·ae -arum *fpl,* volupt·as -atis *f,* ocell·us -i *m; (in address)* mea voluptas, mi ocelle
sweetly *adv* dulce; *(fig)* suaviter
sweetness *s* dulced·o -inis *f*
sweets *spl* cuppedi·a -orum *npl*
swell *s* aest·us -ūs *m*
swell *tr* tumefacere ‖ *intr* tumēre; **to — (up)** *(of limbs)* turgēre, se attollere *(opp.* se summittere)
swelling *s* tum·or -oris *m*
swelter *intr* aestu laborare
sweltering *adj* aestuos·us -a -um
swerve *intr* aberrare
swift *adj* cel·er -eris -ere
swiftness *s* celerit·as -atis *f*
swim *intr* natare; **to — across** tranare
swimmer *s* nata·tor -toris *m* (·trix -tricis *f*)
swimming *s* natati·o -onis *f; (of the head)* vertig·o -inis *f*
swimming meet certam·en -inis *n* natatorum
swimming pool *s* piscin·a -ae *f*
swimsuit *s* vest·is -is *f* balnearis
swindle *s* frau·s -dis *f*
swindle *tr* fraudare
swindler *s* frauda·tor -toris *m* (·trix -tricis *f*)
swine *s* sus, suis *mf*
swing *s* oscill·um -i *n*
swing *tr* librare ‖ *intr* oscillare
swipe *tr (to steal)* surripere
Swiss *adj* Helveti·us -a -um
switch *s (whip)* virgul·a -ae *f,* verb·er -eris *n; (change)* transit·us -ūs *m,* commutati·o -onis *f; (electrical)* epitol·ium -(i)i *n* electricum
switch *tr (to whip)* verberare; *(to change)* commutare; **to — off** disiungere ‖ *intr* transire; **to — from wine to water** transire a vino ad aquam; **to — over to the plebs** transire ad plebem
Switzerland *s* Helveti·a -ae *f*
swivel *tr & intr* vertere, volvere

swivel chair *s* sell·a -ae *f* volvens
swollen *adj* tumid·us -a -um
swoon *s* defecti·o -onis *f* animi
swoon *intr* intermor·ior -i -tuus sum
swoop *s* impet·us -ūs *m*
swoop *intr* **to — down on** involare in *(w. acc);* **to — upon** petere
sword *s* glad·ius -(i)i *m,* ens·is -is *m;* **with fire and —** ferro ignique
swordfish *s* glad·ius -(i)i *m,* xyphi·as -ae *m*
sycamore *s* sycamor·us -i *f*
sycophant *s* sychophant·a -ae *mf*
syllabic *s* syllabic·us -a -um
syllable *s* syllab·a -ae *f;* **—s form words** syllabae faciunt dictiones
syllogism *s* syllogism·us -i *m*
symbol *s* symbol·us -i *m,* sign·um -i *n,* indic·ium -(i)i *n*
symbolic *adj* **to be — of s.th.** signum esse alicuius
symbolically *adv* symbolice
symbolize *tr* repraesentare
symmetrical *adj* congru·ens -entis
symmetry *s* symmetri·a -a *f,* proporti·o -onis *f*
sympathetic *adj* misericor·s -dis
sympathy *s* misericordi·a -ae *f;* **to show — for** commiserari *(w. acc)*
symphony *s* symphoni·a -ae *f,* concent·us -ūs *m*
symposium *s* convent·us -ūs *m; (lit)* collectane·a -orum *npl*
symptom *s* sign·um -i *n,* indic·ium -(i)i *n*
synagogue *s* synagog·a -ae *f*
synchronize *tr* congruentem reddere **‖** *intr* congruere
syndicate *s* societ·as -atis *f*
synod *s* synod·os -i *f*
synonym *s* verb·um -i *n* idem declarans, synonym·um -i *n*
synonymous *adj* idem declaran·s -tis; **a Latin word — with the Greek** verb·um -i *n* Latinum quod idem Graeco valet
synopsis *s* synops·is -is *f,* breviar·ium -(i)i *n*
syntax *s* syntax·is -is *f,* constructi·o -onis *f* verborum
synthesis *s* compositi·o -onis *f; (phil)* rati·o -onis *f* consectaria
synthetic *adj* artificios·us -a -um
syringe *s* clyst·er -eris *m*
system *s* rati·o -onis *f; (phil)* doctrin·a -ae *f*
systematic *adj* ordinat·us -a -um
systematically *adv* certā ratione
systematize *tr* in ordinem redigere

T

tab *s* pittac·ium -(i)i *n; (coll)* rati·o -onis *f* (debiti), impens·a -ae *f;* **to keep —s on** caute observare; **to pick up the —** rem solvere
tab *tr* designare, notare
tabernacle *s* tabernacul·um -i *n*
table *s* mens·a -ae *f; (list)* ind·ex -icis *m,* tabul·a -ae *f;* **at —** apud mensam; **to clear the —** mensam mundare; *(Roman)* mensam auferre; **to set the —** mensam ponere; **to sit down at the —** mensae assidere; **to wait on —s** ad mensas ministrare
tablecloth *s* mantil·e -is *n*
table of contents *s* ind·ex -icis *m* capitum; *(often expressed by the passive verb: —:* **Earthquakes; Chasms, etc.** continenter in hoc libro: De Terrae Motibus; De Terrae Hiatibus, etc.)
tablespoon *s* ligul·a -ae *f*
tablet *s* tabul·a -ae *f; (med)* catapot·ium -(i)i *n*
tableware *s* mensae vas·a -orum *npl*
tabulate *tr* in ordinem disponere
tacit *adj* tacit·us -a -um; *(leg)* licit·us -a -um
tacitly *adv* tacite
taciturn *adj* taciturn·us -a -um
tack *s* clavul·us -i *m*
tack *tr* **to — on** *(in sewing)* assuere; *(to add on)* subicere **‖** *intr (of ships)* reciprocari
tackle *tr* obsistere *(w. dat); (to deal with)* tractare
tackle *s (gear)* apparat·us -ūs *m; (naut)* rudent·es -ium *mpl*
tact *s* urbanit·as -atis *f*
tactful *adj* urban·us -a -um
tactician *s* rei militaris perit·us -i *m*
tactics *spl* belli gerendi rati·o -onis *f; (methods)* rati·o -onis *f* rei gerendae
tadpole *s* ranuncul·us -i *m*
tag *s* appendicul·a -ae *f,* pittac·ium -(i)i *n*
tag *tr* appendiculam *(or* pittacium) affigere *(w. dat); (to touch)* tangere **‖** *intr* **to — along** (con)sequi
tail *s* caud·a -ae *f;* **to turn —** tergum vertere
tail *tr* insequi
taillight *s* lum·en -inis *n* posticum
tailor *tr (to adapt)* aptare, accommodare
tailor *s* vestit·or -oris *m,* vestific·us -i *m* (·a -ae *f*)
tailor shop *s* vestificin·a -ae *f*
taint *s* contagi·o -onis *f; (blemish)* vit·ium -(i)i *n*
taint *tr* inficere; *(fig)* corrumpere
take *tr (in nearly all senses of the English word)* capere; *(w. eagerness or haste)* arripere; *(what is offered)* accipere; *(to require)* requirere; *(to grasp, take hold of)* comprehendere; *(food, drink, poison)* sumere; *(to suppose)* opinari; *(to regard, consider)* accipere, habēre, ducere; *(to endure)* pati; **I can't — it anymore** pati nequeo amplius; **— it easy!** parce *(pl:* parcite)!; **to — a bath** balneo uti; **to — a dislike to** capere odium *(w. gen);* **to — as**

a certainty sumere pro certo; **to — aside** seducere; **to — a trip** iter facere; **to — a walk** spatiari; **to — away (from)** adimere *(w. dat),* auferre *(w. dat or abl or* ab *w. abl);* **to — back** recipere, repetere; **to — by the hand** manu prehendere; **to — captive** capere; **to — charge of** curare; **to — credit for** capere gratiam *(w. gen);* **to — down** *(words of a speaker)* excipere; *(posters, signs)* refigere; **to — flight** fugam capere; **to —** *(a dog)* **for a walk** ducere; **to — for granted** praesumere; **to — from** adimere *(w. dat);* **to — great pains to** in magno negotio habēre *(w. inf);* **to — hold of** *(to grasp)* (com)prehendere; *(of a disease)* capere; **to — in** *(as guest)* recipere; *(to deceive)* decipere, fallere, verba dare *(w. dat);* **to — in hand** suscipere; **to — into consideration** respicere; **to — it hard that …** graviter ferre *(w. acc & inf);* **to — its name from** nomen capere ex *(w. abl);* **to — leave of your senses** a te exire; **to — notice of** observare; **to — off** *(clothes, shoes, ring, locket)* detrahere; **to — on** suscipere; **to — over** *(a position)* occupare; **to — pains to** in magno negotio habēre *(w. inf);* **to — part in** capessere partem *(w. gen);* **to — place** fieri; **to — pleasure in** capere laetitiam ex *(w. abl);* **to — out** *(to produce)* proferre; *(from storage)* promere; **to — out a loan** pecuniam mutuam sumere; **to — out of his pocket** de sinu proferre; **to — pity on** capere misericordiam *(w. gen);* **to — possession of** occupare; **to — the opportunity** capere occasionem; **to — the place of** occupare locum *(w. gen);* **to — to task** exprobrare; **to — up** *(a day)* consumere; *(a task)* suscipere; *(space)* occupare; *(to snatch up)* corripere; *(arms)* capere; **to — (it) upon oneself** sibi sumere, in se conferre; **to — vengeance on** vindicare **II** *intr* **I'm —ing off** apoculo *(coll);* **it would — too long to** longum esset *(w. inf);* **to — after** similis esse *(w. gen, esp. of persons; w. dat, esp. of things);* **to — off** abire, proficisci; *(coll)* apoculare; *(of a plane)* avolare; **to — off from** *(e.g., work)* absistere *(w. abl);* **to — over completely** plane tenēre

take *s* praed·a -ae *f; (earnings, profits)* captur·a -ae *f*

take-off *s* avolati·o -onis *f*

tale *s* fabul·a -ae *f; (short tale)* fabell·a -ae *f;* **to tell —s** blaterare

talent *s* talent·um -i *n; (fig)* ingen·ium -(i)i *n*

talented *adj* ingenios·us -a -um, ingenio praedit·us -a -um

talk *s* serm·o -onis *m;* **idle —** nug·ae -arum *fpl;* **small —** sermuncul·us -i *m*

talk *intr* loqui; **to — back (to)** insolenter respondēre *(w. dat);* **to — tough** durae buccae esse; **to — with** colloqui cum *(w. abl)*

talkative *adj* loqu·ax -acis

talker *s (idle)* blater·o -onis *mf*

talk show *s* spectacul·um -i *n* disputativum

tall *adj* alt·us -a -um, cels·us -a -um; *(person)* procer·us -a -um, long·us -a -um; **to be —** procerā staturā esse, longus esse

tally *s* rati·o -onis *f; (scorecard)* tesser·a -ae *f*

tally *intr* convenire, congruere

tambourine *s* tympan·um -i *n*

tame *adj* mansuet·us -a -um

tame *tr* mansuefacere, domare

tamely *adv* mansuete; *(fig)* ignave

tamer *s* domi·tor -toris *m* (·trix -tricis *f)*

taming *s* domit·us -ūs *m*

tamper *intr* **to — with** *(e.g., the jury)* sollicitare; *(writings)* depravare; *(to falsify)* vitiare

tan *tr* colorare; *(by sun)* adurere **II** *intr* colorari, fuscare

tan *s* adustus col·or -oris *m;* **to get a —** colorari

tangent *s* line·a -ae *f* tangens

tangible *adj* tractabil·is -is -e; *(actual)* solid·us -a -um

tangle *s* nod·us -i *m; (fig)* implicati· -onis *f*

tangle *tr* nodare, implicare **II** *intr* **to — with** se implicare in *(w. abl)*

tank *s* lac·us -ūs *m; (mil)* autocurr·us -ūs *m* armatus

tankard *s* canthar·us -i *m*

tanned *adj* adust·us -a -um, colorat·us -a -um

tantalize *tr* vexare

tantamount *adj* pa·r -ris

tantrum *s* acessi·o -onis *f* irae; **to throw a —** accessione irae efferi

tap *s* levis ict·us -ūs *m,* plag·a -ae *f* mollis

tap *tr* leviter ferire; *(wine, etc.)* relin·o -ere relevi; **to — s.o.'s phone** alicuius sermonem telephonicum clam sublegere

tape *s (adhesive)* taeni·a -ae *f* adhaesiva; *(audiotape)* phonotaeniol·a -ae *f; (audiocasette)* phonocaset·a -ae *f*

tape *tr* in phonotaeniolā imprimere, in phonocasetā imprimere

taper *s* cere·us -i *m*

taper *tr* fastigare **II** *intr* decrescere, fastigari

tape measure *s* taeni·a -ae *f* mensuralis

tape recorder *s* magnetophon·um -i *n*

taper off *intr* decrescere; *(of rain)* detumescere

tapestry *s* tapet·e -is *n*

tapeworm *s* taeni·a -ae *f*

taproom *s* cauponul·a -ae *f*

tar *s* pix, picis *f*

tardily *adv* tarde, lente

tardiness *s* tardit·as -atis *f*

tardy *adj* tard·us -a -um

target *s* scop·us -i *m*

tariff *s* portor·ium -(i)i *n*

tarnish *tr* infuscare **||** *intr* infuscari
tarpaulin *s* stragul·um -i *n*
tarry *intr* commorari
tart *adj* acerb·us -a -um, ac·er -ris -re
tart *s* scriblit·a -ae *f*
task *s* pens·um -i *n;* **to take to —** exprobrare
taste *s (sense)* gustat·us -ūs *m; (flavor)* sap·or -oris *m; (fig)* iudic·ium -(i)i *n;* **lack of good —** deformit·as -atis *f;* **this is not to my —** hoc non mei stomachi est
taste *tr* gustare **||** *intr* sapere; **to — bad, good** male, bene sapere; **to — like** reddere saporem *(w. gen),* sapere *(w. acc)*
tasteful *adj* eleg·ans -antis; *(neat in arrangement)* concinn·us -a -um
tastefully *adv* eleganter
tasteless *adj* insipid·us -a -um; *(fig)* insuls·us -a -um
tastelessly *adv* insulse
tasty *adj* sapid·us -a -um
tattered *adj* pannos·us -a -um
tatters *spl* pann·i -orum *mpl;* **to be in —** pannos·us -a -um esse
taunt *s* convic·ium -(i)i *n*
taunt *tr* conviciari; **to — s.o. with his low birth** ignobilitatem alicui obicere
taut *adj* intent·us -a -um
tavern *s* caupon·a -ae *f*
tavern keeper *s* caup·o -onis *m*
tawdry *adj* vil·is -is -e
tax *s* vectig·al -alis *n;* **to impose a — on** victigal imponere *(w. dat);* **to pay —es** vectigalia pensitare
tax *tr* vectigal imponere *(w. dat);* **to — oneself to the utmost** contendere omnes nervos
taxable *adj* vectigal·is -is -e
tax collector *s* exac·tor -toris *m* (·trix -tricis *f*), publican·us -i *m*
taxi *s* raed·a -ae *f* meritoria
tea *s* the·a -ae *f;* **teacup** pocill·um -i *n* theanum; **teapot** hirni·a -ae *f* theana
teach *tr (w. double acc)* docēre; **to — Latin** Latine docēre
teachable *adj* docil·is -is -e
teacher *s* docen·s -tis *mf,* ludi magis·ter -tri *m* (·tr·a -trae *f*)
teaching *s* doctrin·a -ae *f;* **— assistant** *s* hypodidascul·us -i *m* (·a -ae *f*); **— method** rati·o -onis *f* docendi
team *s (sports)* turm·a -ae *f; (of animals)* iug·um -i *n*
tear *s* lacrim·a -ae *f; (a rent)* scissur·a -ae *f;* **to shed —s** lacrimas profundere
tear *tr* scindere; **I can't — myself away from my books** in libris haereo; **to — apart** discindere; **to — down** revellere; *(a building)* diruere; **to — off** abscindere; **to — open** rescindere; **to — out** evellere; **to — to pieces** (di)laniare, discerpere; **to — up** *(trees, shrubs)* convellere; *(paper)* discindere **||** *intr (to rush)* volare, ruere; **to — along a road** viam vorare
tease *tr* taxare
teaspoon *s* parvum cochle·ar -aris *n*
teat *s* mamm·a -ae *f*
technical *adj* artificios·us -a -um, technic·us -a -um; **— term** verb·um -i *n* proprium unius disciplinae
technique *s* ar·s -tis *f,* technica rati·o -onis *f*
technology *s* officinarum art·es -ium *fpl,* technologi·a -ae *f*
tedious *adj* lent·us -a -um, taedios·us -a -um; **it would be — to** longum est *(w. inf)*
tedium *s* taed·ium -(i)i *n*
teem *intr* scatēre, redundare
tee shirt *s* colob·ium -(i)i *n*
teenager *s* adulesc·ens -entis *mf*
teeth *spl* dent·es -ium *mpl;* **back —** dentes posteriores; **front —** dentes primores
teethe *intr* dentire
teething *s* dentiti·o -onis *f*
telephone *adj* telephonic·us -a -um; **— book** *s* telephonicus ind·ex -icis *m;* **— call** *s* telephonem·a -atis *n;* **— number** numer·us -is *m* telephonicus; **— receiver** auscultabul·um -i *n*
telephone *s* telephon·um -i *n;* **by —** telephonice; **to call s.o. on the —** aliquem per telephonum vocare; **to speak with s.o. on the —** cum aliquo telephonice colloqui; **the — is ringing** telephonum tinnit; **to use a pay —** telephono monetali uti
telephone *tr* per telephonum vocare *(or* compellare)
telephone booth *s* cell·a -ae *f* telephonica
telescope *s* telescop·ium -(i)i *n*
television *s* televisi·o -onis *f; (set)* televisor·ium -(i)i *n;* **to turn on (turn off) the —** televisorium excitare (exstinguere); **to turn down (turn up) the —** vim televisorii remittere (augēre); **to watch —** televisionem spectare
television audience televisor·es -um *mpl*
television broadcast *s* emissi·o -onis *f* televisifica
television channel *s* canal·is -is *m* televisificus
television program *s* programm·a -atis *n* televisificum
television screen *s* quadr·um -i *n* televisificum
television series *s* seri·es -ei *f* televisifica
tell *tr* narrare, referre; *(to show, indicate)* docēre; **— me the truth**! dic mihi verum!; **to — s.o. off** aliquem castigare; **to — s.o. to** *(w. inf)* imperare alicui ut *(w. subj);* **to — you the truth** ut verum dicam **||** *intr (to be effective)* pollēre, valēre
teller *s* numera·tor -toris *m* (·trix -tricis *f*)

telltale *adj* partefaci·ens -entis
temerity *s* temerit·as -atis *f*
temper *s (anger)* iracundi·a -ae *f;* **to have a bad —** summā iracundiā esse; **to keep one's —** iram tenēre; **to lose one's —** iracundiā efferri
temper *tr* temperare
temperament *s* indol·es -is *f*
temperamental *adj* instabil·is -is -e; *(excitable)* fervid·us -a -um
temperance *s* temperanti·a -ae *f*
temperate *adj* temperat·us -a -um
temperature *s* temperatur·a -ae *f;* **the — fell below 32 degrees** temperatura lapsa est subter duos et triginta gradūs; **to run a —** febricitare; **what is the —?** quo gradu stat temperatura?
tempest *s* tempest·as -atis *f,* procell·a -ae *f*
tempestuous *adj* procellos·us -a -um
temple *s* templ·um -i *n; (anat)* temp·us -oris *n*
temporal *adj (earthly)* profan·us -a -um
temporarily *adv* ad tempus
temporary *adj* temporari·us -a -um; **— stadium** stadi·um -i *n* ad tempus exstructum
tempt *tr* temptare; **to — fate** experiri casūs
temptation *s* tentati·o -onis *f*
ten *adj* decem [*indecl*]: **— times** decies
tenable *adj* defensibil·is -is -e
tenacious *adj* ten·ax -acis
tenaciously *adv* tenaciter
tenacity *s* tenacit·as -atis *f*
tenant *s* conduc·tor -toris *m* (·trix -tricis *f*); *(of an apartment)* insulari·us -i *m* (·a -ae *f*)
tend *tr* curare ‖ *intr (to be wont)* solēre; **I — to believe** crediderim [*perf subj*]
tendency *s* inclinati·o -onis *f*
tender *adj* ten·er -eris -ere, moll·is -is -e; *(affectionate)* indulg·ens -entis, am·ans -antis; *(sore)* dol·ens -entis
tender *tr* deferre
tenderly *adv* tenere
tenderness *s (softness)* tenerit·as -atis *f;* *(affection)* indulgenti·a -ae *f*
tendon *s* nerv·us -i *m*
tendril *s (of vine)* pampin·us -i *m; (of plants)* clavicul·us -i *m*
tenement *s* conduct·um -i *n,* insul·a -ae *f*
tenet *s* dogm·a -atis *n*
tenfold *adj* decempl·ex -icis
tennis *s* tenisi·a -ae *f,* tenilud·ium -(i)i *n;* **to play —** tenisiā ludere
tennis ball *s* pil·a -ae *f* tenisiae
tennis court *s* sphaerister·ium -(i)i *n*
tennis match *s* certam·en -inis *f* tenisiae
tennis player *s* teniludi·us -i *m* (·a -ae *f*)
tennis racket *s* reticul·um -i *n* manubriatum
tenor *s (purport)* sens·us -ūs *m; (singer)* cant·or -oris *m* vocis mediae
tense *adj (stretched)* tent·us -a -um; *(anxious)* anxi·us -a -um
tense *s (gram)* temp·us -oris *n*
tension *s* intenti·o -onis *f; (mental strain)* anxiet·as -atis *f*
tent *s* tentor·ium -(i)i *n*
tentative *adj* tent·ans -antis
tenth *adj* decim·us -a -um
tenterhooks *spl* **to be on —** animi pendēre
tenuous *adj* tenu·is -is -e
tenure *s (fixed period)* spat·ium -(i)i *n; (possession)* possessi·o -onis *f; (pol)* imperii temp·us -oris *n; (of a professor)* mun·us -eris *n* perpetuum
tepid *adj* tepid·us -a -um
term *s (word)* appellati·o -onis *f; (limit)* termin·us -i *m; (length of time)* spat·ium -(i)i *n; (semester)* studiorum spatium *n; (math)* termin·us -i *m;* **— of office** spatium (temporis) magistratūs; **on these —s** his condicionibus, his legibus; **to accept (dictate, propose, reject) —s of peace** condiciones pacis accipere (dicere, ferre, repudiare); **to be on friendly —s with a country** in amicitiā populi esse; **to be on good —s with** in gratiā esse cum *(w. abl);* **to come to —s** pacisc·or -i pactus sum; **to stick by the —s** in condicionibus manēre
terminal *adj* extrem·us -a -um
terminal *s* stati·o -onis *f* ultima; *(comput)* terminal·e -is *n*
terminate *tr* terminare ‖ *intr* terminari; *(of words)* cadere
termination *s* terminati·o -onis *f*
termite *s* tered·o -inis *f*
terrace *s* agg·er -eris *m; (patio)* xyst·us -i *m*
terrain *s* locorum sit·us -ūs *m*
terrestrial *adj* terrestr·is -is -e
terrible *adj* terribil·is -is -e
terribly *adv* horrendum in modum
terrific *adj* terrific·us -a -um; *(great)* festiv·us -a -um; **—!** euge!
terrify *tr* terrēre, terrificare
territory *s* a·ger -gri *m,* territor·ium -(i)i *n; (country)* fin·es -ium *mpl*
terror *s* terr·or -oris *m*
terse *adj* press·us -a -um
tersely *adv* presse
test *s* experiment·um -i *n; (exam)* probati·o -onis *f;* **to flunk a —** in probatione cadere; **to pass a —** probationem sustinēre
test *tr* experiri; probare
testament *s* testament·um -i *n;* **New (Old) Testament** Novum (Vetus) Testamentum
testamentary *adj* testamentari·us -a -um
testator *s* testa·tor -toris *m* (·trix -tricis *f*)
testicle *s* testicul·us -i *m*
testify *tr* testificari
testimonial *s* laudati·o -onis *f*
testimony *s (proof)* indicati·o -onis *f; (leg)* testimon·ium -(i)i *n*
test tube *s* catin·us -i *m*
testy *adj* stomachos·us -a -um

tetanus *s* tetan·us -i *m*
tether *s* retinacul·um -i *n*
tether *tr* religare
text *s* verb·a -orum *npl* scriptoris; *(comput)* text·us -ūs *m*
textbook *s* enchirid·ion -(i)i *n,* ars, artis *f*
textile *adj* textil·is -is -e
textile *s* textil·e -is *n*
texture *s* textur·a -ae *f*
than *adv* quam; **less —** minus quam; **more —** plus quam; **other —** alius ac; **sooner —** prius quam
thank *tr* gratias agere *(w. dat);* **no, — you** benigne; **no, — you just the same** tam gratia est; **— heaven!** sit dis gratia!; **— you for** gratias tibi ago ob *(w. acc)*; **— you for helping me** gratias tibi ago quod me iuvisti
thankful *adj* **to be — to** gratiam habere *(w. dat)*
thankfully *adv* grate
thankless *adj* ingrat·us -a -um
thanks *spl* grati·ae -arum *fpl;* **— a lot!** multas gratias!; **— a million!** sescentas gratias!; **— to Caesar, I am free** beneficio Caesaris liber sum; **— to me (you,** *etc.)* meā (tuā, *etc.)* operā; **to give —** gratias agere
thanks *interj* gratias!
thanksgiving *s* gratulati·o -onis *f; (public act)* supplicati·o -onis *f*
Thanksgiving Day Di·es -ei *m* Gratulationis
that *adj* ill·e -a -ud; is, ea id; *(sometimes contemptuous)* ist·e -a -ud
that *pron demonstrative* ill·e -a -ud; is, ea, id; ist·e -a -ud; **that is, if Aquila will allow me** si tamen per Aquilam licerit; **— is to say** videlicet; **— was the life!** illud erat vivere!
that *conj (purpose, result, command)* ut; *(after verbs of fearing)* ne
thatch *s* strament·um -i *n*
thatch *tr* stramento tegere
thaw *tr* (dis)solvere **II** *intr* tabescere
the *article not expressed in Latin; however to express celebrity, use* ill·e -a -ud: **— Hercules of Xenophon** Hercules Xenophontius ille
the *adv* **— … —** quo … eo; **— less he pursued glory, — more it followed him** quo minus gloriam petebat eo magis eum sequebatur
theater *s* theatr·um -i *n;* **— of war** sed·es -is *f* belli
theatrical *adj* theatral·is -is -e
thee *pron* te; **of —** de te; **to —** tibi; **with —** tecum
theft *s* furt·um -i *n*
their *adj* illorum, illarum, illorum; eorum, earum, eorum; **— own** su·us -a -um
them *pron* eos, eas, ea; ill·os -as -a; ist·os -ae -a; **to —** eis, illis, istis
theme *s (topic)* materi·a -ae *f,* argument·um -i *n; (essay)* tractat·us -ūs *m*
themselves *pron refl* se; **to —** sibi
themselves *pron intensive* ips·i -ae -a
then *adv (at that time)* tum, tunc; *(after that)* deinde; *(therefore)* igitur, ergo; **now and —** interdum; **— and there** ilico
thence *adv* inde, illinc
thenceforth *adv* dehinc
theologian *s* theolog·us -i *m* (·a -ae *f*)
theological *adj* theologic·us -a -um
theology *s* theologi·a -ae *f*
theoretical *adj* rational·is -is -e
theorizing *s* ratiocinati·o -onis *f*
theory *s* rati·o -onis *f;* **the — and practice of war** ratio et usus belli
therapist *s* therapeut·a -ae *m* (·ria -riae *f*)
therapy *s* therapi·a -ae *f*
there *adv* ibi; *(thither)* illuc; **— are** sunt; **— is** est
thereabouts *adv* circa, circiter, fere
thereafter *adv* deinde
thereby *adv* eā re, eo
therefore *adv* itaque, igitur, ergo
therefrom *adv* exinde, ex eo
thereupon *adv* subinde
thermometer *s* thermometr·um -i *n*
thesis *s* thes·is -is *f*
they *pron* ei eae ea; illi illae illa; isti istae ista
thick *adj* crass·us -a -um; *(closely packed)* dens·us -a -um, spiss·us -a -um; **through —and thin** per invia
thicken *tr* densare, spissare **II** *intr* crassescere
thicket *s* frutect·um -i *n*
thickly *adv* dense
thickness *s* crassitud·o -inis *f*
thick-headed *adj* obtus·us -a -um
thick-skinned *adj* callos·us -a -um; *(fig)* dur·us -a -um
thief *s* fur, furis *mf;* **an out and out —** tri·fur -furis *mf*
thievery *s* furt·um -i *n*
thigh *s* fem·ur -oris *n;* **to slap the —** femur percutere
thigh bone *s* cox·a -ae *f*
thimble *s* digital·e -is *n*
thin *adj* tenu·is -is -e, exil·is -is -e; *(lean)* ma·cer -cra -crum; **to become —** macrescere
thin *tr* attenuare; **to — out** rarefacere
thine *adj* tu·us -a -um
thing *s* res, rei *f;* **of all —s!** edepol!
think *tr* cogitare; *(to believe, imagine, etc.)* putare, credere, opinari; *(upon mature reflection)* aestimare; *(to give one's opinion on)* censēre; *(to surmise)* suspicari; **that is exactly what I —** ita prorsus existimo; **to — over** reputare, in mente agitare; **to — up** excogitare; **what do you —?** quid censes? **II** *intr* cogitare, putare; **to — better of** sententiam mutare de *(w.*

abl); **to — highly of** magni habēre; **to — ill of Crassus** male opinari de Crasso; **to — of** memorare, recordari
thinker *s* philosoph·us -i *m*
thinking *s* cogitati·o -onis *f*
thinness *s* tenuit·as -atis *f*
third *adj* terti·us -a -um
third *s* tertia par·s -tis *f*
thirdly *adv* tertio
thirst *s* sit·is -is *f*
thirst *intr* sitire; **to — for** *(fig)* appetere
thirstily *adv* sitienter
thirsty *adj* siti·ens -entis
thirteen *adj* tredecim [*indecl*]
thirteenth *adj* terti·us decim·us -a -um
thirtieth *adj* tricesim·us -a -um
thirty *adj* triginta [*indecl*]
this *adj* hic, haec, hoc
thistle *s* cardu·us -i *m*
thither *adv* illuc, eo
thong *s* lor·um -i *n*
thorn *s* spin·a -ae *f;* **crown of —s** coron·a -ae *f* spinea
thorn bush *s* vepr·es -is *m*
thorny *adj* spinos·us -a -um; *(fig)* nodos·us -a -um
thorough *adj* perfect·us -a -um
thoroughly *adv* penitus, prorsus, omnino
thoroughbred *adj* generos·us -a -um
thoroughfare *s* perv·ium -(i)i *n*
those *adj see* **that**
thou *pron* tu
though *conj* quamquam, quamvis
though *adv* tamen
thought *s (act, faculty)* cogitati·o -onis *f; (product of thinking)* cogitat·um -i *n;* **on second —** cum ego recogito
thoughtful *adj (reflecting)* cogitabund·us -a -um; *(careful)* provid·us -a -um; *(kind)* human·us -a -um
thoughtless *adj* inconsult·us -a -um
thoughtlessly *adv* inconsulte, temere
thousand *adj* mille [*indecl*]; **a — times** millies
thousandth *adj* millesim·us -a -um
thrash *tr* verberare
thrashing *s* verber·a -orum *npl*
thread *s* fil·um -i *n; (comput)* seri·es -ei *f* (epistularum electronicarum); **to hang by a —** *(fig)* filo pendēre
thread *tr* inserere
threadbare *adj* pannos·us -a -um; *(worn-out)* detrit·us -a -um
threat *s (act)* minati·o -onis *f;* **—s** min·ae -arum *fpl*
threaten *tr* minari *(w. acc of thing and dat of person);* **to — s.o. with death** comminari necem alicui ‖ *intr* imminēre, impendēre
threatening *adj* min·ax -acis, minitabund·us -a -um
three *adj* tres, tres, tria; **— times** ter
threefold *adj* tripl·ex -icis
three-headed *adj* tric·eps -itis
three-legged *adj* trip·es -edis
thresh *tr* terere
thresher *s* tribul·um -i *n*
threshing *s* tritur·a -ae *f*
threshing floor *s* are·a -ae *f*
threshold *s* lim·en -inis *n*
thrice *adv* ter
thrift *s* parsimoni·a -ae *f*
thriftily *adv* frugaliter
thriftiness *s* frugalit·as -atis *f*
thrifty *adj* parc·us -a -um, frugal·is -is -e
thrill *s (delight)* delectati·o -onis *f*
thrill *tr* commovēre
thrilling *adj* mirific·us -a -um
thrive *intr* vigēre, virēre; *(to prosper)* se bene habēre
thriving *adj* veget·us -a -um, prosp·er -era -erum
throat *s* fauc·es -ium *fpl*
throb *s* palpitati·o -onis *f*
throb *intr* palpitare; *(of a vein)* agitare
throes *spl* dol·or -oris *m,* ang·or -oris *m*
throne *s* sol·ium -(i)i *n; (fig) (regal power)* regn·um -i *n;* **to restore to the —** restituere in regnum; **to succeed to the —** recipere regnum; *(of emperors)* recipere imperium
throng *s* frequenti·a -ae *f*
throng *intr* **to — around** stipare
throttle *tr* strangulare
throttle *s* epitom·ium -(i)i *n*
through *prep* per *(w. acc); (on account of)* ob *(w. acc)*
through *adv render by compound verb with* trans- *or* per-, *e.g.,* **to read —** perlegere; **— and —** omnino
throughout *adv* prorsus
throughout *prep* per *(w. acc)*
throw *tr* iacere, conicere; *(freq)* iactare; *(to hurl)* conicere; *(esp. missiles)* mittere; **to — an apple at s.o.** aliquem malo petere; **to — a stone at s.o.** impingere lapidem alicui; **to — at** conicere ad, in *(w. acc);* **to — away** abicere; **to — back** reicere; **to — down** deicere; **to — food to the dogs** cibum canibus obicere; **to — in the way of** obicere *(w. dat);* **to — into the fire** proicere in ignem; **to — off** *(a rider)* eicere, excutere; *(clothes, bonds)* exuere; *(to mislead)* auferre; **to — oneself at the feet of s.o.** ad pedes alicuius se proicere; **to — oneself down** *(from a height)* se praecipitare; **to — open** patefacere; **to — out** eicere; **to — out of the game** a campo relegare; **to —** *(e.g., a cloak)* **over s.o.** inicere (pallium) alicui; **to — the book at s.o.** *(fig)* summo iure cum aliquo agere; **to — together** conicere in unum; **to — up** evomere ‖ *intr* **to — up** vomere
throw *s* iact·us -ūs *m*
thrush *s* turd·us -i *m*
thrust *s* impet·us -ūs *m,* ict·us -ūs *m*

thrust *tr* trudere, impellere; **to — back** retrudere; **to — off** detrudere; **to — out** extrudere; **to — together** contrudere
thumb *s* poll•ex -icis *m*
thumb tack *s* cuspidiol•a -ae *f* pollice infixa
thump *s* percussi•o -onis *f;* grav•is sonit•us -ūs *m*
thump *tr* tundere
thunder *s* tonitr•us -ūs *m*
thunder *intr* tonare
thunder bolt *s* fulm•en -inis *n*
thunderstruck *adj* attonit•us -a -um
Thursday *s* di•es -ei *m* Iovis
thus *adv* ita, sic; **and —** itaque
thwart *tr* obstare *(w. dat)*
thy *adj* tu•us -a -um
tiara *s* diadem•a -atis *n*
Tiber *s* Tiber•is -is *(acc:* -im) *m*
tick *s (insect)* ricin•us -i *m; (clicking)* levis ict•us -ūs *m*
ticket *s* tesser•a -ae *f; (label)* pittac•ium -(i)i *n;* **one-way —** tessera unius cursūs; **round-trip —** tessera itūs reditūsque
ticket agent *s* tesserari•us -i *m* (•a -ae *f)*
ticket window *s* ostiol•um -i *n* tesserarium
tickle *tr & intr* titillare
tickling *s* titillati•o -onis *f*
ticklish *adj* titillatione affect•us -a -um; *(delicate)* periculos•us -a -um, lubric•us -a -um
tide *s* aest•us -ūs *m*; **high —** aestūs access•us -ūs *m;* **low —** aestūs recess•us -ūs *m*
tidiness *s* munditi•a -ae *f*
tidings *spl* nunt•ius -(i)i *m;* **to bring — of joy** gaudium nuntiare
tidy *adj* mund•us -a -um
tidy up *tr* mundare, ordinare
tie *s* vincul•um -i *n; (necktie)* focal•e -is *n; (of blood, kinship)* necessitud•o -inis *f; (of a score)* aequalit•as -atis *f* punctorum; **it's a —** *(in sports)* pares sunt
tie *tr* (al)ligare; *(in a knot)* nodare; *(to equal)* aequare; **to be tied down** *(e.g., w. business)* impediri; **to — one's hair in a knot** colligere capillos in nodum; **to — back** revincire; **to — up** alligare; *(a wound)* deligare; *(money)* occupare; *(in work, etc.)* impedire
tier *s* ord•o -inis *m*
tie-up *(on highway)* affluenti•a -ae *f* vehiculorum
tiger *s* tigr•is -is *mf;* **—s roar** tigres fremunt
tight *adj (knot, clothes)* strict•us -a -um, art•us -a -um; *(shoe)* restrict•us -a -um; *(tense)* intent•us -a -um; *(stingy)* sordid•us -a -um; **to be in a — spot** in angustiis esse; **to get — on wine** se vino devincire
tighten *tr* adstringere
tight-fisted *adj* adstrict•us -a -um
tightly *adv* arte; **too — bandaged** nimis adstrict•us -a -um
tigress *s* tigr•is -is *(or* -idis) *f*
tile *s* lamin•a -ae *f* fictilis; *(on roof)* tegul•a -ae *f*
till *conj* dum, donec
till *prep* usque ad *(w. acc);* **— late at night** ad multm noctem; **— late in the day** ad multum diem; **till the month of July** in mensem Iulium
till *tr (the soil)* colere
tillage *s* agricultur•a -ae *f*
tiller *s (person)* agricol•a -ae *m; (helm)* gubernacul•um -i *n*
tilt *tr* proclinare
timber *s* materi•a -ae *f*
time *s* temp•us -oris *n; (age, period)* aet•as -atis *f; (leisure)* ot•ium -(i)i *n; (opportunity)* occasi•o -onis *f; (interval)* intervall•um -i *n; (of day)* hor•a -ae *f;* **after so long a —** tanto intervallo; **ahead of —** ante tempus; **a long — already** iamdudum, e.g., **I've been here a long — already** iamdudum adsum; **another —** alias; **around the — of the battle** sub tempus proelii; **at about the same —** sub idem tempus; **at one — ... at another** alias ... alias; **at that —** *(at that hour)* ad id temporis; *(in the past)* tum; **at the right —** ad tempus, tempestive; **at the same —** simul; **at the wrong —** intempestive; **at —s** interdum; **a very short — ago** modo; **before —** *(prematurely)* ante tempus; **for all future —** in posterum; **for a long —** diu; **for a short —** brevi tempore, paulisper; **for a —** parumper; **for some —** aliquamdiu; **for the first —** primum; **for the — being** in tempus; **from that — on** ex eo (tempore); **from — to —** interdum; **I have no —** non est mihi tempus; **in a short —** brevi; **in —** ad tempus, temperi; **it is high — to** tempus maxime est *(w. inf)*; **many —s** saepius; **once upon a —** olim; **on —** tempestive, tempori; **there is no — to cry** non vacat flēre; **there is no — to lose** maturato opus est; **there was a — when** tempus erat cum; **to ask what — it is** horas quaerere *or* inquirere; **to have — for** vacare *(w. dat);* **to make up for lost —** cessata tempora corrigere; **to say what — it is** quotas horas nuntiare; **to see what — it is** horas inspicere; **to waste —** tempus perdere; **to while away the —** tempus fallere; **what — is it?** quota hora est?; **you couldn't have come at a better —** non potuisti magis per tempus advenire
time *tr* clepsydrā *(or* horologio) metiri
timeliness *s* tempestivit•as -atis *f*
timely *adj* tempestiv•us -a -um
timepiece *s* horolog•ium -(i)i *n*

times *(used with numeral adverbs) e.g.,* **ten —** decies; **no more than three —** ter nec amplius
timetable *s* horar·ium -(i)i *n*
timid *adj* timid·us -a -um
timidity *s* timidit·as -atis *f*
tin *s* stann·um -i *n*
tin *adj* stanne·us -a -um
tincture *s* col·or -oris *m*
tinder *s* fom·es -itis *m*
tingle *intr* formicare
tinkle *intr* tinnire
tinsel *s* bracteol·a -ae *f*
tint *tr* tingere
tip *s* ap·ex -icis *m,* cacum·en -inis *n; (of sword, horn)* mucr·o -onis *m; (hint)* indic·ium -(i)i *n; (money)* stip·s -is *f;* **on the — of the tongue** in labris primoribus; **— of the nose** imus nas·us -i *m*
tip *tr (to make pointy)* praefigere; *(to give a tip to)* stipem dare *(w. dat);* **to — over** vergere
tippler *s* pot·or -oris *m*
tipsy *adj* ebriol·us -a -um
tiptoe *adv* in digitos erect·us -a -um
tiptoe *intr* erect·us -a in digitos ambulare
tire *tr* fatigare; **to — out** defatigare ‖ *intr* defatigari; **I — of** me taedet *(w. gen)*
tire *s* canth·us -i *m* cummeus; **to put air in the —** canthum cummeum inflare
tired *adj* fess·us -a -um; **I am sick and — of** me pertaedet *(w. gen);* **— out** defess·us -a -um
tireless *adj* assidu·us -a -um
tiresome *adj* molest·us -a -um
tissue *s* mucin·ium -(i)i *n* chartaceum
tit *(vulg) s* mamm·a -ae *f;* **to give s.o. — for tat** alicui par pari respondēre
titanic *adj* ing·ens -entis
tithe *s* decum·a -ae *f*
titillate *tr* titillare
title *s* titul·us -i *m; (of a book)* inscripti·o -onis *f; (of a person)* appellati·o -onis *f; (claim)* iu·s -ris *n*
title *tr* inscribere
title page *s* ind·ex -icis *m*
titter *s* lenis ris·us -ūs *m*
to *prep often rendered by the dative; (motion, except with names of towns, small islands)* ad *(w. acc),* in *(w. acc); (reaching to)* tenus *(always placed after the case) (w. gen);* **— and fro** huc illuc; **— my, your, his house** ad me, te, eum; **— the country** rus; **up —** usque ad *(w. acc)*
toad *s* buf·o -onis *m*
toast *s (bread)* pan·is -is *m* tostus; *(health)* propinati·o -onis *f;* **to drink a — to** propinare *(w. dat)*
toast *tr* torrēre; *(in drinking)* propinare *(w. dat)*
toaster *s* tostr·um -i *n*
toboggan *s* sclodi·a -ae *f*
toboggan run *s* decurs·us -ūs *m* sclodiae
today *adv* hodie
today *s* hodiernus di·es -ei *m*
toe *s* digit·us -i *m* pedis; **big —** poll·ex -icis *m* (pedis)
toga *s* tog·a -ae *f; (worn by magistrates and freeborn children)* toga praetexta; *(worn by a candidate for office)* toga candida; *(worn by young men on coming of age)* toga virilis *or* toga pura; **to receive the — of manhood** togam virilem sumere
together *adv* simul, unā
toil *s* lab·or -oris *m*
toil *intr* laborare
toilet *s* latrin·a -ae *f* loc·us -i *m* secretus; *(public)* foric·a -ae *f;* **to sit on the —** in sellā familiaricā sedēre
toilet bowl *s* labell·um -i *n* intimum
toilet paper *s* chartul·a -ae *f* hygienica
toilet seat *s* sell·a -ae *f* familiarica
token *s* sign·um -i *n; (memento)* pign·us -eris *n;* **by the same —** eandem ob rem
tolerable *adj* tolerabil·is -is -e; *(fair)* mediocr·is -is -e
tolerably *adv* mediocriter
tolerance *s* patienti·a -ae *f*
tolerant *adj* toler·ans -antis
tolerate *tr* tolerare
toleration *s* tolerati·o -onis *f*
toll *s* vectig·al -alis *n; (at ports)* portor·ium -(i)i *n*
toll booth *s* tabern·a -ae *f* vectigalis rotaris; rotar·ium -(i)i *n*
toll collector *s* exac·tor -toris *m* (·trix -tricis *f*) vectigalis rotaris
toll call *s* telephonem·a -atis *n* longinquum
toll road *s* vi·a -ae *f* vectigalis rotaris
tomato *s* lycopersic·um -i *n*
tomb *s* sepulcr·um -i *n*
tomboy *s* puell·a -ae *f* puerilis
tombstone *s* stel·a -ae *f*
tomorrow *adv* cras; **day after —** perendie; **— morning** cras mane; **— night** cras nocte; **until —** in crastinum
ton *s* duo milia libras; **to have —s of money** nummorum nummos habēre
tone *s* son·us -i *m; (in painting)* col·or -oris *m*
tongs *spl* for·ceps -cipis *mf*
tongue *s* lingu·a -ae *f; (of shoe)* ligul·a -ae *f;* **to hold one's —** linguam continēre; **his name was on the tip of my —** versabatur mihi nomen in primoribus labris
tonsils *spl* tonsill·ae -arum *fpl*
too *adv* nimis, nimium; *(also)* quoque *(always postpositive);* **— bad about Marcus** male de Marco
tool *s* instrument·um -i *n; (dupe)* minis·ter -tri *m;* **—s** *(comput)* instrumenta
toolbar *s (comput)* tabell·a -ae *f* instrumentorum
tooth *s* den·s -tis *m;* **— and nail** *(fig)* toto corpore et omnibus ungulis

toothache *s* dol·or -oris *m* dentium
toothbrush *s* penicul·us -i *m* dentibus purgandis
toothed *adj* dentat·us -a -um
toothless *adj* edentul·us -a -um
toothpaste *s* past·a -ae *f* dentaria
toothpick *s* dentiscalp·ium -(i)i *n*
top *adj* summ·us -a -um
top *s* ap·ex -icis *m; (of tree)* cacum·en -inis *n; (of house)* fastig·ium -(i)i *n; (toy)* turb·o -inis *m;* **at the — of the page** ab summā paginā; **on —** supra; **on — of that** insuper; **— of the head** vert·ex -icis *m;* **— of the mountain** summus mon·s -tis *m*
top *tr* superare; **to — it off** in summo
topcoat *s* superindument·um -i *n*
top-heavy *adj* praegrav·is -is -e a superiore parte
topic *s* res, rei *f,* argument·um -i *n*
topmost *adj* summ·us -a -um
topography *s* regionis descripti·o -onis *f*
topple *tr* evertere ‖ *intr* titubare
topsy-turvy *adv* **everything was —** omnia erant sursum deorsum; **to turn everything —** omnia sursum deorsum versare
torch *s* fax, facis *f*
torment *s* torment·um -i *n; (pain inflicted)* cruciat·us -ūs *m*
torment *tr* cruciare
tormentor *s* carnif·ex -icis *mf*
torn *adj* sciss·us -a -um
tornado *s* turb·o -inis *m*
torrent *s* torr·ens -entis *m*
torrid *adj* torrid·us -a -um
tortoise, tortoise shell *s* testud·o -inis *f*
torture *s* torment·um -i *n (almost always used in the plural); (pain inflicted by way of punishment or cruelty)* cruciat·us -ūs *m;* **instruments of —** torment·a -orum *npl;* **to question under —** tormentis quaerere
torture *tr* torquēre, cruciare
torturer *s* tort·or -oris *m*
toss *s* iact·us -ūs *m*
toss *tr* iactare; **to be —ed about** *(at sea)* fluitare ‖ *intr* iactari
total *adj* tot·us -a -um, univers·us -a -um
total *s* summ·a -ae *f*
totalitarian *adj* ab unā factione dominat·us -a -um
totalitarianism *s* dominati·o -onis *f* tyrannica civitatis ab unā factione
totally *adv* omnino, prorsus
totter *intr* titubare
touch *tr* tangere; *(to stir)* movēre; **to — deeply** commovēre ‖ *intr* inter se contingere; **to — on** attingere
touch *s* tact·us -ūs *m;* **to put the finishing —es to** ultimam *(or* summam) manum imponere *(w. dat)*
touch-and-go *adj* anc·eps -itis
touchdown *s* **to make a —** calcem *(or* cretam) attingere
touching *adj* flexanim·us -a -um
touchstone *s (fig)* obruss·a -ae *f*
touchy *adj (person)* stomachos·us -a -um; *(matter)* lubric·us -a -um
tough *adj* dur·us -a -um; *(hardy)* robust·us -a -um; *(difficult)* difficili·is -is -e
toupee *s* galericul·um -i *n;* **to wear a —** galericulo uti
tour *s (rounds)* circuit·us -ūs *m; (abroad)* peregrinati·o -onis *f;* **to complete a three-year — of duty** triennium militiae explēre
tour bus *s* coenautocinet·um -i *n* perigeticum
tour guide *s* mystagog·us -i *m* (·a -ae *f);* dux, ducis *mf* itinerari·us (-a)
tourist *s* peregrina·tor -toris *m* (·trix -tricis *f)*
tournament *s* certam·en -inis *n*
tow *s* stupp·a -ae *f*
tow *tr* remulco trahere
toward *prep* versus *(w. acc),* ad *(w. acc); (of feelings)* erga *(w. acc),* in *(w. acc); (of time)* sub *(w. acc)*
towel *s* gausapin·um -i *n,* mantel·e -is *n; (hand towel)* manuterg·ium -(i)i *n*
tower *s* turr·is -is *f*
tower *intr* **to — over** imminēre *(w. dat)*
towering *adj* excels·us -a -um
towline *s* remulc·um -i *n*
town *s* oppid·um -i *n; (small town)* oppidul·um -i *n*
town hall *s* curi·a -ae *f*
townsman *s* oppidan·us -i *m*
tow truck *s* remulcicarr·us -i *m*
toy *s* ludibr·ium -(i)i *n*
toy *intr* **to — with** ludere cum *(w. abl)*
trace *s* vestig·ium -(i)i *n; (for horses)* helc·ium -(i)i *n;* **no — of a wound** nulla suspici·o -onis *f* vulneris
trace *tr* indagare; *(to outline)* delineare; **to — back to** repetere ab *(w. abl)*
track *tr* indagare; **to — down** indagare; **to — up** *(e.g., a rug)* maculare
track *s* vestig·ium -(i)i *n; (path)* semit·a -ae *f,* call·es -is *m; (the sport)* cursur·a -ae *f; (course laid out for runners)* curricul·um -i *n; (of wheel)* orbit·a -ae *f; (of railroad)* orbit·a -ae *f* ferriviaria; **to keep — of** conspicere
trackless *adj* avi·us -a -um
tract *s (land; treatise)* tract·us -ūs *m*
tractor *s* tractr·um -i *n*
trade *s* commerc·ium -(i)i *n; (profession)* artific·ium -(i)i *n;* **to carry on — in** commercium *(w. gen)* facere
trade *tr* commutare ‖ *intr* mercaturas facere, negotiari
trader *s* merca·tor -toris *m* (·trix -tricis *f)*
tradesman *s* opif·ex -icis *m*
trademark *s* not·a -ae *f*
trade union *s* syndicat·us -ūs *m*
tradition *s* traditi·o -onis *f,* mo·s -ris *m* maiorum; **there is an old —** ab antiquis traditur

traditional *adj* a maioribus tradit·us -a -um
traffic *s* commerc·ium -(i)i *n; (on street)* transit·us -ūs *m,* commeat·us -ūs *m* vehiculorum; **heavy —** celebrit·as -atis *f* viae *(or* viarum); frequenti·a -ae *f* vehiculorum
traffic cop *s* vigil -is *mf* viatori·us (-a)
traffic jam *s* affluenti·a -ae *f* vehicularia
traffic light *s* semiphor·um -i *n* **(red** rubrum; **yellow** flavum; **green** viride)
tragedian *s (playwright)* tragoed·us -i *m; (actor)* tragicus act·or -oris *m*
tragedy *s* tragoedi·a -ae *f*
tragic *adj (lit & fig)* tragic·us -a -um
tragically *adv* tragice
trail *s* vestig·ium -(i)i *n; (path)* call·es -is *m*
trail *tr* investigare; *(to drag)* trahere ‖ *intr* trahi; *(to lag)* cunctari
trailer home *s* habitacul·um -i *n* remulcatum
train *s (sequence)* seri·es -ei *f,* ord·o -inis *m; (of robe)* peniculament·um -i *n; (retinue)* comitat·us -ūs *m; (rail)* tram·en -inis *n* (ferriviarium); **a through —** tramen directum
train *tr* instituere, exercēre; *(to habituate)* assuefacere ‖ *intr* se exercitare
trainer *s* exerci·tor -toris *m* (·trix -tricis *f); (of gladiators)* lanist·a -ae *m*
training *s* instituti·o -onis *f; (practice)* exercitati·o -onis *f*
train schedule *s* horar·ium -(i)i *n* traminum
train station *s* stati·o -onis *f* ferriviaria
train ticket *s* tesser·a -ae *f* ferriviaria
trait *s* mos, moris *m*
traitor *s* prodi·tor -toris *m* (·trix -tricis *f)*
traitorous *adj* perfid·us -a -um
tramp *s* vagabund·us -i *m* (·a -ae *f),* larifug·a -ae *m; (of feet)* puls·us -ūs *m*
tramp *intr* grad·ior -i gressus sum
trample *tr* proterere; **to — underfoot** conculcare ‖ *intr* **to — on** proterere
trampoline *s* desultor·ium -(i)i *n*
trance *s* stup·or -oris *m;* **in a —** in excessu mentis; **she fell into a —** cecidit super eam mentis excessus
tranquil *adj* tranquill·us -a -um
tranquility *s* tranquillit·as -atis *f*
tranquilize *tr* tranquillare
transact *tr* transigere, agere
transaction *s* negot·ium -(i)i *n*
transatlantic *adj* transatlantic·us -a -um
transcend *tr* superare, antecedere
transcendental *adj* sublim·is -is -e
transcribe *tr* transcribere
transcript *s* exempl·um -i *n*
transcription *s* transcripti·o -onis *f*
transfer *s* translati·o -onis *f; (of property)* alienati·o -onis *f*
transfer *tr* transferre; *(property)* abalienare ‖ *intr* **— to** *(another train, etc.)* transcendere in *(w. acc)*
transference *s* translati·o -onis *f*
transfigure *tr* transfigurare
transform *tr* vertere, commutare
transformation *s* commutati·o -onis *f*
transgress *tr* violare, perfringere
transgression *s* violati·o -onis *f; (deed)* delict·um -i *n*
transgressor *s* viola·tor -toris *m* (·trix -tricis *f)*
transient *adj* transitori·us -a -um
transition *s* transit·us -ūs *m*
transitive *adj* transitiv·us -a -um
transitively *adv* transitive
transitory *adj* transitori·us -a -um
translate *tr* (con)vertere, transferre; **to — into Latin** in Latinum (sermonem) convertere; **to — from Latin to English** ex Latino in Anglicum (con)vertere
translation *s* translat·a -orum *npl; (act of translating)* translati·o -onis *f*
translator *s* interpr·es -etis *mf*
transmission *s* transmissi·o -onis *f*
transmit *tr* transmittere
transmutation *s* transmutati·o -onis *f*
transparency *s* pagin·a -ae *f* pellucida
transparent *adj* pellucid·us -a -um; *(fig)* perspicu·us -a -um
transpire *intr (to happen)* fieri
transplant *tr* transferre, transponere; *(med)* inserere
transport *tr* transportare, transvehere
transport *s* vectur·a -ae *f; (ship)* nav·is -is *f* oneraria; *(rapture)* sublimit·as -atis *f*
transportation *s* vectur·a -ae *f*
transpose *tr* transponere
trap *s* laque·us -i *m,* pedic·a -ae *f; (fig)* insidi·ae -arum *fpl*
trap *tr* irretire; *(fig)* inlaqueare
trappings *spl* apparat·us -ūs *m; (of horse)* phaler·ae -arum *fpl*
trash *s* scrut·a -orum *npl; (fig)* nug·ae -arum *fpl*
trashy *adj (cheap)* vil·is -is -e; *(obscene)* obscen·us -a -um
travel *tr* **to — a road** viā ire ‖ *intr* iter facere; **to — abroad** peregrinari; **to — by car (train, plane, ship)** autoraedā (tramine, aëroplano, navi) vehor vehi vectus sum
travel agency *s* sed·es -is *f* perigetica
travel agent *s* itinerum procura·tor -toris *m* (·trix -tricis *f)*
traveler *s* viat·or -oris *mf; (abroad)* peregrina·tor -toris *m* (·trix -tricis *f)*
traverse *tr* peragrare, lustrare
travesty *s* perversa imitati·o -onis *f*
tray *s* fercul·um -i *n*
treacherous *adj* perfid·us -a -um; **to be on — ground** in lubrico versari
treacherously *adv* perfide
treachery *s* perfidi·a -ae *f*
tread *tr* calcare ‖ *intr* incedere; **to — on** insistere *(w. dat),* calcare
tread *s* incess·us -ūs *m*

treason *s* perduelli·o -onis *f,* maiest·as -atis *f*
treasonable *adj* perfid·us -a -um (contra civitatem)
treasure *s* thesaur·us -i *m,* gaz·a -ae *f*
treasure *tr* fovēre, magni aestimare
treasurer *s* aerari praefect·us -i *m* (·a -ae *f*)
treasury *s* arc·a -ae *f; (of the state)* aerar·ium -(i)i *n; (of the emperor)* fisc·us -i *m*
treat *s* oblectament·um -i *n;* **it's my —** meo sumptu convivium est
treat *tr* uti *(w. abl),* tractare; *(patient)* curare; *(topic)* tractare; *(to entertain)* impensam sumere pro *(w. abl)*
treatise *s* commentati·o -oni *f*
treatment *s* tractati·o -onis *f; (med)* **(for)** curati·o -onis *f (w. gen of illness)*
treaty *s* foed·us -eris *n;* **according to the terms of the —** ex pacto, ex foedere; **to break a —** foedus frangere; **to conclude a —** foedus icere; **to violate a —** foedus violare
treble *adj* tripl·ex -icis; *(of sound)* acut·us -a -um
tree *s* arb·or -oris *f*
treetop cacum·en -inis *n*
trellis *s* cancell·i -orum *mpl*
tremble *intr* tremere; **to — all over** contremere
trembling *adj* tremul·us -a -um
trembling *s* trem·or -oris *m*
tremendous *adj* imman·is -is -e
tremendously *adv* valde, vehementer
tremulous *adj* tremul·us -a -um
trench *s* foss·a -ae *f;* **to dig a —** fossam fodere
trend *s* inclinati·o -onis *f*
trespass *intr* in alienum fundum ingredi (sine domini permissu)
trespass *n* peccat·um -i *n*
tress *s* crin·is -is *m*
trestle *s* fulciment·um -i *n*
trial *s (attempt)* conat·us -ūs *m; (experiment)* experienti·a -ae *f; (test)* probati·o -onis *f; (suffering)* tribulati·o -onis *f; (leg)* quaesti·o -onis *f;* iudic·ium -(i)i *n;* **to be on — for** iudicium de *(w. abl)* subire; **to conduct a —** quaestionem exercēre; **to go to —** in ius ire
trial lawyer *s* ac·tor -toris *m* (·trix -tricis *f*) causarum
triangle *s* triangul·um -i *n*
triangular *adj* triquetr·us -a -um
tribe *s* trib·us -ūs *f*
tribulation *s* tribulati·o -onis *f*
tribunal *s (law court)* iudic·ium -(i)i *n; (platform)* tribun·al -alis *n;* **on the —** pro tribunali
tribune *s* tribun·us -i *m;* **plebeian —** tribunus plebis
tribuneship *s* tribunat·us -ūs *m*
tribunician power *s* tribunicia potest·as -atis *f*
tributary *adj* vectigal·is -is -e
tributary *s (river)* amn·is -is *m* in alium influens
tribute *s* vectig·al -alis *n,* tribut·um -i *n;* **to pay a — to s.o.** aliquem laudibus debitis efferre
trick *s* dol·us -i *m; (feat of skill)* stroph·a -ae *f;* **is this a — ?** num hoc est captio?; **to play a — on s.o.** aliquem ludificari
trick *tr* fallere, deludere
trickle *s* stillicid·ium -(i)i *n*
trickle *intr* stillare
trickster *s* veterat·or -oris *mf*
tricky *adj* dolos·us -a -um; *(difficult)* nodos·us -a -um
tricycle *s* trirot·a -ae *f*
trident *s* trid·ens -entis *m*
triennial *adj* trienn·is -is -e
trifle *s* res, rei *f* parva; *(a little)* paul·um -i *n; (somewhat)* paululum; **—s** nug·ae -arum *fpl*
trifle *intr* nugari
trifling *adj* parv·us -a -um, exigu·us -a -um
trigger *s* ligul·a -ae *f* (sclopeti)
trigger *tr (fig)* facessere
trigonometry *s* trigonometri·a -ae *f*
trill *tr* vibrare
trim *adj* compt·us -a -um
trim *tr* adornare; *(to prune)* putare; *(the hair)* tondēre
trim *s* **to be in —** boni habitūs esse
trimmings *spl* ornat·us -ūs *m*
trinket *s* ornament·um -i *n*
trio *s* trini·o -onis *f*
trip *s* it·er -ineris *n;* **to take a —** iter facere
trip *tr* pedem opponere *(w. dat); (fig)* fallere **||** *intr* pedem offendere; *(fig)* errare, labi
tripartite *adj* tripartit·us -a -um
tripe *s* omas·um -i *n*
triple *adj* tripl·ex -icis
triple *tr* triplicare
triplets *s* trigemin·i -orum *mpl*
tripod *s* trip·us -odis *m* (photographicus)
trireme *s* trirem·is -is *f*
trisyllabic *adj* trisyllab·us -a -um
trite *adj* trit·us -a -um
triumph *s (victory)* victori·a -ae *f; (entry of victorious general)* triumph·us -i *m;* **to celebrate a —** triumphum agere
triumph *intr* triumphare; **to — over** devincere; *(of a general)* triumphare de *(w. abl)*
triumphal *adj* triumphal·is -is -e
triumphant *adj (masc)* vict·or -oris; *(fem)* victr·ix -icis
trivial *adj* lev·is -is -e
triviality *s* nug·ae -arum *fpl*
trolley *s* curr·us -ūs *m* electricus
trombone *s* tub·a -ae *f* ductilis
troop *s* caterv·a -ae *f; (of cavalry)* turm·a -ae *f;* **—s** copi·ae -arum *fpl*
trooper *s (coll)* veteran·us -i *m*
trophy *s* tropae·um -i *n*

tropical *adj* torrid·us -a -um
tropics *spl* zon·a -ae *f* torrida
trot *intr* tolutim ire
trouble *s* mal·um -i *n,* lab·or -oris *m,* aerumn·a -ae *f; (annoyance)* molesti·a -ae *f; (effort, pains)* oper·a -ae *f;* **if it is no —** si grave non erit; **it's not worth the —** non est pretium operae; **to be in —** laborare; **to cause s.o. (big) —** alicui molestiam (gravem) adhibēre; **to get s.o. into —** in aliquem aerumnam obserere; **to have stomach —** stomacho laborare; **to make a heap of — for s.o.** magnum malum alicui dare; **to take the — to ...** operam dare ut *(w. subj);* **what's the —?** quid negoti est?
trouble *tr* vexare, angere; **I don't want to — you** nolo tibi molest·us (-a) esse
troubled *adj* confus·us -a -um; *(times)* turbulent·us -a -um; **— face** vult·us -ūs *m* exercitatus; **to be — with** laborare ex *(w. abl)*
troublemaker *s* turba·tor -toris *m* (·trix -tricis *f*)
troublesome *adj* operos·us -a -um; *(person)* molest·us -a -um
trough *s* alve·us -i *m*
trounce *tr (to punish)* castigare; *(to defeat decisively)* devincere
troupe *s* gre·x -gis *m*
trousers *spl* brac·ae -arum *fpl*
trout *s* truct·a -ae *f*
trowel *s* trull·a -ae *f*
truant *s* cessa·tor -toris *m* (·trix -tricis *f*); **to play —** insciis parentibus a scholā abesse
truce *s* induti·ae -arum *fpl;* **during the —** per indutias; **to agree to a —** indutias cum hostibus pacisci; **to break off a —** indutias tollere
truck *s* autocarr·um -i *n*
truck driver autocarri gubernat·or -oris *m*
trudge *intr* repere; **to — over many places** plura loca calcare
true *adj* ver·us -a -um; *(genuine)* german·us -a -um; *(faithful)* fid·us -a -um; *(exact)* rect·us -a -um; **that's —** verum dicis *or* res ita est
truffle *s* tub·er -eris *n* (cibarium)
truism *s* ver·um -i *n* tritum
truly *adv* vere, profecto
trump *tr* **to — up** effingere
trumpet *s (mil)* tub·a -ae *f,* aes, aeris *n; (for civilian purposes)* buccin·a -ae *f; (of an elephant)* barrit·us -ūs *m*
trumpet *intr (of an elephant)* barrire
trumpeter *s* buccinat·or -oris *m*
truncheon *s* fust·is -is *m*
trundle *intr* volvere
trunk *s (of tree, of body)* trunc·us -i *m; (for clothes)* cist·a -ae *f; (of car)* receptacul·um -i *n* sarcinarum; *(of elephant)* probosc·is -is *f,* man·us -ūs *f*
trust *s* fiduci·a -ae *f,* fid·es -ei *f;* **to put one's — in** (con)fidere *(w. dat)*
trust *tr (persons or acts)* fidere *(w. dat); (esp. words spoken)* credere *(w. dat); (to entrust)* committere; **not — his eyes** fidem oculorum timēre **||** *intr* **to — in** fidere *(w. dat)*
trustee *s* fiduciari·us -i *m* (·a -ae *f*)
trusteeship *s* tutel·a -ae *f*
trustful *adj* credul·us -a -um
trusting *adj* (con)fid·ens -entis
trustingly *adv* fidenter
trustworthiness *s* fid·es -ei *f*
trustworthy *adj* fid·us -a -um; *(witness)* locupl·es -etis
trusty *adj* fid·us -a -um
truth *s (abstract)* verit·as -atis *f; (concrete)* ver·um -i *n;* **in —** vero; **this is the —** haec sunt vera; **to speak the —** verum dicere; **to tell the —** ut verum *(or* vera) dicam *(or* loquar)
truthful *adj* ver·ax -acis
truthfully *adv* veraciter
try *tr* conari, tentare, temptare; *(to put to the test)* experiri; *(leg)* iudicare; *(to hold a judicial inquiry of)* cognoscere; **to — a case (of)** causam cognoscere (de *w. abl);* **to — one's best to (not to)** operam dare ut (ne) *(w. subj);* **to — one's patience** patientiā abuti; **to — to obtain** affectare
trying *adj* incommod·us -a -um, molest·us -a -um
tryout *s* prolusi·o -onis *f*
T-shirt *s* colob·ium -(i)i *n*
tub *s* labr·um -i *n*
tube *s* tubul·us -i *m,* fistul·a -ae *f*
tuberculosis *s* phithis·is -is *f*
tuck *s* plic·a -ae *f*
tuck *tr* **to — up** succingere; **with tunic —ed up** succinct·us -a -um
Tuesday *s* di·es -ei *m* Martis
tufa *s* tof·us *or* toph·us -i *m*
tuft *s* flocc·us -i *m*
tug *s* tract·us -ūs *m; (ship)* nav·is -is *f* tractoria
tug *tr* trahere **||** *intr* **to — at** vellicare
tugboat *s* nav·is -is *f* tractoria
tuition *s* minerv·al -alis *n*
tumble *intr* volvi, corruere
tumbler *s* pocul·um -i *n* vitreum
tumor *s* tum·or -oris *m*
tumult *s* tumult·us -ūs *m*
tumultuous *adj* tumultuos·us -a -um
tuna *s* thunn·us -i *m*
tune *s* cant·us -ūs *m;* **in —** conson·us -a -um; **out of —** abson·us -a -um; **to be out of —** discrepare; **to change one's —** recantare; **to the — of** ad numerum *(w. gen)*
tuneful *adj* canor·us -a -um
tunic *s* tunic·a -ae *f;* **long-sleeved —** tunica *f* manicata; **small —** tunicul·a -ae *f;* **—**

reaching to the ankles tunica *f* talaris; **wearing a —** tunicat·us -a -um
tunnel *s* cunicul·us -i *m*; *(for cars, trains)* spec·us -ūs *m* (autocineticus, ferriviarius)
turban *s* mitr·a -ae *f*
turbid *adj* turbid·us -a -um
turbulence *s* agitati·o -onis *f; (air)* flabr·a -orum *npl* violenta
turbulent *adj* turbulent·us -a -um
turf *s* caesp·es -itis *m*
turgid *adj* turgid·us -a -um
turkey *s* gallopav·o -onis *m;* **to talk —** *(coll)* Latine loqui
turmoil *s* perturbati·o -onis *f;* **mental —** animi commoti·o -onis *f*
turn *s (in the road)* flex·us -ūs *m* viae, anfract·us -ūs *m; (circuit)* circuit·us -ūs *m; (revolution)* conversi·o -onis *f; (change, course)* vicissitud·o -inis *f; (inclination of the mind)* inclinati·o -onis *f;* **a good —** benefic·ium -(i)i *n;* **at every —** omnibus ex partibus; **in —** invicem; **it's your — now** nunc te ordo vocat; **out of —** extra ordinem; **to take a — for the better, worse** in melius, in peius inclinari; **to take —s driving** invicem *(or* per vices, in vices) gubernare
turn *tr* (con)vertere; *(to twist)* torquēre; *(to bend)* flectere; **to — around** circumagere, volvere; **to — aside** deflectere; **to — away** avertere; **to — back** convertere; **to — down** *(to refuse)* recusare, detrectare; **to — into** vertere in *(w. acc);* **to — loose** liberare; **to — off** *(computer, light)* exstinguere; **to — on** *(light)* accendere; *(computer)* excitare; **to — over** *(to hand over)* tradere; *(property)* alienare; *(in the mind)* agitare; *(to upset)* evertere; **to — over a new leaf** se reformare; **to — over the pages of a book** librum evolvere; **to — one's attention to** animadvertere; **to — out** eicere; **to — up** *(w. hoe)* invertere; **to — up the nose** nares corrugare; **to — upside down** quod sursum est, deorsum facere ‖ *intr* verti, versari; **something will turn up, I hope** fiet aliquid, spero; **to — against** disciscere ab *(w. abl);* **to — around** converti; **to — aside** se declinare; **to — away** aversari; **to — back** reverti; **to — into** mutari in *(w. acc),* vertere in *(w. acc);* **to — out** evenire, evadere; **to — out fine** belle cadere; **to — up** *(to occur)* intervenire; *(to show up)* apparēre
turncoat *s* transfug·a -ae *mf*
turnip *s* rap·um -i *n*
turn-off *s* deverticul·um -i *n*
turnout *s* concurs·us -ūs *m*
turnpike *s* autocinetica vi·a -ae *f* quadripertita
turn signal *s* ind·ex -icis *m* directionis
turnstile *s* port·a -ae *f* volubilis
turpentine *s* terebinthina resin·a -ae *f*
turquoise *adj* turcic·us -a -um
turret *s* turricul·a -ae *f*
turtle *s* testud·o -inis *f*
tusk *s* den·s -tis *m*
tutelage *s* tutel·a -ae *f*
tutor *s* domesticus praecep·tor -toris *m,* domestica praecep·trix -tricis *f*
tutor *tr* privatim instituere
TV *(see* **television)**
TV room *s* conclav·e -is *n* televisorio instructum
tweezers *spl* volsell·a -ae *f*
twelfth *adj* duodecim·us -a -um
twelve *adj* duodecim [*indecl*]; **— times** duodecies
twentieth *adj* vicesim·us -a -um
twenty *adj* viginti [*indecl*]; **— times** vicies
twice *adv* bis
twig *s* ramul·us -i *m*
twilight *s (evening)* crepuscul·um -i *n; (early dawn)* dilucul·um -i *n*
twilight *adj* sublucan·us -a -um
twin *adj* gemin·us -a -um
twin *s* gemin·us -i *m* (·a -ae *f),* gemell·us -i *m* (·a -ae *f)*
twine *s* fil·um -i *n*
twine *tr* circumplicare ‖ *intr* **to — around** circumplecti *(w. acc)*
twinge *s* dol·or -oris *m;* **to suffer such —s of conscience that** ita conscientia mentem excitam vexat ut
twinkle *s* nit·or -oris *m,* scintill·a -ae *f; (in one's eyes)* nict·us -ūs *m*
twinkle *intr* micare
twinkling *s (of eye)* nict·us -ūs *m*
twirl *tr* versare, circumagere ‖ *intr* versari
twist *tr* torquēre ‖ *intr* se torquēre
twit *tr* obiurgare
twitch *s* vellicati·o -onis *f*
twitch *tr* vellicare ‖ *intr* formicare
twitter *s* pipul·um -i *n*
twitter *intr* pipilare
two *adj* duo, duae, duo; **— at a time, two each** bin·i -ae -a; **— camps** bina castr·a -orum *npl;* **— times** bis
two-bit *adj (worthless)* sestertiari·us -a -um
two-edged *adj* anc·eps -ipitis; **— ax** bipenn·is -is *f*
two-faced *adj (pej)* bilingu·is -is -e
twofold *adj* dupl·ex -icis
two-footed *adj* bip·es -edis
two-headed *adj* bic·eps -ipitis
two hundred *adj* ducent·i -ae -a
two-pronged *adj* bid·ens -entis
twosome *s* par, paris *n*
two-time *tr* fraudare
two-timer *s* infidel·is is *mf*
two-way *adj* bivi·us -a -um
tycoon *s* magnat·us -i *m*
type *s* exempl·um -i *n; (class)* gen·us -eris *n; (print)* typ·i -orum *mpl;* **that — of person** istius generis homo; **this — of speech** huius generis orati·o -onis *f*

type *tr* dactylographare
typesetter *s* typothet·a -ae *m* (·ria -riae *f*)
typewriter *s* dactylograph·ium -(i)i *n*
typewriter key *s* malleol·us -i *m*
typing *s* dactylphraphica ar·s -tis *f*
typist *s* dactylograph·us -i *m* (·a -ae *f*)
typhoon *s* turb·o -inis *f* violenta
typical *adj* typic·us -a -um
typically *adv* per typum
typify *tr* repraesentare, imaginem *(w. gen)* fingere
typist *s* scrib·a -ae *mf*
tyrannical *adj* tyrannic·us -a -um
tyrannically *adv* tyrannice
tyrannicide *s (act)* tyrannicid·ium -(i)i *n; (person)* tyrannicid·a -ae *m*
tyrant *s* tyrann·us -i *m*
tyranny *s* tyrann·is -idis *f*
tyro *s* tir·o -onis *mf*
Tyrrhenian *adj* Tyrrhenic·us -a -um

U

ubiquitous *adj* ubique praes·ens -entis
udder *s* ub·er -eris *n*
ugh *interj* vah!; heu!
ugliness *s* deformit·as -atis *f*
ugly *adj* deform·is -is -e; **to make —** deformare
uh-oh *interj (when taken by surprise)* attat!; attatae!
ulcer *s* ulc·us -eris *n*
ulcerate *intr* ulcerari
ulcerous *adj* ulceros·us -a -um
ulterior *adj (place)* ulter·ior -ior -ius; *(time)* poster·us -a -um; **— motive** rati·o -onis *f* recondita
ultimate *adj* ultim·us -a -um
ultimately *adv* ad ultimum, denique
ultimatum *s* propositi·o -onis *f* ultima
umbilical cord *s* umbilic·us -i *m*
umbrage *s* **to take — at** aegre ferre
umbrella *s* umbell·a -ae *f*
umpire *s* arbi·ter -tri *m* (·tra -trae *f*)
unabashed *adj* intrepid·us -a -um; *(pej)* impud·ens -entis
unabated *adj* continu·us -a -um
unable *adj* **(to)** nequi·ens -entis *(w. inf);* **— to control his anger** impot·ens -entis irae; **— to keep up with the words of the speaker** male subsequ·ens -entis verba dicentis; **to be — to** non posse *or* nequire *(w. inf)*
unabridged *s* complet·us -a -um
unaccented *adj* accentu car·ens -entis, sine ictu
unacceptable *adj* **(to)** invis·us -a -um *(w. dat)*
unaccompanied *adj* incomitat·us -a -um
unaccomplished *adj* infect·us -a -um
unaccountable *adj* inenodabil·is -is -e
unaccountably *adv* praeter opinionem
unaccustomed *adj* insuet·us -a -um
unacquainted *adj* **— with** ignar·us -a -um *(w. gen),* exper·s -tis *(w. gen)*
unadorned *adj* inornat·us -a -um
unadulterated *adj* mer·us -a -um
unaffected *adj* simpl·ex -icis
unafraid *adj* impavid·us -a -um
unaided *adj* non adiut·us -a -um
unalterable *adj* immutabil·is -is -e
unaltered *adj* immutat·us -a -um
unanimous *adj* unanim·us -a -um
unanimously *adv* consensu omnium, unā voce
unanswerable *adj* irrefragabil·is -is -e
unappeased *adj* implacat·us -a -um
unappreciative *adj* ingrat·us -a -um
unapproachable *adj* inaccess·us -a -um
unarmed *adj* inerm·is -is -e
unasked *adj* iniuss·us -a -um
unassailable *adj* inexpugnabil·is -is -e
unassuming *adj* modest·us -a -um
unattached *adj* vacu·us -a -um, solut·us -a -um; *(unmarried)* cael·eb·s -ebis
unattainable *adj* ardu·us -a -um, inaccess·us -a -um
unattended *adj (unaccompanied)* sine comitatu; *(not cared for)* neglect·us -a -um; **— by pain** privat·us -a -um dolore
unattractive *adj* invenust·us -a -um
unauthorized *adj* illicit·us -a -um
unavailable *adj* non expedit·us -a -um
unavailing *adj* inutil·is -is -e
unavenged *adj* inult·us -a -um
unavoidable *adj* inevitabil·is -is -e
unaware *adj* insci·us -a -um
unbearable *adj* intolerabil·is -is -e
unbeaten *adj* invict·us -a -um
unbecoming *adj* indecor·us -a -um; **it is —** dedecet
unbefitting *adj* indecor·us -a -um
unbend *intr* animum remittere
unbending *adj* inflexibil·is -is -e
unbiased *adj* sine ira et studio
unbidden *adj* iniuss·us -a -um
unbind *tr* revincire
unbleached *adj* crud·us -a -um
unblemished *adj* intact·us -a -um
unblest *adj* infortunat·us -a -um
unbolt *tr* reserare
unborn *adj* nondum nat·us -a -um
unbounded *adj* infinit·us -a -um
unbridled *adj (lit & fig)* infren·is -is -e
unbroken *adj* irrupt·us -a -um; *(of horses)* indomit·us -a -um
unbuckle *tr* refibulare
unburden *tr* exonerare
unburied *adj* inhumat·us -a -um
unbutton *tr* diloricare
uncalled-for *adj* alien·us -a -um
uncanny *adj* mir·us -a -um
uncared-for *adj* neglect·us -a -um
unceasing *adj* assidu·us -a -um
unceasingly *adv* assidue, sine fine

uncertain *adj* incert·us -a -um; **to be —** haerēre, vacillare
uncertainty *s* dubitati·o -onis *f*
unchangeable *adj* immutabil·is -is -e
unchanged *adj* immutat·us -a -um
unchanging *adj* immutat·us -a -um
uncharitable *adj* immisericor·s -dis
unchaste *adj* parum cast·us -a -um
uncivil *adj* inurban·us -a -um
uncivilized *adj* incult·us -a -um
unclasp *tr* refibulare
uncle *s (father's brother)* patru·us -i *m; (mother's brother)* avuncul·us -i *m;* **great —** magnus patruus *(or* avunculus) *m*
unclean *adj* immund·us -a -um
uncombed *adj* inpex·us -a -um
uncomfortable *adj* incommod·us -a -um
uncommon *adj* rar·us -a -um; *(outstanding)* egregi·us -a -um
uncommonly *adv* praeter solitum
uncomplaining *adj* pati·ens -entis
unconcerned *adj* incurios·us -a -um
unconditional *adj* sine exceptione
unconditionally *adv* nullā condicione
unconnected *adj* disiunct·us -a -um
unconquerable *adj* invict·us -a -um
unconscionable *adj* iniqu·us -a -um
unconscious *adj* omni sensu car·ens -entis; **— of** ignar·us -a -um *(w. gen)*, insci·us -a -um *(w. gen)*
unconstitutional *adj* illicit·us -a -um
uncontrollable *adj* impot·ens -entis
uncontrolled *adj* effrenat·us -a -um
unconventional *adj* insolit·us -a -um
unconvinced *adj* **I am — that** non adductus sum ut credam *(w. acc & inf)*
unconvincing *adj* non verisimil·is -is -e
uncooked *adj* crud·us -a -um
uncorrupted *adj* incorrupt·us -a -um
uncouth *adj* inurban·us -a -um
uncover *tr* detegere
uncritical *adj* credul·us -a -um
uncultivated *adj* incult·us -a -um
uncut *adj (hair)* intons·us -a -um; *(wood)* incaedu·us -a -um
undamaged *adj* incolum·is -is -e
undaunted *adj* intrepid·us -a -um
undecided *adj* anc·eps -ipitis; **— whether … or** cunctat·us -a -um utrum … an
undefended *adj* indefens·us -a -um
undefiled *adj* incontaminat·us -a -um
undeniable *adj* haud dubi·us -a -um
under *adv* subter, infra
under *prep (position)* sub *(w. abl); (motion)* sub, subter *(w. acc); (less than)* infra *(w. acc);* **— the appearance of** sub specie *(w. gen);* **— the pretense of** per simulationem *(w. gen)*
underage *adj* impub·es -is
underbid *tr* minoris faciendum conducere
underbrush *s* frutect·um -i *n,* dumet·a -orum *npl*
undercover *adj* abdit·us -a -um, secret·us -a -um
undercover agent *s* emissari·us -i *m* (·a -ae *f)*
undercurrent *s* torr·ens -entis *m* subterfluens; **— of feeling** intimus animi sens·us -ūs *m*
underdone *adj* semicrud·us -a -um
underestimate *tr* minoris aestimare
underfoot *adv* obvi·us -a -um
undergarment *s* subucul·a -ae *f; (worn chiefly by women)* suppar·um -i *n*
undergo *tr* subire; **to — change** se mutare; **to — punishment** poenam dare
underground *adj* subterrane·us -a -um
undergrowth *s* virgult·a -orum *npl*
underhanded *adj* clandestin·us -a -um
underhandedly *adv* clam, furtim
underline *tr* subnotare
underling *s* minis·ter -tri *m*
undermine *tr* subruere; *(fig)* labefactare
underneath *adv* infra, subter
underneath *prep (position)* infra *(w. acc),* sub *(w. abl); (motion)* sub *(w. acc)*
underpants *spl* brac·ae -arum *fpl* interiores
underpass *s* viaeduct·us -ūs *m*
underpin *tr* fulcire
underpinnings *spl* fulciment·a -orum *npl*
underrate *tr* minoris aestimare
undershirt *s* subucul·a -ae *f*
understand *tr* intellegere; *(a language or art)* scire; **do you — now?** iam tenes?; **I don't quite —** non satis intellego; **"ego" is understood if I should say: "sum philosophus"** subauditur "ego" si dicam "philosophus sum"; **to — Latin** Latine scire
understanding *adj* prud·ens -entis
understanding *s* intellect·us -ūs *m; (agreement)* consens·us -ūs *m; (condition)* condici·o -onis *f*
undertake *tr* adire ad *(w. acc),* suscipere; *(to begin)* incipere
undertaker *s* pollinc·tor -toris *m* (·trix -tricis *f)*
undertaking *s* incept·um -i *n*
undervalue *tr* minoris aestimare
underwear *s* subucul·a -ae *f*
underworld *s* infer·i -orum *mpl; (criminals)* inhonest·i -orum *mpl*
undeserved *adj* immerit·us -a -um
undeservedly *adv* immerito
undeserving *adj* **(of)** indign·us -a -um *(w. abl)*
undeveloped *adj* incult·us -a -um
undignified *adj* indecor·us -a -um
undiminished *adj* imminut·us -a -um
undiscernible *adj* impercept·us -a -um
undiscerning *adj* heb·es -etis
undisciplined *adj* immoderat·us -a -um; *(mil)* inexercitat·us -a -um
undisguised *adj* apert·us -a -um
undismayed *adj* interrit·us -a -um

undisputed *adj* cert·us -a -um; **since this is —** cum hoc constet
undistinguished *adj* ignobil·is -is -e
undisturbed *adj* imperturbat·us -a -um; **— peace** immota pa·x -cis *f*
undivided *adj* indivis·us -a -um
undo *tr (knot)* solvere; *(fig)* infectum reddere, irritum facere; *(to ruin)* perdere; **you have undone everything** omnia irrita fecisti
undone *adj (ruined)* perdit·us -a -um; **to be —** *(to be ruined)* perire
undoubted *adj* haud dubi·us -a -um
undoubtedly *adv* haud dubie, nimirum
undress *tr* exuere; **to get undressed** vestimenta exuere **‖** *intr* se exuere
undue *adj (excessive)* nimi·us -a -um; *(unfair)* iniqu·us -a -um
undulate *intr* undare, fluctuare
undulating *adj* undulabund·us -a -um
undulation *s* undarum agitati·o -onis *f*
unduly *adv* nimis, plus aequo
undying *adj* aetern·us -a -um
unearth *tr* effodere; *(fig)* detegere
unearthly *adj* haud mortal·is -is -e, caelest·is -is -e
uneasily *adv* turbate; **to sleep —** male dormire
uneasiness *s* sollicitud·o -inis *f*
uneasy *adj* sollicit·us -a -um
uneducated *adj* indoct·us -a -um
unemployed *adj* otios·us -a -um; **to be —** cessare
unemployment *s* cessati·o -onis *f*
unencumbered *adj* expedit·us -a -um
unending *adj* infinit·us -a -um, perpetu·us -a -um
unendurable *adj* intolerand·us -a -um
unenjoyable *adj* iniucund·us -a -um
unenlightened *adj* inerudit·us -a -um
unenviable *adj* non invidend·us -a -um
unequal *adj* inaequal·is -is -e; **— to** im·par -paris *(w. dat)*
unequalled *adj* singular·is -is -e
unequally *adv* impariter
unerring *adj* cert·us -a -um
unerringly *adv* certe
uneven *adj* iniqu·us -a -um; *(rough)* asp·er -era -erum
unevenness *s* iniquit·as -atis *f*
unexpected *adj* inopinat·us -a -um; *(unforeseen)* improvis·us -a -um
unexpectedly *adv* de improviso
unexplored *adj* inexplorat·us -a -um
unfading *adj* semper rec·ens -entis; *(fig)* perenn·is -is -e
unfailing *adj (friend)* cert·us -a -um; *(waters)* perenn·is -is -e
unfair *adj* iniqu·us -a -um
unfairly *adv* inique
unfaithful *adj* infid·us -a -um; *(adulterous)* adult·er -era -erum
unfamiliar *adj* ignot·us -a -um
unfamiliarity *s* **(with)** imprudenti·a -ae *f* *(w. gen)*
unfashionable *adj* obsolet·us -a -um, non ad morem
unfasten *tr* resolvere, laxare
unfavorable *adj* iniqu·us -a -um; **— and favorable omens** omin·a -um *npl* tristia et laeta
unfavorably *adv* male, inique
unfed *adj* impast·us -a -um
unfeeling *adj* dur·us -a -um
unfetter *tr* vincula demere *(w. dat)*
unfinished *adj* imperfect·us -a -um; *(crude)* rud·is -is -e
unfit *adj* inept·us -a -um; *(not qualified)* inhabil·is -is -e
unfold *tr* explicare; *(story)* enarrare **‖** *intr* patescere
unforeseen *adj* improvis·us -a -um
unforgiving *adj* inexorabil·is -is -e
unfortified *adj* immunit·us -a -um
unfortunate *adj* infel·ix -icis
unfortunately *adv* infeliciter; **—, it rained** male accidit quod pluit
unfounded *adj* van·us -a -um
unfriendliness *s* inimiciti·a -ae *f*
unfriendly *adj* parum amic·us -a -um, inimic·us -a -um; **in an — manner** inimice
unfruitful *adj* infecund·us -a -um; *(ineffective)* irrit·us -a -um
unfurl *tr* pand·o -ere -i pansus *or* passus
unfurnished *adj* imparat·us -a -um, nud·us -a -um
ungainly *adj* inhabil·is -is -e
ungenerous *adj* illiberal·is -is -e
ungentlemanly *adj* inurban·us -a -um
ungird *tr* dis·cingo -cingere -cinxi -cinctus
ungodly *adj* impi·us -a -um; *(wicked)* nefand·us -a -um; *(coll)* immoderat·us -a -um
ungovernable *adj* intractabil·is -is -e
ungraceful *adj* inconcinn·us -a -um
ungracious *adj* illepid·us -a -um
ungrateful *adj* ingrat·us -a -um
ungratefully *adv* ingrate
ungrudging *adj* non invit·us -a -um
ungrudgingly *adv* sine invidia
unguarded *adj* incustodit·us -a -um; *(of words)* inconsult·us -a -um
unhandy *adj* inhabil·is -is -e
unhappily *adv* infeliciter
unhappiness *s* infelicit·as -atis *f*
unhappy *adj* infel·ix -icis
unharness *tr* disiungere
unhealthiness *s* mala valetud·o -inis *f; (of a place)* gravit·as -atis *f*
unhealthy *adj* infirm·us -a -um, morbos·us -a -um; *(place, season, wind)* grav·is -is -e
unheard-of *adj* inaudit·us -a -um
unheeded *adj* neglect·us -a -um
unheroic *adj* ignav·us -a -um
unhesitating *adj* prompt·us -a -um

unhindered *adj* expedit·us -a -um
unhinge *tr* de cardine detrahere; *(fig)* perturbare
unholy *adj* impi·us -a -um
unhoped-for *adj* insperat·us -a -um
unhurt *adj* incolum·is -is -e
unicorn *s* monocer·os -otis *m*
uniform *adj* aequabil·is -is -e, const·ans -antis
uniform *s* ornat·us -ūs *m; (mil)* ornat·us -ūs *m* militaris; **in —** subornat·us -a -um
uniformed *adj* subornat·us -a -um
uniformity *s* aequabilit·as -atis *f*
uniformly *adv* aequabiliter
unify *tr* coniungere, solidare
unilateral *adj* de uno latere tantummodo
unimaginable *adj* supra animi vires
unimaginative *adj* heb·es -etis
unimpaired *adj* inte·ger -gra -grum
unimpeachable *adj* probatissim·us -a -um
unimportant *adj* parv·us -a -um
uninformed *adj* indoct·us -a -um
uninhabitable *adj* inhabitabil·is -is -e
uninhabited *adj* desert·us -a -um
uninjured *adj* incolum·is -is -e
uninspired *adj* non inspirat·us -a -um
unintelligible *adj* incomprehensibil·is -is -e, obscur·us -a -um
uninteresting *adj* ieiun·us -a -um, frigid·us -a -um
uninterrupted *adj* continu·us -a -um
uninviting *adj* iniucund·us -a -um
union *s (act)* coniuncti·o -onis *f; (social)* societ·as -atis *f; (agreement)* consens·us -ūs *m; (marriage)* coniug·ium -(i)i *n; (of workers)* syndicat·us -ūs *m*
unique *adj* unic·us -a -um
unison *s* concent·us -ūs *m;* **to sing in —** unā voce canere
unit *s* unit·as -atis *f,* mon·as -adis *f*
unite *tr* coniungere; *(to make into one)* unire ‖ *intr* coïre, coalescere
united *adj* consociat·us -a -um; **— opposition** *(pol)* conspirati·o -onis *f*
United States (of America) Uniti Statūs (Americae) *(gen:* Unitorum Statuum); Civitat·es -um *fpl* Foederat·ae -arum (Americae)
unity *s* unit·as -atis *f*
universal *adj* universal·is -is -e
universally *adv* universe
universe *s* universit·as -atis *f*
university *s* (studiorum) universit·as -atis *f*
unjust *adj* uniust·us -a -um
unjustly *adv* iniuste
unjustifiable *adj* quod nihil excusationis habet
unkempt *adj* incompt·us -a -um
unkind *adj* inhuman·us -a -um
unkindly *adv* inhumane
unknowingly *adv* inscienter
unknown *adj* ignot·us -a -um; **— to his wife** clam uxorem
unlawful *adj* contra ius, illicit·us -a -um; *(w. reference to state law)* contra legem; **it is — to** nefas est *(w. inf)*
unlawfully *adv* contra legem *(or* leges)
unleavened *adj* non fermentat·us -a -um; **— bread** pan·is -is *m* azymus, panis sine fermento
unless *conj* nisi
unlike *adj* dissimil·is -is -e; **it is not — going** non est dissimile atque ire
unlimited *adj* infinit·us -a -um
unload *tr* exonerare
unlock *tr* reserare; **with the door unlocked** reseratis foribus
unlooked-for *adj* inopinat·us -a -um
unluckily *adv* infeliciter
unlucky *adj* infel·ix -icis; *(omen)* infaust·us -a -um; **— day** di·es -ei *m* ater
unmanageable *adj* intractabil·is -is -e
unmanly *adj* moll·is -is -e
unmannerly *adj* male morat·us -a -um, inurban·us -a -um
unmarried *adj (man)* cael·ebs -ibis; *(woman)* innupta
unmask *tr* detegere
unmatched *adj* singular·is -is -e
unmerciful *adj* immisericor·s -dis
unmercifully *adv* immisericorditer
unmistakable *adj* evid·ens -entis, cert·us -a -um
unmistakably *adv* sine dubio
unmoved *adj* immot·us -a -um
unnatural *adj* contra naturam; *(event)* monstruos·us -a -um; *(deed)* imman·is -is -e
unnaturally *adv* contra naturam
unnecessarily *adv* ex supervacuo
unnecessary *adj* haud necessari·us -a -um
unnerve *tr* debilitare
unnoticed *adj* praetermiss·us -a -um; **to go — by** latēre inter *(w. acc)*
unobjectionable *adj* culpā exper·s -tis
unoccupied *adj* vacu·us -a -um; *(land)* apert·us -a -um; **to be —** vacare
unofficial *adj* privat·us -a -um
unpack *tr* e cistis eximere
unpaid *adj (of money)* debit·us -a -um; *(of service)* gratuit·us -a -um
unpalatable *adj* insuav·is -is -e
unparalleled *adj* singular·is -is -e
unpardonable *adj* cui ignosci non potest, inexcusabil·is -is -e
unpatriotic *adj* immem·or -oris patriae
unpaved *adj* instrat·us -a -um
unpleasant *adj* iniucund·us -a -um
unpleasantly *adv* iniucunde
unpolished *adj* impolit·us -a -um
unpolluted *adj* impollut·us -a -um; *(fig)* intact·us -a -um
unpopular *adj* invis·us -a -um
unpopularity *s* invidi·a -ae *f*
unpracticed *adj* inexpert·us -a -um
unprecedented *adj* inaudit·us -a -um

unprejudiced *adj* aequ·us -a -um
unpremeditated *adj* inconsult·us -a -um, subit·us -a -um
unprepared *adj* imparat·us -a -um
unpretentious *adj* demiss·us -a -um
unprincipled *adj* improb·us -a -um
unproductive *adj* infecund·us -a -um
unprofitable *adj* inutil·is -is -e, van·us -a -um
unprofitably *adv* nullis fructibus
unprotected *adj* indefens·us -a -um
unprovoked *adj* ultro
unpunished *adj* inpunit·us -a -um; **to allow a crime to go —** maleficium impune habēre
unqualified *adj* haud idone·us -a -um; *(complete)* consummat·us -a -um
unquenchable *adj* inexstinct·us -a -um
unquestionable *adj* certissim·us -a -um
unquestionably *adv* facile
unquestioning *adj* credul·us -a -um
unravel *tr* retexere; *(fig)* enodare
unreasonable *adj* absurd·us -a -um
unreasonably *adv* absurde
unrefined *adj* crud·us -a -um
unrelenting *adj* inplacabil·is -is -e
unremitting *adj* assidu·us -a -um
unrepentant *adj* impaenit·ens -entis
unrest *s (outbreak of disorder)* inquietud·o -inis *f*
unrestrained *adj* effrenat·us -a -um
unrighteous *adj* iniust·us -a -um
unripe *adj* immatur·us -a -um
unrivaled *adj* incomparabil·is -is -e
unroll *tr* evolvere
unruffled *adj* immot·us -a -um
unruliness *s* impotenti·a -ae *f*
unruly *adj* impot·ens -entis, turbulent·us -a -um
unsafe *adj* intut·us -a -um
unsalted *adj* insals·us -a -um
unsatisfied *adj* inexplet·us -a -um
unsatisfactory *adj* non idone·us -a -um
unsavory *adj* insipid·us -a -um; *(disreputable)* foed·us -a -um
unscrew *tr* retorquēre
unseal *tr (letter)* resignare; *(a jar)* relinere
unseasonable *adj* intempestiv·us -a -um
unseemly *adj* indecor·us -a -um
unseen *adj* invis·us -a -um
unselfish *adj* suae utilitatis immem·or -oris
unselfishly *adv* liberaliter
unsettle *tr* sollicitare
unsettled *adj* incert·us -a -um; *(of mind)* sollicit·us -a -um
unsettling *adj* sollicit·ans -antis
unshaken *adj* immot·us -a -um
unshaved *adj* irras·us -a -um
unsheathe *tr* destringere
unsightly *adj* turp·is -is -e
unskillful *adj* imperit·us -a -um
unskillfully *adv* imperite
unskilled *adj* imperit·us -a -um
unsophisticated *adj* simpl·ex -icis
unsound *adj* infirm·us -a -um; *(of mind)* insan·us -a -um; *(ill-founded)* van·us -a -um
unsparing *adj (merciless)* inclem·ens -entis; *(lavish)* larg·us -a -um
unsparingly *adv* inclementer; *(lavishly)* large
unspeakable *adj* ineffabil·is -is -e
unstable *adj* instabil·is -is -e; *(fig)* lev·is -is -e, inconst·ans -antis
unstained *adj* pur·us -a -um; *(honor)* intaminat·us -a -um
unsteadily *adv* inconstanter
unsteady *adj* inconst·ans -antis; *(tottering)* caduc·us -a -um
unsubscribe *intr (comput)* cessare
unsuccessful *adj* infel·ix -icis
unsuccessfully *adv* infeliciter
unsuitable *adj* incommod·us -a -um
unsuited *adj* haud idone·us -a -um
unsullied *adj* intaminat·us -a -um
unsuspected *adj* non suspect·us -a -um, praeter suspicionem
untamed *adj* indomit·us -a -um
untasted *adj* ingustat·us -a -um
untaught *adj* indoct·us -a -um
unteachable *adj* indocil·is -is -e
untenable *adj* infirm·us -a -um, quod defendi non potest
unthankful *adj* ingrat·us -a -um
untie *tr* solvere
until *conj* dum, donec, quoad
until *prep* usque ad *(w. acc)*, in *(w. acc)*; **to put off — tomorrow** differre in crastinum; **— late at night** in multam noctem; **— now** adhuc
untimely *adj* intempestiv·us -a -um; *(premature)* praematur·us -a -um
untiring *adj* assidu·us -a -um
untold *adj (numberless)* innumer·us -a -um; *(story)* immemorat·us -a -um
untouched *adj* intact·us -a -um; *(fig)* immot·us -a -um
untrained *adj* inexercitat·us -a -um
untried *adj* intemptat·us -a -um
untrodden *adj* non trit·us -a -um
untroubled *adj* tranquill·us -a -um
untrue *adj* fals·us -a -um; *(disloyal)* infid·us -a -um
untrustworthy *adj* infid·us -a -um
unusual *adj* inusitat·us -a -um
unusually *adv* praeter solitum
unutterable *adj* infand·us -a -um
unvarnished *adj (fig)* nud·us -a -um
unveil *tr* revelare; *(fig)* patefacere
unversed *adj* **— in** imperit·us -a -um *(w. gen)*
unwanted *adj* ingrat·us -a -um; *(superfluous)* supervacane·us -a -um
unwarranted *adj* iniust·us -a -um
unwary *adj* incaut·us -a -um
unwelcome *adj* ingrat·us -a -um

unwieldy *adj* inhabil•is -is -e
unwilling *adj* invit•us -a -um
unwillingly *adv* invite
unwind *tr* revolvere
unwise *adj* imprud•ens -entis
unwisely *adv* imprudenter
unworthily *adv* indigne
unworthiness *s* indignit•as -atis *f*
unworthy *adj* **(of)** indign•us -a -um *(w. abl)*
unwrap *tr* explicare, evolvere
unwritten *adj* non script•us -a -um
unyielding *adj* inflexibil•is -is -e, dur•us -a -um
unyoke *tr* disiungere
up *adv* sursum; (**up** *is often expressed in Latin by the prefix* con-, com- cor-, ex-, sub- *combined with the verb:* **— in the air** *(in uncertaintiy)* in medio relict•us -a -um; **to be — in the air** *(to be undecided)* pendēre; **to eat —** comesse; **to finish —** conficere; **to snatch —** corripere; **to rise —** exsurgere; **to lift —** sublevare; **to charge — the hill** erigere aciem per adversum collem; **to go — the mountains** ire in adversos montes; **to rise — against us** exsurgere adversus *(or* in) nos; **— and down** sursum deorsum; **to run — and down** modo huc modo illuc cursare; **— to** tenus *(w. abl) (always placed after its case, e.g.,* **the water came up to the waist** umbilico tenus aqua erat); **—s and downs** modo sic, modo sic; **— till now** antehac
upbraid *tr* castigare verbis
upbringing *s* educati•o -onis *f*
upheaval *s* eversi•o -onis *f*
uphill *adj* accliv•is -is -e; *(fig)* difficil•is -is -e; **to have an — struggle** clivo laborare
uphill *adv* adversus clivum, in collen
uphold *tr* servare, sustentare
upkeep *s* impens•a -ae *f*
uplift *tr* sublevare
upon *prep (position)* super *(w. abl),* in *(w. abl); (motion)* super *(w. acc),* in *(w. abl); (directly after)* ex *(w. abl),* sub *(w. abl); (converning)* de *(w. abl)*; **— my word** fidem do
upper *adj* super•ior -ior -ius; *(world, air)* super•us -a -um; **an — room** superius cenacul•um -i *n;* **the — classes** superiores *(or* ampliores) ordin•es -um *mpl;* **to get the — hand** superare, vincere
uppermost *adj* summ•us -a -um
upright *adj* erect•us -a -um; *(of character)* honest•us -a -um, inte•ger -gra -grum
uproar *s* tumult•us -ūs *m;* **to be in an —, to cause an —** tumultuari
uproot *tr* eradicare, erurere
ups and downs *spl* **he has his —** ei modo bene, modo male est; **there are —** est modo sic, modo sic
upset *tr* evertere, subvertere; *(to worry)* perturbare, commovēre
upset *adj* percul•us -a -um, commot•us -a -um; **don't be —** noli *(pl:* nolite) perturbari
upset *s (setback)* offensi•o -onis *f; (at polls)* repuls•a -ae *f;* **to suffer an —** offensionem *(or* repulsam) ferre
upside down *adv* **everything was —** omnia erant sursum deorsum; **to turn —** sursum deorsum versare
upstairs *adv (direction)* sursum; *(position)* in superiore tabulato; **to go —** per scalas ascendere
upstairs *s* dom•us -ūs *f* superior
upstairs bedroom *s* cubicul•um -i *n* superius
upstart *s* novus hom•o -inis *m; (pej)* terrae fil•ius -(i)i *m*
upstream *adv* adverso flumine
up to *prep* usque ad *(w. acc),* tenus *(postpositive, w. abl or gen);* **it is — you** ex te pendet
upwards *adv* sursum; **— of** *(of number)* plus quam
urban *adj* urban•us -a -um
urge *tr* urgēre, impellere; **to — on** stimulare, incitare; *(horses)* admittere
urge *s* impuls•us -ūs *m,* animi impet•us -ūs *m*
urgency *s* necessit•as -atis *f*
urgent *adj* inst•ans -antis; grav•is -is -e; **whose need was most —** quibus summa necessitudo erat; **to be —** instare
urgently *adv* vehementer
urging *s* stimul•us -i *m;* **at the — of the consul** consule auctore
urinal *s* matell•a -ae *f,* lasan•um -i *n*
urine *s* urin•a -ae *f*
URL *s (comput)* Universale Rerum Locatr•um -i *n,* inscripti•o -onis *f* interretialis
urn *s* urn•a -ae
us *pron* nos; **of —** nostri; *(partitive)* nostrum; **to —** nobis; **with —** nobiscum
usage *s* us•us -ūs *m; (custom)* consuetud•o -inis *f*
use *s* us•us -ūs *m;* **no —!** frustra!; **in common —** usitat•us -a -um; **it is no —** nihil opus est; ilicet; **to be in —** in usu esse; **to be of —** usui esse; **to be of no —** inutile esse, usum nullum habēre; **to come into —** invalescere, in morem *(or* in usum) venire; **to make — of** uti *(w. abl);* **what's the —?** quid opus est?
use *tr* uti *(w. abl); (to take advantage of)* abuti *(w. abl);* **to — in a sentence** in sententiā ponere; **to — s.th. for** aliquid adhibēre *(w. dat);* **to — up** consumere, exhaurire ‖ *intr* **I used to** solebam *(w. inf)*
used *adj* usitat•us -a -um; *(second-hand)* trit•us -a -um; **— to** *(accustomed to)* assuet•us -a -um *(w. dat)*
useful *adj* util•is -is -e; **to be —** usui esse
usefully *adv* utiliter, commode
useless *adj* inutil•is -is -e

uselessly *adv* frustra
usher *n (in theater)* dissignat•or -oris *m*
usual *adj* solit•us -a -um; **as —** ut solet; **more than —** plus solito; **you were wrong as —** errabas ut solebas *(or* ex consuetudine tuā)
usually *adv* plerumque, fere
usurp *tr* invadere *(w. acc or* in *w. acc),* usurpare
usurpation *s* usurpati•o -onis *f*
usurper *s* usurpa•tor -toris *m* (•trix -tricis *f)*
usury *s* immodica usur•a -ae *f*
utensils *spl* untensil•ia -ium *npl;* **household —** suppel•ex -ectilis *f;* **kitchen —** coquinatori•a -orum *npl*
utility *s* utilit•as -atis *f*
utilize *tr* uti *(w. abl),* adhibēre
utmost *adj* summ•us -a -um
utmost *n* **to do one's —** omnibus viribus contendere
utter *adj* tot•us -a -um
utter *tr* emittere; *(to reveal what is a secret)* proloqui; **she never —ed a word** nullum verbum emisit
utterance *s* dict•um -i *n;* **to give — to one's feelings** exprimere dicendo sensa
utterly *adv* omnino, funditus
uttermost *adj* extrem•us -a -um
uvula *s* uvul•a -ae *f*

V

vacancy *s* vacuit•as -atis *f; (in hotel)* cubicul•um -i *n* vacans
vacant *adj* vacu•us -a -um; *(look, stare)* inan•is -is -e; **to be —** vacare
vacate *tr* vacuefacere
vacation *s* feri•ae -arum *fpl;* **at the beginning (the end of) —** feriis ineuntibus (feriis peractis); **summer —** feriae aestivae; **to be on —** feriat•us -a -um esse; **to spend the —** ferias agere
vaccinate *tr* vaccinum inserere in *(w. acc)*
vaccination *s* vaccinati•o -onis *f*
vaccine *s* vaccin•um -i *n*
vacillate *intr* vacillare
vacillating *adj* vacill•ans -antis
vacuum *s* inan•e -is *n*
vacuum cleaner *s* pulveris hauritor•ium -(i)i *n*
vagabond *s* larifug•a -ae *mf*
vagary *s* libid•o -inis *f*
vagina *s* vagin•a -ae *f*
vagrancy *s* vagati•o -onis *f*
vagrant *adj* vag•us -a -um
vagrant *s* err•o -onis *mf*
vague *adj* vag•us -a -um; *(not fixed)* incert•us -a -um; *(ambiguous)* ambigu•us -a -um
vaguely *adv* incerte
vagueness *s* obscurit•as -atis *f,* abiguit•as -atis *f*
vain *adj (empty)* van•us -a -um; *(proud)* superb•us -a -um; **in —** frustra
vainly *adv* frustra
vainglorious *adj* glorios•us -a -um
valedictorian *s* valedic•ens -entis *mf*
valedictory *s* orati•o -onis *f* valedicens
valentine *s* chartul•a -ae *f* amatoria
valet *s* cubicular•ius -(i)i *m*
valiant *adj* fort•is -is -e
valid *adj* firm•us -a -um
valley *s* vall•es *(or* vall•is) -is *f*
valor *s* fortitud•o -inis *f*
valuable *adj* pretios•us -a -um; **to be —** pretium habēre
valuables *spl* res, rerum *fpl* pretiosae
valuation *s* aestimati•o -onis *f*
value *s* pret•ium -(i)i *n*
value *tr* aestimare; **to — highly** magni aestimare; **to — s.o. for his prowess** aliquem probare a viribus
valueless *adj* vil•is -is -e
valve *s* epistom•ium -(i)i *n*
vampire *s* vespertili•o -onis *m; (fig)* hirud•o -inis *f*
vandal *s* evers•or -oris *m*
vanguard *s (mil)* primum agm•en -inis *n*
vanish *intr* (e)vanescere, diffugere
vanity *s* vanit•as -atis *f*
vanquish *tr* profligare, devincere
vantage *s* commod•um -i *n;* **— point** superior loc•us -i *m*
vapor *s* vap•or -oris *m*
variable *adj* vari•ans -antis
variance *s* differenti•a -ae *f;* **at — with** dissid•ens -entis ab *(w. abl);* **to set the state at —** serere civiles discordias
variation *s* variet•as -atis *f*
varicose vein *s* var•ix -icis *f*
variety *s* variet•as -atis *f*
various *adj* vari•i -ae -a; **in — ways** varie
variously *adv* varie
vary *tr* variare, mutare **||** *intr* variare, mutari
vase *s* vascul•um -i *n*
vast *adj* vast•us -a -um
vastly *adv* valde, maxime
vastness *s* immensit•as -atis *f*
vat *s* cup•a -ae *f*
vault *s (archit)* camer•a -ae *f; (leap)* salt•us -ūs *m; (for valuables)* thesaur•us -i *m*
vault *intr* salire
vaunt *tr* iactare **||** *intr* se iactare
VCR *s* magnetoscop•ium -(i)i *n*
veal *s* vitulin•a -ae *f*
veer *intr* se vertere
vegetable *s* hol•us -eris *n* [*also collective for vegetables*]
vegetable *adj* holitari•us -a -um
vegetable garden *s* hort•us -i *m* holitorius
vegetarian *adj* holerari•us -a -um
vehemence *s* vehementi•a -ae *f*
vehement *adj* vehem•ens -entis; *(violent)* violent•us -a -um

vehemently *adv* vehementer
vehicle *s* vehicul•um -i *n*
Veii *spl* Vei•i -orum *mpl*
veil *s* ric•a -ae *f; (bridal)* flamme•um -i *n; (fig)* integument•um -i *n*
veil *tr* velare
vein *s (anat)* ven•a -ae *f;* **in a similar —** ad similem sententiam
velocity *s* velocit•as -atis *f*
velvet *s* velvet•um -i *n*
vend *tr* vendere
vendetta *s* simult•as -atis *f*
vendor *s* vendi•tor -toris *m* (•trix -tricis *f*)
veneer *s* ligni bracte•a -ae *f; (fig)* speci•es -ei *f*
venerable *adj* venerabil•is -is -e
venerate *tr* venerari
veneration *s* venerati•o -onis *f*
venereal *adj* venere•us -a -um
Venetian blinds *spl* transenn•a -ae *f;* **to open, (close, let down, raise) the —** transennam aperire (claudere, demittere, subvolvere)
vengeance *s* ulti•o -onis *f;* **to take — on s.o.** se vindicare ab *(w. abl);* **with a —** valde, vehementer
venison *s* ferin•a -ae *f*
venom *s* venen•um -i *n*
venomous *adj* venenat•us -a -um
vent *s* spirament•um -i *n*
vent *tr* aperire; **to — one's wrath on** iram erumpere in *(w. acc)*
ventilate *tr* ventilare
ventriloquist *s* ventriloqu•us -i *m* (•a -ae *f*)
venture *s* facin•us -eris *n;* **to risk a —** periculum subire
venture *tr* periclitari; **to — all** dare summam rerum in aleam
venturesome *adj* aud•ax -acis
veracity *s* veracit•as -atis *f*
veranda *s* subdial•ia -ium *npl*
verb *s* verb•um -i *n*
verbal *adj* verbal•is -is -e
verbally *adv* verbo
verbatim *adv* ad verbum
verbose *adj* verbos•us -a -um
verdict *s* sententi•a -ae *f;* **to deliver the —** sententiam pronuntiare; **to give a guilty —** condemnatoriam sententiam ferre; **to give a — of acquittal** absolutoriam sententiam ferre
verge *s* marg•o -inis *m;* **to be on the — of** non procul abesse ut *(w. subj)*
verge *intr* **to — on** non multum distare ab *(w. abl)*
verification *s* confirmati•o -onis *f*
verify *tr* comprobare, confimare
vermilion *adj* minian•us -a -um
vermilion *s* min•ium -(i)i *n*
vermin *spl* bestiol•ae -arum *fpl*
vernacular *s* patrius serm•o -onis *m*
versatile *adj* versatil•is -is -e
verse *s* vers•us -ūs *m*
versed *adj* **(in)** versat•us et exercitat•us -a -um (in *w. abl)*
versification *s* versificati•o -onis *f*
versify *intr* versificare
version *s* translati•o -onis *f;* **to give a literal — of** plane vertere
vertebra *s* vertebr•a -ae *f*
vertex *s* vert•ex -icis *m*
vertical *adj* rect•us -a -um; **a — line** perpendicul•um -i *n*
vertically *adv* ad perpendiculum
very *adj* ips•e -a -um; **on the — day on which** ipso die quo
very *adv* valde, admodum, perquam, maxime, per- *(w. adj or adv);* **— good** optim•us -a -um; **— good!** optime!; **— well!** *(in agreement)* fiat!
vessel *s* vas, vasis *n; (ship)* navig•ium -(i)i *n*
vest *s* thor•ax -acis *m*
vestal virgin *s* virg•o -inis *f* vestalis
vestibule *s* vestibul•um -i *n*
vestige *s* vestig•ium -(i)i *n*
vestment *s* vestiment•um -i *n*
veteran *s* veteran•us -i *m* (•a -ae *f*), emerit•us -i *m* (•a -ae *f*)
veterinarian *s* veterinari•us -i *m* (•a -ae *f*)
veterinary *adj* veterinari•us -a -um
veto *s* intercessi•o -onis *f;* **to interpose a —** intercedere
veto *tr* intercedere *(w. dat)*
vex *tr* vexare
vexation *s* vexati•o -onis *f*
via *prep* per *(w. acc)*
vial *s* phial•a -ae *f*
vibrate *intr* vibrare
vibration *s* vibrat•us -ūs *m*
vicar *s* vicar•ius -(i)i *m; (eccl)* sacerd•os -otis *m*
vicarious *adj* vicari•us -a -um
vice *s (shameful deed)* flagit•ium -(i)i *n; (flaw)* vit•ium -(i)i *n; (tool)* retinacul•um -i *n*
vice admiral *s* classis subpraefect•us -i *m* (•a -ae *f*)
vice chancellor *s* procancellar•ius -(i)i *m* (•ia -iae *f*)
vice president *s* praesidis vicar•ius -(i)i *m* (•ia -iae *f*)
vice principal *s* (scholae) rect•or -oris *m* vicarius, rectr•ix -icis *f* vicaria
viceroy *s* subregul•us -i *m*
vicinity *s* vicini•a -ae *f;* **in the — of** circum *(w. acc)*
vicious *adj* crudel•is -is -e
viciously *adv* crudeliter
vicissitude *s* vicissitud•o -inis *f*
victim *s* victim•a -ae *f;* **to fall — to** obire *(w. dat)*
victimize *tr (to swindle)* circumvenire; *(to assault, kill)* vim inferre *(w. dat)*
victor *s* vict•or -oris *m,* victr•ix -icis *f*

victorious *adj* vict•or -oris, *(of a female)* victr•ix -icis [*used appositively*]; **to be —** vincere
victory *s* victori•a -ae *f;* **news of —** litter•ae -arum *fpl* victrices; **to win a —** victoriam consequi *or* adipisci; **to gain a — over the enemy** ab hoste victoriam reportare
video cassette *s* caset•a -ae *f* magnetoscopica
video cassette recorder (VCR) *s* magnetoscop•ium -(i)i *n*
video game lus•us -ūs *m* magnetoscopicus; **to play —s** lusūs magnetoscopicos ludere
videotape *s* taeniol•a -ae *f* magnetoscopica; **to play** *or* **show a —** taeniolam mangetoscopicam exhibēre
vie *intr* certare, contendere
view *s* aspect•us -ūs *m,* conspect•us -ūs *m; (from above)* despect•us -ūs *m; (from a window)* prospect•us -ūs *m; (opinion)* sententi•a -ae *f;* **almost in — of the city** paene in conspectu urbis; **in my —** meo iudicio; **in — of** pro *(w. abl);* **this is my point of —** hoc sic mihi videtur; **to come into —** apparēre; **to enjoy a — of** conspectu *(w. gen)* uti; **to get a bird's eye — of the city** omnem urbem sub uno aspectu despicere
view *tr* visere, spectare; *(to regard)* intueri
vigil *s* vigili•ae -arum *fpl; (lasting all night)* pervigil•ium -(i)i *n*
vigilance *s* vigilanti•a -ae *f*
vigilant *adj* vigil•ans -antis
vigilantly *adv* vigilanter
vigor *s* vig•or -oris *m*
vigorous *adj* ala•cer -cris -cre
vigorously *adv* alacriter
vile *adj* vil•is -is -e
vilify *tr* infamare
villa *s* vill•a -ae *f;* **my — at Formiae** meum Formian•um -i *n*
village *s* pag•us -i *m,* vic•us -i *m*
villager *s* pagan•us -i *m* (•a -ae *f*)
villain *s* scelest•us -i *m* (•a -ae *f*)
villany *s* nequiti•a -ae *f; (deed)* scel•us -eris *n*
vindicate *tr* vindicare; *(to justify)* probare; *(person)* defendere
vindication *s* vindicati•o -onis *f*
vindictive *adj* ultionis cupid•us -a -um
vine *s* vit•is -is *f*
vine arbor *s* pergul•a -ae *f*
vinegar *s* acet•um -i *n*
vinegar bottle *s* acetabul•um -i *n*
vineyard *s* vine•a -ae *f*
vintage *s* vindemi•a -ae *f*
violate *tr* violare
violation *s* violati•o -onis *f*
violator *s* viola•tor -toris *m* (•trix -tricis *f*)
violence *s* violenti•a -ae *f*
violent *adj* violent•us -a -um
violently *adv* violenter
violin *s* fidicul•a -ae *f;* **to play the —** fidiculā canere
virgin *adj* virg•o -inis *f (used appositively);* **— forest** silv•a -ae *f* intacta
virgin *s* virg•o -inis *f*
virile *adj* viril•is -is -e
virility *s* virilit•as -atis *f*
virtually *adv* fere
virtue *s* virt•us -utis *f; (power)* vis *f;* **by — of** per *(w. acc),* ex *(w. abl)*
virtuous *adj* prob•us -a -um, virtute praedit•us -a -um
virtuously *adv* cum virtute, honeste
virulence *s* vis *f,* gravit•as -atis *f*
virulent *adj* virulent•us -a -um
viscera *spl* viscer•a -um *npl*
visible *adj* visibil•is -is -e; *(striking, noticeable)* manifest•us -a -um
visibly *adv* manifeste
vision *s (sense)* vis•us -ūs *m; (apparition)* visi•o -onis *f*
visionary *s* somni•ans -antis *mf*
visit *s (formal)* salutati•o -onis *f;* **to pay s.o. a —** aliquem visere
visit *tr* visere, visitare; **to go to —** visere
visitor *s* hosp•es -itis *mf*
visor *s* buccul•a -ae *f*
vista *s* prospect•us -ūs *m*
visual *adj* ad visum pertinens, oculorum *[gen]*
visualize *tr* fingere
visually *adv* oculis
vital *adj* vital•is -is -e; *(essential)* necessari•us -a -um
vitally *adv* praecipue
vitality *s* vis *f* vitalis
vitamin *s* vitamin•um -i *n*
vitiate *tr* vitiare, corrumpere
vivacious *adj* viv•ax -acis
vivaciously *adv* vivaciter
vivid *adj* vivid•us -a -um
vividly *adv* vivide
vivify *tr* vivificare
vocabulary *s* verborum copi•a -ae *f; (list of words)* vocabulorum ind•ex -icis *m*
vocal *adj* vocal•is -is -e
vocation *s* vocati•o -onis *f*
vocative *s* vocativ•us -i *m,* cas•us -ūs *m* vocativus
vociferous *adj* clamos•us -a -um
vogue *s* mos, moris *m;* **to be in —** moris esse
voice *s* vox, vocis *f; (of a verb)* gen•us -eris *n;* **what — is "audimur"? it is passive.** cuius generis est "audimur"? est passivi generis [Note: "genus" *in connection with nouns and adjectives means "gender," and in connection with verbs means "voice"*]
void *adj* inan•is -is -e; **— of** vacu•us -a -um *(w. abl)*
void *s* inan•e -is *n*
volatile *adj* volatic•us -a -um, lev•is -is -e

volcanic *adj* vulcani·us -a -um
volcano *s* mon·s -tis *m* flammas et vaporem eructans
volition *s* volunt·as -atis *f*
volley *s* coniect·us -ūs *m; (fig)* tempest·as -atis *f*
volleyball *s* foll·is -is *m* volatilis; *(game)* lus·us -ūs *m* follis volatilis; **to play —** folle volatili ludere
volt *s* volt·ium -(i)i *n*
volume *s (book)* volum·en -inis *n; (quantity)* copi·a -ae *f; (of voice)* magnitud·o -inis *f*
voluminous *adj* voluminos·us -a -um; **— writer** scrip·tor -toris *m* (·trix -tricis *f*) per multa diffusus volumina
voluntarily *adv* suā voluntate, ultro
voluntary *adj* voluntari·us -a -um; *(unpaid)* gratuit·us -a -um
volunteer *s* voluntari·us -i *m* (·a -ae *f*); *(mil)* mil·es -itis *mf* voluntari·us (-a)
volunteer *intr (mil)* sponte nomen dare; **to — to do s.th.** aliquid ultro facere
voluptuous *adj* voluptari·us -a -um
vomit *tr & intr* vomere
vomit *s* vomit·us -ūs *m*
voracious *adj* vor·ax -acis
voraciously *adv* voraciter
vortex *s* vort·ex -icis *m*
vote *s* suffrag·ium -(i)i *n; (fig) (judgment)* sententi·a -ae *f;* **to cast a —** suffragium ferre
vote *tr* **to — down** antiquare ‖ *intr* suffragium ferre; *(of a judge)* sententiam ferre; *(of a senator)* censēre; **to — for** suffragari *(w. dat)*
voter *s* suffraga·tor -toris *m* (·trix -tricis *f*)
voting booth *s* saept·um -i *n*
votive *adj* votiv·us -a -um; **— offering** vot·um -i *n*
vouch *intr* **to — for** testificari, affirmare
voucher *s* testimon·ium -(i)i *n* (per tabellas)
vouchsafe *tr* concedere
vow *s* vot·um -i *n*
vow *tr* vovēre ‖ *intr* spondēre
vowel *s* vocal·is -is *f*
voyage *s* it·er -ineris *n; (by sea)* navigati·o -onis *f*
voyage *intr* iter facere; *(abroad)* peregrinari; *(by sea)* navigare
voyager *s* peregrina·tor -toris *m* (·trix -tricis *f*); *(by sea)* naviga·tor -toris *m* (·trix -tricis *f*)
vulgar *adj* vulgar·is -is -e; *(low)* vil·is -is -e
vulgarity *s* obscenit·as -atis *f*, dicti·o -onis *f* obscena
Vulgate *s* Bibli·a -orum *npl* editionis vulgatae
vulnerable *adj* qui (quae, quod) vulnerari potest; *(of a fortress)* expugnabil·is -is -e
vulture *s* vult·ur -uris *m; (fig)* hom·o -inis *mf* rapax

W

wad *s* fascicul·us -i *m*
waddle *intr* anatis in modum incedere
wade *intr* per vada ire; **to — across** vado transire
waffle *s* vafl·um -i *n*
wag *tr (the tail)* movēre
wage *tr* **to — war** bellum gerere
wager *tr* deponere
wager *s* sponsi·o -onis *f*
wages *spl* merc·es -edis *f;* **to receive (fair, good, low, unfair) —** (aequam, magnam, parvam, iniquam) mercedem accipere
wagon *s* carr·us -i *m; (for agricultural purposes)* plaustr·um -i *n; (toy)* plostell·um -i *n*
wail *intr* plorare
wailing *s* plorat·us -ūs *m*
waist *s* media par·s -tis *f* corporis
wait *intr* exspectare, opperiri; *(not to depart)* manēre; **to — for** exspectare, opperiri; **to — on** ministrare *(w. dat);* **to — on tables** ministrare
wait *s* mor·a -ae *f;* **to lie in — for** insidiari *(w. dat)*
waiter *s* minis·ter -tri *m*
waiting room *s* oec·us -i *m* praestolatorius
waitress *s* ministr·a -ae *f*
waive *tr* remittere
wake *tr* (e somno) excitare ‖ *intr* **to — up** expergisci, evigilare
wake *s* tract·us -ūs *m* aquarum a tergo navis; **in the — of** post *(w. acc)*
wakeful *adj* vig·il -ilis
walk *s (act)* ambulati·o -onis *f; (place)* ambulacr·um -i *n*, xyst·us -i *m; (covered)* portic·us -ūs *f; (gait)* incess·us -ūs *m;* **to go for a —** demabulatum ire
walk *intr* ambulare, incedere; **to — out on** *(coll)* deserere; **to — up and down** deambulare; **to — up to** accedere ad *(w. acc)*
wall *s (inner or outer wall of a house)* pari·es -etis *m; (exterior)* mur·us -i *m;* **—s** *(of town)* moen·ia -ium *npl*, mur·us -i *m*
wall *tr* **to — in** moenibus munire; **to — up** *(w. stones, bricks)* concludere (saxis, lateribus)
wall clock *s* horolog·ium -(i)i *n* parietarium
walled *adj* moenibus munit·us -a -um
wallet *s* per·a -ae *f*
wallop *tr (coll)* percolopare; **to get —ed** vapulare
wallow *intr* volutari
walnut *s* iugl·ans -andis *f*
walnut tree *s* iugl·ans -andis *f*
walrus *s* odoben·us -i *m*
waltz *s* saltati·o -onis *f* in gyrum
waltz *intr* saltare in gyrum
wan *adj* pallid·us -a -um

wander *intr* errare, vagari; **to — about** pervagari; **to — over** pererrare
wanderer *s* err•o -onis *mf*
wandering *s* errati•o -onis *f*
wane *intr* decrescere
want *s (scarcity)* penuri•a -ae *f; (opp:* copia) inopi•a -ae *f; (extreme want)* egest•as -atis *f;* **to be in —, suffer —** egēre
want *tr* velle, cupere; *(to lack)* egēre *(w. abl);* **now what do you —?** quid nunc tibi vis?
wanting *adj (defective)* vitios•us -a -um; *(missing)* abs•ens -entis; **to be —** deficere, deesse
wanton *adj (lewd)* libidinos•us -a -um; *(unwarranted)* iniqu•us -a -um
war *s* **(against, with)** bell•um -i *n* (contra *or* adversus *w. acc);* **civil —** bellum civile *or* domesticum; **foreign —** bellum externum; **in —** bello, belli tempore; **in — and in peace** pace belloque; **offensive —** *(of war yet to be begun)* bellum ultro inferendum; *(of war already begun)* bellum ultro illatum; **to be involved in —** bello implicari; **to bring a — to a successful conclusion** bellum conficere; **to carry on — with** bellum gerere cum *(w. abl);* **to cause a —** bellum movēre; **to conduct a —** *(of a general)* bellum administrare; **to declare — on** bellum indicere *(w. dat);* **to fight a —** bellum gerere; **to go to — with** bellum inferre *(w. dat);* **to settle a — by diplomacy** bellum componere; **to start a — with** bellum inire cum *(w. abl);* **to take part in a —** bellum capessere; **to wage a —** bellum gerere; **— against pirates** bellum piraticum; **— against slaves** bellum servile; **— of extermination** bellum internecium; **— breaks out** bellum exardescit
war *intr* **(against)** bellare (adversus *w. acc)*
warble *intr* canere; *(to twitter)* fritinnire
war cry *s* ululat•us -ūs *m*
ward *s (minor)* pupill•us -i *m* (•a -ae *f*); *(of a city)* regi•o -onis *f;* **— by —** regionatim
ward *tr* **to — off** arcēre, avertere
warden *s* carcerar•ius -(i)i *m* (•ia -iae *f*)
wardrobe *s (place to keep clothes)* vestiar•ium -(i)i *n; (clothes)* vestiment•a -orum *npl*
warehouse *s* horre•um -i *n*
wares *spl* merc•es -ium *fpl*
warfare *s* res, rei *f* bellica, bell•um -i *n*
war-horse *s* equ•us -i *m* bellator
warily *adv* caute
warlike *adj* bellicos•us -a -um
warm *adj* calid•us -a -um; *(just warm)* tepid•us -a -um; *(fig)* fervid•us -a -um; **to be —** calēre; **to become —** calescere, tepescere
warm *tr* calefacere, tepefacere; **to — up** *(food)* recoquere; *(by exercise)* exercēre
warm-hearted *adj* am•ans -antis
warmly *adv* ardenter; *(kindly)* benigne; **— dressed** spissis vestibus involut•us -a -um
warmth *s* cal•or -oris *m; (fig)* ferv•or -oris *m*
warm-up *s* exercitati•o -onis *f*
warn *tr* monēre
warning *s* monit•um -i *n; (lesson)* document•um -i *n*
warp *s* stam•en -inis *n*
warp *tr* torquēre ‖ *intr (of wood)* pandere
warped *adj* pand•us -a -um
warping *s* pandati•o -onis *f*
warrant *tr (to guarantee)* praestare; *(to justify, call for)* probare
warrant *s* mandat•um -i *n;* **— for arrest** praemandat•a -orum *npl*
warranty *s* satisdati•o -onis *f*
warrior *s* bellat•or -oris *m*
warship *s* nav•is -is *f* longa
wart *s* verruc•a -ae *f*
wary *adj* caut•us -a -um
wash *tr* lavare; **to — away** abluere; **to — out** eluere ‖ *intr* lavari
wash *s* lavandari•a -orum *npl;* **to send to the —** ad lavandum dare
wash basin *s* aqual•is -is *m*
wash cloth *s* drapp•us -i *m* lavatorius
washer, washmachine *s* machin•a -ae *f* lavatoria
washing *s* lavati•o -onis *f*
wasp *s* vesp•a -ae *f*
waste *s* detriment•um -i *n; (of time, money)* iactur•a -ae *f*
waste *tr* effundere; *(time, effort)* perdere, terere; **I'm wasting my time** frustra tempus contero; **to — one's breath** *(fig)* operam perdere ‖ *intr* **to — away** tabescere
waste *adj* vast•us -a -um; **to lay —** vastare
waste basket scirpicul•us -i *m* chartarius
wasteful *adj* prodig•us -a -um
wastefully *adv* prodige
wasteland *s* solitud•o -inis *f*
watch *s (timepiece)* horolog•ium -(i)i *n; (guard)* vigili•a -ae *f; (sentry)* excubi•ae -arum *fpl;* **to keep —** excubare; **to keep — over** invigilare *(w. dat),* custodire
watch *tr (to observe)* observare, spectare; *(to guard)* custodire ‖ *intr* cavēre; **hey you, — out!** heus tu, cave!; **to — out for** cavēre *(w. abl or dat or* **ab** *w. abl);* **— out that you don't …** cave ne …
watchful *adj* vigil•ans -antis
watchman *s* vig•il -ilis *m*
watchtower *s* specul•a -ae *f*
watchword *s* tesser•a -ae *f*
water *s* aqu•a -ae *f;* **fresh —** aqua dulcis; **in deep —** *(fig)* artibus in rebus; **rain —** aqua pluvialis; **running —** proflu•ens -entis *f;* **salt —** aqua salsa
water *tr* irrigare; *(animals, plants)* adaquare
water bottle *s* lagoen•a -ae *f* aquaria

water boy *s* aquar·ius -(i)i *m,* aquat·or -oris *m*
water clock *s* clepsydr·a -ae *f*
water closet *s* latrin·a -ae *f,* loc·us -i *m* secretus
watercolor *s* pigment·um -i *n* aquā dilutum
waterfall *s* cataract·a -ae *f*
waterfront *s* lit·us -oris *n; (of city)* naval·ia -ium *npl*
watering can *s* nassitern·a -ae *f*
waterlogged *adj* aquā gravid·us -a -um
watermelon *s* melopep·o -onis *m*
water pipe *s* fistul·a -ae *f* aquaria
waterproof *adj* aquae impervi·us -a -um
waterski *s* nart·a -ae *f* aquaria
waterski *intr* per summas undas natare
watertight *adj* aquae impervi·us -a -um; *(fig)* absolut·us -a -um
watery *adj* aquos·us -a -um
watt *s* vatt·ium -(i)i *n*
wave *s* und·a -ae *f,* fluct·us -ūs *m*
wave *tr (hands, arms)* iactare; *(weapon, flag)* quassare; *(hair)* crispare
waver *intr* labare, nutare, vacillare
wavering *adj* nut·ans -antis, vacill·ans -antis
wavy *adj* und·ans -antis; *(hair)* crisp·us -a -um
wax *s* cer·a -ae *f*
wax *adj* cere·us -a -um
wax *tr* incerare ‖ *intr* crescere
way *adv (coll)* longe, multo
way *s* vi·a -ae *f; (route)* it·er -ineris *n; (manner)* mod·us -i *m; (plan, system, method)* rati·o -onis *f; (habit)* mo·s -ris *m;* **all the — from** usque ab *(w. abl);* **all the — to** usque ad *(w. acc);* **a long — off** longinqu·us -a -um; **by the —** *(incidentally)* obiter; **by — of** per *(w. acc),* viā *(w. gen);* **get out of the —!** abi, apage!; **have it your —!** esto ut lubet!; **if it is not too much out of your —** si tibi non sane devium erit; **I'm in a bad —** mihi male est; **in every —** omnibus modis; **in no —** nullo modo; **in the same —** eodem modo; **in the —** obvi·us -a -um; **in this —** ad hunc modum; **to be a long — off** longe distare; **to be in the — of** obesse *(w. dat);* **to be out of the —** devi·us -a -um esse; **to get in the — of** intervenire *(w. dat);* **to get under —** ancoram solvere; **to give —** *(of a structure)* labare; *(to yield)* concedere; *(mil)* pedem referre; **to get one's own —** pervincere; **to give — to** indulgēre *(w. dat);* **to have one's own —** res pro arbitrio gerere; **to stand in the — of** obstare *(w. dat);* **under —** proced·ens -entis; **— in** ingress·us -ūs *m;* **— out** exit·us -ūs *m;* **what is the quickest (best) — to … ?** quae est brevissima (optima) via ad *(w. acc)?*
wayfarer *s* viat·or -oris *mf*
waylay *tr* insidiari *(w. dat)*
wayward *adj* inconst·ans -antis
we *pron* nos; **— ourselves** *(masc)* nosmet ipsi; *(fem)* nosmet ipsae
weak *adj (in body, mind, resources)* infirm·us -a -um; *(from defects)* debil·is -is -e; *(argument, light, constitution)* tenu·is -is -e; *(senses)* heb·es -etis; *(voice)* exil·is -is -e
weaken *tr* infirmare, debilitare ‖ *intr* hebescere, labare
weakly *adv* infirme
weakness *s* infirmit·as -atis *f,* debilit·as -atis *f; (of mind)* imbecillit·as -atis *f; (flaw)* vit·ium -(i)i *n; (of arguments)* levit·as -atis *f*
wealth *s* diviti·ae -arum *fpl; (resources)* op·es -um *fpl; (store, plenty)* copi·a -ae *f*
wealthy *adj* div·es -itis
wean *tr* ab ubere depellere; *(fig)* **(from)** desuefacere ab *(w. abl)*
weapon *s* tel·um -i *n,* ferr·um -i *n*
wear *tr (clothes)* gerere, gestare; *(to wear regularly)* uti *(w. abl);* **to — out** *(clothes, a person)* conterere ‖ *intr* durare; *(to last)* perferre; **to — out** dilabi
wear *s* trit·us -ūs *m;* **— and tear** intertriment·um -i *n*
weariness *s* lassitud·o -inis *f*
wearisome *adj* operos·us -a -um
weary *adj* fess·us -a -um
weary *tr* fatigare
weasel *s* mustel·a -ae *f; (pej)* hom·o -inis *mf* lucifugus (-a)
weather *s (good or bad)* tempest·as -atis *f,* cael·um -i *n;* **beautiful (clear, cloudless, cloudy, fine, foul, lousy, rainy) —** egregia (clara, suda, nebulosa, serena, foeda, spurca) tempestas; **— conditions** tempestatum habit·us -ūs *m;* **types of —** gener·a -um *npl* tempestatum, tempestat·es -um *fpl*
weather *tr* **to — a storm** procellam durare; *(fig)* res adversas superare
weatherbeaten *adj* tempestate afflict·us -a -um
weather forecast *s* praenuntiati·o -onis *f* tempestatis
weather report *s* renuntiati·o -onis *f* tempestatis
weave *tr* texere
web *s (spider's)* arane·um -i *n; (on a loom)* tel·a -ae *f;* **the Web** Tel·a -ae *f (see* **World Wide Web)**
web site *s* sit·us -ūs *m* interretialis
wed *tr (a woman)* ducere; *(a man)* nubere *(w. dat)* ‖ *intr (of bride)* nubere; *(of groom)* uxorem ducere
wedding *s* nupti·ae -arum *fpl*
wedding *adj* nuptial·is -is -e; **to set the — day** diem nuptiis dicere; **— day** dies -ei *m* nuptiarum; **— gown** vest·is -is *f* nuptialis; **— present** don·um -i *n* nuptiale; **—**

reception conviv·ium -(i)i *n* nuptiale; — **ring** anul·us -i *m* nuptialis
wedge *s* cune·us -i *m*
wedlock *s* matrimon·ium -(i)i *n*
Wednesday *s* di·es -ei *m* Mercurii
weed *s* herb·a -ae *f* mala
weed *tr* eruncare
week *s* hebdom·as -adis *f,* septiman·a -ae *f*
weekday *s* di·es -ei *m* profestus
weekend *s* fin·is -is *m* hebdomadis; **on the** — exeunte hebdomade
weekly *adj* hebdomadal·is -is -e
weekly *adv* septimo quoque die, singulis hebdomadibus
weep *intr* flēre, lacrimare; **to — for** flēre, deplorare
weeping *s* flet·us -ūs *m*
weigh *tr* pendere; *(fig)* examinare; **to — down** degravare; *(fig)* opprimere; **to — out** expendere **||** *intr* **to — much** magni ponderis esse
weight *s* pond·us -eris *n; (heaviness)* grav·it·as -atis *f; (influence)* auctorit·as -atis *f; (importance)* moment·um -i *n*
weight lifting *s* sublati·o -onis *f* libramentorum
weighty *adj* grav·is -is -e
welcome *s* salutati·o -onis *f;* **I gave him a warm** — eum amantissime excepi
welcome *adj* opportunissim·us -a -um; **you're —!** *(after a person says "thank you)* libenter!
welcome *tr* benigne excipere
welcome *interj* salve!; *pl:* salvete!
weld *tr* (con)ferruminare
welfare *s* sal·us -utis *f; (charity)* carit·as -atis *f*
well *s* pute·us -i *m*
well *adj (healthy)* san·us -a -um, salv·us -a -um; **all's** — salva res est; **it is — to** convenit *(w. inf)*; **to be** — valēre; **to get** — convalescere
well *adv* bene, recte; **he is — off** bene se habet; *(fin)* bene aeratus est; **I am doing** — mihi bene est; **very** — optime; — **done!** macte virtute esto!
well *interj* immo; *(all right)* licet; — **now** age ergo; — —! enim vero!
well-behaved *adj* bene morat·us -a -um
well-being *s* sal·us -tis *f*
well-born *adj* generos·us -a -um
well-bred *adj* bene educat·us -a -um
well-deserved *adj* rite merit·us -a -um
well-done *adj* optime fact·us -a -um; *(cooking)* percoct·us -a -um; — **done!** macte virtute esto!
well-heeled *adj* bene aerat·us -a -um
well-known *adj* nobil·is -is -e, not·us -a -um
well-mannered *adj* bene morat·us -a -um
well-off *adj* bene aerat·us -a -um
well-read *adj* litterat·us -a -um
well-spoken *adj* disert·us -a -um
well-supplied *adj* copiosissim·us -a -um
well-timed *adj* opportun·us -a -um
welter *s* congeri·es -ei *f*
werewolf *s* versipell·is -is *m*
west *s* occas·us -ūs *m* (solis); **in the** — ab occidente; **toward the** — in occasum
western *adj* occidental·is -is -e
westward *adv* in occasum, in occidentem versus [versus *is an adverb*]
west wind *s* Zephyr·us -i *m*
wet *adj* uvid·us -a -um; *(through and through)* madid·us -a -um; **to get** — madefieri
wet *tr* madefacere
wet-nurse *s* nutr·ix -icis *f*
whack *tr (coll)* percolopare
whack *s* colaph·us -i *m;* **to give s.o. a** — colaphum alicui ducere
whale *s* balaen·a -ae *f*
wharf *s* naval·e -is *n*
what *adj interrog* qui, quae quod; — **kind of,** — **sort of** qual·is -is -e
what *pron interrog* quid, quidnam; — **about me?** quid de me?; — **do you take me for? a fool?** pro quo me habēs? pro stulto?; — **else?** quid amplius?; quid aliud?; — **else can I do for you?** quid est quod tibi efficere possum amplius?; — **for?** quam ob rem?; — **is it?** *(what's the trouble?)* quid est negoti?; — **is it? out with it!** quid id est? cedo!; — **is this all about?** quid enim?; — **next?** quid deinde?; —**'s that?** *(what did you say?)* quid id est?; —**'s that to you?** quid ad te attinet?; —**'s the matter?** quid est?; — **is the reason why . . .** ? quid est quod *(w. indic);* —**'s up?** quid rei est?; —**'s wrong?** quid est?
whatever *pron* quicquid; —! quidvis!
whatever *adj interrog* quicumque, quaecumque, quodcumque
wheat *s* tritic·um -i *n*
wheedle *tr* blandiri; **to — out of s.o.** eblandiri ex aliquo
wheel *s* rot·a -ae *f;* **the — turns** rota revolvitur
wheelbarrow *s* pab·o -onis *m*
wheelchair *s* sell·a -ae *f* rotalis
when *adv (interrog)* quando
when *conj* cum, ubi, ut; — **first** cum primum; — **joking** inter iocos
whence *adv* unde
whenever *adv* quandocumque, utcumque
where *adv* quā, ubi; *(motion)* quo; **from — ?** unde?; — **are you from?** unde es?; — **on earth** ubinam gentium
whereabouts *s* positi·o -onis *f,* loc·us -i *m* quo
whereas *conj* quandoquidem
whereby *adv* quā viā, quo
wherever *adv (position)* ubicumque, quo in loco; *(direction)* quocumque
wherefore *adv* quare, quamobrem

wherein *adv* in quo, in quibus, ubi
whereof *adv* de quo, de quibus
whereupon *adv* quo facto; *(then)* deinde
wherever *conj* quacumque, ubicumque, sicubi
wherewithall *s* **to have the — to** unde habēre *(w. inf)*
whet *tr* acuere; **to — the appetite** exacuere appetentiam (cibi)
whether *conj (in single indir. ques.)* num, -ne, an; **— ... or** *(in multiple indir. ques.)* utrum ... an, -ne ... an, *or* ... an; *(in disjunctive conditions)* sive ... sive, seu ... seu; **— ... or not** utrum ... necne
whetstone *s* co•s -tis *f*
which *pron interrog* quis, quid; *(of two)* ut•er -ra -rum ‖ *pron rel* qui, quae, quod
which *adj interrog* qui, quae, quod; *(of two)* u•ter -tra -trum ‖ *adj rel* qui, quae, quod
whichever *pron* quicumque, quaecumque, quodcumque; *(of two)* utercumque, utracumque, utrumcumque
whiff *s (slight smell)* od•or -oris *m* exiguus; **to get a — of** subolēre; **— of air** aur•a -ae *f*
while *s* temp•us -oris *n,* spat•ium -(i)i *n;* **after a —** paulo post; **a good — after** aliquanto post; **a long —** diu; **a short — ago, a short — before** paulo ante; **for a short —** paulisper; **for a —** aliquamdiu; **in a little —** in brevi spatio; **once in a —** interdum
while *conj* dum, quoad, donec
while *tr* **to — away the time** tempus fallere
whim *s* arbitr•ium -(i)i *n;* **according to their — and pleasure** ad eorum arbitrium et nutum
whimper *s* vagit•us -ūs *m*
whimper *intr* vagire
whimsical *adj* mobil•is -is -e
whine *intr* plorare
whinny *s* hinnit•us -ūs *m*
whinny *intr* hinnire
whip *s* flagell•um -i *n,* ver•ber -beris *n*
whip *tr* flagellare; *(coll)* superare; **to — out** eripere
whipped cream *s* crem•um -i *n* battutum
whippersnapper *s* frust•um -i *n* pueri
whipping *s* verberati•o -onis *f;* **to get a —** vapulare
whirl *tr* torquēre, rotare ‖ *intr* torquēri, rotari
whirl *s* turb•o -inis *m*
whirlpool *s* vert•ex -icis *m,* gurg•es -itis *m*
whirlwind *s* turb•o -inis *m*
whirr *intr* stridēre, increpare
whisk *tr (to brush lightly)* verrere; **to — away** everrere, eripere ‖ *intr* **to — about** *(to move about quickly)* circumvolitare
whiskbroom *s* scopul•a -ae *f*
whisker *s (of animal)* saet•a -ae *f;* **by a —** vix; **—s** barb•a -ae *f*
whiskey *s* aqu•a -ae *f* vitae
whisper *s* susurr•us -i *m*
whisper *tr & intr* susurrare
whistle *s (sound)* sibil•us -i *m; (pipe)* fistul•a -ae *f; (of wind)* strid•or -oris *m*
whistle *tr* **to — some tune** exsibilare nescio quid ‖ *intr* sibilare; *(of the wind)* stridēre
whit *s* **every — as good** omnino par; **not a — better** nihilo melius
white *adj* alb•us -a -um; *(brilliant)* candid•us -a -um; *(hair)* can•us -a -um; **to be —** albēre, albicare; **to turn —** albescere; *(face)* pallescere; **— bread** pan•is -is *m* candidus
white *s (the color; of an egg, of the eye)* alb•um -i *n;* cand•or -oris *m*
whiten *tr* dealbare, candefacere ‖ *intr* albescere, canescere
whitewash *s* albar•ium -(i)i *n; (fig)* fuc•us -i *m*
whitewash *tr* dealbare; *(fig)* fucare
whither *adv* quo, quorsum
whithersoever *adv* quocumque
whitish *adj* subalb•us -a -um
whittle *tr & intr* ad fastigium secare; *(to carve)* sculpere
whiz *intr* stridēre, increpare; **to — by** praetervolare
whiz *s (sound)* strid•or -oris *m; (brilliant person)* ingen•ium -(i)i *n*
who *pron interrog* quis; **— are you?** quis tu homo es?; **— says so?** quis hoc dicit factum? **— the devil** quis malum ‖ *pron rel* qui, quae
whoa *interj* eho!
whoever *pron* quicumque, quaecumque
whole *adj* tot•us -a -um, cunct•us -a -um, univers•us -a -um; *(unimpaired)* incolum•is -is -e, inte•ger -gra -grum
whole *s* tot•um -i *n;* **on the —** plerumque, ex toto; **taken as a —** in summam
wholehearted *adj* sincer•us -a -um
wholesale *adj* magnari•us -a -um; **to carry on — business** magnariam mercaturam facere
wholesale *adv* acervatim
wholesaler *s* magnarius (-a) negotia•tor -toris *m* (•trix -tricis *f*)
wholesome *adj* salutar•is -is -e
whole-wheat bread *s* autopyr•us -i *m*
wholly *adv* omnino, prorsus
whom *pron* quem; **of —** cuius; **to —** cui; **with —** quocum, cum quo
whoop *s* ululat•us -ūs *m*
whoop *intr* ululatum tollere
whore *s* scort•um-i *n*
whorehouse *s* lupan•ar -aris *n*
whoremonger *s* scortat•or -oris *m*
whose *pron* cuius; *pl:* quorum, quarum, quorum
why *adv* cur, quamobrem, quare; **just —** cur tandem; **that's — ...** quo fit ut *(w. subj);* **— is it that ...** quid est quod *(w.*

indic); — **not?** quid ita non?; *(as an expression of assent; of course)* quippini *or* quidni?; — **say more?** quid plura?; — **so? because …** quid ita? quia … ; — **the devil** cur malum
wick *s* fil·um -i *n*
wicked *adj* improb·us -a -um
wickedly *adv* improbe, sceleste
wickedness *s* improbit·as -atis *f*
wicker *adj* vimine·us -a -um
wicker basket *s* scirpul·us -i *m*
wide *adj* lat·us -a -um; *(spread out)* pass·us -a -um, porrect·us -a -um; **to be — of** aberrare ab *(w. abl)*
wide *adv* late; **far and —** longe et late
wide-awake *adj (fig)* ala·cer -cris -cre
wide-eyed *adj* oculis apertis; *(surprised)* attonit·us -a -um
widely *adv* late; *(among people)* vulgo
widen *tr* dilatare ‖ *intr* dilatari; *(of a country)* se pandere
widespread *adj* divulgat·us -a -um
widow *s* vidu·a -ae *f*
widower *s* vidu·us -i *m*
width *s* latitud·o -inis *f;* **ten feet in —** decem pedes in latitudinem
wield *tr (weapon)* tractare, vibrare; **to — supreme power** plurimum pollēre
wife *s* ux·or -oris *f; (of a slave)* contubernal·is -is *f*
wifely *adj* uxori·us -a -um
wig *s* capillament·um -i *n*
wiggle *tr* torquēre ‖ *intr* se torquēre; *(of a woman)* crisare
wild *adj* fer·us -a -um; *(desolate)* vast·us -a -um; *(mad)* insan·us -a -um; *(uncontrolled)* efferat·us -a -um; *(of trees, plants)* silvestr·is -is -e; *(of land)* incult·us -a -um; *(of disposition)* fer·ox -ocis; — **beast** fer·a -ae *f*, fera besti·a -ae *f*
wild *s* **growing in the —** silvestr·is -is -e; **the —s** incult·a -orum *npl*
wildcat *s* lynx, lyncis *mf*
wildcat *adj (unauthorized)* illicit·us -a -um
wilderness *s* desert·a -orum *npl; (fig)* vastit·as -atis *f*
wild-goose chase *s* vanum incept·um -i *n*
wildly *adv* saeve, ferociter
wildness *s* ferit·as -atis *f*
wile *s* dol·us -i *m*
wiliness *s* callidit·as -atis *f*
will *s* volunt·as -atis *f*, anim·us -i *m; (intent)* proposit·um -i *n; (testament)* testament·um -i *n; (of gods)* nut·us -ūs *m;* **against one's —** invit·us -a -um; **at —** ad libidinem suam; **of one's own free —** suā sponte; **to make a —** testamentum facere
will *tr (a legacy)* legare
willful *adj* consult·us -a -um
willfully *adv* consulto
willing *adj* lib·ens -entis; **to be —** velle
willingly *adv* libenter
willingness *s* volunt·as -atis *f*
willpower *s* vis *f* mentis
willy-nilly *adv* nolens volens
wily *adj* va·fer -fra -frum
win *s* victori·a -ae *f;* **a — on points** praevalenti·a -ae *f* punctorum
win *tr (to attain)* adipisci, consequi; *(to gain)* potiri; *(victory)* reportare, adipisci; **to — a battle** proelio vincere; **to — a bet** sponsione vincere; **to — a court case** iudicio vincere; **to — friends** amicos acquirere; **to — highest honors** amplissimos honores consequi; **to — the hearts of the people** conciliare animos plebis; **to — over** conciliare ‖ *intr* vincere; **to — out** *(to prevail)* praevalēre
wince *intr* **to — with sudden pain** prae dolore subito horrēre
winch *s* sucul·a -ae *f*
wind *s* vent·us -i *m;* **head (tail) —** ventus adversus (secundus); **I got — of it long ago** iam pridem id mihi subolebat
wind *tr* circumvolvere; *(a clock)* intendere; **the plant wound itself around the tree** herba arbori se circumvolvit; **to — up** *(a speech)* concludere, perorare; **to — up one's affairs** res domesticas et familiares in ordinem redigere
winded *adj* anhel·ans -antis
windfall *s (fig)* lucr·um -i *n* insperatum
winding *adj* flexuos·us -a -um
windmill *s* mol·a -ae *f* vento acta
window *s* fenestr·a -ae *f; (of glass)* fenestra vitrea; *(comput)* fenestell·a -ae *f*
windowpane *s* specular·e -is *n*, fenestrae vitr·um -i *n*
window seat *s* sed·es -is *f* fenestralis
windpipe *s* arteri·a -ae *f* aspera
windshield *s* vitr·um -i *n* antiaërium
windshield wiper *s* vitriterg·ium -(i)i *n*
windstorm *s* procell·a -ae *f*
windup *s* fin·is -is *m*, termin·us -i *m; (of a speech)* perorati·o -onis *f*
windy *adj* ventos·us -a -um
wine *s* vin·um -i *n; (undiluted)* mer·um -i *n; (cheap wine)* vapp·a -ae *f;* **dry (light, red, sweet, white) —** austerum (tenue, sanguineum, dulce, album) vinum
wine cellar *s* cellar·ium -(i)i *n* vinarium
wined and dined *adj* prans·us et pot·us -a -um
wine glass hyal·us -i *m* vinarius
wing *s* al·a -ae *f; (of a building)* lat·us -eris *n; (mil)* corn·u -ūs *n*
winged *adj* alat·us -a -um
wink *intr* nictare, connivēre; **to — at** nictare *(w. dat)*
winner *s* vic·tor -toris *m* (·trix -tricis *f*)
winning *adj (fig)* amoen·us -a -um
winnings *spl* lucr·um -i *n*
winter *s* hiem·s -is *f;* **at the beginning (end) of —** ineunte (exeunte) hieme; **in the dead of —** mediā hieme; brumā; **to spend the —** hiemare

winter *intr* hiemare, hibernare
winter *adj* hibern•us -a -um, hiemal•is -is -e; **— clothes** hiberna vestiment•a -orum *npl;* **— time** hiemale temp•us -oris *n*
winter quarters *spl* hibern•a -orum *npl*
wintry *adj* hiemal•is -is -e, brumal•is -is -e
wipe *tr* tergēre; *(lips)* abstergēre; **to be —ed out** *(of a debt)* deperire; **to — away** abstergēre; *(tears)* extergēre; **to — off** *or* **clean** detergēre; **to — out** *(writing)* delēre; **to — the nose** emungere
wire *s* fil•um -i *n* ferreum; *(of silver)* filum argenteum; *(of copper)* filum aëneum
wisdom *s* sapienti•a -ae *f*
wise *adj* sapi•ens -entis, prud•ens -entis
wise *s (way)* mod•us -i *m;* **in no —** nequaquam
wise guy *s* impud•ens -entis *m;* **don't be a —!** ne sis impudens!
wisely *adv* sapienter, prudenter
wish *s (act of wishing)* optati•o -onis *f; (thing wished)* optat•um -i *n; (prayer)* vot•um -i *n;* **according to one's —es** de sententiā; **according to your —es** secundum voluntatem tuam; **best —es to your brother** salutem plurimam fratri tuo; **I give you three —es** tres optationes tibi do
wish *tr* optare, velle, cupere; **to — earnestly** exoptare ‖ *intr* **to — for** exoptare, expetere
wishing *s* optati•o -onis *f*
wisp *s (of hair, grass, etc.)* manipul•us -i *m*
wistful *adj* desiderii plen•us -a -um
wistfully *adv* oculis intentis
wit *s (intellect)* ingen•ium -(i)i *n; (humor)* faceti•ae -arum *fpl; (person)* hom•o -inis *mf* facet•us (•a -ae); **to be at one's —s' end** delirare; **to —** scilicet
witch *s* strig•a -ae *f,* mag•a -ae *f*
witchcraft *s* ar•s -tis *f* magica
with *prep* cum *(w. abl); (at the house of)* apud *(w. acc)*
withdraw *tr* seducere, avocare; *(words)* revocare ‖ *intr* recedere
wither *tr* torrēre ‖ *intr* marcēre
withered *adj* marcid•us -a -um
withhold *tr* retinēre; *(to suppress)* supprimere
within *adv* intus, intra; *(on the inside)* intrinsecus; **— and without** intrinsecus et extrinsecus
within *prep (place, time, the law)* intra *(w. acc); (during a definite period)* inter *(w. acc);* **— a few days** paucis diebus
without *adv* extra, exterius; *(out of doors)* foris; **from —** extrinsecus
without *prep* sine *(w. abl),* absque *(w. abl);* **I could in no way enter — their seeing me** nullo modo introire poteram quin me viderent; **to be —** carēre *(w. abl)*
withstand *tr* resistere *(w. dat),* obsistere *(w. dat)*
witness *s* test•is -is *mf; (to a signature)* obsigna•tor -toris *m* (•trix -tricis *f*); **to bear —** testificari; **to be called as a —** contestari; **to call to —** testari; **trustworthy witness** testis locuples *(gen:* testis locupletis) *mf*
witness *tr* testificari; *(to see)* interesse *(w. dat),* spectare
witticism *s* faceti•a -ae *f*
wittily *adv* facete, festive
witty *adj* facet•us -a -um
wizard *s* mag•us -i *m*
woe *s* luct•us -ūs *m;* **—s** mal•a -orum *npl*
woeful *adj* luctuos•us -a -um
woefully *adv* misere, flebiliter
wolf *s* lup•us -i *m,* lup•a -ae *f;* **wolves howl** lupi ululant
wolf cub *s* lupae catul•us -i *m*
woman *s* muli•er -eris *f,* femin•a -ae *f;* **old —** an•us -ūs *f;* **young —** muliercul•a -ae *f*
womanly *adj* muliebr•is -is -e
womb *s* uter•us -i *m*
wonder *s* admirati•o -onis *f; (astonishing object)* miracul•um -i *n;* **and no —** nec mirum; **seven —s of the world** septem miracula mundi; **to excite —** mirationem facere
wonder *intr* mirari; **I wonder what's up** miror quid hoc sit negoti; **to — at** admirari
wonderful *adj* (ad)mirabil•is -is -e
wonderfully *adv* mirabiliter
wont *adj* **to be — to** solēre *(w. inf)*
woo *tr* petere
wood *s* lign•um -i *n;* **—s** silv•a -ae *f*
wooded *adj* silvos•us -a -um
wooden *adj* ligne•us -a -um
wooden spoon *s* cochle•ar -aris *n* coquinarium
woodland *s* salt•us -ūs *m*
wood nymph *s* Dry•as -adis *f*
woodpecker *s* pic•us -i *m*
woods *spl* silv•a -ae *f*
woody *adj (full of wood fibers)* lignos•us -a -um; *(covered with woods)* silvos•us -a -um, silvestr•is -is -e
wooer *s* proc•us -i *m*
wool *s* lan•a -ae *f;* **to pull the — over s.o.'s eyes** subdol•us (-a) esse adversus aliquem
woolen *adj* lane•us -a -um
word *s (in context)* verb•um -i *n; (out of context)* vocabul•um -i *n; (gram)* dicti•o -onis *f; (spoken)* vox vocis *f,* dict•um -i *n; (promise)* fid•es -ei *f; (news)* nunt•ius -(i)i *m;* **in a —** ad summam; **I want a — with you** paucis te volo; **to break one's —** fidem fallere; **to give one's —** fidem dare; **to keep one's —** fidem praestare; **to send —** muntiare; **why should I take your — for it?** cur tibi credam?; **— for —** ad verbum; **— of honor** fid•es -ei *f;* **—s fail me** mihi verba desunt; quid dicam non invenio; **you took the —s**

right out of my mouth tu quidem ex ore orationem mihi eripuisti; **upon my —** meā fide; **— of honor** fid·es -ei *f*
wordy *adj* verbos·us -a -um
work *s (labor, pains)* oper·a -ae *f; (act of working and thing completed; literary work)* op·us -eris *n; (labor, trouble)* lab·or -oris *m; (employment)* occupati·o -onis *f*, negot·ium -(i)i *n;* **at —** occupat·us -a -um, negotios·us -a -um; **good —s** recte et honeste fact·a -orum *npl;* **one day's work** una opera *f;* **to throw out of —** de negotio deicere
work *tr (to exercise)* exercēre; *(to till)* colere; *(a machine)* administrare; **to — one's way up** proficere; **to — out** solvere; **to — up** elaborare; *(emotion)* efferre; *(fig)* excitare, perturbare **ll** *intr* laborare, operari; *(to function)* fung·or -i functus sum; **to — at** *(or* **on)** operam dare *(w. dat);* **to — out** *(to exercise)* exercitare
worker *s (unskilled)* operari·us -i *m* (·a -ae *f*); *(skilled)* opif·ex -icis *mf; (day laborer)* oper·a -ae *f* [*mostly in the pl*]
workmanship *s* op·us -eris *n*, artific·ium -(i)i *n*
workout *s* exercitati·o -onis *f*
workshop *s* officin·a -ae *f*
world *s (universe)* mund·us -i *m*, summ·a -ae *f* rerum; *(earth)* orb·is -is *m* terrarum; *(mankind)* homin·es -um *mpl;* **next —** vit·a -ae *f* futura; **where in the —** ubi terrarum, ubi gentium; **worst poet in the —** pessimus poeta omnium
worldly *adj* profan·us -a -um
world war *s* bell·um -i *n* mandanum
worldwide *adj* univers·us -a -um, per orbem terrarum pat·ens -entis
World Wide Web (WWW) Tel·a -ae *f* Totius Terrae (TTT)
worm *s* verm·is -is *m;* **earth worm** lumbric·us -i *m*
worm *tr* **to — one's way into** se insinuare in *(w. acc)*
worm-eaten, wormy *adj* vermiculos·us -a -um
worn out *adj (person)* fatigat·us -a -um; *(clothes)* trit·us -a -um
worrisome *adj* molest·us -a -um
worry *s* sollicitud·o -inis *f; (cause)* molesti·a -ae *f*
worry *tr* sollicitare; **don't — yourself to death** ne te crucia **ll** *intr* sollicitari; **don't —!** noli *(pl:* nolite) sollicitari!
worse *adj* pe·ior -ior -ius, deter·ior -ior -ius; **to get —** ingravescere; **to make matters —** res exasperare; **to make —** peiorem reddere, deteriorem reddere; **to turn out for the —** in peius evenire
worse *adv* peius, deterius
worsen *intr* ingravescere
worship *s* cult·us -ūs *m*, venerati·o -onis *f*
worship *tr* colere, venerari
worshipful *adj* rever·ens -entis
worshipper *s* cul·tor -toris *m* (·trix -tricis *f*)
worst *adj* pessim·us -a -um, deterrim·us -a -um; **— of all** maxime alien·us -a -um
worst *adv* pessime
worst *tr* vincere
worth *s (value)* pret·ium -(i)i *n*, aestimati·o -onis *f; (merit)* dignit·as -atis *f; (prestige)* auctorit·as -atis *f;* **man is of little —** hom·o -inis *m* parvi preti est; **of great —** pretios·us -a -um; **of little —** vil·is -is -e
worth *adj* dign·us -a -um *(w. abl);* **a slave — any price** serv·us -i *m* quantivis preti; **he is — a lot of money** divitias maximas habet; **he is — nothing** nihil est; **how much are pigs — here?** quibus hic pretis porci veneunt?; **it is — knowing** est operae pretium cognoscere; **this is — s.th. to me** hoc mihi in lucro est; **to be — a lot** multum valēre
worthless *adj* vil·is -is -e; *(of persons)* nequam [*indecl*]; **completely — fellow** nequissimus hom·o -inis *m*
worthlessness *s* inanit·as -atis *f*
worthwhile *adj* **to be —** operae pretium esse
worthy *adj* **(of)** dign·us -a -um *(w. abl)*
wound *s* vuln·us -eris *n; (fig)* offensi·o -onis *f*
wound *tr* vulnerare; *(fig)* offendere
wounded *adj* sauci·us -a -um
wow *interj (expressing amazement, surprise)* vah!; hui!
wrangle *intr* rixari, altercari
wrangling *s* discordi·a -ae *f*
wrap *tr (to wind)* involvere; **to — oneself** se amicire; **to — the head in his toga** caput obvolvere togā; **to — up** complicare; *(against the cold)* involvere; *(to finish)* conficere, finem facere *(w. dat)*
wrap *s (cloak)* amict·us -ūs *m*
wrapper *s* involucr·um -i *n*
wrapping paper *s* chart·a -ae *f* emporetica
wrath *s* ir·a -ae *f*, iracundi·a -ae *f*
wrathful *adj* iracund·us -a -um
wreak *tr* **to — havoc** stragem dare; **to — vengeance on** ulcisci
wreath *s* sert·um -i *n*, coron·a -ae *f*
wreathe *tr (to twist)* torquēre; *(to adorn with wreathes)* nectere
wreck *s* ruin·a -ae *f; (of ship)* naufrag·ium -(i)i *n;* **he is a —** naufragus est
wreck *tr* frangere; *(fig)* delēre
wren *s* regul·us -i *m*
wrench *s (tool)* forf·ex -icis *f; (twist)* luxati·o -onis *f*
wrench *tr (a limb)* detorquēre, luxare; **to — away** eripere
wrest *tr* extorquēre, eripere
wrestle *intr* luctari
wrestler *s* luct·or -oris *m*
wrestling *s* luctati·o -onis *f*

wrestling match *s* certam·en -inis *n* luctationis
wretch *s* mis·er -eri *m,* miser·a -ae *f*
wretched *adj* mis·er -era -erum
wretchedly *adv* misere
wretchedness *s* miseri·a -ae *f*
wring *tr* contorquēre; **to — the neck** gulam frangere; **—ing his hands** manibus inter se constrictis; **to — out a cloth** linteolum exprimere
wrinkle *s* rug·a -ae *f*
wrinkle *tr* corrugare; **to — the forehead** frontem contrahere
wrinkled *adj* rugos·us -a -um
wrist *s* primoris man·us -ūs *f;* **sleeves reaching all the way down to the —s** manicae prolixae usque in primores manūs
wrist bone *s* carp·us -i *m*
writ *s* mandat·um -i *n*
write *tr* scribere; *(a book)* conscribere; *(poetry, book)* componere; *(history)* perscribere; **to — a program** *(comput)* programma componere; **to — Latin** Latine scribere
writer *s* scrip·tor -toris *m* (·trix -tricis *f)*
writhe *intr* torquēri
writing *s (act)* scripti·o -onis *f; (result)* script·um -i *n,* scriptur·a -ae *f;* **in the —s of Cicero** apud Ciceronem; **—s** script·a -orum *npl*
wrong *s* nefas *n (indecl),* iniuri·a -ae *f,* mal·um -i *n;* **to do —** peccare, male facere
wrong *adj (opp:* erectus) prav·us -a -um; *(incorrect, mistaken)* fals·us -a -um; *(unfair)* iniqu·us -a -um; *(unsuitable)* alien·us -a -um; *(faulty)* vitios·us -a -um; *(morally)* nefas [*indecl*]; **if I have done anything —, I'm sorry** si quid perperam feci, me paenitet; **to be —** errare; **what's — with you?** quid est tecum?
wrong *tr* iniuriam inferre *(w. dat),* offendere
wrongdoing *s* probr·um -i *n,* malefact·um -i *n*
wrongly *adv* perperam, male
wrought *adj* confect·us -a -um
wrought iron *s* ferr·um -i *n* temperatum
wry *adj* contort·us -a -um; *(sharp)* mord·ax -acis, sals·us -a -um

Y

yacht *s* phasel·us -i *m; (smaller model)* cel·ox -ocis *f*
yank *tr (coll)* vellere
yap *intr (to prattle)* garrire; *(to grumble)* gannire
yapping *s (prattle)* garrit·us -ūs *m;* gannit·us -ūs *m*
yard *s* are·a -ae *f* domūs; *(measure)* tres pedes *mpl;* **back yard** area (domūs) postica
yardarm *s* antenn·a -ae *f*
yarn *s (of linen)* fil·um -i *n* lini; *(of wool)* fil·um -i *n* laneum; *(story)* fabul·a -ae *f*
yawn *s* oscitati·o -onis *f*
yawn *intr* oscitare, hiare; *(to gape open)* dehiscere
year *s* ann·us -i *m;* **at the beginning (end) of the —** ineunte (exeunte) anno; **a — from now** ad annum; **a hundred —s from now** ad centum annos; **every —** quotannis; **five —s** quinquenn·ium -(i)i *n;* **for a —** in annum; **four —s** quadrenn·ium -(i)i *n;* **he is twenty —s old** viginti annos natus est; **in his later —s** tempore extremo; **in the — of our Lord** anno Domini; **it's ten —s since the law was passed** decem anni sunt quum lata lex est; **I wish you a happy New Year** Novum Annum laetum tibi exopto; **last —** anno superiore; **next —** anno proximo; **three —s** trienn·ium -(i)i *n;* **twice a —** bis (in) anno; **two —s** bienn·ium -(i)i *n;* **up in —s** aetate provect·us -a -um
yearly *adj* annu·us -a -um
yearly *adv* quotannis
yearn *intr* **to — for** desiderare
yearning *s* **(for)** desider·ium -(i)i *n (w. gen)*
yeast *s* ferment·um -i *n*
yell *s* clam·or -oris *m,* ululat·us -ūs *m*
yell *tr* clamāre ‖ *intr* ululare; *(in pain)* eiulare
yellow *adj (hair, gold, sand, grainfields, honey)* flav·us -a -um; *(teeth)* lurid·us -a -um; *(hair, sand)* fulv·us -a -um
yellowish *adj* subflav·us -a -um
yelp *intr (like a dog)* gannire; *(in pain)* eiulare; **what's he —ing for?** quid ille gannit?
yelp *s* gannit·us -ūs *m; (in pain)* eiulat·us -ūs *m*
yes *adv* ita, sic, sane, oppido *(but the most frequent way in Latin to express a simple yes is to repeat the word emphasized in the question):* **do you want me? Yes.** visne me? Te.; **has he sold her? Yes.** eam vendidit? Vendidit.
yes-man *s* assecl·a -ae *m*
yesterday *adv* heri; **the day before —** nudiustertius [*adv*]; **— evening** heri vesperi; **— morning** heri mane
yet *adv (contrast, after adversative clause)* tamen; *(time)* adhuc; *(w. comparatives)* etiam; **as —** adhuc; **not —** nondum
yew *s* tax·us -i *f*
yield *tr (to produce)* ferre, parere; *(to surrender)* concedere ‖ *intr* cedere; **to — to** cedere *(w. dat)*
yield *s* fruct·us -ūs *m; (profit)* quaest·us -ūs *m*

yipes *interj (to express surprise, fear, dismay)* eheu!
yippee *interj (to express joy, elation)* ehem!
yoke *s* iug•um -i *n; (fig)* servit•us -utis *f*
yoke *tr* coniungere
yokel *s* rustic•us -i *m* (•a -ae *f*)
yolk *s* vitell•us -i *m*
yonder *adv* illic
yonder *adj* ill•e -a -ud
you *pron* tu; *(ye)* vos; **to —** tibi; vobis; **with —** tecum; vobiscum; **— know** [*parenthetical*] enim
young *adj (children)* parv•us -a -um (natu), parvul•us -a -um (natu); *(goat, vine)* novell•us -a -um; **— boy** puerul•us -i *m;* **— bride** nova nupt•a -ae *f;* **— daughter** filiol•a -ae *f;* **— girl** puellul•a -ae *f;* **— lady** muliercul•a -ae *f;* **— man** adulescentul•us -i *m,* adulesc•ens -entis *m; (between the ages of 20 and 40)* iuven•is -is *m*
younger *adj* iun•ior -ior -ius, min•or -or -us (natu)
youngster *s* adulescentul•us -i *m* (•a -ae *f*)
your *adj* tu•us -a -um; *pl:* ves•ter -tra -trum
yourself *pron refl* te; **by —** per te; **to —** tibi; **with —** tecum ‖ *pron intensive* **you —** *(masc)* tu ipse; *(fem)* tu ipsa
yourselves *pron refl* vos; **to —** vobis; **with —** vobiscum ‖ *pron intensive* **you —** *(masc)* vos ipsi; *(fem)* vos ipsae
youth *s (age)* adulescenti•a -ae *f; (collectively)* iuvent•us -utis *f; (young person)* iuven•is -is *mf,* adulesc•ens -entis *mf*
youthful *adj* iuvenil•is -is -e
youthfully *adv* iuveniliter

Z

zany *adj* delir•us -a -um
zeal *s* stud•ium -(i)i *n,* ferv•or -oris *m*
zealot *s* fanatic•us -i *m* (•a -ae *f*)
zealous *adj* studios•us -a -um
zealously *adv* studiose, enixe
zebra *s* zebr•a -ae *f*
zenith *s* vert•ex -icis *m; (fig)* fastig•ium -(i)i *n*
zephyr *s* Zephyr•us -i *m*
zero *s* nihil *n,* nil *n* [*indecl*]
zest *s* sap•or -oris *m; (fig)* gustat•us -ūs *m;* **— for true praise** gustatus *m* verae laudis
zig-zag *adj* tortuos•us -a -um; **— streets** anfract•ūs -uum *mpl* viarum
zip code *s* numer•us -i *n* cursualis
zipper *s* clausur•a -ae *f* tractilis
zither *s* cithar•a -ae *f*
zodiac *s* Zodiac•us -i *m,* signifer orb•is -is *m*
zone *s* zon•a -ae *f,* regi•o -onis *f*
zoo *s* vivar•ium -(i)i *n,* hort•i -orum *mpl* zoölogici
zoology *s* zoölogi•a -ae *f*

Abbreviations

abbr ....abbreviation
abl ....ablative
acc ....accusative
adj ....adjective
adjl ....adjectival
adv ....adverb
advl ....adverbial
anat ....anatomy
archit ....architecture
astr ....astronomy
bot ....botany
biol ....biology
c. ....circa, about
cf. ....confer, compare
cent. ....century
coll ....colloquial
com ....commerce
comp ....comparative
comput ....computer
conj ....conjunction
d. ....died
dat ....dative
defect ....defective verb
dim. ....diminutive
E. ....East(ern)
eccl ....ecclesiastical
educ ....education
euphem ....euphemism
esp. ....especially
expr. ....expressed
f ....feminine noun
fem ....feminine
fig ....figurative
fin ....finance
fl ....floruit, flourished
fpl ....feminine plural noun
fut ....future
gen ....genitive
geog ....geography
geol ....geology
gram ....grammar
hum ....humorous
imperf ......imperfect
impers .....impersonal verb
impv ....imperative
indecl ......indeclinable
indef ....indefinite
indic ....indicative
inf ....infinitive
interj ....interjection
interrog ...interrogative
intr ....intransitive
leg ....legal
lit ....literal
loc ....locative
m ....masculine noun
masc ....masculine
math ....mathematics
mech ....mechanics
med ....medicine
mf ....masculine or feminine noun
mil ....military
mpl ....masculine plural noun
mus ....music
n ....neuter noun
N. ....North(ern)
naut ....nautical
neg. ....negative
neut ....neuter
nom ....nominative
npl ....neuter plural noun
opp ....opposite of
p ....participle
pass ....passive
pej ....pejorative
perf ....perfect
phil ....philosophy
pl ....plural
poet ....poetry
pol ....politics
pp ....past participle
pref ....prefix
prep ....preposition
pres ....present
pron ....pronoun
pros ....prosody
prov ....proverb
refl ....reflexive
rel ....relative
relig ....religion
rhet ....rhetoric
s ....substantive
S. ....South(ern)
sc ....scilicet
singl ....singular
sl ....slang
s.o. ....someone
spl ....substantive plural
s.th. ....something
subj ....subjunctive
suf ....suffix
superl ......superlative
theat ....theater
topog ....topography
tr ....transitive verb
usu ....usually
vbl ....verbal
v defect ....defective verb
v impers ..impersonal verb
vulg ....vulgar
w. ....with
W. ....West(ern)